ASHP best practices

POSITION & GUIDANCE DOCUMENTS OF ASHP

2015-2016 Edition

ashp publications

The ASHP policies in this book, positions and guidance documents, are intended to foster improvements in pharmacy practice and patient care. The content of individual positions and guidance documents should be assessed in the context of your own health system, its policies and procedures, as well as applicable federal and state laws and regulations.

Guidance documents, in particular, evolve because of advances in technology, new knowledge from research, and lessons from experience. Additionally, medication information is constantly evolving because of ongoing research and clinical experience, and it is often subject to interpretation and unique clinical situations. The American Society of Health-System Pharmacists (ASHP) endeavors to ensure the completeness and timeliness of the information presented. However, the reader is advised that the publisher, contributors, editors, and reviewers make no representations concerning the suitability of the information for any purpose, and are not responsible for the immediate currency of the information, for any errors or omissions, or for any consequences arising from the use of these materials. All decisions made within the context of pharmacy practice should be based on the independent judgment of the practitioner.

ASHP is the national professional organization whose more than 40,000 members include pharmacists, student pharmacists, and pharmacy technicians who serve as patient care providers on healthcare teams in acute and ambulatory settings. For over 70 years, ASHP has been on the forefront of efforts to improve medication use and advance healthcare. For more information about the wide array of ASHP activities and the many ways in which pharmacists help people make the best use of medicines, visit ASHP's website, www.ashp.org, or its consumer website, www.safemedication.com.

Editor: Bruce Hawkins

Published by the American Society of Health-System Pharmacists, 7272 Wisconsin Avenue, Bethesda, MD 20814.

ISBN: 978-1-58528-533-4

10 9 8 7 6 5 4 3 2 1

Contents

*Indicates content that has been added or revised since the 2014–2015 edition.

*Indicates content that has been added or revised since the 2014–2015 edition.

Ethics

Formulary Management (Medication-Use Policy Development)

*Indicates content that has been added or revised since the 2014–2015 edition.

Government, Law, and Regulation

*Indicates content that has been added or revised since the 2014–2015 edition.

*Indicates content that has been added or revised since the 2014–2015 edition.

Medication Therapy and Patient Care

ORGANIZATION AND DELIVERY OF SERVICES

*Indicates content that has been added or revised since the 2014–2015 edition.

SPECIFIC PRACTICE AREAS

*Indicates content that has been added or revised since the 2014–2015 edition.

Pharmaceutical Industry

DRUG PRODUCTS, LABELING, AND PACKAGING

MARKETING

*Indicates content that has been added or revised since the 2014–2015 edition.

Pharmacy Management

COMPENSATION AND REIMBURSEMENT

HUMAN RESOURCES

*Indicates content that has been added or revised since the 2014–2015 edition.

*Indicates content that has been added or revised since the 2014–2015 edition.

Page Locator for Guidance Documents by Type and Title

ASHP Statements

ASHP Guidelines

ASHP Report

ASHP Technical Assistance Bulletins

Acknowledgments

ASHP gratefully acknowledges the following organizations and individuals for drafting and reviewing the new and revised guidance documents in this edition.

ASHP Statement on the Roles and Responsibilities of the Pharmacy Executive

Council on Pharmacy Management

Contributing Reviewers:
Karl Kappeler, M.S., FASHP
Michael Nnadi, Pharm.D, MHS
Sam Calabrese, M.B.A., FASHP
Debra Cowan, Pharm.D., FASHP
Bonnie Kirshenbaum, M.S., FASHP, FCSHP
John Lewin, Pharm.D., M.B.A.
Christine Marchese, Pharm.D.
Tricia Meyer, Pharm.D., M.S., FASHP
Brandon Ordway, Pharm.D., M.S.
Roger Woolf, Pharm.D.,
Rusol Karralli, Pharm.D., M.S.
Kelly Sennett, B.S.

ASHP Statement on the Pharmacist's Role in Substance Abuse Prevention, Education and Assistance

Contributors:
Jeffrey N. Baldwin, Pharm.D.
Chelsea Leeper, Pharm.D.

ASHP Statement on the Pharmacist's Role in Clinical Informatics

Author: Mark Siska, M.B.A./TM, B.S.Pharm.

Reviewers:
American Association of Colleges of Pharmacy (AACP)
American Medical Informatics Association, Pharmacoinformatics Working Group Leadership (AMIA-PWGL)
Kansas Council of Health-System Pharmacists (KCHP)
New Hampshire Society of Health-System Pharmacists (NHSHP)
Pharmacy HIT Collaborative (PHITC)
Ernest R. Anderson, Jr., M.S., FASHP
Paul J. Barrett, Pharm.D., MPA, BCPS, FASHP
Janinah Barreto, Pharm.D., M.S.
Carol J. Bickford, Ph.D., RN-BC, CPHIMS
Sarah Bledsoe, Pharm.D.
Lynette R. Bradley-Baker, Ph.D. (AACP)
Max E. Burchett, Jr., Pharm.D.
Gregory Burger, Pharm.D., CPPS (KCHP)
Michelle DeLuca Fraley, Pharm.D., RPD
Barbara Giacomelli, Pharm.D., M.B.A., FASHP
Nancy Hope Goodbar, Pharm.D., BCPS
James Hoffman, Pharm.D., M.S.
Joan Kapusnik-Uner, Pharm.D. FASHP
Janet M Kozakiewiz, M.S., Pharm.D., FASHP
Emily Kirkwold, Pharm.D.
Kabeer Mago, Pharm.D.
Ben McDaniel, Pharm.D.
Karen Michaud, Pharm.D., BCPS
Richard Pacitti, Pharm.D., M.B.A.
Lois F. Parker, B.S.Pharm.
Shea Polk, Pharm.D.
James A. Ponto, M.S., RPh, BCNP, FASHP
Jason J. Schafer, Pharm.D., M.P.H., BCPS
Philip J. Schneider, M.S.
Terry L. Seaton, Pharm.D., FCCP, BCPS (AMIA-PWGL)
Nancy R. Smestad, M.S., CMI
Shelly Spiro, B.S.Pharm., FASCP (PHITC)
Mark St. Cyr, D.Ph., M.P.H.
Craig Stern, RPh, Pharm.D., M.B.A.
Tate N. Trujillo, Pharm.D., BCPS, FCCM, FASHP
Elizabeth Wade, Pharm.D., BCPS (NHSHP)
Jody Jacobson Wedret, FASHP
Marc Willner, Pharm.D.

ASHP Guidelines on Pharmacist Involvement in HIV Care

Authors:
Jason J. Schafer, Pharm.D., M.P.H, BCPS, AAHIVP
Taylor K. Gill, Pharm.D., BCPS, AAHIVP
Elizabeth M. Sherman, Pharm.D., AAHIVP
Ian R. McNicholl, Pharm.D., FCCP, BCPS (AQ-ID), AAHIVP

Reviewers:
American Pharmacists Association (APhA)
Canadian HIV/AIDS Pharmacists Network (CHAP)
HIV Medicine Association (HIVMA)
Society of Infectious Disease Pharmacists
South Carolina Society of Health-System Pharmacists (SCSHP)

Melissa Badowski, Pharm.D., BCPS, AAHIVP
Carol J. Bickford, Ph.D., RN-BC, CPHIMS
Shanna Chan, B.Sc.Pharm., ACPR, AAHIVP (CHAP)
Patrick Clay, Pharm.D. FCCP, CCTI (APhA)

*Review does not imply endorsement.

Natalie Dayneka, B.Sc.Pharm., ACPR, Pharm.D., FCSHP (CHAP)
Heather Easterling, Pharm.D., M.B.A. (SCSHP)
Devon Flynn, Pharm.D., BCPS, AAHIVP
Michelle Foisy, B.Sc.Pharm., Pharm.D., FCSHP, AAHIVP (CHAP)
Patricia Pecora Fulco, Pharm.D., BCPS, FASHP, AAHIVP
Barbara Giacomelli, Pharm.D., M.B.A., FASHP
Pierre Giguère, B.Sc.Pharm., M.Sc. (CHAP)
Christine Hughes, B.Sc.Pharm., Pharm.D, AAHIVP (CHAP)
Tara K. Jellison, Pharm.D., M.B.A., FASHP
Deborah V. Kelly, B.Sc.Pharm., ACPR, Pharm.D, FCSHP, AAHIVP (CHAP)
William Kuykendall, Pharm.D.
Kristina Lantis, Pharmacy Student, Class of 2016
J. Craig Phillips, Ph.D., LLM, RN, ARNP, PMHCNS-BC, ACRN
Carlo Quaia, B.Sc.Pharm., ACPR (CHAP)
James R. Rinehart, R.Ph., M.S., FASHP
Linda Robinson, B.Sc.Pharm., AAHIVE (CHAP)
Nancy Sheehan, B.Sc.Pharm., M.Sc. (CHAP)
Shannon Stone, B.Sc.Pharm., ACPR (CHAP)
Alice Tseng, B.Sc.Pharm., Pharm.D., FCSHP, AAHIVP (CHAP)
Andrea Weddle, M.S.W. (HIVMA)
Jody Jacobson Wedret, FASHP, FCSHP
Deborah Yoong, B.Sc.Pharm., ACPR, Pharm.D. (CHAP)

ASHP Guidelines on Outsourcing Sterile Compounding Services

Revised by: Patricia C. Kienle, M.P.A., FASHP

Contributor: Bona E. Benjamin, B.S.Pharm.

Reviewers:
Darrell Chan, Pharm.D.
Michael Cunningham, Pharm.D.
Kate Douglass, M.S., RN, APN,C, CRNI
Bernadette Henrichs, Ph.D., CRNA, CCRN
Eric Kastango, M.B.A., FASHP
Michael Koch, M.B.A.
Rich Kruzynski, B.S.Pharm., M.B.A.
Kathy Parrinello, Ph.D., RN
James R. Rinehardt, M.S., FASHP
Douglas Smith, Pharm.D.
Ross W. Thompson, M.S., B.S.Pharm.
Tom Woller, M.S., FASHP

ASHP Guidelines: Minimum Standard for Ambulatory Care Pharmacy Practice

Authors:
Jennifer Askew Buxton, Pharm.D., CPP
RoseMarie Babbitt, B.S.Pharm., M.A.
Cyndy A. Clegg, M.H.A.
Sandra F. Durley, Pharm.D.
Kelly T. Epplen, Pharm.D.
Laurel M. Marsden, B.S.Pharm., M.S.H.A.
Bridgette A. Thomas, Pharm.D.
Nathan S. Thompson, B.S.Pharm., M.B.A.

Contributions by:
Section of Ambulatory Care Practitioners Executive Committee
Seena L. Haines, Pharm.D., FASHP, FAPhA, BCACP, BC-ADM, CDE
Gloria P. Sachdev, Pharm.D.
Jennifer Askew Buxton, Pharm.D., CPP
Melanie A. Dodd, Pharm.D., Ph.C., BCPS
Sandra Leal, Pharm.D., FAPhA, CDE
Steven M. Riddle, Pharm.D., BCPS, FASHP
Justine Coffey, J.D., LL.M.

Association and Organization Reviewers:
Academy of Managed Care Pharmacy (AMCP)*
American Association of Critical-Care Nurses (AACN)*
American College of Clinical Pharmacy (ACCP)*
American Geriatric Society*
The Joint Commission (TJC)*
Cindi Brennan, Pharm.D., M.H.A.*
Mark N. Brueckl, M.B.A. (AMCP)*
Anne Burns, Pharm.D.*
Frank P. Castronovo, Jr., Ph.D*
Sharon Connor, Pharm.D.*
Paul F. Davis, B.S.Pharm.*
Ernest Dole, Pharm.D., FASHP*
Melanie A. Dodd, Pharm.D., Ph.C., BCPS*
Scott R. Drab, Pharm.D., CDE, BC-ADM*
Sarah K. Ford, Pharm.D., BCPS, CPP*
Seena L. Haines, Pharm.D., FASHP, FAPhA, BCACP, BC-ADM, CDE*
Deanne L. Hall, Pharm.D., CDE*
Philip E. Johnson, M.S., FASHP*
Tom Kaye, M.B.A., FASHP*
Sandra Leal, Pharm.D., FAPhA, CDE*
Jeff Little, Pharm.D., MPH, BCPS*
Jimmy R. Mitchell, M.S., M.P.H.*
Bruce A. Nelson, M.S.*
Colleen O'Malley, M.S., B.S.Pharm.*
James A. Ponto, M.S., BCNP*
Matt Ransom, Pharm.D., BCACP*
Steven M. Riddle, Pharm.D., BCPS, FASHP*
Christine Ruby, Pharm.D., BCPS*
Gloria P. Sachdev, Pharm.D.*
Paul M. Schyve, M.D. (TJC)
Pamela Shellner, R.N., M.A. (AACN)*
Melissa Somma-McGivney, Pharm.D., CDE*
Richard L. Stambaugh, M.S., Pharm.D., BCPS*
Marc H. Stranz, Pharm.D.*
Megan Wagner, Pharm.D.*
C. Edwin Webb, Pharm.D., M.P.H. (ACCP)*

Jody Jacobson Wedret, FASHP, FCSHP*

ASHP Guidelines on the Design of Database-Driven Clinical Decision Support: Strategic Directions for Drug Database and Electronic Health Records Vendors

Authors:
Bruce W. Chaffee, Pharm.D.
Raymond C. Chan, Pharm.D.
Allen Flynn, Pharm.D.
Michael A. Jones, Pharm.D
Andrew P. Laegeler, M.S., Pharm.D.
Trinh Le, B.S.Pharm., M.S., FASHP
Andrew H. Smith, B.S.Pharm., M.H.A.
David Troiano, B.S.Pharm., MSIA, CPPS

Reviewers:
Marc Willner, Pharm.D.
Gary J. Kerr, M.B.A., Pharm.D.
Lois F. Parker, B.S.
Adrienne Au, Pharm.D., M.S., FASHP
James Ponto, M.S., BCNP, FASHP
Karen Michaud, Pharm.D., BCPS
John Hamiel, Pharm.D.
Philip J. Schneider, M.S.
Christopher J. Scott, Pharm.D.
Steven J. Kelsey, Pharm.D.
Thomas Payne, M.D., FACMI
Greg Burger, Pharm.D.
Toby Clark, M.Sc., FASHP, FFIP
Laura Fochtmann, M.D., MBI
Jody Jacobson Wedret, FASHP, FCSHP
James J. Cimino, M.D., FACP, FACMI
Michelle DeLuca Fraley, Pharm.D.
John Poikonen
Brittany L. Melton, Ph.D., Pharm.D.
Kerry Goldrosen, Pharm.D.
Tejal Gandhi, M.D., M.P.H (NPSF)
Philip Emberley, Pharm.D., M.B.A. (CPA)
Elizabeth Wade, Pharm.D., BCPS (NHSHP)
Howard Strasberg (WKH)

Organization Reviewers:
National Patient Safety Foundation (NPSF)*
Canadian Pharmacists Association (CPA)*
New Hampshire Society of Health-System Pharmacists (NHSHP)*
Wolters Kluwer Health (WKH)*

Introduction

ASHP is the national professional organization whose more than 40,000 members include pharmacists, student pharmacists, and pharmacy technicians who serve as patient care providers on healthcare teams in acute and ambulatory settings. For over 70 years, ASHP has been on the forefront of efforts to improve medication use and advance healthcare. ASHP is also a national accrediting organization for pharmacy residency and pharmacy technician training programs.

The Compendium

ASHP, since its founding, has developed official professional policies in the form of policy positions and guidance documents about pharmacy practice, first for hospitals, and then for the continuum of practice settings in integrated health systems. Since 1984, these policies have been compiled annually in this compendium, a compilation of ASHP policy positions, statements, guidelines, technical assistance bulletins, therapeutic position statements, therapeutic guidelines, and selected ASHP-endorsed documents. *Best Practices* reflects the intent of ASHP's professional policies to foster improvements in pharmacy practice and patient care.

The compendium is organized by topic to help readers quickly locate related documents. The table of contents is structured by topic, and under each topic the relevant ASHP policy positions, statements, guidelines, technical assistance bulletins, and endorsed documents are listed. The therapeutic documents are listed by type. Following the table of contents is a page locator for documents by type and title, and the index lists each document, to assist readers who are accustomed to searching for a specific document by its title.

Origins and Purposes of ASHP's Policy Positions and Guidance Documents

Policy positions generally originate with an ASHP council and are approved by the ASHP Board of Directors and ASHP House of Delegates. Some policy positions originate as House of Delegate resolutions. Statements, guidelines, and technical assistance bulletins originate with an ASHP council or commission. Statements are approved by the Board of Directors and the House of Delegates, because of their broad philosophical nature. Other types of documents are approved by the Board of Directors only. Therapeutic position statements and therapeutic guidelines originate with the ASHP Council on Therapeutics and are approved by the Board of Directors.

There is a gradation in detail among the guidance documents. Policy positions are short pronouncements, intended to address professional practice. Often, principles established in policy positions are elaborated on in statements and guidelines. Statements express basic philosophy, guidelines offer programmatic advice, and technical assistance bulletins offer more detailed programmatic advice. Of the two types of therapeutic documents, therapeutic guidelines are thorough discussions of drug use and therapeutic position statements are concise responses to specific therapeutic issues.

The guidance documents of ASHP represent a consensus of professional judgment, expert opinion, and documented evidence. They provide guidance and direction to ASHP members and pharmacy practitioners and to other audiences who affect pharmacy practice. Their use may help to comply with federal and state laws and regulations, to meet accreditation requirements, and to improve pharmacy practice and patient care. They are written to establish reasonable goals, to be progressive and challenging, yet attainable as "best practices" in applicable health-system settings. They generally do not represent minimum levels of practice, unless titled as such, and should not be viewed as ASHP requirements.

The use of ASHP's guidance documents by members and other practitioners is strictly voluntary. Their content should be assessed and adapted based on independent judgment to meet the needs of local health-system settings.

The need for authoritative guidance in pharmacy practice has grown with changes in health care and with the shifting influences from regulatory, accrediting, risk-management, financing, and other bodies. Because of the complex nature of ASHP guidance documents, ASHP does not typically undertake immediate development of new documents or expedited revisions to existing documents in response to environmental changes. Other ASHP activities and services, such as educational sessions at national meetings and *American Journal of Health-System Pharmacy (AJHP)* articles, provide more timely information that may be helpful, until sufficient experience is gained to serve as the basis for a document.

Definitions

The types of guidance documents included in this compendium are defined as follows:

ASHP Policy Position: A pronouncement on an issue related to pharmacy professional practice, as approved by the Board of Directors and House of Delegates.

ASHP Statement: A declaration and explanation of basic philosophy or principle, as approved by the Board of Directors and the House of Delegates.

ASHP Guideline: Advice on the implementation or operation of pharmacy practice programs, as approved by the Board of Directors.

ASHP Technical Assistance Bulletin: Specific, detailed advice on pharmacy programs or functions as developed by an ASHP staff division in consultation with experts, as approved by the Board of Directors.*

ASHP Therapeutic Guideline: Thorough, systematically developed advice for health-care professionals on appropriate use of medications for specific clinical circumstances, as approved by the Board of Directors.

ASHP Therapeutic Position Statement: Concise statements that respond to specific therapeutic issues of concern to health care consumers and pharmacists, as approved by the Board of Directors.

ASHP-Endorsed Document: Professional policy developed by another organization that offers guidance on some aspect of pharmacy practice or medication use, as approved by the Board of Directors.

**The ASHP Board of Directors voted in November 1997 to discontinue the title "Technical Assistance Bulletin" in ASHP guidance documents, assigning the title "Guidelines" in its place. Over time, the title "Guidelines" will replace the title "Technical Assistance Bulletin" on existing documents when they are revised.*

Development of Guidance Documents

The responsible ASHP council or commission recommends the development of a guidance document after considering whether the topic: a) has generated a need among practitioners for authoritative advice; b) has achieved some stability and there is sufficient experience upon which to base a statement or guideline; c) is relevant to the practice of a significant portion of ASHP's members; d) is within the purview of pharmacy practice in health systems; e) is without other sufficient guidance; and f) does not pose significant legal risks to ASHP. Another consideration is whether ASHP leadership believes that there is room for improvements in practice and that an ASHP document would foster that improvement. The Board of Directors must support the recommendations before developmental processes begin.

The processes used to draft and review new or revised documents vary depending on the body responsible for their development and on the type of document. These processes are described below. Once approved, the document draft becomes an official ASHP policy and is published in *AJHP*, added to ASHP's Web site, and incorporated into the next edition of this compendium. Therapeutic documents are reviewed and revised as needed every three years, and policy positions and practice documents every five years.

ASHP Statements and Guidelines

Any of the ASHP policy-recommending bodies (councils and commissions) may initiate and oversee the development of ASHP statements and guidelines; however, most of them are initiated by the Council on Pharmacy Practice. The development of these documents generally includes the following steps:

1. A group of experts on a given topic volunteers to develop a preliminary draft. Drafters are selected based on demonstrated knowledge of the topic and their practice settings. Most often, the drafters are ASHP members.
2. The draft is sent by ASHP to reviewers who have interest and expertise in the given topic. Reviewers consist of members and selected individuals knowledgeable in the content area, representatives of various ASHP bodies, and other professional organizations. A draft of particular interest to ASHP's membership may be published in *AJHP*, posted on ASHP's Web site, or discussed at an open hearing or in a network forum during an ASHP Summer or Midyear Clinical meeting to solicit comments.
3. Based on the comments, a revised draft is submitted to the appropriate ASHP policy-recommending body for action. When the draft meets the established criteria for content and quality, that body recommends that the Board of Directors approve the document.

ASHP Therapeutic Guidelines and Therapeutic Position Statements

The Council on Therapeutics (COT) has responsibility for the development of ASHP therapeutic guidelines and ASHP therapeutic position statements.

Therapeutic Guidelines—The development of these documents generally includes the following steps:

1. When the COT identifies a topic for therapeutic guidelines development, ASHP formally solicits proposals for a contractual arrangement with an individual, group, or organization to draft the guidelines document and coordinate its review. The contractor will work with a panel of 6–10 experts appointed by ASHP who have diverse backgrounds relevant to the topic.
2. A systematic analysis of the literature is performed, and scientific evidence is evaluated based on predetermined criteria. Recommendations in the document are based on scientific evidence or expert consensus. When expert judgment must be used, the document indicates the scientific reasoning that influenced the decision. Scientific evidence takes precedence over expert judgement. Each recommendation is accompanied by projections of the relevant health and cost outcomes that could result.
3. The expert panel and COT review each draft of the guidelines document and provide comments. This process is repeated until the expert panel and COT are satisfied with the content.
4. ASHP solicits multidisciplinary expert input on the draft. Reviewers consist of members and selected individuals knowledgeable in the content area, representatives of various ASHP bodies, and other professional organizations.
5. Once the above processes are completed, COT recommends that the ASHP Board of Directors approve it.

ASHP Therapeutic Position Statements (TPS)—The development of these documents generally includes the following steps:

1. One or more experts on a given topic are assigned to draft the TPS. Drafters are selected based on demonstrated knowledge of the topic and their practice setting. Most often, the drafters are ASHP members.
2. The proposed draft document is reviewed by COT, which may suggest modifications. This process is repeated until COT is satisfied with the content.

3. ASHP solicits multidisciplinary expert input on the draft. Reviewers consist of members and selected individuals knowledgeable in the content area, representatives of various ASHP bodies, and other professional organizations.
4. Once the above processes are completed, COT finalizes the draft and recommends that the ASHP Board of Directors approve it.

Access to ASHP Positions and Guidance Documents

Besides publishing in *AJHP* and this compendium, policy positions and guidance documents are available through ASHP's Web site at **www.ashp.org.** They are located at the "Policy Positions & Guidelines" heading under "Policy and Practice" on the ASHP Web site (www.ashp.org/bestpractices), where a chronological compendium of policy positions (*ASHP Policy Positions 1982–2015*) is also available.

Opportunities to Be a Part of Guidance Document Development

ASHP members determine the needs for policy guidance documents. They write and review the drafts. And, as members of policy-recommending bodies, the Board of Directors, and House of Delegates, they approve the documents.

ASHP members are encouraged to take an active role in the development of documents by suggesting topic ideas for new documents or modifications to current ones, volunteering to be drafters or reviewers, and completing survey and evaluation forms. Members may comment on or express their interests in participating in the development of documents by contacting the editor at (301) 657-3000 or by e-mail at standards@ashp.org.

Mission Statement of the American Society of Health-System Pharmacists (ASHP)

The mission of pharmacists is to help people achieve optimal health outcomes. ASHP helps its members achieve this mission by advocating and supporting the professional practice of pharmacists in hospitals, health systems, ambulatory clinics, and other settings spanning the full spectrum of medication use. ASHP serves its members as their collective voice on issues related to medication use and public health.

Approved by the ASHP Board of Directors, December 6, 2012.

Vision Statement of the American Society of Health-System Pharmacists (ASHP)

ASHP's vision is that medication use will be optimal, safe, and effective for all people all of the time.

Approved by the ASHP Board of Directors, December 6, 2012.

ASHP Policy Positions, Statements, Guidelines, and Technical Assistance Bulletins

Automation and Information Technology

Automation and Information Technology

Online Pharmacy and Internet Prescribing (1529)
Source: Council on Pharmacy Practice
To support efforts to regulate prescribing and dispensing of medications via the Internet; further,

To support legislation or regulation that requires online pharmacies to list the states in which the pharmacy and pharmacists are licensed, and, if prescribing services are offered, requires that the sites (1) ensure that a legitimate patient-prescriber relationship exists (consistent with professional practice standards) and (2) list the states in which the prescribers are licensed; further,

To support mandatory accreditation of online pharmacies by the National Association of Boards of Pharmacy Verified Internet Pharmacy Practice Sites or Veterinary-Verified Internet Pharmacy Practice Sites; further,

To support appropriate consumer education about the risks and benefits of using online pharmacies; further,

To support the principle that any medication distribution or drug therapy management system must provide timely access to, and interaction with, appropriate professional pharmacist patient-care services.

This policy supersedes ASHP policy 0523.

Risk Assessment of Health Information Technology (1418)
Source: Council on Pharmacy Management
To urge hospitals and health systems to directly involve departments of pharmacy in performing appropriate risk assessment before new health information technology (HIT) is implemented or existing HIT is upgraded, and as part of the continuous evaluation of current HIT performance; further,

To advocate that HIT vendors provide estimates of the resources required to implement and support new HIT; further,

To collaborate with HIT vendors to encourage the development of HIT that improves patient-care outcomes; further,

To advocate for changes in federal law that would recognize HIT vendors' safety accountability.

Interoperability of Patient-Care Technologies (1302)
Source: Council on Pharmacy Management
To encourage interdisciplinary development and implementation of technical and semantic standards for health information technology (HIT) that would promote the interoperability of patient-care technologies that utilize medication-related databases (e.g., medication order processing systems, automated dispensing cabinets, intelligent infusion pumps, electronic health records); further,

To encourage the integration, consolidation, and harmonization of medication-related databases used in patient-care technologies to reduce the risk that outdated, inaccurate, or conflicting data might be used and to minimize the resources required to maintain such databases.

Pharmacist's Role in Health Care Information Systems (1211)
Source: Council on Pharmacy Management
To strongly advocate key decision-making roles for pharmacists in the planning, selection, design, implementation, and maintenance of medication-use information systems, electronic health records, computerized provider order entry systems, and e-prescribing systems to facilitate clinical decision support, data analysis, and education of users for the purpose of ensuring the safe and effective use of medications; further,

To advocate for incentives to hospitals and health systems for the adoption of patient-care technologies; further,

To recognize that design and maintenance of medication-use information systems is an interdisciplinary process that requires ongoing collaboration among many disciplines; further,

To advocate that pharmacists must have accountability for strategic planning and direct operational aspects of the medication-use process, including the successful deployment of medication-use information systems.

This policy supersedes ASHP policy 0921.

Clinical Decision Support Systems (1212)
Source: Council on Pharmacy Management
To advocate for the development of clinical decision support (CDS) systems that are proven to improve medication-use outcomes and that include the following capabilities: (1) alerts, notifications, and summary data views provided to the appropriate people at the appropriate times in clinical workflows, based on (a) a rich set of patient-specific data, (b) standardized, evidence-based medication-use best practices, and (c) identifiable patterns in medication-use data in the electronic health record; (2) audit trails of all CDS alerts, notifications, and follow-up activity; (3) structured clinical documentation functionality linked to individual CDS alerts and notifications; and (4) highly accessible and detailed management reporting capabilities that facilitate assessment of the quality and completeness of CDS responses and the effects of CDS on patient outcomes.

Definition of Meaningful Use of Health Information Technology (1006)
Source: Council on Public Policy
To advocate to policymakers (public and private) that definitions of "meaningful use of health information technology" address interoperability of medication orders and prescriptions, medication decision support and continuous improvement, and quality reporting; further,

To advocate with respect to interoperability of medication orders and prescriptions that (1) a common medication vocabulary be mandated to promote the semantic interoperability of medication use across the continuum of care, because a common vocabulary is essential for comparative effectiveness research and for communicating medication information; and (2) communication of orders and electronic prescriptions must be demonstrated to be functional and semantically interoperable with pharmacy information systems; further,

To advocate with respect to medication decision support and continuous improvement that (1) medication decision support should include but not be limited to allergy, drug interaction (e.g., drug-lab or drug-disease interactions), duplicate therapy, and dose-range checking; and (2) that such a decision-support service must include an ongoing, continuous improvement process to attune the decision-support service to the needs of the providers who use it; further,

To advocate with respect to quality reporting that the ability to quantify improved patient safety, quality outcomes, and cost reductions in the medication-use process is essential, particularly in antimicrobial and adverse event surveillance.

This policy was reviewed in 2014 by the Council on Public Policy and by the Board of Directors and was found to still be appropriate.

Role of Pharmacists in Safe Technology Implementation (1020)

Source: Council on Pharmacy Practice

To affirm the essential role of the pharmacist in the evaluation, implementation, and ongoing assessment of all technology intended to ensure safety, effectiveness, and efficiency of the medication-use process.

This policy was reviewed in 2014 by the Council on Pharmacy Practice and by the Board of Directors and was found to still be appropriate.

Electronic Health and Business Technology and Services (0712)

Source: Council on Pharmacy Practice

To encourage pharmacists to assume a leadership role in their hospitals and health systems with respect to strategic planning for and implementation of electronic health and business technology and services; further,

To encourage hospital and health-system administrators to provide dedicated resources for pharmacy departments to design, implement, and maintain electronic health and business technology and services; further,

To advocate the inclusion of electronic health technology and telepharmacy issues and applications in college of pharmacy curricula.

This policy was reviewed in 2011 by the Council on Pharmacy Practice and by the Board of Directors and was found to still be appropriate.

Electronic Information Systems (0507)

Source: Council on Administrative Affairs

To advocate the use of electronic information systems, with appropriate security controls, that enable the integration of patient-specific data that is accessible in all components of a health system; further,

To support the use of technology that allows the transfer of patient information needed for appropriate medication management across the continuum of care; further,

To urge computer software vendors and pharmaceutical suppliers to provide standards for definition, collection, coding, and exchange of clinical data used in the medication-use process; further,

To pursue formal and informal liaisons with appropriate health care associations to ensure that the interests of patient care and safety in the medication-use process are fully represented in the standardization, integration, and implementation of electronic information systems; further,

To strongly encourage health-system administrators, regulatory bodies, and other appropriate groups to provide health-system pharmacists with full access to patient-specific clinical data.

This policy was reviewed in 2014 by the Council on Pharmacy Practice and by the Board of Directors and was found to still be appropriate.

Computerized Prescriber Order Entry (0105)

Source: Council on Administrative Affairs

To advocate the use of computerized entry of medication orders or prescriptions by the prescriber when (1) it is planned, implemented, and managed with pharmacists' involvement, (2) such orders are part of a single, shared database that is fully integrated with the pharmacy information system and other key information system components, especially the patient's medication administration record, (3) such computerized order entry improves the safety, efficiency, and accuracy of the medication-use process, and (4) it includes provisions for the pharmacist to review and verify the order's appropriateness before medication administration, except in those instances when review would cause a medically unacceptable delay.

This policy was reviewed in 2010 by the Council on Pharmacy Management and by the Board of Directors and was found to still be appropriate.

Telepharmacy (9920)

Source: Council on Professional Affairs

To foster among health-system pharmacists and leaders of the telecommunications industry a common vision for the integration of telecommunication technology into the delivery of pharmaceutical care.

This policy was reviewed in 2008 by the Council on Pharmacy Practice and by the Board of Directors and was found to still be appropriate.

Regulation of Automated Drug Distribution Systems (9813)

Source: Council on Legal and Public Affairs

To work with the Drug Enforcement Administration and other agencies to seek regulatory and policy changes to accommodate automated drug distribution in health systems.

This policy was reviewed in 2012 by the Council on Public Policy and by the Board of Directors and was found to still be appropriate.

ASHP Statement on Bar-Code-Enabled Medication Administration Technology

Position

The American Society of Health-System Pharmacists (ASHP) encourages health systems to adopt bar-code-enabled medication administration (BCMA) technology to improve patient safety and the accuracy of medication administration and documentation. To support the goal of having all medications electronically verified before they are administered, BCMA systems should be used in all areas of health systems in which medications are used. Pharmacists must be involved in the interdisciplinary planning, development, implementation, and management of BCMA systems and must ultimately be responsible for developing and maintaining the infrastructure required to ensure BCMA success. Health systems deploying BCMA programs must provide the funding and staffing necessary to permit pharmacists to fulfill this role.

ASHP urges the Food and Drug Administration (FDA) and other regulatory agencies, standard-setting bodies, contracting entities, health systems, and others to mandate that pharmaceutical manufacturers use symbologies that are readily deciphered by commonly used scanning equipment to code for the National Drug Code (NDC), lot number, and expiration date on all unit dose, unit-of-use, and injectable drug packaging. Pharmaceutical manufacturers should also provide all medications used in health systems in unit dose packages. FDA, pharmaceutical manufacturers and packagers, and the manufacturers of BCMA systems should collaborate to minimize or eliminate the causes of false rejection of valid medication doses. Certain characteristics of the current NDC identification system contribute to the burden of implementing BCMA systems, and ASHP urges stakeholders to participate in efforts to develop a system that more reliably identifies the unique drug (or combination of drugs), strength, dosage form, and route of administration.

Although bar-coding systems are currently a widely used point-of-care technology, ASHP recognizes that other types of machine-readable coding (e.g., radio-frequency identification) may evolve. ASHP supports the use of new technologies that are as effective as or improve upon existing systems and believes the principles outlined in this statement apply to such systems. ASHP urges further research on such systems as well as research that will definitively determine the extent to which BCMA systems reduce preventable medication errors and provide a financial return on investment for health systems.

Background

Since the 1980s, health care practitioners and policymakers have recognized the potential benefits of using bar-coding technology in the medication dispensing and administration process.[1–5] Although there is a consensus of professional judgment and expert opinion on the advancement of BCMA technology, more studies are needed to definitively determine the impact of BCMA systems on medication errors and the finances of health systems. ASHP believes that optimally implemented BCMA systems have tremendous potential to improve patient safety. In addition, the reengineering of the medication-use process required to implement a BCMA system can provide opportunities for performance improvement in patient care and clinical documentation.

A 2005 ASHP survey estimated that only 13.2% of hospitals used a BCMA system.[6] Although this percentage is small, it represents an almost 10-fold increase since 2002.[7] The rapid adoption of BCMA systems presents challenges to health systems, and ASHP believes that pharmacists have a crucial role in responding to those challenges.

Role of the Pharmacist

Pharmacists should take the lead in ensuring that the implementation of BCMA systems and the reengineering of the medication-use system address the complexities of the process and that the goal of improving patient safety is achieved. Poor design and inadequate planning can compromise the effectiveness of a BCMA system and may even introduce new sources of error into the medication-use process.[8] Growing experience with BCMA systems has produced a body of knowledge that will aid hospitals and health systems in the adoption of BCMA systems.[9–12]

Pharmacy leadership needs to engage the chief information officer, chief nursing officer, and other key stakeholders in planning for BCMA systems as early as possible. Pharmacists and nurses should be involved with the preinstallation evaluation and selection of the BCMA system. Allowing end users to provide crucial advice about system design will increase acceptance and utility of the system.

Implementation of a BCMA system must be accompanied by the development of policies and procedures that ensure the system's safety. These policies and procedures should be developed by an interdisciplinary team that includes pharmacists.[10] Pharmacists and nurses should be involved with postinstallation evaluation and system improvement.

The role of nurses as end users of this technology should not be underestimated; nursing involvement is essential to successful system implementation and use. Processes for delivery and storage of medications (e.g., in medicine rooms or bedside storage spaces) should be examined by pharmacists and nurses to avoid workarounds or diversion.

Elements of a BCMA System

Although every hospital and health system will need to develop a BCMA system that meets its own needs, the following general principles should guide the implementation and use of such systems.

Use of the BCMA system should be universal within the health system. To the fullest extent feasible, every patient, care provider, and medication should receive a unique identifier, and that identifier should be used not only to verify care prescribed for a patient but also to document every significant step in the medication-use process.

A process should be in place to ensure simple, secure, and controllable placement and replacement of a patient identification tag. To ensure that there is only one active wristband per patient, this process should discourage the printing of multiple labels.[12] In addition to appropriate human-readable information, machine-readable patient wristbands should contain information (e.g., a photograph or the patient's medical record number) in order to uniquely identify the patient.

The BCMA system should have a secure user-identification system. Every care provider should be assigned and use a unique identifier. The care provider administering a medication should be able to use the BCMA system to verify that the medication to be administered is appropriate for the patient (i.e., confirming that the five rights of medication administration[13] are met). The BCMA system should document the information in the electronic medication administration record.

The pharmacy must be able to ensure that doses received in patient care areas can be scanned without inappropriate rejection and that those scans reliably indicate whether the medication is appropriate for a particular patient. For the implementation of a BCMA system to succeed, the health system must commit the pharmacy resources necessary to verify that each incoming medication is scannable and that the data encoded within its bar code accurately represent the product.

Every medication possible should be packaged in unit doses, and each unit dose package should be labeled with both human-readable medication identification information and a machine-readable code that includes the medication's unique identifier and, when feasible, its lot number and expiration date. Pharmacy information systems must be able to generate bar codes for multiple-component items. Pharmacy departments must develop a validation process for ensuring that every item has a bar code that can be scanned by all equipment supporting the BCMA system, including pharmacy automation systems, automated medication storage and distribution devices, and nursing BCMA scanning units.

An adequate number of scanners should be provided for each patient care area to facilitate scanning at peak times. Scanners should have the capacity to autodiscriminate the variety of symbologies encountered on pharmaceutical and pharmacy-prepared containers.

Finally, contingency plans should exist to ensure patient safety during system downtime. These policies should require that medications administered during downtime are retrospectively documented electronically in the medical record so that decision-support systems accurately reflect clinical trends associated with the patient, medication administration, and medication effects.

Conclusion

ASHP encourages health systems to adopt BCMA technology, with the goal of having all medications electronically verified before they are administered. Pharmacists must ultimately be responsible for developing and maintaining the infrastructure necessary to ensure BCMA success, and health systems deploying BCMA systems must provide the funding and staffing necessary to permit pharmacists to fulfill this role.

ASHP believes that pharmaceutical manufacturers should be required to place machine-readable coding that includes the NDC, lot number, and expiration date on all unit dose, unit-of-use, and injectable drug packaging, using symbologies that are readily deciphered by commonly used scanning equipment. ASHP also urges further research that will definitively determine the extent to which BCMA systems reduce preventable medication errors or provide a financial return on investment for health systems.

References

1. Hokanson JA, Keith MR, Guernsey BG et al. Potential use of barcodes to implement automated dispensing quality assurance programs. *Hosp Pharm.* 1985; 20:327–37.
2. Nold EG, Williams TC. Barcodes and their potential applications in hospital pharmacy. *Am J Hosp Pharm.* 1985; 42:2722–32.
3. Barry GA, Bass GE, Eddlemon JK et al. Bar-code technology for documenting administration of large-volume intravenous solutions. *Am J Hosp Pharm.* 1989; 46:282–7.
4. Lefkowitz S, Cheiken H, Barhart MR. A trial of the use of bar code technology to restructure a drug distribution and administration system. *Hosp Pharm.* 1991; 26:239–42.
5. Meyer GE, Brandell R, Smith JE et al. Use of bar codes in inpatient drug distribution. *Am J Hosp Pharm.* 1991; 48:953–66.
6. Pedersen CA, Schneider PJ, Scheckelhoff DJ. ASHP national survey of pharmacy practice in hospital settings: dispensing and administration—2005. *Am J Health-Syst Pharm.* 2006; 63:327–45.
7. Pedersen CA, Schneider PJ, Scheckelhoff DJ. ASHP national survey of pharmacy practice in hospital settings: dispensing and administration—2002. *Am J Health-Syst Pharm.* 2003; 60:52–68.
8. Patterson ES, Cook RI, Render ML. Improving patient safety by identifying side effects of introducing bar coding in medication administration. *J Am Med Inform Assoc.* 2002; 9:540–53.
9. Patterson E, Rogers M, Render M. Fifteen best practice recommendations for bar-code medication administration in the Veterans Health Administration. *Joint Comm J Qual Saf.* 2004; 30:355–65.
10. Neuenschwander M, Cohen MR, Vaida AJ et al. Practical guide to bar coding for patient medication safety. *Am J Health-Syst Pharm.* 2003; 60:768–79.
11. ASHP Research and Education Foundation Implementing a bar-coded medication safety program: a pharmacist's toolkit. www.ashpfoundation.org/MainMenuCategories/Education/SpecialPrograms/ImplementingaBarCodedMedSafetyProgram.aspx (accessed 2008 Dec 3).
12. Cummings J, Bush P, Smith D et al. Bar-coding medication administration overview and consensus recommendations. *Am J Health-Syst Pharm.* 2005; 62:2626–9.
13. 10 Golden rules for administering drugs safely. In: McGovern K. Preventing medication errors. Springhouse, PA: Springhouse; 1994:2–3.

Suggested Readings or Other Resources

ASHP guidelines on preventing medication errors in hospitals. *Am J Hosp Pharm.* 1993; 50:305–14.

Aspden P, Wolcott J, Bootman JL et al., eds. Preventing medication errors: quality chasm series. Washington, DC: National Academies Press; 2007.

Cohen MR, ed. Medication errors. Washington, DC: American Pharmaceutical Association; 1999.

Johnson CL, Carlson RA, Tucker CL et al. Using BCMA software to improve patient safety in Veterans Administration medical centers. *J Healthc Inf Manage.* 2002; 16:46–51.

Leape LL. Error in medicine. *JAMA.* 1994; 272:1851–7.

Poon EG, Cina JL, Churchill W et al. Medication dispensing errors and potential adverse drug events before and after implementing bar code technology in the pharmacy. *Ann Intern Med.* 2006; 145:426–34.

Puckett F. Medication management component of a point of care information system. *Am J Health-Syst Pharm.* 1995; 52:1305–9.

Developed through the ASHP Section of Pharmacy Informatics and Technology and approved by the ASHP Board of Directors on March 7, 2008, and by the ASHP House of Delegates on June 10, 2008. Supersedes ASHP policy position 0308.

Arash T. Dabestani, Pharm.D., M.H.A. and Alicia B. Perry, Pharm.D., are gratefully acknowledged for drafting versions of this statement.

The bibliographic citation for this document is as follows: American Society of Health-System Pharmacists. ASHP statement on bar-code-enabled medication administration technology. *Am J Health-Syst Pharm.* 2009; 66:588–90.

ASHP Statement on Bar-Code Verification During Inventory, Preparation, and Dispensing of Medications

Position

The American Society of Health-System Pharmacists encourages hospital and health-system pharmacies to incorporate bar-code scanning into inventory management, dose preparation and packaging, and dispensing of medications. The purpose of such scanning is to ensure that drug products distributed, deployed to intermediate storage areas, or used in the preparation of patient doses are the correct products, are in-date, and have not been recalled. Such bar-code scanning should be employed in:

- Stocking of inventory both in the pharmacy and in other locations from which patient medications may be dispensed (e.g., an automated dispensing device),
- Manual packaging of oral solid and liquid medications,
- Compounding, repackaging, and labeling processes (e.g., scanning of source ingredients),
- Retrieving medications from automated dispensing devices, and
- Dispensing from the pharmacy to any location.

Prudent use of bar-coding technology in these processes will enhance patient safety and the quality of care by improving the accuracy of core pharmacy functions, closing potential gaps in the bar-code-assisted medication administration (BCMA) process, and allowing better allocation of pharmacists' knowledge and skills.

Background

Discussion of the role of technology in improving medication safety almost universally focuses on BCMA or computerized provider order entry (CPOE), despite evidence of medication errors that neither CPOE nor BCMA could prevent.[1,2] A number of activities in the medication-use process create opportunities for error outside of medication ordering and administration systems, such as:

- Receiving of inventory from suppliers and stocking of inventory locations from which patient medications may be dispensed (e.g., stocking unit-based automated dispensing devices with medications that may not be delivered to the bedside in their original packaging).
- Packaging of medications, which has become more prevalent as BCMA systems are more widely adopted by health systems and manufacturers have discontinued unit dose packaging of medications.
- Manual packaging of liquid medications in ready-to-administer form.
- The compounding of medications.
- The dispensing of patient-specific medications (e.g., 24-hour medication carts, nurse servers).

In addition, for BCMA to function, a vast majority of doses must be accurately bar coded, meaning there must be a highly reliable relationship between the information in the bar code and the contents of the dose. Additionally, the bar code must be readable by commercially-available scanners. Although doses delivered directly from manufacturer-labeled packages generally meet these conditions, there are numerous drug products that may not:

- Commercial products may lack a readily readable bar code, may have an irregular package shape that confounds the ability of scanning equipment to read the bar code, or may have a bar code in a symbology format that cannot be interpreted by the institution's bar-code scanning software.
- Nurse-prepared medications (e.g., insulin doses, heparin boluses, or syringes pre-drawn in the operating room) may be prepared at a location other than the patient's bedside, with the result that there is no labeling of any kind on the dose when it is administered.
- Compounded medications (e.g., sterile preparations) are often labeled by the pharmacy with a bar code that references a prescription or order number that describes the intended contents of the prescribed dose but provides no assurance that the prescribed contents were actually used in the product's preparation.

Benefits of Bar-Code Verification During Inventory, Preparation, and Dispensing

Initial estimates of the contribution of pharmacy dispensing errors to the overall medication errors were quite low.[3] However, recent reports have suggested that adding bar coding to the pharmacy dispensing process can significantly reduce opportunities for medication errors at the bedside and reduce the occurrence of potential adverse drug reactions.[4-6] Incorporating bar-code scanning in inventory management, dose preparation and packaging, and dispensing can improve patient safety in the following ways:

- Scanning during stocking in the pharmacy or patient-care locations (e.g., loading of an automated dispensing device) can help ensure that the product is placed in the correct location.
- Scanning during the retrieval of medications mitigates the hazards of erroneous medication stocking, which is especially important in the case of automated dispensing devices, where there is a potential risk that caregivers will override controls and remove medications for immediate use.
- Scanning of source ingredients during compounding, repackaging, or labeling processes can ensure that labeled doses contain the appropriate ingredients. Additionally, such scanning creates a reliable link be-

tween the information in the final package's bar code, its contents, and the National Drug Code (NDC) of the source container, which may be required to satisfy billing requirements (e.g., those of the Centers for Medicare & Medicaid Services).

- Scanning on dispensing can help prevent look-alike, sound-alike medication substitution errors that are difficult to visually detect, can identify and remove from distribution drug products whose bar codes are missing or unreadable, and prevent the distribution of expired or recalled products or facilitate retrieval in case of a recall.
- Scanning during any of these activities permits accumulation of an audit trail for each transaction in the inventory, preparation, and dispensing process. This information provides indications of the frequency of error encounter and detection, a record of the amount of time needed to perform selected functions, and evidence of success or failure of manual processes to deliver the correct medication.

Bar-code verification is optimized, and its potential negative impacts on productivity minimized, when the scanning system is configured to use bar codes on bulk packages (e.g., the bar code on an unopened case of unit-dose-packaged tablets) to confirm the contents of each item in the case, especially during batch processes. For patient-specific doses, each individual container used for the dose must be scanned.

The equipment and training costs for a pharmacy-based bar-code scanning implementation is quite small, especially when compared to those of BCMA systems.[7] Pharmacy-based bar-code scanning implementation may be considered a prerequisite for BCMA success, because unreadable bar codes are a significant cause of BCMA implementation failures.[8,9]

Limitations

As with BCMA, adoption of bar code scanning within distribution processes creates the necessity to ensure that the scanning system will recognize and appropriately respond to every bar code it scans. This verification activity is likely to create significant additional work for the pharmacy. Pharmacies planning on implementing such systems must plan for the resources needed to ensure that properly bar-coded products are presented to, and readable by, the scanning system.

In addition, as with other bar-code technology implementations, pharmacy-based bar-code scanning systems will only be beneficial if appropriately deployed. For example, given the need to scan three vials of medication to prepare an IV admixture, such a system cannot distinguish between scanning each vial and scanning the same vial three times, although the latter defeats the purpose of the scanning. Any program of pharmacy-based bar-code scanning should be accompanied by appropriate training, policies, and procedures to promote and optimize safe use of the system, as well as a regular program of auditing to ensure that the program is being properly deployed by staff. Additionally, such programs require hospitals and health systems to compile and maintain a complete database of bar codes in use throughout the institution. The availability of such information in a timely fashion is a well-recognized problem.[10] An incomplete database or the absence of bar codes on drug products can undermine the entire system, as the system cannot properly recognize and evaluate the drug products being scanned. Procedures should address such issues as the expected behavior while scanning occurs, specific prohibited acts, and the penalties associated with known at-risk behavior.[11]

In addition, this statement should not be interpreted to express a preference for bar-code scanning over other forms of automated identification of medications. Currently, bar coding is the least-expensive mechanism to introduce and deploy throughout the medication management cycle.[12] Should other technologies (e.g., radio-frequency identification) demonstrate similar or better capabilities, the principles articulated in this statement will continue to apply.

Validation

As with all such systems, bar coding on dispensing presumes that the scanning software, the scanning hardware, and the associated underlying database are accurate and complete. To ensure accuracy and completeness, organizations using a bar coding process will need to validate both that the software operates as expected and that the underlying database information is correct and reliable. A process will also need to be in place to immediately remediate problems if it is discovered that the hardware, software, or database are not operating properly.

Conclusion

Prudent use of bar-code scanning in inventory management, dose preparation and packaging, and dispensing of medications can enhance patient safety and the quality of care. Such scanning also provides the opportunity to accumulate and use statistics on the pharmacy distributive operation that can direct more appropriate staffing, identify sources of routine error, and generally permit better management of the drug distribution process.

References

1. Wolf R. Preventable medication error responsible for infant deaths. Injury Board.com. Available at: http://dallas.injuryboard.com/medical-malpractice/preventable-medication-error-responsible-for-infant-deaths.aspx?googleid=206592 (accessed 2010 Jan 11).
2. Institute for Safe Medication Practices. Failed check system for chemotherapy leads to pharmacist's no contest plea for involuntary manslaughter. www.ismp.org/Newsletters/acutecare/articles/20090423.asp (accessed 2010 Mar 4).
3. Bates DW, Cullen DJ, Laird N et al. Incidence of adverse drug events and potential adverse drug events. Implications for prevention. ADE Prevention Study Group. *JAMA.* 1995; 274:29–34.
4. Cina J, Fanikos J, Mitton P et al. Medication errors in a pharmacy-based bar-code-repackaging center. *Am J Health-Syst Pharm.* 2006; 63:165–8.
5. Poon EG, Cina JL, Churchill W et al. Medication dispensing errors and potential adverse drug events before and after implementing bar code technology in the pharmacy. *Ann Intern Med.* 2006;145:426–34.

6. Ragan R, Bond J, Major K et al. Improved control of medication use with an integrated bar-code-packaging and distribution system. *Am J Health-Syst Pharm.* 2005; 62:1075–9.
7. Maviglia SM, Yoo JY, Franz C et al. Cost-benefit analysis of a hospital pharmacy bar code solution. *Arch Intern Med.* 2007; 167:788–94.
8. Koppel R, Wetterneck T, Telles JL et al. Workarounds to barcode medication administration systems: their occurrences, causes and threats to patient safety. *J Am Med Inform Assoc.* 2008;15:408–23.
9. Young D. VA pursues bar code quality. *Am J Health-Syst Pharm.* 2004; 61:1312–4.
10. ASHP statement on bar-code-enabled medication administration technology. *Am J Health-Syst Pharm.* 2009; 66:588–90. www.ashp.org/DocLibrary/BestPractices/AutoITStBCMA.aspx. (accessed 2010 Mar 4).
11. ASHP policy position 0910: reporting medication errors. In: Hawkins B, ed. *Best practices for hospital and health-system pharmacy: positions and guidance documents of ASHP.* 2009-2010 ed. Bethesda, MD: American Society of Health-System Pharmacists; 2006:160. www.ashp.org/DocLibrary/BestPractices/MedMisPositions09.aspx (accessed 2010 Mar 08).
12. Cummings J, Bush P, Smith D et al. Bar-coding medication administration: overview and consensus recommendations. *Am J Health-Syst Pharm.* 2005; 62:2626–9.

Suggested Reading

Bates DW, Cullen JC, Laird N et al. Incidence of adverse drug events and potential adverse drug events. *JAMA.* 1995; 274:29–34.

Nold EG, Williams TC. Bar codes and their potential applications in hospital pharmacy. *Am J Hosp Pharm.* 1985; 42:2722–32.

Meyer GE, Brandell R, Smith JE et al. Use of bar codes in inpatient drug distribution. *Am J Hosp Pharm.* 1991; 48:953–66.

Santell JP, Hicks RW, McMeekin J et al. Medication errors: experience of the United States Pharmacopeia (USP) MEDMARX reporting system. *J Clin Pharmacol.* 2003; 43:760–7.

Ness JE, Sullivan SD, Stergachis A. Accuracy of technicians and pharmacists in identifying dispensing errors. *Am J Health-Syst Pharm.* 1994; 51:354–7.

Oswald S, Caldwell R. Dispensing error rate after implementation of an automated pharmacy carousel system. *Am J Health-Syst Pharm.* 2007; 64:1427–31.

Cina J, Fanikos J, Mitton P et al. Medication errors in a pharmacy-based bar-code-repackaging center. *Am J Health-Syst Pharm.* 2006; 63:165–8.

Ambrose PJ, Saya FG, Lovett LT et al. Evaluating the accuracy of technicians and pharmacists in checking unit dose medication cassettes. *Am J Health-Syst Pharm.* 2002; 59:1183–8.

Shane R. Current status of administration of medicines. *Am J Health-Syst Pharm.* 2009; 66:s42–s48.

Blair R. Medication transformation: pharmacists on the floor. A Midwest healthcare system takes bar code technology to new heights, as part of an enterprise initiative to optimize patient safety. *Health Manag Technol.* 2004; 25:26, 28, 30.

Nanji KC, Cina J, Patel N et al. Overcoming barriers to the implementation of a pharmacy bar code scanning system for medication dispensing: a case study. *J Am Med Inform Assoc.* 2009; 16:645–50.

Developed through the ASHP Section of Pharmacy Informatics and Technology and approved by the ASHP Board of Directors on April 15, 2010, and by the ASHP House of Delegates on June 6, 2010.

This statement was drafted by the ASHP Section of Pharmacy Informatics and Technology 2009–2010 Section Advisory Group on Pharmacy Operations Automation (Dennis A. Tribble, Pharm.D.; Ron Burnette, B.S.Pharm., M.B.A.; Dawn M. Biller; Leslie Brookins, M.S.; Richard Capps III, Pharm.D.; Marvin H. Choi; Kavish J. Choudhary, Pharm.D., M.S.; Seth Aaron Cohen, Pharm.D.; Thomas W. Cooley M.B.A.; Arash T. Dabestani, Pharm.D., M.H.A., FABC; Charles De la Torre, M.S., MIS; Doina Dumitru, Pharm.D., M.B.A.; Christopher Fortier, B.S.Pharm.; Barbara Giacomelli, Pharm.D., MBA, FASHP; Staci Hermann, M.S., Pharm.D.; Gary L. Johnson, Jr., Pharm.D., M.H.A.; Seth A. Kuiper, Pharm.D.; Denise Mckenzie, B.S.Pharm.; Rhonda B. McManus, Pharm.D.; Eric C. Nemec, II, Pharm.D.; Beth Prier, Pharm.D., M.S.; Brad Rognrud, M.S., R.Ph.; Kevin A. Scheckelhoff, M.B.A.; Paul M. Seelinger, B.S.Pharm.; Suzanne B. Shea, M.B.A.; David A. Tjhio, M.S., Pharm.D.; Christopher J. Urbanski, M.S.; Gwen Volpe, B.S.Pharm.; Rayburn Brian Vrabel, Pharm.D.; and Robynn P. Wolfschlag, M.B.A.).

ASHP gratefully acknowledges the following organizations and individuals for reviewing drafts of this statement (review does not imply endorsement): American Association of Critical Care Nurses (AACCN); American Nurses Association (ANA); Institute for Safe Medication Practices (ISMP); Rhode Island Society of Health System Pharmacists (RISHP); South Carolina Society of Health-System Pharmacists (SCSHP); Wyoming Society of Health-System Pharmacy (WSHP); Linda Annecchini, M.S.; James L. Besier, Ph.D., FASHP; Carol J. Bickford, Ph.D., RN-BC (ANA); Denny C. Briley, Pharm.D.; Mary E. Burkhardt, M.S., FASHP; Richard Capps, Pharm.D.; William W. Churchill, M.S.; Debra Cowan, Pharm.D.; Michele Danish, Pharm.D, FASHP; Brent I. Fox, Pharm.D., Ph.D.; Karl F. Gumpper, BCNSP, BCPS, FASHP; Kathleen M. Gura, Pharm.D., BCNSP, FASHP; J. Chad Hardy, Pharm.D., M.S.; Robi Hellman, RN, MSN, CNS (AACCN); Matthew R. Keith, B.S.Pharm., FASHP; Stan Kent, M.S.; Thomas E. Kirschling, Pharm.D., M.S.; Jim Lile, Pharm.D.; Jeff Little, Pharm.D., M.P.H.; Donald Lynx, M.B.A., FASHP; Leslie R. Mackowiak, M.S.; Linda Gore Martin, Pharm.D., M.B.A., BCPS (WSHP); Denise McKenzie, CPhT; Joel Melroy, Pharm.D., M.S., BCPS (SCSHP); Ian Orensky, Pharm.D., M.S.; Stephanie C. Peshek, Pharm.D., M.B.A., FASHP; Tommie Peterson, B.S.Pharm.; James Ponto, M.S., BCNP, FASHP; Brad Rognrud, M.S.; Martha J. Roberts, Pharm.D. (RISHP); Richard I. Sakai, Pharm.D., FASHP, FCSHP; Ronald Schneider, B.S.Pharm., M.H.A.; Paul Seelinger, B.S.Pharm.; Suzanne Shea, M.B.A.; Armen Simonian, Pharm.D.; Kirby K. Stiening, B.S.Pharm.; George Taniguchi, Pharm.D., M.P.H., M.A.; Greg Teale, Pharm.D.; Jennifer Thomas, Pharm.D.; Melanie J. Townsend, Pharm.D., BCPS; Dennis A. Tribble, Pharm.D.; Chris L. Tucker, B.S.Pharm.; Chris Urbanski, M.S.; Allen J. Vaida, Pharm.D., FASHP (ISMP); Rayburn B. Vrabel, Pharm.D.; Kelley A. Wasicek, B.S.Pharm.; and Jody Jacobson Wedret, FASHP, FCSHP.

The bibliographic citation for this document is as follows: American Society of Health-System Pharmacists. ASHP statement on bar-code verification during inventory, preparation, and dispensing of medications. *Am J Health-Syst Pharm.* 2011; 68:442–5.

ASHP Statement on the Pharmacist's Role in Clinical Informatics

Position

ASHP believes that pharmacists have the training, knowledge, background, and responsibility to assume a significant role in clinical informatics.

Background

Healthcare organizations continue to invest a significant amount of financial and human resource in health information technology (HIT) initiatives, including advanced clinical systems, electronic health records, business intelligence and analytics tools, and applications that deliver the highest levels of patient safety and value. This growth has led to a considerable demand for HIT workers but more importantly has identified the need for a workforce with training and skills to create a successful and safe interface between HIT and the healthcare delivery system. This workforce must understand healthcare; information and communication technology; and the people, processes, and culture of an organization. The intersection of these skills has commonly been described as the discipline of biomedical and health informatics, more recently termed clinical informatics.[1] Evidence continues to emerge regarding the value a well-trained individual in clinical informatics can bring to an organization faced with implementing highly complex and transformative HIT systems.[2,3]

Pharmacy informatics has grown to be an integral discipline within the clinical informatics domain, centered on the effective management and delivery of medication-related data, information, and knowledge across systems that support the medication-use process. Pharmacists' professional identity, education, training, and experience with medication management make them ideal candidates to play a significant role and fill a critical need in pharmacy informatics. Their firm understanding of core pharmacy operations, clinical practice, the medication-use process, standards, and regulations and their long history of utilizing technology to support medication management provide the essential components for effectively transitioning into this role. Despite the growing number of formally trained pharmacy informaticists, the path and skills required for a career in informatics has varied considerably, emphasizing the need to build core competencies and grow the number of available programs.[4-6] The American Board of Medical Specialties (ABMS) recognition of clinical informatics as a physician subspecialty will likely play an important role in evolving pharmacy informatics beyond its current state to one with a clinical edge, centered on analytics and delivering information and knowledge at the point of care. The ABMS decision may also impact the development of a standardized, interprofessional educational roadmap for individuals seeking a career in pharmacy informatics.[7-9]

Roles and Responsibilities

Pharmacists who practice clinical informatics must collaborate with other healthcare and information technology professionals to promote the safe, efficient, effective, timely, and optimal use of medications. They contribute to the transformation of healthcare by analyzing, designing, implementing, maintaining, and evaluating information and communication systems that improve medication-related outcomes and strengthen the pharmacist-patient relationship. The role of a pharmacy informaticist revolves around their knowledge of pharmacy practice, safe medication use, clinical decision-making, and improving medication therapy outcomes, combined with their understanding of the discipline of informatics and HIT systems.[10] Their primary roles and responsibilities must encompass five broadly defined categories:

> *Data, information, and knowledge management*—Managing medication-related information while promoting integration, interoperability, and information exchange.
>
> *Information and knowledge delivery*—Delivering medication-related information and knowledge throughout the clinical knowledge lifecycle, from the point of knowledge generation through cataloging, embedding knowledge into the workflow, and measuring the usage and effectiveness of that knowledge.
>
> *Practice analytics*—Developing point-of-business analytic solutions for improving decision-making.
>
> *Applied clinical informatics*—Applying user experiences, research, and theoretical informatics principles to improve clinical practice and usability.
>
> *Leadership and management of change*—Leading and participating in the procurement, development, implementation, customization, management, evaluation, and continuous improvement of clinical information systems.

Data, Information, and Knowledge Management. Pharmacy informaticists play a key role in maintaining the data, information, and knowledge assets across all systems that support medication management. They are instrumental in ensuring data quality and safety, minimizing data quality risks, and affirming medication-related data, information, and knowledge management best practices.[10,11] Data quality and information management best practices encompass:

- Providing the appropriate level of data governance and stewardship.
- Adopting standard human and machine interpretable formats.
- Utilizing controlled terminology for integration and interoperability.
- Ensuring that data are accurate, accessible, complete, consistent, current, timely, precise, at appropriate level of granularity, reliable, relevant, conforming, and

understandable across all data quality management domains.

- Ensuring consistent use of maps to internal and external standards and reference data.
- Ensuring that system architecture supports data interchange.
- Ensuring that data, information, and knowledge are audited, measured, and evaluated for effectiveness.
- Ensuring that data, information, and knowledge assets are validated, integrated, normalized, consolidated, and routinely optimized.
- Developing infrastructure for knowledge, metadata, and terminology management.
- Ensuring that information is readily and rapidly understood and accessed within the workflow.
- Ensuring that information and knowledge are centrally managed, collaboratively developed, and easily disseminated and maintained.
- Ensuring that information and knowledge are platform-independent.
- Developing tools to effectively maintain and manage data, information, and knowledge.

Maintenance roles and responsibilities include:

- Corrective maintenance—Taking corrective and educative steps required to correct problems with the utilization of a clinical information system or technology.
- Customized maintenance—Modifying features already in production systems that require updating or modification for user needs. Customized maintenance is essential in clinical information systems, as healthcare is constantly changing (e.g., with new drugs, new treatment guidance, new procedures).
- Enhancement maintenance—Improving the performance of applications and people associated with the use of tools.
- Preventive maintenance—Taking steps in advance to reduce the risk of a problem that includes testing prior to a new release or system upgrade.[12]

Information and Knowledge Delivery. Healthcare delivery is inherently complex and knowledge-dependent, and it is becoming ever more challenging for providers to absorb and assimilate the growing volume and granularity of knowledge needed for safe and effective patient care. The clinical knowledge available is often conflicted, misaligned, and not readily identified or available at the point of care. To serve the needs of any clinical encounter, relevant patient-centered knowledge must be accessible to the person supplying care at the right time in the workflow. Such knowledge can be delivered proactively (before decisions are made), interactively (as decisions are made), or asynchronously or passively as reference information that can be searched online. Pharmacy informatics plays a key role in supporting and overseeing the core processes involving information and knowledge delivery throughout the clinical knowledge lifecycle. This role includes knowledge discovery and creation, knowledge application and delivery, and knowledge asset management.

Knowledge discovery and creation. As technology-driven transactions for results, ordering, documentation, task completion, communication, and patient monitoring continue to grow, so will the amount of data. Pharmacy informatics plays a key role in analyzing these data for the purpose of understanding performance; evaluating process; and reporting, predicting, and harvesting new information to create new knowledge for improving outcomes.

Knowledge application and delivery. Pharmacy informatics is responsible for leveraging knowledge at the right time and place within a provider's workflow to improve caregiver effectiveness, work satisfaction, patient satisfaction, and the quality of care. Pharmacy informatics must continue to evolve to optimize clinical decision support use and develop tools that reduce information overload and provider burden. Pharmacy informatics is responsible for looking beyond the traditional means of delivering knowledge by analyzing process and outcomes data from existing applications to develop and implement new solutions for embedding knowledge into the workflow.[13]

Knowledge asset management. Pharmacy informatics must play a significant role in managing and supporting a healthcare system's technology-enabled medication information and knowledge assets. This role would include assisting with authoring, encoding, cataloging, versioning, updating, disseminating, and maintaining an inventory of medication-related information and knowledge. Despite the emergence of commercial content management systems and groupware, pharmacy informatics must provide the appropriate level of oversight and governance for these activities and play a role in the development of future knowledge asset management systems that support end-to-end knowledge engineering.

Practice Analytics. The healthcare industry has historically generated large amounts of data driven by financial, regulatory, compliance, and patient-care-related activities. These data have primarily been stored in hard copy form, making it difficult to process through traditional database management tools. Paper records have also limited opportunities for effective exchange of information with other healthcare systems or providing actionable insight on reducing costs, improving performance, and making decisions. The recent infusion of financial incentives and regulation involving HIT from the American Recovery and Reinvestment Act (ARRA)[14] has fueled the implementation of technologies across the United States, contributing to an exponential growth of available and useable healthcare data. Healthcare organizations are looking for every opportunity to transform and leverage data into information that provides concise, timely, descriptive, predictive, and prescriptive insight into their business and clinical data. Business intelligence (BI) and analytics (BA) processes and technologies are enabling health systems to improve their performance and maintain their competitive advantage while creating an additional demand for clinical informatics professionals. Pharmacy informatics plays a significant role in all efforts surrounding medication management-related BI and BA activities. Pharmacy informaticists' understanding of basic software and database design, ability to grasp the big picture, and functional knowledge of detail, coupled with their analytical skills, create opportunities to develop evidence-driven answers for practice improvement and performance questions, such as

- How are pharmacists performing in relation to cost, quality, and service?

- How can pharmacists improve performance and safety within and outside their service lines?
- How can pharmacy practice identify patients who are at risk for readmission?
- How can pharmacy practice identify patients requiring medication therapy management services?[15,16]

Pharmacy informatics roles and responsibilities in BI and BA must include:

- Ensuring data are standardized, structured, and modeled to support a data-driven BI and BA culture.
- Creating effective analytics tools that allow for multiple formats and layers of analysis, from summary reports for a population of patients to a practice and at the individual patient-encounter level.
- Development, maintenance, and quality assurance of clinical, operational, and financial dashboards, scorecards, screening, and surveillance tools to guide achievement of treatment and strategic goals.
- Driving analytics to the front line by creating greater end-user accessibility to BI and BA tools.
- Monitoring effectiveness of tools and information to deploy or further develop point of care or analytical systems.

Applied Clinical Informatics. Pharmacy informatics plays a key role in delivering informatics research principles and best practices to the bedside. Through informal and formal partnerships with the research community, pharmacy informaticists must work collaboratively with members of various disciplines to improve the effectiveness, efficiency, and safety of systems that support medication management. They must actively participate in relevant associations and workgroups in the clinical informatics field to maintain their current skills and play a significant role in the following activities:

- Acquiring professional perspective—Understanding and analyzing the history and values of the discipline and its relationship to other fields while demonstrating an ability to read, interpret, and critique the core literature.
- Analyzing problems—Analyzing, understanding, abstracting, and modeling a specific biomedical problem in terms of data, information, and knowledge components.
- Producing solutions—Troubleshooting and effectively analyzing problems to identify and understand the spectrum of possible solutions and generating designs that capture essential aspects of solutions and their components.
- Articulating the rationale—Defending the specific solution and its advantage over competing options.
- Implementing, evaluating, and refining - Carrying out the solution (including obtaining necessary resources and managing projects), evaluating it, and iteratively improving it.
- Innovating—Creating new theories, typologies, frameworks, representations, methods, and processes to address clinical informatics problems.
- Working collaboratively—Teaming effectively with partners within and across disciplines.
- Educating, disseminating, and discussing—Communicating effectively to students and to other audiences in multiple disciplines in persuasive written and oral form.

Leading and Managing Change. To ensure that HIT systems support safe and effective medication use, pharmacy informaticists are expected to lead as well as manage the risks and changes associated with the development, implementation, safety, and use of systems that support medication management. Their knowledge and skills in comprehending and evaluating organizational culture, managing change, working effectively in interdisciplinary teams, communication, synthesizing user requirements, and articulating HIT needs within the context of broader strategic goals allow them to play a significant role in

- Leading health-system, professional, industry, regulatory, standards-setting, and governmental organizations to sound conclusions regarding the use of technology in medication management.
- Leading and managing the evaluation and communication of the potential risks of a newly implemented technology and developing plans to mitigate potential hazards.
- Translating user requirements into safe and effective system designs.
- Implementing project management best practices.
- Attaining key leadership roles within the healthcare technology industry, professional practice associations, and healthcare technology organizations.[4,10,11]

Conclusion

As the scope for development and complexity of systems that support medication management continues to grow, so does the need for individuals to lead, manage, and evaluate them. A pharmacy informaticist is uniquely qualified and possesses the necessary skills to fulfill this need. Their knowledge of pharmacy practice and safe medication use, combined with their understanding of informatics concepts, methods, and tools, provide the framework for effectively leading and participating in the procurement, customization, development, implementation, management, evaluation, and continuous improvement of clinical information systems.

References

1. Hersh W, Margolis A, Quiros F, et al. Building a health informatics workforce in developing countries. *Health Affairs* 2010; 29:274–7.
2. Price Water House Cooper Health Research Institute. Needles in a haystack: Seeking knowledge with clinical informatics. www.pwc.com/us/en/health-industries/publications/needles-in-a-haystack.jhtml (accessed 2015 Jan 9).
3. Kilbridge PM, Classen DC. The informatics opportunities at the intersection of patient safety and clinical informatics *J Am Med Inform Assoc*. 2008; 15:397–407.
4. American Society of Health-System Pharmacists. ASHP statement on the pharmacist's role in informatics. *Am J Health-Syst Pharm*. 2007; 64:200–3.

5. Tribble DA, Poikonen J, Blair J, et al. Whither pharmacy informatics. *Am J Health-Syst Pharm.* 2009; 66:813–5.
6. HIMSS Pharmacy Informatics. What is Pharmacy Informatics? www.himss.org/library/pharmacy-informatics (accessed 2015 Jan 9).
7. American Medical News. Clinical informatics now a subspecialty. www.amednews.com/article/20111010/business/310109962/6/ (accessed 2015 Jan 9).
8. Detmer DE, Lumpkin JR, Williamson JJ. Defining the medical subspecialty of clinical informatics. *J Am Med Informatics Assoc.* 2009; 16:167–8.
9. Safran C, Shabot MM, Munger BS, et al. Program requirements for fellowship education in the subspecialty of clinical informatics. *J Am Med Informatics Assoc.* 2009; 16:158–66.
10. Fox BI, Thrower MR, Felkey BG. *Building Core Competencies in Pharmacy Informatics.* Washington, DC: American Pharmacists Association, 2010.
11. Gardner RM, Overhage JM, Steen EB, et al. AMIA board white paper: core content for the subspecialty of clinical informatics. *J Am Med Inform Assoc.* 2009; 16:153–7.
12. Stratis Health. Health Information Technology Toolkit: Ongoing System Maintenance, Administration, and Data Quality Management. www.stratishealth.org/documents/HITToolkitcoordination/ongoing_system_maintenance.doc (accessed 2015 Jan 9).
13. Sittig DF, Wright A, Simonaitis L, et al. The state of the art in clinical knowledge management: an inventory of tools and techniques. *Int J Med Inform.* 2010; 79:44–57.
14. American Recovery and Reinvestment Act of 2009 (P.L. 111-5, 123 Stat. 115-521). www.gpo.gov/fdsys/pkg/PLAW-111publ5/html/PLAW-111publ5.htm (accessed 2015 Jan 9).
15. The Advisory Board. Business intelligence and analytics in health care: a primer. www.advisory.com/Research/Health-Care-IT-Advisor/Research-Notes/2011/Business-Intelligence-and-Analytics-in-Health-Care (accessed 2015 Jan 9).
16. Sage Growth Partners. The changing role of health analytics for providers. http://sage-growth.com/index.php/2012/02/the-changing-role-of-analytics-for-health-care-providers/ (accessed 2015 Jan 9).

Approved by the ASHP Board of Directors on April 10, 2015 and by the ASHP House of Delegates on June 7, 2015. Developed through the ASHP Section of Pharmacy Informatics and Technology. This statement supersedes the ASHP Statement on the Pharmacist's Role in Informatics dated June 27, 2006.

Mark Siska, M.B.A./TM, B.S.Pharm., is gratefully acknowledged for drafting this statement.

ASHP gratefully acknowledges the contributions of Alan Chung, Pharm.D.; Carol Hope, Pharm.D., M.S.ChemEng., M.S.Biosciences; Beth Breeden, D.Ph., M.S., CPHIT, CPEHR; and the 2013-2014 and 2014-2015 SOPIT Section Advisory Groups on Professional Development to this statement.

ASHP also gratefully acknowledges the following organizations and individuals for reviewing this document (review does not imply endorsement): American Association of Colleges of Pharmacy (AACP); American Medical Informatics Association, Pharmacoinformatics Working Group Leadership (AMIA-PWGL); Kansas Council of Health-System Pharmacists (KCHP); New Hampshire Society of Health-System Pharmacists (NHSHP); Pharmacy HIT Collaborative (PHITC); Ernest R. Anderson, Jr., M.S., FASHP; Paul J. Barrett, Pharm.D., MPA, BCPS, FASHP; Janinah Barreto, Pharm.D., M.S.; Carol J. Bickford, Ph.D., RN-BC, CPHIMS; Sarah Bledsoe, Pharm.D.; Lynette R. Bradley-Baker, Ph.D. (AACP); Max E. Burchett, Jr., Pharm.D.; Gregory Burger, Pharm.D., CPPS (KCHP); Michelle DeLuca Fraley, Pharm.D., RPD; Barbara Giacomelli, Pharm.D., M.B.A., FASHP; Nancy Hope Goodbar, Pharm.D., BCPS; James Hoffman, Pharm.D., M.S.; Joan Kapusnik-Uner, Pharm.D., FASHP; Janet M. Kozakiewiz, M.S., Pharm.D., FASHP; Emily Kirkwold, Pharm.D.; Kabeer Mago, Pharm.D.; Ben McDaniel, Pharm.D.; Karen Michaud, Pharm.D., BCPS; Richard Pacitti, Pharm.D., M.B.A.; Lois F. Parker, B.S.Pharm.; Shea Polk, Pharm.D.; James A. Ponto, M.S., RPh, BCNP, FASHP; Jason J. Schafer, Pharm.D., M.P.H., BCPS; Philip J. Schneider, M.S.; Terry L. Seaton, Pharm.D., FCCP, BCPS (AMIA-PWGL); Nancy R. Smestad, M.S., CMI; Shelly Spiro, B.S.Pharm., FASCP (PHITC); Mark St. Cyr, D.Ph., M.P.H.; Craig Stern, RPh, Pharm.D., M.B.A.; Tate N. Trujillo, Pharm.D., BCPS, FCCM, FASHP; Elizabeth Wade, Pharm.D., BCPS (NHSHP); Jody Jacobson Wedret, FASHP; and Marc Willner, Pharm.D.

Note: This statement had not been published in the *American Journal of Health-System Pharmacy* (*AJHP*) when *ASHP Best Practices 2015–2016* went to press. Some minor editorial differences may exist between this document and the official one that will eventually appear in *AJHP* and subsequent editions of this publication.

ASHP Statement on the Pharmacist's Role with Respect to Drug Delivery Systems and Administration Devices

Technological advances in drug delivery systems and administration devices frequently enable improved control of drug administration. Such advances may offer numerous potential benefits to patients, including improved therapeutic outcomes in disease management, improved patient compliance with drug regimens, and greater efficiency and economy in disease therapy. These advances constitute an important aspect of pharmaceutical knowledge and are routinely incorporated into pharmacy practice as they occur.

A drug delivery system is defined as one in which a drug (one component of the system) is integrated with another chemical, a drug administration device, or a drug administration process to control the rate of drug release, the tissue site of drug release, or both. A drug administration device is an apparatus that is used for introducing a drug to the body or controlling its rate of introduction. Drug delivery systems include (but are not limited to) osmotic pumps, thermal isolation, transdermal patches, lipsomal encapsulation, iontophoresis, phonophoresis, magnetic migration, and implantation. Drug administration devices include (but are not limited to) mechani cal (e.g., balloon-driven), gravity-driven, and electromechanical pumps. Some of the latter are portable, implantable, computer controlled, or patient controlled. Some enable the simultaneous infusion of multiple drugs. Drug administration control devices include plasma concentration monitoring and administration rate monitoring devices, which incorporate computers.

Pharmacists bear a substantial responsibility for ensuring optimal clinical outcomes from drug therapy and are suited by education, training, clinical expertise, and practice activities to assume responsibility for the professional supervision of drug delivery systems and administration devices. As a natural extension of efforts to optimize drug use, pharmacists should participate in organizational and clinical decisions with regard to these systems and devices. Some decisions and activities in which pharmacists should participate follow. Others may be appropriate as well.

1. Research and development of innovative drug delivery systems and administration devices.
2. Evaluation and research to determine the direct and comparative efficacy, safety, and cost-effectiveness of specific drug delivery systems and administration devices.
3. In conjunction with pharmacy and therapeutics committees (or other appropriate medical staff committees), decisions to choose or exclude particular drug delivery systems and administration devices for use in specific organizational settings.
4. Development of organization-specific policies and procedures regarding the acquisition, storage, distribution, use, maintenance, and ongoing product quality control of drug delivery systems and administration devices.
5. Choice of a particular drug delivery system or administration device for use in a specific patient's drug therapy.
6. Direct communication with patients to instruct them in the use of such systems and devices and to gather information necessary to monitor the outcome of their therapy.
7. Monitoring of the ongoing clinical effectiveness and suitability of specific drug delivery systems or administration devices with respect to specific patients and the communication of clinically relevant observations and recommendations to prescribers and other health professionals involved in the patients' care.

Failures or malfunctions of drug administration devices may lead to patient harm. Reports of such problems should be made in accordance with the provisions of the Safe Medical Devices Act of 1990 (PL 101–629).

Recommendations for Additional Reading

Acevedo ML. Electronic flow control. *NITA.* 1983; 6: 105–6.

Akers MJ. Current problems and innovations in intravenous drug delivery. Considerations in using the i.v. route for drug delivery. *Am J Hosp Pharm.* 1987; 44:2528–30.

Alexander MR. Current problems and innovations in intravenous drug delivery. Developing and implementing a contract for electronic infusion devices. *Am J Hosp Pharm.* 1987; 44:2553–6.

Anderson RW, Cohen JE, Cohen MR, et al. Hospital pharmacy symposium on new concepts in parenteral drug delivery. *Hosp Pharm.* 1986; 21:1033–55.

Baharloo M. Iontophoresis and phonophoresis: a role for the pharmacist. *Hosp Pharm.* 1987; 22:730–1.

Block LH, Shukla AJ. Drug delivery in the 1990s. *US Pharm.* 1986; 11(Oct):51–6, 58.

Boothe CD, Talley JR. Mechanical and electronic intravenous infusion devices. Part 1. *Infusion.* 1986; 10:6–8.

Chandrasekaran SK, Benson H, Urquhart J. Methods to achieve controlled drug delivery, the biomedical engineering approach. In: Robinson JR, ed. Sustained and controlled release drug delivery systems. New York: Marcel Dekker; 1978:557–93.

Colangelo A. Current problems and innovations in intravenous drug delivery. Drug preparation techniques for i.v. drug delivery systems. *Am J Hosp Pharm.* 1987; 44:2550–3.

Davis SR. Latest developments in drug delivery systems—abstracts. *Hosp Pharm.* 1987; 22:890–908.

Goodman MS, Wickham R. Venous access devices: oncology nurse overview. *Hosp Pharm.* 1985; 20:495–511.

Holm A, Campbell N. Role of institutional review boards in facilitating research, marketing of drugs and devices, and protecting human subjects. *Drug Dev Ind Pharm.* 1985; 11:1–12.

Juliano RL. Drug delivery systems. New York: Oxford University Press; 1980.

Kelly WN, Christensen LA. Selective patient criteria for the use of electronic infusion devices. *Am J IV Ther Clin Nutr.* 1983; 10(Mar):18, 19, 21, 25, 26, 29.

Kirschenbaum B, Klein S. Pharmacy-coordinated infusion device evaluation. *Am J Hosp Pharm.* 1984; 41:1181–3.

Leff RD. Current problems and innovations in intravenous drug delivery. Features of i.v. devices and equipment that affect i.v. drug delivery. *Am J Hosp Pharm.* 1987; 44:2530–3.

Longer MA, Robinson JR. Sustained-release drug delivery systems. In: Gennaro AR, ed. Remington's pharmaceutical sciences. Easton, PA: Mack Publishing Company; 1985:1644–61.

McFarlane AE. Role for pharmacists in the provision of medical devices. *Aust J Hosp Pharm.* 1986; 16:78.

Mutschler E. Now and future of drug delivery systems. *Pharm Tech.* 1983(Suppl); 7:13–5.

Nahata MC. Current problems and innovations in intravenous drug delivery. Effect of i.v. drug delivery systems on pharmacokinetic monitoring. *Am J Hosp Pharm.* 1987; 44:2538–42.

Piecoro JJ Jr. Current problems and innovations in intravenous drug delivery. Development of an institutional i.v. drug delivery policy. *Am J Hosp Pharm.* 1987; 44:2557–9.

Polack AE, Roberts MS. Drug delivery systems. *Med J Aust.* 1986; 144:311–4.

Rapp RP. Current problems and innovations in intravenous drug delivery. Considering product features and costs in selecting a system for intermittent i.v. drug delivery. *Am J Hosp Pharm.* 1987; 44:2533–8.

Reilly KM. Current problems and innovations in intravenous drug delivery. Problems in administration techniques and dose measurement that influence accuracy of i.v. drug delivery. *Am J Hosp Pharm.* 1987; 44:2545–50.

Reiss RE. Volumetric IV pumps. *Pharm Tech.* 1983(Suppl); 7:46–9.

Self TH, Brooks JB, Lieberman P, et al. The value of demonstration and role of the pharmacist in teaching the correct use of pressurized bronchodilators. *Can Med Assoc J.* 1983; 128:129–31.

Selton MV. Implantable pumps. *CRC Crit Rev Biomed Eng.* 1987; 14:201–40.

Smith KL. Developments in drug delivery systems. *Hosp Pharm.* 1987; 22:905–6.

Talley JR. Mechanical and electronic intravenous infusion devices. Part 2. *Infusion.* 1986; 10:31–4.

Talley JR. Mechanical and electronic intravenous infusion devices. Part 3. *Infusion.* 1986; 10:58–62.

Talsma H, Crommelin DJA. Liposomes as drug delivery systems, part I: preparation. *Pharm Tech.* 1992(Oct); 16:98, 100, 102, 104, 106.

Urquhart J. Implantable pumps in drug delivery. *Pharm Tech.* 1983(Suppl); 7:53–4.

Zenk KE. Current problems and innovations in intravenous drug delivery. Intravenous drug delivery in infants with limited i.v. access and fluid restriction. *Am J Hosp Pharm.* 1987; 44:2542–5.

This statement was reviewed in 1998 by the Council on Professional Affairs and by the ASHP Board of Directors and was found to still be appropriate.

Approved by the ASHP Board of Directors, November 18, 1992, and the ASHP House of Delegates, June 9, 1993. Revised by the ASHP Council on Professional Affairs. Supersedes a previous version approved by the ASHP House of Delegates on June 5, 1989, and the ASHP Board of Directors on November 16, 1988.

The bibliographic citation for this document is as follows: American Society of Hospital Pharmacists. ASHP statement on the pharmacist's role with respect to drug delivery systems and administration devices. *Am J Hosp Pharm.* 1993; 50:1724–5.

ASHP Statement on the Pharmacy Technician's Role in Pharmacy Informatics

Position

The American Society of Health-System Pharmacists (ASHP) believes that specially trained pharmacy technicians can assume important supportive roles in pharmacy informatics. These roles include automation and technology systems management, management of projects, training and education, policy and governance, customer service, charge integrity, and reporting. Such roles require pharmacy technicians to gain expertise in information technology (IT) systems, including knowledge of interfaces, computer management techniques, problem resolution, and database maintenance. This knowledge could be acquired through specialized training or experience in a health science or allied scientific field (e.g., health informatics). With appropriate safeguards and supervision, pharmacy technician informaticists (PTIs) will manage IT processes in health-system pharmacy services, ensuring a safe and efficient medication-use process.

Background

The National Library of Medicine defines health informatics as the "the interdisciplinary study of the design, development, adoption and application of IT-based innovations in healthcare services delivery, management and planning."[1] Health informatics is a discipline at the intersection of information science, health care, and computer science that designs and delivers information to improve clinical care, individual and public health care, and biomedical research. Health informatics optimizes the usability, acquisition, and processing of health-related information, using resources and tools that span the IT spectrum, from people to processes, from information to knowledge, and from algorithms to data. The broad definition of health informatics and the number of disciplines involved present an opportunity for the growth of subspecialties within the field. One of these subspecialties is pharmacy informatics, which has been defined as "the use and integration of data, information, knowledge, technology, and automation in the medication-use process for the purpose of improving health outcomes."[2] ASHP believes that pharmacists have the unique knowledge, expertise, and responsibility to assume a significant role in health informatics.[2] A properly trained and qualified pharmacy technician may assume a supporting role in the field of informatics as well.[3]

The potential for health informatics to improve health outcomes has prompted the health care industry, large health care purchasers, and state and federal governments to undertake sweeping health information technology (HIT) initiatives. These initiatives have greatly increased the demand for a highly skilled HIT workforce. The Bureau of Labor Statistics estimates that 37,700 new medical records and HIT technician jobs will be created between 2010 and 2020.[4] This tremendous increase will affect organizations' ability to recruit and retain the qualified personnel necessary for health care operations. Although not all pharmacy technicians are qualified to fill this pressing need, an emerging cadre of specialized PTIs will help fill these important roles. The purpose of this statement is to provide a preliminary description of the potential roles and responsibilities of the PTI in the evolving HIT landscape as well as the knowledge, skills, and abilities required to assume those roles and responsibilities.

Roles and Responsibilities

In general, the PTI will be a health care professional, working under the supervision of a registered pharmacist, who uses his or her knowledge to influence and adapt IT systems to improve the effectiveness and efficiency of the health system. The roles of PTIs will vary, depending on the needs of the health care institution and the knowledge, skills, and abilities of the individual. A PTI specializing in the management of health-system pharmacy IT services may, for example, perform workflow assessment and optimization in clinical, administrative, educational, or research domains; adapt software controls to existing workflow; provide subject-matter expertise for new technology assessment and usability; or serve as a resource for pharmacist informaticists when mission-critical updates are needed or problems are identified. The areas of responsibility of the PTI will also vary considerably but may include automation and technology systems management, management of projects, end-user training and education, policy and governance, customer service, charge integrity, and reporting.

Automation and Technology Systems Management. With training and experience in health informatics, the PTI can serve as a knowledgeable expert for placement, configuration, monitoring, maintaining, and troubleshooting automation and technology systems and provides users and staff with consultative support. The PTI participates in assessing the functions, benefits, and constraints of technology and automation systems for drug procurement, pharmacy inventory management, prescribing medications, order processing, distribution and dispensing of medications, administering and documenting administration of medications, and effects monitoring. The PTI consults, advises, and educates staff on methods and means to make automation and technology systems more effective and efficient. The PTI's functions include integration of information and workflow processes to achieve successful adoption and application of new technologies to support health care operations and systems.

The PTI provides relevant technological or administrative data to identify, quantify, and resolve organizational or operational problems. PTIs integrate software applications for technological services by: (1) evaluating the unique needs of the specific services in conjunction with the capabilities of the software and coordinating required modifications; (2) reviewing the effectiveness of the systems and procedures to assure optimum benefit to patient-care activities; and (3) determining the cause of and the solution to problems when functionality is compromised.

Using the applicable software manager menu systems and tools, the PTI develops, modifies, and tests components specific to fields and data that individualize or customize applications to user roles or needs while maintaining integrity among multiple software packages. The PTI also provides for the maintenance and updating of site parameters and site-specific files to ensure proper functioning of complex, interrelated, and interdependent software applications, effectively and efficiently managing multiple competing priorities.

Management of Projects. The PTI collaborates with the pharmacist informaticist in managing technology and information systems based on a shared understanding of system requirements, capabilities, and limitations. The PTI serves as an interdisciplinary team member to complete HIT system initiatives using analytical and evaluative techniques to assess the effectiveness of results and other related programs. For example, the PTI may contribute to planning for acquisition and implementation of a technology or automation system by assisting the pharmacist informaticist in developing a plan for the evaluation of the system; writing a request for proposal (RFP) for the system; assessing responses to the RFP; or developing a plan for implementation, testing, or maintenance of the system. The PTI may participate in the implementation of a technology or automation system by contributing to system installation (including supplemental build-outs), testing, and training of staff for use of the system, as well as maintaining the system according to an established plan. The PTI may also participate in development of a contingency plan for failure or compromise of technology or automation systems.

End-user Training and Education. The PTI identifies end-user educational requirements and training needs and develops educational programs, instructional materials, and appropriate tools to educate users and support staff at all levels of the organization. In collaboration with the pharmacist informaticist, the PTI monitors end-user satisfaction to drive enhancements and increase performance. The PTI functions in a supportive role with the pharmacist informaticist to ensure the technological changes are aligned with the organizational needs and participates on process improvement, root cause analysis, and system redesign teams.

Policy and Governance. The PTI maintains state-of-the-art knowledge of changes in technology and the clinical environment to identify, propose, formulate, and support new or revised major technological policies and directives for automation and systems technology. PTIs collaborate with pharmacist informaticists on the structure of programmatic and security requirements for data access in IT to ensure that best practices are applied to operational requirements.

The PTI applies statistical analyses and interprets their significance, including evaluation of the validity of measures used to generate outcomes related to patient management systems. PTIs will work cooperatively with the pharmacist informaticist to develop recommendations for improving clinical data management methods, follow-up procedures, and timely compliance with regulatory guidelines. Finally, the PTI instructs staff members in the proper use of information management tools in compliance with policy, regulations, and best practices.

Customer Service. The PTI maintains an ongoing personal relationship with onsite peers, pharmacist informaticists, technical support staff, administrative staff, and health care professionals within the facility. The PTI will frequently need to contact offsite technical support personnel and clinical and subject-matter experts as needed. External contacts may include contract developers, for whom the PTI can serve as a primary contact and knowledge resource.

Charge Integrity. The PTI maintains appropriate charging controls to ensure accurate patient and third-party billing. The PTI will be engaged with pharmaceutical wholesalers and distributors to validate price files in clinical and automation systems, as well as Healthcare Common Procedure Coding System (HCPCS) coding, units, and quantities. The PTI will also monitor charging and transaction interfaces for errors in charge application, quantities, or amounts.

Reporting. The PTI extracts, compiles, and analyzes standard reports from clinical and automation systems to facilitate organizational and individual decision-making. An advanced PTI customizes reports and provides advanced database management (e.g., via SQL or Microsoft Access) to address organizational needs not addressed through standard reporting tools.

Knowledge, Skills, and Abilities

The PTI is uniquely qualified to serve in these roles because of the combination of technological knowledge, skills, abilities, experience, and training. The PTI will be required to understand IT systems, including interfaces, computer management techniques, problem resolution, and database maintenance. The PTI will need to be familiar with pharmacy, medication, and medical terminologies as well as medication-use workflow processes, including drug procurement, pharmacy inventory, medication ordering, order management, dispensing, drug preparation, distribution, and billing systems.

The PTI will require a thorough knowledge of the clinical environment, including practices, procedures, policies, strengths, and weaknesses in order to effectively use data to track and manage patient care. Thorough and current knowledge of emerging and state-of-the-art technology, regulations, programs, and processes related to health informatics will be necessary for the PTI to propose and formulate administrative and clinical policies and directives, instruct practitioners on the changes and application of new policies and directives, and provide leadership on informatics committees or teams.

The PTI must have practical, in-depth knowledge of automation and software systems that affect clinical practice, as well as knowledge of technologies that may benefit health care delivery processes. The PTI should be able to troubleshoot functionality issues and develop solutions, and to ensure quality management of clinical operations.

The PTI should have comprehensive knowledge of the data life cycle, including data design, collection, and management, in order to input, retrieve, analyze, summarize, and present information effectively. The required knowledge base is extensive and includes usability, data standards, data validation, understanding content relationships, and interoperability among systems.

The PTI should understand common network standards and network architectures and the functions and purposes of common hardware components and configurations. The PTI should also understand the design of safe technology and automation systems. Finally, the PTI should possess the database skills to successfully create patient and medication information data sets and successfully construct reports.

The PTI should be skilled in communicating both orally and in a variety of written media for a variety of audiences, from information technology and clinical experts to end-users. As a specialist with training and experience in health informatics, the PTI guides the evolution of automation technology and processes using creative and well-developed interpersonal skills to achieve effective communication with end users and management.

Conclusion

The ASHP Pharmacy Practice Model Initiative provides several recommendations regarding use of technology to ensure medication safety. Meeting these recommendations will require an expansion of pharmacy resources devoted to the implementation and maintenance of HIT. A trained and educated PTI has unique skill sets that combine technical knowledge with an understanding of medication vocabulary and pharmacy operational workflow. Through these specialized skills, the PTI is able to support and coordinate pharmacy technologies under the direction of the pharmacy department or an accountable pharmacist. The PTI possesses a working knowledge of the technology and automation systems and processes that support the medication-use system and can contribute to ensuring their safety and efficiency.

References

1. National Library of Medicine. Health Services Research Information Central: Health Informatics. www.nlm.nih.gov/hsrinfo/informatics.html (accessed 2012 Dec 13).
2. American Society of Health-System Pharmacists. ASHP statement on the pharmacist's role in informatics. *Am J Health-Syst Pharm.* 2007; 64:200–3.
3. American Society of Health-System Pharmacists. The consensus of the Pharmacy Practice Model Summit. *Am J Health-Syst Pharm.* 2011; 68:1148-52. Available at: www.ajhp.org/content/68/12/1148.full.pdf (accessed 8 March 2013).
4. Bureau of Labor Statistics. Occupational Outlook Handbook: Medical Records and Health Information Technicians. www.bls.gov/ooh/healthcare/medical-records-and-health-information-technicians.htm#tab-6.

Approved by the ASHP Board of Directors on April 12, 2013, and by the ASHP House of Delegates on June 2, 2013. Developed through the ASHP Section of Pharmacy Informatics and Technology.

Nancy R. Smestad, M.S.; Trinh Le, M.S.; Adelaide Quansah-Arku, B.S.B.A.; Karl F. Gumpper, BCNSP, BCPS, FASHP; and Andy Laegeler, Pharm.D., M.S. are gratefully acknowledged for drafting this statement.

The following individuals and organizations are gratefully acknowledged for reviewing this statement (review does not imply endorsement): John A. Armitstead, M.S., FASHP; Mark Banzon, CPhT, PMP; Frank Barnett (Wiregrass Georgia Technical College); Louis D. Barone, Pharm.D., FASHP; Bob Begliomini, Pharm.D., M.B.A., FASHP; Jeff Brittain, Pharm.D., BCPS; Mark P. Chabot, M.H.A., M.B.A.; Bruce Chaffee, Pharm.D.; Sister Mary Louise Degenhart, M.B.A.; Robert Fink, Pharm.D., M.B.A., FASHP, FACHE, BCNSP, BCPS; Patricia C. Kienle, M.P.A., FASHP; Nicole Grimmer; Kathleen M. Gura, Pharm.D., BCNSP, FASHP, FPPAG; Nik Johnson (Academy of Managed Care Pharmacy); Kevin Marvin, M.S., FASHP, FHIMSS; Firouzan (Fred) Massoomi, Pharm.D., FASHP; Lisa McCartney, BAAS, CPhT, PhTR; Michael McGregory, Pharm.D., M.B.A.; Rhonda McManus, Pharm D; Jutia DeVae Merriweather, A.S, B.S., CPhT; Kelly Meyer, B.S, M.Ed, CPhT, PhTR; Timothy O'Connor-Crowe, CPhT, M.P.H., M.S.H.I.; Brandon Ordway, Pharm.D., M.S.; Ashley Overy, Pharm.D.; William Pennington, LVN, CPhT; Curt W. Quap, M.S., FASHP; Catherine Sharafanowich; Steven Silverstein, Pharm.D., BCPS; Lori Stepp, BSE, CPhT; Dennis A. Tribble, Pharm. D., FASHP; David Troiano, M.S.I.A.; James A. Trovato, Pharm.D., M.B.A., BCOP, FASHP; Alan Vogenberg, FASCP; and Deb Wagner, Pharm.D., FASHP.

The bibliographic citation for this document is as follows: American Society of Health-System Pharmacists. ASHP Statement on the Pharmacy Technician's Role in Pharmacy Informatics. *Am J Health-Syst Pharm.* 2014; 71:247–50.

ASHP Statement on Use of Social Media by Pharmacy Professionals

Position

The American Society of Health-System Pharmacists (ASHP) encourages pharmacy professionals working in hospitals and health systems who use social media to do so in a professional, responsible, and respectful manner. Such use may complement and enhance their relationships with patients, caregivers, other members of the health care team, and the public. To achieve that goal, pharmacy professionals should

- Thoroughly consider the purposes and potential outcomes of participation in social media and develop the strategies and skills required to effectively utilize social media to meet their goals, and
- Exercise professional judgment and adhere to professional standards and legal requirements in both private and public social media communications, especially legal and ethical obligations to protect the privacy of personal health information.

Background

The term "social media" may be defined as online tools that allow interaction among individuals. Examples include professional networks such as ASHP Connect, career-building networks such as LinkedIn, and sites such as Facebook and Twitter that are primarily social but which may serve multiple purposes.[1-3] Informational sites regarding medical information that allow for commentary from users and medical professionals (e.g., PharmQD, The Pharmacist Society, Sermo) should also be considered collaborative social media.

Social media have transformed the way people communicate by reducing barriers to the exchange of information, increasing both the amount of communication and the number of people who can participate. Health care organizations (e.g., hospitals, health systems, professional societies, pharmaceutical companies, patient advocacy groups, pharmacy benefit companies) have chosen to use social media for both communication and marketing.

Like other health care professionals, pharmacy professionals have adapted to advancing technology and are using social media to communicate with patients, caregivers, other health care professionals, and the public. Pharmacy professionals (including pharmacy students as professionals in training) should continue to incorporate these new tools into the armamentarium of pharmacy practice and apply them with professional judgment to pursue the goal of helping people make the best use of medications. Social media provide pharmacy professionals with opportunities to educate patients and practitioners, seek advice from and provide advice to colleagues, optimize the medication use of individual patients and populations, promote the role of pharmacists in caring for patients, and engage in debate about issues in health care practice and policy, among other things.[1-5]

Participation in Social Media

Hospitals or health systems that choose to use social media or permit practice-related social media use by staff should have in place policies and procedures that

- Balance the benefits social media provide with the obligations and liabilities they may create, and
- Encourage the development and application of best practices by users of social media.

The details of such policies, procedures, and best practices are beyond the scope of this statement, which has as its purpose to briefly outline some of the considerations that should guide pharmacy professionals' participation in social media.

Pharmacy professionals should carefully consider the purposes and potential outcomes of their participation in social media and develop the strategies and skills required to achieve their goals. They need to be aware of and employ best practices when using social media, because health care practitioners, including pharmacy professionals, are held to a higher standard of professionalism within and outside the workplace than members of the public.[6] Pharmacy professionals who participate in social media should strive for a high degree of professionalism in their communications and ensure that patient privacy is not compromised.

Professionalism

ASHP has long advocated for the adoption of high professional aspirations for pharmacy practice. Pharmacists' responsibilities as professionals include "advancing the well-being and dignity of their patients, acting with integrity and conscience, [and] collaborating respectfully with health care colleagues." [7] The following recommendations for the use of social media represent high professional aspirations, and pharmacy professionals are encouraged to exercise their professional judgment in incorporating them into their practices.

Advancing the Well-Being and Dignity of Patients. The following recommendations can help pharmacy professionals who choose to participate in social media advance the well-being and dignity of patients.

1. Medical advice offered through social media should be provided in accordance with the professional standards of pharmacy practice. For example, pharmacy professionals should provide medical advice only with a complete understanding of the patient's medical conditions and only if they accept the associated liabilities, especially those regarding privacy and the requirements of pharmacy practice. Pharmacy professionals should be aware that providing medical advice may create a pharmacist–patient relationship, with all its attendant obligations and liabilities. All online relationships should conform to the ethical boundaries of an appropriate pharmacist–patient relationship.[8]

2. Pharmacy professionals should be cognizant of both the benefits and limitations of online communication. Social media may serve especially well as a point of initial contact or as a convenient way to maintain contact between patients and care providers, but professionals must recognize when a patient's health care needs would be better met through other means (e.g., phone consultation, office visit).
3. Pharmacy professionals should view social media as a means to not only provide timely and accurate drug information but also to rebut inaccurate, misleading, or outdated information. While the purpose of specific social media content may not always be apparent, pharmacy professionals need to be aware of and alert to the use of social media for marketing and sales purposes.
4. Complaining about or disparaging patients, even in general terms, does not advance the dignity of patients or the profession. Communications that contain patients' identifying information would violate privacy requirements, which are discussed in more detail below. Pharmacy professionals should keep in mind that simply avoiding the name of a patient may not be sufficient to avoid patient identification.

Acting with Integrity and Conscience. The following recommendations are intended to assist pharmacy professionals to act with integrity and conscience in their use of social media.

1. Pharmacy professionals should carefully distinguish between personal and professional information within social media and make conscientious decisions regarding who will have access to personal or professional information. Although some organizations recommend use of a strictly personal page and a separate, strictly practice-related page,[9] professionals will quickly recognize the difficulty of making such distinctions. The higher standards of conduct expected of professionals, even in personal behavior, apply as well to their participation in social media.[6,10]
2. Pharmacy professionals must be conscious that content posted to social media may have consequences on reputations or careers for years to come, reflect poorly upon the pharmacy profession, or undermine patient confidence in the care provided. Postings on social media should be subject to the same professional standards and ethical considerations as other personal or public interactions.
3. The apparent anonymity provided by social media does not release pharmacy professionals from their ethical obligation to disclose potential conflicts of interest, especially when representing themselves as professionals. Some circumstances may require personal identification or disclosure of potential competing interests.[9]
4. Although all pharmacists should use social media in ways that set positive examples for pharmacy students and residents, preceptors and mentors have a special responsibility to model appropriate practices.[7,11]

Collaborating Respectfully with Health Care Colleagues. Although social media can and should be used to promote healthy debate about health care and pharmacy practice, such debate should be conducted in a respectful manner. Reasoned debate sometimes requires constructive criticism, but pharmacy professionals should not use social media to make ad hominem comments or needlessly denigrate specific care providers, institutions, or professions.

Patient Privacy

Health care professionals have long confronted the challenge of "communicat[ing] freely with each other while maintaining patient confidentiality and privacy."[12] Social media, by their very nature, present new issues of privacy and confidentiality by extending the reach of communications. The following recommendations may help pharmacy professionals protect patient privacy and confidentiality as they navigate this new terrain.

1. Pharmacy professionals should continue to adhere to all laws, regulations, standards, and other mandates intended to protect patient privacy and confidentiality in all environments, including social media.[8]
2. Pharmacy professionals should exercise professional judgment and employ established best practices to ensure compliance with privacy requirements when communicating with patients or about specific patient cases on social media.[9,13,14]
3. Pharmacy professionals should select privacy settings in social media accounts that provide the greatest degree of protection for personal information, keeping in mind that privacy settings are not perfect and that information posted online is likely permanent. Continuous self-monitoring of privacy settings is necessary, as social media sites change privacy policies.[10]

Conclusion

Social media are emerging as important modes of communication and are increasingly being used for personal, professional, and business communication, as well as for patient care. As medical professionals held to high standards of personal, professional, ethical, and moral conduct, pharmacy professionals have a responsibility to use social media appropriately.

References

1. Fox BI, Varadarajan R. Use of Twitter to encourage interaction in a multi-campus pharmacy management course. *Am J Pharm Educ.* 2011; 75(5):88.
2. Estus E. Using Facebook within a geriatric pharmacotherapy course. *Am J Pharm Educ.* 2010; 74(8):145.
3. Cain J, Fox BI. Web 2.0 and pharmacy education. *Am J Pharm Educ.* 2009; 73(7):120.
4. Clauson KA, Seamon MJ, Fox BI. Pharmacists' duty to warn in the age of social media. *Am J Health-Syst Pharm.* 2010; 67:1290–3.
5. Mattingly TJ, Cain J, Fink JL. Pharmacists on Facebook: online social networking and the profession. *J Am Pharm Assoc.* 2010; 50:424–7.

6. Williams J, Field C, James K. The effects of a social media policy on pharmacy students' Facebook security settings. *Am J Pharm Educ.* 2011; 75(9):177.
7. American Society of Health-System Pharmacists. ASHP statement on professionalism. *Am J Health-Syst Pharm.* 2008; 65:172–4.
8. University of California, San Diego. Guidelines and best practices for online social media use by student pharmacists. http://pharmacy.ucsd.edu/current/pdf/Social_Media_Guidelines.pdf (accessed 2012 Feb 1).
9. Ohio State Medical Association. Social networking and the medical practice: guidelines for physicians, office staff, and patients. www.osma.org/files/documents/tools-and-resources/running-a-practice/social-media-policy.pdf (accessed 2012 Feb 1).
10. American Medical Association. AMA policy: professionalism in the use of social media. www.ama-assn.org/ama/pub/meeting/professionalism-social-media.shtml (accessed 2012 Feb 1).
11. Kukreja P, Sheehan AH, Riggins J. Use of social media by pharmacy preceptors. *Am J Pharm Educ.* 2011; 75(9):176.
12. American Society of Health-System Pharmacists. ASHP statement on confidentiality of patient health care information. *Am J Health-Syst Pharm.* 2009; 66:411–2.
13. Dimov V. Case reports and HIPAA rules. http://casesblog.blogspot.com/2005/07/case-reports-and-hipaa-rules.html (accessed 2012 Feb 1).
14. Dimov V. How to write a medical blog and not get fired. http://casesblog.blogspot.com/2008/02/how-to-write-medical-blog-and-not-get.html (accessed 2012 Feb 1).

Developed through the ASHP Pharmacy Student Forum and the ASHP Section of Pharmacy Informatics and Technology and approved by the ASHP Board of Directors on April 13, 2012, and by the ASHP House of Delegates on June 10, 2012.

This statement was drafted by Ashley M. Overy, Pharm.D. The following individuals are also acknowledged for their contributions to this statement: Kevin A. Clauson, Pharm.D.; Brent I. Fox, Pharm.D., Ph.D.; Karl F. Gumpper, BCNSP, BCPS, FASHP; Arpit Mehta, Pharm.D.; and David R. Witmer, Pharm.D. The drafters and contributors have declared no potential conflicts of interest.

ASHP gratefully acknowledges the following individuals and organizations for reviewing drafts of this statement (review does not imply endorsement): Academy of Managed Care Pharmacy (AMCP); Paul Barrett, Pharm.D., M.P.A., BCPS, FASHP; Mark Brueckl, M.B.A. (AMCP); Jeff Cain, Ed.D., M.S.; Michael S. Edwards, Pharm.D., M.B.A., BCOP, FASHP; Erin R. Fox, Pharm.D.; Becky Harvey, Pharm.D.; John Hertig, Pharm.D., M.S.; Justin Julius, Pharm.D.; Nishaminy Kasbekar, Pharm.D., FASHP; Linda McElhiney, Pharm.D., FASHP, FIACP; Sean Mirk, Pharm.D.; John F. Mitchell, Pharm.D., FASHP; David B. Moore, M.P.A., CPh.; Linda A. Nelson, Pharm.D.; Agatha Nolen, Ph.D.; James Ponto, M.S., FASHP; Curt W. Quap, M.S., FASHP; Marcus Ravnan, Pharm.D.; Jamie S. Sinclair, M.S., FASHP; Kelly M. Smith, Pharm.D., BCPS, FASHP, FCCP; and Jody Jacobson Wedret, B.S.Pharm., FASHP, FCSHP.

The bibliographic citation for this document is as follows: American Society of Health-System Pharmacists. ASHP statement on use of social media by pharmacy professionals. *Am J Health-Syst Pharm.* 2012; 69:2095–7.

ASHP Guidelines on the Design of Database-Driven Clinical Decision Support: Strategic Directions for Drug Database and Electronic Health Records Vendors

ASHP believes that use of clinical decision support (CDS) tools can make patient care more efficient and effective.[1] Currently available pharmacotherapy CDS systems are not as effective as they need to be at helping all practice settings achieve the goal of safe and effective pharmacotherapy. The focus of these guidelines is commercially available pharmacotherapy warning systems such as drug interaction, allergy, and dose monitoring CDS. Pharmacotherapy warning CDS systems are collectively referred to as "database-driven CDS" in these guidelines. Database-driven alert associations are compiled by drug database vendors and are incorporated as alerts into clinical information systems by electronic health record (EHR) vendors. All practice settings are usually limited in their ability to customize the content of messages or severity levels of alerts created by the drug database or EHR vendors. In contrast, free-form, rule-based alerts are created by users based on coded logic rules using information contained in the EHR database. Although free-form, rule-based alerts are an important tool, these guidelines limit their focus to active, interruptive database warnings. These guidelines outline an approach that would provide all practice settings with the power and flexibility to implement database-driven CDS so that it is a useful tool for improving the quality, cost efficiency, and safety of medication use. Adoption of this functionality by all practice settings is of course critical to meeting the goal of delivering improved, patient-centered care. These database-driven CDS rules should be shareable between all practice settings so that each institution can make the customizations needed for its particular circumstances.

Purpose

The purposes of these guidelines are to describe essential functions and capabilities that should be available to reduce alert fatigue, increase user satisfaction, and increase the effectiveness of these CDS systems; and to advocate for collaboration between health information system vendors, drug database vendors, and the end-user community on design and testing of the CDS systems as well as new algorithmic models for pharmacotherapy warnings.

Background

There are two different types of CDS, passive and active, as well as several types of active CDS (Figure 1).

1. *Passive CDS.* This type of CDS directs the user toward the most appropriate practices unobtrusively; examples include order sets and limited selections in drop-down lists or check boxes. Passive CDS is derived from population data, or more commonly clinical guidelines, and is therefore not patient-specific by nature. It is left to the patient's healthcare provider to make these patient-specific.
2. *Active CDS.* There are two types of active CDS, interruptive and noninterruptive. Active CDS is patient-specific in that it uses at least two pieces of patient data to trigger an alert (e.g., two interacting drugs, or the patient's age and an ordered dose).

Figure 1. Types of clinical decision support (CDS).

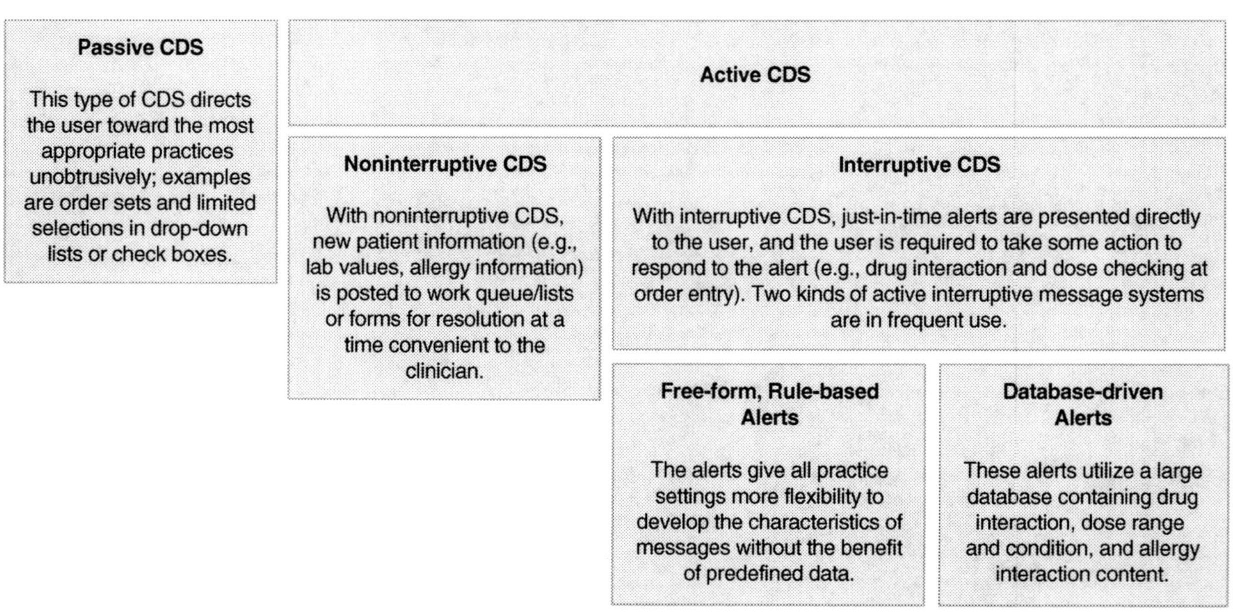

a. *Noninterruptive CDS.* With noninterruptive CDS, new patient information (e.g., lab values, allergy information) is posted to work queue/lists or forms for resolution at a time convenient to the clinician.

b. *Interruptive CDS.* With interruptive CDS, just-in-time alerts are presented directly to the user, and the user is required to take some action to respond to the alert (e.g., drug interaction and dose checking at order entry). Two kinds of active interruptive message systems are in frequent use:

i. *Database-driven alerts.* These alerts utilize a large database containing drug interaction, dose range and condition, and allergy interaction content.

ii. *Free-form, rule-based alerts.* The alerts give all practice settings more flexibility to develop other decision models and the characteristics of patient-specific messages. Ideally, in the future it will be common for free-form CDS rules to be able to access the content of commercially developed pharmacotherapy CDS databases.

Although database-driven CDS systems have been commercially available for over 30 years, most of these systems have not progressed beyond the use of simple rules for drug–drug, drug–food, and drug–allergy checking. Most provide limited logic to determine a patient's true susceptibility to these drug interactions, and some provide limited drug–disease state screening and age-based dose checking.[2] Most currently available database-driven CDS systems have excellent content and can generally inform the right person; however, they have limited options for format, channel, and right time in workflow. These limitations cause a high incidence of false-positive alerts in computerized prescriber-order-entry and pharmacy information systems, which can in turn decrease users' sensitivity to alerts, also known as "alert fatigue." Alert fatigue is more than just an annoyance; it increases the risk of harm to both patients and providers.[2-4] The lack of clinical usefulness of the majority of drug interaction, drug allergy, and dose monitoring tools has been demonstrated by physician alert override rates that exceeded 90% in some studies.[3-8] The relevance and specificity of CDS tools will be improved, and the value of CDS tools enhanced, when the rate of meaningful warnings is increased and the incidence of clinically irrelevant alerts is reduced. Achieving these goals will require more than the currently available simple logic, especially for dose monitoring and mathematical algorithms. These systems also need broader access to the rich patient data that are now available in the EHR.

The meaningful use requirements of the American Recovery and Reinvestment Act[9] contain explicitly stated objectives for CDS, spurring healthcare facilities to invest in new EHR systems with an increased focus on CDS. Although these systems are the most current ones available, many of them continue to use the same simple logic for database-driven CDS. What is needed is more sophisticated logic, such as statistical methods and branching algorithms to reduce the false-positive and false-negative alerts. The Agency for Healthcare Research and Quality recommends that CDS developers consider the CDS Five Rights model, which states "that we can achieve CDS-supported improvements in desired healthcare outcomes if we communicate:

1. The ***right information:*** evidence-based, suitable to guide action, pertinent to the circumstance
2. To the ***right person:*** considering all members of the care team, including clinicians, patients, and their caretakers
3. In the ***right CDS intervention format:*** such as an alert, order set, or reference information to answer a clinical question
4. Through the ***right channel:*** for example, a clinical information system (CIS) such as an electronic medical record (EMR), personal health record (PHR), or a more general channel such as the Internet or a mobile device
5. At the ***right time in workflow:*** for example, at time of decision/action/need."[10]

The Healthcare Standards Organization Health Level Seven (HL7) and the American National Standards Institute have developed and maintain a standard programming language design for clinical informaticists to build medical logic modules capable of sophisticated clinical logic. There are also many HL7 standards (e.g., Arden Syntax, GELLO, HQMF, Infobutton, DSS) that can assist in this endeavor and offer a mechanism across all practice settings around the world to collaborate on the development of effective database-driven CDS.[11] Use of these standards could improve the ability for users to share logic developed to capitalize on the functionality presented below.

ASHP encourages pharmacists, hospital and health-system administrators, drug database vendors, and EHR system vendors to use the recommendations in these guidelines to increase the usefulness and flexibility of database-driven CDS tools. In essence, the goal of their collaborative efforts should be to provide the flexibility and customization capabilities as are currently available in the free-form rules engines provided by most EHR vendors today. This would allow users to build alerts that have greater specificity and higher positive predictive performance.

Essential CDS Capabilities

The following are essential database-driven CDS capabilities that should be available in all EHR systems for any combination of drug database vendor and EHR vendor used by a hospital or health system. These recommendations are not listed in order of feasibility or priority; all are considered vitally important for the development of more patient appropriate care.

1. The institution should be able to configure and/or customize "drug groups" that can be used in alert triggers or criteria. Drug groups should be defined as lists of individual medication products or generic or therapeutic groupings. Individual medication products should be capable of being included in multiple drug groups, and drug groups should be able to subsume other drug groups. The drug group construct should be an option for using the configuration functionality described below. The drug group must have a free-text comment

field of at least 1000 characters to allow the institution to identify the drug group's owner and purpose and to construct a history of changes.

2. Warnings should be available in real time and be capable of being tailored to the specific patient situation using available patient information (e.g., age, gender, weight, laboratory values, radiology procedures, dietary needs, diagnosis, current problem list, location of care delivery) together with information contained in the drug database to construct inclusion and exclusion criteria that make alerts more useful and reduce alert fatigue. The patient information should conform to standard terminology, such as Logical Observation Identifiers Names and Codes (LOINC) for laboratory tests. The drug database vendor should consider developing an external database that translates standard terminologies (e.g., RxNorm, LOINC, Systematized Nomenclature of Medicine, and International Classification of Diseases codes) to an internal dictionary of medical terms used in their knowledge base.
3. Medication-order-specific information (e.g., dosage forms, routes, frequencies, dose, order status, ordering provider) should also be available to be utilized in alert inclusion and exclusion criteria.
4. All practice settings should have the ability to (a) customize how an alert looks (e.g., color, shape, audio, size) to emphasize the criticality or type of warning, and (b) offer response options based on characteristics of the potential harm (e.g., prevalence of problem, extent of risk or severity) (see "Notification System" in Figure 2).
5. All practice settings should have the ability to configure the information displayed in the warnings. The CDS rule development language must enable the rule to build patient-specific alert messages during rule execution. The following five basic types of logic must be supported by the rule development tool kit.
    a. *String handling.* This type of logic allows the rule developer to incorporate useful patient-specific suggestions based on patient information. It also allows displaying of useful data such as allergies, relevant medications, and other patient characteristics or data, in the form of text or structured data values, directly into the warning message, so the information contained in the alert can help the clinician determine the best response to the alert.
    b. *Loop functions.* This type of logic allows alert designers to gather or group all related information into a single warning (e.g., sort through lists of patient data to find relevant drug, lab result, or diagnosis). In addition, the loop functions should allow the use of mathematical algorithms (e.g., statistical methods to test trends of data, calculate glomerular filtration rate, or perform patient scoring).
    c. *Math functions.* This type of logic allows an alert to perform calculations and must include logarithmic and other standard mathematical functions. This will be necessary to perform specialized calculations that are available in but not retrievable from the EHR.
    d. *Trends over time.* This type of logic provides the ability to configure alerts based on trends in data over a defined period of time (e.g., decrease in hemoglobin of 2 grams in 2 days, or increase of hemoglobin A_{1c} > 2.0% in 3 months).
    e. *Conditional statements.* If-then-else statements that direct action based on the result of a Boolean logic statement (AND, OR, NOT). Duration conveniences must allow construction of temporal logic such as:
        1. If age < 6 days then ...
        2. Else if age < 2 years then ...

        In this case, age (a duration) is automatically converted to days and then years.
6. All practice settings should have the ability to configure whether a warning acknowledgment cannot be bypassed (i.e., a "hard stop"), can only be bypassed by documenting a valid reason for bypassing the alert (i.e., a "soft stop"), or can be bypassed without documenting a reason, and whether an additional comment is required by user type and venue (e.g., critical care, ambulatory). If a drop-down menu is utilized, it should specifically relate to the context and content of an alert.
7. Users should be able to take action from the synchronous alert presentation window. Such actions should be specific to the type of alert presented and include at least the following seven choices, by type of user or user category:
    a. Discontinue the conflicting order.
    b. Cancel the order being entered.
    c. Modify the order being entered (e.g., change dose, dosage form, route, frequency, start date, or end date).
    d. Modify the preexisting order (e.g., change dose, dosage form, route, frequency, start date, or end date).
    e. Add monitoring orders (e.g., laboratory tests or other parameters).
    f. Continue with current order as requested.
    g. Suspend the current order (i.e., put it in a held/suspended state).
8. The EHR system should be able to handle logic rules that determine how an alert can be transmitted to the clinician as well as specifying the individuals and/or groups that are to receive the alert. The importance of the alert should also be included in the logic rules for determining who is notified about the alert and how they are notified. The alert notification should be able to be transmitted in any electronic form, depending on the technology available at the institution, including but not limited to the electronic message inbox within the EHR, e-mail (where the alert information is available within the e-mail message), pagers, text message, fax, and printers. Encryption or secured messaging must be utilized to protect patient health information. The alert notification system should include a means of stratifying the alert importance and associating the type of alert notification with the level of the alert (e.g., an alert of moderate importance would be e-mailed to the clinician, whereas a more urgent alert such as a direct allergy match would be sent via text message). This type of stratification would be included in the logic using "if-then" types of statements.

Figure 2. Conceptual schematic of a potential new architecture with a clinical rules engine (CRE). Not shown here is the integrated development environment, where the rules are built by a clinician analyst. CPOE = computerized provider order entry, eMAR = electronic medication administration record, MedIA = medication interaction alert (e.g., drug–drug, drug–allergy, dose check, drug–disease).

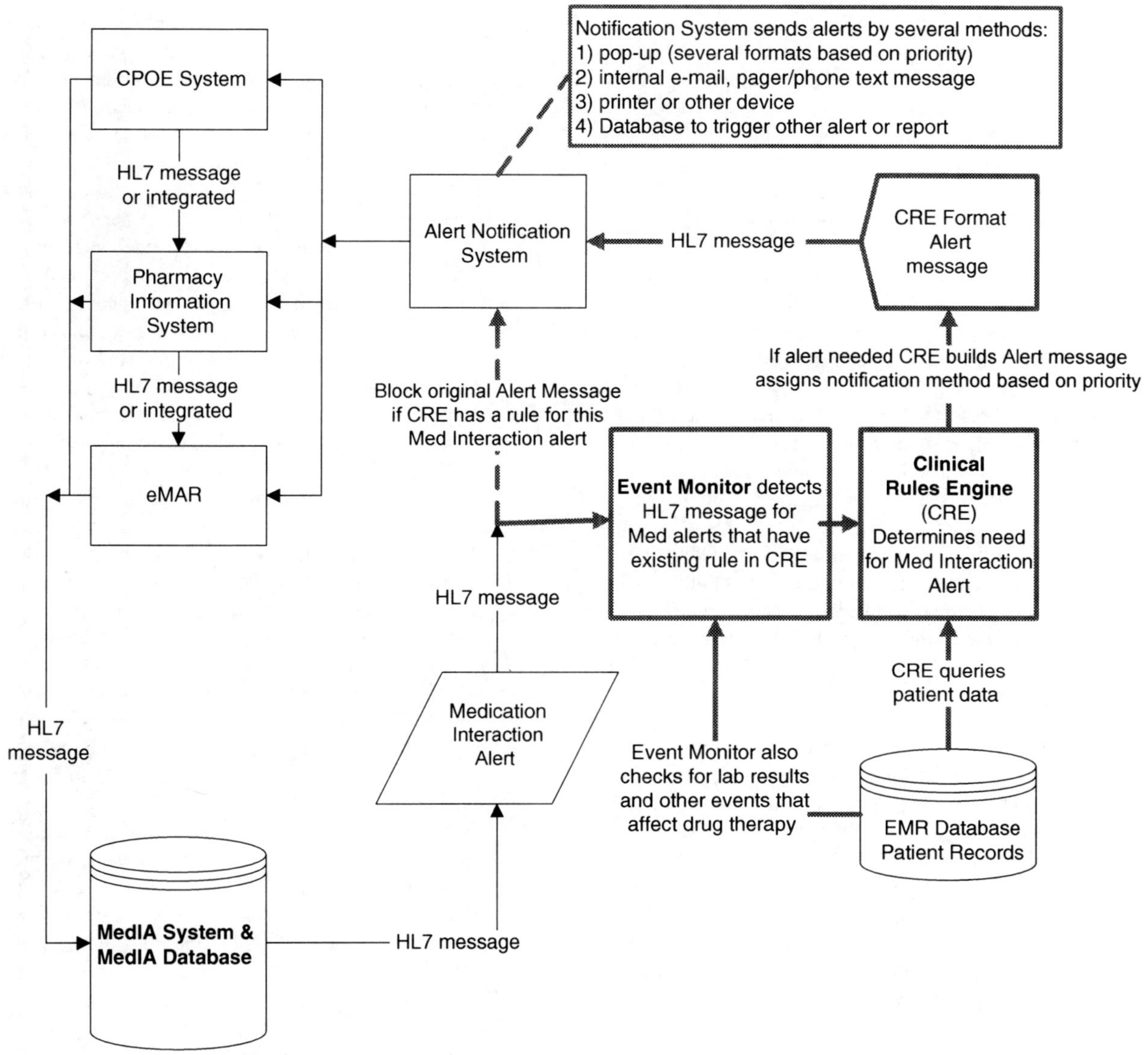

9. The EHR system should provide the capability to allow all practice settings to determine whether end users can customize the conditions under which they must respond to specific alerts within the larger list of alerts assigned to them. Appropriate warnings and audit trails must be in place to support this functionality. Database managers should be able to customize the conditions and options for the user to respond to specific alerts to

a. "Snooze" the alert: delaying a response to the alert, whether globally or for user-identified individual patients for a predetermined amount of time with the ability to limit how many times an alert may be ignored before an action is required.

b. Forward the alert: send the alert to an EHR message box with a time constraint based on the follow-up action needed.

10. The alerts system should allow sub-second response times (i.e., the absence of user waiting for system response) for warning notification and filing user response. Although response time is contingent upon a practice setting's hardware configuration, a short response time is essential to winning user acceptance. Reporting or database updates should not impact real-time system performance.

11. All practice settings should have the capability to configure and record (or track) when an alert notification displays, which implies when the checking occurs (e.g., when the medication is first selected, when a portion of the order information is changed, when the order or group of orders is filed). If an alert is overridden but then the triggering order is discontinued within a certain time period of the alert firing, the data should indicate that the alert had a user response that resulted in discontinuing an order.

12. Clinicians and EHR system managers should have easy access to the supporting data available for each alert viewed in the EHR. Supporting evidence, including citations, should be available as specified in the American Recovery and Reinvestment Act of 2009 Stage 2 meaningful-use requirements.[9] Supporting evidence formats that should be available would include

a. References that are included with the data imports from the various knowledge databases.

b. Internal system policies and protocols.

c. External reference databases or guidelines.

EHR systems should be able to display these references, the quality of the references, and any other supporting evidence provided by the knowledge vendor. EHRs should allow links to external databases or documentation when deemed appropriate by the institution. These links should allow viewing of more details than what is presented in the initial alert. Supporting information should be easily retrieved by the user as part of the typical workflow. Supporting evidence should be formatted so that it could be presented in either a soft- or hard-alert format.

13. If there is additional information located within the EHR that is relevant to the alert, the EHR should provide a link or other means of easily accessing that content as part of the clinician workflow. Examples would include

a. Allergy information.

b. All orders flagged by the alert.

c. Links to orders needed for entry as determined by the alert (e.g., laboratory test, medication).

Setting up links for internal or custom external documents via the EHR alert should be a simple process.

14. The EHR system should provide the ability to invoke the database for synchronous and asynchronous checking based on different system transactions (i.e., not only order entry). Examples include laboratory test values filing to the patient chart, entering of patient information (e.g., diagnosis, problem, allergy), medication administration (see "Event Monitor" in Figure 2), or to delay alert notification to allow completion of orders (e.g., for an aminoglycoside order, allowing time for the practitioner to determine whether serum creatinine, drug levels, or a consult has also been ordered).

15. The CDS system must log all alert warnings and user actions taken in response to the alert (i.e., record alert outcomes). Those alert outcomes should include, at a minimum, the following:

a. User who has received the alert.

b. Users who have viewed the alert.

c. Overridden alerts.

d. Alerts that have occurred and had an action taken on them.

e. Subsequent actions taken from the synchronous alert or view window.

f. Current patient data related to the alert.

g. Communications associated with the alert (e.g., reasons, required responses, comments).

16. All responses entered during the alert session should be available to subsequent users who view either the order or alert via inquiry and as part of subsequent alerts at order verification or other transactions related to the order. The inquiry should provide the ability for a user to check a patient's record for any alerts displayed in the system, including a historical account of all alerts that have displayed for a patient (pertaining to the current or prior inpatient or outpatient visits), including all information mentioned in item 15 above.

17. Data related to user actions in response to alerts and messages must be available within the context of CDS, and standard queries should be available. Data on alerts and responses to those alerts should be exportable to an external database or spreadsheet to support retrospective auditing. Studies are needed to determine if documenting override reasons improves or diminishes alert effectiveness and patient outcomes. Rates of overrides and other simple measures of alert effectiveness can be useful for identifying potential opportunities to improve system performance, but additional studies are needed to document the effect of changes made to CDS alerting rules. The reporting mechanism should facilitate the capture of the chronological history of alerts associated with an order across the multiple users who receive them.

18. Outcome documentation should be consistent across vendor systems so that healthcare organizations can accurately compare and benchmark database-driven CDS outcomes among organizations. To achieve this goal, vendors and CDS researchers may need to establish a consensus database schema for CDS outcomes.

19. The alerts system must facilitate easy identification of any facility-specific custom data that will be affected by modifications that a vendor has made to data or functionality.

20. CDS rules must be easily exportable to a text file. The exported rule must contain rule logic and all documentation contained in the rule. The exported rule does not have to contain external data queries or external destination logic referenced within the rule's logic, as this information is unique to the hospital or health system.

21. The CDS system must allow batch import of CDS rules from standalone files of prespecified types and formats. There must be options to overwrite existing rules and add new rules.

22. The CDS system must allow users to flag alerts for usefulness or intrusiveness so as to give the user a mechanism to provide immediate feedback to the CDS team. This functionality would be an extremely helpful tool to allow for a real-time evaluation tool for CDS, especially when changes are made to a system before the CDS team has a chance to collect and collate data.

Conclusion

Database-driven CDS could have a major impact on the quality, safety, and cost of healthcare. Unfortunately, its potential is largely unfulfilled due to the high number of false-positive warnings produced by most CDS systems. Alert fatigue from these warnings is common among physician and pharmacist users of EHR systems. To realize the promise of CDS, drug database and EHR vendors must work collaboratively to develop CDS systems that offer flexible patient-specific checking, reduce false-positive and false-negative warnings, and provide useful warning information to clinicians. It is of equal importance that all practice settings embrace this new functionality and aggressively use it to improve the specificity and appropriateness of patient care. By giving all practice settings the power to tailor drug database warning systems as they do with their EHR rules engines, the needed specificity to patient factors can be obtained.

References

1. Bates DW, Cohen M, Leape LL, et al. Reducing the frequency of errors in medicine using information technology. *J Am Med Inform Assoc.* 2001; 8:299–308.
2. Kuperman GJ, Reichley RM, Bailey TC. Using commercial knowledge bases for clinical decision support: opportunities, hurdles, and recommendations. *J Am Med Inform Assoc.* 2006; 13:369–71.
3. Kesselheim A, Cresswell K, Phansalkar S, et al. Clinical decision support systems could be modified to reduce "alert fatigue" while still minimizing the risk of litigation. *Health Aff.* 2011; 30:2310–7.
4. Phansalkar S, van der Sijs H, Tucker AD, et al. Drug–drug interactions that should be noninterruptive in order to reduce alert fatigue in electronic health records. *J Am Med Inform Assoc.* 2013; 20:489–93.
5. Lin CP, Payne TH, Nichol WP, et al. Evaluating clinical decision support systems: monitoring CPOE order check override rates in the Department of Veterans Affairs' computerized patient record system. *J Am Med Inform Assoc.* 2008; 15:620–6.
6. Payne TH, Nichol WP, Hoey P, et al. Characteristics and override rates of order checks in a practitioner order entry system. *Proc AMIA Symp.* 2002:602–6.
7. Weingart SN, Toth M, Sands DZ, et al. Physicians' decisions to override computerized drug alerts in primary care. *Arch Intern Med.* 2003; 163:2625–31.
8. Karsh BT. Clinical practice improvement and redesign: how change in workflow can be supported by clinical decision support (June 2009). AHRQ publication no. 09-0054-EF. http://healthit.ahrq.gov/sites/default/files/docs/page/09-0054-EF-Updated_0.pdf (accessed 2014 Sep 26).
9. Centers for Medicare and Medicaid Services. Meaningful use. www.cms.gov/Regulations-and-guidance/Legislation/EHRIncentivePrograms/Meaningful_Use.html (accessed 2014 Sep 26).
10. Agency for Healthcare Research and Quality. Chapter 1: approaching clinical decision support in medication management. Section 2: overview of CDS five rights. Improving medication use and outcomes with clinical decision support: a step-by-step guide. http://healthit.ahrq.gov/ahrq-funded-projects/clinical-decision-support-initiative/chapter-1-approaching-clinical-decision/section-2-overview-cds-five-rights (accessed 2014 Sep 26).
11. Health Level Seven International. HL7 standards—master grid. www.hl7.org/implement/standards/product_matrix.cfm?ref=nav (accessed 2014 Sep 26).

Developed through the ASHP Section of Pharmacy Informatics and Technology Section Advisory Group on Clinical Information Systems. Approved by the ASHP Section of Pharmacy Informatics and Technology Executive Committee on December 6, 2014, and by the ASHP Board of Directors on April 10, 2015.

David Troiano, B.S.Pharm., M.S.I.A., CPPS, is Director of Consulting, Dearborn Advisors, Chicago, IL. Michael A. Jones, Pharm.D., is Informatics Pharmacist for Clinical Decision Support, University of Colorado Hospital, Aurora. Andrew H. Smith, B.S.Pharm., M.H.A., is Pharmacy Clinical Applications Analyst, Novant Health, Winston-Salem, NC. Raymond C. Chan, Pharm.D., is Informatics Residency Coordinator—Information Technology, Sentara HealthCare, Norfolk, VA. Andrew P. Laegeler, M.S., Pharm.D., is Pharmacy Informatics Operations Manager, Harris County Hospital District, Houston, TX. Trinh Le, B.S.Pharm, M.S., FASHP, is Clinical Pharmacy Manager—Informatics, Department of Pharmacy, University of North Carolina Health Care, Chapel Hill. Allen Flynn, Pharm.D., is Solutions Designer, Health Practice Innovators, Ann Arbor, MI. Bruce W. Chaffee, Pharm.D., is Coordinator for Strategic Projects and Adjunct Clinical Associate Professor of Pharmacy, Department of Pharmacy Services, College of Pharmacy, University of Michigan, Ann Arbor.

The bibliographic citation for this document is as follows: American Society of Health-System Pharmacists. ASHP Guidelines on the Design of Database-Driven Clinical Decision Support: Strategic Directions for Drug Database and Electronic Health Records Vendors. *Am J Health-Syst Pharm.* 2015; 72:1499–505.

ASHP Guidelines on Pharmacy Planning for Implementation of Computerized Provider-Order-Entry Systems in Hospitals and Health Systems

Purpose and Scope

The purpose of these guidelines is to provide guidance to pharmacists in hospitals and health systems on planning for, implementing, and enhancing safe computerized provider-order-entry (CPOE) systems. To date, most CPOE guidelines have concentrated on the functionality required of a CPOE system, despite the fact that most CPOE system implementations occur using commercial systems whose functionality is largely pre-determined. These guidelines are intended to help pharmacy directors, managers, informaticists, and project managers successfully engage in this type of CPOE system implementation. CPOE is commonly part of a larger health information technology (IT) plan or system implementation. Though many health care technologies impact patient care and pharmacy practice, this guideline will focus on CPOE only. This document is the first of a planned series of ASHP guidelines on CPOE and related technologies and addresses the planning phase of a health-system CPOE implementation, primarily focusing on acute care and associated ambulatory care clinics. The guideline will focus on using CPOE in the medication-use process, though it is important to realize that CPOE includes all orders for patient care (laboratory, nursing, respiratory, and others). Topics covered in these guidelines include

- Developing an interdisciplinary planning and implementation team,
- Defining the vision, goals, and objectives of the CPOE system,
- Establishing essential metrics to measure the success of CPOE system implementation,
- Understanding current and future workflow in order to reengineer the medication-use process as part of CPOE system implementation,
- Planning for scope and depth of clinical decision support (CDS),
- Determining the functionality that ensures the safety of the CPOE system, and
- Educating and training health care providers to use the CPOE system.

Terms used in these guidelines are defined in the appended glossary. The recommendations presented in these guidelines can be used for strategic planning with the organization's decision-makers, drafting contract provisions, prospectively comparing CPOE systems, and creating an implementation plan. These guidelines should be used in conjunction with other literature on the topic and information from prospective or selected CPOE vendors. Pharmacists should exercise professional judgment in assessing their health system's needs regarding CPOE systems and in adapting these guidelines to meet those needs.

CPOE and the Electronic Health Record

In its 1999 report *To Err is Human*,[1] the Institute of Medicine (IOM) shocked the nation with its estimate of deaths due to medical errors. Two large studies, one conducted in New York[2,3] and the other in Utah and Colorado,[4] revealed adverse events occurring in 2.9% and 3.7% of hospitalizations, respectively. Over half of these adverse events were judged to be preventable. Based on these studies, IOM estimated that 44,000–98,000 Americans die each year due to medical errors in hospitals.[1] Many of these deaths are caused by medication errors or preventable adverse drug events (ADEs).[5,6]

When it was recognized that errors resulting in preventable ADEs involved a wide range of drug classes and most commonly occurred at the prescribing stage,[7] interest in CPOE systems grew. In a second report, *Crossing the Quality Chasm: A New Health System for the 21st Century*,[8] the IOM called for IT, including CPOE, to take a central role in the redesign of the health care system to improve quality, increase efficiency, and reduce errors. In addition to IOM, organizations such as the Leapfrog Group and the National Quality Forum have pushed for hospitals to adopt CPOE.[9,10] The American Recovery and Reinvestment Act of 2009 (Recovery Act) authorizes the Centers for Medicare and Medicaid Services (CMS) to provide reimbursement incentives for eligible professionals and hospitals who are successful in becoming "meaningful users" of certified electronic health record (EHR) technology. This law will likely increase the adoption of CPOE in hospitals and health systems.[11]

CPOE has the potential to affect the ordering of all medications, laboratory tests, medical imaging, nursing orders, and more. Even a basic CPOE system can eliminate illegible and incomplete orders and facilitate efficient order processing through instantaneous transmission of orders to hospital departments such as pharmacy and laboratory. Additionally, CPOE integrated with a pharmacy information system and the electronic medication administration record (eMAR) can nearly eliminate transcription errors, resulting in another potential 6% decrease in ADEs.[7] A homegrown CPOE system has been shown to decrease medication errors by 55–80%.[12,13] There are many reports of improvements in physician practices and patient outcomes with health IT related to ordering,[14-21] but in some reports it is difficult to distinguish whether the benefits were due to CPOE, CDS, the EHR, or a combination of all three. The synergy of the three of these will likely lead to the most significant improvements.[15,16] Although there are many reported benefits to CPOE, there is a growing body of research pointing to new problems introduced by CPOE. These new problems are collectively known as e-iatrogenesis, which is defined as patient harm caused at least in part by the application of health IT.[22] Though the systems themselves may contribute to these problems, design and implementation decisions play a role in the avoidance of these new errors.

More recently, attention has focused on the development of an integrated information system to support the coordination and integration of clinical and business processes. The terminology for such information systems is evolving, with *enterprise information system* sometimes used to describe the broader system that integrates clinical and business systems, and *EHR* used to describe the clinical information system, which may include a patient portal or the ability to link to a personal health record (PHR).[23] CPOE must be viewed in the context of the EHR, which would integrate CPOE, CDS, and departmental information systems and make patient-specific clinical information available to providers.

The EHR is a longitudinal electronic record of patient health information generated by one or more encounters in any care delivery setting.[24] It contains medical histories, medication histories, laboratory test results, diagnostic images, clinical documentation, progress notes, narrative summaries (such as operative reports or consultations), and other information related to patient encounters. EHRs provide the ability to manipulate, organize, and present data in ways that are clinically meaningful during the care planning, ordering, and care processes and allow broad clinician access to patient-specific clinical information, which is important to clinical quality and patient safety. When fully deployed within a facility through protected networks, the EHR serves as an information source and platform to coordinate patient care and communicate with the health care team. In addition, codified data can be used to trigger effective CDS as well as to provide data for continuous quality improvement.

For CPOE to be most useful it must be deployed as part of an EHR and not as a stand-alone module. CPOE is the process of health care providers entering orders and related information directly into the EHR. It places the provider at the center of patient care, allowing direct access and secure sharing of health information.

The EHR, including electronic clinician (e.g., physician, pharmacist, nurse) documentation with CPOE and CDS, is important to support the complex effort needed to improve hospital care.[15,16] The integration of CPOE and CDS within an EHR can create a platform upon which to build and improve the delivery of health care today and in the future. Many organizations implement these in a stepwise fashion because of the enormous work effort and the significant workflow changes required. Although there is no single solution that fits every circumstance, the literature offers many examples for others to follow or avoid.[25–28] Regardless of the vendor, organization size, or other factors that could potentially affect success, there are quite a number of implementation decisions that can increase the likelihood of a clinician-accepted CPOE installation that leads to quality and safety improvements.

Planning for the Transition to CPOE

A successful CPOE implementation starts with a well-organized, realistic plan. In planning for the transition to CPOE, initial tasks include assembling an interdisciplinary planning and implementation team; developing a vision, goals, and objectives for the CPOE system; establishing essential baseline and post-go-live metrics; mapping current physician, pharmacist, and nurse workflows as they relate to the medication-use process; defining the desired medication-use process; and planning for CDS. Project management and change management skills are vital for the conversion to CPOE. Because the enormous change in workflow will affect every clinician, standard project management and change management tools, such as a formal project charter, will help keep the implementation on track and manage expectations. Establishing a plan for communication is important from day 1.

Assembling an Interdisciplinary Planning and Implementation Team

The transition to CPOE is an immense cultural change that will affect every member of the health care team. No individual or department will be exempt from the impact of CPOE. Support for the project at the executive level is a prerequisite. Medical and administrative leadership/sponsorship are instrumental in the development of a clear vision for CPOE. An interdisciplinary team approach to planning and implementation is essential for a safe, well-designed, user-friendly, and successful CPOE system.

Physicians must be central players in the decision-making process, as prescriber buy-in and acceptance is crucial to CPOE success. Key departments (such as pharmacy, nursing, laboratory, radiology, admissions, dietary, and respiratory therapy) must dedicate resources and be involved in the initial effort, including workflow/process analysis and redesign, system analysis, integration between ancillary systems, review of organizational culture, and compliance with regulatory, legal, and reimbursement requirements.

The involvement of pharmacists in the development and implementation of CPOE is essential for several reasons. Pharmacists have the benefit of years of experience with electronic order entry systems. Pharmacists' experience with human factors issues related to the interaction between human and computer is invaluable, even though pharmacy systems may differ from CPOE systems in significant ways. In addition, the medication-order-entry aspect of CPOE systems leads to the most significant increase in patient safety and is likely the most complex part of the system.[21,29–32] The initial decision to purchase a completely integrated CPOE system or develop one that can interface with existing electronic systems (e.g., the pharmacy department's information system) is an important one that would benefit from the pharmacist's perspective. Although the number of successful implementations is increasing on a yearly basis,[33] the complexity of the systems should not be underestimated.

Collaboration among health care staff and the IT department is critical to the selection, implementation, and maintenance of CPOE systems. Although a CPOE system cannot be developed and implemented without IT expertise, the CPOE system is intended to serve the best interests of patients and clinicians. Clinicians and IT staff do not always talk the same language, and differences of opinion are not uncommon. Though difficult at times, these groups must work together for success. IT understands the technical aspects, but physicians, nurses, and pharmacists are best suited to determine how the CPOE system can be implemented to best serve the interests of patients and clinicians.

Recommendations for Team Structure. The organization should carefully consider the structure of the interdisciplinary implementation team, which should include physicians, nurses, pharmacists, IT staff, the chief medical information officer, and staff from all ancillary departments (e.g., laboratory services, respiratory therapy). In addition to front-line practitioners, patient safety and quality improvement staff can help immensely with some of the workflow and design decisions. CPOE systems by definition require ownership by the medical staff. Therefore, prescribers (mainly physicians) must be actively solicited for system requirements and be involved in key decisions. CPOE system design, including the content, the user interface, and the flow of CDS, will be influenced by the vendor's product, but acceptance will ultimately reside with the medical staff.

The team structure for implementing CPOE must take into account the interests and expertise of the following types of individuals:

- *Clinical content experts.* Physicians, pharmacists, mid-level providers, nurses, and practitioners of other disciplines who have clinical knowledge and workflow experience that can help shape the CPOE system to be most useful in the local environment.
- *Medical record content experts.* Health care information management representatives who oversee the legal medical record.
- *Technical experts.* Typically, IT professionals who understand the capabilities of the system, write or configure the software, and test and troubleshoot problems.
- *Front-line users.* Physicians, nurses, pharmacists, and others who care for patients on a regular basis and who will understand the positive and negative implications of each proposal regarding CPOE. CPOE's effects on nurses cannot be overstated. The workflow of incoming information completely changes with the implementation of CPOE. The unit secretary will no longer be the gatekeeper and notifier of new orders. The development of an electronic means to notify nurses of new orders must be considered and incorporated into the nursing workflow to enhance patient care.
- *Project managers.* Individuals responsible for overseeing the completion of project tasks and managing timelines and resources. There may be both a facility project manager and a project manager for the vendor or outside contractor.
- *Workflow analysts.* Team members responsible for analyzing the workflow and processes of patient care, from admission through the entire hospitalization (including transfers, surgeries, and procedures) to discharge.
- *Project sponsors.* Clinician champions and organization leaders who can, with frequent reports from the CPOE team, help overcome the many real and imagined barriers to the CPOE transition and keep the implementation on track.
- *Others.* Ancillary staff whose roles or responsibilities may change with the implementation of CPOE.

Representatives from each of these areas of expertise should work together regularly, in a variety of committees and work group formats. The team should report to a key organizational committee (e.g., the pharmacy and therapeutics [P&T] committee) as well as medical staff or other governance-related bodies. Communication with many formal committees is important as early as possible. The hospital should consider the merits of compensation for time spent away from clinical duties. The health system's existing committee structure may be utilized as oversight authority for CPOE initiatives before, during, and after the system goes live. However, it is highly recommended to create small work groups consisting of physicians, administrators, pharmacists, nurses, and IT personnel to make and approve design decisions and form specific task groups as needed when policy or process issues arise. Quick and timely action will be required during the implementation phase to keep the project moving forward on schedule and in an organized and cohesive manner. This interdisciplinary group should refer matters of policy to existing policy-making committees (e.g., P&T committee, medication safety committee, executive committee, practice guidelines committee, leadership council). The interdisciplinary CPOE committee is not a policymaking committee, but rather a tool to provide structure to existing policies. Some organizations may find it necessary to keep this new formal committee for ongoing oversight of clinical information systems and CDS decision-making.

Pharmacists are needed to provide oversight of medication-use process development. Pharmacist involvement should begin in the initial CPOE planning stages and continue throughout all phases of CPOE development and optimization. The pharmacists that serve on the interdisciplinary team would ideally be relieved of clinical duties to the extent possible in order to commit much of their time to the complex project. Those pharmacists could remain in the pharmacy or be physically relocated to whatever space the interdisciplinary team is allocated. Any pharmacist chosen to serve on the team should be

- A team player,
- Well-respected within and outside the pharmacy department,
- A good communicator,
- Knowledgeable about all facets of the medication-use system, especially the thought process prescribers use to determine a treatment or treatment plan,
- Well-versed in the regulatory and legal requirements of medication management,
- Current on patient safety initiatives and issues, both external and internal to the health system,
- Detail-oriented, with sharp analytical skills,
- Open to new ideas,
- Very interested in informatics,
- Capable of handling stressful situations and limited time lines, and
- Able to differentiate the requirements of an ordering system from those of a dispensing system and translate those requirements for others.

Outside Consultants. External consultants may be used in a variety of roles, including evaluation and vendor selection as well as project management and post-implementation assessments. Use of outside consultants may be warranted if there are insufficient resources, lack of on-site knowledge of the vendor's application, or a desire for a quicker implementation timeline. Consultants add a unique dimension to the team structure in that they have experienced how other hospitals have solved similar problems, can offer a variety of solutions based on their experience from other facilities, and have a network of colleagues they can contact for advice. Having a consultant engaged early in the process can provide continuity to the development and implementation processes.

External consultants should work in conjunction with permanent members of the implementation team. It is important that the permanent members of the team know and understand how the system was designed, how its components fit together, and how each item was built by the consultants. Changes in one part of the system may have intended and unintended downstream effects. Modifications to the system are inevitable, and the on-site team must have the knowledge to understand and execute the necessary future changes. It is detrimental to have this knowledge leave with the consultant when the contract expires. Formal documentation and knowledge transfer meetings should be part of the consultant deliverables.

Allocating Resources. The resources required to manage the transition to a CPOE system will vary, based on a number of factors: the size and complexity of the institution, whether it is an academic or a community setting, types of patients served, current IT infrastructure, the scope of the CPOE project, commitment of implementation project team members, degree of system integration, and other circumstances. There are no general rules about the time, money, or number of employees required for such a transition. Vendors may perform an assessment to help determine the resources that will be required based on the institution's circumstances.

The resources needed should be identified and approved before the project begins, and monitoring of ongoing resource needs and allocation will be necessary. Planning often focuses on capital expenses, underestimating the personnel required to build, test, maintain, improve, and train staff on the use of the system.[29] Having these resources in place is critical to the success of an implementation. During planning and implementation, resource needs may vary, based on project activities. Following implementation, order sets and CDS are integral components of managing care, and the ongoing maintenance to keep the care components current and in line with practice requires ongoing resources. In addition, as the complexity of the system increases with enhancements and user requests, resources needed for ongoing management may increase. Understanding these needs before implementation can help in resource planning.

Developing a Vision for the CPOE System

A vision statement helps describe where the organization wants to be after CPOE implementation and helps define decision-making criteria and the framework for metrics. It is imperative that the CPOE vision align tightly with the vision of the organization as a whole. Large-scale projects should include a clear organizational vision, which might be as simple as increasing patient safety or improving provider access to information. Taking the time to develop these criteria will focus the team throughout the design and implementation processes, help the team communicate the rationale for the necessary change that front-line clinicians will have to make, and lay the groundwork for ongoing measurement.

CPOE is a vital component of the institution's overall patient safety and IT development plans. It is important to establish from the beginning that CPOE is a clinical intervention and not an IT implementation. The implementation team should determine whether there are other issues that may influence CPOE implementation, such as new buildings or other system changes (e.g., pharmacy, bar-coding, or eMAR systems). The team should review and attempt to anticipate trends in regulation or best practices (e.g., from CMS, the Joint Commission, the Institute for Safe Medication Practices, or ASHP) and adopt practices from similar sites that have implemented CPOE. Finally, it should be remembered that CPOE is only one element of the hospital's IT infrastructure. Care should be taken to integrate these disparate systems, with the end result of a complete EHR.

Pharmacy involvement in CPOE development and implementation will be related mainly to medication use within the health system. Pharmacists often have experience with entry of medication orders into a computer system. This experience can be used to help providers adapt to the changes that come with CPOE, but pharmacists should be aware of the differences between ordering medications and verifying and dispensing them. Financial goals, hospital infrastructure, integration, and regulatory compliance also play an important role in the development of a vision for CPOE.

Developing a vision for medication orders in a CPOE system can be divided into three main tasks: defining the goals and objectives for the CPOE system, mapping the current and desired medication-use processes, and determining CPOE system performance requirements to reach those goals. An organization's physicians, nurses, pharmacists, other providers, and administrators can team up to prepare this vision. The vision might include describing how products should be named for easy identification or the configuration of special populations of orders. Consideration should also be given to how medication orders relate to other orders, laboratory test results, allergies, and other clinical information.

Defining Goals and Objectives for the CPOE System

Implementing CPOE is an immense cultural change that involves every part of an organization. After an overarching vision for the components of the CPOE system has been established, the implementation team should reach out to all areas of the institution to develop and explain the goals and objectives of the CPOE system. Widespread understanding and acceptance of these goals and objectives will facilitate development and implementation of the CPOE system. The central goals of a CPOE system typically include improving medication safety and the quality of health care processes.

Medication Safety. Improving the safety of the medication-ordering process should always be in the forefront of any design decision, programming modification, or enhancement to CPOE. The analysis of the existing medication-use process (see "Mapping the Current Medication-use Process" below) should identify any safety deficiencies that can be corrected with CPOE, as well as the strengths of the current processes. The addition of safety features to CPOE will be an ongoing endeavor, as acceptance of the system grows and clinicians realize how the system can improve their practices.

CPOE systems need to be monitored for unexpected safety failures. CPOE can introduce previously unknown safety failures through user interaction with the system, programming changes, or poor system design.[26] To prevent the introduction of new medication errors, careful analysis, review, and testing needs to be conducted with initial implementation and subsequent additions, modifications, and enhancements. Constant surveillance for errors and unanticipated outcomes is an ongoing necessity.[29] This evaluation can also be used to develop the goals and objectives for implementation.

A major impetus behind CPOE is that the deployment of a well-designed CPOE system with effective CDS can reduce medication errors and ADEs. A systematic review of the effects of CPOE with CDS on medication errors and ADEs supports the successful use of CPOE in health care facilities.[18] Many hospitals will implement CPOE to improve patient care, while focusing less on research that explores its impact. Nevertheless, internal systems for tracking medication errors and ADEs should be continually used to assess the impact of CPOE. CPOE could potentially

- Reduce some forms of ADEs or medication errors,
- Qualitatively change some forms of ADEs or medication errors (e.g., an error of omission may become a wrong-time error), and
- Introduce new types of ADEs or medication errors (e.g., a physician may select the wrong drug or wrong patient from a list appearing on the computer screen or inappropriately select a default dose).

Quality of Health Care Processes. In addition to improving medication safety, the goals of CPOE implementation may include such things as decreasing drug or laboratory costs, reducing the time required for pharmacist medication order review, improving data collection, or increasing communication among health care team members. If efficiencies from the direct entry of medication orders by the physician result in time savings in the pharmacy, the pharmacy department could potentially direct more pharmacist resources to patient interaction or areas such as pharmacotherapy consultation, pharmacokinetics, anticoagulation monitoring, drug regimen review, antibiotic streamlining, or intravenous-to-oral (i.v.-to-p.o.) conversions. Such goals will be different for every organization, but it is important to establish them during the planning phase of the project. The transition to CPOE represents a major paradigm shift for most organizations. The organized, goal-oriented institution will benefit from creating concise, measurable goals and objectives.[19]

Establishing Baseline Data

In conjunction with the analysis of the current medication-use process, the interdisciplinary team should develop a clear and complete understanding of the institution's current medication safety data (e.g., medication errors, ADEs) as well as the resources devoted to the manual medication order system.[34,35] It is important to track data for at least three months in advance of implementation to assemble adequate baseline data. These data can then be compared with data from the CPOE system at designated intervals. Data should be tracked over time to assess the impact of the CPOE on the medication-use process. This information can help identify workflow bottlenecks or discrepancies in the CPOE system, providing opportunities for improvement. Examples of data that may change with the implementation of CPOE and CDS include errors related to known drug allergies, ADEs related to drug–drug interactions, prescribing errors related to drug dose, and drugs withheld due to contraindications identified via CDS.

Establishing Post-Go-Live Metrics

Implementation metrics can be used to help measure achievement of organizational goals. Comparing baseline and post-go-live measures can identify which areas have improved and which need further review. Metrics are quantitative, measurable parameters, and may include

- Order entry time (e.g., average time it takes a provider to enter an order[36]),
- Compliance with established evidence-based order sets,
- Number of entered orders,
- Missing doses,
- Pharmacist interventions related to order entry problems,
- Changes to scheduled administration times in the system,
- First dose medication administration turnaround time,
- Assess possible financial indicators of success,
- Frequency of provider contact (e.g., pages for questions or errors on order entry), and
- Documented medication errors.

When reporting these data, the hospital should be careful not to overstate the impact of the CPOE system on patient outcomes. The measures listed above are process measures, not outcome measures. For example, although the CPOE system may have flagged a patient allergy and prevented administration of the medication, it is possible that even without the CPOE system the pharmacist or nurse would have identified the allergy and intervened before the drug was administered.

It is important to identify and report new errors or ADEs introduced by the CPOE system.[22,25,26,31,37–40] The hospital should actively engage clinicians at all levels in open dialogue and reporting of such issues. These reports should be used to make rapid changes in the design of the system in the spirit of continuous quality improvement.

Describing the Current Medication-Use Process And System Design

To ensure that the integrity, safety, and efficiency of the entire current medication process are maintained, if not enhanced, it is important to perform a complete analysis of the current medication-use process. This analysis should include the interdisciplinary workflows associated with medication use for multiple types of medications. The output can be represented in a variety of ways, including flow charts, narrative scenarios, analyzed issue/problem reports, and comparisons of current practices to known best practices.

The analysis of the current medication-use process should consider a variety of medication order types, based on frequency of use or potential impact on patient safety, in all different process settings (e.g., acute care, critical care, emergency department), procedural areas (e.g., diagnostic imaging), and patient populations (e.g., pediatric, geriatric, adult). The project team should consider a representative group of orders that includes the basic types of orders prescribers typically write. How orders are currently entered into the system may not necessarily be intuitive to a physician. Most importantly, the project team should consider how the prescriber currently orders medications and what would make the most sense to the prescriber when ordering electronically. CPOE systems should be designed from the prescribers' perspective, with an eye on how orders flow over the course of their existence, to encompass all facets of medication use, ensuring the process is complete from medication reconciliation through ordering, renewing, and discontinuing. Complex medication orders and/or protocols may need special attention because of current technology limitations or workflow differences. The types of medication orders that should be reviewed and included in the design, as well as the processes across which they should be considered, are listed in Figure 1.

The description of the current medication-use process should be developed from a number of sources: observation, paper order sets, discussion with clinicians, and the knowledge of those who have worked on the organization's previous process-improvement efforts. This process is an opportunity to engage staff pharmacists who service various areas of the organization. Pharmacists often have a broad view of the medication-use process, seeing it from end to end, both receiving orders from physicians and helping address complex administration scheduling issues. The project team should strive to understand the current state of the medication-use process in terms of the components listed in Table 1, which also lists the form best used to represent the component.

Developing the Future Medication-Use Process and System Design

Once the current state of the medication-use process is well understood, one or more instances of the future state (depending on the plan for phasing in the CPOE system) can be designed. This future state should be designed to meet or exceed the current levels of service and other important designated metrics and priorities (e.g. patient safety, first-dose delivery time) and address any desired improvements.

The CPOE system should be designed to support the hospital's ideal medication-use process as much as is possible. The system should be configured to support clinicians and promote improved patient care processes, rather than compromising these processes to accommodate system functionality. It will likely be necessary (and desirable) to change many of the key work processes to ensure that benefits (such as improved medication safety) are achieved. A description of the ideal medication-use process is beyond the scope of these guidelines, but key steps in a typical medication-use process are outlined in Figure 2.

A successful CPOE design is a combination of process, information systems, and supporting technologies that work together to allow the desired improvements to occur. Figures 3-6 list some of the process and technology enhancements that should be considered for incorporation into the new process/technology/system design.

The desired benefits of the CPOE implementation should be clearly identified, and the process and system design should make those benefits possible. The design should include the practices, work processes, and techno-

Figure 1. Types of medication orders and processes that should be reviewed and included in CPOE design.

Medication Order Types

Oral solids
Oral liquids
Topicals
High-risk medications (e.g., anticoagulants, heparin, insulin, or potassium chloride)
Compounded medications, such as triple mix or acetazolamide suspension (e.g., oral swish-and swallow or dermatological preparations made in the pharmacy)
Combination products (e.g., hydrocodone-acetaminophen, multi-drug inhalers)
Combination doses
Respiratory therapy
Total parenteral nutrition
I.V. medications
  Piggy-back i.v.'s
  Continuous infusion medications and titrations
Flushes
Medical staff protocols that include medications
Automated dispensing device overrides
Irrigations
Immunizations
Patient-controlled analgesia, including epidural analgesia
Sliding scale insulin and heparin
Chemotherapy standard and non-standard protocols
Conditional orders
Hemodialysis, peritoneal dialysis, and continuous renal replacement solutions
Investigational medications
Herbal medications
Ophthalmic or otic medications
Injectable medications (e.g., i.v. push, i.m.)
Medications used in operative and procedural areas
Linked or interdependent orders
Medications used for diagnostic imaging

Medication Order Processes

Ordering (physician or other clinician)
Electronic signature, signing of verbal orders
Medication reconciliation
Preparation and labeling
Medication order review
Dispensing and distribution (including interface to automated dispensing devices)
Administration and documentation
Medication schedule changes
Holding orders
Code medications
On-call to operating room or procedures
Future orders
Negative orders (e.g., do not give aspirin)
Charging
Transfer orders

Table 1.

Components of the Medication-use Process and Formats Best Suited to Representing Them

Component	Representation
Activities performed	Process flow chart
Strengths and weaknesses of the current process	Text/table
The person(s) performing the activities	Text
The information needed in order to perform the activitiy	Text
The tools and systems used to perform the activity	Flow chart
The outputs of the activity and where they are sent/recorded	Text
The time/effort used to perform the activities'	Text
The barriers, constraints, reductions in efficiency, and limitations on the activity	Text

logical components in an integrated fashion. General process design principles are listed in Figure 7.

The future state design should be an interdisciplinary effort that considers the entire medication-use process, even though parts of the process may not change or may not change much with CPOE implementation. It is important to maintain the continuity and integrity of the process by making sure that the design of the component activities is compatible and completely accounts for manual or previously automated processes.

The draft future state design is typically done with a small interdisciplinary group of clinicians (the "core team") who understand the current process and the capabilities and limitations of the CPOE system. This group should consist of clinicians who order (physicians, nurse practitioners, and pharmacists), dispense (pharmacists and pharmacy technicians), and administer (nurses and physicians) medications. This core team should have dedicated time for the project, or at least be relieved of their regular staff schedules for the time spent working on the project. The charge of this group is to weave into the system design the following factors:

- Existing work processes and systems,
- Best practices,
- New systems, with consideration for their capabilities and limitations,
- Physical limitations (e.g., space, facility issues, staffing limitations),
- Political issues (e.g., organizational priorities, limited physician cooperation or interest in CPOE),
- Desired benefits and performance improvements, and
- Compliance with regulatory, legal, and reimbursement requirements.

This redesign typically starts with a high-level process flow diagram that describes the activities performed by each member in the medication-use process, coupled with demonstrations of the system capabilities and flow. Through successive iterations, the workflow and system design is brought into increasing levels of detail and expanded to address the factors listed above.[34] Once the core team is satisfied with the design, practicing clinicians can be brought in to validate and improve the design. The clinicians involved in these process redesign sessions should be experienced and practicing clinicians who understand the current process and will likely find the potential issues with the new processes. These process redesign sessions should be as practically focused as possible and should demonstrate prototypes of orders and output from the system. They should provide a forum to discuss what to do and how it will be done. The redesign will likely take at least three or four sessions to cover the necessary detail of all the affected processes. The information gathered from these sessions can then be used to complete the process and system design and build the policy and procedure and training documents.

Failure Mode and Effects Analysis. A safety analysis of the future state design should be done prior to implementation to identify unintended or unidentified consequences.[41] Failure mode and effects analysis (FMEA) is a useful tool to prospectively evaluate the potential risks associated with the new process and identify inconsistencies or omissions that may have the unwanted effect of increasing risk to patient safety rather than reducing it.[41–44]

Other Design Considerations. It should be determined whether there are required elements at provider order entry in order for the pharmacy to verify orders (e.g., patient allergies, weight). Integrated systems start to break down the silos in which physicians, nurses, and pharmacists sometimes practice. There should be one shared field for allergy and weight documentation, so any expected workflow changes need to be discussed prior to implementation. Though it is the right thing to do, this standardization often uncovers workflow issues that were previously hidden in the paper process. The current process for handling allergy conflicts or drug interactions should be examined and it should be determined how users will handle an alert in a critical or time-dependent area, such as the emergency room. It should also be determined whether there is a need for an additional set of elements for order processing (e.g., laboratory or other results).

Medication Use within the Context of CPOE and the EHR. Whether your organization implements CPOE alone or along with other parts of the EHR (such as the eMAR), other parts of the medication-use process will be affected. To meet the long-term goal of a complete EHR, all medication orders should be included in CPOE. Having disparate ordering systems (i.e., manual and electronic systems) causes confusion, creates additional work for health care professionals, and presents risks to patient safety. The hospital

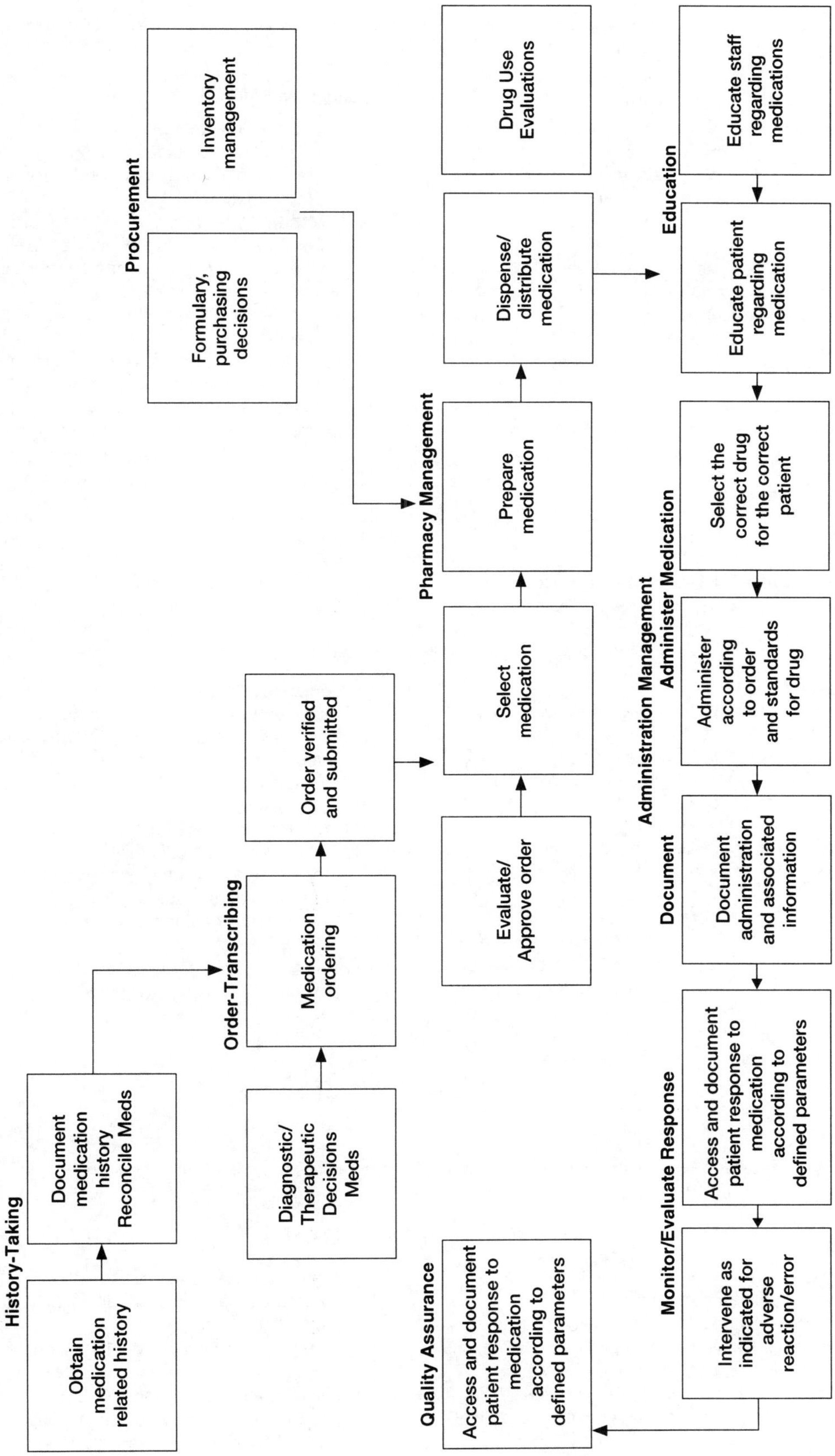

Figure 2. Medication-use process model. Reprinted, with permission, from reference 32. Copyright, VHA, Inc. 2001.

must recognize that CPOE may increase the amount of time the medical staff spends on prescribing medications, at least in the beginning.[45,46] Therefore, there must be considerable dialogue with the medical staff about their role in the overall medication-use process. It is important that they understand that CPOE is an effective way for them to communicate their orders and improve the timeliness, accuracy, and safety of patient care and that efficiency should improve over time.

Figure 3. Potential process and technology interventions in order writing and submission to improve medication safety. Reprinted, with permission, from reference 32. Copyright VHA, Inc. 2001.

Ordering: Order Writing and Submission

Process Interventions

Establish standards for abbreviations
Establish policies that do not accept incomplete or vague orders such as "continue previous medications"
Establish standard protocols for drug dosing and administration
Develop standard order sets to include drug order, time associated tests, and associated medicines
Provide routine staff education on common causes of error
Educate staff on back-up procedures for system down time
Establish policies for routine review and updating of current orders
Monitor the bypass of rules and alerts to complete order
Do not dispense drug prior to written order or verbal order verification unless critical
Minimize verbal order use

Technology Interventions

Implement tools to guide the user:
- Order entry (CPOE) with standard order sets and protocols
- Mandatory fields to complete an order
- Rules-based ordering to include dose adjustment, interaction checking, and accompanying orders

Provide formulary selections
Provide mobile charting devices to allow for ordering at the point of care
Adequate back-up procedures for system down
Updated Mar generated by CPOE or pharmacy sytem on routine basis (minimum every 24 hours)
Automated reminders or alerts for changes in patient status
Automated dispensing units do not dispense drug prior to order verification unless a critical medication

Figure 4. Potential process and technology interventions in medication history-taking and medication reconciliation to improve medication safety. Reprinted, with permission, from reference 32. Copyright VHA, Inc. 2001.

Medication History-Taking and Medication Reconciliation

Process Interventions

Establish procedures for obtaining admission history
Establish minimum data set to include medications, diagnoses, height, weight, and allergies
Establish accountability for obtaining minimum data set
Use standardized templates
Multi-disciplinary clinical documentation
Instruct patient/family on need to bring all current medications with them, including over-the-counter medications
Select and identify "record of truth"
Establish communication links with primary and extended care providers to support transitions in level of care
Replace free text with checklists when appropriate
Establish standard abbreviations for medication recording
Provide wallet cards or other forms to prompt patients to bring complete home medication information

Technology Interventions

Implement tools to guide the user
Clinical documentation with templates and checklists
Prompts for required fields to include minimum data set
Flags to highlight changes in minimum data set from previous data
Improve access to patient record through implementation of computer-based patient record/clinical data repository
Establish communication links with primary and extended care providers to support transitions in level of care
Provide mobile charting devices to allow for documentation at the point of care
Structured for computer-based clinical documentation
Technology adherence to standards

Figure 5. Potential process and technology interventions in pharmacy evaluation of orders to improve medication safety. Reprinted, with permission, from reference 32. Copyright VHA, Inc. 2001.

Pharmacy Evaluation of Orders

Process Interventions

- Establish standards for abbreviations
- Establish policies that do not accept incomplete or vague orders such as "continue previous medications"
- Develop standard order sets to include drug order, associated tests and associated medications
- Provide routine staff education on common causes of error
- Do not dispense drug prior to order evaluation unless critical
- Establish procedures for evaluation of orders and when to clarify

Establish procedures for pharmacy dosing
- Develop procedures for escalating an order that is on hold for clarification

Technology Interventions

- Adequate back-up procedures for system downtime
- Minimize system downtime
- Automated reminders or alerts for patient changes in status

Pharmacy alerts and reminders based on change in lab value, drug-to-drug interaction, dose-checking, drug-to-diagnosis, drug-to-allergy checking
- Targeted alerts that vary by individual receiving them to reduce alert fatigue
- Ability to view online clinical information to include: lab values, clinical documentation and orders
- Interfaces to auto-populate pharmacy system with ADT, laboratory, clinical documentation
- Access to drug knowledge base

Figure 6. Potential process and technology interventions in administering medications to improve medication safety. Reprinted, with permission, from reference 32. Copyright VHA, Inc. 2001. RFID = radio frequency identification.

Administering Medications

Process Interventions

- Standardize medication administration times
- Standardize equipment for IV infusion; minimize number of different kinds of devices
- Provide tools that assist staff in calculating correct rate of infusion
- Stock pre-mixed IV drugs
- Establish standard dose packaging and labeling
- Patients with multiple IV access lines have line clearly marked at distal end
- Distal ports of non-IV tubing incompatible with medication oral syringe
- Standard protocols for the physical assessment prior to administering a specific drug throughout the hospital

Technology Interventions

- MAR with time based schedule
- Electronic MAR
- Automated drug distribution carts at the point of care
- Smart infusion pumps
- Alerts to caregiver to obtain and document clinical information prior to administering a drug
- Bar code/RFID administration systems
- Comprehensive wireless network coverage
- Needleless administration system
- Other medication delivery technologies

Figure 7. General CPOE process design principles.

CPOE Process Design Principles

- Standardization of order entry and management information and workflows across the organization to the degree possible.
- Simplifying processes.
- Creating an effective interdisciplinary, team-based approach (i.e., improving communication).
- Designing mechanisms for reporting and learning from errors.
- Seeking redundancy through use of technology to support clinical decision making.
- Avoiding reliance on memory.
- Using constraints and forcing functions where appropriate.
- Simulating planned and unplanned events for how people interact with each other and technology.
- Planning for failure and designing for recovery.
- Providing access to a core set of integrated clinical information at the time and point of decision-making.

The hospital should provide incentives for prescribers to utilize the system and disincentives for giving verbal orders or continuing to handwrite orders. To facilitate use of the system, prescribers should have access to the CPOE system from multiple venues, including their offices and homes and via wireless computers. If clinicians have the ability to enter orders from multiple locations such as home or office, a defined process should exist to easily reach the prescriber if there is a problem with the order (e.g., non-formulary, lack of availability).

All new orders should be verified by a pharmacist and reviewed by a nurse, and these actions should be documented in the EHR prior to medication administration. The nurse should work directly in the EHR for all clinical documentation, including medication administration. To comply with the "five rights" of medication administration,[47] a workstation must be available close to the patient's bedside with ready access to that patient's relevant information to facilitate resolution of any questions on the medications that arise. Figure 8 lists some design considerations for the workgroup as new workflows are designed for different clinical scenarios.

Computers (both wired and wireless) should be available in sufficient quantities so that no clinician has to wait to use one. It is critical that the technologies used for stationary and mobile computing be matched to the anticipated workflow. It is likely that stationary computers, handheld devices (e.g., personal digital assistants), and tablet and cart-mounted computers will all be needed for some part of medication ordering for various users. If they are not part of an integrated system, the CPOE, eMAR, and pharmacy information systems should be available on the same computer to facilitate switching between systems. Any other technologies that are used by providers (e.g., voice recognition) should not only be on the same computer but ideally available from these devices as well. Users should be able to easily switch between different applications if needed, and clinical data should freely flow between applications so that the pharmacist and other providers have real-time access to the same information.

Planning for CDS

CPOE is an important part of an organization's plan for improved safety and quality. The addition of CDS to the EHR and CPOE is essential for the prevention of adverse events and improvement in patient outcomes.[17,20,21] A full discussion of CDS is beyond the scope of this document. ASHP plans to cover the topic in future guidelines. The purpose of this section is to provide an overview of CDS that will allow incorporation of CDS to be addressed in planning.

CDS can be defined as providing the appropriate clinicians with clinical knowledge and/or patient information intelligently filtered and presented at appropriate times to enhance patient care.[48] CDS has many intervention types, including but not limited to the following[49]:

- Documentation forms/templates (structured guidance, required or restricted fields, checklists),
- Relevant data presentation (optimize decision making by ensuring all pertinent data are considered),
- Order/prescription creation facilitators (pick-lists, pre-completed order sentences and order sets),
- Protocol/pathway support (multistep care plans, link to evidence or protocol, pertinent reference information or institution-specific best practice guidance),

Figure 8. CPOE design considerations.

Design Considerations

How do orders post to the MAR, and what is the relationship between the MAR and intake/output flowsheets?
Are there other documentation flowsheets that are also used or needed (e.g., patient-controlled anesthesia, continuous renal replacement therapy)?
When do orders need to be approved by pharmacy before a nurse can chart or administer the first dose of the medication?
Can nursing staff easily tell when the order has been verified by pharmacy?
Is there a mechanism to have critically needed orders available on the eMAR before pharmacist review?
What medication information is displayed to the nurse for administration (i.e., both brand and generic names)?
How are orders sorted on the MAR (e.g., are as-needed orders separated from scheduled orders)?
Are administration instructions and notes required (e.g., do not administer oral ciprofloxacin with Maalox)? Will they be supplied from the CPOE system or from the pharmacy system?
Are nondrug items needed on the MAR (e.g., wet to dry dressings)? If so, how will these items be entered (i.e., are these orders that pharmacy must review and approve)? Can some type of treatment administration record be created for these items?
Is there a chart on removal from an automated dispensing cabinet or are auto-charting functions in use?
How will the health system develop a bar-coding system for medication administration?
Override rates of alerts by both pharmacists and providers to better set sensitivities for the warning.
Order verification times by pharmacists to determine turn-around times for different priorities of medication ordering.
Compliance to clinical practice guidelines and order sets.
If integration of the CPOE system is available with automated dispensing devices, then monitoring for overrides would be warranted.
Monitoring free-text orderables in the system, to better address the provider's needs and provide guidance for appropriate formulary build.
Does the software provide the ability to designate a medication and document "First Dose Effectiveness"?
How are enteral nutritional supplements and tube feeding supplements documented, ordered, etc?
Does the software provide "Query Tools"?
Will provider, pharmacist, nursing software "Hand Off" IT tools be needed?
Does the software handle "Look-A-Like, Sound-A-Like" medications and due to this aspect should generate medication nomenclature be utilized exclusively?
Does the software provide the functionality for "after hours" entry and how will the review be completed if pharmacy service is closed?
How will MAR/eMAR handle multi-component medication orders?
How will MAR/eMAR process fractional doses of medication package forms?
How will reporting needs be developed and integrated into the system for users? When?
How are co-signatures or verbal order sign-offs obtained?

- Alerts and reminders (drug–drug interactions, therapeutic duplication, drug–disease, allergy alerts, and others), and
- Automated ADE detection based on patient symptoms, labs, diagnostic results, and patient notes.

Because CDS has such a broad definition, the line between CDS and CPOE is not always clear. Basic forms of CDS, such as fully defined order sentences and order sets, are an important aspect of CPOE and can decrease errors while enhancing clinician acceptance of the system.[27,28] This type of basic CDS encourages clinicians to make proper choices initially rather than alerting them to potentially problematic choices after the fact and is an essential part of any CPOE implementation.

An organization must recognize that to realize the benefits of CDS, the CPOE system must be accepted by clinicians and used effectively. Poor design or too many alerts could lead to system rejection or, even worse, unanticipated outcomes such as increased errors or adverse events.[25,26,50–53]

Some CDS, including checks for allergies, drug–drug interactions, drug duplications, and dose ranges, are typically delivered via an interruptive alert to the user or displayed as a passive warning on an order entry screen. Such CDS should be considered before CPOE implementation, but designers should keep in mind that a high number of interruptive alerts may cause clinicians to ignore alerts altogether and may even threaten clinician acceptance of CPOE. The way alerts are prioritized and presented to the user may be as important as which alerts are presented. Alerts for very serious clinical situations may be ignored when lost in a sea of less important ones.[54] Some vendor systems allow clients to change severity levels or even disable some alerts in an effort to bring alert interruptions to a better signal-to-noise ratio and thus decrease the potential for alert fatigue, particularly for physician recipients.[50–52] Ideally, there needs to be an alternative mechanism to provide CDS feedback to prescribers that is not intrusive but still allows the prescriber to know that there may be issues with an order. If ignored, these alerts can be acted upon by the pharmacist.

The strategy for prioritization of CDS should be defined as early as possible, and pharmacists should take a leading role in all medication-related CDS. It is likely that organizations will be eager to implement CDS along with CPOE. Pharmacists should ensure that the CPOE system is implemented with basic CDS, such as order sets and sentences, while using appropriate caution when implementing alerts.[27] Although vendor systems are continuously improving and may allow tiering of alerts, there is typically a significant amount of work necessary to vet any changes and carry out the technical work involved in the customization. The combination of pharmacists' clinical knowledge of drugs and their experience with the interruptive alerts that have been present in pharmacy information systems for years provide pharmacists with a unique understanding of the many implications of implementing medication-related CDS. Pharmacists should work with medical leadership, either through the P&T, informatics, or another interdisciplinary committee, to decide how and when medication-related CDS will be added to CPOE. Pharmacists are well positioned to formulate local evidence criteria, collect information on medication therapy outcomes, and to bring together institutional health providers for the purpose of setting priorities and targeted outcomes where select IT interventions are made. The design, implementation, and optimization of CDS is an exciting area of opportunity for pharmacists now and in the years to come.

Elements of a Safe CPOE System

Minimum Features and Functions. The implementation group and key stakeholders should consider what features and functions of the CPOE system are desired both now and in the future. Starting with a pilot group of users allows experience with the system to build and permits users to work through some process issues before system usage is widespread. Any pilot should be brief, with plans for a roll-out shortly after addressing the major discoveries. A highly sophisticated system may take so long to develop that interest is lost, or it may be too sophisticated or rigid in its initial application to be well accepted.

An important consideration during CPOE implementation is the determination of which functionalities are required for go-live. CPOE will always be a work in progress, and there will be opportunities for modifications and enhancements. At a minimum, the project team should evaluate all existing manual medication ordering processes, including such complex orders as epidurals, patient-controlled analgesia, weight-based dosing, lab-result-dependent dosing, tapering medication doses, total parenteral nutrition, and chemotherapy, along with critical patient safety functionality driven from known internal or external sentinel events. An agreed-upon list of basic functionality should be established in order to ensure a timely yet successful go-live. If some complex or high-risk medication orders will be left on paper at the initial go-live (e.g., chemotherapy), be sure this is well communicated during training. As well, this principle applies to other identified yet unresolved design topics. The project team will to need re-visit these topics for completion in the post-go-live period.

General Features and Functions. The user interface is often a problematic aspect of CPOE. Users have been reported to enter orders for the wrong patient or to select the wrong item (or wrong feature of an order) unintentionally because they did not use selection lists properly or because it is very easy to select the wrong item from a drop-down list.[38] The CPOE user interface should incorporate appropriate human-factors engineering to avoid risk-prone workflows and controls (e.g., memorized mnemonic codes or function keys, long selection lists) that may produce order-entry errors. The order entry functionality should be independent of patient setting (e.g., inpatient, outpatient), and users should be able to combine data (e.g., order history) from all settings without a need for independent searches or screen selections. The system should include an online help function for system navigation and provide notification if another user modifies the patient record while an order session is ongoing, without losing the session. All displays should contain the patient name, patient location, user name, and function in consistent screen locations. The system should support third-party data entry for prescribers by simultaneous display of the same session in multiple locations and default fields where possible or helpful. The CPOE system should permit user definition of data elements and fields that can be attached to any portion of the database. The system should permit user-friendly, error-free medication order processing by providing the functionalities for the CPOE interface and order processing listed in Figure 9.

Levels of Access. The team will need to determine the levels of access or security permitted to staff throughout the hospital. The team may find it easier to begin with the current level of privileges for existing systems.

In general, pharmacists require a high level of access (full access to medication orders, and in some cases the ability place lab orders) because they cover multiple areas; place, alter, or discontinue orders; and may practice under protocols that require monitoring of laboratory test results. There may be different levels of access within the pharmacy department (e.g., actions by a pharmacy student, intern, or resident may need to be reviewed by a senior pharmacist; pharmacy technicians may require different levels of access, depending on duties). Staff may also need off-site or alternative site access.

In addition to pharmacy personnel access, the design team will need to determine levels of access for other staff members. This should include all categories of physicians that practice at the site (e.g., attendings, specialists, consultants, community clinicians with privileges, residents or other trainees, fellows, and medical students). The medical staff office, medical staff executive committees, or P&T committees may be able to make recommendations for appropriate access based on existing policies. Nursing will need to consider similar access issues and ensure compliance with provider practice acts. Ideally, these issues are addressed by existing policies that will only need to be reviewed and implemented. Other ancillary staff will need to be granted access, depending on their need for information and orders that will be built within CPOE and routed to the appropriate department for action.

User Levels and Co-Signatures. The CPOE system should permit restriction of medication orders by user type, individual order, or class of order. Each medication order should indicate the name and user level of the ordering party. The CPOE system should support the entry of unverified orders and the editing and verification of unverified orders, and this function should be role-based and restricted. The system should also support the creation of reminders or inbox messages for orders that require a co-signature. The pending prescriber co-signature name should default into the field from service, team, or coverage schedules, and there should be an option to override the name. The system should provide the ability to require that all orders be countersigned prior to placing a discharge order if the organization wishes to implement this.

Medication Order Status. Considerations regarding medication order status include the following:

Figure 9. Functionalities for CPOE interface and order processing.

CPOE Interface

- Multiple active sessions on one display (i.e., ability to put a current order session on hold and review other information, then return to the original work session without losing the work in progress).
- Side-by-side viewing of active order lists and any system-maintained order list (e.g., a standard order set, personal favorites list, or critical path order set).
- Alignment of orders by department while in side-by-side view.
- Switching between applications on the same display without exiting order functions.
- Utilization of all functions via either keyboard or mouse.
- Forward and backward navigation anywhere in the application.
- Access to the Internet from anywhere in the orders application.
- Access from multiple locations (e.g., sign-on, viewing, data entry, and verification at clinical or remote location).
- Order entry with minimal (<3) screen flips and user definition of defaulted fields.

CPOE Medication Order Processing

- Ability to return user to previous screen.
- Online access to error message documentation.
- Hospital-defined error messages.
- Ability to audit and track all errors and alerts.
- Robust search functionality available from all screens.
- Support for coding all diagnoses, tests, and procedures with institutional, departmental, and user-definable subsets of preferred terms (e.g., the appropriate edition of the International Classification of Diseases,[55] SnoMed CT,[56] or others).
- Ability to establish cross-references for tests or procedures, including:
  - o Information regarding the name of a procedure or test (i.e., the ability to use alternate names for a procedure).
  - o Information regarding indications for, execution of, cost of, and medical literature pertinent to a procedure.
  - o Diagnosis codes that can be restricted based on type of exam or test.
  - o Diagnosis code restrictions that staff can override by direct entry of the code or access to full table for lookup.
  - o Ability to enter a diagnosis code along with reason for exam.
  - o Ability to maintain orders online for the duration of the patient stay and to display the status of the orders (e.g., open, in process, completed, scheduled to expire, expired) during order inquiry.
  - o Ability to store, display, and print patient test instructions as well as preparation instructions for the order.
- Ability to perform global set-up changes (i.e., changes to a master file table element can be optionally set to automatically populate all relevant items throughout the table).
- Ability to update patient service and physician(s).
- Ability to clearly note, flag and color-code order status.
- Option to have active orders remain visible on the same screen while writing new orders.
- Ability to view all orders, including stopped and interrupted (partially entered) orders.
- Automatic assignment of unique order identification numbers used in mapping to other systems, with the order identification number large enough, or based on an algorithm, so that such numbers are not repeated within 5 years.
- Ability to retain multiple order numbers or other unique identifiers from other systems.
- Option to manually update order status, with the ability to restrict such updates to specific order items or specific users or user classes.
- Ability to create user-defined order status.
- One-step cancel/reorder process.
- Discontinue, discontinue/renew, cancel occurrence, and hold order functions.
- Automatic calculations.
- Option to input order information using free text.
- Ability to search for, track, and audit free text orders.
- Ability to drill down for detail from every screen.
- Ability to drill down to the following during the order entry process:
  - o Medication and doses, since initial orders include suspended and discontinued orders.
  - o Termination date and time of current orders.
  - o Allergies (coded).
  - o Patient diagnoses (coded).
  - o Demographic information.
  - o Visit information (medical).
  - o Physicians responsible for the patient (resident, attending, and consultant physicians, at a minimum).
  - o Active and completed orders with dates and times.
  - o Patient location and service.
- Modules with data specific to clinical specialties, including sets for reporting results, CDS, and order sets.

- Whether all orders must be reviewed by a pharmacist before they are active or posted to the MAR.
- If the answer to the above question is yes, the process in which the organization will handle urgent medications that are administered before pharmacist review.
- Should the CPOE system have some medications on override for urgent use? Are these medications always on override or are there alternative methods for ordering them?
- Does the pharmacy have sufficient staff to deal with the volume of orders? Pharmacy will potentially see all changes, i.v. fluid orders, discontinuation orders, and titration orders. Design considerations will need to address the disposition of the orders prior to implementation.
- If a prescriber enters and then changes an order, how are those two orders reconciled into one order?
- How does the system handle an order by a physician assistant or student that requires a co-signature before becoming active?
- Do hold orders need a defined duration to be accepted? Do these orders automatically discontinue if on hold for a certain amount of time?

Except in urgent situations as described by the Joint Commission,[57] a pharmacist should verify every medication order prior to drug dispensing and administration. Once verified by a pharmacist, the order should populate the pharmacy computer system, generate labels and other items necessary for dispensing, release the drug in the automated dispensing device (if applicable), and populate the eMAR as an active order. The order should be available to the eMAR as soon as it is placed, but it should be clear to the nurse whether the pharmacist has verified the order or not.

Order History. The CPOE system should permit viewing of orders from all previous patient encounters regardless of enterprise location, setting, or patient status. The system should be capable of storing and retrieving previous patient order lists and sorting, reporting, and printing patient order lists by date and date range, setting, patient status (e.g., discharge), service, department, and provider.

The system should allow pharmacists to maintain eMARs and permit online updates, provide online capability to automatically generate a hard copy of eMARs for downtime back-up, provide the ability to display and/or print patient medication profiles or eMARs on demand or at a specified time, and include the ability to have multiple formats that are definable by systems-level staff.

Documentation in the eMAR. The CPOE system should seamlessly build the eMAR from orders in real time. Some institutions may want medication administration time changes to be modifiable from the eMAR, and the eMAR may have a bi-directional interface to the pharmacy information system (if it is not an integrated system). The system should provide the ability to enable bar-code medication documentation. Pharmacist order validation should automatically update the eMAR. The pharmacy and nursing departments should work together to ensure that the eMAR is designed to be readable and user-friendly from the nurse's perspective. Pharmacists and nurses should have the ability to add or delete patient allergies, enter special instructions, change administration times, and place medication orders on or remove them from hold or conditional status. Changes made to administration times in the eMAR should back-populate the CPOE and pharmacy information systems.

Medication Orderable Design and Build Considerations

The design and build of the medication orderables are key tasks in implementing the CPOE system. Care should be taken in designing and building the formulary or formularies, as well as the standard orders and order sets that are built from the formulary. The pharmacy department must have direct involvement in this task.

The CPOE formulary cannot be simply a copy of the pharmacy inventory. Prescribers need to have the orderables constructed to match how they order medications (therapeutic entity), rather than how the pharmacy maintains medication inventory (dosage form/product). In addition, care must be exercised when deciding on the default dose, frequency, and route values for items that will be displayed to the prescriber and in developing the construction of standard orders. Medication errors can result from a hurried prescriber accepting the default that he or she assumes must be correct.[25] The CPOE system should be able to generate formulary lists by generic name, trade name, and dosage form.

The CPOE system should allow routine online updating of the formulary and clinical checks of information without system functionality downtime. The system should provide authorized personnel the ability to maintain and display the formulary with pertinent data (e.g., formulary code, generic name, trade name, national drug code [NDC], or American Hospital Formulary Service [AHFS] number), while limiting access to certain formulary data by role. The CPOE system should include the ability to identify whether an i.v. with a medication additive is to be handled as a large-volume i.v. or as a small-volume i.v. for appropriate handling within the pharmacy department for compounding and dispensing. The system should allow the ability to make changes to the medication identifier (NDC or RxNorm identifier), communicate those changes to other systems, and receive changes from other systems.

Build Considerations

IT analysts design and build the system from documents or order sets reviewed and approved by the multidisciplinary group. Standard IT processes should be followed, beginning with the design phase. Once the design has been approved, IT staff should build the system in a test environment. A test environment protects from mishaps in the live (or "production") environment. It is important for the test environment to match the production environment so that testers get a true feel for how the build will work and interact. IT staff should meet with nursing and pharmacy throughout building and testing phases to resolve any issues that may arise.

After the builder is satisfied that the requested build or order set is complete, the builder should then develop a testing plan. The builder should work through the test plan initially and sign off when the build works as designed.

Next, pharmacy and nursing should perform testing. This testing should involve patient scenarios throughout the patient's visit. Pharmacy is integral to this process and should ensure proper medication management and workflow. When the build passes pharmacy and nursing testing, physicians should review, test, and sign off.

When all aspects have been tested and fixed, and any necessary education is completed, the build may be moved to production. Follow-up is critical to ensure the build meets the needs of providers and is not adversely affecting ancillary staff. A mechanism to report issues quickly must be established, so that the implementation team can investigate and resolve them. The CPOE group should maintain reports of problems and review those lists for recurrent issues. Providing feedback and updates to the persons reporting problems is vital to progression of the project. Clinicians need to know they have been heard and resolution is being sought.

Dependent or Joined Orders. Support for dependent or joined orders is important in the case of i.v. medications and the diluent used for administration, two drugs to be taken together, or a drug and a measurement requirement (e.g., digoxin and pulse rate). The CPOE system needs to make it easy for the prescriber to order these types of formulary items. The system should be flexible enough for the prescriber to select the drug form and size or indicate the diluent for an i.v. piggy-back when ordering if so desired or to allow these choices to be made once the order reaches the pharmacy system.

Order Sets. Requiring providers to use a CPOE system requires a change in workflow, and many fear it may increase the time clinicians spend processing orders.[46] Configuring pre-constructed order sentences and order sets prior to implementing CPOE may increase speed, accuracy, and acceptability of CPOE.[27,28,58] Careful deliberation is needed prior to the creation of CPOE order sets, including consideration of how order sets are currently developed and revised (e.g., by department or by individual practitioners), what the process to propose and review order sets is, and what level of medical oversight is in place for order set development and use. It is also important to understand ordering patterns when developing order sets for use by clinicians. Many organizations use this opportunity to improve and standardize across important aspects of care, such as post-operative nausea and vomiting or pain management, as well as move to evidence-based order sets from their legacy order sets.[28]

The system should permit development of specific admission pathways (e.g., order sets capable of including any type of order and intervention) and integrate with data documented elsewhere in the EHR (e.g., medical histories, medication lists, laboratory results, diagnostic images, clinical documentation, progress notes, narrative summaries [such as operative reports or consultations]). Order set availability should be limitable by user, user role, location, service, or patient status or diagnosis. The system should permit an unlimited number of orders within an order set and an unlimited number of order sets within departments, across departments, and with user-definable time parameters. Order sets can include nursing orders, tests, and medications, and should include appropriate laboratory tests at appropriate intervals to assist in monitoring therapy. Though many systems allow users to create and save their own order sets in a favorites list, this flexibility needs to be weighed against the desire to standardize care by allowing hospital-based order sets only.[28] Discontinuation of an order set should trigger the automatic ability to review, edit, or discontinue all linked orders.

Because the CPOE system may permit initiation of standard order sets with a single action (mouse click, keyboard stroke, etc.), order sets' ease of use may lead to inappropriate or excess medications being ordered. Order sets should be allowed to include linked orders, but orders grouped in a standard order set need not be linked. The institution should decide whether all orders in the set are going to be active once they are signed or if prescribers are required to actively check and click on each medication before signing.

The CPOE system should require designation of an owner (i.e., department, service, person, or role) for each order set. CPOE order sets should be reviewed on a periodic basis for therapy updates. Item and service maintenance should be performed at the departmental level, with updates in item or service definition flagged for review by the owner of the standard order set containing that item or service (i.e., the change triggers a report that the order set requires review). The CPOE system should support restriction of departmental or service standard order set creation or editing by role or individual.

The CPOE system should support standard order set maintenance and review by

- Grouping order sets by department/service,
- Dating the creation and review of order sets,
- Providing periodic (user-defined intervals or dates, or as-needed) reporting of standard order sets that require review by owner (department, service, person, or role), and
- Permitting global changes.

Critical Pathways and Protocol Order Sets. Critical pathways and paper-based order sets, a very basic form of CDS already widely used in hospitals, provide a starting point in efforts to standardize care and improve quality and safety through the CPOE system. With the implementation of evidence-based order sets, organizations can provide the prescriber with a direct link to the electronic literature supporting the recommended practice. The work of synthesizing and classifying the available evidence is done by organizations such as the National Guideline Clearinghouse[59] and the Cochrane Database of Systematic Reviews.[60] Organizations may incorporate these guidelines into electronic order sets and critical pathways, in addition to providing the link to give prescribers point-of-care access to the evidence-based literature at the time of order entry.

The CPOE system should support all functions listed under general order sets for critical pathways and protocol order sets. The system should provide a default set of protocols that are available by service and physician and a default set of protocols that are restricted by location. The CPOE system should include an alert system for orders not completed within user-defined time parameters or time parameters required by critical paths or research protocol.

Medication Order Linking. The CPOE system should include the ability to identify orders as linked and sequential or mutually exclusive or time off-set, and to specify intervals, as well as cascade changes in future orders to maintain sequence and timing. It should permit an order stop to automatically bring up any linked orders for re-verification, with the default being to cancel unless re-verified. The system should provide automatic re-sequencing of future orders if any item identified as sequential is moved on the timeline, and it should permit linked orders (i.e., reflexive occurrences that trigger other procedures) that cascade through multiple levels.

Favorites Lists. The CPOE system should permit use of favorites lists by individual user that may include orders for multiple departments (e.g., laboratory, pharmacy, radiology). The system should provide default components of medication prescribing ("Sigs"), such as dose route frequency, and length of order, that are user-definable at the nursing unit level and that have discharge orders or discharge worksheet functionality. The system should provide default Sigs and permit users to save favorite Sigs in user favorites. Users should be able to create favorites lists that include orders from multiple departments on one list. Favorites lists should be fully editable on an ad hoc basis for an active order session, and user-specific favorites lists should be editable by the user. Users should be able to designate any order list as a favorite and may name or rename the list ad hoc (i.e., the save function automatically prompts for name, defaulting to the existing name if available). There should be an option to save an order list as a favorite, either as a new favorite or as a replacement for an existing favorite; that option should be available during any ordering session. Favorites lists should be allowed to contain ordering details that default into the order, and default details should be editable and replaceable during order entry. The CPOE system should support context-specific favorites lists by user, nursing unit, service, and diagnosis, and by combinations of user and diagnosis or by combinations of user, diagnosis, and setting (e.g., outpatient, inpatient). User favorites lists should be copied and shared easily, and the system should allow favorites lists to be built by opening and then editing standard order sets and saving as a favorite. Favorites lists may also include reminders. The system should permit review of favorites lists.

Pharmacy Department Considerations

The ideal CPOE system will have to be integrated with or have a fully functional bi-directional interface with the hospital's pharmacy computer system so that orders entered or modified in one system will populate fields in the other system, avoiding the need for dual order entry. The bi-directional feature of an interface is important because it prevents potentially dangerous discrepancies between data in the pharmacy and EHR systems and removes the transcription step of the medication-use process. In addition, if the distribution and administration components of medication management are not linked, then documentation and billing will not be either, causing more opportunities for error and audit problems.

In their day-to-day interaction with the CPOE system, pharmacists should be working primarily in the pharmacy system, which has all relevant patient information fully integrated with the EHR and CPOE module. The pharmacist's roles include verifying all orders, reviewing and responding to alerts, and clinical monitoring of the patient. The pharmacist should have security privileges to enter and modify orders under protocol (such as formulary or formulation changes).The pharmacist should see all orders within a particular group of orders so that they can see the context in which each individual drug order was prescribed. Additionally, any functionality to help the pharmacist prioritize the review and approval of orders will improve the care of patients.

Pharmacists should receive and work with orders electronically in a queue. Patients with stat orders should appear at the top of the list and be clearly differentiated from less urgent orders. Pharmacists should have the ability to screen their view of orders based on the nursing units they are responsible for on a given shift. At no time should a pharmacist be able to view orders for more than one patient at the same time.

When working with paper orders, pharmacists often gain insight into the medication orders from the context of the surrounding patient care orders. CPOE systems should preserve that context so that pharmacists can view an order in terms of the other therapies, tests, nutrition, and nursing care surrounding it.

Communication Among Departments

The CPOE system should allow for notification of clinicians for pending orders needing signature via e-mail, pager, text message, or inbox message. Pharmacist order notification should be allowed via printout, work queue, e-mail message, system message, or pager. The default method for receiving notification of orders should be definable by the department or service, and the system should support special notification methods for specific services or items different from the departmental or service default, without affecting summary reporting by department. Users should be able to print orders to alternate locations and to send messages, orders, and alerts to additional departments (including information about scheduling and priority of orders) as a single order is being entered or completed. The CPOE system should have an option that order placement generates user-defined worklists. The system should also provide the ability to e-mail patient and preparation instructions and to reference on-call lists.

Education and Training of Health Care Providers

The rate of adoption of the new CPOE system may be directly linked to the extent of training provided to users prior to and during the implementation. One cannot spend too much time training users, as the change the new system entails will be overwhelming. This training can be in the form of formal classroom training, local expert training, or "at-the-elbow" support and training (the type of training typically most welcomed by physicians) during implementation. Organizations may find the most success in using a combination of all three. The more familiar the users are with the system at the time of implementation, the easier the transition will be.

The facility should train and employ a group of prescriber "super users." These users will support the go-live, help the institution refine the CPOE system to be as efficient as possible, and serve as liaisons and CPOE champions to the other members of the medical staff. There should be ongoing, open dialogue with leadership and medical staff members to continually improve the system.

Each training session should be geared toward the type of user, since utilization will differ by clinician type (e.g., physician, respiratory therapist, nurse, pharmacist, laboratory technician). The initial training of users is important, but ongoing training for new users, changes in programming, and functionality require that training be given a high priority after transition to the new system.

Overview of System. The initial introduction to the system should familiarize the user with the layout of the system. It should review toolbars and menus of each application. The first glimpse should include any definitions that are new or to which meanings may be different from the current process.

Accessing Data. This section of training should familiarize the user with the various methods for accessing data. It should provide information on sorting and filtering data. Because access to data will vary based upon the type of user, separating different user types for training purposes at this stage may be beneficial, and this is a good time to discuss security and privileges.

Documenting Information. This section should teach users how to document information pertinent to their practices. These tasks would include adding basic patient information and documentation onto flow sheets, as well as clinical progress notes.

Orders. The training sessions on medication orders will be the most comprehensive. Some users will be limited to ordering tests or procedures specific to their practices. Physicians, nurses, and pharmacists, however, will spend a large percentage of their time in the CPOE system working with orders. Time should be taken to demonstrate each type of order. After the demonstration, users should practice working with all types of orders that they may process in various scenarios. Though documented information may be sparse in test domains, practicing with realistic patient scenarios will provide the best training results and prepare the user for success when using the live CPOE system.

Pilot Project. A pilot with a defined scope is advisable at the beginning of the implementation phase. Organizers should consider the length of the pilot, which patients will be included, what the objectives of the pilot are (i.e., testing system performance, workflow, completeness of ordering), and what happens at the conclusion of the pilot (e.g., more programming, more testing, another pilot, or live rollout). Consideration should be given to type of prescriber/practitioner, order types and number of patient transfers into or out of pilot test area as well as flow of patient information to non-pilot areas. Because user feedback is a valuable objective of the pilot, organizers should develop and use a formal evaluation tool for the pilot clinicians. A time analysis should be performed, comparing how long it takes the pharmacy to process orders with the CPOE system versus their previous workflow. If the time analysis demonstrates a negative impact on workload, the facility may consider making appropriate staffing adjustments. These adjustments will vary, based on the percentage of orders directly entered by the prescriber, and should be continually assessed. True final measurement of process performance capabilities will likely not be realized until implementation processes have been completed and stabilized. A time analysis should also be performed comparing how long it takes CPOE-trained nursing staff to administer and document medications in the CPOE system versus the manual system. This analysis should determine whether time is saved by eliminating manual transcription of orders and manual development and maintenance of MARs. If the time analysis demonstrates a negative impact on workload, the facility should make appropriate staffing adjustments. These adjustments will vary, based on the percentage of orders directly entered by the prescriber, and should be continually assessed.

Conclusion

These guidelines provide guidance to pharmacists in hospitals and health systems on planning for and implementing safe CPOE systems. Pharmacists should utilize their unique knowledge and skills as part of the interdisciplinary CPOE planning and implementation team. Participation by pharmacists is critical in defining the vision, goals, and objectives of the CPOE system; establishing essential metrics to measure the success of CPOE system implementation; re-engineering the medication-use process as part of CPOE system implementation; determining the functionality that ensures the safety of the CPOE system; planning for CDS; and educating and training health care providers to use the CPOE system. Finally, for optimal benefits to patients, organizations should realize that the implementation is merely the beginning and that pharmacists should continue to take a central role in ongoing system optimization and continued CDS implementation.

References

1. Kohn LT, Corrigan JM, Donaldson MS, eds. *To err is human—building a safer health system.* Washington, DC: National Academy Press; 1999.
2. Brennan TA, Leape LL, Laird NM, et al. Incidence of adverse events and negligence in hospitalized patients. Results of the Harvard Medical Practice Study I. *N Engl J Med.* 1991; 324:370–6.
3. Leape LL, Brennan TA, Laird NM, et al. The nature of adverse events in hospitalized patients: Results from the Harvard Medical Practice Study II. *N Engl J Med.* 1991; 324:377–84.
4. Thomas EJ, Studdert DM, Burstin HR, et al. Incidence and types of adverse events and negligent care in Utah and Colorado. *Med Care.* 2000; 38:261–71.
5. Phillips DF, Christenfeld N, Glynn LM. Increase in U.S. medication-error deaths between 1983 and 1993. *Lancet.* 1998; 351:643–4.
6. Bates DW, Spell N, Cullen DJ, et al. The costs of adverse drug events in hospitalized patients. *JAMA.* 1997; 277:307–11.
7. Bates DW, Cullen DJ, Laird N, et al. Incidence of adverse drug events and potential adverse drug events. Implications for prevention. ADE Prevention Study Group. *JAMA.* 1995; 274:29–34.
8. Corrigan JM, Donaldson MD, Kohn LT, et al. Crossing the quality chasm: a new health system for the 21st

century. Washington, DC: National Academy Press; 2001.

9. Birkmeyer JD, Dimick JB. The Leapfrog Group's Patient Safety Practices, 2003: The Potential Benefits of Universal Adoption. Leapfrog Group; February 2004. www.leapfroggroup.org/media/file/Leapfrog-Birkmeyer.pdf (accessed 2009 Jan 22).
10. National Quality Forum (NQF). Safe Practices for Better Healthcare–2009 Update: A Consensus Report. Washington, DC: NQF; 2009.
11. American Recovery and Reinvestment Act of 2009 [ARRA] (P.L. 111-5, 123 Stat. 115-521). http://edocket.access.gpo.gov/2010/E9-31217.htm (accessed 2010 May 19).
12. Bates DW, Teich JM, Lee J, et al. The impact of computerized physician order entry on medication error prevention. *J Am Med Inform Assoc.* 1999; 6:313–21.
13. Bates DW, Leape LL, Cullen DJ, et al. Effect of computerized physician order entry and a team intervention on prevention of serious medication errors. *JAMA.* 1998; 280:1311–6.
14. Hunt DL, Haynes RB, Hanna SE, et al. Effects of computer-based clinical decision support systems on physician performance and patient outcomes: a systemic review. *JAMA.* 1998; 289:1330–46.
15. Amarasingham R, Plantinga L, Diener-West M, et al. Clinical information technologies and inpatient outcomes: a multiple hospital study. *Arch Intern Med.* 2009; 169:108–11.
16. Bates DW. The effects of health information technology on inpatient care. *Arch Intern Med.* 2009; 169:105–7.
17. Wolfstadt JI, Gurwitz JH, Field TS, et al. The effect of computerized physician order entry with clinical decisions support on the rates of adverse drug events: a systematic review. *J Gen Intern Med.* 2008; 23:451–8.
18. Ammenwerth E, Schnell-Inderst P, Machan C, et al. The effect of electronic prescribing on medication errors and adverse drug events: a systematic review. *J Am Med Inform Assoc.* 2008; 15: 585–600.
19. Eslami S, de Keizer NF, Abu-Hanna A. The impact of computerized physician medication order entry in hospitalized patients—a systematic review. *Int J Med Informatics.* 2008; 77:365–76.
20. Teich JM, Merchia PR, Schmiz JL, et al. Effects of computerized physician order entry on prescribing practices. *Arch Intern Med.* 2000; 160:2741–7.
21. Chaudry B, Wang J, Wu S, et al. Systematic review: impact of health information technology on quality, efficiency and costs of medical care. *Ann Intern Med.* 2006; 144:E-12–22.
22. Weiner JP, Kfuri T, Chan K, et al. "e-Iatrogenesis": the most critical unintended consequence of CPOE and other HIT. *J Am Med Inform Assoc.* 2007; 14:387–8.
23. Healthcare Information and Management Systems Society (HIMSS) Enterprise Information Systems Steering Committee. Clinical perspectives on enterprise information technology. www.himss.org/content/files/ClinicalPerspectives_whitepaper_052907.pdf (accessed 2009 Aug 26).
24. Healthcare Information and Management Systems Society (HIMSS). Electronic health record. www.himss.org/ASP/topics_ehr.asp (accessed 2009 Aug 26).
25. Koppel R, Metlay JP, Cohen A, et al. Role of computerized physician order entry systems in facilitating medication errors. *JAMA.* 2005; 293:1197–203.
26. Han YY, Carcillo JA, Venkataraman ST, et al. Unexpected increased mortality after implementation of a commercially sold computerized physician order entry system. *Pediatrics.* 2005; 116:1506–12.
27. Kuperman GJ, Bobb AM, Payne TH, et al. Medication-related clinical decision support in computerized provider order entry systems: a review. *J Am Med Inform Assoc.* 2007; 14:29–40.
28. Bobb AM, Payne TH, Gross PA. Viewpoint: controversies surrounding use of order sets for clinical decision support in computerized provider order entry. *J Am Med Inform Assoc.* 2007; 14:41–7.
29. Bates DW. Computerized physician order entry and medication errors: finding a balance. *J Biomed Informatics.* 2005; 38:259–61.
30. Kaushal R, Shojania KG, Bates DW. Effects of computerized physician order entry and clinical decision support systems on medication safety: a systematic review. *Arch Intern Med.* 2003; 163:1409–16.
31. Bobb A, Gleason K, Husch M, et al. The epidemiology of prescribing errors: the potential impact of computerized prescriber order entry. *Arch Intern Med.* 2004; 164:785–92.
32. Kilbridge PM, Classen DC. A process model of inpatient medication management and information technology interventions to improve patient safety. VHA Research Series, vol. 1. Irving, TX: VHA Inc.; 2001.
33. Pedersen CA, Gumpper KF. ASHP national survey on informatics: Assessment of the adoption and use of pharmacy informatics in U.S. hospitals—2007. *Am J Health-Syst Pharm.* 2008; 65:2244–64.
34. Khajouei R, Jaspers MW. The impact of CPOE medication systems' design aspects on usability, workflow and medication orders: a systematic review. *Methods Inf Med.* 2010; 49:3–19.
35. Niazkhani Z, Pirnejad H, Berg M, et al. The impact of computerized provider order entry systems on inpatient clinical workflow: a literature review. *J Am Med Inform Assoc.* 2009; 16:539–49.
36. Wietholter J, Susan Sitterson S, Allison S. Effects of computerized prescriber order entry on pharmacy order-processing time. *Am J Health-Syst Pharm.* 2009; 66:1394–8.
37. Kaushal R, Jha AK, Franz C, et al. Return on investment for a computerized physician order entry system. *J Am Med Inform Assoc.* 2006; 13:261–6.
38. Campbell EM, Sittig DF, Ash JS, et al. Types of unintended consequences related to computerized provider order entry. *J Am Med Inform Assoc.* 2006; 13:547–56.
39. Campbell EM, Guappone KP, Sittig DF. Computerized provider order entry adoption: implications for clinical workflow. *J Gen Intern Med.* 2009; 24:21–6.
40. Singh H, Mani S, Espadas D, et al. Prescription errors and outcomes related to inconsistent information transmitted through computerized order entry: a prospective study. *Arch Intern Med.* 2009; 169:982–9.

41. Bonnabry P, Despont-Gros C, Grauser D, et al. A risk analysis method to evaluate the impact of a computerized provider order entry system on patient safety. *J Am Med Inform Assoc.* 2008; 15:453–60.
42. Kozakiewicz JM, Benis LJ, Fisher SM, et al. Safe chemotherapy administration: using failure mode and effects analysis in computerized prescriber order entry. *Am J Health-Syst Pharm.* 2005; 62:1813–6.
43. Coles G, Fuller B, Nordquist K, et al. Using failure mode effects and criticality analysis for high-risk processes at three community hospitals. *Jt Comm J Qual Patient Saf.* 2005; 31:132–40.
44. Beuscart-Zéphir MC, Pelayo S, Bernonville S. Example of a human factors engineering approach to a medication administration work system: potential impact on patient safety. *Int J Med Inform.* 2010; 79:e43–57.
45. Kuperman GJ, Gibson RF. Computer physician order entry: benefits, costs, and issues. *Ann Intern Med.* 2003; 139:31–9.
46. Bates DW, Boyle DL, Teich JM. Impact of computerized physician order entry on physician time. *Proc Annu Symp Comput Appl Med Care.* 1994:996.
47. McGovern K. 10 Golden rules for administering drugs safely. In: Preventing medication errors. Springhouse, PA: Springhouse; 1994:2–3.
48. Osheroff JA, Pifer EA, Teich JM, et al. Improving outcomes with clinical decision support: an implementer's guide. Chicago: Healthcare Information and Management Systems Society; 2005.
49. Osheroff J, ed. Improving medication use and outcomes with clinical decision support: a step-by-step guide. Chicago: Healthcare Information and Management Systems Society; 2009.
50. Weingart SN, Toth M, Sands DZ, et al. Physicians' decisions to override computerized drug alerts in primary care. *Arch Intern Med.* 2008; 163:2625–31.
51. Igboechi CA, Ng CL, Yang CS, et al. Impact of computerized prescriber order entry on medication errors at an acute tertiary care hospital. *Hosp Pharm.* 2003; 38:227–31.
52. Hsieh TC, Kuperman GJ, Jaggi T, et al. Characteristics and consequences of drug allergy alert overrides in a computerized physician order entry system. *J Am Med Inform Assoc.* 2004; 11:482–91.
53. Nebeker JR, Hoffman JM, Weir CR, et al. High rates of adverse drug events in a highly computerized hospital. *Arch Intern Med.* 2005; 165:1111–6.
54. Paterno MD, Maviglia SM, Gorman PN, et al. Tiering drug-drug interaction alerts by severity increases compliance rates. *J Am Med Inform Assoc.* 2009; 16:40–6.
55. International classification of diseases, ninth revision, clinical modification (ICD-9-CM). www.cdc.gov/nchs/about/otheract/icd9/abticd9.htm (accessed 2009 Jan 27).
56. SnoMed Clinical Terms (SnoMed CT). www.nlm.nih.gov/research/umls/Snomed/snomed_main.html (accessed 2009 Aug 28).
57. Medication Management Standard MM.4.10—preparing and dispensing. In: Comprehensive accreditation manual for hospitals. Oakbrook Terrace, IL: Joint Commission on the Accreditation of Healthcare Organizations; 2006:MM-10.
58. Payne TH, Hoey PJ, Nichol P, et al. Preparation and use of preconstructed orders, order sets, and order menus in a computerized provider order entry system. *J Am Med Inform Assoc.* 2003; 10:322–9.
59. National Guideline Clearinghouse. www.guideline.gov (accessed 2009 Jan 22).
60. Cochrane Database of Systematic Reviews. www.cochrane.co.uk (accessed 2009 Jan 22).

Appendix—Glossary of Terms and Abbreviations

Adverse drug event (ADE): ASHP defines a significant ADE as any unexpected, unintended, undesired, or excessive response to a drug that
1. Requires discontinuing the drug (therapeutic or diagnostic),
2. Requires changing the drug therapy,
3. Requires modifying the dose (except for minor dosage adjustments),
4. Necessitates admission to a hospital,
5. Prolongs stay in a health care facility,
6. Necessitates supportive treatment,
7. Significantly complicates diagnosis,
8. Negatively affects prognosis, or
9. Results in temporary or permanent harm, disability, or death.

Bar-code-assisted medication administration (BCMA): A methodology involving the use of scanners and software to verify all medications electronically before they are administered to patients. These systems may also document the medication in the eMAR.

Clinical decision support (CDS): Clinical decision support systems are interactive computer programs or other tools, which are designed to assist physicians and other health professionals with decision making tasks usually at the point of care.

Computerized provider-order-entry; alternatively, computerized prescriber-order-entry (CPOE): An electronic system that health care professionals can use to enter drug, treatment, and test orders and transmit the orders directly to the department responsible for fulfilling the order.

e-iatrogenesis: Patient harm caused at least in part by the application of health information technology including but not limited to the systems and/or the design and implementation of the system.

Electronic health record (EHR): An electronic record of health-related information on an individual that conforms to nationally recognized interoperability standards and that can be created, managed, and consulted by authorized clinicians and staff across more than one health care organization.

Electronic medication administration record (eMAR): A version of the medication administration record viewable online and not printed.

Electronic medical record (EMR): An electronic record of health-related information on an individual that can be created, gathered, managed, and consulted by authorized clinicians and staff within one health care organization.

Enterprise information system: Broader system that integrates clinical systems such as an EHR and business systems such a scheduling and/or financial systems and quality reporting systems.

Leadership: Within a health-system, leadership may address three leadership groups: The governing body, the chief executive and other senior managers, and the leaders of the licensed independent practitioners.

Legal medical record (LMR): The legal health record is the documentation of health care services provided to an individual during any aspect of health care delivery in any type of health care organization. It is consumer or patient-centric. The legal health record contains individually identifiable data, stored on any medium, and collected and directly used in documenting health care or health status.

National drug code (NDC): A universal 11-digit product identifier used in the United States for drugs intended for human use. The Drug Listing Act of 1972 requires registered drug establishments to provide the Food and Drug Administration (FDA) with a current list of all drugs manufactured, prepared, propagated, compounded, or processed by it for commercial distribution.

Orderable: An authoritative direction or instruction from a prescriber to perform a task (e.g., a radiology test or administer a medication or treatment).

Medication administration record (MAR): Medication administration record usually handwritten or printed from an electronic pharmacy information system.

Personal health record (PHR): An electronic record of health-related information on an individual that conforms to nationally recognized interoperability standards and that can be drawn from multiple sources while being managed, shared, and controlled by the individual.

RxNorm: RxNorm is a standardized nomenclature for clinical drugs and drug delivery devices and is produced by the National Library of Medicine.

Sponsorship: An identified executive or clinical leader who assumes responsibility for another person or a group during a period of project planning implementation follow-up.

Systematized nomenclature of medicine (SNOMed): A multiaxial, hierarchical classification system. As in any such system, a disease may be located in a body organ, which results in a code in a topography axis and may lead to morphological alterations represented by a morphology code.

Workflow: The flow or progress of work done by a company, industry, department, or person.

Developed through the ASHP Section of Pharmacy Informatics and Technology and approved by the ASHP Board of Directors on September 24, 2010.

A work group of the ASHP Section of Pharmacy Informatics and Technology Section Advisory Group on Clinical Information Systems is gratefully acknowledged for developing these guidelines: Anne M. Bobb, B.S.Pharm.; Jennifer Boehne, Pharm.D.; W. Lynn Ethridge, Pharm.D.; J. Chad Hardy, Pharm.D., M.S.; Randy Herring, B.S.Pharm.; Richard S. Jacobs, Pharm.D.; Michael A. Jones, Pharm.D.; Timothy W. Lynch, Pharm.D., M.S.; Leslie R. Mackowiak, M.S.; Tommy J. Mannino, B.S.; Jayson J. Przybyla, Pharm.D.; Brendan J. Reichert, M.S.; Ranee M. Runnebaum, Pharm.D.; Nancy R. Smestad, M.S.; David L. Troiano, M.B.A., MSIA; Laura L. Tyndall, Pharm.D.; and Lori Wright, Pharm.D.

ASHP also gratefully acknowledges the contributions of the following people: Bruce W. Chaffee, Pharm.D.; Toby Clark, M.Sc., FASHP; Kate Farthing, Pharm.D., BCPS; Burt W. Finkelstein, Pharm.D.; William L. Fritz, M.S., FASHP; Kimberly A. Galt, Pharm.D., FASHP; Barry R. Goldspiel, Pharm.D., FASHP; Frances M. Jordan, M.B.A., FASHP; Renee B. Marino, Pharm.D.; Kevin C. Marvin, M.S., FASHP; Steven Meisel, Pharm.D.; Alicia S. Miller, M.S.; Sandi Mitchell, M.S.I.S., FASHP; Kuldip R. Patel, Pharm.D.; Alicia B. Perry, Pharm.D.; John Poikonen, Pharm.D.; Mark H. Siska, B.S.Pharm.; and Mary Windle, Pharm.D.

ASHP also acknowledges the following organizations and individuals for reviewing drafts of these guidelines (review does not imply endorsement): American Academy of Family Physicians (AAFP); American Association of Critical Care Nurses (AACCN); American Health Information Management Association (AHIMA); American Hospital Association (AHA); California Society of Health-System Pharmacists (CSHP); Healthcare Information and Management Systems Society (HIMSS); Jeanine (Porter) Abrons, Pharm.D., M.S.; Christel Anderson (HIMSS); Dan Buffington; Peggy Brashear, B.S.Pharm.; Tim R. Brown, Pharm.D., FASHP; Dominick A. Caselnova III, M.H.A.; Thomas W. Cooley, M.B.A.; Debby Cowan, Pharm.D.; Michele Danish, Pharm.D., FASHP; Neil Davis; Charlie De la Torre; Robert DeChristoforo, M.S., FASHP; Jean Douglas, Pharm.D.; Brent R. Ekins, Pharm.D., DABA; Elizabeth Fang, Pharm.D.; Tim Lanese, M.B.A., FASHP, CPHIMS; Lisa Gunther Lum, Pharm.D., FASHP, FCSHP; Robi Hellman, RN, MSN, CNS (AACCN); James M. Hoffman, Pharm.D., M.S., BCPS; Carol J. Hope, Pharm.D., M.S.; Amey Hugg; Joan E. Kapusnik-Uner, Pharm.D., FCSHP; Linda L. Kloss, RHIA, FAHIMA (AHIMA); Ronald E. Lay, M.S.; Jeff Little, Pharm.D.; Bob Lobo, Pharm.D.; LTC Eric M. Maroyka, Pharm.D., BCPS; Greg Matsuura, Pharm.D., BCPS; Patrick J. McDonnell, Pharm.D.; Michael McGregory, Pharm.D., M.B.A., BCPS; Robert Moore, B.S.Pharm., BCPS; Susan J. Morikawa, Pharm.D., BCPS; Kevin Olsen, RN, BSN; Peg Panella-Spangler M.S.; Christine Pavlak, M.H.A., FASHP; Stephanie C. Peshek, Pharm.D., FASHP; Tommie Peterson; Minh James Pham, Pharm.D.; James A. Ponto, M.S., BCNP, FASHP; Donald W. Rucker, M.D.; Richard Sakai; Kevin Scheckelhoff; Thomas R. Schafer, Pharm.D., BCPS; Terry Seaton, Pharm.D.; Suzanne Shea; Pamela Shellner, M.A., RN (AACCN); Clyde Spence, Pharm.D., M.B.A.; Richard L. Stambaugh, Pharm.D., M.S., BCPS; Craig S. Stern, Pharm.D., M.B.A.; Scott H. Takahashi, Pharm.D., FCSHP (CSHP); Dennis A. Tribble, Pharm.D.; Jody Jacobson Wedret, FASHP, FCSHP; Rich Umbdenstock (AHA); Ray Vrabel, Pharm.D.; Steven E. Waldren, M.D., M.S. (AAFP); Eric Weber; Barbara White, M.S., PMP, FASHP.

The bibliographic citation for this document is as follows: American Society of Health-System Pharmacists. ASHP guidelines on pharmacy planning for implementation of computerized provider- order-entry systems in hospitals and health systems. *Am J Health-Syst Pharm.* 2011; 68:e9–31.

ASHP Guidelines on Remote Medication Order Processing

Purpose

Because of the complexity of the care that pharmacists provide patients, the American Society of Health-System Pharmacists (ASHP) advocates that patients have 24-hour access to the pharmacist responsible for their care and that the pharmacist be physically accessible to the patient when feasible. ASHP recognizes that such access is not always possible and encourages the development of remotely delivered pharmacist care as a supplement to onsite care.

Medication order review is one aspect of pharmacist patient care. All health-system pharmacies have an obligation to provide a review of medication orders that ensures safe medication use.[1] When onsite pharmacist review is not available, health systems may determine that remote pharmacist review of medication orders is a suitable alternative. The purpose of these guidelines is to describe the policies and procedures that must be in place to safely employ remote medication order processing (RMOP). Health-system policies and procedures regarding RMOP should address quality assurance and safety; access to drug information and hospital policy resources; training and orientation; minimum technical standards and specifications; confidentiality, privacy, and security; regulatory and accreditation standards; and communication and problem resolution. These guidelines also describe some general considerations for RMOP implementation, and Appendix A provides a checklist for assessing implementation readiness. Appendix B contains an outline of a model agreement for RMOP. A glossary of terms used in these guidelines appears in Appendix C.

Because of the rapid pace of change, differences in practice settings and RMOP models, and the complexities of health care organizational arrangements, aspects of these guidelines may not be applicable to all settings. These guidelines are not intended to describe best practices for the operational relationships between satellite and central pharmacies in acute care settings. Readers should also note that these guidelines do not attempt to address all aspects of remotely delivered pharmacist care and should interpret them as limited to the subject of RMOP. These guidelines address remote order verification only when medication order fulfillment occurs through automated medication storage and distribution devices. Remote end verification of the dispensed drug product (e.g., visual approval of the drug product by video camera or other means) is beyond the scope of these guidelines. Health-system administrators and pharmacy managers should therefore exercise their professional judgment in assessing and adapting these guidelines to meet the needs of their particular settings and to comply with the health care organization's policies and procedures.

Models of RMOP Services

The technologies used in RMOP are relatively new and rapidly changing, so different methods for RMOP have evolved, and further evolution should be encouraged. At least two models of RMOP are currently in use: contracted services and supplemental workload balancing, which includes network workload balancing and on-call assistance. Each of these models has unique characteristics that must be considered in planning for its use.

Contracted Services. In this model, a hospital pharmacy that is not continuously open contracts with a larger hospital or a service to provide RMOP when its pharmacy is closed. This model is typically applied when a hospital without 24-hour pharmacy services has sufficient automated dispensing cabinet capacity that RMOP allows nursing staff to keep functioning without having a pharmacist present,[2] although some institutions have developed models for remote verification by pharmacists of dispensing performed by pharmacy technicians at the client site.[3]

Supplemental Workload Balancing. Similar to the model described above, in this case a health system with a number of hospitals relies on the ones that have a 24-hour pharmacy department or on a service to provide RMOP for hospitals whose pharmacies are closed or that experience unanticipated peaks in order processing workload. For example, in an on-call model, a staff pharmacist from the client site or a contracted service is placed on call to help with managing workload. This pharmacist works remotely (sometimes from a home office, where allowed by state regulation) to help the client's pharmacy department manage unanticipated peaks in order processing workload (often on the second or third shift). In this model, the remote pharmacist is responsible for medication order entry and/or review, and medication order fulfillment occurs through the client-site pharmacy.

Quality Assurance and Safety

Medication-use management and safety in the RMOP environment require special efforts in the coordination of quality-assurance, quality-improvement, and patient safety practices between the client site and the remote site. Differences in local practice standards and organizational cultures, combined with unique human factors issues, have the potential to magnify the risk of errors. Quality, safety, and risk management strategies should be jointly examined and agreed on and should address the procedures and communication pathways unique to RMOP systems. These include critical workflow steps and handoffs involved in medication ordering, review, and verification; communication among prescriber, pharmacist, and nurse; and assessing the patient's response to drug therapy and achieving desired therapeutic outcomes.

Review of the Patient's Profile. The remote pharmacist must be able to review the patient's profile for

- Medication history and medication reconciliation reports,
- Diagnosis,
- Allergies and prior adverse drug reactions,

- Height, weight, age (measured versus estimated), and sex,
- Pregnancy status for women of childbearing potential,
- Duplications of drug therapies,
- Potential drug interactions,
- Pertinent laboratory data, and
- Other information as needed.

Clarification of Medication Orders. The remote pharmacist must have a process by which he or she can clarify the medication order with the prescriber. The remote pharmacist must alert other health care providers caring for the patient (e.g., the client nursing and pharmacy staff) of the need for additional review and clarification. There must be a mechanism for the remote pharmacist to readily communicate by phone or leave a note in the patient profile for other health care providers, including the client site pharmacy staff, to clarify the order or otherwise respond within an appropriate period of time. The remote pharmacy must have a mechanism for timely follow-up on medication orders that are pending clarification.

Quality-Assurance and Medication Error Reporting Systems. The remote pharmacy must participate in the client site's quality-assurance and medication error reporting systems. These systems should include the collection and reporting of medication errors and process variances as described below:

- The medication error reporting system should include potential adverse events that reach the patient (with or without harm) and potential adverse events that are intercepted before reaching the patient.
- Medication error reports related to RMOP procedures and communications should be tracked by outcome, type, cause, severity, preventability, and source.
- Corrective action plans should be directed toward the system failures that contributed to or caused the error, variance, or adverse event.
- Policies and procedures should ensure that quality-assurance data and medication error reports are jointly reviewed in a timely manner by pharmacy leadership and safety officers (if applicable) at both the client and remote sites and that relevant information is shared with relevant frontline practitioners at both sites, including remote pharmacists and client-site nursing and pharmacy staff.

The quality-assurance program should include indicators that measure important aspects of RMOP, including measures of (1) timeliness (e.g., elapsed time to receive and verify an order), (2) system performance (e.g., percentage of time information technology systems are not available for RMOP), (3) compliance with contractual requirements, (4) employee satisfaction at the client and remote sites, and (5) unanticipated problems (e.g., breaks in privacy standards, communication and handoff problems).

Handoff Communication. The remote site should have a documented process for handoff communication that meets the requirements of Joint Commission National Patient Safety Goals.[4]

Access to Drug Information and Hospital Policy Resources

Drug Information Resources. Drug information resources are essential tools for health care organizations. Drug information resources, specific to the needs and scope of patients served, are essential for practicing evidence-based medicine in a safe and efficient manner. In health care systems that use RMOP procedures, each institution needs point-of-care access to internal and external drug information systems. Internal drug information resources include the client's formulary, laboratory reference values, newsletters, and drug-use guidelines based on local standards. External drug information resources include commercially available electronic and print media that organize information into full-text and bibliographic retrieval systems.

Drug information resources available in the remote pharmacy should at a minimum meet the state board of pharmacy requirements for both the client and remote pharmacy sites and include the current edition of a drug information reference (hard copy or electronic). Other reference material (hard copy or electronic media) should be available, depending on the scope of care being provided. Recommended clinical and drug information reference materials available in the remote pharmacy include

- Two sources of pediatric dosing information (ideally, one of which is the same resource used by clinicians in the remote pharmacy),
- Internet access to online drug information resources, including the Food and Drug Administration,
- Drug compatibility and drug interaction resources,
- Poison information and poison control resources (at a minimum, the telephone number for a certified poison control center), and
- Drug information center contact number.

Drug information requirements, resources, and staff competencies in the use of drug information systems should be reviewed at least annually to ensure that patient care needs are met.

Hospital Policy and Procedures. The minimum information on client site hospital policies and procedures that the remote pharmacist should have available is

- Client site's pharmacy department's policies and procedures,
- Client site's formulary,
- Client site's relevant nursing department policies and procedures,
- Standard medication administration times,
- Standard drip concentrations or drug protocols,
- High-risk policies including the "Do Not Use" abbreviations list,
- Drug-specific clinical guidelines,
- Restrictions by indication or prescriber,
- Chemotherapy protocols, pain protocols, and anticoagulation protocols,
- Standing or protocol orders,

- Pre- and postoperative antibiotic selection and administration protocols, and other protocols as determined,
- Therapeutic interchange list,
- Client's policies and procedures for processing nonformulary medication orders,
- Client's policies and procedures for handling a clinical message order to alert nursing staff and pharmacy department of the need to address an issue at a future time, and
- Client's pharmacokinetic and renal dosing policies along with written medical staff approval to write orders in the patient's chart if required to comply with these policies.

The remote site must have a procedure that ensures the timely and complete communication of changes in client site hospital policies and procedures, including changes to formularies and medication protocols.

Training and Orientation

Pharmacists, through training and orientation, are competent to review and enter medication orders written by prescribers into a computerized database to maintain a complete patient profile. This patient profile can be used by nurses and other providers to access medications appropriate for their patients. This training and orientation are critical for pharmacists to accurately document and transcribe the appropriate information to maintain an accurate and up-to-date profile. Requirements for training and orientation include the following:

- All education and orientation are documented in a permanent record maintained in the pharmacy department of the remote site (if applicable) and shared with client sites or in the pharmacy department of the client site, as appropriate.
- All pharmacy personnel accessing the pharmacy information system are tested for competency prior to use of the system and annually thereafter.
- When upgrades or significant changes are made to the client site's computer system, the client site will communicate to the remote site the need for follow-up training.
- When significant changes are made to the client site's clinical policies or procedures, the client site will communicate to the remote site the need for follow-up training.
- The client and the remote site must have a process for documenting the remote pharmacist's competencies. If the remote site is responsible for the documentation of those competencies, the client and the remote site must have a system for reporting those competencies to the client.

Minimum Technical Standards and Specifications

The client and the remote site must ensure that the following minimum technical standards and specifications are met:

- The remote site must have access to the client's network or Internet, phone, and scan or fax access to the client.
- The remote site must have the ability to access the client facility via the client's Internet solution or via the client's computer network.
- The remote site must, to the extent possible, have redundant systems in place to ensure RMOP service availability (e.g., computer network and Internet connectivity, other information systems used to facilitate RMOP).
- The remote site must have the ability to operate remotely the client's order transmittal system.
- The systems used by the remote pharmacist to view the patient orders and other medical information must comply with the technical standards set by the Health Insurance Portability and Accountability Act of 1996 and ensure technical and physical safeguarding of patient health care information.

Confidentiality, Privacy, and Security

To ensure the confidentiality, privacy, and security of patient health care information, the following conditions must be met:

- Remote pharmacists must adhere to the client's confidentiality policy.
- The remote site, if a business entity, must have a signed business associate agreement with the client.
- The client must provide individual pharmacist-specific access to the client's hospital computer system.

Regulatory Considerations

State regulation of RMOP varies considerably. The client and the remote site should jointly analyze state regulations governing pharmacy practice at both sites to determine and meet applicable requirements. This analysis should be repeated on a routine basis, as regulations may change. To ensure regulatory compliance, at a minimum the following should be verified and approved by the client and the remote site before implementing RMOP:

- Remote site's approval to operate by the client's state board of pharmacy, if required,
- The policy and procedure manual for the RMOP operation, including but not limited to procedures for handling computer system or connectivity downtime, issue escalation, annual competency renewal verification, and communication between the client site and remote site personnel,
- Copies of all licensure required by the states in which the client and the remote site are located (some states require remote pharmacists to have a consultant license in addition to a state pharmacist license for each hospital for which the pharmacist performs RMOP services), and
- Copies of any hospital job-specific competency requirements for pharmacy personnel.

Communication and Problem Resolution

To ensure the safety of the RMOP service, the client and the remote site must establish effective communication channels between personnel at the two sites. Communication among prescriber, pharmacist, and nurse will be critical to assessing the patient's response to drug therapy and achieving desired therapeutic outcomes. The remote pharmacist must have the ability to immediately contact the prescriber or client site's nursing staff to discuss any concerns identified during review of the patient's information. The client must provide its nursing supervisor with a 24-hour telephone number to contact the remote site or remote pharmacist and encourage nurses to communicate with the remote pharmacist. In the event the nursing supervisor is unable to resolve a problem or concern, the client pharmacist on call is available for consultation and problem resolution if the problem cannot wait until the client pharmacist is on duty again. Patient profile information, including laboratory results, should be communicated to the remote site electronically; oral communication of laboratory results should be limited to exceptional circumstances, and such oral communications should be documented in the patient medical record as soon as possible. Downtime procedures should provide mechanisms for direct communication among the remote pharmacist, nurses, and the prescriber.

Considerations for Implementation

The success of RMOP implementation will depend on a host of specific factors. Below are some considerations that are generally applicable. Appendix A provides a brief checklist for implementation readiness.

- Terms of the contract or agreement should allow flexibility for the number of orders processed, since estimates prior to "go-live" may be inaccurate.
- Early and frequent communication between the client site and the remote site, especially in the first few weeks after go-live, is critical to the success of the implementation and ongoing operation.
- After-hours technical support at both the remote site and the client site will be essential to the success of the implementation and ongoing operation. Plan for information technology support in advance of go-live.
- Education will be required for all nurses at the client site, not just those whose shifts coincide with RMOP coverage. In particular, changes to the client site's override processes will need to be planned in collaboration with nurses.
- The client should implement a mechanism for communication between the remote site and nursing via the electronic medication administration record (eMAR) system. For example, if the remote pharmacist reviews the patient's home medication reconciliation list and identifies items not stocked by the pharmacy, it would be helpful to have a drug dictionary item (e.g., "Pharmacy Note to Nurse") whereby the remote pharmacist can make an entry in the eMAR that informs nurses that the remote pharmacist has reviewed the order but that some action at the client site is required.

Conclusion

ASHP believes that patients should have 24-hour access to the pharmacist responsible for their care and that the pharmacist should be physically accessible to the patient when feasible. Because 24-hour pharmacy services are not achievable in all circumstances, health systems may employ remote pharmacist review and processing of medication orders. The purpose of these guidelines is to describe the policies and procedures that must be in place to safely employ RMOP. Health-system policies and procedures regarding RMOP should address quality assurance and safety; access to drug information and hospital policy resources; training and orientation; minimum technical standards and specifications; confidentiality, privacy, and security; regulatory and accreditation standards; and communication and problem resolution. Given the rapid pace of change in technology, differences in practice settings and RMOP models, and the complexities of health care organizational arrangements, health-system administrators and pharmacy managers should exercise their professional judgment in assessing and adapting these guidelines to their particular settings.

References

1. The Joint Commission. Elements of performance for medication management standard 4.10 (preparing and dispensing). Comprehensive accreditation manual for hospitals. Oakbrook Terrace, IL: The Joint Commission; 2007:MM-10.
2. Stratton TP, Worley MW, Schmidt M, et al. Implementing after-hours pharmacy coverage for critical access hospitals in northeast Minnesota. *Am J Health-Syst Pharm.* 2008; 65:1727–34.
3. Clifton GD, Byer H, Heaton K, et al. Provision of pharmacy services to underserved populations via remote dispensing and two-way videoconferencing. *Am J Health-Syst Pharm.* 2003; 60:2577–82.
4. The Joint Commission. 2009 National Patient Safety Goals: hospital program. www.jointcommission.org/PatientSafety/NationalPatientSafetyGoals/09_hap_npsgs.htm. (accessed 2009 Dec 28).

Appendix A—Checklist/Assessment for Implementation Readiness

1. All automation has been tested and is functional, including
   a. Communication of medication orders (fax machines or scanners)
   b. Computer systems maintaining patient profiles
   c. Connectivity to automated medication dispensing cabinets
   d. Electronic reference resources
   e. Remote connectivity
2. All personnel training for remote site and client site is completed and documented:
   a. Computer systems
   b. Clinical guidelines
   c. Client site pharmacy policies and procedures related to review, authorization, and entry of medication orders
   d. Communication procedures
3. Pre-go-live test of mock patients and scenarios has been performed for
   a. Fax/scan orders
   b. Admission, transfer, and discharge of patient

   c. Medication order entry
   d. Communication procedures
4. System downtime protocols have been well communicated to all applicable personnel at both the remote site and client site (e.g., pharmacy, nursing, information technology, and administrative personnel)
5. Go-live date and service level expectations have been well communicated to all applicable personnel at both the remote site and client site
6. Communication process that includes quality reporting, system changes/availability, and policy and procedure updates as well as shift change communication has been agreed on, established, and well communicated to all applicable personnel at both the remote site and client site

Appendix B—Outline for Model Agreement Between Remote Site and Client

The agreements between a remote site and the client must be approved by both contract office and risk management in both facilities (if applicable). The agreement should include

1. Services to be provided, including the roles of both parties:
   a. Hours of service
   b. Technology requirements
   c. Order processing services
   d. All clinical services provided
   e. Management services
   f. Quality measures
   g. Other services (e.g., vacation, emergency, or other hours of coverage)
   h. Qualification of pharmacy and pharmacists
   i. Security of information
   j. Limitations
   k. Access to records, including information required to review patient profiles
2. Terms and renewal of the agreement
3. Mutual indemnification and insurance
4. Termination of the agreement, including changes in laws or regulations
5. Confidentiality, including requirements set by the Health Insurance Portability and Accountability Act of 1996
6. Limitations of liability
7. No exclusion from federal health care programs
8. Dispute resolution
9. Fees and payment terms:
   a. Hourly rates
   b. Per-order rates
   c. Order volume
   d. Overpayment and underpayment exposure
   e. Penalty charges
   f. Addition of new services
10. Miscellaneous issues, including
   a. Independent contractors
   b. Notices
   c. Compliance with the terms
   d. Rights of the parties
   e. Conflict of laws
   f. Compliance with laws, regulations, guidelines, and accrediting body standards (e.g., Joint Commission)

Appendix C—Glossary

Terms used to describe remote medication order processing (RMOP) practices are evolving and vary considerably. Readers should be alert to these inconsistencies and exercise caution in interpreting the literature. The following terms are used in these guidelines:

Client: The health care organization receiving the RMOP service.

Client Site: The site receiving the RMOP service (the site where the patient is receiving care).

RMOP: Medication order processing provided by a remote pharmacist; this term includes remote order entry and remote order review.

Remote Pharmacist: A licensed pharmacist processing the medication order from the remote site.

Remote Site: The site that is electronically linked to the client site via a computer system and/or a video or auditory communication system approved by the appropriate state board(s) of pharmacy. The remote site may be a licensed pharmacy or other location permitted by the appropriate state board(s) of pharmacy.

Developed through the ASHP Council on Pharmacy Management and approved by the ASHP Board of Directors on September 25, 2009.

ASHP gratefully acknowledges the expert panel that authored these guidelines. At the time of writing, members of the expert panel held the following positions. Bruce Thompson, M.S., was Director of Pharmacy Services, Hennepin County Medical Center, Minneapolis, MN; Greg Conrad was Director, Pharmacy, Willamette Falls Hospital, Oregon City, OR; Michael O. Gum was Pharmacy Director, Presbyterian Hospital, Charlotte, NC; John M. Kessler, Pharm.D., BCPS, was Founder and Chief Clinical Officer, SecondStory Health LLC, Carrboro, NC; Tim Larson was Pharmacy Director, Cardinal Rxe-source Center–Chicago region, Westmont, IL; Dallas Moore, M.S., was Pharmacy Director, American Fork Hospital–Intermountain Healthcare, American Fork, UT; Kelly Morrison was Director of Sales & Marketing, Rxe-source, Cardinal Health, Houston, TX; and Mickey Price was Vice President, Rxe-source, Cardinal Health, Dublin, OH.

The contributions of Stephen R. Novak, M.P.A., FASHP, to these guidelines are gratefully acknowledged. At the time of his contribution, Mr. Novak was Director, Pharmacy Services, Pardee Hospital, Hendersonville, NC. ASHP also acknowledges the following organizations and individuals for reviewing drafts of these guidelines (review does not imply endorsement): Accreditation Council for Pharmacy Education (ACPE); Healthcare Information and Management Systems Society (HIMSS) Pharmacy Informatics Task Force; Emily Alexander, Pharm.D., BCPS; David B. Archer, D.Ph.; David Aresco, B.S.Pharm., FASCP; John A. Armitstead, M.S., FASHP; Darrel W. Box, M.H.A.; Michael Brown, Pharm.D.; Kimberly K. Daugherty, Pharm.D., BCPS; Doug DeJong, M.B.A., FASHP; Mike Dudzik, M.H.A.; Francis J. Dunn, Jr., B.S.Pharm.; Jeanne Ezell, M.S., FASHP; Kelly Guhr, Pharm.D., BCPS; George Hill, M.B.A.; Linda Horton, Pharm.D.; Jody Jacobson Wedret, FASHP, FCSHP; Ken Kester, Pharm.D., J.D.; Patricia Kienle,

M.P.A., FASHP; Nancy Konieczny, M.B.A.; Donald H. Lynx, M.B.A., FASHP; Lynnae M. Mahaney, M.B.A.; Peter G. Mayberry; Roland Patry, Dr.P.H., FASHP; James A. Ponto, M.S., BCNP, FASHP; Cliff Richards, Pharm.D.; Mike Rouse, B.Pharm.(Hons), M.P.S. (ACPE); Terry Seaton, Pharm.D., FCCP, BCPS; Timothy P. Stratton, Ph.D., BCPS, FAPHA; Basil J. Thoppil, M.Sc., Pharm.D.; and Dennis A. Tribble, Pharm.D.

The bibliographic citation for this document is as follows: American Society of Health-System Pharmacists. ASHP guidelines on remote medication order processing. *Am J Health-Syst Pharm.* 2010; 67:672–7.

ASHP Guidelines on the Safe Use of Automated Compounding Devices for the Preparation of Parenteral Nutrition Admixtures

Purpose

Automated compounding devices are frequently used by pharmacists for the extemporaneous preparation of parenteral nutrition admixtures. This continuing shift from manual compounding procedures comes as a result of significant advances in automated technology, as well as in response to changing health care demands to provide admixture compounding in a safer, more efficient, and more accurate manner. Approximately 65% of the hospitals in the United States currently use automated compounding devices for parenteral nutrition admixtures on a daily basis.[a] Compounders are also used for other types of intravenous admixtures and in other settings, including home care and long-term-care facilities; therefore, the overall magnitude of their use may be substantial. As with other automated systems or devices, the benefits can be realized only when the technology is used appropriately. Significant patient harm may occur when safety and quality assurance measures are overlooked or circumvented.[1]

The purpose of these guidelines is to outline the key issues that should be considered to safely and cost-effectively incorporate this technology into the pharmacy operations of health care organizations. The guidelines focus on parenteral nutrition admixtures, but the safety issues are also applicable to the use of compounders for other types of i.v. admixtures. The term "health care organization" is used throughout the guidelines as a general descriptor and is intended to be inclusive of any of the practice settings and types of facilities in which compounders are used, including, for example, home infusion companies. These guidelines should be used in conjunction with the ASHP Guidelines on Quality Assurance for Pharmacy-Prepared Sterile Products and device manufacturers' instruction manuals and training materials. Pharmacists should use professional judgment in assessing their health care organization's needs for automated compounding devices and in adapting these guidelines to meet those needs.

Background

The act of extemporaneously compounding any parenteral formulation is complex and not without inherent risks; therefore, compounding tasks are best performed by personnel most qualified to do so. An incompatible, unstable, or contaminated i.v. infusion may induce significant patient morbidity and even mortality.[1] Pharmacists are specifically educated and legally responsible for performing these tasks safely. Pharmacists are also responsible for training other personnel to perform relatively simple tasks with the least risk possible.

The extemporaneous preparation of multiadditive products, such as parenteral nutrition admixture compounding, should be performed under the direct supervision of a pharmacist and in the appropriate environment.[2] The historical method of compounding these multicomponent admixtures has been to manually use gravity-driven transfers for large-volume additives, such as amino acids, dextrose, lipids, and sterile water. Small-volume additives, such as electrolytes, trace minerals, multivitamins, and drugs, have often been added manually and separately with a syringe. Thus, this compounding method is limited by the visual inspection of volumes transferred between stock containers, as well as by the precision of the calibrations marked on the stock containers or transfer devices.

The manual method of parenteral nutrition admixture compounding is labor-intensive and requires multiple manipulations of infusion containers, sets, syringes, needles, and so forth, which can lead to the extrinsic contamination of the final admixture with sterile and nonsterile contaminants. A sterile contaminant can be particulate matter from elastomeric vial enclosures (needle cores), and nonsterile contaminants can be bacteria and other infectious materials. Minimizing the number of extemporaneous manipulations of the parenteral infusion containers and supplies improves compounding efficiency and reduces the risk of extrinsic contamination and associated sequelae.[3]

The emergence of automated technology as an alternative approach to parenteral nutrition admixture compounding has led to potentially improved compounding accuracy with the use of fluid pump technology and software that controls the compounder pump. Fluid can be delivered from the source container to the final container by using either a volumetric or a gravimetric fluid pumping system. Volumetric systems transfer a specified volume of fluid from a source container to a final container via a rotary peristaltic pump. The tubing is stretched around a rotor and, as the rotor turns, solution is pulled from the source container and pushed toward the final container. Measurements are based on the theory that each rotor movement advances a constant amount of fluid through the system. The total volume delivered is calculated by the volume pulled into the tubing by each rotor movement multiplied by the number of movements. These systems usually incorporate a final check of the *actual* total bag weight by comparing it with a calculated *expected* weight.

In gravimetric systems, measurement of fluid volume delivered from the source container to the final container is determined by weighing the fluid transferred and dividing the weight by the solution's known specific gravity, thereby converting weight to volume. Two types of gravimetric pumps are available: additive and subtractive. With an additive pump, a single load cell is positioned to measure each fluid as it is delivered to the final container. With a subtractive pump, load cells are positioned beneath the source containers to measure each fluid as it is being pumped from its source container. Weight is determined by subtracting the posttransfer weight from the pretransfer weight of the container for each source solution. When all transfers are completed, the system compares the *actual* total bag weight with a calculated *expected* weight.

In addition to the compounder, dedicated software may be used to electronically transfer information to the compounding device. Automated compounding software has additional features that can enhance the management of the parenteral nutrition program. Software issues and their integrity are additional critical components unique to compounder methods and require continuous monitoring to ensure that the operations are correct.[4]

Justification for the Use of Automated Compounding Devices

When is it appropriate to use compounders, and how will decisions affect others within and outside the pharmacy department? It is incumbent upon the pharmacist to ensure that the department is fully knowledgeable about the operation of the compounder and that a minimum acceptable standard of pharmacy practice is met. First, internal decisions need to be made to justify the expenses associated with this technology. Second, policies and procedures should be in place to assess workflow, establish training programs, and standardize compounder use in the specific pharmacy practice setting. Third, changing current compounder contracts may result in more cost than the savings that might appear in the new contracts. Specifically, the initial incorporation of an automated compounder into daily pharmacy practice is a labor-intensive effort, and such transitions can be disruptive and can even increase the risk of errors. This may be particularly true during staff orientation to new devices. Such changes must be carefully reviewed; if they are determined to be worthwhile, a well-coordinated transition plan should be devised beforehand. Whether transition costs (including the potential for unused sets and supplies) can be deferred to the new contract is another factor for consideration.

The principal emphasis associated with using automated compounding devices in health care organizations should be improving patient care and enhancing efficiency while remaining cost-effective. "Cost-effectiveness" is, therefore, a relative term with respect to personnel, as the labor saved is often redirected to other aspects of pharmaceutical care that could also improve patient safety. Time that was previously spent on operations associated with parenteral nutrition admixture compounding can now be aimed at other issues, such as optimization of drug and nutritional therapies, reorganization of product utilization, quality assurance programs, and augmentation of other core pharmaceutical services. Specific objectives related to cost justification of automated compounding devices may include the following:

1. Enhanced efficiency and worker safety during the parenteral nutrition compounding process and patient safety with parenteral use.
2. Reduction in labor associated with manually compounded parenteral nutrition admixtures. Assessment of the overall labor and material costs associated with the current manual compounding methods should include hidden costs such as pharmacists' time to perform calculations, quality assurance checks, and compounder set-up, as well as staff training (initial and on-going).
3. Reduction in waste through more efficient use of base solutions and additives. Inventory can often be reduced by consolidating source solutions to a few high-concentration, large-volume additives.

In some cases in which the cost of implementing automated compounding technology in one facility is prohibitive, health care organizations have opted to explore regional compounding centers or outsourcing to contractors.

Performance Requirements and Responsibilities

The use of automated devices for compounding parenteral nutrition admixtures should be clearly defined by the health care organization and the manufacturer. This includes the ongoing responsibilities of the pharmacy department and those of the manufacturer during and after implementation of the compounder in the pharmacy practice setting.

Three areas need to be clearly defined before choosing an automated compounding system: (1) the system's performance requirements, (2) the manufacturer's responsibilities, and (3) the pharmacy department's responsibilities. The performance requirements of the automated compounding system should ensure that

1. The compounder exceeds the level of accuracy achieved with manual compounding. The automated compounding device should be accurate to within 5% of the amount programmed, with verification of the amount pumped versus the programmed amount for each ingredient.
2. The automated compounding device has inherent safeguards, including the ability to detect inadvertent source-solution mixups; the ability to detect situations that could result in inaccurate deliveries, such as occluded transfer-set tubing and empty source containers; and the ability to keep incompatible source solutions separate.
3. The automated compounding software alerts the user when formulation issues arise.
4. The automated compounding software meets the standards of the American Society for Parenteral and Enteral Nutrition for parenteral nutrition label formats.[5]
5. The automated compounding software assists the pharmacist in producing physicochemically compatible parenteral nutrition formulations.
6. The automated compounding software provides useful clinical information.
7. The automated compounding software integrates with existing pharmacy programs wherever possible to optimize patient care and avoid therapeutic duplications.

The contractual agreement with the manufacturer should provide continuous support of the compounder and software, including information updates, problem solving, and emergency coverage. FDA considers all automated compounding devices class II devices,[6] and as such they must comply with federal regulations. The manufacturer's responsibilities are as follows:

1. The manufacturer should supply, and the pharmacist should verify, that the device is 510K cleared as evidence of compliance with regulatory requirements; that the device meets the fire and safety standards established by Underwriters Laboratories (i.e., is

UL-approved); that the operator's manual and other documentation support recommendations for use; and that accuracy statements and manufacturer claims are valid.

2. The manufacturer should provide 24-hour support for the compounder and its software throughout the life of the contract.
3. The manufacturer should routinely provide the latest version of the compounder software in a timely manner.
4. The manufacturer should ensure adequate availability of compounding supplies.
5. The manufacturer should provide detailed information and instructions on the appropriate use of the compounder and its software. References should be provided when appropriate.
6. The manufacturer should comply with FDA requirements for reporting adverse events.

Within the pharmacy department, specific policies and procedures should be developed that address responsibilities for compounder operations and maintenance, staff training, and monitoring compounder performance at all times. Before selecting and implementing an automated compounder, the pharmacy department should

1. Define and agree on automated compounding system needs and performance requirements.
2. Develop an implementation team with a lead person.
3. Develop a set of policies and procedures.

Control of the Automated Compounding Device in Daily Operations

The pharmacy department is responsible for the use, maintenance, and performance of the automated compounding device, including decisions about who has access to the compounder and its operations. Specific consideration should be given to the following:

1. Only designated pharmacy department personnel should have access to the compounder and its software. The level of access should correspond to the level of authority and expertise of the personnel.
2. Before being granted access to a compounder, pharmacy personnel should pass established competency-standard testing.
3. Access to and use of the compounder by pharmacy support personnel (i.e., pharmacy technicians, students, and other designated support staff) should be directly supervised by an authorized pharmacist.
4. The additive configuration or sequence of the compounder for compounding parenteral nutrition admixtures should not be altered from the established format without the authorization of a designated pharmacist.
5. The compounder should not be used for any purpose other than parenteral nutrition admixture compounding without authorization from a designated pharmacist. If the compounder is used for other extemporaneous drug preparation, this should be done separately from the schedule for parenteral nutrition admixtures.The use of the compounder in this manner will likely require the use of new compounding sets and admixture configurations.

Safety and Efficacy Features

The complexity of automated compounding device functions makes it imperative that the pharmacy department develop a specific plan for ensuring safe and efficacious use at all times. The safety and efficacy features should outline the core principles necessary for carrying out the complex tasks of parenteral nutrition compounding. The plan should identify the minimum standards that are routinely assessed through an established monitoring and surveillance program. Automated compounding devices on the market differ in hardware design, mechanisms of fluid transfer, and software applications. Consequently, sterility and quality assurance testing procedures and measures are also different, including routine assessments of accuracy in the delivery of correct amounts of nutrients. Consideration should be given to the following in accordance with the device manufacturer's specific instructions:

1. Establishing minimum competency standards for all personnel who have access to and operate the compounder. Competency standards should ensure that the compounder user has sufficient expertise to identify errors that may inadvertently bypass quality assurance systems. The competency standards should be reviewed and validated on a routine basis for all personnel operating the compounder.
2. Establishing specific procedures for the operation of the compounder that standardize its use, irrespective of the individual operator. Changes in compounder operations should occur only when authorized and should be communicated to all staff involved in compounding.
3. Including sterility and quality assurance measures to avoid extrinsic contamination and to ensure accurate delivery of parenteral nutrition additives.
4. Ensuring that compounder tubing changes occur at appropriate specified time intervals in accordance with the manufacturer's recommendations.
5. Devising methods for assessing and calibrating the accuracy of the compounder in delivering precise levels of substrates and additives.
6. Developing a contingency plan and a readily available backup system or method for providing uninterrupted parenteral nutrition therapy to patients in the event of compounder failure.
7. Ensuring that adequate amounts of solutions and supplies for automated compounding are on hand.

Quality Assurance Monitoring and Documentation

Automated compounding devices are intended to provide a higher margin of accuracy and to streamline the labor-intensive tasks associated with the manual extemporaneous preparation of large-volume, multiadditive parenteral nutrition admixtures and other admixtures. The compounders are not designed to replace oversight functions, which require the expertise of a pharmacist.

In theory, automated compounding devices provide compounding accuracy superior to that of traditional methods of manual compounding. However, the performance of compounders must be critically challenged by the pharmacist to ensure that their manufacturing specifications are equal to the task. In the pharmaceutical industry, that process is called validation. Ongoing quality assurance measures specified by the device manufacturer for assessing the performance of the compounder, as well as corrective actions, should be clearly delineated in policies separate from those dedicated to operational tasks. "Ongoing" means daily, and whatever measures are determined to be essential should be performed each day because random checks may not detect a more insidious, intermittent flaw that could assume major clinical significance.[7,8]

The pharmacy department may work with other departments to assess the compounder's performance if such expertise is not available within the pharmacy department. For example, portions of parenteral nutrition admixtures may be sent to the health care organization's laboratory to determine dextrose content. However, laboratory methods are usually designed for biological rather than pharmaceutical systems and should be validated to meet USP requirements for the components being tested. If outside departments participate in the quality assurance program, their methods should be appropriately validated in accordance with USP specifications and the results documented within the pharmacy department records on the compounder's performance.

The pharmacy department should develop a monitoring and surveillance plan with output reports that encompasses the principles outlined under the section on safety and efficacy features. The plan should detail specific policies and procedures that will ensure the continuing operation of the automated compounding device at optimum performance levels at all times. The data generated by the monitoring procedures should be reported to the pharmacy director and other appropriate oversight personnel and kept as a permanent record of the compounder's operations. These reports should be regularly reviewed in the assessment of trends and other long-term measures of performance. Specific consideration should be given to

1. Establishing performance standards and continuous quality assurance measures for assessing the compounder's performance and product quality during setup and in-process (during compounding) and end-process testing.
2. Establishing quality assurance testing of user-defined software variables validating that the correct responses to user commands occur.
3. Validating all quality assurance testing before implementation.
4. Establishing a minimum performance standard for each quality assurance test. For example, deviations in the accuracy of delivering a single additive cannot exceed a predetermined percent error without immediate corrective actions.
5. Documenting all quality assurance data on a daily basis. A comprehensive review of the data and documentation of performance trends should be performed at scheduled intervals as necessitated by aseptic conditions. The compounder should have scheduled, routine cleaning and maintenance according to the manufacturer's recommendations to ensure proper operation.

Storage and Inventory

The pharmacy department is responsible for housing the automated compounding device, related disposable supplies, and admixture ingredients. Other departments, such as materials management, may order and store additional supplies for the compounder yet defer to the pharmacy for the selection of the components necessary for proper compounder operation. Specific consideration should be given to

1. Maintaining an adequate inventory of supplies necessary for compounder operation and patient needs.
2. Procuring all large-volume parenteral nutrition components (amino acids, dextrose, and lipids) from one manufacturer unless such combinations have adequate physicochemical data that ensure the stability, compatibility, and safety of the final formulations commensurate with the data for single-source products.[5] Any proposed substitute products should be assessed for compatibility and approved by designated pharmacy personnel qualified to do so and possibly by the pharmacy and therapeutics committee if clinical issues are identified.
3. If a health care organization's contract requires a change in the brand of parenteral products, designated pharmacy personnel should verify that the new products are compatible. If a new product is approved, designated pharmacy personnel should verify that the new product is compatible, add it to the compounder formulary, and revise the admixture requirements and instructions relevant to the compounder's operations.

Education and Training

Pharmacists, by education and training, are competent to safely compound pharmaceuticals, including parenteral nutrition admixtures. Nevertheless, the introduction of automated compounding devices requires specific training of pharmacists as well as other pharmacy personnel in the operation, maintenance, and quality assurance of compounders. Specific consideration should be given to ensuring that

1. Pharmacy administration determines the individuals who will be responsible for education and training in the use of the compounders.
2. All education and training are documented in a permanent record maintained in the pharmacy department and in personnel files.
3. All pharmacy personnel using or supervising compounder operations are tested at regular intervals to ensure that individuals meet the department's minimum competency standards.
4. Retraining, competency assessment, and appropriate documentation accompany upgrades and new versions of the compounder to ensure the continued proficiency of personnel, safety of compounder operations, and adequacy of oversight.

Device Variability

Automated compounding devices are marketed by several manufacturers. Even though there are similarities among compounders, there may be significant differences in the design, accuracy, operation, maintenance, software, and manufacturing support, among other things. The safe operation and supervision of any given compounder depend on adherence to the manufacturer's specific instructions and continuous quality assurance monitoring of compounder performance. The safe and efficient operation of an automated compounding system depends on defined responsibilities for the pharmacy and manufacturer, as well as on strict adherence to policies, procedures, and quality assurance programs.

References

1. Food and Drug Administration. Safety alert: hazards of precipitation associated with parenteral nutrition. *Am J Hosp Pharm.* 1994; 51:1427–8.
2. American Society of Hospital Pharmacists. ASHP technical assistance bulletin on quality assurance for pharmacy-prepared sterile products. *Am J Hosp Pharm.* 1993; 50:2386–98.
3. McClendon RR. A comparative evaluation of methods used to compound parenteral nutrition solutions. *Nutr Support Serv.* 1983; 3:46–9.
4. Driscoll DF. Clinical delivery of nutritional therapy: automated compounders and patient-specific feeding. *Nutrition.* 1996; 12:461–2. Editorial.
5. American Society for Parenteral and Enteral Nutrition National Advisory Group on Standards and Practice Guidelines for Parenteral Nutrition. Safe practices for parenteral nutrition formulations. *JPEN J Parenter Enteral Nutr.* 1998; 22:49–66.
6. Trautman KA. The FDA and worldwide quality system requirements guidebook for medical devices. Milwaukee, WI: ASQ Quality Press; 1997.
7. Driscoll DF. Delivery of nutritional therapy: quality assurance of automated compounding devices. *Nutrition.* 1996; 12:651–2. Editorial.
8. Fields HS. Establishing core performance requirements for automated TPN compounders. *Am J Health-Syst Pharm.* 1996; 53:1607. Letter.

---

[a] Mihalski T, Clintec Nutrition Division, Baxter Healthcare. Personal communication. 1999 Mar 15.

Approved by the ASHP Board of Directors on April 27, 2000. Developed through the ASHP Council on Professional Affairs.

The bibliographic citation for this document is as follows: American Society of Health-System Pharmacists. ASHP guidelines on the safe use of automated compounding devices for the preparation of parenteral nutrition admixtures. *Am J Health-Syst Pharm.* 2000; 57:1343–8.

ASHP Guidelines on the Safe Use of Automated Dispensing Devices

Purpose

The purposes of these guidelines are to (1) propose goals and objectives for the safe use of automated dispensing devices in the medication-use process, (2) provide guidance on the safe use of automated dispensing devices to pharmacists and others involved in the medication-use process, (3) advise vendors of automated dispensing devices about the safety needs of health care professionals who use their systems, and (4) recommend standardization for Health Level 7 (HL7) interfaces between pharmacy information systems and automated dispensing devices. The recommendations presented in these guidelines should be used in conjunction with other literature on the topic and information from prospective or selected automated dispensing device or system vendors, established guidelines, and state and federal regulations. Pharmacists should exercise professional judgment in assessing their health system's needs regarding automated dispensing devices and systems and in adapting these guidelines to meet those needs.

Automated pharmacy systems are designed for centralized filling of individual patient prescriptions and unit-dose medication orders, decentralized dispensing, and other purposes. These guidelines address primarily computer-controlled decentralized medication-dispensing cabinets, which will be referred to as "automated dispensing devices." Since many of the concepts discussed here may be applicable to related technologies, the term "automated pharmacy system" will be used generally and the term "automated dispensing device" will be used specifically. Automated dispensing devices are located in hospital patient care units, surgical suites, emergency rooms, long-term care facilities, physicians' offices, and other settings. Several manufacturers produce automated dispensing devices with a variety of configurations and software capabilities that may interface with the pharmacy or health care organization's information systems.[1,2]

Background

The appropriate, accurate, and timely distribution of medications to patients is a well-established responsibility of pharmacists. In acute care settings in particular, distribution systems have been developed that enable pharmacists to review patient-specific medication orders and oversee the preparation and packaging or selection of these medication doses, as well as the delivery of these medication doses to patient care units. Automation has evolved to ease fulfillment of pharmacists' distributive responsibilities, expand distribution system capabilities, and improve efficiency in distribution.

Automated dispensing devices are an increasingly prevalent component of the medication-use process in health care organizations today. The pharmacy profession's transition to an emphasis on direct patient care, changes in health care systems, and pressures to reduce costs have all created interest in the availability and use of automated dispensing devices. ASHP supports the use of automated dispensing devices when it frees pharmacists from labor-intensive distributive functions, helps improve patient care by both pharmacists and nurses, improves accountability and storage of medications, and improves the accuracy and timeliness of medication product availability. Experience with automated dispensing devices suggests that, when used appropriately, these benefits can be realized.[3–11] When automated dispensing devices are not used appropriately, their complexity, design and function variations, maintenance and education requirements, and other factors can have undesirable effects and compromise patient safety.[12,13] The National Association of Boards of Pharmacy (NABP) includes language on automation in the NABP Model State Pharmacy Act and Model Rules.[14,15] The NABP Model Act uses the term "automated pharmacy systems" and defines them to include, but not be limited to, "mechanical systems that perform operations or activities, other than Compounding or Administration, relative to the storage, packaging, Dispensing, or Distribution of medications, and which collect, control, and maintain all transaction information."[14] Data processing and bar code technologies, although incorporated as integral components of some of these systems, are not considered in the NABP Model Act definition as automated drug distribution technology. The NABP Model Rules suggest specific requirements and options for helping individual states determine which automated pharmacy systems are appropriate for use.[15] These ASHP guidelines reflect and expand on the requirements of the NABP Model Rules.

The use of automated dispensing devices continues to evolve. Some health care organizations deploy one or several devices in selected areas, such as emergency departments, that are floor-stock intensive and where lost charges can be substantial. Some devices are used for selected categories of medications, such as controlled substances, that have time-consuming tracking and documentation requirements. Some organizations deploy devices throughout patient care areas to cover nearly all medications used.

The rapid development of technology applications in health care, including automated dispensing devices, and pressures to expand their use have raised concerns about patient safety, access to medications, and possible legislative and regulatory barriers. While technologies can be designed to minimize opportunities for medication errors, that same design can create other, often unanticipated, opportunities for medication errors. Consideration of the use of automated dispensing devices, like consideration of any other technology, must include serious evaluation of existing and potential opportunities for error and the implementation of mitigating strategies to minimize or prevent such errors. Pharmacists have a professional responsibility to ensure that appropriate policies, procedures, and quality-assurance programs are in place to address the safety, accuracy, security, and patient confidentiality of automated pharmacy systems, including automated dispensing devices.

Goals and Objectives

Goals for the use of automated dispensing devices in the medication-use process should focus on improving patient care and resource use. Specific objectives related to these goals may include the following:

- Information necessary for appropriate medication management and patient care is accurate, accessible, and timely.
- Appropriate medications are readily available and accessible to meet patient needs within safety and security controls.
- Vulnerabilities to medication errors are minimized, and those that remain are identified, documented, and mediated.
- Staff members involved in the medication-use process are safety conscious, accurate, and productive.
- Patients are satisfied with the quality and delivery of care.
- Medication distribution services are facilitated across the continuum of practice settings in the health care system.
- Resource management is improved by linking supply ordering channels to the medication distribution system.
- Billing accuracy is improved by allowing charges and credits to post when medications are dispensed from or returned to the automated dispensing device.

Requirements

Automated dispensing devices should be regarded by users as tools for improving the medication-use process rather than inherent solutions to problems in that process. Consideration should be given to how the technology can be adapted to meet the goals and objectives of the user rather than how the user's systems should be redesigned to fit the automated dispensing device. It is important to consider the recommended workflow for the automated dispensing device while simultaneously reviewing the facility's current workflow and practices to ultimately determine the best practices that will provide safe and efficient patient care while maximizing the safety and efficiency advantages offered by the automated dispensing device.

Before deciding to deploy automated dispensing devices in the medication-use process, an organization should assess its logistical, financial, and cultural circumstances; the safety, patient care, and resource benefits it hopes to gain; and how these benefits would be observed and measured. The organization should also determine if the automated dispensing devices in consideration are capable of producing the desired benefits. Specific consideration should be given to

- Incorporating the use of automated dispensing devices into the organization's strategic planning (i.e., ensuring that automation is compatible with the vision and mission of the organization).
- Assessing the use of automation from a complete systems perspective. Automated dispensing devices should integrate smoothly with other systems and processes, both manual and automated. Interfaces with overall patient care computer systems especially must be considered.
- Establishing performance standards for safety, accuracy, timeliness, and costs.[16]
- Determining the responsibilities of the automated dispensing device vendor and the organization for installation, validation, maintenance, education, operations, and troubleshooting.
- Assessing the impact of automation on organizational culture. Automation has a significant impact on employees, particularly pharmacy technicians and nurses. Optimal preparation and support should be considered.
- Ensuring effective education for the organization's employees who use the automated dispensing device or whose responsibilities are affected by its use.
- Developing an ongoing support plan.

Since the medication-use process involves multiple health care disciplines, selection of automated dispensing devices and establishment of policies and procedures for their use will require decisions that meet the needs of all disciplines involved. However, since pharmacists have a professional and legal responsibility for the safety and integrity of the entire medication-use process, they should provide leadership in the development and maintenance of policies and procedures for the safe use of automated pharmacy systems. Any system or device adopted for drug distribution and control, including automated dispensing devices, should meet the intent of established professional standards and guidelines regarding patient safety. The automated system or device should provide the following inherent safety features of unit-dose drug distribution systems:

- Medications are contained in, and administered from, single-unit or unit-dose packages.
- Medications are dispensed in ready-to-administer form to the extent possible.[17]
- Medications are available for administration to the patient only at the time at which they are to be administered, according to the institution's policy.
- An electronic patient medication profile is concurrently maintained in the pharmacy for each patient and made easily accessible to the pharmacist.
- Medications are accessible to different categories of health care professionals with the ability to limit access based on policy or law.

In addition, the automated systems or devices should ensure safe medication storage, distribution, access, and use wherever they are deployed, including meeting required environmental conditions for the storage and handling of medications. Plans for use of automated dispensing devices should include

- Sufficient quantity and appropriate location of devices to support intended use and efficient work processes,
- Selection of a location that minimizes distractions and interruptions during use,
- Consideration of surrounding work-space to allow efficient device operation and movement of staff,
- Ensuring appropriate ventilation and temperature control, including refrigeration for applicable medications,
- Ensuring adequate infection control policies and procedures are maintained when appropriate for the intended use and placement of the device,

- Ensuring appropriate and sufficient lighting to support the safe and accurate verification of medication orders, reading of medication labels, and administration documentation,
- Establishing proximity of the device to medication information and documentation systems,
- Selection of location or placement of the device that permits only the patient's caregivers access to protected health information, and
- Ensuring power and data connections essential to the operation of the device are included in the facility's emergency backup power and data management systems, so that support and information are provided in a reliable manner during power or data interruptions.

Finally, the automated system or device should comply with applicable federal and state consumer protection laws and regulations. State boards of pharmacy may have different requirements for the use of automated dispensing devices in various practice settings and for obtaining approval for their use.

Override Access to Medications Through Automated Dispensing Devices

All medication distribution systems have medication withdrawal functions that allow nurses and other caregivers limited access to certain medications before order review and approval by a pharmacist, especially in cases of patient emergencies. This function is typically referred to as an "override." Clearly stated organizational policies and criteria for system overrides should be developed that limit access to medications before orders have been reviewed and approved by a pharmacist.[16,18,19] Override access to medications should be limited to cases in which the drug product has been approved by a multidisciplinary committee of physicians, pharmacists, and nurses as having a clinically urgent need for the medication that outweighs the potential risk of medication error.

Subsequent order-based retrieval of the same medication should cause the user to be reminded that an override supply of medication was recently dispensed for the patient. Provision should be made for the retrospective review and reconciliation by a pharmacist of orders that were initiated without a pharmacist's review and approval. Override data (e.g., name of medication, quantity, location of the automated device, any associated adverse drug events) should be routinely reviewed to help evaluate and manage those medications approved for override access. Override data evaluation can aid an organization in improving the outcomes of automated dispensing device use by decreasing medication errors and potential adverse drug events[20] and should be considered part of the routine management process for automated dispensing devices.

Interfaces with Automated Pharmacy Systems

Proper planning should include the development of an interface strategy. Automated pharmacy systems interface with systems for pharmacy information, electronic medical records, admission/discharge/transfer, bar-coded medication administration (BCMA), and materials management for various purposes in support of the medication-use process, including the following:

- Commanding distribution of medications from a pharmacy location,
- Maintaining current data on patient population, including demographics and patient location, for the automated pharmacy system,
- Maintaining a current and accurate patient medication profile for each patient served by the automated pharmacy system,
- Maintaining current formulary information,
- Recording the addition, removal, or dispensing of medications from automated dispensing devices,
- Issuing charges for medications removed or dispensed from automated dispensing devices (if this is the charge method of choice), and
- Integrating with bedside point-of-care systems to assure accurate medication dispensing and patient administration.

Interfaces are effectively used to communicate patient demographic information, medication order information, formulary additions and updates, dispensing/charting information, and inventory management transactions between the automated dispensing device and the pharmacy information system (or pharmacy functionality in a hospital information system). Such interfaces may also pose challenges related to the complexity of their own deployment and maintenance. Their completeness and level of application may also impact the workflow associated with the use of automated dispensing devices. For these reasons, it is important to consider the impact that specific interfaces will have on the hospital and system users.

Interfaces between automated dispensing devices and pharmacy systems can be costly to create and maintain. Most vendors base these interfaces on HL7 standards[21] but do not necessarily interpret and apply the HL7 specifications in the same way. The result is that automated dispensing device interfaces should be easily customizable and thoroughly tested prior to implementation. Pharmacists should consult with other users of the same pharmacy system, automated dispensing device, and interface for advice on functionality and customization.

ASHP believes that the vendor community should work with the HL7 organization to identify one standard message set for communicating key transactions to and from automated dispensing devices to permit interfaces to be more easily implemented and supported. In addition, vendors should be prepared to support XML-based interfaces with the newer Web-based pharmacy applications.

Safety Checks

The pharmacy is responsible for ensuring that the automated pharmacy system operates as designed and is well maintained to prevent errors and system interruptions. All elements of the automated pharmacy system require periodic monitoring, including, as applicable, patient information and medication profiles, computer controls for access, operations of drawers and bins, and transaction records.

Any organization that uses an automated pharmacy system should have a written plan for the safe and effective use of the system. The plan should be developed by the pharmacy and nursing staff, with input from respiratory therapy, medicine, and other disciplines that may be affected by the system.[22,23] The plan should address

- Conformance with industry and government standards as well as accepted practice standards,
- Potential sources of medication errors and the procedures to follow to avoid such errors,
- Limits on access to medications,[24]
- How medications will be packaged and labeled, including standardizing and limiting available concentrations,
- How medications will be safely and securely transported from the pharmacy to the automated dispensing device,
- The use of clinical alerts for high-risk medications,
- How medications will be transported from the automated dispensing device to the patient to reduce risk of administration to the wrong patient or at the wrong time,[16]
- How patient and medication information will be available and displayed while maintaining patient privacy,[16]
- How user privacy, security, and safety will be ensured,
- Procedures for ensuring the security of all stored medications, especially controlled substances, with a process in place to prevent and detect diversion,[25,26]
- Procedures for auditing all system transactions,
- Procedures for avoiding drug product cross-contamination (evident or trace amounts of a liquid or solid drug that may contaminate another drug or package),
- Procedures for identifying and removing medications prior to expiration, and
- Procedures for reporting malfunction or breakdown of the automated dispensing device.

The organization should have a written plan for ensuring the accuracy of (1) medications stored and accessed through an automated pharmacy system and (2) machine-readable identification on medication labels. This plan should provide

- A thorough review of the automated pharmacy system to identify potential sources of error that may be introduced by the system,
- Policies and procedures designed to preclude errors, and
- A quality-assurance program for reviewing override data and medication error data associated with the automated dispensing device and identifying opportunities for improvement, including a process for validating any medications that have been designated as high risk via machine-readable coding on removal.

Any organization that allows external suppliers to replenish medications in the automated pharmacy system should have a written plan for ensuring medication accuracy.[27] When possible, this plan should include the use of machine-readable identification to ensure placement of medications in the appropriate containers within automated dispensing devices, as well as recording that the proper filling was performed. To support this, processes must be in place to ensure that products do not reach the active inventory before confirmation that the product's bar code is accurately loaded into the appropriate cross-reference file. If possible, the machine-readable identification should also be used to ensure that medication supplies are not expired or in immediate danger of expiring.[28] If a hospital utilizes BCMA, all medications present in an automated dispensing device must be encoded with a bar code that will appropriately identify them in the BCMA system.

The organization should have a written contingency plan for maintaining timely medication distribution, security, and documentation when system interruptions occur.

A profile interface in which all medication order information is sent from the pharmacy information system to the automated dispensing device should be present whenever 24/7 pharmacy order entry is available. (For facilities that do not have 24/7 pharmacy order entry, a profile interface should be employed whenever feasible.) A profile interface is important for patient safety because it requires that a pharmacist review medication orders before the caregiver can access the medication from the automated dispensing device. Profiling functionality should include

- Transmission of all components of medication and i.v. orders, including drug, dose and/or infusion rate, route, frequency, dosing schedule, and order start/stop times,
- Ensuring that all patient care areas use the profiling functionality, including ambulatory and outpatient areas such as the emergency department, whenever possible,
- Limiting the variety and quantity of medications that are accessible without pharmacist review (override), and
- The option to require a double-check (witness) at the time of dispensing of an identified high-alert medication from automated devices, especially when pharmacist review and order entry have not occurred.[16]

The organization should include a process for comparing patient allergies with the current medication profile. Automated devices should receive coded allergy information from the pharmacy or hospital information system, which would allow an alert to be displayed when a medication to which a patient is allergic is dispensed.

Monitoring and Surveillance

Pharmacists are legally and organizationally responsible for ensuring that drug supplies are adequately controlled and that medication use is documented within the health care organization. Automated pharmacy systems usually provide options for tracking and accounting for medication use, which can be used to help monitor important data, such as the number of adverse drug events.[29,30] These options often include freestanding computer-controlled access and record keeping for each device, computer-controlled access and record keeping linked to the pharmacy information system, and computer linking among the pharmacy, patient record, and billing information systems. Appropriate interfaces with pharmacy and overall patient care computer systems are critical. Each of these options may require a different level of oversight.

The organization should have a written plan for the monitoring and surveillance of medications accessed through automated pharmacy systems. The plan should be developed by the pharmacy, with input from nursing staff and other clinicians, and communicated to staff members responsible for its implementation. The plan should include[18,25,26,31]

- Identification of the data to be captured and the reports to be generated for monitoring medication use, waste reconciliation, and discrepancies (data and reports may vary by drug categories and requirements for control and accountability),
- Assignment of responsibility for reviewing reports, scheduling the frequency of report reviews, and reporting discrepancies,
- Assignment of responsibility for resolving discrepancies, scheduling the resolution of discrepancies, following up on unresolved discrepancies, and taking action if the discrepancy is not resolved on schedule,
- A description of the process for investigating trends in discrepancies and assigning responsibility for conducting the investigation,
- Appropriate access by personnel, including timely removal of access when no longer employed or credentialed by the facility,
- Determination of frequency of narcotic counts, who will perform them, and who is responsible for verifying that the narcotic counts were completed,
- Examination of charge and credit flow to ensure billing accuracy, and
- Assignment of reviewing overrides to ensure the function is being used appropriately.

Compliance with the plan should be monitored through the organization's quality-assurance program.

Storage and Inventory

The drawer, bin, and pocket configurations of automated dispensing devices vary depending on device design and hospital preferences. Open matrix drawers, pockets that open or light up for a specific drug, and multiple open bins within a cabinet door are just a few of many different configurations available from various vendors. The pharmacy should develop criteria for determining the drug products and quantities that will be stored under different levels of access control in specific configurations of drawers, pockets, or bins. Patient safety should be the primary concern in establishing these criteria. The criteria should address

- The frequency and appropriateness of individual medication use,
- The effective use of reports related to the safe, accurate, and timely withdrawal of medications available through the automated pharmacy system,
- The party responsible for medication safety oversight and administrative control of drug availability in the automated pharmacy system (e.g., the pharmacy and therapeutics committee),[16]
- The identification of drug products that are considered inappropriate for inclusion in automated dispensing devices (e.g., products that have short expiration dates or special preparation or storage requirements, present cross-contamination risks, or are hazardous),
- The need for ongoing monitoring and optimization of the contents of the automated dispensing device by a pharmacist, taking into consideration such matters as evolving therapeutic trends, the differing needs of individual patient care areas, and the capabilities and safety features of the automated pharmacy system,[17]
- Oversight of the positioning of look-alike and sound-alike drugs, high-alert drugs, and drugs with multiple strengths throughout the automated dispensing device as well as procedures to minimize the incorrect restocking of these medications (e.g., keeping these items as far apart as possible),
- Procedures to prevent and/or minimize the return of drugs directly to the automated dispensing device by nursing staff to decrease the potential for error,
- Specification of the individual(s) responsible for adding, modifying, or reviewing formulary items on a regular and ongoing basis to ensure they correctly display and interface map. Tall-man lettering, standardized concentration displays, and form designations are just a few of the many items that need to be maintained for safety,
- Procedures for keeping policies, procedures, and education current,
- Policies addressing drug product integrity, including
    - The importance of accuracy and integrity of product labels,
    - How to handle medications that are removed from an automated dispensing device but not used,
    - How medication waste is accounted for,
    - Checking products for expiration and beyond-use dates,
    - Identifying and following up on tampered products,
    - Storing products, and
    - Procedures for delivering medications to patient care units and individual patients.
- Controls that ensure accurate restocking of automated dispensing devices, such as
    - Access controls on drawers, bins, and pockets, including software restrictions and use of location lights and/or locking bin or pocket systems that support safe access,
    - Process redundancies to ensure correct restocking,[16]
    - Standardization of restocking procedures to limit process variation,[16] and
    - When the system permits, use of bar coding to restock the correct medication in the correct drawer, bin, or pocket, and
- Controlling access to medications to limit the potential for inadvertent selection of the wrong medication, and assuring that each drug has a unique and segregated location within the automated dispensing device so only the specific drug needed is accessible.[16]

Security and Responsibility

Among pharmacy's responsibilities for the medication-use process is preventing threats to patient and employee safety and economic loss through medication misuse, pilferage, and diversion.

Any organization that uses an automated pharmacy system should have a written plan that assigns responsibility for and addresses issues of security. The plan should be developed by the pharmacy, with input from nursing, medicine, and other disciplines that may be affected by the system. The plan should clearly identify that the pharmacist in charge has general responsibility for the automated pharmacy system. The plan should specify who in the pharmacy and elsewhere in the organization has responsibility for computer interface issues; operational problems; the accuracy of medications contained in the system; maintenance of access codes, magnetic cards, and other positive identification methods; and education of users and the determination of skill levels those individuals must achieve.

The specific responsibilities and privileges of all personnel involved in operating or using the automated pharmacy system should be set forth in written policies and procedures. The policies and procedures should minimize the use of temporary user and patient identifications and should describe the circumstances in which these features may be used.

Downtime procedures in case of software or hardware malfunctions, power failures, or planned maintenance affecting normal operations should be developed to ensure medication security, accurate documentation of distribution and administration, and continued patient safety.[16]

Education

Automated pharmacy systems bring together information systems, machines, and humans in highly complex and interdependent relationships. Individuals involved in the use and operation of the system must possess the knowledge and skills required by their level of responsibility and understand the risks associated with the use and foreseeable misuse of automated pharmacy systems.[16] The organization should

- Have procedures in place for ensuring that all staff members who use the automated pharmacy system receive adequate education, both initially and on an ongoing basis,
- Ensure that adequate resources are provided for effective education,
- Ensure that the content of the education programs is continually updated,
- Evaluate staff members to ensure competency in the use of the automated pharmacy system and document the evaluations,
- Share with staff members the lessons learned from the evaluations and discuss medication errors related to the automated pharmacy system and near-miss reports,[16] and
- Include at least one higher-level user group capable of managing and supporting the system and its end users.

Support

When automated dispensing devices are utilized, alternative distribution systems need to be in place to deliver medications in case of failure. The organization must negotiate a service level agreement with the vendor that meets the organization's minimal acceptable downtime requirements. The organization should define the level of support that will be provided internally and ensure that staff are sufficiently educated to deliver the defined level of internal support. The organization will need to negotiate with the vendor the purchase of spare parts needed to optimally recover from mechanical failures.

Conclusion

Automated dispensing devices are increasingly being used in health systems for centralized filling of individual patient prescriptions and unit-dose medication orders, decentralized dispensing, and other purposes. When such devices and the systems that support them are not used appropriately, their complexity, design and function variations, maintenance and education requirements, and other factors can compromise patient safety and have other harmful effects. ASHP supports the appropriate use of automated dispensing devices and has developed these guidelines to provide recommendations to pharmacists and others involved in their use.

References

1. Perini VJ, Vermeulen LC. Comparison of automated medication-management systems. *Am J Hosp Pharm.* 1994; 51:1883–91.
2. ECRI. Automated decentralized pharmacy dispensing systems. *Health Devices.* 1996; 25:436–73.
3. Ray MD, Aldrich LT, Lew PJ. Experience with an automated point-of-use drug distribution system. *Hosp Pharm.* 1995; 30: 18, 20–3, 27–30.
4. Borel JM, Karen LR. Effect of an automated, nursing unit-based drug-dispensing device on medication errors. *Am J Health-Syst Pharm.* 1995; 52:1875–9.
5. Guerrero RM, Nickman NA, Jorgenson JA. Work activities before and after implementation of an automated dispensing system. *Am J Health-Syst Pharm.* 1996; 53:548–54.
6. Schwarz HO, Brodowy BA. Implementation and evaluation of an automated dispensing system. *Am J Health-Syst Pharm.* 1995; 52:823–8.
7. Franklin BD, O'Grady K, Donyai P et al. The impact of a closed-loop electronic prescribing and administration system on prescribing errors, administration errors and staff time: a before-and-after study. *Qual Saf Health Care.* 2007; 16:279–84.
8. Gaunt MJ, Johnston J, Davis MM. Automated dispensing cabinets. Don't assume they're safe; correct design and use are crucial. *Am J Nurs.* 2007; 107:27–8.
9. Crane J, Crane FG. Preventing medication errors in hospitals through a systems approach and technological innovation: a prescription for 2010. *Hosp Top.* 2006; 84:3–8.
10. Chung K, Choi YB, Moon S. Toward efficient medication error reduction: error-reducing information management systems. *J Med Syst.* 2003; 27:553–60.
11. Oren E, Shaffer ER, Guglielmo BJ. Impact of emerging technologies on medication errors and adverse drug events. *Am J Health-Syst Pharm.* 2003; 60:1447–58.
12. Barker KN. Ensuring safety in the use of automated medication dispensing systems. *Am J Health-Syst Pharm.* 1995; 52:2445–7.

13. Tribble DA. How automated systems can (and do) fail. *Am J Health-Syst Pharm.* 1996; 53:2622–7.
14. National Association of Boards of Pharmacy. Model State Pharmacy Act. Article 1, section 105(h), p. 3. www.nabp.net/ftpfiles/NABP01/ModelActFINAL.doc (accessed 2009 Mar 18).
15. National Association of Boards of Pharmacy Model Rules for the Practice of Pharmacy. Section 3(p), pp. 94-95. www.nabp.net/ftpfiles/NABP01/ModelAct FINAL.doc (accessed 2009 Mar 18).
16. Institute for Safe Medication Practices (ISMP). ISMP guidance on the interdisciplinary safe use of automated dispensing cabinets. www.ismp.org/Tools/guidelines/ADC_Guidelines_Final.pdf (accessed 2009 Mar 19).
17. Fanikos J, Erickson A, Munz KE et al. Observations on the use of ready-to-use and point-of-care activated parenteral products in automated dispensing cabinets in U.S. hospitals. *Am J Health-Syst Pharm.* 2007; 64:2037–43.
18. Kowiatek JG, Weber RJ, Skledar SJ et al. Assessing and monitoring override medications in automated dispensing devices. *J Comm J Qual Patient Saf.* 2006; 32:309–17.
19. Kester K, Baxter J, Freudenthal K. Errors associated with medications removed from automated dispensing machines using override function. *Hosp Pharm.* 2006; 41:535–7.
20. Oren E, Griffiths L, Guglielmo J. Characteristics of antimicrobial overrides associated with automated dispensing machines. *Am J Health-Syst Pharm.* 2002; 59:1445–8.
21. Health Level 7 (HL7). HL7 standards. www.hl7.org/Library/standards.cfm (accessed 2009 Mar 19).
22. Novek J, Bettess S, Burke K et al. Nurses' perceptions of the reliability of an automated medication dispensing system. *J Nurs Care Qual.* 2000; 14:1–13.
23. Rebidas D, Smith ST, Denomme P. Redesigning medication distribution systems in the OR. *AORN J.* 1999; 69:184–6,188,190.
24. Botwin KJ, Chan J, Jacobs R et al. Restricted access to automated dispensing machines for surgical antimicrobial prophylaxis. *Am J Health-Syst Pharm.* 2001; 58:797–9.
25. Vigoda MM, Gencorelli FJ, Lubarsky DA. Discrepancies in medication entries between anesthetic and pharmacy records using electronic databases. *Anesth Analg.* 2007; 105:1061–5.
26. Epstein RH, Gratch DM, Grunwald Z. Development of a scheduled drug diversion surveillance system based on an analysis of atypical drug transactions. *Anesth Analg.* 2007; 105:1053–60.
27. Louie C, Brethauer B, Dong D et al. Use of a drug wholesaler to process refills for automated medication dispensing machines. *Hosp Pharm.* 1997; 32:367–75.
28. ASHP 2015 Initiative, Objective 5.1. www.ashp.org/s_ashp/docs/files/2015_Goals_Objectives_0508.pdf (accessed 2010 Jan 6).
29. Romero AV, Malone DC. Accuracy of adverse-drug-event reports collected using an automated dispensing system. *Am J Health-Syst Pharm.* 2005; 62:1375–80.
30. Institute for Safe Medication Practices, McIntosh ST, Petropoulos JB. Using data from automated dispensing units to identify adverse drug reactions. *Am J Health-Syst Pharm.* 2005; 62:2397–400.
31. Klibanov OM, Eckel SF. Effects of automated dispensing on inventory control, billing, workload, and potential for medication errors. *Am J Health-Syst Pharm.* 2003; 60:569–72.

Developed through the ASHP Section of Pharmacy Informatics and Technology and approved by the ASHP Board of Directors on July 21, 2009. These guidelines supersede the ASHP Guidelines on the Safe Use of Automated Medication Storage and Distribution Devices dated April 22, 1998.

A work group of the ASHP Section of Pharmacy Informatics and Technology 2008–2009 Section Advisory Group on Automation and Documentation (Leslie Brookins, M.S.; Ron Burnette, M.B.A.; Thomas W. Cooley, M.B.A.; Paul M. Seelinger, B.S.Pharm.; and Gwen Volpe, B.S.Pharm.) is gratefully acknowledged for revising these guidelines. Other members of the section advisory group included Christopher J. Urbanski, M.S., Chair; Arash T. Dabestani, Pharm.D., M.H.A., FABC, Vice Chair; Jim Besier, Ph.D., FASHP; Kimberly Dove, Pharm.D.; Craig P. Frost, M.B.A.; Rick K. Glabach, B.S.Pharm.; Gary L. Johnson, Jr., Pharm.D., M.H.A.; Denise Mckenzie; Brad Rognrud, M.S.; Charles De la Torre, M.S., M.I.S.; Rayburn Brian Vrabel, Pharm.D.; Matt Marshall, Pharm.D.; Marvin H. Choi (Student Member); Dennis A. Tribble, Pharm.D. (Executive Committee Liaison); and Karl Gumpper, Pharm.D., BCNSP, BCPS.

The bibliographic citation for this document is as follows: American Society of Health-System Pharmacists. ASHP guidelines on the safe use of automated dispensing devices. *Am J Health-Syst Pharm.* 2010; 67:483–90.

Drug Distribution and Control

Drug Distribution and Control

Redistribution of Unused Medications (0611)
Source: Council on Legal and Public Affairs
To advocate that any program for the return and reuse of medications comply with all federal and state laws (including laws regarding controlled substances); further,

To advocate that in order to ensure patient safety and provide an equal standard of care for all patients, such a program should include the following elements: (1) compliance with practice standards, accreditation standards, and laws related to prescription dispensing; (2) a requirement that these medications must not have been out of the possession of a licensed health care professional or his or her designee; (3) protection of the privacy of the patient for whom the prescription was originally dispensed; (4) inclusion of only those drug products that are in their original sealed packaging or in pharmacy-prepared unit-of-use packaging that is not expired and has been properly stored; (5) the presence of a system for identifying medications for the purpose of a drug recall or market withdrawal; (6) a definition of patient eligibility for participation in the program; and (7) adequate compensation of participating pharmacists for any associated costs.

This policy was reviewed in 2010 by the Council on Public Policy and by the Board of Directors and was found to still be appropriate.

Pharmaceutical Counterfeiting (0401)
Source: Council on Professional Affairs
To foster increased pharmacist and public awareness of drug product counterfeiting; further,

To encourage pharmacists to purchase and handle medications in ways that enhance the transparency and integrity of the drug product supply chain; further,

To encourage pharmacists to identify instances of drug product counterfeiting and to respond by assisting the patient in receiving appropriate treatment and monitoring, documenting patient outcomes, and notifying the patient, prescriber, and appropriate state and federal regulatory bodies (e.g., the Food and Drug Administration's MedWatch system); further,

To provide consumers and health professionals with information on how to avoid counterfeit drug products and how to recognize, respond to, and report encounters with suspicious drug products; further,

To foster research and education on the extent, methods, and impact of drug product counterfeiting and on strategies for preventing and responding to drug product counterfeiting.

This policy was reviewed in 2013 by the Council on Pharmacy Practice and by the Board of Directors and was found to still be appropriate.

Pharmacy Drug Theft (0303)
Source: House of Delegates Resolution
To support the development of policies and guidelines for health-system pharmacists designed to deter drug product theft and thereby enhance both the integrity of the drug distribution chain and the safety of the workplace; further,

To encourage the development of systems that limit the diversion and abuse potential of medications, including high-cost drugs and controlled substances, and thereby reduce the likelihood that these products will be targets of theft.

This policy was reviewed in 2013 by the Council on Pharmacy Management and by the Board of Directors and was found to still be appropriate.

Pharmacist's Role in Drug Procurement, Distribution, Surveillance, and Control (0232)
Source: Council on Professional Affairs
To affirm the pharmacist's expertise and responsibility in the procurement, distribution, surveillance, and control of all drugs used within health systems; further,

To encourage the Joint Commission on Accreditation of Healthcare Organizations, other accreditation bodies, and governmental entities to enhance patient safety by supporting the pharmacist's role in drug procurement, distribution, surveillance, and control.

(*Note:* For purposes of this policy, drugs include those used by inpatients and outpatients, large- and small-volume injectables, radiopharmaceuticals, diagnostic agents including radiopaque contrast media, anesthetic gases, blood-fraction drugs, dialysis fluids, respiratory therapy drugs, biotechnologically produced drugs, investigational drugs, drug samples, drugs brought to the setting by patients or family, and other chemicals and biological substances administered to patients to evoke or enhance pharmacologic responses.)

This policy was reviewed in 2011 by the Council on Pharmacy Practice and by the Board of Directors and was found to still be appropriate.

Optimizing the Medication-Use Process (9903)
Source: Council on Administrative Affairs
To urge health-system pharmacists to assume leadership, responsibility, and accountability for the quality, effectiveness, and efficiency of the entire medication-use process (including prescribing, dispensing, administration, monitoring, and education) across the continuum of care; further,

To urge health-system pharmacists to work in collaboration with patients, prescribers, nurses, and other health care providers in improving the medication-use process.

This policy was reviewed in 2013 by the Council on Pharmacy Management and by the Board of Directors and was found to still be appropriate.

ASHP Guidelines on Managing Drug Product Shortages in Hospitals and Health Systems

Purpose

Drug product shortages can adversely affect drug therapy, compromise or delay medical procedures, and result in medication errors.[1,2] Health care professionals are increasingly concerned about the clinical effect that shortages have on patients and the tremendous resources required to address shortages.[3–5] Adverse patient outcomes related to drug product shortages[1,2,6–9] have prompted aggressive management strategies by health care providers and gained the attention of the Joint Commission,[10] the government,[11,12] and the media.[13,14] Drug product shortages adversely affect health-system finances by increasing the cost of delivering patient care, largely through higher drug acquisition and personnel costs.[6] In addition, shortages create a high level of frustration for everyone involved, including purchasing agents, pharmacists, nurses, physicians, and patients.[7]

Managing drug product shortages is particularly complex for practitioners in hospitals and health systems (hereinafter, "health systems"), because these facilities routinely treat patients with acute or emergent conditions, use a significant number of medically necessary or single-source products, and use high-cost new drug technologies. These health care providers are challenged during drug product shortages to ensure the provision of seamless, safe, and therapeutically equivalent drug therapy, preferably at comparable costs. The pharmacy department must take a leadership role in efforts to develop and implement appropriate strategies and processes for informing practitioners of shortages and ensuring the safe and effective use of therapeutic alternatives. Strategic planning is required for managing drug product shortages, just as it is for disasters such as major weather events and mass-casualty incidents.

Because a thorough understanding of why drug product shortages occur is essential for their successful management, these guidelines begin with a description of factors that contribute to or exacerbate shortages. The guidelines then describe a three-phase approach to contingency planning for management of drug product shortages and include strategies for prevention. Given the differences and complexities in health-system organizational arrangements and practice settings, some aspects of these guidelines may not be applicable in all settings. Pharmacy managers should use their professional judgment in assessing and adapting these guidelines to meet their needs.

Contributing Factors

For the purpose of these guidelines, a drug product shortage is defined as a supply issue that affects how the pharmacy prepares or dispenses a drug product or influences patient care when prescribers must use an alternative agent. Shortages can be the result of one or a combination of factors throughout the supply chain. The supply chain includes sources of raw materials, manufacturers, regulators, wholesalers or distributors, prime vendors, group purchasing organizations, and end-user health care systems. The factors that follow contribute to disruptions in the availability of drug products.

Raw and Bulk Material Unavailability. Disruptions in the supply of raw or bulk materials are especially problematic when the primary or sole source experiences production difficulties or discontinues production, affecting multiple manufacturers. An estimated 80% of the raw materials used in pharmaceuticals comes from outside the United States.[4] Availability problems can arise when armed conflict or political upheaval disrupts trade, animal diseases contaminate tissue from which raw materials are extracted, climatic and other environmental conditions depress the growth of plants used to produce raw materials, or raw materials are degraded or contaminated during harvesting, storage, or transport.

Manufacturing Difficulties and Regulatory Issues. Drug product shortages can also occur when the primary or sole manufacturer of a drug product halts or delays production in response to a Food and Drug Administration (FDA) enforcement action concerning noncompliance with current good manufacturing practices (cGMPs). Contributing factors may include antiquated manufacturing equipment, a shift of resources from maintenance of equipment and facilities to research and development, loss of manufacturer personnel experienced in production and compliance issues as a result of company mergers or retirements, cGMP-related problems with subcontractors who supply products to multiple pharmaceutical manufacturers, and limited FDA resources for timely inspections of manufacturing sites.[4] Resolution of these issues is often a lengthy process and may include inspections to ascertain cGMP compliance, issuance of an injunction against the manufacturer, or seizure of products. In some instances, a manufacturer's decision to close a specific manufacturing facility results in unintended drug product shortages. Such was the case when the sole source for hyaluronidase production closed, leaving no supplier.[5]

FDA enforcement actions are intended to protect the public from potentially unsafe drug products. These actions are evaluated by FDA's Center for Drug Evaluation and Research (CDER) drug shortage coordinator to determine if the action might create a shortage of a medically necessary drug product.[12] (FDA's definition of a medically necessary product is discussed in the "Government intervention" section below.) In the event that a significant corrective action involves a medically necessary product, FDA will help the manufacturer return to compliance, consider qualifying additional manufacturing sites, or, in extreme circumstances, permit importation of the product from a foreign manufacturing source once the required quality controls are met.

Voluntary Recalls. Voluntary recalls, generally related to manufacturing problems, can cause shortages, especially when a sole manufacturer's drug product dominates the market supply. Voluntary recalls are generally temporary and occur as a result of a minor lapse in manufacturing procedures that would not be subject to FDA legal action. Recalls usually affect specific lots and are conducted either because of a lack of assurance that the recalled product is safe or for reasons not related to safety, such as technical deficiencies in the drug's labeling. An ethical dilemma could arise when it is predictable that complying with the voluntary recall may cause a drug product shortage in a given health system.

Change in Product Formulation or Manufacturer. Changes in a product's formulation or manufacturer may also delay product availability. One example is the transition from albuterol metered-dose inhalers (MDIs) containing chlorofluorocarbons to MDIs containing hydro-fluoroalkanes in 2006.

Manufacturers' Production Decisions and Economics. Manufacturers' business decisions are based on a variety of factors, including availability of generic products, market size, patent expiration, drug-approval status, regulatory compliance requirements, and anticipated clinical demand. Occasionally, manufacturers temporarily or permanently reduce production quantities of certain drug products as they shift production efforts or reallocate resources to other products. A manufacturer's reasoned, sound business decision to discontinue production of a drug product because of insufficient financial return or a high cost to correct manufacturing issues can cause an unanticipated, serious shortage, especially in the instance of a sole-source or medically necessary product.[15] For example, a shortage of diphtheria and tetanus toxoids and acellular pertussis vaccine adsorbed was precipitated when one of the manufacturers, claiming low revenues, discontinued its product in 2000.[5] Manufacturers are not required to notify FDA of a drug discontinuation unless the product is a sole-source or medically necessary product.[16] For medically necessary drugs, FDA can encourage other manufacturers to produce the product or request that the manufacturer not suspend production until an alternative source is available. However, FDA does not have the authority to require a company to make any product, even if it is medically necessary. Even with advance notice, some agents, such as vaccines or antibiotics, are complex to manufacture, and shortages may result even if other manufacturers are willing and able to produce the product. Similarly, business decisions on the part of wholesale distributors and end-user health systems may contribute to drug product shortages.

Industry Consolidations. Manufacturer mergers often result in decisions to narrow the focus of product lines or move a production line to a new facility, resulting in the discontinuation or delayed availability of drug products. Mergers between two companies that manufacture similar product lines typically result in single-source products. As the number of manufacturers of a product decreases, resiliency in the supply chain also decreases, making product supplies more vulnerable. Many vaccines in the United States are single-source products, in part because of discontinuations and consolidations.

Restricted Drug Product Distribution And Allocation. Most hospitals and health systems obtain the majority of their drug products through wholesale distributors. Restricted distribution methods that bypass the normal supply chain can also create shortages. As the result of either market approval requirements or postmarketing surveillance, manufacturers limit the availability of specific drug products. Only selected suppliers and end users who comply with manufacturer agreements can obtain the product. A manufacturer can also place restrictions on available limited supplies, requiring health systems to order directly from the manufacturer or through a specialty distributor to receive an allocation.

Inventory Practices. Communication and transportation efficiencies throughout the supply chain have allowed inventory reductions at all levels. Most manufacturers, distribution centers, and health systems use "just-in-time" inventory management to reduce the cost of inventory on hand and optimize cash flow. This strategy is recognized as sound business management for all stakeholders, but an unexpected shortage at any point in the supply chain can significantly affect the end user and patient. Some manufacturers and distributors use inventory management strategies that minimize end-of-quarter or end-of-year product inventories or limit shipments based on yearly quotas.

Poor ordering practices, stockpiling before price increases, hoarding caused by rumors of an impending shortage, and unexpected delivery delays may affect inventory levels in individual health systems. Hospitals in rural areas face additional inventory challenges caused by distant distribution centers and the inability to easily borrow an item from a nearby hospital. Drug product shortages may also occur when all hospitals in an area disproportionately use the same wholesaler. Some shortages are wholesaler dependent, as shortages of drugs can occur when contracts with suppliers are delayed.

Unexpected Increases in Demand and Shifts in Clinical Practice. Occasionally, the demand for a drug product unexpectedly increases or exceeds production capacity. This may occur when a new indication is approved for an existing drug product, when usage patterns change in response to new therapeutic guidelines, when a substantial disease outbreak occurs, or when unpredictable factors influence demand. Shortages may be prolonged when the raw materials are limited or manufacturing processes are complex or dependent on a long lead time. For example, when the Centers for Disease Control and Prevention (CDC) recommended annual influenza vaccination for children age 6–59 months in 2006, only one product had FDA-approved labeling for use in children 6–23 months old.[17,18]

Nontraditional Distributors. The increased frequency of drug product shortages has precipitated the development of nontraditional distributors, also known as open-market, gray-market, or alternative distributors. These specialty, licensed distributors or brokers obtain products in short supply for the purpose of reselling them to end users who are unable to obtain them through their normal suppliers. These distributors aggressively market the availability of these products to hospitals, specialty health systems, home care agencies, and physician practices, generally at substantially higher prices. Typically, these distributors have a limited quantity of product, often only enough for one or two patients. Many do not offer a return or refund on a product if it expires or is not used. Especially worrisome is the inability to ascertain the product's pedigree or ensure the reliability of the product's source, which could be outside the United States, and proper handling and storage throughout the chain of custody. The extent to which the activities of such nontraditional distributors contribute to drug product shortages is unknown.

Compounding pharmacies have also pursued the production of drugs that are in short supply. Caution is warranted because preparations from these pharmacies may not meet applicable state or federal standards (e.g., United States Pharmacopeia chapter 797 or FDA labeling requirements). The sources of raw materials used by compounding pharmacies have been questioned, and apparent lapses in quality control have resulted in serious patient injury, including death.[13]

Natural Disasters. Natural disasters can have a profound effect on the availability of drug products. Damage to manufacturing facilities, particularly those that are the sole source of a drug product or category of products, is likely to cause long-term shortages. Damage to manufacturing facilities in Puerto Rico in 1998 from hurricane George caused shortages of several drug products. Fires, hurricanes, tornadoes, and floods are examples of natural disasters that may temporarily compromise drug product supplies. In some instances, these shortages may be exacerbated by an escalated need for certain classes of drug products to care for victims of the disaster. In 2005, areas affected by hurricanes Katrina and Rita were affected by both an increased need for medications and the inability to obtain them.

Phased Approach to Planning for Drug Product Shortages

The discovery of a shortage initiates a cascade of events surrounding drug procurement and therapeutic decision-making (Figure 1). Drug procurement considerations include validating the shortage and its anticipated duration, determining the availability of supplies from alternative sources, locating and procuring alternative supplies (if available), investigating the implications of compounding the product, and researching and providing education about alternative agents and the cost implications of all scenarios. The outcome of this process may prompt an evaluation of the shortage's potential effect on patient care and development of a strategy for effectively communicating the needed information to all professionals involved and to affected patients when warranted.

In an ideal world, there would be a system for warning providers in advance of impending drug product shortages; this would give them ample opportunity to proactively address and manage all aspects and implications of the shortage. In lieu of this ideal, pharmacists, when confronted with the unavailability of a drug product, want information on which to base decisions about meeting patient needs for the product. Segments of the supply chain, especially manufacturers and distributors, have been inconsistent in providing information and assistance to health systems. The difficulty in obtaining information is exacerbated by the many players, complexities, and uncertainties in the supply chain.

The pharmacy department must take a leadership role in managing shortages by developing and implementing appropriate strategies and processes for optimizing the safe

Figure 1. Process for decision-making in the management of drug product shortages.

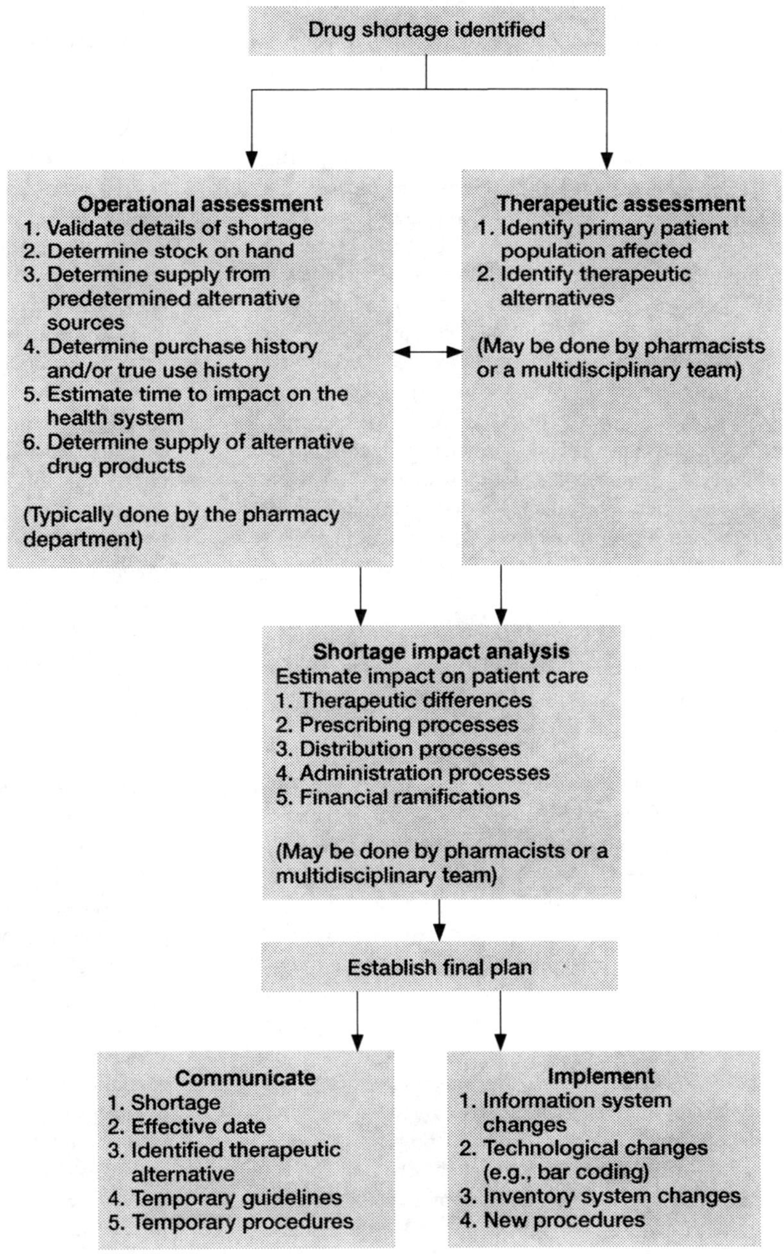

and effective use of therapeutic alternatives. Health systems should develop a contingency planning strategy to prepare for the possibility of a prolonged drug product shortage.[19] Although it often is not possible to predict when shortages will occur, the process for dealing with them can be defined in advance. The health system should identify a point person to implement and monitor this process and establish an organizational approach to decision-making and communication. The institution should determine committee structures and responsibilities for decision-making during each phase of the process (e.g., pharmacy and therapeutics committee, medical executive committee).

Planning can be divided into three phases: identification and assessment, preparation, and contingency. Assessment requires a critical evaluation of the current situation and the potential effect of the shortage on the health system. An effective evaluation examines the reason for the shortage and estimates an end date; both internal and external supply availabilities are assessed.

The preparation phase consists of all activities that can be performed before the actual effects of the shortage are felt. Depending on the health system's inventory, when a back order or other notice is received, there is often lead-time before actual stock depletion. All patients whose treatment depends on the unavailable drug product and alternative therapies should be identified. Since many drug products have limited therapeutic alternatives, outages can have significant patient care and cost consequences. Health systems need to gauge the effect of those consequences on their institutions. Preparation should also include the development of methods for implementation and communication.

The contingency phase involves operations and circumstances for which preparation is limited because of incomplete information, financial constraints, or circumstances beyond the health system's control. For example, biological products are available only in increments and at a very high cost when no therapeutic alternatives are readily available or when shortages are longer than anticipated. Since direct control over availability is not possible, health systems must prepare for a product's unavailability.

Identification and Assessment Phase. The purchasing agent is often the person who identifies a shortage and may be the person responsible for managing drug product shortages. This person must be cognizant of aberrant fluctuations in the health system's supply chain that may indicate a potential shortage (e.g., partial orders filled, one strength difficult to obtain, most manufacturers have no more stock). If the purchasing agent is not a pharmacist, he or she must work with a designated pharmacist.

When a shortage is identified, the point person or his or her designee should conduct an assessment to evaluate its potential effect. A threat analysis using the shortage's expected duration and an assessment of the current inventory and usage patterns can be used to determine the potential consequences of the shortage.

Details and duration of shortage. Pharmacists can contact product manufacturers, distributors, FDA, CDC, and other sources to determine the reason for the shortage and its expected duration. This information may already be available on the ASHP Drug Shortage Resource Center Web site (www.ashp.org/shortages). If not, visitors to the site can report a shortage online. Predictions of when the product will be available help determine the health system's ability to endure the shortage and guide its short- and long-term management strategies.

Although the end result is the same, the time to impact and the duration of effect vary according to the reason for the shortage and where in the supply chain problems occur—from raw materials to manufacturer, manufacturer to wholesaler, or wholesaler to health system. A lack of raw materials may affect several manufacturers of the finished drug product. A manufacturer's problems may affect only its product. Effects on distributors are dependent on their inventory levels.

Inventory on hand. Once a shortage is confirmed, the pharmacy should count the inventory on hand and estimate the time period it will cover. Available inventory includes all supplies of the drug product within the health system, including the pharmacies, inpatient units, ambulatory care clinics, automated medication storage and distribution devices, floor stock, resuscitation carts, and prepared trays.

Based on available quantities and historical usage, the pharmacy should estimate how long the health system can endure a shortage. Usage history can be obtained from procurement and issue records held by distributors, the purchasing department, and the pharmacy department. Billing and automated medication storage and dispensing device records can assist in determining actual usage within the system.

Inventory counts of all alternative drug products should be converted into common measurement units to augment estimates of use. Both current use rates and reduced rates after conservation measures are implemented should be included when assessing how long the available inventory of the shortage drug product and possible alternative products will last.

Threat to patient care and costs. A threat analysis evaluates all factors relevant to the shortage (e.g., duration, current inventory, medical necessity, alternative sources or therapies) to determine the shortage's potential effect on patient care and costs. Shortages affect safe medication practices throughout the medication distribution and administration process within a health system. When considering alternative dosage forms or therapies, pharmacists must consider changes in their procedures for look-alike and sound-alike medications, bar coding, distribution paths, and the effect on automation, contract compliance, and final product preparation.[20] The extent to which a health system will be affected by a given shortage depends on the health system's scope and level of services and its service population.

Preparation Phase. Once an imminent shortage is confirmed, the health system should take steps to prepare for known and potential problems in maintaining patient care and controlling costs.

Therapeutic alternatives. The first step in the preparation phase is to identify therapeutic alternatives to the unavailable drug product. A formal process for identifying and approving therapeutic alternatives for the health system should be established. The health system should make decisions about alternative agents in collaboration with medical, nursing, and pharmacy representatives and obtain approval of the appropriate medical committees. Therapeutic alternatives should be inventoried to ensure adequate supplies to meet new demand. In many cases, supplies of the best alternative agent may be affected by the current shortage.

Communication and patient safety. Information about the drug product shortage, alternative therapies, temporary therapeutic guidelines, and implementation plans should be communicated to clinical staff by the most effective means available within the health system. Communication of this information is essential for ensuring patient safety and preventing medication errors caused by confusion over differences between drug products' dosages, onsets, durations, and other factors. Automated systems and order-entry systems must be updated with changes. Pharmacy department staff responsible for assisting prescribers with medication orders and aiding nursing staff with administration should be thoroughly informed about the alternative therapy decisions and implementation plans. Sustained communication is necessary to reach medical, nursing, and pharmacy staffs working varied shifts or services.

External relationships with other health systems. The preparation phase includes, when applicable, the establishment of collaborative arrangements with other institutions within a regional network or system. Available supplies of a potentially unavailable product and information about alternative therapies should be shared among the facilities. This option is limited for rural hospitals and for area hospitals served by a single wholesaler.

Patient prioritization. When a limited supply of a drug remains available and alternatives for specific patient groups are undesirable, a health system may prioritize the drug for specific patient groups. National organizations (e.g., CDC, medical organizations) may provide guidance on setting patient priorities. Medication-use evaluation data on prescribing and utilization trends, if available for the drug in question, may be useful in developing prioritization criteria to guide appropriate drug use. Such criteria are particularly helpful in dealing with long-term shortages such as with intravenous immunoglobulin. To limit product use for select patients or services in the health system, criteria should be developed by a multidisciplinary team. Communication is essential to ensure that adequate supplies are available to complete courses of therapy. Clear guidelines for prioritization must be provided to assist pharmacists in evaluating the appropriateness of medication orders.

Consultation with risk management and ethics staff members or committees may be useful when supplies are severely limited. For example, during the influenza vaccine shortage of 2004–05, many health systems did not have sufficient product to follow recommended CDC guidelines and further restricted use of the product to specific patient groups.

Stockpiling restraint. Inventory management is a challenge during a shortage. Despite pressure to do otherwise, stockpiling (hoarding) in advance of a feared shortage can occur; this can exacerbate the shortage and divert unneeded supplies away from other health systems with patients in need.[21] Health systems should refrain from stockpiling, which causes two distinct problems:

1. Stockpiling can cause artificial shortages when health systems drain the supply chain and exceed manufacturing capacities, and
2. Increased inventory is costly and may not be absorbed by normal usage if shortages do not occur as anticipated.

Speculative purchasing in response to a potential shortage has drawbacks, depending on the likely cause of the shortage and where it might occur in the supply chain. Problems may arise that pose threats to, but do not reach, end users. This happens when the supply chain, from raw material to finished product, contains several months' supply; the long lead-time allows corrections that avert a shortage.

During shortages, manufacturers and distributors often allocate a product on the basis of past usage. An initial stockpile order generally has no effect on increasing an allocation.

Contingency Phase. Health systems must establish clear guidelines for dealing with situations in which a product is available only from a compounding source or nontraditional source or when a critical drug is not available at all.

Risk management and liability. One potential complication of a shortage is litigation by patients who feel that they have received improper care or suffered unanticipated adverse drug events as a result of delays, prioritization, alternative therapy, or nontraditional drug product sources. This situation is most likely with agents for which no alternatives are available. Even though risk management and legal representatives may have participated in earlier phases of the process, they should be notified immediately when all options for obtaining either the drug product or acceptable alternatives have been exhausted.

Each health system must determine its philosophy on purchasing drugs from the gray-market or compounding pharmacies and on compounding agents inhouse. These decisions should be made before the pressure and emotion of a specific shortage occur. Each option and its potential effect on patient risk should be evaluated. Nontraditional drug product sources (e.g., secondary wholesalers) have extremely limited supplies, and the quality of these products may be questionable, as the provenance of the medication may be unknown. Compounding pharmacies may also present patient risks; several deaths have been associated with improperly sterilized compounded products.[9] Health systems may choose to compound products if they can meet the necessary guidelines; however, obtaining raw materials may be difficult in some cases.

Budget considerations. In the event that the drug product is available only from noncontracted manufacturers or through nontraditional distributors, the increased costs of using these sources should be estimated. Using alternative therapies may also increase costs. The financial implications should be presented through budget channels, with a request and justification for contingency funds. Additional expenditures caused by drug product shortages (e.g., overtime spent in locating product, extra or priority deliveries, inhouse compounding or packaging) must be documented to explain budget variances and to support future budget proposals.

Information coordination and communication. Clear communication with all affected clinicians about the status of a shortage is vital. Some health systems may designate a specific department to manage communications; others may find that a collaborative strategy involving various organizational departments and committees works best. Patients or family members should be counseled when a drug product shortage will delay or compromise care, especially when patients have been stabilized on the drug product and when alternatives may not be as effective (e.g., pain or blood pressure medications). The Joint Commission requires that prescribers potentially affected by drug product shortages be actively alerted.[10]

Strategies for Prevention

Communication with the media, national professional or patient organizations, and government agencies can raise awareness of the shortage and its potential consequences. Notifying ASHP or FDA about a drug product shortage can initiate these efforts. Drawing attention to the shortage may encourage production by other manufacturers, collaborative efforts to develop alternative therapies, and ad hoc training opportunities on the safe and effective use of alternatives.

Government Intervention

FDA is responsible for assisting with drug product shortages to the extent of its authority.[11] Its responsibilities are dispersed among several components of CDER. The extent of FDA's activities depends on whether a shortage meets "medical necessity" criteria. FDA will attempt to prevent or alleviate shortages of medically necessary products. A product is considered to be medically necessary or a medical necessity if it "is used to treat or prevent a serious disease or medical condition, and there is no other available source of that product or alternative drug that is judged by medical staff to be an adequate substitute."[12] Inconvenience to the patient and cost to the patient, institution, and manufacturer are insufficient reasons for classifying a product as a medical necessity.

A determination of medical necessity involves a risk–benefit evaluation of the compromising issue with the product versus the medical need. When FDA has determined that a shortage of a medically necessary product exists, the agency will act within its authority; actions may include discussions with pharmaceutical manufacturers to encourage additional sources, technical assistance to manufacturers experiencing cGMP difficulties, or expedited reviews of drug product marketing applications or cGMP-related improvements. FDA may take these actions whether the cause of the shortage involves business decisions to stop manufacturing the product, voluntary recalls, FDA enforcement actions, or other factors. Information on the availability of medically necessary drug products is posted on CDER's website, and information regarding the availability of blood and vaccine products regulated by FDA's Center for Biologics Evaluation and Research (CBER) is posted on CBER's website. FDA encourages consumers and health care professionals and organizations to report product shortages. Reports of drug product shortages can be made by e-mail via CDER's Drug Shortages website (www.fda.gov/cder/drug/shortages/default.htm), and reports on vaccine and blood product shortages via CBER's Biological Products Shortage website (www.fda.gov/cber/shortage/shortage.htm). FDA's shortage team will obtain information about availability and will work cooperatively with ASHP's drug product shortage team.

Conclusion

Drug product supply issues are becoming more frequent, whether they result from manufacturing difficulties or natural disasters that affect production, reductions in the supply of raw materials, voluntary recalls, manufacturer business decisions, FDA enforcement actions to ensure public safety, or stockpiling that leads to artificial shortages. Although it is impractical to prepare for every potential shortage, proper planning can minimize adverse effects on patient care and health-system costs and prevent problems from escalating into crises. The key to success will undoubtedly be found in the effectiveness of information gathering, teamwork to assess options, and communication with providers, patients, and administrators.

References

1. U.S. Pharmacopeia Center for the Advancement of Patient Safety. Section I: USP medication error analysis; drug shortages affect patient safety. www.usp.org/pdf/EN/patientSafety/capsLink2004-10-01.pdf (accessed 2008 Sep 17).
2. Institute for Safe Medication Practices. Safety briefs: drug shortage causes error. www.bfr06.com/ISMP_12_3.pdf (accessed 2009 Mar 23).
3. Schwartz MA. Prescription drugs in short supply: case histories. New York: Marcel Dekker; 1980.
4. Provisional observations on drug product shortages: effects, causes, and potential solutions. *Am J Health-Syst Pharm.* 2002; 59:2173–82.
5. Fox ER, Tyler LS. Managing drug shortages: seven years' experience at one health system. *Am J Health-Syst Pharm.* 2003; 60:245–53.
6. Baumer AM, Clark AM, Witmer DR et al. National survey of the impact of drug shortages in acute care hospitals. *Am J Health-Syst Pharm.* 2004; 61:2015–22.
7. Institute for Safe Medication Practices. National survey on drug shortages reveals high level of frustration, low regard for safety. www.ismp.org/Newsletters/acutecare/articles/20010321_2.asp (accessed 2009 Mar 23).
8. Institute for Safe Medication Practices. Recent national shortage of fentanyl products presents potential problems when substituting sufentanil. *ISMP Med Saf Alert.* 2001; 6(Feb 7):1.
9. Traynor K. Meningitis deaths linked to drug shortages. www.ashp.org/import/news/HealthSystemPharmacyNews/newsarticle.aspx?id=648 (accessed 2008 Sep 17).
10. Element of performance 7, medication management standard 2.10 (selection and procurement). In: Comprehensive acccreditation manual for hospitals. Oakbrook Terrace, IL: Joint Commission; 2007:MM-7.
11. Jensen V, Kimzey LM,Goldberger MJ. FDA's role in responding to drug shortages. *Am J Health-Syst Pharm.* 2002; 59:1423–5.
12. CDER manual of policies and procedures (MAPP) 6003.1: drug shortage management. Rockville, MD: Food and Drug Administration; 2006.
13. Rubin AJ, Gosselin PG. Shortages of drugs threaten patients. http://articles.latimes.com/2001/may/06/news/mn-60196 (accessed 2009 Mar 23).
14. Szabo L. Shortages of pediatric cancer drugs are common. www.usatoday.com/news/health/2005-07-19-cancer-drugs_x.htm (accessed 2009 Mar 23).
15. Hensley S, Wysocki B. Shots in the dark. As industry profits elsewhere, U.S. lacks vaccines, antibiotics. *Wall St J.* 2005; Nov 8:A1.

16. Food and Drug Administration. Federal Food, Drug, and Cosmetic Act, Sec. 506C (21 U.S.C. 356c). Discontinuance of a life-saving product. www.fda.gov/opacom/laws/fdcact/fdcact5a3.htm#sec506c (accessed 2009 Mar 23).
17. Smith NM, Bresee JS, Shay DK et al. Prevention and control of influenza: recommendations of the Advisory Committee on Immunization Practices (ACIP). *MMWR Recomm Rep.* 2006; 55(RR-10):1–42. [Erratum, MMWR. 2006; 55:800.]
18. FluZone (influenza vaccine) package insert. Swiftwater, PA: Sanofi Pasteur; 2006.
19. Schrand LM, Troester TS, Ballas ZKet al. Preparing for drug shortages: one teaching hospital's approach to the IVIG shortage. *Formulary.* 2001; 36:52,56–9.
20. Pick AM, Massoomi F, Neff WJet al. A safety assessment tool for formulary candidates. *Am J Health-Syst Pharm.* 2006; 63:1269–72.
21. Myers CE. Artificial shortages of drug supplies. *Am J Health-Syst Pharm.* 1999; 56:727. Editorial.

Developed through the ASHP Council on Pharmacy Management and approved by the ASHP Board of Directors on January 15, 2009. These guidelines supersede the ASHP Guidelines on Managing Drug Product Shortages dated March 28, 2001.

ASHP gratefully acknowledges the expert panel that developed these guidelines: Erin R. Fox, Pharm.D.; Annette Birt, M.B.A., M.P.H.; Ken B. James, Pharm.D.; Heather Kokko, Pharm.D.; Sandra Salverson, Pharm.D., BCPS; and Donna L. Soflin, B.S.Pharm.

Erin R. Fox, Pharm.D., is Director, Drug Information Service, University of Utah Hospitals & Clinics, Salt Lake City. Annette Birt, M.B.A., M.P.H., is Pharmacy Communications Manager at Novation, Irving, TX. Ken B. James, Pharm.D., is Supervisor, Drug Information Services, Kaiser-Permanente Medical Center, Santa Clara, CA. Heather Kokko, Pharm.D., is Manager, Pharmacy Support Services, Department of Pharmacy Services, and Clinical Assistant Professor, Medical University of South Carolina. Sandra Salverson, Pharm.D., BCPS, is Drug Information/Infectious Disease Pharmacist, OSF Saint Francis Medical Center, Peoria, IL. Donna L. Soflin is Pharmacy Director, Tri-County Area Hospital, Lexington, NE.

The bibliographic citation for this document is as follows: American Society of Health-System Pharmacists. ASHP guidelines on managing drug product shortages in hospitals and health systems. *Am J Health-Syst Pharm.* 2009; 66:1399–406.

ASHP Guidelines for Selecting Pharmaceutical Manufacturers and Suppliers

Pharmacists are responsible for selecting, from hundreds of manufacturers and suppliers of drugs, those that will enable them to fulfill an important obligation: ensuring that patients receive pharmaceuticals and related supplies of the highest quality and at the lowest cost. These guidelines are offered as an aid to the pharmacist in achieving this goal.

Obligations of the Supplier

Pharmacists may purchase with confidence the products of those suppliers meeting the criteria presented here. Other factors such as credit policies, delivery times, and the breadth of a supplier's product line also must be considered when selecting a supplier.

Technical Considerations

1. On request of the pharmacist, the supplier should furnish
   a. Analytical control data.
   b. Sterility testing data.
   c. Bioavailability data.
   d. Bioequivalency data.
   e. Descriptions of testing procedures for raw materials and finished products.
   f. Any other information that may be indicative of the quality of a given finished drug product.

   Testing data developed by independent laboratories should be identified by the supplier. All information should be supplied at no charge.
2. There should be no history of recurring product recalls indicative of deficient quality control procedures.
3. The supplier should permit visits (during normal business hours) by the pharmacist to inspect its manufacturing and control procedures.
4. All drug products should conform to the requirements of *The United States Pharmacopeia—The National Formulary (USP—NF)* (the most recent edition) unless otherwise specified by the pharmacist. Items not recognized by *USP—NF* should meet the specifications set forth by the pharmacist.
5. To the extent possible, all products should be available in single unit or unit dose packages. These packages should conform to the "ASHP Technical Assistance Bulletin on Single Unit and Unit Dose Packages of Drugs."[1]
6. The name and address of the manufacturer of the final dosage form and the packager or distributor should be present on the product labeling.
7. Expiration dates should be clearly indicated on the package label and, unless stability properties warrant otherwise, should occur in January or July.
8. Therapeutic, biopharmaceutic, and toxicologic information should be available to the pharmacist on request. Toxicity information should be available around the clock.
9. Patient/staff educational materials that are important for proper use of the product should be routinely available.
10. On request, the supplier should furnish proof of any claims made with respect to the efficacy, safety, and superiority of its products.
11. On request, the supplier should furnish, at no charge, a reasonable quantity of its products to enable the pharmacist to evaluate the products' physical traits, including pharmaceutical elegance (appearance and absence of physical deterioration or flaws), packaging, and labeling.

Distribution Policies

1. Whenever possible, delivery of a drug product should be confined to a single lot number.
2. Unless otherwise specified or required by stability considerations, not less than a 12-month interval between a product's time of delivery and its expiration date should be present.
3. The supplier should accept for full credit (based on purchase price), without prior authorization, any unopened packages of goods returned within 12 months of the expiration date. Credits should be in cash or applied to the institution's account.
4. The supplier should ship all goods in a timely manner, freight prepaid, and enclose a packing list with each shipment. All items "out of stock" should be noted, and the anticipated availability of the item should be clearly indicated. There should be no extensive recurrence of back orders.
5. The supplier should warrant title to commodities supplied, warrant them to be free from defects and imperfections and fit for any rational use of the product, and indemnify and hold the purchaser harmless against any and all suits, claims, and expenses, includ-ing attorneys' fees, damages, and injuries or any claims by third parties relating to the products.

Marketing and Sales Policies

1. The supplier should not, without written consent, use the pharmacist's or his or her organization's name in any advertising or other promotional materials or activities.
2. The supplier should honor formulary decisions made by the organization's pharmacy and therapeutics committee, and the supplier's sales representatives should comply with the organization's regulations governing their activities.
3. The supplier should not offer cash, equipment, or merchandise to the organization or its staff as an inducement to purchase its products.
4. Discounts should be in cash or cash credit, not merchandise, and should be clearly indicated on invoices and bills rather than consisting of end-of-year rebates or similar discount practices.
5. In entering into a contract to supply goods, the supplier should guarantee to furnish, at the price specified, any minimum amount of products so stated. If the supplier

is unable to meet the supply commitment, the supplier should reimburse the organization for any excess costs incurred in obtaining the product from other sources. If, during the life of the contract, a price reduction occurs, the lower price should prevail.

6. All parties to the bidding process should respect the integrity of the process and the contracts awarded thereby.

Responsibilities of the Purchaser

It may be desirable to purchase drugs or other commodities on a competitive bid basis. The pharmacist should ensure that competitive bidding procedures conform to the guidelines below:

1. Invitations to bid should be mailed to the suppliers' home offices with copies to their local representatives (if any), unless suppliers specify otherwise.
2. Potential bidders should be given no less than 3 weeks to submit a bid.
3. The opening date for bids should be specified and honored by the purchaser.
4. The language of the invitation to bid should be clear and should indicate the person (and organization address and telephone number) the bidder should contact in the event of questions or problems. Specifications should be complete with respect to products, packagings, and quantities desired.
5. If bidding forms are used, they should contain adequate space for the bidder to enter the information requested.
6. The winning bidder should be notified in writing. Unsuccessful bidders may be informed of who won the award at what price, if they so request.
7. The quantities specified in the invitation to bid should be a reasonable estimate of requirements.
8. If the invitation to bid is offered on behalf of a group of purchasers, the individual members of the group should not engage in bidding procedures of their own and should purchase the goods in question from the winning bidder.

Reference

1. American Society of Hospital Pharmacists. ASHP technical assistance bulletin on single unit and unit dose packages of drugs. *Am J Hosp Pharm.* 1985; 42:378–9.

Approved by the ASHP Board of Directors, November 14, 1990. Revised by the ASHP Council on Professional Affairs. Supersedes previous versions approved November 17–*18, 1983,* and September 22, 1989.

The bibliographic citation for this document is as follows: American Society of Hospital Pharmacists. ASHP guidelines for selecting pharmaceutical manufacturers and suppliers. *Am J Hosp Pharm.* 1991; 48:523–4.

Preparation and Handling

Pharmaceutical Waste (0903)

Source: Council on Pharmacy Practice

To collaborate with regulatory bodies and appropriate organizations to develop standards for the disposal of pharmaceutical hazardous waste as defined in the Resource Conservation and Recovery Act (RCRA), for the purpose of simplifying the disposal of these substances by health systems; further,

To encourage pharmaceutical manufacturers and the Environmental Protection Agency (EPA) to provide guidance and assistance to hospitals and health systems in proper pharmaceutical waste disposal and destruction efforts; further,

To advocate that EPA update the list of hazardous substances under RCRA and establish a process for maintaining a current list; further,

To urge federal, state, and local governments to harmonize regulations regarding disposal of hazardous pharmaceutical waste; further,

To advocate that the Food and Drug Administration standardize labeling of drug products with information relating to appropriate disposal; further,

To promote awareness within hospitals and health systems of pharmaceutical waste regulations; further,

To encourage research on the environmental and public health impacts of drug products and metabolites excreted in human waste; further,

To encourage pharmaceutical manufacturers to streamline packaging of drug products to reduce waste materials.

This policy was reviewed in 2013 by the Council on Pharmacy Practice and by the Board of Directors and was found to still be appropriate.

Safe Disposal of Patients' Home Medications (0614)

Source: Council on Professional Affairs

To minimize the patient safety consequences and public health impact of inappropriate disposal of patients' home medications by working collaboratively with other interested organizations to (1) develop models for patient-oriented medication disposal programs that will minimize accidental poisoning, drug diversion, and potential environmental impact, (2) advocate that the pharmaceutical industry and regulatory bodies support the development and implementation of such models, and (3) educate health professionals, regulatory bodies, and the public regarding safe disposal of unused home medications.

This policy was reviewed in 2010 by the Council on Pharmacy Practice and by the Board of Directors and was found to still be appropriate.

Safe and Effective Extemporaneous Compounding (0616)

Source: Council on Professional Affairs

To affirm that extemporaneous compounding of medications, when done to meet immediate or anticipatory patient needs, is part of the practice of pharmacy and is not manufacturing; further,

To support the principle that medications should not be extemporaneously compounded when they are commercially and readily available in the form necessary to meet patient needs; further,

To encourage pharmacists who compound medications to use only drug substances that have been manufactured in Food and Drug Administration-approved facilities and that meet official United States Pharmacopeia (USP) compendial requirements where those exist; further,

To support the principle that pharmacists be adequately trained and have sufficient facilities and equipment that meet technical and professional standards to ensure the quality of compounded medications; further,

To encourage USP to develop drug monographs for commonly compounded preparations; further,

To educate prescribers and other health care professionals about the potential risks associated with the use of extemporaneously compounded preparations.

This policy was reviewed in 2010 by the Council on Pharmacy Practice and by the Board of Directors and was found to still be appropriate..

Accreditation of Compounding Facilities (0617)

Source: Council on Professional Affairs

To encourage facilities where extemporaneous compounding of medications occurs to seek accreditation by a nationally credible accreditation body.

This policy was reviewed in 2010 by the Council on Pharmacy Practice and by the Board of Directors and was found to still be appropriate.

ASHP Guidelines on Compounding Sterile Preparations

Purpose

The compounding of medications is a fundamental part of pharmacy practice. All compounding personnel, mainly pharmacists and pharmacy technicians, are responsible for compounding and dispensing sterile products and preparations of correct ingredient identity, purity (freedom from physical contaminants, such as precipitates,[1] and chemical contaminants), strength (including stability[2] and compatibility), and sterility and for dispensing them in appropriate containers that are labeled accurately and appropriately for the end user. In contemporary health care organizations, patients receive compounded sterile preparations (CSPs) that are stored for extended periods before use. It has long been recognized that extended storage of CSPs may allow for the growth of a pathological bioburden of microorganisms[3] and that patient morbidity and mortality can result from contaminated or incorrectly compounded sterile preparations.[4–9] When quality monitoring is inadequate, personnel responsible for sterile compounding may not know that inaccurate or contaminated products are dispensed.[10–13]

These guidelines are intended to help compounding personnel prepare CSPs of high quality and reduce the potential for harm to patients and consequences for compounding personnel. The recommendations in these guidelines are based on published data, when available; on expert opinion and procedures used in similar industries; and on applicable regulations and standards. These guidelines are a revision of the 2000 *ASHP Guidelines on Quality Assurance of Pharmacy-Prepared Sterile Products*,[14] with the goals of providing more current recommendations and harmonizing the ASHP guidelines with *United States Pharmacopeia* (*USP*) chapter 797, Pharmaceutical Compounding—Sterile Preparations.[15] To help achieve that harmonization, these guidelines employ the definitions and terminology of *USP* chapter 797 rather than those of the previous guidelines.

Many health care settings also use CSPs prepared by compounding pharmacies. Although these guidelines may be useful in assessing the quality of CSPs prepared by compounding pharmacies, more information on the topic of outsourcing sterile compounding services is available in the *ASHP Guidelines on Outsourcing Sterile Compounding Services*.[16]

Finally, while these guidelines are generally applicable to all personnel who prepare CSPs and all facilities in which CSPs are prepared, pharmacists and other health care professionals responsible for the preparation, selection, and use of CSPs are urged to use professional judgment in interpreting and applying these guidelines to their specific circumstances. Users of these guidelines are cautioned that the information provided is current as of publication and are urged to consult current editions of original sources (e.g., laws, regulations, and applicable standards, including USP compendial standards) to ensure patient safety as well as legal and regulatory compliance.

Legal and Regulatory Considerations

Significant legal and regulatory changes have taken place since publication of the previous ASHP guidelines (Figure 1).

At the time of its publication, section 503A of the U.S. Food and Drug Administration Modernization Act (FDAMA) served to define the limits of legitimate compounding.[18] When section 503A of FDAMA was ruled unconstitutional in 2001, the delineation between compounding and manufacturing reverted to earlier regulations based on the Federal Food, Drug, and Cosmetics Act.[19] Under those regulations, compounding is considered part of the practice of pharmacy and in most states, is governed by state law and regulation. Manufacturing is regulated by the federal government through the auspices of the Food and Drug Administration (FDA). In most cases, extemporaneously compounded preparations must be prepared pursuant to a prescriber's prescription for a specific patient. Some states have specific regulations dealing with CSPs for office use. Some pharmacies whose primary purpose is preparing CSPs for hospitals and other facilities may be registered with the FDA as manufacturers and must adhere to federal good manufacturing practices. Some state boards of pharmacy permit one pharmacy to compound for another pharmacy under central fill regulations. Most pharmacies compound only pursuant to a prescriber's prescription and follow state regulations regarding compounding.

On January 1, 2004, *USP* chapter 797, Pharmaceutical Compounding—Sterile Preparations,[15] became official, replacing *USP* chapter 1206, Sterile Drug Products for Home Use.[20] The change from a chapter numbered above 1000 to a chapter below 1000 marked a change from an advisory standard to an enforceable one. *USP* chapter 797 has since been revised.[15] Some state regulations require full compliance with *USP* chapter 797, some have indirect references to the chapter, some do not mention the chapter, and some have additional regulations.[21] The National Association of Boards of Pharmacy supports the incorporation of compounding regulations into state pharmacy practice legislation by including such wording in the association's Model Rules and Model State Pharmacy Act.[22] State boards of pharmacy should be consulted to determine the current status of sterile compounding regulations, as there are significant differences in regulation among states.

Accreditation Considerations

The Centers for Medicare and Medicaid Services (CMS) Hospital Conditions of Participation and Interpretive Guidelines, the Joint Commission, the American Osteopathic Association's Healthcare Facilities Accreditation Program, and DNV Healthcare's National Integrated Accreditation for Healthcare Organizations all include statements concerning safe practices for storage and preparation of sterile compounds.[23–26] Clinics, long-term care facilities, home care organizations, rehabilitation facilities, and physician offices (all of which come under the purview of *USP* chapter 797[15])

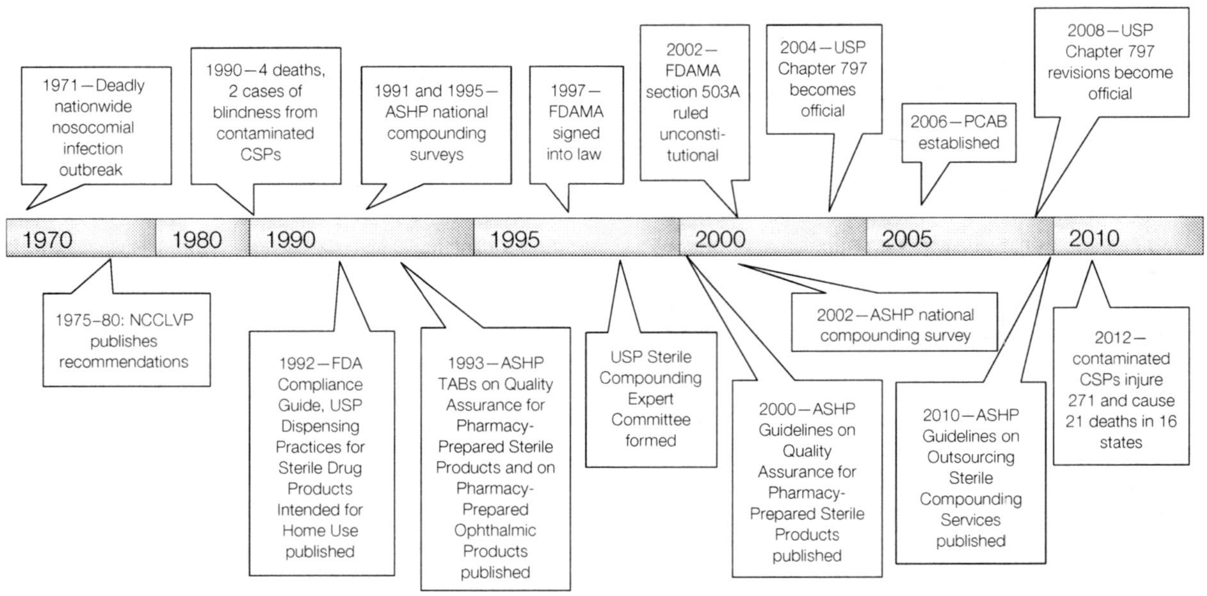

Figure 1. Evolution of Sterile Compounding Standards, 1970—2010. Adapted from *The ASHP Discussion Guide on USP Chapter <797> for Compounding Sterile Preparations.*[17] NCCLVP, National Coordinating Committee on Large Volume Parenterals; CSPs, compounded sterile preparations; USP, United State Pharmacopeia; TAB, technical assistance bulleting; FDAMA, Food and Drug Administration Modernization Act; PCAB, Pharmacy Compounding Accreditation Board.

may all be subject to specific additional governance of sterile compounding practices, depending on the agencies regulating or accrediting the facility. In addition, organizations preparing hazardous drugs[27,28] should comply with National Institute for Occupational Safety and Health (NIOSH) recommendations to ensure that compounding personnel are operating in a safe environment.[29,30]

Other Compounding-Related Guidelines

ASHP provides several guidelines for safe compounding practices[28,31,32] and a discussion guide on *USP* chapter 797[17] and has recognized *USP* chapter 797 as a relevant practice standard in the *ASHP Guidelines: Minimum Standard for Pharmacies in Hospitals.*[33] Other professional organizations also provide guidance on specific aspects of compounding. Standards for prescribing, preparation, administration, and monitoring of parenteral nutrition are available through the American Society for Parenteral and Enteral Nutrition.[34,35] The Institute for Safe Medication Practices provides recommendations for preventing medication errors, including those involving CSPs.[36,37] The Infusion Nurses Society offers standards, professional development, and resources for all aspects of infusion care.[38] The Controlled Environment Testing Association (CETA) provides numerous CETA Application Guides (CAGs) for the proper use, cleaning, and certification of primary engineering controls (PECs) and buffer areas (generally referred to as "cleanrooms").[39–45] *Guidelines for Hand Hygiene in Healthcare Settings,*[46] *Guidelines for Prevention of Intravascular Catheter-Related Infections,*[47] *Guidelines for Environmental Infection Control in Healthcare Facilities,*[48] and *Protect Patients Against Preventable Harm from Improper Use of Single-dose/Single-use Vials,*[49] all from the Centers for Disease Control and Prevention (CDC), serve as the backbone for most infection prevention practices in the United States. Safe infusion, injection, and medication vial practices have been addressed by CMS[50] and the Association for Professionals in Infection Control and Epidemiology,[51] and the Association of periOperative Registered Nurses has recommended practices for medication safety in perioperative settings.[52]

Physical Facilities and Equipment

Design and Functionality Requirements

Facility requirements are intended to establish a safe environment for compounding CSPs. The International Organization for Standardization (ISO) air cleanliness classification of the compounding environment is a critical measure that is affected by facility design.

Primary Engineering Controls (PECs). A PEC is a device or room that provides an ISO Class 5 environment for compounding CSPs. PECs all rely on a special type of high-efficiency particle air (HEPA) filter that is ≥99.99% efficient in removing particles as small as 0.3 microns in size (the most penetrating particle size [MPPS], which refers to the largest-sized particle that may escape the filter, although particles of all sizes may be captured). The unidirectional (horizontal or vertical) HEPA-filtered air must provide sufficient velocity to sweep particles away from the direct compounding area and maintain unidirectional flow during preparation of CSPs. (More information about HEPA filtration and first-air concepts can be found in the ASHP publications *Compounding Sterile Preparations,*[53] *Basics of Aseptic Compounding Technique,*[54] *Getting Started in Aseptic Compounding,*[55] and *Compounding Sterile Preparations: ASHP Video Guide to USP <797>.*[56])

PEC devices include laminar airflow workbenches (LAFWs), biological safety cabinets (BSCs), compounding aseptic isolators (CAIs), and compounding aseptic containment isolators (CACIs) (Table 1). Properly designed, unidirectional airflow CAIs function in a similar manner as LAFWs, but the direct compounding area does not interact with room air because it is within a closed system, with the air sweeping particles away from the compounding site. Smoke tests of PECs assist a facility in verifying unidirectional airflow and lack of turbulence and reverse flows.

CAIs or CACIs located outside of an ISO Class 7 environment must be coupled with documentation from the manufacturer that the device will meet or exceed *USP* chapter 797 standards under these conditions and be dynamically tested on site to USP 797 and CETA requirements. If the CACI used for hazardous drug preparation is located outside the buffer area (see **Architecture**, below), it must be located in a segregated and dedicated area that maintains at least 0.01-inch water column negative pressure and maintains, at a minimum, 12 air changes per hour (ACPH).

Architecture. The sterile compounding area includes a well-lit buffer area and ante area (both are secondary engineering controls) and an area for storage of sterile products and supplies. A buffer area (or "cleanroom") is defined as an area where a PEC is located and where activities such as preparation, compounding, and staging of CSPs occur. This area should provide adequate space for the PEC and may include a limited amount of shelving and/or carts for staging of compounding (not for storing stock). An ante area provides space for hand washing, garbing, and product decontamination; it also serves as a way to further segregate the buffer area from other, less-clean areas of the facility. Water sources, such as sinks or floor drains, are not permitted in the buffer area and should not be immediately adjacent to segregated compounding areas outside of a buffer area. A storage area outside the buffer and ante areas should provide adequate space for placement of sterile products and supplies.

The sterile compounding area (ante and buffer areas) may be constructed of either hard- or soft-walled enclosures, with the zones being delineated by open or closed architecture. Closed architecture is formed by walls and doors between the buffer and ante areas and is required for high-risk compounding (Table 2).

Open architecture has openings between the buffer and ante areas and relies on a defined airflow velocity to divide the two areas, which are marked by a line of demarcation; this type of facility may only be utilized for low- and medium-risk compounding. Demarcation lines should be indicated by colored tiles or other elements integrated into the flooring pattern but may be as simple as marking on the floor.

Table 1.
Primary Engineering Controls (PECs)

PEC Device	Used to Prepare Non-Hazardous CSPs	Used to Prepare Hazardous CSPs
Conventional	Laminar airflow workbench (LAFW)	Class II Biological safety cabinet (BSC)
Isolators	Compounding aseptic isolator (CAI)	Compounding aseptic containment isolator (CACI)

Facilities for preparation of radiopharmaceuticals have some different requirements. Refer to *USP* chapter 797[15] and other relevant standards for specifics.

Facilities without *USP* chapter 797-compliant ante areas and buffer areas may prepare low-risk, non-hazardous CSPs in a PEC within a segregated compounding area. A segregated compounding area is an unclassified space (i.e., an area with no specific ISO classification) and does not include ante or buffer areas. It is required to be separated from activities that are not essential to the preparation of CSPs; not be located adjacent to food preparation sites, warehouses, or construction sites; and not have unsealed windows or doors that connect to the outdoors or high-traffic areas.[15] This architecture type is most often seen in satellite pharmacies, small hospitals, procedural areas, or clinics. The beyond-use dating for sterile preparations compounded in a segregated compounding area cannot exceed 12 hours (see **Expiration and Beyond-Use Dating**).

Buffer Areas

Air Supply. A buffer area differs from an ordinary ventilated room by having the following:

- Increased air supply.
- HEPA filtration (the filtered air should be introduced at the ceiling, with returns mounted low on the walls; ceiling-mounted returns should not be used) including a terminal air filter (a filter at the end of the heating, ventilation, and air conditioning [HVAC] ducting).
- Room pressurization.
- A perforated plate or swirl supply air diffuser (if an air diffuser is necessary); high-induction supply air diffusers should not be used in buffer areas.

Structural components must be coupled with HEPA filtration and air exchanges in order to provide a complete buffer area environment and proper ISO classifications. Buffer areas must meet or exceed ISO Class 7 air cleanliness standards. Ante areas must at least meet ISO Class 8 standards; ante areas opening into a negative pressure preparation area must meet ISO Class 7 standards. The number of ACPH is based upon air/room pressure, velocity or air handler capacity, HEPA flow restriction, duct size, the amount of processing completed on a daily basis, and temperature. ACPH must occur at a minimum of 30 times per hour in buffer and ante areas, but may need to be increased in high-traffic/high-volume areas in order to maintain the room's specified ISO classification (Table 2) under dynamic conditions. Facilities may incorporate the contribution of up to 15 air changes per hour from a LAFW in the total air changes per hours in a nonhazardous buffer area. By design, these devices filter room air as it passes through the HEPA filter.

Airflow within the room should be as steady as possible, having as few interruptions as possible. Within the PEC, it must be unidirectional,[39] with as few interruptions in steady airflow as possible. PEC placement within the room should be well designed, with PECs placed where they are least affected by opened doors, HVAC systems, or personnel traffic. For non-hazardous preparations, positive pressure is required between rooms physically divided by walls or doors (closed architecture style) and should be maintained at a minimum of positive 0.02 inch water column. If a room does not have physical barriers (i.e., has an open architecture

Table 2.
Facilities Features Required for Specific Types of Compounding (Data from *USP* Chapter 797[15] Except as Noted)

	Low-Risk with ≤12-hour BUD (Non-Hazardous)	Low-Risk (Non-Hazardous)	Medium-Risk (Non-Hazardous)	High-Risk (Non-Hazardous)	Hazardous Drugs
Architectural Style[a]	Segregated	Open or closed	Open or closed	Closed	Closed
Buffer zone ISO classification	N/A	ISO Class 7 or better	ISO Class 7 or better	ISO Class 7 or better	ISO Class 7 or better
Ante area ISO classification	N/A	ISO Class 8 (ISO Class 7 if opens into negative pressure area) or better	ISO Class 8 (ISO Class 7 if opens into negative pressure area) or better	ISO Class 8 (ISO Class 7 if opens into a negative pressure area) or better	ISO Class 7 or better
Minimum air exchanges for buffer area[b]	N/A	30	30	30	30
Minimum air exchanges for ante area[c]	N/A	20 if ISO 8; 30 if ISO 7	20 if ISO 8; 30 if ISO 7	20 if ISO 8; 30 if ISO 7	30
Pressure	N/A	Positive	Positive	Positive	Negative

[a]Architectural style ("open" and "closed") is not defined in *USP* chapter 797, but the concept of physical separation of ante areas and buffer rooms is described in the chapter. For the purposes of these guidelines, "closed architecture" indicates that the buffer and ante areas are separated by a door (i.e., are physically separate rooms) and maintain a pressure differential of no less than 0.02-inch water column positive pressure. "Open architecture" indicates that the buffer and ante areas are in one room, not separated by a door (i.e., not physically separated). Displacement airflow is used to separate open architecture spaces, with at least 40 feet per minute of airflow across the entire plane of the opening. A segregated compounding area contains a PEC within a restricted space.

[b]If an ISO Class 5 recirculating device is in place, a minimum of 15 air changes per hour (ACPH) is sufficient if the ACPH is 30 between the device and the area supply HEPA filters.

[c]*USP* chapter 797 does not address the air changes in ISO Class 8 ante areas. The FDA Aseptic Processing Guide[57] recommends a minimum of 20 ACPH to maintain ISO 8. However, this is a minimum value intended for industry. Since ante areas for CSPs include ungowned personnel and other activities, a minimum of 30 ACPH is best practice for ISO Class 8 ante areas and required for ISO 7 ante areas.

style) and relies on a line of demarcation, the displacement airflow concept requiring air velocity of 40 feet per minute (0.2 meter per second) from the buffer area across the entire plane of line of demarcation into the ante area is required. Open architecture is not permitted in areas used for high-risk preparations.

When designing buffer areas, facilities must consider workflow patterns, such as how personnel performing double-checks will affect air quality. If supervisory personnel are not located in the buffer area, movement in and out of the buffer area is likely to increase airflow interruption. Communication devices should be used to minimize traffic between areas, and cameras may be installed to supplement supervision of staff or check compounding accuracy, if permitted by state regulations.

Surfaces. Surfaces of any kind in the buffer area and ante area must be smooth, impervious, and easy to clean, with no cracks or crevices that could trap dust or contaminants. All materials used in the facilities must be non-shedding. Walls and ceilings must be made of either hard plastic or epoxy-painted gypsum board. If ceiling tiles are used, they must be coated with hard polymer and caulked both around the perimeter and around each tile. Ceiling lights must be smooth, mounted flush, and sealed. Floors should be made of wide, heavy-duty sheet vinyl, rubber, or epoxy that is coved around the corners and rolled up onto the walls. Paint must be an epoxy, acrylic, or other non-porous sealant type.

Work surfaces should preferably be stainless steel, but at a minimum are required to be non-porous and easily sanitized. Carts and shelves, ideally made of stainless steel wire, nonporous plastic, or rustproof metal, should be easy to move and clean, if necessary. Office equipment (e.g., computers and components [including washable keyboard and mouse], telephones, printers) placed in the buffer area must be easily cleanable and placed in such a manner that they have no material impact on the ISO air cleanliness classification of the area.

Renovations

To meet requirements for sterile compounding, many facilities choose to renovate existing space rather than construct new facilities. Whether designing a new area or retrofitting one, the specific types (e.g., hazardous or nonhazardous) and risk levels of CSPs that will be prepared in the area should guide the facility design and construction. A plan for how operations will continue without interruption should be devised prior to construction.

Power and Other Utility Interruptions

The facility's emergency management plan should include steps to meet patient-care needs during time of utility interruptions, including the need for CSPs. In some cases, immediate-use procedures may be safely implemented to meet some needs. Methods to identify and safely meet interim compounding needs or address patient-care needs with noncompounded alternatives should be developed, put into standard operating procedures (SOPs), inserviced to staff, and tested as part of the organization's emergency planning process.

Pharmacy Compounding Devices

Pharmacy compounding devices are utilized to increase efficiency while decreasing the potential for human error. Devices that do not create their own ISO Class 5 environment must be located within an ISO Class 5 PEC and adhere to applicable standards for accuracy and precision. All compounding devices must be monitored and validated for accuracy consistent with device manufacturer specifications.

Automated Compounding Devices (ACDs) are utilized to accurately combine multiple drugs and solutions into a single delivery container. These devices are most commonly used for parenteral nutrition preparation, but may be used for cardioplegia solutions, continuous renal replacement therapy, or other complex processes. *ASHP Guidelines on the Safe Use of Automated Compounding Devices for the Preparation of Parenteral Nutrition Admixtures*[32] should be consulted for further details on utilizing ACDs. Accuracy and precision testing for ACDs is required by *USP* chapter 797[15] and incorporate gravimetric, volumetric, and chemical analyses. These analyses, as determined by facility protocol, must be monitored and recorded on a daily basis, with evaluation for outliers occurring at least weekly.

Repeater pumps are devices used to pump a preset volume of fluid in a consistent and reproducible manner. They must be calibrated according to manufacturer specifications, which may depend on the volume and frequency of use.

Robotic systems automate the compounding and labeling of parenteral doses in syringes and bags using an enclosed chamber that must create an ISO Class 5 air cleanliness environment or better.

The proper use of ACDs, repeater pumps, robotic systems, and other compounding equipment used in the preparation of CSPs remains the responsibility of the pharmacist.

Cleaning and Disinfecting

Cleaning with a germicidal detergent and water will remove visible solids or soiling before disinfecting. Disinfecting removes microbial contamination. It is critical that an appropriate germicidal detergent and water be used to clean all surfaces of the buffer and ante areas in addition to all of the PECs. Great care must be exercised to avoid getting the HEPA filters wet during cleaning. Cleaning with a germicidal detergent will leave a residue that needs to be removed from work surfaces (e.g., counter and PEC surfaces). This residue is best removed by using sterile 70% isopropyl alcohol (IPA).

Appendix II of *USP* chapter 797[15] provides information on types of products that can be used for cleaning and disinfecting the ante and buffer areas, including floors, walls, and ceilings. Choice of cleaning and disinfection products should be approved by the organization's appropriate authority (e.g., the Infection Control Committee).

Policies and procedures must be developed to ensure consistent practices, including dilution of cleaning products. Table 3 describes the minimum frequency for cleaning surfaces used to compound low- and medium-risk CSPs in the sterile compounding area.

Table 3.

Minimum Frequency for Cleaning of Specific Sites (Reprinted with Permission from *USP* Chapter 797[15])

Site	Minimum Frequency
ISO Class 5 PEC	Beginning of each shift Before each batch Every 30 minutes when compounding After spills When surface contamination is known or suspected
Counters and easily cleanable work surfaces	Daily
Floors	Daily
Walls	Monthly
Ceilings	Monthly
Storage shelving	Monthly

Environmental Monitoring

Environmental monitoring and related documentation must be completed on a routine basis to ensure adequate environmental and personnel controls are in place to prevent contamination of CSPs. Ensuring a safe compounding environment requires viable and nonviable airborne particle testing, pressure differential or displacement airflow measurement, temperature monitoring, and surface disinfection sampling and assessment. Nonviable particles are particles that do not contain a living organism, such as particles shed from paper or dust. Viable particles are living organisms, such as bacteria or fungal spores, that require nonviable particles to travel. Monitoring of humidity,[39,44] sound,[39] and lighting[39] may also be considered by facilities to enhance the environmental monitoring program.

Each element of the monitoring program must be included in a sampling plan with sample locations, methods of collection, sampling frequency, and other specifics depending on the type of monitoring being performed. The environmental monitoring sampling frequency must occur at a minimum as listed below, with possible additional times based on the type of testing:

- At the commissioning and certification of new facilities and equipment.
- Every six months during routine re-certification of equipment and facilities.
- After any facility or equipment maintenance, including construction or remodeling of adjacent departments or work on shared air handlers.
- At any point when problems are identified with products, preparations, or employee technique or if a CSP is suspected to be the source of a patient infection.

Records of data collected through the monitoring program must be maintained as part of the overall quality assurance program of the facility. The data should be reviewed by management personnel or their designees and by the facility's Infection Control Committee to ensure that the findings of the reports are addressed. Table 4 provides an overview of environmental monitoring requirements.

Table 4.
Environmental Monitoring Requirements (Adapted from *USP* Chapter 797[15])

Parameter	Monitored By	Frequency
Temperature	Compounding personnel or facilities management staff (if electronic monitoring is centralized)	Documented daily (at a minimum)
Pressure differential or velocity across line of demarcation	Compounding personnel	Documented each shift (preferably), daily (at a minimum)
	Qualified certifier	At least every 6 months
Nonviable particles	Qualified certifier	At least every 6 months
Surface sampling	Compounding or laboratory personnel	Periodically, as defined by compounding and infection control personnel, at least every 6 months or after significant changes in procedures or cleaning practices
Electronic device sample of viable particles	Compounding personnel or qualified certifier	At least every 6 months

Table 5.
Controlled Temperatures (Data from *USP* General Notices and Requirements[58])

Storage Condition	Centigrade	Fahrenheit
Room temperature	20 to 25 °C	68 to 77 °F
Cold temperature (refrigerated)	2 to 8 °C	36 to 46 °F
Freezer (frozen)	−25 to −10 °C	−13 to 14 °F

Temperature Monitoring. Any controlled temperature area used for compounding sterile preparations or for storage of sterile products or CSPs must be monitored at least once daily and results documented in a log. The facilities should maintain a comfortable room temperature (20 °C [68 °F] or cooler) for properly garbed compounding personnel. If facilities use continuous temperature recording devices, they must be monitored and documented once daily to ensure they are functioning properly. Controlled temperature ranges are listed in Table 5.

Pressure Differential or Air Displacement. Since positive- and/or negative-pressure rooms are required for sterile compounding, the appropriate differential pressure or air displacement velocities must be maintained. If closed architecture is used, a pressure differential between general, ante, and buffer areas must be monitored. A facility with open architecture design must monitor the differential airflow across the opening between ante and buffer areas.

A pressure gauge or velocity meter must be in place to monitor airflow between relevant areas. Pressure between ISO Class 7 positive-pressure areas and the general area must be at least 5 Pa (0.02-inch water column). Negative pressure areas should have no less than 2.5 Pa (0.01-inch water column) negative pressure to adjacent positive pressure. A monitored pressure indicator must be installed to ensure proper pressurization. If differential airflow is used as a measure, the velocity must be at least 0.2 meter per second (40 feet per minute).

Results of pressure differential and/or velocity of air displacement must be reviewed and documented each shift (at least daily) or by a continuous device with alarms.

Nonviable Airborne Particle Testing Program. Determination of the ISO classification of an area or device is dependent on nonviable particle testing ("certification"), which must be completed by qualified personnel complying with the Certification Guide for Sterile Compounding Facilities (CAG-003-2006).[39] PECs such as LAFWs, BSCs, CAIs, and CACIs must be certified every 6 months and whenever the device is relocated or serviced. Both primary (LAFWs, BSCs, CAIs, and CACIs) and secondary engineering controls (buffer areas and ante areas) must be checked for total particle counts every 6 months according to the manufacturer's specifications or CETA recommendation and when a device or room is relocated or altered. Thresholds for each ISO class are presented in Table 6.

Viable Airborne Particle Testing Program. Classified space (PECs and buffer and ante areas) must undergo routine viable particle testing. The testing plan should include the required sample locations, method of collection, frequency, the volume of air to be tested, and the time of day testing will occur. Testing must occur every 6 months in all compounding areas (PECs, buffer areas, ante areas, and areas adjacent to segregated compounding areas) as part of the overall compounding recertification process. The method of testing must be impaction via an electronic air sampling device, as settling plates alone are not considered an acceptable method.

Sampling plans should be detailed and include all high-traffic locations within the compounding area and any sites prone to contamination. Turbulence caused by airflow disruption, such as within an ISO Class 5 LAFW or doorways, should be included in the testing plan, along with areas where garbing, cleaning, labeling, and staging occur. In segregated compounding areas, sampling should include locations within the ISO Class 5 PEC and other areas in close proximity to the PEC.

Viable particle testing must be performed using a general microbiological growth medium, such as sterile nutrient

Table 6.
Particle Limits for Sterile Compounding Areas (Adapted from *USP* Chapter 797[15])

	Primary Engineering Controls (LAFW, BSC, CAI, CACI)	Buffer Area and Ante-Area Opening into a Negative Pressure Room	Ante-Area Opening Only into a Positive Pressure Room
ISO Class	5	7	8
Limit on number of ≥ 0.5 micron particles/m^3 of air	3,520	352,000	3,520,000

Table 7.
Viable Environmental Monitoring Recommended Action Levels for Microbial Contamination (Adapted from *USP* Chapter 797[15])

ISO Classification	Recommended Action Levels for Microbial Contamination (CFUs/m^3)[a]
5	1[b]
7	10
8 or above	100

[a]CFUs/m^3, colony-forming units per cubic meter.
[b]Samples from ISO Class 5 environments should normally yield no microbiological contaminants.

agar. In facilities that compound high-risk preparations, testing must also be done with a medium that supports fungal growth, such as malt extract. The growth medium should be incubated (outside of the sterile preparation area) according to the manufacturer's recommendations.

Sample data must be reviewed as a means of evaluating control of the compounding environment. Results above recommended action levels (see Table 7) should prompt reevaluation of work practices, cleaning procedures, and HEPA filtration. Any microbial growth that results from viable environment sampling must be identified to the genus level by microbiology personnel. If any highly pathogenic organisms (e.g., gram-negative rods or yeasts) are identified, infection control specialists should immediately be consulted to assist in formulating a response to the situation.

Surface Disinfection Sampling and Assessment. Touch contamination originating from contaminated work surfaces must be minimized and prevented if possible. Surface sampling provides facilities with a snapshot of the effectiveness of their disinfection procedures (including technique and cleaning products) and must be part of the overall quality assurance plan. Using a sterile nutrient agar contact plate for flat surfaces or swabs for equipment and other non-flat surfaces, sampling must be performed in all ISO classified areas on a periodic basis, at a minimum, every 6 months or when significant procedural or cleaning changes are implemented. A specific plan detailing the location of each sample must be devised so that the same locations are repeated with each testing session. Contact plates require pressing a plate directly to the surface being tested, while swabbing requires swabbing an area, submersing the swab in the correct amount of diluent, and then swabbing onto or into a sterile nutrient agar surface. Agar plates will leave a residue on contact surfaces that must be cleaned with sterile water and disinfected with sterile 70% IPA.

Results must be reported in colony-forming units (CFUs) per plate. Reevaluation of work practices and cleaning procedures should occur if the CFU count exceeds the suggested action levels (Table 8). Investigation into the source of contamination should be undertaken, the sources eliminated, and the area cleaned and re-sampled.

Environmental monitoring and quality assurance programs and documentation may be completed by a limited number of personnel in any given facility, but the actions of all compounding personnel may affect these two critical elements of compliance. All compounding personnel should be familiar with all facility policies and procedures specific to CSPs, even if the procedures are not typically their responsibility.

Expiration and Beyond-Use Dating

A manufacturer's expiration date is the date assigned pursuant to manufacturer testing. The drug product is guaranteed by the manufacturer to be safe and effective up to the listed date when products are stored as described in the product labeling.

A beyond-use date (BUD) is the date or time after which administration of a CSP shall not be initiated. As described in previous ASHP guidelines[14] and in *USP* chapter 797,[15] the BUD is determined from the date or time the preparation is compounded, its chemical stability, and the sterility limits described later in these guidelines. Both the stability of the components and the sterility limits described above must be taken into consideration when determining BUDs, and the BUD must be the shorter of the sterility dating or chemical stability dating. Information regarding stability dating procedures and defaults can be found in *USP* chapter 795, Pharmaceutical Compounding—Non-Sterile Preparations,[59] and other published literature sources.[60,61]

Processes such as thin-layer chromatography (TLC) and high-performance liquid chromatographic (HPLC) assays are the most reliable means of determining the stability of a product and should be used in place of theoretical predictions of stability when published literature is not available. The use of commercial reference laboratories that offer qualitative and quantitative testing may serve as a key resource for end-product testing.

Risk Level Classification

In these guidelines, as in previous ASHP guidelines[14] and *USP* chapter 797,[15] CSPs are stratified by potential risk of

Table 8.
Recommended Action Levels for Personnel Testing (Adapted from *USP* Chapter 797[15])

	PEC	Buffer Area	Ante Area
Viable airborne particle testing action levels for contamination (CFUs per cubic meter [1000 L] of air per plate)	>1	>10	>100
Surface sample contamination (CFUs per plate)	>3	>5	>100
Glove fingertip sampling	>3	N/A	N/A

[a]CFUs = colony-forming units.

microbial contamination into three primary categories: low-, medium-, and high-risk CSPs, with an additional category for CSPs intended for immediate use[15] and a sub-category for low-risk CSPs intended for use within 12 hours.[15] The potential risk is based on the danger of exposing multiple patients to microbial bioburden and based on microbial growth factors influenced by product storage time, temperature and product ability to support microbial growth, surface and time exposure of critical sites, and microbial bioburden in the environment. Compounding personnel must determine the appropriate risk level and the appropriate BUD for use based upon chemical stability and the potential for microbial, physical, or chemical contamination during compounding. In making a risk-level determination, compounding personnel must evaluate where the preparation is being made, the number of components or the number of aseptic breaches needed to compound the preparation, and the complexity of the compounding process. When circumstances make risk-level assignment unclear, guidelines for the more stringent risk level should prevail. For examples and a comparison of the risk levels, requirements, and BUDs to be used in risk-level determination, see Table 9.

Low-Risk CSPs

This category encompasses simple admixtures involving closed-system transfer, measuring, and mixing of three or fewer commercially manufactured sterile products (including the infusion solution). Low-risk compounding conditions must include all of the following:

- CSPs are compounded using aseptic technique within an ISO Class 5 PEC (e.g., LAFW, BSC, CAI, or CACI) that is located within an ISO Class 7 buffer area with an ISO Class 8 ante area.
- Each container, including the final container, may not be entered more than twice to prepare the CSP.
- Compounding is limited to aseptic manipulations of disinfected containers using sterile needles and syringes.

Low-Risk CSPs for Use Within 12 Hours. Under limited circumstances, sterile compounding may occur in a segregated compounding area (such as a satellite pharmacy or dedicated sterile compounding space) in which the ISO Class 5 PEC is not located within an ISO Class 7 buffer area. A segregated compounding area is a designated space, either a demarcated area or room, in which compounding is restricted to preparing low-risk, nonhazardous CSPs with a beyond-use time of no more than 12 hours from the time of preparation. All other requirements for low-risk CSPs must be followed, with the exception that the ISO Class 5 PEC is not required to be located within an ISO Class 7 buffer area. The PEC must be separate from other operations, including sinks and other water sources or drains, and away from unsealed windows or doors that connect to high traffic areas, construction, warehouses, or food preparation areas. Distinct labeling for conveying short BUDs should be considered.

Medium-Risk CSPs

This category encompasses preparations requiring more complex compounding processes, including:

- Multiple doses of sterile products combined or pooled to prepare a product that will be administered either to multiple patients (i.e., batching of syringes or large volumes), or one patient on multiple occasions (e.g., preparation for use over several days).[49]
- More than three commercially available sterile products are used to produce the compound.
- More complex compounding processes (e.g., total parenteral nutrition).

All requirements for low-risk compounding regarding location and aseptic technique must be followed.

High-Risk CSPs

High-risk CSPs are those

- Prepared from nonsterile ingredients, including manufactured products not intended for sterile routes of administration;
- Compounded using a nonsterile device prior to terminal sterilization;
- Containing nonsterile water that are stored for more than 6 hours before sterilization;
- Exposed to conditions worse than ISO Class 5 air quality for longer than 1 hour, if they contain or are compounded from sterile contents of commercially manufactured products or CSPs without antimicrobial preservatives;
- Containing bulk ingredients whose chemical purity and content strength are not verified by labeling and documentation from suppliers or by direct determination; or
- Prepared by compounding personnel who are improperly garbed or gloved.

Presterilization procedures for high-risk level CSPs, such as weighing and mixing, shall be completed in no worse than an ISO Class 8 environment.

CSPs in this category must be terminally sterilized before administration to patients. Terminal sterilization is defined by the FDA as the application of a lethal process

Table 9.
CSP Risk Levels and Beyond-Use Dates (BUDs) (Adapted from *USP* Chapter 797[15])[a]

Risk Category	Compounding Location	Garbing Required	Aseptic Technique Required	Examples	BUDs of CSP Stored at: Room Temperature	Refrigerated	Frozen (≤ 10 °C)
Low-risk	ISO Class 5 PEC, ISO Class 7 buffer area, ISO Class 8[b] ante area	Yes	Yes	Reconstitution of a single-dose vial, single preparation of a small volume parenteral, single large volume IV replacement fluids with no more than 3 components	48 hours	14 days	45 days
Low-risk with < 12-hour BUD	ISO Class 5 PEC segregated from other operations	Yes	Yes	Same as low-risk examples, non-hazardous preparations only	12 hours	12 hours	N/A
Medium-risk	ISO Class 5 PEC, ISO Class 7 buffer area, ISO Class 8[b] ante area	Yes	Yes	Batched syringes, total parenteral nutrition, ophthalmic preparations made from sterile products, pooled admixtures, batch-compounded preparations without bateriostatic additives, preparations made using automated compounders or other automated devices, elastomeric pumps	30 hours	9 days	45 days
High-risk	ISO Class 5 PEC, ISO Class 7 buffer area, ISO Class 7 ante area	Yes	Yes	CSPs prepared from bulk, nonsterile components or in final containers which are not sterile; preparations that must be terminally sterilized before administration	24 hours	3 days	45 days
Immediate-use	Medication preparation areas should be clean, uncluttered, and functionally separate[c]	No	Yes	Emergent use preparations such as epidurals prepared by anesthesia for immediate injection or infusion, diagnostics, any non-hazardous preparations that might cause harm due to delays in administration	1 hour	N/A	N/A

[a]ISO = International Organization for Standardization, PEC = primary engineering control, IV = intravenous.
[b]Ante area must be ISO 7 if it opens into a negative pressure buffer area.
[c]*Source*: The Joint Commission. MM.05.01.07, EP2.[24]

(e.g., steam under pressure or autoclaving) to sealed containers for the purpose of achieving a sterility assurance level of less than 10^{-6} or a probability of 1 nonsterile unit per 1 million sterilized units.[57] For CSPs that are heat-labile and cannot be processed as above, sterilization using an alternative method, such as a sterilizing grade 0.22 micron filter, must be done. Filtration only achieves a sterility assurance level of 10^{-3}, which is only 1 nonsterile unit per one thousand filtrated units. All filters used to sterilize CSPs must undergo filter integrity (bubble-point) testing.

Immediate-Use CSPs

The immediate-use category should be reserved for emergent use or situations in which adhering to low-risk compounding procedures would add additional risk due to delays in patient care. Examples of such situations may include cardiopulmonary resuscitation, diagnostic procedures, or short-stability medications that must be prepared immediately before administration outside health care facilities (e.g., in home infusion or emergency care at the accident site or in an ambulance). Immediate-use CSPs do not need to be compounded in an ISO Class 5 environment and garbing and gowning are not required, as long as all of the following criteria are met:

- Hand hygiene per CDC recommendations[46];
- Aseptic technique is followed;
- No hazardous drugs are used;
- Only simple transfer of no more than three sterile, non-hazardous drugs in the manufacturer's original containers are involved in the compounding, and no more than two entries into any one container occur;
- No more than 1 hour elapses from the time compounding commences to the time administration to the patient begins (although best practice dictates that there are no intervening steps between compounding and administration);
- No batching or storage of CSPs occurs; and
- The preparation is labeled with patient identification, names and amounts of all ingredients, name or initials of preparer, and exact 1-hour BUD and time.

If CSPs prepared for immediate use are not administered within 1 hour, they must be properly discarded. All medications must be labeled to meet regulatory and accreditation standards and in accordance with facility policy.

Point-of-Care Activation Systems

Point-of-care (POC) activation systems (i.e., vial/bag systems) create a physical barrier between components (fluid and medication) that can be activated to allow the components to mix. These devices are designed to create a closed system by which the end user activates the components just prior to the administration of the medication. BUDs for these products are based on the individual manufacturer's recommendations for labeling and dating. Table 10 provides a summary of manufacturer-recommended BUDs for POC systems at time of publication. To decrease potential for contamination and errors, POC systems that will be attached and stored for longer than 1 hour prior to activation should be assembled (but not activated) by pharmacy staff within an ISO Class 5 environment. Activation of the devices should be completed at the point of care just prior to administration.

Ampuls, Single-Dose, and Multiple-Dose Containers

Ampuls may not be reused or saved at any time during the compounding process. To minimize particulate contamination, 5 micron filter straws or filter needles must be used when withdrawing contents of ampuls. Refer to the drug labeling for manufacturer's recommendations concerning filtration.

The environmental conditions in which drug vials are entered determine the BUD for the CSP. Single-dose vials are intended to be used to prepare single doses; however, in times of critical need, contents from unopened single-dose/single-use vials may be repackaged for multiple patients.[49] This repackaging should only be performed by qualified health care personnel in accordance with the procedures described in these guidelines and in *USP* chapter 797.[15]

Pharmacy bulk packages (PBPs), a type of vial containing many single doses,[65] must be considered a single-dose vial for purposes of determining BUDs. Manufacturer's information for each PBP contains recommended BUDs, which are usually between 4 and 8 hours.

Multiple-dose vials may be reused or saved up to the manufacturer's recommended BUD, if they are not opened in a direct patient-care area and if facility policy does not require a shorter period.[66] If there is no manufacturer recommendation, multiple-dose vials may be reused or saved up to a maximum of 28 days or for a shorter period dictated by facility policy. Table 11 illustrates the dating for these products based on environmental conditions.

The person who first punctures a multiple-dose container intended for re-use must note the BUD and other information required by facility policy (e.g., his or her initials) on the vial or attached label. A label indicating "use by" clarifies that the date is the BUD rather than the opening date. If a vial lacks a BUD, it should not be used and should be properly discarded.

Table 10.

Beyond-Use Date (BUD) at Room Temperature for Point-of-Care Activated Devices Assembled in ISO Class 5 Environment[a]

Device	Company	BUD[b]	Applicable Products
ADD-Vantage[62]	Hospira	30 days from date diluent removed from overwrap	
Mini-Bag Plus[63]	Baxter	15 days from date diluent removed from overwrap	50 and 100 mL bags
Mini-Bag Plus[63]	Baxter	30 days from date diluent removed from overwrap	100 mL containers docked with the following drugs: cefazolin 1 g, cefuroxime (Zinacef) 750 mg, ceftriaxone (Rocephin) 1 g, aztreonam (Azactam) 1 g, piperacillin and tazobactam (Zosyn) 3.375 g
addEASE[64]	B. Braun	70 days	When connected to 50 mL and 100 mL bags
		56 days	When connected to Excel 250 mL bags

[a]Information is current as of January 2011. The manufacturer's package insert should always be checked for the most current recommendation for dating.

[b]BUD for assembled but not activated system.

Batch Compounding and Sterility Testing

Use of CSPs stored for extended periods of time is guided by the chemical stability of components and the sterility limits of the CSP defined above. If medium-risk batches are prepared and assigned a BUD within those limits, no sterility testing is required. However, if those limits are exceeded, each batch must be tested for sterility according to the requirements of *USP* chapter 71.[67]

Facilities that wish to store CSPs for periods longer than those described above must complete sterility testing for each batch to determine the extended BUD. Each batch of any risk-level CSP intended for storage outside the limits described above must be tested for sterility, according to the requirements of *USP* chapter 71, *Sterility Tests*.[67] The results must be evaluated along with stability data to establish the extended BUD. The policies and procedures of the individual facility must outline the processes used to determine extended BUDs.

Batches of high-risk CSPs prepared as multiple-dose vials intended for administration to multiple patients, batches of high-risk CSPs exposed for more than 12 hours to temperatures of 2 to 8 °C (36 to 46 °F) or for more than 6 hours to temperatures above 8 °C (46 °F) before sterilization, or batches of more than 25 identical, single-dose, high-risk CSPs must undergo sterilization and microbial and bacterial endotoxin (pyrogen) testing prior to dispensing or administration. Sterility testing, as outlined in *USP* chapter 71, must be completed prior to dispensing or administration.[67] *USP* Membrane Filtration, *USP* Direct Inoculation of the Culture Medium, or another testing method that produces verification results statistically comparable with those methods may be utilized.[67]

If sterility testing results are not received prior to dispensing, procedures must be in place for daily observation of the sterility test specimens, immediate recall of dispensed CSPs, and notification of patients and their physicians if microbial or fungal growth is observed. An investigation into the root cause of contamination must occur if sterility testing is positive.

All high-risk CSPs prepared in batches of more than 25 units, with the exception of inhalation or ophthalmic preparations, must be tested to ensure that they do not contain excessive bacterial endotoxins, as described in *USP* chapter 85, Bacterial Endotoxins Test,[68] and *USP* chapter 151, Pyrogen Test.[69] Endotoxin limits (reported in *USP* endotoxin units/hour/kg or units/hour/m^2), if established, are included in the official monograph for the product or may be found in other formula sources. If specific endotoxin limits are not available, default guidance can be found in *USP* chapter 85.[68]

For high-risk preparations, batches of 25 or fewer CSPs do not require sterility testing.[15] However, facilities should consider sterility testing of such CSPs as part of their quality assurance plans to ensure that proper procedures are being followed.

Outsourced CSPs

Outsourcing the preparation of CSPs to pharmacies that specialize in sterile compounding provides an option for facilities that cannot or do not wish to prepare all or some types of CSPs (e.g., radiopharmaceuticals, high-risk CSPs, parenteral nutrition) in their own facility. Facilities considering outsourcing compounding should consult the *ASHP Guidelines on Outsourcing Sterile Compounding Services*.[16] The decision to use CSPs prepared by outside compounding pharmacies should be reviewed and approved by hospital leadership,[23,70] and such use should only occur in accordance with written policies and procedures.

Administration of CSPs

USP chapter 797 does not include any specifications for administration or timing during this crucial period of the drug delivery cycle. CDC provides the most comprehensive guidance regarding administration of intravenous medications, including administration times, frequency of infusion set changes, use of filters, and prevention of catheter-related infections.[38,47]

Personnel

Personnel Responsibilities

The term *compounding personnel* refers to any individual involved in compounding sterile preparations, regardless of profession. Compounding personnel are responsible for ensuring that CSPs are accurately identified, measured, diluted, and mixed and are correctly purified, sterilized, packaged, sealed, labeled, stored, dispensed, distributed, and disposed of if not used. Emphasis should be on the need to

Table 11.

Beyond-Use Dates for Ampuls, Single-Dose, and Multiple-Dose Containers (Adapted from *USP* Chapter 797[15])

Container	Opened and Maintained within an ISO Class 5 Environment	Opened Outside an ISO Class 5 Environment or Taken from ISO Class 5 Conditions to Less Clean Air
Ampuls	One time use; cannot be stored	One time use; cannot be stored
Single-dose vials	One time use, cannot be stored; contents of unopened vial may be repackaged in times of critical need[49]	One time use; cannot be stored
Pharmacy bulk packages	6 hours[a]	Not intended for use outside ISO 5 environment
Multiple-dose vials	28 days[a]	28 days[a]

[a]Unless otherwise specified by manufacturer.

maintain quality standards for the control of processes, components, and environments and for the skill and knowledge of personnel who prepare CSPs.

Accurate identification and inspection of quality and purity of non-sterile chemicals or non-sterile ingredients are necessary for the integrity of the finished preparations. Upon arrival from the manufacturer and subsequently after opening, bulk packages should be inspected for breaks in the package or closure integrity and for proper appearance, color, odor, and texture.

If nonsterile ingredients are not official *USP* or *National Formulary* products, compounding personnel must require a Certificate of Analysis from the manufacturer to accompany the products.[59] Once a product is received from the manufacturer, the date of receipt must be clearly marked on each package. If a manufacturer's expiration date is not provided, chemicals should be given a three-year BUD from the time of opening unless inspection or testing deems the product within drug monograph specification (if available) to be used for a longer time.[59]

Compounding personnel must have an understanding of how combining different agents in a preparation may affect bioavailability, compatibility (visual and chemical), pH, and concentration effects. Factors that influence stability (e.g., temperature, pH, sorption, photolysis, and chemical degradation) must be carefully evaluated and supported by references or appropriate testing.

Compounding personnel must understand and demonstrate competency in aseptic technique and for the products and systems used in CSP preparation, such as needles, syringes, administration sets, fluid containers, and compounding devices. Aseptic principles and techniques are explained in depth in *Compounding Sterile Preparations*[53] and demonstrated in *Basics of Aseptic Compounding Technique*,[54] *Getting Started in Aseptic Compounding*,[55] and *Compounding Sterile Preparations: ASHP's Video Guide to Chapter <797>*.[56] Personnel must understand the types of PECs, HEPA filtration, and airflow concepts that are critical to sterile compounding.

Policies should be developed in conjunction with employee health or infection control personnel to set thresholds for health status fitness for compounding personnel. Compounding personnel with weeping sores, rashes, conjunctivitis, or respiratory infections must not participate in compounding processes until these conditions resolve.

Hygiene and Garbing. Proper preparation for sterile, nonhazardous drug compounding must include effective hand hygiene and garbing procedures. To minimize the number of particles introduced into the sterile compounding area and to minimize the risk of bacteria, all outer jackets and sweaters, visible jewelry, and cosmetics must be removed prior to initiating the handwashing and garbing processes. Personal electronic devices (e.g., cell phones, MP3 players) and any associated attachments must be removed prior to hand hygiene and garbing and should not be used within the sterile compounding area.

Hand hygiene must be performed prior to and after gowning and includes:

- Washing hands, under the fingernails, wrists, and up to the elbow for 30 seconds with a facility-approved agent.
- Drying hands and arms with nonshedding disposable towels or an electronic hand dryer.
- Sanitizing hands with application of a waterless, alcohol-based hand rub (ABHR) with persistent activity prior to donning sterile gloves.

Garbing occurs in the ante area and should be sequenced as follows (from "dirtiest" to "cleanest"):

- Don shoe covers, hair and beard covers, and a mask.
- Perform hand hygiene.
- Don gown, fastened securely at the neck and wrists.
- Sanitize hands using an ABHR and allow hands to dry.
- Enter the buffer area (if facility layout dictates, this step may occur after the following two steps).
- Don sterile powder-free gloves.
- Sanitize the gloves with application of 70% sterile IPA and allow gloves to dry.

Studies support the use of sterile rather than nonsterile gloves in the reduction of initial bioburden.[71] Furthermore, nonsterile gloves run the risk of cross-contamination from hands touching multiple gloves as they are removed from a stock box or container. Gloves must be inspected by personnel on a routine basis during the compounding process to check for tears or holes. The gloves should be disinfected with sterile 70% IPA throughout the compounding process and each time contaminated items are touched.

When high-risk compounding operations prior to terminal sterilization occur, personnel must glove and garb as stated above.

When exiting the compounding area during a work shift, gowns that are not soiled may be removed and retained in the ante area and re-worn during the same work shift. All other garb, including gloves, must be removed and replaced, and proper hand hygiene must be completed before re-entering the compounding area. When CAIs are utilized, compounding personnel must glove and garb as above, unless the manufacturer of the isolator provides written documentation based on environmental testing that any or all of the components of personnel hygiene and garbing are not required based on the PECs of the facility where the device is located.

Proper garb should always be used with CACIs, because personnel will be handling hazardous materials. Vials may be contaminated, even upon delivery,[72–74] and the garb is needed to protect compounding personnel from unexpected drug residue and from inadvertent spills.

Compounding Areas. Compounding personnel must understand the purposes of and relationships between ante, buffer, segregated, and storage areas. A systematic process of entering and exiting the various areas is necessary to minimize contamination. Food, drinks, and gum are prohibited in all of these areas. Since shedding from paper and labels provides a source of nonviable particles, only paper products essential to the compounding process should be allowed in the buffer area. Corrugated cardboard packaging must be eliminated from buffer areas and should be eliminated from ante areas, with all products and components such as needles, syringes, and tubing removed from their outer cardboard packaging and decontaminated by wiping the individual packages (if not in an overwrap) with a suitable disinfectant (e.g.,70% IPA) prior to entering the buffer area.

When used for sterile compounding, items in plastic or foil overwrap should remain in the overwrap until introduced into the ISO Class 5 PEC, at which point they should be opened immediately before placing in the PEC and the overwrap immediately discarded.[75] Items stored in the buffer area but not in an overwrap must be decontaminated again prior to entering the PEC, as items may be stored in a buffer area for an extended period of time and may become contaminated by dust or other particles.

Packaging and Labeling

Packaging and subsequent labeling are critical to patient safety. Packaging must be appropriate to preserve both sterility and stability until the BUD. Proper labeling requires an understanding of compounding risk levels and how to determine BUDs based on both stability and sterility.

Labels for single compounded preparations must, at a minimum, include the following:

- Names of active ingredients,
- Amounts or concentrations of active ingredients,
- BUD and time,
- Storage requirements, and
- Identification of responsible compounding personnel.

Labels for batch-prepared CSPs must also include:

- Control or lot number,
- Appropriate auxiliary labeling (including precautions), and
- Device-specific instructions (when appropriate).

Federal and state regulations and accreditation requirements may necessitate additional label information before the CSP is dispensed to a specific patient.

Verification of compounding accuracy and sterility incorporates physical inspection, ensuring compounding accuracy processes are in place, and (when applicable) sterility and endotoxin testing. Finished preparation evaluation is the responsibility of compounding personnel and should be performed during the compounding process and when the preparation leaves the storage area. Visual inspection should assess particulate matter, coring, cloudiness, leaks, and container and closure integrity.

Compounding accuracy checks must comply with federal and state dispensing regulations and include accuracy of the product or preparation and the labeling. Prescription orders, compounding procedures, records, and materials used to prepare the compounds should be evaluated. A process should be implemented to confirm that the compounding process and end-preparation testing are properly done. Checking procedures should follow facility policy and procedures and may be accomplished via cameras or other devices, by video recordings, or by keeping the used additive containers and syringes with the final product until checked. The check ideally should be performed by someone other than the compounder to decrease confirmation bias. Accuracy can be further verified by weighing when applicable and practical. When using an ACD, specific gravity values must be independently confirmed after being entered to ensure proper volumes are delivered during the compounding process.

Storage of CSPs

Temperatures of areas used for storage on patient-care and procedural units, including room temperature and in refrigerators, freezers, and warmers, must be monitored and recorded daily. On at least a monthly basis, compounding personnel or designated pharmacy personnel should evaluate storage areas for appropriate secure conditions, separation of drugs and food, and proper use and disposal of single- and multiple-dose vials.

Control and Oversight of IV Solutions

Some facilities delegate storage and distribution of parenteral solutions to materials management. Since the products are prescription drugs, the pharmacy must maintain oversight, including selection of appropriate products, package sizes, and forms; safe and secure storage; and temperature control. IV solutions that contain medications (e.g., potassium chloride, heparin, dopamine, dextran, mannitol) or high-risk agents (e.g., sterile water, sodium chloride greater than 0.9%, and parenteral nutrition components) should be stored in and distributed by the pharmacy.

Transporting CSPs

All personnel involved in the handling, transport, or storage of CSPs, whether they are compounding personnel or not, must be properly trained to complete these tasks, and the performance of all personnel, including contractors, must be monitored for compliance with facility policies. Transportation methods for CSPs should be evaluated, as some forms of transportation, such as pneumatic tube systems, may adversely affect stability or integrity. Pneumatic tube delivery may require additional padding around containers to ensure that heat and light exposure and impact are minimized. Some preparations may degrade if shaken, and therefore personnel, including pharmacy and nursing personnel, should be aware of which preparations may not be delivered via a pneumatic tube device.

Hazardous drug transport must incorporate measures to maintain CSP integrity while minimizing the risk of drug residue exposure to patients, personnel, and the environment. These preparations should always be delivered in a bag to prevent leakage or accidental exposure during transport, and they should not be delivered using a pneumatic tube device due to the risk of contamination to the environment if breakage occurs. Cleaning protocols for pneumatic tube systems are inadequate for hazardous drug contamination throughout the system.

Transport may occur outside of the compounding facility to other facilities or directly to patients. In these situations, compounding personnel must ensure physical integrity, sterility, and stability are maintained during transit. Proper packaging must be chosen to prevent contamination, leaks, damage, and temperature variations and to protect the end recipients and transporting personnel from harm. Handling and exposure instructions should be legibly displayed on the outside of shipping containers. BUDs, storage instructions, and disposal instructions for out-of-date preparations must be available to recipients, and recipients must be able to properly store CSPs (e.g., in a refrigerator or freezer, if necessary).

Redispensing CSPs

If facility policy allows redispensing of CSPs, the process must only be done by compounding personnel to ensure continued sterility, purity, and stability. Facilities must determine how to track original preparation and thaw dates (if applicable) and be able to detect product tampering. There must be policies and procedures in place to provide assurance of proper storage conditions for each product or preparation (e.g., refrigeration, protection from light, package integrity) before redispensing. CSPs must not be redispensed if package integrity has been compromised, including temperature variations.

Personnel Responsibilities for Handling, Preparation, and Disposal of Cytotoxic and Other Hazardous Agents

The Occupational Safety and Health Administration (OSHA) requires that employers and employees be made aware of the hazards of all chemicals used in the workplace, including drugs.[76] Compounding personnel of reproductive capability shall confirm in writing that they understand the risks of handling hazardous drugs.[15] Personnel at high risk of exposure to hazardous drugs should be enrolled in a medical surveillance program. In many larger facilities, the employee's health department will determine who should be enrolled. Specific guidance about surveillance for health care workers exposed to hazardous drugs is available from NIOSH,[77] as is a list of drugs NIOSH considers hazardous.[27] The risks of occupational exposure to hazardous drugs and their potential effects on compounding personnel should be conveyed to employees during employee orientation and in an ongoing manner through continuing education and monitoring at least annually. Training and competency programs should be provided in addition to competencies for compounding of non-hazardous sterile drugs, with details of differentiating the garbing, storage, preparation, and disposal procedures for hazardous drugs. *USP* chapter 797 requires that training, at a minimum, include:

- Safe aseptic manipulation practices.
- Negative pressure techniques when compounding.
- Proper utilization of a BSC or CACI.
- Correct use of closed-system transfer devices (CSTDs), if used.
- Containment, cleanup, and disposal procedures for breakages and spills.
- Treatment of personnel contact and inhalation exposure.[15]

OSHA requires more general training on chemical label elements and safety data sheet (SDS) format.[76] When training or evaluating competency, facilities may choose products to objectively evaluate hazardous drug compounding technique. These products utilize dyes or fluorescence to determine personnel technique and assess for spills or hazardous drug exposures.

Definitions of hazardous drugs and proper handling of hazardous drugs, including receiving, distribution, stocking, inventorying, preparation, transport, and disposal, are all concepts discussed in detail in the *ASHP Guidelines on Handling Hazardous Drugs*.[28]

Personnel Responsibilities for Specialty Preparations

Specialty preparations (e.g., allergen extracts, radiopharmaceuticals, and evolving technology and therapeutics such as biologics and nanotechnology) provide specific treatments for patients and require specialized procedures to be followed. Although compounding of intradermal or subcutaneous injections of allergen extracts would ideally occur under conditions for similar risk-level CSPs, they may not necessarily be subject to the same personnel, environmental, and storage requirements as for other CSPs of a similar risk level, as long as the following criteria outlined by *USP* chapter 797,[15] in conjunction with the American Academy of Otolaryngic Allergy and the Joint Council of Allergy, Asthma and Immunology,[78] are met:

- Compounding process involves simple transfer using sterile components and allergen products.
- All allergen extracts contain effective preservatives to prevent microbial growth.
- All hand hygiene, garbing, and gloving procedures for low-risk compounding, with the exception of donning shoe covers, must be followed.
- Ampul necks and vial stoppers are disinfected by wiping with sufficient amounts of sterile 70% IPA to ensure that the critical sites remain wet for 10 seconds and are allowed to dry.
- Direct contact contamination of critical sites is minimized by utilizing aseptic compounding.
- Multiple-dose vials are labeled with the name of one patient and a BUD and storage temperature range based on manufacturer recommendations or published literature. Single-dose extracts are not to be stored for subsequent use after entry.

Nuclear pharmacies are regulated by the Nuclear Regulatory Commission as well as other applicable pharmacy laws and regulations. *USP* chapter 823, Radiopharmaceuticals for Positron Emission Tomography,[79] provides the standards for production facilities. Once the components for use in positron emission tomography are released as finished preparations, handling, manipulation, and use are considered compounding by *USP* chapter 797[15] and for the purposes of these guidelines. Low-risk-level radiopharmaceuticals are those compounded from sterile components with a volume of less than 100 mL for a single-dose injection or no more than 30 mL taken from a multiple-dose container.[15] These radiopharmaceutical preparations must be compounded in an ISO Class 5 PEC within an ISO Class 8 environment.

Non-radiopharmaceuticals compounded in nuclear pharmacies must be compounded under full USP 797 compliant conditions. The radiopharmaceutical exemption in USP chapter 797[15] does not apply to non-radiopharmaceuticals.

The concept of limiting radiation exposure to a level that is as low as reasonably achievable (ALARA) must be adhered to for handling, compounding, and visual inspection of products. Technetium-99m/molybdenum-99 generator system operations and storage must occur within an ISO Class 8 environment and must further comply with all manufacturer's recommendations and federal and state regulations. Manufacturer's guidelines for BUDs should be followed for radiopharmaceutical multiple-dose vials that are compounded with technetium-99m and exposed to ISO Class 5 conditions with no direct contact contamination.

Personnel Compounding Competency

Touch contamination remains the primary cause of microbial contamination in sterile compounding.[71,80] For this reason, personnel training and assessment of competency are of utmost importance to ensure the lowest possible risk for contamination due to human error. For low- and medium-risk operations, training and competency assessment are required initially upon hire or upon transfer to compounding responsibilities, and again at least every 12 months for all staff involved in the compounding of sterile products. High-risk operations require more frequent assessments, and staff must be evaluated upon hire or transfer and again at least every six months.

As part of the training competency assessment, a written test that evaluates knowledge about proper compounding SOPs, aseptic technique, cleaning and garbing, environmental monitoring, calculations, risk levels and BUDs, and quality assurance principles must be successfully completed. Thresholds for passing the written examination should be set by the facility. While written tests assess knowledge, hands-on observation of daily duties assesses for proper technique. Personnel should be able to demonstrate at least the following in a hands-on, witnessed assessment, as applicable to their compounding responsibilities:

- Proper hand hygiene technique (see Appendix III of *USP* chapter 797[15] for a sample assessment form).
- Proper gloving and garbing technique, including successful glove fingertip test (see Appendix III of *USP* chapter 797[15] for a sample assessment form).
- Proper aseptic technique, including successful media-fill test (see Appendix IV of *USP* chapter 797[15] for a sample assessment form).
- Proper cleaning and disinfecting procedures, including successful surface sampling test (see Appendix V of *USP* chapter 797[15] for a sample assessment form and Appendix II for information about cleaning products).
- Competency in the compounding of hazardous drugs.
- Competency in the compounding of allergen extracts.
- Competency in the compounding of radiopharmaceuticals.
- Competency in the use of sterile devices, such as filter needles, injection port adapters, sterile fluid transfer devices, and CSTDs.
- Competency in the use of pharmacy compounding devices.
- Ability to fill pump reservoirs.
- Competency to perform end-product testing and sterilization.

USP chapter 797[15] requires specific assessments to be completed using sterile nutrient agar growth media to test for potential contamination. Personnel-specific examples of this type of testing include media-fill testing of aseptic technique and glove fingertip testing of compounding personnel.

Media-Fill Testing

As described in *USP* chapter 797, the media-fill component of personnel assessment provides an objective evaluation of aseptic technique.[15] Media-fill tests should be customized to mimic the most challenging preparations compounded by personnel on a regular basis in a specific facility. Testing should occur at least every 12 months for personnel who compound low- and medium-risk preparations, while testing at least every 6 months is required for personnel involved in compounding high-risk preparations. The actual testing should take place under conditions that reflect realistic workflow, such as the end of a shift, to simulate a worst-case scenario environment for compounding sterile preparations. Once started, the test should be completed without interruption. Fluid culture media are available commercially for low- and medium-risk evaluations. High-risk assessments may utilize nonsterile nutrient medium in a powder form, which may be diluted and sterilized by filter methods. Finished tests should be incubated per manufacturer's recommendations. If incubators are in the pharmacy, they must be placed outside the sterile compounding area. Ideally, the facility's microbiology services should incubate and read the tests, providing an independent evaluation by qualified individuals. Turbidity in the culture media signifies failure of the media-fill testing and requires retesting of compounding personnel. Personnel who fail these tests will require re-training and may not compound sterile preparations until tests have been repeated with successful results.

Glove Fingertip Testing

Three sets of glove fingertip evaluations must be completed with no growth prior to personnel being allowed to compound sterile preparations. This initial testing involves compounding personnel completing all necessary hand hygiene and garbing procedures (with the exception of applying sterile 70% IPA to gloves). Immediately upon completion of these procedures, the glove fingertip and thumb samples from each hand are placed on sterile nutrient agar plates. The samples should be incubated (such as by the facility's microbiology personnel) according to manufacturer standards. This test must be successfully completed three times initially, then at least every 12 months. Personnel compounding high-risk products must successfully complete the test at least every 6 months. Suggested thresholds for contamination limits can be found in Table 6. Patterns of failures (personnel, media, or facility) must be evaluated as part of the facility's quality assurance plan. Qualified microbiology personnel and the facility's infection control practitioner should be consulted.

Growth Media Requirements

Sterile nutrient agar for media-fill testing, plates for fingertip testing, and surface testing materials are available from multiple vendors. *USP* chapters 797 and 1116 provide specifications and requirements.[15,81] The media-fill testing growth media and viable airborne particle plates should utilize a Soybean-Casein Digest medium, which may also be sold as Tryptic Soy Agar/Broth. The agar plates for glove fingertip testing and surface testing should utilize general nutrient agar with neutralizing agents such as lecithin and polysorbate 80.

SOP Development

SOPs are documents containing detailed, step-by-step instructions on how to perform a task or procedure so that all personnel consistently perform the task or procedure in the same manner. SOPs are part of a good quality assurance program within the pharmacy. They provide assurance that:

- Equipment and facilities are properly maintained in good working order.
- Personnel are properly educated, trained, and evaluated.
- Supplies are received, stored, and disposed of properly and meet compendial standards.
- All tasks and procedures are performed uniformly and documented.

There are several components that should be included in an SOP:

- *Title*—should clearly identify the task.
- *SOP number*—an internal department number assigned by the organization to identify it.
- *Author(s)*—the name of the person or persons who write the SOP so that problems and revisions can be addressed.
- *Date effective*—date when the SOP is implemented into the compounding routine.
- *Authorization signature*—person or committee that approves the SOP.
- *Responsibility*—person- or persons-in-charge who are responsible for making sure that the SOP is performed properly.
- *Purpose of the procedure*—brief explanation of why the SOP is necessary or being implemented.
- *Equipment and supplies required*—list of equipment and supplies needed to perform the SOP.
- *Procedure*—detailed step-by-step explanation that can be easily followed by different individuals with the same results. The instructions should be concise to minimize any required interpretation.
- *References*—references should be listed to support the implementation and use of the SOP.
- *Documentation form*—easily accessible written record or log that demonstrates that the SOP is being performed routinely and properly.
- *Revision*—documentation of the date that an SOP has been reviewed and the name of the reviewer.

USP chapter 797[15] lists and recommends SOPs and should be reviewed to guide the pharmacy department in developing, writing, and implementing SOPs. There should be SOPs written to address tasks or procedures in the following general categories:

- *Personnel*—training, education, skills, competency evaluations, and responsibilities.
- *Facilities*—access, cleaning, maintenance, use, monitoring, and testing.
- *Equipment*—calibration, maintenance, cleaning, certification, verification, and use.
- *Supplies*—ordering, storing, certification, inspection, and disposal.
- *Compounding procedures*—preparation of various sterile compounded medications (e.g., batches, total parenteral nutrition, hazardous drugs, epidural, patient-controlled analgesia, or ophthalmics), formulas, assigning BUDs, handling, and packaging.
- *Safety*—injuries, hazardous spills, and accidental exposures.
- *Quality assurance*—inspection of CSPs, testing of CSPs, BUDs, delivery, and storage of final CSPs, patient monitoring, adverse event reporting, and personnel and environmental monitoring.
- *Administration*—record keeping and management.

All significant procedures performed in a pharmacy should be covered by SOPs and documentation. These procedures should be routinely reviewed and modified for improvements at least annually.

Quality Assurance Program

The purpose of a quality assurance program is to provide a mechanism for monitoring, evaluating, correcting, and improving activities and processes. A quality assurance program should review and analyze objective data and use these data to develop action plans. Facilities should actively work to correct problems detected and improve activities and processes as needed. Any plan designed to correct problems should include follow-up parameters to make certain actions were taken and were effective.

Activities and processes that are identified based on their high frequency, high risk, or problem-prone nature should have specific monitoring and evaluation criteria assigned for objective and measurable assessment. The quality assurance program should encompass any and all activities that are included in previous sections of this document as elements which should be assessed and documented. This includes, but is not limited to:

- Personnel training and assessment,
- Environmental monitoring, and
- Equipment calibration and maintenance.

Specific quality assurance measures, pursuant to each risk level compounded in a facility, include routine cleaning and disinfection and air quality testing, visual confirmation of proper garbing procedures, review of all orders and preparations to ensure accuracy of compounded products, and visual inspection of final CSPs to confirm the absence of particulate matter or leakage.

A critical part of any quality assurance program is proper documentation, corrective action, and follow-up. Institutions must determine how results will be reported and evaluated, including development of action limits and thresholds. Thresholds and follow-up mechanisms must be in place prior to initiating a quality assurance program or immediately after collecting initial benchmark data. Responsible persons for completing these tasks should be identified and trained, if necessary, in the proper execution of the quality assurance plan. Results of monitoring and measurements should be reported within and outside of the department responsible for compounding practices to committees such as Infection Control and Quality Improvement.

If corrective action is needed, the problem should be resolved as soon as possible. Assessment of problems with compounding errors, evident contamination during preparation, quarantine, or patterns of personnel or environmental monitoring outside the established parameters require formal follow-up. A root cause analysis, including participation by other facility experts such as infection control personnel, should be completed.[82] For situations needing more time for corrective measures, an action plan should be developed and followed. Indicators and effectiveness of the quality assurance program should be reassessed annually.

New technologies, procedures, and policies should be incorporated on an as-needed basis. A failure mode and effects analysis of new techniques can serve as a valuable proactive assessment of the ease and value prior to introduction into the compounding process.[83]

References

1. Hasegawa GR. Caring about stability and compatibility. *Am J Hosp Pharm.* 1994; 51:1533–4. [editorial]
2. Stability considerations in dispensing practice (general information chapter 1191). In: The United States pharmacopeia, 34th rev., and The national formulary, 29th ed. Rockville, MD: The United States Pharmacopeial Convention; 2011:742–5.
3. Guynn JB Jr, Poretz DM, Duma RJ. Growth of various bacteria in a variety of intravenous fluids. *Am J Hosp Pharm.* 1973; 30:321–5.
4. Selenic D, Dodson DR, Jensen B, et al. *Enterobacter cloacae* bloodstream infection in pediatric patients traced to a hospital pharmacy. *Am J Health-Syst Pharm.* 2003; 60:1440–6.
5. Hughes CF, Grant AF, Lick BD, et al. Cardioplegic solution: a contamination crisis. *J Thorac Cardiovasc Surg.* 1986; 91:296–302.
6. Dugleaux G, Coutour XL, Hecquard C, et al. Septicemia caused by contaminated parenteral nutrition pouches: the refrigerator as an unusual cause. *J Parenter Enteral Nutr.* 1991; 15:474–5.
7. Sachs GS. Microbial contamination of parenteral nutrition—How could it happen? *J Parenter Enteral Nutr.* 2011; 35:432.
8. Traynor K. Meningitis outbreak challenges hospital pharmacies. *Am J Health-Syst Pharm.* 2012; 69:2024–6.
9. Pierce LR, Gaines A, Varricchio R, et al. Hemolysis and renal failure associated with use of sterile water for injection to dilute 25% human albumin solution. *Am J Health-Syst Pharm.* 1998; 55:1057,1062,1070.
10. Flynn EA, Pearson RE, Barker KN. Observational study of accuracy in compounding i.v. admixtures at five hospitals. *Am J Health-Syst Pharm.* 1997; 54:904–12.
11. Morris AM, Schneider PJ, Pedersen CA, et al. National survey of quality assurance activities for pharmacy-compounded sterile preparations. *Am J Health-Syst Pharm.* 2003; 60:2567–76.
12. Santell JP, Kamalich RF. National survey of quality assurance activities for pharmacy-prepared sterile products in hospitals and home infusion facilities—1995. *Am J Health-Syst Pharm.* 1996; 53:2591–605.
13. Kastango ES, Douglass K. Improving the management, operations and cost effectiveness of sterile-product compounding. *Int J Pharm Compd.* 1999; 3:253–8.
14. American Society of Health-System Pharmacists. ASHP Guidelines on Quality Assurance for Pharmacy-Prepared Sterile Products. *Am J Health-Syst Pharm.* 2000; 57:1150–69.
15. Pharmaceutical compounding—sterile preparations (general information chapter 797). In: The United States Pharmacopeia, 36th rev., and the National Formulary, 31 ed. Rockville, MD: The United States Pharmacopeial Convention; 2013: 361–98.
16. American Society of Health-System Pharmacists. ASHP guidelines on outsourcing sterile compounding services. *Am J Health-Syst Pharm.* 2010; 67:757–65.
17. ASHP Discussion Guide on USP Chapter <797>; 2008. www.ashp.org/s_ashp/docs/files/DiscGuide797-2008.pdf (accessed 2012 Dec 28).
18. Food and Drug Administration Modernization Act of 1997, Pub. L. No. 105-115, 111 Stat. 2296. www.fda.gov/RegulatoryInformation/Legislation/FederalFoodDrugandCosmeticActFDCAct/SignificantAmendmentstotheFDCAct/FDAMA/default.htm (accessed 2012 Dec 28).
19. Office of Regulatory Policy and Office of Compliance, Center for Drug Evaluation and Research (CDER), Food and Drug Administration. Guidance for FDA staff and industry. Compliance policy guides manual. Sec. 460.200. Pharmacy compounding. www.fda.gov/ICECI/ComplianceManuals/CompliancePolicyGuidanceManual/ucm074398.htm (accessed 2012 Dec 28).
20. Sterile drug products for home use (general information chapter 1206). In: The United States pharmacopeia, 23rd rev., and The national formulary, 19th ed. Rockville, MD: The United State Pharmacopeial Convention; 1995:2130–43.
21. Douglas K, Kastango E, Cantor P. State regulations impact USP <797> compliance. *Pharm Purch Prod.* 2012; 9:S18–S21.
22. National Association of Boards of Pharmacy. Model State Pharmacy Act and Model Rules of the National Association of Boards of Pharmacy. www.nabp.net/publications/model-act/ (accessed 2012 Dec 28).
23. CMS Hospital Conditions of Participation and Interpretative Guidelines, Centers for Medicare and Medicaid Services (CMS), Department of Health and Human Services. *State Operations Manual Appendix A—Survey Protocol, Regulations and Interpretive Guidelines for Hospitals,* Rev 78 (12-22-11). Washington, DC: Government Printing Office; 2011. www.cms.gov/Regulations-and-Guidance/Guidance/Manuals/downloads/som107ap_a_hospitals.pdf (accessed 2012 Dec 28).
24. Comprehensive accreditation manual for hospitals: the official handbook. Oakbrook Terrace, IL: The Joint Commission; 2012.
25. American Osteopathic Association. Healthcare Facilities Accreditation Program, 2009 Accreditation Requirements for Healthcare Facilities; 2009.
26. DNV Healthcare. National Integrated Accreditation for Healthcare Organizations (NIAHO), Interpretive Guidelines and Surveyor Guidance, Revision 10; 2012.
27. National Institute for Occupational Safety and Health [NIOSH]. NIOSH List of Antineoplastic and Other Hazardous Drugs in Healthcare Settings 2012. www.cdc.gov/niosh/docs/2012-150/ (accessed 2012 Dec 28).

28. American Society of Health-System Pharmacists. ASHP guidelines on handling hazardous drugs. *Am J Health-Syst Pharm.* 2006; 63:1172–93.
29. National Institute for Occupational Safety and Health [NIOSH]. NIOSH alert: preventing occupational exposure to antineoplastic and other hazardous drugs in health care settings; 2004. www.cdc.gov/niosh/docs/2004-165/#g (accessed 2012 Dec 28).
30. National Institute for Occupational Safety and Health [NIOSH]. Personal protective equipment for health care workers who work with hazardous drugs (NIOSH document 2009-16). www.cdc.gov/niosh/docs/wp-solutions/2009-106/ (accessed 2012 Dec 20).
31. American Society of Hospital Pharmacists. ASHP technical assistance bulletin on pharmacy-prepared ophthalmic products. *Am J Hosp Pharm.* 1993; 50:1462–3.
32. American Society of Health-System Pharmacists. ASHP guidelines on the safe use of automated compounding devices for the preparation of parenteral nutrition admixtures. *Am J Health-Syst Pharm.* 2000; 57:1343–8.
33. American Society of Health-System Pharmacists. ASHP guidelines: minimum standard for pharmacies in hospitals. *Am J Health-Syst Pharm.* 2013; 70:1619–30.
34. ASPEN Task Force for the Revision of Safe Practices for Parenteral Nutrition: Mirtallo J, Canada T, Johnson D, et al. Safe Practices for Parenteral Nutrition. *J Parenter Enteral Nutr.* 2004; 28(6):S39–S70.
35. Bankhead R, Boullata J, Brantley S, et al. Enteral nutrition practice recommendations. *J Parenter Enteral Nutr.* 2009; 33:122–67.
36. Institute for Safe Medication Practices [ISMP]. 2004 ISMP medication safety self assessment for hospitals. Huntington Valley, PA: ISMP; 2004. www.ismp.org/selfassessments/Hospital/2004Hospsm.pdf (accessed 2012 Dec 28).
37. Institute for Safe Medication Practices [ISMP]. Proceedings from the ISMP Sterile Preparation Compounding Safety Summit: Guidelines for SAFE Preparation of Sterile Compounds; 2012. www.ismp.org/tools/guidelines/IVSummit/IVCGuidelines.pdf (accessed 2012 Dec 28).
38. Infusion Nurses Society. Infusion nursing standards of practice. *J Infus Nurs.* 2011; 34(1S):S1–S110.
39. Controlled Environment Testing Association [CETA]. CETA certification guide for sterile compounding facilities (CAG-003-2006) (revised January 31, 2012). www.cetainternational.org/reference/CAG-003-2006v11.pdf (accessed 2012 Dec 28).
40. Controlled Environment Testing Association [CETA]. Servicing hazardous drug compounding primary engineering controls (CAG-005-2007). www.cetainternational.org/reference/CAG005-v15.pdf (accessed 2012 Dec 28).
41. Controlled Environment Testing Association [CETA]. Application guide for the use of surface decontaminants in biosafety cabinets (CAG-004-2007). www.cetainternational.org/reference/CAG0042007i.pdf (accessed 2012 Dec 28).
42. Controlled Environment Testing Association [CETA]. Compounding isolator testing guide (CAG-002-2006) (revised December 2008). www.cetainternational.org/reference/CETACompoundingIsolatorTestingGuide2006.pdf (accessed 2012 Dec 28).
43. Controlled Environment Testing Association [CETA]. Application guide for the use of compounding isolators in compounding sterile preparations in healthcare facilities (CAG-001-2005) (revised December 2008). www.cetainternational.org/reference/ApplicationsGuideBarrierIsolator-CAG-001-2005.pdf (accessed 2012 Dec 28).
44. Controlled Environment Testing Association [CETA]. CETA Certification Matrix for Sterile Compounding Facilities (CAG-008-2010) (updated January 2012). www.cetainternational.org/reference/CAG-008-2010v2.pdf (accessed 2012 Dec 20).
45. Controlled Environment Testing Association [CETA]. CETA Certification Application Guide USP <797> Viable Environmental Sampling & Gowning Evaluation (CAG-009-2011v3). www.cetainternational.org/reference/CAG-009v3.pdf (accessed 2012 Dec 28).
46. Centers for Disease Control and Prevention [CDC]. Guidelines for hand hygiene in healthcare settings. *MMWR* 2002; 51(RR16):1–45. www.cdc.gov/mmwr/preview/mmwrhtml/rr5116a1.htm (accessed 2012 Dec 28).
47. O'Grady NP, Alexander M, Burns LA, et al. 2011 Guidelines for the Prevention of Intravascular Catheter-Related Infections. Centers for Disease Control and Prevention, 2012. www.cdc.gov/hicpac/pdf/guidelines/bsi-guidelines-2011.pdf (accessed 2012 Dec 28).
48. Centers for Disease Control and Prevention [CDC]. Guidelines for Environmental Infection Control in Healthcare Facilities. *MMWR.* 2003; 52(RR10):1–42. www.cdc.gov/mmwr/preview/mmwrhtml/rr5210a1.htm (accessed 2012 Dec 28).
49. Centers for Disease Control and Prevention, National Center for Emerging and Zoonotic Infectious Diseases (NCEZID), Division of Healthcare Quality Promotion (DHQP). Protect Patients Against Preventable Harm from Improper Use of Single-Dose/Single-Use Vials. www.cdc.gov/injectionsafety/CDCposition-SingleUseVial.html (accessed 2012 Dec 28).
50. Centers for Medicare & Medicaid Services [CMS]. Single use of single dose/single use medications to prevent healthcare-associated infections. www.cms.gov/Medicare/Provider-Enrollment-and-Certification/SurveyCertificationGenInfo/Policy-and-Memos-to-States-and-Regions-Items/Survey-and-Cert-Letter-12-35.html (accessed 2012 Dec 28).
51. Dolan SA, Felizardo G, Barnes S, et al. APIC position paper: Safe injection, infusion, and medication vial practices in health care. *Am J Infect Control.* 2010; 38:167–72.
52. Chapter 17. Recommended Practices for Medication Safety. In: Conner R, Blanchard J, Burlingame B, et al. (eds). Perioperative Standards and Recommended Practices. Denver, CO: Association of periOperative Registered Nurses (AORN); 2012:251–300.
53. Buchanan EC, Schneider PJ. Compounding sterile preparations, 3rd ed. Bethesda, MD: American Society of Health-System Pharmacists; 2009.
54. American Society of Health-System Pharmacists [ASHP]. Basics of aseptic compounding technique. Bethesda, MD: ASHP; 2006.

55. Davis K, Sparks J. Getting started in aseptic compounding. Bethesda, MD: American Society of Health-System Pharmacists; 2008.
56. Kienle PC. Compounding sterile preparations: ASHP video guide to chapter <797>. Bethesda, MD: American Society of Health-System Pharmacists; 2009.
57. U.S. Department of Health and Human Services, Food and Drug Administration, Office of Regulatory Affairs. Guidance for industry: sterile drug products produced by aseptic processing—current good manufacturing practice. September 2004. www.fda.gov/downloads/Drugs/GuidanceComplianceRegulatoryInformation/Guidances/UCM070342.pdf (accessed 2012 Dec 28).
58. General notices and requirements. In: The United States pharmacopeia, 34th rev., and The national formulary, 29th ed. Rockville, MD: The United States Pharmacopeial Convention; 2011:11–12.
59. Pharmaceutical compounding—nonsterile preparations (general information chapter 795). In: The United States pharmacopeia, 34th rev., and The national formulary, 29th ed. Rockville, MD: The United States Pharmacopeial Convention; 2011:330–6.
60. Trissel LA. Handbook on injectable drugs. 17th ed. Bethesda, MD: American Society of Health-System Pharmacists; 2013.
61. Bing CD, Nowobilski-Vasilios A. Extended stability for parenteral drugs. 5th ed. Bethesda, MD: American Society of Health-System Pharmacists; 2013:321.
62. Personal communication from Hospira. December 16, 2008.
63. Personal communication from Baxter. December 18, 2008.
64. Personal communication from B. Braun. December 26, 2008.
65. Injections (general information chapter 1). In: The United States pharmacopeia, 34th rev., and The national formulary, 29th ed. Rockville, MD: The United States Pharmacopeial Convention; 2011:33–8.
66. Centers for Disease Control and Prevention, National Center for Emerging and Zoonotic Infectious Diseases (NCEZID), Division of Healthcare Quality Promotion (DHQP). Safe Injection Practices to Prevent Transmission of Infections to Patients. www.cdc.gov/injectionsafety/IP07_standardPrecaution.html (accessed 2013 Jan 30).
67. Sterility tests (general information chapter 71). In: The United States pharmacopeia, 34th rev., and The national formulary, 29th ed. Rockville, MD: The United States Pharmacopeial Convention; 2011:65–70.
68. Bacterial endotoxins test (general information chapter 85). In: The United States pharmacopeia, 34th rev., and The national formulary, 29th ed. Rockville, MD: The United States Pharmacopeial Convention; 2011: 78–82.
69. Pyrogen test (general information chapter 151). In: The United States pharmacopeia, 34th rev., and The national formulary, 29th ed. Rockville, MD: The United States Pharmacopeial Convention; 2011:115–7.
70. Oversight of Care, Treatment, and Services Provided through Contractual Agreement (Standard LD.04.03.09). Comprehensive accreditation manual for hospitals: the official handbook. Oakbrook Terrace, IL: The Joint Commission; 2012.
71. Trissel LA, Gentempo JA, Saenz LM, et al. Effect of two work practice changes on the microbial contamination rates of pharmacy-compounded sterile preparations. *Am J Health-Syst Pharm.* 2007; 64:837–41.
72. Sessink PJ, Boer KA, Scheefhals AP, et al. Occupational exposure to antineoplastic agents at several departments in a hospital: environmental contamination and excretion of cyclophosphamide and ifosfamide in urine of exposed workers. *Int Arch Occup Environ Health.* 1992; 64:105–12.
73. Kiffmeyer TK, Ing KG, Schoppe G. External contamination of cytotoxic drug packing: safe handling and cleaning procedures. *J Oncol Pharm Pract.* 2000; 6:13.
74. Connor TH, Sessink PJ, Harrison BR et al. Surface contamination of chemotherapy drug vials and evaluation of new vial-cleaning techniques: results of three studies. *Am J Health-Syst Pharm.* 2005; 62:475–84.
75. Kastango ES, Wagner JT, Kastango KB, et al. Generation of particulate matter during handling of needle and syringe packaging. *Am J Health-Syst Pharm.* 2008; 65:1443–50.
76. OSHA Hazard Communication Standard (revised 2012). www.osha.gov/dsg/hazcom/index.html. (accessed 2012 Dec 28).
77. National Institute for Occupational Safety and Health [NIOSH]. Medical surveillance for healthcare workers exposed to hazardous drugs. NIOSH Publication No. 2013-103; November 2012. www.cdc.gov/niosh/docs/wp-solutions/2013-103/ (accessed 2012 Dec 28).
78. Joint Council of Allergy, Asthma, and Immunology. Allergen Immunotherapy Extract Preparation Guidelines. www.jcaai.org/file_depot/0-10000000/20000-30000/27387/folder/62846/Allergen_Extract_Preparation_Guidelines.pdf (accessed 2012 Dec 28).
79. Radiopharmaceuticals for positron emission tomography—compounding (general information chapter 823). In: The United States pharmacopeia, 34th rev., and The national formulary, 29th ed. Rockville, MD: The United States Pharmacopeial Convention, 2011:385–9.
80. Thomas M, Sanborn MD, Couldry R. I.V. admixture contamination rates: Traditional practice site versus a class 1000 cleanroom. *Am J Health-Syst Pharm.* 2005; 62:2386–92.
81. Microbiological evaluation of clean rooms and other controlled environments (general information chapter 1116). In: The United States pharmacopeia, 34th rev., and The national formulary, 29th ed. Rockville, MD: The United States Pharmacopeial Convention; 2011: 633–41.
82. Agency for Healthcare Research and Quality Patient Safety Network (AHRQ PSNet). Patient safety primer: root cause analysis. www.psnet.ahrq.gov/primer.aspx?primerID=10 (accessed 2012 Dec 28).
83. DeRosier J, Stalhandske E, Bagian JP, et al. Using health care failure mode and effects analysis: the VA National Center for Patient Safety's prospective risk analysis system. *Jt Comm J Qual Improv.* 2002; 28: 248–67.

Approved by the ASHP Board of Directors on June 2, 2013. Developed through the ASHP Council on Pharmacy Practice. These guidelines supersede the ASHP Guidelines on Quality Assurance for Pharmacy-Prepared Sterile Products dated April 27, 2000.

Patricia C. Kienle, M.P.A., FASHP, is gratefully acknowledged for leading the development of and drafting substantial portions of these guidelines. Linda F. McElhiney, Pharm.D.; Richard B. Osteen, D.Ph.; Ed Troell, M.B.A.; Fred Massoomi, Pharm.D., FASHP; Kathleen Sheehy, M.B.A.; and Angela T. Cassano, Pharm.D., BCPS, are also gratefully acknowledged for their contributions to these guidelines.

ASHP gratefully acknowledges the following individuals for reviewing these guidelines (review does not imply endorsement): Caryn D. Bing, M.S., FASHP; E. Clyde Buchanan, M.S., FASHP; Ryan A. Forrey, Pharm.D., M.S.; Eric S. Kastango, M.B.A., FASHP; Lee B. Murdaugh, Ph.D.; Daryl McCollum, Pharm.D.; Luci A. Power, M.S.; Philip J. Schneider, M.S., FASHP; and James T. Wagner.

The bibliographic citation for this document is as follows: American Society of Health-System Pharmacists. ASHP Guidelines on Compounding Sterile Preparations. *Am J Health-Syst Pharm.* 2014; 71:145–66.

ASHP Guidelines on Handling Hazardous Drugs

In 1990, the American Society of Health-System Pharmacists (ASHP) published its revised technical assistance bulletin (TAB) on handling cytotoxic and hazardous drugs.[1] The information and recommendations contained in that document were current to June 1988. Continuing reports of workplace contamination and concerns for health care worker safety prompted the Occupational Safety and Health Administration (OSHA) to issue new guidelines on controlling occupational exposure to hazardous drugs in 1995.[2,3] In 2004, the National Institute for Occupational Safety and Health (NIOSH) issued the "NIOSH Alert: Preventing Occupational Exposure to Antineoplastic and Other Hazardous Drugs in Health Care Settings."[4] The following ASHP Guidelines on Handling Hazardous Drugs include information from these recommendations and are current to 2004.

Purpose

The purpose of these guidelines is to (1) update the reader on new and continuing concerns for health care workers handling hazardous drugs and (2) provide information on recommendations, including those regarding equipment, that have been developed since the publication of the previous TAB. Because studies have shown that contamination occurs in many settings, these guidelines should be implemented wherever hazardous drugs are received, stored, prepared, administered, or disposed.[2–7]

Comprehensive reviews of the literature covering anecdotal and case reports of surface contamination, worker contamination, and risk assessment are available from OSHA,[2,3] NIOSH,[4] and individual authors.[5–7] The primary goal of this document is to provide recommendations for the safe handling of hazardous drugs.

These guidelines represent the recommendations of many groups and individuals who have worked tirelessly over decades to reduce the potential harmful effects of hazardous drugs on health care workers. The research available to date, as well as the opinions of thought leaders in this area, is reflected in the guidelines. Where possible, recommendations are evidence based. In the absence of published data, professional judgment, experience, and common sense have been used.

Background

Workers may be exposed to a hazardous drug at many points during its manufacture, transport, distribution, receipt, storage, preparation, and administration, as well as during waste handling and equipment maintenance and repair. All workers involved in these activities have the potential for contact with uncontained drug.

Early concerns regarding the safety of workers handling potentially hazardous drugs focused on antineoplastic drugs when reports of second cancers in patients treated with these agents were coupled with the discovery of mutagenic substances in nurses who handled these drugs and cared for treated patients.[8,9] Exposure to these drugs in the workplace has been associated with acute and short-term reactions, as well as long-term effects. Anecdotal and case reports in the literature range from skin-related and ocular effects to flu-like symptoms and headache.[4,5,10–17] Two controlled surveys have reported significant increases in a number of symptoms, including sore throat, chronic cough, infections, dizziness, eye irritation, and headaches, among nurses, pharmacists, and pharmacy technicians routinely exposed to hazardous drugs in the workplace.[18,19] Reproductive studies on health care workers have shown an increase in fetal abnormalities, fetal loss, and fertility impairment resulting from occupational exposure to these potent drugs.[20–23] Antineoplastic drugs and immunosuppressants are some of the types of drugs included on lists of known or suspected human carcinogens by the National Toxicology Program[24] and the International Agency for Research on Cancer.[25] Although the increased incidence of cancers for occupationally exposed groups has been investigated with varying results,[26,27] a formal risk assessment of occupationally exposed pharmacy workers by Sessink et al.[28] estimated that cyclophosphamide causes an additional 1.4–10 cases of cancer per million workers each year. This estimate, which considered workplace contamination and worker contamination and excretion in combination with animal and patient studies, was based on a conservative exposure level. Connor et al.[29] found greater surface contamination in a study of U.S. and Canadian clinical settings than had been reported in European studies conducted by Sessink and colleagues.[30–32] Ensslin et al.[33] reported an almost fivefold greater daily average excretion of cyclophosphamide in their study than that reported by Sessink. These later findings could add 7–50 additional cancer cases per year per million workers to Sessink's estimate. From these and other studies that show variations in work practices and engineering controls,[34,35] it may be assumed that such variations contribute to differences in surface and worker contamination.

Routes of Exposure. Numerous studies showed the presence of hazardous drugs in the urine of health care workers.[30–34,36–41] Hazardous drugs enter the body through inhalation, accidental injection, ingestion of contaminated foodstuffs or mouth contact with contaminated hands, and dermal absorption. While inhalation might be suspected as the primary route of exposure, air sampling studies of pharmacy and clinic environments have often demonstrated low levels of or no airborne contaminants.[30–32,40] Recent concerns about the efficacy of the sampling methods[42] and the possibility that at least one of the marker drugs may be volatile[42–45] and thus not captured on the standard sampling filter leave the matter of inhalational exposure unresolved. Surface contamination studies do, however, suggest that dermal contact and absorption may be a primary route of exposure.[31,46] While some hazardous drugs are dermally absorbed, a 1992 report showed no detectable skin absorption of doxorubicin, daunorubicin, vincristine, vinblastine, or melphalan.[47] An alternative to dermal absorption is that surface contamination transferred to hands may be ingested via the hand-to-mouth route.[48,49] One or more of these routes might be responsible for workers' exposure.

Hazard Assessment. The risk to health care personnel from handling hazardous drugs is the result of a combination of the inherent toxicity of the drugs and the extent to which workers are exposed to the drugs in the course of their daily job activities. Both hazard identification (the qualitative evaluation of the toxicity of a given drug) and an exposure assessment (the amount of worker contact with the drug) are required to complete a hazard assessment. As the hazard assessment is specific to the safety program and safety equipment in place at a work site, a formal hazard assessment may not be available for most practitioners. An alternative is a performance-based, observational approach. Observation of current work practices, equipment, and the physical layout of work areas where hazardous drugs are handled at any given site will serve as an initial assessment of appropriate and inappropriate practices.[4]

Hazardous Drugs as Sterile Preparations

Many hazardous drugs are designed for parenteral administration, requiring aseptic reconstitution or dilution to yield a final sterile preparation. As such, the compounding of these products is regulated as pharmaceutical compounding by the *United States Pharmacopeia (USP)*, chapter 797.[50] The intent of chapter 797 is to protect patients from improperly compounded sterile preparations by regulating facilities, equipment, and work practices to ensure the sterility of extemporaneously compounded sterile preparations. Chapter 797 addresses not only the sterility of a preparation but also the accuracy of its composition. Because many hazardous drugs are very potent, there is little margin for error in compounding.

The initial version of chapter 797, released in early 2004, provided only minimal guidance for the handling of hazardous drugs, limiting this issue to a short discussion of chemotoxic agents in the document's section on aseptic technique. The chapter referred to standards established by the International Organization for Standardization (ISO)[51] that address the acceptable air quality (as measured by particulate counts) in the critical environment but failed to discuss airflow, air exchanges per hour, or pressure gradients of the ISO standards for cleanrooms and associated environments for compounding sterile products. The chapter did not describe the containment procedures necessary for compounding sterile hazardous agents, leaving it to the practitioner to simultaneously comply with the need to maintain a critical environment for compounded sterile products for patient safety while ensuring a contained environment for worker safety. The use of positive-pressure isolators for compounding hazardous drugs or placement of a Class II biological-safety cabinet (BSC) for use with hazardous drugs in a positive-pressure environment may result in airborne contamination of adjacent areas. Engineering assessment of designs of areas where this may occur should be done to address concerns of contaminant dissemination. Because hazardous drugs are also compounded in areas adjacent to patients and their family members (e.g., in chemotherapy infusion centers), inappropriate environmental containment puts them, as well as health care workers, at risk. Because *USP* review is a dynamic and ongoing process, future revisions are likely to address these concerns. Practitioners are encouraged to monitor the process and participate when appropriate.

Definition of Hazardous Drugs

The federal hazard communication standard (HCS) defines a hazardous chemical as any chemical that is a physical or health hazard.[52,53] A health hazard is defined as a chemical for which there is statistically significant evidence, based on at least one study conducted in accordance with established scientific principles, that acute or chronic health effects may occur in exposed employees. The HCS further notes that the term *health hazard* includes chemicals that are carcinogens, toxic or highly toxic agents, reproductive toxins, irritants, corrosives, sensitizers, and agents that produce target organ effects.

A 1990 ASHP TAB proposed criteria to determine which drugs should be considered hazardous and handled within an established safety program.[1] OSHA adopted these criteria in its 1995 guidelines, which were posted on its Web site in 1999.[2,3] The TAB's definition of hazardous drugs was revised by the NIOSH Working Group on Hazardous Drugs for the 2004 alert.[4] These definitions are compared in Table 1.

Each facility should create its own list of hazardous drugs based on specific criteria. Appendix A of the NIOSH alert contains related guidance and a sample list.[4] When drugs are purchased for the first time, they must be evaluated to determine whether they should be included in the facility's list of hazardous drugs. As the use and number of hazardous drugs increase, so too do the opportunities for health care worker exposure. Investigational drugs must be evaluated according to the information provided to the principal investigator. If the information provided is deemed insufficient to make an informed decision, the investigational drug should be considered hazardous until more information is available.

Recommendations

Safety Program. Policies and procedures for the safe handling of hazardous drugs must be in place for all situations in which these drugs are used throughout a facility. A comprehensive safety program must be developed that deals with all aspects of the safe handling of hazardous drugs. This program must be a collaborative effort, with input from all affected departments, such as pharmacy, nursing, medical staff, housekeeping, transportation, maintenance, employee health, risk management, industrial hygiene, clinical laboratories, and safety. A key element of this safety program is the Material Safety Data Sheet (MSDS) mandated by the HCS.[52,53] Employers are required to have an MSDS available for all hazardous agents in the workplace. A comprehensive safety program must include a process for monitoring and updating the MSDS database. When a hazardous drug is purchased for the first time, an MSDS must be received from the manufacturer or distributor. The MSDS should define the appropriate handling precautions, including protective equipment, controls, and spill management associated with the drug. Many MSDSs are available online through the specific manufacturer or through safety-information services.

Drugs that have been identified as requiring safe handling precautions should be clearly labeled at all times during their transport and use. The HCS applies to all workers, including those handling hazardous drugs at the manufac-

Table 1.
Comparison of 2004 NIOSH and 1990 ASHP Definitions of Hazardous Drugs[a]

NIOSH[4]	ASHP[1]
Carcinogenicity	Carcinogenicity in animal models, in the patient population, or both as reported by the International Agency for Research on Cancer
Teratogenicity or developmental toxicity[b]	Teratogenicity in animal studies or in treated patients
Reproductive toxicity[b]	Fertility impairment in animal studies or in treated patients
Organ toxicity at low doses[b]	Evidence of serious organ or other toxicity at low doses in animal models or treated patients
Genotoxicity[c]	Genotoxicity (i.e., mutagenicity and clastogenicity in short-term test systems)
Structure and toxicity profile of new drugs that mimic existing drugs determined hazardous by the above criteria	

[a]NIOSH = National Institute for Occupational Safety and Health, ASHP = American Society of Health-System Pharmacists.
[b]NIOSH's definition contains the following explanation: "All drugs have toxic side effects, but some exhibit toxicity at low doses. The level of toxicity reflects a continuum from relatively nontoxic to production of toxic effects in patients at low doses (for example, a few milligrams or less). For example, a daily therapeutic dose of 10 mg/day or a dose of 1 mg/kg/day in laboratory animals that produces serious organ toxicity, developmental toxicity, or reproductive toxicity has been used by the pharmaceutical industry to develop occupational exposure limits (OELs) of less than 10 micrograms/meter^3 after applying appropriate uncertainty factors. OELs in this range are typically established for potent or toxic drugs in the pharmaceutical industry. Under all circumstances, an evaluation of all available data should be conducted to protect health care workers."
[c]NIOSH's definition contains the following explanation: "In evaluating mutagenicity for potentially hazardous drugs, responses from multiple test systems are needed before precautions can be required for handling such agents. The EPA evaluations include the type of cells affected and *in vitro* versus *in vivo* testing."

turer and distributor levels. Employers are required to establish controls to ensure worker safety in all aspects of the distribution of these drugs.

The outside of the vials of many commercial drugs are contaminated by the time they are received in the pharmacy.[30,54,55] Although the possibility has not been studied, the contamination may extend to the inside of the packing cartons and onto the package inserts placed around the vial within the carton. Such contamination would present an exposure risk to anyone opening drug cartons or handling the vials, including workers receiving open or broken shipping cartons or selecting vials to be repackaged at a distribution point (e.g., a worker at the drug wholesaler selecting hazardous drugs for shipping containers or a pharmacy worker dividing a hazardous drug in a multidose container for repackaging into single-dose containers). These activities may present risks, especially for workers who too often receive inadequate safety training. Housekeepers and patient care assistants who handle drug waste and patient waste are also at risk and are not always included in the safe handling training required by safety programs. Safety programs must identify and include all workers who may be at risk of exposure.

The packaging (cartons, vials, ampuls) of hazardous drugs should be properly labeled by the manufacturer or distributor with a distinctive identifier that notifies personnel receiving them to wear appropriate personal protective equipment (PPE) during their handling. Sealing these drugs in plastic bags at the distributor level provides an additional level of safety for workers who are required to unpack cartons. Visual examination of such cartons for outward signs of damage or breakage is an important first step in the receiving process. Policies and procedures must be in place for handling damaged cartons or containers of hazardous drugs (e.g., returning the damaged goods to the distributor using appropriate containment techniques). These procedures should include the use of PPE, which must be supplied by the employer. As there may be no ventilation protection in the area where damaged containers are handled, the use of complete PPE, including an NIOSH-certified respirator, is recommended.[56,57] As required by OSHA, a complete respiratory program, including proper training and fit testing, must be completed by all staff required to use respirators.[56] Surgical masks do not provide adequate protection from the harmful effects of these drugs.

Labeling and Packaging from Point of Receipt. Drug packages, bins, shelves, and storage areas for hazardous drugs must bear distinctive labels identifying those drugs as requiring special handling precautions. Segregation of hazardous drug inventory from other drug inventory improves control and reduces the number of staff members potentially exposed to the danger. Hazardous drugs should be stored in an area with sufficient general exhaust ventilation to dilute and remove any airborne contaminants.[4] Hazardous drugs placed in inventory must be protected from potential breakage by storage in bins that have high fronts and on shelves that have guards to prevent accidental falling. The bins must also be appropriately sized to properly contain all stock. Care should be taken to separate hazardous drug inventory to reduce potential drug errors (e.g., pulling a look-alike vial from an adjacent drug bin). Because studies have shown that contamination on the drug vial itself is a consideration,[30,54,55] all staff members must wear double gloves when stocking and inventorying these drugs and selecting hazardous drug packages for further handling. All transport of hazardous drug packages must be done in a manner to reduce environmental contamination in the event of accidental dropping. Hazardous drug packages must be placed in sealed containers and labeled with a unique identifier. Carts or other transport devices must be designed with guards to protect against falling and breakage. All individuals transporting hazardous drugs must have safety training that includes spill control and have spill kits immediately accessible. Staff handling hazardous drugs or cleaning areas where hazardous drugs are stored or handled must be trained to recognize the unique identifying labels used to distinguish these drugs and areas. Warning labels and signs must be clear to non-English readers. All personnel who work with or around hazardous drugs must be trained to appropriately perform their jobs using the established precautions and required PPE.[52]

Environment. Hazardous drugs should be compounded in a controlled area where access is limited to authorized personnel trained in handling requirements. Due to the hazardous nature of these preparations, a contained environment where air pressure is negative to the surrounding areas or that is protected by an airlock or anteroom is preferred. Positive-pressure environments for hazardous drug compounding should be avoided or augmented with an appropriately designed antechamber because of the potential spread of airborne contamination from contaminated packaging, poor handling technique, and spills.

Only individuals trained in the administration of hazardous drugs should do so. During administration, access to the administration area should be limited to patients receiving therapy and essential personnel. Eating, drinking, applying makeup, and the presence of foodstuffs should be avoided in patient care areas while hazardous drugs are administered. For inpatient therapy, where lengthy administration techniques may be required, hanging or removing hazardous drugs should be scheduled to reduce exposure of family members and ancillary staff and to avoid the potential contamination of dietary trays and personnel.

Because much of the compounding and administration of hazardous drugs throughout the United States is done in outpatient or clinic settings with patients and their family members near the compounding area, care must be taken to minimize environmental contamination and to maximize the effectiveness of cleaning (decontamination) activities. The design of such areas must include surfaces that are readily cleaned and decontaminated. Upholstered and carpeted surfaces should be avoided, as they are not readily cleaned. Several studies have shown floor contamination and the ineffectiveness of cleaning practices on both floors and surfaces.[29,30,46] Break rooms and refreshment areas for staff, patients, and others should be located away from areas of potential contamination to reduce unnecessary exposure to staff, visitors, and others.

Hazardous drugs may also be administered in nontraditional locations, such as the operating room, which present challenges to training and containment. Intracavitary administration of hazardous drugs (e.g., into the bladder, peritoneal cavity, or chest cavity) frequently requires equipment for which locking connections may not be readily available or even possible. All staff members who handle hazardous drugs should receive safety training that includes recognition of hazardous drugs and appropriate spill response. Hazardous drug spill kits, containment bags, and disposal containers must be available in all areas where hazardous drugs are handled. Techniques and ancillary devices that minimize the risk of open systems should be used when administering hazardous drugs through unusual routes or in nontraditional locations.

Ventilation Controls. Ventilation or engineering controls are devices designed to eliminate or reduce worker exposure to chemical, biological, radiological, ergonomic, and physical hazards. Ventilated cabinets are a type of ventilation or engineering control designed for the purpose of worker protection.[4] These devices minimize worker exposure by controlling the emission of airborne contaminants. Depending on the design, ventilated cabinets may also be used to provide the critical environment necessary to compound sterile preparations. When asepsis is not required, a Class I BSC or a containment isolator may be used to handle hazardous drugs. When sterile hazardous drugs are being compounded, a Class II or III BSC or an isolator intended for aseptic preparation and containment is required.[4] Recommendations for work practices specific to BSCs and isolators are discussed later in these guidelines.

Class II BSCs. In the early 1980s, the Class II BSC was determined to reduce the exposure of pharmacy compounding staff to hazardous preparations, as measured by the mutational response to the Ames test by urine of exposed subjects.[58,59] Studies in the 1990s, using analytical methods significantly more specific and sensitive than the Ames test, indicated that environmental and worker contamination occurs in workplace settings despite the use of controls recommended in published guidelines, including the use of Class II BSCs.[29–35,37–41,60,61] The exact cause of contamination has yet to be determined. Studies have shown that (1) there is contamination on the outside of vials received from manufacturers and distributors,[30,54,55] (2) work practices required to maximize the effectiveness of the Class II BSC are neglected or not taught,[32,46] and (3) the potential vaporization of hazardous drug solutions may reduce the effectiveness of the high-efficiency particulate air (HEPA) filter in providing containment.[42–45] Studies of surface contamination have discovered deposits of hazardous drugs on the floor in front of the Class II BSC, indicating that drug may have escaped through the open front of the BSC onto contaminated gloves or the final product or into the air.[29–32]

Workers must understand that the Class II BSC does not prevent the generation of contamination within the cabinet and that the effectiveness of such cabinets in containing hazardous drug contamination depends on operators' use of proper technique.

Some Class II BSCs recirculate airflow within the cabinet or exhaust contaminated air back into the work environment through HEPA filters.[62] The Class II BSC is designed with air plenums that are unreachable for surface decontamination; the plenum under the work tray collects room dirt and debris that mix with hazardous drug residue when the BSC is operational.[1] Drafts, supply-air louvers, and other laminar flow equipment placed near the BSC can interfere with the containment properties of the inflow air barrier, resulting in contamination of the work environment.[63] More information on the design and use of Class II BSCs is available from the NSF International (NSF)/American National Standards Institute (ANSI) standard 49-04.[62] Recommendations for use of Class II BSCs are listed in Appendix A.

Alternatives to Class II BSCs. Alternatives to the open-front Class II BSC include the Class III BSC, glove boxes, and isolators. By definition, a Class III BSC is a totally enclosed, ventilated cabinet of leak-tight construction.[64] Operations in the cabinet are conducted through fixed-glove access. The cabinet is maintained under negative air pressure. Supply air is drawn into the cabinet through HEPA filters. The exhaust air is treated by double HEPA filtration or by HEPA filtration and incineration. The Class III BSC is designed for use with highly toxic or infectious material. Because of the costs of purchasing and operating a Class III BSC, it is seldom used for extemporaneous compounding of sterile products.

Less rigorous equipment with similar fixed-glove access include glove boxes and isolators. Although standardized definitions and criteria exist for glove boxes, these guidelines currently focus on applications in the nuclear industry and not on compounding hazardous drugs.[65] There are no standardized definitions or criteria for pharmaceutical compounding applications for this equipment and no performance standards determined by an independent organization to aid the purchaser in the selection process. NIOSH recommends that only ventilated engineering controls be used to compound hazardous drugs and that these controls be designed for containment.[4] NIOSH defines these controls and details their use and selection criteria as well as recommendations for airflow, exhaust, and maintenance. NIOSH further differentiates between ventilated engineering controls used for hazard containment that are intended for use with sterile products (aseptic containment) and those for use with nonsterile handling of hazardous drugs.[4]

An isolator may be considered a ventilated controlled environment that has fixed walls, floor, and ceiling. For aseptic use, supply air must be drawn through a high-efficiency (minimum HEPA) filter. Exhaust air must also be high-efficiency filtered and should be exhausted to the outside of the facility, not to the workroom. Workers access the isolator's work area, or main chamber, through gloves, sleeves, and air locks or pass-throughs. Currently available isolators have either unidirectional or turbulent airflow within the main chamber. For compounding sterile preparations, the filtered air and airflow must achieve an ISO class 5 (former FS-209E class 100) environment within the isolator.[50,51,66,67] Isolators for sterile compounding have become increasingly popular as a way to minimize the challenges of a traditional cleanroom and some of the disadvantages of the Class II BSC.[50,68–70] The totally enclosed design may reduce the escape of contamination during the compounding process. The isolator may be less sensitive to drafts and other laminar-airflow equipment, including positive-pressure environments. Issues unique to isolators include pressure changes when accessing the fixed-glove assembly, pressure changes in the main chamber when accessing the antechamber or pass-through, positive- versus negative-pressure isolators used to compound hazardous drugs, and ergonomic considerations associated with a fixed-glove assembly. Many isolators produce less heat and noise than Class II BSCs.[68] The Controlled Environment Testing Association has developed an applications guide for isolators in health care facilities.[71]

Isolators, like Class II BSCs, do not prevent the generation of contamination within the cabinet workspace, and their effectiveness in containing contamination depends on proper technique.[72] The potential for the spread of hazardous drug contamination from the pass-through and main chamber of the isolator to the workroom may be reduced by surface decontamination, but no wipe-down procedures have been studied. Surface decontamination may be more readily conducted in isolators than in Class II BSCs. (See *Decontamination, deactivation, and cleaning* for more information.)

Recirculating isolators depend on high-efficiency (HEPA or ultra-low penetrating air [ULPA]) filters. These filters may not sufficiently remove volatile hazardous drug contamination from the airflow. Isolators that discharge air into the workroom, even through high-efficiency filters, present exposure concerns similar to those of unvented Class II BSCs if there is a possibility that the hazardous drugs handled in them may vaporize. Isolators used for compounding hazardous drugs should be at negative pressure or use a pressurized air lock to the surrounding areas to improve containment. Some isolators rely on a low-particulate environment rather than laminar-airflow technology to protect the sterility of the preparations. Recommendations for use of Class III BSCs and isolators are summarized in Appendix B.

Closed-system drug-transfer devices. Closed-system drug-transfer devices mechanically prevent the transfer of environmental contaminants into the system and the escape of drug or vapor out of the system.[4] ADD-Vantage and Duplex devices are closed-system drug-transfer devices currently available for injectable antibiotics. A similar system that may offer increased environmental protection for hazardous drugs is a proprietary, closed-system drug-transfer device known as PhaSeal. This multicomponent system uses a double membrane to enclose a specially cut injection cannula as it moves into a drug vial, Luer-Lok, or infusion-set connector.

Several studies have shown a reduction in environmental contamination with marker hazardous drugs during both compounding and administration when comparing standard techniques for handling hazardous drugs with the use of PhaSeal.[73–78] It should be noted, however, that PhaSeal components cannot be used to compound all hazardous drugs.

In 1984, Hoy and Stump[79] concluded that a commercial air-venting device reduced the release of drug aerosols during reconstitution of drugs packaged in vials. The testing was limited to visual analysis. The venting device does not lock onto the vial, which allows it to be transferred from one vial to another. This practice creates an opportunity for both environmental and product contamination. Many devices labeled as "chemo adjuncts" are currently available. Many feature a filtered, vented spike to facilitate reconstituting and removing hazardous drugs during the compounding process. However, none of these devices may be considered a closed-system drug-transfer device, and none has been formally studied with the results published in peer-reviewed journals. As other products become available, they should meet the definition of closed-system drug-transfer devices established by NIOSH[4] and should be required to demonstrate their effectiveness in independent studies. Closed-system drug-transfer devices (or any other ancillary devices) are not a substitute for using a ventilated cabinet.

Personal Protective Equipment. *Gloves.* Gloves are essential for handling hazardous drugs. Gloves must be worn at all times when handling drug packaging, cartons, and vials, including while performing inventory control procedures and when gathering hazardous drugs and supplies for compounding a batch or single dose. During compounding in a Class II BSC, gloves and gowns are required to prevent skin surfaces from coming into contact with these agents. Studies of gloves indicate that many latex and nonlatex materials are effective protection against penetration and permeation by most hazardous drugs.[80–84] Recent concerns about latex sensitivity have prompted testing of newer glove materials. Gloves made of nitrile or neoprene rubber and polyurethane have been successfully tested using a battery of antineoplastic drugs.[82–84] The American Society for Testing and Materials (ASTM) has developed testing standards for assessing the resistance of medical gloves to permeation by chemotherapy drugs.[85] Gloves that meet this standard earn the designation of "chemotherapy gloves." Gloves selected for use with hazardous drugs should meet this ASTM standard.

Connor and Xiang[86] studied the effect of isopropyl alcohol on the permeability of latex and nitrile gloves exposed to antineoplastic agents. During the limited study period of 30 minutes, they found that the use of isopropyl alcohol during cleaning and decontaminating did not appear to affect the integrity of either material when challenged with six antineoplastic agents.

In most glove-testing systems, the glove material remains static, in contrast to the stressing and flexing that occur during actual use. In one study designed to examine glove permeability under static and flexed conditions, no significant difference in permeation was reported, except in thin latex examination gloves.[87] Another study, however, detected permeation of antineoplastic drugs through latex gloves during actual working conditions by using a cotton glove under the latex glove.[88] The breakthrough time for cyclophosphamide was only 10 minutes. The authors speculated that the cotton glove may have acted as a wick, drawing the hazardous drug through the outer glove. Nonetheless, under actual working conditions, double gloving and wearing gloves no longer than 30 minutes are prudent practices.

Permeability of gloves to hazardous drugs has been shown to be dependent on the drug, glove material and thickness, and exposure time. Powder-free gloves are preferred because powder particulates can contaminate the sterile processing area and absorb hazardous drug contaminants, which may increase the potential for dermal contact. Hands should be thoroughly washed before donning gloves and after removing them. Care must be taken when removing gloves in order to prevent the spreading of hazardous drug contaminants.

Several studies have indicated that contamination of the outside of gloves with hazardous drug is common after compounding and that this contamination may be spread to other surfaces during the compounding process.[30–33,39] Studies have also shown that hazardous drug contamination may lead to dermal absorption by workers not actively involved in the compounding and administration of hazardous drugs.[30,88] The use of two pairs of gloves is recommended when compounding these drugs. In an isolator, one additional pair of gloves must be worn within the fixed-glove assembly.[68]

Once compounding has been completed and the final preparation surface decontaminated, the outer glove should be removed and contained inside the BSC. The inner glove is worn to affix labels and place the preparation into a sealable containment bag for transport. This must be done within the BSC. In the isolator, the fixed gloves must be surface cleaned before wiping down the final preparation, placing the label onto the preparation, and placing it into the pass-through. The inner gloves should be worn to complete labeling and to place the final preparation into a transport bag in the pass-through. The inner gloves may then be removed and contained in a sealable bag within the pass-through. If the final check is conducted by a second staff member, fresh gloves must be donned before handling the completed preparation.

During batch compounding, gloves should be changed at least every 30 minutes. Gloves (at least the outer gloves) must be changed whenever it is necessary to exit and re-enter the BSC. For aseptic protection of sterile preparations, the outer gloves must be sanitized with an appropriate disinfectant when reentering the BSC. Gloves must also be changed immediately if torn, punctured, or knowingly contaminated. When wearing two pairs of gloves in the BSC, one pair is worn under the gown cuff and the second pair placed over the cuff. When removing the gloves, the contaminated glove fingers must only touch the outer surface of the glove, never the inner surface. If the inner glove becomes contaminated, then both pairs of gloves must be changed. When removing any PPE, care must be taken to avoid introducing hazardous drug contamination into the environment. Both the inner and outer gloves should be considered contaminated, and glove surfaces must never touch the skin or any surface that may be touched by the unprotected skin of others. Gloves used to handle hazardous drugs should be placed in a sealable plastic bag for containment within the BSC or isolator pass-through before disposal as contaminated waste.

If an i.v. set is attached to the final preparation in the BSC or isolator, care must be taken to avoid contaminating the tubing with hazardous drug from the surface of the gloves, BSC, or isolator.

Class III BSCs and isolators are equipped with attached gloves or gauntlets. They should be considered contaminated once the BSC or isolator has been used for compounding hazardous drugs. For compounding sterile preparations, attached gloves or gauntlets must be routinely sanitized per the manufacturer's instructions to prevent microbial contamination. Hazardous drug contamination from the gloves or gauntlets may be transferred to the surfaces of all items within the cabinet. Glove and gauntlet surfaces must be cleaned after compounding is complete. All final preparations must be surface decontaminated by staff, wearing clean gloves to avoid spreading contamination.[68] Recommendations for use of gloves are summarized in Appendix C.

Gowns. Gowns or coveralls are worn during the compounding of sterile preparations to protect the preparation from the worker, to protect the worker from the preparation, or both. The selection of gowning materials depends on the goal of the process. Personal protective gowns are recommended during the handling of hazardous drug preparations to protect the worker from inadvertent exposure to extraneous drug particles on surfaces or generated during the compounding process.

Guidelines for the safe handling of hazardous drugs recommend the use of gowns for compounding in the BSC, administration, spill control, and waste management to protect the worker from contamination by fugitive drug generated during the handling process.[1–4,89,90] Early recommendations for barrier protective gowns required that they be disposable and made of a lint-free, low-permeability fabric with a closed front, long sleeves, and tight-fitting elastic or knit cuffs.[1] Washable garments (e.g., laboratory coats, scrubs, and cloth gowns) absorb fluids and provide no barrier against hazardous drug absorption and permeation. Studies into the effectiveness of disposable gowns in resisting permeation by hazardous drugs found variation in the protection provided by commercially available materials. In an evaluation of polypropylene-based gowns, Connor[91] found that polypropylene spun-bond nonwoven material alone and polypropylene–polyethylene copolymer spun-bond provided little protection against permeation by a battery of aqueous-

and nonaqueous- based hazardous drugs. Various constructions of polypropylene (e.g., spun-bond/melt-blown/spun-bond) result in materials that are completely impermeable or only slightly permeable to hazardous drugs. Connor[91] noted that these coated materials are similar in appearance to several other nonwoven materials but perform differently and that workers could expect to be protected from exposure for up to four hours when using the coated gowning materials. Harrison and Kloos[92] reported similar findings in a study of six disposable gowning materials and 15 hazardous drugs. Only gowns with polyethylene or vinyl coatings provided adequate splash protection and prevented drug permeation. In a subjective assessment of worker comfort, the more protective gowns were found to be warmer and thus less comfortable. These findings agree with an earlier study that found that the most protective gowning materials were the most uncomfortable to wear.[93] Resistance to the use of gowns, especially by nurses during administration of hazardous drugs, has been reported.[94] The lack of comfort could cause resistance to behavioral change.

Researchers have looked at gown contamination with fluorescent scans, high-performance liquid chromatography, and tandem mass spectrometry.[39,95] In one study, researchers scanned nurses and pharmacists wearing gowns during the compounding and administration of hazardous drugs.[95] Of a total of 18 contamination spots detected, 5 were present on the gowns of nurses after drug administration. No spots were discovered on the gowns of pharmacists after compounding. In contrast, researchers using a more sensitive assay placed pads in various body locations, both over and under the gowns used by the subjects during compounding and administration of cyclophosphamide and ifosfamide.[39] Workers wore short-sleeved nursing uniforms, disposable or cotton gowns, and vinyl or latex gloves. More contamination was found during compounding than administration. Contamination found on the pads placed on the arms of preparers is consistent with the design and typical work practices used in a Class II BSC, where the hands and arms are extended into the contaminated work area of the cabinet. Remarkably, one preparer had contamination on the back of the gown, possibly indicating touch contamination with the Class II BSC during removal of the final product. While early guidelines do not contain a maximum length of time that a gown should be worn, Connor's[91] work would support a two- to three-hour window for a coated gown. Contamination of gowns during glove changes must be a consideration. If the inner pair of gloves requires changing, a gown change should be considered. Gowns worn as barrier protection in the compounding of hazardous drugs must never be worn outside the immediate preparation area. Gowns worn during administration should be changed when leaving the patient care area and immediately if contaminated. Gowns should be removed carefully and properly disposed of as contaminated waste to avoid becoming a source of contamination to other staff and the environment.

Hazardous drug compounding in an enclosed environment, such as a Class III BSC or an isolator, may not require the operator to wear a gown. However, because the process of handling drug vials and final preparations, as well as accessing the isolator's pass-throughs, may present an opportunity for contamination, the donning of a gown is prudent. Coated gowns may not be necessary for this use if appropriate gowning practices are established. Recommendations for use of gowns are summarized in Appendix D.

Additional PPE. Eye and face protection should be used whenever there is a possibility of exposure from splashing or uncontrolled aerosolization of hazardous drugs (e.g., when containing a spill or handling a damaged shipping carton). In these instances, a face shield, rather than safety glasses or goggles, is recommended because of the improved skin protection afforded by the shield.

Similar circumstances also warrant the use of a respirator. All workers who may use a respirator must be fit-tested and trained to use the appropriate respirator according to the OSHA Respiratory Protection Standard.[56,57] A respirator of correct size and appropriate to the aerosol size, physical state (i.e., particulate or vapor), and concentration of the airborne drug must be available at all times. Surgical masks do not provide respiratory protection. Shoe and hair coverings should be worn during the sterile compounding process to minimize particulate contamination of the critical work zone and the preparation.[50] With the potential for hazardous drug contamination on the floor in the compounding and administration areas, shoe coverings are recommended as contamination-control mechanisms. Shoe coverings must be removed with gloved hands when leaving the compounding area. Gloves should be worn and care must be taken when removing hair or shoe coverings to prevent contamination from spreading to clean areas. Hair and shoe coverings used in the hazardous drug handling areas must be contained, along with used gloves, and discarded as contaminated waste.

Work Practices. *Compounding sterile hazardous drugs.* Work practices for the compounding of sterile hazardous drugs differ somewhat with the use of a Class II BSC, a Class III BSC, or an isolator. Good organizational skills are essential to minimize contamination and maximize productivity. All activities not requiring a critical environment (e.g., checking labels, doing calculations) should be completed before accessing the BSC or isolator. All items needed for compounding must be gathered before beginning work. This practice should eliminate the need to exit the BSC or isolator once compounding has begun. Two pairs of gloves should be worn to gather hazardous drug vials and supplies. These gloves should be carefully removed and discarded. Fresh gloves must be donned and appropriately sanitized before aseptic manipulation.

Only supplies and drugs essential to compounding the dose or batch should be placed in the work area of the BSC or main chamber of the isolator. BSCs and isolators should not be overcrowded to avoid unnecessary hazardous drug contamination. Luer-Lok syringes and connections must be used whenever possible for manipulating hazardous drugs, as they are less likely to separate during compounding.

Spiking an i.v. set into a solution containing hazardous drugs or priming an i.v. set with hazardous drug solution in an uncontrolled environment must be avoided. One recommendation is to attach and prime the appropriate i.v. set to the final container in the BSC or isolator before adding the hazardous drug. Closed-system drug-transfer devices should achieve a dry connection between the administration set and the hazardous drug's final container. This connection allows the container to be spiked with a secondary i.v. set and the set to be primed by backflow from a primary nonhazardous solution. This process may be done outside the BSC or isolator, reducing the potential for surface contamination of the i.v. set during the compounding process. A new i.v. set must be used with each dose of hazardous drug. Once attached, the i.v. set must never be removed from a hazardous drug dose, thereby preventing the residual fluid in the bag, bottle, or tubing from leaking and contaminating personnel and the environment.

Transport bags must never be placed in the BSC or in the isolator work chamber during compounding to avoid inadvertent contamination of the outer surface of the bag. Final preparations must be surface decontaminated after compounding is complete. In either the BSC or isolator, clean inner gloves must be worn when labeling and placing the final preparation into the transport bag. Handling final preparations and transport bags with gloves contaminated with hazardous drugs will result in the transfer of the contamination to other workers. Don fresh gloves whenever there is a doubt as to the cleanliness of the inner or outer gloves.

Working in BSCs or isolators. With or without ancillary devices, none of the available ventilation or engineering controls can provide 100% protection for the worker. Workers must recognize the limitations of the equipment and address them through appropriate work practices.[1] The effectiveness of Class II BSCs and isolators in containing contamination depends on proper technique.[72] Hazardous drug contamination from the work area of the isolator may be brought into the workroom environment through the pass-throughs or air locks and on the surfaces of items removed from the isolators (e.g., the final preparation). Surface decontamination of the preparation before removal from the isolator's main chamber should reduce the hazardous drug contamination that could be transferred to the workroom, but no wipe-down procedures have been studied. Surface decontamination may be accomplished using alcohol, sterile water, peroxide, or sodium hypochlorite solutions, provided the packaging is not permeable to the solution and the labels remain legible and intact. Recommendations for working in BSCs and isolators are summarized in Appendix E.

<u>BSCs.</u> Class II BSCs use vertical-flow, HEPA-filtered air (ISO class 5) as their controlled aseptic environment. Before beginning an operation in a Class II BSC, personnel should wash their hands, don an inner pair of appropriate gloves, and then don a coated gown followed by a second pair of gloves. The work surface should be cleaned of surface contamination with detergent, sodium hypochlorite, and neutralizer or disinfected with alcohol, depending on when it was last cleaned. For the Class II BSC, the front shield must be lowered to the proper level to protect the face and eyes. The operator should be seated so that his or her shoulders are at the level of the bottom of the front shield. All drugs and supplies needed to aseptically compound a dose or batch should be gathered and sanitized with 70% alcohol or appropriate disinfectant. Avoid exiting and reentering the work area. Being careful not to place any sterile objects below them, i.v. bags and bottles may be hung from the bar. All items must be placed well within the Class II BSC, away from the unfiltered air at the front barrier. By design, the intended work zone within the Class II BSC is the area between the front and rear air grilles. The containment characteristics of the Class II BSC are dependent on the airflow through both the front and back grilles; these grilles should never be obstructed. Due to the design of the Class II BSC, the quality of HEPA-filtered air is lowest at the sides of the work zone, so manipulations should be performed at least six inches away from each sidewall in the horizontal plane. A small waste–sharps container may be placed along the sidewall toward the back of the BSC. One study has suggested that a plastic-backed absorbent preparation pad in a Class II BSC may interfere with airflow,[39] but another study determined that use of a flat firm pad that did not block the grilles of the cabinet had no effect on airflow.[96] The use of a large pad that might block the front or rear grilles must be avoided. In addition, because a pad may absorb small spills, it may become a source of hazardous drug contamination for anything placed upon it. Preparation pads are not readily decontaminated and must be replaced and discarded after preparation of each batch and frequently during extended batch compounding. More information on the design and use of Class II BSCs is available from the NSF/ANSI standard 49-04.[62]

<u>Isolators.</u> For work in an isolator, all drugs and supplies needed to aseptically compound a dose or batch should be gathered and sanitized with 70% alcohol or appropriate disinfectant and readied for placement in the pass-through. A technique described in the literature involves the use of a tray that will fit into the pass-through.[97] A large primary sealable bag is placed over the tray. Labels and a second sealable (transport) bag, which is used to contain the final preparation, are placed into the primary sealable bag on the tray surface. Vials, syringes, needles, and other disposables are placed on top of the sealed bag. The enclosed tray is then taken into the main chamber of the isolator, where the drug and supplies are used to compound the dose. The contaminated materials, including the primary sealable bag, are removed using the closed trash system of the isolator, if so equipped, or sealed into a second bag and removed via the pass-through for disposal as contaminated waste. The dose is then labeled and placed into the second sealable bag for transport.

This technique does not address contamination on the isolator gloves or gauntlets. Additional work practices may include cleaning off the gloves or gauntlets and final preparation after initial compounding and before handling the label and second sealable bag. Care must be taken when transferring products out of the pass-through and disposing of waste through the pass-through or trash chute to avoid accidental contamination.

Aseptic technique. Stringent aseptic technique, described by Wilson and Solimando[98] in 1981, remains the foundation of any procedure involving the use of needles and syringes in manipulating sterile dosage forms. This technique, when performed in conjunction with negative pressure technique, minimizes the escape of drug from vials and ampuls. Needleless devices have been developed to reduce the risk of blood-borne pathogen exposure through needle sticks. None of these devices has been tested for reduction of hazardous drug contamination. The appropriateness of these devices in the safe handling of hazardous drugs has not been determined.

In reconstituting hazardous drugs in vials, it is critical to avoid pressurizing the contents of the vial. Pressurization may cause the drug to spray out around the needle or through a needle hole or a loose seal, aerosolizing the drug into the work zone. Pressurization can be avoided by creating a slight negative pressure in the vial. Too much negative pressure, however, can cause leakage from the needle when it is withdrawn from the vial. The safe handling of hazardous drug solutions in vials or ampuls requires the use of a syringe that is no more than three-fourths full when filled with the solution, which minimizes the risk of the plunger separating from the syringe barrel. Once the diluent is drawn up, the needle is inserted into the vial and the plunger is pulled back (to create a slight negative pressure inside the vial), so that air is drawn into the syringe. Small amounts of diluent should be transferred slowly as equal volumes of air are removed. The needle should be kept in the vial, and the contents should be swirled carefully until dissolved. With the vial inverted, the proper amount of drug solution should be gradually withdrawn while equal volumes of air are exchanged for solution. The exact volume needed must be measured while the needle is in the vial, and any excess drug should remain in the vial. With the vial in the upright position, the plunger should be withdrawn past the original starting point to again induce a slight negative pressure before removing the needle. The needle hub should be clear before the needle is removed.

If a hazardous drug is transferred to an i.v. bag, care must be taken to puncture only the septum of the injection port and avoid puncturing the sides of the port or bag. After the drug solution is injected into the i.v. bag, the i.v. port, container, and set (if attached by pharmacy in the BSC or isolator) should be surface decontaminated. The final preparation should be labeled, including an auxiliary warning, and the injection port covered with a protective shield. The final container should be placed, using clean gloves, into a sealable bag to contain any leakage.[1]

To withdraw hazardous drugs from an ampul, the neck or top portion should be gently tapped.[98] After the neck is wiped with alcohol, a 5-µm filter needle or straw should be attached to a syringe that is large enough that it will be not more than three-fourths full when holding the drug. The fluid should then be drawn through the filter needle or straw and cleared from the needle and hub. After this, the needle or straw is exchanged for a needle of similar gauge and length; any air and excess drug should be ejected into a sterile vial (leaving the desired volume in the syringe); aerosolization should be avoided. The drug may then be transferred to an i.v. bag or bottle. If the dose is to be dispensed in the syringe, the plunger should be drawn back to clear fluid from the needle and hub. The needle should be replaced with a locking cap, and the syringe should be surface decontaminated and labeled.

Training and demonstration of competence. All staff who will be compounding hazardous drugs must be trained in the stringent aseptic and negative-pressure techniques necessary for working with sterile hazardous drugs. Once trained, staff must demonstrate competence by an objective method, and competency must be reassessed on a regular basis.[99]

Preparation and handling of noninjectable hazardous drug dosage forms. Although noninjectable dosage forms of hazardous drugs contain varying proportions of drug to nondrug (nonhazardous) components, there is the potential for personnel exposure to and environmental contamination with the hazardous components if hazardous drugs are handled (e.g., packaged) by pharmacy staff. Although most hazardous drugs are not available in liquid formulations, such formulations are often prescribed for small children and adults with feeding tubes. Recipes for extemporaneously compounded oral liquids may start with the parenteral form, or they may require that tablets be crushed or capsules opened. Tablet trituration has been shown to cause fine dust formation and local environmental contamination.[100] Procedures for the preparation and the use of equipment (e.g., Class I BSCs or bench-top hoods with HEPA filters) must be developed to avoid the release of aerosolized powder or liquid into the environment during manipulation of hazardous drugs. Recommendations for preparation and handling of noninjectable hazardous drug dosage forms are summarized in Appendix F.

Decontamination, deactivation, and cleaning. Decontamination may be defined as cleaning or deactivating. Deactivating a hazardous substance is preferred, but no single process has been found to deactivate all currently available hazardous drugs. The use of alcohol for disinfecting the BSC or isolator will not deactivate any hazardous drugs and may result in the spread of contamination rather than any actual cleaning.[30,47]

Decontamination of BSCs and isolators should be conducted per manufacturer recommendations. The MSDSs for many hazardous drugs recommend sodium hypochlorite solution as an appropriate deactivating agent.[101] Researchers have shown that strong oxidizing agents, such as sodium hypochlorite, are effective deactivators of many hazardous drugs.[102,103] There is currently one commercially available product, SurfaceSafe (SuperGen, Dublin, CA), that provides a system for decontamination and deactivation using sodium hypochlorite, detergent, and thiosulfate neutralizer. A ventilated cabinet that runs continuously should be cleaned before the day's operations begin and at regular intervals or when the day's work is completed. For a 24-hour service, the cabinet should be cleaned two or three times daily. Cabinets used for aseptic compounding must be disinfected at the beginning of the workday, at the beginning of each subsequent shift (if compounding takes place over an extended period of time), and routinely during compounding.

Appropriate preparation of materials used in compounding before introduction into the Class II BSC or the pass-through of a Class III BSC or isolator, including spraying or wiping with 70% alcohol or appropriate disinfectant, is also necessary for aseptic compounding.

The Class II BSC has air plenums that handle contaminated air. These plenums are not designed to allow surface decontamination, and many of the contaminated surfaces (plenums) cannot be reached for surface cleaning. The area under the work tray should be cleaned at least monthly to reduce the contamination level in the Class II BSC (and in isolators, where appropriate).

Surface decontamination may be accomplished by the transfer of hazardous drug contamination from the surface of a nondisposable item to disposable ones (e.g., wipes, gauze, towels). Although the outer surface of vials containing hazardous drugs has been shown to be contaminated with hazardous drugs,[30,54,55] and hazardous drug contamination has been found on the outside of final preparations,[30] no wipe-down procedures have been studied. The amount of hazardous drug contamination placed into the BSC or isolator may be reduced by surface decontamination (i.e., wiping down) of hazardous drug vials. While no wipe-down procedures have been studied, the use of gauze moistened with alcohol, sterile water, peroxide, or sodium hypochlorite solutions may be effective. The disposable item, once contaminated, must be contained and discarded as contaminated waste.

Administration of hazardous drugs. Policies and procedures governing the administration of hazardous drugs must be jointly developed by nursing and pharmacy for the mutual safety of health care workers. These policies should supplement policies designed to protect patient safety during administration of all drugs. All policies affecting multiple departments must be developed with input from managers and workers from the affected areas. Extensive nursing guidelines for the safe and appropriate administration of hazardous drugs have been developed by the Oncology Nursing Society[90,104] and OSHA.[2,3] Recommendations for reducing exposure to hazardous drugs during administration in all practice settings are listed in Appendix G.

Spill management. Policies and procedures must be developed to attempt to prevent spills and to govern cleanup of hazardous drug spills. Written procedures must specify who is responsible for spill management and must address the size and scope of the spill. Spills must be contained and cleaned up immediately by trained workers.

Spill kits containing all of the materials needed to clean up spills of hazardous drugs should be assembled or purchased (Appendix H). These kits should be readily available in all areas where hazardous drugs are routinely handled. A spill kit should accompany delivery of injectable hazardous drugs to patient care areas even though they are transported in a sealable plastic bag or container. If hazardous drugs are being prepared or administered in a nonroutine area (e.g., home setting, unusual patient care area), a spill kit and respirator must be obtained by the drug handler. Signs should be available to warn of restricted access to the spill area.

Only trained workers with appropriate PPE and respirators should attempt to manage a hazardous drug spill. All workers who may be required to clean up a spill of hazardous drugs must receive proper training in spill management and in the use of PPE and NIOSH-certified respirators.

The circumstances and handling of spills should be documented. Staff and nonemployees exposed to a hazardous drug spill should also complete an incident report or exposure form and report to the designated emergency service for initial evaluation.

All spill materials must be disposed of as hazardous waste.[105] Recommendations for spill cleanup procedure are summarized in Appendix I.

Worker contamination. Procedures must be in place to address worker contamination, and protocols for medical attention must be developed before the occurrence of any such incident. Emergency kits containing isotonic eyewash supplies (or emergency eyewashes, if available) and soap must be immediately available in areas where hazardous drugs are handled. Workers who are contaminated during the spill or spill cleanup or who have direct skin or eye contact with hazardous drugs require immediate treatment. OSHA-recommended steps for treatment are outlined in Appendix J.

Hazardous Waste Containment and Disposal. In 1976, the Resource Conservation and Recovery Act (RCRA) was enacted to provide a mechanism for tracking hazardous waste from its generation to disposal.[106] Regulations promulgated under RCRA are enforced by the Environmental Protection Agency and apply to pharmaceuticals and chemicals discarded by pharmacies, hospitals, clinics, and other commercial entities. The RCRA outlines four "characteristics" of hazardous waste[107] and contains lists of agents that are to be considered hazardous waste when they are discarded.[108] Any discarded drug that is on one of the lists (a "listed" waste) or meets one of the criteria (a "characteristic" waste) is considered hazardous waste. The listed drugs include epinephrine, nicotine, and physostigmine, as well as nine chemotherapy drugs: arsenic trioxide, chlorambucil, cyclophosphamide, daunomycin, diethylstilbestrol, melphalan, mitomycin C, streptozocin, and uracil mustard. They require handling, containment, and disposal as RCRA hazardous waste.

The RCRA allows for the exemption of "empty containers" from hazardous waste regulations. Empty containers are defined as those that have held U-listed or characteristic wastes and from which all wastes have been removed that can be removed using the practices commonly employed to remove materials from that type of container and no more than 3% by weight of the total capacity of the container remains in the container.[109] Disposal guidelines developed by the National Institutes of Health (NIH) and published in 1984 coined the term "trace-contaminated" waste using the 3% rule.[110] Note that a container that has held an acute hazardous waste listed in §§261.31, 261.32, or 261.33(e), such as arsenic trioxide, is not considered empty by the 3% rule,[111] and that spill residues from cleanup of hazardous agents are considered hazardous waste.[105]

In addition, many states are authorized to implement their own hazardous waste programs, and requirements under these programs may be more stringent than those of the EPA. State and local regulations must be considered when establishing a hazardous waste policy for a specific facility.

General categories of hazardous waste found in health care settings would include trace-contaminated hazardous waste, bulk hazardous waste, hazardous drugs not listed as hazardous waste, and hazardous waste and mixed infectious–hazardous waste.

Trace-contaminated hazardous drug waste. By the NIH definition of trace chemotherapy waste,[110] "RCRA-empty" containers, needles, syringes, trace-contaminated gowns, gloves, pads, and empty i.v. sets may be collected and incinerated at a regulated medical waste incinerator. Sharps used in the preparation of hazardous drugs should not be placed in red sharps containers or needle boxes, since these are most frequently disinfected by autoclaving or microwaving, not by incineration, and pose a risk of aerosolization to waste-handling employees.

Bulk hazardous drug waste. While not official, the term *bulk hazardous drug waste* has been used to differentiate containers that have held either (1) RCRA-listed or characteristic hazardous waste or (2) any hazardous drugs that are not RCRA empty or any materials from hazardous drug spill cleanups. These wastes should be managed as hazardous waste.

Hazardous drugs not listed as hazardous waste. The federal RCRA regulations have not kept up with drug development, as there are over 100 hazardous drugs that are not listed as hazardous waste, including hormonal agents. In some states, such as Minnesota, these must be managed as hazardous waste. In other states, organizations should manage these drugs as hazardous waste as a best- management practice until federal regulations can be updated.

Hazardous waste and mixed infectious–hazardous waste. Most hazardous waste vendors are not permitted to manage regulated medical waste or infectious waste; therefore, they cannot accept used needles and items contaminated with squeezable, flakable, or drippable blood. Organizations should check carefully with their hazardous waste vendors to ensure acceptance of all possible hazardous waste, including mixed infectious waste, if needed. Once hazardous waste has been identified, it must be collected and stored according to specific EPA and Department of Transportation requirements.[112] Properly labeled, leakproof, and spill-proof containers of nonreactive plastic are required for areas where hazardous waste is generated. Hazardous drug waste may be initially contained in thick, sealable plastic bags before being placed in approved satellite accumulation containers. Glass fragments should be contained in small, puncture-resistant containers to be placed into larger containers approved for temporary storage.

Waste contaminated with blood or other body fluids must not be mixed with hazardous waste. Transport of waste containers from satellite accumulation to storage sites must be done by individuals who have completed OSHA-mandated hazardous waste awareness training.[113,114] Hazardous waste must be properly manifested and transported by a federally permitted hazardous waste transporter to a federally permitted hazardous waste storage, treatment, or disposal facility.[115] A licensed contractor may be hired to manage the hazardous waste program. The waste generator, however, may be held liable for mismanagement of hazardous waste. Investigation of a contractor, including verification of possession and type of license, should be completed and documented before a contractor is engaged. More information on hazardous waste disposal is available at www.hercenter.org.

Alternative Duty and Medical Surveillance. A comprehensive safety program for controlling workplace exposure to hazardous drugs must include engineering controls, training, work practices, and PPE. Such safety programs must be able to identify potentially exposed workers and those who might be at higher risk of adverse health effects due to this exposure. Because reproductive risks have been associated with exposure to hazardous drugs, alternative duty should be offered to individuals who are pregnant, breast-feeding, or attempting to conceive or father a child. Employees' physicians should be involved in making these determinations.

All workers who handle hazardous drugs should be routinely monitored in a medical surveillance program.[2–4,90,104] Medical surveillance involves the collection and interpretation of data for the purpose of detecting changes in the health status of working populations. Medical surveillance programs involve assessment and documentation of symptom complaints, physical findings, and laboratory values (such as a blood count) to determine whether there is a deviation from the expected norms. Descriptions of medical surveillance programs for hazardous drug handlers are presented in the literature.[90,104] NIOSH encourages employees who handle hazardous drugs to participate in medical surveillance programs that are provided in the workplace.[4] Limited resources may preclude the implementation of a comprehensive medical surveillance program for health care workers who are exposed to hazardous drugs. In the absence of an institutional medical surveillance program, NIOSH encourages workers handling hazardous drugs to inform their personal health care providers of their occupation and possible hazardous drug exposure when obtaining routine medical care.[4]

Conclusion

These guidelines represent the recommendations of many groups and individuals who have worked tirelessly over decades to reduce the potential of harmful effects on health care workers exposed to hazardous drugs. No set of guidelines on this topic, however comprehensive, can address all the needs of every health care facility. Health care professionals are encouraged to rely on their professional judgment, experience, and common sense in applying these recommendations to their unique circumstances and to take into account evolving federal, state, and local regulations, as well as the requirements of appropriate accrediting institutions.

References

1. American Society of Hospital Pharmacists. ASHP technical assistance bulletin on handling cytotoxic and hazardous drugs. *Am J Hosp Pharm.* 1990; 47:1033–49.
2. Controlling occupational exposure to hazardous drugs. Chapter 21. In: OSHA technical manual (OSHA Instruction CPL 2-2.20B CH-4). Washington, DC: Directorate of Technical Support, Occupational Safety and Health Administration; 1995.
3. Occupational Safety and Health Administration. Controlling occupational exposure to hazardous drugs. OSHA technical manual, TED 1-0.15A. Section VI. Chapter 2. www.osha.gov/dts/osta/otm/otm_vi/otm_vi_2.html (accessed 2005 Feb 15).
4. National Institute for Occupational Safety and Health. NIOSH alert: preventing occupational exposure to anti-neoplastic and other hazardous drugs in health care settings. www.cdc.gov/niosh/docs/2004-165/ (accessed 2006 Mar 14).
5. Harrison BR. Risks of handling cytotoxic drugs. In: Perry MC, ed. The chemotherapy source book. 3rd ed. Philadelphia: Lippincott, Williams and Wilkins; 2001:566–82.
6. Baker ES, Connor TH. Monitoring occupational exposure to cancer chemotherapy drugs. *Am J Health-Syst Pharm.* 1996; 53:2713–23.
7. Sessink PJ, Bos RP. Drugs hazardous to healthcare workers: evaluation of methods for monitoring occupational exposure to cytostatic drugs. *Drug Saf.* 1999; 20:347–59.
8. Harris CC. The carcinogenicity of anticancer drugs: a hazard in man. *Cancer.* 1976; 37:1014–23.
9. Falck K, Grohn P, Sorsa M et al. Mutagenicity in urine of nurses handling cytostatic drugs. *Lancet.* 1979; 1:1250–1. Letter.
10. Ladik CF, Stoehr GP, Maurer MA. Precautionary measures in the preparation of antineoplastics. *Am J Hosp Pharm.* 1980; 37:1184,1186.
11. Crudi CB. A compounding dilemma: I've kept the drug sterile but have I contaminated myself? *NITA.* 1980; 3:77–8.

12. Crudi CB, Stephens BL, Maier P. Possible occupational hazards associated with the preparation/administration of antineoplastic agents. *NITA*. 1982; 5:264–6.
13. Reynolds RD, Ignoffo R, Lawrence J et al. Adverse reactions to AMSA in medical personnel. *Cancer Treat Rep*. 1982; 66:1885. Letter.
14. Knowles RS, Virden JE. Handling of injectable antineoplastic agents. *Br Med J*. 1980; 281:589–91.
15. McFarlane A. Ophthalmic problems in staff handling cytotoxic drugs. *Aust J Hosp Pharm*. 1986; 16:145. Letter.
16. Curran CF, Luce JK. Ocular adverse reactions associated with adriamycin (doxorubicin). *Am J Ophthalmol*. 1989; 108:709–11.
17. McLendon BF, Bron AJ. Corneal toxicity from vinblastine solution. *Br J Ophthalmol*. 1978; 62:97–9.
18. Valanis BG, Hertzberg V, Shortridge L. Antineoplastic drugs: handle with care. *AAOHN J*. 1987; 35:487–92.
19. Valanis BG, Vollmer WM, Labuhn KT et al. Association of antineoplastic drug handling with acute adverse effects in pharmacy personnel. *Am J Hosp Pharm*. 1993; 50:455–62.
20. Hemminki K, Kyyronen P, Lindholm ML. Spontaneous abortions and malformations in the offspring of nurses exposed to anaesthetic gases, cytostatic drugs, and other potential hazards, based on registered information of outcome. *J Epidemiol Community Health*. 1985; 39:141–7.
21. Selevan SG, Lindbohm ML, Hornung RW et al. A study of occupational exposure to antineoplastic drugs and fetal loss in nurses. *N Engl J Med*. 1985; 313:1173–8.
22. Valanis BG, Vollmer WM, Labuhn KT et al. Occupational exposure to antineoplastic agents and self-reported infertility among nurses and pharmacists. *J Occup Environ Med*. 1997; 39:574–80.
23. Valanis BG, Vollmer WM, Steele P. Occupational exposure to antineoplastic agents: self-reported miscarriages and stillbirths among nurses and pharmacists. *J Occup Environ Med*. 1999; 41:632–8.
24. National Toxicology Program. Report on carcinogens, 11th ed. http://ehis.niehs.nih.gov/roc/toc9.html (accessed 2005 Sep 15).
25. International Agency for Research on Cancer. Monographs database on carcinogenic risks to humans. www-cie.iarc.fr/ (accessed 2004 Nov 1).
26. Skov T, Lynge E, Maarup B et al. Risks for physicians handling antineoplastic drugs. *Lancet*. 1990; 336:1446. Letter.
27. Skov T, Maarup B, Olsen J et al. Leukaemia and reproductive outcome among nurses handling antineoplastic drugs. *Br J Ind Med*. 1992; 49:855–61.
28. Sessink PJ, Kroese ED, van Kranen HJ et al. Cancer risk assessment for health care workers occupationally exposed to cyclophosphamide. *Int Arch Occup Environ Health*. 1995; 67:317–23.
29. Connor TH, Anderson RW, Sessink PJ et al. Surface contamination with antineoplastic agents in six cancer treatment centers in Canada and the United States. *Am J Health-Syst Pharm*. 1999; 56:1427–32.
30. Sessink PJ, Boer KA, Scheefhals AP et al. Occupational exposure to antineoplastic agents at several departments in a hospital: environmental contamination and excretion of cyclophosphamide and ifosfamide in urine of exposed workers. *Int Arch Occup Environ Health*. 1992; 64:105–12.
31. Sessink PJ, Van de Kerkhof MC, Anzion RB et al. Environmental contamination and assessment of exposure to antineoplastic agents by determination of cyclophosphamide in urine of exposed pharmacy technicians: is skin absorption an important exposure route? *Arch Environ Health*. 1994; 49:165–9.
32. Sessink PJ, Wittenhorst BC, Anzion RB et al. Exposure of pharmacy technicians to antineoplastic agents: reevaluation after additional protective measures. *Arch Environ Health*. 1997; 52:240–4.
33. Ensslin AS, Stoll Y, Pethran A et al. Biological monitoring of cyclophosphamide and ifosfamide in urine of hospital personnel occupationally exposed to cytostatic drugs. *Occup Environ Med*. 1994; 51:229–33.
34. Wick C, Slawson MH, Jorgenson JA et al. Using a closed-system protective device to reduce personnel exposure to antineoplastic agents. *Am J Health-Syst Pharm*. 2003; 60:2314–20.
35. Schmaus G, Schierl R, Funck S. Monitoring surface contamination by antineoplastic drugs using gas chromatography–mass spectrometry and voltammetry. *Am J Health-Syst Pharm*. 2002; 59:956–61.
36. Hirst M, Tse S, Mills DG et al. Occupational exposure to cyclophosphamide. *Lancet*. 1984; 1:186–8.
37. Ensslin AS, Pethran A, Schierl R et al. Urinary platinum in hospital personnel occupationally exposed to platinum-containing antineoplastic drugs. *Int Arch Occup Environ Health*. 1994; 65:339–42.
38. Ensslin AS, Huber R, Pethran A et al. Biological monitoring of hospital pharmacy personnel occupationally exposed to cytostatic drugs: urinary excretion and cytogenetics studies. *Int Arch Occup Environ Health*. 1997; 70:205–8.
39. Minoia C, Turci R, Sottani C et al. Application of high performance liquid chromatography/tandem mass spectrometry in the environmental and biological monitoring of health care personnel occupationally exposed to cyclophosphamide and ifosfamide. *Rapid Commun Mass Spectrom*. 1998; 12:1485–93.
40. Nygren O, Lundgren C. Determination of platinum in workroom air and in blood and urine from nursing staff attending patients receiving cisplatin chemotherapy. *Int Arch Occup Environ Health*. 1997; 70:209–14.
41. Pethran A, Schierl R, Hauff K et al. Uptake of antineoplastic agents in pharmacy and hospital personnel. Part I: monitoring of urinary concentrations. *Int Arch Occup Environ Health*. 2003; 76:5–10.
42. Larson RR, Khazaeli MB, Dillon HK. A new monitoring method using solid sorbent media for evaluation of airborne cyclophosphamide and other antineoplastic agents. *Appl Occup Environ Hyg*. 2003; 18:120–31.
43. Opiolka S, Schmidt KG, Kiffmeyer K et al. Determination of the vapor pressure of cytotoxic drugs and its effects on occupational safety. *J Oncol Pharm Practice*. 2000; 6:15. Abstract.
44. Kiffmeyer TK, Kube C, Opiolka S et al. Vapor pressures, evaporation behavior and airborne concentrations of hazardous drugs: implications for occupational safety. *Pharm J*. 2002; 268:331–7.

45. Connor TH, Shults M, Fraser MP. Determination of the vaporization of solutions of mutagenic antineoplastic agents at 23 and 36 °C using a dessicator technique. *Mutat Res.* 2000; 470:85–92.
46. Kromhout H, Hoek F, Uitterhoeve R et al. Postulating a dermal pathway for exposure to antineoplastic drugs among hospital workers. Applying a conceptual model to the results of three workplace surveys. *Ann Occup Hyg.* 2000; 44:551–60.
47. Dorr RT, Alberts DS. Topical absorption and inactivation of cytotoxic anticancer agents in vitro. *Cancer.* 1992; 70(4 suppl):983–7.
48. Bos RP, Leenaars AO, Theuws JL et al. Mutagenicity of urine from nurses handling cytostatic drugs, influence of smoking. *Int Arch Occup Environ Health.* 1982; 50:359–69.
49. Evelo CT, Bos RP, Peters JG et al. Urinary cyclophosphamide assay as a method for biological monitoring of occupational exposure to cyclophosphamide. *Int Arch Occup Environ Health.* 1986; 58:151–5.
50. Pharmaceutical compounding—sterile preparations (general information chapter 797). In: The United States pharmacopeia, 28th rev., and The national formulary, 23rd ed. Rockville, MD: United States Pharmacopeial Convention; 2004:2461–77.
51. Standard 14644-1. Cleanrooms and associated environments—part 1: classification of air cleanliness. 1st ed. Geneva, Switzerland: International Organization for Standardization; 1999.
52. 29 C.F.R. 1910-1200.
53. Occupational Safety and Health Administration. Hazard communication standard: hazard communication—final rule. 29 C.F.R. 1910. *Fed Regist.* 1987; 52:31852–86.
54. Kiffmeyer TK, Ing KG, Schoppe G. External contamination of cytotoxic drug packing: safe handling and cleaning procedures. *J Oncol Pharm Pract.* 2000; 6:13.
55. Connor TH, Sessink PJ, Harrison BR et al. Surface contamination of chemotherapy drug vials and evaluation of new vial-cleaning techniques: results of three studies. *Am J Health-Syst Pharm.* 2005; 62:475–84.
56. 29 C.F.R. 1910.134.
57. National Institute for Occupational Safety and Health. Summary for respirator users. www.cdc.gov/niosh/respsumm.html (accessed 2005 Sep 15).
58. Nguyen TV, Theiss JC, Matney TS. Exposure of pharmacy personnel to mutagenic antineoplastic drugs. *Cancer Res.* 1982; 42:4792–6.
59. Anderson RW, Puckett WH Jr, Dana WJ et al. Risk of handling injectable antineoplastic agents. *Am J Hosp Pharm.* 1982; 39:1881–7.
60. Rubino FM, Floridia L, Pietropaolo AM et al. Measurement of surface contamination by certain antineoplastic drugs using high-performance liquid chromatography: applications in occupational hygiene investigations in hospital environments. *Med Lav.* 1999; 90:572–83.
61. Sessink PJ, Anzion RB, Van den Broeck PH et al. Detection of contamination with antineoplastic agents in a hospital pharmacy department. *Pharm Weekbl Sci.* 1992; 14:16–22.
62. NSF/ANSI standard 49-04: class II (laminar flow) biosafety cabinetry. Ann Arbor, MI: NSF International; 2004.
63. Clark RP, Goff MR. The potassium iodide method for determining protection factors in open-fronted microbiological safety cabinets. *J Appl Bacteriol.* 1981; 51:439–60.
64. National Sanitation Foundation standard 49: Class II (laminar flow) biohazard cabinetry. Ann Arbor, MI: National Sanitation Foundation; 1987.
65. American Glovebox Society. Guidelines for gloveboxes. 2nd ed. Santa Rosa, CA: AGS; AGS-G001-1998.
66. General Services Administration. Federal standard 209e: clean room and work station requirements, controlled environments. Washington, DC: U.S. Government Printing Office; 1992.
67. Food and Drug Administration. Guidance for industry—sterile drug products produced by aseptic processing. Current good manufacturing practice. www.fda.gov/cder/guidance/5882fnl.pdf (accessed 2005 Sep 10).
68. Tillett L. Barrier isolators as an alternative to a cleanroom. *Am J Health-Syst Pharm.* 1999; 56:1433–6.
69. Mosko P, Rahe H. Barrier isolation technology: a labor-efficient alternative to cleanrooms. *Hosp Pharm.* 1999; 34:834–8.
70. Rahe H. Understanding the critical components of a successful cleanroom and barrier isolator project. *Am J Health-Syst Pharm.* 2000; 57:346–50.
71. Controlled Environment Testing Association. CETA applications guide for the use of barrier isolators in compounding sterile preparations in healthcare facilities. www.cetainternational.org/reference/isolator3.pdf (accessed 2005 Sep 10).
72. Mason HJ, Blair S, Sams C et al. Exposure to antineoplastic drugs in two UK hospital pharmacy units. *Ann Occup Hyg.* 2005; 49:603–10.
73. Nygren O, Gustavsson B, Strom L et al. Exposure to anti-cancer drugs during preparation and administration. Investigations of an open and a closed system. *J Environ Monit.* 2002; 4:739–42.
74. Sessink PJ, Rolf ME, Ryden NS. Evaluation of the PhaSeal hazardous drug containment system. *Hosp Pharm.* 1999; 34:1311–7.
75. Sessink PJ. How to work safely outside the biological safety cabinet. *J Oncol Pharm Pract.* 2000; 6:15. Abstract.
76. Connor TH, Anderson RW, Sessink PJ et al. Effectiveness of a closed-system device in containing surface contamination with cyclophosphamide and ifosfamide in an i.v. admixture area. *Am J Health-Syst Pharm.* 2002; 59:68–72.
77. Vandenbroucke J, Robays H. How to protect environment and employees against cytotoxic agents: the UZ Gent experience. *J Oncol Pharm Pract.* 2001; 6:146–52.
78. Spivey S, Connor TH. Determining sources of workplace contamination with antineoplastic drugs and comparing conventional IV drug preparation with a closed system. *Hosp Pharm.* 2003; 38:135–9.

79. Hoy RH, Stump LM. Effect of an air-venting filter device on aerosol production from vials. *Am J Hosp Pharm.* 1984; 41:324–6.
80. Connor TH. Permeability testing of glove materials for use with cancer chemotherapy drugs. *Oncology.* 1995; 52:256–9.
81. Singleton LC, Connor TH. An evaluation of the permeability of chemotherapy gloves to three cancer chemotherapy drugs. *Oncol Nurs Forum.* 1999; 26:1491–6.
82. Gross E, Groce DF. An evaluation of nitrile gloves as an alternative to natural rubber latex for handling chemotherapeutic agents. *J Oncol Pharm Pract.* 1998; 4:165–8.
83. Connor TH. Permeability of nitrile rubber, latex, polyurethane, and neoprene gloves to 18 antineoplastic drugs. *Am J Health-Syst Pharm.* 1999; 56:2450–3.
84. Klein M, Lambov N, Samev N et al. Permeation of cytotoxic formulations through swatches from selected medical gloves. *Am J Health-Syst Pharm.* 2003; 60:1006–11.
85. American Society for Testing and Materials D 6978-05 standard practice for assessment of resistance of medical gloves to permeation by chemotherapy drugs. West Conshohocken, PA: American Society for Testing and Materials; 2005.
86. Connor TH, Xiang Q. The effect of isopropyl alcohol on the permeation of gloves exposed to antineoplastic agents. *J Oncol Pharm Pract.* 2000; 6:109–14.
87. Colligan SA, Horstman SW. Permeation of cancer chemotherapeutic drugs through glove materials under static and flexed conditions. *Appl Occup Environ Hyg.* 1990; 5:848–52.
88. Sessink PJ, Cerna M, Rossner P et al. Urinary cyclophosphamide excretion and chromosomal aberrations in peripheral blood lymphocytes after occupational exposure to antineoplastic agents. *Mutat Res.* 1994; 309:193–9.
89. National Institutes of Health. Recommendations for the safe handling of cytotoxic drugs. www.nih.gov/od/ors/ds/pubs/cyto/index.htm (accessed 2004 Nov 1).
90. Polovich M, White JM, Kelleher LO, eds. Chemotherapy and biotherapy guidelines and recommendations for practice. 2nd ed. Pittsburgh: Oncology Nursing Society; 2005.
91. Connor TH. An evaluation of the permeability of disposable polypropylene-based protective gowns to a battery of cancer chemotherapy drugs. *Appl Occup Environ Hyg.* 1993; 8:785–9.
92. Harrison BR, Kloos MD. Penetration and splash protection of six disposable gown materials against fifteen antineoplastic drugs. *J Oncol Pharm Pract.* 1999; 5:61–6.
93. Laidlaw JL, Connor TH, Theiss JC et al. Permeability of four disposal protective-clothing materials to seven antineoplastic drugs. *Am J Hosp Pharm.* 1985; 42:2449–54.
94. Valanis B, Shortridge L. Self protective practices of nurses handling antineoplastic drugs. *Oncol Nurs Forum.* 1987; 14:23–7.
95. Labuhn K, Valanis B, Schoeny R et al. Nurses' and pharmacists' exposure to antineoplastic drugs: findings from industrial hygiene scans and urine mutagenicity tests. *Cancer Nurs.* 1998; 21:79–89.
96. NuAire. Containment capabilities of a Class II, type A2 BSC using a chemo pad on the worksurface. Technical bulletin. www.nuaire.com/tech_papers/Containment_Capabilities_using_Chemo_Pad.PDF (accessed 2006 Mar 23).
97. Farris J. Barrier isolators and the reduction of contamination in preparation of parenteral products. www.mic4.com/articles/parenteral-products.php (accessed 2006 Mar 23).
98. Wilson JP, Solimando DA. Aseptic technique as a safety precaution in the preparation of antineoplastic agents. *Hosp Pharm.* 1981; 15:575–81.
99. Harrison BR, Godefroid RJ, Kavanaugh EA. Quality-assurance testing of staff pharmacists handling cytotoxic agents. *Am J Health-Syst Pharm.* 1996; 53:402–7.
100. Shahsavarani S, Godefroid RJ, Harrison BR. Evaluation of occupational exposure to tablet trituration dust. Paper presented at ASHP Midyear Clinical Meeting. Atlanta, GA; 1993 Dec 6.
101. Johnson EG, Janosik JE. Manufacturers' recommendations for handling spilled antineoplastic agents. *Am J Hosp Pharm.* 1989; 46:318–9.
102. Benvenuto JA, Connor TH, Monteith DK et al. Degradation and inactivation of antitumor drugs. *J Pharm Sci.* 1993; 82:988–91.
103. Hansel S, Castegnaro M, Sportouch MH et al. Chemical degradation of wastes of antineoplastic agents: cyclophosphamide, ifosfamide, and melphalan. *Int Arch Occup Environ Health.* 1997; 69:109–14.
104. Polovich M, Belcher C, Glynn-Tucker EM et al. Safe handling of hazardous drugs. Pittsburgh: Oncology Nursing Society; 2003.
105. 40 C.F.R. 261.33.
106. Resource Conservation and Recovery Act of 1976. 42 U.S.C. 82 §6901-92.
107. 40 C.F.R. 261.20-24C.
108. 40 C.F.R. 261.3.38D.
109. 40 C.F.R. 261.7.
110. Vaccari PL, Tonat K, DeChristoforo R et al. Disposal of antineoplastic wastes at the National Institutes of Health. *Am J Hosp Pharm.* 1984; 41:87–93.
111. 40 C.F.R. 261.7(b)(1)-(3).
112. 49 C.F.R. 172.0-.123,173,178,179.
113. 29 C.F.R. 1910.120(e)(3)(i).
114. 29 C.F.R. 1910.120(q)(1-6).
115. 40 C.F.R. 260-8,270.

Appendix A—Recommendations for Use of Class II BSCs

1. The use of a Class II BSC must be accompanied by a stringent program of work practices, including training, demonstrated competence, contamination reduction, and decontamination.
2. Only a Class II BSC with outside exhaust should be used for compounding hazardous drugs; type B2 total exhaust is preferred. Total exhaust is required if the hazardous drug is known to be volatile.[4]
3. Without special design considerations, Class II BSCs are not recommended in traditional, positive-pressure cleanrooms, where contamination from hazardous drugs may result in airborne contamination that may spread from the open front to surrounding areas.
4. Consider using closed-system drug-transfer devices while compounding hazardous drugs in a Class II BSC; evidence documents a decrease in drug contaminants inside a Class II BSC when such devices are used.[4]
5. Reduce the hazardous drug contamination burden in the Class II BSC by wiping down hazardous drug vials before placing them in the BSC.

Appendix B—Recommendations for Use of Class III BSCs and Isolators

1. Only a ventilated cabinet appendix to protect workers and adjacent personnel from exposure and to provide an aseptic environment may be used to compound sterile hazardous drugs.
2. Only ventilated cabinets that are designed to contain aerosolized drug product within the cabinet should be used to compound hazardous drugs.
3. The use of a Class III BSC or isolator must be accompanied by a stringent program of work practices, including operator training and demonstrated competence, contamination reduction, and decontamination.
4. Decontamination of the Class III BSC or isolator must be done in a way that contains any hazardous drug surface contamination during the cleaning process.
5. Appropriate decontamination within the cabinet must be completed before the cabinet is accessed via pass-throughs or removable front panels.
6. Gloves or gauntlets must not be replaced before completion of appropriate decontamination within the cabinet.
7. Surface decontamination of final preparations must be done before labeling and placing into the pass-through.
8. Final preparations must be placed into a transport bag while in the pass-through for removal from the cabinet.

Appendix C—Recommendations for Use of Gloves

1. Wear double gloves for all activities involving hazardous drugs. Double gloves must be worn during any handling of hazardous drug shipping cartons or drug vials, compounding and administration of hazardous drugs, handling of hazardous drug waste or waste from patients recently treated with hazardous drugs, and cleanup of hazardous drug spills.
2. Select powder-free, high-quality gloves made of latex, nitrile, polyurethane, neoprene, or other materials that meet the ASTM standard for chemotherapy gloves.
3. Inspect gloves for visible defects.
4. Sanitize gloves with 70% alcohol or other appropriate disinfectant before performing any aseptic compounding activity.
5. Change gloves every 30 minutes during compounding or immediately when damaged or contaminated.
6. Remove outer gloves after wiping down final preparation but before labeling or removing the preparation from the BSC.
7. Outer gloves must be placed in a containment bag while in the BSC.
8. In an isolator, a second glove must be worn inside the fixed-glove assembly.
9. In an isolator, fixed gloves or appendix must be surface cleaned after compounding is completed to avoid spreading hazardous drug contamination to other surfaces.
10. Clean gloves (e.g., the clean inner gloves) should be used to surface decontaminate the final preparation, place the label onto the final preparation, and place it into the pass-through.
11. Don fresh gloves to complete the final check, place preparation into a clean transport bag, and remove the bag from the pass-through.
12. Wash hands before donning and after removing gloves.
13. Remove gloves with care to avoid contamination. Specific procedures for removal must be established and followed.
14. Gloves should be removed and contained inside the Class II BSC or isolator.
15. Change gloves after administering a dose of hazardous drugs or when leaving the immediate administration area.
16. Dispose of contaminated gloves as contaminated waste.

Appendix D—Recommendations for Use of Gowns

1. Gowns should be worn during compounding, during administration, when handling waste from patients recently treated with hazardous drugs, and when cleaning up spills of hazardous drugs.
2. Select disposable gowns of material tested to be protective against the hazardous drugs to be used.
3. Coated gowns must be worn no longer than three hours during compounding and changed immediately when damaged or contaminated.
4. Remove gowns with care to avoid spreading contamination. Specific procedures for removal must be established and followed.
5. Dispose of gowns immediately upon removal.
6. Contain and dispose of contaminated gowns as contaminated waste.
7. Wash hands after removing and disposing of gowns.

Appendix E—Recommendations for Working in BSCs and Isolators

1. The use of a Class II or III BSC or isolator must be accompanied by a stringent program of work practices, including operator training and demonstrated competence, contamination reduction, and decontamination.
2. Do not place unnecessary items in the work area of the cabinet or isolator where hazardous drug contamination from compounding may settle on them.
3. Do not overcrowd the BSC or isolator.
4. Gather all needed supplies before beginning compounding. Avoid exiting and reentering the work area of the BSC or isolator.
5. Appropriate handling of the preparation in the BSC or pass-through of the isolator, including spraying or wiping with 70% alcohol or another appropriate disinfectant, is necessary for aseptic compounding.
6. Reduce the hazardous drug contamination burden in the BSC or isolator by wiping down hazardous drug vials before placing them in the BSC or isolator.
7. Transport bags must never be placed in the BSC or the isolator work chamber during compounding to avoid inadvertent contamination of the outside surface of the bag.
8. Final preparations should be surface decontaminated within the BSC or isolator and placed into the transport bags in the BSC or in the isolator pass-through, taking care not to contaminate the outside of the transport bag.
9. Decontaminate the work surface of the BSC or isolator before and after compounding per the manufacturer's recommendations or with detergent, sodium hypochlorite solution, and neutralizer.
10. Decontaminate all surfaces of the BSC or isolator at the end of the batch, day, or shift, as appropriate to the workflow. Typically, a BSC or isolator in use 24 hours a day would require decontamination two or three times daily. Disinfect the BSC or isolator before compounding a dose or batch of sterile hazardous drugs.
11. Wipe down the outside of the Class II BSC front opening and the floor in front of the BSC with detergent, sodium hypochlorite solution, and neutralizer at least daily.
12. Seal and then decontaminate surfaces of waste and sharps containers before removing from the BSC or isolator.
13. Decontamination is required after any spill in the BSC or isolator during compounding.
14. Seal all contaminated materials (e.g., gauze, wipes, towels, wash or rinse water) in bags or plastic containers and discard as contaminated waste.
15. Decontamination of the Class III BSC or isolator must be done in a way that contains any hazardous drug surface contamination during the cleaning process.
16. Appropriate decontamination within the cabinet must be completed before the cabinet is accessed via the pass-throughs or removable front panels.
17. Gloves or gauntlets must not be replaced before completion of appropriate decontamination within the cabinet.
18. Surface decontamination of final preparations must be done before labeling and placing into the pass-through.
19. Final preparations must be placed into a transport bag while in the pass-through for removal from the cabinet.

Appendix F—Recommendations for Compounding and Handling Noninjectable Hazardous Drug Dosage Forms

1. Hazardous drugs should be labeled or otherwise identified as such to prevent improper handling.
2. Tablet and capsule forms of hazardous drugs should not be placed in automated counting machines, which subject them to stress and may introduce powdered contaminants into the work area.
3. During routine handling of noninjectable hazardous drugs and contaminated equipment, workers should wear two pairs of gloves that meet the ASTM standard for chemotherapy gloves.[85]
4. Counting and pouring of hazardous drugs should be done carefully, and clean equipment should be dedicated for use with these drugs.
5. Contaminated equipment should be cleaned initially with gauze saturated with sterile water; further cleaned with detergent, sodium hypochlorite solution, and neutralizer; and then rinsed. The gauze and rinse should be contained and disposed of as contaminated waste.
6. Crushing tablets or opening capsules should be avoided; liquid formulations should be used whenever possible.
7. During the compounding of hazardous drugs (e.g., crushing, dissolving, or preparing a solution or an ointment), workers should wear nonpermeable gowns and double gloves. Compounding should take place in a ventilated cabinet.
8. Compounding nonsterile forms of hazardous drugs in equipment designated for sterile products must be undertaken with care. Appropriate containment, deactivation, and disinfection techniques must be utilized.
9. Hazardous drugs should be dispensed in the final dose and form whenever possible. Unit-of-use containers for oral liquids have not been tested for containment properties. Most exhibit some spillage during preparation or use. Caution must be exercised when using these devices.
10. Bulk containers of liquid hazardous drugs, as well as specially packaged commercial hazardous drugs (e.g., Neoral [manufactured by Novartis]), must be handled carefully to avoid spills. These containers should be dispensed and maintained in sealable plastic bags to contain any inadvertent contamination.
11. Disposal of unused or unusable noninjectable dosage forms of hazardous drugs should be performed in the same manner as for hazardous injectable dosage forms and waste.

Appendix G—Recommendations for Reducing Exposure to Hazardous Drugs During Administration in All Practice Settings[104]

Intravenous administration

1. The use of gloves, gown, and face shield (as needed for splashing) is required.
2. Gather all necessary equipment and supplies, including PPE.
3. Use needleless systems whenever possible.
4. Use Luer-Lok fittings for all needleless systems, syringes, needles, infusion tubing, and pumps.
5. Needleless systems may result in droplets leaking at connection points; use gauze pads to catch leaks.
6. Designate a workplace for handling hazardous drugs.
7. Have a spill kit and hazardous drug waste container readily available.
8. Procedure for gowning and gloving: Wash hands, don first pair of gloves, don gown and face shield, and then don second pair of gloves. Gloves should extend beyond the elastic or knit cuff of the gown. Double-gloving requires one glove to be worn under the cuff of the gown and the second glove over the cuff.
9. Always work below eye level.
10. Visually examine hazardous drug dose while it is still contained in transport bag.
11. If hazardous drug dose appears intact, remove it from the transport bag.
12. Place a plastic-backed absorbent pad under the administration area to absorb leaks and prevent drug contact with the patient's skin.
13. If priming occurs at the administration site, prime i.v. tubing with an i.v. solution that does not contain hazardous drugs or by the backflow method.
14. Place a gauze pad under the connection at injection ports during administration to catch leaks.
15. Use the transport bag as a containment bag for materials contaminated with hazardous drugs, drug containers, and sets.
16. Discard hazardous drug containers with the administration sets attached; do not remove the set.
17. Wash surfaces that come into contact with hazardous drugs with detergent, sodium hypochlorite solution, and neutralizer, if appropriate.
18. Wearing gloves, contain and dispose of materials contaminated with hazardous drugs and remaining PPE as contaminated waste.
19. Hazardous drug waste container must be sufficiently large to hold all discarded material, including PPE.
20. Do not push or force materials contaminated with hazardous drugs into the hazardous drug waste container.
21. Carefully remove, contain, and discard gloves. Wash hands thoroughly after removing gloves.

Intramuscular or subcutaneous administration

1. The use of double gloves is required.
2. Gather all necessary equipment and supplies, including PPE.
3. Use Luer-Lok safety needles or retracting needles or shields.
4. Syringes should have Luer-Lok connections and be less than three-fourths full.
5. Designate a workplace for handling hazardous drugs.
6. Have a spill kit and hazardous drug waste container readily available.
7. Procedure for gloving: Wash hands; don double gloves.
8. Always work below eye level.
9. Visually examine hazardous drug dose while still contained in transport bag.
10. If hazardous drug dose appears intact, remove it from the transport bag.
11. Remove the syringe cap and connect appropriate safety needle.
12. Do not expel air from syringe or prime the safety needle.
13. After administration, discard hazardous drug syringes (with the safety needle attached) directly into a hazardous drug waste container.
14. Wearing gloves, contain and dispose of materials contaminated with hazardous drugs.
15. Do not push or force materials contaminated with hazardous drugs into the hazardous drug waste container.
16. Carefully remove, contain, and discard gloves.
17. Wash hands thoroughly after removing gloves.

Oral administration

1. Double gloves are required, as is a face shield if there is a potential for spraying, aerosolization, or splashing.
2. Workers should be aware that tablets or capsules may be coated with a dust of residual hazardous drug that could be inhaled, absorbed through the skin, ingested, or spread to other locations and that liquid formulations may be aerosolized or spilled.
3. No crushing or compounding of oral hazardous drugs may be done in an unprotected environment.
4. Gather all necessary equipment and supplies, including PPE.
5. Designate a workplace for handling hazardous drugs.
6. Have a spill kit and hazardous drug waste container readily available.
7. Procedure for gloving: Wash hands and don double gloves.
8. Always work below eye level.
9. Visually examine hazardous drug dose while it is still contained in transport bag.
10. If hazardous drug dose appears intact, remove it from the transport bag.
11. Place a plastic-backed absorbent pad on the work area, if necessary, to contain any spills.
12. After administration, wearing double gloves, contain and dispose of materials contaminated with hazardous drugs into the hazardous drug waste container.
13. Do not push or force materials contaminated with hazardous drugs into the hazardous drug waste container.
14. Carefully remove, contain, and discard gloves.
15. Wash hands thoroughly after removing gloves.

Appendix H—Recommended Contents of Hazardous Drug Spill Kit

1. Sufficient supplies to absorb a spill of about 1000 mL (volume of one i.v. bag or bottle).
2. Appropriate PPE to protect the worker during cleanup, including two pairs of disposable gloves (one outer pair of heavy utility gloves and one pair of inner gloves); nonpermeable, disposable protective garments (coveralls or gown and shoe covers); and face shield.
3. Absorbent, plastic-backed sheets or spill pads.
4. Disposable toweling.
5. At least two sealable, thick plastic hazardous waste disposal bags (prelabeled with an appropriate warning label).
6. One disposable scoop for collecting glass fragments.
7. One puncture-resistant container for glass fragments.

Appendix I—Recommendations for Spill Cleanup Procedure

General

1. Assess the size and scope of the spill. Call for trained help, if necessary.
2. Spills that cannot be contained by two spill kits may require outside assistance.
3. Post signs to limit access to spill area.
4. Obtain spill kit and respirator.
5. Don PPE, including inner and outer gloves and respirator.
6. Once fully garbed, contain spill using spill kit.
7. Carefully remove any broken glass fragments and place them in a puncture-resistant container.
8. Absorb liquids with spill pads.
9. Absorb powder with damp disposable pads or soft toweling.
10. Spill cleanup should proceed progressively from areas of lesser to greater contamination.
11. Completely remove and place all contaminated material in the disposal bags.
12. Rinse the area with water and then clean with detergent, sodium hypochlorite solution, and neutralizer.
13. Rinse the area several times and place all materials used for containment and cleanup in disposal bags. Seal bags and place them in the appropriate final container for disposal as hazardous waste.
14. Carefully remove all PPE using the inner gloves. Place all disposable PPE into disposal bags. Seal bags and place them into the appropriate final container.
15. Remove inner gloves; contain in a small, sealable bag; and then place into the appropriate final container for disposal as hazardous waste.
16. Wash hands thoroughly with soap and water.
17. Once a spill has been initially cleaned, have the area recleaned by housekeeping, janitorial staff, or environmental services.

Spills in a BSC or isolator

1. Spills occurring in a BSC or isolator should be cleaned up immediately.
2. Obtain a spill kit if the volume of the spill exceeds 30 mL or the contents of one drug vial or ampul.
3. Utility gloves (from spill kit) should be worn to remove broken glass in a BSC or an isolator. Care must be taken not to damage the fixed-glove assembly in the isolator.
4. Place glass fragments in the puncture-resistant hazardous drug waste container located in the BSC or discard into the appropriate waste receptacle of the isolator.
5. Thoroughly clean and decontaminate the BSC or isolator.
6. Clean and decontaminate the drain spillage trough located under the Class II BSC or similarly equipped Class III BSC or isolator.
7. If the spill results in liquid being introduced onto the HEPA filter or if powdered aerosol contaminates the "clean side" of the HEPA filter, use of the BSC or isolator should be suspended until the equipment has been decontaminated and the HEPA filter replaced.

Appendix J—OSHA-Recommended Steps for Immediate Treatment of Workers with Direct Skin or Eye Contact with Hazardous Drugs[3]

1. Call for help, if needed.
2. Immediately remove contaminated clothing.
3. Flood affected eye with water or isotonic eyewash for at least 15 minutes.
4. Clean affected skin with soap and water; rinse thoroughly.
5. Obtain medical attention.
6. Document exposure in employee's medical record and medical surveillance log.
7. Supplies for emergency treatment (e.g., soap, eyewash, sterile saline for irrigation) should be immediately located in any area where hazardous drugs are compounded or administered.

Glossary

Antineoplastic drug: A chemotherapeutic agent that controls or kills cancer cells. Drugs used in the treatment of cancer are cytotoxic but are generally more damaging to dividing cells than to resting cells.[4]

Aseptic: Free of living pathogenic organisms or infected materials.[4]

Biological-safety cabinet (BSC): A BSC may be one of several types.[4]

Class I BSC: A BSC that protects personnel and the work environment but does not protect the product. It is a negative-pressure, ventilated cabinet usually operated with an open front and a minimum face velocity at the work opening of at least 75 ft/min. A class I BSC is similar in design to a chemical fume hood except that all of the air from the cabinet is exhausted through a high-efficiency particulate air (HEPA) filter (either into the laboratory or to the outside).

Class II BSC: A ventilated BSC that protects personnel, the product, and the work environment. A Class II BSC has an open front with inward airflow for personnel protection, downward HEPA-filtered laminar airflow for product protection, and HEPA-filtered exhausted air for environmental protection.

Type A1 (formerly type A): These Class II BSCs maintain a minimum inflow velocity of 75 ft/min, have HEPA-filtered down-flow air that is a portion of the mixed down-flow and inflow air from a common plenum, may exhaust HEPA-filtered air back into the laboratory or to the environment through an exhaust canopy, and may have positive-pressure contaminated ducts and plenums that are not surrounded by negative-pressure plenums. They are not suitable for use with volatile toxic chemicals and volatile radionucleotides.

Type A2 (formerly type B3): These Class II BSCs maintain a minimum inflow velocity of 100 ft/min, have HEPA-filtered down-flow air that is a portion of the mixed down-flow and inflow air from a common exhaust plenum, may exhaust HEPA-filtered air back into the laboratory or to the environment through an exhaust canopy, and have all contaminated ducts and plenums under negative pressure or surrounded by negative-pressure ducts and plenums. If these cabinets are used for minute quantities of volatile toxic chemicals and trace amounts of radionucleotides, they must be exhausted through properly functioning exhaust canopies.

Type B1: These Class II BSCs maintain a minimum inflow velocity of 100 ft/min, have HEPA-filtered down-flow air composed largely of uncontaminated, recirculated inflow air, exhaust most of the contaminated down-flow air through a dedicated duct exhausted to the at-mosphere after passing it through a HEPA filter, and have all contaminated ducts and plenums under negative pressure or surrounded by negative-pressure ducts and plenums. If these cabinets are used for work involving minute quantities of volatile toxic chemicals and trace amounts of radionucleotides, the work must be done in the directly exhausted portion of the cabinet.

Type B2 (total exhaust): These Class II BSCs maintain a minimum inflow velocity of 100 ft/min, have HEPA-filtered down-flow air drawn from the laboratory or the outside, exhaust all inflow and down-flow air to the atmosphere after filtration through a HEPA filter without recirculation inside the cabinet or return to the laboratory, and have all contaminated ducts and plenums under negative pressure or surrounded by directly exhausted negative-pressure ducts and plenums. These cabinets may be used with volatile toxic chemicals and radionucleotides.

Class III BSC: A BSC with a totally enclosed, ventilated cabinet of gastight construction in which operations are conducted through attached rubber gloves and observed through a nonopening view window. This BSC is maintained under negative pressure of at least 0.50 in of water gauge, and air is drawn into the cabinet through HEPA filters. The exhaust air is treated by double HEPA filtration or single HEPA filtration–incineration. Passage of materials in and out of the cabinet is generally performed through a dunk tank (accessible through the cabinet floor) or a double-door pass-through box (such as an autoclave) that can be decontaminated between uses.

Chemotherapy drug: A chemical agent used to treat diseases. The term usually refers to a drug used to treat cancer.[4]

Chemotherapy glove: A medical glove that has been approved by FDA for use when handling antineoplastic drugs.[4]

Chemotherapy waste: Discarded items such as gowns, gloves, masks, i.v. tubing, empty bags, empty drug vials, needles, and syringes used while preparing and administering antineoplastic agents.[4]

Closed system: A device that does not exchange unfiltered air or contaminants with the adjacent environment.[4]

Closed-system drug-transfer device: A drug-transfer device that mechanically prohibits the transfer of environmental contaminants into the system and the escape of hazardous drug or vapor concentrations outside the system.[4]

Cytotoxic: A pharmacologic compound that is detrimental or destructive to cells within the body.[4]

Deactivation: Treating a chemical agent (such as a hazardous drug) with another chemical, heat, ultraviolet light, or another agent to create a less hazardous agent.[4]

Decontamination: Inactivation, neutralization, or removal of toxic agents, usually by chemical means.[4] Surface decontamination may be accomplished by the transfer of hazardous drug contamination from the surface of a nondisposable item to disposable ones (e.g., wipes, gauze, towels).

Disinfecting: Removal of viable organism from surfaces using 70% alcohol or other appropriate disinfectant prior to compounding of sterile hazardous drugs.

Engineering controls: Devices designed to eliminate or reduce worker exposures to chemical, biological, radiological, ergonomic, or physical hazards. Examples include laboratory fume hoods, glove bags, retracting syringe needles, sound-dampening materials to reduce noise levels, safety interlocks, and radiation shielding.[4]

Genotoxic: Capable of damaging DNA and leading to mutations.[4]

Glove box: A controlled environment work enclosure providing a primary barrier from the work area. Operations are performed through sealed gloved openings to protect the worker, the ambient environment, and/or the product.[4]

Hazardous drug: Any drug identified by at least one of the following six criteria: carcinogenicity, teratogenicity or developmental toxicity, reproductive toxicity in humans, organ toxicity at low doses in humans or animals, genotoxicity, and new drugs that mimic existing hazardous drugs in structure or toxicity.[4]

Hazardous waste: Any waste that is an RCRA-listed hazardous waste [40 C.F.R. 261.30-.33] or that meets an RCRA characteristic of ignitability, corrosivity, reactivity, or toxicity as defined in 40 C.F.R. 261.21-.24.[4]

Health care settings: All hospitals, medical clinics, outpatient facilities, physicians' offices, retail pharmacies, and similar facilities dedicated to the care of patients.[4]

Health care workers: All workers who are involved in the care of patients. These include pharmacists, pharmacy technicians, nurses (registered nurses, licensed practical nurses, nurses' aides, etc.), physicians, home health care workers, and environmental services workers (housekeeping, laundry, and waste disposal).[4]

HEPA filter: Filter rated 99.97% efficient in capturing particles 0.3-µm in diameter.[4]

Horizontal-laminar-airflow hood (horizontal-laminar-airflow clean bench): A device that protects the work product and the work area by supplying HEPA-filtered air to the rear of the cabinet and producing a horizontal flow across the work area and out toward the worker.[4]

Isolator: A device that is sealed or is supplied with air through a microbially retentive filtration system (HEPA minimum) and may be reproducibly decontaminated. When closed, an isolator uses only decontaminated interfaces (when necessary) or rapid transfer ports for materials transfer. When open, it allows for the ingress and egress of materials through defined openings that have been designed and validated to preclude the transfer of contaminants or unfiltered air to adjacent environments. An isolator can be used for aseptic processing, for containment of potent compounds, or for simultaneous asepsis and containment. Some isolator designs allow operations within the isolator to be conducted through a fixed-glove assembly without compromising asepsis or containment.[4]

Aseptic isolator: A ventilated isolator designed to exclude external contamination from entering the critical zone inside the isolator.[4]

Aseptic containment isolator: A ventilated isolator designed to meet the requirements of both an aseptic isolator and a containment isolator.[4]

Containment isolator: A ventilated isolator designed to prevent the toxic materials processed inside it from escaping to the surrounding environment.[4]

Laboratory coat: A disposable or reusable open-front coat, usually made of cloth or other permeable material.[4]

Material safety data sheet: Contains summaries provided by the manufacturer to describe the chemical properties and hazards of specific chemicals and ways in which workers can protect themselves from exposure to these chemicals.[4]

Mutagenic: Capable of increasing the spontaneous mutation rate by causing changes in DNA.[4]

Personal protective equipment (PPE): Items such as gloves, gowns, respirators, goggles, and face shields that protect individual workers from hazardous physical or chemical exposures.[4]

Respirator: A type of PPE that prevents harmful materials from entering the respiratory system, usually by filtering hazardous agents from workplace air. A surgical mask does not offer respiratory protection.[4]

Risk assessment: Characterization of potentially adverse health effects from human exposure to environmental or occupational hazards. Risk assessment can be divided into five major steps: hazard identification, dose–response assessment, exposure assessment, risk characterization, and risk communication.[4]

Surface decontamination: Transfer of hazardous drug contamination from the surface of nondisposable items to disposable ones (e.g., wipes, gauze, towels). No procedures have been studied for surface decontamination of hazardous drug contaminated surfaces. The use of gauze moistened with alcohol, sterile water, peroxide, or sodium hypochlorite solutions may be effective. The disposable item, once contaminated, must be contained and discarded as hazardous waste.

Ventilated cabinet: A type of engineering control designed for purposes of worker protection (as used in these guidelines). These devices are designed to minimize worker exposures by controlling emissions of airborne contaminants through (1) the full or partial enclosure of a potential contaminant source, (2) the use of airflow capture velocities to capture and remove airborne contaminants near their point of generation, and (3) the use of air pressure relationships that define the direction of airflow into the cabinet. Examples of ventilated cabinets include BSCs, containment isolators, and laboratory fume hoods.[4]

Developed through the ASHP Council on Professional Affairs and approved by the ASHP Board of Directors on January 12, 2006.

These guidelines supersede the ASHP technical assistance bulletin on handling cytotoxic and hazardous drugs (*Am J Hosp Pharm.* 1990; 47:1033–49).

Luci A. Power, M.S., is gratefully acknowledged for leading the revision of these guidelines. ASHP acknowledges the following individuals for their contributions to these guidelines: Thomas H. Connor, Ph.D., CAPT (ret.) Joseph H. Deffenbaugh Jr., M.P.H., CDR Bruce R. Harrison, M.S., BCOP, Dayna McCauley, Pharm.D., BCOP, Melissa A. McDiarmid, M.D., M.P.H., Kenneth R. Mead, M.S., PE, and Martha Polovich, M.N., RN, AOCN.

The bibliographic citation for this document is as follows: American Society of Health-System Pharmacists. ASHP guidelines on handling hazardous drugs. *Am J Health-Syst Pharm.* 2006; 63:1172–93.

ASHP Guidelines on Pharmacy-Prepared Ophthalmic Products

Pharmacists are frequently called on to prepare sterile products intended for ophthalmic administration when a suitable sterile ophthalmic product is not available from a licensed manufacturer. These products may be administered topically or by subconjunctival or intraocular (e.g., intravitreal and intracameral) injection and may be in the form of solutions, suspensions, or ointments.

The sterility of these products, as well as accuracy in the calculation and preparation of doses, is of great importance. Ocular infections and loss of vision caused by contamination of extemporaneously prepared ophthalmic products have been reported.[1,2] Drugs administered by subconjunctival or intraocular injection often have narrow therapeutic indices. In practice, serious errors in technique have occurred in the preparation of intravitreal solutions, which resulted in concentrations up to double the intended amounts.[3] To ensure adequate stability, uniformity, and sterility, ophthalmic products from licensed manufacturers should be used whenever possible.

The following guidelines are intended to assist pharmacists when extemporaneous preparation of ophthalmic products is necessary. These guidelines do not apply to the manufacturing of sterile pharmaceuticals as defined in state and federal laws and regulations. Other guidelines on extemporaneous compounding of ophthalmic products also have been published.[4,5]

1. Before compounding any product for ophthalmic use, the pharmacist should review documentation that substantiates the safety and benefit of the product when administered into the eye. If no such documentation is available, the pharmacist must employ professional judgment in determining suitability of the product for ophthalmic administration.
2. Important factors to be considered in preparing an ophthalmic medication include the following:[6]
   - **a.** Sterility.
   - **b.** Tonicity.
   - **c.** pH, buffering.
   - **d.** Inherent toxicity of the drug.
   - **e.** Need for a preservative.
   - **f.** Solubility.
   - **g.** Stability in an appropriate vehicle.
   - **h.** Viscosity.
   - **i.** Packaging and storage of the finished product.
3. A written procedure for each ophthalmic product compounded should be established and kept on file and should be easily retrievable. The procedure should specify appropriate steps in compounding, including aseptic methods, and whether microbiologic filtration or terminal sterilization (e.g., autoclaving) of the finished product is appropriate.
4. Before preparation of the product is begun, mathematical calculations should be reviewed by another person or by an alternative method of calculation in order to minimize error. This approach is especially important for products, such as intraocular injections, for which extremely small doses are frequently ordered, necessitating multiple dilutions. Decimal errors in the preparation of these products may have serious consequences.
5. Accuracy in compounding ophthalmic products is further enhanced by the use of larger volumes, which tends to diminish the effect of errors in measurement caused by the inherent inaccuracy of measuring devices. Larger volumes, however, also necessitate special attention to adequate mixing procedures, especially for ointments.
6. Strict adherence to aseptic technique and proper sterilization procedures are crucial in the preparation of ophthalmic products. All extemporaneous compounding of ophthalmic products should be performed in a certified laminar airflow hood (or, for preparing cytotoxic or hazardous agents, a biological safety cabinet).[5] Only personnel trained and proficient in the techniques and procedures should prepare ophthalmic products. Quality-assurance principles for compounding sterile products should be followed, and methods should be established to validate all procedures and processes related to sterile product preparation. In addition, the following should be considered:
   - **a.** Ingredients should be mixed in sterile empty containers. Individual ingredients often can first be drawn into separate syringes and then injected into a larger syringe by insertion of the needles into the needle-free tip of the larger syringe. The larger syringe should be of sufficient size to allow for proper mixing of ingredients.
   - **b.** To maximize measurement accuracy, the smallest syringe appropriate for measuring the required volume should be used. When the use of a single syringe would require estimation of the volume (e.g., measuring 4.5 mL in a 5-mL syringe with no mark at the 4.5-mL level), the use of two syringes of appropriate capacities (or two separate syringe "loads") should be considered in order to provide a more accurate measurement.
   - **c.** A fresh disposable needle and syringe should be used at each step to avoid contamination and prevent error due to residual contents.
   - **d.** When multiple dilutions are required, the containers of interim concentrations should be labeled to avoid confusion.
   - **e.** In the preparation of an ophthalmic product from either (1) a sterile powder that has been reconstituted or (2) a liquid from a glass ampul, the ingredients should be filtered through a 5-μm filter to remove any particulate matter.
7. For ophthalmic preparations that must be sterilized, an appropriate and validated method of sterilization should be determined on the basis of the characteristics of the particular product and container. Filtration of thepreparation through a 0.22-μm filter into a sterile final container is a commonly used method; however, this method is not suitable for sterilizing ophthalmic

suspensions and ointments.[7] When an ophthalmic preparation is compounded from a nonsterile ingredient, the final product must be sterilized before it is dispensed. Sterilization by autoclaving in the final container may be possible, provided that product stability is not adversely affected and appropriate quality control procedures are followed.[6]

8. Preservative-free ingredients should be used in the preparation of intraocular injections, since some preservatives are known to be toxic to many of the internal structures of the eye.[6]

9. In the preparation of ophthalmic products from cytotoxic or other hazardous agents, the pharmacist should adhere to established safety guidelines for handling such agents.[8,9]

10. The final container should be appropriate for the ophthalmic product and its intended use and should not interfere with the stability and efficacy of the preparation.[10] Many ophthalmic liquids can be packaged in sterile plastic bottles with self-contained dropper tips or in glass bottles with separate droppers. Ophthalmic ointments should be packaged in sterilized ophthalmic tubes. Injectables that are not for immediate use should be packaged in sterile vials rather than in syringes, and appropriate overfill should be included. All containers should be adequately sealed to prevent contamination.

11. The pharmacist should assign appropriate expiration dates to extemporaneously prepared ophthalmic products; these dates should be based on documented stability data as well as the potential for microbial contamination of the product.[11] The chemical stability of the active ingredient, the preservative, and packaging material should be considered in determining the overall stability of the final ophthalmic product.[12]

12. Ophthalmic products should be clearly and accurately labeled. In some cases, it may be appropriate to label the products with both the weight and concentration of active ingredients and preservatives. Labels should also specify storage and handling requirements and expiration dates. Extemporaneously prepared ophthalmic products dispensed for outpatient use should be labeled in accordance with applicable state regulations for prescription labeling.

References

1. Associated Press. Pittsburgh woman loses eye to tainted drugs; 12 hurt. *Baltimore Sun.* 1990; Nov 9:3A.
2. Associated Press. Eye drop injuries prompt an FDA warning. *N Y Times.* 1990; 140(Dec 9):39l.
3. Jeglum EL, Rosenberg SB, Benson WE. Preparation of intravitreal drug doses. *Ophthalmic Surg.* 1981; 12:355–9.
4. Reynolds LA. Guidelines for preparation of sterile ophthalmic products. *Am J Hosp Pharm.* 1991; 48:2438–9.
5. Reynolds LA, Closson R. Ophthalmic drug formulations. A handbook of extemporaneous products. Vancouver, WA: Applied Therapeutics; (in press).
6. The United States Pharmacopeia, 22nd rev., and The National Formulary, 17th ed. Rockville, MD: The United States Pharmacopeial Convention; 1989:1692–3.
7. Allen LV. Indomethacin 1% ophthalmic suspension. *US Pharm.* 1991; 16(May):82–3.
8. American Society of Hospital Pharmacists. ASHP technical assistance bulletin on handling cytotoxic and hazardous drugs. *Am J Hosp Pharm.* 1990; 47:1033–49.
9. OSHA work-practice guidelines for personnel dealing with cytotoxic (antineoplastic) drugs. *Am J Hosp Pharm.* 1986; 43:1193–204.
10. Ansel HC, Popovich NG. Pharmaceutical dosage forms and drug delivery systems. 5th ed. Philadelphia: Lea & Febiger; 1990:354–7.
11. Stolar MH. Expiration dates of repackaged drug products. *Am J Hosp Pharm.* 1979; 36:170. Editorial.
12. Remington's pharmaceutical sciences. 19th ed. Gennaro AR, ed. Easton, PA: Mack Publishing; 1990:1581–959.

These guidelines were reviewed in 2008 by the Council on Pharmacy Practice and by the Board of Directors and were found to still be appropriate.

Approved by the ASHP Board of Directors, April 21, 1993. Developed by the ASHP Council on Professional Affairs.

The bibliographic citation for this document is as follows: American Society of Hospital Pharmacists. ASHP technical assistance bulletin on pharmacy-prepared ophthalmic products. *Am J Hosp Pharm.* 1993; 50:1462–3.

ASHP Technical Assistance Bulletin on Compounding Nonsterile Products in Pharmacies

Introduction

Pharmacists are the only health care providers formally trained in the art and science of compounding medications.[1,2] Therefore pharmacists are expected, by the medical community and the public, to possess the knowledge and skills necessary to compound extemporaneous preparations. Pharmacists have a responsibility to provide compounding services for patients with unique drug product needs.

This Technical Assistance Bulletin is intended to assist pharmacists in the extemporaneous compounding of nonsterile drug products for individual patients. Included in this document is information on facilities and equipment, ingredient selection, training, documentation and record keeping, stability and beyond-use dating, packaging and labeling, and limited batch compounding. This document is not intended for manufacturers or licensed repackagers.

Facilities and Equipment

Facilities. It is not necessary that compounding activities be located in a separate facility; however, the compounding area should be located sufficiently away from routine dispensing and counseling functions and high traffic areas. The area should be isolated from potential interruptions, chemical contaminants, and sources of dust and particulate matter. To minimize chemical contaminants, the immediate area and work counter should be free of previously used drugs and chemicals. To minimize dust and particulate matter, cartons and boxes should not be stored or opened in the compounding area. The compounding area should not contain dust-collecting overhangs (e.g., ceiling utility pipes, hanging light fixtures) and ledges (e.g., windowsills). Additionally, at least one sink should be located in or near the compounding area for hand washing before compounding operations. Proper temperature and humidity control within the compounding area or facility is desirable.

Work areas should be well lighted, and work surfaces should be level and clean. The work surface should be smooth, impervious, free of cracks and crevices (preferably seamless), and nonshedding. Surfaces should be cleaned at both the beginning and the end of each distinct compounding operation with an appropriate cleaner or solvent. The entire compounding facility should be cleaned daily or weekly (as needed) but not during the actual process of compounding.

Equipment. The equipment needed to compound a drug product depends upon the particular dosage form requested. Although boards of pharmacy publish lists of required equipment and accessories, these lists are not intended to limit the equipment available to pharmacists for compounding.[2] Equipment should be maintained in good working order. Pharmacists are responsible for obtaining the required equipment and accessories and ensuring that equipment is properly maintained and maintenance is documented.

Weighing Equipment. In addition to a torsion balance, pharmacists who routinely compound may need to use a top-loading electronic balance that has a capacity of at least 300 g, a sensitivity of ±1 mg (or 0.1 mg), and 1-mg, 100-mg, 1-g, and 100-g weights for checking. Balances should be maintained in areas of low humidity and should be stored on flat, nonvibrating surfaces away from drafts. At least annually, the performance of balances should be checked according to the guidelines found in *Remington's Pharmaceutical Sciences,*[3] *USP XXII NF XVII: The United States Pharmacopeia–The National Formulary (USP–NF),*[4] or *USP DI Volume III: Approved Drug Products and Legal Requirements*[5] or the instructions of the balance manufacturer. Performance should be documented.

Weights should be stored in rigid, compartmentalized boxes and handled with metal, plastic, or plastic-tipped forceps—not fingers—to avoid scratching or soiling. Since most Class III prescription balances are only accurate to ±5 or 10 mg, Class P weights may be used for compounding purposes.[4] The *USP–NF* recommends that the class of weights used be chosen to limit the error to 0.1%. In practical terms this means that Class P weights can be used for weighing quantities greater than 100 mg.

The minimum weighable quantity must be determined for any balance being used for compounding. To avoid errors of 5% or more on a Class III balance with a sensitivity requirement of 6 mg, quantities of less than 120 mg of any substance should not be weighed. Smaller quantities may be weighed on more sensitive balances. If an amount is needed that is less than the minimum weighable quantity determined for a balance, an aliquot method of measurement should be used.

Measuring Equipment. The pharmacist should use judgment in selecting measuring equipment. The recommendations given in the *USP–NF* General Information section on volumetric apparatus should be followed. For maximum accuracy in measuring liquids, a pharmacist should select a graduate with a capacity equal to or slightly larger than the volume to be measured. The general rule is to measure no less than 20% of the capacity of a graduate. Calibrated syringes of the appropriate size may be preferred over graduated cylinders for measuring viscous liquids such as glycerin or mineral oil, since these liquids drain slowly and incompletely from graduated cylinders. Viscous liquids may also be weighed if this is more convenient, provided that the appropriate conversions from volume to weight are made by using the specific gravity of the liquid. Thick, opaque liquids should be weighed. For example, if a formulation specifies 1.5 mL of a liquid, it is better to use a 3-mL syringe with appropriate graduations to measure 1.5 mL than to use a 10-mL graduated cylinder, since quantities of less than 2.0 mL cannot be accurately measured in a 10-mL graduate. Also, if an opaque, viscous chemical, such as Coal Tar, USP, must be measured, it is more accurate to weigh the substance than to try to read a meniscus on a graduated cylinder or a fill line on a syringe.

For volumes smaller than 1 mL, micropipettes are recommended, in sizes to cover the range of volumes measured. Two or three variable pipettes can usually cover the range from about 50 μL to 1 mL.

Although conical graduates are convenient for mixing solutions, the error in reading the bottom of the meniscus increases as the sides flare toward the top of the graduate.

Therefore, for accurate measurements, cylindrical graduates are preferred. Conical graduates having a capacity of less than 25 mL should not be used in prescription compounding.[4]

Compounding Equipment. Pharmacists need at least two types of mortars and pestles—one glass and one Wedgwood or porcelain. The sizes of each will depend on the drug products being compounded. Glass mortars should be used for liquid preparations (solutions and suspensions) and for mixing chemicals that stain or are oily. Generally, glass mortars should be used for antineoplastic agents. Because of their rough surface, Wedgwood mortars are preferred for reducing the size of dry crystals and hard powder particles and for preparing emulsions. Porcelain mortars have a smoother surface than Wedgwood mortars and are ideal for blending powders and pulverizing soft aggregates or crystals. When Wedgwood mortars are used for small amounts of crystals or powders, the inside surface may first be lightly dusted with lactose to fill any crevices in which the crystals or powders might lodge. If the contact surfaces of the mortar and pestle become smooth with use, rubbing them with a small amount of sand or emery powder may adequately roughen them. Over extended use, a pestle and a mortar become shaped to each other's curvature. Thus, to ensure maximum contact between the surface of the head of each pestle and the interior of its corresponding mortar, pestles and mortars should not be interchanged.[3]

The compounding area should be stocked with appropriate supplies. Although supply selection depends on the types of products compounded, all areas should have weighing papers, weighing cups, or both to protect balance pans and spatulas. Glassine weighing papers (as opposed to bond weighing paper) should be used for products such as ointments, creams, and some dry chemicals. Disposable weighing dishes should also be stocked for substances like Coal Tar, USP.

Each compounding area should have stainless steel and plastic spatulas for mixing ointments and creams and handling dry chemicals. The pharmacist should exercise judgment in selecting the size and type of spatula. Small spatula blades (6 inches long or less) are preferred for handling dry chemicals, but larger spatula blades (>6 inches) are preferred for large amounts of ointments or creams and for preparing compactible powder blends for capsules. Plastic spatulas should be used for chemicals that may react with stainless steel blades. A variety of spatulas should be stocked in the compounding area, including 4-, 6-, and 8-inch stainless steel spatulas (one each) and 4- and 6-inch plastic spatulas (one each). Imprinted spatulas should not be used in compounding, since the imprinted ink on the spatula blade may contaminate the product.

The compounding area should contain an ointment slab, pill tile, or parchment ointment pad. Although parchment ointment pads are convenient and reduce cleanup time, parchment paper cannot be used for the preparation of creams because it will absorb water. Therefore, an ointment slab or pill tile is necessary. If suppositories are compounded, appropriate suppository molds, either reusable or disposable, should be available.

Other useful equipment and supplies may include funnels, filter paper, beakers, glass stirring rods, a source of heat (hot plate or microwave oven), a refrigerator, and a freezer—in some cases, an ultrafreezer capable of maintaining temperatures as low as –80 °C.

Ingredients

Ideally, only USP or NF chemicals manufactured by FDA-inspected manufacturers should be used for compounding. Although chemicals labeled USP or NF meet *USP–NF* standards for strength, quality, and purity for human drug products, the facilities in which the chemicals were manufactured may not meet FDA Good Manufacturing Practice (GMP) standards. In the event that a needed chemical is not available from an FDA-inspected facility, the pharmacist should, by next best preference, obtain a USP or NF product. If that is not available, the pharmacist should use professional judgment and may have to obtain the highest-grade chemical possible. Chemical grades that may be considered in this situation are ACS grade (meeting or exceeding specifications listed for reagent chemicals by the American Chemical Society) and FCC grade (meeting or exceeding requirements defined by the Food Chemicals Codex). Additional professional judgment is especially necessary in cases of chemical substances that have not been approved for *any* medical use. Particularly in these cases, but also in others as needed, the pharmacist, prescriber, and patient should be well informed of the risks involved.

Selection of ingredients may also depend on the dosage form to be compounded. In most cases, the prescriber specifies a particular dosage form, such as a topical ointment, oral solution or rectal suppository. Sometimes, however, the prescriber relies on the pharmacist to decide on an appropriate form. Irrespective of how the drug order is written, the pharmacist should evaluate the appropriateness of ingredients and the drug delivery system recommended. Factors to consider in selecting the dosage form include (1) physical and chemical characteristics of the active ingredient, (2) possible routes of administration that will produce the desired therapeutic effect (e.g., oral or topical), (3) patient characteristics (e.g., age, level of consciousness, ability to swallow a solid dosage form), (4) specific characteristics of the disease being treated, (5) comfort for the patient, and (6) ease or convenience of administration.

In checking the physical form of each ingredient, the pharmacist should not confuse drug substances that are available in more than one form. For example, coal tar is available as Coal Tar, USP, or Coal Tar Topical Solution, USP; phenol is available as Liquified Phenol, USP, or Phenol, USP; sulfur is available as Precipitated Sulfur, USP, or Sublimed Sulfur, USP. If ingredients are liquids, the pharmacist should consider compounding liquid dosage forms such as solutions, syrups, or elixirs for the final product. If ingredients are crystals or powders and the final dosage form is intended to be a dry dosage form, options such as divided powders (powder papers) or capsules should be considered. If ingredients are both liquids and dry forms, liquid formulations such as solutions, suspensions, elixirs, syrups, and emulsions should be considered.

Care must be exercised when using commercial drug products as a source of active ingredients. For example, extended-release or delayed-release products should not be crushed. Also, since chemicals such as preservatives and excipients in commercial products may affect the overall stability and bioavailability of the compounded product, their presence should not be ignored. Information on preservatives and excipients in specific commercial products can be found in package inserts and also in the dosage form section of selected product monographs in *USP DI Volume I*.[6]

If an injectable drug product is a possible source of active ingredient, the pharmacist should check the salt form of the injectable product to make sure it is the same salt form ordered. If it is necessary to use a different salt because of physical or chemical compatibility considerations or product availability, the pharmacist should consult with the prescriber. Some injectable products contain active constituents in the form of prodrugs that may not be active when administered by other routes. For example, if an injectable solution is a possible source of active ingredient for an oral product, the pharmacist must consider the stability of the drug in gastric fluids, the first-pass effect, and palatability. Also, if injectable powders for reconstitution are used, expiration dating may have to be quite short.

Storage

All chemicals and drug products must be stored according to *USP–NF* and manufacturer specifications. Most chemicals and drug products marketed for compounding use are packaged by the manufacturer in tight, light-resistant containers. Chemicals intended for compounding should be purchased in small quantities and stored in the manufacturer's original container, which is labeled with product and storage information. This practice fosters the use of fresh chemicals and ensures that the manufacturer's label remains with the lot of chemical on hand. Certificates of purity for chemical ingredients should be filed for a period of time no less than the state's time requirement for retention of dispensing records.

The manufacturer's label instructions for storage should be followed explicitly to ensure the integrity of chemicals and drug products and to protect employees. Most chemicals and commercial drug products may be stored at controlled room temperature, between 15 and 30 °C (59 and 86 °F); however, the pharmacist should always check the manufacturer's label for any special storage requirements. Storage information provided for specific commercial drug products in *USP DI Volume I* and on product labels follows the definitions for storage temperatures found in the General Notices and Requirements section of *USP–NF*. An acceptable refrigerator maintains temperatures between 2 and 8 °C (36 and 46 °F); an acceptable freezer maintains temperatures between −20 and −10°C (−4 to +14 °F)

To protect pharmacy employees and property, hazardous products such as acetone and flexible collodion must be stored appropriately. Safety storage cabinets in various sizes are available from laboratory suppliers.

Personnel

Compounding personnel include pharmacists and supportive personnel engaged in any aspect of the compounding procedures.

Training. The pharmacist—who is responsible for ensuring that the best technical knowledge and skill, most careful and accurate procedures, and prudent professional judgment are consistently applied in the compounding of pharmaceuticals—must supervise all compounding activities and ensure that supportive personnel are adequately trained to perform assigned functions. Both pharmacists and the compounding personnel they supervise should participate in programs designed to enhance and maintain competence in compounding. Training programs should include instruction in the following areas:

- Proper use of compounding equipment such as balances and measuring devices—including guidelines for selecting proper measuring devices, limitations of weighing equipment and measuring apparatus, and the importance of accuracy in measuring.
- Pharmaceutical techniques needed for preparing compounded dosage forms (e.g., levigation, trituration, methods to increase dissolution, geometric dilution).
- Properties of dosage forms (see Pharmaceutical Dosage Forms in *USP–NF*) to be compounded and related factors such as stability, storage considerations, and handling procedures.
- Literature in which information on stability, solubility, and related material can be found (see suggested references at the end of this document).
- Handling of nonhazardous and hazardous materials in the work area, including protective measures for avoiding exposure, emergency procedures to follow in the event of exposure, and the location of Material Safety Data Sheets (MSDSs) in the facility.[7–10]
- Use and interpretation of chemical and pharmaceutical symbols and abbreviations in medication orders and in product formulation directions.
- Pharmaceutical calculations.

Procedures should be established to verify the ability of staff to meet established competencies. These procedures may include observation, written tests, or quality control testing of finished products.

Attire. Personnel engaged in compounding should wear clean clothing appropriate for the duties they perform. Protective apparel, such as head, face hand, and arm coverings, should be worn as necessary to preclude contamination of products and to protect workers.

Generally, a clean laboratory jacket is considered appropriate attire for most personnel performing nonsterile compounding activities. Personnel involved in compounding hazardous materials should wear safety goggles, gloves, a mask or respirator, double gowns, and foot covers as required, depending on the substance being handled. To avoid microbial contamination of compounded drug products, written policies should be established that address appropriate precautions to be observed if an employee has an open lesion or an illness. Depending on the situation, an affected employee may be required to wear special protective apparel, such as a mask or gloves, or may be directed to avoid all contact with compounding procedures.

Reference Materials

Pharmacists and supportive personnel must have ready access to reference materials on all aspects of compounding (see suggested references at the end of this document). Earlier editions of some references, such as *Remington's Pharmaceutical Sciences,* provide more comprehensive compounding information than do the later editions. Information on compounding extemporaneous dosage forms from commercially available products can sometimes be obtained from the product's FDA-approved labeling (package insert), the manufacturer, a local pharmacy college, or a drug information center. It is essential that the stability and proper storage conditions for extemporaneous products be thoroughly researched. Therefore, the availability of adequate references and appropriate training in the use of the references is important.

Documentation and Record Keeping

Each step of the compounding process should be documented. Pharmacists should maintain at least four sets of records in the compounding area: (1) compounding formulas and procedures, (2) a log of all compounded items, including batch records and sample batch labels (see section on packaging and labeling), (3) equipment-maintenance records, including documentation of checks of balances, refrigerators, and freezers, and (4) a record of ingredients purchased, including certificates of purity for chemicals (see section on ingredient selection) and MSDSs.

Compounding procedures should be documented in enough detail that preparations can be replicated and the history of each ingredient can be traced. Documentation should include a record of who prepared the product (if the compounder is not a pharmacist, the supervising pharmacist should also sign the compounding record); all names, lot numbers, and quantities of ingredients used; the order of mixing, including any interim procedures used (such as preparing a solution and using an aliquot); the assigned beyond-use date; and any special storage requirements (see section on stability and expiration dating). Compounding formulas and procedures should be written in a typeface that can be read easily. If formulas originate from published articles, copies of the articles should be attached to or filed with the written procedures.

Equipment maintenance and calibrations should be documented and the record maintained in an equipment-maintenance record file. Refrigerator and freezer thermometers should be checked and documented routinely, as should alarm systems indicating that temperatures are outside of acceptable limits.

Follow-up contact with patients who have received extemporaneously compounded products is recommended to ascertain that the product is physically stable and that no adverse effects have occurred from use of the product. Documentation of the contact and the findings is recommended.

Stability, Expiration, and Beyond-Use Dating

The *USP–NF*[4] defines stability as the extent to which a dosage form retains, within specified limits and throughout its period of storage and use, the same properties and characteristics that it possessed at the time of its preparation. The *USP–NF* lists the following five types of stability:

- Chemical
- Physical
- Microbiological
- Therapeutic
- Toxicological

Factors affecting stability include the properties of each ingredient, whether therapeutically active or inactive. Environmental factors such as temperature, radiation, light, humidity, and air can also affect stability. Similarly, such factors as particle size, pH, the properties of water and other solvents employed, the nature of the container, and the presence of other substances resulting from contamination or from the intentional mixing of products can influence stability.[4]

Since compounded drug products are intended for consumption immediately or storage for a very limited time, stability evaluation and expiration dating are different for these products than for manufactured drug products. According to criteria for assigning dating in the *USP–NF*[4] General Notices and Requirements section and the Code of Federal Regulations,[11] the pharmacist labeling extemporaneously compounded drug products should be concerned with the beyond-use date as used by *USP–NF* or the expiration date as used by the Code of Federal Regulations. For uniformity, the term *beyond-use date* will be used in the remainder of this bulletin. The beyond-use date is defined as that date after which a dispensed product should no longer be used by a patient.

Determination of the period during which a compounded product may be usable after dispensing should be based on available stability information and reasonable patient needs with respect to the intended drug therapy. When a commercial drug product is used as a source of active ingredient, its expiration date can often be used as a factor in determining a beyond-use date. For stability or expiration information on commercial drug products, the pharmacist can refer to *USP DI Volume I*.[6] If no information is available, the manufacturer should be contacted. When the active ingredient is a USP or NF product, the pharmacist may be able to use the expiration dating of similar commercial products for guidance in assigning a beyond-use date. In addition, the pharmacist can often refer to published literature to obtain stability data on the same active ingredient under varying conditions and in different formulations.[12]

The pharmacist must assess the potential for instability that may result from the new environment for the active ingredients—from the combination of ingredients and the packaging materials. According to *USP–NF*,[4] hydrolysis, oxidation-reduction, and photolysis are the most common chemical reactions that cause instability. When the possibility of such reactions exists, the pharmacist should seek additional stability data or consider other approaches. These could, in extreme cases, include the preparation and dispensing of more than one compounded drug product or the use of alternative methods of dosing. For some drugs, the latter methods might include, for example, crushing a tablet or emptying the contents of a hard gelatin capsule into an appropriate food substance at each dosing time.

In assigning a beyond-use date for compounded drug products, the pharmacist should use all available stability information, plus education and experience in deciding how factors affecting product stability should be weighted. In the absence of stability data to the contrary or any indication of a stability problem, the following general criteria for assigning maximum beyond-use dates are recommended. It must be emphasized that these are *general* criteria. Professional judgment as discussed elsewhere in this section must be used in deciding when these general criteria may not be appropriate.

- When a manufactured final-dosage-form product is used as a source of active ingredient, use no more than 25% of the manufacturer's remaining expiration dating or six months, whichever is less;
- When a USP or NF chemical not from a manufactured final-dosage-form product is used, use no more than six months;

- In other cases, use the intended period of therapy or no more than 30 days, whichever is less.

All compounded products should be observed for signs of instability. Observations should be performed during preparation of the drug product and any storage period that may occur before the compounded drug product is dispensed. A list of observable indications of instability for solid, liquid, and semisolid dosage forms appears in *USP–NF*.

Packaging and Labeling

The packaging of extemporaneously compounded products for ambulatory patients should comply with regulations pertaining to the Poison Prevention Packaging Act of 1970. These regulations can be found in *USP–NF*.[4]

Containers for compounded products should be appropriate for the dosage form compounded. For example, to minimize administration errors, oral liquids should never be packaged in syringes intended to be used for injection.

The drug product container should not interact physically or chemically with the product so as to alter the strength, quality, or purity of the compounded product. Glass and plastic are commonly used in containers for compounded products. To ensure container inertness, visibility, strength, rigidity, moisture protection, ease of reclosure, and economy of packaging, glass containers have been the most widely used for compounded products.[3] Amber glass and some plastic containers may be used to protect light-sensitive products from degradation; however, glass that transmits ultraviolet or violet light rays (this includes green, blue, and clear ["flint"] glass) should not be used to protect light-sensitive products.

The use of plastic containers for compounded products has increased because plastic is less expensive and lighter in weight than glass. Since compounded products are intended for immediate use, most capsules, ointments, and creams should be stable in high-density plastic vials or ointment jars. Only plastic containers meeting *USP–NF* standards should be used.[4] Reclosable plastic bags may be acceptable for selected divided powders that are intended to be used within a short period of time.

Each compounded product should be appropriately labeled according to state and federal regulations. Labels should include the generic or chemical name of active ingredients, strength or quantity, pharmacy lot number, beyond-use date, and any special storage requirements. If a commercial product has been used as a source of drug, the generic name of the product should be used on the label. The trade name should not be used because, once the commercial drug product has been altered, it no longer exists as the approved commercial product. Listing the names and quantities of inactive ingredients on labels is also encouraged. The coining of short names for convenience (e.g., "Johnson's solution") is strongly discouraged; these names provide no assistance to others who may need to identify ingredients (e.g., in emergency circumstances).

Capsules should be labeled with the quantity (micrograms or milligrams) of active ingredient(s) per capsule. Oral liquids should be labeled with the strength or concentration per dose (e.g., 125 mg/5 mL or 10 meq/15 mL). If the quantity of an active ingredient is a whole number, the number should not be typed with a decimal point followed by a zero. For example, the strength of a capsule containing 25 mg of active ingredient should be labeled as 25 mg and not 25.0 mg. In cases where the dosage strength is less than a whole number, a zero should precede the decimal point (e.g., 0.25 µg).[3]

In expressing salt forms of chemicals on a label, it is permissible to use atomic abbreviations. For example, HCl may be used for hydrochloride, HBr for hydrobromide, Na for sodium, and K for potassium.

Vehicles should also be stated on labels, especially if similar products are prepared with different vehicles. For example, if a pharmacist prepares two potassium syrups, one using Syrup, USP, as the vehicle and one using a sugar-free syrup as the vehicle, the name of the vehicle should be included on the labels.

Liquids and semisolid concentrations may be expressed in terms of percentages. When the term "percent" or the symbol "%" is used without qualification for solids and semisolids, percent refers to weight in weight; for solutions or suspensions, percent refers to weight in volume; for solutions of liquids in liquids, percent refers to volume in volume.[4]

Labels for compounded products that are prepared in batches should include a pharmacy-assigned lot number. Assignment of a pharmacy lot number must enable the history of the compounded product to be traced, including the person compounding the product and the product's formula, ingredients, and procedures. Being able to trace the history of a batch is essential in cases of a drug product recall or withdrawal.

In the preparation of labels for batches of compounded products, all extra labels should be destroyed, since pharmacy lot numbers change with each batch. If computers, memory typewriters, or label machines are used to print batch labels, care must be taken to ensure that the memory and printing mechanism have been cleared and the correct information is programmed before any additional labels are made. It is a good practice to run a blank label between each batch of labels to ensure that the memory has been erased or cleared. To document the information printed on each set of labels, a sample label printed for the batch should be attached to the compounded-product log. If labels are sequentially prepared for different drug products, procedures should exist to minimize the risk of mislabeling the compounded products. These procedures should ensure, for example, that labels for one drug product are physically well separated from labels for any other drug product.

Auxiliary labels are convenient for conveying special storage or use information. Auxiliary labels should be attached conspicuously to containers, if possible. If the container is too small for both a general label and an auxiliary label, special storage and use instructions should appear on the label in a format that will emphasize the instructions.

Limited Batch Compounding

The purpose of extemporaneously compounding products is to provide individualized drug therapy for a particular patient. When a pharmacist is repeatedly asked to prepare identical compounded products, it may be reasonable and more efficient for the pharmacist to prepare small batches of the compounded product.

Batch sizes should be consistent with the volume of drug orders or prescriptions the pharmacist receives for the compounded product and the stability of the compounded product. The pharmacist should use judgment in deciding reasonable batch sizes. Product assays should be performed by a chemical analysis laboratory on a regular basis to ensure product consistency among various lots, product uniformity, and stability. Analyses should be repeated every time an ingredient (active or inert) or procedure is changed. Documentation of assay findings should be filed for a period no less than the state's time requirement for the retention of dispensing records.

General Compounding Considerations

To provide the patient with the most stable drug product, the pharmacist should take the following steps upon receiving a prescription order that requires compounding.

First, the pharmacist should determine if a similar commercial product is available. A pharmacist can refer to various reference texts to check the availability of identical or similar products. Package inserts from commercially available products also contain information on inactive ingredients that can be compared with the requested formulation. If there is a commercially manufactured identical product, the local availability of the product should be determined.

When a similar product is commercially available, the pharmacist should determine which ingredients are different from the requested formulation to decide whether or not the commercial product can be used. At this stage, the pharmacist should seek answers to the following questions:

- Are all of the ingredients appropriate for the condition being treated?
- Are the concentrations of the ingredients in the drug order reasonable?
- Are the physical, chemical, and therapeutic properties of the individual ingredients consistent with the expected properties of the ordered drug product?

If the answers to these questions are positive, the pharmacist should consult the prescriber about the possibility of dispensing the commercial product. (In some states, pharmacists may not be required to obtain permission from the prescriber to dispense a commercial product if the formulation is identical to the drug order.) Dispensing a commercial product is preferable to extemporaneously compounding a drug product because commercial products carry the manufacturer's guarantee of labeled potency and stability.

If there is not a commercial product available with the same or similar formulation, the pharmacist should consider asking the prescriber the following questions:

- What is the purpose of the order? There may be another way to achieve the purpose without compounding a product.
- Where did the formula originate (article, meeting, colleague)?
- How will the drug product be used?
- Does the patient have other conditions that must be considered?
- For how long will the drug product be used?

If possible, the pharmacist should obtain a copy of the original formula to determine the extent to which the formulation has been tested for stability. When documentation is not available, the pharmacist should review the ingredients for appropriateness and reasonable concentrations.

For drug products that must be compounded, the pharmacist should closely observe the compounded drug product for any signs of instability. Such observations should be performed during preparation of the drug product and during any storage period that may occur before the compounded drug product is dispensed.

If specific packaging information is not available, a light-resistant, tight container, such as an amber vial or bottle, should be used to maximize stability (see section on packaging and labeling).

The pharmacist should label the compounded drug product, including an appropriate beyond-use date and storage instructions for the patient.

Specific Compounding Considerations

Accepted, proven compounding procedures for products including solutions, suspensions, creams, ointments, capsules, suppositories, troches, emulsions, and powders may be found in reference sources or the pharmacy literature. For additional information, pharmacists should check references cited in this document or consult colleagues or colleges of pharmacy with known expertise in compounding.

Glossary

For the purposes of this document, the following terms are used with the meanings shown.

Active Ingredient: Any chemical that is intended to furnish pharmacologic activity in the diagnosis, cure, mitigation, treatment, or prevention of disease or to affect the structure or function of the body of man or other animals.[4]

Batch: Multiple containers of a drug product or other material with uniform character and quality, within specified limits, that are prepared in anticipation of prescription drug orders based on routine, regularly observed prescribing patterns.

Cold: Any temperature not exceeding 8 °C (46 °F).[4]

Commercially Available Product: Any drug product manufactured by a producer registered with the Department of Health and Human Services as a pharmaceutical manufacturer.

Compounding: The mixing of substances to prepare a drug product.

Container: A device that holds a drug product and is or may be in direct contact with the product.[3]

Cool: Any temperature between 8 and 15 °C (46 and 59 °F).[4]

Drug Product: A finished dosage form that contains an active drug ingredient usually, but not necessarily (in the case of a placebo), in combination with inactive ingredients.[4]

Extemporaneous: Impromptu; prepared without a standard formula from an official compendium; prepared as required for a specific patient.

Inactive Ingredient: Any chemical other than the active ingredients in a drug product.[4]

Manufacturer: Anyone registered with the Department of Health and Human Services as a producer of drug products.[14]

Sensitivity Requirements: The maximal load that will cause one subdivision of change on the index plate in the position of rest of the indicator of the balance.[4]

Stability: The chemical and physical integrity of a drug product over time.[4]

Trituration: The reducing of substances to fine particles by rubbing them in a mortar with a pestle.[3]

Warm: Any temperature between 30 and 40 °C (86 and 104 °F).[4]

Suggested References

Product Availability

American Drug Index
Drug Facts & Comparisons
Physicians' Desk Reference
The Extra Pharmacopoeia (Martindale)
CHEMSOURCES
AHFS Drug Information

Compounding Techniques

Compounding Companion PC-Based Software
King's *Dispensing of Medications*
Remington's Pharmaceutical Sciences
Contemporary Compounding column in *U.S. Pharmacist*

Pharmaceutical Calculations

Stoklosa and Ansel's *Pharmaceutical Calculations*
Math—Use It or Lose It column in *Hospital Pharmacy*
Calculations in Pharmacy column in *U.S. Pharmacist*

Drug Stability and Compatibility

American Journal of Hospital Pharmacy
ASHP's *Handbook on Extemporaneous Formulations*
ASHP's *Handbook on Injectable Drugs*
International Pharmaceutical Abstracts
Journal of the Parenteral Drug Association (now *Journal of Pharmaceutical Science and Technology*)
Canadian Society of Hospital Pharmacists *Extemporaneous Oral Liquid Dosage Preparations*
Pediatric Drug Formulations
Physicians' Desk Reference
Contemporary Compounding column in *U.S. Pharmacist*
AHFS Drug Information
The Merck Index

References

1. Pancorbo SA, Campagna KD, Devenport JK, et al. Task force report of competency statements for pharmacy practice. *Am J Pharm Educ*. 1987; 51:196–206.
2. Allen LV Jr. Establishing and marketing your extemporaneous compounding service. *US Pharm*. 1990; 15(Dec):74–7.
3. Remington's pharmaceutical sciences. 18th ed. Gennaro AR, ed. Easton, PA: Mack Publishing; 1990; 1630–1, 1658, 1660.
4. The United States Pharmacopeia, 22nd rev., and The National Formulary, 17th ed. Rockville, MD: The United States Pharmacopeial Convention; 1989.
5. USP DI Volume III: Approved drug products and legal requirements. 14th ed. Rockville, MD: The United States Pharmacopeial Convention; 1994.
6. USP DI Volume I: Drug information for the health care professional. 14th ed. Rockville, MD: The United States Pharmacopeial Convention; 1994.
7. 29 §C.F.R. 1910. 1200(1990).
8. ASHP technical assistance bulletin on handling cytotoxic and hazardous drugs. *Am J Hosp Pharm*. 1990; 47:1033–49.
9. Feinberg JL. Complying with OSHA's Hazard Communication Standard. *Consult Pharm*. 1991; 6:444, 446, 448.
10. Myers CE. Applicability of OSHA Hazard Communication Standard to drug products. *Am J Hosp Pharm*. 1990; 47:1960–1.
11. 21 C.F.R. §211.137.
12. Connors KA, Amidon GL, Stella VJ. Chemical stability of pharmaceuticals: a handbook for pharmacists. 2nd ed. New York: Wiley; 1986.
13. American Society of Hospital Pharmacists. ASHP guidelines on preventing medication errors in hospitals. *Am J Hosp Pharm*. 1993; 50:305–14.
14. Fitzgerald WL Jr. The legal authority to compound in pharmacy practice. *Tenn Pharm*. 1990; 26(Mar):21–2.

Approved by the ASHP Board of Directors, April 27, 1994. Developed by the Council on Professional Affairs.

The bibliographic citation for this document is as follows: American Society of Hospital Pharmacists. ASHP technical assistance bulletin on compounding nonsterile products in pharmacies. *Am J Hosp Pharm*. 1994; 51:1441–8.

Distribution

Technician-Checking-Technician Programs (0310)

Source: Council on Administrative Affairs

To advocate technician-checking-technician programs (with appropriate quality control measures) in order to permit redirection of pharmacist resources to patient care activities; further,

To advocate state board of pharmacy approval of these programs.

This policy was reviewed in 2012 by the Council on Pharmacy Management and by the Board of Directors and was found to still be appropriate.

Dispensing by Nonpharmacists and Nonprescribers (0010)

Source: Council on Legal and Public Affairs

To reaffirm the position that all medication dispensing functions must be performed by, or under the supervision of, a pharmacist; further,

To reaffirm the position that any relationships that are established between a pharmacist and other individuals in order to carry out the dispensing function should preserve the role of the pharmacist in (a) maintaining appropriate patient protection and safety, (b) complying with regulatory and legal requirements, and (c) providing individualized patient care.

This policy was reviewed in 2014 by the Council on Public Policy and by the Board of Directors and was found to still be appropriate.

ASHP Statement on Pharmacist's Responsibility for Distribution and Control of Drug Products

A fundamental purpose of pharmaceutical services in any setting is to ensure the safe and appropriate use of drug products and drug-related devices. Fulfillment of this responsibility is enhanced through the pharmacist's involvement in all aspects of the use of drugs.[1]

This involvement should include decisions and actions with respect to the evaluation, procurement, storage, distribution, and administration of all drug products. The pharmacist is responsible for development, in consultation with appropriate other professionals, departments, and interdisciplinary committees in the setting, of all drug-use control policies. The pharmacist should be directly responsible for the control and distribution of all stocks of drugs.

The Federal Food, Drug, and Cosmetic Act defines the term *drug* as "(A) articles recognized in the official United States Pharmacopeia, official Homeopathic Pharmacopeia of the United States, or official National Formulary, or any supplement to any of them; and (B) articles intended for use in the diagnosis, cure, mitigation, treatment, or prevention of disease in man or other animals; and (C) articles (other than food) intended to affect the structure or any function of the body of man or other animals; and (D) articles intended for use as a component of any article specified in clauses (A), (B), or (C) of this paragraph; but does not include devices or their components, parts, or accessories."[2]

For purposes of this document, drugs include those used by inpatients and outpatients, large- and small-volume injections, radiopharmaceuticals, diagnostic agents including radiopaque contrast media, anesthetic gases, blood-fraction drugs, dialysis fluids, respiratory therapy drugs, biotechnologically produced drugs, investigational drugs, drug samples, drugs brought to the setting by patients or family, and other chemicals and biological substances administered to patients to evoke or enhance pharmacologic responses.

The pharmacist's responsibility for drug-use control extends throughout the setting served. This purview extends to all pharmacy satellite locations (inpatient and outpatient, including those serving the general public), emergency rooms, surgical and labor and delivery suites (and related areas such as recovery rooms), anesthesiology, nuclear medicine, radiology, dialysis areas, ambulatory care clinics and treatment (including surgery) areas, respiratory therapy areas, central sterile supply centers, blood banks, intensive care areas, cardiac catheterization suites, research areas, and all other areas in which drugs are handled and used. The pharmacist should be responsible for drug-use policies and routine inspection of all drug stocks, even if direct custody and distribution are not possible.

The pharmacist also has an advocacy responsibility with respect to decisions and policies about the use of drug-related devices as they affect drug therapy. As appropriate, the pharmacist may also be assigned direct responsibility for control and distribution of drug-related devices.[3] Drug-related devices include electromechanical pumps, devices for administration of injectable drugs, devices for monitoring plasma drug concentration, and devices for monitoring drug administration rate.

References

1. American Society of Hospital Pharmacists. ASHP guidelines: minimum standard for pharmacies in institutions. *Am J Hosp Pharm.* 1985; 42:372–5.
2. 21 U.S.C. §321 (g) (1).
3. American Society of Hospital Pharmacists. ASHP statement on the pharmacist's role with respect to drug delivery systems and administration devices. *Am J Hosp Pharm.* 1989; 46:802–4.

This statement was reviewed in 2005 by the Council on Professional Affairs and by the Board of Directors and was found to still be appropriate.

Approved by the ASHP Board of Directors, November 16, 1994, and by the ASHP House of Delegates, June 5, 1995. Revised by the ASHP Council on Professional Affairs. Supersedes a previous version dated June 3, 1992.

The bibliographic citation for this document is as follows: ASHP statement on the pharmacist's responsibility for distribution and control of drug products. In: *Practice Standards of ASHP 1996–97.* Deffenbaugh JH, ed. Bethesda, MD: American Society of Health-System Pharmacists; 1996.

ASHP Statement on Unit Dose Drug Distribution

The unit dose system of medication distribution is a pharmacy-coordinated method of dispensing and controlling medications in organized health-care settings.

The unit dose system may differ in form, depending on the specific needs of the organization. However, the following distinctive elements are basic to all unit dose systems: medications are contained in single unit packages; they are dispensed in as ready-to-administer form as possible; and for most medications, not more than a 24-hour supply[a] of doses is delivered to or available at the patient-care area at any time.[1,2]

Numerous studies concerning unit dose drug distribution systems have been published over the past several decades. These studies indicate categorically that unit dose systems, with respect to other drug distribution methods, are (1) safer for the patient, (2) more efficient and economical for the organization, and (3) a more effective method of utilizing professional resources.

More specifically, the inherent advantages of unit dose systems over alternative distribution procedures are

1. A reduction in the incidence of medication errors.
2. A decrease in the total cost of medication-related activities.
3. A more efficient usage of pharmacy and nursing personnel, allowing for more direct patient-care involvement by pharmacists and nurses.
4. Improved overall drug control and drug use monitoring.
5. More accurate patient billings for drugs.
6. The elimination or minimization of drug credits.
7. Greater control by the pharmacist over pharmacy workload patterns and staff scheduling.
8. A reduction in the size of drug inventories located in patient-care areas.
9. Greater adaptability to computerized and automated procedures.

In view of these demonstrated benefits, the American Society of Hospital Pharmacists considers the unit dose system to be an essential part of drug distribution and control in organized health-care settings in which drug therapy is an integral component of health-care delivery.

References

1. Summerfield MR. Unit dose primer. Bethesda, MD: American Society of Hospital Pharmacists; 1983.
2. American Society of Hospital Pharmacists. ASHP technical assistance bulletin on hospital drug distribution and control. *Am J Hosp Pharm.* 1980; 37:1097–1103.

---

[a]In long-term care facilities, a larger supply of medication (e.g., 48 or 72 hours) may be acceptable.

Approved by the ASHP Board of Directors, November 16, 1988, and by the ASHP House of Delegates, June 5, 1989. Supersedes previous versions approved by the House of Delegates on June 8, 1981, and by the Board of Directors on April 19, 1975, and November 13–14, 1980.

The bibliographic citation for this document is as follows: American Society of Hospital Pharmacists. ASHP statement on unit dose drug distribution. *Am J Hosp Pharm.* 1989; 46:2346.

ASHP Technical Assistance Bulletin on Hospital Drug Distribution and Control

Drug control (of which drug distribution is an important part) is among the pharmacist's most important responsibilities. Therefore, adequate methods to assure that these responsibilities are met must be developed and implemented. These guidelines will assist the pharmacist in preparing drug control procedures for all medication-related activities. The guidelines are based on the premise that the pharmacy is responsible for the procurement, distribution, and control of *all* drugs used within the institution. In a sense, the entire hospital is the pharmacy, and the pharmacy service is simply a functional service extending throughout the institution's physical and organizational structures.

It should be noted that, although this document is directed toward hospitals, much of it is relevant to other types of health-care facilities.

Pharmacy Policies, Procedures, and Communications

Policy and Procedure Manuals.[1] The effectiveness of the drug control system depends on adherence to policies (broad, general statements of philosophy) and procedures (detailed guidelines for implementing policy). The importance of an up-to-date policy and procedure manual for drug control cannot be overestimated. All pharmacy staff must be familiar with the manual; it is an important part of orientation for new staff and crucial to the pharmacy's internal communication mechanism. In addition, preparing written policies and procedures requires a thorough analysis of control operations; this review might go undone otherwise.

Drug control begins with the setting of policy. The authority to enforce drug control policy and procedures must come from the administration of the institution, with the endorsement of the medical staff, via the pharmacy and therapeutics (P&T) committee and/or other appropriate committee(s). Because the drug control system interfaces with numerous departments and professions, the P&T committee should be the focal point for communications relating to drug control in the institution. The pharmacist, with the cooperation of the P&T committee, should develop media such as newsletters, bulletins, and seminars to communicate with persons functioning within the framework of the control system.

Inservice Training and Education. Intra- and interdepartmental education and training programs are important to the effective implementation of policies and procedures and the institution's drug control system in general. They are part of effective communication and help establish and maintain professional relationships among the pharmacy staff and between it and other hospital departments. Drug control policies and procedures should be included in the pharmacy's educational programs.

Standards, Laws, and Regulations

The pharmacist must be aware of and comply with the laws, regulations, and standards governing the profession. Many of these standards and regulations deal with aspects of drug control. Among the agencies and organizations affecting institutional pharmacy practice are those described below.

Regulatory Agencies and Organizations. The U.S. government, through its Food and Drug Administration (FDA), is responsible for implementing and enforcing the federal Food, Drug, and Cosmetic Act. The FDA is responsible for the control and prevention of misbranding and of adulteration of food, drugs, and cosmetics moving in interstate commerce. The FDA also sets label requirements for food, drugs, and cosmetics; sets standards for investigational drug studies and for marketing of new drug products; and compiles data on adverse drug reactions.

The U.S. Department of the Treasury influences pharmacy operation by regulating the use of tax-free alcohol through the Bureau of Alcohol, Tobacco and Firearms. The U.S. Department of Justice affects pharmacy practice through its Drug Enforcement Agency (DEA) by enforcing the Controlled Substances Act of 1970 and other federal laws and regulations for controlled drugs.

Another federal agency, the Health Care Financing Administration, has established Conditions of Participation for hospitals and skilled nursing facilities to assist these institutions to qualify for reimbursement under the health insurance program for the aged (Medicare) and for Medicaid.

The state board of pharmacy is the agency of state government responsible for regulating pharmacy practice within the state. Practitioners, institutions, and community pharmacies must obtain licenses from the board to practice pharmacy or provide pharmacy services in the state. State boards of pharmacy promulgate numerous regulations pertaining to drug dispensing and control. (In some states, the state board of health licenses the hospital pharmacy separately or through a license that includes all departments of the hospital.)

Standards and guidelines for pharmaceutical services have been established by the Joint Commission on Accreditation of Hospitals (JCAH)[2] and the American Society of Hospital Pharmacists (ASHP)[3]. The United States Pharmacopeial Convention also promulgates certain pharmacy practice procedures as well as official standards for drugs and drug testing. Professional practice guidelines and standards generally do not have the force of law but rather are intended to assist pharmacists in achieving the highest level of practice. They may, however, be employed in legal proceedings as evidence of what constitutes acceptable practice as determined by the profession itself.

In some instances, both federal and state laws may deal with a specific activity; in such cases, the more stringent law will apply.

The Medication System

Procurement: Drug Selection, Purchasing Authority, Responsibility, and Control.[4–6] The selection of pharmaceuticals is a basic and extremely important professional function of the hospital pharmacist who is charged with making decisions regarding products, quantities, product specifications, and sources of supply. It is the pharmacist's obligation to establish and maintain standards assuring the quality, proper storage, control, and safe use of all pharmaceuticals and related supplies (e.g., fluid administration sets); this responsibility must not be delegated to another individual. Although the actual purchasing of drugs and supplies may be performed by a non-pharmacist, the setting of quality standards and specifications requires professional knowledge and judgment and must be performed only by the pharmacist.

Economic and therapeutic considerations make it necessary for hospitals to have a well-controlled, continuously updated formulary. It is the pharmacist's responsibility to develop and maintain adequate product specifications to aid in the purchase of drugs and related supplies under the formulary system. The *USP–NF* is a good base for drug product specifications; there also should be criteria to evaluate the acceptability of manufacturers and distributors. In establishing the formulary, the P&T committee recommends guidelines for drug selection. However, when his knowledge indicates, the pharmacist must have the authority to reject a particular drug product or supplier.

Although the pharmacist has the authority to select a brand or source of supply, he must make economic considerations subordinate to those of quality. Competitive bid purchasing is an important method for achieving a proper balance between quality and cost when two or more acceptable suppliers market a particular product meeting the pharmacist's specifications. In selecting a vendor, the pharmacist must consider price, terms, shipping times, dependability, quality of service, returned goods policy, and packaging; however, prime importance always must be placed on drug quality and the manufacturer's reputation. It should be noted that the pharmacist is responsible for the quality of all drugs dispensed by the pharmacy.

Records. The pharmacist must establish and maintain adequate recordkeeping systems. Various records must be retained (and be retrievable) by the pharmacy because of governmental regulations; some are advisable for legal protection, others are needed for JCAH accreditation, and still others are necessary for sound management (evaluation of productivity, workloads, and expenses and assessment of departmental growth and progress) of the pharmacy department. Records must be retained for at least the length of time prescribed by law (where such requirements apply).

It is important that the pharmacist study federal, state, and local laws to become familiar with their requirements for permits, tax stamps, storage of alcohol and controlled substances, records, and reports.

Among the records needed in the drug distribution and control system are

- Controlled substances inventory and dispensing records.
- Records of medication orders and their processing.
- Manufacturing and packaging production records.
- Pharmacy workload records.
- Purchase and inventory records.
- Records of equipment maintenance.
- Records of results and actions taken in quality-assurance and drug audit programs.

Receiving Drugs. Receiving control should be under the auspices of a responsible individual, and the pharmacist must ensure that records and forms provide proper control upon receipt of drugs. Complete accountability from purchase order initiation to drug administration must be provided.

Personnel involved in the purchase, receipt, and control of drugs should be well trained in their responsibilities and duties and must understand the serious nature of drugs. All nonprofessional personnel employed by the pharmacy should be selected and supervised by the pharmacist.

Delivery of drugs directly to the pharmacy or other pharmacy receiving area is highly desirable; it should be considered mandatory for controlled drugs. Orders for controlled substances must be checked against the official order blank (when applicable) and against hospital purchase order forms. All drugs should be placed into stock promptly upon receipt, and controlled substances must be directly transferred to safes or other secure areas.

Drug Storage and Inventory Control. Storage is an important aspect of the total drug control system. Proper environmental control (i.e., proper temperature, light, humidity, conditions of sanitation, ventilation, and segregation) must be maintained wherever drugs and supplies are stored in the institution. Storage areas must be secure; fixtures and equipment used to store drugs should be constructed so that drugs are accessible only to designated and authorized personnel. Such personnel must be carefully selected and supervised. Safety also is an important factor, and proper consideration should be given to the safe storage of poisons and flammable compounds. Externals should be stored separately from internal medications. Medications stored in a refrigerator containing items other than drugs should be kept in a secured, separate compartment.

Proper control is important wherever medications are kept, whether in general storage in the institution or the pharmacy or patient-care areas (including satellite pharmacies, nursing units, clinics, emergency rooms, operating rooms, recovery rooms, and treatment rooms). Expiration dates of perishable drugs must be considered in all of these locations, and stock must be rotated as required. A method to detect and properly dispose of outdated, deteriorated, recalled, or obsolete drugs and supplies should be established. This should include monthly audits of all medication storage areas in the institution. (The results of these audits should be documented in writing.)

Since the pharmacist must justify and account for the expenditure of pharmacy funds, he must maintain an adequate inventory management system. Such a system should enable the pharmacist to analyze and interpret prescribing trends and their economic impacts and appropriately minimize inventory levels. It is essential that a system to indicate subminimum inventory levels be developed to avoid "outages," along with procedures to procure emergency supplies of drugs when necessary.

In-House Manufacturing, Bulk Compounding, Packaging, and Labeling.[7,8] As with commercially marketed drug products, those produced by the pharmacy must be accurate in identity, strength, purity, and quality. Therefore, there must be adequate process and finished product controls for all manufacturing/bulk compounding and packaging operations. Written master formulas and batch records (including product test results) must be maintained. All technical personnel must be adequately trained and supervised.

Packaging and labeling operations must have controls sufficient to prevent product/package/label mixups. A lot number to identify each finished product with its production and control history must be assigned to each batch.

The Good Manufacturing Practices of the FDA is a useful model for developing a comprehensive control system.

The pharmacist is encouraged to prepare those drug dosage forms, strengths, and packagings that are needed for optimal drug therapy but that are commercially unavailable. Adequate attention must be given to the stability, palatability, packaging, and labeling requirements of these products.

Medication Distribution (Unit Dose System).[9–11] Medication distribution is the responsibility of the pharmacy. The pharmacist, with the assistance of the P&T committee and the department of nursing, must develop comprehensive policies and procedures that provide for the safe distribution of all medications and related supplies to inpatients and outpatients.

For reasons of safety and economy, the preferred method to distribute drugs in institutions is the *unit dose* system. Although the unit dose system may differ in form depending on the specific needs, resources, and characteristics of each institution, four elements are common to all: (1) medications are contained in, and administered from, single unit or unit dose packages; (2) medications are dispensed in ready-to-administer form to the extent possible; (3) for most medications, not more than a 24-hour supply of doses is provided to or available at the patient-care area at any time; and (4) a patient medication profile is concurrently maintained in the pharmacy for each patient. Floor stocks of drugs are minimized and limited to drugs for emergency use and routinely used "safe" items such as mouthwash and antiseptic solutions.

(1) Physician's drug order: writing the order. Medications should be given (with certain specified exceptions) only on the *written* order of a qualified physician or other authorized prescriber. Allowable exceptions to this rule (i.e., telephone or verbal orders) should be put in written form immediately and the prescriber should countersign the nurse's or pharmacist's signed record of these orders within 48 (preferably 24) hours. Only a pharmacist or registered nurse should accept such orders. Provision should be made to place physician's orders in the patient's chart, and a method for sending this information to the pharmacy should be developed.

Prescribers should specify the date and time medication orders are written.

Medication orders should be written legibly in ink and should include

- Patient's name and location (unless clearly indicated on the order sheet).
- Name (generic) of medication.
- Dosage expressed in the metric system, except in instances where dosage must be expressed otherwise (i.e., units, etc.).
- Frequency of administration.
- Route of administration.
- Signature of the physician.
- Date and hour the order was written.

Any abbreviations used in medication orders should be agreed to and jointly adopted by the medical, nursing, pharmacy, and medical records staff of the institution.

Any questions arising from a medication order, including the interpretation of an illegible order, should be referred to the ordering physician by the pharmacist. It is desirable for the pharmacist to make (appropriate) entries in the patient's medical chart pertinent to the patient's drug therapy. (Proper authorization for this must be obtained.[12]) Also, a duplicate record of the entry can be maintained in the pharmacy profile.

In computerized patient data systems, each prescriber should be assigned a unique identifier; this number should be included in all medication orders. Unauthorized personnel should not be able to gain access to the system.

(2) Physician's drug order: medication order sheets. The pharmacist (except in emergency situations) must receive the physician's original order or a direct copy of the order before the drug is dispensed. This permits the pharmacist to resolve questions or problems with drug orders before the drug is dispensed and administered. It also eliminates errors which may arise when drug orders are transcribed onto another form for use by the pharmacy. Several methods by which the pharmacy may receive physicians' original orders or direct copies are

1. Self-copying order forms. The physician's order form is designed to make a direct copy (carbon or NCR) which is sent to the pharmacy. This method provides the pharmacist with a duplicate copy of the order and does not require special equipment. There are two basic formats:
   a. Orders for medications included among treatment orders. Use of this form allows the physician to continue writing his orders on the chart as he has been accustomed in the past, leaving all other details to hospital personnel.
   b. Medication orders separated from other treatment orders on the order form. The separation of drug orders makes it easier for the pharmacist to review the order sheet.
2. Electromechanical. Copying machines or similar devices may be used to produce an exact copy of the physician's order. Provision should be made to transmit physicians' orders to the pharmacy in the event of mechanical failure.
3. Computerized. Computer systems, in which the physician enters orders into a computer which then stores and prints out the orders in the pharmacy or elsewhere, are used in some institutions. Any such system should provide for the pharmacist's verification of any drug orders entered into the system by anyone other than an authorized prescriber.

(3) Physician's drug order: time limits and changes. Medication orders should be reviewed automatically when the patient goes to the delivery room, operating room, or a different service. In addition, a method to protect patients from indefinite, open-ended drug orders must be provided. This may be accomplished through one or more of the following: (1) routine monitoring of patients' drug therapy by a pharmacist; (2) drug class-specific, automatic stop-order policies covering those drug orders not specifying a number of doses or duration of therapy; and (3) automatic cancellation of all drug orders after a predetermined (by the P&T committee) time interval unless rewritten by the prescriber. Whatever the method used, it must protect the patient, as well as provide for a timely notification to the prescriber that the order will be stopped *before* such action takes place.

(4) Physician's drug order: receipt of order and drug profiles. A pharmacist must review and interpret every medication order and resolve any problems or uncertainties with

it before the drug is entered into the dispensing system. This means that he must be satisfied that each questionable medication order is, in fact, acceptable. This may occur through study of the patient's medical record, research of the professional literature, or discussion with the prescriber or other medical, nursing, or pharmacy staff. Procedures to handle a drug order the pharmacist still believes is unacceptable (e.g., very high dose or a use beyond that contained in the package insert) should be prepared (and reviewed by the hospital's legal counsel). In general, the physician must be able to support the use of the drug in these situations. It is generally advisable for the pharmacist to document actions (e.g., verbal notice to the physician that a less toxic drug was available and should be used) relative to a questionable medication order on the pharmacy's patient medication profile form or other pharmacy document (not in the medical record).

Once the order has been approved, it is entered into the *patient's medication profile.* A medication profile must be maintained in the pharmacy for all inpatients and those outpatients routinely receiving care at the institution. (Note: Equivalent records also should be available at the patient-care unit.) This essential item, which is continuously updated, may be a written copy or computer maintained. It serves two purposes. First, it enables the pharmacist to become familiar with the patient's total drug regimen, enabling him to detect quickly potential interactions, unintended dosage changes, drug duplications and overlapping therapies, and drugs contraindicated because of patient allergies or other reasons. Second, it is required in unit dose systems in order for the individual medication doses to be scheduled, prepared, distributed, and administered on a timely basis. The profile information must be reviewed by the pharmacist *before* dispensing the patient's drug(s). (It also may be useful in retrospective review of drug use.)

Patient profile information should include

- Patient's full name, date hospitalized, age, sex, weight, hospital I.D. number, and provisional diagnosis or reason for admission (the format for this information will vary from one hospital to another).
- Laboratory test results.
- Other medical data relevant to the patient's drug therapy (e.g., information from drug history interviews).
- Sensitivities, allergies, and other significant contraindications.
- Drug products dispensed, dates of original orders, strengths, dosage forms, quantities, dosage frequency or directions, and automatic stop dates.
- Intravenous therapy data (this information may be kept on a separate profile form, but there should be a method for the pharmacist to review both concomitantly).
- Blood products administered.
- Pharmacist's or technician's initials.
- Number of doses or amounts dispensed.
- Items relevant or related to the patient's drug therapy (e.g., blood products) not provided by the pharmacy.

(5) Physician's drug order: records. Appropriate records of each medication order and its processing in the pharmacy must be maintained. Such records must be retained in accordance with applicable state laws and regulations. Any changes or clarifications in the order should be written in the chart. The signature(s) or initials of the person(s) verifying the transcription of medication orders into the medication profile should be noted. A way should be provided to determine, for all doses dispensed, who prepared the dose, its date of dispensing, the source of the drug, and the person who checked it. Other information, such as the time of receipt of the order and management data (number of orders per patient day and the like) should be kept as desired. Medication profiles also may be useful for retrospective drug use review studies.

(6) Physician's drug order: special orders.[5,6,13,14] Special orders (i.e., "stat" and emergency orders and those for nonformulary drugs, investigational drugs, restricted use drugs, or controlled substances) should be processed according to specific written procedures meeting all applicable regulations and requirements.

(7) Physician's drug order: other considerations. The pharmacy, nursing, and medical staffs, through the P&T committee, should develop a schedule of standard drug administration times. The nurse should notify the pharmacist whenever it is necessary to deviate from the standard medication schedule.

A mechanism to continually inform the pharmacy of patient admissions, discharges, and transfers should be established.

(8) Intravenous admixture services.[15] The preparation of sterile products (e.g., intravenous admixtures, "piggybacks," and irrigations) is an important part of the drug control system. The pharmacy is responsible for assuring that all such products used in the institution are (1) therapeutically and pharmaceutically appropriate (i.e., are rational and free of incompatibilities or similar problems) to the patient; (2) free from microbial and pyrogenic contaminants; (3) free from unacceptable levels of particulate and other toxic contaminants; (4) correctly prepared (i.e., contain the correct amounts of the correct drugs); and (5) properly labeled, stored, and distributed. Centralizing all sterile compounding procedures within the pharmacy department is the best way to achieve these goals.

Parenteral admixtures and related solutions are subject to the same considerations presented in the preceding sections on "physician's drug order." However, their special characteristics (e.g., complex preparation or need for sterility assurance) also mandate certain additional requirements concerning their preparation, labeling, handling, and quality control. These are described in Reference 15.

It is important that the pharmacy is notified of any problems that arise within the institution pertaining to the use of intravenous drugs and fluids (infections, phlebitis, and product defects).

(9) Medication containers, labeling, and dispensing: stock containers. The pharmacist is responsible for labeling medication containers. Medication labels should be typed or machine printed. Labeling with pen or pencil and the use of adhesive tape or china marking pencils should be prohibited. A label should not be superimposed on another label. The label should be legible and free from erasures and strikeovers. It should be firmly affixed to the container. The labels for stock containers should be protected from chemical action or abrasion and bear the name, address, and telephone number of the hospital. Medication containers and labels should not be altered by anyone other than pharmacy personnel. Prescription labels should not be distributed outside the pharmacy. Accessory labels and statements (shake well, may not be refilled, and the like) should be used as required. Any container to be used outside the institution should bear its name, address, and phone number.

Important labeling considerations are

1. The metric system should be given prominence on all labels when both metric and apothecary measurement units are given.
2. The names of all therapeutically active ingredients should be indicated in compound mixtures.
3. Labels for medications should indicate the amount of drug or drugs in each dosage unit (e.g., per 5 mL and per capsule).
4. rugs and chemicals in forms intended for dilution or reconstitution should carry appropriate directions.
5. he expiration date of the contents, as well as proper storage conditions, should be clearly indicated.
6. The acceptable route(s) of administration should be indicated for parenteral medications.
7. Labels for large volume sterile solutions should permit visual inspection of the container contents.
8. Numbers, letters, coined names, unofficial synonyms, and abbreviations should not be used to identify medications, with the exception of approved letter or number codes for investigational drugs (or drugs being used in blinded clinical studies).
9. Containers presenting difficulty in labeling, such as small tubes, should be labeled with no less than the prescription serial number, name of drug, strength, and name of the patient. The container should then be placed in a larger carton bearing a label with all necessary information.
10. The label should conform to all applicable federal, state, and local laws and regulations.
11. Medication labels of stock containers and repackaged or prepackaged drugs should carry codes to identify the source and lot number of medication.
12. Nonproprietary name(s) should be given prominence over proprietary names.
13. Amount dispensed (e.g., number of tablets) should be indicated.
14. Drug strengths, volumes, and amounts should be given as recommended in References 11 and 16.

(10) Medication containers, labeling, and dispensing: inpatient medications.[11,16] Drug products should be as ready for administration to the patient as the current status of pharmaceutical technology permits. Inpatient medication containers and packages should conform to applicable *USP* requirements and the guidelines in References 11 and 16.

Inpatient self-care and "discharge" medications should be labeled as outpatient prescriptions (see below).

(11) Medication containers, labeling, and dispensing: outpatient medications.[17] Outpatient medications must be labeled in accordance with state board of pharmacy and federal regulations. As noted, medications given to patients as "discharge medication" must be labeled in the pharmacy (not by nursing personnel) as outpatient prescriptions.

The source of the medication and initials of the dispenser should be noted on the prescription form at the time of dispensing. If feasible, the lot number also should be recorded.

An identifying check system to ensure proper identification of outpatients should be established.

Outpatient prescriptions should be packaged in accordance with the provisions of the Poison Prevention Packaging Act of 1970 and any regulations thereunder. They must also meet any applicable requirements of the *USP*.

Any special instructions to or procedures required of the patient relative to the drug's preparation, storage, and administration should be either a part of the label or accompany the medication container received by the patient. Counseling of the patient sufficient to ensure understanding and compliance (to the extent possible) with his medication regimen must be conducted. Nonprescription drugs, if used in the institution, should be labeled as any other medication.

(12) Delivery of medications. Couriers used to deliver medications should be reliable and carefully chosen.

Pneumatic tubes, dumbwaiters, medication carts, and the like should protect drug products from breakage and theft. In those institutions having automatic delivery equipment, such as a pneumatic tube system, provision must be made for an alternative delivery method in case of breakdown.

All parts of the transportation system must protect medications from pilferage. Locks and other security devices should be used where necessary. Procedures for the orderly transfer of medications to the nurse should be instituted; i.e., drug carts or pneumatic tube carriers should not arrive at the patient-care area without the nurse or her designee acknowledging their arrival.

Medications must always be properly secured. Storage areas and equipment should meet the requirements presented in other sections of these guidelines.

(13) Administration of medications. The institution should develop detailed written procedures governing medication administration. In doing so, the following guidelines should be considered:

1. All medications should be administered by appropriately trained and authorized personnel in accordance with the laws, regulations, and institutional policies governing drug administration. It is particularly important that there are written policies and procedures defining responsibility for starting parenteral infusions, administering all intravenous medications, and adding medications to flowing parenteral fluids. Procedures for drug administration by respiratory therapists and during emergency situations also should be established. Exceptions to any of these policies should be provided in writing.
2. All medications should be administered directly from the medication cart (or equivalent) at the patient's room. The use of unit dose packaged drugs eliminates the need for medication cups and cards (and their associated trays), and they should not be used. A medication should not be removed from the unit dose package until it is to be administered.
3. Medications prepared for administration but not used must be returned to the pharmacy.
4. Medications should be given as near the specified time as possible.
5. The patient for whom the medication is intended should be positively identified by checking the patient's identification band or hospital number or by other means as specified by hospital policy.
6. The person administering the medication should stay with the patient until the dose has been taken. Exceptions to this rule are specific medications which may be left at the patient's bedside upon the physician's written order for self-administration.
7. Parenteral medications that are not to be mixed together in a syringe should be given in different injection sites on the patient or separately injected into the

administration site of the administration set of a compatible intravenous fluid.

8. The pharmacy should receive copies of all medication error reports or other medication-related incidents.
9. A system to assure that patients permitted to self-medicate do so correctly should be established.

(14) Return of unused medication. All medications that have not been administered to the patient must remain in the medication cart and be returned to the pharmacy. Only those medications returned in unopened sealed packages may be reissued. Medications returned by outpatients should not be reused. Procedures for crediting and returning drugs to stock should be instituted. A mechanism to reconcile doses not given with nursing and pharmacy records should be provided.

(15) Recording of medication administration. All administered, refused, or omitted medication doses should be recorded in the patient's medical record according to an established procedure. Disposition of doses should occur immediately after administering medications to each patient and before proceeding to the next patient. Information to be recorded should include the drug name, dose and route of administration, date and time of administration, and initials of the person administering the dose.

Drug Samples and Medical Sales Representatives.[18] The use of drug samples within the institution is strongly discouraged and should be eliminated to the extent possible. They should never be used for inpatients (unless, for some reason, no other source of supply is available to the pharmacy). Any samples used must be controlled and dispensed through the pharmacy.

Written regulations governing the activities of medical sales representatives within the institution should be established. Sales representatives should receive a copy of these rules and their activities should be monitored.

Investigational Drugs.[13] Policies and procedures governing the use and control of investigational drugs within the institution are necessary. Detailed procedural guidelines are given in Reference 13.

Radiopharmaceuticals. The basic principles of compounding, packaging, sterilizing, testing, and controlling drugs in institutions apply to radiopharmaceuticals. Therefore, even if the pharmacy department is not directly involved with the preparation and dispensing of these agents, the pharmacist must ensure that their use conforms to the drug control principles set forth in this document.

"Bring-In" Medications. The use of a patient's own medications within the hospital should be avoided to the extent possible. They should be used only if the drugs are not obtainable by the pharmacy. If they are used, the physician must write an appropriate order in the patient's medical chart. The drugs should be sent to the pharmacy for verification of their identity; if not identifiable, they must not be used. They should be dispensed as part of the unit dose system, not separate from it.

Drug Control in Operating and Recovery Rooms.[19] The institution's drug control system must extend to its operating room complex. The pharmacist should ensure that all drugs used within this area are properly ordered, stored, prepared, and accounted for.

Emergency Medication Supplies. A policy to supply emergency drugs when the pharmacist is off the premises or when there is insufficient time to get to the pharmacy should exist. Emergency drugs should be limited in number to include only those whose prompt use and immediate availability are generally regarded by physicians as essential in the proper treatment of sudden and unforeseen patient emergencies. The emergency drug supply should not be a source for normal "stat" or "p.r.n." drug orders. The medications included should be primarily for the treatment of cardiac arrest, circulatory collapse, allergic reactions, convulsions, and bronchospasm. The P&T committee should specify the drugs and supplies to be included in emergency stocks.

Emergency drug supplies should be inspected by pharmacy personnel on a routine basis to determine if contents have become outdated and are maintained at adequate levels. Emergency kits should have a seal which visually indicates when they have been opened. The expiration date of the kit should be clearly indicated.

Pharmacy Service When the Pharmacy Is Closed. Hospitals provide services to patients 24 hours a day. Pharmaceutical services are an integral part of the total care provided by the hospital, and the services of a pharmacist should be available at all times. Where around the clock operation of the pharmacy is not feasible, a pharmacist should be available on an "on call" basis. The use of "night cabinets" and drug dispensing by nonpharmacists should be minimized and eliminated wherever possible.

Drugs must not be dispensed to outpatients or hospital staff by anyone other than a pharmacist while the pharmacy is open. If it is necessary for nurses to obtain drugs when the pharmacy is closed and the pharmacist is unavailable, written procedures covering this practice should be developed. They generally should provide for a limited supply of the drugs most commonly needed in these situations; the drugs should be in proper single dose packages and a log should be kept of all doses removed. This log must contain the date and time the drugs were removed, a complete description of the drug product(s), name of the (authorized) nurse involved, and the patient's name.

Drugs should not be dispensed to emergency room patients by nonpharmacist personnel if the pharmacy is open. When no pharmacist is available, emergency room patients should receive drugs packaged, to the extent possible, in single unit packages; no more than a day's supply of doses should be dispensed. The use of an emergency room "formulary" is recommended.[20]

Adverse Drug Reactions. The medical, nursing, and pharmacy staffs must always be alert to the potential for, or presence of, adverse drug reactions. A written procedure to record clinically significant adverse drug reactions should be established. They should be reported to the FDA, the involved drug manufacturer, and the institution's P&T committee (or its equivalent). Adverse drug reaction reports should contain

- Patient's age, sex, and race.
- Description of the drug reaction and the suspected cause.
- Name of drug(s) suspected of causing the reaction.
- Administration route and dose.
- Name(s) of other drugs received by patient.
- Treatment of the reaction, if any.

These reports, along with other significant reports from the literature, should be reviewed and evaluated by the P&T committee. Steps necessary to minimize the incidence of adverse drug reactions in the facility should be taken.

Medication Errors. If a medication error is detected, the patient's physician must be informed immediately. A written report should be prepared describing any medication errors of clinical import observed in the prescribing, dispensing, or administration of a medication. This report, in accordance with hospital policy, should be prepared and sent to the appropriate hospital officials (including the pharmacy) within 24 hours.

These reports should be analyzed, and any necessary action taken, to minimize the possibility of recurrence of such errors. Properly utilized, these incident reports will help to assure optimum drug use control. Medication error reports should be reviewed periodically by the P&T committee. (It should be kept in mind that, in the absence of an organized, independent error detection system, most medication errors will go unnoticed.)

The following definitions of medication errors are suggested. A *medication error* is broadly defined as a dose of medication that deviates from the physician's order as written in the patient's chart or from standard hospital policy and procedures. Except for errors of omission, the medication dose must actually reach the patient; i.e., a wrong dose that is detected and corrected before administration to the patient is not a medication error. Prescribing errors (e.g., therapeutically inappropriate drugs or doses) are excluded from this definition.

Following are the nine categories of medication errors:

1. *Omission error:* the failure to administer an ordered dose. However, if the patient refuses to take the medication, no error has occurred. Likewise, if the dose is not administered because of recognized contraindications, no error has occurred.
2. *Unauthorized drug error:* administration to the patient of a medication dose not authorized for the patient. This category includes a dose given to the wrong patient, duplicate doses, administration of an unordered drug, and a dose given outside a stated set of clinical parameters (e.g., medication order to administer only if the patient's blood pressure falls below a predetermined level).
3. *Wrong dose error:* any dose that is the wrong number of preformed units (e.g., tablets) or any dose above or below the ordered dose by a predetermined amount (e.g., 20%). In the case of ointments, topical solutions, and sprays, an error occurs only if the medication order expresses the dosage quantitatively, e.g., 1 inch of ointment or two 1-second sprays.
4. *Wrong route error:* administration of a drug by a route other than that ordered by the physician. Also included are doses given via the correct route but at the wrong site (e.g., left eye instead of right).
5. *Wrong rate error:* administration of a drug at the wrong rate, the correct rate being that given in the physician's order or as established by hospital policy.
6. *Wrong dosage form error:* administration of a drug by the correct route but in a different dosage form than that specified or implied by the physician. Example of this error type include use of an ophthalmic ointment when a solution was ordered. Purposeful alteration (e.g., crushing of a tablet) or substitution (e.g., substituting liquid for a tablet) of an oral dosage form to facilitate administration is generally not an error.
7. *Wrong time error:* administration of a dose of drug greater than $\pm X$ hours from its scheduled administration time, X being as set by hospital policy.
8. *Wrong preparation of a dose:* incorrect preparation of the medication dose. Examples are incorrect dilution or reconstitution, not shaking a suspension, using an expired drug, not keeping a light-sensitive drug protected from light, and mixing drugs that are physically/chemically incompatible.
9. *Incorrect administration technique:* situations when the drug is given via the correct route, site, and so forth, but improper technique is used. Examples are not using Z-track injection technique when indicated for a drug, incorrect instillation of an ophthalmic ointment, and incorrect use of an administration device.

Special Considerations Contributing to Drug Control

Pharmacy Personnel and Management.[21–24] Adequate numbers of competent personnel and a well-managed pharmacy are the keys to an effective drug control system. References 21–24 provide guidance on the competencies required of the pharmacy staff and on administrative requirements of a well-run pharmacy department.

Assuring Rational Drug Therapy: Clinical Services.[21,25] Maximizing rational drug use is an important part of the drug control system. Although all pharmacy services contribute to this goal in a sense, the provision of drug information to the institution's patients and staff and the pharmacy's clinical services are those that most directly contribute to rational drug therapy. They are, in fact, institutional pharmacists' most important contributions to patient care.

Facilities. Space and equipment requirements relative to drug storage have been discussed previously. In addition to these considerations, space and equipment must be sufficient to provide for safe and efficient drug preparation and distribution, patient education and consultation, drug information services, and proper management of the department.

Hospital Committees Important to Drug Control.[26,27] Several hospital committees deal with matters of drug control, and the pharmacist must actively participate in their activities. Among these committees (whose names may vary among institutions) are the P&T committee, infection control committee, use review committee, product evaluation committee, patient care committee, and the committee for protection of human subjects. Of particular importance to the drug control system are the formulary and drug use review (DUR) functions of the P&T committee (although DUR in many institutions may be under a use review or quality-assurance committee).

Drug Use Review.[28] Review of how drugs are prescribed and used is an important part of institutional quality-assurance and drug control systems. DUR programs may be performed retrospectively or, preferably, concurrently or prospectively. They may utilize patient outcomes or therapeutic processes as the basis for judgments about the appropriateness of drug prescribing and use. Depending on the review methodology, the pharmacist should be involved in

1. Preparing, in cooperation with the medical staff, drug use criteria and standards.
2. Obtaining quantitative data on drug use, i.e., information on the amounts and types of drugs used, prescribing patterns by medical service, type of patient, and so forth. These data will be useful in setting priorities for the review program. They also may serve as a measure of the effectiveness of DUR programs, assist in analyzing nosocomial infection and culture and sensitivity data, and help in preparing drug budgets.
3. Reviewing medication orders against the drug use criteria and standards.
4. Consulting with prescribers concerning the results of 3 above.
5. Participating in the followup activities of the review program, i.e., educational programs directed at prescribers, development of recommendations for the formulary, and changes in drug control procedures in response to the results of the review process.

It should be noted that the overall DUR program is a joint responsibility of the pharmacy and the organized medical staff; it is not unilaterally a pharmacy or medical staff function.

Quality Assurance for Pharmaceutical Services.[29] To ensure that the drug control system is functioning as intended, there should be a formalized method to (1) set precise objectives (in terms of outcome and process criteria and standards) for the system; (2) measure and verify the degree of compliance with these standards, i.e., the extent to which the objectives have been realized; and (3) eliminate any noncompliance situations. Such a *quality-assurance program* will be distinct from, though related to, the DUR activities of the department.

Drug Recalls. A written procedure to handle drug product recalls should be developed. Any such system should have the following elements:

1. Whenever feasible, notation of the drug manufacturer's name and drug lot number should appear on outpatient prescriptions, inpatient drug orders or profiles, packaging control records, and stock requisitions and their associated labels.
2. Review of these documents (prescriptions, drug orders, and so forth) to determine the recipients (patients and nursing stations) of the recalled lots. Optimally, this would be done by automated means.
3. In the case of product recalls of substantial clinical significance, a notice should go to the recipients that they have a recalled product. The course of action they should take should be included. In the case of outpatients, caution should be exercised not to cause undue alarm. The uninterrupted therapy of the patients must be assured; i.e., replacement of the recalled drugs generally will be required. The hospital's administration and nursing and medical staffs should be informed of any recalls having significant therapeutic implications. Some situations also may require notifying the physicians of patients receiving drugs that have been recalled.
4. Personal inspection of all patient-care areas should be made to determine if recalled products are present.
5. Quarantine of all recalled products obtained (marked "Quarantined—Do Not Use") until they are picked up by or returned to the manufacturer.
6. Maintenance of a written log of all recalls, the actions taken, and their results.

Computerization.[30] Many information handling tasks in the drug control system (e.g., collecting, recording, storing, retrieving, summarizing, transmitting, and displaying drug use information) may be done more efficiently by computers than by manual systems. Before the drug control system can be computerized, however, a comprehensive, thorough study of the existing manual system must be conducted. This study should identify the data flow within the system and define the functions to be done and their interrelationships. This information is then used as the basis to design or prospectively evaluate a computer system; any other considerations, such as those of the hospital accounting department, are subordinate.

The computer system must include adequate safeguards to maintain the confidentiality of patient records.

A backup system must be available to continue the computerized functions during equipment failure. All transactions occurring while the computer system is inoperable should be entered into the system as soon as possible.

Data on controlled substances must be readily retrievable in written form from the system.

Defective Drug Products, Equipment, and Supplies. The pharmacist should be notified of any defective drug products (or related supplies and equipment) encountered by the nursing or medical staffs. All drug product defects should be reported to the USP–FDA–ASHP Drug Product Defect Reporting Program.

Disposal of Hazardous Substances. Hazardous substances (e.g., toxic or flammable solvents and carcinogenic agents) must be disposed of properly in accordance with the requirements of the Environmental Protection Agency or other applicable regulations. The substances should not be poured indiscriminately down the drain or mixed in with the usual trash.

Unreconstituted vials or ampuls and unopened bottles of oral medications supplied by the National Cancer Institute (NCI) should be returned to the NCI's contract storage and distribution facility.

Other intact products should be returned to the original source for disposition.

Units of anticancer drugs no longer intact, such as reconstituted vials, opened ampuls, and bottles of oral medications, and any equipment (e.g., needles and syringes) used in their preparation require a degree of caution greater than with less toxic compounds to safeguard personnel from accidental exposure. The National Institutes of Health recommends that all such materials be segregated for special destruction procedures. The items should be kept in special containers marked *"Danger—Chemical Carcinogens."* Needles and syringes first should be rendered unusable and then placed in specially marked plastic bags. Care should be taken to prevent penetration and leakage of the bags. Excess liquids should be placed in sealed containers; the original vial is satisfactory. Disposal of all of the above materials should be by incineration to destroy organic material.

Alternate disposal for BCG vaccine products has been recommended by the Bureau of Biologics (BOB). The BOB suggests that all containers and equipment used with BCG vaccines be sterilized prior to disposal. Autoclaving at 121 ^{0}C for 30 minutes will sterilize the equipment.

At all steps in the handling of anticancer drugs and other hazardous substances, care should be taken to safeguard professional and support services personnel from accidental exposure to these agents.

References

1. Ginnow WK, King CM Jr. Revision and reorganization of a hospital pharmacy policy and procedure manual. *Am J Hosp Pharm.* 1978; 35:698–704.
2. Accreditation manual for hospitals 1980. Chicago: Joint Commission on Accreditation of Hospitals; 1979.
3. Publications, reprints and services. Washington, DC: American Society of Hospital Pharmacists; current edition.
4. American Society of Hospital Pharmacists. ASHP guidelines for selecting pharmaceutical manufacturers and distributors. *Am J Hosp Pharm.* 1976; 33:645–6.
5. American Society of Hospital Pharmacists. ASHP guidelines for hospital formularies. *Am J Hosp Pharm.* 1978; 35:326–8.
6. American Society of Hospital Pharmacists. ASHP statement of guiding principles on the operation of the hospital formulary system. *Am J Hosp Pharm.* 1964; 21:40–1.
7. American Society of Hospital Pharmacists. ASHP guidelines for repackaging oral solids and liquids in single unit and unit dose packages. *Am J Hosp Pharm.* 1979; 36:223–4.
8. 21 CFR Parts 210 and 211. Current good manufacturing practices in manufacturing, processing, packing or holding of drugs. April 1979.
9. Sourcebook on unit dose drug distribution systems. Washington, DC: American Society of Hospital Pharmacists; 1978.
10. American Society of Hospital Pharmacists. ASHP statement on unit dose drug distribution. *Am J Hosp Pharm.* 1975; 32:835.
11. American Society of Hospital Pharmacists. ASHP guidelines for single unit and unit dose packages of drugs. *Am J Hosp Pharm.* 1977; 34:613–4.
12. American Society of Hospital Pharmacists. ASHP guidelines for obtaining authorization for pharmacists' notations in the patient medical record. *Am J Hosp Pharm.* 1979; 36:222–3.
13. American Society of Hospital Pharmacists. ASHP guidelines for the use of investigational drugs in institutions. *Am J Hosp Pharm.* 1979; 36:221–2.
14. American Society of Hospital Pharmacists. ASHP guidelines for institutional use of controlled substances. *Am J Hosp Pharm.* 1974; 31:582–8.
15. Recommendations of the National Coordinating Committee on Large Volume Parenterals. Washington, DC: American Society of Hospital Pharmacists; 1980.
16. National Coordinating Committee on Large Volume Parenterals. Recommendations for the labeling of large volume parenterals. *Am J Hosp Pharm.* 1978; 35:49–51.
17. American Society of Hospital Pharmacists. ASHP guidelines on pharmacist-conducted patient counseling. *Am J Hosp Pharm.* 1976; 33:644–5.
18. Lipman AG, Mullen HF. Quality control of medical service representative activities in the hospital. *Am J Hosp Pharm.* 1974; 31:167–70.
19. Evans DM, Guenther AM, Keith TD, et al. Pharmacy practice in an operating room complex. *Am J Hosp Pharm.* 1979; 36:1342–7.
20. Mar DD, Hanan ZI, LaFontaine R. Improved emergency room medication distribution. *Am J Hosp Pharm.* 1978; 35:70–3.
21. American Society of Hospital Pharmacists. ASHP minimum standard for pharmacies in institutions. *Am J Hosp Pharm.* 1977; 34:1356–8.
22. American Society of Hospital Pharmacists. ASHP guidelines on the competencies required in institutional pharmacy practice. *Am J Hosp Pharm.* 1975; 32:917–9.
23. American Society of Hospital Pharmacists. ASHP training guidelines for hospital pharmacy supportive personnel. *Am J Hosp Pharm.* 1976; 33:646–8.
24. American Society of Hospital Pharmacists. ASHP competency standard for pharmacy supportive personnel in organized health care settings. *Am J Hosp Pharm.* 1978; 35:449–51.
25. American Society of Hospital Pharmacists. ASHP statement on clinical functions in institutional pharmacy practice. *Am J Hosp Pharm.* 1978; 35:813.
26. American Society of Hospital Pharmacists. ASHP statement on the pharmacy and therapeutics committee. *Am J Hosp Pharm.* 1978; 35:813–4.
27. American Society of Hospital Pharmacists. ASHP statement on the hospital pharmacist's role in infection control. *Am J Hosp Pharm.* 1978; 35:814–5.
28. Antibiotic use review and infection control: evaluating drug use through patient care audit. Chicago: InterQual, Inc.; 1978.
29. Model quality assurance program for hospital pharmacies, revised. Washington, DC: American Society of Hospital Pharmacists; 1980.
30. Sourcebook on computers in pharmacy. Washington, DC: American Society of Hospitals Pharmacists; 1978.

Developed by the ASHP Council on Professional Affairs. Approved by the ASHP Board of Directors, March 20, 1980. Revised November 1981.

This document contains numerous references to various official ASHP documents and other publications. Inclusion of the latter does not constitute endorsement of their content by the Society; they are, however, considered to be useful elaborations on certain subjects contained herein. To avoid redundancy with other ASHP documents, relevant references are cited in many sections of these guidelines. Most may be obtained from ASHP through its publications catalog

The bibliographic citation for this document is as follows: American Society of Hospital Pharmacists. ASHP technical assistance bulletin on hospital drug distribution and control. *Am J Hosp Pharm.* 1980; 37:1097–103.

ASHP Technical Assistance Bulletin on Repackaging Oral Solids and Liquids in Single Unit and Unit Dose Packages

To maximize the benefits of a unit dose drug distribution system, all drugs must be packaged in single unit or unit dose packages.[a] However, not all drugs are commercially available in single unit (or unit dose) packages. Therefore, the institutional pharmacist must often repackage drugs obtained in bulk containers (e.g., bottles of 500 tablets) into single unit packages so that they may be used in a unit dose system.

Certain precautions must be taken if the quality of drugs repackaged by the pharmacist is to be maintained. The guidelines presented herein will assist the pharmacist in developing procedures for repackaging drugs in a safe and acceptable manner:

1. The packaging operation should be isolated, to the extent possible, from other pharmacy activities.
2. Only one drug product at a time should be repackaged in a specific work area. No drug products other than the one being repackaged should be present in the immediate packaging area. Also, no labels other than those for the product being repackaged should be present in the area.
3. Upon completion of the packaging run, all unused stocks of drugs and all finished packages should be removed from the packaging area. The packaging machinery and related equipment should then be completely emptied, cleaned, and inspected before commencing the next packaging operation.
4. All unused labels (if separate labels are used) should be removed from the immediate packaging area. The operator should verify that none remains in the packaging machine(s). If labels are prepared as part of the packaging operation, the label plate (or analogous part of the printing apparatus) should be removed or adjusted to "blank" upon completion of the run. This will help assure that the correct label is printed during any subsequent run. There should be a procedure to reconcile the number of packages produced with the number of labels used (if any) and destroyed (if any) and the number of units or volume of drug set forth to be packaged.
5. Before beginning a packaging run, an organoleptic evaluation (color, odor, appearance, and markings) of the drug product being repackaged should be made. The bulk container should also be examined for evidence of water damage, contamination, or other deleterious effects.
6. All packaging equipment and systems should be operated and used in accordance with the manufacturer's or other established instructions. There should be valid justification and authorization by the supervisor for any deviation from those instructions on the part of the operator.
7. The pharmacist should obtain data on the characteristics of all packaging materials used. This information should include data on the chemical composition, light transmission, moisture permeability, size, thickness (alone or in laminate), recommended sealing temperature, and storage requirements.
8. Unit dose packages and labels should, to the extent possible, comply with the "ASHP Guidelines for Single Unit and Unit Dose Packages of Drugs."[1]
9. Whenever feasible, a responsible individual, other than the packaging operator, should verify that (a) the packaging system (drug, materials, and machines) is set up correctly and (b) all procedures have been performed properly. Ultimate responsibility for all packaging operations rests with the pharmacist.
10. Control records of all packaging runs must be kept. These records should include the following information: (1) complete description of the product, i.e., name, strength, dosage form, route of administration, etc.; (2) the product's manufacturer or supplier; (3) control number; (4) the pharmacy's control number if different from the manufacturer's; (5) expiration dates of the original container and the repackaged product; (6) number of units packaged and the date(s) they were packaged; (7) initials of the operator and checker (if any); (8) a sample of the label and, if feasible, a sample of the finished package, which should not be discarded until after the expiration date and which should be examined periodically for signs of deterioration; and (9) description (including lot number) of the packaging materials and equipment used.
11. It is the responsibility of the pharmacist to determine the expiration date to be placed on the package, taking into account the nature of the drug repackaged, the characteristics of the package, and the storage conditions to which the drug may be subjected. This date must not be beyond that of the original package.[b]
12. All drugs should be packaged and stored in a temperature- and humidity-controlled environment to minimize degradation caused by heat and moisture. A relative humidity of 75% at 23 °C should not be exceeded. Packaging materials should be stored in accordance with the manufacturer's instructions and any applicable regulations.
13. Written procedures (both general and product specific) governing repackaging operations should be prepared and updated as required. Any deviation from these procedures should be noted and explained on the control record. Operators must understand the procedures (and operation of all packaging equipment) before commencing the run.
14. Applicable FDA and USP requirements concerning the type of package required for specific drug products must be followed.
15. Drugs and chemicals with high vapor pressures should be stored separately from other products to minimize cross contamination.

References

1. American Society of Hospital Pharmacists. ASHP guidelines for single unit and unit dose packages of drugs. *Am J Hosp Pharm.* 1977; 34:613–4.
2. Stolar MH. Expiration dates of repackaged drug products. *Am J Hosp Pharm.* 1979; 36:170. Editorial.

---

[a]A *single unit* package is one which contains one discrete pharmaceutical dosage form, e.g., one tablet or one 5-mL volume of liquid. A *unit dose* package is one which contains the particular dose of drug ordered for the patient. A *single unit* package is a *unit dose (or single dose)* package if it contains that particular dose of drug ordered for the patient.

[b]For specific recommendations on expiration date policy, see Reference 2.

Revised by the ASHP Board of Directors, November 16–17, 1978.

Developed originally by a joint working group of the American Society of Hospital Pharmacists and the American Society of Consultant Pharmacists and representatives of the drug packaging industry. The original document subsequently was approved officially by the Boards of Directors of ASHP and ASCP. FDA reviewed the original document and commended ASHP and ASCP for developing the guidelines.

The bibliographic citation for this document is as follows: American Society of Hospital Pharmacists. ASHP technical assistance bulletin on repackaging oral solids and liquids in single unit and unit dose packages. *Am J Hosp Pharm.* 1983; 40:451–2.

ASHP Technical Assistance Bulletin on Single Unit and Unit Dose Packages of Drugs

Drug packages must fulfill four basic functions:

1. Identify their contents completely and precisely.
2. Protect their contents from deleterious environmental effects (e.g., photodecomposition).
3. Protect their contents from deterioration due to handling (e.g., breakage and contamination).
4. Permit their contents to be used quickly, easily, and safely.

Modern drug distribution systems use single unit packages to a great extent and, in fact, such packages are central to the operation of unit dose systems, intravenous admixture services, and other important aspects of pharmacy practice. These guidelines have been prepared to assist pharmaceutical manufacturers and pharmacists in the development and production of single unit and unit dose packages, the use of which has been shown to have substantial benefits.

A *single unit* package is one that contains one discrete pharmaceutical dosage form, i.e., one tablet, one 2-mL volume of liquid, one 2-g mass of ointment, etc. A *unit dose* package is one that contains the particular dose of the drug ordered for the patient. A single unit package is also a *unit dose* or *single dose* package if it contains the particular dose of the drug ordered for the patient. A unit dose package could, for example, contain two tablets of a drug product.

General Considerations

Packaging Materials. Packaging materials (and the package itself) must possess the physical characteristics required to protect the contents from (as required) light, moisture, temperature, air, and handling. The material should not deteriorate during the shelf life of the contents. Packages should be of lightweight, nonbulky materials that do not produce toxic fumes when incinerated. Materials that may be recycled or are biodegradable, or both, are to be preferred over those that are not. Packaging materials should not absorb, adsorb, or otherwise deleteriously affect their contents. Information should be available to practitioners indicating the stability and compatibility of drugs with various packaging materials.

Shape and Form. Packages should be constructed so that they do not deteriorate with normal handling. They should be easy to open and use, and their use should require little or no special training or experience. Unless the package contains a drug to be added to a parenteral fluid or otherwise used in compounding a finished dosage form, it should allow the contents to be administered directly to the patient (or IPPB apparatus or fluid administration set) without any need for repackaging into another container or device (except for ampuls).

Label Copy. Current federal labeling requirements must be adhered to, with attention also given to the items at right. The desired copy and format are as follows:

Nonproprietary Name
(and proprietary name if to be shown)
Dosage Form (if special or other than oral)
Strength
Strength of Dose and Total Contents Delivered
(e.g., number of tablets and their total dose)
Special Notes (e.g., refrigerate)
Expiration Date
Control Number

1. *Nonproprietary and proprietary names.* The nonproprietary name and the strength should be the most prominent part of the package label. It is not necessary to include the proprietary name, if any, on the package. The name of the manufacturer or distributor should appear on the package. In addition, the name of the manufacturer of the finished dosage form should be included in the product labeling. The style of type should be chosen to provide maximum legibility, contrast, and permanence.
2. *Dosage form.* Special characteristics of the dosage form should be a part of the label, e.g., extended release. Packages should be labeled as to the route of administration if other than oral, e.g., topical use. In a package containing an injection, the acceptable injectable route(s) of administration should be stated on both outer and inner packages, i.e., both on the syringe unit and carton (if any).
3. *Strength.* Strength should be stated in accordance with terminology in the *American Hospital Formulary Service.* The metric system should be used, with dosage forms formulated to provide the rounded-off figures in the *USP* table of approximate equivalents and expressed in the smallest whole number. Micrograms should be used through 999, then milligrams through 999, then grams. Thus, 300 mg, *not* 5 gr, nor 325 mg, nor 0.3 g; 60 mg, *not* 1 gr, nor 0.06 g, nor 64.5 mg, nor 65 mg; 400 mcg, *not* 1/150 gr, nor 0.4 mg, nor 0.0004 g; mL (milliliters) should be used instead of cc (cubic centimeters).
4. *Strength of dose and total contents delivered.* The total contents and total dose of the package should be indicated. Thus, a unit dose package containing a 600-mg dose as two 300-mg tablets should be labeled "600 mg (as two 300-mg tablets)." Likewise, a 500-mg dose of a drug in a liquid containing 100 mg/mL should be labeled "Delivers 500 mg (as 5 mL of 100 mg/mL)."
5. *Special notes.* Special notes such as conditions of storage (e.g., refrigerate), preparation (e.g., shake well or moisten), and administration (e.g., not to be chewed) that are not obvious from the dosage form designation are to be included on the label.
6. *Expiration date.* The expiration date should be prominently visible on the package. If the contents must be reconstituted prior to use, the shelf life of the final product should be indicated. Unless stability data warrant otherwise, expiration dates should fall during January and July to simplify recall procedures.

7. *Control number (lot number).* The control number should appear on the package.

Product Identification Codes. The use of product identification codes, appearing directly on the dosage form, is encouraged.

Evidence of Entry. The package should be so designed that it is evident, when the package is still intact, that it has never been entered or opened.

Specific Considerations

Oral Solids

1. *Blister package.* A blister package should
   - **a.** Have an opaque and nonreflective backing (flat upper surface of package) for printing.
   - **b.** Have a blister (dome or bubble) of a transparent material that is, preferably, flat bottomed.
   - **c.** Be easily peelable.
   - **d.** If it contains a controlled substance, be numbered sequentially for accountability purposes.
2. *Pouch package.* A pouch package should
   - **a.** Have one side opaque and nonreflective for printing.
   - **b.** Be easily deliverable, i.e., large tablets in large pouches, small tablets in small pouches.
   - **c.** Tear from any point or from multiple locations.
   - **d.** If it contains a controlled substance, be numbered sequentially for accountability purposes.
3. The packages should be such that contents can be delivered directly to the patient's mouth or hand.

Oral Liquids

1. The packages should be filled to deliver the labeled contents. It is recognized that overfilling will be necessary, depending on the shape of the container, the container material, and the formulation of the dosage form.
2. The label should state the contents as follows: Delivers ____mg (or g or mcg) in ____mL.
3. If reconstitution is required, the amount of vehicle to be added should be indicated. These directions may take the form of "fill to mark on container" in lieu of stating a specific volume.
4. Syringe-type containers for oral administration should not accept a needle and should be labeled "For Oral Use Only."
5. Containers should be designed to permit administration of contents directly from the package.

Injectables

1. The device should be appropriately calibrated in milliliters and scaled from the tip to the fill line. Calibrated space may be built into the device to permit addition of other drugs. The label should state the contents as follows: Delivers ____mg (or g or mcg) in ____mL.
2. An appropriate size needle may be an integral part of the device. The needle sheath should not be the plunger. The plunger should be mechanically stable in the barrel of the syringe.
3. The device should be of such a design that it is patient ready and assembly instructions are not necessary.
4. The sheath protecting the needle should be a nonpenetrable, preferably rigid material, to protect personnel from injury. The size of the needle should be indicated.
5. The device should be of such a design that easy and visible aspiration is possible. It should be as compact as possible and of such a size that it can be easily handled.

Parenteral Solutions and Additives

1. The approximate pH and osmolarity of parenteral solutions should be stated on the label. The amount of overfill also should be noted. Electrolyte solutions should be labeled in both mEq (or millimole) and mg concentrations. Solutions commonly labeled in terms of percent concentration, e.g., dextrose, should also be labeled in w/v terms.
2. Parenteral fluid container labels should be readable when hanging and when upright or in the normal manipulative position.
3. Drugs to be mixed with parenteral infusion solutions should be packaged into convenient sizes that minimize the need for solution transfers and other manipulations.
4. Partially filled piggyback-type containers should
   - **a.** Be recappable with a tamperproof closure.
   - **b.** Have a hanger.
   - **c.** Have volume markings.
   - **d.** Be designed to minimize the potential for contamination during use.
   - **e.** Contain a partial vacuum for ease of reconstitution.
5. If an administration set is included with the container, it should be compatible with all large volume parenteral delivery systems.

Other Dosage Forms—Ophthalmics, Suppositories, Ointments, etc. Dosage forms other than those specifically discussed above should be adequately labeled to indicate their use and route of administration and should adhere to the above and other required package labeling and design criteria.

Approved by the ASHP Board of Directors, November 14–15, 1984. Revised by the ASHP Council on Clinical Affairs. Supersedes the previous version, which was approved on March 31–April 1, 1977.

The bibliographic citation for this document is as follows: American Society of Hospital Pharmacists. ASHP technical assistance bulletin on single unit and unit dose packages of drugs. *Am J Hosp Pharm.* 1985; 42:378–9.

Education and Training

Education and Training

Developing Leadership Competencies (1518)
Source: Council on Education and Workforce Development
To work with healthcare organization leadership to foster opportunities for pharmacy practitioners to move into leadership roles; further,

To encourage leaders to seek out and mentor pharmacy practitioners in developing administrative, managerial, and leadership skills; further,

To encourage pharmacy practitioners to obtain the skills necessary to pursue administrative, managerial, and leadership roles; further,

To encourage colleges of pharmacy and ASHP state affiliates to collaborate in fostering student leadership skills through development of co-curricular leadership opportunities, leadership conferences, and other leadership promotion programs; further,

To reaffirm that residency programs should develop leadership skills through mentoring, training, and leadership opportunities; further,

To foster leadership skills for pharmacists to use on a daily basis in their roles as leaders in patient care.

This policy supersedes ASHP policy 0509.

Pharmacy Technician Training and Certification (1519)
Source: Council on Education and Workforce Development
To support the position that by the year 2020, the completion of a pharmacy technician training program accredited by ASHP and the Accreditation Council for Pharmacy Education (ACPE) be required to obtain Pharmacy Technician Certification Board certification for all new pharmacy technicians entering the workforce; further,

To foster expansion of ASHP-ACPE accredited pharmacy technician training programs.

This policy supersedes ASHP policies 1015 and 0702.

Cultural Competency and Cultural Diversity (1414)
Source: Council on Education and Workforce Development
To promote the development of cultural competency of pharmacy educators, practitioners, residents, students, and technicians; further,

To educate providers on the importance of providing culturally congruent care to achieve quality care and patient engagement; further,

To foster awareness of the impact that an ethnically and culturally diverse workforce has on improving health care quality.

This policy supersedes ASHP policies 0314 and 0409.

Pharmacy Resident and Student Roles in New Practice Models (1316)
Source: Council on Education and Workforce Development
To promote pharmacy practice and training models that: (1) provide experiential and residency training in team-based patient care; (2) recognize and utilize the skills and knowledge of student pharmacists and residents in providing direct patient care services; (3) augment the patient care services of pharmacists through expanded roles for residents as practitioner learners; and (4) where appropriate, utilize an approach to learning and service in which a supervising pharmacist oversees the services of students, residents, and other pharmacists providing direct patient care; further,

To support the assessment of the impact of these pharmacy practice and training models on the quality of learner experiences and patient care outcomes.

This policy supersedes ASHP policy 1204.

Education and Training in Health Care Informatics (1317)
Source: Council on Education and Workforce Development
To recognize the significant and vast impacts of health-system information systems, automation, and technology changes on safe and effective use of medications; further,

To foster, promote, and lead the development of and participation in formal health care informatics educational programs for pharmacists, pharmacy technicians, and student pharmacists.

Preceptor Skills and Abilities (1201)
Source: Council on Education and Workforce Development
To collaborate with pharmacy organizations on the development of standards to enhance the quality of experiential education and pharmacy residency precepting; further,

To provide tools, education, and other resources to develop preceptor skills.

Qualifications of Pharmacy Technicians in Advanced Roles (1203)
Source: Council on Education and Workforce Development
To recognize that highly trained and skilled pharmacy technicians working in advanced roles regularly perform complex and critical medication-use procedures, and that a safe and effective medication-use process depends significantly on the skills, knowledge, and competency of those pharmacy technicians to perform those tasks; further,

To reaffirm that all pharmacy technicians should complete an ASHP-accredited training program, be certified by the Pharmacy Technician Certification Board, and be licensed by state boards of pharmacy; further,

To advocate that beyond those requirements pharmacy technicians working in advanced roles should have additional training and should demonstrate ongoing competencies specific to the tasks to be performed; further,

To advocate that expansion of pharmacy technician duties into expanded, advanced roles should include consideration of potential risk to patients and that ongoing quality assurance metrics should be established to assure patient safety.

Quality of Pharmacy Education and Expansion of Colleges of Pharmacy (1108)
Source: Council on Education and Workforce Development
To support the Accreditation Council for Pharmacy Education's continuing role of promulgating accreditation standards and guidelines and engaging in sound accreditation processes to ensure quality in the education provided by colleges of pharmacy; further,

To acknowledge that, in addition to a robust curriculum, access to quality experiential educational sites and the availability of qualified faculty (including preceptors and specialty-trained clinical faculty) are essential determinants of the ability to expand enrollment in existing or additional colleges of pharmacy; further,

To oppose expansion of enrollment in existing or new colleges of pharmacy unless well-designed projections demonstrate that such enrollment increases are necessary to maintain a viable pharmacist workforce.

This policy supersedes ASHP policy 0607.

Residency Equivalency (1109)
Source: Council on Education and Workforce Development
To acknowledge the distinct role of ASHP-accredited residency training in preparing pharmacists to be direct patient-care providers; further,

To recognize the importance of clinical experience in developing practitioner expertise; further,

To affirm that there are no objective means to convert or express clinical experience as equivalent to or a substitute for the successful completion of an ASHP-accredited residency.

Pharmacy Internships (1110)
Source: Council on Education and Workforce Development
To encourage the National Association of Boards of Pharmacy to develop standardized pharmacy internship hour requirements that would be used uniformly by all state boards of pharmacy; further,

To support structured requirements, goals, and objectives for pharmacy internship experiences, in alignment with requirements for introductory and advanced pharmacy practice experiences; further,

To promote and expand new staffing models that foster expanded roles for pharmacy interns, providing work experiences that build upon their knowledge and help them develop as future pharmacists.

This policy supersedes ASHP policy 0802.

State-Specific Requirements for Pharmacist Continuing Education (1111)
Source: Council on Education and Workforce Development
To support the standardization of state pharmacist continuing education requirements; further,

To advocate that state boards of pharmacy adopt continuing professional development (CPD) as the preferred model for maintaining pharmacist competence and structure continuing education requirements as a component of CPD.

Innovative Residency Models (1112)
Source: Council on Education and Workforce Development
To support the development of innovative residency models that meet ASHP accreditation requirements.

Employment Classification and Duty Hours of Pharmacy Residents (1008)
Source: Council on Public Policy
To advocate that pharmacy residents should be classified as exempt employees; further,

To advocate that pharmacy residents be subject to duty hour limits (similar to resident physicians) with respect to all clinical and academic activities during their training program in accordance with the Accreditation Council on Graduate Medical Education (ACGME) standards and ASHP accreditation standards for pharmacy residency programs.

This policy was reviewed in 2014 by the Council on Public Policy and by the Board of Directors and was found to still be appropriate.

Interprofessional Education and Training (1014)
Source: Council on Education and Workforce Development
To support interprofessional education as a component of didactic and experiential education in Doctor of Pharmacy degree programs; further,

To support interprofessional education as a part of professional development for pharmacy practitioners and to collaborate with other disciplines to facilitate and promote programs that support this goal; further,

To encourage and support pharmacists' collaboration with other health professionals and health care executives in the development of team-based, patient-centered care models; further,

To foster documentation and dissemination of outcomes achieved as a result of interprofessional education of health care professionals.

This policy was reviewed in 2014 by the Council on Education and Workforce Development and by the Board of Directors and was found to still be appropriate.

Pharmacy Student Experiences in Medically Underserved Areas (0913)
Source: Council on Education and Workforce Development
To encourage colleges of pharmacy to require student learning experiences in traditionally medically underserved areas and with diverse patient populations.

This policy was reviewed in 2013 by the Council on Education and Workforce Development and by the Board of Directors and was found to still be appropriate.

Pharmacy Expertise in the Preparation and Handling of Injectable Medications (0915)
Source: Council on Education and Workforce Development
To encourage colleges of pharmacy to include sterile compounding and aseptic technique instruction in the didactic curriculum and during experiential education; further,

To support the development of postgraduate, curriculum-based sterile compounding training programs to foster an increase in the number of pharmacists with sterile compounding expertise.

This policy was reviewed in 2013 by the Council on Education and Workforce Development and by the Board of Directors and was found to still be appropriate.

Continuing Professional Development (0916)
Source: Council on Education and Workforce Development
To endorse and promote the concept of continuing professional development (CPD), which involves personal self-appraisal, educational plan development, plan implementation, documentation, and evaluation; further,

To continue the development of a variety of mechanisms and tools that pharmacists can use to assess their CPD needs; further,

To encourage individual pharmacists to embrace CPD as a means of maintaining their own professional competence; further,

To encourage pharmacy managers to promote CPD as the model for ensuring the competence of their staff; further,

To collaborate with other pharmacy organizations, state boards of pharmacy, accrediting bodies, and regulatory bodies in the development of effective methods for implementing CPD; further,

To strongly support objective assessment of the impact of CPD on pharmacist competence; further,

To endorse the efforts of colleges of pharmacy and ASHP-accredited pharmacy residency programs to teach the principles, concepts, and skills of CPD.

This policy was reviewed in 2013 by the Council on Education and Workforce Development and by the Board of Directors and was found to still be appropriate.

Pharmacy Residency Training (0917)

Source: Council on Education and Workforce Development

To continue efforts to increase the number of ASHP-accredited pharmacy residency training programs and positions available.

This policy was reviewed in 2013 by the Council on Education and Workforce Development and by the Board of Directors and was found to still be appropriate.

Collaboration Regarding Experiential Education (0804)

Source: Council on Education and Workforce Development

To promote collaboration of health-system teaching sites with the colleges of pharmacy (nationally or regionally), for the purpose of fostering preceptor development, standardization of experiential rotation schedule dates and evaluation tools, and other related matters.

This policy was reviewed in 2012 by the Council on Education and Workforce Development and by the Board of Directors and was found to still be appropriate.

Requirement for Residency (0701)

Source: House of Delegates Resolution

To support the position that by the year 2020, the completion of an ASHP-accredited postgraduate-year-one residency should be a requirement for all new college of pharmacy graduates who will be providing direct patient care.

This policy was reviewed in 2011 by the Council on Education and Workforce Development and by the Board of Directors and was found to still be appropriate.

Residency Programs (0704)

Source: Council on Education and Workforce Development

To strongly advocate that all pharmacy residency programs become ASHP-accredited as a means of ensuring and conveying program quality.

This policy was reviewed in 2012 by the Council on Education and Workforce Development and by the Board of Directors and was found to still be appropriate.

ASHP Guidelines, Statements, and Professional Policies as an Integral Part of the Educational Process (0705)

Source: Council on Education and Workforce Development

To encourage faculties in colleges of pharmacy and preceptors of ASHP-accredited residency training programs to use ASHP statements, guidelines, and professional policies as an integral part of training programs and courses.

This policy was reviewed in 2011 by the Council on Education and Workforce Development and by the Board of Directors and was found to still be appropriate.

Communication Among Health-System Pharmacy Practitioners, Patients, and Other Health Care Providers (0510)

Source: Council on Educational Affairs

To foster effective communication (with appropriate attention to patients' levels of general and health literacy) among health-system pharmacy practitioners, patients, and other health care providers; further,

To develop programs to enable pharmacy students, residents, and health-system pharmacy practitioners to self-assess their levels of health literacy and general communication skills; further,

To develop methods with which pharmacy students, residents, and health-system pharmacy practitioners can assess the level of general and health literacy of patients; further,

To disseminate information about resources for students, residents, and health-system pharmacy practitioners to use in working with patients and others having specific communication needs.

This policy was reviewed in 2014 by the Council on Education and Workforce Development and by the Board of Directors and was found to still be appropriate.

Practice Sites for Colleges of Pharmacy (0315)

Source: Council on Educational Affairs

To encourage practitioner input in pharmacy education; further,

To encourage that institutional and health-system environments be used as sites for experiential training of pharmacy students; further,

To encourage colleges of pharmacy and health systems to define and develop appropriate organizational relationships that permit a balance of patient care and service, as well as educational and research objectives, in a mutually beneficial manner; further,

To include the administrative interests of both the health system and the college of pharmacy in defining these organizational relationships to ensure compatibility of institutional (i.e., health system or university) and departmental (i.e., pharmacy department and department in the college) objectives; further,

To encourage pharmacists and pharmacy leaders to recognize that part of their professional responsibility is the development of new pharmacy practitioners.

This policy was reviewed in 2012 by the Council on Education and Workforce Development and by the Board of Directors and was found to still be appropriate.

Licensure for Pharmacy Graduates of Foreign Schools (0323)

Source: Council on Legal and Public Affairs

To support state licensure eligibility of a pharmacist who has graduated from a pharmacy program accredited by the Accreditation Council for Pharmacy Education (ACPE) or accredited by an ACPE-recognized accreditation program.

This policy was reviewed in 2012 by the Council on Public Policy and by the Board of Directors and was found to still be appropriate.

Public Funding for Pharmacy Residency Training (0325)
Source: Council on Legal and Public Affairs
To support legislation and regulation that ensures public funding for accredited pharmacy residency programs consistent with the needs of the public and the profession; further,

To oppose legislation or regulation involving reimbursement levels for graduate medical education that adversely affects pharmacy residencies at a rate disproportionate to other residency programs.

This policy was reviewed in 2012 by the Council on Public Policy and by the Board of Directors and was found to still be appropriate.

Residency Training for Pharmacists Who Provide Direct Patient Care (0005)
Source: Council on Educational Affairs
To recognize that optimal direct patient care by a pharmacist requires the development of clinical judgment, which can be acquired only through experience and reflection on that experience; further,

To establish as a goal that pharmacists who provide direct patient care should have completed an ASHP-accredited residency or have attained comparable skills through practice experience.

This policy was reviewed in 2014 by the Council on Education and Workforce Development and by the Board of Directors and was found to still be appropriate.

Career Counseling (8507)
Source: Council on Educational Affairs
To urge colleges of pharmacy to develop career counseling programs to make students aware of postgraduate career options, including residency training and career paths in various types of practice; further,

To urge that career counseling occur in a structured manner early in the curriculum and be continued throughout the curriculum; further,

To urge practitioners in various organized health care settings to make themselves available to colleges of pharmacy for participation in both structured and unstructured career counseling.

This policy was reviewed in 2011 by the Council on Education and Workforce Development and by the Board of Directors and was found to still be appropriate.

Definitions of Pharmacy Residencies and Fellowships

Pharmacy residencies (originally termed "internships") began in the early 1930s, primarily for the purpose of training pharmacists for the management of pharmacy services in hospitals. The first nonacademic residency program is believed to have been conducted by Harvey A. K. Whitney at the University of Michigan Hospital.[1] Approximately 10 years later, the first residency program combined with formal graduate studies was created.[2] Developments in these programs eventually led the American Society of Hospital Pharmacists to establish, in 1948, standards for pharmacy internships in hospitals.[3] Those standards defined an internship as "a period of organized training in an accredited hospital pharmacy under the direction and supervision of personnel qualified to offer such training."

Two types of internships were recognized, nonacademic and academic. The nonacademic internship consisted of a period of training in a hospital pharmacy. The academic internship consisted of training in a hospital pharmacy and study in an accredited graduate school associated with a college of pharmacy and leading to a Master of Science degree.

In 1962, following several revisions in the standards, ASHP established an accreditation process and accreditation standards for residencies in hospital pharmacy.[4,5] In this action, the term "internship" was replaced by "residency." A residency was defined as "a postgraduate program of organized training . . ." (and further detailed within the various standards). In 1985, the concept that a resident's training should be *directed* was incorporated into the definition.[6–9] It was also acknowledged that a residency is practice oriented and that it is possible for a residency to focus on a defined (specialized) area.

During the early 1970s, numerous residencies developed in *clinical* practice, leading to the establishment, in 1980, of accreditation standards for clinical pharmacy and specialized residency training.[10,11] In 1986, the American Pharmaceutical Association published a compilation of programmatic essentials for community pharmacy residencies.[12] In that same year, the American College of Apothecaries published specific guidelines for the accreditation of community pharmacy residencies.[13]

Paralleling these developments and fostered by a growing sophistication and clinical thrust in institutional pharmacy practice, postgraduate research-oriented programs (generally termed "fellowships") developed in the 1970s. These programs were conducted primarily in colleges of pharmacy and in academically based health centers to educate and train individuals to conduct pharmacy research. A 1981 survey of fellowship programs reported the existence of 58 fellowships in 19 topic areas.[14] Two-thirds of these fellowships had existed for 3 years or less. The oldest program had existed for less than 9 years. The ASHP Research and Education Foundation initiated clinical fellowships in 1978 and defined a pharmacy fellowship as "a directed, but highly individualized program [that] emphasizes research. The focus of a pharmacy fellowship is to develop the participant's (the fellow's) ability to conduct research in his or her area of specialization."[15,16]

ASHP publishes an annual directory of ASHP-accredited residency programs. In 1985, there were 184 accredited programs.[17] The American College of Clinical Pharmacy publishes an annual listing of residencies and fellowships conducted by its members. In 1985, ACCP reported the availability of 51 such residencies and 83 such fellowships.[18] Another source reported 115 known fellowships in 1986.[19] In that year, there were 12 clinical fellowships sponsored by the ASHP Research and Education Foundation in nine areas of specialization.

By 1986, a lack of conformity had arisen in the use of the terms "residency" and "fellowship," and considerable potential existed for program applicants to be misinformed or misled regarding program purposes and content. In 1986, at the recommendation of the ASHP Commission on Credentialing, ASHP invited six other national pharmacy organizations to discuss the issue and develop consensus definitions for the terms. The definitions and interpretations that follow resulted from that conference. These definitions and interpretations are viewed as accurate for current residencies and fellowships yet sufficiently broad and flexible to allow the development of new types of programs. Education, practice, and research developments may generate changes in residencies and fellowships and ultimately stimulate revisions in the definitions and interpretations.

Residency

Definition. A pharmacy residency is an organized, directed, postgraduate training program in a defined area of phamacy practice.

Interpretation. Residencies exist primarily to train pharmacists in professional practice and management activities. Residencies provide experience in integrating pharmacy services with the comprehensive needs of individual practice settings and provide indepth experiences leading to advanced practice skills and knowledge. Residencies foster an ability to conceptualize new and improved pharmacy services. Within a given residency program, there is considerable consistency in content for each resident. In addition, accreditation standards and program guidelines produced by national pharmacy associations provide considerable program content detail and foster consistency among programs.

A residency is typically 12 months or longer in duration, and the resident's practice experiences are closely directed and evaluated by a qualified practitioner–preceptor. A residency may occur at any career point following an entry-level degree in pharmacy. Individuals planning practice-oriented careers are encouraged to complete all formal academic education before entry into a residency.

Fellowship

Definition. A pharmacy fellowship is a directed, highly individualized, postgraduate program designed to prepare the participant to become an independent researcher.

Interpretation. Fellowships exist primarily to develop competency in the scientific research process, including conceptualizing, planning, conducting, and reporting research. Under the close direction and instruction of a qualified researcher-preceptor, the participant (the fellow) receives a highly individualized learning experience that utilizes research interests and knowledge needs as a focus for his or her education and training. A fellowship graduate should be capable of conducting collaborative research or functioning as a principal investigator.

Fellowships are typically offered through colleges of pharmacy, academic health centers, or specialized health-care institutions. Fellowships are usually offered for predetermined, finite periods of time, often exceeding 12 or even 24 months. Individuals planning research-oriented careers should expect to complete formal education in research design and statistics either before or during a fellowship. A fellowship candidate is expected to possess basic practice skills relevant to the knowledge area of the fellowship. Such skills may be obtained through practice experience or through an appropriate residency and should be maintained during the program.

References

1. Niemeyer G. Ten years of the American Society of Hospital Pharmacists, 1942–1952: education and training. *Bull Am Soc Hosp Pharm.* 1952; 9:363–75.
2. American Society of Hospital Pharmacists. Approval program for internships in hospital pharmacy. *Bull Am Soc Hosp Pharm.* 1955; 12:309–13.
3. American Society of Hospital Pharmacists. Standards for internships in hospital pharmacies. *Bull Am Soc Hosp Pharm.* 1948; 5:233–4.
4. American Society of Hospital Pharmacists. Minimum standard for pharmacy internship in hospitals. *Bull Am Soc Hosp Pharm.* 1955; 12:288–90.
5. American Society of Hospital Pharmacists. Accreditation standard for residency in hospital pharmacy. *Am J Hosp Pharm.* 1963; 20:378–80.
6. American Society of Hospital Pharmacists. Accreditation standard for pharmacy residency in a hospital. *Am J Hosp Pharm.* 1971; 28:189–90.
7. American Society of Hospital Pharmacists. Accreditation standard for pharmacy residency in a hospital. *Am J Hosp Pharm.* 1973; 30:1129.
8. American Society of Hospital Pharmacists. ASHP accreditation standard for pharmacy residency in a hospital (with guide to interpretation). *Am J Hosp Pharm.* 1979; 36:74–80.
9. American Society of Hospital Pharmacists. ASHP accreditation standard for hospital pharmacy training (with guide to interpretation). *Am J Hosp Pharm.* 1985; 42:2008–18.
10. American Society of Hospital Pharmacists. ASHP accreditation standard for residency training in clinical pharmacy (with guide to interpretation). *Am J Hosp Pharm.* 1980; 37:1223–8.
11. American Society of Hospital Pharmacists. ASHP accreditation standard for specialized residency training (with guide to interpretation). *Am J Hosp Pharm.* 1980; 37:1229–32.
12. American Pharmaceutical Association, Academy of Pharmacy Practice. APhA community pharmacy residency program: programmatic essentials. *Am Pharm.* 1986; NS26:35–43.
13. American College of Apothecaries. Guidelines for accreditation of community pharmacy residencies. Memphis, TN: American College of Apothecaries; 1986.
14. Kaul AF, Powell SH, Cyr DA. Postgraduate pharmacy fellowships. *Drug Intell Clin Pharm.* 1981; 15:981–5.
15. ASHP Commission on Credentialing. Statement of definition of pharmacy fellowships and residency. Bethesda, MD: American Society of Hospital Pharmacists; 1981.
16. McConnell W. Fellowship program in critical care pharmacy. In: Majerus TC, Dasta JF, eds. Practice of critical care pharmacy. Rockville, MD: Aspen Systems; 1985:59–68.
17. American Society of Hospital Pharmacists. Residency directory. Accredited pharmacy residency programs and programs participating in the 1986 ASHP resident matching program. Bethesda, MD: American Society of Hospital Pharmacists; 1985.
18. American College of Clinical Pharmacy. Residency and fellowship programs offered by members of the American College of Clinical Pharmacy, 1986–87. Kansas City, MO: American College of Clinical Pharmacy; 1986.
19. Kaul AF, Janosik JE, Powell SH. Postgraduate pharmacy fellowships (1985–86). *Drug Intell Clin Pharm.* 1986; 20:203–8.

Developed by an ad hoc consortium made up of representatives from the American Association of Colleges of Pharmacy (AACP), the American College of Apothecaries (ACA), the American College of Clinical Pharmacy (ACCP), the American Pharmaceutical Association (APhA), the American Society of Consultant Pharmacists (ASCP), the American Society of Hospital Pharmacists (ASHP), and the National Association of Retail Druggists (NARD); the consortium was convened by ASHP and met on August 4, 1986. Approved by the ASHP Board of Directors, November 20, 1986, and subsequently approved by ACCP, APhA, ASCP, ACA, and AACP.

The bibliographic citation for this document is as follows: American Society of Hospital Pharmacists. Definitions of pharmacy residencies and fellowships. *Am J Hosp Pharm.* 1987; 44:1142–4.

Ethics

Ethics

Pharmacist Role in Capital Punishment (1531)
Source: Council on Pharmacy Practice
To acknowledge that an individual's opinion about capital punishment is a personal moral decision; further,

To oppose pharmacist participation in capital punishment; further,

To reaffirm that pharmacists have a right to decline to participate in capital punishment without retribution.

This policy supersedes ASHP policy 8410.

Pharmacist's Role on Ethics Committees (1403)
Source: Council on Pharmacy Practice
To advocate that pharmacists should be included as members of hospital and health-system ethics committees; further,

To encourage pharmacists to actively seek ethics consultations as appropriate; further,

To encourage pharmacists serving on ethics committees to seek advanced training in health care ethics.

Ethical Use of Placebos in Clinical Practice (1116)
Source: Council on Pharmacy Practice
To affirm that the use of placebos in clinical practice is ethically acceptable only when patients have been informed of and agree to such use as a component of treatment; further,

To encourage hospitals and health systems to develop policies and procedures to guide clinicians in making informed decisions regarding the use of placebos; further,

To oppose the use of pharmacologically active substances or medications as placebos.

This policy supersedes ASHP policy 0517.

Pharmacist's Right of Conscience and Patient's Right of Access to Therapy (0610)
Source: Council on Legal and Public Affairs
To recognize the right of pharmacists, as health care providers, and other pharmacy employees to decline to participate in therapies they consider to be morally, religiously, or ethically troubling; further,

To support the proactive establishment of timely and convenient systems by pharmacists and their employers that protect the patient's right to obtain legally prescribed and medically indicated treatments while reasonably accommodating in a nonpunitive manner the right of conscience; further,

To support the principle that a pharmacist exercising the right of conscience must be respectful of, and serve the legitimate health care needs and desires of, the patient, and shall provide a referral without any actions to persuade, coerce, or otherwise impose on the patient the pharmacist's values, beliefs, or objections.

This policy was reviewed in 2014 by the Council on Pharmacy Practice and by the Board of Directors and was found to still be appropriate.

Patient's Right to Choose (0013)
Source: Council on Legal and Public Affairs
To support the right of the patient or his or her representative as allowed under state law to develop, implement, and make informed decisions regarding his or her plan of care; further,

To acknowledge that the patient's rights include being informed of his or her health status, being involved in care planning and treatment, and being able to request or refuse treatment; further,

To support the right of the patient in accord with state law to (a) formulate advance directives and (b) have health care practitioners who comply with those directives.

This policy was reviewed in 2014 by the Council on Public Policy and by the Board of Directors and was found to still be appropriate.

ASHP Position on Assisted Suicide (9915)
Source: Council on Legal and Public Affairs
To remain neutral on the issue of health professional participation in assisted suicide of patients who are terminally ill; further,

To affirm that the decision to participate in the use of medications in assisted suicide is one of individual conscience; further,

To offer guidance to health-system pharmacists who practice in states in which assisted suicide is legal.

This policy was reviewed in 2013 by the Council on Pharmacy Practice and by the Board of Directors and was found to still be appropriate.

Nondiscriminatory Pharmaceutical Care (9006)
Source: Council on Professional Affairs
To adopt the following positions in regard to nondiscriminatory pharmaceutical care:

- All patients have the right to privacy, respect, confidentiality, and high-quality pharmaceutical care.
- No patient should be refused pharmaceutical care or denied these rights based solely on diagnosis.
- Pharmacists must always act in the best interest of individual patients while not placing society as a whole at risk.

This policy was reviewed in 2011 by the Council on Pharmacy Practice and by the Board of Directors and was found to still be appropriate.

ASHP Statement on Leadership as a Professional Obligation

Position

The American Society of Health-System Pharmacists (ASHP) believes that all pharmacists have a professional obligation to serve as leaders in the safe and effective use of medications and encourages pharmacy practitioners, administrators, faculty members, preceptors, and students to advance patient care and strengthen the pharmacy profession by embracing the responsibility to exert leadership in their practices. ASHP urges all pharmacists to accept this responsibility, actively seek the development of leadership skills, and exercise leadership when working with others, including pharmacists, pharmacy technicians, pharmacy students and residents, administrators, other health care professionals, and patients.

ASHP encourages colleges of pharmacy to go beyond management coursework and integrate education on leadership as a practice philosophy throughout the pharmacy curriculum. All pharmacists share the responsibility to mentor pharmacy students, pharmacy residents, other pharmacists, and pharmacy technicians. Pharmacists in formal leadership roles have a specific responsibility to foster the development of leadership skills in pharmacists, facilitate the development of practice models that provide regular opportunities to exercise leadership, and encourage pharmacists to exercise leadership in practice. ASHP also encourages hospital and health-system executives to support the development of leadership skills of all health care professionals.

Leadership in Practice

The ASHP Statement on Professionalism includes leadership as 1 of 10 characteristics of a professional,[1] and the ASHP Statement on the Roles and Responsibilities of the Pharmacy Executive explains the formal leadership roles of the pharmacy executive.[2] Neither of these documents, however, describes the professional obligation every pharmacist has to serve as a leader in the safe and effective use of medications.

Definitions of leadership commonly focus on working toward goals and exerting influence.[3] For example, Nahata[4] stated that leadership "is about a vision, direction, strategies, motivating, and inspiring." The focus on goals and influence guides understanding of the inherent requirement for leadership in pharmacy. The success of current pharmacy practice models and the successful implementation of future models rest on the ability of members of the profession to influence others. In the complex and evolving health care environment, leadership from pharmacists is required to promote and advance the profession and our care for patients. Thus, leadership is not an option—it is a professional obligation.

The ASHP Research and Education Foundation convened a Student and New Practitioner Leadership Task Force that generated a report titled *Leadership as a Professional Obligation*.[5] This 2009 report addressed several issues regarding the current perceptions of leadership in the pharmacy profession, methods for training pharmacy leaders, and the challenges presented by the leadership gap defined by White.[6] The Task Force report noted that leadership and management are different, stating that despite the synonymous use of "management" and "leadership" within the literature, hierarchy does not confer leadership, nor does leadership confer hierarchy. As Covey[7] wrote, "Management works in the system; leadership works on the system." He also further differentiated the concepts of leadership and management, saying, "Effective leadership is putting first things first. Effective management is discipline, carrying it out." Although the two terms are often used synonymously, leadership is a broader and more encompassing concept that extends to a wider array of situations, whereas management has a more specific focus.

The most successful organizations facilitate the development of routine leadership roles and encourage participation in those roles. Frontline pharmacists must exhibit themselves as leaders each time they step into the workplace. The practice of effectively influencing the behavior of physicians, nurses, pharmacy technicians, interns, support staff, and others to optimize medication safety and patient outcomes constitutes successful leadership. Innovative practice models can support the development of both clinical and leadership skills. ASHP encourages these types of practice models and their development.

The obligation to develop practitioners prepared for professional leadership requires colleges of pharmacy to adopt such values. Currently, leadership training is inconsistently present in both academic and practice settings. The Task Force report noted that pharmacy curricula commonly offer elective management courses without addressing fundamental leadership skills in a proactive or longitudinal manner and that the concept of using management training to teach leadership skills has led to further gaps in how new pharmacists perceive leadership.[5] The report emphasized the need for increased focus on leadership training in colleges of pharmacy and recommended that these institutions incorporate formalized leadership training throughout the curriculum in a formal, longitudinal manner and not exclusively through management course work.

White's[6] survey of student and new practitioners demonstrated that they are likely to be mentored by frontline pharmacists, supporting the critical need for expressions of leadership. All pharmacists should take personal responsibility for leadership of the medication-use process and for mentorship of students, residents, and colleagues. Although it is not the exclusive responsibility of formal pharmacy leaders such as pharmacy directors and managers, formal leaders must foster and support pharmacist leadership.

The report of the American Association of Colleges of Pharmacy Argus Commission, *Building a Sustainable System of Leadership Development for Pharmacy*, also argued that leadership is a responsibility for all pharmacists.[8] The report called for integration of leadership throughout pharmacy education and offered a number of specific recommendations. To support leadership development of students and practitioners, the report recommended greater focus on fostering leadership education in pharmacy curricula, in residencies, and in practice sites. To cultivate high-quality candidates to fulfill the pharmacy leadership gap, the report also recommended expansion of didactic leadership training, distance learning programs, the use of social media for networking and mentorship, and an increased focus on the full spectrum of leadership. Colleges should also assess leadership potential during the application and selection process.

Pharmacists also have an obligation to exert leadership and participate in shaping the future of the profession. Participation in professional societies such as ASHP provides opportunities to shape the future of the profession and affords excellent opportunities for the development of leadership skills. Professional organizations such as ASHP also have an obligation to encourage the development of leadership skills and support their development among their memberships.

Conclusion

Leadership is a professional obligation of all pharmacists and not the exclusive responsibility of pharmacists who hold formal leadership roles or titles. All pharmacists should accept the obligation to develop and exert leadership skills to ensure the safe and effective use of medications. Pharmacy schools, professional organizations, and employers should encourage the development of these skills among students and practitioners and should provide both formal training and opportunities for pharmacists to develop leadership capacity.

References

1. American Society of Health-System Pharmacists. ASHP statement on professionalism. *Am J Health-Syst Pharm.* 2008; 65:172–4.
2. American Society of Health-System Pharmacists. ASHP statement on the roles and responsibilities of the pharmacy executive. *Am J Health-Syst Pharm.* 2009; 66:499–502.
3. Holdford DA. Leadership theories and their lessons for pharmacists. *Am J Health-Syst Pharm.* 2003; 60:1780–6.
4. Nahata MC. Balancing leadership and management. *Am J Pharm Educ.* 2001; 65:295–6.
5. American Society of Health-System Pharmacists Research and Education Foundation Center for Health-System Pharmacy Leadership Student and New Practitioner Leadership Task Force. Final report: leadership is a professional obligation (2009). www.ashpfoundation.org/MainMenuCategories/CenterforPharmacyLeadership/AbouttheCenter/StudentNewPractitionerLeadershipTaskForce/SNPFinalReport.aspx (accessed 2011 Mar 23).
6. White SJ. Will there be a pharmacy leadership crisis? An ASHP Foundation Scholar-in-Residence report. *Am J Health-Syst Pharm.* 2005; 62:845–55.
7. Covey SR. *The 7 habits of highly effective people.* New York: Free Press; 1989.
8. Kerr RA, Beck DE, Doss J, et al. Building a sustainable system of leadership development for pharmacy: report of the 2008–09 Argus Commission. *Am J Pharm Educ.* 2009; 73(suppl):S5.

Approved by the ASHP Board of Directors on April 14, 2011, and by the ASHP House of Delegates on June 12, 2011. Developed through the ASHP Council on Pharmacy Management.

Ashley L. Mains, Pharm.D., and David R. Witmer, Pharm.D., are gratefully acknowledged for drafting this statement.

The bibliographic citation for this document is as follows: American Society of Health-System Pharmacists. ASHP statement on leadership as a professional obligation. *Am J Health-Syst Pharm.* 2011; 68:2293–5.

ASHP Statement on Pharmacist's Decision-making on Assisted Suicide

Preamble

Consistent with the intent of the Code of Ethics for Pharmacists "to state publicly the principles that form the fundamental basis of the roles and responsibilities of pharmacists," the American Society of Health-System Pharmacists issues this Statement on Pharmacist Decision-making on Assisted Suicide. The practice of providing competent patients with pharmaceutical means of ending their lives raises issues of professional obligations to patients and to other professionals involved in patient care. We affirm the ASHP policy (9802) that supports the right of a pharmacist to participate or not in morally, religiously, or ethically troubling therapies.

This Statement establishes a framework for pharmacist participation in the legal and ethical debate about the appropriate care of patients at the end of life. This Statement will help pharmacists resolve the growing questions about the ethical obligations of health care professionals to provide care and alleviate suffering. It is hoped that this framework and its use by pharmacists will virtually eliminate a patient's request for assisted suicide.

When asked to evaluate and comment on legislative, regulatory, or judicial actions or on organizational policies of health systems regarding pharmaceutical care, pharmacists should use the principles expressed in this Statement in developing their responses.

Guiding Principles

Professional Tradition. The basic tenet of the profession is to provide care and affirm life. The pharmacy profession is founded on a tradition of patient trust. The trust developed between each patient and members of the health care team makes it important for each professional to examine the moral and ethical issues of patients' requests for assistance in dying. Pharmacists should serve as advocates for the patient throughout the continuum of care.

Respect for Patients. *Patient autonomy.* Pharmacists should ensure the rights of competent patients to know about all legally available treatment options while communicating to patients and their caregivers (including family members if appropriate) the overall duty of health care professionals to preserve life.

Confidentiality. Pharmacists should maintain the confidentiality of all patient information, regardless of whether they agree with the values underlying the patient's choice of treatment or decision to forgo any particular treatment.

Decision-making. Patients' ability to exercise their ethical and legal right to choose or decline treatment is dependent upon pharmacists informing patients and their health care providers about the nature of pharmaceutical options. Those options are constantly changing, given the dynamic aspect of the pharmaceutical marketplace and the evolving nature of hospice care and available palliative treatments.

Health Care Systems. *Collaboration.* Collaboration among members of the health care team must occur at both the patient care and the public policy levels. It is the pharmacist's responsibility to educate members of the health care team about the pharmacotherapeutic options available in treating the patient's condition. Health care team members include the patient, members of the patient's family, and caregivers.

Confidentiality. The patient's right of confidentiality and right to determine his or her therapy, including end-of-life decisions, shall be respected, included, and considered in the decision process in health care systems. Pharmacists should maintain the confidentiality of all patient information, regardless of whether they agree with the values underlying the patient's choice of treatment or decision to forgo any particular treatment.

Covenant with society. Health care is delivered in a system in which each profession makes a contribution on the patient's behalf. An act in one part of the system has consequences in other parts of that system. Each profession has a covenant with society, founded on a relationship of trust with the patient. The trust developed between each patient and members of the health care team makes it important for each professional to examine the moral and ethical issues of patients' requests for assistance in dying.

Barriers to care. Health care professionals must address the following barriers to adequate end-of-life care:

1. Inadequate knowledge and use of pain- and symptom-management therapies.
2. The paucity of published data related to the ingestion of lethal drugs and the outcomes thereof.
3. Insufficient education of health care professionals about end-of-life and palliative care issues.
4. Inadequate recognition that end-of-life care is the responsibility of the entire health care team.
5. Legal and regulatory issues that deter appropriate provision of pain and symptom management.

Professional Obligations. *Conscientious objection.* Pharmacists must retain their right to participate or not in morally, religiously, or ethically troubling therapies. Procedures should be in place to ensure that employers are able to provide care to the patient and provide adequate services to the patient and caregiver. The employer has specific responsibilities, and the employee cannot be a barrier to the employer's ability to fulfill those obligations. Employers must reasonably accommodate the employee pharmacist's right to not participate in morally, religiously, or ethically troubling therapies.

Obligation to the patient. Pharmacists should support appropriate drug therapy to ensure that palliative care and aggressive pain management are available for all patients in need. Pharmacists, as part of their professional responsibility, must offer to provide counseling services to the patient and caregivers and be prepared to provide pharmaceutical care to the patient until the end of life.

Obligation to team members. The pharmacist, as a member of a health care team responsible for the care of a patient, is accountable for providing the team members with detailed information concerning efficacious use of pharmaceutical and other therapies available that may affect the options open to the patient.

As active members of an interdisciplinary team caring for patients, pharmacists must be central participants in all decisions relating to medication management of the patient. Pharmacists should respect the opinions and specific areas of expertise of the other members of the health care team.

Pharmacist education. Pharmacists are often inadequately trained in the care of dying patients. Therefore, pharmacists' education at all levels (undergraduate, graduate, continuing education) should be sensitive to these issues and offer the development of skills and knowledge concerning care of the dying. Pharmacists should make a personal, professional commitment to learn more about end-of-life care.

Recommended Readings

Supreme Court Decisions

1. *Washington v. Glucksberg,* decided June 26, 1997.
2. *Vacco v. Quill,* decided June 26, 1977.
3. Angell M. The Supreme Court and physician-assisted suicide—the ultimate right. *N Engl J Med.* 1997; 336: 50–3.
4. Annas GJ. The bell tolls for a constitutional right to physician-assisted suicide. *N Engl J Med.* 1997; 337:1098–103.
5. Burt RA. The Supreme Court speaks: not assisted suicide but a constitutional right to palliative care. *N Engl J Med.* 1997; 337:1234–6.
6. Gostin LO. Deciding life and death in the courtroom: from *Quinlan to Cruzan, Glucksberg,* and *Vacco*—a brief history and analysis of constitutional protection of the "right to die" *JAMA* 1997; 278:1523–8.
7. Orentlicher D. The Supreme Court and physician-assisted suicide: rejecting assisted suicide but embracing euthanasia. *N Engl J Med.* 1997; 337:1236–9.
8. Palmer LI. Institutional analysis and physicians' rights after *Vacco v. Quill, Cornell J Law Public Policy.* 1998; 7:415–30.

Professional Organization Position Statements/Policies

1. American Bar Association house of delegates. Report of action taken at 1997 annual meeting.
2. American Pharmaceutical Association. Code of Ethics for Pharmacists.
3. American Pain Society. Treatment of pain at the end of life.
4. National League for Nursing. Life-terminating choices: a framework for nursing decision-making.
5. American Medical Association Policy on Physician-Assisted Suicide, 1996.
6. American Nurses Association. Position statement on assisted suicide.
7. American Geriatrics Society. Position statement on the care of dying patients.
8. National Hospice Organization.

Assisted Suicide

1. Dixon KM, Kier KL. Longing for mercy, requesting death: pharmaceutical care and pharmaceutically assisted death. *Am J Health-Syst Pharm.* 1998; 55:578–85.
2. Hamerly JP. Views on assisted suicide: perspectives of the AMA and the NHO. *Am J Health-Syst Pharm.* 1998; 55:543–7.
3. Lee BC. Views on assisted suicide: the aid-in-dying perspective. *Am J Health-Syst Pharm.* 1998; 55: 547–50.
4. Meier DE, Emmons CA, Wallenstein S et al. A national survey of physician-assisted suicide and euthanasia in the United States. *N Engl J Med.* 1998; 338: 1193–201.
5. Mullan K, Allen WL, Brushwood DB. Conscientious objection to assisted death: can pharmacy address this in a systematic fashion? *Ann Pharmacother.* 1996; 30:1185–91.
6. Rupp MT. Issues for pharmacists in assisted patient death. In: Battin MP, Lipman AG, eds. Drug use in assisted suicide and euthanasia. Binghamton, NY: Haworth; 1996.
7. Rupp MT. Physician-assisted suicide and the issues it raises for pharmacists. *Am J Health-syst Pharm.* 1995; 52:1455–60.
8. Rupp MT, Isenhower HL. Pharmacists' attitudes toward physician-assisted suicide. *Am J Hosp Pharm.* 1994; 51:69–74.
9. Stein GC. Assisted suicide: an issue for pharmacists. *Am J Health-Syst Pharm.* 1998; 55:539. Editorial.
10. Van der Maas PJ, van der Wal G, Haverkate I et al. Euthanasia, physician-assisted suicide, and other medical practices involving the end of life in the Netherlands, 1990–1995. *N Engl J Med.* 1996; 335:1699–705.
11. Van der Wal G, van der Maas PJ, Bosma JM et al. Evaluation of the notification procedure for physician-assisted death in the Netherlands. *N Engl J Med.* 1996; 335:1706–11.
12. Vaux KL. Views on assisted suicide: an ethicist's perspective. *Am J Health–Syst Pharm.* 1998; 55:551–3.

End-of-Life Care

1. Foley KM. Competent care for the dying instead of physician-assisted suicide. *N Engl J Med.* 1997; 336:54–8.
2. Quill TE, Lo B, Brock DW. Palliative options of last resort: a comparison of voluntarily stopping eating and drinking, terminal seda-tion, physician-assisted suicide, and voluntary active euthanasia. *JAMA.* 1997; 278:2099–104.
3. Suicide prevention: efforts to increase research and education in palliative care. Washington, DC: General Accounting Office, 1998 Apr; report HEHS-98-128.

Miscellaneous

1. Board of Directors report on the Council on Legal and Public Affairs, ASHP House of Delegates Session—1994.
2. Board of Directors report on the Council on Professional Affairs, ASHP House of Delegates Session—1998.

3. Board of Directors report on the Council on Legal and Public Affairs, ASHP House of Delegates Session—1998.
4. Statement of Attorney General Reno on Oregon's Death with Dignity Act. June 5, 1998.
5. Schnabel J, Schnabel G. Pharmacy information. In: Haley K, Lee M, eds. The Oregon Death With Dignity Act: A Guidebook for Health Care Providers. Portland: Oregon Health Sciences University, Center for Ethics in Health Care; 1998 Mar.

This statement was reviewed in 2013 by the Council on Pharmacy Practice and by the Board of Directors and was found to still be appropriate.

Approved by the ASHP Board of Directors, April 21, 1999, and by the ASHP House of Delegates, June 7, 1999. Developed by the Council on Legal and Professional Affairs.

The bibliographic citation for this document is as follows: American Society of Health-System Pharmacists. ASHP statement on pharmacist's decision-making on assisted suicide. *Am J Health-Syst. Pharm.* 1999; 56:1661–4.

Relevant ASHP Policies

Pharmacist Support for Dying Patients (0307)
Source: Council on Professional Affairs
To support the position that care for dying patients is part of the continuum of care that pharmacists should provide to patients; further,

To support the position that pharmacists have a professional obligation to work in a collaborative and compassionate manner with patients, family members, caregivers, and other professionals to help fulfill the patient care needs, especially the quality-of-life needs, of dying patients of all ages; further,

To support research on the needs of dying patients; further,

To provide education to pharmacists on caring for dying patients, including education on clinical, managerial, professional, and legal issues; further,

To urge the inclusion of such topics in the curricula of colleges of pharmacy.

This policy was reviewed in 2007 by the Council on Pharmacy Practice and by the Board of Directors and was found to still be appropriate.

Pharmacist's Right of Conscience and Patient's Right of Access to Therapy (0610)
Source: Council on Legal and Public Affairs
To recognize the right of pharmacists, as health care providers, and other pharmacy employees to decline to participate in therapies they consider to be morally, religiously, or ethically troubling; further,

To support the proactive establishment of timely and convenient systems by pharmacists and their employers that protect the patient's right to obtain legally prescribed and medically indicated treatments while reasonably accommodating in a nonpunitive manner the right of conscience; further,

To support the principle that a pharmacist exercising the right of conscience must be respectful of, and serve the legitimate health care needs and desires of, the patient, and shall provide a referral without any actions to persuade, coerce, or otherwise impose on the patient the pharmacist's values, beliefs, or objections.

This policy supersedes ASHP policy 9802.

Pharmacist Role in Capital Punishment (1531)
Source: Council on Pharmacy Practice
To acknowledge that an individual's opinion about capital punishment is a personal moral decision; further,

To oppose pharmacist participation in capital punishment; further,

To reaffirm that pharmacists have a right to decline to participate in capital punishment without retribution.

This policy supersedes ASHP policy 8410.

ASHP Statement on Professionalism

Position

Pharmacy is a profession. Despite the challenges to professionalism presented by changes in health care, pharmacists must embrace the responsibilities that stem from their profession's guiding principles. Among those responsibilities are advancing the well-being and dignity of their patients, acting with integrity and conscience, collaborating respectfully with health care colleagues, and seeking justice in the distribution of health care resources.

The American Society of Health-System Pharmacists (ASHP) encourages pharmacy practitioners, administrators, faculty members, preceptors, and students to advance patient care and strengthen the pharmacy profession by promoting professionalism in everyday practice. ASHP urges pharmacists to dedicate themselves to serving the interests of their patients and to practicing with compassion and respect for patients and their families. Pharmacists should commit to working cooperatively with and with respect for other health care providers and to seeking to improve the quality of health care received by the communities in which they work and live. ASHP encourages pharmacists to serve as mentors to students, residents, and colleagues in a manner that fosters the adoption of high professional aspirations for pharmacy practice, high personal standards of integrity and competence, a commitment to serving humanity, habits of analytical thinking and ethical reasoning, and a commitment to lifelong learning.

Background

Between 1995 and 2005, the number of PubMed-indexed articles on professionalism quadrupled, from 50 to approximately 200 per year.[1] Professional associations from the American College of Physicians–American Society of Internal Medicine to the American College of Dentistry have convened task forces, developed white papers and charters, and initiated programs to increase the professionalism of their members.[2–6]

The rising interest in professionalism has been attributed to the perception that changes in health care delivery are eroding the professional standards of health care providers.[2] Among the changes confronting the pharmacy profession are managed care's continuing emphasis on cost containment[7]; increased demand for systems that ensure the safety of medication use[8]; technology-driven changes in pharmacy's core responsibilities, the most important of which is an expansion of the pharmacist's role in patient care[7,9,10]; and a prolonged shortage of pharmacists.[11] As such challenges mount, it is in the best interest of our profession and the public we serve to reaffirm our foundational principles. Hospital and health-system pharmacists must therefore define for themselves the principles that will guide them in their unique practice settings.

Guiding Principles and Responsibilities for Health-System Pharmacy

The use of the term "profession" to describe a group of individuals pursuing an occupation or career is based on the idea that these individuals profess a common purpose.[12] The common purpose of pharmacists is eloquently stated in the eight principles of the Code of Ethics for Pharmacists.[13]

Professing these principles creates responsibilities for pharmacists. Foremost among these responsibilities is the obligation to place the well-being of patients at the center of pharmacy practice. Many of the other principles flow from the covenantal relationship between the pharmacist and the patient. To provide the best possible care, pharmacists dedicate themselves to maintaining professional competence through lifelong learning and contemplation. Professional education and advancing standards of practice can only be achieved through a profession's collective efforts; pharmacists therefore commit themselves to serve not only their patients but also their profession. Finally, pharmacists commit themselves to improving health care institutions not simply for the well-being of individual patients but for the benefit of society as a whole.

Incorporating Professionalism into Practice

ASHP encourages practitioners, administrators, faculty members, preceptors, and pharmacy students to contemplate and to incorporate into their practices the guiding principles set forth in the Code of Ethics for Pharmacists[13] and the following 10 characteristics of a professional:

1. Knowledge and skills of the profession,
2. Commitment to self-improvement of skills and knowledge,
3. Service orientation,
4. Pride in and service to the profession,
5. Covenantal relationship with the patient,
6. Creativity and innovation,
7. Conscience and trustworthiness,
8. Accountability for his or her work,
9. Ethically sound decision-making, and
10. Leadership.[6]

Practicing and aspiring hospital and health-system pharmacists should develop a personal plan for professional development, encourage their colleagues to do the same, and share the results. Continuing education should be viewed as an opportunity to enhance one's practice rather than an obligation to be fulfilled in the most expedient manner.

Much could be done to make practice sites more conducive to professional behavior. Institutions can develop personnel recruitment, orientation, and evaluation systems that encourage professional development (e.g., by offering benefit packages that emphasize professional development rather than salary or by incorporating characteristics of professionalism into job descriptions).[14] Administrators and pharmacists can promote professionalism by improving the pharmacy practice area to reduce environmental barriers to professionalism (e.g., cluttered, isolated, outdated, or cramped working quarters).

One of the fundamental services of a professional is recruiting, nurturing, and securing new practitioners to that profession's ideals and mission.[15] For hospital and health-system pharmacists, professional socialization is especially important because the principles of institutional pharmacy practice are not emphasized in typical pharmacy curricula. Above all else, hospital and health-system pharmacists need to prevent "inconsistent socialization,"[16] in which the principles of professionalism instilled in pharmacy students are undermined by a lack of professionalism in the role models they encounter when they enter practice. Pharmacy departments can avoid inconsistent socialization by promoting a culture of professionalism in the workplace through personnel recruitment and evaluation systems that emphasize professional development.[16] Regardless of the level of support they receive, however, hospital and health-system pharmacists must commit themselves fully to their mentorship responsibilities.

ASHP urges practicing pharmacists to serve as mentors to students, residents, and colleagues in a manner that fosters the adoption of high professional aspirations for pharmacy practice, high personal standards of integrity and competence, a commitment to serve humanity, habits of analytical thinking and ethical reasoning, and a commitment to lifelong learning. Practice sites should designate preceptors, implement preceptor training programs, encourage preceptor adherence to the highest professional standards, solicit student feedback on preceptorship programs, and reward those who participate.[6] Hospitals and health systems should also explore other ways to promote mentorship relationships among staff. Hospital and health-system pharmacists and students can participate in ASHP's Virtual Mentoring Exchange.[17] ASHP encourages pharmacists, particularly new practitioners, to actively seek mentors.

Finally, hospital and health-system pharmacists can advance the cause of professionalism in health care by reinvigorating the mission development processes of their institutions, encouraging those institutions to revise their mission statements to describe how they will address such ethical issues as the treatment of patients, employees, and staff; institutions' responsibilities to their communities, to other institutions, and to their own futures; the need to honor founding traditions and sustaining principles; and the complex interactions of legal and ethical responsibilities and their obligations to meet legislatively and socially defined needs.[18]

In 1976, Anderson[15] called on hospital pharmacists to "create a code that reflects our relationships with all of the different people and conditions under which we practice." The time has come for hospital and health-system pharmacists to join forces with other health care providers and patients to engage what has been called "the new authorities of health care"[18] to attain the kind of health care system our patients deserve and our society demands.

Conclusion

The pharmacy profession's guiding principles are eloquently stated in the Code of Ethics for Pharmacists. Despite the challenges to professionalism presented by changes in health care, pharmacists must embrace the responsibilities that stem from their profession's guiding principles.

References

1. National Center for Biotechnology Information. PubMed online database. www.ncbi.nih.gov/entrez/query.fcgi (accessed 2006 Jun 16).
2. ABIM Foundation, ACP–ASIM Foundation, and European Federation of Internal Medicine. Medical professionalism in the new millennium: a physician charter. *Ann Intern Med.* 2002; 136:243–6.
3. Yeager AL. Dental ethics for the 21st century: learning from the Charter on Medical Professionalism. *J Am Coll Dent.* 2002; 69:53–60.
4. Popp RL, Smith SC Jr. Cardiovascular professionalism and ethics in the modern era. *J Am Coll Cardiol.* 2004; 44:1722–3.
5. American Society of Health-System Pharmacists. 2001 ASHP Leadership Conference on Pharmacy Practice Management Executive Summary. From management to leadership: the building blocks of professionalism. *Am J Health-Syst Pharm.* 2002; 59:661–5.
6. Adapted from: American Pharmaceutical Association Academy of Students of Pharmacy—American Association of Colleges of Pharmacy Council of Deans Task Force on Professionalism. White paper on pharmacy student professionalism. *J Am Pharm Assoc.* 2000; 40:96–102.
7. Zacker C, Mucha L. Institutional and contingency approaches to the reprofessionalization of pharmacy. *Am J Health-Syst Pharm.* 1998; 55:1302–5.
8. Pedersen CA, Schneider PJ, Scheckelhoff DJ. ASHP national survey of pharmacy practice in hospital settings: prescribing and transcribing—2004. *Am J Health-Syst Pharm.* 2005; 62:378–90.
9. Reeder CE, Dickson M, Kozma CM et al. ASHP national survey of pharmacy practice in acute care settings—1996. *Am J Health-Syst Pharm.* 1997; 54: 653–69.
10. Knapp KK, Okamoto MP, Black BL. ASHP survey of ambulatory care pharmacy practice in health systems—2004. *Am J Health-Syst Pharm.* 2005; 62: 274–84.
11. Knapp KK, Quist RM, Walton SM et al. Update on the pharmacist shortage: national and state data through 2003. *Am J Health-Syst Pharm.* 2005; 62:492–9.
12. Knowlton CH, Penna RP. Pharmaceutical care, 2nd ed. Bethesda, MD: American Society of Health-System Pharmacists; 2003:4.
13. Code of ethics for pharmacists. In: Hawkins BH, ed. Best practices for hospital and health-system pharmacy. Bethesda, MD: American Society of Health-System Pharmacists; 2005:103.
14. Hammer DP, Berger BA, Beardsley RS et al. Student professionalism. *Am J Pharm Educ.* 2003; 63:1–29.
15. Anderson RD. 1976 Harvey A.K. Whitney lecture: the peril of deprofessionalization. *Am J Hosp Pharm.* 1977; 34:133–9 [reprinted in *Am J Health-Syst Pharm.* 2004; 61:2373–9].
16. Manasse HR Jr, Stewart JE, Hall RH. Inconsistent socialization in pharmacy—a pattern in need of change. *J Am Pharm Assoc.* 1975; 15:616–21,658.
17. American Society of Health-System Pharmacists. ASHP virtual mentoring exchange. www.ashp.org/virtualmentoring/index.cfm (accessed 2005 Jun 16).

18. Reiser SJ, Banner RS. The Charter on Medical Professionalism and the limits of medical power. *Ann Intern Med.* 2003; 138:844–6.

Approved by the ASHP Board of Directors on January 12, 2007, and by the ASHP House of Delegates on June 26, 2007. Developed through the ASHP Council on Pharmacy Practice.

The bibliographic citation for this document is as follows: American Society of Health-System Pharmacists. ASHP statement on professionalism. *Am J Health-Syst Pharm.* 2008; 65:172–4.

ASHP Guidelines on Pharmacists' Relationships with Industry

In the practice of their profession, pharmacists should be guided only by the consideration of patient care. Pharmacists should neither accept nor retain anything of value that has the potential to affect materially their ability to exercise judgments solely in the interests of patients. A useful criterion in determining acceptable activities and relationships is this: Would the pharmacist be willing to have these relationships generally known? Notwithstanding this responsibility, pharmacists may benefit from guidance in their relationships with industry. To this end, the following suggestions are offered.

Gifts and Hospitality

Gifts, hospitality, or subsidies offered to pharmacists by industry should not be accepted if acceptance might influence, or appear to others to influence, the objectivity of clinical judgment or drug product selection and procurement.

Continuing Education

Providers of continuing education that accept industry funding for programs should develop and enforce policies to maintain complete control of program content.

Subsidies to underwrite the costs of continuing-education conferences, professional meetings, or staff development programs can contribute to the improvement of patient care and are permissible. Payments to defray the costs of a conference should not be accepted directly or indirectly from industry by pharmacists attending the conference or program. Contributions to special or educational funds for staff development are permissible as long as the selection of staff members who will receive the funds is made by the department of pharmacy.

It is appropriate for faculty at conferences or meetings to accept reasonable honoraria and reimbursement for reasonable travel, lodging, and meal expenses. However, direct subsidies from industry should not be accepted to pay the costs of travel, lodging, or other personal expenses of pharmacists attending conferences or meetings, nor should subsidies be accepted to compensate for the pharmacists' time.

Scholarships or other special funds to permit pharmacy students, residents, and fellows to attend carefully selected educational conferences may be permissible as long as the selection of students, residents, or fellows who will receive the funds is made by the academic or training institution.

Consultants and Advisory Arrangements

Consultants who provide genuine services for industry may receive reasonable compensation and accept reimbursement for travel, lodging, and meal expenses. Token consulting or advisory arrangements cannot be used to justify compensating pharmacists for their time, travel, lodging, and other out-of-pocket expenses.

Clinical Research

Pharmacists who participate in practice-based research of pharmaceuticals, devices, or other programs should conduct their activities in accord with basic precepts of accepted scientific methodology. Practice-based drug studies that are, in effect, promotional schemes to entice the use of a product or program are unacceptable.

Disclosure of Information

To avoid conflicts of interest or appearances of impropriety, pharmacists should disclose consultant or speaker arrangements or substantial personal financial holdings with companies under consideration for formulary inclusion or related decisions. To inform audiences fully, speakers and authors should disclose, when pertinent, consultant or speaker and research funding arrangements with companies.

Additional Issues

The advice in this document is noninclusive and is not intended to limit the legitimate exchange of prudent scientific information.

This guideline was reviewed in 2001 by the Council on Legal and Public Affairs and by the ASHP Board of Directors and was found to still be appropriate.

Approved by the ASHP Board of Directors, November 20, 1991. Developed by the ASHP Council on Legal and Public Affairs.

The language used in many of the guidance issues contained in this document was adapted, with permission, from documents developed by the American Medical Association (*JAMA*. 1991; 265:501) and the American College of Physicians (*Ann Intern Med.* 1990; 112:624–6).

The bibliographic citation for this document is as follows: American Society of Hospital Pharmacists. ASHP guidelines on pharmacists' relationships with industry. *Am J Hosp Pharm.* 1992; 49:154.

Code of Ethics for Pharmacists

Preamble

Pharmacists are health professionals who assist individuals in making the best use of medications. This Code, prepared and supported by pharmacists, is intended to state publicly the principles that form the fundamental basis of the roles and responsibilities of pharmacists. These principles, based on moral obligations and virtues, are established to guide pharmacists in relationships with patients, health professionals, and society.

Principles

I. ***A pharmacist respects the covenantal relationship between the patient and pharmacist.***
Interpretation: Considering the patient-pharmacist relationship as a covenant means that a pharmacist has moral obligations in response to the gift of trust received from society. In return for this gift, a pharmacist promises to help individuals achieve optimum benefit from their medications, to be committed to their welfare, and to maintain their trust.

II. ***A pharmacist promotes the good of every patient in a caring, compassionate, and confidential manner.***
Interpretation: A pharmacist places concern for the well-being of the patient at the center of professional practice. In doing so, a pharmacist considers needs stated by the patient as well as those defined by health science. A pharmacist is dedicated to protecting the dignity of the patient. With a caring attitude and a compassionate spirit, a pharmacist focuses on serving the patient in a private and confidential manner.

III. ***A pharmacist respects the autonomy and dignity of each patient.***
Interpretation: A pharmacist promotes the right of self-determination and recognizes individual self-worth by encouraging patients to participate in decisions about their health. A pharmacist communicates with patients in terms that are understandable. In all cases, a pharmacist respects personal and cultural differences among patients.

IV. ***A pharmacist acts with honesty and integrity in professional relationships.***
Interpretation: A pharmacist has a duty to tell the truth and to act with conviction of conscience. A pharmacist avoids discriminatory practices, behavior or work conditions that impair professional judgment, and actions that compromise dedication to the best interests of patients.

V. ***A pharmacist maintains professional competence.***
Interpretation: A pharmacist has a duty to maintain knowledge and abilities as new medications, devices, and technologies become available and as health information advances.

VI. ***A pharmacist respects the values and abilities of colleagues and other health professionals.***
Interpretation: When appropriate, a pharmacist asks for the consultation of colleagues or other health professionals or refers the patient. A pharmacist acknowledges that colleagues and other health professionals may differ in the beliefs and values they apply to the care of the patient.

VII. ***A pharmacist serves individual, community, and societal needs.***
Interpretation: The primary obligation of a pharmacist is to individual patients. However, the obligations of a pharmacist may at times extend beyond the individual to the community and society. In these situations, the pharmacist recognizes the responsibilities that accompany these obligations and acts accordingly.

VIII. ***A pharmacist seeks justice in the distribution of health resources.***
Interpretation: When health resources are allocated, a pharmacist is fair and equitable, balancing the needs of patients and society.

The endorsement of this document was reviewed in 2012 by the Council on Pharmacy Practice and by the Board of Directors and was found to still be appropriate.

 Adopted by the membership of the American Pharmaceutical Association on October 27, 1994. Endorsed by the American Society of Health-System Pharmacists House of Delegates on June 3, 1996 (ASHP Policy 9607). Proceedings of the 47th annual session of the ASHP House of Delegates. *Am J Health-Syst Pharm.* 1996; 53:1805. ASHP Reports.

Formulary Management

(Medication-Use Policy Development)

Formulary Management

Pharmacogenomics (1104)
Source: Council on Therapeutics
To advocate that pharmacists take a leadership role in the therapeutic applications of pharmacogenomics, which is essential to individualized drug therapy; further,

To support research to validate and standardize genetic markers and genetic testing for drug therapy and to support research and other efforts that guide and accelerate the application of pharmacogenomics to clinical practice; further,

To advocate for the inclusion of pharmacogenomic test results in medical and pharmacy records in a format that clearly states the implications of the results for drug therapy and facilitates availability of the genetic information throughout the continuum of care and over a patient's lifetime; further,

To encourage pharmacists to educate prescribers and patients about the use of pharmacogenomic tests and their appropriate application to drug therapy management; further,

To encourage pharmacist education on the use of pharmacogenomics and advocate for the inclusion of pharmacogenomics and its application to therapeutic decision-making in college of pharmacy curricula.

This policy supersedes ASHP policy 0016.

Medications Derived from Biologic Sources (0809)
Source: Council on Pharmacy Practice
To encourage pharmacists to take a leadership role in their health systems for all aspects of the proper use of medications derived from biologic sources, including preparation, storage, control, distribution, administration procedures, safe handling, and therapeutic applications; further,

To facilitate education of pharmacists about the proper use of medications derived from biologic sources.

(*Note:* Section 351(a) of the Public Health Service Act [42 U.S.C. 262(a)] defines *biological product* as follows: a virus, therapeutic serum, toxin, antitoxin, vaccine, blood, blood component or derivative, allergenic product, or analogous product, or arsphenamine or derivative of arsphenamine [or any other trivalent organic arsenic compound], applicable to the prevention, treatment, or cure of a disease or condition of human beings.)

This policy was reviewed in 2012 by the Council on Pharmacy Practice and by the Board of Directors and was found to still be appropriate.

Generic Substitution of Narrow Therapeutic Index Drugs (0817)
Source: Council on Therapeutics
To support the current processes used by the Food and Drug Administration (FDA) to determine bioequivalence of generic drug products, including those with a narrow therapeutic index, and to recognize the authority of the FDA to decide if additional studies are necessary to determine equivalence; further,

To oppose a blanket restriction on generic substitution for any medication or medication class without evidence from well-designed, independent studies that demonstrate inferior efficacy or safety of the generic drug product.

This policy was reviewed in 2012 by the Council on Therapeutics and by the Board of Directors and was found to still be appropriate.

Expression of Therapeutic Purpose of Prescribing (0305)
Source: Council on Professional Affairs
To advocate that the prescriber provide or pharmacists have immediate access to the intended therapeutic purpose of prescribed medications in order to ensure safe and effective medication use.

This policy was reviewed in 2012 by the Council on Pharmacy Practice and by the Board of Directors and was found to still be appropriate.

Appropriate Dosing of Medications in Patient Populations with Unique Needs (0228)
Source: Council on Professional Affairs
To advocate reforms in medication-use systems, including electronic systems, and health care provider education and training that facilitate optimal patient-specific dosing in populations of patients (e.g., pediatrics, geriatrics) with altered pharmacokinetics and pharmacodynamics.

This policy was reviewed in 2011 by the Council on Pharmacy Practice and by the Board of Directors and was found to still be appropriate.

Medication Formulary System Management (0102)
Source: Council on Administrative Affairs
To declare that decisions on the management of a medication formulary system (1) should be based on clinical, ethical, legal, social, philosophical, quality-of-life, safety, and pharmacoeconomic factors that result in optimal patient care, and (2) must include the active and direct involvement of physicians, pharmacists, and other appropriate health care professionals; further,

To declare that decisions on the management of a medication formulary system should not be based solely on economic factors.

This policy was reviewed in 2010 by the Council on Pharmacy Management and by the Board of Directors and was found to still be appropriate.

Gene Therapy (0103)
Source: Council on Administrative Affairs
To declare that health-system decisions on the selection, use, and management of gene therapy agents should be based on the same principles as a medication formulary system in that (1) decisions are based on clinical, ethical, legal, social, philosophical, quality-of-life, safety, and pharmacoeconomic factors that result in optimal patient care and (2) such decisions must include the active and direct involvement of physicians, pharmacists, and other appropriate health care professionals.

This policy was reviewed in 2010 by the Council on Pharmacy Management and by the Board of Directors and was found to still be appropriate.

Role of Pharmacists and Business Leaders in Health Care Services and Policies (9819)
Source: Council on Professional Affairs
To support the principle that business leaders and health professionals must share responsibility and accountability for providing optimal health care services to patients; further,

To support the principle that business leaders should expect practicing pharmacists to formulate policies that affect the prerogative of pharmacists to make optimal care decisions on behalf of patients.

This policy was reviewed in 2013 by the Council on Pharmacy Practice and by the Board of Directors and was found to still be appropriate.

Standardization of Drug Medication Formulary Systems (9601)
Source: Council on Administrative Affairs
To support the concept of a standardized medication formulary system among components of integrated health systems when standardization leads to improved patient outcomes; further,

To include in the formulary-standardization process the direct involvement of the health system's physicians, pharmacists, and other appropriate health care professionals.

This policy was reviewed in 2014 by the Council on Pharmacy Practice and by the Board of Directors and was found to still be appropriate.

Medical Devices (9106)
Source: Council on Legal and Public Affairs
To support public and private initiatives to clarify and define the relationship among drugs, devices, and new technologies in order to promote safety and effectiveness as well as better delivery of patient care.

This policy was reviewed in 2012 by the House of Delegates and by the Board of Directors and was found to still be appropriate.

Therapeutic Interchange (8708)
Source: Council on Legal and Public Affairs
To support the concept of therapeutic interchange of various drug products by pharmacists under arrangements where pharmacists and authorized prescribers interrelate on the behalf of patient care.

This policy was reviewed in 2013 by the Council on Pharmacy Practice and by the Board of Directors and was found to still be appropriate.

ASHP Statement on the Pharmacy and Therapeutics Committee and the Formulary System

Position

American Society of Health-System Pharmacists (ASHP) believes that health systems should develop, organize, and administer a formulary system that follows the principles below in order to optimize patient care by ensuring access to clinically appropriate, safe, and cost-effective medications.

Background

A formulary is a continually updated list of medications and related information, representing the clinical judgment of pharmacists, physicians, and other experts in the diagnosis and treatment of disease and promotion of health.[1] A formulary includes, but is not limited to, a list of medications and medication-associated products or devices, medication-use policies, important ancillary drug information, decision-support tools, and organizational guidelines. The multiplicity of medications available, the complexities surrounding their safe and effective use, and differences in their relative value make it necessary for health systems to have medication-use policies that promote rational, evidence-based, clinically appropriate, safe, and cost-effective medication therapy. The formulary system is the ongoing process through which a health care organization establishes policies on the use of drugs, therapies, and drug-related products and identifies those that are most medically appropriate and cost-effective to best serve the health interests of a given patient population.

Pharmacy and Therapeutics Committee

To be effective, medication-use policies must have the concurrence of individuals involved in the medication-use process. Such consensus is achieved by developing medication-use policies through a properly organized and representative pharmacy and therapeutics (P&T) committee or equivalent body and ensuring that those policies are approved by the organized medical staff.

The P&T committee is composed of actively participating physicians, other prescribers, pharmacists, nurses, administrators, quality-improvement managers, and other health care professionals and staff who participate in the medication-use process. Customarily, P&T member appointments are based on guidance from the medical staff. The P&T committee should serve in an evaluative, educational, and advisory capacity to the medical staff and organizational administration in all matters that pertain to the use of medications (including investigational medications). The P&T committee is a policy-recommending body to the medical staff and the administration of the organization on matters related to the safe and therapeutic use of medications. The P&T committee is responsible to the medical staff as a whole, and its recommendations are subject to approval by the organized medical staff as well as the administrative approval process. The basic policies and procedures that govern the P&T committee's administration of the formulary system should be incorporated, as appropriate, in the health system's medical staff bylaws, medical staff rules and regulations, and other organizational policies.

The overarching purposes of the P&T committee are policy development, communication and education, and formulary management.

Policy Development

The P&T committee formulates policies regarding evaluation, selection, diagnostic and therapeutic use, and monitoring of medications and medication-associated products and devices. The P&T committee should establish and assist in programs and procedures that ensure safe and effective medication therapy (e.g., clinical care plans, treatment guidelines, critical pathways, disease management protocols). Members of the P&T committee, or their representatives from appropriate specialties (including pharmacists), should participate in or direct the development and review of such programs or procedures, which should be kept current.

The P&T committee should participate in performance improvement activities related to procurement, prescribing, dispensing, administering, monitoring, and overall use of medications. The P&T committee should advise the institution, including the pharmacy department, in the implementation of effective medication distribution and control procedures, incorporating technological advances when appropriate. The P&T committee should initiate, direct, and review the results of medication-use evaluation programs to optimize medication use and routinely monitor outcomes (economic, clinical, and humanistic) of formulary decisions. Medication-use evaluation should result in performance-improvement initiatives to improve the medication-use process.

The P&T committee should take actions to prevent, monitor, and evaluate adverse drug reactions and medication errors in the health care setting, including those occurring with biological products and vaccines. Information from these activities should be disseminated to the appropriate health care personnel for informational and educational purposes (e.g., newsletters, memoranda) and, when appropriate, to the Food and Drug Administration (FDA).

The P&T committee should establish clearly defined policies and procedures related to manufacturer sales representatives' activities within the organization.

Communication and Education

The P&T committee ensures that mechanisms are in place to communicate with health care professionals, patients, and payers about all aspects of the formulary system, including changes made to the formulary or policies and how formulary system decisions are made. The P&T committee also recommends or assists in the formulation of educational programs designed to meet the needs of professional staff, patients, families, and caregivers on matters related to medications and medication use. The P&T committee should establish or plan suitable educational programs on matters related to medication use for staff involved in the care of patients and the use of medications.

Formulary Management

Health systems should develop, organize, and administer a formulary system that follows the principles below in order to optimize patient care by ensuring access to clinically appropriate, safe, and cost-effective medications.

Formulary System. The P&T committee is responsible for administering the formulary system. Although the basic organization of each health care setting and its medical staff may influence the specific functions and scope of the P&T committee, key elements of a formulary system that should also be included are the evaluation of the clinical use of medications (including outcomes), the development of policies and quality assurance activities for medication use and administration, and the evaluation and monitoring of adverse drug reactions and medication errors. The formulary system shall be endorsed by the medical staff based on the recommendations of the P&T committee. The medical staff should adapt the principles of the system to fit the needs of the particular organization and affiliated institutions and ambulatory care settings. The organization, often through the pharmacy department, should make certain that all personnel involved in the care of patients and the use of medications in all health-system components are informed about the existence of the formulary system, how to access the formulary, the procedures governing its operation, any changes in those procedures, and other necessary information (e.g., changes in drug product availability). This information may be further disseminated to other interested entities (e.g., affiliated managed care organizations).

Formulary. The P&T committee develops an evidence-based formulary of medications and medication-associated products accepted for use in the organization. The committee also provides timely revision and maintenance for the formulary and promotes the rational, clinically appropriate, safe, and cost-effective use of medications via guidelines, protocols, and other mechanisms. The P&T committee, on an ongoing basis, objectively appraises, evaluates, and selects medications for addition to or deletion from the formulary. The formulary is based on the best clinical evidence available and reflects the current clinical judgment of the medical staff, pharmacists, and other health care experts. The selection of items to be included in the formulary should be based on objective evaluation of their relative economic, clinical, and humanistic outcomes. The decisions should not be based solely on economic factors. The committee should identify potential safety concerns for each medication considered for inclusion in the formulary and should ensure those safety concerns are addressed if the medication is added to the formulary or used in the health system.

The committee should minimize unnecessary duplication of the same basic drug type, drug entity, or drug product. Optimizing the number of drug entities and products available from the pharmacy can produce substantial patient care and financial benefits. These benefits are greatly increased through the use of generic equivalents (drug products considered identical or equivalent by FDA) and therapeutic equivalents (drug products differing in composition or basic drug entity that are considered to have similar pharmacologic and therapeutic activities).[2] The P&T committee must set forth policies and procedures that govern the dispensing of generics and therapeutic equivalents.

The P&T committee, when considering formulary options, should evaluate coordination issues with local health care plans and other organizations' formularies. At a minimum, appropriateness of therapeutic interchange should be evaluated for any formulary decisions that may conflict with known managed care or other health plan formularies.

The formulary should be published and updated regularly. It should also be readily available and accessible at all times, either manually or electronically, to all personnel involved in the care of patients and the use of medications. Medications should be identified in the formulary by their generic names, and prescribers should be strongly encouraged to order medications by their generic names.

The P&T committee should clearly define terminology related to formulary status of medications (e.g., formulary, nonformulary, not stocked at a given site, restricted by criteria specific to a given site), especially in multihospital organizations, and disseminate this information to health care professionals involved in the medication-use process. The P&T committee should establish a procedure for appraisal and use by the medical staff of medications not included in the formulary (i.e., nonformulary medication use).

The pharmacist shall be responsible for specifications for the quality, quantity, and source of supply of all medications, chemicals, biologicals, and pharmaceutical preparations used in the diagnosis and treatment of patients.

Conclusion

ASHP believes that medication-use policies should be developed and implemented in organized health-care systems to promote the rational, evidence-based, clinically appropriate, safe, and cost-effective use of medications. The P&T committee of a health system should develop, organize, and administer a formulary system that follows the principles set forth in this statement in order to optimize patient care.

References

1. Principles of a sound drug formulary system [consensus statement]. In: Hawkins B, ed. Best practices for hospital & health-system pharmacy: positions and guidance documents of ASHP. Bethesda, MD: American Society of Health-System Pharmacists; 2006:110–3.
2. U.S. Department of Health and Human Services. Electronic orange book: approved drug products with therapeutic equivalence evaluations. www.fda.gov/cder/ob/ (accessed 2008 Sep 24).

This statement was reviewed in 2012 by the Council on Pharmacy Practice and by the Board of Directors and was found to still be appropriate.

Approved by the ASHP Board of Directors on January 23, 2008 and by the ASHP House of Delegates on June 10, 2008. Developed through the ASHP Council on Pharmacy Practice. This statement supersedes the ASHP Statement on Pharmacy and Therapeutics Committee dated November 20, 1991, and the ASHP Statement on the Formulary System dated November 18, 1982.

Linda S. Tyler, Pharm.D., FASHP; Mirta Millares, Pharm.D., FCSHP, FASHP; Andrew L. Wilson, Pharm.D., FASHP; Lee C. Vermeulen, Jr., B.S.Pharm., M.S.; J. Russell (Rusty) May, Pharm.D., FASHP; Michael A. Valentino, M.H.S.A.; and Sabrina W. Cole, Pharm.D., are gratefully acknowledged for drafting this statement. The drafters have declared no potential conflicts of interest.

ASHP also acknowledges the following organizations and individuals for reviewing drafts of this statement: Academy of Managed Care Pharmacy (AMCP); American Nurses Association (ANA); American Society for Clinical Pharmacology and Therapeutics (ASCPT); American Society of Consultant Pharmacists (ASCP); Institute for Safe Medication Practices (ISMP); Pharmacy Compounding Accreditation Board (PCAB); Daniel T. Abazia, Pharm.D.; Philip Anderson, Pharm.D., FASHP; Lilian M. Azzopardi, B.Pharm., M.Phil., Ph.D.; Kenneth R. Baker, J.D. (PCAB); James L. Besier, Ph.D., FASHP; J. Lyle Bootman, Ph.D., Sc.D.; David G. Bowyer, B.S.; Maureen Brady, Pharm.D.; Margaret Chrymko, Pharm.D., FASHP; Joseph W. Cranston, Ph.D.; Steven Dzierba, M.S., FASHP; Michael Gaunt, Pharm.D. (ISMP); Pamela C. Hagan, M.S.N., R.N. (ANA); Raymond W. Hammond, Pharm.D., BCPS, FCCP; Eric T. Hola, M.S.; Patricia Kienle, B.S.Pharm., M.P.A., FASHP; Katharine Kiser, Pharm.D.; Thomas L. Kurt, M.D., M.P.H., FACPM, FACMMT, FAACT, FCP, FACE (ASCPT); Timothy R. Lanese, M.B.A., FASHP, FACHE; Rosario (Russ) J. Lazzaro, M.S.; Melvin E. Liter, M.S., Pharm.D.; Patrick M. Malone, Pharm.D., FASHP; Candis M. Morello, Pharm.D., CDE, FCSHP; Richard O'Brocta, Pharm.D., BCPS; Folakemi T. Odedina, Ph.D.; James A. Ponto, M.S., BCNP, FASHP; Curt W. Quap, M.S.; Mike Rouse, B.Pharm., M.P.S.; Marissa Schlaifer, M.S. (AMCP); Shelley Hoppe Schliesser, Pharm.D.; Michele F. Shepherd, Pharm.D., M.S., BCPS, FASHP; Jonalan Smith, Pharm.D. (ASCP); Allen J. Vaida, Pharm.D., FASHP (ISMP); William E. Wade, Pharm.D., FASHP, FCCP; Tom W. Woller, M.S., FASHP; and John L. Woon, Pharm.D., FASHP. (Review does not imply endorsement.)

The bibliographic citation for this document is as follows: American Society of Health-System Pharmacists. ASHP statement on the pharmacy and therapeutics committee and the formulary system. *Am J Health-Syst Pharm.* 2008; 65:2384–6.

ASHP Statement on the Use of Medications for Unlabeled Uses

The freedom and responsibility to make drug therapy decisions that are consistent with patient-care needs is a fundamental precept supported by ASHP. This activity is a professional duty of pharmacists not limited by language in Food and Drug Administration (FDA)-approved product labeling.

The prescribing, dispensing, and administration of FDA-approved drugs for uses, treatment regimens, or patient populations that are not reflected in FDA-approved product labeling often represent a therapeutic approach that has been extensively studied and reported in medical literature. Such uses are *not* indicative of inappropriate usage. Health-care professionals should appreciate the critical need for freedom in making drug therapy decisions and understand the implications of unlabeled uses. ASHP supports third-party reimbursement for FDA-approved drug products appropriately prescribed for unlabeled uses.

Definition of Unlabeled Use

The FDA approves drug products for marketing in the United States. Such a product approved for marketing is often termed an "FDA-approved drug." FDA also approves each drug product's labeling (container label, package insert, and certain advertising); the term "FDA-approved labeling" applies here. Drug uses that are not included in the indications or dosage regimens listed in the FDA-approved labeling are defined as "unlabeled uses." For purposes of this document, unlabeled use includes the use of a drug product in (1) doses, (2) patient populations, (3) indications, or (4) routes of administration that are not reflected in FDA-approved product labeling.

It is important to recognize that FDA cannot approve or disapprove physician prescribing practices of legally marketed drugs. FDA does regulate what manufacturers may recommend about uses in their products' labeling and what manufacturers can include in advertising and promotion.

The sometimes-used term "unapproved use" is a misnomer, implying that FDA regulates prescribing and dispensing activities. This term should be avoided.[1] Other terminology that is sometimes used to describe unlabeled use includes "off-label use," "out-of-label use," and "usage outside of labeling."

According to FDA, unlabeled use encompasses a range of situations that extend from inadequate to carefully conceived investigations, from hazardous to salutary uses, and from infrequent to widespread medical practice. Accepted medical practice often involves drug use that is not reflected in FDA-approved drug-product labeling.[2]

Health-Care Issues Related to Unlabeled Use

Access to Drug Therapies. The prescribing and dispensing of drugs for unlabeled uses are increasing.[3,4] In many clinical situations, unlabeled use represents the most appropriate therapy for patients. Failure to recognize this or, more importantly, regarding such use as "unapproved" or "experimental" may restrict access to necessary drug therapies.

Lack of Practice Standards. Well-defined medical practice standards that differentiate between experimental therapies and established practice will probably always be somewhat lacking, owing to the advancement of medical science and the dynamic nature of medical practice. Standards of practice for certain drug therapies, particularly biotechnologically produced drugs, cancer chemotherapy, and AIDS treatments, are continually evolving. The dynamic nature of these drug therapies makes it difficult for professional societies to review scientific data expediently and to develop standards that remain absolutely current.

Failure of Package Insert and FDA-Approved Labeling to Reflect Current Practice. For FDA-approved product labeling to be modified, scientific data must be submitted by a product's manufacturer to FDA to support any additional indication(s) and dosage regimen(s). Once they are submitted, FDA must review the data and make a decision to permit alteration of the package insert.

Knowing that unlabeled uses are permitted, and knowing that the accumulation and submission of scientific data to FDA to modify labeling is a time-consuming and often expensive process, some pharmaceutical manufacturers elect not to pursue labeling changes. Therefore, a product's labeling sometimes fails to represent the most current therapeutic information for a drug, and situations naturally occur when it is appropriate to prescribe drugs for unlabeled uses.

Pharmacist's Role

ASHP believes that pharmacists in organized health-care settings bear a significant responsibility for ensuring optimal outcomes from all drug therapy. With respect to unlabeled uses, the role of the pharmacist should be to

1. Fulfill the roles of patient advocate and drug information specialist.
2. Develop policies and procedures for evaluating drug orders (prescriptions) and dispensing drugs for unlabeled uses in their own work settings. Such policies and procedures might address the documentation of scientific support, adherence to accepted medical practice standards, or a description of medical necessity.
3. Develop proactive approaches to promote informed decisionmaking by third-party payers for health-care services.

Role of Drug Information Compendia

The Medicare Catastrophic Coverage Act of 1988 (now repealed) included the statements that "in carrying out the legislation, the Secretary [of Health and Human Services] shall establish standards for drug coverage. In establishing such standards, which are based on accepted medical practice, the Secretary shall incorporate standards from such current authoritative compendia as the Secretary may select."[5] Specific compendia recommended were the *AHFS Drug Information,*

AMA Drug Evaluations, and *USP Dispensing Information, Volume I.* Despite the repeal of the Act, some third-party payers have adopted guidelines that endorse these three compendia as authoritative information sources with respect to unlabeled uses for drug products.

Positions on Unlabeled Use

FDA Position. A statement entitled "Use of Approved Drugs for Unlabeled Indications" was published in the *FDA Drug Bulletin* in April 1982 to address the issues of appropriateness and legality of prescribing approved drugs for uses not included in FDA's approved labeling. This statement included the following:

> *The Food, Drug and Cosmetic Act does not limit the manner in which a physician may use an approved drug. Once a product has been approved for marketing, a physician may prescribe it for uses or in treatment regimens or patient populations that are not included in approved labeling. Such "unapproved" or, more precisely, "unlabeled" uses may be appropriate and rational in certain circumstances, and may, in fact, reflect approaches to drug therapy that have been extensively reported in medical literature.*[1]

Other Organizations. Other organizations that have published positions on the issue of unlabeled uses of drug products are the Health Care Financing Administration (HCFA),[6] the Blue Cross and Blue Shield Association of America (BC/BS),[7] and the Health Insurance Association of America (HIAA).[8]

The American Medical Association, American Society of Clinical Oncology, Association of American Cancer Institutes, Association of Community Cancer Centers, Candlelighters Childhood Cancer Foundation, Memorial Sloan Kettering Cancer Center, National Cancer Institute, and the National Institute of Allergy and Infectious Diseases jointly developed a consensus statement and recommendations regarding use and reimbursement of unlabeled uses of drug products.[9]

These statements are consistent with the ASHP position.

Reimbursement Issues

As a cost-containment measure, most third-party payers exclude coverage for experimental therapies. Drug therapy coverage decisions are complicated, because often it is difficult to differentiate among an accepted standard of practice, an evolving standard of practice, and investigational therapies. Data demonstrating medical necessity and improved patient outcome are often difficult to retrieve. Consequently, insurance carriers and managed care providers have sometimes elected to cover only those indications included in FDA-approved drug-product labeling and have frequently denied coverage for unlabeled uses of drug products.

ASHP believes that such coverage denials restrict patients from receiving medically necessary therapies that represent the best available treatment options. A growing number of insurance carriers are following the BC/BS and HIAA guidelines that encourage the use of the three authoritative drug compendia, peer-reviewed literature, and consultation with experts in research and clinical practice to make specific coverage decisions. ASHP supports informed decisionmaking that promotes third-party reimbursement for FDA-approved drug products appropriately prescribed for unlabeled uses.

References

1. Use of approved drugs for unlabeled indications. *FDA Drug Bull.* 1982; 12:4–5.
2. Nightingale SL. Use of drugs for unlabeled indications. *FDA Q Rep.* 1986(Sep); 269.
3. Mortenson LE. Audit indicates many uses of combination therapy are unlabeled. *J Cancer Program Manage.* 1988; 3:21–5.
4. Off-label drugs: initial results of a national survey. Washington, DC: U.S. General Accounting Office. 1991:1–27.
5. PL 100-360, 1988.
6. Health Care Financing Administration. Medicare carriers' manual. Section 2050.5. Washington, DC: U.S. Department of Health and Human Services; 1987 Aug.
7. Statement on coverage recommendation for FDA-approved drugs. Chicago: Blue Cross and Blue Shield Association; 1989 Oct 25.
8. Statement of the Health Insurance Association of America (HIAA) on coverage for unapproved drugs and drug-related costs. Presented to the National Committee to Review Current Procedures for Approval of New Drugs for Cancer and AIDS. 1989 Oct 25.
9. Cancer economics. *Cancer Lett.* 1989; Suppl(Jun):2–3.

Approved by the ASHP Board of Directors, November 20, 1991, and by the ASHP House of Delegates, June 1, 1992. Developed by the Council on Professional Affairs.

The bibliographic citation for this document is as follows: American Society of Hospital Pharmacists. ASHP statement on the use of medications for unlabeled uses. *Am J Hosp Pharm.* 1992; 49:2006–8.

ASHP Guidelines on Medication-Use Evaluation

Medication-use evaluation (MUE) is a performance improvement method that focuses on evaluating and improving medication-use processes with the goal of optimal patient outcomes. MUE may be applied to a medication or therapeutic class, disease state or condition, a medication-use process (prescribing, preparing and dispensing, administering, and monitoring), or specific outcomes.[1] Further, it may be applied in and among the various practice settings of organized health systems.

MUE encompasses the goals and objectives of drug-use evaluation (DUE) in its broadest application, with an emphasis on improving patient outcomes. Use of "MUE," rather than "DUE,"[2] emphasizes the need for a more multifaceted approach to improving medication use. MUE has a common goal with the pharmaceutical care it supports: to improve an individual patient's quality of life through achievement of predefined, medication-related therapeutic outcomes.[3,4] Through its focus on the system of medication use, the MUE process helps to identify actual and potential medication-related problems, resolve actual medication-related problems, and prevent potential medication-related problems that could interfere with achieving optimum outcomes from medication therapy.

In organized health systems, MUE must be conducted as an organizationally authorized program or process that is proactive, criteria based, designed and managed by an interdisciplinary team, and systematically carried out. It is conducted as a collaborative effort of prescribers, pharmacists, nurses, administrators, and other health care professionals on behalf of their patients.

MUE Objectives

Some typical objectives of MUE include

- Promoting optimal medication therapy.
- Preventing medication-related problems.
- Evaluating the effectiveness of medication therapy.
- Improving patient safety.
- Establishing interdisciplinary consensus on medication-use processes.
- Stimulating improvements in medication-use processes.
- Stimulating standardization in medication-use processes.
- Enhancing opportunities, through standardization, to assess the value of innovative medication-use practices from both patient-outcome and resource-utilization perspectives.
- Minimizing procedural variations that contribute to suboptimal outcomes of medication use.
- Identifying areas in which further information and education for health care professionals may be needed.
- Minimizing costs of medication therapy. These costs may be only partly related to the direct cost of medications themselves. When medications are selected and managed optimally from the outset, the costs of complications and wasted resources are minimized, and overall costs are decreased.
- Meeting or exceeding internal and external quality standards (e.g., professional practice standards, accreditation standards, or government laws and regulations).

Steps of the MUE Process

While the specific approach varies with the practice setting and patient population being served, the following common steps occur in the ongoing MUE process:

- Establish organizational authority for the MUE process and identify responsible individuals and groups.
- Develop screening mechanisms (indicators) for comprehensive surveillance of the medication-use system.
- Set priorities for in-depth analysis of important aspects of medication use.
- Inform health care professionals (and others as necessary) in the practice setting(s) about the objectives and expected benefits of the MUE process.
- Establish criteria, guidelines, treatment protocols, and standards of care for specific medications and medication-use processes. These should be based on sound scientific evidence from the medical and pharmaceutical literature.
- Educate health care professionals to promote the use of criteria, guidelines, treatment protocols, and standards of care.
- Establish mechanisms for timely communication among health care professionals.
- Initiate the use of MUE criteria, guidelines, treatment protocols, and standards of care in the medication-use process.
- Collect data and evaluate care.
- Develop and implement plans for improvement of the medication-use process based on MUE findings (if indicated).
- Assess the effectiveness of actions taken, and document improvements.
- Incorporate improvements into criteria, guidelines, treatment protocols, and standards of care, when indicated.
- Repeat the cycle of planning, evaluating, and taking action for ongoing improvement in medication-use processes.
- Regularly assess the effectiveness of the MUE process itself and make needed improvements.

Selecting Medications and Medication-Use Processes for Evaluation

Medications or medication-use processes should be selected for evaluation for one or more of the following reasons:

1. The medication is known or suspected to cause adverse reactions, or it interacts with another medication, food, or diagnostic procedure in a way that presents a significant health risk.
2. The medication is used in the treatment of patients who may be at high risk for adverse reactions.
3. The medication-use process affects a large number of patients or the medication is frequently prescribed.
4. The medication or medication-use process is a critical component of care for a specific disease, condition, or procedure.

5. The medication is potentially toxic or causes discomfort at normal doses.
6. The medication is most effective when used in a specific way.
7. The medication is under consideration for formulary retention, addition, or deletion.
8. The medication or medication-use process is one for which suboptimal use would have a negative effect on patient outcomes or system costs.
9. Use of the medication is expensive.

Indicators Suggesting a Need for MUE Analysis

Certain events (indicators) serve as "flags" of potential opportunities to improve medication use. Some are

- Adverse medication events, including medication errors, preventable adverse drug reactions, and toxicity.
- Signs of treatment failures, such as unexpected readmissions and bacterial resistance to anti-infective therapy.
- Pharmacist interventions to improve medication therapy, categorized by medication and type of intervention.
- Nonformulary medications used or requested.
- Patient dissatisfaction or deterioration in quality of life.

Roles and Responsibilities in the MUE Process

The roles of individual health care professionals in MUE may vary according to practice setting, organizational goals, and available resources. The organizational body (e.g., quality management committee, pharmacy and therapeutics committee) responsible for the MUE process should have, at a minimum, prescriber, pharmacist, nurse, and administrator representation. Other health care professionals should contribute their unique perspectives when the evaluation and improvement process addresses their areas of expertise and responsibility. Temporary working groups may be used for specific improvement efforts.

Pharmacist's Responsibilities in MUE

Pharmacists, by virtue of their expertise and their mission of ensuring proper medication use, should exert leadership and work collaboratively with other members of the health care team in the ongoing process of medication-use evaluation and improvement.[5] Responsibilities of pharmacists in the MUE process include

- Developing an operational plan for MUE programs and processes that are consistent with the health system's overall goals and resource capabilities.
- Working collaboratively with prescribers and others to develop criteria for specific medications and to design effective medication-use processes.
- Reviewing individual medication orders against medication-use criteria and consulting with prescribers and others in the process as needed.
- Managing MUE programs and processes.
- Collecting, analyzing, and evaluating patient-specific data to identify, resolve, and prevent medication-related problems.
- Interpreting and reporting MUE findings and recommending changes in medication-use processes.
- Providing information and education based on MUE findings.

Resources

Some resources helpful in designing and managing an MUE process are listed here.

- The primary professional literature and up-to-date reference texts are key resources necessary for the development of MUE criteria. In general, local consensus should be based on medical and pharmaceutical literature recommendations.
- Published criteria, such as found in *AJHP* and ASHP's *Criteria for Drug Use Evaluation* (volumes 1–4), provide medication-specific criteria that may be adapted for local use.
- Computer software programs, including proprietary programs designed specifically for MUE functions, may be helpful in managing data and reporting.
- External standards-setting bodies, such as the Joint Commission on Accreditation of Healthcare Organizations, publish medication-use indicators that can help to identify portions of the medication-use system that require improvement.

Follow-up Actions in an MUE Process

The MUE process itself should be reviewed regularly to identify opportunities for its improvement. The success of an MUE process should be assessed in terms of improved patient outcomes. Medication-use system changes that evolve from MUE findings should be developed by the departments and medical services with responsibility for providing care, rather than solely through a committee having oversight for MUE (e.g., a pharmacy and therapeutics committee). Typical follow-up actions based on MUE findings include contact with individual prescribers and other health care professionals, information and education (newsletters, seminars, clinical care guidelines) for health care professionals, changes in medication-use systems, and changes in medication-therapy monitoring processes. MUE should be conducted as an ongoing interdisciplinary and collaborative improvement process. Punitive reactions to quality concerns are often counterproductive. It is important to communicate and commend positive achievements (care that meets or exceeds expectations) and improvements.

Pitfalls

Some common pitfalls to avoid in performing MUE activities include the following:[6]

1. Lack of authority. An MUE process that does not involve the medical staff is likely to be ineffective. Authoritative medical staff support and formal organizational recognition of the MUE process are necessary.

2. Lack of organization. Without a clear definition of the roles and responsibilities of individuals involved (e.g., who will develop criteria, who will communicate with other departments, who will collect and summarize data, and who will evaluate data), an MUE process may not succeed.
3. Poor communication. Everyone affected by the MUE process should understand its importance to the health system, its goals, and its procedures. The pharmacist should manage the MUE process and have the responsibility and authority to ensure timely communication among all professionals involved in the medication-use process. Criteria for medication use should be communicated to all affected professionals prior to the evaluation of care. MUE activity should be a standing agenda item for appropriate quality-of-care committees responsible for aspects of medication use.
4. Poor documentation. MUE activities should be well documented, including summaries of MUE actions with respect to individual medication orders and the findings and conclusions from collective evaluations. Documentation should address recommendations made and follow-up actions.
5. Lack of involvement. The MUE process is not a one-person task, nor is it the responsibility of a single department or professional group. Medication-use criteria should be developed through an interdisciplinary consensus process. Lack of administrative support can severely limit the effectiveness of MUE. The benefits of MUE should be conveyed in terms of improving patient outcomes and minimizing health-system costs.
6. Lack of follow-through. A one-time study or evaluation independent of the overall MUE process will have limited success in improving patient outcomes. The effectiveness of initial actions must be assessed and the action plan adjusted if necessary. It is important not to lose sight of the improvement goals.
7. Evaluation methodology that impedes patient care. Data collection should not consume so much time that patient care activities suffer. Interventions that can improve care for an individual patient should not be withheld because of the sampling technique or evaluation methodology.
8. Lack of readily retrievable data and information management. Existing data capabilities need to be assessed and maximum benefit obtained from available computerized information management resources. Deficiencies in information gathering and analysis should be identified and priorities for upgrading information support established.

References

1. Nadzam DM. Development of medication-use indicators by the Joint Commission on Accreditation of Healthcare Organizations. *Am J Hosp Pharm.* 1991; 48:1925–30.
2. American Society of Hospital Pharmacists. ASHP guidelines on the pharmacist's role in drug-use evaluation. *Am J Hosp Pharm.* 1988; 45:385–6.
3. Hepler CD, Strand LM. Opportunities and responsibilities in pharmaceutical care. *Am J Hosp Pharm.* 1990; 47:533–43.
4. American Society of Hospital Pharmacists. ASHP statement on pharmaceutical care. *Am J Hosp Pharm.* 1993; 50:1720–3.
5. Angaran DM. Quality assurance to quality improvement: measuring and monitoring pharmaceutical care. *Am J Hosp Pharm.* 1991; 48:1901–7.
6. Todd MW. Drug use evaluation. In: Brown TR, ed. Handbook of institutional pharmacy practice. 3rd ed. Bethesda, MD: American Society of Hospital Pharmacists; 1992.

Approved by the ASHP Board of Directors, April 24, 1996. Developed by the ASHP Council on Professional Affairs. Supersedes the ASHP Guidelines on the Pharmacist's Role in Drug-Use Evaluation, dated November 19, 1987.

The bibliographic citation for this document is as follows: American Society of Health-System Pharmacists. ASHP guidelines on medication-use evaluation. *Am J Health-Syst Pharm.* 1996; 53:1953–5.

ASHP Guidelines on the Pharmacy and Therapeutics Committee and the Formulary System

Purpose

These guidelines outline the recommended processes and techniques for formulary system management and describe the pharmacist's responsibilities and roles in managing the formulary system in partnership with other health care professionals. These guidelines also provide assistance to pharmacists in the organization and operation of the pharmacy and therapeutics (P&T) committee or equivalent body, evaluation of medications for formularies, and development and implementation of strategies to manage medication use through the formulary system. A glossary of terms is provided in the appendix.

Formulary and Formulary System

A *formulary* is a continually updated list of medications and related information, representing the clinical judgment of physicians, pharmacists, and other experts in the diagnosis, prophylaxis, or treatment of disease and promotion of health. A formulary includes, but is not limited to, a list of medications and medication-associated products or devices, medication-use policies, important ancillary drug information, decision-support tools, and organizational guidelines. A *formulary system* is the ongoing process through which a health care organization establishes policies regarding the use of drugs, therapies, and drug-related products and identifies those that are most medically appropriate and cost-effective to best serve the health interests of a given patient population.[1] Formulary systems are used in many different settings, including hospitals, acute care facilities, home care settings, and long-term-care facilities, as well as by payers such as Medicare, Medicaid, insurance companies, and managed care organizations. Many organizations have policy statements on the use of formularies.[2–8] This document focuses on the use of formulary systems in hospitals and health systems.

Evolution of Formularies

Formulary systems have evolved over time. Modern formularies began as rudimentary drug lists developed by the military in the 1940s and came into more widespread use during the 1950s. Pharmacists, in conjunction with their organizations, developed policies to dispense generic equivalent drugs when a specific brand-name drug was prescribed. Protests from the National Pharmaceutical Council and the American Medical Association (AMA) resulted in state laws prohibiting this activity. Community pharmacies complied, but hospital pharmacies resisted. In the late 1950s, the ASHP minimum standard for pharmacies in hospitals called for the implementation of a formulary system.[9]

During the 1960s, the concept of a hospital formulary continued to grow. Hospitals developed policies that authorized pharmacists to make generic interchanges in an institutional formulary system based on prior consent from physicians.[10] ASHP and the American Hospital Association (AHA) issued joint statements on the legality of formularies.[11,12] AMA and the American Pharmaceutical (later Pharmacists) Association subsequently joined with ASHP and AHA to revise the statements.[13] In 1965, two significant events occurred: (1) Medicare listed formularies as a reimbursement eligibility requirement[14] and (2) the Joint Commission on the Accreditation of Hospitals (now known as the Joint Commission) included an active P&T committee in its accreditation requirements.[15] Even with these actions, formularies were typically no more than lists of drugs stocked by the pharmacy.

By the 1980s, literature describing the clinical and economic value of well-designed formularies had emerged. Evidence from the hospital setting was published first, soon followed by evidence from the ambulatory care environment.[10] This literature led to more widespread acceptance of formularies. In 1986, the Pharmaceutical Research and Manufacturers Association officially accepted the concept of therapeutic interchange in hospitals and opposed its use in other settings.[10] As more evidence emerged, AMA's views on formularies for inpatient and outpatient settings became more closely aligned with those of ASHP. AMA's official policy on drug formularies and therapeutic interchange was first published in 1994[16] and has since been updated several times.[5]

Today, formulary systems are considered an essential tool for health care organizations. Formularies have grown from simple drug lists to comprehensive systems of medication-use policies intended to ensure safe, appropriate, and cost-effective use of pharmaceuticals in patient care.

P&T Committee

The P&T committee is responsible for managing the formulary system. It is composed of actively practicing physicians, other prescribers, pharmacists, nurses, administrators, quality-improvement managers, and other health care professionals and staff who participate in the medication-use process. Customarily, P&T committee member appointments are based on guidance from the medical staff. The P&T committee should serve in an evaluative, educational, and advisory capacity to the medical staff and organizational administration in all matters pertaining to the use of medications (including investigational medications). The P&T committee should be responsible for overseeing policies and procedures related to all aspects of medication use within an institution. The P&T committee is responsible to the medical staff as a whole, and its recommendations are subject to approval by the organized medical staff as well as the administrative approval process. The P&T committee's organization and authority should be outlined in the organization's medical staff bylaws, medical staff rules and regulations, and other organizational policies as appropriate.

Other responsibilities of the P&T committee include medication-use evaluation (MUE), adverse-drug-event monitoring and reporting, medication-error prevention, and development of clinical care plans and guidelines. Information about these activities is available in ASHP guidelines on the topics.[17–20]

P&T committees have been credited with increasing practitioners' knowledge about drug therapy, improving the safety of drug therapy, and improving therapeutic outcomes.[21]

Consideration of patient care and unbiased reviews of the biomedical literature are the cornerstone principles of formulary decision-making. A conflict of interest (COI), financial or otherwise, may interfere with professionals' ability to make evidence-based decisions,[22] and even the appearance of a potential COI can undermine a formulary decision. The P&T committee has a responsibility to its patients and its organization to identify and address COI issues in its decision-making processes. Professionals participating in the P&T committee should disclose financial relationships with pharmaceutical manufacturers, medical supply vendors, other health care provider organizations, and other commercial interests. Some health care organizations exclude heath care professionals with COIs from P&T committee membership, whereas others allow participation in committee discussions but prohibit voting on particular items. Practitioners requesting additions or changes to the formulary should disclose financial relationships with pharmaceutical companies and other potential COIs to the P&T committee.

Finally, the role of pharmaceutical company representatives and medical science liaisons in a health care organization should be carefully considered. Organizational guidelines should define appropriate relationships and interactions with such individuals. At a minimum, these guidelines should address the provision of pharmaceutical samples, indirect or direct funding support, and educational programming regarding formulary and nonformulary medications. Applications for formulary additions should be initiated and completed independently by the requesting health care provider and not by an industry representative or vendor. Refer to ASHP's "Guidelines on Pharmacists' Relationships with Industry" for more information on appropriate interactions with industry.[23]

Managing the Formulary System

Health systems should develop, maintain, and implement a formulary management process. Decisions on the management of a formulary system should be founded on the evidence-based clinical, ethical, legal, social, philosophical, quality-of-life, safety, and economic factors that result in optimal patient care.[24,25] The process must include the active and direct involvement of physicians, pharmacists, and other appropriate health care professionals. This evidence-based process should not be based solely on economic factors. The formulary system should be standardized among components of integrated health systems when standardization leads to improved patient outcomes and safety.

Management of a formulary system is a significant component of a health care organization's ongoing medication-use policy development process. A comprehensive, well-maintained formulary that is tailored to the organization's patient care needs, policy framework, and medication-use systems ensures that the six critical processes identified by the Joint Commission (selection and procurement, storage, ordering and transcribing, preparing and dispensing, administration, and monitoring) work in concert to ensure optimal outcomes.[26] A well-managed formulary system ensures a close relationship among the organization's medication-use policies, the therapies offered by the organization, and the medications routinely stocked in the pharmacy. A formulary also identifies those medications that are most medically appropriate and cost-effective to best serve the health interests of the health system's patient population. The P&T committee should interpret the term *medication* broadly in the context of care delivery to include alternative remedies (herbals and supplements), nonprescription drugs, blood derivatives, contrast media, and other diagnostic and treatment agents.[26]

The formulary system should include review and approval of all policies related to the medication-use process. All medication-use policies, regardless of their origination, should flow through the P&T committee. The organization's medical staff leadership (i.e., the body to which the P&T committee reports) should complete the final policy approval. Policy review and revision should occur as new information becomes available and at regularly established intervals (e.g., annually). Specific medication-use policies should address

- How medications are requested for addition to or deletion from the formulary,
- How medications are reviewed for addition to or deletion from the formulary, including who performs the reviews,
- The process for developing, implementing, and monitoring medication-use guidelines,
- Methods for ensuring the safe prescribing, distribution, administration, and monitoring of medications,
- Methods for selection of suitable manufacturers for specific medications (a pharmacist shall be responsible for specifications for the quality, quantity, and source of supply of all medications, chemicals, biologicals, and pharmaceutical preparations used in the diagnosis and treatment of patients),[27]
- The process for using nonformulary agents within the institution,
- The process for managing drug product shortages,
- The process for developing an organization-specific MUE plan,
- Policies regarding specific medication-use processes (e.g., procurement, prescribing, distribution, administration, monitoring), and
- The process for disseminating medication-use policies and how users will be educated regarding the process.

A formal process to review medication-use policies should be in place. This process may include the use of expert panels or subcommittees of the P&T committee. Expert panels should serve in an advisory role to the P&T committee, and their membership should include recognized experts in their areas of practice. Such panels can be helpful in applying clinical study results to specific patient populations, and panel members can help educate groups of physicians, who ultimately drive prescribing behaviors, about significant formulary changes. User groups, representing those primarily affected by the policy, may also be helpful. The P&T committee may also find subcommittees that address specific therapeutic areas to be beneficial (e.g., antimicrobial, cancer chemotherapy, cardiovascular, adverse-drug-reaction, or biotechnology subcommittees).

The P&T committee should have formal interactions (i.e., communication lines) with other committees whose functions may affect the medication-use process. These committees would include those responsible for developing tools to facilitate medication use (e.g., forms or order set review committee, computerized prescriber-order-entry committee), those concerned with safety or performance improvement (e.g., quality-improvement or patient safety committees), those involved in developing patient care policies (e.g., medical and nursing committees), those involved with investigational medications (e.g., investigational review boards), and other committees whose actions may affect medication use (e.g., nutrition, equipment and supply, or finance committees). Recommendations from other committees, subcommittees of P&T, expert panels, and others should be submitted to the P&T committee for review. P&T committee decisions on recommendations should be communicated to the recommending group in a timely fashion.

Evaluating Medications for Inclusion in the Formulary

The P&T committee should use a structured, evidence-based process in the evaluation of medications for formulary consideration. The P&T committee should be provided with information that reflects a thorough, accurate, and unbiased review and analysis of the evidence available in the scientific literature. The evaluation process should encourage objective consideration of clinical and care delivery information, facilitate communication, foster positive patient outcomes, and support safe and effective medication ordering, dispensing, administration, and monitoring. Decisions made by the P&T committee should support improved patient care outcomes across the continuum of care.

Evidence-Based Evaluation. Inclusion of a medication on a health system's formulary should reflect that an evidence-based evaluation of the relative merits and risks of the medication has been performed and that the institution's P&T committee, with input from appropriate experts, has determined that the medication is appropriate for routine use in the management of the patient population at that institution.

Evidence-based medicine is a systematic approach to the evaluation of biomedical literature and application to clinical practice and should be applied to formulary decision-making for medication product selection.[24] Evidence-based decision-making standardizes and improves the quality of patient care and promotes cost-effective prescribing.[24,25] To practice evidence-based medicine, practitioners must be proficient in retrieving, evaluating, and applying the biomedical literature to clinical practice.

Evidence-based decision-making incorporates the systematic approach to reviewing, evaluating, and applying the biomedical literature to guide formulary decisions. Various types and strengths of evidence (e.g., meta-analyses, randomized clinical trials, case reports, association consensus statements) may be useful in the decision-making process. Although different types of evidence are available for application, those with stronger evidence should be used to drive formulary decisions (e.g., meta-analyses, randomized controlled trials). Other types of evidence have a role in the decision-making process, however, and may be appropriate when stronger evidence is not available. Observational studies (i.e., case–control and cohort studies), case reports, and consensus opinions may be valuable even when stronger evidence is available. Some organizations find it useful to grade evidence when evaluating formulary requests; several tools are available for this purpose.[28–32]

Published evidence and expert opinion are not the only resources available to aid in the formulary decision-making process. Internal data and prescribing and outcomes information may be helpful in formulary decision-making. When published data are not available, it may be appropriate to incorporate expert opinion into the review process. Experts in practice areas sometimes have access to unpublished data or reports that may offer insight into difficult formulary decisions.

The P&T committee should use formulary packets and dossiers prepared by pharmaceutical manufacturers with the utmost caution, since the objectivity of these documents may be challenged. The formulary decision-making process should instead be guided by an independent review of evidence published in the biomedical literature, application of expert opinion, and use of internal data and benchmarking programs.

The information should be provided to the P&T committee in a written document with a standard format (e.g., a drug monograph, drug review, drug-evaluation document). All information provided in the drug-evaluation document should be referenced to the evidence or identified as a conclusion supported by evidence. Any areas of consensus recommendations or opinion should be clearly identified.

Types of Drug Reviews. There are four major types of drug reviews: new drug monographs, reevaluations of previous formulary decisions, therapeutic class reviews, and expedited reviews of newly approved medications. Because of the expertise and training of pharmacists (drug information specialists in particular), pharmacists should play an integral part in the preparation and presentation of the drug review document to the P&T committee.

New drug monographs. When the Food and Drug Administration (FDA) approves a new drug for marketing that is relevant to the health system, a drug monograph should be prepared for formulary consideration by the P&T committee. New chemical entities warrant a thorough evaluation and a written drug monograph. A short (e.g., one-page) summary could be provided along with the full monograph.[33] Some organizations use an executive summary format. A new drug that is significantly similar to other available therapeutic alternatives may be presented in a more abbreviated manner (e.g., an abbreviated monograph) provided that the P&T committee or experts agree that the drug is therapeutically equivalent to agents already available on the formulary.

Addenda to original monographs used to reevaluate previous formulary decisions. Formulary decisions may need to be reassessed based on relevant new information or in light of newly marketed drugs or dosage forms. New data on safety, efficacy, stability, methods of administration, cost, or pharmacoeconomics may warrant a reevaluation of the drug or dosage strengths or formulations stocked by the health system. An addendum to the original monograph summarizing the new information should be developed for evaluation by the P&T committee. The P&T committee may want to establish reassessment dates at the time of formulary review so that the committee can reassess the effect of a formulary decision on quality or cost of care.

Therapeutic class reviews. Review of an entire therapeutic class of drugs should be performed at regular intervals, which may be determined by the P&T committee or influenced by regulatory agencies. A therapeutic class review should include all formulary and nonformulary medications within the class and may include institutional utilization or outcomes data and newly published information. Therapeutic class reviews may lead to formulary removal of therapeutically equivalent drugs or a change in restriction or guideline status for a drug.

Expedited reviews. A process should be available for the P&T committee to conduct an expedited review of a new drug, new indication for a drug, or reevaluation of a previous formulary decision. Criteria should be in place to describe when an expedited review is warranted. For example, approval of a new chemical entity for a disease with no therapeutic alternative may warrant an expedited review to ensure availability of the drug for patients who need it. Likewise, a significant new safety concern may warrant an expedited review for addition of restrictions or removal from the formulary.

Elements of a Drug-Evaluation Document. The drug-evaluation document should present the evidence in a manner that is thorough, is consistent from medication to medication, and provides all necessary facts and analysis to the P&T committee to allow for an informed formulary decision. Document structure may vary, depending on the needs of the specific health system and P&T committee, but the following elements are essential to all such documents:

- Brand and generic names and synonyms,
- FDA approval information, including date and FDA rating,
- Pharmacology and mechanism of action,
- FDA-approved indications,
- Potential non-FDA-approved (off-label) uses,
- Dosage forms and storage,
- Recommended dosage regimens,
- Pharmacokinetic considerations,
- Use in special populations (e.g., children, elderly, patients with renal or liver failure),
- Pregnancy category and use during breast-feeding,
- Comparisons of the drug's efficacy, safety, convenience, and costs with those of therapeutic alternatives (with evidence tables when feasible),
- If information on comparative efficacy is minimal or lacking, data on absolute efficacy (i.e., efficacy versus placebo),
- Clinical trial analysis and critique,
- Medication safety assessment and recommendations (adverse drug reactions; drug–drug and drug–food interactions; specific therapy monitoring requirements; unusual administration, storage, or stability issues; and potential for medication errors, such as look-alike or sound-alike issues), and
- Financial analysis, including pharmacoeconomic assessments.

Formulary status recommendations (e.g., from drug information services or expert groups) may be included in the drug evaluation document. In some organizations, recommendations are not provided in the written document in order to promote an unbiased discussion by the P&T committee. Recommendations should consider the formulary status (addition or rejection) of a medication, as well as the need for restrictions, educational efforts, or policies and procedures to ensure safe and appropriate use within the health system.

Pharmacoeconomic Assessments. Rigorous pharmacoeconomic evaluations can and should be conducted in some cases when reviewing new medications. These evaluations should explicitly state the perspective of the analysis (e.g., patient, health care provider, payer) and should include consideration of all costs and consequences relevant to that perspective. When new medications being considered are found to be therapeutically equivalent to existing alternatives (having equivalent efficacy and safety), then the cost-minimization approach is appropriate. In these circumstances, it is important to consider costs associated with the medication and nonmedication-related costs (e.g., costs of administration, monitoring, prolonged hospital stay, and laboratory test monitoring; costs to patients and providers).

While cost-effectiveness analysis (evaluating the incremental difference in investment necessary to produce an incremental difference in clinical outcome) is another potentially useful analytic approach, it is not often used for formulary decision-making because of its complexity and need for strong evidence or data. The academic value of this approach lies in its ability to show how little (or how much) must be spent to achieve a particular margin of clinical advantage when comparing an alternative that is more expensive but safer or more efficacious. No standards currently exist to determine how much money is reasonable to spend for any given improvement in out-come; however, it is unreasonable to recommend alternatives of lower quality simply to achieve cost savings. This approach can be used to demonstrate how a decrease in clinical outcomes associated with the use of a less expensive agent can be offset by investing the savings achieved in other interventions that produce even greater total benefits.

Cost-utility evaluations (evaluating the incremental difference in investment necessary to produce an incremental difference in quality-of-life-adjusted clinical outcome [e.g., incremental cost per quality-adjusted life years gained for one medication versus another]) may also be beneficial by serving to reflect patient preference in formulary decision-making. However, the same concerns related to the use of cost-effectiveness evaluations apply to this approach.[34–36]

Decision analysis models incorporating local data can be employed when published pharmacoeconomic data are limited or unavailable. Probabilities for each outcome can be extracted from the published literature or drawn from local data sources, which would provide a more relevant local perspective on outcomes. Costs associated with medications and outcomes should reflect those of the health care system.

Pharmacoeconomic analyses published in the medical literature or provided in the manufacturer's formulary dossier should be analyzed carefully before being included as part of the review process. Particular attention should be paid to the assumptions made in these studies. In many situations, assumptions made to simplify economic studies are not valid in particular institutions. Institution-specific costs are often different from the costs used in published studies, and local data should be used when incorporating their results into medication reviews.[37,38]

Even if a formal pharmacoeconomic evaluation is not included in a drug review document, a financial evaluation must be conducted, including consideration of nonmedication-related costs and financial consequences to the pharmacy and to the organization as a whole.

Formulary Exceptions. Exclusion of a medication from a formulary may affect coverage of and access to the medication. In a closed formulary system, for example, only medications listed on the formulary are covered under the patient's drug benefit. Regardless of health-system setting, the formulary system should include an exception process that provides prescribers and patients with timely access to medications that are not on the formulary but are medically necessary for the care of the patient. The underlying principle for such a process is that unique patient needs may not be satisfied by use of the formulary medications. The formulary exception process should generate information on nonformulary medication use that will enable the P&T committee to evaluate trends in such use. Criteria for approval of nonformulary medications should be developed (e.g., allergy to or therapeutic failure of formulary alternative, condition not treatable by formulary medications).

Subformularies. Depending on state regulations, subformularies may be developed and maintained, using the same evidence-based process, to provide lists of appropriate and approved medications for furnishing by nonphysician providers or to specific patient subsets, such as Medicare patients. Health systems must follow specific rules and regulations provided under the U.S. Medicare Modernization Act of 2003 in their evaluation and inclusion of medications in a Medicare formulary for those medications to be covered.[39]

Strategies for Managing Medication Use

Common strategies for managing medication use via the formulary include use of generic drugs, therapeutic interchange, guided-use policies, clinical practice guidelines, and policies for off-label prescribing and the use of research pharmaceuticals. MUE is also important in managing medication use.

Generic Drugs. Optimizing the number of medication entities and products available from the pharmacy can produce substantial patient care and financial benefits. These benefits are greatly increased through the use of generic equivalents (drugs considered bioequivalent by FDA [i.e., AB-rated drug products[40]] and therapeutic equivalents (drug products differing in composition or in their basic drug entity that are considered to have very similar pharmacologic and therapeutic activities). The use of high-quality generic equivalents is encouraged in order to provide the best possible care at an affordable cost. Use of generic drugs that have been deemed bioequivalent by FDA does not require review or approval by the P&T committee, although a review of all new medications for key safety issues (e.g., look-alike, sound-alike concerns) should be conducted to prevent medication errors. For some drug categories, such as those with a narrow therapeutic range, a more thorough evaluation of the bioequivalency data and approval of experts or the P&T committee should be considered before implementing a generic substitution.

The P&T committee must establish policies and procedures governing the dispensing of generic equivalents. These policies and procedures should include the following points:

- The pharmacist is responsible for selecting from available generic equivalents those drugs to be dispensed pursuant to a prescriber's order for a particular medication.
- The prescriber has the option, at the time of prescribing, to specify the brand or supplier of the drug to be dispensed for that particular medication order if considered clinically justified.
- The prescriber's decision should be based on pharmacologic or therapeutic considerations (or both) relative to that patient.

Therapeutic Interchange. Therapeutic interchange is the authorized exchange of therapeutic alternatives in accordance with previously established and approved written guidelines, policies, or protocols within a formulary system.[1] Therapeutic interchange provides pharmacists with the authorization to use a formulary therapeutic alternative in place of a nonformulary medication or a non-preferred formulary medication without having to contact the prescriber. Drugs appropriate for therapeutic interchange are drug products with different chemical structures that are expected to have similar therapeutic effects and safety profiles when administered to patients in therapeutically equivalent doses. The authorization of a therapeutic interchange and notification of the prescriber should occur according to the organization's policy. In some organizations, prescribers agree to the therapeutic interchange process as part of their overall agreement to follow the organization's policies when they are granted prescribing privileges. Other organizations require that the prescriber be notified each time a medication is interchanged. A process should be established for when the prescriber wishes to opt out of the interchange. Adequate educational initiatives should be undertaken to ensure that everyone affected (prescribers, patients, pharmacists, nurses, and other health care professionals) is notified of the therapeutic interchange. Guidelines on therapeutic interchange are available elsewhere.[41]

Guided-Use Strategies. Medications may be added to the formulary with additional processes in place to guide the use of the medications to improve therapeutic outcomes, prevent adverse events, or reduce costs. Examples of strategies to help guide the use of medications in addition to therapeutic interchange may include the following.

Established-use criteria. Patients must meet the established criteria before the medication is dispensed. A process should be developed to cover situations in which the patient does not meet the established criteria, but the medication is nevertheless determined to be medically necessary. This strategy may also be useful when medications are in short supply.

Restricting drug use to a service. A specific service must approve the use of the drug before dispensing. This strategy can be used when inappropriate use or severe adverse effects may occur, and it can also be employed for antimicrobial agents when inappropriate use or overuse can result in resistant organisms and pose a danger to the general patient population or the public.

Limiting use of the drug to specially trained individuals. This strategy may be appropriate when the drug is inherently dangerous and should only be used by individuals with specific training (e.g., restricting use of chemotherapy agents to oncologists).

Designating medications for use in specific areas. Such policies can be helpful when administration of a medication requires special equipment or staff with particular skills to use the medication safely (e.g., limiting neuromuscular blockers to operating rooms and critical care areas).

Approval of medical director (or designee) before drug use. This strategy is particularly appropriate when the P&T committee has reviewed a high-cost medication and determined that the drug has little or no role in the care of patients at that organization but a prescriber would like to use the medication on a nonformulary basis.

Clinical Practice Guidelines. The implementation of medication-use policy decisions is a complicated process that, when properly conducted, can decrease variability in practice and improve patient outcomes, including clinical and economic consequences of care. Many tools are used to reduce practice variability, reduce cost, and improve quality, including order sets, clinical pathways, treatment algorithms, and clinical practice guidelines. While active intervention tools, such as order sets, directly influence prescribing for individual patients, clinical practice guidelines influence prescriber behavior in a passive manner, primarily through education. Like the medication formulary, clinical practice guidelines should reflect current biomedical evidence, although they may also include expert opinion of prescribers within a practice seting. Clinical practice guidelines are developed and disseminated by national and international organizations, but they can also be developed locally. Not all guidelines are equally valuable, however. Policymakers should not assume that guidelines, even those endorsed by respected organizations, are necessarily evidence based and should carefully review guidelines to ensure that they are truly evidence driven and current. Regardless of the source of the synthesis of biomedical evidence that forms the framework for an individual guideline, a locally conducted consensus development process, incorporating local expertise, must be performed if a guideline is to be accepted and followed.

Whether the medication formulary is a reflection of existing clinical practice guidelines in a particular organization or vice versa, it is critical that the guidelines and formulary are consistent. If a specific medication is recommended by a clinical practice guideline, it should in the majority of cases be on the formulary. As formulary changes are made, agents may need to be removed from or replaced in existing guidelines. Guidelines should avoid recommending use of nonformulary medications, and they can be useful in discouraging nonformulary medication use and guiding the appropriate use of nonformulary products when necessary.

Guidelines are frequently developed to address complex or particularly expensive medication therapies. However, complicated specialty therapies that will affect the care of very few patients may not justify the time and resources necessary to develop and maintain a guideline. Guidelines may be medication specific or disease oriented and may overlap in their scope of coverage.

The development of a clinical practice guideline should begin with the synthesis of all available biomedical evidence addressing the guideline topic. In many cases, guidelines from other organizations, both national and local, can be used as a starting point for development. The national guideline clearinghouse sponsored by the Agency for Healthcare Research and Quality is a useful source of previously developed guidelines (www.guideline.gov). The subsequent consensus process, eliciting feedback and input from local stakeholders, is critical. Stakeholders may not reach unanimous agreement about all dimensions of the guideline, but their involvement in its development increases their awareness of it and may create a sense of investment in its goals. Process-of-care and outcomes data from the organization's MUE activities (or, in some organizations, from such sources as the electronic medical records and computerized prescriber-order-entry systems) can also be used to make informed decisions during the consensus process. After the consensus process is completed, the guideline should be reviewed and approved by the P&T committee.

The dissemination and implementation of guidelines in the practice environment must also be carefully executed. Unlike active intervention tools that directly influence behavior, guidelines change behavior only when they are accessed, read, accepted, and put into practice. Exhaustive communication about the availability of guidelines is necessary. The dissemination of guidelines in hardcopy format is common, but electronic distribution (often in the form of a library of guidelines available via the Internet) is more efficient. Given the dynamic nature of the biomedical evidence and the quickening pace of changes in practice, maintaining current practice guidelines is an important challenge. Every guideline should include a time frame for future review and revision. If resources are not available to properly update and revise an older guideline, the guideline should be retired and removed from circulation.

Off-Label Use. The use of a drug prescribed for an indication not specifically approved by FDA is often referred to as off-label use. Off-label use can include the use of pharmaceuticals outside of specified populations, for different diseases or stages of diseases, or by different routes of administration. Other types of off-label use involve changes to dosing or dosing schedules or in chronology or sequence of use.

Before considering off-label use, supporting safety and efficacy evidence must be carefully evaluated and a risk-benefit determination made, especially when alternatives with FDA-approved labeling are available for the intended off-label use.[42] When considering or reviewing off-label use, the P&T committee should use an evidence-based process. The approach to evaluating evidence and benefit developed by the U.S. Preventive Services Task Force is an example.[43,44]

The following principles should guide the off-label use of medications:

1. Off-label pharmaceutical prescribing should be based on published evidence, and patient safety should be the primary consideration.
2. When the off-label use of an agent is expected to occur frequently, the P&T committee should establish protocols guiding that use. The P&T committee should be considered the arbiter of off-label use and should rely on the scientific evidence to guide its decisions.
3. The ultimate responsibility for the safety and efficacy of off-label use resides with the prescriber, who should be familiar with the evidence before considering off-label use, be aware of local protocols for use of the agent, and, when necessary, consult with an appropriately knowledgeable pharmacist.
4. Proper assessment of evidence for off-label use should involve as comprehensive and balanced a review as possible. Selective use of studies to support a position is strongly discouraged and, in the event of a negative

outcome, may not withstand the rigor of a thorough peer review.

Research Pharmaceuticals (Investigational Drugs). An investigational drug is defined as a chemical or biological used in a clinical investigation and can include prescription and nonprescription drugs, nutritional supplements, and herbal preparations. Investigational drug study procedures must be consistent with all applicable laws and regulations. Efforts should be made to ensure that the prescribing and distribution of investigational drugs benefit from the safe medication management systems used for other medications. More information on the management of investigational drugs can be found in other ASHP guidelines.[45,46]

MUE Process. Although distinctions have historically been made among the terms *drug-use evaluation, drug-use review*, and *medication-use evaluation*, they all refer to the systematic evaluation of medication use employing standard, observational quality-improvement methods (e.g., traditional "plan–do–check–act" approach). MUE is a quality-improvement activity, but it can also be considered a formulary system management technique.

MUE methods have traditionally involved establishing evidence-based criteria for medication use and applying those criteria retrospectively to determine the degree to which a particular medication was used in discordance with established criteria. Interventions could then be used to improve prescribing based on those data. As electronic medical records have become increasingly important and more widely available, MUE activities have matured from simple paper-based medical record reviews to sophisticated analyses drawing on multiple sources of data regarding medication use. A more expansive approach to MUE has been described in which not only the use of individual medications but the entire process of care for disease states is examined.[47] The use of quasiexperimental research methods may provide more meaningful information for quality-improvement purposes (e.g., economic, clinical, and humanistic outcomes of greater relevance than arbitrarily set appropriateness criteria).

MUE can be simply informative (collecting data to guide decision-making) or be used to measure the effect of interventions, such as the addition of a new agent to the formulary or the implementation of a new medication-use policy. MUE activities can focus on any dimension of the medication-use process (from medication acquisition to patient monitoring) that presents an opportunity for improvement. While MUE often focuses on problem-prone, high-risk, or high-cost medications, MUE can be used to examine any aspect of medication use that is problematic to the institution conducting the evaluation.

A systematic plan to monitor, evaluate, and improve medication use should be established within the organization.[17] Such a plan is an accreditation requirement for many organizations (e.g., Joint Commission[26]). MUE should be a part of the organization's overall quality-improvement program. MUE activities should be conducted to examine the effect of medication-use policy decisions (particularly those made in the absence of convincing evidence from the biomedical literature) but can also be conducted to inform decision-making (again, particularly when making policy decisions under conditions of uncertainty). Specific projects to evaluate medication use can either involve assessing how an individual medication is used or evaluate medication management of a given disease state. All steps of the medication-use process should be evaluated over time. The P&T committee, or its equivalent, should be involved in the MUE process.

Concurrent evaluation (collecting data during care delivery and sometimes as a component of the care process) is usually preferred over retrospective methods because it allows organizations to select relevant outcomes for collection rather than rely on out-comes routinely documented in patient medical records. For example, quality-of-life measures remain an infrequently documented measure in medical records. Only through concurrent evaluation can that outcome measure be reliably captured. Medications recently added to the formulary should be evaluated, especially if there is the potential for inappropriate use or adverse effects of concern. This review should occur 6–12 months after their addition to the formulary. High-cost, high-use, and problemprone medications are also good candidates for evaluation.

Incorporating Patient Safety Issues in the Decision-Making Process

P&T committees have always addressed medication safety issues. However, as medication errors have received increased scrutiny and more is understood about the process failures that contribute to such errors, P&T committees have more opportunities to address patient safety issues. The P&T committee should systematically address patient safety as part of its deliberations. Opportunities for including patient safety in P&T committee deliberations include the following:

1. When evaluating a medication for inclusion on the formulary, the P&T committee should consider adverse effects, issues in preparation, sound-alike or look-alike potential, and dosing or administration issues. Assessments should be conducted to identify potential safety concerns posed by use of the medication. The P&T committee should make recommendations for managing identified risks.
2. Organizations, in collaboration with the appropriate committees, should undertake projects to proactively assess risk in medication-use processes. The use of high-risk medications or major system changes (e.g., a new computer system, new equipment) offer opportunities to perform proactive risk assessments. Failure mode and effects analysis (FMEA) can be used to structure these assessments. The Joint Commission, Institute for Healthcare Improvement, and National Center on Patient Safety provide information about conducting and examples of FMEA projects on their websites (www.jointcommission.org/, www.ihi.org/, and www.patientsafety.gov).
3. The P&T committee should consistently review medication-event data, including data on near misses, and make recommendations to prevent future events.
4. The P&T committee should conduct targeted quality-improvement projects to improve the safety of specific medications or to evaluate the processes involved.
5. When reviewing policies, the P&T committee should ensure that the policies adequately address the potential risk issues.

6. The P&T committee should champion evidence-based fail-safe techniques (e.g., bar-coding) to prevent medication events.
7. The P&T committee should review information available on patient safety or events reported by other organizations to identify ways to prevent medication events and disseminate the information to health care providers and, when appropriate, patients.

Resources on medication safety should be routinely reviewed to identify potential issues an organization could address. Examples of resources include the Institute for Safe Medication Practices (www.ismp.org), Medwatch (www.fda.gov/medwatch), FDA Patient Safety News (www.accessdata.fda.gov/scripts/cdrh/cfdocs/psn/), and the U.S. Pharmacopeia Patient Safety Program (www.usp.org/hqi/patientSafety/).

Drug Product Shortages

Health systems frequently need to address drug product shortages. Drug product shortages disrupt patient care and the processing of medication orders, increasing the risks presented by all aspects of the medication-use system, including purchasing, storage, pharmacy computer and automation systems, ordering, preparation, administration, and monitoring.

During a drug product shortage, the P&T committee plays an important role in setting organizational priorities. The P&T committee needs to develop strategies to address shortages in a timely manner, including designating appropriate alternatives, identifying strategies for rationing available drug product, establishing use restrictions, and implementing evidence-based review procedures. Therapeutic interchange can be useful in dealing with critical drug product shortages. When necessary, the P&T committee should work collaboratively with other committees and departments, such as risk management or specific medical departments affected by the shortage, to develop effective management plans for addressing shortages. Many organizations include a drug shortage update as a regular agenda item for the P&T committee. Communication with patients and staff is crucial to effectively manage shortages.

More information about managing drug product shortages can be found in the ASHP Guidelines on Managing Drug Product Shortages.[48]

Implementing Medication-Use Policies

Various tools can be used to implement medication-use policies. The policy should be integrated directly into the therapeutic decision-making processes that guide the use of a medication as the health care professional orders it or incorporated into a preprinted order form. Other specific ways of communicating information about a medication-use policy may include the use of

- Inservice education,
- Grand rounds,
- Interactions between pharmacists and prescribers at the time of prescribing or dispensing,
- Staff meetings,
- e-mail,
- Newsletters,
- Mailings,
- Prescriber detailing, and
- Pharmacy or institutional websites.

Pilot or demonstration projects may be beneficial in illustrating the value of a new medication-use policy and may generate data that could justify a decision or help communicate why a specific policy is necessary.

Conclusion

A formulary system is the multidisciplinary, evidence-based process employed by an organization to select and use medications that offer the best therapeutic outcomes while minimizing potential risks and costs for patients. Organizations employ the MUE process to continually improve how medications are used within the organization at all steps in the medication-use process. Medication use is an inherently complex and dangerous process that requires constant evaluation. Organizations need to implement tools and processes necessary to meet the goals of using medications effectively and safely. Professionals involved in the medication-use process need to know and understand how the organization's medication-use policies and processes can be incorporated into their daily work so that medications are used appropriately and safely. Technology offers many opportunities to make those processes more effective. Communicating the actions related to medication use is a constant challenge that organizations need to address.

References

1. Principles of a sound drug formulary system. In: Hawkins B, ed. Best practices for hospital and health-system pharmacy: positions and guidance documents of ASHP. Bethesda, MD: American Society of Health-System Pharmacists; 2006:110–3.
2. American Society of Consultant Pharmacists. ASCP statement on medication formulary principles for older adults. www.ascp.com/resources/policy/upload/Sta01-Formulary%20Older%20Adults.pdf (accessed 2008 Mar 27).
3. American Society of Consultant Pharmacists. ASCP statement on formularies in nursing facilities. www.ascp.com/resources/policy/upload/Sta96-Formularies.pdf (accessed 2008 Mar 27).
4. Laing R, Tisocki K. How to develop a national formulary based on the WHO model formulary. http://whqlibdoc.who.int/hq/2004/WHO_EDM_PAR_2004.8.pdf (accessed 2008 Apr 24).
5. American Medical Association. Policy H-125.991: drug formularies and therapeutic interchange. www.ama-assn.org/apps/pf_new/pf_online?f_n=resultLink&doc=policyfiles/HnE/H-125.991.HTM (accessed 2008 Mar 27).
6. American Medical Association. Policy H-285.965: managed care cost containment involving prescription drugs. www.ama-assn.org/apps/pf_new/pf_online?f_n=resultLink&doc=policyfiles/HnE/H-285.965.HTM (accessed 2008 Mar 27).

7. Academy of Managed Care Pharmacy. AMCP format for formulary submissions, version 2.1. www.fmcpnet.org/cfr/waSys/f.cfc?method=getListFile&id=A2D0F502 (accessed 2008 Mar 27).
8. American Academy of Family Physicians. Patient-centered formularies. www.aafp.org/online/en/home/policy/policies/p/patientcenteredformularies.html (accessed Mar 27).
9. American Society of Hospital Pharmacists. Minimum standard for pharmacies in hospitals. *Am J Hosp Pharm.* 1958; 15:992–4.
10. May JR. Formulary systems. In: DiPiro JT, ed. Encyclopedia of clinical pharmacy. New York: Marcel Dekker; 2002.
11. Willcox AM. The legal basis of the formulary system. *Am J Hosp Pharm.* 1960; 17:603–8.
12. American Society of Hospital Pharmacists, American Hospital Association. Statement of guiding principles on the operation of hospital formularies. *Am J Hosp Pharm.* 1960; 17:609–10.
13. American Society of Hospital Pharmacists, American Hospital Association, American Pharmaceutical Association, et al. Statement of guiding principles on the operation of hospital formularies. *Am J Hosp Pharm.* 1964; 21:40–1.
14. Social Security Administration. Conditions of participation for hospitals. *Am J Hosp Pharm.* 1966; 23:179–80.
15. Lammy PP, Flack HL. Pharmacy and therapeutics committee, consent, and the hospital formulary. *Am J Hosp Pharm.* 1966; 23:662–72.
16. American Medical Association. AMA policy on drug formularies and therapeutic interchange in inpatient and ambulatory patient care settings. *Am J Hosp Pharm.* 1994; 51:1808–10.
17. American Society of Health-System Pharmacists. ASHP guidelines on medication-use evaluation. *Am J Health-Syst Pharm.* 1996; 53:1953–5.
18. American Society of Health-System Pharmacists. ASHP guidelines on adverse drug reaction monitoring and reporting. *Am J Health-Syst Pharm.* 1995; 52:417–9.
19. American Society of Hospital Pharmacists. ASHP guidelines on preventing medication errors in hospitals. *Am J Hosp Pharm.* 1993; 50:305–14.
20. American Society of Health-System Pharmacists. ASHP guidelines on the pharmacist's role in the development, implementation, and assessment of critical pathways. *Am J Health-Syst Pharm.* 2004; 61:939–45.
21. Nair KV, Ascione FJ. Evaluation of P&T committee performance: an exploratory study. *Formulary.* 2001; 36:136–46.
22. Brennan TA, Rothman DJ, Blank L, et al. Health industry practices that create conflicts of interest: a policy proposal for academic medical centers. *JAMA.* 2006; 295:429–33.
23. American Society of Hospital Pharmacists. ASHP guidelines on pharmacists' relationships with industry. *Am J Hosp Pharm.* 1992; 49:154.
24. Nakahiro S. Contemporary issues in formulary management. In: Millares M, ed. Applied drug information: strategies for information management. Vancouver: Applied Therapeutics Inc.; 1998:8.1–8.43.
25. Nakahiro RK, Ho SS, Okamoto MP. Concepts of pharmacoeconomics. In: Millares M, ed. Applied drug information: strategies for information management. Vancouver: Applied Therapeutics Inc.; 1998:7.1–7.37.
26. Comprehensive accreditation manual for accreditation of hospitals. Joint Commission on Accreditation of Healthcare Organizations. Oakbrook Terrace, IL; 2006.
27. ASHP guidelines for selecting pharmaceutical manufacturers and suppliers. *Am J Hosp Pharm.* 1991; 48:523–4.
28. Briss PA, Zaza S, Pappaioanou M., et al. Developing an evidence-based guide to community preventive services—methods. *Am J Prev Med.* 2000; 18(suppl 1):35–43.
29. Atkins D, Best D, Briss PA., et al. Grading quality of evidence and strength of recommendations. *BMJ.* 2004; 328:1490–8.
30. Guyatt G, Gutterman D, Baumann MH., et al. Grading strength of evidence of recommendations and quality of evidence in clinical guidelines: report from an American College of Chest Physicians task force. *Chest.* 2006; 129:174–81.
31. Harbour R, Miller J. A new system for grading recommendations in evidence based guidelines. *BMJ.* 2001; 323:334–6.
32. Corman SL, Skledar SJ, Culley CM. Evaluation of conflicting literature and application to formulary decisions. *Am J Health-Syst Pharm.* 2007; 64:182–5.
33. Sterné SC, Uchida KM, Iteen SA. Improving the presentation of drug information to pharmacy and therapeutics committees for formulary decisions. *Am J Health-Syst Pharm.* 1996; 53:1162–4.
34. Reeder CE. Overview of pharmacoeconomics and pharmaceutical outcomes evaluations. *Am J Health-Syst Pharm.* 1995; 52(19, suppl 4):S5–8.
35. Drummond MF, Sculpher MJ, Torrance GW., et al. Methods for the economic evaluation of health care programmes. 3rd ed. Oxford, England: Oxford Univ. Press; 2005:137–89.
36. Gold MR, Siegel JE, Russell LB, et al., eds. Cost-effectiveness in health and medicine. New York: Oxford Univ. Press; 1996:176–213.
37. Sanchez LA. Applied pharmacoeconomics: evaluation and use of pharmacoeconomic data from the literature. *Am J Health-Syst Pharm.* 1999; 56:1630–8.
38. Ofman JJ, Sullivan SD, Neumann PJ, et al. Examining the value and quality of health economic analyses: implications of utilizing the QHES. *J Manag Care Pharm.* 2003; 9:53–61.
39. U.S. Medicare Prescription Drug, Improvement, and Modernization Act of 2003. Pub. L. No. 108–173.
40. Food and Drug Administration. Electronic orange book: approved drug products with therapeutic equivalence evaluations. www.fda.gov/cder/ob/ (accessed 2008 Mar 27).
41. Gray T, Bertch K, Galt K, et al. Guidelines for therapeutic interchange—2004. *Pharmacotherapy.* 2005; 25:1666–80.

42. American Society of Hospital Pharmacists. ASHP statement on the use of medications for unlabeled uses. *Am J Hosp Pharm.* 1992; 49:2006–8.
43. U.S. Preventive Services Task Force. Strength of recommendations rating guide. www.ahrq.gov/clinic/3rduspstf/ratings.htm (accessed 2008 Mar 27).
44. U.S. Preventive Services Task Force. Current methods of the U.S. Preventive Services Task Force: a review of the process.www.ahrq.gov/clinic/ajpmsuppl/harris2.htm#assessing (accessed 2008 Mar 27).
45. American Society of Hospital Pharmacists. ASHP guidelines for pharmaceutical research in organized health-care settings. *Am J Hosp Pharm.* 1989; 46:129–30.
46. American Society of Health-System Pharmacists. ASHP guidelines on clinical drug research. *Am J Health-Syst Pharm.* 1998; 55:369–76.
47. Vermeulen LC, Beis SJ, Cano SB. Applying outcomes research in improving the medication-use process. *Am J Health-Syst Pharm.* 2000; 57:2277–82.
48. American Society of Health-System Pharmacists. ASHP guidelines on managing drug product shortages. *Am J Health-Syst Pharm.* 2001; 58:1445–50.

Appendix—Glossary of Terms

Formulary: A continually updated list of medications and related information, representing the clinical judgment of physicians, pharmacists, and other experts in the diagnosis, prophylaxis, or treatment of disease and promotion of health.

Formulary System: An ongoing process whereby a health care organization, through its physicians, pharmacists, and other health care professionals, establishes policies on the use of drug products and therapies and identifies drug products and therapies that are the most medically appropriate and cost-effective to best serve the health interests of a given patient population.[1]

Generic Substitution: The substitution of drug products that contain the same active ingredient or ingredients and are chemically identical in strength, concentration, dosage form, and route of administration to the drug product prescribed.[1]

Medication: Any prescription medications, herbal remedies, vitamins, nutraceuticals, nonprescription drugs, vaccines, or diagnostic and contrast agents used to diagnose, treat, or prevent disease and other abnormal conditions and radioactive medications, respiratory therapy treatments, parenteral nutrition, blood derivatives, intravenous solutions (plain or with electrolytes or drugs), or any product designated by the Food and Drug Administration as a drug (including investigational drugs).[26]

Medication-Use Evaluation: A performance-improvement method that focuses on evaluating and improving medication-use processes with the goal of optimal patient outcomes.[17]

Pharmacy and Therapeutics (P&T) Committee: An advisory committee that is responsible for developing, managing, updating, and administering a formulary system.[1]

Therapeutic Alternatives: Drug products with different chemical structures but of the same pharmacologic or therapeutic class and usually have similar therapeutic effects and adverse-reaction profiles when administered to patients in therapeutically equivalent doses.[1]

Therapeutic Interchange: Authorized exchange of therapeutic alternatives in accordance with previously established and approved written guidelines or protocols within a formulary system.[1, 41]

Therapeutic Substitution: The act of dispensing a therapeutic alternative for the drug product prescribed without prior authorization of the prescriber. This is an illegal act because only the prescriber may authorize an exchange of therapeutic alternatives.[1]

These guidelines were reviewed in 2012 by the Council on Pharmacy Practice and by the Board of Directors and were found to still be appropriate.

Approved by the ASHP Board of Directors on January 28, 2008. These guidelines supersede the ASHP Guidelines on Formulary System Management dated November 20, 1991, the ASHP Technical Assistance Bulletin on Drug Formularies dated November 14, 1990, and the ASHP Technical Assistance Bulletin on the Evaluation of Drugs for Formularies dated November 19, 1987. Developed through the ASHP Council on Pharmacy Practice.

ASHP gratefully acknowledges the expert panel that developed these guidelines: Linda S. Tyler, Pharm.D., FASHP; Mirta Millares, Pharm.D., FCSHP, FASHP; Andrew L. Wilson, Pharm.D., FASHP; Lee C. Vermeulen, Jr., B.S.Pharm., M.S.; J. Russell (Rusty) May, Pharm.D., FASHP; Michael A. Valentino, R.Ph. MHSA; and Sabrina W. Cole, Pharm.D.

The bibliographic citation for this document is as follows: American Society of Health-System Pharmacists. ASHP guidelines on the pharmacy and therapeutics committee and the formulary system. *Am J Health-Syst Pharm.* 2008; 65:1272–83.

Principles of a Sound Drug Formulary System

These principles have been endorsed by the following organizations:

- Academy of Managed Care Pharmacy
- Alliance of Community Health Plans
- American Medical Association
- American Society of Health-System Pharmacists
- Department of Veterans Affairs, Pharmacy Benefits Management Strategic Healthcare Group
- National Business Coalition on Health
- U.S. Pharmacopeia

Preamble

A coalition of national organizations representing health care professionals, government, and business leaders formed a working group (see Appendix III) to develop a set of principles specifying the essential components that contribute to a sound drug formulary system. The Coalition was formed in September 1999 in response to the widespread use of drug formularies in both inpatient and outpatient settings and the lack of understanding about formularies among the public. Also, proposed federal legislation that would provide a prescription drug benefit for Medicare beneficiaries has brought increased attention to the appropriate role and management of drug formulary systems within drug benefit programs.

The formulary system, when properly designed and implemented, can promote rational, clinically appropriate, safe, and cost-effective drug therapy. The Coalition has enumerated these principles, however, because it recognizes that patient care may be compromised if a formulary system is not optimally developed, organized, and administered. This document contains "Guiding Principles" that the Coalition believes must be present for a drug formulary system to appropriately serve the patients it covers. The absence of one or more of these "Guiding Principles" should be cause for careful scrutiny of a formulary system. A glossary (see Appendix I) and bibliography (see Appendix II) are included with the "Guiding Principles" to clarify terminology and to provide additional resources, respectively.

The Coalition believes that the presence of consensus-based Formulary System Principles can assist decision-makers who must balance the health care quality and cost equation. Further, the Guiding Principles will be a valuable educational tool for national, state, and local public policy makers, health care system administrators, purchasers and third-party payers, practitioners, and consumers and patient advocates. These parties all have an interest in designing formulary systems that ensure patients have access to rational, clinically appropriate, safe, and cost-effective therapy and which supports an affordable and sustainable drug benefit program.

Definitions

Drug Formulary System. An ongoing process whereby a health care organization, through its physicians, pharmacists, and other health care professionals, establishes policies on the use of drug products and therapies, and identifies drug products and therapies that are the most medically appropriate and cost-effective to best serve the health interests of a given patient population.

Drug Formulary. A continually updated list of medications and related information, representing the clinical judgement of physicians, pharmacists, and other experts in the diagnosis and/or treatment of disease and promotion of health.

Guiding Principles

Formulary system decisions are based on scientific and economic considerations that achieve appropriate, safe, and cost-effective drug therapy.

- Clinical decisions are based on the strength of scientific evidence and standards of practice that include, but are not limited, to the following:
    - Assessing peer-reviewed medical literature, including randomized clinical trials (especially drug comparison studies), pharmacoeconomic studies, and outcomes research data.
    - Employing published practice guidelines, developed by an acceptable evidence-based process.
    - Comparing the efficacy as well as the type and frequency of side effects and potential drug interactions among alternative drug products.
    - Assessing the likely impact of a drug product on patient compliance when compared to alternative products.
    - Basing formulary system decisions on a thorough evaluation of the benefits, risks, and potential outcomes for patients; risks encompass adverse drug events (adverse drug reactions and medication errors, such as those caused by confusing product names or labels).
- Economic considerations include, but are not limited, to the following:
    - Basing formulary system decisions on cost factors only after the safety, efficacy, and therapeutic need have been established.
    - Evaluating drug products and therapies in terms of their impact on total health care costs.
    - Permitting financial incentives only when they promote cost management as part of the delivery of quality medical care. Financial incentives or pressures on practitioners that may interfere with the delivery of medically necessary care are unacceptable.

The formulary system encompasses drug selection, drug utilization review, and other tools to foster best practices in prescribing, dispensing, administration, and monitoring of outcomes.

- The formulary system:
    - Provides drug product selection and formulary maintenance (see above).
    - Provides drug use evaluation (also called drug utilization review) to enhance quality of care for patients by assuring appropriate drug therapy.

- Provides for the periodic evaluation and analysis of treatment protocols and procedures to ensure that they are up-to-date and are consistent with optimum therapeutics.
- Provides for the monitoring, reporting, and analysis of adverse results of drug therapy (e.g., adverse drug reactions, medication errors) to continuously improve the quality of care.

The Pharmacy and Therapeutics (P&T) Committee, or equivalent body, comprised of actively practicing physicians, pharmacists, and other health care professionals, is the mechanism for administering the formulary system, which includes developing and maintaining the formulary and establishing and implementing policies on the use of drug products.

- The Pharmacy and Therapeutics Committee:
  - Objectively appraises, evaluates, and selects drugs for the formulary.
  - Meets as frequently as is necessary to review and update the appropriateness of the formulary system in light of new drugs and new indications, uses, or warnings affecting existing drugs.
  - Establishes policies and procedures to educate and inform health care providers about drug products, usage, and committee decisions.
  - Oversees quality improvement programs that employ drug use evaluation.
  - Implements generic substitution and therapeutic interchange programs that authorize exchange of therapeutic alternatives based upon written guidelines or protocols within a formulary system. (Note: Therapeutic substitution, the dispensing of therapeutic alternates without the prescriber's approval, is illegal and should not be allowed—see Glossary.)
  - Develops protocols and procedures for the use of and access to non-formulary drug products.

Physicians, pharmacists, and other health care professionals provide oversight of the formulary system.

- Health care organization policies should ensure appropriate oversight of the P&T Committee and its decisions by the medical staff or equivalent body.

The formulary system must have its own policies, or adhere to other organizational policies, that address conflicts of interest and disclosure by P&T committee members.

- Formulary system policies should:
  - Require P&T committee members to reveal, by signing a conflict of interest statement, economic and other relationships with pharmaceutical entities that could influence Committee decisions.
  - Exclude product sponsor representatives from P&T committee membership and from attending P&T committee meetings.
  - Require P&T committee members to adhere to the formulary system's policy on disclosure and participation in discussion as it relates to conflict of interest.

The formulary system should include educational programs for payers, practitioners, and patients concerning their roles and responsibilities.

- The formulary system should:
  - Inform physicians, pharmacists, other health care professionals, patients, and payers about the factors that affect formulary system decisions, including cost containment measures; the procedures for obtaining non-formulary drugs; and the importance of formulary compliance to improving quality of care and restraining health care costs.
  - Proactively inform practitioners about changes to the formulary or to other pharmaceutical management procedures.
  - Provide patient education programs that explain how formulary decisions are made and the roles and responsibilities of the patient, especially the importance of patient compliance with drug therapy to assure the success of that therapy.
  - Disclose the existence of formularies and have copies of the formulary readily available and accessible.
  - Provide rationale for specific formulary decisions when requested.

The formulary system should include a well-defined process for the physician or other prescriber to use a non-formulary drug when medically indicated.

- The formulary system should:
  - Enable individual patient needs to be met with non-formulary drug products when demonstrated to be clinically justified by the physician or other prescriber.
  - Institute an efficient process for the timely procurement of non-formulary drug products and impose minimal administrative burdens.
  - Provide access to a formal appeal process if a request for a non-formulary drug is denied.
  - Include policies that state that practitioners should not be penalized for prescribing non-formulary drug products that are medically necessary.

Appendix I—Glossary

Drug Formulary System: An ongoing process whereby a health care organization, through its physicians, pharmacists, and other health care professionals, establishes policies on the use of drug products and therapies, and identifies drug products and therapies that are the most medically appropriate and cost effective to best serve the health interests of a given patient population.

Drug Formulary: A continually updated list of medications and related information, representing the clinical judgement of physicians, pharmacists, and other experts in the diagnosis and/or treatment of disease and promotion of health.

Pharmacy & Therapeutics (P&T) Committee: An advisory committee that is responsible for developing, managing, updating, and administering the drug formulary system.

Generic Substitution: The substitution of drug products that contain the same active ingredient(s) and are chemically identical in strength, concentration, dosage form, and route of administration to the drug product prescribed.

Therapeutic Alternates: Drug products with different chemical structures but which are of the same pharmacological and/or therapeutic class, and usually can be expected to have similar therapeutic effects and adverse reaction profiles when administered to patients in therapeutically equivalent doses.

Therapeutic Interchange: Authorized exchange of therapeutic alternates in accordance with previously established and approved written guidelines or protocols within a formulary system.

Therapeutic Substitution: The act of dispensing a therapeutic alternate for the drug product prescribed without prior authorization of the prescriber. This is an illegal act because only the prescriber may authorize an exchange of therapeutic alternates.

Drug Utilization Review (Drug Use Review, DUR, and Drug Use Evaluation): Process used to assess the appropriateness of drug therapy by engaging in the evaluation of data on drug use in a given health care environment against predetermined criteria and standards.

Appendix II—Bibliography

1. Academy of Managed Care Pharmacy, Concepts in Managed Care Pharmacy Series—Formulary Management (Alexandria, VA: 1998).
2. American Medical Association. Board of Trustees Report PPP, Principles of Drug Utilization Review. In, American Medical Association House of Delegates Proceedings, 140th Annual Meeting. Chicago: American Medical Association; June 1991; 225–7.
3. American Medical Association. Board of Trustees Report 45, Drug Formularies and Therapeutic Interchange. In, American Medical Association House of Delegates Proceedings, 47th Interim Meeting. New Orleans: American Medical Association; December 1993; 155–8.
4. American Medical Association. Council on Ethical and Judicial Affairs Report 2, Managed Care Cost Containment Involving Prescription Drugs. In, American Medical Association House of Delegates Proceedings, 144th Annual Meeting. Chicago: American Medical Association; June 1995; 207–13.
5. American Medical Association. Board of Trustees Report 9, Pharmaceutical Benefits Management Companies. In, American Medical Association House of Delegates Proceedings, 51st Interim Meeting. Dallas: American Medical Association; December 1997; 33–44.
6. American Society of Consultant Pharmacists. Guidelines for the Development of Formulary Systems in Nursing Facilities; July 1996.
7. American Society of Hospital Pharmacists. ASHP Statement on the Formulary System. *Am J Hosp Pharm.* 1983; 40:1384–5.
8. American Society of Hospital Pharmacists. ASHP Guidelines on Formulary System Management. *Am J Hosp Pharm.* 1992; 49:648–52.
9. American Society of Hospital Pharmacists. ASHP Statement on the Pharmacy and Therapeutics Committee. *Am J Hosp Pharm.* 1992; 49:2008–9.
10. American Society of Health-System Pharmacists. ASHP Guidelines on Medication-Use Evaluation. *Am J Health-syst Pharm.* 1996; 53:1953–5.
11. American Society of Hospital Pharmacists. ASHP Technical Assistance Bulletin on Drug Formularies. *Am J Hosp Pharm.* 1991; 48:791–3.
12. American Society of Hospital Pharmacists. ASHP Technical Assistance Bulletin on the Evaluation of Drugs for Formularies. *Am J Hosp Pharm.* 1988; 45:386–7.
13. Covington TR and Thornton JL. The formulary system: A cornerstone of drug benefit management, in A Pharmacist's Guide to Principles and Practices of Managed Care Pharmacy. Ito S and Blackburn S, eds. Foundation for Managed Care Pharmacy, Alexandria VA. 1995:35–49.
14. Dillon MJ. Drug Formulary Management, in Managed Care Pharmacy Practice. Navarro RP ed. Aspen Publishers, Inc., Gaithersburg, MD. 1999:145–65.
15. Hejna CS and Shepherd MD. Pharmacy and therapeutics committee and formulary development, in A Pharmacist's Guide to Principles and Practices of Managed Care Pharmacy. Ito S and Blackburn S, eds. Foundation for Managed Care Pharmacy, Alexandria VA. 1995:27–34.
16. National Committee for Quality Assurance. UM 10 procedures for pharmaceutical management. 2000 Standards for Accreditation of MCOs. 1999:58–60.
17. National Committee for Quality Assurance. UM 10 procedures for pharmaceutical management. 2000 Surveyor Guidelines for the Accreditation of MCOs. 1999:173–82.
18. PCMA Response to American Medical Association Report, I-97, "Pharmaceutical Benefits Management Companies." September 1998.
19. Rucker TD and Schiff GD. Drug formularies: myths-information. *Medical Care.* 1990; 28:928–42. Reprinted in *Hospital Pharmacy,* 1991; 26:507–14.

Appendix III—Coalition Working Group

Academy of Managed Care Pharmacy

Judith A. Cahill, C.E.B.S., Executive Director

Richard Fry, Senior Director, Pharmacy Affairs

American Medical Association

Joseph W. Cranston, Ph.D., Director-Science, Research and Technology

American Society of Health-System Pharmacists

William A. Zellmer, M.P.H., Deputy Executive Vice President

Department of Veterans Affairs

John E. Ogden, Director, Pharmacy Services

Michael A. Valentino, Associate Chief Consultant for Pharmacy Benefits Management

National Business Coalition on Health

Catherine Kunkle, Vice President

U.S. Pharmacopeia

Jacqueline L. Eng, Senior Vice President, Program Development

Keith W. Johnson, Vice President and Director, New and Off-Label Uses

Thomas R. Fulda, Program Director, Drug Utilization Review Programs

Nancy B. Mabie, Assistant Director, Pharmacy Affairs

Observer

AARP

David Gross, Senior Policy Advisor, Public Policy Institute

Public Comment Requested

To ensure that knowledgeable and interested parties beyond the Coalition Working Group had an opportunity to contribute to the Principles development process, a preliminary set of principles was distributed for public comment to 50-plus organizations in February 2000. Comments received were thoroughly reviewed and considered by the Coalition Working Group.

These principles were endorsed by the ASHP Board of Directors on June 4, 2000.

The endorsement of this document was reviewed in 2011 by the Council on Pharmacy Practice and by the Board of Directors and was found to still be appropriate.

Government, Law, and Regulation

Government, Law, and Regulation

Pharmacist Participation in Health Policy Development (1501)
Source: Council on Public Policy
To advocate that pharmacists participate with policymakers and stakeholders in the development of health-related policies at the national, state, and community levels; further,

To develop tools and resources to assist pharmacists in fully participating in health policy development at all levels.

Pharmacist Recognition as a Healthcare Provider (1502)
Source: Council on Public Policy
To advocate for changes in federal (e.g., Social Security Act), state, and third-party payment programs to define pharmacists as healthcare providers; further,

To affirm that pharmacists, as medication-use experts, provide safe, accessible, high-quality care that is cost effective, resulting in improved patient outcomes; further,

To recognize that pharmacists, as healthcare providers, improve access to patient care and bridge existing gaps in healthcare; further,

To collaborate with key stakeholders to describe the covered direct patient-care services provided by pharmacists; further,

To advocate for sustainable compensation and standardized billing processes used by payers for pharmacist services by all available payment programs.

This policy supersedes ASHP policy 1307.

Pharmaceutical Product and Supply Chain Integrity (1503)
Source: Council on Public Policy
To encourage the Food and Drug Administration (FDA) and relevant state authorities to take the steps necessary to ensure that (1) all drug products entering the supply chain are thoroughly inspected and tested to establish that they have not been adulterated or misbranded and (2) patients will not receive improperly labeled and packaged, deteriorated, outdated, counterfeit, adulterated, or unapproved drug products; further,

To encourage FDA and relevant state authorities to develop and implement regulations to (1) restrict or prohibit licensed drug distributors (drug wholesalers, repackagers, and manufacturers) from purchasing legend drugs from unlicensed entities and (2) ensure accurate documentation at any point in the distribution chain of the original source of drug products and chain of custody from the manufacturer to the pharmacy; further,

To advocate for the establishment of meaningful penalties for companies that violate current good manufacturing practices (cGMPs) intended to ensure the quality, identity, strength, and purity of their marketed drug product(s) and raw materials; further,

To advocate for improved transparency so that drug product labeling include a readily available means to retrieve the name and location of the facility that manufactured the specific lot of the product; further,

To advocate that this readily retrievable manufacturing information be available prospectively to aid purchasers in determining the quality of a drug product and its raw materials; further,

To urge Congress and state legislatures to provide adequate funding, or authority to impose user fees, to accomplish these objectives.

This policy supersedes ASHP policy 0907.

Premarketing Comparative Clinical Studies (1506)
Source: Council on Public Policy
To advocate that the Food and Drug Administration have the authority to impose a requirement for comparative clinical trials.

This policy supersedes ASHP policy 0514.

Funding, Expertise, and Oversight of State Boards of Pharmacy (1507)
Source: Council on Public Policy
To advocate appropriate oversight of pharmacy practice and the pharmaceutical supply chain through coordination and cooperation of state boards of pharmacy and other state and federal agencies whose mission it is to protect the public health; further,

To advocate adequate representation on state boards of pharmacy and related agencies by pharmacists who are knowledgeable about all areas of pharmacy practice (e.g., hospitals, health systems, clinics, and nontraditional settings) to ensure appropriate oversight; further,

To advocate for dedicated funds for the exclusive use by state boards of pharmacy and related agencies including funding for the training of state board of pharmacy inspectors and the implementation of adequate inspection schedules to ensure the effective oversight and regulation of pharmacy practice, the integrity of the pharmaceutical supply chain, and protection of the public; further,

To advocate that inspections be performed only by pharmacists competent about the applicable area of practice.

This policy supersedes ASHP policy 0518.

Support for FDA Expanded Access (Compassionate Use) Program (1508)
Source: Council on Public Policy
To advocate that the Food and Drug Administration (FDA) Expanded Access (Compassionate Use) Program be the sole mechanism for patient access to drugs for which an investigational new drug application (IND) has been filed, in order to preserve the integrity of the drug approval process and assure patient safety; further,

To advocate for broader patient access to such drugs under the FDA Expanded Access Program; further,

To advocate that IND applicants expedite review and release of drugs for patients who qualify for the program; further,

To advocate that the drug therapy be recommended by a physician and reviewed and monitored by a pharmacist to assure safe patient care; further,

To advocate for the patient's right to be informed of the potential benefits and risks via an informed consent process, and the responsibility of an institutional review board to review and approve the informed consent and the drug therapy protocol.

Approval of Biosimilar Medications (1509)
Source: Council on Public Policy
To encourage the development of safe and effective biosimilar medications in order to make such medications more affordable and accessible; further,

To encourage research on the safety, effectiveness, and interchangeability of biosimilar medications; further,

To support legislation and regulation to allow Food and Drug Administration (FDA) approval of biosimilar medications; further,

To support legislation and regulation to allow FDA approval of biosimilar medications that are also determined by the FDA to be interchangeable and therefore may be substituted for the reference product without the intervention of the prescriber; further,

To oppose the implementation of any state laws regarding biosimilar interchangeability prior to finalization of FDA guidance; further,

To oppose any state legislation that would require a pharmacist to notify a prescriber when a biosimilar deemed to be interchangeable by the FDA is dispensed; further,

To require postmarketing surveillance for all biosimilar medications to ensure their continued safety, effectiveness, purity, quality, identity, and strength; further,

To advocate for adequate reimbursement for biosimilar medications that are deemed interchangeable; further,

To promote and develop ASHP-directed education of pharmacists about biosimilar medications and their appropriate use within hospitals and health systems; further,

To advocate and encourage pharmacist evaluation and the application of the formulary system before biosimilar medications are used in hospitals and health systems.

This policy supersedes ASHP policy 1409.

Development of Abuse-Resistant Narcotics (1512)
Source: Council on Therapeutics
To advocate that the Food and Drug Administration investigate the efficacy of abuse-resistant formulations in preventing prescription drug abuse.

Quality Patient Medication Information (1513)
Source: Council on Therapeutics
To support efforts by the Food and Drug Administration (FDA) and other stakeholders to improve the quality, consistency, and simplicity of written patient medication information (PMI); further,

To encourage the FDA to work in collaboration with patient advocates and other stakeholders to create evidence-based models and standards, including establishment of a universal literacy level, for PMI; further,

To advocate that research be conducted to validate these models in actual-use studies in pertinent patient populations; further,

To advocate that FDA explore alternative models of PMI content development and maintenance that will ensure the highest level of accuracy, consistency, and currency; further,

To advocate that the FDA engage a single third-party author to provide editorial control of a highly structured, publicly accessible central repository of PMI in a format that is suitable for ready export; further,

To advocate for laws and regulations that would require all dispensers of medications to comply with FDA-established standards for unalterable content, format, and distribution of PMI.

This policy supersedes ASHP policy 1012.

Automatic Stop Orders (1405)
Source: Council on Pharmacy Practice
To advocate that the Centers for Medicare & Medicaid Services (1) remove the requirement in the Hospital Conditions of Participation that all medication orders automatically stop after an arbitrarily assigned period to include other options to protect patients from indefinite, open-ended medication orders, and (2) revise the remainder of the medication management regulations and interpretive guidelines to be consistent with this practice; further,

To affirm that the requirement for automatic stop orders for all medications is a potential source of medication errors and patient harm; further,

To encourage pharmacists to participate in interprofessional efforts to establish standardized methods to assure appropriate duration of therapy.

This policy supersedes ASHP policy 0904.

Federal and State Regulation of Compounding (1406)
Source: Council on Public Policy
To advocate that the applicable compendial standards of the United States Pharmacopeia be included in state and federal laws and regulations that govern compounding by any health professional; further,

To advocate for mandatory state registration of compounding facilities (e.g., pharmacies, physician offices, clinics, ambulatory surgery centers) that provide products for specific patient prescriptions or in anticipation of specific patient prescriptions or medication orders; further,

To advocate for mandatory Food and Drug Administration registration and current good manufacturing practices requirements for outsourcing facilities that compound and sell products without patient-specific prescriptions across state lines; further,

To advocate for improved patient safety and care through education of regulatory inspectors, increased frequency and improved effectiveness of compliance inspections, and enhancing interagency communications; further,

To advocate that state and federal agencies develop standardized definitions and nomenclature relating to sterile and nonsterile compounding, including but not limited to definitions of compounding, manufacturing, repackaging, and relabeling.

This policy supersedes ASHP policy 1308.

340B Drug Pricing Program Sustainability (1407)
Source: Council on Public Policy
To affirm the intent of the federal drug pricing program (the "340B program") to stretch scarce federal resources as far as possible, reaching more eligible patients and providing more comprehensive services; further,

To advocate legislation or regulation that would optimize access to the 340B program in accordance with the intent of the program; further,

To advocate for clarification and simplification of the 340B program and any future federal discount drug pricing programs with respect to program definitions, eligibility, and compliance measures to ensure the integrity of the program; further,

To encourage pharmacy leaders to provide appropriate stewardship of the 340B program by documenting the expanded services and access created by the program; further,

To educate pharmacy leaders and health-system administrators about the internal partnerships and accountabilities and the patient-care benefits of program participation; further,

To educate health-system administrators, risk managers, and pharmacists about the resources (e.g., information technology) required to support 340B program compliance and documentation; further,

To encourage communication and education concerning expanded services and access provided by 340B participants to patients in fulfillment of its mission.

This policy supersedes ASHP policy 0506.

State Prescription Drug Monitoring Programs (1408)
Source: Council on Public Policy
To advocate for mandatory, uniform prescription drug monitoring programs that collect real-time, relevant, and standard information from all dispensing outpatient entities about controlled substances and monitored prescriptions; further,

To advocate that the design of these programs should balance the need for appropriate therapeutic management with safeguards against fraud, misuse, abuse, and diversion; further,

To advocate that such programs be structured as part of electronic health records and exchanges to allow prescribers, pharmacists, and other practitioners to proactively monitor data for appropriate assessment; further,

To advocate for full interstate integration to allow for access by prescribers, pharmacists, and other qualified designees across state lines; further,

To advocate for federal and state funding to establish and administer these programs; further,

To promote research, education, and implementation of best practices in prescription drug monitoring programs.

This policy supersedes ASHP policy 1122.

Access to Oral Contraceptives Through an Intermediate Category of Drug Products (1410)
Source: Council on Therapeutics
To advocate that oral contraceptives be provided only under conditions that ensure safe use, including the availability of counseling to ensure appropriate self-screening and product selection; further,

To support expanded access to these products through a proposed intermediate category of drug products, as described by ASHP policy, that would be available from all pharmacists and licensed health care professionals (including pharmacists) who are authorized to prescribe medications; further,

To advocate that the proposed reclassification of these products be accompanied by coverage changes by third-party payers to ensure that patient access is not compromised and that pharmacists are reimbursed for the clinical services provided.

Expedited Pathways for FDA Drug Approval (1411)
Source: Council on Therapeutics
To support the use of expedited pathways for Food and Drug Administration (FDA) approval of new drugs that expand access to innovative therapies while protecting patient safety; further,

To advocate for the development of unique labeling requirements that would be used on an interim basis to identify products approved by these pathways in order to increase awareness of data limitations and guide clinician use of these drugs until additional evidence becomes available; further,

To advocate that the FDA be diligent in enforcing postmarketing commitments for drug products approved via expedited pathways, including utilizing its existing authority to enforce penalties when these requirements are not met; further,

To encourage research to evaluate the impact of expedited pathways on drug product development and patient care, including drug development timelines and costs, overall health care costs, patient access to care, and the effectiveness and safety of these therapies.

FDA Oversight of Laboratory-Developed Tests (1412)
Source: Council on Therapeutics
To advocate that the Food and Drug Administration be granted increased authority to regulate laboratory-developed tests as medical devices, including tests used for pharmacogenetic testing; further,

To support development of a risk-based framework for regulatory oversight of laboratory-developed tests that promotes innovation while providing a mechanism to ensure that test results are reliable, reproducible, and clinically relevant; further,

To encourage expanded availability of commercially marketed pharmacogenetic tests that would be available for use by laboratory and health care professionals to guide drug therapy.

Regulation of Telepharmacy Services (1310)
Source: Council on Public Policy
To advocate that state governments adopt laws and regulations that standardize telepharmacy practices across state lines and facilitate the use of United States-based telepharmacy services; further,

To advocate that boards of pharmacy and state agencies that regulate pharmacy practice include the following in regulations for telepharmacy services: (1) education and training of participating pharmacists; (2) education, training, certification by the Pharmacy Technician Certification Board, and licensure of participating pharmacy technicians; (3) communication and information systems requirements; (4) remote order entry, prospective order review, verification of the completed medication order before dispensing, and dispensing; (5) direct patient-care services, including medication therapy management services and patient counseling and education; (6) licensure (including reciprocity) of participating pharmacies and pharmacists; (7) service arrangements that cross state borders; (8) service arrangements within the same corporate entity or between different corporate entities; (9) service arrangements for workload relief in the point-of-care pharmacy during peak periods; (10) pharmacist access to all applicable patient information; and (11) development and monitoring of patient safety, quality, and outcomes measures; further,

To identify additional legal and professional issues in the provision of telepharmacy services to and from sites located outside the United States.

This policy supersedes ASHP policy 0716.

Regulation of Centralized Order Fulfillment (1311)
Source: Council on Public Policy
To advocate changes in federal and state laws, regulations, and policies to permit centralized medication order fulfillment within health care facilities under common ownership.

DEA Scheduling of Hydrocodone Combination Products (1314)
Source: Council on Therapeutics
To advocate that the Drug Enforcement Administration (DEA) reschedule hydrocodone combination products to Schedule II based on their potential for abuse and patient harm and to achieve consistency with scheduling of other drugs with similar abuse potential.

DEA Scheduling of Controlled Substances (1315)
Source: Council on Therapeutics
To advocate that the Drug Enforcement Administration (DEA) establish clear, measurable criteria and a transparent process for scheduling determinations; further,

To urge the DEA to use such a process to re-evaluate existing schedules for all substances regulated under the Controlled Substances Act to ensure consistency and incorporate current evidence concerning the abuse potential of these therapies; further,

To monitor the effect of DEA scheduling of products under the Controlled Substances Act and other abuse-prevention efforts (e.g., prescription drug monitoring programs) to assess the impact on patient access to these medications and on the practice burden of health care providers.

Pharmacy Technicians (1216)
Source: Council on Public Policy
To advocate that pharmacy move toward the following model with respect to the evolving pharmacy technician workforce as the optimal approach to protecting public health and safety: (1) development and adoption of uniform state laws and regulations regarding pharmacy technicians, (2) mandatory completion of an ASHP-accredited program of education and training as a prerequisite to pharmacy technician certification, (3) mandatory certification by the Pharmacy Technician Certification Board as a prerequisite to licensure by the state board of pharmacy, and (4) licensure of pharmacy technicians by state boards of pharmacy granting the technician permission to engage in the full scope of responsibilities authorized by the state; further,

To advocate, with respect to certification, as an interim measure until the optimal model is fully implemented, that individuals be required either (1) to have completed an ASHP-accredited program of education and training or (2) to have at least one year of full-time equivalent experience as pharmacy technicians before they are eligible to become certified; further,

To advocate that all pharmacy functions be performed under the general supervision of a licensed pharmacist and that licensed pharmacists and technicians be held accountable for the quality of pharmacy services provided.

(*Note:* Licensure is the process by which an agency of government grants permission to an individual to engage in a given occupation upon finding that the applicant has attained the minimal degree of competency necessary to ensure that the public health, safety, and welfare will be reasonably well protected. Certification is the process by which a nongovernmental agency or association grants recognition to an individual who has met certain predetermined qualifications specified by that agency or association.)

This policy supersedes ASHP policy 0815.

Stable Funding for HRSA Office of Pharmacy Affairs (1219)
Source: Council on Public Policy
To advocate for a sustainable level of funding, including appropriations, sufficient to support the public health mission of the Health Resources and Services Administration (HRSA) Office of Pharmacy Affairs; further,

To support initiatives of the Office of Pharmacy Affairs, including the 340B Drug Pricing Program and innovative pharmacy service models in HRSA-funded programs; further,

To encourage research on the potential impact of any proposed fees or alternative funding sources for the Office of Pharmacy Affairs.

This policy supersedes ASHP policy 0911.

Globalization of Clinical Trials (1223)
Source: Council on Therapeutics
To encourage the Food and Drug Administration (FDA) to use its existing authority to increase monitoring and inspection of foreign clinical trials to ensure the integrity and quality of those studies; further,

To advocate that the FDA expand its oversight of clinical trials conducted abroad by continuing to pursue innovative strategies, such as increased collaboration with foreign regulatory agencies and changes in domestic regulatory processes that support timely submission of foreign clinical trial information; further,

To encourage the FDA to establish a standardized electronic format and reporting standards that would be required for submission of data from foreign clinical trials; further,

To support the ethical treatment of patients in foreign clinical trials in accordance with international standards designed to protect human subjects; further,

To encourage public and private research to study the impact of the globalization of clinical trials on patient care.

Medical Marijuana (1101)
Source: Council on Therapeutics
To oppose state legislation that authorizes the use of medical marijuana until there is sufficient evidence to support its safety and effectiveness and a standardized product that would be subject to the same regulations as a prescription drug product; further,

To encourage research to define the therapeutically active components, effectiveness, safety, and clinical use of medical marijuana; further,

To advocate for the development of processes that would ensure standardized formulations, potency, and quality of medical marijuana products to facilitate research; further,

To encourage the Drug Enforcement Administration to eliminate barriers to medical marijuana research, including review of medical marijuana's status as a Schedule I controlled substance, and its reclassification, if necessary to facilitate research; further,

To oppose the procurement, storage, preparation, or distribution of medical marijuana by licensed pharmacies or health care facilities for purposes other than research; further,

To oppose the smoking of marijuana in settings where smoking is prohibited; further,

To encourage continuing education that prepares pharmacists to respond to patient and clinician questions about the therapeutic and legal issues surrounding medical marijuana use.

(*Note:* As defined by the Congressional Research Service, the term *medical marijuana* refers to uses of botanical marijuana that qualify for a medical use exception under the laws of certain states and under the federal Investigational New Drug Compassionate Access Program. Botanical marijuana includes the whole or parts of the natural marijuana plant and therapeutic products derived therefrom, as opposed to drugs produced synthetically in the laboratory that replicate molecules found in the marijuana plant.)

Agricultural Use of Hormone and Prohormone Therapies (1102)
Source: Council on Therapeutics
To advocate that the Food and Drug Administration and United States Department of Agriculture re-evaluate the agricultural use of hormone and prohormone therapies for purposes of animal growth promotion based on evidence demonstrating potential adverse effects on human health; further,

To encourage additional research to better define the public health impact of using hormone therapies for agricultural purposes.

Direct-to-Consumer Clinical Genetic Tests (1103)
Source: Council on Therapeutics
To support research to validate and standardize genetic markers used in direct-to-consumer clinical genetic tests and guide the application of test results to clinical practice; further,

To encourage the Food and Drug Administration to use existing authority to regulate these tests as medical devices and to work with the National Institutes of Health to expedite establishment of a process to evaluate and approve direct-to-consumer clinical genetic tests; further,

To advocate that direct-to-consumer clinical genetic tests to support disease diagnosis or management of drug therapy be provided to consumers only through the services of appropriate health care professionals that order tests from laboratories that are certified under the Clinical Laboratories Improvement Amendments of 1988 (CLIA); further,

To oppose advertising of direct-to-consumer clinical genetic tests unless such testing includes the established patient-health care provider relationship as a mechanism to provide information and interpretation of test results; further,

To oppose advertising of direct-to-consumer clinical genetic tests unless the following requirements are met: (1) that the relationship between the genetic marker and the disease or condition being assessed is clearly presented, (2) that the benefits and risks of testing are discussed, and (3) that such advertising is provided in an understandable format, at a level of health literacy that allows the intended audience to make informed decisions, and includes a description of the established patient-health care provider relationship as a critical source for information about the test and interpretation of test results; further,

To encourage pharmacists to educate consumers and clinicians on the appropriate use of direct-to-consumer clinical genetic tests for disease diagnosis and drug therapy management.

Drug Product Shortages (1118)
Source: Council on Public Policy
To advocate that the Food and Drug Administration (FDA) have the authority to require manufacturers to report drug product shortages and the reason(s) for the shortage, and to make that information available to the public; further,

To strongly encourage the FDA to consider, in its definition of "medically necessary" drug products, the patient safety risks created by use of alternate drug products during a shortage; further,

To support government-sponsored incentives for manufacturers to maintain an adequate supply of medically necessary drug products; further,

To advocate laws and regulations that would (1) require pharmaceutical manufacturers to notify the appropriate government body at least 12 months in advance of voluntarily discontinuing a drug product, (2) provide effective sanctions for manufacturers that do not comply with this mandate, and (3) require prompt public disclosure of a notification to voluntarily discontinue a drug product; further,

To encourage the appropriate government body to seek the cooperation of manufacturers in maintaining the supply of a drug product after being informed of a voluntary decision to discontinue that product.

This policy supersedes ASHP policy 0319.

Poison Control Center Funding (1121)
Source: Council on Public Policy
To advocate that poison control centers be considered an essential emergency service; further,

To advocate for new and stable funding mechanisms for poison control centers to continue to provide these essential and valuable services; further,

To support the integration and coordination of poison control center services where appropriate.

Health Insurance Coverage for U.S. Residents (1001)
Source: Council on Public Policy
To advocate health insurance for all residents of the United States, including coverage of medications and related pharmacist patient-care services; further,

To advocate that the full range of available methods be used to (1) ensure the provision of appropriate, safe, and cost-effective health care services; (2) optimize treatment outcomes; and (3) minimize overall costs without compromising quality; further,

To advocate that health insurers seek to optimize continuity of care in their design of benefit plans.

This policy was reviewed in 2014 by the Council on Public Policy and by the Board of Directors and was found to still be appropriate.

Risk Evaluation and Mitigation Strategies (1002)

Source: Council on Public Policy

To advocate for research on the impact of the Food and Drug Administration's Risk Evaluation and Mitigation Strategies (REMS) on patient safety, cost effectiveness, and pharmacy workflow; further,

To advocate pharmacist involvement in the development and implementation of REMS; further,

To urge computer software vendors to assist pharmacists in the identification of and compliance with REMS; further,

To advocate that any REMS that include constraint on traditional drug distribution systems be consistent with ASHP policy on restricted drug distribution.

This policy was reviewed in 2014 by the Council on Public Policy and by the Board of Directors and was found to still be appropriate.

FDA Authority on Recalls (1003)

Source: Council on Public Policy

To strongly encourage the Food and Drug Administration (FDA) to develop a standard recall notification process and format to be used by all manufacturers to facilitate the timely removal of recalled drugs; further,

To advocate that such notification should (1) come from a single source, (2) clearly identify the recalled product, (3) explain why the product is being recalled, (4) provide a way to report having the recalled product, (5) give instructions on what to do with the recalled product, and (6) be provided concurrently to all entities in the supply chain; further,

To advocate that the FDA be given the authority to order mandatory recalls of medications; further,

To urge the FDA to require drug manufacturers and the computer software industry to provide bar codes and data fields for lot number, expiration date, and other necessary and appropriate information on all medication packaging, including unit dose, unit-of-use, and injectable drug packaging, in order to facilitate compliance with recalls or withdrawals and to prevent the administration of recalled products to patients; further,

To urge the FDA to encourage postmarketing reporting of adverse events and product quality issues to enhance the recall system.

This policy was reviewed in 2014 by the Council on Public Policy and by the Board of Directors and was found to still be appropriate.

Postmarketing Comparative Clinical and Pharmacoeconomic Studies (1004)

Source: Council on Public Policy

To advocate expansion of comparative clinical and pharmacoeconomic studies on the effectiveness, safety, and cost comparison of marketed medications in order to improve therapeutic outcomes and promote cost-effective medication use; further,

To advocate that such studies compare a particular medication with (as appropriate) other medications, medical devices, or procedures used to treat specific diseases; further,

To advocate adequate funding for the Agency for Healthcare Research and Quality and other federal agencies to carry out such studies; further,

To encourage impartial private-sector entities to also conduct such studies.

This policy was reviewed in 2014 by the Council on Public Policy and by the Board of Directors and was found to still be appropriate.

Regulation of Home Medical Equipment Medication Products and Devices (1007)

Source: Council on Public Policy

To advocate for consistent regulatory oversight of all home medical equipment, with the goals of continuity of care, patient safety, and appropriate pharmacist involvement whenever equipment is used for medication administration; further,

To monitor the impact of the Centers for Medicare & Medicaid Services quality standards on the accreditation of suppliers of medication-related durable medical equipment and supplies.

This policy was reviewed in 2014 by the Council on Public Policy and by the Board of Directors and was found to still be appropriate.

Preservation of Antimicrobials for Medical Treatment (1009)

Source: Council on Therapeutics

To advocate that the Food and Drug Administration (FDA) eliminate future approval of antimicrobials for nontherapeutic uses in agricultural animals that represent a safety risk by contributing to antibiotic resistance; further,

To encourage efforts to phase out and eliminate the nontherapeutic uses of antimicrobials previously approved by the FDA; further,

To support the therapeutic use of antimicrobials in animals only under the supervision of a veterinarian; further,

To encourage the FDA, Centers for Disease Control and Prevention, and other stakeholders to monitor and limit, when effective alternatives are available, the therapeutic use of antimicrobials that are essential to the treatment of critically ill human patients; further,

To advocate for the inclusion of pharmacists in antimicrobial surveillance and related public health efforts based on pharmacists' knowledge of antimicrobial drug products and antimicrobial resistance.

This policy was reviewed in 2014 by the Council on Therapeutics and by the Board of Directors was found to still be appropriate.

Use of Surrogate Endpoints for FDA Approval of Drug Uses (1011)

Source: Council on Therapeutics

To support the continued use of qualified surrogate endpoints by the Food and Drug Administration (FDA) as a mechanism to evaluate the effectiveness and safety of new drugs and new indications for existing therapies, when measurement of definitive clinical outcomes is not feasible; further,

To support efforts by the FDA and other stakeholders to qualify surrogate endpoints; further,

To advocate that the FDA consistently enforce existing requirements that drug product manufacturers complete postmarketing studies for drugs approved based on qualified surrogate endpoints in order to confirm that the expected improvement in outcomes occurs, and to require that these studies be completed in a timely manner.

This policy was reviewed in 2014 by the Council on Therapeutics and by the Board of Directors and was found to still be appropriate.

Regulation of Interstate Pharmacy Practice (0909)
Source: Council on Public Policy
To advocate that state governments, including legislatures and boards of pharmacy, adopt laws and regulations that harmonize the practice of pharmacy across state lines in order to provide a consistent, transparent, safe, and accountable framework for pharmacy practice.

This policy was reviewed in 2013 by the Council on Public Policy and by the Board of Directors and was found to still be appropriate.

Regulation of Dietary Supplements (0811)
Source: Council on Public Policy
To advocate that Congress grant authority to the Food and Drug Administration (FDA) to (1) require that dietary supplements undergo FDA approval for evidence of safety and efficacy; (2) mandate FDA-approved dietary supplement labeling that includes disclosure of excipients; (3) mandate FDA-approved patient information materials that describe safe use in a clear, standardized format, including the potential for interaction with medications and cautions for special populations; and (4) establish and maintain an adverse-event reporting system specifically for dietary supplements, and require dietary supplement manufacturers to report suspected adverse reactions to the FDA; further,

To oppose direct-to-consumer advertising of dietary supplements unless the following criteria are met: (1) federal laws are amended to include all the requirements described above to ensure that dietary supplements are safe and effective; (2) evidence-based information regarding safety and efficacy is provided in a format that allows for informed decision-making by the consumer; (3) the advertising includes a recommendation to consult with a health care professional before initiating use; (4) any known warnings or precautions regarding dietary supplement–medication interactions or dietary supplement-disease interactions are provided as part of the advertising; and (5) the advertising is educational in nature and includes pharmacists as a source of information.

(*Note: Dietary supplement* as used in this policy is defined by the Dietary Supplement Health and Education Act of 1994, as amended; 21 U.S.C. 321.)

This policy was reviewed in 2012 by the Council on Public Policy and by the Board of Directors and was found to still be appropriate.

Medicare Prescription Drug Benefit (0813)
Source: Council on Public Policy
To strongly advocate a fully funded prescription drug program for eligible Medicare beneficiaries that maintains continuity of care and ensures the best use of medications; further,

To advocate that essential requirements in the program include (1) appropriate product reimbursement; (2) affordability for patients, including elimination of coverage gaps; (3) payment for indirect costs and practice expenses related to the provision of pharmacist services, based on a study of those costs; (4) appropriate coverage and payment for patient care services provided by pharmacists; (5) open access to the pharmacy provider of the patient's choice; (6) formularies with sufficient flexibility to allow access to medically necessary drugs; and (7) well-publicized, unbiased resources to assist beneficiaries in enrolling in the most appropriate plan for their medication needs.

(*Note: Fully funded* means the federal government will make adequate funds available to fully cover the Medicare program's share of prescription drug program costs; *eligible means* the federal government may establish criteria by which Medicare beneficiaries qualify for the prescription drug program.)

This policy was reviewed in 2012 by the Council on Public Policy and by the Board of Directors and was found to still be appropriate.

Federal Review of Anticompetitive Practices by Drug Product Manufacturers (0814)
Source: Council on Public Policy
To strongly oppose anticompetitive practices by manufacturers that adversely affect drug product availability and price; further,

To encourage appropriate federal review of these practices.

This policy was reviewed in 2012 by the Council on Public Policy and by the Board of Directors and was found to still be appropriate.

FDA Authority to Prohibit Reuse of Brand Names (0719)
Source: Council on Public Policy
To advocate for Food and Drug Administration authority to prohibit reuse of brand names of prescription and nonprescription drugs when any active component of the product is changed or after any other changes are made in the product that may affect its safe use.

This policy was reviewed in 2011 by the Council on Public Policy and by the Board of Directors and was found to still be appropriate.

Minimum Effective Doses (0602)
Source: Commission on Therapeutics
To advocate that the Food and Drug Administration require manufacturers to identify minimum effective doses for medications and make this information available to health care providers.

This policy was reviewed in 2010 by the Council on Therapeutics and by the Board of Directors and was found to still be appropriate.

Streamlined Licensure Reciprocity (0612)
Source: Council on Legal and Public Affairs
To advocate that state boards of pharmacy grant temporary licensure to pharmacists who are relocating from another state in which they hold a license in good standing, permitting them to engage in practice while their application for licensure reciprocity is being processed; further,

To advocate that the National Association of Boards of Pharmacy collaborate with state boards of pharmacy to streamline the licensure reciprocity process.

This policy was reviewed in 2010 by the Council on Public Policy and by the Board of Directors and was found to still be appropriate.

Postmarketing Safety Studies (0515)

Source: Council on Legal and Public Affairs

To advocate that Congress grant the Food and Drug Administration (FDA) authority to require the manufacturer of an approved drug product or licensed biologic product to conduct postmarketing studies on the safety of the product when the agency deems it to be in the public interest; further,

To advocate that Congress grant FDA broader authority to require additional labeling or withdrawal of the product on the basis of a review of postmarketing studies; further,

To advocate that Congress provide adequate funding to FDA to fulfill this expanded mission related to postmarketing surveillance.

This policy was reviewed in 2014 by the Council on Public Policy and by the Board of Directors and was found to still be appropriate.

Mandatory Registry of Clinical Trials (0516)

Source: Council on Legal and Public Affairs

To advocate disclosure of the most complete information on the safety and efficacy of drug products; further,

To advocate that the Department of Health and Human Services establish a mandatory registry for all Phase II, III, and IV clinical trials that are conducted on drugs intended for use in the United States; further,

To advocate that each clinical trial have a unique identifier; further,

To advocate that all data from registered clinical trials be posted electronically with unrestricted access, and that such posting occur (1) after Food and Drug Administration approval of the related new product but before marketing begins and (2) as soon as possible for trials completed after initial marketing.

This policy was reviewed in 2014 by the Council on Public Policy and by the Board of Directors and was found to still be appropriate.

Importation of Pharmaceuticals (0413)

Source: Council on Legal and Public Affairs

To advocate for the continuation and application of laws and regulations enforced by the Food and Drug Administration and state boards of pharmacy with respect to the importation of pharmaceuticals in order to (1) maintain the integrity of the pharmaceutical supply chain and avoid the introduction of counterfeit products into the United States; (2) provide for continued patient access to pharmacist review of all medications and preserve the patient-pharmacist-prescriber relationship; and (3) provide adequate patient counseling and education, particularly to patients taking multiple high-risk medications; further,

To urge the FDA and state boards of pharmacy to vigorously enforce federal and state laws in relation to importation of pharmaceuticals by individuals, distributors (including wholesalers), and pharmacies that bypass a safe and secure regulatory framework.

This policy was reviewed in 2008 by the Council on Public Policy and by the Board of Directors and was found to still be appropriate.

Intermediate Category of Drugs (0220)

Source: Council on Legal and Public Affairs

To support, with appropriate changes in federal statutes and regulations, the establishment of an intermediate category of drug products that do not require a prescription but are available only from pharmacists and licensed health care professionals who are authorized to prescribe medications; further,

To base such support on the following facts:

1. Some drug products that are potential candidates for switching from prescription-only to nonprescription status raise concerns about patient safety as nonprescription products; these products could be better controlled, monitored, and evaluated by making them available only from pharmacists and licensed health care professionals who are authorized to prescribe medications; and
2. Pharmacists have the education, training, and expertise to help patients make appropriate therapeutic decisions associated with the use of such drug products; further,

To support that the regulatory system for this intermediate category of drug products contain the following features:

1. Drug products appropriate for this intermediate category would be identified through the advice of pharmacists, physicians, and other licensed health professionals who are authorized to prescribe medications, on the basis of the medical conditions to be treated and potential adverse effects (as indicated in FDA-approved labeling);
2. Pharmacists would be able to provide drugs in this intermediate category directly to patients without a prescription, on the basis of appropriate assessment and professional consultation;
3. Licensed health professionals who currently have prescribing authority would continue to have the ability to prescribe medications in this intermediate category; and
4. Data from postmarketing surveillance, epidemiologic studies, and adverse-drug-reaction reporting would be collected to help determine a drug product's eventual movement to nonprescription status, return to prescription-only status, or continuation in the intermediate category.

This policy was reviewed in 2011 by the Council on Public Policy and by the Board of Directors and was found to still be appropriate.

Greater Access to Less Expensive Generic Drugs (0222)

Source: Council on Legal and Public Affairs

To support legislation and regulations that promote greater patient access to less expensive generic drug products.

This policy was reviewed in 2011 by the Council on Public Policy and by the Board of Directors and was found to still be appropriate.

FDA's Public Health Mission (0012)

Source: Council on Legal and Public Affairs

To support the Food and Drug Administration's public health mission of ensuring the safety and effectiveness of drugs, biologics, and medical devices through risk assessment, appropriate product approval, labeling approval, manufacturing oversight, and consultation with health professionals, while deferring to state regulation and professional self-regulation on matters related to the use of drugs, biologics, and medical devices; further,

To support the allocation of sufficient federal resources to allow FDA to meet its defined public health mission; further,

To support the appointment of practicing pharmacists to FDA advisory committees as one mechanism of ensuring that decisions made by the agency incorporate the unique knowledge of the profession of pharmacy for the further benefit of the patient; further,

To support an ongoing dialogue between FDA and ASHP for the purpose of exploring ways to advocate the best use of FDA-regulated products by consumers and health care professionals.

This policy was reviewed in 2014 by the Council on Public Policy and by the Board of Directors and was found to still be appropriate.

Generic Pharmaceutical Testing (9010)

Source: House of Delegates Resolution

To support and foster legislative and regulatory initiatives designed to improve and restore public and professional confidence in the drug approval and regulatory process in which all relevant data are subject to public scrutiny.

This policy was reviewed in 2010 by the Council on Public Policy and by the Board of Directors and was found to still be appropriate.

ASHP Statement on Criteria for an Intermediate Category of Drug Products

Position

The American Society of Health-System Pharmacists (ASHP) supports the establishment of an intermediate category of drug products that would not require a prescription but would be available from a pharmacist after appropriate patient assessment and professional consultation.[1] These drug products would continue to be available by prescription from licensed health care professionals who are authorized to prescribe medications. Drug products appropriate for this intermediate category should have proven public health benefits and be identified by processes that include the input and advice of experts, such as pharmacists, physicians, and other licensed health care professionals. Identification of drug products for inclusion in the intermediate category should be based on the medical condition to be treated and potential adverse effects of the drug. Concerns that patients may not be able to fulfill a substantial self-care role associated with these drug products will be alleviated by taking into consideration the benefits of pharmacist oversight of these drug regimens. Data from postmarketing surveillance, epidemiologic studies, and adverse-drug-reaction reports should be collected and analyzed to evaluate the ongoing safety and effectiveness of drug products placed in this category. This information would be used to determine whether the product would remain in the intermediate category, return to prescription-only status, or move to nonprescription status.

Background

Rationale for Establishing an Intermediate Drug Category. Reclassification of prescription drug products to nonprescription status (e.g., antifungal products used for the treatment of vaginitis, nonsedating antihistamines) has been associated with improvements in patient autonomy, health care knowledge, and self-care behavior.[2-4] However, proposals to reclassify some prescription drug products to nonprescription status have been denied because of concerns about safety and whether patients would be capable of determining if they were suitable candidates for treatment. In 2008, for example, the Food and Drug Administration (FDA) ruled a third time against making lovastatin, a hydroxymethylglutaryl-coenzyme A reductase inhibitor (or statin), available without a prescription,[5] although the predicted public health benefit of increasing the availability of statins was estimated to range between 23,000 and 33,000 coronary heart disease events prevented per 1 million treated for 10 years.[6] ASHP supports inclusion of statins in an intermediate category of drug products that provides the benefit of pharmacist oversight.[7] Other drug products that should be considered for the intermediate category include injectable epinephrine to treat anaphylaxis; inhaled corticosteroids, leukotriene modifiers, and inhaled ß-agonists used in the treatment of asthma; select therapies for osteoporosis and hypertension; and vaccines.

ASHP and other pharmacy organizations have long proposed the creation of an intermediate category of drug products that would bridge the large gap between prescription and nonprescription status.[1,8,9] An intermediate drug category could improve patient access to medications that offer substantial public health benefit but present challenges for safety or effectiveness if used under existing models for nonprescription drug dispensing. Two concerns regarding the use of existing models are that (1) a product's labeling information may be beyond most consumers' capacity to understand (or may be subject to misinterpretation) and (2) monitoring procedures are not readily accessible to patients. Pharmacists' expertise, licensure, and education, which includes instruction on physiology, pharmacology, disease management, and physical assessment, make pharmacists well qualified to help patients make appropriate therapeutic decisions about the use of these drug products.

The terms "behind-the-counter (BTC) drugs" and "pharmacist-only drugs" have also been used to describe the proposed intermediate category of drug products. While an FDA-established BTC category does not currently exist, the term BTC has been used to refer to drug products such as pseudoephedrine and levonorgestrel (marketed as Plan B) that are available for purchase only at the pharmacy counter.[10,11] Implementation of that restriction has largely been a policing action (e.g., to restrict the amount of drug a patient can obtain or to confirm the patient's age). In some instances, these functions are completed by pharmacy support staff under the supervision of a pharmacist. ASHP recommends the use of the terminology intermediate category of drugs to describe drug products appropriate for this category that would be used by patients in conjunction with clinical assessment and consultation provided by pharmacists. Distribution of the aforementioned nonprescription products via an intermediate category model of dispensing could improve appropriate use of those products.

The purpose of this statement is to describe the criteria that should be used to identify drug products for inclusion in an intermediate category. While the practice implications of an intermediate drug category are briefly described, that discussion is beyond the scope of this statement. Pharmacoeconomic analyses should be conducted to assess the overall impact and costs of an intermediate category of drug products on patients, health systems, and health insurers, and new models of reimbursement for pharmacists' services should be developed. It should be noted that a few studies have demonstrated that overall costs to the health system decrease when the cost of these medications is not transferred solely to the patient.[12,13] Alternative reimbursement models, such as insurance coverage for these products, would be necessary to optimize the use of the intermediate category of drug products.

Criteria for an Intermediate Category of Drug Products

Appropriate identification of drug products for inclusion in the intermediate category should address the concerns associated with a substantial self-care role for patients by providing the benefits of pharmacist oversight of these drug therapy regimens (e.g., assessing for appropriate indications, contraindications, precautions, adverse drug events, drug interactions, and therapeutic response). ASHP believes drug products proposed for inclusion in the intermediate category should

- Meet many of the criteria currently used to reclassify prescription drugs to nonprescription status (e.g., the drug product has a well-established benefit:risk ratio and a wide safety margin),
- Have been marketed as a prescription product for a length of time and been used by a number of patients deemed sufficient by FDA to detect serious adverse effects. Likewise, a product could be marketed as a nonprescription product but would benefit from pharmacist oversight because safety and effectiveness concerns have arisen with its nonprescription use,
- Have evidence of effectiveness and safety for the dosage and regimen recommended for the formulation intended for intermediate classification, and
- Be used to prevent or treat a disease, symptom, or condition that can be readily detected by the patient or identified by the pharmacist or other health care provider.

Further, if the drug is used for a condition that requires laboratory or other medical monitoring, the pharmacy should be able to offer testing or have access to the results of that monitoring. Signs and symptoms of deterioration in health and the need for medical attention should be identifiable by the pharmacist or patient, as should signs demonstrating the effectiveness of the drug therapy. If the drug has the potential to rarely cause serious toxicity that can result in death or serious harm, there should be reliable early warning signs that can be readily detected and interpreted by the pharmacist or patient.

Antiinfective agents (systemic or other formulations) for which the emergence of resistance is a concern would not be appropriate for the intermediate category.

In applying these criteria, an independent decision should be made about each individual chemical entity, dosage form, and drug product because differences among various members of a drug class and dosage forms prevent using therapeutic class as a basis for classifying groups of related drug products.

Because drug information is continually evolving, drug products in the intermediate category may be reclassified as prescription or nonprescription medications as new effectiveness and safety information becomes available. Similarly, products could be permanently classified in the intermediate category if ongoing evidence documents the necessity of pharmacist intervention to ensure safe and effective use. The postmarketing surveillance of these medications through the collaboration of FDA and product manufacturers should be supported, in part, by information reported by pharmacists and patients to an established surveillance system, such as MedWatch, or similar reporting mechanisms.

Practice Implications

Implementation of the intermediate drug category would require that an ongoing relationship be established and maintained between the pharmacist and the patient and that documentation of the care provided be available to the patient's other health care providers, upon approval of the patient to provide such information. The exact nature and duration of the patient–pharmacist relationship would depend on the condition being treated and the drug therapy selected. A practice model that includes collaboration among the patient, the pharmacist, and the patient's physician (or other primary care provider) would enhance the use of these drug products and result in improved patient outcomes.

Increased pharmacist time for patient assessment, counseling, and documentation of services provided with these drug products would require reimbursement for these cognitive services. In addition, other conditions and procedures would be necessary to ensure the safety and effectiveness of these therapies, including the following:

- If the drug is to be used in conjunction with other therapies, such as diet and exercise, information about those adjunct therapies should be readily available to the patient from the pharmacist or through recommendation of the pharmacist or other health care provider.
- Patient care services provided by the pharmacist should be documented in the pharmacy record and available for sharing with other health care providers.
- Pharmacists and patients should provide information on actual or suspected adverse effects or drug interactions to programs such as MedWatch for the purposes of drug safety surveillance.
- Pharmacies should adopt standardized processes for the use of medications in the intermediate category that would guide patient triage, treatment, and referral to a physician when necessary. The expertise offered by clinical practice guidelines and professional associations should serve as the basis for these protocols, with appropriate modifications based on the unique characteristics of the patient population at the practice site.
- Pharmacies should adhere to quality measures that would be developed to assess the care provided (similar to those offered by the Pharmacy Quality Alliance) and engage in ongoing quality-improvement activities to assess and improve the quality of services provided.

A detailed discussion of these topics is addressed by other ASHP position and guidance documents, including the ASHP Statement on the Pharmacist's Role in Primary Care[14]; the ASHP Guidelines on Pharmacist-Conducted Patient Education and Counseling[15]; the ASHP Guidelines on the Pharmacist's Role in the Development, Implementation, and Assessment of Critical Pathways[16]; the ASHP Guidelines on Documenting Pharmaceutical Care in Patient Medical Records[17]; and the ASHP Guidelines on Adverse Drug Reaction Monitoring and Reporting.[18]

Conclusion

An intermediate category of drug products would increase patient access to and benefit from drug products that would otherwise be available only by prescription. The use of appropriate criteria for classifying drug products in an intermediate drug category—in conjunction with pharmacist oversight of patient assessment, counseling, and monitoring—would improve public health without compromising patient safety.

References

1. American Society of Health-System Pharmacists. ASHP policy position 0220: intermediate category of drugs. www.ashp.org/DocLibrary/BestPractices/DistributionPositions.aspx (accessed 2008 Dec 3).
2. Brass EP. Implications of a switch from prescription to over-the-counter status for allergy drugs. *Curr Allergy Asthma Rep.* 2004; 4:245–50.
3. Lipsky MS, Waters T. The "prescription-to-OTC switch" movement. Its effects on antifungal vaginitis preparations. *Arch Fam Med.* 1999; 8:297–300.
4. Gurwitz JH, McLaughlin TJ, Fish LS. The effect of an Rx-to-OTC switch on medication prescribing patterns and utilization of physician services: the case of vaginal antifungal products. *Health Serv Res.* 1995; 30:672–85.
5. Merck and Company. Merck receives not approvable letter from FDA for OTC Mevacor (lovastatin) 20 mg. www.merck.com/newsroom/press_releases/product/2008_0125a.html (accessed 2008 Feb 14).
6. Brass EP, Allen SE, Melin JM. Potential impact on cardiovascular public health of over-the-counter statin availability. *Am J Cardiol.* 2006; 97:851–6.
7. American Society of Health-System Pharmacists. ASHP statement on the over-the-counter availability of statins. *Am J Health-Syst Pharm.* 2005; 62:2420–2.
8. National Association of Boards of Pharmacy. Groups advocate various Plan B classifications as FDA delays decision on OTC application. www.nabp.net/ftpfiles/newsletters/NABP/nabp022006.pdf (accessed 2008 Dec 3).
9. American Pharmacists Association. Report of the APhA 2005 House of Delegates. Transition class of drugs. *J Am Pharm Assoc.* 2005; 45:557.
10. Food and Drug Administration. Legal requirements for the sale and purchase of drug products containing pseudoephedrine, ephedrine, and phenylpropanolamine. www.fda.gov/cder/news/methamphetamine.htm (accessed 2008 Dec 3).
11. Food and Drug Administration. Plan B: questions and answers. www.fda.gov/cder/drug/infopage/planB/planBQandA20060824.htm (accessed 2008 Dec 3).
12. West DS, Johnson JT, Hone SH. A 30-month evaluation of the effects on the cost and utilization of proton pump inhibitors from adding OTC to drug benefit coverage in a state employee health plan. *J Manag Care Pharm.* 2006; 12:25–32.
13. Trygstad TK, Hansen RA, Wegner SE. Evaluation of product switching after a state Medicaid program began covering loratadine OTC one year after market availability. *J Manag Care Pharm.* 2006; 12:108–20.
14. American Society of Health-System Pharmacists. ASHP statement on the pharmacist's role in primary care. *Am J Health-Syst Pharm.* 1999; 56:1665–7.
15. American Society of Health-System Pharmacists. ASHP guidelines on pharmacist-conducted patient education and counseling. *Am J Health-Syst Pharm.* 1997; 54:431–4.
16. American Society of Health-System Pharmacists. ASHP guidelines on the pharmacist's role in the development, implementation, and assessment of critical pathways. *Am J Health-Syst Pharm.* 2004; 61:939–45.
17. American Society of Health-System Pharmacists. ASHP guidelines on documenting pharmaceutical care in patient medical records. *Am J Health-Syst Pharm.* 2003; 60:705–7.
18. American Society of Health-System Pharmacists. ASHP guidelines on adverse drug reaction monitoring and reporting. *Am J Health-Syst Pharm.* 1995; 52:417–9.

This statement was reviewed in 2012 by the Council on Therapeutics and by the Board of Directors and was found to still be appropriate.

Developed through the ASHP Council on Therapeutics and approved by the ASHP Board of Directors on March 7, 2008, and by the ASHP House of Delegates on June 10, 2008.

The assistance of Susan R. Dombrowski, B.S.Pharm., M.S., in drafting this statement is gratefully acknowledged.

The bibliographic citation for this document is as follows: American Society of Health-System Pharmacists. ASHP statement on criteria for an intermediate category of drug products. *Am J Health-Syst Pharm.* 2009; 66:502–9.

ASHP Statement on the Over-the-Counter Availability of Statins

The American Society of Health-System Pharmacists (ASHP) believes that existing models for over-the-counter (OTC) dispensing do not provide the safeguards required to ensure the safe and effective use of 3-hydroxy-3-methylglutaryl coenzyme A (HMG-CoA) reductase inhibitors ("statins") as part of a multimodal approach to preventing coronary heart disease (CHD). ASHP supports the goal of more widespread use of CHD-preventive therapies, including statin therapy, and encourages consideration of alternative nonprescription dispensing models for statins that would advance CHD prevention.

Since 1985, ASHP has called for changes in federal statutes and regulations to establish an intermediate category of drug products that do not require a prescription but are available only from pharmacists and other licensed health care professionals authorized to prescribe medications.[1] ASHP believes consideration of OTC reclassification for statins presents an opportunity to explore the creation of such a category of drugs. ASHP has suggested that the regulatory system for such an intermediate category of drug products would allow pharmacists to provide drugs in this intermediate category directly to patients without a prescription, on the basis of appropriate assessment and professional consultation, while ensuring that licensed health professionals who currently have prescribing authority would continue to have the ability to prescribe such medications. ASHP believes that under such a regulatory system, data from postmarketing surveillance, epidemiologic studies, and adverse-drug-reaction reporting should be collected to help determine a drug product's eventual movement to nonprescription status, return to prescription-only status, or continuation in the intermediate category.[1] ASHP believes statins are an ideal candidate for dispensing under such a model.

Background

ASHP supports the use of statins to lower cholesterol and reduce morbidity and mortality in patients at risk for cardiovascular events.[2] Elevated cholesterol, specifically low-density lipoprotein cholesterol (LDL-C), is an important risk factor for the development of CHD. ASHP has recommended that evaluation and management of lipid disorders be guided by the recommendations of the National Cholesterol Education Program (NCEP), the latest of which are contained in the Adult Treatment Panel III (ATP III) guidelines.[3,4] Statins are considered the drug of choice for most patients with dyslipidemia who require lipid-lowering therapy. They are effective in lowering elevated LDL-C, and studies have demonstrated that statins reduce the risk of cardiovascular events in patients without known CHD (primary prevention). In addition, statins have been shown to reduce cardiovascular events and mortality in patients with CHD (secondary prevention). Cardiovascular disease is the leading cause of death for both men and women in the United States, and CHD is responsible for nearly 75% of all deaths from cardiovascular disease.[5] Individuals with multiple cardiovascular risk factors and a low LDL-C derive an absolute benefit in reducing risk of CHD for a given milligram-per-deciliter lowering of LDL-C. However, for individuals with lower LDL-C levels and fewer risk factors for CHD, the benefits of lowering LDL-C level are less dramatic.[6]

Nonprescription Dispensing Models

The efficacy of statins in reducing LDL-C has prompted calls for more widespread use, including suggestions for a reclassification of statins as an OTC medication. Although ASHP does not support reclassification to OTC status as that status is currently constructed, alternative nonprescription models for dispensing these valuable medications should be explored.

To approve a reclassification to OTC status, FDA reviewers must find that (1) a drug is safe and effective in its proposed use(s), (2) the benefits of the drug outweigh its risks, and (3) consumers will be able to use the drug's labeling (e.g., its package insert) to safely use the medication in an OTC setting.[7] ASHP believes a decision to approve nonprescription dispensing models for statins should be based on evidence that, under the proposed model, the target population would receive a clinical benefit in primary prevention of CHD from the medication and patients can safely use the medication to achieve that clinical benefit. To achieve the goal of safe and effective use, any nonprescription dispensing model for statins should

- Identify candidates for appropriate therapeutic interventions, including statin therapy, on the basis of cholesterol levels, other risk factors for CHD events, and the patient's medical and family histories;
- Allow patients and health care providers to monitor response to treatment, including adverse reactions; and
- Maximize the effectiveness of treatment by encouraging adherence to therapy and appropriate interactions with health care professionals.

ASHP believes that before a patient begins statin therapy, a cardiac risk assessment should be performed by a competent health care professional in order to

- Determine the patient's LDL-C value, which can be used as a baseline value if the patient is a candidate for treatment;
- Assess the individual for other cardiovascular risk factors such as smoking, diabetes, hypertension, diet, weight, amount of exercise, and family history of cardiovascular disease; and
- Develop the optimal treatment plan based on ATP III guidelines and the assessment above.

Individuals with two or more risk factors or a family history of cardiovascular disease who have never been evaluated should have a complete medical assessment and appropriate interventions by a physician. If statins are an appropriate therapeutic option, they should be part of a multimodal approach to reducing the overall CHD risk, which would include managing and treating modifiable risk factors such as hypertension, smoking, obesity, diet, and lack of exercise. Diet and exercise therapy should be a fundamental part of all cholesterol-lowering regimens.

Current OTC Model

Statins are not suitable for OTC status as that class is currently regulated. One study has examined the use of statins in a simulated OTC setting. The CUSTOM study[8] was an open-label study designed to observe consumers' initial and continued use of a statin to lower LDL-C. Although the results may indicate that some individuals in the study sample were able to use an OTC statin as directed, the study was, by the investigators' own admission, not designed to evaluate clinical outcomes and therefore not able to demonstrate efficacy. The study certainly did not prove that the existing OTC model would provide the level of counseling required to reduce cardiovascular risk factors other than LDL-C levels.

However encouraging these results might seem, caution should be exercised in extrapolating such information to a larger population, especially information regarding safety. Adverse drug effects should always be assessed, especially if the medications that cause them are easily available to the public. A system that relies on the voluntary reporting of adverse drug effects by patients may be inadequate to protect the public or detect subtle signals. It is imperative that the decision to reclassify a statin to a nonprescription status include a wide margin of safety. After statin therapy starts, ongoing evaluations should assess the patient's response, reassess risk factors, and monitor for and report adverse events. The existing model for OTC medications would place the entire burden for performing this evaluation and reassessment on the patient. Most patients are likely to be unfamiliar with the system used to report an adverse event, if the adverse event is even recognized. Although adverse events from prescription statins are rare, particularly at lower doses, they can occur months or years after therapy is initiated. Since OTC status would encourage wider use of statins, these drugs might be used by individuals with multiple disease states or those taking potentially interacting medications (e.g., cyclosporine, diltiazem, verapamil, macrolide antibiotics, azole antifungals, or protease inhibitors). Because statins are a chronic therapy, new risks may be introduced as the patient's health varies, requiring vigilance on the part of the patient as well as health care providers.

ASHP believes, for these reasons, that reclassification of statins to OTC status as currently constructed is not advisable but that alternative nonprescription models for dispensing these valuable medications should be explored.

Alternative Nonprescription Models

ASHP believes that there are alternatives to prescription-only status that would allow expanded use of statins to reduce cardiovascular events in primary prevention patients. Since 1985, ASHP has had a policy urging changes in federal statutes and regulations to create an intermediate category of drug products that do not require a prescription but are available only from pharmacists and other licensed health care professionals.[1] ASHP believes the regulatory system for this intermediate category of drug products should have the following features:

1. Drug products appropriate for this intermediate category would be identified through the advice of pharmacists, physicians, and other licensed health professionals who are authorized to prescribe medications, on the basis of the medical conditions to be treated and potential adverse effects (as indicated in FDA-approved labeling);
2. Pharmacists would be able to provide drugs in this intermediate category directly to patients without a prescription, on the basis of appropriate assessment and professional consultation;
3. Licensed health professionals who currently have prescribing authority would continue to have the ability to prescribe medications in this intermediate category; and
4. Data from postmarketing surveillance, epidemiologic studies, and adverse-drug-reaction reporting would be collected to help determine a drug product's eventual movement to nonprescription status, return to prescription-only status, or continuation in the intermediate category.[1]

Drugs that would raise safety and efficacy concerns if used as nonprescription products could be better controlled, monitored, and evaluated if they were available only from pharmacists and licensed health care professionals who are authorized to prescribe medications. Pharmacists have the education, training, and expertise to help patients make appropriate therapeutic decisions about the use of such products. ASHP believes statins are a good candidate for dispensing under such a model, much as is done in Great Britain, where simvastatin was approved for "counterprescribing" in May 2004.[9]

Conclusion

ASHP supports nonprescription dispensing models for statins that ensure their safe and effective use as part of a multimodal approach to CHD prevention. Given the complexities of therapies to prevent CHD, ASHP encourages consideration of alternatives to the current model of OTC distribution for statins.

References

1. Policy Position 0220: Intermediate Category of Drugs. In: Best practices for hospital and health-system pharmacy 2004–2005. Positions and practice documents of ASHP. Bethesda, MD: American Society of Health-System Pharmacists; 2004:89.
2. ASHP Therapeutic Position Statement on the Use of Statins in the Prevention of Atherosclerotic Disease in Adults. *Am J Health Syst Pharm.* 2003; 60:593–8.
3. Expert Panel on Detection, Evaluation, and Treatment of High Blood Cholesterol in Adults. Executive summary of the Third Report of the National Cholesterol Education Program (NCEP) Expert Panel on Detection, Evaluation, and Treatment of High Blood Cholesterol in Adults (Adult Treatment Panel III). *JAMA.* 2001; 285:2486–97.

4. National Cholesterol Education Program (NCEP) Expert Panel on Detection, Evaluation, and Treatment of High Blood Cholesterol in Adults (Adult Treatment Panel III). Third Report of the National Cholesterol Education Program (NCEP) Expert Panel on Detection, Evaluation, and Treatment of High Blood Cholesterol in Adults (Adult Treatment Panel III) final report. *Circulation.* 2002; 106:3143–421.
5. American Heart Association. 2002 heart and stroke statistical update. Available at: www.americanheart.org/presenter (accessed 2002 May 14).
6. Grundy SM, Cleeman JI, Merz CN et al. Implications of recent clinical trials for the National Cholesterol Education Program Adult Treatment Panel III Guidelines. *Circulation.* 2004; 110:227–39.
7. Food and Drug Administration, Center for Drug Evaluation and Research, Endocrinologic and Metabolic Drugs Advisory Committee, Questions to the Committee (joint meeting of January 13–14, 2005, to consider new drug application 21-213). Available at: http://www.fda.gov/ohrms/dockets/ac/05/questions/2005-4086S2_02_FDA-Questions.htm (accessed January 26, 2005).
8. Melin JM, Struble WE, Tipping RW et al. A consumer use study of over-the-counter lovastatin (CUSTOM). *Am J Cardiol.* 2004; 94:1243–8.
9. Royal Pharmaceutical Society of Great Britain. Concise version of practice guidance on the sale of OTC simvastatin. July 2004. Available at: http://www.rpsgb.org. uk/pdfs/otcsimvastatincardguid.pdf (accessed January 4, 2005).

This statement was reviewed in 2009 by the Council on Therapeutics and by the Board of Directors and was found to still be appropriate.

Approved by the ASHP Board of Directors on January 6, 2005, and by the ASHP House of Delegates on June 14, 2005. Developed through the ASHP Commission on Therapeutics.

The bibliographic citation for this document is as follows: American Society of Health-System Pharmacists. ASHP statement on the over-the-counter availability of statins. *Am J Health-Syst Pharm.* 2005; 62:2420–2.

ASHP Statement on Principles for Including Medications and Pharmaceutical Care in Health Care Systems

Introduction

The United States government, individual state governments, and private health care systems are moving toward reforming the way that they provide health care to their citizens or beneficiaries. As they do so, policy makers must improve their medication-use systems to address problems of access, quality, and cost of medicines and pharmaceutical care services. This document offers principles for achieving maximum value from the services of the nation's pharmacists.

Although pharmaceuticals and pharmaceutical care are among the most cost-effective methods of health care available, there is evidence that the public is not currently realizing the full potential benefit from these resources. Illnesses related to improper medication use are costing the health care systems in the United States billions of dollars per year in patient morbidity and mortality. Pharmacists are prepared and eager to help other health providers and patients prevent and resolve medication-related problems, and health care systems should facilitate and take advantage of pharmacists' expertise.

These principles are offered to guide health policy makers in their deliberations concerning the inclusion of medications and pharmacists' services in health care systems.

Principles

Principle I. Health care systems must make medications available to patients and provide for pharmaceutical care, which encompasses pharmacists' health care services and health promotional activities that ensure that medications are used safely, effectively, and efficiently for optimal patient outcomes.

Principle II. Careful distinction must be made between policies that affect pharmacist reimbursement and policies that affect pharmacist compensation. Health care systems must reimburse pharmacists for the medications they provide patients (including the costs of drug products, the costs associated with dispensing, and related administrative costs). Health care systems also must compensate pharmacists for the services and care that they provide to patients, which result in improved medication use and which may not necessarily be associated with dispensing.

Principle III. Patients differ in their needs for pharmaceutical care services. The method of compensating pharmacists for their services must recognize the value of the different levels and types of services that pharmacists provide to patients based on pharmacists' professional assessments of patients' needs.

Principle IV. Pharmacists must be enabled and encouraged to use their professional expertise in making medication-related judgments in collaboration with patients and health care colleagues. Health care systems must not erect barriers to pharmacists' exercising professional judgments; nor should health care systems prescribe specific services or therapies for defined types of patients.

Principle V. Pharmacists should have access to relevant patient information to support their professional judgments and activities. Pharmacists should be encouraged and permitted to make additions to medical records for the purpose of adding their findings, conclusions, and recommendations. Pharmacists will respect the confidential nature of all patient information.

Principle VI. Health care systems must be designed to enable, foster, and facilitate communication and collaboration among pharmacists and other care providers to ensure proper coordination of patients' medication therapies.

Principle VII. Quality assessment and assurance programs related to individual patient care should be implemented at local levels through collaborative efforts of health care practitioners rather than through centralized bureaucracies. Quality assessment and assurance procedures for medication use (such as pharmacy and therapeutics committees, formulary systems, drug-use evaluation programs, and patient outcomes analyses) are most effective when the professionals who care for covered patients are involved in the design and implementation of the procedures. Moreover, such programs must recognize local variations in epidemiology, demography, and practice standards. Information related to quality assessment and assurance activities must be held in confidence by all parties.

Principle VIII. Demonstration projects and evaluation studies in the delivery of pharmaceutical care must be enabled, fostered, and implemented. New services, quality assessment and assurance techniques, and innovative medication delivery systems are needed to improve the access to and quality of medication therapy and pharmaceutical care while containing costs.

Principle IX. Health care policies that are intended to influence practices of those associated with pharmacy, such as the pharmaceutical industry or prescribers, should address those audiences directly rather than through policies that affect reimbursement, compensation, or other activities of pharmacists.

This statement was reviewed in 2012 by the Council on Public Policy and by the Board of Directors and was found to still be appropriate.

Approved by the ASHP Board of Directors, November 18, 1992, and by the ASHP House of Delegates, June 7, 1993. Developed by a committee of the Joint Commission of Pharmacy Practitioners and subsequently reviewed and approved by the ASHP Council on Legal and Public Affairs.

The bibliographic citation for this document is as follows: American Society of Hospital Pharmacists. ASHP statement on principles for including medications and pharmaceutical care in health care systems. *Am J Hosp Pharm.* 1993; 50:756–7.

Medication Misadventures

Medication Misadventures

Statutory Protection for Medication-Error Reporting (1505)
Source: Council on Public Policy
To collaborate with other healthcare providers, professions, and stakeholders to advocate and support state and federal legislative and regulatory initiatives that provide liability protection for the reporting of actual and potential medication errors by individuals and healthcare providers; further,

To provide education on the role that patient safety organizations play in liability protection.

This policy supersedes ASHP policy 0011.

Support for Second Victims (1524)
Source: Council on Pharmacy Practice
To acknowledge that the patient is the primary victim in any medical error, unanticipated adverse patient event, or patient-related injury; further,

To acknowledge that involvement by healthcare personnel in such events may cause them to become second victims; further,

To recognize that a just culture and a healthy culture of safety embrace a support system for second victims; further,

To encourage healthcare organizations to establish programs to support second victims; further,

To educate healthcare professionals (including those in training), health organization administrators, and regulatory agencies about the second-victim effect and available resources.

Standardization of Small-Bore Connectors to Avoid Wrong-Route Errors (1530)
Source: Council on Pharmacy Practice
To support the use of medication administration device connectors and fittings that are designed to prevent misconnections and wrong-route errors; further,

To encourage healthcare organizations to prepare for safe transition to use of medication delivery device connectors and adapters that meet International Organization for Standardization standards; further,

To identify and promote the implementation of best practices for preventing wrong-route errors.

This policy supersedes ASHP policy 1018.

Just Culture (1115)
Source: Council on Pharmacy Practice
To recognize that the principles of *just culture* promote an environment in health care organizations in which safety is valued, reporting of safety risks is encouraged, and a fair process is used to hold staff and leaders accountable; further,

To encourage hospitals and health systems to include *just culture* as a component in organizational safety culture surveys and quality improvement initiatives.

Just Culture and Reporting Medication Errors (1021)
Source: Council on Pharmacy Practice
To encourage pharmacists to exert leadership in establishing a just culture in their workplaces and a nonpunitive systems approach to addressing medication errors while supporting a nonthreatening reporting environment to encourage pharmacy staff and others to report actual and potential medication errors in a timely manner; further,

To provide leadership in supporting a single, comprehensive, hospital- or health-system-specific medication error reporting program that (1) fosters a confidential, nonthreatening, and nonpunitive environment for the submission of medication error reports; (2) receives and analyzes these confidential reports to identify system-based causes of medication errors or potential errors; and (3) recommends and disseminates error prevention strategies; further,

To provide leadership in encouraging the participation of all stakeholders in the reporting of medication errors to this program.

(*Note:* A just culture is one that has a clear and transparent process for evaluating errors and separating events arising from flawed system design or inadvertent human error from those caused by reckless behavior, defined as a behavioral choice to consciously disregard what is known to be a substantial or unjustifiable risk.)

This policy was reviewed in 2014 by the Council on Pharmacy Practice and by the Board of Directors and was found to still be appropriate.

Minimizing the Use of Abbreviations (0604)
Source: Council on Administrative Affairs
To support efforts to minimize the use of abbreviations in health care; further,

To collaborate with others in the development of a lexicon of a limited number of standard drug name abbreviations that can be safely used in patient care.

This policy was reviewed in 2010 by the Council on Pharmacy Management and by the Board of Directors and was found to still be appropriate.

Drug Names, Labeling, and Packaging Associated with Medication Errors (0020)
Source: Council on Professional Affairs
To urge drug manufacturers and FDA to involve practicing pharmacists, nurses, and physicians in decisions about drug names, labeling, and packaging to help eliminate (a) look-alike and sound-alike drug names, and (b) labeling and packaging characteristics that contribute to medication errors; further,

To inform pharmacists and others, as appropriate, about specific drug names, labeling, and packaging that have documented association with medication errors.

This policy was reviewed in 2014 by the Council on Pharmacy Practice and by the Board of Directors and was found to still be appropriate.

Medication Errors and Risk Management (0021)
Source: Council on Professional Affairs
To urge that pharmacists be included in health care organizations' risk management processes for the purpose of (a) assessing medication-use systems for vulnerabilities

to medication errors, (b) implementing medication-error prevention strategies, and (c) reviewing occurrences of medication errors and developing corrective actions.

This policy was reviewed in 2014 by the Council on Pharmacy Practice and by the Board of Directors and was found to still be appropriate.

Medication Misadventures (9805)

Source: Council on Administrative Affairs

To affirm that pharmacists must assume a leadership role in preventing, investigating, and eliminating medication misadventures across the continuum of care.

This policy was reviewed in 2013 by the Council on Pharmacy Management and by the Board of Directors and was found to still be appropriate.

Human Factors Concepts (9609)

Source: Council on Professional Affairs

To encourage pharmacists to apply human factors concepts (human errors related to inadequate systems or environment) in the prevention, analysis, and reporting of medication errors; further,

To encourage research (in conjunction with other groups, as appropriate) to identify human factors causes of medication errors and opportunities for their prevention.

This policy was reviewed in 2014 by the Council on Pharmacy Practice and by the Board of Directors and was found to still be appropriate.

ASHP Statement on Reporting Medical Errors

Position

The incidence of death and serious harm caused by mistakes and accidents in health care is unacceptable.[1] This serious public health problem merits top-priority national attention. Addressing this issue will require major reforms and sizable investment of resources throughout the health care system, including the medication use process, which is a particular focus of the American Society of Health-System Pharmacists (ASHP).

ASHP believes that the following steps should be taken as part of a comprehensive national solution to the problem: (1) The establishment of a standardized, uniform nationwide system (with the characteristics noted below) of mandatory reporting of adverse medical events that cause death or serious harm, (2) continued development and strengthening of systems for voluntary reporting of medical errors, and (3) strengthening efforts to implement process changes that reduce the risk of future errors and improve patient care.

The fundamental purpose of reporting systems for medical errors is to learn how to improve the health care delivery process to prevent these errors. Reporting of medical errors must become culturally accepted throughout health care. A major investment of resources will be required in the health care system to apply the lessons derived from the reporting of medical errors. Marshaling those resources is an urgent issue for the governing boards of health care institutions, health care administrators, health professionals, purchasers of health care (including federal and state governments), third party payers, public policy makers, credentialing organizations, the legal profession, and consumers.

Requirements

The primary goal of *mandatory reporting* of adverse medical events that cause death or serious harm should be to foster accountability for health care delivery process changes to prevent errors or adverse medical events. If a patient dies or is seriously harmed because of a mistake or accident in the health care system, the practitioner or institution responsible for the patient's care should report the incident to a designated state health body. Further, states should be obligated to share information based on these reports promptly with a national coordinating body and with national programs that are designed to improve the quality and enhance the safety of patient care.

ASHP's support of a mandatory reporting system is contingent upon the system having the following characteristics:

1. An overall focus on improving the processes used in health care, with the proper application of technical expertise to analyze and learn from reports,
2. Legal protection of confidentiality of patients, health care workers, and the information submitted to the extent feasible while preserving the interest of public accountability,
3. Nonpunitive in the sense that the submission of a report, per se, does not engender a penalty on the reporting institution or practitioner or others involved in the incident,
4. A definition of "serious harm" that concentrates on long-term or irreversible patient harm, so as not to overburden the reporting system,
5. National coordination and strong federal efforts to ensure compliance with standardized methods of reporting, analysis, and follow up, that emphasize process improvement and avoid a culture of blame,
6. Adequate resources devoted to report analysis, timely dissemination of advisories based on report analysis, and development of appropriate quality improvement efforts, and
7. Periodic assessment of the system to ensure that it is meeting its intent and not having serious undesired consequences.

Experience associated with current mandatory state reporting of adverse medical events and mandatory public health reporting of certain infectious diseases should be assessed, and the best practices of such programs should be applied to the new system of mandatory reporting of adverse medical events that cause death or serious harm.

The primary goals of *voluntary reporting* of medical errors should be quality improvement and enhancement of patient safety. Reports by frontline practitioners of errors and "near misses" are a strength of such programs when report analysis and communication lead to prevention of similar occurrences. The public interest will be served if protection is granted to individuals who submit reports to voluntary reporting programs. The Medication Errors Reporting Program operated by the United States Pharmacopeia in cooperation with the Institute for Safe Medication Practices is an important initiative that merits strengthening; this program may be a model for voluntary reporting of other types of medical error.

Reference

1. Institute of Medicine Division of Health Care Services Committee on Quality of Health Care in America. To err is human: building a safer health system. Washington, DC: National Academy Press; 1999.

This statement was reviewed in 2005 by the Council on Professional Affairs and by the Board of Directors and was found to still be appropriate.

Approved by the ASHP House of Delegates, June 5, 2000.

The bibliographic citation for this document is as follows: American Society of Health-System Pharmacists. ASHP statement on reporting medical errors. *Am J Health-Syst Pharm*. 2000; 57:1531–2.

ASHP Statement on the Role of the Medication Safety Leader

Position

The American Society of Health-System Pharmacists (ASHP) believes that medication safety is a fundamental responsibility of all members of the profession of pharmacy. For a medication safety program to succeed, however, it is essential that there be an innovative leader to set a vision and direction, identify opportunities to improve the medication-use system, and lead implementation of error-prevention strategies. The medication safety leader's role includes responsibility for leadership, medication safety expertise, influencing practice change, research, and education. ASHP believes that because of their training, knowledge of the medication-use process, skills, and abilities, pharmacists are uniquely qualified to fill the roles and meet the responsibilities of the medication safety leader in hospitals and health systems.

Background

Hospital and health-system pharmacists have improved pharmacy systems over the past 60 years to reduce the risk that medications could harm patients. Medication safety was at the heart of such historic innovations in pharmacy services as unit-dose systems, decentralized clinical pharmacy services, and intravenous admixture services. The crucial leadership role of pharmacists in medication safety has been summarized as follows:

> Pharmacy leadership is the core of a successful medication safety program. Pharmacy leaders can play an enormously important role in performance improvement. They can be part of the senior leadership team's DNA because their impact and view go far beyond the walls of the pharmacy . . . . Pharmacists can play an important role as leaders to reduce patient safety risks, optimize the safe function of medication management systems, and align pharmacy services with national initiatives that measure and reward quality performance.[1]

The landmark Institute of Medicine (IOM) report *To Err Is Human: Building a Safer Health System*[2] generated major patient safety initiatives by government agencies, regulatory and accrediting bodies, professional and organizational associations, and health care organizations. The Joint Commission National Patient Safety Goals (NPSGs)[3] are an example of a response to the original IOM report. The Pharmacy Practice Model Initiative[4] and the National Quality Forum Safe Practice 18[5] incorporate medication safety principles to ensure optimal patient safety and outcomes.

The medication safety leader (also referred to as a medication safety officer, medication safety manager, or medication safety coordinator, among other titles) is a clinical practitioner designated by an organization to serve as the authoritative expert in safe medication use. Traditionally, the medication safety leader has been a clinical pharmacist or manager within the department of pharmacy, although the position is sometimes filled by a nurse or physician. The medication safety leader may report to the organization's risk-management department, its office of quality, or a senior administrator (e.g., hospital vice president, chief medical officer, chief executive officer). Reporting outside the pharmacy department may foster interdisciplinary approaches to medication safety. Medication safety leadership may encompass a single hospital or a group of organizations (e.g., spanning a health system or at a corporate level of a larger organization). Regardless of organization size, it is critical that the fundamentals of medication safety are the central component of the medication safety leader's job function. Although medication safety leaders may have other responsibilities in smaller institutions, medication safety should remain their core responsibility, and they must be strategically positioned and empowered to lead efforts to reduce the risks of medication use.

The characteristics of a medication safety leader include

1. A strong understanding of the facility's internal systems and processes developed through firsthand experience, observations, medication-use evaluations, interviews, and data analysis for a spectrum of patient populations (e.g., pediatric, geriatric, cardiac, oncology).
2. Clinical expertise and a broad understanding of health care systems and processes to facilitate accurate interpretation of clinical events.
3. Knowledge of and experience with all aspects of the medication-use system, including procurement, prescribing, transcribing, preparation, distribution, administration, documentation, and monitoring.
4. Strong analytical skills and an understanding of statistics, population data, and the concepts of risk and prioritization.
5. Knowledge of performance-improvement methodology and tools, including root cause analysis (RCA), failure mode and effects analysis (FMEA), cause-and-effect diagramming, process-flow mapping, and methods for monitoring projects and measuring the progress of performance-improvement initiatives.
6. Three or more years of posttraining health-system practice experience.
7. Demonstrated leadership skills.
8. Excellent small- and large-group presentation skills.
9. Excellent oral communication skills, especially the ability to communicate to all types of health care providers as individuals as well as in small and large groups.
10. Excellent writing and editing skills.
11. Strong personal belief that resolving the problem of medication errors is a systems issue and not an individual health care provider issue.
12. Ability to function proactively rather than reactively.
13. Strong personal belief in the concept of a "just culture"[6] that enhances transparency, opens participation to all health care professionals, and fosters a "lessons learned" environment in an organization's medication error reporting system.

14. Understanding of concepts and application of safety principles, continuous quality improvement, and human factors engineering.
15. Appropriate assertiveness.
16. A passion for medication safety and improving patient outcomes.
17. Proven success in working with interdisciplinary teams and engaging diverse groups.
18. Strong personal belief in engaging patients as part of the health care team.
19. Eagerness to learn from events outside one's own facility (e.g., through external sources of information) to apply learning about what went wrong in order to identify and remedy possible system weaknesses to prevent patient harm.[7]

The scope of a medication safety leader's responsibilities reaches into every corner of the health care system and encompasses many roles, such as educator, preceptor, mentor, detective, compliance officer, risk manager, engineer, accountant, statistician, computer analyst, and counselor. A typical day may include attending safety rounds, precepting pharmacy students and residents, writing policies, reviewing adverse drug reactions and medication error reports, developing error-prevention strategies, leading process-improvement teams, implementing action items, reviewing smart pump libraries, ensuring safe use of automated medication dispensing systems, assessing the safety of replacement drug products during drug shortages, orienting new professional staff, assisting with medication reconciliation, conducting tracers to ensure compliance with accreditation standards (e.g., Joint Commission medication management standards and NPSGs), working with practitioners to resolve acute events, attending medical staff meetings, and educating the corporate board on the culture of safety. Most medication safety leaders quickly find themselves involved in many projects and committees as well as serving as the contact person when nursing, pharmacy, or medical staff have questions or problems. The medication safety leader needs a solid understanding of patient safety principles and must have the ability to prioritize work activities to have a positive impact on the safety of patient care. The medication safety leader should strive to acquire additional skills crucial to success, such as presentation and communication skills, as well as expertise in process-improvement methodologies such as Six Sigma and Lean. Formalized training in medication safety can be achieved through residency, fellowship, and certificate programs and other methods of continuing education. ASHP supports the expansion of pharmacy education and postgraduate residency training to include an emphasis on medication safety.[8]

Responsibilities of Medication Safety Leaders

Medication safety leaders must collaborate with all types of health care professionals, support staff, and management and consider all components of the medication-use process in both inpatient and clinic settings in order to improve medication safety. The medication safety leader's role includes responsibility for leadership, medication safety expertise, influencing practice change, research, and education.

Leadership. To provide leadership, the medication safety leader will

1. Develop a vision of an ideal safe medication-use system for the organization.
2. Oversee the planning, creation, review, and refinement of a medication safety plan.
3. Proactively develop and lead implementation of error-prevention strategies based on practice standards, literature review, medication safety tools, and analysis of the organization's medication safety data.
4. Participate in the planning, design, and implementation of the organization's medication-use technology and automation systems.
5. Build a culture of safety through "lesson learned" education and communication across the entire organization.
6. Oversee processes to collect information on the organization's medication errors and system failures to ensure that they are captured and barriers to reporting are addressed.
7. Ensure compliance with state and federal regulatory and legal requirements relating to medication safety and assist in the accreditation process by ensuring that the organization's medication-use processes meet applicable medication management standards and NPSGs.

Medication Safety Expertise. In the role of medication safety expert, the medication safety leader will

1. Serve as an authoritative resource on medication safety for the organization.
2. Contribute the medication safety perspective for technology initiatives.
3. Contribute the medication safety perspective to internal and external emergency-preparedness planning.
4. Serve as an internal consultant to investigate medication safety events or issues and develop recommendations for action.
5. Serve as the chair of the medication safety committee, whose duties may include setting the agenda, reviewing general and specific error reports, and examining the progress of projects and initiatives assigned to the medication safety team.
6. Be knowledgeable in the application and use of a variety of quality-improvement methodologies and tools (e.g., FOCUS-PDCA or Lean methodologies, RCA, FMEA).
7. Collect, review, and analyze, as the leader of review teams, the organization's medication-use, medication error, adverse drug reaction, and continuous quality-improvement data (e.g., markers of adverse drug events, smart pump event data, triggers and surveillance information, automated dispensing system and bedside bar-code scanning reports) and use appropriate data analysis techniques to identify needed improvements and develop high-leverage error-reduction strategies.
8. Predict and prepare to manage medication safety issues caused by potential or actual drug product shortages and the use of replacement drug products.
9. Maintain knowledge of trends and developments in the patient safety field through continuous profes-

sional development: reading articles, journals, and related material; attending appropriate seminars, conferences, or educational programs; and using information from the Institute of Safe Medication Practices (ISMP) National Medication Error Reporting Program, the Food and Drug Administration (FDA) MedWatch program, and similar programs.

10. Participate at local and national levels in patient safety and medication safety organizations and initiatives.

Influencing Practice Change. To influence practice change, the medication safety leader will

1. Collaborate with other departments (e.g., pharmacy, risk management, patient safety), hospital or health-system senior leadership, frontline staff, and nursing and medical staff leadership to identify and prioritize safety issues and develop risk-reduction strategies using the methods listed above to identify opportunities to improve medication safety.

2. Manage changes in the medication-use system to enhance medication safety, ensure that appropriate measures are taken to address and resolve medication safety issues, and see that hospital staff and faculty are supported in providing safe care for patients.

3. Work closely with others (e.g., the patient safety officer) to integrate medication safety into the overall strategic plan for patient safety and coordinate medication safety initiatives with organizational patient safety initiatives.

4. Participate in or lead multidisciplinary hospital and health-system committees concerned with medication errors, adverse drug events and reactions, near misses, policy review, safe medication use, new product review, and patient safety to identify risk points and prioritize system improvements to reduce the potential for medication error and patient harm.

5. Consult with and advise specific clinical teams and the hospital and health system generally on opportunities and strategies to improve patient care.

6. Encourage organizationwide medication error reporting through an established and accepted error reporting system that utilizes appropriate error detection methods (e.g., trigger tools) and through other appropriate avenues such as the pharmacy and therapeutics committee, medication safety committee, and patient safety committee.

7. Develop effective methods for spreading best medication-use practices throughout the organization.

8. Use continuous quality-improvement principles to assess and report on the status of efforts to improve medication safety.

9. Periodically review and update clinical decision-support tools to alert staff to high-risk situations and educate staff as needed.

Research and Education. To further research and education regarding medication safety, the medication safety leader will

1. Design and assist in the implementation of education and orientation programs in safe medication use, including

- Development of competency assessment for staff tasks related to medication safety (e.g., use of smart pumps and automated medication dispensing systems),
- Education of health care providers, other pertinent staff, and (as possible) patients to ensure they are competent in safe medication-use practices, and
- Provision of effective ongoing programs and presentations related to safe medication use to diverse audiences (e.g., nursing, pharmacy, respiratory care, and medical staff).

2. Share information about actual or potential medication errors or harm with safety organizations such as ISMP, FDA, drug or product manufacturers, and state error reporting programs.

3. Conduct medication-use safety research through well-designed, externally validated studies and implement evidence-based practices for medication safety.

4. Contribute to the literature on medication safety.

5. Provide medication safety education to pharmacy colleagues, students, and residents, as well as other health care professionals.

6. Integrate medication safety into orientation and training for all health care providers who participate in the medication-use process.

Conclusion

ASHP believes that pharmacists, as experts on medication use, are uniquely qualified to serve as medication safety leaders. Medication safety leaders articulate the vision and direction for improving the safety of the medication-use system to prevent patient harm. The medication safety leader's role includes responsibility for leadership through direction and prioritization, medication safety expertise, influencing practice change, research, and education. Through analysis of the organization's medication safety data and literature review, the medication safety leader will lead development and implementation of proactive error-prevention strategies and build a culture of safety across the organization.

References

1. Burgess LH, Cohen MR, Denham CR. A new leadership role for pharmacists: a prescription for change. *J Patient Saf.* 2010; 6:31–7.
2. Kohn LT, Corrigan JM, Donaldson MS, eds. To err is human: building a safer health system. Washington, DC: National Academy Press; 1999.
3. Joint Commission. Facts about the National Patient Safety Goals. www.jointcommission.org/facts_about_the_national_patient_safety_goals/ (accessed 2012 Nov 3).
4. The consensus of the Pharmacy Practice Model Summit. *Am J Health-Syst Pharm.* 2011; 68:1148–52.
5. National Quality Forum. Safe Practices for Better Healthcare 2009 Update: a consensus report. www.qualityforum.org/publications/reports/safe_practices_2009.aspx (accessed 2012 Jan 31).
6. Marx D. Patient safety and the "just culture": a primer for health care executives. New York: Columbia University Press; 2001.

7. Desired entry characteristics for those to be trained for medication-use safety coordinator positions. www.ashp.org/DocLibrary/Accreditation/Regulations-Standards/RTPEntryCharactMedUseSafety.aspx (accessed 2011 Nov 28).
8. American Society of Health-System Pharmacists. Required educational outcomes, goals, and objectives for postgraduate year two (PGY2) pharmacy residencies in medication-use safety. www.ashp.org/DocLibrary/Accreditation/Regulations-Standards/RTPObjMedicationSafety032608.aspx (accessed 2012 Feb 3).

Suggested Readings

1. Cohen MR, ed. Medication errors. Washington, DC: American Pharmacists Association; 2007.
2. Manasse HR, Thompson KK, eds. Medication safety: a guide for health care facilities. Bethesda, MD: American Society of Health-System Pharmacists; 2005.
3. Hepler CD, Segal R. Preventing medication errors and improving drug therapy outcomes: a management systems approach. Boca Raton, FL: CRC Press; 2003.
4. Joint Commission Resources. Medication use: a systems approach to reducing errors, 2nd ed. Oakbrook Terrace, IL: Joint Commission Resources; 2008.
5. Committee on Quality of Health Care in America, Institute of Medicine. Crossing the quality chasm: a new health system for the 21st century. Washington, DC: National Academy Press; 2001.
6. Committee on Data Standards for Patient Safety, Institute of Medicine. Patient safety: achieving a new standard for care. Washington, DC: National Academy Press; 2004.
7. Committee on the Work Environment for Nurses and Patient Safety, Board on Health Care Services, Institute of Medicine. Page A, ed. Keeping patients safe: transforming the work environment of nurses. Washington, DC: National Academy Press; 2004.
8. Committee on Identifying and Preventing Medication Errors, Board on Health Care Services, Institute of Medicine. Aspden P, Wolcott JA, Bootman JL, et al., eds. Preventing medication errors. Washington, DC: National Academy Press; 2007.

Web Resources

www.ashp.org
www.ismp.org
www.safemedication.com
www.asmso.org
www.ahrq.gov
www.fda.gov/cder/drugSafety.htm
www.ihi.org
www.jointcommission.org/standards_information/npsgs.aspx
www.leapfroggroup.org
www.qualityforum.org
www.nccmerp.org
www.usp.org
www.patientsafety.gov

Approved by the ASHP Board of Directors on April 13, 2012, and by the ASHP House of Delegates on June 10, 2012. Developed through the ASHP Section of Inpatient Care Practitioners Section Advisory Group on Medication Safety and approved by the ASHP Council on Education and Workforce Development on February 21, 2012.

This statement was drafted by Lynn Eschenbacher, Pharm.D., M.B.A., who declared no potential conflicts of interest.

Michael R. Cohen, M.S., Sc.D., FASHP; Deborah Saine, M.S., FASHP; and Allen Vaida, Pharm.D., FASHP are gratefully acknowledged for their contributions to this statement.

ASHP gratefully acknowledges the following individuals and organizations for reviewing drafts of this statement (review does not imply endorsement): American Osteopathic Association (AOA); Emily Alexander, Pharm.D., BCPS; Dean A. Bennett, CPHQ; Jorge Carrillo, Pharm.D., M.S.; Toby Clark, M.Sc., FASHP; John B. Crosby, J.D. (AOA); Jean Douglas, Pharm.D.; Michael S. Edwards, Pharm.D., M.B.A., BCOP, FASHP; Roy Guharoy, Pharm.D.; Becky Harvey, Pharm.D.; John Hertig, Pharm.D., M.S.; James M. Hoffman, Pharm.D., M.S., BCPS; Justin M. Julius, Pharm.D.; Ambra King, Pharm.D.; Joanne Kowiatek, M.P.M., FASHP; Donna Luong, Pharm.D.; Jeannell Mansur, Pharm.D., FASHP; Elaine Mebel, Pharm.D., M.S.; John F. Mitchell, Pharm.D., FASHP; David B. Moore, M.P.A., CPh; Ashley M. Overy, Pharm.D.; Stephanie Peshek, Pharm.D., M.B.A., FASHP; James Ponto, M.S., FASHP; Curt W. Quap, M.S., FASHP; Marcus Ravnan, Pharm.D., FASHP, FCSHP; Jennifer Schultz, Pharm.D., FASHP; Nancy R. Smestad, M.S.; Robert L. Stein, Pharm.D., J.D.; and Jody Jacobson Wedret, B.S.Pharm., FASHP, FCSHP.

The bibliographic citation for this document is as follows: American Society of Health-System Pharmacists. ASHP statement on the role of the medication safety leader. *Am J Health-Syst Pharm.* 2013; 70:448–52.

ASHP Guidelines on Adverse Drug Reaction Monitoring and Reporting

Pharmacists in organized health care systems should develop comprehensive, ongoing programs for monitoring and reporting adverse drug reactions (ADRs).[1] It is the pharmacist's responsibility and professional obligation to report any suspected ADRs. ADR-monitoring and reporting programs encourage ADR surveillance, facilitate ADR documentation, promote the reporting of ADRs, provide a mechanism for monitoring the safety of drug use in high-risk patient populations, and stimulate the education of health professionals regarding potential ADRs. A comprehensive, ongoing ADR program should include mechanisms for monitoring, detecting, evaluating, documenting, and reporting ADRs as well as intervening and providing educational feedback to prescribers, other health care professionals, and patients. Additionally, ADR programs should focus on identifying problems leading to ADRs, planning for positive changes, and measuring the results of these changes. Positive outcomes resulting from an ADR program should be emphasized to support program growth and development.

ASHP does not suggest that there is a predictable rate of incidence or severity of ADRs. The number and severity of ADRs reported in a given organization or setting would vary with the organization's size, type, patient mix, drugs used, and the ADR definition used.

Definitions

ASHP defines a significant ADR as any unexpected, unintended, undesired, or excessive response to a drug that

1. Requires discontinuing the drug (therapeutic or diagnostic),
2. Requires changing the drug therapy,
3. Requires modifying the dose (except for minor dosage adjustments),
4. Necessitates admission to a hospital,
5. Prolongs stay in a health care facility,
6. Necessitates supportive treatment,
7. Significantly complicates diagnosis,
8. Negatively affects prognosis, or
9. Results in temporary or permanent harm, disability, or death.

Consistent with this definition, an *allergic reaction* (an immunologic hypersensitivity, occurring as the result of unusual sensitivity to a drug) and an *idiosyncratic reaction* (an abnormal susceptibility to a drug that is peculiar to the individual) are also considered ADRs.

Several other definitions of ADRs exist, including those of the World Health Organization (WHO),[2] Karch and Lasagna,[3] and the Food and Drug Administration (FDA).[4]

> **WHO:** "Any response to a drug which is noxious and unintended, and which occurs at doses normally used in man for prophylaxis, diagnosis, or therapy of disease, or for the modification of physiological function."
>
> **Karch and Lasagna:** "Any response to a drug that is noxious and unintended, and that occurs at doses used in humans for prophylaxis, diagnosis, or therapy, excluding failure to accomplish the intended purpose."
>
> **FDA:** For reporting purposes, FDA categorizes a *serious adverse event* (events relating to drugs or devices) as one in which "the patient outcome is death, life-threatening (real risk of dying), hospitalization (initial or prolonged), disability (significant, persistent, or permanent), congenital anomaly, or required intervention to prevent permanent impairment or damage."

For perspective, it may be helpful to note events that are not classified as ADRs. A *side effect* is defined by ASHP as an expected, well-known reaction resulting in little or no change in patient management (e.g., drowsiness or dry mouth due to administration of certain antihistamines or nausea associated with the use of antineoplastics). ASHP further defines a side effect as an effect with a predictable frequency and an effect whose intensity and occurrence are related to the size of the dose. Additionally, drug withdrawal, drug-abuse syndromes, accidental poisoning, and drug-overdose complications should not be defined as ADRs.

While individual health care organizations may need to apply ADR surveillance to different degrees for different groups of patients, ASHP believes it would be greatly beneficial if a common definition of ADRs were used in all settings to facilitate reporting, collective surveillance, and ADR-trend research.

Program Features

A comprehensive ADR-monitoring and reporting program should be an integral part of an organization's overall drug-use system. An ADR-monitoring and reporting program should include the following features:

1. The program should establish
   a. An ongoing and concurrent (during drug therapy) surveillance system based on the reporting of suspected ADRs by pharmacists, physicians, nurses, or patients.[5]
   b. A prospective (before drug therapy) surveillance system for high-risk drugs or patients with a high risk for ADRs.
   c. A concurrent surveillance system for monitoring alerting orders. Alerting orders include the use of "tracer" drugs that are used to treat common ADRs (e.g., orders for immediate doses of antihistamines, epinephrine, and corticosteroids), abrupt discontinuation or decreases in dosage of a drug, or stat orders for laboratory assessment of therapeutic drug levels.[6,7]
2. Prescribers, caregivers, and patients should be notified regarding suspected ADRs.
3. Information regarding suspected ADRs should be reported to the pharmacy for complete data collection

and analysis, including the patient's name, the patient's medical and medication history, a description of the suspected ADR, the temporal sequence of the event, any remedial treatment required, and sequelae.

4. High-risk patients should be identified and monitored. High-risk patients include but are not limited to pediatric patients, geriatric patients, patients with organ failure (e.g., hepatic or renal failure), and patients receiving multiple drugs.[6]
5. Drugs likely to cause ADRs ("high-risk" drugs) should be identified, and their use should be monitored. Examples of drugs that may be considered as high risk include aminoglycosides, amphotericin, antineoplastics, corticosteroids, digoxin, heparin, lidocaine, phenytoin, theophylline, thrombolytic agents, and warfarin.[6]
6. The cause(s) of each suspected ADR should be evaluated on the basis of the patient's medical and medication history, the circumstances of the adverse event, the results of dechallenge and rechallenge (if any), alternative etiologies, and a literature review.
7. A method for assigning the probability of a reported or suspected ADR (e.g., confirmed or definite, likely, possible, and unlikely) should be developed to categorize each ADR. Algorithms[8–10] may be useful in establishing the causes of suspected ADRs. Subjective questions and the professional judgment of a pharmacist can be used as additional tools to determine the probability of an ADR. Questions might include the following:
   a. Was there a temporal relationship between the onset of drug therapy and the adverse reaction?
   b. Was there a dechallenge; i.e., did the signs and symptoms of the adverse reaction subside when the drug was withdrawn?
   c. Can signs and symptoms of the adverse reaction be explained by the patient's disease state?
   d. Were there any laboratory tests that provide evidence for the reaction being an ADR?
   e. What was the patient's previous general experience with the drug?
   f. Did symptoms return when the agent was readministered?
8. A method for ranking ADRs by severity should be established.[11]
9. A description of each suspected ADR and the outcomes from the event should be documented in the patient's medical record.
10. Serious or unexpected ADRs should be reported to the Food and Drug Administration (FDA) or the drug's manufacturer (or both).[a]
11. All ADR reports should be reviewed and evaluated by a designated multidisciplinary committee (e.g., a pharmacy and therapeutics committee).
12. ADR-report information should be disseminated to health care professional staff members for educational purposes. Good topics for medical staff education include preventing ADRs and appropriate and effective care for patients who experience ADRs. Educational programs can be conducted as morning "report" discussions, newsletters, "grand rounds" presentations, algorithms for treatment, and multidisciplinary reviews of drug-use evaluations. Patient confidentiality should be preserved.
13. In settings where it is possible, a pharmacy-coordinated ADR team or committee, consisting of a physician, nurse, quality improvement leader, an administrator, and a pharmacist is recommended.[12–15] The team should be charged with adopting a definition for the organization, promoting awareness of the consequences of ADRs, establishing mechanisms for identifying and reporting ADRs, reviewing ADR patterns or trends, and developing preventive and corrective interventions.
14. Continuous monitoring of patient outcomes and patterns of ADRs is imperative. Findings from an ADR-monitoring and reporting program should be incorporated into the organization's ongoing quality improvement activities. The process should include the following:
   a. Feedback to all appropriate health care staff,
   b. Continuous monitoring for trends, clusters, or significant individual ADRs,
   c. Educational efforts for prevention of ADRs, and
   d. Evaluation of prescribing patterns, patient monitoring practices, patient outcomes, and the ADR program's effect on overall and individual patient outcomes.

An overall goal of the ADR process should be the achievement of positive patient outcomes.

Benefits

An ongoing ADR-monitoring and reporting program can provide benefits to the organization, pharmacists, other health care professionals, and patients. These benefits include (but are not limited to) the following:

1. Providing an indirect measure of the quality of pharmaceutical care through identification of preventable ADRs and anticipatory surveillance for high-risk drugs or patients.
2. Complementing organizational risk-management activities and efforts to minimize liability.
3. Assessing the safety of drug therapies, especially recently approved drugs.
4. Measuring ADR incidence.
5. Educating health care professionals and patients about drug effects and increasing their level of awareness regarding ADRs.
6. Providing quality-assurance screening findings for use in drug-use evaluation programs.
7. Measuring the economic impact of ADR prevention as manifested through reduced hospitalization, optimal and economical drug use, and minimized organizational liability.

Role of the Pharmacist

Pharmacists should exert leadership in the development, maintenance, and ongoing evaluation of ADR programs. They should obtain formal endorsement or approval of such programs through appropriate committees (e.g., a pharmacy and therapeutics committee and the executive committee of the medical staff) and the organization's administration. In settings where applicable, input into the design of the program should be obtained from the medical staff, nursing staff, quality improvement staff, medical records department, and risk managers.[8,16–18] The pharmacist should facilitate

1. Analysis of each reported ADR,
2. Identification of drugs and patients at high risk for being involved in ADRs,
3. The development of policies and procedures for the ADR-monitoring and reporting program,
4. A description of the responsibilities and interactions of pharmacists, physicians, nurses, risk managers, and other health professionals in the ADR program,
5. Use of the ADR program for educational purposes,
6. Development, maintenance, and evaluation of ADR records within the organization,
7. The organizational dissemination and use of information obtained through the ADR program,
8. Reporting of serious ADRs to the FDA or the manufacturer (or both), and
9. Publication and presentation of important ADRs to the medical community.

Direct patient care roles for pharmacists should include patient counseling on ADRs, identification and documentation in the patient's medical record of high-risk patients, monitoring to ensure that serum drug concentrations remain within acceptable therapeutic ranges, and adjusting doses in appropriate patients (e.g., patients with impaired renal or hepatic function).

References

1. American Society of Hospital Pharmacists. ASHP technical assistance bulletin on hospital drug distribution and control. *Am J Hosp Pharm.* 1980; 37:1097–103.
2. Requirements for adverse reaction reporting. Geneva, Switzerland: World Health Organization; 1975.
3. Karch FE, Lasagna L. Adverse drug reactions—a critical review. *JAMA.* 1975; 234:1236–41.
4. Kessler DA. Introducing MedWatch, using FDA form 3500, a new approach to reporting medication and device adverse effects and product problems. *JAMA.* 1993; 269:2765–8.
5. Prosser TR, Kamysz PL. Multidisciplinary adverse drug reaction surveillance program. *Am J Hosp Pharm.* 1990; 47:1334–9.
6. Koch KE. Adverse drug reactions. In: Brown TR, ed. Handbook of institutional pharmacy practice. 3rd ed. Bethesda, MD: American Society of Hospital Pharmacists; 1992.
7. Koch KE. Use of standard screening procedures to identify adverse drug reactions. *Am J Hosp Pharm.* 1990; 47:1314–20.
8. Karch FE, Lasagna L. Toward the operational identification of adverse drug reactions. *Clin Pharmacol Ther.* 1977; 21:247–54.
9. Kramer MS, Leventhal JM, Hutchinson TA, et al. An algorithm for the operational assessment of adverse drug reactions. I. Background, description, and instructions for use. *JAMA.* 1979; 242:623–32.
10. Naranjo CA, Busto U, Sellers EM, et al. A method for estimating the probability of adverse drug reactions. *Clin Pharmacol Ther.* 1981; 30:239–45.
11. Hartwig SC, Siegel J, Schneider PJ. Preventability and severity assessment in reporting adverse drug reactions. *Am J Hosp Pharm.* 1992; 49:2229–32.
12. Accreditation Manual for Hospitals. Chicago: Joint Commission on Accreditation of Healthcare Organizations; 1989:121, 180.
13. Keith MR, Bellanger-McCleery RA, Fuchs JE. Multidisciplinary program for detecting and evaluating adverse drug reactions. *Am J Hosp Pharm.* 1989; 46:1809–12.
14. Kimelblatt BJ, Young SH, Heywood PM, et al. Improved reporting of adverse drug reactions. *Am J Hosp Pharm.* 1988; 45:1086–9.
15. Nelson RW, Shane R. Developing an adverse drug reaction reporting program. *Am J Hosp Pharm.* 1983; 40:445–6.
16. Swanson KM, Landry JP, Anderson RP. Pharmacy-coordinated, multidisciplinary adverse drug reaction program. *Top Hosp Pharm Manage.* 1992; 12(Jul):49–59.
17. Flowers P, Dzierba S, Baker O. A continuous quality improvement team approach to adverse drug reaction reporting. *Top Hosp Pharm Manage.* 1992; 12(Jul): 60–7.
18. Guharoy SR. A pharmacy-coordinated, multidisciplinary approach for successful implementation of an adverse drug reaction reporting program. *Top Hosp Pharm Manage.* 1992; 12(Jul):68–74.

---

[a]To report an adverse drug event to the FDA, use the MedWatch program. Reports can be mailed (MedWatch, 5600 Fishers Lane, Rockville, MD 20852–9787), faxed (800-FDA-0178), called in (800-FDA-1088), or reported by modem (800-FDA-7737). An easy-to-use FDA form 3500 can be used. This form should be available from a pharmacy.

Approved by the ASHP Board of Directors, November 16, 1994. Revised by the ASHP Council on Professional Affairs. Supersedes a previous version dated November 16, 1988.

The bibliographic citation for this document is as follows: American Society of Health-System Pharmacists. ASHP guidelines on adverse drug reaction monitoring and reporting. *Am J Health-Syst Pharm.* 1995; 52:417–9.

ASHP Guidelines on Preventing Medication Errors in Hospitals

The goal of drug therapy is the achievement of defined therapeutic outcomes that improve a patient's quality of life while minimizing patient risk.[1] There are inherent risks, both known and unknown, associated with the therapeutic use of drugs (prescription and nonprescription) and drug administration devices. The incidents or hazards that result from such risk have been defined as drug misadventuring, which includes both adverse drug reactions (ADRs) and medication errors.[2] This document addresses medication errors—episodes in drug misadventuring that should be preventable through effective systems controls involving pharmacists, physicians and other prescribers, nurses, risk management personnel, legal counsel, administrators, patients, and others in the organizational setting, as well as regulatory agencies and the pharmaceutical industry.

This document suggests medication error prevention approaches that should be considered in the development of organizational systems and discusses methods of managing medication errors once they have occurred. These guidelines are primarily intended to apply to the inpatient hospital setting because of the special collaborative processes established in the setting [e.g., formulary system, pharmacy and therapeutics (P&T) committee, and opportunity for increased interaction among health-care providers].

Recommendations for practice settings other than hospitals are beyond the scope of this document, although many of the ideas and principles may be applicable.

Medication errors compromise patient confidence in the health-care system and increase health-care costs. The problems and sources of medication errors are multidisciplinary and multifactorial. Errors occur from lack of knowledge, substandard performance and mental lapses, or defects or failures in systems.[3,4] Medication errors may be committed by both experienced and inexperienced staff, including pharmacists, physicians, nurses, supportive personnel (e.g., pharmacy technicians), students, clerical staff (e.g., ward clerks), administrators, pharmaceutical manufacturers, patients and their caregivers, and others. The incidence of medication errors is indeterminate; valid comparisons of different studies on medication errors are extremely difficult because of differences in variables, measurements, populations, and methods.[2]

Many medication errors are probably undetected. The outcome(s) or clinical significance of many medication errors may be minimal, with few or no consequences that adversely affect a patient. Tragically, however, some medication errors result in serious patient morbidity or mortality.[3] Thus, medication errors must not be taken lightly, and effective systems for ordering, dispensing, and administering medications should be established with safeguards to prevent the occurrence of errors. These systems should involve adequately trained and supervised personnel, adequate communications, reasonable workloads, effective drug handling systems, multiple procedural and final product checks by separate individuals, quality management, and adequate facilities, equipment, and supplies.

The pharmacist's mission is to help ensure that patients make the best use of medications.[5] This applies to all drugs used by inpatients or ambulatory patients, including oral or injectable products, radiopharmaceuticals, radiopaque contrast media, anesthetic gases, blood-fraction drugs, dialysis fluids, respiratory therapy agents, investigational drugs, drug samples, drugs brought into the hospital setting by patients, and other chemical or biological substances administered to patients to evoke a pharmacological response.[6]

Through a systems-oriented approach, the pharmacist should lead collaborative, multidisciplinary efforts to prevent, detect, and resolve drug-related problems that can result in patient harm.[1] An understanding of the risk factors associated with medication errors should enable improved monitoring of patients and medications associated with increased risk for serious errors and should enable the development of organizational systems designed to minimize risk.[7] The pharmacist should participate in appropriate organizational committees and work with physicians, nurses, administrators, and others to examine and improve systems to ensure that medication processes are safe.

Types of Medication Errors

Medication errors include prescribing errors, dispensing errors, medication administration errors, and patient compliance errors. Specific types of medication errors are categorized in Table 1, based on a compilation of the literature.[3,7–18]

A *potential error* is a mistake in prescribing, dispensing, or planned medication administration that is detected and corrected through intervention (by another health-care provider or patient) before actual medication administration. Potential errors should be reviewed and tabulated as separate events from errors of occurrence (errors that actually reach patients) to identify opportunities to correct problems in the medication use system even before they occur. Detection of potential errors should be a component of the hospital's routine quality improvement process. Documentation of instances in which an individual has prevented the occurrence of a medication error will help identify system weaknesses and will reinforce the importance of multiple checks in the medication use system.

Recommendations for Preventing Medication Errors

Organizational systems for ordering, dispensing, and administering medications should be designed to minimize error. Medication errors may involve process breakdowns in more than one aspect of a system. This section provides recommendations to the management staff (general and departmental) of hospitals, as well as to individual prescribers, pharmacists, nurses, patients, pharmaceutical manufacturers, and others.

Organizational and Departmental Recommendations. Organizational policies and procedures should be established to prevent medication errors. Development of the policies and procedures should involve multiple departments, including pharmacy, medicine, nursing, risk management, legal counsel, and organizational administration. The following recommendations are offered for organizational management and clinical staff: [3,8,11–14,16,19–29]

Table 1.
Types of Medication Errors[3,7–18,a]

Type	Definition
Prescribing error	Incorrect drug selection (based on indications, contraindications, known allergies, existing drug therapy, and other factors), dose, dosage form, quantity, route, concentration, rate of administration, or instructions for use of a drug product ordered or authorized by physician (or other legitimate prescriber); illegible prescriptions or medication orders that lead to errors that reach the patient
Omission error[b]	The failure to administer an ordered dose to a patient before the next scheduled dose, if any
Wrong time error	Administration of medication outside a predefined time interval from its scheduled administration time (this interval should be established by each individual health care facility)
Unauthorized drug error[c]	Administration to the patient of medication not authorized by a legitimate prescriber for the patient
Improper dose error[d]	Administration to the patient of a dose that is greater than or less than the amount ordered by the prescriber or administration of duplicate doses to the patient, i.e., one or more dosage units in addition to those that were ordered
Wrong dosage-form error[e]	Administration to the patient of a drug product in a different dosage form than ordered by the prescriber
Wrong drug-preparation error[f]	Drug product incorrectly formulated or manipulated before administration
Wrong administration-technique error[g]	Inappropriate procedure or improper technique in the administration of a drug
Deteriorated drug error[h]	Administration of a drug that has expired or for which the physical or chemical dosage-form integrity has been compromised
Monitoring error	Failure to review a prescribed regimen for appropriateness and detection of problems, or failure to use appropriate clinical or laboratory data for adequate assessment of patient response to prescribed therapy
Compliance error	Inappropriate patient behavior regarding adherence to a prescribed medication regimen
Other medication error	Any medication error that does not fall into one of above predefined categories

[a] The categories may not be mutually exclusive because of the multidisciplinary and multifactorial nature of medication errors.

[b] Assumes no prescribing error. Excluded would be (1) a patient's refusal to take the medication or (2) a decision not to administer the dose because of recognized contraindications. If an explanation for the omission is apparent (e.g., patient was away from nursing unit for tests or medication was not available), that reason should be documented in the appropriate records.

[c] This would include, for example, a wrong drug, a dose given to the wrong patient, unordered drugs, and doses given outside a stated set of clinical guidelines or protocols.

[d] Excluded would be (1) allowable deviations based on preset ranges established by individual health care organizations in consideration of measuring devices routinely provided to those who administer drugs to patients (e.g., not administering a dose based on a patient's measured temperature or blood glucose level) or other factors such as conversion of doses expressed in the apothecary system to the metric system and (2) topical dosage forms for which medication orders are not expressed quantitatively.

[e] Excluded would be accepted protocols (established by the pharmacy and therapeutics committee or its equivalent) that authorize pharmacists to dispense alternate dosage forms for patients with special needs (e.g., liquid formulations for patients with nasogastric tubes or those who have difficulty swallowing), as allowed by state regulations.

[f] This would include, for example, incorrect dilution or reconstitution, mixing drugs that are physically or chemically incompatible, and inadequate product packaging.

[g] This would include doses administered (1) via the wrong route (different from the route prescribed), (2) via the correct route but at the wrong site (e.g., left eye instead of right), and (3) at the wrong rate of administration.

[h] This would include, for example, administration of expired drugs and improperly stored drugs.

1. Using the principles of the formulary system, the P&T committee (or its equivalent)—composed of pharmacists, physicians, nurses, and other health professionals—should be responsible for formulating policies regarding the evaluation, selection, and therapeutic use of drugs in organized health-care settings.
2. Care and consideration must be given in hiring and assigning personnel involved in medication ordering, preparation, dispensing, administration, and patient education. Policies and procedures should be developed that ensure adequate personnel selection, training, supervision, and evaluation. This would include the need to ensure proper interviewing, orientation, evaluation of competency, supervision, and opportunities for continuing professional and technical education.
3. Sufficient personnel must be available to perform tasks adequately. Policies and procedures should ensure that reasonable workload levels and working hours are established and rarely exceeded.
4. Suitable work environments should exist for the preparation of drug products. Potential error sources within the work environment, such as frequent interruptions, should be identified and minimized.
5. Lines of authority and areas of responsibility within the hospital should be clearly defined for medication ordering, dispensing, and administration. The system should ensure adequate written and oral communications among personnel involved in the medication use process to optimize therapeutic appropriateness and to enable medications to be prescribed, dispensed, and administered in a timely fashion. All systems should provide for review and verification of the prescriber's original order (except in emergency situations) before a drug product is dispensed by a pharmacist. Any necessary clarifications or changes in a medication order must be resolved with the prescriber before a medication is administered to the patient. Written documentation of such consultations should be made in the patient's medical record or other appropriate record. Nursing staff should be informed of any changes made in the medication order. Changes required to correct incorrect orders should be regarded as potential errors, assuming the changes occurred in time to prevent the error from reaching the patient.
6. There should be an ongoing, systematic program of quality improvement and peer review with respect to the safe use of medications. A formal drug use evaluation (DUE) program, developed and conducted through collaborative efforts among medicine, pharmacy, and nursing, should be integrated and coordinated with the overall hospital quality improvement program. To prevent medication errors, a portion of the DUE program should focus on monitoring

the appropriate use of any drugs associated with a high frequency of adverse events, including specific drug classes (such as antimicrobials, antineoplastic agents, and cardiovascular drugs) and injectable dosage forms (e.g., potassium products, narcotic substances, heparin, lidocaine, procainamide, magnesium sulfate, and insulin). The quality improvement program should include a system for monitoring, reviewing, and reporting medication errors to assist in identifying and eliminating causes of errors (system breakdowns) and preventing their recurrence. Table 2 lists common causes of medication errors, i.e., areas where there may be system breakdowns.

7. Pharmacists and others responsible for processing drug orders should have routine access to appropriate clinical information about patients (including medication, allergy, and hypersensitivity profiles; diagnoses; pregnancy status; and laboratory values) to help evaluate the appropriateness of medication orders.

8. Pharmacists should maintain medication profiles for all patients, both inpatients and ambulatory patients, who receive care at the hospital. This profile should include adequate information to allow monitoring of medication histories, allergies, diagnoses, potential drug interactions and ADRs, duplicate drug therapies, pertinent laboratory data, and other information.

9. The pharmacy department must be responsible for the procurement, distribution, and control of all drugs used within the organization. Adequate hours for the provision of pharmaceutical services must be maintained; 24-hour pharmaceutical service is strongly recommended in hospital settings. In the absence of 24-hour pharmaceutical service, access to a limited supply of medications should be available to authorized nonpharmacists for use in initiating urgent medication orders. The list of medications to be supplied and the policies and procedures to be used (including subsequent review of all activity by a pharmacist) should be developed by the P&T committee (or its equivalent). Items should be chosen with safety in mind, limiting wherever possible medications, quantities, dosage forms, and container sizes that might endanger patients. The use of well-designed night cabinets, after-hours drug carts, and other methods would preclude the need for non-pharmacists to enter the pharmacy. Access to the pharmacy by nonpharmacists (e.g., nurses) for removal of doses is strongly discouraged; this practice should be minimized and eliminated to the fullest extent possible. When 24-hour pharmacy service is not feasible, a pharmacist must be available on an "on-call" basis.

Table 2.
Common Causes of Medication Errors

Ambiguous strength designation on labels or in packaging
Drug product nomenclature (look-alike or sound-alike names, use of lettered or numbered prefixes and suffixes in drug names)
Equipment failure or malfunction
Illegible handwriting
Improper transcription
Inaccurate dosage calculation
Inadequately trained personnel
Inappropriate abbreviations used in prescribing
Labeling errors
Excessive workload
Lapses in individual performance
Medication unavailable

10. The pharmacy manager (or designee), with the assistance of the P&T committee (or its equivalent) and the department of nursing, should develop comprehensive policies and procedures that provide for efficient and safe distribution of all medications and related supplies to patients. For safety, the recommended method of distribution within the organized health-care setting is the unit dose drug distribution and control system.

11. Except in emergency situations, all sterile and nonsterile drug products should be dispensed from the pharmacy department for individual patients. The storage of nonemergency floor stock medications on the nursing units or in patient-care areas should be minimized. Particular caution should be exercised with respect to drug products that have commonly been involved in serious medication errors or whose margin of safety is narrow, such as concentrated forms of drug products that are intended to be diluted into larger volumes (e.g., concentrated lidocaine and potassium chloride for injection concentrate). All drug storage areas should be routinely inspected by pharmacy personnel to ensure adequate product integrity and appropriate packaging, labeling, and storage. It is important that drug products and other products for external use be stored separately from drug products for internal use.

12. The pharmacy director and staff must ensure that all drug products used in the organizational setting are of high quality and integrity. This would include, for example, (1) selecting multisource products supported by adequate bioavailability data and adequate product packaging and labeling, (2) maintaining an unexpired product inventory, and (3) keeping abreast of compendial requirements.

13. The use of a patient's own or "home" medications should be avoided to the fullest extent possible. Use of such medications should be allowed only if there is a need for the patient to receive the therapy, the drug product is not obtainable by the pharmacy, and no alternative therapy can be prescribed. If such medications are used, the prescribing physician must write an appropriate order in the patient's medical record. Before use, a pharmacist should inspect and identify the medication. If there are any unresolved questions with respect to product identity or integrity, the medication must not be used.

14. All discontinued or unused drugs should be returned to the department of pharmacy immediately on discontinuation or at patient discharge. Discharged patients must not be given unlabeled drug products to take home, unless they are labeled for outpatient use by the pharmacy in accordance with state and federal regulations. Discharged patients should be counseled about use of any medications to be used after discharge.

15. It is recommended that there be computerized pharmacy systems in place that enable automated checking for doses, duplicate therapies, allergies, drug interactions, and other aspects of use. Where possible, the use of technological innovations such as bar coding is recommended to help identify patients, products, and care providers. Pharmacy-generated medication administration records or labels are recommended to assist nurses in interpreting and documenting medication activities.

16. Adequate drug information resources should be available for all health-care providers involved in the drug use process.

17. Standard drug administration times should be established for the hospital by the P&T committee (or its equivalent), with input from the departments of nursing and pharmacy. Policies and procedures should allow for deviations from the standard times when necessary. Further, standard drug concentrations and dosage charts should be developed to minimize the need for dosage calculations by staff.

18. The P&T committee (or its equivalent) should develop a list of standard abbreviations approved for use in medication ordering. There should be efforts to prohibit or discourage the use of other abbreviations in medication ordering.

19. A review mechanism should be established through the P&T committee specifying those responsible for data collection and evaluation of medication error reports. The review group should investigate causes of errors and develop programs for decreasing their occurrence. The review group should be composed of representatives from pharmacy, nursing, medicine, quality assurance, staff education, risk management, and legal counsel.

20. The pharmacy department, in conjunction with nursing, risk management, and the medical staff, should conduct ongoing educational programs to discuss medication errors, their causes, and methods to prevent their occurrence. Such programs might involve seminars, newsletters, or other methods of information dissemination.

Recommendations for Prescribers. Prescribing is an early point at which medication errors can arise. It has been estimated that 1% of hospitalized patients suffer adverse events as the result of medical mismanagement[30] and that drug-related complications are the most common type of adverse event.[7] The following recommendations for preventing medication errors are suggested for physicians and other prescribers[3,7,11–16,31]:

1. To determine appropriate drug therapy, prescribers should stay abreast of the current state of knowledge through literature review, consultation with pharmacists, consultation with other physicians, participation in continuing professional education programs, and other means. It is especially crucial to seek information when prescribing for conditions and diseases not typically experienced in the prescriber's practice.

2. Prescribers should evaluate the patient's total status and review all existing drug therapy before prescribing new or additional medications to ascertain possible antagonistic or complementary drug interactions. To evaluate and optimize patient response to prescribed drug therapy, appropriate monitoring of clinical signs and symptoms and of relevant laboratory data is necessary.

3. In hospitals, prescribers should be familiar with the medication ordering system (e.g., the formulary system, participation in DUE programs, allowable delegation of authority, procedures to alert nurses and others to new drug orders that need to be processed, standard medication administration times, and approved abbreviations).

4. Drug orders should be complete. They should include patient name, generic drug name, trademarked name (if a specific product is required), route and site of administration, dosage form, dose, strength, quantity, frequency of administration, and prescriber's name. In some cases, a dilution, rate, and time of administration should be specified. The desired therapeutic outcome for each drug should be expressed when the drug is prescribed. Prescribers should review all drug orders for accuracy and legibility immediately after they have prescribed them.

5. Care should be taken to ensure that the intent of medication orders is clear and unambiguous. Prescribers should

- **a.** Write out instructions rather than using nonstandard or ambiguous abbreviations. For example, write "daily" rather than "q.d.," which could be misinterpreted as q.i.d. (causing a drug to be given four times a day instead of once) or as o.d. (for right eye).
- **b.** Do not use vague instructions, such as "take as directed," because specific instructions can help differentiate among intended drugs.
- **c.** Specify exact dosage strengths (such as milligrams) rather than dosage form units (such as one tablet or one vial). An exception would be combination drug products, for which the number of dosage form units should be specified.
- **d.** Prescribe by standard nomenclature, using the drug's generic name (United States Adopted Name or USAN), official name, or trademarked name (if deemed medically necessary). Avoid the following: locally coined names (e.g., Dr. Doe's syrup); chemical names [e.g., 6-mercaptopurine (instead of mercaptopurine) could result in a sixfold overdose if misinterpreted]; unestablished abbreviated drug names (e.g., "AZT" could stand for zidovudine, azathioprine, or aztreonam); acronyms; and apothecary or chemical symbols.
- **e.** Always use a leading zero before a decimal expression of less than one (e.g., 0.5 mL). Conversely, a terminal zero should never be used (e.g., 5.0 mL), since failure to see the decimal could result in a 10-fold overdose. When possible, avoid the use of decimals (e.g., prescribe 500 mg instead of 0.5 g).
- **f.** Spell out the word "units" (e.g., 10 units regular insulin) rather than writing "u," which could be misinterpreted as a zero.
- **g.** Use the metric system.

6. Written drug or prescription orders (including signatures) should be legible. Prescribers with poor handwriting should print or type medication or prescription orders if direct order entry capabilities for computerized systems are unavailable. A handwritten order should be completely readable (not merely recognizable through familiarity). An illegible handwritten order should be regarded as a potential error. If it leads to an error of occurrence (that is, the error actually reaches the patient), it should be regarded as a prescribing error.

7. Verbal drug or prescription orders (that is, orders that are orally communicated) should be reserved only for those situations in which it is impossible or impractical for the prescriber to write the order or enter it in the computer. The prescriber should dictate verbal orders slowly, clearly, and articulately to avoid confusion. Special caution is urged in the prescribing of drug dosages in the teens (e.g., a 15-mEq dose of potassium chloride could be misheard as a 50-mEq dose). The order should be read back to the prescriber by the recipient (i.e., the nurse or pharmacist, according to institutional policies). When read back, the drug name should be spelled to the prescriber and, when directions are repeated, no abbreviations should be used (e.g., say "three times daily" rather than "t.i.d."). A written copy of the verbal order should be placed in the patient's medical record and later confirmed by the prescriber in accordance with applicable state regulations and hospital policies.
8. When possible, drugs should be prescribed for administration by the oral route rather than by injection.
9. When possible, the prescriber should talk with the patient or caregiver to explain the medication prescribed and any special precautions or observations that might be indicated, including any allergic or hypersensitivity reactions that might occur.
10. Prescribers should follow up and periodically evaluate the need for continued drug therapy for individual patients.
11. Instructions with respect to "hold" orders for medications should be clear.

Recommendations for Pharmacists. The pharmacist is expected to play a pivotal role in preventing medication misuse. The value of pharmacists' interventions to prevent medication errors that would have resulted from inappropriate prescribing has been documented.[7,32,33] Ideally, the pharmacist should collaborate with the prescriber in developing, implementing, and monitoring a therapeutic plan to produce defined therapeutic outcomes for the patient.[1] It is also vital that the pharmacist devote careful attention to dispensing processes to ensure that errors are not introduced at that point in the medication process. The following recommendations are suggested for pharmacists[3,4,8–10,14,16,18–20,28,29]:

1. Pharmacists should participate in drug therapy monitoring (including the following, when indicated: the assessment of therapeutic appropriateness, medication administration appropriateness, and possible duplicate therapies; review for possible interactions; and evaluation of pertinent clinical and laboratory data) and DUE activities to help achieve safe, effective, and rational use of drugs.
2. To recommend and recognize appropriate drug therapy, pharmacists should stay abreast of the current state of knowledge through familiarity with literature, consultation with colleagues and other health-care providers, participation in continuing professional education programs, and other means.
3. Pharmacists should make themselves available to prescribers and nurses to offer information and advice about therapeutic drug regimens and the correct use of medications.
4. Pharmacists should be familiar with the medication ordering system and drug distribution policies and procedures established for the organizational setting to provide for the safe distribution of all medications and related supplies to inpatients and ambulatory patients. In particular, pharmacists should be familiar with all elements that are designed into the system to prevent or detect errors. Actions by any staff that would (even unintentionally) defeat or compromise those elements should serve as "alerts" to the pharmacist that safety may be affected. Any necessary followup action (e.g., education or reeducation of staff) should ensue promptly. Policies and procedures to be followed for "hold" orders should be clear and understood by pharmacy, medical, and nursing staffs.
5. Pharmacists should never assume or guess the intent of confusing medication orders. If there are any questions, the prescriber should be contacted prior to dispensing.
6. When preparing drugs, pharmacists should maintain orderliness and cleanliness in the work area and perform one procedure at a time with as few interruptions as possible.
7. Before dispensing a medication in nonemergency situations, the pharmacist should review an original copy of the written medication order. The pharmacist should ensure that all work performed by supportive personnel or through the use of automated devices is checked by manual or technological means. All processes must conform with applicable state and federal laws and regulations. Pharmacists should participate in, at a minimum, a self-checking process in reading prescriptions, labeling (drug or ingredients and pharmacist-generated labeling), and dosage calculations. For high risk drug products, when possible, all work should be checked by a second individual (preferably, another pharmacist). Pharmacists must make certain that the following are accurate: drug, labeling, packaging, quantity, dose, and instructions.
8. Pharmacists should dispense medications in ready-to-administer dosage forms whenever possible. The unit dose system is strongly recommended as the preferred method of drug distribution. The need for nurses to manipulate drugs (e.g., measure, repackage, and calculate) prior to their administration should be minimized.
9. Pharmacists should review the use of auxiliary labels and use the labels prudently when it is clear that such use may prevent errors (e.g., "shake well," "for external use only," and "not for injection").
10. Pharmacists should ensure that medications are delivered to the patient-care area in a timely fashion after receipt of orders, according to hospital policies and procedures. If medication doses are not delivered or if therapy is delayed for any reason pending resolution of a detected problem (e.g., allergy or contraindications), the pharmacist should notify the nursing staff of the delay and the reason.
11. Pharmacists should observe how medications are actually being used in patient-care areas to ensure that dispensing and storage procedures are followed and to assist nurses in optimizing patient safety.
12. Pharmacy staff should review medications that are returned to the department. Such review processes may reveal system breakdowns or problems that resulted in medication errors (e.g., omitted doses and unauthorized drugs).

13. When dispensing medications to ambulatory patients (e.g., at discharge), pharmacists should counsel patients or caregivers and verify that they understand why a medication was prescribed and dispensed, its intended use, any special precautions that might be observed, and other needed information. For inpatients, pharmacists should make their services available to counsel patients, families, or other caregivers when appropriate.
14. Pharmacists should preview and provide advice on the content and design of preprinted medication order forms or sheets if they are used.
15. Pharmacists should maintain records sufficient to enable identification of patients receiving an erroneous product.

Recommendations for Nurses. By virtue of their direct patient-care activities and administration of medications to patients, nurses—perhaps more than any other health-care providers—are in an excellent position to detect and report medication errors. Nurses often serve as the final point in the checks-and-balances triad (physicians and other prescribers, pharmacists, and nurses) for the medication use process; thus, they play an important role in risk reduction. The following recommendations for preventing medication administration errors are suggested[3,14,16,17,34]:

1. Nurses who practice in organized health-care settings should be familiar with the medication ordering and use system (e.g., participation in DUE activities, order processing, and standard medication administration times).
2. Nurses should review patients' medications with respect to desired patient outcomes, therapeutic duplications, and possible drug interactions. Adequate drug information (including information on medication administration and product compatibilities) should be obtained from pharmacists, nurses, other health-care providers, the literature, and other means when there are questions. There should be appropriate followup communication with the prescriber when this is indicated.
3. All drug orders should be verified before medication administration. Nurses should carefully review original medication orders before administration of the first dose and compare them with medications dispensed. Transcriptions of orders should be avoided to the extent possible and should be recognized as prime opportunities for errors. Doses should not be administered unless the meaning of the original order is clear and unambiguous and there are no questions with respect to the correctness of the prescribed regimen. Nurses should check the identity and integrity (e.g., expiration date and general appearance) of the medications dispensed before administering them. When there are discrepancies, the nurse should contact the pharmacy department and determine the appropriate action.
4. Patient identity should be verified before the administration of each prescribed dose. When appropriate, the patient should be observed after administration of the drug product to ensure that the doses were administered as prescribed and have the intended effect.
5. All doses should be administered at scheduled times unless there are questions or problems to be resolved. Medication doses should not be removed from packaging or labeling until immediately before administration. The administration of medication should bedocumented as soon as it is completed.
6. When standard drug concentrations or dosage charts are not available, dosage calculations, flow rates, and other mathematical calculations should be checked by a second individual (e.g., another nurse or a pharmacist).
7. The drug distribution system should not be circumvented by "borrowing" medications from one patient (or another hospital area) to give to a different patient or by stockpiling unused medications. If there are apparent missing doses, it is important that the pharmacy be contacted for explanation or correction. There may be an important reason why the dose was not sent to the patient-care area (e.g., allergy, contraindication, and questionable dose), and resolution of the potential question or problem may be pending.
8. If there are questions when a large volume or number of dosage units (e.g., more than two tablets, capsules, vials, or ampuls) is needed for a single patient dose, the medication order should be verified. Consult with the pharmacist and prescriber as appropriate.
9. All personnel using medication administration devices (e.g., infusion pumps) should understand their operation and the opportunities for error that might occur with the use of such devices.
10. Nurses should talk with patients or caregivers to ascertain that they understand the use of their medications and any special precautions or observations that might be indicated. Any counseling needed should be provided before the first dose is administered, when possible.
11. When a patient objects to or questions whether a particular drug should be administered, the nurse should listen, answer questions, and (if appropriate) double check the medication order and product dispensed before administering it to ensure that no preventable error is made (e.g., wrong patient, wrong route, and dose already administered). If a patient refuses to take a prescribed medication, that decision should be documented in the appropriate patient records.

Recommendations for Patients and Personal Caregivers. Patients (or their authorized caregivers or designees) have the right to know about all aspects of their care, including drug therapy. When patient status allows, health-care providers should encourage patients to take an active role in their drug use by questioning and learning about their treatment regimens. Generally, if patients are more knowledgeable, anxieties about the uncertainty of treatments can be alleviated and errors in treatment may be prevented. The following suggestions are offered to help patients whose health status allows, and their caregivers, make the best use of medications[3]:

1. Patients should inform appropriate direct health-care providers (e.g., physicians, nurses, and pharmacists) about all known symptoms, allergies, sensitivities, and current medication use. Patients should communicate their actual self-medication practices, even if they differ from the prescribed directions.
2. Patients should feel free to ask questions about any procedures and treatments received.
3. atients should learn the names of the drug products that are prescribed and administered to them, as well as dosage strengths and schedules. It is suggested that

patients keep a personal list of all drug therapy, including prescribed drugs, nonprescription drugs, home remedies, and medical foods. Patients should also maintain lists of medications that they cannot take and the reasons why. This information should be shared with health-care providers. Patients should be assertive in communicating with health-care providers when anything seems incorrect or different from the norm.

4. After counseling from an authorized health-care provider about the appropriateness of the medication, patients should take all medications as directed.

Recommendations for Pharmaceutical Manufacturers and Approval Organizations. Poor designs with respect to drug product packaging and labeling, as well as selection of inappropriate or confusing nomenclature, have been identified as factors that contribute to serious medication errors by practitioners.[4,35–37] Pharmaceutical manufacturers and approval agencies should be responsive to efforts of practitioners to minimize errors. The following guidelines are recommended for the pharmaceutical industry and regulatory authorities[3,4,16,38]

1. Drug manufacturers and the Food and Drug Administration are urged to involve pharmacists, nurses, and physicians in decisions about drug names, labeling, and packaging.
2. Look-alike or sound-alike trademarked names and generic names should be avoided.
3. Similar proprietary appearances of packaging and labeling should be avoided, because look-alike products contribute to medication errors.
4. The use of lettered or numbered prefixes and suffixes in trademarked names is generally discouraged. Lettered prefixes or suffixes could be mistaken for instructions or strength. Commonly used medical abbreviations should never be used in trademarked names (e.g., "HS" could stand for half-strength or a bedtime dose). Numbers as part of trademarked names could be mistaken for quantities to be administered. Coined abbreviations that could be misinterpreted (e.g., MTX, U, and HCTZ) should not be used in trademarked names.
5. Special instructions should be highlighted on labeling, such as the need for dilution before administration.
6. The most prominent items on the product label should be information in the best interest of safety (e.g., product name and strength). Less prominence should be given to company names or logos.
7. Drug manufacturers are encouraged to make dosage forms available commercially in unit dose and unit-of-dispensing containers, as well as bulk packaging, to facilitate their appropriate use in all practice settings.
8. Drug manufacturers must communicate with health-care providers (i.e., pharmacists, physicians, and nurses) when changes are made in product formulations or dosage forms.

Monitoring and Managing Medication Errors

Monitoring Medication Errors. Ongoing quality improvement programs for monitoring medication errors are needed. The difficulty in detecting errors has long been recognized as one of the barriers to studying the problem effectively.[39] Medication errors should be identified and documented and their causes studied in order to develop systems that minimize recurrence.[3,4,7,10,11,14,16,22,40] Several error monitoring techniques exist (e.g., anonymous self-reports, incident reports, critical incident technique, and disguised observation technique) and may be applied as appropriate to determine the rates of errors.[9,40,41] There are differences in the validity of data obtained by the various error monitoring techniques or combined techniques. Program managers should determine the best method for use in their organizations in consideration of utility, feasibility, and cost. Monitoring programs for medication errors should consider the following risk factors[6,10,11,22,40,41]:

1. Work shift (higher error rates typically occur during the day shift).
2. Inexperienced and inadequately trained staff.
3. Medical service (e.g., special needs for certain patient populations, including geriatrics, pediatrics, and oncology).
4. Increased number or quantity of medications per patient.
5. Environmental factors (lighting, noise, and frequent interruptions).
6. Staff workload and fatigue.
7. Poor communication among health-care providers.
8. Dosage form (e.g., injectable drugs are associated with more serious errors).
9. Type of distribution system (unit dose distribution is preferred; floor stock should be minimized).
10. Improper drug storage.
11. Extent of measurements or calculations required.
12. Confusing drug product nomenclature, packaging, or labeling.
13. Drug category (e.g., antimicrobials).
14. Poor handwriting.
15. Verbal (orally communicated) orders.
16. Lack of effective policies and procedures.
17. Poorly functioning oversight committees.

Managing Medication Errors. Medication errors result from problematic processes, but the outcomes of medication errors could range from minimal (or no) patient risk to life-threatening risk. Classification of the potential seriousness and clinical significance of detected medication errors should be based on predefined criteria established by the P&T committee (or its equivalent). The error classification should be based on the original order, standard medication dispensing and administration procedures, dosage forms available, acceptable deviation ranges, potential for adverse consequences and patient harm, and other factors.[6,32,41]

Classification of medication errors should allow for better management of followup activities upon medication error detection. A simple classification of medication errors is the following: (1) clinically significant (includes potentially fatal or severe, potentially serious, and potentially significant errors) or (2) minor.[7,33] Hartwig, Denger, and Schneider defined seven medication error severity levels, as follows[41]:

Level 0—Nonmedication error occurred (potential errors would be classified here).

Level 1—An error occurred that did not result in patient harm.

Level 2—An error occurred that resulted in the need for increased patient monitoring but no change in vital signs and no patient harm.

Level 3—An error occurred that resulted in the need for increased patient monitoring with a change in vital signs but no ultimate patient harm, or any error that resulted in the need for increased laboratory monitoring.

Level 4—An error occurred that resulted in the need for treatment with another drug or an increased length of stay or that affected patient participation in an investigational drug study.[a]

Level 5—An error occurred that resulted in permanent patient harm.

Level 6—An error occurred that resulted in patient death.

Medication error classifications could also be based on probability and severity scales analogous to those used in ADR reporting programs.[42,43]

Determination of the causes of medication errors should be coupled with assessment of the severity of the error. While quality management processes should include programs to decrease the incidence of all medication errors, effort should be concentrated on eliminating the causes of errors associated with greater levels of severity. There should be established mechanisms for tracking drugs or drug classes that are involved in medication errors. Correlations between errors and the method of drug distribution should also be reviewed (e.g., unit dose, floor stock, or bulk medications; premixed or extemporaneously compounded products; and oral or injectable products). These processes will help identify system problems and stimulate changes to minimize the recurrence of errors.

Quality improvement programs should provide guidance for patient support, staff counseling and education, and risk management processes when a medication error is detected. Incident reporting policies and procedures and appropriate counseling, education, and intervention programs should be established in all hospitals. Risk management processes for medication errors should include pharmacists, physicians, and nurses, in addition to risk management specialists, legal counsel, and others as appropriate. The following actions are recommended upon error detection[3,7,10,11,16,17,27,43]:

1. Any necessary corrective and supportive therapy should be provided to the patient.
2. The error should be documented and reported immediately after discovery, in accordance with written procedures. For clinically significant errors, an immediate oral notice should be provided to physicians, nurses, and pharmacy managers. A written medication error report should follow promptly.
3. For clinically significant errors, fact gathering and investigation should be initiated immediately. Facts that should be determined and documented include what happened, where the incident occurred, why the incident occurred, how the incident occurred, and who was involved. Appropriate product evidence (e.g., packaging and labeling) should be retrieved and retained for future reference until causative factors are eliminated or resolved.
4. Reports of clinically significant errors and the associated corrective activities should be reviewed by the supervisor and department head of the area(s) involved, the appropriate organizational administrator, the organizational safety committee (or its equivalent), and legal counsel (as appropriate).
5. When appropriate, the supervisor and the staff members who were involved in the error should confer on how the error occurred and how its recurrence can be prevented. Medication errors often result from problems in systems rather than exclusively from staff performance or environmental factors[2,3,44]; thus, error reports should not be used for punitive purposes but to achieve correction or change.
6. Information gained from medication error reports and other means that demonstrates continued failure of individual professionals to avoid preventable medication errors should serve as an effective management and educational tool in staff development or, if necessary, modification of job functions or staff disciplinary action.
7. Supervisors, department managers, and appropriate committees should periodically review error reports and determine causes of errors and develop actions to prevent their recurrence (e.g., conduct organizational staff education, alter staff levels, revise policies and procedures, or change facilities, equipment, or supplies).
8. Medication errors should be reported to a national monitoring program so that the shared experiences of pharmacists, nurses, physicians, and patients can contribute to improved patient safety and to the development of valuable educational services for the prevention of future errors. Reports of medication errors can be made by telephone to the United States Pharmacopeial Convention, Inc. (USP) Medication Errors Reporting Program (1-800-23ERROR). Reports can be submitted to USP on a confidential basis if the reporter so chooses. Other reporting programs may also be in existence or under development. Reporting programs are intended to track trends and inform practitioners, regulators, and the pharmaceutical industry of potential product and system hazards that have a documented association with medication errors.

References

1. Hepler CD, Strand LM. Opportunities and responsibilities in pharmaceutical care. *Am J Hosp Pharm.* 1990; 47:533–43.
2. Manasse HR Jr. Medication use in an imperfect world: drug misadventuring as an issue of public policy, part 1. *Am J Hosp Pharm.* 1989; 46:929–44.
3. Davis NM, Cohen MR. Medication errors: causes and prevention. Huntingdon Valley, PA: Neil M. Davis Associates; 1981.
4. Zellmer WA. Preventing medication errors. *Am J Hosp Pharm.* 1990; 47:1755–6. Editorial.
5. Zellmer WA. ASHP plans for the future. *Am J Hosp Pharm.* 1986; 43:1921. Editorial.
6. American Society of Hospital Pharmacists. ASHP statement on the pharmacist's responsibility for distribution and control of drugs. *Am J Hosp Pharm.* 1991; 48:1782.
7. Lesar RS, Briceland LL, Delcoure K, et al. Medication prescribing errors in a teaching hospital. *JAMA.* 1990; 263:2329–34.
8. American Society of Hospital Pharmacists. ASHP technical assistance bulletin on hospital drug distribution and control. *Am J Hosp Pharm.* 1980; 37:1097–103.
9. Allan EL, Barker KN. Fundamentals of medication error research. *Am J Hosp Pharm.* 1990; 47:555–71.

10. Betz RP, Levy HB. An interdisciplinary method of classifying and monitoring medication errors. *Am J Hosp Pharm.* 1985; 42:1724–32.
11. Leape LL, Brennan TA, Laird N, et al. The nature of adverse events in hospitalized patients—results of the Harvard medical practice study II. *N Engl J Med.* 1991; 324:377–84.
12. Ingrim NB, Hokanson JA, Guernsey BG, et al. Physician noncompliance with prescription-writing requirements. *Am J Hosp Pharm.* 1983; 40:414–7.
13. Anderson RD. The physician's contribution to hospital medication errors. *Am J Hosp Pharm.* 1971; 28:18–25.
14. Cooper JW. Consulting to long-term care patients. In: Brown TR, Smith MC, eds. Handbook of institutional pharmacy practice. 2nd ed. Baltimore, MD: Williams & Wilkins; 1986:649–61.
15. Bedell SE, Dertz DC, Leeman D, et al. Incidence and characteristics of preventable iatrogenic cardiac arrest. *JAMA.* 1991; 265:2815–20.
16. Fuqua RA, Stevens KR. What we know about medication errors: a literature review. *J Nurs Qual Assur.* 1988; 3:1–17.
17. Intravenous Nurses Society. Intravenous nursing standards of practice. *J Intraven Nurs.* 1990; 13(Apr): Suppl.
18. American Society of Hospital Pharmacists. ASHP statement on the pharmacist's clinical role in organized health care settings. *Am J Hosp Pharm.* 1989; 46:2345–6.
19. American Society of Hospital Pharmacists. ASHP guidelines on the pharmacist's role in drug-use evaluation. *Am J Hosp Pharm.* 1988; 45:385–6.
20. American Society of Hospital Pharmacists. ASHP guidelines: minimum standard for pharmacies in institutions. *Am J Hosp Pharm.* 1985; 42:372–5.
21. American Society of Hospital Pharmacists. ASHP guidelines for obtaining authorization for documenting pharmaceutical care in patient medical records. *Am J Hosp Pharm.* 1989; 46:338–9.
22. Barker KN, Pearson RE. Medication distribution systems. In: Brown TR, Smith MC, eds. Handbook of institutional pharmacy practice. 2nd ed. Baltimore, MD: Williams & Wilkins; 1986:325–51.
23. Cohen MR, Davis NM. Assuring safe use of parenteral dosage forms in hospitals. *Hosp Pharm.* 1990; 25:913–5. Editorial.
24. American Society of Hospital Pharmacists. ASHP statement on the pharmacy and therapeutics committee. *Am J Hosp Pharm.* 1992; 49:2008–9.
25. Barker KN, Pearson RE, Hepler CD, et al. Effect of an automated bedside dispensing machine on medication errors. *Am J Hosp Pharm.* 1984; 41:1352–8.
26. American Society of Hospital Pharmacists. ASHP guidelines for selecting pharmaceutical manufacturers and suppliers. *Am J Hosp Pharm.* 1991; 48:523–4.
27. Joint Commission on Accreditation of Healthcare Organizations. 1992 Accreditation manual for hospitals, vol. 1: standards. Oakbrook Terrace, IL: Joint Commission on Accreditation of Healthcare Organizations; 1991.
28. American Society of Hospital Pharmacists. ASHP guidelines on pharmacist-conducted patient counseling. *Am J Hosp Pharm.* 1984; 41:331.
29. American Society of Hospital Pharmacists. ASHP statement on unit dose drug distribution. *Am J Hosp Pharm.* 1989; 46:2346.
30. Brennan TA, Leape LL, Laird NM, et al. Incidence of adverse events and negligence in hospitalized patients—results of the Harvard medical practice study I. *N Engl J Med.* 1991; 324:370–6.
31. American Society of Hospital Pharmacists. Medication errors: a closer look (videocassette). Bethesda, MD: American Society of Hospital Pharmacists; 1988. 20 min.
32. Folli HL, Poole RL, Benitz WE, et al. Medication error prevention by clinical pharmacists in two children's hospitals. *Pediatrics.* 1987; 19:718–22.
33. Blum KV, Abel SA, Urbanski CJ, et al. Medication error prevention by pharmacists. *Am J Hosp Pharm.* 1988; 45:1902–3.
34. American Society of Hospital Pharmacists and American Nurses Association. ASHP and ANA guidelines for collaboration of pharmacists and nurses in institutional care settings. *Am J Hosp Pharm.* 1980; 37:253–4.
35. Derewicz HJ. Color-coded packaging and medication errors. *Am J Hosp Pharm.* 1978; 35:1344–6. Letter.
36. Myers CE. Color-coding of drug product labels and packages. *Am J Hosp Pharm.* 1988; 45:1660.
37. Clifton GD, Record KE. Color coding of multisource products should be standardized or eliminated. *Am J Hosp Pharm.* 1988; 45:1066. Letter.
38. Proceedings of the 41st annual session of the ASHP House of Delegates. Report of the House of Delegates. *Am J Hosp Pharm.* 1990; 47:1807–17.
39. Barker KN, McConnell WE. The problems of detecting medication errors in hospitals. *Am J Hosp Pharm.* 1962; 19:361–9.
40. McClure ML. Human error—a professional dilemma. *J Prof Nurs.* 1991; 7:207.
41. Hartwig SC, Denger SD, Schneider PJ. A severity-indexed, incident-report based medication-error reporting program. *Am J Hosp Pharm.* 1991; 48:2611–6.
42. Maliekal J, Thornton J. A description of a successful computerized adverse drug reaction tracking program. *Hosp Formul.* 1990; 25:436–42.
43. Miwa LJ, Fandall RJ. Adverse drug reaction program using pharmacist and nurse monitors. *Hosp Formul.* 1986:1140–6.
44. Anderson ER Jr. Disciplinary action after a serious medication error. *Am J Hosp Pharm.* 1987; 44:2690, 2692.

---

[a]The mention of investigational drugs in the definition of level 4 errors (and nowhere else in the levels) may lead some to believe that any error involving an investigational drug should automatically be classified as a level 4 error. However, in discussing this issue at its September 1992 meeting, the ASHP Council on Professional Affairs noted that it is the effect on the patient (for a medication of any type) that really should determine what level of error is involved. Approved by the ASHP Board of Directors, June 23, 1993, reaffirming the version approved November 18, 1992. Developed by the ASHP Council on Professional Affairs.

The bibliographic citation for this document is as follows: American Society of Hospital Pharmacists. ASHP guidelines on preventing medication errors in hospitals. *Am J Hosp Pharm.* 1993; 50:305–14.

ASHP Guidelines on Preventing Medication Errors with Chemotherapy and Biotherapy

Purpose and Definitions

The purposes of these guidelines are to define best practices for the safe use of chemotherapy and biotherapy agents and to assist practitioners in improving their medication-use systems to prevent medication errors and patient harm from these agents. Although the guidelines are intended primarily to address use of chemotherapy and biotherapy agents in cancer treatment, some recommendations may be more broadly applicable across the medication-use system. These guidelines supplement ASHP's Guidelines on Preventing Medication Errors in Hospitals and address error prevention within diverse healthcare settings.[1] Further, these guidelines provide updated general guidance to include a standard definition of a "medication error" and applicable aspects of recommendations from the National Coordinating Council on Medication Error Reporting and Prevention (NCC MERP). NCC MERP's definition of a medication error is:

> any preventable event that may cause or lead to inappropriate medication use or patient harm while the medication is in the control of the healthcare provider, patient, or consumer. Such events may be related to professional practice, healthcare products, procedures, and systems, including prescribing; order communication; product labeling, packaging, and nomenclature; compounding; dispensing; distribution; administration; education; monitoring; and use.[2]

For the purposes of these guidelines, chemotherapy and biotherapy agents are defined as any medication that (1) is listed in section 10:00 of the American Hospital Formulary Service[3] (AHFS) pharmacologic–therapeutic classification system; (2) has at least one FDA-labeled indication to prevent or treat cancer, even if not listed in AHFS 10:00; or (3) is an investigational medication being used to prevent or treat cancer. This definition includes medications administered by any route. For simplicity, the term "chemotherapy" is used throughout these guidelines to refer to any chemotherapy or biotherapy medication that is used for cancer treatment.

The variety of therapies used in the treatment of cancer will only increase as advances are made, and healthcare organizations will confront the challenge of defining the products that require special procedures for safe use. Given the complexity of cancer care, it is recommended that such a list be as inclusive as possible. While these guidelines focus on the safe use of chemotherapy in treating cancer patients, in some situations chemotherapy agents may be used for nonmalignant diseases. In general, these additional safety procedures should apply for all uses of a chemotherapy agent, regardless of indication. Although they are specific to use of chemotherapy for cancer treatment, many of the principles of these guidelines also apply to cancer supportive care (e.g., treatment for pain and nausea). Finally, for organizations that conduct clinical research, investigational chemotherapy agents should be included in all safety systems established for FDA-approved chemotherapy agents.

These guidelines provide wide-ranging recommendations for preventing errors with chemotherapy agents in healthcare organizations, with an emphasis on hospitals, infusion centers, and ambulatory care clinics that offer direct pharmacy services. Nevertheless, it is strongly recommended that the guidance also be adopted by other settings, including physician office practices, home care, and patients self-administering oral and injectable therapies at home. Other guidance on the safe use of chemotherapy in the ambulatory setting has been published by the American Society of Clinical Oncology (ASCO) and the Oncology Nursing Society (ONS).[4] These recommendations cover known procedural, technical, and behavioral elements that could systematically reduce a healthcare organization's vulnerabilities to errors. Given use of an electronic medical record (EMR) increased from 3.8% of hospitals in 2007 to 8% in 2011, and computerized provider order entry (CPOE) use increased from 4% of hospitals in 2005 to 34% of hospitals in 2011,[5] additional information on the unique considerations of using CPOE for chemotherapy ordering has been included in these guidelines.

Strict adherence to good practice recommendations is not sufficient. Because the complexities of chemotherapy use afford unlimited opportunities for system failures, continuous diligence to verify accuracy is critical by all persons responsible for medication-use functions for chemotherapy. These guidelines focus on the medication-use responsibilities shared by and unique to specific professional healthcare disciplines, progressing from general to specific applications. The structure of the guidelines, by necessity, includes the repetition of some material, repeated and enhanced in specific sections and recommendations for different healthcare professionals. With the growth in use and number of oral chemotherapy agents on the market, a greater responsibility for care management is now placed on the patient. It is essential that applicable sections of these guidelines extend to patients so they can participate in protecting their own safety.

The guidelines contain the following major sections:

1. Recommendations for healthcare organizations,
2. Recommendations for multidisciplinary monitoring of medication use and verification,
3. Recommendations for prescribing systems and prescribers,
4. Recommendations for medication preparation and dispensing systems and roles for pharmacists,
5. Recommendations for medication administration systems and roles for nurses,
6. Recommendations for patient education,
7. Recommendations for manufacturers and regulatory agencies, and
8. Recommendations for identifying and managing medication errors.

Because of the complexity of and differences in practice settings and organizational arrangements, aspects of these guidelines may be more applicable to some practice settings than others. Pharmacists, physicians, nurses, and other healthcare providers should use their professional judgment in assessing and adapting the guidance to their own settings. These guidelines focus on safe use of a specific type of high-risk medications at various stages of the medication-use process and should be augmented as appropriate by other clinical and practice guidance, including ASHP statements and guidelines.

Background

Although the rate of medication errors for chemotherapy administered in the inpatient setting is not well documented, estimates of the frequency of errors with adult and pediatric chemotherapy in the ambulatory setting have been published. In one study, the overall chemotherapy error rate was 8.1 errors per 100 clinic visits.[6] For adults, errors were associated with 7.1% of clinic visits, and errors were associated with 18.8% of pediatric clinic visits. Errors occurred across all phases of the medication-use system, but administration (56%) and ordering (36%) errors were most common. Another study found a substantially lower rate (3%) of errors in chemotherapy orders in the outpatient infusion center at a major cancer center.[7] The error rate with oral chemotherapy agents is less well studied, but serious medication errors can occur with these therapies across all phases of the medication-use system.[8,9] Taylor and colleagues[10] documented a 9.9% error rate with oral chemotherapy given to pediatric patients with acute lymphoblastic leukemia. In this study, the errors occurred at the prescribing and administration steps.

Regardless of the exact rate of medication errors for chemotherapy agents, the safe use of these therapies presents unique challenges that demand additional safety systems. Chemotherapy agents often have a narrow therapeutic index, and they are used in complex, multidrug regimens. Complex dose calculations and adjustments are required, such as dosing per body surface area (BSA) and frequent adjustment according to renal function, toxicity, and other clinical parameters. Chemotherapy agents can cause serious toxicities at FDA-approved dosages and with FDA-approved administration schedules. Advocates for safe medication use, including oncology pharmacy specialists, have recommended that healthcare organizations improve their medication-use systems specifically to prevent medication errors with chemotherapy.[11-14]

Chemotherapy-related medication-error prevention remains a priority. Increasingly, many chemotherapy agents are administered outside the inpatient or ambulatory care setting. A growing number of patients are self-administering oral chemotherapy agents at home.[15] Thus, error-prevention strategies should be applicable to the diverse settings in which chemotherapy agents are used.

Surveys have indicated a need for improvement in medication-use systems for chemotherapy agents. One survey of major United States cancer centers indicated that the safety systems routinely used for infused chemotherapy agents are rarely applied to oral chemotherapy agents.[16] Another survey replicated this finding and indicated that many other recommended safety practices for chemotherapy agents are not followed.[17]

Recommendations for Healthcare Organizations

Optimal and comprehensive patient care, especially for patients receiving chemotherapy, requires the participation of multiple healthcare disciplines. Systems are necessary to coordinate the functions throughout the medication-use process of prescribing, preparing, dispensing, and administering of chemotherapy, and for educating and counseling patients.

Healthcare organizations where multiple disciplines are represented should establish committees with representatives from each discipline to develop policies and procedures for the medication-use process and to oversee its operation. These policies and procedures should include educational and competency requirements for persons with medication-use responsibilities; general system requirements that minimize vulnerabilities to errors; and periodic auditing of physicians', pharmacists', and nurses' proficiency with the system. Further, near misses and errors involving both commercial and investigational chemotherapy agents should be analyzed in all settings, and problems in the procedures that place patients at risk should be resolved.

Education, Competency, and Credentialing. All practice settings should establish policies and procedures ensuring that healthcare providers who prescribe, prepare, dispense, and administer chemotherapy and monitor patients receiving those medications are competent to perform those functions. For pharmacists and nurses, specific education and experience or board certification in a practice specialty may be included in the institution's credentialing process.

Employers should evaluate prospective employees' training and previous practice experiences for knowledge and mastery of the skills that are essential prerequisites for working with chemotherapy. Prerequisites for preparing and administering chemotherapy should include discipline-appropriate training in how to safely handle chemotherapy agents to protect themselves, co-workers, and patients. Competency to appropriately educate patients and monitor adherence with prescribed therapy should be assessed. Deficiencies in applicants' training and experience must be identified and remedied before new employees assume patient-care responsibilities. Ongoing training for new and current employees should emphasize collaboration among healthcare providers to ensure optimal patient care, outcomes, and worker safety.

All healthcare providers who prescribe, prepare, dispense, and administer chemotherapy and monitor patients receiving those medications should be oriented in their practice setting before commencing patient-care responsibilities. Orientation should include an introduction of new employees to all the departments, service providers, and functions that affect patient care. Each provider's roles and responsibilities should be identified, and expectations should be clarified about how healthcare providers from different disciplines will communicate and work collaboratively with respect to the chemotherapy medication-use process.

Further, healthcare organizations should require that all personnel who prescribe, prepare, dispense, administer, and handle hazardous drugs or contaminated materials, and all persons who may be exposed to hazardous drugs or contaminated materials in the course of their duties, complete job-appropriate training and evaluation. Employees should demonstrate competence, knowledge, and proficiency in techniques and procedures for safely handling (preventing exposure to oneself, other persons, and the environment, and managing accidental exposure) and disposing of hazardous drugs. Those competencies should be reassessed annually or more frequently if performance problems occur. It is the responsibility of medication-use system administrators and supervisory personnel to know the current government restrictions that limit or prohibit some healthcare providers from preparing and administering chemotherapy medications.

Healthcare providers who participate in the chemotherapy medication-use process and those who monitor patients receiving chemotherapy should be knowledgeable and have current information available about each of the following factors, relative to their scope of practice and job duties, on the chemotherapy used in their practice settings:

1. Names of chemotherapy drug formulations.
2. Indications and uses, and whether they comply with the FDA-approved labeling or approved compendia or are part of an investigational protocol.
3. Routes of administration.
4. Administration schedules.
5. Appropriate dosages, including dose adjustments for toxicity and, when applicable, constraints for the maximum dose of medication that can be safely given during a single administration, over a course of treatment, or cumulatively over a lifetime.
6. Appropriate storage conditions.
7. Potential adverse effects.
8. Potential drug interactions.
9. Procedures to use for handling hazardous substances.
10. Strategies for identifying and mitigating the risks of extravasation.

Every practice setting where cancer patients receive chemotherapy should provide opportunities for continuing professional and technical education related to chemotherapy management. A portion of the annual continuing education programs for healthcare providers specializing in oncology should be related to chemotherapy agents and their uses.

Providers who use drug-delivery devices (e.g., intravenous pumps and infusion controllers) to administer chemotherapy agents should be required to demonstrate competencies related to the clinical application, function (general use, operational limits, alarms), and care of these devices; problems that may occur with the devices; and troubleshooting.

Communication and Access to Information. Many errors occurring in the medication-use process are caused or aggravated by inadequate patient-specific information. Patients' medical records should be organized and made readily accessible for use by all providers who prescribe, dispense, and administer chemotherapy to enable independent confirmation that all prerequisite criteria have been met before commencing treatment. In some cases, individual disciplines may keep additional patient records that supplement the patient's primary medical record. For example, it has historically been the responsibility of pharmacists and pharmacies to maintain patient-specific medication profiles and records of medications that were prescribed and dispensed for each patient. Medication profiles for cancer patients should, at a minimum, include the following information:

1. Patient's name and a unique identifying code or number.
2. A brief medical history that identifies a patient's cancer diagnosis.
3. Known drug-related adverse events, allergies, and medication-, nutrient-, and food-related sensitivities.
4. Vital statistics that may affect treatment intensity, particularly those needed to calculate medication doses, including height, weight, BSA, age, sex, and pertinent laboratory values (e.g., serum creatinine, creatinine clearance, liver transaminases).
5. Data about all prescription, over-the-counter, and complementary and alternative medications used by a patient, including:
   - All relevant dates, including when the medication(s) were:
     - prescribed (if it differs from the date they were prepared and administered),
     - prepared and dispensed (if it differs from the date the medications were administered), and
     - administered (use planned date for patient self-administered agents);
   - Drug identity;
   - Drug dosage and reason(s) for any dose adjustments, as appropriate;
   - Total drug dosage administered per unit interval (e.g., day, week, treatment cycle);
   - Administration route;
   - Administration schedule as a function of the treatment plan (e.g., every 3 hours, days 1, 8, and 15, with the specific treatment dates);
   - Rate of administration (when relevant);
   - Prescribed duration of use (e.g., number of doses to administer; number of treatment hours, days, or weeks); and
   - The product manufacturer's identity, product lot numbers, and (when practicable) expiration dates for drugs dispensed from that facility.
6. Additional ingredients and diluting agents and the amounts used in extemporaneously compounded medications.
7. Primary references that describe the treatment regimen.
8. An up-to-date treatment history, including:
   - The treatment cycle or course number for each treatment repetition,
   - The dates on which a patient last received treatment,
   - How previous treatment was tolerated, and
   - The cumulative amount of drug previously administered for medications with established absolute cumulative dosage limits (e.g., anthracyclines, bleomycin) or constraints against repeated administration as a function of time.

Other settings, such as ambulatory, home, specialty, and managed care organizations are vulnerable to the same communication and interpretation errors that occur in hospitals. These settings and organizational arrangements, however, could introduce additional opportunities for errors of omission and duplication when treatments and other services are provided at multiple locations and by more than one participating provider or group of providers. In hospitals and integrated health systems, patient-specific medical information has traditionally been communicated through a single comprehensive medical record. In contrast, providers in private practice, home care, and managed care organizations generally cannot rely on the availability of a comprehensive medical record, because medication prescribing, preparing, and administering may occur at geographically separate facilities.

Local policies should be developed to ensure that orders for a patient's chemotherapy medications are transmitted accurately and completely, that medication reconciliation takes place at all transitions in care, and that patient confidentiality is protected.[18] Electronic means of communication are recommended to transmit up-to-date, accurate, and comprehensive patient-specific medical information among providers. Thus, data entered into this electronic system by any one provider are immediately available to all. Until a single unifying network becomes available for all healthcare providers, portable printed and electronic records (including an accurate, updated patient medication list) that ensure patient safety and confidentiality must be devised.

Schedule Coordination. Because oncology patients often receive care from more than one healthcare provider, their primary provider, care coordinator, or patient navigator should coordinate patient care with other providers and facilities. Efficient organizational systems should have someone to coordinate a patient's healthcare needs with their various healthcare providers' schedules.

Standardize Medication Ordering. To the extent possible, medication prescribing, preparation, dispensing, and administration should be standardized. Healthcare organizations should adopt and incorporate national standards into their practice. Patient-care facilities should develop and use standardized preprinted medication-order forms or forms that are retrievable from a computerized database for requesting frequently used chemotherapy treatments and treatment-related services. Well-designed standardized, regimen-specific, medication-order forms decrease potential errors by organizing treatment information in a clear, consistent, and uniform format. As discussed further below, CPOE provides standardization opportunities and other potential benefits.

Standardized forms should be developed collaboratively with input from the healthcare providers who prescribe, prepare, and administer chemotherapy medications. Forms should be preprinted with the entire treatment plan and include items such as generic drug names, specifications for drug dosage and dosage modifications as a function of patient-specific variables, and administration routes and schedules. Forms should include the entire treatment plan, including oral medications that may be filled by an outside provider and patient self-administered. Prescription forms should also include space for prescribers to note laboratory test results that affect dosages, administration rates, and treatment duration. These forms may also permit prescribers to schedule laboratory tests and request other services for comprehensive patient care. A multidisciplinary process should be in place for the development, implementation and maintenance of these standard order forms, including independent double checks of the content. (An "independent double check" is a process in which two qualified individuals separately check, alone and apart from each other, an item or action, and then compare results to ensure the desired outcomes.[19]) These forms should include the revision date, as appropriate, to allow everyone involved to identify and validate that they are using the most current version.

Standardized medication-order forms, including prescriptions for oral therapies administered by patients, simplify and expedite medication ordering by requiring prescribers to supply only patient-specific information, such as

1. Patient's name and unique identifying number (e.g., medical record number) or date of birth according to institutional policies regarding patient identification.
2. Date and time the order was generated.
3. Time and date treatments are to be administered.
4. Cycle and day number.
5. Current patient-specific laboratory values (as defined by institutional policy regarding the timeframe for which laboratory test results are considered acceptable to use to determine whether chemotherapy can be initiated).
6. Patient-specific dosing parameters (i.e., height, weight, dosing weight, BSA).
7. Medication generic name.
8. Planned medication dosages and administration rates as a function of patient-specific factors and the calculated doses and rates to be administered.
9. Route of administration (including the venous access device type, if applicable).
10. Patient's allergies and medication and nutrient sensitivities.
11. Prescriber's name and signature.
12. Prescriber's telephone, pager, or fax number (or another means to communicate with the prescriber).

Preprinted forms should specify, by protocol number or publication reference, the treatment that is to be administered.[11,20,21]

For investigational chemotherapy treatments, standardized forms should also include the study name, protocol number, and patient-specific study number, as applicable. Color-coded forms, for example, may be used to designate different types of treatment, such as commercially marketed chemotherapy and investigational medications.

Standardized order forms eliminate many of the issues related to misinterpreting medication orders that are commonly associated with nonstandardized orders; however, healthcare providers must be aware that interpretation errors may still result from illegible handwriting. Multipurpose preprinted forms that list chemotherapy medications alphabetically may also contribute to prescribing errors when two similar drug names appear in close proximity. Since lined paper can obscure the details of a prescriber's orders, preprinted forms should be printed on unlined paper.

Self-replicating forms (e.g., carbon copies, no-carbon required paper) can produce copies that are difficult to read, and these forms should be avoided. Further, poor quality fax transmissions of these order sets should also be avoided. Providers who prepare and administer medications on the basis of a copy of a prescriber's order should be wary of ambiguous notations, artifact markings, and omissions on the copy. Each facility should restrict chemotherapy ordering (e.g., access to medication-order forms) to providers with the appropriate clinical privileges. Healthcare organizations that depend on standardized forms should review all forms on a regularly defined schedule and must ensure that only the most current versions of standardized forms are available and that obsolete forms are recalled and destroyed.

CPOE. CPOE should be implemented to further enhance the safety of the chemotherapy-use process. CPOE offers an opportunity to introduce new safety features into the chemotherapy prescribing process, but implementation of CPOE for chemotherapy providers appears to lag other areas.[5,22,23]

CPOE provides many of the same safety and convenience features as preprinted orders, such as order legibility, standardization across practitioners, chemotherapy scheduling and sequencing, and inclusion of support care medications and some patient demographics. CPOE also provides additional benefits that are not available with a paper system. For example, the ability to control user access to various sections of the system can be very useful in managing prescriber privileges, especially to limit which staff may order chemotherapy or prescribe specific investigational drugs. CPOE improves efficiency by allowing data to be accessed by different providers in different locations at the same time, and it serves as a guide for the ordering provider via clinical decision support features and serves to structure workflow (i.e., specific steps in subsequent preparation, dispensing, and administration). CPOE provides benefits over a paper system, including additional safety checks not possible with paper, but diligence by the prescriber and careful independent checks of the resulting orders are still essential when using CPOE for chemotherapy.

CPOE for chemotherapy must be implemented with great care. CPOE represents a major change in an organization's chemotherapy use process and workflow, and it may introduce new errors that may not have existed in the traditional handwritten process.[24] In a well-established and mature chemotherapy-use system, one must be certain that the dramatic changes produced by CPOE do not threaten the safety of the chemotherapy-use process during the implementation period.

To gain the benefits of CPOE, there are several key principles of implementation and continued development that must be considered, such as standardization, reduction in ambiguity, safety over convenience, and an evaluation of workflow effects.[25,26] When feasible, formal process redesign methods should be applied before implementing CPOE for chemotherapy. Given the patient safety risks involved, a formal failure modes and effects analysis (FMEA) should be considered, as such an approach has been successfully used.[23,27] When reviewing the capabilities of a CPOE system, pertinent patient data must be available to all providers. These data include provider notes, laboratory values, flow sheets that show prior chemotherapy and medications administered, and consent forms, among others. Workflow should be considered when determining how data are displayed and in what order the data are presented. This workflow begins at the point the order is entered by the prescriber, followed by pharmacist review, nurse review, drug administration, and the documentation of the effect on the patient. The number and type of checks required to verify the order should be reviewed with consideration of the CPOE capabilities and workflow. Some institutional chemotherapy policies dictate a final review and approval (informally known as "OK to Give" or final sign-off) of the chemotherapy order by an attending physician or other senior clinician.

Clinical decision support is another important consideration for CPOE.[26] Clinical decision support can guide the prescriber through various phases of the ordering process and include specific chemotherapy considerations based on individual patient parameters, such as laboratory values, comorbid conditions, hydration requirements, and the need for supportive care medications (e.g., antiemetics). Appropriate alerts, such as allergies, drug interactions, duplicate therapies, and maximum doses, should be incorporated as appropriate and be consistent with the institution's overall plan for implementing clinical decision support alerts. The duration of the order set, a cycle or specific weeks of therapy, should be standardized, and clear criteria to treat or continue treatment must be documented for the patient to continue treatment.

Users should plan for improvements and alterations to the CPOE system after implementation. Changes should be considered by a multidisciplinary team and include provider feedback as well as data from continuous monitoring of the order entry process, including safety reporting and near-miss data. Continuous review and improvement are multidisciplinary processes and need to include both clinicians and information systems staff.[28]

Implementing CPOE for chemotherapy is an important step, and CPOE should be leveraged to provide guidance for prescribers ordering chemotherapy. By definition, the prescriber is entering orders directly into the system, and safety can be improved because there is usually no intermediary who must interpret the orders and enter them into another information system. Since CPOE clearly reflects and communicates the intent of the prescriber, properly planned CPOE should give prescribers the ability to select a specific regimen or protocol that delineates the necessary information to produce a clear and accurate drug regimen.[28] These custom ordering screens are typically called "order sets" or "templates," and they are essential to safely using CPOE for chemotherapy.[23]

Depending on the system and resources devoted to order sets, additional information (e.g., requirements for laboratory values, supportive care, dose reductions, or dose-limiting parameters) may be part of the order sets. Information such as dosing (e.g., mg/kg or mg/m^2, diluents, or concentration, if appropriate) should be part of the order set to facilitate dose verification by the pharmacist. The system may also be able to prevent ordering the wrong route of administration or append a warning message to specific orders, averting such potentially deadly mistakes as inadvertently prescribing vincristine intrathecally.

Transitioning complex order sets from paper to a CPOE system poses various challenges. Care must be taken in designing ordering templates, because an undetected design error may result in multiple mistakes. Prescribers and investigators (in the case of an investigational protocol ordering set) should be involved in the checking of the template, and ideally they should be asked to sign off on the particular ordering screens before they are put into wide use. The building of these orders sets is not a simple process, especially pediatric order sets and investigational drug regimens.[29]

Cancer chemotherapy often includes a complicated sequencing of drugs and scheduling of the regimen. Growth factors need to be scheduled at the proper time to be effective and not interfere with the mechanism of action of the chemotherapy or biotherapy regimen. Unfortunately, if there is a delay in the scheduled administration times, some systems may not allow a simple click or two to reschedule multiple days and doses, in contrast to older methods in which a prescriber could just write "delay chemotherapy by 6 hours."

If possible, the CPOE system and electronic health record should allow for an electronic check and documentation of the independent checks by the pharmacist, nurse, and any others involved in the chemotherapy use process. A notation in the system alerting the nurse or prescriber that the order is under review by the pharmacist is very helpful. Systems should allow senior physician final approval (i.e., "OK to give" or final sign-off) before action is taken by the pharmacy.

Careful thought is necessary and critical when using a CPOE system, and the potential for error still exists. Prior to order entry, the prescriber must consider whether a dose reduction is needed based on a change in laboratory values or organ function. If an investigational protocol is involved, the prescriber must select the correct cycle or dose level, if dose escalation is necessary. CPOE systems may be able to guide the prescriber, but they cannot make the correct choice for him or her. Another potential source of error is the autocalculation feature of some systems. The system can utilize the latest height and weight to calculate BSA or use the patient's weight to calculate the proper dose. However, an incorrect height or weight entry can result in a dosing error. It is easy for prescribers to miss small but significant changes that could result from data entry errors. Systems may be able to prevent data entry error by displaying an alert when data differ from a previous entry by a certain percentage or final dose amount.

Emergency contingency plans for how to communicate chemotherapy orders in the event the CPOE is not available (e.g., power outage, system failure) should be developed and tested. Whenever possible, the contingency plan should replicate the CPOE process (e.g., paper orders replicating CPOE screens) as much as possible to minimize introduction of new risks. Training and awareness of the emergency contingency plan should be part of the orientation and annual competency plan for all providers.

Implementation of a CPOE system presents many new challenges for the health (or patient) care team. Although remotely entering orders in a CPOE system may be convenient for some, it may also reduce the face-to-face contact of writing in the chart during rounds or while on the patient-care unit, reducing the opportunity for personal interactions between healthcare professionals. While CPOE has been shown to prevent prescribing errors, it is not a panacea, and diligence and independent checks are still essential to a safe chemotherapy process using CPOE. Knowing some of its pitfalls in advance will aid in the design and use of all the features available in a CPOE system, especially for high-risk therapies such as chemotherapy. The success of CPOE depends on having high-level administrative, clinical, financial, and information technology support. It is critical front-line staff have a significant role in the development, implementation, and monitoring of CPOE.[28]

Verbal Orders for Chemotherapy Medications. Except for discontinuing treatment, medication-use systems should not permit healthcare providers to use or accept verbal orders to commence or modify a chemotherapy medication.[11,12,30] Verbal communication for chemotherapy orders, whether face-to-face or over the telephone, circumvent an essential checkpoint in the order-verification process, whether they are communicated directly to persons who prepare medications or received and reported by one or more intermediaries.[31]

Stat Orders for Chemotherapy Medications. It is rarely necessary to begin chemotherapy treatment as quickly as possible (i.e., "stat"). In general, stat orders for chemotherapy may compromise essential order-verification safeguards and are almost never appropriate. Except for urgently required treatments, chemotherapy medication preparation and administration should be scheduled when staffing is adequate to ensure that appropriate safety checks are performed during compounding, verification, and administration. It is essential that patient care is not compromised under any circumstances.

Standardize Dosage Calculation. Medication-use systems should establish whether drug dosages should be routinely calculated as a function of actual, ideal (lean), or adjusted body weight and develop standardized criteria that direct dosage calculation as a function of this weight. ASCO has produced guidelines for dosing chemotherapy in obese patients that suggest using actual body weight if the intent is cure.[32] Institutions should consider this information when deciding on dose calculation standards. Institutions should also define policies for other situations, such as in pediatric or hematopoietic stem cell transplant patients, where adjusted-weight dosing is used, or when cure is not the goal. Investigational protocols may specify treatment parameters different from institutional parameters. In all cases, the treatment plans and medication orders should indicate whether patients' actual or ideal body weight was used in calculating drug dosages and identify the equation from which dosages were calculated.

Methods should be standardized for calculating BSA and ideal body weight, rounding calculated results (e.g., drug dosages and administration rates), and changing dosages and administration rates in response to changes in patients' weight and stature. For dosage and administration rates calculated from pharmacokinetic data, the mathematical equations that describe how calculated values were derived should appear in the treatment plans and medication orders.

Standardize the Content of Medication Orders. Standards should be established for the content of an acceptable medication order, requirements for patient-specific measurements, and data that must be included on medication-order forms.[33,34] The following standards are recommended:

1. All orders for patient-care services should be clearly dated and timed.
2. When ordering chemotherapy medications, the generic drug name (as approved by the United States Adopted Names [USAN] program) should be used. Brand names are not acceptable unless they aid in identifying combination drug products or a particular

drug formulation (e.g., to distinguish between liposomal and nonliposomal product formulations).

3. The dosage form should be specified.
4. Orders for medications should include the patient-specific data from which drug doses are calculated (height, weight, BSA, laboratory test results). When drug dosages and schedules are modified for current or anticipated pathologies, treatment plans and medication orders should explicitly identify the factors on which treatment modifications are based. If the order is for chemotherapy as part of the clinical trial, identifying information for the protocol should be included in the order.
5. Drug dosages and calculated doses should be expressed in metric notation. The word units should never be abbreviated in medication orders where drug dosages and administration rates are expressed in biological activity units (e.g., aldesleukin, asparaginase, bleomycin). Leading zeros (e.g., 0.3 mg) should be used for numbers less than one. Trailing zeros should never be used.
6. Medication orders should specify the drug dosage and calculated dose according to the "container rule" (i.e., the specified and calculated dose is the amount prepared in and administered from a single container).[20]
7. Administration vehicle solutions and volumes should be specified, unless standard solutions and volumes have been established.
8. The administration route should be specified.
9. The administration rate should be specified, when relevant.
10. The administration schedule and the duration of treatment should be specified. Treatment plans and medication orders should specify the interval between repeated doses, the days on which each dose is to be given within a treatment cycle or course, and the total length of a treatment cycle or course.
11. The dates and times when drug administration is to commence, or the temporal sequence in which each medication is to be administered, should be specified. When 1200 is written as 12 a.m. or 12 p.m., it may be incorrectly interpreted. Directions indicating events for 1200 should be written as 12:00 noon or 12:00 midnight, or expressed in the 24-hour system.
12. The medical record should contain a justification for the chemotherapy treatment plan (e.g., a reference to FDA product labeling, the primary literature, institutionally approved guidelines, national consensus guidelines, or an investigational protocol); similar information may be included in the medication order to provide additional clarification.
13. Although healthcare providers have traditionally used abbreviations, acronyms, and nicknames to describe chemotherapy medications and treatment regimens, the practice is potentially dangerous and should be avoided. Abbreviations for drug names, scheduling information, and directions for medication use should be prohibited in medication orders. Nonstandard abbreviations, Latin abbreviations, and apothecaries' weights and measures should not be used in orders for chemotherapy medications. Whenever possible, measurement units should be expressed in metric notation.

Therefore, a medication order that complies with these recommendations would appear as follows for a patient with a BSA of 2 m^2: Methotrexate injection 100 mg/m^2/dose = 200 mg in 100 mL 5% dextrose injection/dose, administer by continuous intravenous infusion over 24 hours, every 48 hours for three doses days 1, 3, and 5. Start at 0800 on April 1, 2014.

Establish Dosage Limits and Acceptable Routes of Administration. Medication-use systems should include utilization limits for chemotherapy medications. Constraints should be developed to limit maximum chemotherapy drug dosages and administration routes and schedules. Multidisciplinary peer review should be completed before established drug administration limits are exceeded.[11,12] These constraints should include the maximum amount of a chemotherapy drug that may be administered as a single dose, the maximum amount that may be administered during a defined time interval (including maximum administration rates for parenterally administered medications and maximum dose per day for oral therapy), and the routes by which each drug should be administered.[35] For example, some institutions cap the dose of vincristine at 2 mg or limit the lifetime dose of doxorubicin to 550 mg/m^2 in patients with normal cardiac function.

Constraints for dosage and administration rate may be defined by treatment regimens and protocols and may vary among protocols. In contrast, the types of treatments administered in some practice settings may be consistently similar, permitting the establishment of absolute maximum dose limits within that practice setting.

Limits should also be established for the maximum amount of a chemotherapy drug that may be administered during one treatment course or cycle and, when appropriate, the maximum amount of drug that may be administered to a single patient within his or her lifetime.[11] In addition, dosage limits should be established for chemotherapy medications used in specific combination regimens (defined for each drug) in which clinical toxicities may be exacerbated by combining agents with overlapping adverse-effect profiles.

Chemotherapy drug-use limits should appear prominently in printed treatment descriptions (e.g., protocol summaries, care maps, schematic treatment diagrams) and on printed medication-order forms and computer-based medication-order templates. Active clinical decision support that alerts healthcare providers whenever an order for chemotherapy medications exceeds defined limits would be ideal.[36] For patients who receive chemotherapy medications for which cumulative dosage limits have been established, cumulative dosage data should be constantly updated in their permanent medical records and in any supplementary records. Patients' cumulative dosage data should be audited and independently confirmed by healthcare providers when verifying orders for chemotherapy medications.[11,37]

In each healthcare organization, the medication-use system should include a multidisciplinary committee that oversees matters related to medication-use limits. The committee should proactively develop and establish policies and procedures for resolving disagreements related to patient treatment among providers; whether medications should be prepared, dispensed, and administered if a discrepancy cannot be resolved; and how medication-use-related disputes are to be resolved. Committee membership should comprise all providers who have responsibilities in the medication-use process in the organization.[11]

Investigational Chemotherapy Medications. Cancer patients often receive investigational (i.e., experimental) anticancer treatments at facilities participating in clinical trials. Consideration must be given to ensure that the same safety precautions and checks that are used for FDA-approved chemotherapy therapies apply similarly to prescribing, preparing, dispensing, and administering oral and parenteral investigational medications and monitoring patients who receive those therapies.

Facility administrators should ensure that adequate staff is maintained to support an investigational drug program.[31] Ideally, nurses and pharmacists should be involved early in the process of developing clinical protocols involving the use of commercially marketed and investigational chemotherapy medications.[38] Early involvement helps ensure that chemotherapy regimens are expressed in a fashion to mitigate errors, and investigational medications are prepared and administered in accordance with local policies and procedures. Nurses and pharmacists should be voting members on regulatory and review committees that evaluate the scientific and ethical treatment of patients receiving chemotherapy medications and monitor investigational therapies (e.g., institutional review boards).[11]

Because a protocol governs and supplies the rules for drug use in clinical trials, an up-to-date copy of the study protocol should be available for review at all sites where medications are prepared and administered. All staff should be informed through inservice education programs before new protocols are implemented. Inservice programs and study-related information should be provided by persons associated with the investigational study (e.g., principal investigator, associate investigators, protocol chairperson, study-coordinating personnel). If an investigational protocol is to be conducted at more than one site within a health system, procedures should be developed to ensure that up-to-date information is available at all study sites where patients receive protocol-directed care.

Procedures for supplying healthcare providers with information about patients' dose assignments, drug dosage, and schedule modifications should also be devised. A separate procedure should be established allowing independent dose-checking activity among all disciplines involved in the medication-use process for investigational drugs.

Intrathecal Administration. Administration of chemotherapy via the intrathecal route is necessary for certain treatment regimens. Given the high risk associated with intrathecal administration (e.g., vincristine intrathecal administration is fatal), specific considerations apply to intrathecal administration of chemotherapy:

1. Prescribing should be limited to providers with institutional privileges to prescribe chemotherapy.
2. Drug labels should clearly indicate that the chemotherapy is only intended for intrathecal administration, including ancillary labels. Vinca alkaloid drugs must contain label warnings to avoid intrathecal administration.
3. Medications that will be administered intrathecally should be placed in separate bags from medications administered by other routes (e.g., intravenous, subcutaneous, intramuscular) in the pharmacy. Upon delivery to the unit, intrathecal medications should be stored separately from medications with other routes of administration.
4. Providers administering intrathecal chemotherapy should do so in a setting that has been designated for that procedure. An independent double check by two qualified individuals should be completed prior to administration.

Recommendations for Multidisciplinary Monitoring of Medication Use and Verification

Independent medication-order verification is an essential safeguard that ensures the accuracy and appropriateness of medical treatment. It is imperative that healthcare providers resolve any questions related to medication orders before treatment commences. Providers should recognize that medication-order verification and other system safeguards ensure patients' safety.[11,20,37] Lack of information about patients and their medications has been described as the most frequent cause of medication errors.[24,39] In order to independently verify prescribers' orders for medications, all persons who prepare and administer chemotherapy medications and those who monitor patients who have received chemotherapies should also have access to complete, up-to-date copies of treatment protocols and patient-specific data, including home medication lists.[11,30,37] Drug information and reference materials should be readily available to all persons who provide patient care.

Each healthcare provider has a responsibility to share information with other providers and consultants to ensure patient safety and an optimal treatment outcome. Policies that regulate treatment verification standards should describe how prescribers, medically responsible and senior authorizing physicians, pharmacists and pharmacy technicians, nurses, and other persons who are responsible for transcribing and transmitting medication orders should interact and communicate information.

Providers who prescribe, prepare, dispense, and administer chemotherapy medications should perform independent double checks at defined points in the chemotherapy use process. Treatment-verification systems may incorporate computerized medication-order safety checks but should also include independent manual double checks.[11,31] Ideally, computerized systems (e.g., CPOE) are used to calculate and verify dosages and the rate and route of administration for chemotherapy drug orders and to screen medication orders for compliance with dosage limits. In addition to facilitating chemotherapy-order processing, computer software can also serve as a double check on prescribers' orders. Systems requiring pharmacists to transcribe prescribers' medication orders into a computerized or manual drug-ordering system should have a second person, preferably a pharmacist, recheck all order-processing documents and product labeling before a drug product is dispensed. In situations in which a pharmacist is not available, a prescriber or nurse may serve as the second check.

Providing medications to patients includes five discrete steps: prescribing, preparation, dispensing, administration, and monitoring. The ideal verification system has ten established checkpoints to ensure that an chemotherapy drug is accurately prescribed, prepared, dispensed, and administered to the patient for whom it was intended (Figure 1). Different individuals should complete each check so that no single person bears responsibility for checking his or her own work.

Prescribing Chemotherapy Medications (Checkpoint 1). Healthcare providers who prescribe, prepare, and administer chemotherapy drugs should be familiar with the entire treatment regimen. A prescriber should order all the medications necessary for the entire treatment regimen, including hydration and supportive care orders, at the same time and prior to administration of any of the medications. When prescribing chemotherapy regimens based on a patient's weight (or BSA, which relies on weight), weight data and trends in patient weight should be evaluated to be sure the correct information is used. In CPOE, order sets may assist in completing all relevant orders of a treatment regimen at the same time. Requiring all treatment details in advance ensures that orders can be checked for completeness and accuracy and compliance with planned treatment.

Institutions should establish policies regarding whether chemotherapy may be prescribed by physicians-in-training (e.g., medical fellows) and nonphysician healthcare providers with prescribing privileges (e.g., nurse practitioners, physician assistants). If the institution allows prescriptions by these individuals, these orders should be verified by at least one medically responsible person, other than the prescriber, who is knowledgeable about medical oncology.

When orders for chemotherapy drugs must be countersigned by a second medically responsible individual, the person who countersigns the medication orders should critically evaluate each order for a chemotherapy treatment. This is checkpoint 1. The orders should be compared with patient-specific data and verified against original reference sources that describe the treatment regimen (e.g., a published article,

Figure 1. Medication-order verification system. These established checkpoints ensure a chemotherapy medication is accurately prescribed, prepared, dispensed, administered, and monitored.

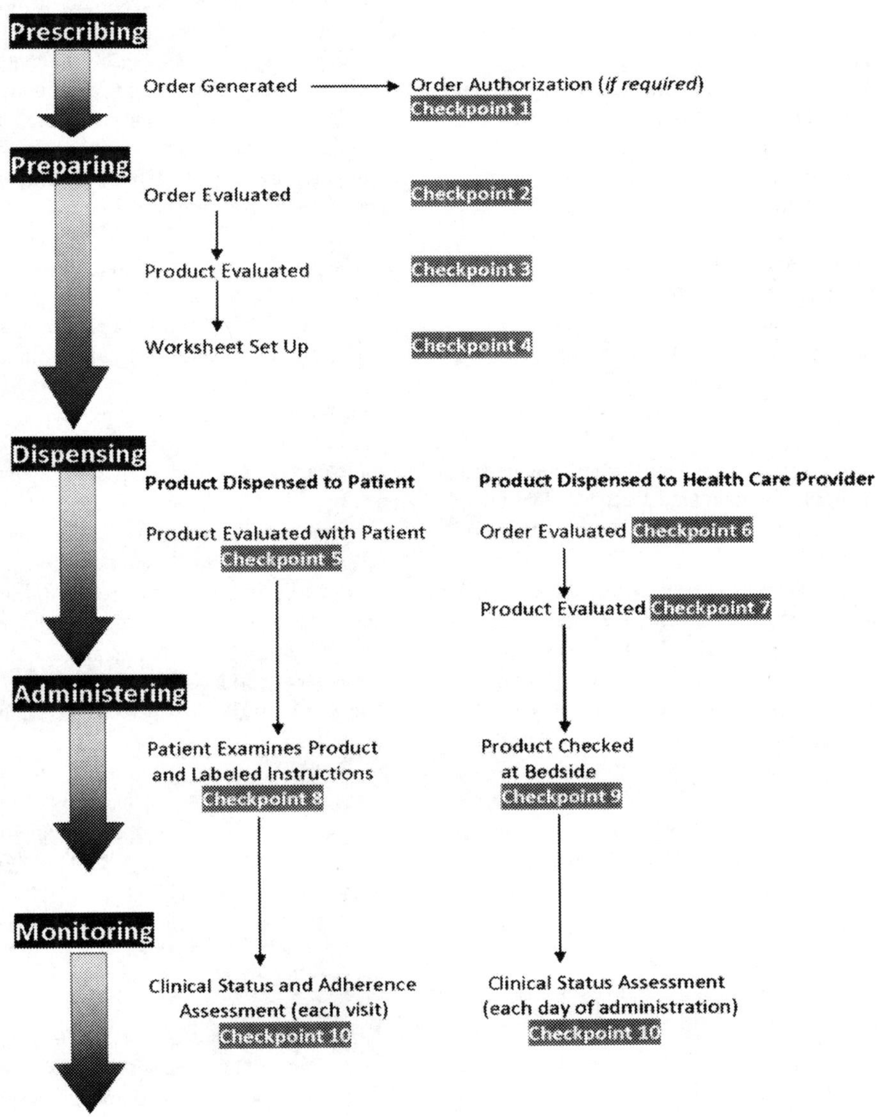

validated standard reference text, investigational protocol). If the patient is taking part in an investigational study, verification of enrollment onto the trial and of informed consent should be reviewed.

Preparing Chemotherapy Medications (Checkpoints 2–4). Checkpoint 2 requires persons receiving a prescriber's order for chemotherapy medications to review the original medication orders and independently verify them against published standards (e.g., product package labeling, reports published in professional journals, treatment protocols, standard reference textbooks) and determine appropriateness based on patient-specific information. The dose per container and the total course dose should be verified at this checkpoint.

Because erroneous information sometimes appears in published information, orders for noninvestigational chemotherapy medications should be verified against the primary reference in which the specific treatment was described (e.g., published reports, study protocols, meeting proceedings). If a primary reference is not available, the treatment regimen should be confirmed with a resource that previously had been validated as accurately describing the planned treatment (locally compiled handbooks, guides, and compendia) or at least two alternative publications, including reviews and reference textbooks.[11,34] Investigational drug doses and administration schedules must be verified against a study protocol that was approved by all relevant regulatory agencies and study sponsors (e.g., institutional review board, National Cancer Institute, FDA). Protocol amendments should be distributed immediately and be readily available for reference. In addition, order templates should be updated as soon as possible, especially for drug dose or preparation changes.

Although preprinted order forms and CPOE preclude the necessity of repeatedly verifying drug names, dosages, routes, and schedules, all medication orders should be evaluated for completeness, compliance with the planned regimen, and, during repeated courses, deviations from previous treatments by following these recommendations:

1. The date a patient was last treated and the next planned treatment date should be compared to ensure that an appropriate interval has elapsed since treatment was last administered.
2. Measurements from which a patient's medication dosage and administration rate are calculated should be confirmed (e.g., height, weight, BSA). Institutions should develop policies and procedures regarding when patient-specific data (e.g., height, weight, BSA) should be re-measured. It is important to review trends in height and weight as a double check to ensure there were no errors in documentation.
3. Appropriate laboratory test and physical assessment values should be evaluated and primary treatment references should be consulted to determine whether they are within acceptable ranges or if treatment modifications are indicated.
4. A patient's allergy, drug sensitivity, and adverse drug effect histories and his or her current medication profile should be evaluated for potential drug interactions with planned chemotherapy treatment.

For patients who receive treatment in clinical trials in which more than one primary or ancillary treatments are prescribed (e.g., dose- and duration-escalating studies), treatment assignment and dosage and administration schedule modifications should be confirmed with at least one person directly associated with the clinical trial, other than the prescriber (e.g., the principal investigator, an associate investigator, research nurses or pharmacists, a study coordinator or chairperson). The prescriber should be consulted when expected treatment modifications were not ordered or when nonstandard modifications were prescribed.

Instructions for diluents, drug administration sequence and duration, number of doses, and starting date and time should be checked. To ensure that appropriate ancillary and supportive medications that facilitate chemotherapy drug delivery and those required by protocol have been prescribed and are complete and accurate (e.g., premedications, hydration, cytoprotectant and "rescue" medications, antiemetics, hematopoietic growth factors), their orders should be reviewed and confirmed. Discrepancies between prescribed medications and planned treatment should be brought to the prescriber's attention and resolved before medication preparation proceeds.

At checkpoint 3, after treatment orders have been verified, all work related to medication-order processing and preparation accuracy should be routinely documented in a standardized format, either on paper or electronically. Drug preparation work sheets (sometimes referred to as work cards or admixture or compounding logs, sheets, and cards) identify the drug products prepared for each patient and the persons who prepared and checked the medications. Although layout and design may vary among work sheets, and data may be organized as a continuous log in which each drug product appears on separate, consecutive lines or as a separate record for each patient, all work sheets should detail the techniques used in preparing the drug products. They should also identify special preparation and dispensing information, such as the indication of special product containers, requirements for filtration, the need for special diluents, intermediate dilution steps, and how and when administration sets should be attached to the drug product container. Order processing, drug preparation, and processing records should be confirmed by a second individual (preferably a pharmacist).[11,12] The calculations written on preparation work sheets should be independently verified by a second healthcare provider who did not prepare the work sheet. Independent verification should include checking the work sheet for completeness and accuracy of content, with particular attention given to special preparation instructions. A checklist, whether paper or electronic, that identifies the necessary elements in chemotherapy drug preparation may be a helpful reference (Figure 2).[11] Technology can serve as a surrogate checklist, if practitioners follow procedures in using appropriately developed and applied software.

At checkpoint 4, drug products should be checked, after preparation, against both the preparation work sheet and the original order by an individual who was not involved in preparing the work sheet. Checklists may also be helpful for this step.[11]

Dispensing Chemotherapy Medications (Checkpoint 5). Checkpoint 5 requires persons dispensing medications to patients or caregivers for outpatient use to verify a patient's

Figure 2. Chemotherapy drug preparation checklists.

Checklist for Initial Setup of Chemotherapy Drug Work Card

This form should be completed on paper or electronically by the pharmacist checking the work card. Place check mark (or N/A) in each space after each check is completed. Your check marks and initials at the bottom of this work sheet are your personal assurance that you checked all these items for accuracy in the setup and transcription of information onto the work card. Each drug requires a separate checklist.

Patient ___________________ Drug _______________

Start date _____________

Administration time _____________

Stop date _____________

Duration _____________

Correct drug name _____________

Number of doses ______

Dose _____________

Drug concentration _____________

Drug volume _____________

Diluent _____________

Volume of diluent ______Overfill ______Drug in overfill ____

Expiration time _____________

Special delivery devices (tubing, cassette, container, etc.)

Correct route of administration _________________________

Correct line type, as appropriate ______________________

Correct mixing instructions (special directions, e.g., "Do Not Filter") _____________

Auxiliary label information (e.g., "Do Not Refrigerate," "Use In-line Filter," "For Intrathecal Use Only") ___________

Correct total volume _____________

Pharmacist's initials ______________ Date ______________

This record should remain with the work card for the duration of the order and be saved for the supervisor for review after discontinuation of the order.

Supervisor's initials ______________ Date ______________

Continued on next page

identity when a medication is dispensed. Patients who self-administer their medications or personal caregivers should visually examine the medication, confirm whether its appearance meets their expectations, and compare its instructions with information they received from their healthcare providers (e.g., a chemotherapy calendar).

Dispensing and Administering Chemotherapy Medications (Checkpoints 6–9). At checkpoint 6, before starting treatment, each chemotherapy medication should be checked independently against the prescriber's orders by at least two individuals who are trained and competent to administer chemotherapy medications. All dosage- and administration-rate-related calculations should be independently verified. This includes any infusion pump rate settings, which should be checked at the initiation of each container of the infusion, periodically throughout the infusion, and whenever a new nurse assumes care for the patient. Healthcare providers should routinely confirm that the medication will be administered to the intended patient by comparing a patient's name and unique identifying code or number with medication labels (e.g., alpha–numeric characters or bar codes) and that a drug product's identity, ancillary components (e.g., additional medications, diluent, and vehicle solutions), route of administration, and schedule are correct.

At checkpoint 7, healthcare providers should examine the medication container and note whether the content's general appearance is what was expected. Many parenteral chemotherapy products have distinctive colors, and product coloration should be confirmed before administration.

At checkpoint 8, patients who self-administer their medications (or receive it from personal caregivers) should carefully read the container's label to confirm the product's identity and review its instructions for use (schedule of dosing, whether to take with or without food) each time they take a medication.

At checkpoint 9, patients should be encouraged to ask questions about their treatment before its administration and compare its appearance and medication label with information they received about the treatment. Patient identification using two identifiers should occur prior to chemotherapy administration. Whenever possible, barcode-driven administration should be used.[40]

In ambulatory care practice, it is common for patients to receive parenteral chemotherapy medications in a setting where a physician and a nurse (or other healthcare profes-

Figure 2 (*continued*)

Checklist for Preparing and Labeling Chemotherapy Drugs

For each order you check, verify that each element is correct with a check mark.

Patient ________________________ Drug ____________

Date _____________

Label check

Patient name is same as on front of work card __________

Drug name on label matches drug name written on back of work card ____________

Dose on label matches dose written on back of work card_____________

Diluent on label matches diluent written on back of work card _____________

Volume of diluent on label matches volume of diluent on back of work card _______

Correct date to prepare _____________

Expiration date and time _____________

Correct time (expiration date not greater than administration time) _____________

For each drug/additive

Correct drug used ________Proper protocol supply ____

Drug concentration in each vial _____________

Additives, such as sodium bicarbonate solution, for which large stock bottles are used (which remain in hood) are visually checked, lot number is verified, and technician is asked to verify volume used ____________

Drug volume for dose verified ____________

Drug lot number on each vial matches lot number written on work card _____________

Calculations are checked _____________

Drug has not expired _____________

For each diluent

Correct diluent ______Volume of diluent _____

Diluent has not expired _____________

Special instructions followed

Air purged from bag ____

Tubing affixed/primed to end of line ________

Diluent for reconstitution _______

Correct container _____Proper overfill ___Drug in overfill ___

Final miscellaneous steps

Chemotherapy work card checklist is in card pocket _____

Solution is inspected for impurities/floaters_____________

Label is initialed (on left-hand side of label just below last additive or drug) **after** being affixed to correct admixture _____________

Total volume to be infused _____ Red chemo i.v. seal _____

"Caution chemo" label ____ Other auxiliary labeling ____

Zip-lock bag __________

Work card is initialed _____________

Pharmacist's initials ___________ Date _____________

Supervisor's initials ___________ Date _____________

sional) complete all tasks related to prescribing, preparing, administering, and monitoring treatment without a pharmacist's participation. Under these circumstances, the healthcare providers involved should perform independent double checks and be involved in the entire process. The person preparing chemotherapy medications should work from written orders.

Monitoring (Checkpoint 10). Chemotherapy agents are usually expected to produce adverse events, so it is sometimes difficult to detect possible medication errors resulting from failure at one of the prior checkpoints. However, a vigilant healthcare team might discover a potential error sooner if they are knowledgeable about the expected adverse effects and are vigilant for either exaggerated or unexpected adverse effects.

For all chemotherapy agents administered at a healthcare institution, the patient's clinical status should be assessed on each day of chemotherapy administration. Vital signs should be taken and a standardized assessment for possible toxicities should be performed.

For oral chemotherapy agents, assurance that patients understand how to take their chemotherapy medicine should be assessed initially and then at each patient encounter. An assessment for adherence should be performed at each clinic visit. Patients should be taught how to recognize and report expected and unexpected toxicities.

Recommendations for Prescribing Systems and Prescribers

Chemotherapy prescribing is complicated by numerous medical publications that report indications, dosages, and administration schedules inconsistent with FDA-approved product labeling. Chemotherapy treatments frequently involve off-label uses based on preliminary reports, promising information from abstracts, and compendia information. Prescribers must exercise great care in correctly interpreting this information and clearly communicating orders for chemotherapy medications with other healthcare providers.

Health-system administrators should require orders for all chemotherapy medications and other high-risk drugs prescribed by physicians-in-training or nonphysician prescribers to be countersigned by a senior physician with expertise in the specialty to safeguard against errors in interpretation and prescribing. Healthcare providers seeking privileges for prescribing chemotherapy drugs should complete an orientation to local policies and procedures related to prescribing chemotherapy before they are permitted to order them for patient care.

Healthcare providers should locally develop standardized dosage and administration schedule modifications for each chemotherapy medication. Treatment modifications may be appropriate for patients with the following characteristics: (1) preexisting pathologies that predispose a patient to adverse effects from treatment with particular chemotherapies (e.g., withholding or decreasing bleomycin dosages in patients with preexisting pulmonary dysfunction or cardiotoxic agents in patients with congestive heart failure); (2) a history of severe, prolonged, or cumulative adverse effects after previous chemotherapy treatments; (3) impaired physiological function that predisposes patients to altered pharmacodynamic responses (e.g., renal or hepatic impairment); (4) low or decreased performance status; and (5) patients on multiple medications with a potential for a drug interaction with a particular chemotherapy.

Healthcare providers should also establish for their institutions standardized guidelines for prescribing drugs that are routinely administered concomitantly with chemotherapy medications. Medication-use guidelines for supportive care and ancillary agents (e.g., antiemetics, hydration, chemoprotectants) should be made accessible to all healthcare providers who prescribe, prepare, and administer chemotherapy drugs and for persons who perform clinical monitoring.

When generating medication orders in a setting where preprinted ordering forms, CPOE, and other electronic and mechanical means (e.g., e-prescribing) are not available, prescribers should legibly print the names of medications, dosages, routes of administration, and administration schedules in plain block letters and Arabic numerals. Medication orders should include the indications for which they are prescribed (e.g., for sore mouth, for nausea, for chronic lymphocytic leukemia).

When chemotherapy treatment (ordering, preparing, and administering) is coordinated at a single location, it is the prescriber's responsibility (or in the conduct of clinical trials, it is the principal investigator's responsibility) to provide information about the treatment (e.g., protocols, publication reprints) to those who prepare and administer medications and monitor patient outcomes. It remains the prescriber's responsibility to answer questions and provide information to other healthcare providers when treatment is implemented in a place that is geographically separate from the prescriber's location. Prescribers, clinical investigators, and medically responsible staff should provide to healthcare providers who prepare and administer chemotherapy medications a complete printed (or electronically reproduced) copy of the treatment regimen.

General Guidelines for Prescribing Chemotherapy Medications.[11,13,20,41] The following are general guidelines for prescribing chemotherapy drugs:

1. Instructions for medication regimens should be explicit, complete, clear, and easy to follow. Treatment regimens should be described accurately and consistently in all written, published, or circulated materials in which chemotherapy medication use is described.
2. The patient's medical record should contain a justification for the chemotherapy treatment plan (e.g., FDA product labeling, a primary literature reference, institutionally approved guidelines, national consensus guidelines, or an investigational protocol).
3. Medication-use systems should require healthcare providers to use standardized vocabulary and nomenclature for describing treatment with chemotherapy medications. "Tall Man" lettering should be used for written and electronic orders.
4. Prescribers should use uniform and consistent notations to express quantifiable amounts (dosage, concentration, volume, and time).
5. Prescribers should never trail a whole number with a decimal point followed by a zero (e.g., write "5 mg," not "5.0 mg").
6. When writing amounts less than one, the expression should be written with a leading zero preceding the decimal point (e.g., "0.125 mg").
7. All treatment plans and medication orders should identify the dosage (as a function of body weight, BSA, or other dosing factors) and the calculated dose. Total course dose should be included in circumstances in which a single infusion container is designed to provide multiple days of treatment (e.g. 7-day cladridine infusion).
8. When treatment day enumeration is arbitrary, day 1 typically describes the day treatment commences. In contrast, hematopoietic progenitor-cell transplantation regimens often include day 0, and significant treatment-related events before and after a progenitor-cell graft is administered are distinguished by negative (minus) and positive (plus) prefixes, respectively.
9. All medications that are a part of the treatment regimen (e.g., oral chemotherapies) should be included, indicating where the product will be filled or dispensed.

10. Recommendations for proper medication storage should also be included. Cancer patients must often travel long distances to receive care, so guidance and support (provision of coolers and ice packets for refrigerated medications) to properly store medications when in transit as well as at home.

In some cases, CPOE can be used to promote best practices (e.g., eliminating the use of trailing and leading zeros [items 4 and 5 above]).

Specific Recommendations for Parenterally Administered Medications.[20] Healthcare providers should adhere to the following guidelines for parenteral chemotherapy drugs:

1. In treatment plans and orders, doses should be expressed as the total amount of medication to be administered from a single container (i.e., the total amount of medication per syringe, bag, or other container).
2. For medication admixtures that can be prepared in more than one way, practitioners should institute *a priori*, standard, and consistent methods directing how each medication will be prepared and administered.
3. When a medication with extended stability is administered from a single container for more than 24 hours, a prescriber's order for treatment should specify the amount of medication to be administered during each 24-hour interval.[20] For example, a medication order for a patient with a BSA of 2 m^2 should read: Drug XYZ (8 mg/m^2/day × 3 days) 48 mg in 150 mL 0.9% sodium chloride injection by continuous intravenous infusion over 72 hours. Start on 04/01/2001 at 0800 (total dose/cycle = 48 mg).

Specific Recommendations for Orally Administered Chemotherapy Medications.[20,42] Prescribing orally administered chemotherapy agents presents unique challenges for healthcare providers due to the greater responsibility placed upon patients to manage their own care and patients' perception that these agents may be less dangerous than parentally administered agents. Healthcare providers should adhere to the following recommendations when oral medications are the prescribed chemotherapy treatment or when oral chemotherapy is included as part of the treatment regimen:

1. In treatment plans and medication orders, drug doses and schedules should be described as the amount of medication to be taken per dose, not as a total daily dose that is to be taken in divided doses.
2. In treatment plans, medication orders, and instructions to a patient, the number of doses to be administered or taken should be clearly identified.
3. Doses for solid orally administered dosage forms should specify whether and how doses are to be rounded to the nearest capsule or tablet strength. If the calculated dose can't be provided based on the available dosage forms, the following alternatives can be considered:
   a. whether tablet formulations should be broken (if not a hazardous drug);
   b. whether an alternative dosage method or formulation is appropriate; or
   c. whether alternate day dosing is appropriate based on the pharmacokinetic and pharmacodynamic properties of the medication. The goal of alternate day dosing is to fulfill the total weekly dose rather than giving the exact daily dose (e.g., if an agent is to be given 175 mg daily for 2 weeks, but the drug is only available in 50 mg capsules, consider alternate day dosing by giving 200 mg on one day and 150 mg on the next day). If alternate day dosing is used, then instructions that say "take X tablets on odd days and X tablets on even days" should be avoided, as two consecutive odd days may occur when transitioning from one month to another. For example: January 31 and February 1.
4. Only the quantity needed to cover the administration period until the next clinical evaluation should be ordered.
5. If appropriate, instructions should address how medications are to be taken with respect to food ingestion and indicate whether particular types of food may affect medication activity.
6. Oral chemotherapy medication orders should be included with parenteral chemotherapy orders to allow for appropriate screening and safety checks.
7. Oral chemotherapy medication orders should be included on the patient's home medication list to allow for appropriate screening and safety checks.
8. Oral chemotherapy medication orders should be communicated to the pharmacist for appropriate screening and safety checks.
9. Patient instructions should address what to do if a dose is missed.
10. Patients should be provided with explicit instructions regarding what adverse effects to expect, which ones require a telephone call to a provider, and who and where to call.
11. Instructions should describe safe handling, storage, and disposal of oral chemotherapy.
12. Essential ancillary medications and supportive care that accompany a chemotherapy treatment regimen should be explicitly identified.
13. Refills on oral chemotherapy medications should be discouraged, when feasible.
14. Patients should be appropriately educated regarding access and cost issues (e.g., regarding specialty pharmacies, prior authorization, out-of-pocket costs, and options for pharmaceutical manufacturer or copay assistance).

Recommendations for Medication Preparation and Dispensing Systems and Roles for Pharmacists

For each practice setting, persons representing the various healthcare disciplines that prescribe, prepare, and administer chemotherapy medications should participate in planning and managing local medication-use systems.

Standardized Medication Preparation Guidelines. Healthcare providers should establish standardized guidelines for reconstituting, diluting, admixing, packaging, and labeling commonly used chemotherapy and other medications that are routinely administered with chemotherapy. Each practice facility should also establish a standardized method for labeling multidose vials and reconstituted drug products. Standardized medication preparation guidelines should be prominently displayed (e.g., as a chart) for easy accessibility in areas where orders are processed and medications prepared. Policies should be developed for prescribing of oral chemotherapy that are not being dispensed by the health system. Instructions for patient counseling, safe handling, and disposal should be included in these policies.

Policies and procedures should be developed for situations in which medications are prepared at facilities that are geographically removed from where treatment is administered. Procedural protocols should describe requirements for medication packaging, storage conditions during transportation, duration of transport, and handling after delivery. Medication couriers should receive training in organizational policies for handling medications and should immediately report when conditions and handling practices deviate from procedural standards. In addition, handling procedures should ensure patient confidentiality and provide guidelines for emergency situations, such as hazardous-drug spills.

Persons who prepare and dispense chemotherapy medications should ensure timely drug delivery to patients and patient-care areas after receiving written orders. If dispensing is delayed for any reason, healthcare providers awaiting the medications should be notified.[11]

Quality Assurance and Improvement. In collaboration with healthcare providers who prescribe and administer medications, pharmacists and persons who prepare and dispense chemotherapy should take the initiative in developing and managing quality-assurance and quality improvement programs for their medication-use systems. These programs should include surveillance and reporting systems, FMEAs, and root-cause analysis, when appropriate, that track potential and actual medication errors, evaluate the proximal causes of errors among processes and systems, and identify preventive measures.[11,43] The major advantage of multidisciplinary participation is that each discipline's perspectives and methods for conceptualizing system flaws and solutions can be incorporated in designing strategies for preventing medication errors. Confidential reporting is essential to the success of a medication-error surveillance and reporting system. Only by understanding what causes and contributes to errors can the number of errors be reduced. In designing a medication-error surveillance and reporting system, strategic emphasis should be placed on understanding why errors occur and not on blaming or censuring personnel.[44] Further, proactive assessment of the chemotherapy-use process should be conducted.

Orientation on Medication-Error Reduction. Pharmacy supervisors and managers should develop an orientation program about medication errors commonly associated with chemotherapy medications for training of pharmacy personnel who prepare and dispense chemotherapy. Pharmacists should develop ongoing interprofessional educational programs that focus awareness on potential medication errors with chemotherapy medications, strategies for preventing errors, and local and national medication-error reporting and evaluation systems for all practitioners who have direct patient contact.

Pharmacists should engage the support of medical and nursing administrators and supervisors to encourage their staff (particularly those in professional training programs) to complete chemotherapy medication-error awareness programs.[30] Educational programs should be discipline specific. Program content should include medication-error case scenarios, problem-solving to prevent and mitigate medication errors, and discussion about the effects that medication errors have on patients' quality of life and the health system.[11,31]

Standardized Drug Procurement and Storage. Pharmacists who select and procure drugs should strive to minimize or eliminate look-alike drug product containers and limit the availability of different vial sizes for parenteral medications whenever possible.[12] Frequent additions to the variety of available drug products and changes among alternative manufacturers' drug products can contribute to medication-use errors and should be avoided. If it is necessary to change manufacturers, healthcare organizations should develop a process to ensure staff are educated about the new product and that computer systems have the appropriate manufacturer's information. When practical, drug products with similar names and packaging should not be stored next to each other. Medication-use systems that involve a formulary should separate nonformulary products from those that are on the formulary. Healthcare providers should familiarize themselves with chemotherapy drugs that are not on formulary before prescribing, preparing, and administering them.

Standardized Medication Preparation and Dispensing. Chemotherapy medications should be dispensed in ready-to-administer dosage forms whenever possible. Generally, chemotherapy for intermittent parenteral administration should be prepared so that each medication container has only one dose. The risk of incorrect medication use is increased when the amount of drug dispensed in a single container exceeds the amount to be administered during a 24-hour period. It is essential that individuals and committees responsible for developing and overseeing medication-use systems establish guidelines on whether prescribers may order chemotherapy preparations to be administered from a single container for more than 24 hours. In all practices where parenteral drugs with extended stability (more than 24 hours) are sanctioned, it is imperative that the duration of their use is clearly labeled and that healthcare providers are trained to correctly prescribe, prepare, and administer them.[20]

When preparing a chemotherapy admixture, a quantity of medication that most closely approximates the prescribed dose should be segregated from other drug supplies. For treatment regimens that include two or more drugs, especially when medications are to be administered by different routes, the medications should be physically segregated during preparation and when administered. Compounded medications should be prepared one at a time, using standardized techniques whenever possible.

The chemotherapy preparation process should include an independent double check by two separate individuals of the correct drug, diluents, administration containers, and volume measurements before the solutions are transferred to the final administration container. A person other than the individual who selected the components of the preparation (drug and diluent) and measured the volume of diluent solutions used to reconstitute the medications should visually confirm the correct product(s) and measurement(s) before the solutions are transferred from the measuring device to the drug vial for reconstituted drugs and to the final administration container. Post hoc or proxy methods for checking medication preparation, including pulling back syringe plungers to demonstrate the volume of fluid that was injected into the secondary container, should not be used as the sole method for verifying chemotherapy product preparation. Verification may be accomplished by direct visual inspection; remote monitoring through telepharmacy applications (with pictures); or by weighing syringes, other transfer devices, and intermediate product containers before fluid transfer is completed. Whenever possible, methods that allow direct observation of product preparation should be used. The actual original medication vials and diluents that were used during preparation must be present for inspection during the verification process.

Technologies to automate the preparation of sterile products, including chemotherapy, are emerging. Some robotic technologies enclose and automate the entire production process, and these products may provide a variety of benefits to institutions with a sufficient volume of chemotherapy to justify their substantial cost. A more common technology organizes information, manages workflow, adds new checks, and documents parenteral drug therapy preparation through a combination of computer software, barcodes, and cameras. In these systems, the components of a chemotherapy preparation are verified with bar code technology and pictures before preparation, and pictures of the preparation are stored. These systems add additional double checks with the barcode technology and improve documentation of the preparation and other relevant information such as product lot number. In some settings, the photos taken through this technology enable the pharmacist to check chemotherapy preparation outside the sterile area. Like other technologies, automation for parenteral therapies must be carefully implemented to be certain the new technology is not eliminating checks in the process. For example, bar coding the components of a chemotherapy dose does not eliminate the need to check the components of the chemotherapy before they are admixed.

Standardized Medication Labeling. Strict procedures should be established for standardizing medication labeling. A uniform, systematic labeling method should be used, especially when multiple drugs are prepared for a single patient. Medication labels should be mechanically printed (not handwritten). Chemotherapy medications should be labeled immediately after preparation. Oral medications should also be sealed with child-resistant or poisoning-prevention closures.

Chemotherapy agents are administered parenterally by many routes other than the intravenous route (e.g., intrathecally, intrahepatically, intrapleurally, intraarterially). Inadvertent administration by the wrong route can result in serious or fatal consequences (e.g., administering vincristine intrathecally is fatal). Medication-use systems should include policies and procedures that clearly distinguish medications administered by the intravenous route from those intended for administration by other routes. Auxiliary labels may facilitate distinguishing among medications that are administered by particular delivery methods.

Labels for oral dosage forms, rectal suppositories, and topically applied unit-dose products should include *all* of the following information:

1. Patient's name, unique identifying code or number, and location within a treatment facility (when applicable).
2. Date (with or without specifying time) the medication was dispensed.
3. Generic drug name.
4. Dosage form and strength.
5. Amount of medication per dose (when the container dispensed holds more than one dose).
6. Administration route.
7. Detailed instructions to the patient for self-administering the medication (including a dosing calendar when appropriate).
8. Supplemental administration instructions (e.g., starting and completion dates and times; number of doses to administer; cautionary information about when medications are to be taken in relation to food ingestion and other medications; and instructions and warnings regarding administration route, handling precautions, storage conditions, and container closures).
9. The quantity dispensed within each container (the number of tablets, capsules, or suppositories, packaged in a single container).

Labels for injectable dosage form containers should include *all* of the following information:

1. Patient's name, unique identifying code or number, and location within a treatment facility (when applicable).
2. Generic drug name.
3. The amount of medication per container and, when a product container holds more than one dose (e.g., multiple doses for intermittent administration), the amount of medication per dose).[20]
4. How much overfill is added to a container when excess medication and fluid volumes are added to displace air from the tubing lumen ("dead space") in administration sets.
5. Route of administration (for example, medications prescribed for administration other than by the intravenous route—especially those for intrathecal administration— should bear ancillary labels that distinctively identify the intended administration route).
6. The name and amount of all drug additives in a chemotherapy admixture.
7. Diluent (vehicle fluid) name.
8. The volume of fluid to be administered. Adding overfill to the container should be discouraged, but when unavoidable, both the volume to administer and the overfill volume should be specified. Proper education for nurses administering these products is essential to ensure that patients do not receive additional drug.
9. Administration rate and duration. Ideally, both administration rate and duration should be specified. Because administration rates can be calculated from the volume to be administered and duration of administration, duration is the essential component.

10. Supplemental administration instructions, such as starting and completion dates and times; prohibitions about when medications are not to be administered in relation to other medications; and instructions and warnings regarding administration (e.g., information about special requirements for administration sets, including inline filtration, warnings to avoid intrathecal administration with vinca alkaloid drugs, and hazardous-drug warning labels).
11. When it is necessary to prepare more than one medication intended for sequential administration, the container labels should be numbered. The sequence in which each container is to be used and the total number of containers (e.g., bag 1 of 3, bottle 3 of 7) should be indicated.
12. Date (with or without specifying time) the medication was ordered or prepared. Investigational compounds, in particular, should be labeled with the date and time they were prepared.
13. Expiration date and time after which a medication should no longer be used (i.e., beyond-use date and time).
14. Cautionary warnings as required for hazardous drug products.[45]
15. Storage specifications.
16. The name (with or without specifying location or telephone number) of the institution, pharmacy, or practice from which a medication was dispensed and the prescriber's identity.

Credentialing Pharmacists for Chemotherapy Medication-Use Programs. Pharmacy managers and supervisors should require pharmacist employees to complete training and demonstrate competencies related to chemotherapy medication use, evaluating medication orders, preparing chemotherapy medications, safe handling procedures, error surveillance and reporting programs, and local policies as a prerequisite to pharmacist credentialing. Healthcare organizations should periodically reassess pharmacist employees' competencies related to their responsibilities, increasing the frequency of reassessment if performance problems occur.[14]

Roles for Pharmacists. Among primary healthcare providers, pharmacists generally are best positioned to ensure that medications are used rationally and safely and increase others' awareness about medication errors and how to prevent them. Pharmacists should participate in all aspects of patient care related to chemotherapy treatment, including developing policies for safe and appropriate medication use and other services consistent with pharmacist patient care.[11,30] Pharmacists should participate with other primary healthcare providers in multidisciplinary groups that develop, implement, and periodically reevaluate practice-specific procedures and processes for verifying chemotherapy medication orders, resolving procedural questions related to confirming and processing medication orders, and evaluating and resolving disputes among healthcare providers.

Each organization should establish a minimum acceptable level of pharmacist participation in the error-prevention elements of patient care, such as proactively reviewing medication orders, screening laboratory results, providing drug information and patient counseling, and reviewing drug storage conditions.[11,46]

The following roles are recommended for pharmacist participation:

1. Educating healthcare providers about medication errors.
2. Independently verifying medication dosages, routes of administration, and schedules.
3. Participating in multidisciplinary efforts to establish drug-specific utilization constraints that limit maximum doses, administration rates, and administration schedules for chemotherapy medications.
4. Participating in multidisciplinary efforts to standardize the prescribing vocabulary and the development, implementation, and maintenance of standardized order sets.
5. Participating in multidisciplinary efforts to educate patients, their families, and personal caregivers.
6. Participating in multidisciplinary efforts to develop adherence programs and monitor patient adherence to prescribed regimens, including recommendations for supportive care to treat and or mitigate adverse events associated with chemotherapy agents.
7. Participating in multidisciplinary efforts to assist patients with accessing medications (e.g., prior authorization, manufacturer assistance programs, copay assistance programs, coping with drug shortages).
8. Improving communication among healthcare providers and among healthcare providers, patients, and caregivers.
9. Working with pharmaceutical or equipment manufacturers on medication-specific safety strategies.

Drug Information Resources and Education for Providers. Pharmacists should help ensure the availability of up-to-date references on the appropriate use of chemotherapy drugs for all healthcare providers involved in medication use.[11,31] Drug information resources should provide information about:

- Drug products' FDA-approved labeling, compendia-supported indications, and investigational uses.
- Drug-specific precautionary warnings and information about adverse effects, particularly dosage- and schedule-limiting effects.
- Potential interactions with other drugs, disease states, and foods.
- Administration methods, including drug admixture stability and compatibility data.
- Usual adult and pediatric dosages.
- Dosage recommendations for single- and multiple-treatment courses.
- Treatment modifications for persons with concurrent pathologies or end-organ impairment.
- Safety Data Sheets.
- Pharmacokinetically based dosing and monitoring guidelines.

Information and guidelines for handling chemotherapy extravasations and hypersensitivity reactions, including the use of antidotes, should be developed by a multidisciplinary team and be readily available.

Pharmacists should develop and provide discipline-specific educational materials about chemotherapy medication use to healthcare providers who prescribe, prepare, and administer chemotherapy medications. The instructional tools developed for each professional healthcare discipline should complement the materials developed for the other disciplines.[11]

When new chemotherapies, treatment regimens, or treatment protocols are introduced, pharmacists should assume a continuous, proactive leadership role in developing educational programs and materials for healthcare providers, patients, and caregivers.[11,31] Pharmacists should assess the competency of individuals assigned primary responsibility for chemotherapy education to confirm their ability to effectively communicate medication-related information.

For patients whose care is transferred from oncologists to nonspecialist practitioners, oncology pharmacy specialists should develop and provide drug monographs, medication-use summaries, and other treatment-related materials describing how oral and parenteral chemotherapy medications and treatment regimens are to be accomplished.[12,30] The need is especially acute among organizations and practitioners who provide local care for patients enrolled in clinical trials or receiving investigational chemotherapy treatments.

Treatment Protocols. Oncology pharmacy specialists should participate in developing treatment protocols for standard treatments and clinical investigations. In practice settings where chemotherapy medications and treatment regimens are used routinely, pharmacists should initiate the development of tools that standardize the way medications are ordered, thereby facilitating accurate and appropriate prescribing, order interpretation and verification, and medication processing and dispensing.[31,47] Pharmacists should lead initiatives to standardize drug preparation procedures, including reconstitution, dilution, and drug admixture methods for commonly used parenteral chemotherapy medications.[12]

CPOE. Pharmacists should work with information systems personnel, computer programmers, and software vendors to develop CPOE systems. System requirements should include mechanisms for standardizing medication orders, decreasing opportunities for error by minimizing data entry, and screening orders for medication doses and administration schedules that exceed established limits. Pharmacists should advocate for and participate in establishing maximum safe chemotherapy dosage and scheduling limits with physicians, nurses, and other primary healthcare providers. Pharmacists should guide the appropriate use of clinical decision support in CPOE systems for chemotherapy and the medication management process.

Vocabulary and Nomenclature. Pharmacists are uniquely qualified to lead multidisciplinary efforts to develop and implement clear, detailed, standardized vocabulary and nomenclature for chemotherapy treatment regimens, medication orders, and administration instructions. Pharmacists should participate in the early stages of protocol development for standard treatments and clinical investigations to ensure that pharmacotherapeutic regimens are clearly described, easily understood, and incorporate standardized language, content, abbreviations, and units of measure.[11,20,30]

Patient Education and Counseling. Pharmacists should ensure that educational materials used for patient education are comprehensive and routinely updated. When meeting or interviewing patients, their family members, or other home-based caregivers (e.g., completing medication-use and allergy histories, screening blood pressure, performing ongoing treatment response assessment, dispensing medications), pharmacists should provide medication education and counseling. They should verify that patients and their caregivers understand the following:

1. The purpose of the medication and its intended use.
2. The appropriate use and safe handling of medications (e.g., don't place oral chemotherapy agents in a pill box, keep away from children) and administration devices.
3. Appropriate temperature and safe storage conditions.
4. Special precautions to prevent exposure to hazardous materials that may be present in patients' clothing, linens, body fluids, and excreta during and after treatment.
5. The potential interactions with other medications and foods.
6. The critical need for good medication adherence practices.
7. What to do if a dose is missed.
8. Dosing calendars or other supplemental information to improve adherence.
9. Common and possible adverse effects associated with the medication.
10. Methods for preventing, managing, and reporting adverse effects.
11. What to do if potentially serious adverse effects occur, including when to contact a provider, who to contact, and how to reach them.[11,36]
12. How to properly dispose of the medication, container, and supplies.
13. Access and cost issues (specialty pharmacies, prior authorization, out-of-pocket costs, options for pharmaceutical manufacturer or copay assistance, drug shortages).

Pharmacists should provide educational materials to patients and suggest supplemental and alternative information resources, such as the National Cancer Institute information services department (1-800-4-CANCER and www.cancer.gov), the American Cancer Society, libraries, and bookstores.[11] If pharmacists are not available to provide chemotherapy patient education, they should assist in competency assessment of those assigned primary responsibility for that education.

Advocates for Patients' Rights. Pharmacists should encourage patients and their caregivers to participate in their own care and advise patients how to protect themselves from medication errors. Pharmacists should advise patients that they are entitled to satisfactory answers from their healthcare providers. Pharmacists should encourage patients to double-check the details of their treatment, including drug names and dosages, and to request dosage recalculation if their biological measurements change. Pharmacists who participate in developing treatment plans and protocols should ensure that consent-for-treatment forms contain accurate, complete information to secure patients' informed consent. Pharmacists should help to prepare treatment consent forms; provide patients with an accurate and detailed description of their treatment plan in clear, unambiguous, and easily understood language and answers to their questions about the treatment and alternative treatment options; and assess patients' understanding of expected and possible outcomes. Pharmacists should also describe their role as primary care providers and the care they provide.[11,12]

Clinical Intervention, Analysis, and Performance Improvement. In addition to dispensing medications, pharmacists can help improve the quality of patient care by implementing a proactive clinical intervention program and documenting healthcare providers' deviations from planned chemotherapy treatments. Longitudinal data collection, analysis, and reporting can reveal system flaws that contributed to (or failed to prevent) prescribing errors, suggest targets for quality improvement, and validate pharmacists' interventions.

Pharmacists should proactively work with other primary care providers to establish medication-use reporting and surveillance programs. Committees established for this purpose should include representatives from medical, nursing, pharmacy, and risk-management disciplines. Programs should continually evaluate local medication-use systems to identify potential problems and solutions related to medication use and prevent medication errors.[11,43] Such programs in institutions should seek endorsement from appropriate local multidisciplinary committees (e.g., pharmacy and therapeutics, medical executive, and clinical practice committees).

Feedback for Pharmaceutical Manufacturers and Regulators. Pharmacists should work with pharmaceutical manufacturers and the FDA to eliminate ambiguous, confusing, and potentially misleading drug product and treatment information from published resources (e.g., product packaging, package inserts, official compendia, and promotional information). Pharmacists working in the pharmaceutical manufacturing industry should proactively identify preventable causes of product-user errors and adverse effects associated with product labeling, packaging, and promotion.[48] Pharmacists' voluntary participation in national reporting programs can increase the awareness of medication errors and promote error prevention throughout the healthcare system. These aggregate data promote changes in product identity, packaging, labeling, commercial information, and marketing practices that are subject to manufacturers' control and governmental regulation.[11,41]

Recommendations for Medication Administration Systems and Roles for Nurses

Nurses are often the last link in the chain of healthcare providers who provide treatment with chemotherapy medications. To safeguard patients from mistakes that have potentially lethal consequences, evidence-based systems have evolved that promote safety and include[4]:

- Requirements for credentialing persons who administer chemotherapy medications.
- Tools and methods to facilitate documentation and identification of correct medication use.
- Independent verification of medication orders.
- Independent double check of the final product and infusion pump settings.
- Accurate documentation of medication use and effects on patient care.
- Strict compliance with regulations and practice standards.
- Patient education regarding medication safety.

Credentialing Nurses for Chemotherapy Medication-Use Programs. Organizational policies and procedures should require nurse employees to complete training and demonstrate nursing care-related competencies, such as administering chemotherapy medications, caring for patients who have received chemotherapy medications, and knowledge of local policies. Specialty certification (e.g., ONS Oncology Certified Nurse credential, ONS Chemotherapy and Biotherapy Provider Card) is highly encouraged. Nurses may be required to complete additional training and competency assessments before they are permitted to administer experimental medications. Training usually combines didactic and supervised practical instruction. Didactic instruction generally includes training about specific chemotherapy agents, appropriate dosages and dosage ranges, adverse effects and clinical toxicities, administration techniques, and safe handling. Technical experience in administering chemotherapy medications requires demonstrating competence with administering intravenous medications. Healthcare organizations should periodically (at least annually, but more frequently if performance problems occur) reassess nurses' competencies related to their responsibilities.

Standardized Medication Administration Practices. In collaboration with the multidisciplinary team, nurses within an organization should standardize chemotherapy administration practices. It should be determined whether intravenous chemotherapy agents should be infused as a primary or secondary infusion across the organization. Institutions should establish cut-off times to initiate nonurgent chemotherapy administration in relation to the need for adequate staffing.

Medication safety technologies should be implemented to enhance the chemotherapy administration process. ASHP encourages health systems to adopt bar-code-enabled medication administration (BCMA) technology to improve patient safety and the accuracy of medication administration and documentation.[39] Infusion pumps that provide dose and infusion-rate warnings (often called "smart pumps") should also be implemented. Because of unique challenges from chemotherapy (e.g., BSA-based dosing), some organizations' pumps may not immediately provide warnings for chemotherapy, and care must be taken to make enhancements to the technology to accommodate chemotherapy. Appropriate use of both of these technologies provides new checks in the chemotherapy administration process.

Standardized Tools for Recording Medication Administration. Nurses with a variety of experiences have devised and contributed to designing tools to facilitate the prevention of drug administration errors, such as standardized work sheets used to calculate medication dosages and administration rates and checklists of pertinent laboratory results and physiological measurements. Treatment flow sheets provide easily interpretable information about when a patient's previous treatments were administered, whether dosages and medication delivery deviated from planned treatment, and the cumulative amount of medication administered. Thoughtfully designed treatment flow sheets may become part of a patient's permanent medical record and can be an invaluable resource for patient care.

Checking Orders and Equipment for Administering Chemotherapy Medications. Medication orders for chemotherapy require documentation of independent double-checks by two individuals prior to administration.[4] These individuals should be different than the individual who prepared the product. In addition, nurses should evaluate and confirm the functional integrity of vascular access devices (and devices for other administration routes), medication pumps, and other devices that control medication delivery. For adjustable and programmable mechanical and electronic devices, mechanical adjustments or electronic programming for delivering the correct dose at the appropriate rate should be independently verified with another healthcare provider who is knowledgeable about the delivery device before it is used to administer medications.

Recording and Tracking Chemotherapy Use. After medications have been administered, it is a nurse's responsibility to manually or electronically record the activity. The documentation should be in a standardized format and include the patient's name, the names of all medications administered, dosages, administration routes, rates of administration, the date and time administration began, the duration of administration or time that treatment was completed, and whether adverse effects were observed or reported by the patient during or after administration. Communications with patients, other healthcare providers, and personal caregivers should be documented in an objective, chronological narrative style, reporting the dates and times the events occurred, the names of involved persons, and how questions and problems were resolved.

Clinical Intervention, Analysis, and Performance Improvement. Nurses and other personnel should immediately report to medically responsible personnel and their supervisors any instance in which medications were used incorrectly and the events attributable to the error. In response to discovering a medication-use error, a provider's primary responsibility is to ensure the patient's safety. Subsequently, the error and related circumstances should be recorded in accordance with specific policies and procedures. Medication-use error reports (also called occurrence, safety, or incident reports) should be written in an objective, chronological, narrative style without editorial remarks and speculative comments. Comprehensive occurrence reports are useful in discovering and evaluating system flaws and may provide the impetus for improving medication-use systems.

To prevent medication errors, nurses and other personnel who administer chemotherapy medications must comply with policies and procedures that define standards of practice. It is important, however, to periodically reevaluate practice standards in order to assess how well a medication-use system functions, make appropriate changes, and, ultimately, improve patient safety and the quality of care.

Healthcare providers administering chemotherapy medications should not deviate from guidelines for ordering, preparing, and administering chemotherapy agents. Examples of inappropriate practice include borrowing medications from a patient's drug supply to give to another patient and preparing agents without the proper facilities or staff. Medication administration schedules should be followed as closely as possible; providers and caregivers should strive to comply with treatment plans. Drug administration should be documented promptly after it is completed, and providers administering chemotherapy medications should rigorously comply with local requirements for documenting treatment. To prevent the inadvertent duplication of treatment, it is recommended that one individual assume the primary responsibility for each patient during a work period (shift or tour of duty). When one individual cannot assume primary responsibility for each patient during a work period, appropriate hand-off communication is essential.

Nurses and Patient Education. Nurses who administer chemotherapy medications have a prominent role in educating patients about their chemotherapy. Nurses should encourage patients and their personal caregivers to ask questions about their treatment. Patient education guidelines may be included in treatment maps and clinical care plans.

Recommendations for Patient Education

Well-informed patients (and their authorized caregivers) are the vital last link in the safety chain to prevent errors related to chemotherapy medications. Patients are entitled to know all pertinent facts about the medications they receive during their treatment. Healthcare providers charged with educating patients should have demonstrated competency to accurately perform this function. Healthcare providers have an obligation to encourage patients to ask questions and to provide answers.

The following suggestions are offered to help patients and their caregivers ensure optimal outcomes from the cancer therapy medications.

Multifocal Medication Education. Patients need multifocal education about the purpose, adverse effects, schedules, routes of administration, and descriptions (e.g., colors, shapes) for all the medications they will receive during their treatment. This includes the chemotherapy regimen, including both oral and intravenous therapy, and all ancillary and supportive medications, such as antiemetics and medications that hasten bone marrow recovery. In order to ensure patients receive the appropriate education to manage their therapy or its side effects, it is imperative that roles of the various healthcare professionals are defined and that responsibility for primary patient education versus reinforcement of key information is clearly delineated. When patients are well informed and the information they receive is reinforced by nurses, pharmacists, and other caregivers, they are better prepared to detect a misinterpreted medication order and assertively question conflicting information.[49] Healthcare professionals should be sensitive to the emotional aspects of patients with cancer when planning medication education. Education should take place at a time when a patient is able to listen and understand. Medication education should not be attempted when patients are sedated or confused as a result of medications or immediately after receiving their cancer diagnosis.

Patients should participate in their care by asking questions about their cancer treatment and related medications and by confirming the regimen with their nurse before receiving treatment. Healthcare providers should make educational materials available in counseling and treatment areas to encourage patients to learn more about their cancer therapies.

Health-System Procedures Education. Patients should understand the health system's plan for chemotherapy medication-error prevention. They should become familiar with their providers' routine procedures for checking medication orders so that they can understand the safeguards that have been established and why delays may occur before their treatment can be started. For example, patients can remind the person administering chemotherapy to compare medication labels with a patient's identity and can verify their height and weight each time they are measured.

Patient Participation in a Medication-Use System. Patients (or their caregivers) should be knowledgeable about their medications and the ways in which the medications are to be administered according to their treatment plan. In some circumstances, patients should be encouraged to take responsibility for some of their care to help improve their quality of life. Examples include self-administering medications, maintaining the patency of vascular access devices, giving themselves a subcutaneous injection, and troubleshooting a problem with the portable infusion pump. Patients should demonstrate their ability to perform these functions if they are included in the therapy plan. Competency and readiness for self-administration should be assessed for patients prescribed oral chemotherapy.

Each patient should be given a detailed treatment calendar that clearly identifies his or her treatment plan. They should be encouraged to keep their calendar with them to compare the expected treatment with what is being dispensed and administered.

Patients' Responsibilities. Patients should be taught and empowered to detect and to seek help in managing adverse effects that may occur during their cancer treatment. Healthcare providers should be promptly informed about adverse effects experienced during a chemotherapy cycle before the next cycle commences. Patients should keep a list of the medications that they may self-administer to treat these adverse effects. Patients should be encouraged and taught how to report medication errors and near misses that occur as a result of self-administration. Safe handling, storage, and disposal of oral chemotherapy should be taught to the patient or their caregiver.

It is important for healthcare providers to be able to determine potential interactions between a patient's nonchemotherapy medications and the chemotherapy they are to receive. Therefore, patients should be requested to provide to their healthcare team members a list of all medications they are using, including over-the-counter preparations, dietary supplements, and other complementary and alternative medicines. In general, use of any medication should be discussed with their healthcare providers before initiating therapy.

Recommendations for Manufacturers and Regulatory Agencies

Pharmaceutical manufacturers have a responsibility to exercise care in designing product packaging and labeling, determining dosage strengths and dosage forms, and in promoting their products, as these features may contribute to errors in prescribing, product selection, preparation, and administration. Companies that market chemotherapy agents should develop and support educational programs that encourage safe and accurate prescribing, preparation, administration, handling, storage, and disposal of their products. The following guidelines address some of the major areas.

Product Naming, Packaging, Labeling, and Drug Dosage Strengths/Forms. Companies should avoid trademarking drug names that look or sound similar to those of other drug products. Proprietary drug names for new products and product formulations should not be similar to existing generic and proprietary names. Manufacturers should avoid appending letters and numbers to drug names, as this practice can result in potential confusion with dosage strengths, medication quantities, and the amount of medication to be administered.

Product packaging and labeling should provide clear, easily distinguished features to identify a drug and the amount of drug per dosage unit (e.g., tablet, capsule, wafer) and within a product container (e.g., vials, bags, bottles, prefilled syringes). It is particularly important that a drug product's USAN-approved generic name appear more prominently than other information on the product label. Drug names should be printed on both the front and back of the containers and packaging of parenteral drugs; "Tall Man" characters should be used to distinguish between similar drug names. Container labels for drugs that are in solution and for those that require reconstitution or dilution before they are used should identify the total drug content in mass units (or biological activity units) rather than concentration.[49] Product packaging and labeling that include both mass and concentration values should be designed to display mass units more prominently. Product packaging should include a bar code on inner and outer packaging.

Labels should be unique and well designed. Distinguishing colors and contrasting hues facilitate identifying and distinguishing drug products and products in different strengths and concentrations. Warnings and special or unique instructions should be prominently displayed on product packaging and labeling. Unique labeling and packaging techniques should be used to prevent product misidentification and to warn about dosing errors and unique characteristics that predispose medication users to potentially serious or life-threatening toxicities. Examples include the unique way that the Platinol-AQ brand of cisplatin injection (Bristol-Myers Squibb, Princeton, NJ) is packaged to prevent misidentification with carboplatin and the cautionary statements on vials containing vincristine sulfate injection that warn against using the entire contents of a vial for a single patient (on bulk packages) and that intrathecal administration may be fatal.

A statement that declares a drug's approved routes of administration is optional and may or may not appear on product packaging. If the agent is approved for administration by only one route, it must be clearly indicated.

Appropriate storage temperatures or conditions should be clearly visible on drug labeling and packaging.

Drug labeling and packaging must identify the manufacturer's product lot or control number.

Drugs that must be reconstituted and diluted before clinical use should include reconstitution instructions that identify appropriate diluents and volumes.

A manufacturer's drug product preparation date (for experimental drugs) or an expiration date should be clearly visible on the product label.

Special instructions (e.g., "Shake Well," "Do Not Shake," "Albumin Required") and instructions for dilution should appear on product labeling. In cases where important information will not fit on a product label, a package insert, or "pull-away" label may be required as part of the labeling and packaging.

In the case of oral chemotherapy agents, careful consideration should be given to dosage forms and strengths provided. Often patients must combine multiple strengths of a medication to receive their prescribed dosage, thereby increasing the opportunity for a medication error. Many oncology patients have difficulty swallowing and cannot take solid dosage forms. Manufacturers should be responsive to dosing practice patterns and other patient-specific needs of oncology patients that become apparent after medications are released into the market.

Product changes should be widely communicated to prescribers, pharmacists, nurses, and other healthcare providers involved in drug prescribing, preparation, and administration.

Package inserts and product information that describe medical indications, medication doses, administration schedules, safe handling, disposal, and product use should not include abbreviations. This is especially important for drugs used in complex treatment regimens.

Educational Materials and Programs. Pharmaceutical manufacturers and drug product sponsors should be encouraged to provide educational materials and programs that promote and encourage safe use of their drug products. Programs should clearly explain the indications appearing on FDA-approved labeling, dosages, methods for preparation, administration routes and schedules, and safe handling and disposal. Treatment descriptions should be standardized and consistent with guidelines designed to prevent medication-use errors.[20] Medication names and administration information should not be abbreviated in educational and promotional materials.

Restricted Drug Distribution. Chemotherapy agents, particularly newer oral chemotherapy agents, may be subject to restricted distribution. Restricted drug distribution products are available only through a select distribution program in which only prescribers and patients registered with the program are able to prescribe, administer, and receive the product.[50] Restricted distribution can occur due to decisions made by pharmaceutical manufacturers or as a result of Risk Evaluation and Mitigation Strategies (REMS).[51] There are circumstances in which properly implemented constraints on the traditional drug distribution system are appropriate.[52] The primary safety concern is that restricted distribution may adversely affect continuity of care. For example, when patients receive medications from various sources (clinic, local pharmacy, specialty pharmacy), it is difficult to establish a comprehensive medication list for screening of drug interactions, therapeutic duplications, and other important aspects of medication management. Delays in therapy could result when patients must wait for medications to be shipped to their home from a specialty pharmacy. Receiving prescriptions by mail does not allow for a face-to-face interaction between the patient and the pharmacist, where patient concerns and educational deficits may be identified. In addition, specialty pharmacies may not have access to the patient's complete health record and this may compromise the specialty pharmacist's ability to properly verify the order. Given these challenges, when patients can only obtain chemotherapy through a restricted drug distribution system, pharmacists and other providers should proactively provide relevant information to patients and specialty pharmacies to coordinate care. Follow up, such as phone calls, should be conducted to verify that the patient receives the chemotherapy and understands proper use. The ASHP Task Force on Caring for Patients Served by Specialty Suppliers provided recommendations for effectively managing restricted-distribution drugs and other aspects of working with specialty suppliers.[50] The National Comprehensive Cancer Network (NCCN) has also commented on specialty pharmacies and their effects on patient care and medication safety regarding chemotherapy.[53]

Regulatory Oversight. Regulatory agencies have a responsibility to review product packaging, labeling, and advertising to ensure that their content accurately reflects safety and efficacy data and conforms with language that has been approved by the FDA. A key component in those reviews should be that the product packaging and labeling facilitate safe and appropriate use and prevent users from making errors in selecting, preparing, and administering a drug product. Pharmacists should be consulted in screening proprietary drug names, product packaging, and labeling before drug products are approved for commercial use.

Recommendations for Identifying and Managing Medication Errors

Medication-use errors with chemotherapy are distinguished from errors with other types of drugs in two important ways, both of which relate to the inherent toxicity of chemotherapy agents. Individually and categorically, the therapeutic index for chemotherapy drugs is less than that for any other class of drugs. Adverse effects are an expected pharmacodynamic consequence attendant with chemotherapy use, and clinical toxicities may occur and persist at substantially lower dosages and schedules than are therapeutically used. The second characteristic that distinguishes chemotherapy from many other types of drugs is that subtherapeutic doses ("underdoses") of chemotherapy can severely complicate further treatment. Subtherapeutic doses of chemotherapy medications may not only fail to provide a therapeutic benefit but may also compromise patients' ultimate response to therapy by delaying effective treatment until adverse effects are resolved or contributing to cumulative, long-term patient harm from adverse effects. It should be noted that chemotherapy treatments are almost always repeated, and the effect of a medication-use error may not be apparent until long after the error occurs. Consequently, if treatment plans and medication orders are not verified during each treatment cycle, errors may be compounded during repeated cycles and go undetected throughout an entire treatment course. With the increased responsibility placed upon patients to manage oral therapies, it is likely that medication errors will occur with self-administration. Patients should be educated and encouraged to report medication errors to their healthcare providers, who in turn should report the error through the institutional reporting system. Patient reported errors should be handled with the same concern and diligence as an error that occurred in the hospital, clinic, or physician's office.

In addition to the actions already set forth in the ASHP Guidelines on Preventing Medication Errors in Hospitals,[1] the following actions are recommended after detecting a medication error[6]:

1. Implement monitoring and interventions for controlling injurious effects and ensuring patient safety.
2. Determine whether an error could have previously occurred during prior treatment in the same patient and in other patients. Medication preparation work sheets or logs and drug administration records should be evaluated. Unexpected toxicities and an apparent or unaccountable lack of therapeutic and adverse effects should be investigated when it is suspected that a medication error has occurred.
3. Seek the advice of healthcare professionals from various disciplines. The diverse perspective of providers in other disciplines may facilitate discovering and understanding the circumstances that allowed a medication error to occur.
4. Determine whether an immediate temporary or stopgap change in policy or procedure is necessary to prevent recurrence of an error while the proximal cause is being analyzed.
5. Provide immediate professional counseling and support for employees implicated in causing or contributing to an error that results in serious patient harm. Counseling and support should be offered to all personnel who learn that they have been involved in a medication error without regard for how recently the error occurred.
6. Establish procedures to inform and follow up with patients and their families about a medication error.
7. Understand that reporting medication errors and adverse drug reactions is a responsibility that should be shared by all healthcare providers. However, health systems may designate a person or committee to be specifically responsible for reporting and investigating medication errors and adverse drug reactions. In investigational drug studies, a study's principal investigator must report serious adverse events to the trial's sponsors (the drug manufacturer and the investigational new drug application holder) and to the institutional review board that oversees study conduct. Investigational drug sponsors are required to report to the FDA serious adverse effects associated with investigational agents, even if they are caused by a medication-use error. While reporting of medication errors in investigational studies to the institutional review board and the FDA occur, it is imperative they also be reported through the institutional reporting system or committee so that system and process improvement can occur in the setting of investigational studies.
8. Encourage practitioners to report medication errors to a national medication-error tracking program. This allows other providers to learn how medication errors occur and how they can be prevented. Reporting mechanisms for medication-use systems should be standardized by policy. Mechanisms must be developed for ongoing, interprofessional analysis and use of information that is reported to medication-error databases.[54]

Categorizing Medication Errors. In practice settings where a variety of disciplines provide patient care, serious potential and actual errors should be reported to an oversight committee composed of representatives of all the disciplines that provide care. By standardizing the way medication errors are reported, comparisons between reports and databases are facilitated, error trends are more easily identified, and system-based solutions can be developed.[55] Continuous oversight by a multidisciplinary quality-assurance committee promotes continuity and permits all primary patient-care providers to evaluate system flaws and develop and improve the quality of processes and systems that safeguard patient care.[43] Medication-use oversight committees are advised to review medication-error reports from systems other than their own and evaluate their local medication-use system for design characteristics that may permit similar errors.[30,38]

The ASHP Guidelines on Preventing Medication Errors in Hospitals[1] recommend adopting a system for categorizing medication-error severity, such as the one developed by Myers and Hartwig, et al.[54,55] Although this system is generally applicable to errors of occurrence with chemotherapy drugs, it categorizes errors by severity and prioritizes them without consideration for the frequency at which repeated errors occur. Accordingly, errors with the highest severity ranking receive the greatest efforts toward remediation. In contrast, potential errors are assigned a "zero" ranking, the lowest severity level, as they do not reach patients. By relegating potential errors to the lowest priority category, this outcome severity-based system risks trivializing system-design flaws. Errors discovered before they reach patients could cause devastating consequences, yet serious nascent errors are often transformed into potential errors only by serendipitous discovery. Therefore, potential errors should be distinguished from errors of occurrence and subcategorized based on their potential to cause harm.[54,55] However, potential errors should not be taken less seriously than errors of occurrence. When serious potential errors are discovered, the systems and processes that contributed to the errors should be evaluated and their proximal causes identified. The greatest efforts toward remediation of potential errors and errors of occurrence should be concentrated on eliminating the causes of errors that could have and had, respectively, the greatest adverse effects on patients' health.

NCC MERP's definition for medication errors includes any event that may cause or lead to inappropriate medication use.[2] The definition is complemented by the NCC MERP Taxonomy of Medication Errors, a comprehensive expandable tool intended for use in developing databases and analyzing medication-error reports.[56] The Taxonomy provides standardized language and structure for recording and tracking medication-error-related data for errors of occurrence and potential errors. NCC MERP permits interested persons to adopt it as it is presented or adapt it for use in a particular practice setting.

Conclusion

The use of chemotherapy and biotherapy agents presents healthcare organizations with distinct safety challenges that require additional precautions to prevent medication errors. These guidelines provide best practices for the safe use of chemotherapy and biotherapy agents to help practitioners improve their medication-use systems to prevent medication errors and patient harm from these agents. The guidelines describe the medication-use responsibilities shared by and unique to specific professional healthcare disciplines, progressing from general to specific applications. Although the guidelines focus on the safe use of chemotherapy in treatment of cancer patients, in general the recommendations apply for all uses of a chemotherapy agent, regardless of indication. These wide-ranging recommendations focus on preventing errors with chemotherapy agents in hospitals and ambulatory care clinics that offer direct pharmacy services, but the guidance may also be useful in other settings. Because of the complexity of and differences between practice settings and organizational arrangements, aspects of these guidelines may be more applicable to some practice settings than others. Healthcare providers should use their professional judgment in assessing and adapting the recommendations to their own circumstances, keeping in mind that these guidelines address a specific aspect of the medication-use process and should be augmented as appropriate by other clinical and practice guidance.

References

1. American Society of Hospital Pharmacists. ASHP guidelines on preventing medication errors in hospitals. *Am J Hosp Pharm.* 1993; 50:305–14.
2. National Coordinating Council on Medication Error Reporting and Prevention. About medication errors. www.nccmerp. org (accessed 2001 Jun 4).
3. McEvoy GK, ed. AHFS drug information. Section 10:00. Bethesda, MD: American Society of Health-System Pharmacy; 2013.
4. Neuss MN, Polovich M, McNiff K, et al. 2013 updated American Society of Clinical Oncology/Oncology Nursing Society chemotherapy administration safety standards including standards for the safe administration and management of oral chemotherapy. *J Oncol Pract.* 2013 (Mar 1); 9:5s–13s.
5. Pedersen CA, Schneider PJ, Scheckelhoff DJ. ASHP national survey of pharmacy practice in hospital settings: Dispensing and administration—2011. *Am J Health-Syst Pharm.* 2012; 69:768–85.
6. Walsh KE, Dodd KS, Seetharaman K, et al. Medication errors among adults and children with cancer in the outpatient setting. *J Clin Oncol.* 2009; 27:891–6.
7. Gandhi TK, Bartel SB, Shulman LN, et al. Medication safety in the ambulatory chemotherapy setting. *Cancer.* 2005; 104:2477–83.
8. Weingart SN, Toro J, Spencer J, et al. Medication errors involving oral chemotherapy. *Cancer.* 2010; 116:2455–64.
9. Weingart SN, Spencer J, Buia S, et al. Medication safety of five oral chemotherapies: a proactive risk assessment. *J Oncol Pract.* 2011; 7:2–6.
10. Taylor JA, Winter L, Geyer LJ, et al. Oral outpatient chemotherapy medication errors in children with acute lymphoblastic leukemia. *Cancer.* 2006; 107:1400–06.
11. Cohen MR, Anderson RW, Attilio RM, et al. Preventing medication errors in cancer chemotherapy. *Am J Health-Syst Pharm.* 1996; 53:737–46.
12. Attilio RM. Caring enough to understand: the road to oncology medication error prevention. *Hosp Pharm.* 1996; 31:17–26.
13. Beckwith MC, Tyler LS. Preventing medication errors with antineoplastic agents, part 1. *Hosp Pharm.* 2000; 35:511–23.
14. Beckwith MC, Tyler LS. Preventing medication errors with antineoplastic agents, part 2. *Hosp Pharm.* 2000; 35:732–47.
15. Weingart SN, Brown E, Bach PB, et al. NCCN Task Force Report: Oral chemotherapy. *J Natl Compr Canc Netw.* 2008; 6(Suppl 3):S1–S14.
16. Weingart SN, Flug J, Brouillard D, et al. Oral chemotherapy safety practices at US cancer centers: questionnaire survey. *BMJ.* 2007; 334:407.
17. Johnson PE, Chambers CR, Vaida AJ. Oncology medication safety: a 3D status report. *J Oncol Pharm Pract.* 2008; 14:169–80.
18. American Society of Health-System Pharmacists. ASHP statement on medication reconciliation. [in press]
19. Institute for Safe Medication Practices [ISMP]. Independent double checks: undervalued and misused. ISMP Medication Safety Alert - Acute Care. June 13, 2013. www.ismp.org/newsletters/acutecare/showarticle.asp?id=51 (accessed 2013 Oct 23).
20. Kohler DR, Montello MJ, Green L, et al. Standardizing the expression and nomenclature of cancer treatment regimens. *Am J Health-Syst Pharm.* 1998; 55:137–44.
21. ISMP Guidelines for Standard Order Sets. www.ismp. org/tools/guidelines/StandardOrderSets.asp (accessed 2012 Aug 12).
22. Pedersen CA, Gumpper KF. ASHP national survey on informatics: assessment of the adoption and use of pharmacy informatics in U.S. hospitals—2007. *Am J Health-Syst Pharm.* 2008; 65:2244–64.
23. Hoffman JM, Baker DK, Howard SC, et al. Safe and successful implementation of CPOE for chemotherapy at a children's cancer center. *J Natl Compr Canc Netw.* 2011; 9:S36–S50.
24. Koppel R, Metlay JP, Cohen A, et al. Role of computerized physician order entry systems in facilitating medication errors. *JAMA.* 2005; 293:1197–203.
25. Shulman LN, Miller RS, et al. Principles of Safe Practice Using an Oncology HER System for Chemotherapy Ordering, Preparation, and Administration, Part 1 of 2. *J Oncol Pract.* 2008; 4:203–6.
26. Shulman LN, Miller RS, et al. Principles of Safe Practice Using an Oncology HER System for Chemotherapy Ordering, Preparation, and Administration, Part 2 of 2. *J Oncol Pract.* 2008; 4:254–7.
27. Kim GR, Chen AR, Arceci RJ, et al. Error reduction in pediatric chemotherapy: computerized order entry

and failure modes and effects analysis. *Arch Pediatr Adolesc Med.* 2006; 160:495–8.

28. American Society of Health-System Pharmacists. ASHP guidelines on pharmacy planning for implementation of computerized provider-order-entry systems in hospitals and health systems. *Am J Health-Syst Pharm.* 2011; 68:e9–31.
29. Baker DK, Hoffman JM, Hale G, et al. Analysis of Patient Safety: Converting Complex Pediatric Chemotherapy Ordering Processes from Paper to Electronic System. *Advances in Patient Safety: New Directions and Alternative Approaches.* Volumes 1-4, AHRQ Publication Nos. 08-0034 (1-4). July 2008. Agency for Healthcare Research and Quality, Rockville, MD. www.ahrq.gov/downloads/pub/advances2/vol2/Advances-Baker_107.pdf (accessed 2012 Sep 26).
30. Kloth DD. Assuring safe care for cancer patients through an organized multidisciplinary team effort. *Hosp Pharm.* 1997; 32(suppl 1):S21–5.
31. Fischer DS, Alfano S, Knobf MT, et al. Improving the cancer chemotherapy use process. *J Clin Oncol.* 1996; 14:3148–55.
32. Griggs JL, Mangu PB, Anderson H, et al. Appropriate chemotherapy dosing for obese adult patients with cancer: American Society of Clinical Oncology Practice Guidelines. *J Clin Oncol.* 2012; 30:1553–61.
33. Lajeunesse JD. Quality assurance methods in chemotherapy production. *Hosp Pharm.* 1997; 32(suppl 1): S8–13.
34. Attilio RM. Strategies for reducing chemotherapy-related medication errors: improving the chemotherapy prescribing, dispensing, and administration process, and the patient's role in ensuring safety. *Hosp Pharm.* 1997; 32(suppl 1):S14–20.
35. Institute for Safe Medication Practices. Guideline for Maximum Adult Dose Limits of Parenteral Chemotherapy. www.medpathways.info/medpathways/tools/content/1_F.pdf (accessed 28 Mar 2013).
36. Hutcherson DA, Gammon DC. Preventing errors with antineoplastic agents: a pharmacist's approach. *Hosp Pharm.* 1997; 32:194–202, 209.
37. United Kingdom Joint Council for Clinical Oncology. Quality control in cancer chemotherapy. Managerial and procedural aspects. Oxford, England: Royal College of Physicians of London, 1994.
38. Cohen MR. Enhancing chemotherapy safety through medication system improvements. *Hosp Pharm.* 1997; 32(suppl 1):S1–7.
39. Leape LL, Bates DW, Cullen DJ, et al. Systems analysis of adverse drug events. *JAMA.* 1995; 274:35–43.
40. American Society of Health-System Pharmacists. ASHP statement on barcode-enabled medication administration technology. *Am J Health-Syst Pharm.* 2009; 66:588–90.
41. USP Quality Review. National council focuses on coordinating error reduction efforts. Rockville, MD: United States Pharmacopeial Convention, 1997 Jan.
42. Goodin S, Griffith N, Chen B, et al. Safe handling of oral chemotherapeutic agents in clinical practice: recommendations from an international pharmacy panel. *J Oncol Prac.* 2011; 7:7–12.
43. Top-priority actions for preventing adverse drug events in hospitals. Recommendations of an expert panel. *Am J Health-Syst Pharm.* 1996; 53:747–51.
44. Pepper GA. Errors in drug administration by nurses. *Am J Health-Syst Pharm.* 1995; 52:390–5.
45. OSHA Training and Education Directive 1.15—Controlling exposure to hazardous drugs. Section V. Chap. 3. Washington, D.C.: U.S. Department of Labor, 1995 Sep 22.
46. Waddell JA, Solimando DA Jr, Strickland WR, et al. Pharmacy staff interventions in a medical center hematology–oncology service. *J Am Pharm Assoc.* 1998; 38:451–6.
47. Thorn DB, Sexton MG, Lemay AP, et al. Effect of a cancer chemotherapy prescription form on prescription completeness. *Am J Hosp Pharm.* 1989; 46:1802–6.
48. Lesar TS, Lomaestro BM, Pohl H. Medication-prescribing errors in a teaching hospital. A 9-year experience. *Arch Intern Med.* 1997; 157:1569–76.
49. Cohen MR. Drug product characteristics that foster drug-use-system errors. *Am J Health-Syst Pharm.* 1995; 52:395–9.
50. American Society of Health-System Pharmacists. Report of the ASHP Task Force on Caring for Patients Served by Specialty Suppliers. *Am J Health-Syst Pharm.* 2010; 67:1650–8.
51. Stubbings JA, Joshi R, Hoffman JM. Risk evaluation and mitigation strategies (REMS): Challenges and opportunities for pharmacists. *Am J Health-Syst Pharm.* 67:1447–54, 2010.
52. ASHP policy position 0714: restricted drug distribution systems. In: Hawkins B, ed. Best practices for hospital and health-system pharmacy: positions and guidance documents of ASHP. 2011–2012 ed. Bethesda, MD: American Society of Health-System Pharmacists; 2011:338. www.ashp.org/DocLibrary/BestPractices/MarketingPositions.aspx (accessed 2012 Jun 07).
53. Schwartz RN, Eng KJ, Frieze DA, et al. National Comprehensive Cancer Network Task Force Report: Specialty Pharmacy. *J Natl Compr Canc Network.* 2010; 8 (Suppl 4):S1–12.
54. Myers CE. Needed: an interdisciplinary approach to drug misadventures. *Am J Health-Syst Pharm.* 1995; 52:367. [editorial]
55. Hartwig SC, Denger SD, Schneider PJ. Severity-indexed, incident report-based medication error-reporting program. *Am J Hosp Pharm.* 1991; 48:2611–6.
56. National Coordinating Council for Medication Error and Reporting (NCC MERP). NCC MERP taxonomy of medication errors (1998). www.nccmerp.org/pdf/taxo2001-07-31.pdf (accessed 2012 Sep 10).

Developed through the ASHP Council on Pharmacy Practice and approved by the ASHP Board of Directors on April 10, 2014. These guidelines supersede ASHP Guidelines on Preventing Medication Errors with Antineoplastic Agents dated April 19, 2002.

Barry Goldspiel, Pharm.D., BCPS, BCOP, FASHP, FISOPP, is Chief, Clinical Pharmacy Specialist Section, Clinical Center Pharmacy Department, National Institutes of Health, Bethesda, MD. James M. Hoffman, Pharm.D., M.S., BCPS, is Medication Outcomes and Safety Officer, Pharmaceutical Sciences, St. Jude Children's

Research Hospital, Memphis, TN. Niesha L. Griffith, M.S., FASHP, is Director of Pharmacy and Infusion Services, Arthur G. James Cancer Hospital and Richard J. Solove Research Institute, The Ohio State University, Columbus. Susan Goodin, Pharm.D., BCOP, FASHP, FCCP, is Executive Director, Statewide Affairs, Rutgers Cancer Institute of New Jersey, New Brunswick, and Professor of Medicine, Division of Medical Oncology, Robert Wood Johnson Medical School, New Brunswick. Robert DeChristoforo, M.S., FASHP, is Chief, Clinical Center Pharmacy Department, National Institutes of Health. CAPT Michael Montello, Pharm.D., M.B.A., is Associate Branch Chief for Clinical Trials Technology and Pharmacist Consultant, Clinical Investigations Branch, National Cancer Institute (NCI) Cancer Therapy Evaluation Program, Bethesda, and Project Officer, NCI Cancer Trials Support Unit, Bethesda. Judy L. Chase, Pharm.D., FASHP, is Director, Clinical Pharmacy Services, University of Texas M. D. Anderson Cancer Center, Houston. Sylvia Bartel, M.P.H., is Director of Pharmacy and Clinical Support Services, Dana-Farber Cancer Institute, Boston, MA. Jharana Tina Patel, Pharm.D., is Quality Assurance Officer, Clinical Center, National Institutes of Health.

The Hematology/Oncology Pharmacy Association (HOPA) is gratefully acknowledged for reviewing and endorsing these guidelines.

ASHP also gratefully acknowledges the following organizations and individuals for reviewing these guidelines (review does not imply endorsement): Academy of Medical-Surgical Nurses (AMSN); American Nurses Association (ANA); Society of Hospital Pharmacists of Australia (SHPA); Carol Bickford, Ph.D., RN-BC, CPHIMS (ANA); Jeff Brittain, Pharm.D., BCPS; Melissa Dinolfo, Pharm.D., BCOP; Paul S. Driver, Pharm.D., BCPS, FASHP; Glenn T. Etow, Pharm.D.; Jennifer Hagen, Pharm.D.; John Hamiel, Pharm.D.; Mark Holdsworth, Pharm.D., BCOP; Lisa M. Holle, Pharm.D., BCOP (HOPA); Sean Keefe, Pharm.D., BCOP; Jim Lile, Pharm.D.; Neil J. MacKinnon, M.S.Pharm., Ph.D.; Shannon Manzi, Pharm.D.; Patrick McDonnell, Pharm.D.; Cham Nguyen, Pharm.D.; Robert S. Oakley, M.S., FASHP; Karen M. O'Leary, B.S.Pharm. (SHPA); N. Pauline Thomas Parks, M.S.; Nisha Pherwani, Pharm.D., BCOP; Judy Pi, Pharm.D., BCOP; Carol Rollins, M.S., Pharm.D., BCNSP; Andrea N. Sikora, Pharm.D.; Sue Stott, B.S. (AMSN); Thomas V. Thomas, Pharm.D.; Dennis Tribble, Pharm.D.; Siu-Fun Wong, Pharm.D., FASHP, FCSHP; Arlene Wright; Daisy Yang, Pharm.D.; and Maria L. Zarambo, Pharm.D.

The authors have declared no potential conflicts of interest.

The bibliographic citation for this document is as follows: Goldspiel B, Hoffman JM, Griffith NL, et al. ASHP guidelines on preventing medication errors with chemotherapy and biotherapy. *Am J Health-Syst Pharm.* 2015; 72:e6–35.

Medication Therapy and Patient Care

Organization and Delivery of Services

Patient Adherence Programs as Part of Health Insurance Coverage (1504)

Source: Council on Public Policy

To advocate for the pharmacist's role in patient medication adherence programs that are part of health insurance plans; further,

To advocate those programs that (1) maintain the direct patient pharmacist relationship; (2) are based on the pharmacist's knowledge of the patient's medical history, indication for the prescribed medication, and expected therapeutic outcome; (3) use a communication method desired by the patient; (4) are consistent with federal and state regulations for patient confidentiality; and (5) permit dispensing of partial fills or overfills of prescription medications in order to synchronize medication refills and aid in medication adherence.

This policy supersedes ASHP policy 0116.

Complementary and Alternative Medicine in Patient Care (1511)

Source: Council on Therapeutics

To promote awareness of the impacts of complementary and alternative (CAM) products on patient care, particularly drug interactions, medication safety concerns, and the risk of contamination and variability in active ingredient content; further,

To advocate for the documentation of CAM products in the health record to improve patient safety; further,

To advocate for the inclusion of information about CAM products and their characteristics in medication-related databases; further,

To provide education on the impacts of CAM products on patient care in healthcare organizations; further,

To foster the development of up-to-date and readily available resources about CAM products.

Impact of Insurance Coverage Design on Patient Care Decision (1520)

Source: Council on Pharmacy Management

To advocate that all health insurance policies be designed and coverage decisions made in a way that preserves the patient–practitioner relationship; further,

To oppose provisions in health insurance policies that interfere with established drug distribution and clinical services designed to ensure patient safety, quality, and continuity of care; further,

To advocate for the inclusion of hospital and health-system outpatient and ambulatory care services in health insurance coverage determinations for their patients.

This policy supersedes ASHP policy 1017.

Pharmacist's Role in Population Health Management (1523)

Source: Council on Pharmacy Management

To recognize the importance of medication management in patient-care outcomes and the vital role of pharmacists in population health management; further,

To encourage healthcare organizations to engage pharmacists and pharmacy leaders in identifying appropriate patient cohorts, anticipating their healthcare needs, and implementing the models of care that optimize outcomes for patients and the healthcare organization; further,

To encourage the development of complexity index tools and resources to support the identification of high-risk, high-cost, and other patient cohorts to facilitate patient-care provider panel determinations and workload balancing; further,

To promote collaboration among members of the interprofessional healthcare team to develop meaningful measures of individual patient and population care outcomes; further,

To advocate for education to prepare pharmacists for their role in population health management.

Standardization of Doses (1525)

Source: Council on Pharmacy Practice

To recognize that standardization of medication doses reduces medication errors and improves information technology interoperability, operational efficiency, and transitions of care; further,

To encourage development of universal standardized doses for specific patient populations; further,

To encourage healthcare organizations to adopt standardized doses and to promote publication and education about best practices.

Standardization of Oral Liquid Medication Concentrations (1401)

Source: Council on Pharmacy Practice

To advocate for the development of nationally standardized drug concentrations for oral liquid medications; further,

To encourage all health care providers and organizations to standardize concentrations of oral liquid medications; further,

To promote effective instruction of patients and caregivers on how to properly measure and administer oral liquid medications.

Documentation of Patient-Care Services in the Permanent Health Record (1419)

Source: Council on Pharmacy Management

To advocate for public and organizational policies that support pharmacist documentation of patient-care services in the permanent patient health record to ensure accurate and complete documentation of the care provided to patients and to validate the impact of pharmacist patient care on patient outcomes and total cost of care; further,

To advocate that electronic health records be designed with a common documentation space to accommodate all health care team members and support the communication needs of pharmacy.

This policy supersedes ASHP policy 0407.

Standardization of Intravenous Drug Concentrations (1306)

Source: Council on Pharmacy Practice

To develop nationally standardized drug concentrations and dosing units for commonly used high-risk drugs that are given as continuous infusions to adult and pediatric patients; further,

To encourage all hospitals and health systems to use infusion devices that interface with their information systems and include standardized drug libraries with dosing limits, clinical advisories, and other patient-safety-enhancing capabilities; further,

To encourage interprofessional collaboration on the adoption and implementation of standardized drug concentrations and dosing units in hospitals and health systems.

This policy supersedes ASHP policy 0807.

Medication Overuse (1312)
Source: Council on Therapeutics
To define medication overuse as use of a medication when the potential risks of using the drug outweigh the potential benefits for the patient; further,

To recognize that medication overuse is inappropriate and can result in patient harm and increased overall health care costs; further,

To advocate that pharmacists take a leadership role in interprofessional efforts to minimize medication overuse.

Drug-Containing Devices (1313)
Source: Council on Therapeutics
To recognize that use of drug-containing devices (also known as combination devices) has important clinical and safety implications for patient care; further,

To advocate that use of such devices be documented in the patient's medical record to support clinical decision-making; further,

To encourage pharmacists to participate in interprofessional efforts to evaluate and create guidance on the use of these products through the pharmacy and therapeutics committee process to ensure patient safety and promote cost-effectiveness; further,

To advocate that the Food and Drug Administration (FDA) and device manufacturers increase the transparency of the FDA approval process for drug-containing devices, including access to data used to support approval; further,

To encourage research that evaluates the clinical and safety implications of drug-containing devices to inform product development and guide clinical practice.

Qualifications and Competencies Required to Prescribe Medications (1202)
Source: Council on Education and Workforce Development
To affirm that prescribing is a collaborative process that includes patient assessment, understanding of the patient's diagnoses, evaluation and selection of available treatment options, monitoring to achieve therapeutic outcomes, patient education, and adherence to safe and cost-effective prescribing practices; further,

To affirm that safe prescribing of medications, performed independently or collaboratively, requires competent professionals who complement each others' strengths at each step; further,

To explore the creation of prescribing standards that would apply to all who initiate or modify medication orders or prescriptions and that would facilitate development of competencies and training of prescribers; further,

To encourage research on the effectiveness of current educational processes designed to train prescribers.

Transitions of Care (1208)
Source: Council on Pharmacy Management
To recognize that continuity of patient care is a vital requirement in the appropriate use of medications; further,

To strongly encourage pharmacists to assume professional responsibility for ensuring the continuity of care as patients move from one setting to another (e.g., ambulatory care to inpatient care to home care); further,

To encourage the development, optimization, and implementation of information systems that facilitate sharing of patient-care data across care settings and providers; further,

To advocate that payers and health systems provide sufficient resources to support effective transitions of care; further,

To encourage the development of strategies to address the gaps in continuity of pharmacist patient care services.

This policy supersedes ASHP policy 0301.

Pharmacist Prescribing in Interprofessional Patient Care (1213)
Source: Council on Pharmacy Practice
To define pharmacist prescribing as follows: patient assessment and the selection, initiation, monitoring, adjustment, and discontinuation of medication therapy pursuant to diagnosis of a medical disease or condition; further,

To advocate that health care delivery organizations establish credentialing and privileging processes that delineate the scope of pharmacist prescribing within the hospital or health system and to ensure that pharmacists who prescribe are competent and qualified to do so.

Pharmacist's Role in Team-Based Care (1215)
Source: Council on Pharmacy Practice
To recognize that pharmacist participation in interprofessional health care teams as the medication-use expert increases the capacity and efficiency of teams for delivering high-quality care; further,

To advocate to policymakers, payers, and other stakeholders for the inclusion of pharmacists as care providers within team-based care; further,

To assert that pharmacists are responsible for coordinating the care they provide with that provided by other members of the health care team and are accountable to the patient and to the health care team for the outcomes of that care; further,

To urge pharmacists on health care teams to collaborate with other team members in establishing quality measures for care provided by those teams.

Collaborative Drug Therapy Management (1217)
Source: Council on Public Policy
To pursue the development of federal and state legislative and regulatory provisions that authorize collaborative drug therapy management by pharmacists; further,

To advocate expansion of federal and state legislative and regulatory provisions that optimize pharmacists' ability to provide the full range of professional services within their scope of expertise; further,

To acknowledge that as part of these advanced collaborative practices, pharmacists, as active members in team-based care, must be responsible and accountable for medication-related outcomes; further,

To support affiliated state societies in the pursuit of state-level collaborative drug therapy management authority for pharmacists.

This policy supersedes ASHP policy 9812.

Medication Adherence (1222)
Source: Council on Therapeutics
To recognize that improving medication adherence should be a key component of strategies to improve the quality and safety of patient care only when adherence improvement efforts include the following as required elements: (1) assessing the appropriateness of therapy, (2) providing patient education, and (3) ensuring patient comprehension of information necessary to support safe and appropriate use of prescribed therapies; further,

To advocate that pharmacists, because of their distinct knowledge, skills, and abilities, should take a leadership role in multidisciplinary efforts to develop, implement, monitor, and maintain effective strategies for improving medication adherence; further,

To recognize that clinicians, patients, and caregivers share accountability for the outcomes of medication therapies, and that the central role patients and their caregivers have in disease management includes responsibility for following instructions for safe and effective medication use; further,

To encourage development, evaluation, and dissemination of models that improve adherence, including those that combine existing strategies that have demonstrated effectiveness; further,

To discourage practices that inhibit education of or lead patients to decline education and clinical information regarding their medication therapy; further,

To support the development of mechanisms to document medication adherence interventions, including information technology solutions; further,

To advocate for payment models that facilitate an expanded role for pharmacists in medication adherence efforts.

Patient-Reported Outcomes Tools (1107)
Source: Council on Therapeutics
To advocate for expanded use of validated patient-reported outcomes (PRO) tools in clinical research and direct patient care; further,

To support development of validated PRO tools that are sensitive to differences in cultural and health literacy; further,

To encourage additional research on PRO tools, including studies to assess their correlation to overall patient outcomes; further,

To educate clinicians and patients about the appropriate use of PRO tools.

Pharmacist Accountability for Patient Outcomes (1114)
Source: Council on Pharmacy Practice
To affirm that pharmacists are obligated by their covenantal relationship with patients to ensure that medication use is safe and effective; further,

To declare that pharmacists, pursuant to their authority over a specialized body of knowledge, are autonomous in exercising their professional judgment and accountable as professionals and health care team members for safe and effective medication therapy outcomes; further,

To encourage pharmacists to define practices and associated measures of effectiveness that support their accountability for patient outcomes; further,

To promote pharmacist accountability as a fundamental component of pharmacy practice to other health care professionals, standards-setting and regulatory organizations, and patients.

Pharmacists' Role in Medication Reconciliation (1117)
Source: Council on Pharmacy Practice
To affirm that an effective process for medication reconciliation reduces medication errors and supports safe medication use by patients; further,

To advocate that pharmacists, because of their distinct knowledge, skills, and abilities, should take a leadership role in interdisciplinary efforts to develop, implement, monitor, and maintain effective medication reconciliation processes; further,

To encourage community-based providers, hospitals, and health systems to collaborate in organized medication reconciliation programs to promote overall continuity of patient care; further,

To declare that pharmacists have a responsibility to educate patients and caregivers on their responsibility to maintain an up-to-date and readily accessible list of medications the patient is taking and that pharmacists should assist patients and caregivers by assuring the provision of a personal medication list as part of patient counseling, education, and maintenance of an individual medical record.

This policy supersedes ASHP policy 0620.

Medication Therapy Management (1005)
Source: Council on Public Policy
To support medication therapy management (MTM) services as defined in Section 3503 of the Patient Protection and Affordable Care Act (PL 111-148); further,

To affirm that MTM is a partnership between the patient (or a caregiver) and a pharmacist, in collaboration with other health care professionals, that promotes the safe and effective use of medications.

This policy was reviewed in 2014 by the Council on Public Policy and by the Board of Directors and was found to still be appropriate.

Patient Access to Pharmacy Services in Small and Rural Hospitals (1022)
Source: Council on Pharmacy Practice
To advocate that critical-access hospitals (CAHs) and small and rural hospitals meet national medication management and patient safety standards, regardless of size or location; further,

To provide resources and tools to assist pharmacists who provide services to CAHs and small and rural hospitals in meeting standards related to safe medication use.

This policy was reviewed in 2014 by the Council on Pharmacy Practice and was found to still be appropriate.

Scope and Hours of Pharmacy Services (1023)
Source: Council on Pharmacy Practice
To support the principle that all patients should have 24-hour access to a pharmacist responsible for their care, regardless of hospital size or location; further,

To advocate alternative methods of pharmacist review of medication orders (such as remote review) before drug administration when onsite pharmacist review is not available; further,

To support the use of remote medication order review systems that communicate pharmacist approval of orders electronically to the hospital's automated medication distribution system; further,

To promote the importance of pharmacist access to pertinent patient information, regardless of proximity to patient.

This policy was reviewed in 2014 by the Council on Pharmacy Practice and was found to still be appropriate.

Health-System Use of Medications and Administration Devices Supplied Directly to Patients (0806)

Source: Council on Pharmacy Management

To encourage hospitals and health systems not to permit administration of medications brought to the hospital or clinic by the patient or caregiver when storage conditions or the source cannot be verified unless it is determined that the risk of not using such a medication exceeds the risk of using it; further,

To support care models in which medications are prepared for patient administration by the pharmacy and are obtained from a licensed, verified source; further,

To encourage hospitals and health systems not to permit the use of medication administration devices with which the staff is unfamiliar (e.g., devices brought in by patients) unless it is determined that the risk of not using such a device exceeds the risk of using it; further,

To advocate adequate reimbursement for preparation, order review, and other costs associated with the safe provision and administration of medications and use of related devices.

This policy was reviewed in 2012 by the Council on Pharmacy Management and by the Board of Directors and was found to still be appropriate.

Pharmacist's Leadership Role in Anticoagulation Therapy Management (0816)

Source: Council on Therapeutics

To advocate that pharmacists provide leadership in the interdisciplinary development, implementation, maintenance, effectiveness monitoring, and assurance of continuity of care of anticoagulation management programs; further,

To advocate that pharmacists be responsible for coordinating the individualized care of patients within anticoagulation management programs; further,

To encourage pharmacists who participate in anticoagulation programs to educate patients, caregivers, prescribers, and staff about anticoagulant medication uses, drug interactions, adverse effects, the importance of adhering to therapy, and recommended laboratory testing and other monitoring.

This policy was reviewed in 2012 by the Council on Therapeutics and by the Board of Directors and was found to still be appropriate.

Standard Drug Administration Schedules (0707)

Source: Council on Pharmacy Management

To support the principle that standard medication administration times should be based primarily on optimal pharmacotherapeutics, with secondary consideration of workload, caregiver preference, patient preference, and logistical issues; further,

To encourage the development of hospital-specific or health-system-specific standard administration times through an interdisciplinary process coordinated by the pharmacy; further,

To encourage information technology vendors to adopt these principles in system design while allowing flexibility to meet site-specific patient needs.

This policy was reviewed in 2011 by the Council on Pharmacy Management and by the Board of Directors and was found to still be appropriate.

Universal Influenza Vaccination (0601)

Source: Commission on Therapeutics

To advocate universal administration of influenza vaccinations to the United States population.

This policy was reviewed in 2010 by the Council on Therapeutics and by the Board of Directors and was found to still be appropriate.

Integrated Team-Based Approach for the Pharmacy Enterprise (0619)

Source: Council on Professional Affairs

To advocate a high level of coordination of all components of the pharmacy enterprise in hospitals and health systems for the purpose of optimizing (1) the value of drug therapy and (2) medication-use safety; further,

To encourage pharmacy department leaders to develop and maintain patient-centered practice models that integrate into a team all components of the pharmacy enterprise, including general and specialized clinical practice, drug-use policy, product acquisition and inventory control, product preparation and distribution, and medication-use safety and other quality initiatives.

This policy was reviewed in 2010 by the Council on Pharmacy Practice and by the Board of Directors and was found to still be appropriate.

Health Care Quality Standards and Pharmacy Services (0502)

Source: Council on Administrative Affairs

To advocate that health care quality improvement programs adopt standard quality measures that are developed with the involvement of pharmacists, are evidence-based, and promote the demonstrated role of pharmacists in improving patient outcomes.

This policy was reviewed in 2014 by the Council on Pharmacy Practice and by the Board of Directors and was found to still be appropriate.

Health-System Facility Design (0505)

Source: Council on Administrative Affairs

To advocate the development and the inclusion of contemporary pharmacy specifications in national and state health care design standards to ensure adequate space for safe provision of pharmacy products and patient care services; further,

To promote pharmacist involvement in the design-planning and space-allocation decisions of health care facilities.

This policy was reviewed in 2014 by the Council on Pharmacy Management and by the Board of Directors and was found to still be appropriate.

Mandatory Tablet Splitting for Cost Containment (0525)
Source: Council on Professional Affairs
To oppose mandatory tablet splitting for cost containment in ambulatory care; further,

To encourage pharmacists, when voluntary tablet splitting is considered, to collaborate with patients, caregivers, and other health care professionals to determine whether tablet splitting is appropriate on the basis of the patient's ability to split tablets and the suitability of the medication (e.g., whether it is scored or is an extended-release product); further,

To urge pharmacists to promote dosing accuracy and patient safety by ensuring that patients are educated on how to properly split tablets; further,

To encourage further research by the United States Pharmacopeia and the Food and Drug Administration on the impact of tablet splitting on product quality.

This policy was reviewed in 2014 by the Council on Pharmacy Practice and by the Board of Directors and was found to still be appropriate.

Performance Improvement (0202)
Source: Council on Administrative Affairs
To encourage pharmacists to establish performance improvement processes within their practice settings that measure both operational and patient outcomes; further,

To encourage pharmacists to use contemporary performance improvement techniques and methods for ongoing improvement in their services; further,

To support pharmacists in their development and implementation of performance-improvement processes.

This policy was reviewed in 2011 by the Council on Pharmacy Management and by the Board of Directors and was found to still be appropriate.

Pharmacy Benefits for the Uninsured (0101)
Source: Council on Administrative Affairs
To support the principle that all patients have the right to receive care from pharmacists; further,

To declare that health system pharmacists should play a leadership role in ensuring access to pharmacists' services for indigent or low-income patients who lack insurance coverage and for patients who are underinsured; further,

To advocate better collaboration among health systems, community health centers, state and county health departments, and the federal Health Resources and Services Administration (HRSA) in identifying and addressing the needs of indigent and low-income patients who lack insurance coverage and of patients who are underinsured.

This policy was reviewed in 2010 by the Council on Pharmacy Management and by the Board of Directors and was found to still be appropriate.

Patient Satisfaction (0104)
Source: Council on Administrative Affairs
To encourage pharmacists to establish mechanisms within their practice settings that measure the level of satisfaction patients have with pharmacy services and with the outcomes of their drug therapy; further,

To construct such mechanisms in a manner that will (1) provide a system for monitoring trends in the quality of pharmacy services to patients, (2) increase recognition of the value of pharmacy services, and (3) provide a basis for making improvements in the process and outcomes of pharmacy services; further,

To facilitate a dialogue with and education of national patient satisfaction database vendors on the role and value of clinical pharmacy services.

This policy was reviewed in 2010 by the Council on Pharmacy Management and by the Board of Directors and was found to still be appropriate.

Pharmacist Validation of Information Related to Medications (9921)
Source: Council on Professional Affairs
To support consultation with a pharmacist as a primary means for consumers to validate publicly available information related to medications.

This policy was reviewed in 2013 by the Council on Pharmacy Practice and by the Board of Directors and was found to still be appropriate.

Collaborative Drug Therapy Management Activities (9801)
Source: House of Delegates Resolution
To support the participation of pharmacists in collaborative drug therapy management, which is defined as a multidisciplinary process for selecting appropriate drug therapies, educating patients, monitoring patients, and continually assessing outcomes of therapy; further,

To recognize that pharmacists participate in collaborative drug therapy management for a patient who has a confirmed diagnosis by an authorized prescriber; further,

To recognize that the activities of a pharmacist in collaborative drug therapy management may include, but not be limited to, initiating, modifying, and monitoring a patient's drug therapy; ordering and performing laboratory and related tests; assessing patient response to therapy; counseling and educating a patient on medications; and administering medications.

This policy was reviewed in 2012 by the Council on Pharmacy Practice and by the Board of Directors and was found to still be appropriate.

Medication Administration by Pharmacists (9820)
Source: Council on Professional Affairs
To support the position that the administration of medicines is part of the routine scope of pharmacy practice; further,

To support the position that pharmacists who administer medicines should be skilled to do so; further,

To support the position that pharmacists should be participants in establishing procedures in their own work settings with respect to the administration of medicines (by anyone) and monitoring the outcomes of medication administration.

This policy was reviewed in 2012 by the Council on Pharmacy Practice and by the Board of Directors and was found to still be appropriate.

ASHP Statement on Confidentiality of Patient Health Care Information

The American Society of Health-System Pharmacists (ASHP) believes that all medical information is sensitive and should be given the utmost protection. ASHP supports the adoption into federal law of a minimum standard for protection of individually identifiable patient health information and believes that states should retain the ability to adopt standards that are more stringent than federal law.

ASHP believes that patients should have the right to access and review their medical records and the ability to correct factual errors in those records. Patients should also have the right to know who has access to their medical records and to authorize how their medical information will be used.

The Health Insurance Portability and Accountability Act of 1996 (HIPAA) requires health systems to have written policies and procedures in place to guard against the unauthorized collection, use, or disclosure of individually identifiable patient health information and provide notice of such policies to their patients. All health-system personnel should be trained to understand and comply with those privacy standards.

ASHP strongly believes that pharmacists must have access to patient health records in order to provide quality care and ensure the safe use of medications. Within health systems, all authorized practitioners should be encouraged to communicate freely with each other while maintaining patient confidentiality and privacy. This includes pharmacists practicing across the continuum of practice settings in order to maintain continuity of care. Pharmacists recognize that with access to the patient's health record comes the pharmacist's professional responsibility to safeguard the patient's rights to privacy and confidentiality. Uniquely identifiable patient information should not be exchanged without the patient's authorization for any reason not directly related to treatment, payment, health care operations, or research conducted under an appropriately constituted institutional review board (IRB). ASHP advocates strict governmental protections, with appropriate civil or criminal penalties for violations, to prevent disclosure of individually identifiable patient information outside the health system (i.e., to an unauthorized third party) for any purposes not directly related to treatment, payment, health care operations, or research conducted under an appropriately constituted IRB.

Pharmacists participate extensively in research on drugs. ASHP believes that all research data must be recorded and stored in such a way that the subjects' rights of privacy and confidentiality are protected. IRBs have a responsibility to determine when informed consent is necessary and to establish procedures for obtaining informed consent. Patients should receive a statement describing the parties who may have access to patient-identifiable information (e.g., institutional personnel, business associates, researchers, personnel from study sponsors, employees of government agencies that monitor compliance with regulations). Patient authorization requirements under the privacy regulations of HIPAA must be followed, and patients always have the right to withdraw their consent at any time.

ASHP believes that there is no potential for a breach of patient confidentiality when patient information is aggregated for use in legitimate research or statistical measurement and is not uniquely identifiable. Therefore, specific authorization by individual patients for access to this information is not needed.

ASHP believes that pharmacy residency programs and other training programs must implement policies and procedures to ensure the confidentiality of patient medical records while allowing pharmacy students and residents access to these records in the course of their training and presentation of their research.

This statement was reviewed in 2013 by the Council on Public Policy and by the Board of Directors and was found to still be appropriate.

Developed through the ASHP Council on Public Policy and approved by the ASHP Board of Directors on February 22, 2008, and by the ASHP House of Delegates on June 10, 2008.

This statement supersedes the ASHP Statement on the Confidentiality of Patient Health Care Information dated April 21, 1999.

The bibliographic citation for this document is as follows: American Society of Health-System Pharmacists. ASHP statement on confidentiality of patient health care information. *Am J Health-Syst Pharm.* 2009; 66:411–2.

ASHP Statement on the Health-System Pharmacist's Role in National Health Care Quality Initiatives

Position

The American Society of Health-System Pharmacists (ASHP) believes that pharmacists who practice in hospitals and health systems ("health-system pharmacists") have a critical leadership role in national health care quality-improvement initiatives. Health-system pharmacists possess the knowledge of drug therapy and medication-use systems required to successfully implement quality-assurance and improvement programs. These pharmacists should use their authority over and accountability for medication management systems to align medication use in hospitals and health systems with the national health care quality agenda.

Background

Major reports from the Institute of Medicine (IOM) have demonstrated that the quality and safety environment across the health care industry needs significant transformation. *The Urgent Need to Improve Health Care Quality*[1] suggested that the quality of the health care system in the United States could be accurately measured and that the quality of care was being compromised by the underuse, overuse, and misuse of health care entities. *Crossing the Quality Chasm*[2] built a compelling case that the American health care delivery system requires major restructuring and proposed goals for improving six key dimensions of health care quality: safety, timeliness, effectiveness, efficiency, equity, and patient centeredness (the "STEEP" framework). To achieve these aims, IOM called for fundamental reforms, including new payment methodologies, public reporting, and transparency of quality-improvement data.

Since the release of these reports, health care policymakers, providers, purchasers, payers, consumers, and others have responded in ways that are beginning to change the U.S. health care delivery system. These changes are influenced by a growing number of private and public organizations, including the Joint Commission, Centers for Medicare and Medicaid Services (CMS), National Quality Forum, National Priorities Partnership, Agency for Healthcare Research and Quality, Institute for Healthcare Improvement, and American Health Quality Association, among others. These organizations, alone or in collaboration, identify health care quality measures to set the national health care quality agenda. These quality measures are collected and reported through both mandatory and voluntary reporting systems, and the outcome measurements of a health system may be linked to reimbursement (e.g., through CMS pay-for-performance programs).

Responsibilities of Health-System Pharmacists

Many national health care quality measures are related to medication use.[3] Health-system pharmacists are strategically positioned to integrate practices and procedures that support these quality measures into the medication-use system. To help align medication use in hospitals and health systems with the national health care quality agenda, health-system pharmacists should

- Become familiar with the organizations that influence the national health care quality agenda and monitor those organizations for changes in medication-use-related quality measures.
- Participate in the development, implementation, and evaluation of national and state health care quality-improvement initiatives related to medication use.
- Collaborate with other health care professionals to evaluate medication-use practices in their organizations and develop and implement programs that optimize patient outcomes, improve medication use, and align with the national health care quality agenda, including expanding the scope and reach of pharmacists' services when appropriate.
- Collect, analyze, and report data that measure health care quality related to medication use, and support the public availability of those data.
- Integrate and align information systems in their organizations with the national health care quality agenda.
- Educate other health care practitioners, health care executives, and the public about medication-related health care quality-improvement initiatives and the critical role pharmacists have in those initiatives (e.g., by publishing articles about innovative pharmacy services that improve patient outcomes or medication use).
- Encourage national pharmacy organizations to support, guide, and provide education related to the national health care quality agenda.

Conclusion

The number of mandatory and voluntary health care quality measures related to the use of medications is large and growing. As medication-use experts, health-system pharmacists have a responsibility to become knowledgeable about national health care quality-improvement initiatives and to align their practices accordingly. Because health-system pharmacists possess knowledge of drug therapy and medication-use systems and have authority over and accountability for medication management systems, they have a fundamental leadership role in the development, implementation, and evaluation of health care quality-improvement initiatives.

References

1. Chassin MR, Galvin RW. The urgent need to improve health care quality. Institute of Medicine National Roundtable on Health Care Quality. *JAMA.* 1998; 280:1000–5.
2. Institute of Medicine Committee on Quality of Health Care in America. Crossing the quality chasm: a new health system for the 21st century. Washington, DC: National Academy Press; 2001:43–56.

3. Bohenek WS, Grossbart SR. Pharmacists' role in improving quality of care. *Am J Health-Syst Pharm.* 2008; 65:1566–70.

This policy was reviewed in 2013 by the Council on Pharmacy Practice and by the Board of Directors and was found to still be appropriate.

Approved by the ASHP Board of Directors on April 17, 2009, and by the ASHP House of Delegates on June 16, 2009. Developed through the ASHP Council on Pharmacy Practice.

The contributions of Wayne S. Bohenek, Pharm.D., M.S., FASHP, and Jamie S. Sinclair, M.S., to this statement are gratefully acknowledged. The following organizations and individuals are acknowledged for reviewing draft versions of this statement (review does not imply endorsement): Academy of Managed Care Pharmacy (AMCP); Accreditation Council for Pharmacy Education (ACPE); American Pharmacists Association (APhA); South Carolina Society of Health-Systems Pharmacists (SCSHSP); John A. Armitstead, M.S., FASHP; Cathy Baker, Pharm.D.; Frank Briggs, Pharm.D., M.P.H.; Kimberly K. Daugherty, Pharm.D., BCPS; Jeanne Ezell, M.S., FASHP; Linda Gore Martin, Pharm.D., M.B.A., BCPS; Jody Jacobson Wedret, FASHP, FCSHP; Patricia Kienle, M.P.A., FASHP; Julie Kuhle, B.S.Pharm.; Greg Polk, M.B.A.; James A. Ponto, M.S., BCNP, FASHP; Mike Rouse, B.Pharm.(Hons), M.P.S. (ACPE); Marissa Schlaifer, M.S. (AMCP); Sue Skledar, M.P.H., FASHP; Darren M. Triller, Pharm.D.; and Bradley White, Pharm.D., R.N. (SCSHSP).

The bibliographic citation for this document is as follows: American Society of Health-System Pharmacists. ASHP statement on the health-system pharmacist's role in national health care quality initiatives. *Am J Health-Syst Pharm.* 2010; 67:578–9.

ASHP–SHM Joint Statement on Hospitalist–Pharmacist Collaboration

Position

The American Society of Health-System Pharmacists (ASHP) and the Society for Hospital Medicine (SHM) believe that the rapidly emerging hospitalist model of inpatient care offers new and significant opportunities to optimize patient care through collaboration among hospitalists, hospital pharmacists (hereinafter, "pharmacists"), and other health care providers. The emerging model of care allows for deeper professional relationships among health care providers and promotes a shared interest in and responsibility for direct patient care, indirect patient care, and service activities. ASHP and SHM encourage hospitalists, pharmacists, and health care executives to seek out ways to foster collaboration between hospitalists and pharmacists.

The purpose of this consensus statement is to promote an understanding of the ways hospitalists and pharmacists can jointly optimize the care provided to patients in hospitals, examine opportunities for improving hospitalist–pharmacist alliances that enhance patient care, suggest future directions for collaboration, and identify aspects of such collaboration that warrant further research.

Background

Increases in health care spending and the expanding influence of managed care in the late 1980s and early 1990s resulted in calls for more efficient health care. The movement toward greater efficiency resulted in more emphasis on ambulatory care, fewer hospital admissions, shortened hospital stays, and an overall increase in the acuity of illness of hospitalized patients. The emphasis on ambulatory care increased the number and complexity of physician office visits, and the changing characteristics of office- and hospital-based care placed significant demands on primary care physicians and contributed to the rise of hospital medicine.

In 1996, the term "hospitalist" was introduced to the health care lexicon.[1] A hospitalist was defined as an inpatient physician who manages the care of hospitalized patients and facilitates the transfer of their care back to the primary care physician. The Society of Hospital Medicine has since defined a hospitalist as a physician whose primary professional focus is the general medical care of hospitalized patients and whose activities may include patient care, teaching, research, and leadership related to hospital medicine.[2]

The past decade has seen rapid growth in the number of hospitalists and the use of hospitalists by U.S. hospitals.[3] In 2005, 70% of hospitals with more than 200 beds used hospitalist services, and there were over 16,000 hospitalists in practice.[4] An estimated 20,000 hospitalists were practicing at over 2,600 U.S. hospitals in 2007.[5]

Initially, many physicians expressed concern about the potential for hospitalists to interfere in the relationship between the patient and the primary care physician, as well as about the potential negative impact on continuity of care.[6] However, subsequent studies demonstrated increasing acceptance of hospitalists by primary care physicians, with as many as 89% considering the hospitalist model to be superior to the historical model of hospital care being provided by primary care physicians or by specialists working on rotations.[7,8] Numerous studies demonstrate the value of hospitalists in improving quality of care, decreasing hospital costs and length of stay, and reducing hospital readmissions.[9–21]

As early as 1921, hospital pharmacists in the American Pharmaceutical Association (now the American Pharmacists Association) had formed a committee to address their distinct concerns. During the 1930s, hospital pharmacists began to organize state organizations and to adhere to a set of minimum standards of practice. In 1942, the American Society of Hospital Pharmacists (now the American Society of Health-System Pharmacists [ASHP]) was formed to establish minimum standards of pharmaceutical services in hospitals, provide interchange among pharmacists, promote new pharmaceutical techniques, and aid the medical profession in extending the economic and rational use of medications.[22] As of 2005, there were approximately 50,000 pharmacists practicing in U.S. hospitals.[23]

The modern mission of hospital pharmacy departments is to ensure optimal outcomes from the use of medicines.[24] Although the focus of hospital pharmacy has traditionally been on the safe dispensing of medications, direct patient care by pharmacists (clinical pharmacy) has always been a component of hospital pharmacy practice. Following the rise of pharmaceutical care in the 1980s,[25] these pharmacist services have expanded greatly. It has been estimated that 35–40% of hospital pharmacists are devoted to providing clinical services.[23] A systematic review in 2006 documented improved outcomes when clinical pharmacists interacted with the health care team on patient rounds, interviewed patients, reconciled medications, and provided discharge counseling and follow-up.[26] These findings support those of other studies in which specific clinical pharmacy services were associated with improved therapeutic and economic outcomes.[27–31]

Opportunities for Collaboration Between Pharmacists and Hospitalists

Pharmacists and hospitalists have shared interests that provide strong incentives for collaboration. All health care professionals share, first, a commitment to and responsibility for providing safe and effective patient care. Physicians, pharmacists, and other health care providers have long collaborated in providing direct patient care. The emerging hospitalist model of care offers more opportunities for collaboration because pharmacists and hospitalists also share interest in and responsibility for indirect patient care and service activities—developing the institutional policies, processes, and infrastructure that support patient care.

Direct patient care activities typically performed by hospitalists include obtaining patient histories, conducting physical examinations, making diagnoses, developing treatment plans, monitoring patients' responses to therapy, performing follow-up hospital visits, participating in family meetings, and providing discharge instructions.[32] Specific clinical pharmacy services that have been associated with improved health care outcomes include providing drug information, managing medication protocols and adverse drug reactions, participating in medical rounds, gathering admission medication histories, interviewing patients, reconciling patient medications, and providing discharge counseling and follow-up.[26–31]

Pharmacists should be involved in the care of hospitalized patients and can collaborate with hospitalists in numerous ways, including

- Providing consultative services that foster appropriate, evidence-based medication selection (e.g., during rounds),
- Providing drug information consultation to physicians, nurses, and other clinicians,
- Managing medication protocols under collaborative practice agreements,
- Assisting in the development of treatment protocols,
- Monitoring therapeutic responses (including laboratory test results),
- Continuously assessing for and managing adverse drug reactions,
- Gathering medication histories,
- Reconciling medications as patients move across the continuum of hospital care, and
- Providing patient and caretaker education, including discharge counseling and follow-up.

Both hospitalists and pharmacists have a responsibility for ensuring continuity as patients move across settings of care.

In addition to their direct patient care activities, hospitalists add value through their efforts in hospital service activities, student and resident education, and research. Typical service activities include participating in quality-improvement and safety initiatives, developing institutional guidelines and protocols for the treatment of specific diseases, serving on hospital committees (e.g., the pharmacy and therapeutics [P&T] committee), and working with others to introduce new technologies to the hospital setting.[33,34]

Pharmacists also participate in hospital service activities, student and resident education, and research. For example, pharmacists serve on the P&T committee and are directly involved in managing the formulary system that guides an institution's medication use. As medication experts, pharmacists contribute to the development and implementation of patient care guidelines and other medication-use policies. Pharmacist expertise is also integral to many quality-improvement efforts (e.g., surgical infection prophylaxis) and to technology initiatives (e.g., bedside medication scanning and computerized prescriber-order-entry systems). Pharmacist provision of inservice education on medications and medication use is invaluable for all health care providers.

These overlapping responsibilities provide hospitalists and pharmacists with opportunities to collaborate on activities that can have a profound effect on care in the hospital. Hospitalists and pharmacists can work together to ensure that care is evidence-based, cost-effective, and adherent to national guidelines; establish an institutional culture of safety; develop and implement quality-improvement initiatives; meet accreditation standards; and, in many cases, foster the institution's education and research initiatives. Health professional education and research offer the opportunities to improve patient care provided not just by a single hospital but by other facilities as well.

Opportunities to Improve Collaboration

ASHP and SHM believe that there are opportunities for improving collaboration between hospitalists and pharmacists. Barriers to collaboration include real and perceived professional boundaries, poor integration of technology systems, inadequate pharmacist and hospitalist staffing, time constraints, inadequate funding and resources, lack of third-party compensation for clinical pharmacy services, and the competing obligations weighing on both professions.

Real and perceived professional boundaries can be addressed by clear communication and by enhanced interdisciplinary educational opportunities for all members of the health care team.[35–38] ASHP and SHM believe that, while hospitalists should serve as the primary leaders of hospital care teams, all health care professionals should be willing to assume a leadership role in treating patients and, when appropriate, accept leadership by other team members. Like all members of the care team, pharmacists require timely access to hospitalists for consultation, as well as access to patient information. The vital flow of information and communication among health care providers should be conducive to collaborating and improving patient outcomes. ASHP and SHM believe that properly applied, well-integrated technologies (e.g., electronic medical records and personal digital assistants with clinical decision support systems, including drug information) can enhance communication among all members of the health care team.

Hospitalists and pharmacists can work together to overcome limitations created by inadequate funding and staffing by providing evidence to health care executives of the value of clinical pharmacist positions and pharmacist–hospitalist collaboration. This evidence should examine the impact of these positions and such collaboration on therapeutic, safety, humanistic, and economic outcomes. Collaboration among all members of the health care team would also be encouraged by reforming the current fee-for-service reimbursement practices to base payment for care delivery on overall treatment goals (e.g., a payment rate based on diagnosis).

Conclusion

An interdisciplinary approach to health care that includes physicians, pharmacists, nurses, and other health care professionals will improve the quality of patient care. Hospitalists and pharmacists need to collaborate with each other and with other health care professionals to optimize outcomes in hospitalized patients. ASHP and SHM believe that hospitalist–pharmacist alliances should be encouraged and that the systems and technologies that enable collaboration, and the incentives for such collaboration, should be enhanced.

References

1. Wachter RM, Goldman L. The emerging role of "hospitalists" in the American health care system. *N Engl J Med.* 1996; 335:514–7.

2. Society of Hospital Medicine. Definition of a hospitalist. www.hospitalmedicine.org/Content/NavigationMenu/AboutSHM/DefinitionofaHospitalist/Definition_of_a_Hosp.htm (accessed 2007 May 29).
3. Kralovec PD, Miller JA, Wellikson L, et al. The status of hospital medicine groups in the United States. *J Hosp Med.* 2006; 1:75–80.
4. AHA hospital statistics. Chicago: American Hospital Association; 2005.
5. Hospital medicine specialty shows 20 percent growth. SHM analysis of 2005 American Hospital Association survey data. www.hospitalmedicine.org/AM/Template.cfm?Section=Press_Releases&Template=/CM/ContentDisplay.cfm&ContentID=12507 (accessed 2007 May 29).
6. Sox HC. The hospitalist model: perspectives of the patient, the internist, and internal medicine. *Ann Intern Med.* 1999; 130:368–72.
7. Auerbach AD, Nelson EA, Lindenauer PK, et al. Physician attitudes toward and prevalence of the hospitalist model of care: results of a national survey. *Am J Med.* 2000; 109:648–53.
8. Fernandez A, Grumbach K, Goitein L, et al. Friend or foe? How primary care physicians perceive hospitalists. *Arch Intern Med.* 2000; 160:2902–8.
9. Wachter RM, Katz P, Showstack J, et al. Reorganizing an academic medical service: impact on cost, quality, patient satisfaction, and education. *JAMA.* 1998; 279:1560–5.
10. Diamond HS, Goldberg E, Janosky JE. The effect of full-time faculty hospitalists on the efficiency of care at a community teaching hospital. *Ann Intern Med.* 1998; 129:197–203.
11. Stein MD, Hanson S, Tammaro D, et al. Economic effects of community versus hospital-based faculty pneumonia care. *J Gen Intern Med.* 1998; 13:774–7.
12. Craig DE, Hartka L, Likosky WH, et al. Implementation of a hospitalist system in a large health maintenance organization: the Kaiser Permanente experience. *Ann Intern Med.* 1999; 130:355–9.
13. Freese RB. The Park Nicollet experience in establishing a hospitalist system. *Ann Intern Med.* 1999; 130:350–4.
14. Rifkin WD, Connor DS, Silver A, et al. Comparison of hospitalists and primary care internists in the care of patients with pneumonia. *J Gen Intern Med.* 1999; 14(suppl):S118.
15. Rifkin WD, Connor DS, Silver A, et al. Comparing hospitalists' and community-based primary care physicians' care of patients with pneumonia. *J Gen Intern Med.* 2001; 16(suppl):S215.
16. Davis KM, Koch KE, Harvey JK, et al. Effects of hospitalists on cost, outcomes, and patient satisfaction in a rural health system. *Am J Med.* 2000; 108:621–6.
17. Halpert AP, Pearson SD, LeWine HE, et al. The impact of an inpatient physician program on quality, utilization, and satisfaction. *Am J Manag Care.* 2000; 6:549–55.
18. Bellet PS, Whitaker RC. Evaluation of a pediatric hospitalist service: impact on length of stay and hospital charges. *Pediatrics.* 2000; 105:478–84.
19. Landrigan C, Srivastava R, Muret-Wagstaff S, et al. Outcomes of hospitalization in pediatric patients insured by HMOs: comparison of care by hospitalists and traditional academic providers. *Pediatr Res.* 2000; 47:204A. Abstract.
20. Srivastava R, Landrigan C, Muret-Wagstaff S, et al. Impact of a managed care hospitalist system in academic pediatrics. *Pediatr Res.* 2000; 47:228A. Abstract.
21. Srivastava R, Landrigan C, Muret-Wagstaff S, et al. Cost savings for patients with acute conditions cared for by pediatric hospitalists in a tertiary care center. *Pediatr Res.* 2001; 49:125A. Abstract.
22. Zellmer WA. Overview of the history of pharmacy in the United States. In: Brown TR, ed. Handbook of institutional pharmacy practice. Bethesda, MD: American Society of Health-System Pharmacists; 2006:19–32.
23. Pedersen CA, Schneider PJ, Scheckelhoff DJ. ASHP national survey of pharmacy practice in hospital settings: dispensing and administration—2005. *Am J Health-Syst Pharm.* 2006; 63:327–45.
24. Zellmer WA. Perspectives on Hilton Head. *Am J Hosp Pharm.* 1986; 43:1439–43.
25. American Society of Hospital Pharmacists. ASHP statement on pharmaceutical care. *Am J Hosp Pharm.* 1993; 50:1720–3.
26. Kaboli PJ, Hoth AB, McClimon BJ, et al. Clinical pharmacists and inpatient medical care: a systematic review. *Arch Intern Med.* 2006; 166:955–64.
27. Bond CA, Raehl CL, Franke T. Interrelationships among mortality rates, drug costs, total cost of care, and length of stay in United States hospitals: summary and recommendations for clinical pharmacy services and staffing. *Pharmacotherapy.* 2001; 21:129–41.
28. Bond CA, Raehl CL, Franke T. Clinical pharmacy services, hospital pharmacy staffing, and medication errors in United States hospitals. *Pharmacotherapy.* 2002; 22:134–47.
29. Bond CA, Raehl CL. Clinical pharmacy services, pharmacy staffing, and adverse drug reactions in United States hospitals. *Pharmacotherapy.* 2006; 26:735–47.
30. Schumock GT, Butler MG, Meek PD, et al. Evidence of the economic benefit of clinical pharmacy services: 1996–2000. *Pharmacotherapy.* 2003; 23:113–32.
31. Kucukarslan SN, Peters M, Mlynarek M, et al. Pharmacists on rounding teams reduce preventable adverse drug events in hospital general medicine units. *Arch Intern Med.* 2003; 163:2014–8.
32. O'Leary KJ, Liebovitz DM, Baker DW. How hospitalists spend their time: insights on efficiency and safety. *J Hosp Med.* 2006; 1:88–93.
33. Hauer KE, Wachter RM. Implications of the hospitalist model for medical students' education. *Acad Med.* 2001; 76:324–30.
34. Plauth WH III, Pantilat SZ, Wachter RM, et al. Hospitalists' perceptions of their residency training needs: results of a national survey. *Am J Med.* 2001; 111:247–54.
35. Committee on the Health Professions Education Summit. Health professions education: a bridge to quality. Washington, DC: National Academy Press; 2003.
36. Cooper H, Carlisle C, Gibbs T, et al. Developing an evidence base for interdisciplinary learning: a systematic review. *J Adv Nurs.* 2001; 31:228–37.

37. Horsburgh M, Lamdin R, Williamson E. Multiprofessional learning: the attitudes of medical, nursing, and pharmacy students to shared learning. *Med Educ.* 2001; 35:876–83.
38. Crawford GB, Price SD. Team working: palliative care as a model of interdisciplinary practice. *Med J Aust.* 2003; 179:S32–4.

This statement was reviewed in 2012 by the Council on Pharmacy Practice and by the Board of Directors and was found to still be appropriate.

Approved by the ASHP Council on Pharmacy Practice on September 24, 2007, by the ASHP Board of Directors on September 27, 2007, by the SHM Board of Directors on September 26, 2007. Developed through the American Society of Health-System Pharmacists Research and Education Foundation through a sponsorship from sanofi-aventis, Inc.

Daniel J. Cobaugh, Pharm.D., FAACT, DABAT (Corresponding Author, ASHP); Alpesh Amin, M.D., MBA, FACP (Corresponding Author, SHM); Thomas Bookwalter, Pharm.D. (ASHP, SHM); Mark Williams, M.D., FACP (SHM), Patricia Grunwald, Pharm.D. (ASHP); Cynthia LaCivita, Pharm.D. (ASHP); and Bruce Hawkins, B.A., B.S. (ASHP) are gratefully acknowledged for drafting this statement.

The bibliographic citation for this document is as follows: American Society of Health-System Pharmacists. ASHP–SHM joint statement on hospitalist–pharmacist collaboration. *Am J Health-Syst Pharm.* 2008; 65:260–3.

ASHP Statement on Pharmaceutical Care

The purpose of this statement is to assist pharmacists in understanding pharmaceutical care. Such understanding must precede efforts to implement pharmaceutical care, which ASHP believes merit the highest priority in all practice settings.

Possibly the earliest published use of the term pharmaceutical care was by Brodie in the context of thoughts about drug use control and medication-related services.[1,2] It is a term that has been widely used and a concept about which much has been written and discussed in the pharmacy profession, especially since the publication of a paper by Hepler and Strand in 1990.[3–5] ASHP has formally endorsed the concept.[6] With varying terminology and nuances, the concept has also been acknowledged by other national pharmacy organizations.[7,8] Implementation of pharmaceutical care was the focus of a major ASHP conference in March 1993.

Many pharmacists have expressed enthusiasm for the concept of pharmaceutical care, but there has been substantial inconsistency in its description. Some have characterized it as merely a new name for clinical pharmacy; others have described it as anything that pharmacists do that may lead to beneficial results for patients.

ASHP believes that pharmaceutical care is an important new concept that represents growth in the profession beyond clinical pharmacy as often practiced and beyond other activities of pharmacists, including medication preparation and dispensing. All of these professional activities are important, however, and ASHP continues to be a strong proponent of the necessity for pharmacists' involvement in them. In practice, these activities should be integrated with and culminate in pharmaceutical care provided by individual pharmacists to individual patients.

In 1992, ASHP's members urged the development of an officially recognized ASHP definition of pharmaceutical care.[9] This statement provides a definition and elucidates some of the elements and implications of that definition. The definition that follows is an adaptation of a definition developed by Hepler and Strand.[3]

Definition

The mission of the pharmacist is to provide pharmaceutical care. Pharmaceutical care is the direct, responsible provision of medication-related care for the purpose of achieving definite outcomes that improve a patient's quality of life.

Principal Elements

The principal elements of pharmaceutical care are that it is *medication related*; it is *care* that is *directly provided* to the patient; it is provided to produce *definite outcomes*; these outcomes are intended to improve the patient's *quality of life*; and the provider accepts personal *responsibility* for the outcomes.

Medication Related. Pharmaceutical care involves not only medication therapy (the actual provision of medication) but also decisions about medication use for individual patients. As appropriate, this includes decisions *not* to use medication therapy as well as judgments about medication selection, dosages, routes and methods of administration, medication therapy monitoring, and the provision of medication-related information and counseling to individual patients.

Care. Central to the concept of care is caring, a personal concern for the well-being of another person. Overall patient care consists of integrated domains of care including (among others) medical care, nursing care, and pharmaceutical care. Health professionals in each of these disciplines possess unique expertise and must cooperate in the patient's overall care. At times, they share in the execution of the various types of care (including pharmaceutical care). To pharmaceutical care, however, the pharmacist contributes unique knowledge and skills to ensure optimal outcomes from the use of medications.

At the heart of any type of patient care, there exists a one-to-one relationship between a caregiver and a patient. In pharmaceutical care, the irreducible "unit" of care is one pharmacist in a direct professional relationship with one patient. In this relationship, the pharmacist provides care directly to the patient and for the benefit of the patient.

The health and well-being of the patient are paramount. The pharmacist makes a direct, personal, caring commitment to the individual patient and acts in the patient's best interest. The pharmacist cooperates directly with other professionals and the patient in designing, implementing, and monitoring a therapeutic plan intended to produce definite therapeutic outcomes that improve the patient's quality of life.

Outcomes. It is the goal of pharmaceutical care to improve an individual patient's quality of life through achievement of definite (predefined), medication-related therapeutic outcomes. The outcomes sought are

1. Cure of a patient's disease.
2. Elimination or reduction of a patient's symptomatology.
3. Arresting or slowing of a disease process.
4. Prevention of a disease or symptomatology.

This, in turn, involves three major functions: (1) identifying potential and actual medication-related problems, (2) resolving actual medication-related problems, and (3) preventing potential medication-related problems. A medication-related problem is an event or circumstance involving medication therapy that actually or potentially interferes with an optimum outcome for a specific patient. There are at least the following categories of medication-related problems[3]:

- *Untreated indications.* The patient has a medical problem that requires medication therapy (an indication for medication use) but is not receiving a medication for that indication.
- *Improper drug selection.* The patient has a medication indication but is taking the wrong medication.
- *Subtherapeutic dosage.* The patient has a medical problem that is being treated with too little of the correct medication.
- *Failure to receive medication.* The patient has a medical problem that is the result of not receiving a medication (e.g., for pharmaceutical, psychological, sociological, or economic reasons).
- *Overdosage.* The patient has a medical problem that is being treated with too much of the correct medication (toxicity).

- *Adverse drug reactions.* The patient has a medical problem that is the result of an adverse drug reaction or adverse effect.
- *Drug interactions.* The patient has a medical problem that is the result of a drug–drug, drug–food, or drug–laboratory test interaction.
- *Medication use without indication.* The patient is taking a medication for no medically valid indication.

Patients may possess characteristics that interfere with the achievement of desired therapeutic outcomes. Patients may be noncompliant with prescribed medication use regimens, or there may be unpredictable variations in patients' biological responses. Thus, in an imperfect world, intended outcomes from medication-related therapy are not always achievable.

Patients bear a responsibility to help achieve the desired outcomes by engaging in behaviors that will contribute to—and not interfere with—the achievement of desired outcomes. Pharmacists and other health professionals have an obligation to educate patients about behaviors that will contribute to achieving desired outcomes.

Quality of Life. Some tools exist now for assessing a patient's quality of life. These tools are still evolving, and pharmacists should maintain familiarity with the literature on this subject.[10,11] A complete assessment of a patient's quality of life should include both objective and subjective (e.g., the patient's own) assessments. Patients should be involved, in an informed way, in establishing quality-of-life goals for their therapies.

Responsibility. The fundamental relationship in any type of patient care is a mutually beneficial exchange in which the patient grants authority to the provider and the provider gives competence and commitment to the patient (accepts responsibility).[3] Responsibility involves both moral trustworthiness and accountability.

In pharmaceutical care, the direct relationship between an individual pharmacist and an individual patient is that of a professional covenant in which the patient's safety and well-being are entrusted to the pharmacist, who commits to honoring that trust through competent professional actions that are in the patient's best interest. As an accountable member of the health-care team, the pharmacist must document the care provided.[4,7,12,13] The pharmacist is personally accountable for patient outcomes (the quality of care) that ensue from the pharmacist's actions and decisions.[1]

Implications

The idea that pharmacists should commit themselves to the achievement of definite outcomes for individual patients is an especially important element in the concept of pharmaceutical care. The expectation that pharmacists personally accept responsibility for individual patients' outcomes that result from the pharmacists' actions represents a significant advance in pharmacy's continuing professionalization. The provision of pharmaceutical care represents a maturation of pharmacy as a clinical profession and is a natural evolution of more mature clinical pharmacy activities of pharmacists.[14]

ASHP believes that pharmaceutical care is fundamental to the profession's purpose of helping people make the best use of medications.[15] It is a unifying concept that transcends all types of patients and all categories of pharmacists and pharmacy organizations. Pharmaceutical care is applicable and achievable by pharmacists in all practice settings. The provision of pharmaceutical care is not limited to pharmacists in inpatient, outpatient, or community settings, nor to pharmacists with certain degrees, specialty certifications, residencies, or other credentials. It is not limited to those in academic or teaching settings. Pharmaceutical care is not a matter of formal credentials or place of work. Rather, it is a matter of a direct personal, professional, responsible relationship with a patient to ensure that the patient's use of medication is optimal and leads to improvements in the patient's quality of life.

Pharmacists should commit themselves to continuous care on behalf of individual patients. They bear responsibility for ensuring that the patient's care is ongoing despite work-shift changes, weekends, and holidays. An important implication is that a pharmacist providing pharmaceutical care may need to work as a member of a team of pharmacists who provide backup care when the primary responsible pharmacist is not available. Another is that the responsible pharmacist should work to ensure that continuity of care is maintained when a patient moves from one component of a health-care system to another (e.g., when a patient is hospitalized or discharged from a hospital to return to an ambulatory, community status). In the provision of pharmaceutical care, professional communication about the patient's needs between responsible pharmacists in each area of practice is, therefore, essential. ASHP believes that the development of recognized methods of practicing pharmaceutical care that will enhance such communication is an important priority for the profession.

Pharmaceutical care can be conceived as both a purpose for pharmacy practice and a purpose of medication use processes. That is, a fundamental professional reason that pharmacists engage in pharmacy practice should be to deliver pharmaceutical care. Furthermore, the medication use systems that pharmacists (and others) operate should be designed to support and enable the delivery of pharmaceutical care by individual pharmacists. ASHP believes that, in organized health-care settings, pharmaceutical care can be most successfully provided when it is part of the pharmacy department's central mission and when management activity is focused on facilitating the provision of pharmaceutical care by individual pharmacists. This approach, in which empowered frontline staff provide direct care to individual patients and are supported by managers, other pharmacists, and support systems, is new for many pharmacists and managers.

An important corollary to this approach is that pharmacists providing pharmaceutical care in organized health-care settings cannot provide such care alone. They must work in an interdependent fashion with colleagues in pharmacy and other disciplines, support systems and staff, and managers.[7] It is incumbent on pharmacists to design work systems and practices that appropriately focus the efforts of all activities and support systems on meeting the needs of patients. Some patients will require different levels of care, and it may be useful to structure work systems in light of those differences.[16,17] ASHP believes that the provision of pharmaceutical care and the development of effective work systems to document and support it are major priorities for the profession.

In the provision of pharmaceutical care, pharmacists use their unique perspective and knowledge of medication therapy to evaluate patients' actual and potential medication-related problems. To do this, they require direct access to clinical information about individual patients. They make judgments regarding medication use and then advocate optimal medication use for individual patients in cooperation with other professionals and in consideration of their unique professional knowledge and evaluations. Pharmaceutical care includes the active participation of the patient (and designated caregivers such as family members) in matters pertinent to medication use.

The acknowledgment of pharmacists' responsibility for therapeutic outcomes resulting from their actions does not contend that pharmacists have exclusive authority for matters related to medication use. Other health-care professionals, including physicians and nurses, have valuable and well-established, well-recognized roles in the medication use process. The pharmaceutical care concept does not diminish the roles or responsibilities of other health professionals, nor does it imply any usurping of authority by pharmacists. Pharmacists' actions in pharmaceutical care should be conducted and viewed as collaborative. The knowledge, skills, and traditions of pharmacists, however, make them legitimate leaders of efforts by health-care teams to improve patients' medication use.

Pharmaceutical care requires a direct relationship between a pharmacist and an individual patient. Some pharmacists and other pharmacy personnel engage in clinical and product-related pharmacy activities that do not involve a direct relationship with the patient. Properly designed, these activities can be supportive of pharmaceutical care, but ASHP believes it would be confusing and counterproductive to characterize such activities as pharmaceutical care. ASHP believes that clinical and product-related pharmacy activities are essential, however, and are as important as the actions of pharmacists interacting directly with patients.

Pharmaceutical educators must teach pharmaceutical care to students.[18] Providers of continuing education should help practicing pharmacists and other pharmacy personnel to understand pharmaceutical care. Students and pharmacists should be taught to conceptualize and execute responsible medication-related problem-solving on behalf of individual patients. Curricula should be designed to produce graduates with sufficient knowledge and skills to provide pharmaceutical care competently.[8,18] Initiatives are under way to bring about these changes.[8] Practicing pharmacists must commit their time as preceptors and their workplaces as teaching laboratories for the undergraduate and postgraduate education and training necessary to produce pharmacists who can provide pharmaceutical care.[8]

Research is needed to evaluate various methods and systems for the delivery of pharmaceutical care.

Pharmaceutical care represents an exciting new vision for pharmacy. ASHP hopes that all pharmacists in all practice settings share in this vision and that the pharmaceutical care concept will serve as a stimulus for them to work toward transforming the profession to actualize that vision.

References

1. Brodie DC. Is pharmaceutical education prepared to lead its profession? The Ninth Annual Rho Chi Lecture. *Rep Rho Chi.* 1973; 39:6–12.
2. Brodie DC, Parish PA, Poston JW. Societal needs for drugs and drug-related services. *Am J Pharm Educ.* 1980; 44:276–8.
3. Hepler CD, Strand LM. Opportunities and responsibilities in pharmaceutical care. *Am J Hosp Pharm.* 1990; 47:533–43.
4. Penna RP. Pharmaceutical care: pharmacy's mission for the 1990s. *Am J Hosp Pharm.* 1990; 47:543–9.
5. Pierpaoli PG, Hethcox JM. Pharmaceutical care: new management and leadership imperatives. *Top Hosp Pharm Manage.* 1992; 12:1–18.
6. Oddis JA. Report of the House of Delegates: June 3 and 5, 1991. *Am J Hosp Pharm.* 1991; 48:1739–48.
7. American Pharmaceutical Association. An APhA white paper on the role of the pharmacist in comprehensive medication use management; the delivery of pharmaceutical care. Washington, DC: American Pharmaceutical Association; 1992 Mar.
8. Commission to Implement Change in Pharmaceutical Education. A position paper. Entry-level education in pharmacy: a commitment to change. *AACP News.* 1991; Nov (Suppl):14
9. Oddis JA. Report of the House of Delegates: June 1 and 3, 1992. *Am J Hosp Pharm.* 1992; 49:1962–73.
10. Gouveia WA. Measuring and managing patient outcomes. *Am J Hosp Pharm.* 1992; 49:2157–8.
11. MacKeigan LD, Pathak DS. Overview of health-related quality-of-life measures. *Am J Hosp Pharm.* 1992; 49:2236–45.
12. Galinsky RE, Nickman NA. Pharmacists and the mandate of pharmaceutical care. *DICP Ann Pharmacother.* 1991; 21:431–4.
13. Angaran DM. Quality assurance to quality improvement: measuring and monitoring pharmaceutical care. *Am J Hosp Pharm.* 1991; 48:1901–7.
14. Hepler CD. Pharmaceutical care and specialty practice. *Pharmacotherapy.* 1993; 13:64S–9S.
15. Zellmer WA. Expressing the mission of pharmacy practice. *Am J Hosp Pharm.* 1991; 48:1195. Editorial.
16. Smith WE, Benderev K. Levels of pharmaceutical care: a theoretical model. *Am J Hosp Pharm.* 1991; 48:540–6.
17. Strand LM, Cipole RJ, Morley PC., et al. Levels of pharmaceutical care: a needs-based approach. *Am J Hosp Pharm.* 1991; 48:547–50.
18. O'Neil EH. Health professions education for the future: schools in service to the nation. San Francisco, CA: Pew Health Profession Commission; 1993.

This statement was reviewed in 1998 by the Council on Professional Affairs and the ASHP Board of Directors and was found to still be appropriate.

Approved by the ASHP Board of Directors, April 21, 1993, and by the ASHP House of Delegates, June 9, 1993. Developed by the ASHP Council on Professional Affairs.

The bibliographic citation for this document is as follows: American Society of Hospital Pharmacists. ASHP statement on pharmaceutical care. *Am J Hosp Pharm.* 1993; 50:1720–3.

ASHP Guidelines on Documenting Pharmaceutical Care in Patient Medical Records

Purpose

The professional actions of pharmacists that are intended to ensure safe and effective use of drugs and that may affect patient outcomes should be documented in the patient medical record (PMR). These guidelines describe the kinds of information pharmacists should document in the PMR, how that information should be documented, methods for obtaining authorization for pharmacist documentation, and the important role of training and continuous quality improvement (CQI) in documentation.

Background

Pharmaceutical care is the direct, responsible provision of medication-related care for the purpose of achieving definite outcomes that improve a patient's quality of life.[1] A core principle of pharmaceutical care is that the pharmacist accepts professional responsibility for patient outcomes.[2] Integrating pharmaceutical care into a patient's overall health care plan requires effective and efficient communication among health care professionals. As an integral member of the health care team, the pharmacist must document the care provided. Such documentation is vital to a patient's continuity of care and demonstrates both the accountability of the pharmacist and the value of the pharmacist's services. Moreover, because clinical services (e.g., those incident to a physician's services) are generally considered reimbursable only when they are necessary for the medical management of a patient and when the service provided and the patient's response are carefully documented, thorough documentation may increase the likelihood of reimbursement. Early implementation of such documentation practices may help health-system pharmacies cope with documentation requirements in the event pharmacists' clinical services become reimbursable.

The PMR's primary purpose is to convey information for use in patient care; it serves as a tool for communication among health care professionals. Information in the PMR may also be used in legal proceedings (e.g., as evidence), education (e.g., for training students), research (e.g., for evaluating clinical drug use), and quality assurance evaluations (e.g., to ascertain adherence to practice standards).[3]

Clinical recommendations made by a pharmacist on behalf of the patient, as well as actions taken in accordance with these recommendations, should be documented in a permanent manner that makes the information available to all the health care professionals caring for the patient. ASHP believes that, to ensure proper coordination of patients' medication therapies, health care systems must be designed to enable, foster, and facilitate communication and collaboration among health care providers.[2] Health care systems must not erect barriers to that communication or to the exercise of the professional judgment of health care providers.

Although telephone calls and other oral communication may be necessary for immediate interventions, they do not allow for the dissemination of information to care providers who are not a part of the conversation. Such interventions should be documented in the PMR as soon as possible after the acute situation has settled. For less urgent and routine recommendations, timely documentation is also preferred, because delays in response to telephone calls or pager messages may lead to miscommunicated or undocumented recommendations. Unofficial, temporary, or removable notes placed in the PMR do not provide a standard of acceptable communication or documentation and therefore are discouraged. Documentation that is not a part of the PMR (e.g., documentation in pharmacy records) may provide a degree of risk reduction; however, such documentation does not provide important information to other care providers and can interrupt continuity of care when the patient is discharged or transferred.

Documenting Pharmaceutical Care

Pharmacists should be authorized and encouraged to make notations in the PMR for the purpose of documenting their findings, assessments, conclusions, and recommendations.[2] ASHP believes that all significant clinical recommendations and resulting actions should be documented in the appropriate section of the PMR. The pharmacy department should establish policies and procedures for documenting information in the PMR. Such policies and procedures will help pharmacists exercise good judgment in determining what information to document in the PMR and how to present it.

Examples of information a pharmacist may need to document in the PMR include, but are not limited to, the following:

1. A summary of the patient's medication history on admission, including medication allergies and their manifestations.
2. Oral and written consultations provided to other health care professionals regarding the patient's drug therapy selection and management.
3. Physicians' oral orders received directly by the pharmacist.
4. Clarification of drug orders.
5. Adjustments made to drug dosage, dosage frequency, dosage form, or route of administration.
6. Drugs, including investigational drugs, administered.
7. Actual and potential drug-related problems that warrant surveillance.
8. Drug therapy-monitoring findings, including
    a. The therapeutic appropriateness of the patient's drug regimen, including the route and method of administration.
    b. Therapeutic duplication in the patient's drug regimen.
    c. The degree of patient compliance with the prescribed drug regimen.
    d. Actual and potential drug–drug, drug–food, drug–laboratory test, and drug–disease interactions.
    e. Clinical and pharmacokinetic laboratory data pertinent to the drug regimen.
    f. Actual and potential drug toxicity and adverse effects.

   g. Physical signs and clinical symptoms relevant to the patient's drug therapy.
9. Drug-related patient education and counseling provided.

Documentation by pharmacists should meet established criteria for legibility, clarity, lack of judgmental language, completeness, need for inclusion in the PMR (versus an alternative form of communication), appropriate use of a standard format (e.g., SOAP [subjective, objective, assessment, and plan] or TITRS [title, introduction, text, recommendation, and signature]), and how to contact the pharmacist (e.g., a telephone or pager number).[4]

The authority to document pharmaceutical care in the PMR comes with a responsibility to ensure that patient privacy and confidentiality are safeguarded and the communication is concise and accurate. Local, state, and federal guidelines and laws (including the Health Insurance Portability and Accountability Act of 1996 [HIPAA]) and risk management sensitivities should be considered. Nonjudgmental language should be used, with care taken to avoid words that imply blame (e.g., *error, mistake, misadventure,* and *inadvertent*) or substandard care (e.g., *bad, defective, inadequate, inappropriate, incorrect, insufficient, poor, problem,* and *unsatisfactory*).[3] Facts should be documented accurately, concisely, and objectively; such documentation should reflect the goals established by the medical team.

Documentation of a formal consultation solicited by a physician or other health care provider may include direct recommendations or suggestions as appropriate. However, unsolicited informal consultations, clinical impressions, findings, suggestions, and recommendations should generally be documented more subtly, with indirect recommendations presented in a way that allows the provider to decline the suggestion without incurring a liability. For example, the phrase "may want to consider" creates an opportunity for the suggestion to be acted upon or not, depending on presenting clinical factors.

Obtaining Authorization to Document Pharmaceutical Care

The authority to document pharmaceutical care in the PMR is granted by the health care organization in accordance with organizational and medical staff policies. Although documenting pharmaceutical care in the PMR is a pharmacist's professional responsibility, physicians and other health care professionals may not be accustomed to or open to this practice.

The following steps are recommended for obtaining authorization to document pharmaceutical care in the PMR:

1. Determine the existing organizational and medical staff policies regarding authority for documentation in the PMR. These policies may provide specific guidance on how to proceed.
2. Ascertain whether other nonphysician and nonnurse providers in the organization or affiliated organizations have been granted authority to document patient care activities in the PMR. If so, consult them regarding the process used to establish the authority.
3. Identify physicians in the organization who are willing to support documentation of pharmaceutical care in the PMR.
4. Identify the committees in the organization whose recommendations or decisions will be required to establish authority for pharmacists to document pharmaceutical care in the PMR. Determine the necessary sequence of these approvals. Committees typically involved include the pharmacy and therapeutics (P&T) committee, the executive committee of the medical staff, a quality-assurance committee (e.g., the CQI committee), and the medical records committee.
5. Determine the accepted method and format for submitting a proposal requesting authority to document pharmaceutical care in the PMR. In some organizations, a written proposal may be required. If so, determine the desired format (length, style, and necessary justification) and deadlines for proposal submission. An oral presentation to the deciding bodies may be required. If so, determine in advance the desired presentation format and supporting materials desired by these bodies.
6. Draft a written plan describing
   a. Examples of information to be documented in the PMR. It may be helpful to describe how this important information may be lost or miscommunicated if it is not documented in the PMR.
   b. The locations within the PMR where documentation will be made and any special format or forms proposed. New forms will have to comply with HIPAA regulations and will require review and approval by specific organizational or medical staff committees. To achieve the goal of effective communication among all the members of the health care team, compartmentalization of the PMR should be avoided.
   c. The persons who will be documenting pharmaceutical care in the PMR (i.e., pharmacists, residents, or students). If pharmacy residents or students will be making notations in the PMR, procedures regarding authority and cosignatures will also have to be described.
7. Review the draft plan with the chair of the P&T committee, the director of nursing, the director of medical records, and other appropriate administrative personnel, such as the organization's risk management officer and legal counsel.
8. Seek the endorsement and recommendation of the P&T committee.
9. In appropriate sequence, seek the endorsement or decision of any other committees necessary for ultimate approval. Monitor the proposal's course through the various committees and provide assistance, clarification, or additional data as necessary.
10. When the final approving body grants PMR documentation authority, participate in the required policy development and the communication of the new policy to the individuals or departments in the organization that will be affected by the change (e.g., nurses, the medical staff, the quality-assurance staff, and the medical records department).

Training and CQI

Pharmacist documentation in the PMR is a skill that requires ongoing training and evaluation.[4] A temporary committee may be formed to manage the initial training required to implement pharmacist documentation in the PMR. That committee may consider offering presentations by physicians or other members of the health care team to provide their perspective on how to effectively communicate using the PMR. The information in those presentations may be reinforced by workshops on documentation skills. Presentation and workshop topics may include the choice of communication method (i.e., when documentation in the PMR is preferred to other means of communication), the documentation format (e.g., SOAP or TITRS), documentation etiquette, and legal requirements.[4] Documentation skills should be demonstrated before a pharmacist is allowed to make notations in the PMR.[4] The ASHP Clinical Skills Program is another tool for training pharmacists to use the PMR.[3]

Documentation of pharmaceutical care should also be one of the many functions addressed in CQI efforts. Pharmacy department CQI efforts should include the development of quality indicators that can be used to evaluate pharmacist documentation in the PMR.[4] Other CQI efforts might analyze and improve systemwide policies and procedures for documenting medication use.[5] Periodic review of organizational policies and procedures will allow for their revision in response to changes in health care and advances in technology, including the availability of an electronic PMR.[6,7]

References

1. Hepler CD, Strand LM. Opportunities and responsibilities in pharmaceutical care. *Am J Hosp Pharm.* 1990; 47:533–43.
2. American Society of Hospital Pharmacists. ASHP statement on pharmaceutical care. *Am J Hosp Pharm.* 1993; 50:1720–3.
3. Shepherd MF. Professional conduct and use of patient medical records. In: ASHP Clinical Skills Program, module 1: reviewing patient medical charts. Bethesda, MD: American Society of Hospital Pharmacists; 1992:38–41.
4. Lacy CF, Saya FG, Shane RR. Quality of pharmacists' documentations in patients' medical records. *Am J Health-Syst Pharm.* 1996; 53:2171–5.
5. Matuschka P. Improving documentation of preoperative antimicrobial prophylaxis. *Am J Health-Syst Pharm.* 1998; 55:993–4.
6. Lau A, Balen RM, Lam R,, et al. Using a personal digital assistant to document clinical pharmacy services in an intensive care unit. *Am J Health-Syst Pharm.* 2001; 58:1229–32.
7. Gordon W, Malyuk D, Taki J. Use of health-record abstracting to document pharmaceutical care activities. *Can J Hosp Pharm.* 2000; 53:199–205.

These guidelines were reviewed in 2008 by the Council on Pharmacy Practice and by the Board of Directors and were found to still be appropriate.

Approved by the ASHP Board of Directors, February 20, 2003. Revised by the ASHP Council on Professional Affairs. Supercedes the ASHP Guidelines for Obtaining Authorization for Documenting Pharmaceutical Care in Patient Medical Records dated November 16, 1988.

The bibliographic citation for this document is as follows: American Society of Health-System Pharmacists. ASHP guidelines on documenting pharmaceutical care in patient medical records. *Am J Health-Syst Pharm.* 2003; 60:705–7.

ASHP Guidelines on Pharmacist-Conducted Patient Education and Counseling

Purpose

Providing pharmaceutical care entails accepting responsibility for patients' pharmacotherapeutic outcomes. Pharmacists can contribute to positive outcomes by educating and counseling patients to prepare and motivate them to follow their pharmacotherapeutic regimens and monitoring plans. The purpose of this document is to help pharmacists provide effective patient education and counseling.

In working with individual patients, patient groups, families, and caregivers, pharmacists should approach education and counseling as interrelated activities. ASHP believes pharmacists should educate and counsel all patients to the extent possible, going beyond the minimum requirements of laws and regulations; simply offering to counsel is inconsistent with pharmacists' responsibilities. In pharmaceutical care, pharmacists should encourage patients to seek education and counseling and should eliminate barriers to providing it.

Pharmacists should also seek opportunities to participate in health-system patient-education programs and to support the educational efforts of other health care team members. Pharmacists should collaborate with other health care team members, as appropriate, to determine what specific information and counseling are required in each patient care situation. A coordinated effort among health care team members will enhance patients' adherence to pharmacotherapeutic regimens, monitoring of drug effects, and feedback to the health system.

ASHP believes these patient education and counseling guidelines are applicable in all practice settings—including acute inpatient care, ambulatory care, home care, and long-term care—whether these settings are associated with integrated health systems or managed care organizations or are freestanding. The guidelines may need to be adapted; for example, for use in telephone counseling or for counseling family members or caregivers instead of patients. Patient education and counseling usually occur at the time prescriptions are dispensed but may also be provided as a separate service. The techniques and the content should be adjusted to meet the specific needs of the patient and to comply with the policies and procedures of the practice setting. In health systems, other health care team members share in the responsibility to educate and counsel patients as specified in the patients' care plans.

Background

The human and economic consequences of inappropriate medication use have been the subject of professional, public, and congressional discourse for more than two decades.[1–5] Lack of sufficient knowledge about their health problems and medications is one cause of patients' nonadherence to their pharmacotherapeutic regimens and monitoring plans; without adequate knowledge, patients cannot be effective partners in managing their own care. The pharmacy profession has accepted responsibility for providing patient education and counseling in the context of pharmaceutical care to improve patient adherence and reduce medication-related problems.[6–9]

Concerns about improper medication use contributed to the provision in the Omnibus Budget Reconciliation Act of 1990 (OBRA '90) that mandated an offer to counsel Medicaid outpatients about prescription medications. Subsequently, states enacted legislation that generally extends the offer-to-counsel requirement to outpatients not covered by Medicaid. Future court cases may establish that pharmacists, in part because of changing laws, have a public duty to warn patients of adverse effects and potential interactions of medications. The result could be increased liability for pharmacists who fail to educate and counsel their patients or who do so incorrectly or incompletely.[10]

Pharmacists' Knowledge and Skills

In addition to a current knowledge of pharmacotherapy, pharmacists need to have the knowledge and skills to provide effective and accurate patient education and counseling. They should know about their patients' cultures, especially health and illness beliefs, attitudes, and practices. They should be aware of patients' feelings toward the health system and views of their own roles and responsibilities for decision-making and for managing their care.[11]

Effective, open-ended questioning and active listening are essential skills for obtaining information from and sharing information with patients. Pharmacists have to adapt messages to fit patients' language skills and primary languages, through the use of teaching aids, interpreters, or cultural guides if necessary. Pharmacists also need to observe and interpret the nonverbal messages (e.g., eye contact, facial expressions, body movements, vocal characteristics) patients give during education and counseling sessions.[12]

Assessing a patient's cognitive abilities, learning style, and sensory and physical status enables the pharmacist to adapt information and educational methods to meet the patient's needs. A patient may learn best by hearing spoken instructions; by seeing a diagram, picture, or model; or by directly handling medications and administration devices. A patient may lack the visual acuity to read labels on prescription containers, markings on syringes, or written handout material. A patient may be unable to hear oral instructions or may lack sufficient motor skills to open a child-resistant container.

In addition to assessing whether patients know *how* to use their medications, pharmacists should attempt to understand patients' attitudes and potential behaviors concerning medication use. The pharmacist needs to determine whether a patient is willing to use a medication and whether he or she intends to do so.[13,14]

Environment

Education and counseling should take place in an environment conducive to patient involvement, learning, and acceptance—one that supports pharmacists' efforts to establish caring relationships with patients. Individual patients, groups, families, or caregivers should perceive the counseling environment as comfortable, confidential, and safe.

Education and counseling are most effective when conducted in a room or space that ensures privacy and opportunity to engage in confidential communication. If such an isolated space is not available, a common area can be restructured to maximize visual and auditory privacy from other patients or staff. Patients, including those who are disabled, should have easy access and seating. Space and seating should be adequate for family members or caregivers. The design and placement of desks and counters should minimize barriers to communication. Distractions and interruptions should be few, so that patients and pharmacists can have each other's undivided attention.

The environment should be equipped with appropriate learning aids, e.g., graphics, anatomical models, medication administration devices, memory aids, written material, and audiovisual resources.

Pharmacist and Patient Roles

Pharmacists and patients bring to education and counseling sessions their own perceptions of their roles and responsibilities. For the experience to be effective, the pharmacist and patient need to come to a common understanding about their respective roles and responsibilities. It may be necessary to clarify for patients that pharmacists have an appropriate and important role in providing education and counseling. Patients should be encouraged to be active participants.

The pharmacist's role is to verify that patients have sufficient understanding, knowledge, and skill to follow their pharmacotherapeutic regimens and monitoring plans. Pharmacists should also seek ways to motivate patients to learn about their treatment and to be active partners in their care. Patients' role is to adhere to their pharmacotherapeutic regimens, monitor for drug effects, and report their experiences to pharmacists or other members of their health care teams.[12,15] Optimally, the patient's role should include seeking information and presenting concerns that may make adherence difficult.

Depending on the health system's policies and procedures, its use of protocols or clinical care plans, and its credentialing of providers, pharmacists may also have disease management roles and responsibilities for specified categories of patients. This expands pharmacists' relationships with patients and the content of education and counseling sessions.

Process Steps

Steps in the patient education and counseling process will vary according to the health system's policies and procedures, environment, and practice setting. Generally, the following steps are appropriate for patients receiving new medications or returning for refills[12–21]:

1. Establish caring relationships with patients as appropriate to the practice setting and stage in the patient's health care management. Introduce yourself as a pharmacist, explain the purpose and expected length of the sessions, and obtain the patient's agreement to participate. Determine the patient's primary spoken language.
2. Assess the patient's knowledge about his or her health problems and medications, physical and mental capability to use the medications appropriately, and attitude toward the health problems and medications. Ask open-ended questions about each medication's purpose and what the patient expects, and ask the patient to describe or show how he or she will use the medication.

   Patients returning for refill medications should be asked to describe or show how they have been using their medications. They should also be asked to describe any problems, concerns, or uncertainties they are experiencing with their medications.
3. Provide information orally and use visual aids or demonstrations to fill patients' gaps in knowledge and understanding. Open the medication containers to show patients the colors, sizes, shapes, and markings on oral solids. For oral liquids and injectables, show patients the dosage marks on measuring devices. Demonstrate the assembly and use of administration devices such as nasal and oral inhalers. As a supplement to face-to-face oral communication, provide written handouts to help the patient recall the information.

   If a patient is experiencing problems with his or her medications, gather appropriate data and assess the problems. Then adjust the pharmacotherapeutic regimens according to protocols or notify the prescribers.
4. Verify patients' knowledge and understanding of medication use. Ask patients to describe or show how they will use their medications and identify their effects. Observe patients' medication-use capability and accuracy and attitudes toward following their pharmacotherapeutic regimens and monitoring plans.

Content

The content of an education and counseling session may include the information listed below, as appropriate for each patient's pharmacotherapeutic regimen and monitoring plan.[8,9,20] The decision to discuss specific pharmacotherapeutic information with an individual patient must be based on the pharmacist's professional judgment.

1. The medication's trade name, generic name, common synonym, or other descriptive name(s) and, when appropriate, its therapeutic class and efficacy.
2. The medication's use and expected benefits and action. This may include whether the medication is intended to cure a disease, eliminate or reduce symptoms, arrest or slow the disease process, or prevent the disease or a symptom.
3. The medication's expected onset of action and what to do if the action does not occur.
4. The medication's route, dosage form, dosage, and administration schedule (including duration of therapy).
5. Directions for preparing and using or administering the medication. This may include adaptation to fit patients' lifestyles or work environments.
6. Action to be taken in case of a missed dose.
7. Precautions to be observed during the medication's use or administration and the medication's potential risks in relation to benefits. For injectable medications and administration devices, concern about latex allergy may be discussed.
8. Potential common and severe adverse effects that may occur, actions to prevent or minimize their occurrence, and actions to take if they occur, including notifying the prescriber, pharmacist, or other health care provider.
9. Techniques for self-monitoring of the pharmacotherapy.

10. Potential drug–drug (including nonprescription), drug–food, and drug–disease interactions or contraindications.
11. The medication's relationships to radiologic and laboratory procedures (e.g., timing of doses and potential interferences with interpretation of results).
12. Prescription refill authorizations and the process for obtaining refills.
13. Instructions for 24-hour access to a pharmacist.
14. Proper storage of the medication.
15. Proper disposal of contaminated or discontinued medications and used administration devices.
16. Any other information unique to an individual patient or medication.

These points are applicable to both prescription and nonprescription medications. Pharmacists should counsel patients in the proper selection of nonprescription medications.

Additional content may be appropriate when pharmacists have authorized responsibilities in collaborative disease management for specified categories of patients. Depending on the patient's disease management or clinical care plan, the following may be covered:

1. The disease state: whether it is acute or chronic and its prevention, transmission, progression, and recurrence.
2. Expected effects of the disease on the patient's normal daily living.
3. Recognition and monitoring of disease complications.

Documentation

Pharmacists should document education and counseling in patients' permanent medical records as consistent with the patients' care plans, the health system's policies and procedures, and applicable state and federal laws. When pharmacists do not have access to patients' medical records, education and counseling may be documented in the pharmacy's patient profiles, on the medication order or prescription form, or on a specially designed counseling record.

The pharmacist should record (1) that counseling was offered and was accepted and provided or refused and (2) the pharmacist's perceived level of the patient's understanding.[9] As appropriate, the content should be documented (for example, counseling about food–drug interactions). All documentation should be safeguarded to respect patient confidentiality and privacy and to comply with applicable state and federal laws.[10]

References

1. Smith MC. Social barriers to rational drug therapy. *Am J Hosp Pharm.* 1972; 29:121–7.
2. Priorities and approaches for improving prescription medicine use by older Americans. Washington, DC: National Council on Patient Information and Education; 1987.
3. Manasse HR Jr. Medication use in an imperfect world: drug misadventuring as an issue of public policy, part 1. *Am J Hosp Pharm.* 1989; 46:929–44.
4. Manasse HR Jr. Medication use in an imperfect world: drug misadventuring as an issue of public policy, part 2. *Am J Hosp Pharm.* 1989; 46:1141–52.
5. Johnson JA, Bootman JL. Drug-related morbidity and mortality: a cost-of-illness model. *Arch Intern Med.* 1995; 155:1949–56.
6. Summary of the final report of the Scope of Pharmacy Practice Project. *Am J Hosp Pharm.* 1994; 51:2179–82.
7. Hepler CD, Strand LM. Opportunities and responsibilities in pharmaceutical care. *Am J Hosp Pharm.* 1990; 47:533–42.
8. Hatoum HT, Hutchinson RA, Lambert BL. OBRA 90: patient counseling—enhancing patient outcomes. *US Pharm.* 1993; 18(Jan):76–86.
9. OBRA '90: a practical guide to effecting pharmaceutical care. Washington, DC: American Pharmaceutical Association; 1994.
10. Lynn NJ, Kamm RE. Avoiding liability problems. *Am Pharm.* 1995; NS35(Dec):14–22.
11. Herrier RN, Boyce RW. Does counseling improve compliance? *Am Pharm.* 1995; NS35(Sep):11–2.
12. Foster SL, Smith EB, Seybold MR. Advanced counseling techniques: integrating assessment and intervention. *Am Pharm.* 1995; NS35(Oct):40–8.
13. Bond WS, Hussar DA. Detection methods and strategies for improving medication compliance. *Am J Hosp Pharm.* 1991; 48:1978–88.
14. Felkey BG. Adherence screening and monitoring. *Am Pharm.* 1995; NS35(Jul):42–51.
15. Herrier RN, Boyce RW. Establishing an active patient partnership. *Am Pharm.* 1995; NS35(Apr):48–57.
16. Boyce RW, Herrier RN, Gardner M. Pharmacist-patient consultation program, unit I: an interactive approach to verify patient understanding. New York: Pfizer Inc.; 1991.
17. Pharmacist-patient consultation program, unit II: counseling patients in challenging situations. New York: Pfizer Inc.; 1993.
18. Pharmacist-patient consultation program, unit III: counseling to enhance compliance. New York: Pfizer Inc.; 1995.
19. Boyce RW, Herrier RN. Obtaining and using patient data. *Am Pharm.* 1991; NS31(Jul):65–70.
20. Herrier RN, Boyce RW. Communicating risk to patients. *Am Pharm.* 1995; NS35(Jun):12–4.
21. APhA special report: medication administration problem solving in ambulatory care. Washington, DC: American Pharmaceutical Association; 1994.

This guideline was reviewed in 2011 by the Council on Pharmacy Practice and by the ASHP Board of Directors and was found to still be appropriate.

Approved by the ASHP Board of Directors, November 11, 1996. Revised by the ASHP Council on Professional Affairs. Supersedes the ASHP Statement on the Pharmacist's Role in Patient-Education Programs dated June 3, 1991, and ASHP Guidelines on Pharmacist-Conducted Patient Counseling dated November 18, 1992.

The bibliographic citation for this document is as follows: American Society of Health-System Pharmacists. ASHP guidelines on pharmacist-conducted patient education and counseling. *Am J Health-Syst Pharm.* 1997; 54:431–4.

ASHP Guidelines on the Pharmacist's Role in the Development, Implementation, and Assessment of Critical Pathways

Purpose

The purpose of these guidelines is (1) to describe the pharmacist's role in the development, implementation, and assessment of critical pathways (CPs) and (2) to help pharmacists prepare for that responsibility. Because pharmacotherapy is a central component of many CPs, pharmacists should take leadership roles in the development, implementation, and assessment of CPs. By assuming leadership roles, pharmacists can help improve patient outcomes, contribute to cost-effective patient care, and promote multidisciplinary approaches to patient care and performance improvement. Although pharmacist involvement in the early stages of CP development is crucial to success, CP development is generally cyclical, and pharmacists should seek opportunities to become involved at any stage in the cycle of CP development, implementation, and assessment.

Summary of guidelines. Because pharmacotherapy is a central component of many critical pathways, pharmacists should take leadership roles in their development, implementation, and assessment.

Pharmacists can improve the development of critical pathways by ensuring the evidence-based selection of medications, establishing measures for monitoring patients for drug efficacy and adverse effects, and evaluating the proposed critical pathway for patient safety.

Pharmacists can improve the implementation of critical pathways by documenting processes and outcomes, ensuring proper patient selection and medication use, monitoring patients for drug efficacy and adverse effects, and providing for continuity of care. Pharmacists can improve the assessment of critical pathways by measuring and analyzing processes and outcomes, disseminating the results of those analyses, and reviewing the critical pathways' pharmacotherapy to keep pace with changes in best practices.

Background

The development of CPs has been stimulated by the desire to improve patient outcomes by applying evidence-based clinical practice guidelines; increased interest in measuring and improving the quality of health care, including continuous-quality-improvement (CQI) initiatives; and managed care and other market-driven health care reforms. CPs can be defined as patient care management plans that delineate key steps along an optimal treatment timeline to achieve a set of predetermined intermediate and ultimate goals for patients who have clearly defined diagnoses or require certain procedures.[1] CPs have also been called care guides, clinical pathways, clinical care plans, and care maps.[2] CPs derive from the industrial engineering concept of critical paths[3] and were originally associated with inpatient acute care and used primarily by nurses. CPs have evolved to incorporate the spectrum of patient care providers and settings and to include CQI concepts.[4] CPs and similar tools are developed in many facilities for many purposes.[5–20] Although dismissed by some critics as "cookbook medicine," CPs have in some cases been shown to improve patient outcomes[21–26] and to reduce health care expenses.[27–36] ASHP believes that carefully developed and skillfully managed CPs can improve the care of patients across the spectrum of health-system settings, as well as improve the allocation of scarce health care resources.

Typical CP Process

Each health system will use a process of CP development, implementation, and assessment that meets its own needs within its own structure, culture, practice settings, and policies and procedures, but these processes do share common elements. Typically, once a disease or procedure is selected for CP development, a multidisciplinary team analyzes its current management (including process variances, costs, and outcomes), evaluates the scientific literature, and develops a plan of care. The planned actions for each discipline on the health care team are mapped on a timeline for the specific disease or procedure.[37] Pharmacists perform the following functions in a typical CP: oversee the selection of medications by using an evidence-based approach, develop the criteria for medication selection or dosages, monitor patients for drug efficacy and adverse effects (or establish parameters for monitoring), and ensure continuity of care across the health system. The following describes common steps in the development, implementation, and assessment of CPs.[3]

1. *Select diagnoses and procedures.* Diagnoses and procedures selected for CP development usually include those with high process variability, high cost, high patient volume, and high risk. CPs can be developed for common or specialized diagnoses (e.g., myocardial infarction, diabetes mellitus) or procedures (e.g., transurethral prostatectomy, coronary artery bypass grafting), for diagnoses that are likely to cause changes in health status (e.g., uncontrolled asthma), and for diseases requiring complicated pharmacotherapeutic regimens (e.g., AIDS). The criteria for selection should be developed with input from administrative and clinical leaders to ensure institutionwide acceptance and should be based on scientific evidence.
2. *Appoint a development team.* The development team should include key health care providers from all organizational components involved in the CP. The importance of a multidisciplinary approach to CP development cannot be overemphasized. If possible, consideration should be given to including a patient representative on the CP development team. Although insurance carriers and managed care providers may not have representatives on the development team, their protocols or guidelines should be evaluated by the team for inclusion in the CP as appropriate.

3. *Conduct a search of the scientific literature.* A literature and database search conducted early in the process will help identify measures for assessing current processes and outcomes and will help ensure an evidence-based approach to the CP.
4. *Document current processes and outcomes.* The current processes, costs, variances, and outcomes need to be documented, usually through flow charting of the current process, retrospective chart review, and benchmarking. Benchmarking may be internal or external to the health system. Depending on the health system's resources, benchmarking may rely on chart review or may use computerized databases that compare physicians' use of resources, health-system costs, and outcomes for specific diagnosis-related groups. This step identifies the health system's practice and compares it with published clinical guidelines that are preferably consensus based (e.g., guidelines from the Agency for Healthcare Research and Quality or the American Heart Association). The team developing the CP should use an evidence-based approach to identify, discuss, and resolve the gaps between clinical guidelines and current local practice. Input from the practitioners who will be involved in the CP is crucial to the success of this process evaluation and CP development in general.
5. *Develop the CP.* Multidisciplinary, standardized development of the CP ensures integration of care and elimination of duplication and oversights. The CP should state its goals, define actions essential to achieving those goals, provide for patient education, outline assessment of patient safety, identify measures of conformance and outcomes, and describe required documentation. The actions and resources required for implementation should be discussed and agreed upon by all disciplines involved.
   a. Goals and outcomes
      - Define the specific goals or measurable outcomes of the CP (e.g., decreased length of stay, decreased ventilator time, reduced overall patient cost, decreased pain scores, early ambulation).
      - Select the areas of focus or categories of actions essential to achieving the goals and outcomes. To ensure consistency and continuity, these areas of focus should be standardized for all CPs developed within a health system; examples of focus areas are treatments, medications, and patient education and counseling.
      - Determine the appropriate time frame. This will vary according to the disease or procedure being addressed and the practice setting (e.g., emergency room, ambulatory care clinic, acute care hospital). The time frame may be specified in minutes, hours, days, or phases. A workload assessment may be required to develop appropriate time frames.
      - Define the activity for the focus area under the appropriate time frame (e.g., "pharmacist provides medication-use education and counseling on discharge day").
   b. Patient education
      - Modify the CP, using lay terms in the patient's primary language, to educate the patient about activities to be performed, time frames, and expected outcomes. In some practice settings, the patient may be an active partner in CP decision-making and implementation.
   c. Patient safety
      - Identify potential risks to the patient that may arise from use of the CP. For example, the CP could be subjected to the institution's failure-mode and effects analysis, or the medication safety self-assessment tool of the Institute for Safe Medication Practices could be used to assess the safety of the practices outlined in the CP.[38]
   d. Monitoring
      - Identify measures of conformance and variance so that the CP and the resulting outcomes can be continuously improved. Variances are deviations from the CP that may be positive or negative, avoidable or unavoidable, consequential or inconsequential. Sources of variances include patient responses to medications, physician decisions, and system breakdowns.
   e. Documentation
      - Develop a single, multidisciplinary work sheet or other tool that describes the CP's actions and time frames and provides spaces for documenting that actions were performed.[12] Describe how this tool will be used and how data will be collected.
6. *Obtain approval for the CP and educate participants.* To ensure global acceptance among all health care provider groups, the CP should be approved by appropriate committees, especially those of the medical staff. The impact of CP implementation on practitioner workloads will require careful consideration, and departmental policies or procedures may need to be modified. The pharmacy and therapeutics (P&T) committee should review pharmacotherapeutic issues associated with the CP early enough during development that therapeutic concerns can be addressed as they arise rather than after the CP is implemented. After the CP is approved, all health care team members involved in the care of the patients affected by the CP should be educated about the anticipated outcomes, specific actions and time frames, and professional responsibilities associated with the CP.
7. *Implement the CP.* After the necessary education and training of providers, the CP is available for use. Starting the CP as a pilot project for a small number of patients may provide valuable initial assessments that will facilitate wider implementation. Staff members should be designated to identify patients suitable for the CP and to guide their enrollment and the CP's use. Patients enrolled in a CP are assigned to a health care team whose members have specific responsibilities for actions and time frames.
8. *Assess the CP.* Because not all consequences of a CP are foreseeable, CPs require periodic assessment. Assessments after a few days or weeks of use may gauge only the feasibility of the CP and not its success in achieving desired goals, but they should identify unexpected problems that may require modifications to the CP. Surveys of health care practitioners may be useful in such initial assessments. Assessments after a few months of use may provide an initial perspective

on the CP's success but may not be sufficient to fully evaluate outcomes. Assessments after longer periods should produce evidence supporting the CP's original goals. Regular analysis of the results and variances, as well as new information (e.g., new indications for medications) and technologies (e.g., new pharmacotherapy), provides data for a root-cause analysis and continuous improvement of the CP.

9. *Disseminate the results of the assessment.* The results of the assessment should be shared not just with health-system managers or members of the CP development or oversight committees but with all staff involved in the CP. Widespread dissemination allows for more suggestions for improvement from all members of the health care team and encourages acceptance of any alterations in the CP required by the assessment. Publishing the results in a journal, sharing the experience with a practice network, or presenting the results at a meeting expands the general pool of knowledge concerning CPs.

Pharmacist Involvement

These guidelines suggest actions to help prepare pharmacists and pharmacy departments for involvement in the development, implementation, and assessment of CPs at various levels of care and in different practice settings. The applicability of these guidelines depends on a pharmacist's or pharmacy department's current level of involvement in patient care and CPs. Pharmacists should focus on incorporating contemporary pharmaceutical care principles (e.g., assessing medication orders, developing pharmacotherapeutic regimens and monitoring plans, educating and counseling patients, calculating doses according to pharmacokinetic principles, conducting medication-use evaluations [MUEs], and managing anticoagulation therapy) in the development, implementation, and assessment of CPs.[39–42]

Preparing for Involvement in CP Development. Pharmacists should learn about their health system's approach to CP development and assess their readiness for involvement. They should

1. Review the health system's current strategic plan with respect to CPs. Because CPs are inherently collaborative, pharmacists should try to understand this strategic plan from the perspective of other health care providers, seeking advice from them when necessary. When reviewing the strategic plan, pharmacists should also consider the needs of specific patient populations served by their institutions.
2. Educate the pharmacy staff on the purposes and processes of CP development and the contents of CPs. The patient care decisions required in CPs demand clinical knowledge, and the pharmacotherapy involved should be based on evidence in the scientific literature. This clinical knowledge is fundamental to the CP. An effective contributor to the CP process needs to first acquire the clinical knowledge on which the CP is based and then use CQI, teamwork, negotiation, and administrative skills to develop, implement, and assess the CP.
3. Discuss CP experiences with pharmacy colleagues within and outside the health system. Pharmacists should create a forum within the health system for ongoing dialogue about CPs; for example, CPs could be made a regular agenda item for the P&T committee meeting and for other multidisciplinary clinical and departmental meetings.
4. Monitor pharmacy, nursing, quality management, health-system, health care, and management literature for ideas on CP development, implementation, and assessment. CPs from other institutions may be used as examples of and frameworks for mapping care, but they should not be adopted directly, because acceptance and use are greater when CPs are developed or adapted by their users.
5. Identify opportunities for contributing, through the provision of pharmaceutical care, to the health system's patient care delivery and improvement efforts.

Initiating Involvement. Pharmacists should begin their involvement in the CP process in ways most appropriate to their health system's structure, culture, practice settings, and policies and procedures. Involvement may vary substantially from one health system to another, but in general pharmacists should

1. Develop relationships with nursing, medical, dietary, laboratory, quality management, risk management, respiratory care, and other personnel through routine meetings, nursing and medical forums, and other multidisciplinary opportunities. These relationships should be used to promote pharmacists' contributions to collaborative patient care. The pharmacy department should support the use of CPs as an effective way to integrate and align services, processes, and costs.
2. Support or initiate the implementation of a multidisciplinary team for CP development and oversight and ensure that the pharmacy department and the P&T committee are represented on the oversight committee.
3. Seek leadership roles on the health system's CP oversight committee and development teams but be willing to accept subordinate roles. For example, pharmacists should be willing to lead or assist with literature evaluation for the health system's CP development teams.
4. Identify qualities required for the pharmacist's role and develop a consistent process for selecting the most appropriate pharmacists to participate on the various CP development teams.
5. Ensure the ongoing involvement of the P&T committee in the CP process. The P&T committee can facilitate the process by
   - Reviewing and endorsing the pharmacotherapy proposed for inclusion in each CP.
   - Establishing a standing P&T subcommittee or liaison position to assist CP development teams. The subcommittee or liaison would have the opportunity to educate the CP team about the formulary process, the process for MUE, the appropriate use of restricted medications, and other critical medication-use issues.
   - Publishing CPs and information about the health system's experiences with CPs in the P&T committee newsletter.
   - Developing the drug therapy portion of the CP assessment into an MUE.
6. Emphasize to pharmacists, other health care providers, and health-system administrators pharmacists' responsibility for implementing CP steps that involve pharmacotherapeutic regimens and monitoring, medication distribution, and patient education and counseling.

7. Initiate, after appropriate approvals, the development of the pharmacotherapeutic components of CPs.
8. Offer to evaluate and adapt the pharmacotherapeutic components of existing protocols and guidelines for CPs under development. Maintain a pharmacotherapy database to facilitate CP updates when new medications and pharmacotherapeutic alternatives become available.
9. Develop patient education and counseling materials for the pharmacotherapeutic components of CPs and develop plans for pharmacists or other members of the health care team to provide education and counseling to patients.
10. Advocate the development and use of preprinted medication orders (hard copy or electronic) and consistent use of terminology (e.g., generic drug names, decimals and units of measurement, and standardized terms and abbreviations) within the CP.
11. Be proactive in anticipating alternative processes or drug regimens that may be required in unusual circumstances, such as drug shortages.

Maintaining Involvement. Pharmacists' continued involvement in CPs will depend on their ability to demonstrate their contributions to patient care delivery and improvement to the CP oversight committee and development teams and to the health system's administration. To accomplish this, pharmacists can

1. Monitor the literature of pharmacy, nursing, quality management, health systems, health care, and management for ideas on CP development, implementation, and assessment.
2. Identify new areas for CP development on the basis of medication-use data (e.g., medication error data and MUE findings).
3. Incorporate CPs into the pharmacy department's culture by building responsibilities and performance expectations for CP development, implementation, and assessment into pharmacists' job descriptions.
4. Identify and train pharmacy staff on their roles and responsibilities for implementing the pharmaceutical care components of CPs.
5. Provide objective clinical input that is based on scientific evidence.
6. Ensure consistent use of terminology (e.g., generic drug names, decimals and units of measurement, and standardized terms and abbreviations), rational medication use, and appropriate monitoring. This could be done by the P&T committee or by a pharmacist who coordinates and reviews the pharmacotherapeutic efforts of all CPs.
7. Maintain good working relationships with CP development teams. The pharmacist member should be confident, assertive, cooperative, and effective in communicating with other health care providers.
8. Develop and maintain clinical and management skills through ongoing self-education.

Contributing to the CQI Aspects of CPs. The pharmacist should ensure that the pharmaceutical care actions of the CP contribute to patient satisfaction, desired clinical outcomes, and financial goals by

1. Monitoring the literature for best-practice results relating to specific disease states (as defined by federal diagnosis-related-group classification) and comparing these results with the health system's experience.
2. Ensuring that an internal system of CP tracking and therapeutic review is in place for the rapid insertion of new, more effective therapies into the CP and that CPs are integrated into the institution's CQI processes.
3. Assisting the development of patient satisfaction surveys.
4. Monitoring the results of the CPs and using them to perform MUEs.[42] Since patients enrolled in CPs are receiving predetermined pharmacotherapeutic regimens and monitoring, this is an excellent opportunity to perform disease- and outcome-oriented MUEs. The pharmacist should review the variances and outcomes associated with the CP, determine the effects of pharmacotherapy, and use this analysis to modify the CP. The pharmacotherapeutic component must be specific enough (e.g., specifying the medication and dosage) that its influence on the outcomes can be determined with confidence.
5. Ensuring that CPs are updated when there are changes in institutional practices (e.g., formulary changes) or when external practices change (e.g., guidelines are revised, dosage or monitoring recommendations are revised).

Ensuring the Continuity of a CP. Many CPs require continuity of care across various levels of care and practice settings. Such CPs should specify referral patterns among the levels of care and practice settings. To help accomplish this, pharmacists can

1. Ensure that members of all organizational components are included in the development and assessment of the CP as appropriate for the particular disease or procedure. Included might be personnel in the emergency department, the operating room, the intensive care unit, the step-down unit, the general nursing unit, the rehabilitation unit, the long-term-care facility, the ambulatory care clinic, the laboratory, and the home care service.
2. Develop relationships with ambulatory care, home care, and long-term-care pharmacists and other health care providers to foster the seamless provision of pharmaceutical care by inviting pharmacist members of managed care organizations to participate in CP development, exchanging CPs with the managed care organizations, and creating work teams to ensure the continuity of care.
3. Organize interdisciplinary sharing of information (e.g., recent laboratory test results) and documentation that are useful to all health care providers.
4. Develop a plan to communicate and monitor both internal and external CPs so that pharmacists have a full understanding of the CP process and can evaluate and adjust the CP as necessary when new therapeutic modalities emerge. Optimize this by using electronic and Internet technology to rapidly insert new pharmacotherapies into CPs when appropriate and evaluate which pharmacotherapies are included in which CPs to ensure consistency in medication management.
5. Initiate dialogue among pharmacists to ensure the continuity of the individual patient's CP. For example, when a patient is admitted, the hospital pharmacist should, if necessary and with the patient's permission, contact the patient's community pharmacist or managed care company to obtain information as allowed

under local, state, and federal laws (e.g., the Health Insurance Portability and Accessibility Act). The pharmacist should document an accurate medication history (prescription and nonprescription products, dietary supplements, and home remedies), the patient's history of adverse drug reactions and allergies, the patient's medication-taking behaviors (adherence, health beliefs, and social and cultural issues), and any self-monitoring. This does not obviate the requirement for the pharmacist to establish a professional relationship with the patient and to obtain information directly. When the patient is discharged, the hospital pharmacist could (in accordance with the institution's policies and procedures and with the patient's permission) prepare an original discharge summary or append to the physician's discharge summary any necessary notes regarding medications. An appropriate member of the discharge team should forward the discharge summary to relevant health care providers (e.g., physicians, home care nurses, and community or home care pharmacists). The summary should include the patient's chief complaint, the patient's height and weight, a history of the present illness (including the hospital course), pregnancy and lactation status, prescription and nonprescription medications on admission and at discharge, patient education and counseling, the monitoring plan (including patient self-monitoring and a plan for long-term monitoring of the patient's pharmacotherapeutic regimen), and a person to contact if the patient has questions. The pharmacist should check any discharge prescriptions against the indications listed in the discharge summary.

The Pharmacist's Responsibility

Carefully developed and skillfully managed CPs can improve the quality of care and the allocation of health care resources. Because pharmacotherapy is a central component of many CPs, pharmacists can help improve patient outcomes, contribute to cost-effective patient care, and promote team approaches to patient care and performance improvement by incorporating contemporary pharmaceutical care principles, activities, and services into the development, implementation, and assessment of CPs. Health systems will develop CPs in ways that are most appropriate to their patient populations, organizational structure, culture, and environment, so it is the responsibility of health-system pharmacists to identify opportunities to become involved in and improve the CPs in their institutions.

References

1. Darer J, Pronovost P, Bass E. Use and evaluation of critical pathways in hospitals. *Eff Clin Pract.* 2002; 5:114–9.
2. Lumsdon K, Hagland M. Mapping care. *Hosp Health Netw.* 1993; 67:34–40.
3. Coffey RJ, Richards JS, Remmert CS,, et al. An introduction to critical paths. *Qual Manag Health Care.* 1992; 1:45–54.
4. Jaggers LD. Differentiation of critical pathways from other health care management tools. *Am J Health-Syst Pharm.* 1996; 53:311–3.
5. Koch KE. Opportunities for pharmaceutical care with critical pathways. *Top Hosp Pharm Manag.* 1995; 14:1–7.
6. Stevenson LL. Critical pathway experience at Sarasota Memorial Hospital. *Am J Health-Syst Pharm.* 1995; 52:1071–3.
7. Gousse GC, Rousseau MR. Critical pathways at Hartford Hospital. *Am J Health-Syst Pharm.* 1995; 52:1060–3.
8. Shane R, Vinson B. Use of critical pathways and indicators in pharmacy practice. *Top Hosp Pharm Manag.* 1995; 14:55–67.
9. Gouveia WA, Massaro FJ. Critical pathway experience at New England Medical Center. *Am J Health-Syst Pharm.* 1995; 52:1068–70.
10. Saltiel E. Critical pathway experience at Cedars-Sinai Medical Center. *Am J Health-Syst Pharm.* 1995; 52:1063–8.
11. Nelson SP. Critical pathways at University of Iowa Hospitals and Clinics. *Am J Health-Syst Pharm.* 1995; 52:1058–60.
12. Marrie TJ, Lau CY, Wheeler SL,, et al. A controlled trial of a critical pathway for treatment of community-acquired pneumonia. CAPITAL Study Investigators. Community-Acquired Pneumonia Intervention Trial Assessing Levofloxacin. *JAMA.* 2000; 283:749–55.
13. Cannon CP, Hand MH, Bahr R,, et al. Critical pathways for management of patients with acute coronary syndromes: an assessment by the National Heart Attack Alert Program. *Am Heart J.* 2002; 143:777–89.
14. Jones S. A clinical pathway for pediatric gastroenteritis. *Gastroenterol Nurs.* 2003; 26:7–18.
15. Nierman DM. A structure of care for the chronically critically ill. *Crit Care Clin.* 2002; 18:477–91.
16. Kercsmar CM, Myers TR. Clinical pathways in treatment of asthma. *Curr Opin Allergy Clin Immunol.* 2002; 2:183–7.
17. Mavroukakis SA, Muehlbauer PM, White RL Jr,, et al. Clinical pathways for managing patients receiving interleukin 2. *Clin J Oncol Nurs.* 2001; 5:207–17.
18. Zevola DR, Raffa M, Brown K. Using clinical pathways in patients undergoing cardiac valve surgery. *Crit Care Nurse.* 2002; 22:31–9, 44–50.
19. Rymer MM, Summers D, Soper P. Development of clinical pathways for stroke management: an example from Saint Luke's Hospital, Kansas City. *Clin Geriatr Med.* 1999; 15:741–64.
20. Bisanz A, DeJesus Y, Saddler DA. Development, implementation, and ongoing monitoring of pathways for the treatment of gastrointestinal cancer at a comprehensive cancer center. *Gastroenterol Nurs.* 1999; 22:107–14.
21. Sesperez J, Wilson S, Jalaludin B,, et al. Trauma case management and clinical pathways: prospective evaluation of their effect on selected patient outcomes in five key trauma conditions. *J Trauma.* 2001; 50:643–9.
22. Mamolen NL, Brenner PS. The impact of a burn wound education program and implementation of a clinical pathway on patient outcomes. *J Burn Care Rehabil.* 2000; 21:440–5.

23. Crane M, Werber B. Critical pathway approach to diabetic pedal infections in a multidisciplinary setting. *J Foot Ankle Surg.* 1999; 38:30–3.
24. Baker CM, Miller I, Sitterding M., et al. Acute stroke patients comparing outcomes with and without case management. *Nurs Case Manag.* 1998; 3:196–203.
25. Holtzman J, Bjerke T, Kane R. The effects of clinical pathways for renal transplant on patient outcomes and length of stay. *Med Care.* 1998; 36:826–34.
26. Petitta A, Kaatz S, Estrada C., et al. The transition to medication system performance indicators. *Top Hosp Pharm Manag.* 1995; 14:20–6.
27. Johnson KB, Blaisdell CJ, Walker A., et al. Effectiveness of a clinical pathway for inpatient asthma management. *Pediatrics.* 2000; 106:1006–12.
28. Philbin EF, Rocco TA, Lindenmuth NW., et al. The results of a randomized trial of a quality improvement intervention in the care of patients with heart failure. The MISCHF Study Investigators. *Am J Med.* 2000; 109:443–9.
29. Murphy M, Noetscher C, Lagoe R. A multihospital effort to reduce inpatient lengths of stay for pneumonia. *J Nurs Care Qual.* 1999; 13:11–23.
30. Dzwierzynski WW, Spitz K, Hartz A., et al. Improvement in resource utilization after development of a clinical pathway for patients with pressure ulcers. *Plast Reconstr Surg.* 1998; 102:2006–11.
31. Boykin JV Jr, Crossland MC, Cole LM. Wound healing management: enhancing patient outcomes and reducing costs. *J Healthc Resour Manag.* 1997; 15:22,24–6.
32. Leibman BD, Dillioglugil O, Abbas F., et al. Impact of a clinical pathway for radical retropubic prostatectomy. *Urology.* 1998; 52:94–9.
33. Bailey R, Weingarten S, Lewis M., et al. Impact of clinical pathways and practice guidelines on the management of acute exacerbations of bronchial asthma. *Chest,* 1998; 113:28–33.
34. Uchiyama K, Takifuji K, Tani M., et al. Effectiveness of the clinical pathway to decrease length of stay and cost for laparoscopic surgery. *Surg Endosc.* 2002; 16:1594–7.
35. Wilson SD, Dahl BB, Wells RD. An evidence-based clinical pathway for bronchiolitis safely reduces antibiotic overuse.*Am J Med Qual.* 2002; 17:195–9.
36. Smith DM, Gow P. Towards excellence in quality patient care: a clinical pathway for myocardial infarction. *J Qual Clin Pract,* 1999; 19:103–5.
37. Kirk JK, Michael KA, Markowsky SJ., et al. Critical pathways: the time is here for pharmacist involvement. *Pharmacotherapy.* 1996; 16:723–33.
38. Institute for Safe Medication Practices. Medication safety self-assessment. www.ismp.org/pages/mssacaprdf.html (accessed 2003 May 16).
39. American Society of Hospital Pharmacists. ASHP statement on pharmaceutical care. *Am J Hosp Pharm.* 1993; 50:1720–3.
40. American Society of Hospital Pharmacists. ASHP statement on principles for including medications and pharmaceutical care in health care systems. *Am J Hosp Pharm.* 1993; 50:756–7.
41. American Society of Health-System Pharmacists. ASHP guidelines on a standardized method for pharmaceutical care. *Am J Health-Syst Pharm.* 1996; 53:1713–6.
42. American Society of Health-System Pharmacists. ASHP guidelines on medication-use evaluation. *Am J Health-Syst Pharm.* 1996; 53:1953–5.

These guidelines were reviewed in 2009 by the Council on Pharmacy Practice and by the Board of Directors and were found to still be appropriate.

Approved by the ASHP Board of Directors on April 15, 2004. Developed by the ASHP Council on Professional Affairs. Supersedes the "ASHP guidelines on the pharmacists' role in the development of clinical care plans" dated November 16, 1996.

The bibliographic citation for this document is as follows: American Society of Health-System Pharmacists. ASHP guidelines on the pharmacist's role in the development, implementation, and assessment of critical pathways. *Am J Health-Syst Pharm.* 2004; 61:939–45.

ASHP Guidelines on a Standardized Method for Pharmaceutical Care

Need for a Standardized Method

The purpose of this document is to provide pharmacists with a standardized method for the provision of pharmaceutical care in component settings of organized health systems. Since the introduction of the pharmaceutical care concept[1] and the development of the ASHP Statement on Pharmaceutical Care,[2] considerable variation in pharmacists' provision of pharmaceutical care has been noted. ASHP believes pharmacists need a standardized method for providing pharmaceutical care.

This document describes a standardized method based on functions that all pharmacists should perform for individual patients in organized health systems. The use of this method would foster consistency in the provision of pharmaceutical care in all practice settings. It would support continuity of care both within a practice setting (e.g., among pharmacists on different work shifts caring for an acutely ill inpatient) and when a patient moves among practice settings (e.g., when an inpatient is discharged to home or ambulatory care). Further, a standardized method would establish consistent documentation so that patient-specific and medication-related information could be shared from pharmacist to pharmacist and among health professionals.

The need to identify the functions involved in pharmaceutical care and the critical skills necessary to provide it was discussed at the San Antonio consensus conference in 1993.[3] Functions for the provision of pharmaceutical care were identified by the practitioner task force of the Scope of Pharmacy Practice Project.[4] Those functions have been defined in more detail in the pharmacotherapy series of the ASHP Clinical Skills Program.[5–9]

These Guidelines are not specific to any practice setting. ASHP believes this standardized method can be used in acute care (hospitals), ambulatory care, home care, long-term care, and other practice settings. Functions can be tailored as appropriate for a given practice setting. It is recognized that the degree of standardization and tailoring appropriate for a given work site will depend on the practice environment, the organization of services (e.g., patient-focused or department-focused), working relationships with other health professionals, the health system's and patient's financial arrangements, and the health system's policies and procedures. ASHP believes the use of the systematic approaches encouraged by these guidelines will assist pharmacists in implementing and providing pharmaceutical care in their work sites.

Functions of Pharmaceutical Care

ASHP believes that a standardized method for the provision of pharmaceutical care should include the following:

- Collecting and organizing patient-specific information,
- Determining the presence of medication-therapy problems,
- Summarizing patients' health care needs,
- Specifying pharmacotherapeutic goals,
- Designing a pharmacotherapeutic regimen,
- Designing a monitoring plan,
- Developing a pharmacotherapeutic regimen and corresponding monitoring plan in collaboration with the patient and other health professionals,
- Initiating the pharmacotherapeutic regimen,
- Monitoring the effects of the pharmacotherapeutic regimen, *and*
- Redesigning the pharmacotherapeutic regimen and monitoring plan.

These major functions have been adapted, in part, from the pharmacotherapy series of the ASHP Clinical Skills Program and the final report of the ASHP Model for Pharmacy Practice Residency Learning Demonstration Project.

Collecting and Organizing Pertinent Patient-Specific Information. Information should be collected and used as a patient-specific database to prevent, detect, and resolve the patient's medication-related problems and to make appropriate medication-therapy recommendations. The database should include the following sections, each containing specific types of information to the extent that it is relevant to medication therapy:

Demographic

- Name
- Address
- Date of birth
- Sex
- Religion and religious affiliation
- Occupation

Administrative

- Physicians and prescribers
- Pharmacy
- Room/bed numbers
- Consent forms
- Patient identification number

Medical

- Weight and height
- Acute and chronic medical problems
- Current symptoms
- Vital signs and other monitoring information
- Allergies and intolerances
- Past medical history
- Laboratory information
- Diagnostic and surgical procedures

Medication therapy

- Prescribed medications
- Nonprescription medications
- Medications used prior to admission
- Home remedies and other types of health products used
- Medication regimen
- Compliance with therapy
- Medication allergies and intolerances
- Concerns or questions about therapy

Assessment of understanding of therapy
Pertinent health beliefs

Behavioral/lifestyle
Diet
Exercise/recreation
Tobacco/alcohol/caffeine/other substance use or abuse
Sexual history
Personality type
Daily activities

Social/economic
Living arrangement
Ethnic background
Financial/insurance/health plan

Objective and subjective information should be obtained directly from patients (and family members, other caregivers, and other health professionals as needed). A physical assessment should be performed as needed. In addition, information can be obtained by reviewing the patient's health record and other information sources.

Information in the patient's health record should be understood, interpreted, and verified for accuracy before decisions are made about the patient's medication therapy. With access to the patient's health record comes the professional responsibility to safeguard the patient's rights to privacy and confidentiality. The Privacy Act of 1974,[10] professional practice policies,[11,12] and policies and procedures of organized health systems provide guidance for the pharmacist in judging the appropriate use of patient-specific information.

The patient (as well as family members, caregivers, and other members of the health care team as needed) should be interviewed. This is necessary for the pharmacist to establish a direct relationship with the patient, to understand the patient's needs and desired outcome, to obtain medication-related information, and to clarify and augment other available information. Pharmacists in many practice settings, including ambulatory care, may need to perform physical assessments to collect data for assessing and monitoring medication therapy.

Information, including clinical laboratory test results, gathered or developed by other members of the health care team may not be in the patient's health record. Therefore, to ensure that the patient information is current and complete, other sources should be checked. Other sources may include medication profiles from other pharmacies used by the patient.

Although it is ideal to have a comprehensive database for all patients, time and staffing limitations may necessitate choices regarding the quantity of information and the number of patients to follow. Choices could be determined by the health system's policies and procedures, by clinical care plans, or by disease management criteria in the patient's third-party health plan.

Systems for recording patient-specific data will vary, depending on pharmacists' preferences and practice settings. Electronic documentation is recommended. Some information may already be in the patient's health record. Therefore, when authorized, the additional information gathered by the pharmacist should be recorded in the patient's health record so that it can be shared with other health professionals. Abstracted summaries and work sheets may also be useful.

Determining the Presence of Medication-Therapy Problems. Conclusions should be drawn from the integration of medication-, disease-, laboratory test-, and patient-specific information. The patient's database should be assessed for any of the following medication-therapy problems:

- Medications with no medical indication,
- Medical conditions for which there is no medication prescribed,
- Medications prescribed inappropriately for a particular medical condition,
- Inappropriate medication dose, dosage form, schedule, route of administration, or method of administration,
- Therapeutic duplication,
- Prescribing of medications to which the patient is allergic,
- Actual and potential adverse drug events,
- Actual and potential clinically significant drug–drug, drug–disease, drug–nutrient, and drug–laboratory test interactions,
- Interference with medical therapy by social or recreational drug use,
- Failure to receive the full benefit of prescribed medication therapy,
- Problems arising from the financial impact of medication therapy on the patient,
- Lack of understanding of the medication therapy by the patient, and
- Failure of the patient to adhere to the medication regimen.

The relative importance of problems must be assessed on the basis of specific characteristics of the patient or the medication. Checklists, work sheets, and other methods may be used to determine and document the presence of medication-therapy problems. The method should be proactive and should be used consistently from patient to patient.

Summarizing Patients' Health Care Needs. The patient's overall needs and desired outcomes and other health professionals' assessments, goals, and therapy plans should be considered in determining and documenting the medication-related elements of care that are needed to improve or prevent deterioration of the patient's health or well-being.

Specifying Pharmacotherapeutic Goals. Pharmacotherapeutic goals should reflect the integration of medication-, disease-, laboratory test-, and patient-specific information, as well as ethical and quality-of-life considerations. The goals should be realistic and consistent with goals specified by the patient and other members of the patient's health care team. The therapy should be designed to achieve definite medication-related outcomes and improve the patient's quality of life.

Designing a Pharmacotherapeutic Regimen. The regimen should meet the pharmacotherapeutic goals established with the patient and reflect the integration of medication-, disease-, laboratory test-, and patient-specific information; ethical and quality-of-life considerations; and pharmacoeconomic principles. It should comply with the health system's medication-use policies, such as clinical care plans and disease management plans. The regimen should be designed for optimal medication use within both the health system's and the patient's capabilities and financial resources.

Designing a Monitoring Plan for the Pharmacotherapeutic Regimen. The monitoring plan should effectively evaluate achievement of the patient-specific pharmacotherapeutic goals and detect real and potential adverse effects. Measurable, observable parameters should be determined for each goal. Endpoints should be established for assessing whether the goal has been achieved. The needs of the patient, characteristics of the medication, needs of other health care team members, and policies and procedures of the health care setting will influence the monitoring plan.

Developing a Pharmacotherapeutic Regimen and Corresponding Monitoring Plan. The regimen and plan developed in collaboration with the patient and other health professionals should be systematic and logical and should represent a consensus among the patient, prescriber, and pharmacist. The approach selected should be based on consideration of the type of practice setting, its policies and procedures, practice standards, and good professional relations with the prescriber and patient. The regimen and monitoring plan should be documented in the patient's health record to ensure that all members of the health care team have this information.

Initiating the Pharmacotherapeutic Regimen. Depending on the regimen and plan, the pharmacist could, as appropriate, implement all or portions of the pharmacotherapeutic regimen. Actions should comply with the health system's policies and procedures (e.g., prescribing protocols) and correspond to the regimen and plan. Orders for medications, laboratory tests, and other interventions should be clear and concise. All actions should be documented in the patient's health record.

Monitoring the Effects of the Pharmacotherapeutic Regimen. Data collected according to the monitoring plan should be sufficient, reliable, and valid so that judgments can be made about the effects of the pharmacotherapeutic regimen. Changes in patient status, condition, medication therapy, or nonmedication therapy since the monitoring plan was developed should be considered. Missing or additional data should be identified. Achievement of the desired endpoints should be assessed for each parameter in the monitoring plan. A judgment should be made about whether the pharmacotherapeutic goals were met. Before the pharmacotherapeutic regimen is adjusted, the cause for failure to achieve any of the pharmacotherapeutic goals should be determined.

Redesigning the Pharmacotherapeutic Regimen and Monitoring Plan. Decisions to change the regimen and plan should be based on the patient's outcome. When clinical circumstances permit, one aspect of the regimen at a time should be changed and reassessed. Recommendations for pharmacotherapeutic changes should be documented in the same manner used to document the original recommendations.

Pharmacist's Responsibility

An essential element of pharmaceutical care is that the pharmacist accepts responsibility for the patient's pharmacotherapeutic outcomes. The same commitment that is applied to designing the pharmacotherapeutic regimen and monitoring plan for the patient should be applied to its implementation. The provision of pharmaceutical care requires monitoring the regimen's effects, revising the regimen as the patient's condition changes, documenting the results, and assuming responsibility for the pharmacotherapeutic effects.

References

1. Hepler CD, Strand LM. Opportunities and responsibilities in pharmaceutical care. *Am J Hosp Pharm.* 1990; 47:533–43.
2. American Society of Hospital Pharmacists. ASHP statement on pharmaceutical care. *Am J Hosp Pharm.* 1993; 50:1720–3.
3. Implementing pharmaceutical care. Proceedings of an invitational conference conducted by the American Society of Hospital Pharmacists and the ASHP Research Foundation. *Am J Hosp Pharm.* 1993; 50: 1585–656.
4. Summary of the final report of the Scope of Pharmacy Practice Project. *Am J Hosp Pharm.* 1994; 51:2179–82.
5. Shepherd MF. Clinical skills program pharmacotherapy series module 1. Reviewing patient medical charts. Bethesda, MD: American Society of Hospital Pharmacists; 1992.
6. Mason N, Shimp LA. Clinical skills program pharmacotherapy series module 2. Building a pharmacist's patient data base. Bethesda, MD: American Society of Hospital Pharmacists; 1993.
7. Mason N, Shimp LA. Clinical skills program–module 3. Constructing a patient's drug therapy problem list. Bethesda, MD: American Society of Hospital Pharmacists; 1993.
8. Jones WN, Campbell S. Clinical skills program pharmacotherapy series module 4. Designing and recommending a pharmacist's care plan. Bethesda, MD: American Society of Hospital Pharmacists; 1994.
9. Frye CB. Clinical skills program pharmacotherapy series module 5. Monitoring the pharmacist's care plan. Bethesda, MD: American Society of Hospital Pharmacists; 1994.
10. PL 93-579. 5 U.S.C.A. 552a (88 Stat. 1896).
11. ASHP guidelines for obtaining authorization for documenting pharmaceutical care in patient medical records. *Am J Hosp Pharm.* 1989; 46:338–9.
12. Principles of practice for pharmaceutical care. Washington, DC: American Pharmaceutical Association; 1995.

Approved by the ASHP Board of Directors, April 24, 1996. Developed by the ASHP Council on Professional Affairs.

The bibliographic citation for this document is as follows: American Society of Health-System Pharmacists. ASHP guidelines on a standardized method for pharmaceutical care. *Am J Health-Syst Pharm.* 1996; 53:1713–6.

Specific Practice Areas

Naloxone Availability (1510)
Source: Council on Therapeutics
To recognize the potential public health benefits of naloxone for opioid reversal; further,

To support efforts to safely expand access to naloxone; further,

To advocate that individuals other than licensed healthcare professionals be permitted access to naloxone after receiving education; further,

To foster education on the role of naloxone in opioid reversal and its proper administration, safe use, and appropriate follow-up care; further,

To support state efforts to authorize pharmacists' prescribing authority for naloxone for opioid reversal.

Safety and Effectiveness of Ethanol Treatment for Alcohol Withdrawal Syndrome (1514)
Source: Council on Therapeutics
To oppose the use of oral or intravenous ethanol for the prevention or treatment of alcohol withdrawal syndrome (AWS) because of its poor effectiveness and safety profile; further,

To support hospital and health-system efforts that prohibit the use of oral or intravenous ethanol therapies to treat AWS; further,

To educate clinicians about the availability of alternative therapies for AWS.

This policy supersedes ASHP policy 1010.

Chemotherapy Parity (1516)
Source: Council on Therapeutics
To advocate that all insurance payers design plans so that patient cost sharing for chemotherapy be equivalent regardless of route of administration; further,

To continue to foster the development of best practices, including adherence monitoring strategies, and education on the safe use and management of chemotherapy agents regardless of route of administration.

Documentation of Penicillin Allergy as a Component of Antimicrobial Stewardship (1517)
Source: Council on Therapeutics
To advocate involvement of pharmacists in the clarification of penicillin allergy, intolerance, and adverse drug events; further,

To advocate for documentation of penicillin allergy, intolerance, reactions, and severity in the medical record to facilitate optimal antimicrobial selection; further,

To recommend the use of penicillin skin testing in appropriate candidates when clinically indicated to optimize antimicrobial selection.

Prescription Drug Abuse (1526)
Source: Council on Pharmacy Practice
To affirm that pharmacists have leadership roles in recognition, prevention, and treatment of prescription drug abuse; further,

To promote education on prescription drug abuse, misuse, and diversion-prevention strategies.

Pharmacist's Role in Urgent and Emergency Situations (1527)
Source: Council on Pharmacy Practice
To affirm that pharmacists should participate in planning and providing emergency treatment team services; further,

To advocate that pharmacists participate in decision-making about the medications and supplies used in medical emergencies; further,

To advocate that pharmacists serve in all emergency responses, and that those pharmacists receive appropriate training and maintain appropriate certifications.

Safe Use of Radiopharmaceuticals (1402)
Source: Council on Pharmacy Practice
To affirm that radiopharmaceuticals require the same standards for safe medication use as other medications, including but not limited to standards for procurement, storage and control, prescribing, preparation, dispensing, administration, documentation, clinical and regulatory monitoring, disposal, and formulary consideration; further,

To advocate that pharmacy departments, in cooperation with departments of nuclear medicine, radiology, and radiation safety, provide oversight of radiopharmaceuticals to assure safe use; further,

To advocate for incorporation of information on radiopharmaceuticals into college of pharmacy curricula and increased pharmacy continuing education on radiopharmaceuticals.

Safe Use of Fentanyl Transdermal System Patches (1404)
Source: Council on Pharmacy Practice
To advocate for enhanced consumer education and product safety requirements for fentanyl transdermal system patches; further,

To encourage manufacturers of fentanyl transdermal system patches to collaborate with pharmacists and other stakeholders to identify and implement packaging, labeling, and formulation changes that prevent accidental exposure and facilitate safe disposal.

Education About Performance-Enhancing Substances (1305)
Source: Council on Pharmacy Practice
To encourage pharmacists to engage in community outreach efforts to provide education to athletes on the risks associated with the use of performance-enhancing substances; further,

To encourage pharmacists to advise athletic authorities and athletes on the dangers of performance-enhancing substances and other products that are prohibited in competition; further,

To advocate for the role of the pharmacist in all aspects of sports doping control.

This policy supersedes ASHP policy 0710.

Pharmacists' Role in Immunization (1309)
Source: Council on Public Policy
To affirm that pharmacists have a role in improving public health and increasing patient access to immunizations by

promoting and administering appropriate immunizations to patients and employees in all settings; further,

To collaborate with key stakeholders to support the public health role of pharmacists and student pharmacists in the administration of adult and pediatric immunizations; further,

To advocate that states grant pharmacists and appropriately supervised student pharmacists the authority to initiate and administer all adult and pediatric immunizations; further,

To advocate that pharmacists and student pharmacists who have completed a training and certification program acceptable to state boards of pharmacy and meeting the standards established by the Centers for Disease Control and Prevention may provide such immunizations; further,

To advocate that state and federal health authorities establish centralized databases for documenting administration of immunizations that are accessible to all health care providers; further,

To advocate that state and federal health authorities require pharmacists and other immunization providers to report their documentation to these centralized databases, if available; further,

To strongly encourage pharmacists to educate all patients, their caregivers, parents, guardians, and health care providers about the importance of immunizations for disease prevention; further,

To encourage pharmacists to seek opportunities for involvement in disease prevention through community immunization programs; further,

To advocate for the inclusion of pharmacist-provided immunization training in college of pharmacy curricula.

This policy supersedes ASHP policies 1220 and 0213.

Pharmacist's Role in Accountable Care Organizations (1214)

Source: Council on Pharmacy Practice

To recognize that pharmacist participation in collaborative health care teams improves outcomes from medication use and lowers costs; further,

To advocate to health policymakers, payers, and other stakeholders for the inclusion of pharmacists as health care providers within accountable care organizations (ACOs) and other models of integrated health care delivery; further,

To advocate that pharmacist-provided care (including care coordination services) be appropriately recognized in reimbursement models for ACOs; further,

To advocate that pharmacists be included as health care providers in demonstration projects for ACOs; further,

To encourage comparative effectiveness research and measurement of key outcomes (e.g., clinical, economic, quality, access) for pharmacist services in ACOs; further,

To encourage pharmacy leaders to develop strategic plans for positioning pharmacists in key roles within ACOs.

Criteria for Medication Use in Geriatric Patients (1221)

Source: Council on Therapeutics

To support medication therapy management, including assessment of physiologic and pharmacokinetic factors, as a central component of providing safe and effective drug therapy to geriatric patients; further,

To oppose use of the Beers criteria or similar criteria by the Centers for Medicare & Medicaid Services and other accreditation and quality improvement entities as the sole indicator to assess the appropriateness of prescribing for geriatric patients based on known limitations in the evidence evaluating the association between use of medications listed in such criteria and subsequent adverse drug events; further,

To advocate for the development, refinement, and validation of new criteria that consider drug-, disease-, and patient-specific factors and demonstrate the ability to decrease the occurrence of adverse drug events in geriatric patients; further,

To support research to assess the clinical application of existing and proposed criteria, including assessment of their correlation to patient outcomes and strategies for implementation; further,

To encourage inclusion of validated criteria in clinical decision support systems and other information technologies to facilitate prescribing for geriatric patients; further,

To acknowledge that such criteria are intended as a guide and should not replace the clinical judgment of pharmacists and other clinicians.

Tobacco and Tobacco Products (1224)

Source: Council on Therapeutics

To discourage the use, distribution, and sale of tobacco and tobacco products in and by pharmacies; further,

To advocate for tobacco-free environments in hospitals and health systems; further,

To seek, within the bounds of public law and policy, to eliminate the use and distribution of tobacco and tobacco products in meeting rooms and corridors at ASHP-sponsored events; further,

To promote the role of pharmacists in tobacco-cessation counseling and medication therapy management; further,

To join with other interested organizations in statements and expressions of opposition to the use of tobacco and tobacco products.

This policy supersedes ASHP policy 0713.

Safe and Effective Use of IV Promethazine (1105)

Source: Council on Therapeutics

To recognize intravenous (IV) promethazine as a treatment alternative in limited clinical circumstances; further,

To support health-system efforts to restrict use of IV promethazine by encouraging alternate routes of administration or use of therapeutic alternatives when appropriate; further,

To encourage health systems to establish medication-use processes that reflect nationally recognized best practices to limit the potential for patient harm when IV promethazine use is medically necessary.

Pain Management (1106)

Source: Council on Therapeutics

To advocate fully informed patient and caregiver participation in pain management decisions as an integral aspect of patient care; further,

To advocate that pharmacists actively participate in the development and implementation of health-system pain management policies and protocols; further,

To support the participation of pharmacists in pain management, which is a multidisciplinary, collaborative process for selecting appropriate drug therapies, educating patients, monitoring patients, and continually assessing outcomes of therapy; further,

To advocate that pharmacists lead efforts to prevent inappropriate use of pain therapies, including engaging in strategies to detect and address patterns of abuse and misuse; further,

To encourage the education of pharmacists, pharmacy students, and other health care providers regarding the principles of pain management and methods to minimize drug diversion.

This policy supersedes ASHP policy 0306.

Pharmacist's Role in Providing Care for an Aging Population (0902)

Source: Council on Pharmacy Practice

To encourage expansion of geriatric health care services; further,

To foster expanded roles for pharmacists in caring for geriatric patients; further,

To support successful innovative models of team-based, interdisciplinary geriatric care; further,

To increase training of pharmacists in caring for geriatric patients within college of pharmacy curricula, in ASHP-accredited postgraduate-year-one residencies, and through the expansion of the number of ASHP-accredited postgraduate-year-two geriatric pharmacy residency programs.

This policy was reviewed in 2013 by the Council on Pharmacy Practice and by the Board of Directors and was found to still be appropriate.

Pharmacist Role in the Health Care (Medical) Home (0908)

Source: Council on Public Policy

To advocate to health policymakers, payers, and other stakeholders for the inclusion of pharmacists as a care provider within the health care (medical) home model; further,

To ensure that there are appropriate reimbursement mechanisms for the care that pharmacists provide (including care coordination services) within the health care home model; further,

To advocate to the Centers for Medicare & Medicaid Services that pharmacists be included in demonstration projects for the health care home model; further,

To encourage comparative effectiveness research and measurement of key outcomes (e.g., clinical, economic, quality, access) for pharmacist services in the health care home model.

This policy was reviewed in 2013 by the Council on Public Policy and by the Board of Directors and was found to still be appropriate.

Safe and Effective Use of Heparin in Neonatal Patients (0912)

Source: Council on Therapeutics

To support the development and use of nationally standardized concentrations of heparin when used for maintenance and flush of peripheral and central venous lines in neonatal patients; further,

To advocate that hospitals and health systems use manufacturer-prepackaged heparin flush products to improve the safe use of heparin in neonatal patients.

This policy was reviewed in 2013 by the Council on Therapeutics and by the Board of Directors and was found to still be appropriate.

Pharmacist Support for Dying Patients (0307)

Source: Council on Professional Affairs

To support the position that care for dying patients is part of the continuum of care that pharmacists should provide to patients; further,

To support the position that pharmacists have a professional obligation to work in a collaborative and compassionate manner with patients, family members, caregivers, and other professionals to help fulfill the patient care needs, especially the quality-of-life needs, of dying patients of all ages; further,

To support research on the needs of dying patients; further,

To provide education to pharmacists on caring for dying patients, including education on clinical, managerial, professional, and legal issues; further,

To urge the inclusion of such topics in the curricula of colleges of pharmacy.

This policy was reviewed in 2012 by the Council on Pharmacy Practice and by the Board of Directors and was found to still be appropriate.

Interventions to Reduce High-Risk Behavior in Intravenous Drug Users (9711)

Source: House of Delegates Resolution

ASHP supports the use of needle and syringe exchange programs, drug abuse treatment, and community outreach programs for substance abusers to reduce the risk of transmission of the human immunodeficiency virus (HIV), hepatitis B virus, and hepatitis C virus in intravenous drug users.

This policy was reviewed in 2011 by the Council on Pharmacy Practice and by the Board of Directors and was found to still be appropriate.

Primary and Preventive Care (9407)

Source: Council on Professional Affairs

To support primary and preventive care roles for pharmacists in the provision of pharmaceutical care; further,

To collaborate with physician, nursing, and health-system administrator groups in pursuit of these goals.

This policy was reviewed in 2011 by the Council on Pharmacy Practice and by the Board of Directors and was found to still be appropriate.

ASHP Statement on the Pharmacist's Role in Antimicrobial Stewardship and Infection Prevention and Control

Position

The American Society of Health-System Pharmacists (ASHP) believes that pharmacists have a responsibility to take prominent roles in antimicrobial stewardship programs and participate in the infection prevention and control programs of health systems. This responsibility arises, in part, from pharmacists' understanding of and influence over antimicrobial use within the health system. Further, ASHP believes that the pharmacist's ability to effectively participate in antimicrobial stewardship and infection prevention and control efforts can be realized through clinical endeavors focused on proper antimicrobial utilization and membership on multidisciplinary work groups and committees within the health system. These efforts should contribute to the appropriate use of antimicrobials, ultimately resulting in successful therapeutic outcomes for patients with infectious diseases, and reduce the risk of infections for other patients and health care workers.

Background

Antimicrobial stewardship is utilized in practice settings of health systems to improve patient outcomes while minimizing the unintended consequences of antimicrobial use. The goals of antimicrobial stewardship programs include attenuating or reversing antimicrobial resistance, preventing antimicrobial-related toxicity, and reducing the costs of inappropriate antimicrobial use and health care-associated infections. Guidelines published by the Infectious Diseases Society of America and the Society for Healthcare Epidemiology of America and endorsed by ASHP and other organizations describe an evidence-based approach to antimicrobial stewardship in health systems and the important role pharmacists with infectious diseases training have in leading stewardship efforts.[1]

Identifying and reducing the risks of developing, acquiring, and transmitting infections among patients, health care workers, and others are an important part of improving patient outcomes. In order to maximize outcomes, antimicrobial stewardship should be used in combination with infection prevention and control practices.[1] Most health systems maintain an infection prevention and control program directed by a multidisciplinary committee. The specific program and responsibilities of the infection prevention and control committee (or its equivalent) may differ among health systems.

Typically, the infection prevention and control committee develops organizational policies and procedures addressing

1. The management and provision of patient care and employee health services regarding infection or infection prevention and control.
2. The education of staff, patients, family members, and other caregivers in the prevention and control of infections.
3. Surveillance systems to track the occurrence and transmission of infections.
4. Surveillance systems to track the use of antimicrobials and the development of antimicrobial resistance.
5. Promotion of evidence-based practices and interventions to prevent the development of infections.

Responsibilities of Pharmacists

Pharmacists' responsibilities for antimicrobial stewardship and infection prevention and control include promoting the optimal use of antimicrobial agents, reducing the transmission of infections, and educating health professionals, patients, and the public.

Promoting Optimal Use of Antimicrobial Agents. An important clinical responsibility of the pharmacist is to ensure the optimal use of antimicrobial agents throughout the health system. Functions related to this responsibility may include

1. Encouraging multidisciplinary collaboration within the health system to ensure that the prophylactic, empirical, and therapeutic uses of antimicrobial agents result in optimal patient outcomes. These activities may include antimicrobial-related patient care (e.g., aiding in appropriate selection, optimal dosing, rapid initiation, and proper monitoring and de-escalation of antimicrobial therapies) as well as the development of restricted antimicrobial-use procedures, therapeutic interchange, treatment guidelines, and clinical care plans.[2]
2. Working within the pharmacy and therapeutics committee (or equivalent) structure, which may include infectious disease-related subcommittees, to ensure that the number and types of antimicrobial agents available are appropriate for the patient population served. Such decisions should be based on the needs of special patient populations and microbiological trends within the health system. High priority should be given to developing antimicrobial-use policies that result in optimal therapeutic outcomes while minimizing the risk of the emergence of resistant strains of microorganisms.
3. Operating a multidisciplinary, concurrent antimicrobial stewardship program that uses patient outcomes to assess the effectiveness of antimicrobial-use policies throughout the health system.
4. Generating and analyzing quantitative data on antimicrobial drug use to perform clinical and economic outcome analyses.
5. Working with the microbiology laboratory personnel to ensure that appropriate microbial susceptibility tests are reported on individual patients in a timely manner, and collaborating with the laboratory, infectious diseases specialists, and infection preventionists in compiling susceptibility reports (at least annually) for

distribution to prescribers within the health system to guide empirical therapy.

6. Utilizing information technology to enhance antimicrobial stewardship through surveillance, utilization and outcome reporting, and the development of clinical decision-support tools.
7. Facilitating safe medication management practices for antimicrobial agents by utilizing efficient and effective systems to reduce potential errors and adverse drug events.

Reducing the Transmission of Infections. Pharmacists should participate in efforts to prevent or reduce the transmission of infections among patients, health care workers, and others within all of the health system's applicable practice settings. This may be accomplished through

1. Participating in the infection prevention and control committee (or its equivalent).
2. Establishing internal pharmacy policies, procedures, and quality-control programs to prevent contamination of drug products prepared in or dispensed by the pharmacy department. This is of paramount importance in the preparation and handling of sterile products.[3] Other considerations include (but are not limited to) provisions for cleaning pharmaceutical equipment (e.g., laminar-airflow hoods and bulk-compounding equipment) and establishment of appropriate personnel policies (e.g., limiting the activities of staff members who exhibit symptoms of a viral respiratory illness or other infectious condition).
3. Encouraging the use of single-dose packages of sterile drug products rather than multiple-dose containers, except in sterile environments.
4. Recommending proper labeling, dating, and storage of sterile products and multiple-dose sterile-product containers (if used).
5. Encouraging routine immunization (e.g., influenza vaccination) of hospital staff and others who impact the patient care environment, and promoting periodic screening for selected transmissible diseases (e.g., tuberculosis) in accordance with health-system policy and federal, state, or local regulations.
6. Promoting adherence to standard precautions by health care workers, patients, and others who impact the patient care environment.[4]
7. Collaborating in the development of guidelines for risk assessment, treatment, and monitoring of patients and health care workers who have been in contact with persons with a transmissible infectious disease.
8. Striving for zero tolerance of health care-associated infections, including surgical site infections, catheter-associated bloodstream infections, catheter-associated urinary tract infections, and ventilator-associated pneumonia.

Educational Activities. The pharmacist's role includes providing education and information about antimicrobial stewardship and infection prevention and control to health professionals, patients, and members of the public who come in contact with the health system's practice settings. Incorporating active intervention techniques, such as formulary restriction and preauthorization, enhances the effectiveness of educational activities in the patient care setting.[1] Specific activities may include

1. Providing clinical conferences, newsletters, and other types of educational forums for health professionals on topics such as antimicrobial use and resistance, decontaminating agents (disinfectants, antiseptics, and sterilants), aseptic technique and procedures, and sterilization methods.
2. Educating and counseling inpatients, ambulatory care patients, home care patients, and their families and caregivers in the following areas: adherence to prescribed directions for antimicrobial use, storage and handling of medications and administration devices, and other infection prevention and control procedures (e.g., medical waste disposal).
3. Participating in public health education and awareness programs aimed at controlling the spread of infectious diseases by
   a. Promoting prudent use of antimicrobials,
   b. Providing immunization access for children and adults, an
   c. Promoting appropriate infection prevention and control measures (e.g., proper hand hygiene techniques).
4. Providing exposure to antimicrobial stewardship and infection prevention and control practices through experiential and didactic training for practicing health-system pharmacists, students, residents, and research fellows.

Education and Training of Pharmacists

ASHP recognizes that the current shortage of pharmacists with advanced training in infectious diseases and the limited number of training opportunities may require pharmacists without such training to assume some of the responsibilities described above. ASHP supports the expansion of pharmacy education and postgraduate residency training on infectious diseases in order to develop an adequate supply of pharmacists trained to deliver these essential services.

Conclusion

ASHP believes that pharmacists have a responsibility to take prominent roles in antimicrobial stewardship and infection prevention and control programs in health systems. Pharmacists should participate in antimicrobial stewardship and infection prevention and control efforts through clinical endeavors focused on proper antimicrobial utilization and membership on relevant multidisciplinary work groups and committees within the health system.

References

1. Dellit TH, Owens RC, McGowen JE, et al. Infectious Diseases Society of America and the Society for Healthcare Epidemiology of America guidelines for developing an institutional program to enhance antimicrobial stewardship. *Clin Infect Dis.* 2007; 44:159–77.

2. American Society of Health-System Pharmacists. ASHP guidelines on the pharmacist's role in the development, implementation, and assessment of critical pathways. *Am J Health-Syst Pharm.* 2004; 61:939–45.
3. American Society of Health-System Pharmacists. ASHP guidelines on quality assurance for pharmacy-prepared sterile products. *Am J Health-Syst Pharm.* 2000; 57:1150–69.
4. Siegel JD, Rhinehart E, Jackson M, et al. 2007 guideline for isolation precautions: preventing transmission of infectious agents in healthcare settings, June 2007. www.cdc.gov/ncidod/dhqp/pdf/guidelines/Isolation2007.pdf (accessed 2009 Feb 18).

Suggested Readings

Centers for Disease Control and Prevention. Guideline for disinfection and sterilization in healthcare facilities, 2008. Accessed 15 December 2008. www.cdc.gov/ncidod/dhqp/pdf/guidelines/Disinfection_Nov_2008.pdf.

Centers for Disease Control and Prevention [CDC]. Guidelines for environmental infection control in health-care facilities: recommendations of CDC and the Healthcare Infection Control Practices Advisory Committee (HICPAC). *MMWR.* 2003; 52(No. RR-10):1–48.

Diekema DJ, Doebbeling BN. Employee health and infection control. *Infect Control Hosp Epidemiol.* 1995; 16:292–301.

Gardner P, Schaffner W. Immunization of adults. *N Engl J Med.* 1993; 328:1252–8.

Goldmann DA, Weinstein RA, Wenzel RP, et al. Strategies to prevent and control the emergence and spread of antimicrobial-resistant microorganisms in hospitals. A challenge to hospital leadership. *JAMA.* 1996; 275: 234–40.

Kollef M, Shapiro S, Fraser V, et al. A randomized trial of ventilator circuit changes. *Ann Intern Med.* 1995; 123: 168–74.

MacDougall C, Polk RE. Antimicrobial stewardship programs in health care systems. *Clin Microbiol Rev.* 2005 Oct; 18(4):638–56.

Sepkowitz KA. Occupationally acquired infections in health care workers. *Ann Intern Med.* 1996; 125:826–34,917–28.

Shlaes DM, Gerding DN, John JF Jr., et al. SHEA and IDSA Joint Committee on the Prevention of Antimicrobial Resistance: guidelines for the prevention of antimicrobial resistance in hospitals. *Clin Infect Dis.* 1997; 25:584–99.

This statement was reviewed in 2013 by the Council on Pharmacy Practice and by the Board of Directors and was found to still be appropriate.

Approved by the ASHP Board of Directors on April 17, 2009, and by the ASHP House of Delegates on June 16, 2009. Developed through the ASHP Council on Pharmacy Practice. This statement supersedes the ASHP Statement on the Pharmacist's Role in Infection Control dated June 3, 1998.

Curtis D. Collins, Pharm.D., M.S., is gratefully acknowledged for drafting this statement.

The bibliographic citation for this document is as follows: ASHP Statement on the Pharmacist's Role in Antimicrobial Stewardship and Infection Prevention and Control. *Am J Health-Syst Pharm.* 2010; 67:575–7.

ASHP Statement on the Pharmacist's Role in Clinical Pharmacogenomics

Position

The American Society of Health-System Pharmacists (ASHP) believes that pharmacogenomic testing can improve medication-related outcomes across the continuum of care in all health-system practice settings. These improvements include reduction in suboptimal clinical outcomes, decreased cost of treatment, better medication adherence, more appropriate selection of therapeutic agents, decreased length of treatment, and enhanced patient safety.[1-3] Because of their distinct knowledge, skills, and abilities, pharmacists are uniquely positioned to lead inter-professional efforts to develop processes for ordering pharmacogenomic tests and for reporting and interpreting test results. They are also uniquely qualified to lead efforts to guide optimal drug selection and drug dosing based on those results. Pharmacists therefore have a fundamental responsibility to ensure that pharmacogenomic testing is performed when needed and that the results are used to optimize medication therapy.[1] Pursuant to this leadership role, pharmacists share accountability with other hospital and health-system leaders, such as physicians, laboratory professionals, and genetic counselors, for the ongoing implementation and application of pharmacogenomics across the continuum of care. Because test results will have implications throughout a patient's lifetime, all pharmacists should have a basic understanding of pharmacogenomics in order to provide appropriate patient-care recommendations. Some advanced pharmacist functions in applying clinical pharmacogenomics may require specialized education, training, or experience. ASHP encourages pharmacist education on the use of pharmacogenomics and advocates inclusion of pharmacogenomics and its application to the therapeutic decision-making process in college of pharmacy curricula and Board of Pharmacy Specialties certification programs.

Background

Clinical pharmacogenomics uses genetic information to guide optimal drug selection and drug dosing for patients to maximize therapeutic effects, improve outcomes, and minimize toxicity.[2] Pharmacogenomic testing can be performed reactively or preemptively. Reactive testing generally occurs when a patient is experiencing adverse effects unexplained by dose or drug-drug or drug-disease interactions, or when the use of a high-risk drug is anticipated and the patient's genotype is obtained in anticipation of starting therapy. In contrast, preemptive testing occurs when patients are screened for multiple pharmacogenomic variants prior to developing an indication for specific pharmacotherapy.

Application of pharmacogenomic information requires an understanding of how genetic variations impact the pharmacokinetic and pharmacodynamic properties of a drug in specific diseases and patient populations, as well as an understanding of molecular pathways. The influence of factors such as age, sex, diet, pathophysiologic conditions, and current medication use, as well as their relationship to genetic variability, must also be understood. As awareness of individual genetic variation grows due to improved access to lower-cost testing and availability of evidence-based consensus guidelines in pharmacogenomics,[4] the development of patient-individualized therapeutic regimens should include an assessment of patients' pharmacogenomic profiles in addition to allergy and adverse reaction history, drug interactions, dietary and lifestyle factors, patterns of adherence, and other therapeutic drug-monitoring parameters.[5] The FDA provides a list of drugs for which pharmacogenomic markers are included in the drug labeling,[6] and the Clinical Pharmacogenetics Implementation Consortium (CPIC) has published ASHP-endorsed therapeutic guidelines for multiple drug-gene pairs.[7,8]

The pharmacist's patient-care functions include appropriate and cost-conscious medication selection and monitoring, which now increasingly include pharmacogenomic profile assessment. The purpose of this statement is to describe pharmacists' responsibilities and accountabilities in the field of pharmacogenomics.

Pharmacists' Responsibilities

Pharmacists' responsibilities for pharmacogenomics include promoting the optimal use and timing of pharmacogenomic tests; interpreting clinical pharmacogenomic test results; and educating other pharmacists, fellow health care professionals, patients, and the public about the field of pharmacogenomics. The following are responsibilities that should be part of any clinical pharmacogenomics service:

- Advocating for the rational and routine use of pharmacogenomic testing.
- Providing test result interpretation and clinical guidance for return of results to providers and patients in collaboration with other health care professionals (e.g., physicians, laboratory professionals, and genetic counselors).
- Optimizing medication therapy based on pharmacogenomic test results.
- Educating and providing information on the clinical application of pharmacogenomics to health professionals, patients, and members of the public.
- Supporting and participating in research, consortia, and networks that guide and accelerate the application of pharmacogenomics to clinical practice.

Using these responsibilities as a guide, ASHP has developed the following recommendations for pharmacists' functions in pharmacogenomics.

Pharmacists' Functions

A pharmacist's functions in clinical pharmacogenomics will vary, depending on education, training, experience, and the needs of the practice setting. All pharmacists should have a basic understanding of pharmacogenomics in order to provide patient care that incorporates pharmacogenomic recommendations. Elements of a basic understanding of pharmacogenomics should enable pharmacists to perform the following functions:

- Recommending or scheduling pharmacogenomic testing to aid in the process of drug and dosage selection.
- Designing a patient-specific drug and dosage regimen based on the patient's pharmacogenomic profile that also considers the pharmacokinetic and pharmacodynamic properties of the drug. These factors should be combined in the regimen design along with other pertinent patient-specific factors such as comorbidities, other drug therapy, demographics, and laboratory data to optimize patient outcomes.
- Educating patients, pharmacists, and other health care professionals about pharmacogenomic principles and appropriate indications for clinical pharmacogenomic testing, including the cost-effective use of pharmacogenomic testing.[9]
- Communicating pharmacogenomic-specific drug therapy recommendations to the health care team, including documentation of interpretation of results in the patient's health record.[10]

Pharmacists with specialized education, training, or experience in pharmacogenomics should also assume the following additional functions:

- Developing pharmacogenomic-specific clinical decision support tools in electronic health record systems that guide prescribers on the appropriate use and dosing of medicines based on a patient's pharmacogenomic profile.[11-13]
- Developing a process, including patient-specific educational materials, to explain to patients the importance and significance of their pharmacogenomic test results, not only in the short term but also over the patient's lifetime.
- Developing institutional guidelines and processes for implementation of a clinical pharmacogenomic service.
- Establishing a process for communicating patient-specific results, including documentation of the results in the patient's health record.
- Establishing a mechanism for revisable reporting (reinterpretation of findings based on evolving science) over the course of the patient's care with the institution and beyond.
- Developing processes to document improved patient outcomes and economic benefits resulting from clinical pharmacogenomics.
- Serving as an expert consultant on a clinical pharmacogenomics service.
- Contributing to the evaluation and implementation of clinical pharmacogenomic testing as an integral part of medication therapy.
- Promoting collaborative relationships with other health care professionals and departments involved in drug therapy to encourage the development and appropriate use of pharmacogenomic principles in patient care.
- Applying collaborative drug therapy management principles to a clinical pharmacogenomics service, including advocating for the reimbursement of pharmacogenomic tests and pharmacist interpretation by health insurance plans.
- Developing and planning pharmacogenomic-specific advanced training opportunities for pharmacists and other health care professionals.
- Actively contributing to the body of knowledge in pharmacogenomics by publishing articles on the topic in the biomedical literature.
- Designing and conducting pharmacogenomic research.

Conclusion

ASHP believes that pharmacists have a responsibility to take a prominent role in the clinical application of pharmacogenomics. This emerging science should be spearheaded in many institutions by pharmacists to promote safe, effective, and cost-efficient medication practices.

References

1. Swen JJ, Nijenhuis M, de Boer A, et al. Pharmacogenetics: from bench to byte—an update of guidelines. *Clin Pharmacol Ther.* 2011; 89(5):662–73.
2. Manolio TA, Chisholm RL, Ozenberger B, et al. Implementing genomic medicine in the clinic: the future is now. *Genet Med.* 2013; 15(4):258–67.
3. Wu AC, Fuhlbrigge AL. Economic evaluation of pharmacogenetic tests. *Clin Pharmacol Ther.* 2008; 84(2):272–4.
4. Relling MV, Klein TE. CPIC: Clinical Pharmacogenetics Implementation Consortium of the Pharmacogenomics Research Network. *Clin Pharmacol Ther.* 2011; 89(3):464–7.
5. ASHP policy position 1104: Pharmacogenomics. In: Hawkins B, ed. Best practices for hospital and health-system pharmacy: positions and guidance documents of ASHP. 2013–2014 ed. Bethesda, MD: American Society of Health-System Pharmacists; 2013:162. http://www.ashp.org/DocLibrary/BestPractices/FormularyPositions.aspx (accessed 2014 Jun 19).
6. Table of Pharmacogenomic Biomarkers in Drug Labeling. http://www.fda.gov/drugs/scienceresearch/researchareas/pharmacogenetics/ucm083378.htm (accessed 2014 Jun 19).
7. Clinical Pharmacogenetics Implementation Consortium [CPIC]. Drug-Gene Pairs. www.pharmgkb.org/page/cpicGeneDrugPairs (accessed 2014 Jun 19).
8. American Society of Health-System Pharmacists. Endorsed Documents. http://www.ashp.org/menu/PracticePolicy/PolicyPositionsGuidelinesBestPractices/BrowsebyDocumentType/EndorsedDocuments.aspx (accessed 2014 Jun 19).
9. Feero WG, Kuo GM, Jenkins JR, et al. Pharmacist education in the era of genomic medicine. *J Am Pharm Assoc.* 2012; 52:e113–e121.
10. Hicks JK, Crews KR, Hoffman JM, et al. A clinician-driven automated system for integration of pharma-

cogenetic interpretations into an electronic medical record. *Clin Pharmacol Ther.* 2012; 92(5):563–6.

11. Welch BM, Kawamoto K. Clinical decision support for genetically guided personalized medicine: a systematic review. *J Am Med Inform Assoc.* 2013; 20(2):388–400.
12. Pulley JM., et al. Operational implementation of prospective genotyping for personalized medicine: the design of the Vanderbilt PREDICT project. *Clin Pharmacol Ther.* 2012; 92(1):87–95.
13. Bell GC, Crews KR, Wilkinson MR, et al. Development and use of active clinical decision support for preemptive pharmacogenomics. *J Am Med Inform Assoc.* 2013. DOI: 10.1136/anuajnl-2013-001993 [Epub ahead of print].

Developed through the ASHP Section of Clinical Specialists and Scientists Section Advisory Group on Emerging Sciences, and approved by the ASHP Board of Directors on April 10, 2014, and by the ASHP House of Delegates on June 1, 2014.

Cyrine-Eliana Haidar, Pharm.D., BCPS, BCOP; James M. Hoffman, Pharm.D., M.S., BCPS; and Samuel G. Johnson, Pharm.D., FCCP, BCPS (AQ-Cardiology) are gratefully acknowledged for drafting this statement. Mary V. Relling, Pharm.D., and Kristine R. Crews, Pharm.D., BCPS, are gratefully acknowledged for their review of and contributions to the statement.

The following individuals are gratefully acknowledged for reviewing this statement (review does not imply endorsement): Manju T. Beier, Pharm.D., CGP; Gillian C. Bell, Pharm.D.; Larisa H. Cavallari, Pharm.D., BCPS; J. Kevin Hicks, Pharm.D., Ph.D.; Shannon Manzi, Pharm.D.; Darius Mason, Pharm.D., BCPS; Teresa Vo, Pharm.D.; and Kristin Weitzel, Pharm.D., CDE, FAPhA.

The bibliographic citation for this document is as follows: American Society of Health-System Pharmacists. ASHP statement on the pharmacist's role in clinical pharmacogenomics. *Am J Health-Syst Pharm.* 2015; 72:579–81.

ASHP Statement on the Pharmacist's Role in Clinical Pharmacokinetic Monitoring

The American Society of Health-System Pharmacists (ASHP) believes that clinical pharmacokinetic monitoring is a fundamental responsibility of all pharmacists providing pharmaceutical care. Clinical pharmacokinetic monitoring is an integral component of pharmaceutical care for selected patients based on their specific pharmacotherapy, disease states and related factors, and treatment goals. ASHP believes that clinical pharmacokinetic monitoring is essential to achieving positive outcomes for these patients across the continuum of care and in all practice settings of health systems. Examples of such outcomes include decreased mortality, decreased length of treatment, decreased length of hospital stay, decreased morbidity (either improved symptoms of disease or improved recuperation), and decreased adverse effects from drug therapy.

Background

Clinical pharmacokinetics is the process of applying pharmacokinetic principles to determine the dosage regimens of specific drug products for specific patients to maximize pharmacotherapeutic effects and minimize toxic effects. Application of these principles requires an understanding of the absorption, distribution, metabolism, and excretion characteristics of specific drug products in specific diseases and patient populations. The influence of factors such as age, sex, diet, pathophysiologic conditions, and concomitant use of other drug products must also be understood. The development of patients' individualized dosage regimens should be based on integrated findings from monitoring both the drug concentration-versus-time profiles in biological fluids and the pharmacologic responses to these drug products.

Within the pharmaceutical care process, pharmacists' clinical functions include appropriate and cost-conscious therapeutic drug monitoring and provision of clinical pharmacokinetic assessments. Clinical pharmacokinetic monitoring is necessary when the range between minimal effectiveness and toxicity is narrow and the results of the drug assay provide significant information for clinical decision-making. In the absence of drug concentration measurements, patient-specific characteristics and physiological markers should be used to provide clinical pharmacokinetic assessments and make dosage-regimen recommendations.

Responsibilities

The following responsibilities should be part of clinical pharmacokinetic services or monitoring conducted by pharmacists:

1. Designing patient-specific drug dosage regimens based on the pharmacokinetic and pharmacologic characteristics of the drug products used, the objectives of drug therapy, concurrent diseases and drug therapy, and other pertinent patient factors (e.g., demographics, laboratory data) that improve the safety and effectiveness of drug therapy and promote positive patient outcomes.
2. Recommending or scheduling measurements of drug concentrations in biological fluids (e.g., plasma, serum, blood, cerebrospinal fluid) or tissues in order to facilitate the evaluation of dosage regimens.
3. Monitoring and adjusting dosage regimens on the basis of pharmacologic responses and biological fluid and tissue drug concentrations in conjunction with clinical signs and symptoms or other biochemical variables.
4. Evaluating unusual patient responses to drug therapy for possible pharmacokinetic and pharmacologic explanations.
5. Communicating patient-specific drug therapy information to physicians, nurses, and other clinical practitioners and to patients orally and in writing, and including documentation of this in the patient's health record.
6. Educating pharmacists, physicians, nurses, and other clinical practitioners about pharmacokinetic principles and appropriate indications for clinical pharmacokinetic monitoring, including the cost-effective use of drug concentration measurements.
7. Developing quality assurance programs for documenting improved patient outcomes and economic benefits resulting from clinical pharmacokinetic monitoring.
8. Promoting collaborative relationships with other individuals and departments involved in drug therapy monitoring to encourage the development and appropriate use of pharmacokinetic principles in pharmaceutical care.

Pharmacists with specialized education, training, or experience may have the opportunity to assume the following additional responsibilities:

1. Designing and conducting research to expand clinical pharmacokinetic knowledge and its relationship to pharmacologic responses, exploring concentration–response relationships for specific drugs, and contributing to the evaluation and expansion of clinical pharmacokinetic monitoring as an integral part of pharmaceutical care.
2. Developing and applying computer programs and point-of-care information systems to enhance the accuracy and sophistication of pharmacokinetic modeling and applications to pharmaceutical care.
3. Serving as an expert consultant to pharmacists with a general background in clinical pharmacokinetic monitoring.

Readers are referred to ASHP's more thorough publications on the subject of clinical pharmacokinetic monitoring, including *Clinical Pharmacokinetics Pocket Reference* and *Concepts in Clinical Pharmacokinetics: A Self-Instructional Course.*

This statement was reviewed in 2013 by the Council on Pharmacy Practice and by the Board of Directors and was found to still be appropriate.

Approved by the ASHP Board of Directors, November 15, 1997, and by the ASHP House of Delegates, June 3, 1998. Revised by the ASHP Council on Professional Affairs. Supersedes a previous version approved by the House of Delegates on June 5, 1989.

The bibliographic citation for this document is as follows: American Society of Health-System Pharmacists. ASHP statement on the pharmacist's role in clinical pharmacokinetic monitoring. *Am J Health-Syst Pharm.* 1998; 55:1726–7.

ASHP Statement on the Pharmacist's Role in Hospice and Palliative Care

Position

The American Society of Health-System Pharmacists (ASHP) believes that pharmacists have a pivotal role in the provision of hospice and palliative care and that pharmacists should be integral members of all hospice interdisciplinary teams. Pharmacists practicing in U.S. health systems have been active in defining and providing palliative care since the introduction of hospice through a demonstration project supported by the National Cancer Institute and conducted in New Haven, Connecticut, between 1974 and 1977.[1]

Palliative care has been defined by the World Health Organization (WHO) as "the active total care of patients whose disease is not responsive to curative treatment."[2] WHO notes that control of pain, other symptoms, and psychological, social, and spiritual problems is paramount. The goal of palliative care is achievement of the best quality of life for patients and their families.

Pharmaceutical care is defined as the direct, responsible provision of medication-related care for the purpose of achieving definite outcomes that improve a patient's quality of life.[3] Medication therapy is the cornerstone of most—but not all—symptom control in palliative care. The goals of palliative care and pharmaceutical care are consistent, with the latter being a necessary component of good palliative care.

Hospice is a philosophy and program that delivers palliative care. Hospice care is provided by an interdisciplinary team, which provides expert medical care, pain management, and emotional and spiritual support expressly tailored to the patient's wishes. Emotional and spiritual support are also extended to the family of the patient. In U.S. hospice programs, care is usually provided in the patient's home or in a homelike setting operated by a hospice program. Hospice and palliative care share the same core values and philosophies.

The purpose of this statement is to describe pharmacist's responsibilities and to promote understanding of the various ways in which pharmacists provide or contribute to the provision of care to patients who might be nearing the end of life.

Background

Currently, there are over 3100 operational or planned hospice programs in the 50 states, the District of Columbia, Puerto Rico, and Guam.[4] According to the National Hospice and Palliative Care Organization, 42% of hospices were freestanding in 2000 and 33% were affiliated with hospitals, 22% with home health agencies, and 9% with hospital systems. Over 700,000 patients were served in 2000, and that number is growing annually. In that same year, 73% of hospices were nonprofit, 20% were for-profit institutions, and 7% were run by government.

In 2000, 2.4 million Americans died from all causes. Hospices admitted approximately 700,000 patients. Of those, 600,000 died while under hospice care. Patients are discharged from hospices typically because of stabilization of disease, moving to an area or facility not served by a hospice, and patient and family preference. Over half of patients who die of cancer in the United States are cared for by a hospice. Hospices across the country are caring for increasing numbers of patients with cardiac disease, AIDS, renal disease, end-stage pulmonary disease, dementia, amyotrophic lateral sclerosis, Parkinson's disease, and other degenerative neurologic diseases.

Hospice care is covered by Medicare Part A, private health insurance, and Medicaid in most states for patients who meet certain criteria. Any Medicare beneficiary who has a terminal illness with a prognosis of less than six months is, if the disease runs its normal course as certified by the attending physician and the hospice medical director, eligible for the hospice Medicare benefit.[5] Ninety-one percent of U.S. hospices have met Medicare certification requirements to provide this benefit to Medicare beneficiaries at no cost to the beneficiaries. Many hospices receive charitable contributions to cover the cost of care for terminally ill patients who cannot afford to pay for their care.

Palliative care should be provided in conjunction with curative care at the time of diagnosis of a potentially terminal illness. Palliative care alone may be indicated when attempts at a cure are judged to be futile. Admissions to hospice and palliative care programs often come too late for optimal services to be provided.[6] The mean length of stay is 50 days, and the median is 25 days.[4] Many hospice patients die within days to a week after admission to a program.

A nationwide Gallup survey conducted in 1996 indicated that 9 out of 10 adults, if terminally ill and with six months or less to live, would prefer to be cared for at home. A majority of adults would be interested in a comprehensive program of care, such as hospice. When asked to name their greatest fear associated with death, most respondents cited being a burden to family and friends. Pain was the second most common fear. Effective hospice programs address these concerns.

Pharmaceutical services provided by pharmacists in U.S. hospices were surveyed qualitatively and quantitatively in 1979 and 1991.[7,8]

While many pharmacists continue to serve hospice programs as volunteer consultants to the interdisciplinary team, a growing number of those who work with hospice programs are now considered integral staff and are paid for their services. Inhouse pharmacies have increased since the mid-1990s, and the number continues to grow. A hospice that can support its own pharmacy typically has an average daily census of 200 patients. Most pharmacists who provide pharmaceutical services to hospice programs are not employed directly by the hospices but by a provider of pharmaceutical services, such as a home health pharmacy or hospital. Many are employees of pharmacies that have contracts with hospices to provide drug products and services. In recent years, specialized hospice pharmacy services have been developed in several parts of the United States, and such programs are growing rapidly.

The Hospice Interdisciplinary Team. According to Medicare hospice regulations, a hospice interdisciplinary team should include a doctor of medicine or osteopathy, a registered nurse, a social worker, and a pastoral or other counselor.

Many other professionals and support persons often serve on such teams. In addition, Medicare regulations state that the hospice must "employ a licensed pharmacist; or have a formal agreement with a licensed pharmacist to advise the hospice on ordering, storage, administration, disposal, and recordkeeping of drugs and biologicals." According to the two published surveys of pharmacist activities in hospices, the hospice pharmacist typically is a full member of the interdisciplinary team.[7,8]

By regulation, a patient's plan of care must be reviewed and updated at specified intervals. If a hospice has more than one team, then it must designate the team by which a particular patient will be cared for. Hospice teams typically meet for one or two hours two to four times a month to review patients' care, status, and needs. Treatment plan modifications, determinations of need for additional services, and planning for consultations with specialists, changes in care settings, imminent death, and other important events are discussed. Education and training are often provided at these meetings as well.

The hospice medical director is a doctor of medicine or osteopathy who is responsible for the medical component of the patient's care. The director also serves as a consultant to the patient's primary care physicians and the hospice program staff. Pharmacists coordinate pharmacotherapy by making recommendations for appropriate therapy, educating patients and the hospice team about medications, monitoring therapeutic responses, and performing other medication-related functions. Adjusting drug therapy in accordance with treatment algorithms is a new role for pharmacists in some hospice and palliative care settings.

A registered nurse coordinates the implementation of each patient's plan of care. After certified nursing assistants, who may provide personal care on a daily basis, nurses make the largest number of home visits. Social workers are responsible for the psychosocial care of patients and their families, and they arrange bereavement care for families after patients die. The volunteer director recruits, trains, and coordinates volunteers—another essential component of hospice care. Volunteers provide needed relief for family caregivers and a broad range of services to patients and their families.

Chaplains address spiritual and existential issues. Hospice chaplaincy is typically nondenominational and is often provided in coordination with patients' own clergy. Other frequent participants in team meetings include nursing assistants, home health aides, dietitians, physical therapists, occupational therapists, speech therapists, and hospice administrative personnel. Students and postgraduate trainees from a variety of professions, including pharmacy, often attend as well.

Value of the Pharmacist's Care. Most hospice and palliative care is reimbursed through a capitation plan. Therefore, fees for service generally do not apply. Pharmacists can improve the cost-effectiveness of pharmacotherapy for symptom control in hospice care through patient-specific monitoring for drug therapy outcomes, recommending alternative drug products and dosage forms, minimizing duplicative and interacting medications, compounding medications extemporaneously, improving drug storage and transportation, and educating staff, patients, and families about the most efficient ways of handling and using medications. Systems for documenting these activities and determining cost-effectiveness and the cost–benefit and cost–utility ratios of medications used in the care of terminally ill patients are needed. Avoidance of admissions to hospitals or long-term-care facilities through improved symptom control is a highly desirable and cost-effective outcome of pharmaceutical care for hospice and palliative care patients.

The Pharmacist's Responsibilities

High-quality hospice and palliative care requires both traditional and expanded pharmacist activities, including a variety of clinical, educational, administrative, and support responsibilities:

1. *Assessing the appropriateness of medication orders and ensuring the timely provision of effective medications for symptom control.* Pharmacists maintain patient medication profiles and monitor all prescription and nonprescription medication use for safety and effectiveness. Pharmacists provide patients with essential medications within a time frame that ensures continuous symptom control (especially pain relief) and avoids the need for emergency medical services.
2. *Counseling and educating the hospice team about medication therapy.* Pharmacists attend hospice team meetings to advise other team members about medication therapy, including dosage forms, routes of administration, costs, and availability of various drug products. This is done through regularly scheduled educational sessions. Pharmacists develop and maintain a library of contemporary references about medications, dietary supplements, and alternative and complementary therapies. Pharmacists advise members of the hospice team about the potential for toxicity from and interactions with dietary supplements and alternative and complementary therapies.
3. *Ensuring that patients and caregivers understand and follow the directions provided with medications.* Pharmacists ensure that all medication labeling is complete and understandable by patients and their caregivers. Hospice pharmacists communicate with patients, either through the team or in person, about the importance of adhering to the prescribed drug regimen. Pharmacists explain the differences among addiction, dependence, and tolerance and dispel patient and caregiver misconceptions about addiction to opiate agonists. Pharmacists ensure the availability of devices and equipment to permit accurate measurement of liquid dosage forms by patients and their caregivers. Pharmacists counsel patients about the role and potential toxicity of alternative and complementary therapies. When needed, hospice pharmacists visit patients' homes to communicate directly with patients and their caregivers and to make necessary assessments.
4. *Providing efficient mechanisms for extemporaneous compounding of nonstandard dosage forms.* Hospice pharmacists communicate with pharmaceutical manufacturers to determine the availability of nonstandard dosage forms. Medication-compounding needs in hospice care include the preparation of dosage forms to ease administration (e.g., concentrated sublingual solutions, topical medications), flavoring medications to promote compliance, eliminating or adjusting ingredients that patients cannot tolerate, and preparing or changing drug concentrations. Whenever possible, pharmacists compound formulations for which stability and bioavailability data are available.

5. *Addressing financial concerns.* Hospice benefits usually cover medications. However, patients may lack insurance coverage or benefits may not cover medications that are not considered strictly palliative. Pharmacists communicate with pharmaceutical manufacturers to obtain medications through patient assistance programs.
6. *Ensuring safe and legal disposal of all medications after death.* Medications dispensed to patients are "owned" by the patients and, in most states, cannot be used for other patients. Medications remaining in patients' homes fall under a variety of hazard categories. Pharmacists are able to assist families with the removal of the medications from the home in compliance with federal and state drug control and environmental protection laws and regulations.
7. *Establishing and maintaining effective communication with regulatory and licensing agencies.* Because hospice patients often require large quantities of controlled substances, open communication with both state and federal controlled-substance agencies is important. Pharmacists ensure compliance with laws and regulations pertaining to medications.

Pharmacists' Scope of Practice

The pharmacist may have a range of practice privileges that vary in their level of authority and responsibility. Pharmacists who participate in hospice and palliative care should meet the health care organization's competency requirements to ensure that they provide appropriate quality and continuity of patient care. They should demonstrate required knowledge and skills, which may be obtained through practice-intensive continuing education and pharmacy practice and specialty residencies.

The specific practice of pharmacists should be defined within a scope-of-practice document or a similar tool or protocol developed by the health care organization. The scope-of-practice document defines activities that pharmacists would provide within the context of collaborative practice as a member of the interdisciplinary team, as well as limitations where appropriate. The document should indicate referral and communication guidelines, including the documentation of patient encounters and methods for sharing patient information with collaborating medical providers.

Also included in the scope-of-practice document should be references to activities that will review the quality of care provided and the methods by which the pharmacist will maintain continuing professional competency for functions encompassed by the scope-of-practice document. A process should be in place, and responsible parties identified, to review and update the scope-of-practice document as appropriate.

Documentation of Services

As members of the interdisciplinary health care team, pharmacists should have access to patients' health records and authority to make entries necessary for the team's coordinated care of the patient. With access to the patient's health record comes the pharmacist's professional responsibility to safeguard the patient's rights to privacy and confidentiality. Patients should be informed that pharmacists, as well as other members of the team, have access to their records.

Pharmacists should routinely sign patient-review records at interdisciplinary team meetings. Pharmacist documentation in patient records should include drug therapy recommendations, monitoring of medication effects, patient and family education and counseling activities, and other activities as indicated. Medication profiles should be maintained and should include information about prescription and nonprescription drug products, dietary supplements, and alternative and complementary therapies. Pharmacists also should maintain detailed formulation files for all extemporaneously compounded dosage forms. Other records should be maintained in compliance with applicable federal and state laws and regulations.

References

1. Lipman AG. Drug therapy in terminally ill patients. *Am J Hosp Pharm.* 1975; 32:270–6.
2. World Health Organization Expert Committee. Cancer pain relief and palliative care. Technical report series 804. Geneva, Switzerland: World Health Organization; 1990.
3. American Society of Hospital Pharmacists. ASHP statement on pharmaceutical care. *Am J Hosp Pharm.* 1993; 50:1720–3.
4. National Hospice and Palliative Care Organization. NHPCO facts and figures on hospice care in America. www.nhpco.org (accessed 2002 Apr 11).
5. Gage B, Miller SC, Coppola K et al. Important questions for hospice in the next century. www.aspe.hhs.gov/daltcp/Reports/impques.htm#execsum (accessed 2001 Nov 27).
6. Lipman AG. Evidence-based palliative care. *J Pharm Care Pain Symptom Control.* 1999; 7(4):1–9.
7. Berry JI, Pulliam CC, Caiola SM et al. Pharmaceutical services in hospices. *Am J Hosp Pharm.* 1981; 38:1010–4.
8. Arter SG, Berry JI. The provision of pharmaceutical care to hospice patients: results of the National Hospice Pharmacist Survey. *J Pharm Care Pain Symptom Control.* 1993; 1(1):25–42.

Suggested Readings

1. Lipman AG, Berry JI. Pharmaceutical care of terminally ill patients. *J Pharm Care Pain Symptom Control.* 1995; 3(2):31–56.
2. Arter SG, Lipman AG. Hospice care: a new opportunity for pharmacists. *J Pharm Pract.* 1990; 3:28–33.
3. Lipman AG. Pain management in the home care and hospice patient. *J Pharm Pract.* 1990; 3:1–11.
4. Wilkins C. Pharmacy and hospice: a personal experience. *Consult Pharm.* 1988; 3:462–5.
5. Arter SG, DuBe J, Mahoney J.Hospice care and the pharmacist. *Am Pharm.* 1987; NS27:616–24.
6. Murphy DH. The delicate art of caring: treating the whole person. *Am Pharm.* 1984; NS24:388–90.
7. Quigley JL, Quigley MA, Gumbhir AK. Pharmacy and hospice: partners in patient care. *Am Pharm.* 1982; NS22:420–3.
8. Berry JI. Pharmacy services in hospice organizations. *Hosp Formul.* 1982; 17:1333–8.
9. Mullan PA. Pharmacy and hospice: opportunities for service. *Am Pharm.* 1982; NS22:424–6.
10. Oliver CH. Pharmacy and hospice: talk with the dying patient. *Am Pharm.* 1982; NS22:429–33.

11. DuBe JE. Hospice care and the pharmacist. *US Pharm.* 1981; Apr:25–38.
12. Gable FB. Death with dignity: the pharmacist's role in hospice care. *Apothecary.* 1980; Sep/Oct:62–7.
13. Hammel MI, Trinca CE. Patient needs come first at Hillhaven hospice: pharmacy services essential for pain control. *Am Pharm.* 1978; NS18:655–7.
14. Nee D. Pharmacy practice in a hospice setting. *Fla Pharm Today.* 1995; Apr:19–23.

Approved by the ASHP Board of Directors in April 2002 and ASHP House of Delegates in June 2002. Developed through the ASHP Council on Professional Affairs.

The bibliographic citation for this document is as follows: American Society of Health-System Pharmacists. ASHP statement on the pharmacist's role in hospice and palliative care. *Am J Health-Syst Pharm.* 2002; 59:1770–3.

ASHP Statement on the Pharmacist's Role in Medication Reconciliation

Position

The American Society of Health-System Pharmacists (ASHP) believes that an effective process for medication reconciliation reduces medication errors and supports safe medication use by patients. ASHP encourages hospitals and health systems, including community-based providers and managed care systems, to collaborate in organized, multidisciplinary medication reconciliation programs to promote continuity of patient care. ASHP further believes that pharmacists, because of their distinct knowledge, skills, and abilities, are uniquely qualified to lead interdisciplinary efforts to establish and maintain an effective medication reconciliation process in hospitals and across health systems. Pharmacists should lead or assume key roles in the following essential components of medication reconciliation: developing policies and procedures, implementing and continuously improving medication reconciliation processes, training and assuring the continuing competency of those involved in medication reconciliation, providing operational and therapeutic expertise in the development of information systems that support medication reconciliation, and advocating for medication reconciliation programs in the community. Pursuant to their leadership role, pharmacists share accountability with other hospital and health-system leaders for the ongoing success of medication reconciliation processes across the continuum of care.

Background

The term "medication reconciliation" is defined by the Joint Commission as "the process of comparing the medications a patient is taking (and should be taking) with newly ordered medications" in order to resolve discrepancies or potential problems.[1] The goals of medication reconciliation are to obtain and maintain accurate and complete medication information for a patient and use the information within and across the continuum of care to ensure safe and effective medication use. Although it is sometimes associated with survey and accreditation activities, medication reconciliation is an important component of patient safety and has demonstrated effectiveness in preventing adverse drug events. When organizations do not consistently and reliably reconcile patient medications across the continuum of care, medication errors and adverse drug events occur: approximately half of all hospital-related medication errors and 20% of all adverse drug events have been attributed to poor communication at the transitions and interfaces of care.[2,3]

In 1999, the Institute of Medicine report *To Err Is Human: Building a Safer Health System*[4] identified medication errors as the most common type of health-system error, contributing to several thousand deaths each year. The fiscal impact of these errors is also significant. With reported costs of $2595–4685 per adverse drug event, drug-related morbidity and mortality were estimated to cost over $177 billion in 2000 alone.[5]

Reports and studies such as these had a profound impact on the medical community, and the call for action was immediate. Organizations such as the Institute for Healthcare Improvement, the Agency for Healthcare Research and Quality, and the Joint Commission launched initiatives for performance improvement and established higher expectations through new regulatory standards for improved communication between providers and patients and across health care systems.

In 2005, the Joint Commission made medication reconciliation a focus of one of its National Patient Safety Goals. The initial goal included a number of detailed and specific requirements, which made implementation challenging and resulted in numerous findings of noncompliance during survey. In response, the Joint Commission affirmed the importance of the goal but suspended it in 2009 and 2010 for extensive revision. After a comprehensive literature review and analysis of data collected by surveyor teams, a modified goal was released in 2011, and scoring of the goal began in July 2011.[6] The revised goal sets an expectation for maintaining accurate medication information at critical risk points in the medication-use process while allowing organizations latitude to define processes and encouraging performance improvement.

The purpose of this statement is to describe pharmacists' responsibilities and accountabilities in medication reconciliation practices.

Pharmacists' Responsibilities

When performed by pharmacists, medication reconciliation can reduce the frequency and severity of hospital medication errors that could potentially result in patient harm.[7] Pharmacists have demonstrated high rates of patient interventions; interventions per patient; and documentation of medications, medication interactions, drug-related admissions, and previous drug failures.[8]

ASHP and the American Pharmacists Association began a collaborative effort in 2007 and 2008 to create a shared vision for the role of the pharmacist in medication reconciliation processes.[9] That vision recognizes that pharmacists should take a leadership role in improving medication reconciliation, acting as both advocates and medication experts, to provide information to and educate patients and health care providers. Specifically, pharmacists' responsibilities were described as including but not being limited to

- Providing leadership in designing and managing patient-centered medication reconciliation systems,
- Educating patients and health care professionals about the benefits and limitations of the medication reconciliation process, and
- Serving as patient advocates throughout transitions of care.

Using this vision as a guide, ASHP has developed the following recommendations for pharmacists' functions in medication reconciliation activities.

Pharmacists' Functions

Although medication reconciliation is required at key transitions of care, activities associated with medication reconciliation should be considered part of ongoing care provided to a patient. Beyond active participation in medication reconciliation activities, pharmacists have five fundamental functions in medication reconciliation: developing policies and procedures regarding medication reconciliation processes, implementing and continuously improving those processes, training and assuring the continuing competency of those involved in medication reconciliation, providing operational and therapeutic expertise in the development of information systems that support medication reconciliation, and advocating for medication reconciliation programs in the community. The extent of pharmacist involvement in these functions will depend on the resources available.

Policy and Procedure Development. Pharmacists should provide leadership and participate in establishing policies and procedures that encourage (a) provision of patient care services that include medication reconciliation processes, (b) implementation and operation of an evidence-based medication reconciliation system that optimizes available resources, (c) education of organization staff on the importance of medication reconciliation as a patient safety initiative, and (d) promotion of medication reconciliation as a focus of performance-improvement activities.

Implementation and Performance Improvement. Pharmacists should lead or participate in organizational implementation of and performance-improvement efforts regarding medication reconciliation activities. These activities may include but are not limited to (a) establishing a medication reconciliation implementation task force or redesign team, (b) creating a vision and expectations for medication reconciliation activities, (c) securing executive-level commitment to or sponsorship of medication reconciliation resource needs, (d) identifying barriers that are preventing, or potential barriers that may prevent, safe and effective medication reconciliation procedures within their practice model, as well as possible solutions, (e) guiding workflow development that integrates operational and clinical needs, (f) establishing roles and responsibilities of health care providers in medication reconciliation processes, including pharmacy technicians, pharmacy students, and other medical support personnel, (g) ensuring that competency-based training for all personnel involved in medication reconciliation procedures is established, (h) creating or assisting in the development of standardized documentation templates for medication lists and reconciliation, (i) ensuring that established procedures meet regulatory requirements and organizational policy, and (j) developing a method for ongoing medication reconciliation system evaluation.

Training and Competency Assurance. Pharmacists should lead or participate in (a) identifying all health care providers and support staff involved in medication reconciliation activities, (b) creating competency training and skills assessment that are specific to each staff member's roles and responsibilities in medication reconciliation (e.g., conducting a medication interview, taking a medication history, performing medication reconciliation), (c) providing education and performing assessments to ensure the competency of those who document and perform medication reconciliation activities, and (d) providing didactic or simulated training for medication history and reconciliation procedures.

Information Systems Development. As more organizations adopt computerized provider order entry, electronic medical records, and other information systems, pharmacists should ensure that the systems support medication reconciliation throughout the continuum of care. Consideration should be given to establishing methods for data extraction from the medical record that allow for internal and external reporting of measures related to medication reconciliation.

Advocacy. Pharmacists should provide information about medication reconciliation to health care providers, patients, and the community, and they should evaluate the effectiveness of these advocacy efforts on the medication reconciliation process. Activities may include clinical grand rounds, professional conferences, patient counseling, and mass communications such as newsletters and public service announcements. These efforts should (a) demonstrate the effectiveness of sound medication reconciliation processes in improving patient safety and reducing health care costs, (b) emphasize the importance of timely and accurate communication of medication information between patients and their health care providers, (c) clarify and describe the important role of technology and electronic medical records that support medication reconciliation documentation and reconciliation, (d) provide strategies for preventing medication adverse events related to overuse, misuse, omission, duplication, or other discrepancies found during medication reconciliation processes, (e) highlight the importance of completing a full and accurate medication history, including supplement use, prior to prescribing or administering a new medication, and (f) describe opportunities for pharmacist extenders, such as pharmacy technicians and students, to participate in medication reconciliation activities.

Resource Constraints. Although the literature demonstrates the important role of pharmacists in successful medication reconciliation processes across the continuum of care, significant resources are needed to perform medication reconciliation skillfully and efficiently, which suggests opportunities for expanding the roles of pharmacy residents, students, and technicians. When properly trained, these individuals can participate in the documentation of medication histories, which should then be reviewed by the pharmacist for accuracy prior to medication reconciliation, as described in the ASHP Pharmacy Practice Model Initiative Summit Recommendations.[10] In one study, potential errors due to incomplete or incorrect information, illegible orders, and serious drug interactions were reduced by 82% by having pharmacy technicians obtain medication histories.[11]

When confronted with limited resources, pharmacists should at a minimum participate in and guide interdisciplinary efforts to develop and define policies and procedures for their organizations, standardize workflows for electronic documentation, promote safe practices to the community, and, most importantly, engage health care leadership in efforts to ensure medication reconciliation processes are successful.

Conclusion

An effective process for medication reconciliation reduces medication errors and supports safe medication use. Pharmacists are uniquely qualified to lead interdisciplinary efforts to establish and maintain an effective medication reconciliation process in hospitals and across health systems and should lead or assume key roles in the essential components of medication reconciliation. Because of their crucial role, pharmacists share accountability with other hospital and health-system leaders for the ongoing success of medication reconciliation processes across the continuum of care.

References

1. Joint Commission. National Patient Safety Goals effective January 1, 2012. NPSG.03.06.01. www.jointcommission.org/assets/1/6/NPSG_Chapter_Jan2012_HAP.pdf (accessed 2012 Feb 2).
2. Barnsteiner JH. Medication reconciliation: transfer of medication information across settings: keeping it free from error. *J Infus Nurs.* 2005; 28(suppl 2):31–6.
3. Rozich J, Roger R. Medication safety: one organization's approach to the challenge. *J Clin Outcomes Manag.* 2001; 8:27–34.
4. Kohn LT, Corrigan JM, Donaldson MS, eds. To err is human: building a safer health system. Washington, DC: National Academy Press; 1999.
5. Bates DW, Spell N, Cullen DJ, et al. The cost of adverse drug events in hospitalized patients. *JAMA.* 1997; 277:307–11.
6. Joint Commission. 2011 National Patient Safety Goals. www.jointcommission.org/standards_information/npsgs.aspx. (accessed 2011 Dec 13).
7. Gleason KM, Groszek JM, Sullivan C, et al. Reconciliation of discrepancies in medication histories and admission orders of newly hospitalized patients. *Am J Health-Syst Pharm.* 2004; 61:1689–95.
8. Gurwich EL. Comparison of medication histories acquired by pharmacists and physicians. *Am J Hosp Pharm.* 1983; 40:1541–2.
9. Chen D, Burns A. ASHP–APhA Medication Reconciliation Initiative Workgroup Meeting, February 12, 2007: summary and recommendations. www.ashp.org/s_ashp/docs/files/MedRec_ASHP_APhA_Wkgrp_MtgSummary.pdf (accessed 2012 Feb 1).
10. American Society of Health-System Pharmacists. Pharmacy Practice Model Initiative Summit recommendations. Recommendation D3a. February 1, 2011. www.ashp.org/DocLibrary/PPMI/Summit-Recommendations.aspx (accessed 2012 Feb 1).
11. Michels R, Meisel S. Program using pharmacy technicians to obtain medication histories. *Am J Health-Syst Pharm.* 2003; 60:1982–6.

Approved by the ASHP Board of Directors on April 13, 2012, and by the ASHP House of Delegates on June 10, 2012. Developed through the ASHP Council on Pharmacy Practice.

This statement was drafted by Michelle M. Thoma, Pharm.D., who declared no potential conflicts of interest.

ASHP gratefully acknowledges the following individuals and organizations for reviewing drafts of this statement (review does not imply endorsement): Academy of Managed Care Pharmacy (AMCP); Paul Barrett, Pharm.D., M.P.A., BCPS, FASHP; Julie Cooper, Pharm.D., BCPS; Jean Douglas, Pharm.D.; Michael S. Edwards, Pharm.D., M.B.A., BCOP, FASHP; Kristine M. Gleason, B.S.Pharm.; Kayla Hansen, Pharm.D., M.S.; Becky Harvey, Pharm.D.; John Hertig, Pharm.D., M.S.; Justin Julius, Pharm.D.; Nishaminy Kasbekar, Pharm.D., FASHP; Carlo Lupano, B.S.Pharm., M.B.A., CCP; Ashley M. Overy, Pharm.D.; Fred J. Pane, B.S.Pharm., FASHP; Barbara Petroff, M.S., FASHP; James Ponto, M.S., FASHP; Curt W. Quap, M.S., FASHP; Elizabeth Sampsel, Pharm.D., M.B.A., BCPS (AMCP); Jamie S. Sinclair, M.S., FASHP; Richard L. Stambaugh, Pharm.D., M.S., BCPS; Robert L. Stein, Pharm.D., J.D.; and Jeffrey Stroup, Pharm.D., BCPS, AAHIVE.

The bibliographic citation for this document is as follows: American Society of Health-System Pharmacists. ASHP statement on the pharmacist's role in medication reconciliation. *Am J Health-Syst Pharm.* 2013; 70:453–6.

ASHP Statement on the Pharmacist's Role in Primary Care

Position

The American Society of Health System Pharmacists (ASHP) believes that pharmacists have a role in meeting the primary care needs of patients by fulfilling their responsibilities to provide pharmaceutical care and, in states where it is authorized, through their expanded responsibilities in collaborative drug therapy management.

Pharmaceutical care is the direct, responsible provision of medication-related care for the purpose of achieving definite outcomes that improve a patient's quality of life.[1] Pharmacists establish relationships with patients to ensure the appropriateness of medication therapy and patients' understanding of their therapy, and to monitor the effects of that therapy. In collaborative drug therapy management, pharmacists enter agreements with physicians and other prescribers that may authorize pharmacists, for patients who have a confirmed diagnosis, to select appropriate medication therapies and regimens and adjust them on the basis of patients' responses.

National and international organizations, states, and health care organizations, among others, may have differing or overlapping definitions of primary care. Primary care is a concept intended to improve the quality of care received by everyone in the United States.[2] For the purposes of this document, primary care is defined as the provision of integrated, accessible health care services by clinicians who are accountable for addressing a majority of personal health care needs, developing a sustained partnership with patients, and practicing in the context of family and community. Primary care services should be comprehensive, coordinated, and continuously provided over time by individuals or a team of health care professionals according to the patient's needs. Services should be accessible to patients by telephone or at sites of care provision. Clinicians who provide these services are responsible for the quality of care, the satisfaction of patients, and the efficient use of resources, as well as for their own ethical behavior.[3]

Practice elements of pharmaceutical care and collaborative drug therapy management are consistent with the intents and evolving forms of primary care. ASHP supports the development of definitions and working models of primary care that recognize and incorporate the services of pharmacists for meeting primary care needs of patients. In general, pharmacists contribute to the provision of primary care through the delivery of pharmaceutical care and in collaboration with other health care providers.[4–9] Furthermore, pharmacists may directly provide a limited range of primary care functions in addition to those encompassed by pharmaceutical care, either independently or in collaboration with other members of a primary care team.[10,11] High-quality, coordinated, and continuous medication management for patients should be measurable as a result of the provision of pharmaceutical care within a primary care delivery model. The benefits to patients are valuable access to medication information, the prevention and resolution of medication-related problems, improved outcomes, and increased satisfaction.[12] Pharmacists are able to use medication-related encounters with patients to provide information and either resolve or make a referral for other health care needs.

The purposes of this statement are to promote understanding of the various ways in which pharmacists provide or contribute to the provision of primary care in integrated health systems and to clarify future directions for pharmacists in efforts to expand patient care services in primary care.

Background

Changes in the nation's health care system, especially the growth of managed care and integrated health systems, are stimulating adoption of primary care as a way of meeting basic health care needs and managing access to specialty services. Integrated health systems are organized to deliver acute, intermediate, long-term, home, and ambulatory care. They are intended to seamlessly provide care across practice settings through appropriate use of individual health professionals and teams.[13] Integrated systems offer opportunities for pharmacists and other health care providers to detect and respond to the medication-related needs of patients in transition between settings (e.g., from inpatient to ambulatory care). As integrated systems expand to offer more intensive ambulatory care services and cover broader geographic areas, primary care will become more prominent. Improving patients' access to and continuity of care, implementing disease management, and focusing on quality-related outcomes contribute to optimizing drug costs within the total costs of patient care.[14] Pharmacists involved in primary care contribute to all of these.

Pharmacists participate in primary care services in a variety of practice settings within integrated health systems, including the acute (inpatient), physician office, clinic, pharmacy, long-term, and home settings. A growing number of acute care hospitals have pharmacists participating in patient care activities in ambulatory care clinics and hospital-based home health care services.[15] Along with other providers, pharmacists are expanding and further defining practice models to meet the pharmaceutical and primary care needs of patients throughout the continuum of care.

Responsibilities

Pharmacists involved in primary care participate with other team members in the management of patients for whom medications are a focus of therapy. Pharmacists' responsibility is to optimize patients' medication therapy. Primary care pharmaceutical services should be designed to support the various components of the medication-use process (ordering, dispensing, administering, monitoring, and educating) as individual steps or as they relate to one another in the continuum of care. Pharmacists should evaluate all components of the medication-use process to optimize the potential for positive patient outcomes.

Functions. In general, pharmacists who participate in providing primary care to individual patients perform the following functions in collaboration with physicians and other members of the primary care team:

- Perform patient assessment for medication-related factors.

- Order laboratory tests necessary for monitoring outcomes of medication therapy.
- Interpret data related to medication safety and effectiveness.
- Initiate or modify medication therapy care plans on the basis of patient responses.
- Provide information, education, and counseling to patients about medication-related care.
- Document the care provided in patients' records.
- Identify any barriers to patient compliance.
- Participate in multidisciplinary reviews of patients' progress.
- Communicate with payers to resolve issues that may impede access to medication therapies.
- Communicate relevant issues to physicians and other team members.

Expanded Functions. Expanded primary care functions of pharmacists include all the functions previously described as well as:

- Provide individualized health promotion and disease prevention, including administration of immunizations where this is legally and organizationally authorized.
- Perform limited physical assessment and supervise medication therapy with appropriate collaborative drug therapy management authority.

Pharmacists' Scope of Practice. The pharmacist may have a range of practice privileges that vary in their extent of authority and responsibility. Pharmacists who participate in collaborative primary care practice should meet the health care organization's competency requirements to ensure that they provide appropriate quality and continuity of patient care. They should demonstrate required knowledge and skills that may be obtained through practice-intensive continuing education and pharmacy practice and specialty residencies. The specific practice of pharmacists who participate in collaborative primary care should be defined within a scope-of-practice document or a similar tool developed by the health care organization. The scope-of-practice document defines activities that pharmacists would provide within the context of collaborative primary care practice, as well as limitations where appropriate. The document should indicate referral and communication guidelines, including the documentation of patient encounters and methods for sharing patient information with collaborating medical providers. Also included should be references to activities that will review the quality of care provided and the methods by which the pharmacist will maintain continuing professional competency for functions within the scope-of-practice document. A process should be in place to review and update the scope-of-practice document as appropriate.

Description of Services Provided. The services offered by the pharmacist range from consulting with the health care team to providing direct support of the patient while working in collaboration with the health care team. The pharmacist provides medication therapy outcomes management as part of the patient's ongoing care. The level of intensity of services varies as the patient's needs change. For chronic illnesses, services may range from health maintenance care to active management of treatment; for acute illnesses, services may range from facilitating access to medical care to providing initial management. In this context, health maintenance may include counseling (e.g., abuse of alcohol, tobacco, and other drugs; use of seat belts) and ordering screening procedures (e.g., blood lipids and glucose, fecal occult blood). The complexity of services provided varies according to patient need and support from within the integrated health system.

Areas of primary care pharmacy practice that have previously been demonstrated to be cost-effective and to improve outcomes include participation on primary care teams and primary care clinics for medication monitoring and refill in the management of general or specific pharmacotherapy (e.g., for asthma, hypertension, dyslipidemia, anticoagulation, dermatologic diseases, diabetes, and psychotherapeutics).[16–23]

Documentation of Pharmacists' Care. Pharmacists in each setting should routinely document the quantity and quality of services provided and the estimated effect on patient outcomes. Pharmacists must safeguard patients' rights to privacy and confidentiality. Patient information should be shared only with members of the health care team and others with authorized access as needed for the care of patients.

Methods for referral to other health care providers and documentation of care provided should be defined and must occur as a routine part of the daily functions of a pharmacist's practice. When more than one pharmacist is involved in delivering care, practice standards for the group should be adopted and should serve as a guide for all. Pharmacists must also establish methods of communication among themselves in order to provide and ensure continuity of pharmaceutical care on behalf of patients served.

Value of Pharmacist's Care. Methods for obtaining compensation or economic and professional credit for value-added services must continue to be addressed. Structures designed to measure the practitioner's effectiveness as part of an innovative team should be instituted. The pharmacy profession should embrace these activities in the form of well-structured research. Integrated health systems will need to receive adequate support to expand the availability of pharmacists to provide pharmaceutical care as an essential component of primary care.

References

1. American Society of Health System Pharmacists. ASHP statement on pharmaceutical care. *Am J Hosp Pharm.* 1993; 50:1720–3.
2. Rubin E. Beyond the rhetoric: ensuring the availability of primary care. Report of an AHC/FASHP retreat. *Am J Pharm Educ.* 1993; 57:191–3.
3. Donaldson MS, Yordy KD, Lohr KN, et al., eds. Primary care: America's health in a new era. Committee on the Future of Primary Care, Division of Health Services, Institute of Medicine. Washington, DC: National Academy Press; 1996.
4. Koecheler JA, Abramowitz PW, Swim SE, et al. Indicators for the selection of ambulatory patients who warrant pharmacist monitoring. *Am J Hosp Pharm.* 1989; 46:729–32.
5. Lobas LH, Lepinski PW, Abramowitz PW. Effects of pharmaceutical care on medication cost and quality of patient care in an ambulatory-care clinic. *Am J Hosp Pharm.* 1992; 49:1681–8.
6. Chrischelles EQ, Helling DK, Aschoff CR. Effect of clinical pharmacy services on the quality of family

practice physician prescribing and medication costs. *Drug Intell Clin Pharm.* 1989; 23:417–21.

7. Monson R, Bond CA, Schuna A. Role of the clinical pharmacist in improving drug therapy: clinical pharmacists in outpatient therapy. *Arch Intern Med.* 1981; 141:1441–4.
8. Bond CA, Monson R. Sustained improvement in drug documentation, compliance, and disease control: a four-year analysis of an ambulatory care model. *Arch Intern Med.* 1984; 114:1159–62.
9. Jameson J, VanNoord G, Vanderwoud K. The impact of a pharmacotherapy consultation on the cost and outcome of medical therapy. *J Fam Pract.* 1995; 41:469–72.
10. Dong BJ, Echaves SA, Brody RV, et al. Pharmacist provision of preventive health services in a hypertension clinic. *Am J Health-Syst Pharm.* 1997; 54:564–6.
11. Furmaga EM. Pharmacist management of a hyperlipidemia clinic. *Am J Hosp Pharm.* 1993; 50:91–5.
12. Galt KA, Skrabal MA, Abdouch I, et al. Using patient expectations and satisfaction data to design a new pharmacy service model in a primary care clinic. *J Manage Care Pharm.* 1997; 3:531–40.
13. American Society of Health-System Pharmacists. Vision statement. American Society of Health-System Pharmacists. *Am J Health-Syst Pharm.* 1996; 53:174.
14. Chamberlain MA. The vertically integrated pharmacy department. *Am J Health-Syst Pharm.* 1998; 55:669–75.
15. Raehl CL, Bond CA, Pitterle ME. Ambulatory pharmacy services affiliated with acute care hospitals. *Pharmacotherapy.* 1993; 13:618–25.
16. Chandler C, Barriuso P, Rozenberg-Ben- Dror K, et al. Pharmacists on a primary care team at a Veterans Affairs medical center. *Am J Health-Syst Pharm.* 1997; 54:1280–7.
17. Oke TO. Primary health care services with a functional ambulatory care clinical pharmacy in a low income housing project clinic. *J Natl Med Assoc.* 1994; 86:465–8.
18. Alsuwaidan S, Malone DC, Billups SJ, et al. Characteristics of ambulatory care clinics and pharmacists in Veterans Affairs medical centers. *Am J Health-Syst Pharm.* 1998; 55:68–72.
19. Libby EA, Laub JJ. Economic and clinical impact of a pharmacy-based antihypertensive replacement program in primary care. *Am J Health-Syst Pharm.* 1997; 54:2079–83.
20. Konzem SL, Morreale AP, Kaplan LA. Pharmacist-managed primary care dermatology clinic. *Hosp Pharm.* 1996; 31:823–5,834.
21. Wilson Norton JL, Gibson DL. Establishing an outpatient anticoagulation clinic in a community hospital. *Am J Health-Syst Pharm.* 1996; 53:1151–7.
22. Lacro JP, Kodsi A, Dishman B, et al. Primary care role of psychopharmacists in an ambulatory care setting. *Calif J Health-Syst Pharm.* 1995; 7:9–10.
23. Galt KA. Cost avoidance, acceptance, and outcomes associated with a pharmacotherapy consult clinic in a Veteran's Affairs medical center. *Pharmacotherapy.* 1998; 18:1103–11.

Approved by the ASHP Board of Directors, April 21, 1999, and by the ASHP House of Delegates, June 7, 1999. Developed by the Council on Professional Affairs.

Kimberly A. Galt, Pharm.D., FASHP, Richard F. Demers, and Richard N. Herrier, Pharm.D., are gratefully acknowledged for drafting this document.

The bibliographic citation for this document is as follows: American Society of Health-System Pharmacists. ASHP statement on the pharmacist's role in primary care. *Am J Health-Syst Pharm.* 1999; 56:1665–7.

ASHP Statement on the Pharmacist's Role in Substance Abuse Prevention, Education, and Assistance

Position

The American Society of Health-System Pharmacists (ASHP) believes that pharmacists have the unique knowledge, skills, and responsibilities for assuming an important role in substance abuse prevention, education, and assistance. Pharmacists, as health care providers, should be actively involved in reducing the negative effects that substance abuse has on society, health systems, and the pharmacy profession. Further, ASHP supports efforts to rehabilitate pharmacists and other health-system employees whose mental or physical impairments are caused by substance abuse.

Background

The term "substance abuse" is commonly used to describe the hazardous or addictive use of psychoactive substances with either addictive, typically depressing or stimulating, or perception distorting properties. The American Psychiatric Association's *Diagnostic and Statistical Manual of Mental Disorders*, 5th edition (DSM-5) includes substance use disorders, typically considered addictions with severity categories, and substance-induced disorders, typically intoxication or withdrawal, in its "Substance-Related and Addictive Disorders" chapter.[1] Examples include alcohol, tobacco, "street" drugs (e.g., marijuana, lysergic acid diethylamide [LSD], phencyclidine [pcp], cocaine, methamphetamine, methylenedioxymethamphetamine [MDMA], inhalants, gammahydroxybutyrate [GHB], heroin, K2/Spice, salvia, bath salts), and the nonmedical use or the overuse of psychoactive and other prescription and nonprescription drugs (e.g., hydrocodone, oxycodone, ketamine, methadone, dextromethorphan).

Substance abuse is a major societal problem. The 2012 National Household Survey on Drug Use and Health (NSDUH), a primary source of statistical information on drug abuse in the U.S. population, estimated that (a) 23.9 million Americans (or 9.2% of the population 12 years of age or older) had used an illicit drug* in the past month, (b) 2.8 million Americans were classified with dependence or abuse of both illicit drugs and alcohol, (c) 4.5 million had dependence or abuse of illicit drugs but not alcohol, and (d) 14.9 million Americans were dependent on alcohol.[2] A 2001-2002 study conducted using DSM-IV criteria in the U.S. suggested of substance abuse/dependence disorders suggested a lifetime prevalence of alcohol use disorders of 30.3%, of drug use disorders of 10.3%, of alcohol dependence (alcoholism) of 12.5% (17.4% for men; 8.0% for women)[3] and of other drug dependence ("drug addiction"), excluding tobacco, at 2.6% (3.3% for men; 2.0% for women).[4] Studies suggest that the prevalence of drug abuse among health professionals appears to be similar to that in the general population.[5-7] Given their access, however, health professionals abuse prescription drugs more often and "street" drugs less often than does the general population.

Substance abuse frequently coexists with and complicates other psychiatric disorders, and it is a common and often unrecognized cause of physical morbidity. Intravenous drug abuse is a major factor in the spread of human immunodeficiency virus (HIV) and hepatitis. Alcohol is a major factor in cirrhosis of the liver, and tobacco is a key contributor to emphysema and lung cancer. Collectively, substance abuse contributes significantly to morbidity and mortality in our population and to the cost of health care.

Substance abuse is also a serious workplace problem. The 2012 NSDUH reported that approximately 14.6 million Americans reporting past month illicit drug use were currently employed full- or part-time.[2] Substance abuse by employees of health care organizations leads to reduced productivity, increased absenteeism, drug diversion, and, almost certainly, increased accidents and medication misadventures. Consequently, it affects the quality of patient care, liability, and operational and health care costs.

The abuse, or non-medical use, of prescription medications has also become a prevalent issue. Nonmedical use of prescription drugs among youths aged 12 to 17 and young adults aged 18 to 25 in 2012 was the second most prevalent illicit drug use category, with marijuana being first.[2] The survey also found that over half of all prescription drug abusers had obtained the prescription medication "from a friend or relative for free" as compared to the 3.9% who had obtained the medication from a drug dealer or other stranger.

Pharmacists have unique, comprehensive knowledge about the safe and effective use of medications and about the adverse effects of their inappropriate use. The provision of pharmaceutical care to individual patients involves pharmacists assessing the appropriateness of pharmacotherapy, counseling, and monitoring medication-use outcomes. Health-system pharmacists have responsibilities for ensuring a safe and effective medication-use system, including legal and organizational responsibilities for medication distribution and control across the continuum of practice settings within health care organizations. With this combination of knowledge and organizational responsibilities, pharmacists are prepared to serve in leadership and service roles in substance abuse prevention and education and assist in a variety of patient care, employee health, and community activities.

Responsibilities

The scope of substance abuse responsibilities of pharmacists varies with the health care organization's mission, policies

*The National Survey on Drug Use and Health obtains information on nine categories of illicit drug use: use of marijuana, cocaine, heroin, hallucinogens, and inhalants, as well as the nonmedical use of prescription-type pain relievers, tranquilizers, stimulants, and sedatives.

and procedures, patient population, and community. The responsibilities listed below should be adapted to meet local needs and circumstances. Each responsibility is intended to be applicable to any substance of abuse; therefore, specific substances are generally not mentioned. Pharmacists should be involved in substance abuse prevention, education, and assistance by performing the following activities:

Prevention

1. Participating in or contributing to the development of substance abuse prevention and assistance programs within health care organizations. A comprehensive program should consist of (a) a written substance abuse policy; (b) an employee education and awareness program; (c) a supervisor training program; (d) an employee assistance program; (e) peer support systems, such as pharmacist recovery networks; and (f) drug testing.[8]
2. Participating in public substance abuse education and prevention programs (e.g., in primary and secondary schools, colleges, churches, and civic organizations) and stressing the potential adverse health consequences of the misuse of legal and use of illegal drugs.
3. Opposing the sale of alcohol and tobacco products by pharmacists and in pharmacies.
4. Establishing a multidisciplinary controlled-substance inventory system, in compliance with statutory and regulatory requirements, that discourages diversion and enhances accountability. Where helpful, for example, procedures might require the purchase of controlled substances in tamper-evident containers and maintenance of a perpetual inventory and ongoing surveillance system.
5. Working with local, state, and federal authorities in controlling substance abuse, including participation in state prescription drug monitoring programs, encouraging participation in appropriate prescription disposal programs, complying with controlled-substance reporting regulations, and cooperating in investigations that involve the misuse of controlled substances, especially diversion from a health care organization.
6. Working with medical laboratories to (a) identify substances of abuse by using drug and poison control information systems, (b) establish proper specimen collection procedures based on knowledge of the pharmacokinetic properties of abused substances, and (c) select proper laboratory tests to detect the suspected substances of abuse and to detect tampering with samples.
7. Discouraging prescribing practices that enable or foster drug abuse behavior (e.g., prescribing a larger quantity of pain medication than is clinically needed for treatment of short-term pain).
8. Collaboration with outpatient and ambulatory care providers to prevent substance abuse after discharge.

Education

1. Providing information and referral to support groups appropriate to the needs of people whose lives are affected by their own or another person's substance abuse or dependency.
2. Providing recommendations about the appropriate use of mood-altering substances to health care providers and the public, including those persons recovering from substance dependency and their caregivers.[9]
3. Fostering the development of undergraduate and graduate college of pharmacy curricula and pharmacy technician education on the topic of substance abuse prevention, education, and assistance.[10]
4. Providing substance abuse education to fellow pharmacists, other health care professionals, and other employees of their health care organization.
5. Instructing drug abuse counselors in drug treatment programs about the pharmacology of abused substances and medications used for detoxification.
6. Promoting and providing alcohol risk-reduction education and activities.
7. Maintaining professional competency in substance abuse prevention, education, and assistance through formal and informal continuing education.
8. Providing post-graduate training in addictions, pain management, and palliative care where feasible.
9. Conducting research on substance abuse and addiction.
10. Educating patients about the correct storage, handling, and proper disposal of prescription medications.

Assistance

1. Assisting in the identification of patients, coworkers, and other individuals who may be having problems related to their substance abuse, and referring them to the appropriate people for evaluation and treatment.
2. Participating in multidisciplinary efforts to support and care for the health care organization's employees and patients who are recovering from substance dependency.
3. Supporting and encouraging the recovery of health professionals with alcoholism or other drug addictions. Major elements of an employer's support program might include (a) a willingness to hire or retain employees; (b) participating in monitoring and reporting requirements associated with recovery or disciplinary contracts; (c) maintaining an environment supportive of recovery; (d) establishing behavioral standards and norms among all employees that discourage the abuse of psychoactive substances, including alcohol; and (e) participating in peer assistance programs.
4. Collaborating with other health care providers in the development of the pharmacotherapeutic elements of drug detoxification protocols.
5. Providing pharmaceutical care to patients being treated for substance abuse and dependency.
6. Maintaining knowledge of professional support groups (e.g., state- and national-level pharmacist recovery networks) and other local, state, and national organizations, programs, and resources available for preventing and treating substance abuse (see "Other Resources").
7. Refusing to allow any student or employee, including health professionals, to work, practice, or be onsite for rotations within the health care organization while his or her ability to safely perform his or her responsibilities is impaired by drugs, including al-

cohol. The refusal should follow the organization's policies and procedures, the principles of ethical and responsible pharmacy practice, and statutory requirements. Practice should not be precluded after appropriate treatment and monitoring, if approved by the treatment provider or contract monitor (or both, when applicable).

References

1. American Psychiatric Association. Diagnostic and statistical manual of mental disorders. 5th ed. Arlington, VA: American Psychiatric Association; 2013. http://www.dsm.psychiatryonline.org/ (accessed 2014 Jun 26).
2. Substance Abuse and Mental Health Services Administration. Results from the 2012 National Survey on Drug Use and Health: Summary of national findings; NSDUH Series H-46, HHS publication no. (SMA) 13-4795.Rockville, MD: Substance Abuse and Mental Health Services Administration; 2013.
3. Hasin DS, Stinson FS, Ogburn E, et al. Prevalence, correlates, disability, and comorbidity of DSM-IV alcohol abuse and dependence in the United States. *Arch Gen Psychiatry*. 2007; 64:830–42.
4. Comton WM, Thomas YF, Stinson FS, et al. Prevalence, correlates, disability, and comorbidity of DSM-IV drug abuse and dependence in the United States. *Arch Gen Psychiatry*. 2007; 64:566–76.
5. McAuliffe WE, Santangelo SL, Gingras J, et al. Use and abuse of controlled substances by pharmacists and pharmacy students. *Am J Hosp Pharm*. 1987; 44:311–7.
6. Sullivan E, Bissell L, Williams E. Chemical dependency in nursing: the deadly diversion. Menlo Park, CA: Addison-Wesley; 1988.
7. Bissell L, Haberman PW, Williams RL. Pharmacists recovering from alcohol and other drug addictions: an interview study. *Am Pharm*. 1989; NS29(6):19–30. [Erratum, *Am Pharm*. 1989; NS29(9):11.]
8. Substance Abuse and Mental Health Services Administration. Making your workplace drug-free: a kit for employers. DHHS publication no. SMA07-4230. Rockville, MD: Substance Abuse and Mental Health Services Administration; 2007. http://store.samhsa.gov/shin/content//SMA07-4230/SMA07-4230.pdf (accessed 2014 Jun 24).
9. Davis NH. Dispensing and prescribing cautions for medical care during recovery from alcohol and drug addiction. *J Pharm Pract*. 1991; 6:362–8.
10. DeSimone EM, Kissack JC, Scott DM, et al. Curricular guidelines for pharmacy: substance abuse and addictive disease. http://www.aacp.org/resources/education/Documents/CurricularGuidelinesforPharmacy-SubstanceAbuseandAddictiveDisease.pdf (accessed 2014 May 27).

Other Resources

1. Hogue MD, McCormick DD, eds. Points of light: a guide for assisting chemically dependent health professional students. Washington, DC: American Pharmaceutical Association; 1996.
2. AACP Special Committee on Substance Abuse and Pharmacy Education. American Association of Colleges of Pharmacy guidelines for the development of addiction and related disorders policies for colleges and schools of pharmacy. http://www.aacp.org/career/grants/Documents/Guidelines%20for%20the%20Development%20of%20Addiction%20and%20Related%20Disorders%20Policies%20for%20Schools%20and%20Colleges%20of%20Pharmacy.pdf (accessed 2014 Jun 24).
3. Tucker DR, Gurnee MC, Sylvestri MF, et al. Psychoactive drug use and impairment markers in pharmacy students. *Am J Pharm Educ*. 1988; 52:42–7.
4. Miederhoff PA, Voight FB, White CE. Chemically impaired pharmacists: an emerging management issue. *Top Hosp Pharm Manage*. 1987; 7(Nov):75–83.
5. Kriegler KA, Baldwin JN, Scott DM. A study of alcohol and other drug use behaviors and risk factors in health profession students. *J Am Coll Health*. 1994; 42:259–65.
6. Haberman P. Alcoholism in the professions. Troy, MI: Performance Resource; 1991.
7. Bissell L, Royce JE. Ethics for addiction professionals. Center City, MN: Hazelden Foundation; 1994.
8. Colvin R. Prescription drug addiction: the hidden epidemic. Omaha, NE: Addicus; 2002.
9. Crosby L, Bissell L. To care enough: intervention with chemically-dependent colleagues. Minneapolis: Johnson Institute; 1989.
10. Johnson VE. Intervention: how to help someone who doesn't want help. A step-by-step guide for families and friends of chemically-dependent persons. Minneapolis: Johnson Institute; 1989.
11. Rinaldi RC, Steindler EM, Wilford BB, et al. Clarification and standardization of substance abuse terminology. *JAMA*. 1988; 259:555–7.
12. Brown ME, Trinkoff AM, Christen AG, et al. Impairment issues for health care professionals: review and recommendations. *Subst Abus*. 2002; 23S:155–65.
13. Dole EJ, Tommasello AC. Recommendations for implementing effective substance abuse education in pharmacy practice. *Subst Abus*. 2002; 23S:263–71.
14. Lafferty L. Hunter TS, Marsh WA. Knowledge, attitudes and practices of pharmacists concerning prescription drug abuse. *J Psychoactive Drugs*. 2006; 38(3):229–32
15. Baldwin JN, Scott DM, Agrawal S, et al. Assessment of alcohol and other drug use behaviors in health professions students. *Subst Abus*. 2006; 27(3):25–35.
16. American Pharmacists Association. Pharmacists' role in addressing opioid abuse, addiction, and diversion. *J Am Pharm Assoc*. 2014; 54:e5–e15.
17. Lord S, Downs G, Furtaw P, et al. Nonmedical use of prescription opioids and stimulants among student pharmacists. *J Am Pharm Assoc*. 2009; 49:519–28.
18. American Pharmacists Association. Addiction and substance abuse in the pharmacy professions: From discovery to recovery. *Pharmacy Today*. 2013; 19(8):62–72.
19. Merlo LJ, Cummings SM, Cottler LB. Recovering substance-impaired pharmacists' views regarding occupational risks for addiction. *J Am Pharm Assoc*. 2012; 52:480–91.

20. Baldwin JN. Substance abuse care. In: Allen LV, ed. Remington: the science and practice of pharmacy. 22nd ed. London, UK: Pharmaceutical Press; 2013:2613–9.
21. Kenna GA, Baldwin JN, Trinkoff A, et al. Substance use disorders in health care professionals. In: Johnson BA, ed. Addiction medicine: science and practice. New York, NY: Springer; 2011:1375–98.
22. Baldwin JN, Scott DM, DeSimone EM, et al. Substance use attitudes and behaviors at three pharmacy colleges. *Subst Abus.* 2011; 32:27–35.
23. National Clearinghouse for Alcohol and Drug Information (NCADI). The clearinghouse is a federally funded service that assists in finding information on all aspects of substance abuse. Many publications and educational materials are available free of charge from NCADI. Telephone, 800-729-6686; Website, http://store.samhsa.gov/home
24. Center for Substance Abuse Prevention (CSAP) Workplace Helpline (for employers). Telephone, 800-967-5752; e-mail, dwp@samhsa.hhs.gov.
25. National Association of State Alcohol and Drug Abuse Directors (NASADAD). The association coordinates and encourages cooperative efforts between the federal government and state agencies on substance abuse. NASADAD serves as a resource on state drug programs and can provide contacts in each state. Website, www.nasadad.org.
26. Community organizations are available to help with drug or alcohol problems. Treatment counselors may be valuable in developing assistance policies and in providing professional education about treatment and referral systems. Community drug abuse prevention organizations may be helpful in prevention efforts, including community drug education. Check your local telephone directory under headings such as Alcoholism Information and Treatment, Drug Abuse Information and Treatment, and Counselors.
27. Twelve-step groups (usually available locally unless otherwise noted; listed telephone numbers and Websites are for national headquarters):
    a. Adult Children of Alcoholics (ACA); for adults who, as children, lived with alcoholic parents. Telephone, 562-595-7831; Website, www.adultchildren.org.
    b. Al-Anon; provides information on alcoholism and alcohol abuse and refers callers to local Al-Anon support groups established to help people affected by others' alcohol misuse. Telephone, 757-563-1500; Website, www.al-anon.org.
    c. Alateen; for adolescents affected by alcoholics. Website, www.al-anon.alateen.org/for-alateen.
    d. Alcoholics Anonymous (AA); provides information and support to recovering alcoholics. Telephone, 212-870-3400; Website, www.alcoholics anonymous.org.
    e. Cocaine Anonymous (CA); for individuals with cocaine dependencies. Telephone, 310-559-5833; Website, www.ca.org.
    f. International Doctors in Alcoholics Anonymous (IDAA) includes pharmacists in recovery regardless of degree (a national group that has an annual conference and recovery resources for doctoral degree health professionals). Website is www.idaa.org. IDAA Executive Director contact is executive@idaa.org.
    g. Nar-Anon; for helping people affected by another's drug misuse. Telephone, 800-477-6291; e-mail wso@nar.anon.org.
    h. Narcotics Anonymous (NA); provides information and support to recovering substance abusers. Telephone, 818-773-9999; Website, www.na.org.
28. Advocacy and professional substance abuse education:
    a. Pharmacist Recovery Networks (PRNs) exist in most states in the U.S. to assist pharmacists (and often also pharmacy technicians and sometimes pharmacy students) with addictions or in addiction recovery. The www.usaprn.org website includes information about these programs by state as well as information about other recovery-related resources.
    b. The Pharmacy Section (cosponsored by APhA and APhA Academy of Students of Pharmacy) of the University of Utah School on Alcoholism and Other Drug Dependencies was a one-week seminar held each summer until 2014 (options are being considered to establish the School at another site beginning in 2015) for learning to deal with substance abuse problems as they affect the profession. Consult www.usaprn.org for updates and current status of the School.

Approved by the ASHP Board of Directors on April 10, 2015, and by the ASHP House of Delegates June 7, 2015. Developed through the ASHP Council on Pharmacy Practice. This statement supersedes a previous version dated June 2, 2013.

Jeffrey N. Baldwin, Pharm.D. and Chelsea Leeper, Pharm.D., are gratefully acknowledged for revising this statement.

Note: This statement had not been published in the *American Journal of Health-System Pharmacy* (*AJHP*) when *ASHP Best Practices 2015–2016* went to press. Some minor editorial differences may exist between this document and the official one that will eventually appear in *AJHP* and subsequent editions of this publication.

ASHP Statement on Pharmacy Services to the Emergency Department

Position

The American Society of Health-System Pharmacists (ASHP) believes every hospital pharmacy department should provide its emergency department (ED) with the pharmacy services that are necessary for safe and effective patient care. Although the nature of these services will vary with each institution's needs and resources, the pharmacist's role may include

- Working with emergency physicians, emergency nurses, and other health care professionals to develop and monitor medication-use systems that promote safe and effective medication use in the ED, especially for high-risk patients and procedures,
- Collaborating with emergency physicians, emergency nurses, and other health care professionals to promote medication use in the ED that is evidence based and aligned with national quality indicators,
- Participating in the selection, implementation, and monitoring of technology used in the medication-use process,
- Providing direct patient care as part of the interdisciplinary emergency care team,
- Participating in or leading emergency-preparedness efforts and quality-improvement initiatives,
- Educating patients, caregivers, and health care professionals about safe and effective medication use, and
- Conducting or participating in ED-based research.

ASHP supports the expansion of pharmacy education and postgraduate residency training to include an emphasis on emergency care.

The purposes of this statement are to promote understanding of the pharmacist's contributions to the care of patients in the ED and to suggest future roles for pharmacists in providing that care.

Background

EDs across the nation treat approximately 114 million patients annually.[1] EDs are overcrowded because of a high percentage of uninsured patients, increased patient volume, increased complexity of patients in the ED, and a hospital bed shortage that frequently results in the boarding of inpatients in the ED. The combination of interruptions, intense pressure, and a fast-paced environment can lead to medication errors and fewer error interceptions.[1] The Institute of Medicine (IOM) has estimated that as many as 98,000 people die each year as a result of medical errors and that adverse drug events (ADEs) occurred in 3.7% of hospitalizations.[2] Hafner et al.[3] reported a similar frequency of ADEs in the ED. Chin et al.[4] found that 3.6% of patients received an inappropriate medication in the ED and 5.6% were prescribed an inappropriate medication at discharge.

Pharmacy services in the ED have been documented since the 1970s.[5-8] These services initially focused on inventory control, cost containment, and participation on resuscitation teams but have since expanded to include clinical pharmacy services.[9] The effectiveness of clinical pharmacy services has been well documented in other settings. The participation of pharmacists in intensive care units and on internal medicine teams has improved patient outcomes by reducing preventable ADEs by 66% and 78%, respectively.[10-12] Similar effectiveness with pharmacist participation on emergency medicine teams has also been documented.[13] Despite this evidence, the 2005 ASHP national survey found that only 3.5% of the hospitals surveyed had a pharmacist assigned to the ED for any period of time, and only 5% had a formal policy requiring that pharmacists review and approve medication orders before administration in EDs.[14]

Pharmacy Services in the ED

All health care professionals share a commitment to and responsibility for providing safe and effective patient care. These shared objectives provide strong incentives for collaboration. Pharmacists and other health care professionals can collaborate in developing and monitoring medication-use systems that promote safe and effective medication use in the ED, including medication use in high-risk ED patients and procedures. By working together, pharmacists and other health care professionals can ensure that medication use in the ED is evidence based, cost-effective, and adherent to national guidelines; develop and implement emergency-preparedness plans and quality-improvement efforts; and, in many cases, foster the institution's education and research initiatives. The department of pharmacy should assume a leadership role in ensuring these collaborations.

When making decisions regarding pharmacy services to the ED, hospital leadership should consider the ED's need for medication therapy management services, medication-allergy assessment and clarification, medication-interaction assessment, reporting of and intervention on medication errors and ADEs, timely provision of drug information, and participation in formulary decision making. Institutions should also keep in mind the Joint Commission's pharmacist first-review requirement[15] and national patient safety goals,[16] the hospital's quality indicators related to medication selection, timing, and delivery; the potential effects of patient flow and technology on medication safety in the ED; and contributions pharmacists can make to continuity of care from ED admission through hospital discharge.

Patient Care. The IOM report, Hospital-Based Emergency Care: At the Breaking Point, recommends the inclusion of clinical pharmacists on the ED care team to ensure patients' medication needs are appropriately met, to lead system changes in order to reduce or eliminate medication errors, and to evaluate the cost effectiveness of medication therapy for the patient and hospital.[1] As part of the interdisciplinary ED care team, pharmacists can provide care to critically ill patients by

- Participating in resuscitation efforts,
- Providing consultative services that foster appropriate evidence-based medication selection,
- Providing consultation on patient-specific medication dosage and dosage adjustments,
- Providing drug information consultation to emergency physicians, emergency nurses, and other clinicians,
- Monitoring for patient allergies and drug interactions,
- Monitoring patient therapeutic responses (including laboratory values),
- Continuously assessing for and managing adverse drug reactions, and
- Gathering or reviewing medication histories and reconciling patients' medications.

In addition, pharmacists can provide care to ambulatory patients in the ED by

- Modifying medication regimens based on collaborative-practice agreements for the management of specific patient populations that return to the ED,
- Providing vaccination screening, referral, and administration,
- Offering patient and caregiver education, including discharge counseling and follow-up, and
- Providing information on obtaining medications through patient assistance programs, care funds, and samples.

The boarding of patients in the ED until an inpatient bed becomes available poses challenges for patients, caregivers, and health care professionals. The department of pharmacy should work with the health care professionals involved in the care of these patients to provide a seamless medication-use process.

Emergency-Preparedness Planning. ASHP believes that all hospital and health-system pharmacists must assertively exercise their responsibilities to prepare for and respond to disasters.[17] ASHP has insisted that emergency-response planners at the federal, regional, state, and local levels call on pharmacists to participate in the full range of planning issues related to pharmaceuticals. Hospital emergency-preparedness plans, including ED components, must be developed with the assistance of departments of pharmacy. Pharmacists should play a pivotal role in emergency-preparedness planning and as members of the health care team that provides care to victims. Ensuring the efficacy and safety of the medication-use process is a natural role for pharmacists because treatment of disaster victims almost always involves the use of pharmacologic agents.[18,19]

Quality-Improvement Initiatives. The department of pharmacy can collaborate with other health care professionals on a variety of quality-improvement initiatives in the ED, including

- Guiding the development of evidence-based treatment protocols, algorithms, and clinical pathways that are congruent with nationally accepted practice guidelines and quality indicators,
- Assisting in the development, implementation, and assessment of various technologies used throughout the ED's medication-use process,
- Conducting failure mode and effects analysis and root-cause analysis on error-prone aspects of the medication-use process,
- Participating in ED-based and hospitalwide committees (e.g., pharmacy and therapeutics, infection control, disaster) whose decisions affect medication use in the ED,
- Maintaining compliance with standards of national accrediting bodies, such as the Joint Commission, and
- Assisting in surveillance and reporting of adverse drug reactions.

Education. The pharmacy department should support the pharmacist's role in providing education and information to health care professionals, patients, and the public in ED service areas. Specific activities could include

- Conducting educational forums for health care professionals and students on topics such as emergency preparedness, disaster management, poisoning prevention and treatment, immunizations, and use of medications in the ED and emergency situations,
- Providing health literacy-sensitive education to patients and caregivers regarding medication use, disease-state management, and prevention strategies, and
- Offering ED-based educational opportunities to pharmacy students and residents.

The ED offers an enormous number of services, activities, and opportunities to train future pharmacists in all aspects of the medication-use process. Students and residents could participate in longitudinal experiences in ED-based services such as clinics, community services (e.g., health fairs), and satellite pharmacies and could study topics as varied as cultural follow-up, ADE monitoring and reporting, or toxicology services. Introductory experiences could focus on student training on specific skills or competencies, such as taking medication histories, medication reconciliation, or discharge counseling. Residency training of pharmacists in emergency care would provide more rewarding educational experiences, foster pharmacist involvement in emergency-medicine research, and ultimately improve the quality of patient care. Such residencies should meet ASHP-accredited residency quality standards.[20] Achievement of the goals, objectives, and expected outcomes of such training would be supported by around-the-clock or on-call clinical pharmacist services in the ED.

ED-Based Research. Research on and publications about ED pharmacy, though plentiful, usually focus on specific clinical settings, such as toxicology, drug interactions, and infectious disease epidemiology. The literature lacks a broad representation of the varied scope and range of ED pharmacy practices. ASHP believes that there should be more research and publications regarding medication use in the ED and ED-based pharmacy activities. Studies that generate data on therapeutic, safety, humanistic, and economic outcomes of pharmacist-mediated process changes are urgently needed.

Professional Development of Pharmacists in Emergency Care

ASHP believes there should be an increase in the number of ED-based training opportunities for pharmacists, pharmacy students, and residents. Schools and colleges of pharmacy are encouraged to provide ED-based educational opportunities for students. Hospitals and health systems are encouraged to support ED-based educational programs that produce experts in the field. Postgraduate training of pharmacists will provide a pipeline of clinicians, educators, leaders, and scientists who are experts in and committed to quality emergency care.

Conclusion

Every pharmacy department should provide the ED with the pharmacy services required to ensure safe and effective patient care. These services must be tailored to match each institution's needs and resources; therefore, pharmacy departments must decide the best way to safely provide medications to ED patients. ASHP supports the expansion of pharmacy education and postgraduate residency training to include emphasis on emergency care in order to develop an adequate supply of pharmacists who are trained to deliver these essential pharmacy services.

References

1. Institute of Medicine of the National Academies. Hospital-based emergency care: at the breaking point. www.iom.edu/CMS/3809/16107/35007.aspx (accessed 2006 Sep 5).
2. Kohn LT, Corrigan JM, Donaldson MS, eds. To err is human: building a safer health system. Washington, DC: National Academy Press; 1999:26.
3. Hafner JW Jr, Belknap SM, Squillante MD, et al. Adverse drug events in emergency department patients. *Ann Emerg Med.* 2002; 39:258–67.
4. Chin MH, Wang LC, Jin L, et al. Appropriateness of medication selection for older persons in an urban academic emergency department. *Acad Emerg Med.* 1999; 6:1232–42.
5. Elenbaas RM, Waeckerle JF, McNabney WK. The clinical pharmacist in emergency medicine. *Am J Hosp Pharm.* 1977; 34:843–6.
6. Schwerman E, Schwartau N, Thompson CO, et al. The pharmacist as a member of the cardiopulmonary resuscitation team. *Drug Intell Clin Pharm.* 1973; 7:299–308.
7. Kasuya A, Bauman JL, Curtis RA, et al. Clinical pharmacy on-call program in the emergency department. *Am J Emerg Med.* 1986; 4:464–7.
8. Powell MF, Solomon DK, McEachen RA. Twenty-four hour emergency pharmaceutical services. *Am J Hosp Pharm.* 1985; 42:831–5.
9. Fairbanks RJ, Hays DP, Webster DF, et al. Clinical pharmacy services in an emergency department. *Am J Health-Syst Pharm.* 2004; 61:934–7.
10. Leape LL, Cullen DJ, Clapp MD, et al. Pharmacist participation on physician rounds and adverse drug events in the intensive care unit. *JAMA.* 1999; 282:267–70. [Erratum, JAMA. 2000; 283:1293.]
11. Kane SL, Weber RJ, Dasta JF. The impact of critical care pharmacists on enhancing patient outcomes. *Intensive Care Med.* 2003; 29:691–8.
12. Kucukarslan SN, Peters M, Mlynarek M, et al. Pharmacists on rounding teams reduce preventable adverse drug events in hospital general medicine units. *Arch Intern Med.* 2003; 163:2014–8.
13. Ling JM, Mike LA, Rubin J, et al. Documentation of pharmacist interventions in the emergency department. *Am J Health-Syst Pharm.* 2005; 62:1793–7.
14. Pedersen CA, Schneider PJ, Scheckelhoff DJ. ASHP national survey of pharmacy practice in hospital settings: dispensing and administration—2005. *Am J Health-Syst Pharm.* 2006; 63:327–45.
15. Medication Management Standard MM.4.10—preparing and dispensing. In: Comprehensive accreditation manual for hospitals. Oakbrook Terrace, IL: Joint Commission on the Accreditation of Healthcare Organizations: 2006:MM-10.
16. Joint Commission. National patient safety goals. www.jointcommission.org/PatientSafety/NationalPatientSafetyGoals (accessed 2007 May 25).
17. American Society of Health-System Pharmacists. ASHP statement on the role of health-system pharmacists in emergency preparedness. *Am J Health-Syst Pharm.* 2003; 60:1993–5.
18. Burda AM, Sigg T. Pharmacy preparedness for incidents involving weapons of mass destruction. *Am J Health-Syst Pharm.* 2001; 58:2274–84.
19. Setlak P. Bioterrorism preparedness and response: emerging role for health-system pharmacists. *Am J Health-Syst Pharm.* 2004; 61:1167–75.
20. American Society of Health-System Pharmacists. ASHP residency accreditation regulations and standards. www.ashp.org/Import/ACCREDITATION/Residency Accreditation/RegulationsStandards.aspx (accessed 2008 Sep 24).

Developed through the ASHP Council on Pharmacy Practice and approved by the ASHP Board of Directors on September 28, 2007, and by the ASHP House of Delegates on June 10, 2008.

Roshanak Aazami, Pharm.D.; Elizabeth A. Clements, Pharm.D.; Daniel J. Cobaugh, Pharm.D., FACCT, DABAT; and Frank P. Paloucek, Pharm.D., are gratefully acknowledged for drafting this statement. The ASHP Section of Clinical Specialists and Scientists Section Advisory Group on Emergency Care is also gratefully acknowledged for reviewing drafts and providing advice on the development of this statement.

The drafters have declared no conflict of interest.

The bibliographic citation for this document is as follows: American Society of Health-System Pharmacists. ASHP statement on pharmacy services to the emergency department. *Am J Health-Syst Pharm.* 2008; 65:2380–3.

ASHP Statement on Racial and Ethnic Disparities in Health Care

Position

Health disparities continue to be a major public health problem confronting the U.S. health care system. These disparities arise from a complex set of factors, including social and economic inequality, cultural and linguistic barriers, and persistent racial and ethnic discrimination. Evidence continues to emerge, however, that some health disparities are attributable to differences in the quality of health care provided to different racial and ethnic groups. The American Society of Health-System Pharmacists (ASHP) believes that all patients, regardless of race, ethnicity, sex, age, sexual orientation, religion, physical or mental disability (or impairment), education, socioeconomic status, diagnosis, or limitations in access, have the right to high-quality health care that reflects knowledge of, sensitivity to, and respect for their differences.

Pharmacists who practice in hospitals and health systems ("health-system pharmacists"), working individually and in coordination with interested organizations and other health care professionals, can play a leading role in building culturally competent systems of care to reduce racial and ethnic disparities in health care by

- Increasing awareness of these disparities among health care providers, health-system administrators, legislators, regulators, third-party payers, and the public,
- Promoting a more diverse and culturally competent health care work force and environment,
- Ensuring effective communication with patients and among providers,
- Fostering consistent use of multidisciplinary teams and evidence-based guidelines for patient care,
- Collecting and reporting data on health care access, utilization, and outcomes by racial and ethnic minorities and measuring progress toward reducing health care disparities, and
- Researching, identifying, and disseminating best practices for providing culturally competent care and reducing disparities in health care.

Background

The Institute of Medicine (IOM) defines racial and ethnic disparities in health care as "racial or ethnic differences in the quality of healthcare that are not due to access-related factors or clinical needs, preferences, and appropriateness of intervention."[1] IOM states that "evidence of racial and ethnic disparities in healthcare is . . . remarkably consistent across a range of illnesses and healthcare services." More than 600 articles documenting racial or ethnic variations in health care have been published in the past three decades.[2] With the majority of U.S. population growth between now and 2050 expected to come from racial and ethnic minority Americans and immigrants, our health care system must soon learn how to address the effects that race and ethnicity can have on health care. Eliminating health disparities is so important that it is one of only two overarching goals for the Healthy People 2010 objectives.[3]

Culture has been defined by IOM as "the accumulated store of shared values, ideas (attitudes, beliefs, values, and norms), understandings, symbols, material products, and practices of a group of people."[1] Ethnicity refers to "a shared culture and way of life, especially as reflected in language, folkways, religious and other institutional forms, material culture such as clothing and food, and cultural products such as music, literature, and art." [1] An ethnic group is a collection of people "socially distinguished or set apart, by others or by itself, primarily on the basis of cultural or national-origin characteristics."[1] Like ethnicity, race has been described as a sociocultural concept used to distinguish groups of people (in this case, those who share certain physical characteristics) and treat them differently.

ASHP recognizes the need to address all forms of health disparities and believes that health-system pharmacists can take an important step in addressing these broader disparities by assuming a leadership role in the national campaign to eliminate racial and ethnic disparities in health care. Health-system pharmacists, like other health professionals, have espoused a tradition of nondiscriminatory health care practice.[4,5] Because medication therapy management is central to many of the health disparities cited by IOM (e.g., treatment for pain, HIV infection, diabetes, end-stage renal disease, kidney transplantation),[1] health-system pharmacists have opportunities to directly address these disparities. As health-system administrators and members of multidisciplinary health care teams, health-system pharmacists have an important role to play in implementing the institutional changes necessary to eliminate racial and ethnic disparities in health care. ASHP believes that health-system pharmacists have a professional and moral responsibility to address racial and ethnic disparities in health care.

General Principles

The following three principles should guide the actions of health-system pharmacists in efforts to eliminate racial and ethnic disparities in health care: (1) all patients have the right to high-quality care, (2) medication-use practices should reflect knowledge of, sensitivity to, and respect for the race and culture of the patient, and (3) health-system pharmacists have a vital role to play in eliminating racial and ethnic disparities in health care.

All Patients Have the Right to High-Quality Care. A long-standing policy position of ASHP holds that "all patients have the right to . . . high-quality pharmaceutical care."[4] ASHP believes that all patients have the right to receive care from pharmacists and that health-system pharmacists should play a leadership role in ensuring patient access to pharmacists' services.[6] The Code of Ethics for Pharmacists issued by the American Pharmacists Association states that the pharmacist "places concern for the well-being of the patient at the center of professional practice" and "seeks justice in the distribution of health resources."[5] Racial and ethnic disparities in health care are antithetical to the core principles of pharmacy and must be eliminated.

Medication-Use Practices Should Reflect Knowledge of, Sensitivity to, and Respect for the Race and Culture of the Patient. Culture strongly influences how a person interacts with the world. Failing to account for the patient's race or cultural beliefs and values in health care decisions can lead to negative health consequences. Providers may miss screening opportunities because they are unfamiliar with the prevalence of conditions among racial or ethnic groups. They may fail to consider different responses to medications that exist in different populations. Potential harmful interactions between medications and traditional remedies used by the patient may be overlooked. Finally, miscommunication due to cultural, linguistic, or literacy differences between providers and patients regarding symptoms, medications, supplements, or the use of devices may lead to faulty diagnoses, unnecessary laboratory testing, medication-related errors, decreased adherence to therapy, or missed opportunities for early detection and preventive measures.[7]

The Code of Ethics for Pharmacists states that "in all cases" the pharmacist "respects personal and cultural differences among patients."[5] Clinicians who want to provide the best care for their patients must understand the role of culture and its potential impact on health outcomes and the provider–patient relationship.

Health-System Pharmacists Have a Vital Role to Play in Eliminating Racial and Ethnic Disparities in Health Care. In their roles as medication-use experts, patient care providers, and health-system administrators, health-system pharmacists have the knowledge, skills, and opportunities to contribute to efforts to eliminate racial and ethnic disparities in health care.

Pharmacists' Roles in Eliminating Disparities

IOM has made recommendations to eliminate racial and ethnic disparities in health care.[1] The IOM recommendations most relevant to health-system pharmacists are listed in the appendix. ASHP would add to that list that pharmacists can and should engage in research on disparities in health care. ASHP encourages all health care professionals and administrators to embrace these recommendations and urges health-system pharmacists to take the following actions to help eliminate health care disparities.

Increase Awareness of Disparities. One elemental barrier to eliminating racial and ethnic disparities in health care may be a lack of awareness of their existence and their impact on society. Polls show that a significant majority of Americans believe that African Americans receive the same quality of health care as whites,[1,8] despite ample evidence to the contrary.[1] Efforts to eliminate racial and ethnic disparities in health care must begin with the acknowledgment that there is a problem. Health-system pharmacists should lead efforts to increase awareness of health disparities among health care providers, health-system administrators, legislators, regulators, third-party payers, and the public. Pharmacists can increase awareness of health disparities by encouraging their health care organizations to make the elimination of disparities in health care a key component of the organization's mission. They can help their institutions foster an environment that promotes input from and involvement by all members of the organization in addressing this component of the organizational mission. In addition, pharmacists can help develop inhouse and community programs to promote cultural understanding and appreciation of the importance of diversity. They can also partner with community groups, governmental agencies, health care provider organizations, payers, and others to increase awareness of specific diseases among certain populations and encourage innovation and creativity in evaluating and disseminating approaches to eliminating disparities in health care.

Create a More Diverse Health Care Work Force. Increased racial and ethnic diversity among health care professionals may be associated with improved access to care for racial and ethnic minority patients, greater patient choice of and satisfaction with health care professionals, more effective patient–clinician communication, and enhanced educational experiences for students in the health professions.[9] Racial and ethnic diversity in the health care work force has been well correlated with the delivery of quality care to diverse patient populations. For minority patients, racial concordance between patient and physician is associated with greater patient satisfaction and higher self-rated quality of care.[10] Spanish-speaking patients, for example, report more satisfaction with care from Spanish-speaking providers.[11]

In 2002, the American Hospital Association's Commission on Workforce for Hospitals and Health Systems reported that although the national labor force is becoming more diverse, hospital employees remain disproportionately female and Caucasian.[12] The Commission recommended working aggressively to develop a work force that more fully represents changing U.S. demographics. IOM has also cited a continuing shortage of minorities among health care professionals.[9]

ASHP is committed to developing a diverse work force of health-system pharmacists.[13] In June 2003, the ASHP Board of Directors established the Ad Hoc Committee on Ethnic Diversity and Cultural Competence, which has recommended six major goals and developed long-term strategic action plans for each goal.[14] ASHP members are encouraged to participate in these efforts and to monitor their progress at ASHP's Health Disparities Web Resource Center (www.ashp.org/s_ashp/cat1c.asp?CID=4266&DID=7523).

Promote Culturally Competent Care and Services. Many cultures take a different approach to health than is found in allopathic ("western") medicine. Perceptions of illness and disease vary by culture, and culture may influence a person's health-seeking behavior, approach to seeking out health care providers, and treatment preferences. As allopathic medicine increasingly emphasizes evidence-based approaches, health care practitioners will more frequently confront the cultural divide between the demands of their profession and the closely held beliefs of their patients. Cultural competency is rapidly becoming a quality and risk management issue for hospitals and health systems. ASHP is committed to developing a culturally sensitive, competent, and respectful work force.[15]

The Department of Health and Human Services (HHS) states that a culturally competent health care practitioner is

- Knowledgeable about cultural differences and their impact on attitudes and behaviors,
- Sensitive, understanding, nonjudgmental, and respectful in dealings with peoples whose culture is different from one's own, and
- Flexible and skillful in responding and adapting to different cultural contexts and circumstances.[16]

HHS's Office of Minority Health has developed a set of standards for culturally and linguistically appropriate services in health care to provide a consistent and comprehensive approach to cultural and linguistic competence in health care.[17] These standards offer a framework for implementing services and organizational structures to help health care organizations and providers, including pharmacists, respond to the cultural and linguistic issues presented by diverse populations. ASHP believes these standards should be used to assess staff competence and to guide organizations' educational programming and strategic planning. Education on cultural competency issues is encouraged in preceptor training sessions, residency standards, and leadership orientation at ASHP and affiliate levels. The Accreditation Council for Pharmaceutical Education now requires that schools and colleges of pharmacy include cultural competency in their curricula.[18] Approaches to the subject could include standalone courses in health disparities and cultural competence, inclusion of traditional healers in the educational process, and infusion of the concept of cultural competence throughout the curriculum (e.g., through case studies that include diverse populations). ASHP believes that experiential learning should also include practice experiences with racial and ethnic minorities, medically underserved populations, and patient populations whose cultures incorporate the use of traditional healers and complementary or alternative medicine (e.g., folk medicine, home remedies).

The Code of Ethics for Pharmacists states that "A pharmacist maintains professional competence."[5] ASHP believes that cultural competence is among the competencies that pharmacists, residents, fellows, students, and technicians have an obligation to develop and maintain.

Ensure Effective Communication with Patients and Among Providers. The Code of Ethics for Pharmacists states that "a pharmacist communicates with patients in terms that are understandable."[5] ASHP guidelines recommend that pharmacists "know about their patients' cultures, especially health and illness beliefs, attitudes, and practices," and "adapt messages to fit patients' language skills and primary languages, through the use of teaching aids, interpreters, or cultural guides if necessary."[19] Persons with the most health problems and the greatest need for self-management skills often have the poorest health literacy. Health-system pharmacists providing direct patient care should be able to assess the health literacy of patients and provide appropriate education.[20]

Lack of interpretation services or culturally and linguistically appropriate health education materials is associated with patient dissatisfaction, poor comprehension and compliance, and ineffective or lower quality of patient care.[21–23] Health care providers rely heavily on the use of the written word to communicate, a circumstance that contributes to health care disparities.[1] When interpretation services are used, practitioners should ensure their quality. Fluency in language is not necessarily sufficient to provide adequate interpretation of the complex concepts involved in medical decision-making. Interpretation by family members also raises issues of patient confidentiality and autonomy.

Communication with patients needs to be culturally and linguistically appropriate. For example, although Spanish is the primary language of many cultures, simply translating educational material into Spanish may not provide the cultural context to make the education effective.

Health-system pharmacists should also utilize their medication-use expertise to help their institutions and communities develop culturally and linguistically appropriate public education campaigns. These campaigns could address health risks prevalent in racial and ethnic minority populations served by the hospital and explain preventive measures and health care services available to those populations.

Health care professionals also need to recognize that racial and cultural differences may affect communication among providers. Health-system pharmacists should take steps to ensure that provider-to-provider communication is effective and reflects the respect for colleagues expressed in the Code of Ethics for Pharmacists.[5]

Utilize Multidisciplinary Teams and Evidence-Based Guidelines. Multidisciplinary team approaches to health care improve health outcomes for majority and minority patients being treated for a range of diseases.[1] ASHP believes pharmacists should be integral participants in the development of multidisciplinary action plans for patient care, disease management plans, and health management plans.[24] Evidence-based guidelines "offer the advantages of consistency, predictability, and objectivity,"[1] but their use must be balanced with the need for clinical flexibility, especially when there is evidence of different outcomes or responses among racial or ethnic groups.

Collect and Monitor Data on Health Disparities. Standardized collection of data regarding access to medications, drug utilization, and medical and cost-effectiveness outcomes from medication therapy management by racial and ethnic minorities would promote research on disparities in health care and help institutions monitor the progress of their efforts to eliminate those disparities.[25] Pharmacists should be active partners with health care administrators and other health professionals in developing measures of progress against health care disparities in institutional performance measures, which should be a key component of the organization's mission.[26]

Research Disparities in Health Care. Health-system pharmacists can research, identify, and disseminate best practices for providing culturally competent care and reducing disparities in health care. Priority areas for research include racial and ethnic groups' access to medications, drug utilization, and medical and cost-effectiveness outcomes from medication therapy management. Pharmacists must keep pace with research regarding disparities in health care, programs to provide culturally competent care to patients, and new educational approaches to improving patient care. It is also important that pharmacy develop researchers to investigate health care disparities and cutting-edge practitioners to translate those research findings into practice.

Conclusion

ASHP believes racial and ethnic disparities in health care are antithetical to the core principles of pharmacy. All patients have the right to high-quality health care that reflects knowledge of, sensitivity to, and respect for their differences. Health-system pharmacists, working individually and in coordination with interested organizations and other health care professionals, can and must play a vital role in efforts to eliminate racial and ethnic disparities in health care.

References

1. Smedley BD, Stith AY, Nelson AR, eds. Unequal treatment: confronting racial and ethnic disparities in health care. Washington, DC: National Academy Press; 2003.
2. Rubenstein LS. Racial disparities and health: Physicians for Human Rights testimony to Congressional Black Caucus. March 18, 2003. www.phrusa.org/research/methics/caucus_0303.html (accessed 2006 Dec 1).
3. U.S. Department of Health and Human Services. Healthy People 2010. www.healthypeople.gov/default.htm (accessed 2005 Nov 4).
4. ASHP policy position 9006: nondiscriminatory pharmaceutical care. In: Hawkins B, ed. Best practices for hospital and health-system pharmacy: positions and guidance documents of ASHP. Bethesda, MD: American Society of Health-System Pharmacists; 2006:82.
5. American Pharmacists Association. Code of Ethics for Pharmacists. www.pharmacist.com/AM/PrinterTemplate.cfm?Section=Search1&template=/CM/HTMLDisplay.cfm&ContentID=2903 (accessed 2008 Jan 7).
6. ASHP policy position 0101: pharmacy benefits for the uninsured. In: Hawkins B, ed. Best practices for hospital and health-system pharmacy: positions and guidance documents of ASHP. Bethesda, MD: American Society of Health-System Pharmacists; 2006:161.
7. Brach C, Fraser I. Can cultural competency reduce racial and ethnic health care disparities? A review and conceptual model. *Med Care Res Rev.* 2000; 57(suppl 1):181–217.
8. Harvard Forums on Health. Americans speak out on disparities in health care. www.phsi.harvard.edu/health_reform/poll_media_report_disparities.pdf (accessed 2004 Dec 10).
9. Committee on Institutional and Policy-Level Strategies for Increasing the Diversity of the U.S. Healthcare Workforce. In the nation's compelling interest: ensuring diversity in the health care workforce. Washington, DC: National Academy Press; 2004.
10. Saha S, Komaromy M, Koepsell TD, et al. Patient-physician racial concordance and the perceived quality and use of health care. *Arch Intern Med.* 1999; 159:997–1004.
11. Morales LS, Cunningham WE, Brown JA, et al. Are Latinos less satisfied with communication by health care providers? *J Gen Intern Med.* 1999; 14:409–17.
12. American Hospital Association Commission on Workforce for Hospitals and Health Systems. In our hands: how hospital leaders can build a thriving workforce. www.aha.org/aha/key_issues/workforce/commission/InOurHands.html (accessed 2004 Dec 10).
13. ASHP policy position 0409: cultural diversity among health care providers. In: Hawkins B, ed. Best practices for hospital and health-system pharmacy: positions and guidance documents of ASHP. Bethesda, MD: American Society of Health-System Pharmacists; 2006:253.
14. Report of the ASHP Ad Hoc Committee on Ethnic Diversity and Cultural Competence. *Am J Health-Syst Pharm.* 2005; 62:1924–30.
15. ASHP policy position 0314: cultural competence. In: Hawkins B, ed. Best practices for hospital and health-system pharmacy: positions and guidance documents of ASHP. Bethesda, MD: American Society of Health-System Pharmacists; 2006:75.
16. Department of Health and Human Services Administration on Aging. Achieving cultural competence: a guidebook for providers of services to older Americans and their families. www.aoa.gov/prof/adddiv/cultural/CC-guidebook.pdf (accessed 2004 Dec 10).
17. U.S. Department of Health and Human Services. Final report: national standards for culturally and linguistically appropriate services in health care (2001). www.omhrc.gov/omh/programs/2pgprograms/finalreport.pdf (accessed 2004 Dec 10).
18. Accreditation standards and guidelines for the professional program in pharmacy leading to the doctor of pharmacy degree. Chicago: Accreditation Council for Pharmaceutical Education; 2006.
19. American Society of Health-System Pharmacists. ASHP guidelines on pharmacist-conducted patient education and counseling. *Am J Health-Syst Pharm.* 1997; 54:431–4.
20. ASHP policy position 0510: communication among health-system pharmacy practitioners, patients, and other health care providers. In: Hawkins B, ed. Best practices for hospital and health-system pharmacy: positions and guidance documents of ASHP. Bethesda, MD: American Society of Health-System Pharmacists; 2006:74.
21. Erizinger S. Communication between Spanish-speaking patients and their doctors in medical encounters. *Cult Med Psychiatry.* 1991; 15:91–101.
22. Carrasquillo O, Orav EJ, Brennan TA, et al. Impact of language barriers on patient satisfaction in an emergency department. *J Gen Intern Med.* 1999; 14:82–7.
23. Perez-Stable EJ, Napoles-Springer A, Miramontes JM. The effects of ethnicity and language on medical outcomes of patients with hypertension or diabetes. *Med Care.* 1997; 35:1212–9.
24. ASHP policy position 9804: multidisciplinary action plans for patient care. In: Hawkins B, ed. Best practices for hospital and health-system pharmacy: positions and guidance documents of ASHP. Bethesda, MD: American Society of Health-System Pharmacists; 2006:161.
25. Ver Ploeg M, Perrin E, eds. Eliminating health disparities: measurement and data needs. Washington, DC: National Academy Press; 2004.

26. The Commonwealth Fund. Enhancing public hospitals' reporting of data on racial and ethnic disparities in care. www.cmwf.org/publications/publications_show.htm?doc_id=452681&#doc452681 (accessed 2007 Jan 31).

Appendix—Institute of Medicine Recommendations Most Pertinent to Hospital and Health-System Pharmacy Practice[1]

General Recommendations

Recommendation 2-1. Increase awareness of racial and ethnic disparities in healthcare among the general public and key stakeholders.

Recommendation 2-2. Increase healthcare providers' awareness of disparities.

Legal, Regulatory, and Policy Interventions

Recommendation 5-3. Increase the proportion of underrepresented U.S. racial and ethnic minorities among healthcare professionals.

Health-System Interventions

Recommendation 5-6. Promote the consistency and equity of care through use of evidence-based guidelines.

Recommendation 5-9. Support the use of interpretation services where community need exists.

Recommendation 5-11. Implement multidisciplinary treatment and preventive care teams.

Patient Education and Empowerment

Recommendation 5-12. Implement patient education programs to increase patients' knowledge of how to best access care and participate in treatment decisions.

Cross-Cultural Education in the Health Professions

Recommendation 6-1. Integrate cross-cultural education into the training of all current and future health professionals.

Data Collection and Monitoring

Recommendation 7-1. Collect and report data on healthcare access and utilization by patients' race, ethnicity, socioeconomic status, and, where possible, primary language.

Recommendation 7-2. Include measures of racial and ethnic disparities in performance measurement.

Recommendation 7-3. Monitor progress toward the elimination of healthcare disparities.

Recommendation 7-4. Report racial and ethnic data by OMB categories, but use subpopulation groups where possible.

Developed through the ASHP Council on Pharmacy Practice and approved by the ASHP Board of Directors on April 16, 2007, and by the ASHP House of Delegates on June 24, 2007.

The bibliographic citation for this document is as follows: American Society of Health-System Pharmacists. ASHP statement on racial and ethnic disparities in health care. *Am J Health-Syst Pharm.* 2008; 65:728–33.

This statement was reviewed in 2011 by the Council on Pharmacy Practice and by the Board of Directors and was found to still be appropriate.

ASHP Statement on the Role of Health-System Pharmacists in Emergency Preparedness

The United States has experienced and remains vulnerable to many events that cause large numbers of casualties. The tragic events of September 11, 2001, and the subsequent anthrax exposures and deaths also awakened the nation to the threat of homeland terrorist attacks.

As the United States began to enhance counterterrorism measures in response to the homeland terrorist attacks of September 11, 2001, it became clear that hospital and health-system pharmacists have an essential role in emergency preparedness.

Position

The American Society of Health-System Pharmacists (ASHP) believes that hospital and health-system pharmacists must assertively exercise their responsibilities in preparing for and responding to disasters, and the leaders of emergency planning at the federal, regional, state, and local levels must call on pharmacists to participate in the full range of issues related to pharmaceuticals. For the purposes of this Statement, disasters include natural disasters (e.g., floods, hurricanes, tornadoes, earthquakes, and forest fires); industrial accidents (e.g., explosions, fires, chemical releases, radiation escape from nuclear power plants, and airplane or train crashes); and terrorist attacks with weapons of mass destruction (WMD), including biological and chemical agents and radiological, nuclear, and explosive devices.

General Principles

1. On the basis of their education, training, experience, and legal responsibilities, pharmacists should have a key role in the planning and execution of (a) pharmaceutical distribution and control and (b) drug therapy management of patients during disasters.
2. The expertise of the pharmacist should be sought in (a) developing guidelines for the diagnosis and treatment of casualties and exposed individuals, (b) selecting pharmaceuticals and related supplies for national and regional stockpiles and local emergency inventories in emergency-preparedness programs, (c) ensuring proper packaging, storage, handling, labeling, and dispensing of emergency supplies of pharmaceuticals, (d) ensuring appropriate deployment of emergency supplies of pharmaceuticals, and (e) ensuring appropriate education and counseling of individuals who receive pharmaceuticals from an emergency supply in response to a disaster.
3. Pharmacists should be in a position to advise public health officials on appropriate messages to convey to the public about the use of essential pharmaceuticals in response to disasters, giving consideration to issues such as adverse effects, contraindications, the effectiveness of alternative pharmaceuticals, and the potential development of drug-resistant infectious agents.
4. In the event of a disaster, pharmacists should be called on to collaborate with physicians and other prescribers in managing the drug therapy of individual victims.

Advice to Hospital and Health-System Pharmacy Directors

Every hospital and health-system pharmacy director (or designee) should

1. Become well informed about the local history of and potential for natural disasters and industrial accidents, as well as the threat of terrorist attacks with WMD, including potential agents that could be used and the related diagnostic and treatment issues;
2. Become thoroughly informed of federal, regional, state, local, and institutional plans for emergency-preparedness, especially those related to the distribution, control, and use of pharmaceuticals;
3. Ensure that the pharmaceutical components of the institution's emergency plans are coordinated with the overall local preparedness plans involving other institutions, community pharmacies, and wholesalers, as well as coordinated with federal, regional, and state plans;
4. Ensure that the appropriate pharmaceuticals and related equipment and supplies are in stock at the institution, consistent with the overall local emergency-preparedness plan, which should account for the interim between the occurrence of a disaster and the receipt of federal or state assistance;
5. Ensure that information about the appropriate use of pharmaceuticals in response to a disaster is available to the health professionals in the institution;
6. Ensure that the institution does not engage in stockpiling of pharmaceuticals without regard to local emergency-preparedness plans that are designed to meet the needs of the whole community; and
7. Ensure that pharmacy personnel are trained to implement the institution's emergency plans.

Advice to Hospital and Health-System Pharmacists

Every hospital and health-system pharmacist should

1. Become well informed about the local history of and potential for natural disasters and industrial accidents, as well as the threat of terrorist attacks with WMD, including potential agents that could be used and the related diagnostic and treatment issues;
2. Become thoroughly informed of local and institutional plans for emergency preparedness, especially those related to the distribution, control, and use of pharmaceuticals;
3. Share with professional colleagues and patients evidence-based information on pharmaceuticals used to respond to disasters;
4. Act assertively to prevent and allay panic and irrational responses to disasters;

5. Strongly discourage individuals from developing personal stockpiles of pharmaceuticals for use in the event of chemical, biological, or nuclear terrorism;
6. Consider volunteering in advance of a disaster to assist in (a) distributing emergency supplies of pharmaceuticals, (b) dispensing and administering medications and immunizations, and (c) managing the drug therapy of individual victims; and
7. Develop and maintain first-aid skills and complete and maintain basic cardiac life support (BCLS) certification. BCLS certification may be required for administering injectable medications, such as vaccines.

Advice to Hospital and Health-System Administrators

Hospital and health-system administrators should

1. Ask the pharmacy director to participate in preparing the institution's emergency-preparedness plan and to consider participating in the development of local, state, regional, and federal emergency-preparedness plans;
2. Consult with the pharmacy director to coordinate the institution's participation in the building of emergency pharmaceutical supplies for use in the community;
3. Refrain from building institutional stockpiles of pharmaceuticals that are not coordinated with the local plan;
4. Encourage local preparedness-planning officials to involve pharmacists in the full range of issues related to pharmaceuticals; and
5. Encourage and enable pharmacy personnel employed by the institution to participate in local, state, regional, and federal emergency-preparedness planning and to volunteer for community service in the event of a disaster.

Advice to Emergency-Preparedness Planners

Emergency-preparedness planners at the federal, regional, state, and local levels should

1. Consult with qualified pharmacists in all areas in which the pharmacist's expertise would contribute to the creation and execution of workable plans;
2. Inform pharmacists, through national and state pharmacy organizations, of plans for deployment of emergency pharmaceutical supplies so that appropriate plans can be made at the local level; and
3. Consult with qualified pharmacists on messages that should be conveyed to the public about the appropriate use of pharmaceuticals in the event of a disaster.

Advice to State Societies of Health-System Pharmacists

State societies of health-system pharmacists should

1. Offer their assistance to state and local emergency-preparedness planning officials, especially in identifying qualified pharmacists to participate in emergency-preparedness planning;
2. Advise their members of information unique to the state regarding pharmacists' participation in emergency-preparedness planning and deployment efforts; and
3. Establish a volunteer network of health-system pharmacists for deployment in the event of a terrorist attack.

Commitments Made by ASHP

In support of the efforts of health-system pharmacists in emergency preparedness and counterterrorism, ASHP will

1. Maintain an electronic communications network of hospital pharmacy department directors that can be used to transmit urgent information related to emergency preparedness and counterterrorism;
2. Disseminate promptly to ASHP members important new information related to pharmacist involvement in emergency preparedness and counterterrorism;
3. Disseminate to ASHP members and others in the health care community timely evidence-based information about pharmaceuticals used when responding to disasters; and
4. Meet with government officials and others when necessary to clarify promptly important issues that affect the involvement of health-system pharmacists in emergency preparedness and counterterrorism.

This statement was reviewed in 2013 by the Council on Pharmacy Practice and by the Board of Directors and was found to still be appropriate.

Approved by the ASHP Board of Directors on February 21, 2003, and by the ASHP House of Delegates on June 1, 2003. Developed through the ASHP Council on Professional Affairs. Supersedes the ASHP Statement on the Role of Health-System Pharmacists in Counterterrorism approved by the ASHP Board of Directors, November 27, 2001, and revised and approved (as the ASHP Statement on the Role of Health-System Pharmacists in Emergency Preparedness) by the ASHP House of Delegates and the ASHP Board of Directors, June 2, 2002.

The bibliographic citation for this document is as follows: American Society of Health-System Pharmacists. ASHP statement on the role of health-system pharmacists in emergency preparedness. *Am J Health-Syst Pharm.* 2003; 60:1993–5.

ASHP Statement on the Role of Health-System Pharmacists in Public Health

Position

Pharmacists who practice in hospitals and health systems (health-system pharmacists) play a vital role in maintaining and promoting public health. The American Society of Health-System Pharmacists (ASHP) believes that all health-system pharmacists have a responsibility to participate in global, national, state, regional, and institutional efforts to promote public health and to integrate the goals of those initiatives into their practices. Furthermore, health-system pharmacists have a responsibility to work with public health planners to ensure their involvement in public health policy decision-making and in the planning, development, and implementation of public health efforts.

The primary objectives of this statement are to (1) increase awareness of health-system pharmacists' contributions to public health, (2) describe the role of health-system pharmacists in public health planning and promotion, and (3) identify new opportunities for health-system pharmacists' involvement in future public health initiatives. This statement does not provide an exhaustive review of health-system pharmacists' public health activities. Its intent is to stimulate dialogue about the role that health-system pharmacists can play in providing care that improves public health in the United States.

Background

Public health has been defined simply as "what we as a society do to assure the conditions in which people can be healthy."[1] In contrast to medicine, public health initiatives "emphasize the prevention of disease and the health needs of the population as a whole."[2]

Public health services have been characterized as occurring on two levels: the planning ("macro") level and the implementation ("micro" or "provider") level.[3] Macro-level public health services focus on the well-being of the population as a whole and emphasize the assessment and prioritization of a community's health-related needs as well as planning to address those needs. Such services include working with community representatives in identifying health-related community problems; setting community health priorities; formulating community health programs and policies; managing, administering, and evaluating community health-promotion programs; educating the community in ways that promote public health; and researching, presenting, and publishing information about public health activities.[3] These macro-level activities are carried out by public health professionals with varying backgrounds, degrees, and interests.

Micro-level public health services include all the activities required to implement public health initiatives. Many of these services are performed on a provider-to-patient or a program-to-population basis, usually with a specific health-related outcome in mind.[4] Examples of such services include disease screening, immunization, counseling for at-risk populations, and tobacco-cessation programs.

One concept underlying many public health activities is prevention, which is commonly categorized into three types: primary prevention (reducing the actual incidence and occurrence of diseases, injuries, and disability), secondary prevention (decreasing the severity or progression of the disease, injury, and disability), and tertiary prevention (treatment or rehabilitation to return the disease, injury, or disability to the initial or baseline state).[5] Public health efforts on the macro and micro levels can fall anywhere along the prevention spectrum and can reinforce each other. For example, Healthy People 2010 (a macro-level public health policy) aims to reduce the number of hospital admissions attributable to drug therapy management problems (primary prevention).[6] Policies implemented by individual hospitals (on the micro level) will allow clinicians to quickly identify such adverse drug events (ADEs) and prevent them from worsening (secondary prevention), as well as treat the affected patients (tertiary prevention). Pooling and evaluating these clinical experiences can lead to the development of dispensing guidelines or utilization studies that could be used as a primary prevention tool on the macro level.

The health-system pharmacist's role in public health, and the distinction between individualized patient care and public health efforts, can be illustrated by several examples. Providing optimal pharmacotherapy to a single patient has great value. Nonetheless, lessons learned from the management of individual patients can have an even greater impact when they result in practice guidelines or health policies that affect the larger population. Such policy development requires careful evaluation and synthesis of health information using epidemiologic principles. Similarly, identification of a specific ADE is an important patient care service routinely performed by health-system pharmacists. The pharmacoepidemiologic study of ADEs across a population, coupled with action to prevent or mitigate such events, can have a significant impact on public health. Counseling a patient on the proper use of a medication helps that patient. When that knowledge is systematically evaluated and used to develop better behavioral outcomes, general public health can be improved. Finally, a health-system pharmacist who dispenses medications as a member of an emergency-response team has a limited impact on public health. However, the same health-system pharmacist working with emergency-preparedness planners to develop policies and programs that ensure proper utilization of the full range of pharmacy services during a disaster can have an enormous effect on the health of the affected population.

Public Health Activities of Health-System Pharmacists

In 1981, the American Public Health Association (APHA) outlined the public health role of the pharmacist in a pioneering statement.[7] This succinct policy position, building on a previous APHA publication,[8] declared that pharmacists were an underutilized resource in promoting public health and described an array of functions that could be performed by pharmacists, from providing direct personal health care services to planning for health care for communities or wider geographic areas. In 2004, the American Association of Colleges of Pharmacy recognized the important role pharmacists can play in public health by including population-based care and public health in its Center for Advancement in Pharmaceutical Education (CAPE) Educational Outcomes.[9] These outcomes also emphasized the pharmacist's role in the public health components of "health improvement, wellness, and disease prevention" and the need for pharmacist involvement to ensure the "availability of effective, quality health and disease prevention services," as well as the urgency to "develop public health policy."[9]

The public health duties that an individual health-system pharmacist performs will vary, based on the individual's experience, abilities, training, and work setting. ASHP believes that all health-system pharmacists, working alone or in collaboration with health care colleagues and administrators, can contribute to the promotion of public health. ASHP believes that health-system pharmacists have specific public-health-related responsibilities in infection control[10]; substance abuse prevention, education, and treatment[11]; immunization[12]; tobacco cessation[13]; and emergency preparedness and response.[14] The following are examples of other activities that health-system pharmacists can engage in to promote public health:

- Providing population-based care,
- Developing disease prevention and control programs (including medication safety programs) in their institutions and communities,
- Developing health-education policies and programs within their institutions that address the needs of patients, other health care professionals, community leaders, and the public,
- Collaborating with state and local authorities, including local and state health departments and boards of health, to address local and regional health care needs (including environmental hazard and emergency-preparedness programs),
- Advocating for sound legislation, regulations, and public policy regarding disease prevention and management, and
- Engaging in population-based research and initiating campaigns to disseminate new knowledge.

Population-Based Care. The Institute of Medicine, in *Crossing the Quality Chasm: A New Health System for the 21st Century*, presented the problems of health care quality in the United States and provided recommendations for change.[15] Subsequent follow-up reports, including *Priority Areas for National Action: Transforming Health Care Quality*, have provided additional direction related to population-based care.[16] The CAPE Educational Outcomes recommended that pharmacists engage in both patient-centered and population-based care, suggesting that a core competency of pharmacists is the ability to develop "population-specific, evidence-based disease management programs and protocols based upon analysis of epidemiologic and pharmacoeconomic data, medication use criteria, medication use review and risk reduction strategies."[9]

Over the past two decades, the expanding role of health-system pharmacists in patient care has allowed them to support public health efforts by designing and providing disease management programs. ASHP urges health-system pharmacists to build on this foundation by leading their institutions' efforts to provide population-based care. By working with their health care colleagues through such institutional mechanisms as the pharmacy and therapeutics committee and using tools such as medication-use evaluation, health-system pharmacists can contribute to population-specific, evidence-based disease management programs tailored to fit the needs of the institutions and communities they serve. Health-system pharmacists can participate in quality reviews and ensure that evidence-based treatments are used for all patients to help alleviate health care disparities.

Disease Prevention and Medication Safety. Health-system pharmacists can be involved in disease prevention and control in many ways. For example, they can help develop institutional screening programs to check immunization status and identify undiagnosed medical conditions (e.g., hypertension, diabetes, hyperlipidemia, depression). The health-system pharmacist's role in medication safety and error prevention is in keeping with the national public health goals outlined in the federal government's Healthy People 2010 initiative, which include reducing the number of hospital admissions resulting from drug therapy mismanagement and fostering programs to intercept counterfeit medications.[6] Medication reconciliation programs are one example of the tools pharmacists can encourage their facilities to use to achieve these goals.

Health Education. Health-system pharmacists can promote public health by developing patient education programs on safe and effective medication use[17] and other public health-related topics, such as tobacco cessation, exercise, and healthy nutrition. Pharmacists should support the education and training of the population at an early age, such as through school health programs, to help children develop good health behaviors that can continue into adulthood. Furthermore, health-system pharmacists can improve society's use of medications by educating their health care colleagues about safe and effective medication use. Health-system pharmacists can also use their knowledge and expertise to educate community leaders (e.g., legislators, regulators, public officeholders, school officials, religious leaders) about and involve them in public health initiatives.

Public Health Policy. Health-system pharmacists should be encouraged to participate in public health policy development, from local boards of health to national programs. By linking disease prevalence, drug utilization, and the determinants of disease, health-system pharmacists can place prevention within a larger context. Drugs play a central role in health, and health policy, especially policy directed at chronic disease, must be formulated with a better understanding of the relationship of drug therapy to the many other factors that affect disease outcomes. Since medication use increases as patients age, health-system pharmacists will face increasing responsibilities to ensure appropriate and cost-effective medication use as the average age of the U.S. population rises.

Health-system pharmacist participation in emergency planning and service delivery is critical. Requirements for new and enlarged inventories of specialized pharmaceuticals to provide prophylaxis and treatment to communities during emergencies are growing. The Centers for Disease Control and Prevention's Strategic National Stockpile (SNS) program, for example, includes 12-hour push packages, vendor-managed inventory, "chempacks," vaccines, and medical supplies.[18] Hospital and health-system pharmacies are essential in planning for accommodation of supplies, such as antibiotics and antidotes needed in the initial 24 hours following a crisis, before state and federal assets become available. Community-based planning efforts for mass immunization, prophylaxis, and treatment, including pandemic response to biological, chemical, radiological, or explosive agents, are an ongoing process, as is planning for utilization of the SNS. Medication management is a critical component of all these contingencies, yet many of the plans do not address pharmacy participation. Involvement of health-system pharmacists is critically important to reliably address medication issues.

ASHP encourages pharmacists to serve on National Disaster Medical System assistance teams (http://ndms.dhhs.gov), the National Pharmacy Response Team (www.ndms.dhhs.gov/nprt.html), or local units of the Medical Reserve Corps (www.medicalreservecorps.gov) to assist in distributing emergency supplies of pharmaceuticals, dispensing and administering medications and immunizations, and managing the drug therapy of individual victims.[14] The development, implementation, and revision of local emergency operations plans, which include public health management of emergencies, require pharmacist input. Health-system pharmacists need to be actively involved in planning for procurement, distribution, and dispensing of medications, as well as ongoing management of patient medication issues.

Pharmacists should also work with health-system administrators to develop policies and initiatives that heighten awareness of the applicable laws and best management practices in the proper handling and disposal of hazardous drugs.

As medication-use experts and experienced health-system administrators, health-system pharmacists can and should contribute to the development of public-health-related legislation and regulation and should be involved in public program oversight and administration. Legislators, regulators, and program managers at all levels of government should be educated to utilize this expertise. Health-system pharmacists, as individuals and through their professional associations, state and local boards of health, and state boards of pharmacy, are encouraged to participate in legislative, regulatory, and oversight processes.

Research and Training. To assume a greater responsibility in public health, health-system pharmacists must receive adequate education and training. Pharmacy curricula should include advanced coursework in public health and research design. Health-system pharmacists need to be proficient in research methodology, pharmacoepidemiology, and biostatistics and their applications to public health decision-making. Knowledge and experience in the design, conduct, and interpretation of clinical studies (both observational and experimental) are essential. Health-system pharmacists have the opportunity to participate in collaborative research and serve on institutional review boards, data monitoring and safety committees, and expert medication advisory committees. Experiential and didactic training for practicing health-system pharmacists, students, residents, and research fellows should include exposure to research in public health policy, pharmacoepidemiology, pharmacoeconomics, health-related quality of life, and evidence-based medicine. Health-system pharmacists should also work directly with public health policymakers and other key stakeholders, such as professional organizations, medical centers, academic institutions, governmental agencies, and third-party payers, to promote optimal pharmacotherapy.

Future Roles

Revolutionary progress in basic biomedical sciences, including human genomics, stem-cell biology, immunology, biomedical engineering, and bioinformatics, has provided an unprecedented supply of information for improving human health. The rapidly emerging fields of population genetics and pharmacogenomics highlight the significance of molecular techniques in the clinical diagnostic laboratory and the potential for application in patient-directed pharmacotherapy. Medication-prescribing decisions will increasingly rely on the results of genotyping of drug-metabolizing enzymes. New technology and practices will allow health-system pharmacists to reduce treatment failures and prevent adverse drug reactions through the proper application of pharmacogenetic principles.[19] Advances in informatics will permit aggregation and application of population- and patient-specific clinical data in ways that will encourage development of population-specific, evidence-based disease management programs. As medication-use experts, health-system pharmacists will need to apply these new tools not simply to improve patient-specific pharmacotherapy but to advance public health. Similarly, innovations in medication delivery technology will allow more complex therapies to be administered outside institutional settings. Patients, caregivers, and health professionals will require education about the safe use of such technologies, as will the legislators and other officials responsible for regulating their use.

Conclusion

Health-system pharmacists play a vital role in maintaining and promoting public health. ASHP believes that all health-system pharmacists have a responsibility to participate in global, national, state, regional, and institutional efforts to promote public health and to integrate them into their practices and that health-system pharmacists should be involved in public health policy decision-making and in the planning, development, and implementation of public health efforts. Health-system pharmacists can improve public health by providing population-based care; developing disease prevention and control programs; providing health education; collaborating with state and local authorities to address local and regional health care needs, including emergency preparedness and response; advocating for sound legislation, regulations, and public policy regarding disease prevention and management; and engaging in public health research.

References

1. Committee for the Study of the Future of Public Health. The future of public health. Washington, DC: National Academies Press; 1988:1.
2. Higher education for public health. New York: Milbank Memorial Fund; 1976.
3. Bush PJ, Johnson KW. Where is the public health pharmacist? *Am J Pharm Educ.* 1979; 43:249–53.
4. Bush PJ, ed. The pharmacist role in disease prevention and health promotion. Bethesda, MD: ASHP Research and Education Foundation; 1983:3.
5. Ives TJ, DerMarderosian AH. Pharmacists and public health. In: Hendrickson R, Beringer P, DerMarderosian AH, et al., eds. Remington: the science and practice of pharmacy. 21st ed. Philadelphia: Lippincott Williams & Wilkins; 2006:51.
6. Office of Disease Prevention and Health Promotion. Healthy People 2010. www.healthypeople.gov/document/HTML/Volume2/17Medical.htm (accessed 2007 Dec 27).
7. American Public Health Association. APHA policy 8024: the role of the pharmacist in public health. *Am J Public Health.* 1981; 71:213–6.
8. Cain RM, Kahn JS. The pharmacist as a member of the health team. *Am J Public Health.* 1971; 61:2223–8.
9. Center for Advancement in Pharmaceutical Education (CAPE) Educational Outcomes 2004. www.aacp.org/Docs/MainNavigation/Resources/6075_CAPE2004.pdf (accessed 2007 Nov 27).
10. American Society of Health-System Pharmacists. ASHP statement on the pharmacist's role in infection control. *Am J Health-Syst Pharm.* 1998; 55:1724–6.
11. American Society of Health-System Pharmacists. ASHP statement on the pharmacist's role in substance abuse prevention, education, and assistance. *Am J Health-Syst Pharm.* 2003; 60:1995–8.
12. American Society of Health-System Pharmacists. ASHP guidelines on the pharmacist's role in immunization. *Am J Health-Syst Pharm.* 2003; 60:1371–7.
13. American Society of Health-System Pharmacists. ASHP therapeutic position statement on smoking cessation. *Am J Health-Syst Pharm.* 1999; 56:460–4.
14. American Society of Health-System Pharmacists. ASHP statement on the role of health-system pharmacists in emergency preparedness. *Am J Health-Syst Pharm.* 2003; 60:1993–5.
15. Committee on Quality of Health Care in America. Crossing the quality chasm: a new health system for the 21st century. Washington, DC: National Academy Press; 2001.
16. Adams K, Corrigan JM, eds. Priority areas for national action: transforming health care quality. Washington, DC: National Academies Press; 2003.
17. American Society of Health-System Pharmacists. ASHP guidelines on pharmacist-conducted patient education and counseling. *Am J Health-Syst Pharm.* 1997; 54:431–4.
18. Centers for Disease Control and Prevention. Strategic National Stockpile. www.bt.cdc.gov/stockpile/ (accessed 2007 Nov 20).
19. Spear BB, Health-Chiozzi M, Huff J. Clinical applications of pharmacogenetics. *Trends Mol Med.* 2001; 7:201–4.

Other Resources

Pharmacists looking for further involvement in public health have many options. First, training and competence in public health disciplines are invaluable in understanding the field of public health and its applications to pharmacy practice. Accredited schools of public health offer traditional didactic classes, and some have courses or continuing education available on-line that will give the beginner a clearer understanding of the four traditional areas of public health practice: health administration and policy, health education, biostatistics, and epidemiology. Pharmacists who wish to pursue a degree in public health can also do so online at a growing number of schools of public health (www.asph.org/document.cfm?page=718).

Pharmacists with an interest in federal public health initiatives can start with one of three main points of access. The first is the Centers for Disease Control and Prevention (www.cdc.gov), the largest repository of documents, program descriptions, and contacts in the realm of prevention. Major efforts aimed at disease surveillance, infectious disease control, immunization, health education, chronic disease maintenance, and disease-related data management provide an ample and readily available source of information. The second major source of information is the Office of Disease Prevention and Health Promotion (http://odphp.osophs.dhhs.gov), which provides access to Healthy People 2010, a health information clearinghouse, national dietary guidelines, and information about health observances. Finally, the Agency for Healthcare Research and Quality (www.ahrq.gov) provides information on evidence-based clinical practice, the Guide to Clinical Preventive Services (www.ahrq.gov/clinic/pocketgd.htm), and quality measurement of health care. Virtually the entire realm of public health within the U.S. Public Health Service can be accessed or linked via these three websites.

State government websites provide public health information for their respective states. State entities serve as the main policymaking entity for public health priorities and strategies, provide a conduit for federal public health dollars, and are the main repository of health information and data for the state. States often organize a range of advisory groups, task forces, and planning committees whose output shapes their public health agenda. These entities also provide input and direction for state legislative bodies to address, legislate, and fund.

On the local level, boards of health serve as the main government entities involved in public health. Aside from their usual routine of immunizations and restaurant inspections, these boards serve as the policymakers for disaster response and provision of primary care to underserved populations. They receive federal and state dollars that are used to fund public health efforts. They are closest to the general population both in their makeup and in their efforts at improving the public's health. Pharmacists interested in learning more about public health and the types of activities that community public health agencies are involved in can register for a free interactive tutorial at www.nynj-phtc.org/orientation.

Below is a list of websites that provide information related to public health.

Public Health Organizations

- World Health Organization (www.who.int)
- Pan American Health Organization (www.paho.org)
- American Public Health Association (www.apha.org)
- Association of State and Territorial Health Officials (www.astho.org)
- National Association of County and City Health Officials (www.naccho.org)
- Public Health Foundation (www.phf.org)
- Association of Schools of Public Health (www.asph.org)

Federal Health Agencies

- U.S. Department of Health and Human Services (www.dhhs.gov)
- Office of the Surgeon General, Public Health Priorities (www.surgeongeneral.gov/publichealthpriorities.html)
- Centers for Disease Control and Prevention (www.cdc.gov)
- Food and Drug Administration (www.fda.gov)
- Health Resources and Services Administration (www.hrsa.gov)
- National Institutes of Health (www.nih.gov)
- Agency for Healthcare Research and Quality (www.ahrq.gov)
- Environmental Protection Agency (www.epa.gov)

Developed through the ASHP Council on Pharmacy Practice and approved by the ASHP Board of Directors on January 12, 2007, and by the ASHP House of Delegates on June 24, 2007.

The bibliographic citation for this document is as follows: American Society of Health-System Pharmacists. ASHP statement on the role of health-system pharmacists in public health. *Am J Health-Syst Pharm.* 2008; 65:462–7.

This statement was reviewed in 2011 by the Council on Pharmacy Practice and by the Board of Directors and was found to still be appropriate.

ASHP Statement on the Use of Dietary Supplements

Position

The American Society of Health-System Pharmacists (ASHP) believes that the widespread, indiscriminate use of dietary supplements presents substantial risks to public health and that pharmacists have an opportunity and a professional responsibility to reduce those risks. ASHP recognizes that patients may choose to use legally available dietary supplements, but believes that the decision to use substances that may be pharmacologically active should always be based on reliable information about their safety and efficacy. The current regulatory framework governing dietary supplements does not provide consumers or health care providers with sufficient information on safety and efficacy to make informed decisions. Furthermore, standards for product quality are currently inadequate. ASHP recognizes the concerns raised by the dietary supplement industry regarding regulating dietary supplements as nonprescription drugs because of the industry's inability to patent product ingredients. Still, ASHP urges Congress to amend the Dietary Supplement Health and Education Act of 1994 (DSHEA) to require that the Food and Drug Administration (FDA) develop a regulatory scheme to ensure that dietary supplements are safe and effective. ASHP believes that dietary supplements, at a minimum, should (1) receive FDA approval for evidence of safety and efficacy, (2) meet manufacturing standards for identity, strength, quality, purity, packaging, and labeling, and (3) undergo mandatory postmarketing reporting of adverse events, including drug interactions.

ASHP strongly encourages in vitro and clinical studies of interactions between dietary supplements and medications. Because of the demonstrated risk of these interactions, ASHP discourages the concurrent use of dietary supplements and drug therapy, especially those therapies for which failure may have irreversible consequences (e.g., immunosuppressive therapy, cancer chemotherapy, treatment for human immunodeficiency virus infection, anticoagulation therapy, and hormonal contraceptive therapy).

ASHP believes that the criteria used to evaluate dietary supplements for inclusion in health-system formularies should be as rigorous as those established for nonprescription drugs and that the self-administered use of dietary supplements during a health-system stay may increase risks to patients and liabilities to health care professionals and institutions.

ASHP urges pharmacists and other health care practitioners to integrate awareness of dietary supplement use into everyday practice and encourages pharmacists to increase efforts to prevent interactions between dietary supplements and drugs. ASHP also supports the education of pharmacists and other health care practitioners in the taxonomy, formulation, pharmacology, and pharmacokinetics of dietary supplements and believes that such education should be required in college of pharmacy curricula.

Background

Dietary supplements are defined in DSHEA as products "intended to supplement the diet" that contain vitamins, minerals, herbs or other botanicals, amino acids; "a dietary substance for use by man to supplement the diet by increasing the total daily intake"; or "a concentrate, metabolite, constituent, extract, or combinations of these ingredients."[1]

Evidence of variability in dietary supplement content[2–8] has spurred efforts to standardize products. Current federal regulations regarding the manufacture of dietary supplements are not adequate.[9] Some manufacturers voluntarily follow good manufacturing practices (GMPs) devised by their own trade groups (e.g., the National Nutritional Foods Association GMP Certification Program[10]), and the U.S. Pharmacopeia (USP) has created voluntary standards for a handful of dietary supplements.[11] Manufacturers that wish to carry the "USP approved" seal on their product labels have to subject their products to testing by USP. The creation of these voluntary programs reflects a widespread concern, even on the part of dietary supplement manufacturers, that production processes must be regulated. Although FDA has had the authority to establish dietary supplement GMPs for almost a decade, it issued its first proposed rule on the topic in 2003.[12]

DSHEA does not require FDA to review evidence of the efficacy or safety of dietary supplements, so manufacturers have no burden to prove that their products are effective or safe. Although dietary supplement labeling cannot claim activity in the treatment of a specific disease or condition, claims that suggest an effect on the "structure or function of the body" are allowed.[1] For example, dietary supplements containing echinacea can be labeled as supporting immune health (as a "function") but cannot be labeled as preventing or ameliorating colds (treating a disease). Regardless of this distinction between function and treatment, consumers are bombarded by the lay press (and even some scientific literature) with what can only be described as specific-disease indications for dietary supplements (e.g., glucosamine for osteoarthritis, black cohosh for menopausal symptoms, and St. John's wort for depression).

The health claims allowed in dietary supplement labeling by current interpretation of DSHEA create further confusion for consumers. FDA's attempt to hold these health claims to the same scientific standard required for conventional foods was struck down in *Pearson* v. *Shalala*, so FDA must permit dietary supplement labels to carry "qualified" health claims based on equivocal scientific evidence.[13]

Although DSHEA does require that dietary supplements be safe, it does not require prospective testing to ensure safety. To remove a product from the market, FDA must prove that the product is unsafe. Under DSHEA, some dietary supplements that were banned from the U.S. market because of concerns about their safety have been allowed to return (e.g., sassafras tea, dehydroepiandrosterone). Demonstrably unsafe products have made their way onto the market, and fatal adverse reactions have been reported.[14,15]

Establishing the safety record of dietary supplements has been complicated by the lack of systematically collected data about their adverse reactions. The MedWatch system has been used to a limited extent to report adverse events related to dietary supplement use, but, nine years after the passage of DSHEA, FDA is still developing an adverse-reaction-reporting system for dietary supplements. Despite the limited data, however, the number of case reports of interactions between dietary supplements and medications is growing.[16–21] The safety of dietary supplements for special populations (e.g., children, pregnant women, people with impaired organ or immunologic function) has also not been demonstrated.

Dangers to Public Health

It has been estimated that 40% of the U.S. population uses dietary supplements often and that almost twice as many have used at least 1 of the estimated 29,000 dietary supplements on the market.[22] Out-of-pocket expenditures on dietary supplements total approximately $18 billion annually.[23] Such widespread and indiscriminate use of dietary supplements presents five dangers to the public health:

1. Some dietary supplements are inherently unsafe when ingested orally (e.g., chaparral, ephedra, comfrey, tiractricol, aristolochic acid, pennyroyal).[24–28]
2. Lax regulation of dietary supplement manufacturing presents the risk of contamination or adulteration with harmful substances, including carcinogens,[29–32] and of dangerous variability in active ingredient content among products.[2–8]
3. The use of dietary supplements may compromise, delay, or supplant treatment with therapies of proven efficacy.[16–21,25]
4. Dietary supplements may present dangers to special populations (e.g., children, pregnant women, patients undergoing surgery, patients with impaired organ or immunologic function).
5. Spending on dietary supplements represents an enormous health-related expenditure of unsubstantiated value.[33]

Since the mid-19th century, the federal government has exercised its responsibility to protect Americans from hazardous or adulterated foods and medicines. ASHP believes that, with the passage and implementation of DSHEA, the federal government has abandoned its duty to create a regulatory scheme for dietary supplements that adequately protects the health of consumers. Under DSHEA, consumers and health care practitioners are not provided with the information they need to use dietary supplements safely. To reduce the dangers posed by the current regulatory framework, Congress should amend DSHEA to

1. Require that dietary supplements undergo FDA approval for evidence of safety and efficacy,
2. Mandate FDA-approved dietary supplement labeling that describes safe use in a clear, standardized format, including the potential for interaction with medications and cautions for special populations,
3. Require FDA to promulgate and enforce GMPs for dietary supplements,
4. Require that dietary supplements meet FDA-established standards for identity, strength, purity, and quality, and
5. Empower FDA to establish and maintain an adverse-event-reporting system specifically for dietary supplements, and require dietary supplement manufacturers to report suspected adverse reactions to FDA.

Implications for Practice

Although examples of persons rejecting potentially life-saving medical interventions in favor of alternative therapies can be found in the medical and lay press,[34] the presumption that most users of dietary supplements reject traditional treatments is unfounded. One survey found that most individuals who use alternative therapies for a specific symptom or disease are also receiving care and prescription medications from a physician or surgeon.[35] In a more recent nationwide survey, almost 20% of adults taking prescription drugs reported that they were taking at least one dietary supplement, not including vitamin or mineral supplements.[36]

Pharmacists and other health care practitioners therefore have an opportunity to reduce the risks associated with dietary supplement use. Health care providers face unfamiliar challenges in this effort, however, because much of the information they typically use to establish pharmaceutical treatment regimens is lacking for dietary supplements. Product content is not standardized, therapeutic goals are vague, and evidence of efficacy and safety is absent or ambiguous. ASHP believes that pharmacists, as medication-use experts and accessible members of the health care team, are uniquely qualified and positioned to counsel patients using or considering the use of dietary supplements. Despite their professional responsibility to provide patients with sound advice, pharmacists (like other health care providers) are frustrated by the lack of reliable information about the safety and efficacy of dietary supplements. Pharmacists have shown that they can improve medication safety by identifying and preventing adverse drug events,[37] and they could play a similar role in preventing adverse events due to dietary supplement use if they had sound, evidence-based professional resources.

Incorporate Awareness of Dietary Supplement Use into Practice. ASHP urges pharmacists and other health care practitioners to integrate awareness of dietary supplement use into everyday practice. ASHP believes that all health systems should have an institutional policy regarding the use of dietary supplements. Such policies should allow pharmacists and other health care practitioners to exercise their professional judgment and try to balance patient autonomy and institutional concerns.

Patient Counseling. Although most consumers of alternative therapies also take prescription medications,[35] one survey found that 72% of respondents who used alternative therapies did not report that use to their health care providers.[38] Pharmacists and other health care practitioners must therefore routinely inquire about a patient's current or planned use of dietary supplements, providing examples so that patients understand what is meant (e.g, asking "Do you use dietary supplements, such as St. John's wort or gingko?").[39] This information will allow pharmacists and other health care practitioners to counsel the patient about dietary supplement use and monitor for adverse reactions and drug interactions.

When counseling patients about dietary supplements, the concept of *caveat emptor* (buyer beware) must be emphasized because the content and safety of dietary supplements are not well regulated. ASHP believes that all pharmacists, at a minimum, should be familiar with the pharmacology and pharmacokinetics of common dietary supplements that might contraindicate concurrent use with a therapeutic regimen (i.e., proven and potential pharmacokinetic and pharmacodynamic interactions with prescription and nonprescription medications) to the extent that sound evidence exists. To provide informed counsel to patients using or considering the use of dietary supplements, pharmacists further need to be familiar with the following:

- The typical uses of common dietary supplements and the scientific literature regarding their efficacy and safety,
- The proven and potential interactions between common dietary supplements and prescription and nonprescription medications,
- The methods of therapeutic monitoring for common dietary supplements, including signs and symptoms of potential adverse effects and toxicities,
- The proven and potential effects of certain disease states on supplement absorption, distribution, and elimination, and
- The safety of using dietary supplements before or after surgery.

Despite the shortcomings of the data on dietary supplements, the limited references on the topic that are available should be consulted.[40–45]

Patients stabilized on a combination of a supplement and medication should be cautioned not to suddenly discontinue the use of either without first consulting with the prescriber. The potential for adverse effects from an interaction exists both when a dietary supplement is discontinued and when it is initiated.

Dietary supplement sales have a very high potential for profit. Despite the expectation that pharmacies should receive a profit from the sale of products, professional ethics mandate that any recommendations or purchasing suggestions be made with the well-being of the customer or patient as the primary concern. Pharmacists should also review promotional and reference materials promulgated in or by their workplaces to ensure that these materials are evidence based and not misleading or deceptive. The scientific literature about the safety and efficacy of dietary supplements is updated continually. Pharmacists have a responsibility to continually monitor that literature and incorporate the evolving knowledge into their care for and advice to patients.

Inclusion in Formularies. ASHP believes that the criteria used to evaluate dietary supplements for inclusion in health-system formularies should be as rigorous as those established for prescription and nonprescription drugs. The Joint Commission on Accreditation of Healthcare Organizations (JCAHO) has recommended that medical staff weigh the patient care implications of dietary supplements with the same rigor applied to prescription and nonprescription medications,[46] and all JCAHO medication management standards apply to dietary supplements, as well as prescription and nonprescription drugs.[47] ASHP believes that the decision to include any product in a health-system formulary should be based on comparative data regarding efficacy, adverse effects, cost, and potential therapeutic advantages and deficiencies.[48] The lack of definitive evidence of efficacy and safety and the demonstrated variability in product content make most dietary supplements unsuitable for inclusion in health-system formularies.[49] More research is needed to determine the relative effectiveness of dietary supplements and their safety for all patient populations, especially drug–supplement interactions.

The shortcomings that make most dietary supplements unsuitable for inclusion in formularies also argue strongly against their self-administered use by patients during a health-system stay. ASHP believes that the use of self-administered medications should be avoided to the extent possible[50] and that pharmacists should identify all drug products before their use.[15] There is currently no way to definitively determine the content of dietary supplements brought into health systems. In addition, discontinuing supplement use may be advisable as part of the diagnostic workup, and the possibility that supplement use may have contributed to hospitalization should be considered.

If an institution decides, as a matter of patient autonomy, to allow the use of dietary supplements, such use should require a prescribed order for the specific dietary supplement in the patient medical record and pharmacist review and verification of the order. Health systems should be aware that the use of dietary supplements may expose patients to risks, and the health system and staff should take steps to reduce potential liability (e.g., require patients to sign a liability waiver for dietary supplement use) and decrease those risks.

Conclusion

Current regulation of the manufacture and labeling of dietary supplements fails to address substantial risks to the public health. As the activity of some dietary supplements has become apparent, so have their dangers and the shortcomings of the current regulatory framework. These laws and regulations should be revised, with the primary goal of providing consumers and health care practitioners with the information they need to use dietary supplements safely and effectively. In short, dietary supplements should be regulated in a manner that ensures that they are safe and effective. Regardless of the shortcomings of the current regulatory framework, pharmacists have an opportunity and a professional responsibility to reduce the risks presented by dietary supplement use.

References

1. Dietary Supplement Health and Education Act of 1994 (SB 784). http://thomas.loc.gov/ (accessed 2003 Apr 1).
2. Gurley BJ, Wang P, Gardner SF. Ephedrine-type alkaloid content of nutritional supplements containing *Ephedra sinica* (Ma-huang) as determined by high performance liquid chromatography. *J Pharm Sci.* 1998; 87:1547–53.
3. Harkey MR, Henderson GL, Gershwin ME, et al. Variability in commercial ginseng products: an analysis of 25 preparations. *Am J Clin Nutr.* 2001; 73:1101–6.
4. Parasrampuria J, Schwartz K, Petesch R. Quality control of dehydroepiandrosterone dietary supplement products. *JAMA.* 1998; 280:1565. Letter.
5. Feifer AH, Fleshner NE, Klotz L. Analytical accuracy and reliability of commonly used nutritional supplements in prostate disease. *J Urol.* 2002; 168:150–4.
6. De los Reyes GC, Koda RT. Determining hyperforin and hypericin content in eight brands of St. John's wort. *Am J Health-Syst Pharm.* 2002; 59:545–7.
7. Glisson JK, Rogers HE, Abourashed EA, et al. Clinic at the health food store? Employee recommendations and product analysis. *Pharmacotherapy.* 2003; 23:64–72.
8. Gurley BJ, Gardner SF, Hubbard MA. Content versus label claims in ephedra-containing dietary supplements. *Am J Health-Syst Pharm.* 2000; 57:963–9.
9. Fontanarosa PB, Rennie D, DeAngelis CD. The need for regulation of dietary supplements—lessons from ephedra. *JAMA.* 2003; 289:1568–70. Editorial.

10. National Nutritional Foods Association. NNFA GMP certification program overview. www.nnfa.org/services/science/gmp.htm (accessed 2003 Dec 12).
11. U.S. Pharmacopeia. U.S. Pharmacopeia dietary supplement verification program. www.usp-verified.org (accessed 2004 May 13).
12. Food and Drug Administration. Current good manufacturing practice in manufacturing, packing, or holding dietary ingredients and dietary supplements. Proposed rule. *Fed Regist.* 2003; 68:12157–263.
13. *Pearson* v. *Shalala,* 164 F.3d 650 (D.C. Cir. 1999).
14. Food and Drug Administration. Illnesses and injuries associated with the use of selected dietary supplements. www. cfsan.fda.gov/~dms/ds-ill.html (accessed 2003 Feb 14).
15. Palmer ME, Haller C, McKinney PE, et al. Adverse events associated with dietary supplements: an observational study. *Lancet.* 2003; 361:101–6.
16. Williamson EM. Drug interactions between herbal and prescription medicines. *Drug Saf.* 2003; 26:1075–92.
17. Fugh-Berman A. Herb–drug interactions. *Lancet.* 2000; 355: 134–8.
18. Yue QY, Bergquist C, Gerdén B. Safety of St. John's wort *(Hypericum perforatum). Lancet.* 2000; 355:576–7. Letter.
19. Brazier NC, Levine MA. Drug–herb interaction among commonly used conventional medicines: a compendium for health care professionals. *Am J Ther.* 2003; 10:163–9.
20. Izzo AA, Ernst E. Interactions between herbal medicines and prescribed drugs: a systematic review. *Drugs.* 2001; 61:2163–75.
21. Piscitelli SC, Burstein AH, Chaitt D, et al. Indinavir concentrations and St. John's wort. *Lancet.* 2000; 355:547–8. Letter. [Erratum, *Lancet.* 2001;357:1210.]
22. Office of the Inspector General. Dietary supplement labels: key elements. Report OEI-01-01-00120. http://oig.hhs.gov/oei/reports/oei-01-01-00120.pdf (accessed 2004 May 13).
23. Annual overview of the nutrition industry VII. *Nutr Bus J.* 2002; 7(May/Jun):1–11.
24. Food and Drug Administration. Dietary supplements: warnings and safety information. www.cfsan.fda.gov/~dms/ds~warn.html (accessed 2004 May 21).
25. De Smet PA. Herbal remedies. *N Engl J Med.* 2002; 347:2046–56.
26. Blumenthal M, ed. The complete German Commission E monographs—therapeutic guide to herbal medicines. Austin, TX: American Botanical Council; 1998:116,125–6.
27. Nortier JL, Martinez MC, Schmeiser HH, et al. Urothelial carcinoma associated with the use of a Chinese herb (*Aristolochia fangchi*). *N Engl J Med.* 2000; 342:1686–92.
28. Shekelle PG, Hardy ML, Morton SC, et al. Efficacy and safety of ephedra and ephedrine for weight loss and athletic performance: a meta-analysis. *JAMA.* 2003; 289:1537–45.
29. Slifman NR, Obermeyer WR, Musser SM, et al. Contamination of botanical dietary supplements by *Digitalis lanata. N Engl J Med.* 1998; 339:806–11.
30. Food and Drug Administration. Letter to health care professionals: FDA concerned about botanical products, including dietary supplements, containing aristolochic acid. http://vm.cfsan.fda.gov/~dms/ds-botl2.html (accessed 2003 Apr 1).
31. De Smet PA. Toxicological outlook on the quality assurance of herbal remedies. In: De Smet PA, Keller K, Hansel R, et al., eds. Adverse effects of herbal drugs. Vol. 1. Berlin: Springer-Verlag; 1992:1–72.
32. De Smet PA. The safety of herbal products. In: Jonas WB, Levin JS, eds. Essentials of complementary and alternative medicine. Philadelphia: Lippincott Williams & Wilkins; 1999:108–47.
33. De Smet PA. Health risks of herbal remedies. *Drug Saf.* 1995; 13:81–93.
34. Eisenberg DM, Davis RB, Ettner SL, et al. Trends in alternative medicine use in the United States, 1990–1997: results of a follow-up national study. *JAMA.* 1998; 280:1569–75.
35. Astin JA. Why patients use alternative medicine: results of a national study. *JAMA.* 1998; 279:1548–53.
36. Kaufman DW, Kelly JP, Rosenberg L, et al. Recent patterns of medication use in the ambulatory adult population of the United States: the Slone survey. *JAMA.* 2002; 287:337–44.
37. Leape LL, Cullen DJ, Clapp M, et al. Pharmacist participation on physician rounds and adverse drug events in the intensive care unit. *JAMA.* 1999; 282:267–70.
38. Eisenberg DM, Kessler RC, Van Rompay MI, et al. Perceptions about complementary therapies relative to conventional therapies among adults who use both: results from a national survey. *Ann Intern Med.* 2001; 135:344–51.
39. Ang-Lee MK, Moss J, Yuan CS. Herbal medicines and perioperative care. *JAMA.* 2001; 286:208–16.
40. Chambliss WG, Hufford CD, Flagg ML, et al. Assessment of the quality of reference books on botanical dietary supplements. *J Am Pharm Assoc.* 2002; 42:723–34.
41. Haller CA, Anderson IB, Kim SY, et al. An evaluation of selected herbal reference texts and comparison to published reports of adverse herbal events. *Adverse Drug React Toxicol Rev.* 2002; 21:143–50.
42. Kemper KJ, Amata-Kynvi A, Sanghavi D, et al. Randomized trial of an internet curriculum on herbs and other dietary supplements for health care professionals. *Acad Med.* 2002; 77:882–9.
43. Sweet BV, Gay WE, Leady MA, et al. Usefulness of herbal and dietary supplement References. *Ann Pharmacother.* 2003; 37:494–9.
44. Office of Dietary Supplements. International Bibliographic Information on Dietary Supplements (IBIDS) database. http://ods.od.nih.gov/showpage.aspx? pageid=48 (accessed 2003 Dec 11).
45. Memorial Sloan-Kettering Cancer Center. AboutHerbs Web site. www.mskcc.org/mskcc/html/11570.cfm (accessed 2003 Dec 11).
46. Rich DS. Ask the Joint Commission: understanding JCAHO requirements for hospital pharmacies. St. Louis: Facts and Comparisons; 2002:132–3.
47. Medication management standards. In: Comprehensive accreditation manual for hospitals, 2004 update. Oakbrook Terrace, IL: Joint Commission on Accreditation of Healthcare Organizations; 2004:MM1–20.
48. American Society of Hospital Pharmacists. ASHP technical assistance bulletin on the evaluation of drugs for formularies. *Am J Hosp Pharm.* 1988; 45:386–7.

49. Ansani NT, Ciliberto NC, Freedy T. Hospital policies regarding herbal medicines. *Am J Health-Syst Pharm.* 2003; 60:367–70.
50. American Society of Hospital Pharmacists. ASHP technical assistance bulletin on hospital drug distribution and control. *Am J Hosp Pharm.* 1980; 37:1097–1103.
51. American Society of Health-System Pharmacists. ASHP guidelines: minimum standard for pharmacies in hospitals. *Am J Health-Syst Pharm.* 1995; 52:2711–7.

This statement was reviewed in 2014 by the Council on Pharmacy Practice and by the Board of Directors and was found to still be appropriate.

Approved by the ASHP Board of Directors on April 14, 2004, and by the ASHP House of Delegates on June 20, 2004. Developed through the ASHP Council on Professional Affairs. Supersedes ASHP policies 0223, 0304, and 0324.

The bibliographic citation for this document is as follows: American Society of Health-System Pharmacists. ASHP statement on the use of dietary supplements. *Am J Health-Syst Pharm.* 2004; 61:1707–11.

ASHP Guidelines on Emergency Medicine Pharmacist Services

Emergency medicine (EM) is an ever-changing, rapidly evolving practice specialty. The formal emergency department (ED) has its roots in the 1950s, when full-time emergency services were established in the United States.[1] Since then, the rate of mortality from accidental and traumatic injuries has significantly declined as a result of the development of regional trauma centers and improved training in the care of trauma patients.[2,3] The first descriptions of pharmacy services provided in the ED appeared in the 1970s.[4–6] These early reports detail services primarily related to medication distribution. Since that time, the literature has detailed the development of EM pharmacy services as they evolved to address changing needs in the ED.[7–23] In recent years, the number of EM pharmacists (EMPs) has dramatically increased,[24] likely as a result of several factors, including an increased focus on preventing medication errors in the ED and the EMP's role in error prevention, changing medication management standards from regulatory and accrediting agencies, and emerging literature on a variety of critical illnesses that emphasizes the need for early, goal-directed therapy. Furthermore, initial research indicates that ED health care providers highly value the services provided by EMPs.[25]

Purpose

In 2008, ASHP published a statement on services that the pharmacy department should provide to the ED.[26] These guidelines extend beyond the scope of that document and are intended to define the role of the EMP, to suggest goals for providing services to meet institution-specific needs, and to establish a definition of best practices for the ED. These guidelines are based on the primary literature, therapeutic and practice guidelines, national standards, and the consensus of experts in the field of EM pharmacy practice.

Two levels of EMP services are described: essential services, which should be the basis of the practice specialty, and desirable services, which would optimize pharmacotherapy outcomes through the highest level of practice, teaching, and research and should be considered in addition to essential services. The services are further delineated by either a direct patient care or an administrative focus.

The services provided by EMPs will depend on the level of services provided by the ED. Optimal EMP coverage would provide consistent pharmacy services through a physical presence in the ED 24 hours per day, seven days per week. However, such coverage is not possible in every institution, nor may it be ideal based on institutional needs. Coverage and services provided by EMPs will therefore vary from institution to institution and should be designed to best meet the needs of the institution's emergency and pharmacy departments. In concert with ED and pharmacy administrators and providers, each EMP should use his or her professional judgment to individually weigh the factors that determine which services should be provided. These factors include the patient populations served, the number of pharmacists and time dedicated to services provided to the ED, whether corresponding duties are required of EMPs in other areas of the hospital, and the extent of time provided for administrative duties and obligations outside the ED. Finally, it should be noted that the many services described in these guidelines could not be provided by a single EMP. When used in these guidelines, the phrase "the EMP" should not be interpreted to imply that a single EMP could or should be expected to provide every service detailed herein.

The target audience for these guidelines includes EMPs, health-system administrators, physicians, emergency nurses and other emergency clinical staff, accreditors, and regulators. In addition, pharmacists and health-system administrators may find these guidelines helpful in establishing new pharmacy services in the ED. Because some of these readers may not require as much detail as others, the services are briefly summarized in Appendix A. Those seeking more information should consult the appended list of recommended readings, references, and resources (Appendix B).

Essential Direct Patient Care Roles of EMPs

The essential direct patient care roles of EMPs include optimizing medication use through participation in direct patient care rounds, medication order review, medication therapy monitoring, participation in procedures that utilize high-risk medications, resuscitation, medication procurement and preparation, provision of medication information, and documentation of associated interventions.

Direct Patient Care Rounds. Because the large majority of medication errors occur in the prescribing and administration phases of the medication-use process, it is critical for EMPs to be involved in direct patient care activities, including medication selection and the prescribing process.[22,27–29] For the purposes of these guidelines, rounding is broadly defined as conducting bedside patient care evaluations; working as a visible, well-integrated member of the multidisciplinary ED team; and participating in traditional rounding services when applicable (e.g., in EDs with EM residency programs for physicians). When conducting patient care rounds, EMPs should focus on providing direct patient care; they will be most effective in doing this when physically present in the ED. EMPs, in collaboration with other ED providers, should be accountable for ensuring optimized medication therapy regimens and therapeutic outcomes based on emerging literature, treatment guidelines, and quality measures established by accrediting bodies. Depending on the number of patients seen in the ED and the number of pharmacists dedicated to the ED, EMPs should create a triage system to focus their patient care efforts on patients with critical illnesses or urgent needs, on high-risk patient populations, or on specific classes of medications most associated with medication errors.

Medication Order Review. Medication order review in the ED must comply with federal, state, and local regulations and accreditation requirements. The Joint Commission's standards state that all medication orders should undergo prospective order review by a pharmacist prior to administration of the medication to the patient, with three exceptions: (1) in an emergency situation, (2) if a delay in administration would harm the patient, and (3) if a licensed independent practitioner is present to oversee the ordering, preparation, and administration of the medication.[30] Although many medication orders in the ED fall under the above exceptions, the level of assessment during medication order review should be consistent with that provided for patients elsewhere in the hospital. The process through which ED medication orders are reviewed should be determined by each institution based on its needs, staffing structure, and systems, as well as the interpretation of requirements by regulatory and accrediting organizations.

The role of an EMP in medication order review will vary, depending on the number of patient visits per day, particularly during peak patient utilization; the hours of EMP coverage; and the method of medication order entry. The role of an EMP should not focus on the medication order review process alone but rather should parallel the role of other pharmacy specialists providing direct patient care services within the institution.[24,31–33] A process should be developed to ensure that other pharmacists are accountable to review those orders that are not reviewed by an EMP.[3] Medication order review by EMPs may be performed in a manner other than traditional medication order review. When at the bedside, an EMP is able to quickly complete a review of medication orders and make medication selection and dosing recommendations based on patient-specific factors. Having a physical presence in the ED provides EMPs with the information needed to prioritize patient orders based on need and time demands. To allow EMPs to review medication orders while maintaining a physical presence in the ED, institutions should consider employing portable hand-held technology for use by the ED patient care team, including EMPs.

The majority of medication orders in the ED are one-time orders, so an EMP's intervention is most valuable if performed prior to medication administration. Ideally, all orders for high-risk medications would receive prospective review, but optimal medication use in the ED requires a balance between ensuring patient safety and preventing delays in patient care. EMPs should develop a triage system to focus the medication order review process on high-risk medications, high-risk patient populations, and emergent situations. When evaluating medication orders, EMPs should focus on key factors such as appropriateness of the medication and dose, potential medication interactions, and patient-specific factors (e.g., age, weight, medication allergies, disease states, current clinical condition).[30] If time and other patient care activities allow, EMPs may be involved in the review process of routine medication orders, including cost-saving initiatives, formulary compliance, and therapeutic substitutions.

In an institution with computerized provider order entry (CPOE), centrally located or designated pharmacists could work collaboratively with the EMP to assist in the medication order review process for routine ED medication orders, as well as admitting orders for boarded patients. If time permits, EMP participation in CPOE medication database maintenance should also be considered. In an institution that relies on written medication orders, a process should be developed to address the medication order review process through collaboration between the pharmacy and emergency departments. An alert system should be developed to notify the EMP to any medication orders requiring immediate pharmacist intervention, while all other routine medication orders would be sent to the central pharmacy for review, processing, and preparation.

Medication Therapy Monitoring. The development and assessment of monitoring parameters related to medication therapy are essential steps in the medication-use process; they will determine whether the therapy selected was safe and effective, was suboptimal, or failed and whether changes to the regimen are needed. Research on pharmacist participation in monitoring medication therapy has demonstrated improved clinical outcomes in a variety of settings, including the treatment, management, and monitoring of chronic disease states such as diabetes mellitus, hypertension, and hyperlipidemia, and from therapeutic medication monitoring of antimicrobial and anticoagulant therapy in the hospital setting.[34–37]

Several medication classes administered in the ED exert an immediate therapeutic effect and therefore can be monitored shortly after administration. EMPs should be familiar with the pharmacokinetic parameters of medications commonly administered in the ED, as well as the recommended monitoring parameters associated with each therapeutic agent. Monitoring should also be provided for medications the patient has taken prior to arrival in the ED, whether administered by emergency medical services or by the patient as part of a home medication regimen. Medication therapy monitoring should include both subjective (e.g., patient-reported pain score) and objective (e.g., blood pressure, heart rate) elements.

EMPs should provide recommendations for monitoring parameters for both the effectiveness and safety of medications administered in the ED. Much of this assessment can be completed by EMPs and used in combination with information gathered from the patient's medical record. EMPs should subsequently suggest revisions to medication regimens based on the results of monitoring parameters and the established goals for therapy. In addition, EMPs should incorporate medication therapy monitoring parameters in the development of treatment protocols used in the ED, and they may provide education to other health care providers regarding appropriate monitoring of medication therapies.

Patient Care Involving High-Risk Medications and Procedures. A number of high-risk medications and procedures are utilized in the ED. A procedure may be considered high risk for a variety of reasons. Procedures performed on patients considered at high risk due to critical illness or instability may qualify, or the procedure may involve medications with a narrow therapeutic index or with serious potential for adverse effects (i.e., high-alert medications).[38] EMPs should be present at the bedside to assist in the delivery of patient care involving high-risk medications or procedures. Participation should include assisting in the appropriate selection of medications and corresponding doses, preparation of medications, and patient monitoring.

EMPs should also participate in efforts to improve the safety of procedures that utilize high-risk medications. EMPs should evaluate current processes associated with the use of high-risk medications and should assist in the development of processes and systems to improve current practices and prevent potential harm and errors. The EMP's role may include assisting in the development of policies and protocols, with a focus on appropriate medication selection, use, monitoring, and management. Several recommendations for reducing errors associated with high-risk medications and procedures have been suggested.[29,39–41] For example, use of medication infusion systems with smart infusion technology software and double checks on high-alert medications may be considered.[39,40] In addition, EMPs should provide education and training related to high-risk medications to ED health care providers.

Resuscitation. EMPs should be present during all resuscitations in the ED. Initial evaluations of the role of EMPs in the resuscitation of trauma patients have revealed improved patient safety by decreasing preventable adverse medication events and expedited time to medication administration.[7,42–44] The role of EMPs in resuscitation may vary, depending on such factors as the clinical scenario or the practice setting, but may involve preparing medications for immediate administration; ensuring appropriate medication selection and dose; ensuring appropriate administration of medications; obtaining medications that are not readily available in the ED; making recommendations for alternative routes of administration when appropriate; answering medication information questions; assisting physicians with differential diagnosis, particularly when related to a potential medication-related cause; and completing resuscitation documentation.[45,46] In addition, EMPs should ensure that processes are in place to maintain an appropriate and readily available supply of emergency medications in the ED.

Toxicologic emergencies present resuscitation scenarios in which the knowledge of EMPs is highly valuable. Pharmacist involvement in toxicologic emergencies has been described for more than 30 years.[47,48] EMPs should be familiar with the recognition and treatment of patients experiencing a toxicologic emergency, including recognition of characteristic physical signs and symptoms noted in the physical examination, laboratory parameters, and other diagnostic evaluations (e.g., toxidromes), that can result from a wide range of substances, including prescription and over-the-counter medications, illicit drugs, natural occurring poisons (e.g., those from plants, mushrooms, or envenomations), and various chemicals.[49] When a patient with a suspected toxicologic emergency presents to the ED, EMPs should assist in obtaining a thorough and accurate medication history and a history of present illness, as well as in identifying potential causative agents; should assist in the selection and administration of specific antidotes and other supportive therapies; may assist in the preparation of antidotes; and should provide recommendations for monitoring antidote effectiveness and safety. These services should be provided in collaboration with clinical and medical toxicologists, when available, or local and regional poison control centers. Finally, EMPs should serve as a resource to the pharmacy department in ensuring that an adequate inventory of toxicologic antidotes is available in the institution.[50]

In preparing to become a member of the resuscitation team, EMPs should seek out training and certification in the conditions applicable to their practice settings. Several training opportunities and certification programs are available, including but not limited to the American Stroke Association National Institutes of Health Stroke Scale, American Heart Association (AHA) Basic Life Support (BLS), AHA Advanced Cardiac Life Support (ACLS), AHA Pediatric Advanced Life Support (PALS), American College of Surgeons Advanced Trauma Life Support, American Academy of Clinical Toxicology Advanced HAZMAT Life Support (AHLS), and board certification as a Diplomate of the American Board of Applied Toxicology (DABAT). At a minimum, all EMPs should achieve and maintain up-to-date certification in BLS, ACLS, and PALS.

Medication Procurement and Preparation. Medication procurement in the ED presents challenges that differ significantly from those in other areas of the hospital. Because of the urgent treatment needs of patients in the ED, several critical medications must be readily available. EMPs should be an integral part of the medication procurement and preparation process for medications used in the ED, as dispensing medications is one of the five stages of the medication-use process that EMPs can impact to prevent medication errors.[29] EMPs may serve as consultants to the pharmacy department and ED regarding the development or revision of processes associated with medication procurement, or they may play a more active role in medication procurement and preparation.

The options available for medication procurement vary widely among EDs and depend on such factors as patient volume and acuity, the physical limitations of the ED, and processes established by the pharmacy department. Medications may be available in automated dispensing cabinets, in emergency kits, from the inpatient central pharmacy department, or from a satellite pharmacy within the ED. A satellite pharmacy with compounding ability may best serve the needs of an ED by providing prompt preparation of medications, though this is not considered a requirement. While a sterile room for preparation of intravenous medications may not be a possibility for most EDs, a laminar flow hood would aid in the preparation of most intravenous medication requests. In an ED with no satellite pharmacy, the central pharmacy should have processes in place to assist with rapid preparation and delivery of medications.[26] In this model, EMPs should work with the central pharmacy to ensure understanding of urgent medication needs. Finally, EMPs should be competent and responsible for preparation of medications needed for emergency use at the bedside as an exception to the *United States Pharmacopeia* 797 standards.[51] Competency should include methods of compounding, knowledge of potential medication interactions, intravenous medication compatibility, rates of administration, and skill in using references on these topics.

A full review of medications used in the ED, including commonly used medications, high-risk medications, and antidotes, should be performed regularly (e.g., annually or as required by institution policy). EMPs should be involved in the decision-making process regarding which medications will be made available immediately within the ED.[52] Medications identified as appropriate and necessary for frequent use in the ED should be stored in automated dispensing cabinets or another location as designated safe by the institution, with appropriate alerts to prevent medication errors.[52] EMPs may assist in the evaluation and management of these medications, including monitoring for appropriate usage, inventory levels, and medication storage according to both hospital and regulatory body requirements. Optimization of available medications should be based on changes in prescribing practices, guideline or protocol recommendations, medication availability, and formulary changes. Inventory and storage replacement should be maintained by technician support and should not be the responsibility of EMPs.

Finally, EMPs should be involved with the institution's formulary review and process-improvement committees to assist with medication reviews of new formulary agents and for revisions to the current formulary regarding medications used in the ED. Further, data from medication-use evaluations, safety monitoring, and monitoring for adherence to national quality indicators should be used to assist in evaluating medication procurement and preparation processes.

Medication Information. The most common cause of medication errors is a lack of information related to medication therapy.[53] Provision of medication information is therefore a vital role in the practice of all pharmacists, including EMPs. Numerous studies in the ED demonstrate that medication information is an important service provided by EMPs.[9,10,25,54] A survey of pharmacy departments revealed that only 50.4% of respondents provide medication information services to the ED.[54] In addition, ED health care providers report that they are more likely to utilize the resources of a pharmacist when that pharmacist is located in the ED rather than the central pharmacy department.[25] These statistics suggest a strong role in medication information for the EMP.

The medication information needs of the ED cover a broad spectrum of clinical scenarios and may include questions related to medication selection, dose, and administration; adverse medication reactions; intravenous compatibility; medication interactions; and identification of unknown medications.[55] EMPs should ensure that access to appropriate primary, secondary, and tertiary references is available as needed to respond to medication information requests. EMPs must be able to quickly and accurately retrieve the answers to medication information questions using readily available resources, programs for personal digital assistants, textbooks, or electronic resources to provide urgently needed medication information.

Documentation. Research on pharmacist interventions in the inpatient setting has demonstrated improvement in patient outcomes through optimized pharmacotherapy regimens, improved monitoring of medication therapy, and avoidance of adverse medication events.[36] In addition, pharmacist participation in patient care has been shown to significantly reduce the costs associated with medication therapy.[56,57] Research has detailed EMP interventions in the ED, describing improvements to the medication-use process and patient care by EMPs recommending improvements in medication therapy, serving as a medication information resource, and improving patient safety.[4,5,9,11,13,18,20,22,58] Several of these publications have shown dramatic cost avoidance.[8,17,19,21,23] More detailed studies on the role of EMPs in managing specific disease states and a definitive evaluation of improvement in patient outcomes are needed.

EMPs should be diligent in documenting interventions provided during patient care and other activities (e.g., education). They should regularly review intervention documentation to identify trends, which may indicate a need to educate ED health care providers or change medication-use procedures. Finally, cost-avoidance documentation may provide the justification needed for further expansion of EMP services.

Health care institutions should support EMPs by providing the means to document interventions. Different media have been used to document interventions, including personal digital assistants, software programs on institutional intranets, and manual paper systems.[59–64] Electronic systems offer more complete, readily retrievable documentation and shorter entry times than manual systems, without the risk of loss associated with paper records.[65,66] In addition, electronic documentation systems offer the benefit of associating cost avoidance with the documented intervention.[19] Although determining true cost avoidance can be difficult, there is research available to provide some guidance for quantifying the cost avoidance of pharmacist interventions.[6,10,56,57,67–69] In addition to these benefits, electronic documentation of EMP interventions may improve communication with other health care providers caring for the patient after admission (e.g., "hand-off") if the documentation system allows the documentation to follow the patient.

Desirable Direct Patient Care Roles of EMPs

Desirable direct patient care roles of EMPs include the care of boarded patients, obtaining medication histories, and medication reconciliation.

Care of Boarded Patients. ED overcrowding is a common occurrence.[70,71] Not only are more patients seeking primary care services in the ED, but a significant number of EDs have closed over the past decade, increasing ED patient volumes.[72,73] Because there are many obstacles and processes that hinder the timely transfer of admitted patients from the ED to an inpatient bed,[74] overcrowding in the ED often results in bottlenecks that force EDs to provide care to patients for long periods of time while they await admission or physical transfer to an inpatient bed or to another institution for a different level of care ("boarding").[75] The needs of a boarded patient can vary from simple requests for as-needed medications to such complex needs as critical care management.

Processes should be developed, based on institutional resources, to designate the pharmacist who will be accountable for providing care to boarded patients (i.e., an EMP or the pharmacist assigned to the area to which the patient will be admitted). The EMP's primary role in ensuring the safety and effectiveness of the medication-use process of the ED should not be compromised to provide care for boarded patients if alternatives exist. When staffing levels are insufficient (e.g., when only a single EMP is present in the ED) or when the boarding area is physically separated from the ED, the responsibility of caring for boarded patients should be assigned to the inpatient pharmacist. (Ideally, to ensure continuity of care, the inpatient pharmacist would be the same pharmacist responsible for providing care to the patient after admission.) The services provided to boarded patients by EMPs will depend on the level of services offered by the institution. At a minimum, EMPs should review the medication profile of critical patients, with a focus on high-risk medications, medication dosing and procurement, and monitoring, as necessary. When it is necessary to initiate an admitting order for a boarded patient, the responsible pharmacist should review medications administered in the ED and those taken prior to arrival at the ED to prevent duplications in therapy.

Medication Histories and Medication Reconciliation. Research on medication reconciliation has identified several barriers to obtaining an accurate medication history in the ED.[76–82] In many cases, ED staff are required to contact multiple sources, including primary care physician offices, pharmacies, and family members, to obtain a medication history, and even these burdensome efforts may not result in an accurate home medication list. There have been significant changes in medication reconciliation practices, with the most recent recommendations from The Joint Commission that complete medication reconciliation needs only be performed by the receiving unit for patients admitted to the hospital and that "screening" reconciliations be performed in the ED, unless otherwise requested by the treating physician.[30]

Although research has shown that pharmacists are the providers who obtain the most accurate home medication list,[83–85] dedicating a pharmacist solely to medication reconciliation is not the best allocation of pharmacist resources in the ED. EMPs should assist in the development and implementation of a risk-stratification protocol for identifying and determining which ED patients need a medication history. In general, medication histories may be obtained for patients with known or suspected toxicologic emergencies, with known or suspected adverse events from home medications, or with complicated medication histories that will influence ED clinical decision-making.

Auxiliary pharmacy staff (pharmacy students hired through work/study programs and pharmacy technicians) can also be effective in obtaining accurate home medication histories; when possible, they should be incorporated into medication reconciliation procedures.[86–89] Quality reviews of medication histories completed by pharmacy technicians should be conducted to assess accuracy and to provide guidance for further training opportunities.

Essential Administrative Roles of EMPs

The administrative duties of EMPs will vary, depending on such factors as the availability of other EMPs to provide direct patient care activities in the ED or to distribute committee involvement among other EMPs. The essential administrative roles of EMPs include involvement in medication and patient safety initiatives, quality-improvement activities, professional leadership, and emergency preparedness.

For EMPs to succeed in fulfilling their administrative responsibilities without compromising patient care in the ED, pharmacy management must provide support that will allow EMPs to participate in committee meetings, pursue related projects, and develop proposals with action plans. Ideally, another pharmacist would be made available to provide coverage for direct patient care activities in the ED.

Medication and Patient Safety. EMPs play an important role in monitoring and ensuring patient and medication safety in the ED. The environment of the ED is naturally at high risk for patient and medication safety lapses. EMPs should encourage and assist in maintaining a safe environment for medication and patient safety, which should be continuously reviewed for potential process improvements. This review can include proactive and continuous monitoring of medication practices; identification of errors and high-risk medications for monitoring; addressing hazardous conditions with potential for harm; and documentation and review of medication errors, adverse medication events, and near misses.[22,27,28,90]

Medication errors that occur in the ED should be reviewed by EMPs in collaboration with other health care providers and hospital executives to identify potential sources of error, contributing factors related to the error, and potential solutions for preventing similar errors. Performance of a root cause analysis could identify potential error trends or system failures and contribute to the development of safe medication practices and processes for prevention of future events. In addition, a review of medication errors should result in education and future policy or guideline development. Finally, EMPs should be responsible for the development and provision of education to ED health care providers on the source of the error, the risks associated with the error, and ways to prevent similar errors in the future.

Quality-Improvement Initiatives. As a practitioner in the ED setting, an EMP is able to recognize those aspects of patient care, medication safety, compliance with hospital and regulatory policies, and adherence to national practice recommendations and guidelines that could be improved. EMPs or other pharmacy representatives should be extensively involved with quality-improvement initiatives in the ED. Involvement with a multidisciplinary committee of ED health care providers and hospital administrators will provide EMPs with an avenue for improving the quality of care in the ED.

EMPs should participate in ongoing efforts to optimize pharmacotherapy regimens through medication-use evaluations and through the development and implementation of medication-use guidelines and pathways. A medication-use evaluation may be beneficial in reviewing medications commonly used in the ED, as well as those medications associated with errors.[91,92] The results of a medication-use evaluation can be used to further guide education for other ED health care providers.

Leadership Duties and Professional Service. The leadership role of EMPs should include responsibilities to both the pharmacy department and ED. Involvement in administrative processes of both departments allows EMPs to serve as a liaison between the groups to support joint endeavors. This role would ideally include participation in departmental meetings, medication-use committees, quality-improvement and process-improvement committees, medication safety committees, and research meetings for both departments. Involvement in such meetings ensures that the needs of both departments are met and provides EMPs with an avenue for improving both patient care and medication use. In addition, involvement in ED-specific research projects increases pharmacy involvement, pharmacy publication and recognition, and grant funding potential.

Membership and active participation in local, state, and national professional pharmacy organizations are essential for the continued growth of the practice of EM pharmacy. As a relatively young area of practice, EM pharmacy is continually developing and growing. One way to support this development and strengthen the presence of EM pharmacy is through participation in professional organizations. At the local level, EMPs may collaborate to develop a local support network for training and research and can provide new practitioners with avenues for learning. At the state level, legislative and professional advocacy may help educate government officials and other health care professionals about EM pharmacy practice. At the national level, collaboration among EMPs increases the strength as a group, serves to challenge existing programs to improve, assists new programs in their development, and allows collaboration as a group to affect the stature, practice, and further development of EM pharmacy practice. A final source of support for the development of the profession is involvement with national EM organizations. Traditionally designed for physicians, nurses, and emergency medical technicians, EM organizations provide an avenue for education, networking, and publication for EMPs.

Emergency Preparedness. As experts in pharmacology and toxicology, EMPs have the skills and knowledge to serve as active participants in emergency situations, such as natural disasters; disease outbreaks; biological, radiological, or chemical exposures; and acts of terrorism. It is essential that EMPs, in conjunction with the department of pharmacy, participate in emergency preparedness planning.[93,94] Planning and involvement should occur at a minimum at the institutional level, with participation potentially expanding to include local, state, and national emergency preparedness efforts. Knowledge of local, state, and national emergency preparedness plans, programs, and support systems is paramount in the development of institution-specific emergency preparedness plans. These plans and programs should be used to develop recommendations and policies regarding decontamination, medication acquisition, stockpiles, storage, distribution, and use.[93]

Actively participating in emergency preparedness events will strengthen the knowledge and skills EMPs need to effectively lead in emergency situations. EMPs and executives in the pharmacy department should work together in the development of pharmacy-specific plans to coincide with institution-specific plans. Education of ED and pharmacy staff related to emergency preparedness should be among the responsibilities of EMPs.

To further develop strengths in emergency preparedness, EMPs should seek out training and certification in emergency preparedness, such as certification for AHLS, Basic Disaster Life Support, Advanced Disaster Life Support, and the National Incident Management System.

Desirable Administrative Roles of EMPs

Education of pharmacists and other health care providers, pharmacy students and residents, and ED patients and their caregivers and participation in research are desirable administrative roles for EMPs.

Education. The role of EMPs in education can be variable and broad, and it has been mentioned in conjunction with other responsibilities throughout these guidelines. It is desirable for EMPs to participate in the education of other health care providers, including pharmacists and pharmacy staff, pharmacy students, pharmacy residents, physicians, medical residents, midlevel practitioners, nurses, and emergency medical support personnel. The types and levels of education will vary with patient care and administrative workload.

Provision of education to ED health care staff should, at a minimum, include information on the appropriate use of medications, improvement in quality and effective medication use, and patient and medication safety. Education may include formal sessions (e.g., in-service or didactic presentation at a conference) or participation in courses such as BLS, ACLS, or PALS. Participation in formal education sessions may strengthen the relationship with other ED health care providers and serves as a method of continuous learning for EMPs. Informal education may also be provided through interaction in the ED, particularly at the bedside, which is a time-efficient, effective tool for education of staff.

Participation in the didactic and experiential education of doctor of pharmacy students is also a desirable activity that supports the development of the profession. Precepting pharmacy residents in EM learning experiences supports the overall development of direct patient care practitioners and provides exposure to the practice of EM pharmacy. To support the continued development of EM pharmacy services, the development of EM residency training programs is highly desirable. With the expansion of EM pharmacy service locations and hours and the increasing role of EMPs in administrative activities, the need for additional qualified pharmacists increases. New EMPs should focus on developing current services with plans to develop advanced (e.g., postgraduate year two) residency training programs after the program is established and the practice experience is significant. Additionally, education and development of currently practicing pharmacists are desirable, as education and development of existing pharmacists will provide additional EMP coverage.

Having medication therapy expertise, EMPs are uniquely qualified to provide medication education and information to patients and their caregivers in the ED and should play a key role in the delivery of medication information. In some cases, the education of ED patients and their families and caregivers may be independently considered among the essential roles of the EMP. EMPs may develop a system of triage for patient education so that counseling is focused on patients who will be discharged from the ED with a new or high-risk medication or on patients whose visit to the ED was the result of a medication adverse event or error. In addition to developing a triage system for identifying the patients with the greatest need for education, EMPs may also rely on other ED health care providers to identify patients in need of medication education. The medication education provided to patients and caregivers in the ED is diverse and may include information related to the use of a new device, the importance of medication adherence, or a potential adverse medication event. Education can include oral or written materials and should be documented in the patient's medical record. EMPs should confirm patient and caregiver understanding of the medication education provided.

Research and Scholarly Activity. The Institute of Medicine has described three aspects of emergency care research.[95] These aspects include EM research, defined as research conducted in either the prehospital or ED setting by EM specialists; trauma and injury control research, defined as the research of the acute management of traumatic injury; and research contributions that affect the ED but are attributed to other practice specialties. EM research can be further subdivided into basic science, clinical, and health services research. A number of research priorities in the prehospital and ED settings have been described.[96–100]

There is also an urgent need for research in EM pharmacy, both for pharmacotherapy and pharmacy practice. Such research would be facilitated by the development of a practice-based research network, which is a group of practitioners located locally, regionally, or nationally that collaborates on pursuits of scholarly activity.[101] Practice research networks can be effective, as a larger group of researchers represents a larger patient population that is more diverse than a single medical center. Practice-based research networks have been successful in other areas of practice and among a wide variety of health care practitioners, including interdisciplinary health care teams.

The role of the pharmacist in research has been described and can be applied to the ED setting.[102,103] EMPs may participate in ongoing clinical and practice-based research being conducted in the institution, including identifying a research question, providing assistance with patient recruitment and randomization, assisting with research medications, and completing data collection and analysis. EMPs could also assist in securing funding for conducting research in the ED, and, after the completion of research projects, EMPs could participate in the scholarly activities related to research efforts.

Conclusion

EMPs provide many vital services within the ED. The central role of the EMP is to improve patient outcomes by improving patient safety, preventing medication errors, and providing optimized pharmacotherapy regimens and therapeutic outcomes through participation in direct patient care activities and quality-improvement initiatives in the ED. In addition, EMPs can provide education to members of the pharmacy department and other health care providers, as well as patients and their caregivers, and EMPs may participate in research and scholarly activities in the ED.

References

1. Institute of Medicine of the National Academies Committee on the Future of Emergency Care in the United States Health System. Historical development of hospital-based emergency and trauma care. In: Hospital-based emergency care: at the breaking point. Washington, DC: National Academy Press; 2006:353–64.
2. Cales RH, Trunkey DD. Preventable trauma deaths. A review of trauma care systems development. *JAMA.* 1985; 254:1059–63.
3. Gruen RL, Jurkovich GJ, McIntyre LK, et al. Patterns of errors contributing to trauma mortality: lessons learned from 2,594 deaths. *Ann Surg.* 2006; 244:371–80.
4. Elenbaas RM, Waeckerle JF, McNabney WK. The clinical pharmacist in emergency medicine. *Am J Hosp Pharm.* 1977; 34:843–6.
5. Elenbaas RM. Role of the pharmacist in providing clinical pharmacy services in the emergency department. *Can J Hosp Pharm.* 1978; 31:123–5.
6. Spigiel RW, Anderson RJ. Comprehensive pharmaceutical services for the emergency room. *Am J Hosp Pharm.* 1979; 36:52–6.
7. Patanwala AE, Hays D. Pharmacist's activities on a trauma response team in the emergency department. *Am J Health-Syst Pharm.* 2010; 67:1536–8.
8. Fairbanks RJ, Hays DP, Webster DF, et al. Clinical pharmacy services in an emergency department. *Am J Health-Syst Pharm.* 2004; 61:934–7.
9. Wymore ES, Casanova TJ, Broekemeier RL, et al. Clinical pharmacist's daily role in the emergency department of a community hospital. *Am J Health-Syst Pharm.* 2008; 65:395–6, 398–9.
10. Whalen FJ. Cost justification of decentralized pharmaceutical services for the emergency room. *Am J Hosp Pharm.* 1981; 38:684–7.
11. Culbertson V, Anderson RJ. Pharmacist involvement in emergency room services. *Contemp Pharm Pract.* 1981; 4:167–76.
12. Powell MF, Solomon DK, McEachen RA. Twenty-four hour emergency pharmaceutical services. *Am J Hosp Pharm.* 1985; 42:831–5.
13. Kasuya A, Bauman JL, Curtis RA, et al. Clinical pharmacy on-call program in the emergency department. *Am J Emerg Med.* 1986; 4:464–7.
14. Schauben JL. Comprehensive emergency pharmacy services. *Top Hosp Pharm Manage.* 1988; 8:20–8.
15. Laivenieks N, McCaul K, O'Brodovich M. Clinical pharmacy services provided to an emergency department. *Can J Hosp Pharm.* 1992; 45:113–5.
16. Berry NS, Folstad JE, Bauman JL, et al. Clinical pharmacy services provided to an emergency department. *Ann Pharmacother.* 1992; 26:476–80.
17. Levy DB. Documentation of clinical and cost-saving pharmacy interventions in the emergency room. *Hosp Pharm.* 1993; 28:630–4, 653.
18. Mialon PJ, Williams P, Wiebe RA. Clinical pharmacy services in a pediatric emergency department. *Hosp Pharm.* 2004; 39:121–4.
19. Ling JM, Mike LA, Rubin J, et al. Documentation of pharmacist interventions in the emergency department. *Am J Health-Syst Pharm.* 2005; 62:1793–7.
20. Weant KA, Sterling E, Winstead PS, et al. Establishing a pharmacy presence in the ED. *Am J Emerg Med.* 2006; 24:514–5.
21. Lada P, Delgado G Jr. Documentation of pharmacists' interventions in an emergency department and associated cost avoidance. *Am J Health-Syst Pharm.* 2007; 64:63–8.
22. Brown JN, Barnes CL, Beasley B, et al. Effect of pharmacists on medication errors in an emergency department. *Am J Health-Syst Pharm.* 2008; 65:330–3.
23. Aldridge VE, Park HK, Bounthavong M, et al. Implementing a comprehensive, 24-hour emergency department pharmacy program. *Am J Health-Syst Pharm.* 2009; 66:1943–7.
24. Pederson CA, Schneider PJ, Scheckelhoff DJ. ASHP national survey of pharmacy practice in hospital settings: dispensing and administration—2008. *Am J Health-Syst Pharm.* 2009; 66:926–46.
25. Fairbanks RJ, Hildebrand JM, Kolstee KE, et al. Medical and nursing staff highly value clinical pharmacists in the emergency department. *Emerg Med J.* 2007; 24:716–8.
26. American Society of Health-System Pharmacists. ASHP statement on pharmacy services to the emer-

gency department. *Am J Health-Syst Pharm.* 2008; 65:2380–3.

27. Patanwala AE, Warholak TL, Sanders AB, et al. A prospective observational study of medication errors in a tertiary care emergency department. *Ann Emerg Med.* 2010; 55:522–6.
28. Flynn EA, Barker K, Barker B. Medication-administration errors in an emergency department. *Am J Health-Syst Pharm.* 2010; 67:347–8.
29. Peth HA. Medication errors in the emergency department: a systems approach to minimizing risk. *Emerg Med Clin N Am.* 2003; 21:141–58.
30. The Joint Commission. 2011 comprehensive accreditation manual for hospitals: the official handbook. Oakbrook Terrace, IL: Joint Commission Resources; 2011.
31. Bond CA, Raehl CL, Franke T. Clinical pharmacy services and hospital mortality rates. *Pharmacotherapy.* 1999; 19:556–64.
32. Bond CA, Raehl CL. Clinical pharmacy services, pharmacy staffing, and hospital mortality rates. *Pharmacotherapy.* 2007; 27:481–93.
33. Bond CA, Raehl CL. Clinical pharmacy services, pharmacy staffing, and adverse drug reactions in United States hospitals. *Pharmacotherapy.* 2006; 26:735–47.
34. Tully MP, Seston EM. Impact of pharmacists providing a prescription review and monitoring service in ambulatory care or community practice. *Ann Pharmacother.* 2000; 34:1320–31.
35. Coast-Senior EA, Kroner BA, Kelley CL, et al. Management of patients with type 2 diabetes by pharmacists in primary care clinics. *Ann Pharmacother.* 1998; 32:636–41.
36. Kaboli PJ, Hoth AB, McClimon BJ, et al. Clinical pharmacist and inpatient medical care: a systematic review. *Arch Intern Med.* 2006; 166:955–64.
37. Chisholm-Burns MA, Graff Zivin JS, Lee JK, et al. Economic effects of pharmacists on health outcomes in the United States: a systematic review. *Am J Health-Syst Pharm.* 2010; 67:1624–34.
38. Institute for Safe Medication Practices. ISMP's list of high-alert medications (2008). www.ismp.org/Tools/highalertmedications.pdf (accessed 2010 Oct 20).
39. The Joint Commission. High-alert medications and patient safety. *Sentinel Event Alert.* 1999; 11:1–3.
40. Wilson K, Sullivan M. Preventing medication errors with smart infusion technology. *Am J Health-Syst Pharm.* 2004; 61:177–83.
41. Federico F. Preventing harm from high-alert medications. *Jt Comm J Qual Patient Saf.* 2007; 33:537–42.
42. Kalina M, Tinkoff G, Gleason W, et al. A multidisciplinary approach to adverse drug events in pediatric trauma patients in an adult trauma center. *Pediatr Emerg Care.* 2009; 25:444–6.
43. Kelly-Pisciotti SJ, Hays DP, O'Brien TE, et al. Pharmacists enhancing patient safety during trauma resuscitations. Presented at the American Society of Health-System Pharmacists Midyear Clinical Meeting. Las Vegas, NV: Dec 2009.
44. Acquisto NM, Hays DP, Fairbanks RJ, et al. The outcomes of emergency pharmacist participation during acute myocardial infarction. *J Emerg Med.* Epub ahead of print. 2010 Aug 31 (DOI 10.1016/j.jemermed.2010.6.011).
45. Draper HM, Eppert JA. Association of pharmacist presence on compliance with advanced cardiac life support guidelines during in-hospital cardiac arrest. *Ann Pharmacother.* 2008; 42:469–74.
46. Shimp LA, Mason NA, Toedter NM, et al. Pharmacist participation in cardiopulmonary resuscitation. *Am J Health-Syst Pharm.* 1995; 52:980–4.
47. Czajka PA, Skoutakis VA, Wood GC, et al. Clinical toxicology consultation by pharmacists. *Am J Hosp Pharm.* 1979; 36:1087–9.
48. Roberts RW, Russell WL. A pharmacist-based toxicology service. 1978. *Ann Pharmacother.* 2007; 41:1719–24.
49. Bronstein AC, Spyker DA, Cantilena LR, et al. 2008 annual report of the American Association of Poison Control Centers' National Poison Data System (NPDA): 26th annual report. *Clin Tox.* 2009; 47:911–1084.
50. Dart RC, Borron SW, Caravati EM, et al. Expert consensus guidelines for stocking antidotes in hospitals that provide emergency care. *Ann Emerg Med.* 2009; 54:386–94.
51. U.S. Pharmacopeial Convention. USP <797> guidebook to pharmaceutical compounding—sterile preparations. 2nd ed. Rockville, MD: U.S. Pharmacopeial Convention; 2008.
52. American Society of Health-System Pharmacists. ASHP guidelines on the safe use of automated dispensing devices. *Am J Health-Syst Pharm.* 2010; 67:483–90.
53. Leape LL, Bates DW, Cullen DJ, et al. Systems analysis of adverse drug events. *JAMA.* 1995; 274:35–43.
54. Thomasset KB, Faris R. Survey of pharmacy services provision in the emergency department. *Am J Health-Syst Pharm.* 2003; 60:1561–4.
55. Rosenberg JM, Koumis T, Nathan JP, et al. Current status of pharmacist-operated drug information centers in the United States. *Am J Health-Syst Pharm.* 2004; 61:2023–32.
56. McMullin ST, Hennenfent JA, Ritchie DJ, et al. A prospective, randomized trial to assess the cost impact of pharmacist-initiated interventions. *Arch Intern Med.* 1999; 159:2306–9.
57. Kinky DE, Erush SC, Laskin MS, et al. Economic impact of a drug information service. *Ann Pharmacother.* 1999; 33:11–6.
58. Rothschild JM, Churchill W, Erickson A, et al. Medication errors discovered by emergency department pharmacists. *Ann Emerg Med.* 2010; 55:513–21.
59. Reilly JC, Wallace M, Campbell MM. Tracking pharmacist interventions with a hand-held computer. *Am J Health-Syst Pharm.* 2001; 58:158–61.
60. Silva MA, Tataronis GR, Maas B. Using personal digital assistants to document pharmacist cognitive services and estimate potential reimbursement. *Am J Health-Syst Pharm.* 2003; 60:911–5.
61. Simonian AI. Documenting pharmacist interventions on an intranet. *Am J Health-Syst Pharm.* 2003; 60:151–5.
62. Lau A, Balen RM, Lam R, et al. Using a personal digital assistant to document clinical pharmacy services in

an intensive care unit. *Am J Health-Syst Pharm.* 2001; 58:1229–32.

63. Bosinski TJ, Campbell L, Schwartz S. Using a personal digital assistant to document pharmacotherapeutic interventions. *Am J Health-Syst Pharm.* 2004; 61:931–4.
64. Mason RN, Pugh CB, Boyer SB, et al. Computerized documentation of pharmacists' interventions. *Am J Hosp Pharm.* 1994; 51:2131–8.
65. Schumock GT, Hutchinson RA, Bilek BA. Comparison of two systems for documenting pharmacist interventions in patient care. *Am J Hosp Pharm.* 1992; 49:2211–4.
66. Zimmerman CR, Smolarek RT, Stevenson JG. A computerized system to improve documentation and reporting of pharmacists' clinical interventions, cost savings, and workload activities. *Pharmacotherapy.* 1995; 15:220–7.
67. Mutnick AH, Sterba KJ, Peroutka JA, et al. Cost savings and avoidance from clinical interventions. *Am J Health-Syst Pharm.* 1997; 54:392–6.
68. Schneider PJ, Gift MG, Lee YP, et al. Cost of medication-related problems at a university hospital. *Am J Health-Syst Pharm.* 1995; 52:2415–8.
69. Kopp BJ, Mrsan M, Erstad BL, et al. Cost implications of and potential adverse events prevented by interventions of a critical care pharmacist. *Am J Health-Syst Pharm.* 2007; 64:2483–7.
70. Olshaker JS, Rathlev NK. Emergency department over-crowding and ambulance diversion: the impact and potential solutions of extended boarding of admitted patients in the emergency department. *J Emerg Med.* 2006; 30:351–6.
71. Andrulis DP, Kellermann A, Kintz EA, et al. Emergency departments and crowding in United States teaching hospitals. *Ann Emerg Med.* 1991; 20:980–6.
72. Brennan TA, Leape LL, Laird NM, et al. Incidence of adverse events and negligence in hospitalized patients: results of the Harvard medical practice study I. *New Engl J Med.* 1991; 324:370–6.
73. Weiss SJ, Ernst AA, Nick TG. Comparison of the national emergency department overcrowding scale and the emergency department work index for quantifying emergency department crowding. *Acad Emerg Med.* 2006; 13:513–8.
74. Kulstad EB, Sikka R, Sweis RT, et al. ED overcrowding is associated with an increased frequency of medication errors. *Am J Emerg Med.* 2010; 28:304–9.
75. American College of Emergency Physicians. Emergency department crowding: high impact solutions. www.acep.org/practres.aspx?id=32050 (accessed 2010 Oct 20).
76. Santel JP. Reconciliation failures lead to medication errors. *Jt Comm J Qual Patient Saf.* 2006; 32:225–9.
77. Tam VC, Knowles SR, Cornish PL, et al. Frequency, type, and clinical importance of medication history errors at admission to hospital: a systematic review. *Can Med Assoc J.* 2005; 173:510–5.
78. Cornish PL, Knowles SR, Marchesano R, et al. Unintended medication discrepancies at the time of hospital admission. *Arch Intern Med.* 2005; 165:424–9.
79. Gleason KM, Groszek JM, Sullivan C, et al. Reconciliation of discrepancies in medication histories and admission orders of newly hospitalized patients. *Am J Health-Syst Pharm.* 2004; 61:1689-95.
80. Miller SL, Miller S, Balon J, et al. Medication reconciliation in a rural trauma population. *Ann Emerg Med.* 2008; 52:483–91.
81. Schenkel S. The unexpected challenges of accurate medication reconciliation. *Ann Emerg Med.* 2008; 52:493–5.
82. Eppert HD, Eppert JA. In response to "the unexpected challenges of accurate medication reconciliation." *Ann Emerg Med.* 2009; 53:548–9.
83. Carter MK, Allin DM, Scott LA, et al. Pharmacist-acquired medication histories in a university hospital emergency department. *Am J Health-Syst Pharm.* 2006; 63:2500–3.
84. Reeder TA, Mutnick A. Pharmacist- versus physician-obtained medication histories. *Am J Health-Syst Pharm.* 2008; 65:857–60.
85. Nester TM, Hale LS. Effectiveness of a pharmacist-acquired medication history in promoting patient safety. *Am J Health-Syst Pharm.* 2002; 59:2221–5.
86. Lubowski TJ, Cronin LM, Pavelka RW, et al. Effectiveness of a medication reconciliation project conducted by PharmD students. *Am J Pharm Educ.* 2007; 71:94.
87. Mersfelder TL, Bickel RJ. Inpatient medication history verification by pharmacy students. *Am J Health-Syst Pharm.* 2008; 65:2273–5.
88. Michels RD, Meisel SB. Program using pharmacy technicians to obtain medication histories. *Am J Health-Syst Pharm.* 2003; 60:1982–6.
89. Hayes BD, Donovan JL, Smith BS, et al. Pharmacist-conducted medication reconciliation in an emergency department. *Am J Health-Syst Pharm.* 2007; 64:1720–3.
90. Ratz Y, Shafir I, Berkovitch S, et al. The importance of the pharmacist in reporting adverse drug reactions in the emergency department. *J Clin Pharm.* 2010; 50:1217–21.
91. American Society of Health-System Pharmacists. ASHP guidelines on medication-use evaluation. *Am J Health-Syst Pharm.* 1996; 53:1953–5.
92. American Society of Health-System Pharmacists. ASHP guidelines on the pharmacist's role in the development, implementation, and assessment of critical pathways. *Am J Health-Syst Pharm.* 2004; 61:939–45.
93. American Society of Health-System Pharmacists. ASHP statement on the role of health-system pharmacists in emergency preparedness. *Am J Health-Syst Pharm.* 2003; 60:1993–5.
94. Setlak P. Bioterrorism preparedness and response: emerging role for health-system pharmacists. *Am J Health-Syst Pharm.* 2004; 61:1167–75.
95. Institute of Medicine of the National Academies Committee on the Future of Emergency Care in the United States Health System. Enhancing the emergency care research base. In: Hospital-based emergency care: at the breaking point. Washington, DC: National Academy Press; 2006:291–320.
96. Aghababian RV, Barsan WG, Bickell WH, et al. Research directions in emergency medicine. *Am J Emerg Med.* 1996; 14:681–3.

97. Maio RF, Garrison HG, Spaite DW, et al. Emergency medical services outcomes project I (EMSOP I): prioritizing conditions for outcomes research. *Ann Emerg Med.* 1999; 33:423–32.
98. Seidel JS, Henderson D, Tittle S, et al. Priorities for research in emergency medical services for children: results of a consensus conference. *Ann Emerg Med.* 1999; 33:206–10.
99. Becker LB, Weisfeldt ML, Weil MH, et al. The PULSE initiative: scientific priorities and strategic planning for resuscitation research and life saving therapies. *Circulation.* 2002; 105:2562–70.
100. Hoyt DB, Holcomb J, Abraham E, et al. Working group on trauma research program summary report: National Heart Lung Blood Institute (NHLBI), National Institute of General Medical Sciences (NIGMS), and National Institute of Neurological Disorders and Stroke (NINDS) of the National Institutes of Health (NIH), and the Department of Defense (DOD). *J Trauma.* 2004; 57:410–5.
101. Lipowsi EE. Pharmacy practice-based networks: Why, what, who, and how. *J Am Pharm Assoc.* 2008; 48:142–52.
102. American Society of Hospital Pharmacists. ASHP statement on pharmaceutical research in organized health-care settings. *Am J Hosp Pharm.* 1991; 48:1781.
103. Fagan SC, Touchette D, Smith JA, et al. The state of science and research in clinical pharmacy. *Pharmacotherapy.* 2006; 26:1027–40.

Appendix A—Summary of Recommendations

Essential Direct Patient Care Roles of EMPs

Direct patient care rounds: It is critical for EMPs to be accountable for and involved in direct patient care activities, including medication selection and the prescribing process. EMPs should focus on providing direct patient care and will be most effective in doing this when physically present in the ED, working as visible and well-integrated members of the multidisciplinary ED team.

Medication order review: Review of medication orders in the ED should provide the same level of assessment provided to patients elsewhere in the hospital. The role of an EMP in medication order review will vary, depending on site-specific factors. The EMP should develop a triage system to focus the medication order review process on high-risk medications, high-risk patient populations, and emergent situations. The EMP must not be the sole party responsible for ensuring that medication order review occurs in the ED; the pharmacy department should ensure that adequate processes are in place to ensure that all medication orders are reviewed in compliance with federal, state, and local regulations and accreditation requirements. Each institution should strive to identify the optimal balance between accountability for prospective medication order review and direct patient care activities in the ED.

Medication therapy monitoring: EMPs should ensure that medication therapy administered in the ED is safe and effective by designing monitoring plans for medications administered both in the ED and prior to arrival. EMPs should subsequently provide recommendations for modifications to medication regimens based on the results of monitoring parameters and established goals for therapy.

Patient care involving high-risk medications and procedures: Whenever possible, EMPs should be present at the patient's bedside to assist in the delivery of patient care that utilizes high-risk medications or procedures. EMPs should review the use of high-risk medications in the ED and should assist in the development of processes and procedures to improve patient safety and avoid errors. In addition, EMPs should provide education to ED health care providers related to the use of high-risk medications.

Resuscitation: EMPs should be present during all resuscitations in the ED, including trauma, cardiopulmonary arrest, and toxicologic emergencies. In the resuscitation setting, EMPs should prepare medications for immediate administration, ensure the appropriate administration and dose of medications, obtain medications that are not readily available in the ED, make recommendations for alternative routes of medication administration, answer medication information questions, assist with differential diagnosis, and complete resuscitation documentation. EMPs should be familiar with the recognition and treatment of toxicologic emergencies and should assist in identifying causative agents, with the selection and administration of antidotes and other supportive therapies, and with recommendations for monitoring antidote therapy in conjunction with toxicologists and poison control centers. EMPs should seek training programs relevant to the conditions treated in their EDs.

Medication procurement and preparation: Although the role of EMPs will vary, depending on the needs and resources of the institution, EMPs should be an integral part of the medication procurement and preparation process in the ED. EMPs should be involved in selecting medications stocked in the ED, should ensure safe storage and usage of these medications, should ensure timely turnaround for medications obtained from the central pharmacy, and may assist in the preparation of urgently needed medications. EMPs should be involved with the institution's formulary review and process-improvement committees to assist with formulation of policies regarding medications used in the ED.

Medication information: Medication information is a vital role of EMPs. The medication information needs of the ED cover a broad spectrum of clinical scenarios and patient cases. EMPs should ensure access to appropriate primary, secondary, and tertiary references as needed to respond to medication information requests and must be able to quickly and accurately retrieve the answers to medication information questions using those resources.

Documentation: EMPs should document interventions provided in the ED to allow measurement of improvement in patient outcomes and potential cost avoidance. EMPs should regularly review intervention documentation to identify trends, which may indicate a need to educate ED health care providers or change medication-use procedures. Health care institutions should support EMPs by providing means to document those interventions.

Desirable Direct Patient Care Roles of EMPs

Care of boarded patients: Based on institutional resources, processes should be developed to identify the pharmacist accountable for providing care to boarded patients. These processes should not compromise the EMP's primary role in ensuring safe and effective use of medications for new patients presenting to the ED. When possible, responsibility for the care of boarded patients should be assigned to the pharmacist who will be responsible for providing care to the patient after admission to ensure continuity of care. At a minimum, the responsible pharmacist should review the medication profile of critical patients, review any high-risk medications, assist with medication dosing, assist with medication procurement, and provide monitoring as necessary.

Medication histories and medication reconciliation: EMPs may assist in the development of a risk-stratification protocol for determining which medication histories will be obtained in the ED. In general, a focus on patients with known or suspected toxicologic emergencies, with known or suspected adverse events from home medication regimens, or with complicated medication histories that will influence ED clinical decision-making should be considered.

Essential Administrative Roles of EMPs

Medication and patient safety: In collaboration with physicians, nurses, and hospital executives, EMPs should assist in reporting medication errors, reviewing reported medication errors, and identifying error trends. EMPs should further assist in developing safe medication practices and processes for prevention of errors, assist in implementing system improvements, and provide staff education when needed.

Quality-improvement initiatives: EMPs or other pharmacy representatives should be extensively involved with quality-improvement initiatives in the ED. EMPs should participate in ongoing efforts to optimize pharmacotherapy regimens through medication-use evaluation and development of medication-use guidelines and pathways.

Leadership duties and professional service: The leadership duties and professional service of EMPs may include involvement at the hospital level, which provides EMPs with an avenue for improving both patient care and medication use. Involvement with local, state, and national professional pharmacy organizations, as well as with other professional health care organizations, will allow for collaboration, leading to further development of EM pharmacy practice and the role of the EMP as an integral member of the ED health care team.

Emergency preparedness: The role of EMPs in emergency preparedness should include education, training, and certification; knowledge of federal, state, and local emergency preparedness and response policies; involvement with institutional emergency preparedness policy development; planning of and participation in planned disaster drills; and education of pharmacy and ED staff.

Desirable Administrative Roles of EMPs

Education: It is desirable that EMPs provide education to fellow pharmacists; other health care providers; pharmacy students and residents; and ED patients, their families, and caregivers.

Research and scholarly activity: There is an urgent need for research in EM pharmacy, both for pharmacotherapy and pharmacy practice. EMPs can be valuable researchers in the ED and should be encouraged to participate in the completion of research projects and scholarly activities. The establishment of pharmacy practice research networks to facilitate the completion of pharmacy-based research projects in the ED setting should also be encouraged.

Appendix B—Recommended Readings, References, and Resources

The following list represents suggested readings that would be useful to readers and should be considered in addition to those references and resources provided in the guidelines. The suggested readings are categorized into applicable categories and are then listed in alphabetical order by the primary author. For additional resources related to specific areas of emergency medicine pharmacist (EMP) service development, implementation, and best practices, please refer to the ASHP Section of Clinical Specialists and Scientists Section Advisory Group on Emergency Care Internet Resource Center (www.ashp.org/EmergencyCare.aspx). In addition to these resources and references, interested parties should seek out relevant resources and references related to local, regional, state, and national regulatory and accrediting agencies.

Internet Resources

1. American Society of Health-System Emergency Medicine Pharmacist Practice Internet Resource Center. www.ashp.org/EmergencyCare.aspx
2. American Society of Health-System Pharmacy Medication Reconciliation Toolkit. www.ashp.org/Import/PRACTICEANDPOLICY/PracticeResourceCenters/PatientSafety/ASHPMedicationReconciliationToolkit_1.asp
3. Institute for Healthcare Improvement: Prevent Adverse Drug Events (Medication Reconciliation). www.ihi.org/IHI/Programs/Campaign/ADEsMedReconciliation.htm

Primary Literature

Initial descriptions of EMP services

1. Berry NS, Folstad JE, Bauman JL, et al. Follow-up observations on 24-hour pharmacotherapy services in the emergency department. *Ann Pharmacother.* 1992; 26:476–80.
2. Culbertson V, Anderson RJ. Pharmacist involvement in emergency room services. *Contemp Pharm Pract.* 1981; 4:164–76.
3. Elenbaas RM. Role of the pharmacist in providing clinical pharmacy services in the emergency department. *Can J Hosp Pharm.* 1978; 31:123–5.
4. Elenbaas RM, Waeckerle JF, McNabney WK. The clinical pharmacist in emergency medicine. *Am J Hosp Pharm.* 1977; 34:843–6.

5. High JL, Gill AW, Silvernale DJ. Clinical pharmacy in an emergency medicine setting. *Contemp Pharm Pract.* 1981; 4:227–30.
6. Kasuya A, Bauman JL, Curtis RA, et al. Clinical pharmacy on-call program in the emergency department. *Am J Emerg Med.* 1986; 4:464–7.
7. Laivenieks N, McCaul K, O'Brodovich M. Clinical pharmacy services provided to an emergency department. *Can J Hosp Pharm.* 1992; 45:113–5.
8. Powell MF, Solomon DK, McEachen RA. Twenty-four hour emergency pharmaceutical services. *Am J Hosp Pharm.* 1985; 42:831–5.
9. Schauben JL. Comprehensive emergency pharmacy services. *Top Hosp Pharm Manage.* 1988; 8:20–8.
10. Spigiel RW, Anderson RJ. Comprehensive pharmaceutical services in the emergency department. *Am J Hosp Pharm.* 1979; 36:52–6.
11. Whalen FJ. Cost justification of decentralized pharmaceutical services for the emergency room. *Am J Hosp Pharm.* 1981; 38:684–7.
12. Whalen FJ. Cost containment of emergency room prescriptions. *Am J Hosp Pharm.* 1982; 39:312–3.

Recent descriptions of EMP services

13. Aldridge VE, Park HK, Bounthavong M, et al. Implementing a comprehensive, 24-hour emergency department pharmacy program. *Am J Health-Syst Pharm.* 2009; 66:1943–7.
14. American Society of Health-System Pharmacists. ASHP statement on pharmacy services to the emergency department. *Am J Health-Syst Pharm.* 2008; 65:2380–3.
15. Bednall R, McRobbie D, Duncan J, et al. Identification of patients attending accident and emergency who may be suitable for treatment by a pharmacist. *Fam Pract.* 2003; 20:4–7.
16. Cohen V, Jellinek SP, Hatch A, et al. Effect of clinical pharmacists on care in the emergency department: a systematic review. *Am J Health-Syst Pharm.* 2009; 66:1353–61.
17. Fairbanks RJ, Hays DP, Webster DF, et al. Clinical pharmacy services in an emergency department. *Am J Health-Syst Pharm.* 2004; 61:934–7.
18. Fairbanks RJ, Hildebrand JM, Kolstee KE, et al. Medical and nursing staff highly value clinical pharmacists in the emergency department. *Emerg Med J.* 2007; 24:716–9.
19. Mialon PJ, Williams P, Wiebe RA. Clinical pharmacy services in a pediatric emergency department. *Hosp Pharm.* 2004; 39:121–4.
20. Patanwala AE, Hays D. Pharmacist's activities on a trauma response team in the emergency department. *Am J Health-Syst Pharm.* 2010; 67:1536–8.
21. Szczesiul JM, Fairbanks RJ, Hildebrand JM, et al. Survey of physicians regarding clinical pharmacy services in academic emergency departments. *Am J Health-Syst Pharm.* 2009; 66:576–9.
22. Thomasset KB, Faris R. Survey of pharmacy services provision in the emergency department. *Am J Health-Syst Pharm.* 2003; 60:1561–4.
23. Weant KA, Sterling E, Winstead PS, et al. Establishing a pharmacy presence in the ED. *Am J Emerg Med.* 2006; 24:514–5.
24. Witsil JC, Aazami R, Murtaza UI, et al. Strategies for implementing emergency department pharmacy services: results from the 2007 ASHP Patient Care Impact Program. *Am J Health-Syst Pharm.* 2010; 67:375–9.
25. Wymore ES, Casanova TJ, Broekemeirer RL, et al. Clinical pharmacist's daily role in the emergency department of a community hospital. *Am J Health-Syst Pharm.* 2008; 65:395–6, 398–9.

Resuscitation

26. Acquisto NM, Hays DP, Fairbanks RJ, et al. The outcomes of emergency pharmacist participation during acute myocardial infarction. *J Emerg Med.* 2010 [epub ahead of print 2010 Aug 31].
27. Draper HM, Eppert JA. Association of pharmacist presence on compliance with advanced cardiac life support guidelines during in-hospital cardiac arrest. *Ann Pharmacother.* 2008; 42:469–74.
28. Schwerman E, Schwartau N, Thompson CO, et al. The pharmacist as a member of the cardiopulmonary resuscitation team. *DICP.* 1973; 7:299–308.
29. Shimp LA, Mason NA, Toedter NM, et al. Pharmacist participation in cardiopulmonary resuscitation. *Am J Health-Syst Pharm.* 1995; 52:980–4.

Toxicology

30. Czajka PA, Skoutakis VA, Wood GC, et al. Clinical toxicology consultation by pharmacists. *Am J Hosp Pharm.* 1979; 36:1087–9.
31. Dart RC, Borron SW, Caravati EM, et al. Expert consensus guidelines for stocking antidotes in hospitals that provide emergency care. *Ann Emerg Med.* 2009; 54:386–94.
32. Roberts RW, Russell WL. A pharmacist-based toxicology service. 1978. *Ann Pharmacother.* 2007; 41:1719–24.

Automated medication dispensing systems

33. American Society of Health-System Pharmacists. ASHP guidelines on the safe use of automated dispensing devices. *Am J Health-Syst Pharm.* 2010; 67:483–90.
34. Conners GP, Hays D. Emergency department drug orders: does drug storage location make a difference? *Ann Emerg Med.* 2007; 50:414–8.
35. Gordon JO, Hadsall RS, Schommer JC. Automated medication-dispensing system in two hospital emergency departments. *Am J Health-Syst Pharm.* 2005; 62:1917–23.

Documentation and cost avoidance

36. Bosinski TJ, Campbell L, Schwartz S. Using a personal digital assistant to document pharmacotherapeutic interventions. *Am J Health-Syst Pharm.* 2004; 61:931–4.
37. Kopp BJ, Mrsan M, Erstad BL, et al. Cost implications of and potential adverse events prevented by interventions of a critical care pharmacist. *Am J Health-Syst Pharm.* 2007; 64:2483–7.
38. Lada P, Delgado G Jr. Documentation of pharmacists' interventions in an emergency department and associated cost avoidance. *Am J Health-Syst Pharm.* 2007; 64:63–8.

39. Lau A, Balen RM, Lam R, et al. Using a personal digital assistant to document clinical pharmacy services in an intensive care unit. *Am J Health-Syst Pharm.* 2001; 58:1229–32.
40. Levy DB. Documentation of clinical and cost-saving pharmacy interventions in the emergency room. *Hosp Pharm.* 1993; 28:624–7, 630–4, 653.
41. Ling JM, Mike LA, Rubin J, et al. Documentation of pharmacist interventions in the emergency department. *Am J Health-Syst Pharm.* 2005; 62:1793–7.
42. Mason RN, Pugh CB, Boyer SB, et al. Computerized documentation of pharmacists' interventions. *Am J Hosp Pharm.* 1994; 51:2131–8.
43. McMullin ST, Hennenfent JA, Ritchie DJ, et al. A prospective, randomized trial to assess the cost impact of pharmacist-initiated interventions. *Arch Intern Med.* 1999; 159:2306–9.
44. Mutnick AH, Sterba KJ, Peroutka JA, et al. Cost savings and avoidance from clinical interventions. *Am J Health-Syst Pharm.* 1997; 54:392–6.
45. Reilly JC, Wallace M, Campbell MM. Tracking pharmacist interventions with a hand-held computer. *Am J Health-Syst Pharm.* 2001; 58:158–61.
46. Schumock GT, Hutchinson RA, Bilek BA. Comparison of two systems for documenting pharmacist interventions in patient care. *Am J Hosp Pharm.* 1992; 49:2211–4.
47. Schneider PJ, Gift MG, Lee YP, et al. Cost of medication-related problems at a university hospital. *Am J Health-Syst Pharm.* 1995; 52:2415–8.
48. Simonian AI. Documenting pharmacist interventions on an intranet. *Am J Health-Syst Pharm.* 2003; 60:151–5.
49. Silva MA, Tataronis GR, Maas B. Using personal digital assistants to document pharmacist cognitive services and estimate potential reimbursement. *Am J Health-Syst Pharm.* 2003; 60:911–5.
50. Zimmerman CR, Smolarek RT, Stevenson JG. A computerized system to improve documentation and reporting of pharmacists' clinical interventions, cost savings, and workload activities. *Pharmacotherapy.* 1995; 15:220–7.

Medication histories and medication reconciliation

51. Ajdukovic M, Crook M, Angley C, et al. Pharmacist elicited medication histories in the emergency department: identifying patient groups at risk of medication misadventure. *Pharm Pract.* 2007; 5:162–8.
52. Akwagyriam I, Goodyer LI, Harding L, et al. Drug history taking and the identification of drug related problems in an accident and emergency department. *J Accid Emerg Med.* 1996; 13:166–8.
53. Carter MK, Allin DM, Scott LA, et al. Pharmacist-acquired medication histories in a university hospital emergency department. *Am J Health-Syst Pharm.* 2006; 63:2500–3.
54. Cornish PL, Knowles SR, Marchesano R, et al. Unintended medication discrepancies at the time of hospital admission. *Arch Intern Med.* 2005; 165:424–9.
55. Gleason KM, Groszek JM, Sullivan C, et al. Reconciliation of discrepancies in medication histories and admission orders of newly hospitalized patients. *Am J Health-Syst Pharm.* 2004; 61:1689–95.
56. Hayes BD, Donovan JL, Smith BS, et al. Pharmacist-conducted medication reconciliation in an emergency department. *Am J Health-Syst Pharm.* 2007; 64:1720–3.
57. Lubowski TJ, Cronin LM, Pavelka RW, et al. Effectiveness of a medication reconciliation project conducted by PharmD students. *Am J Pharm Educ.* 2007; 71:94.
58. Mersfelder TL, Bickel RJ. Inpatient medication history verification by pharmacy students. *Am J Health-Syst Pharm.* 2008; 65:2273–5.
59. Michels RD, Meisel SB. Program using pharmacy technicians to obtain medication histories. *Am J Health-Syst Pharm.* 2003; 60:1982–6.
60. Miller SL, Miller S, Balon J, et al. Medication reconciliation in a rural trauma population. *Ann Emerg Med.* 2008; 52:483–91.
61. Nester TM, Hale LS. Effectiveness of a pharmacist-acquired medication history in promoting patient safety. *Am J Health-Syst Pharm.* 2002; 59:2221–5.
62. Reeder TA, Mutnick A. Pharmacist- versus physician-obtained medication histories. *Am J Health-Syst Pharm.* 2008; 65:857–60.
63. Santel JP. Reconciliation failures lead to medication errors. *Jt Comm J Qual Patient Saf.* 2006; 32:225–9.
64. Schenkel S. The unexpected challenges of accurate medication reconciliation. *Ann Emerg Med.* 2008; 52:493–5.
65. Tam VC, Knowles SR, Cornish PL, et al. Frequency, type, and clinical importance of medication history errors at admission to hospital: a systematic review. *Can Med Assoc J.* 2005; 173:510–5.

Medication and patient safety

66. Bizovi KE, Beckley BE, McDade MC, et al. The effect of computer-assisted prescription writing on emergency department prescription errors. *Acad Emerg Med.* 2002; 9:1168–75.
67. Brown JN, Barnes CL, Beasley B, et al. Effect of pharmacists on medication errors in an emergency department. *Am J Health-Syst Pharm.* 2008; 68:330–3.
68. Case LL, Paparella S. Safety benefits of a clinical pharmacist in the emergency department. *J Emerg Nurs.* 2007; 33:564–6.
69. Federico F. Preventing harm from high-alert medications. *Jt Comm J Qual Patient Saf.* 2007; 33:537–42.
70. Flynn E, Barker K, Barker B. Medication-administration errors in an emergency department. *Am J Health-Syst Pharm.* 2010; 67:347–8.
71. Gruen RL, Jurkovich GJ, McIntyre LK, et al. Patterns of errors contributing to trauma mortality: lessons learned from 2,594 deaths. *Ann Surg.* 2006; 244:371–80.
72. The Joint Commission. High-alert medications and patient safety. *Sentinel Event Alert.* 1999; 11:1–3.
73. Juarez A, Gacki-Smith J, Bauer MR, et al. Barriers to emergency departments' adherence to four medication safety-related Joint Commission National Patient Safety Goals. *Jt Comm J Qual Patient Saf.* 2009; 35:49–59.
74. Kraus DM, Stifter J, Hatoum HT. Program to improve nurses' knowledge of pediatric emergency medications. *Am J Hosp Pharm.* 1991; 48:97–101.
75. Kulstad EB, Sikka R, Sweis RT, et al. ED overcrowding is associated with an increased frequency of medication errors. *Am J Emerg Med.* 2010; 28:304–9.

76. Peth HA. Medication errors in the emergency department: a systems approach to minimizing risk. *Emerg Med Clin N Am.* 2003; 21:141–58.
77. Risser DT, Rice MM, Salisbury ML, et al. The potential for improved teamwork to reduce medical errors in the emergency department. *Ann Emerg Med.* 1999; 34:373–83.
78. Rothschild JM, Churchill W, Erickson A, et al. Medication errors discovered by emergency department pharmacists. *Ann Emerg Med.* 2010; 55:513–21.
79. Schenkel S. Promoting patient safety and preventing medical error in emergency departments. *Acad Emerg Med.* 2000; 7:1204–22.
80. Taylor D, Walsham N, Taylor SE, et al. Potential for interaction between prescription drugs and complementary and alternative medicines amongst patients in the emergency department. *Pharmacotherapy.* 2006; 26:634–40.
81. Patanwala AE, Warholak TL, Sanders AB, et al. A prospective observational study of medication errors in a tertiary care emergency department. *Ann Emerg Med.* 2010; 55:522–6.
82. Wilson K, Sullivan M. Preventing medication errors with smart infusion technology. *Am J Health-Syst Pharm.* 2004; 61:177–83.

Adverse medication events

83. Aparasu RR. Drug-related injury visits to hospital emergency departments. *Am J Health-Syst Pharm.* 1998; 55:1158–61.
84. Croskerry P, Shapiro M, Campbell S, et al. Profiles in patient safety: medication errors in the emergency department. *Acad Emerg Med.* 2004; 11:289–99.
85. Dennehy CE, Kishi DT, Louie C. Drug-related illness in emergency department patients. *Am J Health-Syst Pharm.* 1996; 53:1422–6.
86. Hafner JW, Belknap SM, Squillante MD, et al. Adverse drug events in the emergency department. *Ann Emerg Med.* 2002; 39:258–67.
87. Kalina M, Tinkoff G, Gleason W, et al. A multidisciplinary approach to adverse drug events in pediatric trauma patients in an adult trauma center. *Pediatr Emerg Care.* 2009; 25:444–6.
88. Ratz Y, Shafir I, Berkovitch S, et al. The importance of the pharmacist in reporting adverse drug reactions in the emergency department. *J Clin Pharmacol.* 2010; 50:1217–21.
89. Schneitman-McIntire O, Farnen TA, Gordon N, et al. Medication misadventures resulting in emergency department visits at an HMO medical center. *Am J Health-Syst Pharm.* 1996; 53:1416–22.
90. Smith KM, McAdams JW, Frenia ML, et al. Drug-related problems in emergency department patients. *Am J Health-Syst Pharm.* 1997; 54:295–8.

Quality-improvement initiatives

91. American Society of Health-System Pharmacists. ASHP guidelines on medication-use evaluation. *Am J Health-Syst Pharm.* 1996; 53:1953–5.
92. American Society of Health-System Pharmacists. ASHP guidelines on the pharmacist's role in the development, implementation, and assessment of critical pathways. *Am J Health-Syst Pharm.* 2004; 61:939–45.

Emergency preparedness

93. American Society of Health-System Pharmacists. ASHP statement on the role of health-system pharmacists in emergency preparedness. *Am J Health-Syst Pharm.* 2003; 60:1993–5.
94. Burda AM, Sigg T. Pharmacy preparedness for incidents involving weapons of mass destruction. *Am J Health-Syst Pharm.* 2001; 58:2274–84.
95. Cohen V. Organization of a health-system pharmacy team to respond to episodes of terrorism. *Am J Health-Syst Pharm.* 2003; 60:1257–63.
96. Setlak P. Bioterrorism preparedness and response: emerging role for health-system pharmacists. *Am J Health-Syst Pharm.* 2004; 61:1167–75.

Research

97. Aghababian RV, Barsan WG, Bickell WH, et al. Research directions in emergency medicine. *Am J Emerg Med.* 1996; 14:681–3.
98. American Society of Hospital Pharmacists. ASHP statement on pharmaceutical research in organized health-care settings. *Am J Hosp Pharm.* 1991; 48:1781.
99. Becker LB, Weisfeldt ML, Weil MH, et al. The PULSE initiative: scientific priorities and strategic planning for resuscitation research and life saving therapies. *Circulation.* 2002; 105:2562-70.
100. Fagan SC, Touchette D, Smith JA, et al. The state of science and research in clinical pharmacy. *Pharmacotherapy.* 2006; 26:1027–40.
101. Lipowsi EE. Pharmacy practice-based networks: why, what, who, and how. *J Am Pharm Assoc.* 2008; 48:142–52.
102. Maio RF, Garrison HG, Spaite DW, et al. Emergency medical services outcomes project I (EMSOP I): prioritizing conditions for outcomes research. *Ann Emerg Med.* 1999; 33:423–32.
103. Seidel JS, Henderson D, Tittle S, et al. Priorities for research in emergency medical services for children: results of a consensus conference. *Ann Emerg Med.* 1999; 33:206–10.

Textbooks

1. Cohen V. Safe and effective medication use in the emergency department. Bethesda, MD: American Society of Health-System Pharmacists; 2009.
2. Institute of Medicine of the National Academies Committee on the Future of Emergency Care in the United States Health System. Hospital-based emergency care: at the breaking point. Washington, DC: National Academy Press; 2006.
3. Institute of Medicine of the National Academies Committee on the Future of Emergency Care in the United States. Hospital-based emergency care: at the breaking point. Washington, DC: National Academy Press; 2006.

Developed through the ASHP Section of Clinical Specialists and Scientists Advisory Group on Emergency Care and approved by the ASHP Board of Directors on July 8, 2011.

Heather Draper Eppert, Pharm.D., BCPS, and Alison Jennett Reznek, Pharm.D., BCPS, are gratefully acknowledged for authoring these guidelines. The authors and ASHP gratefully acknowledge Roshanak (Roshy) Aazami, Pharm.D., BCPS, Emergency Medicine Pharmacist, Cedars-Sinai Medical Center, for her substantial contribution and dedication to the completion of these guidelines.

The bibliographic citation for this document is as follows: American Society of Health-System Pharmacists. ASHP guidelines on emergency medicine pharmacist services. *Am J Health-Syst Pharm.* 2011; 68:e81–95.

ASHP Guidelines on Pharmacist Involvement in HIV Care

Background and Purpose

The epidemic of human immunodeficiency virus (HIV) infection in the United States has changed dramatically since its initial recognition in 1981.[1] Early in the epidemic, the incidence of HIV reached over 130,000 new cases per year, and death as a result of acquired immunodeficiency syndrome (AIDS) was an almost certain prognosis for those infected.[2] Significant advances in the strategies to prevent HIV transmission and in the medical care of patients with HIV infection led to significant reductions in both HIV transmission events and AIDS-related deaths over time. Among these advancements was an understanding of HIV infection pathophysiology, identification of HIV transmission modes, development of public health interventions targeting behavioral changes in high-risk populations, and identification of novel HIV medication targets leading to advances in HIV treatment and eventually combination-antiretroviral therapy (ART). Because the application of ART in particular can significantly suppress HIV replication, restoring a patient's immune function, it has resulted in a significant decline in HIV-related mortality. As a result, patients on long-term therapy that maintain viral suppression can now manage their infection as a chronic illness and are likely to experience a near-normal life expectancy.[3]

Despite remarkable advances in HIV treatment and prevention, the HIV epidemic in the United States has persisted. While the annual incidence of AIDS and AIDS-related deaths initially declined following the introduction of ART in 1995, the annual number of new HIV infections, AIDS diagnoses, and AIDS-related deaths has remained constant since 2000.[4] From 2000 to 2011, there were 45,000–55,000 new HIV infections every year in the U.S. and nearly 15,000 deaths annually as a result of AIDS. These statistics indicate that significant challenges remain for public health officials and HIV care providers to properly address the HIV epidemic. Furthermore, while long-recognized challenges to successful HIV care remain relevant (e.g., lack of early diagnosis, inadequate linkage to and retention in care, poor adherence to ART, stigma and public perception, and disparities in access to care for disenfranchised or socially marginalized populations), new challenges to successful HIV care and prevention are emerging (e.g., HIV in an aging population, the application of novel prevention methods such as pre-exposure prophylaxis, the optimal timing of ART initiation, and management of special patient populations with HIV infection).[5-9]

As the HIV epidemic in the U.S. evolves and new challenges to successful care and prevention emerge, healthcare providers—including pharmacists—are expanding their roles to ensure optimal patient care.[10,11] Pharmacists have long been recognized as essential members of the HIV patient care team, and their involvement in managing HIV-infected patients has been associated with improved outcomes. Pharmacist activities such as helping the team in selecting individualized HIV treatment regimens, providing patient counseling, monitoring for treatment responses and adverse effects, evaluating regimens for potential drug-drug interactions, and identifying opportunities for regimen simplification are associated with better viral load reductions and CD4 cell responses, improved ART adherence, simpler regimens, and reductions in medication errors.[12-16] To address emerging challenges, pharmacists will need to apply their traditional expertise within an interdisciplinary healthcare framework in multiple practice settings (inpatient, community, and ambulatory care) as well as identify and establish new roles in evolving areas of care including HIV testing and diagnosis, medication therapy management (MTM), transitions of care, patient retention, acute HIV treatment, pre-exposure prophylaxis (PrEP), and initiating ART in key populations, such as those with acute opportunistic infections, hepatitis co-infections, and solid organ transplantation. In developing these roles, it will be essential for pharmacists to remain highly engaged in the rapidly changing field of HIV using reliable resources such as aidsinfo.gov, the U.S. Department of Health and Human Services HIV management guidelines, and other resources that are listed in the Appendix.

In 2003, ASHP published a statement on the pharmacist's role in the care of patients with HIV infection.[17] These current guidelines extend beyond the scope of that document and are intended to provide guidance for all pharmacists and other healthcare professionals involved in the care of patients with HIV. Pharmacists may also find these guidelines helpful in establishing or expanding their services in an HIV practice setting. Using primary literature, therapeutic and practice guidelines, national standards, and the consensus of experts in the field of HIV pharmacy practice, these guidelines describe the available evidence for traditional pharmacist roles and identify new areas of emerging significance in which pharmacists can establish novel roles to meet the current and future challenges of the U.S. HIV epidemic. Specifically, these guidelines address in detail the involvement of pharmacists in the following ten key aspects of HIV prevention, care, and treatment for patients:

- HIV testing,
- treatment of HIV infection,
- treatment of HIV in key patient populations,
- HIV treatment failure,
- management of HIV disease state complications,
- treatment and prevention of opportunistic infections,
- prevention of HIV infection,
- HIV education,
- social services and HIV infection, and
- professional engagement.

Pharmacist Involvement in HIV Testing

The need for expanded HIV testing in the U.S. is demonstrated by the fact that one in six individuals with HIV in the United States is unaware of their infection and may therefore present an increased risk of transmission to others.[18] Recommendations from both the Centers for Disease Control and Prevention (CDC) and the U.S. Preventive Services Task Force (USPTF) stress the importance of routine "opt-out" HIV testing for adults in all healthcare settings, under which all patients are informed about and undergo testing for HIV unless they specifically decline.[19,20] Ubiquity and flexible hours make pharmacies ideal HIV testing locations. Pharmacists, as advocates for public health, should be involved with HIV testing initiatives through recommending HIV testing, providing and/or counseling on HIV tests, and assisting healthcare providers with test interpretation.

HIV testing and early HIV diagnoses improve access to HIV treatment that prolongs life, preserves health, and prevents transmission to others. To ensure timely HIV testing, pharmacists should recommend HIV testing according to recommendations set forth by CDC and USPTF and must be knowledgeable about the signs and symptoms of early HIV infection and the behaviors placing an individual at risk for HIV infection. The CDC and the U. S. Department of Health and Human Services (DHHS) maintain website resources with updated HIV testing recommendations, risk behaviors and common symptoms of early HIV infection (www.cdc.gov/hiv/; www.aids.gov). Pharmacists referring patients for testing should be knowledgeable about community HIV testing sites. The CDC maintains a list of free HIV testing sites (hivtest.cdc.gov, or 800-232-4636). The pharmacist should support routine HIV testing and help educate patients infected with HIV about how to modify their behavior to prevent disease transmission.

HIV testing may not be easily accessible for patients with limited access to healthcare. Community pharmacies are addressing this issue and improving patient access to HIV testing by offering onsite rapid HIV testing and counseling services.[21,22] Pharmacists in community and outpatient settings perform point-of-care HIV tests, provide pre- and post-test counseling, counsel patients with a positive result about confirmatory testing, and facilitate linkage to care.[23] CDC is developing a toolkit for HIV testing in community pharmacies and retail clinics, and the Michigan Pharmacists Association offers an accredited certificate course for pharmacists focused on point-of-care testing in community pharmacies.[24] These training modules set forth a curriculum designed to support pharmacists in the administration of point-of-care HIV testing, including competencies in pre- and post-test counseling, performing, reading, and interpreting the HIV test, and identifying sites for linkage to care and confirmatory testing. Where state legislation doesn't permit pharmacists to perform these activities, these guidelines can be used to advocate for change and improve and standardize pharmacist care nationally. Expanding HIV testing to pharmacies serves to eliminate barriers and reduce stigma by providing convenient, ubiquitous access to testing. Interest in pharmacy-based HIV testing initiatives has been documented from the perspectives of both pharmacy staff and patients.[25-28] The readiness of pharmacies to provide these services calls attention to their ideal accessibility to both urban and rural communities and to hard-to-reach populations not integrated into the formal healthcare system.

In 2012, the first point-of-care home HIV test became available for sale in community pharmacies. The OraQuick In-Home HIV Test provides results in as little as twenty minutes using a sample obtained by swabbing the test strip along the gum lines.[29] This test joined the already available over-the-counter Home Access HIV-1 Test System, which uses a mailed dried blood spot and provides telephone results in as little as one day. Community pharmacists should stock over-the-counter HIV test kits and be able to educate individuals about the proper method for administering and interpreting the tests, as well as taking action on either reactive or non-reactive test results.

In addition to recommending and providing HIV testing, clinical pharmacists can assist healthcare providers with interpreting HIV test results. HIV infection can be diagnosed by serologic assays that detect antibodies against HIV and by assays that detect HIV antigens or ribonucleic acid (RNA). Reactive screening tests are always confirmed by a supplemental test. Pharmacists' expertise is useful when clinicians are faced with discordant HIV test results, especially during the window period from exposure to seroconversion. Clinicians may have questions about which additional tests are necessary. New HIV diagnostic algorithms incorporating the use of fourth generation HIV testing assays are increasingly implemented within US institutions following updated recommendations from CDC.[30] Pharmacists should familiarize themselves with evolving HIV testing diagnostics and, to this end, CDC maintains a website of HIV testing recommendations (www.cdc.gov/hiv/guidelines/testing.html). At the Clinician Consultation Center, clinical pharmacists practicing in HIV medicine and physicians are on staff to assist with healthcare provider telephone inquiries regarding HIV testing.[31,32]

HIV testing is the first step in linking persons to HIV care and prevention. Pharmacists should encourage HIV testing as part of routine care and familiarize themselves with testing methods performed at local medical facilities, pharmacies, or at home. Pharmacist endorsement of HIV testing is important for expansion of HIV prevention and treatment services.

Pharmacist Involvement in HIV Treatment

Patient Assessment and Laboratory Testing. As ambulatory care transitions to the patient-centered medical home model, it is becoming increasingly important for pharmacists to be able to provide both comprehensive HIV care and primary care for HIV-positive patients. A pharmacist should therefore be familiar with both HIV and primary care management guidelines (see Appendix) and ensure that laboratory testing and monitoring of patients with HIV include parameters specific to HIV as well as primary care. It is also essential that pharmacists have the ability to interpret laboratory test results and provide or recommend appropriate treatment or additional testing when necessary in collaboration with the patient care team. Pharmacists should understand how certain laboratory test results may influence the management of HIV (e.g., the presence of baseline dyslipidemia, renal dysfunction, or hepatitis B co-infection among other conditions may influence the selection of antiretroviral agents or perhaps the timing of ART initiation). Among the laboratory tests that should be obtained at baseline in a patient with HIV are CD4 cell count; viral load; HIV genotype test; hepatitis, tuberculosis, and sexually transmitted infection testing; varicella, cytomegalovirus, and toxoplasmosis serologies; complete blood count with differential; chemistry and liver panels; and fasting lipid profile.[33,34] Many of these values will require periodic assessment or ongoing monitoring, particularly the HIV viral load and CD4 cell count to assess HIV disease progression or treatment response. Following the initiation of ART, the HIV viral load and CD4 cell count are closely monitored, though over time the frequency of monitoring may decline once a patient demonstrates a durable virologic and immunologic response. For example, after receiving ART for two years and consistently achieving HIV RNA suppression and a CD4 cell count of greater than 500 cells/mm^3, viral load monitoring can be extended to every six months and CD4 cell count monitoring is considered optional.[35] Pharmacists should be intimately familiar with laboratory values that require periodic assessment or ongoing monitoring in HIV-positive patients and ensure that appropriate assessment and monitoring occurs. Specific laboratory testing may also be necessary prior to the use of specific antiretroviral agents (e.g., if abacavir is considered for therapy, an HLA B5701 test is required to determine a patient's risk for abacavir hypersensitivity; for maraviroc, HIV tropism must be assessed).

Initiating and Maintaining Antiretroviral Therapy. In initiating ART, current HIV management guidelines state that treatment should be offered to all patients regardless of CD4 cell count to reduce the risk of HIV transmission and disease progression. Treatment is no longer based on the patient's CD4 cell count but rather on the patient's willingness and interest in starting and adhering to his or her first ART regimen.[35] The pharmacist, as part of the healthcare team, should contribute to assessing a patient's willingness to initiate ART and provide a readiness assessment. This assessment should include the identification of potential adherence barriers such as substance abuse, depression, or an unstable social or housing situation. Once identified, the pharmacist should help patients and providers resolve adherence barriers, providing ongoing adherence assessments and barrier management as necessary. This role includes monitoring for side effects following ART initiation and implementing side effect management strategies with the patient and provider to improve regimen tolerability and maintain ART adherence.

In selecting an initial ART regimen, convenience, patient preference, cost, comorbidities, baseline viral load, CD4 cell count, potential for side effects, resistance testing, and concomitant medications need to be considered.[35] Performing a thorough medication history and assessing for potential drug interactions in particular are essential functions of the pharmacist.

Antiretroviral agents may interact with other antiretrovirals, concomitant medications, food, nutrients, or herbal supplements. These interactions may be complex, occurring through multiple mechanisms, and may result in diminished treatment efficacy or an increased risk for toxicity. Drug interactions that are not clinically relevant, will not cause patient harm, or impact treatment outcomes may also occur. The pharmacist is uniquely positioned to evaluate potential drug interactions using appropriate resources and determine the clinical significance of each interaction identified. To ensure the safety and efficacy of a patient's initial ART regimen and other medications, the pharmacist should perform thorough initial and ongoing assessments of potential drug interactions, including prescription and nonprescription medicines, recreational drugs, and all nutritional and herbal supplements. The results of this assessment should be communicated to the healthcare team and used to help determine the most appropriate ART regimen for the patient. When nonprescription medication, food, or nutritional supplement interactions are identified, the pharmacist should educate the patient and ensure their understanding of any safety and efficacy concerns that may be present.

To ensure the accurate assessment of drug interactions, the pharmacist should consult primary resources specific to HIV medications as well as the primary drug interaction literature when necessary. Because drug interaction literature is constantly expanding and may be difficult to access for efficient decision-making, the pharmacist should identify alternative resources that are current, reliable, easily accessible, and that provide an efficient assessment of drug interaction information. These sources include (but are not limited to) the U.S. Department of Health and Human Services HIV Treatment Guidelines for Adults and Adolescents (http://aidsinfo.nih.gov/guidelines), the UCSF HIV InSite Drug Interaction Database (http://arv.ucsf.edu), the University of Liverpool HIV Drug Interactions website and mobile application (www.hiv-druginteractions.org/), and the Toronto General Hospital Immunodeficiency Clinic website (www.hivclinic.ca/main/drugs_interact.html) (see Appendix). Since drug interactions are considered a subset of medication errors, preventing drug interactions should lead to better patient outcomes. Patients with HIV are at high risk of medication errors, and the identification and correction of these errors by pharmacists has been instrumental in improving the care of HIV-positive patients.[36-39]

Pharmacist Involvement in HIV Treatment of Key Patient Populations

The management of HIV infection can pose unique challenges in key patient populations. These populations include women and children, patients with comorbid conditions or co-infections, patients receiving solid organ transplantation, and patients who are immigrants or refugees. These populations often have specific medical and/or medication needs and regularly require coordinated interdisciplinary care. Pharmacists are essential members of these interdisciplinary teams and can help to ensure optimal patient outcomes.

Women. Women account for 20% of all new HIV infections annually in the U.S., and nearly 25% of all persons living with HIV in the U.S. are women. The majority of women living with HIV and those that are newly infected in the U.S. are between the ages of 13 and 45, or child-bearing age.[40,41] The proper use of ART in women of child-bearing age requires several important considerations. First, it is important for pharmacists and other healthcare practitioners to identify patients who should receive preconception counseling, including all women of child-bearing age in HIV-concordant or serodiscordant relationships. To accomplish this, pharmacists should first be familiar with resources related to preconception counseling in HIV-positive women, including the DHHS Guidelines for the Treatment of HIV-Infected Pregnant Women and Prevention of Perinatal Transmission (see Appendix).[42] Additionally, pharmacists should be engaged in the decision-making process with patients and providers regarding the use of ART to prevent HIV transmission. As part of the healthcare team, pharmacists can initiate discussions with HIV patients regarding fertility, including a patient's potential desire to become pregnant or their desire to initiate or maintain contraceptive methods such as hormonal contraception. Multiple complex drug interactions exist between ART agents and commonly used oral hormonal contraceptives. It is therefore essential for pharmacists to identity potential drug interactions and provide proper counseling to patients prior to initiating ART.[35] In contrast, for patients who express a desire to become pregnant or are inconsistent with contraception, the proper selection of an ART regimen that is safe during pregnancy becomes very important.

The initiation of ART is indicated for all HIV-infected pregnant women regardless of CD4 cell count as a means to prevent vertical HIV transmission. Pharmacists should be knowledgeable about current treatment guidelines for the use of ART antepartum and intrapartum for the mother as well as postpartum for the infant, including the safety and efficacy of individual antiretroviral agents as well the recommendations for preferred ART combinations.[42] When appropriate, pharmacists should report outcomes of ART exposures to The Antiviral Pregnancy Registry (www.apregistry.com/), which monitors for the teratogenic effects of antiretrovirals.

Pharmacists should be acutely aware of the importance of careful and frequent monitoring for ART efficacy, tolerability, and adherence for pregnant patients. They should also be aware of physiologic changes that could impact the pharmacokinetics and dosing of certain ART agents, particularly in the third trimester of pregnancy.[42] Pharmacists should also consider the pregnancy-related safety of concomitant agents that are often prescribed to patients with HIV infection, including agents used for the treatment or prevention of opportunistic infections. Postpartum, pharmacists should reinforce DHHS recommendations for women to abstain from breastfeeding, even in the presence of a fully suppressive ART regimen.[42] Pharmacists should also continue to provide adherence support and encouragement for HIV-positive women dealing with the challenges associated with being a new mother.

Pediatric Patients. To make meaningful contributions to the management of established HIV infection in infants and children, pharmacists must first develop interprofessional partnerships with pediatric HIV specialty care providers. They must also have a thorough understanding of the differing immunologic and virologic patterns associated with HIV infection in children and how they compare to adults and adolescents. For example, within weeks to months following acute HIV infection, very high HIV RNA levels decline rapidly in adults, whereas high RNA levels persist in perinatally infected infants for prolonged periods, decreasing slowly over years following the first year of life.[43,44] The different virologic pattern in infants likely reflects an immature but developing immune system's relative inability to contain viral replication compared to that of an adult. Immunologically, while declines in CD4 cell counts and percentages are expected to occur in both adults and children with advancing HIV infection, absolute CD4 cell counts in children under 5 years old are generally higher than their adult counterparts. However, the risk of disease progression associated with specific CD4 cell counts and/or percentages varies with the age of the child. For any given CD4 cell count or percentage, younger children, particularly those in the first year of life, face a higher risk of disease progression than other children and adults.[45-48] As a result, pharmacists and other specialty care providers must consider the age of the child in addition to HIV-specific laboratory values when determining the risk of disease progression and the need to initiate ART.

As with adults, treatment of pediatric HIV infection is a dynamic field with constant change and progression, requiring pharmacists to be aware of constantly evolving guidelines and treatment recommendations. This is particularly true for data regarding the use of specific antiretroviral agents in young children. Pharmacists must be aware of existing and emerging data describing the efficacy and safety of specific antiretroviral agents in this population. Pharmacists must also be knowledgeable about the pharmacokinetic differences that occur in children as a result of developing physiology and maturation of organs involved in the metabolism and clearance of medications.[49] These factors, in addition to developmental differences in absorption and body composition, often require that children receive higher weight-based dosing of antiretroviral agents than adults. In addition to weight, pharmacists must also be acutely aware and knowledgeable about antiretroviral agent-specific dosing recommendations that consider body surface area, age, and pubertal development staging.[50]

When treatment decisions are made, pharmacists must not only ensure proper regimen selection and dosing, but they must also take active roles in educating children (when appropriate) and caregivers about HIV infection and provide ongoing adherence counseling.[50] Adolescents face multiple barriers that can affect the initiation and maintenance of ART and other aspects of HIV care, including fear, denial, depression, substance abuse, concomitant mental illness, and lack of social and familial support.[51] Healthcare providers, including pharmacists, must work to establish trust and build strong relationships with patients and their caregivers while utilizing patient-care strategies that minimize barriers to adherence. For example, regimen fatigue can occur in young children who have been receiving ART since early childhood and can result in poor adherence, virologic resistance, and the need to implement increasingly complex ART regimens.[52] Working with pediatric HIV specialty providers, pharmacists can help to reduce regimen fatigue through the provision of ongoing adherence support as well as the selection or simplification of regimens to minimize the number of required pills, volumes of prescribed liquids, frequency of doses, and presence of drug interactions or side effects. Pharmacists are also uniquely aware of the availability of alternative dosage formulations and delivery systems and are equipped to recommend methods to improve the palatability of crushed pills or liquid formulations to minimize treatment aversion due to offending taste.

Finally, pharmacists must be sensitive to the many psychosocial components of care that may be present in the pediatric HIV population. These include the housing status of the child and caregiver; the child's attendance at school or daycare; the presence of substance abuse, mental health or other behavioral issues; and the HIV infection disclosure status of the child.[52-54] When contributing to the care of pediatric HIV patients, pharmacists may be helpful in identifying psychosocial issues that require intervention and possible referral to specialty providers, or to social services and child protective services when appropriate. These interventions can be essential to the overall health and well-being of children as well as their success in managing their HIV infection. Pharmacists may also serve as important information resources as children transition into adolescence and approach their sexual debut. Counseling on contraceptive methods, safe sex, and preventing HIV transmission should occur regularly and should be delivered by members of the healthcare team, including the pharmacist.

Patients with Comorbid Conditions. Comorbidities are common among patients with HIV. Compared to the general population, those with HIV infection are more likely to have cardiovascular disease, hypertension, renal failure, osteoporosis, diabetes, and certain cancers. Not only do these conditions and others appear to occur more commonly in patients with HIV, they also tend to appear earlier in patients with HIV and at times progress more rapidly than in the general population, likely due to complex interactions between host risk factors, HIV infection, and ART exposure.[55] As a result, it is increasingly important to not only provide effective ART to ensure viral suppression and immune reconstitution but also to provide comprehensive primary care for patients with HIV. Furthermore, due to the success of combination ART regimens in reducing AIDS-related mortality over the years, the HIV population is getting older; it is estimated that more than half of all patients with HIV in the U.S. are over the age of 50.[56]

Effective management of the changing HIV population will require pharmacists and other healthcare providers specializing in HIV care to maintain proficient knowledge and clinical skills in the screening, prevention, diagnosis, treatment, and monitoring of a variety of primary care conditions. Conversely, pharmacists practicing in primary care settings will likely encounter an increasing number of patients with HIV, which will require them to develop the knowledge and skills to be increasingly proficient in the management of this infection. Regardless of practice setting, pharmacists should be acutely aware of disease management similarities with the general population and potential differences for patients with HIV. They should also understand the potential contributions HIV and ART can have in the development of certain primary care disease states. For example, HIV infection and certain antiretroviral agents can contribute to dyslipidemia, insulin resistance, kidney disease, liver disease, and lipodystrophy.[57-60] They also can contribute to bone loss and an increased risk of osteoporosis and fragility fractures.[61-63] Pharmacists can play key roles in understanding the links between HIV, ART, and these disease states; educate patients and other healthcare providers; encourage disease state screenings; implement prevention programs; and ensure proper disease state diagnosis and management according to available treatment guidelines. They can also assist in the selection or adjustment of HIV treatment regimens that account for a patient's baseline risk or current diagnosis of primary care conditions that can be exacerbated by certain antiretroviral agents.

Other comorbidities that commonly present in patients with HIV, such as mental health conditions and substance abuse, may require special attention by pharmacists and other healthcare professionals. Depression is among the most common mental health conditions diagnosed in patients with HIV and is one of the strongest predictors of poor patient adherence and treatment outcomes.[64] Substance abuse including illicit drug use as well as mental health conditions including major depression can affect medication adherence and lead to poor patient outcomes.[65-67] The management of depression and substance abuse problems in patients with HIV is similar to the general population but pharmacists must be aware of the potential for drug interactions between ART and antidepressants as well as agents used in the management of substance abuse.

It is often necessary to properly manage mental health conditions and substance abuse problems before patients are able to initiate and maintain successful ART.[68] As a result, healthcare providers, including pharmacists, need to be active in the screening processes for mental health and substance abuse problems and provide a means of linking patients as necessary to appropriate specialty care and support services. Ongoing and close collaboration with specialty services, particularly in substance abuse treatment settings, is therefore necessary, as pharmacists can identify and prevent possible drug-drug interactions between substance abuse treatment medications and ART.[69] For example, methadone is a common pharmacologic agent used for the management of opioid addiction. Because multiple cytochrome P450 enzymes are involved in methadone metabolism, it is also subject to several interactions with antiretroviral agents. These interactions can increase methadone concentrations, and therefore toxicity, or they can decrease methadone concentrations, and trigger opioid withdrawal. Pharmacists need to educate providers about these potential interactions, assist in ART selection and/or adjustment process, and work in collaboration with substance abuse treatment programs to ensure successful HIV and substance abuse management.

Finally, many recreational drugs, including methylenedioxymethamphetamine (MDMA), gamma-hydroxybutyric acid (GHB), ketamine, and methamphetamine, are metabolized in part by cytochrome P450 enzymes and can therefore interact with certain antiretroviral agents. Overdoses as a result of these interactions have been reported, and pharmacists can educate providers and identify opportunities to counsel patients as a means of prevention.[70]

Patients with Hepatitis B Co-infection. Approximately 10% of patients with HIV in the U.S. also have chronic hepatitis B virus (HBV) infection.[71] Compared to patients with HBV infection alone, those with HIV co-infection can have a faster progression to end-stage liver disease, cirrhosis, and hepatocellular carcinoma.[72] Pharmacists involved in HIV care should be familiar with the treatment recommendations for both infections and be acutely aware that certain medications have activity against both infections. More specifically, tenofovir, lamivudine, and emtricitabine are all active against both HIV and HBV, which can be important in decision-making when treatment for either infection is indicated. For example, tenofovir is a preferred agent for treating HBV infection and can be used as a single agent for management of infection. However, in a co-infected patient, initiating tenofovir alone will lead to HIV resistance. As a result, if HBV or HIV treatment is indicated in a co-infected patient, a full ART regimen should be initiated, usually with the combination of tenofovir plus emtricitabine or lamivudine as the nucleoside reverse transcriptase inhibitor backbone.[35] If tenofovir cannot be used, entecavir is often used for the management of HBV. Of note, entecavir is not an effective agent for treating HIV, but it does have some anti-HIV activity and when used alone in co-infection could result in the selection of HIV resistance.[73] As a result, if entecavir is initiated for the management of HBV infection in a co-infected patient, it must be used in addition to a fully suppressive HIV medication regimen.

In addition to concerns regarding the proper selection of antiviral agents, pharmacists should strongly encourage patients to remain adherent to therapies, as acute HBV treatment discontinuations can cause serious hepatocellular damage due to spontaneous HBV reactivation. Pharmacists can also educate patients about avoiding hepatotoxins, including acetaminophen, and encourage patients to abstain from alcohol or identify patients with alcohol dependence that require referrals to specialty care. Finally, pharmacists should recommend an evaluation of immunity to the hepatitis A virus for all co-infected patients. Those not immune to hepatitis A should receive vaccination.

Patients with Hepatitis C Co-infection. Nearly 25% of patients with HIV infection in the U.S. are also infected with hepatitis C virus (HCV).[74] Like HBV, HCV progresses more rapidly in patients with HIV, resulting in twice the risk of HCV-related death in patients with co-infection compared to those with HCV infection alone.[75]

The initiation of ART may slow the progression of liver disease in co-infected patients, so current HIV treatment guidelines recommend considering the initiation of ART in this population regardless of CD4 cell count.[35,75] However, in HIV treatment-naive patients with higher CD4 cell counts (>500 cells/mm^3), some clinicians may choose to defer ART until HCV therapy is complete in order to avoid the complications of combined HIV and HCV treatment (i.e., large pill burden, drug interactions, and overlapping toxicities).[35] In patients with lower CD4 cell counts, combined treatment is more likely and pharmacists can play a key role in identifying and managing treatment complications. For instance, currently available direct-acting antiviral agents for HCV have significant drug interactions with multiple antiretroviral agents, including HIV protease inhibitors, elvitegravir/cobicistat, and non-nucleoside reverse transcriptase inhibitors. Pharmacists should contribute to HIV and/or HCV treatment regimen selection when combined treatment is indicated in order to avoid significant interactions that can lead to treatment failure and drug toxicity. Pharmacists can also recommend self-care strategies for side effects and report serious adverse effects back to the prescriber.

Adherence is also essential for optimal HIV and HCV treatment outcomes. As part of an interprofessional team, pharmacists should provide counseling to ensure patients understand what are often complex regimens, including proper administration (e.g., food requirements), the importance of adherence, the benefits and goals of therapy, and the recognition and management of treatment-related side effects. This level of pharmacist involvement has been shown to improve overall adherence and response to therapy in HIV and HCV mono-infected patients and may be particularly beneficial in patients with co-infection.[76,77] Furthermore, because the field of HCV medicine is evolving rapidly, it is increasingly essential for pharmacists to maintain a heightened awareness of evolving HCV treatment guidelines (available at: www.hcvguidelines.org) and newly available HCV medications including those in development and their potential impact on the management of HIV co-infection.[78] Although an increasing number of medicines available for the treatment of HCV will create opportunities to improve patient outcomes, they may also lead to additional challenges in treating co-infected patients that will require pharmacist intervention and management.

Additional roles for pharmacists in treating HIV-HCV co-infection include the evaluation of patient immunity to hepatitis A virus (HAV) and HBV infection and the recommendation or provision of HAV and HBV immunizations as necessary. As with patients with HBV, pharmacists should educate patients with HCV infection about avoiding hepatotoxins and encourage patients to abstain from alcohol, or pursue specialized care for the treatment of alcohol abuse.

Patients Undergoing Solid Organ Transplantation. Increasing numbers of patients with HIV infection are receiving solid organ transplantation, a practice previously considered controversial or infeasible. The increasing ability to provide transplantation for patients with HIV infection is largely the result of advances in the management of HIV, having a better understanding of the effects of HIV and transplant-associated immune suppression, and accumulating clinical trial data demonstrating the viability of transplantation in the HIV population.[79,80]

Irrespective of concomitant HIV infection, the process of solid organ transplantation is complex and requires interdisciplinary collaboration. The presence of HIV infection only increases the complexity of the process by introducing additional variables to consider during screening and during pre- and post-transplantation management. For example, protocols for liver and kidney transplantation often include thresholds for CD4 cell count levels and usually require patients to have a sustained undetectable HIV viral load.[81] Pharmacists, in addition to other members of the healthcare team, can contribute to the screening process by reviewing criteria with patients and providing essential adherence counseling to help patients achieve CD4 cell count and viral load goals.

During pre-transplantation management, pharmacists should contribute to the selection and/or adjustment of antiretroviral regimens in anticipation of drug-drug interactions that can occur following transplantation. For instance, nearly all patients will receive proton pump inhibitor medications for stomach acid suppression after transplantation. As a result, ART regimens that contain medications requiring an acidic environment for adequate absorption (e.g., atazanavir and rilpivirine) may need to be avoided. In addition, pharmacists should anticipate antiretroviral drug-drug interactions with post-transplantation immunosuppressing agents. Allograft rejection has been reported to occur at a higher rate in patients with concurrent HIV infection; one of the causes may be inadequate exposure to immune-suppressing agents as a result of interactions with ART agents.[82,83] Both HIV protease inhibitors and non-nucleoside reverse transcriptase inhibitors can cause complex interactions with commonly used immunosuppressive agents such as calcineurin inhibitors (e.g., tacrolimus and sirolimus) and cyclosporine. Pharmacists should provide close monitoring of immunosuppressive drug levels and recommend dosing adjustments as necessary to achieve stable therapeutic concentrations. Proper interdisciplinary communication should also occur between HIV specialty pharmacists, transplant pharmacy specialists, and other members of the HIV and transplantation healthcare teams. Communication will help ensure proper awareness and management of potential drug-drug interactions.

The primary indications for solid organ transplantation in patients with HIV are end-stage kidney disease due to HIV-associated nephropathy (HIVAN) and advanced liver disease due to HBV or HCV co-infection.[81] The presence of viral hepatitis adds to the complexity of both pre- and post-transplantation management. Pharmacists should be acutely aware of the differences in managing these infections in transplantation patients, including the differing roles of antiviral therapy. For example, patients with HBV infection should continue to receive antiviral agents after transplantation to prevent a hepatitis flare and will also receive therapy with HBV immune globulin.[84] Patients with HCV may not require antiviral therapy initially, but recurrent infection is common and can adversely impact transplantation outcomes.[81,85,86] As a result, patients should be followed closely following transplantation to identify recurrent HCV infection and the need to initiate therapy.

During the post-transplantation stage, pharmacists should ensure that the use of medications toxic to transplanted organs is limited. They should also work closely with patients to develop strategies to maintain medication adherence to complex drug regimens. At the very least, these post-transplantation regimens will include antiretroviral agents, immunosuppressive agents, and antibiotics for opportunistic infection prophylaxis. The inclusion of the pharmacist on the transplantation team has been shown to improve patient adherence to these complex regimens and may be essential to the overall success of the patient following transplantation.[87]

Finally, pharmacists must be aware of the role of post-transplantation opportunistic infection prophylaxis. Although patients generally receive prophylaxis against *Pneumocystis jirovecii*, opportunistic infections and other AIDS-defining conditions are uncommonly reported following transplantation.[83,88] Importantly, the risk of infection may change following the administration of thymoglobulin for the treatment of acute rejection. Thymoglubulin has been associated with prolonged CD4 cell declines, loss of cytotoxic antiviral T-cell responses, and the development of severe bacterial infections.[89,90] To address these risks, pharmacists must have a thorough understanding of anti-rejection medications, their impact on CD4 cells, and the need for increased monitoring and/or additional prophylaxis to reduce a patient's risk of severe infection.

Immigrant and Refugee Populations. In January 2010, the restriction on immigration to the United States for non-U.S. citizens living with HIV was lifted.[91] The restriction had been in place for more than 20 years and its removal not only helped to reduce social barriers, discrimination, and stigma for immigrants and refugees with HIV, it also aligned the domestic position of the U.S. with its increasing efforts to combat HIV and AIDS internationally.

While there are many positive implications from the removal of the immigration restriction, there are now also challenges for U.S. healthcare professionals to ensure that immigrants and refugees living with HIV consistently receive proper care. For example, the removal of the immigration restriction also removed mandatory HIV testing as a part of the immigration process. The CDC estimates that lifting the ban will allow an additional 4,275 persons with HIV to enter the U.S. each year.[91,92] At least some of these immigrants will have missed opportunities for early HIV diagnosis and entry into care. Furthermore, although the CDC recommends HIV screening for all immigrants and refugees, these patients will encounter barriers to healthcare as they enter the U.S. (e.g., lack of familiarity with the U.S. healthcare system) that not only limit their opportunities to receive HIV testing but also proper primary care services.[93] Pharmacists can assist in overcoming these barriers by being knowledgeable of the local medical clinics and organizations serving immigrant and refugee populations and helping to link patients into care as necessary.

As patients enter into care, additional barriers may need to be addressed prior to performing HIV testing. These include language differences, cultural beliefs regarding HIV and healthcare in general, and mistrust regarding confidentiality and disclosure of HIV status.[94] Pharmacists must be sensitive to these issues and help reduce barriers whenever possible. Language barriers can be addressed through use of interpreters. Patients should receive HIV education and counseling in their primary spoken language, and interpreters should be medically knowledgeable so they can explain the complexities of HIV infection and the importance of testing. Pharmacists should be sensitive to situations in which a patient declines the use of an interpreter for fear of disclosure within their community and seek alternative translation methods if they are available (family member or close friend). The delivery of information to the patient in their primary language and in a safe environment is paramount as it not only helps to ensure patient understanding but can also be helpful in developing a trusting patient-provider relationship.

When providing HIV education and prevention counseling, pharmacists should also be particularly sensitive to the HIV risk profiles that may be present in immigrant populations. Specifically, foreign-born persons with HIV are more likely than those in the U.S. to be women who have acquired HIV through heterosexual contact.[95] Pharmacists should also be aware of conditions heightening HIV risk for refugees, such as sexual abuse, violence, and gender inequality.[93,96] Failure to recognize these issues may limit the patient's engagement in care as well as the pharmacist's ability to provide proper counseling or referral to social services.

When testing is performed, it is important for pharmacists and other healthcare providers to follow CDC recommendations specific to the refugee population.[93] These include specific recommendations for screening adults and adolescents as well as pregnant women and children from endemic areas. Also included are recommendations for screening patients at risk for HIV-2. Pharmacists should have an understanding of the testing for HIV-2 infection as well as groups of HIV-1 infection that are endemic in certain countries and may not be detected with assays commonly used in the U.S.

Finally, pharmacists, as part of an interprofessional team, should be involved in the ART selection process for HIV-positive refugees and immigrants. They should provide ongoing HIV education and adherence counseling using an interpreter as well as ongoing evaluations for potential drug-drug interactions. Patients should be assessed for co-infections endemic to their home countries and receive proper treatment and/or opportunistic infection prophylaxis when necessary. Patients may encounter financial difficulty, and pharmacists should pursue available services that can assist patients in paying for their medications.

Pharmacist Involvement in the Management of HIV Treatment Failure

Once an ART regimen is initiated it is critical to monitor the success of therapy via routine assessment of the CD4 cell count and HIV viral load. Pharmacists can play a key role in interpreting test results to detect possible treatment failure. Treatment failure may be defined immunologically by identifying a significant CD4 cell count decline or virologically by finding a significant quantity of virus when full viral load suppression is expected. In identifying potential treatment failure, monitoring trends in viral load are essential as a single detectable viral load is not generally sufficient to diagnose treatment failure. These viral "blips" occur when a previously undetectable viral load becomes detectable but does not exceed 200 copies/mL and generally reduces to undetectable levels again with subsequent testing. Increasing viral loads over time or a viral load > 200 copies/mL are suggestive of treatment failure. Pharmacists can reduce the chances of unnecessary ART regimen changes in response to viral load blips by monitoring the viral load trend and understanding the definitions of virologic failure. If true failure is identified, pharmacists should then work with other members of the healthcare team to identify the cause of the regimen failure.

Most treatment failures may be attributed to three main reasons: nonadherence, pharmacokinetic complications, and ART resistance. Pharmacists, especially those with specialized training in adherence assessment, interventions, and motivational interviewing, can help determine which of these reasons may have contributed to valid ART failure. Many factors lead to non-adherence, including medication intolerance and adverse effects, depression, substance use, psychosocial factors, lack of social support, housing insecurity or homelessness and patient beliefs. The pharmacist should work with the patient to assess and resolve any barriers to ART adherence. Strategies for improving adherence include utilizing an interprofessional team approach, establishing a rapport with the patient, proactively identifying adherence barriers prior to regimen initiation, assessing for medication intolerance and adverse effects, providing mental health and social resources for the patient, assessing adherence at every pharmacy visit, involving the patient in regimen selection, providing adherence aids such as pill boxes and calendars, and assisting the patient in setting a cell phone alert or text message.[97] Literature has shown that virologic failure has been rescued and the initial ART regimen preserved with pharmacist involvement and adherence interventions.[35]

Pharmacokinetic complications may also contribute to HIV treatment failure. Malabsorption, alterations in drug distribution, and drug-drug and drug-herbal interactions may all cause subtherapeutic antiretroviral concentrations and lead to HIV resistance and ART failure. Pharmacists should be aware of and monitor for these factors and suggest treatment alternatives. Although not routinely recommended, therapeutic drug monitoring may be obtained in specific clinical situations and pharmacists may assist in the interpretation of antiretroviral drug levels.[35,98]

Once ART adherence and pharmacokinetic complications have been assessed, attention should then focus on ART resistance testing. An HIV genotype and other specific medication tests (as needed) should be obtained to determine the presence of viral mutations. Specialized pharmacists involved in HIV care should be fully versed in ordering appropriate resistance tests, including the appropriate timing of particular tests, as well as in interpreting test results. Pharmacists thus serve an important role in the review and interpretation of viral genotypes. This role requires an understanding of primary and secondary mutations, polymorphisms, and the accumulation of mutations to a critical number that will contribute to ART failure. Pharmacists should be familiar with resources available to assist with HIV resistance mutation assessment including the Stanford University HIV Drug Database and International AIDS Society-USA online repository (see Appendix).[99] With knowledge of the viral genotype, mutation patterns, and associated antiretroviral medications, pharmacists can be a resource for the healthcare team in determining treatment options. Pharmacists should apply the results of genotype testing as well as consider clinical guideline recommendations, ART regimen history, adverse effects, pill burden, and patient preference to provide a new ART regimen for a patient. Pharmacists should be involved in any ART regimen change with the goal of reestablishing viral suppression and improving the CD4 cell count.

Pharmacist Involvement in the Management of HIV Disease State Complications

Long-term complications of HIV infection have become an area of focus as patients with HIV live longer. Historically, research and treatment efforts have revolved around antiretroviral-related medication toxicities and little has been known about the long-term consequences of being infected with HIV. However, recent literature has identified that being chronically infected with HIV can lead to end-organ toxicities, thrombotic complications, non-AIDS-defining cancers, and metabolic abnormalities.[100] Pharmacists can play a key role in the identification and treatment of these emerging complications.

The mechanism by which HIV infection causes organ toxicity remains unclear. One postulated theory is that the virus causes a prolonged state of immune system activation that can lead to inflammation, endothelial dysfunction, and accelerated atherosclerosis, resulting in organ damage.[101] This prolonged inflammatory state may lead to the generation of free radicals and oxidative stress in various organs.[102] Another possible mechanism is via a hypercoagulable state that is seen in patients with HIV. Evidence supports a depletion of proteins C and S, leading to enhanced thrombosis and subsequent disease complications.[101,103] The extent of contribution of the virus itself in these conditions is unknown and the increased disease incidence may be a combination of the effects of the virus, ART, and the longevity of HIV-infected patients. Organ toxicity, via a variety of mechanisms, may be seen in virtually all organ systems, but most research has been in HIV-associated cardiovascular, renal, hepatic, and neurological toxicities.

HIV and Cardiovascular Disease. In the cardiovascular system, HIV infection has been linked to coronary artery disease and cardiomyopathy. Cardiovascular disease is now the third-most common cause of death in HIV-infected patients in the U.S., and literature has shown that patients with HIV have a greater incidence of myocardial infarction than non-infected patients.[104,105] In addition to myocardial infarction, cardiomyopathy in the form of systolic dysfunction has been seen in 10–20% and diastolic dysfunction in 48% of HIV-infected individuals.[106,107] The mechanism underlying this increase in cardiovascular disease is thought to be a combination of HIV infection, treatment with ART, and the increased lifespan of HIV-infected patients.[105] Known inflammatory markers associated with cardiovascular risk are elevated in HIV disease, leading to chronic inflammation, endothelial dysfunction, and accelerated atherosclerosis and thrombosis.[108] Additionally, adverse effects of ART, specifically protease inhibitors, include metabolic abnormalities such as hyperlipidemia and hyperglycemia that heighten the risk of cardiovascular complications.[109] Pharmacists are vitally important in assisting with control of risk factors and improving the cardiovascular risk of patients living with HIV.

Pharmacists should be actively involved in controlling the cardiovascular risk factors of patients living with HIV. Pharmacists should recommend annual cardiovascular risk assessments that include a lipid profile, fasting glucose, hemoglobin A1c (HbA1c) and blood pressure assessment. Specifically, pharmacists who practice in the ambulatory care setting may advocate for complete care via pharmacist-directed outpatient clinics based on physician collaborative practice agreements. Most research on pharmacist impact has been conducted in pharmacist-managed outpatient lipid, hypertension, diabetes, and heart failure clinics. Pharmacists in these settings may conduct risk assessment screening, limited physical examinations, laboratory monitoring, medication adjustments, and patient education. While not specific to the HIV disease state, incorporation of a pharmacist into outpatient clinics has been shown to have a significant reduction in cardiovascular events, low-density lipoprotein (LDL) cholesterol, blood pressure, HbA1c, and improved utilization of mortality-reducing heart failure medications.[110-114] Pharmacist patient care may be conducted by facilitating in-person clinic visits or via telephone consultations.[115] In addition, the benefits of pharmacist management of cardiovascular risk factors in the patient-centered medical home model have been demonstrated.[116,117] Pharmacists practicing in the community setting should recommend routine blood pressure monitoring at all pharmacy visits and assist in appropriate selection and training of diabetes supplies such as glucose meters and test strips.[33] Community pharmacists should perform routine medication profile review and recommend selection of safe and effective over-the-counter medications and herbal products. Pharmacists may also be proactive by recommending and overseeing the use of patient self-monitoring treatment journals documenting changes in blood pressure and glucose control. Finally, inpatient pharmacists may facilitate increased use of medication prescriptions for cardiovascular risk reduction at hospital discharge. In all practice settings, pharmacists should be familiar with lipid, blood pressure, and blood glucose treatment goals and guidelines and should directly apply those guidelines to assist in decreasing the cardiovascular risk in HIV-infected patients. In addition, pharmacists should routinely monitor and recommend lifestyle modifications, including smoking cessation, diet modification, and exercise adherence, as these have also been shown to decrease cardiovascular risk in patients with HIV.[118-120]

In addition to controlling risk factors, pharmacists should minimize exposure of direct cardiotoxic medications and to other medications that have adverse effects on the lipid profile. Abacavir, a nucleoside reverse transcriptase inhibitor, has been linked with possible increased risk of myocardial infarction.[121,122] While literature is conflicting regarding this adverse effect, pharmacists should be cognizant of this possibility and recommend alternative antiretroviral therapies as appropriate. Additionally, pharmacists involved in HIV management may recommend an ART regimen that may have a less detrimental lipid effect.[123]

HIV and Renal Disease. HIV infection is associated with nephropathy in the form of both acute kidney injury and chronic renal failure.[124] Acute kidney injury has been found to be more common among HIV-infected patients than the general patient population and is associated with poor outcomes.[125] Acute kidney injury presents in many forms, but pre-renal failure and acute tubular necrosis are most common. Postulated mechanisms of HIV-induced acute renal failure include medication-induced toxicities, specifically nephrolithiasis with atazanavir and indinavir, Fanconi's Syndrome with tenofovir, and dehydration from opportunistic infections.[125] Pharmacists are vital in the management of HIV-induced renal toxicities and should review the serum creatinine and urinary analysis for the development of acute renal toxicity.[33] Pharmacists should readily identify contributing nephrotoxic medications that may compound nephrotoxicity and recommend possible discontinuation and therapeutic alternatives. In addition, pharmacists should be familiar with common medications used in the treatment of HIV that interfere with the tubular section of creatinine, such as cobicistat, rilpivirine, dolutegravir, ritonavir, and trimethoprim-sulfamethoxazole.[126] These medications, although not inherently nephrotoxic, may increase the serum creatinine and complicate the renal assessment of patients on these antiretroviral medications.

Patients with HIV may also present with chronic forms of nephrotoxicity. Perhaps the most widely recognized form of renal failure in HIV disease is HIV-associated nephropathy (HIVAN). HIVAN is most common among patients of African descent and is a significant contributor to chronic renal failure. ART has been shown to aid in the reversal of HIV nephropathy by suppressing viral replication in the kidney, and pharmacists should advocate for prompt initiation of ART in these circumstances.[127,128] HIV infection may also enhance other common risk factors for chronic kidney disease, such as diabetes and hypertension. As with cardiovascular toxicity, pharmacists should assist in glucose and blood pressure control and additionally recommend therapies such as angiotensin-converting enzyme (ACE) inhibitors or angiotensin receptor blockers that are thought to delay the progression of kidney failure.[129,130]

For patients with renal failure, pharmacists should take responsibility for ensuring appropriate dose adjustments of renally eliminated medications, including antiretroviral medications and other medications on a patient's profile (see Appendix).[35] Active pharmacist involvement in ensuring proper doses of renally eliminated medications has been demonstrated to decrease adverse effects and result in cost savings.[131] Medication renal dose adjustment is especially important in advanced nephropathy requiring dialysis. Pharmacists should be familiar with various dialysis modalities and their effects on medication removal. Pharmacists should then pair this with knowledge of specific medication renal elimination characteristics to ensure safe and effective medication regimens.

Finally, pharmacists knowledgeable about HIV may recommend ART that minimizes nephrotoxicity, taking into consideration the HIV genotype and laboratory markers of HIV disease. Alteration of a patient's ART to minimize renal involvement can lead to enhanced safety and simplification of the HIV regimen. In addition, pharmacists should aim to minimize renal toxicity of all medications prescribed, with the goal of providing a safe and effective complete medication profile.

HIV and Hepatic Disease. As with HIV-associated nephrotoxicity, pharmacists should be cognizant of HIV hepatotoxicity. Although the majority of literature revolves around mechanisms such as medication-induced hepatotoxicity, co-infection with viral hepatitis, and alcohol injury, there is some evidence that HIV infection alone may contribute to accelerated liver damage.[132] Pharmacists should first routinely monitor liver function tests to detect the presence of hepatic toxicity. If clinically significant elevations in hepatic function tests are detected, pharmacists should identify and limit all medications that may induce hepatic injury. Many classes of antiretroviral medications have been linked to hepatotoxicity, including non-nucleoside reverse transcriptase inhibitors and protease inhibitors. Specifically, nevirapine, maraviroc, and tipranavir have boxed warnings for hepatotoxicity, and ART regimens may need to be altered for patients being treated with those medications. If toxicity progresses to advanced liver failure and cirrhosis, pharmacists need to recognize that altered drug metabolism may occur and monitor for medication toxicities and possible treatment failure.[133] Pharmacists should also recommend testing for viral hepatitis, as co-infection has been known to accelerate liver decline.[130] Pharmacists may also recognize current alcohol and illicit drug use and facilitate admission into treatment programs if necessary.[133] In addition, recognizing that alcohol and illicit drug consumption may alter medication adherence, pharmacists should reinforce the importance of medication adherence and adopt adherence strategies that are acceptable to patients. Finally, pharmacists should recommend hepatic dose adjustment of medications for which adjustment has been identified (see Appendix).

HIV and Neurologic Disease. Neurotoxicity and central nervous system disorders are recognized complications of HIV infection. HIV-associated neurocognitive disorders (HAND) classifies certain neurologic HIV complications, including mental slowing, memory loss, motor disorders, and behavioral abnormalities.[134] These progressive symptoms lead to a decline in cognitive function that may eventually develop into HIV dementia. HAND complications occur in approximately half of patients diagnosed with HIV and represent a substantial cause of morbidity and mortality.[134-136] Although the known incidence of HAND is high, this estimate may be conservative, as HAND is often unrecognized and may be under-diagnosed. Pharmacists should be alert to symptoms of possible cognitive decline. If such symptoms are recognized, communication and facilitation with the patient's provider is recommended.

Several theories about the mechanism of HAND have been postulated, with most suggesting that the chronic inflammation state caused by HIV infection generates free radicals that inflict neuronal damage. There is no correlation between the development of HAND and HIV plasma concentration, current CD4 count, or the presence of effective ART.[134,136] The development of HAND has been associated with a low CD4 nadir, however.[137] This association reinforces the need for early initiation of ART to prevent low CD4 levels and protect against the development of neurotoxicity. No other therapy has been shown to prevent or improve HAND, so pharmacists can contribute to the care of these patients by focusing on early and effective utilization of ART.[102, 138]

HAND and its complications have serious ramifications on other aspects of HIV care. Decreased neurologic function has been linked to poor patient adherence to ART and other therapies, unemployment, lack of transportation, and increased reliance on financial assistance for medications.[139] Pharmacists should work closely with their patients to create personalized medication adherence programs and provide access to medication assistance programs. Ensuring safe and effective use of medications is the pharmacists' highest priority in caring for these patients.

Other HIV-associated neurologic complications include peripheral neuropathy and ischemic stroke. Peripheral neuropathy is the most frequently reported neurologic diagnosis in HIV-positive patients and usually responds to medications typically used to treat neuropathic pain.[136] Common causes of peripheral neuropathy in HIV-infected patients include neurotoxic medications (such as didanosine), diabetes, alcohol use, and nutritional deficiencies (such as B_{12}). Pharmacists should assess for the development and progression of peripheral neuropathy and recommend appropriate therapeutic treatment options.

Hospital admissions for ischemic stroke in HIV-infected patients have increased 43% over the last decade in the U.S. The higher incidence of ischemic stroke is thought to be caused by a combination of accelerated atherosclerosis and thrombosis.[101] Pharmacists should play an active role in assisting in the medication selection of acute stroke treatment. Because stroke patients often suffer from dysphagia, necessitating use of short- and long-term enteral feeding tubes, pharmacists should be familiar with guidelines for proper administration of medications via enteral tubes (e.g., determining whether a medication may be crushed and the implications of the site of enteral medication absorption) (see Appendix).[140,141] After an acute stroke episode, pharmacists should be involved in assisting patients with the selection of secondary prevention medications (e.g., antiplatelet and lipid therapies) to minimize drug interactions and maximize the safety and efficacy of the patient's entire medication regimen. Pharmacists should also be aggressive in helping manage modifiable risk factors, such as hypertension, diabetes, and hyperlipidemia. Literature demonstrates that interdisciplinary teams including active pharmacist intervention improve management of ischemic stroke risk factors.[142] Pharmacists should encourage intensive management of these risk factors and other lifestyle modifications, such as smoking cessation, exercise regimens, and weight management programs.

In addition to physiologic causes, medications are another important consideration in the neurological state of the patient with HIV. Pharmacists should review the medication profile for all medications that may affect cognitive function, such as opioid narcotics and benzodiazepines. Certain antiretroviral medications, including efavirenz, have also been associated with CNS abnormalities. The pharmacist should be alert to and aim to minimize the neurological adverse effects of medications in patients experiencing HIV-associated neurotoxicity and recommend appropriate therapeutic alternatives.

HIV and Malignancy. AIDS-associated malignancies are a well-documented complication of HIV, but HIV-infected patients also face increased incidence of other cancer types.[143] Collectively, these cancers are termed "non-AIDS-defining cancers" and include cancers such as Hodgkin's lymphoma and malignancies of the lung, kidney, anus, liver, and skin.[144,145] Guidelines for identification of these cancers overall mimic recommendations for the general population; however, some, such as cervical cancer, require more frequent monitoring, and pharmacists should recommend routine cancer screening when appropriate.

Cancer treatment in patients with HIV presents a challenge to pharmacists and practitioners, as the need to balance cancer cure must be weighed against the risk of chemotherapy-enhanced immunosuppression and resulting opportunistic infections. Given their expertise in drug-drug interaction and toxicity management, pharmacists are uniquely qualified to assist in chemotherapy and ART selection. Pharmacists should be knowledgeable in drug interactions between ART and chemotherapy agents and assist with regimen selections for both disease states that minimize toxicity while ensuring efficacy (see Appendix). In addition, pharmacists can aid in the initiation of appropriate opportunistic infection prophylaxis. Finally, more research is needed on the interaction between cancer, chemotherapy, HIV disease, and ART. Pharmacists should be a key component in future research teams where research is desperately needed to ensure safe and appropriate patient care.

HIV and Endocrine Disease. Patients living with HIV are also at risk for the development of traditional endocrine disorders related to HIV disease, including lipodystrophy, hypogonadism, and HIV wasting syndrome. These conditions are thought to be caused by mitochondrial toxicity and alterations in levels of growth hormone accelerated by adverse effects of antiretroviral medications, specifically protease inhibitors.[146,147] Lipodystrophy consists of an increase in visceral fat and decrease in subcutaneous fat stores, particularly in the face and extremities.[147] Low levels of testosterone may lead to hypogonadism, sexual dysfunction, and muscle wasting in HIV-infected individuals.[148] Some patients with HIV suffer from HIV wasting syndrome due in part to increased energy expenditure that leads to a decrease in lean body mass and total body mass index.[149] New agents are being investigated for treatment of these disorders, and pharmacists caring for patients living with HIV should be knowledgeable about available recommended therapies.[150,151] Specifically, pharmacists may assist in testosterone formulation selection, contraindication assessment, laboratory monitoring, and counseling on proper testosterone administration and adverse effects.[152-154] Pharmacists should also minimize ART agents that have adverse metabolic effects and recommend appropriate alternatives.[147] In addition, pharmacists should work closely with dietitians to ensure appropriate nutrition support for the complete care of the HIV-infected patient.[154] Morphologic complications may have detrimental physical and psychological effects on patients, which may decrease adherence to ART. Pharmacists should be cognizant of morphologic complications, recommend medical and lifestyle modifications as appropriate, and work with patients and providers to maximize treatment and adherence to HIV therapies.

In addition to traditional endocrine complications, alterations in bone metabolism have become a significant endocrine complication of HIV. HIV infection leads to earlier and more frequent loss of bone density than non-infected individuals, leading to increased incidence of osteopenia, osteoporosis and fractures.[155] Like other chronic HIV complications, this is due to traditional risk factors, effects of the virus itself and use of certain antiretroviral therapies, specifically tenofovir.[156] Specific screening recommendations have been developed for patients with HIV, and pharmacists should be informed of these recommendations and take an active role in screening patients for this complication.[157] Pharmacists should also be versed on appropriate osteoporosis treatments and recommend vitamin supplementation and pharmacologic therapy when warranted. In addition, pharmacists should aid in recommending nonpharmacologic strategies for prevention of bone loss, including reducing alcohol intake, smoking cessation, and advocating for healthy body weight.

As patients with HIV live longer, more information will emerge regarding the role of chronic HIV disease state complications. What is already evident is that proper recognition and treatment of cardiovascular, renal, hepatic, neurological, malignant, and endocrine complications is desperately needed to fully care for HIV-infected patients. Pharmacists are integral to the medical team that must care for the whole patient, including HIV infection itself and long-term complications of HIV disease.

Pharmacist Involvement in Opportunistic Infections

Opportunistic infections contribute significantly to the morbidity and mortality of HIV-infected individuals. Although effective ART has reduced the incidence of opportunistic infections, prevention, recognition, and treatment of those infections continue to be of utmost importance in this patient population.[158] The complexity of prophylaxis and treatment of opportunistic infections in HIV patients requires an interdisciplinary approach. Pharmacists can be involved in the prevention and treatment of HIV-associated opportunistic infections by providing recommendations on the initiation or discontinuation of opportunistic infection prophylaxis, the recognition and diagnosis of active opportunistic infections, treatment and dosing recommendations for active opportunistic infections, and the timing of ART initiation. Through these interventions pharmacists play a key role in improving the medication management of individuals with HIV disease.

Pharmacists may first intervene with recommendations for when to initiate opportunistic infection prophylaxis. Medication prophylaxis for various opportunistic infections is offered to individuals with advanced HIV disease. Primary prophylaxis aims to prevent the first occurrence of an opportunistic infection; secondary prophylaxis is geared toward preventing disease recurrence.[159] The decision to initiate prophylaxis is therefore dependent on the patient's CD4 cell count and the patient's history of an active opportunistic infection. Pharmacists should be familiar with and recommend specific prophylactic agents and alternative regimens for patients with medication allergies. Published guidelines that can help pharmacists in making recommendations regarding appropriate prophylactic medications and when to initiate primary and secondary opportunistic infection prophylaxis are available (see Appendix).[160]

The recognition of when to discontinue prophylaxis is as important as its initiation. Literature supports the safety of discontinuation of opportunistic infection prophylaxis when the CD4 cell count rises above a threshold for a defined period of time while on effective ART.[159-161] Pharmacists familiar with discontinuation recommendations may intervene to discourage inappropriate continuation of drug therapy. Discontinuation of opportunistic infection prophylaxis may lead to a decrease in side effects and drug-drug interactions, limit drug resistance, lower pill burden, increase rates of adherence, and provide cost savings.[159]

Pharmacists also play a vital role in the recognition and treatment of active opportunistic infections. Pharmacists aid in the diagnosis of opportunistic infections via symptom recognition and testing recommendations. Once a patient is diagnosed, pharmacists can contribute to the treatment of opportunistic infections by offering evidence-based recommendations on anti-infective drug selection and dosing, monitoring medication efficacy and toxicity, preventing and recognizing drug-drug and drug-nutrient interactions, and making literature-based recommendations on total treatment duration.[160]

After an opportunistic infection has been diagnosed and treatment initiated, pharmacists should be active in determining the optimal timing of ART initiation. The decision regarding ART initiation is complex and must weigh the benefits of ART against the possibility of the complication of immune reconstitution inflammatory syndrome. Although some literature has shown that early ART initiation is paramount in improving survival and decreasing AIDS progression by improved immune functioning, other studies have demonstrated that ART may not improve or may perhaps be detrimental in certain types of opportunistic infections.[162-164] Current guidelines provide recommendations on when to initiate ART in specific types of opportunistic infections and can help guide patients, pharmacists, and other healthcare providers in this decision-making process.[160,165] Pharmacists can assist other HIV care practitioners by providing evidence-based recommendations regarding the initiation of ART in the setting of an active opportunistic infection and contributing to the selection of an ART treatment regimen that avoids interactions with the anti-infective medication regimen.

Patients with opportunistic infections are on complex medication regimens and often require hospitalization. Pharmacists practicing in the inpatient setting play a key role in the appropriate care of these patients by preventing and resolving medication-related errors. Patients with HIV specifically have a high rate of medication errors due to the complexity and alteration of medication regimens, the necessity of transitions of care, and the need for their care to be provided by practitioners that may be unfamiliar with ART and HIV complications.[166] The inpatient setting provides pharmacists a unique venue for impact in the care of HIV-infected patients, and literature has shown that pharmacist involvement specifically in this patient population decreases medication relation errors.[167] Pharmacists should be involved in admission and discharge medication reconciliation, provide patient discharge medication education, and assist with the transition of the patient to outpatient care.

HIV and Immunization. Immunization, as disease prevention, is important in the care of patients with HIV, as immunodeficiency creates enhanced susceptibility to infection acquisition. Pharmacists should be aware of current immunization recommendations for HIV-infected patients and work to assure appropriate and timely routine immunization (see Appendix). Additionally, pharmacists should also be active immunization advocates by facilitating pharmacist-administered immunization programs.

The Advisory Committee on Immunization Practices (ACIP) publishes annual immunization recommendations for all patients, including specific recommendations for those with HIV infection. It is generally accepted that inactivated vaccines are considered safe for HIV-infected patients; some live vaccines may be administered based on a patient's CD4 cell count. Patients with HIV should be immunized against infections such as influenza, pneumococcus, hepatitis A, hepatitis B, and tetanus/diphtheria.[168] In addition, certain immunizations may require different dosages in HIV-infected patients. Pharmacists should be aware of the immunization status of their patients and provide recommendations regarding safe and effective vaccine administration.

Effective seroprotective antibody levels after immunization are a concern in patients with HIV. Immunization is most effective at high CD4 cell counts and may be delayed until the CD4 count is above 200 cells/mm^3. There are situations, however, in which delay is not feasible, as patients with HIV may receive pneumococcal vaccination upon HIV diagnosis and an annual influenza vaccination regardless of CD4 cell count.[169] In addition, certain live vaccines are now being safely administered if the CD4 cell count is near normal levels. Pharmacists should aid HIV care practitioners in the appropriate timing of immunizations to enhance adequate immune response while balancing the safety of vaccine administration.

After determination of immunization needs and timing, pharmacists in the community and clinic settings may also directly administer immunizations. Pharmacist-managed immunization programs improve access to vaccine administration and corresponding immunization rates.[170] Pharmacist immunization administration privileges vary by type of vaccine, patient age, and immunization training requirements, so pharmacists should practice in accordance with state and local regulations. Pharmacists certified or licensed in immunization administration should take an active role in immunizing patients with HIV. Documentation of vaccine administration and communication of immunization status to prescribers and other practitioners should be completed to bridge the continuum of HIV patient care.[171]

Pharmacist Involvement in HIV Prevention

HIV prevention requires an interdisciplinary approach involving pharmacists as active members of the healthcare team. Active pharmacist participation in prevention initiatives can help prevent transmission and reduce the rate of HIV infection. Pharmacists play a key role in HIV prevention through both pharmacological and behavioral interventions.

High viral load is a risk factor for HIV transmission.[35] By reinforcing ART adherence, and subsequently lowering a patient's HIV viral load, the risk of HIV transmission can be reduced. The benefits of ART for prevention have been demonstrated in various populations, including pregnant women, HIV-serodiscordant partners, and geographic communities. Because the risk of mother-to-child transmission is strongly associated with a higher HIV viral load, the use of ART in pregnancy has dramatically reduced the incidence of perinatally acquired HIV infections and is recommended by DHHS guidelines.[42] Decreases in HIV viral load via ART are also associated with decreased heterosexual transmission, as demonstrated in both observational studies and randomized trials.[173-175] Based on these results, DHHS guidelines recommend ART be offered to those at risk of transmitting HIV to sexual partners, including heterosexuals and other risk groups.[35] In addition to the benefits of ART for preventing HIV transmission in serodiscordant couples, data have shown that widespread use of ART may benefit entire communities via reductions in community viral load and decreased numbers of new infections.[176,177]

Medication adherence is the key to maximizing the full benefits of ART. Pharmacist involvement in antiretroviral medication adherence is perhaps the most well-documented prevention intervention in the literature and, as shown in a systematic review, is associated with statistically significant adherence improvements and positive impact on viral suppression.[178] Pharmacist involvement in direct patient-care efforts focused on adherence extend well beyond required prescription counseling and may include providing practical and social support to motivate adherence, educating to enhance patient self-efficacy, regularly monitoring adherence, collaborating with other healthcare professionals, recognizing and managing side effects, making recommendations regarding self-management, advocating for patients with insurance issues, and instructing on the use of adherence-enhancing tools.[178-180] The DHHS adult HIV guidelines provide evidence-based recommendations on assessing and monitoring adherence and outline strategies to help patients maintain high levels of adherence.[35] Identifying patients with adherence challenges requiring attention and implementing methods to enhance adherence are essential roles for all members of the treatment team, including pharmacists.

Although ART adherence is an essential component of HIV prevention among HIV-infected individuals, it is also a necessary factor for prevention among HIV-exposed individuals taking pre- or post-exposure prophylaxis. Pre-exposure prophylaxis (PrEP) is the use of antiretroviral medications by higher-risk, uninfected individuals before and during periods of risk to prevent HIV acquisition. Currently, the fixed-dose combination tablet of tenofovir/emtricitabine taken orally is the only FDA-approved product for PrEP; however, ongoing studies are examining use of other antiretroviral agents in various dosage forms. When responding to patient inquiries regarding PrEP, pharmacists should be familiar with clinical practice guidelines on the use of PrEP in high-risk populations published by CDC and make informed and appropriate recommendations about PrEP safety, efficacy, acquisition, and need for routine follow-up HIV testing.[181] Pharmacists practicing in community settings that sell barrier methods, or those who fill prescriptions for PrEP or medications used to treat sexually transmitted infections, can help identify patients who may benefit from PrEP and link them to PrEP prescribers in the community. The success of PrEP is largely dependent on high levels of medication adherence. To date, five clinical trials have demonstrated the efficacy of PrEP for HIV prevention in various patient populations, with improved efficacy for adherent individuals.[182-186] Notably, other PrEP studies have been halted early due to futility, primarily attributed to lower medication adherence.[187,188] Pharmacists have the opportunity to assist with developing PrEP protocols for newer prevention modalities and, with appropriate training and resources, pharmacists can improve patient understanding, promote medication adherence, and enhance PrEP efficacy.[189,190] Pharmacists are well positioned to play a key role in helping patients make choices about PrEP, managing their therapy, and developing policy.

Post-exposure prophylaxis (PEP) is the short-term use of antiretroviral medications by uninfected individuals following an HIV exposure. CDC has published guidelines for the implementation of HIV post-exposure prophylaxis following both occupational and non-occupational exposures.[191,192] Effective perinatal ART is also thought of as a form of PEP, and pharmacists are involved in prevention of mother-to-child transmission.[193] Opportunities for pharmacist involvement in PEP varies by setting and may include developing institutional protocols, dispensing initial PEP doses, counseling patients on PEP medications, identifying drug interactions, and coordinating follow-up testing. An important resource for pharmacists and other healthcare providers is the Clinician Consultation Center, which provides national expert telephone consultation, free of charge, surrounding PrEP, PEP, and perinatal HIV infection (www.nccc.ucsf.edu). The use of antiretroviral chemoprophylaxis for preventing HIV after accidental or occupational exposure and in maternal-to-fetal transmission has become a widely accepted method to combat HIV, and pharmacists can effectively contribute to these initiatives.

HIV testing, in addition to ensuring early entry into care for HIV-infected individuals, is also an effective HIV prevention strategy. Pharmacists should be an entry point for early HIV testing; they should recognize HIV risk factors and signs and symptoms of HIV/AIDS, and recommend testing, whether it is provided on site in community pharmacies or as a take-home test. Pharmacists should link those who test negative with effective prevention measures, including PrEP. For patients who test positive, pharmacists should ensure that patients access medical care.

Decreasing circulation of contaminated syringes in and beyond the intravenous drug user (IDU) community is a central HIV prevention strategy.[194] Pharmacists can play an integral role in providing HIV prevention and health services to IDU populations by counseling IDUs regarding syringe access and disposal and addiction treatment programs. The literature documents pharmacist participation in providing and encouraging use of sterile syringes and injection equipment, providing patient counseling on harm-reduction strategies (e.g., substance abuse treatment, safe injection and disposal practices, and safe sex practices), and supporting local syringe exchange programs.[194,195] In some areas, IDUs have the option of purchasing syringes from a pharmacy without a prescription. Such policies are controversial, however, and ultimately the decision to sell syringes without a prescription belongs to the individual pharmacist. Pharmacists should be aware of syringe replacement programs in their community and provide appropriate information to IDUs when requested. Providing HIV-related services to IDUs may not only limit HIV transmission but may also present an opportunity to expand healthcare services to a population that is historically underserved and may have limited access to other healthcare services.

Pharmacists should be knowledgeable about behavioral interventions to reduce HIV transmission, although documentation of pharmacists' delivery of behavioral interventions is still nascent. Pharmacists should provide educational messages and materials, advise patients on prevention methods (e.g., condom promotion, safer sex practices, and drug-use counseling), and deliver behavioral risk-reduction counseling.

Pharmacists' unique position in society allows them to contribute to HIV prevention efforts. Pharmacist involvement includes both traditional roles (providing ART education and ensuring legal access to sterile needles and syringes) and innovative roles (developing PrEP protocols and delivering behavioral interventions). As HIV prevention becomes increasingly important, the pharmacist's role will continue to expand within the healthcare team.

Pharmacist Involvement in HIV Education

Pharmacists are extensively involved in providing education to patients and providers about medication-related care, assessing the patient's readiness and ability to adhere to ART, providing initial or follow-up education on HIV-related disease and complications as well as antiretroviral medications, and evaluating adherence to a therapeutic regimen. Pharmacists perform these tasks within an interprofessional healthcare environment. As medication experts, pharmacists play a role in education of patients, communities, and healthcare workers.

A central pharmacist role is patient education and provision of medication counseling to patients and communities. A recent systematic review documents the positive impact of pharmacist-conducted medication adherence education on clinical patient outcomes.[38] Education about medication indication, dose, route, frequency, potential adverse effects, and the importance of adherence should occur at every patient encounter. For returning patients, medication understanding and adherence should be reassessed not just for antiretroviral medications but for all medications. Through patient educational initiatives, pharmacists can assure optimal pharmacotherapy, adherence, and successful outcomes.

Pharmacists often act as an educational liaison between the patient and the medical provider. Pharmacist tasks can include helping with the selection of the optimal ART regimen, assisting patients in overcoming adherence issues, counseling patients, identifying and advising on potential drug-drug interactions, recognizing and managing medication side effects, and providing information on clinically oriented questions. Because HIV management is complex and involves coordination of multi-drug therapies, pharmacists should support providers and assist prescribers and patients in attaining specific disease state goals. Pharmacists have expertise in medication dosing, adverse effects, drug-drug interactions, and medication adherence, and they serve as useful drug information sources for provider and patient inquiries.

Pharmacists practicing in HIV medicine should educate healthcare team members, provide in-service training to healthcare staff, and conduct community seminars for patients, caregivers, and the public on HIV, ART, drug interactions, and adherence. As a leader in HIV medication use, the pharmacist should train colleagues and the next generation of providers by teaching pharmacy students and residents. Trainee education could expand to other health professions, including medical students and residents, nursing students, especially those in advanced degree programs, mid-level provider students, and allied health professions students as well as those receiving advanced training in the field of infectious diseases. Teaching may be clinical in nature (e.g., experiential rotations) or didactic training in a classroom setting.

Emphasis on the importance of keeping current with the rapidly evolving HIV field is vital for both practicing clinicians and future providers. Whatever the setting, pharmacists should continue to serve as a liaison between patients and providers to remain knowledgeable and credible within the field and to interact with colleagues in the HIV field at an interprofessional level. It is important to stay active and to be part of the exchange of information and clinical experience with other connected providers and trainees.

Pharmacist Social Services Involvement

Access to healthcare, including prescription medications, is a growing problem as the cost of healthcare rises. The cost of medications and copayments are major predictors of adherence to medication therapy regimens.[197,198] Many programs are available to assist with healthcare costs, but eligibility guidelines and application processes can be complicated. Pharmacists are well poised to assist patients in overcoming these obstacles, making medications more accessible and reducing costs to individuals and healthcare entities.

Pharmacists are in an ideal position to educate patients, monitor adherence with therapy, and help patients work through drug-related problems. Pharmacists should monitor refills – both for availability and for timeliness – and notify the prescriber of any concerns. Pharmacists also have an important role in being aware when prior authorization requirements exist for medications and how to facilitate approval to prevent delays in medication access for patients.[199] Pharmacists should ensure all antiretroviral medications and medications for opportunistic infection treatment and prophylaxis can be ordered for stock quickly and easily to minimize delays in medication access. Pharmacists can also ensure an adequate stock is available for the most common regimens. Likewise, pharmacists in all settings can play a significant role in medication reconciliation during care transitions.[200] Pharmacists should assist other healthcare providers in providing seamless care transitions (from outpatient care to institutional care, during hospitalization, and at the time of discharge) to prevent medication errors.[201] Pill burden, side effects, and demands on time and attention pose considerable obstacles to adherence; helping patients obtain their medications in a timely manner removes one major obstacle.

Pharmacists should assist patients at risk of nonadherence due to limited financial means. Patients often misunderstand available insurance benefits, and pharmacists can support patients by reviewing drug formularies, suggesting cost-effective options, and relaying this information to the prescriber. Pharmacists must know how to access national, state, and local resources. For patients with prescription drug insurance but difficulty affording copayments, or for patients lacking insurance, the pharmacist should confirm all medications are necessary and identify less-expensive alternatives. Many antiretroviral medication manufacturers offer prescription copay cards that reduce a patient's out-of-pocket costs. Pharmaceutical manufacturers also offer patient assistance programs (PAPs) to ease the financial burden of medications. Eligibility criteria and enrollment requirements for PAPs vary, but they generally include documentation of limited income, lack of prescription drug coverage, and ineligibility for public assistance. Although PAP applications usually require both the prescriber's and the patient's signature, pharmacists can assist in the application process.[197,198] Pharmacists should also be aware of pharmacies—local or mail order—that offer special generic retail pricing, which is sometimes less than insurance copayments.

Pharmacists should have the knowledge to effectively help low-income patients gain access to national and state-level prescription drug programs for which they may be eligible, including Medicare Part D, Ryan White AIDS Drug Assistance Programs (ADAPs), and Medicaid. Medicare Part D is designed to offer the beneficiary a choice between prescription drug plans, and many pharmacists offer Part D plan selection assistance to help beneficiaries obtain optimal drug coverage.[202] ADAPs are available in each state, guaranteeing antiretroviral medication prescription assistance to low-income and under- and uninsured HIV-infected patients. The Patient Protection and Affordable Care Act will expand health insurance program eligibility and provide opportunities for pharmacists to assist with care coordination and expand their scopes of practice.[203] Although pharmacists cannot choose prescription drug plans for patients, pharmacists should serve as a resource to help patients understand their options to ensure continued access to antiretroviral medications.

Pharmacist Professional Involvement

Although pharmacists have a role in direct HIV patient care, there are other ways pharmacists can assist the HIV patient population. Pharmacists should be active in extracurricular professional involvement, which can be achieved via organizational membership, HIV pharmacist certification, advocacy initiatives, volunteer positions, and participation in clinical research. These areas represent possible opportunities for pharmacists to supplement clinical roles.

In recent years, HIV-focused professional organizations have expanded to include pharmacist membership. State and regional AIDS Education and Training Centers have embraced pharmacist involvement and many provide education, networking, and faculty appointments for pharmacists involved in HIV care. On a national scale, the American Academy of HIV Medicine (AAHIVM) encourages pharmacist membership and invites pharmacists to serve as active members in organizational leadership and committees. Several national HIV organizations also have pharmacist-specific registration, programming, and continuing education credit opportunities at their educational conventions. Internationally, the Canadian HIV/AIDS Pharmacist Network (CHAP) strives to connect pharmacists involved in HIV care and provides educational information to its members. In addition, the International Association of Providers of AIDS Care has expanded to recognize pharmacists as part of the HIV treatment team. Pharmacists involved in HIV care should strive to be active members of professional organizations, attend organizational meetings, provide meeting lectures on HIV clinical updates, participate in the sharing of HIV information via pharmacist networks, and support enhanced pharmacist membership in these organizations (see Appendix).

The creation of pharmacist HIV credentialing programs highlights the importance of having pharmacists knowledgeable about and trained in the treatment of HIV disease. The American Academy of HIV Medicine HIV Pharmacist credential (AAHIVP) is offered to pharmacists who have completed certain requirements, such as evidence of direct HIV patient care, HIV continuing education, and successful completion of the AAHIVP credentialing exam.[204] Other institutions also offer specific pharmacist HIV certificate programs. Pharmacists should investigate certification opportunities, seek the knowledge and skills necessary to be certified HIV providers, and lead the pharmacy profession in the care of the HIV patient (see Appendix).

Pharmacists should also be aware of local and national policy issues surrounding HIV care. The world of HIV changes rapidly, and many challenges require legislative or regulatory action. Pharmacists should be advocates for HIV patients by being familiar with current HIV legislation and national HIV programs such as the Ryan White Program. Pharmacists should also contact local and national policymakers to ensure proper education about HIV issues, be involved in HIV advisory panels, provide expert testimony, and participate in advocacy initiatives to assist in the development of laws that best serve HIV patients. Through these opportunities, pharmacists can steer policy development and actively advocate for HIV patients.

There are also many opportunities for pharmacists to volunteer for HIV-related activities. Locally, pharmacists can volunteer in their communities by participating in fundraising events such as AIDS walks, auctions, and other functions in which proceeds go to fund local HIV programs. Many communities are in need of pharmacists to serve in free medical and dental clinics, where underserved patients receive access to much-needed HIV care. Pharmacists can also choose to volunteer outside of their communities, through programs such as Doctors Without Borders that focus on delivering HIV care and medications to developing countries.[205] There are numerous volunteer opportunities that benefit HIV patients outside of medical settings, and pharmacists should dedicate time to serving in these capacities.

Finally, pharmacists should play an active role in HIV clinical research. Pharmacists should be knowledgeable about ongoing clinical research trials on topic areas such as new antiretroviral medications, disease state complications, and prevention strategies that will shape the future of HIV care. Pharmacists can serve in a variety of capacities as part of HIV clinical research teams, as principal or co-investigators, in recruitment and consent of trial participants, and in facilitation of clinical research trials within their practice settings.[206] Permissible scope of pharmacist involvement in clinical research varies by state, and pharmacists should be familiar with laws that define pharmacist activity. Pharmacists may also be involved in research by publishing case reports, serving on institutional review boards, acting as consultants in HIV clinical research trials, and serving as research mentors to other practitioners caring for patients with HIV. With over 30 antiretroviral medications available, and more in the investigational pipeline, pharmacists can have an integral role in facilitating the introduction of safe and effective HIV medications and clinical research.

Pharmacist involvement in the care of the HIV patient extends beyond the bedside to include other types of professional activity. Through organizational membership, HIV pharmacist certification, advocacy initiatives, volunteer positions, and participation in clinical research, pharmacists should be true advocates in all aspects of HIV patient care. Pharmacists are a tremendous resource that should be mobilized and each pharmacist has a responsibility to be an active proponent for the advancement of HIV care.

Conclusion

HIV medicine is a dynamic field that has evolved dramatically since its inception. It continues to evolve today, providing both opportunities and challenges to delivering optimal patient care. These challenges and opportunities should be met with interprofessional efforts that identify and optimize the roles of all healthcare team members, including pharmacists, as a means to provide comprehensive care and improve patient outcomes. The pharmacist in particular is uniquely capable of contributing to all components of HIV care by being highly accessible to both patients and providers in a variety of healthcare settings. Their expert drug therapy knowledge and clinical skills provide an avenue for proficient clinical consultation with other healthcare providers as well as effective patient interactions through counseling and education. Furthermore, given their training and skill set, pharmacists are well positioned to help meet the current and future challenges of HIV medicine, including the delivery of comprehensive primary care to an aging HIV patient population as well as identification and management of the long-term complications of HIV infection and ART. Given the ongoing evolution of HIV medicine, pharmacists must continue to evolve their roles as a part of the healthcare team to identify and meet the future needs of HIV-positive patients. This goal can be achieved through continuous assessment of the role of the HIV pharmacist, the development and maintenance of HIV specialty pharmacist training programs and expert certification, and the continued collaboration with other healthcare providers, patients, activist groups, and professional HIV medicine and pharmacy organizations.

References

1. Centers for Disease Control and Prevention. *MMWR*. 1981; 30(25):305–8.
2. Hall HI, Song R, Rhodes P, et al. Estimation of HIV incidence in the United States. *JAMA*. 2008; 300:520–9.
3. Rodger AJ, Lodwick R, Schecter M, et al. Mortality in well controlled HIV in the continuous antiretroviral therapy arms of the SMART and ESPRIT trials compared with the general population. *AIDS*. 2013; 27(6):973–9.
4. Centers for Disease Control and Prevention. Estimates of new HIV infections in the United States, 2006-2009. August 2011. Available at: http://www.cdc.gov/nchhstp/newsroom/docs/HIV-Infections-2006–2009.pdf. Accessed October 16, 2012.
5. El-Sadr WM, Mayer KH, Adimora AA. The HIV epidemic in the United States: A time for action. *JAIDS*. 2010; 55:S63.
6. Millet GA, Crowley JS, Koh H, et al. A way forward: The national HIV/AIDS strategy and reducing HIV incidence in the United States. *JAIDS*. 2010; 55:S144–S147.
7. El-Sadr WM, Mayer KH, Hodder SL. AIDS in America – Forgotten but not gone. *New Engl J Med*. 2010; 362:967–70.
8. Moore RD. Epidemiology of HIV Infection in the United States: Implications for Linkage to Care. *Clin Infect Dis*. 2011; 52:S208–S213.
9. Centers for Disease Control and Prevention. U.S. Department of Health and Human Services. *MMWR*. 2011; 60(47):1618–23.
10. Smith M, Bates DW, Bodenheimer TS. Pharmacists belong in accountable care organizations and integrated care teams. *Health Aff*. 2013; 11: 1963–70.
11. Smith M, Bates DW, Bodenhimer TS, et al. Why pharmacists belong in the medical home. *Health Aff*. 2010; 5: 906–13.
12. Henderson KC, Hindman J, Johnson SC, et al. Assessing the effectiveness of pharmacy-based adherence interventions on antiretroviral adherence in persons with HIV. AIDS Patient Care STDs 2011; 25(4):221–8.
13. Ma A, Chen D, Chau F, et al. Improving adherence and clinical outcomes through an HIV pharmacist's interventions. *AIDS Care*. 2010; 22(10):1189–94.
14. March K, Mak M, Louie SG. Effects of pharmacists' interventions on patient outcomes in an HIV primary care clinic. *Am J Health-Syst Pharm*. 2007; 64(24):2574–8.
15. Merchen BA, Gerzenshtein L, Scarsi KK, et al. HIV-specialized pharmacists' impact on prescribing errors in hospitalized patients on antiretroviral therapy [abstract H2-794]. 51st Interscience Conference on Antimicrobial Agents and Chemotherapy. Chicago, IL: 2011 Sep 17–20.
16. Heelon M, Skiest D, Tereso G, et al. Effect of a clinical pharmacist's intervention on duration of antiretroviral-related errors in hospitalized patients. *Am J Health-Syst Pharm*. 2007; 64(19):2064–8.
17. American Society of Health-System Pharmacists. ASHP statement on the pharmacist's role in the care of patients with HIV infection. *Am J Health-Syst Pharm*. 2003; 60(19):1998–2003.
18. Centers for Disease Control and Prevention. Monitoring selected national HIV prevention and care objectives by using HIV surveillance data—United States and 6 dependent areas—2011. HIV Surveillance Supplemental Report 2013; 18(No. 5). http://www.

cdc.gov/hiv/library/reports/surveillance/. Published October 2013. Accessed November 24, 2014.

19. Branson BM, Handsfield HH, Lampe MA, et al. Revised recommendations for HIV testing of adults, adolescents, and pregnant women in health-care settings. *MMWR Recomm Rep.* 2006; 55:1–17.
20. Moyer VA on behalf of the U.S. Preventive Services Task Force. Screening for HIV: U.S. Preventive Services Task Force Recommendation Statement. *Ann Intern Med.* 2013; 159:210–8.
21. Weidle PJ, Lecher S, Botts LW, et al. HIV testing in community pharmacies and retail clinics: a model to expand access to screening for HIV infection. *J Am Pharm Assoc.* (2003) 2014; 54(5):486–92.
22. Darin KM, Klepser ME, Klepser DE, et al. Pharmacist-provided rapid HIV testing in two community pharmacies. *J Am Pharm Assoc.* (2003). 2014 Nov 21; e7–e14. [Epub ahead of print].
23. Sherman EM, Elrod S, Allen D, et al. Pharmacist testers in multidisciplinary health care team expand HIV point-of-care testing program. *J Pharm Pract.* 2014; 27(6):578–81.
24. Michigan Pharmacists Association. Community pharmacy based rapid diagnostic testing certificate course and train-the trainer program. http://www.michigan-pharmacists.org/resources/pointofcare. Accessed December 2, 2014.]
25. Amesty S, Blaney S, Crawford ND, et al. Pharmacy staff characteristics associated with support for pharmacy-based HIV testing. *J Am Pharm Assoc.* 2012; 52:472–9.
26. Deas CM, McCree DH. Pharmacists and HIV/AIDS prevention: Review of the literature. *J Am Pharm Assoc.* 2010; 50:411–5.
27. Lutnick A, Case P, Kral AH. Injection drug users' perspectives on placing HIV prevention and other clinical services in pharmacy settings. *J Urban Health.* 2012; 89:354–64.
28. Darin KM, Scarsi KK, Klepser DG, et al. Consumer interest in community pharmacy HIV screening services. *J Am Pharm Assoc.* (2003). 2014; Nov 21:e1–e6. [Epub ahead of print]
29. U.S. Food and Drug Administration [press release]. FDA approves first over-the-counter home-use rapid HIV test. Accessed at www.fda.gov/NewsEvents/Newsroom/PressAnnouncements/ucm310542.htm, August 9, 2012.
30. Centers for Disease Control and Prevention and Association of Public Health Laboratories. Laboratory testing for the diagnosis of HIV infection: updated recommendations. Available at http://stacks.cdc.gov/view/cdc/23447. Published June 27, 2014. Accessed December 4, 2014.
31. Waldura JF, Neff S, Goldschmidt RH. Teleconsultation for clinicians who provide human immunodeficiency virus care: experience of the National HIV Telephone Consultation Service. *Telemed J E Health.* 2011; 17:472–7.
32. Neff S, Goldschmidt RH. State Human Immunodeficiency Virus Testing Laws. *Arch Intern Med.* 2008; 168:1717–8.
33. Aberg JA, Gallant JE, Ghanem KG, et al. Primary care guidelines for the management of persons infected with human immunodeficiency virus: 2013 update by the HIV Medicine Association of the Infectious Disease Society of America. *Clin Infect Dis.* 2013 Nov 13 [epub ahead of print].
34. U.S. Department of Health and Human Services. Health Resources and Services Administration, HIV/AIDS Bureau. Guide for HIV/AIDS Clinical Care, 2011. http://hab.hrsa.gov/deliverhivaidscare/clinical-guide11.
35. Panel on Antiretroviral Guidelines for Adults and Adolescents. Guidelines for the use of antiretroviral agents in HIV-1-infected adults and adolescents. Department of Health and Human Services. Available at http://aidsinfo.nih.gov/ContentFiles/AdultandAdolescentGL.pdf.
36. Yehia BR, Mehta JM, Ciuffetelli D, et al. Antiretroviral medication errors remain high but are quickly corrected among hospitalized HIV-infected adults. *Clin Infect Dis.* 2012; 55:593–9.
37. Liao TV, Rab S, Armstrong WS. Evaluation of medication errors in patients infected with human immunodeficiency virus treated with antiretroviral therapy. *Am J Health-Syst Pharm.* 2012; 69:1461–2.
38. Saberi P, Dong BJ, Johnson MO, et al. The impact of HIV clinical pharmacists on HIV treatment outcomes: a systematic review. *Patient Pref Adherence.* 2012; 6: 297–322.
39. Kauffman Y, Nair V, Herist K, et al. HIV medication therapy management services in community pharmacies. *J Am Pharm Assoc.* 2012; 52:e287–91.
40. Centers for Disease Control and Prevention. U.S. Department of Health and Human Services. Monitoring selected national HIV prevention and care objectives by using HIV surveillance data—United States and 6 U.S. dependent areas—2010. HIV Surveillance Supplemental Report 2012; 17(No. 3, part A). http://www.cdc.gov/hiv/surveillance/resources/reports/2010supp_vol17no3/index.htm
41. Centers for Disease Control and Prevention. U.S. Department of Health and Human Services. Estimated HIV incidence in the United States, 2007–2010. HIV Surveillance Supplemental Report 2012; 17(No. 4). http://www.cdc.gov/hiv/topics/surveillance/resources/reports/#supplemental.
42. Panel on Treatment of HIV-Infected Pregnant Women and Prevention of Perinatal Transmission. Recommendations for Use of Antiretroviral Drugs in Pregnant HIV-1-Infected Women for Maternal Health and Interventions to Reduce Perinatal HIV Transmission in the United States. Available at http://aidsinfo.nih.gov/contentfiles/lvguidelines/PerinatalGL.pdf
43. Palumbo PE, Kwok S, Waters S, et al. Viral measurement by polymerase chain reaction-based assays in human immunodeficiency virus-infected infants. *J Pediatr.* Apr 1995; 126(4):592–5.
44. Shearer WT, Quinn TC, LaRussa P, et al. Viral load and disease progression in infants infected with human immunodeficiency virus type 1. Women and Infants Transmission Study Group. *N Engl J Med.* May 8 1997; 336(19):1337–42.
45. HIV Paediatric Prognostic Markers Collaborative Study. Predictive value of absolute CD4 cell count for

disease progression in untreated HIV-1-infected children. *AIDS*. Jun 12 2006; 20(9):1289–94.
46. Dunn D. HIV Paediatric Prognostic Markers Collaborative Study. Short-term risk of disease progression in HIV-1-infected children receiving no antiretroviral therapy or zidovudine monotherapy: a meta-analysis. *Lancet*. Nov 15 2003; 362(9396):1605–11.
47. Dunn D, Woodburn P, Duong T, et al. Current CD4 cell count and the short-term risk of AIDS and death before the availability of effective antiretroviral therapy in HIV-infected children and adults. *J Infect Dis*. Feb 1 2008; 197(3):398–404.
48. Boyd K, Dunn DT, Castro H, et al. HIV Paediatric Prognostic Markers Collaborative Study. Discordance between CD4 cell count and CD4 cell percentage: implications for when to start antiretroviral therapy in HIV-1 infected children. *AIDS*. May 15, 2010; 24(8):1213–7.
49. Kearns GL, Abdel-Rahman SM, Alander SW, et al. Developmental pharmacology-drug disposition, action, and therapy in infants and children. *N Engl J Med*. Sep 18 2003; 349(12):1157–67.
50. Panel on Antiretroviral Therapy and Medical Management of HIV-Infected Children. Guidelines for the Use of Antiretroviral Agents in Pediatric HIV Infection. Available at http://aidsinfo.nih.gov/contentfiles/lvguidelines/pediatricguidelines.pdf. Accessed May 1, 2013.
51. Murphy DA, Sarr M, Durako SJ, et al. Barriers to HAART adherence among human immunodeficiency virus-infected adolescents. *Arch Pediatr Adolesc Med*. Mar 2003; 157(3):249–55.
52. Merzel C, Vandevanter N, Irvine M. Adherence to antiretroviral therapy among older children and adolescents with HIV: a qualitative study of psychosocial contexts. *AIDS Patient Care STDs*. Dec 2008; 22(12):977–87.
53. Mellins CA, Brackis-Cott E, Dolezal C, et al. The role of psychosocial and family factors in adherence to antiretroviral treatment in human immunodeficiency virus-infected children. *Pediatr Infect Dis J*. Nov 2004; 23(11):1035–41.
54. Malee K, Williams P, Montepiedra G, et al. Medication adherence in children and adolescents with HIV infection: associations with behavioral impairment. *AIDS Patient Care STDs*. Mar 2011; 25(3):191–200.
55. Guaraldi G, Orlando G, Zona S, et al. Premature age-related comorbidities among HIV-infected persons compared with the general population. *Clin Infect Dis*. 2011; 53(11):1120–6.
56. Centers for Disease Control and Prevention Fact Sheet: HIV/AIDS among Persons Aged 50 and Older. http://www.cdc.gov/hiv/topics/over50/resources/factsheets/over50.htm
57. Anuurad E, Semrad A, Berglund L. Human immunodeficiency virus and highly active antiretroviral therapy–associated metabolic disorders and risk factors for cardiovascular disease. *Met Synd Relat Disord*. 2009; 5:401–9.
58. Kotler DP. HIV and antiretroviral therapy: lipid abnormalities and associated cardiovascular risk in HIV-infected patients. *J Acquir Immune Defic Syndr*. 2008; 49:S79–S85.
59. Gupta SK, Eustace JA, Winston JA, et al. Guidelines for the management of chronic kidney disease in HIV-infected patients: recommendations of the HIV Medicine Association of the Infectious Diseases Society of America. *Clin Infect Dis*. 2005; 40:1559–85.
60. Dube MP. Disorders of glucose metabolism in patients infected with Human Immunodeficiency Virus. *Clin Infect Dis*. 2000; 31:1467–75.
61. Triant VA, Brown TT, Lee H, et al. Fracture prevalence among human immunodeficiency virus (HIV)-infected versus non HIV-infected patients in a large U.S. health care system. *J Clin Endocrinol Metab*. 2008; 93:3499–504.
62. Young B, Dao CN, Buchacz K, et al. Increased rates of bone fracture among HIV-infected persons in the HIV Outpatient Study (HOPS) compared with the US general population, 2000–2006. *Clin Infect Dis*. 2011; 52:1061–8.
63. Bedimo R, Maalouf NM, Zhang S, et al. Osteoporotic fracture associated with cumulative exposure to tenofovir and other antiretroviral agents. *AIDS*. 2012; 26:825–31.
64. Do AN, Rosenberg ES, Beer L, et al. Excess burden of depression among HIV-infected persons receiving medical care in the United States: data from the medical monitoring project and behavioral risk factor surveillance system. *PloS One*. 2014; 9:e92842.
65. Hicks PL, Mulvey KP, Chander G, et al. The impact of illicit drug use and substance abuse treatment on adherence to HAART. *AIDS Care*. 2007; 19(9):1134–40.
66. Cofrancesco J, Jr., Scherzer R, Tien PC, et al. Illicit drug use and HIV treatment outcomes in a US cohort. *AIDS*. 2008; 22(3):357–65.
67. Tucker JS, Burman MA, Sherbourne CD, et al. Substance use and mental health correlates of nonadherence to antiretroviral medications in a sample of patients with human immunodeficiency virus infection. *Am J Med*. 2003; 114:573–80.
68. Morris JD, Golub ET, Mehta SH, et al. Injection drug use and patterns of highly active antiretroviral therapy use: an analysis of ALIVE, WIHS, and MACS cohorts. *AIDS Res Ther*. 2007; 4:12.
69. Gruber VA, McCance-Katz EF. Methadone, buprenorphine, and street drug interactions with antiretroviral medications. *Curr HIV/AIDS Rep*. 2010; 7(3):152–60.
70. Bruce RD, Altice FL, Gourevitch MN, et al. A review of pharmacokinetic drug interactions between drugs of abuse and antiretroviral medications: implications and management for clinical practice. *Exp Rev of Clin Pharmacol*. 2008; 1(1):115–27.
71. Spradling PR, Richardson JT, Buchacz K, et al. Prevalence of chronic hepatitis B virus infection among patients in the HIV Outpatient Study, 1996-2007. *J Viral Hepat*. 2010; 17:879–86.
72. Thio CL, Seaberg EC, Skolasky R, Jr, et al. HIV-1, hepatitis B virus, and risk of liver-related mortality in the Multicenter Cohort Study (MACS). *Lancet*. 2002; 360(9349):1921–6.
73. McMahon MA, Jilek BL, Brennan TP, et al. The HBV drug entecavir - effects on HIV-1 replication and resistance. *N Engl J Med*. 2007; 356(25):2614–21.
74. Sulkowski MS, Mast EE, Seeff LB, et al. Hepatitis C virus infection as an opportunistic disease in persons

infected with human immunodeficiency virus. *Clin Infect Dis*. 2000; 30(Suppl 1):S77–S84.

75. Macias J, Berenguer J, Japon MA, et al. Fast fibrosis progression between repeated liver biopsies in patients coinfected with human immunodeficiency virus/hepatitis C virus. *Hepatology*. 2009; 50:1056–63.
76. Marino EL, Alvarez-Rubio L, Miro S, et al. Pharmacist intervention in treatment of patients with genotype 1 chronic hepatitis C. *J Manag Care Pharm*. 2009; 15:147–50.
77. Rosenquist A, Best BM, Miller TA, et al. Medication therapy management services in community pharmacy: a pilot program in HIV specialty pharmacies. *J Eval Clin Pract*. 2010; 16:1142–6.
78. AASLD/IDSA/IAS–USA. Recommendations for testing, managing, and treating hepatitis C. http://www.hcvguidelines.org. Accessed December 26, 2014.
79. Stock PG, Barin B, Murphy B, et al. Outcomes of kidney transplantation in HIV-infected recipients. *N Engl J Med*. 2010; 363:2004–14.
80. Terrault NA, Roland ME, Schiano T, et al. Outcomes of liver transplant recipients with hepatitis C and human immunodeficiency virus coinfection. *Liver Transpl*. 2012; 18:716–26.
81. Blumberg EA, Stock P, and the AST Infectious Diseases Community of Practice. Solid organ transplantation in the HIV-infected patient. *Am J Transplant*. 2009; 9(suppl 4):S131–5.
82. Roland ME, Barin B, Carlson L, et al. HIV-infected liver and kidney transplant recipients: 1- and 3-year outcomes. *Am J Transplant*. 2008; 8:355–65.
83. Stock P, Roland M, Hanto D, et al. Early and unexpected results in a multicenter study of kidney transplant recipients. *Am J Transplant*. 2009; 9(suppl 2):197.
84. Terrault NA, Carter JT, Carlson L, et al. Outcome of patients with Hepatitis B virus and human immunodeficiency virus infections referred for liver transplantation. *Liver Transpl*. 2006; 12:801–7.
85. De Vera ME, Vorchik I, Tom K, et al. Survival of liver transplant patients coinfected with HIV and HCV is adversely impacted by recurrent Hepatitis C. *Am J Transplant*. 2006; 6:2983–93.
86. DuClos-Vallee J-C, Feray JC, Sebagh M, et al. Survival and recurrence of hepatitis C after liver transplantation in patients coinfected with human immunodeficiency virus and hepatitis C virus. *Hepatology*. 2008; 47:407–17.
87. Chisholm MA, Mulloy LL, Jaqadeesan M, et al. Impact of clinical pharmacy services on renal transplant patients' compliance with immunosuppressive medications. *Clin Transplant*. 2001; 15:330–6.
88. Roland ME, Barin B, Carlson L, et al. HIV-infected liver and kidney transplant recipients: 1- and 3-year outcomes. *Am J Transplant*. 2008; 8:355–65.
89. Gasser O, Bihl F, Sanghavi S, et al. treatment-dependent loss of polyfunctional CD8+ T-cell responses in HIV-infected kidney transplant recipients is associated with herpesvirus reactivation. *Am J Transplant*. 2009; 9:794–803.
90. Carter JT, Melcher ML, Carlson LL, et al. Thymoglobulin-associated CD4+ T-cell depletion and infection risk in HIV-infected renal transplant recipients. *Am J Transplant*. 2006; 6:753–60.
91. Centers for Disease Control and Prevention, U.S. Department of Health and Human Services. Medical examination of aliens—removal of human immunodeficiency virus infection from definition of communicable diseases of public health significance. Final Rule. *Fed Regist*. 2009; 74:56547–62.
92. Winston SE, Beckwith CG. The impact of removing the immigration ban on HIV-infected persons. *AIDS Patient Care STDs*. 2011; 25:709–11.
93. Centers for Disease Control and Prevention, U.S. Department of Health and Human Services, National Center for Emerging and Zoonotic Infectious Diseases. Screening for HIV infection during the refugee domestic medical examination. Division of Global Migration and Quarantine, April 1, 2012.
94. Akinsete OO, Sides T, Hirigoyen D, et al. Demographic, clinical, and virologic characteristics of African-born persons with HIV/AIDS in a Minnesota hospital. *AIDS Patient Care STDs*. 2007; 21:356–65.
95. Tassy Prosser A, Tang T, Hall HI. HIV persons born outside the United States, 2007-2010. *JAMA*. 2012; 308:601–7.
96. Tanaka Y, Kunni O, Hatano T, et al. Knowledge, attitude, and practice (KAP) of HIV prevention and HIV infection risks among Congolese refugees in Tanzania. *Health Place*. 2008:14:434–52.
97. Thompson MA, Mugavero MJ, Amico KR, et al. Guidelines for improving entry into and retention in care and antiretroviral adherence for persons with HIV: Evidence-based recommendations from an international association of physicians in AIDS care panel. *Ann Intern Med*. 2012; 146:817–33.
98. Kredo T, Van der Walt JS, Siegfried N, et al. Therapeutic drug monitoring of antiretrovirals for people with HIV (review). *Cochrane Database Syst Rev*. 2009, Issue 3. Art No.: CD007268. DOI: 10.1002/14651858.CD007268.pub2.
99. Liu TF, Shafer RW. Web resources for HIV Type 1 Genotype-Resistance Test Interpretation. *Clin Infect Dis*. 2006; 42:1608–18.
100. Neuhaus J, Angus B, Kowalska JD, et al. Risk of all-cause mortality associated with nonfatal AIDS and serious non-AIDS events among adults infected with HIV. *AIDS*. 2010; 24:697–706.
101. Benjamin LA, Bryer A, Emsley HC, et al. HIV infection and stroke: current perspectives and future directions. *Lancet Neurol*. 2012; 11:878–90.
102. Schifitto G, Zhang J, Evans SR, et al. A multicenter trial of selegiline transdermal system for HIV-associated cognitive impairment. *Neurology*. 2007; 69:1314–21.
103. Auerbach E, Aboulafia DM. Venous and arterial thromboembolic complications associated with HIV infection and highly active antiretroviral therapy. *Semin Thromb Hemost*. 2012; 38(8):830–8.
104. Friis-Moller N, Sabin CA, Weber R, et al. Combination antiretroviral therapy and the risk of myocardial infarction. *N Engl J Med*. 2003; 349:1993–2003.
105. Boccara F, Mary-Krause M, Teiger E, et al. Acute coronary syndrome in human immunodeficiency virus-

infected patients: characteristics and 1 year prognosis. *Eur Heart J.* 2001; 32:41–50.

106. Dakin CL, O'Conner CA, Patsdaughter CA. HAART to heart: HIV-related cardiomyopathy and other cardiovascular complications. *AACN Clin Issues.* 2006; 17:18–29.
107. Reinsch N, Neuhasu K, Esser S, et al. Prevalence of cardiac diastolic dysfunction in HIV-infected patients: results of the HIV-HEART study. *HIV Clin Trials.* 2010; 11:156–62.
108. Calmy A, Gayet-Ageron A, Montecucco F, et al. HIV increases markers of cardiovascular risk: results from a randomized, treatment interruption trial. *AIDS* 2009; 23:929–39.
109. El-Sadr WM, Lundgren JD, Neaton JD, et al. CD4+ count-guided interruption of antiretroviral treatment. *N Engl J Med.* 2006; 335:2283–96.
110. Bunting BA, Smith BH, Sutherland SE. The Ashville Project: Clinical and economic outcomes of a community-based long-term medication therapy management program for hypertension and dyslipidemia. *J Am Pharm Assoc.* 2008; 48:23–31.
111. Till LT Jr., Voris JC, Bourne Horst J. Assessment of clinical pharmacist management of lipid-lowering therapy in a primary care setting. *J Managed Care Pharm.* 2003; (9)3:269–73.
112. Simpson SH, Majjumdar SR, Tsuyuki RT, et al. Effect of adding pharmacists to primary care teams on blood pressure control in patients with type 2 diabetes. *Diabetes Care.* 2011; 34:20–26.
113. Morello CM, Zadvornky EB, Cording MA, et al. Development and clinical outcomes of pharmacist-managed diabetes care clinics. *Am J Health-Syst Pharm.* 2006; 63:1325–31.
114. Gerber J, Parra D, Beckey NP, et al. Optimizing drug therapy in patients with cardiovascular disease: the impact of pharmacist-managed pharmacotherapy clinics in a primary care setting. *Pharmacotherapy.* 2002; 22:738–47.
115. Doler NM, Dolder CR. Comparison of a pharmacist-managed lipid clinic: In-person versus telephone. *J Am Pharm Assoc.* 2010; 50:375–8.
116. Pape GA, Hunt JS, Butler KL, et al. Team-based care approach to cholesterol management in diabetes mellitus. *Arch Intern Med.* 2011; 17:1480–6.
117. Johnson KA, Chen S, Cheng IN, et al. The impact of clinical pharmacy services integrated into medical homes on diabetes-related clinical outcomes. *Ann Pharmacother.* 2010; 44:1877–86.
118. Petoumenos K, Worm S, Reiss P, et al. Rates of cardiovascular disease following smoking cessation in patients with HIV infection: results from the D:A:D study. *HIV Medicine.* 2011; 12:412–21.
119. Mutimura E, Crowther NJ, Cade TW, et al. Exercise training reduces central adiposity and improves metabolic indices in HAART-treated HIV-positive subjects in Rwanda: a randomized control trial. *AIDS Res Hum Retroviruses.* 2008; 24(1):15–21.
120. Lima EM, Cualandro DM, Yu PC, et al. Cardiovascular prevention in HIV patients: results from a successful intervention program. *Atherosclerosis.* 2009; 204(1):299–32.
121. Sabin C, Worm SW, Weber R. Use of nucleoside reverse transcriptase inhibitors and risk of myocardial infarction in HIV-infected patients enrolled in the D:A:D study: a multi-cohort collaboration. *Lancet.* 2008; 372:1417–26.
122. SMART Study Group. CD4+ count-guided interruption of antiretroviral treatment. *N Engl J Med.* 2006; 355(22):2283–96.
123. Friis-Moller N, Reiss P, Sabin CA, et al. Class of antiretroviral drugs and the risk of myocardial infarction. *N Engl J Med.* 2007; 356:1723–35.
124. Yongmei L, Skilpak MG, Grunfeld C, et al. Incidence and risk factors for acute kidney injury in HIV infection. *Am J Nephrol.* 2012; 35:327–34.
125. Wyatt CM, Stenger M. The kidney in HIV infection: beyond HIV-associated nephropathy. *Top Antivir Med.* 2012; 20(3):106–10.
126. Maggi P, Montinaro V, Mussino C, et al. Novel antiretroviral drugs and renal function monitoring of HIV patients. *AIDS Rev.* 2014; 16(3) [Epub ahead of print]
127. Atta MG, Gallant JE, Rahman MH, et al. Antiretroviral therapy in the treatment of HIV-associated nephropathy. *Nephrol Dial Transplant.* 2006; 21:2809–13.
128. Kalayjian RC, Franceschini N, Gupta SK, et al. Suppression of HIV-1 replication by antiretroviral therapy improves renal function in persons with low CD4 cell counts and chronic kidney disease. *AIDS.* 2008; 22:481–7.
129. Choi AI, Yongmei L, Deeks SG, et al. Association between kidney function and albuminuria with cardiovascular events in HIV-infected persons. *Circulation.* 2010; 121:651–8.
130. Appelbaum JS, McCormick WC, et al. Executive Summary: recommended treatment strategies for clinicians managing older patients with HIV. HIV & Aging Consensus Project. April 2013.
131. Hassan Y, Al-Ramahi RJ, Aziz NA, et al. Impact of a renal drug dosing service on dose adjustment in hospitalized patients with chronic kidney disease. *Ann Pharmacother.* 2009; 43(10):1598–605.
132. Mendes-Correa MC, Andrade Jr HF, Fumica Takakura C, et al. Hepatic ultrastructural mitochondrial changes prior to antiretroviral therapy in HIV-infected patients in Brazil. *J Int Assoc Physicians AIDS Care.* 2001; 27(5):426–31.
133. Neuman MG, Schneider M, Nanau RM, et al. HIV-antiretroviral therapy induced liver, gastrointestinal and pancreatic injury. *Int J Hepatology.* 2012; 760706:1–23.
134. Simioni S, Cavassini M, Annoni JM, et al. Cognitive dysfunction in HIV patients despite long-standing suppression of viremia. *AIDS.* 2010; 24:1243–50.
135. Heaton RK, Clifford DB, Franklin DR Jr., et al. HIV-associated neurocognitive disorders persist in the era of potent antiretroviral therapy. CHARTER Study. *Neurology.* 2010; 75:2087–96.
136. Mateen FJ, Shinohara RT, Carone M, et al. Neurological disorders incidence in HIV+ and HIV- men: multicenter AIDS cohort study, 1996-2011. *Neurology.* 2012; 79:1873–80.
137. Ellis RJ, Badiee J, Vaida F, et al. CD4 nadir is a predictor of HIV neurocognitive impairment in the era

of combination antiretroviral therapy. *AIDS.* 2011; 25:1747–51.

138. Schifitto G, Navia BA, Yiannoutsos CT, et al. Memantine and HIV-associated cognitive impairment: a neuropsychological and proton magnetic resonance spectroscopy study. *AIDS.* 2007; 21(14):1877–86.
139. Gomes da Silva MM. Neurologic complications of HIV in the HAART era: where are we? *Braz J Infect Dis.* 2012; 16:373–8.
140. Prohaska ES, King AR. Administration of antiretroviral medication via enteral tubes. *Am J Health-Syst Pharm.* 2012; 69(24):2140–6.
141. Nyberg CR, Patterson BY, Williams MM. When patients cannot take pills: antiretroviral drug formulations for managing adult HIV infection. *Top Antivir Med.* 2011; 19(3):126–31.
142. Chiu CC, Wu SS, Lee PY, et al. Control of modifiable risk factors in ischemic stroke outpatients by pharmacist intervention: an equal allocation stratified randomized study. *J Clin Pharm Ther.* 2008; 33:529–35.
143. Patel P, Hanson DL, Sullivan PS, et al. Incidence of types of cancer among HIV-infected persons compared with the general population in the United States, 1992-2003. *Ann Intern Med.* 2008; 148(10):728–36.
144. Deeken JF, Tjen-A-Looi, A, Rudek MA, et al. The rising challenge of non-AIDS-defining cancers in HIV-infected patients. *Clin Infect Dis.* 2012; 55(9):1228–35.
145. Engels EA, Biggar RJ, All HI, et al. Cancer risk in people infected with human immunodeficiency virus in the United States. *Int J Cancer.* 2008; 123(1):187–94.
146. Falutz J. Management of fat accumulation in patients with HIV infection. *Curr HIV/AIDS Rep.* 2011; 8:297–9.
147. Chen D, Misra A, Garg A. Lipodystropy in human immunodeficiency virus-infected patients. *J Clin Endocrinol Metab.* 2002; 87:4845–56.
148. Poretsky L, Can S, Zumoff B. Testicular dysfunction in human immunodeficiency virus-infected men. *Metabolism.* 1995; 44:946–53.
149. Kosmiski L. Energy expenditure in HIV infection. *Am J Clin Nutr.* 2011; 94(suppl):1677S–82S.
150. Falutz J, Mamputu JC, Potvin D, et al. Effects of tesamorelin (TH9507), a growth hormone-releasing factor analog, in human immunodeficiency virus-infected patients with excess abdominal fat: a pooled analysis of two multicenter, double-blind placebo-controlled phase 3 trials with safety extension data. *J Clin Endocrinol Metab.* 2010; 95:4291–304.
151. Hadigan C, Corcoran C, Basgoz N, et al. Metformin in the treatment of HIV lipodystrophy syndrome. *JAMA.* 2000; 284:472–7.
152. Kong A, Edmonds P. Testosterone therapy in HIV wasting syndrome: systemic review and meta-analysis. *Lancet Infect Dis.* 2002; 2:692–9.
153. Sardar P, Jha A, Roy D, et al. Therapeutic effects of nandrolone and testosterone in adult male HIV patients with AIDS wasting syndrome (AWS): a randomized, double-blind, placebo-controlled trial. *HIV Clin Trials.* 2010; 11:220–9.
154. Gold J, Batterham MJ, Rekers H, et al. Effects of nandrolone decanoate compared to placebo or testosterone on HIV-associated wasting. *HIV Medicine.* 2006; 7:146–55.
155. Guaraldi G, Orlando G, Zona S, et al. Premature age-related comorbidities among HIV-infected person compared with the general population. *Clin Infect Dis.* 2011; 53:110–6.
156. Schafer JJ, Manlangit K, Squires KE. Bone health and human immunodeficiency virus infection. *Pharmacotherapy.* 2013; 33(6):665–82.
157. McComsey GA, Tebas P, Shane E, et al. Bone disease in HIV infection: a practical review and recommendations for HIV care providers. *Clin Infect Dis.* 2010; 51:937–46.
158. Redondo Sanchez C, Poza Cisneros G, Galera Penaranda G, et al. Changes in hospitalizations due to opportunistic infections, chronic conditions and other causes among HIV patients (1989–2011). A study in a HIV unit. *J Int AIDS Soc.* 2012; 15(Suppl 4):180–9.
159. Hermsen ED, Wynn HE, McNabb J. Discontinuation of prophylaxis for HIV-associated opportunistic infections in the era of highly active antiretroviral therapy. *Am J Health-Syst Pharm.* 2004; 61:245–56.
160. Panel on Opportunistic Infections in HIV-Infected Adults and Adolescents. Guidelines for the prevention and treatment of opportunistic infections in HIV-infected adults and adolescents: recommendations from the Centers for Disease Control and Prevention, the National Institutes of Health, and the HIV Medical Association of the Infectious Diseases Society of America. Available at http://aidsinfo.nih.gov/contentfiles/lvguidelines/adult_oi.pdf. Accessed 5/9/2013.
161. Foisy MM, Akai PS. Pharmaceutical care for HIV patients on directly observed therapy. *Ann Pharmacother.* 2004 Apr; 38(4):550–6.
162. Zolopa AR, Andersen J, Komarow L, et al. Early antiretroviral therapy reduces AIDS progression/death in individuals with acute opportunistic infections: a multicenter randomized strategy trial. *PLoS ONE.* 2009; 4(5):e5575. Doi:10.1371/journal.pone.0005575.
163. Grant PM, Zolopa AR. When to start ART in the setting of acute AIDS-related opportunistic infections: the time is now! *Curr HIV/AIDS Rep.* 2012 Sep; 9(3):251–8.
164. Bisson GP, Molefi M, Bellamy S, et al. Early versus delayed antiretroviral therapy and cerebrospinal fluid fungal clearance in adults with HIV and cryptococcal meningitis. *Clin Infect Dis.* 2013; 53(8):1165–73.
165. Blanc FX, Sok T, Laureillard D, et al. Earlier versus later start of antiretroviral therapy in HIV-infected adults with tuberculosis. *N Engl J Med.* 2011; 365:1471–81.
166. Yehia BR, Mehta JM, Ciuffetelli D, et al. Antiretroviral medication errors remain high but are quickly corrected among hospitalized HIV-infected adults. *Clin Infect Dis.* 2012; 55:593–9.
167. Eginger KH, Yarborough LL, DeVito Inge L, et al. Medication errors in HIV-infected hospitalized patients: A pharmacist's impact. *Ann Pharmacother.* 2013; 47:953–60.
168. Bridges CB, Woods L, Coyne-Beasley T. Advisory committee on immunization practices (ACIP) recommended immunization schedule for adults ages 19 and older–United States, 2013. *MMWR.* 2013; Jan 28:9–17.

169. Stenger M, Spach DH. Immunizations for HIV-infected adults: indications, timing and response. *Top HIV Med*. 2006; 14(5)154–8.
170. Higginbothan S, Stewart A, Pfaizgraf A. Impact of a pharmacists immunizer on adult immunization rates *J Am Pharm Assoc*. 2012; 52:367–71.
171. Skelton JB. Pharmacist-provided immunization compensation and recognition: White paper summarizing APhA/AMCP stakeholder meeting. *J Am Pharm Assoc*. 2011; 51:704–12.
172. Centers for Disease Control and Prevention. U.S. Department of Health and Human Services. HIV prevention in the United States: at a critical crossroads. Aug 2009. Available from: http://www.cdc.gov/hiv/resources/reports/hiv_prev_us.htm
173. Cohen MS, Chen YQ, McCauley M, et al. Prevention of HIV-1 infection with early antiretroviral therapy. *N Engl J Med*. 2011; 365:493–505.
174. Bunnell R, Ekwaru JP, Soldberg P, et al. Changes in sexual behavior and risk of HIV transmission after antiretroviral therapy and prevention interventions in rural Uganda. *AIDS*. 2006; 20:85–92.
175. Sullivan P, Kayitenkore K, Chomba E, et al. Is the reduction of HIV transmission while prescribed antiviral therapy (ARVT) different for men and women? Results from discordant couples in Rwanda and Zambia. Abstract WEAC101 presented at the 5th IAS Conference on HIV Pathogenesis, Treatment, and Prevention. Capetown, South Africa; 2009 July.
176. Das M, Chu PL, Santos GM, et al. Decreases in community viral load are accompanied by reductions in new HIV infections in San Francisco. *PLoS One*. 2010; 5:e11068.
177. Montaner JS, Lima VD, Barrios R, et al. Association of highly active antiretroviral therapy coverage, population viral load, and yearly new HIV diagnoses in British Columbia, Canada: a population-based study. *Lancet*. 2010; 376:532–9.
178. Saberi P, Dong BJ, Johnson MO, et al. The impact of HIV clinical pharmacists on HIV treatment outcomes: a systematic review. *Patient Prefer Adherence*. 2012; 6:297–322.
179. Cocohoba JM, Althoff KN, Cohen M, et al. Pharmacist counseling in a cohort of women with HIV and women at risk for HIV. *Patient Prefer Adherence*. 2012; 6:457–63.
180. Kibicho J, Owczarzak J. Pharmacists' strategies for promoting medication adherence among patients with HIV. *J Am Pharm Assoc*. 2011; 51:746–55.
181. Centers for Disease Control and Prevention, U.S. Public Health Service. Preexposure prophylaxis for the prevention of HIV infection in the United States—2014: a clinical practice guideline. Available at: http://www.cdc.gov/hiv/pdf/PrEPguidelines2014.pdf. Accessed December 5, 2014.
182. Abdool KQ, Abdool Karim SS, Frolich JA. Effectiveness and safety of tenofovir gel, an antiretroviral microbicide for the prevention of HIV infection in women. *Science*. 2010; 329:1168–74.
183. Grant RM, Lama JR, Anderson PL, et al. Preexposure chemoprophylaxis for HIV prevention in men who have sex with men. *N Engl J Med*. 2010; 363(27):2587–99.
184. Baeten JM, Donnell D, Ndase P, et al. Antiretroviral prophylaxis for HIV prevention in heterosexual men and women. *N Engl J Med*. 2012; 367:399–410.
185. Thigpen MC, Kebaabetswe PM, Paxton LA, et al. Antiretroviral preexposure prophylaxis for heterosexual HIV transmission in Botswana. *N Engl J Med*. 2012; 367:423–34.
186. Choopanya K, Martin M, Suntharasamai P, et al. Antiretroviral prophylaxis for HIV infection in injecting drug users in Bangkok, Thailand (the Bangkok Tenofovir Study): a randomized, double-blind, placebo controlled phase 3 trial. *Lancet*. 2013; 381:2083–90.
187. Van Damme L, Corneli A, Ahmed K, et al. Preexposure prophylaxis for HIV infection among African women. *N Engl J Med*. 2012; 367:411–22.
188. Marrazzo J, Ramjee G, Nair G, et al. Pre-exposure prophylaxis for HIV in women: daily oral tenofovir, oral tenofovir/emtricitabine, or vaginal tenofovir gel in the VOICE Study (MTN 003) [Abstract]. Presented at the 20th Conference on Retroviruses and Opportunistic Infections; March 3–6, 2013; Atlanta, GA.
189. Bruno C, Saberi P. Pharmacists as providers of HIV pre-exposure prophylaxis. *Int J Clin Pharm*. 2012; 34:803–6.
190. Shaeer KM, Sherman EM, Shafiq S, et al. Exploratory survey of Florida pharmacists' experience, knowledge, and perception of HIV pre-exposure prophylaxis. *J Am Pharm Assoc*. 2014; 54(6):610–7.
191. Kuhar DT, Henderson DK, Struble KM, et al. Updated US public health service guidelines for the management of occupational exposures to human immunodeficiency virus and recommendations for postexposure prophylaxis. *Infect Control Hosp Epidemiol*. 2013; 34:875–93.
192. Centers for Disease Control and Prevention. Antiretroviral postexposure prophylaxis after sexual, injection-drug use, or other nonoccupational exposure to HIV in the United States: recommendations from the U.S. Department of Health and Human Services. *MMWR*. 2005; 54 (No. RR-2).
193. Foisy M, Highes C. Role of the pharmacist in perinatal management of HIV disease. *Am J Health-Syst Pharm*. 2011; 68:2116–22.
194. Nacopoulos AG, Lewtas AJ, Ousterhout MM. Syringe exchange programs: impact on injection drug users and the role of the pharmacist from a US perspective. *J Am Pharm Assoc*. 2010; 50:148–57.
195. Janulis P. Pharmacy nonprescription syringe distribution and HIV/AIDS: a review. *J Am Pharm Assoc*. 2012; 52:787–97.
196. Sherman EM, Cocohoba JM, Neff SE, et al. Health care provider satisfaction with telephone consultations provided by pharmacists and physicians at the National HIV/AIDS clinicians' consultation center. *Ann Pharmacother*. 2011; 45:1499–505.
197. Bartlett D, Evans P, Sullivan M. Effect of a pharmacist-run call center on medication access for ambulatory care patients. *Am J Health-Syst Pharm*. 2009; 66:1666–8.
198. Sarrafizadeh M, Waite NW, Hobson E, et al. Pharmacist-facilitated enrollment in medication assis-

tance programs in a private ambulatory care clinic. *Am J Health-Syst Pharm.* 2004; 61:1816–20.

199. Raper JL, Willig JH, Lin HY, et al. Uncompensated medical provider costs associated with prior authorization for prescription medications in an HIV clinic. *Clin Infect Dis.* 2010 Sep 15; 51(6):718–24.
200. American College of Clinical Pharmacy. Improving care transitions: current practice and future opportunities for pharmacists. *Pharmacotherapy.* 2012; 32:e326–37.
201. Li EH, Foisy MM. Antiretroviral and medication errors in hospitalized HIV-positive persons. *Ann Pharmacother.* 2014; 48(8):998–1010.
202. Cutler TW, Stebbins MR, Smith AR, et al. Promoting access and reducing expected out-of-pocket prescription drug costs for vulnerable Medicare beneficiaries: a pharmacist-directed model. *Med Care.* 2011; 49(4):343–7.
203. Matzke GR. Health care reform 2011: opportunities for pharmacists. *Ann Pharmacother.* 2012; 46:S27–32.
204. American Academy of HIV Medicine. Credentialing. Available from: http://www.aahivm.org/about.
205. Traynor K. U.S. Pharmacists respond to global AIDS crisis. *Am J Health-Syst Pharm.* 2005; 1110–5.
206. Okubanjo T. Pharmacists as investigators in FDA-related drug trials. *Am J Health-Syst Pharm.* 2008; 1010–1.

Appendix

Website Resources

General HIV Care and Treatment Information

- U.S. Department of Health and Human Services AIDSinfo Web site (www.aidsinfo.nih.gov)
- Clinical Care Options HIV–in Practice (www.inpractice.com/Textbooks/HIV.aspx)

Clinical Practice Guidelines and Recommendations

- U.S. Department of Health and Human Services AIDSinfo Web site (www.aidsinfo.nih.gov)
- International Antiviral Society—USA (www.iasusa.org/guidelines)
- World Health Organization (www.who.int/hiv/pub/guidelines/en/)
- European AIDS Clinical Society (eacsociety.org/Guidelines.aspx)

Antiretroviral Information (Drug Interactions, Renal/Hepatic Dose Adjustments and Crushing/Liquid Formulations)

- U.S. Department of Health and Human Services AIDSinfo Web site (www.aidsinfo.nih.gov)
- University of Liverpool Drug Interaction Database and Mobile Application (www.hiv-druginteractions.org/)
- Toronto General Hospital Immunodeficiency Clinic website (www.hivclinic.ca/main/drugs_interact.html and www.hivclinic.ca/main/drugs_extra.html)
- HIV Insite (hivinsite.ucsf.edu)
- Clinician Consultation Center, Antiretroviral Drug Tables (nccc.ucsf.edu/clinical-resources/hiv-aids-resources/pharmacy)
- Florida/Caribbean AIDS Education and Training Center Antiretroviral Therapy Pocket Cards (fcaetc.org/treatment-guidelines.php)

HIV Resistance Testing and Mutations

- HIV Drug Resistance Database–Stanford University (www.hivdb.stanford.edu)
- International Antiviral Society–USA (www.iasusa.org/resistance_mutations/mutations_figures.pdf)

Immunizations

- Centers for Disease Control and Prevention (www.cdc.gov/vaccines/schedules/hcp/index.html)

Professional Organizations

- American Academy of HIV Medicine (www.aahivm.org)
- British HIV Association (www.bhiva.org)
- HIV Medicine Association (www.hivma.org)
- International Association of Providers of AIDS Care (www.iapac.org)
- International AIDS Society (www.iasociety.org)

Information Exchange

- The Canadian HIV/AIDS Pharmacists Network (hivclinic.ca/chap/)
- National AIDS Treatment Advocacy Project (natap.org)
- American College of Clinical Pharmacy, HIV Practice and Research Network (http://www.accp.com/about/prns.aspx)

Clinical Trials

- U.S. Department of Health and Human Services AIDSinfo Web site (www.aidsinfo.nih.gov)

Hotlines and Clinical Consultation

- Clinicians Consultation Center (nccc.usf.edu)
    - Pre-Exposure Prophylaxis (855) 448-7737
    - Post-Exposure Prophylaxis (888) 448-4911
    - HIV/AIDS Management (800) 933-3413
    - Perinatal HIV/AIDS (888) 448-8765

HIV Certificate and Credentialing Programs

- American Academy of HIV Medicine, HIV Pharmacist Credentialing (www.aahivm.org/about)
- University of Buffalo School of Pharmacy and Pharmaceutical Sciences (tdm.pharm.buffalo.edu/hiv_cert_main/)

Continuing Education for Pharmacists

- Clinical Care Options–HIV (www.clinicaloptions.com/HIV.aspx)
- International Antiviral Society–USA (iasusa.org)
- American Academy of HIV Medicine (aahivm.org)
- AIDS Education and Training Centers (aidsetc.org)

Approved by the ASHP Board of Directors on September 17, 2015. Developed through the ASHP Section of Clinical Specialists and Scientists.

These guidelines supersede the ASHP Statement on the Pharmacist's Role in HIV Care dated June 1, 2003.

Jason J. Schafer, Pharm.D., M.P.H, BCPS, AAHIVP; Taylor K. Gill, Pharm.D., BCPS, AAHIVP; Elizabeth M. Sherman, Pharm.D., AAHIVP; and Ian R. McNicholl, Pharm.D., FCCP, BCPS (AQ-ID), AAHIVP are gratefully acknowledged for authoring these guidelines. The authors have declared no potential conflicts of interest.

ASHP gratefully acknowledges the following organizations and individuals for reviewing these guidelines (review does not imply endorsement): American Pharmacists Association (APhA); Canadian HIV/AIDS Pharmacists Network (CHAP); HIV Medicine Association (HIVMA); Society of Infectious Disease Pharmacists; South Carolina Society of Health-System Pharmacists (SCSHP); Melissa Badowski, Pharm.D., BCPS, AAHIVP; Carol J. Bickford, Ph.D., RN-BC, CPHIMS; Shanna Chan, B.Sc.Pharm., ACPR, AAHIVP (CHAP); Patrick Clay, Pharm.D. FCCP, CCTI (APhA); Natalie Dayneka, B.Sc.Pharm., ACPR, Pharm.D., FCSHP (CHAP); Heather Easterling, Pharm.D., M.B.A. (SCSHP); Devon Flynn, Pharm.D., BCPS, AAHIVP; Michelle Foisy, B.Sc.Pharm., Pharm.D., FCSHP, AAHIVP (CHAP); Patricia Pecora Fulco, Pharm.D., BCPS, FASHP, AAHIVP; Barbara Giacomelli, Pharm.D., M.B.A., FASHP; Pierre Giguère, B.Sc.Pharm., M.Sc. (CHAP); Christine Hughes, B.Sc. Pharm., Pharm.D, AAHIVP (CHAP); Tara K. Jellison, Pharm.D., M.B.A., FASHP; Deborah V. Kelly, B.Sc.Pharm., ACPR, Pharm.D, FCSHP, AAHIVP (CHAP); William Kuykendall, Pharm.D.; Kristina Lantis, Pharmacy Student, Class of 2016; J. Craig Phillips, Ph.D., LLM, RN, ARNP, PMHCNS-BC, ACRN; Carlo Quaia, B.Sc. Pharm., ACPR (CHAP); James R. Rinehart, R.Ph., M.S., FASHP; Linda Robinson, B.Sc.Pharm., AAHIVE (CHAP); Nancy Sheehan, B.Sc.Pharm., M.Sc. (CHAP); Shannon Stone, B.Sc.Pharm., ACPR (CHAP); Alice Tseng, B.Sc.Pharm., Pharm.D., FCSHP, AAHIVP (CHAP); Andrea Weddle, M.S.W. (HIVMA); Jody Jacobson Wedret, FASHP, FCSHP; and Deborah Yoong, B.Sc.Pharm., ACPR, Pharm.D. (CHAP).

Note: These guidelines had not been published in the *American Journal of Health-System Pharmacy* (*AJHP*) when *ASHP Best Practices* 2015–2016 went to press. Some minor editorial differences may exist between this document and the official one that will eventually appear in *AJHP* and subsequent editions of this publication.

ASHP Guidelines on the Pharmacist's Role in Immunization

Purpose

Pharmacists can play an important role in disease prevention by advocating and administering immunizations. Such activities are consistent with the preventive aspects of pharmaceutical care and have been part of pharmacy practice for over a century.[1,2] These guidelines address the pharmacist's role in promoting and conducting proper immunization of patients in all organized health care settings. The pharmacist's role in promoting disease prevention through participation in community efforts is also discussed.

Background

Each year, an average of 90,000 Americans die of vaccine-preventable infections such as influenza, pneumococcal disease, and hepatitis B.[3,5] Most of these people visited health care providers in the year preceding their deaths but were not vaccinated.[6–11] Influenza and pneumonia, considered together, are the fifth leading cause of death for Americans 65 years of age or older.[12] Although vaccination rates for U.S. children at the time they enter school exceed 95%, nearly 25% do not complete their primary series by the age of two years.[13] Most American adults are inadequately vaccinated, particularly against pneumococcal disease, influenza, hepatitis B, tetanus, and diphtheria.[6] Tens of millions of Americans remain susceptible to potentially deadly infections despite the availability of effective vaccines.

This long-standing failure to adequately immunize the U.S population helped prompt the inclusion of immunization as a leading health indicator for Healthy People 2010.[14] The renewed focus on immunization and the potential for increased vaccination needs in response to threats of bioterrorism should stimulate pharmacists, as well as other health care providers, to reassess what they and their institutions can do to improve immunization rates in their communities. Pharmacists can contribute to this effort by administering immunizations where scope of practice allows and by promoting immunization in other ways.

Immunization Administration

As health care providers, pharmacists can administer vaccines or host other health care professionals who can administer vaccines. Pharmacists must understand the legal and professional mechanisms by which authorization to administer vaccines is granted, as well as the additional responsibilities and considerations that accompany this expanded role. The feasibility of vaccine administration by pharmacists within a particular practice site or health care system can be determined by analyzing the issues of legal authority, training, and program structure.

Legal Authority. The pharmacist's authority to administer vaccines is determined by each state's laws and regulations governing pharmacy practice. At least 36 states permit vaccine administration by pharmacists as part of the scope of pharmacy practice.[15] The American College of Physicians–American Society of Internal Medicine supports pharmacists as sources of immunization information, hosts of immunization sites, and immunizers.[16] Vaccine administration may occur pursuant to individual prescription orders or through standing orders or protocols. The Centers for Disease Control and Prevention (CDC) Advisory Committee on Immunization Practices recommends the use of standing orders to improve adult immunization rates.[17] Its recommendations encourage pharmacists, among other providers, to establish standing-order programs in long-term-care facilities, home health care agencies, hospitals, clinics, workplaces, and managed care organizations. The Centers for Medicare and Medicaid Services (CMS) no longer requires a physician order for influenza or pneumoccocal immunizations administered in participating hospitals, long-term-care facilities, or home health care agencies.[18] Development of state-specific protocols or standing-order programs can be facilitated through partnerships with state pharmacy associations, boards of pharmacy, and health departments.

Training. Although legal authority to administer vaccines may be granted through pharmacy practice acts, pharmacists must achieve competency in all aspects of vaccine administration. A comprehensive training program should address the following:

1. The epidemiology of and patient populations at risk for vaccine-preventable diseases,
2. Public health goals for immunization (e.g., local, regional, state, and federal goals),
3. Vaccine safety (e.g., risk–benefit analysis),
4. Screening for contraindications and precautions of vaccination in each patient,
5. Vaccine stability and transportation and storage requirements,
6. Immunologic drug interactions,
7. Vaccine dosing (including interpreting recommended immunization schedules and patient immunization records and determining proper dosing intervals and the feasibility of simultaneous administration of multiple vaccines),
8. Proper dose preparation and injection technique,
9. Signs and symptoms of adverse reactions to vaccines, adverse reaction reporting, and emergency procedures, such as basic and advanced cardiac life support (BCLS and ACLS),
10. Documentation,
11. Reporting to the primary care provider or local health department, and
12. Billing.

Live and videotaped programming is available through some state and national pharmacy associations and offered in many college of pharmacy curricula. Information regarding immunizations can change rapidly. To maintain competency, pharmacists must have access to current immunization references (e.g., CDC's National Immunization Program publications, including the "Pink Book"[19]) and continuing-education programs to stay abreast of evolving guidelines and recommendations.

Program Structure. A vaccine administration program requires a solid infrastructure of appropriately trained staff, physical space, and written policies and procedures to ensure appropriate vaccine storage and handling, patient screening and education, and documentation. The structure of a vaccine administration program must also provide for storage and disposal of injection supplies, disposal of and prevention of exposure to biological hazards as dictated by the Occupational Safety and Health Administration (OSHA), and emergency procedures (e.g., BCLS and ACLS). Pharmacists should be fully immunized to protect their health and the health of their patients.[20]

Reimbursement. Immunization has repeatedly been shown to be cost-effective[21–24]; it may be the most cost-effective practice in medicine. However, third-party reimbursement policies often do not provide coverage for recommended vaccines despite this evidence. A major exception is Medicare Part B, which not only covers immunization services for its participants but also recognizes and compensates pharmacists as mass immunization providers. Enrollment as a Medicare provider is required to bill for covered services. Provider status can be obtained through local Medicare offices, which also process CMS claims for reimbursement (CMS-1500 claims). The CMS Web site (www.cms.hhs.gov) is a useful source for billing information. Pharmacists should continue to closely monitor other immunization reimbursement policies and advocate third-party coverage for immunizations as a cost-effective preventive measure. For patients without insurance coverage, requesting out-of-pocket payments from the patient remains a viable option for pharmacists to obtain compensation for their immunization services.

Immunization Promotion

Pharmacists who do not administer vaccines can promote immunization through six types of activities: (1) history and screening, (2) patient counseling, (3) documentation, (4) formulary management, (5) administrative measures, and (6) public education.[25,26] These promotional activities can also be integrated into or accompany a pharmacy-based immunization program.

History and Screening. Pharmacists can promote proper immunization by identifying patients in need of immunization. Tasks that support this objective include gathering immunization histories, encouraging use of vaccine profiles, issuing vaccination records to patients,[27–34] preventing immunologic drug interactions,[35,36] and screening patients for immunization needs.[28–33,37–39]

Immunization screening should be a component of all clinical routines, regardless of the practice setting. All health care institutions should implement consistent, systematic monitoring systems and quality indicators to ensure that all patients are assessed for immunization adequacy before they leave the facility. The health care provider designated to identify patient immunization needs should have the authority, knowledge, and responsibility to provide or arrange for the immunization service.[40] Clinics that provide treatment for a large number of patients at high risk for contracting vaccine-preventable diseases (e.g., diabetic, asthmatic, heart disease, and geriatric clinics) have a particular obligation to employ immunization screening and ensure appropriate vaccine use.

Screening for immunization needs may be organized in several ways; prototype screening forms are available.[39,41] Pharmacists should seek out leadership roles in some or all of the following forms of immunization screening.

Occurrence screening. With this type of screening, vaccine needs are identified at the time of particular events, such as hospital or nursing home admission or discharge, ambulatory care or emergency room visits, mid-decade birthdays (e.g., years 25, 35, and 45),[42,43] and any contact with a health care delivery system for patients under 8 years or over 50 years of age.

Diagnosis screening. This screening reviews the vaccine needs of patients with conditions that increase their risk of preventable infections. Diagnoses such as diabetes, asthma, heart disease, acute myocardial infarction, congestive heart failure, chronic obstructive pulmonary disease, hemophilia, thalassemia, most types of cancer, sickle cell anemia, chronic alcoholism, cirrhosis, human immunodeficiency virus infection, and certain other disorders should prompt specific attention to the patient's vaccine needs.[12,33,42] The immunization rate for patients diagnosed with community-acquired pneumonia is considered a marker for quality by some accrediting bodies. Incorporating assessment of vaccination status into an institution's critical pathways has been shown to improve vaccination rates.[44]

Procedure screening. Immunization needs are assessed on the basis of medical or surgical procedures using this type of screening. These procedures include splenectomy, heart or lung surgery, organ transplantation, antineoplastic therapy, radiation therapy, immunosuppression of other types, dialysis, and prescription of certain medications used to treat conditions that increase patients' risk of preventable infections.[45,46] When designing and implementing automated prescription databases, pharmacy managers should consider specifications that allow retrieval of lists of patients receiving drugs that suggest the need for immunization.[33,37]

Periodic mass screening. This type of screening is a comprehensive assessment of immunization adequacy in selected populations at a given time. Such screening may be conducted, for example, during autumn influenza programs or outbreaks of certain vaccine-preventable illnesses (e.g., measles and meningococcal disease).[29,32,33] Schools and other institutions can perform mass screening when registering new students or residents. Mass screening may also be appropriate in areas where no comprehensive immunization program has been conducted recently. This type of screening helps improve vaccine coverage rates at a given time, but long-term benefits are much greater when such intermittent programs are combined with ongoing comprehensive screening efforts. Several states, including South Dakota, New Jersey, and Oklahoma, have enacted laws requiring that influenza and pneumococcal vaccines be offered annually to residents of nursing homes.

Occupational screening. This screening method focuses on the immunization needs of health care personnel whose responsibilities place them at risk of exposure to certain vaccine-preventable diseases or bring them into contact with high-risk patients (i.e., patients with those conditions listed in the *Diagnosis screening* section above). Health care providers who have contact with these patients should receive an annual influenza vaccination. Health care employers frequently provide immunization screening and vaccination of employees as part of employee health programs. OSHA requires that health care employers provide hepatitis B vaccination at no cost, on a voluntary basis, to all employees at risk for occupational exposure to blood borne pathogens.[47] Depending on their risk of exposure, it may be advisable for members of the pharmacy staff to receive hepatitis B vaccination.

Screening for contraindications and precautions. After candidates for immunization have been identified, they should be screened for contraindications and precautions. A CDC-reviewed contraindication screening questionnaire is available.[48]

Patient Counseling. Patients in need of immunization should be advised of their infection risk and encouraged to accept the immunizations they need. Patient concerns about vaccine safety and efficacy should be discussed and addressed.[49,50] Health care providers can influence patients' attitudes regarding immunization.[51,52] Physicians should be informed of their patients' need for vaccination if standing orders or collaborative practice agreements are not in place. Patients who need immunizations should be vaccinated during the current health care contact unless valid contraindications exist. Delaying vaccination until a future appointment increases the risk that the patient will not be vaccinated.

Advising patients of their need for immunization can take several forms. In the ambulatory care setting, individualized or form letters can be mailed to patients, patients can be called by telephone, or an insert can be included with prescriptions informing patients of their infection risk and the availability and efficacy of vaccines.[30,33,53–55] Adhesive reminder labels can also be affixed to prescription containers for drugs used to treat conditions that may indicate the need for vaccination against influenza and pneumococcal disease (e.g., digoxin, warfarin, theophylline, and insulin[33]); these labels would be analogous to labels currently in widespread use (e.g., "Shake well" and "Take with food or milk"). Such labels might read, "You may need flu or pneumonia vaccine: Ask your doctor or pharmacist." Chart notes, consultations, messages to patients, one-on-one conversations, and similar means can be used to communicate with inpatients and institutional patients.[28,31,56]

Federal law requires that health care providers who administer diphtheria, tetanus, pertussis, measles, mumps, rubella, varicella, polio, *Haemophilus influenzae* type B, hepatitis B, and pneumococcal conjugate vaccines give the most recent version of the CDC-developed Vaccine Information Statement (VIS) to the adult or the parent or legal guardian of the child to be vaccinated.[57] VISs are available in many languages from state or local health departments or the CDC.[58] VISs are also available for other commonly used vaccines, such as influenza, pneumococcal polysaccharide, hepatitis A, meningococcal, and anthrax vaccines. Pharmacists should also ensure that informed consent is obtained in a manner that complies with state laws.[20]

Documentation. The National Childhood Vaccine Injury Act of 1986 (NCVIA) requires all health care providers who administer vaccines to maintain permanent vaccination records and to report occurrences of certain adverse events specified in the act.[57,59] The recipient's permanent medical record (or the equivalent) must state the date the vaccine was administered, the vaccine's manufacturer and lot number, and the name, address, and title of the person administering the vaccine. Pharmacists in organized health care settings may encourage compliance with this requirement by providing reminder notices each time doses of vaccines are dispensed.[60] Automated databases that allow for long-term storage of patient immunization information may provide an efficient method for maintaining and retrieving immunization records.[39] Efforts to develop electronic vaccination registries, especially for children, are under way by states collaborating with CDC.[61]

NCVIA also mandates that selected adverse effects noted after any inoculation be reported to the Vaccine Adverse Event Reporting System (www.vaers.org).[57,59,62] Because pharmacists have experience with adverse-drug-reaction reporting, they can take the lead in developing and implementing a program to meet this requirement, even if they are not responsible for administering the vaccine.

Patients should maintain personal immunization records that document all immunization experiences and function as a backup if the clinicians' immunization records are lost. Several personal immunization record forms are available. Public Health Service Form 731 (International Certificate of Vaccination), colloquially called the "yellow shot record," is used to document vaccines indicated for international travel but can also serve as a patient's personal record of vaccinations. The Immunization Action Coalition distributes a standard adult immunization record card developed in collaboration with CDC.[63] In addition, each state and the District of Columbia prints its own uniform immunization record form for pediatric immunizations, which may also be a suitable personal patient record. It has been recommended that adults carry personal immunization records in their wallets.[46]

Formulary Management. Formulary systems in organized health care settings should include vaccines, toxoids, and immune globulins available for use in preventing diseases in patients and staff. Decisions by the pharmacy and therapeutics committee (or its equivalent) on immunologic drug choices require consideration of relevant immunologic pharmaceutics, immunopharmacology, and disease epidemiology. Because of their expertise and training, pharmacists are well equipped to provide information and recommendations on which these decisions may be based.

It is the pharmacist's responsibility to develop and maintain product specifications to aid in the purchase of drugs under the formulary system.[64,65] The pharmacist should establish and maintain standards to ensure the quality, proper storage, and proper use of all pharmaceuticals dispensed. Pharmacists must choose between single dose or multidose containers of vaccines on the basis of efficiency, safety, economic, and regulatory considerations. Pharmacists in institutions should develop guidelines on the routine stocking of immunologic drugs in certain high-use patient care areas.

Proper transportation and storage are an important consideration for immunologic drugs, including vaccines, because many require storage at refrigerated or frozen temperatures. Pharmacists have an important responsibility to maintain the "cold chain" in the handling of these drugs. Detailed references on this topic have been published.[66–73] Storage considerations include the conditions in all areas in which immunologic drugs are kept, as well as a method for ensuring that immunologic drugs received by the pharmacy have been transported under suitable conditions.

It is important that methods be established for detecting and properly disposing of outdated and partially administered immunologic agents. Live viral (e.g., varicella, yellow fever, and smallpox) and live bacterial (e.g., bacille Calmette-Guérin) vaccines should be disposed of in the same manner as other infectious biohazardous waste.

Administrative Measures. Pharmacists on key committees (e.g., infection control and risk management) in organized health care settings can promote adequate immunization delivery among staff and patients by encouraging the development of sound organizational policies on immunization. Health care organizations should develop policies and protocols that address the following:

1. Hepatitis B preexposure prophylaxis for health care workers at risk for exposure to blood products and other contaminated items,[45,74–76]
2. Hepatitis B postexposure (e.g., needle stick) prophylaxis for previously unvaccinated patients, health care personnel, and personnel who have been vaccinated but do not have a previously documented serologic response,[45,74–76]
3. Rabies preexposure and postexposure prophylaxis,[77]
4. Wound management guidelines designed to prevent tetanus and diphtheria,[78,79]
5. Valid contraindications to vaccination to ensure patient safety and minimize inappropriate exclusions from vaccination,[78,80,81]
6. Requirements for employee immunization against measles, rubella, influenza, and other diseases,[42,82]
7. Tuberculosis screening of patients and staff,[83,84]
8. Immunization of persons at high risk (e.g., patients with diabetes, asthma, heart disease, and pregnant or immunocompromised patients). Current authoritative guidelines on this subject should be consulted,[42,46,58,85,86] and
9. Emergency measures in the event of vaccine-related adverse reactions. Such measures should address the availability of epinephrine and other emergency drugs, as well as BCLS and ACLS.

Public Education. Pharmacists have ample opportunities to advance the public health through immunization advocacy. Pharmacists can facilitate disease prevention strategies, because many potential victims of influenza and pneumococcal disease visit pharmacies and are seen by pharmacists daily. Pharmacists can lead local activities in observance of National Adult Immunization Week each October.[37] Working with local public health departments, state or national immunization coalitions, and other groups (e.g., state or local parent—teacher, diabetes, heart, lung, or retired persons' associations), pharmacists can promote vaccination among high-risk populations. Newsletters, posters, brochures, and seminars may be used to explain the risk of preventable infections to pharmacy staff, other health care personnel, and patients. Excellent resources are available from the Immunization Action Coalition and the National Coalition for Adult Immunization.

References

1. Hepler CD, Strand LM. Opportunities and responsibilities in pharmaceutical care. *Am J Hosp Pharm.* 1990; 47:533–43.
2. Grabenstein JD. Pharmacists and immunization: increasing involvement over a century. *Pharm Hist.* 1999; 41:137–52.
3. Prevention and control of influenza: recommendations of the Advisory Committee on Immunization Practices. *MMWR Recomm Rep.* 2002; 51(RR-3):1–31.
4. Prevention of pneumococcal disease: recommendations of the Advisory Committee on Immunization Practices (ACIP). *MMWR Recomm Rep.* 1997; 46(RR-8):1–24.
5. Thompson WW, Shay DK, Weintraub E, et al. Mortality associated with influenza and respiratory syncytial virus in the United States. *JAMA.* 2003; 289:179–86.
6. Williams WW, Hickson MA, Kane MA, et al. Immunization policies and vaccine coverage among adults. The risk for missed opportunities. *Ann Intern Med.* 1988; 108:616–25.
7. Fedson DS, Harward MP, Reid RA, et al. Hospital-based pneumococcal immunization. Epidemiologic rationale from the Shenandoah study. *JAMA.* 1990; 264:1117–22.
8. Fedson DS. Influenza and pneumococcal immunization strategies for physicians. *Chest.* 1987; 91:436–43.
9. Fedson DS. Improving the use of pneumococcal vaccine through a strategy of hospital-based immunization: a review of its rationale and implications. *J Am Geriatr Soc.* 1985; 33:142–50.
10. Magnussen CR, Valenti WM, Mushlin AI. Pneumococcal vaccine strategy. Feasibility of a vaccination program directed at hospitalized and ambulatory patients. *Arch Intern Med.* 1984; 144:1755–7.
11. Vondracek TG, Pham TP, Huycke MM. A hospital-based pharmacy intervention program for pneumococcal vaccination. *Arch Intern Med.* 1998; 158:1543–7.
12. Bratzler DW, Houck PM, Jiang H, et al. Failure to vaccinate Medicare inpatients: a missed opportunity. *Arch Intern Med.* 2002; 162:2349–56.
13. Barker L, Luman E, Zhao Z, et al. National, state, and urban area vaccination coverage levels among children aged 19–35 months—United States, 2001. *MMWR. Morb Mortal Wkly Rep.* 2002; 51(30):664–6.
14. Office of Disease Prevention and Health Promotion. Healthy people 2010. www.healthypeople.gov (accessed 2003 Mar 12).
15. American Pharmaceutical Association. States where pharmacists can immunize. www.aphanet.org/pharmcare/immunofact.html (accessed 2003 Mar 6).
16. Keely JL. Pharmacist scope of practice. *Ann Intern Med.* 2002; 136:79–85.
17. Use of standing orders programs to increase adult vaccination rates: recommendations of the Advisory Committee on Immunization Practices (ACIP). *MMWR Recomm Rep.* 2000; 49(RR01):15–26.
18. 42 C.F.R. §482–4.
19. Centers for Disease Control and Prevention. Epidemiology and prevention of vaccine-preventable diseases. 7th ed. Atlanta: U.S. Department of Health and Human Services; 2003.
20. Grabenstein JD. High expectations: standards and guidelines for immunization delivery. *Hosp Pharm.* 2000; 35:841–51.
21. Sisk JE, Moskowitz AJ, Whang W, et al. Cost-effectiveness of vaccination against pneumococcal bacteremia among elderly people. *JAMA.* 1997; 278:1333–9.
22. Van den Oever R, de Graeve D, Hepp B, et al. Pharmacoeconomics of immunisation: a review. *Pharmacoeconomics.* 1993; 3:286–308.
23. Nichol KL, Lind A, Margolis KL, et al. The effectiveness of vaccination against influenza in healthy, working adults. *N Engl J Med.* 1995; 333:889–93.
24. Nichol KL, Margolis KL, Wuorenma J, et al. The efficacy and cost-effectiveness of vaccination against influ-

enza among elderly persons living in the community. *N Engl J Med.* 1994; 331:778–84.
25. Grabenstein JD. Immunizations: what's a health-system pharmacy to do? Part 1. *Hosp Pharm.* 1998; 33:742,745–50,753.
26. Grabenstein JD. Immunizations: what's a health-system pharmacy to do? Part 2. *Hosp Pharm.* 1998; 33:870–2,876–80.
27. Huff PS, Hak SH, Caiola SM. Immunizations for international travel as a pharmaceutical service. *Am J Hosp Pharm.* 1982; 39:90–3.
28. Spruill WJ, Cooper JW, Taylor WJR. Pharmacist-coordinated pneumonia and influenza vaccination program. *Am J Hosp Pharm.* 1982; 39:1904–6.
29. Grabenstein JD, Smith LJ, Carter DW, et al. Comprehensive immunization delivery in conjunction with influenza vaccination. *Arch Intern Med.* 1986; 146:1189–92.
30. Williams DM, Daugherty LJ, Aycock DG, et al. Effectiveness of improved targeting efforts for influenza immunization in an ambulatory-care setting. *Hosp Pharm.* 1987; 22:462–4.
31. Morton MR, Spruill WJ, Cooper JW. Pharmacist impact on pneumococcal vaccination rates in long-term-care facilities. *Am J Hosp Pharm.* 1988; 45:73. Letter.
32. Grabenstein JD, Smith LJ, Watson RR, et al. Immunization outreach using individual need assessments of adults at an Army hospital. *Public Health Rep.* 1990; 105:311–6.
33. Grabenstein JD, Hayton BD. Pharmacoepidemiologic program for identifying patients in need of vaccination. *Am J Hosp Pharm.* 1990; 47:1774–81.
34. Grabenstein JD. Get it in writing: documenting immunizations. *Hosp Pharm.* 1991; 26:901–4.
35. Grabenstein JD. Drug interactions involving immunologic agents. Part I. Vaccine–vaccine, vaccine–immunoglobulin, and vaccine–drug interactions. *DICP.* 1990; 24:67–81.
36. Grabenstein JD. Drug interactions involving immunologic agents. Part II. Immunodiagnostic and other immunologic drug interactions. *DICP.* 1990; 24:186–93.
37. Grabenstein JD. Pneumococcal pneumonia: don't wait, vaccinate. *Hosp Pharm.* 1990; 25:866–9.
38. Grabenstein JD, Casto DT. Recommending vaccines to your patients' individual needs. *Am Pharm.* 1991; NS31:58–67.
39. Grabenstein JD. Immunization delivery: a complete guide. St. Louis: Facts and Comparisons; 1997.
40. Fedson DS, Houck P, Bratzler D. Hospital-based influenza and pneumococcal vaccination: Sutton's law applied to prevention. *Infect Control Hosp Epidemiol.* 2000; 21:692–9.
41. Immunization Action Coalition. Do I need any vaccinations today? www.immunize.org/catg.d/4036need.htm (accessed 2003 Mar 12).
42. Guide for adult immunization. 3rd ed. Philadelphia: American College of Physicians; 1994.
43. Slobodkin D, Zielske PG, Kitlas JL, et al. Demonstration of the feasibility of emergency department immunization against influenza and pneumococcus. *Ann Emerg Med.* 1998; 32:537–43.
44. Robke JT, Woods M, Heitz S. Pharmacist impact on pneumococcal vaccination rates through incorporation of immunization assessment into critical pathways in an acute care setting. *Hosp Pharm.* 2002; 37:1050–4.
45. Hepatitis B virus: a comprehensive strategy for eliminating transmission in the United States through universal childhood vaccination. Recommendations of the Immunization Practices Advisory Committee (ACIP). *MMWR Recomm Rep.* 1991; 40 (RR-13):1–25.
46. Canadian National Advisory Committee on Immunization. Canadian immunization guide. 5th ed. Ottawa, Ont.: Ministry of National Health and Welfare; 1998.
47. 29 C.F.R. §1910.1030.
48. Immunization Action Coalition. Screening questionnaire for adult immunization. www.immunize.org/catg.d/p4065scr.pdf (accessed 2003 Mar 12).
49. Grabenstein JD, Wilson JP. Are vaccines safe? Risk contamination applied to vaccination. *Hosp Pharm.* 1999; 34:713–4,717–8,721–3,727–9.
50. Kirk JK, Grabenstein JD. Interviewing and counseling patients about immunizations. *Hosp Pharm.* 1991; 26:1006–10.
51. Nichol KL, MacDonald R, Hauge M. Factors associated with influenza and pneumococcal vaccination behavior among high-risk adults. *J Gen Intern Med.* 1996; 11:673–7.
52. Gene J, Espinola A, Cabezas C, et al. Do knowledge and attitudes about influenza and its immunization affect the likelihood of obtaining immunization? *Fam Pract Res J.* 1992; 12:61–73.
53. Grabenstein JD, Hartzema AG, Guess HA, et al. Community pharmacists as immunization advocates: a clinical pharmacoepidemiologic experiment. *Int J Pharm Pract.* 1993; 2:5–10.
54. Grabenstein JD, Guess HA, Hartzema AG. People vaccinated by pharmacists: Descriptive epidemiology. *J Am Pharm Assoc.* 2001; 41:46–52.
55. Grabenstein JD, Guess HA, Hartzema AG, et al. Effect of vaccination by community pharmacists among adult prescription recipients. *Med Care.* 2001; 39:340–8.
56. Casto DT. Prevention, management, and control of influenza: roles for the pharmacist. *Am J Med.* 1987; 82(suppl 6A):64–7.
57. Health Services & Resources Administration. Vaccine injury table. *Fed Regist.* 1997; 62:7685–90.
58. Centers for Disease Control and Prevention. Vaccine Information Statements. www.cdc.gov/nip/publications/vis (accessed 2003 Mar 27).
59. Update on adult immunization. Recommendations of the Immunization Practices Advisory Committee (ACIP). *MMWR Recomm Rep.* 1991; 40(RR-12): 1–94.
60. Grabenstein JD. Compensation for vaccine injury: balancing society's need and personal risk. *Hosp Pharm.* 1995; 30:831–2,834–6.
61. Grabenstein JD. Vaccination records must be available to be used. *J Am Pharm Assoc.* 2000; 40:113.
62. Kapit RM, Grabenstein JD. Adverse events after immunization: reports and results. *Hosp Pharm.* 1995; 30:1031–2,1035–6,1038,1041.
63. Immunization Action Coalition. Adult immunization record card. www.immunize.org/adultizcards/index.htm (accessed 2003 Mar 12).
64. American Society of Hospital Pharmacists. ASHP technical assistance bulletin on hospital drug distribution and control. *Am J Hosp Pharm.* 1980; 37:1097–103.
65. ASHP statement on the pharmacist's responsibility for distribution and control of drug products. In:

Deffenbaugh JH, ed. Best practices for health-system pharmacy. Positions and guidance documents of ASHP. 2002–2003 ed. Bethesda, MD: American Society of Health-System Pharmacists; 2002:91.

66. Grabenstein JD. ImmunoFacts: vaccines and immunologic drugs. 28th ed. St Louis: Facts and Comparisons; 2002.
67. Centers for Disease Control and Prevention. Vaccine management: recommendations for handling and storage of selected biologicals. www.cdc.gov/nip/publications/vac_mgt_book.htm (accessed 2003 Mar 27).
68. Casto DT, Brunell PA. Safe handling of vaccines. *Pediatrics.* 1990; 87:108–12.
69. Ross MB. Additional stability guidelines for routinely refrigerated drug products. *Am J Hosp Pharm.* 1988; 45:1498–9. Letter.
70. Sterchele JA. Update on stability guidelines for routinely refrigerated drug products. *Am J Hosp Pharm.* 1987; 44:2698, 2701. Letter.
71. Miller LG, Loomis JH Jr. Advice of manufacturers about effects of temperature on biologicals. *Am J Hosp Pharm.* 1985; 42:843–8.
72. Vogenberg FR, Souney PF. Stability guidelines for routinely refrigerated drug products. *Am J Hosp Pharm.* 1983; 40:101–2.
73. Wolfert RR, Cox RM. Room temperature stability of drug products labeled for refrigerated storage. *Am J Hosp Pharm.* 1975; 32:585–7.
74. Update: recommendations to prevent hepatitis B virus transmission—United States. *MMWR Morb Mortal Wkly Rep.* 1995; 44:574–5.
75. Update: recommendations to prevent hepatitis B virus transmission—United States. *MMWR Morb Mortal Wkly Rep.* 1999; 48:33–4.
76. Prevention of hepatitis A through active or passive immunization: recommendations of the Advisory Committee on Immunization Practices (ACIP). *MMWR Recomm Rep.* 1999; 48(RR-12):1–37.
77. Human rabies prevention—United States, 1999. Recommendations of the Advisory Committee on Immunization Practices (ACIP). *MMWR Recomm Rep.* 1999; 48(RR-1):1–21.
78. Diphtheria, tetanus, and pertussis: recommendations for vaccine use and other preventive measures. Recommendations of the Immunization Practices Advisory Committee (ACIP). *MMWR Recomm Rep.* 1991; 40(RR-10):1–28.
79. Grabenstein JD. Stop buying tetanus toxoid (with one exception). *Hosp Pharm.* 1990; 25:361–2.
80. Pertussis vaccination: use of acellular pertussis vaccines among infants and young children. Recommendations of the Advisory Committee on Immunization Practices (ACIP). *MMWR Recomm Rep.* 1997; 46(RR-7):1–25.
81. American Academy of Pediatrics Committee on Infectious Diseases. The relationship between pertussis vaccine and brain damage: reassessment. *Pediatrics.* 1991; 88:397–400.
82. Immunization of health-care workers: recommendations of the Advisory Committee on Immunization Practices (ACIP) and the Hospital Infection Control Practices Advisory Committee (HICPAC). *MMWR Recomm Rep.* 1997; 46(RR-18):1–42.
83. Screening for tuberculosis and tuberculosis infection in high-risk populations: recommendations of the Advisory Council for the Elimination of Tuberculosis. *MMWR Recomm Rep.* 1995; 44(RR-11):19–34.
84. Anergy skin testing and tuberculosis [corrected] preventive therapy for HIV-infected persons: revised recommendations. *MMWR Recomm Rep.* 1997; 46(RR-15):1–10.
85. Health information for international travel, 2001–02. Washington, DC: Government Printing Office; 2001.
86. American College of Obstetricians and Gynecologists committee opinion. Immunization during pregnancy. *Obstet Gynecol.* 2003; 101:207–12.

These guidelines were reviewed in 2013 by the Council on Pharmacy Practice and by the Board of Directors and were found to still be appropriate.

Developed through the ASHP Council on Professional Affairs and approved by the ASHP Board of Directors on May 31, 2003.

The bibliographic citation for this document is as follows: American Society of Health-System Pharmacists. ASHP guidelines on the pharmacist's role in immunization. *Am J Health-Syst Pharm.* 2003; 60:1371–7.

ASHP Guidelines on the Pharmacist's Role in Providing Drug Information

Background and Rationale

The provision of drug information (DI) is among the fundamental professional responsibilities of all pharmacists. Recent practice trends, including increased provision of medication therapy management services and efforts to obtain provider status, have placed pharmacists in increasingly complex patient-care roles and necessitated a higher level of competence by all pharmacists in meeting DI needs. Drug information may be patient specific, academic (for educational purposes), or population based (to aid in the decision-making process for evaluating medication use for groups of patients). The goal of providing carefully evaluated, evidence-based recommendations to support specific medication-use practices is to enhance the quality of patient care, improve patient outcomes, and ensure the prudent use of resources. The primary focus of these guidelines is to describe contemporary DI activities, including the application of a systematic approach, appropriate documentation methods, and use of high-quality DI resources. This information is intended to assist pharmacists in providing optimal DI services in a variety of practice settings, including hospitals and health systems, outpatient care centers, managed care environments, medical communication departments, and university or academic-based drug information centers. Some of the activities described in these guidelines are the subjects of other American Society of Health-System Pharmacists (ASHP) policy and guidance documents, which should be referred to for additional information. Pharmacists providing DI should use professional judgment in assessing ASHP's policy and guidance documents and in adapting them to meet their health care organizations' and patients' needs and circumstances.

Drug Information Activities

To be an effective provider of DI, the pharmacist must exercise excellent oral and written communication skills and be able to

1. Anticipate and evaluate the DI needs of patients and health care professionals;
2. Obtain appropriate and complete background information as described under the section Systematic Approach for Responding to Drug Information Requests;
3. Use a systematic approach to address DI needs by effectively searching, retrieving, and critically evaluating the literature (i.e., assessment of study design, statistics, bias, limitations, applicability); and
4. Appropriately synthesize, communicate, document, and apply pertinent information to the patient care situation.[1,2]

A variety of DI activities may be performed by pharmacists, depending on the particular practice setting and need. Every pharmacist should have the skills to perform the following DI activities[2,3]:

1. Providing DI to patients, caregivers, and health care professionals.
2. Creating and maintaining currency of a variety of print and online educational resources for patients (e.g., tip sheets, pamphlets) and health care professionals (e.g., in-service documents, newsletters) on topics such as optimal medication use, general health, or select clinical questions.
3. Educating health care professionals on safe and effective medication-use policies and processes, including development of resources to communicate this information.
4. Leading or participating in continuing education services for health care professionals.
5. Precepting and educating pharmacy students and residents.
6. Participating in quality improvement research projects and drug cost analyses.
7. Contributing to the biomedical literature and providing peer review for other contributors.

Some activities may be more appropriate for pharmacists with additional expertise and training in DI, such as those who have completed a postgraduate year two (PGY2) drug information residency. Drug information specialists often perform DI activities that overlap with other pharmacists and health care professionals. However, as a result of their advanced training and experience, DI specialists may be able to more efficiently retrieve, evaluate, and disseminate information in order to develop evidence-based recommendations and assist in patient care decisions.[2] Many DI specialists are also involved in medication-safety activities and collaborate with experts in informatics. These activities are highlighted in other ASHP statements.[4,5] Specific activities of the DI specialist may include some or all of the following[2,6-11]:

1. Providing information when there is not sufficient time for other health care professionals to appropriately research the DI question, when there is a knowledge gap, or when the question requires more thorough research.
2. Establishing and maintaining a formulary based on scientific evidence of efficacy and safety, pharmacoeconomics, and institution-specific factors.
3. Coordinating programs to support population-based medication practices that maximize patient outcomes (e.g., development of pharmacotherapeutic guidelines, medication-use evaluation criteria, and therapeutic interchange protocols).
4. Developing and participating in efforts to prevent medication errors and adverse drug events, including surveillance, ensuring institutional compliance to Risk Evaluation and Mitigation Strategies

(REMS), and leading reporting and analysis programs (e.g., MedWatch).

5. Monitoring and assessing the clinical significance of medication safety alerts communicated by the FDA, drug manufacturers, and other sources.
6. Performing health outcome and comparative effectiveness analyses.
7. Coordinating investigational drug services, including participating on institutional review boards (IRBs), evaluating protocols, and providing DI to patients, caregivers, and health care professionals.
8. Managing drug shortages, including identifying alternative treatments, developing protocols for restrictive use, and addressing formulary concerns.
9. Developing clinical decision support tools such as order sets, dosing protocols, and order-entry alerts.
10. Maintaining DI and medication-use policy-related intranet resources.
11. Precepting or providing advanced DI education and training to interprofessional and pharmacy students and residents.
12. Coordinating selection and purchase of pharmacy and institution-wide DI resources.
13. Participating in various fee-for-service projects (e.g., formulary support, database development, training programs) for clients.
14. Planning and delivering academic detailing programs.

Although the above activities may be best suited for pharmacists with advanced DI training, many institutions lack a formal DI specialist. Therefore, other pharmacists may be involved in more in-depth DI activities, depending on their level of expertise. For example, preparing drug monographs for pharmacy and therapeutics committees was once considered almost exclusively the responsibility of the DI specialist. As pharmacy practice has evolved, the expertise and knowledge of all pharmacy practitioners have been integrated into this process.

Today, depending on the institution, pharmacists without specialized DI training may prepare monographs, assist in the design of medication-use evaluation criteria, participate in medication monitoring activities, or educate health care professionals on appropriate medication use. If available, a DI specialist may serve in an oversight role by editing and providing feedback on these projects or providing general DI support to pharmacists involved in direct patient care. Moreover, a DI specialist may be involved in implementation and follow-up of medication-use policies and formulary changes as part of a larger medication policy management program, which may include interpreting the impact of legislation, regulation, and public policy on medication utilization.

Systematic Approach for Responding to Drug Information Requests

A systematic approach for responding to DI requests was first introduced by Watanabe, et al. in 1975.[12] This approach has been modified and expanded over the years to ensure that all relevant information is considered prior to formulating a response.[1,13] The importance of gathering pertinent patient data and understanding the context of a question prior to answering a DI request is described in the literature.[14-16] Of note, a full systematic approach may not be practical for all requests, especially for urgent clinical needs in the direct patient care setting. In addition, consideration should be given to the ethical and legal aspects of responding to DI requests, including patient privacy concerns.[1]

A systematic approach may be outlined as follows.[1,13]

1. *Identify the requestor.* In order to obtain complete information and develop a response with the appropriate perspective, consider the health literacy and professional background of the requestor.
2. *Define the true question and information need.* Identify the true question and information needed by asking probing questions of the requestor. For example, "Why is the question being asked?" and "Does the question pertain to a specific patient?" may help reveal important details of the true question.[1] This kind of information helps in optimizing the search process and assessing the appropriate time frame of response need.
3. *Obtain complete background information.* Obtain more complete background information, including examining the medical record for patient data, if applicable, to individualize the response to meet the requestor's need.
4. *Categorize the question.* Classify requests as patient-specific or academic and by type of question (e.g., product availability, adverse drug event, compatibility, compounding/formulation, dosage/administration, drug interaction [drug-drug, drug-disease, drug-laboratory], drug product identification, pharmacokinetics, therapeutic use/efficacy [FDA approved vs. unlabeled indications], safety in pregnancy/nursing toxicity/poisoning) to aid in tailoring the search strategy and selecting resources.
5. *Perform a systematic search.* Perform a systematic search of appropriate tertiary, secondary, and primary resources, including electronic resources, as necessary.
6. *Analyze the information.* Evaluate, interpret, and combine information from the resources used. Other information needs should be anticipated as a result of the information gathered.
7. *Disseminate the information.* Provide an oral or written response, or both, as needed by the requestor that specifically applies the information to the particular situation. The information, its urgency, and its purpose may influence the method of response. Supporting documentation (e.g., primary literature) should be included when possible.
8. *Document.* Document the request, information resources used, the information found in each source, time spent on the response, and the response itself as appropriate for the request and the practice setting.
9. *Follow-up.* Perform a follow-up assessment to determine the utility of the information provided and whether the information resulted in changes in medication-use practices or patient outcomes.

Documentation and Quality Assessment

Numerous methods of documenting pharmacist interventions, including the provision of DI, have been described in the literature. Drug information centers are moving toward increased use of electronic documentation systems, which have helped to increase the depth and quantity of documentation, as well as provide increased efficiency and cost savings.[17-21] In addition, an electronic system can promote a standardized and systematic approach and provides a readily retrievable archive that can be used to rapidly search previously answered questions.[22,23] Documentation of DI services should incorporate elements identified through the systematic approach. The ASHP Guidelines on Documenting Pharmaceutical Care in Patient Medical Records states that "the professional actions of pharmacists that are intended to ensure safe and effective use of drugs and that may affect patient outcomes should be documented in the patient medical record."[24] Therefore, if the DI request is patient-specific, it is appropriate, but not always necessary, to document the request and response in the patient's medical record. Documentation is critical to appropriate patient care, highlights the value of pharmacist services, demonstrates accountability, provides a basis for quality assessment and performance improvement, and details an appropriate systematic approach in case a medico-legal dispute arises from a DI request. Consequently, even academic or population-based DI activities should be appropriately documented. Despite the importance of assessing the quality of drug-related information provided by pharmacists, there is currently no standardized method described in the literature. However, some DI centers have reported use of double-check systems prior to providing a response, random retrospective audits by a DI specialist or another individual, obtaining feedback from the requestor, and conducting an internal review by a committee as methods of quality assessment.[25]

Resources

It is important for pharmacists to use appropriate and credible resources. The amount of medical knowledge has grown substantially and access to information has changed dramatically over the last few decades. Traditional print resources are rapidly being replaced by electronic databases (both online and included in health information management systems), online resources, and mobile applications.[26] The internet and mobile technology have allowed for convenient and quick access to medical information. However, pharmacists should critically evaluate all resources prior to use to ensure that they are accurate, current, and unbiased.

General principles to consider when critically evaluating medical information available on the internet have been published.[27] Pharmacists should work closely with others within the organization to ensure that up-to-date resources, including representative primary (e.g., peer-reviewed original studies), secondary (e.g., indexing or abstracting services such as MEDLINE and International Pharmaceutical Abstracts), and tertiary resources (e.g., electronic databases, textbooks, review articles, clinical practice guidelines) are available to assist in answering a variety of DI requests. Pharmacists should be familiar with the features of each resource; familiarity makes searching more efficient so that more time can be devoted to analyzing, applying, and communicating the information.

The following factors should be considered when purchasing DI resources, including electronic subscriptions, for the pharmacy department or practice setting:

1. Features of the resource (e.g., frequency of updates, qualifications and affiliations of authors, year of publication, type of information, organization of material, method of delivery, cost).
2. Practice setting (e.g., type of facility and needs of health care professionals within that environment, state-specific regulatory requirements).
3. Accessibility of the resource (e.g., location of print resources, number of users allowed by subscription).

Keeping Current

Pharmacists are challenged with keeping up to date with an increasing number of new drugs and literature.[3] Drug information and literature evaluation skills are crucial for building clinical knowledge and providing evidence-based recommendations. It is the responsibility of the pharmacist to commit to lifelong learning and make an effort to keep abreast of advances both in the methods of delivering DI and the information itself. In addition to keeping up to date with clinical knowledge, it is important for pharmacists to keep current on changes in pharmacy practice as the health care system evolves. Recommendations for staying current include the following:

1. Subscribe to table of contents of or full access to relevant journals, as appropriate.
2. Subscribe to appropriate email listservers (e.g., Food and Drug Administration Drug Information Updates, National Guideline Clearinghouse, Centers for Disease Control and Prevention, Medline Plus).
3. Receive email alerts from relevant health-related websites (e.g., MedWatch, Medline Plus).
4. Bookmark important websites and check regularly for updates (e.g., Institute for Safe Medication Practices, ASHP Drug Shortages Resource Center).
5. Choose pertinent continuing education activities and methods that challenge learning.
6. Maintain active membership in local, state, and national pharmacy associations/societies.
7. Pursue board certification from the Board of Pharmacy Specialties.

Conclusion

All pharmacists are involved in the provision of DI, which includes a broad array of activities. A systematic approach should be considered for all DI requests, and pharmacists should document their services to demonstrate accountability and justify the value of pharmacist care. Increased availability of medical information, both due to increased knowledge and technological advances, has not changed the overall process of DI practice. It is important for pharmacists to select appropriate resources and keep current on new literature and new tools to address a variety of DI requests.

References

1. Malone PM, Kier KL, Stanovich JE. Drug information: a guide for pharmacists, 4th ed. New York: McGraw-Hill; 2012.
2. Bernknopf AC, Karpinski JP, McKeever AL, et al. Drug information: from education to practice. *Pharmacotherapy*. 2009; 29:331–46.
3. Wang F, Troutman WG, Seo T, et al. Drug information education in doctor of pharmacy programs. *Am J Pharm Educ*. 2006; 70(3):51.
4. American Society of Health-System Pharmacists. ASHP statement on the role of the medication safety leader. *Am J Health-Syst Pharm*. 2013; 70:448–52.
5. American Society of Health-System Pharmacists. ASHP statement on the pharmacist's role in informatics. *Am J Health-Syst Pharm*. 2007; 64:200–3.
6. American Society of Health-System Pharmacists. ASHP accreditation standards for postgraduate year one (PGY1) pharmacy residency programs. http://www.ashp.org/DocLibrary/Accreditation/ASD-PGY1-Standard.aspx (accessed 2013 May 9).
7. American Society of Health-System Pharmacists. ASHP accreditation standards for postgraduate year two (PGY2) pharmacy residency programs. http://www.ashp.org/DocLibrary/Accreditation/ASD-PGY2-Standard.aspx (accessed 2013 May 9).
8. Rosenberg JM, Schilit S, Nathan JP, et al. Update on the status of 89 drug information centers in the United States. *Am J Health-Syst Pharm*. 2009; 66:1718–22.
9. Powell L, Pepper M. Reviewing the pharmacy department's drug information activities. *Am J Health-Syst Pharm*. 2000; 57:2260–1.
10. American Society of Health-System Pharmacists. ASHP guidelines on managing drug product shortages in hospitals and health systems. *Am J Health-Syst Pharm*. 2009; 66:1399–1406.
11. Wisniewski CS, Robert S, Ball S. Collaboration between a drug information center and an academic detailing program. *Am J Health-Syst Pharm*. 2014; 71:128–33.
12. Watanabe AS, McCart G, Shimomura S, et al. Systematic approach to drug information requests. *Am J Hosp Pharm*. 1975; 32:1282–5.
13. Nathan JP. Drug information—the systematic approach: continuing education article. *J Pharm Pract*. 2013; 26:78–84.
14. Calis KA, Anderson DW, Auth DA, et al. Quality of pharmacotherapy consultations provided by drug information centers in the United States. *Pharmacotherapy*. 2000; 20:830–6.
15. Beaird SL, Coley RM, Blunt JR. Assessing the accuracy of drug information responses from drug information centers. *Ann Pharmacother*. 1994; 28:707–11.
16. Halbert MR, Kelly WN, Miller DE. Drug information centers: lack of generic equivalence. *Drug Intell Clin Pharm*. 1977; 11:728–35.
17. Wisniewski CS, Pummer TL, Krenzelok EP. Documenting drug information questions using software for poison information documentation. *Am J Health-Syst Pharm*. 2009; 66:1039–43.
18. Simonian AI. Documenting pharmacist interventions on an intranet. *Am J Health-Syst Pharm*. 2003; 60:151–5.
19. Nurgat ZA, Al-Jazairi AS, Abu-Shraie N, et al. Documenting clinical pharmacist intervention before and after the introduction of a web-based tool. *Int J Clin Pharm*. 2011; 33:200–7.
20. Abe AM. Implementation of a cloud computing system for documenting drug information consultation requests and responses. Poster presented at: ASHP Midyear Clinical Meeting; December 2012; Las Vegas, NV.
21. Brown JN. Cost savings associated with a dedicated drug information service in an academic medical center. *Hosp Pharm*. 2011; 46:680–4.
22. Erbele SM, Heck AM, Blankenship CS. Survey of computerized documentation system use in drug information centers. *Am J Health-Syst Pharm*. 2001; 58:695–7.
23. Cheng SC. Computerized tools that standardize the systematic approach to researching drug information requests. Poster presented at: ASHP Midyear Clinical Meeting; December 2006; Anaheim, CA.
24. American Society of Health-System Pharmacists. ASHP guidelines on documenting pharmaceutical care in patient medical records. *Am J Health-Syst Pharm*. 2003; 60:705–7.
25. Rosenberg JM, Koumis T, Nathan JP, et al. Current status of pharmacist-operated drug information centers in the United States. *Am J Health-Syst Pharm*. 2004; 61:2023–32.
26. Fass JA, Carvajal M, Polen H, et al. Knowledge, use, and decision-making considerations for drug information resources in community and hospital pharmacies. Poster presented at: ASHP Midyear Clinical Meeting; December 2012; Las Vegas, NV.
27. Grossman S, Zerilli T. Health and medication information resources on the World Wide Web. *J Pharm Pract*. 2013; 26:85–94.

Developed through the ASHP Council on Therapeutics and approved by the ASHP Board of Directors on April 10, 2014. These guidelines supersede the ASHP Guidelines on the Provision of Medication Information by Pharmacists dated April 24, 1996.

Shadi Ghaibi, Pharm.D., BCPS, is Pharmacist, Drug Information and Medication Safety, Intermountain Medical Center, Murray, UT. Heather Ipema, Pharm.D., BCPS, is Clinical Assistant Professor; and Michael Gabay, Pharm.D., J.D., BCPS, is Clinical Associate Professor, Pharmacy Practice, University of Illinois at Chicago, Chicago.

ASHP gratefully acknowledges contributions made to these guidelines by the following individuals: Karim Calis, Pharm.D., M.P.H., FASHP, FCCP; Erin Fox, Pharm.D.; Randy Hatton, Pharm.D., BCPS, FCCP; Corinne Johnson, Pharm.D., M.B.A.; Joe Jordan, Pharm.D.; Mandy Leonard, Pharm.D., BCPS; Michelle W. McCarthy, Pharm.D., FASHP; Genevieve Ness, Pharm.D.; Jennifer Riggins, Pharm.D.; Ryan Rodriguez, Pharm.D., BCPS; and Sheri VanOsdol, Pharm.D., BCPS.

ASHP also gratefully acknowledges the following organizations and individuals for reviewing these guidelines (review does not imply endorsement): American Pharmacists Association (APhA); Institute for Safe Medication Practices (ISMP); Joseph Aloi, Pharm.D., BCPS; Jason Babby, Pharm.D., BCPS; Linda Banares, Pharm.D., BCACP; Sara J. Beis, M.S., FASHP; John D. Bowman, B.S.Pharm., M.S., BCPS, FASHP; Susan Teil Boyer, M.S., FASHP; Jamie N. Brown, Pharm.D., BCPS; William Budris, B.S.Pharm.; Juan Hincapie Castillo, Pharm.D.; Erin S. Christensen, Pharm.D., BCPS; Jason C. Cooper, Pharm.D.; Michelle C. Corrado, Pharm.D., M.H.A.; Paul Driver, Pharm.D., BCPS, FASHP; Steven Dzierba, Pharm.D., M.S., FASHP; Lauren Ellison, Pharm.D.; Margo Farber, Pharm.D.; Leah Frantzen, Pharm.D., BCPS; Kelli Garrison, Pharm.D., BCPS; Kelly N. Glover, Pharm.D.; Conor Hanrahan, Pharm.D., BCPS; Joe Jordan, Pharm.D., BCPS; Julie P. Karpinski, Pharm.D., BCPS; Tim Lanese, M.B.A.; Ashley Lewis, Pharm.D.; Gregory Light, Pharm.D. (candidate); Jim Lile, Pharm.D., FMPA, FASHP; Patrick M. Malone, Pharm.D., FASHP; Jeannell Mansur, Pharm.D., FASHP, FSMSO; Shannon Manzi, Pharm.D., NREMT; Linda Gore Martin, Pharm.D., M.B.A., BCPS; Theresa Mays, B.S., Pharm.D., BCOP, FASHP; Leslie McCament-Mann, Ph.D.; John F. Mitchell, Pharm.D., FASHP; Ruth W. Ndungi, Pharm.D.; Genevieve Ness, Pharm.D.; James A. Owen, Pharm.D., BCPS (APhA); Frank P. Paloucek, Pharm.D., DABAT, FASHP; Fred J. Pane, B.S.Pharm., FASHP; Lois F. Parker, B.S.; Peter Pascale, M.S.; Stephanie C. Peshek, Pharm.D., M.B.A., M.S.Ed., FASHP; James Ponto, M.S., BCNP, FASHP; William H. Puckett, M.S., M.B.A., FASHP; Curt W. Quap, M.S., FASHP; Dan Rackham, Pharm.D., BCPS; James R. Rinehart, M.S., FASHP; Martha M. Rumore, M.S., Pharm.D, J.D., FAPhA; Sam Shimomura, Pharm.D., CGP, FASHP; Sarah J. Steinhardt, Pharm.D., J.D., M.S.; Allen J. Vaida, Pharm.D., FASHP (ISMP); Kristina Ward, Pharm.D., BCPS; Jody Jacobson Wedret, FASHP, FCSHP; Tom Westerkamp, M.S.; Phipson Wu, Pharm.D., BCPS; and Kristi Yamasaki, Pharm.D.

The authors have declared no potential conflicts of interest.

The bibliographic citation for this document is as follows: Ghaibi S., Ipema H., Gabay M. ASHP guidelines on the pharmacist's role in providing drug information. *Am J Health-Syst Pharm.* 2015; 72:573–7.

ASHP Guidelines for Providing Pediatric Pharmaceutical Services in Organized Health Care Systems

Patient care consists of integrated domains of care, including medical care, nursing care, and pharmaceutical care. The provision of pharmaceutical care involves not only medication therapy but decisions about medication selection, dosages, routes and methods of administration, medication therapy monitoring, and the provision of medication-related information and counseling to individual patients.[1] The pediatric patient population poses some unique challenges to the pharmaceutical care provider in terms of these medication-related activities. These challenges include the lack of published information on the therapeutic uses and monitoring of drugs in pediatric patients; the lack of appropriate commercially available dosage forms and concentrations of many drugs for pediatric patients; and the resulting need to develop innovative ways of ensuring that the patient receives the drug in a manner that allows the intended therapeutic effect to be realized.[2] These guidelines are intended to assist pharmacists in meeting the special needs of the pediatric patient in any organized health care setting.

General Principles

The pharmacy service should be organized in accordance with the principles of good management. It should be under the direction of a pharmacist and be provided with sufficient physical facilities, personnel, and equipment to meet the pharmaceutical care needs of the pediatric population. Resources necessary for compounding and testing alternative doses and dosage forms of commercially available products are essential. The pharmacy should comply with all applicable federal, state, and local laws, codes, statutes, and regulations.[3] The setting should meet applicable accreditation criteria of the Joint Commission on Accreditation of Healthcare Organizations. Organizations such as the National Association of Children's Hospitals and Related Institutions, the American Academy of Pediatrics, and the Pediatric Pharmacy Administrative Group are useful sources of further information on pediatric health care services.

Orientation and Training Programs

Orientation, training, and staff development programs for pharmacists providing services to pediatric patients should emphasize dosage calculations, dosage-form selection appropriate to the patient's age and condition, and specialized drug preparation and administration techniques. Pharmacists should be familiar with the pharmacokinetic and pharmacodynamic changes that occur with age (e.g., in volume of distribution, protein binding, renal elimination, metabolism, muscle mass, and fluid requirements) and with disease-specific conditions that might affect drug choice or administration (e.g., short-gut syndrome, lactose intolerance). A sensitivity to the nature, frequency, and severity of medication-related errors in the pediatric population is important for all pharmacy personnel.[4]

Inpatient Services

A lack of availability of commercially prepared dosage forms, combined with the documented risk of calculation errors, requires the use of comprehensive unit dose drug distribution systems and intravenous (i.v.) admixture services for pediatric patients. Appropriate dosage standardization in both oral and parenteral drug distribution systems may facilitate the provision of these services.

Unit Dose System. The pediatric unit dose system must meet the original intent of these systems, which is to minimize errors and provide drugs to the patient care areas in ready-to-administer form. Multidose containers and stock medications should be avoided. An extemporaneous preparation service should facilitate the preparation and packaging of medications according to sound compounding principles.

I.V. Admixture Service. The drugs provided by the i.v. admixture service should include all i.v. push, i.v. minibag, intramuscular, and subcutaneous doses; large-volume injections; antineoplastic agents; parenteral nutrient fluids; ophthalmic products; peritoneal dialysis solutions; and irrigation fluids. Knowledge of pediatric fluid requirements and limitations, drug administration techniques and devices, and acceptable volumes for intramuscular injection is critical. Care should be taken when making dilutions to maximize concentrations of drug products (when safe to do so) for fluid-sensitive patients, as well as to minimize hyperosmolar solutions that might lead to destruction of vasculature or, in the neonate, intraventricular hemorrhage. Quality controls for both manually prepared and computer-driven preparation should exist to ensure that each product contains the ingredients ordered and that they are properly labeled. Knowledge of products that contain benzyl alcohol and the risks of this substance in neonates is essential in a pediatric i.v. admixture service.

The labels of all products should be evaluated for legibility, clarity of expression, and their potential for leading to a medication error.[5] Labels should include the drug name; the drug concentration; the route of administration; the expiration date or time; appropriate instructions for administration, additional preparation, and storage; and the lot number (if a batch-prepared product).[6]

Ambulatory Care Services

Ambulatory care pharmacy services should be attentive to the unique drug needs of the pediatric patient. These include the need for special dosage forms (e.g., liquids and chewable tablets), measuring devices, and detailed counseling on drug administration. When product stability is a problem, caregivers may have to be taught how to prepare an appropriate dosage form in the home. Consideration must be given to taste and the need for an extra prescription container to be taken to school or daycare. Children should be included whenever possible in discussions concerning their medications. In the ambulatory care setting, the pharmacist is well positioned to play a role in preventive health care, including poison prevention and immunization.[7]

Drug Information

Drug information services should provide the pharmacist practicing in the pediatric setting with information unique to the pediatric population. References should include pediatric medical texts and current information on pediatric dosages, extemporaneous formulations, drug compatibilities and stability, poison control, and drug effects during pregnancy and lactation. Drug information should be available in areas where decisions are being made about drug therapy. Literature supporting the use of drugs for unlabeled uses in pediatric patients should also be available.[8] Pharmacists should provide other health care professionals with information on new and investigational drugs, adverse effects of and contraindications to drug therapy, compatibility and stability information, dosage computations, pharmacokinetics, and drug interactions. This may be accomplished through educational presentations, seeing patients in conjunction with other caregivers ("rounding"), and printed materials (e.g., newsletters).

Therapeutic Drug Monitoring

Therapeutic drug monitoring enables assessment of therapeutic outcomes and recognition at the earliest moment of an undesirable response to a drug. Both desired and undesired effects should be documented. The person performing therapeutic drug monitoring should take into consideration the age-related differences in dosage when recommending or reviewing drug therapy.

Pharmacokinetic Services

For both oral and injectable drugs, pharmacokinetic services should ensure that the drug has been administered appropriately before samples are taken for the measurement of serum drug concentrations. The frequency and timing of sampling should also be monitored to avoid excessive and traumatic sampling in children. Knowledge of age-related differences in absorption, distribution, metabolism, and elimination is essential for the pharmacist who is involved in pharmacokinetic services for pediatric patients. The collection and publication of accurate pharmacokinetic data on the pediatric population are encouraged.

Patient and Caregiver Education

Pharmacists should counsel and educate patients and caregivers about their medications, including the purpose of each medication, dosage instructions, potential drug interactions, potential adverse effects, and any specific age-related issues (e.g., compounding and diluting techniques, measuring and administration instructions). Caregivers should be informed of any drug products for which crushing, chewing, dividing, or diluting should be avoided. Suggestions about masking the taste of an unpleasant medication should also be provided. Administration of products, including ophthalmics, otics, inhalers, and injectables, should be demonstrated. The prevention of accidental ingestion of medications should also be emphasized. The benefits of educational programs are best realized when a cooperative multidisciplinary approach is used. Sharing of pertinent information by all participants is fundamental to the success of patient education services.[9]

Medication Errors

Systems for the recognition, documentation, and prevention of medication errors are essential for the pediatric population. Pharmacist participation in quality-improvement committees and the participation of pharmacists, nurses, physicians, and risk managers are important in minimizing medication errors in pediatric patients. The development and enforcement of policies and procedures for minimizing medication errors are essential. Pediatric patients are especially vulnerable to errors caused by mistakes in calculations. Pharmacists should recognize that since some commercially available products are available in strengths that can be potentially toxic to a pediatric patient, special scrutiny of these products is necessary.[5]

Adverse Drug Reactions

Pediatric patients frequently have the same kinds of adverse drug reactions that adults have, but adverse reactions in the pediatric population may be harder to recognize or of greater or lesser intensity. The lack of literature on newly introduced therapeutic agents makes it imperative to monitor experience with new drugs initially used in the pediatric population. Comprehensive adverse drug reaction monitoring and reporting programs are important in reducing the occurrence of these reactions in pediatric patients.[10]

Drug-Use Evaluation

Drug-use evaluation should be directed at drugs with a low therapeutic index that require extensive monitoring, those that are responsible for serious medication errors in the institution, and those that are found to be associated with high frequency of preventable adverse drug reactions. Cost-related issues may also become important in the evaluations, since many expensive drugs are not available in package sizes appropriate for the pediatric patient.

Research

Pediatric patients have long been recognized as "therapeutic orphans" because of a relative absence of therapeutic trials in this patient population. The reasons for this are numerous and include ethical issues, potential adverse publicity, possible litigation, methodological hurdles, and an inability to justify such studies for economic reasons. Nonetheless, the need for timely and effective research on medication safety, efficacy, and practical application in the pediatric population is compelling. The paucity of pediatric drug information, the impact of new drug delivery systems, the expansion of adult diseases (such as AIDS) into the pediatric population, and expanded applications of new and established therapeutic agents are all areas warranting additional research. The pediatric pharmacist can be directly involved in collaboration with other health care providers in conducting pediatric research. Examples of pediatric research topics include, but are not limited to, the following:

- Safety and efficacy of drug products in pediatric patients;
- Pharmacokinetics and pharmacodynamics of new medications;
- Stability, safety, and efficacy of extemporaneously compounded sterile and nonsterile drug products;
- Safety and efficacy of administration techniques;
- Comparative evaluations of medications addressing treatment regimens, outcomes of therapy, and their relative costs;
- Behavioral and socioeconomic compliance issues in pediatric pharmaceutical care; and
- New and existing pharmacy drug distribution systems and services for pediatric patients.

Examples of direct involvement include

- Serving as a member of an institutional review board;
- Maintenance, oversight, and dissemination of all information on investigational drug studies and comparative trials involving medications in the pediatric population; and
- Maintenance, coordination, and oversight of policies and procedures involving investigational drug studies and comparative trials involving medications in the pediatric population.

References

1. American Society of Hospital Pharmacists. ASHP statement on pharmaceutical care. *Am J Hosp Pharm.* 1993; 50:1720–3.
2. Pediatric Pharmacy Administration Group Committee on Pediatric Pharmacy Practice. Pediatric pharmacy practice guidelines. *Am J Hosp Pharm.* 1991; 48:2475–7.
3. American Society of Hospital Pharmacists. ASHP guidelines: minimum standard for pharmacies in institutions. *Am J Hosp Pharm.* 1985; 42:372–5.
4. Folli HL, Poole RL, Benitz WE, et al. Medication error prevention by clinical pharmacists in two children's hospitals. *Pediatrics.* 1987; 79:718–22.
5. American Society of Hospital Pharmacists. ASHP guidelines on preventing medication errors in hospitals. *Am J Hosp Pharm.* 1993; 50:305–14.
6. American Society of Hospital Pharmacists. ASHP technical assistance bulletin on single unit and unit dose packages of drugs. *Am J Hosp Pharm.* 1985; 42:378–9.
7. American Society of Hospital Pharmacists. ASHP technical assistance bulletin on the pharmacist's role in immunization. *Am J Hosp Pharm.* 1993; 50:501–5.
8. American Society of Hospital Pharmacists. ASHP statement on the use of medications for unlabeled uses. *Am J Hosp Pharm.* 1992; 49:2006–8.
9. American Society of Hospital Pharmacists. ASHP guidelines on pharmacist-conducted patient counseling. *Am J Hosp Pharm.* 1993; 50:505–6.
10. American Society of Hospital Pharmacists. ASHP guidelines on adverse drug reaction monitoring and reporting. *Am J Hosp Pharm.* 1989; 46:336–7.

Approved by the ASHP Board of Directors, April 27, 1994. Developed by the ASHP Council on Professional Affairs.

The bibliographic citation for this document is as follows: American Society of Hospital Pharmacists. ASHP guidelines for providing pediatric pharmaceutical services in organized health care systems. *Am J Hosp Pharm.* 1994; 51:1690–2.

ASHP Guidelines on Surgery and Anesthesiology Pharmaceutical Services

Purpose

In hospitals, surgery and anesthesiology generally have been without direct pharmacist involvement. Drugs have been available through a stock-distribution system maintained by operating-room (OR) personnel, and documentation of controlled-substance use has often been handled by personnel other than those administering the drugs. More important, without direct pharmacist involvement, patient-related issues that are best addressed by a pharmacist usually have been handled by other health care personnel out of necessity. ASHP believes that pharmaceutical services (including drug-use control) to these areas should be provided by pharmacists, ideally with their direct presence. In many hospitals this is accomplished through an onsite satellite pharmacy.[1–5]

The purpose of these guidelines is to help pharmacists identify services they could provide in the areas of surgery and anesthesiology, decide on the scope of these services, and develop performance improvement plans. In addition, the appendix provides guidance for justifying and implementing a satellite pharmacy. Some topics outlined in these guidelines are the subject of other ASHP practice standards, which should be referred to for additional information and guidance. Pharmacists should use professional judgment in assessing their organization's needs for pharmaceutical services in surgery and anesthesiology. The guidance should be adapted, as applicable, to meet those needs.

The term "surgery and anesthesiology pharmaceutical services" should not be interpreted too literally. Many satellite pharmacies serving surgery and anesthesiology areas also serve other areas. These may include cystoscopy and endoscopy suites, cardiac catheterization laboratories or suites, preoperative holding areas, postanesthesia care units (PACUs), labor and delivery rooms, freestanding surgical centers, and critical care areas. In general, these satellite pharmacies are termed "OR satellite pharmacies" and the pharmacist an "OR pharmacist." The guidelines do not distinguish among terms, because terms may be applied differently in various settings. The terms "satellite pharmacy" and "the pharmacist" are used in their broadest senses.

Pharmaceutical Services

The successful establishment of pharmaceutical services in surgery and anesthesiology will depend to a large extent on the OR pharmacist's ability to positively affect drug-use management, take a leadership role in all aspects of cost containment, and contribute to improving patient care and outcomes.

The performance of many activities and services may be improved in surgery and anesthesiology through the establishment of pharmaceutical services. Often these include the following:

1. Drug preparation and distribution;
2. Drug inventory control;
3. Waste reduction;
4. Drug cost reduction;
5. Improved revenue generation through accurate patient billing;
6. Improved documentation of drugs administered to patients;[6]
7. Clinical activities;
8. Formulary management;
9. Drug accountability and control, including adherence to organizational drug-use guidelines;
10. Quality assurance and continuous quality improvement;
11. Compliance with standards of the Joint Commission on Accreditation of Healthcare Organizations (JCAHO);
12. Informational, educational, and research activities;
13. Involvement with the use of drug administration devices; and
14. Enhanced interdisciplinary decision-making.

Drug Preparation and Distribution

In most ORs, the drug preparation and distribution functions can be improved by pharmacy personnel practicing in this setting. These activities should not be so labor-intensive as to exclude cognitive services being provided by the pharmacist. Technicians should be assigned most of the drug preparation and distribution activities, under the supervision of a pharmacist. Drug preparation and distribution can be accomplished in various ways. For non-anesthesiology drugs and drugs that are not case specific, a secure general supply of predetermined medications in limited quantities (e.g., in cart or cassette) can be provided, with the understanding that these drugs may be used for any patient. Anesthesiology medications could be supplied by case or by daily stock replenishment (e.g., an "anesthesia cart"). Increasingly, automated medication storage and distribution devices (e.g., Pyxis Medstation [Cardinal Health]) are being used to supply medications to the anesthesiology, nursing, and surgery staffs. With these devices, automatic and more accurate patient charging is often realized and pharmacy staff spend less time in distribution activities. The methods chosen may depend on the preferences and needs of the anesthesiologists and surgery staff, available resources, and whether there is a satellite pharmacy. The choice should be based on the method that will provide accurate and timely delivery of medications to meet the needs of patients. The common objectives for all methods, however, are reducing the time spent by nursing and anesthesiology staff in gathering and preparing medications and maximizing patient safety by limiting the selection of drugs, quantities, and dosage forms.

Drug Accountability and Control

The pharmacist should be responsible for all drugs and controlled substances dispensed and distributed in the setting. Pharmacy technicians could be assigned most of the responsibility for these daily activities. If there is a satellite pharmacy, all drug inventories, to the extent possible, should be centralized there. Minimal drug stock should be kept in each surgical suite. Ideally, the satellite pharmacy should be staffed whenever the surgery and anesthesiology areas are normally staffed. If the satellite pharmacy is not open 24 hours a day, it may be necessary to establish an after-hours drug supply (e.g., a cart). The pharmacist should decide the drugs and quantities required for this supply and the accountability system to be used. The supply levels should be checked and replenished daily. With an OR pharmacy, trends in drug use or disappearance are more easily identified, noted, and reconciled. Systems to track drugs used, to adjust par levels as needed, and to monitor drug expiration dates should be devised.

Clinical Services

Provision of clinical services should be a major focus of pharmacists practicing in the surgery and anesthesiology areas. These services may be similar to those provided to all other patient care areas. Clinical services can be provided by a pharmacist even without a satellite pharmacy.

To make effective clinical contributions, the pharmacist should be familiar with all drugs used in the setting, including drugs for general and regional anesthesia, neuromuscular blockade, analgesia, preoperative management, hemodynamic control, diagnosis and manipulation during surgery, prevention of infection, treatment of intraoperative emergencies, control of bleeding, and postoperative nausea and vomiting (PONV). Knowledge may be gained by observation of surgery and anesthesia procedures, attendance at anesthesia and surgery conferences, assigned topics to be presented by each pharmacy team member, review of pertinent literature, and direct clinical involvement in patient care. Clinical services may include the following[7]:

Medication-Use Management. The pharmacist is especially suited to taking a leadership role in medication-use management in the OR. This could be accomplished through the development of pharmaceutical practice guidelines and critical pathways for select surgical procedures, including intraoperative drug use. Guidelines are routinely developed for the neuromuscular blocking agents, synthetic opioids, propofol, antiemetic agents, volatile inhalation agents, and anti-infectives for surgical prophylaxis. Additional guidelines could be developed on the basis of organizational needs. It has been demonstrated that pharmaceutical practice guidelines for anesthesia-related medications reduce costs without adversely affecting patient outcomes.[8–10] With or without established guidelines, the presence of an OR satellite pharmacy allows the pharmacist to reinforce the appropriate use of agents dispensed from the pharmacy and to monitor patient outcomes.

Medication-Regimen Review. Whenever possible, medication requests from surgery or anesthesiology staff should be evaluated before the drug is dispensed for appropriateness (e.g., allergies, disease states, adherence to pharmaceutical practice guidelines), dose, route of administration, timing of administration, and cost compared with other therapeutic alternatives. The pharmacist should review the surgery schedule and routinely screen patient profiles or charts before surgery for allergies (e.g., antimicrobials, narcotics, latex) and notify appropriate personnel of pertinent findings. In addition, doses, timing, and choices of prophylactic antimicrobials should be monitored. Profiles or charts should also be reviewed whenever possible for potential perioperative drug—drug or drug—disease interactions and for proper continuation of maintenance medications and discontinuation of unnecessary medications postoperatively.

Medication-Use Evaluation. The pharmacist should take a leadership role in the performance of medication-use evaluations by establishing criteria, collecting data, analyzing the data, making recommendations, and performing follow-up. Data collection is often more easily accomplished prospectively or concurrently by coordination with surgery and anesthesiology staff. High-cost or high-use medications are good starting places for medication-use evaluations in the OR. Medication-use evaluations are especially useful for assessing compliance with established guidelines. In organizations with automated anesthesia record keepers, collection and manipulation of medication-use information is greatly facilitated.[11]

Drug Information. The pharmacist should provide timely and accurate drug information in response to known needs and random inquiries. Inquiries may originate from any type of staff, including surgery and recovery-room staff, anesthesia staff, residents, nurses, perfusionists, and students. Drug information may be provided in oral or written form, as appropriate. The preparation of responses could require detailed literature searches with accompanying interpretations. The satellite pharmacy should maintain a body of pharmaceutical literature containing current primary, secondary, and tertiary literature sources. Scientific and professional practice journals in pharmacy, anesthesiology, and surgery should be directly available or readily accessible to support clinical decision-making for patients in the OR. Online drug information and access to the Internet should also be readily available to OR pharmacists. Reference texts should be current and should provide detailed information in at least the following areas: drug action, adverse effects, dosages, drugs of choice, efficacy, formulations, incompatibilities, indications for use, drug interactions, laws and regulations, pharmacology, pediatric medication administration (if applicable), nonprescription drugs, drug use during pregnancy and lactation, pathophysiology, pharmacokinetics, toxicology, surgery, and anesthesia. The pharmacist may also develop and distribute a newsletter and make available specific articles of interest to others in the setting. The pharmacist should have access to a formal drug information center.

Formulary System. The pharmacist should continually evaluate the organization's formulary and advise the medical staff and pharmacy and therapeutics (P&T) committee about drug efficacy, adverse-effect experiences, cost, and ongoing need for formulary agents. OR pharmacists can enforce P&T committee-approved restrictions on anesthesiology and surgery drugs and educate OR personnel on these restrictions.

Drug Research. The pharmacist should strive to initiate and participate in research related to drug use in surgery and anesthesia. Pharmacists could be principal investigators or could support the studies of others (e.g., perform randomization, prepare drugs, assist in study design and data collection). Because the OR is one of the most medication-intensive areas of a hospital, it is an excellent setting for pharmacoeconomic analyses and outcome studies.[12–14] These studies are best accomplished when they are collaborative. Given that newer anesthetic agents are often more expensive than older ones, studies are useful for learning whether a higher drug cost will result in a lower total cost for the patient.

Adverse-Drug-Reaction Monitoring and Reporting. The pharmacist should monitor, detect, document, report, and recommend appropriate management of adverse drug reactions that occur in the OR. OR health care providers should be asked to report suspected adverse drug reactions to the OR pharmacist for follow-up.

Education. Educational presentations on drug-related topics should be made regularly by the pharmacist to surgery and anesthesiology residents and staff, nursing staff, pharmacy staff, and other personnel. This could include information on drugs added to the organization's formulary, drug precautions, periodic reviews of drugs used during cardiac and respiratory arrest, pain management, and the management of malignant hyperthermia and latex allergy. The pharmacist should also educate OR personnel about drugs used in the setting, giving special attention to the synthetic opiods neuromuscular blocking agents, anesthetic gases, intravenous anesthetic agents, local anesthetics, antiemetics, and antimicrobials (surgical prophylaxis).

Formal educational rotations in the satellite pharmacy may be conducted for undergraduate and graduate pharmacy students, pharmacy residents, or pharmacy fellows. Specific learning and experiential goals and objectives should be developed. The student should learn about satellite pharmacy services and preoperative, intraoperative, and postoperative medication therapy through didactic instruction, observation, project participation, and selected readings. Rotations should be coordinated with the anesthesiology and nursing departments.

Rounds. When possible, the pharmacist should be an active participant with anesthesia, surgery, and PACU staff in patient care rounds. The pharmacist may limit rounds to specific types of patients (e.g., cardiothoracic surgery, transplant) for whom the pharmacist's preoperative or postoperative involvement may be most beneficial. The pharmacist should participate in anesthesia grand rounds, morbidity and mortality reviews, and other scheduled educational sessions as appropriate. Pharmacy grand rounds could be conducted by pharmacy staff to provide detailed drug information or to supplement anesthesia grand round topics.

Pain Management. The pharmacist should participate actively in epidural anesthesia, patient-controlled analgesia, and other pain-management programs. Participation could include the development of such a program, identification of appropriate patients, patient education, drug preparation, educational presentations to other staff, and participation in rounds with acute-pain-management teams as time permits.

Participation in Emergency Life Support. The pharmacist should be authorized to participate in the medication therapy for cardiac or respiratory arrests that occur in the OR. At a minimum, the pharmacist should have current certification in basic cardiac life support (BCLS) procedures and, preferably, training in advanced cardiac life support (ACLS). The pharmacist should also participate in the treatment of malignant hyperthermia by preparing and maintaining malignant hyperthermia emergency kits and preparing and administering medications used to treat malignant hyperthermia.

Pharmacokinetic Management and Consultation. The pharmacist should participate in the pharmacokinetic management of patients and should serve as a consultant to surgery and anesthesiology staff on pharmacokinetic of medications dosing.

Compliance with JCAHO Standards. The presence of pharmacy personnel in the surgery and anesthesiology areas, especially with an established satellite pharmacy, could help to ensure adherence to Joint Commission standards. Specifically, pharmacy plays a key role in compliance with the standards related to the medication-use process. These include reviewing medication orders; considering patient information when preparing and dispensing medication(s); ensuring pharmaceutical services are available when the pharmacy department is closed or pharmacy personnel are not available; controlling the preparation and dispensing of medication(s) (drugs should be secure from tampering, safe from patient-to-patient contamination, and properly labeled); ensuring that emergency medications are consistently available, controlled, and secure in the pharmacy and patient care areas; and monitoring the effects of medications on patients.

Documentation of Clinical Activities. The pharmacist should document clinical activities and identify activities leading to improved patient outcomes and cost reductions. This type of information is critical in order for the pharmacist to prove his or her value and the ongoing need for the services provided. The pharmacist is responsible for safeguarding the patient's rights to privacy and the confidentiality of the patient's clinical information.

Controlled Substances

All controlled-substance procedures should comply with applicable federal and state laws and regulations as well as the organization's policies and procedures. Procedures for the satellite pharmacy and the surgery and anesthesiology areas served should address the following:

1. Controlled substances (and other drugs) to be monitored;
2. Methods of distribution;
3. Records;
4. Ordering;
5. Storage, access, and inventory control;
6. Reconciliation and disposal;
7. Discrepancy reporting and disciplinary action; and
8. Performance of quality control checks.

The goal of the controlled-substance system is to prevent diversion yet be practical enough that patient care is not adversely affected. The system should limit exposure to controlled substances, be accountable and consistent, and contain an educational component for health care personnel.[15]

Controlled Substances (and Other Drugs) to Be Monitored. The pharmacist should be responsible for monitoring the use of all controlled substances. As required (e.g., because of abuse or diversion potential), drugs other than controlled substances (e.g., ketamine) could also be handled according to procedures similar or identical to those used for controlled substances.

Methods of Distribution

One of two primary methods could be used for distribution of controlled substances in the OR: a per-case method or a daily-supply method.

A per-case system is advantageous in that it minimizes the quantity of controlled substances available to the anesthesiologist and the anesthetist at any one time and allows for a good audit trail. Its major disadvantage is that it is very time intensive for an organization that performs many surgeries per day. This time may be better spent by the pharmacist in clinical activities.

Daily distribution of controlled substances is less time intensive and can be accomplished from a central pharmacy or an OR satellite pharmacy. Its disadvantages are that greater amounts of controlled substances are dispensed at one time and that these substances need to be kept secure throughout the day.

The various advantages and disadvantages of each method must be considered and the appropriate system selected on an organization-specific basis.

To the extent possible, controlled substances should be distributed only in response to signed orders or oral requests from prescribers. Given the urgency often present during surgical procedures, the necessity for prescribers to devote undivided attention to anesthesia procedures, and the use of sterility-safeguard procedures during surgery, it may not always be possible to comply with such a requirement. When it is possible, the organization's standard physician-order sheet or a special controlled-substance request form developed specifically for use in the surgical suite could be used. A par level of controlled substances needed per type of case or for the day could be devised; requests for controlled substances beyond this would be treated as special orders. Whatever the methods used, clear documentation that all controlled substances used were administered to the patient should be signed by the responsible prescribers at the end of each surgical procedure. Ideally, unused controlled substances drawn up by the anesthesiologist should be returned to the satellite pharmacy and wasted by the pharmacist. Alternatively, controlled substances could be disposed of by the anesthesiologist in the presence of a witness, with both parties documenting the disposal. No matter the system, disposal of contaminated controlled substances (e.g., with blood or other body fluid) should occur in the OR and be properly documented.

Records

Records should be kept of the following:

1. Controlled substances dispensed;
2. Controlled-substance inventories;
3. Controlled substances returned (including controlled substances drawn up but not used), and records reconciliation;
4. Controlled substances disposed; and
5. Controlled-substance use, categorized by prescriber.

If the satellite pharmacy does not provide 24-hour services, the documentation procedures for after-hours use should be as similar as possible to those used when the satellite pharmacy is staffed. This will help ensure staff efficiency and familiarity with the record-keeping requirements after hours. Forms specific to the setting and to the after-hours circumstance may have to be developed.

Ordering

The pharmacist should be responsible for ordering all controlled substances for the satellite pharmacy. Once received, the controlled substances should be added to the satellite pharmacy's stock and recorded in inventory records. If the satellite pharmacy does not provide 24-hour services, the pharmacist is responsible for ensuring that adequate supplies are available in a secure, specially designated after-hours location. The pharmacist should maintain controlled-substance inventory amounts sufficient only to meet the needs of the OR for a reasonable time. This time should depend on the frequency and timeliness with which controlled substances are available from the central pharmacy. Less inventory is required, for example, if controlled substances are ordered on a daily basis rather than less often. The inventory system should be perpetual in order to provide the most current record of controlled substances on hand.

Shortly after the initial opening of a satellite pharmacy and after drug use has stabilized, stock levels should be reassessed and adjusted as needed. During ordering, the pharmacist should note developing trends in use. Nonformulary controlled substances should be dispensed only by special request.

Storage, Access, and Inventory Control

Controlled substances should be stored in a locked space (e.g., cabinet, drawer, cart) within the satellite pharmacy. These storage spaces should remain locked when controlled substances are not being dispensed. Access to the space should be limited to satellite pharmacy personnel. If 24-hour satellite pharmacy services are not provided, a separate locked after-hours storage space will be required. Kits of after-hours controlled substances may be useful. No matter how they are configured or located, all after-hours supplies should be checked and all records reconciled by satellite pharmacy staff on the first working day after the after-hours supplies are entered.

If possible, one person per shift should be identified as being responsible for controlled substances (and related procedures) when the satellite pharmacy is not open. That person should have access (key or code) to locked after-hours supplies. This approach enables more consistent record keeping, limits the number of people with access to after-hours supplies, and enables more reliable monitoring of controlled-substance use. Individuals often assigned this responsibility include an "in-charge" nurse or the "first-call" anesthesiology resident.

Controlled-substance inventories should be verified by physical count at least once daily. If the satellite pharmacy is open for two shifts, an end-of-shift count by the morning pharmacist is recommended. The use of automated medication storage and distribution devices for controlled substances may be a timesaving benefit for maintaining a perpetual inventory. Unscheduled audits of controlled substances in the satellite pharmacy should be done by staff not normally assigned to this setting. The results should be documented.

Reconciliation and Disposal

A thorough system for reconciling controlled-substance use should be developed and include the following components[16–18]:

1. *Comparison of quantities dispensed with quantities documented as administered.* The quantity of controlled substances returned to the satellite pharmacy should be compared with the quantity dispensed. The amount dispensed should equal the amount returned (unopened and partially filled containers and partially used syringes) plus the amount documented as administered.
2. *Verification of use through review of the anesthesia record.* The anesthesia record should be reviewed to ensure that the amount documented as administered (in records returned to the satellite pharmacy) is identical to the amount documented in the patient's anesthesia record. This verification is ideally done for all cases but may be done by periodic audits of randomly selected cases if anesthesia records are not readily available for every case.
3. *Qualitative testing of returned controlled substances.* To verify that unadulterated drug is contained in partially used containers returned to the satellite pharmacy, a refractometer or other device can be used. It is important to randomly audit controlled-substance returns in order to detect trends in diversion. The organization's legal department should be consulted to make sure such testing is permitted.

The pharmacist should account for all controlled substances dispensed and should report all discrepancies to internal and external authorities as required.

Disposal of controlled substances (e.g., partially used syringes) should be done in the satellite pharmacy by a member of the pharmacy staff in the presence of a witness. This action should be documented in the satellite pharmacy's controlled-substance records.

Communication and Education

It is important that there are open lines of communication among the pharmacist, the chair of anesthesiology (or designee), and the head surgical nurse to allow sharing of information indicative of diversion (e.g., behavioral change). In addition, periodic continuing education for all members of the OR team on the potential for substance abuse may sensitize staff to this problem.[15]

Performance Improvement

The pursuit of continuous improvement in the quality of services provided should be a philosophy of practice of the pharmacist and the satellite pharmacy staff.[19] In that light, many activities may be seen as pertinent to performance improvement efforts. Some of these are the following:

1. Adverse-drug-reaction monitoring and reporting,
2. Medication-error monitoring and reporting,
3. Medication histories,
4. Periodic inspections of all drug storage sites,
5. Drug therapy monitoring related to improved patient outcome (e.g., decreased time in the PACU, decreased frequency of PONV),
6. Medication-use evaluations,
7. Drug-interaction monitoring,
8. Controlled-substance monitoring,
9. Quality control of compounded parenterals (e.g., cardioplegic solutions) and batch-prepared syringes,
10. Medication-waste monitoring, and
11. Allergy and patient demographic monitoring.

Some of these activities should not be difficult to implement in a satellite pharmacy, because ongoing procedures should already be developed for the organization overall. Sometimes, it may be necessary to develop new programs or variations of existing ones tailored to the surgery and anesthesiology areas.

Other Activities

Policies and Procedures. If there is a satellite pharmacy, the pharmacist should develop and maintain policies and procedures for the satellite pharmacy and its services. There should be policies and procedures for the preparation of drug kits (if applicable), medication distribution systems, controlled-substance handling, hours of operation, preparation of parenteral products, expiration-date checking and monthly inspections, recycling of products, monitoring of drug inventory levels, staff training, quality assurance activities, and after-hours drug distribution.

Interdisciplinary Interfaces. The pharmacist should function as a liaison between the pharmacy department and all staff in the setting served, including anesthesiology, nursing, and surgery staff; perfusionists; and management staff. The pharmacist should represent the pharmacy department on appropriate interdisciplinary committees charged with evaluating or making recommendations about services and medication selection and use in the surgery and anesthesiology areas. A committee specifically designed to focus on pharmacy matters may be appropriate.

Financial Analysis. The pharmacist should document drug costs, service costs, revenues, and savings attributable to the satellite pharmacy and the activities (clinical and distributive) of its staff. If there is no OR satellite pharmacy, some of the aforementioned items will not need to be included in the analysis. Financial reports should be prepared periodically (e.g., quarterly, annually) and provided to the hospital administration and the departments of anesthesiology, surgery, and pharmacy.

The Pharmacy Technician's Role

Pharmacy technicians assigned to the satellite pharmacy should be trained to perform their assigned functions. It is critical and appropriate for the technician to do most of the drug distribution-related activities in the satellite pharmacy. Within the total work force of pharmacy technicians in the organization, it is desirable to have some technicians trained as available back-up staff for the satellite pharmacy. Technicians should be trained and certified by the Pharmacy Technician Certification Board or equivalent. In general, technician training and experience should include parenteral drug preparation, drug distribution procedures, physician-order interpretation, anesthesia and OR record interpretation, computer order entry, and controlled-substance record keeping. Specific training should include a review of the following:

1. Procedures unique to surgical suites, including special apparel (e.g., caps, masks, foot covers) and restricted movements and areas within surgical suites;
2. Surgical-suite terms, including abbreviations and acronyms used to name surgical procedures;

3. Drug classes, indications for use, and proper handling of drugs routinely used in surgical suites (e.g., special packaging, preservative requirements for spinal and epidural drugs, infusion concentrations);
4. Controlled-substance procedures;
5. Emergency drugs typically used in surgical suites; and
6. A review of the role of the pharmacy technician in the OR pharmacy area.

Typical activities performed by pharmacy technicians in the satellite pharmacy under the supervision of the pharmacist are drug distribution, controlled-substance handling, sterile drug preparation, drug ordering and restocking, orientation and training of new staff, and quality assurance activities. Each of these will be discussed in greater detail.

Drug Distribution. The technician could distribute medications to storage sites in the setting and prepare per-case or per-prescriber kits of medications and distribute these after they have been checked by the pharmacist. If automated medication storage and distribution devices are used, the technician is responsible for all activities associated with restocking these. Given the nature of surgical procedures and the urgency of the need for the requested medications, distribution would be required in response to oral requests. The pharmacist should screen such requests to ensure proper choices of drugs for specific patients. The technician should be trained to ask about patient allergies and relay this information to the pharmacist before preparing a medication. The technician also should be taught which situations must be handled by the pharmacist (e.g., drug information, dose calculations).

The technician could return unused drugs to stock and charge patients or departments for medications used.

Another technician function could be to check and replenish after-hours drug supplies and charge medications used to appropriate patients or departments.

The technician could be responsible for monthly inspections of drug storage areas and drug supply areas in the satellite pharmacy. Technicians should be assigned their own inspection zone when drugs are stored in many places.

Controlled Substances. Other responsibilities of the technician could be the distribution of controlled substances and the creation of appropriate records according to the distribution procedures of the satellite pharmacy and according to federal and state laws and regulations. Typical activities could include helping with inventory counts, maintaining perpetual inventory records, disposing of controlled substances with the pharmacist, and participating in audits, assays, and preparation of reports.

Sterile Drug Preparation. The technician could aseptically compound, package, and label sterile drugs—for injection and for irrigation—and document all products made. Appropriate records of drug name, diluent, lot numbers, and expiration dates of batch-prepared products should be maintained by the technician.

Drug Ordering and Restocking of the Pharmacy Satellite. In addition, technicians could routinely order replenishment supplies of drugs for the satellite pharmacy, check supplies delivered in response to the orders, and place the stock in appropriate places. Requests for odd medications or unusual trends in medication demand should be reported to the pharmacist for further review.

Orientation and Training of New Staff. Helping with the orientation and training of new staff (including other technicians and pharmacy students) could also be a responsibility of the technician. An orientation checklist, workflow sheets, and task lists are helpful training tools. An OR pharmacy student module would be a helpful teaching tool for students on rotation in the satellite pharmacy.

Quality Assurance. The technician could be involved in quality assurance activities of the satellite pharmacy. Such activities may include regular controlled-substance audits or assays, microbiological monitoring of parenteral drugs prepared, and inspections of drug supplies (e.g., expiration dates).

Summary

Pharmaceutical services in surgery and anesthesiology should be the standard of practice in health care organizations across the United States. Although not essential, an onsite satellite pharmacy would help in the provision of these services. A majority of distribution-related activities should be done by technicians. The availability of automated devices and other technology may lessen, to some extent, the time devoted to drug distribution. It is important for the OR pharmacist to concentrate on the provision of clinical services, such as medication-use management, drug information services, medication-use evaluations, formulary management, and pharmacoeconomic analyses of anesthesia- related medications. These activities provide the best opportunity for the pharmacist to contribute to improving patient care and outcomes and containing costs. Finally, pharmaceutical services in surgery and anesthesiology should be periodically assessed for patient care and financial effectiveness.

References

1. Powell PJ, Maland L, Bair JN, et al. Implementing an operating room pharmacy satellite. *Am J Hosp Pharm.* 1983; 40:1192–8.
2. Opoien D. Establishment of surgery satellite pharmacy services in a large community hospital. *Hosp Pharm.* 1984; 19:485–90.
3. Keicher PA, McAllister JC III. Comprehensive pharmaceutical services in the surgical suite and recovery room. *Am J Hosp Pharm.* 1985; 42:2454–62.
4. Buchanan EC, Gaither MW. Development of an operating room pharmacy substation on a restricted budget. *Am J Hosp Pharm.* 1986; 43:1719–22.
5. Vogel DP, Barone J, Penn F, et al. Ideas for action: the operating room pharmacy satellite. *Top Hosp Pharm Manag.* 1986; 6:63–80.
6. Donnelly AJ. Multidisciplinary approach to improving documentation of medications used during surgical procedures. *Am J Hosp Pharm.* 1989; 46:724–8.
7. Shafer AS. Clinical pharmacy practice in the operating room. *J Pharm Pract.* 1993; 6:165–70.
8. Gora-Harper ML, Hessel E II, Shadick D. Effect of prescribing guidelines on the use of neuromuscular blocking agents. *Am J Health-Syst Pharm.* 1995; 52:1900–4.
9. Freund PR, Borolle TA, Posner KL, et al. Cost-effective reduction of neuromuscular-block drug expenditures. *Anesthesiology.* 1997; 87:1044–9.

10. Lubarsky DA, Glass PSA, Ginsberg B, et al. The successful implementation of pharmaceutical practice guidelines. *Anesthesiology.* 1997; 86:1145–60.
11. Lubarsky DA, Sanderson IC, Gilbert WC, et al. Using an anesthesia information management system as a cost containment tool. *Anesthesiology.* 1997; 86:1161–9.
12. Lorighlin KA, Weingarten CM, Nagelhout J, et al. A pharmacoeconomic analysis of neuromuscular blocking agents in the operating room. *Pharmacotherapy.* 1996; 16:942–50.
13. DeMonaco HJ, Shah AS. Economic considerations in the use of neuromuscular blocking drugs. *J Clin Anesth.* 1994; 6:383–7.
14. Tang J, Watcha MF, White PF. A comparison of costs and efficacy of ondansetron and droperidol as prophylactic antiemetic therapy for elective outpatient gynecologic procedures. *Anesth Analg.* 1996; 83:304–13.
15. Castellano FC. Developing methods for preventing and detecting substance abuse in the operating room: a disease approach. *J Pharm Pract.* 1993; 6:159–64.
16. Satterlee GB. System for verifying use of controlled substances in anesthesia. *Am J Hosp Pharm.* 1989; 46:2506–8.
17. Shovick VA, Mattei TJ, Karnack CM. Audit to verify use of controlled substances in anesthesia. *Am J Hosp Pharm.* 1988; 45:1111–3.
18. Gill DL, Goodwin SR, Knudsen AK, et al. Refractometer screening of controlled substances in an operating room satellite pharmacy. *Am J Hosp Pharm.* 1990; 47:817–8.
19. Hawkins PR. Quality improvement: pharmacy involvement in the operating room. *J Pharm Pract.* 1993; 6:171–6.

Appendix— Justifying and Implementing an Operating-Room Satellite Pharmacy

Justification of the need for a satellite pharmacy is a critical step in establishing pharmaceutical services in surgery and anesthesiology.[1,2]

The pharmacist's ability to positively affect medication-use management, to take a leadership role in all aspects of cost containment, and to contribute to improved patient care and outcomes must be highlighted.

Familiarization with Surgery and Anesthesiology Pharmaceutical Services. As an initial step, the person in charge of the project should become familiar with typical surgery and anesthesiology satellite pharmacy services. Review of pertinent literature, discussions with pharmacists in other organizations, and site visits to established satellite pharmacies are methods of accomplishing this step. The site visit is especially useful, because it can reinforce and further define information gained by other means. At the conclusion of this step, the pharmacist should have a realistic view of the types and scope of services typically provided.

Obtaining Support. If justification is to be successful, the support of key individuals from the major departments affected by the service should be obtained.[1] In most organizations, these are hospital administration, anesthesiology (anesthesiologists and certified registered nurse anesthetists), and surgery, operating-room (OR), and postanesthesia care unit nursing.

The support of the anesthesiology department is necessary because this department represents the major users of medications in the OR and has significant patient care responsibilities in this setting. Support for pharmaceutical services from anesthesiology department administration is important for the success of the project. If the request for satellite pharmacy services originates in the anesthesiology department, the justification process may be simpler and more collaborative. Data gathered during the preliminary review of the site and information obtained from the literature can be used when the project is discussed with anesthesiology administration. It may be valuable to solicit the support of any anesthesiologists who have been especially receptive to pharmacy involvement. Many anesthesiologists have had positive experiences with OR pharmaceutical services at other organizations. The proposal for a satellite pharmacy might then be presented jointly by pharmacy personnel and anesthesiologists. Once formalized, the proposal should be presented to hospital administration. The administration's opinion will provide some guidance on how to facilitate the approval process for the satellite pharmacy.

If conceptual support from these groups is obtained, development of a more formal proposal can begin. If there are still concerns about the benefits gained from OR satellite pharmacy services, it may be helpful to propose an interim step to expose more hospital staff to OR pharmaceutical services in order to keep the process moving forward. One possible approach is to suggest that a pilot project be conducted involving several ORs or one specific surgical specialty. The establishment of a permanent satellite pharmacy would depend on favorable results from the pilot project.

Initial Assessment of Setting. A general review of the surgery and anesthesiology areas to be served by the satellite pharmacy should be done after staff have become familiar with the project. At this time, it is not essential that detailed information be obtained. Useful information to collect includes the following:

1. All locations and quantities of drugs stored in the setting,
2. The location and storage of controlled substances,
3. Controlled-substance accountability systems used,
4. Drug preparation and distribution procedures used in the setting,
5. Billing systems used for all drugs,
6. Stock replenishment and rotation systems used, and
7. The role (or potential role) of automation in the involved areas.

The collection of this information could be speeded by a tour of the area and by inquiries through nurses, anesthesiologists, supply technicians, surgeons, and other OR personnel (e.g., perfusionists).

Formal Proposal. The development of a formal proposal is an important part of the justification process. It is essential that the proposal be well organized and factual. The writers of the proposal should expect the proposal to be examined in great detail by hospital administration and others during the decision-making process. The proposal should expand upon the information obtained in the initial review of the surgery and anesthesiology areas. Information that should be in the proposal includes the following:

1. The dollar value of current drug inventory,
2. The dollar value of drugs used per period (e.g., per year),

3. The dollar value of patient charges currently generated,
4. The estimated dollar value of increased revenue,
5. The average cost of drugs used per surgical case,
6. An estimated cost of drug waste per period,
7. The general quality and completeness of controlled-substance records,
8. The number of controlled-substance discrepancies reported per month,
9. The number of reports of drug-related incidents received per month,
10. The time personnel in the setting currently spend performing pharmacy-related activities,
11. The time pharmacy personnel currently spend performing activities for the setting, and
12. Opportunities for collaborative efforts by pharmacy–anesthesiology, pharmacy–nursing, pharmacy–perfusion, and pharmacy–surgery in drug-use management (e.g., development of pharmaceutical practice guidelines, performance of medication-use evaluations).

Collection of this information could be helped through the formation of a multidisciplinary team. Representatives of the departments of pharmacy, anesthesiology, nursing, and surgery should be included. This approach has several benefits. Data collection can be expedited, because the expertise of each individual can be used. The value of a satellite pharmacy will be continually reinforced to these individuals, and all groups will have input into the decision-making process.

A formal proposal should be prepared once the required information has been collected. Minimally, the proposal should contain the following sections[1]:

1. Introduction;
2. Statement of problems and anticipated benefits (and beneficiaries);
3. Summary of the proposed services;
4. Cost–benefit analysis, including staffing, estimated cost savings, revenue projections, and inventory savings; and
5. Implementation plan.

During preparation of these sections, it is important to be as specific as possible and to assign dollar values whenever these are available. The proposal should be endorsed by the members of the multidisciplinary team and should be submitted to the administration by the director of pharmacy. Careful planning, data collection, analysis, and presentation of the information gathered will make approval more likely.

Implementation. Implementation should begin as soon as possible after administrative approval.[1] Implementation steps should be planned and executed in a clear, concise manner. To guide planning, an implementation time line should be developed (e.g., Gantt chart), listing the steps to be taken, the task force member responsible for each step, and the expected amount of time required for each activity. The amount of time required for each activity may vary from organization to organization, but the order in which the steps should be performed will be reasonably standard.

The major implementation steps and an approximate order in which they should be completed are as follows[1]:

1. Obtain a formal commitment of space,
2. Assign a project leader (who should be responsible for the project's development and need not be the pharmacist who will be assigned to staff the satellite pharmacy; often, it is valuable for the project leader to be a supervisor or assistant director),
3. Identify construction and equipment needs,
4. Oversee construction work,
5. Obtain and install equipment,
6. Draft policies and procedures (e.g., controlled-substance accountability, medication distribution system, inventory control),
7. Develop job descriptions,
8. Select staff (pharmacists and support personnel),
9. Design and print forms,
10. Formalize policies and procedures,
11. Determine satellite pharmacy drug-stock levels,
12. Train staff,
13. Identify back-up and relief staff and orient them to the setting,
14. Educate nursing staff,
15. Educate anesthesiology department staff,
16. Educate surgeons,
17. Open the satellite pharmacy for operation,
18. Determine future goals for service, and
19. Determine systems for periodic analyses of the impact of the program.

Many of these steps can be expedited by a close working relationship with members of the anesthesiology and nursing departments.

The satellite pharmacy's services should be monitored and evaluated on an ongoing basis through workload statistics, data on controlled-substance discrepancies, financial data, and patient outcomes data. In addition, the satisfaction levels of the nursing and anesthesiology staffs should be assessed before the program is implemented, six months after implementation, and yearly after that.

References

1. Vogel DP, Barone J, Penn F, et al. Ideas for action: the operating room pharmacy satellite. *Top Hosp Pharm Manage.* 1986; 6:63–80.
2. Ziter CA, Dennis BW, Shoup LK. Justification of an operating-room satellite pharmacy. *Am J Hosp Pharm.* 1989; 46:1353–61.

These guidelines were reviewed in 2003 by the Council on Professional Affairs and by the Board of Directors and were found to still be appropriate.

Approved by the ASHP Board of Directors November 14, 1998. Developed through the ASHP Council on Professional Affairs. Supersedes the ASHP Technical Assistance Bulletin on Surgery and Anesthesiology Pharmaceutical Services dated November 14, 1990.

The bibliographic citation for this document is as follows: American Society of Health-System Pharmacists. ASHP guidelines on surgery and anesthesiology pharmaceutical services. *Am J Health-Syst Pharm.* 1999; 56:887–95.

Pharmaceutical Industry

Drug Products, Labeling, and Packaging

Excipients in Drug Products (1528)
Source: Council on Pharmacy Practice
To advocate that manufacturers remove unnecessary, potentially allergenic excipients from all drug products; further,

To advocate that manufacturers declare the name and derivative source of all excipients in drug products on the official label; further,

To advocate that vendors of medication-related databases incorporate information about excipients; further,

To foster education on the allergenicity of excipients and documentation in the patient medical record of allergic reactions to excipients.

This policy supersedes ASHP policy 0808.

Ensuring Effectiveness, Safety, and Access to Orphan Drug Products (1413)
Source: Council on Therapeutics
To encourage continued research on and development of orphan drug products; further,

To advocate for the use of innovative strategies and incentives to expand the breadth of rare diseases addressed by this program; further,

To encourage postmarketing research to support the safe and effective use of these drug products for approved and off-label indications; further,

To urge health policymakers, payers, and pharmaceutical manufacturers to develop innovative ways to ensure patient access to orphan drug products.

This policy supersedes ASHP policy 0715.

Standardized Clinical Drug Nomenclature (0920)
Source: Council on Pharmacy Management
To encourage federal agencies, the pharmaceutical industry, pharmacy and medical software providers, and purveyors of clinical data repositories and drug databases to explore the potential benefits of supplementing or modifying the National Drug Code with a coding system that can be used effectively to support patient care, research, and financial management; further,

To encourage that such a coding system encompass prescription drug products, nonprescription medications, and dietary supplements and include both active and inactive ingredients.

This policy was reviewed in 2013 by the Council on Pharmacy Management and by the Board of Directors and was found to still be appropriate.

Standardizing Prefixes and Suffixes in Drug Product Names (0720)
Source: Council on Public Policy
To collaborate with others, including the United States Pharmacopeia and the Food and Drug Administration, in standardizing and defining the meaning of prefixes and suffixes for prescription and nonprescription drugs to prevent medication errors and ensure patient safety.

This policy was reviewed in 2011 by the Council on Public Policy and by the Board of Directors and was found to still be appropriate.

Elimination of Surface Contamination on Vials of Hazardous Drugs (0618)
Source: Council on Professional Affairs
To advocate that pharmaceutical manufacturers eliminate surface contamination on vials of hazardous drugs; further,

To inform pharmacists and other personnel of the potential presence of surface contamination on the vials of hazardous drugs; further,

To encourage health care organizations to adhere to published standards and regulations to protect workers from undue exposure to hazardous drugs.

This policy was reviewed in 2010 by the Council on Pharmacy Practice and by the Board of Directors and was found to still be appropriate.

Mandatory Labeling of the Presence of Latex (0501)
Source: Section of Inpatient Care Practitioners
To urge the Food and Drug Administration to mandate that manufacturers of medications and medication-device combination products include labeling information on whether any component of the product, including its packaging, contains natural rubber latex.

This policy was reviewed in 2014 by the Council on Pharmacy Practice and by the Board of Directors and was found to still be appropriate.

Ready-to-Use Packaging for All Settings (0402)
Source: Council on Professional Affairs
To advocate that pharmaceutical manufacturers provide all medications used in ambulatory care settings in unit-of-use packages; further,

To urge the Food and Drug Administration to support this goal; further,

To encourage pharmacists to adopt unit-of-use packaging for dispensing prescription medications to ambulatory patients; further,

To support continued research on the safety benefits and patient adherence associated with unit-of-use packaging and other dispensing technologies.

(*Note:* A *unit-of-use* package is a container–closure system designed to hold a specific quantity of a drug product for a specific use and intended to be dispensed to a patient without any modification except for the addition of appropriate labeling.)

This policy was reviewed in 2013 by the Council on Pharmacy Practice and by the Board of Directors and was found to still be appropriate.

Unit Dose Packaging Availability (0309)
Source: Council on Administrative Affairs
To advocate that pharmaceutical manufacturers provide all medications used in health systems in unit dose packages; further,

To urge the Food and Drug Administration to support this goal in the interest of public health and patient safety.

This policy was reviewed in 2012 by the Council on Pharmacy Management and by the Board of Directors and was found to still be appropriate.

Drug Shortages (0002)

Source: Council on Administrative Affairs

To declare that pharmaceutical manufacturers, distributors, group purchasing organizations, and regulatory bodies, when making decisions that may create drug product shortages, should strive to prevent those decisions from compromising the quality and safety of patient care.

This policy was reviewed in 2014 by the Council on Pharmacy Practice and by the Board of Directors and was found to still be appropriate.

Pediatric Dosage Forms (9707)

Source: Council on Professional Affairs

To support efforts that stimulate development of pediatric dosage forms of drug products.

This policy was reviewed in 2012 by the Council on Pharmacy Practice and by the Board of Directors and was found to still be appropriate.

Use of Color to Identify Drug Products (9608)

Source: Council on Professional Affairs

To support the reading of drug product labels as the most important means of identifying drug products; further,

To oppose reliance on color by health professionals and others to identify drug products; further,

To oppose actions by manufacturers of drug products and others to promulgate reliance on color to identify drug products.

This policy was reviewed in 2013 by the Council on Pharmacy Practice and by the Board of Directors and was found to still be appropriate.

Expiration Dating of Pharmaceutical Products (9309)

Source: House of Delegates Resolution

To support and actively promote the maximal extension of expiration dates of pharmaceutical products as a means of reducing health care costs and to recommend that pharmaceutical manufacturers review their procedures to accomplish this end.

This policy was reviewed in 2011 by the Council on Pharmacy Practice and by the Board of Directors and was found to still be appropriate.

Tamper-Evident Packaging on Topical Products (9211)

Source: House of Delegates Resolution

ASHP should support the standardization and requirement of tamper-evident packaging on all topical products, including all dermatologicals and nonprescription products.

This policy was reviewed in 2011 by the Council on Pharmacy Practice and by the Board of Directors and was found to still be appropriate.

Drug Nomenclature (9011)

Source: House of Delegates Resolution

To work with the FDA, USP, and pharmaceutical industry to assure that drug products are named in a manner that clearly and without confusion permits identification of ingredients' strengths and changes.

This policy was reviewed in 2013 by the Council on Public Policy and by the Board of Directors and was found to still be appropriate.

Codes on Solid Dosage Forms of Prescription Drug Products (8709)

Source: Council on Legal and Public Affairs

To support efforts requiring manufacturers of solid dosage form prescription drug products to imprint a readily identifiable code indicating the manufacturer of the drug product and the product's ingredients; further,

To make information on transition of the codes readily available.

This policy was reviewed in 2011 by the Council on Public Policy and by the Board of Directors and was found to still be appropriate.

Elimination of Apothecary System (8613)

Source: Council on Professional Affairs

To recommend to all health professions and to the Pharmaceutical Manufacturers Association (PMA) [now the Pharmaceutical Research and Manufacturers of America (PhRMA)] that the apothecary system be eliminated in referring to dosage quantities and strengths.

This policy was reviewed in 2011 by the Council on Pharmacy Practice and by the Board of Directors and was found to still be appropriate.

Size, Color, and Shape of Drug Products (8310)

Source: Council on Legal and Public Affairs

To approve the authority of manufacturers to copy the size, shape, and color of generically equivalent drug products as a means of promoting better patient compliance (rational drug therapy), but only when the source and identity of the product are readily ascertainable from a uniform mark or symbol on the product.

This policy was reviewed in 2012 by the Council on Public Policy and by the Board of Directors and was found to still be appropriate.

Marketing

Identification of Prescription Drug Coverage and Eligibility for Patient Assistance Programs (1521)
Source: Council on Pharmacy Management
To advocate that pharmacists or pharmacy technicians ensure that the use of patient assistance programs is optimized and documented to promote continuity of care and patient access to needed medications; further,

To advocate that patient assistance programs should incorporate the pharmacist–patient relationship, including evaluation by a pharmacist as part of comprehensive medication management; further,

To support the principle that medications provided through manufacturer patient assistance programs should be stored, packaged, labeled, dispensed, and recorded using systems that ensure the same level of safety as prescription-based programs that incorporate a pharmacist–patient relationship.

This policy supersedes ASHP policy 0603.

Manufacturer-Sponsored Patient Assistance Programs (1420)
Source: Council on Pharmacy Management
To encourage pharmaceutical manufacturers to extend their patient assistance programs (PAPs) to serve the needs of both uninsured and underinsured patients; further,

To advocate that pharmaceutical manufacturers and PAP administrators enhance access to and availability of such programs by standardizing application criteria, processes, and forms, and by automating PAP application processes through computerized programs, including Web-based models; further,

To advocate expansion of PAPs to include high-cost drugs used in inpatient settings; further,

To encourage pharmacists and pharmaceutical manufacturers to work cooperatively to ensure that essential elements of pharmacist patient care are included in these programs.

This policy supersedes ASHP policies 0404 and 9703.

Direct-to-Consumer Advertising of Prescription and Nonprescription Medications (1119)
Source: Council on Public Policy
To oppose direct-to-consumer advertising unless it is educational in nature about prescription drug therapies for certain medical conditions and appropriately includes pharmacists as a source of information; further,

To oppose direct-to-consumer advertising of specific prescription drug products unless the following requirements are met: (1) that such advertising is delayed until postmarketing surveillance data are collected and assessed, (2) that the benefits and risks of therapy are presented in an understandable format at an acceptable literacy level for the intended population, (3) that such advertising promotes medication safety and allows informed decisions, (4) that a clear relationship between the medication and the disease state is presented, (5) that no such advertising or marketing information for prescription or nonprescription medication is directed toward minors, and (6) that such advertising include mechanisms that direct consumers to a medication adverse event reporting system (AERS); further,

To advocate that the Food and Drug Administration require an AERS reporting link in direct-to-consumer advertising material available on the Internet; further,

To support the development of legislation or regulation that would require nonprescription drug advertising to state prominently the benefits and risks associated with product use that should be discussed with the consumer's pharmacist or physician.

This policy supersedes ASHP policy 0609.

Regulation of Off-label Promotion and Marketing (1120)
Source: Council on Public Policy
To advocate for authority for the Food and Drug Administration to regulate the promotion and dissemination of information about off-label uses of medications by manufacturers; further,

To advocate that such promotion and dissemination be permitted only if manufacturers submit a supplemental new drug application for new use within a reasonable time after initial dissemination of information about off-label uses.

Pharmaceutical Distribution Systems (1016)
Source: Council on Pharmacy Management
To support wholesaler/distribution business models that meet the requirements of hospitals and health systems with respect to timely delivery of products, minimizing short-term outages and long-term product shortages, managing and responding to product recalls, fostering product-handling and transaction efficiency, preserving the integrity of products as they move through the supply chain, and maintaining affordable service costs.

This policy was reviewed in 2014 by the Council on Pharmacy Management and by the Board of Directors and was found to still be appropriate.

Restricted Drug Distribution (0714)
Source: Council on Public Policy
To affirm support for the current system of drug distribution in which prescribers and pharmacists exercise their professional responsibilities on behalf of patients; further,

To acknowledge that there may be limited circumstances in which constraints on the traditional drug distribution system may be appropriate if the following principles are met: (1) the requirements do not interfere with the continuity of care for the patient; (2) the requirements preserve the pharmacist–patient relationship; (3) the requirements are based on scientific evidence fully disclosed and evaluated by prescribers, pharmacists, and others; (4) there is scientific consensus that the requirements are necessary and represent the least restrictive means to achieve safe and effective patient care; (5) the costs of the product and any associated product or services are identified for purposes of reimbursement, mechanisms are provided to compensate providers for special services, and duplicative costs are avoided; (6) all requirements are stated in functional, objective terms so that any provider who meets the criteria may participate in the care of patients; and (7) the requirements do not interfere with the professional practice of pharmacists, prescribers, and others; further,

To advocate that the Food and Drug Administration (FDA) be granted the authority to consult with practicing pharmacists and others when the establishment of a restricted distribution system is contemplated for a drug product; further,

To advocate that FDA be granted the authority to require that manufacturers disclose all of the considerations that led to the establishment of a restricted distribution system for a specific product; further,

To advocate that FDA be granted the authority to require that manufacturers include in each restricted distribution system a mechanism that will ensure medication reconciliation and continuity of care as patients transition from one level or site of care to another; further,

To advocate that FDA be granted the authority to require manufacturers to conduct a follow-up assessment of the impact of a restricted drug distribution system.

This policy was reviewed in 2011 by the Council on Public Policy and by the Board of Directors and was found to still be appropriate.

Drug Samples (9702)

Source: Council on Legal and Public Affairs

To oppose drug sampling or similar drug marketing programs that (1) do not provide the elements of pharmaceutical care, (2) result in poor drug control, allowing patients to receive improperly labeled and packaged, deteriorated, outdated, and unrecorded drugs, (3) provide access to prescription drugs by unauthorized, untrained personnel, (4) may encourage inappropriate prescribing habits, or (5) may increase the cost of treatment for all patients.

This policy was reviewed in 2011 by the Council on Public Policy and by the Board of Directors and was found to still be appropriate.

ASHP Guidelines for Pharmacists on the Activities of Vendors' Representatives in Organized Health Care Systems

For purposes of this document, vendors' representatives are defined as agents who promote products and provide information and services to health care providers on behalf of manufacturers and suppliers. The narrow focus of this document is on those vendors who serve and interact with settings with respect to drug products, drug-related devices, and other equipment, supplies, and services purchased by pharmacies.

Each individual setting should develop its own specific policies and procedures relating to the activities of vendors' representatives. Such policies and procedures should supplement and complement applicable federal, state, and local laws and regulations (for example, statutes that address prescription drug-product sampling). The ASHP Guidelines on Pharmacists' Relationships with Industry, the ASHP Guidelines for Selecting Pharmaceutical Manufacturers and Suppliers, and setting-specific conflict-of-interest policies may be helpful in the development of policies and procedures.[1,2] The policies and procedures should be developed by the setting's pharmacy and therapeutics committee (or equivalent body) and approved by higher authorities in the setting as required. Depending on the individual setting, policies and procedures may be useful in the following areas.

1. *A defined scope of applicability.* The vendors' representatives to which any policies and procedures apply should be defined by the individual setting. For example, if the policies and procedures are applicable only to drug-product vendors' representatives and not to those promoting medical–surgical supplies, packaging equipment, or drug administration devices, this should be clearly stated.
2. *Orientation of representatives.* In some individual settings, vendors' representatives receive an orientation packet upon their initial visit to the setting. Such a packet might contain a copy of the setting's policies and procedures, a medical staff directory, and the formulary. Some settings provide a formal orientation program that includes meeting key individuals and touring the setting.
3. *Directory.* In some individual settings, a file of current vendor-contact information is maintained in the pharmacy. A form for recording such information might include the following:
   - The vendor's name and address;
   - The name, address, telephone number, and answering service number (if any), and drug-product assignment (purview) of each representative;
   - The name, address, and telephone number of the representative's manager;
   - The names, telephone numbers, and emergency telephone numbers of the vendor's directors of distribution, sales, and product information (titles may vary); and
   - The names and telephone numbers of the vendor's medical director and research director (titles may vary).
4. *Availability of vendor-contact information to professionals in the setting.* In some individual settings, the pharmacy department provides the setting's professional staff with the information in item 3, upon request.
5. *Registration while on premises.* In some individual settings, vendors' representatives register with the pharmacy department or other designated department upon each visit to the setting. At such time, the vendors' representatives document the time, purpose, and location of their appointments. In many settings, during the registration process, the representative is provided with a dated name badge to be prominently worn along with the representative's current vendor-supplied name tag (if any).
6. *Locations permitted.* In some individual settings, restriction (if any) from patient care and pharmacy storage and work areas in the setting are specified in the policies and procedures. Meetings with professional staff are conducted in areas convenient to staff and generally in non-patient-care areas.
7. *Appointments and purposes.* In some individual settings, representatives are encouraged to schedule appointments with appropriate pharmacy department staff to
   - Provide information useful for product evaluation. Representatives might be asked to include balanced scientific literature (journal reprints, for example) on drug-product safety and efficacy, as well as documentation of likely cost benefits.
   - Provide timely information on the vendor's products and services.
   - Facilitate procurement and crediting transactions.
   - Obtain and provide information necessary to support the setting's formulary system.
   - Facilitate informational activities for the pharmacy staff and other health care professionals with respect to the vendor's products.
8. *Exhibits.* In some individual settings, the pharmacy department provides opportunities for vendors' representatives to distribute informational material by arranging for organized, scheduled exhibits. Policies and procedures about the times, places, content, and conduct of such events are established.
9. *Dissemination of promotional materials.* In some individual settings, there are policies and procedures about the dissemination (by vendors' representatives) of information on formulary and nonformulary products, including the designation of appropriate categories of recipients of the information (e.g., attending physicians, department chairmen, house staff physicians). Representatives may be asked to promptly provide the pharmacy department with copies of all informational and promotional materials disseminated in the setting. The Food and Drug Administration (FDA) prohibits

the advertising and promotion of drug products for uses not reflected in FDA-approved product labeling ("unlabeled uses").[3] Pharmacists and other health care professionals should be aware of these laws and regulations when evaluating the content of promotional materials.

10. *Samples.* In some individual settings, there are policies and procedures with respect to product samples. ASHP urges that the use of drug samples within the institution be eliminated to the extent possible.[4,5]

11. *Noncompliance.* In some individual settings, policies and procedures exist to address noncompliance with the policies and procedures by either vendors' representatives or professional staff.

Each setting should have policies and procedures concerning research to be conducted on its premises. Pharmacists and vendors' representatives should clearly differentiate research from sales and promotional activities, applying appropriate policies and procedures accordingly.[6] Generally, scientific research involving drug products is coordinated through research departments of product manufacturers rather than through sales and promotional representatives.

References

1. American Society of Hospital Pharmacists. ASHP guidelines on pharmacists' relationships with industry. *Am J Hosp Pharm.* 1992; 49:154.
2. American Society of Hospital Pharmacists. ASHP guidelines for selecting pharmaceutical manufacturers and suppliers. *Am J Hosp Pharm.* 1991; 48:523–4.
3. American Society of Hospital Pharmacists. ASHP statement on the use of medications for unlabeled uses. *Am J Hosp Pharm.* 1992; 49:927–8.
4. American Society of Hospital Pharmacists. ASHP guidelines: minimum standard for pharmacies in institutions. *Am J Hosp Pharm.* 1985; 42:372–5.
5. Greenberg RB. The Prescription Drug Marketing Act of 1987. *Am J Hosp Pharm.* 1988; 45:2118–26.
6. American Society of Hospital Pharmacists. ASHP guidelines for pharmaceutical research in organized health-care settings. *Am J Hosp Pharm.* 1989; 46:129–30.

This guideline was reviewed in 1998 by the Council on Professional Affairs and by the ASHP Board of Directors and was found to still be appropriate.

Approved by the ASHP Board of Directors, November 17, 1993. Developed by the Council on Professional Affairs.

The bibliographic citation for this document is as follows: American Society of Hospital Pharmacists. ASHP guidelines for pharmacists on the activities of vendors' representatives in organized health care systems. *Am J Hosp Pharm.* 1994; 51:520–1.

Pharmacy Management

Pharmacy Management

Disposition of Illicit Substances (1522)

Source: Council on Pharmacy Management

To advocate that healthcare organizations be required to develop procedures for the disposition of illicit substances brought into a facility that ensure compliance with applicable laws and accreditation standards; further,

To advocate that healthcare organizations be required to include pharmacy leaders in formulating such procedures.

Pharmacy Department Business Partnerships (1416)

Source: Council on Pharmacy Management

To recognize that a key objective of pharmacy departments is to provide comprehensive medication management across the continuum of patient care, and that pharmacy leaders should proactively evaluate potential business partnerships against this objective; further,

To recognize that hospitals and health-system pharmacy leaders must ensure that business partners meet all applicable patient safety and accountability standards; further,

To provide education and tools for pharmacy leaders to aid in the evaluation of and development of business partnerships; further,

To educate health-system administrators on the importance of pharmacy leadership in evaluating and developing pharmacy-related business partnerships; further,

To encourage health-system pharmacy leaders to consider evolving health care financing systems when evaluating and developing business partnerships.

Integration of Pharmacy Services in Multifacility Health Systems (1417)

Source: Council on Pharmacy Management

To advocate that pharmacists are responsible for organizational efforts to standardize and integrate pharmacy services throughout the entire pharmacy enterprise in multifacility health systems and integrated delivery networks; further,

To educate health-system administrators about the importance of pharmacy leadership in setting system-wide policy regarding the safe and effective use of medications; further,

To advocate for the regulations and resources needed to support efforts to achieve optimal patient health outcomes in multifacility organizations.

This policy supersedes ASHP policy 1210.

Proliferation of Accreditation Organizations (1303)

Source: Council on Pharmacy Management

To advocate that health care accreditation organizations include providers and patients in their accreditation and standards development processes; further,

To encourage health care accreditation organizations to adopt consistent standards for the medication-use process, based on established principles of patient safety and quality of care; further,

To encourage hospitals and health systems to include pharmacy practice leaders in decisions about seeking recognition by specific accreditation organizations.

Workload Monitoring and Reporting (0901)

Source: House of Delegates Resolution

To strongly discourage the use of pharmacy workload and productivity measurement systems ("pharmacy benchmarking systems") that are based solely upon dispensing functions (e.g., doses dispensed or billed) or a variant of patient days, because such measures do not accurately assess pharmacy workload, staffing effectiveness, clinical practice contributions to patient care, or impacts on costs of care, and therefore these measurement systems are not valid and should not be used; further,

To advocate the development and implementation of pharmacy benchmarking systems that accurately assess the impact of pharmacy services on patient outcomes and total costs of care; further,

To define pharmacy workload as all activities related to providing pharmacy patient care services; further,

To continue communications with health-system administrators, consulting firms, and professional associations regarding the value of pharmacists' services and the importance of using valid, comprehensive, and evidence-based measures of pharmacy workload and productivity; further,

To encourage practitioners and vendors to develop and use a standard protocol for collecting and reporting pharmacy workload data and patient outcomes; further,

To advocate to health-system administrators, consulting firms, and vendors of performance-measurement services firms the development and implementation of pharmacy benchmarking systems that accurately assess the impact of pharmacy services on patient outcomes and total costs of care.

This policy was reviewed in 2013 by the Council on Pharmacy Management and by the Board of Directors and was found to still be appropriate.

Pharmacist Leadership of the Pharmacy Department (0918)

Source: Council on Pharmacy Management

To affirm the importance of an organizational structure in hospitals and health systems that places administrative, clinical, and operational responsibility for the pharmacy department under a pharmacist leader; further,

To affirm the role of the pharmacist leader in oversight and supervision of all pharmacy personnel; further,

To recognize the supporting role of nonpharmacists in leadership and management roles within pharmacy departments.

This policy was reviewed in 2013 by the Council on Pharmacy Management and by the Board of Directors and was found to still be appropriate.

Pharmacy Staff Fatigue and Medication Errors (0504)

Source: Council on Administrative Affairs

To encourage pharmacy managers to consider workload fatigue, length of shifts, and similar performance-altering factors when scheduling pharmacy staff, in order to ensure safe pharmacy practices; further,

To oppose state or federal laws or regulations that mandate or restrict work hours for pharmacy staff; further,

To support research on the effects of shift length, fatigue, and other factors on the safe practice of pharmacy.

This policy was reviewed in 2014 by the Council on Pharmacy Management and by the Board of Directors and was found to still be appropriate.

ASHP Statement on the Roles and Responsibilities of the Pharmacy Executive

Position

The American Society of Health-System Pharmacists (ASHP) believes that complex hospitals and health systems benefit from having a pharmacy executive responsible for the strategic planning, design, operation, and improvement of their organization's medication management system. This individual (sometimes referred to as the "chief pharmacy officer" but hereafter "the pharmacy executive") must be properly positioned within the organization to ensure the best utilization of his or her expertise in all decisions regarding medication management. To promote effective communication, collaboration, and teamwork with peers, the pharmacy executive should

- Have a title internally consistent with others reporting at that organizational level,
- Report directly to the organization's principal executive (e.g., chief executive officer [CEO], chief operating officer [COO]),
- Be involved in the organization's strategic planning regarding all components of the medication management process across the continuum of care,
- Participate in regularly scheduled healthcare executive-level meetings (e.g., CEO, COO, chief financial officer [CFO], chief medical officer [CMO], and chief nursing officer [CNO]),
- Be a member of the medical executive committee (or its equivalent), and
- Engage in regular, direct communication with health system leadership and the board of directors about medication management system performance.

Background

Hospitals and health systems are complex organizations. Executive-level decisions that affect the medication management system are made at a rapid pace, often with profound implications for patient care, patient safety, and the health system's fiscal well-being. The pharmacy executive must be properly positioned within an organization to ensure the best utilization of his or her expertise in decision-making that affects the policies, procedures, and systems that support safe, effective, and efficient medication management. The quality and timeliness of information exchange improves significantly when pharmacy leadership reports directly to the principal executive rather than through multiple layers of management. Pharmacy leaders can more actively engage in critical decision-making and will be more effective in helping the health system anticipate and address rapid change.

Significant changes in pharmacy practice, healthcare, and health-system management over the past 20 years have dramatically transformed the traditional role of the pharmacy director.[1] More widespread use of the title "chief pharmacy officer" was first proposed in 2000 in an attempt to enhance the contribution pharmacy makes to patient care by creating organizational parity between the pharmacy executive and other chief officers (e.g., chief nursing, medical, and information officers).[2] When the pharmacy executive works collaboratively with others at this executive level, the pharmacy department is better positioned to effectively contribute to the organization's strategic initiatives and address system-wide issues regarding medications and medication management.

Qualifications and Responsibilities of the Pharmacy Executive

The pharmacy executive is a professionally competent, legally qualified pharmacist. He or she must be thoroughly knowledgeable about and have experience in hospital pharmacy practice and management. Additional qualifications might include completion of a pharmacy residency program accredited by ASHP, an advanced management degree (e.g., M.B.A., M.H.A.), or an administrative specialty residency.

What distinguishes the pharmacy executive from the established director of pharmacy position is a deeper knowledge of the organization's operations as well as a greater degree of involvement in the organization's strategic planning and decision-making processes. The pharmacy executive provides the organization with pharmacy's unique clinical and business perspectives in discussions and decisions related to changes in the medication management system.[3] He or she has experience leading evidence-based clinical decision-making about drug use, controlling pharmaceutical expenses while maximizing patient benefit through the formulary system. The pharmacy executive has in-depth knowledge of the pharmaceutical supply chain, clinical therapeutics, physician prescribing habits, medication management systems, medication-use policy, and the technology used to deliver and support patient care and about how those issues affect the overall success of the organization. The pharmacy executive understands the relationships between third-party requirements, coding, documentation, billing equations, pricing updates, and organizational resources and can provide quality assurance for all these functions, improving financial performance.[4]

The pharmacy executive's responsibilities include but are not limited to the following: strategic planning; designing, managing, measuring and improving the medication management system; ensuring quality outcomes through performance-improvement activities; leading drug-utilization efforts; optimizing use of information systems and technology; managing the pharmaceutical supply chain, pharmacy department financial operations, and human resources; ensuring compliance with regulatory and accreditation requirements; fulfilling the organization's research and educational missions; and providing institutional representation and leadership.[5,8] The pharmacy executive fulfills these responsibilities through his or her own actions, proper delegation to competent individuals on his or her staff, and collaborative efforts with other healthcare professionals.

Strategic Planning. The pharmacy executive assesses the ever-changing healthcare environment for emerging trends that will influence the pharmacy enterprise. He or she identifies opportunities to leverage pharmacy expertise to improve quality, safety, patient experience, access across the continuum of care and the economic performance of the organization. It is also the pharmacy executive's responsibility to continually assess healthcare related trends and discoveries to ensure the value of pharmacy and pharmacists is advocated for and advanced in overall efforts to improve patient care.[6,7]

Optimizing Medication Management and Advancing Pharmacy Practice. The pharmacy executive is responsible for ensuring that pharmacists participate as the interdisciplinary team members who are responsible for patients' medication-related outcomes. He or she ensures that pharmacy is responsible for developing and ensuring compliance with evidence-based prescribing criteria that support effective, safe and fiscally responsible treatment. The pharmacy executive will ensure collaboration outside of the walls of the institution, fostering pharmacist communication with patients and outpatient providers following discharge to ensure continuity of medication therapy and monitoring of patient outcomes. With the expanded role of the pharmacist in drug therapy management, he or she is responsible for the professional development of the pharmacy team in order to support this advanced role.

Advancing the Application of Information Technology in the Medication Management System. The pharmacy executive provides leadership at the organizational level regarding planning, purchasing, implementing and maintaining information systems that support patient care. He or she is responsible for the adoption of a long-term perspective and commits themselves to achieving the patient-safety innovations made feasible by Electronic Health Records (EHRs) and other clinical applications: Computerized provider order entry (CPOE), clinical decision support (CDS), automated medication reconciliation, bar-coded medication administration (BCMA), medication surveillance, telepharmacy, and smart infusion pumps. The pharmacy executive will leverage technology to advance pharmacist clinical practice through implementation of processes that allow pharmacist work load to be more heavily devoted to patient-care activities and ensuring that the EHR supports drug therapy management services. He or she will leverage technology capabilities to improve the safety of medications, specifically those identified as high-risk. The pharmacy executive will utilize technology enabled medication management data to capture and report pharmacy metrics and to drive improvements in patient care and outcomes. He or she will ensure CDS systems support processes for the enhancement of medication-related decisions and actions with pertinent, organized clinical knowledge and patient information to improve health and healthcare delivery. The pharmacy executive will ensure that appropriately trained and qualified pharmacy team members are available to safely develop, implement and maintain medication related technology. Use of technology to increase the safety and efficiency of medication distribution, including automated dispensing units (ADU), carousels, and compounding automation should also be leveraged.[8]

Medication System Management and Improvement. The pharmacy executive is responsible for overseeing the design, implementation, and management of a safe and effective medication management system. He or she ensures that systems are developed and improved based on evidence and best practices, operate effectively and efficiently across the continuum of care, and are continuously evaluated and improved using contemporary quality-improvement methods. The pharmacy executive provides leadership at the organizational level to ensure that pharmacists are positioned to improve the quality, safety and efficiency of medication management throughout the health system. The pharmacy executive (or his or her designee) should be a member of all of the institution's key committees responsible for performance-improvement activities related to medication management and patient safety. The pharmacy executive and his or her staff must be intimately involved in all improvement initiatives involving medication management. The pharmacy executive should give particular attention to patients in high-risk areas (as identified by organizations such as the Centers for Medicare and Medicaid Services, the Joint Commission and other accreditation organizations) to ensure that pharmacy services meet patient care needs and that drug therapy is as safe, effective, and economical as possible. Safe handling of hazardous medications throughout the medication process (preparation, administration, and disposal) is assured. The pharmacy executive is responsible for developing plans for the continued operation of medication management systems and for the provision of pharmaceutical services during emergencies and disasters.

Quality Outcomes. With a greater percentage of reimbursement being tied to quality outcomes, the pharmacy executive is responsible for leveraging pharmacy expertise in support of value based purchasing, including leading core measures initiatives involving medication therapy, playing an active role in reducing readmissions, and owning the process for medication related customer satisfaction indicators. He or she will take steps to ensure that pharmacists in the department are highly skilled at communicating with patients through assessment of individual pharmacist competency in this area and implementation of professional development plans. The pharmacy executive will identify and implement specific ways that the pharmacy enterprise can contribute to the patient experience related to the care they receive at admission, during the stay and at discharge. He or she takes a leadership role in program development to reduce drug-related hospital readmissions through patient education about the appropriate management of medications, embedding pharmacy in the care transitions process and implementing programs such as medication history technicians and bedside delivery of discharge prescriptions. The pharmacy leader also commits to continuously improve the organizations medication reconciliation process at all care transitions.

Drug-Utilization Management. The pharmacy executive collaborates with peers to develop drug-utilization and formulary initiatives that optimize therapeutic outcomes, reduce the risk of drug-related problems, and ensure the use of cost-effective pharmacotherapy throughout the health system. The pharmacy executive ensures there is pharmacist representation on the pharmacy and therapeutics committee(s) of the health system as an active voting participant. He or she identifies inappropriate utilization and leads efforts to modify practices to improve medication management. The pharmacy executive (or a designee) is a member and active participant of the antimicrobial stewardship committee, anti-coagulation, pain and other specialized teams to ensure that stewardship principles are applied to the prescribing, dispensing, and administration of these agents.

Supply Chain Management. The pharmacy executive is responsible for oversight of all pharmaceutical contracting, procurement, receiving, security, inventory control, diversion prevention, and distribution policies across the continuum, including outsourced sterile products, alternate distribution channels utilized during drug shortages, reverse distribution and other methods of pharmaceutical waste disposal. He or she ensures that the methods used to contract and obtain products are safe, cost-effective, and timely. The pharmacy executive is also responsible for emergency preparedness of the supply chain, including strategies to ensure ongoing safe and effective patient care during drug product shortages through the collaborative development of alternatives to treatment and restricted use guidelines.

Financial Management. The pharmacy executive manages the health-system pharmacy's financial performance within the context of the broader health system. He or she develops budgets aligned with organizational and departmental objectives and monitors financial performance appropriately, performing financial audits and analysis as needed to ensure accurate, appropriate, and timely recording and classification of actual revenue capture and expenses. The pharmacy executive evaluates medication expenditure patterns and reimbursement trends, including the potential development of value-based approaches to pharmaceutical reimbursement. He or she seeks opportunities to implement medication related services that can improve the financial health of the organization, such as retail pharmacy and ambulatory infusion. He or she ensures that the pharmacy department has the expertise to manage the clinical and financial implications of specialty pharmaceutical products. The pharmacy executive may be called upon to provide guidance in areas outside of the traditional pharmacy arena, including management of drug expenditures in the self-insured employee population and in payer shared risk arrangements that include medication management incentives.

Managing the Pharmacy Workforce. The pharmacy executive manages the health-system pharmacy's workforce efforts. These efforts include determining the appropriate number, type and qualification of staff required to meet patient care needs, satisfy regulatory and accrediting requirements, achieve the organization's mission and advance pharmacy practice. In order to accomplish this task, he or she implements standards and development programs to advance the use of pharmacy technicians within the organization, allowing the redeployment of pharmacists' time to drug therapy management activities. The pharmacy executive works with state and federal regulatory agencies to support this expansion in the role of the pharmacy technician. He or she develops programs that fully leverage the use of students and residents within the organization, which includes participating in the development of student and resident standards to ensure that education and training reflects the needs of patients and health systems, and to further expand the capability of the pharmacy enterprise. The pharmacy executive ensures effective and timely staff recruitment, orientation, training, education, mentoring, career development, performance review, and retention efforts.

Regulatory and Accreditation Compliance. The pharmacy executive ensures continued compliance with all national, state, and local regulations related to medications and their management. He or she is responsible for the implementation of Board of Pharmacy, Drug Enforcement Agency, Centers for Medicare and Medicare Services, The Joint Commission and other medication management accreditation standards; for maintaining ASHP accreditation, where applicable (e.g., residency and technician training); and for the implementation of best practices. When applicable, the pharmacy executive is responsible for compliance oversight of the 340B program for the covered entity, all covered outpatient departments and contract pharmacy arrangements.

Research and Educational Missions. The pharmacy executive has an integral role in supporting the organization's research and educational missions by overseeing investigational drug services, fostering staff and resident research, participation in organizational grant funding applications and managing student and residency educational programs.

Institutional Representation and Leadership. The pharmacy executive demonstrates the personal leadership qualities and business acumen essential to operate effectively within the health system and to advance the profession and practice of pharmacy. He or she serves as the primary pharmacy representative on relevant committees of the organization's leaders to ensure that medication management systems and pharmaceutical services meet the needs of patients and health care providers across the continuum of care. The pharmacy executive assumes a leadership role within the profession through active participation in local, state, and national professional associations.

Conclusion

Complex hospital and health systems should have a pharmacy executive responsible for the strategic planning, design, operation, and improvement of the organization's medication management system. This individual must be properly positioned within the organization to ensure the best utilization of his or her expertise in all decisions regarding medication management.

References

1. Nold EG, Sander WT. Role of the director of pharmacy: the first six months. *Am J Health-Syst Pharm.* 2004; 61:2297–310.
2. Godwin HN. Achieving best practices in health-system pharmacy: eliminating the 'practice gap.' *Am J Health-Syst Pharm.* 2000; 57:2212–3.

3. Anderson RW. Health-system pharmacy: new practice framework and leadership model. *Am J Health-Syst Pharm.* 2002; 59:1163–72.
4. Mitchell CL, Anderson ER, Braun L. Billing for inpatient hospital care. *Am J Health-Syst Pharm.* 2003; 60(suppl 6):8–11.
5. Ivey MF. Rationale for having a chief pharmacy officer in a health care organization. *Am J Health-Syst Pharm.* 2005; 62:975–8.
6. The consensus of the Pharmacy Practice Model Summit. *Am J Health-Syst Pharm.* 2011; 68:1148–52; doi:10.2146/ajhp110060.
7. CPO Perspectives Scott Knoer; Stewardship of the pharmacy enterprise *Am J Health-Syst Pharm.* 2014; 71:1204–9; doi:10.2146/ajhp140170.
8. CPO Perspectives Thomas W. Woller, Scott Knoer, and Rowell Daniels; Strategic considerations for centralization of services across the pharmacy enterprise. *Am J Health-Syst Pharm.* 2015; 72:74–7; doi:10.2146/ajhp140401.

Approved by the ASHP Board of Directors on April 10, 2015, and by the ASHP House of Delegates on June 7, 2015. Developed through the ASHP Council on Pharmacy Management. This statement supersedes a previous version dated June 10, 2008.

Karl Kappeler, M.S., FASHP; Michael Nnadi, Pharm.D, MHS; Sam Calabrese, M.B.A., FASHP; Debra Cowan, Pharm.D., FASHP; Bonnie Kirshenbaum, M.S., FASHP, FCSHP; John Lewin, Pharm.D., M.B.A.; Christine Marchese, Pharm.D.; Tricia Meyer, Pharm.D., M.S., FASHP; Brandon Ordway, Pharm.D., M.S.; Roger Woolf, Pharm.D.; Rusol Karralli, Pharm.D., M.S.; and Kelly Sennett, B.S., are gratefully acknowledged for revising this statement.

Note: This statement had not been published in the *American Journal of Health-System Pharmacy* (*AJHP*) when *ASHP Best Practices **2015–2016*** went to press. Some minor editorial differences may exist between this document and the official one that will eventually appear in *AJHP* and subsequent editions of this publication.

ASHP Statement on Standards-Based Pharmacy Practice in Hospitals and Health Systems

Position

Pharmacy practice leaders in hospitals and health systems have a distinguished history of advancing health-system pharmacy practice beyond the minimum required by law, regulation, and accreditation. The American Society of Health-System Pharmacists (ASHP) supports those efforts by developing and disseminating a comprehensive body of evidence-based, peer-reviewed descriptions of best practices in health-system pharmacy. ASHP believes that pharmacists who practice in hospitals and health systems ("health-system pharmacists") and pharmacy leaders in health systems can continuously improve the delivery of patient care by regularly assessing compliance with ASHP best practices, identifying gaps in practice, establishing practice improvement priorities appropriate for their unique circumstances, and working to close the targeted gaps.

Purpose

The purpose of this statement is to promote understanding of how health-system pharmacists use ASHP best practices to develop and promote in health systems a standard of practice that exceeds what is required by law, regulation, or accreditation.

Standards-Based Pharmacy Practice

A standard is "a statement that defines the performance expectations, structures, or processes that must be in place for an organization to provide safe and high quality care, treatment, and service."1 In health care, practice standards serve as guideposts for a profession and as a way of communicating to peers, patients, policymakers, other professionals, and the public the roles and responsibilities of members of the profession. Practice standards also provide a benchmark for evaluating the quality of services and patient care.

Health-system pharmacists, like other health care professionals, practice under a number of mandated standards. These standards include state board of pharmacy regulations, public health requirements, Drug Enforcement Administration regulations, Joint Commission accreditation standards, Centers for Medicare and Medicaid Services conditions of participation, and the standards of other accrediting bodies and professional associations. Individual health care organizations also develop their own interdisciplinary practice policies and standards of care related to medication use, with health-system pharmacists serving as key participants in their development.

ASHP members have invested decades of effort in developing and maintaining an extensive body of policy positions, statements, and guidelines (hereinafter "ASHP best practices") that serve as a guide for effective, high-quality pharmacy practice in hospitals and health systems.[2] This comprehensive set of policies is unique in pharmacy.

ASHP best practices reinforce health-system pharmacists' established roles in health care and encourage development of responsibilities that answer the growing need and public demand for expanded involvement of pharmacists in patient care. ASHP best practices are based on professional and scientific literature and are developed with input from ASHP members, the public, regulatory bodies, other professional associations, and representatives of other health care disciplines. Peer groups of ASHP expert members systematically review ASHP best practices and compare them with the existing literature, the changing expectations of society, and changes in the professional and ethical challenges faced by health-system pharmacists. A compilation of these documents is published annually as *Best Practices for Hospital and Health-System Pharmacy* and made available to the public (www.ashp.org/bestpractices).

Most ASHP best practices represent the professional beliefs and aspirations of pharmacists practicing in health systems, based on evidence and expert opinion. Only three ASHP guidelines describe a minimum level of practice that all hospital pharmacy departments should consistently provide; these guidelines are designated as ASHP minimum standards.[3-5] Institutions that offer ASHP-accredited residencies are required to meet ASHP best practices to ensure the quality of the educational experience.

ASHP best practices represent a commitment by ASHP members to advancing the standard of pharmacy practice. ASHP believes that all health-system pharmacists have a role to play in raising health-system pharmacy practice to a level consistent with the best practices that have been developed and have gained acceptance by a peer-reviewed, consensus-based process. Practicing pharmacists and pharmacy leaders in health systems should use their professional judgment to regularly assess compliance with ASHP best practices, identify gaps in practice in their settings, establish practice improvement priorities appropriate for their unique circumstances, and work to close those practice gaps to ensure continuous improvement in the delivery of patient care.

Conclusion

Health-system pharmacy practice leaders have a long tradition of striving to advance practice beyond the minimum required by law, regulation, and accreditation. ASHP best practices embody those aspirations and provide health-system pharmacists with a means to continuously improve the delivery of patient care.

References

1. Comprehensive accreditation manual for hospitals. Oakbrook Terrace, IL: Joint Commission; 2007:GL-22.
2. Zellmer WA. Overview of the history of hospital pharmacy in the United States. In: Brown TR, ed. Handbook of institutional pharmacy practice. 4th ed.

Bethesda, MD: American Society of Health-System Pharmacists; 2006:19–32.

3. American Society of Health-System Pharmacists. ASHP guidelines: minimum standard for pharmacies in hospitals. *Am J Health-Syst Pharm.* 1995; 52:2711–7.
4. American Society of Health-System Pharmacists. ASHP guidelines: minimum standards for home care pharmacies. *Am J Health-Syst Pharm.* 1999; 56:629–38.
5. American Society of Health-System Pharmacists. ASHP guidelines: minimum standard for pharmaceutical services in ambulatory care. *Am J Health-Syst Pharm.* 1999; 56:1744–53.

Developed through the ASHP Council on Pharmacy Management and approved by the ASHP Board of Directors on March 7, 2008, and by the ASHP House of Delegates on June 10, 2008.

Scott Mark, Pharm.D., M.S., M.Ed., CHE, FASHP, FABC, is gratefully acknowledged for drafting this statement.

The bibliographic citation for this document is as follows: American Society of Health-System Pharmacists. ASHP statement on standards-based pharmacy practice in hospitals and health systems. *Am J Health-Syst Pharm.* 2009; 66:409–10.

ASHP Guidelines on Medication Cost Management Strategies for Hospitals and Health Systems

Because medication costs comprise the majority of health-system pharmacy budgets and continue to increase faster than other health care expenditures,[1] drug costs are a constant target for cost containment initiatives. The purpose of these guidelines is to provide guidance on medication-cost-management strategies.

These guidelines recommend techniques to manage drug costs in hospitals and health systems. The guidelines focus on drug use in inpatient settings and hospital clinics, where health-system pharmacies typically have responsibility for purchasing and distributing drugs. Strategies for other settings, such as managed care and ambulatory care settings, and strategies for revenue optimization are beyond the scope of this document. Although revenue optimization and medication cost management are complementary approaches to improving the financial performance of pharmacy departments, revenue optimization is best addressed through literature specific to that topic[2,3] and is not extensively reviewed in this document.

These guidelines examine methods for nonlabor pharmaceutical cost containment, focusing primarily on variable costs (costs dependent on patient volume) and direct drug costs. Fixed and indirect costs, such as labor to prepare or administer medication, nonpharmaceutical materials, and overhead, are also beyond the scope of these guidelines. There is also not an attempt to consider the impact of drug costs and drug-cost-management strategies on other hospital departments (e.g., laboratory, respiratory care) or on the total health care costs once the patient leaves the acute care setting. Although not discussed here, these shifts in drug costs are important to consider as drug therapies influence other health care costs, and pharmacists should lead efforts to promote the value medications provide across the hospital and health care system.

A broad range of drug-cost-management strategies exist throughout hospitals and health systems. Some approaches are relatively straightforward and can be implemented within the pharmacy. Other approaches are more complex and require high-level strategic planning and extensive collaboration throughout the hospital. Successful drug cost management requires systematic attention to and integration of both approaches. Because of the different nature of various drug-cost-management activities, these guidelines present information at different levels of complexity appropriate to the approach being described.

When selecting and implementing drug-cost-management strategies, it is essential that pharmacists remain mindful of patient safety and the quality of patient care.

Drug-cost-containment initiatives must never compromise the department's ability to provide the best possible care to patients. In many cases, it is prudent and necessary to monitor and evaluate the safety and outcomes of drug-cost-management projects. Fortunately, many drug-cost-containment strategies have little or no potential for detrimental effects on patient care, and efforts to improve the quality of drug use often coincide with cost-containment initiatives.

Trends in Medication Expenditures

Senior hospital administrators have recognized the importance of drug costs to the fiscal status of health systems. For example, a health care consultancy reported that in 1996, "managing hospital drug utilization and expenditures" was not ranked in the top 20 concerns for hospital CEOs.[4] When the survey was repeated in 2000; however, hospital CEOs ranked drug costs as their seventh most important concern. The 2000 survey also reported that among hospitals' greatest financial challenges, drug and technology costs were second only to decreased reimbursement, and hospital CEOs said that drugs offered the single greatest opportunity for cost savings.[4] Although somewhat dated, these data illustrate that drug-expenditure management presents health systems with an important challenge that is recognized by senior hospital administration.

Four primary factors drive growth in overall drug expenditures: price, utilization, mix, and innovation.[1]

Price inflation is an increase in the unit price of existing medications. Utilization is an increase in use of a drug, such as an increase in number of users, days of therapy, or dose per day of therapy. Mix changes when newer, more expensive therapies are used in place of older, less expensive but equally effective drugs. Finally, a blend of the utilization and mix factors increases drug expenditures when expensive, new medications become available to treat conditions previously untreatable with drug therapy (i.e., innovative therapy).

The United States spent over $250 billion dollars on prescription drugs in 2005, but total drug costs represent a relatively small portion of total U.S. health care spending (approximately 11%).[5] However, double-digit increases in prescription drug expenditures have been common (e.g., 15% in 2000, 18% in 2001, 12% in 2002, 11% in 2003, and 9% in 2004).[1,4,6] The rate of drug-expenditure growth has frequently been higher than inflation, increases in wages, and other health care spending, including spending for hospitals, physician services, and total health care expenditures. However, with the exception of 26% growth in 2001, the recent rate of growth in hospital drug expenditures has been less than the growth of total drug expenditures. Hospital drug expenditures grew 4.9% in 2000, 26% in 2001, 9.7% in 2002, 6.3% in 2003, 7.9% in 2004, and 5.7% in 2005.[1,5–7] However, the rate of growth in clinic drug expenditures has consistently exceeded the growth of total drug expenditures. Clinic drug expenditures grew 24.6% in 2000, 23% in 2001, 21.3% in 2002, 22.2% in 2003, 13.5% in 2004, and 12.4% in 2005.[1,5,7]

While the rate of increase in prescription drug expenditures moderated somewhat between 2004 and 2006, drug-expenditure growth remains substantial. Long-range forecasts suggest that the rate of increase in total prescription drug expenditures will continue to exceed the rate of increase for total health care expenditures through 2014. Because drug expenditures are the largest component of every health-system pharmacy's operating budget and often a meaningful portion of the entire hospital operating budget, drug expenses attract significant attention from hospital leaders. For these reasons, it is apparent that drug-expenditure-management will remain an area of focus and responsibility for health-system pharmacists for the foreseeable future.[8]

Systematic Approach to Medication-Cost-Management Measures

A systematic approach to planning and prioritizing specific drug cost management strategies is essential when implementing initiatives that will influence drug expenditures in a health system. Annual financial planning (i.e., budgeting) is the most common planning approach, and specific drug-cost-management strategies should be considered a part of the budgeting process. However, longer-term strategic and programmatic planning activities also have an important role in managing drug expenditures.

A systematic approach to drug-cost containment requires specific and detailed data on both health-system drug purchases and actual drug-use patterns. Data must underlie all types of planning to manage medication expenditures. Systems should be established to have ready access to the data and continually review and monitor these data.

It is essential to interact and collaborate consistently with physician leaders from various specialties to successfully plan, prioritize, and implement medication-cost management efforts. Physician involvement must be sought during the annual financial planning process and when doing strategic or programmatic planning related to drug expenditures. Appropriate physician representatives must also be engaged in specific drug-cost-management initiatives. During the annual financial planning process, physicians can provide important information related to drug costs, such as anticipated use of key drugs in the pipeline, programmatic or new service implementation, anticipated recruitment of specialists who may require high-cost agents, projections for use of high-priority drugs, and insights for drug cost containment. Pharmacy leaders can also use this opportunity to update physicians on the pharmacy department's recent accomplishments and goals for the future.

Drug Budgeting. Although a complete discussion of the drug-budgeting process is beyond the scope of this document, several important suggestions are provided below. A general approach to systematically developing the annual drug budget is outlined in Table 1.[7] At the beginning of each calendar year, the *American Journal of Health-System Pharmacy* publishes a projection of drug expenditures for that year.[1,5–7]

Annual drug budgeting is a challenging exercise. Unanticipated situations that result in extreme increases in drug expenditures will likely occur and the pharmacy director should be prepared to explain those situations. Better data and more experience will improve a department's ability to forecast institutional drug expenditures. Regardless of the drug budget's accuracy in forecasting the institution's drug expenditures, a well-planned drug budget should help the department understand drug use patterns and identify opportunities for drug cost management. Specific reports that can be helpful in understanding drug use will be described below.

During the annual financial planning process, it is important to identify and focus on key drug expenditures. The Pareto Principle, or 80/20 rule, applies to drug budgeting and states that in nearly all cases, a few vital factors are important and many are trivial. A relatively small number of drugs (50–60) typically account for 80% of most hospital drug budgets. Therefore, budgeting and cost-containment efforts should focus on those drugs, and the cost-management plan should especially concentrate on those top drugs for which it is feasible to influence prescribing patterns. Much of this document focuses on the need to develop a cost-containment plan after initial estimates of drug costs are completed (Table 1).

Table 1.
Steps for Developing Annual Drug Budget[7]

Collect and review data (e.g., drug purchase data, drug utilization data, workload and productivity data, other financial statements).
Develop budget for high-priority agents (top 50–60 drugs).
Identify relevant new drugs and build new agent budget.
Budget for nonformulary drugs and lower-priority drugs.
Establish a drug cost containment plan (identify drugs going off patent, opportunities for therapeutic interchange or protocol development).
Finalize and present the total drug budget.
Continue the budgeting process throughout the year through constant vigilance and monitoring of drug use.

Medication-cost-management projects should be carefully selected and prioritized as part of an ongoing financial planning process. Because drug-cost containment strategies must be customized to each health system's unique characteristics, a global assessment of the pharmacy department and the hospital must be conducted to identify opportunities for drug-cost-management. This assessment must go beyond a qualitative assessment of opportunities and must include retrieval and analysis of both drug purchase and drug-utilization data. Pharmacy departments may need to obtain and develop resources, such as personnel and software, to analyze these data.

Despite the need to customize the strategy and tactics to fit the needs of different hospitals and health systems, a systematic approach to identifying, prioritizing, and implementing medication-cost containment initiatives is necessary and can be applied in any setting. A clearly defined list of cost-containment targets should be established during each financial planning cycle. To be successful, the number of initiatives should be manageable and should focus on the institution's top expenditures. In many situations, multiple approaches for cost containment will be necessary.

The foundation for effective cost-management strategies, and the first stage of the systematic approach, begins with determining current costs of medications, both as ongoing expenses and those held as assets in inventory. Understanding and tracking key medication-cost indicators on an ongoing basis is necessary to determine the opportunities for medication-cost reduction. Examples of these indicators may include:

- Medication inventory per adjusted patient day
- Medication inventory turnover rate
- Contract coverage percentage
- Contract compliance percentage
- Intravenous-to-oral dosage ratio
- Volume-adjusted total medication costs (e.g., cost per adjusted patient day, discharge, etc.)

- Volume-adjusted drug category costs (e.g., antibiotics, anesthesia-related drugs, etc.)
- Descending-order total purchase histories, tracked over time

In addition, the use of external benchmarks may provide assistance in identifying medication-cost-reduction opportunities. External benchmarks may be available as a component of services provided by consulting organizations, the pharmacy's drug wholesaler or group-purchasing organization (GPO), or from professional published data. Benchmark data should be used with care; however, because there may be important limitations to the applicability of the data to a specific site. For example, difficulties may exist in adjusting the data for the specific pharmacy practice, such as models and intensity of services, and in finding an appropriate peer group.[9]

After cost-management opportunities are identified, they need to be quantified. Dollar values should be assigned to each opportunity, including inventory reduction, improvement in inventory turns, improving contract compliance, therapeutic interchange of various agents, and others. A specific goal and action plan should be set for each drug-cost-management target. For example, one goal might be to reduce expenditures for a drug class by 8% by establishing a contract for a new, preferred agent and implementing a therapeutic interchange program to shift use to the new agent. Alternatively, the goal might be to slow the rate of increase in use of a particular drug or drug class (e.g., based on current patterns, use of this drug class is expected to grow 15% in the next fiscal year, but the goal of interventions is to limit the rate of increase to 10%). Monitoring is essential, so drug cost containment targets should be consistently measured and evaluated. Identifying and quantifying the opportunities must be completed before prioritization and in-depth evaluation begins.

Assessment and Prioritization. Once opportunities for cost management have been identified and quantified, assessment and prioritization can occur. There are many methods of prioritization, but most of them contain two key elements: determining the potential benefit and estimating the relative ease or difficulty of attaining the benefit. Even though potential benefit may be clear-cut, the degree of difficulty is often hard to establish. Important points to consider when determining the relative degree of difficulty and likelihood of achieving benefits from a given drug-cost-management opportunity include (1) the amount of time pressure (the time available until the cost reductions occur), (2) key stakeholder (e.g., nurse, physician) sensitivity and willingness to collaborate, (3) extent of leadership support for the initiative, (4) resources required, and (5) existing level of expertise within the organization for the specific cost-management opportunity.

Drug-cost management strategies that are under the direct and exclusive purview of the pharmacy department (e.g., purchasing, inventory management, and waste reduction approaches) are generally easier to implement and provide more immediate benefits. These activities, however, often provide smaller or one-time financial benefits. Utilization management tactics (e.g., clinical practice guidelines and therapeutic interchange) generally provide greater financial benefits, but these efforts have correspondingly higher degrees of difficulty and complexity.

Because of the relative ease of implementation, cost-containment opportunities in areas that are primarily under the department's control will usually be pursued first. After these initiatives are underway, more complex techniques that require collaboration with the medical staff and others should be pursued.

These guidelines are structured so that the cost-management techniques are presented in the order in which health systems often implement them. Components of a cost-management program are listed in Table 2. An appendix that lists specific cost management opportunities is also provided. It is important to note that although these guidelines are separated into sections on purchasing and inventory management and medication-use management, both activities are integral and indivisible to drug-cost management planning and the practice of pharmacy in hospitals and health systems.

Purchasing and Inventory Management

When selecting drug-cost-containment initiatives, purchasing and inventory management procedures should be considered first.

Drug Product Costs and Procurement. At the most fundamental level, drug costs are a function of unit costs and

Table 2.
Components of a Cost-Management Program[a]

Pharmacy-Directed Activities
Purchasing
GPO contracts
Facility contracts
Wholesaler contracts
Inventory management
Wholesaler ordering programs
Storage
Waste reduction
I.V. product waste
Returns
Interdisciplinary Activities
Medication utilization program
Clinical pharmacy services
Assessment of drug costs
Medical staff support
Formulary management
Therapeutic interchange
Guideline (protocol) development
Pharmacist interventions
Plan implementation and analysis
Reimbursement & Charging
Reimbursement
340B programs
CMS (DRG class)
Commercial insurance (payer mix)
Outpatient infusion center
Charging
Coding and processing
Indigent care programs

[a]GPO = group purchasing organization, CMS = Centers for Medicare and Medicaid Services, DRG = diagnosis-related group.

utilization. Drug-unit costs are a function of acquisition costs (contracted or non-contracted), the external (in-bound) distribution fee, inventory management costs, and internal distribution costs.

Contracting. There are three main avenues for purchasing pharmaceuticals at discounted rates: GPO contracts, facility contracts, and wholesaler own-use contracts. All facilities should seek to maximize savings available from use of generic products, and some may have other considerations, such as use of 340B or indigent care programs.

GPO contracts. GPOs utilize the aggregate purchasing power of many facilities in negotiating pricing agreements with manufacturers. Most hospitals are members of a GPO. While there are GPOs that focus exclusively on drugs, the majority of GPOs offer contracts for medical and surgical supplies, food, and other support products and services in addition to pharmaceuticals. Most GPOs make their contract portfolio available to members via hard copy, and some GPOs have contract portfolios available on secure internet sites. Considerations in contracting with a GPO are listed in Table 3. It is also important to have routine surveillance, preferably an automated service, that ensures that contract prices are applied to all purchases.

GPOs are funded by one of two means. First, most, if not all, GPOs collect a contract administrative fee (CAF) from the manufacturers or distributors with which they contract. The CAF is rarely greater than 3% of the dollar volume of product purchased through the contract. Some GPOs return a portion or all of the CAF to its members. If any or all of the CAF for a particular drug product is returned to the facility by the GPO, it should be taken into account when calculating the net cost of the drug. The second method by which GPOs are funded is direct payment of fees by members to the GPO. In this arrangement, all of the CAF is returned to the facility.

Contracts through GPOs consider not only the unit cost of the pharmaceutical but also include the allowable distribution methods for the pharmaceutical, payment terms, returns policies, and supplier performance requirements. Many GPO contracts, especially those for multi-source generics, include simple line-item pricing, which only requires the purchaser to buy and pay for the product. Other contracts are more complicated, with incentive rebates for all purchases or rebates for achieving volume or market share targets.

Typically, market share agreements are utilized when two or more products can be used to treat the same disease and no generic equivalent exists. The incentive, such as a rebate, a lock-in of a current discount, or achievement of a higher discount, is contingent upon attaining a given market share for a particular product in the institution's market basket. To achieve the greatest financial advantage from the contract (lowest net drug cost), the pharmacy must work with the medical staff. This process requires a careful evaluation of comparative efficacy and safety of the product and its alternatives.

Some GPOs have multiple products on contract within categories of pharmaceuticals, allowing the facility to receive discounted pricing on similar agents when prescribing practices are not standardized to one agent. More aggressive GPOs will sometimes contract for a single agent within a particular class (e.g., for one fluoroquinolone or one liposomal amphotericin B product to the exclusion of others) in order to gain the maximum value for its members.

Successful use of GPO contracts requires a constructive and collaborative relationship between the member, the GPO, the manufacturer, and the distributor (i.e., wholesaler). Potential advantages of GPO contracts are listed in Table 4.

In addition to the contracting portfolio, GPOs offer services such as lost savings and compliance reports, rebate and contract administrative fee reports, clinical utilization management programs, and letters of commitment.

Lost savings and compliance reports. These reports provide data and analysis of missed savings opportunities in the user's purchase history (e.g., items purchased off-contract when a generically equivalent alternative item was on-contract). These reports may also indicate the compliance level, or the amount of purchases on-contract versus the amount of purchases that could have been made on-contract (drugs purchased on-contract plus the value of drugs purchased off-contract when alternatives were on-contract). These reports should be reviewed monthly to determine if purchasing practices are effective.

Rebate and contract administration fee report. These reports tally the amount of rebates and contract administration fees generated by the facility's purchases of specific products under contact. When evaluating the costs of two or more equivalent products, it is important to include any applicable rebates to arrive at net cost.

Clinical utilization management programs. These programs assist facilities in managing the utilization of various drug products and classes, often through evaluation and

Table 3.
Considerations in Group Purchasing Organization (GPO) Contracting

Fees (e.g., contract administrative fee)
Allowable distribution methods
Payment terms
Return policies
Supplier performance requirements
Rebates
Market-share agreements
Single-agent contracts
GPO services (e.g., lost savings and compliance reports, rebate and contract administration fee reports, clinical utilization management programs)
Letters of commitment

Table 4.
Potential Advantages of Group Purchasing Organization Contracts[10,11]

Standardization of products
Reduction of contract labor costs for institutions
Enhancement of member institution's purchasing program
Enhancement of information sharing
Enhancement of purchasing expertise
Protracted periods of price protection
Coordination of contracting and budgeting process
Reduction of duplication of purchasing efforts among institutions
Assistance identifying alternative or secondary products during drug shortage

comparison of product efficacy, safety, and cost, as well as therapeutic interchange programs.

Letters of commitment. Letters of commitment (LOC) available through GPOs should be evaluated and taken advantage of when appropriate. The LOCs usually contain requirements for the pharmacy to do one or more of the following in order to gain lower pricing or rebates:

- Declare that a particular drug is on formulary.
- Declare that a particular drug will be on formulary and will not be restricted.
- Achieve a target periodic volume.
- Achieve a target market share relative to competitive drugs for a given period of time.

The LOC may not require significantly more purchasing of the drug. If LOC requirements do not conflict with formulary and utilization management strategies, the LOC should be signed if there is a reasonable chance of meeting the requirements.

Facility contracts. The alternative to GPO contracting is individual contracting. This type of contracting may be done at the facility or the health-system level. In some cases, equal or better pricing than GPOs can be obtained by individual facilities when contracting, especially large facilities or integrated delivery networks (IDNs). Opportunities for better pricing through individual contracting may exist for specialized health systems (e.g., those focused on oncology or transplantation), that purchase a large volume of a selected drug and are able to commit to maintaining a market share for the drug.

It is important to carefully evaluate the benefits of individual contracting and its influence on the collective bargaining power of the GPO. Continual use of individual contracts that are in contravention to GPO contracts, in theory, will eventually erode the GPO's ability to consistently contract aggressively for its members. Because of larger GPO volume, manufacturers often will not offer the same pricing or other terms to individual facilities or IDNs that they offer to GPOs. Another factor to consider with individual contracting is that a facility may require contracts to be reviewed by attorneys, whereas the GPO acts as the contracting agent of the facility, obviating the need for legal review of each contract by the facility's counsel. Finally, the amount of time required to negotiate, write, and maintain an individual contract should be weighed against the incremental value gained over what a GPO contract would offer. In many situations, it may be more efficient and productive to voice contract concerns to GPO representatives and become involved in GPO committees rather than write multiple, individual contracts outside the GPO.

Some drug contracts, especially for sole-source awards to generic manufacturers, call for the manufacturer to reimburse the pharmacy for the difference in cost when the pharmacy must purchase a product off-contract because the manufacturer was not able to supply the contracted product. The manufacturer-unable-to-supply reimbursement process is time-consuming and the requirements can be rigid, but submitting reimbursement to manufacturers under these provisions can return additional funds to the pharmacy.

Wholesaler own-use contracts. Wholesalers are also able to take advantage of special pricing on certain branded and generic drugs and offer those products to their customers in the wholesaler's proprietary contract portfolio. This creates margin for the wholesalers that can be used to fund distribution discounts. Wholesalers also take advantage of cash discounts and quick-payment terms from manufacturers to increase their margin and to offer discounts to customers.

Generic Drug Savings Maximization. The expiration of patents on widely used branded drugs can result in large reductions in drug expenditures. It is important to be mindful of the opportunities presented by the first-time introduction of generics on high-spend branded drugs, both in budgeting and implementing rapid and effective uptake of generics when they are introduced.

Budgeting. There are several sources for monitoring patent expiration dates (off-patent dates) for branded drugs, including www.drugpatentwatch.com and the GPO. The GPO may also be able to estimate the potential initial savings from contracting for generic drugs that are first-time introductions. It is also important to determine when the first-time generic product will be available from multiple manufacturers. The initial savings differential between the branded and generic versions may be small because a single generic manufacturer often has a period of exclusivity before the generic drug becomes available from multiple sources. In some cases the savings may be so insignificant that health systems will choose to remain with the branded drug for safety reasons and consistency in product supply. Changing products several times within a short period of time could confuse caregivers, so pharmacy managers should weigh the benefits and risks of making such changes.

Operational considerations. Swift uptake of the generic product is necessary to maximize the savings after a branded drug comes off-patent and multiple generic versions are available. The following steps should be taken during any product conversion, but they are particularly important when converting from a brand name product to a first-time generic equivalent product.

- Contracting. Be sure that the health system has access to contract pricing on a generic product on the first date that the drug is available as a multisource item. The contract pricing will usually be through the health system's GPO, but in some cases, the health system may write its own contract for the generic product.
- Contract Price Loading. The contract pricing for the product must be loaded at the wholesaler with enough notice to become effective. Up to 30 days notice may be required before the contract pricing becomes effective through the wholesaler. Although the manufacturer or GPO typically send the contract information to the wholesalers, when the hospital or health system directly contracts for the generic drug, the contract information should be sent directly to the wholesaler by the hospital or health system.
- Demand Matching. Work with the wholesaler to ensure that there will be a sufficient supply of the generic product at the local wholesaler distribution center to match current purchases of the branded product, a process called demand matching. Wholesalers will need at least 30 days notice on demand matching to ensure sufficient stock of the generic product on the off-patent date. Working with the wholesaler on demand matching also improves overall supply chain management

by allowing the wholesaler to draw down inventory of products that will be in less demand.

- Autosubstitution. Some wholesalers allow pharmacies to institute autosubstitution rules in the wholesaler ordering system to substitute a preferred generic product for a branded product or non-preferred generic products. This process maximizes savings and contract compliance. Care must be exercised in creating autosubstitution rules to ensure correct product-to-product substitution in chemical entity, dosage form, package size, package form (unit dose, bulk oral, liquid), and so forth, especially in cases in which a brand-name drug goes off-patent. Autosubstitution rules may also be implemented in the wholesaler ordering system for medication safety reasons (e.g., reduction of sound-alike and look-alike drugs) in addition to savings optimization or contract compliance.

Other Considerations. Pharmacy managers should explore whether the hospital can obtain pharmaceuticals at advantageous pricing using 340B (disproportionate share) programs. Because hospitals and health systems must meet specific criteria to be designated as a 340B facility, pharmacy managers should collaborate with the chief financial officer and financial services department to determine if they can access 340B pricing for pharmaceuticals. Detailed descriptions of the qualifications and benefits of 340B programs are also available through the Health Resources and Services Administration Office of Pharmacy Affairs www.hrsa.gov/opa/; the Pharmacy Services Support Center, pssc.aphanet.org/; the Safety Net Hospitals for Pharmaceutical Access, safetynetrx.org; and ASHP 340B Information Site www.ashp.org/s_ashp/cat1c.asp? CID=3813&DID=6225.

Pharmaceutical manufacturers also continue to offer indigent patient care programs for select drugs for qualified patients on an individual basis. Although substantial savings can be realized through replacement drugs at no charge, the process can be arduous and complex. There are independent consulting services that specialize in assisting with coordination of the program for hospitals and typically require payment as a percentage of the savings. Patients eligible for Medicaid and other regional or local low-income health insurance do not usually qualify for the indigent care programs sponsored by the pharmaceutical industry.

Wholesalers and Distribution Fees. Most hospital pharmacies purchase 80% or more (by dollar volume) of their pharmaceutical needs from a drug distributor (wholesaler). Hospital pharmacies can lower their costs by ensuring that the distribution fee mark-up is as low as possible. To understand the cost that wholesalers charge for drugs, and the distribution fee charged to hospital pharmacies, it is necessary to understand wholesalers' revenue streams and expense drivers.

The adoption of the prime-vendor system, in which a pharmacy procures a very large portion of its pharmaceutical needs from one supplier, has led to great efficiencies in the pharmaceutical supply chain. Through these efficiencies, wholesalers are able to offer low incremental fees to their customers for distribution of pharmaceuticals. In many cases, they are able to offer discounts to the contracted price of the drug or "cost-minus" discounts to the wholesale acquisition cost of the drug if it is not contracted.

Through automated inventory, stock replacement, and order fulfillment, wholesalers have streamlined the delivery process and lowered pharmaceutical costs in the supply chain. In the past, wholesalers increased their margins through speculative buying, which is buying pharmaceuticals in large quantities and holding them past the date of future manufacturer price increases. The products would then be sold to customers at the higher price. These practices have reportedly decreased since 2004.[12] However, at the same time that speculative buying decreased, the wholesale drug industry instituted inventory management agreements with manufacturers, who in return for agreements regarding product supply and demand, pay the wholesalers a negotiated fee based on the percentage of the volume that the wholesalers purchase from them. These methods of creating margin through increasing revenue and decreasing expenses can be translated into a cost-minus fee structure for the hospital that is purchasing from the wholesalers.

Individual hospital factors that influence wholesaler fee structure. Several characteristics of individual hospital-pharmacy purchasing can affect a wholesaler's revenue and expenses and result in higher or lower distribution fees. To some degree, a higher purchasing volume results in a lower distribution fee. However, other factors, including deliveries per week, dollars per drop, dollars per line extension, numbers of delivery sites per location, payment terms, and special services, must also be considered. These factors should be considered collectively and not in isolation. In addition, most major wholesalers have supply, automation, and other service and equipment divisions, and an institutional contract with multiple divisions can provide additional savings.

Deliveries per week. The fewer deliveries from the wholesaler per week, the lower the expenses for the wholesaler, which can reduce the wholesaler distribution fee to the pharmacy. Some large hospitals have up to 11 deliveries per week, but other large hospitals are able to manage inventory so that patient care can be well-maintained with only 5. Inventory and patient care can be well maintained at less than five deliveries per week at small hospitals. Fewer deliveries may require additional purchasing discipline, but some wholesalers have programs to help pharmacies improve their purchasing practices.

Dollars per drop. This factor is important to wholesalers because the higher the number of delivery locations (drops), the higher the wholesalers' cost, and vice versa. For a given dollar value of pharmaceuticals purchased, a wholesaler's expenses are lower, and margin is higher, for a lower number of delivery points. This margin can be translated into lower distribution fees for the pharmacies, particularly for IDNs of multiple pharmacies.

Dollars per line extension. For each line of products on an invoice that a wholesaler fills and delivers to a pharmacy, there is an associated cost. The dollars per line extension is the total dollars purchased by a pharmacy over a given period of time divided by the number of lines of products ordered over the same period of time. Pharmacies with higher dollars per line extension purchased can sometimes have lower distribution costs than pharmacies with lower dollars per line extension because it costs relatively less for the wholesaler to service the pharmacy with the higher dollars per line extension.

Secondary wholesalers. Secondary wholesaler relationships should be avoided if inventory levels meet patient care needs. Purchases from secondary wholesalers usually carry a much higher distribution fee. Such purchases also result in a higher primary wholesaler distribution fee because there are decreases for the pharmacy in its dollars per drop, dollars per line extension, and total volume. Wholesalers are increasingly requiring pharmacies to meet a minimum monthly volume to maintain an account, and the costs of maintaining the minimum volume at a significantly higher distribution fee can be prohibitive.

Expanding the use of the wholesaler within the health system may offer additional opportunities for cost savings. Hospital departments such as radiology, the clinical laboratory, interventional cardiology, and anesthesiology may procure pharmaceuticals directly from the manufacturer through the purchasing or materials management departments. Utilizing the pharmaceutical wholesaler for these products through a separate purchasing account does not change the process of procurement or distribution but reduces the unit cost through application of the wholesaler discount. Because some of these products may be relatively costly (e.g., contrast agents, blood factors, or anesthetic gases), there is a potential for additional savings if these purchases push the hospital into a higher tier of the wholesaler cost structure. Pharmacy directors should communicate with other department managers to determine how pharmaceuticals are purchased, and it is usually best if all drug purchases are managed by the pharmacy.

Payment method and frequency. Payment method and frequency can also affect the distribution fee. Many wholesalers offer a lower distribution fee to hospitals that pay by electronic fund transfer (EFT). Pharmacy managers should work with their accounts-payable departments to establish EFT, which is usually a more efficient method of payment for both the hospital and the wholesaler. In addition, the more frequent the payment, the lower the wholesaler distribution fee will generally be. Since 2004, the amount of speculative buying has waned and large discounts for more frequent payments have decreased. However, many wholesalers offer terms based on prepayment, or placing funds on deposit with the wholesaler, and then paying invoices on a go-forward basis. The advantage in lower distribution fee is clear, but this gain must be balanced against the time value of money for having the funds on deposit with the wholesaler rather than drawing a return for the health system.

Most GPOs have wholesaler-distribution agreements for use by their members. However, because of higher-than-average dollars per drop, dollars per line extension, and discipline in number of deliveries per week, large hospitals and health systems can often get better pricing and terms by dealing directly with wholesalers rather than through GPO wholesaler agreements.

Other wholesaler tools. Most wholesalers provide pharmacies with access to computer software or Web-based solutions for product ordering, reporting, and inventory management. The programs will allow the buyer to check for lower-priced alternatives and contract compliance prior to placing orders. Pharmacy managers should work with their wholesaler representatives to be sure that these features are available and utilized.

Some wholesalers produce contract compliance reports. These reports can be used to gauge the effectiveness of purchasing practices. Pharmacy managers should check with their wholesalers to determine if these reports are available. If they are, they should be reviewed monthly for opportunities to improve contract purchasing.

Some wholesalers have automatic substitution programs to assist pharmacy buyers in selecting the correct product when multiple generic alternatives exist. These programs allow the pharmacy manager to direct purchases of less-preferred products (as determined by the pharmacy management) to more-preferred items. For example, if one brand of unit dose acetaminophen 325-mg tablet is on contract as a sole-source award, the autosubstitution program can allow for inadvertent orders for noncontract unit dose acetaminophen 325-mg tablets to be substituted with the preferred version. Such programs may not be available from all wholesalers, and they should receive careful consideration before being implemented.

Inventory Management. Inventory management is a balancing act. It involves meeting patient and internal customer needs while committing the least amount of dollars possible to drugs on the shelves or in automated cabinets. The rate of inventory turnover (defined as total annual drug expenses divided by the dollar value of the inventory assessed on an annual basis) is dependent on many factors. Typically, the pharmacies of smaller hospitals will have a lower drug inventory turnover (8–10 turns per year) than the pharmacies of larger hospitals (12–18 turns per year or higher) and some specialty hospitals.

Many wholesalers' ordering programs provide systematic methods for asset management (i.e., inventory value optimization and increasing turnover). Wholesaler representatives can assist in the initial setup of these programs. Inventory items should be divided into high-, medium-, and low-value products, and the minimum and maximum inventory levels for at least the high- and medium-value products should be established. At the same time, reorder points and reorder quantities should be established for at least the high- and medium-value products. Systematic use of these programs can decrease the time required for the ordering process and increase inventory turns. The minimum and maximum levels, as well as the reorder points and reorder quantities, should be reviewed on a routine schedule and revised when necessary.

When seeking to increase inventory turns, storage in the central pharmacy and automated dispensing cabinets should also be considered. Configuring pharmacy storage locations so that each drug product has only one storage location in the central pharmacy sometimes helps to free capital by reducing inventory. Automated cabinet inventories should be regularly reviewed for appropriate turnover. Most cabinet systems have report capabilities to optimize both the products and the quantities that should be in a particular cabinet based on the dispensing philosophy devised by pharmacy and nursing departments. Cabinet manufacturers have product specialists that consult with pharmacy management to optimize use of the cabinets.

I.V. product waste. Many pharmacies waste a significant quantity of drugs, particularly unused IV solutions, and many do not have an accurate valuation of the amount of waste because it is only sporadically monitored. Table 5 lists strategies for reduction of IV product waste.

Returns. Most pharmacies use a third party (reverse distributors or returns companies) to process wasted and expired drugs. However, not all pharmacies completely track

Table 5.
Strategies for Reducing I.V. Product Waste

Establish policies that are based on the most recent literature for maximum i.v. bag hang-times and i.v. set change frequency.
Institute an i.v.-to-oral switch program for both cost reduction and patient care benefits.
Periodically audit the amount of i.v. admixtures being wasted and log the date and time of waste, date and time of preparation, the i.v. fluid type and drug admixed, quantity of products, and the cost of the products. Review the log and determine the most common occurrences.
Reduce i.v. batch sizes (creating more, smaller batches) and reduce the amount of time between preparation of the i.v. dose and the actual administration time.
Routinely monitor the status of i.v. drips that are adjusted.
Routinely return all unused i.v. admixtures to the i.v. preparation area as soon as possible.
Consider the use of manufacturer premixed products where advantageous, both economically and for patient care.
Compare the quality, economic, and regulatory (e.g., *USP* chapter 797) differences within your practice site between different administration methods such as i.v. syringe infusion, i.v. intermittent infusion (i.v. piggyback), and volumetric drip chambers.
Establish standard concentrations, dosages, and base solutions for i.v. admixtures.
Ensure that there is an efficient process for communicating changes in i.v. admixtures (e.g., rate, fluid, dosage) or discontinuation.
Reduce total parenteral nutrition use by employing enteral nutrition when possible, and establish standardized total parenteral nutrient base solutions, hang times, and related policies and procedures.

and trend the drugs that are most commonly wasted, the dollar value of the expired and wasted drugs, or whether credits were received. The pharmacy manager and pharmacy buyer should work together to utilize reports from the reverse distributor to determine the opportunities for reducing the amount of expired and wasted drugs and insuring that all credits due to the pharmacy from the manufacturers are received.

Medication Utilization Management

Planning and Developing a Medication Utilization Management Program. An effective plan for medication utilization management must provide the health system with a road map for continuous improvement in pharmaceutical expense management, with specific goals and outcome measures of success. It is important to acknowledge that although one purpose of medication-utilization-management is to add economic value, the quality and safety of patient care are foremost in the mission of pharmacy services and should never be compromised for cost. Medication-utilization-management must integrate evidence-based science with the standards of medical practice within the health system.

Before embarking on a comprehensive medication-utilization-management plan, goals must be established, a reporting structure delineated, roles identified, measurement tools developed, and implementation procedures established. The successful plan is dependent on many levels of commitment, including commitment to administrative and clinical pharmacy management, the medical staff, and senior health-system management. The director of pharmacy provides leadership by facilitating the efforts of the medical staff, setting priorities for the clinical pharmacy staff, and cultivating the support of senior leadership. Clinical pharmacists with advanced training and education must have dedicated time to develop and implement the cost management initiatives. They must also be empowered to monitor the program and educate other staff to participate in therapeutic interchange, medication utilization review, and other interventions while encouraging the infusion of fresh ideas for pharmaceutical cost management.

Role of Clinical Pharmacy Services in Drug Cost Management. Clinical pharmacy services, activities in which pharmacists provide direct patient care, are an important foundation for a successful medication-utilization-management program that is focused on managing drug costs. Clinical pharmacy services have demonstrated an overall positive financial impact. In a systematic review of original assessments of clinical pharmacy services from 1988 to 1995, Schumock et al.[13] reported that 89% of 104 studies reviewed reported positive financial results. In the seven studies of clinical pharmacy services where sufficient information was available to calculate a benefit-to-cost ratio, the median benefit-to-cost ratio was 4.09:1. Therefore, in these studies, every dollar invested in clinical pharmacy services returned four dollars. The systematic review was updated in 2003 to review published assessments of clinical pharmacy services from 1995 to 2000, and once again, the value of clinical pharmacy services was demonstrated.[14] For this five-year period, benefit-to-cost ratios could be determined from 16 studies, and when these studies were combined, the median benefit:cost ratio was 4.68:1.

Some specific types of clinical pharmacy services have also been associated with decreased drug costs. Bond et al.[15] have used an extensive database of the outcomes of clinical pharmacy services to show that drug information services, medication admission histories, and drug protocol management are associated with lower drug costs.

In addition, clinical pharmacists' active involvement is crucial to the success of many drug-cost-management ini-tiatives. Many of the drug-cost-containment techniques can only be successful with diligent and often daily support from clinical pharmacists. For example, successful implementation of a clinical practice guideline as a drug-cost-management technique will require the expertise of the department's clinical pharmacists to develop the guideline, and will also require the pharmacy staff's consistent enforcement of the guideline in their interactions with prescribers. Similarly, it will often be the clinical pharmacist's responsibility to routinely carry out the hospital's therapeutic interchange policies.

Assessment of Drug Costs

A successful pharmaceutical-cost-management program must be data driven. GPOs, wholesalers, distributors, pharmaceutical manufacturers, and supply-chain divisions of multi-hospital systems need to track costs in a variety of ways. Advances in information technology have made drug usage data more accessible and sophisticated, and effort should be spent to manage and analyze these data. Pharmacy management must also take advantage of the data available in its own facility through the materials management department, purchasing department, and finance department. Internal and external data sources are the foundation for the decision-making process for medication-utilization-management and must be examined closely prior to setting goals for cost-management initiatives.

Because each health system has a unique mix of patients, services, and centers of excellence, the drug-cost-assessment process must be customized to create a priority list of initiatives that will provide the greatest value. Key reports that should be considered are listed in Table 6. Once the formulas for denominator data are established as consistent across many facilities, a multihospital health system can effectively benchmark drug costs.

Medical Staff Support. Any program that involves altering prescribing patterns to improve the cost-effectiveness of drug therapy requires the support and engagement of the medical staff. Although health systems have the ability to negotiate discounted unit prices for pharmaceuticals, the efforts of the GPOs and the increased availability of generics have leveled the expense of many high-cost drug products used in hospitals. Cost-management programs have therefore become increasingly dependent on the hospital's ability to manage utilization and prescribing, which will ultimately influence market share and drug pricing. Several effective strategies that can harness physician knowledge, cultivate a collaborative relationship, and facilitate ownership of the process by the medical staff are described in Table 7.

Once the medical staff is engaged and there is a commitment from senior management for the medication-utilization-management program, a detailed procedure for initiative generation can be established. Key steps include the following:

- Designating clinical sub-groups based on categories of the initiatives,
- Identifying the lead physicians, clinical pharmacists, and other key practitioners for each group,
- Using evidence-based studies and the drug assessment data to make decisions,
- Defining the types and categories of the initiatives,
- Creating a dashboard and a clear and concise reporting format for communicating progress,
- Facilitating the infusion of ideas through brainstorming and other effective meeting and group techniques, and
- Defining measurable outcomes and benchmarks for evaluation.

Table 6.
Key Reports to Consider in Assessing Drug Costs

Report	Considerations
Wholesaler purchasing reports	For 80/20 analysis, by therapeutic class, and of top 200 drugs; drugs with multiple strengths and sizes need to be aggregated; wholesalers can also provide monthly trending reports and benchmarks from their customers.
Direct (nonwholesaler) purchase reports	Available from the purchasing or finance departments.
Interdepartmental purchasing reports	Available from materials management or other departments that have internal transfers.
Cost (total drug costs or specific drugs) per medical service or hospital area	Drug-utilization data will be needed to produce this report.
Cost per drug-related group reports	Available from internal sources (ideally) or fee-based external vendors; distinction must be made between using cost or charge data.
Cost per occupied bed, adjusted patient day, admission, discharge, or case mix index adjusted patient day	Adjusted patient days are calculated with a standard financial formula that modifies patient days with a ratio of outpatient to inpatient revenue to correct for volume changes and severity of illness.[16] External and internal benchmarking is dependent on these kinds of reports.
Pharmacy-adjusted patient days	Calculated using the same ratio of outpatient to inpatient revenue but for drugs only, and may also add specificity and value to comparative data.
Cost per case, procedure, or admission (e.g., surgical case, cardiac procedure, dialysis admission)	These are important based on the patient mix and the drugs that comprise the greatest costs within the health system. Physician participation in the dissemination of the data is essential.

Formulary Management. The guiding principles of a sound formulary management system are well described in two documents,[17,18] and are concisely summarized in the following statement: a well-managed formulary system ensures a close relationship between the organization's medication-use policies, the therapies offered by the organization, and the medication routinely stocked by the pharmacy.[18] Although the primary goal of a formulary system is to promote safe and effective drug therapy, it can be a valuable cost management tool and has inherent medical staff support through the actions of the pharmacy and therapeutics (P&T) committee. The medication-utilization-management program is highly dependent on an effective formulary system. Key aspects of formulary management in cost-management efforts are described in Table 8. Once again, the efforts of clinical pharmacists are crucial to successful implementation of the formulary system.

Methods of Pharmaceutical Cost Management. Pharmaceutical cost-management initiatives are typically categorized by therapeutic class or group or by method of implementation. The latter is usually subdivided into three or four different types: therapeutic interchange (therapeutic substitution), guideline (protocol)

Table 7.
Strategies to Involve Medical Staff in Cost-Management Efforts

Enlist the pharmacy and therapeutic (P&T) committee to review medication-utilization management issues as a standing agenda item.
Identify the centers of excellence and work with individual chiefs of service to gain support.
Meet with key medical staff departments and divisions, including infectious diseases, anesthesiology, cardiology, and oncology, as well as intensivists, hospitalists, and interventionalists as appropriate.
Develop prescriber reports on the targeted high-cost drugs and discuss methods for cost reduction.
Provide continuous feedback to the P&T committee and individual departments and divisions on cost management successes.
Provide hospitalwide expenditure data on the top 50 items to the P&T committee.
Utilize evidence-based research to propose changes in medication utilization.
Identify physician champions for specific initiatives.
Create a consistent procedure for developing prescribing guidelines, protocols, care paths, and preprinted orders.

Table 8.
Key Aspects of Formulary Management in Cost-Management Efforts

Policy for formulary drug addition and deletion through evidence-based product selection, including efficacy, safety, and pharmacoeconomic assessments
Policy for the use and monitoring of non-formulary medications
Policy for medication-use evaluation
Limitation on combination, sustained-release, and long-acting products
Policy for therapeutic interchange and prescribing guidelines
Reduction of drugs in the same therapeutic group or class
Periodic house cleaning to reduce under-used and discontinued line items
Policy for drug restriction
Procedure for consistently monitoring the use of new agents particularly if there are specific guidelines for use
System to provide the formulary electronically with timely updated information
Off-label or ad hoc use of medications
Restricted use (by indication, prescriber, patient care area, patient)
Dose adjustment or discontinuation based on clinical triggers or end points
Injectable to oral conversion
Therapeutic equivalence

development, and pharmacist interventions (clinical and operational), such as parenteral-to-oral conversions, renal-dose adjustments, drug restrictions, repackaging, dosage-form changes, waste reduction, and others. Although the terms are sometimes used interchangeably, therapeutic group refers to a broad classification (e.g., anesthetic agents, anti-infectives, or chemotherapeutic agents), whereas therapeutic class is a narrower designation (e.g., beta-lactam antibiotics, volatile anesthetic gases, serotonin antagonists). If the decision is made to use therapeutic class, then each of the methods of implementation are used as appropriate within the medication categories. An example would be selecting third-generation cephalosporins utilizing a therapeutic interchange for cefotaxime and ceftriaxone (therapeutic interchange method). Third-generation cephalosporins may also be the preferred class of antibiotics within a pneumonia protocol (guidelines method). Examples of using the implementation method rather than the therapeutic class would be to select several drug classes for therapeutic interchange, some for guideline development, and some for other intervention types.

Therapeutic interchange. ASHP defines therapeutic interchange (TI) as "an authorized exchange of therapeutic alternatives in accordance with previously established and approved written guidelines or protocols within a formulary system."[17] This definition stipulates that the interchange is between two or more drugs that are not generic equivalents. Although FDA defines the term *therapeutic equivalent* to include generically equivalent products, therapeutic interchange or substitution in the hospital setting generally refers to drugs that are not generically identical.

The American College of Clinical Pharmacy (ACCP) Guidelines for Therapeutic Interchange[19] contain a more recent definition of TI:

> Therapeutic interchange is defined as the dispensing of a drug that is therapeutically equivalent to but chemically different from the drug originally prescribed. Although usually of the same pharmacological class, drugs appropriate for therapeutic interchange may differ in chemistry or pharmacokinetic properties, and may possess different mechanism of action, adverse-reaction, toxicity, and drug interaction profiles. In most cases, the interchanged drugs have close similarity in efficacy and safety profiles.

The ACCP guidelines also describe a comprehensive five-part process for health-system TI implementation, with an emphasis on patient safety; an extensive review of drug classes appropriate for therapeutic interchange, including specific evidence-based examples; discussion of legal and regulatory issues; viewpoints of other professional organizations, including the American Medical Association, the American College of Physicians, and the Pharmaceutical Research and Manufacturers of America; and medical and pharmaceutical literature references.

The health system, through the action of the P&T committee, must decide on the general policy for a TI program, particularly regarding the authority and autonomy of the pharmacy staff. The committee may define TI as an automatic conversion by the pharmacist, may require contact with the prescriber before the change can occur, or may employ a combination of both. The prescriber may be informed orally before the drug is dispensed or through written communication in the medical record. Most commonly, TI implies pharmacist autonomy once the P&T committee has sanctioned the policy, but there may be exceptions based on the level of clinical judgment required. A survey of the prevalence of TI conducted in 2002 revealed that the vast majority (88%) of hospitals use TI programs, and most of those did not require the pharmacist to contact the prescriber before making the conversion.[20]

Categories of drugs that offer modest savings with minimal challenge include various non-prescription groups, such as antacids, vitamins, nonsteroidal antiinflammatory drugs, topical products, and cold and cough remedies. To make significant gains in pharmaceutical cost savings, the health system must consider the drug classes that comprise the greatest proportion of drug expenditures, such as colony-stimulating factors, antiinfectives, cardiac agents, and drugs used in critical care settings. An abundance of literature supports the success of TI programs, both in terms of quality patient outcomes and economic benefit. Based on the literature, therapeutic classes offering the most opportunity for success with the medical staff, as well as significant cost savings, include histamine-2 antagonists, fluoroquinolones, hydroxymethylglutaryl–coenzyme A reductase inhibitors, serotonin antagonists, colony-stimulating factors, low molecular weight heparins, and proton pump inhibitors.[20–27] Although it is not the intent of these guidelines to delineate an exhaustive list of all potential TI opportunities, the appendix contains examples of the TIs that have proven successful.

Most of the evaluative studies on TI initiatives focus on the economic value and quality improvement related to standardization and formulary management. As the popularity of TI programs increases in the acute care, managed care, and ambulatory settings, an associated risk may also increase due to substitutions along the continuum of care and patient confusion regarding drug classes and duplicative therapy.[28,29] The Joint Commission standard requiring medication reconciliation can be partially traced to anecdotal reports of the potential for medication errors as a result of TI programs in various health care settings.[29] Pharmacists can play a vital role in supporting medication-reconciliation activities through medication history assessments and discharge counseling.[30,31]

Guidelines. A variety of terms are used to describe these tools, including prescribing guidelines, therapeutic position statements, therapeutic guidelines, clinical practice guidelines, protocols, or pathways. There may be subtle differences beween these tools, but they all seek to enhance patient safety, reduce variation in medical practice, and increase standardization.

Guidelines can focus on a disease state, a therapeutic class, or a specific drug.[32] Published guidelines are available for many drugs and drug classes.[33,34] The Agency for Health Care Research and Quality maintains an extensive online collection of published guidelines at www.guideline.gov. A 2004 ASHP survey found that 83% of U.S. hospitals use guidelines that include medications.[35] Successful implementation of such general guidelines often requires customization to meet the needs of individual health systems, however. For example, local guidelines should be developed that reflect the best available evidence, incorporate the opinions of local prescriber experts when necessary, and are applicable within the context of the individual health system.

Guidelines are also an important step leading to rules-based computerized prescriber order entry (CPOE), which is recommended by NQF in its 2006 Safe Practices.[36] CPOE facilitates guideline adherence during the ordering process.

Steps to implementing an effective pharmaceutical cost-containment program using drug-specific or drug class guidelines mirror those for TI and include:

- Utilization of evidence-based criteria,
- Adoption of published, evidence-based, and peer-reviewed guidelines from national organizations,
- Solicitation of thought leaders and clinical experts (e.g., physician specialists, chiefs of service, chief medical officers),
- Review and approval of the P&T committee,
- Education of clinical staff,
- Ongoing support from front line clinical pharmacist staff,
- Use of quantifiable measures, and
- Utilization of medication-use evaluation (MUE) to determine compliance.

The last step is an important distinction between TI and guidelines because what is approved by the medical staff and what is done in practice may differ. Conducting periodic MUEs with the approved criteria can determine the thoroughness and consistency of the guidelines and ultimately the success of this component of cost management. It should also be emphasized that although guidelines can be used to reduce drug costs, improving quality of care may require more spending rather than less.

When guidelines reduce inappropriate prescribing, drug costs will also be reduced. Due to the complex uses of some drugs and drug classes, such as low-molecular-weight heparins, guidelines may be more practical and effective in managing drug costs than TI and other approaches.[37] Drotrecogin alfa was one costly agent for which guidelines became the standard of care in most acute care settings.[38–40] Other successful guideline efforts have been demonstrated with a number of drugs and drug classes, such as third-generation cephalosporins,[41] statins,[42] antifungals,[43, 44] albumin,[45] and serotonin-receptor antagonists.[46] Drug shortages can also be an impetus for the development and implementation of guidelines, as was the case with the use of parenteral pantoprazole, which may be used inappropriately and at a much higher cost in place of histamine-2 antagonists for stress ulcer prophylaxis.[47] Although volatile anesthetic agents are often a top-20 item in the pharmaceutical budget and offer a unique challenge for guidelines or TI implementation, accurate evaluation of cost savings can be accomplished by using the hourly cost to maintain a minimum alveolar concentration.[48]

Implementation of Medication Utilization Management Initiatives. Careful thought and attention to the implementation is required to successfully influence drug expenditures through medication utilization initiatives, and multifaceted interventions are often necessary. The active involvement and support of clinical pharmacists and the medical staff are crucial to effective implementation of these initiatives. It is necessary to seek out ways to integrate or hard-wire initiatives such as guidelines and TI into the care provided at the bedside. For example, passive guideline dissemination (e.g., simply posting to the hospital's intranet site) is rarely successful. Protocols, order sets, and pathways that reflect the evidence in the guideline should be used to integrate the guideline into daily patient care. The growing use of CPOE systems and other technologies can also be leveraged to implement medication-utilization-management endeavors. CPOE can be used to guide prescribing in such straightforward ways as leading prescribers to select formulary products or recommended dosing frequencies.[49] CPOE can also promote efficient medication use through more complex scenarios such as prompting therapeutic interchanges or requiring prescribers to follow interactive prescribing guidelines. For example, one institution established guidelines for activated protein C use and utilized an interactive computer order entry algorithm to implement the guideline.[50]

Data Analysis. To ensure the validity of the medication-utilization-management program, regardless of the method of implementation, the estimated and actual cost savings calculations must be grounded in accurate and consistent data analysis. Unfortunately, there is no standard regarding a method to determine the pharmaceutical cost savings with programs such as TI. Hospitals have struggled for years to balance practical considerations while striving for accuracy and completeness.[20] Hospitals have to decide early in the process whether to consider indirect costs such as devices and other non-pharmaceuticals, price changes during the review period, general drug price inflation, volume changes, and labor costs.

Equivalent doses for all drug alternatives for each TI must be established based on scientific evidence and current practice standards, which may not be the same as FDA-approved manufacturers' recommendations. Most of the references cited for TI above list the therapeutic equivalence for the drugs in a specific class. *Days of therapy* is the common method to compare equivalent costs of drug therapy within a therapeutic class, particularly for antibiotics and other classes that include scheduled drugs that are dosed multiple times per day. For classes that include drugs with extended half-lives and durations of action, weeks of therapy or cost per course of therapy may be more appropriate. Examples include colony-stimulating factors (e.g., epoetin versus darbopoetin and filgrastim versus pegfilgrastim). Correcting for equivalent strengths, sizes, and units of packaging is another important step in cost-savings calculations, particularly for liquid and parenteral products. The number of standard doses available from a container of liquid medication or a large volume parenteral medication varies based on the size of the container. Medical staff input is important in determining equivalent doses, particularly if there is a divergence between manufacturer's recommendations and published literature on dosing.

Once the methodology of data analysis is established, a drug savings matrix should be developed. This becomes the primary monitoring document that tracks the progress of each initiative based on the changes in utilization. Purchase data is the typical source for maintaining the cost savings matrix, but it is essential to adjust and scrub the data before matrix input. It is important to maintain a consistent common denominator. Utilization increases in certain targeted drugs may be due to patient volume and may be appropriate. Correcting for volume with denominator data and using effective MUE programs will assist with determining actual cost increases. The elements of a standard drug-savings matrix spreadsheet include the initiatives (TI and guidelines), savings targets, baseline purchase dollars corrected for volume, current purchase dollars (after implementation) corrected for volume, and actual savings monthly and year-to-date. It is important to be accurate and include both wholesaler and direct purchases, rebates, and wholesaler discounts.

To maintain commitment to and focus on the process, it is paramount to provide consistent feedback regarding the changes in the cost savings matrix to the P & T committee. Some health systems also establish a reporting structure to another oversight committee, such as a value analysis group or similar body that has overall responsibility for non-labor cost management.

Conclusion

Medication costs continue to rise and will continue to be a target for cost management. Drug costs make up a majority of health-system pharmacy budgets, and budgeting for these expenses is an important function, but longer-term programmatic and policy planning is also essential for successful cost management. An effective plan for medication utilization management must provide the health system with a road map for continuous improvement in pharmaceutical expense containment with specific goals and outcome measures of success. Gathering the data to understand drug expenditures and drug-use patterns is a prerequisite for cost-savings efforts, and constant vigilance and monitoring of these data are required.

A relatively small number of drugs usually makes up the majority of the drug budget. Cost-management efforts focused on these drugs will generally offer the best return. Cost-management strategies that fall completely under the pharmacy department's control (e.g., purchasing and inventory strategies) will be easiest to implement and should be pursued first. Strategies that require an interdisciplinary effort (e.g., use of protocols or guidelines, therapeutic interchange, IV-to-PO switches) can be led by pharmacists with the proper clinical background. Clinical pharmacy services, such as participation in rounds, pharmacokinetic monitoring, and renal dose adjustment, can also reduce drug expenses.

Cost management efforts should be coordinated. The programs should contain a clearly defined and manageable list of cost containment targets with a goal and specific targets for each initiative. Results should be measured and evaluated, and this information should be shared with the interdisciplinary team involved in the effort as well as with health-system administration.

When selecting and implementing drug-cost-management strategies, pharmacists must keep patient safety and the quality of patient care in mind. Cost-management initiatives must never compromise the pharmacy department's ability to provide the best possible care. Fortunately, there are many drug-cost-management opportunities that have little or no potential for detrimental effects on patient care, and efforts to improve appropriate use of a drug or drug class often also offer opportunities for cost containment.

References

1. Hoffman JM, Shah ND, Vermeulen LC, et al. Projecting future drug expenditures—2006. *Am J Health-Syst Pharm.* 2006; 63:123–38.
2. Vogenberg FR, ed. Understanding pharmacy reimbursement. Bethesda, MD: American Society of Health-System Pharmacists; 2005:17–42.
3. ASHP Practice Resource Center for Pharmaceutical Reimbursement. www.ashp.org/s_ashp/cat1c.asp?CID=490&DID=532 (accessed 2007 Sep 10).
4. Clinical Initiative Center interviews. The Advisory Board Company. Washington, DC 2000:20–1.
5. Hoffman JM, Shah ND, Vermeulen LC, et al. Projecting future drug expenditures—2007. *Am J Health-Syst Pharm.* 2007; 64:298–314.

6. Hoffman JM, Shah ND, Vermeulen LC, et al. Projecting future drug expenditures 2004. *Am J Health-Syst Pharm.* 2004; 61:145–58.
7. Hoffman JM, Shah ND, Vermeulen LC, et al. Projecting future drug expenditures 2005. *Am J Health-Syst Pharm.* 2005; 62:149–67.
8. Heffler S, Smith S, Keehan S, et al. U.S. health spending projections for 2004–2014. *Health Aff (Millwood).* 2005; W5:74-WS-85.
9. Rough S, Saenz R. Benchmarking and productivity monitoring: practical strategies for pharmacy managers. www.ashp.org/s_ashp/docs/files/2004Leadership Summary.pdf (accessed 2007 Sep 10).
10. May BE, Herrick JD. Evaluation of drug-procurement alternatives. *Am J Hosp Pharm.* 1984; 41:1373–8.
11. Wetrich JG. Group purchasing: an overview. *Am J Hosp Pharm.* 1987; 44:1581–92.
12. Yost RD. New economics of the pharmaceutical supply chain. *Am J Health-Syst Pharm.* 2005; 62:525–6.
13. Schumock GT, Meek PD, Ploetz PA, et al. Economic evaluations of clinical pharmacy services—1988–1995. *Pharmacotherapy.* 1996; 16:1188–208.
14. Schumock GT, Butler MG, Meek PD, et al. Evidence of the economic benefit of clinical pharmacy services: 1996–2000. *Pharmacotherapy.* 2003; 23:113–32.
15. Bond CA, Raehl CL, Patry RL. Evidence-based core clinical pharmacy services in United States hospitals in 2020: services and staffing. *Pharmacotherapy.* 2004; 24:427–40.
16. Bond CA, Raehl CL. Clinical and economic outcomes of pharmacist-managed aminoglycoside or vancomycin therapy. *Am J Health-Syst Pharm.* 2005; 62:1596–605.
17. Coalition Working Group. Principles of a sound drug formulary system. In: Hawkins BH, ed. Best practices for hospital & health-system pharmacy. Bethesda, MD: American Society of Health-System Pharmacists; 2005:125–8.
18. American Society of Hospital Pharmacists. ASHP guidelines on formulary system management. *Am J Hosp Pharm.* 1992; 49:648–52.
19. Gray T, Bertch K, Galt K, et al. Guidelines for therapeutic interchange - 2004. *Pharmacotherapy.* 2005; 25:1666–80.
20. Schachtner JM, Guharoy R, Medicis JJ, et al. Prevalence and cost savings of therapeutic interchange among U.S. hospitals. *Am J Health-Syst Pharm.* 2002; 59:529–33.
21. Goldwater SH, Milkovich G, Morrison AJ Jr, et al. Comparison of therapeutic interchange with standard educational tools for influencing fluoroquinolone prescribing. *Am J Health-Syst Pharm.* 2001; 58:1740–5.
22. Grace KA, Swiecki J, Hyatt R, et al. Implementation of a therapeutic-interchange clinic for HMG-CoA reductase inhibitors. *Am J Health-Syst Pharm.* 2002; 59:1077–82.
23. Steiner MA, Yorgason RZ, Vermeulen LC, et al. Patient outcomes after therapeutic interchange of dolasetron for granisetron. *Am J Health-Syst Pharm.* 2003; 60: 1023–8.
24. Stull DM, Bilmes R, Kim H, et al. Comparison of sargramostim and filgrastim in the treatment of chemotherapy-induced neutropenia. *Am J Health-Syst Pharm.* 2005; 62:83–7.
25. Bollinger KA, Vermeulen LC, Davis SN, et al. Comparative effectiveness of low-molecular-weight heparins after therapeutic interchange. *Am J Health-Syst Pharm.* 2000; 57:368–72.
26. Nelson WW, Vermeulen LC, Geurkink EA, et al. Clinical and humanistic outcomes in patients with gastroesophageal reflux disease converted from ome-prazole to lansoprazole. *Arch Intern Med.* 2000; 160:2491–6.
27. Sodorff MM, Galt KA, Galt MA, et al. Patient perceptions of a proton pump inhibitor therapeutic interchange program across the continuum of care. *Pharmacotherapy.* 2002; 22:500–12.
28. Carroll NV. Formularies and therapeutic interchange: the health care setting makes a difference. *Am J Health-Syst Pharm.* 1999; 56:467–72.
29. Rodehaver C, Fearing D. Medication reconciliation in acute care: ensuring an accurate drug regimen on admission and discharge. *Jt Comm J Qual Patient Saf.* 2005; 31:406–13.
30. Gleason KM, Groszek JM, Sullivan C, et al. Reconciliation of discrepancies in medication histories and admission orders of newly hospitalized patients. *Am J Health-Syst Pharm.* 2004; 61:1689–95.
31. Saunders SM, Tierney JA, Forde JM, et al. Implementing a pharmacist-provided discharge counseling service. *Am J Health-Syst Pharm.* 2003; 60:1101,6,9.
32. American Society of Health-System Pharmacists. ASHP guidelines on the pharmacist's role in the development, implementation, and assessment of critical pathways. *Am J Health-Syst Pharm.* 2004; 61:939–45.
33. American Society of Health-System Pharmacists therapeutic position statements. www.ashp.org/s_ashp/cat1c.asp?CID=516&DID=558 (accessed 2007 Sep 10).
34. American Society of Health-System Pharmacists therapeutic guidelines. www.ashp.org/s_ashp/cat1c.asp?CID=516&DID=559 (accessed 2007 Sep 10).
35. Pedersen CA, Schneider PJ, Scheckelhoff DJ. ASHP national survey of pharmacy practice in hospital settings: prescribing and transcribing—2004. *Am J Health-Syst Pharm.* 2005; 62:378–90.
36. Safe practices for better healthcare: 2006 Update: A Consensus Report. Washington, DC: National Quality Forum (NQF). 2006:22.
37. Schumock GT, Nutescu EA, Walton SM, et al. Survey of hospital policies regarding low-molecular-weight heparins. *Am J Health-Syst Pharm.* 2002; 59:534–8.
38. Bernard GR, Vincent JL, Laterre PF, et al. Efficacy and safety of recombinant human activated protein C for severe sepsis. *N Engl J Med.* 2001; 344:699–709.
39. Matthay MA. Severe sepsis—a new treatment with both anticoagulant and antiinflammatory properties. *N Engl J Med.* 2001; 344:759–62.
40. Thompson CA. High-cost sepsis drug forces pharmacists to weigh patients' future. *Am J Health-Syst Pharm.* 2002; 59:692,697. News.
41. Dranitsaris G, Spizzirri D, Pitre M, et al. A randomized trial to measure the optimal role of the pharmacist in promoting evidence-based antibiotic use in acute care hospitals. *Int J Technol Assess Health Care.* 2001; 17:171–80.

42. Fugit RV, Resch ND. Conversion of patients from simvastatin to lovastatin in an outpatient pharmacy clinic. *Am J Health-Syst Pharm.* 2000; 57:1703–8.
43. Mazzola JL, Belliveau PP, Cheeseman SH. Guidelines for liposomal amphotericin B. *Am J Health-Syst Pharm.* 2003; 60:1480–1.
44. Bower AN, Tang HM, Guglielmo BJ. Compliance in two medical centers with criteria for use of caspofungin and lipid-based amphotericin B. *Am J Health-Syst Pharm.* 2004; 61:915–20.
45. Vermeulen LC Jr, Ratko TA, Erstad BL, et al. A paradigm for consensus. The University Hospital Consortium guidelines for the use of albumin, nonprotein colloid, and crystalloid solutions. *Arch Intern Med.* 1995; 155:373–9.
46. Lucarelli CD. Formulary management strategies for type 3 serotonin receptor antagonists. *Am J Health-Syst. Pharm.* 2003; 60:(10, suppl)S4–S11.
47. Devlin JW. Proton pump inhibitors for acid suppression in the intensive care unit: formulary considerations. *Am J Health-Syst Pharm.* 2005; 62:(10, suppl 2):24–30.
48. Chernin EL. Pharmacoeconomics of inhaled anesthetic agents: considerations for the pharmacist. *Am J Health-Syst Pharm.* 2004; 61:(suppl 4)S18–S22.
49. Teich JM, Merchia PR, Schmiz JL, et al. Effects of computerized physician order entry on prescribing practices. *Arch Intern Med.* 2000; 160:2741–7.
50. Fischer MA, Lilly CM, Churchill WW, et al. An algorithmic computerised order entry approach to assist in the prescribing of new therapeutic agents: case study of activated protein C at an academic medical centre. *Drug Saf.* 2004; 27:1253–61.

Appendix—Therapeutic Interchanges, Prescribing Guidelines, and Other Interventions

Therapeutic Interchanges

The following are some examples of drugs and drug classes for which health systems have successfully implemented therapeutic interchange protocols:

Angiotensin-converting-enzyme inhibitors
Adenosine–dipyridamole for cardiac stress test
Amphotericin, lipid-based
Angiotensin-receptor blockers
Benzodiazepine hypnotics
Beta-lactamase inhibitor antibiotics
Cephalosporins: first- (oral), second-, and third-generation
Cholesterol-lowering agents
Colony-stimulating factors (filgrastim and sargramostim, darbopoetin and epoetin alfa)
Fluroquinolones
Glycoprotein IIb/IIIa inhibitors
Hepatitis B vaccine, pediatric strength
Histamine H_2-receptor antagonists
Inhaled and intranasal corticosteroids
I.V. immune globulin
Insulins – various, including insulin aspart and insulin lispro
Iron products, injectable
Low-molecular-weight heparins
Narcotic analgesics (fentanyl group) in anesthesia
Neuromuscular blocking agents
Nonbenzodiazepine hypnotics
Proton-pump inhibitors
Respiratory agents (tiotropium interchanged with albuterol–ipratropium [Combivent, Boehringer Ingelheim], albuterol–ipratropium [Duoneb, Day] interchanged with individual drugs)
Respiratory spacers
Selective serotonin-reuptake inhibitors
Serotonin-receptor antagonists
Surfactants for newborns
Thrombolytics
Viscoelastic agents

Generic Substitutions

Generic products should be used routinely with few exceptions. The following are particularly important for cost savings:

Amiodarone
Fluconazole injection
Megestrol
Milrinone
Pamidronate
Propofol

Prescribing Guidelines

The following are some examples of drugs, drug classes, and diseases for which health-systems have developed prescribing guidelines, protocols, or pathways in collaboration with the medical staff and nursing staff.

Albumin
Anesthesia gas, low flow and guidelines for selection
Antibiotic surgical prophylaxis
Antibiogram and antibiotic guidelines
Antifungal (injectable) agents (voriconazole, itraconazole, caspofungin)
Aprotinin dosing
Carbapenems
Chemotherapy-induced nausea and vomiting
Colony-stimulating factor guidelines/monitoring
Drotrecogin alfa
Fosphenytoin
Heparin-induced thrombocytopenia
Intensive care unit sedation protocol
I.V. immune globulin
Levalbuterol
Nesiritide
Octreotide
Pneumonia protocol
Postoperative nausea and vomiting
Proton-pump inhibitors (i.v.)
Venous thromboembolism, use of anticoagulants in acute coronary syndrome
Ziprasidone injection

Interventions—Other

Other initiatives or activities that pharmacists can collaborate with the medical staff to reduce drug costs.

Cost per case in anesthesia
Antibiotic monitoring, laboratory reporting of sensitivities
Antibiotic restrictions
Eptifibatide waste reduction
Epoetin alfa waste reduction, prepare syringes
Pegfilgrastim is used in outpatients only

Approved by the ASHP Board of Directors on January 17, 2008. These guidelines supersede the ASHP Technical Assistance Bulletin on Assessing Cost-Containment Strategies dated September 27, 1991. Developed through the ASHP Council on Pharmacy Management.

ASHP gratefully acknowledges the expert panel that developed these guidelines: Michael Rubino, M.S., FASHP; James M. Hoffman, Pharm.D., M.S., BCPS; Larry J. Koesterer, M.B.A.; and Robert G. Swendrzynski, M.S.

The bibliographic citation for this article is as follows: American Society of Health-System Pharmacists. ASHP guidelines on medication cost management strategies for hospitals and health systems. *Am J Health-Syst Pharm.* 2008; 65:1368–84.

ASHP Guidelines on Outsourcing Pharmaceutical Services

Purpose

Health-system pharmacy, as an essential component in health care organizations, is challenged by changes in the structure and financing of health care to reduce costs and improve performance. One option being used to achieve these goals is outsourcing. Outsourcing is a formal arrangement by which a health care organization contracts with an outside company to obtain selected pharmaceutical services or comprehensive management of the organization's pharmacy. Through this arrangement, the organization negotiates a contract with a company to access its expertise, technologies, and resources.

ASHP believes that the organization's pharmacist-in-charge (e.g., a pharmacy director) must take complete responsibility for patient outcomes from all medication-related activities performed at or for the organization's work sites, whether they are carried out by the organization's or contractor's onsite staff or by the contractor off site. This responsibility should be explicitly stated in all outsourcing contracts.

Health care organizations considering outsourcing pharmaceutical services should have a clear understanding of what they want to accomplish. Consideration should include, at the least, an internal needs assessment, a cost analysis, and a careful review of possible contractors. The organization should examine the potential long-term consequences of outsourcing as well as the short-term outcomes expected during a contract's performance period.

The purpose of these guidelines is to provide an overview of factors and processes for health care organizations to consider when exploring outsourcing. The ideas presented in this document could be used for strategic planning with the organization's decision-makers, for drafting contract provisions, for comparing prospective contractors, for preparing for contract negotiations, or for evaluating a contractor's performance. These guidelines may be applied, for example, to independent and networked acute care hospitals, ambulatory care clinics, and home care providers.

This document includes ideas about reasons for outsourcing and reasons for not outsourcing, services available from contractors, the outsourcing process and outsourcing arrangements, and evaluation of contractor performance. The appendix provides a topical list of contract provisions, some of which relate to specific pharmaceutical services, pharmacy practices, or administrative functions that may be the subject of other ASHP practice standards. Organizations should refer to pertinent ASHP practice standards for additional information on which to base their contract provisions, agreements, and decisions. This document addresses representative outsourcing options and contract agreements and is not intended to cover all situations. Managers of pharmacy and health care organizations should use their professional judgment about applicability to their own needs and circumstances.

Environment

Various environmental influences and market forces that may contribute to outsourcing being considered as an option include the following.

Organizational and Operational

- Re-engineering and downsizing initiatives
- Consolidation and integration of health systems and departments within health systems
- Elimination of or reduction in the size of traditional departments
- Reorganization around patient-focused care
- Implementation of automated pharmacy systems and the attendant need to reorganize medication distribution functions

Staffing

- Shortage of nurses and other health care professionals
- Shortage of pharmacists with specific experience and capabilities

Financial and Cost-Control

- Restricted budgets
- Increased operating costs
- Increased drug costs
- Increased emphasis on measuring performance in terms of staffing and costs instead of clinical outcomes

Quality

- Increased expectations of and pressures from accreditation organizations and consumer groups to improve the quality of patient care

Governmental and Regulatory

- Increased numbers of individuals dependent on federal, state, and local governments for health care
- Reduced ability of federal, state, and local governments to finance health care
- Increased government controls on reimbursement for health care

Competitive

- Increased competition among health care organizations
- Increased competition among suppliers of pharmaceutical products and related services

Purposes of Outsourcing

Health care organizations that conduct in-depth assessments may decide that outsourcing either is or is not a good option for meeting their needs. Reasons for their decision will vary according to a variety of factors.

Reasons Health Care Organizations Outsource Pharmaceutical Services. Organizations tend to outsource pharmaceutical services when guided by a careful assessment of their capabilities of providing services themselves, when unsuccessful in using their own resources to provide services, or, in some cases, when influenced by a consultant. Contracting with an outsourcing firm may produce one or more of the following results.

Organizational and operational

- Ease the consolidation of pharmaceutical services in integrated health systems
- Resolve operational inefficiencies (e.g., by improving medication distribution systems, designing new pharmacy workspaces, reducing medication dispensing and administration errors, and improving computer and information systems)
  - Enable the organization to acquire additional resources and expertise to carry out other changes (e.g., reallocation of existing staff to pharmaceutical care roles in patient care areas)
  - Provide educational programs for patients and their families and for health care staff

Staffing

- Help the organization to staff hard-to-fill pharmacy positions
- Allow the organization to reach optimal staffing levels for achieving productivity targets

Financial and cost-control

- Control or reduce the cost of the organization's services
- Control or reduce labor costs (e.g., by shifting the cost of employees, benefits, and liabilities to a contractor)
- Enable the organization to acquire a contractor who will share the risks associated with operating the pharmaceutical services
- Avoid the cost of purchasing and maintaining pharmacy equipment
- Avoid the cost of physical remodeling (e.g., by using an offsite contractor to provide specific services for which remodeling would be required)
- Increase the organization's financial operating margin (e.g., by allowing the organization to purchase drugs in bulk quantities, use group purchasing contracts, decrease lost charges, improve billing accuracy, decrease drug diversion and pilferage, improve drug formularies, and transfer drug inventory, equipment, and supply activities to a contractor)

Quality

- Enable the organization to maintain or improve the quality of patient care (e.g., by expanding clinical services and pharmaceutical care, establishing new services, and obtaining specialized expertise in pharmaceutical care)
- Provide support for the medical and nursing staffs and improve physician–nursing–pharmacy collaboration

Governmental and regulatory

- Correct regulatory and accreditation problems relating to pharmaceutical services
- Ensure continuing compliance with accreditation and certification standards

Competitive

- Enhance the organization's image
- Allow the organization to gain an edge on competitors through improvements in service, quality, or price

Reasons Health Care Organizations Do Not Outsource Pharmaceutical Services. An organization's choice to continue providing its own pharmaceutical services may be based on one or more of the following reasons.

Organizational and operational

- A belief that pharmaceutical services are well managed and are provided as effectively as or better than they could be by a contractor
- Negative experiences with outsourcing contractors (pharmacy or nonpharmacy) or awareness of other organizations' negative experiences with such contractors
- Concern that the decision to outsource pharmaceutical services can be reversed only with great difficulty
- A belief that the organization's needs are currently met cost-effectively and that changes are therefore unnecessary
- Concern about losing short-term and long-term control over decisions about pharmaceutical services
- Concern about reduced involvement of pharmacy leadership in organizationwide initiatives (e.g., development and implementation of information systems, clinical care plans or pathways, and disease management)

Staffing

- Concern that staff will be reduced to unacceptable levels
- Concern about potentially alienating relationships between pharmacists and other health care staff

Financial and cost-control

- An assessment that outsourcing would increase rather than decrease costs
- Concern that high-cost drugs might be excluded from contract agreements
- Concern that the organization may not be able to recapitalize pharmaceutical services if outsourcing is unsuccessful

Quality

- Concern that conflicting values and priorities of the outsourcing contractor and the organization will reduce quality
- Concern that clinical quality could be reduced as a result of a loss of continuity of pharmacy staffing and relationships with medical and nursing staffs

Professional responsibility

- Concern that outsourcing will confuse or dilute the on-site pharmacists' ultimate professional authority and responsibility for all medication-related activities and outcomes at the site

Pharmaceutical Services Provided by Contractors

Some contractors manage and provide comprehensive pharmaceutical services. Other contracors focus more on providing specialty services or carrying out specific tasks (e.g., drug information services, offsite preparation of sterile products). The needs of the health care organization should guide the identification of potential contractors with the appropriate expertise and capabilities. Examples of services that may be available from contractors follow. (This list is likely to grow over time.)

Organizational and Operational

- Development of pharmacy policies, procedures, and processes
- Pharmacy record-keeping systems
- Productivity reviews
- Feasibility studies on expanding services (e.g., outpatient dispensing and home infusion)
- Unit dose medication distribution
- Pharmacy-based or offsite preparation of sterile products
- Pharmacokinetic monitoring and dosage determinations
- Medication therapy monitoring (e.g., for appropriate and effective use)
- Investigational drug programs
- Patient profile reviews
- Medication therapy-related consultation with physicians, nurses, and other health care professionals
- Assessment of patients' nutritional needs
- Guidance in purchasing and implementing automated pharmacy equipment
- Educational programs for patients, families, and caregivers
- Drug information services
- Packaging and repackaging of pharmaceuticals

Staffing

- Competency assessment and performance review
- Management, operational, and clinical training
- Recruitment and retention assistance

Financial and Cost-Control

- Billing
- Inventory control
- Formulary management

Quality

- Performance improvement (including improvement of medication use and reduction of medication errors)
- Quality assurance

Outsourcing Process

After the health care organization has completed an internal assessment of its needs and capabilities and decided to explore outsourcing, it should identify and contact reputable and experienced contractors. Some organizations simply identify prospective contractors and ask them to submit a proposal. A more thorough approach is to require prospective contractors to respond to a request for proposals (RFP). Although a formal RFP (and the contractor's formal proposal based on the RFP) may not be necessary, the information found in typical RFPs and proposals may be helpful for making a decision about outsourcing.

Contents of RFPs. RFPs often include the following information.

- A description of the organization (including statistical information)
- The organization's financial status (e.g., a current balance sheet and audited financial statement, the pharmacy's financial status)
- A description of the process the organization will use to select the contractor
- The organization's standard terms and conditions for contracting for services
- The names and telephone numbers of individuals in the organization who are involved in the outsourcing decision (the director of pharmacy should be included)
- A description of the specific outsourced services required of the contractor (e.g., pharmacy workspace design, intravenous admixture preparation, and implementation of an automated pharmacy system) and performance-measurement criteria or targets
- The date(s) on which the contractor can inspect the facility and the pharmacy
- The number of copies of the proposal to submit
- The name and address of the individual to whom the proposal is to be delivered
- Acceptable method(s) for delivery of the proposal (e.g., mail, delivery service, courier)
- A statement that the organization reserves the right to cancel its solicitation for services and reject any and all proposals
- A deadline date and time for receipt of the proposal
- The date on which the contractor would be expected to initiate services
- The date by which the selected contractor must provide a written contract
- Other requirements related to the proposal (e.g., that it be typewritten, that it include reference to an RFP number [if any], that it be signed by an officer of the firm who is authorized to contract)

Contents of Proposals. RFPs often require contractors to submit the following information with their proposals.

- A brief history of the contractor, including its mission, vision, and values
- The location of the contractor's offices and other facilities that would provide services to the organization
- The names, addresses, telephone numbers, and résumés or background information on the individual(s) who will provide the services
- Evidence that the contractor can provide qualified staff who are licensed or eligible for licensure by federal, state, and local agencies and a history of turnover in management, pharmacist, and support staff
- A history of the results of Joint Commission on Accreditation of Healthcare Organizations (JCAHO), Health Care Financing Administration, National Committee for Quality Assurance, state, or other accreditation or regulatory surveys conducted in the contractor's sites
- Proof of professional liability, general liability, and workers'-compensation insurance coverage (including the name, address, and telephone number of the insurance company) and a history of claims filed against the contractor
- Minimum-experience requirements (e.g., years of experience in providing outsourced pharmacy-management services, total number of clients served, current number of clients)

- A list of the requested services that the contractor can provide
- A list of the requested services that the contractor cannot provide and the reasons for the contractor's inability to provide them
- Evidence of organizational and staff experience and competence (including nature and extent) in the services the contractor can provide (e.g., pharmaceutical care, specialty clinical practice, antineoplastic medication preparation, enteral and parenteral nutrition solution preparation), as pertinent
- A copy of a standard or proposed contract
- A list of all fees and charges that would be billed under the contract and the detailed methods for their calculation, as well as a billing schedule
- A description of reports that the contractor will be expected to submit to the organization
- Information relating to the contractor's financial status and stability (e.g., balance sheets and audited financial statements for the past three years, bank references, lists of principal equity owners)
- The names, addresses, and telephone numbers of current clients receiving similar services
- The names, addresses, and telephone numbers of other clients served within the past two years and the reasons for all, if any, terminations of services
- Written references and copies of annual performance-improvement reports from clients of a similar size with similar types of patients

Visits to Contractors and Their Clients. Contractors should allow the organization's representatives to visit their corporate offices and production facilities and to tour pharmacies in the facilities of other clients. The contractor should provide ample opportunity for the organization's representatives to confer with the contractor's corporate and pharmacy staff.

Evaluating Proposals. A decision to outsource pharmaceutical services should be collaborative and should involve, as appropriate, the governing board, the chief executive officer (CEO), the chief financial officer (CFO), the chief operating officer (COO), the chief of the medical staff, the chair of the pharmacy and therapeutics committee, the director of nursing (DON), the director of pharmacy, and department heads, for example. The organization should scrutinize the following factors when evaluating proposals.

- Services offered versus services requested (including the contractor's ability to enhance current services)
- Professional experience (e.g., years of service; number, size, and types of clients; knowledge of the client's business)
- Financial stability (e.g., ability to absorb start-up expenses and to commit the resources needed to effect change)
- References and reputation (e.g., client-satisfaction reports, reputation in the health care industry, commitment to improving patient care)
- Technology or automated pharmacy systems (e.g., up-to-date hardware, proprietary software, the capability to interface with the organization's information systems)
- Education and training (e.g., internal and external continuing-education programs, educational allowances for professional and technical staff)
- Additional qualities (e.g., high employee morale, confidentiality, creativity, sensitivity to minorities and the community, willingness to share risks and rewards)
- Cost aspects of services (e.g., cost-effectiveness, ability to affect economies of scale)

The organization should assign an evaluation rating to each proposal. Ratings should be weighted appropriately with respect to professional services, experience, references, and cost of services. The organization should base its decision to outsource pharmaceutical services on its assessment of the contractor's ability to meet the organization's needs and fulfill the terms of the contract.

Negotiating the Contract. The organization should carefully review the proposal and clarify the provisions of the contract. Assistance from the organization's risk-management and legal counsel may be necessary. Negotiations can ensure a contract that best meets the needs of the organization and the contractor.

Signing the Contract. In some organizations the director of pharmacy may be authorized to sign contracts for outsourced services. If this is not the case, the director of pharmacy should be fully involved in negotiating the contract and advising the authorized signer(s).

Outsourcing Arrangement

The health care organization and the contractor should agree on the outsourcing arrangement that best meets their needs. Several outsourcing options are available to health care organizations. Variations and combinations of these options are common. The contract should clearly describe the outsourcing arrangement. Examples of outsourcing arrangements include the following.

Consulting. The contractor acts as a pharmacy consultant to the organization. Some consulting arrangements are limited to an assessment of all pharmaceutical services or to specific aspects of pharmaceutical services (e.g., clinical pharmacy services, productivity, compliance with JCAHO standards). Other consulting arrangements may include advising the pharmacy and helping it to improve its services.

Onsite Advisor. The contractor provides a full-time onsite advisor to the organization's director of pharmacy. The advisor works with the director of pharmacy and others, as needed, to carry out programs that will fulfill the contract provisions.

Management of Specific Pharmaceutical Services. The contractor provides one or more specific services (e.g., i.v. admixture preparation, drug information, stock replenishment, medication distribution). Services may be provided onsite or at an offsite location.

Comprehensive Management. The contractor assumes complete responsibility for operating the pharmacy and may provide some or all of the pharmacy staff.

Contract Provisions

A contract that meets the needs of the health care organization and of the contractor is the foundation for a successful relationship. Contracts should include provisions of the outsourcing arrangement that describe agreements between the organization and the contractor concerning their respective responsibilities. These provisions will vary depending on the kind and scope of services outsourced. For example, contractors who prepare sterile products at an offsite location will not require onsite pharmacy space and utilities. Also, the assignment of responsibilities may vary. A contract may specify that the organization will purchase all drugs. Conversely, another contract may assign this responsibility to the contractor. See the appendix for examples of contract provisions.

Evaluation of Contractor's Performance

Health care organizations should evaluate and document their contractor's performance and assess their contractor's compliance with the terms of the contract. Objective and subjective evaluations should be regular (e.g., quarterly or annually). Evaluations should address all measurable standards of performance that are specified in the contract. Evaluations should be multidisciplinary and should involve, for example, the CEO, CFO, COO, DON, and medical staff representatives, as appropriate. An evaluation may include an assessment of how well the contractor performed the following functions.

- Improved the quality of patient care
- Responded to the organization's needs
- Helped the organization to achieve its financial and patient-outcome goals
- Evaluated the productivity and performance of pharmacy staff
- Provided continuing education for pharmacy staff
- Implemented and improved pharmacy clinical programs
- Improved pharmacy processes (e.g., medication dispensing and delivery)
- Reduced and controlled pharmacy costs without compromising patient care
- Worked and communicated effectively with the organization's staff and resolved interdepartmental problems
- Participated effectively in the organization's performance-improvement program

Suggested Reading

1. Curtis FR, Stai HC. Contract pharmacy services. In: Brown TR, ed. Handbook of institutional pharmacy practice, 3rd ed. Bethesda, MD: American Society of Hospital Pharmacists; 1992: 299–306.
2. Talley CR. Outsourcing drug distribution. *Am J Health-Syst Pharm.* 1997; 54:37. Editorial.
3. Schneider PJ. Outsourcing: a key to professional survival. *Am J Health-Syst Pharm.* 1997; 54:41–3.
4. Lazarus HL. Outsourcing: a success story. *Am J Health-Syst Pharm.* 1997; 54:43–4.
5. Puckett WH. Outsourcing: taking the first step. *Am J Health-Syst Pharm.* 1997; 54:45–8.
6. Kolar GR. Outsourcing: route to a new pharmacy practice model. *Am J Health-Syst Pharm.* 1997; 54:48–52.
7. Eckel FM. Outsourcing: at odds with pharmacy's professional foundation. *Am J Health-Syst Pharm.* 1997; 54:52–5.
8. Gates DM, Smolarek RT, Stevenson JG. Outsourcing the preparation of parenteral nutrient solutions. *Am J Health-Syst Pharm.* 1996; 53:2176–8.
9. Burruss RA, Carroll NV, Schraa C, et al. Outsourcing inpatient IV compounding: expense and medication error implications. *Pharm Pract Manage Q.* 1996; 16(3):52–9.
10. McAllister JC III. Collaborating with re-engineering consultants: maintaining resources for the future. *Am J Health-Syst Pharm.* 1995; 52:2676–80.
11. Anderson RJ. Clinical service contracts between hospital pharmacy departments and colleges of pharmacy. *Am J Hosp Pharm.* 1991; 48:1994–7.
12. Murphy JE, Ward ES, Job ML. Implementing and maintaining a private pharmacokinetics practice. *Am J Hosp Pharm.* 1990; 47:591–7.
13. Souhrada L. Contract management. *Hospitals.* 1990; 64(8):66–8.
14. Wagner M. Basic pitfalls can undermine hospital–service firm relationship. *Mod Healthc.* 1993; 23(8):32.
15. Wagner M. Contract-managed pharmacy departments are just the prescription at some hospitals. *Mod Healthc.* 1988; 18(8):36–40.

Appendix—Contract Provisions

The following are examples of contract provisions that, among others, the organization and contractor might adapt as needed and include in a contract, depending on the scope of services being considered. In addition, a contract would include provisions about the specific pharmaceutical services to be provided by the contractor. The language in contract provisions should be adapted to meet the needs of the health care organization and to comply with the organization's contracting policies and applicable laws and regulations.

Accreditation and Certification: A contract may include a requirement that services meet or exceed applicable accreditation and certification standards. These include, but are not limited to, the standards (or requirements) of the following organizations.

- Joint Commission on Accreditation of Healthcare Organizations
- American Osteopathic Association
- Health Care Financing Administration
- National Committee for Quality Assurance

After-Hours Pharmaceutical Services when 24-Hour Services Are Not Provided: The contractor may agree, for example, to provide an after-hours stock of drug products for authorized staff to use in filling urgent medication orders. In addition, the contractor may agree to ensure that a pharmacist is on call or available to return to the facility to provide pharmaceutical services.

Automation: A contract may outline responsibilities for the purchase or lease and the use of automated medication storage and distribution equipment and software associated with the equipment.

Choice of Law: There may be a statement that the contract is governed by the laws of the state in which patient care is provided.

Compensation for Contractor's Services: There may be compensation arrangements, which vary greatly but are often based on one or more of the following principles.

- Management fee(s)
- Fee per item dispensed or service performed
- Fixed fee per patient per patient day, admission, discharge, adjusted patient day, adjusted admission, or adjusted discharge

Besides agreeing on a compensation arrangement, the organization and the contractor may agree on ways for the contractor to share the financial risk of contract performance with the organization; these might include guarantees or incentives for meeting targets and penalties for underperformance.

Computer Equipment and Information Systems: A contract may outline responsibilities for the purchase, ownership, and maintenance of computer equipment and related software. Agreements might extend to personal computers used by pharmacy staff. There should be clear agreement about access to and use of data generated by the information system.

Confidentiality: There may be a requirement that information not generally available to the public (e.g., financial statements, medical records, market information) be kept confidential. Both parties must agree to safeguard access to computer databases and patient records to ensure that the patient's rights to privacy and confidentiality is protected. Use of the information should be limited solely to purposes specified in the contract.

Contractor Reports: The content and regularity of performance reports that the contractor will submit to the organization may be specified.

Controlled Substances: Responsibilities may be assigned for the procurement and security of controlled substances in compliance with Drug Enforcement Administration (DEA) and state regulations. For example, the organization may be required to

- Register with the DEA and any state equivalent for each site involved
- Assume complete responsibility for record keeping and security of controlled substances throughout the facility
- Ask the contractor to maintain proper records and provide adequate security for controlled substances as required by federal, state, and local laws and regulations and
- Verify that the contractor maintains proper records and provides adequate security for controlled substances

It may be necessary for the organization to grant power of attorney to the contractor to order and purchase controlled substances.

Similarly, the contractor may be required to

- Ensure that all registrations are current
- Order and maintain an adequate stock of controlled substances
- Ensure compliance with record-keeping and security requirements
- Inform the organization of problems with compliance

Cost Control: A contract may include objectives, methods, and performance measures for controlling costs.

Cytotoxic and Hazardous Drug Products: Responsibilities for ensuring the safety of the organization's staff and patients during the preparation and distribution of cytotoxic and hazardous drug products may be assigned. Either the organization or the contractor should provide a hazardous-materials handling program, including staff training, that meets Occupational Safety and Health Administration (OSHA) requirements.

Drug Inventory Disposition upon Termination of the Contract: A provision for the disposition of the drug inventory is based on inventory ownership. In cases in which the drug inventory may be purchased by either party, a mutually acceptable, independent appraiser could decide the purchase price. Legal advice may be needed to ensure that purchases comply with the Prescription Drug Marketing Act and other applicable laws and regulations.

Drug Inventory Ownership: If the contractor purchases the organization's inventory, a mutually acceptable, independent appraiser could decide the purchase price. Expired and other unusable drugs should be excluded from the purchase. The contractor could agree to obtain credit for the organization for expired and other unusable drugs if credit is obtainable. Legal advice may be needed to ensure that purchases comply with the Prescription Drug Marketing Act and other applicable laws and regulations.

Drug Ordering: A contract may assign responsibilities for selecting vendors and purchasing drug supplies for the organization. The contract should specify that all drugs used must be subject to approval by the organization's pharmacy and therapeutics (P&T) committee or its equivalent. The organization should understand how purchasing discounts are accounted for, recorded, and distributed. The impact of removing pharmacy items from group purchasing programs should be clear also.

Early Termination: There may be conditions for early termination of the contract.

Extension of Period of Performance: Conditions for extending the period of performance may be included in the contract.

Forms: Responsibilities for the design, approval, purchase, and storage of forms may be assigned.

Formulary System: A contract may assign responsibilities for evaluation of medications, collaboration with the P&T committee, and provision of formulary-related information services.

Hours of Pharmacy Operation: A contract may specify hours of operation that meet or exceed legal requirements and that are sufficient to serve patients' needs.

Laws, Rules, and Regulations: Requirements for services to meet or exceed federal, state, and local laws, rules, and regulations may be specified. These include but are not limited to those of FDA, DEA, OSHA, and the state board of pharmacy. The pharmacy should maintain (e.g., display, file) the appropriate licenses, permits, and records of equipment maintenance and certification. Any contractor required to be licensed as a manufacturer must be so licensed. The organization may agree to allow the contractor to act on the organization's behalf in communicating with the state board of pharmacy and other regulatory agencies.

Liability Insurance: Responsibilities for maintaining liability insurance coverage for the acts of employees may be assigned. The contract might specify, for example, that the contractor must maintain adequate liability insurance coverage for the acts of its employees.

Nondiscrimination: There might be a requirement that the contractor abide by all laws and regulations relating to discrimination in appointments, promotions, and terminations.

Ownership of Equipment, Fixtures, and Supplies: A contract may specify ownership of equipment, fixtures, and supplies and responsibilities for ensuring that equipment is maintained and certified according to applicable practice standards, laws, and regulations.

Performance Improvement: Responsibilities for establishing any performance-improvement programs and integrating them with the organization's performance-improvement activities may be included. Performance-improvement programs might be appropriate, for example, for the ordering, dispensing, and administering of medications and for the monitoring of medication effects and misadventures, including adverse drug reactions and adverse drug events.

Period of Performance: The contract might specify the period for which the contractor will provide services to the organization.

Pharmacy Staff Education and Training: Responsibilities for required ongoing staff education and training may be specified. For example, there might be an agreement that the contractor's staff will participate in the organization's education and training programs. In addition, the contractor may agree to provide specific training to ensure that all pharmacy personnel can perform any duties imposed by contractor-implemented functions.

Pharmacy Staff Employment: There may be a provision for the employment of pharmacists and technical and support personnel; this may specify those who will be employed by the organization and those who will be employed by the contractor. Whether employed by the organization or by the contractor, all staff should be competent and legally qualified. The organization should retain the right to assess, accept, or reject the performance of any of the contractor's staff who are used at the organization's work sites.

Pharmacy Staff Expenses: Responsibilities for any personnel expenses may be assigned. A contract might specify, for example, that the organization will be responsible for the salary, wages, and benefits of its employees whereas the contractor will be responsible for such expenses for its own employees. The contract might also allocate expenses for parking, meal discounts, and similar privileges for employees.

Pharmacy Staff Levels: There may be a requirement that the staffing levels for the contracted services be sufficient to meet the organization's needs.

Pharmacy Staff Orientation: A contract may assign responsibilities for orientation of all new pharmacy staff members to the organization and to the pharmacy, according to the organization's requirements.

Pharmacy Staff Performance: Responsibilities for pharmacy staff competency assessments and performance evaluations and for ensuring that assessments and evaluations are based on criteria in the individual's job description may be assigned.

Policies and Procedures: Responsibilities may be assigned for developing policies and procedures covering the outsourced services, all of which should comply with applicable laws, regulations, and accreditation or certification standards. The contract should specify that the policies and procedures must not conflict with those of the organization.

Purchasing and Accounts Payable: Responsibilities for maintaining the pharmacy's purchasing and accounts-payable functions, including ordering drugs, monitoring costs, and authorizing payment to vendors, might be specified.

Record Maintenance: A contract may assign responsibilities for maintaining and storing records. The contract should specify that all pertinent records must be kept for the time required by law and by the organization.

Space: Responsibilities for space required by the contractor to provide onsite services might be outlined. The organization should agree to provide space for the provision of onsite contractor services that is acceptable to the contractor and within the guidelines of the agencies that regulate the practice of pharmacy. Organizations might agree to provide the following facilities, depending on the contract's scope of services.

- Adequate square footage
- Space for preparing, compounding, packaging, and storing drugs under proper conditions
- Space for receiving and storing intravenous fluids and supplies
- Refrigerators and freezers
- Adequate space for maintaining and storing pharmacy records
- Laminar-airflow hoods and biological safety cabinets (if needed)

Sterile Products: A contract might include requirements for the quality of sterile products provided by the contractor. The contractor should ensure that sterile products (e.g., large-volume intravenous admixtures, total parenteral nutrient solutions) are prepared and labeled in a suitable environment by trained and competent employees. The contractor should provide quality-control information periodically and on demand. For services that involve deliveries, the contract should specify order cutoff and delivery times, any penalties for late deliveries, and arrangements for after-hours or emergency services and deliveries.

Successors: The rights of each party in the event that the organization or contractor merges or transfers its business or assets to a successor may be included in a contract.

Utilities: A contract may assign responsibility for utilities required by the contractor to provide onsite services. These utilities may include the following, as appropriate.

- Electrical service
- Water
- Heating and air conditioning
- Plumbing
- Janitorial services
- Internal and external telephone services (allowance might be made for a private external telephone line for the contractor)
- Security
- Waste disposal

These guidelines were reviewed in 2013 by the Council on Pharmacy Management and by the Board of Directors and were found to still be appropriate.

Approved by the ASHP Board of Directors, April 22, 1998. Developed through the Council on Administrative Affairs.

The bibliographic citation for this document is as follows: American Society of Health-System Pharmacists. ASHP guidelines on outsourcing pharmaceutical services. *Am J Health-Syst Pharm.* 1998; 55:1611–7.

ASHP Guidelines on Outsourcing Sterile Compounding Services

Purpose

The purpose of these guidelines is to provide an overview of factors and processes for healthcare organizations to consider when contracting with compounding pharmacies or outsourcing facilities to obtain sterile compounding services. These guidelines describe services available from compounding pharmacies or outsourcing facilities, reasons for outsourcing and reasons for not outsourcing, the outsourcing process and outsourcing arrangements, and recommendations for evaluating a contractor's performance. The guidelines also provide a topical list of contract provisions, some of which relate to practices that are the subject of other ASHP guidelines. Organizations should refer to pertinent ASHP guidelines for additional information on which to base their contract provisions, agreements, and decisions.[1-3] The concepts presented in this document could be used for strategic planning with the organization's decision-makers, assisting in assessing the quality of compounded sterile preparations or products, drafting contract provisions, comparing prospective contractors, preparing for contract negotiations, and evaluating contractor performance.

This document addresses representative outsourcing options and contract agreements and is not intended to cover all situations. Managers of pharmacy and healthcare organizations should use their professional judgment about applicability to their own needs and circumstances.

Services Provided by Vendors of Outsourced Sterile Compounding Services

The Drug Quality and Security Act (DQSA) of 2013 dramatically changed federal regulation of pharmacy compounding.[4] The DQSA amended the federal Food, Drug, and Cosmetic (FD&C) Act, carving out a safe harbor for traditional, prescription-based compounding pharmacies (called "503A compounding pharmacies" for the section of the FD&C Act that regulates them, or, more simply, "compounding pharmacies") and creating a new category of drug establishment, Human Drug Compounding Outsourcing Facilities. These facilities (frequently referred to as "registered 503B outsourcing facilities" for the section of the FD&C Act that regulates them, or, more simply, "outsourcing facilities") are permitted to engage in the manufacture and interstate shipment of larger quantities of compounded sterile drug products without prescriptions or medication orders. (For the purposes of these guidelines, both types of entities are referred to as "vendors of outsourced sterile compounding services" or, simply, "vendors.") The regulatory changes spawned by the DQSA have significant implications for compounding pharmacies, outsourcing facilities, and their customers. Healthcare organizations considering outsourcing sterile compounding services need to have a clear understanding of how these two distinct types of entities are regulated (Table 1).

Compounding Pharmacies. Section 503A clarified the FD&C Act for activities described as traditional patient-specific compounding (sometimes now called "503A compounding"). Healthcare organization pharmacies fall into this category, as do other pharmacies that fill prescriptions or medication orders within a prescriber–pharmacist–patient professional relationship. All 503A compounding pharmacies, except those in federal facilities, are regulated by state boards of pharmacy; however, they may also be subject to Food and Drug Administration (FDA) inspection under the agency's authority to enforce section 503A of the FD&C Act. The agency's expectations for compliance are specified in the FDA *Compliance Policy Guide* (CPG) *on Pharmacy Compounding of Human Drug Products Under Section 503A of the Federal Food, Drug, and Cosmetic Act.*[5] In addition to current regulatory requirements, such as prescriptions or medication orders for compounded preparations and compliance with applicable *United States Pharmacopeia* (*USP*) chapters on compounding (i.e., *USP* chapters 795 and 797),[8,9] inspectors may look for implementation of additional CPG recommendations. The services provided by compounding pharmacies are limited by the existing requirement for individual prescriptions or medication orders and may be further limited by forthcoming regulation of distribution across state lines,[7] state and federal restrictions on office-use preparations, and other limitations of section 503A.

Outsourcing Facilities. Section 503B outsourcing facilities are not required by federal regulation to be licensed pharmacies or to fill prescriptions or medication orders; however, a licensed pharmacist must supervise compounding. Outsourcing facilities are federally regulated by FDA, which has established guidance documents for the industry that will be updated as necessary. Outsourcing facilities must comply with applicable Current Good Manufacturing Practices (CGMPs) established under section 503B by FDA,[6] which differ from those for manufacturers. States may establish additional requirements with which outsourcing facilities must comply. All outsourcing facilities are inspected by FDA. The frequency of reinspections is determined by a risk-based schedule. Inspection findings are documented on form FDA-483, Inspectional Observations. A form FDA-483 is used to notify the entity of any concerns or potential violations and provide an opportunity for correction before enforcement action.[10] The compounding facility may work with inspectors to resolve issues during the inspection or respond in writing with a corrective action plan, usually within 15 days. The contents of these forms are publicly available.[11] However, findings in FDA-483 reports do not represent a final determination of noncompliance, nor is information available indicating that the findings have been satisfactorily resolved.

Healthcare organization pharmacy leaders must be aware of the quality standards that should be expected from outsourcing facilities.[12,13] In a letter sent to hospitals in January 2014, FDA encouraged healthcare organizations

Table 1.

Differences Between Compounding Pharmacies and Outsourcing Facilities[a]

Variable	Section 503A Compounding Pharmacies	Section 503B Registered Outsourcing Facilities
Regulatory authority	State boards of pharmacy	FDA, according to guidelines established by federal legislation; states may add requirements
Applicable standards	*USP* compounding standards; FDA Compliance Policy Guide on Pharmacy Compounding of Human Drug Products Under Section 503A of the Federal Food, Drug, and Cosmetic Act[5]	Applicable section 503B-specific FDA Current Good Manufacturing Practice[6]; subject to additional state requirements
FDA inspection	Subject to FDA inspection under authority to enforce section 503A	Subject to risk-based FDA inspection and enforcement procedures
State inspection	Subject to state board of pharmacy inspection	May be subject to state inspection if state law imposes additional requirements

Limitations on services	• May only dispense pursuant to an individual prescription or medication order for an identified patient
	• Anticipatory compounding of "limited quantities" is permitted, but a prescription or medication order is required before dispensing[5]
	• FDA limitations on interstate distribution, either 5% or 30%, depending on whether the state has entered into an MOU with FDA[b]
	• May not compound
	  • Drugs that present demonstrable difficulties for compounding
	  • Copies of FDA-approved products
	  • Drugs using certain prohibited bulk substances
		• Not required to be a licensed pharmacy or obtain prescriptions for specific patients
		• May compound and maintain inventory of compounded products in anticipation of customer orders
		• No federal limit on interstate commerce; some state regulations may apply
		• Compounding from bulk APIs only allowed for drugs on approved list
		• May compound copies of FDA-approved products from bulk substances if on FDA shortage list

Office-use compounding	Not yet addressed in FDA guidance[5]	Permitted; resale prohibited but "resale" does not include administration or dispensing by the purchaser[4]
Labeling requirements	As mandated by state law and regulation	Must include "Office use," "This is a compounded drug," and "Not for resale"

[a]FDA = Food and Drug Administration, ***USP* = *United States Pharmacopeia***, MOU = memorandum of understanding, API = active pharmaceutical ingredient.

[b]At the time of writing, FDA had not issued final guidance on interstate distribution by section 503A facilities but had proposed a 30% limit on interstate distribution of compounded sterile preparations by section 503A compounding pharmacies in states that had entered into an MOU with FDA and a 5% limit in states that had not entered into an MOU.[7]

to purchase compounded sterile drugs from FDA-registered outsourcing facilities.[14] Although FDA usually inspects an outsourcing facility soon after registration (unless the facility has been inspected previously), pharmacy leaders should be aware that registration does not necessarily mean that a particular outsourcing facility has been inspected and found to meet FDA standards. FDA's website listing registered outsourcing (503B) facilities provides dates of the initial and most recent registration as an outsourcing facility; the end date of the last FDA inspection related to compounding; whether an FDA-483 was issued; whether FDA action was taken, if any, based on the last inspection; and whether the outsourcing facility intends to compound sterile drugs from nonsterile bulk active pharmaceutical ingredients (APIs).[15] Pharmacy leaders should bear in mind that FDA or state inspections only reflect conditions at one particular time and should consider a facility's history as well as its most recent results.

Environmental Influences Affecting Outsourcing Decision

There are various environmental influences and market forces that may contribute to a facility's decision to consider outsourcing sterile compounding services. A list of some of those considerations follows.

Organizational and Operational

- Elimination of or reduction in the size of traditional pharmacy departments, re-engineering, and downsizing initiatives.
- Limited available physical or technological resources (e.g., sterile compounding area, inventory storage area, engineering controls) to provide the specific desired services.

- Consolidation and integration of health systems and departments within health systems, including pressure to provide pharmacy services to acquired entities (e.g., physician practices).
- Implementation of automated pharmacy systems and the attendant need to reorganize medication preparation and distribution functions.
- Inability to cost-effectively perform in-house testing to establish extended beyond-use dating for sterile preparations.
- Federal restriction under section 503A of the DQSA on the distribution of compounded sterile preparations from a central site in the healthcare organization to other campuses of the same system.[a]

Staffing

- Shortage of pharmacy personnel with specific experience and capabilities, especially regarding sterile preparation.
- Lack of resources, experience, or investment to effectively train staff on sterile compounding and aseptic technique.

Financial and Cost Control

- Restricted budgets.
- Increased operating costs.
- Increased drug costs.
- Increased emphasis on measuring performance in terms of staffing and costs.

Drug Shortages

- Unavailability of medications or specific dosage forms.
- Conservation of limited supplies of available medications.

Quality Assurance

- Increased expectations of and pressures from payers, regulatory agencies, accreditation organizations, and consumer groups to improve the quality of patient care, reduce the incidence of hospital infections, and demonstrate compliance with applicable standards and regulations.

Governmental and Regulatory

- Increased federal and state interest in standards for sterile compounding (i.e., *USP* chapter 797[9]).

Competitive

- Increased competition among healthcare organizations.
- Increased competition among suppliers of pharmaceutical products and related services.

Purposes of Outsourcing

Healthcare organizations should conduct an in-depth assessment to decide whether outsourcing is a good option for meeting their needs. Reasons for their decision will vary according to a variety of factors, some of which are outlined below. As with use of other contracted services, hospital leadership must be included in the decision-making process for outsourcing. A decision to outsource sterile compounding services should be collaborative and may involve, as appropriate, the governing board, chief executive officer (CEO), chief financial officer (CFO), chief operating officer (COO), chief of the medical staff, chair of the pharmacy and therapeutics (P&T) committee, director of pharmacy, director of nursing, legal counsel, medication safety officer, risk management director, and department heads.

Reasons Healthcare Organizations Outsource Sterile Compounding Services. Organizations tend to outsource sterile compounding services when guided by a careful assessment of their capabilities of providing services themselves, when unsuccessful in using their own resources to provide those services, or, in some cases, on the advice from a qualified consultant. Contracting with a compounding pharmacy or outsourcing facility may produce one or more of the following results.

Organizational and Operational

- Resolve operational inefficiencies (e.g., batch compounding, staff scheduling, high-demand periods).
- Provide compounded sterile preparations outside the scope of those routinely provided (e.g., complex or rarely compounded sterile preparations).
- Enable the organization to reallocate resources and expertise to carry out other priorities (e.g., reassignment of existing staff to roles in patient care areas).

Staffing

- Allow organizations to acquire quality compounded sterile preparations or products without hiring for hard-to-fill pharmacy positions and to concentrate on other staffing priorities.
- Allow the organization to reach optimal staffing levels for achieving quality and productivity targets.

Financial and Cost Control

- Control or reduce the cost of the organization's services (e.g., by shifting costs associated with sterile compounding services from fixed to variable).
- Control or reduce labor costs (e.g., by shifting responsibility for employees, benefits, and liabilities to a compounding pharmacy or outsourcing facility).
- Enable the organization to acquire a business partner to share the risks and other associated liability by delineating and contracting for the responsibilities associated with operating sterile compounding services.
- Minimize the cost of facility remodeling or maintenance (e.g., to meet *USP* chapter 797[9] or chapter 800[16] requirements).

Quality Assurance

- Provide consistent and high-quality pharmacy and sterile compounding services, including documented or extended beyond-use dating[b] and batch-level sterility, potency, and endotoxin testing.

- Enable the organization to maintain or improve the quality of patient care (e.g., by expanding clinical services or establishing new services).
- Enhance patient safety by providing more medications in a dose-specific, ready-to-administer form.
- Provide support for the medical and nursing staffs and improve prescriber–nursing–pharmacy collaboration.
- Improve organizational procedures by learning from contractors' experience and knowledge, especially with technologies used to improve safety (e.g., labeling, barcoding, or tamper-evident technologies).

Governmental and Regulatory

- Assist and ensure compliance with legal, regulatory, certification, and accreditation requirements.

Reasons Healthcare Organizations Do Not Outsource Sterile Compounding Services. An organization's choice to continue providing its own sterile compounding services may be based on one or more of the following reasons.

Organizational and Operational

- The organization demonstrates that its sterile compounding services meet the requirements and standards of *USP* chapter 797[9]; comply with applicable local, state, and federal regulations; are cost-effective, well managed, and provided as efficiently as or better than services that could be provided by a compounding pharmacy or an outsourcing facility.
- Negative experiences with outsourcing other clinical services, or awareness of other organizations' negative experiences with such outsourcing.
- Concern about time delays in receiving compounded sterile preparations or products, especially ones that are needed urgently or have poor stability or short beyond-use dates (BUDs).
- Concern that the contractor may experience interruptions in service, perhaps with little notice, due to quality-control issues not related to services provided to the organization.
- Concern that the decision to outsource sterile compounding services can be reversed only with great difficulty.
- Concern about losing short- and long-term control over decisions regarding or expertise in sterile compounding services.

Staffing

- Concern that staff will be reduced to unacceptable levels.

Financial and Cost Control

- An assessment that outsourcing would increase rather than decrease costs.
- Concern that high-cost drugs might be excluded from contract agreements.
- Concern that the organization may not be able to recapitalize sterile compounding services if outsourcing is unsuccessful.

Quality Assurance

- Concern that conflicting values and priorities of the contractor and the organization will reduce quality.
- Loss of direct control over quality-assurance procedures for the compounding process.
- Concern about the qualifications or competencies of contractors' pharmacy staff.

Governmental and Regulatory

- Legal, regulatory, certification, and accreditation requirements may hinder operational efficiencies.

Outsourcing Process

The needs of the healthcare organization should guide the identification of potential vendors of outsourced sterile compounding services with the appropriate expertise and capabilities. Among the services that may be available from such vendors are the preparation of implantable and external pump cartridges; total parenteral nutrition; cardiovascular solutions; anesthesia syringes and solutions; dialysis, irrigation, or cardioplegia solutions; continuous renal replacement therapy, hydration, and oxytocin solutions; antibiotics; ophthalmic injectables and solutions; chemotherapy preparations; and analgesic preparations (patient-controlled analgesia, epidural, or regional nerve-block devices).

After the healthcare organization has completed an internal assessment of its needs and capabilities and decided to explore outsourcing, it should identify and contact vendors of outsourced sterile compounding services.

Organizations that are part of a larger network (e.g., an integrated delivery network) may explore options that are available to them through the network or from other organizations in the network. A health system may be exempt from registering as a 503B entity if it compounds medications for the health system's own patients in response to a prescription or medication order or in a "limited quantity" in anticipation of such prescriptions or orders, based on a history of such prescriptions or orders, as long as the pharmacy complies with state laws.[5] This exemption is expected to be clarified by FDA in the future.[13]

Many organizations begin to identify prospective contractors through a request for information (RFI). The RFI should provide

- A short history of the prospective contractor, including number of years in business, number and location of facilities, approximate number of customers served, and approximate volume of compounded sterile products or preparations delivered per month or year.
- The prospective contractor's regulatory status (i.e., compounding pharmacy or registered outsourcing facility) and applicable licensure or registration information (e.g., pharmacy license number).
- Whether the prospective contractor compounds sterile preparations or products from nonsterile bulk APIs (for registered outsourcing facilities, this information is available on FDA Registered Outsourcing Facilities website).[15]

- Description of products and services typically available (e.g., customer support, website), value-added services available (e.g., clinical support), and typical ordering process and turnaround times.
- Representative prices for specified compounded sterile products or preparations and services at an annual unit demand.
- Whether the prospective contractor has any contracts with group purchasing organizations.
- A description of the prospective contractor's backup facility capabilities and business continuity and disaster recovery plans.
- Whether the prospective contractor has ever been the subject of an enforcement or accreditation action.

After prospective contractors have been identified through RFIs, many organizations require them to respond to a more detailed request for proposal (RFP). Although a formal RFP (and the contractor's formal proposal based on the RFP) may not always be necessary, the information found in typical RFPs and prospective contractor responses or proposals is often helpful in making a systematic decision about outsourcing.

Contents of RFPs. RFPs often include the following information:

- A description of the demographics of the organization making the RFP (e.g., number of hospitals, bed sizes, typical census).
- A description of the process the organization will use to select the contractor.
- The organization's standard terms and conditions for contracting for services or, if available, a sample contract from the organization.
- The names and telephone numbers of individuals in the organization who are involved in the outsourcing decision (the organization's director of pharmacy should be included).
- A description of the specific services required of the contractor (e.g., desired drugs, strengths, concentrations, diluents, container systems, annual demand) and performance-measurement criteria or targets. Special packaging, handling, and delivery procedures for hazardous drugs should be included.
- A request for documentation of follow-up and correction of any enforcement or accreditation findings.
- The dates on which the organization's representatives can inspect the contractor's facility, with reasonable notice. (Inspections by the organization's representatives will be more important when contracting with vendors that are not regularly inspected by FDA or state inspectors.)
- The number of copies of the proposal to submit.
- The name and address of the individual to whom the proposal is to be delivered.
- Acceptable methods for delivery of the proposal (e.g., e-mail, mail, delivery service, courier).
- A statement that the organization reserves the right to cancel its solicitation for services and reject any and all proposals for any reason or for no reason.
- A deadline date and time for receipt of the proposal.
- The date on which the contractor would be expected to initiate services.
- The date by which the selected contractor must provide a written contract.
- Other requirements related to the proposal (e.g., that it be in a specific file format, include reference to an RFP number [if any], or be signed by an officer of the firm who is authorized to contract or his or her designee).

Contents of Responses or Proposals. RFPs should require prospective contractors to submit the following information with their responses or proposals:

- A brief history of the contractor, including its mission, vision, and values.
- A history of the results of all regulatory or accreditation surveys conducted of the contractor's sites, including copies of significant regulatory actions.
- The location of the contractor's offices and other facilities that would provide services to the organization.
- The contractor's regular business hours or hours of operation and emergency and after-hours contact information.
- The names, addresses, telephone numbers, and resumés or background information on individuals who will provide the services.
- Assurance that all pharmacists employed at the compounding facility are licensed as required and that all technicians involved in the compounding process are registered (if required by the state or by the healthcare organization's policy).
- Evidence of the following documentation regarding the contractor:
    - Proof and description of coverage of current liability insurance.
    - Current accreditation or certification certificates, if applicable.
    - State pharmacy licensure or other appropriate licenses.
    - Registration with FDA as an outsourcing facility, which can be obtained on FDA's registered outsourcing facilities webpage.[15]
    - Proof of FDA registration as a device manufacturer, if applicable.
    - Current Drug Enforcement Administration (DEA) registration, consistent with federal and state regulations.
    - Licensure of pharmacists employed and verification that they are in good standing, are on file, and available for review.
    - Registration of pharmacy technicians employed and verification that they are in good standing, are on file, and available for review, if applicable.
    - Pharmacist and pharmacy technician notarized statements stating that they have never been convicted of a drug-related misdemeanor or felony or proof of background check, are on file, and available for review.
    - Pharmacist and pharmacy technician training manual are on file and available for review.
    - Standard operating procedures manual are on file and available for review.
    - Certificates of analysis for nonsterile ingredients used in compounding are on file and available for review, if applicable.

  - Policies and procedures for stability testing are on file and available for review.
  - Policies and procedures for sterility assurance testing are on file and available for review.
  - Policies and procedures for pyrogen testing are on file and available for review, if applicable.
  - Examples of batch reports for products being considered for outsourcing are on file and available for review.
  - Examples of the quality-control and quality-assurance reports.
  - Stability documents and clinical references, as well as any materials that are used to determine BUDs on file and available for review. (Because studies used to establish BUDs are sometimes considered proprietary, compounding service providers may require a nondisclosure agreement.)
- Proof of professional liability, general liability, and workers' compensation insurance coverage (including the name, address, and telephone number of the insurance company).
- Experience (e.g., years of experience in providing sterile compounding services, total number of clients served, current number of clients).
- A list of the requested services that the contractor can provide and the normal terms of service, including but not limited to normal delivery cycles, availability and cost of emergency preparation and delivery, remedies for failure to perform to the contract, specific goods and services to be provided, and the infrastructure available at the compounding site for electronic ordering.
- A list of the requested sterile compounding services that the contractor cannot provide and the reasons for its inability to provide them.
- Expectation statements to assist in meeting the Centers for Medicare and Medicaid Services (CMS) requirements[17] and accreditation organization standards[18-23] related to contracted services, if applicable.
- A copy of a standard or proposed contract.
- A list of all fees and charges, including shipping, handling, and delivery charges, and any fees associated with order changes that would be billed under the contract and the billing methodology for their calculation.
- A billing schedule and a copy of a sample bill for each of the preparations compounded by the contractor.
- A description of a routine delivery schedule (e.g., daily by a specified time) and options for nonroutine delivery (e.g., later the same day, after-hours, weekends, holidays, during emergencies).
- Examples of reports that the contractor will be expected to submit to the organization.
- The process for requesting new preparations from the contractor.
- The contractor's policy on unannounced inspections by its customers.
- The names, addresses, and telephone numbers of
  - Current clients of a similar size or those receiving similar types of compounded preparations or products, with written references and copies of annual performance-improvement reports, if possible.
  - Reference accounts currently served.

Additional information to obtain from the prospective contractor but not necessarily contained in the proposal may include

- Whether the contractor has had product liability lawsuits filed against it for preparations it compounded. If so, the contractor should be asked to provide a description of the lawsuits filed, the file date of the lawsuits, and the outcome, though such information is sometimes sealed as part of a settlement or decision and may not be disclosable.
- A description of the contractor's formal procedures for conducting recalls and whether there have ever been recalls of any of its compounded preparations. If the contractor has ever recalled any of its compounded preparations, it should be asked to provide the dates of recall, a description of the preparations recalled, and the reasons for the recall. Outsourcing facilities must comply with the specific requirements of FDA for 503B entities, which include having procedures for putting into place corrective and preventive actions.[6]
- Information related to the delivery process and backup planning when severe or catastrophic events happen (e.g., severe weather).

Visits to Contractors and Their Clients. Outsourcing facilities and compounding pharmacies should allow the organization's representatives to visit their corporate offices and compounding facilities. The contractor should provide ample opportunity for the organization's representatives to confer with the contractor's corporate, pharmacy, and compounding staff. During the evaluation phase, the organization's representative should expect to give notice of a visit, but after a contract has been signed the contractor should allow unannounced inspections, provided that the visit will be conducted in a manner that does not interfere with daily activity or compromise the state of microbial control.

For outsourcing facilities, the FDA inspection report and documentation of follow-up and correction of any enforcement or accreditation findings should be reviewed in advance of the visit. For compounding pharmacies, the healthcare organization should, in addition to requesting any FDA or state inspection reports and any applicable accreditation reports, assess the contractor's compliance with *USP* chapter 797 using a standard tool, such as the ASHP Research and Education Foundation's contractor assessment tool for outsourcing sterile products preparation.[24]

Evaluating Proposals. A decision to outsource sterile compounding services should be collaborative and may involve, as appropriate, the organization's governing board, CEO, CFO, COO, chief of the medical staff, chair of the P&T committee, director of pharmacy, director of nursing, legal counsel, medication safety officer, risk management director, and department heads, for example. The organization should scrutinize the following factors when evaluating proposals:

- Services offered versus services requested (including the contractor's potential to enhance currently offered sterile compounding services or customize to the organization's needs).

- Professional experience (e.g., years of service; number, size, and types of clients; knowledge of the organization's operations).
- Quality management program, specifically as it relates to facility cleaning and validation, environmental monitoring, staff training, and competency assessment.
- Financial stability (e.g., ability to absorb startup expenses and to commit the resources needed to initiate service).
- References and reputation.
- Information systems and other technological infrastructure (e.g., the capability to interface with the organization's information and drug delivery systems, such as infusion pumps or barcode-assisted medication administration systems).
- Demonstrated commitment to continually integrating technology and knowledge to improve patient safety.
- Education and training of the contractor's staff (e.g., internal and external continuing-education programs, educational allowances for professional and technical staff).
- The organization's and the contractor's policies on specific compounding practices (e.g., references with real-time stability data supporting beyond-use dating, compliance with standards and regulations, use of USP–National Formulary-grade ingredients or FDA-approved products in accordance with the organization's intended use).
- Risk-assessment program to ensure that medication errors are not introduced by new or increased outsourced compounding activities and that the medications dispensed are compatible with the client's medication administration devices (e.g., automated distribution devices, barcode labeling, smart pumps).
- Knowledge of the regulatory requirements and accreditation standards that the organization must meet and willingness to assist the organization in meeting these standards.
- Inventory and supply chain issues (e.g., the organization's and contractor's back-order policies, the contractor's ability to produce drug products in shortage through validated compounding procedures).
- Emergency-preparedness implications (e.g., the abilities of the organization and the contractor to deliver services in the event of a disaster).
- Additional qualities (e.g., high employee morale, confidentiality, creativity, dedication to the community, collaborative spirit).
- Cost aspects of services (e.g., cost-effectiveness, ability to achieve economies of scale).

The contractor should, at a minimum, be able to

- Provide assurance that each compounded sterile preparation or product meets applicable state and federal labeling requirements and is sterile and free of endotoxins (when required) and unintended particulate matter, according to professionally established and accepted quality-monitoring data.
- If the contractor is extending beyond-use dates longer than defined in *USP* chapter 797,[9] confirm the validity of those beyond-use dates with stability and strength,[25] sterility, and endotoxin testing that is available for review.
- If the contractor is compounding high-risk preparations or products, provide documentation of the end product–testing processes used to determine that the preparations or products are sterile, free of endotoxins and unintended particulate matter, and (for preparations or products made from bulk APIs) meet the strength requirements of the drug.
- Deliver appropriate preparations or products in tamper-resistant packaging and in containers that will maintain the sterility and stability of the drugs. All products must be shipped under proper storage temperatures and (when required) protection from light.

The organization should assign an evaluation rating to each proposal. Ratings should be weighted appropriately with respect to services, experience, references, and cost. The organization should base its decision to outsource sterile compounding services on its assessment of the contractor's ability to meet the organization's needs and fulfill the terms of the contract.

Outsourcing Arrangement. The healthcare organization and the contractor should agree on the outsourcing arrangement that best meets their needs. The contract should clearly describe all aspects of the outsourcing arrangement. The healthcare organization's pharmacy should

- Ensure that the proper body of the healthcare organization (e.g., the organization's P&T committee) has developed a formal process to identify which preparations will (and which preparations will not) be prepared by the contractor, based on the organization's assessment of the therapeutic needs of patients and logistical considerations associated with outsourcing.
- Establish the components of the medication orders or prescriptions for preparations that will be compounded by an outside facility.
- Determine whether patient consent must be obtained for use of preparations compounded outside the healthcare organization's pharmacy, consistent with state board of pharmacy regulations and prevailing law.
- Determine a method for identifying patients receiving the contractor's preparations or products.
- Ensure that the contract and the contractor's facility have been reviewed by all the necessary bodies in the pharmacy's healthcare organization (e.g., the organization's risk management team, legal counsel, P&T and infection control committees, epidemiology department).
- Determine how to handle situations in which a patient presents with a compounded medication that is not available from the healthcare organization's pharmacy or the contractor under the existing contract (e.g., medication in an implantable device, i.v. push medication, i.v. infusion) and that has not been previously considered by the P&T committee. Considerations include what the process will be for:
    - Having the P&T committee consider outsourcing the compounding of such medications to

another contractor with which the healthcare organization has an agreement.

- Acquiring certain compounded medications if the contractor already under contract cannot or will not prepare them and how the associated liability risks will be addressed (e.g., how the healthcare organization's pharmacy will negotiate an agreement with another contractor from which the preparation or product is available) until the P&T committee decision is obtained regarding such medications.

Negotiating the Contract. The healthcare organization should carefully review the proposal and clarify the provisions of the contract. Active participation by the healthcare organization's risk management team and legal counsel is highly recommended. Negotiations can ensure a contract that best meets the needs of the healthcare organization and the contractor. ASHP believes that the healthcare organization's pharmacist-in-charge (e.g., a pharmacy director) must take responsibility for patient outcomes from all medication-related activities performed at or for the organization's work sites, whether they are carried out by the organization's staff or by contractors. This responsibility should be explicitly stated in all outsourcing contracts.

The signed contract between the parties should at a minimum

- Describe the term length of the contract and the processes for the contractor's billing to the healthcare organization, including methods of determining the charge for the compounded items, payment terms, and processes for resolution of disputed invoices.
- Contain a confidentiality clause and a Health Insurance Portability and Accountability Act business associate agreement, if applicable.
- Establish the pharmacy's right to unannounced inspections of the premises where compounding occurs, including the right to inspect quality-control reports, provided that the visit will be conducted in a manner that does not interfere with daily activity or compromise the microbial state of control.
- Describe the method of communicating the medication order or prescription from the healthcare organization's pharmacy to the contractor (e.g., telephone, fax, computer transmission, hard copy, controlled-substance ordering system).
- Protect both parties from liabilities created by errors made by the other party and delineate the obligations of both parties.[26]
- Establish recall procedures that comply with hospital policy mandates and prevailing law should a preparation or product need to be recalled by the contractor.
- Address documentation, regulatory and accreditation compliance, sterile compounding process, and compounded preparation or product considerations.
- Describe the pertinent situations and processes for the return, credit, or destruction of compounded preparations or products with the contractor.
- Describe any requirements regarding the submission of quality reports by the contractor.
- Describe the procedures for resolving preparation or delivery issues encountered by the organization or the contractor.
- Describe the expectations to be met by the contractor. These expectations must comply with CMS Hospital Conditions of Participation for Contracted Services requirements,[17] which state (in part) that "The governing body must ensure that a contractor of services . . . furnishes services that permit the hospital to comply with all applicable conditions of participation and standards for the contracted services." Hospital accreditation organizations (Joint Commission,[18] DNV GL Healthcare,[19] the Healthcare Facilities Accreditation Program,[20] and the Center for Improvement in Healthcare Quality[21]) and other accreditation organizations (e.g., Accreditation Commission for Health Care's Pharmacy Compounding Accreditation Board,[22] National Association of Boards of Pharmacy Verified Pharmacy Program[23]) have additional standards that must be addressed.

Both operational and quality expectations should be defined by the organization, such as expectations that

- Delineate routine sterile compounding turnaround times (e.g., from receipt of the request, medication order, or prescription by the contractor to delivery to the healthcare organization) and describe acceptable deviations from the agreed-upon schedules (e.g., raw product availability problems, unique end-product testing requirements, compounded preparation stability characteristics, nonroutine and emergency delivery requests).
- Describe the specific drugs provided, documentation flow, delivery methods, security considerations, and time frames for the provision of controlled substances by the contractor.
- Describe any special processes, documentation flow, delivery methods, security considerations, and time frames for the provision of hazardous drugs by the contractor.
- Describe the frequency of quality statements provided to the healthcare organization, such as quarterly summaries of facility, personnel, and environmental monitoring.

Signing the Contract. In some organizations, the director of pharmacy may be authorized to sign contracts for outsourced services. If this is not the case, the director of pharmacy must be fully involved in negotiating the contract and advising the authorized signers.

Contract Provisions

A contract that meets the needs of the healthcare organization and of the contractor is the foundation for a successful relationship. Contracts should specifically describe the respective responsibilities of the organization and the contractor. See the appendix for examples of contract provisions.

Evaluation of the Contractor's Performance

The healthcare organization must evaluate and document the contractor's performance and assess the contractor's compliance with the terms of the contract. The contractor should regularly submit quality reports, and the organization must regularly perform objective and subjective evaluations (e.g., quarterly, annually). Evaluations should address all measurable standards of performance specified in the contract. Evaluations should be led by the director of pharmacy, be multidisciplinary, and should involve, for example, the CEO, CFO, COO, director of nursing, and medical staff representatives, as appropriate. An evaluation may include an assessment of how well the contractor has

- Helped improve the quality of patient care.
- Responded to the organization's needs (e.g., invoicing, process adjustment).
- Met its contractual obligations, including timely and complete deliveries of products.
- Provided clear and concise quality metric data ensuring compliance with state and federal regulations and patient-safety standards.
- Helped the organization achieve its financial and patient-outcome goals.
- Improved the productivity and performance of pharmacy staff.
- Improved medication management processes (e.g., medication dispensing and delivery).
- Reduced and controlled medication costs without compromising patient care.
- Worked and communicated effectively with the organization's staff and resolved problems.

Handling Performance or Quality Issues

The contractor should provide the healthcare organization with information at least quarterly on its compliance with contract requirements and other information needed for the organization's quality-assurance programs. A mechanism should be in place for resolving preparation or delivery issues (e.g., delivery to the wrong location, late deliveries).

Conclusion

These guidelines offer an overview of factors and processes for healthcare organizations to consider when exploring the outsourcing of pharmacy sterile compounding. Such considerations include an internal needs assessment, a cost analysis, a careful review of prospective outsourcing facilities and compounding pharmacies, and an examination of the potential long-term consequences of outsourcing as well as the short-term outcomes expected during a contract's performance period. The ideas presented can be used for strategic planning, drafting of initial contract provisions, comparing prospective contractors, preparing for contract negotiations, or evaluating a contractor's performance. These guidelines are intended to address representative outsourcing options and contract agreements and may not be applicable to all situations. Managers of pharmacy and healthcare organizations should exercise professional judgment about applicability to their own needs and circumstances.

---

[a]At the time of writing, FDA had not issued final guidance on interstate distribution by 503A facilities.[7]

[b]Draft CGMP limits on BUDs for 503B outsourcing facilities may present challenges to those purchasing them. For sterile preserved drugs, the longest permissible BUD is 30 days beyond completion of a sterility test. If a sterility test is completed before release, the BUD must not exceed 14 days (at USP controlled room temperature or refrigerated) beyond completion of the test (e.g., for a 14-day sterility test, the BUD could not exceed 28 days). For terminally sterilized products without a sterility test, the BUD cannot exceed 14 days. And for aseptically processed products without a sterility test, the BUD cannot exceed 24 hours at USP controlled room temperature or 3 days refrigerated. BUDs for frozen products are considerably longer.[6]

References

1. American Society of Health-System Pharmacists. ASHP guidelines on outsourcing pharmaceutical services. *Am J Health-Syst Pharm.* 1998; 55:1611–7.
2. American Society of Health-System Pharmacists. ASHP guidelines on compounding sterile preparations. *Am J Health-Syst Pharm.* 2014; 71:145–66.
3. American Society of Hospital Pharmacists. ASHP guidelines for selecting pharmaceutical manufacturers and suppliers. *Am J Hosp Pharm.* 1991; 48:523–4.
4. Drug Quality and Security Act (November 27, 2013). www.govtrack.us/congress/bills/113/hr3204/text (accessed 2015 Jan 20).
5. Food and Drug Administration. FDA guidance on pharmacy compounding of human drug products under section 503A of the Federal Food, Drug, and Cosmetic Act (July 2014). www.fda.gov/downloads/Drugs/GuidanceComplianceRegulatoryInformation/Guidances/UCM377052.pdf (accessed 2015 Jan 20).
6. Food and Drug Administration. FDA guidance for industry: Current Good Manufacturing Practice—interim guidance for human drug compounding outsourcing facilities under section 503B of the FD&C Act (July 2014). www.fda.gov/downloads/drugs/guidancecomplianceregulatoryinformation/guidances/ucm403496.pdf (accessed 2015 Jan 20).
7. Food and Drug Administration. FDA draft memorandum of understanding addressing certain distributions of compounded human drug products (February 12, 2015). www.fda.gov/downloads/Drugs/GuidanceComplianceRegulatoryInformation/PharmacyCompounding/UCM434233.pdf (accessed 2015 Feb 24).
8. General chapter 795: pharmaceutical compounding—nonsterile preparations. In: The United States pharmacopeia, 38th rev., and The national formulary, 33rd ed. Rockville, MD: United States Pharmacopeial Convention; 2014:560–7.
9. General chapter 797: pharmaceutical compounding—sterile preparations. In: The United States pharmacopeia, 38th rev., and The national formulary, 33rd ed. Rockville, MD: United States Pharmacopeial Convention; 2014:567–611.
10. Food and Drug Administration. FDA inspections, compliance, enforcement, and criminal investigations: FDA Form 483—frequently asked questions. www.fda.gov/ICECI/Inspections/ucm256377.htm (accessed 2015 Feb 24).
11. Food and Drug Administration. FDA pharmacy inspections and related records. www.fda.gov/

AboutFDA/CentersOffices/OfficeofGlobalRegulatoryOperationsandPolicy/ORA/ORAElectronicReadingRoom/ucm431393.htm (accessed 2015 Apr 1).

12. Kastango E, Douglass K. Quality standards for large scale sterile compounding facilities (May 2014). www.clinicaliq.com/images/stories/clinicaliq_compounding%20quality%20standards.pdf (accessed 2015 Jan 20).
13. Kastango ES. Impact of the US Drug Quality and Security Act. www.pppmag.com/article_print.php?articleid=1595 (accessed 2015 Feb 24).
14. Food and Drug Administration. Letter to hospital/purchaser from Margaret A. Hamburg, M.D., Commissioner of Food and Drugs (January 8, 2014). www.fda.gov/downloads/drugs/guidancecompliance regulatoryinformation/pharmacycompounding/ucm380599.pdf (accessed 2015 Jan 20).
15. Food and Drug Administration. Registered outsourcing facilities. www.fda.gov/drugs/guidancecompliance regulatoryinformation/pharmacycompounding/ucm378645.htm (accessed 2015 Mar 16).
16. United States Pharmacopeial Convention. General chapter 800 hazardous drugs—handling in healthcare settings. www.usp.org/usp-nf/notices/general-chapter-hazardous-drugs-handling-healthcare-settings (accessed 2015 Feb 24).
17. Centers for Medicare and Medicaid Services. Conditions of participation for hospitals, §482.12 (e), (e)(1), and (e)(2). http://cms.hhs.gov/Regulations-and-Guidance/Guidance/Manuals/downloads/som107ap_a_hospitals.pdf (accessed 2015 Jan 20).
18. Joint Commission. Standard LD.04.03.09. Comprehensive accreditation manual for hospitals (update 2, November 2014). Oakbrook Terrace, IL: Joint Commission Resources; 2014.
19. National Integrated Accreditation for Healthcare Organizations (NIAHO) interpretive guidelines and surveyor guidance–version 11. Milford, OH: DNV GL Healthcare USA; 2014:20–1.
20. Accreditation requirements 01.00.29, 01.00.30, and 01.01.13. 2012 accreditation requirements for acute care facilities. Chicago: American Osteopathic Association, Healthcare Facilities Accreditation Program; 2012.
21. Accreditation standards for acute care hospitals (October 2014) Round Rock, TX: Center for Improvement in Healthcare Quality; 2014:3.
22. Pharmacy Compounding Accreditation Board, Accreditation Commission for Health Care. Pharmacy accreditation. www.achc.org/programs/pharmacy (accessed 2014 Jul 24).
23. National Association of Boards of Pharmacy. Verified Pharmacy Program. www.nabp.net/programs/licensure/verified-pharmacy-program (accessed 2015 Apr 1).
24. ASHP Research and Education Foundation. Outsourcing sterile products preparation: contractor assessment tool, 2011. www.ashpfoundation.org/MainMenuCategories/PracticeTools/SterileProductsTool/SterileProductsAssessmentTool.aspx (accessed 2015 Jan 20).
25. Allen LV, Bassani GS, Elder EJ, et al. Strength and stability testing for compounded preparations. www.usp.org/sites/default/files/usp_pdf/EN/2014-01-13_strength_versus_stability_testing_for_compounded_preparations_3.pdf (accessed 2015 Apr 1).
26. Food and Drug Administration. FDA draft guidance for industry: adverse event reporting for outsourcing facilities under section 503B of the Federal Food, Drug, and Cosmetic Act. www.fda.gov/downloads/Drugs/GuidanceCompliance RegulatoryInformation/Guidances/UCM434188.pdf (accessed 2015 Apr 1).

Suggested Readings

Allen LV. Quality assurance in pharmaceutical compounding, part 2: documentation and verification. *Int J Pharm Compound.* 2012; 16:230–4.

Donnelly AJ, Kienle PC, Lake RT et al. The Drug Quality and Security Act: a new reality for the practice of outsourcing compounded sterile preparations. *Pharm Pract News.* 2014; 41(suppl):1–8.

Douglass K, Kastango ES. Consolidation of pharmacy compounding services: an alternative to outsourcing. *Int J Pharm Compound.* 2001; 5:140–4.

Eberts MW, Cecere DA, Mark S. Ensuring the safety of sterile admixtures prepared outside of the institution. *Hosp Pharm.* 2013; 48:248–52.

Fiebert L. Adjusting to the new world of outsourced compounding. www.pppmag.com/download.php?file=documents/V11N7/pdfs/ppp_1407_outsourcedcompounding.pdf (accessed 2014 Nov 28).

Gates DM, Smolarek RT, Stevenson JG. Outsourcing the preparation of parenteral nutrient solutions. *Am J Health-Syst Pharm.* 1996; 53:2176–8.

Kastango ES. Sterile-product preparations: mix or buy? *Int J Pharm Compound.* 2001; 5:59–63.

Kastango ES. Impact of the US Drug Quality and Security Act. www.pppmag.com/article_print.php?articleid=1595 (accessed 2015 Feb 24).

Kastango E, Douglass K. Quality standards for large scale sterile compounding facilities (May 2014). www.clinicaliq.com/images/stories/clinicaliq_compounding%20quality%20standards.pdf (accessed 2015 Jan 20).

Myers CE. History of sterile compounding in U.S. hospitals: learning from the tragic lessons of the past. *Am J Health-Syst Pharm.* 2013; 70:1414–27.

Ponto JA. Outsourcing radiopharmaceutical services. *Am J Health-Syst Pharm.* 1998; 55:2537.

Souhrada L. Contract management. *Hospitals.* 1990; 64:66–8.

Timko RJ, Crooker PE. Pharmaceutical compounding or pharmaceutical manufacturing: a regulatory perspective. *Int J Pharm Compound.* 2014; 18:101–11.

Wagner M. Basic pitfalls can undermine hospital–service firm relationship. *Mod Healthcare.* 1993; 23:32.

Appendix—Contract Provisions

The following are examples of contract provisions that, among others, the organization and a contractor might adapt as needed and include in a contract, depending on the scope of services being considered. In addition, a contract would include provisions about the specific compounding services to be provided by the contractor. The language in contract provisions should always be adapted to meet the specific needs of the healthcare organization and to comply with the organization's contracting policies and applicable laws and regulations.

In reviewing the following list of suggested contract provisions, attention should be paid to the fact that listed provisions are not intended and should not be considered all-inclusive and do not constitute legal advice but rather are provided solely to convey general information related to legal issues commonly addressed in contracts for the outsourcing of sterile compounding services. The purpose of enumerating the following possible contract provisions is to provide a general understanding of the types of provisions that may be included in a contract. Because laws vary from jurisdiction to jurisdiction and are subject to varying interpretations, healthcare organizations considering outsourcing sterile compounding services should consult with professional legal counsel in their relevant jurisdictions regarding the drafting of contracts.

Accreditation and Certification. A contract should include a requirement that services meet or exceed applicable accreditation and certification standards. These include, but are not limited to, the standards (or requirements) of the following organizations:

- Centers for Medicare and Medicaid Services[17]
- Joint Commission[18]
- DNV GL Healthcare[19]
- American Osteopathic Association[20]
- Center for Improvement in Healthcare Quality[21]
- Pharmacy Compounding Accreditation Board[22]
- National Association of Boards of Pharmacy Verified Pharmacy Program[23]

After-Hours Access. This section describes the process and extent of access to off-site contractor resources after normal business hours.

Choice of Law. The contract should state by which state law the contract is governed.

Confidential Information. This section describes what information is considered confidential and actions that are required to prevent unauthorized distribution of such information. Both parties must agree to safeguard access to computer databases and patient records to ensure that the patients' rights to privacy and confidentiality are protected. Use of the information should be limited solely to purposes specified in the contract.

Contractor. The outsourcing facility or compounding pharmacy contracted by the healthcare organization to provide sterile compounding services.

Contractor Indemnification. This section describes in detail the indemnities the contractor owes the healthcare organization, such as

Contractor shall indemnify and defend customer and its affiliates, and each of their respective officers, directors, trustees, employees, agents, and representatives (collectively, the "customer indemnities") and hold them harmless from and against any and all losses on account of any claims asserted by a third party in connection with, arising from, or related to (a) any of the acts or omissions related to the services and/or products provided pursuant to this contract attached hereto, (b) breach of contractor's representations and warranties, (c) injuries to persons, including death, or damage to property caused by contractor's agents, servants, or employees, or in any way attributable to contractor's performance of this contract, and (d) any breach of any laws or regulations in connection with contractor's performance of services or provision of products pursuant to the contract.

Contractor Reports. The content and regularity of performance reports that the contractor will submit to the organization may be specified.

Contractor's Performance Responsibilities. The contractor's responsibilities and commitments associated with proper federal (if necessary) and state licensure and regulatory requirements for all the preparations or products it compounds are outlined in this section (e.g., labeling). It further describes the contractor's responsibilities to operate in accordance with applicable Current Good Manufacturing Practices, *United States Pharmacopeia* (*USP*) compounding standards, Drug Enforcement Administration (DEA) requirements (as applicable), and company standard operating procedures.

Customer Responsibilities. This section describes the healthcare organization pharmacy's responsibilities for affirming that it has all required state, local, and federal licenses associated with the receipt of services being provided by the contractor. It may also describe the healthcare organization's responsibilities for determining clinical appropriateness of any compounded preparation or product it purchases from the contractor as well as the procedures to be used to ensure the traceability of compounded preparations or products.

Extension of Period of Performance. Conditions for extending the period of performance should be included in the contract.

Force Majeure. This section describes when neither party shall be liable for nonperformance or delays related to causes that are beyond one's reasonable control.

Forms. Responsibilities for the design, approval, purchase, and storage of forms may be assigned.

General Provisions. This section outlines a myriad of other contractual items, such as contract assignment, process for adding or changing compounding services, reference to other agreements, and reference to other applicable terms outside the services agreement.

Hazardous Drug Preparations or Products. Responsibilities for ensuring the safety of the organization's staff and patients during delivery and distribution of hazardous drug preparations or products may be assigned. Either the organization or the contractor must provide a hazardous materials handling program, including staff training, that meets ASHP guidelines, Occupational Safety and Health Administration (OSHA) requirements, and *USP* compounding standards.

Indemnification. This section describes specific conditions under which, and responsibilities for which, both parties will hold each other harmless for, and potentially defend, the actions of the other.

Information Transfer. This section describes the mechanisms by which the organization transfers orders and other information to the contractor.

Laws, Rules, and Regulations. Requirements for services to meet or exceed federal, state, and local laws, rules, and regulations may be specified. These include but are not limited to those of the Food and Drug Administration, DEA, OSHA, USP, and the state board of pharmacy. The contractor should maintain (e.g., display, file) the appropriate licenses, permits, and records of equipment maintenance and certification. Any contractor required to be registered as an outsourcing facility must be so registered.

Liability Insurance. This section describes the responsibility for maintaining liability insurance coverage. The contract might specify, for example, the specific level and types of liability insurance coverage that the healthcare organization and the contractor must maintain.

Payment Terms. This section describes the agreed-upon number of days from receipt of an invoice by the healthcare organization's pharmacy until payment is due to the contractor.

Period of Performance. This section specifies the period for which the contractor will provide services to the organization.

Policies and Procedures. This section describes the required written policies and procedures covering the outsourced services, all of which should comply with applicable laws, regulations, and accreditation or certification standards. The contract should specify that the policies and procedures must not conflict with those of the organization.

Pricing. The price of each service the hospital pharmacy is interested in purchasing from the contractor, along with conditions and methodology for price increases, is described in this section, which may be an addendum to the contract. Shipping, handling, and delivery charges for both routine and nonroutine deliveries should also be detailed.

Purchase Volume Requirements. This section establishes a mutual understanding of annual purchase volume commitments between the healthcare organization's pharmacy and the contractor.

Record Maintenance. The contract should specify that all pertinent records must be kept for the time required by law and by the organization and describe how, where, and by whom the records will be maintained.

Staff Education and Training. Responsibilities for required ongoing staff training may be specified. For example, there might be a clause in the contract that the contractor's staff will participate in some of the organization's education and training programs. In addition, the contractor may agree to provide specific training to ensure that all contractor and healthcare organization personnel can perform the duties created by the contractor's services.

Successors. The rights of each party in the event that the healthcare organization or contractor merges or transfers its business or assets to a successor are described in this section.

Term of Agreement. This section communicates the length of time the agreement is in effect between the healthcare organization and the contractor, including renewals.

Termination. This section describes how and when the contract will end or be terminated, including early termination. It should also address any penalties that may be appropriate or when the contract may be ended without penalty.

Developed through the ASHP Council on Pharmacy Management and approved by the ASHP Board of Directors on June 6, 2015. These guidelines supersede the ASHP Guidelines on Outsourcing Sterile Compounding Services dated January 14, 2010.

The revision of this document was led by Patricia C. Kienle, M.P.A., FASHP. The contributions of Bona E. Benjamin, B.S.Pharm., to this document are gratefully acknowledged.

The following individuals are gratefully acknowledged for reviewing draft versions of these guidelines (review does not imply endorsement): Darrell Chan, Pharm.D.; Michael Cunningham, Pharm.D.; Kate Douglass, M.S., RN, APN, CRNI; Bernadette Henrichs, Ph.D., CRNA, CCRN; Eric Kastango, M.B.A., FASHP; Michael Koch, M.B.A.; Rich Kruzynski, B.S.Pharm., M.B.A.; Kathy Parrinello, Ph.D., RN; James R. Rinehardt, M.S., FASHP; Douglas Smith, Pharm.D.; Ross W. Thompson, M.S., B.S.Pharm.; and Tom Woller, M.S., FASHP.

The drafters have declared no potential conflicts of interest.

The bibliographic citation for this document is as follows: American Society of Health-System Pharmacists. ASHP guidelines on outsourcing sterile compounding services. *Am J Health-Syst Pharm.* 2015; In press.

Compensation and Reimbursement

Payer Processes for Payment Authorization and Coverage Verification (1301)
Source: Council on Pharmacy Management
To advocate that public and private payers collaborate with each other and with health care providers to create standardized and efficient processes for authorizing payment or verifying coverage for care; further,

To advocate that payment authorization and coverage verification processes (1) facilitate communication among patients, providers, and payers prior to therapy; (2) provide timely payment or coverage decisions; (3) facilitate access to information that allows the pharmacist to provide prescribed medications and medication therapy management to the patient; and (4) foster continuity in patient care.

This policy supersedes ASHP policy 1206.

Drug Product Reimbursement (1304)
Source: Council on Pharmacy Management
To pursue, in collaboration with public and private payers, the development of improved methods of reimbursing pharmacies for the costs of drug products dispensed, compounding and dispensing services, and associated overhead; further,

To educate pharmacists about those methods.

This policy supersedes ASHP policy 0207.

Revenue Cycle Compliance and Management (1205)
Source: Council on Pharmacy Management
To encourage pharmacists to serve as leaders in the development and implementation of strategies to optimize medication-related revenue cycle compliance, which includes billing, finance, and prior authorization, for the health care enterprise; further,

To advocate for the development of consistent billing and reimbursement policies and practices by both government and private payers; further,

To advocate that information technology (IT) vendors enhance the capacity and capability of IT systems to support and facilitate medication-related billing and audit functions; further,

To investigate and publish best practices in medication-related revenue cycle compliance and management.

This policy supersedes ASHP policy 9902.

Value-Based Purchasing (1209)
Source: Council on Pharmacy Management
To support value-based purchasing reimbursement models when they are appropriately structured to improve health care quality, patient satisfaction, and clinical outcomes, and encourage medication error reporting and quality improvement; further,

To encourage pharmacists to actively lead in the design and interdisciplinary implementation of medication-related value-based purchasing initiatives.

This policy supersedes ASHP policy 0708.

Reimbursement for Unlabeled Uses of FDA-Approved Drug Products (0206)
Source: Council on Administrative Affairs
To support third-party reimbursement for FDA-approved drug products appropriately prescribed for unlabeled uses.

This policy was reviewed in 2011 by the Council on Pharmacy Management and by the Board of Directors and was found to still be appropriate.

Human Resources

Credentialing, Privileging, and Competency Assessment (1415)

Source: Council on Education and Workforce Development

To support the use of post-licensure credentialing, privileging, and competency assessment to practice pharmacy as a direct patient-care practitioner; further,

To advocate that all post-licensure pharmacy credentialing programs meet the guiding principles established by the Council on Credentialing in Pharmacy; further,

To recognize that pharmacists are responsible for maintaining competency to practice in direct patient care.

This policy supersedes ASHP policy 0006.

Financial Management Skills (1207)

Source: Council on Pharmacy Management

To foster the systematic and ongoing development of management skills for health-system pharmacists in the areas of (1) health-system economics, (2) business plan development, (3) financial analysis, (4) metrics for clinical and distributive services, (5) pharmacoeconomic analysis, (6) diversified pharmacy services, (7) compensation for pharmacists' patient-care services, and (8) revenue cycle compliance and management; further,

To encourage colleges of pharmacy to incorporate these management areas in course work and experiential education; further,

To encourage financial management skills development in pharmacy residency training programs and new practitioner orientation.

This policy supersedes ASHP policy 0508.

Board Certification for Pharmacists (1225)

Source: Section of Clinical Specialists and Scientists

To support the principle that pharmacists who practice where a pharmacy specialty has been formally recognized by the profession should become board certified in the appropriate specialty area; further,

To recognize the Board of Pharmacy Specialties (BPS) as an appropriate organization through which specialties are formally recognized and specialty pharmacy certification should occur; further,

To advocate prioritization for recognition of new specialties in those areas where sufficient numbers of postgraduate year two residency training programs are established and where adequate numbers of pharmacists are completing accredited training programs to prepare them to practice in the specialty area; further,

To advocate for standardization of credentialing eligibility and recertification requirements to include consistent requirements for advanced postgraduate residency training; further,

To promote a future vision encouraging accredited training as an eventual prerequisite for board certification; further,

To encourage BPS to be sensitive to the needs of current practitioners as prerequisites evolve; further,

To actively encourage and support the development of effective training and recertification programs that prepare specialists for certification examination and ensure the maintenance of core competencies in their area of specialization.

Professional Socialization (1113)

Source: Council on Education and Workforce Development

To encourage pharmacists to serve as mentors to students, residents, and colleagues in a manner that fosters the adoption of: (1) high professional standards of pharmacy practice, (2) high personal standards of integrity and competence, (3) a commitment to serve humanity, (4) analytical thinking and ethical reasoning, (5) a commitment to continuing professional development, and (6) personal leadership skills.

This policy supersedes ASHP policy 0110.

Credentialing and Privileging by Regulators, Payers, and Providers for Collaborative Drug Therapy Management (0905)

Source: Council on Public Policy

To advocate expansion of collaborative drug therapy management (CDTM) practices in which the prescriber and the licensed pharmacist agree upon the conditions under which the pharmacist initiates, monitors, and adjusts a patient's drug therapy; further,

To acknowledge that as a step toward the goal of universal recognition of and payment for pharmacist CDTM services, public or private third-party payers may require licensed pharmacists to demonstrate their competence to provide CDTM, before the payers authorize them to engage in or be paid for such clinical services; further,

To support (1) the development (as a professional initiative by pharmacist associations rather than as a government activity) of national standards for determining a pharmacist's competence to provide CDTM and (2) the appropriate use of these standards by clinical privileging systems, government authorities, and public or third-party payers; further,

To support the use of clinical privileging by hospitals and health systems to assess a licensed pharmacist's competence to engage in CDTM within the hospital or health system; further,

To advocate that state boards of pharmacy apply the principles of continuous quality improvement in assessing the quality, safety, and outcomes of CDTM.

(*Note: Privileging* is the process by which an oversight body of a health care organization or other appropriate provider body, having reviewed an individual health care provider's credentials and performance and found them satisfactory, authorizes that individual to perform a specific scope of patient care services within that setting.)

This policy was reviewed in 2013 by the Council on Public Policy and by the Board of Directors and was found to still be appropriate.

Intimidating or Disruptive Behaviors (0919)

Source: Council on Pharmacy Management

To affirm the professional responsibility of the pharmacist to ensure patient safety by communicating with other health care personnel to clarify and improve medication management; further,

To advocate that hospitals and health systems adopt zero-tolerance policies for intimidating or disruptive behaviors; further,

To encourage hospitals and health systems to develop and implement education and training programs for all health care personnel to encourage effective communication and discourage intimidating or disruptive behaviors; further,

To encourage colleges of pharmacy and residency training programs to incorporate training in communications and managing intimidating or disruptive behaviors; further,

To collaborate with other organizations to advocate codes of conduct that minimize intimidating or disruptive behavior in hospitals and health systems.

This policy was reviewed in 2013 by the Council on Pharmacy Management and by the Board of Directors and was found to still be appropriate.

Education, Prevention, and Enforcement Concerning Workplace Violence (0810)
Source: Council on Public Policy
To advocate that federal, state, and local governments recognize the risks and consequences of workplace violence in the pharmacy community and enact appropriate criminal penalties; further,

To collaborate with federal, state, and local law enforcement and other government authorities on methods for early detection and prevention of workplace violence; further,

To encourage all workplace environments to develop and implement a policy for pharmacy personnel that (1) educates about prevention and deterrence of workplace violence, (2) identifies escalating situations that can lead to violence and instructs employees on protection and self-defense, and (3) provides continued support and care to heal personnel who were directly or indirectly involved in an incident of workplace violence; further,

To encourage the health care community to develop and maintain a communication network to share information about incidents of potential and real workplace violence.

This policy was reviewed in 2012 by the Council on Public Policy and by the Board of Directors and was found to still be appropriate.

Appropriate Staffing Levels (0812)
Source: Council on Public Policy
To advocate that pharmacists at each practice site base the site's pharmacist and technician staffing levels on patient safety considerations, taking into account factors such as (1) acuity of care, (2) breadth of services, (3) historical safety data, and (4) results of research on the relationship between staffing patterns and patient safety; further,

To advocate that regulatory bodies not mandate specific, uniform pharmacy personnel ratios but rather ensure that site-specific staffing levels optimize patient safety; further,

To encourage additional research on the relationship between pharmacy staffing patterns and patient safety.

This policy was reviewed in 2012 by the Council on Public Policy and by the Board of Directors and was found to still be appropriate.

Image of and Career Opportunities for Hospital and Health-System Pharmacists (0703)
Source: Council on Education and Workforce Development
To sustain and enhance the public information program promoting the professional image of hospital and health-system pharmacists to the general public, public policymakers, payers, other health care professionals, and hospital and health-system decision-makers; further,

To provide ASHP informational and recruitment materials identifying opportunities for pharmacy careers in hospitals and health systems.

This policy was reviewed in 2012 by the Council on Education and Workforce Development and by the Board of Directors and was found to still be appropriate.

Influenza Vaccination Requirements to Advance Patient Safety and Public Health (0615)
Source: Council on Professional Affairs
To advocate that hospitals and health systems require health care workers to receive an annual influenza vaccination except when (1) it is contraindicated, or (2) the worker has religious objections, or (3) the worker signs an informed declination; further,

To encourage all hospital and health-system pharmacy personnel to be vaccinated against influenza; further,

To encourage hospital and health-system pharmacists to take a lead role in developing and implementing policies and procedures for vaccinating health care workers and in providing education on the patient safety benefits of annual influenza vaccination; further,

To work with the federal government and others to improve the vaccine development and supply system in order to ensure a consistent and adequate supply of influenza virus vaccine.

This policy was reviewed in 2010 by the Council on Pharmacy Practice and by the Board of Directors and was found to still be appropriate.

Staffing for Safe and Effective Patient Care (0201)
Source: Council on Administrative Affairs
To encourage pharmacy managers to work in collaboration with physicians, nurses, health-system administrators, and others to outline key pharmacist services that are essential to safe and effective patient care; further,

To encourage pharmacy managers to be innovative in their approach and to factor into their thinking legal requirements, accreditation standards, professional standards of practice, and the resources and technology available in individual settings; further,

To support the following principles:

- Sufficient qualified staff must exist to ensure safe and effective patient care;
- During periods of staff shortages, pharmacists must exert leadership in directing resources to services that are the most essential to safe and effective patient care;
- Within their own organizations, pharmacists should develop contingency plans to be implemented in the event of insufficient staff—actions that will preserve services that are the most essential to safe and effective patient care and will, as necessary, curtail other services; and

- Among the essential services for safe and effective patient care is pharmacist review of new medication orders before the administration of first doses; in settings where patient acuity requires that reviews of new medication orders be conducted at any hour and similar medication-use decisions be made at any hour, there must be 24-hour access to a pharmacist.

This policy was reviewed in 2011 by the Council on Pharmacy Management and by the Board of Directors and was found to still be appropriate.

Image of and Career Opportunities for Pharmacy Technicians (0211)
Source: Council on Educational Affairs
To promote the image of pharmacy technicians as valuable contributors to health care delivery; further,

To develop and disseminate information about career opportunities that enhance the recruitment and retention of qualified pharmacy technicians.

This policy was reviewed in 2011 by the Council on Education and Workforce Development and by the Board of Directors and was found to still be appropriate.

Pharmacist Recruitment and Retention (0218)
Source: Council on Legal and Public Affairs
To support federal and state incentive programs for new pharmacy graduates to practice in underserved areas; further,

To provide information and educational programming on strategies used by employers for successful recruitment and retention of pharmacists and pharmacy technicians; further,

To conduct regular surveys on trends in the health-system pharmacy work force, including retention rates for pharmacists and pharmacy technicians.

This policy was reviewed in 2011 by the Council on Public Policy and by the Board of Directors and was found to still be appropriate.

Professional Development as a Retention Tool (0112)
Source: Council on Educational Affairs
To recognize that pharmacy department staff development is an essential component of staff recruitment and retention as well as quality of work life; further,

To recognize that staff development encompasses more than formal inservice or external programs and includes informal learning among colleagues, mentoring, and other types of learning; further.

To strongly encourage pharmacy directors and health-system administrators to support staff development programs as an important benefit that aids in recruiting and retaining qualified practitioners; further,

To assist pharmacy directors with staff development initiatives by providing a variety of educational programs, services, and resource materials.

This policy was reviewed in 2010 by the Council on Education and Workforce Development and by the Board of Directors and was found to still be appropriate.

Drug Testing (9103)
Source: Council on Legal and Public Affairs
To recognize the use of pre-employment drug testing or drug testing for cause during employment based on defined criteria and with appropriate validation procedures; further,

To support employer-sponsored drug programs that include a policy and process that promote the recovery of impaired individuals.

This policy was reviewed in 2011 by the Council on Public Policy and by the Board of Directors and was found to still be appropriate.

Employee Testing (9108)
Source: Council on Legal and Public Affairs
To oppose the use of truth-verification testing such as polygraphs as routine employment practices because of the possible interference with the rights of individuals; further,

To recognize the limited use of such testing during employment where such testing may protect the rights of individuals against false witness.

This policy was reviewed in 2011 by the Council on Public Policy and by the Board of Directors and was found to still be appropriate.

ASHP Guidelines on the Recruitment, Selection, and Retention of Pharmacy Personnel

Purpose

These guidelines are intended to assist pharmacy managers in the recruitment, selection, and retention of qualified employees. The pharmacy manager working in an organized health care system will usually have to work with the system's human resources department and within the framework of the specific recruitment, selection, and hiring policies of the organization.

Recruitment

Position Descriptions. Well-developed job descriptions are extremely important in addressing many personnel issues. They are often used to establish salary ranges, define performance expectations, and write performance evaluations, but they can also be crucial tools in a successful recruitment effort.[1] The position description should contain detailed information on the knowledge, skills, experience, and abilities that an acceptable candidate should possess. The following information may be included in a position description:

- Position title and position control number (if applicable),
- Duties, essential job functions, and responsibilities of the position,
- Education, training, experience, and licensure required,
- Knowledge, skills, and abilities required to perform assigned duties,
- Reporting relationships,
- Pay grade and salary range (optional),
- Education and training required to maintain competence, and
- Other specifications of the position that may be required to meet legal requirements (e.g., the Americans with Disabilities Act) or the objectives of the organization (e.g., residency or certification requirements).

[*Note:* A variety of sample job descriptions can be found in Section 7.3 of the *Pharmacy Management Toolkit: Tools of the Trade for Pharmacy Managers and Directors* (CD-ROM) and in module 1 of *Competence Assessment Tools for Health-System Pharmacies* (online and print versions), both available from ASHP.]

A revised position description should be reviewed with staff members currently in that position and with the supervisor of that position. In many workplaces, human resources departments maintain a file of position descriptions and may require approval of all position descriptions in the organization. Procedures specific to the workplace should be followed. Staff with legal expertise should review revised position descriptions to determine compliance with organizational and legal requirements.

Recruitment Sources. Recruitment processes will depend on the type of position being filled. Strategies for filling a support staff position may not be appropriate when searching for a management candidate and vice versa. A recruitment plan should be developed for each position being filled. This plan should incorporate strategies that have worked in the past while allowing for innovative ideas. Organizations that recruit frequently or have very limited candidate pools should consider a continuous recruitment plan so that a list of prospective candidates is available even before an opening occurs.

Recruitment of individuals from within the department or the organization (e.g., from another department) creates internal growth opportunities and may result in greater employee retention and staff loyalty. Internal recruitment may also be less disruptive and expensive. To facilitate internal recruitment, notice of a vacant position can be posted within the organization before the information is made available to outsiders. Posting can be accomplished by various means, including memoranda, e-mail, voice mail, newsletters, announcements at staff meetings, and bulletin boards.

Recruitment of outside candidates expands the number of potential candidates and the experience available to the organization. It brings in new talent and discourages a reliance on seniority as the primary basis for promotion. Budgetary constraints and the urgency to fill a position may affect the recruitment method selected for external candidates. When recruitment of individuals outside the organization becomes necessary, the following methods should be considered:

- Advertisements in professional journals, newspapers, state professional society newsletters, and electronic bulletin boards,
- Personnel placement services provided by national or state professional societies,
- Oral and written recommendations from colleagues. Some organizations offer a "finder's fee" for hires that result from an employee referral,
- Personal discussion or correspondence with potential candidates,
- Recruitment visits to colleges of pharmacy or to facilities that conduct technician-training programs,
- Professional recruiting firms, which typically charge the organization a percentage of the position's annual salary. In addition, recruitment advertising companies offer access to a list of job seekers for a fee,
- Familiarizing students with the organization by offering summer jobs or participating in college of pharmacy experiential rotations,
- Tuition assistance programs for students in exchange for future work commitments,
- A "prospect list" of individuals applying for previous job openings, which can often be supplied by the human resources department,
- Internet-job-site postings,
- Community job fairs and local or state welfare-to-work programs, and
- Organization-sponsored events such as continuing-education sessions, award presentations, or community outreach programs.

The ability to recruit qualified candidates will depend on a multitude of factors, including the financial stability and location of the organization, the area's cost of living, the organization's compensation program (including salary, fringe benefits, and raise structure), the position's schedule and reporting structure, opportunities for professional growth and advancement, and the reputation and scope of pharmaceutical services offered. Only some of these factors are within the pharmacy manager's control.

Preinterview Information. The applicant's correspondence, resumé or curriculum vitae, letters of recommendation, academic records, and completed application form (if any) should be carefully evaluated on the basis of the position description to determine the suitability of the candidate for an interview.

There are certain legal restrictions on the type of information that may be requested from candidates on an application form. In general, an application form may request only information that relates directly to the evaluation of the applicant's ability to perform the job for which he or she is applying. If an application form different from that of the organization is used, it is advisable to have the human resources and legal departments review it before distribution to potential candidates.

Selection

Initial Screening Interview. An initial screening interview may be necessary if several qualified candidates have been identified. The screening interview is generally a brief interview conducted by the human resources department or the direct supervisor for the position; it offers a quick assessment of the suitability of the candidate for the position. This interview is often conducted by telephone, especially if the candidate lives far away. The screening interview should be documented and included in the applicant's file.

The Interview Process. A successful interview process is one that matches the best available candidate with a specific position. The process should allow the interviewers to predict the future performance of candidates as accurately as possible. One style of interview is the individual interview—one interviewer and one interviewee. Individual interviews offer the advantages of simplicity, ease of scheduling, and consistency of perspective. Because they are less intimidating to the candidate than group interviews, individual interviews may allow the interviewer to more accurately evaluate the applicant and provide the applicant with more opportunities to ask questions. The disadvantage of an individual interview is that it does not allow for multiple viewpoints and therefore increases the chance that something will be overlooked.

Another style, team interviewing, involves a group of interviewers. Members of the team may interview the candidate individually and then pool their results or they may interview the candidate as a group. The well-prepared team approach offers multiple perspectives within a standardized evaluation scheme. Its disadvantages are extra time consumed to train the team and conduct interviews and the intimidating effect it may have on candidates. Its advantage is that it incorporates more individuals into the process of analyzing a candidate's qualifications.[2] Team interviews foster the ideal of teamwork, and the involved employees share responsibility for the success or failure of the person hired. They also provide an opportunity to observe the candidate's ability to interact with groups, which may be important if the position will require that type of activity.

The composition of the interview team will depend on the position being filled. The team should include people with a common interest in the outcome of the selection process and people who have been in the organization long enough to share with the applicant some history of the organization and the department.[2]

Characteristics of an effective interview process include the following:

- Prior to the interview, the manager should provide the following to the candidate: information about the health-system institution, department, city, and state (if the applicant is not from the area); an agenda for the interview; the position description; travel directions to the facility; and clarification of expenses that will be incurred or reimbursed.
- The interview should be carefully planned. Consider the availability of those who need to participate in the process and allow adequate time for each event, including a tour of the facility (if needed).
- Interviewers should be well prepared. Preinterview information submitted by the candidate should be distributed to and reviewed by participants in advance of an interview.
- Carefully planned, open-ended questions should be developed in advance. Literature can be consulted to obtain sample questions and questions that are inadvisable or prohibited by law.[2–5] Human resources departments can usually assist in developing questions. (Refer to the appendix for sample questions.)
- To the extent possible, a core group of questions should be asked of all candidates as a means of comparing them. This does not negate the need to investigate different areas for each candidate or to pursue specific questions that surface during the interview.
- Questions should focus on predetermined criteria for the position and the qualifications of the candidates. The goal is to match the best candidate with the vacant position. Questions should focus on past performance, which is often a good indicator of future performance. In addition to questions regarding professional competency, the interview should contain questions that will help determine whether the applicant's attitudes and behaviors will be suitable for the job. Behavior-based selection criteria should be used when possible.
- The interviewer should give the candidate a realistic view of the position, including both favorable and unfavorable information. If the candidate is "oversold" on the position, dissatisfaction may set in when the truth becomes apparent.
- Performance standards and methods used for evaluation should be fully explained, and opportunities for professional growth should be presented.
- A description of employee benefits (e.g., medical insurance, vacation, sick leave, retirement benefits, and holidays) should be provided, either by the manager or by the human resources department.
- The initial salary and salary range for the position should be discussed with the candidate.
- The employee work schedule should be reviewed with the candidate.
- Any additional services or covered expenses the department offers should be outlined. Examples of these services of covered expenses include serving as a

provider of continuing-education programs, travel expenses and time off for continuing-education programs, payment of professional membership fees, and any other benefits that would attract the candidate to the position.
- A tour of the department should be provided.
- If the candidate is not from the area, a tour of the region should be given. Employees of the department or a real estate agency may show a candidate the area and describe the housing market and local schools.
- A follow-up letter is sent to the candidate after the interview to express thanks for interest in the position and the organization and to advise the candidate of the next steps. Timely and well-organized communication between recruiters and candidates is essential to a successful recruitment effort.

Each interview should be documented to keep track of each candidate's responses and to avoid confusion later. Documentation could include interview questions and the candidate's responses or simply a rating of the candidate's responses to specific questions. One person may be designated to collect and collate comments from a group interview. Documentation should occur immediately after the interview.[2] When considering a potential employee, the interviewer should examine punctuality, completeness and accuracy of the resumé or curriculum vitae, communication skills, compensation expectations, skills and knowledge pertinent to the position, and optimal fit with coworkers. The recruitment team should agree in advance on a systematic method for selecting the successful candidate.

Background Verification. The accuracy of information provided by the candidate should be verified by the human resources department. Information may be obtained from the following sources:

- Personal reference letters provided by the applicant,
- Letters of reference provided by previous employers or preceptors (with the applicant's permission),
- State board of pharmacy records,
- Academic records, and
- Legal background searches (when permitted by law and/or by the applicant).

Job Offer. The job offer should be made as quickly as possible after the interview process is completed. Offers should be made to candidates with enthusiasm and should include a deadline for response. Information about candidate selection should be kept confidential until the offer has been accepted. The organization may have specific policies and procedures regarding job offers.[2]

The salary offered to a candidate will usually be competitive with salaries for similar jobs in other organizations in the same market and compatible with the organization's existing salary structure. The market may vary, depending on the position. For example, the market for a pharmacy technician may be local, whereas the market for a pharmacist or pharmacy manager may be regional or national. To preserve equity within the organization, the salary offered to a candidate generally should be consistent with salaries of staff currently in that position. When exceptions are considered, it may become necessary to reassess the compensation of existing staff.

In addition to salary, other commitments made to a candidate should be expressed in writing as part of the formal job offer. These may include the following:

- Date on which employment will begin,
- Supervisor's name and position,
- Position description,
- Performance standards and evaluation system,
- Next performance review date,
- Next compensation increase date,
- Expected work schedule and whether it is subject to change depending on future needs of the department,
- Employee benefits (e.g., insurance, vacation, tuition assistance, sick leave, holidays, and retirement and pension benefits),
- Miscellaneous commitments (e.g., employment bonus, relocation expenses, licensure reimbursement, payment for professional association memberships, and payment for attendance at professional education programs), and
- Potential drug screening (as applicable and in keeping with the law) or employee physical examination and the dates of these activities.

Retention

Staff turnover is costly. The time required to recruit and train new employees has been shown to cause a temporary loss of productivity in the workplace.[6] Staff turnover also has a negative impact on staff morale, which may further reduce productivity and increase turnover. Because individuals have varied needs and wants that may change over time, there is no consistent formula for managers to apply to ensure employee retention.[7-9] Each organization's experience will depend on such factors as the age of employees, the employees' stages in life and career, the organizational structure, the work environment, and the work itself.

Retention may compete with recruitment. For example, creating staff positions with exclusively morning shifts may help retention but hurt recruitment, because fewer candidates are interested in evening shifts. When competing issues arise, pharmacy managers must balance them with the short- and long-term departmental goals and the current demand for employment.

Each organization should identify and assess retention factors by examining the unique aspects of the respective department and organization. For example, a committee broadly representing the organization could be established to determine major retention factors. On the basis of this assessment, a retention plan should be developed. The plan should be reviewed periodically as the needs of employees change; employee surveys may help determine these. The following factors may be considered in analyzing staff retention:

- *Training period.* The department should devote sufficient time and attention to training. Prepare for the new employee's first day by providing him or her with key material in advance and by developing an organized training schedule. Introduce the new employee to key people on the first day and have everyone in the department introduce themselves during the orientation period. Communicate with the new employee regularly during the training period and throughout the first three months.[10] Sufficient training time ensures that the new employee is comfortable in the new work environment and decreases the likelihood that he or she will become frustrated in the new position. Some organizations have developed a structured mentoring program in which a new employee is paired with a senior employee during the training period.

- *Intent to stay.* In several studies, this factor was the best predictor of staff retention.[11] Employees can simply be asked whether they intend to stay. Replies will reflect employee perceptions and should be considered in light of behavior (i.e., the actual turnover rate). Replies also may be influenced by the employees' fear of reprisal.
- *Job satisfaction.* Job satisfaction is a measure of the degree to which individuals like their jobs, their work environment, and relationships with their coworkers. Job satisfaction is important to retention, although the relationship may be direct or indirect. Employees can be asked how satisfied they are with their jobs; there are many survey instruments to assist pharmacy managers and directors in performing this task.[12] Job dissatisfaction does not necessarily lead to staff turnover if other factors are more important to the individual.[13,14]
- *Pay and benefits.* These refer to the remuneration for work performed and the organization's overall benefit plan. Pay may be hourly (a wage) or salaried and may include overtime premiums or bonuses and incentive plans. A benefit plan may include life, medical, dental, disability, and liability insurance; tuition payments; retirement packages; paid organizational membership dues; sick leave; paid vacation; child care; and prescription benefits. The value of specific benefits to an employee will likely change over time. Many organizations offer a benefits plan that gives the employee the option of choosing benefits individually suited to stages in his or her life and career.
- *Performance management.* Performance appraisal is a periodic assessment of an employee's performance throughout the year. Performance appraisal is only one step in a performance management process that includes appraisal, ongoing feedback, goal setting, and development. This process is important to the success of the manager, the employee, and the organization. The goal of performance management is to share information that will help the employee grow, both personally and professionally, and improve the organization. Periodic discussions with the employee are necessary to provide and receive feedback and to avoid surprises at the time of the scheduled performance appraisal.[15] Direct observation and evaluation by supervisors and coworkers can contribute to a meaningful appraisal.
- *Recognition and awards.* Employees often feel that recognition is lacking in the workplace.[7–10] New supervisors or managers should receive training in employee recognition, which includes both formal and informal feedback mechanisms, from structured employee of the month (or year) programs to a simple thank-you given in private or at a department meeting. Managers should identify how employees want to be recognized, through employee surveys or informal discussions.[10] Methods of employee recognition include

    - Thank-you notes,
    - Commendations,
    - Acknowledgment at department meetings,
    - Organization-wide events during National Pharmacy Week,
    - Employee of the month, quarter, or year,
    - Support for attendance at a professional meeting, and
    - Small awards such as movie tickets or gift certificates for coffee.[16]

- *Promotion opportunities.* These may be in the form of formal promotions, career advancement programs, training opportunities, or special project or committee appointments. Flat organizational structures provide fewer formal opportunities for staff promotion. Employees who have made personal investments in the organization—through expanded responsibilities associated with promotion—may have stronger feelings of loyalty that translate into increased retention. Succession planning is a key organizational strategy that ensures the availability of future leaders.
- *Job design.* This refers to the general tasks that an employee performs—the content of the work. Job design includes autonomy, the complexity of tasks, and the support and tools provided to the employee. Studies have found that job content is more highly correlated with retention as the level of an employee's education increases.[11] Motivational theories suggest that the job itself can motivate intrinsically and that success in the job can lead to increased employee satisfaction.
- *Peer relations.* This refers to working relationships with peers, nurses, physicians, and technical support staff. Peer relations are often rated highly as a reason for staying with an organization. It is difficult to predict during the interview process how a candidate's peer relations will develop, but past behaviors and discussion of hypothetical scenarios can provide some insight.
- *Kinship responsibilities.* This refers to family considerations, such as child care needs, spouse-employment transfers, and care for elderly relatives. Child and elder care needs are important for working parents. These considerations are also difficult to screen for during the interview process, and they will change over time. Legal restrictions prevent recruiters from asking some questions; the organization's human resources department should be able to offer advice on this issue.
- *Opportunity.* This refers to other options in the job market. Obviously, tight job markets (a relative lack of alternative positions) increase retention, whereas open job markets (those with many other open positions) may increase turnover. Managers should always be attentive to retaining good employees, but in open job markets they need to be especially attentive.
- *Staff-development opportunities.* This refers to job training, educational opportunities, and tuition reimbursement or other educational and personal growth opportunities for staff. Training and educational opportunities can affect recognition and awards, promotion opportunities, job design, and peer relations, so they can have a big impact on employee retention.
- *Management style.* This refers to the organizational structure and prevalent management style in the organization (e.g., on the spectrum from autocratic to participatory). The accessibility of management staff may be a factor as well as the extent to which staff input is encouraged. Each employee will prefer a particular management style; no one style will work equally well for all employees. Managers must be sensitive to the management styles that are effective for their staff.
- *Employee coaching.* This refers to the manager's mentorship role. Managers should provide feedback to employees regarding performance, teach specific job-related skills, hold formal and informal career discussions with employees, help employees achieve greater

self-awareness, advise employees on how best to prepare for career options, and assist employees in preparing a yearly career-development plan.[10] In addition, it is important that managers recognize and acknowledge the employee's contributions to the health system.

- *Management survey.* This refers to the organization's commitment to identifying opportunities for improving management. Such opportunities can be identified by surveying employees about their manager's performance. The survey should be conducted by each manager's supervisor. Managers should also complete the survey to see how their rating compares with that of their staff. Action plans should be established on the basis of the survey results.[10] Such "360-degree" surveys should be managed with caution, however; they may create animosity and foster unhealthy relationships between management and staff.
- *Physical working conditions.* This refers to the physical characteristics and safety of the workplace, such as space, equipment, noise levels, parking accommodations, and cleanliness.
- *Scheduling.* This refers to opportunities for varied scheduling, vacation time, shift rotation, job sharing, flexible hours, and part-time work.
- *Motivation.* Extrinsic motivators for change (such as salary, promotion, and recognition) can affect behavior, but they cannot change values and attitudes.[17] In the workplace, change occurs most readily when people are motivated by the desire to bring their professional activities in line with their personal and professional values and beliefs. Living vision and value statements offer employees an opportunity to shape an inspiring organizational culture. Although each employee's motivations will be different, some theories of motivation can help managers understand what contributes to job satisfaction. Maslow's[14] hierarchy of needs, for example, states that employees will be happiest when they are working toward self-actualization, which requires that their more basic needs for security, esteem, belonging, and knowledge be satisfied first. Herzberg et al.'s[18] motivation/hygiene theory explains that employees cannot be motivated by the "hygiene" aspects of their work (organization policies, supervision, salary, peer relations, and working conditions), but that dissatisfaction with those aspects can interfere with motivating factors (the work itself, responsibility, achievement, recognition, and advancement).
- *Exit interview.* An interview should be scheduled with a director of the department, the human resources department, and the exiting employee. The director should ask in-depth questions to identify why the employee is leaving. The exit interview should explore the employee's opinion of the company, department, his or her direct manager as well as any other issues the employee may have for leaving. Pharmacy managers should validate and share this information with the appropriate management staff to decrease the likelihood that another employee may leave for a similar reason.[14]

References

1. Poremba AC. Determining the department's staffing: writing job descriptions. In: Pharmacy management toolkit: tools of the trade for pharmacy managers and directors [CD-ROM]. Bethesda, MD: American Society of Health-System Pharmacists; 2001.
2. Nimmo CM, ed. Human resources management. ACCRUE level II. Bethesda, MD: American Society of Hospital Pharmacists; 1991.
3. Yate M. Hiring the best. 3rd ed. Holbrook, MA: Adams; 1990.
4. Wilson R. Conducting better job interviews. Hauppauge, NY: Barrons; 1991.
5. Smart B. The smart interviewer. New York: Wiley; 1989.
6. Donovan L. The shortage. *RN.* 1980; 8:21–7.
7. Smith SN, Stewart JE, Grussing PG. Factors influencing the rate of job turnover among hospital pharmacists. *Am J Hosp Pharm.* 1986; 43:1936–41.
8. Porter LW, Stears RM. Organizational work and personal factors in employee turnover and absenteeism. *Psychol Bull.* 1973; 80:151–76.
9. Loveridge CE. Contingency theory: explaining staff nurse retention. *J Nurs Adm.* 1988; 18:22–5.
10. Branham FL. Keeping the people who keep you in business. 1st ed. New York: Amacon; 2001.
11. Cavanagh SJ. Predictions of nursing staff turnover. *J Adv Nurs.* 1990; 15:373–80.
12. Section 7.5: employee satisfaction. In: Pharmacy management toolkit: tools of the trade for pharmacy managers and directors [CD-ROM]. Bethesda, MD: American Society of Health-System Pharmacists; 2001.
13. Johns G. Organizational behavior: understanding life at work. Glenview, IL: Scott, Foresman; 1983.
14. Maslow AH. Motivation and personality. 2nd ed. New York: Harper & Rowe; 1970.
15. Chrymko MM. How to do a performance appraisal. *Am J Hosp Pharm.* 1991; 48:2600–1.
16. Nelson B. 1001 ways to reward employees. New York: Workman Publishing; 1994.
17. Nimmo CM, Holland RW. The practice change model: an innovative pharmacy-specific approach to motivating staff change. In: Pharmacy management toolkit: tools of the trade for pharmacy managers and directors [CD-ROM]. Bethesda, MD: American Society of Health-System Pharmacists; 2001.
18. Herzberg F, Mausner B, Snyderman BB. The motivation to work. 2nd ed. New York: Wiley; 1959.

Appendix—Sample Questions to Ask of Job Candidates[2]

Questions for Experienced Pharmacists and Technicians

- How did you become interested in pharmacy?
- What skills or traits do you think a pharmacist needs to be successful?
- What is the single greatest contribution you have made in your present (or most recent) position?
- What is something you have recommended or tried in your present (or most recent) position that did not work? Why didn't it?
- How are you evaluated in your present (most recent) job?
- What would your present (most recent) employer say are your strong points? Your weak points?
- Why did you (do you want to) leave your last (present) job?

- Do you prefer working on a team or alone? Why?
- What part of the job did you like the best and least?

Questions for Recent College of Pharmacy Graduates

- What was your most rewarding college experience?
- Why did you want to study pharmacy?
- What would you change about your college experience if you could?
- Do you think your grades accurately reflect your academic achievements?
- What subjects did you like most and least? Why?

General Questions

- What qualities are you looking for in your next supervisor?
- What supervisory style do you think you have?
- What are your long-term career goals?
- How does this position fit in with your long-term career goals?
- What are you looking for in your next position that has been lacking in previous positions?

Subjects About Which You May Not Ask

- Race,
- National origin,
- Religion,
- Age,
- Marital or family status,
- Child care arrangements or childbearing plans,
- Arrest records (although convictions related to drug use would be appropriate),
- Credit rating and other financial information (unless the position involves financial responsibilities),
- Military discharge status, unless resulting from a military conviction, and
- General information that would point out handicaps or health problems unrelated to job performance.

Approved by the ASHP Board of Directors, September 27, 2002. Revised by the ASHP Council on Administrative Affairs. Supersedes the ASHP Technical Assistance Bulletin on the Recruitment, Selection, and Retention of Pharmacy Personnel dated April 27, 1994.

The bibliographic citation for this document is as follows: American Society of Health-System Pharmacists. ASHP guidelines on the recruitment, selection, and retention of pharmacy personnel. *Am J Health-Syst Pharm.* 2003; 60:587–93.

ASHP Long-Range Vision for the Pharmacy Work Force in Hospitals and Health Systems

Ensuring the Best Use of Medicines in Hospitals and Health Systems

Executive Summary

The ASHP Vision for the Pharmacy Workforce in Hospitals and Health Systems expresses a vision for building the workforce capacity of pharmacy departments in hospitals and health systems to meet the growing challenges related to optimizing the use of medicines in those settings.

Challenges

The scientific knowledge about drugs and the professional knowledge about pharmacy service delivery expand continuously. Many patients in hospitals and health systems in the United States have serious, complex, and urgent health problems that require advanced diagnostic evaluations, intricate medical procedures, and aggressive care. Medication use in hospitals and health systems is a prominent therapy for virtually all patients, and it is inherently complex and dangerous.

Pharmacy Functions

The objective of the overall pharmacy function in hospitals and health systems is to support sound patient care through the safe, evidence-based, and cost-beneficial use of medicines. Hospitals and health systems—in part because of demands by the government and external quality bodies—will require that pharmacists and pharmacy technicians possess and maintain sound credentials attesting to their competence to handle the tasks assigned to them. The overall pharmacy function in hospitals and health systems includes:

- Reviewing individual patients' medication orders for safety and effectiveness and taking corrective action as indicated.
- Collaboratively managing medication therapy for individual patients.
- Educating patients and caregivers about medications and their use.
- Leading continuous improvements in the medication-use process.
- Leading the interdisciplinary and collaborative development of medication-use policies and procedures.
- Acquiring quality drug products from trusted supply sources.
- Preparing medications in the doses and dosage forms needed.
- Distribution of medications to inpatients and outpatients.
- Ensuring the availability of quality drug information.
- Influencing drug administration policies, procedures, and the use of related devices.
- Conducting quality reviews of medication utilization in the hospital's or health system's population of patients and seeking improvements where indicated.
- Leading and influencing decisions about medication-related informatics, other technology (including drug administration devices), and automated processes in medication use.

The most effective pharmacy departments coordinate and integrate these functions into a cohesive whole, bringing together a team of pharmacists, pharmacy technicians, and others that have differentiated roles in management, patient care, medication-use policy, quality improvement, informatics, and drug product preparation and distribution.

Vision for Teamwork. Overall medication-use processes (which include prescribing, order review, dispensing, administration, monitoring, and adjusting therapy based on patient response) will be carried out by interdisciplinary teams, and pharmacists will continue to be the only health professionals with the depth and breadth of knowledge about, and the interest to focus their full time leadership attention on, the use of medicines.

Vision for Technology. Hospitals and health systems will continue to be technology-intensive environments. Shortages of pharmacists and pharmacy technicians qualified for work in hospitals and health systems are expected to be chronic. Technology will not eliminate these shortages. The use of technology will remain incomplete and nonstandardized (an important safety issue in itself) for some time.

Vision for Pharmacists' Responsibilities. Increasingly, pharmacists will apply their time to direct, interdisciplinary patient care to ensure the best use of medicines by individual patients. A growing number of pharmacists will work in highly specialized therapeutic areas. The expanded use of uniformly educated and certified pharmacy technicians will permit a larger portion of a pharmacy department's pharmacist staff to focus on direct patient care activities.

Credentials

Licensure alone will be insufficient for pharmacy practice in hospitals and health systems.

Vision for Residencies. Hospital and health-system employers will expect all entry-level pharmacists to have completed an ASHP-accredited first-year postgraduate pharmacy residency. First-year residency programs in hospitals and health systems concentrate on developing pharmacists that understand the organizational environment, can work in that environment to provide clinical care to individual patients, are capable of interdisciplinary professional work at both an organizational and clinical level, understand the internal and external standards of quality that apply, and are adept at measuring and documenting metrics of success to manage quality.

Vision for Specialty Certification. Second-year ASHP-accredited postgraduate residencies will be required for pharmacists caring for highly specialized and complex patients. These programs prepare pharmacists to effectively interface with specialized physicians and nurses and manage pharmacy services and informatics. Pharmacists who provide services in an area in which specialty certification exists will be expected to be certified in that specialty.

Vision for Leadership. All hospital and health-system pharmacists will be required to refresh their credentials continuously and to engage actively in personal continuing professional development. Strong leadership will be required to provide and sustain comprehensive professional vision for pharmacy departments. Pharmacy managers will possess credentials appropriate to the scope of services and the size and complexity of the setting, including, in many cases, advanced graduate degrees in pharmacy or nonpharmacy disciplines. Pharmacy departments will be headed by pharmacists; nonpharmacist managers will handle many tasks that do not require the expertise or judgment of a pharmacist.

Vision for Pharmacy Technicians. Pharmacy technicians eventually will be defined in laws and regulations as those individuals working under a pharmacist's responsibility that (a) have completed an ASHP-accredited pharmacy technician training program, (b) are certified by the Pharmacy Technician Certification Board, and (c) are registered with state boards of pharmacy.

Achieving the Vision

ASHP is assessing what it and others need to do to achieve this vision for the pharmacy workforce in hospitals and health systems. Future programs and advocacy of ASHP will be based on this assessment.

Introduction

Medication use in hospitals and health systems is complex and inherently risky. The American Society of Health-System Pharmacists (ASHP) believes it is inevitable that public policymakers, hospital and health-system administrators, and others will seek to modify the roles and required credentials for the pharmacy work force in those settings to ensure that medication use is safe, effective, and appropriate. ASHP believes the decisions will be best guided by a long-range vision about the pharmacy work force for those settings.

This vision is consistent with the ASHP Vision Statement for Pharmacy Practice in Hospitals and Health Systems,[1] the ASHP Health-System Pharmacy 2015 Initiative,[2] and the future vision of pharmacy practice[3] developed by the Joint Commission of Pharmacy Practitioners. This document serves as

- An expression of ASHP's continuing aim to support the development of competence building, sound credentials, and credentialing and privileging processes for pharmacists and pharmacy technicians in hospitals and health systems,
- A guide for ASHP in its long-term development of policies, education, publications, and activities to help pharmacists and pharmacy technicians develop and maintain the competence and credentials needed to work in hospitals and health systems, and
- An advocacy tool to stimulate public policymakers, external quality standards groups, hospital and health-system trustees and administrators, hospital and health-system pharmacy directors, and leaders in other collaborative health professions to ensure that the pharmacy work force in hospitals and health systems is appropriately competent, has the appropriate credentials, and is appropriately privileged on the basis of credentialing processes.

Hospitals and Health Systems

Hospitals and health systems include individual hospitals, multiple-hospital systems, health maintenance organization clinics, hospital-affiliated predischarge and postdischarge clinics, hospital-based ambulatory care pharmacies, home care services, rehabilitation facilities, skilled-nursing facilities, and assisted-living facilities. Common to all of these settings are the health-system characteristics of (1) an interdependent and interdisciplinary work force, (2) collaboratively developed and evidence-based medication-use processes, (3) a governance structure that is accountable for safe, effective, and appropriate patient care, (4) multiple levels of care with continuity of care among these levels, and (5) an ongoing assessment of performance using externally established quality standards and accreditation requirements.

The Overall Pharmacy Function in Hospitals and Health Systems. Pharmacists and pharmacy departments bear professional and legal responsibility for all medication-use activities in hospitals and health systems. That responsibility is abundantly clear in professional standards, statutes, regulations, court precedents, and external quality standards. The overall pharmacy function in hospitals and health systems will continue to include

- Leading the interdisciplinary and collaborative development of medication-use policies and procedures within the setting, including pharmacy and therapeutics committee policies and therapeutic protocols,
- Reviewing patients' medication orders for safety and effectiveness,
- Collaboratively managing medication therapy for individual patients,
- Educating patients and caregivers about medications and their use,
- Leading continuous improvements in the quality of medication-use processes,
- Acquiring quality drug products from trusted supply sources,

- Preparing medications in the doses and dosage forms needed,
- Distributing medications to inpatients and outpatients,
- Integrating the work of staff in clinical and other functions to ensure coordinated attention to safe, effective, and appropriate care,
- Functioning as a gatekeeper with respect to the quality of drug information available to caregivers throughout the setting as a means to support up-to-date, evidence-based care,
- Influencing drug administration policies and procedures and the use of related devices,
- Conducting quality reviews of medication utilization in the hospital or health system's population of patients, and
- Leading and influencing decisions about medication-related informatics, other technology (including drug administration devices), drug administration, and automated medication-use processes.

Differentiation and Teamwork. In hospitals and health systems, the overall pharmacy function will be accomplished via a differentiated pharmacy work force that includes managers, pharmacists practicing in direct inpatient and outpatient clinical roles, pharmacists and pharmacy technicians in inpatient and outpatient drug preparation and logistical distribution, pharmacists leading informatics and other technology activities, pharmacy technicians, business and operations managers, and other personnel, including informatics assistants, secretarial and administrative assistants, clerks, stock-handling personnel, and couriers. Differentiation in the pharmacy work force will increase with the size and scope of hospitals and health systems. Differentiation will be most pronounced in academic health centers where there are additional missions of education and research. Overall medication-use processes will be conducted by interdisciplinary teams. Pharmacists will continue to be the only health professionals with the depth and breadth of knowledge about—and the interest to focus their full-time leadership attention on—the safe, effective, and appropriate use of medicines.

Technology. Hospitals and health systems will continue to be technology-intensive environments. Many of the technologies, including those for automated medication delivery, pharmaceutical compounding, pharmaceutical packaging and labeling, automated distribution and vending, bedside verification, drug administration (e.g., infusion pumps), electronic drug information, electronic communications, and electronic patient records, will influence medication use. Automation and information technology will be increasingly integrated into medication-use processes. Pharmacists with technology and informatics expertise will influence the choice and use of technologies to ensure patient safety, effectiveness of care, and efficiency.[4] As new technologies evolve, pharmacists will ensure that these preserve and enhance medication-use safety, effectiveness, and appropriateness.

Leadership. Ongoing pharmacy leadership and management will be required to provide and sustain a comprehensive professional vision and evidence-based medication use via an integrated and interdisciplinary work force and to apply limited resources to activities that will be the most effective. Leadership and management will be required at all levels, including clinical practice, to ensure that the overall pharmacy function successfully influences the care of patients. In successful pharmacy departments, middle management positions will exist, and qualified personnel at all levels will be mentored for leadership and advanced-level positions. Hospitals and health systems in which this does not occur will be vulnerable to lapses in quality when inevitable turnover occurs in top management positions. Therefore, ongoing investment in succession planning will be essential. In large hospitals and multiple-facility systems, some pharmacists will be corporate-level directors (e.g., vice presidents). Some will have responsibility for departments in addition to pharmacy.

Pharmacies and pharmacy departments in hospitals and health systems will continue to be headed by pharmacists. In most cases, major positions below the department head level are currently occupied by pharmacists. However, it is likely that nonpharmacists will increasingly be employed below the department head level to handle various tasks that do not require the expertise or judgment of a pharmacist. These tasks may include secondary management, finance, personnel administration, quality assurance, informatics and technology, and supply and distribution logistics. Nonpharmacist positions of these types may be more common in large, complex hospitals and health systems where a differentiated work force is more necessary and possible.

Experiential Learning. Hospital and health-system pharmacists and pharmacy technicians will attain their knowledge, skills, and abilities in various ways. All pharmacists and pharmacy technicians will receive on-the-job orientation, training, and experiences that hone their knowledge and skills necessary for specific workplaces. New pharmacy college graduates will continue to be prepared primarily to deliver individual patient care. They will have in-depth knowledge about medications, their pharmacology, and their therapeutic uses. The Accreditation Council for Pharmacy Education's (ACPE's) accreditation standards for doctor of pharmacy degree programs require colleges to include experiential education in community pharmacy, ambulatory care, a hospital or health-system pharmacy, and inpatient or acute care general medicine.[5] These learning experiences are expected primarily to involve direct patient care rather than learning to navigate and fully influence the interdisciplinary and multidepartmental aspects of medication use within hospitals and health systems. Concerns exist about the capacity of hospitals and health systems to accommodate the growing volume of pharmacy students needing this experiential education. Most new graduates entering hospital and health-system practice will continue to require substantial further education in order to fully function in those settings. As a means to achieve that education, they should—at minimum—complete an ASHP-accredited pharmacy residency. Some hospitals and health systems may create mechanisms for existing staff to enroll in such residencies.

Pharmacists' Responsibilities

In hospitals and health systems, all pharmacists will be responsible for error prevention, patient safety, and patient outcomes related to medication therapy. Many will work at various supervisory and management levels in the acquisition, preparation, and dispensing of drug products, operating facilities and equipment for those activities, ensuring the supply and integrity of drug products, providing evidence-based drug information to other professionals and patients, managing the technology applied to medication use, monitoring the quality of pharmacy services, and conducting medication-use-safety activities. Some pharmacists will be engaged in sterile compounding. Some will influence the selection and management of technology and information systems for medication use. Depending on the role of the hospital and health system in education, some pharmacists will educate and train pharmacy students, residents, and pharmacy technicians. All pharmacists will appropriately balance their roles as employees of the setting and their autonomous public professional obligations on behalf of patients.

Increasingly, and dependent partly on the expanded use of uniformly trained and educated pharmacy technicians certified by the Pharmacy Technician Certification Board (PTCB), pharmacists will apply their time to direct, interdisciplinary, and collaborative drug therapy to ensure that the medication therapy of individual patients is effective, evidence based, safe, and cost-effective.[6] Some pharmacists will work in highly specialized clinical areas. Specialists will train and support generalist pharmacists. To ensure a high level of coordination by all components of the pharmacy function in hospitals and health systems and appropriate medication use and safety, the work of clinical pharmacists will be integrated with other aspects of the overall medication-use process. Depending on the volume of clinical work required, most pharmacists will have some ongoing work assignments and responsibilities in medication distribution. Hospitals and health systems will require that all clinical pharmacists and faculty of colleges of pharmacy working in their facilities be credentialed through the routine processes used for all other pharmacy staff and be managed by the department of pharmacy.

Throughout the work setting, the acquisition of patient medication histories and the provision of discharge medication information to patients and downstream caregivers will be managed by pharmacists. This will facilitate continuity of care, reconciliation of medication regimens, and avoidance of medication-related problems. Pharmacists will ensure that necessary clinical monitoring of laboratory test values occurs pertinent to medication use for individual patients. They will engage in disease prevention activities on behalf of patients. Pharmacists will influence the selection of authoritative, evidence-based drug information that is made available to all caregivers in the workplace. They will engage in interdisciplinary development of systemwide policies, procedures, and therapeutic protocols about medica-tion use. They will engage in medication-related public health activities on behalf of their communities.

Medication-Use Process. Pharmacists will continuously improve and collaboratively redesign medication-use processes to optimize patient safety and improve patients' health-related quality of life. They will ensure that medication-use processes incorporate system characteristics of interdependency, checks, and immediate safety feedback mechanisms. In addition to caring for individual patients, pharmacists will ensure that the outcomes of medication therapy are assessed and managed on both a systemwide and patient population basis.

Interpersonal Skills. Pharmacists in hospitals and health systems will possess exceptional interpersonal skills, work well in interdisciplinary teams, and lead the development of medication-use policies and procedures to meet patients' needs. They will possess competence in caring for and effectively interacting with patients from a variety of cultures. They will engage in behavior and activities that promote the pharmacy profession and will represent the profession in a positive light and promote its goals.

Proliferation of Potent and Complex Medications

The scientific knowledge about drugs and the professional and managerial knowledge about pharmacy service delivery expand continuously. Further, many patients in hospitals and health systems in the United States have serious, complex, and urgent health problems that require advanced diagnostic evaluations, intricate medical procedures, and aggressive care. Even for nonurgent care, medication use in hospitals and health systems is a prominent (or at least adjunct) therapy for virtually all patients, and it is inherently complex and dangerous. The medications used are among the most potent, and many require complex administration procedures. Many of these medications are injectable products that pose both inherent pharmacologic and infection-control challenges and must be handled by individuals in multiple disciplines, some of whom have little education and training about medications. Even more potent and riskier medications are anticipated in the future, and medication use in hospitals and health systems is expected to become even more intense and complex. Medications for patient groups with specific genomic characteristics will evolve.

Public Demand

Medication-use problems (particularly errors) are well documented,[7–25] but the public is not yet sufficiently aware that there is available a professional (the pharmacist) with the expertise and interest to help prevent those problems and better ensure optimum medication therapy in hospitals and health systems.[26–34] However, an increasing public awareness and debate is evolving about medication-use safety and costs, including the cost of preventable errors.[35–44] This will ultimately function as an important driver of public demand that pharmacists and pharmacy technicians in hospitals and health systems be competent to achieve (and manage the achievement of) desired patient outcomes with respect to medication use.

Sound Credentials Required for Pharmacy Personnel in Hospitals and Health Systems

ASHP believes that every pharmacist and pharmacy technician working in hospitals and health systems will be required to possess and maintain sound credentials attesting to their competence. Hospitals and health systems will engage in ongoing systematic assessments of the credentials and experience of all pharmacists and pharmacy technicians.[45,46] Some local policies may, with good reason, allow privileges for some pharmacists and pharmacy technicians who lack specific formal credentials; some of these practitioners may have well-documented experience and competence. As an ongoing investment in the safety and evidence-based effectiveness of medication use, hospitals and health systems will develop incentives to stimulate pharmacy staff to obtain desired credentials. Mechanisms will exist for acquisition of necessary credentials by entry-level pharmacists and pharmacy technicians and those in practice that aspire to expand their roles.

Residencies. ASHP believes that a variety of sound credentials will exist for pharmacists who practice in hospitals and health systems. ASHP-accredited postgraduate residency training exists to equip entry-level practitioners with the knowledge and skills they need to function safely and effectively and to successfully influence medication-use policies and procedures in their workplaces. First-year ASHP-accredited postgraduate residency programs in hospitals and health systems concentrate on developing pharmacists who (1) understand that organizational environment, (2) can work in that environment to provide clinical care to individual patients, (3) understand the academic health center environment (if the residency is conducted there), (4) are capable of interdisciplinary professional work at both an organizational and clinical level, (5) understand both the internal and external standards of quality that apply, and (6) are adept at measuring and documenting the metrics of success that are necessary for the management of quality in hospitals and health systems.[47–49]

Second-year ASHP-accredited postgraduate residencies are of several types. Some develop pharmacists capable of the care of highly specialized and complex patients, capable of effectively interacting with specialized physicians and nurses and conducting collaborative research. Others focus on hospital and health-system pharmacy management or informatics.[50,51,a]

Individuals enrolled in ASHP-accredited residency programs are licensed pharmacists. Similar to residencies in medicine, pharmacy residencies are intense, structured, "learn-by-doing" experiences that involve close work with preceptors and mentors. Pharmacy residents are fully accountable for the outcomes of their clinical and operational actions. Residencies are not "learn-by-observing" experiences, and they differ from internships, which are intended only to bring learners to a minimal competency for academic graduation or licensure. Among the benefits of residency training is the development of clinical skills and competency for work and leadership in hospitals and health systems. It is conceivable that future medication-use residencies may evolve that enroll pharmacists, physicians, and nurses and are conducted in an interdisciplinary fashion.

Hospital and health-system employers will expect new entry-level pharmacists in hospitals and health systems to have completed an ASHP-accredited first-year postgraduate pharmacy residency. ASHP believes that licensure alone will be insufficient for practice in hospitals and health systems.

Specialty Credentials. For some roles, pharmacists will be required to have completed ASHP-accredited second-year postgraduate pharmacy residencies for specialized clinical activities, informatics, and top management positions. Pharmacists who spend the majority of their time practicing clinical specialties for which there is available certification by the Board of Pharmaceutical Specialties (BPS) or the American Society of Consultant Pharmacists (ASCP) Commission for Certification in Geriatric Pharmacy will be expected to be certified or to be working with appropriate promptness to become certified.[52,b] They will be expected to maintain the certification. Other sound certification credentials may evolve.

Continuous Professional Development. Hospital and health-system administrators, public policymakers, and pharmacists will insist that up-to-date, evidence-based medication use occurs in hospitals and health systems. Effective, evidence-based interdisciplinary care of hospital and health-system patients requires currentness in professional knowledge and skills. Therefore, all pharmacists will be required to refresh their credentials continuously and to engage actively in personal continuing professional development. Professionally motivated pharmacists will seek out some of the updating of their knowledge and skills on their own. In order to sustain pharmacy work force competence, hospitals and health systems will financially support staff development and will allow paid work time for it. The extent to which pharmacists and pharmacy technicians engage in activities to sustain and expand their competence will be a factor in ongoing local assessments of their credentials and their continued employment.

Evolving Credentials. Additional competence-building mechanisms will evolve to educate and train pharmacists for specific tasks in hospitals and health systems, including those involving complex and high-risk services for which in-depth knowledge is necessary. Sound credentials will evolve for those tasks, and pharmacists will be expected to obtain those credentials to do that work. Examples of special certification roles include diabetes education, advanced cardiac life support, emergency department care, handling of biological products and products hazardous to workers, sterile compounding, distribution logistics, informatics, and clinical research.

Current sound credentials specific for pharmacists include the following:

- Doctor of pharmacy degrees awarded by colleges of pharmacy accredited by ACPE. The current entry-level degree awarded by all colleges of pharmacy is the Doctor of Pharmacy degree. Until recently, colleges of pharmacy awarded bachelor of science degrees as the entry-level degree, which also are sound credentials,
- Graduate degrees in pharmacy,
- National Association of Boards of Pharmacy License Examination for state board of pharmacy licensure,
- Certification by BPS,[b]
- Certification by the ASCP Commission for Certification in Geriatric Pharmacy,[b] and
- Graduation from an ASHP-accredited pharmacy residency program.

Parallel with these sound credentials there likely will be purported "credentials" that are based on unsound approaches lacking ensured validity and depth. ASHP supports only sound credentials. In their own quality and liability interests, hospitals and health systems will come to understand that there is a quality spectrum of pharmacy credentials and will insist on sound credentials for their pharmacy staff. The multiorganizational Council on Credentialing in Pharmacy (CCP) has created guiding principles for sound certification programs in pharmacy.[53]

Additional sound credentials in pharmacy may be recognized in the future, particularly for clinical specialties. BPS now certifies pharmacists in five specialties: pharmacotherapy (plus two "added qualifications" in infectious diseases and cardiology), nuclear pharmacy, nutrition support pharmacy, psychiatric pharmacy practice, and oncology pharmacy practice.[c] More BPS added qualifications may evolve. Hospitals and health systems will require pharmacists working in those areas to attain them. The Department of Veterans Affairs has established a mechanism for credentialing and privileging pharmacists to perform some tasks, including medication prescribing.[54–57] Privileging is defined as

> *the process by which an oversight body of a health care organization or other appropriate provider body, having reviewed an individual health care provider's credentials and performance and found them satisfactory, authorizes that individual to perform a specific scope of patient care services within that setting.*[45]

It is conceivable that legislatures and regulatory bodies may establish additional required pharmacist licenses for specific activities.

Leadership Credentials. All pharmacy managers (whether pharmacists or nonpharmacists) will possess credentials appropriate to the scope of services and the size and complexity of the setting. Some pharmacists, particularly in large and complex settings and multiple-facility organizations, will have corporate-level administrative appointments higher than the department head level. Individuals with that authority will have sufficient management experience to have developed the skills and talents for that role and will possess appropriate advanced credentials, which may include graduation from an ASHP-accredited second-year postgraduate residency in management or advanced graduate degrees in pharmacy or nonpharmacy disciplines. The ASHP Research and Education Foundation has created a Center on Health-System Pharmacy Leadership. It is possible that this may lead to an available certification for pharmacy leaders in hospitals and health systems.

Pharmacy Technicians

In the pharmacy profession and in laws and regulations, pharmacy technicians eventually will be defined as those individuals working under a pharmacist who (1) have completed an ASHP-accredited pharmacy technician training program,[58–60] (2) are certified by PTCB, and (3) are registered with state boards of pharmacy. Other support staff will be employed in pharmacies in hospitals and health systems, but they will not be defined in laws and regulations as pharmacy technicians. All pharmacy technicians will be required to participate in continuing education offered by accredited providers of such continuing education. ACPE conducts a process to accredit such providers.

Role of Technicians. Most pharmacy technicians will be engaged in drug-product acquisition, preparation, dispensing, and distribution under the physical supervision of pharmacists. Some pharmacy technicians will manage aspects of product acquisition and supply logistics. Some will manage the use of technology and quality assurance activities. Some will supervise other pharmacy technicians. Some will assist pharmacists in collecting and screening routine patient-specific clinical laboratory data and routine screening of clinical monitoring data to identify out-of-range findings that warrant pharmacist attention. Some will manage aspects of informatics.

Technician Credentials. Additional competence-building mechanisms will evolve to educate and train pharmacy technicians for specific tasks in hospitals and health systems, including those involving complex and high-risk services for which in-depth knowledge is necessary. Hospitals and health systems will require pharmacy technicians to obtain those credentials to do that work. Pharmacy technicians will continue to work under the supervision of pharmacists and will not be sanctioned to work independently. Although legislatures and regulatory bodies may establish licenses for pharmacy technicians, these will not be licenses for independent, unsupervised practice. Telepharmacy arrangements may evolve in which a supervising pharmacist may be physically remote from a pharmacy technician.

Sound credentials for pharmacy technicians currently include graduation from an ASHP-accredited pharmacy technician training program and certification by PTCB.

For pharmacy technicians, there also exists a spectrum in the quality of education and training available (some of which is unsound). Hospitals and health systems will be diligent in insisting on sound credentials. All pharmacy technicians will be registered with state boards of pharmacy.

Entry-Level Staff

Some entry-level staff will lack all the competencies and credentials needed to work fully in hospitals and health systems. Employers will require them to build competence and acquire appropriate credentials promptly. The initial work assignments of entry-level staff may be somewhat restricted until completion of the necessary competence building and acquisition of credentials.

Assumptions and Expectations

This vision is based on the following assumptions and expectations:

1. As scientific pharmacologic advances increase, mortality from various diseases will decrease. People will live longer and will have chronic conditions and more temporary acute conditions for which they will increasingly use hospital and health-system services. They will use more medications, necessitating greater numbers of qualified pharmacists and pharmacy technicians.
2. For reasons of quality assurance and compliance with accreditation requirements (such as Joint Commission standards[61]), hospitals and health systems will insist that pharmacists and pharmacy technicians demon-

strate that they are competent to perform the tasks set forth in their job descriptions.

3. Hospitals and health systems will establish systematic and ongoing processes to assess the competence and credentials of pharmacists and pharmacy technicians. Many hospitals and health systems will develop their own tools for assessing employee competence and credentials. Some will use external validation methods, such as BPS certification and graduation from an ASHP-accredited residency.
4. The quality of patient care in hospitals and health systems will be enhanced by pharmacists and pharmacy technicians with appropriate credentials.
5. To ensure safe, effective, and coordinated patient care, clinical and other pharmacy activities in hospitals and health systems will be staffed, conducted, and managed in an integrated fashion.
6. The public will increasingly wish to be able to distinguish pharmacists who are qualified to provide medication therapy management services from those who are not.
7. Governments and quality-standards organizations, such as the Joint Commission, will eventually insist on appropriate credentials for pharmacists and pharmacy technicians in hospitals and health systems.
8. Medicare provider status will evolve for pharmacists with appropriate credentials, enabling payment to hospitals and health systems for their medication therapy management. Medicare payments to hospitals and health system will be contingent on active local credentialing and privileging processes for all major health care workers in hospitals and health systems, including pharmacists.
9. Specialization will increase, and hospitals and health systems will look to sound credentials as indications of pharmacists' specialized competencies.
10. BPS will be urged to develop additional clinical credentialing processes in cooperation with professional associations.
11. In the face of shortages of qualified pharmacists and pharmacy technicians for hospital and health-system work, and in the face of the increasing need for qualified workers, accreditation bodies for hospitals and health systems will become increasingly insistent that the pharmacists and pharmacy technicians in those settings have appropriate credentials.
12. Compared with the chronic shortage of pharmacists across the entire pharmacy profession, the shortage of pharmacists competent to work in hospitals and health systems will continue to be more severe.[62–68]
13. The demographics of the pharmacy work force in hospitals and health systems are changing, and hospital and health-system employers will need to respond resourcefully and creatively to adjust to those changes.[69]
14. State laws and regulations will continue to require that pharmacists be graduates of colleges accredited by ACPE. However, some hospital and health-system employers in the United States will consider hiring graduates of foreign pharmacy schools. A process exists for foreign graduates to achieve a foreign pharmacy graduate equivalency certification.[70] Given that licensure alone will not be sufficient for successful work in hospitals and health systems, and given the advanced credentials needed for hospital and health-system work, this avenue for recruitment will not likely be very effective for those settings.
15. Graduation from an ASHP-accredited pharmacy residency will become a minimum requirement by employers for pharmacists to work in hospitals and health systems.[d]
16. Graduation from an ASHP-accredited pharmacy technician training program, certification by PTCB, and registration with a state board of pharmacy will become minimum requirements for pharmacy technicians to practice in hospitals and health systems.[d]
17. Greater quality and consistency in the education and training of pharmacy technicians will allow for expanded roles for pharmacy technicians, similar to those seen in U.S. military facilities and to the legal allowances for the work of pharmacy technicians in several European and Nordic countries.
18. The demand for qualified pharmacy technicians with appropriate credentials will increase in the United States. State requirements for the credentials of pharmacy technicians are advancing rapidly.
19. Hospital and health-system pharmacy departments will continue to employ supportive personnel who are not legally defined as pharmacy technicians and are not legally authorized to perform the same functions as pharmacy technicians.
20. Technology will not eliminate pharmacy work-force shortages in hospitals and health systems. Moreover, the use of technology will remain incomplete and nonstandardized (an important safety issue in itself) for some time.
21. As health care becomes increasingly collaborative and multidisciplinary, pharmacists' knowledge about medications will continue to be different from and more complete than that of other health care professionals.

Some Implications

Embedded in the following implications are numerous priorities that will influence ASHP's ongoing and long-term actions with respect to the pharmacy work force in hospitals and health systems. Other actions will evolve as well.

- Hospital and health-system trustees, administrators, and human resource, risk-management, and legal departments must be helped to understand that only qualified pharmacists and pharmacy technicians with appropriate credentials must comprise the pharmacy work force in hospitals and health systems.
- Mechanisms must be developed to help hospital and health-system employers readily discern sound pharmacy credentials from unsound ones.[53,71]
- Model local credentialing and privileging processes must be developed and implemented to assist hospitals and health systems in assessing whether pharmacists and pharmacy technicians possess the necessary credentials for the functions assigned to them.
- Colleges of pharmacy and pharmacies in hospitals and health systems must better articulate and integrate their respective roles in preparing graduates for ASHP-accredited pharmacy practice residencies.
- Since patient care in hospitals and health systems is inherently interdisciplinary, the education of pharma-

cists must be conducted in a more interdisciplinary manner.

- Sound credentials are needed for various subdepartment-level activities within hospitals and health systems (e.g., sterile compounding). ASHP and CCP should lead a prompt identification of the primary activities and develop a time-certain call for the profession to develop corresponding training and credentials for those activities.
- Public policymakers must be helped to understand the need for qualified pharmacists and pharmacy technicians within hospitals and health systems and to support mechanisms to educate and train practitioners for those roles.
- In cooperation with professional associations, BPS should expand the credentials for pharmacy practice and the number of pharmacists certified.
- Pharmacy technicians must receive uniform education and training before becoming PTCB certified.
- Pharmacy technicians must be registered with state boards of pharmacy.
- The National Association of Boards of Pharmacy should establish model laws and regulations to support state requirements for uniform education and training for pharmacy technicians and for PTCB certification of all pharmacy technicians.

Definitions

In this document, the following definitions apply, as published in 2006 by CCP.[71]

- ***Accreditation:*** Process by which a private association, organization or government agency, after initial and periodic evaluations, grants recognition to an organization, site or program that has met certain established criteria.
- ***Certification:*** Voluntary process by which a nongovernmental agency or an association grants recognition to an individual who has met certain predetermined qualifications specified by that organization. This formal recognition is granted to designate to the public that the individual has attained the requisite level of knowledge, skill, and/or experience in a well-defined, often specialized, area of the total discipline. Certification usually requires initial assessment and periodic reassessments of the individual's knowledge, skills and/or experience.
- ***Credential:*** Documented evidence of qualifications. Pharmacist credentials include diplomas, licenses, certificates, and certifications. For pharmacy technicians . . . CPhT . . . indicates certification by the Pharmacy Technician Certification Board. Credentials are reflected in a variety of abbreviations that pharmacists place after their names (e.g., Pharm.D. for "doctor of pharmacy," an earned academic degree; R.Ph. for "registered pharmacist," which indicates state licensure; and acronyms such as BCNSP for "Board-Certified Nutrition Support Pharmacist," which indicates that an individual has demonstrated advanced knowledge or skill in a specialized area of pharmacy).
- ***Credentialing:*** Process by which an organization or institution obtains, verifies, and assesses a pharmacist's qualifications to provide patient care services. [Similarly, credentialing can be applied to pharmacy technicians.]

---

[a]Federal funding is available to help support ASHP-accredited first-year residencies in hospitals caring for Medicare patients. To address the growing need in hospitals and health systems for pharmacists with advanced credentials, ASHP is seeking similar funding (which previously existed) for ASHP-accredited second-year residencies. ASHP is the accrediting body for pharmacy residencies. In early 2007, there were 714 ASHP-accredited postgraduate residency programs (481 first-year programs and 233 second-year programs). These programs graduate approximately 1400 residents per year. More ASHP-accredited residencies and residency graduates are needed to fulfill the work-force needs in hospitals and health systems.

[b]The processes used by BPS and ASCP for designating specialties and assessing the knowledge of individuals applying for certification are different.

[c]As of early 2007, BPS is engaged in a practice analysis in ambulatory care, which could lead to a sixth designation or "added qualifications."

[d]While this evolves to become a requirement by employers, a natural transition period will exist when pharmacists and pharmacy technicians who have achieved competence and successful experience in hospitals and health systems will continue to be employed.

References

1. American Society of Health-System Pharmacists. ASHP vision statement for pharmacy practice in hospitals and health systems. www.ashp.org/s_ashp?cat1c.asp?CID=2911&DID=4029 (accessed 2007 Mar 13).
2. American Society of Health-System Pharmacists. ASHP Health-System Pharmacy 2015 Initiative. www.ashp.org/s_ashp/quart1.asp?CID=218&DID=255 (accessed 2006 Dec 14).
3. Joint Commission of Pharmacy Practitioners. JCPP future vision of pharmacy practice, final version. www.aacp.org/Docs/MainNavigation/Resources/6725_JCPPFutureVisionofPharmacyPracticeFINAL.pdf (accessed 2006 Nov 28).
4. American Society of Health-System Pharmacists. ASHP statement on the pharmacist's role in informatics. *Am J Health-Syst Pharm.* 2007; 64:200–3.
5. Accreditation Council for Pharmacy Education. Accreditation standards and guidelines. www.acpe-accredit.org/standards/default.asp (accessed 2006 Dec 14).
6. Pharmacy Technician Certification Board. Pharmacy technician certification board (PTCB) announces milestone: 250,000 certified pharmacy technicians (CPhT). www.ptcb.org/AM/Template.cfm?Section=Home1&CONTENTID=2196&TEMPLATE=/CM/ContentDisplay.cfm (accessed 2007 Mar 13).
7. Leape LL, Bates DW, Cullen DJ, et al. Systems analysis of adverse drug events. *JAMA.* 1995; 274:35–43.
8. Bates DW, Boyle DL, Vander Vliet MB, et al. Relationship between medication errors and adverse drug events. *J Gen Intern Med.* 1995; 10:199–205.

9. Johnson JA, Bootman JL. Drug-related morbidity and mortality and the economic impact of pharmaceutical care. *Am J Health-Syst Pharm.* 1997; 54:554–8.
10. Bootman JL, Harrison DL, Cox E. The health care cost of drug-related morbidity and mortality in nursing facilities. *Arch Intern Med.* 1997; 157:2089–96.
11. Johnson JA, Bootman JL. Drug-related morbidity and mortality. A cost-of-illness model. *Arch Intern Med.* 1995; 155:1949–56.
12. Classen DC, Pestotnik SL, Evans RS, et al. Adverse drug events in hospitalized patients. *JAMA.* 1997; 277:301–6.
13. Bates DW, Spell N, Cullen DJ, et al. The costs of adverse drug events in hospitalized patients. *JAMA.* 1997; 277:307–11.
14. Lesar TS, Briceland L, Stein DS. Factors related to errors in medication prescribing. *JAMA.* 1997; 277:312–7.
15. Allan EL, Barker KN. Fundamentals of medication error research. *Am J Hosp Pharm.* 1990; 47:555–71.
16. Lesar TS, Lomaestro BM, Pohl H. Medication-prescribing errors in a teaching hospital. A 9-year experience. *Arch Intern Med.* 1997; 157:1569–76.
17. Bates DW, Cullen DJ, Laird N, et al. Incidence of adverse drug events and potential adverse drug events. Implications for prevention. *JAMA.* 1995; 274:29–34.
18. Lazarou J, Pomeranz BH, Corey PN. Incidence of adverse drug reactions in hospitalized patients: a meta-analysis of prospective studies. *JAMA.* 1998; 279:1200–5.
19. Cohen MR, Proulx SM, Crawford SY. Survey of hospital systems and common serious medication errors. *J Healthc Risk Manag.* 1998; 18(1):16–27.
20. Barker KN, Flynn EA, Pepper GA, et al. Medication errors observed in 36 health care facilities. *Arch Intern Med.* 2002; 162:1897–903.
21. Ernst FR, Grizzle AJ. Drug-related morbidity and mortality: updating the cost-of-illness model. *J Am Pharm Assoc.* 2001; 41:192–9.
22. Budnitz DS, Pollock DA, Weidenbach KN, et al. National surveillance of emergency department visits for outpatient adverse drug events. *JAMA.* 2006; 296:1858–66.
23. Manasse HR Jr. Medication use in an imperfect world: drug misadventuring as an issue of public policy, part 1. *Am J Hosp Pharm.* 1989; 46:929–44.
24. Manasse HR Jr. Medication use in an imperfect world: drug misadventuring as an issue of public policy, part *2. Am J Hosp Pharm.* 1989; 46:1141–52.
25. Davis TC, Wolf MS, Bass PF III, et al. Literacy and misunderstanding prescription drug labels. *Ann Intern Med.* 2006; 145:887–94.
26. American Society of Health-System Pharmacists. Understanding and preventing drug misadventures. A multidisciplinary invitational conference sponsored by the ASHP Research and Education Foundation in cooperation with the American Medical Association, the American Nurses Association, and the American Society of Hospital Pharmacists. *Am J Health-Syst Pharm.* 1995; 52:369–416.
27. American Society of Health-System Pharmacists. Top-priority actions for preventing adverse drug events in hospitals. Recommendations of an expert panel. *Am J Health-Syst Pharm.* 1996; 53:747–51.
28. American Society of Hospital Pharmacists. ASHP guidelines on preventing medication errors in hospitals. *Am J Hosp Pharm.* 1993; 50:305–14.
29. Leape LL, Cullen DJ, Clapp MD, et al. Pharmacist participation on physician rounds and adverse drug events in the intensive care unit. *JAMA.* 1999; 282:267–70. [Erratum, *JAMA.* 2000; 283:1293.]
30. Kucukarslan SN, Peters M, Mlynarek M, et al. Pharmacists on rounding teams reduce preventable adverse drug events in hospital general medicine units. *Arch Intern Med.* 2003; 163:2014–8.
31. Schnipper JL, Kirwin JL, Cotugno MC, et al. Role of pharmacist counseling in preventing adverse drug events after hospitalization. *Arch Intern Med.* 2006; 166: 565–71.
32. Pearlman MD. Patient safety in obstetrics and gynecology: an agenda for the future. *Obstet Gynecol.* 2006; 108:1266–71.
33. Kaboli PJ, Hoth AB, McClimon BJ, et al. Clinical pharmacists and inpatient medical care: a systematic review. *Arch Intern Med.* 2006; 166:955–64.
34. Manasse HR Jr, Thompson KK. Medication safety: a guide for health care facilities. Bethesda, MD: American Society of Health-System Pharmacists; 2006.
35. Kohn LT, Corrigan JM, Donaldson MS, eds. To err is human: building a safer health system. Washington, DC: National Academy Press; 1999.
36. Committee on Quality of Health Care in America. Crossing the quality chasm: a new health system for the 21st century. Washington, DC: National Academy Press; 2001.
37. Greiner AC, Knebel E, eds. Health professions education: a bridge to quality. Washington, DC: National Academies Press; 2003.
38. Aspden P, Wolcott JA, Bootman JL, et al., eds. Prevent-ing medication errors: quality chasm series. Washing-ton, DC: National Academies Press; 2006.
39. Food and Drug Administration. Strategies to reduce medication errors: working to improve medication safety. www.fda.gov/fdac/special/testtubetopatient/safety.html (accessed 2006 Dec 15).
40. Food and Drug Administration. FDA's new drug safety initiative. www.fda.gov/cder/drugSafety.htm (accessed 2006 Dec 15).
41. National Quality Forum. Safe practices for better healthcare. www.qualityforum.org/projects/completed/safe_practices (accessed 2006 Dec 15).
42. National Quality Forum. Improving use of prescription medications. www.qualityforum.org/projects/completed/medications.asp (accessed 2006 Dec 15).
43. Joint Commission on Accreditation of Healthcare Organizations. Patient safety practices. An online resource for improving patient safety. www.jointcommission.org/PatientSafety/PSP (accessed 2006 Dec 15).
44. Joint Commission on Accreditation of Healthcare Organizations. 2007 National Patient Safety Goals. www.jointcommission.org/PatientSafety/NationalPatientSafetyGoals (accessed 2006 Dec 15).
45. American Society of Health-System Pharmacists. Policy: role of licensing, credentialing, and privileging in collaborative drug therapy management (0318).

www.ashp.org/s_ashp/bin.asp?CID=6&DID=4086&DOC=FILE.PDF (accessed 2006 Dec 14).

46. Galt KA. Credentialing and privileging for pharmacists. *Am J Health-Syst Pharm.* 2004; 61:661–70.
47. American Society of Health-System Pharmacists. Accreditation standards: postgraduate year one (PGY1) pharmacy residency programs. www.ashp.org/rtp/starting/ practice-residencies.cfm (accessed 2006 Nov 28).
48. American Society of Health-System Pharmacists. PGY1 educational goals and objectives. www.ashp.org/rtp/starting/specialized-residencies.cfm (accessed 2006 Nov 28).
49. Teeters JL, Brueckl M, Burns A, et al. Pharmacy residency training in the future: a stakeholder's roundtable discussion. *Am J Health-Syst Pharm.* 2005; 62:1817–20.
50. American Society of Health-System Pharmacists. ASHP accreditation standard for postgraduate year two (PGY2) pharmacy residency programs. www.ashp.org/s_ashp/docs/files/RTP_PGY2AccredStandard.pdf (accessed 2007 Mar 13).
51. American Society of Health-System Pharmacists. PGY2 educational goals and objectives. www.ashp.org/rtp/Starting/PGY2.cfm (accessed 2006 Nov 28).
52. Board of Pharmaceutical Specialties. Recognized specialties. www.bpsweb.org (accessed 2006 Dec 14).
53. Council on Credentialing in Pharmacy. Guiding principles for certification of individuals in pharmacy. www.pharmacycredentialing.org/ccp/Files/CCP%20Guiding%20Principles%20for%20Certification%20Adopted%20January%202006.pdf (accessed 2006 Nov 28).
54. Department of Veterans Affairs. Credentialing and privileging. VHA handbook 1100.19. www1.va.gov/VHAPUBLICATIONS/ViewPublication.asp?pub_ID=357 (accessed 2006 Dec 15).
55. Department of Veterans Affairs. VHA Directive 2001-022. Implementation of VEPRO, VHA's national credentials databank. www1.va.gov/vhapublications/ViewPublication.asp?pub_ID=87 (accessed 2006 Dec 15).
56. American Society of Health-System Pharmacists. Medication prescribing authority for VA pharmacists to continue for 2 years. www.ashp.org/s_ashp/sec_news_article.asp?CID=167&DID=2024&id=2864 (accessed 2006 Dec 15).
57. Clause S, Fudin J, Mergner A, et al. Prescribing privileges among pharmacists in Veterans Affairs medical centers. *Am J Health-Syst Pharm.* 2001; 58:1143–5.
58. American Society of Health-System Pharmacists. ASHP accreditation standard for pharmacy technician training programs. www.ashp.org/emplibrary/Accreditation%20Standard%20for%20Pharmacy%20Technician%20Training%202005%20.pdf (accessed 2006 Nov 27).
59. American Society of Health-System Pharmacists. ASHP-accredited technician training program directory. www.ashp.org/directories/technicians/directory-intro.cfm (accessed 2006 Nov 27).
60. American Society of Health-System Pharmacists. Model curriculum for pharmacy technician training. 2nd ed. www.ashp.org/technician/model_curriculum/index.cfm (accessed 2006 Nov 28).
61. Joint Commission on Accreditation of Healthcare Organizations. Standards. www.jointcommission.org/Standards (accessed 2006 Dec 14).
62. American Hospital Association. The state of America's hospitals—taking the pulse. Findings from the 2006 AHA Survey of Hospital Leaders. www.aha.org/aha/content/2006/PowerPoint/StateHospitalsChartPack2006.PPT (accessed 2006 Dec 15).
63. Department of Health and Human Services. The pharmacist workforce: a study of the supply and demand for pharmacists. http://bhpr.hrsa.gov/healthworkforce/reports/pharmacist.htm (accessed 2007 Mar 13).
64. American Society of Health-System Pharmacists. 2004 ASHP Pharmacy Staffing Survey results. www.ashp.org/emplibrary/04ASHPRxStaffSurvey.pdf (accessed 2006 May 3).
65. Knapp DA. Professionally determined need for pharmacy services in 2020. *Am J Pharm Educ.* 2002; 66:421–9.
66. White SJ. Will there be a pharmacy leadership crisis? An ASHP Foundation Scholar-in-Residence report. *Am J Health-Syst Pharm.* 2005; 62:845–55.
67. Mott DA, Doucette WR, Gaither CA, et al. A ten-year trend analysis of pharmacist participation in the workforce. *Am J Pharm Educ.* 2002; 66:223–33.
68. Speedie MK, Manasse HR Jr. Pharmacists, pharmaceuticals and policy issues related to the workforce in pharmacy. Submitted for publication.
69. Report of the ASHP Task Force on Pharmacy's Changing Demographics. *Am J Health-Syst Pharm.* 2007; 64:1311–9.
70. National Association of Boards of Pharmacy. Foreign Pharmacy Graduate Equivalency Examination. www.nabp.net/index.html?target=/competency/intro.asp& (accessed 2007 Jan 4).
71. Council on Credentialing in Pharmacy. Credentialing in pharmacy. www.pharmacycredentialing.org/ccp/Files/CCPWhitePaper2006.pdf (accessed 2006 Nov 28).

Developed through the ASHP Council on Education and Workforce Development and approved by the ASHP Board of Directors on January 11, 2007.

The bibliographic citation for this document is as follows: American Society of Health-System Pharmacists. ASHP long-range vision for the pharmacy work force in hospitals and health systems. *Am J Health-Syst Pharm.* 2007; 64:1320–30.

Practice Settings

Practice Settings

Use of Two Patient Identifiers in the Outpatient Setting (1024)
Source: Council on Pharmacy Practice
To encourage the use of two identifiers to confirm patient identity when transferring filled prescriptions to the possession of the patient or patient's agent in outpatient settings.

This policy was reviewed in 2014 by the Council on Pharmacy Practice and by the Board of Directors and was found to still be appropriate.

Home Intravenous Therapy Benefit (0414)
Source: Council on Legal and Public Affairs
To support the continuation of a home intravenous therapy benefit under federal and private health insurance plans, and expand the home infusion benefit under Medicare Part B at an appropriate level of reimbursement for pharmacists' patient care services provided, medications, supplies, and equipment.

This policy was reviewed in 2008 by the Council on Public Policy and by the Board of Directors and was found to still be appropriate.

ASHP Guidelines on Home Infusion Pharmacy Services

Background and Purpose

Background. Home infusion services are provided by a variety of organizations, including hospitals, community pharmacies, home health agencies, hospices, and specialized infusion companies. Patients receive care in non-inpatient settings, such as their homes and ambulatory infusion centers, or in alternative-site settings, such as skilled-nursing facilities. Home infusion pharmacies may provide one or more of several service lines:

- Infusion therapies (e.g., intravenous, subcutaneous, intrathecal, epidural);
- Specialty pharmacy services;
- Ambulatory infusion center services;
- Home health nursing;
- Private duty nursing;
- Respiratory equipment and clinical respiratory services;
- Hospice services;
- Home medical equipment and supplies (with or without oxygen service); or
- Enteral products and supplies.

It should be noted that different aspects of home infusion can be provided by different organizations. When services are shared among providers, pharmacists have a professional responsibility to ensure that all patient care responsibilities are defined, understood, agreed upon, coordinated, and documented in advance by all providers. These guidelines apply to the provision of home infusion services by pharmacists practicing in all health care settings.

Purpose. The purposes of these guidelines are to define the role of the pharmacist in providing home infusion care to patients and to outline minimum requirements (indicated by use of the word "shall") and best practices for the operation and management of services provided by pharmacies in the home or alternative-site setting. In broad terms, home infusion includes the provision of specialized, complex pharmaceutical products; development and execution of plans to manage the medication therapy of patients; and clinical assessment and monitoring of patients in their homes. These services generally include home infusion therapy; other injectable drug therapy; parenteral and enteral nutrition therapy; and occasionally preparation of other sterile preparations, compounds, or products. As the number and types of therapies administered in the home and alternative sites expand, the resources and support required to provide these therapies will expand as well. Specific and unique pharmacist education and training in drug product admixtures and administration techniques, equipment operation and maintenance, patient monitoring, and patient and family education are required to ensure successful outcomes. These guidelines outline the pharmacist's role in providing these services and products. They are not intended to apply to home health or previously mentioned services that do not involve the provision of home infusion pharmacy services.

Many of the activities included in these guidelines are the subjects of other American Society of Health-System Pharmacists (ASHP) policy and guidance documents, which should be referred to for additional information. Pharmacists practicing in home infusion should use professional judgment in assessing ASHP's policy and guidance documents and in adapting them to meet their health care organizations' and patients' needs and circumstances.

To ensure the safe, appropriate, and effective use of medications in the home, home infusion pharmacies should develop comprehensive services to address factors unique to home infusion. Caregivers such as family members, who often have no health care experience, should be trained if deemed safe and appropriate to properly administer, store, and dispose of medications supplies and biohazard waste; operate medication administration devices; and monitor patients as necessary. Many medications must be aseptically compounded, often in quantities sufficient for a week's use, and delivered under conditions that will ensure that product potency and purity are maintained. Vascular access for infused therapies should be maintained for the intended duration of treatment, which may range from days to years. Medication administration devices should be selected and maintained to accurately and safely administer a variety of therapeutic regimens. Potential complications should be anticipated, and a proactive individualized plan of care should be established for monitoring, detecting, and managing complications, including those related to equipment, enteral and parenteral access, compliance, response to therapy, and patient and family education. Economic considerations should be taken into account so that care is provided in the most cost-effective manner. Home infusion pharmacies should have an effective organizational structure with the flexibility to meet the changing needs of patients, as well as to keep pace with the rapid growth of the industry and changes in health systems. As health care providers in the home setting, pharmacists must be concerned with the outcomes of therapy and not just the provision of services. Effective management is necessary to ensure that quality outcomes of therapy are achieved. While the scope of pharmacy services is likely to vary from site to site, depending upon the needs of the patients served, these criteria are strongly linked to patient outcomes; neglect of any one area may compromise quality.

Practice Management

Mission and Goals of the Home Infusion Organization. The pharmacy or its affiliated organization shall have a written mission statement that reflects patient safety, quality of care, and operational responsibilities. The statement should be consistent with the mission of the parent home infusion organization and/or health system, if applicable. The development and prioritization of goals, objectives, and work plans shall be consistent with the pharmacy's mission statement. The mission should be understood by employees, contract staff, and other participants (e.g., students and residents) in the pharmacy's activities.

Laws and Regulations. The home infusion pharmacy shall comply with all applicable local, state, and federal laws and regulations. Laws and regulations change frequently, so it is imperative to remain up to date on these changes so that the pharmacy remains in compliance. The pharmacy shall maintain written or computerized documentation of compliance regarding procurement, storage, and distribution of drug products, patient information, and related safety regulations from applicable state boards of pharmacy, the federal Food and Drug Administration (FDA), the United States Pharmacopeia (USP), the Drug Enforcement Administration (DEA), the Centers for Medicare & Medicaid Services (CMS), the Occupational Safety and Health Administration (OSHA), the National Institute for Occupational Safety and Health (NIOSH), and the Environmental Protection Agency (EPA), among others. Pharmacy management of patient information shall conform to the Health Insurance Portability and Accountability Act of 1996[1] (HIPAA) and to the parent organization's policies and procedures. Pharmacies that participate in Medicare Part D plans shall comply with government regulations for Medicare Part D, which may include annual compliance training regarding Medicare fraud and abuse. Appropriate business licenses, permits, and tax stamps should also be available.

Licensure. Professional staff shall maintain pharmacist licensure applicable to their practice. Policies and procedures should be available to ensure that health care providers meet applicable state licensure and home infusion organization authorization, if required, for prescribing medications.

Many states require pharmacies with out-of-state pharmacy licenses to also have a pharmacist licensed in the state of the prescription recipient. Pharmacies dispensing drugs across state lines shall comply with out-of-state licensure requirements, as well as other state and federal interstate laws and regulations. The pharmacy director shall have a process in place for validating current licensure of all professional staff, and the source(s) of this validation shall also be verified. In locations in which pharmacy technicians are required to be registered and/or certified, such registration and/or certification shall be validated annually or as required by law or regulation.

Accreditation. Accreditation provides patients, referral sources, and payers the assurance that the pharmacy meets a basic level of quality in patient care. Accreditation may be required by some payers and is recommended for the home infusion pharmacy. Accrediting bodies may include the Joint Commission, Community Health Accreditation Program (CHAP), Pharmacy Compounding Accreditation Board (PCAB), Healthcare Quality Association on Accreditation (HQAA), Accreditation Commission for Healthcare (ACHC), and Medicare.

Practice Standards and Guidelines. Appropriate practice standards and guidelines of professional pharmacy organizations such as ASHP should be assessed and utilized as appropriate to the scope of pharmacy services provided. The standards of other professional clinical organizations, such as the American Society for Parenteral and Enteral Nutrition (A.S.P.E.N.), the Infusion Nurses Society (INS), the Infectious Diseases Society of America (IDSA), and the Oncology Nursing Society (ONS), should also be assessed and used when applicable to the home infusion organization, its scope of services, and the population served. Such practice standards and guidelines should be adapted into the organization's policies and procedures when appropriate.

Policies and Procedures Manual. A policies and procedures manual governing the scope of the home infusion pharmacy services (e.g., administrative, operational, clinical, quality performance and/or improvement, infection control, drug preparation and dispensing, equipment maintenance) shall be properly maintained and available. The manual should be reviewed and revised annually or whenever necessary to reflect changes in procedures specific to the sites where the pharmacy's products and services are provided. All personnel should be familiar with the contents of the manual. Appropriate mechanisms should be established to ensure compliance with the policies and procedures.

Human Resources

The responsibilities and related competencies for home infusion pharmacy employees should be clearly defined in written position descriptions for all job categories.

Director of Home Infusion Pharmacy Services. Effective leadership and practice management skills are necessary for pharmacists' delivery of care that meets the needs of patients and the health system and results in continuous improvement in patient outcomes. These guidelines use the term *director of home infusion pharmacy services* (or, more simply, *director*) to indicate the person responsible for managing those services. Depending on the health system's organizational structure and other factors, designations such as manager or pharmacist-in-charge may also be used.

The director of the home infusion pharmacy services must work in collaboration with appropriate health-system leaders to create a long-term vision for the home infusion pharmacy department that is consistent with that of the health system. Depending on the size and scope of the setting, these functional responsibilities may be assigned to a single person or a team. It is the responsibility of the director to monitor the status of the goals set forth in the department's vision, provide feedback to the pharmacy team as necessary, and support the team's implementation of the core functions of the pharmacy practice.

Home infusion pharmacy services should be managed by a professionally competent, legally qualified pharmacist. In addition to the requirements for a staff pharmacist, the director shall be thoroughly knowledgeable about home infusion pharmacy practice and management. Completion of a pharmacy residency program and/or home infusion experience is desirable.

The director shall be responsible for

- Establishing the mission, vision, goals, and scope of services of the pharmacy on the basis of the needs of the patients served, the needs of the health system, and developments and trends in health care;
- Developing, implementing, evaluating, and updating plans and activities to fulfill the mission, vision, goals, and scope of services of the pharmacy;
- Ensuring the development and implementation of policies and procedures that provide safe and effective medication use for the patients served by the institution;

- Mobilizing and managing the resources, both human and financial, necessary for the optimal provision of pharmacy services;
- Overseeing contracts (for example vendors, home health agencies, payers, etc.);
- Ensuring that pharmacy services are delivered in compliance with applicable state and federal laws and regulations, as well as national practice standards; and
- Ensuring all technology and automation used throughout the medication use process is implemented, maintained, and utilized to promote patient safety.

A part-time or contract director shall have the same obligations and responsibilities as a full-time director. The director, in carrying out these responsibilities, should supervise an adequate number of competent, qualified personnel.

Home Infusion Pharmacists. Pharmacists who provide home infusion services shall have an active license to practice pharmacy issued by the applicable state board of pharmacy and other credentials as required by local, state, or federal laws and regulations. Some states require special licensure or training for preparing sterile preparations. Pharmacists dispensing medications to patients who reside in other states may also be subject to laws and regulations in those states; additional licensure may be required. The pharmacist should be knowledgeable about all applicable federal and state laws and regulations. The pharmacist is responsible for:

- Day-to-day supervision of dispensing sterile preparations and delivery activities;
- Drug information provided to nurses, physicians, patients, and caregivers;
- Clinical monitoring, care planning, and assessment of home infusion patients;
- Maintaining a professional image and demeanor in both appearance and actions;
- Maximizing work efficiency and patient safety through the use of technology;
- Maintaining confidentiality of patient and proprietary information; and
- Utilizing support personnel effectively.

Technicians and Other Support or Clinical Staff. Sufficient support personnel (pharmacy technicians, clinical staff [e.g., nurses, dietitians, respiratory therapists], and customer service, procurement, delivery, clerical, and administrative personnel) should be available to facilitate the delivery of home infusion pharmacist care and services. Pharmacy technicians should have completed an accredited pharmacy technician training program and be certified by the Pharmacy Technician Certification Board (PTCB). The pharmacy should hire pharmacy technician trainees without those qualifications only if those individuals (1) are required to both successfully complete an accredited pharmacy technician training program and successfully complete PTCB certification within 12 months of employment or as required by law or regulation, and (2) are limited to positions with lesser responsibilities until they successfully complete such training and certification. The pharmacy should require ongoing PTCB certification as a condition of continued employment. Appropriate supervisory controls should be maintained and documented, consistent with federal and state laws and regulations. In states in which registration of pharmacy technicians and/or special licensure or training is required for specific responsibilities (e.g., preparing sterile preparations), the pharmacy shall ensure that such requirements are met.

Pharmacy technicians are responsible for compounding sterile and nonsterile preparations in a manner to ensure patient safety, managing drug inventory, contacting patients about scheduled deliveries, and other duties as assigned. Customer service staff may be tasked with contacting patients about scheduled deliveries, communication with customers (e.g., other suppliers, patients, families, referral sources), and other duties as assigned. Drivers and/or warehouse managers may be responsible for delivery of medication to the patient, processing of initial paperwork to be signed, storage of medication in the home, observation of quantities of medications and supplies left in the home, and/or communication with the pharmacist if there are any questions or concerns. Intake personnel, insurance verification staff, and/or billers take referrals, determine insurance coverage, obtain authorizations or precertifications and renew them as needed, bill payers for services provided, and follow up on rejected claims.

Staffing, Work Schedules, and Assignments. The director should ensure that work schedules, procedures, and assignments make the best use of pharmacy personnel and other resources. Resources should be sufficient to ensure patient safety. Flex time, weekend options, exempt and nonexempt status, shift differentials, and on-call pay and responsibilities should all be considered when creating a staffing plan.

Recruitment and Selection of Personnel. Personnel should be recruited and selected on the basis of the requirements stated in the established job description, the candidates' job-related qualifications, and their prior performance. The pharmacy director should assist in identifying the relevant professional and technical qualifications for each job description and should participate in candidate interviews and final selection. The organization should have a human resources manual stating the requirements for reference checks, criminal background checks, and primary source verification of professional licenses. In addition, it should be organization policy that the Office of the Inspector General (OIG) List of Excluded Individuals/Entitites[2] is checked to ensure that potential candidates for employment have not been excluded from federally funded health care programs. Employees' professional licenses and the OIG List of Excluded Individuals/Entities should be verified at least annually.

Recruitment for home infusion pharmacy positions can be a challenge, especially when the pharmacist labor market is tight. Home infusion pharmacy practice is a unique practice setting with which many pharmacists are not familiar, especially new graduates. Infusion pharmacy practice training in college of pharmacy curricula varies, so recruiting staff with home infusion experience may not be possible. Creative recruitment techniques, such as hiring part-time pharmacists to cover open positions and offering on-site training, may help recruitment.

Orientation and Training. All employees shall be oriented to the type(s) of care and services provided by the organization. There should be an established procedure for orienting new personnel to the pharmacy, the parent organization, the health system(s) that the home infusion pharmacy serves, respective staff positions, and the patient populations served. All employees should understand the roles and responsibilities of others in the organization and should be oriented and demonstrate proficiency on equipment they are expected to operate or support as part of their duties. Employees should be knowledgeable about the supplies and equipment that are delivered to the patient. All personnel should possess the education and training needed to fulfill their responsibilities, including specific knowledge related to home infusion. All personnel should participate in continuing education programs and activities relevant to home infusion practice as necessary to maintain or enhance their competence.[3]

A home infusion organization is responsible for helping teach employees, patients, family members, and caregivers about standard safety precautions. The pharmacist should ensure that the home infusion organization provides appropriate education for its employees and patients, including education about appropriate disposal and handling of medical waste, procedures for preventing and managing needle and sharps stick injuries,[4] handling of cytotoxic and hazardous medications,[5] and material safety data sheets (MSDSes).[6] The pharmacist should be a key resource in the development of such educational programs. The pharmacist should assume an active role in the home infusion organization's infection-control activities.

Pharmacists should receive training as necessary to ensure that they possess the knowledge and skills required for the provision of home infusion services. They should participate in ongoing continuing education activities to update and enhance their knowledge and skills related to home infusion. Pharmacists should also participate in an ongoing competence assessment program as part of an overall staff development program. A valid assessment of competence should consider the pharmacist's responsibilities and the types and ages of patients served. The assessment should be conducted and documented on an ongoing basis for all pharmacists. When appropriate, pharmacists should assist in training and in continuing education programs for other home infusion providers.

Performance Evaluation, Contribution Management, and Competency Assessment. Policies and procedures should define the ongoing performance evaluations, contribution management, and competency assessments of home infusion pharmacy personnel. All home infusion pharmacy personnel should receive regular and timely evaluations. Performance should be evaluated on the basis of position description requirements and expected competencies. ASHP guidelines[7] and *USP* Chapter 797[8] describe requirements for initial and ongoing assessment of compounding knowledge and skills. Competency assessments should include practical skills (e.g., aseptic technique challenge), clinical competencies (e.g., assessing patients, developing a plan to manage patient care, and executing the plan), equipment competencies, and patient teaching competencies, if appropriate (i.e., if the employee will be instructing patients). Monitoring clinical outcomes is a critical part of the home infusion pharmacist's roles.

Financial Management

Budget Management. The home infusion pharmacy should have a budget that is consistent with the health system's financial management process and supports the scope of and demand for pharmacy services. Oversight of workload and financial performance should be managed in accordance with the health system's requirements. Management should provide for the determination and analysis of pharmacy service costs, the determination and analysis of capital equipment costs, and the determination and analysis of new project growth.

The pharmacy budget processes should enable the analysis of pharmacy services by unit of service and other parameters appropriate to the organization (e.g., organization-wide costs by medication therapy, clinical service, specific disease management categories, and patient third-party enrollment). The director should have an integral part in the organization's financial management process.

Health-System Integration. Other functional units within the health system should factor the cost of pharmacy services being provided by the home infusion pharmacy into their departmental budget when appropriate.

Third-Party Contract Review. In conjunction with the organization's legal department, the pharmacy director's team should review third-party payer contracts to ensure that reimbursement is appropriate for services being rendered and that terms of the contracts are in the best interests of the patient and the health system. The pharmacy should contract with third-party payers that are relevant to the pharmacy's patient population.

Drug and Supply Expenditures. Specific policies and procedures for managing drug expenditures should address such methods as competitive bidding, group purchasing, utilization review programs, inventory management, and cost-effective patient services.

Manufacturers and Suppliers. Criteria for selecting drug product manufacturers and suppliers should be established by the pharmacy to ensure the quality of drug products and the best prices, and that vendors are able to supply products in the volume required.

Reimbursement. The director of the pharmacy or home infusion organization should be knowledgeable about reimbursements for home infusion pharmaceutical services, medications, supplies, durable medical equipment, and, if applicable, nursing services. Processes should exist for routine verification of patient reimbursement benefits and for counseling patients about their anticipated financial responsibility for planned therapies. A process should also exist for responding to service requests from medically indigent patients.

The director of the pharmacy or home infusion organization should also be responsible for policies regarding drug procurement, drug expenditures, inventory management, determination and analysis of pharmacy service costs, capital equipment acquisition, budgeting (including analysis of budgetary variances, patient revenue projections, and justification of personnel commensurate with workload productivity), and payer audits.

Medication Use and Drug Information Services

Medication-Use Policy Development. Medication-use policy decisions should be founded on the evidence-based clinical, ethical, legal, social, philosophical, quality-of-life, safety, and economic factors that result in optimal patient care. Committees within the organization (e.g., pharmacy and therapeutics, infection control) that make decisions concerning medication use should include the active and direct involvement of physicians, pharmacists, and other appropriate health care professionals. The pharmacy should actively participate on committees whose decisions could affect the quality, safety, effectiveness, or cost of pharmacy services or the medication-use process.

Medication Therapy Decisions. The pharmacist's prerogatives to initiate, monitor, and modify medication therapy for individual patients, consistent with laws, regulations, home infusion organization policy, and clinical protocols, should be clearly delineated and approved by the home infusion organization's authorized leadership.

Formulary. An independent home infusion provider does not have to abide by a formulary; drugs are dispensed according to the orders of the physicians in its service area. A hospital- or health-system-based infusion pharmacy may have to abide by the same formulary restrictions as the rest of the hospital or health system. The home infusion pharmacist should have a mechanism for providing input to the formulary committee.[9] The pharmacy should have access to specialty medications distributed through closed network systems when needed to support consistent delivery of patient care and medication reconciliation.

Selection of Medications. Policies and procedures addressing the selection of medications should be available. These policies should be based on clinical appropriateness and USP standards. For bulk powders, USP or chemical standards for purity should be applied. Selection criteria should also include safety (including clinical and labeling safety such as manufacturer use of "tall man" lettering), efficacy, and ability to detect counterfeit medications.

Drug Information. The home infusion pharmacist should provide accurate, comprehensive, and patient-specific drug information to patients, caregivers, other pharmacists, physicians, nurses, and other health care providers as appropriate, both proactively and in response to requests associated with the delivery of pharmacy patient care, educational programs, and publications. Pharmacists should provide concise, applicable, and timely responses to requests for drug information from health care providers and home infusion patients. Responses to general and patient-specific drug information requests should be accurate and prompt. Drug information requests and responses should be documented and monitored for accuracy and timeliness as part of performance improvement activities. Policies and procedures should be in place for reviewing responses to requests for drug information for the purpose of performance improvement and education.

Adequate information about a medication's therapeutic use, dosage, potential adverse effects, and safe administration in the home, including storage and stability requirements, should be supplied before the medication is administered. Information about the stability of drugs for home infusion should address administration via a variety of alternative delivery devices, such as portable infusion pumps, syringe pumps, implantable infusion devices, elastomeric infusion pumps, and common peripheral and central-line administration devices.

Adequate space, resources, and information handling and communication technology shall be available to facilitate the provision of drug and related information to patients, caregivers, health care providers, multidisciplinary team members, and referring physicians. The director shall identify a core library (hard copy or electronic) appropriate for a home infusion pharmacy practice setting and ensure that those resources are readily available to users. Drug information sources should include current professional and scientific periodicals, Web-based research tools (e.g., AHFS-DI, MicroMedex, Lexi-Comp Online), the latest editions of drug compendia and textbooks in appropriate pharmaceutical and biomedical subject areas, and any references required by state boards of pharmacy. Availability of drug information on electronic media is desirable. Information may be accessed and provided in conjunction with medical libraries and other resources.

Available information sources should support research on patient care issues, facilitate provision of patient care, and promote safety in the medication-use process. When possible, a pharmacist should have a role within the health system for addressing complex drug information questions presented by professional staff (e.g., pharmacists, nurses, physicians).

If applicable, pharmacists should have access to information on all investigational studies and similar research projects involving medications and medication-related devices used by the organization. Pharmacists should, following the organization's procedures, provide pertinent written information (to the extent known) about the safe and proper use of investigational drugs, including possible adverse effects, to family members, nurses, pharmacists, physicians, and other health care providers involved in the care of patients admitted to the investigational drug protocols. Pharmacist representation on the health system's institutional review board is preferred.[10,11]

Education and Mentoring of Staff, Students, and Providers. The home infusion pharmacy staff should provide in-service education to physicians, nurses, pharmacy technicians, and other practitioners on home infusion pharmacy-related issues. They should also provide, to the extent possible in their organizations, student experiential education, externship, and internship training, as well as postgraduate residency training. Home infusion pharmacy staff also have a responsibility to keep the home infusion organization's staff informed about the use of medications on an ongoing basis through appropriate consultations, publications, and presentations. Pharmacists should ensure the timely dissemination of drug product recall notices, safety alerts, market withdrawals, and labeling changes.

Administration Devices, Delivery Systems, and Automated Dispensing Devices. Home infusion pharmacists should provide leadership and advice in organizational and clinical decisions about the selection of drug delivery systems, administration devices, and automated compounding and dispensing devices, and should participate in the evaluation, use, and monitoring of these systems and devices.[12] The potential for medication errors associated with such systems and devices should be thoroughly evaluated. Policies and procedures should be available for the certification (calibration) and maintenance of equipment and devices. Equipment should be adequately maintained and certified in compliance with applicable standards, laws, and regulations. Equipment maintenance and certification should be documented.

Preventive and Postexposure Immunization Programs. The pharmacy should participate in the development of policies and procedures concerning preventive and postexposure programs for infectious diseases (including, but not limited to, human immunodeficiency virus infection, tuberculosis, and hepatitis) for patients and employees.

Substance Abuse Programs. The pharmacy should assist in the development of, and participate in, substance abuse prevention, education, and employee and patient assistance programs.[13]

Development of Patient Care Services. The home infusion pharmacy services team should be involved in the development, implementation, and evaluation of new or changing patient care services within the organization, such as the development of new clinic sites or new service areas or lines. In reviewing the potential for new services, both the value added to patient care by the new service and the financial and logistical implications of the new service should be considered. These efforts should promote the continuity of pharmacist patient care across the continuum of care, practice settings, and geographically dispersed facilities.

Committee Involvement. The director and other pharmacy staff should contribute to the organization's goals through effectively participating in or leading committees and informal work groups. The pharmacist should be involved in the home infusion organization's initiatives to develop model clinical protocols and assessments that develop pharmacist care plans, pathways, or disease management guidelines to ensure that pharmacist care elements are included.[14] Clinical protocols should be used whenever appropriate to maximize the safety of medication use in the home.

A pharmacist should be a member of and actively participate on committees responsible for establishing policies and procedures for medication use, patient care, and performance improvement, among other things.[9] Pharmacists should also participate in the activities of similar committees of a parent home infusion organization or health system, as applicable.

The director or a designee should be a member of the home infusion organization's or health system's institutional review board, if applicable.

Drug Procurement and Management

The home infusion pharmacy should be responsible for the proper acquisition, compounding, dispensing, storage, delivery, and administration of all drug products used in the treatment of the organization's patients, as well as the proper use of related equipment and supplies. Policies and procedures governing medication procurement and management should be developed by the pharmacy in collaboration with other appropriate organization staff and committees.

Selection of Medications and Management of Supplies and Inventory. Policies and procedures governing selection of medications and management of supplies and inventory should be developed by the pharmacy director in collaboration with other appropriate home infusion organization staff members.

Procurement through Wholesalers, Manufacturers, or Group Purchasing Organizations. Each pharmacy should have a primary drug wholesaler for routine stock orders and a local source (e.g., a local hospital) for obtaining medications it does not have in stock. Group purchasing organizations (GPOs) may be used to control purchasing costs for drugs and supplies. Policies and procedures should address procurement and management of medications that must be obtained directly from the manufacturer or a limited set of distributors to ensure safe and proper pedigree of pharmaceutical products.[15,16]

Storage and Stock Levels. Each pharmacy should determine the appropriate level of stock required to serve the local patient population and manage its physical inventory for maximum cost control and operational efficiency.

Returns, Recalls, and Backorders. Procedures should be in place for responding to drug and device product returns, recalls, and backorders; for identifying patients who received or used a recalled product; and for removing the drug or device product from the pharmacy or home when the recall is at the user level. All stocks of medications stored in the home infusion pharmacy or in the organization's facilities should be inspected routinely to ensure the absence of recalled, outdated, unusable, or mislabeled products. Inspections should include identification of storage conditions that could compromise medication integrity, storage arrangements that might contribute to medication errors, and storage locations that might be vulnerable to drug diversion efforts.

Drug Shortages. There shall be policies and procedures for managing drug product shortages. The pharmacy's inventory management system should be designed to detect subminimum inventory levels and alert the pharmacy to potential shortages, and pharmacy staff should monitor reliable sources of information regarding drug product shortages (e.g., the ASHP[17] and FDA[18] drug shortages web resource centers). The pharmacy should develop strategies for identifying alternative therapies, working with suppliers, collaborating with physicians and other health care providers, and conducting an awareness campaign in the event of a drug product shortage.[19]

Compounding. The home infusion pharmacist is responsible for assuring appropriate techniques are used for preparing and dispensing medications, following the home infusion pharmacy's policies and procedures and accepted standards of practice. Double checks are a good practice in many steps of the pharmacy dispensing process. The pharmacy should have a process by which all high-risk calculations are checked for accuracy by a second clinician. Pediatric medications (e.g., doses), parenteral nutrition (PN), chemotherapy, pain management, and inotropes are examples of high-risk therapies. It is also good practice that the pharmacist who processed a new order should not be the same person who checks the order for accuracy and completeness. In addition to double checks on calculations, there should be visual double checks on all medications listed as high-alert medications by the Institute for Safe Medication Practices (ISMP) (e.g., heparin, insulin, chemotherapy agents, PN additives).[20]

Compounding Sterile Preparations. Compounding of sterile preparations should comply with applicable practice standards, accreditation standards, and pertinent state and federal laws and regulations. If these services are being provided by another pharmacy, the pharmacist should have reasonable assurance that these standards are being met by the pharmacy providing the service.[21]

Home infusion pharmacists are responsible for ensuring the quality of sterile preparations intended for use in the home. Guidance is available from various sources for developing an adequately designed and equipped facility, training and validating employees, validating and documenting compounding procedures, practicing aseptic technique, monitoring the work environment, maintaining the facility and equipment, ensuring the quality of prepared preparations, and developing policies and procedures.[7,8]

Stability and Compatibility Issues. Home infusion pharmacies are often required to assign extended beyond-use dates to sterile preparations so that a multiple-day supply of medications can be dispensed and delivered. However, pharmacists should take into account circumstances that may affect the medication's potency and stability, including:

- Delivery of sterile preparations to the home, either by the pharmacy's own vehicles or by a common carrier;
- Storage of sterile preparations in the home before use;
- Manipulation of sterile preparations in the home environment to add ingredients (such as vitamins) and to set up tubing and filters for administration; and
- Administration of preparations at temperatures that are warmer than controlled room temperature because of administration in outdoor or non-air-conditioned environments or the use of ambulatory infusion pumps worn close to the body.

The home infusion pharmacist should consult *USP* Chapter 797[8] and other appropriate resources to establish an appropriate beyond-use date. Applying published stability data can introduce inaccuracies if the intended conditions of use differ greatly from the reported conditions. Pharmacists should maintain a record of the resources used for establishing beyond-use dates. A table or chart of accepted beyond-use dates, formulations, and conditions of use for commonly prepared preparations may be helpful in ensuring that assigned dates are consistent and appropriate. Patients should be trained to check preparations for current beyond-use dates prior to their use.

Labeling. Medications for home use should be labeled so that patients and caregivers can easily understand instructions for drug storage, preparation, and administration. Auxiliary labels should be used as necessary. When manipulation of medications is required before administration, labeling should clearly state current contents and the steps for measuring, reconstituting, or adding other ingredients. Labels for compounded medications should state the total content of the medication or nutrient per container so that it can be clearly known in case the patient is transferred to another treatment setting. If medications are to be administered with an infusion device, pump settings should be included on the label. All labels shall conform to the requirements of the law. Home infusion pharmacies should adopt the list of prohibited abbreviations as another safety precaution to ensure that patients and caregivers receive clear instructions for drug use.

Packaging and Delivery. Policies and procedures should be available to ensure product integrity and temperature control during home delivery or patient pickup of supplies and drugs. The pharmacist should ensure that the delivery of medications and supplies to the patient occurs in a timely manner to avoid interruptions in drug therapy. Furthermore, the pharmacist should ensure that storage conditions during delivery and while in the patient's home are consistent with the recommendations for storing the product and beyond-use dating. The temperature of home refrigerators or freezers in which medications are stored should be within acceptable limits and should be monitored by the patient or caregiver. The pharmacist should ensure that an adequate inventory of medications and ancillary supplies is available in the patient's home. It may be appropriate to provide additional inventory for unforeseen circumstances in which extra doses or supplies may be required (e.g., waste, breakage, and emergencies). The pharmacist is responsible for providing sufficient quantities of medications and supplies to the patient, so that the ordered dosing regimen is maintained in the home setting without missed doses due to lack of drugs or supplies. Delivery to the patient should also include inventory management to avoid excessive accumulation of supplies and drugs. Excesses may indicate poor compliance, inadequate patient training, failure to assess patient needs, or ineffective inventory management by the patient. When common carriers are used, the pharmacy is responsible for ensuring that the carrier can provide timely delivery, proper handling, and external temperature control. Delivery personnel should know the shipping requirements for each package. If products are packaged so that product labels containing storage instructions are concealed, an exterior label specifying the storage conditions shall be used. To protect patient confidentiality, prescription labels with medication names and directions should not be used to label boxes. Box labels should include only the patient's name and address, the storage requirements, and delivery instructions. Additional precautions (i.e., double bagging, using at least one leak-proof container, and cushioning) should be used to safeguard hazardous products from breaking and leaking. The delivery person, patient, and caregiver shall be trained to recognize and manage accidental spills. Packages containing hazardous products should have appropriate precautionary labels.

Products should be delivered in appropriate packaging to ensure that labeled storage requirements are met during transit under the expected environmental conditions. The pharmacy should develop and follow written procedures for packaging; these procedures should include privacy-protection considerations. Product confirmation after delivery should be used to ensure that the packaging procedures and materials used were effective in maintaining product integrity and temperature control during transit. The stability of refrigerated products at room temperature should be taken into account in the development of packaging procedures. A few refrigerated products have extended stability at room temperature and may be safely delivered without refrigerated packaging. Products that are stable for 24 hours or less at room temperature should always be delivered in temperature-controlled packaging (coolers, ice packs, etc.).

Hazardous Drugs. Policies and procedures for the definition, storing, handling, and disposing of hazardous drug products should be available to ensure patient and employee safety in compliance with applicable local, state, and federal laws and regulations. Receipt, storage, and disposal of hazardous substances shall comply with all applicable federal, state, and local laws and regulations, including the Resource Conservation and Recovery Act (RCRA), as well as applicable guidance (e.g., ASHP guidelines,[22] *USP* Chapter 797[8]). Hazardous drug products should be stored in a negative pressure compounding room whenever possible. Additional storage precautions may include placement on a lower shelf or containment in a resealable plastic bag. Employees should be specially trained, and their handling and disposal of these products should be monitored. Spill kits should be available in locations where hazardous drugs are handled, and all personnel who handle these agents should be trained on using the kits.[4,22]

Controlled Substances. Policies and procedures for the storage, distribution, use, and accountability of controlled substances should be available to ensure appropriate use and to prevent diversion in compliance with applicable local, state, and federal laws and regulations. Controlled substances shall be kept in a secure and locked storage area that meets the requirements of state law. Pharmacists should be aware of the ways drugs can be diverted. Employees should be carefully screened before hire. Processes should be in place to minimize the risk of drug diversion and allow detection should diversion occur. Policies or procedures for activities such as ordering, receiving product, and conducting inventories should assure proper supervision and limit opportunities for a single individual to control the entire process.

Drug Samples. The use of drug samples should be eliminated to the fullest extent possible. If samples are permitted, the pharmacy should control these products to ensure proper storage, records, labeling, and product integrity.

Patient Care

Pharmaceutical care, defined as the responsible provision of drug therapy for the purpose of achieving definite outcomes that improve a patient's quality of life, has been adopted by much of the pharmacy profession.[23] The concept of pharmaceutical care is evolving into a more comprehensive, patient-focused model of pharmacist-provided care, sometimes termed *pharmacist patient care*. The principal elements of such care are the same: it is *medication related*; it is *care* that is *directly provided* to the patient; it is provided to produce *definite outcomes*; these outcomes are intended to improve the patient's *quality of life*; and the provider accepts personal *responsibility* for the outcomes.[23]

The mission of the pharmacist is to help people make the best use of medications. At a minimum, pharmacists are responsible for assessing the legal and clinical appropriateness of medication orders (or prescriptions), educating and counseling patients on the use of their medications, monitoring the effects of medication therapy, and maintaining patient profiles and other records. In the home infusion care setting, these responsibilities are best accomplished through the provision of pharmacist-provided patient care in which pharmacists are responsible for establishing relationships with patients and providers that will facilitate coordination and continuity of care, improve access to care, and improve patient outcomes.

Preadmission Assessment. The pharmacist, alone or in collaboration with other home infusion health care providers (e.g., nurses), should ensure that each patient referred for home infusion is assessed for appropriateness on the basis of admission criteria, including the following:

- The patient, family, and caregiver agree with provision of infusion services in the home;
- The patient or caregiver is willing and able to be educated about the correct administration of medications;
- The pharmacy can provide this education in a manner that the patient, family and caregiver can understand;
- The home environment is conducive to the provision of home infusion services (e.g., electricity and running water are present, and the home is clean and safe);
- The home infusion provider has reasonable geographic access to the patient;
- There is psychosocial and family support (e.g., caregiver requirements and financial concerns are manageable, and the family environment is suitable);
- There is ongoing prescriber involvement in the assessment and treatment of the patient;
- The medical condition and prescribed medication therapy are suitable for home infusion services, and there is a prognosis with clearly defined outcome goals;
- The indication, dosage, and route and method of administration of medications are appropriate; and
- Appropriate laboratory tests are ordered for monitoring the patient's response to medications.

Using the information collected during the preadmission assessment, the pharmacist, in conjunction with the other health care providers involved in the patient's care and the patient or caregiver, will determine the patient's appropriateness for home infusion services. The conclusions of the assessment should be communicated to all parties and appropriately documented.

Initial Patient Database and Assessment. The complete patient database should be documented in the patient's home infusion record in a timely manner. This database should include, at a minimum, the following:

- The patient's name, address, telephone number, and date of birth;

- The person to contact in the event of an emergency, including the legal guardian or representative, if applicable;
- Information on the existence, content, and intent of an advance directive, if applicable;
- The patient's height, weight, and gender;
- All diagnoses;
- The location and type of termination site of the vascular access device and internal and external catheter lengths, if applicable;
- Pertinent laboratory test results;
- Pertinent medical history and physical findings;
- Nutrition screening test results;
- An accurate history of allergies;
- Initial and ongoing pharmaceutical assessments;
- A detailed medication profile, including all medications (prescription and nonprescription), immunizations, home remedies, and investigational and nontraditional therapies;
- The prescriber's name, address, and telephone number and any other pertinent information (e.g., Drug Enforcement Administration number, National Provider Identifier [NPI]);
- Other agencies and individuals involved in the patient's care and directions for contacting them;
- A history of medication use; and
- A care plan and a list of drug-related problems, if any.

To obtain this information, the pharmacist could use the medical record; laboratory test results; direct communication with the patient, caregiver, nurse, and prescriber; and direct observation. When the pharmacist cannot directly observe the patient, the patient's home infusion nurse or other appropriate health care provider could provide the results of direct observation and physical assessment. If a shared-service agreement exists among multiple providers, the pharmacist should ensure that this agreement specifies the responsibilities of each provider for obtaining and sharing pertinent patient information.

Medication Reconciliation. Pharmacists should prepare or have access to comprehensive medication histories for each patient, including prescription drugs, nonprescription drugs, and alternative therapies. A pharmacist-conducted medication history for each patient is desirable; however, another appropriate health care provider (e.g., home infusion nurse, pharmacy technician) may obtain and maintain current medication histories, provided this information is accessible to the pharmacist and other health care providers.

Development of Care Plans. The pharmacist, in collaboration with the patient or caregiver and other health care providers, is responsible for developing an appropriate and individualized care plan for each patient. The pharmacist's contribution to the care plan should be based on information obtained from the initial pharmacy assessment and other relevant information obtained from the nurse, prescriber, patient, and caregivers. At a minimum, the pharmacist's contribution to the care plan should include the following:

- A description of actual or potential drug therapy problems and their proposed solutions;
- A description of desired outcomes of the drug therapy provided;
- A proposal for patient education and counseling; and
- A plan specifying proactive objective and subjective monitoring (e.g., vital signs, laboratory tests, physical findings, patient response, toxicity, adverse reactions, and noncompliance) and the frequency with which monitoring is to occur.

The care plan should be developed at the start of therapy and regularly reviewed and updated; the degree of detail of the plan should be based on the complexity of drug therapy and the patient's condition. Updates or changes to the plan, as they occur, should be communicated to other health care providers involved in the patient's care, to the patient, and to caregivers. The care plan and updates should be a part of the patient's record.

Clinical Monitoring. The pharmacist is responsible, in collaboration with other health care providers, for ongoing clinical monitoring of the patient's drug therapy according to the care plan and for appropriately documenting and communicating the results of all pertinent monitoring activities to other health care providers involved in the patient's care. The pharmacist is also responsible for ensuring that relevant information is obtained from the patient, the caregiver, and other health care providers and for documenting this information in the patient's home infusion record.

Pharmacists may, in collaboration with prescribers and others, wish to develop clinical monitoring protocols for various therapies that could be individualized in specific care plans. Pharmacists may receive laboratory test results before other health care providers. In such cases, the pharmacist is responsible for communicating the test results to the prescriber and other health care providers. The pharmacist should provide an interpretive analysis of the information and recommendations for dosage adjustments and for continuation or discontinuation of drug therapy. The pharmacist should ensure that sufficient laboratory test results are readily available for monitoring the patient's therapy. In shared-service arrangements, clinical monitoring responsibilities should be delineated.

The patient, the family, the caregiver, and all health care providers involved in the patient's care should have access to a pharmacist 24 hours a day. The pharmacist is responsible for providing a summary of all relevant clinical information to another pharmacist providing coverage for that patient (e.g., an on-call pharmacist) before transferring patient care responsibilities.

Patient Consultation and Education. Home infusion pharmacists will primarily consult patients or caregivers over the telephone. Home visits should be considered for enhancing compliance or simplifying complex drug-related patient issues.

The home infusion pharmacist, or the home infusion nurse as the agent, should ensure that the patient, caregiver, and other health care providers understand the proper use and administration of medications provided, including vascular access and infusion devices, as required. The home infusion pharmacist, or the nurse as the agent, should explain to the patient or the patient's agent the directions for use and any additional information.

The pharmacist is responsible for ensuring that the patient or caregiver receives appropriate education and counseling about the patient's medication therapy.[24] The pharmacist should verify that the patient or caregiver understands the therapy. Other health care providers may be involved in the education and counseling. A home infusion pharmacist should be readily accessible if questions or problems arise. Supplementary written information should be provided to reinforce oral communications. Contingencies should be available to provide education, counseling, and written materials to patients whose understanding of English may be compromised. Depending on the need, this might require access to interpreters or bilingual pharmacists. Patients who have hearing and sight impairments will potentially need other support or communication resources.

Professional judgment is required to determine what information should be included in patient education and counseling. The following should be considered:

- A description of medication therapy, including drug, dose, route of administration, dosage interval, and duration of therapy;
- The goals of medication therapy and indicators of progress toward those goals;
- Self-assessment techniques for monitoring the effectiveness of therapy;
- The importance of following the therapeutic plan;
- Proper aseptic technique;
- Hand hygiene;
- Proper care of the vascular-access device and site, if applicable;
- Precautions and directions for administering medications;
- Inspection of medications, containers, and supplies prior to use;
- Equipment use, maintenance, and troubleshooting;
- Home inventory management and procedures for securing additional supplies and medications when needed;
- Potential adverse effects, drug–drug interactions, drug–nutrient interactions, contraindications, adverse reactions, and the management of those events;
- Special precautions and directions for the preparation, storage, handling, and disposal of drugs, supplies, and biomedical waste;
- Information on contacting health care providers involved in the patient's care;
- Examples of situations that should be brought to the attention of the pharmacist or other health care providers involved in the patient's care (e.g., missed doses, doses not given at the proper time, and low supplies); and
- Emergency procedures.

Patient counseling and education should be performed in accordance with applicable state regulations and documented in the patient's home infusion record.

Communication with Patients and Caregivers. Effective communication among pharmacists, patients, and caregivers is also essential to ensuring high-quality care. The pharmacist providing home infusion services should establish free and open channels of communication with patients and caregivers. The pharmacist should contact the patient or the caregiver, as appropriate, to

- Obtain information needed for the initial pharmacy assessment;
- Provide supplemental patient education and counseling as needed;
- Assess compliance with drug therapy;
- Assess progress toward the goal of therapy;
- Inform the patient how to contact the pharmacist when needed; and
- Assess drug therapy problems (e.g., failure to respond to therapy and adverse drug events).

All contacts with the patient should be documented in the patient's home infusion record.

Communication with Physicians, Prescribers, Nurses, and Other Health Care Providers. Effective communication among pharmacists and other health care providers is essential to ensuring continuous, coordinated care. The pharmacist should ensure that effective channels of communication about care are in place, including shared-service arrangements (e.g., regarding pain assessments and laboratory test data). Oral and written communication methods can be used for communicating patient information. All relevant clinical communication should be documented in the patient's home infusion record. The pharmacist is responsible for protecting the patient's privacy and confidentiality while communicating this information to other health care providers. Personnel involved in the care of the patient should meet regularly to discuss the clinical status of the patient and any operational issues related to the patient's care.

Medication Administration. Policies and procedures on the administration of medications should be available. Only personnel who are authorized by the home infusion organization and are appropriately trained and licensed should be permitted to administer medications to a patient. Pharmacists, where legally permitted, may be authorized to administer medications after receiving appropriate training.

Emergency Medical Care. The home infusion pharmacist should participate in decisions about the emergency care of patients at home, including the development of protocols for using emergency drugs in the home. Policies and procedures should exist within the organization for providing appropriate levels of patient care during emergency situations 24 hours a day, including access to the pharmacist responsible for the care, when appropriate. Appropriately trained pharmacists should have an authorized role in responding to medical emergencies. The pharmacy should participate in the development of policies and procedures to ensure availability of, access to, and security of emergency medications.

Discharge from Home Infusion. When patients have completed therapy as ordered, they should be discharged from service. Items that should be documented in the medical record upon discharge include the patient's response to therapy and status at discharge.

Transfer to Another Care Setting. The pharmacist should ensure continuity of pharmacist care to and from the home and other patient-care settings. The pharmacist should routinely contribute to processes ensuring that each patient receives pharmacist care regardless of transitions that occur across different health care settings (for example, among different components of a health system and different types of home infusion services). When home infusion patients are admitted to a hospital, the home infusion pharmacy should inform the hospital about (1) the medications the patient is currently receiving from the home infusion pharmacy and (2) known allergies. The home infusion pharmacy should recognize hospital policy when considering whether properly stored medications and medical equipment from the home can be used during the home infusion patient's hospitalization.

Documentation in the Home Infusion Medical Record. Clinical actions and recommendations by pharmacists that are intended to ensure safe and effective use of medications and that have a potential effect on patient outcomes should be documented in patients' home infusion medical records. Pharmacists should provide oral or written consultations to other health professionals regarding medication therapy selection and management. Consultations should be documented in the patient's home infusion medical record. The pharmacy should have an ongoing process for consistent documentation (and reporting to physicians, administrators, and others) of pharmacist care and patient outcomes resulting from medication therapy and other pharmacy actions. Patient privacy and confidentiality should be protected at all times.

A home infusion record should be developed and used for documenting the home infusion services provided to each patient. Written organizational policies and procedures should address the security of home infusion records and specify personnel authorized to review patient records and to make entries. The need to maintain confidentiality of patient information should be stressed to all personnel. The pharmacist is responsible for documenting all pharmacy clinical activities in the patient's record in a timely manner. General clinician-oriented forms are preferred over specific nursing, pharmacy, and other health care professional forms to minimize duplication of information. It may be advisable for organizations that provide multiple home infusion services (e.g., pharmacy, nursing, respiratory therapy, dieticians) to use a single home infusion record for documenting all clinical information regarding each patient. The patient's record should be accessible at all times to authorized personnel involved in the care of the patient, but confidentiality should be maintained.

Selection of Products, Devices, and Ancillary Supplies. The pharmacist, in collaboration with other health care providers and the patient, is responsible for selecting infusion devices, ancillary drugs (e.g., heparin lock flush solution, 0.9% sodium chloride flush), and ancillary supplies (e.g., dressing kits, syringes, and administration sets). Pharmacists should be thoroughly trained and knowledgeable in the selection, proper use, and maintenance of these devices, drugs, and supplies. Factors involved in the selection of devices and ancillary supplies may include the following:

- The stability and compatibility of prescribed medications in infusion device reservoirs;
- The ability of an infusion device to accommodate the appropriate volume of medication and diluent, and to deliver the prescribed dose at the appropriate rate;
- The ability of the patient or caregiver to learn to operate an infusion device;
- The potential for patient complications and noncompliance;
- Patient preference;
- Nursing or caregiver experience with therapies and selected devices;
- Prescriber preferences;
- Cost considerations; and
- The safety features of infusion devices.

Patient's Own Medications. Drug products and related devices not dispensed by the home infusion pharmacy that are to be used during the patient's course of therapy should be documented in the patient's home infusion medical record. When home infusion patients are known to be admitted to a hospital or other extended care facility, the home infusion pharmacy should inform the hospital about the medications the patient is currently receiving from the home infusion pharmacy and about any known allergies. The home infusion pharmacy should recognize hospital policy when considering whether properly stored medications and medical equipment from the home can be used during the home infusion patient's hospitalization.

Emergency Medications. The home infusion pharmacist, in consultation with the prescriber, should determine when emergency medications and supplies (e.g., anaphylaxis "kits") should be dispensed to home infusion patients. When standing orders for ancillary drugs or supplies or standardized treatment protocols are used, the pharmacist should review each protocol to determine its appropriateness for the patient.

Performance Improvement Activities

The home infusion pharmacy should have an ongoing, systematic program for assessing pharmacist patient care, and pharmacists should be active participants in performance improvement activities. A performance improvement program for home infusion should monitor patient satisfaction and outcomes, and the program should also include appropriate quality control measures for compounding sterile preparations and other activities. Performance improvement activities based on assessments should be integrated with the health system's overall performance improvement activities, as applicable. The performance improvement team should work with frontline staff to implement systems that include proper checks and balances focused on protecting against human error. Performance improvement initiatives should be focused on error reporting trends and high-risk functions such as dispensing high-alert medications.

Benchmarking. As part of the performance improvement program, operational and outcomes data should be benchmarked with those of other home infusion pharmacy services of similar size and scope. The results, including follow-up actions for improvement, should be documented and provided to the organization's managers, the frontline staff using the system, and others as appropriate.

Clinical Outcomes. Most accrediting bodies and some regulatory agencies require the home infusion pharmacy to monitor clinical patient outcomes. Common measures that are tracked routinely by home infusion companies include the rate of catheter-related infections, adverse drug reactions, medication errors, warehouse/delivery errors, equipment malfunctions, and unplanned hospitalizations. In addition, the organization should have an infection control program in which both staff and patient infection (communicable diseases) rates are monitored. The organization may also select outcomes that are monitored over a short time as a specific process is improved.

Medication Error Reporting. Medication error monitoring and prevention should be part of every pharmacy's performance improvement program. Information about strategies to prevent medication errors is available from several sources, including ISMP, which produces regular newsletters on this topic.

All pharmacies should have processes in place that are designed to prevent and detect medication errors before they leave the pharmacy. If an error does occur, the pharmacy director and staff should determine how and why the error happened, and what can be done to prevent similar errors from occurring. Medication errors should be reported to voluntary national reporting systems and, as required, to accrediting organizations or regulatory agencies. Reports should be documented, analyzed, trended and reviewed consistent with National Coordinating Council for Medication Error Reporting and Prevention (NCCMERP) standards.

Patient Satisfaction. Most accrediting bodies require the home infusion pharmacy to measure patient satisfaction with treatment and services. This function can be performed in-house by mailing questionnaires to the patient, or it can be outsourced to a contractor. Patient satisfaction surveys that are returned should be reviewed for both positive and negative comments so that corrective action can be targeted to service issues.

Medication-Use Evaluation. An ongoing program of monitoring drug utilization and costs should be in place to ensure that medications are used appropriately, safely, and effectively, and to increase the probability of desired outcomes within defined populations of patients. The medication-use policy committee should define specific parameters for evaluation (e.g., disease state, pharmacologic category, high-use/high-cost drug products, high-alert medications) as appropriate for the organization. Through this ongoing evaluation, areas in need of improvement in medication prescribing and management can be identified and targeted for intervention.

Adverse Drug Event Reporting. The home infusion pharmacist should take a leadership role in the development of a program for reporting and monitoring all adverse drug events and device-related events, including adverse drug reactions and medication errors. The pharmacist should ensure that the prescriber is notified promptly of any suspected adverse drug events. Adverse drug events should serve as outcome indicators of quality, and the monitoring of adverse drug events should be a part of the organization's ongoing performance improvement program. Relevant trends should be integrated into staff development and in-service education programs for pharmacists and nurses to improve the quality of care and patient outcomes. Serious adverse drug reactions and device-related problems should be reported promptly to the manufacturer and to the Food and Drug Administration's MedWatch program.[25]

Operations

Hours of Operation. Home infusion pharmacy services shall be available 24 hours a day, seven days a week. A pharmacist should be available for consultation or dispensing after hours. Home infusion pharmacy staff may be supplemented by knowledgeable and experienced part-time or on-call personnel to extend pharmacy services coverage.

Pharmacy Security and After-Hours Access. Only authorized pharmacy personnel should have access to the pharmacy area. Other home infusion organization personnel may be in the pharmacy area only when an authorized pharmacist is present, in accordance with the home infusion organization's policies or as required by laws and regulations. In an emergency situation in which a pharmacist is not present, such as a fire or security alarm, policies and procedures should guide safe access to the pharmacy area and provide for notification of the pharmacist in charge or a designee.

Emergency Preparedness and Business Continuity Planning. Policies and procedures should be available that include a plan for providing pharmacy services in case of an area-wide disaster affecting the home infusion pharmacy or patients' home infusion settings. Appropriately trained pharmacists and representatives from the pharmacy team should be members of emergency preparedness teams and participate in drills. Patients should be informed about what to do to safely continue needed home therapies in the event of a disaster. The health system's business continuity plan should address the provision of pharmacy services in non-emergency situations, such as information system failures or disruptions of the drug procurement process.[19,26]

Communications. Staff meetings should be conducted on a regular basis for various purposes, which may include:

- Brief daily meeting to review on-call issues, upcoming referrals, and current daily plan;
- Hand-off communications to and from evening staff or on-call personnel;
- In-services regarding updates to policies or procedures, law, regulation, or services;
- Review of new medications;
- Analysis of sales and marketing efforts;
- Performance improvement functions;
- Team building among the staff; or
- Interdisciplinary meetings or case conferences to communicate the pharmacist's care plan for a patient (with patients, caregivers, physicians, prescribers, or other health professionals).

Equipment Management. Equipment may be owned, leased, or rented by the infusion pharmacy. It is usually most cost-effective to lease-purchase infusion pumps that are used in high volume. Pumps with specialized uses (e.g., micro-infusers) may be used less frequently and may be rented as needed.

Equipment may be purchased or rented from a properly qualified vendor. Routine maintenance (i.e., basic safety checks, alarm testing, and accuracy validation) is performed between patient use, and preventive maintenance for medical equipment is defined by the manufacturer for each specific device. The manufacturer's preventive maintenance recommendations should be followed, and all equipment should be maintained so that the preventive maintenance is not overdue during patient use. Technical repair of medical equipment should be done by a properly qualified service technician. Home infusion pharmacies typically do not have the capacity to employ staff on site with the technical certification required for equipment preventive maintenance or repair. Outsourcing these functions is usually the most efficient and cost-effective way to maintain equipment in good working order.

Records Storage and Maintenance. Adequate space should be available for maintaining and storing records, including medication profiles and other patient information, management information, equipment maintenance sheets, controlled-substances inventory sheets, and MSDSes, among others, to ensure compliance with laws, regulations, accreditation requirements, and sound management practices. Patient records shall be secure. Records shall be retained according to applicable laws and regulations, which may vary by state and by Centers for Medicare & Medicaid Services (CMS) participation guidelines. There may be additional record retention requirements for specific patient population (e.g., pediatric patients) medical records in some states and according to accreditation standards.

Information Technology. Computer resources should be used to maintain patient medication profiles, perform necessary patient billing procedures, manage drug product inventories, and interface with other available computerized systems to obtain patient-specific clinical information for drug therapy monitoring and other clinical functions and to facilitate the continuity of care after patients transfer to and from other care settings.

Home Infusion Medical Record Systems. A patient medication profile should be maintained by all home infusion pharmacies regardless of where the dispensing of medications takes place. The home infusion medical record should include assessment and care planning documents, progress notes, laboratory test results, and other patient information related to determining the appropriateness of medications and monitoring their effects. The system should provide safeguards against the improper manipulation or alteration of records and provide an audit trail.

An automated information system is preferred, but the system may be manual, automated, or a combination of the two. If an automated information system is used, an auxiliary record-keeping procedure should be available for documenting medication information in case the automated system is inoperative, and a daily data backup system should be in place.

Hazardous Waste Management and Disposal. There are many ways to dispose of hazardous waste generated by the pharmacy. In addition to the established waste management companies, there are also mail-back services. For the traditional services, it is important to follow the company's requirements. Since much of the waste eventually is sent to dump sites, waste that needs to be incinerated should be discarded separately. The companies that provide mail-back service also incinerate all the waste they receive, so it is not necessary to separate the waste. It is also important that the pharmacist understand the OSHA and RCRA requirements regarding management and disposal of hazardous substances. There should be a designated area for hazardous waste, including sharps. Spill kits should be readily available in locations where hazardous substances are handled, and all personnel who handle these agents should be trained on using these kits.[4,22]

Facilities

To ensure optimal operational performance and quality patient care, adequate space, equipment, and supplies should be available for all professional and administrative functions related to medication use. These resources should be located in areas that facilitate the provision of services to patients, nurses, prescribers, and other health care providers and should be integrated with the home infusion organization's communications, delivery, or transportation systems. Facilities should be constructed, arranged, and equipped to promote safe and efficient work and to avoid damage to or deterioration of drug products.

Ambulatory Infusion Center or Infusion Suite. Pharmacies that have an on-site (ambulatory) infusion suite must include appropriate access to the facility (e.g., handicapped parking, sidewalk ramp) and other internal design features (e.g., restroom grab bar) according to the Americans with Disabilities Act. Local building code regulations may also apply. Accreditation standards for home care organizations typically include a section on infusion suites and cover such items as patient access, facility safety checks, nursing procedures, and room sanitation. State and local authorities may have additional regulations for ambulatory treatment centers; these should be researched before planning to offer ambulatory treatment services.

Home Infusion Pharmacies. Designated space and equipment for compounding and packaging sterile preparations should be available.[7,8] The compounding environment should be monitored and maintained on an ongoing basis. Appropriate facility space, equipment, and supplies for compounding hazardous preparations should be available.[7,8,22] Adequate facilities and equipment should be established for decontaminating, cleaning, and maintaining infusion devices, including durable medical equipment.

General Work Area. The pharmacy work area should allow pharmacists to observe work being done by support staff (telephone calls to patients, computer data entry, compounding, etc.). Pharmacies should consider having an area dedicated to the function of checking compounded preparations and other prescriptions that is out of the main traffic pattern and where the checking pharmacist is not distracted by noise, telephones, or conversation.

Stockroom and Storage Areas. Facilities should be available for storing and preparing medications in the home infusion pharmacy under proper conditions of sanitation, temperature, light, moisture, ventilation, segregation, and security to ensure medication integrity and personnel safety and to prevent drug diversion.[27] Adequate refrigeration and freezer capacity should be provided within the secure pharmacy area.

Office and Meeting Space. Office and meeting areas should be available for administrative, clinical, technical, and reimbursement staff. Ideally, interdisciplinary team members from pharmacy, nursing, and reimbursement are located within a proximate space.

Cleanroom and Anteroom (Compounding Area). The home infusion pharmacy should follow all applicable federal, state, and local requirements, including USP Chapter 797,[8] for building and maintaining the pharmacy's compounding facilities. Options for building out a cleanroom include purchase of a modular prefabricated unit or building out an existing space with only those materials needed to bring the facility into compliance with laws, regulation, and guidance. Design and organization of the cleanroom should allow for the pharmacist's view of compounding activities through a large window or clear wall and efficient flow of materials and compounding documents into the cleanroom for processing and out of the cleanroom for the checking/verification step.

Sterile medications shall be compounded within a primary engineering control such as a laminar flow hood or a compounding aseptic containment isolator. Compounding facilities shall be cleaned and maintained following federal, state, and local laws or regulations as well as applicable guidance (e.g., ASHP guidelines, *USP* Chapter 797).[7,8] Environmental monitoring of the compounding facilities shall be ongoing and should include all elements required by federal, state, and local laws or regulations as well as applicable guidance (e.g., ASHP guidelines, USP 797).[7,8]

References

1. Health Insurance Portability and Accountability Act of 1996. Pub. L. No. 104-191. www.cms.hhs.gov/HIPAAGenInfo/Downloads/HIPAALaw.pdf (accessed 12 February 2011).
2. U.S. Department of Health and Human Services Office of Inspector General Exclusions Program. http://oig.hhs.gov/fraud/exclusions.asp (accessed 12 January 2011).
3. American Society of Hospital Pharmacists. ASHP statement on continuing education. *Am J Hosp Pharm.* 1990; 47:1855.
4. United States Department of Labor Occupational Safety & Health Administration. http://osha.gov/SLTC/bloodbornepathogens/index.html (accessed 12 February 2011).
5. National Institute of Occupational Safety and Health. NIOSH List of Antineoplastic and Other Hazardous Drugs in Healthcare Settings 2010. www.cdc.gov/niosh/docs/2010-167/pdfs/2010-167.pdf (accessed 12 February 2011).
6. United States Department of Labor Occupations Safety & Health Administration, Hazard Communication: Foundation of Workplace Chemical Safety Program. www.osha.gov/dsg/hazcom/index.html (accessed 12 February 2011).
7. American Society of Health-System Pharmacists. ASHP guidelines on quality assurance for pharmacy-prepared sterile products. *Am J Health-Syst Pharm.* 2000; 57:1150–69.
8. Pharmaceutical compounding—sterile preparations (general information chapter 797). In: The United States pharmacopeia, 34th rev., and The national formulary, 29th ed. Rockville, MD: The United States Pharmacopeial Convention; 2011: 336–73.
9. American Society of Health-System Pharmacists. ASHP guidelines on the pharmacy and therapeutics committee and the formulary system. *Am J Health-Syst Pharm.* 2008; 65:1272–83.
10. American Society of Health-System Pharmacists. ASHP guidelines on clinical drug research. *Am J Health-Syst Pharm.* 1998; 55:369–76.
11. American Society of Hospital Pharmacists. ASHP guidelines for pharmaceutical research in organized health-care settings. *Am J Hosp Pharm.* 1989; 46:129–30.
12. American Society of Health-System Pharmacists. ASHP guidelines on the safe use of automated dispensing devices. *Am J Health-Syst Pharm.* 2010; 67:483–90.
13. American Society of Health-System Pharmacists. ASHP statement on the pharmacist's role in substance abuse prevention, education, and assistance. *Am J Health-Syst Pharm.* 2014; 71:243–6.
14. American Society of Health-System Pharmacists. ASHP guidelines on the pharmacist's role in the development, implementation, and assessment of critical pathways. *Am J Health-Syst Pharm.* 2004; 61:939–45.
15. American Society of Hospital Pharmacists. ASHP guidelines for selecting pharmaceutical manufacturers and suppliers. *Am J Hosp Pharm.* 1991; 48:523–4.
16. American Society of Health-System Pharmacists. ASHP guidelines on medication cost management strategies for hospitals and health systems. *Am J Health-Syst Pharm.* 2008; 65:1368–84.
17. American Society of Health-System Pharmacists (ASHP). ASHP Drug Shortages Resource Center. www.ashp.org/shortages (accessed 21 Mar 2013).
18. U.S. Food and Drug Administration. Drug shortages. www.fda.gov/cder/drug/shortages/ (accessed 21 Mar 2013).
19. American Society of Health-System Pharmacists. ASHP guidelines on managing drug product shortages in hospitals and health systems. *Am J Health-Syst Pharm.* 2009; 66:1399–406.
20. Institute for Safe Medication Practices (ISMP). ISMP's List of High-Alert Medications. www.ismp.org/tools/highalertmedications.pdf (accessed 21 Mar 2013).
21. American Society of Health-System Pharmacists. ASHP guidelines on outsourcing sterile compounding services. *Am J Health-Syst Pharm.* 2010; 67:757–65.
22. American Society of Health-System Pharmacists. ASHP guidelines on handling hazardous drugs. *Am J Health-Syst Pharm.* 2006; 63:1172–93.
23. Hepler CD, Strand LM. Opportunities and responsibilities in pharmaceutical care. *Am J Hosp Pharm.* 1990;47:533–43.

24. American Society of Health-System Pharmacists. ASHP guidelines on pharmacist-conducted patient education and counseling. *Am J Health-Syst Pharm.* 1997; 54:431–4.
25. American Society of Health-System Pharmacists. ASHP guidelines on adverse drug reaction monitoring and reporting. *Am J Health-Syst Pharm.* 1995; 52:417–9.
26. American Society of Health-System Pharmacists. ASHP statement on the role of health-system pharmacists in emergency preparedness. *Am J Health-Syst Pharm.* 2003; 60:1993–5.
27. American Society of Hospital Pharmacists. ASHP technical assistance bulletin on hospital drug distribution and control. *Am J Hosp Pharm.* 1980; 37:1097–103.

Approved by the ASHP Board of Directors on June 28, 2013. Developed through the ASHP Section of Ambulatory Care Practitioners Section Advisory Group on Home Infusion. These guidelines supersede the ASHP Guidelines on the Pharmacist's Role in Home Care dated April 27, 2000, and the ASHP Guidelines: Minimum Standard for Home Care Pharmacies dated November 14, 1998.

Barbara J. Petroff, M.S., FASHP; Donald Filibeck, Pharm.D., M.B.A.; Anna Nowobilski-Vasilios, Pharm.D., M.B.A., CNSC, BCNSP, FASHP; R. Stephen Olsen, Pharm.D.; Carol J. Rollins, Pharm.D., M.S., RD, BCNSP; and Cathy Johnson, B.S.Pharm., are gratefully acknowledged for authoring these guidelines.

ASHP gratefully acknowledges the contributions of the following individuals to these guidelines: Mitra Gavgani, Pharm.D.; Brian G. Swift, Pharm.D., M.B.A.; Lisa Linn Siefert, B.S.Pharm., ASQ-CQM, FASHP; Kelly Rogers, B.S.Pharm.; and Caryn M. Bing, M.S., FASHP.

ASHP also gratefully acknowledges the following organizations and individuals for reviewing these guidelines (review does not imply endorsement): Academy of Managed Care Pharmacy (AMCP); American Academy of Ambulatory Care Nursing (AAACN); American Society for Parenteral and Enteral Nutrition (ASPEN); Infusion Nurses Society; Rhode Island Society of Health-System Pharmacists; Jeanette Spain Adams, Ph.D., RN, ACNS, BC, CRNI; Mary Alexander, M.A., RN, CRNI, CAE, FAAN; Dominick A. Caselnova III, B.S.Pharm., M.H.A., FASHP; Toby Clark, M.Sc., FASHP; Sharon M. Durfee, B.S.Pharm., BCNSP; Michael Edwards, Pharm.D., M.B.A., BCOP, FASHP; Allen Flynn, Pharm.D., CPHIMS, CHS; Peggi Guenter, Ph.D., RN, CNSN (ASPEN); Kathleen M. Gura, Pharm.D., BCNSP, FASHP, FPPAG; Richelle Hamblin, RN, M.S.N., CRNI (AAACN); John Hertig, Pharm.D., M.S.; Tim Lanese, M.B.A., FASHP; Jay Lewandowski, Pharm.D.; Mary R. Monk-Tutor, Ph.D., FASHP; Richard D. Paoletti, M.B.A., FASHP; Susan M. Paschke, M.S.N., RN-BC, NEA-BC (AAACN); Stephanie Peshek, Pharm.D., M.B.A., FASHP; Nicole Pilch, Pharm.D., MSCR, BCPS; James A. Ponto, M.S., BCNP, FASHP; Tony Powers, Pharm.D.; Curt W. Quap, M.S., FASHP; Armando Riggi, Pharm.D.; Jean S. Rutledge, Ph.D.; Elizabeth Sampsel, Pharm.D., M.B.A., BCPS (AMCP); Robert A. Smaglia, B.S.Pharm.; Nancy R. Smestad, M.S.; Rex Speerhas, CDE, BCNSP; Melisa Tong, Pharm.D.; and Kristine Widboom.

The bibliographic citation for this document is as follows: American Society of Health-System Pharmacists. ASHP Guidelines on Home Infusion Pharmacy Services. *Am J Health-Syst Pharm.* 2014; 71:325–41.

ASHP Guidelines: Minimum Standard for Ambulatory Care Pharmacy Practice

In recent years, there has been an increasing emphasis in health systems on the provision of ambulatory care services. Payers have created incentives to decrease hospitalization rates and length of stay, making way for a new shift toward pay-for-performance, outcomes-based reimbursement, and accountable care. There is also an increasing focus in medicine on preventive health, patient education, and care transitions. Yet, the number of patients with multiple chronic medical conditions that require longitudinal and integrated care management across a continuum of care settings is growing. Appropriate medication therapy in the ambulatory care setting is often the most common and most cost-effective form of treatment, yet the consequences of adverse drug events (ADEs) and the inappropriate use of medications in this setting can be catastrophic.[1] Ambulatory care pharmacy services are therefore an essential component of any comprehensive healthcare delivery system.

Pharmacists have become integral members of healthcare teams in a variety of settings, such as patient-centered medical homes, community health centers, long-term care facilities, hospital outpatient departments, and freestanding pharmacies, among others; the care they provide has enabled patients, other providers, and payers to achieve their clinical, humanistic, and economic goals.[2,3] There is growing recognition and understanding that ambulatory care pharmacy services extend far beyond the dispensing of medications and include direct patient care and the design and management of complex medication regimens and care delivery systems. Current evidence demonstrates that the inclusion of pharmacists practicing in ambulatory care settings on the healthcare team improves quality of care, enhances patient outcomes, and contributes to cost avoidance.[4] Most states now allow pharmacists to provide direct patient care services under a physician–pharmacist collaborative agreement, further supporting the expansion of ambulatory care pharmacy services.

The primary purpose of these guidelines is to outline the minimum requirements for the operation and management of services for patients in this rapidly evolving ambulatory care setting. The elements of service that are critical to optimal, safe, and effective medication use in the ambulatory setting include (1) leadership and practice management, (2) patient care, (3) drug distribution and control, and (4) facilities, equipment, and other resources. Although the scope of pharmacy services will vary from site to site, depending on the needs of the patients served and the resources available, these elements are directly linked to improved patient, population, and health-system outcomes. Specific attention to each element is essential to delivering patient care of the highest quality. As providers of care to patients in ambulatory care settings, pharmacists should be concerned with and take responsibility for the outcomes of their services in addition to the provision of these services. Care should also extend into and be coordinated with care providers in other settings; therefore, these guidelines should be used, as applicable, in conjunction with minimum standards for other practice settings. Rather than including detailed advice in this document, readers should refer to other referenced documents that address many of the outlined topics for additional information and guidance. Aspects of these guidelines may not be applicable in some settings due to differences in settings and organizational arrangements and complexity. Pharmacists practicing in ambulatory care settings should use their professional judgment in assessing and adapting these guidelines to meet the needs of their own practice settings.

These guidelines are intended to be a comprehensive overview of current minimum requirements for the operation and management of services for patients in the ambulatory care setting. These guidelines are complemented by the ASHP/ASHP Foundation Ambulatory Conference and Summit consensus recommendations,[5] which provide a long-term vision for aspirational and forward-thinking pharmacy practice models that will ensure that pharmacists participate as members of the ambulatory healthcare team who are responsible and accountable for patient and population outcomes.

Standard I. Practice Management

Effective leadership and practice management skills are necessary for the delivery of pharmacy services in a manner consistent with the health system's and the patient's needs. Such leadership should foster continuous improvement in patient care outcomes. The management of ambulatory care pharmacy services should focus on the pharmacist's value and responsibilities as a patient care provider and leader of the pharmacy enterprise through the development of organizational structures that support this mission. Development of such structures will require communication and collaboration with other departments and services throughout the health system that support ambulatory care, which every member of the pharmacy team should cultivate at every opportunity.

A. Pharmacy and Pharmacist Services

Pharmacy Mission, Goals, and Scope of Services. Ambulatory care pharmacy services should have a written mission statement that, at a minimum, reflects both pharmacy patient care and service responsibilities. The mission should be consistent with the mission of the health system. The development and prioritization of goals, objectives, and work should be consistent with the mission statement. The mission statement may also incorporate consensus-based national goals, such as those expressed in the recommendations from the ASHP Pharmacy Practice Model Initiative.[6]

Ambulatory care pharmacy services should also maintain a written document describing the scope of pharmacy services. These services should be consistent with the health system's scope of services and should be applied in all practice sites. The mission, goals, and scope of services should be clearly communicated to everyone involved in the provision of pharmacy services.

Practice Standards and Guidelines. The standards and regulations of all relevant government bodies (e.g., state boards of pharmacy, departments of health) shall be met. The practice standards and guidelines of the American Society of Health-System Pharmacists, the Joint Commission, the National Committee for Quality Assurance, and other appropriate accrediting bodies should be assessed and adapted, as applicable. Guidelines set forth by other independent organizations such as the Institute for Safe Medication Practices (ISMP) should be assessed and adapted as applicable. The health system and the pharmacy should strive to meet these standards, regardless of the particular financial and organizational arrangements by which pharmacy services are provided to the health system and its patients. Pharmacists practicing in ambulatory care settings should play a critical role in ensuring that the health system adheres to medication-related national quality indicators and evidence-based practice guidelines.

B. Laws and Regulations

Compliance with local, state, and federal laws and regulations applicable to the ambulatory care pharmacy shall be required. The pharmacy shall maintain relevant documentation of compliance with requirements concerning procurement, distribution, and disposal of drug products; security of patient information; and workplace safety from the state board of pharmacy, Food and Drug Administration (FDA), Drug Enforcement Administration (DEA), Centers for Medicare and Medicaid Services (CMS), Occupational Safety and Health Administration, and others. Ambulatory care pharmacies dispensing medications across state boundaries shall comply with out-of-state licensure requirements as well as other state and federal interstate laws and regulations. Pharmacists practicing in ambulatory care settings may enter into prescriptive authority and collaborative practice agreements that are state specific in scope. Finally, pharmacists practicing in ambulatory care settings should be knowledgeable about reimbursement rules and compliance and billing requirements.

C. Policies and Procedures

Policies and Procedures Manual. A policy and procedures manual governing the scope of the ambulatory care pharmacy services being provided (e.g., administrative, operational, and clinical) should be available and consistent with current department processes. The manual should be reviewed and revised on a regular basis to reflect changes in policies and procedures, the scope of services, organizational arrangements, objectives, or practices. All personnel should be familiar with and adhere to the contents of the manual. Appropriate mechanisms should be established to ensure compliance with all policies and procedures.

Personnel Safety. Ambulatory care pharmacy personnel should be involved in the health system's plans for emergency response, infection prevention and control, management of hazardous substances and waste, and incident reporting. All pharmacy staff shall be familiar with these plans.

Emergency Preparedness. Policies and procedures should exist for providing pharmacy services during facility, local, or areawide disasters affecting the organization's patients. Appropriately trained pharmacists and representatives from the pharmacy team should be members of emergency preparedness teams and participate in drills. Patients should be informed about what to do to safely continue medication therapy in the event of a disaster.[7]

The health system's business continuity plan should consider the provision of pharmacist patient care services in emergency situations. Factors to consider should include system failures and breakdowns in the drug procurement process.

Medical Emergencies. Policies and procedures should exist within the organization for providing appropriate levels of patient care during emergency situations 24 hours a day, including access to the pharmacist responsible for patient care, when appropriate. Pharmacists in the ambulatory care setting are an essential part of both rapid-response teams and resuscitation teams. Appropriately trained pharmacists should have an authorized role in responding to medical emergencies. The pharmacy should participate in the development of policies and procedures to ensure the availability of, access to, and security of emergency medications, including antidotes.

Preventive and Postexposure Immunization Programs. If appropriate, the pharmacy team should participate in the development of policies and procedures concerning preventive and wellness programs and postexposure programs for infectious diseases (e.g., human immunodeficiency virus, tuberculosis, hepatitis) for patients and employees. As appropriate, pharmacists should promote the use of immunizations and, when legally allowed, participate as active immunizers.[8]

Substance Abuse Programs. If appropriate, the pharmacy team should assist in the development of and participate in the health system's substance abuse education, prevention, identification, and organization-sponsored programs for staff and patients.[9]

D. Human Resources

Position Descriptions. Areas of responsibility within the scope of pharmacy services shall be clearly defined. The responsibilities and related competencies of pharmacy personnel shall be clearly defined in written position descriptions. Pharmacists should be responsible for the provision of patient care and for the supervision and management of support staff. Sufficient support staff (pharmacy technicians, clerical) should be employed to facilitate the provision of care. Technicians should be responsible for aspects of drug procurement, dialogue with third-party payers, support of pharmacists' patient care activities, and preparation of prescription orders for a pharmacist's clinical review.

Director of Ambulatory Care Pharmacy Services. These guidelines use the term *director of ambulatory care pharmacy services* (or, more simply, *director*) to indicate the person responsible for managing these services. Depending on the health system's organizational structure and other factors, designations such as manager or pharmacist-in-charge may also be used. Ambulatory care pharmacy services shall be managed by a professionally competent, legally qualified pharmacist. The director should be knowledgeable about and have experience in all aspects of pharmacy care for ambulatory care patients. Completion of an advanced management degree (e.g., M.B.A., M.H.A., M.S., M.P.H.), a residency, or both is desirable. Completion of an ASHP-accredited postgraduate year 1 (PGY1) residency should be considered a minimum competency, while completion of an ASHP-accredited postgraduate year 2 (PGY2) residency would be optimal.

The director of ambulatory care pharmacy services shall be responsible for

- Establishing the mission, vision, goals, and scope of services of the ambulatory care pharmacy practice setting on the basis of the needs of the patients served, the needs of the health system, and developments and trends in healthcare and pharmacy practice,
- Developing, implementing, evaluating, and updating plans and activities to fulfill the mission, vision, goals, and scope of services,
- Actively working with health-system leadership to develop and implement policies and procedures that provide safe and effective medication use for all patients served by the organization,
- Ensuring the development and implementation of policies and procedures that provide safe and effective medication use for the patients served by the organization,
- Mobilizing and managing the resources, both human and financial, necessary for the optimal provision of pharmacy services, and
- Ensuring that patient care services provided by pharmacists and other pharmacy personnel are delivered in compliance with applicable state and federal laws and regulations as well as national practice standards.

A part-time director shall have the same obligations and responsibilities as a full-time director.[10,11]

The ambulatory care pharmacy team should be a cross-functional group whose skills set includes operations management, clinical care, financial management, process improvement, and informatics. Depending on the size and scope of the setting, these functional responsibilities may be assigned to a single person or a team. It is the responsibility of the director to monitor the status of the goals set forth in the vision, provide feedback to the pharmacy team as necessary, and support the team's implementation of the core functions of the pharmacy practice.

Pharmacist Licensure and Certification. All pharmacists must possess a current state license to practice pharmacy. Functional responsibilities may mandate additional degrees (M.S., M.B.A., M.H.A., M.P.H.), certificates, or credentials (e.g., Board of Pharmacy Specialties certification). Pharmacists who provide direct patient care and drug therapy management should be certified through the most appropriate Board of Pharmacy Specialties certification process. As appropriate, these pharmacists should also be privileged and credentialed by the health system.

Technician Requirements. The ambulatory care setting shall adhere to all state guidelines regarding pharmacy technician registration, certification, and licensure, as applicable. All pharmacy technicians should successfully complete a training course approved by the ambulatory care site that includes education on at least the following topics: the prescription-dispensing process, patient service skills, patient and employee safety, and pharmacy technician duties and responsibilities as defined by the board of pharmacy for that state. Pharmacy technicians should have completed an ASHP-accredited pharmacy technician training program and be certified by the Pharmacy Technician Certification Board (PTCB). The pharmacy should hire pharmacy technician trainees without those qualifications only if those individuals (1) are required to both successfully complete an ASHP-accredited pharmacy technician training program and successfully complete PTCB certification within 24 months of employment and (2) are limited to positions with lesser responsibilities until they successfully complete such training and certification. The pharmacy should require ongoing PTCB certification as a condition of continued employment.

Education and Training. All personnel should possess the education and training needed to fulfill their job responsibilities. All personnel should participate in relevant continuing-education programs, staff development programs, and other activities as necessary to maintain or enhance their competence. Both the ambulatory care pharmacy department and the health system should make available to personnel, as appropriate, training and education on new processes, procedures, and methods of patient care.[12] For pharmacists, ASHP-accredited PGY1 residency should be considered a minimum competency, while completion of an ASHP-accredited PGY2 residency would be optimal.

Recruitment, Selection, and Retention of Personnel. Qualities to consider in recruitment include completion of one or two years of postgraduate residency training, board certification, previous participation in a collaborative practice environment, and other credentials and privileges as appropriate. An ASHP-accredited PGY1 residency should be considered a minimum competency, while completion of an ASHP-accredited PGY2 residency would be optimal. Personnel should be recruited and selected on the basis of requirements in established position descriptions. Criteria used in the selection process should include the candidate's performance of similar job-specific duties, education history relevant to job-specific duties, and willingness to contribute to achieving the mission of the department and the health system. The director should assist in identifying the professional and technical requirements that a candidate must meet to qualify for the position. Clinical specialist positions are a necessary part of any health system in order to advance practice, education, and research activities. An employee retention plan is desirable.[13]

Orientation of Personnel. Personnel who are new to either a specific position or the organization should be oriented to their position through an established and structured procedure. During the orientation process, personnel should be trained in their new job functions by an employee knowledgeable in the work assigned. During the orientation period, the trainer's normal workload should be reduced in order to provide dedicated instruction time to the person being oriented, particularly in distributive settings. The orientation period of new personnel should be tailored to both the new employee's needs and the functions of the employee's position. Evaluation of the effectiveness of orientation programs should be done in conjunction with the competency assessment required before a new hire can assume full responsibility for the new position.

Work Schedules and Assignments. Assignments of pharmacists and pharmacy technicians should be clearly defined to allow the optimal use of personnel and resources. Work schedules should take into account peak demand times for pharmacist-provided patient care. Sufficient personnel should be available to ensure the safe and timely delivery of pharmacy services. Hours of operation should be designed to meet the needs of the patient population given the available resources of the health system.

Performance Evaluation and Job-Specific Competencies. Scheduled periodic evaluations of performance should occur for all pharmacy personnel. Performance should be evaluated on the basis of position description requirements and expected competencies, and the evaluation format should be consistent with that used by the health system. Evaluations should include comments from professional and technical staff as well as other members of the healthcare team. Pharmacy staff should meet the expectations defined in their position descriptions for adequate performance of their duties. The director should ensure that an ongoing competency assessment program is in place for all staff, and each staff member should have a continuous professional development plan.

E. Facilities, Equipment, and Other Resources

Pharmacy. To ensure optimal performance and quality patient care, adequate space, equipment, and other resources should be available for all professional, administrative, distributive, and direct patient care functions. Patient care areas, which include the pharmacy counter, counseling rooms, and clinic offices or examination rooms where direct patient care is provided, should ensure proper patient confidentiality, promote safe and efficient patient care, and contain all tools and supplies necessary for the provision of such care. Pharmacy services operations shall be located in areas that facilitate the provision of services to patients and healthcare providers. Distributive areas should be constructed, arranged, and equipped to promote safe and efficient workflow for staff and patients and to ensure medication integrity. All facilities shall be designed to comply with applicable state and federal guidelines.

Medication Storage and Preparation Areas. Facilities should exist for the preparation and storage of drug products and medications under proper conditions of sanitation, temperature, light, moisture, ventilation, segregation, and security throughout the pharmacy and other patient care areas. Monitored, adequate refrigerator and freezer capacity should be available within the secure pharmacy area and, as necessary, in nonpharmacy areas.

Compounding and Packaging Areas. There shall be suitable facilities to enable the compounding, preparation, packaging, and labeling of sterile and nonsterile drug products, including hazardous drug products, in accordance with established quality-assurance procedures. The work environment should promote orderliness and efficiency and minimize the potential for medication errors and contamination of products.[14-19]

Patient Care and Counseling Areas. A designated area should be available for private patient care and counseling by pharmacists to enhance patients' knowledge and understanding of and adherence to prescribed medication therapy regimens and monitoring plans, to provide disease state management and patient care services, and to foster continuity of care. Space should accommodate the pharmacist and patient and, as appropriate, parents, caregivers, or chaperones. These areas should be stocked with relevant supplies and equipment, including computers, drug references, monitoring equipment, and other necessary tools.[20]

Office and Meeting Areas. Adequate office and meeting areas should be available for administrative, educational, and training activities. These areas should be stocked with relevant supplies and equipment, including computers, drug references, and other necessary tools.

Automated Systems. Automated mechanical systems and software can promote safe, accurate, and efficient medication ordering and preparation, drug distribution, and clinical monitoring. Barcode technology that is associated with any of these systems provides an additional level of safety. The potential for medication errors with any of these systems should be thoroughly understood, evaluated, and eliminated to the greatest extent possible. Organizations should have policies and procedures for the evaluation, selection, use, calibration, monitoring, and maintenance of all automated pharmacy systems.[21,22] The greatest benefits to safety and productivity are seen with robust functionality, proper system maintenance, and the prevention of workarounds.

Automated systems and devices should interface with pharmacy-based systems and support and augment the medication-use process. The replenishment of dispensing equipment should be overseen by pharmacists or by technicians who have been certified as part of a technician-checking program, depending on specific state board requirements. Calibration, maintenance, and certification as required by applicable standards, laws, and regulations should be continual and documented. All automated systems shall include adequate safeguards to maintain the confidentiality and security of patient records, and there shall be procedures to provide essential patient care services in case of equipment failure or downtime.

Health Information Technology. A comprehensive pharmacy computer system shall be employed and should be integrated to the fullest extent possible with other health-system information systems and software. Computer resources should be used to support clerical functions, maintain patient medication profile records, provide clinical decision support, perform necessary patient-billing procedures, manage drug product inventories, provide drug information, access the patient medical record, manage electronic prescribing, and interface with other computerized systems to obtain patient-specific clinical information for medication therapy monitoring and other clinical functions and to facilitate the continuity and transitions of care to and from other care settings.

Pharmacy-based systems experts who act as resources and consultants in maintaining current systems, planning for implementations and upgrades, and assisting in performance improvement and evaluation are critical to the success of informatics implementation and use.

Record and Equipment Maintenance. Adequate space should exist for maintaining and storing records (e.g., prescription records, equipment maintenance, controlled substances inventory) to ensure compliance with laws, regulations, accreditation requirements, and sound management practices. Appropriate licenses, permits, tax stamps, and other documents shall be on display or on file as required by law or regulation. All equipment shall be adequately maintained and certified in accordance with applicable standards, laws, and regulations. Equipment maintenance and certification shall be documented.

F. Managing Financial Resources

Budget Management. The pharmacy shall have a budget that is consistent with the health system's financial management process and supports the scope of and demand for pharmacy services. Oversight of workload and financial performance should be managed in accordance with the health system's requirements. Management should provide for the determination and analysis of pharmacy service costs, capital equipment costs, and new project growth.

The ambulatory care pharmacy budget processes should enable the analysis of pharmacy services by unit of service and other parameters appropriate to the organization (e.g., organizationwide costs by medication therapy, clinical service, specific disease management categories, and patient third-party enrollment). The director should have an integral part in the organization's financial management process.

Health-System Integration. Other functional units within the health system should factor the cost of pharmacy services being provided by the ambulatory care pharmacy into the departmental budget when appropriate.

Third-Party Contract Review. In conjunction with the organization's legal or contracting department, the pharmacy director's team should review third-party payer contracts to ensure that reimbursement is appropriate for services being rendered (including dispensing, patient care, and disease state management services) and the terms of the contract are in the best interest of the patient and the health system. The organization, pharmacy, or pharmacist should contract with third-party payers that are relevant to the ambulatory care pharmacy's patient population.

Revenue, Reimbursement, and Compensation. The director should be knowledgeable about revenues for pharmacy services, including reimbursement for medication dispensing, patient care, and disease state and drug therapy management services. Processes should exist for the routine verification of payment from third-party payers.

Drug Expenditures. Specific policies and procedures for managing drug expenditures should address such methods as utilization review programs, inventory management, and cost-effective care for patients with limited income and resources. The pharmacy department should use practices such as competitive bidding, group purchasing, and specialized pricing (e.g., 340B Drug Pricing Program) when applicable to develop a responsible drug purchasing model.

G. Committee Involvement

A pharmacist representative from the ambulatory care pharmacy team shall be a member of and actively participate on committees responsible for establishing and implementing medication-related policies and procedures, ambulatory care leadership, the provision of patient care, informatics, and performance improvement, as appropriate. Members of the pharmacy team should take part in staff recognition, patient service programs, and other programs as identified in the ambulatory care pharmacy service. Members of the pharmacy team should participate in the activities of similar committees of the health system, as applicable

Standard II. Managing the Medication-Use Process

A. Medication-Use Policy Development

Medication-use policy decisions should be founded on the evidence-based clinical, ethical, legal, social, philosophical, quality-of-life, safety, and economic factors that result in optimal patient care. Committees within the organization that make decisions concerning medication use (e.g., pharmacy and therapeutics, infection control) should include the active and direct involvement of physicians, pharmacists, other appropriate healthcare professionals, and patients, where appropriate. Pharmacists practicing in ambulatory care settings should actively participate on committees whose decisions could affect the quality, safety, effectiveness, or cost of pharmacy services or the medication-use process. Institutional and health-system pharmacists and pharmacy technicians shall be members of an interprofessional team accountable and responsible for medication reconciliation, patient counseling, and medication-related outcomes by establishing a medication-related continuity-of-care process for all patients. Pharmacists practicing in ambulatory care settings should be actively involved in the development, maintenance, and updating of medication-use policies, including tracking and trending of health-system antibiotic resistance patterns.

B. Formulary Management and Integration

Both the patients' diseases and the medications authorized for use by patients' third-party prescription drug programs should be taken into account when determining the ambulatory care pharmacy's inventory. The pharmacy should have access to specialty medications distributed through closed-network systems when needed to support consistent delivery of patient care and medication reconciliation.

Health systems should maintain a formulary that is efficacious and cost-effective. This formulary should be developed with feedback from professional healthcare providers (pharmacists, physicians, social workers, case managers). When possible, charity programs (patient assistance programs, copayment foundations) should be accessed to help patients with limited income and resources to procure their medications.

C. Clinical Care Plans and Disease State Management

Pharmacists in their scope of practice should be involved as part of an interprofessional team in the development and implementation of clinical care plans with prescriptive authority in the healthcare setting (clinical practice guidelines, critical pathways) and disease state management programs involving collaborative drug therapy management (CDTM) agreements and treatment protocols. In addition, medication therapy management (MTM) services should be developed to assist with collaborative patient care. Emphasis should be placed on clinical care plans, primary care, and medication treatment protocols that cover dosage calculations and limits and medications frequently associated with adverse (potential and actual) events, including medication errors.[23,24] Primary care protocols should consider whole-patient needs for health promotion and disease prevention measures as well as appropriate patient assessments, comprehensive management of chronic disease states, management of medication-related care problems, and referrals for acute medical care. The targeting of diseases should consider the prevalence of the disease in the population served by the organization and the potential impact on clinical and economic outcomes.[25]

D. Drug Information

Policies and procedures should be in place for reviewing responses to requests for drug information for the purpose of performance improvement, safety, and education. Pharmacists should provide accurate, comprehensive, and patient-specific drug information to patients, caregivers, other pharmacists, physicians, nurses, and other healthcare providers as appropriate, both proactively and in response to requests associated with the delivery of pharmacist-provided patient care, educational programs, and publications. Expertise in evaluating literature on drugs should be considered essential to the provision of drug therapy management.

Drug information sources should include current professional and scientific periodicals, Web-based research tools (e.g., AHFS-DI, MicroMedex, Lexicomp Online), and the latest editions of reference books in appropriate pharmaceutical and biomedical subject areas that can be easily accessed. Available sources should support research on patient care issues, facilitate the provision of patient care, and promote safety in the medication-use process. When possible, a pharmacist should play a role in addressing complex drug information questions presented by professional staff within the health system (e.g., pharmacists, nurses, physicians).

E. Development of Patient Care Services

Pharmacists who practice in ambulatory care settings should be involved in the development, implementation, and evaluation of new or changing patient care services and drug therapy management services within the organization, such as the development of new clinic or office sites, medical homes, or accountable care organizations. In reviewing the potential for new services, both the value added to patient care by the new service and the financial and logistical implications of the new service should be considered. These efforts should promote the continuity of pharmacist-provided patient care across the continuum of care, practice settings, and geographically dispersed facilities, particularly for newly discharged patients. New services should be developed when opportunities arise for earlier involvement in medication therapy decisions (e.g., clinic rounds) and for continuity between patient encounters for the purpose of assessing therapy success, tolerance, toxicity, and adherence.

Standard III. Drug Product Procurement and Inventory Management

The pharmacy or contracted network pharmacies should be responsible for the procurement, distribution, and control of all drug products used in the treatment of the organization's patients. The pharmacy is responsible for the development of policies and procedures governing medication distribution and control. Policies and procedures should be developed in collaboration with other appropriate professionals, departments, and interprofessional committees of the organization.[26]

A. Purchasing and Maintaining the Availability of Drug Products

Drug Product Acquisition and Availability. Drug products approved for routine use should be purchased, stored, and available in sufficient quantities to meet the needs of ambulatory care patients. Drug products not approved for routine use but necessary to meet the needs of specific patients or categories of patients should be obtained in response to orders, according to established policies and procedures.

Pharmaceutical Manufacturers and Suppliers. Criteria for selecting pharmaceutical manufacturers and suppliers shall be established to ensure that patients receive pharmaceuticals and related supplies of the highest quality and at the lowest cost.[27] Although these duties may be delegated in part to a group purchasing organization, the pharmacy maintains sole responsibility for ensuring the quality of drug products used in the hospital.[27,28]

Pharmaceutical Manufacturers' Representatives. Policies and procedures should be developed governing the activities of manufacturers' representatives or vendors of drug products (including related supplies and devices) within the pharmacy, ambulatory care setting, and organization.[29] Representatives should not be permitted access to patient care areas and should be provided with written guidance on permissible activities. All promotional materials and activities shall be reviewed and approved by the pharmacy.[29-31]

B. Managing Inventory

Medication Storage. Medication storage areas must have proper environmental controls (i.e., proper temperature, light, humidity, conditions of sanitation, ventilation, and segregation), be secure, and be constructed so that drugs are accessible only to authorized personnel.[32] Adequate inventory controls must be maintained to allow proper inventory levels of medications based on utilization.

Drug Shortages. There should be policies and procedures for managing drug shortages, and pharmacy staff should monitor reliable sources of information regarding drug product shortages (e.g., drug shortages Web resource centers of ASHP[33] and FDA[34]). The pharmacy should develop strategies for identifying alternative therapies, working with suppliers, collaborating with physicians and other healthcare providers, and conducting an awareness campaign in the event of a drug shortage.[35]

Samples. The use of drug product samples should be prohibited to the extent possible.[32] However, if samples are permitted under certain circumstances, policies and procedures for their storage, control, and distribution should be in place. The pharmacy should oversee procurement, storage, and distribution of these products to ensure proper storage, record-keeping maintenance, product integrity, and compliance with all applicable packaging and labeling laws, regulations, standards, and patient education requirements. Pharmacists should be involved in the organization's efforts to secure safe and effective low-cost medications for low-income patients.[32,36]

Patient Care Area Stock. Inventory of drug products held in nonpharmacy areas (e.g., nursing station, clinic, physicians' offices) for direct administration to ambulatory care patients should be minimal. To the extent possible, medications administered to patients in nonpharmacy areas should be prepared by the pharmacy. If this is not possible, automated medication dispensing machines should be used to dispense medications to patients. The list of medications to be accessible and the policies and procedures regarding their use shall be developed by an interprofessional committee of physicians, pharmacists, and nurses.[36] Access to medications should be limited to cases in which the committee determines that an urgent clinical need for the medication outweighs the potential patient safety risks of making the medication accessible. A separate assessment should occur for every location where a medication may be stocked.

Controlled Substances. Policies and procedures should ensure the distribution of controlled substances and other medications with the potential for abuse. Policies and procedures should be consistent with applicable laws and regulations and should include methods for preventing and detecting diversion.[33]

Emergency Medications and Devices. The pharmacy should ensure the availability, access, and security of emergency medications, including antidotes. The telephone number of the local poison information center should be posted at or near all telephones for staff access. Pharmacists should have an authorized role in responding to medical emergencies.

All emergency medications should be stored in sealed containers that enable the staff to readily determine that the contents are complete and have not expired. All emergency medications should be available, controlled, and secured in the patient procedure areas.

Patient's Own Medications. Drug products and related devices brought into the organization by patients shall be identified by the pharmacy and documented on the patient's medical record if the medications are to be used. These medications shall be administered only pursuant to a prescriber's order and according to policies and procedures, which should ensure the pharmacist's identification and validation of the integrity as well as the secure and appropriate storage and management of such medications.

C. Drug Product Storage Area Inspections

All stocks of drug products, whether located within or outside the pharmacy area, should be inspected routinely and managed by pharmacy and location staff to ensure the absence of outdated, unusable, recalled, or mislabeled products. Storage conditions that would foster medication deterioration, storage arrangements that might contribute to medication errors, and other safety issues shall be assessed, documented, and corrected.[33]

D. Drug Recall and New Prescribing Information

Written procedures should exist for the timely intervention and dissemination of information regarding drug recalls. Procedures should include an established process for removing from use any drugs or devices subjected to a recall, notifying appropriate healthcare professionals, identifying any patients who may have been exposed to the recalled medication, and, if necessary, communicating available alternative therapies to prescribers. The pharmacy shall be notified of any defective drug products or related supplies and equipment encountered by nursing or medical staff. All drug product defects should be reported to FDA's MedWatch program.[33]

Standard IV. Patient Care

Pharmacists play an integral role in the provision of pharmaceutical care, which is defined as the responsible provision of drug therapy for the purpose of achieving definite outcomes that improve a patient's quality of life.[37] The concept of pharmaceutical care has evolved into a comprehensive, patient-focused model of pharmacist-provided care. The principal elements of pharmaceutical care are that it is medication related, is directly provided to the patient, and is provided to produce definite outcomes; these outcomes are intended to improve the patient's quality of life, and the provider must accept personal responsibility for the outcomes.[37] In 2008, a joint working group consisting of members and leadership from the American College of Clinical Pharmacy, the American Pharmacists Association, and the American Society of Health-System Pharmacists created a definition of ambulatory care practice as part of a petition to the Board of Pharmacy Specialties requesting recognition of ambulatory care pharmacy practice as a specialty. The definition described ambulatory care pharmacy practice as a specialty in medication use for preventive and chronic care:

> Ambulatory care pharmacy practice is the provision of integrated, accessible healthcare services by pharmacists who are accountable for addressing medication needs, developing sustained partnerships with patients, and practicing in the context of family and community. This is accomplished through direct patient care and medication management for ambulatory patients, long-term relationships, coordination of care, patient advocacy, wellness and health promotion, triage and referral, and patient education and self-management.[38-40]

The mission of the pharmacist is to help people make the best use of medications. At a minimum, pharmacists are responsible for assessing the legal and clinical appropriateness of medication orders (or prescriptions), educating and counseling patients on the use of their medications, monitoring the effects of medication therapy, and maintaining patient profiles and other records. In the ambulatory care setting, these responsibilities are best accomplished through the provision of pharmacist-provided patient care, whether in the context of collaborative agreements with physicians or independent of such agreements. Pharmacists are responsible for establishing relationships with patients and providers who will facilitate the coordination and continuity of care, improve access to care, and improve patient outcomes.

Providing Comprehensive Patient Care. The addition of clinical pharmacy services to healthcare teams has produced significant cost savings to the healthcare system and improved patient satisfaction, medication safety, and therapy outcomes.[4] Clinical pharmacy services are designed to improve patients' access to care, provide disease management, and focus on quality-related outcomes.

Recommendation B9 from the ASHP Pharmacy Practice Model Initiative specifically states that "for hospitals and health systems that provide ambulatory care services, drug-therapy management should be available from a pharmacist for each outpatient."[6] Furthermore, many of the PPMI recommendations support the comprehensive care of patients by pharmacists practicing in ambulatory care settings through transitions of care; quality, safety, and financial outcomes; and facilitating continuity of care and medication reconciliation.

Interprofessional care models are accepted and promoted by the medical community. The American College of Physicians and the American Society of Internal Medicine have stated that "collaborative drug therapy is one of the best examples of how pharmacists work with physicians. It is designed to maximize the patient's health-related quality of life, reduce the frequency of avoidable drug-related problems, and improve the societal benefits of pharmaceuticals."[41] In addition, governmental agencies support the work of pharmacists in the provision of direct patient care. The Medicare Modernization Act of 2003[42] mandated that MTM services be offered by prescription drug plans to Medicare beneficiaries at high risk for ADEs.[43] While neither the legislation nor the final CMS regulation provided guidance on the design or reimbursement structure for MTM services, CMS stated that these programs should be "patient-focused services aimed at improving therapeutic outcomes that are developed in conjunction with practicing pharmacists."[42] The Centers for Disease Control and Prevention endorsed pharmacists as integral members of the interprofessional healthcare team and supports the pharmacist's role in providing MTM services to improve patient outcomes.[44] The strongest statement about pharmacist-delivered direct patient care to date was presented in a report to the U.S. Surgeon General.[4] This report described how innovative models of care that include pharmacists as members of the healthcare team can help to improve safety, access, quality, and cost while improving outcomes. Lastly, as the Patient Protection and Affordable Care Act is fully implemented, the involvement of pharmacists practicing in ambulatory care settings will be critical in the establishment of accountable care organizations. These integrated systems of care will heavily rely on the expertise of pharmacists to support safe and appropriate medication use.

Patient Care and Disease State Management Services. The purpose of a direct patient care or disease state management service is to optimize therapeutic outcomes for patients. Such services may include elements designed to promote enhanced patient understanding, increase patient adherence, and detect ADEs. Possible services may include performing a comprehensive medication review (comprehensive or targeted) to identify, resolve, and prevent medication-related problems (including ADEs); performing patient health status assessments; formulating medication treatment plans; selecting, initiating, modifying, discontinuing, or administering medication therapy; managing high-cost and specialty medications; administering antibiotic stewardship programs; evaluating and monitoring patient response to drug therapy; documenting the care delivered for and communicating essential information to the patient's other primary care providers; providing education and training designed to enhance patient understanding and appropriate use of his or her medications; providing information, support services, and resources designed to enhance patient adherence with his or her therapeutic regimens; coordinating and integrating MTM services within the broader healthcare management services being provided to the patient; and selecting, initiating, modifying, discontinuing, or administering medication therapy under state-approved CDTM agreements.

Relationships with Patients. Successful disease state and medication management begins with the relationship between the patient and the pharmacist. Pharmacists practicing in ambulatory care settings who provide direct patient care should develop and maintain a rapport with and the trust of the patient and the caregiver. The pharmacist should coordinate all aspects of the individual's pharmacist-provided patient care, serve as a patient advocate, and encourage patients to take responsibility for their health. The pharmacist should be flexible and adapt to patient-specific variables such as the patient's perception of how an illness or symptoms affect his or her life and the patient's readiness for change.

Relationships with Providers: CDTM Agreements. Almost every state has amended its pharmacy practice act to allow for the expansion of pharmacists' scope of practice. Pharmacists should actively participate in medication therapy decision-making and management through collaboration with patients, caregivers, physicians, and other healthcare providers. By participating in CDTM, the pharmacist takes an active role in the initiation, management, and monitoring of medication therapy based on pharmacokinetic parameters, genetic characteristics of the patient, serum concentrations of medications, laboratory values, and other patient-related health and social factors in order to take responsibility and have authority for achieving desired therapeutic outcomes. PPMI recommendation B14 states that, when possible through credentialing and privileging processes, pharmacists should include in their scope of practice prescribing as part of the collaborative practice team.[6] A collaborative care agreement between the pharmacist and physician or other healthcare provider must comply with applicable laws and regulations and the organization's policies and procedures.

Patient History and Medication Reconciliation. Upon patient presentation for ambulatory care services, a pharmacist should obtain a patient and medication history and update and validate the patient's current medication list. Pharmacists should be integral in identifying, developing, reviewing, and approving new medications by conducting a patient-specific medication review before first-dose administration and evaluating patient response to therapy. The history should include pertinent demographic information;

known health problems and diseases; applicable measurements and laboratory values; known drug allergies and ADEs; behavioral, lifestyle, and socioeconomic influences on healthcare; and a comprehensive list of prescription and nonprescription medications and related medical devices currently being used. The current medication list should be maintained and updated during subsequent patient encounters in both the inpatient and ambulatory care settings. Pharmacists should routinely contribute to processes that ensure that each patient's care is maintained, regardless of transitions across the continuum of care and practice settings (e.g., between inpatient and community pharmacies or home care services). Moreover, pharmacists are uniquely positioned to aid in establishing a patient medication complexity index, which includes severity of illness, number of medications, and comorbidities.

Medication Therapy Assessment. Pharmacists practicing in ambulatory care settings must ensure safe and effective medication therapy. The assessment should include the appropriateness of the prescribed medication for the patient's diagnosis and history, identification of medication-related problems, and interventions for resolution. In addition, the assessment should produce a plan for monitoring patient adherence, therapeutic and adverse effects, and patient outcomes.

Medication Therapy Monitoring. The pharmacist should monitor patients' understanding of and adherence to the medication therapy plan as well as its effects and outcomes. During subsequent encounters, pharmacists should obtain appropriate information from patients, assess their progress, and identify and resolve problems. All interventions and assessments of the care plan should be documented and made available to all providers participating in the patient's care.

Documentation of Care Plan and Coordination of Care. Pharmacists should maintain a comprehensive care plan, preferably as a component of an interprofessional CDTM agreement. The care plan should be documented in the patient's medical record and be accessible to other healthcare professionals involved in patient care. The pharmacist is responsible for communicating the plan to the patient and other healthcare providers. The care plan should document the patient's medical and medication history, medication therapy assessment, and medication therapy regimen, including drug name, strength, and route of administration, indication for therapy, goal of therapy, monitoring parameters, and proposed length of therapy.

Pharmacist Skills and Competency. Pharmacists participating in direct patient care activities should demonstrate competency in the areas of care provided. Postdoctoral residency training, board certification, and continuing-education certification programs should be completed by all pharmacists and documented in a retrievable format. PPMI recommendation B10 states that pharmacists who provide drug therapy management should be certified through the most appropriate Board of Pharmacy Specialties certification process.[6] Examples of minimum requirements include demonstration of proficient communication skills, basic physical assessment, laboratory interpretation, and disease- and age-specific competencies. Minimum requirements for level of education, experience, or postgraduate training may be established for specific responsibilities or positions. Pharmacists in frontline practice should not be limited to competency in drug distribution and reactive order processing, and pharmacists engaged specifically in drug therapy management must have an understanding of and responsibility for the medication-use and delivery systems. Individual pharmacists must maintain competence in and accept responsibility for both the clinical and distributive activities of the pharmacy department. A model for ongoing evaluation, which may include peer review, should be developed to ensure that pharmacists remain competent.

Outcomes. Outcome measurements used to quantify the impact of the interventions of pharmacists practicing in ambulatory care settings can be divided into three categories: clinical, economic, and humanistic. Clinical outcomes may include rates of medication adherence, ADEs, and achievement and maintenance of evidence-based therapeutic goals. Examples of economic outcomes include hospitalization rates, emergency room visits, census growth, and revenue generation. Humanistic outcomes may include provider satisfaction, patient satisfaction, and measurements of impact on patient quality of life and personal productivity.

Patient Confidentiality. Policies and procedures for access to and dissemination of confidential patient information must meet all applicable legal and regulatory requirements, including those of the Health Insurance Portability and Accountability Act,[45] and be made readily available.

Standard V. Preparing, Packaging, and Labeling Medications

A. Preparing Medications

Preparation. The pharmacist should prepare or supervise the preparation of, in a timely and accurate manner, drug formulations, strengths, dosage forms, and packages prescribed.

Extemporaneous Compounding. Drug formulations, dosage forms, strengths, and packaging that are not available commercially but are deemed necessary for patient care should be prepared by appropriately trained personnel in accordance with applicable standards and regulations (e.g., FDA, United States Pharmacopeia [USP], state boards of pharmacy). Adequate quality-control and quality-assurance procedures should exist for these operations. Written master formulas and batch records (including product test results, as appropriate) shall be maintained, and a lot number or other method to identify each finished product with its production and control history shall be assigned to each batch. Commercially available products should be used to the maximum extent possible.[14,15,17,18,46-48]

Compounded Sterile Preparations. Sterile compounding is regulated by various state and federal agencies and shall meet all applicable laws and regulations. When possible, manufactured sterile preparations should be preferred to compounding in the pharmacy. Whenever compounded sterile preparations are prepared, properly-trained staff shall use appropriate techniques to avoid contamination and assure quality; this includes but is not limited to the following:

(1) using aseptic technique; (2) maintaining clean, uncluttered, and functionally separate areas for product preparation to minimize the possibility of contamination; (3) using a primary engineering control that provides an International Organization for Standardization class 5 environment while preparing any intravenous admixture, any sterile preparation made from nonsterile ingredients, or any sterile preparation that will not be used within 1 hour; and (4) visually inspecting the integrity of the medications. *USP* Chapter 797[18] and the ASHP Guidelines on Quality Assurance for Pharmacy-Prepared Sterile Products[14] further define the compounding of sterile preparations and should be consulted by those responsible for this area of practice.

All sterile medications for use in the ambulatory care facility or for use by patients in the home should be prepared in a suitable environment by appropriately trained personnel and labeled appropriately for the user. Quality-control and quality-assurance procedures for the preparation of sterile products should exist, including annual competency assessment of the preparer's aseptic technique. For additional guidance regarding therapy in the patient home, refer to ASHP Guidelines on Home Infusion Pharmacy Services.[49]

Hazardous Drug Products. All hazardous drug products for use in the ambulatory care facility or for use by patients in the home should be prepared in a suitable environment by appropriately trained personnel and labeled appropriately for the user.[16] Special precautions, equipment, supplies (spill and eyewash kits), and training for storage, handling, and disposal of hazardous drug products should be in place to ensure the safety of personnel, patients, visitors, the community, and the environment. Quality-control and quality-assurance procedures for the preparation of hazardous products should be in place. Institutional policy should address the risk to personnel handling hazardous drug products, including periodic monitoring of personnel for adverse effects.[16]

B. Packaging and Labeling Medications

Packaging. Medications dispensed to ambulatory care patients should be packaged and labeled in compliance with applicable federal and state laws and regulations and with USP and other standards. When feasible, dispensing in unopened manufacturers' containers and in tamper-evident packaging is desirable. Packaging materials should be selected that preserve the integrity, cleanliness, and potency of compounded and commercially available drug products. Containers, including unit dose packages, for patients' home use shall comply with the Poison Prevention Packaging Act.[50]

Labeling. At a minimum, labels for patient home use of medications shall comply with applicable federal and state laws and regulations. Generally, labels contain the name, address, and telephone number of the pharmacy; date of dispensing; serial number of the prescription; patient's full name; name, strength, and dosage form of the medication; directions to the patient for use of the medication; name of the prescriber; precautionary information; authorized refills; and initials (or name) of the responsible pharmacist. Other information may be required by individual state laws and regulations.

Standard VI. Medication Delivery

A. Dispensing Medications

Prescribing. Policies and procedures should be available to ensure that healthcare providers have applicable state and federal licensure and, if required, organizational authorization for prescribing medications. Medications should be administered and dispensed to ambulatory care patients only after receiving the spoken, written, faxed, or electronic prescription of an authorized prescriber. Spoken orders should be limited to nonroutine and emergency situations and should be strongly discouraged for drug products and regimens prone to medication errors and other ADEs. A pharmacist should, as soon as possible, reduce spoken orders to writing and verify them using the Joint Commission read-back procedure.

Pharmacists practicing in ambulatory care settings should advocate and foster healthcare provider conformance with the formulary, clinical care plans, disease state management programs, and standardized Joint Commission–approved terminology and abbreviations. Pharmacists practicing in ambulatory care settings should advocate the development and use of electronic prescribing systems (direct order entry by the prescriber).

Therapeutic Purpose. Before dispensing any medication, the pharmacist should substantiate the indication for which the medication was prescribed. Prescribers should be encouraged to routinely communicate the condition being treated or the therapeutic purpose with all medication orders.

Medication Orders. Medication orders (or prescriptions) shall contain at a minimum the following information: patient name and address; medication name, dose, frequency, route, and quantity or duration; prescriber name, address, and telephone number; and prescriber DEA number for controlled substances. All medication orders shall be reviewed for legality and clinical appropriateness by a pharmacist before being dispensed. Any questions should be resolved with the prescriber, and any approved changes to the prescription shall be documented in a written notation on the face of the prescription. Information concerning changes should be appropriately communicated to the patient, caregiver, and other involved healthcare providers.

Drug Delivery Systems and Administration Devices. Pharmacists should provide leadership and advice in organizational and clinical decision-making regarding drug delivery systems and administration devices and should participate in the evaluation, use, and monitoring of these systems and devices. The potential for medication errors associated with such systems and devices should be thoroughly evaluated. Follow-up and education of staff should occur after systems errors are discovered to prevent future systems errors.

Mail Distribution. The pharmacy may mail medications to patients, preferably as part of a comprehensive pharmaceutical care program that gives patients access to a pharmacist. Mailed medications shall conform to all federal and state laws and regulations. Outer mailing packages and medication containers should protect the medication from heat, humidity, and other environmental conditions that can affect stability.[51] A toll-free telephone service that is answered during normal business hours should be provided to enable communication between a patient or the patient's physician and a pharmacist with access to the patient's records. The pharmacy should have procedures for investigating, replacing, and reporting, as required, medications lost during delivery. Special requirements for mailing controlled substances vary according to state laws and regulations.

Standard VII. Evaluating the Effectiveness of the Medication-Use System

A. Assessing Pharmacy Services and Practices

Documentation and Measurement of Patient Care, Interventions, and Outcomes. An ongoing process should be in place for consistent documentation and measurement (and reporting to medical staff, administrators, and others) of pharmacist interventions, patient outcomes from MTM (including patient satisfaction with the care provided and quality of life), and pharmacists' contributions to patient care.[52] Documenting pharmacy plans and recommendations in the patient's medical record is important for providing continuity of care between healthcare providers, communicating care plans, and underscoring the professional and legal responsibility a pharmacist assumes when making patient-specific recommendations and modifications in medication regimens. Participating in this program is an essential part of the role of every pharmacist practicing in ambulatory care settings. An electronic medical record should be used for documentation and measurement whenever possible, and the record should be designed to align pharmacists' documentation outlining care provided as well as a method to trace and ensure the quality of care provided with signed recommendations and follow-up notes in the patient's medical record.

Performance Improvement. The ambulatory care pharmacy service should have an ongoing, systematic program for assessing pharmacist-provided patient care.[53] Performance improvement activities based on assessments should be integrated with the health system's overall performance improvement activities, as applicable. The performance improvement team should work with frontline staff to implement systems that include proper checks and balances focused on protecting against human error. Performance improvement initiatives should be focused on error reporting trends and high-risk functions such as dispensing high-alert medications.

As part of the performance improvement program, operational and outcomes data should be benchmarked with those of other ambulatory care pharmacy services of similar size and scope. The results, including follow-up actions for improvement, should be documented and provided to the organization's managers, the frontline staff using the system, and others as appropriate.

B. Improving the Medication-Use Process

Medication-Use Evaluation. An ongoing program of both prospective and retrospective monitoring of drug utilization and costs should be in place to ensure that medications are used appropriately, safely, and effectively and to increase the probability of desired outcomes within defined populations of patients. Proactive and continuous quality-improvement strategies aid in risk mitigation of medication-use systems. Pharmacists practicing in ambulatory care settings should play an integral role in this program. The medication-use policy committee should define specific variables for evaluation (disease state, pharmacologic category, high-use/high-cost drug products, high-alert medications, high-risk therapies, problem-prone regimens) as appropriate for the organization. Through this ongoing evaluation, areas in need of improvement in medication prescribing and management can be identified and targeted for intervention.

Medication Safety. Ambulatory care pharmacy services should be part of the health system's program for preventing medication errors and ADEs. The health system's medication safety team should be a cross-functional group of employees (e.g., pharmacists, physicians, nurses) and patients, when applicable. Pharmacists who practice in ambulatory care settings are an essential part of this medication safety team. The medication safety program should foster a just culture for error reporting. The medication safety team should

- Use a systems-based approach to review errors,
- Review near-miss medication errors (i.e., errors that did not cause patient harm but, if repeated, could cause patient harm),
- Analyze the root cause of medication errors, and
- Work with frontline staff to implement systems that include proper checks and balances focused on protecting against human error and mitigating risk.

The occurrence of medication errors should be reported to voluntary national reporting systems (e.g., USP Medication Errors Reporting Program, ISMP, and FDA MedWatch) to help prevent similar errors from occurring in other practice settings. Serious medication errors that result in temporary or permanent harm, disability, or death should be reported to the appropriate regulatory agency or accrediting body.

Patient Safety. Ambulatory care pharmacy services should be part of a health system's program to encourage patients' participation in and accountability for their care. Patient education should be sensitive to the individual patient's health literacy. To maximize the benefits of medication therapy and reduce the potential for errors, the program should encourage patients to ask questions about their medications and should emphasize adherence to their therapy plan. Pharmacist–patient dialogue, pamphlets, and videos should be used to teach patients how to ask questions about their medications. This process is particularly important for recently discharged patients.

Antimicrobial Stewardship and Infection Prevention and Control. There shall be policies and procedures to promote the optimal use of antimicrobial agents, reduce the transmission of infections, and educate health professionals, patients, and the public about these topics. Pharmacists should participate in antimicrobial stewardship and infection prevention and control efforts through clinical endeavors focused on proper antimicrobial utilization and membership on relevant interprofessional work groups and committees within the health system.

Pharmacists should monitor patients' laboratory reports of microbial sensitivities or applicable diagnostic markers and advise prescribers if microbial resistance is suspected, evaluate trends in microbial prescribing relative to changes in microbial resistance patterns, and assist in developing prescribing patterns to help minimize the development of drug resistance.[54]

Integration of Population-Based and Patient-Specific Activities. A mechanism should be in place for ensuring that the clinical and economic findings of population-based activities are appropriately incorporated into daily patient-specific practice. Population-based activities provide insight and guidance for the treatment of the average patient; however, all variables identified in the patient-specific encounter should be considered in therapeutic decision-making for individual patients.[55]

Standard VIII. Research

The pharmacist should initiate, participate in, and support clinical and practice-related research appropriate to the goals, objectives, and resources of the specific health system.

Policies and Procedures. The pharmacist shall ensure that policies and procedures for the safe and proper use of investigational drugs and medication-related devices are established and followed and that these policies and procedures meet all applicable laws and regulations. There shall be a procedure to ensure that informed consent is obtained from the patient before the first dose of the study drug is administered.[56,57]

Procurement, Distribution, and Control of Investigational Drugs. The pharmacy shall be responsible for overseeing the procurement, distribution, and control of all investigational drugs. Investigational drugs shall be approved for use by an institutional review board and shall be dispensed and administered to consenting patients according to an approved protocol.[38,56,57]

Institutional Review Board. A pharmacist shall be a member of the hospital's institutional review board (or equivalent body), if one exists.[56]

Drugs Not Approved by FDA. The pharmacy should seek and obtain documented authorization from appropriate committees (e.g., pharmacy and therapeutics committee) for the pharmacologic use of any chemical substance that has not received FDA approval for use as a drug. Documentation should exist to ensure that appropriate risk-management measures (e.g., obtaining informed consent) have been taken.

Information Regarding Investigational Drugs. The pharmacy shall have access to information on all investigational studies and similar research projects involving medications and medication-related devices used in the hospital. The pharmacy shall provide pertinent written information (to the extent known) about the safe and proper use of investigational drugs, including possible adverse effects and adverse drug reactions, to nurses, pharmacists, physicians, and other healthcare professionals called on to prescribe, dispense, and administer these medications.[56,57]

References

1. Johnson JA, Bootman JL. Drug-related morbidity and mortality, a cost-of-illness model. *Arch Intern Med.* 1995; 155:1949–56.
2. Lewis RK, Carter BL, Glover DG, et al. Comprehensive services in an ambulatory care pharmacy. *Am J Health-Syst Pharm.* 1995; 52:1793–7.
3. Segarra-Newnham M, Soisson KT. Provision of pharmaceutical care through comprehensive pharmacotherapy clinics. *Hosp Pharm.* 1997; 32:845–50.
4. Giberson S, Yoder S, Lee MP. Improving patient and health system outcomes through advanced pharmacy practice. A report to the U.S. Surgeon General (December 2011). www.usphs.gov/corpslinks/pharmacy/documents/2011AdvancedPharmacyPracticeReporttotheUSSG.pdf (accessed 2013 Mar 18).
5. American Society of Health-System Pharmacists. ASHP/ASHP Foundation Ambulatory Conference and Summit: consensus recommendations (March 4, 2014). www.ashpmedia.org/amcare14/docs/preliminary_recommendations_2014-03-04.pdf (accessed 2014 Jul 8).
6. The consensus of the Pharmacy Practice Model Summit. *Am J Health-Syst Pharm.* 2011; 68:1148–52.
7. American Society of Health-System Pharmacists. ASHP statement on the role of health-system pharmacists in emergency preparedness. *Am J Health-Syst Pharm.* 2003; 60:1993–5.
8. American Society of Health-System Pharmacists. ASHP guidelines on the pharmacist's role in immunization. *Am J Health-Syst Pharm.* 2003; 60:1371–7.
9. American Society of Health-System Pharmacists. ASHP statement on the pharmacist's role in substance abuse prevention, education, and assistance (2013). www.ashp.org/DocLibrary/BestPractices/SpecificStSubstance.aspx (accessed 2013 Jul 29).
10. Crane VS, Hatwig CA, Hayman JN, et al. Developing a management planning and control system for ambulatory pharmacy resources. *Pharm Pract Manag Q.* 1998; 18:52–71.
11. Rosum RW. Planning for an ambulatory care service. *Am J Health-Syst Pharm.* 1997; 54:1584–7.
12. American Society of Hospital Pharmacists. ASHP statement on continuing education. *Am J Hosp Pharm.* 1990; 47:1855.
13. American Society of Health-System Pharmacists. ASHP guidelines on the recruitment, selection, and retention of pharmacy personnel. *Am J Health-Syst Pharm.* 2003; 60:587–93.
14. American Society of Health-System Pharmacists. ASHP guidelines on quality assurance for pharmacy-prepared sterile products. *Am J Health-Syst Pharm.* 2000; 57:1150–69.
15. American Society of Hospital Pharmacists. ASHP technical assistance bulletin on compounding nonsterile products in pharmacies. *Am J Hosp Pharm.* 1994; 51:1441–8.

16. American Society of Health-System Pharmacists. ASHP guidelines on handling hazardous drugs. *Am J Health-Syst Pharm.* 2006; 63:1172–93.
17. American Society of Hospital Pharmacists. ASHP guidelines for repackaging oral solids and liquids in single unit and unit dose packages. *Am J Hosp Pharm.* 1983; 40:451–2.
18. Pharmaceutical compounding—sterile preparations (general information chapter 797). In: The United States pharmacopeia, 34th rev., and The national formulary, 29th ed. Rockville, MD: United States Pharmacopeial Convention; 2011: 336–73.
19. Pharmaceutical compounding—nonsterile preparations (general information chapter 795. In: The United States pharmacopeia, 34th rev., and The national formulary, 29th ed. Rockville, MD: United States Pharmacopeial Convention; 2011:330–6.
20. American Society of Health-System Pharmacists. ASHP guidelines on pharmacist-conducted patient education and counseling. *Am J Health-Syst Pharm.* 1997; 54:431–4.
21. American Society of Health-System Pharmacists. ASHP guidelines on the safe use of automated dispensing devices. *Am J Health-Syst Pharm.* 2010; 67:483–90.
22. Glover DG. Automated medication dispensing devices. *J Am Pharm Assoc.* 1997; NS37:353–60.
23. Kernodle SJ. Improving health care with clinical practice guidelines and critical pathways: implications for pharmacists in ambulatory practice. *Pharm Pract Manag Q.* 1997; 17:76–89.
24. LaCalamita S. Role of the pharmacist in developing critical pathways with warfarin therapy. *J Pharm Pract.* 1997; 10:398–410.
25. Curtiss FR. Lessons learned from projects in disease management in ambulatory care. *Am J Health-Syst Pharm.* 1997; 54:2217–29.
26. American Society of Health-System Pharmacists. ASHP statement on the pharmacist's responsibility for distribution and control of drug products. In: Hawkins BH, ed. Best practices for hospital and health-system pharmacy, 2013–2014 edition. Bethesda, MD: American Society of Health-System Pharmacists; 2013:125.
27. American Society of Hospital Pharmacists. ASHP guidelines for selecting pharmaceutical manufacturers and suppliers. *Am J Hosp Pharm.* 1991; 48:523–4.
28. American Society of Health-System Pharmacists. ASHP guidelines on medication cost management strategies for hospitals and health systems. *Am J Health-Syst Pharm.* 2008; 65:1368–84.
29. American Society of Hospital Pharmacists. ASHP guidelines for pharmacists on the activities of vendors' representatives in organized health care systems. *Am J Hosp Pharm.* 1994; 51:520–1.
30. American Society of Hospital Pharmacists. ASHP guidelines on pharmacists' relationships with industry. *Am J Hosp Pharm.* 1992; 49:154.
31. PhRMA code on interactions with healthcare professionals. Washington, DC: Pharmaceutical Research and Manufacturers of America; 2004 Jan.
32. American Society of Hospital Pharmacists. ASHP guidelines on hospital drug and distribution control. *Am J Hosp Pharm.* 1980; 37:1097–103.
33. American Society of Health-System Pharmacists. ASHP Drug Shortages Resource Center. www.ashp.org/shortages (accessed 2013 Jul 17).
34. Food and Drug Administration. Drug shortages. www.fda.gov/cder/drug/shortages (accessed 2013 Apr 3).
35. American Society of Health-System Pharmacists. ASHP guidelines on managing drug product shortages in hospitals and health systems. *Am J Health-Syst Pharm.* 2009; 66:1399–406.
36. American Society of Health-System Pharmacists. ASHP guidelines on the pharmacy and therapeutics committee and the formulary system. *Am J Health-Syst Pharm.* 2008; 65:1272–83.
37. American Society of Hospital Pharmacists. ASHP statement on pharmaceutical care. *Am J Hosp Pharm.* 1993; 50:1720–3.
38. Lewis RK, Lasack NL, Lambert BL, et al. Patient counseling—a focus on maintenance therapy. *Am J Health-Syst Pharm.* 1997; 54:2084–98.
39. Hepler CD, Strand LM. Opportunities and responsibilities in pharmaceutical care. *Am J Hosp Pharm.* 1990; 47:533–43.
40. Brennan C, Goode JV, Haines ST, et al. A petition to the Board of Pharmaceutical Specialties requesting recognition of ambulatory care pharmacy practice as a specialty (November 2008). www.accp.com/docs/positions/petitions/BPS_Ambulatory_Care_Petition.pdf (accessed 2015 Mar 19).
41. Keely JL, for the American College of Physicians–American Society of Internal Medicine. Pharmacist scope of practice. *Ann Intern Med.* 2002; 136:79–85.
42. Medicare Prescription Drug, Modernization, and Improvement Act of 2003, Pub. L. No. 108–173 (2003).
43. Academy of Managed Care Pharmacy. Sound medication therapy management programs: 2006 consensus document. www.pharmacist.com/sites/default/files/files/mtm_sound_programs_2006.pdf (accessed 2013 Jul 17).
44. Centers for Disease Control and Prevention. A program guide for public health: partnering with pharmacists in the prevention and control of chronic diseases. www.cdc.gov/dhdsp/programs/spha/docs/pharmacist_guide.pdf (accessed 2015 Mar 19).
45. Health Insurance Portability and Accountability Act of 1996. Pub. L. No. 104-191. www.cms.hhs.gov/HIPAAGenInfo/Downloads/HIPAALaw.pdf (accessed 2013 Jul 17).
46. American Society of Health-System Pharmacists. ASHP guidelines: minimum standard for pharmacies in hospitals (2012). www.ashp.org/DocLibrary/BestPractices/SettingsGdlMinHosp.aspx (accessed 2013 Jul 17).
47. American Society of Hospital Pharmacists. ASHP technical assistance bulletin on single unit and unit dose packages of drugs. *Am J Hosp Pharm.* 1985; 42:378–9.
48. Pharmaceutical compounding—nonsterile preparations (general information chapter 795). In: The United States pharmacopeia, 35th rev., and The na-

tional formulary, 30th ed. Rockville, MD: United States Pharmacopeial Convention; 2011:344–50.

49. American Society of Health-System Pharmacists. ASHP guidelines on home infusion pharmacy services. *Am J Health-Syst Pharm.* 2014; 71:325–41.
50. Poison Prevention Packaging Act, 15 U.S.C. 1471–6.
51. General notices and requirements—preservation, packaging, storage, and labeling. In: The United States pharmacopeia, 30th rev., and The national formulary, 25th ed. Rockville, MD: United States Pharmacopeial Convention; 2007:9–12.
52. Borgsdorf LR, Mian JS, Knapp KK. Pharmacist-managed medication review in a managed care system. *Am J Hosp Pharm.* 1994; 51:772–7.
53. MacKinnon N. Performance measures in ambulatory pharmacy. *Pharm Pract Manage Q.* 1997; 17:52–62.
54. American Society of Health-System Pharmacists. ASHP statement on the pharmacist's role in antimicrobial stewardship and infection prevention and control. *Am J Health-Syst Pharm.* 2010; 67:575–7.
55. Mutnick AH, Sterba KJ, Szymusiak-Mutnick BA. Integration of quality assessment and a patient-specific intervention/outcomes program. *Pharm Pract Manage Q.* 1998; 17:25–36.
56. American Society of Health-System Pharmacists. ASHP guidelines on clinical drug research. *Am J Health-Syst Pharm.* 1998; 55:369–75.
57. American Society of Hospital Pharmacists. ASHP guidelines for pharmaceutical research in organized health-care settings. *Am J Hosp Pharm.* 1989; 46:129–30.

Developed through the ASHP Section of Ambulatory Care Practitioners and approved by the ASHP Board of Directors on September 19, 2014. These guidelines supersede the ASHP Guidelines: Minimum Standard for Pharmaceutical Services in Ambulatory Care dated April 21, 1999.

JENNIFER ASKEW BUXTON, PHARM.D., CPP, is Deputy Director, Pharmacy Services, Cape Fear Clinic, Wilmington, NC; at the time of writing she was Manager of Outpatient/Employee Pharmacy Services, New Hanover Regional Medical Center, Wilmington. ROSEMARIE BABBITT, B.S.PHARM., M.A., is Vice President, Federal Contracts and Grants, American Pharmacists Association, Washington, DC; at the time of writing she was Associate Director, Pharmacy Services, Parkland Health and Hospital System, Dallas, TX. CYNDY A. CLEGG, B.S.PHARM., M.H.A., is Director, Retail and Home Care Pharmacy, Swedish Medical Center, Edmonds, WA; at the time of writing she was Assistant Director, Ambulatory Pharmacy Services, Harborview Medical Center, Seattle, WA, and Clinical Associate Professor, University of Washington School of Pharmacy, Seattle. SANDRA F. DURLEY, PHARM.D., is Associate Director, Ambulatory Care Pharmacy Department, and Clinical Assistant Professor, University of Illinois at Chicago (UIC), Chicago. KELLY T. EPPLEN, PHARM.D., BCACP, FASHP, is Associate Professor of Clinical Pharmacy Practice, James L. Winkle College of Pharmacy, University of Cincinnati, Cincinnati, OH; at the time of writing she was Clinical Coordinator, Ambulatory Pharmacy Services, Health Alliance, Greater Cincinnati, Florence, KY. LAUREL M. MARSDEN, B.S.PHARM., M.S.H.A., is Assistant Director of Pharmacy, Virginia Commonwealth University Health System, Richmond. BRIDGETTE A. THOMAS, PHARM.D., is Clinical Applications Manager, Johns Hopkins Outpatient Pharmacy, Baltimore, MD. NATHAN S. THOMPSON, B.S.PHARM., M.B.A., is Director, Outpatient Pharmacy, Johns Hopkins Home Care Group, Baltimore.

The contributions of the Section of Ambulatory Care Practitioners Executive Committee (Seena L. Haines, Pharm.D., FASHP, FAPhA, BCACP, BC-ADM, CDE; Gloria P. Sachdev, Pharm.D.; Jennifer Askew Buxton, Pharm.D., CPP; Melanie A. Dodd, Pharm.D., Ph.C., BCPS; Sandra Leal, Pharm.D., FAPhA, CDE; Steven M. Riddle, Pharm.D., BCPS, FASHP; and Justine Coffey, J.D., LL.M.) to this document are gratefully acknowledged.

The following organizations and individuals are acknowledged for reviewing draft versions of these Guidelines (review does not imply endorsement): Academy of Managed Care Pharmacy (AMCP); American Association of Critical-Care Nurses (AACN); American College of Clinical Pharmacy (ACCP); American Geriatric Society; Joint Commission; Cindi Brennan, Pharm.D., M.H.A.; Mark N. Brueckl, M.B.A. (AMCP); Anne Burns, Pharm.D.; Frank P. Castronovo, Jr., Ph.D.; Sharon Connor, Pharm.D.; Paul F. Davis, B.S.Pharm.; Ernest Dole, Pharm.D., FASHP; Melanie A. Dodd, Pharm.D., Ph.C., BCPS; Scott R. Drab, Pharm.D., CDE, BC-ADM; Sarah K. Ford, Pharm.D., BCPS, CPP; Seena L. Haines, Pharm.D., FASHP, FAPhA, BCACP, BC-ADM, CDE; Deanne L. Hall, Pharm.D., CDE; Philip E. Johnson, M.S., FASHP; Tom Kaye, M.B.A., FASHP; Sandra Leal, Pharm.D., FAPhA, CDE; Jeff Little, Pharm.D., M.P.H., BCPS; Jimmy R. Mitchell, M.S., M.P.H.; Bruce A. Nelson, M.S.; Colleen O'Malley, M.S., B.S.Pharm.; James A. Ponto, M.S., BCNP; Matt Ransom, Pharm.D., BCACP; Steven M. Riddle, Pharm.D., BCPS, FASHP; Christine Ruby, Pharm.D., BCPS; Gloria P. Sachdev, Pharm.D.; Paul M. Schyve, M.D. (Joint Commission); Pamela Shellner, B.S.N., M.A., RN (AACN); Melissa Somma-McGivney, Pharm.D., CDE; Richard L. Stambaugh, M.S., Pharm.D., BCPS; Marc H. Stranz, Pharm.D.; Megan Wagner, Pharm.D.; C. Edwin Webb, Pharm.D., M.P.H. (ACCP); and Jody Jacobson Wedret, B.S.Pharm., FASHP, FCSHP.

The bibliographic citation for this document is as follows: American Society of Health-System Pharmacists. ASHP Guidelines: minimum standard for ambulatory care pharmacy practice. *Am J Health-Syst Pharm.* 2015; 72:1221–36.

ASHP Guidelines: Minimum Standard for Pharmacies in Hospitals

Purpose

The following minimum standard guidelines are intended to serve as a basic guide for the provision of pharmacy services in hospitals. These guidelines outline a minimum level of services that most hospital pharmacy departments should consistently provide. The reader is strongly encouraged to review the American Society of Health-System Pharmacy (ASHP) guidance documents referenced throughout these guidelines for more detailed descriptions. Certain elements of these guidelines may be applicable to other health care settings or may be useful in evaluating the scope and quality of pharmacy services.

Elements of Care

The mission of pharmacists is to help people make the best use of medications.[1] Therefore, pharmacists shall be concerned with not only the provision but the outcomes of pharmacy services. The elements of pharmacy services that are critical to safe, effective, and cost-conscious medication use in a hospital include (1) practice management, (2) medication-use policy development, (3) optimizing medication therapy, (4) drug product procurement and inventory management, (5) preparing, packaging, and labeling medications, (6) medication delivery, (7) monitoring medication use, (8) evaluating the effectiveness of the medication-use system, and (9) research. Although the scope of pharmacy services will vary from site to site, depending upon the needs of patients and the hospital as well as the resources available, these core elements are inextricably linked to successful outcomes. Failure to provide any of these services may compromise the quality of patient care.

Terminology

In these guidelines, the term "shall" is used to indicate a minimum standard of practice set forth in this document, in other ASHP policies, or in requirements established by laws, regulations, accrediting bodies, or other binding authorities. The term "should" is used to indicate a best practice that is strongly encouraged by ASHP but which may not be applicable to all institutions or in all circumstances.

Standard I. Practice Management

Effective leadership and practice management skills are necessary for the delivery of pharmacy services in a manner consistent with the hospital's and patients' needs. Such leadership should foster continuous improvement in patient care outcomes. The management of pharmacy services should focus on the pharmacist's responsibilities as a patient care provider and leader of the pharmacy enterprise through the development of organizational structures that support that mission. Development of such structures will require communication and collaboration with other departments and services throughout the hospital, which every member of the pharmacy team should cultivate at every opportunity.

A. Pharmacy and Pharmacist Services

Pharmacy Mission, Goals, and Scope of Services. The pharmacy shall have a written mission statement that reflects both patient care and operational responsibilities. Other aspects of the pharmacy's mission may require definition as well (e.g., educational and research responsibilities). The mission statement shall be consistent with the mission of the hospital and, if applicable, aligned with the health system of which the hospital is a component. The development, prioritization, and implementation of the pharmacy's goals should be consistent with the mission statement. Determination of short- and long-term goals and the undertaking of implementation activities should be performed in collaboration with institutional leadership and other hospital staff (e.g., pharmacy, nursing, and medical staff), and these should be integrated with the goals of the hospital. The mission statement may also incorporate consensus-based national goals, such as those expressed in the recommendations from the ASHP Pharmacy Practice Model Initiative.[2]

The pharmacy shall also maintain a written document describing the scope of pharmacy services. These services should be consistent with the hospital's scope of services and should be applied throughout the hospital in all practice sites.

The mission, goals, and scope of services shall be clearly communicated to everyone involved in the provision of pharmacy services, including pharmacists, residents, students, technicians, and support staff.

24-Hour Pharmacy Services. Adequate hours of operation for the provision of needed pharmacy services shall be maintained; 24-hour pharmacy services should be provided when possible. Twenty-four hour pharmacy services should be employed in all hospitals with clinical programs that require intensive medication therapy (e.g., transplant programs, open-heart surgery programs, neonatal intensive care units, and trauma centers). When 24-hour pharmacy services are not feasible, a pharmacist shall be available on an on-call basis. Remote medication order processing may be employed (to the extent permitted by law and regulation) to help provide pharmacy services but is not a substitute for an on-call pharmacist.[3] Automated drug dispensing equipment and computer databases are also not a substitute for the skills and knowledge of a pharmacist and should not be considered alternatives to 24-hour pharmacy services.[4]

After-Hours Pharmacy Access. In the absence of 24-hour pharmacy services, access to a limited supply of medications shall only be available to authorized, licensed health care professionals for use in carrying out urgent medication orders. Access to such medications shall be carefully monitored and documented, and after-hours access shall be reviewed regularly to ensure appropriate use. The list of medications to be accessible and the policies and procedures to be used (including subsequent review of all activity by a pharmacist) shall be developed by a multidisciplinary committee of physicians, pharmacists, and nurses (e.g., by the pharmacy and therapeutics [P&T] committee or its equivalent).[5] Access to medications should be limited to cases in which the P&T committee (or its equivalent) determines that the urgent clinical need for the medication outweighs the potential risks of making the medication accessible. The potential safety risks of medications should be considered in the decision to make them accessible, and medications, quantities, dosage forms, and container sizes that might endanger patients should be limited whenever possible.

Routine after-hours access to the pharmacy by nonpharmacists for access to medications shall not be permitted. The use of well-designed night cabinets, after-hours medication carts, automated dispensing devices,[6] and other methods precludes the need for nonpharmacists to enter the pharmacy.[4]

Practice Standards and Guidelines. The standards and regulations of all relevant government bodies (e.g., state boards of pharmacy, departments of health) shall be met. The practice standards and guidelines of ASHP, appropriate accrediting bodies (e.g., Joint Commission, American Osteopathic Association Healthcare Facilities Accreditation Program, Det Norske Veritas), and the Centers for Medicare and Medicaid Services shall be viewed as applicable, and the hospital should strive to meet all applicable standards.

B. Laws and Regulations

Applicable local, state, and federal laws and regulations shall be met, and relevant documentation of compliance shall be maintained.

C. Policies and Procedures

Policy and Procedures Manual. There shall be a policy and procedures manual governing pharmacy functions (e.g., administrative, operational, and clinical), and all pharmacy personnel shall follow those policies and procedures. The manual may include a statement of the pharmacy's mission, philosophy, or values (e.g., the pharmacy's mission or vision statement), but it should concentrate on operational policies and procedures to guide and direct all pharmacy services. The pharmacy's policies and procedures should be consistent with the hospital's policies and procedures, and the manual should be reviewed by a designated medical staff committee for potential conflicts and other medical issues. The manual shall be reviewed by pharmacy staff on a regular basis and revised as necessary to reflect changes in procedures, organization, objectives, or practices. The manual shall be accessible to pharmacy department personnel as well as other hospital employees (e.g., through the hospital's intranet), and all pharmacy personnel should be familiar with its contents. Appropriate mechanisms to ensure compliance with the policies and procedures should be established.

Personnel Safety. Pharmacy employees should be involved in the development of the hospital's plans for emergency response, infection prevention and control, management of hazardous substances and waste, and incident reporting, and all pharmacy staff shall receive education about those plans.

Emergency Preparedness. Facility emergency preparedness plans shall describe the role of pharmacy staff in emergency response (including evacuation), and the facility's business continuity plan shall include procedures for providing safe and efficient pharmacy services in case of emergencies. Appropriately trained pharmacists should be members of emergency preparedness teams and participate in applicable preparations and drills.[7] The pharmacy shall establish, in conjunction with the hospitalwide emergency plan, policies and procedures for the safe and orderly evacuation of pharmacy personnel in the event of an emergency in the hospital.

Medical Emergencies. The pharmacy shall participate in hospital decisions about the contents of code carts, emergency medication kits and trays, and the role of pharmacists in medical emergencies. Pharmacists should serve on cardiopulmonary resuscitation teams, and such pharmacists should receive appropriate training and maintain appropriate certifications (e.g., Basic Life Support, Advanced Cardiopulmonary Life Support, Pediatric Acute Life Support).

Immunization Programs. The pharmacy shall participate in the development of hospital policies and procedures concerning preventive and postexposure immunization programs for patients and hospital employees.[8] When practical, pharmacists should participate as active immunizers for hospital and health-system-based preventive immunization programs (e.g., influenza).

Substance Abuse Programs. The pharmacy shall assist in the development of and participate in hospital substance abuse education, prevention, identification, treatment, and employee assistance programs.[9]

D. Human Resources

Position Descriptions. Areas of responsibility within the scope of pharmacy services shall be clearly defined. The responsibilities and related competencies of professional and supportive personnel shall be clearly defined in written position descriptions. These position descriptions shall be reviewed and revised as required by the hospital's policies. Position descriptions should reflect more general aspects of performance (e.g., communication, motivation, teamwork) in addition to specific responsibilities and competencies.

Director of Pharmacy. The pharmacy shall be managed by a professionally competent, legally qualified pharmacist. The director of pharmacy should be thoroughly knowledgeable about and have experience in hospital pharmacy practice and management. An advanced management degree (e.g., M.B.A., M.H.A., or M.S.) or an administrative specialty residency[10] is desirable.

The director of pharmacy shall be responsible for

- Establishing the mission, vision, goals, and scope of services of the pharmacy based on the needs of the patients served, the needs of the hospital (and any health system of which the hospital may be a component), and developments and trends in health care and hospital pharmacy practice,
- Developing, implementing, evaluating, and updating plans and activities to fulfill the mission, vision, goals, and scope of services of the pharmacy,

- Actively working with or as a part of hospital or health-system leadership to develop and implement policies and procedures that provide safe and effective medication use for the patients served by the institution,
- Mobilizing and managing the resources, both human and financial, necessary for the optimal provision of pharmacy services, and
- Ensuring that patient care services provided by pharmacists and other pharmacy personnel are delivered in adherence to applicable state and federal laws and regulations, hospital privileging requirements, and national practice standards.

A part-time director of pharmacy shall have the same obligations and responsibilities as a full-time director.

Pharmacists. The pharmacy shall employ an adequate number of competent, legally qualified pharmacists to meet the specific medication-use needs of the hospital's patients. Pharmacists hired on a temporary or contract basis shall meet the same requirements as those employed by the hospital.

Support Personnel. Sufficient support personnel (e.g., pharmacy technicians and clerical or secretarial personnel) shall be employed to facilitate pharmacy services. Support positions shall have a written job description that includes a statement of the competencies required for that position. Support staff shall be properly trained and supervised, and professional development programs for them are desirable. Pharmacy technicians should have completed an ASHP-accredited pharmacy technician training program, should be certified by the Pharmacy Technician Certification Board, and shall meet the requirements of applicable laws and regulations. Pharmacy technicians working in advanced roles should have additional training and demonstrate competencies specific to the tasks to be performed.

Education and Training. All personnel shall possess the education and training required to fulfill their responsibilities and shall participate in relevant continuing-education programs and activities as necessary to maintain or enhance their competence.[11]

Recruitment, Selection, and Retention of Personnel. Personnel should be recruited and selected by the pharmacy director on the basis of job-related qualifications and prior performance. An employee retention plan is desirable.[12]

Orientation of Personnel. There shall be an established, structured procedure for orienting new personnel to the pharmacy, the hospital, and their respective positions.[9] Evaluation of the effectiveness of orientation programs should be done in conjunction with the competency assessment required before a new hire can assume full responsibility for the new position.

Work Schedules and Assignments. The director of pharmacy shall ensure that work schedules, procedures, and assignments optimize the use of personnel and resources. There shall be a written departmental staffing plan that addresses how patients' needs will be met during periods of staff shortages and fluctuation in workload and/or patient acuity. Remote medication order processing may be employed to help address staff shortages or workload fluctuations.[3]

Performance Evaluation. There shall be procedures for regularly scheduled evaluation of the performance of pharmacy personnel. The evaluation format should be consistent with that used by the hospital. The competencies of the position shall be well defined in the position description, short- and long-term goals should be established for each employee, and the employee's competency shall be assessed regularly. The pharmacy director shall ensure that an ongoing competency assessment program is in place for all staff, and each staff member should have a continuous professional development plan.

Effective Communication. There should be established methods for communicating important information to staff in a timely manner (e.g., electronic communications, staff meetings, newsletters, bulletin boards). The pharmacy should establish appropriate mechanisms to regularly assess the effectiveness of such communications.

Ethical Conduct. Standards of ethical conduct shall be established, and there shall be procedures for educating all pharmacy staff regarding these standards. The institution's conflict-of-interest and ethical conduct policies shall be clearly communicated to all staff, with appropriate staff acknowledgement of conformance with these policies.[13]

E. Facilities

Pharmacy. Adequate space, equipment, and supplies shall be available for all professional and administrative functions relating to pharmacy services. These resources shall meet all applicable laws and regulations; shall be located in areas that facilitate the provision of services to patients, nurses, prescribers, and other health care providers; and shall be integrated with the hospital's communication and delivery or transportation systems.

Medication Storage and Preparation Areas. There shall be suitable facilities to enable the receipt, storage, and preparation of medications under proper conditions of sanitation, temperature, light, moisture, ventilation, segregation, and security to ensure medication integrity and personnel safety throughout the hospital.[4]

Compounding Areas. There shall be suitable facilities to enable the compounding, preparation, and labeling of sterile and nonsterile products, including hazardous drug products, in accordance with established quality-assurance procedures. The work environment should promote orderliness and efficiency and minimize the potential for medication errors and contamination of products.[14–20]

Patient Assessment and Consultation Area. In outpatient settings, a private area for pharmacist–patient consultations shall be available to confidentially enhance patients' knowledge of and adherence to prescribed medication regimens.[21]

Office and Meeting Space. Adequate office and meeting areas shall be available for administrative, educational, and training activities.

Automated Systems. There shall be policies and procedures for the evaluation, selection, use, calibration, monitoring, and maintenance of all automated pharmacy systems. Automated mechanical systems and software can promote safe, accurate, and efficient medication ordering and preparation, drug distribution, and clinical monitoring. Use of such systems and software shall be structured so as to not hinder the pharmacist's review of (and opportunity to intervene in) medication orders before the administration of first doses. The maintenance, calibration, and certification of all automated systems shall be performed and documented as required by all applicable laws, regulations, and standards.[6,22,23] All automated systems shall include adequate safeguards to maintain the confidentiality and security of patient records, and there shall be procedures to provide essential patient care services in case of equipment failure or downtime.

Information Technology. A comprehensive pharmacy computer system shall be employed and should be integrated to the fullest extent possible with other hospital information systems and software, including computerized provider-order-entry, medication administration, electronic health record, and patient billing systems. Computer resources should be used to support clerical functions, maintain patient medication profile records, provide clinical decision support, perform necessary patient billing procedures, manage drug product inventories, provide drug information, access the patient medical record, manage electronic prescribing, and interface with other computerized systems to obtain patient-specific clinical information for medication therapy monitoring and other clinical functions and to facilitate the continuity of care to and from other care settings. Pharmacists should be involved in the development and maintenance of order sets, templates, and dose ranges used in computerized provider-order-entry and clinical decision-support systems. Pharmacy computer systems should be integrated with the hospital's clinical, financial, and administrative information systems. All computer systems shall include adequate safeguards to maintain the confidentiality and security of patient records, and a backup system should be available to continue essential computerized functions (e.g., those that support patient care) during equipment failure.

Drug Information. Adequate space, current resources, and information-handling and communication technology shall be available to facilitate the provision of drug information. The department of pharmacy shall select its drug information resources, and pharmacists shall play a leadership role in the selection of drug information resources used by other health care providers in the hospital. Up-to-date, objective drug information shall be available, including current print or electronic periodicals, newsletters, best-practices guidelines, and recent editions of reference books in appropriate pharmaceutical and biomedical subject areas. Electronic drug information databases are preferred because they are frequently updated and can be made available to all health care professionals, but sufficient access to print information shall be available in case of equipment failure or downtime. Electronic and print drug information may be supplemented with medical libraries and other available resources. Appropriate drug information resources shall be readily accessible to pharmacists located in patient care areas.

Electronic databases and convenient methods of data dissemination (e.g., e-mail and handheld devices) are desirable. If such tools are employed, they should be made available to all health care practitioners who require access to the data.

Record Maintenance. All records shall be maintained in accordance with applicable laws, regulations, and institutional policies. Adequate space shall exist for maintaining and storing records (e.g., equipment maintenance, controlled substances inventory, and material safety data sheets) to ensure compliance with laws, regulations, accreditation requirements, and sound management practices. Appropriate licenses and permits shall be on display or on file as required by law or regulation. Equipment shall be adequately maintained and certified in accordance with applicable practice standards, laws, and regulations. There shall be documentation of equipment maintenance and certification.

F. Committee Involvement

A pharmacist shall be a member of and actively participate in hospital and health-system committees responsible for establishing and implementing medication-related policies and procedures as well as those committees responsible for the provision of patient care, including the P&T, infection-prevention and control, patient care, medication-use evaluation, medication safety, nutrition, and pain management committees (or their equivalents), as well as the institutional review board, quality-improvement, and information technology committees (or their equivalents).[5,24–26]

Standard II. Medication-Use Policy Development

A. Policy Development

All committees that make decisions concerning medication management and use shall have at least one pharmacist as a member. This includes the P&T, infection-control, patient care, medication-use evaluation, medication safety, nutrition, pain management, and information technology committees, as well as the institutional review board (or their equivalents).[5,24–26] Pharmacists shall be involved in the development, implementation, and assessment of care plans (protocols, critical pathways, disease statement management programs, or clinical practice guidelines), standing orders, and order sets that involve medication therapy.[27]

B. Formulary Management

Formulary. A well-controlled formulary of approved medications shall be maintained and regularly updated by the P&T committee (or its equivalent). The impact of and compliance with the formulary should be periodically reviewed (e.g., through drug-utilization reviews), and the P&T committee should regularly review the formulary for safety information. The P&T committee shall be responsible for developing and maintaining written criteria for drug product selection, which shall address formulary requests for medications intended for use in special populations (e.g., pediatric or geriatric populations). The P&T committee shall be responsible for developing and maintaining adequate product specifications to aid in the purchase of medications and related supplies. The pharmacy shall disseminate the formulary by electronic (preferred) or other means to meet the needs of all health care professionals.

There shall be policies and procedures that address the use of dietary supplements and other alternative therapies.

There shall be policies and procedures for the procurement, control, and use of nonformulary medications required for patient care.[5]

Medication Therapy Monographs. Medication therapy monographs for medications under consideration for formulary addition or deletion shall be made available to the P&T committee for use in the decision-making process. These monographs should be based on evidence gathered through review and evaluation of the pertinent literature. Each monograph shall include a comparative therapeutic, economic, and risk assessment (inclusive of black-box warnings) of each medication. The risk assessment should address the likelihood of an error occurring and the risk of injury should that error occur.[5]

Nondrug Substances. There shall be policies and procedures that describe how the pharmacy shall seek and obtain documented authorization from appropriate medical staff and hospital committees prior to the medical use of any chemical substance that has not received Food and Drug Administration (FDA) approval for use as a drug or medical nutrition therapy. All chemical or biological substances whose administration is intended for pharmacological or medical effect or as a substitute for or complement to approved drugs shall be under the control of the pharmacy. Documentation shall exist to ensure that appropriate risk management measures (e.g., obtaining informed consent) have been taken.

C. Drug Information

Drug Information Requests. The pharmacist shall provide patient-specific drug information and accurate and comprehensive information about drugs and drug therapy to health professionals, patients, and patients' caregivers as appropriate. Responses to general and patient-specific drug information requests shall be provided in an accurate and timely manner by a pharmacist, and there should be a process for assessing and ensuring the quality of responses.[28]

Dissemination of Drug Information. Pharmacists shall keep the hospital's staff and health care providers informed about the use of medications on an ongoing basis through appropriate publications, presentations, and programs. Pharmacists shall ensure timely dissemination of drug product information (e.g., recall notices, labeling changes, and changes in product availability). Electronic communications (e.g., websites, email newsletters, intranet postings) are preferred because of their timeliness and accessibility.[28]

Standard III. Optimizing Medication Therapy

An important responsibility of the pharmacist is optimizing medication use. Pharmacists, in collaboration with medical and nursing staff, shall develop policies and procedures based on demonstrated best practices for ensuring the quality of medication therapy. Clinical imperatives should be the primary determinants of medication-use decisions.

A. Creating a Relationship with the Patient

Pharmacist Role in Direct Patient Care. Hospital and pharmacy department policies should encourage pharmacists to provide direct patient care to the greatest extent possible in both inpatient and outpatient settings. Hospital and pharmacy department policies should encourage pharmacists to engage in medication therapy management,[29] collaborative drug therapy management, immunization, medication ordering and administration, and other patient care activities to the extent permitted by law, regulation, and hospital requirements.

Continuity of Care. Pharmacists should assume responsibility for continuity of care for patients' medication therapy. Pharmacists and pharmacy departments should take a leadership role in developing and implementing policies and procedures for admissions, discharges, and transfers so that patients' medication therapy is well managed regardless of patient transitions across care settings (e.g., among different components of a health system or between inpatient and community pharmacies or home care services).

Patient Confidentiality. Systems shall be in place to ensure that patient confidentiality is maintained in accordance with applicable laws and regulations. All pharmacy personnel shall respect and protect patient confidentiality by safeguarding access to all patient information. Patient information shall be shared only with authorized health professionals and others authorized within the hospital or health system as needed for the care of patients.[30] Pharmacy personnel should periodically receive training in how to comply with patient confidentiality laws and regulations.

B. Acquiring Essential Patient Data

Pharmacists should obtain, prepare, or have immediate access to comprehensive medication histories for each patient, from the patient's medical record or other databases (e.g., a medication profile), or both. A pharmacist-conducted medication history for each patient is desirable. Electronic medical records should be constructed so that medication histories and other data required for medication management, including medication reconciliation, are available to all health professionals caring for a patient.

C. Consulting With Other Health Professionals About Medication Therapy

Pharmacist's Consultations. Pharmacists should provide oral and written consultations to other health professionals regarding medication therapy selection and management.[30]

Medical Record Documentation. There shall be policies and procedures for pharmacist review of and documentation in patients' medical records. Recommendations made by the pharmacist and actions taken in response to those recommendations should be documented in the patient's medical record so that other health care providers have access to that information.[30]

Medication Therapy Decisions. The pharmacist's prerogatives to initiate, monitor, and modify medication therapy for individual patients, and to order laboratory tests to exercise those responsibilities, consistent with laws, regulations, and hospital policy, shall be clearly delineated and approved by the appropriate committee (e.g., P&T, patient care, or medical executive committee).

Standard IV. Drug Product Procurement and Inventory Management

The pharmacy shall be responsible for the procurement, distribution, and control of all drug products used in the hospital for inpatient and ambulatory patients. Policies and procedures governing these functions shall be developed by the pharmacy with input from other appropriate hospital staff and committees.[4]

A. Selecting Sources of Pharmaceutical Products

Medication Acquisition. There shall be policies and procedures for managing medication acquisition. These policies and procedures should address such issues as formulary development (including initial evaluation for formulary consideration, medication-utilization review programs, and therapeutic interchange), competitive bidding, group purchasing, best practices, medication shortages, outsourcing, and cost-effective patient services. Benchmarking of medication costs should be performed to determine whether medication expenses and the change in medication expenses over time are consistent with industry standards.[4,31,32]

Pharmaceutical Manufacturers And Suppliers. Criteria for selecting drug product manufacturers and suppliers shall be established by the pharmacy to ensure the highest quality of and the best price for drug products. Although these duties may be delegated in part to a group purchasing organization, the pharmacy maintains the sole responsibility for ensuring the quality of drug products used in the hospital.[31,32]

Pharmaceutical Manufacturers' Representatives. There shall be written policies governing the activities of manufacturers' representatives or vendors of drug products (including related supplies and devices) within the hospital. Representatives should not be permitted access to patient care areas and should be provided with written guidance on permissible activities within the hospital. All promotional materials and activities shall be reviewed and approved by the pharmacy.[33]

B. Managing Inventory

Medication Storage. Medications shall be received, stored, and prepared under proper conditions of sanitation, temperature, light, moisture, ventilation, segregation, and security to ensure medication integrity and personnel safety.[4]

Drug Shortages. There shall be policies and procedures for managing drug product shortages. The pharmacy's inventory management system should be designed to detect subminimum inventory levels and alert the pharmacy to potential shortages, and pharmacy staff should monitor reliable sources of information regarding drug product shortages (e.g., the ASHP[34] and FDA[35] drug shortages web resource centers). The pharmacy should develop strategies for identifying alternative therapies, working with suppliers, collaborating with physicians and other health care providers, and conducting an awareness campaign in the event of a drug product shortage.[36]

Samples. The use of medication samples shall be eliminated to the extent possible. Medication samples shall never be used for inpatient treatment. If use of samples is otherwise permitted, there shall be policies and procedures to ensure their safe use. The pharmacy shall oversee the procurement, storage, and distribution of these products to ensure proper storage, maintenance of records, product integrity, and compliance with all applicable packaging and labeling laws, regulations, standards, and patient education requirements. Pharmacists should be involved in hospital efforts to secure safe and effective low-cost medications for low-income patients (e.g., through manufacturer patient assistance programs).[4,5,33]

Patient Care Area Stock. The proper use of automated dispensing devices reduces the need for medications to be stored in nonpharmacy areas.[6] Storage of medications in nonpharmacy areas (e.g., patient care and procedural areas) shall to the extent possible be limited to medications for emergency use and routinely used personal care items (e.g., mouthwash and antiseptic solutions). The list of medications to be accessible and the policies and procedures regarding their use shall be developed by a multidisciplinary committee of physicians, pharmacists, and nurses (e.g., the P&T committee).[5] Access to medications should be limited to cases in which the committee determines that the urgent clinical need for the medication outweighs the potential patient-safety risks of making the medication accessible. A separate assessment should occur for every location where a medication may be stocked.

Controlled Substances. There shall be policies and procedures to ensure control of the distribution and use of controlled substances and other medications with a potential for abuse. These policies and procedures shall be consistent with applicable laws and regulations and shall include methods for preventing and detecting diversion.[4]

Patient's Own Medications. Drug products and related devices brought into the hospital by patients shall be identified by pharmacy and documented in the patient's medical record if the medications are to be used during hospitalization. They shall be administered only pursuant to a prescriber's order and according to hospital policies and procedures, which should ensure the pharmacist's identification and validation of medication integrity as well as the secure and appropriate storage and management of such medications.

C. Inspecting Storage Areas and Inventory Items

All stocks of medications shall be inspected routinely to ensure the absence of outdated, unusable, recalled, or mislabeled products. Storage conditions that would foster medication deterioration, storage arrangements that might contribute to medication errors, and other safety issues shall be assessed, documented, and corrected.[4]

D. Returning Recalled, Expired, and Other Unusable Items

There shall be a written procedure for the timely handling and documentation of a drug product recall. These procedures should include an established process for removing from use any drugs or devices subjected to a recall, notifying appropriate health care professionals, identifying patients who may have been exposed to the recalled medication, and, if necessary, communicating available alternative therapies to prescribers. The pharmacy shall be notified of any defective drug products or related supplies and equipment encountered by the nursing or medical staffs. All drug product defects should be reported to the FDA's MedWatch reporting program.[4]

Standard V. Preparing, Packaging, and Labeling Medications

A. Preparing Medications

Compounding. Drug formulations, dosage forms, strengths, and packaging that are not available commercially but are needed for patient care shall be prepared by appropriately trained personnel in accordance with applicable practice standards and regulations. The pharmacy shall provide adequate quality-assurance procedures for these operations. Written master formulas and batch records (including product test results, as appropriate) shall be maintained, and a lot number or other method to identify each finished product with its production and control history shall be assigned to each batch.[14–20]

Sterile Preparations. When possible, manufactured sterile preparations should be preferred to compounding in the pharmacy. All sterile medications shall be prepared and labeled in a suitable environment by appropriately trained personnel in accordance with established quality-assurance and expiration dating procedures.[14,19] The use of sterile medications compounded outside the pharmacy should be avoided to the extent possible; when they are used, there shall be procedures for aseptic preparation, quality assurance, expiration dating, and ongoing competency evaluations for compounding personnel.[14,19,37] Sterile compounding outside the pharmacy or satellite pharmacies (e.g., on nursing units) should be minimized and occur only in emergency situations.[14,19]

Hazardous Drug Products. There shall be policies and procedures that describe special precautions, equipment, and training for preparation, handling, storage, and disposal of hazardous drug products and products used in their preparation. These policies and procedures shall be consistent with applicable laws and regulations and should be adequate to ensure the safety of staff, patients, visitors, the community, and the environment.[17]

B. Packaging Medications

Unit Dose Packaging. Whenever possible, medications shall be available for inpatient use in single-unit packages and in a ready-to-administer form. Manipulation of medications before administration (e.g., withdrawal of doses from containers, reconstitution of powdered drug products, labeling of containers, and splitting of tablets) by final users should be minimized.[15]

Bar-Coding of Unit Dose Packaging and Point of Care Administration. Unit dose packages should contain a bar code and that code should be used in inventory management, dose preparation and packaging, dispensing, and administration. It is the responsibility of the pharmacy department to ensure the quality of all aspects of bar-code medication administration, including scanability of bar codes and database management.[38,39]

Standard VI. Medication Dispensing and Delivery

A. Medication Dispensing

Prescribing. Medications shall be prescribed by individuals who have been granted appropriate clinical privileges in the hospital and are legally permitted to order medications. The pharmacy shall advocate and foster practitioners' conformance with standardized, approved, and safe terminology and abbreviations to be used throughout the hospital when prescribing medications and discourage use of nonstandard and unapproved terminology and abbreviations.[4]

Diagnostic or Therapeutic Purpose. Pharmacists should have immediate access to the patient's diagnosis or the intended therapeutic or medical purpose of medications.

Medication Orders. All patient medication orders shall be contained in the patient's medical record. A direct copy of the prescriber's order, either hard copy (including facsimile) or prescriber-entered electronic transmission (preferred method), shall be received by the pharmacist. Oral orders should be avoided to the extent possible. When oral orders are necessary, they shall follow the organization's established procedures for their use and documentation. Order transmittal safeguards should be used to ensure the security of the prescriber's order. Appropriate records of each medication order and its processing in the pharmacy shall be maintained in accordance with applicable laws and regulations.

A system shall exist to ensure that medication orders are not inappropriately continued.[4]

Review of Medication Orders. All medication orders shall be prospectively reviewed by a pharmacist and assessed in relation to pertinent patient and clinical information before the first dose is administered or made available in an automated dispensing device, except in emergent situations in which the treatment of the patient would be significantly compromised by the delay that would result from pharmacist review of the order. There shall be a procedure for retrospective review of these orders.

Any questions regarding an order shall be resolved with the prescriber prior to administration, and any action taken as a result of this intervention should be documented in the patient's medical record. Information concerning changes shall be communicated to the appropriate health professionals caring for the patient.[4]

B. Medication Delivery and Administration

Drug Delivery Systems, Administration Devices, and Automated Distribution Devices. The pharmacy shall have responsibility for developing policies, procedures, and quality-assurance programs regarding drug delivery systems, administration devices, and automated distribution devices that ensure safety, accuracy, security, and patient confidentiality. The potential for medication errors associated with such systems and devices should be thoroughly evaluated.[4,6] Pharmacy personnel shall supervise the stocking and documentation of medications in automated dispensing devices.[6] Whenever possible, automated dispensing cabinets should employ profile-based technology integrated with remote medication order-entry capabilities.

Medication Administration. Only personnel who are authorized by the hospital in accordance with applicable laws and regulations and appropriately trained shall be permitted to administer medications to a patient. All administered, refused, or omitted medication doses should be recorded in the patient's medical record according to an established procedure, and all medications that have not been administered should be returned to the pharmacy. No medication should be administered to a patient unless medical and nursing personnel have been provided with adequate information about, and are familiar with, its therapeutic use, method of administration, potential adverse effects, and dosage.

Standard VII. Monitoring Medication Use

A. Reviewing Patient Responses to Medication Therapy
Medication therapy monitoring shall be conducted by pharmacists. Medication therapy monitoring includes a proactive assessment of patient problems and an assessment of

- **a.** The therapeutic appropriateness of the patient's medication regimen.
- **b.** Therapeutic duplication or omissions in the patient's medication regimen.
- **c.** The appropriateness of the dose of the medication, as well as the route, method, and frequency of administration of the medication.
- **d.** Patient adherence to the prescribed medication regimen.
- **e.** Medication–medication, medication–food, medication–dietary supplement, medication–laboratory test, and medication–disease interactions.
- **f.** Adverse drug reactions and other undesired effects.[40]
- **g.** Patient medication allergies and sensitivities.
- **h.** Clinical and pharmacokinetic laboratory data to evaluate the efficacy and safety of medication therapy and to anticipate toxicity and adverse effects.
- **i.** Physical signs and clinical symptoms relevant to the patient's medication therapy.
- **j.** Assessment of the effectiveness of the patient's medication therapy.

B. Educating and Counseling Patients and Family
Pharmacists shall be available to participate in patient education. Pharmacists should help to ensure that all patients are given adequate information about the medications they receive in order to help patients participate in their own health care decisions and encourage adherence to medication regimens. Patient education activities shall be coordinated with the nursing, medical, and other clinical staff as needed. Medication-related material developed by other services and departments as well as commercial sources should be reviewed by the pharmacy staff for accuracy, currency, literacy appropriateness, and completeness. If necessary, interpretative language services (written or oral) should be made available to patients.[21]

Standard VIII. Evaluating the Effectiveness of the Medication-Use System

There shall be an ongoing, systematic program for quality assessment and improvement of pharmacy services and the medication-use system. The program should include routinely evaluating the literature for new technologies or successful practices that have been demonstrated to enhance safety in other organizations to determine if such technologies or practices can improve the hospital's medication-use system. This program should be integrated with the hospital's or health system's quality assessment and quality improvement activities. Quality-improvement activities related to the selection, prescription, procurement, storage, preparation, dispensing, distribution, administration, documentation, monitoring, and use of medications shall be routinely performed in cooperation with other health care providers. Feedback to appropriate individuals or entities about the quality achieved shall be provided.

A. Assessing Pharmacy Services and Practices
Documentation of Pharmacist-Provided Patient Care Services and Medication Therapy Outcomes. The pharmacy shall have an ongoing process for consistent documentation of the patient care services provided by pharmacists and patient outcomes from medication therapy.[30]

Workload and Financial Performance. A process shall exist to routinely monitor and document workload and financial performance. Metrics should encompass the full scope of patient care services provided by pharmacists and the pharmacy enterprise. This process should provide for the determination and analysis of hospital and systemwide costs of medication therapy. A pharmacist should be an integral part of the hospital's leadership teams (e.g., administrative, financial).

B. Improving the Medication-Use Process
Medication-Use Evaluation. There shall be an ongoing program for monitoring drug utilization and costs to ensure that medications are used appropriately, safely, and effectively and to increase the probability of desired patient outcomes. The P&T committee (or its equivalent) should define specific parameters for evaluation (e.g., disease state, pharmacological category, or high-use/high-cost drug products) as appropriate for the organization. Through the ongoing evaluation of medication use, areas in need of improvement in medication prescribing and management can be identified and targeted for intervention.[32,41]

Medication Safety. Pharmacists should provide leadership to and participate in collaborative, multidisciplinary efforts to prevent, detect, and resolve drug-related problems that can result in patient harm. Pharmacists and other appropriate hospital personnel shall establish and regularly revise policies and procedures regarding medication error and adverse event prevention and reporting. Monitoring, detecting, review, and analysis of the hospital and health system's medication errors and near-misses should be an ongoing process in a just culture environment,[42] and corresponding corrective actions should be documented. An ongoing program for preventing, monitoring, resolving, and reporting adverse drug events shall be developed.[40] A pharmacist shall participate in appropriate organizational committees and work with physicians, nurses, administrators, and others to examine and improve systems to ensure that medication-use processes are safe.[41]

Antimicrobial Stewardship and Infection Prevention and Control. There shall be policies and procedures to promote the optimal use of antimicrobial agents, reduce the transmission of infections, and educate health professionals, patients, and the public about these topics. Pharmacists should participate in antimicrobial stewardship and infection-prevention and control efforts through clinical endeavors focused on proper antimicrobial utilization and membership on relevant multidisciplinary work groups and committees within the health system.

Pharmacists should monitor patients' laboratory reports of microbial sensitivities or applicable diagnostic markers and advise prescribers if microbial resistance is suspected, evaluate trends in microbial prescribing relative to changes in microbial resistance patterns, and assist in developing prescribing patterns to help minimize the development of drug resistance.[24]

Standard IX. Research

The pharmacist should initiate, participate in, and support clinical and practice-related research appropriate to the goals, objectives, and resources of the specific hospital.

Policies and Procedures. The pharmacist shall ensure that policies and procedures for the safe and proper use of investigational drugs and medication-related devices are established and followed and that these policies and procedures meet all applicable laws and regulations. There shall be a procedure to assure that informed consent is obtained from the patient before the first dose of the study drug is administered.[5,44,45]

Procurement, Distribution, and Control of Investigational Drugs. The pharmacy shall be responsible for overseeing the procurement, distribution, and control of all investigational drugs. Investigational drugs shall be approved for use by an institutional review board and shall be dispensed and administered to consenting patients according to an approved protocol.[5,44,45]

Institutional Review Board. A pharmacist shall be a member of the hospital's institutional review board (or equivalent body), if one exists.[44]

Information Regarding Investigational Drugs. The pharmacy shall have access to information on all investigational studies and similar research projects involving medications and medication-related devices used in the hospital. The pharmacy shall provide pertinent written information (to the extent known) about the safe and proper use of investigational drugs, including possible adverse effects and adverse drug reactions, to nurses, pharmacists, physicians, and other health care professionals called upon to prescribe, dispense, and administer these medications.[44,45]

References

1. American Society of Health-System Pharmacists. Mission statement of the American Society of Health-System Pharmacists. *Am J Health-Syst Pharm.* 2001; 58:1524.
2. American Society of Health-System Pharmacists. The consensus of the Pharmacy Practice Model Summit. *Am J Health-Syst Pharm.* 2011; 68:1148–52.
3. American Society of Health-System Pharmacists. ASHP guidelines on remote medication order processing. *Am J Health-Syst Pharm.* 2010; 67:672–7.
4. American Society of Hospital Pharmacists. ASHP technical assistance bulletin on hospital drug distribution and control. *Am J Hosp Pharm.* 1980; 37:1097–103.
5. American Society of Health-System Pharmacists. ASHP guidelines on the pharmacy and therapeutics committee and the formulary system. *Am J Health-Syst Pharm.* 2008; 65:1272–83.
6. American Society of Health-System Pharmacists. ASHP guidelines on the safe use of automated dispensing devices. *Am J Health-Syst Pharm.* 2010; 67:483–90.
7. American Society of Health-System Pharmacists. ASHP statement on the role of health-system pharmacists in emergency preparedness. *Am J Health-Syst Pharm.* 2003; 60:1993–5.
8. American Society of Health-System Pharmacists. ASHP guidelines on the pharmacist's role in immunization. *Am J Health-Syst Pharm.* 2003; 60:1371–7.
9. American Society of Health-System Pharmacists. ASHP statement on the pharmacist's role in substance abuse prevention, education, and assistance. *Am J Health-Syst Pharm.* 2003; 60:1995–8.
10. American Society of Health-System Pharmacists. ASHP residency accreditation. www.ashp.org/menu/Accreditation/ResidencyAccreditation.aspx (accessed 2012 Jan 10).
11. American Society of Hospital Pharmacists. ASHP statement on continuing education. *Am J Hosp Pharm.* 1990; 47:1855.
12. American Society of Health-System Pharmacists. ASHP guidelines on the recruitment, selection, and retention of pharmacy personnel. *Am J Health-Syst Pharm.* 2003; 60:587–93.
13. American Pharmacists Association. Code of Ethics for Pharmacists. www.pharmacist.com/AM/Template.cfm?Section=Search1&template=/CM/HTMLDisplay.cfm&ContentID=2903 (accessed 2012 Jan 10).
14. American Society of Health-System Pharmacists. ASHP guidelines on quality assurance for pharmacy-prepared sterile products. *Am J Health-Syst Pharm.* 2000; 57:1150–69.
15. American Society of Hospital Pharmacists. ASHP technical assistance bulletin on single unit and unit

dose packages of drugs. *Am J Hosp Pharm.* 1985; 42:378–9.

16. American Society of Hospital Pharmacists. ASHP technical assistance bulletin on compounding nonsterile products in pharmacies. *Am J Hosp Pharm.* 1994; 51:1441–8.
17. American Society of Health-System Pharmacists. ASHP guidelines on handling hazardous drugs. *Am J Health-Syst Pharm.* 2006; 63:1172–93.
18. American Society of Hospital Pharmacists. ASHP technical assistance bulletin on repackaging oral solids and liquids in single unit and unit dose packages. *Am J Hosp Pharm.* 1983; 40:451–2.
19. Pharmaceutical compounding—sterile preparations (general information chapter 797). In: The United States pharmacopeia, 34th rev., and The national formulary, 29th ed. Rockville, MD: United States Pharmacopeial Convention; 2011:336–73.
20. Pharmaceutical compounding—nonsterile preparations (general information chapter 795). In: The United States pharmacopeia, 34th rev., and The national formulary, 29th ed. Rockville, MD: United States Pharmacopeial Convention; 2011:330–6.
21. American Society of Health-System Pharmacists. ASHP guidelines on pharmacist-conducted patient education and counseling. *Am J Health-Syst Pharm.* 1997; 54:431–4.
22. American Society of Health-System Pharmacists. ASHP guidelines on the safe use of automated compounding devices for the preparation of parenteral nutrition admixtures. *Am J Health-Syst Pharm.* 2000; 57:1343–8.
23. American Society of Health-System Pharmacists. ASHP guidelines on pharmacy planning for implementation of computerized provider order entry systems in hospitals and health systems. *Am J Health-Syst Pharm.* 2011; 68:e9–e31.
24. American Society of Health-System Pharmacists. ASHP statement on the pharmacist's role in antimicrobial stewardship and infection prevention and control. *Am J Health-Syst Pharm.* 2010; 67:575–7.
25. American Society of Health-System Pharmacists. ASHP statement on the pharmacist's role in informatics. *Am J Health-Syst Pharm.* 2007; 64:200–3.
26. American Society of Health-System Pharmacists. ASHP statement on the roles and responsibilities of the pharmacy executive. *Am J Health-Syst Pharm.* 2009; 66:499–502.
27. American Society of Health-System Pharmacists. ASHP guidelines on the pharmacist's role in the development, implementation, and assessment of critical pathways. *Am J Health-Syst Pharm.* 2004; 61:939–45.
28. American Society of Health-System Pharmacists. ASHP guidelines on the provision of medication information by pharmacists. *Am J Health-Syst Pharm.* 1996; 53:1843–5.
29. Office of the Law Revision Counsel, United States House of Representatives. USC*prelim*. 42 U.S.C. Sec. 299b-35(c), MTM services to eligible individuals. http://uscode.house.gov/lawrevisioncounsel.shtml (accessed 2012 Apr 24).
30. American Society of Health-System Pharmacists. ASHP guidelines on documenting pharmaceutical care in patient medical records. *Am J Health-Syst Pharm.* 2003; 60:705–7.
31. American Society of Hospital Pharmacists. ASHP guidelines for selecting pharmaceutical manufacturers and suppliers. *Am J Hosp Pharm.* 1991; 48:523–4.
32. American Society of Health-System Pharmacists. ASHP guidelines on medication cost management strategies for hospitals and health systems. *Am J Health-Syst Pharm.* 2008; 65:1368–84.
33. American Society of Hospital Pharmacists. ASHP guidelines for pharmacists on the activities of vendors' representatives in organized health care systems. *Am J Hosp Pharm.* 1994; 51:520–1.
34. American Society of Health-System Pharmacists. ASHP Drug Shortages Resource Center. www.ashp.org/shortages (accessed 2012 Jan 11).
35. Food and Drug Administration. Drug shortages. www.fda.gov/cder/drug/shortages/ (accessed 2012 Jan 11).
36. American Society of Health-System Pharmacists. ASHP guidelines on managing drug product shortages in hospitals and health systems. *Am J Health-Syst Pharm.* 2009; 66:1399–406.
37. American Society of Health-System Pharmacists. ASHP guidelines on outsourcing sterile compounding services. *Am J Health-Syst Pharm.* 2010; 67:757–65.
38. American Society of Health-System Pharmacists. ASHP statement on bar-code-enabled medication administration technology. *Am J Health-Syst Pharm.* 2009; 66:588–90.
39. American Society of Health-System Pharmacists. ASHP statement on bar-code verification during inventory, preparation, and dispensing of medications. *Am J Health-Syst Pharm.* 2011; 68:442–5.
40. American Society of Health-System Pharmacists. ASHP guidelines on adverse drug reaction monitoring and reporting. *Am J Health-Syst Pharm.* 1995; 52:417–9.
41. American Society of Health-System Pharmacists. ASHP guidelines on medication-use evaluation. *Am J Health-Syst Pharm.* 1996; 53:1953–5.
42. Khatri N, Brown GD, Hicks LL. From a blame culture to a just culture in health care. *Health Care Manage Rev.* 2009; 34(4):312–22.
43. American Society of Hospital Pharmacists. ASHP guidelines on preventing medication errors in hospitals. *Am J Hosp Pharm.* 1993; 50:305–14.
44. American Society of Health-System Pharmacists. ASHP guidelines on clinical drug research. *Am J Health-Syst Pharm.* 1998; 55:369–76.
45. American Society of Hospital Pharmacists. ASHP guidelines for pharmaceutical research in organized health-care settings. *Am J Hosp Pharm.* 1989; 46:129–30.

Developed through the ASHP Council on Pharmacy Practice and approved by the ASHP Board of Directors on April 13, 2012.

This document supersedes a previous version approved by the ASHP Board of Directors on September 22, 1995.

ASHP gratefully acknowledges the contributions made by the following individuals to various drafts of these guidelines: Thomas S. Brenner, B.S.Pharm., FASHP; Harold N. Godwin, M.S., FASHP, FAPhA; William A. Gouveia, M.S., FASHP; Brian D. Hodgkins, Pharm.D., FCSHP, FASHP; Stanley S. Kent, M.S., FASHP; Patricia C. Kienle, M.P.A., FASHP; Harold J. Kornfuhrer, B.S.Pharm., FASHP; Emory S. Martin III, Pharm.D., BCPS; J. Russell May, Pharm.D., FASHP; Gerald E. Meyer, Pharm.D., M.B.A., FASHP; Thomas E. O'Brien, Pharm.D., M.S., FASHP; Sherri L. Ramsey, D.Ph., BCPS; Frank G. Saya, Pharm.D., FCSHP, FASHP; Donna L. Soflin, B.S.Pharm., FASHP; David K. Solomon, Pharm.D., FASHP; Kasey K. Thompson, Pharm.D., M.S.; and Billy W. Woodward, B.S.Pharm.

ASHP also gratefully acknowledges the following organizations and individuals for reviewing drafts of these guidelines (review does not imply endorsement): American Nurses Association (ANA); Institute for Safe Medication Practices (ISMP); Rhode Island Society of Health-System Pharmacists (RISHP); South Carolina Society of Health-System Pharmacists (SCSHP); Wyoming Society of Health-System Pharmacy (WSHP); Tuesday Adams, RN-C, WCC; John A. Armitstead, M.S., FASHP; Phil Ayers, Pharm.D., BCNSP; Ronald Barnes, M.S.; Paul J. Barrett, Pharm.D., BCPS; Carol J. Bickford, Ph.D., RN-BC, CPHIMS (ANA); P. Justin Boyd, Pharm.D., BCPS, CDM; Tim Brown, Pharm.D., BCACP; Margaret Chrymko, Pharm.D.; Toby Clark, M.Sc., FASHP; Wayne F. Conrad, Pharm.D., FASHP; Gayle A. Cotchen, Pharm.D., M.B.A.; Debra Lynn Painter Cowan, Pharm.D., FASHP; Arash Dabestani, Pharm.D., M.H.A., FASHP, FABC; Denise F. Daly, Pharm.D., BCPS; Tina H. Denetclaw, Pharm.D., BCPS; Deanna Dossey, Pharm.D.; William L. Fritz, M.S., FASHP; Daphne Hsu Galang, RPhT, CPhT, B.S., M.H.A.; Michael A. Gillette, Pharm.D., BCPS, BCACP; Kathleen M. Gura, Pharm.D., BCNSP, FASHP, FPPAG; Reginald L. Hain, B.S.Pharm.; Thomas G. Hall, Pharm.D.; George Hatfield, Pharm.D.; Jesse Hogue, Pharm.D.; Andrew Jarrell, Pharm.D.; Jack G. Kitrenos, Pharm.D., FASHP; Jamie Kuo, Pharm.D.; Jim Lile, Pharm.D.; Charles "Kurt" Mahan, Pharm.D., Ph.C.; Linda Gore Martin, Pharm.D., M.B.A., BCPS (WSHP); Justine Medina, M.S., RN; Dayna Mitchell, Pharm.D., BCPS; Holly Monatt, Pharm.D., BCPS; Selma Morrison; Robert J. Moura, M.S.; Jonathan M. Mundy, M.B.A. (RISHP); Bruce A. Nelson, M.S.; Beth Norman, M.S., RN, CNS, ACNS-BC; Robert S. Oakley, M.S.; Fred J. Pane, B.S.Pharm., FASHP; Shreya Parekh, Pharm.D.; Jennifer Phillips, Pharm.D.; James Ponto, BCNP, FASHP; Curt W. Quap, M.S., FASHP; Todd Rowland, Pharm.D.; Renee B. Sager, Pharm.D.; Joseph Sceppa, M.S., M.B.A.; Nicole Shumiloff, Pharm.D.; Nancy R. Smestad, M.S.; Carolyn M. Smith, Pharm.D., M.B.A., BCPS (SCSHP); William E. Smith, Pharm.D., M.P.H., Ph.D., FASHP; Richard L. Stambaugh, Pharm.D., M.S., BCPS; Therese Staublin, Pharm.D.; Marc Stranz, Pharm.D.; Timothy P. Stratton, Ph.D.; Pamela Swarny, Pharm.D., J.D.; Jane Tennis, B.S.Pharm., M.B.A.; Sherry Umhoefer, M.B.A.; Allen J. Vaida, Pharm.D., FASHP (ISMP); Jody Jacobson Wedret, FASHP, FCSHP; Roger Woolf, Pharm.D.; and Kevin Zak, Pharm.D.

The bibliographic citation for this document is as follows: American Society of Health-System Pharmacists. ASHP guidelines: minimum standard for pharmacies in hospitals. *Am J Health-Syst Pharm.* 2013; 70:1619–30.

ASHP Guidelines on Pharmaceutical Services in Correctional Facilities

Introduction

Pharmaceutical services in correctional facilities encompass many aspects of community, hospital, and consultant pharmacy practice. These guidelines are intended to address some of the unique aspects of pharmacy practice and services in correctional facilities. Some correctional facilities may not require, or be able to obtain, the services of a pharmacist. However, the concepts, principles, and recommendations contained in this standard are applicable to all correctional facilities, regardless of size or type. Thus, the part-time pharmacy director or consultant pharmacist has the same basic obligations and responsibilities as his or her fulltime counterpart in larger settings. This document should serve as a guide for the provision of pharmaceutical services in correctional institutions.

Administration

Pharmaceutical services are an integral part of health care provided in correctional institutions. The pharmacist is usually responsible for multiple tasks ranging from the management of the pharmacy to the direct provision of services to inmate-patients. Two primary management responsibilities pertain to human and fiscal resources.

Personnel[1]

- Sufficient support personnel should be available to maximize the use of pharmacists in tasks requiring professional judgment. Appropriate supervisory controls for support personnel should be maintained. The use of pharmacy technicians graduated from ASHP-accredited pharmacy technician training programs is recommended. Pharmacy technicians should be certified by the Pharmacy Technician Certification Board.
- All personnel should possess the education and training needed to carry out their responsibilities. The competence of all staff may be enhanced through relevant continuing education. Credentialing of eligible staff as Certified Correctional Health Professionals through the National Commission on Correctional Health Care is recommended.
- A pharmacist should be available, at a minimum, on a consulting basis; the pharmacist should visit each facility no less than monthly. If the only pharmaceutical services provided are those of a consultant pharmacist, the consultant pharmacist should assume the role of pharmacy director.
- If the pharmacist is an employee of a contract vendor, he or she should be designated as the pharmacy director and assume the associated obligations and responsibilities.
- Health care services should be available to inmate-patients 24 hours a day. Pharmacist services should also be available, at least on an "on call" basis.
- Other pertinent guidelines of the American Society of Health-System Pharmacists, the National Commission on Correctional Health Care, and the American Correctional Association should be followed, and requirements set by federal, state, and local laws and regulations with respect to personnel should be met.

Fiscal Resources

Pharmacists serving correctional institutions should strive to manage expenses while providing optimal care to the inmate-patients. The pharmacist should

- Work with the administrators of the correctional institution to establish a budget for the operation of the pharmacy.
- Consider factors unique to each institution for the development of the budget (e.g., total inmate capacity, average daily inmate population, demographics of the inmate population).
- Make allowances for the disproportionate amount of chronic communicable disease in the prison population and the regional variability of diseases.
- Apply the ASHP Technical Assistance Bulletin on Assessing Cost-Containment Strategies for Pharmacies in Organized Health-Care Settings, as appropriate.[2]

Policies and Procedures

A policies and procedures manual specifically written to address aspects of pharmacy practice in the correctional facility should exist.

- All policies and procedures should conform to federal, state, and local laws and regulations.
- The pharmacy director should be familiar with the Standards for Health Services promulgated by the National Commission on Correctional Health Care and the standards of the American Correctional Association.
- The pharmacy director should be familiar with the constitutional rights of inmate-patients, current literature about inmates' rights, and court rulings affecting the practice of correctional health care in general and correctional pharmacy in particular. Attention to these concepts should be reflected in the manual.
- The pharmacy director should be familiar with current literature, laws, and regulations governing confidentiality, consent, and other areas of correctional health care that diverge from more traditional standards of pharmacy practice. Attention to these should be reflected in the manual.
- Transportation of inmate-patients' medications within and among facilities should be addressed.
- Security of drug products, entry into the pharmacy during the absence of a pharmacist, use of night cabinets, emergency supplies of medications, and disaster services should be addressed.
- Policies and procedures on the pharmacy's role in preparing lethal injections for capital punishment should exist.

Administrative Reports

Administrative reports generated by the pharmacy department will vary from facility to facility depending on the level of pharmaceutical services provided. Reports should include

- The amounts and cost of drugs and services furnished
- Destruction of unusable or outdated medications
- Inventory value and quantities
- Records of formal meetings with administrators, physicians, nurses, and other staff and any changes implemented as a result of those meetings
- Minutes of pharmacy and therapeutics committee meetings
- Medication administration records
- Reports of quality-control and quality-improvement activities
- Reports generated as required by applicable state laws regulating the practice of pharmacy. (While often not specifically written for the practice of correctional pharmacy, these laws are nonetheless usually pertinent to pharmacy practice within the correctional setting.)

Facilities

The pharmacy should be located within or in an area contiguous to the space provided for other health care services. Facilities should be adequate to accommodate appropriate security of all drug products, especially controlled substances.[3]

Purchasing, Distribution, and Control of Medications

Purchasing, distribution, and control of medications are essential elements of any pharmacy operation. Adequate methods to ensure that these responsibilities are met should exist.

Purchasing

- The pharmacy director should be responsible for choosing the sources from which to obtain drug products.[4]
- The pharmacy director should ensure that all medications meet applicable legal requirements. Guidance on the obligations of drug product suppliers and purchasers appears in the ASHP Guidelines for Selecting Pharmaceutical Manufacturers and Suppliers.[5]
- The pharmacy director should ensure that medications purchased from sources other than manufacturers or wholesalers (e.g., other pharmacies, contract providers) meet all applicable legal requirements. All suppliers should be able, at the request of the pharmacy director, to provide data on the quality of products.
- To the extent possible, all drug products should be contained in single-unit or unit dose packages.

Distribution

The pharmacist is responsible for the distribution and control of all drug products (including diagnostics and drug-related devices).

- A unit dose drug distribution and control system is recommended.
- The system employed should focus on patient safety and result in a minimal incidence of medication errors and adverse drug reactions. Ongoing processes for the monitoring and reporting of adverse drug reactions and the detection and prevention of medication errors should exist.
- The system employed should be cost-effective.
- The system employed should foster drug-control and drug-use monitoring.
- The system employed should foster patient compliance, recovery of drugs because of expired orders, and ultimate destruction of all unusable and outdated medications.
- Inmates should not be used in the distribution process.
- Patient confidentiality should be ensured in the distribution process (e.g., patients receiving medications for the treatment of AIDS).

Drug Storage

- The pharmacy director should ensure the proper security of medications stored in each location.
- The pharmacy director should ensure that drug products are stored in accordance with manufacturer or USP requirements.
- The pharmacy director should ensure that stored drug products are not expired.

Control

- A process for the recovery of medications dispensed to inmate-patients after the discontinuance of orders or in compliance with automatic stop orders should exist.
- A process for minimizing and eliminating unauthorized use of medications by anyone other than the intended patient (e.g., exchange of medications between inmates) should exist.
- A process for minimizing and eliminating pilferage should exist.
- A process for monitoring and preventing the dispensing of unusually large quantities of medications should exist.
- A process for preventing the dispensing of sufficient doses of any medication to enable potential suicide should exist. Individuals who are evaluated as high risks for suicide should be identified.
- A process for the security and dispensing of controlled substances should exist.
- The pharmacy director, in conjunction with the facility's medical staff and other responsible health authorities, should maintain policies and procedures for the routine review and renewal of medication orders and for any automatic discontinuance of orders.
- Access to patients' medication records should be limited to authorized personnel only. Complete access by the pharmacist should be ensured.
- A process for pharmacist review of medication orders to ensure patient safety and appropriateness of medication should exist. Medication orders (except in emergency situations) should be reviewed by the pharmacist before the first dose is dispensed.

Medication Administration

While medication administration is traditionally the responsibility of nurses, in the correctional setting some or all of this responsibility may be assigned to other personnel.

- The pharmacy director should be familiar with standards of the National Commission on Correctional Health Care with respect to medication administration by non-health-care personnel, and policies and procedures specifically addressing such administration should exist.
- The pharmacy director should participate in development of medication administration forms and ensure that all relevant information is incorporated into the forms.
- The pharmacy director should regularly educate all personnel involved in medication administration. These educational programs should include information on proper administration, indications, monitoring for adverse effects and allergic reactions, documentation, accountability, confidentiality, and the importance of compliance. Inmates who repeatedly refuse to take medications should be counseled by a pharmacist.
- Policies should be developed regarding the administration of medication to inmate-patients assigned to jobs or on work-release programs.
- Policies and procedures should be developed to ensure continuity of therapy upon release. Released inmates should have access to a limited supply of medications; either the drugs should be provided upon release or released inmates should have a prescription order transmitted to the pharmacy of their choice.

Documentation

- Medication administration records should be reviewed by the pharmacist at least monthly for proper documentation of medication administration.
- Review of the medication administration record should include assessments of documentation of medications administered, doses, frequency of administration, compliance, start and stop dates, and medication allergies.
- Pharmacist interventions should be documented in patients' medical records.
- The pharmacist should document refills in accordance with state laws and regulations.
- Policies and procedures should exist for documenting the transportation of medication among separate sites in correctional facilities, including accountability from pickup to drop off.
- A consistent pattern of refusal by an inmate-patient to take medication should be documented in the patient's medical record.
- Policies and procedures should exist for the proper documentation of the receipt, placement in inventory, dispensing, administration, and destruction of controlled substances.

Emergency Services

- A pharmacist should educate medical and correctional personnel on the proper use of medications stocked for emergency use.
- A pharmacist should be available on an on-call basis in case of emergencies.
- Policies and procedures for the use of emergency kits of medications in life-threatening situations should exist. These kits should be maintained by a pharmacist.
- The pharmacy director should maintain policies and procedures for accessibility of medications in case of riots or other emergency situations.
- The pharmacy director, in conjunction with the medical director or other responsible health authority and the correctional institution's administrator, should develop policies and the procedures that complement the standards of the National Commission on Correctional Health Care regarding emergency services.

Therapeutic Policies

- The pharmacy director should be a member of the pharmacy and therapeutics committee or its equivalent.
- A formulary should exist in accordance with the ASHP Statement on the Formulary System, the ASHP Guidelines on Formulary System Management, the ASHP Technical Assistance Bulletin on Drug Formularies, and the ASHP Technical Assistance Bulletin on the Evaluation of Drugs for Formularies.[6–9]
- Drug products selected for formulary inclusion should serve the needs of the inmate-patient population and at the same time be as cost-effective as possible. The pharmacy director should ensure that cost is not the only determinant for drug product selection.
- Procedures should exist for the provision of nonformulary medications when necessary.
- The pharmacy director should, in conjunction with the facility's medical staff, maintain policies and procedures for the use of investigational medications that ensure adherence to the rights of inmate-patients.
- The pharmacy director should, in conjunction with the facility's psychiatrist or medical director, maintain policies and procedures for the use of psychotropic medications.
- The pharmacy director should be familiar with laws and regulations governing the treatment of patients with AIDS and make appropriate procedural allowances for the treatment of these patients.
- The pharmacist should have input into decisions about infection control policies and procedures pertinent to medication use.

Quality Improvement

- The pharmacy director should encourage the development of and participate in an ongoing quality improvement process that includes drug-use evaluation and drug-regimen review.

Drug Information

- A program should exist for regular education of health care and pertinent non-health-care personnel with respect to medication use.
- An up-to-date resource library that includes current publications and those required by law and regulation should be maintained by the pharmacy.
- The pharmacist should provide drug consultations as required to nurses, physician assistants, physicians, and any others involved in initiating, executing, and monitoring medication therapy.
- The pharmacist should educate and counsel inmate-patients on the proper use of medications.

Research

- Policies and procedures for the use of investigational drugs within the correctional facility should exist. (Additional guidance on pertinent policies and procedures can be found in the ASHP Guidelines for the Use of Investigational Drugs in Organized Health-Care Settings.[10])
- The pharmacy director should adhere to the Federal Regulations on Medical Research in Correctional Facilities (45 C.F.R. 46, revised March 6, 1983) when devising policies and procedures for use of investigational drugs.
- Information on issues that affect pharmacy practice within the correctional environment (e.g., criminology, medical-legal issues, endemic patient population) should be maintained.

References

1. American Society of Hospital Pharmacists. ASHP guidelines: minimum standard for pharmacies in institutions. *Am J Hosp Pharm.* 1985; 42:372–5.
2. American Society of Hospital Pharmacists. ASHP technical assistance bulletin on assessing cost-containment strategies for pharmacies in organized health-care settings. *Am J Hosp Pharm.* 1992; 49:155–60.
3. American Society of Hospital Pharmacists. ASHP technical assistance bulletin on use of controlled substances in organized health-care settings. *Am J Hosp Pharm.* 1993; 50:155–501.
4. American Society of Hospital Pharmacists. ASHP technical assistance bulletin on drug distribution and control. *Am J Hosp Pharm.* 1980; 37:1097–103.
5. American Society of Hospital Pharmacists. ASHP guidelines for selecting pharmaceutical manufacturers and suppliers. *Am J Hosp Pharm.* 1991; 48:523–4.
6. American Society of Hospital Pharmacists. ASHP guidelines on formulary system management. *Am J Hosp Pharm.* 1992; 49:648–52.
7. American Society of Hospital Pharmacists. ASHP technical assistance bulletin on drug formularies. *Am J Hosp Pharm.* 1991; 48:791–3.
8. American Society of Hospital Pharmacists. ASHP technical assistance bulletin on the evaluation of drugs for formularies. *Am J Hosp Pharm.* 1988; 45:386–7.
9. American Society of Hospital Pharmacists. ASHP statement on the formulary system. *Am J Hosp Pharm.* 1983; 1384–5.
10. American Society of Hospital Pharmacists. ASHP guidelines for the use of investigational drugs in organized health-care settings. *Am J Hosp Pharm.* 1991; 48:315–9.

These guidelines were reviewed in 2008 by the Council on Pharmacy Practice and by the Board of Directors and were found to still be appropriate.

Approved by the ASHP Board of Directors, April 26, 1995. Developed by the Council on Professional Affairs. Drafted for council review by Ronald L. Rideman.

The bibliographic citation for this document is as follows: American Society of Health-System Pharmacists. ASHP guidelines on pharmaceutical services in correctional facilities. *Am J Health-Syst Pharm.* 1995; 52:1810–3.

Research

Research

Research on Drug Use in Obese Patients (1515)
Source: Council on Therapeutics
To encourage drug product manufacturers to conduct pharmacokinetic and pharmacodynamic research in obese patients to facilitate safe and effective dosing of medications in this patient population, especially for medications most likely to be affected by obesity; further,

To encourage manufacturers to include in the Food and Drug Administration (FDA) – approved labeling detailed information on characteristics of individuals enrolled in drug dosing studies; further,

To advocate that the FDA develop guidance for the design and reporting of studies that support dosing recommendations in obese patients; further,

To advocate for increased enrollment and outcomes reporting of obese patients in clinical trials of medications; further,

To encourage independent research on the clinical significance of obesity on drug use, as well as the reporting and dissemination of this information via published literature, patient registries, and other mechanisms.

This policy supersedes ASHP policy 1013.

Institutional Review Boards and Investigational Use of Drugs (0711)
Source: Council on Pharmacy Practice
To support mandatory education and training on human subject protections and research bioethics for members of institutional review boards (IRBs), principal investigators, and all others involved in clinical research; further,

To advocate that principal investigators discuss their proposed clinical drug research with representatives of the pharmacy department before submitting a proposal to the IRB; further,

To advocate that IRBs include pharmacists as voting members; further,

To advocate that IRBs inform pharmacy of all approved clinical research involving drugs within the hospital or health system; further,

To advocate that pharmacists act as liaisons between IRBs and pharmacy and therapeutics committees in the management and conduct of clinical drug research studies; further,

To strongly support pharmacists' management of the control and distribution of drug products used in clinical research.

This policy was reviewed in 2011 by the Council on Therapeutics and by the Board of Directors and was found to still be appropriate.

Clinical Investigations of Drugs Used in Elderly and Pediatric Patients (0229)
Source: Council on Professional Affairs
To advocate increased enrollment of pediatric and geriatric patients in clinical trials of new medications; further,

To encourage pharmacodynamic and pharmacokinetic research in geriatric and pediatric patients to facilitate the safe and effective use of medications in these patient populations.

This policy was reviewed in 2011 by the Council on Therapeutics and by the Board of Directors and was found to still be appropriate.

ASHP Statement on Pharmaceutical Research in Organized Health-Care Settings

Pharmacy practice is grounded in the physicochemical, biological, and socioeconomic sciences. Hence, the continued and future success and self-esteem of the profession are dependent on the expanded knowledge base that can be produced through dynamic and rigorous scientific research and development. This research, to be meaningful and productive in terms of pharmacy's needs and goals in organized health-care settings, must include the participation of pharmacists practicing in those settings.

Pharmacists in organized health-care settings function in cooperation with other health-care professionals. They contribute a unique expertise to the drug-related aspects of patient care and take personal professional responsibility for the outcomes from the pharmaceutical care they provide to patients. Improvements in drug therapy depend on new knowledge generated by scientific research. Thus, pharmacists in organized health-care settings have a professional obligation to participate actively in and increase pharmacy-related and drug-related research efforts.[1,2]

Reflecting the collaborative nature of contemporary health care, this research should be multidisciplinary to be most beneficial. Thus, ASHP encourages pharmacists with a researchable idea or problem to seek the advice and active participation of people and organizations with scientific expertise such as

- College faculty (especially college of pharmacy faculty).
- Other staff and departments within the setting.
- Staff and departments in other health-care organizations.
- Industrial research personnel and laboratories.

It also is appropriate for pharmacists to function as principal investigators in research projects.

ASHP encourages pharmacists to increase their involvement in the following kinds of scientific research and development:

- Pharmaceutical research, including the development and testing of new drug dosage forms and drug preparation and administration methods and systems.
- Clinical research, such as the therapeutic characterization, evaluation, comparison, and outcomes of drug therapy and drug treatment regimens.
- Health services research and development, including behavioral and socioeconomic research such as research on cost–benefit issues in pharmaceutical care.
- Operations research, such as time and motion studies and evaluation of new and existing pharmacy programs and services.

This research will be a critical contribution of pharmacy to health care and must be fostered by all facets of the profession.

References

1. American Society of Hospital Pharmacists. ASHP guidelines for pharmaceutical research in organized healthcare settings. *Am J Hosp Pharm.* 1989; 46:129–30.
2. American Society of Hospital Pharmacists. ASHP guidelines for the use of investigational drugs in organized healthcare settings. *Am J Hosp Pharm.* 1991; 48:315–9.

Approved by the ASHP Board of Directors, November 14, 1990, and the ASHP House of Delegates, June 3, 1991. Revised by the ASHP Council on Professional Affairs. Supersedes a previous statement, "ASHP Statement on Institutional Pharmacy Research," approved by the ASHP House of Delegates on June 3, 1985, and the ASHP Board of Directors on November 14–15, 1984.

The bibliographic citation for this document is as follows: American Society of Hospital Pharmacists. ASHP statement on pharmaceutical research in organized health-care settings. *Am J Hosp Pharm.* 1991; 48:1781.

ASHP Guidelines on Clinical Drug Research

Purpose

The use of drug products to manage diseases and improve patients' quality of life is increasing as more effective and safer agents become available. Research to develop these agents is occurring in health system practice settings throughout the world. The credibility of this research and the protection of human subjects is a major responsibility of all health professionals involved.

ASHP believes pharmacists should play a pivotal role in the management of drugs used in the conduct of clinical research.[1–3] Pharmacists have become essential components of health system infrastructures supporting clinical research with both approved drugs and investigational drugs.[a,b] Pharmacists' roles in clinical research generally fall into one of two categories: (1) drug storage, preparation, and record keeping, frequently through an investigational drug service, and (2) serving as a principal investigator or a subinvestigator, manager, or coordinator within a research team that may include other health care professionals, research sponsors, monitors, contract research organizations, institutional review boards (IRBs), and institutional administrators.

The purposes of this document are to (1) outline the principles of clinical research, (2) describe the roles of participants in clinical research, (3) define pharmacists' roles in the use of drugs in clinical research, and (4) provide guidance to pharmacists and others responsible for the medication management component of clinical research. ASHP believes these guidelines are applicable to clinical research conducted in any health-system practice setting. These guidelines are an interpretation of federal laws, regulations, and standards for pharmacy practice in health systems. They should be used in conjunction with the applicable federal and state laws and regulations, not as a substitute for them. This document uses the term *shall* when the content is based on law or regulation and the term *should* for advice based on other guidelines, professional judgment, or expert opinion.

Background

The United States has benefited from a system for researching and marketing drug products that is codified in federal and state laws and regulations. The federal Food, Drug, and Cosmetic Act and its amendments[4] regulate drug product quality, safety, and effectiveness. The Food and Drug Administration (FDA) is the federal agency charged with enforcing the act and promulgating regulations for its implementation. FDA regulations concerning the conduct of clinical research with drug products of particular relevance for health-system pharmacists include Title 21 Code of Federal Regulations (CFR) Part 50, Protection of Human Subjects; Title 21 CFR Part 56, Institutional Review Boards; and Title 21 CFR Part 312, Investigational New Drug Application. Also applicable are the Department of Health and Human Services regulations in Title 45 CFR Part 46, Protection of Human Subjects. Requirements for and guidance on compliance with regulations are provided in FDA Information Sheets.

FDA has also published the Good Clinical Practice Consolidated Guideline[5] that was prepared under the auspices of the International Conference on Harmonisation of Technical Requirements for Registration of Pharmaceuticals for Human Use. The guideline offers a unified standard for designing, conducting, recording, and reporting trials that involve the participation of human subjects in the United States, Japan, and the European Union. In particular, the guideline provides a clearer understanding of behavioral and compliance standards for regulated drug research.

Basic Principles

The institutional components and practice settings of health systems participating in clinical drug research shall develop mechanisms, generally in the form of policies and procedures, for the approval, planning, and implementation of protocols. Good clinical practices, consistent with national and international standards, are the cornerstone of drug research in humans. Principles consistent with good clinical practices include the following:

1. An organization participating in human drug research studies shall ensure that such studies contain adequate safeguards for human subjects, its staff, and the scientific integrity of the study. There shall be written policies and procedures for the approval, management, and control of research involving investigational (not FDA-approved) drugs and post-marketing studies of FDA-approved drugs used in a research protocol. All research team members shall be fully informed about and comply with these policies and procedures.
2. The clinical trial shall have adequate prior information to justify use of human subjects, have a clearly defined protocol, and have received IRB approval before implementation.
3. All drug studies shall meet accepted ethical, legal, and scientific standards and be conducted by appropriately qualified investigators. Investigator qualifications, such as prior training and experience in research and with certain disease states, are required to be reviewed by IRBs, study sponsors, and FDA if the research will be submitted under an investigational new drug application (IND).
4. Every member of the research team shall be qualified by experience or training to perform his or her respective role.
5. All subjects must freely provide informed consent (documented in writing) before treatment with study drugs is begun. Accurate and complete information about the study's objectives, risks, and benefits must be provided before consent is obtained from the subject or his or her legally authorized representative. No unreasonable inducements (i.e., coercion or undue influence) shall be offered to subjects to encourage their participation in the study.
6. All clinical trial data shall be recorded and the records stored in such a way that the subject's rights of privacy and confidentiality are protected. All records shall be managed in a way that permits accurate reporting, verification, and retrieval after archiving.
7. Qualified pharmacists and other nonphysicians may serve as principal investigators as long as medical decisions made for the subjects are always the responsibility of a qualified physician or dentist.

Health-System Organization and Oversight

The health system should have processes for the administration of research that ensure that the aforementioned principles are upheld and the following responsibilities are met.

1. The health system shall be able to review and approve a protocol in the context of federal, state, and local laws and regulations. The health system should consider whether its own sponsored research or intellectual property development of drugs requires an IND for drugs not commercially available and approved drugs for unlabeled uses. An IND may be required if proposed research on the use of a marketed drug is intended to support the sponsor's change in drug labeling, advertising, or indications for use; a significant increase in risk; or a change in dosage level or route of administration. The health system should consult FDA for guidance.
2. The health system should have a mechanism for review and approval of the financial aspects of drug research, whether the study is sponsored by government agencies, foundations, or the pharmaceutical industry or is not sponsored.[6] Financial aspects may include contractual agreements stipulating cost recovery for resources, intellectual property agreements, insurance provisions, indemnification terms, and conflict-of-interest statements. Cost identification, allocation, and recovery mechanisms are imperative items for review and approval.
3. As required by federal regulation, clinical research shall be reviewed and approved by an IRB or equivalent committee (21 CFR 56.109). This committee shall evaluate each proposed clinical research study in terms of human subject protections and compliance with recognized ethical, legal, and scientific standards. No clinical study may be initiated unless approved in writing by the committee. Spoken IRB approval may be granted in emergency situations for a single subject's access to an investigational drug, but emergency use shall be reported to the IRB within five days; subsequent use requires full IRB review. Studies on the use of drugs in emergency or critical care settings do not in themselves qualify for single-subject approval and emergency exemption. Specific regulations govern research in the emergency setting and should be consulted in preparing protocols, IRB submissions, and consent procedures.[c,7]

    Treatment IND protocols are also subject to IRB review and approval. These protocols permit patient access to investigational drugs through a special program established by a sponsor. The physician and patient must agree that use of the agent may be in the patient's best interest and must document this agreement on a consent form.

    The IRB shall monitor approved studies to ensure that they are carried out appropriately and that the protocols are reassessed at least annually. Health system policies and procedures shall provide guidance on the conversion of human subjects to other therapies in the event that approval of an existing protocol is withdrawn by the IRB. The investigational-drug pharmacist, pharmacy director, or pharmacy director's designee should be a member of the IRB and should be consulted by the committee whenever drug studies are reviewed.
4. Investigational drugs shall be used only under the supervision of the principal investigator or authorized subinvestigators, all of whom shall be members of the professional staff. The determination of qualifications for investigators is the responsibility of the sponsor, IRB, and FDA when appropriate. Properly qualified pharmacists with experience and training in research may serve as principal investigators or subinvestigators.
5. The principal investigator or designee is responsible for obtaining informed consent from each subject who is eligible for participation in the study (i.e., meets inclusion and exclusion criteria).[c] The informed consent process shall conform to current federal and state regulations. IRB approval of the consent form (and assent form for minors) is required. Review by legal counsel may be desirable. The following points shall be included in the consent document and in an accompanying oral explanation by the investigator:
    - **a.** That the trial involves research.
    - **b.** The nature and purpose of the study and its expected benefits and foreseeable risks or discomforts. The name and telephone number of the principal investigator and persons to contact for questions about the study or drug.
    - **c.** A balanced description of the alternative treatments available, including their respective risks and benefits.
    - **d.** A general description of the study procedures, identification of any procedures that are experimental, expected length of therapy with the drug, and the subject's responsibilities. The name(s) of the investigational drug(s), including brand and generic names of commercial products.
    - **e.** A statement that (1) participation is voluntary, (2) the subject may withdraw from the study at any time, (3) refusal to participate in or withdrawal from the study will involve no penalty or loss of benefits to which the subject is otherwise entitled, and (4) the principal investigator may remove the subject from the study if circumstances warrant. The investigator shall supply any new information that may affect a subject's desire to continue in a study.
    - **f.** The name and signature of the subject (or his or her legally authorized representative), the name and signature of the principal investigator or subinvestigator, and the name and signature of the person presenting the consent form, with lines for each to personally date the signature.
    - **g.** A statement of who will have access to any study records that contain subject identifiers, including monitoring personnel from the study sponsor or FDA who may inspect the records to assess compliance with the study protocol and all regulations, or institutional personnel auditing the quality of clinical research or financial transactions.
    - **h.** Compensation or treatment available for a research-related injury.
    - **i.** Anticipated payments to subjects, pro rata terms, or expenses subjects may incur. Any costs for which the subject will be responsible.

    The consent form shall be as detailed as is practical, with the goal of minimizing the amount of information that must be presented orally yet enabling comprehension by most persons reading the form. For non-English-speaking subjects the consent form shall be in the subject's own language when feasible, or adequate interpretation shall be provided. For children able to read, an assent form shall be used to document their participation in the research process. The subject (or his or her representative) must have adequate time to read the consent form before signing it and shall receive a copy of the signed and dated form, along with any amendments to it. The subject shall retain a copy of the consent form. Additional copies of the consent form shall be kept on file as required by the sponsor, the IRB, the individual health system, and the medical records department.

Under certain protocols, patient drug or medical information may be collected from existing medical or pharmacy records. Pharmacists and investigators should consult the IRB to determine protocol-review and informed-consent requirements for any proposed studies.

6. The principal investigator is responsible for the proper maintenance of case report forms and all other study records required by the health system, the sponsor, and FDA.

7. The health system's medication-use system shall contain the following elements concerning drugs used in clinical research:

a. Drugs shall be properly packaged in accordance with all applicable federal and state laws, regulations, and standards (e.g., FDA, *The United States Pharmacopeia and The National Formulary* [*USP–NF*], and the Poison Prevention Packaging Act).

b. Drugs shall be labeled properly to ensure their safe use by the research and institutional staff and the subject.

c. There shall be a mechanism to ensure that sufficient supplies of the drugs will be always available for the duration of the study.

d. A mechanism shall be in place to allow the pharmacist or other designated health care provider, in a medical emergency during a randomized and blinded trial, to break the blinding code and reveal the identity of the study drug to other health care professionals. A reason to break the blind might be the need for a treatment decision that can be made only with knowledge of drug assignment.

e. Nurses, pharmacists, physicians, and other health care practitioners (e.g., respiratory therapists, physician assistants) called on to administer or dispense investigational drugs should have adequate written information about (1) pharmacology (particularly adverse effects), (2) storage requirements, (3) method of dose preparation and administration, (4) disposal of unused drug, (5) precautions to be taken, including handling recommendations, (6) authorized prescribers, (7) human subject safety monitoring guidelines, and (8) any other material pertinent to safe and proper use of investigational drugs. These health care providers should be informed about the overall study objectives and procedures and shall have available a complete copy of the protocol for reference. Under all circumstances, investigational drugs shall be safely controlled, administered, and destroyed.

f. Bulk supplies of the investigational drug shall be properly stored and adequately secured. When practical, all bulk supplies shall be stored in the pharmacy to ensure that storage, dispensing, accountability, and security are in compliance with federal and state laws and regulations and with standards used by the pharmacy department.

g. There shall be a method for ensuring that only an authorized practitioner or designee prescribes the investigational drug.

h. Records of the amount of investigational drug received from the sponsor and of its disposition (e.g., amounts dispensed to subjects or returned to sponsor) shall be maintained. These records shall be retained as required by regulation. Generally, records shall be maintained for at least two years after the date of an approved new-drug application (NDA) for the indication that is being investigated or, if the application is not approved or no application is filed, for at least two years after the investigation is discontinued and FDA is notified. Institutions should consider retaining records indefinitely. For studies involving international sites, records shall be maintained for 15 years after study closure. The sponsor may also request that records be stored longer than the minimum required time.

i. If the subject is to receive the investigational drug at another facility, suitable arrangements shall be made for transfer of the drug. Sufficient information for safe use of the investigational drug, including copies of the subject's signed consent form, the study protocol, and the IRB approval letter, shall accompany the drug. The responsibilities of the facility to which the drug is transferred are based on whether that facility is providing care incidental to or as a participant in the research protocol.[8]

j. The institution's records on investigational-drug studies should be designed so that various descriptive reports (e.g., names of all drugs under study, names of subjects who have received a given drug) can be generated conveniently and expeditiously. Once a study is closed, a copy of all pharmacy-related records should be provided to the principal investigator for storage. For its own records, the pharmacy should have a mechanism for long-term storage. The drug control responsibilities previously described shall be assigned to a pharmacist. If a pharmacist is not available, the investigator shall make arrangements to comply with these standards.

Pharmaceutical Services

A pharmacist should be responsible for ensuring that procedures for the control of drugs used in clinical research are developed and implemented. Each health system should develop a structure and procedures specific to its own needs and organization.

1. A copy of the IRB-approved research protocol and investigator's brochure or drug data sheet (see item 2 below), or both, and all amendments should be kept by a pharmacist.

2. Using the protocol and additional information (if needed) supplied by the principal investigator and sponsor, the pharmacist should prepare an investigational-drug data sheet that concisely summarizes for the medical, nursing, and pharmacy staffs information pertinent to use of the drug. This communication should contain, at a minimum

- **a.** Drug designation and common synonyms.
- **b.** Dosage forms and strengths.
- **c.** Usual dosage range, including dosage schedule and route of administration.
- **d.** Indications pursued in this study.
- **e.** Expected therapeutic effect to be studied.
- **f.** Expected and potential adverse effects, including symptoms of toxicity and their treatment.
- **g.** Drug–drug and drug–food interactions.
- **h.** Contraindications.
- **i.** Storage requirements.
- **j.** Instructions for dosage preparation and administration, including stability and handling guidelines.
- **k.** Instructions for disposition of unused doses.
- **l.** Names and telephone numbers of principal and authorized subinvestigators and study coordinators.

Confidential copies should be distributed to the appropriate pharmacy staff and all areas within the health system where the investigational drug will be administered and the subjects monitored. Through the pharmacy or health-system computer system, this information can be made available to all staff members who need it. It is staff members' responsibility to become familiar with the information in these data sheets and to not share the information with persons who do not need it.

3. When it is practical, investigational-drug supplies should be stored in a pharmacy. When the drug is stored outside a pharmacy (e.g., small quantities in the investigator's office or in clinics where the drug is administered), methods used by the investigator responsible for the drug shall be audited by a pharmacist to ensure that storage, dispensing, accountability, and security comply with federal and state laws and regulations and with institutional policy.

4. The pharmacist shall maintain a perpetual inventory record for investigational drugs stored in the pharmacy. This record shall contain the drug's name, dosage form and strength, lot number, and expiration date; the name, address, and telephone number of the sponsor; the protocol number; and any other information needed for ordering the drug. Space shall be provided for recording data on the disposition of the drug (amounts received, transferred, wasted, or dispensed, with dates; the names of or codes for persons receiving the drug; and the names of prescribers), the amount currently on hand, the minimum reorder level, and the recorder's initials. The inventory record shall reflect drug doses that were dispensed but not administered and were returned to the pharmacist. These records are commonly audited by the sponsor, the sponsor's representatives, or FDA.[9,10]

5. The dispensing of investigational drugs should be integrated with the rest of the medication-use system, including, but not limited to, order review, profile maintenance, packaging, labeling, delivery, and quality-assurance procedures. However, prescription labels for investigational drugs shall be marked "investigational drug" or otherwise distinguished from other labels. The label should also include an alert to any possible hazards. There shall be a method for verifying that a valid, signed consent has been obtained. The investigational drug shall be dispensed only on the order of an authorized investigator or designee.

6. Educating patients and monitoring therapy (including adverse drug reaction monitoring) are two clinical functions that are particularly important and applicable to investigational drugs. The protocol should specify the provision of these functions by the pharmacists, the authorized investigator(s), and other members of the research team.

7. At the conclusion of the study, the pharmacist shall return, transfer, or dispose of all unused investigational drugs according to the specific instructions provided by the sponsor and in accordance with applicable regulations.

8. The pharmacist should prepare an annual or semiannual descriptive summary of investigational-drug use for the pharmacy director and pharmacy and therapeutics committee. This summary should include the number of studies in progress, a list of all drugs studied during the previous period, and a financial statement.

9. Drug costs and other expenses associated with drug studies (e.g., costs of record keeping and drug administration) should be properly allocated and reimbursed. Policies and procedures should address the role pharmacists play in billing sponsors, subjects, and third-party payers for services and goods related to research. In general, sponsors and health systems cannot charge subjects for an investigational drug. Sponsors may petition FDA for an exception. Health systems may charge subjects for drug preparation and other services necessary to deliver a final product, as is customary for delivery of services within the practice setting and when sponsors do not reimburse for this service. The anticipated costs of research should be described in the consent form. Subjects must be advised that they or their third-party payers are responsible for these charges and that a third-party payer may refuse to pay for charges related to research.

10. The investigational drugs shall be stored under appropriate environmental control in a limited-access area separate from routine drug stocks and shall be inventoried on a regular basis.

11. Pharmacists may be confronted with circumstances related to a patient who is receiving an investigational drug provided by an investigator at a nonaffiliated practice setting and is admitted to their own practice setting for care incidental to the research protocol. Pharmacists should have a policy for managing investigational drugs under those circumstances that meets FDA guidelines.[8]

12. Pharmacists must ensure the scientific integrity of drug studies by managing access to treatment-assignment records in blinded studies and by ensuring that the correct drug was dispensed. The pharmacist, investigator, and sponsor must agree on a procedure for unblinding treatment assignment in emergencies.

13. Pharmacists who are assigned to manage investigational drugs may at times have to delegate certain dispensing activities to other pharmacists within the health system. To ensure continuity of quality dispensing services, the responsible pharmacist should design and implement procedures for educating other members of the pharmacy staff about the protocol and dispensing requirements. Often this can be accomplished by personal instruction and by preparing written directives and references for use by other pharmacists when they are called upon to dispense an investigational drug.

14. Pharmacists managing investigational drugs are in a unique position to monitor patient adherence to medication regimens. Because of the requirement that medication dispensed and returned be accounted for, pharmacists can readily surmise whether study patients are consuming the medication in the prescribed manner. At a minimum, pharmacists should counsel the investigator's research staff with regard to patient adherence. Pharmacists' skills in patient counseling should be used to support the investigators' efforts to encourage patients to adhere to their protocols.

Pharmaceutical Research Sponsors, Monitors, and Contract Research Organizations

The pharmaceutical company, or any study sponsor, that supports the use of investigational drugs in health systems should receive reliable and valid data. The following recommendations will serve as a guide to the pharmaceutical industry or other study sponsors to ensure that investigational drug use is managed appropriately and that studies are conducted effectively, efficiently, and safely.

1. Drugs shall be properly packaged in accordance with all applicable federal and state laws, regulations, and standards (e.g., FDA, *USP–NF*, and the Poison Prevention Packaging Act).

2. Drugs shall be properly labeled in accordance with applicable laws, regulations, and standards. If possible, ample space shall be left on the drug product container for further labeling by the pharmacist. Expiration dates and lot numbers should also be noted on the label.

3. A 24-hour telephone number should be available to study personnel, including the principal investigator and the pharmacy department. In the event of an emergency, information should be available pertaining to (1) adverse effects and their treatment, (2) emergency protocol management and dosing and administration guidelines, (3) the ability to break a "blinded code" to determine the treatment regimen, and (4) the mechanism for procuring a supply of medication under an emergency-use protocol.

4. Company representatives should be designated to handle routine requests, such as those for additional forms and resupply of investigational drugs. If possible, direct telephone or fax access should be available to expedite requests.

5. Investigational drugs should be shipped to the principal investigator in care of a pharmacist. The following information about procurement should also be supplied to the pharmacist:

- **a.** Name and telephone number of the sponsor's study monitor or field representative responsible for drug ordering.
- **b.** Estimated time for fulfillment of orders.
- **c.** Limits on quantities that can be ordered.
- **d.** Special ordering instructions.
- **e.** How the order is to be shipped (e.g., specific package-shipping firms).
- **f.** Disposition of invoice or drug receipt form once the drug is received.

6. The following information should be supplied by a sponsor or investigator to the pharmacist, preferably in an investigator's brochure, as applicable:

- **a.** Storage conditions required before and after preparation.
- **b.** Amounts and types of diluents for reconstitution and administration and the resulting final concentration of active drug.
- **c.** Stability of the prepared (i.e., ready-to-administer, reconstituted, or diluted) product and compatibility with drug delivery systems, diluents or i.v. fluids, containers, i.v. tubing, and filters.
- **d.** Known compatibility or incompatibility with other products.
- **e.** Light sensitivity.
- **f.** Filtration needs.
- **g.** Expiration dates or retest dates.
- **h.** Special instructions for preparation and administration.
- **i.** Acceptable and recommended routes and methods of administration, including rates of infusion for injectable products.
- **j.** Known adverse effects during or after administration (e.g., pain, phlebitis, and nausea) and how to avoid and treat them.
- **k.** Usual dosage regimens and highest dose tested for specific disease states, including dosage expressions for prescribing and labeling that could minimize misreading and misinterpretation.
- **l.** Contraindications.
- **m.** Drug interactions.
- **n.** Special precautions for storage, handling, and disposal of the drugs, including cytotoxic and hazardous drugs. For all hazardous drugs, the pharmacy department must be supplied with material safety data sheets.
- **o.** Pharmacology, including mechanism of action.
- **p.** Pharmacokinetic characteristics.

7. If all unused drugs are to be returned to the sponsor, information regarding storage and return procedures should be provided to the pharmacist. Drugs that are contaminated, outdated, or otherwise unsuitable should be returned to the sponsor or destroyed according to the institution's policies and procedures and applicable laws and regulations. These options should be agreed on beforehand by the sponsor and the pharmacist.

8. A complete current copy of the research protocol and investigator's brochure should be supplied to the pharmacist. Additional educational materials for use in informing pharmacists, physicians, and nurses about the investigational drug and research protocol should also be provided.

9. An appropriate allotment of research funds should be designated as reimbursement for

- **a.** Personnel.
- **b.** Storage facilities.
- **c.** Equipment.
- **d.** Ancillary products, such as diluents, syringes, and needles.
- **e.** Forms and miscellaneous clerical materials.

f. Computer and other data-processing costs.
g. Other expenses attributable to the pharmacist's involvement in the study.
h. Apportioned pharmacy overhead costs.

10. Sponsors should respond to requests for information from pharmacists involved in treating patients without formal research approval at that institution. This may occur, for example, when a patient is hospitalized (e.g., in an emergency) at a facility other than his or her usual care site.

11. When seeking marketing approval for an investigational drug, sponsors should consult pharmacists, physicians, and others involved in their investigational-drug studies for information. Because of their experience with the drug, these practitioners can supply valuable suggestions for labeling, packaging, palatability, routes of administration, and other dosage form characteristics, as well as information regarding patient monitoring and education.

12. The sponsor of an investigational drug study should provide final closure details within six months of trial completion. This includes prompt notification of closure, directions for drug disposition, and final audits of all study records.

13. These recommendations should also apply to the postmarketing approval of drugs under study for new indications or diseases.

References

1. Stolar MH, ed. Pharmacy-coordinated investigational drug services. Revised ed. Bethesda, MD: American Society of Hospital Pharmacists; 1986.
2. American Society of Health-System Pharmacists. ASHP guidelines: minimum standard for pharmacies in hospitals. *Am J Health-Syst Pharm.* 1995; 52:2711–7.
3. American Society of Hospital Pharmacists. ASHP statement on the use of medications for unlabeled uses. *Am J Hosp Pharm.* 1992; 49:2006–8.
4. Federal Food, Drug, and Cosmetic Act (21 U.S.C. 301 et seq.) 1938, as amended.
5. Food and Drug Administration, Department of Health and Human Services. International conference on harmonisation; good clinical practice consolidated guideline. *Fed Regist.* 1997; 62:25692–709.
6. Wermeling DP, Piecoro LT, Foster TS. Financial impact of clinical research on a health system. *Am J Health-Syst Pharm.* 1997; 54:1742–51.
7. Bailey EM, Habowski SR. How to apply for emergency use of an investigational agent. *Am J Health-Syst Pharm.* 1996; 53:208–10.
8. Food and Drug Administration. Use of investigational products when subjects enter a second institution. IRB operations and clinical investigation information sheet. http://www.fda.gov/oc/oha/useofinv.html (accessed August 25, 1997).
9. Food and Drug Administration. Institutional review board inspections. IRB operations and clinical investigation information sheet. http://ww.fda.gov/oc/oha/institut.html (accessed August 25, 1997).
10. Food and Drug Administration. Inspections of clinical investigators. IRB operations and clinical investigation information sheet. http://ww.fda.gov/oc/oha/inspect.html (accessed August 25, 1997).

Suggested Internet Source

Food and Drug Administration information for clinical investigators. http://www.fda.gov/cder/about/smallbiz/clinical_investigator.htm.

Glossary[d]

Adverse Drug Reaction (ADR): In preapproval clinical experience with a new medicinal product or its new usages, particularly since the therapeutic dose(s) may not be established, all noxious and unintended responses to a medicinal product related to any dose should be considered adverse drug reactions. "Responses to a medicinal product" means that a causal relationship between a medicinal product and an adverse event is at least a reasonable possibility (i.e., that the relationship cannot be ruled out).

An ADR to a marketed medicinal product is a response to a drug that is noxious and unintended and that occurs at doses normally used in humans for prophylaxis, diagnosis, or therapy of diseases or for modification of physiological function.

Adverse Event (AE): An AE is any untoward medical event that occurs in a patient or clinical investigation subject administered a pharmaceutical product and that does not necessarily have a causal relationship to this treatment. An AE can therefore be any unfavorable and unintended sign (including an abnormal laboratory finding), symptom, or disease temporally associated with the use of a medicinal (investigational) product, whether or not related to the medicinal (investigational) product.

Audit: A systematic and independent examination of trial-related activities and documents to determine whether the evaluated trial-related activities were conducted and the data were recorded, analyzed, and accurately reported according to the protocol, sponsor's standard operating procedures, good clinical practice, and the applicable regulatory requirements.

Audit Report: A written evaluation by the sponsor's auditor of the results of the audit.

Case Report Form: A printed, optical, or electronic document designed to record all of the protocol-required information to be reported to the sponsor on each trial subject.

Clinical Trial or Study: Any investigation in human subjects that is intended to discover or verify the clinical, pharmacologic, or other pharmacodynamic effects of an investigational product, to identify any adverse reactions to an investigational product, or to study absorption, distribution, metabolism, and excretion of an investigational product with the object of ascertaining its safety, efficacy, or both. (The terms clinical trial and clinical study are synonymous.)

Clinical Trial/Study Report: A written description of a trial or study of any therapeutic, prophylactic, or diagnostic agent conducted in humans, in which the clinical and statistical description, presentations, and analyses are fully integrated into a single report.

Contract Research Organization: A person or organization (commercial, academic, or other) contracted by the sponsor to perform one or more of a sponsor's trial-related duties and functions.

Direct Access: Permission to examine, analyze, verify, and reproduce any records and reports that are important in the evaluation of a clinical trial. Any party (e.g., domestic and foreign regulatory authorities, sponsors, monitors, and auditors) with direct access should take all reasonable precautions within the constraints of the applicable regulatory requirements to maintain the confidentiality of subjects' identities and sponsors' proprietary information.

Documentation: All records, in any form (including but not limited to written, electronic, magnetic, and optical records and scans, roentgenograms, and electrocardiograms) that describe or record the methods, conduct, or results of a trial, the factors affecting a trial, and the actions taken.

Essential Documents: Documents that individually and collectively permit evaluation of the conduct of a study and the quality of the data produced.

Good Clinical Practice: A standard for the design, conduct, performance, monitoring, auditing, recording, analysis, and reporting of clinical trials that provides assurance that the data and reported results are credible and accurate and that the rights, integrity, and confidentiality of trial subjects are protected.

Independent Ethics Committee: An independent body (institutional, regional, national, or supranational review board or committee), constituted of medical or scientific professionals and nonmedical or nonscientific members, whose responsibility it is to ensure the protection of the rights, safety, and well-being of human subjects involved in a trial and to provide public assurance of that protection by, among other things, reviewing and approving or providing favorable opinion on the trial protocol and the suitability of the investigators, the facilities, and the methods and material to be used in obtaining and documenting informed consent of the trial subjects.

Informed Consent: A process by which a subject voluntarily confirms his or her willingness to participate in a particular trial, after having been informed of all aspects of the trial that are relevant to the decision to participate. Informed consent is documented by means of a written, signed, and dated form.

Investigator's Brochure: A compilation of clinical and nonclinical data on an investigational product that are relevant to the study of the product in human subjects.

Monitoring: Overseeing the progress of a clinical trial and ensuring that it is conducted, recorded, and reported in accordance with the protocol, standard operating procedures, good clinical practice, and the applicable regulatory requirements.

Monitoring Report: A written report from the monitor to the sponsor after each site visit or other trial-related communication, according to the sponsor's standard operating procedures.

Protocol: A document that describes the objectives, design, methods, statistical considerations, and organization of a trial. The protocol usually also gives the background and rationale for the trial, but these could be provided in other protocol-referenced documents. (Throughout the ICH GCP Guideline, the term protocol refers to protocol and protocol amendments.)

Serious Adverse Event or Serious Adverse Drug Reaction: Any untoward medical event that occurs in a patient or subject receiving a drug at any dose and results in death, is life-threatening, requires inpatient hospitalization or prolongation of existing hospitalization, results in persistent or significant disability or incapacity, or is a congenital anomaly or birth defect.

Source Data: All information in original records and certified copies of original records of clinical findings, observations, or other activities in a clinical trial that is necessary for the reconstruction and evaluation of the trial. Source data are contained in source documents (original records or certified copies).

Source Documents: Original documents, data, and records (e.g., hospital records, clinical and office charts, laboratory notes, memoranda, subjects' diaries or evaluation checklists, pharmacy dispensing records, recorded data from automated instruments, copies or transcriptions certified after verification as being accurate and complete, microfiches, photographic negatives, microfilm or magnetic media, roentgenograms, and subject files and records kept at the pharmacy, the laboratories, and the medicotechnical departments involved in the clinical trial).

Sponsor: An individual, a company, an institution, or an organization that takes responsibility for the initiation, management, or financing of a clinical trial.

Sponsor–Investigator: An individual who both initiates and conducts, alone or with others, a clinical trial, and under whose immediate direction the investigational product is administered to, dispensed to, or used by a subject. The term does not include any person other than an individual (e.g., it does not include a corporation or an agency). The obligations of a sponsor-investigator include both those of a sponsor and those of an investigator.

---

[a]In this document investigational drugs are defined as those that are being considered for but have not yet received marketing approval by FDA for human use and those that have FDA approval for at least one indication but are being studied for new indications, new routes of administration, or new dosage forms.

[b]The principles and procedures described here are applicable to all clinical drug studies, not just those involving investigational drugs.

[c]In certain emergency situations, prior consent may be waived (21 CFR 50.24).

[d]Definitions selected from reference 5.

These guidelines were reviewed in 2003 by the Council on Professional Affairs and by the Board of Directors and were found to still be appropriate.

Approved by the ASHP Board of Directors, November 15, 1997. Developed by the ASHP Council on Professional Affairs. Supersedes the ASHP Guidelines for the Use of Investigational Drugs in Organized Health-Care Settings, dated November 14, 1990.

The bibliographic citation for this document is as follows: American Society of Health-System Pharmacists. ASHP guidelines on clinical drug research. *Am J Health-Syst Pharm.* 1998; 55:369–76.

ASHP Guidelines for Pharmaceutical Research in Organized Health-Care Settings

The promotion of research in the health and pharmaceutical sciences and in pharmaceutical services is a purpose of the American Society of Hospital Pharmacists, as stated in its Charter.[1] In keeping with this purpose, pharmacists in organized health-care settings should understand the (1) basic need for research and systematic problem solving in pharmacy practice; (2) fundamental scientific approach; (3) basic components of a research plan; (4) process of documenting and reporting findings; and (5) responsibilities of investigators with respect to patients, employers, grantors, and science in general.

In its purest form, scientific research is the systematic, controlled, empirical, and critical investigation of hypothetical propositions (theories) about presumed relationships among natural phenomena.[2] Aspects of the research process (e.g., problem definition, systematic data gathering, interpretation, and reporting), however, are also applicable to resolving specific practice problems. Independent, intraprofessional, and interdisciplinary collaborative research and problem solving are encouraged.

Need

Since pharmacy is based on the theories of the pharmaceutical, medical, and social sciences, pharmacy's advancement is linked to advancement in those sciences. Scientific inquiry, through formal research and systematic problem solving, leads to an expansion of knowledge and thus to advancement. Both research and systematic problem solving in organized health-care settings are needed for developing knowledge in pharmaceutics and drug therapy and for evaluation, modification, and justification of specific practices. Therefore, an understanding of the research process is important to pharmacists in such settings.

Primary areas for research by pharmacists in organized health-care settings are those in which pharmacists possess special expertise or unique knowledge. These areas include drug therapy, pharmaceutics, bioavailability, pharmacy practice administration, sociobehavioral aspects of pharmaceutical service systems, and application of information handling and computer technology to pharmacy practice.

The Scientific Approach

Aspects of the scientific approach may be applied to formal research and systematic problem solving. The scientific approach consists of four basic steps:

1. ***Problem—Obstacle—Idea.***[3] The scientist experiences an obstacle to understanding or curiosity as to why something is as it is. The scientist's first step is to express the idea in some reasonably manageable form, even if it is ill defined and tentative.
2. ***Hypothesis.*** The scientist looks back on experience for possible solutions—personal experience, the literature, and contacts with other scientists. A tentative proposition (hypothesis) is formulated about the relationship between two or more variables in the problem; for example, "If such and such occurs, then so and so results."
3. ***Reasoning—Deduction.*** The scientist deduces the consequences of the formulated hypothesis. The scientist may find that the deductions reveal a new problem that is quite different from the original one. On the other hand, deductions may lead to the conclusion that the problem cannot be solved with existing technical tools. Such reasoning can help lead to wider, more basic, and more significant problems as well as to more narrow (testable) implications of the original hypothesis.
4. ***Observation—Test—Experiment.*** If the problem has been well stated, the hypotheses have been adequately formulated, and the implications of the hypotheses have been carefully deduced, the next step is to test the relationships expressed by the hypotheses, that is, the relationships among the variables. All testing is for one purpose: putting the relationships among the variables to an empirical test. It is not the hypotheses that are tested but the deduced implications of the hypotheses. On the basis of the research evidence, each hypothesis is either accepted or rejected.

Components of a Research Plan

Formal research frequently requires the development of a written plan (protocol or proposal). In funded research, the plan may take the form of a grant application. A typical plan might include

1. A problem statement.
2. A review of available literature on the subject.
3. The objectives for the project, including the hypotheses and the to-be-tested relationships among variables.
4. A description of the methodology to be used.
5. A description of statistical analyses to be applied to the data collected.
6. A budget and time frame for the project (where applicable).
7. The expected applicability of the research findings.

Documentation and Reporting

The structure of a research report is similar to the structure of a research plan. A typical outline is as follows:

1. Problem.
   - a. Theories, hypotheses, and definitions.
   - b. Previous research: the literature.
2. Methodology.
   - a. Sample and sampling method.
   - b. Experimental procedures and instrumentation.
   - c. Measurement of variables.
   - d. Statistical methods of analysis.
   - e. Pretesting and pilot studies.
3. Results, interpretation, and conclusions.

The statement of the problem sets the general stage for the reader and may be in question form. A common practice is to state the broader, general problem and then to state the hypotheses, both general and specific. All important variables should be defined, both in general and in operational terms, giving a justification for the definitions used, if needed.

The general and research literature related to the problem is discussed to explain the theoretical rationale of the problem, to tell the reader what research has and has not been carried out on the problem, and to show that this particular investigation has not been conducted before (except in the case of validating research).

The methodology section should meticulously describe what was done so as to enable another investigator to reproduce the research, reanalyze the data, and arrive at unambiguous conclusions about the adequacy of the methods. This section should tell what samples were used, how they were selected, and why they were selected. The means of measurement of the variables should be described. The data analysis methods should be outlined and justified. Where pilot studies and pretesting were used, they should be described.

Results and data should be condensed and expressed in concise form. Limitations and weaknesses of the study should be discussed. The question of whether the data support the hypotheses must be foremost in the mind of the report writer. Everything written should relate the results and data to the problem and the hypotheses.

Investigators' Responsibilities

Investigators bear a general responsibility to be scientifically objective in their research inquiries, conclusions, and reports. They bear a responsibility for being methodical and meticulous in the gathering of research data. They also bear both a fiduciary and a reporting responsibility to employers and grantors. In general, employee investigators are at least partially responsible to their employer organizations in the choice of research topics. Research funded from sources outside an investigator's organization may impose additional contractual obligations on the investigator and the organization.

In research involving patients, investigators are responsible for protecting patients from harm while the patients are participating in the research. All research involving patients should be reviewed and approved, before initiation, by an institutional review board. Written, informed consent should be obtained from every patient participating in each research project.[4] Meticulous recordkeeping is required regarding the clinical experience of patients participating in research projects.

Employee investigators bear responsibility for helping their organizations differentiate true, objective research from product marketing trials and promotions that may purport to be research projects. Grants for bona fide research typically bear a direct cost-recovery relationship to projects and typically involve the direct transfer of grant funds from grantors to the employee investigator's employer organization. Specific institutional policies vary widely, but employee investigators can generally better fulfill their fiduciary responsibilities when funds are not distributed directly from grantors to investigators. In keeping with their fiduciary responsibilities and their responsibility to be scientifically objective, investigators should be wary of arrangements in which prospective grantors offer inducements of value (gifts, trips, experiences, publicity, publications, etc.) to investigators, institutions, or patients before, during, or after the completion of proposed projects.

Investigators should make legitimate efforts to document publicly the findings of research in scientific, objectively refereed publications.

References

1. American Society of Hospital Pharmacists. Governing documents of the American Society of Hospital Pharmacists. Bethesda, MD: American Society of Hospital Pharmacists; 1984.
2. Kerlinger F. Foundations of behavioral research. New York: Holt, Rinehart and Winston; 1964:13.
3. Dewey J. How we think. Boston: Heath; 1933:106–18, as adapted to the scientific framework by Kerlinger, op cit., p 13–5.
4. American Society of Hospital Pharmacists. ASHP guidelines for the use of investigational drugs in institutions. *Am J Hosp Pharm.* 1983; 40:449–51.

Approved by the ASHP Board of Directors, September 30, 1988. Developed by the Council on Professional Affairs. Supersedes the "ASHP Guidelines for Scientific Research in Institutional Pharmacy" approved on November 15, 1977.

The bibliographic citation for this document is as follows: American Society of Hospital Pharmacists. ASHP guidelines for pharmaceutical research in organized health-care settings. *Am J Hosp Pharm.* 1989; 46:129–30.

ASHP
Therapeutic Position Statements

ASHP Therapeutic Position Statement on the Cessation of Tobacco Use

Position

The American Society of Health-System Pharmacists (ASHP) discourages all use of tobacco products and supports evidence-based tobacco-control policies and activities that reduce the prevalence of tobacco use. ASHP strongly encourages health care providers to take an active role in promoting the health of their patients by systematically integrating into routine patient care (a) the identification of tobacco users and (b) the delivery of evidence-based tobacco-cessation interventions. ASHP recommends behavioral and pharmacologic therapies for cessation, advocates their use for all patients attempting to quit smoking (except when medically contraindicated or in specific populations for which there is insufficient evidence of effectiveness), and advises that these therapeutic interventions be reimbursed under health insurance plans.

To enable more effective and consistent identification of tobacco use and drug interactions with smoking, ASHP urges that all patient records, including those in electronic medical records and pharmacy information technology systems, include a designated field for the collection of tobacco-use data and that this field be integrated within the system such that clinically significant drug interactions with tobacco products are identified. Schools that offer health professional degree programs are encouraged to integrate comprehensive tobacco-cessation training as part of their core curricula, and licensed clinicians are advised to participate in continuing-education programs as necessary to acquire and maintain tobacco-cessation counseling skills. Given the established dangers of secondhand smoke exposure, ASHP supports legislation promoting smoke-free environments for the employees and patrons of all workplaces and public venues. Furthermore, because the sale of tobacco products contradicts the clinician's role in promoting health, ASHP strongly opposes the sale or distribution of tobacco products in all establishments where health care services are rendered.

Epidemiology of Tobacco Use

As the former U.S. Surgeon General C. Everett Koop stated in 1982, "Cigarette smoking is the chief single, avoidable cause of death in our society and the most important public health issue of our time."[1] This statement remains true today, nearly three decades later. The Centers for Disease Control and Prevention (CDC) estimates that nearly 438,000 Americans die each year from smoking,[2] and approximately 50,000 persons die annually due to involuntary exposure to tobacco smoke.[3] Cigarettes are the only marketed consumable product that, when used as intended, will contribute to the death of half or more of its users.[4]

While cigarettes are, by far, the most frequently used form of tobacco in the United States, other forms of smoked tobacco (e.g., cigars, clove cigarettes [kreteks], pipe tobacco, bidis, hookah) and smokeless tobacco (e.g., chewing tobacco, snuff) can also lead to dependence and should be addressed by clinicians. Despite the proven negative health consequences of tobacco use and the fact that approximately 70% of smokers want to quit,[5] 20.8% of the U.S. adult population continues to smoke either every day (16.7%) or some days (4.1%).[6] In 2006, more men (23.9%) than women (18.0%) were smokers.[6] The prevalence of smoking also varied by race or ethnicity (non-Hispanic American Indian/Alaska Native, 32.4%; non-Hispanic white, 21.9%; non-Hispanic black, 23.0%; Hispanic, 15.2%; non-Hispanic Asian, 10.4%), education level (higher education is associated with a lower prevalence), and poverty level (20.4% of individuals living at or above the federal poverty level; 30.6% of individuals living below the poverty level).[6] An estimated 44.3% of cigarettes smoked in the United States are by persons with mental illness.[7]

Smoking prevalence varies across the nation. In 2006, the highest median prevalence of smoking was evident in Kentucky (28.6%) and the lowest was in Utah (9.8%).[8] Because most teens who smoke at least monthly continue to smoke in adulthood,[9] tobacco-use trends among youth are viewed as a key indicator of future national health trends.[10] In 2007, an estimated 21.6% of 12th graders (23.1% of males and 19.6% of females) had smoked one or more cigarettes in the past 30 days.[11] The prevalence of smoking has declined among adolescents over the past decade; however, the downward trend has largely diminished among 12th graders in recent years.

In the past decade, the prevalence of cigarette smoking has decreased while the per-capita consumption of cigars has increased.[12] However, beginning in 2005, there has been a slight trend toward decreased cigar use. In 2007, the prevalence of cigar smoking (one or more cigars in the past month) among persons 12 years or older was 5.4%.[13] Cigar weight and nicotine content vary widely, with most cigars ranging in weight from 1 to 22 g. In comparison, a typical U.S. cigarette weighs <1 g. The nicotine content in 10 commercially available cigars studied in 1996 ranged from 10 to 444 mg.[14] Cigarette brands sold by major manufacturers in the United States have a lower and less-variable total nicotine content, ranging from 11.9 to 14.5 mg of nicotine per cigarette.[15] As such, it is possible for one large cigar to contain as much tobacco as an entire pack of cigarettes and to deliver enough nicotine to establish and maintain dependence.[14]

In 2007, an estimated 8.1 million Americans 12 years of age or older (3.2%) had used smokeless tobacco in the past month; men (6.3%) were more likely than were women (0.4%) to be users.[13] The prevalence of smokeless tobacco use is highest among individuals ages 18–25 years and is substantially higher among American Indians, Alaskan Natives, and residents of the southern United States and rural areas.[13,16] While sales of most forms of smokeless tobacco (e.g., looseleaf, plug, twist) have declined since the mid-1980s, moist snuff sales have increased steadily since the late 1980s.[12]

An enormous economic burden accompanies tobacco use. Each pack of cigarettes smoked costs society $7.18 ($3.45 for associated medical care and $3.73 for productivity losses), for a total of $157 billion in annual health-related economic losses.[17] The lifelong smoker (e.g., one pack per day for 50 years) spends more than $100,000 on his or her smoking habit in addition to the associated medical care costs of tobacco use.

Extensive evidence implicates tobacco as the primary known preventable cause of death in the United States. As such, ASHP strongly supports evidence-based tobacco-control initiatives that aim to reduce the prevalence of tobacco use by (a) preventing the initiation of tobacco use and (b) promoting and maintaining cessation. Tobacco-control initiatives (e.g., those described in each state's comprehensive cancer control plan) should comply with recommendations set forth by CDC as delineated in the "Best Practices for Comprehensive Tobacco Control Programs"[18] and the "Guide to Community Preventive Services: Tobacco Use Prevention and Control."[19]

Nicotine Pharmacology

Tobacco products are carefully engineered formulations that optimize the delivery of nicotine, a chemical that meets established criteria for an addictive substance.[20] Once absorbed, nicotine induces a variety of central nervous system, cardiovascular, and metabolic effects. Within seconds after inhalation, nicotine reaches the brain and stimulates the release of various neurotransmitters including dopamine, which induces nearly immediate feelings of pleasure and relieves nicotine-withdrawal symptoms. This rapid dose response reinforces the need to repeat the administration of nicotine, thereby perpetuating smoking behavior.[21] The short half-life ($t_{½}$ = 2 hours) of nicotine generally necessitates frequent dosing throughout the day, and tobacco users become adept at titrating nicotine intake to maintain pleasure and arousal, modulate mood, and avoid withdrawal symptoms.[21]

When nicotine is discontinued, the following withdrawal symptoms may develop: irritability, impatience, anxiety, difficulty concentrating, restlessness, hunger, depression, insomnia, and cravings.[22-24] Most physical withdrawal symptoms generally manifest within 24–48 hours after quitting and gradually dissipate over two to four weeks[23]; however, strong cravings for tobacco can persist for months or even years.[25] The nicotine levels generated by smokeless tobacco are similar to those of smoking, although their onset of action is less rapid. Upon quitting, smokeless tobacco users experience withdrawal symptoms similar to those of smokers.[26] Although nicotine is the dependence-causing component of tobacco, it is not directly responsible for the myriad of negative health consequences of tobacco use.

Health Consequences of Tobacco Use and Exposure to Secondhand Smoke

Smoking. According to the 2004 Surgeon General's report on the health consequences of smoking,[27] smoking harms nearly every organ of the body, is causally associated with numerous diseases (Table 1), and reduces the health of smokers in general. In addition to contributing to the development of disease, smoking also can lead to exacerbation or reduced control of existing conditions such as hypertension, diabetes mellitus, and asthma. On average, men and women lose 13.2 and 14.5 years of life because of smoking, respectively.[17] Between 1997 and 2001, an estimated 437,902 annual U.S. deaths were attributable to smoking. Of these deaths, 158,529 (36.2%) were due to cancer, 137,979 (31.5%) to cardiovascular disease, and 101,454 (23.2%) to respiratory disease.[2]

Table 1.
Diseases and Other Adverse Health Effects Caused by Smoking[27]

Cancers
Acute myeloid leukemia
Bladder
Cervical
Esophageal
Gastric
Kidney
Laryngeal
Lung
Oral cavity and pharyngeal
Pancreatic
Cardiovascular diseases
Abdominal aortic aneurysm
Coronary heart disease (angina pectoris, ischemic heart disease, myocardial infarction)
Cerebrovascular disease (transient ischemic attacks, stroke)
Peripheral arterial disease
Pulmonary diseases
Acute respiratory illnesses
Upper respiratory tract (rhinitis, sinusitis, laryngitis, pharyngitis)
Lower respiratory tract (bronchitis, pneumonia)
Chronic respiratory illnesses
Chronic obstructive pulmonary disease
Respiratory symptoms: cough, phlegm, wheezing, dyspnea
Poor asthma control
Reduced lung function in infants exposed in utero to maternal smoking
Reproductive effects
Reduced fertility in women
Pregnancy and pregnancy outcomes
Preterm or premature rupture of membranes
Placenta previa
Placental abruption
Preterm delivery
Low infant birth weight
Infant mortality (sudden infant death syndrome)
Other effects
Cataract
Osteoporosis (reduced bone density in postmenopausal women, increased risk of hip fracture)
Periodontitis
Peptic ulcer disease (in patients who are infected with *Helicobacter pylori*)
Adverse surgical outcomes
Poor wound healing
Respiratory complications

Smokeless Tobacco. Users of smokeless forms of tobacco are often under the mistaken impression that these formulations are a "safe" alternative to smoking cigarettes. In addition to cosmetic effects such as halitosis and staining of the teeth, smokeless tobacco use is associated with serious health effects, including cancer, soft tissue alterations (e.g., leukoplakia), and periodontal effects.[16] Smokeless tobacco contains high concentrations of carcinogens, which have direct contact with mucosal tissues over prolonged periods of time. The most serious consequence of smokeless tobacco use is an increased risk of developing oral and pharyngeal cancers, and the risk appears to be dose related, in that heavy, longtime users are more likely to develop oral cancer than are nonusers. The health effects of smokeless tobacco with regard to cardiovascular disease are not well understood, and published data are conflicting.[28-30] Although smokeless tobacco products do not confer many of the risks associated with the inhalation of combusted tobacco (e.g., pulmonary disease, lung cancer), these products do impose harm and should not be recommended as aids for smoking cessation, because safer, effective products (i.e., medications with FDA-approved labeling for use in smoking cessation) are available.[31]

Secondhand Smoke Exposure. Exposure to secondhand smoke results in an estimated 50,000 deaths annually, in addition to contributing to numerous diseases among nonsmoking children and adults.[3] Major conclusions of the Surgeon General's report "The Health Effects of Involuntary Exposure to Tobacco Smoke" included the following:

1. Many millions of Americans, both children and adults, are still exposed to secondhand smoke in their homes and workplaces despite substantial progress in tobacco control,
2. Secondhand smoke exposure causes disease and premature death in children and adults who do not smoke,
3. Children exposed to secondhand smoke are at an increased risk for sudden infant death syndrome (SIDS), acute respiratory infections, ear problems, and more severe asthma; smoking by parents causes respiratory symptoms and slows lung growth in their children,
4. Exposure of adults to secondhand smoke has immediate adverse effects on the cardiovascular system and causes coronary heart disease and lung cancer,
5. The scientific evidence indicates that there is no risk-free level of exposure to secondhand smoke, and
6. Eliminating smoking in indoor spaces fully protects nonsmokers from exposure to secondhand smoke; separating smokers from nonsmokers, cleaning the air, and ventilating buildings cannot eliminate exposures of nonsmokers to secondhand smoke.

Supplementing the evidence presented in the Surgeon General's report,[3] the California Environmental Protection Agency in January 2006 designated secondhand smoke as a "toxic air contaminant" and, in addition to noting the tobacco-related diseases described in the Surgeon General's report, specified that exposure to smoke is associated with breast cancer in younger, primarily premenopausal women.[32]

Drug Interactions with Tobacco Smoke. Various substances in tobacco interact with several commonly prescribed drugs.[33,34] It is widely recognized that polycyclic aromatic hydrocarbons (PAHs), the products of the incomplete combustion of tobacco, are largely responsible for the majority of drug interactions with smoking. PAHs are found in appreciably large quantities in tobacco smoke and are potent inducers of hepatic microsomal (cytochrome P-450) enzymes CYP1A1, CYP1A2, and possibly CYP2E1. Although other substances in tobacco smoke such as acetone, pyridines, benzene, nicotine, carbon monoxide, and heavy metals (e.g., cadmium) might also interact with hepatic enzymes, their effects appear to be less significant.[34] To enable more effective screening for tobacco use and drug interactions with smoking, all patient records, including those stored and accessed via medical records and pharmacy information technology systems, should include a designated field for collection of tobacco-use data. This field should be integrated into the system so that relevant drug interactions with tobacco smoke can be identified.

Health Benefits of Smoking Cessation

Quitting smoking produces immediate as well as long-term benefits, reducing the risk of developing diseases caused by smoking and improving health in general.[35] Some benefits are incurred almost immediately—within the first 24 hours—after quitting. Within two weeks to three months after quitting, circulation improves, walking becomes easier, and lung function increases up to 30%. Within 1 year, the excess risk of coronary heart disease is decreased to half that of a smoker, and after 5–15 years, stroke risk is reduced to a rate similar to that of people who have never smoked. Ten years after quitting, an individual's chance of dying of lung cancer is approximately half that of continuing smokers. In addition, the risk for mouth, throat, esophagus, bladder, kidney, or pancreatic cancer is decreased. Fifteen years after quitting, an individual's risk of coronary heart disease is reduced to a rate similar to that of people who have never smoked. Quitting at ages 30, 40, 50, and 60 has been shown to be associated with 10, 9, 6, and 3 years of life gained, respectively.[4] Thus, the benefits of quitting the use of tobacco are significant. It is never too late to quit to incur health benefits, but there are clear advantages to quitting earlier.

Strategies for Promoting Tobacco Cessation

Because of the immense societal burden that smoking imposes, tobacco use and dependence should be addressed during each clinical encounter. Routine screening for tobacco-use status enables clinicians to prevent the initiation of tobacco use among nonusers, facilitate cessation among current users, and promote continued abstinence among former users.

For most smokers, the quitting process is characterized by a series of quit attempts and subsequent relapses. On average, former smokers report 10.8 quit attempts over a period of 18.6 years before achieving long-term cessation.[36] Most quit attempts are undertaken without assistance, and approximately 95% of attempts end in relapse.[37]

Given the decades of strong, consistent findings in support of the efficacy and cost-effectiveness of both behavioral and pharmacologic interventions to facilitate tobacco cessation, ASHP recommends the use of evidenced-based behavioral and pharmacologic strategies for all patients attempting to quit smoking (except when medically contraindicated or in specific populations for which there is insufficient evidence of effectiveness [e.g., pregnant women, smokeless tobacco users, light smokers, adolescents]). Treatment for tobacco dependence is highly cost-effective relative to other medical interventions (e.g., periodic mammography screening, treatment for hypertension and hyperlipidemia) and should be made available to all tobacco users.[37] In accordance with recommendations set forth in the 2008 clinical practice guideline, Treating Tobacco Use and Dependence,[37] ASHP recommends that (1) all insurance plans include counseling and evidence-based pharmacotherapy treatments as a reimbursable benefit and (2) clinicians be reimbursed for providing treatment for tobacco dependence, just as they are reimbursed for treatment of other chronic conditions.

Data consistently reveal that behavioral interventions (e.g., counseling from a health care provider) and pharmacotherapy, used either alone or in combination, increase patients' odds for quitting their use of tobacco.[37] In a meta-analysis of 29 studies, it was determined that patients who receive a tobacco-cessation intervention from a nonphysician clinician or a physician clinician are 1.7 and 2.2 times as likely to quit (for at least five months), respectively, compared with patients who do not receive an intervention from a clinician.[37] Estimates of the efficacy of various behavioral and pharmacotherapy treatment strategies are shown in Table 2.

As delineated in the clinical practice guideline, clinicians should routinely screen for tobacco use and apply appropriate interventions (Figure 1), addressing five key components for comprehensive tobacco-cessation counseling (the 5 A's): (1) asking patients about tobacco use, (2) advising tobacco users to quit, (3) assessing their willingness to make a quit attempt, (4) assisting patients with quitting, and (5) arranging follow-up care (Appendix A). To increase the odds for success, patients who are not ready to quit should receive tailored motivational interventions that address the 5 R's[37] (Appendix B). Patients who are ready to quit should be provided with a treatment plan that includes behavioral counseling plus pharmacotherapy (as appropriate) and follow-up counseling.

Clinicians should become familiar with local community-based resources for tobacco cessation, including group programs and telephone counseling.[37] When expertise, practice site logistics, or time constraints do not afford an opportunity to provide comprehensive tobacco-cessation counseling, clinicians should apply a truncated 5 A's model whereby they *ask* about tobacco use, *advise* tobacco users to quit, and then *refer* patients to appropriate cessation providers or programs. With the October 2004 introduction of a national toll-free quit line number (1-800-QUIT-NOW), all residents of the United States can receive tobacco-cessation counseling at no cost. In clinical trials, telephone counseling services for smoking cessation have been shown to be effective among the patients

Table 2.
Efficacy of Treatment Methods for Tobacco Use and Dependence[a,b]

Treatment Method	Estimated Odds Ratio[c] (95% CI)	Estimated Abstinence[d] Rate (95% CI)
Behavioral interventions		
Advice to quit		
No advice to quit	1.0	7.9
Physician advice to quit	1.3 (1.1–1.6)	10.2 (8.5–12.0)
Clinician intervention		
No counseling by a clinician	1.0	10.2
Counseling by a nonphysician	1.7 (1.3–2.1)	15.8 (12.8–18.8)
Counseling by a physician	2.2 (1.5–3.2)	19.9 (13.7–26.2)
Format of smoking cessation counseling		
No format	1.0	10.8
Self-help	1.2 (1.0–1.3)	12.3 (10.9–13.6)
Proactive telephone counseling[e]	1.2 (1.1–1.4)	13.1 (11.4–14.8)
Group counseling	1.3 (1.1–1.6)	13.9 (11.6–16.1)
Individual counseling	1.7 (1.4–2.0)	16.8 (14.7–19.1)
Pharmacotherapy		
Placebo	1.0	13.8
First-line agents		
Bupropion SR	2.0 (1.8–2.2)	24.2 (22.2–26.4)
Nicotine gum (6–14 wk)	1.5 (1.2–1.7)	19.0 (16.5–21.9)
Nicotine inhaler	2.1 (1.5–2.9)	24.8 (19.1–31.6)
Nicotine lozenge (2 mg)	2.0 (1.4–2.8)	24.2[f]
Nicotine patch (6–14 wk)	1.9 (1.7–2.2)	23.4 (21.3–25.8)
Nicotine nasal spray	2.3 (1.7–3.0)	26.7 (21.5–32.7)
Varenicline (2 mg/day)	3.1 (2.5–3.8)	33.2 (28.9–37.8)
Second-line agents		
Clonidine	2.1 (1.2–3.7)	25.0 (15.7–37.3)
Nortriptyline	1.8 (1.3–2.6)	22.5 (16.8–29.4)
Combination therapy		
Patch (>14 weeks) + *ad lib* nicotine	3.6 (2.5–5.2)	36.5 (28.6–45.3)
Nicotine patch + bupropion SR	2.5 (1.9–3.4)	28.9 (23.5–35.1)
Nicotine patch + nortriptyline	2.3 (1.3–4.2)	27.3 (17.2–40.4)
Nicotine patch + nicotine inhaler	2.2 (1.2–3.6)	25.8 (17.4–36.5)

[a]Reprinted from reference 43, with permission.
[b]Data from reference 37.
[c]Estimated relative to referent group. CI = confidence interval.
[d]Abstinence percentages for specified treatment method.
[e]A quitline that responds to incoming calls and makes outbound follow-up calls. After an initial request by the smoker or via a fax-to-quit program, the clinician initiates telephone contact to counsel the patient.
[f]One qualifying randomized trial; 95% CI not reported.

Figure 1. Assessing readiness to quit.[38] Algorithm for treating tobacco use.

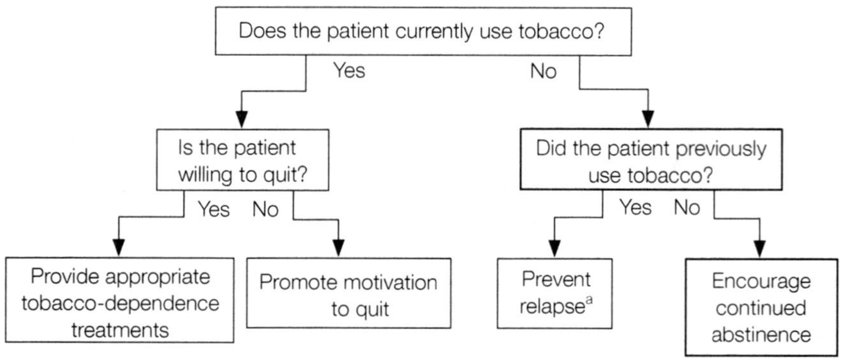

[a]Relapse-prevention interventions are not necessary for adults who have not used tobacco for many years.

who use them.[37-39] These positive results have been shown to translate into real-world effectiveness,[40] as evidenced in several meta-analytic reviews.[37,38,41,42]

Even the busiest of clinicians can serve an important role by spending approximately one minute per patient to identify tobacco users and to provide referrals to the quit line for more comprehensive counseling. When patients indicate a willingness to set a quit date in the next month, clinicians should consider a proactive approach whereby they obtain the patient's permission to contact the quit line directly on the patient's behalf as opposed to their providing a passive referral (by simply offering the patient contact information for the quit line).[38]

Pharmacotherapy for Cessation. All patients attempting to quit using tobacco should be encouraged to use effective pharmacotherapies (Table 3) for smoking cessation,[43] except when medically contraindicated or in specific populations in which there is insufficient evidence of effectiveness (e.g., pregnant women, smokeless tobacco users, light smokers, adolescents).[37] Currently, the agents with approved FDA labeling for smoking cessation include five nicotine-replacement therapy (NRT) dosage forms, sustained-release bupropion, and varenicline. Pharmacologic agents that have not received FDA approval for use in smoking cessation but have demonstrated efficacy are clonidine and nortriptyline.[37]

NRT. Formulations of NRT products currently available in the United States include nicotine gum, lozenge, transdermal patch, nasal spray, and oral inhaler (Table 3). These agents improve quit rates by reducing the symptoms of nicotine withdrawal, enabling the patient to focus on behavior modification and coping with the psychological aspects of quitting. In addition, because the onset of action with NRT is not as rapid as that of nicotine obtained through tobacco (Figure 2), patients become less accustomed to the nearly immediate, reinforcing effects of tobacco. Patients using NRT are approximately two times as likely to quit smoking than are those receiving placebo.[37]

For selected patients with cardiovascular disease,[37] NRT should be used with caution, because nicotine can increase the heart rate and blood pressure and also act as a coronary vasoconstrictor.[44] Despite these effects, randomized, controlled trials have found no significant increase in the incidence of cardiovascular events or mortality among patients with cardiovascular disease receiving NRT when compared with that of patients receiving placebo.[45-47] However, because these studies specifically excluded patients with severe, underlying cardiac diseases, the clinical practice guideline[37] recommends that because of a lack of safety data in these higher-risk populations, NRT should be used with caution among patients who have experienced a myocardial infarction within the past two weeks and among those with serious arrhythmias or unstable angina.[37] A large observational study of more than 33,000 patients found that NRT use was not associated with an increased risk of myocardial infarction, stroke, or death.[48] Because the serum concentrations of nicotine achieved with the recommended dosages of NRT are generally much lower than those attained with smoking, most experts have concluded that the risks associated with NRT use in patients with cardiovascular disease are minimal relative to the risks of continued tobacco use.[44,49-52]

Other conditions for which NRT should be used with caution include active temporomandibular joint disease, pregnancy, and lactation. Patients with active temporomandibular joint disease should not use nicotine gum because doing so might exacerbate their condition. FDA classifies prescription formulations of nicotine as pregnancy category D, indicating that there is evidence of risk to the human fetus. Accordingly, none of the NRT formulations have received FDA approval for use during pregnancy. Although NRT may pose a risk to the developing fetus, it is arguably less than the risks associated with continued smoking.[53] However, because NRT has the potential to cause fetal harm and because of insufficient evidence supporting its efficacy in pregnant women, the 2008 clinical practice guideline does not recommend use during pregnancy.[37] Nicotine is secreted in breast milk[53] and, while the risk is slight, clinicians should be aware that the nursing infant is at risk for nicotine toxicity, especially if the mother concomitantly smokes and uses NRT.

Sustained-Release Bupropion. The first nonnicotine medication FDA approved for smoking cessation was sustained-release bupropion (Zyban, GlaxoSmithKline, Philadelphia). This agent, which was originally marketed as an antidepressant, is hypothesized to promote smoking cessation by inhibiting the reuptake of dopamine and norepinephrine in the central nervous system[54] and may function as a nicotinic acetylcholine-receptor antagonist.[55] The neurochemical effects are believed to modulate the dopamine reward pathway and reduce the cravings for nicotine and symptoms of withdrawal.[37] Bupropion is effective in smokers with or without a history of major depression,[56] suggesting that the mechanism of action is independent of the agent's antidepressant effects. Clinical trials involving almost 10,000 participants have confirmed the effectiveness of sustained-release bupropion as an aid to tobacco cessation; a recent meta-analysis of 31 trials concluded that the odds of tobacco abstinence at six or more months was 1.9 (sustained-release bupropion relative to placebo, 95% CI, 1.7–2.2).[57] Patients receiving sustained-release bupropion are approximately two times more likely to quit smoking than are patients receiving placebo.[44]

Bupropion is contraindicated in patients (1) with a seizure disorder, (2) with a history of anorexia or bulimia nervosa, (3) who are using another formulation of bupropion (Wellbutrin, Wellbutrin SR, Wellbutrin XL), (4) who have used a monoamine oxidase inhibitor within the past 14 days, and (5) who are undergoing abrupt discontinuation of alcohol or sedatives (including benzodiazepines).[58] In clinical trials for smoking cessation, the frequency of seizures with bupropion was <0.1% (seven seizures among 8000 bupropion-treated patients).[57] This frequency is comparable to the report rate of seizures (0.1%) when sustained-release bupropion was used in the treatment of depression.[59] For this reason, bupropion should be used with extreme caution in patients with a history of seizures, those who have experienced cranial trauma, and those receiving medications known to lower the seizure threshold or those with underlying severe hepatic cirrhosis. In addition, caution should be exercised in patients with certain depressive or psychiatric disorders. FDA has recently reclassified bupropion as a pregnancy category C drug, meaning that either (1) animal studies have demonstrated that the drug exerts animal-teratogenic or embryocidal effects, but there are no controlled studies in women, or (2) no studies are available in either animals or women. The pregnancy category reclassification resulted after the reanalysis of preclinical animal data demonstrated an increased incidence of fetal malformations and skeletal variations in rabbits receiving dosages approximately twofold higher than the maximum recommended human dose (on a milligram per square meter basis) of bupropion. The manufacturer continues to recommend that bupropion be used during pregnancy only if clearly needed.[58]

Varenicline. A partial agonist selective for the $\alpha_4\beta_2$ nicotinic acetylcholine receptor, varenicline (Chantix, Pfizer, Inc., New York, NY) was approved in May 2006 for use as an aid to smoking cessation. The drug's efficacy in smoking cessation is believed to be the result of low-level agonist activity at the receptor site combined with the competitive inhibition of nicotine binding. The partial agonist activity induces modest receptor stimulation that attenuates the symptoms of nicotine withdrawal. In addition, by blocking the ability of nicotine to activate $\alpha_4\beta_2$ nicotinic acetylcholine receptors, varenicline inhibits the surges of dopamine release that are believed to be responsible for the reinforcement and reward associated with smoking.[60]

Data from meta-analyses suggest that the use of varenicline significantly increases long-term smoking-abstinence rates relative to placebo and sustained-release bupropion.[37,61] FDA has classified varenicline as a pregnancy category C drug. The manufacturer recommends varenicline use during pregnancy only if the potential benefit justifies the potential risk to the fetus.[62]

In February 2008, FDA issued a public health advisory to alert health care providers about reports of serious neuropsychiatric symptoms in patients attempting to quit smoking while using varenicline, including changes in behavior, depressed mood, agitation, and suicidal ideation and behavior. The warnings and precautions sections of the drug's prescribing information have been updated, and FDA recommends that (1) patients tell their health care providers about any history of psychiatric illness before starting varenicline and (2) clinicians and patients monitor for changes in mood and behavior during treatment with varenicline.[63]

Second-Line Agents. Second-line agents that have not received an FDA indication for smoking cessation include the prescription medications clonidine and nortriptyline.[37] Controlled trials suggest that these agents are effective in treating tobacco dependence (Table 2), but they have a greater incidence of adverse effects and should be reserved for patients unable to quit with medications approved for smoking cessation.[37]

Combination Therapy. Certain combinations of medications have been shown to be effective smoking-cessation treatments. In the previous guideline, combination therapy was recommended only for patients unable to quit after monotherapy with a first-line agent. Based on data from eight clinical trials, the 2008 clinical practice guideline recommends that clinicians consider using combinations of first-line agents for patients who are willing to quit.[37] Combination NRT involves the use of a long-acting formulation (e.g., nicotine patch) along with a short-acting formulation (i.e., gum, lozenge, inhaler, or nasal spray). The long-acting formulation, which delivers nicotine at relatively constant levels, is used to prevent the onset of severe withdrawal symptoms; the short-acting formulation, which delivers nicotine at a more rapid rate, is used as needed to control the withdrawal symptoms that may occur during potential relapse situations (e.g., after meals, during times of stress, when around other smokers).

Controlled trials suggest that the nicotine patch in combination with short-acting NRT formulations (i.e., gum, nasal spray, or inhaler) significantly increases quit rates relative to placebo.[37] Similar results have been observed in trials using combination therapy with sustained-release bupropion and the nicotine patch. Results from an open-label trial suggest that a more-aggressive approach consisting of triple agent NRT (e.g., inhaler, patch, and nasal spray) with or without sustained-release bupropion is safe and effective among highly dependent smokers.[64] Clinicians should be aware that while the combination of the nicotine patch and sustained-release bupropion has been approved by FDA, the concurrent use of two NRT products is not FDA-approved for tobacco cessation. Furthermore, the optimal combinations, dosages, and duration of dual NRTs are currently unknown. The safety and effectiveness of varenicline used with sustained-release bupropion or NRT have not been established. Pilot data suggest that patients receiving both varenicline and the nicotine patch are more likely to experience adverse effects (nausea, headache, vomiting, dizziness, dyspepsia, and fatigue) than are those receiving the patch alone.[62]

Smoke-Free Environments

Smoking initiation and cessation result from the interplay of numerous factors, including but not limited to environmental influences.[21] Smokers in one's environment can both promote initiation and inhibit cessation.

Data on state-specific trends in smoke-free working environments indicate that 73.4% of employees who work indoors were covered by a smoke-free workplace policy,

Table 3.
Medications with FDA-Approved Indications for Smoking Cessation[43,a]

Product Name and Availability	Precautions	Dosing	Administration and Pt Information
Nicorette gum, generic, nonprescription, 2 or 4 mg	Pregnancy[c] (Category D), breastfeeding, recent (≤2 wk) MI, serious underlying arrhythmia, serious or worsening angina pectoris, TMJ disease	≥25 cigarettes/day: 4 mg, <25 cigarettes/day: 2 mg Wk 1–6: 1 piece every 1–2 hr, wk 7–9: 1 piece every 2–4 hr, wk 10–12: 1 piece every 4–8 hr Maximum, 24 pieces/day Duration, up to 12 wk	Chew each piece slowly, park between cheek and gum when peppery or tingling sensation appears (~15–30 chews), resume chewing when taste or tingle fades, repeat chew/park steps until most of the nicotine is gone (taste or tingle does not return; generally 30 min), park in different areas of mouth, no food or beverages 15 min before or during use
Commit lozenges, generic nonprescription, 2 or 4 mg	Pregnancy[c] (Category D), breastfeeding, recent (≤2 wk) MI, serious underlying arrhythmia, serious or worsening angina pectoris	First cigarette ≤30 min after waking: 4 mg, first cigarette >30 min after waking: 2 mg Wk 1–6: 1 lozenge every 1–2 hr, wk 7–9: 1 lozenge every 2–4 hr, wk 10–12: 1 lozenge every 4–8 hr Maximum, 20 lozenges/day Duration, up to 12 wk	Allow to dissolve slowly (20-30 min), nicotine release may cause a warm, tingling sensation, do not chew or swallow, occasionally rotate to different areas of the mouth, no food or beverages 15 min before or during use
Nicoderm CQ transdermal patch, nonprescription, 24-hr release; 7,14, or 21 mg	Pregnancy[c] (Category D), breastfeeding, recent (≤2 wk) MI, serious underlying arrhythmia, serious or worsening angina pectoris	>10 cigarettes/day: 21 mg/day × 6 wk, 14 mg/day × 2 wk, 7 mg/day × 2 wk ≤10 cigarettes/day: 14 mg/day × 6 wk, 7 mg/day × 2 wk Duration: 8–10 wk	May wear patch for 16 hr if pt has sleep disturbances (remove at bedtime)
Generic patch (formerly Habitrol), prescription or nonprescription, 24-hour release; 7,14, or 21 mg	Pregnancy[c] (Category D), breastfeeding, recent (≤2 wk) MI, serious underlying arrhythmia, serious or worsening angina pectoris	>10 cigarettes/day: 21 mg/day × 4 wk, 14 mg/day × 2 wk, 7 mg/day × 2 wk ≤10 cigarettes/day: 14 mg/day x 6 wk, 7 mg/day × 2 wk Duration: 8–10 wk	May wear patch for 16 hr if pt has sleep disturbances (remove at bedtime)
Nicotrol NS, metered spray, prescription, 0.5 mg nicotine in 50 μL aqueous nicotine solution	Pregnancy[c] (Category D), breastfeeding, recent (≤2 wk) MI, serious underlying arrhythmia, serious or worsening angina pectoris, underlying chronic nasal disorders (rhinitis, nasal polyps, sinusitis), severe reactive airway disease	1–2 doses/hr (8–40 doses/day) 1 dose = 2 sprays (1 in each nostril); each spray delivers 0.5 mg of nicotine Maximum of 5 doses/hr or 40 doses/day Duration, 3–6 mo	For best results, initially use at least 8 doses/day; pts should not sniff, swallow, or inhale through nose as spray is administered

Adverse Effects	Advantages	Disadvantages	Cost/Day[b]
Mouth/jaw soreness, hiccups, dyspepsia, hypersalivation, effects associated with incorrect chewing technique (lightheadedness, nausea/ vomiting, throat and mouth irritation)	Might satisfy oral cravings, may delay weight gain; pts can adjust therapy to manage withdrawal symptoms; available in a variety of flavors	Gum chewing may not be socially acceptable, might be problematic for patients with significant dental work; pts must use proper chewing technique to minimize adverse effects	2 mg: \$3.28–\$6.58 (9 pieces), 4 mg: \$4.31–\$6.58 (9 pieces)
Nausea, hiccups, cough, heartburn, headache, flatulence, insomnia	Might satisfy oral cravings, might delay weight gain, easy to use and conceal; pts can adjust therapy to manage withdrawal symptoms; available in a variety of flavors	Adverse gastrointestinal effects (nausea, hiccups, heartburn) might be bothersome; need for frequent dosing can compromise adherence	2 mg or 4 mg: \$3.66–\$5.26 (9 pieces)
Local skin reactions (erythema, pruritus, burning), headache, sleep disturbances (insomnia), abnormal or vivid dreams (associated with nocturnal nicotine absorption)	Provides consistent nicotine levels over 24 hr; easy to use and conceal; once-daily administration associated with fewer adherence problems	Pts cannot adjust dosage; allergic reactions to adhesive might occur, pts with dermatological conditions should not use patch	\$1.90–\$3.89 (1 patch)
Local skin reactions (erythema, pruritus, burning), headache, sleep disturbances (insomnia), abnormal or vivid dreams (associated with nocturnal nicotine absorption)	Provides consistent nicotine levels over 24 hr; easy to use and conceal; once-daily administration associated with fewer adherence problems	Pts cannot adjust dosage; allergic reactions to adhesive might occur, pts with dermatological conditions should not use patch	\$1.90–\$3.89 (1 patch)
Nasal or throat irritation (hot, peppery, or burning sensation), rhinitis, tearing, sneezing, cough, headache	Pts can adjust therapy to manage withdrawal symptoms	Nasal or throat irritation may be bothersome; dependence can result; pts must wait 5 min before driving or operating heavy machinery; pts with chronic nasal disorders or severe reactive airway disease should not use spray; need for frequent dosing can compromise adherence	\$3.72 (8 doses)

Continued on next page

Table 3. *(continued)*
Medications with FDA-Approved Indications for Smoking Cessation[43,a]

Product Name and Availability	Precautions	Dosing	Administration and Pt Information
Nicotrol inhaler, prescription, 10-mg cartridge delivers 4 mg inhaled nicotine vapor	Pregnancy[c] (Category D), breastfeeding, recent (≤2 wk) MI, serious underlying arrhythmia, serious or worsening angina pectoris, bronchospastic disease	6–16 cartridges/day for up to 6 mo, individualized dosing Duration, 3–6 mo	Initially, use at least 6 cartridges/day; best effects with continuous puffing for 20 min; nicotine in cartridge depleted after 20 min of active puffing; pt should inhale into back of throat or puff in short breaths; do not inhale into lungs (like a cigarette) but "puff" as if lighting a pipe; open cartridge retains potency for 24 hr
Zyban (bupropion SR), generic and prescription, 150-mg sustained-release tablets	Pregnancy[c] (Category C), breastfeeding, concomitant therapy with medications or medical conditions known to lower the seizure threshold, severe hepatic cirrhosis *Contraindications:* Seizure disorder, concomitant bupropion (e.g., Wellbutrin) therapy, current or prior diagnosis of bulimia or anorexia nervosa, simultaneous abrupt discontinuation of alcohol or sedatives (including benzodiazepines), MAOI therapy in previous 14 days	150 mg p.o. every morning x 3 days, then increase to 150 mg p.o. twice daily; not to exceed 300 mg/day Duration: 7–12 wk, with maintenance up to 6 mo in selected patients	Treatment should be initiated while pt is still smoking; set quit date 1–2 wk after initiation of therapy; allow at least 8 hr between doses; avoid bedtime administration to minimize insomnia; dose tapering not necessary; can be used safely with NRT
Chantix (varenicline), prescription, 0.5- and 1-mg tablets	Pregnancy[c] (Category C), breastfeeding, severe renal impairment (dosage adjustment is necessary), safety and efficacy have not been established in patients with serious psychiatric illness	Days 1–3: 0.5 mg p.o. every morning, days 4–7: 0.5 mg p.o. twice daily, wk 2–12:1 mg p.o. twice daily Duration: 12 wks; an additional 12-wk course may be used in selected patients	Pts should begin therapy 1 wk before quit date; take dose after eating with full glass of water; dose tapering is not necessary; nausea and insomnia are side effects that are usually temporary

[a]Reprinted from reference 43, with permission. For complete prescribing information, please refer to the manufacturers' package inserts. FDA = Food and Drug Administration, MI = myocardial infarction, TMJ = temporomandibular joint, NRT = nicotine-replacement therapy, MAOI = monoamine oxidase inhibitor.

according to a survey of 14 states conducted in 2005.[65] Smoke-free workplaces have been shown to not only protect individuals from secondhand smoke but also to reduce the prevalence of smoking.[66] In a simulation study, smoke-free workplace policies were estimated to be approximately nine times more cost-effective per patient than are programs that provide NRT at no cost.[67]

Over the past few years, numerous cities and states have adopted clean indoor air laws in workplaces.[68] Nationally, the effects of transitioning all workplaces to smoke-free environments would yield an estimated 4.5% decrease in the overall prevalence of smoking.[66] In its first year of implementation, a nationwide smoke-free workplace policy would produce an estimated 1.3 million new quitters, 1500 fewer myocardial infarctions, 350 fewer strokes, and a direct saving of nearly $60 million in medical costs.[69] Given this substantial impact on public health, ASHP supports the implementation of smoke-free policies for the employees and patrons of all workplaces and public venues, including but not limited to offices, restaurants, bars, bowling alleys, and casinos, and for establishments where health care services are rendered. ASHP also strongly supports smoke-free campuses for all health care institutions and facilities. In practice, clinicians should educate patients about the dangers of secondhand smoke and encourage patients who continue to smoke to do so outdoors.

The Clinician's Role

To ensure that all future clinicians have received adequate training for treating tobacco use and dependence, schools offering health-profession courses or degrees are advised to incorporate comprehensive tobacco-cessation training as part of the required curriculum for all students.[37] Licensed clinicians who have not received the formal training necessary to provide comprehensive tobacco-cessation counseling are encouraged

Adverse Effects	Advantages	Disadvantages	Cost/Day[b]
Mouth or throat irritation, unpleasant taste, cough, headache, rhinitis, dyspepsia, hiccups	Pts can adjust therapy to manage withdrawal symptoms; mimics hand-to-mouth ritual of smoking	Initial throat or mouth irritation can be bothersome; cartridges should not be stored in very warm conditions or used in very cold conditions; pts with underlying bronchospastic disease must use inhaler with caution; need for frequent dosing can compromise adherence	$5.29 (6 cartridges)
Insomnia, dry mouth, nervousness/difficulty concentrating, rash, constipation, seizures (risk is 1/1,000 [0.1%])	Easy to use; oral formulation might be associated with fewer compliance problems; can be used with NRT; might be beneficial in patients with depression	Seizure risk is increased; several contraindications and precautions can preclude use	$3.62–$7.40 (2 tablets)
Nausea, sleep disturbances (insomnia, abnormal dreams), constipation, flatulence, vomiting, neuropsychiatric symptoms (behavior changes, agitation, depressed mood, suicidal ideation or behavior)	Easy to use; oral formulation might be associated with fewer compliance problems; offers new mechanism of action for pts who have not succeeded with other agents	May induce nausea in up to one third of pts; postmarketing surveillance data indicate potential for neuropsychiatric symptoms	$4.49–$4.75 (2 tablets)

[b]Average wholesale price from Medi-Span Electronic Drug File. Indianapolis, IN; Wolters Kluwer Health, September 2008.

[c]The U.S. clinical practice guideline states that pregnant smokers should be encouraged to quit without medication based on insufficient evidence and hypothetical concerns with safety. Pregnant smokers should be offered cessation counseling interventions that exceed minimal advice to quit.[37]

to complete continuing-education programs. Furthermore, clinicians should systematically integrate the identification of tobacco users and the delivery of evidence-based tobacco-use cessation interventions into routine patient care. In the absence of time or expertise to provide comprehensive cessation counseling, clinicians should—at a minimum—ask patients about tobacco use, advise patients to quit, and refer these patients to external resources such as the toll-free quit line (1-800-QUIT-NOW) or a group program.[37] Because higher quit rates result when patients receive assistance from multiple health care providers,[37] clinicians are encouraged to work in tandem with other providers as part of a team approach to helping patients quit smoking. Table 4 provides useful online links to assist clinicians in tobacco-control initiatives.

Given that the sale of tobacco contradicts both the clinician's role in promoting health and the pharmacist's code of ethics,[70] ASHP strongly opposes the sale or distribution of tobacco products in all establishments where health care services are rendered (e.g., hospitals, clinics, retail chain and community pharmacies).[71] For more than three decades, the pharmacy profession has repeatedly voiced opposition to the sale of tobacco products in pharmacies,[72] including formal resolutions from state and national organizations. Notably, few licensed pharmacists (estimated at $<2\%$)[73] and pharmacy students (3.5%)[74] are in favor of tobacco sales in pharmacies. Given this overwhelming lack of support, members of the profession are advised to insist that tobacco sales no longer occur in the environments where pharmaceutical care is rendered. Furthermore, in accordance with a 2003 resolution set forth by the American Association of Colleges of Pharmacy, ASHP encourages colleges and schools of pharmacy to give preference as clerkship sites to those pharmacies that choose not to sell tobacco products.[74]

Figure 2. Plasma nicotine concentrations for nicotine-containing products. Reprinted with permission from reference 43.

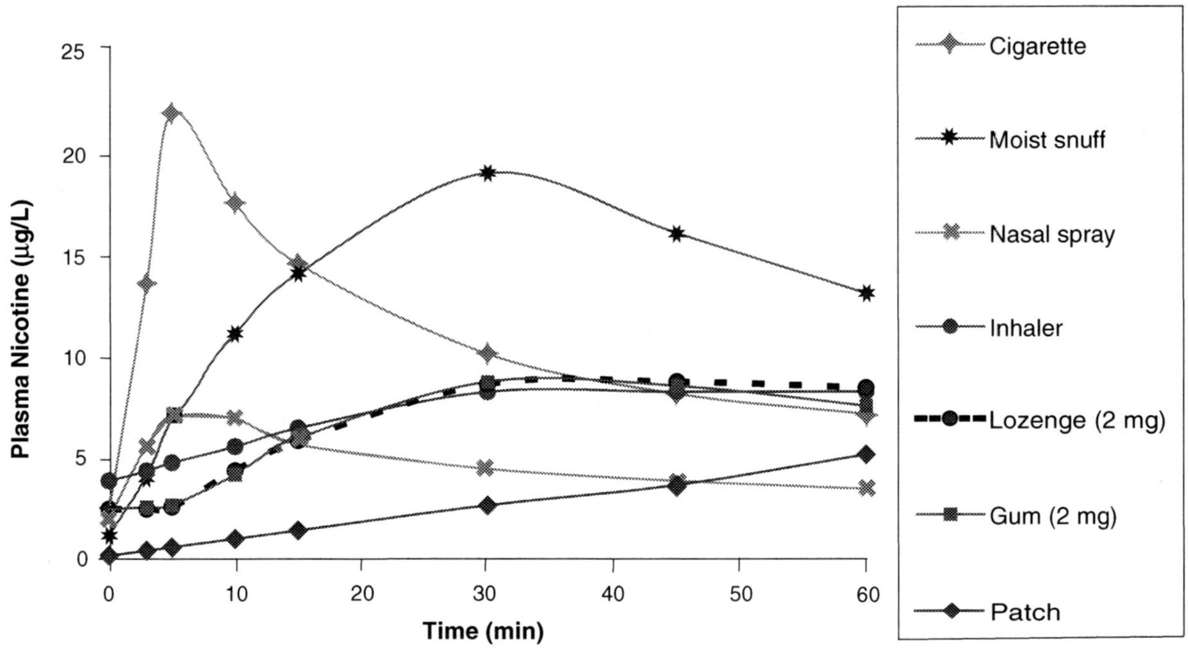

Conclusion

Given the extensive body of data implicating tobacco as the primary known preventable cause of death in the United States, ASHP strongly supports evidence-based tobacco-control initiatives that aim to reduce the prevalence of tobacco use. These efforts should address a continuum of services, activities, and policies ranging from the integration of tobacco-cessation counseling as a routine component of patient care to the adoption of clean indoor air laws. ASHP believes that the active involvement of health care providers is crucial to effective tobacco control at the population level and that the pharmacy profession—as a primary and accessible point of contact between the health care system and the public (including the medically underserved)—has a unique opportunity to serve as a cornerstone for the nation's tobacco-control efforts.

References

1. The health consequences of smoking: cancer. A report of the Surgeon General. http://profiles.nlm.nih.gov/NN/B/C/D/W/_/nnbcdw.pdf (accessed 2008 Jul 16).
2. Centers for Disease Control and Prevention. Annual smoking-attributable mortality, years of potential life lost, and productivity losses—United States, 1997-2001. *MMWR.* 2005; 54:625–8.
3. U.S. Department of Health and Human Services. 2006 Surgeon General's report: the health consequences of involuntary exposure to tobacco smoke. www.cdc.gov/tobacco/data_statistics/sgr/sgr_2006/index.htm (accessed 2008 Jul 16).
4. Doll R, Peto R, Boreham J, et al. Mortality in relation to smoking: 50 years' observations on male British doctors. *BMJ.* 2004; 328:1519.
5. Centers for Disease Control and Prevention. Cigarette smoking among adults—United States, 2000. *MMWR.* 2002; 51:642–5.
6. Centers for Disease Control and Prevention. Cigarette smoking among adults—United States, 2006. *MMWR.* 2007; 56:1157–61.
7. Lasser K, Boyd JW, Woolhandler S, et al. Smoking and mental illness: a population-based prevalence study. *JAMA.* 2000; 284:2606–10.
8. Centers for Disease Control and Prevention. State-specific prevalence of cigarette smoking among adults and quitting among persons aged 18-35 years—United States, 2006. *MMWR.* 2007; 56:993–6.
9. U.S. Department of Health and Human Services. 1994 Surgeon General's report—preventing tobacco use among young people. www.cdc.gov/tobacco/data_statistics/sgr/sgr_1994/index.htm (accessed 2008 Aug 13).
10. U.S. Department of Health and Human Services. Healthy People 2010. Vol. I and II. www.healthypeople.gov/publications/ (accessed 2008 Jul 16).
11. Johnston LD, O'Malley PM, Bachman JG, et al. Teen smoking resumes decline. www.monitoringthefuture.org/data/07data.html#2007data-cigs (accessed 2008 May 21).
12. U.S. Department of Agriculture. Tobacco outlook. Report TBS-263. http://usda.mannlib.cornell.edu/usda/ers/TBS//2000s/2007/TBS-10-24-2007.pdf (accessed 2008 Aug 13).
13. Substance Abuse and Mental Health Services Administration Offices of Applied Studies (2008). Results from the 2007 National Survey on Drug Use and Health: National findings (DHHS publication no. SMA 08-4343). Rockville, MD.
14. Henningfield JE, Fant RV, Radzius A, et al. Nicotine concentration, smoke pH and whole tobacco aqueous

Table 4.
Tobacco-Cessation Resources

Resource	Contact Information
Governmental agencies	
Centers for Disease Control and Prevention	www.cdc.gov
Environmental Protection Agency	www.epa.gov
Federal Trade Commission	www.ftc.gov
Office of the Surgeon General	www.surgeongeneral.gov
National Institutes of Health	www.nih.gov
National Cancer Institute	www.cancer.gov
National Heart, Lung, and Blood Institute	www.nhlbi.nih.gov
National Institute on Drug Abuse	www.nida.nih.gov
Organizations	
American Cancer Society	www.cancer.org
American Heart Association	www.americanheart.org
American Legacy Foundation	www.americanlegacy.org
American Lung Association	www.lungusa.org
American Society of Health-System Pharmacists	www.ashp.org/s_ashp/tobacco
Campaign for Tobacco-Free Kids	www.tobaccofreekids.org
Global Network of Pharmacists Against Tobacco	www.fip.org/pharmacistsagainsttobacco
North American Quitline Consortium	www.naquitline.org
Society for Research on Nicotine & Tobacco	www.srnt.org
University of California Smoking Cessation Leadership Center	smokingcessationleadership.ucsf.edu
University of California Tobacco-Related Disease Research Program	www.trdrp.org
World Health Organization	www.who.int
Documents	
Clinical Practice Guideline for Treating Tobacco Use and Dependence	www.surgeongeneral.gov/tobacco
Legacy Tobacco Industry Documents Archive	www.legacy.library.ucsf.edu
Pharmacologic aids for cessation—online support	
Committed Quitters Program	
Nicorette gum	www.nicorette.com
Nicoderm patch	www.nicodermcq.com
Commit lozenge	www.commitlozenge.com
GETQUIT Support Plan	
Chantix	www.chantix.com
Helping Hand Program	
Nicotrol nasal spray and inhaler	www.nicotrol.com
Smoke-Free Program	
Generic patch (formerly Habitrol)	www.habitrol.com
Nonpharmaceutical cessation support and programs	
QuitKey (handheld computer for scheduled gradual reduction of smoking)	www.quitkey.com
QuitNet (comprehensive online tobacco-cessation support program)	www.quitnet.com
Rx for Change: Clinician-Assisted Tobacco Cessation (evidence-based tobacco-cessation training materials for educating health professional students and licensed clinicians)	rxforchange.ucsf.edu
Tobacco-Free Nurses (national program focused on helping nurses and student nurses to stop smoking)	www.tobaccofreenurses.org
Toll-free quit lines (telephone counseling for cessation, available at no cost to all callers)	1-800-QUIT-NOW

pH of some cigar brands and types popular in the United States. *Nicotine Tob Res.* 1999; 1:163–8.

15. Connolly GN, Alpert HR, Wayne GF, et al. Trends in nicotine yield in smoke and its relationship with design characteristics among popular US cigarette brands, 1997-2005. *Tob Control.* 2007; 16:e5.
16. Ebbert JO, Carr AB, Dale LC. Smokeless tobacco: an emerging addiction. *Med Clin North Am.* 2004; 88:1593–605.
17. Centers for Disease Control and Prevention. Annual smoking-attributable mortality, years of potential life lost, and economic costs—United States, 1995–1999. *MMWR.* 2002; 51:300–3.

18. Best practices for comprehensive tobacco control programs—2007. Atlanta: Centers for Disease Control and Prevention; 2007.
19. Task Force on Community Preventive Services. The guide to community preventive services: tobacco use prevention and control. *Am J Prev Med.* 2001; 20(suppl 2):1–88.
20. U.S. Department of Health and Human Services. The health consequences of smoking: nicotine addiction: a report of the Surgeon General. http://profiles.nlm.nih.gov/NN/B/B/Z/D/_/nnbbzd.pdf (accessed 2008 Jul 16).
21. Benowitz NL. Clinical pharmacology of nicotine: implications for understanding, preventing and treating tobacco addiction. *Clin Pharm Ther.* 2008; 83:531–41.
22. Hughes JR, Gust SW, Skoog K, et al. Symptoms of tobacco withdrawal: a replication and extension. *Arch Gen Psychiatry.* 1991; 48:52–9.
23. Hughes JR. Effects of abstinence from tobacco: valid symptoms and time course. *Nicotine Tob Res.* 2007; 9:315–327.
24. American Psychiatric Association. Diagnostic and statistical manual of mental disorders, 4th edition. Washington, DC: American Psychiatric Publishing; 1994.
25. Benowitz NL. Cigarette smoking and nicotine addiction. *Med Clin North Am.* 1992; 76:415–37.
26. Hatsukami DK, Gust SW, Keenan RM. Physiologic and subjective changes from smokeless tobacco withdrawal. *Clin Pharmacol Ther.* 1987; 41:103–7.
27. Centers for Disease Control and Prevention. U.S. 2004 Surgeon General's report—the health consequences of smoking. www.cdc.gov/tobacco/data_statistics/sgr/sgr_2004/index.htm (accessed 2008 Jul 16).
28. Henley SJ, Thun MJ, Connell C, et al. Two large prospective studies of mortality among men who use snuff or chewing tobacco (United States). *Cancer Causes Control.* 2005; 16:347–58.
29. Hergens MP, Ahlbom A, Andersson T, et al. Swedish moist snuff and myocardial infarction among men. *Epidemiology.* 2005; 16:12–16.
30. Gupta R, Gurm H, Bartholomew JR. Smokeless tobacco and cardiovascular risk. *Arch Intern Med.* 2004; 164:1845–9.
31. Henley SJ, Connell CJ, Richter P, et al. Tobacco-related disease mortality among men who switched from cigarettes to spit tobacco. *Tob Control.* 2007; 16:22–8.
32. California Environmental Protection Agency. Proposed identification of environmental tobacco smoke as a toxic air contaminant: executive summary. www.arb.ca.gov/regact/ets2006/ets2006.htm (accessed 2008 Oct 1).
33. Kroon LA. Drug interactions with smoking. *Am J Health-Syst Pharm.* 2007; 64:1917–21.
34. Zevin S, Benowitz NL. Drug interactions with tobacco smoking. *Clin Pharmacokinet.* 1999; 36:425–38.
35. U.S. Department of Health and Human Services. The benefits of smoking cessation. A report of the surgeon general (DHHS publication no. CDC 90-8416). U.S. Department of Health and Human Services, Public Health Service, Centers for Disease Control and Prevention and Health Promotion, Office on Smoking and Health. 1990.
36. Hazelden Foundation. Survey on current and former smokers—1998. www.hazelden.org/web/public/smokers 1998.page (accessed 2008 Aug 13.).
37. Fiore MC, Jaen CR, Baker TB, et al. Treating tobacco use and dependence—2008 update. Clinical practice guideline. www.surgeongeneral.gov/tobacco/treating_tobacco_use08.pdf (accessed 2008 Jul 16).
38. Stead L, Perera R, Lancaster T. Telephone counselling for smoking cessation. *Cochrane Database Syst Rev.* 2006; 3:CD002850.
39. Ossip-Klein DJ, McIntosh S. Quitlines in North America: evidence base and applications. *Am J Med Sci.* 2003; 326:201–5.
40. Zhu SH, Anderson CM, Tedeschi GJ, et al. Evidence of real-world effectiveness of a telephone quitline for smokers. *N Engl J Med.* 2002; 347:1087–93.
41. Lichtenstein E, Glasgow RE, Lando HA, et al. Telephone counseling for smoking cessation: rationales and meta-analytic review of evidence. *Health Educ Res.* 1996; 11:243–57.
42. Hopkins DP, Briss PA, Ricard CJ, et al. Reviews of evidence regarding interventions to reduce tobacco use and exposure to environmental tobacco smoke. *Am J Prev Med.* 2001; 20(2, suppl):16–66.
43. Rx for Change: clinician-assisted tobacco cessation. http://rxforchange.ucsf.edu (accessed 2008 Oct 1).
44. Benowitz NL. Cigarette smoking and cardiovascular disease: pathophysiology and implications for treatment. *Prog Cardiovasc Dis.* 2003; 46:91–111.
45. Working Group for the Study of Transdermal Nicotine in Patients with Coronary Artery Disease. Nicotine replacement therapy for patients with coronary artery disease. *Arch Intern Med.* 1994; 154:989–95.
46. Joseph AM, Norman SM, Ferry LH, et al. The safety of transdermal nicotine as an aid to smoking cessation in patients with cardiac disease. *N Engl J Med.* 1996; 335:1792–8.
47. Tzivoni D, Keren A, Meyler S, et al. Cardiovascular safety of transdermal nicotine patches in patients with coronary artery disease who try to quit smoking. *Cardiovasc Drugs Ther.* 1998; 12:239–44.
48. Hubbard R, Lewis S, Smith C, et al. Use of nicotine replacement therapy and the risk of acute myocardial infarction, stroke, and death. *Tob Control.* 2005; 14:416–21.
49. McRobbie H, Hajek P. Nicotine replacement therapy in patients with cardiovascular disease: guidelines for health professionals. *Addiction.* 2001; 96:1547–51.
50. Joseph AM, Fu SS. Safety issues in pharmacotherapy for smoking in patients with cardiovascular disease. *Prog Cardiovasc Dis.* 2003; 45:429–41.
51. Benowitz NL, Gourlay SG. Cardiovascular toxicity of nicotine: implications for nicotine replacement therapy. *J Am Coll Cardiol.* 1997; 29:1422–31.
52. Meine TJ, Patel MR, Washam JB, et al. Safety and effectiveness of transdermal nicotine patch in smokers admitted with acute coronary syndromes. *Am J Cardiol.* 2005; 95:976–8.
53. Benowitz NL, Dempsey DA. Pharmacotherapy for smoking cessation during pregnancy. *Nicotine Tob Res.* 2004;6(Suppl 2):S189–202.
54. Ascher JA, Cole JO, Colin J, et al. Bupropion: a review of its mechanism of antidepressant activity. *J Clin Psychiatry.* 1995; 56:395–401.

55. Slemmer JE, Martin BR, Damaj MI. Bupropion is a nicotinic antagonist. *J Pharmacol Exp Ther.* Oct 2000; 295:321–7.
56. Hayford KE, Patten CA, Rummans TA, et al. Efficacy of bupropion for smoking cessation in smokers with a former history of major depression or alcoholism. *Br J Psychiatry.* 1999; 174:173–8.
57. Hughes J, Stead L, Lancaster T. Antidepressants for smoking cessation. *Cochrane Database Syst Rev.* 2007(1):CD000031.
58. Zyban (bupropion hydrochloride) package insert. Research Triangle Park, NC: GlaxoSmithKline, Inc.; 2007 Aug.
59. Dunner DL, Zisook S, Billow AA, et al. A prospective safety surveillance study for bupropion sustained-release in the treatment of depression. *J Clin Psychiatry.* 1998; 59:366–73.
60. Foulds J. The neurobiological basis for partial agonist treatment of nicotine dependence: varenicline. *Int J Clin Pract.* May 2006; 60:571–6.
61. Cahill K, Stead LF, Lancaster T. Nicotine receptor partial agonists for smoking cessation. *Cochrane Database Syst Rev.* 2008(3):CD006103.
62. Chantix (varenicline) package insert. New York: Pfizer, Inc.; 2008 May.
63. Food and Drug Administration. Varenicline information. www.fda.gov/cder/drug/infopage/varenicline/default.htm (accessed 2008 May 22).
64. Bars MP, Banauch GI, Appel D, et al. Tobacco Free With FDNY: the New York City Fire Department World Trade Center Tobacco Cessation Study. *Chest.* 2006; 129:979–87.
65. State-specific prevalence of current cigarette smoking among adults and second hand smoke rules and policies in homes and workplaces, United States, 2005. *MMWR.* 2006; 55:1148–51.
66. Fichtenberg CM, Glantz SA. Effect of smoke-free workplaces on smoking behaviour: systematic review. *BMJ.* 2002; 325:188.
67. Ong MK, Glantz SA. Free nicotine replacement therapy programs vs implementing smoke-free workplaces: a cost-effectiveness comparison. *Am J Public Health.* 2005; 95:969–75.
68. American Nonsmokers' Rights Foundation. States, commonwealths, and municipalities with 100% smokefree laws in workplaces, restaurants or bars. www.no-smoke.org/pdf/100ordlist.pdf (accessed 2008 Aug 13).
69. Ong MK, Glantz SA. Cardiovascular health and economic effects of smoke-free workplaces. *Am J Med.* 2004; 117:32–8.
70. American Pharmacists Association. Code of ethics for pharmacists. http://www.pharmacist.com/AM/Template.cfm?Section=Code_of_Ethics_for_Pharmacists&Template=/CM/HTMLDisplay.cfm&ContentID=5420 (accessed 2008 Aug 13).
71. American Society of Health-System Pharmacists. ASHP policy position 0713: tobacco and tobacco products. http://www.ashp.org/s_ashp/docs/files/BP07/HR_Positions.pdf (accessed 2008 Aug 13).
72. Davis RM. Tobacco sales in pharmacies: mixing good drugs and bad drugs. *Tob Control.* 1992; 1:84–96.
73. Hudmon KS, Prokhorov AV, Corelli RL. Tobacco cessation counseling: pharmacists' opinions and practices. *Patient Educ Couns.* 2006; 61:152–60.
74. Hudmon KS, Corelli RL, Fenlon CM, et al. Pharmacy student perceptions of tobacco sales in pharmacies and suggested methods for promoting tobacco-free experiential sites. *Am J Pharm Educ.* 2006; 70:75.

Appendix A—The 5 A's of Tobacco Cessation Counseling[37]

Step	Action	Strategies for Implementation
Ask—Systematically identify all tobacco users at every visit	Implement a system that ensures that, for every patient at every clinic visit, tobacco use status is queried and documented.[a]	Expand the vital signs to include tobacco use, or use an alternative universal identification system.[b] VITAL SIGNS Blood Pressure: _______ Pulse: ___ Weight: _____ Temperature: ______ Respiratory Rate: _______ Tobacco Use (circle one): Current Former Never
Advise—Strongly urge all tobacco users to quit	In a clear, strong, and personalized manner, urge every tobacco user to quit.	Advice should be: • Clear—"It is important that you quit smoking (or using chewing tobacco) now, and I can help you." "Cutting down while you are ill is not enough." "Occasional or light smoking is still dangerous." • Strong—"As your clinician, I need you to know that quitting smoking is the most important thing you can do to protect your health now and in the future. The clinic staff and I will help you." • Personalized—Tie tobacco use to current symptoms and health concerns, and/or its social and economic costs, and/or the impact of tobacco use on children and others in the household. "Continuing to smoke makes your asthma worse, and quitting may dramatically improve your health." "Quitting smoking may reduce the number of ear infections your child has."

Continued on next page

Appendix A—The 5 A's of Tobacco Cessation Counseling[37] *(continued)*

Step	Action	Strategies for Implementation
Assess—Determine willingness to make a quit attempt	Assess every tobacco user's willingness to make a quit attempt at the time.	Assess patient's willingness to quit: "Are you willing to give quitting a try?" • If the patient is willing to make a quit attempt at the time, provide assistance. —If the patient will participate in an intensive treatment, deliver such a treatment or link/refer to an intensive intervention. —If the patient is a member of a special population (e.g., adolescent, pregnant smoker, racial/ethnic minority), consider providing additional information. • If the patient clearly states that he or she is unwilling to make a quit attempt at the time, provide an intervention shown to increase future quit attempts.
Assist—Aid the patient in quitting (provide counseling and medication)	Help the patient with a quit plan.	STAR: A patient's preparations for quitting: • **S**et a quit date. Ideally, the quit date should be within 2 weeks. • **T**ell family, friends, and coworkers about quitting, and request understanding and support. • **A**nticipate challenges to the upcoming quit attempt, particularly during the critical first few weeks. These include nicotine withdrawal symptoms. • **R**emove tobacco products from your environment. Prior to quitting, avoid smoking in places where you spend a lot of time (e.g., work, home, car). Make your home smoke-free.
	Recommend the use of approved medication, except when contraindicated or with specific populations for which there is insufficient evidence of effectiveness.	Recommend the use of medications found to be effective. Explain how these medications increase quitting success and reduce withdrawal symptoms. The first-line medications include: bupropion SR, nicotine gum, nicotine inhaler, nicotine lozenge, nicotine nasal spray, nicotine patch, and varenicline; second-line medications include: clonidine and nortriptyline. There is insufficient evidence to recommend medications for certain populations (e.g., pregnant women, smokeless tobacco users, light smokers, adolescents).
	Provide practical counseling (problem solving/skills training).	• Abstinence: Striving for total abstinence is essential. Not even a single puff after the quit date. • Past quit experience: Identify what helped and what hurt in previous quit attempts. Build on past success. • Anticipate triggers or challenges in the upcoming attempt. Discuss challenges/triggers and how the patient will successfully overcome them (e.g., avoid triggers, alter routines). • Alcohol: Because alcohol is associated with relapse, the patient should consider limiting/abstaining from alcohol while quitting. (Note that reducing alcohol intake could precipitate withdrawal in alcohol-dependent persons.) • Other smokers in the household: Quitting is more difficult when there is another smoker in the household. Patients should encourage housemates to quit with them or to not smoke in their presence.
	Provide intratreatment social support.	Provide a supportive clinical environment while encouraging the patient in his or her quit attempt. "My office staff and I are available to assist you." "I'm recommending treatment that can provide ongoing support."
	Provide supplementary materials, including information on quitlines.	• Sources: Federal agencies, nonprofit agencies, national quitline network (1-800-QUIT-NOW), or local/state/tribal health departments/quitlines. • Type: Culturally/racially/educationally/age-appropriate for the patient. • Location: Readily available at every clinician's workstation.
Arrange—Ensure follow-up contact	Arrange for follow-up contacts, either in person or via telephone.	• Timing: Follow-up contact should begin soon after the quit date, preferably during the first week. A second follow-up contact is recommended within the first month. Schedule further follow-up contacts as indicated. • Actions during followup contact: For all patients, identify problems already encountered and anticipate challenges in the immediate future. Assess medication use and problems. Remind patients of quitline support (1-800-QUIT-NOW). Address tobacco use at next clinical visit (treat tobacco use as a chronic disease). • For patients who are abstinent, congratulate them on their success. If tobacco use has occurred, review circumstances and elicit recommitment to total abstinence. Consider use of or link to more intensive treatment.

[a]Repeated assessment is not necessary in the case of the adult who has never used tobacco or has not used tobacco for many years and for whom this information is clearly documented in the medical record.

[b]Alternatives to expanding the vital signs include using tobacco use status stickers on all patient charts or indicating tobacco use status via electronic medical records or computerized reminder systems.

Appendix B—Enhancing Motivation to Quit: The 5 R's of Tobacco-Cessation Counseling[37]

Relevance

Encourage the patient to indicate why quitting is personally relevant, being as specific as possible. Motivational information has the greatest impact if it is relevant to a patient's disease status or risk, family or social situation (e.g., having children in the home), health concerns, age, gender, and other important patient characteristics (e.g., prior quitting experience, personal barriers to cessation).

Risks

The clinician should ask the patient to identify potential negative consequences of tobacco use. The clinician may suggest and highlight those that seem most relevant to the patient. The clinician should emphasize that smoking low-tar/low-nicotine cigarettes or use of other forms of tobacco (e.g., smokeless tobacco, cigars, and pipes) will not eliminate these risks. Examples of risks are:

- Acute risks: Shortness of breath, exacerbation of asthma, increased risk of respiratory infections, harm to pregnancy, impotence, infertility.
- Long-term risks: Heart attacks and strokes, lung and other cancers (e.g., larynx, oral cavity, pharynx, esophagus, pancreas, stomach, kidney, bladder, cervix, and acute myelocytic leukemia), chronic obstructive pulmonary diseases (chronic bronchitis and emphysema), osteoporosis, long-term disability, and need for extended care.
- Environmental risks: Increased risk of lung cancer and heart disease in spouses; increased risk for low birthweight, sudden infant death syndrome (SIDS), asthma, middle ear disease, and respiratory infections in children of smokers.

Rewards

The clinician should ask the patient to identify potential benefits of stopping tobacco use. The clinician may suggest and highlight those that seem most relevant to the patient. Examples of rewards include:

- Improved health
- Food will taste better
- Improved sense of smell
- Saving money
- Feeling better about oneself
- Home, car, clothing, breath will smell better
- Setting a good example for children and decreasing the likelihood that they will smoke
- Having healthier babies and children
- Feeling better physically
- Performing better in physical activities
- Improved appearance, including reduced wrinkling/aging of skin and whiter teeth

Roadblocks

The clinician should ask the patient to identify barriers or impediments to quitting and provide treatment (problem solving counseling, medication) that could address barriers. Typical barriers might include:

- Withdrawal symptoms
- Fear of failure
- Weight gain
- Lack of support
- Depression
- Enjoyment of tobacco
- Being around other tobacco users
- Limited knowledge of effective treatment options

Repetition

The motivational intervention should be repeated every time an unmotivated patient visits the clinic setting. Tobacco users who have failed in previous quit attempts should be told that most people make repeated quit attempts before they are successful.

Developed by the ASHP Council on Therapeutics and approved by the ASHP Board of Directors on June 30, 2008.

Karen Suchanek Hudmon, Dr.P.H., M.S., and Robin L. Corelli, Pharm.D., are gratefully acknowledged for authoring this therapeutic position statement. Dr. Suchanek Hudmon is Associate Professor, Department of Pharmacy Practice, Purdue University School of Pharmacy and Pharmaceutical Sciencs, West Lafayette, IN. Dr. Corelli is Professor of Clinical Pharmacy, Department of Clinical Pharmacy, University of California San Francisco, San Francisco.

The following individuals are acknowledged for reviewing draft versions of this statement: John R. Hughes, M.D., Connie C. Revell, M.A., Mary H. Zimmerman, BCPS, CACP, Thomas P. Houston, M.D., FAAFP, FACPM, Candice Garwood, Pharm.D., BCPS, Karen Gunning, Pharm.D., BCPS, Carol Southard, R.N., M.S.N., Frank Vitale, M.A., Alan J. Zillich, Pharm.D., Laura B. Hanson, Pharm.D., Daniel A. Hussar, Ph.D., and the American Nurses Association.

The bibliographic citation for this document is as follows: American Society of Health-System Pharmacists. ASHP therapeutic position statement on the cessation of tobacco use. *Am J Health-Syst Pharm.* 2008; 65:2055–72.

ASHP Therapeutic Position Statement on the Institutional Use of 0.9% Sodium Chloride Injection to Maintain Patency of Peripheral Indwelling Intermittent Infusion Devices

Statement of Position

0.9% Sodium chloride injection is a safe and effective indwelling solution for maintaining catheter patency of peripheral indwelling intermittent infusion devices (PIIIDs) in adults and children age one year or older. ASHP supports the use of 0.9% sodium chloride injection in preference to heparin-containing flush solutions (heparin flush) in the institutional setting, on the basis of clinical evidence indicating that 0.9% sodium chloride injection (1) is as effective as heparin flush in maintaining the patency of PIIIDs when blood is not aspirated into the device, (2) is safer to use than heparin flush because of a lower potential for adverse effects, (3) avoids drug incompatibilities associated with heparin flush, and (4) is a cost-effective alternative to heparin flush. Because of limited and conflicting available scientific evidence to date, this recommendation is not applicable to children under the age of one year or patients in the home or other outpatient settings. This document is not applicable to catheters used for central venous or arterial access (including peripherally inserted central catheters and midline catheters) and the maintenance of patency in indwelling venipuncture devices used to obtain blood samples. Further research on PIIID patency in the aforementioned patient populations and settings is warranted.

Background

PIIIDs, often referred to as "saline locks" and frequently and inappropriately called "heparin locks," are used to provide convenient i.v. access in patients who require intermittent i.v. administration of medications without a continuous infusion of i.v. fluids. The advantages of PIIIDs include patient mobility and comfort and reduced fluid load.[1–4] PIIIDs most commonly consist of an intravenously inserted catheter attached to a short external cannula with a resealable injection port that is designed to facilitate multiple needle entries; thus, these devices eliminate the unnecessary trauma of multiple venipunctures.[4] A problem frequently encountered with PIIIDs is the loss of patency because of clot formation within the catheter. To prevent clot formation, catheters are commonly flushed after each administration of i.v. medication and every 8–12 hours when the device is not in use.[5] Because of heparin's anticoagulant effects, diluted solutions of heparin in 0.9% sodium chloride injection (e.g., 10 or 100 units/mL) have traditionally been used to periodically flush and fill these devices and prevent the formation of clots. Diluted heparin solutions are used to maintain patency while avoiding the systemic effects associated with therapeutic doses of heparin.[6]

However, due to the aforementioned concerns regarding heparin administration and the potential for medication dose error, many clinicians preferentially began using sodium chloride for flushes even before evidence was available that supported the use of sodium chloride instead of heparin.

Efficacy

Studies have indicated that 0.9% sodium chloride injection alone is as effective as heparin-containing solutions in maintaining PIIID patency.[7–16] In several randomized, double-blind studies in which PIIIDs composed principally of fluoroethylene propylene (Teflon) were used, 0.9% sodium chloride injection for flushing was associated with patency rates similar to those achieved with flush solutions containing heparin sodium 10 or 100 units/mL.[10–12] The frequency of phlebitis associated with the use of these solutions was also similar.[7,8,17–19] The type of solution used to maintain PIIID patency may not be as important as the positive pressure maintained in the i.v. line by the capped (sealed) injection device, which appears to prevent blood reflux and clot formation in the devices.[8,19] Several studies provide a scientific basis for using heparin flush,[6,20,21] but most published research supports 0.9% sodium chloride injection as an effective alternative to heparin flush in maintaining the patency of PIIIDs. However, 0.9% sodium chloride or heparin flush may not be the appropriate flush solution when flushing drugs that may not be compatible with 0.9% sodium chloride or heparin. Specific examples of such drugs include liposomal amphotericin B, doxorubicin, and i.v. immune globulin.[22] These drugs may need to be "preflushed" with another compatible solution such as 5% dextrose injection before and after administering the incompatible drug. In addition, the size of the i.v. catheter in pediatric patients appears to be a contributing factor in determining success with 0.9% sodium chloride for maintaining the patency of PIIIDs. Evidence supports the use of 0.9% sodium chloride flushes over heparin in pediatric patients,[23–27] and 0.9% sodium chloride injection is the preferred solution mentioned in the available nursing guidelines on infusion standards.[28]

One survey found that in neonates, it was common practice to flush catheter devices with heparin 1–2 units/mL,[29] and the literature supports the use of heparin 0.5 unit/mL added to continuous infusions through peripheral lines.[30] Concentrations of heparinized 0.9% sodium chloride injection 1–10 units/mL for flushing have been studied in neonatal patients, with no significant difference in catheter life or patency between 0.9% sodium chloride injection and heparinized 0.9% sodium chloride injection.[31–33] A limitation of these studies is small sample size, indicating low statistical power. Despite the lack of evidence-based literature supporting the superiority of heparin over 0.9% sodium chloride injection or vice versa for neonatal peripheral i.v. flushes, current guidelines published by the National Association of Neonatal Nurses state that heparinized 0.9% sodium chloride 0.5 unit/mL should be used to flush peripheral i.v. catheters using 0.2–0.5 mL every three to four hours.[34] If using 0.9% sodium chloride injection in pediatric patients, avoid bacteriostatic 0.9% sodium chloride, especially in neonates.

One trial of pregnant women demonstrated significantly increased efficacy and decreased complication rates with heparin-infused catheters compared with those flushed with 0.9% sodium chloride.[35] A subsequent study of pregnant women found no significant differences in the number of patent catheters or in complications with catheters flushed with either heparin or 0.9% sodium chloride.[36] However, the authors from both studies noted that their sample sizes were small and not powered sufficiently to detect a significant difference in patency or complications, possibly affecting the true clinical significance of their results. While published data from pregnant patients are conflicting, common practice is to use 0.9% sodium chloride flushes for peripheral i.v. catheters in this patient population.

Adverse Effects of Heparin Flush

Heparin, even when used in small doses, may elicit adverse reactions in some patients. The potential for bleeding complications increases when patients receive multiple unmonitored heparin flushes.[37] Repeated injections of heparin, even in small doses, can alter activated partial thromboplastin time.[38] Allergic reactions are an inherent risk of using heparin. Although rare, heparin-flush-associated thrombocytopenia and hemorrhage have been reported.[37,39–41] The risks of these adverse effects may be avoided by using 0.9% sodium chloride injection instead of heparin flush. Heparin is incompatible with many anthracyclines, including daunorubicin and doxorubicin, as well as benzodiazepines such as diazepam and midazolam.[22]

Cost Implications

Enhanced quality of patient care should be the primary reason for deciding to use 0.9% sodium chloride injection for flushing. Secondarily, the choice of 0.9% sodium chloride injection may avoid substantial costs associated with drugs, related supplies, and staff time.[9]

Summary

Because current therapeutic evidence supports the efficacy of 0.9% sodium chloride injection in maintaining PIIID patency and due to the inherent risks associated with heparin, ASHP believes that the use of 0.9% sodium chloride injection is appropriate for maintaining the patency of PIIIDs in adults and children age one year or older in institutional settings. Because of limited and conflicting scientific evidence available to date, this recommendation is not applicable to neonates, patients in the home or other outpatient settings, catheters used for central venous or arterial access (including peripherally inserted central catheters and midline catheters), which was beyond the scope of this therapeutic position statement, and the maintenance of patency in indwelling venipuncture devices used to obtain blood samples.

References

1. Millam DA. Intermittent devices. *NITA.* 1981; 4:142–5.
2. Larkin M. Heparin locks. *NITA.* 1979; 2:18–9.
3. Thomas RB, Salter FJ. Heparin locks: their advantages and disadvantages. *Hosp Formul.* 1975; 10:536–8.
4. Deeb EN, Di Mattia PE. How much heparin in the lock? *Am J IV Ther.* 1976; 3:22–6.
5. Tuten SH, Gueldner SH. Efficacy of sodium chloride versus dilute heparin for maintenance of peripheral intermittent intravenous devices. *Appl Nurs Res.* 1991; 2:63–71.
6. Hanson RL, Grant AM, Majors KR. Heparin-lock maintenance with ten units of sodium heparin in one milliliter of normal saline solution. *Surg Gynecol Obstet.* 1976; 142:373–6.
7. Barrett PJ, Lester RL. Heparin versus saline flushing solutions in a small community hospital. *Hosp Pharm.* 1990; 25:115–8.
8. Dunn DL, Lenihan SF. The case for the saline flush. *Am J Nurs.* 1987; 87:798–9.
9. Fry B. Intermittent heparin flushing protocols. A standardization issue. *J Intraven Nurs.* 1992; 15:160–3.
10. Epperson EL. Efficacy of 0.9% sodium chloride injection with and without heparin for maintaining indwelling intermittent injection sites. *Clin Pharm.* 1984; 3:626–9.
11. Garrelts JC, LaRocca J, Ast D, et al. Comparison of heparin and 0.9% sodium chloride injection in the maintenance of indwelling intermittent i.v. devices. *Clin Pharm.* 1989; 8:34–9.
12. Hamilton RA, Plis JM, Clay C, et al. Heparin sodium versus 0.9% sodium chloride injection for maintaining patency of in-dwelling intermittent infusion devices. *Clin Pharm.* 1988; 7:439–43.
13. Shearer J. Normal saline versus dilute heparin flush: a study of peripheral intermittent i.v. devices. *NITA.* 1987; 10:425–7.
14. Miracle V, Fangman B, Kayrouz P, et al. Normal saline vs. heparin lock flush solution: one institution's findings. *Ky Nurse.* 1989; 37(Jul–Aug):1, 6–7.
15. Ashton J, Gibson V, Summers S. Effects of heparin versus saline solution on intermittent infusion device irrigation. *Heart Lung.* 1990; 19:608–12.
16. Hook ML, Ose P. Heparin vs. normal saline. *J Intraven Nurs.* 1990; 13:150–1. Letter.
17. Garrelts JC. White clot syndrome and thrombocytopenia: reasons to abandon heparin i.v. lock flush solution. *Clin Pharm.* 1992; 11:797–9.
18. Weber DR. Is heparin really necessary in the lock and, if so, how much? *DICP.* 1991; 25:399–407.
19. Goode CJ, Titler M, Rakel B, et al. A meta-analysis of effects of heparin flush and saline flush: quality and cost implications. *Nurs 2Res.* 1991; 40:324–30.
20. Cyganski JM, Donahue JM, Heaton JS. The case for the heparin flush. *Am J Nurs.* 1987; 87:796–7.
21. Holford NH, Vozeh S, Coates P, et al. More on heparin lock. *N Engl J Med.* 1977; 296:1300–1. Letter.
22. Trissel LA. Handbook on injectable drugs. 16th ed. Bethesda, MD: American Society of Health-System Pharmacists; 2011.

23. Mok E, Kwong TK, Chan MF. A randomized controlled trial for maintaining peripheral intravenous lock in children. *Int J Nurs Pract.* 2007; 13:33–45.
24. Hanrahan KS, Kleiber C, Fagan CL. Evaluation of saline for iv locks in children. *Pediatr Nurs.* 1994; 20:549–52.
25. Kleiber C, Hanrahan K, Fagan CL, et al. Heparin vs saline for peripheral i.v. locks in children. *Pediatr Nurs.* 1993; 19:405–9.
26. Danek G, Noris EM. Pediatric iv catheters: efficacy of saline flush. *Pediatr Nurs.* 1992; 18:111–3.
27. LeDuc K. Efficacy of normal saline solution versus heparin solution for maintaining patency of peripheral intravenous catheters in children. *J Emerg Nurs.* 1997; 23:306–9.
28. Intravenous Nurses Society. Infusion nursing standards of practice. *J Infus Nurs.* 2011; 34:37–72.
29. Romanowski GL, Zenk KE. Intravenous flush solutions for neonates. Paper presented at ASHP Midyear Clinical Meeting. New Orleans, LA; 1991 Dec 10.
30. Klenner AF, Fusch C, Rakow A, et al. Benefit and risk of heparin for maintaining peripheral venous catheters in neonates: a placebo-controlled trial. *J Pediatr.* 2003; 143:741–5.
31. Shah PS, Ng E, Sinha AK. Heparin for prolonging peripheral intravenous catheter use in neonates. *Cochrane Database Syst Rev.* 2005; 4:CD002774.
32. Goldberg M, Sankaran R, Givelichan L, et al. Maintaining patency of peripheral intermittent infusion devices with heparinized saline and saline. *Neonatal Intensive Care.* 1999; 12:18–22.
33. Heilskov J. A randomized trial of heparin and saline for maintaining intravenous locks in neonates. *J Soc Pediatr Nurs.* 1998; 3:111–6.
34. Altimier L, Brown B, Tedeschi L. NANN guidelines for neonatal nursing policies, procedures, competencies, and clinical pathways. 4th ed. Glenview, IL: National Association of Neonatal Nurses; 2006.
35. Meyer BA, Little CJ, Thorp JA, et al. Heparin versus normal saline as a peripheral line flush in maintenance of intermittent intravenous lines in obstetric patients. *Obstet Gynecol.* 1995; 85:433–6.
36. Niesen KM, Harris DY, Parkin LS, et al. The effects of heparin versus normal saline for maintenance of peripheral intravenous locks in pregnant women. *J Obstet Gynecol Neonatal Nurs.* 2003; 32:503–8.
37. Passannante A, Macik BG. The heparin flush syndrome: a cause of iatrogenic hemorrhage. *Am J Med Sci.* 1988; 296:71–3.
38. Heparin sodium monograph. In: McEvoy GK, ed. *AHFS Drug Information.* Bethesda, MD: American Society of Health-System Pharmacists; 2006:2616.
39. Heeger PS, Backstrom JT. Heparin flushes and thrombocytopenia. *Ann Intern Med.* 1986; 105:143. Letter.
40. Doty JR, Alving BM, McDonnell DE, et al. Heparin-associated thrombocytopenia in the neurosurgical patient. *Neurosurgery.* 1986; 19:69–72.
41. Cines DB, Tomaski A, Tannenbaum S. Immune endothelial-cell injury in heparin-associated thrombocytopenia. *N Engl J Med.* 1987; 316:581–9.

Approved by the ASHP Board of Directors on April 13, 2012. Developed through the Council on Therapeutics.

This document supersedes the ASHP therapeutic position statement on the institutional use of 0.9% sodium chloride injection to maintain patency of peripheral indwelling intermittent infusion devices approved by the ASHP Board of Directors on January 12, 2006.

Kim W. Benner, Pharm.D., BCPS, FASHP, and Amber J. Lucas, Pharm.D., BCPS, FASHP, are gratefully acknowledged for authoring this document.

The bibliographic citation for this document is as follows: American Society of Health-System Pharmacists. ASHP therapeutic position statement on the institutional use of 0.9% sodium chloride injection to maintain patency of peripheral indwelling intermittent infusion devices. *Am J Health-Syst Pharm.* 2012; 69:1252–4.

ASHP Therapeutic Position Statement on the Role of Pharmacotherapy in Preventing Venous Thromboembolism in Hospitalized Patients

Position

Hospitals should develop formal policies, guidelines, practices, and procedures to address the appropriate prevention of venous thromboembolism (VTE). In addition, all hospitalized patients should be assessed for risk for both VTE and bleeding to determine if pharmacologic, mechanical, or combination VTE prophylaxis should be initiated. Patients should also be reassessed following any pertinent clinical changes. In at-risk patients without contraindications (i.e., risk for bleeding, active bleeding, or allergy), pharmacologic thromboprophylaxis should be initiated as soon as possible and within the first 24 hours of arrival at the hospital. Mechanical methods should be used when pharmacologic prophylaxis is contraindicated. Active interdisciplinary, multifaceted VTE prevention programs, in contrast to passive strategies, should be used to improve appropriate VTE prophylaxis within hospitals. These programs should incorporate provider, staff, and patient education; audits and feedback; hospital guidelines and policies; clinical decision-support software; monitoring for appropriate anticoagulant use; and provider reminders. Guidelines and policies need to be individualized at the hospital level, depending on the degree to which pharmacy, providers, nursing, and other staff are involved. The National Quality Forum (NQF) and the Joint Commission recommend creating policies and guidelines regarding anticoagulation. This is also a key recommendation of the American College of Chest Physicians (ACCP). Pharmacy professionals should actively participate in the development, implementation, and monitoring of anticoagulation and VTE prophylaxis programs. In addition, because pharmacologic prophylaxis is the primary method to prevent VTE, pharmacy professionals should take a leadership role in these hospital programs.

Background

Burden of Disease and Pharmacologic Prophylaxis. VTE comprises pulmonary embolism (PE) and deep vein thrombosis (DVT). Despite a wealth of information regarding the mortality and morbidity associated with VTE, hospitals worldwide continue to do poorly at preventing VTE events for at-risk patients. Between 60,000[1] and 300,000[2] deaths occur annually in the United States from PE, and as many as 200,000 of those deaths occur in U.S. hospitals.[3] Approximately 70% of fatal PEs are first detected postmortem.[4,5] Furthermore, up to 2,000,000 new DVTs occur annually within the United States.[1] VTE occurs in approximately 64.4% of surgical patients and 41.5% of medical patients.[6] PE is the most preventable cause of death among all causes for patients; therefore, VTE prevention is the best strategy for improving patient safety in U.S. hospitals.[7,8] In the absence of thromboprophylaxis, 1 in 10 hospital deaths is attributed to PE.[9] Recurrent VTE occurs in 7% of patients at six months,[10] increasing to up to 30% at 8–10 years[11,12] for patients despite treatment for the initial VTE. The risk of developing VTE rises sharply when the number of risk factors increases.[13] At 1 year after the initial VTE, the mortality rates associated with PE and DVT are particularly high in patients older than 65 years (39% and 21%, respectively).[14] The risk of recurrent VTE continues for up to 90 days after hospitalization.[15,16]

Approximately 60% of VTE events[17] and 75% of autopsy-confirmed fatal PE[18–21] occur in nonsurgical patients. More importantly, PE and proximal DVT are occurring more frequently in medical patients than in surgical patients.[22] This increase may be partially attributable to medical patients having historically lower rates of thromboprophylaxis compared with surgical patients. In addition, VTE prophylaxis for surgical patients has been studied for approximately 50 years, whereas well-designed studies for medical patients began surfacing in the mid-1990s. In placebo-controlled studies, VTE events have been reduced by 50–65% in acutely ill patients when prophylaxis was used.[23–25] Examples of avoided morbidity associated with VTE are recurrent VTE, postthrombotic syndrome (PTS), congestive heart failure, and pulmonary hypertension. PTS is the term used to describe signs and symptoms that may occur as a long-term complication of DVT and includes swelling, pain, edema, venous ectasia, and skin induration of the affected limb.[26] In severe PTS, patients may have painful, intractable leg ulcers, which decrease mobility and require additional medical care.[26] PTS is associated with an annualized cost as high as $11,667[27] and can lead to loss of quality of life and functional status. After a symptomatic DVT, the overall incidence of PTS is 20–50%, and severe PTS occurs in 5–10% of patients.[28] Within 2 years after the development of PE, chronic thromboembolic pulmonary hypertension occurs in approximately 3.8% of patients.[29] Results from clinical trials have shown that when pharmacologic prophylaxis is administered at appropriate doses and durations in medical patients, the breakthrough occurrence of VTE is clinically uncommon (2.8–5.6%).[23–25] The use of thromboprophylaxis has been shown to reduce mortality in both primary studies and meta-analyses.[25,30,31] This position statement focuses on key issues and guideline recommendations for the prevention of VTE in hospitalized patients augmented by health-system pharmacists.

Current Hospital Performance and Barriers. Globally, 41.5% of surgical patients and 60.5% of medical patients at risk for VTE do not receive appropriate prophylaxis therapy.[6] The concept of "appropriate VTE prophylaxis" has recently emerged and denotes appropriate drug, dose, and duration of therapy. Recent studies have demonstrated appropriate prophylaxis rates of only 13–33% in hundreds of U.S. hospitals.[32–35]

Barriers to VTE prophylaxis include concerns about bleeding complications; underestimation of the VTE risk; gaps in provider knowledge of VTE prevention; lack of knowledge regarding recommendations and standards; heterogeneous patient populations; perceived difficulties in risk assessment; lack of familiarity, agreement, or confidence with guidelines; belief that implementing guidelines is ineffective in improving outcomes; resistance to changing established practice patterns; need for approval and funding to implement guidelines; and lack of clarity and ease of use of guidelines.[36–38]

National Impact and Readmissions. Currently, VTE has an estimated financial burden of $13.5 billion–$69.3 billion per year in the United States, with $4.5 billion–$39.3 billion of this being preventable with pharmacist-driven or other VTE prevention programs.[39,40] Because of the gravity of the problem and poor performance of U.S. hospitals, many of the leading U.S. organizations began to prioritize VTE as a top initiative for improvement within the last decade. Some of these organizations include NQF, the Agency for Healthcare Research and Quality, the Institute for Healthcare Improvement, the Joint Commission, the Centers for Disease Control and Prevention (CDC), and the Centers for Medicaid and Medicare Services (CMS).[41]

Interestingly, a 2007 study found that approximately 5.3% of patients previously hospitalized for a DVT or PE are readmitted within one year for VTE.[42] A clear trend of hospital readmission occurred within the first 30 days of the initial event for these patients, with 27.1% readmitted for a DVT and 44.3% readmitted for a PE.[42]

Guidelines and Quality Measures

Many national and international guidelines exist for appropriate, evidence-based treatment of VTE prophylaxis. These include the ACCP guidelines, which were last updated in 2012,[43–45] and the International Union of Angiology guidelines from June 2006.[46] Oncology-specific guidelines, such as those created by the American Society of Clinical Oncology (ASCO)[47] and the National Comprehensive Cancer Network (NCCN),[48] are also available and are very specific about contraindications for prophylaxis, which is helpful to the practicing clinician. ASCO and NCCN guidelines were updated in 2007 and 2011, respectively.

Both the Joint Commission and CMS have initiated quality measures to promote VTE prophylaxis in hospitalized patients. In 2008, the Joint Commission implemented a National Patient Safety Goal that focuses on anticoagulation management in the hospital setting for both medical and surgical patients.[49] CMS also added DVT and PE after total knee replacement (TKR) or total hip replacement (THR) procedures to a list of conditions whose associated costs will not be reimbursed if acquired during a hospital stay.[50] The Joint Commission collaborated with NQF on the development of these measures to promote VTE prophylaxis, which were piloted in U.S. hospitals and then endorsed by NQF in 2008.[51] In October 2009, the Joint Commission made available a core measure set for VTE (Table 1), focusing on prophylaxis, treatment, and one outcome measure of "preventable" VTE.[52] Hospitals may choose this VTE core measure set as one of four required core measure sets on which to report.[52] However, because these measures alone do not give detailed recommendations on VTE prophylaxis, hospitals should base their guidelines, policies, practices, and recommendations on the most recent edition of the ACCP guidelines. At this time, only 60 of approximately 5000 acute care hospitals are reporting on the VTE core measure set. Therefore, hospitals should also adopt the Joint Commission's VTE measure set for core measure reporting to aid in improving patient care and reduce health care costs.

Mechanical Methods of Prophylaxis in Hospitalized Patients. While the focus of this manuscript is pharmacologic prophylaxis, pharmacists should familiarize themselves with mechanical methods of prophylaxis to make appropriate recommendations for patients when a pharmacologic contraindication exists. Mechanical methods of prophylaxis may be dynamic, static, or a combination of the two. Dynamic methods include intermittent pneumatic compression (IPC) devices, sequential compression devices, and venous foot pumps. Static methods include graduated compression stockings, elastic stockings, and thromboembolic deterrent hose. Mechanical methods of prophylaxis have been shown to only reduce the rates of DVT, not PE or death, in contrast with pharmacologic prophylaxis.[8] A 2005 meta-analysis of IPC device use in surgical patients found a 60% risk reduction in DVT with no substantial reduction in PE risk, compared with no prophylaxis ($p < 0.001$).[53,54]

Inferior vena cava filters (IVCFs) are an alternative static method of mechanical prophylaxis. To date, IVCFs have been shown to reduce recurrent PE at the expense of an increased risk of DVT in the absence of anticoagulation.[55] Hospitals should use IVCFs for patients with confirmed proximal DVT who have an absolute contraindication to full-dose anticoagulation (e.g., patients with active bleeding) or who have not responded to standard anticoagulant regi-

Table 1.

The Joint Commission Venous Thromboembolism (VTE) National Hospital Inpatient Quality Measures[a]

Set Measure ID #	Measure Short Name
VTE-1	Venous thromboembolism prophylaxis
VTE-2	Intensive care unit venous thromboembolism prophylaxis
VTE-3	Venous thromboembolism patients with anticoagulant overlap therapy
VTE-4	Venous thromboembolism patients receiving unfractionated heparin therapy with dosages/platelet count monitoring by protocol
VTE-5	Venous thromboembolism discharge instructions
VTE-6	Incidence of potentially preventable venous thromboembolism

[a]Reprinted from the *Specifications Manual for National Hospital Inpatient Quality Measures,* version 4.1, March 2012, a collaborative work of the Centers for Medicare and Medicaid Services and the Joint Commission. This manual is periodically updated, and users of the manual must update their software and associated documentation based on the published manual production timelines.

mens (e.g., patients who developed recurrent thromboembolism despite full-dose anticoagulant therapy) or in high-risk patients who have major surgery planned in the very near future. Once the absolute contraindication to anticoagulation subsides or the major surgery is completed, treatment with an appropriate anticoagulant should be initiated or resumed, depending on the clinical scenario.[8]

The health care team should ensure patients' compliance with mechanical methods of VTE prophylaxis throughout their hospitalization, as compliance is the most important determinant of efficacy.[56] Most devices used for mechanical VTE prophylaxis should be used for a minimum of 20 hours per day to be effective. Because of these compliance issues, hospitals and physicians should attempt to use mobile, battery-powered IPC devices that have the ability to record and report the hours the devices are used.[8,43–45] Mechanical methods of prophylaxis should be reserved for patients who are actively bleeding or at high risk for bleeding, with inclusion of such documentation in the patient record, or possibly as an adjunct to pharmacologic methods of prophylaxis.[8] Studies have demonstrated greater reductions in VTE rates among certain groups of patients (i.e., trauma patients, patients with spinal cord injury, and high-risk patients undergoing TKR, THR, hip fracture surgery, neurosurgery, and elective spine surgery) receiving combination pharmacologic and mechanical VTE prophylaxis compared with pharmacologic prophylaxis alone.[8]

Health-system pharmacists should evaluate patients for potential contraindications to anticoagulation therapies. They should also familiarize themselves with the specific mechanical methods available at their institution, which could be used in patients with such contraindications.

Risk Stratification and Identification

Most hospitalized patients have at least one risk factor for VTE, and approximately 40% have multiple risk factors.[8] Common risk factors for VTE are listed in Table 2, and DVT rates among various patient groups are presented in Table 3.[57] Most critically ill patients have multiple risk factors for VTE. Risk factors that may precede admission to a critical care unit may include trauma, active infection (e.g., sepsis), recent surgery, active malignancy, stroke, advanced age, congestive heart failure, respiratory failure, history of VTE, and pregnancy. In addition, patients admitted to critical care units have an increased risk of developing VTE due to immobilization, placement of central venous lines, sepsis, pharmacologic paralysis, mechanical ventilation, vasopressor use, and the need for surgical procedures and dialysis.[8,58]

PE is the second most common cause of death in patients with cancer.[8] Patients with hematologic malignancies, lung cancer, and gastrointestinal cancer have the highest rates of VTE. Within the first three months after being diagnosed with cancer, patients have an approximate 50-fold increased risk of developing a VTE compared with patients with no cancer.[59] Even during therapeutic anticoagulation after a VTE, fatal PE outnumbers fatal bleeding events in an approximate 3:1 ratio.[60] Certain cancer treatments, including chemotherapy, hormonal manipulation, erythropoiesis, and the presence of a central venous catheter, are also risk factors for VTE.[8] Chemotherapy is associated with an approximate sixfold increased risk of VTE,[61–63] with specific drugs contributing to higher VTE rates, including tamoxifen, anastrozole, letrozole, exemestane, bevacizumab, thalidomide, and lenalidomide.[64–73] Tamoxifen is associated with a higher rate

Table 2.

Venous Thromboembolism (VTE) Risk Factors[8,57]

Risk Factor Category	Risk Factors
Common general risk factors	Previous VTE; surgery; trauma; thrombophilia; obesity (body mass index of >25 kg/m^2); acute hospitalization for medical illness; immobility or lower-extremity paresis; active or occult malignancy; cancer therapy, such as radiotherapy, hormonal therapy, chemotherapy, or angiogenesis inhibitors; venous compression from sources such as tumor, hematoma, or arterial abnormality; increasing age; pregnancy and the postpartum period; estrogen-containing oral contraceptives or hormone- replacement therapy; selective estrogen-receptor modulators; erythropoiesis-stimulating agents; inflammatory bowel disease; nephrotic syndrome; myeloproliferative disorders; paroxysmal nocturnal hemoglobinuria; central venous catheterization
Specific medical risk factors	
High risk	History of deep venous thrombosis or pulmonary embolism, family history of thrombosis, acute infection, active malignancy, age >75 yr, stroke, myocardial infarction, congestive heart failure, prolonged immobility (≥4 days), pregnancy or postpartum period, acute or chronic lung disease, acute inflammatory disease, inflammatory bowel disease, shock
Probable risk	High-dose estrogen therapy, obesity (body mass index of >25 kg/m^2), varicose veins, heparin-induced thrombocytopenia, congenital or acquired thrombophilia, antithrombin deficiency, positive lupus anticoagulant, antiphospholipid antibodies, protein S or C deficiency, positive factor V Leiden, elevated anticardiolipin antibodies, positive prothrombin gene mutation 20210A
Possible risk	Paraproteinemia, Behçet's disease, disorders of plasminogen and plasminogen activation, nephrotic syndrome, polycythemia, elevated serum homocysteine levels, dysfibrinogenemia, myeloproliferative disorders, age ≥ 41 yr, sepsis (<1 mo)

Table 3.

Frequency of DVT Associated with Various Patients Groups and Conditions in the Absence of Prophylaxis[8,57,a]

Patient Group or Condition	Frequency of DVT, %
General medical patients	10–26
Myocardial infarction	17–34
Stroke	11–75
Congestive heart failure	20–40
Medical intensive care	25–42
Critical care patients	10–80
General surgical patients	15–40
Major gynecological surgery	15–40
Major urologic surgery	15–40
Neurosurgery	15–40
Major orthopedic surgery of the hip or knee[b]	40–60
Trauma	40–80
Spinal cord injury	60–80

[a]DVT = deep venous thrombosis.
[b]Total knee or hip replacement or hip fracture surgery.

of VTE than the aromatase inhibitors anastrozole, letrozole, and exemestane.[74–77]

Furthermore, surgical patients with cancer have at least twice the risk of developing a postoperative DVT and three times the risk of developing a fatal PE as compared with patients with no cancer undergoing the same surgeries.[8] VTE recurrence rates are high both during anticoagulation and after anticoagulation has been discontinued.[78–81] Patients with cancer who develop a VTE have a substantial reduction in survival compared with cancer patients who do not develop a VTE.[82-84]

Research into other risk factors for VTE continues,[85–87] though validation of these risk factors will be needed. Risk-assessment models (RAMs) have been developed for the hospitalized patient and have proved useful in identifying patients at risk for VTE and bleeding.[8] The health-system pharmacist should take initiative and lead the collaborative implementation of RAMs within the hospital.

Several methods of risk assessment to reduce hospital-acquired VTE exist. Some methods may use one process or form for all patients being evaluated, while others may use specific processes or forms for specific patient groups. Both methods can be computerized (i.e., using electronic alerts) or completed manually. RAMs could also be based on a scoring system (i.e., positive points for specific risk factors and negative points for contraindications) or they could assess risk factors by patient groups based on guideline recommendations.[8]

Several RAMs have been proposed for hospitalized patients, incorporating both predisposing and exposing risk factors (e.g., major surgery, acute medical illness).[88–92] For example, Caprini et al.[88] developed a RAM for both hospitalized surgical and medical patients, with the surgical RAM being validated in 2009,[90] and Cohen et al.[90] developed an algorithm-based RAM for medical patients. Another recent, predictive, evidence-based, weighted-risk scoring system was developed from the large International Medical Prevention Registry on Venous Thromboembolism (IMPROVE) database for medical patients.[92] The risk scores were derived from the hazard ratios of seven independent clinical risk factors for VTE. The Padua prediction score is another RAM that uses 11 risk factors to determine VTE risk in the medical patient and categorizes a patient's VTE risk as low or high.[93] For all patients, the risk of bleeding should be determined using a group-appropriate RAM or guideline-delineated risk factors. A clear advantage of the IMPROVE RAM is that its derivation is evidence based, whereas the Padua prediction score is not.[91] Collectively, these RAMs further validate the concept of weighted scoring, demonstrating that all VTE risk factors are not equally associated with VTE risk.

Because risk factors are not weighted equally, clinicians should carefully examine risk factors to determine the individual care needed for each patient. Furthermore, efforts should be made to maximize the number of risk factors assessed with the RAM, as this will capture a greater number of patients at risk for VTE and maximize the sensitivity of the model.[94]

Although a review of all risk-assessment programs to reduce VTE is beyond the scope of this position statement, several reviews reiterate key characteristics that are essential to such programs.[94–97] Risk-assessment programs should be multifaceted, and those involved in such programs should provide active interventions instead of merely handing out guidelines or placing incomplete risk-assessment forms in patient charts. These programs should also educate and remind health care providers about the need for VTE prophylaxis, educate patients, use audit and feedback for the program itself and for individuals ignoring alerts (i.e., alert fatigue), monitor for inappropriate use of thromboprophylaxis, and use clinical decision-support software, either electronically or manually.

Pharmacist-driven VTE programs have helped improve the care received by hospitalized patients.[39,98–102] The implementation of one such program led to a significant increase in appropriate type, dose, and duration of prophylaxis while also significantly reducing "preventable" VTE events (relative risk reduction = 74%, $p = 0.0006$).[39] Another pharmacist-driven program significantly increased optimal VTE prophylaxis among hospitalized nonsurgical patients from 11% to 44% ($p<0.001$). The program consisted of presentations, newsletters, and VTE prophylaxis recommendations made during clinical pharmacy rounds.[98] In addition, a multidisciplinary program that included pharmacists in the surgical intensive care unit achieved substantial reductions in both hospital-acquired and preventable VTE.[103] Lastly, the use of a simple, nonscoring, three-tiered (low, moderate, or high) VTE RAM led to an 86% reduction in preventable hospital-acquired VTE over three years.[104] This RAM was modular and embedded into computerized provider-order-entry (CPOE) order sets but was not a pharmacist-driven program.

Efficacy of Antithrombotic Prophylaxis and Recommendations

Heparins and Fondaparinux. Three prospective, randomized, placebo-controlled studies have been conducted to evaluate the efficacy of low-molecular-weight heparins (LMWHs) and fondaparinux for VTE prophylaxis in medical patients. These include the MEDENOX[23] (enoxaparin), PREVENT[24] (dalteparin), and ARTEMIS[25] (fondaparinux) trials. The number needed to treat to avoid a VTE ranged from 11 to 45 in these studies. Major bleeding rates were 1.7%, 0.49%, and 0.2% in the MEDENOX, PREVENT, and ARTEMIS trials, respectively. The three studies demonstrated significant relative risk reductions of 63%, 55%, and 49.5% for VTE, respectively, with no significant differences in major bleeding rates. In the United States, enoxaparin and dalteparin have Food and Drug Administration (FDA)-approved indications for VTE prophylaxis in acutely ill medical patients; fondaparinux does not. Fondaparinux does carry this indication in certain European Union countries. In the recent PROTECT trial, investigators randomized critical care patients to dalteparin 5000 units daily or unfractionated heparin (UFH) 5000 units twice daily and found no significant difference in the rate of proximal DVT, major bleeding, or inhospital death. However, there was a significant reduction in the occurrence of PE with dalteparin as compared with UFH.[105]

According to a recent systematic review conducted by the American College of Physicians (ACP), the use of heparin in medical patients to prevent VTE decreases the rate of pulmonary embolism but does not decrease mortality and leads to more bleeding complications.[106,107] No differences in risks or benefits were found between the types of heparin used, though there was a nonsignificant difference favoring LMWH over UFH for PE (odds ratio, 0.67; confidence interval [CI], 0.45–1.00; $p = 0.053$; $I^2 = 0\%$). The use of mechanical devices led to adverse outcomes and did not demonstrate any benefit. Therefore, in medical and stroke patients, ACP currently recommends assessing the risks of VTE and bleeding before starting VTE prevention and only using pharmacologic prophylaxis if the risk of VTE is greater than the risk of bleeding. In addition, ACP recommends against using mechanical devices to prevent VTE.[106–108] These recommendations are similar to those of ACCP, which recommends an LMWH, a UFH two or three times daily, or fondaparinux for patients not at risk of bleeding but at risk of VTE. However, ACCP does recommend mechanical means of prophylaxis, such as IPC devices and graduated compression stockings for patients at risk of bleeding and VTE. ACCP analyses did not note any substantial difference in bleeding, VTE, or heparin-induced thrombocytopenia between UFH two and three times daily.[43] Because ACCP guidelines are in their ninth edition and ACP guidelines are newly released, we recommend using ACCP guidelines. Key guideline recommendations for the medical patient are listed in Table 4.

Warfarin versus LMWHs and Fondaparinux. Because of its slow onset of action, variable responses among patients, drug–drug and drug–food interactions, lower efficacy compared with LMWHs, need for frequent monitoring, and complexity of both inhospital and postdischarge supervision, warfarin has largely been abandoned as thromboprophylaxis in Europe. Similarly, the ACCP guidelines concluded that LMWHs, and likely fondaparinux by indirect comparison, are more effective than warfarin in preventing inhospital VTE and should be preferred.[8] Health-system pharmacists should continue to educate themselves on emerging evidence on the use of thromboprophylactic agents. They should also familiarize themselves with the risks, benefits, and duration of use in relation to transitions among levels of care.

Optimal Duration for Thromboprophylaxis

With the average length of stay in U.S. hospitals being approximately 5 days,[109] the recommended duration of prophylaxis in studies and within drug labeling is often not reached. Studies have suggested that the inappropriate duration of therapy is a major cause for failure to receive appropriate thromboprophylaxis among hospitalized patients.[15,33] ACCP guidelines advocate extended thromboprophylaxis of up to 35 days with an LMWH in patients undergoing major orthopedic surgery (especially hip fracture repair and hip replacement) and up to 28 days in patients with active cancer undergoing surgery for their cancer.[8] Recent results from the EXCLAIM study suggest that there is a high-risk subgroup of hospitalized medical patients (namely, women, patients with advanced age, or patients with complete immobility) who may benefit from extended outpatient thromboprophylaxis.[110] Results from two recent trials evaluating the use of rivaroxaban and apixaban in VTE prophylaxis did not demonstrate additional benefits with either drug when used for approximately one month.[111,112] Further studies are needed to determine whether the use of thromboprophylaxis for the duration recommended in the drug labeling is safe and improves outcomes in medical patients. The VTE Discharge Alert Trial is currently assessing if a human alert to physicians within 48 hours of planned patient discharge has any effect on increasing postdischarge prophylaxis or reducing VTE within 90 days of hospital admission in the medical patient. Major bleeding events within 30 days of hospital admission are also being monitored.[113] At a minimum, for the majority of at-risk patients, the optimal duration of prophylaxis is the length of the hospital stay if exposing risk factors are still present while considering the primary diagnosis and predisposing risk factors. Importantly, no studies evaluating the impact of ambulation on VTE have been conducted. A recent study found that despite timely ambulation, medical patients were still at risk of VTE, and this risk was substantially reduced with enoxaparin prophylaxis.[114] Therefore, patient ambulation or mobility should not be used as a reason to discontinue, or restrict, prophylaxis during hospitalization. Currently, ACCP guidelines recommend against extending the duration of thromboprophylaxis beyond the hospital stay or period of patient immobilization in the medical patient.[43]

Safety of Antithrombotic Prophylaxis

One of the major adverse events that can occur with the use of heparin is heparin-induced thrombocytopenia (HIT). HIT is an antibody-mediated adverse effect of heparin that is strongly associated with venous and arterial thrombosis. HIT is diagnosed when any of the following events occurs in association with the presence of HIT antibodies: an otherwise unexplained decrease in platelet count, venous or arterial thrombosis, skin lesions at heparin injection sites, and acute systemic reactions (fever or chills, tachycardia, hypertension, dyspnea, cardiopulmonary arrest) that occur after i.v. heparin bolus administration.[115] Although HIT can occur with a prophylactic dose of both LMWH and UFH, it happens about threefold more frequently with UFH than with LMWH and incurs approximately $41,133 of additional costs per case.[116,117] Because the occurrence of HIT

Table 4.

Existing Guideline Recommendations for Thromboprophylaxis of Hospitalized Medical and Critical Care Patients[a]

Group and Recommendations	Modality and Grade of Recommendation(s)
American College of Chest Physicians (2012)	
Acutely ill hospitalized medical patients at low risk of thrombosis: Do not use pharmacologic prophylaxis or mechanical prophylaxis.	No thromboprophylaxis
Acutely ill hospitalized medical patients at increased risk of thrombosis: Provide anticoagulant thromboprophylaxis with LMWH, low-dose UFH twice or three times daily, or fondaparinux and suggests against extending the duration of thromboprophylaxis beyond the period of patient immobilization or acute hospital stay.	Grade 1B[b]
Acutely ill hospitalized medical patients at increased risk of thrombosis who are bleeding or are at high risk for major bleeding: Use mechanical thromboprophylaxis using GCSs or IPC.	Grade 2C
Critically ill patients: Use LMWH or low-dose UFH for thromboprophylaxis.	Grade 2C
Critically ill patients who are bleeding or are at high risk for major bleeding: Use mechanical thromboprophylaxis with GCSs and/or IPC at least until the bleeding risk decreases.	Grade 2C
American College of Physicians (2011)	
Recommends assessment of the risk for thromboembolism and bleeding in medical (including stroke) patients before initiation of prophylaxis of VTE	Grade: strong recommendation; moderate-quality evidence
Recommends pharmacologic prophylaxis with heparin or a related drug for VTE in medical (including stroke) patients unless the assessed risk for bleeding outweighs the likely benefits	Grade: strong recommendation; moderate-quality evidence
Recommends against the use of mechanical prophylaxis with GCSs for prevention of VTE	Grade: strong recommendation; moderate-quality evidence
Policy implication: The American College of Physicians does not support the application of performance measures in medical (including stroke) patients that promote universal VTE prophylaxis regardless of risk.	
International Union of Angiology (2006)	
Acutely ill medical patients (patients older than 40 years with acute medical illness and/or reduced mobility with one of the following morbidities: acute heart failure NYHA class III/IV, respiratory disease [respiratory failure with or without ventilation or exacerbation of respiratory disease], active cancer requiring therapy, acute infective disease including severe infection and sepsis, rheumatic disease, ischemic stroke, or acute myocardial infarction) should be considered for prophylaxis. Patients with acute medical illness with reduced mobility and one of the following risk factors—history of VTE, malignant disease, or older than 75 years—should also be considered for prophylaxis.	UFH 5000 units three times daily (grade A), enoxaparin 40 mg once daily (grade A), dalteparin 5000 units once daily (grade A), fondaparinux 2.5 mg once daily (grade B)
National Comprehensive Cancer Network (2011) Cancer patients	LMWH, UFH 5000 units three times daily
American Society of Clinical Oncology (2007) Hospitalized medical patients	LMWH, UFH 5000 units three times daily

[a]LMWH = low-molecular-weight heparin, UFH = unfractionated heparin, GCSs = graduated compression stockings, IPC = intermittent pneumatic compression, NYHA = New York Heart Association, VTE = venous thromboembolism.

[b]Fondaparinux is not approved by the Food and Drug Administration for medical prophylaxis in the United States.

is more frequent with UFH, overall costs are likely reduced by using LMWH over UFH. Taking into consideration that HIT may be a serious, limb-threatening and life-threatening complication, LMWH may be favored over UFH. Only a limited number of case reports of fondaparinux-induced thrombocytopenia have been reported, and this may be an advantage of fondaparinux over LMWH and UFH. The new oral agents will likely also have an advantage over UFH and LMWH with regard to HIT and may be a useful alternative in patients with a history of HIT.

Major and minor bleeding can also occur with the use of prophylactic LMWH, warfarin, fondaparinux, and UFH. Overall, pharmacologic means of VTE prophylaxis carry a slightly higher risk of bleeding than placebo or mechanical means, but major bleeding rates are negligible with prophylactic doses in well-controlled clinical trials.[23–25,118–121] In studies evaluating the safety and efficacy of VTE prophylaxis in medical and surgical patients, the rate of major bleeding was between 0.2% and 2.7% among patients given pharmacologic prophylaxis.

One recent meta-analysis in medical patients demonstrated no difference in major bleeding between pharmacologic prophylaxis and placebo and also showed a reduction in fatal PE with pharmacologic prophylaxis versus placebo.[122] Another meta-analysis concluded that the use of UFH was associated with substantially higher rates of major bleeding than LMWH.[123] A meta-analysis and two primary studies have also demonstrated lower rates of injection-site hematoma with LMWH than UFH.[124,125] Bleeding rates with fondaparinux appear comparable to those with LMWHs for both the medical and surgical patient.[40,116]

Patient groups at high risk for bleeding include those with serious comorbid diseases, especially active malignancy or cerebrovascular, kidney, heart, and liver disease; older patients; those receiving concurrent antithrombotic medications, including antiplatelets and fibrinolytics; patients with thrombocytopenia (<100,000 mm^3), a hemoglobin concentration of <13 g/dL (in surgical patients), severe renal insufficiency (creatinine clearance [CLcr] of <30 mL/min), active or recent peptic ulcer disease, recent gastrointestinal or major bleeding, uncontrolled arterial hypertension (systolic blood pressure of >200 mm Hg, diastolic blood pressure of >120 mm Hg, or both), or bacterial endocarditis; and those who have undergone spinal tap or epidural anesthesia within 12 hours.[43–45,126]

A bleeding RAM from the IMPROVE registry was developed and can be accessed at http://omnifik.com/dev/improve/bleeding/.[127] Risk factors for bleeding continue to be discovered and are individualized by patient group. Contraindications to VTE prophylaxis should be agreed on at the institution and pharmacy levels.

The overall avoidance of a substantial number of VTE events and their subsequent morbidity is what makes VTE prophylaxis so persuasive and important. A recent review concluded that mortality rates associated with PE were substantially higher than those associated with major bleeding from the use of anticoagulants, further supporting the focus on the prevention of the initial PE.[128] The initial cost of prophylaxis reduces overall costs by avoiding VTE and its associated morbidity. By and large, there is strong evidence that appropriately dosed thromboprophylaxis has an advantageous and favorable risk:benefit ratio.[8,46]

Recommendations

Most hospitalized patients have multiple risk factors for VTE. Patients at high risk include those in critical care, as well as burn, trauma, surgical, and cancer patients. All hospitalized patients, including patients in critical care or with burns, should be assessed for the risk of VTE using a RAM. Importantly, patients should be reassessed every 24–48 hours, or with pertinent clinical changes, for new or resolved VTE, bleeding risk factors, and contraindications to prophylaxis. According to these risks, patients should be given an LMWH, a UFH, or fondaparinux prophylactically. However, if there is a contraindication to pharmacologic prophylaxis (e.g., active bleeding, high risk of bleeding, allergy [including HIT within 100 days]), with inclusion of such documentation in the patient records, mechanical methods should be used for prophylaxis. Providers should refer to current ACCP guidelines and NCCN/ASCO guidelines for detailed recommendations for VTE prophylaxis for hospitalized patients. Special considerations for trauma, surgical, and cancer patients as well as for obese patients, patients with renal impairment, or pregnant patients are discussed below.

Major Trauma Patients. Trauma patients, including those with acute spinal cord injury, are among those with the highest risk of developing VTE. Recommendations are to administer thromboprophylaxis to all trauma patients.[55] One meta-analysis concluded that UFH alone as thromboprophylaxis in trauma patients was not any more effective than not using thromboprophylaxis.[129] Therefore, according to ACCP guidelines, LMWH is preferred over UFH in trauma patients. One trial demonstrated that UFH combined with mechanical ankle flexion devices was superior to UFH alone in orthopedic trauma patients.[130] Therefore, if used in this patient population, UFH should be combined with mechanical methods and not used alone. For patients undergoing rehabilitation, prophylaxis is recommended to continue with LMWH or warfarin (target International Normalized Ratio [INR] of 2.5 [range, 2–3]) until the risk of VTE subsides, until full ambulation, or for up to three months in trauma patients with spinal cord injury.[8,46]

Patients with Cancer. VTE prevention in this group is particularly important, not only because patients with cancer have a higher risk of VTE but because VTE is often more difficult to diagnose and treat in this population.[8] Patients who are confined to a bed and with an active malignancy should receive prophylaxis with an LMWH, a UFH, or fondaparinux.[8,46] If there is a contraindication to pharmacologic prophylaxis, graduated compression stockings or an IPC device should be used, with strong attention paid to compliance.[8] Although patients with cancer have a particularly increased risk of developing VTE, they continue to have the lowest rates of appropriate VTE prophylaxis.[32–35,131]

VTE prophylaxis should be initiated in cancer patients with solid tumors and additional VTE risk factors, including previous venous thrombosis, immobilization, and the use of hormonal therapy, angiogenesis inhibitors, thalidomide, and lenalidomide.[43] Agents of choice include UFH and LMWH. Additional studies are needed to evaluate anticoagulants in patients with cancer who do not have a traditional indication for thromboprophylaxis, such as those with recent cancer now in remission or undergoing outpatient chemotherapy.[8,46] Agreement on contraindications differs between key organizations and international experts, with some suggesting that pharmacologic prophylaxis be used with platelet counts as low as 5,000 per microliter and others suggesting a low of 50,000.[47] For more information on when to administer prophylaxis to cancer patients, refer to ACCP, NCCN, and ASCO guidelines.

Surgical Patients. An abundance of trials involving surgical patients have demonstrated substantial reductions in VTE with UFH, LMWH, fondaparinux, and warfarin over placebo or equivalence or noninferiority to other effective anticoagulants.[8,44–46] Because the number of surgical studies is so expansive and recommendations vary by patient group, readers are referred to the 2012 ACCP guidelines for specific details. ACCP guidelines include recommendations and background on

- General, vascular, laparoscopic, gynecological, urologic, bariatric, thoracic, and coronary bypass surgery; abdominal–pelvic surgery (including gastrointestinal); major trauma,

- THR, TKR, knee arthroscopy, hip fracture surgery, timing of thromboprophylaxis initiation, screening for DVT before hospital discharge, and duration of thromboprophylaxis for the aforementioned major orthopedic surgeries,
- Isolated lower-extremity injuries distal to the knee, and
- Craniotomy and spinal surgery.

The following key points should be considered when initiating thromboprophylaxis for surgical patients:

1. Aspirin and warfarin, with a target INR of 2.5, may be used for the orthopedic population.
2. Select mechanical methods may be used alone for THR; TKR; hip fracture surgery; gynecologic, urologic, laparoscopic, or coronary artery bypass surgical groups; elective spine surgery; and neurosurgery.[8]
3. LMWH, fondaparinux, and three times daily UFH are typically options for surgical patients with multiple VTE risk factors (i.e., high risk), with LMWH and fondaparinux being preferred over three times daily UFH in many high-risk surgical groups.[8]
4. LMWH, fondaparinux, and twice-daily UFH are options in most moderate-risk surgical groups.[8]
5. The combination of IPC with pharmacologic prophylaxis typically conveys a 60% further risk reduction in VTE events.[8]
6. LMWH is the preferred agent in THR, TKR, and hip fracture surgery if patients do not have an increased risk of bleeding.

Obese Patients. Although more studies are needed, evidence supports the use of weight-based prophylactic dosing of LMWHs in obese patients (i.e., body mass index of >30 kg/m^2). Studies assessing anti-Xa levels at both treatment and prophylactic dosages demonstrated appropriate anti-Xa levels and no accumulation of drug. Appropriate anti-Xa levels have been reported in obese patients receiving enoxaparin, tinzaparin, and dalteparin dosed based on total body weights of up to 144, 165, and 190 kg, respectively.[132–136] One meta-analysis verified that major bleeding rates were not increased in obese patients who received weight-based LMWH when compared with nonobese individuals.[137]

Nadroparin and enoxaparin have been studied in prospective studies of obese patients undergoing bariatric surgery and orthopedic surgery.[138–142] Of note, nadroparin is not available in the United States. The usual recommended prophylactic doses of these agents may be inadequate for VTE prophylaxis in obese patients. For LMWHs, ACCP guidelines recommend using weight-based dosing for obese patients.[8] For enoxaparin, the specific dosing that appeared to be more favorable in bariatric surgery was 40 mg twice daily, though this may still be inadequate in some patients, and higher dosing may be more beneficial.[142] Although dosing suggestions are not yet well-defined in the literature, enoxaparin 0.5 mg/kg every 12–24 hours (e.g., depending on the level of obesity, with every-12-hour administration used for patients with higher body mass indexes) has been used successfully for prophylaxis at some centers.[143–145] Dosage increases of up to 30% have also been suggested.[145]

Patients with Renal Impairment. Several studies have assessed the effects of LMWHs in patients with renal impairment. Tinzaparin and dalteparin offer the most convincing data that these drugs may not accumulate in patients with severe renal impairment in both prophylactic and treatment doses.[147–154] However, one recent study comparing tinzaparin with UFH for the treatment of VTE in elderly patients with renal insufficiency found increased mortality in the tinzaparin group.[155] The trial was stopped early because of these interim results, though the increased mortality was not related to increased bleeding or VTE. There were nonsignificant trends for tinzaparin-treated patients having higher rates of VTE than those receiving UFH[155]; thus, more data are needed. Of note, tinzaparin production was recently discontinued in the United States.[156]

The recent Dalteparin's Influence on Renally Compromised anti-Ten-A (DIRECT) trial was a prospective study of 120 critically ill patients with a CLcr of <30 mL/min, who had at least one trough anti-Xa level measured.[150] The investigators analyzed the safety of prophylactic dosages of dalteparin and found no bioaccumulation of the drug in the patients. Interestingly, 62% of patients had acute renal failure at some point during their prophylactic regimen. These data suggest that in critically ill patients with severe renal insufficiency, VTE prophylaxis with dalteparin is unlikely to contribute to bleeding and is not associated with an excessive anticoagulant effect due to bioaccumulation.[150] Enoxaparin, however, has shown accumulation when used at treatment dosages.[157–161]

Because there is conflicting evidence regarding the accumulation of LMWHs in renally impaired patients, further studies are needed. At this time, ACCP recommends using an alternative agent or dosage-adjusted LMWH in patients who are renally impaired (CLcr of <30 mL/min). Because laboratory results are not immediately available on admission, it is important for pharmacists to review patients' history to determine if their LMWH dose needs to be adjusted or if they should be switched to another agent. Twice-daily UFH 5000 units is an appropriate option in both hemodialysis patients and patients with severe renal impairment in the absence of contraindications. A recent review with recommendations by Nutescu and colleagues[146] addressed LMWH use in both renal impairment and obesity across a wide array of patients.

Pregnant Patients. Pregnancy itself is a risk factor for the development of VTE. VTE in this patient population is complicated, and a thorough clinical history and risk assessment should be sought to determine antepartum and postpartum prophylaxis needs. In general, an LMWH is preferred over a UFH for the prevention and treatment of VTE because of UFH's increased risks of HIT and osteoporosis. At-risk pregnant patients should receive appropriate VTE prophylaxis per ACCP guidelines. For women undergoing cesarean delivery with at least one major or two minor risk factors, LMWH should be used or mechanical prophylaxis for patients with contraindications to LMWH. For women undergoing cesarean delivery with multiple additional risk factors, LMWH should be combined with mechanical methods until discharge. For selected high-risk patients, extended prophylaxis should be considered. Readers are referred to the ACCP guidelines for recommendations regarding the prevention of VTE in pregnant patients.[162]

Emerging Anticoagulant Options

At present, dabigatran, rivaroxaban, and warfarin are the only oral anticoagulants available, though dabigatran and rivaroxaban have only recently gained approval for stroke prevention in nonvalvular atrial fibrillation.[163–166] Dabigatran does not have other indications at this time, and its efficacy is based on the recently published RELY trial, which demonstrated that dabigatran was superior to warfarin with a similar rate of bleeding at a dosage of 150 mg twice daily.[165] Although warfarin has been the only oral anticoagulant available for more than five decades, it has several disadvantages when used for VTE prophylaxis in hospitalized patients, as discussed above. The development of new anticoagulants has focused on finding new oral formulations, specifically targeting single procoagulant complexes critical to the coagulation process, including blocking the initiation of coagulation, preventing the propagation of coagulation, and inhibiting thrombin.[167,168] There are several types of monotargeted oral anticoagulants: direct inhibitors of activated factors IXa and Xa, which are involved in the propagation of coagulation, and direct inhibitors of thrombin activity, which target factor IIa. Rivaroxaban and dabigatran have recently been approved by FDA. The approval of apixaban, however, has been delayed due to FDA's request for additional information.

Rivaroxaban. Rivaroxaban is an oral, reversible, once-daily factor Xa inhibitor that has an oral bioavailability of 80% and a half-life of 7–11 hours; it is 67% renally cleared.[164] Rivaroxaban is a substrate for P-glycoprotein 1 transporter, located in the gut and kidneys, and is also metabolized via cytochrome P-450 isoenzyme 3A4 (CYP3A4), so the use of strong inducers or inhibitors of this isoenzyme should be avoided in patients receiving rivaroxaban. The safety and efficacy of rivaroxaban for VTE prevention after TKR and THR have been evaluated in four Phase III studies (RECORD trials) in Europe and the United States.[169–172] The RECORD 1 and 2 trials were conducted in patients undergoing TKR; the RECORD 3 and 4 trials were conducted in those undergoing THR. Rivaroxaban was found to be superior to enoxaparin for preventing VTE and all-cause mortality with similar bleeding rates. In two of the four RECORD trials, rivaroxaban was superior to enoxaparin in the prevention of symptomatic VTE. The agent is approved for these indications in Europe and Canada and has recently gained FDA approval for the same indications within the United States.[164] In the Phase III MAGELLAN study, the safety and efficacy of extended prophylaxis with oral rivaroxaban (10 mg daily for 31–39 days) were compared to short-term prophylaxis with subcutaneous enoxaparin (40 mg daily for 6–14 days) for the prevention of VTE in medical patients. The results of this study indicate the superiority of rivaroxaban over enoxaparin at day 35 for the composite endpoint of asymptomatic proximal DVT, symptomatic DVT, symptomatic nonfatal PE, and VTE-related death. However, this came at the cost of substantially more major bleeding events.[109] The relative risk of bleeding compared with enoxaparin at 10 and 35 days was 2.3 ($p < 0.001$) and 2.5 ($p < 0.001$), respectively. Because of these safety results, the risk:benefit ratio of rivaroxaban in medical patients is questionable. In the ROCKET-AF study, based on the primary endpoint of stroke or systemic embolism in patients with nonvalvular atrial fibrillation, rivaroxaban was found to be noninferior to warfarin (hazard ratio, 0.88; 95% CI, 0.74–1.03; $p < 0.001$) ($p = 0.12$ for superiority). Rivaroxaban received FDA approval for VTE prevention in TKR, THR, and atrial fibrillation in 2011. However, because of the safety data and higher rates of clinically relevant bleeding, its use in medical patients cannot be recommended at this time.

Apixaban. Apixaban is a new, reversible, direct-acting oral pyrazole-based factor Xa inhibitor that is 25% renally cleared, is 60% bioavailable, and has a half-life of 9–14 hours. The drug is also cleared via the CYP3A4 isoenzyme system; therefore, strong inducers and inhibitors will need to be avoided. Apixaban is currently in advanced stages of testing for the prevention and treatment of thrombotic disorders. It binds to the active site of factor Xa without requiring antithrombin.[167,168]

Currently, there are several multinational Phase III studies of apixaban being conducted for the prevention of thrombotic events, including DVT and PE, in patients undergoing knee or hip replacement surgery. The results for one of these trials (ADVANCE-1) showed that the primary endpoint (symptomatic or asymptomatic DVT, PE, or death from any cause) occurred in 9.0% of apixaban recipients (2.5 mg twice daily), compared with 8.9% of those treated with enoxaparin (30 mg twice daily) in TKR.[173,174] Despite being numerically similar, these figures did not meet the statistical criteria for apixaban noninferiority. The ADVANCE-2 trial was conducted in patients undergoing TKR. The results demonstrated that apixaban (2.5 mg twice daily) was superior to enoxaparin 40 mg subcutaneously once daily for VTE prevention without increased bleeding. The ADVANCE-3 trial was conducted in patients undergoing THR, and its results demonstrated that apixaban was superior to enoxaparin for VTE prevention at 35 days postsurgery with a similar rate of bleeding. In the ADOPT study of apixaban for VTE prevention in medical patients, apixaban showed substantially increased major bleeding at 30 days without demonstrating superiority on the primary composite VTE efficacy endpoint.[168] These results are similar to those of the MAGELLAN trial mentioned above. The agent is also in Phase II clinical testing in patients with metastatic cancer.[174]

Dabigatran. Dabigatran is a potent, competitive, reversible direct thrombin (factor IIa) inhibitor with 80% renal excretion, a 14 to 17-hour half-life, and 6% oral bioavailability.[163] Dabigatran inhibits free thrombin, fibrin-bound thrombin, and thrombin-induced platelet aggregation. It is also a substrate of Pgp1; therefore, strong inducers and inhibitors should be avoided.[167,168] Dabigatran has completed Phase III clinical trials in Europe and the United States to evaluate its potential in thromboembolic disorders. It was approved for marketing by FDA in October 2010 for the prevention of stroke and systemic embolism in patients with nonvalvular atrial fibrillation. It has also been approved by the European Medicines Agency for primary prevention of VTE in adult patients who have undergone elective hip or knee replacement and has been subsequently launched in the United Kingdom and Germany.[168]

Three Phase III trials (RE-MODEL, RE-NOVATE, RE-MOBILIZE) have been undertaken to study dabigatran versus enoxaparin in the prevention of major VTE and VTE-related mortality after both knee and hip replacement surgery. The RE-MODEL (TKR) and RE-NOVATE (THR) met noninferiority criteria versus enoxaparin 40 mg daily, but the

RE-MOBILIZE (TKR) failed to meet noninferiority criteria against enoxaparin 30 mg twice daily. Rates of major bleeding were comparable between the treatment groups.[173,174]

Potential Benefits and Limitations of Emerging Agents. The new oral anticoagulants are considered to be more convenient and simpler to use than vitamin K antagonists, because routine measuring of anticoagulant effects and dose adjustment are not required. Their oral route of administration as compared with injectables is favorable and may improve adherence and simplify postdischarge prophylaxis. Ecarin clotting time, thrombin time, activated partial thromboplastin time, and activated clotting time have theoretical potential to be used for measures of anticoagulant effect of dabigatran, whereas factor Xa levels and prothrombin time have the potential to measure the anticoagulant effect of apixaban and rivaroxaban. In addition, direct thrombin inhibitor measurement assays and reversal agents are under development for dabigatran. Most of these agents undergo renal clearance, which could lead to drug accumulation in patients with renal impairment.

Currently, there are no antidotes for rivaroxaban, apixaban, or dabigatran to rapidly reverse drug effects if required. This is also a current limitation shared by fondaparinux. LMWH can be partially reversed by protamine, whereas UFH can be fully reversed with protamine. Because these novel oral anticoagulants have longer half-lives than UFH and LMWH, any adverse effects caused by direct inhibition of thrombin or factor Xa will continue for several hours or days after the cessation of therapy.

Cost-Effectiveness of Antithrombotic Prophylaxis

For the initial hospital admission, the costs of DVT and PE are $9,805 and $14,146, respectively, and readmission costs for the same events are $11,862 (DVT cost significantly higher, $p = 0.006$) and $14,722, respectively.[42] With the cost of prophylaxis for approximately 10 days being $20–$250 for most pharmacologic agents, cost efficacy for pharmacologic prophylaxis is well established. A median of 10 days is a common duration of therapy for prophylaxis used in many medical and surgical trials not requiring an extended duration of therapy. A minimum duration of 10 days is also recommended for THR, TKR, and hip fracture surgery patients. Length of hospitalization and hospital costs have also been found to be substantially increased for patients who develop VTE.[175,176] One retrospective analysis demonstrated that total costs were not different for patients who were given prophylaxis with LMWH versus UFH, though VTE rates were substantially lower with LMWH versus UFH.[177] Two other studies found lower total costs of LMWH versus UFH[178,179] and cost-effectiveness of primary prophylaxis to prevent VTE over no prophylaxis.[111] With the introduction of generic enoxaparin and future agents—including a generic fondaparinux, dabigatran, apixaban, and rivaroxaban—the cost of VTE prophylaxis will likely continue to decrease.

Monitoring Antithrombotic Prophylaxis

Although the incidence of HIT with LMWH and UFH varies by patient group, HIT occurs much more frequently (i.e., threefold) with the use of UFH compared with LMWH. Postoperative orthopedic, cardiac, and vascular surgery patients receiving UFH for one to two weeks for thromboprophylaxis have the highest risk of HIT, ranging from 1% to 5%.[115] In this patient group, platelet count should be monitored at least every other day between postoperative days 4 and 14 or until UFH is stopped (if before day 14), whichever occurs first.[115] The risk of HIT is lower (0.1–1%) among postoperative patients receiving an LMWH or intravascular catheter UFH flushes and medical or obstetric patients receiving LMWH after previously receiving UFH. For these patients, platelet monitoring should occur at least every two or three days from day 4 to 14, or until the UFH or LMWH is stopped (if before day 14), whichever comes first.[115] When the estimated risk of HIT is less than 0.1%, the risk is described as "rare." Patients in this group include medical and obstetric patients receiving only LMWH or medical patients receiving only intravascular catheter UFH flushes, and platelet monitoring is not recommended.

Because LMWH and fondaparinux are cleared renally, pharmacists play an integral role in monitoring the safety and efficacy of therapy. They should pay close attention to patients' renal function and make appropriate dosage changes or modify prophylaxis to other appropriate regimens in collaborative environments. This may be accomplished by measuring anti-Xa levels.

Summary

Despite decades of evidence showing that pharmacologic and mechanical means can help prevent VTE in hospitalized at-risk patients, current national and international prevention strategies remain suboptimal. National organization positions are shifting to include omission of appropriate care as an adverse event or adverse drug event. Therefore, omission of VTE prophylaxis in a patient who develops a VTE is considered an adverse drug event if pharmacologic prophylaxis was indicated or as an adverse event if mechanical prophylaxis was indicated. To date, no adverse-drug-event studies are including "omission" of VTE prophylaxis as an adverse drug event. Inclusion of this adverse drug event will substantially increase the financial implications of adverse drug events nationally.

Future studies are needed in VTE prevention, including elicitation of the optimal duration of thromboprophylaxis (especially after hospital discharge because of the short lengths of stay in U.S. hospitals), the optimal use of currently approved agents for prophylaxis, the impact of preventable VTE as an adverse event or adverse drug event, and validation of individual scoring methods, especially in hospitalized settings. Hospital pharmacy leadership and proactive engagement are driving forces to ensure appropriate prophylactic management of VTE in hospitalized patients.

Recent data revealed that inhospital, pharmacy-driven VTE prevention programs can increase the use of appropriate thromboprophylaxis and reduce VTE events. VTE prophylaxis programs and anticoagulation management, especially in hospitalized settings, are opportunities that pharmacists can take advantage of in their respective health care settings to reduce unnecessary morbidity and mortality from this disease. Because of their expertise in pharmacotherapy, pharmacists are poised to take a leadership role in VTE prevention programs to positively affect patient care within hospitals and beyond.

References

1. Hirsh J, Hoak J. Management of deep vein thrombosis and pulmonary embolism. *Circulation.* 1996; 93:2212–45.
2. Heit JA, Cohen AT, Anderson FA Jr, on behalf of the VTE Impact Assessment Group. Estimated annual number of incident and recurrent, non-fatal and fatal venous thromboembolism (VTE) events in the US. *Blood.* 2005; 106:11. Abstract.
3. Cohen AT, Agnelli G, Anderson FA, et al. Venous thromboembolism (VTE) in Europe. The number of VTE events and associated morbidity and mortality. *Thromb Haemost.* 2007; 98:756–64.
4. Sandler DA, Martin JF. Autopsy proven pulmonary embolism in hospital patients: are we detecting enough deep vein thrombosis? *J R Soc Med.* 1989; 82:203–5.
5. Stein PD, Henry JW. Prevalence of acute pulmonary embolism among patients in a general hospital and at autopsy. *Chest.* 1995; 108:978–81.
6. Cohen AT, Tapson VF, Bergmann J, et al. Venous thromboembolism risk and prophylaxis in the acute hospital care setting (ENDORSE study): a multinational cross-sectional study. *Lancet.* 2008; 371:387–94.
7. Shojania KG, Duncan BW, McDonald KM, et al. Making health care safer: a critical analysis of patient safety practices. AHRQ Publication No. 01-E058. Rockville, MD: Agency for Healthcare Research and Quality; 2001.
8. Geerts WH, Bergqvist D, Pineo GF, et al. Prevention of venous thromboembolism. *Chest.* 2008; 133(suppl): 381S–453S.
9. Anderson FA Jr, Wheeler HB, Goldberg RJ, et al. A population-based perspective of the hospital incidence and case fatality rates of deep vein thrombosis and pulmonary embolism. The Worcester DVT Study. *Arch Intern Med.* 1991; 151:933–8.
10. White RH. The epidemiology of venous thromboembolism. *Circulation.* 2003; 107:14–8.
11. Prandoni P, Lensing AW, Cogo A, et al. The long-term clinical course of acute deep venous thrombosis. *Ann Intern Med.* 1996; 125:1–7.
12. Heit JA, Mohr DN, Silverstein MD, et al. Predictors of recurrence after deep vein thrombosis and pulmonary embolism: a population-based cohort study. *Arch Intern Med.* 2000; 160:761–8.
13. Anderson FA Jr, Spencer FA. Risk factors for venous thromboembolism. *Circulation.* 2003; 107:I9–16.
14. Kniffin WD Jr, Baron JA, Barrett J, et al. The epidemiology of diagnosed pulmonary embolism and deep venous thrombosis in the elderly. *Arch Intern Med.* 1994; 154:861–6.
15. Spencer FA, Gore KM, Lessard D, et al. Patient outcomes after deep vein thrombosis and pulmonary embolism: the Worcester Venous Thromboembolism Study. *Arch Intern Med.* 2008; 168:425–30.
16. Edelsberg J, Hagiwara M, Taneja C, et al. Risk of venous thromboembolism among hospitalized medically ill patients. *Am J Health-Syst Pharm.* 2006; 63(suppl 6):S16–22.
17. Goldhaber SZ, Tapson VF. A prospective registry of 5,451 patients with ultrasound-confirmed deep vein thrombosis. *Am J Cardiol.* 2004; 93:259–62.
18. Nielsen HK, Bechgaard P, Nielsen FP, et al. 178 fatal cases of pulmonary embolism in a medical department. *Acta Med Scand.* 1981; 209:351–5.
19. Hauch O, Jorgensen LN, Khattar SC, et al. Fatal pulmonary embolism associated with surgery: an autopsy study. *Acta Chir Scand.* 1990; 156:747–9.
20. Sperry KL, Key CR, Anderson RE. Toward a population-based assessment of death due to pulmonary embolism in New Mexico. *Hum Pathol.* 1990; 21:159–65.
21. Cohen AT, Edmondson RA, Phillips MJ, et al. The changing pattern of venous thromboembolic disease. *Haemostasis.* 1996; 26:65–71.
22. Piazza G, Seddighzadeh A, Goldhaber SZ. Double trouble for 2,609 hospitalized medical patients who developed deep vein thrombosis: prophylaxis omitted more often and pulmonary embolism more frequent. *Chest.* 2007; 132:554–61.
23. Samama MM, Cohen AT, Darmon JY, et al. A comparison of enoxaparin with placebo for the prevention of venous thromboembolism in acutely ill medical patients. *N Engl J Med.* 1999; 341:793–800.
24. Leizorovicz A, Cohen AT, Turpie AG, et al. Randomized, placebo-controlled trial of dalteparin for the prevention of venous thromboembolism in acutely ill medical patients. *Circulation.* 2004; 110:874–9.
25. Cohen AT, Davidson BL, Gallus AS, et al. Efficacy and safety of fondaparinux for the prevention of venous thromboembolism in older acute medical patients: randomised placebo controlled trial. *BMJ.* 2006; 332:325–9.
26. Ashrani AA, Heit JA. Incidence and cost burden of post-thrombotic syndrome. *J Thromb Thrombolysis.* 2009; 28:465–76.
27. MacDougall DA, Feliu AL, Boccuzzi SJ, et al. Economic burden of deep-vein thrombosis, pulmonary embolism, and post-thrombotic syndrome. *Am J Health-Syst Pharm.* 2006; 63(suppl 6):S5–15.
28. Kahn S, Ginsberg JS. Relationship between deep venous thrombosis and the postthrombotic syndrome. *Arch Intern Med.* 2004; 164:17–26.
29. Pengo V, Lensing AW, Prins MH, et al. Incidence of chronic thromboembolic pulmonary hypertension after pulmonary embolism. *N Engl J Med.* 2004; 350:2257–64.
30. Sagar S, Massey J, Sanderson JM. Low-dose heparin prophylaxis against fatal pulmonary embolism. *Br Med J.* 1975; 4:257–9.
31. Burleigh E, Wang C, Foster D, et al. Thromboprophylaxis in medically ill patients at risk for venous thromboembolism. *Am J Health-Syst Pharm.* 2006; 63(suppl 6):S23–9.
32. Yu HT, Dylan ML, Lin J, et al. Hospitals' compliance with prophylaxis guidelines for venous thromboembolism. *Am J Health-Syst Pharm.* 2007; 64:69–76.
33. Amin A, Stemkowski S, Lin J, et al. Thromboprophylaxis rates in US medical centers: success or failure? *J Thromb Haemost.* 2007; 5:1610–6.
34. Amin A, Stemkowski S, Lin J, et al. Appropriate thromboprophylaxis in hospitalized cancer patients. *Clin Adv Hematol Oncol.* 2008; 6:910–20.

35. Amin A, Spyropoulos AC, Dobesh P, et al. Are hospitals delivering appropriate VTE prevention? The venous thromboembolism study to assess the rate of thromboprophylaxis (VTE start). *J Thromb Thrombolysis*. 2010; 29:326–39.
36. Geerts WH, Pineo GF, Heit JA, et al. Prevention of venous thromboembolism: the Seventh ACCP Conference on Antithrombotic and Thrombolytic Therapy. *Chest*. 2004; 126(suppl):338S–400S.
37. Khorana AA. The NCCN clinical practice guidelines on venous thromboembolic disease: strategies for improving VTE prophylaxis in hospitalized cancer patients. *Oncologist*. 2007; 12:1361–70.
38. Cabana MD, Rand CS, Powe NR, et al. Why don't physicians follow clinical practice guidelines? A framework for improvement. *JAMA*. 1999; 282:1458–65.
39. Mahan CE, Hussein MA, Amin AN, et al. Venous thromboembolism pharmacy intervention management program with an active, multifaceted approach reduces preventable venous thromboembolism and increases appropriate prophylaxis. *Clin Appl Thromb Hemost*. 2012; 18:45–58.
40. Mahan CE, Borrego ME, Woersching AL, et al. Venous thromboembolism: annualised United States models for total, hospital-acquired and preventable costs utilising long-term attack rates. *Thromb Haemost*. 2012; 108:291–302.
41. Centers for Disease Control and Prevention. National Center on Birth Defects and Developmental Disabilities strategic plan 2011–2015. www.cdc.gov/NCBDDD/AboutUs/documents/NCBDDD_StrategicPlan_2-10-11.pdf (accessed 2012 Feb 27).
42. Spyropoulos AC, Lin J. Direct medical costs of venous thromboembolism and subsequent hospital readmission rates: an administrative claims analysis from 30 managed care organizations. *J Manag Care Pharm*. 2007; 13:475–86.
43. Kahn SR, Lim W, Dunn AS, et al. Prevention of venous thromboembolism in non-surgical patients. *Chest*. 2012; 141(suppl 2):e195s–226s.
44. Gould MK, Garcia DA, Wren SM, et al. Prevention of venous thromboembolism in nonorthopedic surgical patients. *Chest*. 2012; 141(suppl 2):e227s–77s.
45. Falck-Ytter Y, Francis CW, Johanson NA, et al. Prevention of venous thromboembolism in orthopedic surgery patients. *Chest*. 2012; 141(suppl 2):e278s–325s.
46. Cardiovascular Disease Educational and Research Trust, Cyprus Cardiovascular Disease Educational and Research Trust, European Venous Forum, et al. Prevention and treatment of venous thromboembolism. International consensus statement (guidelines according to scientific evidence). *Int Angiol*. 2006; 25:101–61.
47. Lyman GH, Khorana AA, Falanga A, et al. American Society of Clinical Oncology guideline: recommendations for venous thromboembolism prophylaxis and treatment in patients with cancer. *J Clin Oncol*. 2007; 25:5490–505.
48. National Comprehensive Cancer Network. NCCN clinical practice guidelines in oncology. Venous thromboembolic disease, version 2.2011. www.nccn.org/professionals/physician_gls/PDF/vte.pdf (accessed 2012 Feb 27).
49. Joint Commission. National Patient Safety Goals effective January 1, 2012. www.jointcommission.org/standards_information/npsgs.aspx (accessed 2012 Feb 27).
50. Centers for Medicare and Medicaid Services. Fact sheet: Medicare takes new steps to help make your hospital stay safer. www.cms.hhs.gov/apps/media/press/factsheet.asp?Counter=3227&intNumPerPage=10&checkDate=&checkKey=&srchType=1&numDays=3500&srchOpt=0&srchData=&keywordType=All&chkNewsType=6&intPage=&showAll=&pYear=&year=&desc=&cboOrder=date (accessed 2008 Aug 4).
51. National Quality Forum. National voluntary consensus standards for prevention and care of venous thromboembolism: policy, preferred practices and performance measures. www.qualityforum.org/Projects/s-z/VTE_Phase_I/Venous_Thromboembolism_%28VTE%29_I.aspx (accessed 2012 Feb 27).
52. Joint Commission. Performance measurement initiatives. Specifications manual for national hospital inpatient quality measures. www.jointcommission.org/specifications_manual_for_national_hospital_inpatient_quality_measures.aspx (accessed 2012 Feb 27).
53. Urbankova J, Quiroz R, Kucher N, et al. Intermittent pneumatic compression and deep vein thrombosis prevention. *Thromb Haemost*. 2005; 94:1181–5.
54. Lacut K, Bressollette L, Le Gal G, et al. Prevention of venous thrombosis in patients with acute intracerebral hemorrhage. *Neurology*. 2005; 65:865–9.
55. Mismetti P, Rivron-Guillot K, Quenet S, et al. A prospective long-term study of 220 patients with a retrievable vena cava filter for secondary prevention of venous thromboembolism. *Chest*. 2007; 131:223–9.
56. Morris R, Woodcock JP. Evidence-based compression prevention of stasis and deep vein thrombosis. *Ann Surg*. 2004; 239:162–71.
57. Spyropoulos AC, Mahan CE. Prevention of venous thromboembolism in medical patients. In: Fang MC, ed. Inpatient anticoagulation. Hoboken, NJ: Wiley-Blackwell; 2011.
58. Cook D, Crowther M, Meade M, et al. Deep venous thrombosis in medical-surgical critically ill patients: prevalence, incidence, and risk factors. *Crit Care Med*. 2005; 33:1565–71.
59. Blom JW, Doggen CJ, Osanto S, et al. Malignancies, prothrombotic mutations, and the risk of venous thrombosis. *JAMA*. 2005; 293:715–22.
60. Monreal M, Falgá C, Valdés M, et al. Fatal pulmonary embolism and fatal bleeding in cancer patients with venous thromboembolism: findings from the RIETE registry. *J Thromb Haemost*. 2006; 4:1950–6.
61. Heit JA, Silverstein MD, Mohr DN, et al. Risk factors for deep vein thrombosis and pulmonary embolism: a population-based case-control study. *Arch Intern Med*. 2000; 160:809–15.
62. Haddad TC, Greeno EW. Chemotherapy-induced thrombosis. *Thromb Res*. 2006; 118:555–68.
63. Khorana AA, Francis CW, Culakova E, et al. Risk factors for chemotherapy-associated venous thromboem-

bolism in a prospective observational study. *Cancer.* 2005; 104:2822–9.

64. Hussein MA. Thromboembolism risk reduction in multiple myeloma patients treated with immunomodulatory drug combinations. *Thromb Haemost.* 2006; 95:924–30.
65. Johnson DH, Fehrenbacher L, Novotny WF, et al. Randomized phase II trial comparing bevacizumab plus carboplatin and paclitaxel with carboplatin and paclitaxel alone in previously untreated locally advanced or metastatic non-small cell lung cancer. *J Clin Oncol.* 2004; 22:2184–91.
66. Zangari M, Barlogie B, Anaissie E, et al. Deep vein thrombosis in patients with multiple myeloma treated with thalidomide and chemotherapy: effects of prophylactic and therapeutic anticoagulation. *Br J Haematol.* 2004; 126:715–21.
67. Barlogie B, Tricot G, Anaissie E, et al. Thalidomide and hematopoietic-cell transplantation for multiple myeloma. *N Engl J Med.* 2006; 354:1021–30.
68. El Accaoui RN, Shamseddeen WA, Taher AT. Thalidomide and thrombosis: a meta-analysis. *Thromb Haemost.* 2007; 97:1031–6.
69. Fisher B, Costantino J, Redmond C, et al. A randomized clinical trial evaluating tamoxifen in the treatment of patients with mode-negative breast cancer who have estrogen receptor-positive tumors. *N Engl J Med.* 1989; 320:479–84.
70. Fisher B, Costantino JP, Wickerham DL, et al. Tamoxifen for prevention of breast cancer: report of the National Surgical Adjuvant Breast and Bowel Project P-1 study. *J Natl Cancer Inst.* 1998; 90:1371–88.
71. Fisher B, Costantino JP, Wickerham DL, et al. Tamoxifen for the prevention of breast cancer: current status of the National Surgical Adjuvant Breast and Bowel Project P-1 study. *J Natl Cancer Inst.* 2005; 97:1652–62.
72. Lee AY, Levine MN. Venous thromboembolism and cancer: risks and outcomes. *Circulation.* 2003; 107:I-17–21.
73. Saphner T, Tormey DC, Gray R. Venous and arterial thrombosis in patients who received adjuvant therapy for breast cancer. *J Clin Oncol.* 1991; 9:286–94.
74. Thürlimann B, Keshaviah A, Coates AS, et al. A comparison of letrozole and tamoxifen in postmenopausal women with early breast cancer. *N Engl J Med.* 2005; 353:2747–57.
75. Baum M, Budzar AU, Cuzick J, et al. Anastrozole alone or in combination with tamoxifen versus tamoxifen alone for adjuvant treatment of postmenopausal women with early breast cancer: first results of the ATAC randomised trial. *Lancet.* 2002; 359:2131–9.
76. Bonnetere J, Buzdar A, Nabholtz JM, et al. Anastrozole is superior to tamoxifen as first-line therapy in hormone receptor positive advanced breast carcinoma: results of two randomized trials designed for combined analysis. *Cancer.* 2001; 92:2247–58.
77. Coombes RC, Hall E, Gibson LJ, et al. A randomized trial of exemestane after two to three years of tamoxifen therapy in postmenopausal women with primary breast cancer. *N Engl J Med.* 2004; 350:1081–92.
78. Prandoni P, Lensing AW, Piccioli A, et al. Recurrent venous thromboembolism and bleeding complications during anticoagulant treatment in patients with cancer and venous thrombosis. *Blood.* 2002; 100:3484–8.
79. Elting LS, Escalante CP, Cooksley C, et al. Outcomes and cost of deep venous thrombosis among patients with cancer. *Arch Intern Med.* 2004; 164:1653–61.
80. Blom JW, Vanderschoot JP, Oostindier MJ, et al. Incidence of venous thrombosis in a large cohort of 66,329 cancer patients: results of a record linkage study. *J Thromb Haemost.* 2006; 4:529–35.
81. Descourt R, Le Gal G, Couturaud F, et al. Recurrent venous thromboembolism under anticoagulant therapy: a high risk in adenocarcinoma? *Thromb Haemost.* 2006; 95:912–3.
82. Chew HK, Wun T, Harvey D, et al. Incidence of venous thromboembolism and its effect on survival among patients with common cancers. *Arch Intern Med.* 2006; 166:458–64.
83. Sorensen HT, Mellemkjaer L, Olsen JH, et al. Prognosis of cancers associated with venous thromboembolism. *N Engl J Med.* 2000; 343:1846–50.
84. Alcalay A, Wun T, Khatri V, et al. Venous thromboembolism in patients with colorectal cancer: incidence and effect on survival. *J Clin Oncol.* 2006; 24:1112–8.
85. Ageno W, Prandoni P, Romualdi E, et al. The metabolic syndrome and the risk of venous thrombosis: a case-control study. *J Thromb Haemost.* 2006; 4:1914–8.
86. Ageno W, Becattini C, Brighton T, et al. Cardiovascular risk factors and venous thromboembolism: a meta-analysis. *Circulation.* 2008; 117:93–102.
87. Masopust J, Maly R, Andrys C, et al. Markers of thrombogenesis are activated in unmedicated patients with acute psychosis: a matched case control study. *BMC Psychiatry.* 2011; 11:2.
88. Lutz L, Haas S, Hach-Wunderle V, et al. [Venous thromboembolism in internal medicine: risk assessment and pharmaceutical prophylaxis: publication for the specialist forum.] *Med Welt.* 2002; 53:231–4. In German.
89. Caprini JA, Arcelus JI, Reyna JJ. Effective risk stratification of surgical and nonsurgical patients for venous thromboembolic disease. *Semin Hematol.* 2001; 38(suppl 5):12–9.
90. Bahl V, Hu HM, Henke PK, et al. A validation study of a retrospective venous thromboembolism risk scoring method. *Ann Surg.* 2010; 251:344–50.
91. Cohen AT, Alikhan R, Arcelus JI, et al. Assessment of venous thromboembolism risk and the benefit of thromboprophylaxis in medical patients. *Thromb Haemost.* 2005; 94:750–9.
92. Spyropoulos AC, Anderson FA Jr, Fitzgerald G, et al. Predictive and associative models to identify hospitalized medical patients at risk for venous thromboembolism. *Chest.* 2011; 140:706–14.
93. Barbar S, Noventa F, Rossetto V, et al. A risk assessment model for the identification of hospitalized medical patients at risk for venous thromboembolism: the Padua Prediction Score. *J Thromb Haemost.* 2010; 8:2450–7.
94. Mahan CE, Spyropoulos AC. Venous thromboembolism prevention: a systematic review of methods to

increase prophylaxis and decrease events in the hospitalized patient. *Hosp Pract.* 2010; 38:97–108.

95. Tooher R, Middleton P, Pham C, et al. A systematic review of strategies to improve prophylaxis for venous thromboembolism in hospitals. *Ann Surg.* 2005; 241:397–415.
96. Michota FA. Bridging the gap between evidence and practice in venous thromboembolism prophylaxis: the quality improvement process. *J Gen Intern Med.* 2007; 22:1762–70.
97. Cohn SL. Prophylaxis of venous thromboembolism in the US: improving hospital performance. *J Thromb Haemost.* 2009; 7:1437–45.
98. Dobesh PP, Stacy ZA. Effect of a clinical pharmacy education program on improvement in the quantity and quality of venous thromboembolism prophylaxis for medically ill patients. *J Manag Care Pharm.* 2005; 11:755–62.
99. Bauer JB, Chun DS, Karpinski TA. Pharmacist-led program to improve venous thromboembolism prophylaxis in a community hospital. *Am J Health-Syst Pharm.* 2008; 65:1643–7.
100. Sobieraj DM. Development and implementation of a program to assess medical patients' need for venous thromboembolism prophylaxis. *Am J Health-Syst Pharm.* 2008; 65:1755–60.
101. Cronin M, Hill T, Reich DA, et al. Implementation of a multidisciplinary, pharmacy-led, thromboprophylaxis program in total-joint arthroplasty patients. *Am J Health-Syst Pharm.* 2009; 66:171–5.
102. Galanter WL, Thambi M, Rosencranz H, et al. Effects of clinical decision support on venous thromboembolism risk assessment, prophylaxis, and prevention at a university teaching hospital. *Am J Health-Syst Pharm.* 2010; 67:1265–73.
103. Stein J, Chesson M, Killian A, et al. Combined effect of multidisciplinary bedside rounding and real-time visualization of prophylaxis status on hospital acquired VTE in a surgical intensive care unit. Paper presented at 2011 Southern Hospital Medicine Annual Meeting. Grapevine, TX; 2011 May 11.
104. Maynard GA, Morris TA, Jenkins IH. Optimizing prevention of hospital-acquired venous thromboembolism (VTE): prospective validation of a VTE risk assessment model. *J Hosp Med.* 2010; 5:8–10.
105. Cook D, Meade M, Guyatt G, et al. Dalteparin vs unfractionated heparin in critically ill patients. *N Engl J Med.* 2011; 364:1305–14.
106. Lederle FA. Venous thromboembolism prophylaxis in hospitalized medical patients and those with stroke: a background review for an American College of Physicians clinical practice guideline. *Ann Intern Med.* 2011; 155:602–15.
107. Baker DW, Qaseem A. Evidence-based performance measures: preventing unintended consequences of quality measurement. *Ann Intern Med.* 2011; 155:625–32.
108. Qaseem A, Chou R, Humphrey L, et al. Venous thromboembolism prophylaxis in hospitalized patients: a clinical practice guideline from the American College of Physicians. *Ann Intern Med.* 2011; 155:625–32.
109. Centers for Disease Control and Prevention. Quick stats: average length of hospital stay, by diagnostic category—United States, 2003. *MMWR.* 2005; 54:680.
110. Hull RD, Schellong SM, Tapson VF, et al. Extended-duration venous thromboembolism (VTE) prophylaxis in acutely ill medical patients with recent reduced morbidity: the EXCLAIM study. *Ann Intern Med.* 2010; 153:8–18.
111. Goldhaber SZ. Apixaban versus enoxaparin for thromboprophylaxis in medically ill patients. *N Engl J Med.* 2011; 365:2167–77.
112. American College of Cardiology. Rivaroxaban compares favorably with enoxaparin in preventing venous thromboembolism in acutely ill patients without showing a net clinical benefit. www.cardiosource.org/News-Media/Media-Center/News-Releases/2011/04/MAGELLAN.aspx (accessed 2012 Feb 27).
113. ClinicalTrials.gov. VTE Discharge Alert Trial.:http://clinicaltrials.gov/ct2/show/NCT00853463 (accessed 2012 Feb 27).
114. Amin AN, Girard F, Samama MM. Does ambulation modify venous thromboembolism risk in acutely ill medical patients? *Thromb Haemost.* 2010; 104:955–61.
115. Warkentin TE, Greinacher A, Koster A, et al. Treatment and prevention of heparin-induced thrombocytopenia. *Chest.* 2008; 133:340–80.
116. Hirsh J, Bauer KA, Donati MB, et al. Parenteral anticoagulants: American College of Chest Physicians evidence-based clinical practice guidelines (8th edition). *Chest.* 2008; 133(suppl):141S–159S.
117. Creekmore FM, Oderda GM, Pendleton RC, et al. Incidence and economic implications of heparin-induced thrombocytopenia in medical patients receiving prophylaxis for venous thromboembolism. *Pharmacotherapy.* 2006; 26:1438–45.
118. Mcleod RS, Geerts WH, Sniderman KW, et al. Subcutaneous heparin versus low-molecular-weight heparin as thromboprophylaxis in patients undergoing colorectal surgery: results of the Canadian colorectal DVT prophylaxis trial: a randomized, double-blind trial. *Ann Surg.* 2001; 233:438–44.
119. Colwell CW Jr, Collis DK, Paulson R, et al. Comparison of enoxaparin and warfarin for the prevention of venous thromboembolic disease after total hip arthroplasty: evaluation during hospitalization and three months after discharge. *J Bone Joint Surg Am.* 1999; 81:932–40.
120. Leclerc JR, Geerts WH, Desjardins L, et al. Prevention of venous thromboembolism after knee arthroplasty: a randomized, double-blind trial comparing enoxaparin with warfarin. *Ann Intern Med.* 1996; 124:619–26.
121. Turpie AG, Bauer KA, Eriksson BI, et al. Fondaparinux vs enoxaparin for the prevention of venous thromboembolism in major orthopedic surgery: a meta-analysis of 4 randomized double-blind studies. *Arch Intern Med.* 2002; 162:1833–40.
122. Dentali F, Douketis JD, Gianni M, et al. Meta-analysis: anticoagulant prophylaxis to prevent symptomatic venous thromboembolism in hospitalized medical patients. *Ann Intern Med.* 2007; 146:278–88.
123. Mismetti P, Laporte-Simitsidis S, Tardy B, et al. Prevention of venous thromboembolism in internal

medicine with unfractionated or low-molecular-weight heparins: a meta-analysis of randomised clinical trials. *Thromb Haemost.* 2000; 83:14–9.

124. Kleber FX, Witt C, Vogel G, et al Randomized comparison of enoxaparin with unfractionated heparin for the prevention of venous thromboembolism in medical patients with heart failure or severe respiratory disease. *Am Heart J.* 2003; 145:614–21.
125. Lechler E, Schramm W, Flosbach CW. The venous thrombotic risk in non-surgical patients: epidemiological data and efficacy/safety profile of a low-molecular-weight heparin (enoxaparin). *Haemostasis.* 1996; 26(suppl 2):49–56.
126. Cheer SM, Dunn CJ, Foster R. Tinzaparin sodium: a review of its pharmacology and clinical use in the prophylaxis and treatment of thromboembolic disease. *Drugs.* 2004; 64:1479–502.
127. Decousus H, Tapson VF, Vergmann JF, et al. Factors at admission associated with bleeding risk in medical patients: findings from IMPROVE. *Chest.* 2011; 139:69–79.
128. Mahan CE, Spyropoulos AC. Venous thromboembolism prophylaxis with unfractionated heparin in the hospitalized medical patient: the case for thrice daily over twice daily dosing. *Intern Emerg Med.* 2010; 5:299–306.
129. Velmahos GC, Kern J, Chan LS, et al. Prevention of venous thromboembolism after injury: an evidence-based report; part I. Analysis of risk factors and evaluation of the role of vena caval filters. *J Trauma.* 2000; 49:132–9.
130. Fuchs S, Heyse T, Rudofsky G, et al. Continuous passive motion in the prevention of deep-vein thrombosis: a randomised comparison in trauma patients. *J Bone Joint Surg Br.* 2005; 87:1117–22.
131. Tapson VF, Decousus H, Pini M, et al. Venous thromboembolism prophylaxis in acutely ill hospitalized medical patients: findings from the International Medical Prevention Registry on Venous Thromboembolism. *Chest.* 2007; 132:936–45.
132. Sanderink G, Liboux A, Jariwala N, et al. The pharmacokinetics and pharmacodynamics of enoxaparin in obese volunteers. *Clin Pharmacol Ther.* 2002; 72:308–18.
133. Wilson S, Wilbur K, Burton E, et al. Effect of patient weight on the anticoagulant response to adjusted therapeutic dosage of low-molecular-weight heparin for the treatment of venous thromboembolism. *Haemostasis.* 2001; 31:42–8.
134. Smith J, Canton E. Weight-based administration of dalteparin in obese patients. *Am J Health-Syst Pharm.* 2003; 60:683–7.
135. Al-Yaseen E, Wells PS, Anderson J, et al. The safety of dosing dalteparin based on actual body weight for the treatment of acute venous thromboembolism in obese patients. *J Thromb Haemost.* 2005; 3:100–2.
136. Hainer J, Barrett J, Assaid C, et al. Dosing in heavy-weight/obese patients with the LMWH tinzaparin: a pharmacodynamic study. *Thromb Haemost.* 2002; 87:817–23.
137. Spinler S, Inverso S, Cohen M, et al. Safety and efficacy of unfractionated heparin versus enoxaparin in patients who are obese and patients with severe renal impairment: analysis from the ESSENCE and TIMI 11B studies. *Am Heart J.* 2003; 146:33–41.
138. Samama M, Verhill C, Carchy L. Relation between weight, obesity, and frequency of deep venous thrombosis after enoxaparin in orthopedic surgery. *Thromb Haemost.* 1995; 73:977.
139. Frederiksen S, Hedenbro J, Norgren L. Enoxaparin effect depends on body-weight and current doses may be inadequate in obese patients. *Br J Surg.* 2003; 90:547–8.
140. Heizmann M, Baerlocher G, Steinmann F, et al. Anti-Xa activity in obese patients after double standard dose of nadroparin for prophylaxis. *Thromb Res.* 2002; 106:179–81.
141. Kalfarentzos F, Stavropoulou F, Yarmenitis S, et al. Prophylaxis of venous thromboembolism using two different doses of low-molecular-weight heparin (nadroparin) in bariatric surgery: a prospective randomized trial. *Obes Surg.* 2001; 11:670–6.
142. Scholten D, Hoedema R, Scholten S. A comparison of two different prophylactic dose regimens of low molecular weight heparin in bariatric surgery. *Obes Surg.* 2002; 12:19–24.
143. Freeman A, Horner T, Pendleton RC, et al. Prospective comparison of three enoxaparin dosing regimens to achieve target anti-factor Xa levels in hospitalized, medically ill patients with extreme obesity. *Am J Hematol.* 2012; 87:740–3.
144. Rondina MT, Wheeler M, Rodgers GM, et al. Weight-based dosing of enoxaparin for VTE prophylaxis in morbidly obese, medically ill patients. *Thromb Res.* 2010; 125:220–3.
145. Ludwig KP, Simons HJ, Mone M, et al. Implementation of an enoxaparin protocol for venous thromboembolism prophylaxis in obese surgical intensive care unit patients. *Ann Pharmacother.* 2011; 45:1356–62.
146. Nutescu EA, Spinler SA, Wittkowsky A, et al. Low-molecular-weight heparins in renal impairment and obesity: available evidence and clinical practice recommendations across medical and surgical settings. *Ann Pharmacother.* 2009; 43:1064–83.
147. Siguret V, Pautas E, Fevrier M, et al. Elderly patients treated with tinzaparin administered once daily (175 anti-Xa IU/kg): anti-Xa and anti-IIa activities over 10 days. *Thromb Haemost.* 2000; 84:800–4.
148. Rabbat CG, Cook DJ, Crowther MA, et al. Dalteparin thromboprophylaxis for critically ill medical-surgical patients with renal insufficiency. *J Crit Care.* 2005; 20:357–63.
149. Tincani E, Mannucci C, Casolari B, et al. Safety of dalteparin for the prophylaxis of venous thromboembolism in elderly medical patients with renal insufficiency: a pilot study. *Haematologica.* 2006; 91:976–9.
150. Douketis JD, Cook D, Meade M, et al. Prophylaxis against deep vein thrombosis in critically ill patients with severe renal insufficiency with the low-molecular-weight heparin dalteparin—an assessment of safety and pharmacodynamics: the DIRECT study. *J Arch Intern Med.* 2008; 168:1805–12.
151. Shprecher AR, Cheng-Lai A, Madsen EM, et al. Peak antifactor Xa activity produced by dalteparin treatment in patients with renal impairment compared with controls. *Pharmacotherapy.* 2005; 25:817–22.

152. Mahe I, Aghassarian M, Drouet L, et al. Tinzaparin and enoxaparin given at prophylactic dose for eight days in medical elderly patients with impaired renal function. *Thromb Haemost.* 2007; 97:581–6.
153. Lim W, Dentali F, Eikelboom W, et al. Meta-analysis: low-molecular-weight heparin and bleeding in patients with severe renal insufficiency. *Ann Intern Med.* 2006; 144:673–84.
154. Cestac P, Bagheri H, Lapeyre-Mestre M, et al. Utilisation and safety of low molecular weight heparins: prospective observational study in medical inpatients. *Drug Saf.* 2003; 26:197–207.
155. Tinzaparin: excess mortality in elderly patients with renal failure. Unfractionated heparin is best in this setting. *Prescrire Int.* 2009; 18:216.
156. American Society of Health-System Pharmacists. Tinzaparin sodium injection. www.ashp.org/DrugShortages/NotAvailable/bulletin.aspx?id=749 (accessed 2012 Oct 12).
157. Brophy D, Wazny L, Behr T, et al. The pharmacokinetics of subcutaneous enoxaparin in end-stage renal disease. *Pharmacotherapy.* 2001; 21:169–74.
158. Becker R, Spencer F, Gibson M, et al. Influence of patient characteristics and renal function on factor Xa inhibition pharmacokinetics and pharmacodynamics after enoxaparin administration in non-ST-segment elevation acute coronary syndromes. *Am Heart J.* 2002; 143:753–9.
159. Chow S, Zammit K, West K, et al. Correlation of antifactor Xa concentrations with renal function in patients on enoxaparin. *J Clin Pharmacol.* 2003; 43:586–90.
160. Sanderink G, Guimart C, Ozoux ML, et al. Pharmacokinetics and pharmacodynamics of the prophylactic dose of enoxaparin once daily over 4 days in patients with renal impairment. *Thromb Res.* 2002; 105:225–31.
161. Gerlach A, Pickworth K, Seth S, et al. Enoxaparin and bleeding complications: a review in patients with and without renal insufficiency. *Pharmacotherapy.* 2000; 20:771–5.
162. Bates SM, Greer IA, Pabinger I, et al. Venous thromboembolism, thrombophilia, antithrombotic therapy, and pregnancy: American College of Chest Physicians Evidence-Based Clinical Practice Guidelines (8th edition). *Chest.* 2008; 133(suppl):844S–886S.
163. Boehringer Ingelheim. Pradaxa (dabigatran etexilate) prescribing information. www.pradaxa.com (accessed 2012 Oct 2).
164. Janssen Pharmaceuticals. Xarelto (rivaroxaban) prescribing information. www.xarelto-us.com (accessed 2012 Oct 2).
165. Connelly S, Ezekowitz MD, Yusuf S, et al. Dabigatran versus warfarin in patients with atrial fibrillation. *N Engl J Med.* 2009; 361:1139–51.
166. Patel MR, Mahaffey KW, Garg J, et al. Rivaroxaban versus warfarin in nonvalvular atrial fibrillation. *N Engl J Med.* 2011; 365:883–91.
167. Mahan CE, Fanikos J. New antithrombotics: the impact on global health care. *Thromb Res.* 2011; 127:518–24.
168. Weitz JI, Eikelboom JW, Samama MM. New antithrombotic drugs: Antithrombotic Therapy and Prevention of Thrombosis, 9th edition: American College of Chest Physicians Evidence-Based Clinical Practice Guidelines. *Chest.* 2012; 141(suppl):e120S–51S.
169. Eriksson BI, Borris LC, Friedman RJ, et al. Rivaroxaban versus enoxaparin for thromboprophylaxis after hip arthroplasty. *N Engl J Med.* 2008; 358:2765–75.
170. Kakkar AK, Brenner B, Dahl OE, et al. Extended duration rivaroxaban versus short-term enoxaparin for the prevention of venous thromboembolism after total hip arthroplasty: a double-blind, randomised controlled trial. *Lancet.* 2008; 372:31–9.
171. Lassen MR, Ageno W, Borris LC, et al. Rivaroxaban versus enoxaparin for thromboprophylaxis after total knee arthroplasty. *N Engl J Med.* 2008; 358:2776–86.
172. Turpie AG, Lassen MR, Davidson BL, et al. Rivaroxaban versus enoxaparin for thromboprophylaxis after total knee arthroplasty (RECORD 4): a randomised trial. *Lancet.* 2009; 373:1673–80.
173. Merli G, Spyropoulos A, Caprini J. Use of emerging oral anticoagulants in clinical practice. *Ann Surg.* 2009; 250:219–28.
174. Gomez-Outes A, Lecumberri R, Pozo C, et al. New anticoagulants: focus on venous thromboembolism. *Curr Vasc Pharmacol.* 2009; 7:309–29.
175. Ollendorf DA, Vera-Llonch M, Oster G. Cost of venous thromboembolism following major orthopedic surgery in hospitalized patients. *Am J Health-Syst Pharm.* 2002; 59:1750–4.
176. Mcgarry LJ, Stokes ME, Thompson D. Outcomes of thromboprophylaxis with enoxaparin vs. unfractionated heparin in medical inpatients: a retrospective database analysis. *Thromb J.* 2006; 4:17.
177. Weinberg R, Lichtig LK, Caprini JA, et al. Cost implications of using unfractionated heparin or enoxaparin in medical patients at risk for venous thromboembolic events. *P&T.* 2006; 31:322–3.
178. Deitelzweig SB, Becker R, Lin J, et al. Comparison of the two-year outcomes and costs of prophylaxis in medical patients at risk of venous thromboembolism. *Thromb Haemost.* 2008; 100:810–20.

Approved by the ASHP Board of Directors on April 13, 2012. Developed through the ASHP Council on Therapeutics.

The following individuals are acknowledged for reviewing draft versions of this statement: Kathleen Achor, Jill Bates, Pharm.D., M.S., BCOP; Tim Brown, Pharm.D.; Debra Cowan, Pharm.D.; Michele Danish, Pharm.D., FASHP; Jean B. Douglas Pharm.D., FASHP; Stuart T. Haines, Pharm.D., BCPS, FASHP; Jody Jacobson Wedret, B.S.Pharm., FASHP, FCSHP; Patrick McDonnell, Pharm.D.; Nicole L. McMaster-Baxter, Pharm.D., M.S., BCPS; Fred Meister, Pharm.D.; Charles D. Ponte, Pharm.D., DPNAP, FCCP, FAPhA, FASHP; James A. Ponto, M.S., B.S.Pharm., FASHP; and Kay Ryan, M.S., M.B.A.

Charles E. Mahan, Pharm.D., Ph.C., is Director of Outcomes Research, New Mexico Heart Institute, Albuquerque, NM. Alex C. Spyropoulos, M.D., FACP, FCCP, FRCPC, is Associate Professor of Medicine, Division of Hematology/Oncology, James P. Wilmot Cancer Center, University of Rochester Medical Center, Rochester, NY.

Dr. Mahan is a participant in the Traveling Fellowship Program for the North American Thrombosis Forum. Dr. Spyropoulos serves on the advisory board of Johnson and Johnson, Pfizer, and Bristol-Myers Squibb and on the steering committee of Bayer and Eisai. He also serves on the data safety monitoring board of Portola.

The bibliographic citation for this document is as follows: American Society of Health-System Pharmacists. ASHP therapeutic position statement on the role of pharmacotherapy in preventing venous thromboembolism in hospitalized patients. *Am J Health-Syst Pharm.* 2012; 69:2174–90.

ASHP Therapeutic Position Statement on Strategies for Identifying and Preventing Pneumococcal Resistance

Position

The American Society of Health-System Pharmacists (ASHP) supports the establishment of state and national surveillance systems to track the prevalence of drug-resistant *Streptococcus pneumoniae* so that appropriate antimicrobial regimens can be used to treat infections caused by this common community-acquired pathogen.

ASHP supports continued educational efforts to promote the rational use of antimicrobials as a strategy for preventing the development of drug-resistant bacteria.

ASHP supports pharmacist leadership and involvement on antimicrobial stewardship teams and the addition of antimicrobial stewardship as a core component of pharmacy services.

ASHP supports the pharmacist in administration of vaccines for all persons at risk for acquiring pneumococcal disease. ASHP encourages the development of pharmacy-based programs to increase pneumonia vaccination rates of at-risk patients. Use of pneumococcal vaccines is a reliable strategy to decrease the morbidity and mortality associated with invasive infections due to *S. pneumoniae*.

Background

S. pneumoniae, also known as pneumococcus, is the most common cause of community-acquired, bacterial, respiratory-tract infections. It is a frequent cause of meningitis, otitis media, and community-acquired pneumonia. Infections caused by *S. pneumoniae* have been associated with increased morbidity and mortality, especially in children under two years of age and elderly adults. Infections caused by *S. pneumoniae* have historically been successfully treated with a variety of antimicrobials, including penicillin, cephalosporins, and erythromycin. In the early 1990s, the first reports of penicillin-nonsusceptible *S. pneumoniae* (PNSP) began to appear in the United States; these strains include both intermediately resistant and resistant strains of *S. pneumoniae*. To date, reports of increasing resistance of *S. pneumoniae* to penicillin and cephalosporins continue. In the late 1990s, reports of increasing resistance to trimethoprim–sulfamethoxazole, macrolides, and fluoroquinolones began to appear. Many isolates developed resistance to multiple classes of drugs and became known as multidrug-resistant *S. pneumoniae* (MDRSP). The increasing prevalence of MDRSP has created a challenge for health care providers in treating this common community-acquired pathogen.

The clinical significance of drug-resistant *S. pneumoniae* on treatment outcomes is unclear. Most of the available data on clinical outcomes are from retrospective reviews, case–control studies, and case reports. There is evidence that meningitis due to PNSP does not respond to treatment with either penicillin or standard doses of cephalosporins, leading to poor clinical outcomes.[1] In contrast, there does not appear to be a significant difference in clinical outcome, primarily mortality, when pneumonia or other nonmeningeal infections due to PNSP are treated with penicillin or cephalosporins. On the contrary, macrolides and fluoroquinolones with poor in vitro activity against *S. pneumoniae* have been associated with poor clinical outcomes and even treatment failures. It is likely that clinical outcomes are dependent on the mechanism and degree of resistance, the site of infection, and the pharmacokinetic and pharmacodynamic characteristics of the antimicrobial agents used in treatment.

Definitions. The Clinical and Laboratory Standards Institute (CLSI), previously known as the National Committee for Clinical Laboratory Standards, revised the definitions of *S. pneumoniae* susceptibility to several antimicrobials in its 2002 standards. Since that time, there have been two sets of interpretive criteria for *S. pneumoniae* isolates for i.v. penicillin and i.v. cephalosporins, depending on whether meningeal disease is present. *S. pneumoniae* resistant to penicillin is defined in terms of the minimum inhibitory concentration (MIC) of penicillin. Strains in a patient with meningeal disease may be distinguished as susceptible (MIC < 0.06 μg/mL) or resistant (MIC ≥ 0.12 μg/mL). Strains in a patient with nonmeningeal disease may be characterized as susceptible (MIC ≤ 2 μg/mL), intermediately resistant (MIC $= 4$ μg/mL), or highly resistant (MIC ≥ 8 μg/mL).[2] CLSI accounted for the pharmacokinetic and pharmacodynamic factors of a drug in redefining susceptibility breakpoints. The definition of MDRSP is a strain resistant to three or more classes of antibacterials (where those antibacterials may have activity).

Epidemiology. Numerous national and international surveillance studies have been conducted to determine the prevalence of *S. pneumoniae* resistance.[3–7] Although many of these surveillance studies have discontinued the annual collection of data, the Active Bacterial Core Surveillance, known as the ABCs, remains active in the United States.[8] These networks used similar methodologies and specimens: clinical isolates of *S. pneumoniae* from sterile body sites or the respiratory tract, with susceptibility testing in accordance with CLSI standards. Although these studies showed differing resistance rates to the antimicrobials tested, some common trends emerged. The incidence of strains highly resistant to penicillin has surpassed that of intermediately resistant strains. The rates of resistance to non-β-lactams have also increased: the prevalence of macrolide resistance is 20–30%, and trimethoprim–sulfamethoxazole resistance ranges between 24% and 38%. *S. pneumoniae* resistance to levofloxacin is hovering around less than 1%. ABCs personnel evaluate the incidence and susceptibility of invasive *S. pneumoniae* infections in the United States.[8] This surveillance group does not distinguish resistance based on location of disease (i.e., meningeal versus nonmeningeal). For the 2010 isolates, the rates of strains intermediately resistant and highly resistant to penicillin were similar (5.5% and

5.1%, respectively).[8] Resistance to macrolides was 25.7%, which greatly surpassed the intermediately resistant strains (0.5%), leaving 73.8% of strains susceptible. Trimethoprim–sulfamethoxazole susceptibility was slightly higher than the macrolides, at 77.6%, and tetracycline susceptibility was higher at 84.9%. Fluoroquinolone (levofloxacin specifically) resistance remained low at 0.3%, and vancomycin remained universally susceptible (100%). Previously, there were reports from Canada[9] and the Centers for Disease Control and Prevention (CDC)[10] of increasing resistance of *S. pneumoniae* to fluoroquinolones. Most fluoroquinolone-resistant isolates are resistant to other antimicrobials. Fluoroquinolone-resistant organisms are more likely to be found in persons over age 65 years, as this population has the highest usage rate of fluoroquinolones.

Persons at Risk. The greatest risk factor for becoming infected with a drug-resistant strain of *S. pneumoniae* is prior antimicrobial use. Other risk factors include carriage of *S. pneumoniae*, daycare attendance, exposure to children who attend daycare, severe medical comorbidities, immunosuppression, and high alcohol intake.[1] Smoking has been identified as a risk factor for developing invasive *S. pneumoniae* infections.[11] The risk of invasive *S. pneumoniae* infections is 4-fold if the patient is a smoker and 2.5-fold if the patient is exposed to secondhand smoke.[11] The risk of invasive disease declines over time for persons who have stopped smoking.

Mechanisms of Resistance. Resistance of *S. pneumoniae* to β-lactams is due to genetic mutations leading to alterations in three or four of the five high-molecular-weight penicillin-binding proteins (PBPs).[12] The degree of *S. pneumoniae* resistance is dependent on which PBPs are involved and the affinity of the β-lactam agent to the PBP. The differences in expression of these PBPs explain the differences in susceptibility to a variety of β-lactams.

S. pneumoniae resistance to macrolides occurs primarily through two mechanisms: active drug efflux (M phenotype) or ribosomal modification (MLS_B phenotype).[13] Active drug efflux confers resistance to all macrolide agents, whereas ribosomal modification confers resistance not only to the macrolides but also to lincosamides (e.g., clindamycin) and streptogramins. Almost 100% of macrolide-resistant *S. pneumoniae* found in the United States is attributable to ribosomal modification via methylation.[13]

Resistance of *S. pneumoniae* to fluoroquinolones is primarily a result of the mutations of the *parC* and *gyrA* genes, though efflux pumps may also play a role.[14] Alterations in the *parC* subunit of topoisomerase IV result in the reduced susceptibility of *S. pneumoniae* to gatifloxacin, levofloxacin, and moxifloxacin. This single-step mutation is difficult to detect clinically because isolates with a *parC* mutation are reported as susceptible using standard laboratory testing. This is concerning because isolates with single-step mutations are the progenitors for fully drug-resistant strains of *S. pneumoniae*, which have additional mutations in the *gyrA* subunit of DNA gyrase.

Establishment of Surveillance Systems

Surveillance systems are an integral component of combating bacterial resistance. The data gathered from surveillance systems can be used for many purposes, including identifying and tracking global outbreaks, identifying new strains and resistance profiles, setting public health policy, heightening awareness of health care providers to local resistance patterns that may affect the routine care of patients, and determining appropriate treatment for infections.

Health systems should develop a mechanism for the local surveillance of bacterial resistance and participate in state and national surveillance programs when available. Ideally, the surveillance system should identify trends in bacterial susceptibility patterns and correlate them with antimicrobial use in both health systems and communities.[15] The clinical microbiology laboratory, pharmacy, infection prevention, and information technology departments play important roles in maintaining an active surveillance system.

At a national level, data acquired through surveillance systems such as those used by CDC and the World Health Organization (WHO) can aid in the research and development of policies and treatment guidelines for pneumococcal disease. State and local surveillance is also essential, as national trends may not reflect trends within specific regions. On a local level, surveillance programs can help raise provider and public awareness of drug-resistant *S. pneumoniae* and direct patient care on an institutional level and potentially on the unit level. Institutional antibiograms should be updated annually, and microbiological data used for diagnosis should be stored in a way that will facilitate resistance surveillance.[16,17] Surveillance data may also be useful for tracking the impact of interventions, such as formulary changes and antimicrobial stewardship interventions, targeting the inappropriate or unnecessary use of antibiotics.

Rational Use of Antimicrobials

There is an abundance of literature showing the relationship between antimicrobial-use patterns and the development of bacterial resistance.[18–21] However, the bulk of this literature thus far has been generated from hospital or institutional studies and has little bearing on PNSP. Since *S. pneumoniae* is primarily a community-acquired pathogen, antimicrobial use in the outpatient setting has the greatest influence on its susceptibility profile. Few studies have shown a relationship between outpatient prescription use or antimicrobial stewardship interventions and *S. pneumoniae* susceptibility patterns. In the United States, Diekema and colleagues[22] found a positive correlation between high usage rates of outpatient β-lactam agents and the decreased penicillin susceptibility of *S. pneumoniae*. No correlation was found between the use of other antimicrobial classes (e.g., macrolides, tetracyclines, fluoroquinolones) and the decreased penicillin susceptibility of *S. pneumoniae*. More recently, Hicks et al.[23] reviewed outpatient antimicrobial prescription data (penicillins, cephalosporins, macrolides, and trimethoprim–sulfamethoxazole) and found a consistent relationship between higher prescription rates and increased rates of *S. pneumoniae* nonsusceptibility to the respective antimicrobial class. This study also found that when comparing sites with high versus low antimicrobial prescription rates for the same class of antimicrobials, macrolide and cephalosporin prescriptions were both associated with serotype 19A, despite yearly decreases in outpatient antimicrobial prescribing rates. Both of these studies were large, retrospective database studies and did not account for patient adherence to antimicrobial regimens. However, these studies demonstrated that antimicrobial use in the community is substantial and plays a role in the development of microbial resistance.

Approximately 50% of prescriptions for antimicrobials are unnecessary or inappropriate.[24] These agents are usually prescribed for treatment of the common cold, upper-respiratory-tract infections, acute rhinosinusitis, and bronchitis, ailments often caused by viruses that do not respond to antibacterials. Recent clinical practice guidelines from the Infectious Diseases Society of America for acute bacterial rhinosinusitis in children and adults acknowledged the difficulty in distinguishing between viral and bacterial etiologies. To decrease inappropriate antibacterial use, the guidelines recommend initiating antibacterials only if the patient has symptoms that are persistent and not improving (duration of ≥10 days), severe (≥3–4 days), or worsening or "double sickening" (subsequent worsening of symptoms or additional symptoms after earlier improvement). Prescribers for patients who do not yet meet the criteria for antibacterial treatment of rhinosinusitis will occasionally give a prescription for antibacterials with the instructions to fill and take the medication if symptoms are persistent. Pharmacists can assist patients in making appropriate decisions on antimicrobial use by counseling patients on the appropriate timing of initiating antibacterials as well as the importance of completing the prescribed treatment course. In addition, empirical antibacterial selection should not include amoxicillin, macrolides, trimethoprim–sulfamethoxazole, or monotherapy with second- or third-generation cephalosporins due to high rates of resistance in *S. pneumoniae*. Finally, a shorter course of antibacterial treatment (5–7 days) is recommended for adults, compared with the 10–14 days recommended for children. Several national organizations,[15,24] CDC, and WHO have advocated antimicrobial stewardship as a mechanism to limit the development of bacterial resistance.[25,26] One of the cornerstones of antimicrobial stewardship is the appropriate use of antimicrobials. Pharmacists should take active roles in antimicrobial stewardship programs, and the infectious diseases pharmacist is considered a core member of the antimicrobial stewardship team.[24,27]

In 1995, CDC launched the National Campaign for Appropriate Antibiotic Use in the Community, which, in 2003, was renamed Get Smart: Know When Antibiotics Work campaign.[28] This campaign was launched in response to growing antimicrobial resistance with respiratory pathogens and aims to reduce the rise of antimicrobial resistance through the promotion of appropriate prescribing, decrease the demand for antimicrobials to treat viral respiratory infections, and increase patient adherence with antimicrobials prescribed for upper-respiratory-tract infections. This program provides a wealth of information for the antimicrobial stewards and the public to help increase awareness at their facilities and includes promotional material for inpatient, outpatient, and long-term-care settings.

Vaccination

Pneumococcal infection has been associated with 2.4 million days of hospitalization and approximately 5000 deaths annually in the United States.[29] As vaccination may contribute to a reduction in these numbers and because hospitalization is an underutilized opportunity for vaccination, the Joint Commission (in collaboration with the Centers for Medicare and Medicaid Services) in January 2012 expanded the pneumococcal vaccination process measure to include all patients regardless of diagnosis. This measure evaluates if, before hospital discharge, patients age 6 years or older were screened for pneumococcal vaccine status and received the pneumococcal vaccine if appropriate. Infections caused by *S. pneumoniae* continue to cause significant morbidity and mortality despite the availability of effective vaccines.

The 23-valent pneumococcal polysaccharide vaccine (PPSV23), the 13-valent pneumococcal conjugate vaccine (PCV13), and the 7-valent pneumococcal conjugate vaccine (PCV7) have been shown to be highly effective in providing protection against the most commonly isolated pneumococcal serotypes that cause human disease, including those serotypes known to be antimicrobial resistant. While the use of these vaccines will not prevent the development of drug-resistant *S. pneumoniae*, they will likely prevent invasive infection caused by a drug-resistant organism. PPSV23 is recommended for all adults age 65 years or older and other adults with certain comorbid conditions.[30] It may also be

Table 1.

Patients Who Should Receive the 13-Valent Pneumococcal Conjugate Vaccine (PCV13)

Risk Group	Underlying Medical Condition
Immunocompetent persons	Cerebrospinal fluid leak Cochlear implant
Immunocompromised persons	Congenital or acquired immune deficiency Human immunodeficiency virus infection Chronic renal failure Nephrotic syndrome Leukemia Lymphoma Hodgkin disease Generalized malignancy Iatrogenic immunosuppression (diseases requiring treatment with immunosuppressive drugs, including long-term systemic corticosteroids and radiation therapy) Solid organ transplant Multiple myeloma
Persons with functional or anatomical asplenia	Sickle cell disease or other hemaglobinopathy Congenital or acquired asplenia

given to select groups of high-risk patients over 2 years of age (such as those with cochlear implants) as long as it is administered at least eight weeks after administration of the last dose of PCV7 or PCV13. This PPSV23 vaccine does not produce an adequate immunologic response in children under 2 years old and should not be used in that population. PCV7 was added to the standard recommended pediatric vaccines in October 2000.[31] PCV13 was added in 2010. The PCV series should be given to all children beginning at age 2 months. A single supplemental dose of PCV13 is recommended for all children age 14–59 months and for children age 60–71 months with certain underlying medical conditions who have already received an age-appropriate PCV7 series.[32] The CDC National Immunization Program has established recommendations for pneumococcal vaccine administration.[30,32]

PPSV23 was licensed in the early 1980s and has demonstrated good immunogenicity in both young and older adults; however, an individual will not develop an immune response to all 23 pneumococcal serotypes.[33] The reason for

Table 2.

Medical Conditions or Other Indications for Administration of 13-Valent Pneumococcal Conjugate Vaccine (PCV13), and Indications for 23-Valent Pneumococcal Polysaccharide Vaccine (PPSV23) Administration and Revaccination for Adults Age 19 Years or Older[24,a]

	PCV13	PPSV23	
Risk Group and Underlying Medical Condition	**Recommended**	**Recommended**	**Revaccination 5 Years After First Dose**
Immunocompetent persons			
Chronic heart disease[b]		X	
Chronic lung disease[c]		X	
Diabetes mellitus		X	
Cerebrospinal fluid leak	X	X	
Cochlear implant	X	X	
Alcoholism		X	
Chronic liver disease, cirrhosis		X	
Cigarette smoking		X	
Persons with functional or anatomic asplenia			
Sickle cell disease or other hemaglobinopathy	X	X	X
Congenital or acquired asplenia	X	X	X
Immunocompromised persons			
Congenital or acquired immunodeficiency[d]	X	X	X
Human immunodeficiency virus infection	X	X	X
Chronic renal failure	X	X	X
Nephrotic syndrome	X	X	X
Leukemia	X	X	X
Lymphoma	X	X	X
Hodgkin disease	X	X	X
Generalized malignancy	X	X	X
Iatrogenic immunosuppression[e]	X	X	X
Solid organ transplant	X	X	X
Multiple myeloma	X	X	X

[a]All adults age ≥65 years should receive a dose of PPSV23, regardless of previous history of vaccination with pneumococcal vaccine.
[b]Including congestive heart failure and cardiomyopathies, excluding hypertension.
[c]Including chronic obstructive pulmonary disease, emphysema, and asthma.
[d]Includes B- (humoral) or T-lymphocyte deficiency, complement deficiencies (particularly C1, C2, C3, and C4 deficiencies), and phagocytic disorders (excluding chronic granulomatous disease).
[e]Diseases requiring treatment with immunosuppressive drugs, including long-term systemic corticosteroids and radiation therapy.

this is unclear. Despite the vaccine's long-standing availability and documented effectiveness, approximately 64% of eligible persons actually receive it.[34] One of the Healthy People 2020 goals is for 90% of eligible adults to receive the pneumococcal vaccine.[35] This is an excellent opportunity for pharmacists to improve the vaccination rate of older adult patients and help promote national health care goals.

Revaccination with PPSV23 is recommended for adults over age 65 years if the first dose was administered when they were under 65 years old at the time of vaccination and at least 5 years has elapsed since the first dose.[30] In addition, persons younger than 65 years with immunocompromising conditions may receive a one-time revaccination if 5 years has elapsed since the first dose of PPSV23. Revaccination with PPSV23 results in a somewhat blunted immune response and is associated with increased injection-site reactions.[33]

PCV7 for children has been available since February 2000. Use of this vaccine has been shown to decrease the carriage rate of *S. pneumoniae* and the incidence of invasive pneumococcal disease, acute otitis media, and pneumonia in vaccinated populations.[36,37] The rate of vaccine-specific serotype *S. pneumoniae* carriage in vaccinated children remains below the rate for nonvaccinated children over prolonged periods of time. Widespread vaccination of children with PCV7 has shown a "herd effect" in decreasing the carriage rate of *S. pneumoniae* in children, who are an important vector for the transmission of *S. pneumoniae* to other children and adults.[36] This is similar to what was seen with widespread use of the *Haemophilus influenzae* type B vaccine and the marked decrease in *H. influenzae*-related infections.

PCV13 for children and adults has been available since February 2010 and has taken the place of the discontinued PCV7. All children age 2–59 months should have routine immunization with PCV13.[32] CDC has established routine and catch-up schedules for vaccination. Recommendations by the CDC Advisory Committee on Immunization Practices for the use of PCV13 in adults were established in 2012.[30] Patients who have immunocompromising conditions should receive PCV13 in addition to PPSV23 (Tables 1 and 2). Screening and vaccination should occur in all appropriate adult patients. Timing of PCV13 and PPSV23 administration is important to ensure maximal immune response. If the person has never received a dose of PCV13 or PPSV23, he or she should receive a dose of PCV13 followed by a dose of PPSV23 at least eight weeks later. If the patient has received one or more doses of PPSV23, the patient should receive one dose of PCV13 at least one year after the last dose of PPSV23.

Health care institutions should develop robust programs to increase pneumococcal vaccination rates as pneumococcal disease continues to contribute to a significant amount of morbidity and mortaility in the United States. More than 65% of patients with severe pneumococcal disease have been hospitalized in the preceding—three to five years, but few have received vaccine.[34] Most people who succumb to preventable infections have visited a health care provider in the preceding year but were not vaccinated.[38–42] Clinicians should ensure that patients receive proper immunizations,[43,44] and pharmacists can promote vaccination efforts by serving as educators, facilitators, and vaccinators. Currently, all 50 states allow pharmacists to administer vaccines, and 49 states allow pharmacists to administer pneumococcal vaccines.[45] Variability exists among the states regarding patient age limitations and pharmacist-administered vaccines, with 13 states authorizing pharmacists to vaccinate patients of any age.[46] Although vaccinations are typically administered in the ambulatory care setting, clinicians must also seize opportunities to vaccinate hospitalized patients (Figure 1). Pharmacists have demonstrated that they can increase the number of persons receiving needed vaccines in both inpatient and ambulatory care settings.[47]

Summary

The incidence of MDRSP continues to increase, causing significant morbidity and mortality. Health care providers should seize the opportunity to promote the judicious use of antimicrobials and vaccinate patients with the pneumococcal vaccines as a means to lessen this significant health problem. Pharmacists are poised to play a key role in patient care by assessing for the need and administering vaccines in compliance with the current guidelines. A pharmacist should have a key role on the antimicrobial stewardship team.

References

1. Pallares R, Fenoll A, Liñares J, for the Spanish Pneumococcal Infection Study Network. The epidemiology of antibiotic resistance in *Streptococcus pneumoniae* and the clinical relevance of resistance to cephalosporins, macrolides and fluoroquinolones. *Int J Antimicrob Agents.* 2003; 22(suppl 1):S15–24.
2. Performance standards for antimicrobial susceptibility testing; 23rd informational supplement. Wayne, PA: Clinical and Laboratory Standards Institute; 2013.
3. Centers for Disease Control and Prevention. ABCs report: *Streptococcus pneumoniae,* 2001. www.cdc.gov/abcs/reports-findings/survreports/spneu01.html (accessed 2013 Nov 20).
4. Jacobs MR, Felmingham D, Appelbaum PC, et al. The Alexander Project 1998–2000: susceptibility of pathogens isolated from community-acquired respiratory tract infection to commonly used antimicrobial agents. *J Antimicrob Chemother.* 2003; 52:229–46.
5. Doern G, Rybak MJ. Activity of telithromycin against *Streptococcus pneumoniae* resistant to penicillin, macrolides and fluoroquinolones isolated from respiratory tract infections: PROTEK US year 2 (2001–2002). Presented at 43rd Annual Interscience Conference on Antimicrobial Agents and Chemotherapy. Chicago, IL; 2003 Sep.
6. Doern GV, Heilmann KP, Huynh HK, et al. Antimicrobial resistance among clinical isolates of *Streptococcus pneumoniae* in the United Stated during 1999–2000, including a comparison of resistance rates since 1994–1995. *Antimicrob Agents Chemother.* 2001; 45:1721–9.
7. Karlowsky JA, Thornsberry C, Jones ME, et al. Factors associated with relative rates of antimicrobial resistance among *Streptococcus pneumoniae* in the United States: results from the TRUST surveillance program (1998–2002). *Clin Infect Dis.* 2003; 36:963–70.
8. Centers for Disease Control and Prevention. ABCs report: *Streptococcus pneumoniae,* 2010. www.cdc.gov/abcs/reports-findings/survreports/spneu10.html (accessed 2013 Nov 20).

Figure 1. Example pneumococcal vaccine administration pathway with notification for adult patients. PCV13 = 13-valent pneumococcal conjugate vaccine, PPSV23 = 23-valent pneumococcal polysaccharide vaccine, CDC = Centers for Disease Control and Prevention.

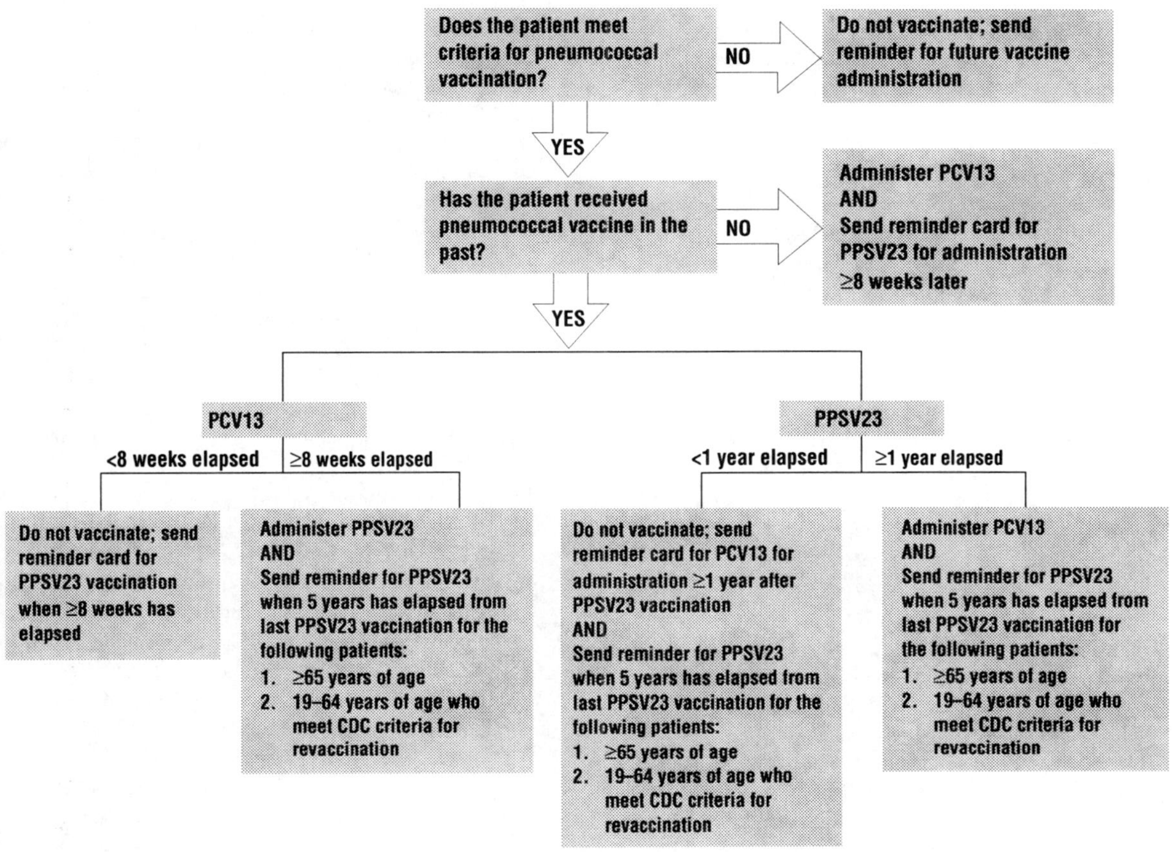

9. Chen DK, McGeer A, de Azavedo JC, et al. Decreased susceptibility of *Streptococcus pneumoniae* to fluoroquinolones in Canada. *N Engl J Med.* 1999; 341:233–9.
10. Centers for Disease Control and Prevention. Resistance of *Streptococcus pneumoniae* to fluoroquinolones—United States, 1995–1999. *MMWR.* 2001; 50:800–4.
11. Nuorti JP, Butler JC, Farley MM, et al. Cigarette smoking and invasive pneumococcal disease. *N Engl J Med.* 2000; 342:681–9.
12. Appelbaum PC. Resistance among *Streptococcus pneumoniae*: implications for drug selection. *Clin Infect Dis.* 2002; 34:1613–20.
13. Lynch JP, Martinez FJ. Clinical relevance of macrolide-resistant *Streptococcus pneumoniae* for community-acquired pneumonia. *Clin Infect Dis.* 2002; 34(suppl 1):S27–46.
14. Hooper DC. Fluoroquinolone resistance among gram-positive cocci. *Lancet Infect Dis.* 2002; 2:530–8.
15. Shales DM, Gerding DN, John JF. et al. Society for Healthcare Epidemiology of America and Infectious Diseases Society of America Joint Committee on Prevention of Antimicrobial Resistance: guidelines for the prevention of antimicrobial resistance in hospitals. *Clin Infect Dis.* 1997; 25:584–99.
16. Analysis and presentation of cumulative antimicrobial susceptibility test data; approved guideline, third edition. CLSI document M39-A3. Wayne, PA: Clinical and Laboratory Standards Institute; 2009.
17. World Health Organization. Surveillance standards for antimicrobial resistance. http://whqlibdoc.who.int/hq/2002/WHO_CDS_CSR_DRS_2001.5.pdf (accessed 2013 Nov 20).
18. Davies J, Davies D. Origins and evolution of antibiotic resistance. *Microbiol Mol Biol Rev.* 2010; 74:417–33.
19. Freire-Moran L, Aronsson B, Manz C, et al. Critical shortage of new antibiotics in development against multidrug-resistant bacteria-Time to react is now. *Drug Resist Updat.* 2011; 14:118–24.
20. Peleg AY, Hooper DC. Hospital-acquired infections due to gram-negative bacteria. *N Engl J Med.* 2010; 362:1804–13.
21. Meyer E, Schwab F, Schroeren-Boersch B, et al. Dramatic increase of third-generation cephalosporin-resistant E. coli in German intensive care units: secular trends in antibiotic drug use and bacterial resistance, 2001 to 2008. *Crit Care.* 2010; 14:R113.
22. Diekema DJ, Brueggemann AB, Doern GV. Antimicrobial-drug use and changes in resistance in *Streptococcus pneumoniae. Emerg Infect Dis.* 2000; 6:552–6.
23. Hicks LA, Chien YW, Taylor TH Jr, et al. Outpatient antibiotic prescribing and nonsusceptible *Streptococcus*

pneumoniae in the United States, 1996–2003. *Clin Infect Dis.* 2011; 53:631–9.

24. Dellit TH, Owens RC, McGowan JE Jr, et al. Infectious Diseases Society of America and the Society for Healthcare Epidemiology of America guidelines for developing an institutional program to enhance antimicrobial stewardship. *Clin Infect Dis.* 2007; 44:159–77.
25. Centers for Disease Control and Prevention. Public health action plan to combat antimicrobial resistance. www.cdc.gov/drugresistance/actionplan/introduction_overview.html (accessed 2014 Jan 23).
26. Leung E, Weil DE, Raviglione M, et al. The WHO policy package to combat antimicrobial resistance. *Bull World Health Organ.* 2011; 89:390–2.
27. ASHP statement on the pharmacist's role in antimicrobial stewardship and infection prevention and control. *Am J Health-Syst Pharm.* 2010; 67:575–7.
28. Centers for Disease Control and Prevention. About the Get Smart campaign. www.cdc.gov/getsmart/campaign-materials/about-campaign.html (accessed 2013 Nov 20).
29. Specifications manual for national hospital inpatient quality measures discharges 07-01-12 (3Q12) through 12-31-12 (4Q12). Oakbrook Terrace, IL: Joint Commission; 2011.
30. Centers for Disease Control and Prevention. Recommended adult immunization schedule—United States, 2013. www.cdc.gov/vaccines/schedules/downloads/adult/adult-schedule.pdf (accessed 2013 Nov 20).
31. Centers for Disease Control and Prevention. Preventing pneumococcal disease among infants and young children: recommendations of the Advisory Committee on Immunization Practices (ACIP). *MMWR.* 2000; 49(RR-9):1–35.
32. Centers for Disease Control and Prevention. Birth—18 years and "catch-up" immunization schedules; Uniteed States, 2013. www.cdc.gov/vaccines/schedules/hcp/child-adolescent.html (accessed 2013 Nov 21).
33. Artz AS, Ershler WB, Longo DL. Pneumococcal vaccination and revaccination of older adults. *Clin Microbiol Rev.* 2003; 16:308–18.
34. Centers for Disease Control and Prevention. Epidemiology and prevention of vaccine-preventable diseases. The pink book: course textbook. www.cdc.gov/vaccines/pubs/pinkbook/pneumo.html#vaccines (accessed 2013 Nov 20).
35. Department of Health and Human Services. Healthy People 2020. www.healthypeople.gov (accessed 2012 Sep 27).
36. Dagan R, Fraser D. Conjugate pneumococcal vaccine and antibiotic-resistant *Streptococcus pneumoniae*: herd immunity and reduction of otitis morbidity. *Pediatr Infect Dis J.* 2000; 19(suppl):S79–88.
37. Whitney CG, Farley MM, Hadler J, et al. Decline in invasive pneumococcal disease after the introduction of protein-polysaccharide conjugate vaccine. *N Engl J Med.* 2003; 348:1737–46.
38. Williams WW, Hickson MA, Kane MA, et al. Immunization policies and vaccine coverage among adults. The risk for missed opportunites. *Ann Intern Med.* 1988; 108:616–25.
39. Fedson DS, Hickson MA, Kane MA, et al. Hospital-based pneumococcal immunization. Epidemiologic rationale from the Shenandoah study. *JAMA.* 1990; 264:1117–22.
40. Fedson DS. Influenza and pneumococcal immunization strategies for physicians. *Chest.* 1987; 91:436–43.
41. Magnussen CR, Valenti WM, Mushlin AI. Pneumococcal vaccine strategy. Feasibility of a vaccination program directed at hospitalized and ambulatory patients. *Arch Intern Med.* 1984; 144:1755–7.
42. Vondracek TG, Pham TP, Huycke MM. A hospital-based pharmacy interventions program for pneumococcal vaccination. *Arch Intern Med.* 1998; 158:1543–7.
43. American Society of Health-System Pharmacists. ASHP guidelines on the pharmacist's role in immunization. *Am J Health-Syst Pharm.* 2003; 60:1371–7.
44. Grabenstein JD, Bonasso J. Health-system pharmacists' role in immunizing adults against pneumococcal disease and influenza. *Am J Health-Syst Pharm.* 1999; 56(suppl 2):S2–24.
45. Immunization Action Coalition. States authorizing pharmacists to vaccinate. www.immunize.org/laws/pharm.asp (accessed 2012 Dec 27).
46. American Pharmacists Association. Pharmacist administered vaccines. www.pharmacist.com/sites/default/files/files/PharmacistIMZAuthority_June18_2012%20%5BRead-Only%5D.pdf (accessed 2012 Dec 27).
47. Noped JC, Schomberg R. Implementing an inpatient pharmacy-based pneumococcal vaccination program. *Am J Health-Syst Pharm.* 2001; 58:1852–5.

Kimberly A. Couch, Pharm.D., M.A., FIDSA, FASHP, is President, Infectious Diseases Pharmacy Associates, Stevensville, MD, and Clinical Pharmacist, Complete Rx, Seaford, DE. Teresa Geide, Pharm.D., BCPS, CGP, is Clinical Pharmacy Specialist, Infectious Diseases, Orlando Veterans Affairs Medical Center, Orlando, FL.

Developed through the ASHP Council on Therapeutics and approved by the ASHP Board of Directors on August 2, 2013.

The following individuals are acknowledged for reviewing draft versions of this statement: Arthur Chaput; Steven Dzierba, Pharm.D., M.S., FASHP; Kathleen M. Gura, Pharm.D., BCNSP, FASHP, FPPAG; Mojdeh Heavner, Pharm.D., BCPS; Jody Jacobson Wedret, B.S.Pharm., FASHP, FCSHP; Kristi Kuper, Pharm.D., BCPS; Fred Meister, Pharm.D., FASHP; Robert J. Moura, B.S.Pharm., M.S.; Michael Postelnick, B.S.Pharm, BCPS-AQ Infectious Diseases; and Michael Powell, B.S.P., M.S.P., FASHP.

The authors have declared no potential conflicts of interest.

This document supersedes the ASHP therapeutic position statement for identifying and preventing pneumococcal resistance approved by the ASHP Board of Directors on April 15, 2004.

The bibliographic citation for this document is as follows: American Society of Health-System Pharmacists. ASHP therapeutic position statement on strategies for identifying and preventing pneumococcal resistance. *Am J Health-Syst Pharm.* 2014; 71:417–24.

Therapeutic Monitoring of Vancomycin in Adult Patients: A Consensus Review of the American Society of Health-System Pharmacists, the Infectious Diseases Society of America, and the Society of Infectious Diseases Pharmacists

Vancomycin is a glycopeptide antibiotic that has been in clinical use for nearly 50 years as a penicillin alternative to treat penicillinase-producing strains of *Staphylococcus aureus*. It is one of the most widely used antibiotics in the United States for the treatment of serious gram-positive infections involving methicillin-resistant *S. aureus* (MRSA).[1] Early use of vancomycin was associated with a number of adverse effects, including infusion-related toxicities, nephrotoxicity, and possible ototoxicity. Upon further investigation, it appears that the impurities in early formulations of vancomycin caused many of these adverse events.[1-4] Its overall use was curtailed significantly with the development of semisynthetic penicillins (e.g., methicillin, oxacillin, nafcillin) that were considered less toxic.[1-4] However, the steady rise in the number of MRSA infections since the early 1980s has once again brought vancomycin into the forefront as the primary treatment for infections caused by this organism.

Over the years, vancomycin has been one of the most studied antibiotics. Extensive pharmacokinetic studies in a variety of patient populations and the availability of commercial drug assays have allowed clinicians to target serum vancomycin concentrations precisely in a relatively narrow range. This approach has been advocated to lessen the potential for nephrotoxicity and ototoxicity and to achieve therapeutic concentrations. However, it should be noted that the practice of routine monitoring and adjusting of serum vancomycin drug concentrations has been the subject of intense debate for many years.[5-9] The controversy has resulted from conflicting evidence regarding the use of serum vancomycin concentrations to predict and prevent drug-induced toxicity and as a measure of effectiveness in treating infections. Further, data derived from more recent studies appear to suggest that vancomycin has little potential for nephrotoxicity or ototoxicity when used at conventional dosages (e.g., 1 g every 12 hours [15 mg/kg every 12 hours]), unless it is used concomitantly with known nephrotoxic drugs or at very high dosages.[10-12] This consensus review evaluates the scientific data and controversies associated with serum vancomycin monitoring and provides recommendations based on the available evidence.

This is a consensus statement of the American Society of Health-System Pharmacists (ASHP), the Infectious Diseases Society of America (IDSA), and the Society of Infectious Diseases Pharmacists (SIDP). Consensus committee members were assigned key topics regarding vancomycin that contribute to current knowledge about patient monitoring. A draft document addressing these areas that included specific recommendations was reviewed by all committee members. After peer review by members of ASHP, IDSA, and SIDP, the committee met to review the submitted comments and recommendations. After careful discussion and consideration of these suggestions, the document was revised and circulated among the committee and supporting organizations for final comment. This consensus review represents the opinion of the majority of committee members.

A search of PubMed was conducted using the following search terms: vancomycin pharmacokinetics, pharmacodynamics, efficacy, resistance, and toxicity. All relevant and available peer-reviewed studies in the English language published between 1958 and 2008 were considered. Studies were rated by their quality of evidence, and the subsequent recommendations were graded using the classification schemata of the Canadian Medical Association (Table 1).[13] Recommendations of the expert panel are presented in Table 2.

Potential limitations of this review include the facts that few prospective or randomized trials of vancomycin monitoring were available and that most of the published literature regarding vancomycin monitoring described observational studies in patients with *S. aureus* infection. Vancomycin monitoring in pediatric patients is beyond the scope of this review.

Table 1.
Definitions of Levels and Grades for Recommendations[13]

Quality Indicator	Type of Evidence
Level of evidence	
I	Evidence from at least one properly randomized, controlled trial
II	Evidence from at least one well-designed clinical trial, without randomization; from cohort or case-controlled analytic studies (preferably from more than one center); from multiple time series; or from dramatic results from uncontrolled experiments
III	Evidence from opinions of respected authorities, based on clinical experience, descriptive studies, or reports of expert committees
Grade of recommendation	
A	Good evidence to support a recommendation for use
B	Moderate evidence to support a recommendation for use
C	Poor evidence to support a recommendation for use

Overview of Vancomycin Pharmacokinetic and Pharmacodynamic Properties

Sophisticated pharmacokinetic techniques such as Bayesian and noncompartmental modeling have been used to derive pharmacokinetic parameters for vancomycin. The serum vancomycin concentration–time profile is complex and has been characterized as one-, two-, and three-compartment pharmacokinetic models. In patients with normal renal function, the α-distribution phase ranges from 30 minutes to 1 hour, and the β-elimination half-life ranges from 6 to 12 hours. The volume of distribution is 0.4–1 L/kg.[14-18]

While reports of the degree of vancomycin protein binding have varied, a level of 50–55% is most often stated.[19,20] Penetration of vancomycin into tissues is variable and can be affected by inflammation and disease state. For example, with uninflamed meninges, cerebral spinal fluid vancomycin concentrations ranging from 0 to approximately 4 mg/L have been reported, whereas concentrations of 6.4–11.1 mg/L have been reported in the presence of inflammation.[21] Penetration into skin tissue is significantly lower for patients with diabetes (median, 0.1 mg/L; range, 0.01–0.45 mg/L) compared with nondiabetic patients based on the median ratio of tissue vancomycin to plasma vancomycin concentrations (median, 0.3 mg/L; range, 0.46–0.94 mg/L).[21] Vancomycin concentrations in lung tissue ranging from 5% to 41% of serum vancomycin concentrations have been reported in studies of healthy volunteers and patients.[5,6,22,23] Epithelial lining fluid (ELF) penetration in critically injured patients is highly variable, with an overall blood:ELF penetration ratio of 6:1.[23,24]

Selection of Pharmacokinetic and Pharmacodynamic Monitoring Parameters

A variety of pharmacokinetic and pharmacodynamic monitoring parameters have been proposed for vancomycin, including time (t) the concentration of vancomycin remains above the minimum inhibitory concentration (MIC), the ratio of the area under the serum drug concentration-versus-time curve and the MIC, and the ratio of the maximum serum drug concentration (C_{max}) and the MIC. These parameters are abbreviated t>MIC, AUC/MIC, and C_{max}/MIC, respectively. Reviews of pharmacokinetics and pharmacodynamics have recommended the AUC/MIC as the preferred parameter based in part on data from animal models, in vitro studies, and limited human studies.[6,25-28] Studies by Ackerman et al.,[29] Löwdin et al.,[30] and Larsson et al.[31] demonstrated that vancomycin kills *S. aureus* and *Staphylococcus epidermidis* in a concentration-independent fashion. By simulating free vancomycin peak concentrations of 40, 20, 10, and 5 mg/L in an in vitro chemostat model with a normal vancomycin terminal half-life of six hours, Larsson et al.[31] found no difference in the corresponding bacterial kill curves for *S. aureus*.

Using neutropenic mouse models, investigators have concluded that the AUC/MIC is the pharmacodynamically linked parameter for measuring vancomycin's effectiveness in treating *S. aureus*, including methicillin-susceptible *S. aureus* (MSSA), MRSA, and vancomycin-intermediate *S. aureus* (VISA) strains.[6,25] (Note: The total AUC/MIC and the free vancomycin AUC/MIC [AUC × 50% protein binding/MIC] have been interchangeably reported for vancomycin. Unless designated *f*AUC/MIC, this consensus review refers to total AUC/MIC.)

Craig and Andes[32] recently evaluated the use of free vancomycin AUC_{0-24hr}/MIC (*f*AUC/MIC) as the primary parameter for predicting vancomycin activity against VISA, heteroresistant VISA (hVISA), and MSSA in the murine neutropenic mouse model. They found that the *f*AUC/MIC requirement varied depending on the vancomycin MIC and was a function of bacterial density at the site of infection, with a lower *f*AUC/MIC needed for a lower bacterial inoculum. Of interest, the dose required for a 2 log colony-forming unit/g kill was 2.5 times higher for hVISA strains than for VISA and vancomycin-susceptible *S. aureus* strains. The researchers concluded that vancomycin dosages of 500 mg every 6 hours or 1 g every 12 hours provide *f*AUC/MIC values of 100–250 and suggested that values around 500 may enhance the therapeutic effectiveness of vancomycin in humans.

Moise-Broder et al.[33] explored the use of AUC/MIC in predicting clinical and microbiological success in treating ventilator-associated *S. aureus* pneumonia. These investigators suggested an average AUC/MIC of 345 for a successful clinical outcome and a ratio of 850 for a successful microbiological outcome. For pathogens with an MIC of 1 mg/L, an AUC/MIC of approximately 250 can be achieved in most patients with 1 g every 12 hours based on a patient with an actual body weight (ABW) of 80 kg and normal renal function (i.e., creatinine clearance [CL_{cr}] = 100 mL/min), but obtaining a target AUC/MIC of 850 would require much higher dosages for most patients.

Summary: *Based on these study results, an AUC/MIC ratio of ≥400 has been advocated as a target to achieve clinical effectiveness with vancomycin. Animal studies and limited human data appear to demonstrate that vancomycin is not concentration dependent and that the AUC/MIC is a predictive pharmacokinetic parameter for vancomycin.*

Impact of Dosing Strategies on Pharmacokinetic and Pharmacodynamic Parameters

The initial clinical dosing strategies for vancomycin were developed in the late 1950s before the emergence of antibiotic pharmacodynamics.[34] Published data on the pharmacodynamics of vancomycin against specific bacterial pathogens or infections are very limited, with much of the available data generated from in vitro or animal models. This is partly due to the drug's generic status, which discourages manufacturers from conducting well-controlled scientific investigations that would provide additional and clarifying pharmacodynamic data. It is recommended that dosages be calculated based on ABW. There are limited data on dosing in obese patients; however, initial dosages should be based on ABW and adjusted based on serum vancomycin concentrations to achieve therapeutic levels.[17]

Vancomycin is ideally suited from a pharmacokinetic and pharmacodynamic perspective for intermittent administration based on the usual susceptibility of staphylococci and streptococci (MIC values of ≤1 mg/L), the most commonly used dosage regimen for vancomycin (1 g every 12 hours), and the concentration-independent nature of the drug. As a

Table 2.
Summary of Expert Panel Recommendations for Vancomycin Therapeutic Drug Monitoring (TDM)[a]

Variable	Recommendation	Level of Evidence and Grade of Recommendation	Section of Consensus Review
Recommended TDM Parameters			
Optimal monitoring parameter	Trough serum vancomycin concentrations are the most accurate and practical method for monitoring efficacy.	IIB	Therapeutic vancomycin drug monitoring, Peak versus trough concentrations
Timing of monitoring	Troughs should be obtained just prior to the next dose at steady-state conditions (just before the fourth dose).	IIB	Therapeutic vancomycin drug monitoring, Peak versus trough concentrations
Optimal trough concentration (see also Optimal trough concentration—complicated infections)	Minimum serum vancomycin trough concentrations should always be maintained above 10 mg/L to avoid development of resistance. For a pathogen with an MIC of 1 mg/L, the minimum trough concentration would have to be at least 15 mg/L to generate the target AUC:MIC of 400.	IIIB	Therapeutic vancomycin drug monitoring, Optimal trough concentrations
Optimal trough concentration—complicated infections (bacteremia, endocarditis, osteo-myelitis, meningitis, and hospital-acquired pneumonia caused by *Staphylococcus aureus*)	Vancomycin serum trough concentrations of 15–20 mg/L are recommended to improve penetration, increase the probability of obtaining optimal target serum concentrations, and improve clinical outcomes.	IIIB	Therapeutic vancomycin drug monitoring, Optimal trough concentrations
Dosing Regimen			
Dosing to achieve optimal trough concentrations	Doses of 15–20 mg/kg (as actual body weight) given every 8–12 hr are recommended for most patients with normal renal function to achieve the suggested serum concentrations when the MIC is ≤1 mg/L. In patients with normal renal function, the targeted AUC:MIC of >400 is not achievable with conventional dosing methods if the MIC is ≥2 mg/L in a patient with normal renal function.	IIIB	Therapeutic vancomycin drug monitoring, Optimal trough concentrations
Loading doses—complicated infections	In seriously ill patients, a loading dose of 25–30 mg/kg (based on actual body weight) can be used to facilitate rapid attainment of target trough serum vancomycin concentration.	IIIB	Therapeutic vancomycin drug monitoring, Optimal trough concentrations
Continuous vs. intermittent dosing	Continuous infusion regimens are unlikely to substantially improve patient outcome when compared to intermittent dosing.	IIA	Impact of dosing strategies on pharmacokinetic and pharmacodynamic parameters
TDM for Vancomycin-Induced Nephrotoxicity			
Definition	A minimum of two or three consecutive documented increases in serum creatinine concentrations (defined as an increase of 0.5 mg/dL or a ≥50% increase from baseline, whichever is greater) after several days of vancomycin therapy.	IIB	Vancomycin toxicity; Incidence, mechanism, and definition of nephrotoxicity

Continued on next page

Table 2. *(continued)*

Summary of Expert Panel Recommendations for Vancomycin Therapeutic Drug Monitoring (TDM)[a]

Variable	Recommendation	Level of Evidence and Grade of Recommendation	Section of Consensus Review
Criteria for monitoring	Data do not support using peak serum vancomycin concentrations to monitor for nephrotoxicity.	IIB	Vancomycin toxicity, Role of therapeutic drug monitoring in preventing nephrotoxicity
	Trough monitoring is recommended for patients receiving aggressive dosing (i.e., to achieve sustained trough levels of 15–20 mg/L) and all patients at high risk of nephrotoxicity (e.g., patients receiving concurrent nephrotoxins).	IIIB	Vancomycin toxicity, Role of therapeutic drug monitoring in preventing nephrotoxicity
	Monitoring is also recommended for patients with unstable (i.e., deteriorating or significantly improving) renal function and those receiving prolonged courses of therapy (more than three to five days).	IIB	Vancomycin toxicity, Role of therapeutic drug monitoring in preventing nephrotoxicity
Frequency of monitoring	Frequent monitoring (more than one trough before the fourth dose) for short course or lower intensity dosing (to attain target trough concentrations below 15 mg/L) is not recommended.	IIB	Vancomycin toxicity, Role of therapeutic drug monitoring in preventing nephrotoxicity
	All patients on prolonged courses of vancomycin (exceeding three to five days) should have at least one steady-state trough concentration obtained no earlier than at steady state (just before the fourth dose) and then repeated as deemed clinically appropriate.	IIB	Vancomycin toxicity, Role of therapeutic drug monitoring in preventing nephrotoxicity
	There are limited data supporting the safety of sustained trough concentrations of 15–20 mg/L. Clinical judgment should guide the frequency of trough monitoring when the target trough is in this range. Once-weekly monitoring is recommended for hemodynamically stable patients. More frequent or daily trough monitoring is advisable in patients who are hemodynamically unstable.	IIIB	Vancomycin toxicity, Role of therapeutic drug monitoring in preventing nephrotoxicity
TDM for Vancomycin-Induced Ototoxicity			
Criteria for monitoring	Monitoring for ototoxicity is not recommended for patients receiving vancomycin monotherapy.	IIIB	Vancomycin toxicity, Incidence of ototoxicity and role of therapeutic drug monitoring for prevention of vancomycin-induced hearing loss
	Monitoring should be considered for patients receiving additional ototoxic agents, such as aminoglycosides.	IIIB	Vancomycin toxicity, Incidence of ototoxicity and role of therapeutic drug monitoring for prevention of vancomycin-induced hearing loss

[a]MIC = minimum inhibitory concentration, AUC = area under the concentration-versus-time curve.

result, the likelihood of maintaining free or unbound serum vancomycin concentrations in excess of the bacterial MIC for the entire dosing interval is usually 100% with standard intermittent i.v. infusions for typical staphylococci and streptococci.

Despite the absence of clinical data supporting *t*>MIC as a predictive parameter for clinical effectiveness, continuous-infusion strategies have been suggested as a possible means to optimize the serum vancomycin concentration and improve effectiveness. Using a randomized crossover study design in intensive care unit (ICU) patients, James et al.[35] found no significant difference between intermittent and continuous administrations when measuring killing activity in vitro, although the ability to maintain serum bactericidal titers above 1:8 was better with a continuous infusion. In a similarly designed study in healthy subjects, Lacy et al.[36] found virtually no difference in activity as measured by bactericidal titers between continuous and intermittent infusions. Further, in a randomized study, Wysocki et al.[37,38] evaluated 160 patients with severe staphylococcal infections. No difference in patient outcome was observed between those receiving intermittent or continuous infusion vancomycin. Vancomycin differs from β-lactam antibiotics, which typically have short half-lives and often require shorter dosage intervals or continuous infusion to optimize therapy. Therefore, based on the available evidence, there does not appear to be any difference in patient outcomes between vancomycin administered by continuous infusion or by intermittent administration.

Summary and recommendations: *Vancomycin dosages should be calculated on ABW. For obese patients, initial dosing can be based on ABW and then adjusted based on serum vancomycin concentrations to achieve therapeutic levels. Continuous infusion regimens are unlikely to substantially improve patient outcome when compared with intermittent dosing. (Level of evidence = II, grade of recommendation = A.)*

Therapeutic Vancomycin Drug Monitoring

Peak versus Trough Concentrations. Over the years, serum vancomycin concentration monitoring practices have varied. Early suggestions, such as those of Geraci,[39] who recommended peak serum vancomycin concentrations of 30–40 mg/L and trough concentrations of 5–10 mg/L, likely did not appreciate the multiexponential decline in the serum vancomycin concentration-versus-time curve.

How Geraci defined peak concentration is unclear. In addition, the pharmacodynamic properties of vancomycin had not been evaluated at the time these recommendations were made. Because the AUC/MIC has been found to correlate with efficacy in experiments conducted with in vitro or animal models, this evidence has led some clinicians to question the relevance of monitoring peak serum vancomycin concentrations.[6] Consequently, some clinicians have decreased the extent of pharmacokinetic monitoring for this antibiotic.[40] However, because it can be difficult in the clinical setting to obtain multiple serum vancomycin concentrations to determine the AUC and subsequently calculate the AUC/MIC, trough serum concentration monitoring, which can be used as a surrogate marker for AUC, is recommended as the most accurate and practical method to monitor vancomycin.

Summary and recommendation: *Trough serum vancomycin concentrations are the most accurate and practical method for monitoring vancomycin effectiveness. Trough concentrations should be obtained just before the next dose at steady-state conditions. (Level of evidence = II, grade of recommendation = B.) (Note: Steady-state achievement is variable and dependent on multiple factors. Trough samples should be obtained just before the fourth dose in patients with normal renal function to ensure that target concentrations are attained.)*

Optimal Trough Concentrations. While Geraci's[39] recommendation for trough concentration was not based on prospective clinical trial data, the benchmark total drug concentration of 5–10 mg/L is likely to fall short of achieving the desired overall vancomycin exposure in many types of infection and isolates with higher (but susceptible) MICs. Therefore, targeting higher trough serum vancomycin concentrations should increase the likelihood of achieving more effective overall antibiotic exposures (i.e., AUC/MIC) and assist in addressing the trend of higher vancomycin MIC values in these organisms.

In recently published guidelines for hospital-acquired, ventilator-associated, and health-care-associated pneumonia, the American Thoracic Society (ATS) suggested an initial vancomycin dosage of 15 mg/kg every 12 hours in adults with normal renal function.[41] ATS acknowledged that vancomycin was a concentration-independent (time-dependent) killer of gram-positive pathogens but had lower penetration into the ELF and respiratory secretions. ATS further recommended that trough serum vancomycin concentrations be maintained at 15–20 mg/L. However, based on pharmacokinetic dosing principles for patients with a normal body weight and normal renal function, it is unlikely that vancomycin 15 mg/kg every 12 hours will produce trough concentrations of 15–20 mg/L. Furthermore, there are no data indicating that achieving these trough concentrations over time is well tolerated and safe.

In an attempt to evaluate the use of targeted trough concentrations of 15–20 mg/L, Jeffres et al.[42] retrospectively evaluated 102 patients with health-care-associated MRSA pneumonia. Overall mortality was 31% (32 patients). There were no significant differences in mean ± S.D. calculated trough serum vancomycin concentrations (13.6 ± 5.9 mg/L versus 13.9 ± 6.7 mg/L) or mean ± S.D. calculated AUC (351 ± 143 mg · hr/L versus 354 ± 109 mg · hr/L) between survivors and nonsurvivors. In addition, no relationship was found between trough serum vancomycin concentrations or AUC and hospital mortality. Although no significant differences were found between survivors and nonsurvivors in terms of trough serum vancomycin concentrations and AUCs, several factors should be noted. For instance, a sample size calculation was not predetermined; therefore, the potential for a Type II error is possible. There was also large variability in both vancomycin trough concentrations (range, 4.2–29.8 mg/L) and AUCs (range, 119–897 mg · hr/L), which may account for the lack of significant findings. Time to achieve targeted serum vancomycin concentrations was not measured and may be a critical factor in determining patient outcome. In addition, because a disk-diffusion method was used for susceptibility testing, organism MIC could not be determined. Therefore, only the AUC, not the AUC/MIC, was evaluated as a potential predictor of success or failure.

Although the results of this study are of interest, additional prospective studies are needed to confirm these data.

Relationship between trough vancomycin concentrations, resistance, and therapeutic failure. While vancomycin is considered a bactericidal antibiotic, the rate of bacterial kill is slow when compared with that of β-lactams, and vancomycin's activity is affected by the bacterial inoculum. Large bacterial burdens in the stationary growth phase or in an anaerobic environment pose a significant challenge to the speed and extent of vancomycin's bactericidal activity.[43-46]

In recent years, VISA or glycopeptide-intermediate susceptible *S. aureus* (GISA) and vancomycin-resistant *S. aureus* (VRSA) have appeared and raised questions about the overall utility of this antibiotic. (Note: The terms VISA and GISA are often used interchangeably. For the purpose of this consensus review, VISA will be used throughout.) Although infection with these organisms is infrequent, there is fear that the organisms could become more prevalent if the high rate of use and exposure pressure of vancomycin continues.[47] The discovery of inducible hVISA (i.e., strains with MIC values in the susceptible range of 0.5–2 mg/L in patients whose therapy with standard dosages of vancomycin has failed) raises further questions regarding current dosing guidelines and the overall use of this antibiotic. Concerns are related to treatment failures and the inability to easily detect hVISA isolates in clinical settings.[48-50]

In 2006, the Clinical and Laboratory Standards Institute (CLSI) lowered the susceptibility and resistance breakpoints for the MIC of vancomycin from ≤4 to ≤2 mg/L for "susceptible," from 8–16 to 4–8 mg/L for "intermediate," and from ≥32 to ≥16 mg/L for "resistant."[51] The decision to move the breakpoints was primarily based on clinical data indicating that patients were less likely to be successfully treated with vancomycin if the *S. aureus* MIC was ≤4 mg/L.[51] Despite the change in susceptibility and resistance breakpoints, two reports have suggested that patients with *S. aureus* isolates having vancomycin MICs of 1–2 mg/L are less likely to be successfully treated with vancomycin compared with patients with *S. aureus* isolates that demonstrate greater susceptibility.[52,53] However, this information alone does not address whether the use of higher concentrations of vancomycin would improve overall effectiveness. Low serum vancomycin concentrations may also create problems, as there appears to be a direct correlation between low serum vancomycin levels and the emergence of hVISA, VISA, or both, at least with certain genotypes of MRSA.[54] In addition, studies have suggested that trough serum vancomycin concentrations of <10 mg/L may predict therapeutic failure and the potential for the emergence of VISA or VRSA.[54,55]

Studies of MRSA and hVISA bacteremia have revealed significantly higher rates of morbidity in patients infected with hVISA.[50,55,56] These patients were more likely to have high bacterial load infections, low initial trough serum vancomycin concentrations, and treatment failure.[56] Jones[57] recently reported that approximately 74% of hVISA strains and 15% of wild-type *S. aureus* strains were tolerant (minimum bactericidal concentration of ≥32 mg/L) to the effects of vancomycin, which contributes to a low probability of success in patients harboring these organisms.

Sakoulas et al.[52] reported a significant correlation between vancomycin susceptibilities and patient outcome. Treatment of bloodstream infections caused by MRSA strains having a vancomycin MIC of ≤0.5 mg/L had an overall success rate of 55.6%, while treatment of patients infected with MRSA strains having a vancomycin MIC of 1–2 mg/L had a success rate of only 9.5% ($p = 0.03$). (Treatment failure was defined as persistent signs or symptoms of infection [e.g., fever, leukocytosis], new signs or symptoms of infection, or worsening of signs or symptoms of infection in patients receiving at least five days of therapy with targeted trough serum vancomycin concentrations of 10–15 mg/L). However, this was a relatively small study ($n = 30$) of MRSA bacteremic patients who were refractory to vancomycin therapy and were enrolled in compassionate-use drug trials. In a more recent study of patients with MRSA bacteremia ($n = 34$), Moise et al.[58] demonstrated that patients with MRSA isolates with a vancomycin MIC of 2 mg/L had significantly higher median days to organism eradication, longer treatment with vancomycin, and a significantly lower overall likelihood of organism eradication. Hidayat et al.[53] evaluated the use of high-dosage vancomycin intended to achieve unbound trough serum vancomycin concentrations of at least four times the MIC in patients with MRSA infections. Of the 95 patients evaluated with MRSA pneumonia or bacteremia, or both, 51 (54%) had vancomycin MIC values of 1.5 or 2 mg/L. Although an initial response of 74% was demonstrated in patients achieving the desired target MIC, a high percentage of patients infected with strains having an MIC of 1.5 or 2 mg/L had a poorer response (62% versus 85%) and significantly higher infection-related mortality (24% versus 10%) compared with patients infected with low-MIC strains (0.5, 0.75, or 1 mg/L), despite achieving target trough serum vancomycin concentrations of 15–20 mg/L. The data from these two studies suggest that *S. aureus* isolates with MICs of 1–2 mg/L that are still within the susceptible range may be less responsive to vancomycin therapy. Soriano et al.[59] evaluated the influence of vancomycin MIC on outcome in a total of 414 episodes of MRSA bacteremic patients. MIC evaluations were determined by Etest methodology. Among several factors that predicted poor outcome, *S. aureus* isolates with an MIC of 2 mg/L were significantly associated with increased mortality. Based on the low probability of achieving an appropriate targeted vancomycin concentration exposure (AUC/MIC), the authors suggested that vancomycin should not be considered an optimal treatment approach for infection due to strains with a vancomycin MIC of >1 mg/L when using trough serum vancomycin concentrations of >10 mg/L as a target.

Lodise et al.[60] evaluated the relationship between vancomycin MIC and treatment failure among 92 adult non-neutropenic patients with MRSA bloodstream infections. Vancomycin failure was defined as 30-day mortality, 10 or more days of bacteremia on vancomycin therapy, or recurrence of MRSA bacteremia within 60 days of vancomycin discontinuation. Classification and regression tree analysis found that a vancomycin MIC breakpoint of ≥1.5 mg/L was associated with an increased probability of treatment failure. The 66 patients with a vancomycin MIC of ≥1.5 mg/L had a 2.4-fold higher rate of treatment failure compared with patients with a vancomycin MIC of ≤1 mg/L (36.4% versus 15.4%, respectively; $p = 0.049$). Poisson regression analysis determined that a vancomycin MIC of ≥1.5 mg/L was independently associated with treatment failure ($p = 0.01$). Based on these findings, the investigators suggested that an alternative therapy should be considered.

An analysis of a large surveillance database of 35,458 *S. aureus* strains by Jones[57] found that the MIC required to inhibit the growth of 50% of organisms or the MIC required to inhibit the growth of 90% of organisms (MIC^{90}) for vancomycin is 1 mg/L.[57] The Centers for Disease Control and Prevention 2005 U.S. Surveillance Network data of vancomycin susceptibility reported that 16.2% of 241,605 *S. aureus* isolates had an MIC of 2 mg/L.[51] Regional variability exists, and an MIC^{90} of 2 mg/L has recently been reported by several institutions. For example, Mohr and Murray[61] reported that as many as 30% of 116 MRSA blood culture isolates collected from the Texas Medical Center over a one-year period had a vancomycin MIC of 2 mg/L. There have been recent reports of significant shifts in bacterial susceptibility to vancomycin over a five-year surveillance period.[62-64] Increasing *S. aureus* MIC values, coupled with reports of failure rates associated with a vancomycin MIC of 2 mg/L, have raised the question of whether the breakpoint for vancomycin resistance should be lowered even further.[65]

New information is emerging regarding the importance of the accessory gene regulator (*agr*), a global quorum-sensing regulator in *S. aureus* that is responsible for orchestrating the expression of adherence factors, biofilm production, tolerance to vancomycin, and virulence factors.[66] The *agr* locus has been a subject of intense study because there appears to be a relationship between polymorphism in this gene cluster and patient response to vancomycin therapy. Several studies have determined that all VISA strains reported to date from the United States belong to *agr* group II. The *agr* group II includes the USA 100 MRSA clones that are predominately associated with nosocomial infections, and these strains have been associated with vancomycin treatment failure.[33,67] Sakoulas et al.[67,68] have determined in in vitro studies that the emergence of hVISA or VISA may occur when *S. aureus* isolates with a down-regulated or defective *agr* locus are exposed to suboptimal vancomycin concentrations. In a series of in vitro experiments, MRSA belonging to *agr* group II with a defective *agr* locus exposed to vancomycin concentrations of <10 mg/L produced heteroresistant-like characteristics similar to VISA strains with subsequent MIC increases from 1 to 8 mg/L.[67] This phenomenon was recently demonstrated in a patient with chronic renal failure undergoing hemodialysis who experienced recurrent MRSA bacteremia over a 30-month period.[54] The patient was treated repeatedly with vancomycin at trough serum concentrations that always exceeded 10 mg/L. Despite frequent recurrences of bacteremia with the same isolate, the isolate remained susceptible to vancomycin. The genetic background of this organism was found to be similar to other VISA strains belonging to *agr* group II. When the isolate was subjected to vancomycin concentrations of <10 mg/L under laboratory conditions, it quickly demonstrated characteristics similar to VISA strains with a subsequent increased MIC.

Tsuji et al.[69] used an in vitro pharmacodynamic model to evaluate *S. aureus agr* groups I–IV exposed to optimal and suboptimal vancomycin doses over a three-day period. In this study, low vancomycin exposures equivalent to total trough serum vancomycin concentrations of 1.5–10 mg/L and an AUC/MIC of 31–264 produced increases in the MIC to the range considered to be VISA by the current CLSI vancomycin breakpoints. Although resistance was produced in both *agr* functional and defective strains, the likelihood of resistance was fourfold to fivefold higher in *agr*-defective isolates. Subsequently, the investigators determined that as many as 48% of hospital-associated MRSA had a dysfunctional *agr* locus, making this finding potentially clinically relevant and warranting further evaluation.[70]

Summary and recommendation: *Based on evidence suggesting that* S. aureus *exposure to trough serum vancomycin concentrations of <10 mg/L can produce strains with VISA-like characteristics, it is recommended that trough serum vancomycin concentrations always be maintained above 10 mg/L to avoid development of resistance. (Level of evidence = III, grade of recommendation = B.)*

Correlating dosing with optimal AUC/MIC and trough concentrations. As mentioned previously, an isolate's vancomycin MIC is an important parameter for determining the potential success of a given dosage regimen. Therefore, an actual vancomycin MIC value should ideally be obtained from the clinical microbiology laboratory. Currently, some clinical microbiology laboratories may be limited in their ability to report vancomycin MIC values, depending on the methodology (disk diffusion or automated microdilution) used to determine antimicrobial susceptibility. In some instances, supplemental Etest methods may be used to obtain this information.

As previously stated, an AUC/MIC of ≥400 has been promoted as the target predictive of successful therapy (i.e., organism eradication). Based on this information, a simple evaluation of standard dosing practices (e.g., 1 g every 12 hours) for an individual with normal renal function (CLcr of ≥100 mL/min) and average weight (80 kg) would only yield a 24-hour drug AUC of approximately 250 mg · hr/L. Unless the pathogen had a vancomycin MIC of ≤0.5 mg/L, this dosage regimen would not generate the targeted AUC/MIC of ≥400. For a pathogen with an MIC of 1 mg/L, the minimum trough serum vancomycin concentration would have to be at least 15 mg/L to obtain the target AUC/MIC. Using the vancomycin pharmacokinetic data generated by Jeffres et al.[42] in patients receiving vancomycin for the treatment of MRSA pneumonia, Mohr and Murray[61] determined by Monte Carlo simulation that the probability of achieving an AUC/MIC of ≥400 would be 100% if the *S. aureus* MIC for vancomycin was 0.5 mg/L but 0% if the MIC was 2 mg/L. Using a similar one-compartment model of vancomycin and a Monte Carlo simulation integrating *S. aureus* MIC values, del Mar Fernández de Gatta Garcia et al.[71] reported that a daily dosage of 3–4 g of vancomycin would be required to provide 90% probability of attaining a target AUC/MIC of 400 with an MIC of 1 mg/L. For VISA strains, a vancomycin daily dose of ≥5 g would be required to provide a high probability of target AUC/MIC attainment for this pathogen. For susceptible *S. aureus*, total daily doses of ≥40 mg/kg would likely be required for typical patients. Use of these larger dosages of vancomycin should be carefully monitored for the desired clinical outcome and the absence of drug-induced toxicity. The use of a nomogram is an alternative method for dosage adjustments; however, the majority of published nomograms in clinical use have been proven to be inaccurate, and most have not been clinically validated.[72] In addition, no published nomogram to date has been constructed to achieve trough serum vancomycin concentrations of 15–20 mg/L.

Loading doses have also been suggested for critically ill patients to attain target trough serum vancomycin levels earlier. In a small study of critically ill patients with serious *S. aureus* infections, a vancomycin loading dose of 25 mg/kg infused at a rate of 500 mg/hr was found to be safe without producing toxic peak serum drug levels.[73] While this approach is not currently supported by evidence from large randomized clinical trials, vancomycin loading doses can be considered in the treatment of serious MRSA infections.[63,74]

Summary and recommendations: *Based on the potential to improve penetration, increase the probability of optimal target serum vancomycin concentrations, and improve clinical outcomes for complicated infections such as bacteremia, endocarditis, osteomyelitis, meningitis, and hospital-acquired pneumonia caused by* S. aureus, *total trough serum vancomycin concentrations of 15–20 mg/L are recommended. Trough serum vancomycin concentrations in that range should achieve an AUC/MIC of ≥400 in most patients if the MIC is ≤1 mg/L. (Level of evidence = III, grade of recommendation = B.)*

In order to achieve rapid attainment of this target concentration for seriously ill patients, a loading dose of 25–30 mg/kg (based on ABW) can be considered. (Level of evidence = III, grade of recommendation = B.)

A targeted AUC/MIC of ≥400 is not achievable with conventional dosing methods if the vancomycin MIC is ≥2 mg/L in a patient with normal renal function (i.e., CL_{cr} of 70–100 mL/min). Therefore, alternative therapies should be considered.

Vancomycin dosages of 15–20 mg/kg (based on ABW) given every 8–12 hours are required for most patients with normal renal function to achieve the suggested serum concentrations when the MIC is ≤1 mg/L. It should be noted that currently available nomograms were not developed to achieve these targeted endpoints. Individual pharmacokinetic adjustments and verification of serum target achievement are recommended. When individual doses exceed 1 g (i.e., 1.5 and 2 g), the infusion period should be extended to 1.5–2 hours. (Level of evidence = III, grade of recommendation = B.)

Vancomycin Toxicity

Vancomycin was initially dubbed "Mississippi mud" because of the brown color of early formulations, which were about 70% pure. The impurities are thought to have contributed to the incidence of adverse reactions.[7,75,76] In the 1960s, purity increased to 75% and in 1985 to 92–95% for Eli Lilly's vancomycin product.[74] Concurrently, a decrease in the reporting of serious adverse events occurred.

The most common vancomycin adverse effects are unrelated to serum drug concentration and include fever, chills, and phlebitis.[7] Red man syndrome may be associated with histamine release and manifests as tingling and flushing of the face, neck, and upper torso. It is most likely to occur when larger dosages are infused too rapidly (>500 mg over ≤30 minutes).[7,77,78] Vancomycin should be administered intravenously over an infusion period of at least 1 hour to minimize infusion-related adverse effects. For higher dosages (e.g., 2 g), the infusion time should be extended to 1.5–2 hours. Less frequent adverse events, such as neutropenia, also appear unrelated to serum drug concentrations.[79,80]

Vancomycin has long been considered a nephrotoxic and ototoxic agent. Excessive serum drug concentrations have been implicated, and it was assumed that monitoring of serum concentrations would allow interventions that decrease toxicity.

Incidence, Mechanism, and Definition of Nephrotoxicity. A review of the literature published from 1956 through 1986 identified 57 cases of vancomycin-associated nephrotoxicity, with over 50% of those cases identified within the first six years of vancomycin use when the product was relatively impure.[75] The rate of nephrotoxicity attributable to vancomycin monotherapy varied from 0% to 17% and from 7% to 35% with concurrent administration of aminoglycosides.[81-85] A review of the literature available through 1993, conducted by Cantu et al.,[8] identified 167 cases of vancomycin-related nephrotoxicity. However, the lack of clear-cut examples of vancomycin-induced nephrotoxicity (when the drug was used alone) was striking. The researchers determined that the frequency of nephrotoxicity due to vancomycin monotherapy was 5–7%. No evidence supported maintaining serum vancomycin concentrations within a given range to prevent nephrotoxicity. However, another study identified older age, longer treatment courses, and higher trough serum vancomycin concentrations (30–65 mg/L) as risk factors for vancomycin-induced nephrotoxicity.[81] Although the definition of vancomycin-induced nephrotoxicity has varied, a reasonable composite from the literature defines this adverse effect as an increase of >0.5 mg/dL (or a ≥50% increase) in serum creatinine over baseline in consecutively obtained daily serum creatinine values or a drop in calculated CL_{cr} of 50% from baseline on two consecutive days in the absence of an alternative explanation.[10,12,53,86-88]

The exact mechanism and incidence of vancomycin nephrotoxicity have been investigated in animals and humans. The filtration and energy-dependent transport mechanisms found in the proximal tubular epithelium render the kidneys susceptible to toxicant-induced injury.[89] Vancomycin exposure in renal proximal tubule epithelial cells results in increased cell proliferation. The stimulation of oxygen consumption and the increase in ATP concentrations support the role of vancomycin as a stimulant of oxidative phosphorylation.[89] In rats, antioxidants protect kidneys against vancomycin-induced injury, in theory, by inhibiting free oxygen radical production.[90] Human data suggest toxicity from vancomycin (or aminoglycosides) is not confined to the proximal tubule but may also involve the medullary region (loop of Henle and collecting duct) of the nephron.[91] Vancomycin destruction of glomeruli and necrosis of the proximal tubule are thought to be due to oxidative stress.[92]

In humans, nephrotoxicity due to vancomycin monotherapy with typical dosage regimens is uncommon, is usually reversible, and occurs with an incidence only slightly above what is reported with other antimicrobials not considered to be nephrotoxic.[11,83,93-96] Investigators have administered a wide dosing range of vancomycin monotherapy to rats without appreciable renal injury.[97,98] Renal impairment in rats was observed when concurrent aminoglycosides were administered[97-99] or if very high dosages of vancomycin were used (350 mg/kg twice daily for four days).[98] Wood et al.[100] investigated the influence of vancomycin on tobramycin-induced nephrotoxicity in rats and found that toxicity occurred earlier and was more severe with concurrent aminoglycoside and vancomycin therapy. Histological evidence of tubular necrosis occurred earlier and the percentage of necrotic cells was higher in rats receiving combination therapy compared with animals administered tobramycin alone. Indeed, animals receiving vancomycin alone lacked evidence of nephrotoxicity. Enhanced renal accumulation of tobramycin was not evident in animals receiving both vancomycin and tobramycin. In fact, animals receiving the combination had lower renal tobramycin concentrations than did animals receiving tobramycin alone. Increased enzymuria and crystalluria were seen in rats and may suggest toxicity after vancomycin administration.[101-104] However, these markers are very sensitive and could reflect transient hypotension due to rapid administration rather than toxicity.[8] Enzymuria in humans was minimally affected during five days of vancomycin therapy.[105]

Data regarding concurrent vancomycin and aminoglycoside administration in humans provide conflicting information, with some reports indicating that the combination augments aminoglycoside-induced nephrotoxicity,[11,76,81,83,91,94,106,107] and others indicating no effect.[81,83,85,86,96,108-111] Rybak et al.[10] found that patients given vancomycin and an aminoglycoside were 6.7-fold more likely to develop nephrotoxicity than those receiving vancomycin alone. Vancomycin administration for more than 21 days was an additional risk factor ($p = 0.007$). Bertino et al.[107] found vancomycin to be an independent risk factor for aminoglycoside nephrotoxicity in a review of 1489 patients who prospectively received individualized pharmacokinetic monitoring. However, vancomycin use was not associated with increased risk when assessed in a multivariate model in this study. Most of the available data suggest a 3- to 4-fold increase in nephrotoxicity when aminoglycosides are combined with vancomycin.[81,83,93,94] Synergistic toxicity may also occur when vancomycin is used with other nephrotoxic agents (e.g., amphotericin B, certain chemotherapy agents) or used to treat certain diseases (e.g., sepsis, liver disease, obstructive uropathy, pancreatitis).[40,86,93]

Vancomycin administered either as a single, large, 30-mg/kg once-daily dose or in two divided doses did not influence nephrotoxicity significantly ($p = 0.71$).[112] However, "high-dose" (defined as a total daily dose of 40 mg/kg, either as a continuous infusion or divided every 12 hours, resulting in a mean ± S.D. concentration of 24.4 ± 7.8 mg/L) was found to be less nephrotoxic than "standard-dose" intermittent therapy (defined as 10 mg/kg every 12 hours, resulting in a mean ± S.D. trough serum vancomycin concentration of 10.0 ± 5.3 mg/L) ($p = 0.007$) by other investigators.[113] It should be noted that the average age of patients in this later investigation was 60 years; their average weight was not provided.

Human trials have suggested that trough serum vancomycin concentrations of >10 mg/L are associated with an increased risk of nephrotoxicity.[10,76,83,85,86] No correlation has been observed between peak vancomycin concentrations and nephrotoxicity.[10] Zimmermann et al.[114] found no correlation between nephrotoxicity and initial serum creatinine concentration, length of hospital stay, or duration of vancomycin therapy. However, the researchers did find that serum vancomycin concentrations were significantly higher in those patients who eventually developed nephrotoxicity. In that study, no patient who maintained trough serum vancomycin concentrations of <20 mg/L developed nephrotoxicity. It is noteworthy that 21 (57%) of 37 patients consistently had trough serum vancomycin concentrations of >20 mg/L and yet did not develop nephrotoxicity. Recent guidelines have recommended target trough serum vancomycin concentrations of 15–20 mg/L.[41] However, the safety of higher trough vancomycin concentrations over a prolonged period has not been sufficiently studied.

Lee-Such et al.[115] conducted a retrospective chart review of patients over age 18 years who received vancomycin for at least 14 days and had an available baseline serum creatinine concentration and a CL_{cr} of >30 mL/min (calculated by Cockroft-Gault equation). Patients were categorized by trough serum vancomycin concentrations (≤15 mg/L [$n = 19$] or ≥15.1 mg/L [$n = 40$]). Nephrotoxicity was defined as a rise in serum creatinine of ≥0.5 mg/dL above baseline. The median maximum serum creatinine percentage increase was 0.0% (range, –31.3 to 30.0) in the low-trough-concentration group and 17.2% (range, –36.4 to 133) in the high-concentration group ($p = 0.0045$). There were no significant correlations between percent change in serum creatinine and duration of vancomycin therapy, highest trough concentration, or average daily dose. The frequency of nephrotoxicity was 0% in the low-trough-concentration group and 15% in the high-trough-concentration group. The investigators could not discern if higher vancomycin levels were a cause or an indicator of worsening renal function. In addition, a single trough vancomycin concentration of >15 mg/L placed a patient in the high-concentration group, but such a level could be due to a variety of clinical or operational factors not related to vancomycin-induced toxicity. Finally, the use of pressors and concurrent nephrotoxins was poorly described but could provide additional concurrent risk for renal dysfunction. Further details are lacking, as the data are currently available only in abstract form.

Jeffres et al.[87] conducted a similar but prospective investigation of 94 patients with health-care-associated pneumonia. Nephrotoxicity was defined as a 0.5-mg/dL increase from baseline in serum creatinine or an increase of ≥50% in serum creatinine from baseline during vancomycin therapy. Patients were stratified based on vancomycin trough concentrations of <15 mg/L ($n = 43$) or ≥15 mg/L ($n = 51$). Overall, 40 patients (42.6%) met the criteria for nephrotoxicity. The maximal serum creatinine concentration observed occurred after the maximum serum vancomycin concentration by at least 24 hours in 34 patients (85.0%). Patients who developed nephrotoxicity were more likely to have higher steady-state mean trough serum vancomycin concentrations (20.8 mg/L versus 14.3 mg/L, respectively; $p < 0.001$), trough serum vancomycin concentrations of >15 mg/L (67.5% versus 40.7%, $p = 0.01$), and a longer duration (≥14 days) of vancomycin therapy (45.0% versus 20.4%, $p = 0.011$) than those who did not develop nephrotoxicity.

Hidayat et al.[53] prospectively investigated the efficacy and toxicity of adjusting vancomycin troughs to achieve an unbound concentration of at least four times the MIC. Patients received vancomycin for 72 hours or more. Nephrotoxicity was defined as a 0.5-mg/dL or ≥50% increase from the baseline serum creatinine concentration in two consecutive laboratory analyses. For nephrotoxicity analysis, groups were divided based on trough serum vancomycin concentrations (<15 or ≥15 mg/L). Nephrotoxicity occurred only in the ≥15-mg/L group (11 of 63 patients [12%] versus 0 of 24 patients in the <15-mg/L group [$p = 0.01$]) and was predicted by the use of concurrent nephrotoxic agents ($p < 0.001$). By controlling for age, admission to ICUs, Acute Physiology and Chronic Evaluation II score, trough serum vancomycin level, and duration of therapy, multivariate analysis demonstrated concurrent nephrotoxins to be the strongest predictor of vancomycin nephrotoxicity. Without concurrent nephrotoxins, nephrotoxicity occurred in only 1 (2%) of 44 patients with a trough concentration of ≥15 mg/L versus 0 of 24 patients in the <15-mg/L group.

Lodise et al.[12] retrospectively examined the relationship between vancomycin dosage and rate of nephrotoxicity at a single institution. Nephrotoxicity was defined as an increase in serum creatinine of 0.5 mg/dL or an increase of 50%, whichever was greater, on at least two consecutive days during the period from initiation of vancomycin or linezolid therapy to 72 hours after completion of therapy. Linezolid usage was also included as a nonvancomycin comparator group. A significant difference in nephrotoxicity was noted among patients receiving vancomycin ≥4 g/day (34.6%), vancomycin <4 g/day (10.9%), and linezolid (6.7%) ($p = 0.001$). The relationship between high-dosage vancomycin and nephrotoxicity persisted in the multivariate analyses that controlled for potential confounding covariates. The multivariate analyses also demonstrated that patient total weight of ≥101.4 kg, estimated CL_{cr} of ≤86.6 mL/min, and ICU residence at the start of therapy each independently influenced the time to nephrotoxicity. In a secondary analysis, a significant relationship was found between the vancomycin AUC and nephrotoxicity. Specifically, a vancomycin AUC of ≥952 mg · L/hr was associated with a higher probability of vancomycin-related nephrotoxicity.

Nguyen et al.[88] retrospectively investigated patients receiving vancomycin between January and December 2006 at a single institution. Patients included were age ≥18 years, receiving vancomycin for at least 72 hours, and had at least one serum vancomycin value obtained. Hemodialysis patients were excluded. Nephrotoxicity was defined as an increase of >0.5 mg/dL over baseline in serum creatinine for two consecutive assays. Creatinine levels were followed until patient discharge. Patients were divided based on trough serum vancomycin concentration attainment of 5–15 mg/L ($n = 130$) or >15 mg/L ($n = 88$). The rate of nephrotoxicity was 6.2% in the lower-trough group and 18.2% in the higher-trough group ($p < 0.01$). Multivariate analysis indicated that the main predictors of nephrotoxicity were an elevated overall average trough concentration and duration of therapy.

Investigations, such as those described herein, are intriguing but often limited by small sample size, retrospective design, and questionable methodology. Additional data are needed, including the timing of the relationship between high vancomycin levels and nephrotoxicity (i.e., which one precedes the other). In addition, while statistically relevant, the clinical significance of minor and transient changes in creatinine or CL_{cr} can be debated. The effect of a 0.5-mg/dL increase in serum creatinine concentration would be greater in a patient with a lower initial CL_{cr} value than in one with a higher baseline CL_{cr} value.

Summary and recommendation: *There are limited data suggesting a direct causal relationship between toxicity and specific serum vancomycin concentrations. In addition, data are conflicting and characterized by the presence of confounding nephrotoxic agents, inconsistent and highly variable definitions of toxicity, and the inability to examine the time sequence of events surrounding changes in renal function secondary to vancomycin exposure.*

A patient should be identified as having experienced vancomycin-induced nephrotoxicity if multiple (at least two or three consecutive) high serum creatinine concentrations (increase of 0.5 mg/dL or ≥50% increase from baseline, whichever is greater) are documented after several days of vancomycin therapy in the absence of an alternative explanation. (Level of evidence = II, grade of recommendation = B.)

Role of Therapeutic Drug Monitoring in Preventing Nephrotoxicity. Because vancomycin is eliminated via glomerular filtration, a decrease in the glomerular filtration rate from any cause will increase the serum vancomycin concentration and make the association between renal dysfunction and trough concentrations difficult to assess.[8]

Some investigators have found vancomycin therapeutic drug monitoring to be associated with decreased nephrotoxicity. Other factors associated with decreased toxicity include shorter courses of therapy, less total dosage in grams of the drug, and a decreased length of hospital stay.[7,12,116,117] However, Darko et al.[7] found therapeutic drug monitoring to be cost-effective only in patients in ICUs, those receiving other nephrotoxins, and, possibly, oncology patients.

Summary and recommendations: *Available evidence does not support monitoring peak serum vancomycin concentrations to decrease the frequency of nephrotoxicity. (Level of evidence = I, grade of recommendation = A.)*

Monitoring of trough serum vancomycin concentrations to reduce nephrotoxicity is best suited to patients receiving aggressive dosing targeted to produce sustained trough drug concentrations of 15–20 mg/L or who are at high risk of toxicity, such as patients receiving concurrent nephrotoxins. (Level of evidence = III, grade of recommendation = B.)

Monitoring is also recommended for patients with unstable renal function (either deteriorating or significantly improving) and those receiving prolonged courses of therapy (over three to five days). (Level of evidence = II, grade of recommendation = B.)

All patients receiving prolonged courses of vancomycin should have at least one steady-state trough concentration obtained (just before the fourth dose). Frequent monitoring (more than a single trough concentration before the fourth dose) for short-course therapy (less than five days) or for lower-intensity dosing (targeted to attain trough serum vancomycin concentrations below 15 mg/L) is not recommended. (Level of evidence = II, grade of recommendation = B.)

There are limited data to support the safety of sustained trough serum vancomycin concentrations of 15–20 mg/L. When this target range is desired, obtaining once-weekly trough concentrations in hemodynamically stable patients is recommended. Frequent (in some instances daily) trough concentration monitoring is advisable to prevent toxicity in hemodynamically unstable patients. The exact frequency of monitoring is often a matter of clinical judgment. (Level of evidence = III, grade of recommendation = B.)

Data on comparative vancomycin toxicity using continuous versus intermittent administration are conflicting and no recommendation can be made.

Incidence of Ototoxicity and Role of Therapeutic Drug Monitoring for Prevention of Vancomycin-Induced Hearing Loss. Vancomycin-induced hearing loss is controversial. Vancomycin has not been found to be ototoxic in animal models.[97,98,100,118,119] Early literature attributed ototoxic events to impurities or to concurrent ototoxic agents.[119] Early studies indicated that other ototoxic agents, such as the aminoglycosides kanamycin and streptomycin, may have additive or synergistic toxicity when used in combination with vancomycin.[120] The frequency of ototoxicity in humans has been reported to range from 1% to 9%[3,8,48,121-124] and to be associated with serum vancomycin concentrations above 40 mg/L.[7,125] This most likely represents an inflated occurrence rate due to impurities associated with the older formulation or poor documentation of cause and effect as they relate to serum concentrations. The true risk of ototoxicity from vancomycin monotherapy is low without concurrent therapy with ototoxic agents.[77]

Severe ototoxicity induced by vancomycin is rare and characterized as damage to the auditory nerve that initially affects high-frequency sensory hairs in the cochlea, then the middle- and low-frequency hairs, and eventually can lead to total hearing loss.[75] High-tone deafness occurs before low-tone deafness at all frequencies and is permanent. Inability to hear high-frequency sounds and tinnitus are ominous signs that should result in discontinuation of vancomycin.[126,127] Also rare is reversible ototoxicity such as tinnitus, which can occur with or without high-tone deafness.[33,120,127] Investigation of pediatric pneumococcal meningitis noted that early vancomycin administration (relative to ceftriaxone administration) was associated with a substantially increased risk of hearing loss due to the effects of rapid bacterial killing by both antimicrobials and the resultant host inflammatory response.[128] However, toxicity did not correlate with vancomycin concentrations.

In 1958, Geraci et al.[129] described hearing loss in two patients with serum vancomycin concentrations of 80–100 mg/L. That report generated an impetus to monitor peak serum concentrations. However, Cantu et al.[8] reviewed 53 published cases of vancomycin-attributed ototoxicity and concluded that vancomycin was rarely ototoxic as a single agent. In addition, ototoxicity was fully reversible when other ototoxic agents were not involved.

Bailie and Neal[75] reviewed 28 cases of ototoxicity reported between 1956 and 1986, most of which involved vancomycin preparations with higher levels of impurities. Patients with severe renal dysfunction were found to be more susceptible to developing ototoxicity when their dosage regimen was not adjusted. The researchers were unable to correlate mild ototoxicity with excessive peak or trough serum vancomycin concentrations or prevention of ototoxicity by monitoring serum concentrations.

A lack of correlation between serum vancomycin levels and the development of ototoxicity has also been observed in cancer patients.[75] Of 742 patients analyzed, ototoxicity occurred in 18 (6%) of 319 patients (95% CI, 4–9%) who were receiving concurrent ototoxic agents (including aminoglycosides, cisplatin, loop diuretics, aspirin, and nonsteroidal antiinflammatory agents) and in 12 (3%) of 423 patients (95% CI, 2–5%) not treated with other ototoxic agents. All clinical ototoxicity resolved within three weeks after vancomycin discontinuation.

Summary and recommendation: *Monitoring serum vancomycin levels to prevent ototoxicity is not recommended because this toxicity is rarely associated with monotherapy and does not correlate with serum vancomycin concentrations. Monitoring may be more important when other ototoxic agents, such as aminoglycosides, are administered. (Level of evidence = III, grade of recommendation = B.)*

Summary

In general, pharmacodynamic dosing of antibiotics may significantly augment antibiotic performance. There seems to be little difference in the pharmacodynamics of intermittently or continuously dosed vancomycin. This consensus panel review supports that vancomycin is a concentration-independent killer of gram-positive pathogens and that the AUC/MIC is likely the most useful pharmacodynamic parameter to predict effectiveness. In many clinical settings where it may be difficult to obtain multiple serum vancomycin concentrations to determine the AUC and subsequently the AUC/MIC, trough serum vancomycin concentration monitoring can be recommended as the most accurate and practical method to monitor serum vancomycin levels. Increasing trough serum vancomycin concentrations to 15–20 mg/L to obtain an increased AUC/MIC of ≥400 may be desirable but is currently not supported by clinical trial data. Target attainment of an AUC/MIC of ≥400 is not likely in patients with *S. aureus* infections who have an MIC of ≥2 mg/L; therefore, treatment with alternative agents should be considered. Higher trough serum vancomycin levels may also increase the potential for toxicity, but additional clinical experience will be required to determine the extent of this potential.

References

1. Moellering RC Jr. Vancomycin: a 50-year reassessment. *Clin Infect Dis.* 2006; 42(suppl 1):S3–4.
2. Levine DP. Vancomycin: a history. *Clin Infect Dis.* 2006; 42(suppl 1):S5–12.
3. Murray BE, Nannini EC. Glycopeptides (vancomycin and teicoplanin), streptogramins (quinupristin-dalfopristin), and lipopeptides (daptomycin). In: Mandell GL, Bennett JE, Dolin R, eds. Mandell, Douglas and Bennett's principles and practice of infectious diseases. 6th ed. Oxford: Churchill Livingstone; 2005:417–40.
4. Virgincar N, MacGowan A. Glycopeptides (dalabavancin, oritavancin, teicoplanin, vancomycin). In: Yu VL, Edwards G, McKinnon PS et al., eds. Antimicrobial therapy and vaccines. Volume II: antimicrobial agents. 2nd ed. Pittsburgh: ESun Technologies; 2004:181–99.
5. Stevens DL. The role of vancomycin in the treatment paradigm. *Clin Infect Dis.* 2006; 42(suppl 1):S51–7.
6. Rybak MJ. The pharmacokinetic and pharmacodynamic properties of vancomycin. *Clin Infect Dis.* 2006; 42(suppl 1):S35–9.
7. Darko W, Medicis JJ, Smith A. Mississippi mud no more: cost-effectiveness of pharmacokinetic dosage adjustment of vancomycin to prevent nephrotoxicity. *Pharmacotherapy.* 2003; 23:643–50.
8. Cantu TG, Yamanaka-Yuen NA, Leitman PS. Serum vancomycin concentrations: reappraisal of their clinical value. *Clin Infect Dis.* 1994; 18:533–43.
9. Moellering RC Jr. Monitoring serum vancomycin levels: climbing the mountain because it is there? *Clin Infect Dis.* 1994; 18:544–6.

10. Rybak MJ, Albrecht LM, Boike SC, et al. Nephrotoxicity of vancomycin alone and with an aminoglycoside. *J Antimicrob Chemother.* 1990; 25:679–87.
11. Rybak MJ, Abate BJ, Kang SL, et al. Prospective evaluation of the effect of an aminoglycoside dosing regimen on rates of observed nephrotoxicity and ototoxicity. *Antimicrob Agents Chemother.* 1999; 43:1549–55.
12. Lodise TP, Lomaestro B, Graves J, et al. Larger vancomycin doses (≥4 grams/day) are associated with an increased incidence of nephrotoxicity. *Antimicrob Agents Chemother.* 2008; 52:1330–6.
13. Canadian Task Force on the Periodic Health Examination. The periodic health examination. *Can Med Assoc J.* 1979; 121:1193–254.
14. Rodvold KA, Blum RA, Fischer JH, et al. Vancomycin pharmacokinetics in patients with various degrees of renal function. *Antimicrob Agents Chemother.* 1988; 32:848–52.
15. Matzke GR, McGory RW, Halstenson CE, et al. Pharmacokinetics of vancomycin in patients with various degrees of renal function. *Antimicrob Agents Chemother.* 1984; 25:433–7.
16. Rotschafer JC, Crossley K, Zaske DE, et al. Pharmacokinetics of vancomycin: observations in 28 patients and dosage recommendations. *Antimicrob Agents Chemother.* 1982; 22:391–4.
17. Blouin RA, Bauer LA, Miller DD, et al. Vancomycin pharmacokinetics in normal and morbidly obese subjects. *Antimicrob Agents Chemother.* 1982; 21:575–80.
18. Golper TA, Noonan HM, Elzinga L, et al. Vancomycin pharmacokinetics, renal handling, and nonrenal clearances in normal human subjects. *Clin Pharmacol Ther.* 1988; 43:565–70.
19. Ackerman BH, Taylor EH, Olsen KM, et al. Vancomycin serum protein binding determination by ultrafiltration. *Drug Intell Clin Pharm.* 1988; 22:300–3.
20. Albrecht LM, Rybak MJ, Warbasse LH, et al. Vancomycin protein binding in patients with infections caused by *Staphylococcus aureus*. *DICP.* 1991; 25:713–5.
21. Skhirtladze K, Hutschala D, Fleck T, et al. Impaired target site penetration of vancomycin in diabetic patients following cardiac surgery. *Antimicrob Agents Chemother.* 2006; 50:1372–5.
22. Cruciani M, Gatti G, Lazzarini L, et al. Penetration of vancomycin into human lung tissue. *J Antimicrob Chemother.* 1996; 38:865–9.
23. Georges H, Leroy O, Alfandari S, et al. Pulmonary disposition of vancomycin in critically ill patients. *Eur J Clin Microbiol Infect Dis.* 1997; 16:385–8.
24. Lamer C, de Beco V, Soler P, et al. Analysis of vancomycin entry into pulmonary lining fluid by bronchoalveolar lavage in critical ill patients. *Antimicrob Agents Chemother.* 1993; 37:281–6.
25. Craig WA. Basic pharmacodynamics of antibacterials with clinical applications to the use of beta-lactams, glycopeptides, and linezolid. *Infect Dis Clin North Am.* 2003; 17:479–501.
26. Craig WA. Pharmacokinetic/pharmacodynamic parameters: rationale for antimicrobial dosing of mice and men. *Clin Infect Dis.* 1998; 26:1–10.
27. Drusano GL. Antimicrobial pharmacodynamics: critical interactions of bug and drug. *Nature Rev Microbiol.* 2004; 2:289–300.
28. Rybak MJ. Pharmacodynamics: relation to antimicrobial resistance. *Am J Med.* 2006; 119(6, suppl 1):S37–44.
29. Ackerman BH, Vannier AM, Eudy EB. Analysis of vancomycin time-kill studies with *Staphylococcus* species by using a curve stripping program to describe the relationship between concentration and pharmacodynamic response. *Antimicrob Agents Chemother.* 1992; 36:1766–9.
30. Löwdin E, Odenholt I, Cars O. In vitro studies of pharmacodynamic properties of vancomycin against *Staphylococcus aureus* and *Staphylococcus epidermidis*. *Antimicrob Agents Chemother.* 1998; 42:2739–44.
31. Larsson AJ, Walker KJ, Raddatz JK, et al. The concentration-independent effect of monoexponential and biexponential decay in vancomycin concentrations on the killing of *Staphylococcus aureus* under aerobic and anaerobic conditions. *J Antimicrob Chemother.* 1996; 38:589–97.
32. Craig WA, Andes DR. In vivo pharmacodynamics of vancomycin against VISA, heteroresistant VISA (hVISA) and VSSA in the neutropenic murine thigh-infection model. Paper presented at 46th Interscience Conference on Antimicrobial Agents and Chemotherapy. San Francisco, CA: 2006 Sep.
33. Moise-Broder PA, Sakoulas G, Eliopoulos GM, et al. Accessory gene regulator group II polymorphism in methicillin-resistant *Staphylococcus aureus* is predictive of failure of vancomycin therapy. *Clin Infect Dis.* 2004; 38:1700–5.
34. The development of vancomycin. In: Cooper GL, Given DB. Vancomycin: a comprehensive review of 30 years of clinical experience. New York: Park Row; 1986:1–6.
35. James JK, Palmer SM, Levine DP, et al. Comparison of conventional dosing versus continuous-infusion vancomycin therapy for patients with suspected or documented gram-positive infections. *Antimicrob Agents Chemother.* 1996; 40:696–700.
36. Lacy MK, Tessier PR, Nicolau DP, et al. Comparison of vancomycin pharmacodynamics (1 g every 12 or 24 h) against methicillin-resistant staphylococci. *Int J Antimicrob Agents.* 2000; 15:25–30.
37. Wysocki M, Thomas F, Wolff MA, et al. Comparison of continuous with discontinuous intravenous infusion of vancomycin in severe MRSA infections. *J Antimicrob Chemother.* 1995; 35:352–4.
38. Wysocki M, Delatour F, Faurisson F, et al. Continuous versus intermittent infusion of vancomycin in severe staphylococcal infections: prospective multicenter randomized study. *Antimicrob Agents Chemother.* 2001; 45:2460–7.
39. Geraci J. Vancomycin. *Mayo Clin Proc.* 1977; 52:631–4.
40. Karam CM, McKinnon PS, Neuhauser MM, et al. Outcome assessment of minimizing vancomycin monitoring and dosing adjustments. *Pharmacotherapy.* 1999; 19:257–66.
41. American Thoracic Society, Infectious Diseases Society of America. Guidelines for the management of adults with hospital-acquired, ventilator-associated, and healthcare-associated pneumonia. *Am J Respir Crit Care Med.* 2005; 171:388–416.

42. Jeffres MN, Isakow W, Doherty JA, et al. Predictors of mortality for methicillin-resistant *Staphylococcus aureus* health-care-associated pneumonia: specific evaluation of vancomycin pharmacokinetic indices. *Chest.* 2006; 130:947–55.
43. LaPlante KL, Rybak MJ. Impact of high-inoculum *Staphylococcus aureus* on the activities of nafcillin, vancomycin, linezolid, and daptomycin, alone and in combination with gentamicin, in an in vitro pharmacodynamic model. *Antimicrob Agents Chemother.* 2004; 48:4665–72.
44. Lamp KC, Rybak MJ, Bailey EM, et al. In vitro pharmacodynamic effects of concentration, pH, and growth phase on serum bactericidal activities of daptomycin and vancomycin. *Antimicrob Agents Chemother.* 1992; 36:2709–14.
45. Peetermans WE, Hoogeterp JJ, Hazekamp-van Dokkum AM, et al. Antistaphylococcal activities of teicoplanin and vancomycin in vitro and in an experimental infection. *Antimicrob Agents Chemother.* 1990; 34:1869–74.
46. Svensson E, Hanberger H, Nilsson LE. Pharmacodynamic effects of antibiotics and antibiotic combinations on growing and nongrowing *Staphylococcus epidermidis* cells. *Antimicrob Agents Chemother.* 1997; 41:107–11.
47. Cosgrove SE, Carroll KC, Perl TM. *Staphylococcus aureus* with reduced susceptibility to vancomycin. *Clin Infect Dis.* 2004; 39:539–45.
48. Liu C, Chambers HF. *Staphylococcus aureus* with heterogeneous resistance to vancomycin: epidemiology, clinical significance, and critical assessment of diagnostic methods. *Antimicrob Agents Chemother.* 2003; 47:3040–5.
49. Moore MR, Perdreau-Remington F, Chambers HF. Vancomycin treatment failure associated with heterogeneous vancomycin-intermediate *Staphylococcus aureus* in a patient with endocarditis and in the rabbit model of endocarditis. *Antimicrob Agents Chemother.* 2003; 47:1262–6.
50. Howden BP, Johnson PD, Ward PB, et al. Isolates with low-level vancomycin resistance associated with per sistent methicillin-resistant *Staphylococcus aureus* bacteremia. *Antimicrob Agents Chemother.* 2006; 50:3039–47.
51. Tenover FC, Moellering RC Jr. The rationale for revising the Clinical and Laboratory Standards Institute vancomycin minimal inhibitory concentration interpretive criteria for *Staphylococcus aureus*. *Clin Infect Dis.* 2007; 44:1208–15.
52. Sakoulas G, Moise-Broder PA, Schentag J, et al. Relationship of MIC and bactericidal activity to efficacy of vancomycin for treatment of methicillin-resistant *Staphylococcus aureus* bacteremia. *J Clin Microbiol.* 2004; 42:2398–402.
53. Hidayat LK, Hsu DI, Quist R, et al. High-dose vancomycin therapy for methicillin-resistant *Staphylococcus aureus* infections: efficacy and toxicity. *Arch Intern Med.* 2006; 166:2138–44.
54. Sakoulas G, Gold HS, Cohen RA, et al. Effects of prolonged vancomycin administration on methicillin-resistant *Staphylococcus aureus* (MRSA) in a patient with recurrent bacteraemia. *J Antimicrob Chemother.* 2006; 57:699–704.
55. Howden BP, Ward PB, Charles PG, et al. Treatment outcomes for serious infections caused by methicillin-resistant *Staphylococcus aureus* with reduced vancomycin susceptibility. *Clin Infect Dis.* 2004; 38:521–8.
56. Charles PG, Ward PB, Johnson PD, et al. Clinical features associated with bacteremia due to heterogeneous vancomycin-intermediate *Staphylococcus aureus*. *Clin Infect Dis.* 2004; 38:448–51.
57. Jones RN. Microbiological features of vancomycin in the 21st century: minimum inhibitory concentration creep, bactericidal/static activity, and applied breakpoints to predict clinical outcomes or detect resistant strains. *Clin Infect Dis.* 2006; 42(suppl 1):S13–24.
58. Moise PA, Sakoulas G, Forrest A, et al. Vancomycin in vitro bactericidal activity and its relationship to efficacy in clearance of methicillin-resistant *Staphylococcus aureus* bacteremia. *Antimicrob Agents Chemother.* 2007; 51:2582–8.
59. Soriano A, Marco F, Martinez JA, et al. Influence of vancomycin minimum inhibitory concentration on the treatment of methicillin-resistant *Staphylococcus aureus* bacteremia. *Clin Infect Dis.* 2008; 46:193–200.
60. Lodise TP, Graves J, Graffunder E, et al. Relationship between vancomycin MIC and failure among patients with methicillin-resistant *Staphylococcus aureus* bacteremia treated with vancomycin. *Antimicrob Agents Chemother.* 2008; 52:3315–20.
61. Mohr JF, Murray BE. Point: vancomycin is not obsolete for the treatment of infection caused by methicillin-resistant *Staphylococcus aureus*. *Clin Infect Dis.* 2007; 44:1536–42.
62. Rhee KY, Gardiner DF, Charles M. Decreasing in vitro susceptibility of clinical *Staphylococcus aureus* isolates to vancomycin at the New York Hospital: quantitative testing redux. *Clin Infect Dis.* 2005; 40:1705–6.
63. Wang G, Hindler JF, Ward KW, et al. Increased vancomycin MICs for *Staphylococcus aureus* clinical isolates from a university hospital during a 5-year period. *J Clin Microbiol.* 2006; 44:3883–6.
64. Steinkraus G, White R, Friedrich L. Vancomycin MIC creep in non-vancomycin-intermediate *Staphylococcus aureus* (VISA), vancomycin-susceptible clinical methicillin-resistant *S. aureus* (MRSA) blood isolates from 2001-05. *J Antimicrob Chemother.* 2007; 60:788–94.
65. Deresinski S. Counterpoint: vancomycin and *Staphylococcus aureus*—an antibiotic enters obsolescence. *Clin Infect Dis.* 2007; 44:1543–8.
66. Novick RP. Autoinduction and signal transduction in the regulation of staphylococcal virulence. *Mol Microbiol.* 2003; 48:1429–49.
67. Sakoulas G, Eliopoulos GM, Moellering RC Jr, et al. *Staphylococcus aureus* accessory gene regulator (agr) group II: is there a relationship to the development of intermediate-level glycopeptide resistance? *J Infect Dis.* 2003; 187:929–38.
68. Sakoulas G, Eliopoulos GM, Fowler VG Jr, et al. Reduced susceptibility of *Staphylococcus aureus* to vancomycin and platelet microbicidal protein correlates with defective autolysis and loss of accessory gene regulator (agr) function. *Antimicrob Agents Chemother.* 2005; 49:2687–92.
69. Tsuji BT, Rybak MJ, Lau KL, et al. Evaluation of accessory gene regulator (agr) group and function in the

proclivity towards vancomycin intermediate resistance in *Staphylococcus aureus*. *Antimicrob Agents Chemother.* 2007; 51:1089–91.
70. Tsuji BT, Rybak MJ, Cheung CM, et al. Community- and health care-associated methicillin-resistant *Staphylococcus aureus*: a comparison of molecular epidemiology and antimicrobial activities of various agents. *Diagn Microbiol Infect Dis.* 2007; 58:41–7.
71. Del Mar Fernández de Gatta Garcia M, Revilla N, Calvo MV, et al. Pharmacokinetic/pharmacodynamic analysis of vancomycin in ICU patients. *Intensive Care Med.* 2006; 33:279–85.
72. Murphy JE, Gillespie DE, Bateman CV. Predictability of vancomycin trough concentrations using seven approaches for estimating pharmacokinetic parameters. *Am J Health-Syst Pharm.* 2006; 63:2365–70.
73. Wang JT, Fang CT, Chen YC, et al. Necessity of a loading dose when using vancomycin in critically ill patients. *J Antimicrob Chemother.* 2001; 47:246. Letter.
74. Mohammedi I, Descloux E, Argaud L, et al. Loading dose of vancomycin in critically ill patients: 15 mg/kg is a better choice than 500 mg. *Int J Antimicrob Agents.* 2006; 27:259–62.
75. Bailie GR, Neal D. Vancomycin ototoxicity and nephrotoxicity. A review. *Med Toxicol Adverse Drug Exp.* 1988; 3:376–86.
76. Elting LS, Rubenstein EB, Kurtin D, et al. Mississippi mud in the 1990s: risks and outcomes of vancomycin-associated toxicity in general oncology practice. *Cancer.* 1998; 83:2597–607.
77. Wilhelm MP, Estes L. Symposium on antimicrobial agents—part XII. *Vancomycin. Mayo Clinic Proc.* 1999; 74:928–35.
78. Rybak MJ, Boike SC. Monitoring vancomycin therapy. *Drug Intell Clin Pharm.* 1986; 20:757–61.
79. Henry K, Steinberg I, Crossley KB. Vancomycin-induced neutropenia during treatment of osteomyelitis in an outpatient. *Drug Intell Clin Pharm.* 1986; 20:783–5.
80. Koo KB, Bachand RL, Chow AW. Vancomycin-induced neutropenia. *Drug Intell Clin Pharm.* 1986; 20:780–2.
81. Farber BF, Moellering RC Jr. Retrospective study of the toxicity of preparations of vancomycin from 1974 to 1981. *Antimicrob Agents Chemother.* 1983; 23:138–41.
82. Mellor JA, Kingdom J, Cafferkey M, et al. Vancomycin toxicity: a prospective study. *J Antimicrob Chemother.* 1985; 15:773–80.
83. Sorrell TC, Collignon PJ. A prospective study of adverse reactions associated with vancomycin therapy. *J Antimicrob Chemother.* 1985; 16:235–41.
84. Cimino MA, Rotstein C, Slaughter RL, et al. Relationship of serum antibiotic concentrations to nephrotoxicity in cancer patients receiving concurrent aminoglycoside and vancomycin therapy. *Am J Med.* 1987; 83:1091–7.
85. Downs NJ, Neihart RE, Dolezal JM, et al. Mild nephrotoxicity associated with vancomycin use. *Arch Intern Med.* 1989; 149:1777–81.
86. Pauly DJ, Musa DM, Lestico MR, et al. Risk of nephrotoxicity with combination vancomycin-aminoglycoside antibiotic therapy. *Pharmacotherapy.* 1990; 10:378–82.
87. Jeffres MN, Isakow W, Doherty JA, et al. A retrospective analysis of possible renal toxicity associated with vancomycin in patients with health care-associated methicillin-resistant *Staphylococcus aureus* pneumonia. *Clin Ther.* 2007; 29:1107–15.
88. Nguyen M, Wong J, Lee C, et al. Nephrotoxicity associated with high dose vs standard dose vancomycin therapy. Paper presented at 47th Interscience Conference on Antimicrobial Agents and Chemotherapy. Chicago, IL; 2007 Sep.
89. King DW, Smith MA. Proliferative responses observed following vancomycin treatment in renal proximal tubule epithelial cells. *Toxicol In Vitro.* 2004; 18:797–803.
90. Celik I, Cihangiroglu M, Ilhan N, et al. Protective effects of different antioxidants and amrinone on vancomycin-induced nephrotoxicity. *Basic Clin Pharmacol Toxicol.* 2005; 97:325–32.
91. Le Moyec L, Racine S, Le Toumelin P, et al. Aminoglycoside and glycopeptide renal toxicity in intensive care patients studied by proton magnetic resonance spectroscopy of urine. *Crit Care Med.* 2002; 30:1242–5.
92. Nishino Y, Takemura S, Minamiyama Y, et al. Inhibition of vancomycin-induced nephrotoxicity by targeting superoxide dismutase to renal proximal tubule cells in the rat. *Redox Rep.* 2002; 7:317–9.
93. Hailemeskel B, Namanny M, Wutoh A. Frequency of nephrotoxicity with vancomycin and aminoglycoside therapy. *Hosp Pharm.* 1999; 12:1417–20.
94. Salama SE, Rotstein C. Prospective assessment of nephrotoxicity with concomitant aminoglycoside and vancomycin therapy. *Can J Hosp Pharm.* 1993; 46:53–9.
95. Malacarne P, Bergamasco S, Donadio C. Nephrotoxicity due to combination antibiotic therapy with vancomycin and aminoglycosides in septic critically ill patients. *Chemotherapy.* 2006; 52:178–84.
96. Cunha BA, Mohan SS, Hamid N, et al. Cost-ineffectiveness of serum vancomycin levels. *Eur J Clin Microbiol Infect Dis.* 2007; 26:509–11.
97. Wold JS, Turnipseed SA. Toxicity of vancomycin in laboratory animals. *Rev Infect Dis.* 1981; 3(suppl):S224–9.
98. Aronoff GR, Sloan RS, Dinwiddie CB Jr, et al. Effects of vancomycin on renal function in rats. *Antimicrob Agents Chemother.* 1981; 19:306–8.
99. Beauchamp D, Pellerin M, Gourde P, et al. Effects of daptomycin and vancomycin on tobramycin nephrotoxicity in rats. *Antimicrob Agents Chemother.* 1990; 34:139–47.
100. Wood CA, Kohlhepp SJ, Kohnen PW, et al. Vancomycin enhancement of experimental tobramycin nephrotoxicity. *Antimicrob Agents Chemother.* 1986; 30:20–4.
101. Marre R, Schulz E, Anders T, et al. Renal tolerance and pharmacokinetics of vancomycin in rats. *J Antimicrob Chemother.* 1984; 14:253–60.
102. Fauconneau B, De Lemos E, Pariat C, et al. Chrononephrotoxicity in rat of a vancomycin and gentamicin combination. *Pharmacol Toxicol.* 1992; 71:31–6.
103. Marre R, Schulz E, Hedtke D, et al. Influence of fosfomycin and tobramycin on vancomycin-induced nephrotoxicity. *Infection.* 1985; 13:190–2.

104. Kacew S, Hewitt WR, Hook JB. Gentamicin-induced renal metabolic alterations in newborn rat kidney: lack of potentiation by vancomycin. *Toxicol Appl Pharmacol.* 1989; 99:61–71.
105. Rybak MJ, Frankowski JJ, Edwards DJ, et al. Alanine aminopeptidase and beta 2-microglobulin excretion in patients receiving vancomycin and gentamicin. *Antimicrob Agents Chemother.* 1987; 31:1461–4.
106. European Organization for Research and Treatment of Cancer (EORTC) International Antimicrobial Therapy Cooperative Group and the National Cancer Institute of Canada-Clinical Trials Group. Vancomycin added to empirical combination antibiotic therapy for fever in granulocytopenic cancer patients. *J Infect Dis.* 1991; 163:951–8. [Erratum, *J Infect Dis.* 1991; 164:832.]
107. Bertino JS Jr, Booker LA, Franck PA, et al. Incidence of and significant risk factors for aminoglycoside-associated nephrotoxicity in patients dosed by using individualized pharmacokinetic monitoring. *J Infect Dis.* 1993; 167:173–9.
108. Karp JE, Dick JD, Angelopulos C, et al. Empiric use of vancomycin during prolonged treatment-induced granulocytopenia: randomized, double-blind, placebo-controlled clinical trial in patients with acute leukemia. *Am J Med.* 1986; 81:237–42.
109. Goren MP, Baker DK Jr, Shenep JL. Vancomycin does not enhance amikacin-induced tubular nephrotoxicity in children. *Pediatr Infect Dis J.* 1989; 8:278–82.
110. Nahata MC. Lack of nephrotoxicity in pediatric patients receiving concurrent vancomycin and aminoglycoside therapy. *Chemotherapy.* 1987; 33:302–4.
111. Goetz MB, Sayers J. Nephrotoxicity of vancomycin and aminoglycoside therapy separately and in combination. *J Antimicrob Chemother.* 1993; 32:325–34.
112. Cohen E, Dadashev A, Drucker M, et al. Once-daily versus twice-daily intravenous administration of vancomycin for infections in hospitalized patients. *J Antimicrob Chemother.* 2002; 49:155–60.
113. Boffi El Amari E, Vuagnat A, Stern R, et al. High versus standard dose vancomycin for osteomyelitis. *Scand J Infect Dis.* 2004; 36:712–7.
114. Zimmermann AE, Katona BG, Plaisance KI. Association of vancomycin serum concentrations with outcomes in patients with gram-positive bacteremia. *Pharmacotherapy.* 1995; 15:85–91.
115. Lee-Such SC, Overholser BR, Munoz-Price LS. Nephrotoxicity associated with aggressive vancomycin therapy. Paper presented at 46th Interscience Conference on Antimicrobial Agents and Chemotherapy. San Francisco, CA; 2006 Sep.
116. Welty TE, Copa AK. Impact of vancomycin therapeutic drug monitoring on patient care. *Ann Pharmacother.* 1994; 28:1335–9.
117. Iwamoto T, Kagawa Y, Kojima M. Clinical efficacy of therapeutic drug monitoring in patients receiving vancomycin. *Biol Pharm Bull.* 2003; 26:876–9.
118. Davis RR, Brummett RE, Bendrick TW, et al. The ototoxic interaction of viomycin, capreomycin and polymyxin B with ethacrynic acid. *Acta Otolaryngol.* 1982; 93:211–7.
119. Tange RA, Kieviet HL, von Marle J, et al. An experimental study of vancomycin-induced cochlear damage. *Arch Otorhinolaryngol.* 1989; 246:67–70.
120. Traber PG, Levine DP. Vancomycin ototoxicity in a patient with normal renal function. *Ann Intern Med.* 1991; 95:458–60.
121. Brummett RE, Fox KE. Vancomycin- and erythromycin-induced hearing loss in humans. *Antimicrob Agents Chemother.* 1989; 33:791–6.
122. Dangerfield HG, Hewit WL, Monzon OT, et al. Clinical use of vancomycin. *Antimicrob Agents Chemother.* 1960; 61:428–37.
123. Kirby WM, Perry DM, Bauer AW. Treatment of staphylococcal septicemia with vancomycin: report of thirty-three cases. *N Engl J Med.* 1960; 262:49–55.
124. Waisbren BA, Kleinerman L, Skemp J, et al. Comparative clinical effectiveness and toxicity of vancomycin, ristocetin, and kanamycin. *Arch Intern Med.* 1960; 106:179–93.
125. Saunders NJ. Why monitor peak vancomycin concentrations? *Lancet.* 1994; 344:1748–50.
126. Fekety R. Vancomycin. *Med Clin North Amer.* 1982; 66:175–81.
127. Reynolds JE, ed. Martindale, the extra pharmacopoeia. 28th ed. London: Pharmaceutical Press; 1982.
128. Buckingham SC, McCullers JA, Lujan-Zilbermann J, et al. Early vancomycin therapy and adverse outcomes in children with pneumococcal meningitis. *Pediatrics.* 2006; 117:1688–94.
129. Geraci JE, Heilman FR, Nichols DR, et al. Antibiotic therapy of bacterial endocarditis. VII. Vancomycin for acute micrococcal endocarditis; preliminary report. *Proc Staff Meet Mayo Clin.* 1958; 33:172–81.

Developed through the ASHP Council on Therapeutics and approved by the ASHP Board of Directors on June 26, 2008, the Infectious Diseases Society of America's Board of Directors on June 16, 2008, and the Society of Infectious Diseases Pharmacists' Board of Directors on June 25, 2008.

Michael Rybak, Pharm.D., M.P.H. is Professor of Pharmacy and Medicine, and Director, Anti-Infective Research Laboratory, Eugene Applebaum College of Pharmacy and Health Science, Wayne State University (WSU), Detroit, MI. Ben Lomaestro, Pharm.D., is Senior Clinical Pharmacy Specialist in Infectious Diseases, Albany Medical Center, Albany, NY. John C. Rotschafer, Pharm.D., is Professor, Department of Experimental and Clinical Pharmacology, College of Pharmacy, University of Minnesota, Minneapolis. Robert Moellering Jr., M.D., is Shields Warren-Mallinckrodt Professor of Medical Research, Harvard Medical School, and Physician, Department of Medicine, Beth Israel Deaconess Medical Center, Boston, MA. William Craig, M.D., is Professor Emeritus, University of Wisconsin School of Medicine and Public Health, School of Medicine and Public Health, University of Wisconsin, Madison. Marianne Billeter, Pharm.D., BCPS, is Manager of Clinical Pharmacy Services at Ochsner Medical Center, New Orleans, LA. Joseph R. Dalovisio, M.D., is Chairman, Department of Infectious Diseases, Ochsner Health System, New Orleans. Donald P. Levine, M.D., is Professor of Medicine and Chief, Division of General Internal Medicine, WSU.

The following individuals are acknowledged for reviewing draft versions of this statement: Diane M. Cappelletty, Pharm.D.; Douglas N. Fish, Pharm.D., FCCP, FCCM, BCPS; William L. Greene, B.S., Pharm.D., BCPS, FASHP; David J. Ritchie, Pharm.D., FCCP,

BCPS; Annette M. Rowden, Pharm.D., BCPS; and Lynda J. Thompson, Pharm.D.

The authors have declared no potential conflicts of interest.

The bibliographic citation for this document is as follows: American Society of Health-System Pharmacists. Therapeutic monitoring of vancomycin in adult patients: A consensus review of the American Society of Health-System Pharmacists, the Infectious Diseases Society of America, and the Society of Infectious Diseases Pharmacists. *Am J Health-Syst Pharm.* 2009; 66:82–98.

ASHP Therapeutic Position Statement on the Use of Second-Generation Antipsychotic Medications in the Treatment of Adults with Psychotic Disorders

Position

The American Society of Health-System Pharmacists (ASHP) recognizes that schizophrenia, schizoaffective disorder, and other psychotic disorders are serious mental illnesses that can significantly affect an individual's perceptual, behavioral, affective, and cognitive functions. These conditions are usually chronic and recurrent, necessitating continuous treatment over the patient's lifetime. Individuals with these disorders frequently require lengthy and expensive hospitalizations, as well as a variety of ongoing rehabilitative and supportive services that can impose a significant burden on society. In addition, high rates of suicidal behavior and completed suicides have been observed in patients with psychotic disorders. The management of these disorders typically requires long-term treatment with antipsychotic medications, the use of adjunctive pharmacologic treatments, and ongoing psychosocial and supportive interventions to reduce morbidity and mortality.

ASHP encourages health professionals to consider the use of second-generation ("atypical" or "novel") antipsychotics as first-line drug treatments for individuals with psychotic disorders. Second-generation antipsychotics share the common pharmacologic action of dual serotonin–dopamine antagonism. While the acquisition costs of these agents are greater than those of older drugs, randomized controlled trials and naturalistic studies have demonstrated that second-generation antipsychotics effectively treat the symptoms of psychotic disorders while providing a tolerability profile that improves treatment adherence and reduces the severity of short- and long-term adverse motor effects. Second-generation antipsychotics have also been found to have improved profiles for cognitive impairments in schizophrenia, relative to older agents, allowing for opportunities toward psychosocial rehabilitation. There is also evidence that the use of these agents improves outcomes in patients with chronic psychotic disorders compared with older antipsychotics, specifically reducing the rates of symptom relapse and inpatient rehospitalization. However, it should be noted that second-generation antipsychotics are associated with significant treatment risks, such as adverse cardiovascular and metabolic effects, that should be carefully considered during treatment initiation and throughout the course of therapy.

Background

Schizophrenia and schizoaffective disorder are serious, chronic mental illnesses that affect perceptual, behavioral, and cognitive functioning. The *DSM-IV-TR* established criteria for five main subtypes of schizophrenia and for schizoaffective disorder.[1] Individuals with schizophrenia generally exhibit a mixture of positive, negative, and cognitive symptoms with varying intensity throughout the course of their illness (Table 1). Schizoaffective disorder differs from schizophrenia in that recurrent mood episodes (mania or depression) occur over a substantial period of time over the course of the illness in addition to chronic psychotic symptoms. These two disorders have been studied together in many clinical trials and will be considered together for the purpose of this document.

It has been estimated that the worldwide lifetime frequency of psychotic disorders is about 1%.[2,3] Onset of the first severe psychotic symptoms in a patient with schizophrenia usually occurs between the late teens and mid-30s, with onset in males peaking between ages 15 and 30 and females exhibiting a later onset, between ages 20 and 35.[4,5] Late-onset schizophrenia, occurring after 40 years of age, may have an otherwise similar course to typical adult-onset schizophrenia. Prodromal symptoms of psychosis occurring in children and adolescents (e.g., apathy, social withdrawal) may be present before the first psychotic break, but the full symptoms of these disorders are rare in this population. Because these illnesses frequently have their symptom onset in early adulthood and are characterized by a wide range of symptoms, they usually cause significant, progressive impairment in the social, occupational, and academic functioning of affected individuals.

Table 1.
Positive, Negative, and Cognitive Symptoms of Schizophrenia

Positive Symptoms	Negative Symptoms	Cognitive Symptoms
Hostility	Emotional withdrawal	Impaired attention
Excitement	Uncooperativeness	Impaired short-term memory
Hallucinations	Blunted affect	Impaired executive functioning
Delusions	Inappropriate affect	Impaired verbal fluency
Suspiciousness	Poverty of thought	
Grandiosity	Social withdrawal	
Conceptual disorganization	Lack of spontaneity	
	Poor abstract thinking	

Pharmacologic Characteristics of Antipsychotic Drugs

The effectiveness of first-generation antipsychotic agents, whose primary mechanism of action was blockade of postsynaptic dopamine type 2 (D_2) receptors in the brain, led to the initial hypothesis regarding dopamine's role in schizophrenia. While it is apparent that increased dopamine in the mesolimbic pathway is responsible for the positive symptoms of schizophrenia, it is now understood that psychotic disorders frequently involve numerous neurochemical abnormalities. Psychosis has been observed in individuals with idiopathic[6] and drug-induced[7] hypofunction of the glutamate system. In addition, the high rate of nicotine dependence in individuals with psychotic disorders–up to 88% in one study[8]—has led to the identification and study of acetylcholine-receptor abnormalities in the pathophysiology of schizophrenia.[9]

The ideal drug for the treatment of psychotic disorders would have several important characteristics. It would provide effective relief and prevention of acute positive symptoms of schizophrenia. Other ideal characteristics would include effective relief of affective, cognitive, and negative symptoms; minimal short- and long-term adverse effects; few drug interactions; and low acquisition cost. Although no antipsychotic agent currently available completely fits all these criteria, second-generation antipsychotics offer many benefits not achieved with traditional antipsychotics.

First-generation antipsychotic agents primarily exert their therapeutic effects through the blockade of postsynaptic D_2 receptors in the mesolimbic pathway, thereby reducing positive symptoms over time. However, these drugs are not selective in their activity. Blockade of dopamine in other areas of the brain often leads to acute extrapyramidal motor effects (e.g., dystonias, parkinsonism), tardive dyskinesia, increased levels of serum prolactin, and exacerbation of negative symptoms. Although occurring infrequently at standard doses, an array of adverse neurologic, cardiovascular, and dermatologic effects are associated with these agents.

Second-generation antipsychotic drugs share the common pharmacologic action of dual serotonin–dopamine antagonism (Table 2). Aripiprazole differs slightly in that it functions as a partial agonist at dopamine receptors, reducing dopamine activity in the mesolimbic pathway.[10,11] Antagonism of serotonin type 2 (5-HT_2) receptors increases the release of endogenous dopamine.[12] This increase in dopamine decreases the likelihood of extrapyramidal motor symptoms and elevated prolactin levels without significantly reducing the beneficial effects against positive symptoms of psychosis. Theoretically, this property of the newer drugs may also help to improve the negative symptoms of schizophrenia.

Efficacy for Psychotic Symptoms

Second-generation antipsychotic agents have been demonstrated to be at least as effective as the traditional antipsychotic agents in the treatment of positive symptoms of schizophrenia when used in appropriate therapeutic doses. The newer antipsychotics also demonstrate benefits for affective symptoms, cognition, and psychosocial functioning not seen with the older agents.

Clozapine, the first second-generation antipsychotic introduced in the United States, has an established level of efficacy for use in individuals with psychotic disorders resistant to treatment with other antipsychotics. Kane et al.[13] conducted the landmark trial that demonstrated the superior efficacy of clozapine in individuals with treatment-resistant psychosis. This trial enrolled only patients whose psychosis was treatment resistant, defined as not responding to at least three periods of treatment in the preceding five years with antipsychotic agents from two different chemical classes at dosages equivalent to 1000 mg/day of chlorpromazine for six weeks. The previous antipsychotic trials must have failed to provide periods of good functioning or significant symptomatic relief. A six-week trial of haloperidol (mean dosage, 61 mg/day) and benztropine followed to confirm lack of drug response. Participants whose psychosis did not respond to haloperidol were randomized to receive clozapine (up to 900 mg/day) or chlorpromazine (up to 1800 mg/day) with benztropine. Using a priori criteria, response rates were 30% for patients treated with clozapine versus 4% for the chlorpromazine group. The authors found that improvements in the Brief Psychiatric Rating Scale total scores and clinical global impression (CGI) were three times greater in patients treated with clozapine.

The landmark clinical studies used in the evaluation of second-generation antipsychotics are summarized in Table 3. In general, these trials lasted four to six weeks and assessed the efficacy of these agents in the treatment of acute psychotic disorders. Because of the study designs employed, no assumptions can be made regarding the efficacy of these agents for long-term prevention of psychotic relapse, for comorbid substance abuse or mood disorders, or in other complex clinical situations. The medical literature suggests that all currently available second-generation antipsychotic agents are superior to placebo and at least as effective as the traditional antipsychotics in the reduction of positive symptoms of schizophrenia. With long-term therapy, second-generation antipsychotics may also have beneficial effects on negative symptoms; however, these benefits have not been consistently demonstrated in the four- to six-week clinical trials.

The Clinical Antipsychotic Trials of Intervention Effectiveness (CATIE) was a multicenter clinical study sponsored by the National Institute of Mental Health.[25] The first phase of this study, conducted between January 2001 and December 2004, involved 1460 patients with chronic schizophrenia age 18–65 years. Patients were randomized to treatment for up to 18 months with one of four available second-generation antipsychotics (olanzapine, quetiapine, risperidone, or ziprasidone) or perphenazine, a traditional antipsychotic. The primary outcome measured was time to discontinuation of treatment for any cause, including lack of efficacy, intolerable adverse effects, or patient's decision to end treatment. Treatment with olanzapine at a mean modal dosage (MMD) of 20.1 mg/day was associated with a significantly longer median duration of treatment (9.2 months) compared with quetiapine (4.6 months; MMD, 543.4 mg/day), risperidone

Table 2.
Second-Generation Antipsychotics Currently Available in the United States

Drug (Trade Name)	Manufacturer	Year Approved
Clozapine (Clozaril)	Novartis	1989
Risperidone (Risperdal)	Janssen Pharmaceutica	1993
Olanzapine (Zyprexa)	Eli Lilly	1996
Quetiapine (Seroquel)	AstraZeneca	1997
Ziprasidone (Geodon)	Pfizer	2001
Aripiprazole (Abilify)	Bristol-Myers Squibb	2002
Paliperidone (Invega)	Janssen Pharmaceutica	2006

Table 3.
Major Efficacy Trials of Second-Generation Antipsychotics[13–24]

Ref.	Patient Population	Treatment	Duration (wk)	Results[a]
13	268 inpatients with schizophrenia refractory to treatment with adequate trials with at least three agents from two different chemical classes, after nonresponse to 6-wk trial of haloperidol	Clozapine 500–900 mg/day vs. chlorpromazine 1000–1800 mg/day + benztropine (up to 6 mg/day)	6	BPRS total, CGI: Improvement with clozapine 3 times greater than with chlorpromazine ($p < 0.001$). Patient improvement (20% reduction in BPRS and either CGI of ≤3 or BPRS total of ≤35: Clozapine, 30%; chlorpromazine, 4% ($p < 0.001$).
14	39 outpatients with schizophrenia with history of residual symptoms after at least two 6-wk trials of neuroleptics from different classes, after nonresponse to 6-wk trial of fluphenazine	Clozapine 200–600 mg/day vs. haloperidol 10–30 mg/day + benztropine (up to 4 mg/day)	10	BPRS positive symptoms: Improvement with clozapine greater than with haloperidol ($p = 0.05$). SANS: Improvement with clozapine, worsening with haloperidol ($p = 0.04$). Clinical response rate: Clozapine, 44.4%; haloperidol, 5.5% ($p = 0.017$).
15	388 inpatients with schizophrenia	Risperidone 2, 6, 10, and 16 mg/day; haloperidol 20 mg/day; placebo	8	Clinical improvement (20% reduction in PANSS): Greater improvement in patients receiving risperidone 6 and 16 mg vs. haloperidol. Clinical improvement (Kane et al. criteria): Risperidone 6, 10, and 16 mg superior to placebo ($p < 0.05$).
16	135 patients with schizophrenia	Risperidone 2, 6, 10, and 16 mg/day; haloperidol 20 mg/day; placebo	8	Clinical improvement (20% reduction in PANSS): Greater improvement in patients receiving risperidone 2, 6, 10, and 16 mg and haloperidol recipients vs. placebo. PANSS—negative subscale: Only risperidone 6 mg superior to placebo.
17	400 patients with schizophrenia	Risperidone long-acting injection 25, 50, and 75 mg every 2 wk vs. placebo	12	Improvement in PANSS and CGI (LOCF) significant for all groups vs. placebo.
18	335 patients with schizophrenia	Olanzapine-L (2.5–7.5 mg/day), olanzapine-M (7.5–12.5 mg/day), olanzapine-H (12.5–17.5 mg/day), haloperidol 10–20 mg/day, placebo	6	CGI, BPRS: Olanzapine-M, olanzapine-H, and haloperidol groups significantly improved vs. placebo. SANS: Olanzapine-H group demonstrated significant improvement vs. haloperidol.
19	152 inpatients with schizophrenia	Olanzapine 1 and 10 mg/day vs. placebo	6	BPRS total, PANSS-negative score: Olanzapine 10-mg group superior to placebo. Olanzapine 1-mg group showed no improvement over placebo for any efficacy measure.
20	361 hospitalized patients with schizophrenia	Quetiapine 75, 150, 300, 600, and 750 mg/day; haloperidol 12 mg/day; placebo	6	BPRS total: Significant improvement from baseline vs. placebo noted in all treatment groups except quetiapine 75 mg. SANS: Significant improvement vs. placebo noted in quetiapine 300 mg and haloperidol groups.

(Continued on next page)

Table 3 *(continued)*

Ref.	Patient Population	Treatment	Duration (wk)	Results[a]
21	286 hospitalized patients with schizophrenia	Quetiapine-H (up to 750 mg/day), quetiapine-L (up to 250 mg/day), placebo	6	BPRS total, CGI, SANS: Quetiapine-H demonstrated significant improvement over placebo. Quetiapine-L group did not show superiority to placebo for any efficacy measure.
22	302 patients with schizophrenia or schizoaffective disorder	Ziprasidone 80 mg/day(40 mg b.i.d.) and 160 mg/day (80 mg b.i.d.), placebo	6	BPRS, PANSS, CGI: Both active treatment groups demonstrated significant improvement over placebo. MADRS: Subset of ziprasidone 160-mg group with depressive symptomatology demonstrated improvement vs. placebo.
23	139 patients with schizophrenia or schizoaffective disorder	Ziprasidone 40 and 120 mg/day, placebo	4	BPRS total, CGI: Ziprasidone 120-mg group demonstrated significant improvement.
24	414 patients with schizophrenia or schizoaffective disorder	Aripiprazole 15 and 30 mg/day, haloperidol 10 mg/day, placebo	4	PANSS total: Significant improvement with all active treatment groups at 2 wk. CGI: Scores in LOCF analysis superior to placebo for all active treatment groups.

[a]BPRS = Brief Psychiatric Rating Scale, CGI = clinical global impression, SANS = Schedule for the Assessment of Negative Symptoms, PANSS = Positive and Negative Syndrome Scale, MADRS = Montgomery–Asberg Depression Rating Scale, LOCF = last observation carried forward.

(4.8 months; MMD, 3.9 mg/day), perphenazine (5.6 months; MMD, 20.8 mg/day), and ziprasidone (3.5 months; MMD, 112.8 mg/day). For patients remaining on the assigned treatment over the course of the study, overall psychopathology as assessed by the Positive and Negative Syndrome Scale and the CGI showed improvement over time. Notably, the traditional antipsychotic perphenazine demonstrated comparable efficacy to the second-generation comparators across all measures.

There are several concerns that need to be considered regarding CATIE. First, within the 18-month study period, 74% of the patients discontinued their initial assigned drug therapy. Second, patients with preexisting tardive dyskinesia were not assigned to perphenazine and may have been less likely to exhibit adverse motor effects during the study. Finally, 30% of the patients receiving olanzapine experienced weight gain and adverse metabolic effects, including elevated blood glucose, cholesterol, triglyceride, and glycosylated hemoglobin levels. CATIE compared a single traditional antipsychotic, perphenazine, given at a low dosage to several second-generation antipsychotics. While the data generated from this study are helpful for determining differences in effectiveness between the assigned regimens and comparing important adverse effect issues, they support the widely held notion that the selection of antipsychotic drugs should be an individualized process.

Neurocognitive Effects

Impaired cognitive functioning has long been observed as a core feature of psychotic disorders. These impairments are relatively stable over the natural course of the illness, regardless of the frequency of acute exacerbations of psychotic symptoms.[26] Furthermore, cognitive impairment may have a greater impact on psychosocial functioning than any other feature of schizophrenia.[27,28]

Many domains of cognition, including attention, short-term memory, and executive function, are affected by schizophrenia.[26] Treatment with traditional antipsychotic drugs, while relieving positive symptoms of psychosis, do little to improve cognitive functioning. The concomitant use of anticholinergic drugs intended to prevent or treat extrapyramidal symptoms that accompany antipsychotic therapy may actually worsen some cognitive functions.[29]

Second-generation antipsychotics can play an important role in facilitating the psychosocial rehabilitation of individuals with psychotic disorders by improving cognition. These agents have been shown to improve scores on assessments representing a broad range of cognitive functions. A lower degree of binding to dopamine-D_2 receptors, as well as 5-HT_2 antagonism, in the mesocortical pathway may contribute to the beneficial effects on cognition. The individualized receptor-binding properties of second-generation antipsychotics may contribute to differential improvements in various cognitive domains in individuals with psychotic disorders.

In a 14-week study of individuals with treatment-resistant schizophrenia, risperidone and olanzapine improved executive function, declarative memory, and attention.[30] Clozapine has been shown to positively affect executive function and working memory in numerous studies.[31-33] In an open-label study of 255 clinically stable patients, aripiprazole and olanzapine improved working memory from baseline after eight weeks of treatment, while aripiprazole showed a greater improvement than olanzapine in verbal learning at weeks 8 and 26.[34]

Adverse Effects

One of the primary advantages of second-generation antipsychotics in the chronic treatment of psychotic disorders is the improved tolerability profile over older antipsychotics. Adverse effects related to dopamine blockade in the central nervous system tend to occur less frequently in individuals treated with second-generation antipsychotics compared with those receiving traditional antipsychotics. However, the newer drugs have been associated with different problems that can affect drug therapy.

Motor Symptoms. Treatment with conventional antipsychotics has long been associated with both acute and chronic adverse motor effects. Acute extrapyramidal symptoms—dystonia, pseudoparkinsonism, and akathisia (a syndrome of subjective anxiety and restlessness)—are thought to be related to drug-induced blockade of dopamine receptors in the nigrostriatal pathway in the brain. Second-generation antipsychotics, possibly through a combination of 5-HT_2-receptor antagonism and rapid dissociation from D_2 receptors,[35] produce antipsychotic effects with a lower likelihood of acute extrapyramidal symptoms.[36]

Tardive dyskinesia, a potentially irreversible chronic motor disorder caused by long-term exposure to dopamine antagonists, has been another serious concern with conventional antipsychotics. Though not completely eliminating the risk, second-generation antipsychotics have been shown to have a lower risk of treatment-emergent tardive dyskinesia with maintenance treatment. Using data pooled from three controlled comparative studies, Tollefson et al.[37] reported that 50 (7.1%) of 707 olanzapine-treated patients manifested symptoms of tardive dyskinesia during the trials, compared with 32 (16.2%) of 197 individuals treated with haloperidol ($p < 0.001$). In a nine-month prospective study of outpatients age 45 years or older, the risk of developing tardive dyskinesia was over four times greater for patients treated with haloperidol than for those receiving risperidone ($p = 0.045$).[38] Similar results have been found in other controlled and noncontrolled studies of risperidone, olanzapine, and quetiapine.[39-41]

Clozapine appears to have an especially favorable profile for the prevention and management of antipsychotic-induced movement disorders. In comparative trials, clozapine exhibited little to no evidence of inducing treatment-emergent extrapyramidal symptoms.[13,42,43] The risk of tardive dyskinesia associated with clozapine treatment also appears to be minimal.[44] In fact, clozapine has been used to successfully treat preexisting tardive dyskinesia. Remission of symptoms has been reported in some, but not all, cases of preexisting tardive dyskinesia treated with clozapine.[45-47] In addition, withdrawal of clozapine in patients with tardive dyskinesia has resulted in either maintenance of reduced movements[46] or worsening of dyskinesias. The inconsistent nature of tardive dyskinesia treatment makes prevention of this syndrome a very important consideration in the pharmacotherapy of psychotic disorders.[48]

Prolactin Elevation. Dopamine antagonists may elevate serum prolactin levels by decreasing the prolactin inhibitory effects of dopamine in the hypothalamus. Prolactin elevation has been reported to cause an irregular or suppressed menstrual cycle,[49] galactorrhea,[50] gynecomastia, and sexual dysfunction[51] in the short term. With long-term elevation of plasma prolactin levels, suppression of estrogen and testosterone may occur. These effects may lead to a decrease in bone mineral density and to osteoporosis.[52]

The degree of prolactin elevation that an antipsychotic agent may exert appears to be related to its dopamine- and serotonin-binding properties. Significant prolactin elevation and its associated adverse effects can occur with moderate-to-high doses of the traditional antipsychotics and risperidone.[52] Risperidone has been consistently associated with the greatest degree of prolactin elevation among the second-generation antipsychotics.[53,54] In a prospective trial, olanzapine was found to cause a low and transient increase in prolactin levels across its dosage range, compared with the significant, persistent hyperprolactinemia associated with haloperidol.[55] The effect of quetiapine treatment across its dosage range on plasma prolactin levels was comparable to placebo, while significant elevations were associated with haloperidol.[20] Similarly, aripiprazole has been shown to be comparable to placebo for prolactin elevation.[24] Antipsychotic-associated prolactin elevation has been successfully managed by switching to an antipsychotic agent with a lower propensity toward increasing prolactin.[56,57]

Weight Gain. The metabolic effects of antipsychotic drug therapy have become a source of concern for clinicians and patients. Psychotic disorders and antipsychotic drug treatment have long been associated with comorbid obesity[58] and its related conditions: type 2 diabetes mellitus[59,60] and cardiovascular disease.[61] In addition, drug treatments[62] and lifestyle changes[63,64] aimed at weight reduction may be ineffective or difficult to implement in this population.

Varying degrees of weight gain have been reported with chronic use of traditional and second-generation antipsychotics. Among the traditional antipsychotics, loxapine[65] and molindone[66,67] are notable for weight-loss or weight-neutral profiles. Of the second-generation antipsychotics, ziprasidone and aripiprazole have been associated with the lowest likelihood for causing weight gain. A large meta-analysis by Allison et al.[68] was conducted to compare the weight gain associated with the use of various antipsychotic drugs that were approved or under investigation in the United States. Table 4 lists estimated weight gain after 10 weeks of treatment on drugs for which sufficient data are available. Clozapine and olanzapine were associated with more weight gain than all other agents included in this review. The small weight loss associated with placebo may have been due to discontinuation of antipsychotic therapy as the subjects entered the studies.

The antipsychotic agents also appear to differ in the duration and rate of weight changes. In one study, weight increases with continuous clozapine treatment occurred until about 46 months of treatment, with the greatest amount of weight being gained during the first 12 months.[69] Weight gain with olanzapine may plateau after 4-5 months.[70]

Table 4.
Estimated Body Weight Changes at 10 Weeks in Patients Receiving Antipsychotics[68]

Treatment	Weight Gain (kg)
Placebo	–0.74
Molindone	–0.39
Ziprasidone	0.04
Fluphenazine	0.43
Haloperidol	1.08
Risperidone	2.10
Chlorpromazine	2.58
Thioridazine-mesoridazine	3.19
Olanzapine	4.15
Clozapine	4.45

Diabetes Mellitus. New-onset hyperglycemia and diabetes mellitus have also been observed with antipsychotic treatment. In some instances, the initial presentation consists of life-threatening diabetic ketoacidosis or hyperosmolar coma.[71] Frequently, clinically significant weight gain does not occur before the diagnosis of diabetes.[72] Koller et al.[73] reviewed cases of hyperglycemic episodes associated with risperidone and haloperidol reported to the Food and Drug Administration's (FDA's) MedWatch surveillance program. Of the 131 cases of hyperglycemia associated with antipsychotic monotherapy with risperidone, 78 were clearly identified as newly diagnosed hyperglycemia. In the cases for which adequate data were available, 71% of cases with preexisting hyperglycemia and 48% of cases of new-onset hyperglycemia occurred within the first three months of risperidone monotherapy.

Sernyak et al.[74] conducted a large analysis of a national sample of patients treated for schizophrenia in Veterans Affairs medical centers to investigate a possible association between the use of antipsychotic medications and development of diabetes mellitus. Patients were identified as being treated with clozapine, olanzapine, quetiapine, risperidone, or traditional antipsychotics. When the patients were stratified by age, significantly higher rates of comorbid diabetes were found in patients treated with second-generation antipsychotics. Overall, clozapine, olanzapine, and quetiapine were most frequently implicated. The strongest relationships were found in individuals less than 40 years of age.

Plasma glucose regulation in individuals receiving antipsychotics and in healthy controls was assessed using oral glucose tolerance tests.[75] Olanzapine-treated patients demonstrated significantly elevated plasma glucose levels while fasting and at 15, 45, and 75 minutes postload compared with controls and patients treated with traditional antipsychotics. Clozapine-treated patients had significant elevations while fasting and at 75 minutes postload compared with controls and patients receiving traditional antipsychotics. With risperidone, the elevations in plasma glucose were seen in the fasting state and at 45 and 75 minutes postload and were significantly higher compared with healthy controls.

Dyslipidemias. Hyperlipidemia is another significant cardiac risk associated with second-generation antipsychotic treatment. Increases in serum triglycerides and low-density lipoproteins with second-generation antipsychotics have not always correlated with significant weight gain.[76]

A retrospective analysis of long-term inpatients treated with risperidone and olanzapine was conducted to determine trends of various metabolic values.[77] The investigator reported that the average increase in triglyceride concentrations was 104.8 mg/dL with olanzapine versus 31.7 mg/dL with risperidone after one year. Total cholesterol increased by 30.7 mg/dL with olanzapine and 7.2 mg/dL with risperidone. A naturalistic study of clozapine treatment revealed a significant increase in serum triglyceride level over five years of treatment.[69] In CATIE, olanzapine was associated with the greatest exposure-adjusted increases in serum cholesterol and triglycerides.[25]

In November 2003, a consensus panel that included experts from the American Diabetes Association, American Psychiatric Association, American Association of Clinical Endocrinologists, and the North American Association for the Study of Obesity was convened. Using data collected during a comprehensive literature review and presentations from representatives from the pharmaceutical industry and FDA, the consensus panel developed a statement outlining the metabolic risks of treatment with second-generation antipsychotics.[78] The panel recommended careful consideration of metabolic risks whenever second-generation antipsychotics are initiated, especially in high-risk patients. The panel also recommended considering switching antipsychotics in patients who gain 5% or more of their initial weight, experience worsening hyperglycemia, or develop worsening hyperlipidemia.

Cardiac Toxicity. Certain traditional and second-generation antipsychotics have been associated with clinically significant prolongation of the corrected Q-T (Q-Tc) interval, which may lead to torsades de pointes, a fatal ventricular arrhythmia. The risk of cardiac mortality associated with psychotropic drug treatment is particularly troublesome because of its spontaneous and unpredictable nature.

The traditional antipsychotics thioridazine, mesoridazine, pimozide, and droperidol have been implicated in numerous cases of sudden unexpected death.[79] Electrocardiographic data have revealed that patients receiving droperidol and thioridazine are more likely to have an abnormally long Q-Tc interval.[80] Numerous reports of patient fatalities and the availability of safer alternatives have prompted FDA to recommend that thioridazine, mesoridazine, pimozide, and droperidol only be used as alternative agents with extreme caution.

Although regulatory scrutiny for cardiac assessment heightened during the development of second-generation antipsychotics, these agents are generally associated with a low risk of electrocardiographic abnormalities. Ziprasidone was found to be associated with modest Q-Tc prolongation during its premarketing studies. A comparative study that sought to determine the extent of Q-Tc prolongation seen with the target therapeutic dosages of haloperidol, risperidone, olanzapine, quetiapine, and ziprasidone was later presented to FDA.[81] Thioridazine was also assessed in this study at half its maximum recommended dosage. Thioridazine was associated with an average Q-Tc-interval increase of 35.6 milliseconds. Of the second-generation agents included in this study, ziprasidone was associated with the greatest mean increase in the Q-Tc interval—20.3

milliseconds. Haloperidol-treated subjects had an average Q-Tc-interval increase of 4.7 seconds, the smallest change observed in this study. Coadministration of other interacting drugs (e.g., cytochrome P-450 isoenzyme inhibitors) did not lead to significant changes in Q-Tc measurement. Ziprasidone's labeling warned of its greater potential of Q-Tc-interval prolongation and discouraged use in patients with electrolyte abnormalities, cardiac comorbidity, or concomitant use of metabolic inhibitors.[82]

Clozapine has been associated with treatment-emergent myocarditis and cardiomyopathy. Myocarditis associated with clozapine treatment presents as an acute inflammation of the myocardium, which may lead to congestive heart failure.[83] With over 180,000 patient exposures to clozapine during the first 10 years of its clinical use in the United States, FDA received 28 reports of myocarditis, including 18 deaths.[84] The greatest risk of fatal events appears to exist during the first month of therapy. Cardiomyopathy associated with clozapine is an insidious process characterized by ventricular dilatation, impaired contraction, and symptoms of congestive heart failure.[83] A total of 41 cases of cardiomyopathy, including 10 deaths, were reported to FDA between 1989 and 1999.[84]

Cerebrovascular Events. The use of second-generation antipsychotics for the treatment of dementia-related agitation and psychosis in elderly patients is an unlabeled use that is generally supported by efficacy data in published controlled clinical trials.[85] However, post hoc analyses of the safety data for these trials revealed an elevated risk of cerebrovascular adverse events (CVAEs), including stroke and transient ischemic attacks, among patients treated with second-generation antipsychotics. These data led FDA to issue a public health advisory warning of the potential for fatal CVAEs in patients with dementia being treated with second-generation antipsychotics. The manufacturers of second-generation antipsychotic agents were also requested to place a black-box warning describing this treatment risk on the labeling of these products.

A closer look at the applicable safety data reveals that the patients in the dementia trials were often at elevated risk for CVAEs because of advanced age, poor control of chronic cardiovascular disease, and the underlying etiology of the dementia.[86] Cases of CVAEs included nonspecific events, such as hypotensive episodes, periods of unresponsiveness, and slurred speech. For example, the pooled results of six placebo-controlled randomized studies of risperidone for the treatment of behavioral disturbances in patients with dementia revealed 33 CVAEs (3.3%) in 1009 subjects receiving the drug. The frequency of CVAEs was 1.1% (8 of 712) among placebo-treated patients ($p = 0.004$). However, serious CVAEs (fatal events, life-threatening events, or CVAEs associated with hospitalization or disability) occurred in 15 (1.5%) of 1009 patients treated with risperidone and 4 (0.6%) of 712 patients treated with placebo, a difference that failed to reach statistical significance. Furthermore, most patients experiencing stroke had risk factors, including hypertension, atrial fibrillation, and previous strokes.[86]

The nature of this type of safety data makes it difficult to determine causality. It has been postulated that the adverse effects of sedation, hypotension, pseudoparkinsonism, and enhanced platelet aggregation may contribute to the observed increase in CVAEs.[86] In addition, these findings have not been widely observed among patients with psychotic disorders. It would therefore be advisable to consider stroke prophylaxis in all elderly patients receiving antipsychotic drugs, particularly high-risk patients.

Hematologic Toxicity, Respiratory Depression, and Seizures. Despite its superior efficacy for treatment-resistant psychotic disorders, the use of clozapine has remained restricted due to the potential of severe adverse effects not commonly seen with other antipsychotics. Agranulocytosis has been estimated to occur in 1–2% of patients treated with clozapine.[87] Episodes tend to occur between two and six months after initiation of treatment.[88] Fatal infectious complications may occur as a result of reduced white blood cell count. Clozapine-induced agranulocytosis can be reversed with the prompt discontinuation of treatment.

In the United States, clozapine is available only under the surveillance of one of the national manufacturer-operated registries that monitor weekly complete blood counts from individuals taking this agent. Consistent monitoring has resulted in a markedly reduced rate of agranulocytosis and mortality associated with clozapine-induced agranulocytosis.[89] Furthermore, the continual monitoring mandated by the clozapine registry programs likely allows for improved treatment adherence and outcomes.[90]

Other toxicities that are more common with clozapine than with other second-generation antipsychotics are respiratory depression and seizures. Respiratory collapse has been associated with rapid dosage adjustment and concomitant benzodiazepine use. It is therefore recommended that clozapine dosage be gradually adjusted from the starting dose if the patient is new to clozapine treatment or if two or more days have elapsed since the last dose. A dose-related reduction of the seizure threshold has been observed with clozapine.[91] Precautions should be taken for patients with seizure disorders receiving clozapine treatment.

Drug Selection and Dosing Considerations

With the notable exception of clozapine, the principal differences among the available second-generation antipsychotics lie in their adverse-effect profiles and dosage forms. Selection of an initial treatment for a patient whose psychosis is not considered to be treatment resistant should be individualized based on the patient's specific tolerability and compliance concerns.[92] Individuals with a sensitivity to extrapyramidal symptoms may benefit from quetiapine or aripiprazole. Patients with preexisting obesity or diabetes mellitus may benefit from an initial trial with ziprasidone or aripiprazole. The availability of orally disintegrating formulations of olanzapine, risperidone, and aripiprazole; liquid formulations of risperidone and aripiprazole; and a long-acting injectable formulation of risperidone provides options for patients with a history of poor treatment adherence or who have difficulty taking standard oral tablets or capsules. The traditional antipsychotics may be an initial choice for those who are at low risk for movement disorders[25] or for whom the newer drugs may be cost-prohibitive.

The importance of appropriate dosing of second-generation antipsychotics was highlighted in an analysis conducted by Love et al.[93] Results of the premarketing studies for risperidone suggested that the dose–efficacy curve peaked at 6 mg/day, leading to the recommendation on the product labeling that risperidone be adjusted to this dosage over the first three days of treatment. After the introduction of risperidone to the mass market, numerous reports[94–96] demonstrated that the optimal dosage of risperidone for efficacy was between 4 and 6 mg/day, a dosage range not assessed in the original large efficacy studies. Aggregate computerized pharmacy records from state inpatient psychiatry facilities in Maryland revealed significantly higher discharge rates for patients receiving 2–4 mg/day than for those receiving 6 mg/day. It is now recommended that clinicians attempt to stabilize patients on risperidone 2–4 mg/day before initiating a trial at higher dosages.[93]

In general, clinical studies suggest that for most of the other second-generation antipsychotics indicated for first-line treatment, a more linear dose–response curve is applicable. Patients may require dosage adjustment to 10–20 mg/day of olanzapine, 300–800 mg/day of quetiapine, 80–160 mg/day of ziprasidone, or 10–30 mg/day of aripiprazole for control of acute psychotic symptoms.[13–24] Maintenance therapy can frequently be achieved with lower dosages, thereby reducing toxicity. Special populations, such as the elderly or individuals with hepatic impairment, may require lower doses due to increased sensitivity to adverse effects. In some individuals with a history of suboptimal response to antipsychotic treatment, additional benefit has been gained using second-generation antipsychotics with doses higher than the maximum recommended in the product labeling.[97]

In the event of nonresponse to an initial trial of antipsychotic medication, most treatment guidelines recommend sequential trials of second-generation antipsychotics with a minimum of three weeks duration at therapeutic doses.[98–100] A trial of clozapine is generally warranted for patients who demonstrate a suboptimal response to two or more trials with first-line antipsychotic agents. Traditional antipsychotics may also have a role for patients who fail treatment with second-generation antipsychotics. In addition, the adjunctive use of antidepressants, mood stabilizers, or anxiolytics may be beneficial in selected patients. The combined use of more than one antipsychotic drug is a controversial and costly practice.[101] Very little published evidence supports the use of multiple oral antipsychotics, except when attempting to transition a patient from one agent to another.[102]

Patient Monitoring

Frequent and continuous monitoring is necessary for individuals treated with antipsychotics in order to assess for therapeutic response and adverse effects. For the second-generation antipsychotics intended for first-line use, the recommended minimum trial duration is three weeks after adjustment to a recommended therapeutic dose. A longer trial is generally warranted for clozapine. Gradual reductions in the severity of psychotic symptoms (e.g., suspiciousness, hallucinations) are expected with adequate treatment.

Monitoring for metabolic adverse effects of second-generation antipsychotic therapy should consist of regular assessments of body weight, glucose levels, and lipid values (Table 5).[103] Treatment with clozapine requires weekly assessments of complete blood count and absolute neutrophil count for the first six months. If no evidence of neutropenia or granulocytopenia is found, the monitoring frequency can be reduced to every two weeks for the next six months and then every four weeks thereafter.

Despite the lower propensity for causing adverse motor effects, all patients receiving second-generation antipsychotics should be monitored for symptoms of dystonia, parkinsonism, akathisia, and tardive dyskinesia.[103] Patients should be evaluated for acute extrapyramidal symptoms weekly until two weeks after dose stabilization when antipsychotics are initiated or adjusted. Assessments for tardive dyskinesia should be conducted at least once yearly for individuals receiving continuous treatment with antipsychotics.[103]

Measurement of antipsychotic plasma levels is not clinically indicated, except to assess for treatment adherence or suspected drug interactions. However, a minimum plasma clozapine concentration of 350 ng/mL has been correlated with treatment response among patients whose psychosis has been identified as treatment resistant.[104,105] In a study of the use of therapeutic drug monitoring in long-term treatment with clozapine, relapse was more frequently associated with a decrease from a stable drug level than maintenance of a threshold minimum concentration.[106]

Treatment Outcomes

Schizophrenia and related disorders are characterized by chronic courses and periodic exacerbations. Exacerbations in the positive symptoms of schizophrenia may precipitate costly hospitalizations and may result in encounters with the legal system, while the negative and cognitive symptoms affect independent functioning, employment, and quality of life. Hospitalizations in specialty psychiatric facilities may

Table 5.
Monitoring Guidelines for Patients Treated with Second-Generation Antipsychotics

Assessment	Monitoring Frequency
Fasting blood glucose	All drugs: Baseline, then monthly for the first 3 mo and every 6 mo thereafter. More frequent assessments are indicated for individuals noted to be gaining weight.
Weight assessment	All drugs: Baseline and monthly thereafter. (Self-monitoring of weight should be encouraged.)
Electrocardiogram	Clozapine and ziprasidone: Baseline and annually thereafter. More frequent assessments may be indicated in patients over age 50 yr and in patients with a history of cardiac arrhythmias.
Complete blood count with differential	Clozapine: Weekly for the first 6 mo. Every other wk for the next 6 mo, and every 4 wk thereafter if no abnormalities are noted.
Fasting total cholesterol, low- and high-density lipoproteins, and triglycerides	All drugs: Baseline and every 2 yr thereafter if no abnormalities are noted. Every 6 mo for individuals noted to have hyperlipidemia or receiving lipid-lowering therapy.

result in lengths of stay measured in months or years. Thus, the single greatest component of the cost of schizophrenia is the cost of hospital stay. In contrast, drugs are thought to account for less than 10% of the direct costs of treating these illnesses.

Studies addressing the effect of second-generation antipsychotics on hospitalization have repeatedly found that these agents reduce the length of stay and readmission rate compared with conventional antipsychotics. Rabinowitz et al.[107] calculated a two-year rehospitalization rate of 31–33% for patients discharged from inpatient psychiatric hospitalization receiving olanzapine or risperidone, compared with a 48% rate for patients discharged on conventional antipsychotics ($p = 0.02$). In a landmark double-blind trial of risperidone versus haloperidol, Csernansky et al.[108] measured relapse by examining rehospitalization, signs of clinical decompensation, and increasing requirements for supervision. They found significantly lower relapse rates at one year and longer times to relapse with risperidone treatment. FDA accepted this trial as sufficient evidence to allow the manufacturer to indicate in the product labeling the drug's efficacy in delaying relapse.

A variety of studies have focused on the cost of second-generation antipsychotics in comparison with each other[109,110] and conventional agents.[111] In general, the generically available first-generation antipsychotics are less expensive than the newer second-generation agents. However, when overall costs of care are calculated, second-generation antipsychotics often demonstrate lower hospital utilization, improved symptomatic control, and fewer adverse effects, resulting in lower or equal total costs for the second-generation agents versus first-generation antipsychotics.[112]

While most studies examining outcomes with second-generation antipsychotics have focused on cost, hospitalization, and relapse, fewer have examined issues related to quality of life. Chouinard and Albright[113] addressed these issues by conducting a cost–utility analysis of risperidone versus haloperidol in association with a randomized clinical trial. Patients taking risperidone gained almost three quality-adjusted life years over those who received haloperidol. Franz et al.[114] conducted quality-of-life interviews with patients receiving conventional antipsychotics, clozapine, risperidone, or zotepine (not available in the United States). Patients receiving second-generation antipsychotics had a significantly higher total quality of life than those receiving conventional agents. They also demonstrated significantly superior ratings in the domains of physical well-being, social life, and everyday life.

Secondary depression is also a major problem in schizophrenia, and suicide is a leading cause of death in this population.[115] It has been estimated that about 10% of patients with psychotic disorders die by suicide.[116,117] In addition to having favorable effects on mood symptoms, there are indications that second-generation antipsychotics may also reduce suicide rates in some populations, with clozapine demonstrating a particular benefit in this regard.[118] In a study of 980 patients with schizophrenia or schizoaffective disorder at high risk for suicide, treatment with clozapine was associated with a significantly lower rate of suicide attempts and hospitalizations to prevent suicide compared with olanzapine (20.8% versus 28.8%, $p < 0.005$).[119]

Second-generation antipsychotics likely produce beneficial outcomes through a variety of effects. Compared with conventional antipsychotics and placebo, second-generation antipsychotics demonstrate improved efficacy for psychotic and cognitive symptoms. In controlled trials, these agents produce fewer disabling extrapyramidal adverse effects, such as akathisia and parkinsonism. These effects result in improved adherence to prescribed regiments, less interference with socialization and occupational function, and a feeling of improved well-being compared with the effects of conventional antipsychotics.

Summary

Psychotic disorders are chronic illnesses that impart a considerable burden on patients, families, and society. Although no known drug therapies can cure these illnesses, antipsychotic agents are a mainstay for the management of acute illness and prevention of relapse. The second-generation antipsychotics—risperidone, olanzapine, quetiapine, ziprasidone, aripiprazole, and paliperidone—offer numerous advantages over the older agents, including a lower risk of extrapyramidal motor symptoms and elevated serum prolactin levels, as well as improvements in cognitive symptoms. These advantages have led to improved long-term outcomes and cost-effectiveness, despite the higher acquisition costs of these drugs. Clozapine has demonstrated a unique level of efficacy for individuals with treatment-resistant psychotic disorders and for individuals at high risk for suicide and is very valuable in these subgroups, despite the additional adverse hematologic and cardiovascular effects. Metabolic adverse effects, including weight gain, glucose abnormalities, and hyperlipidemias, cause significant concern for patients receiving second-generation antipsychotics and must be managed proactively by clinicians. Health care professionals in all settings should play an active role in assisting in the selection of an appropriate antipsychotic agent, ensuring appropriate monitoring, and providing counseling to ensure that patients remain compliant with treatment. Additional readings and resources are listed in the appendix.

References

1. Schizophrenia and other psychotic disorders. In: American Psychiatric Association. DSM-IV-TR: diagnostic and statistical manual of mental disorders, 4th ed., text revision. Washington, DC: American Psychiatric Press; 2000.
2. Keith SJ, Regier DA, Rae DS. Schizophrenic disorders. In: Robins LN, Regier DA, eds. Psychiatric disorders in America: the Epidemiologic Catchment Area Study. New York: Free Press; 1991: 33–52.
3. Kessler RC, McGonagle KA, Zhao S, et al. Lifetime and 12-month prevalence of DSM-III-R psychiatric disorders in the United States: results from the National Comorbidity Survey. *Arch Gen Psychiatry.* 1994; 52:8–19.
4. Loranger AW. Sex differences in age at onset of schizophrenia. *Arch Gen Psychiatry.* 1984; 41:157–61.
5. Hafner H, Maurer K, Loeffler W, et al. The influence of age and sex on the onset and early course of schizophrenia. *Br J Psychiatry.* 1993; 162:80–6.
6. Kim JS, Kornhuber HH, Schmid-Burgk W, et al. Low cerebrospinal fluid glutamate in schizophrenia patients

and a new hypothesis on schizophrenia. *Neurosci Lett.* 1980; 20:379–82.

7. Krystal JH, Karper LP, Seibyl JP, et al. Subanesthetic effects of the noncompetitive NMDA antagonist, ketamine, in humans: psychotomimetic, perceptual, cognitive, and neuroendocrine responses. *Arch Gen Psychiatry.* 1994; 51:199–214.
8. Hughes JR, Hatsukami DK, Mitchell JE, et al. Prevalence of smoking among psychiatric outpatients. *Am J Psychiatry.* 1986; 143:993–7.
9. Dalack GW, Healy DJ, Meador-Woodruff JH. Nicotine dependence in schizophrenia: clinical phenomena and laboratory findings. *Am J Psychiatry.* 1998; 155:1490–501.
10. Stahl SM. Dopamine system stabilizers, aripiprazole, and the next generation of antipsychotics, part I: "Goldilocks" actions at dopamine receptors. *J Clin Psychiatry.* 2001; 62:841–2.
11. Stahl SM. Dopamine system stabilizers, aripiprazole, and the next generation of antipsychotics, part II: illustrating their mechanism of action. *J Clin Psychiatry.* 2001; 62:923–4.
12. Kapur S, Remington G. Serotonin–dopamine interaction and its relevance to schizophrenia. *Am J Psychiatry.* 1996; 153:466–76.
13. Kane J, Honigfeld G, Singer J, et al. Clozapine for the treatment-resistant schizophrenic, a double-blind comparison with chlorpromazine. *Arch Gen Psychiatry.* 1988; 45:789–96.
14. Breier A, Buchanan RW, Kirkpatrick B, et al. Effects of clozapine on positive and negative symptoms in outpatients with schizophrenia. *Am J Psychiatry.* 1994; 152:20–6.
15. Marder SR, Meibach RC. Risperidone in the treatment of schizophrenia. *Am J Psychiatry.* 1994; 151:825–35.
16. Chouinard G, Jones B, Remington G, et al. A Canadian multi-center placebo-controlled study of fixed doses of risperidone and haloperidol in the treatment of chronic schizophrenic patients. *J Clin Psychopharmacol.* 1993; 13:25–40.
17. Kane JM, Eerdekens M, Lindenmayer JP, et al. Long-acting injectable risperidone: efficacy and safety of the first long-acting atypical antipsychotic. *Am J Psychiatry.* 2003; 160:1125–32.
18. Beasley CM, Tollfeson G, Tran P, et al. Olanzapine versus placebo and haloperidol: acute phase results of the North American double-blind olanzapine trial. *Neuropsychopharmacology.* 1996; 14:111–23.
19. Beasley CM, Sanger T, Satterlee W, et al. Olanzapine vs placebo: results of a double-blind, fixed-dose olanzapine trial. *Psychopharmacology.* 1996; 124:159–67.
20. Arvanitis LA, Miller BG. Multiple fixed doses of "Seroquel" (quetiapine) in patients with acute exacerbation of schizophrenia: a comparison with haloperidol and placebo. *Biol Psychiatry.* 1997; 42:233–46.
21. Small JG, Hirsch SR, Arvanitis LA, et al. Quetiapine in patients with schizophrenia: a high- and low-dose double-blind comparison with placebo. *Arch Gen Psychiatry.* 1997; 54:549–57.
22. Daniel DG, Zimbroff DL, Potkin SG, et al. Ziprasidone 80 mg/day and 160 mg/day in the acute exacerbation of schizophrenia and schizoaffective disorder: a 6-week placebo-controlled trial. *Neuropsychopharmacology.* 1999; 20:491–505.
23. Keck P Jr, Buffenstein A, Ferguson J, et al. Ziprasidone 40 and 120 mg/day in the acute exacerbation of schizophrenia and schizoaffective disorder: a 4-week placebo-controlled trial. *Psychopharmacology.* 1998; 140:173–84.
24. Kane JM, Carson WH, Saha AR, et al. Efficacy and safety of aripiprazole and haloperidol versus placebo in patients with schizophrenia and schizoaffective disorder. *J Clin Psychiatry.* 2002; 63:763–71.
25. Lieberman JA, Stroup TS, McEvoy JP, et al. Effectiveness of antipsychotic drugs in patients with chronic schizophrenia. *N Engl J Med.* 2005; 353:1209–23.
26. Sharma T, Antonova L. Cognitive function in schizophrenia: deficits, functional consequences, and future treatment. *Psychiatr Clin North Am.* 2003; 26:25–40.
27. Green MF. What are the functional consequences of neurocognitive deficits of schizophrenia? *Am J Psychiatry.* 1996; 153:321–30.
28. Liddle PF. Cognitive impairment in schizophrenia: its impact on social functioning. *Acta Psychiatr Scand Suppl.* 2000; 400:11–6.
29. Spohn HE, Strauss ME. Relation of neuroleptic and anticholinergic medication to cognitive functions in schizophrenia. *J Abnorm Psychol.* 1989; 98:367–80.
30. Bilder RM, Goldman RS, Volavka J, et al. Neurocognitive effects of clozapine, olanzapine, risperidone, and haloperidol in patients with chronic schizophrenia or schizoaffective disorder. *Am J Psychiatry.* 2002; 159:1018–28.
31. Hagger C, Buckley P, Kenny JT, et al. Improvement in cognitive functions and psychiatric symptoms in treatment-refractory schizophrenic patients receiving clozapine. *Biol Psychiatry.* 1993; 34:702–12.
32. Grace J, Bellus SB, Raulin ML, et al. Long-term impact of clozapine and psychosocial treatment on psychiatric symptoms and cognitive functioning. *Psychiatr Serv.* 1996; 47:41–5.
33. Buchanan RW, Holstein C, Breier A. The comparative efficacy and long-term effect of clozapine on neuropsychological test performance. *Biol Psychiatry.* 1994; 36:717–25.
34. Cornblatt B, Kern RS, Carson WH, et al. Neurocognitive effects of aripiprazole versus olanzapine in stable psychosis. Presented at 23rd Collegium Internationale Neuropsychopharmacologicum Congress. Montreal, Canada; 2002 Jun.
35. Stahl SM. "Hit-and-run" actions at dopamine receptors, part 1: mechanism of action of second-generation antipsychotics. *J Clin Psychiatry.* 2001; 62:670–1.
36. Leucht S, Pitschel-Walz G, Abraham D, et al. Efficacy and extrapyramidal side-effects of the new antipsychotics olanzapine, quetiapine, risperidone, and sertindole compared to conventional antipsychotics and placebo: a meta-analysis of randomized controlled trials. *Schizophr Res.* 1999; 35:51–68.
37. Tollefson GD, Beasley CM, Tamura RN, et al. Blind, controlled, long-term study of the comparative incidence of treatment-emergent tardive dyskinesia with olanzapine or haloperidol. *Am J Psychiatry.* 1997; 154:1248–54.

38. Jeste DV, Lacro JP, Bailey A, et al. Lower incidence of tardive dyskinesia with risperidone compared with haloperidol in older patients. *J Am Geriatr Soc.* 1999; 47:716–9.
39. Jeste DV, Okamoto A, Napolitano J, et al. Low incidence of persistent tardive dyskinesia in elderly patients with dementia treated with risperidone. *Am J Psychiatry.* 2000; 157:1150–5.
40. Beasley CM, Dellva MA, Tamura RN, et al. Randomised double-blind comparison of the incidence of tardive dyskinesia in patients with schizophrenia during long-term treatment with olanzapine or haloperidol. *Br J Psychiatry.* 1999; 174:23–30.
41. Farah A. Reduction of tardive dyskinesia with quetiapine. *Schizophr Res.* 2001; 47:309–10. Letter.
42. Povlssen UJ, Noring U, Fog R, et al. Tolerability and therapeutic effect of clozapine: a retrospective investigation of 216 patients treated with clozapine for up to 12 years. *Acta Psychiatr Scand.* 1985; 71:176–85.
43. Kurz M, Hummer M, Oberbauer H, et al. Extrapyramidal side effects of clozapine and haloperidol. *Psychopharmacology.* 1995; 118:52–6.
44. Casey DE. Clozapine: neuroleptic-induced EPS and tardive dyskinesia. *Psychopharmacology.* 1989; 99: S47–53.
45. Lieberman JA, Saltz BL, Johns CA, et al. The effects of clozapine on tardive dyskinesia. *Br J Psychiatry.* 1991; 158:503–10.
46. Spivak B, Mester R, Abesgaus J, et al. Clozapine treatment for neuroleptic-induced tardive dyskinesia, parkinsonism, and chronic akathisia in schizophrenic patients. *J Clin Psychiatry.* 1997; 58:318–22.
47. Tamminga CA, Thaker GK, Moran M, et al. Clozapine in tardive dyskinesia: observations from human and animal model studies. *J Clin Psychiatry.* 1994; 55(suppl B):102–6.
48. Ahmed S, Chengappa KN, Naidu VR, et al. Clozapine withdrawal-emergent dystonias and dyskinesias: a case series. *J Clin Psychiatry.* 1998; 59:472–7.
49. Dickson RA, Seeman MV, Corenblum B. Hormonal side effects in women: typical versus second-generation antipsychotic treatment. *J Clin Psychiatry.* 2000; 61(suppl 3):10–5.
50. Windgassen K, Wesselman U, Schulze-Monking H. Galactorrhea and hyper-prolactinemia in schizophrenic patients on neuroleptics: frequency and etiology. *Neuropsychobiology.* 1996; 33:142–6.
51. Arana GW. An overview of side effects caused by typical antipsychotics. *J Clin Psychiatry.* 2000; 61(suppl 8):5–11.
52. Petty RG. Prolactin and antipsychotic medications: mechanisms of action. *Schizophr Res.* 1999; 35(suppl): S67–73.
53. Volavka J, Czobor P, Cooper TB, et al. Prolactin levels in schizophrenia and schizoaffective disorder patients treated with clozapine, olanzapine, risperidone, or haloperidol. *J Clin Psychiatry.* 2004; 65:57–61.
54. Breier AF, Malhotra AK, Su T, et al. Clozapine and risperidone in chronic schizophrenia: effects on symptoms, parkinsonian side effects, and neuroendocrine response. *Am J Psychiatry.* 1999; 156:294–8.
55. Crawford AM, Beasley CM, Tollefson GD. The acute and long-term effect of olanzapine compared with placebo and haloperidol on serum prolactin concentrations. *Schizophr Res.* 1997; 26:41–54.
56. David SR, Taylor CC, Kinon BJ, et al. The effects of olanzapine, risperidone, and haloperidol on plasma prolactin levels in patients with schizophrenia. *Clin Ther.* 2000; 22:1085–96.
57. Bunker MT, Marken PA, Schneiderhan ME, et al. Attenuation of antipsychotic-induced hyperprolactinemia with clozapine. *J Child Adolesc Psychopharmacol.* 1997; 7:65–9.
58. Allison DB, Fontaine KR, Heo M, et al. The distribution of body mass index among individuals with and without schizophrenia. *J Clin Psychiatry.* 1999; 60:215–20.
59. Mukherjee S, Decina P, Bocola V, et al. Diabetes mellitus in schizophrenic patients. *Compr Psychiatry.* 1996; 37:68–73.
60. Brambilla F, Guastalla A, Guerrini A, et al. Glucose-insulin metabolism in chronic schizophrenia. *Dis Nerv Syst.* 1976; 37:98–103.
61. Tsuang MT, Perkins K, Simpson JC. Physical diseases in schizophrenia and affective disorder. *J Clin Psychiatry.* 1983; 44:42–6.
62. Borovicka MC, Fuller MA, Konicki PE, et al. Phenylpropanolamine appears not to promote weight loss in patients with schizophrenia who have gained weight during clozapine treatment. *J Clin Psychiatry.* 2002; 63:345–8.
63. Ball MP, Coons VB, Buchanan RW. A program for treating olanzapine-related weight gain. *Psychiatr Serv.* 2001; 52:967–9.
64. Green AI, Patel JK, Goisman RM, et al. Weight gain from novel antipsychotic drugs: need for action. *Gen Hosp Psychiatry.* 2000; 22:224–35.
65. Doss FW. The effect of antipsychotic drugs on body weight: a retrospective review. *J Clin Psychiatry.* 1979; 40:528–30.
66. Parent MM, Roy S, Sramek J, et al. Effect of molindone on weight change in hospitalized schizophrenic patients. *Drug Intell Clin Pharm.* 1986; 20:873–5.
67. Gardos G, Cole JO. Weight reduction in schizophrenics by molindone. *Am J Psychiatry.* 1977; 134:302–4.
68. Allison DB, Mentore JL, Heo M, et al. Antipsychotic-induced weight gain: a comprehensive research synthesis. *Am J Psychiatry.* 1999; 156:1686–96.
69. Henderson DC, Cagliero E, Gray C, et al. Clozapine, diabetes mellitus, weight gain, and lipid abnormalities: a five-year naturalistic study. *Am J Psychiatry.* 2000; 157:975–81.
70. Beasley CM, Tollefson GD, Tran PV. Safety of olanzapine. *J Clin Psychiatry.* 1997; 58(suppl 10):13–7,19–21.
71. Muench J, Carey M. Diabetes mellitus associated with second-generation antipsychotic medications: new case report and review of the literature. *J Am Board Fam Pract.* 2001; 14:278–82.
72. Jin H, Meyer JM, Jeste DV. Phenomenology of and risk factors for new onset diabetes mellitus associated with second-generation antipsychotics: an analysis of 45 published cases. *Ann Clin Psychiatry.* 2002; 14:59–64.

73. Koller EA, Cross JT, Doraiswamy PM, et al. Risperidone-associated diabetes mellitus: a pharmacovigilance study. *Pharmacotherapy.* 2003; 23:735–44.
74. Sernyak MJ, Leslie DL, Alarcon RD. Association of diabetes mellitus with use of second-generation neuroleptics in the treatment of schizophrenia. *Am J Psychiatry.* 2002; 159:561–6.
75. Newcomer JW, Haupt DW, Fucetola R. Abnormalities in glucose regulation during antipsychotic treatment of schizophrenia. *Arch Gen Psychiatry.* 2002; 59:337–45.
76. Meyer JM. Novel antipsychotics and severe hyperlipidemia. *J Clin Psychopharm.* 2001; 21:369–74.
77. Meyer JM. A retrospective comparison of weight, lipid, and glucose changes between risperidone- and olanzapine-treated inpatients: metabolic outcomes after 1 year. *J Clin Psychiatry.* 2002; 63:425–33.
78. American Diabetes Association, American Psychiatric Association, American Association of Clinical Endocrinologists, et al. Consensus development conference on antipsychotic drugs and obesity and diabetes. *Diabetes Care.* 2004; 27:596–601.
79. Mehtonen OP, Aranko K, Malkonen L, et al. A survey of sudden death associated with the use of antipsychotic or antidepressant drugs: 49 cases in Finland. *Acta Psychiatr Scand.* 1991; 84:58–64.
80. Reilly JG, Ayis SA, Ferrier IN, et al. QTc-interval abnormalities and psychotropic drug therapy in psychiatric patients. *Lancet.* 2000; 355:1048–52.
81. Food and Drug Administration. Briefing document for Zeldox capsules (ziprasidone HCl). www.fda.gov/ohrms/dockets/ac/00/backgrd/3619b1a.pdf (accessed 2007 Jan 16).
82. Geodon (ziprasidone hydrochloride) prescribing information. New York: Pfizer Inc.; 2006 Nov.
83. Merrill DB, Dec GW, Goff DC. Adverse cardiac effects associated with clozapine. *J Clin Psychopharmacol.* 2005; 25:32–41.
84. La Grenade L, Graham D, Trontell A. Myocarditis and cardiomyopathy associated with clozapine use in the United States. *N Engl J Med.* 2001; 345:224–5.
85. Sink KM, Holden KF, Yaffe K. Pharmacological treatment of neuropsychiatric symptoms of dementia: a review of the evidence. *JAMA.* 2005; 293:596–608.
86. Herrmann N, Lanctot KL. Do atypical antipsychotics cause stroke? *CNS Drugs.* 2005; 19:91–103.
87. Lieberman JA, Johns CA, Kane JM, et al. Clozapine-induced agranulocytosis: non-cross-reactivity with other psychotropic drugs. *J Clin Psychiatry.* 1988; 49:271–7.
88. Alvir JJ, Lieberman JA, Safferman AZ, et al. Clozapine-induced agranulocytosis—incidence and risk factors in the United States. *N Engl J Med.* 1993; 329:162–7.
89. Honigfeld G, Arellano F, Sethi J, et al. Reducing clozapine-related morbidity and mortality: 5 years of experience with the Clozaril National Registry. *J Clin Psychiatry.* 1998; 59(suppl 3):3–7.
90. Munro J, O'Sullivan D, Andrews C, et al. Active monitoring of 12,760 clozapine recipients in the UK and Ireland: beyond pharmacovigilance. *Br J Psychiatry.* 1999; 175:576–80.
91. Silvestri RC, Bromfield EB, Khoshbin S. Clozapine-induced seizures and EEG abnormalities in ambulatory psychiatric patients. *Ann Pharmacother.* 1998; 32:1147–51.
92. Sprague DA, Loewen PS, Raymond CB. Selection of atypical antipsychotics for the management of schizophrenia. *Ann Pharmacother.* 2004; 38:313–9.
93. Love RC, Conley RR, Kelly DL, et al. A dose-outcome analysis of risperidone. *J Clin Psychiatry.* 1999; 60:771–5.
94. Moller HJ, Bauml J, Ferrero F, et al. Risperidone in the treatment of schizophrenia: results of a study of patients from Germany, Austria and Switzerland. *Eur Arch Psychiatry Clin Neurosci.* 1997; 246:291–6.
95. Philipo M. Neuroleptic treatment long term: results with risperidone. Presented at 21st Collegium Internationale Neuro Psychopharmacologicum Congress. Glasgow, Scotland; 1998 Jul.
96. Sajatovic M, Ramirez LF, Belton J, et al. Health resource utilization and risperidone therapy in patients with serious mental illness. Presented at 21st Collegium Internationale Neuro-Psychopharmacologicum Congress. Glasgow, Scotland; 1998 Jul.
97. Volavka J, Czobor P, Sheitman B, et al. Clozapine, olanzapine, risperidone, and haloperidol in the treatment of patients with chronic schizophrenia and schizoaffective disorder. *Am J Psychiatry.* 2002; 159:255–62.
98. Miller AL, Hall CS, Buchanan RW, et al. The Texas medication algorithm project—antipsychotic algorithm for schizophrenia: 2003 update. *J Clin Psychiatry.* 2004; 65:500–8.
99. Lehman AF, Lieberman JA, Dixon LB, et al. Practice guideline for the treatment of patients with schizophrenia, second edition. *Am J Psychiatry.* 2004; 161(2 suppl):1–56.
100. Lehman AF, Steinwachs DM. Translating research into practice: the schizophrenia patient outcomes research team (PORT) treatment recommendations. *Schizophr Bull.* 1998; 24:1–10.
101. Stahl SM. Antipsychotic polypharmacy: squandering precious resources? *J Clin Psychiatry.* 2002; 63:93–4.
102. Casey DE, Saha AR, Ali MW, et al. Switching to aripiprazole monotherapy. Presented at 23rd Collegium Internationale Neuropsycholpharmacologicum Congress. Montreal, Canada. 2002 Jun.
103. Marder SR, Essock SM, Miller AL, et al. Physical health monitoring of patients with schizophrenia. *Am J Psychiatry.* 2004; 161:1334–49.
104. Perry PJ, Miller DD, Arndt SV, et al. Clozapine and norclozapine plasma concentrations and clinical response of treatment refractory schizophrenic patients. *Am J Psychiatry.* 1991; 148:231–5.
105. Kronig MH, Munne RA, Szymanski S, et al. Plasma clozapine levels and clinical response for treatment refractory schizophrenic patients. *Am J Psychiatry.* 1995; 152:179–82.
106. Gaertner I, Gaertner HJ, Vonthein R, et al. Therapeutic drug monitoring of clozapine in relapse prevention: a five-year prospective study. *J Clin Psychopharmacol.* 2001; 21:305–10.
107. Rabinowitz J, Lichtenberg P, Kaplan Z, et al. Rehospitalization rates of chronically ill schizophrenic patients discharged on a regimen of risperi-

done, olanzapine, or conventional antipsychotics. *Am J Psychiatry.* 2001; 158:266–9.

108. Csernansky JG, Mahmoud R, Brenner R. A comparison of risperidone and haloperidol for the prevention of relapse in patients with schizophrenia. *N Engl J Med.* 2002; 346:16–22.
109. Barbui C, Lintas C, Percudani M. Head-to-head comparison of the costs of atypical antipsychotics: a systematic review. *CNS Drugs.* 2005; 19:935–50.
110. Mladsi DM, Grogg AL, Irish WD, et al. Pharmacy cost evaluation of risperidone, olanzapine, and quetiapine for the treatment of schizophrenia in acute care inpatient settings. *Curr Med Res Opin.* 2004; 20:1883–93.
111. Coley KC, Carter CS, DaPos SV, et al. Effectiveness of antipsychotic therapy in a naturalistic setting: a comparison between risperidone, perphenazine, and haloperidol. *J Clin Psychiatry.* 1999; 60:850–6.
112. Rosenheck R, Cramer J, Allan E, et al. Cost-effectiveness of clozapine in patients with high and low levels of hospital use. *Arch Gen Psychiatry.* 1999; 56:565–72.
113. Chouinard G, Albright PS. Economic and health state utility determinations for schizophrenic patients treated with risperidone or haloperidol. *J Clin Psychopharmacol.* 1997; 17:298–307.
114. Franz M, Lis S, Pluddemann K, et al. Conventional versus second-generation neuroleptics: subjective quality of life in schizophrenic patients. *Br J Psychiatry.* 1997; 170:422–5.
115. Roy A. Depression, attempted suicide, and suicide in patients with chronic schizophrenia. *Psychiatr Clin North Am.* 1986; 9:193–206.
116. Radomsky ED, Haas GL, Mann JJ, et al. Suicidal behavior in patients with schizophrenia and other psychotic disorders. *Am J Psychiatry.* 1999; 156:1590–5.
117. Cohen LJ, Test MA, Brown RL. Suicide and schizophrenia: data from a prospective community treatment study. *Am J Psychiatry.* 1990; 147:602–7.
118. Meltzer HY, Okayli G. Reduction of suicidality during clozapine treatment of neuroleptic-resistant schizophrenia: impact on risk-benefit assessment. *Am J Psychiatry.* 1995; 152:183–90.
119. Meltzer HY, Alphs L, Green AI, et al. Clozapine treatment for suicidality in schizophrenia: International Suicide Prevention Trial (InterSEPT). *Arch Gen Psychiatry.* 2003; 60:82–91.

Appendix—Additional Readings and Resources

Andreasen NC. Scale for the assessment of negative symptoms (SANS). *Br J Psychiatry.* 1989; 155(suppl 7):53–8.

Barnes TR. A rating scale for drug-induced akathisia. *Br J Psychiatry.* 1989; 154:672–6.

Kay SR, Fiszbein A, Opler LA. The positive and negative syndrome scale (PANSS) for schizophrenia. *Schizophr Bull.* 1987; 13:261–76.

Lane RD, Glazer WM, Hansen TE, et al. Assessment of tardive dyskinesia using the Abnormal Involuntary Movements Scale. *J Nerv Ment Dis.* 1985; 173:353–7.

Lehman AF, Kreyenbuhl J, Buchanan RW, et al. The Schizophrenia Patient Outcomes Research Team (PORT): updated treatment recommendations 2003. *Schizophr Bull.* 2004; 30:193–217.

Montgomery SA, Asberg M. A new depression scale designed to be sensitive to change. *Br J Psychiatry.* 1979; 134:382–9.

CGI: clinical global impressions. In: Guy W, Bonato RR, eds. Manual for the ECDEU assessment battery. 2nd ed. Chevy Chase, MD: National Institute of Mental Health; 1970:12-1–12-6.

Overall JE, Gorham DR. The Brief Psychiatric Rating Scale. *Psychol Rep.* 1962; 10:799–812.

Simpson GN, Angus JW. A rating scale for extrapyramidal side effects. *Acta Psychiatr Scand Suppl.* 1970; 212:11–9.

Approved by the ASHP Board of Directors on June 24, 2006. Developed through the ASHP Council on Therapeutics.

Jason M. Noel, Pharm.D., BCPP, is gratefully acknowledged for authoring this therapeutic position statement. At the time of publication, Dr. Noel was Assistant Professor, University of Maryland School of Pharmacy, Baltimore, and Director of Clinical Pharmacy Services, Rosewood Center, Owings Mills, MD.

Marshall E. Cates, Pharm.D., BCPP, FASHP; Beth Dubisar, Pharm. D.; Julie A. Dopheide, Pharm.D., BCPP; W. Kennedy Klugh, Pharm. D.; Dan LeGrady, Pharm.D., FNIH; Rex S. Lott, Pharm.D.; Lisa Mican, Pharm.D.; Virginia Stauffer, Pharm.D.; and the American Academy of Nurse Practitioners are acknowledged for reviewing drafts of this document.

The bibliographic citation for this document is as follows: Noel JM. ASHP therapeutic position statement on the use of second-generation antipsychotic medications in the treatment of adults with psychotic disorders. *Am J Health-Syst Pharm.* 2007; 64:863–76.

ASHP Therapeutic Guidelines

Clinical Practice Guidelines for Antimicrobial Prophylaxis in Surgery

These guidelines were developed jointly by the American Society of Health-System Pharmacists (ASHP), the Infectious Diseases Society of America (IDSA), the Surgical Infection Society (SIS), and the Society for Healthcare Epidemiology of America (SHEA). This work represents an update to the previously published ASHP Therapeutic Guidelines on Antimicrobial Prophylaxis in Surgery,[1] as well as guidelines from IDSA and SIS.[2,3] The guidelines are intended to provide practitioners with a standardized approach to the rational, safe, and effective use of antimicrobial agents for the prevention of surgical-site infections (SSIs) based on currently available clinical evidence and emerging issues.

Prophylaxis refers to the prevention of an infection and can be characterized as primary prophylaxis, secondary prophylaxis, or eradication. Primary prophylaxis refers to the prevention of an initial infection. Secondary prophylaxis refers to the prevention of recurrence or reactivation of a preexisting infection. Eradication refers to the elimination of a colonized organism to prevent the development of an infection. These guidelines focus on primary perioperative prophylaxis.

Guidelines Development and Use

Members of ASHP, IDSA, SIS, and SHEA were appointed to serve on an expert panel established to ensure the validity, reliability, and utility of the revised guidelines. The work of the panel was facilitated by faculty of the University of Pittsburgh School of Pharmacy and University of Pittsburgh Medical Center Drug Use and Disease State Management Program who served as contract researchers and writers for the project. Panel members and contractors were required to disclose any possible conflicts of interest before their appointment and throughout the guideline development process. Drafted documents for each surgical procedural section were reviewed by the expert panel and, once revised, were available for public comment on the ASHP website. After additional revisions were made to address reviewer comments, the final document was approved by the expert panel and the boards of directors of the above-named organizations.

Strength of Evidence and Grading of Recommendations. The primary literature from the previous ASHP Therapeutic Guidelines on Antimicrobial Prophylaxis in Surgery[1] was reviewed together with the primary literature published between the date of the previous guidelines, 1999, and June 2010, identified by searches of MEDLINE, EMBASE, and the Cochrane Database of Systematic Reviews. Particular attention was paid to study design, with greatest credence given to randomized, controlled, double-blind studies. There is a limited number of adequately powered randomized controlled trials evaluating the efficacy of antimicrobial prophylaxis in surgical procedures. Guidelines development included consideration of the following characteristics: validity, reliability, clinical applicability, flexibility, clarity, and a multidisciplinary nature as consistent with ASHP's philosophy on therapeutic guidelines.[4] The limitations of the evidence base are noted within each individual procedure section of the guidelines. Published guidelines with recommendations by experts in a procedure area (e.g., American College of Obstetricians and Gynecologists [ACOG]) and noted general guidelines (e.g., Centers for Disease Control and Prevention [CDC], Scottish Intercollegiate Guidelines Network, *Medical Letter*, SIS, SHEA/IDSA) were also considered.[2,3,5–11]

Recommendations for the use of antimicrobial prophylaxis are graded according to the strength of evidence available. The strength of evidence represents only support for or against prophylaxis and does not apply to the antimicrobial agent, dose, or dosage regimen. Studies supporting the recommendations for the use of antimicrobial therapy were classified as follows:

- Level I (evidence from large, well-conducted, randomized, controlled clinical trials or a meta-analysis),
- Level II (evidence from small, well-conducted, randomized, controlled clinical trials),
- Level III (evidence from well-conducted cohort studies),
- Level IV (evidence from well-conducted case–control studies),
- Level V (evidence from uncontrolled studies that were not well conducted),
- Level VI (conflicting evidence that tends to favor the recommendation), or
- Level VII (expert opinion or data extrapolated from evidence for general principles and other procedures).

This system has been used by the Agency for Healthcare Research and Quality, and ASHP, IDSA, SIS, and SHEA support it as an acceptable method for organizing strength of evidence for a variety of therapeutic or diagnostic recommendations.[4] Each recommendation was categorized according to the strength of evidence that supports the use or nonuse of antimicrobial prophylaxis as category A (levels I–III), category B (levels IV–VI), or category C (level VII).

When higher-level data are not available, a category C recommendation represents a consensus of expert panel members based on their clinical experience, extrapolation from other procedures with similar microbial or other clinical features, and available published literature. In these cases, the expert panel also extrapolated general principles and evidence from other procedures. Some recommendations include alternative approaches in situations in which panel member opinions were divided.

A major limitation of the available literature on antimicrobial prophylaxis is the difficulty in establishing significant differences in efficacy between prophylactic antimicrobial agents and controls (including placebo, no treatment, or other antimicrobial agents) due to study design and low SSI rates for most procedures. A small sample size increases the likelihood of a Type II error; therefore, there may be no apparent difference between the antimicrobial agent and placebo when in fact the antimicrobial has a beneficial effect.[12]

A valid study is placebo controlled and randomized with a sufficient sample in each group to avoid a Type II error. Of note, prophylaxis is recommended in some cases due to the severity of complications of postoperative infection (e.g., an infected device that is not easily removable) necessitating precautionary measures despite the lack of statistical support.

Summary of Key Updates. These guidelines reflect substantial changes from the guidelines published in 1999.[1] Highlights of those changes are outlined here.

Preoperative-dose timing. The optimal time for administration of preoperative doses is within 60 minutes before surgical incision. This is a more-specific time frame than the previously recommended time, which was "at induction of anesthesia." Some agents, such as fluoroquinolones and vancomycin, require administration over one to two hours; therefore, the administration of these agents should begin within 120 minutes before surgical incision.

Selection and dosing. Information is included regarding the approach to weight-based dosing in obese patients and the need for repeat doses during prolonged procedures.[13–18] Obesity has been linked to an increased risk for SSI. The pharmacokinetics of drugs may be altered in obese patients, so dosage adjustments based on body weight may be warranted in these patients. For all patients, intraoperative redosing is needed to ensure adequate serum and tissue concentrations of the antimicrobial if the duration of the procedure exceeds two half-lives of the drug or there is excessive blood loss during the procedure (Table 1). Recommendations for selection of antimicrobial agents for specific surgical procedures and alternative agents (e.g., for patients with allergies to β-lactam antimicrobials) are provided in Table 2.

Duration of prophylaxis. New recommendations for a shortened postoperative course of antimicrobials involving a single dose or continuation for less than 24 hours are provided. Further clarity on the lack of need for postoperative antimicrobial prophylaxis based on the presence of indwelling drains and intravascular catheters is included.

Common principles. A section addressing concepts that apply to all types of surgical procedures has been added. Expanded and new recommendations are provided for plastic, urology, cardiac, and thoracic procedures, as well as clarity on prophylaxis when implantable devices are inserted. The latest information on the use of mupirocin and on the role of vancomycin in surgical prophylaxis is summarized in these updated guidelines.

Application of Guidelines to Clinical Practice. Recommendations are provided for adult (age 19 years or older) and pediatric (age 1–18 years) patients. These guidelines do not specifically address newborn (premature and full-term) infants. While the guidelines do not address all concerns for patients with renal or hepatic dysfunction, antimicrobial prophylaxis often does not need to be modified for these patients when given as a single preoperative dose before surgical incision.

The recommendations herein may not be appropriate for use in all clinical situations. Decisions to follow these recommendations must be based on the judgment of the clinician and consideration of individual patient circumstances and available resources.

These guidelines reflect current knowledge of antimicrobial prophylaxis in surgery. Given the dynamic nature of scientific information and technology, periodic review, updating, and revisions are to be expected.

Special Patient Populations. *Pediatric patients.* Pediatric patients undergo a number of procedures similar to adults that may warrant antimicrobial prophylaxis. Although pediatric-specific prophylaxis data are sparse, available data have been evaluated and are presented in some of the procedure-specific sections of these guidelines. Selection of antimicrobial prophylactic agents mirrors that in adult guidelines, with the agents of choice being first- and second-generation cephalosporins, reserving the use of vancomycin for patients with documented β-lactam allergies.[19,20] While the use of a penicillin with a β-lactamase inhibitor in combination with cefazolin or vancomycin and gentamicin has also been studied in pediatric patients, the number of patients included in these evaluations remains small.[20–23] As with adults, there is little evidence supporting the use of vancomycin, alone or in combination with other antimicrobials, for routine perioperative antimicrobial prophylaxis in institutions that have a high prevalence of methicillin-resistant *Staphylococcus aureus* (MRSA). Vancomycin may be considered in children known to be colonized with MRSA and, in one retrospective historical cohort study, was shown to decrease MRSA infections.[21] Mupirocin use has been studied in and is efficacious in children colonized with MRSA, but there are limited data supporting its use perioperatively.[24–30] However, there is little reason to think that the impact and effect would be any different in children, so its use may be justified. Additional studies in this setting are needed to establish firm guidelines.

Unless noted in specific sections, all recommendations for adults are the same for pediatric patients, except for dosing. In most cases, the data in pediatric patients are limited and have been extrapolated from adult data; therefore, nearly all pediatric recommendations are based on expert opinion. In some sections, pediatric efficacy data do not exist and thus are not addressed in these guidelines. Fluoroquinolones should not be routinely used for surgical prophylaxis in pediatric patients because of the potential for toxicity in this population. The same principle of preoperative dosing within 60 minutes before incision has been applied to pediatric patients.[20–23] Additional intraoperative dosing may be needed if the duration of the procedure exceeds two half-lives of the antimicrobial agent or there is excessive blood loss during the procedure.[19,21] As with adult patients, single-dose prophylaxis is usually sufficient. If antimicrobial prophylaxis is continued postoperatively, the duration should be less than 24 hours, regardless of the presence of intravascular catheters or indwelling drains.[19,22,23,31,32] There are sufficient pharmacokinetic studies of most agents to recommend pediatric dosages that provide adequate systemic exposure and, presumably, efficacy comparable to that demonstrated in adults. Therefore, the pediatric dosages provided in these guidelines are based largely on pharmacokinetic data and the extrapolation of adult efficacy data to pediatric patients. Because few clinical trials have been conducted in pediatric surgical patients, strength of evidence criteria have not been applied to these recommendations. With few exceptions (e.g., aminoglycoside dosages), pediatric dosages should not exceed the maximum adult recommended dosages. Generally, if dosages are calculated on a milligram-per-kilogram basis for

Table 1.

Recommended Doses and Redosing Intervals for Commonly Used Antimicrobials for Surgical Prophylaxis

Antimicrobial	Recommended Dose: Adults[a]	Recommended Dose: Pediatrics[b]	Half-life in Adults With Normal Renal Function, hr[19]	Recommended Redosing Interval (From Initiation of Preoperative Dose), hr[c]
Ampicillin–sulbactam	3 g (ampicillin 2 g/ sulbactam 1 g)	50 mg/kg of the ampicillin component	0.8–1.3	2
Ampicillin	2 g	50 mg/kg	1–1.9	2
Aztreonam	2 g	30 mg/kg	1.3–2.4	4
Cefazolin	2 g, 3 g for pts weighing ≥120 kg	30 mg/kg	1.2–2.2	4
Cefuroxime	1.5 g	50 mg/kg	1–2	4
Cefotaxime	1 g[d]	50 mg/kg	0.9–1.7	3
Cefoxitin	2 g	40 mg/kg	0.7–1.1	2
Cefotetan	2 g	40 mg/kg	2.8–4.6	6
Ceftriaxone	2 g[e]	50–75 mg/kg	5.4–10.9	NA
Ciprofloxacin[f]	400 mg	10 mg/kg	3–7	NA
Clindamycin	900 mg	10 mg/kg	2–4	6
Ertapenem	1 g	15 mg/kg	3–5	NA
Fluconazole	400 mg	6 mg/kg	30	NA
Gentamicin[g]	5 mg/kg based on dosing weight (single dose)	2.5 mg/kg based on dosing weight	2–3	NA
Levofloxacin[f]	500 mg	10 mg/kg	6–8	NA
Metronidazole	500 mg	15 mg/kg Neonates weighing <1200 g should receive a single 7.5-mg/kg dose	6–8	NA
Moxifloxacin[f]	400 mg	10 mg/kg	8–15	NA
Piperacillin–tazobactam	3.375 g	Infants 2–9 mo: 80 mg/kg of the piperacillin component Children >9 mo and ≤40 kg: 100 mg/kg of the piperacillin component	0.7–1.2	2
Vancomycin	15 mg/kg	15 mg/kg	4–8	NA
Oral antibiotics for colorectal surgery prophylaxis (used in conjunction with a mechanical bowel preparation)				
Erythromycin base	1 g	20 mg/kg	0.8–3	NA
Metronidazole	1 g	15 mg/kg	6–10	NA
Neomycin	1 g	15 mg/kg	2–3 (3% absorbed under normal gastrointestinal conditions)	NA

[a]Adult doses are obtained from the studies cited in each section. When doses differed between studies, expert opinion used the most-often recommended dose.

[b]The maximum pediatric dose should not exceed the usual adult dose.

[c]For antimicrobials with a short half-life (e.g., cefazolin, cefoxitin) used before long procedures, redosing in the operating room is recommended at an interval of approximately two times the half-life of the agent in patients with normal renal function. Recommended redosing intervals marked as "not applicable" (NA) are based on typical case length; for unusually long procedures, redosing may be needed.

[d]Although FDA-approved package insert labeling indicates 1 g,14 experts recommend 2 g for obese patients.

[e]When used as a single dose in combination with metronidazole for colorectal procedures.

[f]While fluoroquinolones have been associated with an increased risk of tendinitis/tendon rupture in all ages, use of these agents for single-dose prophylaxis is generally safe.

[g]In general, gentamicin for surgical antibiotic prophylaxis should be limited to a single dose given preoperatively. Dosing is based on the patient's actual body weight. If the patient's actual weight is more than 20% above ideal body weight (IBW), the dosing weight (DW) can be determined as follows: DW = IBW + 0.4(actual weight – IBW).

Table 2.

Recommendations for Surgical Antimicrobial Prophylaxis

Type of Procedure	Recommended Agents[a,b]	Alternative Agents in Patients with β-Lactam Allergy	Strength of Evidence[c]
Cardiac			
Coronary artery bypass	Cefazolin, cefuroxime	Clindamycin,[d] vancomycin[d]	A
Cardiac device insertion procedures (e.g., pacemaker implantation)	Cefazolin, cefuroxime	Clindamycin, vancomycin	A
Ventricular assist devices	Cefazolin, cefuroxime	Clindamycin, vancomycin	C
Thoracic			
Noncardiac procedures, including lobectomy, pneumonectomy, lung resection, and thoracotomy	Cefazolin, ampicillin–sulbactam	Clindamycin,[d] vancomycin[d]	A
Video-assisted thoracoscopic surgery	Cefazolin, ampicillin–sulbactam	Clindamycin,[d] vancomycin[d]	C
Gastroduodenale			
Procedures involving entry into lumen of gastrointestinal tract (bariatric, pancreaticoduodenectomy[f])	Cefazolin	Clindamycin or vancomycin + aminoglycoside[g] or aztreonam or fluoroquinolone[h-j]	A
Procedures without entry into gastrointestinal tract (antireflux, highly selective vagotomy) for high-risk patients	Cefazolin	Clindamycin or vancomycin + aminoglycoside[g] or aztreonam or fluoroquinolone[h-j]	A
Biliary tract			
Open procedure	Cefazolin, cefoxitin, cefotetan, ceftriaxone,[k] ampicillin–sulbactam[h]	Clindamycin or vancomycin + aminoglycoside[g] or aztreonam or fluoroquinolone[h-j] Metronidazole + aminoglycoside[g] or fluoroquinolone[h-j]	A
Laparoscopic procedure			
Elective, low-risk[l]	None	None	A
Elective, high-risk[l]	Cefazolin, cefoxitin, cefotetan, ceftriaxone,[k] ampicillin–sulbactam[h]	Clindamycin or vancomycin + aminoglycoside[g] or aztreonam or fluoroquinolone[h-j] Metronidazole + aminoglycoside[g] or fluoroquinolone[h-j]	A
Appendectomy for uncomplicated appendicitis	Cefoxitin, cefotetan, cefazolin + metronidazole	Clindamycin + aminoglycoside[g] or aztreonam or fluoroquinolone[h-j] Metronidazole + aminoglycoside[g] or fluoroquinolone[h-j]	A
Small intestine			
Nonobstructed	Cefazolin	Clindamycin + aminoglycoside[g] or aztreonam or fluoroquinolone[h-j]	C
Obstructed	Cefazolin + metronidazole, cefoxitin, cefotetan	Metronidazole + aminoglycoside[g] or fluoroquinolone[h-j]	C
Hernia repair (hernioplasty and herniorrhaphy)	Cefazolin	Clindamycin, vancomycin	A

Table 2. *(continued)*

Type of Procedure	Recommended Agents[a,b]	Alternative Agents in Patients with β-Lactam Allergy	Strength of Evidence[c]
Colorectal[m]	Cefazolin + metronidazole, cefoxitin, cefotetan, ampicillin–sulbactam,[h] ceftriaxone + metronidazole,[n] ertapenem	Clindamycin + aminoglycoside[g] or aztreonam or fluoroquinolone[h-j] metronidazole + aminoglycoside[g] or fluoroquinolone[h-j]	A
Head and neck			
Clean	None	None	B
Clean with placement of prosthesis (excludes tympanostomy tubes)	Cefazolin, cefuroxime	Clindamycin[d]	C
Clean-contaminated cancer surgery	Cefazolin + metronidazole, cefuroxime + metronidazole, ampicillin–sulbactam	Clindamycin[d]	A
Other clean-contaminated procedures with the exception of tonsillectomy and functional endoscopic sinus procedures	Cefazolin + metronidazole, cefuroxime + metronidazole, ampicillin–sulbactam	Clindamycin[d]	B
Neurosurgery			
Elective craniotomy and cerebrospinal fluid-shunting procedures	Cefazolin	Clindamycin,[d] vancomycin[d]	A
Implantation of intrathecal pumps	Cefazolin	Clindamycin,[d] vancomycin[d]	C
Cesarean delivery	Cefazolin	Clindamycin + aminoglycoside[g]	A
Hysterectomy (vaginal or abdominal)	Cefazolin, cefotetan, cefoxitin, ampicillin–sulbactam[h]	Clindamycin or vancomycin + aminoglycoside[g] or aztreonam or fluoroquinolone[h-j] Metronidazole + aminoglycoside[g] or fluoroquinolone[h-j]	A
Ophthalmic	Topical neomycin–polymyxin B–gramicidin or fourth-generation topical fluoroquinolones (gatifloxacin or moxifloxacin) given as 1 drop every 5–15 min for 5 doses[o] Addition of cefazolin 100 mg by subconjunctival injection or intracameral cefazolin 1–2.5 mg or cefuroxime 1 mg at the end of procedure is optional	None	B
Orthopedic			
Clean operations involving hand, knee, or foot and not involving implantation of foreign materials	None	None	C
Spinal procedures with and without instrumentation	Cefazolin	Clindamycin,[d] vancomycin[d]	A
Hip fracture repair	Cefazolin	Clindamycin,[d] vancomycin[d]	A

Table 2. *(continued)*

Type of Procedure	Recommended Agents[a,b]	Alternative Agents in Patients with β-Lactam Allergy	Strength of Evidence[c]
Implantation of internal fixation devices (e.g., nails, screws, plates, wires)	Cefazolin	Clindamycin,[d] vancomycin[d]	C
Total joint replacement	Cefazolin	Clindamycin,[d] vancomycin[d]	A
Urologic			
Lower tract instrumentation with risk factors for infection (includes transrectal prostate biopsy)	Fluoroquinolone,[h-j] trimethoprim–sulfamethoxazole, cefazolin	Aminoglycoside[g] with or without clindamycin	A
Clean without entry into urinary tract	Cefazolin (the addition of a single dose of an aminoglycoside may be recommended for placement of prosthetic material [e.g., penile prosthesis])	Clindamycin,[d] vancomycin[d]	A
Involving implanted prosthesis	Cefazolin ± aminoglycoside, cefazolin ± aztreonam, ampicillin–sulbactam	Clindamycin ± aminoglycoside or aztreonam, vancomycin ± aminoglycoside or aztreonam	A
Clean with entry into urinary tract	Cefazolin (the addition of a single dose of an aminoglycoside may be recommended for placement of prosthetic material [e.g., penile prosthesis])	Fluoroquinolone,[h-j] aminoglycoside[g] with or without clindamycin	A
Clean-contaminated	Cefazolin + metronidazole, cefoxitin	Fluoroquinolone,[h-j] aminoglycoside[g] + metronidazole or clindamycin	A
Vascular[p]	Cefazolin	Clindamycin,[d] vancomycin[d]	A
Heart, lung, heart–lung transplantation[q]			
Heart transplantation[r]	Cefazolin	Clindamycin,[d] vancomycin[d]	A (based on cardiac procedures)
Lung and heart–lung transplantation[r,s]	Cefazolin	Clindamycin,[d] vancomycin[d]	A (based on cardiac procedures)
Liver transplantation[q,t]	Piperacillin–tazobactam, cefotaxime + ampicillin	Clindamycin or vancomycin + aminoglycoside[g] or aztreonam or fluoroquinolone[h-j]	B
Pancreas and pancreas–kidney transplantation[r]	Cefazolin, fluconazole (for patients at high risk of fungal infection [e.g., those with enteric drainage of the pancreas])	Clindamycin or vancomycin + aminoglycoside[g] or aztreonam or fluoroquinolone[h-j]	A

Table 2. *(continued)*

Type of Procedure	Recommended Agents[a,b]	Alternative Agents in Patients with β-Lactam Allergy	Strength of Evidence[c]
Plastic surgery	Cefazolin	Clindamycin or vancomycin + aminoglycoside[g] or aztreonam or fluoroquinolone[h-j]	A
Clean with risk factors or clean-contaminated	Cefazolin, ampicillin–sulbactam	Clindamycin,[d] vancomycin[d]	C

[a]The antimicrobial agent should be started within 60 minutes before surgical incision (120 minutes for vancomycin or fluoroquinolones). While single-dose prophylaxis is usually sufficient, the duration of prophylaxis for all procedures should be less than 24 hours. If an agent with a short half-life is used (e.g., cefazolin, cefoxitin), it should be readministered if the procedure duration exceeds the recommended redosing interval (from the time of initiation of the preoperative dose [see Table 1]). Readministration may also be warranted if prolonged or excessive bleeding occurs or if there are other factors that may shorten the half-life of the prophylactic agent (e.g., extensive burns). Readministration may not be warranted in patients in whom the half-life of the agent may be prolonged (e.g., patients with renal insufficiency or failure).

[b]For patients known to be colonized with methicillin-resistant *Staphylococcus aureus*, it is reasonable to add a single preoperative dose of vancomycin to the recommended agent(s).

[c]Strength of evidence that supports the use or nonuse of prophylaxis is classified as A (levels I–III), B (levels IV–VI), or C (level VII). Level I evidence is from large, well-conducted, randomized controlled clinical trials. Level II evidence is from small, well-conducted, randomized controlled clinical trials. Level III evidence is from well-conducted cohort studies. Level IV evidence is from well-conducted case–control studies. Level V evidence is from uncontrolled studies that were not well conducted. Level VI evidence is conflicting evidence that tends to favor the recommendation. Level VII evidence is expert opinion.

[d]For procedures in which pathogens other than staphylococci and streptococci are likely, an additional agent with activity against those pathogens could be considered. For example, if there are surveillance data showing that gram-negative organisms are a cause of surgical-site infections (SSIs) for the procedure, practitioners may consider combining clindamycin or vancomycin with another agent (cefazolin if the patient is not β-lactam allergic; aztreonam, gentamicin, or single-dose fluoroquinolone if the patient is β-lactam allergic).

[e]Prophylaxis should be considered for patients at highest risk for postoperative gastroduodenal infections, such as those with increased gastric pH (e.g., those receiving histamine H_2-receptor antagonists or proton-pump inhibitors), gastroduodenal perforation, decreased gastric motility, gastric outlet obstruction, gastric bleeding, morbid obesity, or cancer. Antimicrobial prophylaxis may not be needed when the lumen of the intestinal tract is not entered.

[f]Consider additional antimicrobial coverage with infected biliary tract. See the biliary tract procedures section of this article.

[g]Gentamicin or tobramycin.

[h]Due to increasing resistance of *Escherichia coli* to fluoroquinolones and ampicillin–sulbactam, local population susceptibility profiles should be reviewed prior to use.

[i]Ciprofloxacin or levofloxacin.

[j]Fluoroquinolones are associated with an increased risk of tendonitis and tendon rupture in all ages. However, this risk would be expected to be quite small with single-dose antibiotic prophylaxis. Although the use of fluoroquinolones may be necessary for surgical antibiotic prophylaxis in some children, they are not drugs of first choice in the pediatric population due to an increased incidence of adverse events as compared with controls in some clinical trials.

[k]Ceftriaxone use should be limited to patients requiring antimicrobial treatment for acute cholecystitis or acute biliary tract infections which may not be determined prior to incision, not patients undergoing cholecystectomy for noninfected biliary conditions, including biliary colic or dyskinesia without infection.

[l]Factors that indicate a high risk of infectious complications in laparoscopic cholecystectomy include emergency procedures, diabetes, long procedure duration, intraoperative gallbladder rupture, age of >70 years, conversion from laparoscopic to open cholecystectomy, American Society of Anesthesiologists classification of 3 or greater, episode of colic within 30 days before the procedure, reintervention in less than one month for noninfectious complication, acute cholecystitis, bile spillage, jaundice, pregnancy, nonfunctioning gallbladder, immunosuppression, and insertion of prosthetic device. Because a number of these risk factors are not possible to determine before surgical intervention, it may be reasonable to give a single dose of antimicrobial prophylaxis to all patients undergoing laparoscopic cholecystectomy.

[m]For most patients, a mechanical bowel preparation combined with oral neomycin sulfate plus oral erythromycin base or with oral neomycin sulfate plus oral metronidazole should be given in addition to i.v. prophylaxis.

[n]Where there is increasing resistance to first- and second-generation cephalosporins among gram-negative isolates from SSIs, a single dose of ceftriaxone plus metronidazole may be preferred over the routine use of carbapenems.

[o]The necessity of continuing topical antimicrobials postoperatively has not been established.

[p]Prophylaxis is not routinely indicated for brachiocephalic procedures. Although there are no data in support, patients undergoing brachiocephalic procedures involving vascular prostheses or patch implantation (e.g., carotid endarterectomy) may benefit from prophylaxis.

[q]These guidelines reflect recommendations for perioperative antibiotic prophylaxis to prevent SSIs and do not provide recommendations for prevention of opportunistic infections in immunosuppressed transplantation patients (e.g., for antifungal or antiviral medications).

[r]Patients who have left-ventricular assist devices as a bridge and who are chronically infected might also benefit from coverage of the infecting microorganism.

[s]The prophylactic regimen may need to be modified to provide coverage against any potential pathogens, including gram-negative (e.g., *Pseudomonas aeruginosa*) or fungal organisms, isolated from the donor lung or the recipient before transplantation. Patients undergoing lung transplantation with negative pretransplantation cultures should receive antimicrobial prophylaxis as appropriate for other types of cardiothoracic surgeries. Patients undergoing lung transplantation for cystic fibrosis should receive 7–14 days of treatment with antimicrobials selected according to pretransplantation culture and susceptibility results. This treatment may include additional antibacterial or antifungal agents.

[t]The prophylactic regimen may need to be modified to provide coverage against any potential pathogens, including vancomycin-resistant enterococci, isolated from the recipient before transplantation.

children weighing more than 40 kg, the calculated dosage will exceed the maximum recommended dosage for adults; adult dosages should therefore be used.

Patients with prosthetic implants. For patients with existing prosthetic implants who undergo an invasive procedure, there is no evidence that antimicrobial prophylaxis prevents infections of the implant. However, updated guidelines from the American Heart Association (AHA) suggest that prophylaxis may be justified in a limited subset of patients for the prevention of endocarditis.[11]

Common Principles and Procedure-Specific Guidelines. The Common Principles section has been developed to provide information common to many surgical procedures. These principles are general recommendations based on currently available data at the time of publication that may change over time; therefore, these principles need to be applied with careful attention to each clinical situation. Detailed information pertinent to specific surgical procedures is included in the procedure-specific sections of these guidelines.

In addition to patient- and procedure-specific considerations, several institution-specific factors must be considered by practitioners before instituting these guidelines. The availability of antimicrobial agents at the institution may be restricted by local antimicrobial-use policy or lack of approval for use by regulatory authorities. Medications that are no longer available or not approved for use by the Food and Drug Administration (FDA) are so noted. Local resistance patterns should also be considered in selecting antimicrobial agents and are discussed in the colonization and resistance patterns section of the Common Principles section.

Requirements for Effective Surgical Prophylaxis

Appendix A lists the wound classification criteria currently used by the CDC National Healthcare Safety Network (NHSN) and Healthcare Infection Control Practices Advisory Committee (HICPAC).[33–35]

Criteria for defining an SSI have also been established by NHSN (Appendix B).[8,36] These definitions assist in evaluating the importance of providing antimicrobial prophylaxis and the potential consequences of infection, including the need for treatment. Some criteria vary slightly by procedure.

Although antimicrobial prophylaxis plays an important role in reducing the rate of SSIs, other factors such as attention to basic infection-control strategies,[37] the surgeon's experience and technique, the duration of the procedure, hospital and operating-room environments, instrument-sterilization issues, preoperative preparation (e.g., surgical scrub, skin antisepsis, appropriate hair removal), perioperative management (temperature and glycemic control), and the underlying medical condition of the patient may have a strong impact on SSI rates.[5,8] These guidelines recognize the importance of these other factors but do not include a discussion of or any recommendations regarding these issues beyond the optimal use of prophylactic antimicrobial agents. Patient-related factors associated with an increased risk of SSI include extremes of age, nutritional status, obesity, diabetes mellitus, tobacco use, coexistent remote body-site infections, altered immune response, corticosteroid therapy, recent surgical procedure, length of preoperative hospitalization, and colonization with microorganisms. Antimicrobial prophylaxis may be justified for any procedure if the patient has an underlying medical condition associated with a high risk of SSI or if the patient is immunocompromised (e.g., malnourished, neutropenic, receiving immunosuppressive agents).

Antimicrobial prophylaxis may be beneficial in surgical procedures associated with a high rate of infection (i.e., clean-contaminated or contaminated procedures) and in certain clean procedures where there are severe consequences of infection (e.g., prosthetic implants), even if infection is unlikely. While prophylactic antimicrobials are not indicated for some clean surgical procedures,[8] available data suggest that the relative risk reduction of SSI from the use of antimicrobial prophylaxis is the same in clean and in higher-risk procedures.[38] The decision to use prophylaxis depends on the cost of treating and the morbidity associated with infection compared with the cost and morbidity associated with using prophylaxis. Antimicrobial prophylaxis is justified for most clean-contaminated procedures. The use of antimicrobial agents for dirty procedures (Appendix A) or established infections is classified as treatment of presumed infection, not prophylaxis. See the procedure-specific sections for detailed recommendations.

Quality-Improvement Efforts. National, state, local, and institutional groups have developed and implemented collaborative efforts to improve the appropriateness of surgical antimicrobial prophylaxis. Various process and outcomes measures are employed, and results are disseminated. Institutional epidemiology and infection-control programs, state-based quality-improvement campaigns (e.g., the Michigan Surgical Quality Collaborative, the Washington State Surgical Clinical Outcomes Assessment Program[39,40]), CDC, NHSN, the National Surgical Quality Improvement Program, the Joint Commission, and the National Quality Forum have been instrumental in developing programs to prevent SSIs.

Over the past decade or more, several organizations, payers, and government agencies, including the Centers for Medicare and Medicaid Services (CMS), have established national quality-improvement initiatives to further improve the safety and outcomes of health care, including surgery.[41–47] One area of focus in these initiatives for patients undergoing surgical procedures is the prevention of SSIs. The performance measures used, data collection and reporting requirements, and financial implications vary among the initiatives. The Surgical Care Improvement Project (SCIP) began in 2002 as the Surgical Infection Prevention (SIP) project, focusing on the timing, selection, and duration of prophylactic antimicrobial agents.[41,42] The SIP project was expanded to SCIP to include additional process measures surrounding patient safety and care during surgical procedures, including glucose control, venous thromboembolism prophylaxis, hair removal, and temperature control. Similar measures have been adopted by the Joint Commission.[43] The Physicians Quality Reporting System was established in 2006 to provide financial incentives to physicians meeting performance standards for quality measures, including surgery-related measures similar to those reported for SCIP and the Joint Commission.[44] Data are required to be collected by institutions and reported to payers.[42,44,46] Data for CMS and the Physicians Quality Reporting System measures are displayed on public websites to allow consumers to compare performance among hospitals. Institutional data collection and reporting are required, with financial incentives tied to performance to varying degrees, including payment for reporting, payment increases for meeting or exceeding minimum levels of performance, payment reduction for poor performance, and lack of payment for the development of surgical complications, such as mediastinitis.

Quality-improvement initiatives and mandated performance reporting are subject to change, so readers of these guidelines are advised to consult their local or institutional quality-improvement departments for new developments in requirements for measures and data reporting that apply to their practice.

Cost Containment. Few pharmacoeconomic studies have addresed surgical antimicrobial prophylaxis; therefore, a cost-minimization approach was employed in developing these guidelines. The antimicrobial agent recommendations are based primarily on efficacy and safety. Individual institutions must consider their acquisition costs when implementing these guidelines.

Additional cost savings may be realized through collaborative management by pharmacists and surgeons to select the most cost-effective agent and minimize or eliminate postoperative dosing.[48–50] The use of standardized antimicrobial order sets, automatic stop-order programs, and educational initiatives has been shown to facilitate the adoption of guidelines for surgical antimicrobial prophylaxis.[51–58]

Common Principles

Ideally, an antimicrobial agent for surgical prophylaxis should (1) prevent SSI, (2) prevent SSI-related morbidity and mortality, (3) reduce the duration and cost of health care (when the costs associated with the management of SSI are considered, the cost-effectiveness of prophylaxis becomes evident),[51,52] (4) produce no adverse effects, and (5) have no adverse consequences for the microbial flora of the patient or the hospital.[53] To achieve these goals, an antimicrobial agent should be (1) active against the pathogens most likely to contaminate the surgical site, (2) given in an appropriate dosage and at a time that ensures adequate serum and tissue concentrations during the period of potential contamination, (3) safe, and (4) administered for the shortest effective period to minimize adverse effects, the development of resistance, and costs.[8,59,60]

The selection of an appropriate antimicrobial agent for a specific patient should take into account the characteristics of the ideal agent, the comparative efficacy of the antimicrobial agent for the procedure, the safety profile, and the patient's medication allergies. A full discussion of the safety profile, including adverse events, drug interactions, contraindications, and warnings, for each antimicrobial agent is beyond the scope of these guidelines. Readers of these guidelines should review the FDA-approved prescribing information and published data for specific antimicrobial agents before use. For most procedures, cefazolin is the drug of choice for prophylaxis because it is the most widely studied antimicrobial agent, with proven efficacy. It has a desirable duration of action, spectrum of activity against organisms commonly encountered in surgery, reasonable safety, and low cost. There is little evidence to suggest that broad-spectrum antimicrobial agents (i.e., agents with broad in vitro antibacterial activity) result in lower rates of postoperative SSI compared with older antimicrobial agents with a narrower spectrum of activity. However, comparative studies are limited by small sample sizes, resulting in difficulty detecting a significant difference between antimicrobial agents; therefore, antimicrobial selection is based on cost, safety profile, ease of administration, pharmacokinetic profile, and bactericidal activity.

Common Surgical Pathogens

The agent chosen should have activity against the most common surgical-site pathogens. The predominant organisms causing SSIs after clean procedures are skin flora, including *S. aureus* and coagulase-negative staphylococci (e.g., *Staphylococcus epidermidis*).[61] In clean-contaminated procedures, including abdominal procedures and heart, kidney, and liver transplantations, the predominant organisms include gram-negative rods and enterococci in addition to skin flora. Additional details on common organisms can be found in procedure-specific sections of these guidelines.

Recommendations for the selection of prophylactic antimicrobials for various surgical procedures are provided in Table 2. Adult and pediatric dosages are included in Table 1. Agents that are FDA-approved for use in surgical antimicrobial prophylaxis include cefazolin, cefuroxime, cefoxitin, cefotetan, ertapenem, and vancomycin.[62–67]

Trends in Microbiology. The causative pathogens associated with SSIs in U.S. hospitals have changed over the past two decades. Analysis of National Nosocomial Infections Surveillance (NNIS) System data found that the percentage of SSIs caused by gram-negative bacilli decreased from 56.5% in 1986 to 33.8% in 2003.[68] *S. aureus* was the most common pathogen, causing 22.5% of SSIs during this time period. NHSN data from 2006 to 2007 revealed that the proportion of SSIs caused by *S. aureus* increased to 30%, with MRSA comprising 49.2% of these isolates.[61] In a study of patients readmitted to U.S. hospitals between 2003 and 2007 with a culture-confirmed SSI, the proportion of infections caused by MRSA increased significantly from 16.1% to 20.6% ($p < 0.0001$).[69] MRSA infections were associated with higher mortality rates, longer hospital stays, and higher hospital costs compared with other infections.

Spectrum of Activity. Antimicrobial agents with the narrowest spectrum of activity required for efficacy in preventing infection are recommended in these guidelines. Alternative antimicrobial agents with documented efficacy are also listed herein. Individual health systems must consider local resistance patterns of organisms and overall SSI rates at their site when adopting these recommendations. Resistance patterns from organisms causing SSIs—in some cases procedure-specific resistance patterns—should take precedence over hospitalwide antibiograms.

Vancomycin. In 1999, HICPAC, an advisory committee to CDC and the Secretary of the Department of Health and Human Services, collaborated with other major organizations to develop recommendations for preventing and controlling vancomycin resistance.[70] The recommendations are echoed by these and other guidelines.[6,7,41,71] Routine use of vancomycin prophylaxis is not recommended for any procedure.[8] Vancomycin may be included in the regimen of choice when a cluster of MRSA cases (e.g., mediastinitis after cardiac procedures) or methicillin-resistant coagulase-negative staphylococci SSIs have been detected at an institution. Vancomycin prophylaxis should be considered for patients with known MRSA colonization or at high risk for MRSA colonization in the absence of surveillance data (e.g., patients with recent hospitalization, nursing-home residents, hemodialysis patients).[5,41,72] In institutions with SSIs attributable to community-associated MRSA, antimicrobial agents with known in vitro activity against this pathogen may be considered as an alternative to vancomycin.

Each institution is encouraged to develop guidelines for the proper use of vancomycin. Although vancomycin is commonly used when the risk for MRSA is high, data suggest that vancomycin is less effective than cefazolin for preventing SSIs caused by methicillin-susceptible *S. aureus* (MSSA).[73,74] For this reason, vancomycin is used in combination with cefazolin at some institutions with both MSSA and MRSA SSIs. For procedures in which pathogens other than staphylococci and streptococci are likely, an additional agent with activity against those pathogens should be considered. For example, if there are surveillance data showing that gram-negative organisms are a cause of SSIs for the procedure, practitioners may consider combining vancomycin with another agent (cefazolin if the patient does not have a β-lactam allergy; an aminoglycoside [gentamicin or tobramycin], aztreonam, or single-dose fluoroquinolone if the patient has a β-lactam allergy). The use of vancomycin for MRSA prophylaxis does not supplant the need for routine surgical prophylaxis appropriate for the type of procedure. When vancomycin is used, it can almost always be used as a single dose due to its long half-life.

Colonization and Resistance. A national survey determined that *S. aureus* nasal colonization in the general population decreased from 32.4% in 2001–02 to 28.6% in 2003–04 ($p < 0.01$), whereas the prevalence of colonization with MRSA increased from 0.8% to 1.5% ($p < 0.05$) during the same time periods.[75] Colonization with MRSA was independently associated with health care exposure among men, having been born in the United States, age of >60 years, diabetes, and poverty among women. Similarly, children are colonized with *S. aureus* and MRSA, but colonization varies by age. Children under 5 years of age have the highest rates, mirroring rates seen in patients over age 60 years.[76] The rates drop in children between 5 and 14 years of age and gradually increase to rates seen in the adult population. Lo et al.[77] reported that in a large cohort of children, 28.1% were colonized with *S. aureus* between 2004 and 2006. Between 2007 and 2009, 23.3% of children were colonized with *S. aureus*, but the proportion of children colonized with MRSA had increased from 8.1% in 2004 to 15.1% in 2009.

Surgical antimicrobial prophylaxis can alter individual and institutional bacterial flora, leading to changes in colonization rates and increased bacterial resistance.[78–84] Surgical prophylaxis can also predispose patients to *Clostridium difficile*-associated colitis.[81] Risk factors for development of *C. difficile*-associated colitis include longer duration of prophylaxis or therapy and use of multiple antimicrobial agents.[85] Limiting the duration of antimicrobial prophylaxis to a single preoperative dose can reduce the risk of *C. difficile* disease.

The question of what antimicrobial surgical prophylaxis to use for patients known to be colonized or recently infected with multidrug-resistant pathogens cannot be answered easily or in a manner that can be applied uniformly to all patient scenarios. Whether prophylaxis should be expanded to provide coverage for these pathogens depends on many factors, including the pathogen, its antimicrobial susceptibility profile, the host, the procedure to be performed, and the proximity of the likely reservoir of the pathogen to the incision and operative sites. While there is no evidence on the management of surgical antimicrobial prophylaxis in a patient with past infection or colonization with a resistant gram-negative pathogen, it is logical to provide prophylaxis with an agent active against MRSA for any patient known to be colonized with this gram-positive pathogen who will have a skin incision; specific prophylaxis for a resistant gram-negative pathogen in a patient with past infection or colonization with such a pathogen may not be necessary for a purely cutaneous procedure. Similarly, a patient colonized with vancomycin-resistant enterococci (VRE) should receive prophylaxis effective against VRE when undergoing liver transplantation but probably not when undergoing an umbilical hernia repair without mesh placement. Thus, patients must be treated on a case-by-case basis, taking into account multiple considerations.

Patients receiving therapeutic antimicrobials for a remote infection before surgery should also be given antimicrobial prophylaxis before surgery to ensure adequate serum and tissue levels of antimicrobials with activity against likely pathogens for the duration of the operation. If the agents used therapeutically are appropriate for surgical prophylaxis, administering an extra dose within 60 minutes before surgical incision is sufficient. Otherwise, the antimicrobial prophylaxis recommended for the planned procedure should be used. For patients with indwelling tubes or drains, consideration may be given to using prophylactic agents active against pathogens found in these devices before the procedure, even though therapeutic treatment for pathogens in drains is not indicated at other times. For patients with chronic renal failure receiving vancomycin, a preoperative dose of cefazolin should be considered instead of an extra dose of vancomycin, particularly if the probable pathogens associated with the procedure are gram-negative. In most circumstances, elective surgery should be postponed when the patient has an infection at a remote site.

Allergy to β-Lactam Antimicrobials. Allergy to β-lactam antimicrobials may be a consideration in the selection of surgical prophylaxis. The β-lactam antimicrobials, including cephalosporins, are the mainstay of surgical antimicrobial prophylaxis and are also the most commonly implicated drugs when allergic reactions occur. Because the predominant organisms in SSIs after clean procedures are gram-positive, the inclusion of vancomycin may be appropriate for a patient with a life-threatening allergy to β-lactam antimicrobials.

Although true Type 1 (immunoglobulin E [IgE]-mediated) cross-allergic reactions between penicillins, cephalosporins, and carbapenems are uncommon, cephalosporins and carbapenems should not be used for surgical prophylaxis in patients with documented or presumed IgE-mediated penicillin allergy. Confusion about the definition of true allergy among patients and practitioners leads to recommendations for alternative antimicrobial therapy with the potential for a lack of efficacy, increased costs, and adverse events.[86,87] Type 1 anaphylactic reactions to antimicrobials usually occur 30–60 minutes after administration. In patients receiving penicillins, this reaction is a life-threatening emergency that precludes subsequent use of penicillins.[88] Cephalosporins and carbapenems can safely be used in patients with an allergic reaction to penicillins that is not an IgE-mediated reaction (e.g., anaphylaxis, urticaria, bronchospasm) or exfoliative dermatitis (Stevens-Johnson syndrome, toxic epidermal necrolysis), a life-threatening hypersensitivity reaction that can be caused by β-lactam antimicrobials and other medications.[88,89] Patients should be carefully questioned about their history of antimicrobial allergies to determine whether a true allergy exists before selection of agents for prophylaxis. Patients with allergies to cephalosporins, penicillins, or both have been excluded from many clinical trials. Alternatives to β-lactam antimicrobials are provided in Table 2 based mainly on the antimicrobial activity profiles against predominant procedure-specific organisms and available clinical data.

Drug Administration

The preferred route of administration varies with the type of procedure, but for a majority of procedures, i.v. administration is ideal because it produces rapid, reliable, and predictable serum and tissue concentrations.

Timing of Initial Dose. Successful prophylaxis requires the delivery of the antimicrobial to the operative site before contamination occurs. Thus, the antimicrobial agent should be administered at such a time to provide serum and tissue concentrations exceeding the minimum inhibitory concentration (MIC) for the probable organisms associated with the procedure, at the time of incision, and for the duration of the procedure.[41,90] In 1985, DiPiro et al.[91] demonstrated that higher serum and tissue cephalosporin concentrations at the time of surgical incision and at the end of the procedure were achieved when the drugs were given intravenously at the time of anesthesia induction compared with administration in the operating room. The average interval between antimicrobial administration and incision was 17–22 minutes[91] (Dellinger EP, personal communication, 2011 May).

A prospective evaluation of 1708 surgical patients receiving antimicrobial prophylaxis found that preoperative administration of antimicrobials within 2 hours before surgical incision decreased the risk of SSI to 0.59%, compared with 3.8% for early administration (2–24 hours before surgical incision) and 3.3% for any postoperative administration (any time after incision).[92] In a study of 2048 patients undergoing coronary bypass graft or valve replacement surgery receiving vancomycin prophylaxis, the rate of SSI was lowest in those patients in whom an infusion was started 16–60 minutes before surgical incision.[93] This time interval (16–60 minutes before incision) was compared with four others, and the rates of SSIs were significantly lower when compared with infusions given 0–15 minutes before surgical incision ($p < 0.01$) and 121–180 minutes before incision ($p = 0.037$). The risk of infection was higher in patients receiving infusions 61–120 minutes before incision (odds ratio [OR], 2.3; 95% confidence interval [CI], 0.98–5.61) and for patients whose infusions were started more than 180 minutes before surgical incision (OR, 2.1; 95% CI, 0.82–5.62).[93]

In a large, prospective, multicenter study from the Trial to Reduce Antimicrobial Prophylaxis Errors (TRAPE) study group, the timing, duration, and intraoperative redosing of antimicrobial prophylaxis and risk of SSI were evaluated in 4472 patients undergoing cardiac surgery, hysterectomy, or hip or knee arthroplasty.[94] The majority of patients (90%) received antimicrobial prophylaxis per the SCIP guidelines.[41] Patients were assigned to one of four groups for analysis. Group 1 ($n = 1844$) received a cephalosporin (or other antimicrobial with a short infusion time) administered within 30 minutes before incision or vancomycin or a fluoroquinolone within one hour before incision. Group 2 ($n = 1796$) received a cephalosporin 31–60 minutes before incision or vancomycin 61–120 minutes before incision. Group 3 ($n = 644$) was given antimicrobials earlier than recommended, and group 4 ($n = 188$) received their initial antimicrobial doses after incision. The infection risk was lowest in group 1 (2.1%), followed by group 2 (2.4%) and group 3 (2.8%). The risk of infection was highest in group 4 (5.3%, $p = 0.02$ compared with group 1). When cephalosporins and other antimicrobials with short infusion times were analyzed separately ($n = 3656$), the infection rate with antimicrobials administered within 30 minutes before incision was 1.6% compared with 2.4% when antimicrobials were administered 31–60 minutes before incision ($p = 0.13$).

In a multicenter Dutch study of 1922 patients undergoing total hip arthroplasty, the lowest SSI rate was seen in patients who received the antimicrobial during the 30 minutes before incision.[95] The highest risk for infection was found in patients who received prophylaxis after the incision.

It seems intuitive that the entire antimicrobial dose should be infused before a tourniquet is inflated or before any other procedure that restricts blood flow to the surgical site is initiated; however, a study of total knee arthroplasties compared cefuroxime given 10–30 minutes before tourniquet inflation with cefuroxime given 10 minutes before tourniquet deflation and found no significant difference in SSI rates between the two groups.[96]

Overall, administration of the first dose of antimicrobial beginning within 60 minutes before surgical incision is recommended.[41,94,97] Administration of vancomycin and fluoroquinolones should begin within 120 minutes before surgical incision because of the prolonged infusion times required for these drugs. Because these drugs have long half-lives, this early administration should not compromise serum levels of these agents during most surgical procedures. Although the recent data summarized above suggest lower infection risk with antimicrobial administration beginning within 30 minutes before surgical incision, these data are not sufficiently robust to recommend narrowing the optimal window to begin infusion to 1–30 minutes before surgical incision. However, these data do suggest that antimicrobials can be administered too close to the time of incision. Although a few articles have suggested increased infection risk with administration too close to the time of incision,[93,96,97] the data presented are not convincing. In fact, all of these articles confirm the increased rate of SSI for antimicrobials given earlier than 60 minutes before incision. In one article, the infection rate for patients given an antimicrobial within 15 minutes of incision was lower than when antimicrobials were given 15–30 minutes before incision.[97]

In another article, small numbers of patients were reported, and an assertion of high infection rates for infusion within 15 minutes of incision was made, but no numeric data or p values were provided.[98] In a third article, only 15 of over 2000 patients received antimicrobials within 15 minutes before incision.[93] Earlier studies found that giving antimicrobials within 20 minutes of incision and as close as 7 minutes before incision resulted in therapeutic levels in tissue at the time of incision.[41,90,91,94,97,98]

Dosing. To ensure that adequate serum and tissue concentrations of antimicrobial agents for prophylaxis of SSIs are achieved, antimicrobial-specific pharmacokinetic and pharmacodynamic properties and patient factors must be considered when selecting a dose. One of the earliest controlled studies of antimicrobial prophylaxis in cardiac surgery found a lower rate of infection in patients with detectable concentrations of the drug in serum at the end of surgery compared with patients in whom the drug was undetectable.[99] In another study, higher levels of antimicrobial in atrial tissue at the time of starting the pump for open-heart surgery were associated with fewer infections than were lower antimicrobial concentrations.[100] In patients undergoing colectomy, infection levels were inversely related to the serum gentamicin concentration at the time of surgical closure.[17] In general, it seems advisable to administer prophylactic agents in a manner that will ensure adequate levels of drug in serum and tissue for the interval during which the surgical site is open.

Weight-based dosing. The dosing of most antimicrobials in pediatric patients is based on body weight, but the dosing of many antimicrobials in adults is not based on body weight, because it is safe, effective, and convenient to use standardized doses for most of the adult patient population. Such standardized doses avoid the need for calculations and reduce the risk for medication errors. However, in obese patients, especially those who are morbidly obese, serum and tissue concentrations of some drugs may differ from those in normal-weight patients because of pharmacokinetic alterations that depend on the lipophilicity of the drug and other factors.[101] Limited data are available on the optimal approach to dosing of antimicrobial agents for obese patients.[102,103] If weight-based dosing is warranted for obese patients, it has not been determined whether the patient's ideal body weight or total (i.e., actual) body weight should be used. In theory, using the ideal body weight as the basis for dosing a lipophilic drug (e.g., vancomycin) could result in subtherapeutic concentrations in serum and tissue, and the use of actual body weight for dosing a hydrophilic drug (e.g., an aminoglycoside) could result in excessive concentrations in serum and tissue. Pediatric patients weighing more than 40 kg should receive weight-based doses unless the dose or daily dose exceeds the recommended adult dose.[104]

Conclusive recommendations for weight-based dosing for antimicrobial prophylaxis in obese patients cannot be made because data demonstrating clinically relevant decreases in SSI rates from the use of such dosing strategies instead of standard doses in obese patients are not available in the published literature.

In a small, nonrandomized, two-phase study of morbidly obese adults undergoing gastroplasty and normal-weight adults undergoing upper abdominal surgery, blood and tissue concentrations of cefazolin after the administration of a 1-g preoperative dose were consistently lower in morbidly obese patients than in the normal-weight patients.[101] The concentrations in morbidly obese patients also were lower than the MICs needed for prophylaxis against gram-positive cocci and gram-negative rods. In the second phase of the study, adequate blood and tissue cefazolin concentrations were achieved in morbidly obese patients receiving preoperative doses of cefazolin 2 g, and the rate of SSIs was significantly lower in these patients compared with morbidly obese patients receiving 1-g doses during the first phase of the study.

While the optimal cefazolin dose has not been established in obese patients, a few pharmacokinetic studies have investigated the cefazolin concentrations in serum and tissue during surgical procedures.[13,105] Two small pharmacokinetic studies found that administering 1- or 2-g doses of cefazolin may not be sufficient to produce serum and tissue concentrations exceeding the MIC for the most common pathogens. In a small, single-center study, 38 adults undergoing Roux-en-Y gastric bypass surgery were classified by body mass index (BMI) in one of three groups.[13] All patients were given cefazolin 2 g i.v. 30–60 minutes before the incision, followed by a second 2-g i.v. dose three hours later. The mean serum drug concentration before the second dose of cefazolin was lower than the resistance breakpoint in all three BMI groups. Serum drug concentrations were lower in patients with a high BMI than in patients with lower BMI values. Tissue drug concentrations were lower than a targeted concentration of 8 μg/mL at all measurement times, except the time of skin closure in the patients with the lowest BMIs. These results suggest that a 1-g dose of cefazolin may be inadequate for obese patients undergoing gastric bypass surgery. A weakness of the literature on drug dosing in morbidly obese patients is the practice of reporting results by BMI rather than weight.

Doubling the normal dose of cephalosporins or making fewer adjustments based on renal dysfunction may produce concentrations in obese patients similar to those achieved with standard doses in normal-weight patients.[103] Considering the low cost and favorable safety profile of cefazolin, increasing the dose to 2 g for patients weighing more than 80 kg and to 3 g for those weighing over 120 kg can easily be justified.[41] For simplification, some hospitals have standardized 2-g cefazolin doses for all adult patients.

Gentamicin doses have been compared for prophylaxis only in colorectal surgery, where a single dose of gentamicin 4.5 mg/kg in combination with metronidazole was more effective in SSI prevention than multiple doses of gentamicin 1.5 mg/kg every eight hours.[16,17] In obese patients who weigh 20% above their ideal body weight, the dose of gentamicin should be calculated using the ideal body weight plus 40% of the difference between the actual and ideal weights.[106] If gentamicin will be used in combination with a parenteral antimicrobial with activity against anaerobic agents for prophylaxis, it is probably advisable to use 4.5–5 mg/kg as a single dose.[16] This dose of gentamicin has been found safe and effective in a large body of literature examining the use of single daily doses of gentamicin for therapeutic indications.[106–113] When used as a single dose for prophylaxis, the risk of toxicity from gentamicin is very low.

Obese patients are often underrepresented in clinical trials and are not currently considered a special population for whom FDA requires separate pharmacokinetic studies during antimicrobial research and development by the drug manufacturer. Obesity has been recognized as a risk factor for SSI; therefore, optimal dosing of antimicrobial prophylaxis is needed in these patients.[114] While a BMI of >30 kg/m^2 is commonly used to define obesity, the body fat percentage (>25% in men and >31% in women) may better predict SSI risk, because the BMI may not reflect body composition. In a recent prospective cohort study of 590 patients undergoing elective surgery, there was no significant difference in SSI rates in nonobese and obese patients when the BMI was used to define obesity (12.3% versus 11.6%, respectively).[115] However, when the body fat percentage (determined by bioelectrical impedance analysis) was used as the basis for identifying obesity (>25% in men and >31% in women), obese patients had a fivefold-higher risk of SSI than did nonobese patients (OR, 5.3; 95% CI, 1.2–23.1; $p = 0.03$). These findings suggest that body fat percentage is a more sensitive and precise measurement of SSI risk than is the BMI.

Redosing. Intraoperative redosing is needed to ensure adequate serum and tissue concentrations of the antimicrobial if the duration of the procedure exceeds two half-lives of the antimicrobial or there is excessive blood loss (i.e., >1500 mL).[17,41,94,116–121] The redosing interval should be measured from the time of administration of the preoperative dose, not from the beginning of the procedure. Redosing may also be warranted if there are factors that shorten the half-life of the antimicrobial agent (e.g., extensive burns). Redosing may not be warranted in patients in whom the half-life of the antimicrobial agent is prolonged (e.g., patients with renal insufficiency or renal failure). See Table 1 for antimicrobial-specific redosing recommendations.

Duration. The shortest effective duration of antimicrobial administration for preventing SSI is not known; however, evidence is mounting that postoperative antimicrobial administration is not necessary for most procedures.[6,7,41,122–124] The duration of antimicrobial prophylaxis should be less than 24 hours for most procedures. Cardiothoracic procedures for which a prophylaxis duration of up to 48 hours has been accepted without evidence to support the practice is an area that remains controversial. The duration of cardiothoracic prophylaxis in these guidelines is based on expert panel consensus because the available data do not delineate the optimal duration of prophylaxis. In these procedures, prophylaxis for the duration of the procedure and certainly for less than 24 hours is appropriate.

A 1992 meta-analysis of studies comparing first-generation cephalosporins and antistaphylococcal antimicrobials (e.g., penicillins) with second-generation cephalosporins in patients undergoing cardiothoracic surgery found a reduction in the rate of SSI with second-generation cephalosporins but no benefit from continuing surgical prophylaxis beyond 48 hours.[125] Reports published in 1980,[126] 1993,[127] 1997,[128] and 2000[129] involving seven studies that compared single-dose prophylaxis or prophylaxis only during the operation with durations of one to four days failed to show any reduction in SSIs with the longer durations of prophylaxis. In a more-recent observational four-year cohort study of 2641 patients undergoing coronary artery bypass graft (CABG) surgery, the extended use of antimicrobial prophylaxis (>48 hours) instead of a shorter duration of prophylaxis (<48 hours) failed to reduce the risk of SSI (OR, 1.2; 95% CI, 0.8–1.6).[130] Moreover, prolonged prophylaxis was associated with an increased risk of acquired antimicrobial resistance (cephalosporin-resistant Enterobacteriaceae and VRE) compared with short-term prophylaxis (OR, 1.6; 95% CI, 1.1–2.6).

There are no data to support the continuation of antimicrobial prophylaxis until all indwelling drains and intravascular catheters are removed.[19,31,32,41,131–134]

Topical Administration of Irrigations, Pastes, and Washes

I.V. and oral antimicrobial administration are the main focus of these guidelines, and these routes of administration are used for most surgical procedures addressed by these guidelines, with the exception of ophthalmic procedures, for which topical administration is the primary route of administration. Limited high-quality data are available regarding the use of antimicrobial irrigations, pastes, and washes that are administered topically. Studies published in the early 1980s demonstrated that prophylactic topical administration of antimicrobials in the surgical incision during various non-ophthalmic procedures is superior to placebo but not superior to parenteral administration, and topical administration does not increase the efficacy of parenteral antimicrobials when used in combination for prophylaxis.[135–138] Additional high-quality data on the safety and efficacy of topical antimicrobial administration as an adjunct to i.v. administration are needed to determine the role of topical antimicrobial prophylaxis.

One area of interest for topical administration of antimicrobials, mainly gentamicin and vancomycin, is application to the sternum during cardiac procedures in combination with i.v. agents to prevent mediastinitis. This strategy has been evaluated in cohort and randomized controlled studies.[139–142] While the studies found a significantly lower rate of SSI with topical antimicrobials compared with standard prophylaxis,[140] placebo,[142] and a historical control,[139] a smaller, randomized, placebo-controlled study found no difference between groups.[141]

More recently, implantable gentamicin collagen sponges failed to show any efficacy in reducing SSIs in a large prospective study of patients undergoing cardiac surgery and resulted in an increased infection rate in patients undergoing colectomy.[143,144] The safety and efficacy of topical antimicrobials have not been clearly established; therefore, routine use of this route cannot be recommended in cardiac or other procedures.[145]

Preoperative Screening and Decolonization

S. aureus is the most common pathogen causing SSIs, accounting for 30% of SSIs in the United States. Colonization with *S. aureus*, primarily in the nares, occurs in roughly one in four persons and increases the risk of SSI by 2- to 14-fold.[146–152] A national survey assessing nasal colonization with *S. aureus* in the general population conducted from 2001 through 2004 found that while the rate of colonization with *S. aureus* decreased from 32.4% in 2001–02 to 28.6% in 2003–04 ($p < 0.01$), the rate of colonization with MRSA increased from 0.8% to 1.5% ($p < 0.05$).[75]

Preoperative screening for *S. aureus* carriage and decolonization strategies have been explored as means to reduce the rate of SSIs. Anterior nasal swab cultures are most commonly used for preoperative surveillance, but screening additional sites (pharynx, groin, wounds, rectum) can increase detection rates.[153] Such preoperative surveillance swabs that can be cultured on selective or nonselective media or sent for rapid polymerase chain reaction (PCR)-based screening can be used to identify colonized patients in the preoperative period. When properly used, all of these techniques can identify MSSA and MRSA. However, not all PCR-based systems will identify both MRSA and MSSA so verification with the laboratory is needed. While many studies have focused specifically on MRSA screening in high-risk hospitalized patients in an effort to prevent MRSA SSI and hospital-acquired infections, the risk of developing an SSI remains elevated for any *S. aureus* carrier. While some authors advocate screening for MRSA carriage in the general population, the data supporting universal screening in the surgical population are more controversial.[154,155] Screening has been advocated to both identify candidates for *S. aureus* decolonization and inform the selection of optimal prophylactic antimicrobials, such as the addition of vancomycin for those colonized with MRSA.

FDA has approved intranasal mupirocin to eradicate MRSA nasal colonization in adult patients and health care workers.[156] It is noted in the prescribing information that there are insufficient data to support use in prevention of autoinfection of high-risk patients from their own nasal colonization with *S. aureus*. However, additional data have demonstrated that the use of intranasal mupirocin in nasal carriers of *S. aureus* decreases the rate of *S. aureus* infections.[157,158] One meta-analysis of seven studies focused on surgical patients only[157]; the other meta-analysis of nine studies included high-quality studies in dialysis patients.[158]

Recent studies have confirmed that *S. aureus* decolonization of the anterior nares decreases SSI rates in many surgical patients.[159] The data are most compelling in cardiac and orthopedic surgery patients. There are fewer data in general surgery patients. A large, randomized controlled trial of general, cardiac, and neurosurgical patients *(n* = 3864) revealed that prophylactic intranasal application of mupirocin did not significantly reduce the overall rate of *S. aureus* SSIs (2.3% in the mupirocin group versus 2.4% in the control group) but did decrease the rate of *S. aureus* SSI among *S. aureus* carriers (3.7% in the mupirocin group versus 5.9% in the control group).[160]

Another randomized controlled trial found no significant difference in the rate of postoperative *S. aureus* SSIs among cardiac surgery patients receiving intranasal mupirocin and those receiving placebo, but the study was limited by the small numbers of patients *(n* = 257) and reported SSIs *(n* = 5).[161] Among elective orthopedic patients undergoing implantation and other procedures, a randomized clinical trial demonstrated a nonsignificant reduction in the rate of postoperative *S. aureus* SSIs in patients receiving mupirocin *(n* = 315, 3.8%) compared with those receiving placebo *(n* = 299, 4.7%).[150]

A recent randomized, double-blind, placebo-controlled, multicenter study conducted in the Netherlands found that the use of mupirocin nasal ointment and chlorhexidine baths in identified *S. aureus* carriers reduced the risk of hospital-associated *S. aureus* infections.[162] In the study, a real-time PCR assay was used to rapidly identify *S. aureus* nasal carriers; all of the *S. aureus* isolates were susceptible to methicillin. Deep SSIs occurred in 0.9% of the mupirocin–chlorhexidine-treated group (4 of 441 patients) versus 4.4% of the placebo group (16 of 367 patients) (relative risk, 0.21; 95% CI, 0.07–0.62). The reduction in superficial SSIs was less marked (1.6% versus 3.5%; relative risk, 0.45; 95% CI, 0.18–1.11). It is plausible that this approach would be beneficial in a setting of MRSA, but it has not been proven.

Most studies conclude that the use of preoperative intranasal mupirocin in colonized patients is safe and potentially beneficial as an adjuvant to i.v. antimicrobial prophylaxis to decrease the occurrence of SSIs. However, the optimal timing and duration of administration are not standardized. In most studies, mupirocin was used for five days before the operation. While *S. aureus* resistance to mupirocin has been detected,[148,162] raising concerns about the potential for widespread problems with resistance from routine use of this agent, resistance has only rarely been seen in the preoperative setting. Low-level resistance is associated with an increased rate of failure of decolonization and has been seen in institutions that use standardized mupirocin decolonization protocols.[163] Therefore, when decolonization therapy (e.g., mupirocin) is used as an adjunctive measure to prevent *S. aureus* SSI, surveillance of susceptibility of *S. aureus* isolated from SSIs to mupirocin is recommended.[164] While universal use of mupirocin is discouraged, specific recommendations for the drug's use can be found in the cardiac and orthopedic sections of these guidelines.

Future Research

Additional research is needed in several areas related to surgical antimicrobial prophylaxis. The risks and benefits of continuing antimicrobial prophylaxis after the conclusion of the operative procedure, including dosing and duration, need to be further evaluated. Insight is needed to make specific recommendations for intraoperative repeat dosing, weight-based dosing in obese patients, and timing of presurgical antimicrobials that must be administered over a prolonged period (e.g., vancomycin, fluoroquinolones). Additional clarification is needed regarding targeted antimicrobial concentrations and intraoperative monitoring of antimicrobial serum and tissue concentrations to optimize efficacy. The role of topical administration of antimicrobial agents as a substitute for or an adjunct to i.v. antimicrobial prophylaxis needs to be further evaluated. Additional data are needed to guide the selection of antimicrobial agents for prophylaxis, particularly combination regimens, for patients with allergies to β-lactam antimicrobials. Data are also needed to devise strategies to optimize antimicrobial prophylaxis in patients and facilities with a high risk or high prevalence of resistant organisms implicated in SSIs (e.g., MRSA). Optimal strategies for screening for *S. aureus* and decolonization for certain procedures need to be identified. Finally, outcomes studies are needed to assess the impact of using quality measures and pay-for-performance incentives designed to reduce surgical morbidity and mortality.

Cardiac Procedures

Background. Cardiac procedures include CABG procedures, valve repairs, and placement of temporary or permanent implantable cardiac devices, including ventricular assist devices (VADs). SSIs, including mediastinitis and sternal wound infection, are rare but serious complications after cardiac procedures. In patients undergoing CABG, the mean frequency of SSIs depending on NHSN SSI risk index category ranges from 0.35 to 8.49 per 100 operations when donor sites are included.[165] The mean frequency of SSIs depending on NHSN SSI risk index category for patients undergoing CABG with only chest incisions ranges from 0.23 to 5.67 per 100 operations.[165] Most of these infections are superficial in depth. Patient-related and procedure-related risk factors for SSIs after cardiac procedures have been identified from several single-center cohort and case–control studies.[117,128,166–176] These include diabetes,[166,169,171–175] hyperglycemia,[177–182] peripheral vascular disease,[171,172,174] chronic obstructive pulmonary disease,[166,174,175] obesity (BMI of >30 kg/m^2),[166–168,171,173–176] heart failure,[171,172] advanced age,[117,128,166,172] involvement of internal mammary artery,[168–172] reoperation,[169–171] increased number of grafts,[171] long duration of surgery,[117,166,167,176] and *S. aureus* nasal colonization.[146,160]

Patients requiring extracorporeal membrane oxygenation (ECMO) as a bridge to cardiac or lung transplantation should be treated with a similar approach. If there is no history of colonization or previous infection, the general recommendations for SSI antimicrobial prophylaxis for the specific procedure should be followed. For ECMO patients with a history of colonization or previous infection, changing the preoperative antimicrobial prophylaxis to cover these pathogens must be considered, weighing whether the pathogen is relevant to SSIs in the planned procedure.

Organisms. Almost two thirds of organisms isolated in both adult and pediatric patients undergoing cardiac procedures are gram-positive, including *S. aureus*, coagulase-negative *staphylococcus*, and, rarely, *Propionibacterium acnes*. Gram-negative organisms are less commonly isolated in these patients and include *Enterobacter* species, *Pseudomonas aeruginosa*, *Escherichia coli*, *Klebsiella pneumoniae*, *Proteus mirabilis*, and *Acinetobacter* species.[93,139,146,183–192]

Efficacy. The SSI rate in cardiac procedures is low, but there are potential consequences if infection occurs. Multiple studies have found that antimicrobial prophylaxis in cardiac procedures lowers the occurrence of postoperative SSI up to fivefold.[125]

Choice of agent. Cephalosporins have been the most studied antimicrobials for the prevention of SSIs in cardiac procedures. Both first-generation (cefazolin) and second-generation (cefamandole and cefuroxime) cephalosporins have been shown to be effective in reducing SSI in cardiac surgery; however, the superiority of one class over another has not been proven.[125,127,193–199]

A meta-analysis comparing cephalosporins with glycopeptides (e.g., vancomycin) as antimicrobial prophylaxis regimens for cardiac procedures found a higher frequency of postoperative chest and deep-chest SSIs and a trend toward an increased risk of gram-positive SSI in the glycopeptide group but a lower frequency of SSIs caused by resistant gram-positive pathogens.[72] The routine use of vancomycin for the prevention of SSIs is not recommended, based on limited evidence of efficacy and concerns of increased glycopeptide resistance of microorganisms.[8,116] There is no clear evidence to support the use of vancomycin, alone or in combination with other antimicrobials, for routine antimicrobial prophylaxis in institutions that have a high prevalence of MRSA.[8,11,41,72,73,116,200] Vancomycin should be considered in patients who are colonized with MRSA.[41,116,201] The accepted alternative antimicrobial for β-lactam-allergic patients undergoing cardiac procedures is vancomycin or clindamycin for gram-positive coverage.[41,116,201,202] The addition of an aminoglycoside, aztreonam, or a fluoroquinolone may be prudent when gram-negative pathogens are a concern.[8,116]

Mupirocin. The proportion of infections related to *S. aureus* among patients undergoing cardiac surgery and the increase in MRSA as a cause of SSIs at some institutions have led to investigations of methods for preoperative eradication, particularly with intranasal mupirocin.[203] Readers are referred to the Common Principles section of these guidelines for discussion of the use of intranasal mupirocin. Of note, the data demonstrated a 45% reduction in *S. aureus* SSIs with the use of preoperative mupirocin among patients known to be colonized with *S. aureus* who undergo cardiac procedures.[157,193] Institutions should monitor for mupirocin resistance periodically.

Topical administration. Additional information on topical administration of antimicrobials can be found in the Common Principles section of these guidelines. Use of topical antimicrobials, mainly gentamicin or vancomycin, applied to the sternum during cardiac procedures in combination with i.v. agents to prevent mediastinitis has been evaluated in both cohort[139] and randomized controlled studies.[140–142] While the studies found a significantly lower rate of SSIs with topical antimicrobials compared with standard prophylaxis,[140] placebo,[142] and a historical control,[139] a smaller randomized, placebo-controlled study found no difference between groups.[141] More recent studies of gentamicin collagen sponges failed to show any efficacy in a large prospective study of cardiac surgery.[143] The safety and efficacy of topical antimicrobials have not been clearly established and therefore cannot be recommended for routine use in cardiac procedures.[139–142]

Cardiopulmonary bypass. Cardiopulmonary bypass (CPB) is a common surgical technique in cardiac procedures that alters the volume of distribution and bioavailability of medications administered during the procedure.[116,204,205] Several small cohort or comparative studies[128,204–213] have evaluated the serum and tissue concentrations of several routinely used antimicrobial prophylactic agents (i.e., cefazolin, cefuroxime, gentamicin, and vancomycin) in patients undergoing CPB during cardiac procedures. Until further clinical outcomes data and well-designed studies become available to inform alternative dosing strategies, routinely used doses of common antimicrobial agents should be used in patients undergoing CPB during cardiac procedures.

Duration. The optimal duration of antimicrobial prophylaxis for cardiac procedures continues to be evaluated. Data support a duration ranging from a single dose up to 24 hours postoperatively.[41,99,131,191,214–217] No significant differences were found in several small studies in patients undergoing cardiac procedures between these dosing strategies in patients primarily receiving first- or second-generation cephalosporins. Although a recent meta-analysis suggested the possibility of increased efficacy with cardiac surgical prophylaxis extending beyond 24 hours, the authors noted that the findings were limited by the heterogeneity of antimicrobial regimens used and the risk of bias in the published studies.[218] The comparisons of varying durations were performed with different antimicrobials with differing efficacy and do not support longer durations. Consequently, this meta-analysis does not provide evidence to support changing the currently accepted prophylaxis duration of less than 24 hours, particularly given the evidence from studies involving noncardiac operations. The currently accepted duration of prophylaxis for cardiac procedures is less than 24 hours, but prophylaxis should be continued for the duration of the procedure.[41,59,126–129,131,201]

Two small studies did not support the continuation of antimicrobial prophylaxis until intravascular catheters or intraaortic balloon pumps were removed, due to a lack of influence on infections or catheter colonization compared with short-course (24 hours) cefazolin or cefuroxime.[219,220] The practice of continuing antimicrobial prophylaxis until all invasive lines, drains, and indwelling catheters are removed cannot be supported due to concerns regarding the development of drug-resistant organisms, superinfections, and drug toxicity.[41,131]

Pediatric Efficacy. The rate of SSI in pediatric cardiac procedures is sometimes higher than in adult patients.[20,31,221] Significant risk factors in pediatric patients with a mediastinal SSI included the presence of other infections at the time of the procedure, young age (newborns and infants), small body size, the duration of the procedure (including CPB time), the need for an intraoperative blood transfusion, an open sternum postoperatively, the need for a reexploration procedure, the length of stay in the intensive care unit, an NNIS/NHSN risk score of 2, and the performance of emergency procedures.[20,31,221]

The organisms of concern in pediatric patients are the same as those in adult patients.[20,21,31,221] However, MRSA is rarely a concern in this population as a risk factor for SSI.[221] Pediatric patients considered at high risk for MRSA infection are those with preoperative MRSA colonization or a history of MRSA infection, neonates younger than one month of age, and neonates under three months of age who have been in the hospital since birth or have a complex cardiac disorder.[21] Strategies such as intranasal mupirocin and changes in antimicrobial prophylactic agent to vancomycin led to decreased rates of MRSA carriage and the absence of MRSA infections in one time-series evaluation; however, the overall clinical impact of these efforts is still unclear.[21,221]

No well-controlled studies have evaluated the efficacy of antimicrobial prophylaxis in pediatric patients undergoing cardiac procedures. Therefore, the efficacy of antimicrobial prophylaxis is extrapolated from adult studies and should be considered the standard of care for pediatric cardiac surgery patients.[19]

No well-designed studies or consensus has established the appropriate doses for common antimicrobial prophylactic agents for use in pediatric cardiac patients. Antibiotic doses have been extrapolated from guidelines for the prevention of bacterial endocarditis.[11] In recent evaluations, doses of cefazolin have ranged from 25 to 50 mg/kg,[19–21,31] and vancomycin doses have ranged from 10 to 20 mg/kg.[19–21,31,222–226] Gentamicin doses used in studies have included 2.5[20] and 5 mg/kg[22]; however, the study authors[22] felt that the higher dose was excessive. The expert panel recognizes that the usual total daily dose for pediatric patients older than six months can be 6.5–7.5 mg/kg and that dosing schedules for younger patients may be complicated.

Recommendations. For patients undergoing cardiac procedures, the recommended regimen is a single preincision dose of cefazolin or cefuroxime with appropriate intraoperative redosing (Table 2). Currently, there is no evidence to support continuing prophylaxis until all drains and indwelling catheters are removed. Clindamycin or vancomycin is an acceptable alternative in patients with a documented β-lactam allergy. Vancomycin should be used for prophylaxis in patients known to be colonized with MRSA. If organizational SSI surveillance shows that gram-negative organisms cause infections for patients undergoing these operations, practitioners should combine clindamycin or vancomycin with another agent (cefazolin if the patient is not β-lactam allergic; aztreonam, aminoglycoside, or single-dose fluoroquinolone if the patient is β-lactam allergic). Mupirocin should be given intranasally to all patients with documented *S. aureus* colonization. (Strength of evidence for prophylaxis = A.)

Cardiac Device Insertion Procedures

Background. Antimicrobial prophylaxis is the standard of care for patients undergoing cardiac implantable device insertion (e.g., pacemaker implantation).[227] Based on available data and perceived infection risk, antimicrobial prophylaxis is not routinely recommended for cardiac catheterization or transesophageal echocardiogram.[228]

NHSN has reported a mean SSI rate after pacemaker placement of 0.44 per 100 procedures.[165] This rate may underestimate the risk of late SSI and complications.[229] Risk factors for device-related infection after implantation of cardioverter–defibrillator systems or pacemakers identified in two large, prospective, multicenter cohort studies[230,231] and a large case–control study[232] included fever within 24 hours before implantation, temporary pacing before implantation, and early reintervention for hematoma or lead replacement[230]; corticosteroid use for more than one month during the preceding year and more than two leads in place compared with two leads[232]; and development of pocket hematoma.[231] In all of the evaluations, antimicrobial prophylaxis was found to be protective against device-related infection.[230–232] Limited data are available on the efficacy and optimal dose and duration of antimicrobial prophylaxis in patients undergoing implantation of a new pacemaker, pacing system, or other cardiac device.

A meta-analysis of 15 prospective, randomized, controlled, mainly open-label studies evaluated the effectiveness of systemic antimicrobial prophylaxis compared with controls (no antimicrobials) on infection rates after pacemaker implantation.[227] Antibiotics included penicillins or cephalosporins with a duration ranging from a single preoperative dose to four days postoperatively. A consistent and significant protective effect of antimicrobial prophylaxis was found and encouraged the routine use of antimicrobial prophylaxis in patients undergoing permanent pacemaker implantation. A prospective, single-center cohort study found a low rate (1.7%) of SSI complications with a single 2-g dose of cefazolin in patients undergoing implantation of a new pacemaker, pulse-generator replacement, or upgrading of a preexisting pacing system.[233] A notable limitation of the study was the exclusion of patients with temporary percutanous cardiac stimulators who are at high risk of infection.

A large, randomized, double-blind, placebo-controlled study found a significantly lower rate of SSI with a single 1-g dose of cefazolin (0.64%) compared with placebo (3.28%) ($p = 0.016$) given immediately before device implantation or generator replacement in a permanent pacemaker, implantable cardioverter defibrillator, or cardiac resynchronization device in a surgical operating room.[231] The expert panel noted that the cefazolin dose was not adjusted for patient weight. Recently, AHA produced evidence-based guidelines that recommend the use of a single dose of a preoperative antimicrobial.[229]

VADs are increasingly used to bridge patients to transplantation or to support individuals who do not respond to medical therapy for congestive heart failure. Very limited data exist on infection rates, and there are no published studies that demonstrate the effectiveness of preoperative antimicrobial therapy. Using 2006–08 data from the Interagency Registry for Mechanically Assisted Circulatory Support, Holman and colleagues[234] reported that most infections related to mechanical cardiac support devices were bacterial (87%), with the remainder associated with fungal (9%), viral (1%), protozoal (0.3%), or unknown (2%) causes. Driveline infections are primarily caused by staphylococcal species from the skin. Fungal organisms also play an important role in VAD infections, most notably *Candida* species, and carry a high risk of mortality. A recent survey of antimicrobial surgical prophylaxis with VADs illustrates the variability and lack of consensus with regimens, using anywhere from one to four drugs for a duration of 24–72 hours.[235] Immediate postoperative infections are caused by gram-positive organisms. Complications from long-term infections should not be confused with immediate postprocedure SSIs.[236] Based on the consensus of the expert panel, antimicrobial prophylaxis for replacement of a VAD due to ongoing or recent infection should incorporate coverage directed at the offending organism or organisms. While many centers use vancomycin plus ciprofloxacin plus fluconazole, this practice is not based on the published evidence.

Recommendation. A single dose of cefazolin or cefuroxime is recommended for device implantation or generator replacement in a permanent pacemaker, implantable cardioverter defibrillator, or cardiac resynchronization device. (Strength of evidence for prophylaxis = A.) There is limited evidence to make specific recommendations for VADs, and each practice should tailor protocols based on pathogen prevalence and local susceptibility profiles. Clindamycin or vancomycin is an acceptable alternative in patients with a documented β-lactam allergy. Vancomycin should be considered for prophylaxis in patients known to be colonized with MRSA.

Thoracic Procedures

Background. Noncardiac thoracic procedures include lobectomy, pneumonectomy, thoracoscopy, lung resection, and thoracotomy. In addition to SSIs, postoperative nosocomial pneumonia and empyema are of concern after thoracic procedures.[237]

NHSN has reported that the rate of infection associated with thoracic surgery ranges from 0.76% to 2.04%.[165] Studies have found that the reported rate of SSIs after thoracic procedures in patients receiving antimicrobial prophylaxis ranged from 0.42% to 4%.[238–241] One study found an SSI rate of 14% when prophylaxis was not used.[239] The reported rates of pneumonia and empyema with antimicrobial prophylaxis are 3–24% and 0–7%, respectively.[237,239–244]

Video-assisted thoracoscopic surgery (VATS) is commonly used for thoracic procedures. In some settings, VATS constitutes one third or more of all thoracic surgical procedures.[245] Since VATS uses small incisions, the rate of SSIs is lower compared with the rate associated with open thoracic surgical procedures.[246] A prospective cohort study ($n = 346$) confirmed a low rate of SSIs (1.7%) after minimally invasive VATS procedures.[240] An additional prospective study of 988 lung resection patients confirmed that the SSI rate was significantly lower (5.5%) in VATS patients than in open thoracotomy patients (14.3%).[247] Furthermore, SSI correlated with the duration of surgery, serum albumin, concurrent comorbidity, age, and forced expiratory volume in one second. Antimicrobial prophylaxis recommendations in this section refer to both open thoracotomy and VATS procedures. Based on available data and perceived infection risk, antimicrobial prophylaxis is not routinely recommended for chest tube insertion.

Results of a prospective cohort and case–control study revealed the following independent risk factors for pneumonia after thoracic procedures: extent of lung resection, intraoperative bronchial colonization, chronic obstructive pulmonary disease, BMI of >25 kg/m^2, induction therapy (chemotherapy, radiotherapy, or chemoradiotherapy), advanced age (≥75 years old), and stage III or IV cancer.[243,244]

Organisms. The organisms reported from SSIs in patients undergoing thoracic procedures were *S. aureus* and *S. epidermidis*.[237] Organisms isolated in patients with postoperative pneumonia included gram-positive (*Streptococcus* and *Staphylococcus* species), gram-negative (*Haemophilus influenzae*, *Enterobacter cloacae*, *K. pneumoniae*, *Acinetobacter* species, *P. aeruginosa*, and *Moraxella catarrhalis*), and fungal (*Candida* species) pathogens.[237,239–243]

Efficacy. Antimicrobial prophylaxis is the standard of care for patients undergoing noncardiac thoracic surgery, including pulmonary resection.[11,201,237] One randomized, double-blind, placebo-controlled, single-center study of patients in Spain undergoing pulmonary resection, persistent pneumothorax without thoracotomy tube before surgery, and non-pulmonary thoracic surgical procedures, excluding those involving the esophagus and exploratory thoracotomies, compared a single dose of cefazolin 1 g i.v. and placebo given 30 minutes before the procedure.[239] The study was stopped early due to the significant difference in SSI rates between groups (1.5% with cefazolin versus 14% with placebo, $p < 0.01$). No differences in the rates of pneumonia and empyema were seen between groups, but these were not endpoints of the study.

Choice of agent. There is no clear optimal choice for antimicrobial prophylaxis in thoracic procedures. The need to consider pneumonia and empyema as well as SSIs after thoracic procedures has been raised in the literature.[237,241–244] There are a limited number of small, single-center, randomized controlled or cohort studies that evaluated several antimicrobial agents. One small, randomized controlled study and one cohort study found that ampicillin–sulbactam was significantly better than cephalosporins (cefazolin and cefamandole) for preventing pneumonia.[242,243] No statistically significant difference was found between cefuroxime and cefepime in the rate of postoperative SSI, pneumonia, or empyema in a small, randomized controlled study in patients undergoing elective thoracotomy.[241] Lower rates of infections and susceptibility of all organisms were noted with cefuroxime compared with cefepime. Therefore, the study authors concluded that cefuroxime was marginally more effective and was more cost-effective than cefepime.

Duration. No clear consensus on the duration of antimicrobial prophylaxis has been established. Studies have evaluated different dosing strategies for cephalosporins or penicillins, with most studies using single doses given preoperatively within 60 minutes before surgical incision.[237,239,240,242,244] Studies found differing results when comparing agents given for 24 hours (cefepime, ampicillin–sulbactam) and 48 hours (cefuroxime, cefamandole); however, these findings may be attributable to the different antimicrobials tested.[241,243] Additional discussion on dosing is provided in the Common Principles section of these guidelines.

Recommendations. In patients undergoing thoracic procedures, a single dose of cefazolin or ampicillin–sulbactam is recommended (Appendix B). Clindamycin or vancomycin is an acceptable alternative in patients with a documented β-lactam allergy. Vancomycin should be used for prophylaxis in patients known to be colonized with MRSA. If organizational SSI surveillance shows that gram-negative organisms are associated with infections during these operations or if there is risk of gram-negative contamination of the surgical site, practitioners should combine clindamycin or vancomycin with another agent (cefazolin if the patient is not β-lactam allergic; aztreonam, aminoglycoside, or single-dose fluoroquinolone if the patient is β-lactam allergic). (Strength of evidence for prophylaxis for VATS = C; strength of evidence for prophylaxis for other thoracic procedures = A.)

Gastroduodenal Procedures

Background. The gastroduodenal procedures considered in these guidelines include resection with or without vagotomy for gastric or duodenal ulcers, resection for gastric carcinoma, revision required to repair strictures of the gastric outlet, percutaneous endoscopic gastrostomy (PEG) insertion, perforated ulcer procedures (i.e., Graham patch repair), pancreaticoduodenectomy (Whipple procedure), and bariatric surgical procedures (gastric bypass, gastric banding, gastroplasty, other restrictive procedures, biliopancreatic diversion). Studies specifically addressing antimicrobial prophylaxis for gastroesophageal reflux disease procedures (Nissen fundoplication) or highly selective vagotomy for ulcers (usually done laparoscopically) could not be identified. Antireflux procedures and highly selective vagotomy are clean procedures in contrast to essentially all other gastroduodenal procedures that are clean-contaminated. Other procedures that are generally performed using laparoscopic or endoscopic techniques (e.g., endoscopic retrograde cholangiopancreatography) are not specifically discussed in this document. Natural orifice transluminal endoscopic surgery (NOTES) is a developing operative technique using natural orifices (e.g., vagina, anus, mouth, stomach) for entry into the abdomen that leaves no visible scar.[248] No studies on antimicrobial prophylaxis using NOTES have been published. SSI rates reported in patients not receiving antimicrobial prophylaxis were 6% after vagotomy and drainage, 13% after gastric ulcer procedures, 6.8–17% after procedures for gastric cancer,[249–253] 8% for pancreaticoduodenectomy,[254] and 23.9–26% after PEG insertion.[255,256]

The stomach is an effective barrier to bacterial colonization; this is at least partially related to its acidity. The stomach and the duodenum typically contain small numbers of organisms ($<10^4$ colony-forming units [CFU]/mL), the most common of which are streptococci, lactobacilli, diphtheroids, and fungi.[257,258] Treatment with agents that increase gastric pH increases the concentration of gastric organisms.[259–261] Alterations in gastric and duodenal bacterial flora as a result of increases in gastric pH have the potential to increase the postoperative infection rate.[262,263]

The risk of postoperative infection in gastroduodenal procedures depends on a number of factors, including the gastroduodenal procedure performed. Patients who are at highest risk include those with achlorhydria, including those receiving pharmacotherapy with histamine H_2-receptor antagonists or proton-pump inhibitors,[264] gastroduodenal perforation, decreased gastric motility, gastric outlet obstruction, morbid obesity, gastric bleeding, or cancer.[265] Similar to other types of surgical procedures, risk factors for SSIs related to gastroduodenal procedures include long procedure duration,[252,266,267] performance of emergency procedures,[250,261] greater than normal blood loss,[251,252] American Society of Anesthesiologists (ASA) classification of ≥3, and late administration of antimicrobials.[268]

Organisms. The most common organisms cultured from SSIs after gastroduodenal procedures are coliforms (*E. coli*, *Proteus* species, *Klebsiella* species), *staphylococci*, *streptococci*, *enterococci*, and occasionally *Bacteroides* species.[101,269–276]

Efficacy. Randomized controlled trials have shown that prophylactic antimicrobials are effective in decreasing postoperative infection rates in high-risk patients after gastroduodenal procedures. The majority of available studies were conducted in single centers outside of the United States. Relative to other types of gastrointestinal tract procedures, the number of clinical trials evaluating antimicrobial prophylaxis for gastroduodenal procedures is limited. In placebo-controlled trials, infection rates ranged from 0% to 22% for patients receiving cephalosporins or penicillins and from 1.7% to 66% for patients receiving placebo.[270,271,273–275,277–284] The difference was significant in most studies.

Data support antimicrobial prophylaxis for patients undergoing PEG insertion.[264,285–287] A Cochrane review of systemic antimicrobial prophylaxis for PEG procedures that included 11 randomized controlled trials and 1196 patients found a statistically significant reduction in peristomal infections with antimicrobial prophylaxis (OR, 0.35; 95% CI, 0.23–0.48).[288] Two meta-analyses found statistically significant decreases in SSIs with antimicrobial prophylaxis compared with placebo or controls, from 23.9–26% to 6.4–8%, respectively.[255,256] Most well-designed, randomized controlled studies found a significant decrease in postoperative SSIs or peristomal infections with single i.v. doses of a cephalosporin or penicillin, ranging from 11% to 17%, compared with from 18% to 66% with placebo or no antimicrobials.[279–282,288] Conflicting results have been seen in studies evaluating the use of preoperative patient MRSA screening, decontamination washes and shampoos, five-day preoperative treatment with intranasal mupirocin, and single-dose teicoplanin preoperative prophylaxis to decrease postoperative MRSA infections during PEG insertion.[289,290]

While there have been no well-designed clinical trials of antimicrobial prophylaxis for patients undergoing bariatric surgical procedures, treatment guidelines support its use based on morbid obesity and additional comorbidities as risk factors for postoperative infections.[264,291] There is no consensus on the appropriate antimicrobial regimen; however, higher doses of antimicrobials may be needed for adequate serum and tissue concentrations in morbidly obese patients.[13,268,291]

A notable risk factor for SSIs after esophageal and gastroduodenal procedures is decreased gastric acidity and motility resulting from malignancy or acid-suppression therapy.[264,276] Therefore, antimicrobial prophylaxis is indicated for patients undergoing gastric cancer procedures (including gastrectomy) and gastroduodenal procedures related to gastric and duodenal ulcer disease or bariatric surgery or pancreaticoduodenectomy. Evaluations of practice for pancreaticoduodenectomy show that antimicrobials are typically given due to concerns of bile contamination. Prophylaxis for gastroduodenal procedures that do not enter the gastrointestinal tract, such as antireflux procedures, should be limited to high-risk patients due to lack of data supporting general use in all patients. Furthermore, laparoscopic antireflux procedures are associated with very low SSI rates (0.3%) compared with open antireflux procedures (1.4%), just as laparoscopic gastric bypass procedures are associated with lower rates than in open procedures (0.4% versus 1.2%).[292]

Choice of agent. The most frequently used agents for gastroduodenal procedures were first-generation[271,273,277,278,284,293–297] and second-generation[269,270,274,275,280,293,294,298] cephalosporins. No differences in efficacy between first- and second-generation cephalosporins were found. Amoxicillin–clavulanate[279,282,283,299] and ciprofloxacin[269,300] were also evaluated with similar results. Relatively few studies have compared the efficacy of different agents in reducing postoperative infection rates.

One meta-analysis recommended using a single dose of an i.v. broad-spectrum antimicrobial for SSI prophylaxis in these patients,[256] while another found no differences between penicillin- or cephalosporin-based regimens and three-dose or single-dose regimens.[255] In a comparative study, oral or i.v. ciprofloxacin and i.v. cefuroxime were similarly effective in upper gastrointestinal procedures, including gastrectomy, vagotomy, and fundoplication.[300] No differences in efficacy were seen between ceftriaxone and combination ceftriaxone and metronidazole for PEG insertion in pediatric patients.[301] An open-label study found a significant decrease in local peristomal and systemic infection (i.e., pneumonia) after PEG insertion after a single 1-g i.v. dose of ceftriaxone was given 30 minutes before surgery when compared with placebo (13.3% and 36.3%, respectively; $p < 0.05$).[281] No differences were noted between cefotaxime and piperacillin–tazobactam for PEG SSIs.[288] Ampicillin–sulbactam and cefazolin had equal efficacy in gastrectomy.[253] One study found that piperacillin–tazobactam in combination with ciprofloxacin or gentamicin was the most active regimen against bacteria recovered from bile in pancreatoduodenectomy patients.[302]

Duration. The majority of studies evaluated a single dose of cephalosporin or penicillin.[256,279–284,288,290,297] The available data indicate that single-dose and multiple-dose regimens are similarly effective. Three studies compared single- and multiple-dose regimens of cefamandole,[294] amoxicillin–cluvulanate,[299] and ampicillin–sulbactam and cefazolin.[253] There were no significant differences in SSI rates. Multiple-dose regimens of first-generation (cefazolin) or second-generation (cefotiam) cephalosporins of four days, operative day only, and three days in duration did not differ in overall SSI rates.[295]

Recommendations. Antimicrobial prophylaxis in gastroduodenal procedures should be considered for patients at highest risk for postoperative infections, including risk factors such as increased gastric pH (e.g., patients receiving acid-suppression therapy), gastroduodenal perforation, decreased gastric motility, gastric outlet obstruction, gastric bleeding, morbid obesity, ASA classification of ≥3, and cancer.

A single dose of cefazolin is recommended in procedures during which the lumen of the intestinal tract is entered (Table 2). (Strength of evidence for prophylaxis = A.) A single dose of cefazolin is recommended in clean procedures, such as highly selective vagotomy, and antireflux procedures only in patients at high risk of postoperative infection due to the presence of the above risk factors. (Strength of evidence for prophylaxis = C.) Alternative regimens for patients with β-lactam allergy include clindamycin or vancomycin plus gentamicin, aztreonam, or a fluoroquinolone. Higher doses of antimicrobials are uniformly recommended in morbidly obese patients undergoing bariatric procedures. Higher doses of antimicrobials should be considered in significantly overweight patients undergoing gastroduodenal and endoscopic procedures.

Biliary Tract Procedures

Background. Biliary tract procedures include cholecystectomy, exploration of the common bile duct, and choledochoenterostomy. These guidelines pertain only to patients undergoing biliary tract procedures with no evidence of acute biliary tract infection and to patients with community-acquired acute cholecystitis of mild-to-moderate severity. As noted in the Common Principles section, patients receiving therapeutic antimicrobials for an infection before surgery should be given additional antimicrobial prophylaxis before surgery.

These guidelines do not address patients requiring biliary tract procedures for more-severe infections, including community-acquired acute cholecystitis with severe physiological disturbance, advanced age, or immunocompromised state; acute cholangitis; and health-care-associated or nosocomial biliary infections. These biliary tract infections are treated as complicated intraabdominal infections.[303] All patients with a suspected biliary tract infection who undergo biliary tract surgery should receive preoperative i.v. antimicrobials.

The majority of published literature regarding SSIs in biliary tract procedures focuses on cholecystectomy.

The overall reported rate of postoperative infection in open biliary tract procedures with antimicrobial prophylaxis is 1–19%.[292,304–311] Infection rates after laparoscopic cholecystectomy range from 0% to approximately 4% in patients without antimicrobial prophylaxis[308,312–320] and from 0% to 7% with prophylaxis.[292,304–323] Several studies found that laparoscopic cholecystectomy SSI rates were significantly lower than those associated with open cholecystectomy.[292,306–311]

Risk factors associated with postoperative SSIs after biliary procedures include performance of emergency procedures,[305] diabetes,[305,306,311,315,317] longer procedure duration (over 120 minutes),[305,317,324] intraoperative gallbladder rupture,[305] age of >70 years,[6,311,315,317,325] open cholecystectomy,[7,311] conversion of laparoscopic to open cholecystectomy,[7] higher ASA classification (≥3),[306,310,317] episode of biliary colic within 30 days before the procedure,[315,316] reintervention in less than a month for noninfectious complications,[310] acute cholecystitis,[6,7,306] bile spillage,[7] jaundice,[6,7,306] pregnancy,[7] nonfunctioning gallbladder,[6] and immunosuppression.[7]

The biliary tract is usually sterile. Patients with bacteria in the bile at the time of surgery may be at higher risk of postoperative infection[305,326,327]; however, some studies have found no association between the presence of bacteria in the bile and infection.[305,315,316,319,321] Obesity (a BMI of >30 kg/m^2) was found to be a risk factor in some studies[306] but not in others.[315,319] Laparoscopic cholecystectomy was associated with a significantly decreased risk for SSI.[292,310,324,325]

Organisms. The organisms most commonly associated with infection after biliary tract procedures include *E. coli, Klebsiella* species, and enterococci; less frequently, other gram-negative organisms, streptococci, and staphylococci are isolated.[305,306,312,315,316,318,319,321,326,328–338] Anaerobes are occasionally reported, most commonly *Clostridium* species.

Recent studies have documented increasing antimicrobial resistance in the causative pathogens in biliary tract infections and other intra-abdominal infections, with up to 40% of *E. coli* isolates resistant to ampicillin–sulbactam and fluoroquinolones.[339–341] Due to this increasing resistance of *E. coli* to fluoroquinolones and ampicillin–sulbactam, local population susceptibility profiles should be reviewed to determine the optimal antimicrobials for SSI prevention in biliary tract procedures.

Efficacy. Numerous studies have evaluated the use of prophylactic antimicrobials during biliary tract procedures, with a focus on laparoscopic cholecystectomy. Laparoscopic cholecystectomy has replaced open cholecystectomy as the standard of practice because of the reduction in recovery time and shorter hospital stay. The majority of studies of antimicrobial prophylaxis for laparoscopic cholecystectomy were underpowered and varied in control groups used (placebo, active, or no treatment), follow-up (from 30 to 60 days, while some studies did not clearly define length of time), and how SSIs were detected and reported.[308,312–316,318,319,321,322] Some studies included patients who were converted from laparoscopic to open cholecystectomy and others did not.

A large, multicenter, quality-assurance study in Germany assessed the effectiveness of antimicrobial prophylaxis in laparoscopic and open cholecystectomies.[308] This study included 4477 patients whose antimicrobial choice and dosage regimens were at the discretion of the medical center and surgeon. Antimicrobials used included first-, second-, and third-generation cephalosporins or penicillins alone or in combination with metronidazole, gentamicin, or both metronidazole and gentamicin. The most common cephalosporin used was ceftriaxone, allowing its data to be separated from data for other antimicrobials. Antimicrobial prophylaxis was administered to 2217 patients (ceftriaxone [n = 787 laparoscopic and n = 188 open] and other antimicrobials [n = 229 laparoscopic and n = 229 open]); none was given to 1328 laparoscopic and 932 open cholecystectomy patients. Significantly lower overall infectious complications occurred in patients receiving antimicrobial prophylaxis (0.8% ceftriaxone and 1.2% other antimicrobials), compared with 5% of those who received no prophylaxis ($p < 0.05$). The overall rates of infectious complications were 0.6%, 0.8%, and 3.3% in patients undergoing laparoscopic cholecystectomy receiving ceftriaxone, other antimicrobials, and no prophylaxis, respectively, and 1.6%, 3.9%, and 7.4%, respectively, for patients undergoing open cholecystectomy. Significantly lower rates of SSIs and postoperative pneumonia were noted in patients receiving antimicrobials compared with those who did not receive prophylaxis ($p < 0.05$). SSI rates were significantly decreased in laparoscopic cholecystectomy patients who received ceftriaxone (0.1%) or other antimicrobials (0.2%) compared with those who received no antimicrobial prophylaxis (1.6%). SSI rates were significantly decreased in open cholecystectomy patients who received ceftriaxone (1.0%) or other antimicrobials (2.6%) compared with those who received no antimicrobial prophylaxis (4.4%). The study authors concluded that antimicrobial prophylaxis should be administered to all patients undergoing cholecystectomy, regardless of approach. The study had several limitations, including lack of randomization, lack of adequate controls, and lack of clear definition of patient selection for the antimicrobial regimens. The statistical analysis was not clearly defined. The study appears to have compared only the use and lack of use of antimicrobials (with ceftriaxone and other antimicrobials combined for analysis) and did not specifically compare the laparoscopic and open approaches.

The findings of this study contrast with those of several other published studies. A meta-analysis of 15 randomized controlled studies evaluated the need for antimicrobial prophylaxis in elective laparoscopic cholecystectomy for patients at low risk of infection.[313] Low risk was defined as not having any of the following: acute cholecystitis, a history of acute cholecystitis, common bile duct calculi, jaundice, immune suppression, and prosthetic implants. A total of 2961 patients were enrolled in the studies, including 1494 who received antimicrobial prophylaxis, primarily with cephalosporins, vancomycin, fluoroquinolones, metronidazole, and amoxicillin–clavulanate, and 1467 controls receiving placebo or no treatment. No significant difference was found in the rates of infectious complications (2.07% in patients receiving antimicrobial prophylaxis versus 2.45% in controls) or SSIs (1.47% in patients receiving antimicrobial prophylaxis versus 1.77% in controls). The authors of the meta-analysis concluded that antimicrobial prophylaxis was not necessary for low-risk patients undergoing elective laparoscopic cholecystectomy. An additional meta-analysis of 9 randomized controlled trials (n = 1437) also concluded that prophylactic antimicrobials do not prevent infections in low-risk patients undergoing laparoscopic cholecystectomy.[342]

A small, prospective, nonrandomized study compared the use of cefotaxime 1 g i.v. during surgery with an additional two i.v. doses given eight hours apart after surgery (n = 80) with no antimicrobial prophylaxis (n = 86) in patients undergoing elective laparoscopic cholecystectomy with accidental or incidental gallbladder rupture and spillage of bile.[317] Patients who had spillage of gallstone calculi or whose operations were converted to open operations were excluded from the study. The rate of SSIs did not significantly differ between treatment groups (2.5% with antimicrobials versus 3.4% without antimicrobial prophylaxis). Based on results of multivariate analysis, routine antimicrobial prophylaxis was not recommended for these patients unless they were diabetic, were older than 60 years, or had an ASA classification of ≥3 or the duration of the procedure exceeded 70 minutes.

Current data do not support antimicrobial prophylaxis for low-risk patients undergoing elective laparoscopic cholecystectomies or those with incidental or accidental gallbladder rupture. Antimicrobial prophylaxis should be considered for patients at high risk of infection, including those undergoing open cholecystectomy, as described above, or who are considered to be at high risk for conversion to an open procedure.

Choice of agent. The data do not indicate a significant difference among first-, second-, and third-generation cephalosporins. First-generation,[307,308,312,315,319,323,330,336,338,343,344] second-generation,[308,314,315,318,323,327–329,331,332,335,344–352] and third-generation[308,309,315–317,321,322,332,333,338,349,353,354] cephalosporins have been studied more extensively than other antimicrobials. Limited data are available for ampicillin with gentamicin,[355] piperacillin,[356] amoxicillin–clavulanate,[305,338,351,354] ciprofloxacin,[320,333,352,357] and cephalosporins or penicillins alone or in combination with metronidazole, gentamicin, or both metronidazole and gentamicin.[308]

Several studies have compared first-generation cephalosporins with second- or third-generation agents.[315,336,338,344–347,353,358] With one exception,[347] there was no significant difference in efficacy among agents. Other studies found no significant differences in efficacy between ampicillin and cefamandole,[335] ciprofloxacin and ceftriaxone,[333] amoxicillin–clavulanate and cefotaxime,[354] amoxicillin–clavulanate and cefamandole,[351] ceftriaxone and ceftazidime,[321] and oral and i.v. ciprofloxacin and i.v. cefuroxime.[352,357] One study found that i.v. ampicillin–sulbactam was associated with significantly lower rates of infection compared with cefuroxime[306] and that patients treated with oral ceftibuten had significantly lower infection rates than those who received amoxicillin–clavulanate.[338]

Duration. The effect of duration of prophylaxis on outcome has been evaluated. A single dose of a cephalosporin was compared with multiple doses in several studies; no significant differences in efficacy were found.[327,329,330,348,349,353,359] The largest study compared one dose of cefuroxime with three doses in 1004 patients with risk factors for infection who were undergoing biliary tract surgery.[327] There was no significant difference in the rates of minor or major SSIs between the single- and multiple-dose groups. In the majority of studies, one dose of an antimicrobial was administered at induction of anesthesia,[306,312,338,352,354] within 30 minutes before incision,[338] or 1[315,316,320,321] or 2[338] hours before incision. Additional doses were given as follows: one dose 12 hours after administration of the initial dose,[352] two doses 12 and 24 hours after administration of the initial dose,[338] two doses every 6[338] or 8[317,319] hours after surgery, and one dose 24 hours after surgery[315] and five days after surgery.[352] In one study, a second dose of amoxicillin–clavulanate or cefotaxime was administered for procedures lasting longer than 4 hours.[354]

Recommendations. A single dose of cefazolin should be administered in patients undergoing open biliary tract procedures (Table 2). (Strength of evidence for prophylaxis = A.) Alternatives include ampicillin–sulbactam and other cephalosporins (cefotetan, cefoxitin, and ceftriaxone). Alternative regimens for patients with β-lactam allergy include clindamycin or vancomycin plus gentamicin, aztreonam, or a fluoroquinolone; or metronidazole plus gentamicin or a fluoroquinolone.

Antimicrobial prophylaxis is not necessary in low-risk patients undergoing elective laparoscopic cholecystectomies. (Strength of evidence against prophylaxis for low-risk patients = A.) Antimicrobial prophylaxis is recommended in patients undergoing laparoscopic cholecystectomy who have an increased risk of infectious complications. Risk factors include performance of emergency procedures, diabetes, anticipated procedure duration exceeding 120 minutes, risk of intraoperative gallbladder rupture, age of >70 years, open cholecystectomy, risk of conversion of laparoscopic to open cholecystectomy, ASA classification of ≥3, episode of biliary colic within 30 days before the procedure, reintervention in less than a month for noninfectious complications of prior biliary operation, acute cholecystitis, anticipated bile spillage, jaundice, pregnancy, nonfunctioning gallbladder, and immunosuppression. Because some of these risk factors cannot be determined before the surgical intervention, it may be reasonable to give a single dose of antimicrobial prophylaxis to all patients undergoing laparoscopic cholecystectomy. (Strength of evidence for prophylaxis for high-risk patients = A.)

Appendectomy Procedures

Background. Cases of appendicitis can be described as complicated or uncomplicated on the basis of the pathology. Patients with uncomplicated appendicitis have an acutely inflamed appendix. Complicated appendicitis includes perforated or gangrenous appendicitis, including peritonitis or abscess formation. Because complicated appendicitis is treated as a complicated intra-abdominal infection,[303] it has not been addressed separately in these guidelines. All patients with a suspected clinical diagnosis of appendicitis, even those with an uncomplicated case, should receive appropriate preoperative i.v. antimicrobials for SSI prevention, which, due to the common microbiology encountered, requires similar antimicrobial choices to those used to treat complicated appendicitis.

Approximately 80% of patients with appendicitis have uncomplicated disease.[59] SSI has been reported in 9–30% of patients with uncomplicated appendicitis who do not receive prophylactic antimicrobials, though some reports suggest lower complication rates in children with uncomplicated appendicitis.[165,360–365] Mean SSI rates for appendectomy reported in the most recent NHSN report (2006–08) were 1.15%

(60 of 5211) for NHSN risk index categories 0 and 1 versus 3.47% (23 of 663) for NHSN risk index categories 2 and 3.[165] Laparoscopic appendectomy has been reported to produce lower rates of incisional (superficial and deep) SSIs than open appendectomy in adults and children in multiple meta-analyses and several randomized clinical trials.[292,310,366–371] However, the rate of organ/space SSIs (i.e., intra-abdominal abscesses) was significantly increased with laparoscopic appendectomy.

Organisms. The most common microorganisms isolated from SSIs after appendectomy are anaerobic and aerobic gram-negative enteric organisms. *Bacteroides fragilis* is the most commonly cultured anaerobe, and *E. coli* is the most frequent aerobe, indicating that the bowel flora constitute a major source for pathogens.[59,372,373] Aerobic and anaerobic streptococci, *Staphylococcus* species, and *Enterococcus* species also have been reported. *P. aeruginosa* has been reported infrequently.

Efficacy. Antibiotic prophylaxis is generally recognized as effective in the prevention of postoperative SSIs in patients undergoing appendectomy when compared with placebo.[374]

Choice of agent. Randomized controlled trials have failed to identify an agent that is clearly superior to other agents in the prophylaxis of postappendectomy infectious complications. An appropriate choice for SSI prophylaxis in uncomplicated appendicitis would be any single agent or combination of agents that provides adequate gram-negative and anaerobic coverage. The second-generation cephalosporins with anaerobic activity and a first-generation cephalosporin plus metronidazole are the recommended agents on the basis of cost and tolerability. Given the relatively equivalent efficacy between agents, a cost-minimization approach is reasonable; the choice of agents should be based on local drug acquisition costs and antimicrobial sensitivity patterns.

A wide range of antimicrobials have been evaluated for prophylaxis in uncomplicated appendicitis. The most commonly used agents were cephalosporins. In general, a second-generation cephalosporin with anaerobic activity (cefoxitin or cefotetan) or third-generation cephalosporins with partial anaerobic activity (cefotaxime) were effective, with postoperative SSI rates of <5% in most studies.[364,375–381]

Piperacillin 2 g was comparable to cefoxitin 2 g in a well-controlled study.[381] Metronidazole used alone was less effective than cefotaxime, with infection rates above 10%.[376] However, when metronidazole was combined with cefazolin, ampicillin,[382] or gentamicin,[378,383] the post-operative SSI rates were 3–6%.

A double-blind, randomized, controlled trial was conducted at two hospitals to evaluate the effect of metronidazole, which is effective against most anaerobes, and cefazolin, which is effective against many aerobic organisms, singly and in combination, on the rate of sepsis after appendectomy.[384] Patients were randomized into one of four groups: metronidazole and placebo, cefazolin and placebo, metronidazole and cefazolin, or double placebo. Patients with generalized peritonitis were excluded for ethical reasons. Treatment was started before the procedure and continued every 8 hours for 24 hours. All patients in the trial were followed for about two weeks after discharge from the hospital, and their surgical sites were inspected. A total of 271 patients were assessed. Sepsis rates at the two hospitals were similar. Patients who received both cefazolin and metronidazole had a significantly lower infection rate compared with the other groups.[384] Consistent with the antibacterial spectrum of the agents, a prospective study of antimicrobial prophylaxis for colorectal procedures found that the combination of metronidazole with aztreonam did not show adequate coverage of gram-positive organisms.[385] The Common Principles section of these guidelines provides additional considerations for weight-based dosing.

Duration. In most of the studies of second- or third-generation cephalosporins or metronidazole combinations, a single dose[376–378,380,383] or two or three doses[364,379,382] were given. Although direct comparisons were not made, there was no discernible difference in postoperative SSI rates between single-dose and multidose administration in most studies. A randomized trial specifically comparing different durations of regimens found no statistical difference between a single preoperative dose, three doses (preoperative dose plus two additional doses), or a five-day regimen.[386] A large cohort study found that single doses of metronidazole and gentamicin in patients undergoing open appendectomy were effective and sufficient in decreasing the SSI rate.[387]

Pediatric Efficacy. In pediatric patients, as with adults, preoperative determination of complicated versus uncomplicated appendicitis is difficult. A comprehensive review is not provided here, but this topic has been addressed by SIS.[388]

Two pediatric studies demonstrated no difference in SSI rates between placebo and several antimicrobials. The first study compared metronidazole, penicillin plus tobramycin, and piperacillin.[389] The second study compared single-dose metronidazole and single-dose metronidazole plus cefuroxime.[390] A meta-analysis including both adult and pediatric studies found that for pediatric patients, antimicrobial prophylaxis trended toward being beneficial, but the results were not statistically significant.[374] A retrospective chart review questioned the routine need for antimicrobial prophylaxis in children with simple appendicitis, due to relatively low infection rates in children not receiving prophylaxis.[365] However, these and other study authors have suggested antimicrobial prophylaxis may be considered due to the morbidity associated with infectious complications (e.g., prolonged hospitalization, readmission, reoperation) and due to the inability to preoperatively identify appendicitis.

As a single agent, metronidazole was no more effective than placebo in two double-blind studies that included children 10 years of age or older[360] and 15 years of age or older.[363] In a randomized study that included pediatric patients, ceftizoxime and cefamandole were associated with significantly lower infection rates and duration of hospitalization than placebo.[391] Both cefoxitin and a combination of gentamicin and metronidazole were associated with a lower rate of postoperative infection in a randomized study that included pediatric patients younger than 16 years.[378] Second-generation cephalosporins with anaerobic activity (cefoxitin or cefotetan) and third-generation cephalosporins with anaerobic activity (cefotaxime) were effective, with postoperative infection rates of <5% in two studies that included pediatric patients younger than 12 years.[364,378,379] A single dose of gentamicin with clindamycin was found to be safe and effective in children with simple appendicitis.[392]

Recommendations. For uncomplicated appendicitis, the recommended regimen is a single dose of a cephalosporin with anaerobic activity (cefoxitin or cefotetan) or a single dose of a first-generation cephalosporin (cefazolin) plus metronidazole (Table 2). For β-lactam-allergic patients, alternative regimens include (1) clindamycin plus gentamicin, aztreonam, or a fluoroquinolone and (2) metronidazole plus gentamicin or a fluoroquinolone (ciprofloxacin or levofloxacin). (Strength of evidence for prophylaxis = A.)

Small Intestine Procedures

Background. Small intestine procedures, or small bowel surgery as defined by NHSN, include incision or resection of the small intestine, including enterectomy with or without intestinal anastomosis or enterostomy, intestinal bypass, and strictureoplasty; it does not include small-to-large bowel anastomosis.

The risk of SSI in small bowel surgery is variable. The Surgical Site Infection Surveillance Service in England (data collected by 168 hospitals in 13 categories of surgical procedures between 1997 and 2002) reported an SSI rate of 8.9% (94 of 1056).[393] Mean SSI rates for small bowel procedures reported in the most recent NHSN report (2006–08) were 3.44% for NHSN risk index category 0 versus 6.75% for NHSN risk index categories 1, 2, and 3. A study of 1472 patients undergoing bowel surgery (small bowel and colon) at 31 U.S. academic medical centers between September and December 2002 found an SSI rate of 8.7% for all wound categories. For patients with clean-contaminated wounds, the SSI rate was 7.9%; for those with contaminated or dirty-infected wounds, the SSI rates were 12.0% and 20.4%, respectively.[394]

In a study of 178 penetrating stomach and small bowel injuries, 94% of which were operated on within six hours of presentation, SSIs occurred in nearly 20% of cases. When associated colon injuries were excluded, SSIs occurred in 16% of gastric injuries and 13% of small bowel injuries. Although 74% of patients received antimicrobials, the specific timing of antimicrobial administration was not provided.[395] Other studies of small bowel injury confirm similar SSI rates.[396–400]

Antimicrobial prophylaxis is recommended for small bowel surgery, based on inferring effectiveness from other clean-contaminated procedures. No specific prospective randomized studies could be identified that addressed antimicrobial prophylaxis for small bowel surgery. Antimicrobial prophylaxis for small bowel surgical procedures related to a diagnosis of complicated intra-abdominal infection is not addressed separately in these guidelines, as antimicrobial therapy for established intraabdominal infection should be initiated preoperatively.

Organisms. The most common microorganisms isolated from SSIs after small bowel surgery are aerobic gram-negative enteric organisms. Among the species isolated from patients with SSI after small intestine surgery are gram-negative bacilli of gastrointestinal enteric origin (aerobic and anaerobic) and gram-positive species, such as streptococci, staphylococci, and enterococci, which is consistent with similar studies.[401] *E. coli* is the most frequently identified aerobe, indicating that the bowel flora constitute a major source of pathogens. Aerobic and anaerobic streptococci, *Staphylococcus* species, and *Enterococcus* species also have been reported.

The microbiology of 2280 SSIs after upper or lower abdominal surgery conducted from 1999 to 2006 was described in the Prevalence of Infections in Spanish Hospitals (EPINE) study.[402] The most frequent microorganisms isolated were *E. coli* (28%), *Enterococcus* species (15%), *Streptococcus* species (8%), *P. aeruginosa* (7%), and *S. aureus* (5%; resistant to methicillin, 2%). The microbiology of SSIs after upper abdominal tract surgery did not show any significant differences compared with SSIs of the lower tract, though there were relatively more staphylococci, *K. pneumoniae*, *Enterobacter* species, *Acinetobacter* species, and *Candida albicans* isolates and fewer *E. coli*, *B. fragilis*, and *Clostridium* species in the upper abdominal surgery group.[402]

Efficacy. Antibiotic prophylaxis is generally recognized as effective in the prevention of postoperative SSIs in patients undergoing small bowel surgery when compared with placebo. However, there are no prospective placebo-controlled trials to definitively establish the efficacy of prophylactic antimicrobials in this patient population.

Choice of agent. The antimicrobials selected for prophylaxis must cover the expected pathogens for the small intestine. The microbial ecology of the proximal small intestine (i.e., jejunum) is similar to that of the duodenum, whereas the microbial flora of the ileum are similar to those of the colon. In patients with small intestine obstruction, the microbial flora are similar to those of the colon.

No randomized controlled trials have confirmed that one antimicrobial agent is superior to other agents for SSI prophylaxis in small bowel surgery. An appropriate antimicrobial choice for SSI prophylaxis in small bowel surgery is any single agent or combination of agents that provides adequate coverage for the small intestinal microbes. In patients with small bowel obstruction, additional coverage of anaerobic bacteria is also desirable.

For small intestine procedures with no evidence of obstruction, a first-generation cephalosporin (cefazolin) is recommended. For patients with small intestine obstruction, a first-generation cephalosporin with metronidazole or a second-generation cephalosporin with anaerobic activity (cefoxitin or cefotetan) is the recommended agent. The choice of agents should be based on local drug acquisition costs and antimicrobial sensitivity patterns. The Common Principles section of these guidelines provides additional considerations for weight-based dosing.

Duration. Preoperative dosing of antimicrobials for SSI prevention, with additional intraoperative antimicrobial dosing dependent on the duration of the operation and no postoperative dosing, is recommended for patients undergoing small bowel surgery.

Pediatric Efficacy. In pediatric patients, as with adults, antimicrobial prophylaxis for SSI prevention in small bowel surgery is recommended.

Recommendations. For small bowel surgery without obstruction, the recommended regimen is a first-generation cephalosporin (cefazolin) (Table 2). For small bowel surgery with intestinal obstruction, the recommended regimen is a cephalosporin with anaerobic activity (cefoxitin or cefotetan) or the combination of a first-generation cephalosporin (cefazolin) plus metronidazole. For β-lactam-allergic patients, alternative regimens include (1) clindamycin plus gentamicin, aztreonam, or a fluoroquinolone and (2) metronidazole plus gentamicin or a fluoroquinolone (ciprofloxacin or levofloxacin). (Strength of evidence for prophylaxis = C.)

Hernia Repair Procedures (Hernioplasty and Herniorrhaphy)

Background. All patients who undergo hernioplasty (prosthetic mesh repair of hernia) or herniorrhaphy (suture repair of hernia) should receive appropriate preoperative i.v. antimicrobials for SSI prevention. The risk of SSIs is higher in hernioplasty compared with herniorrhaphy.[403] There is a significant risk of requiring prosthetic mesh removal in hernioplasty patients who develop an SSI, and determination of whether mesh placement will be required for hernia repair is not always possible in the preoperative period.

Mean SSI rates for herniorrhaphy reported in the most recent NHSN report (2006–08) were 0.74% (21 of 2852) for NHSN risk index category 0, 2.42% (81 of 3348) for NHSN risk index category 1, and 5.25% (67 of 1277) for NHSN risk index categories 2 and 3.[165]

A Cochrane meta-analysis of 17 randomized trials *(n* = 7843; 11 hernioplasty trials, 6 herniorrhaphy trials) in elective open inguinal hernia repair reported SSI rates of 3.1% versus 4.5% in the antimicrobial prophylaxis and control groups, respectively (OR, 0.64; 95% CI, 0.50–0.82).[404] The subgroup of patients with herniorrhaphy had SSI rates of 3.5% and 4.9% in the prophylaxis and control groups, respectively (OR, 0.71; 95% CI, 0.51–1.00). The subgroup of patients with hernioplasty had SSI rates of 2.4% and 4.2% in the prophylaxis and control groups, respectively (OR, 0.56; 95% CI, 0.38–0.81).

A meta-analysis of nine randomized trials of open hernioplasty for inguinal hernia documented SSI rates of 2.4% (39 of 1642) in the antimicrobial group and 4.2% (70 of 1676) in the control group. Antibiotics showed a protective effect in preventing SSI after mesh inguinal hernia repair (OR, 0.61; 95% CI, 0.40–0.92). Antibiotic prophylaxis did reduce the rate of SSI in hernia patients undergoing mesh hernioplasty.[405]

Based on the results of these two systematic reviews, preoperative antimicrobial prophylaxis for SSI prevention is recommended for both herniorrhaphy and hernioplasty. Compared with open hernia repair, laparoscopic hernia repair has been reported to produce lower rates of incisional (superficial and deep) SSIs in randomized clinical trials.[406–408] In a recent multicenter randomized trial of laparoscopic versus open ventral incisional hernia repair *(n* = 162), SSI was significantly less common in the laparoscopic group than in the open repair group (2.8% versus 21.9%; OR, 10.5; 95% CI, 2.3–48.2; $p = 0.003$).[409] A meta-analysis of eight randomized trials comparing laparoscopic and open incisional or ventral hernia repair with mesh revealed that laparoscopic hernia repair was associated with decreased SSI rates (relative risk, 0.22; 95% CI, 0.09–0.54) and a trend toward fewer infections requiring mesh removal.[410]

Organisms. The most common microorganisms isolated from SSIs after herniorrhaphy and hernioplasty are aerobic gram-positive organisms. Aerobic streptococci, *Staphylococcus* species, and *Enterococcus* species are common, and MRSA is commonly found in prosthetic mesh infections.[411]

Efficacy. Antibiotic prophylaxis is generally recognized as effective when compared with placebo in the prevention of postoperative SSIs in patients undergoing herniorrhaphy and hernioplasty.

Choice of agent. Randomized controlled trials have failed to identify an agent that is clearly superior to other agents for SSI prophylaxis in hernia repair. A first-generation cephalosporin is the recommended agent on the basis of cost and tolerability. The Common Principles section of these guidelines provides additional considerations for weight-based dosing.

Duration. Based on the evidence to date, a single preoperative dose of antimicrobial is recommended in hernioplasty and herniorrhaphy, with redosing as recommended in the Common Principles section of these guidelines (if the procedure duration exceeds the recommended redosing interval from the time of initiation of the preoperative dose or if there is prolonged or excessive bleeding).

Recommendations. For hernioplasty and herniorrhaphy, the recommended regimen is a single dose of a first-generation cephalosporin (cefazolin) (Table 2). For patients known to be colonized with MRSA, it is reasonable to add a single preoperative dose of vancomycin to the recommended agent. For β-lactam-allergic patients, alternative regimens include clindamycin and vancomycin. (Strength of evidence for prophylaxis = A.)

Colorectal Procedures

Background. SSIs have been reported to occur in approximately 4–10% of patients undergoing colon procedures, 3–7% in small bowel procedures, and 3–27% in patients after rectal procedures, based on the risk index.[165] However, when patients are followed carefully in clinical trials, rates tend to be considerably higher (17–26%).[412] Other septic complications, such as fecal fistula, intra-abdominal abscesses, peritonitis, and septicemia, are serious concerns but are much less common.[413] Infectious complication rates range from 30% to 60% without antimicrobial prophylaxis[59,414] and are <10% with appropriate antimicrobial prophylaxis. A pooled analysis of clinical trials of antimicrobial prophylaxis in colon procedures demonstrated that antimicrobial use significantly reduced mortality rates (11.2% for control versus 4.5% for treatment) and SSI rates.[415]

The type and duration of the procedure can affect the risk of infection. Rectal resection is associated with a higher risk of infection than is intraperitoneal colon resection.[416–418] Other risk factors include extended procedure duration (e.g., >3.5 hours),[59,412,418,419] impaired host defenses,[418] age of >60 years,[418] hypoalbuminemia,[419,420] bacterial or fecal contamination of the surgical site,[418,420] inadvertent perforation or spillage,[412,421] corticosteroid therapy,[419] perioperative transfusion of packed red blood cells,[394,418] hypothermia,[422] hyperglycemia,[423,424] and obesity.[412,418]

Organisms. The infecting organisms in colorectal procedures are derived from the bowel lumen, where there are high concentrations of organisms. *B. fragilis* and other obligate anaerobes are the most frequently isolated organisms from the bowel, with concentrations 1,000–10,000 times higher than those of aerobes.[425] *E. coli* is the most common aerobe. *B. fragilis* and *E. coli* comprise approximately 20–30% of the fecal mass. They are the most frequently isolated pathogens from infected surgical sites after colon procedures.

Efficacy. Results from randomized controlled trials and a Cochrane review of 182 studies of over 30,000 patients support the routine use of prophylactic antimicrobials in all patients undergoing colorectal procedures.[426]

Choice of agent. The agent chosen for antimicrobial prophylaxis in colorectal procedures should have activity against the anaerobic and aerobic floras of the bowel. The most appropriate regimen for antimicrobial prophylaxis for colorectal procedure (e.g., oral, i.v, oral–i.v. combination) and the optimal choice of antimicrobial agent have not been fully resolved.

Oral regimens. The efficacy of oral prophylactic antimicrobial agents has been established in studies only when used with mechanical bowel preparation (MBP). A variety of oral agents administered after MBP have been evaluated for prophylaxis for colorectal procedures. The most common combinations include an aminoglycoside (neomycin and, less often, kanamycin, which is only available in injectable form in the United States) plus a medication with anaerobic activity, usually erythromycin[427–434] or metronidazole.[432,433,435–439] In placebo-controlled studies, the oral combination was significantly more effective than placebo in reducing SSIs.[427,433,434,439,440] Postoperative SSI rates were 0–11% with neomycin plus erythromycin[427–432] and 2–13% with neomycin and metronidazole.[436–438] Combinations of neomycin and tetracycline,[440] neomycin and clindamycin,[436] and neomycin and tinidazole[441] have also been used successfully, with postoperative SSI rates of <10%. The use of metronidazole as a single agent appears to be less effective, with reported SSI rates of 12–15%.[442–444]

Oral antimicrobials have been compared with i.v. agents in a few studies. Oral neomycin plus oral erythromycin was similarly effective as i.v. cefoxitin in one study[429] but inferior in another[445] and was similarly effective as i.v. ceftriaxone plus i.v. metronidazole in patients undergoing elective colorectal procedures.[431] The addition of i.v. cefamandole to oral neomycin plus oral erythromycin did not improve efficacy.[430] In one of these studies, oral neomycin and erythromycin were more effective than i.v. cefoxitin for procedures lasting longer than 4 hours.[445] A randomized controlled study was stopped early due to the significantly higher rate of infection in the oral neomycin and erythromycin group (41%) compared with the single-dose i.v. metronidazole and ceftriaxone group (9.6%) ($p < 0.01$).[446] Similarly, a study of oral metronidazole and kanamycin compared with the same medications given intravenously found an increased rate of postoperative sepsis (36% versus 6.5%, respectively) ($p < 0.001$), greater numbers of *E. coli* resistant to kanamycin, more bacterial overgrowth, and antimicrobial-associated pseudomembranous colitis in the oral group.[447] However, the oral antimicrobials were not given on a schedule expected to be effective, as they were discontinued 36 hours before the procedure. The fact that oral antibiotics were given for three days rather than less than one day, as is the current practice, was suggested as a possible reason for the resistance and colitis observed.

I.V. regimens. A wide range of i.v. antimicrobials have been evaluated for prophylaxis in colorectal procedures. Cephalosporins are the most common agents, usually administered as a single agent. The majority of studies found that single-agent first-generation cephalosporins (cefazolin and cephalothin)[445,448–451] were ineffective, with postoperative SSI rates ranging from 12% to 39%.[448,449] The lack of efficacy is likely due to their lack of *B. fragilis* activity. The combination of cefazolin and metronidazole provides adequate coverage of pathogens and may be a cost-effective prophylaxis strategy.[6,41]

Second-generation cephalosporins with anaerobic activity, such as cefoxitin and cefotetan, have been widely evaluated. In single-agent therapy, SSI rates ranged from 0% to 17%[91,417,445,452–459]; however, more than half of the studies found SSI rates of >10%.

Third-generation agents, cefotaxime and ceftriaxone, have been evaluated in a few trials; postoperative SSI rates were 8–19% with single-agent use.[456,460,461] In some studies, second- or third-generation cephalosporins were combined with other i.v. agents, most commonly metronidazole.[452,459–462] However, in all but one of these studies, a combination of a second- or third-generation cephalosporin plus metronidazole was no more effective than the cephalosporin alone. The use of third- or fourth-generation cephalosporins for routine antimicrobial prophylaxis is not recommended as use may lead to development of resistant organisms.[6,41,444,463] However, in institutions where there is increasing gram-negative resistance from isolates to first- and second-generation cephalosporins, a single dose of ceftriaxone plus metronidazole may be preferred over routine use of carbapenems.

Three small studies, with under 200 patients each, found i.v. ampicillin–sulbactam or amoxicillin–clavulanate to be as effective as i.v. combinations of gentamicin and metronidazole,[464] gentamicin and clindamycin,[465] and cefotaxime and metronidazole for preventing SSIs in elective colorectal procedures.

A randomized controlled study of adult patients undergoing elective colon or rectal procedures evaluated the use of a single high dose of gentamicin 4.5 mg/kg i.v. plus metronidazole 500 mg i.v. in sequential order over 30 minutes compared with multiple standard doses of gentamicin 1.5 mg/kg plus metronidazole given preoperatively and every 8 hours for 24 hours postoperatively.[16] All patients underwent MBP before surgery. Patients with a serum creatinine concentration exceeding 1.7 mg/L were excluded from the study. No statistically significant differences were seen in deep and superficial incisional SSI rates between groups. Significantly fewer superficial SSIs were seen in the single-dose group compared with the multidose group in procedures lasting longer than 3.5 hours (22.2% versus 55%, $p = 0.021$). A pharmacodynamic study of these patients found the gentamicin concentration at the time of surgical-site closure as the strongest independent factor for infection.[17] Of note, the infection rate was 80% in 10 patients with gentamicin concentrations of <0.5 mg/L.

Other i.v. agents that have been evaluated either alone or in combination include aminoglycosides,[464,466–469] clindamycin,[466] ampicillin,[467,469–471] penicillins plus β-lactamase inhibitors,[464,465,468,472,473] doxycycline,[470,474–476] piperacillin,[91,473] imipenem,[462] and ciprofloxacin.[300]

Ertapenem, a broad-spectrum carbapenem, is approved by FDA for the prophylaxis of SSIs after elective colorectal procedures.[67] Cefotetan is also FDA approved for surgical prophylaxis in clean-contaminated procedures (e.g., gastrointestinal procedures) in adult patients undergoing elective colon or rectal procedures.[62] A large, multicenter, randomized controlled study compared a single 1-g i.v. dose of ertapenem with cefotetan 2 g i.v. infused within 60 minutes before surgical incision.[412] All patients received MBP preoperatively. SSI rates were significantly lower in the ertapenem group versus cefotetan in the per-protocol (18.1% and 31.1%, respectively) and the modified intent-to-treat (17.1% and 50.9%) populations. Ertapenem was found to be superior to cefotetan for SSI prevention. Although not statistically significant, higher rates of skin-related events (i.e., pruritis and rash), gastrointestinal events, and *C. difficile* infection were seen in the ertapenem group. The study authors concluded that ertapenem is an acceptable alternative to cefotetan and cefoxitin. Routine use of ertapenem for surgical prophylaxis remains controversial due to theoretical concerns regarding increases in resistant organisms and a potential increase in adverse events.[477]

Alternative agents for patients with a high likelihood of past serious adverse event or allergy to β-lactams include (1) clindamycin plus an aminoglycoside, aztreonam, or a fluoroquinolone and (2) metronidazole plus an aminoglycoside or a fluoroquinolone.[41]

Combination oral and i.v. regimens. Combinations of oral and i.v. antimicrobials have been used in an attempt to further reduce postoperative infection rates. Regimens include oral neomycin and erythromycin plus i.v. administration of a cephalosporin,[416,417,429,445,449,478,479] metronidazole,[480,481] and gentamicin plus clindamycin.[466] Postoperative SSI rates in these studies ranged from 0% to 7%. With one exception,[416] there was no significant difference between oral neomycin–erythromycin plus an i.v. antimicrobial and oral neomycin–erythromycin alone.[429,449,466,478] When combination oral and i.v. agents were compared with i.v. agents alone, combination therapy was favored in five of six studies[417,429,445,449,480,482]; the difference was significant in three.[417,449,482] The most recent Cochrane review found that the infection rate was significantly lower with the combination of oral plus i.v. prophylaxis when compared with i.v. alone (relative risk, 0.55; $p = 0.000084$) or with oral prophylaxis alone (relative risk, 0.34; $p = 0.024$).[426] A recent report of over 2000 patients recorded prospectively in the Michigan Surgical Quality Collaborative—Colectomy Best Practices Project and analyzed retrospectively revealed a significantly lower rate of postoperative infections when 370 colectomy patients received MBP and oral antimicrobial prophylaxis compared with propensity-matched patients receiving i.v. prophylaxis alone.[483]

A multicenter, randomized, controlled study of 491 patients who received MBP plus oral antimicrobials (kanamycin and erythromycin) with i.v. cefmetazole (not available in the United States but noted by the expert panel to have a similar spectrum of activity as cefotetan) or i.v. cefmetazole alone found no difference in SSI between groups for colon procedures.[484] However, the combination of oral and i.v. antimicrobials was significantly better than i.v. alone for rectal procedures, particularly abdominoperineal excision. Another study found the postoperative SSI rates after rectal resection were 23% and 11%, respectively, for patients receiving i.v. cefoxitin and cefoxitin plus oral neomycin and erythromycin.[417]

The safety and tolerability of oral antimicrobials have been investigated in two studies. One case–control study found an increased incidence of *C. difficile* colitis among patients with oral plus i.v. antimicrobials and MBP compared with i.v. antimicrobials and MBP alone.[485] However, another case–control study found a lower rate (not statistically significant) of *C. difficile* infection in patients who had received oral antimicrobials compared with those who had not (1.6% versus 2.9%, $p = 0.09$).[486] A randomized controlled study of 300 patients undergoing elective colorectal procedures found significantly higher rates of nausea and vomiting among patients receiving three doses of oral antimicrobials (neomycin and metronidazole, 44% and 31%, respectively) in combination with i.v. cefoxitin and MBP compared with regimens including one dose of oral antimicrobials (18% and 11%, respectively) and no oral antimicrobials (13% and 9%, respectively).[487] No difference was noted between groups for rates of abdominal pain, SSIs, or intraabdominal abscesses. An increased number of gastrointestinal adverse events was also reported in another comparative study in the combination oral and i.v. group (2.9%) compared with the i.v.-only group (2.1%), although the results were not statistically significant.[484] Overall, the evidence suggests that the combination of oral antimicrobials with MBP in addition to i.v. prophylactic antimicrobials reduces the rate of postoperative infections compared with i.v. antimicrobials alone without MBP, although the addition of oral antimicrobials increases gastrointestinal symptoms.

Duration. Single and multiple doses were compared in several studies.[454–456,461,471,475] However, only two of these studies compared single doses with multiple doses of the same antimicrobial.[471,475] There was no significant difference in infection rates between single-dose and multidose administration. One study found a single dose of cefotaxime plus metronidazole was significantly more effective than three doses of cefotaxime alone.[461] The most recent Cochrane review found no benefit to extending the duration of prophylaxis ($p = 0.58$).[426] Generally, antimicrobial prophylaxis should be continued for no more than 24 hours and can typically be stopped when the procedure is completed and the surgical site is closed.[6,41,444] No evidence supports greater efficacy for doses given after the completion of the procedure. Additional discussion on this topic is found in the Common Principles section of these guidelines.

Consideration should be given to an additional dose of the i.v. antimicrobial if an agent with a short half-life is used and the procedure duration exceeds the recommended redosing interval (starting from the time of initiation of the preoperative dose) and if intraoperative blood loss occurs.[6,41,120,418,444,445] No significant difference was seen in SSI rates with single-dose cefazolin, single-dose cefotetan, and cefazolin given as one preoperative dose and a second dose three hours later for procedures with a duration of less than three hours.[118] SSI rates were significantly higher with a single dose of cefazolin for procedures with a duration of greater than three hours. Using an agent with a longer half-life can decrease the necessity to redose the antimicrobial during long procedures.

Pediatric Efficacy. No well-controlled studies have evaluated the efficacy of antimicrobial prophylaxis in pediatric patients undergoing colorectal procedures. However, there is no reason to suspect that prophylaxis efficacy would be different. The safety, efficacy, tolerability, and cost-effectiveness of intestinal lavage have been demonstrated in two studies of 20 and 21 pediatric patients.[488,489]

Recommendations. A single dose of second-generation cephalosporin with both aerobic and anaerobic activities (cefoxitin or cefotetan) or cefazolin plus metronidazole is recommended for colon procedures (Table 2). In institutions where there is increasing resistance to first- and second-generation cephalosporins among gram-negative isolates from SSIs, the expert panel recommends a single dose of ceftriaxone plus metronidazole over routine use of carbapenems. An alternative regimen is ampicillin–sulbactam. In most patients, MBP combined with a combination of oral neomycin sulfate plus oral erythromycin base or oral neomycin sulfate plus oral metronidazole should be given in addition to i.v. prophylaxis. The oral antimicrobial should be given as three doses over approximately 10 hours the afternoon and evening before the operation and after the MBP. Alternative regimens for patients with β-lactam allergies include (1) clindamycin plus an aminoglycoside, aztreonam, or a fluoroquinolone and (2) metronidazole plus an aminoglycoside or a fluoroquinolone. Metronidazole plus aztreonam is not recommended as an alternative because this combination has no aerobic gram-positive activity.[385] (Strength of evidence for prophylaxis = A.)

Head and Neck Procedures

Background. Elective procedures of the head and neck are predominantly clean or clean-contaminated.[490] Clean procedures include thyroidectomy and lymph node excisions. Clean-contaminated procedures include all procedures involving an incision through the oral or pharyngeal mucosa, ranging from parotidectomy, submandibular gland excision, tonsillectomy, adenoidectomy, and rhinoplasty to complicated tumor-debulking and mandibular fracture repair procedures requiring reconstruction. The frequency of SSIs reported for clean procedures without antimicrobial prophylaxis is <1%.[491,492] In contrast, infection rates in patients undergoing complicated head and neck cancer surgery are quite high, with infection occurring in 24–87% of patients without antimicrobial prophylaxis.[493–497] While many of these head and neck cancer procedures are clean-contaminated, these procedures can fall into different wound classifications. Head and neck cancer patients often have many of the risk factors for infection mentioned below.[498]

Postoperative SSI rates are affected by age, nutritional status, and the presence of concomitant medical conditions such as diabetes mellitus, anemia, and peripheral vascular disease.[496,499–504] Use of tobacco,[498,505] alcohol,[505,506] or drugs of abuse[507] has also been associated with a higher risk of postoperative infection, particularly in patients with mandibular fracture. The hospital course, including length of hospitalization before operation, duration of antimicrobial use before operation, length of operation, presence of implants, and previous tracheotomy can also affect postoperative SSI rates.[496,497,501–504,508] In patients with cancer, preoperative radiation and chemotherapy as well as the stage of the malignancy may also affect infection risk.[497,498,502–504] Procedure-related risk factors for infection include radical or bilateral neck dissections[501,508] and reconstruction with myocutaneous flaps or microvascular-free flaps.[497–499,508]

Organisms. The normal floras of the mouth and the oropharynx are responsible for most infections that follow clean-contaminated head and neck procedures.[6,8,496,498,499,506,509–519] Anaerobic and aerobic bacteria are abundant in the oropharynx. As a result, postoperative SSIs are usually polymicrobial and involve both aerobic and anaerobic bacteria. The predominant oropharyngeal organisms include various streptococci (aerobic and anaerobic species), other oral anaerobes including *Bacteroides* species (but not *B. fragilis*), *Peptostreptococcus* species, *Prevotella* species, *Fusobacterium* species, *Veillonella* species, Enterobacteriaceae, and staphylococci. Nasal flora includes *Staphylococcus* species and *Streptococcus* species.

Efficacy. *Clean procedures.* Systemic administration of prophylactic antimicrobials has not been proven effective in reducing SSI rates in patients undergoing clean procedures of the head and neck and are not recommended for routine use.[6–8,497,520] One randomized, double-blind, multicenter study of 500 patients undergoing thyroid procedures for goiter or carcinoma found no difference in postoperative SSI rates in those who received antimicrobial prophylaxis (0.8%) and those who did not (0.4%).[491]

Clean-contaminated procedures. Based on the best available evidence, current guidelines and review articles recommend the use of antimicrobial prophylaxis for the majority of clean-contaminated procedures.[6–8,497,520,521] However, antimicrobial prophylaxis did not lower infection risk in randomized controlled trials of patients undergoing adenoidectomy, tonsillectomy,[522,523] and septoplasty,[524] and systematic reviews have not recommended prophylaxis for these procedures.[7,525,526]

The efficacy of antimicrobial prophylaxis is best established for head and neck cancer surgery. Several small randomized, controlled trials found high infection rates in placebo groups (24–78%) and markedly lower infection rates in the prophylaxis groups (5.8–38%) using a variety of regimens, including cefazolin, third-generation cephalosporins, and ampicillin plus cloxacillin. Although these studies were small, the results are concordant, and the high infection rates allowed the studies to reach statistical significance despite the small sample sizes. Similar results were reported in several additional small, uncontrolled studies.[500,527–529]

Choice of agent. Several randomized, single-center studies have compared antimicrobial regimens for clean-contaminated procedures. In one study, 189 patients undergoing head and neck cancer procedures were randomized to receive cefazolin 1 g (n = 92) or amoxicillin–clavulanate (n = 97), both given within one hour of incision and every eight hours postoperatively for three doses.[511] The postoperative SSI rates were 24% with cefazolin and 21% with amoxicillin–clavulanate; there was no statistically significant difference in infection rates in this underpowered study. Two studies have compared ampicillin–sulbactam to clindamycin and yielded discordant results. One study of 242 patients (169 evaluable) undergoing head and neck cancer procedures compared ampicillin–sulbactam 1.5 g (n = 119) and clindamycin 600 mg (n = 123) given within one to two hours of incision and every six hours postoperatively for a total of four doses.[510] No difference in SSIs was found, with 15 infections reported in each group (13% for the ampicillin–sulbactam group and 12% for the clindamycin group). There was no significant difference in adverse events between groups. There was a higher rate of *C. difficile*-positive patients in the clindamycin group *(n* = 7) than in the ampicillin–sulbactam group *(n* = 1), with no reported statistical analysis. Another study of 212 patients undergoing clean-contaminated head and neck oncology surgery found significantly fewer infections in the ampicillin–sulbactam group (13.3%) compared with the clindamycin group (27.1%) (p = 0.02).[530] A greater number of gram-negative pathogens were recovered from patients randomized to the clindamycin group. The combination of gentamicin and clindamycin was superior to cefazolin in one older clinical trial.[531]

Duration. Studies of clean-contaminated head and neck procedures found no difference in efficacy between regimens of 24 hours and longer regimens of three, five, or seven days.[499–501,505,507,512,524,531–534] Limited data exist on single-dose prophylaxis in these procedures.

One study of patients undergoing free-flap reconstruction after head and neck procedures found a significantly lower rate of acquisition and infection with MRSA in patients receiving short-term cefuroxime and metronidazole (one dose during induction of anesthesia and one dose eight hours postoperatively) compared with long-term therapy (same antimicrobials with additional doses every eight hours for up to five days) ($p = 0.005$ and $p = 0.01$, respectively, for acquisition and infection).[535]

Recommendations. *Clean procedures.* Antimicrobial prophylaxis is not required in patients undergoing clean surgical procedures of the head and neck. If there is placement of prosthetic material, a preoperative dose of cefazolin or cefuroxime is reasonable, though there are few data supporting the efficacy of prophylaxis in this setting (Table 2). A reasonable alternative for patients with β-lactam allergies is clindamycin. (Strength of evidence against prophylaxis without prosthesis placement = B; strength of evidence for prophylaxis with prosthesis placement = C.)

Clean-contaminated procedures. Antimicrobial prophylaxis has not been shown to benefit patients undergoing tonsillectomy or functional endoscopic sinus procedures. The preferred regimens for patients undergoing other clean-contaminated head and neck procedures are (1) cefazolin or cefuroxime plus metronidazole and (2) ampicillin–sulbactam. Clindamycin is a reasonable alternative in patients with a documented β-lactam allergy. The addition of an aminoglycoside to clindamycin may be appropriate when there is an increased likelihood of gram-negative contamination of the surgical site. (Strength of evidence for prophylaxis in cancer surgery patients = A; strength of evidence for prophylaxis for other clean-contaminated procedures except tonsillectomy and functional endoscopic sinus procedures = B.)

Neurosurgery Procedures

Background. Nosocomial central nervous system (CNS) infections do not often occur but have potentially serious consequences and poor outcomes, including death.[536] One of the greatest risks for these infections in children and adults is undergoing a neurosurgical procedure. A classification system for neurosurgery, validated by Narotam et al.,[537] divides procedures into five categories: clean, clean with foreign body, clean-contaminated, contaminated, and dirty. Risk factors for postoperative infections after neurological procedures include an ASA classification of ≥2,[538] postoperative monitoring of intracranial pressure[538,539] or ventricular drains[536,538] for five or more days, cerebrospinal fluid (CSF) leak,[539–541] procedure duration of more than two to four hours,[540,542–544] diabetes,[544] placement of foreign body,[536] repeat or additional neurosurgical procedures,[538,541–543] concurrent (remote, incision, or shunt) or previous shunt infection,[536,539,545,546] and emergency procedures.[542,545]

Organisms. Data from most published clinical trials indicate that SSIs are primarily associated with gram-positive bacteria, *S. aureus*, and coagulase-negative *staphylococci*.[6,8,537–545,547–554] Several cohort studies revealed high rates (up to 75–80% of isolates) of MRSA[540–543,548–552] and coagulase-negative staphylococci among patients undergoing a variety of neurosurgical procedures.[539,540,543,549] Other skin organisms such as *P. acnes* may be seen after CSF shunt placement, craniotomy, and other procedures.[536,555,556] Gram-negative bacteria have also been isolated as the sole cause of postoperative neurosurgical SSIs in approximately 5–8% of cases and have been isolated in polymicrobial infections.[537–539,541–545,547–550,552,553]

Efficacy. *Clean procedures.* Antimicrobial prophylaxis is recommended for adult and pediatric patients undergoing craniotomy and spinal procedures.[7,520] One meta-analysis of six studies found decreased odds of meningitis in patients undergoing craniotomy who received antimicrobial prophylaxis (1.1%) versus no prophylaxis (2.7%) (p = 0.03).[557] Two cohort studies[540,543] in patients undergoing craniotomy at the same institution found that antimicrobial prophylaxis with cloxacillin or amoxicillin–clavulanate, clindamycin for β-lactam-allergic patients, and other antimicrobials (not detailed) had a significantly lower infection rate (5.8%) than no prophylaxis (9.7%) ($p < 0.0001$).[543] A significantly lower infection rate of 4.6% was seen in low-risk patients (clean craniotomy, no implant) with antimicrobial prophylaxis compared with those without prophylaxis (4.6% versus 10%, $p < 0.0001$). A significantly lower rate of scalp infections, bone flap osteitis, and abscess or empyema was seen with antimicrobial prophylaxis compared with no prophylaxis. Antimicrobial prophylaxis demonstrated no difference in postoperative meningitis[540,543] and infection rates in high-risk patients (those undergoing emergency, clean-contaminated, and dirty procedures or reoperation or with operative times exceeding four hours).[543]

Prospective studies involving large numbers of patients have also demonstrated lower neurosurgical postoperative infection rates when antimicrobial prophylaxis is used.[558–561] One such study of patients undergoing craniotomy, spinal, or shunting procedures was stopped early because of an excessive number of SSIs in the placebo group.[562]

Choice of agent. Studies of clean neurosurgical procedures reported antimicrobial regimens including clindamycin,[540,543,557] vancomycin,[542,557] cefotiam (not marketed in the United States),[557] piperacillin,[557] cloxacillin,[540,543,557] oxacillin,[542,557] cefuroxime,[547] cefotaxime,[548] sulfamethoxazole–trimethoprim,[548] cefazolin,[542,544] penicillin G,[542] and amoxicillin–clavulanate.[540,542,543] A meta-analysis found no significant difference in the rates of postcraniotomy meningitis with various antimicrobial regimens (single-dose regimens of clindamycin, vancomycin, or cefotiam; three doses of piperacillin; four doses of cloxacillin; and six doses of oxacillin).[557]

A randomized, open-label, multicenter study of 613 adult patients undergoing elective craniotomy, shunt, or stereotactic procedures found no difference in single doses of cefotaxime and trimethoprim–sulfamethoxazole in postoperative abscess formation, SSIs, and shunt infections.[548]

Duration. The majority of studies included single doses of antimicrobials; therefore, the use of single-dose antimicrobial prophylaxis given within 60 minutes before surgical incision in patients undergoing neurosurgery is generally recommened.[6,7,520,540,543,547,548,557,563]

Efficacy for CSF-Shunting Procedures. Antimicrobial prophylaxis is recommended for adults undergoing placement of a CSF shunt.[7] Prophylaxis in patients undergoing ventriculostomy or intraventrical prophylaxis at the time of ventriculoperitoneal shunt insertion has shown some benefit in reducing infection but remains controversial due to limited evidence.[6,7]

Because CNS infections after shunting procedures are responsible for substantial mortality and morbidity, especially in children, the possible role of prophylactic antimicrobials in such procedures has been studied in numerous small, well-conducted, randomized controlled trials.[564–571] Meticulous surgical and aseptic techniques and short procedure times were determined to be important factors in lowering infection rates after shunt placement. Although the number of patients studied in each trial was small, two meta-analyses of these data demonstrated that antimicrobial prophylaxis use in CSF-shunting procedures reduced the risk of infection by approximately 50%.[572,573]

Intrathecal pump placement involves the implantation of a permanent intrathecal catheter to allow instillation of medication. CNS infections may occur after these procedures, which are performed in both pediatric and adult populations. Several retrospective series have reported infection rates of 4.5–9% after intrathecal baclofen pump placement.[574–576] There are minimal published trial data regarding appropriate prophylaxis for intrathecal pump procedures. It has been suggested that prophylaxis for intrathecal pump procedures be managed similarly to prophylaxis for CSF-shunting procedures.[577]

There is no consensus on the use of antimicrobial prophylaxis in patients with extraventricular drains (EVDs) or intracranial pressure monitors.[134] An international survey of neurosurgeons and critical care medicine and infectious diseases specialists illustrates the difference in practices. The majority of neurosurgeons used or recommended the use of antimicrobial prophylaxis with EVDs (73.5%) and other monitoring devices (59%), compared with rates of 46–59% for critical care medicine specialists and 35% for infectious diseases specialists. The majority of specialists did not recommend or use antimicrobial-coated EVD catheters.

Two randomized controlled studies comparing antimicrobial-impregnated shunts to standard, non-antimicrobial-impregnated shunts along with antimicrobial prophylaxis with i.v. cephalosporin found a decrease in rates of shunt infections[549] and a significant decrease in CSF infection with antimicrobial-impregnated shunts.[545] At this time, routine use of antimicrobial-impregnated devices is not recommended; additional well-designed studies are needed to establish their place in therapy.[7,578]

Choice of agent. In CSF-shunting procedures, no single antimicrobial agent has been demonstrated to have greater efficacy than others.[546,548,551–554,579] There is a lack of data on the necessity of antimicrobials with CNS penetration relating to prevention of infection in CNS shunting procedures.

Duration. The majority of studies support the use of single-dose prophylaxis regimens or regimens with a duration of 24–48 hours postoperatively.[6–8,520,539,546,549–552,579] There is a lack of data evaluating the continuation of EVDs with and without antimicrobial prophylaxis. The international survey mentioned above asked respondents to indicate their recommended duration for antimicrobial prophylaxis with EVDs as either periprocedural, for 24 hours, for the first three days, for the entire time the device is in place, or other.[135] The respondents from the specialties of neurosurgery, neurocritical care, and critical care had similar results, with 28–31% using or recommending periprocedural antimicrobials, 4–10% for 24 hours, 2–4% for the first three days, 43–64% for the entire time the device is in place, and 0–14% for other. The infectious diseases specialists reported rates of 62%, 19%, 4%, 12%, and 4%, respectively.

One retrospective single-center cohort study of 308 patients with EVDs placed for three days or more received antimicrobial prophylaxis for the duration of EVD use (n = 209) compared with patients receiving cefuroxime 1.5 g i.v. every eight hours for three doses or less frequently periprocedurally (timing not clearly defined in article) (n = 99).[580] The overall rate of bacterial ventriculitis was 3.9%, with 8 patients (3.8%) in the extended-use group and 4 patients (4%) in the short-term prophylaxis group, the difference of which was not significant. The study authors concluded that there was no benefit to the use of a prolonged duration of antimicrobial prophylaxis.

Pediatric Efficacy for CSF-Shunting Procedures. Antimicrobial prophylaxis is recommended for children undergoing a CSF-shunting procedure.[7] The efficacy of antimicrobial prophylaxis is extrapolated from adult studies.

A retrospective pediatric study of 384 CSF-shunting procedures found a lower infection rate in patients who received antimicrobials (2.1%) compared with those who did not (5.6%), but this difference failed to reach statistical significance.[581] Two randomized, prospective studies that included pediatric patients did not demonstrate a significant difference in infection rates between the control group and the groups that received cefotiam[571] (not available in the United States) or methicillin.[568] A randomized, double-blind, placebo-controlled study that included pediatric patients undergoing ventriculoperitoneal shunt surgeries failed to demonstrate that the use of perioperative sulfamethoxazole–trimethoprim reduced the frequency of shunt infection.[564]

Other studies have demonstrated efficacy for prophylactic antimicrobials.[566,582] A single-center, randomized, double-blind, placebo-controlled trial of perioperative rifampin plus trimethoprim was performed in pediatric patients.[582] Among patients receiving rifampin plus trimethoprim, the infection rate was 12%, compared with 19% in patients receiving placebo. The study was ended because of the high infection rates before significance could be achieved. Infection rates at the study institution had been 7.5% in the years before the study. An open-label randomized study, including pediatric patients, demonstrated a lower infection rate in a group receiving oxacillin (3.3%) than in a control group (20%).[566]

Recommendations. A single dose of cefazolin is recommended for patients undergoing clean neurosurgical procedures, CSF-shunting procedures, or intrathecal pump placement (Table 2). Clindamycin or vancomycin should be reserved as an alternative agent for patients with a documented β-lactam allergy (vancomycin for MRSA-colonized patients). (Strength of evidence for prophylaxis = A.)

Cesarean Delivery Procedures

Background. Approximately 1.2 million infants are born by cesarean delivery in the United States annually.[583] The infection rate after cesarean delivery has been reported to be 4–15%,[583] though recent NHSN data showed an infection rate of 2–4%.[165]

Postpartum infectious complications are common after cesarean delivery. Endometritis (infection of the uterine lining) is usually identified by fever, malaise, tachycardia, abdominal pain, uterine tenderness, and sometimes abnormal or foul-smelling lochia.[584] Fever may also be the only symptom of endometritis.

Endometritis has been reported to occur in up to 24% of patients in elective cesarean delivery and up to approximately 60% of patients undergoing nonelective or emergency section.[584,585] Risk factors for endometritis include cesarean delivery, prolonged rupture of membranes, prolonged labor with multiple vaginal examinations, intrapartum fever, and low socioeconomic status.[585,586] Patients with low socioeconomic status may have received inadequate prenatal care.

The factor most frequently associated with infectious morbidity in postcesarean delivery is prolonged labor in the presence of ruptured membranes. Intact chorioamniotic membranes serve as a protective barrier against bacterial infection. Rupture of the membrane exposes the uterine surface to bacteria from the birth canal. The vaginal fluid with bacterial flora is drawn into the uterus when it relaxes between contractions during labor. Women undergoing labor for more than six to eight hours in the presence of ruptured membranes should be considered at high risk for developing endometritis.[587] Other risk factors for SSIs after cesarean delivery include systemic illness, poor hygiene, obesity, and anemia.[587,588]

Organisms. The normal flora of the vagina include staphylococci, *streptococci, enterococci, lactobacilli*, diphtheroids, *E. coli*, anaerobic streptococci (*Peptococcus* species and *Peptostreptococcus* species), *Bacteroides* species (e.g., *Bacteroides bivius, B. fragilis*), and *Fusobacterium* species.[584,587,589–592] Endometritis infections are often polymicrobial and include aerobic streptococcus (particularly group B β-hemolytic streptococcus and enterococci), gram-negative aerobes (particularly *E. coli*), gram-negative anaerobic rods (particularly *B. bivius*), and anaerobic *cocci* (*Peptococcus* species and *Peptostreptococcus* species). *Ureaplasma urealyticum* has been commonly isolated from endometrial and surgical-site cultures. Additional commonly isolated organisms from SSIs include *Staphylococcus* species and enterococci.

Efficacy. While the use of antimicrobial prophylaxis in low-risk procedures (i.e., those with no active labor and no rupture of membranes) has been brought into question by the results of several randomized, placebo-controlled studies that found no reduction in infectious complications (fever, SSI, urinary tract infection, or endometritis) with the use of prophylaxis, the majority of these evaluations were underpowered and included administration of antimicrobial prophylaxis at cord clamping.[593–599] However, the efficacy of antimicrobial prophylaxis in cesarean delivery has been shown in several studies and two meta-analyses for both elective and nonelective procedures. Therefore, prophylaxis is recommended for all patients undergoing cesarean delivery.[584,592]

One meta-analysis that reviewed 7 placebo-controlled randomized trials in low-risk elective cesarean delivery found that prophylaxis was associated with a significant decrease in endometritis and fever.[592] A larger meta-analysis of 81 randomized trials with 11,937 women undergoing both elective and nonelective cesarean delivery found that antimicrobial prophylaxis was associated with a significant reduction in risk of fever, endometritis, SSI, urinary tract infection, and serious infection.[585] The relative risk for endometritis in elective cesarean section was 0.38 (95% CI, 0.22–0.64) in those receiving antimicrobial prophylaxis compared to those receiving no prophylaxis.

Choice of agent. Although several different antimicrobials used alone or in combination for antimicrobial prophylaxis during cesarean delivery have been evaluated, the use of first-generation cephalosporins (specifically cefazolin) has been advocated by ACOG and the American Academy of Pediatrics (AAP), based on their efficacy, narrow spectrum of activity, and low cost.[584] This recommendation is supported by a meta-analysis of 51 randomized controlled trials comparing at least two antimicrobial regimens that concluded that ampicillin and first-generation cephalosporins have similar efficacy.[600]

Newer prospective randomized controlled and cohort studies have evaluated the addition of metronidazole, azithromycin,[601–603] or doxycycline[601] to a first- or second-generation cephalosporin to extend the spectrum of activity against common organisms isolated from endometrial and surgical-site cultures, specifically *U. urealyticum* and *Mycoplasma* species. These studies found significantly lower rates of postoperative infections (including endometritis and SSI) and a shorter duration of hospital stay compared with prophylaxis with a first- or second-generation cephalosporin alone.[601–604] Antibiotic administration occurred either postoperatively or after cord clamping in these studies. Further study, particularly with preoperative antimicrobial administration, is needed to confirm these preliminary findings and establish a place in therapy for this practice.

Timing. Historically, administration of antimicrobials in cesarean delivery was delayed until after cord clamping.[600,605,606] The principal reasons were to avoid suppression of the neonate's normal bacterial flora that could promote the selection of resistant organisms and concern that the antimicrobials could potentially mask neonatal infection, complicating evaluation of neonatal sepsis. However, more contemporary data support the administration of antimicrobial prophylaxis before surgical incision to protect against bacterial contamination of the surgical site and decrease the risk of infection. The practice of antimicrobial prophylaxis administration before surgical incision is endorsed by ACOG and AAP.[584,607] See the Common Principles section of these guidelines for additional discussion on antimicrobial timing.

A meta-analysis of three randomized controlled trials and two nonrandomized controlled studies provided evidence that preoperative antimicrobial administration significantly decreased the rate of endometritis compared with administration after cord clamping (3.9% and 8.9%, respectively; $p = 0.012$).[605] A lower SSI rate was also seen with preoperative antimicrobial administration (3.2% versus 5.4%), though this difference was not significant. The overall rate of infection-related morbidity was also significantly lower. No differences between the groups were seen in neonatal outcomes, including sepsis, sepsis workups, and neonatal intensive care unit admissions. The largest study included in this meta-analysis was a prospective, randomized, controlled, double-blind, single-center, double-dummy study of 357 patients comparing cefazolin 1 g i.v. given preoperatively and after cord clamping, which had results consistent with the overall meta-analysis.[606]

In a recent randomized trial of more than 1100 women undergoing cesarean section between 2004 and 2010, Witt and colleagues[608] found no difference in SSI rates for patients having antimicrobial administration before surgical incision compared with those who received antimicrobial prophylaxis at the time of cord clamping. All patients received a single dose of cefazolin 2 g.

Duration. A meta-analysis of 51 studies found that multidose regimens provided no apparent benefit over single-dose regimens.[600] The use of single-dose prophylaxis is supported by ACOG and AAP for procedures lasting less than two hours.[584] Additional intraoperative doses may be warranted for patients with excessive blood loss or for whom the duration of the procedure is extended.

For additional discussion of dosing, see the Common Principles section of these guidelines.

Recommendation. The recommended regimen for all women undergoing cesarean delivery is a single dose of cefazolin administered before surgical incision (Table 2). (Strength of evidence for prophylaxis = A.) For patients with β-lactam allergies, an alternative regimen is clindamycin plus gentamicin.

Hysterectomy Procedures

Background. Hysterectomy is second only to cesarean delivery as the most frequently performed major gynecological procedure in the United States, with over 600,000 hysterectomies performed annually.[609] Uterine fibroid tumors account for 40% of all presurgical diagnoses leading to hysterectomy.[609] Other common diagnoses are dysfunctional uterine bleeding, genital prolapse, endometriosis, chronic pelvic pain, pelvic inflammatory disease, endometrial hyperplasia, and cancer.

Hysterectomy involves the removal of the uterus and, occasionally, one or two fallopian tubes, the ovaries, or a combination of ovaries and fallopian tubes.[610] Radical hysterectomy entails removal of the uterus, fallopian tubes, and ovaries and extensive stripping of the pelvic lymph nodes in patients with extension of their cancer. Hysterectomies are performed by a vaginal or abdominal approach using a laparoscopic- or robot-assisted method. During a vaginal hysterectomy, the procedure is completed through the vagina with no abdominal incision. Abdominal hysterectomy involves an abdominal incision. Laparoscopic and robotic methods involve small incisions and require additional equipment, increased operator experience, and increased length of procedures.[611,612] In the United States, between 2000 and 2004, the abdominal approach for hysterectomy was used in 67.9% of surgical procedures and the vaginal approach in 32.1%. Of hysterectomies performed via the vaginal approach, 32.4% also used laparoscopy.[609] The ACOG Committee on Gynecologic Practice recommends vaginal hysterectomy as the approach of choice for benign disease, based on evidence of better outcomes and fewer complications.[613] Laparoscopic abdominal hysterectomy is an alternative when the vaginal route is not indicated or feasible.[613,614] Of note, ACOG has stated that the supracervical approach—removal of the uterus with preservation of the cervix—should not be recommended as a superior technique for hysterectomy due to the lack of advantage in postoperative complications, urinary symptoms, or sexual function and the increased risk of future trachelectomy to remove the cervical stump.[615]

Infections after hysterectomy include superficial and organ/space (vaginal cuff infection, pelvic cellulitis, and pelvic abscess) SSIs.[589] The reported SSI rates between January 2006 and December 2008 in the United States, based on NNIS risk index category, were 0.73–1.16 per 100 procedures for vaginal hysterectomy and 1.10–4.05 per 100 procedures for abdominal hysterectomy.[165] A multicenter surveillance study found a mean infection rate of 2.53% associated with all types of hysterectomy and a significantly lower mean rate of infection with laparoscopic versus abdominal hysterectomies (1.15% versus 3.44%, respectively).[325]

Risk factors for infection after vaginal or abdominal hysterectomy include longer duration of surgery, young age, diabetes, obesity, peripheral vascular disease, collagen disease, anemia, transfusion, poor nutritional status, and previous history of postsurgical infection.[590,616–622] The depth of subcutaneous tissue is also a significant risk factor for infection after abdominal hysterectomy.[623] Additional risk factors for infection after radical hysterectomy for cervical cancer include the presence of malignancy, prior radiation therapy, and the presence of indwelling drainage catheters.[619,620]

Organisms. The vagina is normally colonized with a wide variety of bacteria, including gram-positive and gram-negative aerobes and anaerobes. The normal flora of the vagina includes staphylococci, streptococci, enterococci, lactobacilli, diphtheroids, *E. coli*, anaerobic streptococci, *Bacteroides* species, and *Fusobacterium* species.[589,624] Postoperative vaginal flora differs from preoperative flora; the amount of enterococci, gram-negative bacilli, and *Bacteroides* species increases postoperatively. Postoperative changes in flora may occur independently of prophylactic antimicrobial administration and are not by themselves predictive of postoperative infection.[589,625,626] Postoperative infections associated with vaginal hysterectomy are frequently polymicrobial, with enterococci, aerobic gram-negative bacilli, and *Bacteroides* species isolated most frequently. Postoperative SSIs after abdominal and radical hysterectomies are also polymicrobial; gram-positive cocci and enteric gram-negative bacilli predominate, and anaerobes are frequently isolated.[626,627]

Efficacy. A meta-analysis of 25 randomized controlled trials demonstrated the efficacy of antimicrobial prophylaxis, including first- and second-generation cephalosporins and metronidazole, in the prevention of infections after abdominal hysterectomy.[628] The infection rates were 21.1% with placebo or no prophylaxis and 9.0% with any antimicrobial. Another meta-analysis found that the rate of postoperative infection (surgical and pelvic sites) in women undergoing vaginal hysterectomy who received placebo or no prophylactic antimicrobial ranged from 14% to 57%, which was significantly higher than the 10% rate reported with antimicrobials.[629]

Malignant disease as the reason for hysterectomy is a common exclusion from studies of antimicrobial prophylaxis. Older, prospective, placebo-controlled studies found a lower rate of SSIs with antimicrobial prophylaxis after radical hysterectomy.[619,630–633] The applicability of these results is limited by small sample size and the inclusion of antimicrobials not available in the United States. Radical hysterectomy is primarily completed through an abdominal approach but can also be performed by a vaginal approach and using laparoscopic or robotic methods.[634] Therefore, antimicrobial prophylaxis would be warranted, regardless of approach. No placebo-controlled studies have been conducted to evaluate the efficacy of antimicrobial prophylaxis when used for laparoscopic hysterectomy.

Choice of agent. Cephalosporins are the most frequently used and studied antimicrobials for prophylaxis in vaginal and abdominal hysterectomies. Studies directly comparing different cephalosporins have found no significant differences in rates of infection in vaginal hysterectomy and have indicated that first-generation cephalosporins (primarily cefazolin) are equivalent to second- and third-generation agents.[635–644] In abdominal hysterectomy, no significant differences in the rates of serious infections were noted between second- and third-generation cephalosporin regimens.[641,645–649] Few comparisons have been made between second-generation cephalosporins and cefazolin. Cefazolin has been at least as effective in preventing infectious complications as second- and third-generation cephalosporins.[636,650–652] However, one double-blind controlled study of 511 women undergoing abdominal hysterectomy found that the risk of major SSIs requiring antimicrobial therapy was significantly higher in the group receiving preoperative cefazolin 1 g (11.6%; relative risk, 1.84; 95% CI, 1.03–3.29) than in those treated with cefotetan 1 g (6.3%).[617] A multicenter, randomized, double-blind, active- and placebo-controlled study compared single doses of ampicillin, cefazolin, and placebo administered to women undergoing elective total abdominal hysterectomy at two centers in Thailand.[653] The study found a significantly lower rate of infection, including superficial and deep SSIs, urinary tract infections, vaginal cuff infection, and pneumonia, with cefazolin (10.3%) compared with placebo (26.9%) and ampicillin (22.6%). No difference was seen between ampicillin and placebo. The study authors concluded that cefazolin was more effective than ampicillin for elective total abdominal hysterectomy.

A randomized controlled study of 511 patients undergoing laparoscopic gynecological procedures at one center in Italy compared single doses of amoxicillin–clavulanate 2.2 g and cefazolin 2 g i.v. administered 20–30 minutes before the procedure.[654] A second dose was given if the surgery lasted over three hours or there was extensive blood loss (>1500 mL). No significant differences in the rates of any postoperative infection, including SSIs, were found between groups. The statistical power of the study was not stated.

In light of the organisms encountered in the vaginal canal and comparative studies conducted among different classes of cephalosporins, cefazolin, cefotetan, cefoxitin, cefuroxime, and ampicillin–sulbactam have been supported as appropriate first-line choices for prophylaxis during vaginal or abdominal hysterectomy.[6,9,41] Alternative agents for patients with a history of immediate hypersensitivity to penicillin include either clindamycin or metronidazole plus an aminoglycoside or a fluoroquinolone (ciprofloxacin, levofloxacin, or moxifloxacin) or aztreonam (with clindamycin only).

Duration. Studies comparing single doses of one antimicrobial with multidose regimens of a different antimicrobial have shown the two regimens to be equally effective in reducing the postoperative infection rate in women undergoing vaginal and abdominal hysterectomies.[635–643,645–650,655–663] The limited comparative trials involving single-dose cefazolin[637,654,655,664] or ampicillin–sulbactam[654,663] indicate that a single dose of antimicrobial is sufficient prophylaxis for SSIs for vaginal hysterectomy. Single doses of cefotetan, ceftizoxime, or cefotaxime appear to be as effective as multiple doses of cefoxitin.[644–649,665] A second dose of antimicrobial is warranted when the procedure lasts three hours or longer or if blood loss exceeds 1500 mL.[9,654]

Recommendation. The recommended regimen for women undergoing vaginal or abdominal hysterectomy, using an open or laparoscopic approach, is a single dose of cefazolin (Table 2). Cefoxitin, cefotetan, or ampicillin–sulbactam may also be used. Alternative agents for patients with a β-lactam allergy include (1) either clindamycin or vancomycin plus an aminoglycoside, aztreonam, or a fluoroquinolone and (2) metronidazole plus an aminoglycoside or a fluoroquinolone. (Strength of evidence for prophylaxis = A.)

Ophthalmic Procedures

Background. Ophthalmic procedures include cataract extractions, vitrectomies, keratoplasties, intraocular lens implantation, glaucoma procedures, strabotomies, retinal detachment repair, laser in situ keratomileusis, and laser-assisted subepithelial keratectomy. Most of the available data regarding antimicrobial prophylaxis involve cataract procedures. The goal of prophylaxis is primarily to reduce acute postoperative endophthalmitis, defined as severe intraocular inflammation due to infection, which can lead to loss of vision if untreated.[666] Since 2000, the reported frequency of endophthalmitis after ophthalmic procedures is low worldwide, ranging from 0% to 0.63%.[667–680] The reported time from procedure to diagnosis of endophthalmitis ranges from one day to six weeks, with the majority of infections identified within one week.[666,669,671,673,674,681–683]

Potential risk factors for postoperative ophthalmic infections include preoperative factors such as diabetes,[666] active ocular infection or colonization,[666,684] lacrimal drainage system infection or obstruction, age of >85 years,[685] and immunodeficiency.[684] Procedure-related risk factors include clear corneal incisions (as opposed to scleral tunnel incisions),[680,686] any surgical complication, vitreous loss,[684] posterior capsule tear,[681,684,685] silicone intraocular lens implantation,[677,680] and the nonuse of facemasks in the operating theater.[681]

Organisms. Among organisms isolated from patients developing postoperative endophthalmitis after cataract procedure, approximately 25–60% were coagulase-negative *Staphylococcus* species, primarily *S. epidermidis*.[668,670,671,673,674,678,683,684,686] Other gram-positive organisms identified included *S. aureus*, *Streptococcus* species, *Enterococcus* species, *P. acnes*, and *Corynebacterium* species. Gram-negative organisms isolated included *Serratia* species, *Klebsiella* species, *P. mirabilis*, and *P. aeruginosa*. These organisms represent the normal flora isolated preoperatively in a number of studies.[675,687–693]

Efficacy. Data on antimicrobial prophylaxis efficacy in ophthalmic procedures to prevent endophthalmitis are limited; however, prophylaxis is common.[684] The low rate of postoperative endophthalmitis makes it difficult to complete an adequately powered study to show efficacy of antimicrobial prophylaxis in ophthalmic procedures; therefore, surrogate markers of eradication of normal flora bacteria and reduction of bacterial count on the conjunctiva, lower and upper eyelids, eyelashes, and inner canthus (corner of the eye) preoperatively and postoperatively are used. Many of the available studies are flawed with retrospective or uncontrolled design, inadequate follow-up, variations in surgical techniques (including disinfection, antimicrobial prophylaxis strategies, and methods for performing procedures), and limited reporting of clinical outcomes.

The large, randomized, partially-masked, placebo-controlled, multinational, multicenter study conducted by the European Society of Cataract and Refractive Surgeons (ESCRS) compared the rate of postoperative endophthalmitis in over 16,600 patients undergoing routine cataract procedures at 24 centers in Europe randomized to one of four perioperative prophylaxis groups.[679,680,694] Patients received no antimicrobial prophylaxis, intracameral cefuroxime at the end of the procedure alone, perioperative levofloxacin 0.5% ophthalmic solution given within the hour before the procedure, or both intracameral cefuroxime and perioperative levofloxacin. All patients had the eye area disinfected with povidone–iodine 5% preoperatively and received topical levofloxacin postoperatively. The study was stopped after an interim analysis due to results of a multivariate analysis indicating that patients not receiving intracameral cefuroxime were approximately five times more likely to develop endophthalmitis. The study has been questioned for its high rate of endophthalmitis, selection of cefuroxime due to gaps in gram-negative coverage, unknown drug concentrations in the aqueous humor, risks of hypersensitivity, the lack of a commercially available preparation, the lack of a subconjunctival cefuroxime treatment group, selection of topical levofloxacin, and methods for statistical analysis.[695–697]

Two single-center, historical-controlled studies in hospitals in Spain reported decreases in acute postoperative endophthalmitis among patients undergoing cataract procedure with intracameral cefazolin added to the previous routine prophylaxis of preoperative eyelid cleansing with soap for three days[670] and povidone–iodine eye area preparation,[670,674] topical antimicrobial, and corticosteroid preparations given at the end of the procedure and postoperatively. One study found a significant decrease and a relative risk reduction of 88.7% in postoperative endophthalmitis with intracameral cefazolin.[670] The other found a decrease from 0.63% to 0.055% in postoperative endophthalmitis with intracameral cefazolin.[674] No statistical analysis was performed in this study.

A retrospective cohort study of patients undergoing cataract procedure at one center in Canada between 1994 and 1998 found no significant difference in the rate of postoperative endophthalmitis with preoperative topical antimicrobials compared with none.[668] A significant decrease in endophthalmitis was seen with subconjunctival administration of antimicrobials at the end of the procedure compared with no antimicrobials.

Several prospective studies have shown decreases in ocular flora, measured by bacterial isolate and CFU counts, with preoperative antimicrobial irrigation,[675] topical antimicrobials,[687,688,691,692,698–700] and intracameral antimicrobials.[682] These studies did not report rates of endophthalmitis, limiting the application of the results.

Choice of agent. Along with careful site preparation and disinfection, the ideal antimicrobial prophylaxis agent should be bactericidal against common pathogens of postoperative endophthalmitis and be used safely in the eye.[6,8,684] There is no consensus on the agent of choice for antimicrobial prophylaxis in ophthalmic procedures, and no agent is FDA-approved for this indication. There are limited studies evaluating the efficacy of a particular choice of antimicrobial prophylaxis for ophthalmic surgeries. The most efficacious antimicrobial cannot be determined from the available data due to study flaws and a lack of direct comparisons. Local ocular flora resistance patterns should be monitored to aid in the selection of appropriate agents for prophylaxis.[683,689,701]

Based on the available literature, use of povidone–iodine as a preoperative antiseptic agent is recommended to decrease ocular microbes and thereby prevent endophthalmitis.[6,684,702] Povidone–iodine 5% or 10% is instilled in the conjunctival sac and applied topically to the ocular skin surface.[703] The most effective protocol has not been established, as povidone–iodine is frequently used in combination with other antimicrobials.[670,674,675,678,687,704] Chlorhexidine has been used as an effective alternative to povidone–iodine, particularly in patients who are iodine allergic.[682,703]

Ophthalmic surgeons surveyed in the United Kingdom reported that commonly used antimicrobial prophylactic agents included cephalosporins, aminoglycosides, vancomycin, chloramphenicol, neomycin alone or in combination with polymyxin, and fluoroquinolones.[695,703] A similar survey of members of the American Society of Cataract and Refractive Surgery found that over 90% of respondents used fluoroquinolones (mainly fourth-generation agents), vancomycin, and cephalosporins.[697] These antimicrobials have been recommended in practice guidelines.[6]

Cephalosporins, specifically cefazolin, cefuroxime, and ceftazidime, have been shown to be safe and effective in decreasing postoperative endophthalmitis when added to regimens of povidone–iodine and topical antimicrobials.[670,674,677,679,680,699] Vancomycin has been shown to decrease cultures and reach adequate concentrations to prevent and treat most corneal pathogens.[675,705] Aminoglycosides alone[687] or in combination with an antiseptic agent (chlorhexidine)[682] showed no significant difference in the reduction of culture results compared with an antiseptic alone (povidone–iodine or chlorhexidine)[682,690] and no antimicrobial prophylaxis.

A randomized controlled study compared the antimicrobial activity and safety of trimethoprim 0.1%–polymyxin B sulfate 10,000 units/mL ophthalmic solution and tobramycin 0.3% ophthalmic solution in patients undergoing cataract procedures.[692] All patients received one drop and a subconjunctival injection of corticosteroids and gentamicin postoperatively followed by one drop of study medication four times daily for five to seven days. No significant differences were seen between groups for positive culture results from conjunctiva at baseline, at procedure, or at postoperative days 5–7 or in lid margin culture at baseline and postoperative days 5–7. A higher rate of positive cultures at procedure was seen in the trimethoprim–polymyxin group (37 of 59 cultures, 63%) compared with 13 (41%) of 32 cultures in the tobramycin group ($p = 0.043$). Both medications eradicated the majority of bacteria on the day of procedure and postoperative days 5–7. Aqueous humor concentrations did not achieve the MICs of *S. aureus* or *S. epidermidis* and were undetectable for polymyxin B sulfate. The adverse events of irritation and allergic reaction were experienced by three patients in the trimethoprim–polymyxin group. The study authors concluded that there was no difference between trimethoprim and tobramycin in ocular flora reduction.

A randomized controlled study compared conjunctiva and contact lens culture results after treatment with tobramycin 0.3% versus ofloxacin 0.3% ophthalmic solutions in patients undergoing photorefractive keratectomy.[693] No differences were seen among preoperative, postoperative, or contact lens cultures between treatment groups. Although not statistically significant, logistic regression found that cultures from patients treated with tobramycin were two times more likely to be positive than those treated with ofloxacin. The study had low power and did not compare baseline and posttreatment culture results for any treatment group.

Fluoroquinolones have been found in studies to significantly decrease the ocular culture results from baseline[667,673,691,698,700,706]; achieve aqueous humor, vitreal, and corneal tissue concentrations adequate to prevent and treat common ocular pathogens[705,707–710]; and result in improved ocular measurements (i.e., visual acuity, epithelial cell counts, and epithelial healing).[711–716] A retrospective multicenter case series of 20,013 patients who underwent uncomplicated cataract surgeries and received fourth-generation fluoroquinolones preoperatively and postoperatively reported the rates of postoperative endophthalmitis.[673] Endophthalmitis occurred in 9 (0.06%) of 16,209 surgeries in patients treated with gatifloxacin 0.3% ophthalmic solution (95% CI, 0.03–0.1%) and in 5 (0.1%) of 3,804 surgeries in patients treated with moxifloxacin 0.5% ophthalmic solution (95% CI, 0.05–0.3%). There were no significant differences in efficacy between agents.

In a retrospective cross-sectional study conducted over a 10-year period with third- and fourth-generation fluoroquinolones, significantly lower rates of endophthalmitis were reported for the fourth-generation agents moxifloxacin and gatifloxacin (0.56 per 1000 cataract surgeries) than for the third-generation agents ciprofloxacin and ofloxacin (1.97 per 1000 surgeries) ($p = 0.0011$).[671]

Route. There is no consensus on the most effective route of antimicrobial administration for the prevention of endophthalmitis. The routes of antimicrobial administration used in ophthalmic procedures include preoperative topical antimicrobial ophthalmic drops, addition of antimicrobials to the irrigation solution, instillation of antimicrobials intracamerally at the end of surgery, subconjunctival injection of antimicrobials, and postoperative topical application of antimicrobials.[6,684,702,717]

The ESCRS randomized controlled study mentioned above found that patients not receiving intracameral cefuroxime were approximately six times more likely to develop postoperative endophthalmitis.[679,680,694] Surveys of the impact of the ESCRS study findings found that there was an increase in the use of intracameral over subconjunctival cefuroxime based on preliminary study results.[703] For respondents who had not adopted this practice, the reported reasons for not using intracameral cefuroxime included the need for further study, concerns about risk and cost of therapy, the lack of a subconjunctival comparator group, the high rate of endophthalmitis in the control groups, concerns about statistical analysis, and questions regarding the selection of cefuroxime due to gaps in ophthalmic pathogen coverage.[695,697] There is no commercially available cefuroxime formulation for intracameral administration, which was reported as one of the main barriers to use of this route. Concerns regarding compounded intracameral antimicrobials expressed by survey respondents included inflammation, dilution errors, corneal endothelial injury, and the risk for bacterial contamination and infection.

A retrospective cohort study compared the efficacy of intracameral cefuroxime versus subconjunctival cefuroxime in reducing the rate of endophthalmitis after cataract procedures at one center in northeast England.[718] A total of 19,425 patients received antimicrobial prophylaxis with preoperative povidone–iodine 5% in the conjunctival sac and subconjunctival injection of cefuroxime 50 mg at the end of the procedure, and 17,318 patients received intracameral cefuroxime 1 mg at the end of the procedure. There were two groups of patients excluded from the analysis: protocol violators who received no prophylaxis and patients who were enrolled in the ESCRS study. The overall rate of endophthalmitis in analyzed patients was 35 cases in 36,743 procedures (0.95 per 1,000 cases). Of these, 27 occurred in the subconjunctival cefuroxime group (1.39 per 1,000 cases), and 8 occurred in the intracameral group (0.46 per 1,000 cases) (OR, 3.01; 95% CI, 1.37–6.63; $p = 0.0068$).

Several studies found a lower rate of endophthalmitis with the addition of intracameral cephalosporins (cefazolin and cefuroxime) at the end of the surgical procedure after routine perioperative and postoperative topical antimicrobial prophylaxis regimens.[670,674] A case–control study revealed a 5.7 times increased likelihood of developing postoperative endophthalmitis with topical antimicrobial prophylaxis only (including gentamicin 0.3% and chlorhexidine 0.05%) compared with the addition of intracameral cefuroxime 1 mg to the regimen in cataract procedure.[677] Both intracameral cephalosporins and moxifloxacin have been shown as safe, with no adverse events and no effects on visual acuity and endothelial cell counts.[670,674,699,715,716]

One study involving healthy adult volunteers found that orally administered levofloxacin and moxifloxacin achieved adequate aqueous humor concentrations to provide activity against gram-positive and most gram-negative ocular pathogens without adverse events.[707]

The addition of subconjunctival antimicrobials to existing topical antimicrobial prophylaxis regimens has also been shown to reduce the rate and risk of endophthalmitis in intraocular procedures compared with topical antimicrobials alone.[668,681,686] Topical antimicrobials have been shown to be safe and effective in lowering rates of endophthalmitis,[671,673] decreasing bacterial organisms and CFUs in conjunctiva,[667,675,691,692,698,700] and achieving adequate concentrations to be effective against most ocular pathogens,[705,706,708–710,719] with no notable adverse events.[711–714]

Duration and timing. There are a lack of clear evidence and no consensus on the appropriate duration and timing of antimicrobial prophylaxis in ophthalmic procedures.[6,684] Commonly reported times of antimicrobial prophylaxis include preoperatively, intraoperatively, at the end of the procedure, and postoperatively.[684] Few studies have investigated the differences between the timing and duration of antimicrobial prophylaxis regimens. Many of the regimens are used in combination, making it difficult to determine the optimal timing and duration. Preoperative antimicrobial timing reported in the literature has ranged from one to multiple drops within an hour preoperatively on the day of the procedure[671,673,679,680,692–694,698,703,709,710,716] or one to three days before the procedure.[667,698,700,703,708,710,712,714]

Two topical moxifloxacin regimens were compared for conjunctival bacterial flora and aqueous humor concentrations in a randomized controlled study of patients undergoing cataract procedures.[691,719] In one regimen, patients were administered moxifloxacin 0.5% four times a day beginning one day before the procedure plus one drop two hours before the procedure (total of five drops before the procedure); the other group received moxifloxacin 0.5% two hours before surgery and every 15 minutes for the first hour of the procedure (total of five drops). There were no cases of postoperative endophthalmitis up to six months after the procedure in any patient. Administration of moxifloxacin on the day of the procedure was found to result in a significant decrease in median CFU compared with baseline and was found (based on change in log CFU) to be more effective than antimicrobial administration on the day before the procedure. Mean aqueous humor concentrations of moxifloxacin at the beginning of the procedure were significantly higher in the group who received the drug on the day of the procedure.

A small, randomized controlled study compared aqueous humor concentrations of levofloxacin and ciprofloxacin in patients undergoing a cataract procedure with routine phacoemulsification given as (1) one or two drops four times daily for two days before the procedure, with the last dose given immediately before bedtime on the night before the procedure, (2) five doses (one or two drops) delivered every 10 minutes in the hour before the procedure, or (3) a combination of both dosing strategies.[706] Aqueous humor concentrations of levofloxacin were significantly higher than those of ciprofloxacin. Significantly higher doses of drug were delivered to the aqueous humor in the group receiving same-day prophylaxis than in patients receiving levofloxacin or ciprofloxacin two days before surgery. No cases of endophthalmitis or ocular or systemic toxicities were reported.

A randomized controlled study compared the effectiveness of topical ofloxacin in the reduction or elimination of conjunctival bacterial flora when given as one drop every five minutes for three applications one hour before the procedure alone (control group) or combined with ofloxacin one drop four times daily for three days (study group) before cataract procedures.[688] No differences in positive conjunctival cultures were seen between groups five days before topical antimicrobials or before the administration of ofloxacin on the day of the procedure. Significantly higher positive culture rates were seen in the control group than in the study group one hour after the administration of the preoperative antimicrobial and before povidone–iodine, immediately before the procedure, and at the conclusion of the procedure. Mean CFU counts did not significantly differ five days preoperatively and immediately before the procedure but were significantly higher in the control group at all other time points. Neither outcomes of endophthalmitis nor patient compliance with antimicrobial use was reported. The study's authors concluded that three days of topical ofloxacin was more effective than administration just one hour before the procedure in reducing the number of positive bacterial cultures at several time points perioperatively.

Numerous studies have evaluated the efficacy of intracameral and subconjunctival injections of antimicrobials given at the end of surgery.[6,674,677,679–682,697,699,703,716,718] The most commonly reported dose of intracameral cefuroxime was 1 mg,[677,679,680,682,699,718] and the most commonly reported subconjunctival dose was 50 mg.[718] Doses of 2.5 or 1 mg of intracameral cefazolin were studied,[670,674] as were 250- and 500-μg doses of intracameral moxifloxacin.[715,716] Postoperative dosing strategies reported in the literature include four times daily for 3–7 days[667,670,671,673–675,679,680,692,711,712,715] and for up to 15 days[713,714] or until the bottle was empty.[716]

Despite the lack of well-controlled trials, the consequences of bacterial endophthalmitis support the use of prophylactic antimicrobials. No definitive studies have clearly delineated superiority of antimicrobial route, timing, or duration.

Recommendation. Due to the lack of robust data from trials, specific recommendations cannot be made regarding choice, route, or duration of prophylaxis. As a general principle, the antimicrobial prophylaxis regimens used in ophthalmic procedures should provide coverage against common ocular pathogens, including *Staphylococcus* species and gram-negative organisms, particularly *Pseudomonas* species.

Preoperative antisepsis with povidone–iodine is recommended, based on available evidence. Appropriate topical antimicrobials include commercially available neomycin–polymyxin B–gramicidin solution or fluoroquinolones (particularly fourth-generation agents) given as one drop every 5–15 minutes for five doses within the hour before the start of the procedure (Table 2). The addition of subconjunctival cefazolin 100 mg or intracameral cefazolin 1–2.5 mg or cefuroxime 1 mg at the end of the procedure is optional. While some data have shown that intracameral antimicrobials may be more effective than subconjunctival antimicrobials, there are no commercially available antimicrobials approved for these routes of administration. (Strength of evidence for prophylaxis = B.)

Orthopedic Procedures

Background. Orthopedic procedures considered in these guidelines include clean orthopedic procedures (not involving replacement or implantations), spinal procedures with or without instrumentation, repair of hip fractures, implantation of internal fixation devices (screws, nails, plates, and pins), and total-joint-replacement procedures. Grade III open fractures (extensive soft tissue damage and crushing) are often associated with extensive surgical-site contamination and are routinely managed with empirical antimicrobial treatment and surgical debridement, for which guidelines have been published separately.[720] Available guidelines recommend that antimicrobial prophylaxis in grade I (clean wound with ≤1-cm laceration) and grade II (clean wound with >1-cm laceration without extensive soft tissue damage) open fractures be handled similarly to other clean orthopedic procedures.[721–724]

Between 2006 and 2008, SSIs were reported nationally, based on risk category, in approximately 0.7–4.15 per 100 procedures for patients undergoing spinal fusion, 0.72–2.3 per 100 procedures in patients undergoing laminectomy, 0.67–2.4 per 100 procedures in patients undergoing hip prosthesis, and 0.58–1.60 per 100 procedures in patients undergoing knee prosthesis.[165] Postoperative SSI is one of the most costly complications of orthopedic procedures due to hospital readmissions, extended hospital length of stay, the need for additional procedures (often removal and reimplantation of implanted hardware), convalescent or nursing home care between procedures, and significant increases in direct hospital costs (e.g., prolonged antimicrobial therapy).[725,726] Studies have found that the estimated economic impact of one deep SSI was $100,000 in hospital costs alone after hip arthroplasty and $60,000 after knee arthroplasty.[727–731]

In light of the serious consequences, antimicrobial prophylaxis is well accepted in procedures involving the implantation of foreign materials.[8,732] Prophylaxis is also indicated in spinal procedures without instrumentation, where an SSI would pose catastrophic risks.[726,733–738]

Organisms. Skin flora are the most frequent organisms involved in SSIs after orthopedic procedures. The most common pathogens in orthopedic procedures are *S. aureus*, gram-negative bacilli, coagulase-negative staphylococci (including *S. epidermidis*), and β-hemolytic streptococci.[739–743] Spinal procedures may be complicated by polymicrobial infection that includes gram-negative bacteria.[740]

A contributing factor to SSIs in arthroplasty is the formation of bacterial biofilm, particularly with *S. aureus* and *S. epidermidis*, on inert surfaces of orthopedic devices. Bacterial biofilm confers antimicrobial resistance and makes antimicrobial penetration difficult.[744–748]

There is increasing concern regarding the emergence of SSIs due to resistant microorganisms, specifically VRE and MRSA in surgical patients. Several studies have investigated MRSA colonization and SSIs and evaluated the effect of decolonization, including the use of topical mupirocin, in orthopedic procedures.[150,157,741,749–753] Mupirocin decolonization protocols as an adjunct to i.v. cephalosporin prophylaxis in orthopedic patients resulted in significant decreases in nasal MRSA carriage[150,751] and overall SSIs.[157,750–752] Preoperative decolonization with intranasal mupirocin may have utility in patients undergoing elective orthopedic procedures who are known to be colonized or infected with either MRSA or MSSA.[150,151,157,741,749–755] Readers are referred to additional discussion in the Common Principles section of these guidelines.

Clean Orthopedic Procedures Not Involving Implantation of Foreign Materials

Background. In clean orthopedic procedures, such as knee, hand, and foot procedures, and those not involving the implantation of foreign materials, the need for antimicrobial prophylaxis is not well established.[738,749,756] Antimicrobial prophylaxis in patients undergoing diagnostic and operative arthroscopic procedures is controversial.[6,757–760] The risks of SSI and long-term sequelae are low for procedures not involving implantation.

Efficacy. The efficacy of antimicrobial prophylaxis in clean orthopedic procedures was first investigated in the middle part of the 20th century. A number of these studies and reviews have since been found to be flawed, as patients were not randomized to treatment groups and the timing and duration of antimicrobial prophylaxis were not studied.[761,762] Further, patients were administered prophylactic antimicrobials after the surgical procedure, which may have led to invalid results. The low rate of infection and absence of serious morbidity failed to justify the expense or potential for toxicity and resistance associated with routine use of antimicrobial prophylaxis in the setting of clean orthopedic procedures.

Recommendations. Antimicrobial prophylaxis is not recommended for patients undergoing clean orthopedic procedures, including knee, hand, and foot procedures, arthroscopy, and other procedures without instrumentation or implantation of foreign materials. (Strength of evidence against prophylaxis = C.) If the potential for implantation of foreign materials is unknown, the procedure should be treated as with implantation.

Spinal Procedures with and without Instrumentation

Background. Data support the use of antimicrobial prophylaxis for orthopedic spinal procedures with and without instrumentation, including fusions, laminectomies, and minimally invasive disk procedures, to decrease the rate of postoperative spinal infection.[8,543,563,732,733,739,763–766] SSIs after orthopedic spinal procedures, including minimally invasive disk procedures, are associated with high morbidity. Invasion of the epidural space in organ/space SSIs is of particular concern after spinal procedures.[8,145,767]

SSI rates vary with the complexity of the procedure. One retrospective, multicenter study of 1274 adult patients found an overall SSI rate of 0.22% with antimicrobial prophylaxis after minimally invasive spinal procedures (i.e., any spinal procedures performed through a tubular retractor-type system).[768] Procedures included simple decompressive procedures (such as microscopic or endoscopic discectomy or foraminotomy or decompression of stenosis), minimally invasive arthrodeses with percutaneous instrumentation, and minimally invasive intradural procedures. The SSI rate in patients receiving antimicrobial prophylaxis undergoing spinal procedures with instrumentation has ranged from 2.8%

to 9.7%.[165,764,765,769,770] Monosegmental instrumentation has a reported SSI rate of <2%, compared with 6.7% for instrumentation at multiple levels.[771]

Several case–control studies of adults undergoing spinal procedures with and without instrumentation have found the following notable patient-related risk factors for SSI: prolonged preoperative hospitalization,[771] diabetes,[767,772–775] elevated serum glucose concentration (>125 mg/dL preoperatively [within 30 days] or >200 mg/dL postoperatively),[773] older age,[767,776] smoking and alcohol abuse,[776] previous procedure complicated by infection,[774–776] and obesity.[770–775,777] Procedure-related risk factors include extended duration of procedure (defined in studies as two to five hours or greater than five hours,[775] greater than three hours,[771] and greater than five hours[776]), excessive blood loss (>1 L),[771,775] staged procedure,[776] multilevel fusions,[777] foreign-body placement (e.g., screw, rod, plate),[767] combined anterior and posterior fusion,[776] and suboptimal antimicrobial timing (>60 minutes before or after incision).[773] A significant decrease in SSIs was seen with procedures at the cervical spine level[772,773] or with an anterior surgical approach.[775]

Efficacy. Despite the lack of comparative studies evaluating prophylaxis for spinal procedures with and without instrumentation (implantation of internal fixation devices), antimicrobial prophylaxis is recommended due to the associated morbidity and assumed costs of SSIs.[771] A meta-analysis of six studies with 843 patients undergoing spinal procedures (types of procedures were not differentiated in the analysis) demonstrated an overall effectiveness of antimicrobial prophylaxis.[732] Antimicrobials studied included single-dose or multidose regimens of <24 hours' duration of cephaloridine (a first-generation cephalosporin no longer available in the United States), vancomycin and gentamicin, cefazolin with and without gentamicin, piperacillin, and oxacillin. The pooled SSI rate with antimicrobial prophylaxis was 2.2%, compared with 5.9% in controls (OR, 0.37; 95% CI, 0.17–0.78; $p < 0.01$). One randomized controlled study of 1237 adult patients undergoing spinal procedures to repair a herniated disk (hemilaminectomy, laminectomy, flavectomy, spondylosyndesis) found no significant difference in the rate of SSIs between single-dose cefuroxime 1.5 g i.v. (1.3%) and placebo (2.9%) given within 60 minutes before surgical incision. No significant difference was seen between treatment groups for incisional SSIs (0.98% and 1.12%, respectively) or deep SSIs (0.33% and 0.32%, respectively), but the difference in organ/space infections was significant between groups (0% and 1.44%, respectively; $p < 0.01$).[778]

Choice of agent. There is no clearly superior antimicrobial agent or regimen for spinal procedures.[563,769] The antimicrobials most often studied for prophylaxis in orthopedic procedures are first-generation cephalosporins, particularly cefazolin. Cefazolin has been noted as a suitable agent for spinal procedures with its spectrum of activity (e.g., against *Staphylococcus* species and gram-negative bacilli such as *E. coli*) and adequate tissue[121] and disk concentrations.[779,780]

Second- and third-generation cephalosporins offer no major advantages over first-generation agents. Their routine use is not recommended due to their higher cost and potential to promote resistance, particularly among health-care-associated gram-negative bacilli.[8] Broader coverage may be considered for instrumented fusion due to the risk of polymicrobial infections, including those caused by gram-negative bacteria.[563,769]

Clindamycin and vancomycin have adequate activity against the most common pathogens involved in orthopedic procedures and would be acceptable alternatives under certain circumstances, such as prophylaxis for patients with a β-lactam allergy. Vancomycin should be included with cefazolin or used as an alternative agent for routine antimicrobial prophylaxis for patients who are known to be colonized with MRSA.[6,8,41,733,781]

Duration. The majority of available studies of antimicrobial prophylaxis in spinal procedures have used single doses or regimens of <24 hours' duration.[732] There is no high-quality evidence supporting a duration of >24 hours,[782] and some sources recommend only a single preoperative dose.[8,769,778]

Pediatric Efficacy. While no studies have evaluated the efficacy of antimicrobial prophylaxis in pediatric patients undergoing spinal procedures with or without instrumentation, the incidence and risk factors for SSIs in this population have been reported. The frequencies of SSIs in pediatric patients undergoing spinal fusion were 3.5% (<18 years old),[783] 3.8% (<19 years old),[784] 4.4% (ages 1–22 years old), and 5.2% (<17 years old)[764] for varying conditions, including Scheuermann's kyphosis,[784] myelodysplasia,[764] idiopathic scoliosis,[783,785] neuromuscular scoliosis,[785] kyphosis,[783] and spondylolisthesis.[783] The majority of patients in studies reporting antimicrobial prophylaxis received cefazolin, vancomycin, or clindamycin.[764,783,785]

Risk factors for SSIs after spinal procedures with instrumentation in a pediatric population include myelodysplasia,[764] procedure at the sacral spine, obesity,[785] ASA classification of >2, a complex medical condition (including spinal bifida, cerebral palsy, Marfan syndrome, achondroplasia, osteogenesis imperfecta, other unspecified genetic disease, muscular dystrophy, spinal muscular atrophy, or other debilitating myopathies),[783] and previous spinal procedures. One study found a decreased risk of infection with hypothermia (core body temperature of <35.5 °C for the duration of the procedure).[785]

Two studies found suboptimal antimicrobial prophylaxis as a risk factor for SSIs in spinal procedures.[764,783] Optimal antimicrobial prophylaxis was defined as cefazolin 20 mg/kg (up to 2 g) given within 30 minutes[764] or 60 minutes[783] before surgical incision, vancomycin 10 mg/kg (up to 1 g) given within 60 minutes[783] or 150 minutes[764] before surgical incision, or clindamycin 10 mg/kg (up to 600 mg) given within 60 minutes before surgical incision.[783] Intraoperative redosing was defined as appropriate for cefazolin if administered for procedures lasting more than four hours and for vancomycin or clindamycin for procedures lasting more than six hours in one study[783] and for cefazolin administered every eight hours in the other study.[764] A third study found that use of clindamycin as the perioperative antimicrobial increased the risk of SSI.[785]

Recommendations. Antimicrobial prophylaxis is recommended for orthopedic spinal procedures with and without instrumentation. The recommended regimen is cefazolin (Table 2). (Strength of evidence for prophylaxis in orthopedic spinal procedures = A.) Clindamycin and vancomycin should be reserved as alternative agents as described in the

Common Principles section. If there are surveillance data showing that gram-negative organisms are a cause of SSIs for the procedure, practitioners may consider combining clindamycin or vancomycin with another agent (cefazolin if the patient is not β-lactam allergic; aztreonam, gentamicin, or single-dose fluoroquinolone if the patient is β-lactam allergic). Mupirocin should be given intranasally to all patients known to be colonized with *S. aureus*.

Hip Fracture Repair

Background. Data support the use of antimicrobial prophylaxis for hip fracture repair to reduce the rate of SSIs, particularly in procedures that involve internal fixation (e.g., nails, screws, plates, wires). SSIs after hip fracture repair can result in extensive morbidity, including prolonged and repeated hospitalization, sepsis, persistent pain, device replacement, and possible death.[726,739,786–790]

Efficacy. The efficacy of antimicrobial prophylaxis in hip fracture repair has been illustrated in two meta-analyses.[787,788] One meta-analysis of 15 hip fracture procedure trials (the majority of procedures involved closed, proximal femoral, or trochanteric fractures with internal fixation) demonstrated that any dose and duration of prophylaxis are superior to no prophylaxis with respect to preventing SSIs (deep and superficial SSIs were analyzed together).[787] The rate of SSIs was 10.4% in controls versus 5.39% in treatment groups. A second meta-analysis of 22 studies reiterated the efficacy of antimicrobial prophylaxis in fracture procedures.[788] The analysis included the same hip fracture studies examined in the first meta-analysis, with additional studies of long-bone fracture repair (i.e., closed ankle fracture and other closed fractures, some noted with internal fixation). This second meta-analysis reviewed 10 studies of 1896 patients receiving a preoperative and two or more postoperative doses of a parenteral antimicrobial compared with a placebo or with no treatment. The authors found a relative risk of deep SSIs of 0.36 (95% CI, 0.21–0.65) and a relative risk of superficial SSIs of 0.48 (95% CI, 0.28–0.81) associated with antimicrobial use.

Choice of agent. The antimicrobials most often studied for prophylaxis in orthopedic procedures are first-generation cephalosporins due to their ease of administration, low cost, and safety profile.[787,788,791] Second- and third-generation cephalosporins have not been shown to offer clear advantages over first-generation agents. These agents are not recommended for routine use due to their higher cost, potential to promote resistance, and association with adverse events (e.g., *C. difficile*-associated diarrhea).[8,790,792]

Alternative regimens may be needed for institutions with highly resistant organisms, such as MRSA or *C. difficile*. Success in decreasing rates of *C. difficile*-associated disease and mortality was seen in a single-center study with the antimicrobial prophylaxis regimen change from three doses of cefuroxime[790,792] to a single preoperative dose of cefuroxime plus gentamicin.[792] In another study, *C. difficile*-associated disease decreased after the prophylaxis regimen was changed from cefuroxime to amoxicillin–clavulanate.[790]

Clindamycin and vancomycin have adequate activity against the most common pathogens involved in orthopedic procedures and would be acceptable alternatives under certain circumstances, such as prophylaxis for patients with a β-lactam allergy. Vancomycin should be included with cefazolin or used as an alternative agent for routine antimicrobial prophylaxis for patients who are known to be colonized with MRSA.[6,8,41,733,781]

Duration. For effective prophylaxis, the MIC of the antimicrobial needs to be exceeded at the target site from the moment of incision until surgical-site closure.[788] Two meta-analyses demonstrating the efficacy of antimicrobial prophylaxis in long-bone and hip fracture procedures also showed that multiple perioperative doses did not offer an advantage over a single preoperative dose.[787,788] These studies support a duration of antimicrobial prophylaxis of ≤24 hours.

Recommendations. The recommended regimen in hip fracture repair or other orthopedic procedures involving internal fixation is cefazolin. Clindamycin and vancomycin should be reserved as alternative agents, as described in the Common Principles section. If there are surveillance data showing that gram-negative organisms are a cause of SSIs for the procedure, practitioners may consider combining clindamycin or vancomycin with another agent (cefazolin if the patient is not β-lactam allergic; aztreonam, gentamicin, or single-dose fluoroquinolone if the patient is β-lactam allergic). Mupirocin should be given intranasally to all patients with documented colonization with *S. aureus*. (Strength of evidence for prophylaxis = A.)

Total Joint Replacement

Background. In 2005, more than 750,000 hip or knee replacements were performed in the United States.[793] The reported frequency of SSIs complicating hip, knee, elbow, ankle, or shoulder replacement ranges from 0.6% to 12%.[743,786,794–797] SSI rates as high as 11% after hip replacement and 12% after elbow replacement have been reported.[786,797] However, for hip and knee replacements, the most common joint arthroplasties, infection rates are typically less than 2%.[165]

The introduction of antimicrobial prophylaxis, stringent infection-control protocols, and the use of ultraclean operating rooms has led to a substantial reduction in SSI rates (to ≤1%).[734,786,796,798,799] Postoperative prosthetic joint infection is an organ/space SSI that occurs early (within 3 months postoperatively), is delayed (3–12 months postoperatively), or occurs late (>12 months after surgery).[748] These infections frequently require removal of the prosthesis, a prolonged course of antimicrobials, and one- or two-stage reimplantation of the prosthesis and may result in permanent disability.[796,800] Studies have shown an estimated economic impact of one deep SSI of $100,000 in hospital costs alone after hip arthroplasty and $60,000 after knee arthroplasty.[727–731]

Common risk factors for prosthetic joint infection[748] include advanced age; obesity; diabetes mellitus; corticosteroid use; malignancy; rheumatoid arthritis; previous arthroplasty on the same joint; arthroplasty undertaken to treat a fracture; type of joint replaced (e.g., risk is greater for the knee than the hip); perioperative surgical-site complications, including superficial SSI; hematoma; and persistent surgical-site drainage. Operative risk factors include ASA classification of ≥3, duration of procedure exceeding the 75th percentile for the procedure or exceeding three hours, surgical site classified as contaminated or dirty, and no systemic antimicrobial prophylaxis. Excluding the presence of a systemic antimicrobial, patients with these operative risk factors are at the greatest risk of developing an SSI.

A contributing factor to SSIs in arthroplasty is the formation of bacterial biofilm, particularly with *S. aureus* and *S. epidermidis*, on inert surfaces of orthopedic devices to confer antimicrobial resistance and difficulty in antimicrobial penetration.[744–748]

Efficacy. The majority of studies that have evaluated antimicrobial prophylaxis in joint replacements have been conducted in patients undergoing total hip or total knee arthroplasty.[801] There is a lack of efficacy data involving elbow, shoulder, and ankle arthroplasty; however, the same antimicrobial prophylaxis principles can be applied. In light of the serious potential consequences, antimicrobial prophylaxis is well accepted in procedures involving the implantation of foreign materials.[8,543,732,733]

A meta-analysis supports the use of antimicrobial prophylaxis for SSI reduction in patients undergoing total joint replacement.[801] Of the 26 randomized controlled studies examined, 24 included patients undergoing total hip or total knee arthroplasty. The meta-analysis noted that the studies did not clearly state if the arthroplasties were primary or revision. The SSIs were defined as visible purulent exudates at the surgical site (deep or superficial) in the included studies. Seven studies (n = 3065 patients) pooled to compare antimicrobial prophylaxis with placebo found a relative risk reduction of SSIs of 81%.

Choice of agent. There are no data supporting superiority of one class of antimicrobials over another for antimicrobial prophylaxis in total joint replacement. A meta-analysis of studies, mainly in total hip or total knee replacement, found no difference in SSIs between cephalosporins with teicoplanin (not available in the United States) in five studies with 2625 patients, cephalosporins and penicillin derivatives in three studies of 386 patients, and first- and second-generation cephalosporins in eight studies of 2879 patients.[801] Selection should be based on cost, availability, and local resistance patterns. First-generation cephalosporins are the agents most commonly studied and used for antimicrobial prophylaxis in joint replacement procedures.

Clindamycin and vancomycin have adequate activity against the most common pathogens involved in orthopedic procedures and would be acceptable alternatives under certain circumstances, such as prophylaxis for patients with a β-lactam allergy. Vancomycin should be included with cefazolin or used as an alternative agent for routine antimicrobial prophylaxis in institutions that have a high prevalence of MRSA SSIs and for patients who are known to be colonized with MRSA.[6,8,41,733,781] Readers are referred to the section on implantation of internal fixation devices for further discussion of antimicrobial prophylaxis choice.

Antimicrobial-laden bone cement. The use of antimicrobial-laden bone cement in conjunction with i.v. antimicrobial prophylaxis is common worldwide, particularly for the prevention of infection in primary hip and knee arthroplasties.[802–806] FDA has approved premixed aminoglycoside (i.e., gentamicin and tobramycin) in bone cement products for use in hip, knee, or other joints in second-stage revision of total joint arthroplasty.[807] The products are not approved for prophylaxis in primary joint replacement procedures. While antimicrobial bone cement has not been shown to be superior to i.v. antimicrobials,[808,809] there is evidence that supports the combination of using antimicrobial-laden bone cement together with systemic antimicrobial prophylaxis.

Although the evidence for the prophylactic use of antimicrobial-laden bone cement in primary joint arthroplasty looks favorable, a recent multicenter evaluation of risk factors for SSI in patients undergoing total hip arthroplasty did not find that use of antimicrobial-laden bone cement reduced the risk for infection.[95] In addition, questions remain regarding the risk for antimicrobial resistance and allergy, as well as the increased cost.[41,802–807,810–813] Readers are referred to reviews of this topic for additional information about tissue penetration, clinical application, and safety.[805,810–815]

Duration. The duration of prophylaxis in joint replacement procedures has been controversial. More recent data and clinical practice guidelines do not support prophylaxis beyond 24 hours.[6,41,133,723] Studies involving total hip replacement have used antimicrobials for 12 hours to 14 days postoperatively.[726,734–737,816] A duration of 24 hours was supported in a randomized trial of 358 patients undergoing total hip arthroplasty, total knee arthroplasty, or hip fracture repair that compared prophylaxis that lasted 24 hours versus 7 days of either nafcillin or cefazolin started 20 minutes before the procedure.[816] The difference in SSI rates between groups was not significant. There is no evidence of benefit of antimicrobial administration until all drains or catheters are removed.[32,41,133]

Recommendations. The recommended regimen for patients undergoing total hip, elbow, knee, ankle, or shoulder replacement is cefazolin. Clindamycin and vancomycin should be reserved as alternative agents, as described in the Common Principles section. If there are any surveillance data showing that gram-negative organisms are a cause of SSIs for the procedure, practitioners may consider combining clindamycin or vancomycin with another agent (cefazolin if the patient is not β-lactam allergic; aztreonam, gentamicin, or a single-dose fluoroquinolone if the patient is β-lactam allergic). Mupirocin should be given intranasally to all patients with documented colonization with *S. aureus*. (Strength of evidence for prophylaxis = A.)

Urologic Procedures

Background. The goals of antimicrobial prophylaxis in urologic procedures are the prevention of bacteremia and SSIs and the prevention of postoperative bacteriuria.[59] Postoperative urinary tract infections (UTIs) are the main concern for morbidity in patients after urologic procedures.[817,818] Bacteriuria, defined as $>10^3$ or $>10^4$ CFU/mL in symptomatic UTI and $>10^5$ CFU/mL in asymptomatic bacteriuria, within 30 days postoperatively is a frequent primary outcome in urologic procedure studies.[819–825] The benefits of preventing postoperative bacteriuria are not clearly known.[825]

In addition to general risk factors discussed in the Common Principles section of these guidelines, urologic-specific risk factors include anatomic anomalies of the urinary tract,[818] urinary obstruction,[826] urinary stone,[817,825,826] and indwelling or externalized catheters.[817,818,822,826] Preoperative UTI, particularly if recurrent, is recognized as a high-risk factor for postoperative infection, which is typically treated before procedures and is a common exclusion criterion from studies of efficacy of antimicrobial prophylaxis in urologic procedures.[817,826–828] Additional urologic operation-specific risk factors include length of postoperative catheterization,[829] mode of irrigation (closed versus open), and postoperative pyuria.[821]

Organisms. *E. coli* is the organism most commonly isolated in patients with postoperative bacteriuria; however, other gram-negative bacilli and enterococci may also cause infection.[818,821,827,830–839] Organisms such as *S. aureus*, coagulase-negative *Staphylococcus* species, and group A *Streptococcus* species are also a concern in procedures entering the skin with or without entering the urinary tract.[818,827,830–832,838,840,841] There is also some concern with biofilm-forming bacteria (*S. epidermidis* and *P. aeruginosa*) in patients with prosthesis implantation.[842]

Efficacy. The efficacy of antimicrobial prophylaxis in select urologic procedures has been investigated in several clinical trials. Of note, many of these placebo-controlled studies have excluded patients with risk factors for infection, those requiring antimicrobial prophylaxis for another indication (e.g., infective endocarditis), and those with preoperative UTI or bacteriuria.

The efficacy of antimicrobial prophylaxis in clean procedures among patients at low risk of complications has been variable. One randomized, placebo-controlled study of oral antimicrobials in 2083 patients undergoing flexible cystoscopy found a positive urine culture (bacteriuria with $>10^5$ CFU/mL) in 9.1% of patients receiving placebo, 4.6% of patients receiving trimethoprim, and 2.8% of patients receiving ciprofloxacin.[839] The rates of bacteriuria compared with baseline were significantly higher with placebo and significantly lower with use of antimicrobials compared with placebo. A randomized, placebo-controlled study of 517 patients undergoing prostate brachytherapy found no significant difference in postimplantation epididymitis with or without antimicrobial prophylaxis (0.4% and 1.5%, respectively).[843] A meta-analysis of eight randomized, placebo-controlled or no-treatment-controlled studies with 995 patients undergoing urodynamic studies found a decrease in bacteriuria with antimicrobial prophylaxis (OR, 0.39; 95% CI, 0.24–0.61).[820] The number needed to treat was 13 to prevent one episode of asymptomatic bacteriuria using a pooled rate of 13.7% for bacteriuria. One study found that not using antimicrobial prophylaxis was a significant risk factor for bacteriuria caused by urinary dynamic studies.[821]

Antimicrobial prophylaxis has been studied in urologic procedures involving entry into the gastrointestinal tract, with the majority of the literature on transurethral resection of the prostate (TURP) and prostate biopsy. Two large meta-analyses have suggested prophylactic antimicrobials may be effective in all patients undergoing TURP, including low-risk patients and those with preoperatively sterile urine.[844,845] One meta-analysis of 32 trials with 4260 patients found that prophylactic antimicrobials decreased the combined bacteriuria ($>10^5$ CFU/mL) event rate from 26% to 9.1%, for a relative risk reduction of 65% (95% CI, –55 to –72), and the combined clinical septicemia episode rate from 4.4% to 0.7% in TURP patients, including low-risk patients.[846] Another meta-analysis of 28 trials that included a total of 4694 patients found prophylactic antimicrobials decreased the post-TURP rate of bacteriuria, fever, and bacteremia, as well as the need for additional postoperative antimicrobials.[847] An additional multicenter, open-label, randomized, active- and placebo-controlled trial in patients with sterile urine undergoing TURP found a decreased rate of bacteriuria (≥5 CFU/mL) with antimicrobial prophylaxis (21% with levofloxacin and 20% with sulfamethoxazole–trimethoprim) compared with placebo (30%) ($p = 0.009$).[822]

Three randomized, placebo-controlled studies of patients undergoing transrectal needle biopsy of the prostate found significant differences in infectious complications (including bacteriuria, positive urine cultures, and UTI) in patients treated with single doses of oral antimicrobial prophylaxis compared with placebo.[819,837,838] These three studies support the routine use of antimicrobial prophylaxis in all patients undergoing transrectal needle biopsy of the prostate. Of note, all patients undergoing transrectal needle biopsy of the prostate received a cleansing enema before the procedure.[819,837,838] Use of MBP has been reported in urologic procedures that involve entering the gastrointestinal tract (e.g., urinary diversion).[844,846]

The use of antimicrobial prophylaxis in patients undergoing extracorporeal shock wave lithotripsy (ESWL) and ureterorenoscopy is supported by the results of a meta-analysis[847] and a small randomized controlled trial.[848] The meta-analysis included eight randomized controlled trials with 885 patients and six clinical case series involving 597 patients undergoing ESWL.[845] The overall rate of UTI in the randomized controlled trials ranged from 0% to 7.7% with antimicrobial prophylaxis and from 0% to 28% in the control groups (relative risk, 0.45; 95% CI, 0.22–0.93). A randomized, placebo-controlled study of 113 patients undergoing ureterorenoscopy found a rate of postoperative bacteriuria of 1.8% with antimicrobial prophylaxis and 12.5% without ($p = 0.0026$).[848] No patients had symptomatic UTI or inflammation complications of the urogenital tract postoperatively.

There are no studies of antimicrobial prophylaxis in major open or laparoscopic procedures (cystectomy, radical prostatectomy, and nephrectomy); therefore, data have been extrapolated from other major intraabdominal procedures.

Choice of agent. No single antimicrobial regimen appears superior for urologic procedures. A wide range of antimicrobial regimens, including cephalosporins,[658,835,836,843,849–855] aminoglycosides,[856,857] piperacillin–tazobactam,[849,858,859] trimethoprim–sulfamethoxazole,[822,838,860] trimethoprim,[839] nitrofurantoin,[861] and fluoroquinolones,[819,821,822,824,831,835–837,839,840,843,848,851,853–855,862,863] have been evaluated in urologic procedures. The efficacy of fluoroquinolones for antimicrobial prophylaxis in urologic surgical procedures has been well established. One study found better reduction of bacteriuria with either ciprofloxacin or trimethoprim compared with placebo,[839] while other studies found no difference in efficacy between a fluoroquinolone and sulfamethoxazole–trimethoprim, both of which were better than placebo.[822,838] No differences were found in studies between oral or i.v. fluoroquinolones (ciprofloxacin or ofloxacin) compared with i.v. or intramuscular cephalosporins (ceftriaxone, cefotaxime, or cefazolin) and intramuscular penicillin (piperacillin–tazobactam) in various urologic procedures.[835,836,851,854,855,858] In several studies, fluoroquinolones were administered orally, which appears to be feasible in patients undergoing procedures not involving opening the urinary or gastrointestinal tract, when the i.v. route would be preferred.[822,836,838,851,855,858]

Recently, resistance to fluoroquinolones has been emerging; the fact that most of the literature was published before resistance became prevalent should be considered, since resistance may decrease the relevance of these studies.[836,846,847,858,864] Local resistance patterns to fluoroquinolones, particularly with *E. coli*, should be evaluated to help guide antimicrobial selection.

Broad-spectrum antimicrobials, such as third-generation cephalosporins and carbapenems, are no more effective than first- or second-generation cephalosporins, aminoglycosides, or oral agents (trimethoprim–sulfamethoxazole, nitrofurantoin, or fluoroquinolones) and should be reserved for patients with active infection or who require additional coverage for intestinal organisms.[6,826,827] Their routine use is not recommended due to their higher cost and potential to promote resistance, particularly among health-care-associated gram-negative bacilli.[8]

Duration. While longer durations of postoperative prophylaxis (up to three weeks) have been studied,[856,858,860,861] more-recent data support the use of shorter durations (i.e., a single dose or less than 24 hours' duration) in urologic procedures.[658,817,818,823,824,826,831,832,834,836,846,853,857,859,862,865,866] Based on bioavailability, oral antimicrobial prophylaxis should be administered 1–2 hours before surgical incision or start of the procedure.[817,819–822,824,826,836,838,840,848,851,855]

Pediatric Efficacy. Limited data on antimicrobial prophylaxis are available for pediatric patients undergoing urologic procedures. One prospective, open-label, nonrandomized study of boys undergoing hypospadias repair with tabularized incision plate urethroplasty allocated patients to receive cefonicid (no longer available in the United States) with one i.v. dose before the procedure only or the addition of oral cephalexin three times daily starting on postoperative day 1 until 2 days after catheter removal (median, 8.3 days).[833] More patients in the single-dose group had bacteriuria and complications (urethrocutaneous fistula and meatal stenosis); however, the rate of infection and infection-related complications did not significantly differ between groups.

Recommendations. No antimicrobial prophylaxis is recommended for clean urologic procedures in patients without risk factors for postoperative infections. Patients with preoperative bacteriuria or UTI should be treated before the procedure, when possible, to reduce the risk of postoperative infection. For patients undergoing lower urinary tract instrumentation with risk factors for infection, the use of a fluoroquinolone or trimethoprim–sulfamethoxazole (oral or i.v.) or cefazolin (i.v. or intramuscular) is recommended (Table 2). For patients undergoing clean urologic procedures without entry into the urinary tract, cefazolin is recommended, with vancomycin or clindamycin as an alternative for those patients allergic to β-lactam antimicrobials. For patients undergoing clean urologic procedures with entry into the urinary tract, cefazolin is recommended, with alternative antimicrobials to include a fluoroquinolone, the combination of an aminoglycoside plus metronidazole, or an aminoglycoside plus clindamycin. For clean-contaminated procedures of the urinary tract (often entering the gastrointestinal tract), antimicrobials as recommended for elective colorectal surgery are recommended. This would generally include the combination of cefazolin with or without metronidazole, cefoxitin, or, for patients with β-lactam allergy, a combination of either a fluoroquinolone or aminoglycoside given with either metronidazole or clindamycin. The medical literature does not support continuing antimicrobial prophylaxis until urinary catheters have been removed. See the colorectal procedures section of these guidelines for recommendations pertaining to procedures entering the gastrointestinal tract. (Strength of evidence for prophylaxis = A.)

Vascular Procedures

Background. Infection after vascular procedures occurs with low frequency but can be associated with extensive morbidity and mortality.[867,868] Postoperative infections involving vascular graft material can result in limb loss and life-threatening conditions.[868] As a result, antimicrobial prophylaxis is widely used in procedures that involve implantation of prosthetic material and procedures for which there is greater risk of infection, such as aneurysm repair, thromboendarterectomy, and vein bypass.[6,41,867,869] Patients undergoing brachiocephalic procedures (e.g., carotid endarterectomy, brachial artery repair) without implantation of prosthetic graft material do not appear to benefit from routine antimicrobial prophylaxis.[6,41,867,870]

Risk factors for postoperative SSI in patients undergoing vascular procedures include lower-extremity sites, delayed procedures after hospitalization, diabetes mellitus, and a history of vascular or aortocoronary bypass procedures.[871,872] Currently, prospective data from well-designed studies on prophylaxis for endovascular stenting do not exist. However, if prophylaxis is desired, the same antimicrobials and short duration of therapy used for open vascular procedures should be given. Risk factors that warrant consideration of prophylaxis in patients undergoing endovascular stenting include prolonged procedures (more than two hours), reintervention at the surgical site within seven days, vascular stent placement in the groin through a hematoma or sheath, procedures in immunosuppressed patients, and the presence of another intravascular prosthesis.[873–877]

Organisms. The predominant organisms involved include *S. aureus*, *S. epidermidis*, and enteric gram-negative bacilli. MRSA is an emerging organism of concern.

Several studies evaluated the rate of colonization, carriage, and infection with MRSA in patients undergoing various vascular procedures.[878–884] Independent risk factors for MRSA infection included MRSA colonization, open abdominal aortic aneurysm, tissue loss, and lower-limb bypass.[878] Patients who have or develop MRSA infections before vascular procedures have increased risk of inhospital death, intensive care unit admission, repeat surgeries, increased length of stay, and delayed wound healing, compared with patients without infections.[880–883]

Efficacy. Prophylactic antimicrobials decrease the rate of infection after procedures involving the lower abdominal vasculature and procedures required to establish dialysis access. The follow-up time for patients with late surgical-site complications was at least once after hospital discharge (not further defined) for most studies,[829,865,871,885–887] at one month,[869,871,888,889] at six months,[872] and at three years.[138]

A meta-analysis of 10 randomized controlled trials in patients undergoing peripheral arterial reconstruction with biological or prosthetic graft procedures found an overall consistent reduction in SSIs with systemic antimicrobial prophylaxis compared with placebo (relative risk, 0.25; 95% CI, 0.17–0.38; $p < 0.00001$).[890] An overall reduction was found among 5 studies evaluating early graft infection (relative risk, 0.31; 95% CI, 0.11–0.85; $p = 0.02$), though no individual study found a significant reduction in SSIs.

The largest study included in the meta-analysis above was a randomized, prospective, double-blind, placebo-controlled study of patients undergoing peripheral vascular procedures ($n = 462$). The infection rate was significantly lower with cefazolin than with placebo (0.9% and 6.8%, respectively).[885] Four deep graft infections were observed in the placebo group; none occurred in the patients who received cefazolin. No infections were observed in patients who underwent brachiocephalic ($n = 103$), femoral artery ($n = 56$), or popliteal ($n = 14$) procedures.

Patients undergoing vascular access procedures for hemodialysis may benefit from the administration of antistaphylococcal antimicrobials. A placebo-controlled study of 408 patients undergoing permanent vascular access placement demonstrated an upper-extremity prosthetic polytetrafluoroethylene graft infection rate of 6% with placebo compared with 1% with vancomycin ($p = 0.006$).[869]

Choice of agent. Cefazolin remains the preferred and most cost-effective prophylactic agent for use in vascular procedures.[6,8,41,872,886,887] There was no significant difference in infection rates between cefazolin and cefuroxime in patients undergoing abdominal aortic and lower-extremity peripheral vascular procedures,[886] between cefazolin and cefamandole (no longer available in the United States) in patients undergoing aortic or infrainguinal arterial procedures,[887] or between cefazolin and ceftriaxone in patients undergoing arterial reconstruction involving infraclavicular sites.[872]

A multicenter, randomized, double-blind, prospective trial of 580 patients undergoing arterial procedures involving the groin who received either two doses of ciprofloxacin 750 mg orally or three doses of cefuroxime 1.5 g i.v. on the day of the procedure found an SSI rate of 9.2% (27 patients) and 9.1% (26 patients), respectively, within 30 days of the procedure.[889] Although oral ciprofloxacin was shown to be as effective as i.v. cefuroxime, this study did not address concerns about resistance with routine use of fluoroquinolones.[891] Therefore, i.v. cefazolin remains the first-line agent for this indication. The efficacy of oral agents for prophylaxis needs to be further evaluated.

There are limited data regarding the choice of an antimicrobial for β-lactam-allergic patients undergoing vascular procedures. The main alternative agents are vancomycin and clindamycin, since prophylaxis is largely directed against gram-positive cocci. Vancomycin can also be used for prophylaxis in institutions with MRSA or methicillin-resistant *S. epidermidis* (MRSE) clusters or in patients with β-lactam allergy.[6,8,41] Clindamycin may be an acceptable alternative to vancomycin, though local antimicrobial resistance patterns should be taken into account.

An aminoglycoside may be added to vancomycin for the addition of aerobic gram-negative bacilli coverage if the procedure involves the abdominal aorta or a groin incision, due to the potential for gastrointestinal flora. See the Common Principles section of these guidelines for further discussion of the use of vancomycin. Alternative antimicrobials for β-lactam-allergic patients receiving vancomycin may include a fluoroquinolone or aztreonam.[6]

Duration. A meta-analysis of three randomized controlled studies involving vascular procedures, including lower-limb reconstruction and open arterial procedures, found no additional benefit of continuing prophylactic antimicrobials for over 24 hours postoperatively compared with no more than 24 hours (relative risk, 1.28; 95% CI, 0.82–1.98).[890]

A randomized, double-blind study compared infection rates of a one-day and a three-day course of cefuroxime with placebo in 187 patients undergoing peripheral vascular procedures.[888] The infection rates were 16.7%, 3.8%, and 4.3% in the placebo, one-day, and three-day groups, respectively. The difference in the infection rates between the one- and three-day groups was not significant.

A randomized controlled study compared one day and five days of amoxicillin–clavulanate 1.2 g in 100 patients undergoing 108 lower-limb reconstruction procedures.[892] No difference was seen in the postoperative SSI rate between groups (9 patients [16%] and 12 patients [23%], respectively). The study authors selected the agent based on extended spectrum of activity and good tissue penetration. However, they concluded that due to the high rate of infection observed, the use of antimicrobial prophylaxis might not be as effective as once thought.

A randomized controlled study compared ticarcillin–clavulanate 3.1 g given as a single dose at induction of anesthesia with multiple doses given at induction and every 6 hours postoperatively until venous access lines were removed or a maximum of 20 doses (total of five days) in patients undergoing open arterial procedures.[893] Significantly more SSIs occurred in the single-dose group (28 [18%] of 153 patients) compared with the multidose group (15 [10%] of 149 patients) (relative risk, 2; 95% CI, –1.02 to 3.92; $p = 0.041$). Ticarcillin–clavulanate has a short duration of action and is not recommended as a routine agent for antimicrobial prophylaxis. Practice guidelines recommend single-dose prophylaxis in vascular procedures or a maximum duration of therapy of 24 hours postoperatively, regardless of the presence of invasive drains.[6,41]

Recommendations. The recommended regimen for patients undergoing vascular procedures associated with a higher risk of infection, including implantation of prosthetic material, is cefazolin (Table 2). (Strength of evidence for prophylaxis = A.) Clindamycin and vancomycin should be reserved as alternative agents as described in the Common Principles section of these guidelines. If there are surveillance data showing that gram-negative organisms are a cause of SSIs for the procedure, practitioners may consider combining clindamycin or vancomycin with another agent (cefazolin if the patient is not β-lactam allergic; aztreonam, gentamicin, or single-dose fluoroquinolone if the patient is β-lactam allergic), due to the potential for gastrointestinal flora exposure.

Heart, Lung, and Heart–Lung Transplantation

Background. Solid-organ transplant recipients are at high risk for infections due to the complexity of the surgical procedures, donor- or recipient-derived infections, reactivation of recipient-associated latent infections, preoperative recipient colonization, exposure to community pathogens, and opportunistic infections due to immunosuppression.[894–897] Infections occur more frequently in the first year after transplantation, due to aggressive immunosuppression. Transplant recipients with infections are commonly asymptomatic or have nonspecific symptoms or sequelae of infection, which makes detection and diagnosis of infections difficult.[855,857,894] Postoperative infections caused by bacterial, viral, and fungal pathogens, including SSIs, UTIs, bloodstream infections, and pneumonia, are of greater concern within the first month after transplantation.[895–897] Opportunistic infections that result from immunosuppression typically occur after the first month of transplantation. It is routine for transplant recipients to receive antimicrobial prophylaxis to prevent opportunistic infections.[894–897] A discussion of the prophylactic strategies for prevention of cytomegalovirus (CMV) infection, herpes simplex virus infection, pneumocystis, UTI in kidney transplant recipients, *Aspergillus* infection in lung transplant recipients, and other opportunistic infections outside of the immediate posttransplantation period is beyond the scope of these guidelines.

Few well-designed, prospective, comparative studies of antimicrobial prophylaxis have been conducted with patients undergoing solid-organ transplantation, and no formal recommendations are available from expert consensus panels or professional organizations; however, there are reviews that provide guidance.[8,41,894]

The recommendations given for each of the solid-organ transplant procedures are intended to provide guidelines for safe and effective surgical prophylaxis based on the best available literature. Antimicrobial surgical prophylaxis practice will vary considerably among transplantation centers throughout the United States, based on the organ involved, preexisting recipient and donor infections, and local antimicrobial susceptibilities.[894–897]

Heart Transplantation. *Background.* Heart transplantation is an option for selected patients with end-stage cardiac disease. In 2007, the United Network for Organ Sharing (UNOS) reported that 2209 heart transplants were performed in the United States, including 327 in children (<18 years of age).[898] The mean graft survival rate 10 years after heart transplantation is approximately 49%. Infection continues to be an important cause of morbidity and mortality after heart transplantation and is a primary cause of death in approximately 14% of patients within the first year after transplantation.[899]

Despite the large number of heart transplantation procedures performed, few studies have specifically examined postoperative SSI rates in this population. General cardiothoracic procedures have been associated with SSI rates ranging from 9% to 55% in the absence of antimicrobial prophylaxis.[214,900,901] Studies of general cardiothoracic procedures, including heart transplantation, found SSIs, particularly mediastinitis, in 3–6% of patients who received antimicrobial prophylaxis.[170,902] The frequency was highest in heart transplant recipients. The SSI rates reported in patients undergoing heart transplantation who received antimicrobial prophylaxis ranged from 5.8% to 8.8%, including mediastinitis in 3–7% of patients.[903,904]

Several independent risk factors for SSIs after cardiac and thoracic procedures have been identified (see the cardiac and thoracic sections of this article). Heart transplantation has been identified as an independent risk factor for SSIs.[170] Other independent risk factors for SSIs in heart transplantation include age,[905] receipt of ciprofloxacin alone for prophylaxis,[906] positive wire cultures,[907] a BMI of >30 kg/m^2, female sex,[908] previous cardiac procedures, previous left VAD placement, and hemodynamic instability requiring inotropic support.[903,904] Unfavorable functional outcomes were seen in patients who developed infections within the first year after heart transplantation associated with lung, bloodstream, and CMV infections.[909] Independent predictors of mortality in heart transplant recipients included serum creatinine levels, amyloid etiology, history of hypertension, pulmonary infection, and CNS infection. Additional predisposing factors for infection in heart transplantation include exposure to pathogens from the donor or transplant recipient, the time from organ recovery to reperfusion, and the immunosuppressive regimens used.[897,904,910] Similar risk factors for infection are noted in pediatric transplant recipients, with the addition of a naive immune system to several pathogens, most notably viruses, as well as incomplete primary immunization series.[897]

Patients with an indwelling VAD at the time of heart transplantation have additional prophylaxis concerns. Recipients who do not have a driveline infection and have no history of either colonization or infection should receive prophylaxis as described for recipients without a VAD in place. Patients with a history of colonization or previous infection should have the antimicrobial sensitivities of that organism considered when choosing the SSI prophylactic regimen administered, though the duration should still be less than 24 hours. Heart transplant recipients with an active VAD driveline infection at the time of heart transplantation should be given appropriate antimicrobials specifically for the treatment of that infection. This intervention will usually determine the actual perioperative prophylaxis regimen as well as the duration of therapy beyond the period of prophylaxis.

Patients requiring ECMO as a bridge to heart transplantation should be treated with a similar approach. If there is no history of colonization or previous infection, then the general recommendations for SSI antimicrobial prophylaxis for the specific procedure should be followed. In ECMO patients with a history of colonization or previous infection, changing the preoperative antimicrobial prophylaxis to cover these pathogens must be considered, weighing whether the pathogen is relevant to SSIs in the planned procedure.

Because heart transplantation is similar to other cardiac and thoracic procedures, similar considerations regarding the need for antimicrobial prophylaxis apply (see the cardiac and thoracic sections).[911] These guidelines do not address antimicrobial prophylaxis for infective endocarditis. Readers are referred to the current guidelines for prevention of infective endocarditis from AHA.[11,228]

Organisms. As with other types of cardiothoracic procedures, gram-positive organisms, mainly *Staphylococcus* species, are the primary pathogens that cause SSI after heart transplantation.[902,905–907,912,913] MRSA was reported in 12–21% of SSIs in several cohort studies.[903,905,906] Vancomycin-resistant *Enterococcus faecalis* was noted in 15% of infections in one cohort study.[903] Other gram-positive pathogens (e.g., coagulase-negative staphylococci, *Enterococcus* species)[903,905–907,913] and gram-negative organisms (e.g., Enterobacteriaceae, *P. aeruginosa*, *Stenotrophomonas maltophilia*) are also a concern for SSIs in heart transplant recipients, as are *Candida* species.[903,906]

Efficacy. Despite the paucity of literature on antimicrobial prophylaxis for the prevention of SSIs in heart transplantation, the efficacy noted in other cardiac surgical procedures has made it the standard of practice during transplantation.[896]

No randomized controlled trials have specifically addressed the use of antimicrobial prophylaxis in heart transplantation. In an open-label noncomparative study, the SSI rate was 4.5% among 96 patients administered cefotaxime plus floxacillin preoperatively and for 72 hours after cardiac procedures.[912] This rate of infection was similar to that seen in other cardiothoracic, nonheart transplantation procedures in which antimicrobial prophylaxis was used.

Choice of agent. Antimicrobial prophylaxis for heart transplantation should be similar to that used for other types of cardiothoracic procedures.[911] First- and second-generation cephalosporins are considered to be equally efficacious and are the preferred agents. There appear to be no significant differences in efficacy among prophylactic regimens using agents such as cefazolin and cefuroxime.[914] The use of antistaphylococcal penicillins, either alone or in combination with aminoglycosides or cephalosporins, failed to demonstrate superior efficacy to that of cephalosporin monotherapy (see the cardiac and thoracic sections) in other cardiothoracic procedures.

Several cohort studies examined antimicrobial prophylactic agents used for patients undergoing heart transplantation but did not evaluate efficacy.[902,903,905,906] Ciprofloxacin alone was found to be an independent risk factor for incisional SSIs.[906]

Duration. There is no consensus on the optimal duration of antimicrobial prophylaxis in cardiothoracic procedures, including heart transplantation. Cohort evaluations of patients undergoing heart transplantation reported durations of antimicrobial prophylaxis with cefazolin or vancomycin of 24 or 48 hours postoperatively.[902,903,905] Data from cardiothoracic procedures also support a range of prophylaxis durations, from a single dose to 24 or 48 hours postoperatively.[41,131] The currently accepted duration for these procedures, which do not include transplantation, is 24–48 hours postoperatively.[41,59,131,201] The duration of antimicrobial prophylaxis for patients who do not have their chest primarily closed is unclear; most centers continue prophylaxis until the chest is closed, but there is no evidence to support this practice.

Pediatric efficacy. No randomized controlled studies have specifically addressed antimicrobial prophylaxis for heart transplantation in pediatric patients. Infants are at risk for mediastinitis caused by gram-negative as well as gram-positive organisms. Pediatric patients undergoing heart transplantation should be treated according to recommendations for other types of cardiothoracic procedures. The recommended regimen for pediatric patients undergoing cardiothoracic procedures is cefazolin 25–50 mg/kg i.v. within 60 minutes before surgical incision and every 8 hours for up to 48 hours. Cefuroxime 50 mg/kg i.v. within 60 minutes before surgical incision and every 8 hours for up to 48 hours is an acceptable alternative. Vancomycin 10–20 mg/kg i.v. over 60–120 minutes, with or without gentamicin 2 mg/kg i.v., should be reserved as an alternative on the basis of guidelines from HICPAC for routine antimicrobial prophylaxis in institutions that have a high prevalence of MRSA, for patients who are colonized with MRSA, or for patients with a true β-lactam allergy.[8] Additional doses may be needed intraoperatively for procedures >4 hours in duration, for patients with major blood loss, or for extended use of CPB depending on the half-life of the prophylactic antimicrobial. Fluoroquinolones are not routinely recommended in pediatric patients.

Recommendations. Based on data for other types of cardiothoracic procedures, antimicrobial prophylaxis is indicated for all patients undergoing heart transplantation (see cardiac and thoracic sections). The recommended regimen is a single dose of cefazolin (Table 2). There is no evidence to support continuing prophylaxis until chest and mediastinal drainage tubes are removed. Alternatives include vancomycin or clindamycin with or without gentamicin, aztreonam, or a single fluoroquinolone dose. (Strength of evidence for prophylaxis = A.) The optimal duration of antimicrobial prophylaxis for patients who do not have their chest primarily closed is unclear. No recommendation is made for these patients. Patients who have left VADs as a bridge and who are chronically infected might also benefit from coverage of the infecting microorganism.

Lung and Heart–Lung Transplantation. *Background.* Lung transplantation is an accepted option for a variety of end-stage, irreversible lung diseases. The most common diseases for which lung transplantation is performed are idiopathic pulmonary fibrosis, chronic obstructive pulmonary disease, emphysema, cystic fibrosis, α-1-antitrypsin deficiency, and idiopathic pulmonary arterial hypertension.[915,916] UNOS reported that in the United States in 2007, 1468 lung transplantations and 31 heart–lung transplantations were conducted in adults, and 52 lung transplantations and 3 heart–lung transplantations were performed in children.[898,917] Ten-year survival rates were reported as 29.7% of double-lung, 17.5% of single-lung, and 25.8% of heart–lung transplant recipients.[899] The reported three-year survival rate for pediatric lung transplant recipients was 57%.[89]

Infections are the most common complications after lung and heart–lung transplantations.[899,915,918,919] In an analysis of UNOS data over an 18-year period, infection was the number one cause of death within the first year of transplantation, occurring in 24.8% of lung and 18.3% of heart–lung transplant recipients.[899] Among the top 10 primary causes of death within the first year after lung and heart–lung transplantations were sepsis, pneumonia, fungal infection (lung only), and CMV infection.[899] A study of two cohorts of patients undergoing heart, lung, and heart–lung transplantations who received antimicrobial prophylaxis evaluated the rate of SSIs and mediastinitis.[904,908] The rate of SSI among all transplant recipients was 12.98%, with the majority of infections (72%) being organ/space infections, followed by deep incisional infections (17%) and superficial incisional infections (10%).[908] The overall rate of mediastinitis in a similar cohort was 2.7%, with rates of 5.2% in heart–lung transplant recipients and 3.2% in bilateral lung transplant recipients.[904] Pneumonia was reported in 26.4% of transplantation patients overall, with rates of 20.7% in lung transplant recipients and 40% in heart–lung transplant recipients.[908] A cohort of lung transplant recipients reported a rate of 2.2 episodes of pneumonia per patient during a median follow-up period of 412 days (range, 1–1328 days).[920]

Bronchial anastomotic infections, especially fungal infections, can be serious and are potentially fatal in lung transplant recipients.[921,922] The lung allocation score (LAS) is a rating system adopted by the Organ Procurement and Transplant Network and UNOS in 2005 to improve organ allocation and transplantation outcomes. The LAS is based on the risk of death while on the waiting list for transplantation and the expected 1-year survival after transplantation. Patients with a low LAS are unlikely to undergo transplantation. A study of lung transplant recipients age 12 years or older revealed a higher rate of infection and other morbidities and a lower 1-year survival rate in patients with a high LAS at the time of transplantation than in patients with a low LAS at the time of transplantation.[923] Thus, the potential for bronchial anastomotic infection and a poor posttransplantation outcome needs to be considered in patients undergoing lung transplantation. Among lung transplantation patients, risk factors for nosocomial infections included α-1-antitrypsin deficiency and repeat transplantation. Risk factors for pneumonia included colonized or infected donor bronchus and perfusate and preoperative colonization with gram-negative rods. Risk factors for mortality among the transplant recipients were cystic fibrosis, nosocomial infection, and ventilation before transplantation.[908] Risk factors for mediastinitis after heart, lung, and heart–lung transplantation were degree of immunosuppression, impaired renal function, previous sternotomy, and reexploration due to bleeding.[904] There was a positive association between pretransplantation colonizing microorganisms from suppurative lung disease patients and pneumonia after transplantation.[920] Transplantation alters the physiological function of lungs, including the impairment of mucociliary clearance and interruption of the cough reflex, leading to a higher risk of pulmonary infections.[896]

In patients requiring ECMO as a bridge to lung transplantation who have no history of colonization or previous infection, the general recommendations for SSI antimicrobial prophylaxis for the procedure should be followed. In ECMO patients with a history of colonization or previous infection, changing the preoperative antimicrobial prophylaxis to cover these pathogens must be considered, weighing whether the pathogen is relevant to SSIs in the planned procedure.

Organisms. While gram-positive and gram-negative organisms are of concern in heart transplantation, there is increased concern regarding gram-negative and fungal pathogens in mediastinitis and pneumonia in patients undergoing lung transplantation.[894,904,908] The most frequent organisms found in SSIs or mediastinitis in two cohort studies were *P. aeruginosa*,[904,908] *Candida* species, *S. aureus* (including MRSA),[908] enterococci, coagulase-negative staphylococci (e.g., *S. epidermidis*), *Burkholderia cepacia*,[904] *E. coli*, and *Klebsiella* species.

Patients undergoing lung transplantation are also at risk for bacterial or fungal pneumonia due to colonization or infection of the lower and upper airways of the donor, recipient, or both.[915] Organisms reported to cause pneumonia in lung transplantation patients include *P. aeruginosa*,[894,896,904,908,920] *S. aureus* (including MRSA),[894,896,904,908] *B. cepacia*,[896,904,908] *Enterobacter* species,[908] *S. maltophilia*, *Klebsiella* species,[904,908] *S. epidermidis*,[904] *E. coli*, *Aspergillus* species,[920] and VRE.[894] Similarly, organisms frequently seen in pediatric lung infections are nonfermenting gram-negative bacteria, such as *Pseudomonas* species, *Stenotrophomonas* species, *Alcaligenes* species, and fungi, including *Aspergillus* species.[897]

The donor lung appears to be a major route of transmission of pathogens; 75–90% of bronchial washings from donor organs are positive for at least one bacterial organism.[920,924,925] Organ recipients may also be the source of infection of the transplanted organ. This is particularly true in patients with cystic fibrosis because of the frequent presence of *P. aeruginosa* in the upper airways and sinuses before transplantation.[896,919] These pathogens are often multidrug resistant, likely due, in large part, to frequent administration of broad-spectrum antimicrobials during the course of the disease. Multidrug-resistant strains of *B. cepacia* and *S. maltophilia* may be a problem in cystic fibrosis patients in some transplantation centers.[919,926]

Efficacy. Although much has been published about general infectious complications associated with lung transplantation, no randomized controlled trials regarding antimicrobial prophylaxis for lung or heart–lung transplantation have been published; however, antimicrobial prophylaxis is considered standard practice in these patients.[896] Antimicrobial prophylaxis is routinely administered to patients undergoing lung or heart–lung transplantation, with the aim of preventing pneumonia as well as SSIs. The rate of pneumonia within the first two weeks postoperatively has reportedly been decreased from 35% to approximately 10% by routine antimicrobial prophylaxis.[927–929] Improvements in surgical technique and postoperative patient care are also important factors in the apparently lower rates of pneumonia after lung transplantation.

Choice of agent. No formal studies have addressed optimal prophylaxis for patients undergoing lung transplantation. Antimicrobial prophylaxis for lung and heart–lung transplantation should generally be similar to that used for other cardiothoracic procedures (see the cardiac and thoracic sections). First- and second-generation cephalosporins are considered equally efficacious and are the preferred agents for these procedures. However, prophylactic regimens should be modified to include coverage for any potential bacterial pathogens, including gram-negative and fungal organisms, that have been isolated from the recipient's airways or the donor lung through preoperative cultures.[894,896,904,908,915,920] Patients with end-stage cystic fibrosis should receive antimicrobials on the basis of the known susceptibilities of pretransplant isolates, particularly *P. aeruginosa*, *B. cepacia* complex, and *Aspergillus* species.

Antimicrobial prophylaxis regimens reported in cohort evaluations of thoracic transplantation, including lungs, have varied.[904,908,920] One study used ceftazidime, floxacillin, tobramycin, and itraconazole in these patients.[908] In addition, all patients received nebulized amphotericin B and oral itraconazole as antifungal prophylaxis. Another cohort study used cefepime for lung transplant recipients without known colonization; for those with known colonization, the selection of agents was based on organism susceptibility.[920] A third cohort reported use of metronidazole and aztreonam as prophylaxis for patients with a septic lung (positive sputum culture).[904]

Antifungal prophylaxis should be considered, especially when pretransplantation cultures reveal fungi in the donor lung[915] or the recipient's airway. There is no consensus on the appropriate antifungal agent for lung transplant recipients.[894,896,930] Selection is recommended based on patient risk factors for infection (e.g., cystic fibrosis) and colonization, pretransplantation and posttransplantation cultures, and local fungus epidemiology.[894,896,897,930] Because of the serious nature of fungal infections in the early posttransplantation period and the availability of antifungal agents, prophylaxis should be considered when *Candida* or *Aspergillus* species are isolated from the donor lung[915] or recipient's airway.

Duration. No well-conducted studies have addressed the optimal duration of antimicrobial prophylaxis for lung or heart–lung transplantation. In the absence of positive cultures from the donor or the recipient, prophylactic regimens of 48–72 hours and no longer than 7 days have been reported.[896,904,905,931] In patients with positive pretransplantation cultures from donor or recipient organs or patients with positive cultures after transplantation, postoperative antimicrobial treatment for 7–14 days or longer has been reported, particularly for patients with cystic fibrosis and previous *P. aeruginosa* and multidrug-resistant infections.[896,915,919] Such antimicrobial administration is viewed as treatment and not as surgical prophylaxis. Treatment may include additional antibacterial agents or antifungal agents.

Recommendations. Based on data from other types of cardiothoracic procedures, all adult patients undergoing lung transplantation should receive antimicrobial prophylaxis, because of the high risk of infection. Patients with negative pretransplantation cultures should receive antimicrobial prophylaxis as appropriate for other types of cardiothoracic procedures.

The recommended regimen is a single dose of cefazolin (Table 2). There is no evidence to support continuing prophylaxis until chest and mediastinal drainage tubes are removed. Alternatives include vancomycin with or without gentamicin, aztreonam, and a single fluoroquinolone dose. (Strength of evidence for prophylaxis = A.) The optimal duration of antimicrobial prophylaxis for patients who do not have their chest primarily closed is unclear. No recommendation is made for these patients.

The prophylactic regimen should be modified to provide coverage against any potential pathogens, including gram-negative (e.g., *P. aeruginosa*) and fungal organisms, isolated from the donor lung or the recipient pretransplantation. The prophylactic regimen may also include antifungal agents for *Candida* and *Aspergillus* species based on patient risk factors for infection (e.g., cystic fibrosis) and colonization, pretransplantation and posttransplantation cultures, and local fungus epidemiology. Patients undergoing lung transplantation for cystic fibrosis should receive treatment for at least seven days with antimicrobials selected according to pretransplantation culture and susceptibility results. (Strength of evidence for prophylaxis = B.)

Liver Transplantation

Background. Liver transplantation is a lifesaving procedure for many patients with end-stage hepatic disease for whom there are no other medical or surgical options.[932,933] In 2007, UNOS reported that 6494 liver transplantations were performed in the United States, 96% of which had a cadaveric donor and 4% had a living-related donor source.[934] These liver transplantations were performed in 5889 adults and 605 pediatric (<18 years old) patients. Reported 1-year patient survival rates for adults ranged from 76.9% to 95%[932,935–938] and from 80% to 91.7% for pediatric patients.[934,939–942] Survival at 3 and 5 years ranged from 68.5% to 80.9%[934] and from 61.6% to 76.5%[932,933] in adult patients, respectively. In pediatric patients, 3- and 5-year survival ranged from 73.2% to 86%[897,934,941] and from 69.2% to 80.1%,[934] respectively. One-year graft survival rates ranged from 74.2% to 94% in adults[934–936,938] and from 72.1% to 86.1% in pediatric patients.[934,941,942] Graft survival at 3 and 5 years ranged from 58.9% to 75.5% and from 51.6% to 70.5%, respectively, in adults and from 62.5% to 77.6% and from 68.4% to 71.4%, respectively, in pediatric patients.[934,941] No significant differences were noted in graft or patient survival between cadaveric and living-related donors in adult and pediatric liver transplant recipients.[934] Infection remains a major cause of morbidity and mortality in liver transplant recipients. Infections may occur in 31–83% of patients within three months of transplantation and are the cause of death in 4–53% of patients.[934,936,940,943–950] These rates are highly variable and do not seem to have changed despite advances in surgical technique and medical management. SSIs within 30 days after transplantation ranged from 4% to 48% with antimicrobial prophylaxis in several cohort and controlled studies.[935–938,941,942,948,949,951–964] Superficial SSIs are seen most often within the first two to three weeks postoperatively, whereas organ/space infections and deep infections are seen after three to four weeks.

Liver transplantation is often considered to be the most technically difficult of the solid-organ transplantation procedures. Surgical procedures lasting longer than 8–12 hours have been consistently identified as one of the most important risk factors for early infectious complications, including SSIs, intraabdominal infections, and biliary tract infections.[896,938,939,945,947,957] Other important risk factors for infectious complications related to liver transplantation surgery include previous hepatobiliary surgery,[896,939,945,947,952,963] previous liver or kidney transplantation,[937,951,952,965] and surgical complications such as anastomotic leakage.[896,938,939,945,947,951,952] Patient-related risk factors for infection after liver transplantation include antimicrobial use within three to four months before transplantation,[935,954] low pretransplantation serum albumin concentration,[938,958,963] high pretransplantation serum bilirubin concentration,[939,945,947] ascites,[938] obesity,[963] diabetes, and hemochromatosis.[966] Procedure-related risk factors for infection include transfusion of >4 units of red blood cells,[896,951] bacterial contamination due to entry into the gastrointestinal tract,[963] surgical incision method,[963] and use of muromonab-CD3 within the first week after transplantation.[938]

Organisms. The pathogens most commonly associated with early SSIs and intraabdominal infections are those derived from the normal flora of the intestinal lumen and the skin. Aerobic gram-negative bacilli, including *E. coli*,[935,937,939,940,942,945,947–949,951,967,968] *Klebsiella* species,[933,936,937,939,940,945,947–949,967–969] *Enterobacter* species,[936,939,940,942,945,947,952,959,964,967,968] *Acinetobacter baumannii*,[935–937,942,951] and *Citrobacter* species,[939,940,945,947,952,959,967,968] are common causes of SSIs and intraabdominal infections and account for up to 65% of all bacterial pathogens. Infections due to *P. aeruginosa* may also occur but are much less common in the early postoperative period.[936,937,939,940,942,945,947,948,952,959,969] Enterococci are particularly common pathogens and may be responsible for 20–46% of SSIs and intraabdominal infections.[894,933,935,937,938,940,943,945–947,951,952,955,964,965,969] *S. aureus* (frequently MRSA) and coagulase-negative staphylococci are also common causes of postoperative SSIs.[936–938,940,942,943,945–949,955,957–961,964,965,970,971] *Candida* species commonly cause both early and late postoperative infections.[933,936,937,940,942,943,945–947,949,951,969]

Several studies have noted increasing concern about antimicrobial resistance based on detection of resistant organisms, including *E. coli*,[935,937] *Enterococcus* species,[933,937,964,965] *Enterobacter* species,[964] *Klebsiella* species,[933,937] coagulase-negative staphylococci,[937,964] and *S. aureus*.[937,948,957–961,970] General information on antimicrobial resistance is provided in the Common Principles section of these guidelines. Of specific concern to the transplantation community is the emergence of multidrug-resistant *A. baumannii*,[972] carbapenem-resistant Enterobacteriaceae,[973,974] *K. pneumoniae* carbapenemase-producing organisms,[975] and *C. difficile*.[976–978]

Efficacy. Although there remains a high rate of infection directly related to the liver transplantation procedure, there are few well-controlled studies concerning optimal antimicrobial prophylaxis. In evaluating the efficacy of prophylactic regimens, it is important to differentiate between early infections (occurring within 14–30 days after surgery) and late infections (occurring more than 30 days after surgery). Infections occurring in the early postoperative period are most commonly associated with biliary, vascular, and abdominal surgeries involved in the transplantation procedure itself and are thus most preventable with prophylactic antimicrobial regimens.[939,940,943,945] The frequency of these infections varies from 10% to 55% despite antimicrobial prophylaxis.[939,940,943,945,979] It is difficult to assess the efficacy of prophylactic regimens in reducing the rate of infection, because prophylaxis has been routinely used in light of the complexity of the surgical procedure; therefore, reliable rates of infection in the absence of prophylaxis are not available. No controlled studies have compared prophylaxis with no prophylaxis.

Choice of agent. Antimicrobial prophylaxis should be directed against the pathogens most commonly isolated from early infections (i.e., gram-negative aerobic bacilli, staphylococci, and enterococci). Traditional prophylactic regimens have therefore consisted of a third-generation cephalosporin (usually cefotaxime, because of its antistaphylococcal activity) plus ampicillin.[936,937,943,944,946–948,951,952,954,962,965,967,979] The use of cefoxitin and ampicillin–sulbactam, cefotaxime and ampicillin–sulbactam and gentamicin,[957–959] cefuroxime and metronidazole,[971] ceftriaxone and metronidazole,[980] cefotaxime and metronidazole,[953] ceftriaxone and ampicillin,[949] ceftizoxime alone,[955] cefotaxime and tobramycin,[956] cefoxitin alone,[960,961] cefazolin alone,[951] amoxicillin–clavulanate and gentamicin,[970] amoxicillin–clavulanate alone,[951] glycopeptides and antipseudomonal penicillin,[951] quinolone and amoxicillin–clavulanate or glycopeptide,[951] vancomycin and aztreonam,[951,981] and piperacillin–tazobactam[964,970] has also been reported. Alternative prophylaxis regimens for β-lactam-allergic patients have included cefuroxime and metronidazole,[970] clindamycin and gentamicin or aztreonam,[948,960–962] ciprofloxacin and metronidazole,[970] and vancomycin or ciprofloxacin.[936] Imipenem alone was used in one study for patients with renal failure.[956] The efficacy of these regimens compared with cefotaxime plus ampicillin is difficult to assess due to different definitions of infection used in the available studies and variability of study design (many single-center cohort studies) in different countries. One prospective nonrandomized study found no difference in the frequency of SSIs in orthotopic liver transplant recipients with cefazolin alone and amoxicillin–clavulanate alone, both given one hour before surgical incision, with a second dose given in cases of significant bleeding or surgery lasting over six hours, as antimicrobial prophylaxis.[935] The study did find a significantly higher rate of *A. baumannii* in the cefazolin group than the amoxicillin–clavulanate group. The routine use of vancomycin as antimicrobial prophylaxis is not recommended because of the risk of developing vancomycin-resistant organisms,[8,950] but vancomycin may be reserved for centers with an MRSA or MRSE cluster.[8,950,957–959] No randomized controlled studies have been conducted to compare the efficacy of other antimicrobial prophylactic regimens in the prevention of early postoperative infections. For patients known to be colonized with MRSA, VRE, or resistant gram-negative pathogens, it is reasonable to consider prophylaxis specifically targeted at these organisms. See the Common Principles section for further discussion.

Postoperative infections with *Candida* species after liver transplantation are common, particularly in the abdomen, and are frequently considered organ/space SSIs. For this reason, the use of antifungal prophylaxis in the perioperative period has become common. Efficacy has been demonstrated for fluconazole,[964–984] lipid complex amphotericin B,[985–987] and caspofungin.[988] Finally, one meta-analysis found a decreased risk of fungal infection and death associated with fungal infection, though not overall mortality, among patients given antifungal prophylaxis.[989] Universal antifungal prophylaxis is probably not necessary, since the risk of invasive candidiasis is low in uncomplicated cases. Instead, prophylaxis is generally reserved for patients with two or more of the following risk factors: need for reoperation, retransplantation, renal failure, choledochojejunostomy, and known colonization with *Candida* species.[15] Risk is also increased with prolonged initial procedure or transfusion of >40 units of cellular blood products, but this cannot be predicted before the procedure.

Selective bowel decontamination to eliminate aerobic gram-negative bacilli and yeast from the bowel before the transplantation procedure has been evaluated in several studies and a meta-analysis.[936,943,949,955,956,967,968,980,990,991] These studies used combinations of nonabsorbable antibacterials (aminoglycosides, polymyxin B or E), antifungals (nystatin, amphotericin B), and other antimicrobials (cefuroxime in suspension) administered orally and applied to the oropharyngeal cavity in combination with systemically administered antimicrobials. Results are conflicting, with no differences in patient outcomes (e.g., infection rates, mortality) or cost and concerns of increasing gram-positive infections with potential resistance in several studies[939,955,956,980,991] and others with positive results.[936,949] Two randomized controlled studies found significantly fewer bacterial infections with early enteral nutrition plus lactobacillus and fibers.[971,980] Based on currently available data, the routine use of selective bowel decontamination or lactic acid bacteria and fibers in patients undergoing liver transplantation is not recommended.

Duration. No studies have assessed the optimal duration of antimicrobial prophylaxis in liver transplantation. Although antimicrobials have been administered in studies for five days[937,944,946,949,957–959] and seven days,[964] the majority of recent studies have limited the duration of prophylaxis to 72 hours,[981] 48 hours,[936,943,945,952,955,956,960,961,967,970,979,980,991] 36 hours,[981] 24 hours,[935,948,962,970] and a single dose,[963] with no apparent differences in early infection rates. A prospective, nonrandomized, controlled study found no difference in bacterial infections within the first three months after liver transplantation in patients receiving cefotaxime and ampicillin as short-term antimicrobial prophylaxis for two to three days, compared with long-term prophylaxis for five to seven days.[954] Of note, 5 of the 11 patients in the long-term prophylaxis group had detectable *C. difficile* toxin B in the feces and developed enteritis. No patients in the short-term group had detectable *C. difficile*. Two recent review articles noted that antimicrobial prophylaxis duration should be less than three days.[896,950]

Pediatric Efficacy. There are few data specifically concerning antimicrobial prophylaxis in liver transplantation in pediatric patients. The combination of cefotaxime plus ampicillin has been reportedly used in children undergoing living-related donor liver transplantation; the efficacy of this regimen appeared to be favorable.[946] A small, retrospective, single-center cohort study reported outcomes of children undergoing liver, heart, small bowel, or lung transplantation receiving piperacillin–tazobactam 120–150 mg/kg/day beginning before surgical incision and continuing for 48 hours postoperatively and found favorable results, with a superficial SSI rate of 8% and no deep SSIs.[992]

Recommendations. The recommended agents for patients undergoing liver transplantation are (1) piperacillin–tazobactam and (2) cefotaxime plus ampicillin (Table 2). (Strength of evidence for prophylaxis = B.) For patients who are allergic to β-lactam antimicrobials, clindamycin or vancomycin given in combination with gentamicin, aztreonam, or a fluoroquinolone is a reasonable alternative. The duration of prophylaxis should be restricted to 24 hours or less. For patients at high risk of *Candida* infection, fluconazole adjusted for renal function may be considered. (Strength of evidence for prophylaxis = B.)

Pancreas and Pancreas-Kidney Transplantation

Background. Pancreas transplantation is an accepted therapeutic intervention for type 1 diabetes mellitus; it is the only therapy that consistently achieves euglycemia without dependence on exogenous insulin.[993–997] Simultaneous pancreas–kidney (SPK) transplantation is an accepted procedure for patients with type 1 diabetes and severe diabetic nephropathy. In 2007, UNOS reported that 469 pancreas transplantations and 862 SPK transplantations were performed in the United States, of which 60 and 4 patients, respectively, were under age 18 years.[998] Pancreas graft 1-year survival rates ranged from 70.2% to 89%, and the 3-year rates ranged from 48% to 85.8%.[998–1002] Patient survival with pancreas transplantation has been reported between 75% and 97% at 1 year and between 54% and 92.5% at 3 years.[998] Allograft survival is higher in recipients of SPK transplantations, with allograft survival rates of 86.1–95.1% at 1 year and 54.2–92.5% at 3 years. Reported patient survival rates in SPK are 91.7–97.6% at 1 year and 84.4–94.1% at 3 years. During pancreas transplantation, surgical complications with portal-hepatic drainage significantly decreased the 1-year and 3-year survival rates to 48% and 44%, respectively, in one cohort study.[999]

Infectious complications are a major source of morbidity and mortality in patients undergoing pancreas or SPK transplantation; the frequency of SSI is 7–50% with antimicrobial prophylaxis.[993–997,1000–1009] The majority of SSIs occurred within the first 30 days to three months after transplantation.[1000–1002,1005,1008,1009] UTIs are also a significant concern during the same time frame, with rates ranging from 10.6% to 49% in pancreas transplant recipients who received antimicrobial prophylaxis, and are much more common in recipients with bladder drainage compared with enteric drainage.[1000–1008]

Pancreas and SPK transplantation patients may be at increased risk of SSIs and other infections because of the combined immunosuppressive effects of diabetes mellitus and the immunosuppressive drugs used to prevent graft rejection.[995,1000] Other factors associated with increased SSI rates include prolonged operating and ischemic times (>4 hours), organ donor age of >55 years, and enteric rather than bladder drainage of pancreatic duct secretions.[895,995,1000] Prolonged organ preservation time (>20 hours) was shown to increase the risk of complications, including duodenal leaks and decreased graft survival in cadaveric pancreas transplant recipients.[1003] Risk factors for UTI are reviewed in the kidney transplant section.

Organisms. A majority of superficial SSIs after pancreas or SPK transplantation are caused by *Staphylococcus* species (both coagulase-positive and coagulase-negative) and gram-negative bacilli (particularly *E. coli* and *Klebsiella* species).[993–997,1000–1002,1004–1006,1009–1011] Deep SSIs also are frequently associated with gram-positive (*Enterococcus* species, *Streptococcus* species, and *Peptostreptococcus* species) and gram-negative organisms (*Enterobacter* species, *Morganella* species, and *B. fragilis*), as well as *Candida* species.[993–997,1000–1002,1004–1006,1009–1011] Although anaerobes are occasionally isolated, the necessity for specific treatment of anaerobes in SSIs after pancreas transplantation remains unclear.

Efficacy. Although no placebo-controlled studies have been conducted, several open-label, noncomparative, single-center studies have suggested that antimicrobial prophylaxis substantially decreases the rate of superficial and deep SSIs after pancreas or SPK transplantation. SSI rates were 7–33% with various prophylactic regimens,[995,1000–1002,1004,1005] compared with 7–50% for historical controls in the absence of prophylaxis.[1009,1010] The reason for the wide disparity in infection rates observed with prophylaxis is not readily apparent but may include variations in SSI definitions, variations in antimicrobial prophylaxis, immunosuppression protocols, and variations in surgical techniques.[999–1002,1005,1007,1008]

Choice of agent. Because of the broad range of potential pathogens, several studies have used multidrug prophylactic regimens, including imipenem–cilastatin plus vancomycin[995]; tobramycin, vancomycin, and fluconazole[1010]; cefotaxime, metronidazole, and vancomycin[1012]; cefotaxime, vancomycin, and fluconazole[1008]; ampicillin and cefotaxime[1007]; and piperacillin–tazobactam and fluconazole.[1006]

HICPAC recommendations for SSI prevention include limiting the use of vancomycin unless there is an MRSA or MRSE cluster or as an alternative for β-lactam-allergic patients, though transplantation procedures were not specifically covered in the guidelines.[8] Limited data are available on the use of vancomycin as antimicrobial prophylaxis in kidney or pancreas transplantation, or both. A small, randomized, active-controlled, single-center study evaluated the impact of vancomycin-containing antimicrobial prophylaxis regimens in kidney and pancreas (alone or SPK) transplant recipients on the frequency of gram-positive infections.[1004] Renal transplantation patients received either vancomycin and ceftriaxone or cefazolin, and pancreas transplantation patients received either vancomycin and gentamicin or cefazolin and gentamicin. There was no statistically significant difference in the risk of developing gram-positive infections between antimicrobial prophylaxis regimens with and without vancomycin. The study was not powered to detect a difference in efficacy between the antimicrobial regimens. For patients known to be colonized with MRSA, VRE, or resistant gram-negative pathogens, it is reasonable to consider prophylaxis targeted specifically for these organisms. See the Common Principles section for further discussion.

An evaluation of the surgical complications of pancreas transplant recipients with portal-enteric drainage found an intraabdominal infection rate of 12% in the 65 patients undergoing SPK transplantation and no cases in those undergoing pancreas transplantation alone.[999] All patients received either cefazolin 1 g i.v. every eight hours for one to three days, or vancomycin if the patient had a β-lactam allergy.

One study evaluated SSI rates in SPK transplantation after single-agent, single-dose prophylaxis with cefazolin 1 g i.v. to donors and recipients, as well as cefazolin 1-g/L bladder and intraabdominal irrigation in the recipient.[1009] Superficial SSIs developed in 2 patients (5%), and deep SSIs associated with bladder anastomotic leaks or transplant pancreatitis occurred in 4 additional patients (11%). This study reported similar SSI rates as with multidrug, multidose regimens.

Based on the regularity of isolation of *Candida* species from SSIs after pancreas transplantation and the frequent colonization of the duodenum with yeast, fluconazole is commonly added to prophylactic regimens. Although never studied in a randomized trial, a lower fungal infection rate was found in one large case series with the use of fluconazole (6%) compared with no prophylaxis (10%).[1013] Although enteric drainage of the pancreas has been identified as a risk factor for postoperative fungal infections, many institutions use fluconazole for prophylaxis with bladder-drained organs as well. In settings with a high prevalence of non-*albicans Candida* species, a lipid-based formulation of amphotericin B has been recommended in infectious diseases guidelines from the American Society of Transplantation and the American Society of Transplant Surgeons.[15]

Duration. Studies evaluating the use of antimicrobial prophylaxis regimens in pancreas and SPK transplantation, summarized above, ranged from a single preoperative dose of cefazolin to multidrug regimens of 2–5 days' duration.[995,1005,1009,1010,1012] More recent studies reported monotherapy regimens with cefazolin or vancomycin,[999] amoxicillin–clavulanate,[1001,1002] and piperacillin–tazobactam[1000–1002] 1–7 days in duration, with the majority using the regimen 48–72 hours after transplantation. The duration of fluconazole ranged from 7 to 28 days.[1002]

Recommendations. The recommended regimen for patients undergoing pancreas or SPK transplantation is cefazolin (Table 2). (Strength of evidence for prophylaxis = A.) For patients who are allergic to β-lactam antimicrobials, clindamycin or vancomycin given in combination with gentamicin, aztreonam, or a fluoroquinolone is a reasonable alternative. The duration of prophylaxis should be restricted to 24 hours or less. The use of aminoglycosides in combination with other nephrotoxic drugs may result in renal dysfunction and should be avoided unless alternatives are contraindicated. (Strength of evidence for prophylaxis = C.) For patients at high risk of *Candida* infection, fluconazole adjusted for renal function may be considered.

Kidney Transplantation

Background. In 2007, UNOS reported that 16,628 kidney transplantations were performed in the United States; of these, 796 patients were younger than 18 years.[998] The rate of postoperative infection after this procedure has been reported to range from 10% to 56%, with the two most common infections being UTIs and SSIs.[1004,1014–1024] Graft loss due to infection occurs in up to 33% of cases.[1017,1023] One study of adult and pediatric kidney transplant recipients (both living-related and cadaveric donor sources) found patient survival rates at 7 years after transplantation of 88.9% and 75.5%, respectively, and graft survival of 75% and 55.5%, respectively.[1025] No patients developed an SSI. Mortality associated with postoperative infections is substantial and ranges from approximately 5% to 30%.[1015,1017,1019,1022,1026,1027]

The frequency of SSIs in kidney transplant recipients has ranged from 0% to 11% with antimicrobial prophylaxis[1023–1025,1028,1029] to 2% to 7.5% without systemic prophylaxis.[1030,1031] The majority of these infections were superficial in nature and were detected within 30 days after transplantation.[1023,1028–1030] Risk factors for SSI after kidney transplantation include contamination of organ perfusate[1027]; pretransplantation patient-specific factors, such as diabetes,[1029,1030] chronic glomerulonephritis,[1030] and obesity[1027,1030,1032]; procedure-related factors, such as ureteral leakage and hematoma formation[1027]; immunosuppressive therapy[1024,1027,1029]; and postoperative complications, such as acute graft rejection, reoperation, and delayed graft function.[1030] In one study, the frequency of SSI was 12% in patients receiving immunosuppression with azathioprine plus prednisone but only 1.7% in patients receiving cyclosporine plus prednisone.[1033] A significant difference in SSI rates was noted after kidney transplantation between immunosuppression regimens including mycophenolate mofetil (45 [3.9%] of 1150 patients) versus sirolimus (11 [7.4%] of 144 patients).[1029] Sirolimus-containing immunosuppression was found to be an independent risk factor for SSIs. These recommendations refer to kidney transplant recipients; recommendations for living kidney donors can be found in the discussion of nephrectomy in the urologic section.

Organisms. Postoperative SSIs in kidney transplant recipients are caused by gram-positive organisms, particularly *Staphylococcus* species (including *S. aureus* and *S. epidermidis*) and *Enterococcus* species, gram-negative organisms, *E. coli, Enterobacter* species, *Klebsiella* species, *P. aeruginosa*, and yeast with *Candida* species.[1004,1014–1021,1023,1024,1026,1028,1030,1034] One study site in Brazil reported a high level of antimicrobial resistance.[1030] Organisms recovered from infections included MRSA (77%), methicillin-resistant coagulase-negative *Staphylococcus* (53.5%), extended-spectrum β-lactamase-producing *K. pneumoniae* (80%), and carbapenem-resistant *P. aeruginosa* (33.3%). Another center in Brazil reported a significant difference in resistance to broad-spectrum antimicrobials in pathogens isolated in UTIs from cadaveric kidney transplant recipients ($n = 21$, 19.1%) compared with living-related donor kidney transplant recipients ($n = 2$, 3.7%) ($p = 0.008$).[1024] One center in the United States reported 94% susceptibility to vancomycin of *Enterococcus* species within the first month after transplantation, while *E. coli*, cultured most commonly more than six months after transplantation, was 63% resistant to sulfamethoxazole–trimethoprim.[1023] This resistance may be related to the routine use of sulfamethoxazole–trimethoprim in prophylaxis of *Pneumocystis carinii* pneumonia and UTI.

Efficacy. A number of studies have clearly demonstrated that antimicrobial prophylaxis significantly decreases postoperative infection rates in patients undergoing kidney transplantation. These have included at least one randomized controlled trial[1014] and many prospective and retrospective studies comparing infection rates with prophylaxis and historical infection rates at specific transplantation centers.[1015–1018,1021,1033–1035] Based on the available literature, the routine use of systemic antimicrobial prophylaxis is justified in patients undergoing kidney transplantation.

Two studies that evaluated a triple-drug regimen consisting of an aminoglycoside, an antistaphylococcal penicillin, and ampicillin found infection rates of <2%, compared with 10–25% with no antimicrobial prophylaxis.[1018,1019] More specifically, infection rates in patients without antimicrobial prophylaxis (45 cadaveric and 44 living-related donors) were 10.1% in total (8.9% and 11.4%, respectively), compared with 1.5% in total (1.5% and 0%, respectively) with antimicrobial prophylaxis.[1018] Infection rates were as high as 33% in living-related patients with no antimicrobial prophylaxis and 0–1% in both cadaveric and living-related transplant recipients with antimicrobial prophylaxis.[1021] Piperacillin plus cefuroxime was also shown to be efficacious; infection rates were 3.7%, compared with 19% in cadaveric transplant recipients not receiving prophylaxis.[1018] Several studies have shown that single-agent prophylaxis with an antistaphylococcal penicillin,[1029,1034] a first-generation cephalosporin,[1016,1017,1023,1024,1029] a second-generation cephalosporin,[1028,1035,1036] or a third-generation cephalosporin (e.g., cefoperazone, cefotaxime, ceftriaxone)[1024,1029,1033,1037] can reduce postoperative infection rates to 0–8.4%. All studies included cadaveric transplant recipients, whereas living-related transplant recipients were also included in select studies.[1017,1024,1028,1036] Where compared directly, infection rates between cadaveric and living-related transplant recipients receiving antimicrobial prophylaxis were not statistically different.[1024]

Choice of agent. The available data do not indicate a significant difference between single-drug and multidrug antimicrobial regimens.[1014,1018,1021] In addition, there appears to be no significant differences between single-agent regimens employing antistaphylococcal penicillins and first-, second-, or third-generation cephalosporins.[1016,1017,1033–1035,1037] Studies have directly compared antimicrobial regimens in a prospective, controlled fashion. Single-agent prophylaxis with both cefazolin and ceftriaxone has been reported to result in SSI rates of 0%.[1016,1024,1037]

A survey of 101 kidney transplant centers in 39 countries reported that 65% of the centers used single antimicrobial prophylaxis regimens, 20.8% used two-drug regimens, and 3% used three drugs; no prophylaxis was used in 11% of centers.[1036] Cephalosporins were used in 68 centers (55 alone, 7 in combination with penicillin, and 6 with other antimicrobials). Penicillins were used by 28 centers (13 alone, 7 with cephalosporin, and 8 with other antimicrobials). Other antimicrobials (specifics were not reported) were used in 2 centers as the single agent.

As noted above, HICPAC recommendations for SSI prevention include limiting the use of vancomycin to situations in which there is an MRSA or MRSE cluster or as an alternative for β-lactam-allergic patients.[8] Transplantation procedures were not specifically covered in the guidelines.

Duration. Studies have used various prophylactic regimens, ranging from a single-drug cephalosporin regimen, administered as a single preoperative dose or for up to 24 hours postoperatively, to multidrug regimens of two to five days' duration.[981,1004,1014–1018,1021,1023,1024,1028,1029,1033,1036,1038] Cefazolin for 24 hours was equivalent to seven days of surgical prophylaxis in living-related kidney transplant donors.[1039] There appear to be no significant differences in SSI rates between single-dose, 24-hour, and multidose regimens; therefore, the duration of antimicrobial should be restricted to 24 hours.

Pediatric Efficacy. Although pediatric patients were included in studies demonstrating the efficacy of antimicrobial prophylaxis, there are few data specific to pediatric patients.

One cohort of 96 pediatric patients who underwent 104 renal transplants (63% cadaveric and 37% living-related donors) ranged in age from six months to 18 years (mean age, 8.2 ± 5.5 years).[1040] Antimicrobial prophylaxis included one dose of cefotaxime 30-mg/kg i.v. bolus at the start of the procedure and cefotaxime 90 mg/kg/day in three divided doses during the intensive care unit stay, which averaged one to two days. No SSIs were reported.

Recommendations. The recommended agent for patients undergoing kidney transplantation is cefazolin (Table 2). (Strength of evidence for prophylaxis = A.) For patients who are allergic to β-lactam antimicrobials, clindamycin or vancomycin given in combination with gentamicin, aztreonam, or a fluoroquinolone is a reasonable alternative. The duration of prophylaxis should be restricted to 24 hours or less. The use of aminoglycosides in combination with other nephrotoxic drugs may result in renal dysfunction and should be avoided unless alternatives are contraindicated. (Strength of evidence for prophylaxis = C.) For patients at high risk of *Candida* infection, fluconazole adjusted for renal function may be considered.

Plastic Surgery and Breast Procedures

Background. Plastic surgery encompasses a broad range of procedures focused on reconstructive, dermatological, and cosmetic procedures.[1041] The primary goal of these procedures is to restore function to the affected area, with a secondary goal of improving appearance. The scope of procedures ranges from simple primary surgical-site closure, skin grafts, and skin flaps to composite tissue transplantations. Composite tissue transplantation for tissue reconstruction of the knee joint, larynx, uterus, abdominal wall, hand, face, and penis has been performed in a small number of patients.[1042,1043]

Most dermatological, breast (reduction and reconstructive), clean head and neck, and facial procedures have an associated SSI rate of <5%.[1044–1053] Oral procedures, such as wedge excision of lip or ear, flaps on the nose,[1046,1054] and head and neck flaps, have SSI rates of approximately 5–10%.[1053,1055–1060] In addition to general risk factors as described in the Common Principles section, factors that increase the risk of postoperative infectious complications for plastic surgery procedures include implants,[1061] skin irradiation before the procedure, and procedures below the waist.[1062,1063]

Organisms. The most common organisms in SSIs after plastic surgery procedures are *S. aureus*,[1045,1049,1050,1053,1054,1056,1063–1068] other staphylococci, and streptococci.[1045,1054,1064,1066,1067] Procedures involving macerated, moist environments (e.g., under a panus or axilla of an obese individual), below the waist, or in patients with diabetes are associated with a higher rate of infection with gram-negative organisms such as *P. aeruginosa*,[1068] *Serratia marcescens*, or Enterobacteriaceae, including *E. coli*,[1065,1068] *Klebsiella* species,[1068] and *P. mirabilis*.[1065]

Efficacy. The efficacy of antimicrobial prophylaxis in select plastic surgery procedures has been investigated in several clinical trials and cohort studies.

Most placebo-controlled and retrospective studies for many clean plastic surgery procedures have found that antimicrobial prophylaxis does not significantly decrease the risk of infection. These studies have evaluated head and neck procedures (facial bone fracture, tumor excision and reconstruction, radical neck dissection, rhinoplasty),[1049] flexor tendon injury repairs,[1051] augmentation mammoplasty using periareolar submuscular technique,[1052] carpal tunnel,[1069] and breast procedures (reduction mammoplasty, lumpectomy, mastectomy, axillary node dissection).[1056,1058,1070,1071]

However, a Cochrane review of seven randomized, placebo-controlled trials of 1984 patients undergoing breast cancer procedures (axillary lymph node dissection and primary nonreconstructive surgery) evaluated the effectiveness of preoperative or perioperative antimicrobial prophylaxis ($n = 995$) compared with placebo or no treatment ($n = 989$) in reducing the rate of postoperative infections.[1072] Pooled study results revealed a significant difference in SSI rates with antimicrobial prophylaxis (80 [8%] of 995), compared with 10.5% (104 of 989) for no antimicrobial prophylaxis (relative risk, 0.72; 95% CI, 0.53–0.97). Review authors concluded that antimicrobial prophylaxis is warranted to decrease the risk of SSIs in nonreconstructive breast cancer procedures.

Guidelines also support no antimicrobial prophylaxis in patients undergoing clean facial or nasal procedures without an implant.[7] For patients undergoing facial or nasal procedures with an implant, antimicrobial prophylaxis should be considered.[7]

A randomized, double-blind, controlled trial of 207 patients evaluated the use of three antimicrobial prophylaxis regimens in patients undergoing abdominoplasty procedures.[1066] The reported SSI rates were 13% for patients receiving no antimicrobial prophylaxis, 4.3% for those receiving preoperative antimicrobials only, and 8.7% for those receiving one preoperative dose and three days of postoperative antimicrobials. There was a significantly lower infection rate in the group receiving preoperative antimicrobials only compared with the placebo group ($p < 0.05$). The infection rate was slightly but not significantly higher in patients who received postoperative antimicrobials.

Choice of agent. There is no consensus on the appropriate antimicrobial agent to use for prophylaxis in plastic surgery procedures.[1055,1073] Agents with good gram-positive coverage and, depending on the site of surgery, activity against common gram-negative organisms are recommended for patients undergoing clean plastic surgery procedures with risk factors (listed in the Common Principles section and the background discussion of this section) or clean-contaminated procedures. Cefazolin or ampicillin–sulbactam is sufficient in most cases, with clindamycin and vancomycin as alternatives for patients with β-lactam allergy. There are no studies assessing the impact of MRSA on patients undergoing plastic surgery procedures or regarding the need to alter prophylaxis regimens in patients without known colonization with MRSA. When vancomycin or clindamycin is used and if a gram-negative organism is highly suspected, practitioners should consider adding cefazolin if the patient is not β-lactam allergic; if the patient is β-lactam allergic, the addition of aztreonam, gentamicin, or single-dose fluoroquinolone should be considered. If the surgical site involves the ear, an antipseudomonal fluoroquinolone may be considered to cover *Pseudomonas* species.[1045]

Although oral agents such as cephalexin, amoxicillin, clindamycin, and azithromycin have been recommended in reviews of antimicrobial prophylaxis in clean dermatological surgery, there is no evidence that supports their use.[13,1045,1046,1054]

Duration. Antimicrobial prophylaxis should be limited to the shortest duration possible to prevent SSIs (even if a drain or a catheter is left in place or an implant is inserted), limit adverse events, and prevent antimicrobial resistance.[8,512,1047,1048,1054,1056]

Multiple studies have found no significant differences in SSI rates after breast surgery with single-dose preoperative cephalosporin compared with extended-duration regimens that last from one to five days postoperatively.[1048,1054,1056]

A randomized, single-blind, controlled trial of 74 patients undergoing surgical ablation of head and neck malignancies with immediate free-flap reconstruction found no significant differences in SSI rate between clindamycin 900 mg i.v. every eight hours for 3 doses compared with 15 doses.[1057] Both groups were given clindamycin 900 mg i.v. immediately preoperatively, in addition to the postoperative regimens.

In a controlled study, 200 patients undergoing septorhinoplasty were randomized to a single preoperative dose of amoxicillin–clavulanate 2.2 g i.v. administered 30 minutes before surgical incision only ($n = 100$) or in combination with postoperative oral amoxicillin–clavulanate 1000 mg twice daily for seven days.[533] There was no significant difference in infection rates between the group receiving only a preoperative dose (0%) and the combination group (3%). There was a higher rate of adverse events (nausea, diarrhea, skin rash, and pruritus) among the combination group compared with the group receiving only a preoperative dose ($p = 0.03$). The study authors recommended the use of a single preoperative i.v. dose of amoxicillin–clavulanate for endonasal septorhinoplasty.

Pediatric Efficacy. Limited data on antimicrobial prophylaxis are available for pediatric patients undergoing plastic surgery procedures. There is no consensus among surgeons regarding the use of antimicrobial prophylaxis in the repair of cleft lip and palate.[1074] The occurrence of postoperative infections after these procedures is 1.3%.[1075] No controlled trials have evaluated the use of antimicrobial prophylaxis in these procedures.

Recommendations. Antimicrobial prophylaxis is not recommended for most clean procedures in patients without additional postoperative infection risk factors as listed in the Common Principles section of these guidelines and the background discussion of this section. Although no studies have demonstrated antimicrobial efficacy in these procedures, expert opinion recommends that patients with risk factors undergoing clean plastic procedures receive antimicrobial prophylaxis. The recommendation for clean-contaminated procedures, breast cancer procedures, and clean procedures with other risk factors is a single dose of cefazolin or ampicillin–sulbactam (Table 2). (Strength of evidence for prophylaxis = C.) Alternative agents for patients with β-lactam allergy include clindamycin and vancomycin. If there are surveillance data showing that gram-negative organisms cause SSIs for the procedure, the practitioner may consider combining clindamycin or vancomycin with another agent (cefazolin if the patient is not β-lactam allergic; aztreonam, gentamicin, or single-dose fluoroquinolone if the patient is β-lactam allergic). Postoperative duration of antimicrobial prophylaxis should be limited to less than 24 hours, regardless of the presence of indwelling catheters or drains.

References

1. American Society of Health-System Pharmacists. ASHP therapeutic guidelines on antimicrobial prophylaxis in surgery. *Am J Health-Syst Pharm.* 1999; 56:1839–88.
2. Dellinger EP, Gross PA, Barrett TL, et al. Quality standard for antimicrobial prophylaxis in surgical procedures. *Clin Infect Dis.* 1994; 18:422–7.
3. Page CP, Bohnen JM, Fletcher JR, et al. Antimicrobial prophylaxis for surgical wounds: guidelines for clinical care. *Arch Surg.* 1993; 128:79–88.
4. Dotson LR, Witmer DR. Development of ASHP therapeutic guidelines. *Am J Health-Syst Pharm.* 1995; 52:254–5.
5. Anderson DJ, Kaye KS, Classen D, et al. Strategies to prevent surgical site infections in acute care hospitals. *Infect Control Hosp Epidemiol.* 2008; 29(suppl 1):S51–61.
6. Antimicrobial prophylaxis for surgery. *Treat Guidel Med Lett.* 2009; 7:47–52.
7. Scottish Intercollegiate Guidelines Network. Antibiotic prophylaxis in surgery. www.sign.ac.uk/pdf/sign104.pdf (accessed 2009 Jul 30).
8. Mangram AJ, Horan TC, Pearson ML, et al. Guideline for prevention of surgical site infection. *Infect Control Hosp Epidemiol.* 1999; 20:250–78.
9. American College of Obstetricians and Gynecologists. Antibiotic prophylaxis for gynecologic procedures. ACOG practice bulletin no. 104. *Obstet Gynecol.* 2009; 113:1180–9.
10. AAP Comittee on Fetus and Newborn, ACOG Committee on Obstetric Practice, eds. Guidelines for perinatal care. 6th ed. Elk Grove Village, IL: American Academy of Pediatrics and American College of Obstetricians and Gynecologists; 2008.
11. Wilson W, Taubert KA, Gewitz M, et al. Prevention of infective endocarditis: guidelines from the American Heart Association: a guideline from the American Heart Association Rheumatic Fever, Endocarditis, and Kawasaki Disease Committee, Council on Cardiovascular Disease in the Young, and the Council on Clinical Cardiology, Council on Cardiovascular Surgery and Anesthesia, and the Quality of Care and Outcomes Research Interdisciplinary Working Group. *Circulation.* 2007; 116:1736–54.
12. Freiman JA, Chalmers TC, Smith H, et al. The importance of beta, the type II error and sample size in the design and interpretation of the randomized control trial. *N Engl J Med.* 1978; 299:690–4.
13. Edmiston CE, Krepel C, Kelly H, et al. Perioperative antibiotic prophylaxis in the gastric bypass patient: do we achieve therapeutic levels? *Surgery.* 2004; 136:738–47.
14. Claforan (cefotaxime sodium) for injection package insert. Bridgewater, NJ: Sanofi Aventis; 2009 Jul.
15. Pappas PG, Silveira FP. *Candida* in solid organ transplant recipients. *Am J Transplant.* 2009; 9(suppl 4):S173–9.
16. Zelenitsky SA, Silverman RE, Duckworth H, et al. A prospective, randomized, double-blind study of single high dose versus multiple standard dose gentamicin both in combination with metronidazole for colorectal surgical prophylaxis. *J Hosp Infect.* 2000; 46:135–40.
17. Zelenitsky SA, Ariano RE, Harding GK, et al. Antibiotic pharmacodynamics in surgical prophylaxis: an association between intraoperative antibiotic concentrations and efficacy. *Antimicrob Agents Chemother.* 2002; 46:3026–30.
18. Rybak MJ, Lomaestro BM, Rotschafer JC, et al. Vancomycin therapeutic guidelines: a summary of consensus recommendations from the Infectious Diseases Society of America, the American Society of Health-System Pharmacists, and the Society of Infectious Diseases Pharmacists. *Clin Infect Dis.* 2009; 49:325–7.
19. Alphonso N, Anagnostopoulos PV, Scarpace S, et al. Perioperative antibiotic prophylaxis in paediatric cardiac surgery. *Cardiol Young.* 2007; 17:12–25.

20. Maher KO, VanDerElzen K, Bove EL, et al. A retrospective review of three antibiotic prophylaxis regimens for pediatric cardiac surgical patients. *Ann Thorac Surg.* 2002; 74:1195–200.
21. Kato Y, Shime N, Hashimoto S, et al. Effects of controlled perioperative antimicrobial prophylaxis on infectious outcomes in pediatric cardiac surgery. *Crit Care Med.* 2007; 35:1763–8.
22. Haessler D, Reverdy ME, Neidecker J, et al. Antibiotic prophylaxis with cefazolin and gentamicin in cardiac surgery for children less than ten kilograms. *J Cardiothorac Vasc Anesth.* 2003; 17:221–5.
23. Vargas MR, Danton MH, Javaid SM, et al. Pharmacokinetics of intravenous flucloxacillin and amoxicillin in neonatal and infant cardiopulmonary bypass surgery. *Eur J Cardiothorac Surg.* 2004; 25:256–60.
24. Milstone AM, Budd A, Shepard JW, et al. Role of decolonization in a comprehensive strategy to reduce methicillin-resistant *Staphylococcus aureus* infections in the neonatal intensive care unit: an observational cohort study. *Infect Control Hosp Epidemiol.* 2010; 31:558–60.
25. Chua AN, Goldstein SL, Bell D, et al. Topical mupirocin/sodium hypochlorite reduces peritonitis and exit-site infection rates in children. *Clin J Am Soc Nephrol.* 2009; 4:1939–43.
26. Paglialonga F, Esposito S, Edefonti A, et al. Catheter-related infections in children treated with hemodialysis. *Pediatr Nephrol.* 2004; 19:1324–33.
27. Shiojima T, Ohki Y, Nako Y, et al. Immediate control of a methicillin-resistant *Staphylococcus aureus* outbreak in a neonatal intensive care unit. *J Infect Chemother.* 2003; 9:243–7.
28. Romance L, Nicolle L, Ross J, et al. An outbreak of methicillin-resistant *Staphylococcus aureus* in a pediatric hospital—how it got away and how we caught it. *Can J Infect Control.* 1991; 6:11–3.
29. Hayakawa T, Hayashidera T, Katsura S, et al. Nasal mupirocin treatment of pharynx-colonized methicillin resistant *Staphylococcus aureus*: preliminary study with 10 carrier infants. *Pediatr Int.* 2000; 42:67–70.
30. Liu CC, Hor LI, Wu YH, et al. Investigation and elimination of epidemic methicillin-resistant *Staphylococcus aureus* in a neonatal intensive care unit. *Min Kuo Hsiao Erh Ko I Hsueh Hui Tsa Chih.* (Chinese Medical Journal) 1993; 34:285–93.
31. Nateghian A, Taylor G, Robinson JL. Risk factors for surgical site infections following open-heart surgery in a Canadian pediatric population. *Am J Infect Control.* 2004; 32:397–401.
32. Bratzler DW, Houck PM, Richards C, et al. Use of antimicrobial prophylaxis for major surgery: baseline results from the National Surgical Infection Prevention Project. *Arch Surg.* 2005; 140:174–82.
33. National Healthcare Safety Network. Patient safety component manual: surgical site infection (SSI) event. www.cdc.gov/nhsn/PDFs/pscManual/9pscSSIcurrent.pdf (accessed 2011 Apr 5).
34. Horan TC, Gayness RP, Martone WJ, et al. CDC definitions of nosocomial surgical site infections, 1992: a modification of CDC definitions of surgical wound infections. *Infect Control Hosp Epidemiol.* 1992; 13:606–8.
35. National Healthcare Safety Network. Patient safety component manual: key terms. www.cdc.gov/nhsn/PDFs/pscManual/16pscKeyTerms_current.pdf (accessed 2012 Oct 23).
36. Horan TC, Andrus M, Dudeck MA. CDC/NHSN surveillance definition of health care-associated infection and criteria for specific types of infections in the acute care setting. *Am J Infect Control.* 2008; 36:309–32.
37. Ehrenkranz NJ, Pfaff SJ. Mediastinitis complicating cardiac operations: evidence of postoperative causation. *Rev Infect Dis.* 1991; 13:803–14.
38. Bowater RJ, Stirling SA, Lilford RJ. Is antibiotic prophylaxis in surgery a generally effective intervention? Testing a generic hypothesis over a set of meta-analyses. *Ann Surg.* 2009; 249:551–6.
39. Englesbe MJ, Dimick JB, Sonnenday CJ, et al. The Michigan Surgical Quality Collaborative: will a statewide quality improvement initiative pay for itself? *Ann Surg.* 2007; 246:1100–3.
40. Flum DR, Fisher N, Thompson J, et al. Washington state's approach to variability in surgical processes/outcomes: Surgical Clinical Outcomes Assessment Program (SCOAP). *Surgery.* 2005; 138:821–8.
41. Bratzler DW, Houck PM, for the Surgical Infection Prevention Guidelines Writers Workgroup. Antimicrobial prophylaxis for surgery: an advisory statement from the national surgical infection prevention project. *Clin Infect Dis.* 2004; 38:1706–15.
42. Fry DE. Surgical site infections and the Surgical Care Improvement Project (SCIP): evolution of national quality measures. *Surg Infect.* 2008; 9:579–84.
43. Watson DS. National patient safety goals and implementation. *AORN J.* 2009; 90:123–7.
44. Myles JL, Shamanski F, Witte D. The Physicians Quality Reporting Initiative: measure, development, implementation and current procedural terminology coding. *Adv Anat Pathol.* 2010; 17:49–52.
45. Callcut RA, Breslin TM. Shaping the future of surgery: the role of private regulation in determining quality standards. *Ann Surg.* 2006; 243:304–12.
46. Bratzler DW. The Surgical Infection Prevention and Surgical Care Improvement Projects: promises and pitfalls. *Am Surg.* 2006; 72:1010–6.
47. DePalma RG. Surgical quality programs in the Veterans Health Administration. *Am Surg.* 2006; 72:999–1004.
48. Gómez MI, Acosta-Gnass SI, Mosqueda-Barboza L, et al. Reduction in surgical antibiotic prophylaxis expenditure and the rate of surgical site infection by means of a protocol that controls the use of prophylaxis. *Infect Control Hosp Epidemiol.* 2006; 27:1358–65.
49. Bond CA, Raehl CL. Clinical and economic outcomes of pharmacist-managed antimicrobial prophylaxis in surgical patients. *Am J Health-Syst Pharm.* 2007; 64:1935–42.
50. Hermsen ED, Smith Shull S, Puumala SE, et al. Improvement in prescribing habits and economic outcomes associated with the introduction of a

standardized approach for surgical antimicrobial prophylaxis. *Infect Control Hosp Epidemiol.* 2008; 29:457–61.

51. Alerany C, Campany D, Monterde J, et al. Impact of local guidelines and an integrated dispensing system on antibiotic prophylaxis quality in a surgical centre. *J Hosp Infect.* 2005; 60:111–7.
52. Allerberger F, Gareis R, Jindrák V, et al. Antibiotic stewardship implementation in the EU: the way forward. *Expert Rev Anti Infect Ther.* 2009; 7:1175–83.
53. Voit SB, Todd JK, Nelson B, et al. Electronic surveillance system for monitoring surgical antimicrobial prophylaxis. *Pediatrics.* 2005; 116:1317–22.
54. Kritchevsky SB, Braun BI, Bush AJ, et al. The effect of a quality improvement collaborative to improve antimicrobial prophylaxis in surgical patients: a randomized trial. *Ann Intern Med.* 2008; 149:472–80.
55. Potenza B, Deligencia M, Estigoy B, et al. Lessons learned from the institution of the Surgical Care Improvement Project at a teaching medical center. *Am J Surg.* 2009; 198:881–8.
56. Parker BM, Henderson JM, Vitagliano S, et al. Six sigma methodology can be used to improve adherence for antibiotic prophylaxis in patients undergoing noncardiac surgery. *Anesth Analg.* 2007; 104:140–6.
57. Rosenberg AD, Wambold D, Kraemer L, et al. Ensuring appropriate timing of antimicrobial prophylaxis. *J Bone Joint Surg Am.* 2008; 90:226–32.
58. Manniën J, Van Kasteren ME, Nagelkerke NJ, et al. Effect of optimized antibiotic prophylaxis on the incidence of surgical site infection. *Infect Control Hosp Epidemiol.* 2006; 27:1340–6.
59. Gorbach SL, Condon RE, Conte JE Jr, et al. Evaluation of new anti-infective drugs for surgical prophylaxis. *Clin Infect Dis.* 1992; 15(suppl 1):S313–38.
60. Källman J, Friberg Ö. Antibiotic prophylaxis in cardiac surgery—general principles. *APMIS.* 2007; 115:1012–5.
61. Hidron AI, Edwards JR, Patel J, et al., for the National Healthcare Safety Network Team and participating National Healthcare Safety Network facilities. Antimicrobial-resistant pathogens associated with healthcare-associated infections: annual summary of data reported to the National Healthcare Safety Network at the Centers for Disease Control and Prevention, 2006–2007. *Infect Control Hosp Epidemiol.* 2008; 29:996–1011.
62. Cefotetan package insert. Shaumburg, IL: Abraxis Pharmaceutical Products; 2007 Jul.
63. Cefazolin package insert. Shaumburg, IL: Abraxis Pharmaceutical Products; 2006 Jul.
64. Cefoxitin package insert. Shaumburg, IL: APP Pharmaceuticals, LLC; 2008 Feb.
65. Sterile vancomycin package insert. Shaumburg, IL: APP Pharmaceuticals, LLC; 2008 Apr.
66. Cefuroxime package insert. Shaumburg, IL: APP Pharmaceuticals; 2008 Nov.
67. Invanz (ertapenem injection) package insert. Whitehouse Station, NJ: Merck; 2010 Mar.
68. Gaynes R, Edwards JR. National Nosocomial Infections Surveillance System: overview of nosocomial infections caused by gram-negative bacilli. *Clin Infect Dis.* 2005; 41:848–54.
69. Weigelt JA, Lipsky BA, Tabak UP, et al. Surgical site infections: causative pathogens and associated outcomes. *Am J Infect Control.* 2010; 38:112–20.
70. Centers for Disease Control and Prevention. Recommendations for preventing the spread of vancomycin resistance. Recommendations of the Hospital Infection Control Practices Advisory Committee (HICPAC). www.cdc.gov/mmwr/PDF/RR/RR4412.PDF (accessed 2012 Dec 9).
71. Gould FK, Brindle R, Chadwick PR, et al. Guidelines (2008) for the prophylaxis and treatment of methicillin-resistant *Staphylococcus aureus* (MRSA) infections in the United Kingdom. *J Antimicrob Chemother.* 2009; 63:849–61.
72. Bolon MK, Morlote M, Weber SG, et al. Glycopeptides are no more effective than β-lactam agents for prevention of surgical site infection after cardiac surgery: a meta-analysis. *Clin Infect Dis.* 2004; 38:1357–63.
73. Finkelstein R, Rabino G, Mashiah T, et al. Vancomycin versus cefazolin prophylaxis for cardiac surgery in the setting of a high prevalence of methicillin-resistant staphylococcal infections. *J Thorac Cardiovasc Surg.* 2002; 123:326–32.
74. Bull AL, Worth LJ, Richards MJ. Impact of vancomycin surgical prophylaxis on the development of methicillin-sensitive *Staphylococcus aureus* surgical site infections: report from Australian surveillance data (VICNISS). *Ann Surg.* Epub ahead of print. 2012 Jul 20 (DOI 10.1097/SLA.0b013e31825fa398).
75. Gorwitz RJ, Kruszon-Moran D, McAllister SK, et al. Changes in the prevalence of nasal colonization with *Staphylococcus aureus* in the United States, 2001–2004. *J Infect Dis.* 2008; 197:1226–34.
76. Milstone AM, Carroll KC, Ross T, et al. Community-associated methicillin-resistant *Staphylococcus aureus* strains in pediatric intensive care unit. *Emerg Infect Dis.* 2010; 16:647–55.
77. Lo WT, Wang CC, Lin WJ, et al. Changes in the nasal colonization with methicillin-resistant *Staphylococcus aureus* in children: 2004–2009. *PLoS One.* 2010; 5:e15791.
78. Roberts NJ, Douglas RG. Gentamicin use and *Pseudomonas* and *Serratia* resistance: effect of a surgical prophylaxis regimen. *Antimicrob Agents Chemother.* 1978; 13:214–20.
79. Kriesel D, Savel TG, Silver AL, et al. Surgical antibiotic prophylaxis and *Clostridium difficile* toxin positivity. *Arch Surg.* 1995; 130:989–93.
80. Privitera G, Scarpellini P, Ortisi G, et al. Prospective study of *Clostridium difficile* intestinal colonization and disease following single-dose antibiotic prophylaxis surgery. *Antimicrob Agents Chemother.* 1991; 35:208–10.
81. Jobe BA, Grasley A, Deveney KE, et al. *Clostridium difficile* colitis: an increasing hospital-acquired illness. *Am J Surg.* 1995; 169:480–3.
82. Morris JG, Shay DK, Hebden JN. Enterococci resistant to multiple antimicrobial agents, including vancomycin: establishment of endemicity in a university medical center. *Ann Intern Med.* 1995; 123:250–9.
83. Sastry V, Brennan PJ, Levy MM. Vancomycin-resistant enterococci: an emerging problem in immu-

nosuppressed transplant recipients. *Transplant Proc.* 1995; 27:954–5.

84. Rhinehart E, Smith NE, Wennersten C. Rapid dissemination of beta-lactamase producing aminoglycoside resistant *Enterococcus faecium* among patients and staff on an infant-toddler surgical ward. *N Engl J Med.* 1990; 323:1814–8.
85. Cohen SH, Gerding DN, Johnson S, et al. Clinical practice guidelines for *Clostridium difficile* infection in adults: 2010 update by the Society for Healthcare Epidemiology of America (SHEA) and the Infectious Diseases Society of America (IDSA). *Infect Control Hosp Epidemiol.* 2010; 31:431–55.
86. Salkind AR, Cuddy PG, Foxworth JW. Is this patient allergic to penicillin? An evidence-based analysis of the likelihood of penicillin allergy. *JAMA.* 2001; 285:2498–505.
87. Frumin J, Gallagher JC. Allergic cross-sensitivity between penicillin, carbapenem, and monobactam antibiotics: what are the chances? *Ann Pharmacother.* 2009; 43:304–15.
88. Cunha BA. Antibiotic selection in the penicillin-allergic patient. *Med Clin North Am.* 2006; 90:1257–64.
89. Pichichero ME. Use of selected cephalosporins in penicillin-allergic patients: a paradigm shift. *Diagn Microbiol Infect Dis.* 2007; 57:13s–18s.
90. Galandiuk S, Polk HC Jr, Jagelman DG, et al. Re-emphasis of priorities in surgical antibiotic prophylaxis. *Surg Gynecol Obstet.* 1989; 169:218–22.
91. DiPiro JT, Vallner JJ, Bowden TA, et al. Intraoperative serum and tissue activity of cefazolin and cefoxitin. *Arch Surg.* 1985; 120:829–32.
92. Classen DC, Evans RS, Pestotnik SL, et al. The timing of prophylactic administration of antibiotics and the risk of surgical-wound infection. *N Engl J Med.* 1992; 326:281–6.
93. Garey KW, Dao T, Chen H, et al. Timing of vancomycin prophylaxis for cardiac surgery patients and the risk of surgical site infections. *J Antimicrob Chemother.* 2006; 58:645–50.
94. Steinberg JP, Braun BI, Hellinger WC, et al. Timing of antimicrobial prophylaxis and the risk of surgical site infection: results from the Trial to Reduce Antimicrobial Prophylaxis Errors. *Ann Surg.* 2009; 250:10–6.
95. Van Kasteren ME, Mannien J, Ott A, et al. Antibiotic prophylaxis and the risk of surgical site infections following total hip arthroplasty: timely administration is the most important factor. *Clin Infect Dis.* 2007; 44:921–7.
96. Soriano A, Bori G, Garcia-Ramiro S, et al. Timing of antibiotic prophylaxis for primary total knee arthroplasty performed during ischemia. *Clin Infect Dis.* 2008; 46:1009–14.
97. Weber WP, Marti WR, Zwahlen M, et al. The timing of surgical antimicrobial prophylaxis. *Ann Surg.* 2008; 247:918–26.
98. Dellinger EP. What is the ideal time for administration of antimicrobial prophylaxis for a surgical procedure? *Ann Surg.* 2008; 247:927–8.
99. Goldman DA, Hopkins CC, Karchmer AW, et al. Cephalothin prophylaxis in cardiac valve surgery. A prospective, double-blind comparison of two-day and six-day regimens. *J Thorac Cardiovasc Surg.* 1977; 73:470–9.
100. Platt R, Munoz A, Stella J, et al. Antibiotic prophylaxis for cardiovascular surgery. Efficacy with coronary artery bypass. *Ann Intern Med.* 1984; 101:770–4.
101. Forse RA, Karam B, MacLean LD, et al. Antibiotic prophylaxis for surgery in morbidly obese patients. *Surgery.* 1989; 106:750–6.
102. Falagas ME, Karageorgopoulos DE. Adjustment of dosing of antimicrobial agents for bodyweight in adults. *Lancet.* 2010; 375:248–51.
103. Pai MP, Bearden DT. Antimicrobial dosing considerations in obese adult patients. Insights from the Society of Infectious Diseases Pharmacists. *Pharmacotherapy.* 2007; 27:1081–91.
104. Johnson PN, Miller JL, Boucher EA, for the Pediatric Pharmacy Advisory Group Advocacy Committee. Medication dosing in overweight and obese children. www.ppag.org/obesedose (accessed 2010 Nov 22).
105. Koopman E, Nix DE, Erstad BL, et al. End-of-procedure cefazolin concentrations after administration for prevention of surgical-site infection. *Am J Health-Syst Pharm.* 2007; 64:1927–34.
106. Bauer LA, Edwards WA, Dellinger EP, et al. Influence of weight on aminoglycoside pharmacokinetics in normal weight and morbidly obese patients. *Eur J Clin Pharmacol.* 1983; 24:643–7.
107. Bailey TC, Little JR, Littenberg B, et al. A meta-analysis of extended-interval dosing versus multiple daily dosing of aminoglycosides. *Clin Infect Dis.* 1997; 24:786–95.
108. Barza M, Ioannidis JP, Cappelleri JC, et al. Single or multiple daily doses of aminoglycosides: a meta-analysis. *BMJ.* 1996; 312:338–45.
109. Blaser J, Konig C. Once-daily dosing of aminoglycosides. *Eur J Clin Microbiol Infect Dis.* 1995; 14:1029–38.
110. Murry KR, McKinnon PS, Mitrzyk B, et al. Pharmacodynamic characterization of nephrotoxicity associated with once-daily aminoglycoside. *Pharmacotherapy.* 1999; 19:1252–60.
111. Nicolau DP, Freeman CD, Belliveau PP, et al. Experience with a once-daily aminoglycoside program administered to 2,184 adult patients. *Antimicrob Agents Chemother.* 1995; 39:650–5.
112. Rao SC, Ahmed M, Hagan R. One dose per day compared to multiple doses per day of gentamicin for treatment of suspected or proven sepsis in neonates. *Cochrane Database Syst Rev.* 2006; 1:CD005091.
113. Zhanel GG, Ariano RE. Once daily aminoglycoside dosing: maintained efficacy with reduced nephrotoxicity? *Ren Fail.* 1992; 14:1–9.
114. Anaya DA, Dellinger EP. The obese surgical patient: a susceptible host for infection. *Surg Infect.* 2006; 7:473–80.
115. Waisbren E, Rosen H, Bader AM, et al. Percent body fat and prediction of surgical site infection. *J Am Coll Surg.* 2010; 210:381–9.
116. Engelman R, Shahian D, Shemin R, et al. The Society of Thoracic Surgeons practice guideline series: anti-

biotic prophylaxis in cardiac surgery, part II: antibiotic choice. *Ann Thorac Surg.* 2007; 83:1569–76.
117. Zanetti G, Giardina R, Platt R. Intraoperative redosing of cefazolin and risk for surgical site infection in cardiac surgery. *Emerg Infect Dis.* 2001; 7:828–31.
118. Scher KS. Studies on the duration of antibiotic administration for surgical prophylaxis. *Am Surg.* 1997; 63:59–62.
119. Markantonis SL, Kostopanagiotou G, Panidis D, et al. Effects of blood loss and fluid volume replacement on serum and tissue gentamicin concentrations during colorectal surgery. *Clin Ther.* 2004; 26:271–81.
120. Morita S, Nishisho I, Nomura T, et al. The significance of the intraoperative repeated dosing of antimicrobials for preventing surgical wound infection in colorectal surgery. *Surg Today.* 2005; 35:732–8.
121. Swoboda SM, Merz C, Kostuik J, et al. Does intraoperative blood loss affect antibiotic serum and tissue concentrations? *Arch Surg.* 1996; 131:1165–72.
122. DiPiro JT, Cheung RP, Bowden TA, et al. Single-dose systemic antibiotic prophylaxis of surgical wound infections. *Am J Surg.* 1986; 152:552–9.
123. Fonseca SN, Kunzle SR, Junqueira MJ, et al. Implementing 1-dose antibiotic prophylaxis for prevention of surgical site infection. *Arch Surg.* 2006; 141:1109–13.
124. McDonald M, Grabsch E, Marshall C, et al. Single-versus multiple-dose antimicrobial prophylaxis for major surgery: a systematic review. *Aust N Z J Surg.* 1998; 68:388–96.
125. Kreter B, Woods M. Antibiotic prophylaxis for cardiothoracic operations. Meta-analysis of thirty years of clinical trials. *J Thorac Cardiovasc Surg.* 1992; 104:590–9.
126. Austin TW, Coles JC, Burnett R, et al. Aortocoronary bypass procedures and sternotomy infections: a study of antistaphylococcal prophylaxis. *Can J Surg.* 1980; 23:483–5.
127. Galbraith U, Schilling J, Von Segesser LK, et al. Antibiotic prophylaxis in cardiovascular surgery: a prospective, randomized, comparative trial of one-day cefazolin vs single-dose cefuroxime. *Drugs Exp Clin Res.* 1993; 19:229–34.
128. Kriaras I, Michalopoulos A, Michalis A, et al. Antibiotic prophylaxis in cardiac surgery. *J Cardiovasc Surg.* 1997; 38:605–10.
129. Kriaras I, Michalopoulos A, Turina M, et al. Evolution of antimicrobial prophylaxis in cardiovascular surgery. *Eur J Cardiothorac Surg.* 2000; 18:440–6.
130. Harbarth S, Samore MH, Lichtenberg D, et al. Prolonged antibiotic prophylaxis after cardiovascular surgery and its effect on surgical site infections and antimicrobial resistance. *Circulation.* 2000; 101:2916–21.
131. Edwards FH, Engelman R, Houck P, et al. The Society of Thoracic Surgeons practice guideline series: antibiotic prophylaxis in cardiac surgery, part I: duration. *Ann Thorac Surg.* 2006; 81:397–404.
132. Lee KR, Ring JC, Leggiadro RJ. Prophylactic antibiotic use in pediatric cardiovascular surgery: a surgery of current practice. *Pediatr Infect Dis J.* 1995; 14:267–9.
133. American Academy of Orthopaedic Surgeons. Information statement: recommendations for the use of intravenous antibiotic prophylaxis in primary total joint arthroplasty. www.aaos.org/about/papers/advistmt/1027.asp (accessed 2008 May 13).
134. McCarthy PJ, Patil S, Conrad SA, et al. International and specialty trends in the use of prophylactic antibiotics to prevent infectious complications after insertion of external ventricular drainage devices. *Neurocrit Care.* 2010; 12:220–4.
135. Hares MM, Hegarty MA, Warlow J, et al. A controlled trial to compare systemic and intra-incisional cefuroxime prophylaxis in high risk gastric surgery. *Br J Surg.* 1981; 68:276–80.
136. Moesgaard F, Lykkegaard Nielsen M. Failure of topically applied antibiotics, added to systemic prophylaxis, to reduce perineal wound infection in abdominoperineal excision of the rectum. *Acta Chir Scand.* 1988; 154:589–92.
137. Pitt HA, Postier RG, Gadacz TR, et al. The role of topical antibiotics in "high-risk" biliary surgery. *Surgery.* 1982; 91:518–24.
138. Pitt HA, Postier RG, Mcgowan WA, et al. Prophylactic antibiotics in vascular surgery. Topical, systemic, or both. *Ann Surg.* 1980; 192:356–64.
139. Schersten H. Modified prophylaxis for preventing deep sternal wound infection after cardiac surgery. *APMIS.* 2007; 115:1023–6.
140. Friberg Ö, Svedjeholm R, Söderquist B, et al. Local gentamicin reduces sternal wound infections after cardiac surgery: a randomized controlled trial. *Ann Thorac Surg.* 2005; 79:153–62.
141. Eklund AM, Valtonen M, Werkkala KA. Prophylaxis of sternal wound infections with gentamicin-collagen implant: randomized controlled study in cardiac surgery. *J Hosp Infect.* 2005; 59:108–12.
142. Vander Salm TJ, Okike ON, Pasque MK, et al. Reduction of sternal infection by application of topical vancomycin. *J Thorac Cardiovasc Surg.* 1989; 98:618–22.
143. Bennett-Guerrero E, Ferguson TB Jr, Lin M, et al. Effect of an implantable gentamicin-collagen sponge on sternal wound infections following cardiac surgery: a randomized trial. *JAMA.* 2010; 304:755–62.
144. Bennett-Guerrero E, Pappas TN, Koltun WA, et al. Gentamicin-collagen sponge for infection prophylaxis in colorectal surgery. *N Engl J Med.* 2010; 363:1038–49.
145. McHugh SM, Collins CJ, Corrigan MA, et al. The role of topical antibiotics used as prophylaxis in surgical site infection prevention. *J Antimicrob Chemother.* 2011; 66:693–701.
146. Goodman J, Schaffner W, Collins H, et al. Infection after cardiovascular surgery. *N Engl J Med.* 1968; 278:117–23.
147. Perl TM. Prevention of *Staphylococcus aureus* infections among surgical patients: beyond traditional perioperative prophylaxis. *Surgery.* 2003; 134:s10–7.
148. Kluytmans JA, Mouton JW, Ijzerman EP, et al. Nasal carriage of *Staphylococcus aureus* as a major risk factor for wound infections after cardiac surgery. *J Infect Dis.* 1995; 171:216–9.

149. Kluytmans JA, Mouton JW, Vanden-Bergh MF, et al. Reduction of surgical-site infections in cardiothoracic surgery by elimination of nasal carriage of *Staphylococcus aureus*. *Infect Control Hosp Epidemiol.* 1996; 17:780–5.
150. Kalmeijer MD, Coertjens H, Van Nieuwland-Bollen PM, et al. Surgical site infections in orthopedic surgery: the effect of mupirocin nasal ointment in a double-blind, randomized, placebo-controlled study. *Clin Infect Dis.* 2002; 35:353–8.
151. Hacek DM, Robb WJ, Paule SM, et al. *Staphylococcus aureus* nasal decolonization in joint replacement surgery reduces infection. *Clin Orthop Relat Res.* 2008; 466:1349–55.
152. White A, Smith J. Nasal reservoir as the source of extranasal staphylococci. *Antimicrob Agents Chemother.* 1963; 161:679–83.
153. Lauderdale TL, Wang JT, Lee WS, et al. Carriage rates of methicillin-resistant *Staphylococcus aureus* (MRSA) depend on anatomic location, the number of sites cultured, culture methods, and the distribution of clonotypes. *Eur J Clin Microbiol Infect Dis.* 2010; 29:1553–9.
154. Jain R, Kralovic SM, Evans ME. Veterans Affairs initiative to prevent *Staphylococcus aureus* infections. *N Engl J Med.* 2011; 364:1419–30.
155. Harbarth S, Fankhauser C, Schrenzel J, et al. Univeral screening for methicillin-resistant *Staphylococcus aureus* at hospital admission and nosocomial infection in surgical patients. *JAMA.* 2008; 299:1149–57.
156. Bactroban (mupirocin calcium ointment, 2%) nasal package insert. Research Triangle Park, NC: GlaxoSmithKline; 2009 Apr.
157. Kallen AJ, Wilson CT, Larson RJ. Perioperative intranasal mupirocin for the prevention of surgical-site infections: systematic review of the literature and meta-analysis. *Infect Control Hosp Epidemiol.* 2005; 26:916–22.
158. Van Rijen M, Bonten M, Wenzel R, et al. Mupirocin ointment for preventing *Staphylococcus aureus* infections in nasal carriers. *Cochrane Database Syst Rev.* 2008; 4:CD006216.
159. Hebert C, Robicsek A. Decolonization therapy in infection control. *Curr Opin Infect Dis.* 2010; 23:340–5.
160. Perl TM, Cullen JJ, Wenzel RP, et al. Intranasal mupirocin to prevent postoperative *Staphylococcus aureus* infections. *N Engl J Med.* 2002; 346:1871–7.
161. Konvalinka A, Errett L, Fong IW. Impact of treating *Staphylococcus aureus* nasal carriers on wound infections in cardiac surgery. *J Hosp Infect.* 2006; 64:162–8.
162. Bode LG, Kluytmans JA, Wertheim HF, et al. Preventing surgical-site infections in nasal carriers of *Staphylococcus aureus*. *N Engl J Med.* 2010; 362:9–17.
163. Lee AS, Macedo-Vinas M, Francois P, et al. Impact of combined low-level mupirocin and genotypic chlorhexidine resistance on persistent methicillin-resistant *Staphylococcus aureus* carriage after decolonization therapy: a case-control study. *Clin Infect Dis.* 2011; 52:1422–30.
164. Muto CA, Jernigan JA, Ostrowsky BE, et al. SHEA guideline for preventing nosocomial transmission of multidrug-resistant strains of *Staphylococcus aureus* and *Enterococcus*. *Infect Control Hosp Epidemiol.* 2003; 24:362–86.
165. Edwards JR, Peterson KD, Mu Y, et al. National Healthcare Safety Network (NHSN) report: data summary for 2006 through 2008. *Am J Infect Control.* 2009; 37:783–805.
166. Kutsal A, Ibrisim E, Catav Z, et al. Mediastinitis after open heart surgery. Analysis of risk factors and management. *J Cardiovasc Surg.* 1991; 32:38–41.
167. Abboud CS, Way SB, Baltar VT. Risk factors for mediastinitis after cardiac surgery. *Ann Thorac Surg.* 2004; 77:676–83.
168. Crabtree TD, Codd JE, Fraser VJ, et al. Multivariate analysis of risk factors for deep and superficial sternal infection after coronary artery bypass grafting at a tertiary care medical center. *Semin Thorac Cardiovasc Surg.* 2004; 16:53–61.
169. Kohli M, Yuan L, Escobar M, et al. A risk index for sternal surgical wound infection after cardiovascular surgery. *Infect Control Hosp Epidemiol.* 2003; 24:17–25.
170. Lepelletier D, Perron S, Bizouarn P, et al. Surgical-site infection after cardiac surgery: incidence, microbiology and risk factors. *Infect Control Hosp Epidemiol.* 2005; 26:466–72.
171. Lu JC, Grayson AD, Jha P, et al. Risk factors for sternal wound infection and mid-term survival following coronary artery bypass surgery. *Eur J Cardiothorac Surg.* 2003; 23:943–9.
172. Tang GH, Maganti M, Weisel RD, et al. Prevention and management of deep sternal wound infection. *Semin Thorac Cardiovasc Surg.* 2004; 16:62–9.
173. Jakob HG, Borneff-Lipp M, Bach A, et al. The endogenous pathway is a major route for deep sternal wound infection. *Eur J Cardiothorac Surg.* 2000; 17:154–60.
174. Rahmanian PB, Adams DH, Castillo JG, et al. Impact of body mass index on early outcome and late survival in patients undergoing coronary artery bypass grafting or valve surgery or both. *Am J Cardiol.* 2007; 100:1702–8.
175. Vuorisalo S, Haukipuro K, Pokela R, et al. Risk features for surgical-site infections in coronary artery bypass surgery. *Infect Control Hosp Epidemiol.* 1998; 19:240–7.
176. Segers P, De Jong AP, Kloek JJ, et al. Risk control of surgical site infection after cardiothoracic surgery. *J Hosp Infect.* 2006; 62:437–45.
177. Zerr KJ, Furnary AP, Grunkemeier GL, et al. Glucose control lowers the risk of wound infection in diabetics after open heart operations. *Ann Thorac Surg.* 1997; 63:356–61.
178. Furnary AP, Zerr KJ, Grunkemeier GL, et al. Continuous intravenous insulin infusion reduces the incidence of deep sternal wound infection in diabetic patients after cardiac surgical procedures. *Ann Thorac Surg.* 1999; 67:352–62.
179. Dellinger EP. Preventing surgical-site infections: the importance of timing and glucose control. *Infect Control Hosp Epidemiol.* 2001; 22:604–6.

180. Latham R, Lancaster AD, Covington JF, et al. The association of diabetes and glucose control with surgical-site infections among cardiothoracic surgery patients. *Infect Control Hosp Epidemiol.* 2001; 22:607–12.
181. Furnary AP, Gao G, Grunkemeier GL, et al. Contin-uous insulin infusion reduces mortality in patients with diabetes undergoing coronary artery bypass grafting. *J Thorac Cardiovasc Surg.* 2003; 125:1007–21.
182. Gandhi GY, Nuttall GA, Abel MD, et al. Intraoperative hyperglycemia and perioperative outcomes in cardiac surgery patients. *Mayo Clin Proc.* 2005; 80:862–6.
183. Dohmen PM. Influence of skin flora and preventive measures on surgical site infection during cardiac surgery. *Surg Infect.* 2006; 7:S13–7.
184. Kittle C, Reed W. Antibiotics and extracorporeal circulation. *J Thorac Cardiovasc Surg.* 1961; 41:34–48.
185. Slonim R, Litwak R, Gadboys H, et al. Antibiotic prophylaxis of infection complicating open-heart operations. *Antimicrob Agents Chemother.* 1963; 3:731–5.
186. Garey KW, Amrutkar P, Dao-Tran TK, et al. Economic benefit of appropriate timing of vancomycin prophylaxis in patients undergoing cardiovascular surgery. *Pharmacotherapy.* 2008; 28:699–706.
187. Garey KW, Lai D, Dao-Tran TK, et al. Interrupted time series analysis of vancomycin compared to cefuroxime for surgical prophylaxis in patients undergoing cardiac surgery. *Antimicrob Agents Chemother.* 2008; 52:446–51.
188. Cimochowski GE, Harostock MD, Brown R, et al. Intranasal mupirocin reduces sternal wound infection after open heart surgery in diabetics and nondiabetics. *Ann Thorac Surg.* 2001; 71:1572–9.
189. Zangrillo A, Landoni G, Fumagalli L, et al. Methicillin-resistant *Staphylococcus* species in a cardiac surgical intensive care unit: a 5-year experience. *J Cardiothorac Vasc Anesth.* 2006; 20:31–7.
190. Fekety F, Cluff L, Sabiston D, et al. A study of antibiotic prophylaxis in cardiac surgery. *J Thorac Cardiovasc Surg.* 1969; 57:757–63
191. Conte J, Cohen S, Roe B, et al. Antibiotic prophylaxis and cardiac surgery: a prospective double-blind comparison of single-dose versus multi-dose regimens. *Ann Intern Med.* 1972; 76:943–9.
192. Firor W. Infection following open-heart surgery, with special reference to the role of prophylactic antibiotics. *J Thorac Cardiovasc Surg.* 1967; 53:371–8.
193. Slama T, Sklar S, Misinski J, et al. Randomized comparison of cefamandole, cefazolin and cefuroxime prophylaxis in open-heart surgery. *Antimicrob Agents Chemother.* 1986; 29:744–7.
194. Kaiser A, Petracek M, Lea J, et al. Efficacy of cefazolin, cefamandole, and gentamicin as prophylactic agents in cardiac surgery. *Ann Surg.* 1987; 206:791–7.
195. Conklin C, Gray R, Neilson D, et al. Determinants of wound infection incidence after isolated coronary artery bypass surgery in patients randomized to receive prophylactic cefuroxime or cefazolin. *Ann Thorac Surg.* 1988; 46:172–7.
196. Wellens F, Pirlet M, Larbuisson R, et al. Prophylaxis in cardiac surgery: a controlled, randomized comparison between cefazolin and cefuroxime. *Eur J Cardiothorac Surg.* 1995; 9:325–9.
197. Townsend TR, Reitz BA, Bilker WB, et al. Clinical trial of cefamandole, cefazolin, and cefuroxime for antibiotic prophylaxis in cardiac operations. *J Thorac Cardiovasc Surg.* 1993; 106:664–70.
198. Curtis JJ, Boley TM, Walls JT, et al. Randomized, prospective comparison of first- and second-generation cephalosporins as infection prophylaxis for cardiac surgery. *Am J Surg.* 1993; 166:734–7.
199. Doebbeling BN, Pfaller MA, Kuhns KR, et al. Cardiovascular surgery prophylaxis: a randomized, controlled comparison of cefazolin and cefuroxime. *J Thorac Cardiovasc Surg.* 1990; 99:981–9.
200. Vuorisalo S, Pokela R, Syrjälä H. Comparison of vancomycin and cefuroxime for infection prophylaxis in coronary artery bypass surgery. *Infect Control Hosp Epidemiol.* 1998; 19:234–9.
201. Baddour LM, Bettmann MA, Bolger AF, et al. Nonvalvular cardiovascular device-related infections. *Circulation.* 2003; 108:2015–31.
202. Chamber CE, Eisenhauer MD, McNicol LB, et al. Infection control guidelines for the cardiac catheterization laboratory: society guidelines revisited. *Catheter Cardiovasc Interv.* 2006; 67:78–86.
203. Van Rijen M, Bonten M, Wenzel R, et al. Mupirocin ointment for preventing *Staphylococcus aureus* infections in nasal carriers. *Cochrane Database Syst Rev.* 2008; 4:CD006216.
204. Ortega GM, Martí-Bonmatí E, Guevara SJ, et al. Alteration of vancomycin pharmacokinetics during cardiopulmonary bypass in patients undergoing cardiac surgery. *Am J Health-Syst Pharm.* 2003; 60:260–5.
205. Nascimento JW, Carmona MJ, Strabelli TM, et al. Systemic availability of prophylactic cefuroxime in patients submitted to coronary artery bypass grafting with cardiopulmonary bypass. *J Hosp Infect.* 2005; 59:299–303.
206. Vuorisalo S, Pokela R, Syrjälä H. Is single-dose antibiotic prophylaxis sufficient for coronary artery bypass surgery? An analysis of peri- and postoperative serum cefuroxime and vancomycin levels. *J Hosp Infect.* 1997; 37:237–47.
207. Fellinger EK, Leavitt BJ, Hebert JC. Serum levels of prophylactic cefazolin during cardiopulmonary bypass surgery. *Ann Thorac Surg.* 2002; 74:1187–90.
208. Caffarelli AD, Holden JP, Baron EJ, et al. Plasma cefazolin levels during cardiovascular surgery: effects of cardiopulmonary bypass and profound hypothermic circulatory arrest. *J Thorac Cardiovasc Surg.* 2006; 131:1338–43.
209. Hutschala D, Skhirtladze K, Kinstner C, et al. In vivo microdialysis to measure antibiotic penetration into soft tissue during cardiac surgery. *Ann Thorac Surg.* 2007; 84:1605–10.
210. Waltrip T, Lewis R, Young V, et al. A pilot study to determine the feasibility of continuous cefazolin infusion. *Surg Infect.* 2002; 3:5–9.
211. Nascimento JW, Carmona MJ, Strabelli TM, et al. Perioperative cefuroxime pharmacokinetics in cardiac surgery. *Clinics.* 2007; 62:257–60.

212. Lewis DR, Longman TJ, Wisheart JD, et al. The pharmacokinetics of a single dose of gentamicin (4 mg/kg) as prophylaxis in cardiac surgery requiring cardiopulmonary bypass. *Cardiovasc Surg.* 1999; 7:398–401.
213. Kitzes-Cohen R, Farin D, Piva G, et al. Pharmacokinetics of vancomycin administered as prophylaxis before cardiac surgery. *Ther Drug Monit.* 2000; 22:661–7.
214. Austin T, Coles J, McKenzie P, et al. Cephalothin prophylaxis and valve replacement. *Ann Thorac Surg.* 1977; 23:333–6.
215. Sisto T, Laurikka J, Tarkka MR. Ceftriaxone vs cefuroxime for infection prophylaxis in coronary bypass surgery. *Scand J Thorac Cardiovasc Surg.* 1994; 28:143–8.
216. Nooyen SM, Overbeek BP, Brutel De La Riviere A, et al. Prospective randomised comparison of single-dose versus multiple-dose cefuroxime for prophylaxis in coronary artery bypass grafting. *Eur J Clin Microbiol Infect Dis.* 1994; 13:1033–7.
217. Tamayo E, Gualis J, Flórez S, et al. Comparative study of single-dose and 24-hour multiple-dose antibiotic prophylaxis for cardiac surgery. *J Thorac Cardiovasc Surg.* 2008; 136:1522–7.
218. Mertz D, Johnstone J, Loeb M. Does duration of perioperative antibiotic prophylaxis matter in cardiac surgery? A systematic review and meta-analysis. *Ann Surg.* 2011; 254:48–54.
219. Sandoe JA, Kumar B, Stoddart B, et al. Effect of extended perioperative antibiotic prophylaxis on intravascular catheter colonization and infection in cardiothoracic surgery patients. *J Antimicrob Chemother.* 2003; 52:877–9.
220. Niederhäuser U, Vogt M, Vogt P, et al. Cardiac surgery in a high-risk group of patients: is prolonged postoperative antibiotic prophylaxis effective? *J Thorac Cardiovasc Surg.* 1997; 114:162–8.
221. Huddleston CB. Mediastinal wound infections following pediatric cardiac surgery. *Semin Thorac Cardiovasc Surg.* 2004; 16:108–12.
222. McEvoy GK, Snow EK, Miller J, et al., eds. AHFS drug information. Bethesda, MD: American Society of Health-System Pharmacists; 2011.
223. Johns Hopkins Hospital, Arcara K, Tschudy M, Lee CK, eds. Harriet Lane handbook, 19th edition. Philadelphia: Elsevier, Inc.; 2012.
224. Lance LL, Lacey CF, Goldman MP, et al., eds. Quick-look drug book, 18th edition. Baltimore, MD: Lippincott Williams & Wilkins; 2011.
225. Lexi-Comp Online. Hudson, OH: Lexi-Comp, Inc.; 2011.
226. Smith KM, Riche DM, Henyan NN, eds. Handbook of clinical drug data. 11th ed. New York: McGrawHill; 2010.
227. Da Costa A, Kirkorian G, Cucherat M, et al. Antibiotic prophylaxis for permanent pacemaker implantation: a meta-analysis. *Circulation.* 1998; 97:1796–801.
228. Nishimura RA, Carabello BA, Faxon DP, et al. ACC/AHA 2008 guideline update on valvular heart disease: focused update on infective endocarditis: a report of the American College of Cardiology/American Heart Association Task Force on Practice Guidelines. *Circulation.* 2008; 118:887–96.
229. Baddour LM, Epstein AE, Erickson CC, et al. American Heart Association Rheumatic Fever, Endocarditis, and Kawasaki Disease Committee; Council on Cardiovascular Disease in Young; Council on Cardiovascular Surgery and Anesthesia; Council on Cardiovascular Nursing; Council on Clinical Cardiology; Interdisciplinary Council on Quality of Care; American Heart Association. Update on cardiovascular implantable electronic device infections and their management: a scientific statement from the American Heart Association. *Circulation.* 2010; 121:458–77.
230. Klug D, Balde M, Pavin D, et al. Risk factors related to infections of implanted pacemakers and cardioverter-defibrillators: results of a large prospective study. *Circulation.* 2007; 116:1349–55.
231. De Oliveira JC, Martinelli M, Nishioka SA, et al. Efficacy of antibiotic prophylaxis before the implantation of pacemakers and cardioverter-defibrillators: results of a large, prospective, randomized, double-blinded, placebo-controlled trial. *Circ Arrhythm Electrophysiol.* 2009; 2:29–34.
232. Sohail MR, Uslan DZ, Khan AH, et al. Risk factor analysis of permanent pacemaker infection. *Clin Infect Dis.* 2007; 45:166–73.
233. Bertaglia E, Zerbo F, Zardo S, et al. Antibiotic prophylaxis with a single dose of cefazolin during pacemaker implantation: incidence of long-term infective complications. *PACE.* 2006; 29:29–33.
234. Holman WL, Pae WE, Teutenberg JJ, et al. INTERMACS: interval analysis of registry data. *J Am Coll Cardiol.* 2009; 208:755–61.
235. Walker PC, DePrestel DD, Miles NA, et al. Surgical infection prophylaxis for left ventricular assist device implantation. *J Card Surg.* 2011; 26:440–3.
236. Califano S, Pagani FD, Malani PN. Left ventricular assist device-associated infections. *Infect Dis Clin North Am.* 2012; 26:77–87.
237. Radu DM, Jauréguy F, Seguin A, et al. Postoperative pneumonia after major pulmonary resections: an unsolved problem in thoracic surgery. *Ann Thorac Surg.* 2007; 84:1669–74.
238. Cardo D, Horan T, Andres M, et al. National Nosocomial Infections Surveillance (NNIS) system report: data summary from January 1992 through June 2004. *Am J Infect Control.* 2004; 32:470–85.
239. Aznar R, Mateu M, Miró JM, et al. Antibiotic prophylaxis in non-cardiac thoracic surgery: cefazolin versus placebo. *Eur J Cardiothorac Surg.* 1991; 5:515–8.
240. Rovera F, Imperatori A, Militello P, et al. Infections in 346 consecutive video-assisted thoracoscopic procedures. *Surg Infect.* 2003; 4:45–51.
241. Turna A, Kutlu CA, Ozalp T, et al. Antibiotic prophylaxis in elective thoracic surgery: cefuroxime versus cefepime. *Thorac Cardiov Surg.* 2003; 51:84–8.
242. Boldt J, Piper S, Uphus D, et al. Preoperative microbiologic screening and antibiotic prophylaxis in pulmonary resection operations. *Ann Thorac Surg.* 1999; 68:208–11.

243. Schussler O, Dermine H, Alifano M, et al. Should we change antibiotic prophylaxis for lung surgery? Postoperative pneumonia is the critical issue. *Ann Thorac Surg.* 2008; 86:1727–34.
244. Shiono S, Yoshida J, Nishimura M, et al. Risk factors of postoperative respiratory infections in lung cancer surgery. *J Thorac Oncol.* 2007; 2:34–8.
245. Imperatori A, Rotolo N, Gatti M, et al. Peri-operative complications of video-assisted thoracoscopic surgery (VATS). *Int J Surg.* 2008; 6:S78–81.
246. Solaini L, Prusciano F, Bagioni P, et al. Video-assisted thoracic surgery (VATS) of the lung: analysis of intraoperative and postoperative complications over 15 years and review of the literature. *Surg Endosc.* 2008; 22:298–310.
247. Imperatori A, Rovera F, Rotolo N, et al. Prospective study of infection risk factors in 988 lung resections. *Surg Infect.* 2006; 7:S57–60.
248. Chamberlain RS, Sakpal SV. A comprehensive review of single-incision laparoscopic surgery (SILS) and natural orifice transluminal endoscopic surgery (NOTES) techniques for chelecystectomy. *J Gastrointest Surg.* 2009; 13:1733–40.
249. Cruse PJ, Foord R. The epidemiology of wound infection: a ten-year prospective study of 62,939 wounds. *Surg Clin North Am.* 1980; 60:27–40.
250. Petrosillo N, Drapeau CM, Nicastri E, et al. Surgical site infections in Italian hospitals: a prospective multicenter study. *BMC Infect Dis.* 2008; 8:34.
251. Watanabe A, Kohnoe S, Shimabukuro R, et al. Risk factors associated with surgical site infection in upper and lower gastrointestinal surgery. *Surg Today.* 2008; 38:404–12.
252. Yasuda K, Shiraishi N, Adachi Y, et al. Risk factors for complications following resection of large gastric cancer. *Br J Surg.* 2001; 88:873–7.
253. Mohri Y, Tonouchi H, Kobayashi M, et al. Randomized clinical trial of single- versus multiple-dose antimicrobial prophylaxis in gastric cancer surgery. *Br J Surg.* 2007; 94:683–8.
254. Yeo CJ, Cameron JL, Sohn TA, et al. Pancreaticoduodenectomy with or without extended retroperitoneal lymphadenectomy for periampullary adenocarcinoma: comparison of morbidity and mortality and short-term outcome. *Ann Surg.* 1999; 229:613–24.
255. Jafri NS, Mahid SS, Minor KS, et al. Meta-analysis: antibiotic prophylaxis to prevent peristomal infection following percutaneous endoscopic gastrostomy. *Aliment Pharmacol Ther.* 2007; 25:647–56.
256. Sharma VK, Howden CW. Meta-analysis of randomized, controlled trials of antibiotic prophylaxis before percutaneous endoscopic gastrostomy. *Am J Gastroenterol.* 2000; 95:3133–6.
257. Gorbach SL, Plaut AG, Nahas L, et al. Studies of intestinal microflora: II. Microorganisms of the small intestine and their relations to oral fecal flora. *Gastroenterology.* 1967; 53:856–67.
258. Gorbach SL. Intestinal microflora. *Gastroenterology.* 1971; 60:1110–29.
259. Ruddell WS, Axon AT, Findlay JM, et al. Effect of cimetidine on the gastric bacterial flora. *Lancet.* 1980; 1:672–4.
260. Driks MR, Craven DE, Bartolome RC, et al. Nosocomial pneumonia in intubated patients given sucralfate as compared with antacids or histamine type 2 blockers. *N Engl J Med.* 1987; 317:1376–82.
261. Long J, Desantis S, State D, et al. The effect of antisecretagogues on gastric microflora. *Arch Surg.* 1983; 118:1413–5.
262. Sjostedt S, Levin P, Malmborg AS, et al. Septic complications in relation to factors influencing the gastric microflora in patients undergoing gastric surgery. *J Hosp Infect.* 1989; 12:191–7.
263. Feretis CB, Contou CT, Papoutsis GG, et al. The effect of preoperative treatment with cimetidine on postoperative wound sepsis. *Am Surg.* 1984; 50:594–8.
264. Antimicrobial prophylaxis in surgery. *Treat Guidel Med Lett.* 2006; 4:83–8.
265. LoCiero J, Nichols RL. Sepsis after gastroduodenal operations; relationship to gastric acid, motility, and endogenous microflora. *South Med J.* 1980; 73:878–80.
266. Pessaux P, Msika S, Atalla D, et al. Risk factors for postoperative infectious complications in noncolorectal abdominal surgery: a multivariate analysis based on a prospective multicenter study of 4718 patients. *Arch Surg.* 2003; 138:314–24.
267. Imai E, Ueda M, Kanao K, et al. Surgical site infection surveillance after open gastrectomy and risk factors for surgical site infection. *J Infect Chemother.* 2005; 11:141–5.
268. Christou NV, Jarand J, Sylvestre JL, et al. Analysis of the incidence and risk factors for wound infections in open bariatric surgery. *Obes Surg.* 2004; 14:16–22.
269. McArdle CS, Morran CG, Pettit L, et al. Value of oral antibiotic prophylaxis in colorectal surgery. *Br J Surg.* 1995; 82:1046–8.
270. Nichols RL, Webb WR, Jones JW, et al. Efficacy of antibiotic prophylaxis in high risk gastroduodenal operations. *Am J Surg.* 1982; 143:94–8.
271. Stone HH. Gastric surgery. *South Med J.* 1977; 70:S35–7.
272. Morris DL, Yound D, Burdon DW, et al. Prospective randomized trial of single-dose cefuroxime against mezlocillin in elective gastric surgery. *J Hosp Infect.* 1984; 5:200–4.
273. Lewis RT, Allan CM, Goodall RG, et al. Discriminate use of antibiotic prophylaxis in gastroduodenal surgery. *Am J Surg.* 1979; 138:640–3.
274. Lewis RT, Allan CM, Goodall RG, et al. Cefamandole in gastroduodenal surgery: a controlled prospective, randomized, double-blind study. *Can J Surg.* 1982; 25:561–3.
275. Mitchell NJ, Evans DS, Pollock D. Pre-operative, single-dose cefuroxime antimicrobial prophylaxis with and without metronidazole in elective gastrointestinal surgery. *J Antimicrob Chemother.* 1980; 6:393–9.
276. Uchiyama K, Takifuji K, Tani M, et al. Prevention of postoperative infections by administration of antimicrobial agents immediately before surgery for patients with gastrointestinal cancers. *Hepatogastroenterology.* 2007; 54:1487–93.

277. Pories WJ, Van Rij AM, Burlingham BT, et al. Prophylactic cefazolin in gastric bypass surgery. *Surgery.* 1981; 90:426–32.
278. Polk H, Lopez-Meyer J. Postoperative wound infection: a prospective study of determinant factors and prevention. *Surgery.* 1969; 66:97–103.
279. Saadeddin A, Freshwater DA, Fisher NC, et al. Antibiotic prophylaxis for percutaneous endoscopic gastrostomy for non-malignant conditions: a double-blind prospective randomized controlled trial. *Aliment Pharmacol Ther.* 2005; 22:565–70.
280. Ahmad I, Mouncher A, Abdoolah A, et al. Antibiotic prophylaxis for percutaneous endoscopic gastrostomy—a prospective, randomized, double-blind trial. *Aliment Pharmacol Ther.* 2003; 18:209–15.
281. Dormann AJ, Wigginghaus B, Risius H, et al. Antibiotic prophylaxis in percutaneous endoscopic gastrostomy (PEG)—results from a prospective randomized multicenter trial. *Z Gastroenterol.* 2000; 38:229–34.
282. Preclik G, Grüne S, Leser HG, et al. Prospective, randomized, double blind trial of prophylaxis with single dose of co-amoxiclav before percutaneous endoscopic gastrostomy. *BMJ.* 1999; 319:881–4.
283. Panigrahi H, Shreeve DR, Tan WC, et al. Role of antibiotic prophylaxis for wound infection in percutaneous endoscopic gastrostomy (PEG): result of a prospective double-blind randomized trial. *J Hosp Infect.* 2002; 50:312–5.
284. Sturgis TM, Yancy W, Cole JC, et al. Antibiotic prophylaxis in percutaneous endoscopic gastrostomy. *Am J Gastroenterol.* 1996; 91:2301–4.
285. Banerjee S, Shen B, Baron TH, for the American Society for Gastrointestinal Endoscopy Standards of Practice Committee. Antibiotic prophylaxis for GI endoscopy. *Gastrointest Endosc.* 2008; 67:791–8.
286. Rey JR, Axone A, Budzynska A, et al. Guidelines of the European Society of Gastrointestinal Endoscopy (E.S.G.E.) antibiotic prophylaxis for gastrointestinal endoscopy. *Endoscopy.* 1998; 30:318–24.
287. Allison MC, Sandoe JA, Tighe R, et al., for the Endoscopy Committee of the British Society of Gastroenterology. Antibiotic prophylaxis in gastrointestinal endoscopy. *Gut.* 2009; 58:869–80.
288. Gossner L, Keymling J, Hahn EG, et al. Antibiotic prophylaxis in percutaneous endoscopic gastrostomy (PEG): a prospective randomized clinical trial. *Endoscopy.* 1999; 31:119–24.
289. Rao GG, Osman M, Johnson L, et al. Prevention of percutaneous endoscopic gastrostomy site infections caused by methicillin-resistant *Staphylococcus aureus*. *J Hosp Infect.* 2004; 58:81–3.
290. Thomas S, Cantrill S, Waghorn DJ, et al. The role of screening and antibiotic prophylaxis in the prevention of percutaneous gastrostomy site infection caused by methicillin-resistant *Staphylococcus aureus*. *Aliment Pharmacol Ther.* 2007; 25:593–7.
291. Sauerland S, Angrisani L, Belachew M, et al. Obesity surgery. Evidence-based guidelines of the European Association for Endoscopic Surgery (EAES). *Surg Endosc.* 2005; 19:200–21.
292. Varela JE, Wilson SE, Nguyen NT. Laparoscopic surgery significantly reduces surgical-site infections compared with open surgery. *Surg Endosc.* 2010; 24:270–6.
293. Ueno T, Yamamoto K, Kawaoka T, et al. Current antibiotic prophylaxis in pancreatoduodenectomy in Japan. *J Hepatobiliary Pancreat Surg.* 2005; 12:304–9.
294. Stone HH, Haney BH, Kolb LD, et al. Prophylactic and preventive antibiotic therapy. Timing, duration and economics. *Ann Surg.* 1979; 189:691–9.
295. Kusachi S, Sumiyama Y, Nagao J, et al. Prophylactic antibiotics given within 24 hours of surgery, compared with antibiotics given for 72 hours perioperatively, increased the rate of methicillin-resistant *Staphylococcus aureus* isolated from surgical site infections. *J Infect Chemother.* 2008; 14:44–50.
296. Imamura H, Furukawa H, Iijima S, et al. Multicenter phase II study of antimicrobial prophylaxis in low-risk patients undergoing distal gastrectomy for gastric cancer. *Gastric Cancer.* 2006; 9:32–5.
297. Alexander JW, Rahn R. Prevention of deep wound infection in morbidly obese patients by infusion of an antibiotic into the subcutaneous space at the time of wound closure. *Obes Surg.* 2004; 14:970–4.
298. Radhakrishnan NV, Shenoy AH, Cartmill I, et al. Addition of local antiseptic spray to parenteral antibiotic regimen reduces the incidence of stomal infection following percutaneous endoscopic gastrostomy: a randomized controlled trial. *Eur J Gastroenterol Hepatol.* 2006; 18:1279–84.
299. Bates T, Roberts JV, Smith K, et al. A randomized trial of one versus three doses of augmentin as wound prophylaxis in at-risk abdominal surgery. *Postgrad Med J.* 1992; 68:811–6.
300. McArdle CS, Morran CG, Anderson JR, et al. Oral ciprofloxacin as prophylaxis in gastroduodenal surgery. *J Hosp Infect.* 1995; 30:211–6.
301. Rawat D, Srivistava A, Thomson M. Antibody prophylaxis for children undergoing percutaneous endoscopic gastrostomy. *J Pediatr Gastroenterol Nutr.* 2005; 40:234–5.
302. Cortes A, Sauvanet A, Bert F, et al. Effect of bile contamination on immediate outcomes after pancreaticoduodenectomy for tumor. *J Am Coll Surg.* 2006; 202:93–9.
303. Solomkin JS, Mazuski JE, Bradley JS, et al. Diagnosis and management of complicated intra-abdominal infection in adults and children: guidelines by the Surgical Infection Society and the Infectious Diseases Society of America. *Surg Infect.* 2010; 11:79–109.
304. Meijer WS, Schmitz PI, Jeekel J. Meta-analysis of randomized, controlled clinical trials of antibiotic prophylaxis in biliary tract surgery. *Br J Surg.* 1990; 77:282–90.
305. Den Hoed PT, Boelhouwer RU, Veen HF, et al. Infections and bacteriological data after laparoscopic and open gallbladder surgery. *J Hosp Infect.* 1998; 39:27–37.
306. Dervisoglou A, Tsiodras S, Kanellakopoulou K, et al. The value of chemoprophylaxis against *Enterococcus* species in elective cholecystectomy: a randomized study of cefuroxime vs ampicillin/sulbactam. *Arch Surg.* 2006; 141:1162–7.

307. Cainzos M, Sayek I, Wacha H, et al. Septic complications after biliary tract stone surgery: a review and report of the European Prospective Study. *Hepatogastroenterology.* 1997; 44:959–67.
308. Lippert H, Gastinger J. Antimicrobial prophylaxis in laparoscopic and conventional cholecystectomy. *Chemotherapy.* 1998; 44:355–63.
309. Siddiqui K, Khan AF. Comparison of frequency of wound infection: open vs laparoscopic cholecystectomy. *J Ayub Med Coll Abbottabad.* 2006; 18:21–4.
310. Romy S, Eisenring MC, Bettschart V, et al. Laparoscope use and surgical site infections in digestive surgery. *Ann Surg.* 2008; 247:627–32.
311. Rotermann M. Infection after cholecystectomy, hysterectomy or appendectomy. *Health Rep.* 2004; 15:11–23.
312. Chang WT, Lee KT, Chuang SC, et al. The impact of prophylactic antibiotics on postoperative infection complication in elective laparoscopic cholecystectomy: a prospective randomized study. *Am J Surg.* 2006; 191:721–5.
313. Zhou H, Zhang J, Wang Q, et al. Meta-analysis: antibiotic prophylaxis in elective laparoscopic cholecystectomy. *Aliment Pharmacol Ther.* 2009; 29:1086–95.
314. Dobay KJ, Freier DT, Albear P. The absent role of prophylactic antibiotics in low-risk patients undergoing laparoscopic cholecystectomy. *Am Surg.* 1999; 65:226–8.
315. Higgins A, London J, Charland S, et al. Prophylactic antibiotics for elective laparoscopic cholecystectomy: are they necessary? *Arch Surg.* 1999; 134:611–4.
316. Tocchi A, Lepre L, Costa G, et al. The need for antibiotic prophylaxis in elective laparoscopic cholecystectomy: a prospective randomized study. *Arch Surg.* 2000; 135:67–70.
317. Guzmán-Valdivia G. Routine administration of antibiotics to patients suffering accidental gallbladder perforation during laparoscopic cholecystectomy is not necessary. *Surg Laparosc Endosc Percutan Tech.* 2008; 18:547–50.
318. Harling R, Moorjani N, Perry C, et al. A prospective, randomized trial of prophylactic antibiotics versus bag extraction in the prophylaxis of wound infection in laparoscopic cholecystectomy. *Ann R Coll Surg Engl.* 2000; 82:408–10.
319. Illig KA, Schmidt E, Cavanaugh J, et al. Are prophylactic antibiotics required for elective laparoscopic cholecystectomy? *J Am Coll Surg.* 1997; 184:353–6.
320. Zurbuchen U, Ritz JP, Lehmann KS, et al. Oral vs intravenous antibiotic prophylaxis in elective laparoscopic cholecystectomy—an exploratory trial. *Langenbecks Arch Surg.* 2008; 393:479–85.
321. Al-Abassi AA, Farghaly MM, Ahmed HL, et al. Infection after laparoscopic cholecystectomy: effect of infected bile and infected gallbladder wall. *Eur J Surg.* 2001; 167:268–73.
322. Farello GA, Cerofolini A. Antimicrobial prophylaxis with ceftriaxone in laparoscopic cholecystectomy: a 7-year clinical experience involving 3,603 patients. *J Chemother.* 2000; 12(suppl 3):17–22.
323. McGuckin M, Shea JA, Schwartz JS. Infection and antimicrobial use in laparoscopic cholecystectomy. *Infect Control Hosp Epidemiol.* 1999; 20:624–6.
324. Biscione FM, Couto RC, Pedrosa TM, et al. Comparison of the risk of surgical site infection after laparoscopic cholecystectomy and open cholecystectomy. *Infect Control Hosp Epidemiol.* 2007; 28:1103–6.
325. Brill A, Ghosh K, Gunnarsson C, et al. The effects of laparoscopic cholecystectomy, hysterectomy, and appendectomy on nosocomial infection risks. *Surg Endosc.* 2008; 22:1112–8.
326. Cainzos M, Potel J, Puente JL. Prospective, randomized, controlled study of prophylaxis with cefamandole in high-risk patients undergoing operations upon the biliary tract. *Surg Gynecol Obstet.* 1985; 160:27–32.
327. Meijer WS, Schmitz PI. Prophylactic use of cefuroxime in biliary tract surgery: randomized, controlled trial of single versus multiple dose in high-risk patients. *Br J Surg.* 1993; 80:917–21.
328. Grant MD, Jones RC, Wilson SE, et al. Single-dose cephalosporin prophylaxis in high-risk patients undergoing surgical treatment of the biliary tract. *Surg Gynecol Obstet.* 1992; 174:347–54.
329. Lapointe RW, Roy AF, Turgeon PL, et al. Comparison of single-dose cefotetan and multidose cefoxitin as intravenous prophylaxis in elective, open biliary tract surgery: a multicentre, double-blind, randomized study. *Can J Surg.* 1994; 37:313–8.
330. Strachan CJ, Black J, Powis SJ, et al. Prophylactic use of cephazolin against wound sepsis after cholecystectomy. *Br Med J.* 1977; 1:1254–6.
331. Berne TV, Yellin AE, Appleman MD, et al. Controlled comparison of cefmetazole with cefoxitin for prophylaxis in elective cholecystectomy. *Surg Gynecol Obstet.* 1990; 170:137–40.
332. Wilson SE, Hopkins JA, Williams RA. A comparison of cefotaxime versus cefamandole in prophylaxis for surgical treatment of the biliary tract. *Surg Gynecol Obstet.* 1987; 164:207–12.
333. Kujath P. Antibiotic prophylaxis in biliary tract surgery. Ciprofloxacin versus ceftriaxone. *Am J Med.* 1989; 87(5A):255S–257S.
334. Garibaldi RA, Skolnck D, Maglio S, et al. Postcholecystectomy wound infection. *Ann Surg.* 1986; 204:650–4.
335. Levi JU, Martinez OV, Hutson DG, et al. Ampicillin versus cefamandole in biliary tract surgery. *Am Surg.* 1984; 50:412–7.
336. Kellum JM, Duma RJ, Gorbach SL, et al. Single-dose antibiotic prophylaxis for biliary surgery. *Arch Surg.* 1987; 122:918–22.
337. Muller EL, Pitt HA, Thompson JE, et al. Antibiotics in infections of the biliary tract. *Surg Gynecol Obstet.* 1987; 165:285–92.
338. Jewesson PJ, Stiver G, Wai A, et al. Double-blind comparison of cefazolin and ceftizoxime for prophylaxis against infections following elective biliary tract surgery. *Antimicrob Agents Chemother.* 1996; 40:70–4.
339. Montravers P, Lepape A, Dubreuil L, et al. Clinical and microbiological profiles of community-acquired

and nosocomial intra-abdominal infections: results of the French prospective, observational EBIIA study. *J Antimicrob Chemother.* 2009; 63:785–94.

340. Baquero F, Hsueh PR, Paterson DL, et al. In vitro susceptibilities of aerobic and facultatively anaerobic gram-negative bacilli isolated from patients with intra-abdominal infections worldwide: 2005 results from Study for Monitoring Antimicrobial Resistance Trends (SMART). *Surg Infect.* 2009; 10:99–104.
341. Chow JW, Satishchandran V, Snyder TA, et al. In vitro susceptibilities of aerobic and facultative gram-negative bacilli isolated from patients with intra-abdominal infections worldwide: the 2002 Study for Monitoring Antimicrobial Resistance Trends (SMART). *Surg Infect.* 2005; 6:439–48.
342. Choudhary A, Bechtold ML, Puli SR, et al. Role of prophylactic antibiotics in laparoscopic cholecystectomy: a meta-analysis. *J Gastrointest Surg.* 2008; 12:1847–53.
343. Stone HH, Hooper CA, Kolb LD, et al. Antibiotic prophylaxis in gastric, biliary and colonic surgery. *Ann Surg.* 1976; 184:443–52.
344. Sirinek KR, Schauer PR, Yellin AE, et al. Single-dose cefuroxime versus multiple-dose cefazolin as prophylactic therapy for high-risk cholecystectomy. *J Am Coll Surg.* 1994; 178:321–5.
345. Drumm J, Donovan IA, Wise R. A comparison of cefotetan and cefazolin for prophylaxis against wound infection after elective cholecystectomy. *J Hosp Infect.* 1985; 6:277–80.
346. Crenshaw CA, Glanges E, Webber CE, et al. A prospective, randomized, double-blind study of preventive cefamandole therapy in patients at high risk for undergoing cholecystectomy. *Surg Gynecol Obstet.* 1981; 153:546–52.
347. Leaper DJ, Cooper MJ, Turner A. A comparison trial between cefotetan and cephazolin for wound sepsis prophylaxis during elective upper gastrointestinal surgery with an investigation of cefotetan penetration into the obstructed biliary tree. *J Hosp Infect.* 1986; 7:269–76.
348. Maki DG, Lammers JL, Aughey DR. Comparative studies of multiple-dose cefoxitin vs. single-dose cefonicid for surgical prophylaxis in patients undergoing biliary tract operations or hysterectomy. *Rev Infect Dis.* 1984; 6(suppl 4):S887–95.
349. Garcia-Rodriquez JA, Puig-LaCalle J, Arnau C, et al. Antibiotic prophylaxis with cefotaxime in gastroduodenal and biliary surgery. *Am J Surg.* 1989; 158:428–32.
350. Targarona EM, Garau J, Munoz-Ramos C, et al. Single-dose antibiotic prophylaxis in patients at high risk for infection in biliary surgery: a prospective and randomized study comparing cefonicid with mezlocillin. *Surgery.* 1990; 107:327–34.
351. Krige JE, Isaacs S, Stapleton GN, et al. Prospective, randomized study comparing amoxicillin-clavulanic acid and cefamandole for the prevention of wound infection in high-risk patients undergoing elective biliary surgery. *J Hosp Infect.* 1992; 22(suppl A):33–41.
352. Agrawal CS, Sehgal R, Singh RK, et al. Antibiotic prophylaxis in elective cholecystectomy: a randomized, double blind study comparing ciprofloxacin and cefuroxime. *Indian J Physiol Pharmacol.* 1999; 43:501–4.
353. Kellum JM, Gargano S, Gorbach SL, et al. Antibiotic prophylaxis in high-risk biliary operations: multicenter trial of single preoperative ceftriaxone versus multidose cefazolin. *Am J Surg.* 1984; 148:15–21.
354. Tonelli F, Mazzei T, Novelli A, et al. Amoxicillin/clavulanic acid versus cefotaxime for antimicrobial prophylaxis in abdominal surgery: a randomized trial. *J Chemother.* 2002; 14:366–72.
355. McLeish AR, Keighley MR, Bishop HM. Selecting patients requiring antibiotics in biliary surgery by immediate Gram stains of bile at surgery. *Surgery.* 1977; 81:473–7.
356. Krajden S, Yaman M, Fuksa M, et al. Piperacillin versus cefazolin given perioperatively to high-risk patients who undergo open cholecystectomy: a double-blind, randomized trial. *Can J Surg.* 1993; 36:245–50.
357. McArdle CS. Oral prophylaxis in biliary tract surgery. *J Antimicrob Chemother.* 1994; 33:200–2.
358. Plouffe JF, Perkins RL, Fass RJ, et al. Comparison of the effectiveness of moxalactam and cefazolin in the prevention of infection in patients undergoing abdominal operations. *Diagn Microbiol Infect Dis.* 1985; 3:25–31.
359. Katz S, Glicksman A, Levy Y, et al. Cefuroxime prophylaxis in biliary surgery: single versus triple dose. *Israel J Med Sci.* 1993; 29:673–6.
360. Ahmed ME, Ibrahim SZ, Arabi YE, et al. Metronidazole prophylaxis in acute mural appendicitis: failure of a single intra-operative infusion to reduce wound infection. *J Hosp Infect.* 1987; 10:260–4.
361. Donovan IA, Ellis D, Gatehouse D, et al. One-dose antibiotic prophylaxis against wound infection after appendectomy: a randomized trial of clindamycin, cefazolin sodium and a placebo. *Br J Surg.* 1979; 66:193–6.
362. Gilmore OJ, Martin TD. Aetiology and prevention of wound infection in appendectomy. *Br J Surg.* 1974; 62:567–72.
363. Keiser TA, Mackenzie RL, Feld LN. Prophylactic metronidazole in appendectomy: a double-blind controlled trial. *Surgery.* 1983; 93:201–3.
364. Winslow RE, Rem D, Harley JW. Acute nonperforating appendicitis: efficacy of brief antibiotic prophylaxis. *Arch Surg.* 1983; 118:651–5.
365. Tonz M, Schmid P, Kaiser G. Antibiotic prophylaxis for appendectomy in children: critical appraisal. *World J Surg.* 2000; 24:995–8.
366. Wilson AP. Antibiotic prophylaxis and infection control measures in minimally invasive surgery. *J Antimicrob Chemother.* 1995; 36:1–5.
367. Aziz O, Athanasiou T, Tekkis PP. Laparoscopic versus open appendectomy in children: a meta-analysis. *Ann Surg.* 2006; 243:17–27.
368. Khan MN, Fayyad T, Cecil TD, et al. Laparoscopic versus open appendectomy: the risk of postoperative infectious complications. *JSLS.* 2007; 11:363–7.

369. Hansen J, Smithers MB, Schache D, et al. Laparoscopic versus open appendectomy: prospective randomised trial. *World J Surg.* 1996; 20:17–21.
370. Sauerland S, Lefering R, Neugebauer EA. Laparoscopic versus open surgery for suspected appendicitis. *Cochrane Database Syst Rev.* 2004; 4:CD001546.
371. Hemmila MR, Birkmeyer NJ, Arbabi S, et al. Introduction to propensity scores: a case study on the comparative effectiveness of laparoscopic vs open appendectomy. *Arch Surg.* 2010; 145:939–45.
372. Stone HH. Bacterial flora of appendicitis in children. *J Pediatr Surg.* 1976; 11:37–42.
373. Keighley MR. Infection: prophylaxis. *Br Med Bull.* 1988; 44:374–402.
374. Andersen BR, Kallehave FL, Andersen HK. Antibiotics versus placebo for prevention of postoperative infection after appendicectomy. *Cochrane Database Syst Rev.* 2005; 3:CD001439.
375. Helmer KS, Robinson EK, Lally KP, et al. Standardized patient care guidelines reduce infectious morbidity in appendectomy patients. *Am J Surg.* 2002; 183:608–13.
376. Lau WY, Fan ST, Yiu TF, et al. Prophylaxis of post-appendectomy sepsis by metronidazole and cefotaxime: a randomized, prospective and double-blind trial. *Br J Surg.* 1983; 70:670–2.
377. Lau WY, Fan ST, Chu KW, et al. Randomized, prospective, and double-blind trial of new beta-lactams in the treatment of appendicitis. *Antimicrob Agents Chemother.* 1985; 28:639–42.
378. Lau WY, Fan ST, Chu KW, et al. Cefoxitin versus gentamicin and metronidazole in prevention of post-appendectomy sepsis: a randomized, prospective trial. *J Antimicrob Chemother.* 1986; 18:613–9.
379. O'Rourke MG, Wynne MJ, Morahan RJ, et al. Prophylactic antibiotics in appendectomy: a prospective, double-blind, randomized study. *Aust N Z J Surg.* 1984; 54:535–41.
380. Liberman MA, Greason KL, Frame S, et al. Single-dose cefotetan or cefoxitin versus multiple-dose cefoxitin as prophylaxis in patients undergoing appendectomy for acute nonperforated appendicitis. *J Am Coll Surg.* 1995; 180:77–80.
381. Salam IM, Abu Galala KH, el Ashaal YI, et al. A randomized prospective study of cefoxitin versus piperacillin in appendicectomy. *J Hosp Infect.* 1994; 26:133–6.
382. Lau WY, Fan ST, Yiu TF, et al. Prophylaxis of postappendectomy sepsis by metronidazole and ampicillin: a randomized, prospective and double-blind trial. *Br J Surg.* 1983; 70:155–7.
383. Al-Dhohayan A, Al-Sebayl M, Shibl A, et al. Comparative study of Augmentin versus metronidazole/gentamicin in the prevention of infections after appendectomy. *Eur Surg Res.* 1993; 25:60–4.
384. Morris WT, Innes DB, Richardson RA, et al. The prevention of post-appendicectomy sepsis by metronidazole and cefazolin: a controlled double-blind trial. *Aust N Z J Surg.* 1980; 50:429–33.
385. Morris DL, Wilson SR, Pain J, et al. A comparison of aztreonam/metronidazole and cefotaxime/metronidazole in elective colorectal surgery: antimicrobial prophylaxis must include gram-positive cover. *J Antimicrob Chemother.* 1990; 25:673–8.
386. Mui LM, Ng CS, Wong SK, et al. Optimum duration of prophylactic antibiotics in acute non-perforated appendicitis. *Aust N Z J Surg.* 2005; 75; 425–8.
387. Kasatpibal N, Nørgaard M, Sørensen HT, et al. Risk of surgical site infection and efficacy of antibiotic prophylaxis: a cohort study of appendectomy patients in Thailand. *BMC Infect Dis.* 2006; 6:111.
388. Nadler EP, Gaines BA. The Surgical Infection Society guidelines on antimicrobial therapy for children with appendicitis. *Surg Infect.* 2008; 9:75–83.
389. Kizilcan F, Tanyel FC, Buyukpamukcu N, et al. The necessity of prophylactic antibiotics in uncomplicated appendicitis during childhood. *J Pediatr Surg.* 1992; 27:586–8.
390. Soderquist-Elinder C, Hirsch K, Bergdahl S, et al. Prophylactic antibiotics in uncomplicated appendicitis during childhood: a prospective randomized study. *Eur J Pediatr Surg.* 1995; 5:282–5.
391. Browder W, Smith JW, Vivoda LM, et al. Nonperforative appendicitis: a continuing surgical dilemma. *J Infect Dis.* 1989; 159:1088–94.
392. Emil S, Laberge JM, Mikhail P, et al. Appendicitis in children: a ten-year update of therapeutic recommendations. *J Pediatr Surg.* 2003; 38:236–42.
393. Leong G, Wilson J, Charlett A. Duration of operation as a risk factor for surgical site infection: comparison of English and US data. *J Hosp Infect.* 2006; 63:255–62.
394. Walz MJ, Paterson CA, Seligowski JM, et al. Surgical site infection following bowel surgery: a retrospective analysis of 1446 patients. *Arch Surg.* 2006; 141:1014–8.
395. Salim A, Teixeira PG, Inaba K, et al. Analysis of 178 penetrating stomach and small bowel injuries. *World J Surg.* 2008; 32:471–5.
396. Witzke JD, Kraatz JJ, Morken JM, et al. Stapled versus hand sewn anastomoses in patients with small bowel injury: a changing perspective. *J Trauma.* 2000; 49:660–6.
397. Kirkpatrick AW, Baxter KA, Simons RK, et al. Intraabdominal complications after surgical repair of small bowel injuries: an international review. *J Trauma.* 2003; 55:399–406.
398. Brundage SI, Jurkovich GJ, Hoyt DB, et al. Stapled versus sutured gastrointestinal anastomoses in the trauma patient: a multicenter trial. *J Trauma.* 2001; 51:1054–61.
399. Hackam DJ, Ali J, Jastaniah SS. Effects of other intraabdominal injuries on the diagnosis, management, and outcome of small bowel trauma. *J Trauma.* 2000; 49:606–10.
400. Guarino J, Hassett JM Jr, Luchette FA. Small bowel injuries: mechanisms, patterns, and outcome. *J Trauma.* 1995; 39:1076–80.
401. Schnuriger B, Inaba K, Eberle BM, et al. Microbiological profile and antimicrobial susceptibility in surgical site infections following hollow viscus injury. *J Gastrointest Surg.* 2010; 14:1304–10.
402. Múñez E, Ramos A, Espejo TÁ, et al. [Microbiology of surgical site infections in abdominal tract surgery patients]. *Cir Esp.* 2011; 89:606–12. In Spanish.

403. Den Hartog D, Dur AH, Tuinebreijer WE, et al. Open surgical procedures for incisional hernias. *Cochrane Database Syst Rev.* 2008; 3:CD006438.
404. Sanchez-Manuel FJ, Lozano-García J, Seco-Gil JL. Antibiotic prophylaxis for hernia repair. *Cochrane Database Syst Rev.* 2012; 2:CD003769.
405. Yin Y, Song T, Liao B, et al. Antibiotic prophylaxis in patients undergoing open mesh repair of inguinal hernia: a meta-analysis. *Am Surg.* 2012; 78:359–65.
406. Goodney PP, Birkmeyer CM, Birkmeyer JD. Short-term outcomes of laparoscopic and open ventral hernia repair: a meta-analysis. *Arch Surg.* 2002; 137: 1161–5.
407. Sajid MS, Bokhari SA, Mallick AS, et al. Laparoscopic versus open repair of incisional/ventral hernia: a meta-analysis. *Am J Surg.* 2009; 197:64–72.
408. Kaafarani HM, Kaufman D, Reda D, et al. Predictors of surgical site infection in laparoscopic and open ventral incisional herniorrhaphy. *J Surg Res.* 2010; 163:229–34.
409. Itani KM, Hur K, Kim LT, et al. Comparison of laparoscopic and open repair with mesh for the treatment of ventral incisional hernia: a randomized trial. *Arch Surg.* 2010; 145:322–8.
410. Forbes SS, Eskicioglu C, McLeod RS, et al. Meta-analysis of randomized controlled trials comparing open and laparoscopic ventral and incisional hernia repair with mesh. *Br J Surg.* 2009; 96:851–8.
411. Sanchez VM, Abi-Haidar YE, Itani KM. Mesh infection in ventral incisional hernia repair: incidence, contributing factors, and treatment. *Surg Infect.* 2011; 12:205–9.
412. Itani KM, Wilson SE, Awad SS, et al. Ertapenem versus cefotetan prophylaxis in elective colorectal surgery. *N Engl J Med.* 2006; 335:2640–51.
413. Bartlett S, Burton R. Effects of prophylactic antibiotics on wound infection after elective colon and rectal surgery. *Am J Surg.* 1983; 145:300–9.
414. Burton RC. Postoperative wound infection in colon and rectal surgery. *Br J Surg.* 1973; 60:363–8.
415. Baum M, Anish D, Chalmers T, et al. A survey of clinical trials of antibiotic prophylaxis in colon surgery: evidence against further use of no treatment controls. *N Engl J Med.* 1981; 305:795–9.
416. Coppa G, Eng K, Gouge T, et al. Parenteral and oral antibiotics in elective colorectal surgery: a prospective randomized trial. *Am J Surg.* 1983; 145:62–5.
417. Coppa G, Eng K. Factors involved in antibiotic selection in elective colon and rectal surgery. *Surgery.* 1988; 104:853–8.
418. Glenny AM, Song F. Antimicrobial prophylaxis in colorectal surgery. *Qual Health Care.* 1999; 8:132–6.
419. Suding P, Jensen E, Abramson MA, et al. Definitive risk factors for anastomotic leaks in elective open colorectal resection. *Arch Surg.* 2008; 143:907–12.
420. Svensson LG. Prophylactic antimicrobial administration. *S Afr J Surg.* 1985; 23:55–62.
421. Hojer H, Wetterfors J. Systemic prophylaxis with doxycycline in surgery of the colon and rectum. *Ann Surg.* 1978; 187:362–8.
422. Kurz A, Sessler DI, Lenhardt R, for the Study of Wound Infection and Temperature Group. Perioperative normothermia to reduce the incidence of surgical-wound infection and shorten hospitalization. *N Engl J Med.* 1996; 334:1209–15.
423. Ata A, Lee J, Bestle SL, et al. Postoperative hyperglycemia and surgical site infection in general surgery patients. *Arch Surg.* 2010; 145:858–64.
424. McConnell YJ, Johnson PM, Porter GA. Surgical site infections following colorectal surgery in patients with diabetes: association with postoperative hyperglycemia. *J Gastrointest Surg.* 2009; 13:508–15.
425. Nichols RL. Prophylaxis for intraabdominal surgery. *Rev Infect Dis.* 1984; 6(suppl 1):S276–82.
426. Nelson RL, Glenny AM, Song F. Antimicrobial prophylaxis for colorectal surgery. *Cochrane Database Syst Rev.* 2009; 1:CD001181.
427. Clarke J, Condon R, Bartlett J, et al. Preoperative oral antibiotics reduce septic complications of colon operations: results of a prospective randomized, double-blind clinical study. *Ann Surg.* 1977; 186:251–9.
428. Nichols R, Broldo P, Condon P, et al. Effect of preoperative neomycin-erythromycin intestinal preparation on the incidence of infectious complications following colon surgery. *Ann Surg.* 1973; 178:453–62.
429. Stellato T, Danziger L, Gordon N, et al. Antibiotics in elective colon surgery: a randomized trial of oral, systemic, and oral/systemic antibiotics for prophylaxis. *Am Surg.* 1990; 56:251–4.
430. Petrelli N, Contre DC, Herrera L, et al. A prospective randomized trial of perioperative prophylactic cefamandole in elective colorectal surgery for malignancy. *Dis Colon Rectum.* 1988; 31:427–9.
431. Kling PA, Dahlgren S. Oral prophylaxis with neomycin and erythromycin in colorectal surgery; more proof for efficacy than failure. *Arch Surg.* 1989; 124:705–7.
432. Lewis RT, Goodall RG, Marien B, et al. Is neomycin necessary for bowel preparation in surgery of the colon? Oral neomycin plus erythromycin versus erythromycin–metronidazole. *Dis Colon Rectum.* 1989; 32:265–70.
433. Wapnick S, Gunito R, Leveen HH, et al. Reduction of postoperative infection in elective colorectal surgery with preoperative administration of kanamycin and erythromycin. *Surgery.* 1979; 85:317–21.
434. Bartlett J, Condon R, Gorbach S, et al. Veterans Administration Cooperative Study on bowel preparation for elective colorectal operations: impact of oral antibiotic regimen on colonic flora, wound irrigation cultures and bacteriology of septic complications. *Ann Surg.* 1978; 188:249–54.
435. Wolff B, Beart R, Dozios R, et al. A new bowel preparation for elective colon and rectal surgery: a prospective, randomized clinical trial. *Arch Surg.* 1988; 123:895–900.
436. Gahhos FN, Richards GK, Hinchey EJ, et al. Elective colon surgery: clindamycin versus metronidazole prophylaxis. *Can J Surg.* 1982; 25:613–6.
437. Dion YM, Richards GK, Prentis JJ, et al. The influence of oral metronidazole versus parenteral preoperative metronidazole on sepsis following colon surgery. *Ann Surg.* 1980; 192:221–6.
438. Beggs FD, Jobanputra RS, Holmes JT. A comparison of intravenous and oral metronidazole as prophylactic in colorectal surgery. *Br J Surg.* 1982; 69:226–7.

439. Goldring J, McNaught W, Scott A, et al. Prophylactic oral antimicrobial agents in elective colonic surgery: a controlled trial. *Lancet.* 1975; 2:997–9.
440. Washington J, Dearing W, Judd E, et al. Effect of preoperative antibiotic regimen on development of infection after intestinal surgery. *Ann Surg.* 1974; 180:567–72.
441. Peruzzo L, Savio S, De Lalla F. Systemic versus systemic plus oral chemoprophylaxis in elective colorectal surgery. *Chemioterapia.* 1987; 6:601–3.
442. Willis A, Fergunson I, Jones P, et al. Metronidazole in prevention and treatment of *Bacteroides* infections in elective colonic surgery. *Br Med J.* 1977; 1:607–10.
443. Hagen TB, Bergan T, Liavag I. Prophylactic metronidazole in elective colorectal surgery. *Acta Chir Scand.* 1980; 146:71–5.
444. Song F, Glenny AM. Antimicrobial prophylaxis in colorectal surgery: a systematic review of randomized controlled trials. *Br J Surg.* 1998; 85:1232–41.
445. Kaiser A, Herrington J, Jacobs J, et al. Cefoxitin vs erythromycin, neomycin and cefazolin in colorectal surgery: importance of the duration of the operative procedure. *Ann Surg.* 1983; 198:525–30.
446. Weaver M, Burdon DW, Youngs DJ, et al. Oral neomycin and erythromycin compared with single-dose systemic metronidazole and ceftriaxone prophylaxis in elective colorectal surgery. *Am J Surg.* 1986; 151:437–42.
447. Keighley MR, Arabi Y, Alexander-Williams J, et al. Comparison between systemic and oral antimicrobial prophylaxis in colorectal surgery. *Lancet.* 1979; 1:894–7.
448. Lewis RT, Allan CM, Goodall RG, et al. Are first-generation cephalosporins effective for antibiotic prophylaxis in elective surgery of the colon? *Can J Surg.* 1983; 26:504–7.
449. Condon RE, Bartlett JG, Nichols RL, et al. Preoperative prophylactic cephalothin fails to control septic complications of colorectal operations: results of a controlled clinical trial. *Am J Surg.* 1979; 137:68–74.
450. McDermott F, Polyglase A, Johnson W, et al. Prevention of wound infection in colorectal resections by preoperative cephazolin with and without metronidazole. *Aust N Z J Surg.* 1981; 51:351–3.
451. Jones RN, Wojeski W, Bakke J, et al. Antibiotic prophylaxis to 1,036 patients undergoing elective surgical procedures. A prospective randomized comparative trial of cefazolin, cefoxitin, and cefotaxime in a prepaid medical practice. *Am J Surg.* 1987; 153:341–6.
452. Morton A, Taylor E, Wells G. A multicenter study to compare cefotetan alone with cefotetan and metronidazole as prophylaxis against infection in elective colorectal operations. *Surg Gynecol Obstet.* 1989; 169:41–5.
453. Hoffman C, McDonald P, Watts J. Use of perioperative cefoxitin to prevent infection after colonic and rectal surgery. *Ann Surg.* 1981; 193:353–6.
454. Periti P, Mazzei T, Tonelli F. Single-dose cefotetan vs multiple dose cefoxitin. *Rectum.* 1989; 32:121–7.
455. Jagelman D, Fabian T, Nichols R, et al. Single-dose cefotetan versus multiple dose cefoxitin as prophylaxis in colorectal surgery. *Am J Surg.* 1988; 155:71–6.
456. Shatney CH. Antibiotic prophylaxis in elective gastrointestinal tract surgery: a comparison of single-dose preoperative cefotaxime and multiple-dose cefoxitin. *J Antimicrob Chemother.* 1984; 14(suppl B):241–5.
457. Arnaud JP, Bellissant E, Boissel P, et al. Single-dose amoxycillin-clavulanic acid vs cefotetan for prophylaxis in elective colorectal surgery: a multicentre, prospective, randomized study. *J Hosp Infect.* 1992; 22(suppl A):23–32.
458. Periti P, Tonelli F, Mazzei T, et al. Antimicrobial chemoimmunoprophylaxis in colorectal surgery with cefotetan and thymostimulin: prospective, controlled, multicenter study. *J Chemother.* 1993; 5:37–42.
459. Skipper D, Karran SJ. A randomized, prospective study to compare cefotetan with cefuroxime plus metronidazole as prophylaxis in elective colorectal surgery. *J Hosp Infect.* 1992; 21:73–7.
460. Lumley JW, Siu SK, Pillay SP, et al. Single-dose ceftriaxone as prophylaxis for sepsis in colorectal surgery. *Aust N Z J Surg.* 1992; 62:292–6.
461. Hakansson T, Raahave D, Hansen OH, et al. Effectiveness of single-dose prophylaxis with cefotaxime and metronidazole compared with three doses of cefotaxime alone in elective colorectal surgery. *Eur J Surg.* 1993; 159:177–80.
462. Karran SJ, Sutton G, Gartell P, et al. Imipenem prophylaxis in elective colorectal surgery. *Br J Surg.* 1993; 80:1196–8.
463. Fukatsu K, Saito H, Matsuda T, et al. Influences of type and duration of antimicrobial prophylaxis on an outbreak of methicillin-resistant *Staphylococcus aureus* and on the incidence of wound infection. *Arch Surg.* 1997; 132:1320–5.
464. AhChong K, Yip AW, Lee FC, et al. Comparison of prophylactic ampicillin/sulbactam with gentamicin and metronidazole in elective colorectal surgery: a randomized clinical study. *J Hosp Infect.* 1994; 27:149–54.
465. Kwok SP, Lau WY, Leung KL, et al. Amoxicillin and clavulanic acid versus cefotaxime and metronidazole as antibiotic prophylaxis in elective colorectal resectional surgery. *Chemotherapy.* 1993; 39:135–9.
466. Barbar MS, Hirxberg BC, Rice C, et al. Parenteral antibiotics in elective colon surgery? A prospective, controlled clinical study. *Surgery.* 1979; 86:23–9.
467. Madsen M, Toftgaard C, Gaversen H, et al. Cefoxitin for one day vs ampicillin and metronidazole for three days in elective colorectal surgery: a prospective, randomized, multicenter study. *Dis Colon Rectum.* 1988; 31:774–7.
468. Blair J, McLeod R, Cohen Z, et al. Ticarcillin/clavulanic acid (Timentin) compared to metronidazole/netilmicin in preventing postoperative infection after elective colorectal surgery. *Can J Surg.* 1987; 30:120–2.
469. Mendes Da Costa P, Kaufman L. Amikacin once daily plus metronidazole versus amikacin twice daily plus metronidazole in colorectal surgery. *Hepatogastroenterology.* 1992; 39:350–4.

470. Roland M. Prophylactic regimens in colorectal surgery: an open randomized consecutive trial of metronidazole used alone or in combination with ampicillin or doxycycline. *World J Surg.* 1986; 10:1003–8.
471. Juul PZ, Klaaborg KE, Kronborg O. Single or multiple doses of metronidazole and ampicillin in elective colorectal surgery: a randomized trial. *Dis Colon Rectum.* 1987; 30:526–8.
472. University of Melbourne Colorectal Group. A comparison of single-dose Timentin with mezlocillin for prophylaxis of wound infection in elective colorectal surgery. *Dis Colon Rectum.* 1989; 32:940–3.
473. Stewart M, Taylor EW, Lindsay G. Infection after colorectal surgery: a randomized trial of prophylaxis with piperacillin versus sulbactam/piperacillin. *J Hosp Infect.* 1995; 29:135–42.
474. Bergman L, Solhaug JH. Single-dose chemoprophylaxis in elective colorectal surgery. *Ann Surg.* 1987; 205:77–81.
475. Goransson G, Nilsson-Ehle I, Olsson S, et al. Single- versus multiple-dose doxycycline prophylaxis in elective colorectal surgery. *Acta Chir Scand.* 1984; 150:245–9.
476. Andaker L, Burman LG, Eklund A, et al. Fosfomycin/metronidazole compared with doxycycline/metronidazole for the prophylaxis of infection after elective colorectal surgery: a randomized, double-blind, multi-centre trial in 517 patients. *Eur J Surg.* 1992; 158:181–5.
477. Sexton DJ. Carbapenems for surgical prophylaxis? *N Engl J Med.* 2006; 355:2693–5.
478. Condon RE, Bartlett J, Greenlee H, et al. Efficacy of oral and systemic antibiotic prophylaxis in colorectal operations. *Arch Surg.* 1983; 118:496–502.
479. Condon RE. Preoperative antibiotic bowel preparation. *Drug Ther.* 1983; 83:29–37.
480. Hinchey E, Richards G, Lewis R, et al. Moxalactam as single agent prophylaxis in the prevention of wound infection following colon surgery. *Surgery.* 1987; 101:15–9.
481. Jagelman DG, Fazio VW, Lavery IC, et al. A prospective, randomized, double-blind study of 10% mannitol mechanical bowel preparation combined with oral neomycin and short-term, perioperative, intravenous Flagyl as prophylaxis in elective colorectal resections. *Surgery.* 1985; 98:861–5.
482. Lewis RT. Oral versus systemic antibiotic prophylaxis in elective colon surgery: a randomized study and meta-analysis send a message from the 1990s. *Can J Surg.* 2002; 45:173–80.
483. Englesbe MJ, Brooks L, Kubus J, et al. A statewide assessment of surgical site infection following colectomy: the role of oral antibiotics. *Ann Surg.* 2010; 252:514–20.
484. Kobayashi M, Mohri Y, Tonouchi H, et al. Randomized clinical trial comparing intravenous antimicrobial prophylaxis alone with oral and intravenous antimicrobial prophylaxis for the prevention of a surgical site infection in colorectal cancer surgery. *Surg Today.* 2007; 37:383–8.
485. Wren SM, Ahmed N, Jamal A, et al. Preoperative oral antibiotics in colorectal surgery increase the rate of *Clostridium difficile* colitis. *Arch Surg.* 2005; 140:752–6.
486. Krapohl GL, Phillips LR, Campbell DA, et al. Bowel preparation for colectomy and risk of *Clostridium difficile* infection. *Dis Colon Rectum.* 2011; 54:810–7.
487. Espin-Basany E, Sanchez-Garcia JL, Lopez-Cano M, et al. Prospective, randomised study on antibiotic prophylaxis in colorectal surgery. Is it really necessary to use oral antibiotics? *Int J Colorectal Dis.* 2005; 20:542–6.
488. Sondheimer JM, Sokol RJ, Taylor S, et al. Safety, efficacy, and tolerance of intestinal lavage in pediatric patients undergoing diagnostic colonoscopy. *J Pediatr.* 1991; 119:148–52.
489. Tuggle DW, Hoelzer DJ, Tunell WP, et al. The safety and cost-effectiveness of polyethylene glycol electrolyte solution bowel preparation in infants and children. *J Pediatr Surg.* 1987; 22:513–5.
490. Weber RS, Callender DL. Antibiotic prophylaxis in clean-contaminated head and neck oncologic surgery. *Ann Otol Rhinol Laryngol.* 1992; 101:16–20.
491. Avenia N, Sanguinetti A, Cirocchi R, et al. Antibiotic prophylaxis in thyroid surgery: a preliminary multicentric Italian experience. *Ann Surg Innov Res.* 2009; 3:10.
492. Johnson JT, Wagner RL. Infection following uncontaminated head and neck surgery. *Arch Otolaryngol Head Neck Surg.* 1987; 113:368–9.
493. Saginur R, Odell PF, Poliquin JF. Antibiotic prophylaxis in head and neck cancer surgery. *J Otolaryngol.* 1988; 17:78–80.
494. Mandell-Brown M, Johnson JT, Wagner RL. Cost-effectiveness of prophylactic antibiotics in head and neck surgery. *Otolaryngol Head Neck Surg.* 1984; 92:520–3.
495. Johnson JT, Yu VL, Myers EN, et al. Efficacy of two third-generation cephalosporins in prophylaxis for head and neck surgery. *Arch Otolaryngol.* 1984; 110:224–7.
496. Callender DL. Antibiotic prophylaxis in head and neck oncologic surgery: the role of gram-negative coverage. *Int J Antimicrob Agents.* 1999; 12(suppl 1):s21–7.
497. Simo R, French G. The use of prophylactic antibiotics in head and neck oncological surgery. *Curr Opin Otolaryngol Head Neck Surg.* 2006; 14:55–61.
498. Lotfi CJ, Cavalcanti Rde C, Costa e Silva AM, et al. Risk factors for surgical-site infections in head and neck cancer surgery. *Otolaryngol Head Neck Surg.* 2008; 138:74–80.
499. Liu SA, Tung KC, Shiao JY, et al. Preliminary report of associated factors in surgical site infection after major head and neck neoplasm operations—does the duration of prophylactic antibiotic matter? *J Laryngol Otol.* 2008; 122:403–8.
500. Sepehr A, Santos BJ, Chou C, et al. Antibiotics in head and neck surgery in the setting of malnutrition, tracheotomy, and diabetes. *Laryngoscope.* 2009; 119:549–53.
501. Coskun H, Erisen L, Basut O. Factors affecting wound infection rates in head and neck surgery. *Otolaryngol Head Neck Surg.* 2000; 123:328–33.

502. Robbins KT, Favrot S, Hanna D, et al. Risk of surgical site infection in patients with head and neck cancer. *Head Neck.* 1990; 12:143–8.
503. Tabet JC, Johnson JT. Wound infection in head and neck surgery: prophylaxis, etiology and management. *J Otolaryngol.* 1990; 19:197–200.
504. Girod DA, McCulloch TM, Tsue TT, et al. Risk factors for complications in clean-contaminated head and neck surgical procedures. *Head Neck.* 1995; 17:7–13.
505. Miles BA, Potter JK, Ellis E III. The efficacy of postoperative antibiotic regimens in the open treatment of mandibular fractures: a prospective randomized trial. *J Oral Maxillofac Surg.* 2006; 64:576–82.
506. Penel N, Fournier C, Roussel-Delvallez M, et al. Prognostic significance of surgical site infections following major head and neck cancer surgery: an open non-comparative prospective study. *Support Care Cancer.* 2004; 12:634–9.
507. Lovato C, Wagner JD. Infection rates following perioperative prophylactic antibiotics versus postoperative extended regimen prophylactic antibiotics in surgical management of mandibular fractures. *J Oral Maxillofac Surg.* 2009; 67:827–32.
508. Strauss M, Saccogna PW, Allphin AL. Cephazolin and metronidazole prophylaxis in head and neck surgery. *J Laryngol Otol.* 1997; 111:631–4.
509. Simons JP, Johnson JT, Yu VL, et al. The role of topical antibiotic prophylaxis in patients undergoing contaminated head and neck surgery with flap reconstruction. *Laryngoscope.* 2001; 111:329–35.
510. Johnson JT, Kachman K, Wagner RL, et al. Comparison of ampicillin/sulbactam versus clindamycin in the prevention of infection in patients undergoing head and neck surgery. *Head Neck.* 1997; 19:367–71.
511. Skitarelić N, Morović M, Manestar D. Antibiotic prophylaxis in clean-contaminated head and neck oncological surgery. *J Craniomaxillofac Surg.* 2007; 35:15–20.
512. Andrews PJ, East CA, Jayaraj SM, et al. Prophylactic vs. postoperative antibiotic use in complex septorhinoplasty surgery: a prospective, randomized, single-blind trial comparing efficacy. *Arch Facial Plast Surg.* 2006; 8:84–7.
513. Becker GD, Welch WD. Quantitative bacteriology of closed-suction wound drainage in contaminated surgery. *Laryngoscope.* 1990; 100:403–6.
514. Johnson JT, Yu VL. Role of aerobic gram-negative rods, anaerobes, and fungi in surgical site infection after head and neck surgery: implications for antibiotic prophylaxis. *Head Neck.* 1989; 11:27–9.
515. Rubin J, Johnson JT, Wagner RL, et al. Bacteriologic analysis of surgical site infection following major head and neck surgery. *Arch Otolaryngol Head Neck Surg.* 1988; 114:969–72.
516. Brown BM, Johnson JT, Wagner RL. Etiologic factors in head and neck surgical site infections. *Laryngoscope.* 1987; 97:587–90.
517. Penel N, Fournier C, Lefebvre D, et al. Multivariate analysis of risk factors for surgical site infection in head and neck squamous cell carcinoma surgery with opening of mucosa. Study of 260 surgical procedures. *Oral Oncol.* 2005; 41:294–303.
518. Brook I. Microbiology and management of post-surgical wounds infection in children. *Pediatr Rehabil.* 2002; 5:171–6.
519. Brook I. Microbiology and principles of antimicrobial therapy for head and neck infections. *Infect Dis Clin N Am.* 2007; 21:355–91.
520. National Institute for Health and Clinical Excellence. Surgical site infection (clinical guideline 74) 2008. www.nice.org.uk/CG74 (accessed 2012 Dec 9).
521. Andreasen JO, Jensen SS, Schwartz O, et al. A systematic review of prophylactic antibiotics in the surgical treatment of maxillofacial fractures. *J Oral Maxillofac Surg.* 2006; 64:1664–8.
522. O'Reilly BJ, Black S, Fernandes J, et al. Is the routine use of antibiotics justified in adult tonsillectomy? *J Laryngol Otol.* 2003; 117:382–5.
523. Lee WC, Duignan MC, Walsh RM, et al. An audit of prophylactic antibiotic treatment following tonsillectomy in children. *J Laryngol Otol.* 1996; 110:357–9.
524. Caniello M, Passerotti GH, Goto EY, et al. Antibiotics in septoplasty: is it necessary? *Braz J Otorhinolaryngol.* 2005; 71:734–8.
525. Dhiwakar M, Eng CY, Selvaraj S, et al. Antibiotics to improve recovery following tonsillectomy: a systematic review. *Otolaryngol Head Neck Surg.* 2006; 134:357–64.
526. Dhiwakar M, Clement WA, Supriya M, et al. Antibiotics to reduce post-tonsillectomy morbidity. *Cochrane Database Syst Rev.* 2008; 2:CD005607.
527. Fennessy BG, Harney M, O'Sullivan MJ, et al. Antimicrobial prophylaxis in otorhinolaryngology/head and neck surgery. *Clin Otolaryngol.* 2007; 32:204–7.
528. Seven H, Sayin I, Turgut S. Antibiotic prophylaxis in clean neck dissections. *J Laryngol Otol.* 2004; 118:213–6.
529. Slattery WH III, Stringer SP, Cassisi NJ. Prophylactic antibiotic use in clean, uncontaminated neck dissection. *Laryngoscope.* 1995; 105:244–6.
530. Weber RS, Raad I, Frankenthaler R, et al. Ampicillin-sulbactam vs clindamycin in head and neck oncologic surgery. The need for gram-negative coverage. *Arch Otolaryngol Head Neck Surg.* 1992; 118:1159–63.
531. Johnson JT, Myers EN, Thearle PB, et al. Antimicrobial prophylaxis for contaminated head and neck surgery. *Laryngoscope.* 1984; 94:46–51.
532. Righi M, Manfredi R, Farneti G, et al. Short-term versus long-term antimicrobial prophylaxis in oncologic head and neck surgery. *Head Neck.* 1996; 18:399–404.
533. Rajan GP, Fergie N, Fischer U, et al. Antibiotic prophylaxis in septorhinoplasty? A prospective, randomized study. *Plast Reconstr Surg.* 2005; 116:1995–8.
534. Abubaker AO, Rollert MK. Postoperative antibiotic prophylaxis in mandibular fractures: a preliminary randomized, double-blind, and placebo-controlled clinical study. *J Oral Maxillofac Surg.* 2001; 59:1415–9.
535. Avery CM, Ameerally P, Castling B, et al. Infection of surgical wounds in the maxillofacial region

and free flap donor sites with methicillin-resistant *Staphylococcus aureus*. *Br J Oral Maxillofac Surg.* 2006; 44:217–21.
536. Gantz NM. Nosocomial central nervous system infections. In: Mayhall CG, ed. Hospital epidemiology and infection control. 3rd ed. Philadelphia: Lippincott Williams and Wilkins; 2004.
537. Narotam PK, van Dellen JR, du Trevou MD, et al. Operative sepsis in neurosurgery: a method of classifying surgical case. *Neurosurgery.* 1994; 34:409–16.
538. Kourbeti IS, Jacobs AV, Koslow M, et al. Risk factors associated with postcraniotomy meningitis. *Neurosurgery.* 2007; 60:317–26.
539. Rebuck JA, Murry KR, Rhoney DH, et al. Infection related to intracranial pressure monitors in adults: analysis of risk factor and antibiotic prophylaxis. *J Neurol Neurosurg Psychiatry.* 2000; 69:381–4.
540. Korinek AM, Baugnon T, Golmard JL, et al. Risk factors for adult nosocomial meningitis after craniotomy: role of antibiotic prophylaxis. *Neurosurgery.* 2006; 58:126–33.
541. Lietard C, Thébaud V, Besson G, et al. Risk factors for neurosurgical site infections: an 18-month prospective survey. *J Neurosurg.* 2008; 109:729–34.
542. Korinek AM, for the French Study Group of Neurosurgical Infections SEHP C-CLIN Paris-Nord. Risk factors for neurosurgical site infections after craniotomy: a prospective multicenter study of 2944 patients. *Neurosurgery.* 1997; 41:1073–81.
543. Korinek AM, Golmard JL, Elcheick A, et al. Risk factors for neurosurgical site infections after craniotomy: a critical reappraisal of antibiotic prophylaxis on 4578 patients. *Br J Neurosurg.* 2005; 19:155–62.
544. Valentini LG, Casali C, Chatenoud L, et al. Surgical site infections after elective neurosurgery: a survey of 1747 patients. *Neurosurgery.* 2007; 61:88–96.
545. Zabramski JM, Whiting D, Darouiche RO, et al. Efficacy of antimicrobial-impregnated external ventricular drain catheters: a prospective, randomized controlled trial. *J Neurosurg.* 2003; 98:725–30.
546. Biyani N, Grisaru-Soen G, Steinbok P, et al. Prophylactic antibiotics in pediatric shunt surgery. *Childs Nerv Syst.* 2006; 22:1465–71.
547. Holloway KL, Smith KW, Wilberger JE, et al. Antibiotic prophylaxis during clean neurosurgery: a large, multicenter study using cefuroxime. *Clin Ther.* 1996; 18:84–94.
548. Whitby M, Johnson BC, Atkinson RL, et al. The comparative efficacy of intravenous cefotaxime and trimethoprim/sulfamethoxazole in preventing infection after neurosurgery: a prospective, randomized study. *Br J Neurosurg.* 2000; 14:13–18.
549. Govender ST, Nathoo N, van Dellen JR. Evaluation of an antibiotic-impregnated shunt system for the treatment of hydrocephalus. *J Neurosurg.* 2003; 99:831–9.
550. Tacconelli E, Cataldo MA, Albanese A, et al. Vancomycin versus cefazolin prophylaxis for cerebrospinal shunt placement in a hospital with a high prevalence of methicillin-resistant *Staphylococcus aureus*. *J Hosp Infect.* 2008; 69:337–44.
551. Wong GK, Poon WS, Lyon D, et al. Cefepime vs ampicillin/sulbactam and aztreonam as antibiotic prophylaxis in neurosurgical patients with external ventricular drain: result of a prospective randomized controlled clinical trial. *J Clin Pharm Ther.* 2006; 31:231–5.
552. Ragal BT, Browd SR, Schmidt RH. Surgical shunt infection: significant reduction when using intraventricular and systemic antibiotic agents. *J Neurosurg.* 2006; 105:242–7.
553. Sarguna P, Lakshmi V. Ventriculoperitoneal shunt infections. *Indian J Med Microbiol.* 2006; 24:52–4.
554. Langley JM, Gravel D, Moore D, et al. Study of cerebrospinal fluid shunt-associated infections in the first year following placement, by the Canadian Nosocomial Infection Surveillance Program. *Infect Control Hosp Epidemiol.* 2009; 30:285–8.
555. Nisbet M, Briggs S, Ellis-Pegler R, et al. *Propionibacterium acnes*: an under-appreciated cause of post-neurosurgical infection. *J Antimicrob Chemother.* 2007; 60:1097–103.
556. Conen A, Walti LN, Merlo A, et al. Characteristics and treatment outcome of cerebrospinal fluid shunt-associated infections in adults: a retrospective analysis over an 11-year period. *Clin Infect Dis.* 2008; 47:73–82.
557. Barker FG II. Efficacy of prophylactic antibiotics against meningitis after craniotomy: a meta-analysis. *Neurosurgery.* 2007; 60:887–94.
558. Haines SJ, Goodman ML. Antibiotic prophylaxis of postoperative neurosurgical wound infection. *J Neurosurg.* 1982; 56:103–5.
559. Quartey GR, Polyzoidis K. Intraoperative antibiotic prophylaxis in neurosurgery: a clinical study. *Neurosurgery.* 1981; 8:669–71.
560. Savitz MH, Katz SS. Prevention of primary wound infection in neurosurgical patients: a 10-year study. *Neurosurgery.* 1986; 18:685–8.
561. Blomstedt GC, Kytta J. Results of a randomized trial of vancomycin prophylaxis in craniotomy. *J Neurosurg.* 1988; 69:216–20.
562. Shapiro M, Wald U, Simchen E, et al. Randomized clinical trial of intraoperative antimicrobial prophylaxis of infection after neurosurgical procedures. *J Hosp Infect.* 1986; 8:283–95.
563. Watters WC III, Baisden J, Bono CM, et al. Antibiotic prophylaxis in spine surgery: an evidence-based clinical guideline for the use of prophylactic antibiotics in spine surgery. *Spine J.* 2009; 9:142–6.
564. Wang EL, Prober CG, Hendrick BE. Prophylactic sulfamethoxazole and trimethoprim in ventriculoperitoneal shunt surgery. A double-blind, randomized, placebo-controlled trial. *JAMA.* 1984; 251:1174–7.
565. Blomstedt GC. Results in trimethoprim-sulfamethoxazole prophylaxis in ventriculostomy and shunting procedures. *J Neurosurg.* 1985; 62:694–7.
566. Djindjian M, Fevrier MJ, Ottervbein G, et al. Oxacillin prophylaxis in cerebrospinal fluid shunt procedures: results of a randomized, open study in 60 hydrocephalic patients. *Surg Neurol.* 1986; 24:178–80.

567. Blum J, Schwarz M, Voth D. Antibiotic single-dose prophylaxis of shunt infections. *Neurosurg Rev.* 1989; 12:239–44.
568. Schmidt K, Gjerris F, Osgaard O, et al. Antibiotic prophylaxis in cerebrospinal fluid shunting: a prospective randomized trial in 152 hydrocephalic patients. *Neurosurgery.* 1985; 17:1–5.
569. Griebel R, Khan M, Tan L. CSF shunt complications: an analysis of contributory factors. *Childs Nerv Syst.* 1985; 1:77–80.
570. Lambert M, MacKinnon AE, Vaishnav A. Comparison of two methods of prophylaxis against CSF shunt infection. *Z Kinderchir.* 1984; 39(suppl):109–10.
571. Zentner J, Gilsbach J, Felder T. Antibiotic prophylaxis in cerebrospinal fluid shunting: a prospective randomized trial in 129 patients. *Neurosurg Rev.* 1995; 18:169–72.
572. Haines SJ, Walters BC. Antibiotic prophylaxis for cerebrospinal fluid shunts: a meta-analysis. *Neurosurgery.* 1994; 34:87–92.
573. Langley JM, LeBlanc JC, Drake J, et al. Efficacy of antimicrobial prophylaxis in placement of cerebrospinal fluid shunts: meta-analysis. *Clin Infect Dis.* 1993; 17:98–103.
574. Borowski A, Littleton AG, Borkhuu B, et al. Complications of intrathecal baclofen pump therapy in pediatric patients. *J Pediatr Orthop.* 2010; 30:76–81.
575. Motta F, Buonaguro V, Stignani C. The use of intrathecal baclofen pump implants in children and adolescents: safety and complications in 200 consecutive cases. *J Neurosurg.* 2007; 107(suppl):32–5.
576. Fjelstad AB, Hommelstad J, Sorteberg A. Infections related to intrathecal baclofen therapy in children and adults: frequency and risk factors. *J Neurosurg Pediatr.* 2009; 4:487–93.
577. Follett KA, Boortz-Marx RL, Drake JM, et al. Prevention and management of intrathecal drug delivery and spinal cord stimulation system infections. *Anesthesiology.* 2004; 100:1582–94.
578. Ratilal BO, Costa J, Sampaio C. Antibiotic prophylaxis for surgical introduction of intracranial ventricular shunts. *Cochrane Database Syst Rev.* 2006; 3:CD005365.
579. Arnaboldi L. Antimicrobial prophylaxis with ceftriaxone in neurosurgical procedures: a prospective study of 100 patients undergoing shunt operations. *Chemotherapy.* 1996; 42:384–90.
580. Alleyne CH, Hassan M, Zabramski JM. The efficacy and cost of prophylactic and periprocedural antibiotics in patients with external ventricular drains. *Neurosurgery.* 2000; 47:1124–9.
581. Shurtleff DB, Stuntz JT, Hayden PW. Experience with 1201 cerebrospinal fluid shunt procedures. *Pediatr Neurosci.* 1985-1986; 12:49–57.
582. Walters BC, Goumnerova L, Hoffman HJ, et al. A randomized, controlled trial of perioperative rifampin/trimethoprim in cerebrospinal fluid shunt surgery. *Childs Nerv Syst.* 1992; 8:253–7.
583. Martin JA, Hamilton BE, Sutton PD, et al. Births: final data for 2006. *Natl Vital Stat Rep.* 2009; 57:1–104.
584. Obstetric and medical complications. In: American Academy of Pediatrics and American College of Obstetricians and Gynecologists. Guidelines for perinatal care. 6th ed. Elk Grove Village, IL: American Academy of Pediatrics; 2008:175–204.
585. Hofmeyr GJ, Smaill F. Antibiotic prophylaxis for cesarean section. *Cochrane Database Syst Rev.* 2002; 3:CD000933.
586. Killian C, Graffunder EM, Vinciguerra T, et al. Risk factors for surgical-site infections following cesarean section. *Infect Control Hosp Epidemiol.* 2001; 22:613–7.
587. Faro S. Infectious disease relations to cesarean section. *Obstet Gynecol Clin North Am.* 1989; 16:363–71.
588. Olsen MA, Butler AM, Willers DM, et al. Risk factors for surgical site infection after low transverse cesarean section. *Infect Control Hosp Epidemiol.* 2008; 29:477–84.
589. Hemsell DL. Infections after gynecologic surgery. *Obstet Gynecol Clin North Am.* 1989; 16:381–400.
590. Faro S. Antibiotic prophylaxis. *Obstet Gynecol Clin North Am.* 1989; 16:279–89.
591. Tita AT, Rouse DJ, Blackwell S, et al. Emerging concepts in antibiotic prophylaxis for cesarean delivery: a systematic review. *Obstet Gynecol.* 2009; 113:675–82.
592. Chelmow D, Ruehli MS, Huang E. Prophylactic use of antibiotics for nonlaboring patients undergoing cesarean delivery with intact membranes: a meta-analysis. *Am J Obstet Gynecol.* 2001; 184:656–61.
593. Duff P, Smith PN, Keiser JF. Antibiotic prophylaxis in low-risk cesarean section. *J Reprod Med.* 1982; 27:133–8.
594. Apuzzio JJ, Reyelt C, Pelosi MA, et al. Prophylactic antibiotics for cesarean section: comparison of high- and low-risk patients for endometritis. *Obstet Gynecol.* 1982; 59:693–8.
595. Duff P. Prophylactic antibiotics for cesarean delivery: a simple cost-effective strategy for prevention of postoperative morbidity. *Am J Obstet Gynecol.* 1987; 157:794–8.
596. Jakobi P, Weissman A, Sigler E, et al. Post-cesarean section febrile morbidity. Antibiotic prophylaxis in low-risk patients. *J Reprod Med.* 1994; 39:707–10.
597. Rizk DE, Nsanze H, Mabrouk MH, et al. Systemic antibiotic prophylaxis in elective cesarean delivery. *Int J Gynaecol Obstet.* 1998; 61:245–51.
598. Rouzi AA, Khalifa F, Ba'aqeel H, et al. The routine use of cefazolin in cesarean section. *Int J Gynecol Obstet.* 2000; 69:107–12.
599. Bagratee JS, Moodley J, Kleinschmidt I, et al. A randomized controlled trial of antibiotic prophylaxis in elective caesarean delivery. *Br J Obstet Gynaecol.* 2001; 108:143–8.
600. Hopkins L, Smaill F. Antibiotic prophylaxis regimens and drugs for cesarean section. *Cochrane Database Syst Rev.* 1999; 2:CD001136.
601. Andrews WW, Hauth JC, Cliver SP, et al. Randomized clinical trial of extended spectrum antibiotic prophylaxis with coverage for *Ureaplasma urealyticum* to reduce post-cesarean delivery endometritis. *Obstet Gyncol.* 2003; 101:1183–9.

602. Tita AT, Hauth JC, Grimes A, et al. Decreasing incidence of postcesarean endometritis with extended-spectrum antibiotic prophylaxis. *Obstet Gynecol.* 2008; 111:51–6.
603. Tita AT, Owen J, Stamm A, et al. Impact of extended-spectrum antibiotic prophylaxis on incidence of postcesarean surgical wound infection. *Am J Obstet Gynecol.* 2008; 199:303.e1–e3.
604. Meyer NL, Hosier KV, Scott K, et al. Cefazolin versus cefazolin plus metronidazole for antibiotic prophylaxis at cesarean section. *South Med J.* 2003; 96:992–5.
605. Costantine MM, Rahman M, Ghulmiyah L, et al. Timing of perioperative antibiotics for cesarean delivery: a metaanalysis. *Am J Obstet Gynecol.* 2008; 199:301.e1–e6.
606. Sullivan SA, Smith T, Chang E, et al. Administration of cefazolin prior to skin incision is superior to cefazolin at cord clamping in preventing postcesarean infectious morbidity: a randomized, controlled trial. *Am J Obstet Gynecol.* 2007; 196:455.e1–e5.
607. Committee Opinion No. 465: antimicrobial prophylaxis for cesarean delivery: timing of administration. *Obstet Gynecol.* 2010; 116:791–2.
608. Witt A, Döner M, Petricevic L, et al. Antibiotic prophylaxis before surgery vs after cord clamping in elective cesarean delivery: a double-blind, prospective, randomized, placebo-controlled trial. *Arch Surg.* 2011; 146:1404–9.
609. Whiteman MK, Hillis SD, Jamieson DJ, et al. Inpatient hysterectomy surveillance in the United States, 2000-2004. *Am J Obstet Gynecol.* 2008; 198:34.e1–e7.
610. Schorge JO, Schaffer JI, Halvorson LM, et al. Surgeries for benign gynecologic conditions. Chap. 41. In: Schorge JO, Schaffer JI, Halvorson LM, et al., eds. Williams gynecology. New York: McGraw-Hill Professional; 2008.
611. Drahonovsky J, Haakova L, Otcenasek M, et al. A prospective randomized comparison of vaginal hysterectomy, laparoscopically assisted vaginal hysterectomy, and total laparoscopic hysterectomy in women with benign uterine disease. *Eur J Obstet Gynecol.* 2009; 148:172–6.
612. Sokol AI, Green IC. Laparoscopic hysterectomy. *Clin Obstet Gynecol.* 2009; 52:304–12.
613. ACOG Committee Opinion No. 444: choosing the route of hysterectomy for benign disease. *Obstet Gynecol.* 2009; 114:1156–8.
614. Nieboer TE, Johnson N, Lethaby A, et al. Surgical approach to hysterectomy for benign gynaecological disease. *Cochrane Database Syst Rev.* 2009; 3:CD003677.
615. American College of Obstetricians and Gynecologists. ACOG Committee Opinion No. 388: supracervical hysterectomy. *Obstet Gynecol.* 2007; 110:1215–7.
616. Jennings RH. Prophylactic antibiotics in vaginal and abdominal hysterectomy. *South Med J.* 1978; 71:251–4.
617. Hemsell D, Johnson ER, Hemsell PG, et al. Cefazolin is inferior to cefotetan as single-dose prophylaxis for women undergoing elective total abdominal hysterectomy. *Clin Infect Dis.* 1995; 20:677–84.
618. Goosenberg J, Emich JP Jr, Schwarz RH. Prophylactic antibiotics in vaginal hysterectomy. *Am J Obstet Gynecol.* 1969; 105:503–6.
619. Marsden DE, Cavanagh D, Wisniewski BJ, et al. Factors affecting the incidence of infectious morbidity after radical hysterectomy. *Am J Obstet Gynecol.* 1985; 152:817–21.
620. Mann W, Orr J, Shingleton H, et al. Perioperative influences on infectious morbidity in radical hysterectomy. *Gynecol Oncol.* 1981; 11:207–12.
621. Löfgren M, Poromaa IS, Stjerndahl JH, et al. Postoperative infections and antibiotic prophylaxis for hysterectomy in Sweden: a study by the Swedish National Register for Gynecologic Surgery. *Acta Obstet Gynecol Scand.* 2004; 83:1202–7.
622. Olsen MA, Higham-Kessler J, Yokoe DS, et al. Developing a risk stratification model for surgical site infection after abdominal hysterectomy. *Infect Control Hosp Epidemiol.* 2009; 30:1077–83.
623. Soper DE, Bump RC, Hurt GW. Wound infection after abdominal hysterectomy: effect of the depth of subcutaneous tissue. *Am J Obstet Gynecol.* 1995; 173:465–71.
624. Soper DE. Infections of the female pelvis. In: Mandell GL, Bennett JE, Dolin R, eds. Mandell, Douglas and Bennett's principles and practice of infectious diseases. 7th ed. New York: Churchill Livingstone; 2009:1514–6.
625. Ohm MJ, Galask RP. The effect of antibiotic prophylaxis on patients undergoing vaginal operations. II. Alterations of microbial flora. *Am J Obstet Gynecol.* 1975; 123:597–604.
626. Ohm MJ, Galask RP. The effect of antibiotic prophylaxis on patients undergoing total abdominal hysterectomy. II. Alterations of microbial flora. *Am J Obstet Gynecol.* 1976; 125:448–54.
627. Appelbaum P, Moodley J, Chatterton S, et al. Metronidazole in the prophylaxis and treatment of anaerobic infection. *S Afr Med J.* 1978; 1:703–6.
628. Mittendorf R, Aronson MP, Berry RE, et al. Avoiding serious infections associated with abdominal hysterectomy: a meta-analysis of antibiotic prophylaxis. *Am J Obstet Gynecol.* 1993; 169:1119–24.
629. Duff P. Antibiotic prophylaxis for abdominal hysterectomy. *Obstet Gynecol.* 1982; 60:25–9.
630. Miyazawa K, Hernandez E, Dillon MB. Prophylactic topical cefamandole in radical hysterectomy. *Int J Gynaecol Obstet.* 1987; 25:133–8.
631. Micha JP, Kucera PR, Birkett JP, et al. Prophylactic mezlocillin in radical hysterectomy. *Obstet Gynecol.* 1987; 69:251–4.
632. Sevin B, Ramos R, Lichtinger M, et al. Antibiotic prevention of infection complicating radical abdominal hysterectomy. *Obstet Gynecol.* 1984; 64:539–45.
633. Rosenshein NB, Ruth JC, Villar J, et al. A prospective randomized study of doxycycline as a prophylactic antibiotic in patients undergoing radical hysterectomy. *Gynecol Oncol.* 1983; 15:201–6.
634. Zakashansky K, Bradley WH, Nezhat FR. New techniques in radical hysterectomy. *Curr Opin Obstet Gynecol.* 2008; 20:14–9.

635. Hemsell D, Menon M, Friedman A. Ceftriaxone or cefazolin prophylaxis for the prevention of infection after vaginal hysterectomy. *Am J Surg.* 1984; 148:22–6.
636. Hemsell DL, Johnson ER, Bawdon RE, et al. Ceftriaxone and cefazolin prophylaxis for hysterectomy. *Surg Gynecol Obstet.* 1985; 161:197–203.
637. Soper D, Yarwood R. Single-dose antibiotic prophylaxis in women undergoing vaginal hysterectomy. *Obstet Gynecol.* 1987; 53:879–82.
638. Rapp RP, Connors E, Hager WD, et al. Comparison of single-dose moxalactam and a three-dose regimen of cefoxitin for prophylaxis in vaginal hysterectomy. *Clin Pharm.* 1986; 5:988–93.
639. Roy S, Wilkins J. Single-dose cefotaxime versus 3- to 5-dose cefoxitin for prophylaxis of vaginal or abdominal hysterectomy. *J Antimicrob Chemother.* 1984; 14(suppl B):217–21.
640. Roy S, Wilkins J, Hemsell DL, et al. Efficacy and safety of single-dose ceftizoxime vs. multiple-dose cefoxitin in preventing infection after vaginal hysterectomy. *J Reprod Med.* 1988; 33(suppl 1):149–53.
641. Roy S, Wilkins J, Galaif E, et al. Comparative efficacy and safety of cefmetazole or cefoxitin in the prevention of postoperative infection following vaginal and abdominal hysterectomy. *J Antimicrob Chemother.* 1989; 23 (suppl D):109–17.
642. Mercer LJ, Murphy HJ, Ismail MA, et al. A comparison of cefonicid and cefoxitin for preventing infections after vaginal hysterectomy. *J Reprod Med.* 1988; 33:223–6.
643. Hemsell DL, Heard ML, Nobles BJ, et al. Single-dose cefoxitin prophylaxis for premenopausal women undergoing vaginal hysterectomy. *Obstet Gynecol.* 1984; 63:285–90.
644. McGregor JA, Phillips LE, Dunne JT, et al. Results of a double-blind, placebo controlled clinical trial program of single-dose ceftizoxime versus multiple-dose cefoxitin as prophylaxis for patients undergoing vaginal and abdominal hysterectomy. *J Am Coll Surg.* 1994; 178:12–31.
645. Orr JW Jr, Varner RE, Kilgore LC, et al. Cefotetan versus cefoxitin as prophylaxis in hysterectomy. *Am J Obstet Gynecol.* 1986; 154:960–3.
646. Orr JW Jr, Sisson PF, Barrett JM, et al. Single center study results of cefotetan and cefoxitin prophylaxis for abdominal or vaginal hysterectomy. *Am J Obstet.* 1988; 158(3 pt 2):714–6.
647. Berkeley AS, Orr JW, Cavanagh D, et al. Comparative effectiveness and safety of cefotetan and cefoxitin as prophylactic agents in patients undergoing abdominal or vaginal hysterectomy. *Am J Surg.* 1988; 155:81–5.
648. Berkeley AS, Freedman KS, Ledger WJ, et al. Comparison of cefotetan and cefoxitin prophylaxis for abdominal and vaginal hysterectomy. *Am J Obstet Gynecol.* 1988; 158:706–9.
649. Gordon SF. Results of a single center study of cefotetan prophylaxis in abdominal or vaginal hysterectomy. *Am J Obstet Gynecol.* 1988; 158:710–4. [Erratum, *Am J Obstet Gynecol.* 1989; 160:1025.]
650. Campillo F, Rubio JM. Comparative study of single-dose cefotaxime and multiple doses of cefoxitin and cefazolin as prophylaxis in gynecologic surgery. *Am J Surg.* 1992; 164(suppl):12S–15S.
651. Berkeley AS, Haywork SD, Hirsch JC, et al. Controlled, comparative study of moxalactam and cefazolin for prophylaxis of abdominal hysterectomy. *Surg Gynecol Obstet.* 1985; 161:457–61.
652. Tuomala RE, Fischer SG, Munoz A, et al. A comparative trial of cefazolin and moxalactam as prophylaxis for preventing infection after abdominal hysterectomy. *Obstet Gynecol.* 1985; 66:372–6.
653. Chongsomchai C, Lumbiganon P, Thinkhamrop J, et al. Placebo-controlled, double-blind, randomized study of prophylactic antibiotics in elective abdominal hysterectomy. *J Hosp Infect.* 2002; 52:302–6.
654. Cormio G, Di Fazio F, Lorusso F, et al. Antimicrobial prophylaxis in laparotomic gynecologic surgery: a prospective randomized study comparing amoxicillin-clavulanic acid with cefazolin. *J Chemother.* 2002; 14:618–22.
655. Lett WJ, Ansbacher R, Davison BL, et al. Prophylactic antibiotics for women undergoing vaginal hysterectomy. *J Reprod Med.* 1977; 19:51–4.
656. Hamod KA, Spence MR, Roshenshein NB, et al. Single and multidose prophylaxis in vaginal hysterectomy: a comparison of sodium cephalothin and metronidazole. *Am J Obstet Gynecol.* 1980; 136:976–9.
657. Hemsell DL, Johnson ER, Heard MC, et al. Single dose piperacillin versus triple dose cefoxitin prophylaxis at vaginal and abdominal hysterectomy. *South Med J.* 1989; 82:438–42.
658. Turano A. New clinical data on the prophylaxis of infections in abdominal, gynecologic, and urologic surgery. *Am J Surg.* 1992; 164(suppl):16S–20S.
659. D'Addato F, Canestrelli M, Repinto A, et al. Perioperative prophylaxis in abdominal and vaginal hysterectomy. *Clin Exp Obstet Gynecol.* 1993; 20:95–101.
660. Gonen R, Hakin M, Samberg I, et al. Short-term prophylactic antibiotic for elective abdominal hysterectomy: how short? *Eur J Obstet Gynecol Reprod Biol.* 1985; 20:229–34.
661. Scarpignato C, Labruna C, Condemi V, et al. Comparative efficacy of two different regimens of antibiotic prophylaxis in total abdominal hysterectomy. *Pharmatherapeutica.* 1980; 2:450–5.
662. Hemsell DL, Hemsell PG, Heard ML, et al. Preoperative cefoxitin prophylaxis for elective abdominal hysterectomy. *Am J Obstet Gynecol.* 1985; 153:225–6.
663. Triolo O, Mancuso A, Pantano F. Amoxycillin/clavulanate prophylaxis in gynecologic surgery. *Int J Gynaecol Obstet.* 2004; 85:59–61.
664. Su HY, Ding DC, Chen DC, et al. Prospective randomized comparison of single-dose versus 1-day cefazolin for prophylaxis in gynecologic surgery. *Acta Obstet Gynecol Scand.* 2005; 84:384–9.
665. Tchabo JG, Cutting ME, Butler C. Prophylactic antibiotics in patients undergoing total vaginal or abdominal hysterectomy. *Int Surg.* 1985; 70:349–52.

666. Read RW. Endophthalmitis. In: Yanoff M, Duker JS, eds. Ophthalmology. 3rd ed. St. Louis: Mosby; 2009.

667. Bucci FA, Amico LM, Evans RE. Antimicrobial efficacy of prophylactic gatifloxacin 0.3% and moxifloxacin 0.5% in patients undergoing phacoemulsification surgery. *Eye Contact Lens.* 2008; 34:39–42.

668. Colleaux KM, Hamilton WK. Effect of prophylactic antibiotics and incision type on the incidence of endophthalmitis after cataract surgery. *Can J Ophthalmol.* 2000; 35:373–8.

669. Eifrig CW, Flynn HW Jr, Scott IU, et al. Acute-onset postoperative endophthalmitis: review of incidence and visual outcomes (1995–2001). *Ophthalmic Surg Lasers.* 2002; 33:373–8.

670. Garat M, Moser CL, Martín-Baranera M, et al. Prophylactic intracameral cefazolin after cataract surgery: endophthalmitis risk reduction and safety results in a 6-year study. *J Cataract Refract Surg.* 2009; 35:637–42.

671. Jensen MK, Fiscella RG, Moshirfar M, et al. Third- and fourth-generation fluoroquinolones: retrospective comparison of endophthalmitis after cataract surgery performed over 10 years. *J Cataract Refract Surg.* 2008; 34:1460–7.

672. Mollan SP, Mollan AJ, Konstantinos C, et al. Incidence of endophthalmitis following vitreoretinal surgery. *Int Ophthalmol.* 2009; 29:203–5.

673. Moshirfar M, Feiz V, Vitale AT, et al. Endophthalmitis after uncomplicated cataract surgery with the use of fourth-generation fluoroquinolones: a retrospective observational case series. *Ophthalmology.* 2007; 114:686–91.

674. Romero P, Méndez I, Salvat M, et al. Intracameral cefazolin as prophylaxis against endophthalmitis in cataract surgery. *J Cataract Refract Surg.* 2006; 32:438–41.

675. Soto AM, Mendívil MP. The effect of topical povidone-iodine, intraocular vancomycin, or both on aqueous humor cultures at the time of cataract surgery. *Am J Ophthalmol.* 2001; 131:293–300.

676. Taban M, Behrens A, Newcomb RL, et al. Incidence of acute endophthalmitis following penetrating keratoplasty. *Arch Ophthalmol.* 2005; 123:605–9.

677. Wejde G, Samolov B, Seregard S, et al. Risk factors for endophthalmitis following cataract surgery: a retrospective case-control study. *J Hosp Infect.* 2005; 61:251–6.

678. Wu PC, Li M, Chang SJ, et al. Risk of endophthalmitis after cataract surgery using different protocols for povidone-iodine preoperative disinfection. *J Ocul Pharmacol Ther.* 2006; 22:54–61.

679. Barry P, Seal DV, Gettinby G, et al. ESCRS study of prophylaxis of postoperative endophthalmitis after cataract surgery: preliminary report of principal results from a European multicenter study. *J Cataract Refract Surg.* 2006; 32:407–10.

680. ESCRS Endophthalmitis Study Group. Prophylaxis of postoperative endophthalmitis following cataract surgery: results of the ESCRS multicenter study and identification of risk factors. *J Cataract Refract Surg.* 2007; 33:978–88.

681. Kamalarajah S, Ling R, Silvestri G, et al. Presumed infectious endophthalmitis following cataract surgery in the UK: a case-control study of risk factors. *Eye.* 2007; 21:580–6.

682. Montan PG, Setterquist H, Marcusson E, et al. Preoperative gentamicin eye drops and chlorhexidine solution in cataract surgery: experimental and clinical results. *Eur J Ophthalmol.* 2000; 10:286–92.

683. Recchia FM, Busbee BG, Pearlman RB, et al. Changing trends in the microbiologic aspects of postcataract endophthalmitis. *Arch Ophthalmol.* 2005; 123:341–6.

684. American Academy of Ophthalmology. Cataract in the adult eye, preferred practice pattern. http://one.aao.org/CE/PracticeGuidelines/PPP_Content.aspx?cid=a80a87ce-9042-4677-85d7-4b876deed276 (accessed 2012 Dec 9).

685. Hatch WV, Cernat G, Wong D, et al. Risk factors for acute endophthalmitis after cataract surgery: a population-based study. *Ophthalmology.* 2009; 116:425–40.

686. Lertsumitkul S, Myers PC, O'Rourke MT, et al. Endophthalmitis in the western Sydney region: a case-control study. *Clin Experiment Ophthalmol.* 2001; 29:400–5.

687. De Kaspar HM, Chang RT, Singh K, et al. Prospective randomized comparison of 2 different methods of 5% povidone-iodine applications for anterior segment intraocular surgery. *Arch Ophthalmol.* 2005; 123:161–5.

688. Ta CN, Egbert PR, Singh K, et al. Prospective randomized comparison of 3-day versus 1-hour preoperative ofloxacin prophylaxis for cataract surgery. *Ophthalmology.* 2002; 109:2036–41.

689. Fernández-Rubio E, Urcelay JL, Cuesta-Rodriguez T. The antibiotic resistance pattern of conjunctival bacteria: a key for designing a cataract surgery prophylaxis. *Eye.* 2009; 23:1321–8.

690. Gelfand YA, Mezer E, Linn S, et al. Lack of effect of prophylactic gentamicin treatment on intraocular and extraocular fluid cultures after pars plana vitrectomy. *Ophthalmic Surg Lasers.* 1998; 29:497–501.

691. Vasavada AR, Gajjar D, Raj SM, et al. Comparison of 2 moxifloxacin regimens for preoperative prophylaxis: prospective randomized triple-masked trial. Part 2: residual conjunctival flora. *J Cataract Refract Surg.* 2008; 34:1383–8.

692. Osher RH, Amdahl LD, Cheetham JK. Antimicrobial efficacy and aqueous humor concentration of preoperative and postoperative topical trimethoprim/polymyxin B sulfate versus tobramycin. *J Cataract Refract Surg.* 1994; 20:3–8.

693. Barequet IS, Jabbur NS, Barron Y, et al. Perioperative microbiologic profile of the conjunctiva in photoreactive keratectomy. *J Refract Surg.* 2001; 17:55–62.

694. Seal DV, Barry P, Gettinby G, et al. ESCRS study of prophylaxis of postoperative endophthalmitis after cataract surgery: case for a European multicenter study. *J Cataract Refract Surg.* 2006; 32:396–406.

695. Gore DM, Anjunawela RI, Little BC. United Kingdom survey of antibiotic prophylaxis practice after publication of the ESCRS endophthalmitis study. *J Cataract Refract Surg.* 2009; 35:770–3.

696. O'Brien TP, Arshinoff SA, Mah FS. Perspective on antibiotics for postoperative endophthalmitis prophylaxis: potential role of moxifloxacin. *J Cataract Refract Surg.* 2007; 33:1790–800.
697. Chang DF, Braga-Mele R, Mamalis N, et al. Prophylaxis of postoperative endophthalmitis after cataract surgery: results of the 2007 ASCRS member survey. *J Cataract Refract Surg.* 2007; 33:1801–5.
698. De Kaspar HM, Kreutzer TC, Aguirre-Romo I, et al. A prospective randomized study to determine the efficacy of preoperative topical levofloxacin in reducing conjunctival bacterial flora. *Am J Ophthalmol.* 2008; 145:136–42.
699. Montan PG, Wejde G, Setterquist H, et al. Prophylactic intracameral cefuroxime: evaluation of safety and kinetics in cataract surgery. *J Cataract Refract Surg.* 2002; 28:982–7.
700. Chisari G, Cavallaro G, Reibaldi M, et al. Presurgical antimicrobial prophylaxis: effect on ocular flora in healthy patients. *Int J Clin Pharmacol Ther.* 2004; 42:35–8.
701. Park SH, Lim JA, Choi JS, et al. The resistance patterns of normal ocular bacterial flora to 4 fluoroquinolone antibiotics. *Cornea.* 2009; 28:68–72.
702. Ciulla TA, Starr MB, Masket S. Bacterial endophthalmitis prophylaxis for cataract surgery: an evidence-based update. *Ophthalmology.* 2002; 109:13–26.
703. Gordon-Bennett P, Karas A, Flanagan D, et al. A survey of measures used for the prevention of postoperative endophthalmitis after cataract surgery in the United Kingdom. *Eye.* 2008; 22:620–7.
704. Ta CN, Singh K, Egbert PR, et al. Prospective comparative evaluation of povidone-iodine (10% for 5 minutes versus 5% for 1 minute) as prophylaxis for ophthalmic surgery. *J Cataract Refract Surg.* 2008; 34:171–2.
705. Cahane M, Ben Simon GJ, Barequet IS, et al. Human corneal stromal tissue concentration after consecutive doses of topically applied 3.3% vancomycin. *Br J Ophthalmol.* 2004; 88:22–4.
706. Bucci FA. An in vivo study comparing the ocular absorption of levofloxacin and ciprofloxacin prior to phacoemulsification. *Am J Ophthalmol.* 2004; 137:308–12.
707. García-Sáenz MC, Arias-Puente A, Fresnadillo-Martinez MJ, et al. Human aqueous humor levels of oral ciprofloxacin, levofloxacin and moxifloxacin. *J Cataract Refract Surg.* 2001; 27:11969–74.
708. Hariprasad SM, Blinder KJ, Shah GK, et al. Penetration pharmacokinetics of topically administered 0.5% moxifloxacin ophthalmic solution in human aqueous and vitreous. *Arch Ophthalmol.* 2005; 123:39–44.
709. Holland EJ, McCarthy M, Holland S. The ocular penetration of levofloxacin 1.5% and gatifloxacin 0.3% ophthalmic solutions in subjects undergoing corneal transplant surgery. *Curr Med Res Opin.* 2007; 23:2955–60.
710. Costello P, Bakri SJ, Beer PM, et al. Vitreous penetration of topical moxifloxacin and gatifloxacin in humans. *Retina.* 2006; 26:191–5.
711. Burka JM, Bower KS, Vanroekel RC, et al. The effect of fourth-generation fluoroquinolones gatifloxacin and moxifloxacin on epithelial healing following photorefractive keratectomy. *Am J Ophthalmol.* 2005; 140:83–7.
712. Durrie DS, Trattler W. A comparison of therapeutic regimens containing moxifloxacin 0.5% ophthalmic solution and gatifloxacin 0.3% ophthalmic solution for surgical prophylaxis in patients undergoing LASIK or LASEK. *J Ocul Pharmacol Ther.* 2005; 21:236–41.
713. Campos M, Ávila M, Wallau A, et al. Efficacy and tolerability of a fixed-dose moxifloxacin-dexamethasone formulation for topical prophylaxis in LASIK: a comparative, double-masked clinical trial. *Clin Ophthalmol.* 2008; 2:331–8.
714. Freitas LL, Soriano E, Muccioli C, et al. Efficacy and tolerability of a combined moxifloxacin/dexamethasone formulation for topical prophylaxis and reduction of inflammation in phacoemulsification: a comparative, double masked clinical trial. *Curr Med Res Opin.* 2007; 23:3123–30.
715. Lane SS, Osher RH, Masket S, et al. Evaluation of the safety of prophylactic intracameral moxifloxacin in cataract surgery. *J Cataract Refract Surg.* 2008; 34:1451–9.
716. Espiritu CR, Caparas VL, Bolinao JG. Safety of prophylactic intracameral moxifloxacin 0.5% ophthalmic solution in cataract surgery patients. *J Cataract Refract Surg.* 2007; 33:63–8.
717. Olson RJ. Reducing the risk of postoperative endophthalmitis. *Surv Ophthalmol.* 2004; 49(suppl 2):s55–61.
718. Yu-Wai-Man P, Morgan SJ, Hildreth AJ, et al. Efficacy of intracameral and subconjunctival cefuroxime in preventing endophthalmitis after cataract surgery. *J Cataract Refract Surg.* 2008; 34:447–51.
719. Vasavada AR, Gajjar D, Raj SM, et al. Comparison of 2 moxifloxacin regimens for preoperative prophylaxis: prospective randomized triple-masked trial. Part 1: aqueous concentration of moxifloxacin. *J Cataract Refract Surg.* 2008; 34:1379–82.
720. Eron LJ. Prevention of infection following orthopedic surgery. *Antibiot Chemother.* 1985; 33:140–64.
721. Gosselin RA, Roberts I, Gillespie WJ. Antibiotics for preventing infection in open limb fractures. *Cochrane Database Syst Rev.* 2004; 1:CD003764.
722. Hauser CJ, Adams CA Jr, Eachempati SR, et al. Surgical Infection Society guideline: prophylactic antibiotic use in open fractures: an evidence-based guideline. *Surg Infect.* 2006; 7:379–405.
723. Jaeger M, Maier D, Kern WV, et al. Antibiotics in trauma and orthopedic surgery—a primer of evidence-based recommendations. *Injury.* 2006; 37:s74–80.
724. Luchette FA, Bone LB, Born CT, et al. Practice management guidelines for prophylactic antibiotic use in open fractures. www.east.org/tpg/openfrac.pdf (accessed 2008 May 26).
725. Whitehouse JD, Friedman ND, Kirkland KB, et al. The impact of surgical-site infections following orthopedic surgery at a community hospital and university hospital: adverse quality of life, excess length of stay and extra cost. *Infect Control Hosp Epidemiol.* 2002; 23:183–9.

726. Boyd RJ, Burke JF, Colton T. A double-blind clinical trial of prophylactic antibiotics in hip fractures. *J Bone Joint Surg.* 1973; 55:1251–8.
727. Sculco TP. The economic impact of infected joint arthroplasty. *Orthopaedics.* 1995; 18:871–3.
728. Kurtz SM, Lau E, Schmier J, et al. Infection burden for hip and knee arthroplasty in the United States. *J Arthroplasty.* 2008; 23:984–91.
729. Bozic KJ, Ries MD. The impact of infection after total hip arthroplasty on hospital and surgeon resource utilization. *J Bone Joint Surg Am.* 2005; 87:1746–51.
730. Hebert CK, Williams RE, Levy RS, et al. Cost of treating an infected total knee replacement. *Clin Orthop Related Res.* 1996; 331:140–5.
731. Anderson DJ, Kaye KS, Schmader KE, et al. Clinical and financial outcomes due to methicillin resistant *Staphylococcus aureus* surgical site infection: a multi-center matched outcomes study. *PLoS One.* 2009; 4:e8305.
732. Brown EM, Path FR, Pople IK, et al. Prevention of postoperative infection in patients undergoing spinal surgery. *Spine.* 2004; 29:938–45.
733. Barker FG II. Efficacy of prophylactic antibiotic therapy in spinal surgery: a meta-analysis. *Neurosurgery.* 2002; 51:391–401.
734. Ericson C, Lidgren L, Lindberg L. Cloxacillin in the prophylaxis of postoperative infections of the hip. *J Bone Joint Surg.* 1973; 55:808–13 .
735. Pollard JP, Hughes SP, Scott JE, et al. Antibiotic prophylaxis in total hip replacement. *Br Med J.* 1979; 1:707–9.
736. Burnett JW, Gustilo RB, Williams DN, et al. Prophylactic antibiotics in hip fractures. *J Bone Joint Surg.* 1980; 62:457–62.
737. Tengve B, Kjellander J. Antibiotic prophylaxis in operations on trochanteric femoral fractures. *J Bone Joint Surg.* 1978; 60:97–9.
738. Pavel A, Smith RL, Ballard A, et al. Prophylactic antibiotics in clean orthopedic surgery. *J Bone Joint Surg.* 1974; 56:777–82.
739. Boxma H, Broekhuizen T, Patka P, et al. Randomised controlled trial of single-dose antibiotic prophylaxis in surgical treatment of closed fractures: the Dutch Trauma Trial. *Lancet.* 1996; 347:1133–7.
740. Weinstein MA, McCabe JP, Cammisa FP Jr. Postoperative spinal wound infection: a review of 2,391 consecutive index procedures. *J Spinal Disord.* 2000; 13:422–6.
741. Trampuz A, Zimmerli W. Antimicrobial agents in orthopedic surgery: prophylaxis and treatment. *Drugs.* 2006; 66:1089–105.
742. Yamaguchi K, Adams RA, Morrey BF. Infection after total elbow arthroplasty. *J Bone Joint Surg Am.* 1998; 80:481–91.
743. Bohsali KI, Wirth MA, Rockwood CA Jr. Complications of total shoulder arthroplasty. *J Bone Joint Surg Am.* 2006; 88:2279–92.
744. Meehan J, Jamali AA, Nguyen H. Prophylactic antibiotics in hip and knee arthroplasty. *J Bone Joint Surg Am.* 2009; 91:2480–90.
745. Costerton JW, Stewart PS, Greenberg EP. Bacterial biofilms: a common cause of persistent infections. *Science.* 1999; 284:1318–22.
746. Costerton JW. Biofilm theory can guide the treatment of device-related orthopaedic infections. *Clin Orthop Related Res.* 2005; 437:7–11.
747. Lewis K. Riddle of biofilm resistance. *Antimicrob Agents Chemother.* 2001; 45:999–1007.
748. Matthews PC, Berendt AR, McNally MA, et al. Diagnosis and management of prosthetic joint infection. *BMJ.* 2009; 338:1378–83.
749. Prokuski L. Prophylactic antibiotics in orthopaedic surgery. *J Am Acad Orthop Surg.* 2008; 16:283–93.
750. Gernaat-Van Der Sluis AJ, Hoogenboom-Verdegaal AM, Edixhoven PJ, et al. Prophylactic mupirocin could reduce orthopedic wound infections: 1044 patients treated with mupirocin compared with 1260 historical controls. *Acta Orthop Scand.* 1998; 69:412–4.
751. Wilcox MH, Hall J, Pike H, et al. Use of perioperative mupirocin to prevent methicillin resistant *Staphylococcus aureus* (MRSA) orthopedic surgical site infections. *J Hosp Infect.* 2003; 54:196–201.
752. Coskun D, Aytac J. Decrease in *Staphylococcus aureus* surgical-site infection rates after orthopaedic surgery after intranasal mupirocin ointment. *J Hosp Infect.* 2004; 58:90–1.
753. Van Rijen MM, Bonten M, Wenzel RP, et al. Intranasal mupirocin for reduction of *Staphylococcus aureus* infections in surgical patients with nasal carriage: a systematic review. *J Antimicrob Chemother.* 2008; 61:254–61.
754. Rao N, Cannella B, Crossett LS, et al. A preoperative decolonization protocol for *Staphylococcus aureus* prevents orthopaedic infections. *Clin Orthop Relat Res.* 2008; 466:1343–8.
755. Kim DH, Spencer M, Davidson SM, et al. Institutional prescreening for detection and eradication of methicillin-resistant *Staphylococcus aureus* in patients undergoing elective orthopaedic surgery. *J Bone Joint Surg Am.* 2010; 92:1820–6.
756. Zgonis T, Jolly GP, Garbalosa JC. The efficacy of prophylactic intravenous antibiotics in elective foot and ankle surgery. *J Foot Ankle Surg.* 2004; 43:97–103.
757. Kurzweil PR. Antibiotic prophylaxis for arthroscopic surgery. *Arthroscopy.* 2006; 22:452–4.
758. Wieck JA, Jackson JK, O'Brien TJ, et al. Efficacy of prophylactic antibiotics in arthroscopic surgery. *Orthopedics.* 1997; 20:133–4.
759. Bert JM, Giannini D, Nace L. Antibiotic prophylaxis for arthroscopy of the knee: is it necessary? *Arthroscopy.* 2007; 23:4–6.
760. Babcock HM, Carroll C, Matava M, et al. Surgical site infections after arthroscopy: outbreak investigation and case control study. *Arthroscopy.* 2003; 19:172–81.
761. Olix ML, Klug TJ, Coleman CR, et al. Prophylactic antibiotics in elective operations on bones, joints, and tendons. *Surg Forum.* 1960; 10:818–9.
762. Tachdjian MO, Compere EL. Postoperative wound infections in orthopedic surgery: evaluation and prophylactic antibiotics. *J Int Coll Surg.* 1957; 28:797–805.

763. Beiner JM, Grauer J, Kwon BK, et al. Postoperative wound infections of the spine. *Neurosurg Focus.* 2003; 15:1–5.
764. Labbé AC, Demers AM, Rodrigues R, et al. Surgical-site infection following spinal fusion: a case-control study in a children's hospital. *J Infect Control Hosp Epidemiol.* 2003; 24:591–5.
765. Lonstein J, Winter R, Moe J, et al. Wound infection with Harrington instrumentation and spine fusion for scoliosis. *Clin Orthop Relat Res.* 1973; 96:222–33.
766. Dimick JB, Lipsett PA, Kostuik JP. Spine update: antimicrobial prophylaxis in spine surgery: basic principles and recent advances. *Spine.* 2000; 25:2544–8.
767. Kanafani ZA, Dakdouki GK, El-Dbouni O, et al. Surgical site infections following spinal surgery at a tertiary care center in Lebanon: incidence, microbiology, and risk factors. *Scand J Infect Dis.* 2006; 38:589–92.
768. O'Toole JE, Eichholz KM, Fessler RG. Surgical site infection rates after minimally invasive spinal surgery. *J Neurosurg Spine.* 2009; 11:471–6.
769. Hellbusch LC, Helzer-Julin M, Doran SE, et al. Single-dose vs multiple-dose antibiotic prophylaxis in instrumented lumbar fusion—a prospective study. *Surg Neurol.* 2008; 70:622–7.
770. Pull Ter Gunne AF, van Laarhoven CJ, Cohen DB. Incidence of surgical site infection following adult spinal deformity surgery: an analysis of patient risk. *Eur Spine J.* 2010; 19:982–8.
771. Wimmer C, Gluch H, Franzreb M, et al. Predisposing factors for infection in spine surgery: a survey of 850 spinal procedures. *J Spinal Disord.* 1998; 11:125–8.
772. Friedman ND, Sexton DJ, Connelly SM, et al. Risk factors for surgical site infection complicating laminectomy. *Infect Control Hosp Epidemiol.* 2007; 28:1060–5.
773. Olsen MA, Nepple JJ, Riew D, et al. Risk factors for surgical site infection following orthopaedic spinal operations. *J Bone Joint Surg Am.* 2008; 90:62–9.
774. Hollenbeak CS, Lave JR, Zeddies T, et al. Factors associated with risk of surgical wound infections. *Am J Med Qual.* 2006; 21(suppl):29S–34S.
775. Pull Ter Gunne AF, Cohen DB. Incidence, prevalance, and analysis of risk factors for surgical site infection following adult spinal surgery. *Spine.* 2009; 34:1422–8.
776. Fang A, Hu SS, Endres N, et al. Risk factors for infection after spinal surgery. *Spine.* 2005; 30:1460–5.
777. Patel N, Bagan B, Vadera S, et al. Obesity and spine surgery: relations to perioperative complications. *J Neurosurg Spine.* 2007; 6:291–7.
778. Petignat C, Francioli P, Harbarth S, et al. Cefuroxime prophylaxis is effective in noninstrumented spine surgery: a double-blind, placebo-controlled study. *Spine.* 2008; 33:1919–24.
779. Walters R, Moore R, Fraser R. Penetration of cefazolin in human lumbar intervertebral disk. *Spine.* 2006; 31:567–70.
780. Rimoldi RL, Haye W. The use of antibiotics for wound prophylaxis in spinal surgery. *Orthop Clin North Am.* 1996; 27:47–52.
781. American Academy of Orthopaedic Surgeons. Information statement: the use of prophylactic antibiotics in orthopaedic medicine and the emergence of vancomycin-resistant bacteria. www.aaos.org/about/papers/advistmt/1016.asp (accessed 2008 May 13).
782. Dobzyniak MA, Fischgrund JS, Hankins S, et al. Single versus multiple dose antibiotic prophylaxis in lumbar disc surgery. *Spine.* 2003; 28:453–5.
783. Milstone AM, Maragakis LL, Townsend T, et al. Timing of preoperative antibiotic prophylaxis: a modifiable risk factor for deep surgical site infections after pediatric spinal fusion. *Pediatr Infect Dis J.* 2008; 27:704–8.
784. Coe JD, Smithe JS, Berven S, et al. Complications of spinal fusion for Scheuermann kyphosis: a report of the Scoliosis Research Society Morbidity and Mortality Committee. *Spine.* 2010; 35:99–103.
785. Linam WM, Margolis PA, Staat MA, et al. Risk factors associated with surgical site infection after pediatric posterior spinal fusion procedure. *Infect Control Hosp Epidemiol.* 2009; 30:109–16.
786. Fitzgerald RH. Infections of hip prosthesis and artificial joints. *Infect Dis Clin North Am.* 1989; 3:329–38.
787. Southwell-Keely JP, Russo RR, App B, et al. Antibiotic prophylaxis in hip fracture surgery: a meta-analysis. *Clin Orthop Relat Res.* 2004; 410:179–84.
788. Gillespie WJ, Walenkamp G. Antibiotic prophylaxis for surgery for proximal femoral and other closed long bone fractures. *Cochrane Database Syst Rev.* 2001; 1:CD000244.
789. Hahnel J, Burdekin H, Anand S. Re-admissions following hip fracture surgery. *Ann R Coll Surg Engl.* 2009; 91:591–5.
790. Gulihar A, Nixon M, Jenkins D, et al. *Clostridium difficile* in hip fracture patients: prevention, treatment and associated mortality. *Injury.* 2009; 40:746–51.
791. Cunha BA, Gossling HR, Pasternak HS, et al. The penetration characteristics of cefazolin, cephalothin, and cephradine into bone in patients undergoing total hip replacement. *J Bone Joint Surg.* 1977; 59:856–9.
792. Starks I, Ayub G, Walley G, et al. Single-dose cefuroxime with gentamicin reduces *Clostridium difficile*-associated disease in hip-fracture patients. *J Hosp Infect.* 2008; 70:21–6.
793. DeFrances CJ, Hall MJ. 2005 National Hospital Discharge Survey. *Adv Data.* 2007; 385:1–19.
794. Glazebrook MA, Arsenault K, Dunbar M. Evidence-based classification of complications in total ankle arthroplasty. *Foot Ankle Int.* 2009; 30:945–9.
795. Gougoulias N, Khanna A, Maffulli N. How successful are current ankle replacements? A systematic review of the literature. *Clin Orthop Relat Res.* 2010; 468:199–208.
796. Blom AW, Brown J, Taylor AH, et al. Infection after total knee arthroplasty. *J Bone Joint Surg Br.* 2004; 86:688–91.
797. Kasten MD, Skinner HB. Total elbow arthroplasty. An 18-year experience. *Clin Orthop Relat Res.* 1993; 290:177–88.
798. Periti P, Stringa G, Mini E, et al. Comparative multicenter trial of teicoplanin versus cefazolin for antimicrobial prophylaxis in prosthetic joint implant surgery. *Eur J Clin Microbiol Infect Dis.* 1999; 18:113–9.

799. Minnema B, Vearncombe M, Augustin A, et al. Risk factors for surgical-site infection following primary total knee arthroplasty. *Infect Control Hosp Epidemiol.* 2004; 25:477–80.
800. Blom AW, Taylor AH, Pattison G, et al. Infection after total hip arthroplasty. *J Bone Joint Surg Br.* 2003; 85:956–9.
801. AlBuhairan B, Hind D, Hutchinson A. Antibiotic prophylaxis for wound infections in total joint arthroplasty. *J Bone Joint Surg Br.* 2008; 90:915–9.
802. Fish DN, Hoffman HM, Danziger LH. Antibiotic impregnated cement use in U.S. hospitals. *Am J Hosp Pharm.* 1992; 49:2469–74.
803. Malik MH, Gambhir AK, Bale L, et al. Primary total hip replacement: a comparison of a nationally agreed guide to practice and current surgical technique as determined by the North West Regional Arthroplasty Registry. *Ann R Coll Surg Engl.* 2004; 86:113–8.
804. Bourne RB. Prophylactic use of antibiotic bone cement: an emerging standard—in the affirmative. *J Arthroplasty.* 2004; 19(suppl 1):69–72.
805. Engesaeter LB, Lie SA, Espehaug B, et al. Antibiotic prophylaxis in total hip arthroplasty: effects of antibiotic prophylaxis systemically and in bone cement on the revision rate of 22,170 primary hip replacements followed 0 to 14 years in the Norwegian Arthroplasty Register. *Acta Orthop Scand.* 2003; 74:644–51.
806. Espehaug B, Engesaeter LB, Vollset SE, et al. Antibiotic prophylaxis in total hip arthroplasty: review of 10,905 primary cemented total hip replacements reported to the Norwegian Arthroplasty Register, 1987 to 1995. *J Bone Joint Surg Br.* 1997; 79:590–5.
807. Jiranek WA, Hanssen AD, Greenwald AS. Antibiotic-loaded bone cement for infection prophylaxis in total joint replacement. *J Bone Joint Surg.* 2006; 88:2487–500.
808. McQueen MM, Hughes SP, May P, et al. Cefuroxime in total joint arthroplasty. Intravenous or in bone cement. *J Arthroplasty.* 1990; 5:169–72.
809. Josefsson G, Kolmert L. Prophylaxis with systematic antibiotics versus gentamicin bone cement in total hip arthroplasty. A ten-year survey of 1,688 hips. *Clin Orthop Relat Res.* 1993; 292:210–4.
810. Hanssen AD, Osmon DR. The use of prophylactic antimicrobial agents during and after hip arthroplasty. *Clin Orthop Relat Res.* 1999; 369:124–38.
811. Jiranek W. Antibiotic-loaded cement in total hip replacement: current indications, efficacy, and complications. *Orthopedics.* 2005; 28(suppl):s873–7.
812. Diefenbeck M, Mückley T, Hofman GO. Prophylaxis and treatment of implant-related infections by local application of antibiotics. *Injury.* 2006; 37(suppl 2):S95–104.
813. Hanssen AD. Prophylactic use of antibiotic bone cement: an emerging standard—in opposition. *J Arthroplasty.* 2004; 19(suppl 1):73–7.
814. Block JE, Stubbs HA. Reducing the risk of deep wound infection in primary joint arthroplasty with antibiotic bone cement. *Orthopedics.* 2005; 28:1334–45.
815. Wininger DA, Fass RJ. Antibiotic-impregnated cement and beads for orthopedic infections. *Antimicrob Chemother.* 1996; 40:2675–9.
816. Nelson CL, Green TG, Porter RA, et al. One day versus seven days of preventive antibiotic therapy in orthopedic surgery. *Clin Orthop Relat Res.* 1983; 176:258–63.
817. Matsumoto T, Kiyota H, Matsukawa M, et al. Japanese guidelines for prevention of perioperative infections in urological field. *Int J Urol.* 2007; 14:890–909.
818. Wolf JS Jr, Bennett CJ, Dmochowski RR, et al. Best practice policy statement on urologic surgery antimicrobial prophylaxis. *J Urol.* 2008; 179:1379–90.
819. Kapoor DA, Klimberg IW, Malek GH, et al. Single-dose oral ciprofloxacin versus placebo for prophylaxis during transrectal prostate biopsy. *Urology.* 1998; 52:552–8.
820. Latthe PM, Foon R, Toozs-Hobson P. Prophylactic antibiotics in urodynamics: a systematic review of effectiveness and safety. *Neurourol Urodyn.* 2008; 27:167–73.
821. Kartal ED, Yenilmez A, Kiremitci A, et al. Effectiveness of ciprofloxacin prophylaxis in preventing bacteriuria caused by urodynamic study: a blind, randomized study of 192 patients. *Urology.* 2006; 67:1149–53.
822. Wagenlehner FM, Wagenlehner C, Schinzel S, et al. Prospective, randomized, multicentric, open, comparative study on the efficacy of a prophylactic single dose of 500 mg levofloxacin versus 1920 mg trimethoprim/sulfamethoxazole versus a control group in patients undergoing TUR of the prostate. *Eur Urol.* 2005; 47:549–56.
823. Takeyama K, Takahashi S, Maeda T, et al. Comparison of 1-day, 2-day, and 3-day administration of antimicrobial prophylaxis in radical prostatectomy. *J Infect Chemother.* 2007; 13:320–3.
824. Briffaux R, Coloby P, Bruyere F, et al. One preoperative dose randomized against 3-day antibiotic prophylaxis for transrectal ultrasonography-guided prostate biopsy. *BJU Int.* 2008; 103:1069–73.
825. Bootsma AM, Pes MP, Geerlings SE, et al. Antibiotic prophylaxis in urologic procedures: a systematic review. *Eur Urol.* 2008; 54:1270–86.
826. Grabe M, Bishop MC, Bjerklund-Johansen TE, et al. Guidelines on urological infections. www.uroweb.org (accessed 2010 Mar 18).
827. Yamamoto S, Kanamaru S, Kunishima Y, et al. Perioperative antimicrobial prophylaxis in urology: a multi-center prospective study. *J Chemother.* 2005; 17:189–97.
828. Hamasuna R, Betsunoh H, Sueyoshi T, et al. Bacteria of preoperative urinary tract infections contaminate the surgical fields and develop surgical site infections in urologic operations. *Int J Urol.* 2004; 11:941–7.
829. Richter S, Lang R, Zur F, et al. Infected urine as a risk factor for postprostatectomy wound infection. *Infect Control Hosp Epidemiol.* 1991; 12:147–9.
830. Carson CC. Diagnosis, treatment and prevention of penile prosthesis infection. *Int J Impot Res.* 2003; 15(suppl 5):S139–46.

831. Schaeffer AJ, Montorsi F, Scattoni V, et al. Comparison of a 3-day with a 1-day regimen of an extended-release formulation of ciprofloxacin as antimicrobial prophylaxis for patients undergoing transrectal needle biopsy of the prostate. *BJU Int.* 2007; 100:51–7.

832. Hara N, Kitamura Y, Saito T, et al. Perioperative antibiotics in radical cystectomy with ileal conduit urinary diversion: efficacy and risk of antimicrobial prophylaxis on the operation day alone. *Int J Urol.* 2008; 15:511–5.

833. Meir DB, Livne PM. Is prophylactic antimicrobial treatment necessary after hypospadias repair? *J Urol.* 2004; 171:2621–2.

834. Doğan HS, Şahin A, Çetinkaya Y, et al. Antibiotic prophylaxis in percutaneous nephrolithotomy: prospective study in 81 patients. *J Endourol.* 2002; 16:649–53.

835. Cox CE. Comparison of intravenous ciprofloxacin and intravenous cefotaxime for antimicrobial prophylaxis in transurethral surgery. *Am J Med.* 1989; 87(suppl 5A):252S–254S.

836. Cam K, Kayikci A, Akman Y, et al. Prospective assessment of the efficacy of single dose versus traditional 3-day antimicrobial prophylaxis in 12-core transrectal prostate biopsy. *Int J Urol.* 2008; 18:997–1001.

837. Aron M, Rajeev TP, Gupta NP. Antibiotic prophylaxis for transrectal needle biopsy of the prostate: a randomized controlled study. *BJU Int.* 2000; 85:682–5.

838. Isen K, Küpeli B, Sinik Z, et al. Antibiotic prophylaxis for transrectal biopsy of the prostate: a prospective randomized study of the prophylactic use of single dose oral fluoroquinolone versus trimethoprim-sulfamethoxazole. *Int Urol Nephrol.* 1999; 31:491–5.

839. Johnson MI, Merrilees D, Robson WA, et al. Oral ciprofloxacin or trimethoprim reduces bacteriuria after flexible cystoscopy. *BJU Int.* 2007; 100:826–9.

840. Yokoyama M, Fujii Y, Yoshida S, et al. Discarding antimicrobial prophylaxis for transurethral resection of bladder tumor: a feasibility study. *Int J Urol.* 2009; 16:61–3.

841. Takeyama K, Matsukawa M, Kunishima Y, et al. Incidence of and risk factors for surgical site infections in patients with radical cystectomy with urinary diversion. *J Infect Chemother.* 2005; 11:177–81.

842. Gomelsky A, Dmochowski RR. Antibiotic prophylaxis in urologic prosthetic surgery. *Curr Pharm Des.* 2003; 9:989–96.

843. Hoffelt SC, Wallner K, Merrick G. Epididymitis after prostate brachytherapy. *Urology.* 2004; 63:293–6.

844. Ferguson KH, McNeil JJ, Morey AF. Mechanical and antibiotic bowel preparation for urinary diversion surgery. *J Urol.* 2002; 167:2352–6.

845. Pearle MS, Roehrborn CG. Antimicrobial prophylaxis prior to shock wave lithotripsy in patients with sterile urine before treatment: a meta-analysis and cost-effectiveness analysis. *Urology.* 1997; 49:679–86.

846. Berry A, Barratt A. Prophylactic antibiotic use in transurethral prostatic resection: a meta analysis. *J Urol.* 2002; 167:571–7.

847. Qiang W, Jianchen W, MacDonald R, et al. Antibiotic prophylaxis for transurethral prostatic resection in men with preoperative urine containing less than 100,000 bacteria per ml: a systematic review. *J Urol.* 2005; 173:1175–81.

848. Knopf HJ, Graff H, Schulze H. Perioperative antibiotic prophylaxis in ureteroscopic stone removal. *Eur Urol.* 2003; 44:115–8.

849. Brewster SF, MacGowan AP, Gingell JC. Antimicrobial prophylaxis for transrectal prostatic biopsy: a prospective, randomized trial of cefuroxime versus piperacillin/tazobactam. *Br J Urol.* 1995; 76:351–4.

850. DeBessonet DA, Merlin AS. Antibiotic prophylaxis in elective genitourinary tract surgery: a comparison of single-dose preoperative cefotaxime and multiple-dose cefoxitin. *J Antimicrob Chemother.* 1984; 14(suppl B):271–5.

851. Christiano AP, Hollowell CM, Kim H, et al. Double-blind randomized comparison of single-dose ciprofloxacin versus intravenous cefazolin in patients undergoing outpatient endourologic surgery. *Urology.* 2000; 55:182–5.

852. Bhatia NN, Karram MM, Bergman A. Role of antibiotic prophylaxis in retropubic surgery for stress urinary incontinence. *Obstet Gynecol.* 1989; 74:637–9.

853. Terai A, Ichioka K, Kohei N, et al. Antibiotic prophylaxis in radical prostatectomy: 1-day versus 4-day treatments. *Int J Urol.* 2006; 13:1488–93.

854. Gombert ME, DuBouchet L, Aulicino TM, et al. Brief report: intravenous ciprofloxacin versus cefotaxime prophylaxis during transurethral surgery. *Am J Med.* 1989; 87(suppl 5A): 250S–251S.

855. Klimberg IW, Malek GH, Cox CE. Single-dose oral ciprofloxacin compared with cefotaxime and placebo for prophylaxis during transurethral surgery. *J Antimicrob Chemother.* 1999; 43(suppl A):77–84.

856. Gibbons RP, Stark RA, Gorrea RJ, et al. The prophylactic use—or misuse—of antibiotics in transurethral prostatectomy. *J Urol.* 1978; 119:381–3.

857. Ramsey E, Sheth NK. Antibiotic prophylaxis in patients undergoing prostatectomy. *Urology.* 1983; 21:376–8.

858. Cormio L, Berardi B, Callea A, et al. Antimicrobial prophylaxis for transrectal prostatic biopsy: a prospective study of ciprofloxacin vs. piperacillin/tazobactam. *BJU Int.* 2002; 90:700–2.

859. Sakura M, Kawakami S, Yoshida S, et al. Prospective comparative study of single dose versus 3-day administration of antimicrobial prophylaxis in minimum incision endoscopic radical prostatectomy. *Int J Urol.* 2008; 15:328–31.

860. Hills NH, Bultitude MI, Eykyn S. Co-trimoxazole in prevention of bacteriuria after prostatectomy. *Br Med J.* 1976; 2:498–9.

861. Matthew AD, Gonzales R, Jeffords D, et al. Prevention of bacteriuria after transurethral prostatectomy with nitrofurantoin macrocrystals. *J Urol.* 1978; 120:442–3.

862. Hammarsten J, Lindqvist K. Norfloxacin as prophylaxis against urethral strictures following transurethral resection of the prostate: an open, prospective, randomized study. *J Urol.* 1993; 150:1722–4.
863. Siracusano S, Knez R, Tiberio A, et al. The usefulness of antibiotic prophylaxis in invasive urodynamics in postmenopausal female subjects. *Int Urogynecol J.* 2008; 19:939–42.
864. Patel U, Kirby R. Infections after prostate biopsy and antibiotic resistance. *BJU Int.* 2008; 101:1201–4.
865. Hall JC, Christiansen KJ, England P, et al. Antibiotic prophylaxis for patients undergoing transurethral resection of the prostate. *Urology.* 1996; 47:852–6.
866. Liu GG, Nguyen T, Nichol MB. An economic analysis of antimicrobial prophylaxis against urinary tract infection in patients undergoing transurethral resection of the prostate. *Clin Ther.* 1999; 21:1589–603.
867. Burnakis TG. Surgical antimicrobial prophylaxis: principles and guidelines. *Pharmacotherapy.* 1984; 4:248–71.
868. Homer-Vanniasinkam S. Surgical site and vascular infections: treatment and prophylaxis. *Int J Infect Dis.* 2007; 11:S17–22.
869. Zibari GB, Gadallah MF, Landreneau M, et al. Preoperative vancomycin prophylaxis decreases incidence of postoperative hemodialysis vascular access infections. *Am J Kidney Dis.* 1997; 30:343–8.
870. Naylor AR, Payne D, London NJ, et al. Prosthetic patch infection after carotid endarterectomy. *Eur J Vasc Endovasc Surg.* 2002; 23:11–6.
871. Richet HM, Chidiac C, Prat A, et al. Analysis of risk factors for surgical wound infections following vascular surgery. *Am J Med.* 1991; 91:171S–172S.
872. Ross CB, Wheeler WG II, Jones MJ, et al. Ceftriaxone versus cefazolin in peripheral arterial operations: a randomized, prospective trial. *South Med J.* 1997; 90:16–22.
873. Ryan JM, Ryan BM, Smith TP. Antibiotic prophylaxis in interventional radiology. *J Vasc Interv Radiol.* 2004; 15:547–56.
874. McDermott VG, Schuster MG, Smith TP. Antibiotic prophylaxis in vascular and interventional radiology. *Am J Roentgenol.* 1997; 169:31–8.
875. Beddy P, Ryan JM. Antibiotic prophylaxis in interventional radiology—anything new? *Tech Vasc Interv Radiol.* 2006; 9:69–76.
876. Malek AM, Higashida RT, Reilly LM, et al. Subclavian arteritis and pseudoaneurysm formation secondary to stent infection. *Cardiovasc Interv Radiol.* 2000; 23:57–60.
877. Venkatesan AM, Kundu S, Sacks D, et al. Practice guideline for adult antibiotic prophylaxis during vascular and interventional radiology procedures. *J Vasc Interv Radiol.* 2010; 21:1611–30.
878. Thompson M. An audit demonstrating a reduction in MRSA infection in a specialized vascular unit resulting from a change in infection control protocol. *Eur J Vasc Endovasc Surg.* 2006; 31:609–15.
879. Morange-Saussier V, Giraudeau B, van der Mee N, et al. Nasal carriage of methicillin-resistant *Staphylococcus aureus* in vascular surgery. *Ann Vasc Surg.* 2006; 20:767–72.
880. Taylor MD, Napolitano LM. Methicillin-resistant *Staphylococcus aureus* infections in vascular surgery: increasing prevalence. *Surg Infect.* 2004; 5:180–7.
881. Grimble SA, Magee TR, Galland RB. Methicillin resistant *Staphylococcus aureus* in patients undergoing major amputation. *Eur J Vasc Endovasc Surg.* 2001; 22:215–8.
882. Nasim A, Thompson MM, Naylor AR, et al. The impact of MRSA on vascular surgery. *Eur J Vasc Endovasc Surg.* 2001; 22:211–4.
883. Cowie SE, Ma I, Lee SK, et al. Nosocomial MRSA infection in vascular surgery patients: impact on patient outcome. *Vasc Endovasc Surg.* 2005; 39:327–34.
884. Fawley WN, Parnell P, Hall J, et al. Surveillance for mupirocin resistance following introduction of routine peri-operative prophylaxis with nasal mupirocin. *J Hosp Infect.* 2006; 62:327–32.
885. Kaiser A, Clayton KR, Mulherin JL, et al. Antibiotic prophylaxis in vascular surgery. *Ann Surg.* 1978; 188:283–9.
886. Edwards WH, Kaiser AB, Kernodle DS, et al. Cefuroxime versus cefazolin as prophylaxis in vascular surgery. *J Vasc Surg.* 1992; 15:35–42.
887. Edwards WH Jr, Kaiser AB, Tapper S, et al. Cefamandole versus cefazolin in vascular surgical wound infection prophylaxis: cost-effectiveness and risk factors. *J Vasc Surg.* 1993; 18:470–5.
888. Hasselgren PO, Ivarson L, Risberg B, et al. Effects of prophylactic antibiotics in vascular surgery. A prospective, randomized, double-blind study. *Ann Surg.* 1984; 200:86–92.
889. Risberg B, Drott C, Dalman P, et al. Oral ciprofloxacin versus intravenous cefuroxime as prophylaxis against postoperative infection in vascular surgery: a randomized double-blind, prospective multicentre study. *Eur J Endovasc Surg.* 1995; 10:346–51.
890. Stewart AH, Eyers PS, Earnshaw JJ. Prevention of infection in peripheral arterial reconstruction: a systematic review and meta-analysis. *J Vasc Surg.* 2007; 46:148–55.
891. Murray BE. Problems and dilemmas of antimicrobial resistance. *Pharmacotherapy.* 1992; 12:86–93.
892. Earnshaw JJ, Slack RC, Hopkinson BR, et al. Risk factors in vascular surgical sepsis. *Ann R Coll Surg Engl.* 1988; 70:139–43.
893. Hall JC, Christiansen KJ, Goodman M, et al. Duration of antimicrobial prophylaxis in vascular surgery. *Am J Surg.* 1998; 175:87–90.
894. Fishman JA. Infection in solid-organ transplant recipients. *N Engl J Med.* 2007; 357:2601–14.
895. Fischer SA. Infections in the transplant recipient. *Med Health R I.* 2002; 85:125–7.
896. Soave R. Prophylaxis strategies for solid-organ transplantation. *Clin Infect Dis.* 2001; 33(suppl 1):s26–31.
897. Keough WL, Michaels MG. Infectious complications in pediatric solid organ transplantation. *Pediatr Clin North Am.* 2003; 50:1451–69.
898. United Network for Organ Sharing. Organ Procurement and Transplantation Network data (as

of September 5, 2008). http://optn.transplant.hrsa.gov/data/ (accessed 2012 Dec 9).

899. Cai J. Thoracic transplantation in the United States: an analysis of UNOS registry data. *Clin Transplant.* 2006; 41–56.
900. Fong I, Baker C, McKee D. The value of prophylactic antibiotics in aorta-coronary bypass operations. *J Thorac Cardiovasc Surg.* 1979; 78:908–13.
901. Penketh A, Wansbrough-Jones M, Wright E, et al. Antibiotic prophylaxis for coronary artery bypass graft surgery. *Lancet.* 1985; 1:1500.
902. Muñoz P, Menasalvas A, Bernaldo de Quirós JC, et al. Postsurgical mediastinitis: a case-control study. *Clin Infect Dis.* 1997; 25:1060–4.
903. Filsoufi F, Rahmanian PB, Castillo JG, et al. Incidence, treatment strategies and outcome of deep sternal wound infection after orthotopic heart transplantation. *J Heart Lung Transplant.* 2007; 26:1084–90.
904. Abid Q, Nkere UU, Hasan A, et al. Mediastinitis in heart and lung transplantation: 15 years experience. *Ann Thorac Surg.* 2003; 75:1565–71.
905. Carrier M, Perrault LP, Pellerin M, et al. Sternal wound infection after heart transplantation: incidence and results with aggressive surgical treatment. *Ann Thorac Surg.* 2001; 72:719–24.
906. Ramos A, Asensio A, Muñoz E, et al. Incisional surgical infection in heart transplantation. *Transpl Infect Dis.* 2008; 10:298–302.
907. Sénéchal M, LePrince P, Tezenas du Montcel S, et al. Bacterial mediastinitis after heart transplantation: clinical presentation, risk factors and treatment. *J Heart Lung Transplant.* 2004; 23:165–70.
908. Mattner F, Fischer S, Weissbrodt H, et al. Postoperative nosocomial infections after lung and heart transplantation. *J Heart Lung Transplant.* 2007; 26:241–9.
909. Van De Beek D, Kremer WK, Del Pozo JL, et al. Effect of infectious diseases on outcome after heart transplant. *Mayo Clin Proc.* 2008; 83:304–8.
910. Keay S. Cardiac transplantation: pre-transplant infectious diseases evaluation and post-transplant prophylaxis. *Curr Infect Dis Rep.* 2002; 4:285–92.
911. Kaiser AB. Use of antibiotics in cardiac and thoracic surgery. In: Sabiston DC Jr, Spencer FC, eds. Surgery of the chest. 6th ed. Philadelphia: W. B. Saunders; 1995:98–116.
912. Khaghani A, Martin M, Fitzgerald M, et al. Cefotaxime and flucloxacillin as antibiotic prophylaxis in cardiac transplantation. *Drugs.* 1988; 35(suppl 2):124–6.
913. Montoya JG, Giraldo LF, Efron B, et al. Infectious complications among 620 consecutive heart transplant patients at Stanford University Medical Center. *Clin Infect Dis.* 2001; 33:629–40.
914. Petri WA Jr. Infections in heart transplant recipients. *Clin Infect Dis.* 1994; 18:141–8.
915. Trulock EP. Lung transplantation. *Am J Respir Crit Care Med.* 1997; 155:789–818.
916. U.S. Department of Health and Human Services. Organ Procurement and Transplantation Network/ Scientific Registry of Transplant Recipients annual report. Table 12.4. Transplant recipient characteristics, 1999 to 2008. Recipients of deceased donor lungs. 2009 May 4. http://optn.transplant.hrsa.gov/ar2009/1204_rec-dgn_lu.htm (accessed 2011 Mar 17).
917. Hosenpud JD, Novick RJ, Bennett LE, et al. The registry of the International Society for Heart and Lung Transplantation: thirteenth official report. *J Heart Lung Transplant.* 1996; 15:655–74.
918. Davis RD Jr, Pasque MK. Pulmonary transplantation. *Ann Surg.* 1995; 221:14–28.
919. Kotloff RM, Zuckerman JB. Lung transplantation for cystic fibrosis. Special considerations. *Chest.* 1996; 109:787–98.
920. Campos S, Caramori M, Teixeira R, et al. Bacterial and fungal pneumonia after lung transplantation. *Transplant Proc.* 2008; 40:822–4.
921. Krishnam MS, Suh RD, Tomasian A, et al. Postoperative complications of lung transplantation: radiologic findings along a time continuum. *Radiographics.* 2007; 27:957–74.
922. Helmi M, Love RB, Welter D, et al. *Aspergillus* infection in lung transplant recipients with cystic fibrosis: risk factors and outcomes comparison to other types of transplant recipients. *Chest.* 2003; 123:800–8.
923. Russo MJ, Iribarne A, Hong KN, et al. High lung allocation score is associated with increased morbidity and mortality following transplantation. *Chest.* 2010; 137:651–7.
924. Dowling RD, Zenati M, Yousem S, et al. Donor-transmitted pneumonia in experimental lung allografts. *J Thorac Cardiovasc Surg.* 1992; 103:767–72.
925. Low DE, Kaiser LR, Haydock DA, et al. The donor lung: infectious and pathologic factors affecting outcome in lung transplantation. *J Thorac Cardiovasc Surg.* 1993; 106:614–21.
926. Steinbach S, Sun L, Jiang RZ, et al. Transmissibility of *Pseudomonas cepacia* infection in clinic patients and lung-transplant recipients with cystic fibrosis. *N Engl J Med.* 1994; 331:981–7.
927. Dauber JH, Paradis IL, Dummer JS. Infectious complications in pulmonary allograft recipients. *Clin Chest Med.* 1990; 11:291–308.
928. Deusch E, End A, Grimm M, et al. Early bacterial infections in lung transplant recipients. *Chest.* 1993; 104:1412–6.
929. Paradis IL, Williams P. Infection after lung transplantation. *Semin Respir Infect.* 1993; 8:207–15.
930. Husain S, Zaldonis D, Kusne S, et al. Variation in antifungal prophylaxis strategies in lung transplantation. *Transpl Infect Dis.* 2006; 8:213–8.
931. Noyes BE, Kurland G, Orenstein DM. Lung and heart-lung transplantation in children. *Pediatr Pulmonol.* 1997; 23:39–48.
932. Moreno R, Berenguer M. Post-liver transplantation medical complications. *Ann Hepatol.* 2006; 5:77–85.
933. Muiesan P, Vergani D, Mieli-Vergani G. Liver transplantation in children. *J Hepatol.* 2007; 46:340–8.
934. United Network for Organ Sharing. Organ Procurement and Transplantation Network: data. http://optn.transplant.hrsa.gov/data/. Based on OPTN data as of September 26, 2008.

935. García Prado ME, Matia EC, Ciuro FP, et al. Surgical site infection in liver transplant recipients: impact of the type of perioperative prophylaxis. *Transplantation.* 2008; 85:1849–54.
936. Kuo PC, Bartlett ST, Lim JW, et al. Selective bowel decontamination in hospitalized patients awaiting liver transplantation. *Am J Surg.* 1997; 174:745–9.
937. Kim YJ, Kim SI, Wie SH, et al. Infectious complications in living-donor liver transplant recipients: a 9-year single-center experience. *Transplant Infect Dis.* 2008; 10:316–24.
938. Hollenbeak CS, Alfrey EJ, Souba WW. The effect of surgical site infections on outcomes and resource utilization after liver transplantation. *Surgery.* 2001; 130:388–95.
939. Kibbler CC. Infections in liver transplantation: risk factors and strategies for prevention. *J Hosp Infect.* 1995; 30(suppl):209–17.
940. Wade JJ, Rolando N, Hayllar K, et al. Bacterial and fungal infections after liver transplantation: an analysis of 284 patients. *Hepatology.* 1995; 21:1328–36.
941. Shepherd RW, Turmelle Y, Nadler M, et al. Risk factors for rejection and infection in pediatric liver transplantation. *Am J Transplant.* 2008; 8:396–403.
942. Hollenbeak CS, Alfrey EJ, Sheridan K, et al. Surgical site infections following pediatric liver transplantation: risks and costs. *Transpl Infect Dis.* 2003; 5:72–8.
943. Arnow PM, Carandang GC, Zabner R, et al. Randomized controlled trial of selective bowel decontamination for prevention of infections following liver transplantation. *Clin Infect Dis.* 1996; 22:997–1003.
944. Colonna JO II, Drew WJ, Brill JE, et al. Infectious complications in liver transplantation. *Arch Surg.* 1988; 123:360–4.
945. George DL, Arnow PM, Fox AS, et al. Bacterial infection as a complication of liver transplantation: epidemiology and risk factors. *Rev Infect Dis.* 1991; 13:387–96.
946. Uemoto S, Tanaka K, Fujita S, et al. Infectious complications in living related liver transplantation. *J Pediatr Surg.* 1994; 29:514–7.
947. Kusne S, Dummer JS, Singh N, et al. Infections after liver transplantation. An analysis of 101 consecutive cases. *Medicine.* 1988; 67:132–43.
948. Singh N, Paterson DL, Gayowski T, et al. Predicting bacteremia and bacteremic mortality in liver transplant recipients. *Liver Transpl.* 2000; 6:54–61.
949. Hjortrup A, Rasmussen A, Hansen BA, et al. Early bacterial and fungal infections in liver transplantation after oral selective bowel decontamination. *Transplant Proc.* 1997; 29:3106–10.
950. Villacian JS, Paya CV. Prevention of infections in solid organ transplant recipients. *Transpl Infect Dis.* 1999; 1:50–64.
951. Asensio A, Ramos A, Cuervas-Mons V, et al. Effect of antibiotic prophylaxis on the risk of surgical site infection in orthotopic liver transplant. *Liver Transpl.* 2008; 14:799–805.
952. Arnow PM, Zachary KC, Thistlethwaite JR, et al. Pathogenesis of early operative site infections after orthotopic liver transplantation. *Transplantation.* 1998; 65:1500–3.
953. Mattner F, Kola A, Fischer S, et al. Impact of bacterial and fungal donor organ contamination in lung, heart-lung, heart and liver transplantation. *Infection.* 2008; 36:207–12.
954. Barkholt LM, Andersson J, Ericzon BG, et al. Stool cultures obtained before liver transplantation are useful for choice of perioperative antibiotic prophylaxis. *Transplant Int.* 1997; 10:432–8.
955. Hellinger WC, Yao JD, Alvarez S, et al. A randomized, prospective, double-blinded evaluation of selective bowel decontamination in liver transplantation. *Transplantation.* 2002; 73:1904–9.
956. Zwaveling JH, Maring JK, Klompmaker IJ, et al. Selective decontamination of the digestive tract to prevent postoperative infection: a randomized placebo-controlled trial in liver transplant patients. *Crit Care Med.* 2002; 30:1204–9.
957. Hashimoto M, Sugawara Y, Tamura S, et al. Impact of new methicillin-resistant *Staphylococcus aureus* carriage postoperatively after living donor liver transplantation. *Transplant Proc.* 2007; 39:3271–5.
958. Hashimoto M, Sugawara Y, Tamura S, et al. Bloodstream infection after living donor liver transplantation. *Scand J Infect Dis.* 2008; 40:509–16.
959. Hashimoto M, Sugawara Y, Tamura S, et al. *Pseudomonas aeruginosa* infection after living-donor liver transplantation in adults. *Transpl Infect Dis.* 2009; 11:11–9.
960. Bert F, Galdbart JO, Zarrouk V, et al. Association between nasal carriage of *Staphylococcus aureus* and infection in liver transplant recipients. *Clin Infect Dis.* 2000; 31:1295–9.
961. Bert F, Bellier C, Lassel L, et al. Risk factors for *Staphylococcus aureus* infection in liver transplant recipients. *Liver Transpl.* 2005; 11:1093–9.
962. Chang FY, Singh N, Gayowski T, et al. *Staphylococcus aureus* nasal colonization and association with infections in liver transplant recipients. *Transplantation.* 1998; 65:1169–72.
963. Mehrabi A, Fonouni H, Wente M, et al. Wound complications following kidney and liver transplantation. *Clin Transplant.* 2006; 20(suppl 17):97–110.
964. Kawecki D, Chmura A, Pacholczyk M, et al. Surgical site infections in liver recipients in the early post-transplantation period: etiological agents and susceptibility profiles. *Transplant Proc.* 2007; 39:2800–6.
965. Bedini A, Codeluppi M, Cocchi S, et al. Gram-positive bloodstream infections in liver transplant recipients: incidence, risk factors, and impact on survival. *Transplant Proc.* 2007; 39:1947–9.
966. Dar FS, Faraj W, Zaman MB, et al. Outcome of liver transplantation in hereditary hemochromatosis. *Transplant Int.* 2009; 22:717–24.
967. Arnow PM, Furmaga K, Flaherty JP, et al. Microbiological efficacy and pharmacokinetics of prophylactic antibiotics in liver transplant patients. *Antimicrob Agents Chemother.* 1992; 36:2125–30.
968. Gorensek MJ, Carey WD, Washington JA II, et al. Selective bowel decontamination with quinolones and nystatin reduces gram-negative and fungal infec-

tions in orthotopic liver transplant recipients. *Cleve Clin J Med.* 1993; 60:139–44.

969. Piselli P, Zanfi C, Corazza V, et al. Incidence and timing of infections after liver transplant in Italy. *Transplant Proc.* 2007; 39:1950–2.
970. Desai D, Desai N, Nightingale P, et al. Carriage of methicillin-resistant *Staphylococcus aureus* is associated with an increased risk of infection after liver transplantation. *Liver Transpl.* 2003; 9:754–9.
971. Rayes N, Seehofer D, Theruvath T, et al. Supply of pre- and probiotics reduces bacterial infection rates after liver transplantation—a randomized, double-blind trial. *Am J Transplant.* 2005; 5:125–30.
972. Reid GE, Grim SA, Aldeza CA, et al. Rapid development of *Acinetobacter baumannii* resistance to tigecycline. *Pharmacotherapy.* 2007; 27:1198–201.
973. Chen H, Zhang Y, Chen YG, et al. Sepsis resulting from *Enterobacter aerogenes* resistant to carbapenems after liver transplantation. *Hepatobiliary Pancreat Dis Int.* 2009; 8:320–2.
974. Chen YG, Zhang Y, Yu YS, et al. In vivo development of carbapenem resistance in clinical isolates of *Enterobacter aerogenes* producing multiple ß-lactamases. *Int J Antimicrob Agents.* 2008; 32:302–7.
975. Bennett JW, Herrera ML, Lewis JS II, et al. KPC-2-producing *Enterobacter cloacae* and *Pseudomonas putida* coinfection in a liver transplant recipient. *Antimicrob Agents Chemother.* 2009; 53:292–4.
976. Carignan A, Allard C, Pépin J, et al. Risk of *Clostridium difficile* infection after perioperative antibacterial prophylaxis before and during an outbreak of infection due to a hypervirulent strain. *Clin Infect Dis.* 2008; 46:1838–46.
977. Stelzmueller I, Goegele H, Biebl M, et al. *Clostridium difficile* in solid organ transplantation—a single-center experience. *Dig Dis Sci.* 2007; 52:3231–6.
978. Hashimoto M, Sugawara Y, Tamura S, et al. *Clostridium difficile*-associated diarrhea after living donor liver transplantation. *World J Gastroenterol.* 2007; 13:2072–6.
979. Bion JF, Badger I, Crosby HA, et al. Selective decontamination of the digestive tract reduces gram-negative pulmonary colonization but not systemic endotoxemia in patients undergoing elective liver transplantation. *Crit Care Med.* 1994; 22:40–9.
980. Rayes N, Seehofer D, Hansen S, et al. Early enteral supply of lactobacillus and fiber versus selective bowel decontamination: a controlled trial in liver transplant recipients. *Transplantation.* 2002; 74:123–8.
981. González-Segura C, Pascual M, Garcia Huete L, et al. Donors with positive blood culture: could they transmit infections to the recipients? *Transplant Proc.* 2005; 37:3664–6.
982. Lumbreras C, Cuervas-Mons V, Jara P, et al. Randomized trial of fluconazole versus nystatin for the prophylaxis of *Candida* infection following liver transplantation. *J Infect Dis.* 1996; 174:583–8.
983. Winston DJ, Pakrasi A, Busuttil RW. Prophylactic fluconazole in liver transplant recipients. A randomized, double-blind, placebo-controlled trial. *Ann Intern Med.* 1999; 131:729–37.
984. Sharpe MD, Ghent C, Grant D, et al. Efficacy and safety of itraconazole prophylaxis for fungal infections after orthotopic liver transplantation: a prospective, randomized, double-blind study. *Transplantation.* 2003; 76:977–83.
985. Castroagudin JF, Ponton C, Bustamante M, et al. Prospective interventional study to evaluate the efficacy and safety of liposomal amphotericin B as prophylaxis of fungal infections in high-risk liver transplant recipients. *Transplant Proc.* 2005; 37:3965–7.
986. Lorf T, Braun F, Ruchel R, et al. Systemic mycoses during prophylactical use of liposomal amphotericin B (Ambisome) after liver transplantation. *Mycoses.* 1999; 42:47–53.
987. Tollemar J, Hockerstedt K, Ericzon BG, et al. Liposomal amphotericin B prevents invasive fungal infections in liver transplant recipients. A randomized, placebo-controlled study. *Transplantation.* 1995; 59:45–50.
988. Fortun J, Martin-Davila P, Montejo M, et al. Prophylaxis with caspofungin for invasive fungal infections in high-risk liver transplant recipients. *Transplantation.* 2009; 87:424–35.
989. Cruciani M, Mengoli C, Malena M, et al. Antifungal prophylaxis in liver transplant patients: a systematic review and meta-analysis. *Liver Transpl.* 2006; 12:850–8.
990. Weisner RH, Hermans PE, Rakela J, et al. Selective bowel decontamination to decrease gram-negative aerobic bacterial and candidal colonization and prevent infection after orthotopic liver transplantation. *Transplantation.* 1988; 45:570–4.
991. Safdar N, Said A, Lucey MR. The role of selective digestive decontamination for reducing infection in patients undergoing liver transplantation: a systematic review and meta-analysis. *Liver Transpl.* 2004; 10:817–27.
992. Wiesmayr S, Stelzmueller I, Mark W, et al. Experience with the use of piperacillin-tazobactam in pediatric non-renal solid organ transplantation. *Pediatr Transplant.* 2007; 11:38–48.
993. Barker RJ, Mayes JT, Schulak JA. Wound abscesses following retroperitoneal pancreas transplantation. *Clin Transplant.* 1991; 5:403–7.
994. Douzdjian V, Abecassis MM, Cooper JL, et al. Incidence, management, and significance of surgical complications after pancreas-kidney transplantation. *Surg Gynecol Obstet.* 1993; 177:451–6.
995. Everett JE, Wahoff DC, Statz C, et al. Characterization and impact of wound infection after pancreas transplantation. *Arch Surg.* 1994; 129:1310–7.
996. Ozaki CF, Stratta RJ, Taylor RJ, et al. Surgical complications in solitary pancreas and combined pancreas-kidney transplantations. *Am J Surg.* 1992; 164:546–51.
997. Sollinger HW, Ploeg RJ, Eckhoff DE, et al. Two hundred consecutive simultaneous pancreas-kidney transplants with bladder drainage. *Surgery.* 1993; 114:736–44.
998. United Network for Organ Sharing. Organ Procurement and Transplantation Network: data. http://optn.transplant.hrsa.gov/data/. Based on OPTN data as of October 2, 2008.

999. Reddy KS, Stratta RJ, Shokouh-Amiri MH, et al. Surgical complications after pancreas transplantation with portal-enteric drainage. *J Am Coll Surg.* 1999; 189:305–13.
1000. Berger N, Wirmsberger R, Kafka R, et al. Infectious complications following 72 consecutive enteric-drained pancreas transplants. *Transpl Int.* 2006; 19:549–57.
1001. Bonatti H, Berger N, Kafka R, et al. Experience with ATG short course high dose induction therapy in a series of 112 enteric drained pancreatic transplants. *Ann Transplant.* 2002; 7:22–7.
1002. Berger N, Guggenbichler S, Steurer W, et al. Bloodstream infection following 217 consecutive systemic-enteric drained pancreas transplants. *BMC Infect Dis.* 2006; 6:127.
1003. Humar A, Kandawamy R, Drangstveit MB, et al. Prolonged preservation increases surgical complications after pancreas transplants. *Surgery.* 2000; 127:545–51.
1004. Pfundstein J, Roghmann MC, Schwalbe RS, et al. A randomized trial of surgical antimicrobial prophylaxis with and without vancomycin in organ transplant patients. *Clin Transplant.* 1999; 13:245–52.
1005. Smets YF, van der Pijl JW, van Dissel JT, et al. Infectious disease complications of simultaneous pancreas-kidney transplantation. *Nephrol Dial Transplant.* 1997; 12:764–71.
1006. Michalak G, Kwiatkowski A, Bieniasz M, et al. Infectious complications after simultaneous pancreas-kidney transplantation. *Transplant Proc.* 2005; 37:3560–3.
1007. Linhares MM, Gonzalez AM, Triviño T, et al. Simultaneous pancreas-kidney transplantation: infectious complications and microbiological aspects. *Transplant Proc.* 2004; 36:980–1.
1008. Bassetti M, Salvalaggio PR, Topal J, et al. Incidence, timing and site of infections among pancreas transplant recipients. *J Hosp Infect.* 2004; 56:184–90.
1009. Barone GW, Hudec WA, Sailors DM, et al. Prophylactic wound antibiotics for combined kidney and pancreas transplants. *Clin Transplant.* 1996; 10:386–8.
1010. Freise CE, Stock PG, Roberts JP, et al. Low postoperative wound infection rates are possible following simultaneous pancreas-kidney transplantation. *Transplant Proc.* 1995; 27:3069–70.
1011. Smets YF, van der Pijl JW, van Dissel JT, et al. Major bacterial and fungal infections after 50 simultaneous pancreas-kidney transplantations. *Transplant Proc.* 1995; 27:3089–90.
1012. Douzdjian V, Gugliuzza KK. Wound complications after simultaneous pancreas-kidney transplants: midline versus transverse incision. *Transplant Proc.* 1995; 27:3130–2.
1013. Bartlett ST. Pancreatic transplantation after thirty years: still room for improvement. *J Am Coll Surg.* 1996; 183:408–10.
1014. Cohen J, Rees AJ, Williams G. A prospective randomized controlled trial of perioperative antibiotic prophylaxis in renal transplantation. *J Hosp Infect.* 1988; 11:357–63.
1015. Hoy WE, May AG, Freeman RB. Primary renal transplant wound infections. *N Y State J Med.* 1981; 81:1469–73.
1016. Kohlberg WI, Tellis VA, Bhat DJ, et al. Wound infections after transplant nephrectomy. *Arch Surg.* 1980; 115:645–6.
1017. Muakkassa WF, Goldman MH, Mendez-Picon G, et al. Wound infections in renal transplant patients. *J Urol.* 1983; 130:17–9.
1018. Novick AC. The value of intraoperative antibiotics in preventing renal transplant wound infections. *J Urol.* 1981; 125:151–2.
1019. Ramos E, Karmi S, Alongi SV, et al. Infectious complications in renal transplant recipients. *South Med J.* 1980; 73:752–4.
1020. Rubin RH, Wolfson JS, Cosimi AB, et al. Infection in the renal transplant recipient. *Am J Med.* 1981; 70:405–11.
1021. Tilney NL, Strom TB, Vineyard GC, et al. Factors contributing to the declining mortality rate in renal transplantation. *N Engl J Med.* 1978; 299:1321–5.
1022. Muñoz P. Management of urinary tract infections and lymphocele in renal transplant recipients. *Clin Infect Dis.* 2001; 33(suppl 1):S53–7.
1023. Alangaden GJ, Thyagarajan R, Gruber SA, et al. Infectious complications after kidney transplantation: current epidemiology and associated risk factors. *Clin Transplant.* 2006; 20:401–9.
1024. Dantas SP, Kuboyama RH, Mazzali M, et al. Nosocomial infections in renal transplant patients: risk factors and treatment implications associated with urinary tract and surgical site infections. *J Hosp Infect.* 2006; 63:117–23.
1025. Celik A, Sifil A, Cavdar C, et al. Outcome of renal transplantation: 7-year experience. *Transplant Proc.* 2001; 33:2657–9.
1026. Lai MK, Huang CC, Chu SH, et al. Surgical complications in renal transplantation. *Transplant Proc.* 1994; 26:2165–6.
1027. Schmaldienst S, Hoerl WH. Bacterial infections after renal transplantation. *Nephron.* 1997; 75:140–53.
1028. Maraha B, Bonten H, van Hooff H, et al. Infectious complications and antibiotic use in renal transplant recipients during a 1-year follow-up. *Clin Microbiol Infect.* 2001; 7:619–25.
1029. Ramos A, Asensio A, Muñoz E, et al. Incisional surgical site infection in kidney transplantation. *Urology.* 2008; 72:119–23.
1030. Menezes FG, Wey SB, Peres CA, et al. Risk factors for surgical site infection in kidney transplant recipients. *Infect Control Hosp Epidemiol.* 2008; 29:771–3.
1031. Stephan RN, Munschauer CE, Kumar MS. Surgical wound infection in renal transplantation. Outcome data in 102 consecutive patients without perioperative systemic antibiotic coverage. *Arch Surg.* 1997; 132:1315–9.
1032. Sawyer RG, Pelletier SJ, Pruett TL. Increased early morbidity and mortality with acceptable long-term function in severely obese patients undergoing liver transplantation. *Clin Transplant.* 1999; 13:126–30.

1033. Koyle MA, Glasscock RJ, Ward HJ, et al. Declining incidence of wound infection in cadaveric renal transplant recipient. *Urology.* 1988; 31:103–6.

1034. Judson RT. Wound infection following renal transplantation. *Aust N Z J Surg.* 1984; 54:223–4.

1035. Del Rio G, Dalet F, Chechile G. Antimicrobial prophylaxis in urologic surgery: does it give some benefit? *Eur Urol.* 1993; 24:305–12.

1036. Midtvedt K, Hartmann A, Midtvedt T, et al. Routine perioperative antibiotic prophylaxis in renal transplantation. *Nephrol Dial Transplant.* 1998; 13:1637–41.

1037. Capocasale E, Mazzoni MP, Tondo S, et al. Antimicrobial prophylaxis with ceftriaxone in renal transplantation. Prospective study of 170 patients. *Chemotherapy.* 1994; 40:435–40.

1038. Wakelin SJ, Casey J, Robertson A, et al. The incidence and importance of bacterial contaminants of cadaveric renal perfusion fluid. *Transplant Int.* 2005; 17:680–6.

1039. Zomorrodi A, Buhluli A. Is antibiotic usage necessary after donor nephrectomy? A single center experience. *Saudi J Kidney Dis Transpl.* 2008; 19:200–5.

1040. Pape L, Offner G, Ehrich JH, et al. A single center clinical experience in intensive care management of 104 pediatric renal transplantations between 1998 and 2002. *Pediatr Transplant.* 2004; 8:39–43.

1041. Thorne CH. Techniques and principles in plastic surgery. In: Thorne CH, Beasley RW, Aston SJ, et al., eds. Grabb and Smith's plastic surgery. 6th ed. Philadelphia: Lippincott Williams and Wilkins; 2007.

1042. Chełmoński A, Jabłecki J, Sycz Z. Composite allotransplantations of knee joint, larynx, uterus, abdominal wall, face and penis. *Ann Transplant.* 2007; 12:5–11.

1043. Bonatti H, Brandacher G, Margreiter R, et al. Infectious complications in three double hand recipients: experience from a single center. *Transplant Proc.* 2009; 41:517–20.

1044. Babcock MD, Grekin RC. Antibiotic use in dermatologic surgery. *Dermatol Clin.* 2003; 21:337–48.

1045. Messingham MJ, Arpey CJ. Updates on the use of antibiotics in cutaneous surgery. *Dermatol Surg.* 2005; 31:1068–78.

1046. Wright TI, Baddour LM, Berbari EF, et al. Antibiotic prophylaxis in dermatologic surgery: advisory statement 2008. *J Am Acad Dermatol.* 2008; 59:464–73.

1047. Throckmorton AD, Boughey JC, Boostrom SY, et al. Postoperative prophylactic antibiotics and surgical site infection rates in breast surgery patients. *Ann Surg Oncol.* 2009; 16:2464–9.

1048. Khan UD. Breast augmentation, antibiotic prophylaxis, and infection: comparative analysis of 1,628 primary augmentation mammoplasties assessing the role and efficacy of antibiotics prophylaxis duration. *Aesthetic Plast Surg.* 2010; 34:42–7.

1049. Baran CN, Sensöz Ö, Ulusoy MG. Prophylactic antibiotics in plastic and reconstructive surgery. *Plast Reconstr Surg.* 1999; 103:1561–6.

1050. Mekako AI, Chetter IC, Coughlin PA, et al., on behalf of the Hull Antibiotic pRophylaxis in varicose VEin Surgery Trialists (HARVEST). Randomized clinical trial of co-amoxiclav versus no antibiotic prophylaxis in varicose vein surgery. *Br J Surg.* 2010; 97:29–36.

1051. Stone JF, Davidson JS. The role of antibiotics and timing of repair in flexor tendon injuries of the hand. *Ann Plast Surg.* 1998; 40:7–13.

1052. LeRoy J, Given KS. Wound infection in breast augmentation: the role of prophylactic perioperative antibiotics. *Aesthetic Plast Surg.* 1991; 15:303–5.

1053. Stewart KJ, Stewart DA, Coghlan B, et al. Complications of 278 consecutive abdominoplasties. *J Plast Reconstr Aesth Surg.* 2006; 59:1152–5.

1054. Rosengren H, Dixon A. Antibacterial prophylaxis in dermatologic surgery: an evidence-based review. *Am J Clin Dermatol.* 2010; 11:35–44.

1055. Landes G, Harris PG, Lemaine V, et al. Prevention of surgical site infection and appropriateness of antibiotic prescribing habits in plastic surgery. *J Plast Reconstr Aesthet Surg.* 2008; 61:1347–56.

1056. Ahmadi AH, Cohen BE, Shayani P. A prospective study of antibiotic efficacy in preventing infection in reduction mammaplasty. *Plast Reconstr Surg.* 2005; 116:126–31.

1057. Carroll WR, Rosenstiel D, Fix JR, et al. Three-dose vs. extended-course clindamycin prophylaxis for free-flap reconstruction of the head and neck. *Arch Otolaryngol Head Neck Surg.* 2003; 129:771–4.

1058. Serletti JM, Davenport MS, Herrera HR, et al. Efficacy of prophylactic antibiotics in reduction mammoplasty. *Ann Plast Surg.* 1994; 33:476–80.

1059. Halpern AC, Leyden JJ, Dzubow LM, et al. The incidence of bacteremia in skin surgery of the head and neck. *J Am Acad Dermatol.* 1988; 19:112–6.

1060. Samra S, Sawh-Martinez R, Barry O, et al. Complication rates of lipoabdominoplasty versus traditional abdominoplasty in high-risk patients. *Plast Reconstr Surg.* 2010; 125:683–90.

1061. Olsen MA, Lefta M, Dietz JR, et al. Risk factors for surgical site infection after major breast operation. *J Am Coll Surg.* 2008; 207:326–35.

1062. Dixon AJ, Dixon MP, Dixon JB. Prospective study of skin surgery in patients with and without known diabetes. *Dermatol Surg.* 2009; 35:1035–40.

1063. Wahie S, Lawrence CM. Wound complications following diagnostic skin biopsies in dermatology inpatients. *Arch Dermatol.* 2007; 143:1267–71.

1064. Gravante G, Araco A, Sorge R, et al. Wound infections in post-bariatric patients undergoing body contouring abdominoplasty: the role of smoking. *Obes Surg.* 2007; 17:1325–31.

1065. Rey JE, Gardner SM, Cushing RD. Determinants of surgical site infection after breast biopsy. *Am J Infect Control.* 2005; 33:126–9.

1066. Sevin A, Senen D, Sevin K, et al. Antibiotic use in abdominoplasty: prospective analysis of 207 cases. *J Plast Reconstr Aesthet Surg.* 2007; 60:379–82.

1067. Gravante G, Caruso R, Araco A, et al. Infections after plastic procedures: incidences, etiologies, risk factors, and antibiotic prophylaxis. *Aesthetic Plast Surg.* 2008; 32:243–51.

1068. Bertin ML, Crowe J, Gordon SM. Determinants of surgical site infection after breast surgery. *Am J Infect Control.* 1998; 26:61–5.

1069. Harness NG, Inacio MC, Pfeil FF, et al. Rate of infection after carpal tunnel release surgery and effect of antibiotic prophylaxis. *J Hand Surg*. 2010; 35:189–96.
1070. Platt R, Zucker JR, Zaleznik DF, et al. Perioperative antibiotic prophylaxis and wound infection following breast surgery. *J Antimicrob Chemother*. 1993; 31(suppl B):43–8.
1071. Kompatscher P, von Planta A, Spicher I, et al. Comparison of the incidence and predicted risk of early surgical site infections after breast reduction. *Aesthetic Plast Surg*. 2003; 27:308–14.
1072. Bunn F, Cunningham ME, Handscomb K. Prophylactic antibiotics to prevent surgical site infection after breast cancer surgery. *Cochrane Database Syst Rev*. 2006; 2:CD005360.
1073. Perrotti JA, Castor SA, Perez PC, et al. Antibiotic use in aesthetic surgery: a national survey and literature review. *Plast Reconstr Surg*. 2002; 109:1685–93.
1074. Smyth AG, Knepil GJ. Prophylactic antibiotics and surgery for primary clefts. *Br J Oral Maxillofac Surg*. 2008; 46:107–9.
1075. Cocco JF, Antonetti JW, Burns JL, et al. Characterization of the nasal, sublingual and oropharyngeal mucosa microbiota in cleft lip and palate individuals before and after surgical repair. *Cleft Palate Craniofac J*. 2010; 47:151–5.

Appendix A—National Healthcare Safety Network Criteria for Classifying Wounds[35]

Clean: An uninfected operative wound in which no inflammation is encountered and the respiratory, alimentary, genital, or uninfected urinary tracts are not entered. In addition, clean wounds are primarily closed and, if necessary, drained with closed drainage. Operative incisional wounds that follow nonpenetrating (blunt) trauma should be included in this category if they meet the criteria.

Clean-Contaminated: Operative wounds in which the respiratory, alimentary, genital, or urinary tracts are entered under controlled conditions and without unusual contamination. Specifically, operations involving the biliary tract, appendix, vagina, and oropharynx are included in this category, provided no evidence of infection or major break in technique is encountered.

Contaminated: Open, fresh, accidental wounds. In addition, operations with major breaks in sterile technique (e.g., open cardiac massage) or gross spillage from the gastrointestinal tract and incisions in which acute, nonpurulent inflammation is encountered are included in this category.

Dirty or Infected: Includes old traumatic wounds with retained devitalized tissue and those that involve existing clinical infection or perforated viscera. This definition suggests that the organisms causing postoperative infection were present in the operative field before the operation.

Appendix B—National Healthcare Safety Network Criteria for Defining a Surgical-Site Infection (SSI)[8,36]

Superficial Incisional SSI: Occurs within 30 days postoperatively and involves skin or subcutaneous tissue of the incision and at least one of the following: (1) purulent drainage from the superficial incision, (2) organisms isolated from an aseptically obtained culture of fluid or tissue from the superficial incision, (3) at least one of the following signs or symptoms of infection: pain or tenderness, localized swelling, redness, or heat, and superficial incision is deliberately opened by surgeon and is culture-positive or not cultured (a culture-negative finding does not meet this criterion), and (4) diagnosis of superficial incisional SSI by the surgeon or attending physician.

Deep Incisional SSI: Occurs within 30 days after the operative procedure if no implant is left in place or within one year if implant is in place and the infection appears to be related to the operative procedure, involves deep soft tissues (e.g., fascial and muscle layers) of the incision, and the patient has at least one of the following: (1) purulent drainage from the deep incision but not from the organ/space component of the surgical site, (2) a deep incision spontaneously dehisces or is deliberately opened by a surgeon and is culture-positive or not cultured and the patient has at least one of the following signs or symptoms: fever (>38 °C) or localized pain or tenderness (a culture-negative finding does not meet this criterion), (3) an abscess or other evidence of infection involving the deep incision is found on direct examination, during reoperation, or by histopathologic or radiologic examination, and (4) diagnosis of a deep incisional SSI by a surgeon or attending physician.

Organ/Space SSI: Involves any part of the body, excluding the skin incision, fascia, or muscle layers, that is opened or manipulated during the operative procedure. Specific sites are assigned to organ/space SSI to further identify the location of the infection (e.g., endocarditis, endometritis, mediastinitis, vaginal cuff, and osteomyelitis). Organ/space SSI must meet the following criteria: (1) infection occurs within 30 days after the operative procedure if no implant is in place or within 1 year if implant is in place and the infection appears to be related to the operative procedure, (2) infection involves any part of the body, excluding the skin incision, fascia, or muscle layers, that is opened or manipulated during the operative procedure, and (3) the patient has at least one of the following: (a) purulent drainage from a drain that is placed through a stab wound into the organ/space, (b) organisms isolated from an aseptically obtained culture of fluid or tissue in the organ/space, (c) an abscess or other evidence of infection involving the organ/space that is found on direct examination, during reoperation, or by histopathologic or radiologic examination, and (d) diagnosis of an organ/space SSI by a surgeon or attending physician.

The following individuals are acknowledged for their significant contributions to this manuscript: Sandra I. Berríos-Torres, M.D.; Rachel Bongiorno-Karcher, Pharm.D.; Colleen M. Culley,

Pharm.D., BCPS; Susan R. Dombrowski, M.S., B.S.Pharm.; and Susan J. Skledar, B.S.Pharm., M.P.H., FASHP.

Financial support provided by Emory University, Johns Hopkins University, Northwestern University, Rush University, University of Colorado, University of Michigan, University of Oklahoma, University of Nebraska, University of Virginia, University of Washington, and West Virginia University.

Dr. Bratzler is a consultant for Telligen; Dr. Dellinger has received honoraria for participation on advisory boards and consultation for Merck, Baxter, Ortho-McNeil, Targanta, Schering-Plough, WebEx, Astellas, Durata, Pfizer, Applied Medical, Rib-X, 3M, the American Hospital Association, Premier Inc., Oklahoma Foundation for Medical Quality, and the Hospital Association of New York State; Dr. Perl serves on the advisory boards of Hospira and Pfizer and has received a grant from Merck; Dr. Auwaerter serves on the advisory panel of Genentech; Dr. Fish serves on the advisory board and speakers' bureau of Merck; and Dr. Sawyer serves as a consultant for Pfizer, Merck, Wyeth, 3M, and Ethicon and has received an R01 grant from the National Institute of General Medical Sciences and a T32 grant from the National Institute of Allergy and Infectious Diseases. Drs. Bolon, Napolitano, Olsen, Steinberg, Slain, and Weinstein have declared no potential conflicts of interest.

The bibliographic citation for this article is as follows: Bratzler DW, Dellinger EP, Olsen KM, et al. Clinical practice guidelines for antimicrobial prophylaxis in surgery. *Am J Health-Syst Pharm.* 2013; 70:195–283.

Clinical Practice Guidelines for Sustained Neuromuscular Blockade in the Adult Critically Ill Patient

The decision to treat a patient in the intensive care unit (ICU) with neuromuscular blocking agents (NMBAs) (for reasons other than the placement of an endotracheal tube) is a difficult one that is guided more commonly by individual practitioner preference than by standards based on evidence-based medicine. Commonly cited reasons for the use of NMBAs in the ICU are to facilitate mechanical ventilation or different modes of mechanical ventilation and to manage patients with head trauma or tetanus. Independent of the reasons for using NMBAs, we emphasize that all other modalities to improve the clinical situation must be tried, using NMBAs only as a last resort.

In 1995 the American College of Critical Care Medicine (ACCM) of the Society of Critical Care Medicine (SCCM) published guidelines for the use of NMBAs in the ICU. The present document is the result of an attempt to reevaluate the literature that has appeared since the last guidelines were published and, based on that review, to update the recommendations for the use of NMBAs in the ICU. Appendix A summarizes our recommendations. Using methods previously described to evaluate the literature and grade the evidence, the task force reviewed the physiology of the neuromuscular receptor, the pharmacology of the NMBAs currently used in the ICU, the means to monitor the degree of blockade, the complications associated with NMBAs, and the economic factors to consider when choosing a drug.

Neuromuscular Junction in Health and Disease

The neuromuscular junction consists of a motor nerve terminus, the neurotransmitter acetylcholine, and the postsynaptic muscle endplate (Figure 1). The impulse of an action potential causes the release of acetylcholine from synaptic vesicles (each containing about 10,000 molecules of acetylcholine) diffusing across the 20-nm gap to the postsynaptic endplate. The motor endplate contains specialized ligand-gated, nicotinic acetylcholine receptors (nAChRs), which convert the chemical signal (i.e., binding of two acetylcholine molecules) into electrical signals (i.e., a transient permeability change and depolarization in the postsynaptic membrane of striated muscle).

There are depolarizing and nondepolarizing NMBAs. Depolarizing NMBAs physically resemble acetylcholine and, therefore, bind and activate acetylcholine receptors. Succinylcholine is currently the only available depolarizing NMBA and is not used for long-term use in ICUs.

Nondepolarizing NMBAs also bind acetylcholine receptors but do not activate them—they are competitive antagonists. The difference in the mechanism of action also accounts for different effects in certain diseases. If there is a long-term decrease in acetylcholine release, the number of acetylcholine receptors within the muscle increases. This upregulation causes an increased response to depolarizing NMBAs but a resistance to nondepolarizing NMBAs (i.e., more receptors must be blocked). Conditions in which there are fewer acetylcholine receptors (e.g., myasthenia gravis) lead to an increase in sensitivity to nondepolarizing NMBAs.

Adult skeletal muscle retains an ability to synthesize both the mature adult nAChR as well as an immature nAChR variant in which a gamma subunit is substituted for the normal epsilon subunit. Synthesis of immature (fetal) receptors may be triggered in the presence of certain diseases (e.g., Guillain-Barré syndrome, stroke) and other conditions producing loss of nerve function. These immature nAChRs are distinguished by three features. First, immature receptors are not localized to the muscle endplate but migrate across the entire membrane surface.[2] Second, the immature receptors are metabolically short-lived (<24 hours) and more ionically active, having a 2- to 10-fold longer channel "open time." Lastly, these immature receptors are more sensitive to the depolarizing effects of such drugs as succinylcholine and more resistant to the effects of competitive antagonists, such as pancuronium. This increase in the number of immature acetylcholine receptors may account for the tachyphylaxis seen with NMBAs and some of the complications associated with their use. For the remainder of this document, only nondepolarizing NMBAs will be discussed.

Pharmacology of Neuromuscular-Receptor Blockers

Aminosteroidal Compounds. The aminosteroidal compounds include pancuronium, pipecuronium, vecuronium, and rocuronium (Tables 1 and 2).[3–11]

Pancuronium. Pancuronium, one of the original NMBAs used in ICUs, is a long-acting, nondepolarizing compound that is effective after an intravenous bolus dose of 0.06–0.1 mg/kg for up to 90 minutes. Though it is commonly given as an i.v. bolus, it can be used as a continuous infusion[12] by adjusting the dose to the degree of neuromuscular blockade that is desired (Table 1). Pancuronium is vagolytic (more than 90% of ICU patients will have an increase in heart rate of ≥10 beats/min), which limits its use in patients who cannot tolerate an increase in heart rate.[12] In patients with renal failure or cirrhosis, pancuronium's neuromuscular blocking effects are prolonged because of its increased elimination half-life and the decreased clearance of its 3-hydroxypancuronium metabolite that has one-third to one-half the activity of pancuronium.

Pipecuronium. Pipecuronium is another long-acting NMBA with an elimination half-life of about two hours, similar to pancuronium's. Khuenl-Brady and colleagues[13] conducted an open-label evaluation of pipecuronium compared with pancuronium in 60 critically ill patients to determine the minimum doses required for ventilatory management. The administration of 8 mg of either drug followed by intermittent boluses of 4–6 mg when needed resulted in optimal paralysis. Patients were paralyzed for a mean duration of 62.6 hours (45–240 hours) and 61.5 hours (46–136 hours) with pancuronium and pipecuronium, respectively. No adverse effects were attributed to either drug. Perhaps because of this lack of difference and because there are no recent studies examining pipecuronium's use in the ICU, most clinicians continue to use the more familiar drug, pancuronium.

Figure 1. Neuromuscular Junction. Schematic model of the organization and structure of the neuromuscular junction, with focus and enlargement on the postsynaptic membrane. Agrin is the nerve-derived protein that triggers receptor clustering during synapse formation. Receptor aggregation appears to occur in distinct steps, however, initiated with acetylcholine receptors (AChR) localized together by rapsyn. Meanwhile, D-dystroglycan, the extracellular component of dystrophin-associated glycoprotein complex (DGC), is the agrin receptor which transduces final AChR clustering. This process utilizes the structural organization of additional proteins like utrophin, which stabilize the mature, immobile domains by interaction with the underlying cytoskeleton (actin). When completed, this process concentrates AChR density 1000-fold compared to typical muscle membrane. ACh = acetylcholine, MuSK = muscle-specific-receptor kirase, MASC = MuSK-accessory specificity component. (Reprinted with permission, from Wall MH, Prielipp RC. Monitoring the neuromuscular junction. In: Lake C, Blitt CD, Hines RL, eds. Clinical Monitoring: Practical Applications for Anesthesia and Critical Care. Philadelphia: W.B. Saunders, 2000, Figure 10-3.)

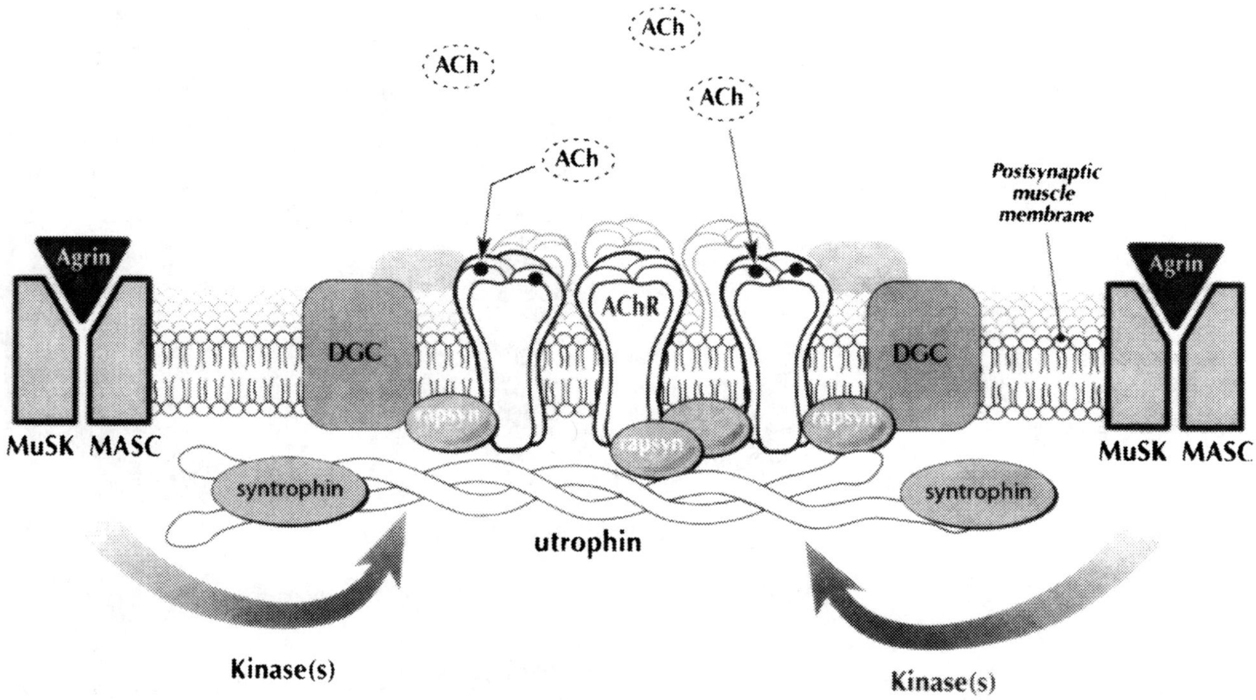

Vecuronium. Vecuronium is an intermediate-acting NMBA that is a structural analogue of pancuronium and is not vagolytic. An i.v. bolus dose of vecuronium 0.08–0.1 mg/kg, produces blockade within 60–90 seconds that typically lasts 25–30 minutes. After an i.v. bolus dose, vecuronium is given as a 0.8–1.2-µg/kg/min continuous infusion, adjusting the rate to the degree of blockade desired. Because up to 35% of a dose is renally excreted, patients with renal failure will have decreased drug requirements. Similarly, because up to 50% of an injected dose is excreted in bile, patients with hepatic insufficiency will also have decreased drug requirements to maintain adequate blockade. The 3-desacetylvecuronium metabolite has 50% of the pharmacologic activity of the parent compound, so patients with organ dysfunction may have increased plasma concentrations of both the parent compound and the active metabolite, which contributes to the prolongation of blockade if the dose is not adjusted. Vecuronium has been reported to be more commonly associated with prolonged blockade once discontinued, compared with other NMBAs[a]. Members of the task force believe that vecuronium is being used with decreased frequency in the ICU.

Vecuronium has been studied in open-label prospective trials.[14,15] In one of these studies, the mean infusion rate for vecuronium was 0.9 ± 0.1 µg/kg/min for a mean duration of 80 ± 7 hours. Recovery of a train-of-four (TOF) ratio of ≥0.7 was significantly longer than with cisatracurium.[15] Recovery time averaged 1–2 hours but ranged from ≤30 minutes to more than 48 hours.

Although Rudis, et al.[14] observed no difference in the incidence of prolonged blockade between patients receiving vecuronium with and without concomitant administration of corticosteroids, the opinion of the task force was that patients receiving vecuronium and corticosteroids were at increased risk of prolonged weakness once the drug was discontinued.

Rocuronium. Rocuronium is a newer nondepolarizing NMBA with a monoquaternary steroidal chemistry that has an intermediate duration of action and a very rapid onset. When given as a bolus dose of 0.6–1 mg/kg, blockade is almost always achieved within two minutes, with maximum blockade occurring within three minutes. Continuous infusions are begun at 10 µg/kg/min.[8] Rocuronium's metabolite, 17-des-acetylrocuronium, has only 5–10% activity compared with the parent compound.

Sparr, Khuenl-Brady, and colleagues[8,9] studied the dose requirements, recovery times, and pharmacokinetics of rocuronium in 32 critically ill patients, 27 of whom were given intermittent bolus doses, and 5 received a continuous infusion. The median duration of drug administration was 29 hours and 63.4 hours in the bolus dose and infusion groups, respectively. The mean dose of rocuronium required to maintain 80% blockade was 0.34 mg/kg, and the median infusion rate required to maintain one twitch of the TOF was 0.54 mg/kg/hr. The median time from the last bolus dose to the appearance of TOF response was 100 minutes; in the infusion group, the TOF response returned 60 minutes after the infusion was stopped.

Rapacuronium. Rapacuronium, a propionate analogue of vecuronium, was marketed as a nonde polarizing NMBA as an alternative to succinylcholine. It was withdrawn from the market on March 27, 2001, because of reports of morbidity (bronchospasm) and mortality associated with its use.

Table 1.
Selected Neuromuscular Blocking Agents[a] for ICU Use

	Benzylisoquinolinium Drugs				
Variable	D-Turbocurarine (Curare)	Cisatracurium (Nimbex)	Atracurium (Tracrium)	Doxacurium (Nuromax)	Mivacurium (Mivacron)
Introduced (yr)	1942	1995	1983	1991	1992
ED_{95}[b] dose (mg/kg)	0.51	0.05	0.25	0.025–0.03	0.075
Initial dose (mg/kg)	0.1–0.2	0.1–0.2	0.4–0.5	0.025–0.05	0.15–0.25
Duration (min)	80	45–60	25–35	120–150	10–20
Infusion described	. . .	Yes	Yes	Yes	Yes
Infusion dose (μg/kg/min)	. . .	2.5–3	4–12	0.3–0.5	9–10
Recovery (min)	80–180	90	40–60	120–180	10–20
% Renal excretion	40-45	Hofmann elimination	5–10 (uses Hofmann elimination)	70	Inactive metabolites
Renal failure	Increased duration	No change	No change	Increased duration	Increased duration
% Biliary excretion	10–40	Hofmann elimination	Minimal (uses Hofmann elimination)	Insufficient data	. . .
Hepatic failure	Minimal change to mild increased effect	Minimal to no change	Minimal to no change	. . .	Increased duration
Active metabolites	No	No	No, but can accumulate laudanosine	. . .	No
Histamine release hypotension	Marked	No	Minimal but dose dependent	No	Minimal but dose dependent
Vagal block tachycardia	Minimal	No	No	No	No
Ganglionic blockade hypotension	Marked	No	Minimal to none	No	No
Prolonged ICU block	. . .	Rare	Rare	Insufficient data	Insufficient data

	Aminosteroidal Drugs			
	Pancuronium (Pavulon)	Vecuronium (Norcuron)	Pipecuronium (Arduan)	Rocuronium (Zemuron)
Introduced (yr)	1972	1984	1991	1994
ED_{95}[b] dose (mg/kg)	0.05	0.05	0.05	0.3
Initial dose (mg/kg)	0.06–0.1	0.08–0.1	0.085–0.1	0.6–1
Duration (min)	90–100	35–45	90–100	30
Infusion described	Yes	Yes	No	Yes
Infusion dose (μg/kg/min)	1–2	0.8–1.2	0.5–2	10–12
Recovery (min)	120–180	45–60	55–160	20–30
% Renal excretion	45–70	50	50+	33
Renal failure	Increased effect	Increased effect, especially metabolites	Increased duration	Minimal
% Biliary excretion	10–15	35–50	Minimal	<75
Hepatic failure	Mild increased effect	Variable, mild	Minimal	Moderate
Active metabolites	Yes, 3-OH and 17-OH-pancuronium	Yes, 3-desacetyl–vecuronium	Insufficient data	No
Histamine release hypotension	No	No	No	No
Vagal block tachycardia	Modest to marked	No	No	Some at higher doses
Ganglionic blockade hypotension	No	No	No	No
Prolonged ICU block	Yes	Yes	Insufficient data	Insufficient data

[a]Based on drugs for use in a 70-kg man. Modified with permission from Prielipp and Coursin. Reference 3.
[b]ED_{95} = effective dose for 95% of patients studied.

Benzylisoquinolinium Compounds. The benzylisoquinolinium compounds include D-tubocuranine, atracurium, cisatracurium, doxacurium, and mivacurium (Tables 1 and 3).[12,15,16,31]

D-Tubocurarine. Tubocurarine was the first nondepolarizing NMBA to gain acceptance and usage in the ICU. This long-acting benzylisoquinolinium agent is rarely used in ICUs because it induces histamine release and autonomic

Table 2.
ICU Studies of Aminosteroidal Drugs[a]

Reference	Type of Study	Patients	Results	Level of Evidence
4	Prospective, observational, cohort	**30**	Median time to recovery with pancuronium was 3.5 hr in infusion group vs. 6.3 hr in the bolus dose group.	3
5	Prospective, open-label	25 PICU	Increased infusion requirements for pancuronium with anticonvulsants.	3
6	Prospective, open-label	6	Vecuronium clearance increased in 3 and decreased in 2 patients. V_D did not change.	3
7	Survey	. . .	Neuromuscular blockade monitored clinically with only 8.3% using TOF. All respondents indicated concomitant use of sedatives and/or opioids (75%).	5
8	Prospective, open-label	30 SICU	25 trauma patients received rocuronium 50-mg i.v. bolus dose followed by maintenance doses of 25 mg whenever TOF = 2, five patients were on continuous infusion at 25 mg/hr. Duration 1–5 days, recovery approximately 3 hr, and plasma clearance similar between groups.	3
9	Prospective, open-label	32	An initial dose of rocuronium 50 mg followed by maintenance doses of 25 mg with TOF = 2 (n = 27) or by continuous infusion to maintain TOF (n = 5). Pharmacokinetic data tabulated. Crossover with patients reported by Khuenl-Brady, et al.[8]	3
10	Prospective, randomized, controlled	20 CABG	Pancuronium (n = 10) was compared to rocuronium (n = 10). Incidence of residual block higher with pancuronium than rocuronium. No effect on time to extubation.	2
11	Prospective, open-label	12 ICU	12 patients, 4 with MODS. Patients given 0.6-mg/kg bolus dose of rocuronium followed by repeated bolus (n = 2) or continuous infusion (n = 10) started at 10–12 µg/kg/min and adjusted to TOF = 1–4. No evidence of prolonged blockade.	3

[a]PICU = pediatric intensive care unit, SICU = surgical intensive care unit, CABG = coronary artery bypass grafting, ICU = intensive care unit, TOF = train-of-four, V_D = volume of distribution, MODS = multiple organ dysfunction syndrome.

Table 3.
ICU Studies of Benzylisoquinolinium Drugs[a]

Reference	Type of Study	Patients	Dose	Results	Level of Evidence
16	Review	. . .	. . .	Review of pharmacokinetics	5
17	Prospective, open-label, controlled	14 with hepatic failure vs. 11 controls	Cisatracurium 0.1-mg/kg i.v. bolus dose	V_D greater in liver patients but no differences in elimination $t_{½}$ or in duration of action	5
18	Prospective, randomized, single-blind	20 ICU	Cisatracurium (n = 12) 0.25 mg/kg/hr Atracurium (n = 8) 0.62 mg/kg/hr	Similar mean recovery time	2
19	Prospective, randomized	12 ICU	Cisatracurium 0.1-mg/kg bolus dose + 0.18-mg/kg/hr infusion Atracurium: 0.5 mg/kg + 0.6-mg/kg/hr infusion	Measured V_D, Cl, $T_{½}$. Laudanosine concentration was lower in patients on cisatracurium	2
20	Randomized, open-label	61 ICU	Cisatracurium (n = 26) 0.1-mg/kg bolus, followed by an infusion of 3 µg/kg/min; 14 pts infusion only Atracurium (n = 18) 0.5 mg/kg bolus followed by an infusion of 10 µg/kg/min; 3 pts infusion only Infusion adjusted to one twitch	118 ± 19 min recovery no change in HR, BP, and ICP with bolus	3

(Continued on Next Page)

Table 3 *(continued)*

Reference	Type of Study	Patients	Dose	Results	Level of Evidence
15	Prospective, randomized, double-blind, multicenter	58 ICU	Cisatracurium 2.5-µg/kg/min Vecuronium 1-µg/kg/min	Recovery profiles were significantly different with more prolonged recovery noted for vecuronium. TOF monitoring could not eliminate prolonged recovery and myopathy	1
21	Prospective, blinded, cross-over	14 with brain injury	Cisatracurium 0.15 mg/kg bolus Atracurium 0.75 mg/kg bolus	No change in ICP, CPP, CBF, MAP, $ETCO_2$, and HR and no histamine-related symptoms, with $3 \times ED_{95}$ cisatracurium. With $3 \times ED_{95}$ tracurium, ICP, CPP, CBF, and MAP decreased within 2–4 min. Five patients had typical histamine reaction; excluding these five patients, there was no difference in any variable compared with cisatracurium	2
22	Observational, prospective, open-label	24 with brain injury	0.1 or 0.2-mg/kg cisatracurium bolus dose	No change from baseline in ICP, CPP, MAP, $ETCO_2$, HR, and CBF velocity in both groups	5
23	Case	. . .	. . .	. . .	4
24	Case	. . .	. . .	. . .	4
25	Review	. . .	. . .	. . .	4
26	Editorial	. . .	. . .	. . .	4
27	Review	. . .	. . .	. . .	5
28	Review	. . .	. . .	. . .	5
12	Multicenter, prospective, double-blind, randomized	40 critically ill	Doxacurium 0.04-mg/kg bolus dose, 0.025-mg/kg maintenance; pancuronium: 0.07 mg/kg bolus dose, 0.05-mg/kg maintenance	No difference in adverse reactions or onset of blockade; pancuronium had a more prolonged and variable recovery time	1
29	Prospective, open-label	8 mechanical ventilated ICU with HD monitoring and pHi <7.35	Doxacurium: 0.03-mg/kg load; 0.03-mg/kg/hr infusion	$DO_2 + VO_2$ decreased, pHi increased; VO_2 is decreased and pHi increased. NMBA causes redistribution of blood flow to splanchnic beds	5
30	Prospective, open-label study	8 ICU with traumatic head injury	Doxacurium 0.05 mg/kg then 0.25 µg/kg/min	No significant effect in HR, BP, ICP. No adverse effects	5
31	Case report	4 with atracurium tachyphylaxis	Doxacurium 0.25–0.75 µg/kg/min	No tachyphylaxis noted	5

[a]ICU = intensive care unit, TOF = train-of-four, V_D = volume of distribution, HR = heart rate, BP = blood pressure, ICP = intracranial pressure, CPP = cerebral perfusion pressure, CBF = cerebral blood flow, MAP = mean arterial pressure, NMBA = neuromuscular blocking agent, $ETCO_2$ = end tidal carbon dioxide, ED_{95} = effective dose for 95% of patients studied, HD = hemodynamic flow, pHi = gastric mucosal pH, DO_2 = oxygen delivery, VO_2 = oxygen consumption, CBF = cerebral blood flow.

ganglionic blockade. Hypotension is rare, however, when the agent is administered slowly in appropriate dosages (e.g., 0.1–0.2 mg/kg). Metabolism and elimination are affected by both renal and hepatic dysfunction.

Atracurium. Atracurium is an intermediate-acting NMBA with minimal cardiovascular adverse effects and is associated with histamine release at higher doses. It is inactivated in plasma by ester hydrolysis and Hofmann elimination so that renal or hepatic dysfunction does not affect the duration of blockade.

Laudanosine is a breakdown product of Hofmann elimination of atracurium and has been associated with central nervous system excitation. This has led to concern about the possibility of precipitating seizures in patients who have received extremely high doses of atracurium or who are in hepatic failure (laudanosine is metabolized by the liver). There has been only one report of a surgical patient who had a seizure while receiving atracurium.[32]

Atracurium has been administered to various critically ill patient populations, including those with liver failure,[17] brain injury,[21] or multiple organ dysfunction syndrome (MODS), to facilitate mechanical ventilation. In these reports, atracurium infusion rates varied widely, but they typically ranged from 10 to 20 µg/kg/min with doses adjusted to clinical endpoints or by TOF monitoring. Infusion durations ranged from ≤24 hours to >200 hours. Recovery of normal neuromuscular activity usually occurred within one to two hours after stopping the infusions and was independent of organ function. Long–term infusions have been associated with the development of tolerance, necessitating significant dose increases or conversion to other NMBAs.[31,33] Atracurium has been associated with persistent neuromuscular weakness as have other NMBAs.[34–38]

Cisatracurium. Cisatracurium, an isomer of atracurium, is an intermediate-acting benzyliso-quinolinium NMBA that is increasingly used in lieu of atracurium. It produces few, if any, cardiovascular effects and has a lesser tendency to produce mast cell degranulation than atracurium. Bolus doses of 0.1–0.2 mg/kg result in paralysis in an average of 2.5 minutes, and recovery begins at approximately 25 minutes; maintenance infusions should be started at 2.5–3 µg/kg/min. Cisatracurium is also metabolized by ester hydrolysis and Hofmann elimination, so the duration of blockade should not be affected by renal or hepatic dysfunction. Prolonged weakness has been reported following the use of cisatracurium.[38]

Cisatracurium has been compared with atracurium and vecuronium for facilitating mechanical ventilation in several open-label prospective trials.[15,18–21] Cisatracurium infusion rates ranged from 2 to 8 μg/kg/min and were adjusted to clinical endpoints or to TOF count. Infusion durations varied from 4 to 145 hours. Recovery of a TOF ratio >0.7 occurred within 34–85 minutes after drug discontinuation and was independent of organ function. These recovery times are similar to those seen with atracurium[18,21] and less than those observed with vecuronium.[15]

Doxacurium. Doxacurium, a long-acting benzylisoquinolinium agent, is the most potent NMBA currently available. Doxacurium is essentially free of hemodynamic adverse effects. Initial doses of doxacurium 0.05–0.1 mg/kg may be given with maintenance infusions of 0.3–0.5 μg/kg/min and adjusted to the degree of blockade desired. An initial bolus dose lasts an average of 60–80 minutes. Doxacurium is primarily eliminated by renal excretion. In elderly patients and patients with renal dysfunction, a significant prolongation of effect may occur.

Murray and colleagues[12] conducted a prospective, randomized, controlled, multicenter comparison of intermittent doses of doxacurium and pancuronium in 40 critically ill patients requiring neuromuscular blockade to optimize mechanical ventilation or to lower intracranial pressure (ICP). Patients were given another bolus dose based on TOF monitoring and were paralyzed for a mean duration of 2.6 days with doxacurium or 2.2 days with pancuronium. There was a clinically significant increase in heart rate after the initial bolus dose of pancuronium compared with baseline (120 ± 23 versus 109 ± 22 beats/min, respectively) without any differences after the initial dose of doxacurium (107 ± 21 versus 109 ± 21 beats/min, respectively). Once the drugs were discontinued, the pancuronium group had a more prolonged and variable recovery time (279 ± 229 min) than the doxacurium group (135 ± 46 min).

Mivacurium. Mivacurium is one of the shortest-acting NMBAs currently available. It consists of multiple stereoisomers and has a half-life of approximately two minutes, allowing for rapid reversal of the blockade. There are little data to support its use as a continuous infusion in the ICU.

Indications

NMBAs are indicated in a variety of situations (Table 4).[8,9,12–15,17–21,30,39,42] There have been no studies randomizing patients who are considered candidates for NMBAs to a placebo versus an NMBA. We therefore reviewed many studies comparing one NMBA to another to assess the clinical indications for enrolling patients in these studies. The most common indications for long-term administration of NMBAs included facilitation of mechanical ventilation, control of ICP, ablation of muscle spasms associated with tetanus, and decreasing oxygen consumption (Figure 2). NMBAs are often used to facilitate ventilation and ablate muscular activity in patients with elevated ICP or seizures but have no direct effect on either condition. Patients who are being treated for seizures who also take NMBAs should have electroencephalographic monitoring to ensure that they are not actively seizing while paralyzed.

With the exception of atracurium and cisatracurium, which need to be given continuously because of their short half-lives, bolus administration of NMBAs offers potential advantages for controlling tachyphylaxis; monitoring for accumulation, analgesia, and amnesia; and limiting complications related to prolonged or excessive blockade; and improving economics. However, in many ICUs, NMBAs are administered continuously, achieving adequate paralysis and faster recovery with TOF monitoring.

Facilitate Mechanical Ventilation. Numerous reports have described the use of NMBAs to facilitate mechanical ventilation. Most of the reports are limited to case studies, small prospective open-label trials, and small randomized open-label and double-blind trials enrolling a wide variety of critically ill patients to whom NMBAs were given to prevent respiratory dysynchrony, stop spontaneous respiratory efforts and muscle movement, improve gas exchange, and facilitate inverse ratio ventilation. However, none of these reports compared NMBAs to placebos.

Manage Increased ICP. The data supporting the use of NMBAs to control ICP are limited to a case report and an open-label trial. Prielipp[30] evaluated doxacurium use in eight patients with severe head injury in an open-label prospective study. NMBAs were given to facilitate ventilation or to manage brain injuries. Patients received an initial bolus injection of doxacurium 0.05 mg/kg followed by a continuous infusion of 0.25 μg/kg/min adjusted to maintain one twitch of the TOF. Doxacurium had no effect on ICP, heart rate, or blood pressure. Infusion rates were similar at the beginning (1 ± 0.1 mg/hr) and at the end (1.3 ± 0.2 mg/hr) of the study. TOF responses returned at 118 minutes; a TOF ratio of 0.7 was measured at 259 ± 24 minutes. No adverse events were reported.

McClelland, et al.[40] treated three patients with atracurium for four to six days to manage increased ICP. patients could undergo a neurologic examination within minutes after discontinuing atracurium. No adverse events were reported. There have been no controlled studies evaluating the role of NMBAs in the routine management of increased ICP.

Treat Muscle Spasms. Case studies describe the use of NMBAs in the treatment of muscle contractures associated with tetanus, drug overdoses, and seizures; many were published before 1994.

Anandaciva and Koay[41] administered a continuous rocuronium infusion to control muscle tone in patients with tetanus. Muscle spasms recurred at an infusion rate of 8 μg/kg/min, and neither administering a bolus dose of 0.9 mg/kg nor increasing the infusion rate to 10 μg/kg/min controlled the muscle contractures but did increase heart rate. Switching to a different NMBA could control the spasms.

Decrease Oxygen Consumption. Freebairn, et al.[42] evaluated the effects of vecuronium on oxygen delivery, oxygen consumption, oxygen extraction ratios, and gastric intramucosal pH in a randomized, placebo-controlled crossover trial in 18 critically ill patients with severe sepsis. Although the infusion of vecuronium achieved an adequate level of paralysis and improved respiratory compliance, it did not alter intramucosal pH, oxygen consumption, oxygen delivery, or oxygen extraction ratios.

Recommended Indications

There are no prospective, randomized, controlled trials assigning patients to an NMBA versus a placebo with a goal

Table 4.
Indications for the Long-Term Use of Neuromuscular Blocking Agents in Critically Ill Patients[a]

Indication	Agents (*n*)	Study Design	Underlying Diseases	Reference	Level of Evidence
Facilitate Mechanical Ventilation					
Facilitate management	Cisatracurium (40), atracurium (21)	Randomized, open-label	Hepatic failure, sepsis, cardiogenic shock, ARDS	20	2
Beneficial to management	Cisatracurium (12), atracurium (8)	Randomized, single-blind	Cardiac arrest, respiratory failure, postneurosurgery, trauma, multiorgan failure, asthma, cardiogenic shock	18	2
Facilitate management	Cisatracurium (6), atracurium (6)	Randomized, open-label	Multiple	19	2
Facilitate management	Cisatracurium (28), vecuronium (30)	Randomized, double-blind	Head trauma, intracranial hemorrhage, trauma, ARDS, sepsis, hepatic or renal failure, tetanus	15	2
Optimize mechanical ventilation, increase ICP	Doxacurium (19), pancuronium (21)	Prospective, randomized, double-blind	Not reported	12	2
Facilitate mechanical ventilation	Pipecuronium (30), pancuronium (30)	Prospective, open-label	Head injury, multiple trauma, sepsis, multiorgan failure	13	3
Facilitate mechanical ventilation; dose-finding pharmacokinetic study	Rocuronium (32)	Prospective, open-label	Respiratory failure, multiple trauma, blunt brain trauma	9	3
Facilitate mechanical ventilation; dose-finding pharmacokinetic study	Rocuronium (30)	Prospective, open-label	Multiple trauma and/or blunt brain trauma	8	3
Deterioration in gas exchange	Vecuronium and atracurium (1)	Case report	Respiratory failure in a kidney/pancreas transplant patient	39	5
Control ICP					
Facilitate mechanical ventilation and/or management of traumatic brain injury	Doxacurium (8)	Prospective, open-label	Severe head injury	30	3
Control ICP	Atracurium (4)	Case report	Severe head injury	40	5
Control Muscle Spasms					
Control tetanospasms	Rocuronium (1)	Case report	Tetanus	41	5
Decrease Oxygen Consumption					
Determine effect on oxygen delivery, consumption, and gastric intramucosal pH	Vecuronium (18)	Prospective, randomized, controlled, cross-over	Severe sepsis and septic shock	42	2

[a]ARDS = acute respiratory distress syndrome, ICP = intracranial pressure.

Figure 2. Use of neuromuscular blocking agents (NMBAs) in the ICU.

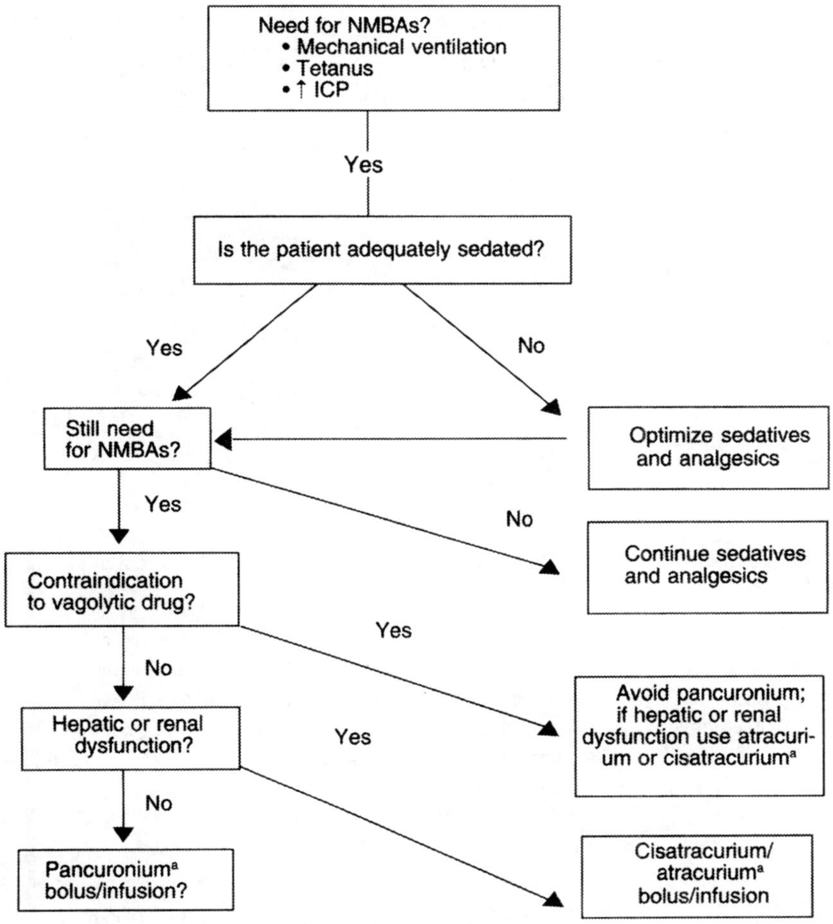

[a]Monitor train-of-four ratio, protect eyes, position patient to protect pressure points, and address deep venous thrombosis prophylaxis. Reassess every 12–24 hours for continued NMBA indication.

of documenting if such patients could be managed by means other than NMBA therapy.

> *Recommendation: NMBAs should be used for an adult patient in an ICU to manage ventilation, manage increased ICP, treat muscle spasms, and decrease oxygen consumption only when all other means have been tried without success. (Grade of recommendation = C)*

Recommended Drugs

There has, in essence, been no study since the last guidelines were published that questions the use of pancuronium for the majority of patients in an ICU. Those prospective, randomized, controlled trials (PRCTs) that have been conducted do not clearly show the benefits of using newer agents or any other agents instead of pancuronium.

There are no well-designed studies with sufficient power to make this a level A recommendation, but there is evidence in the literature that patients on pancuronium fare as well as or better than patients receiving any other NMBA.

The two adverse effects of pancuronium that are commented on frequently are vagolysis and an increase in heart rate. Therefore, patients who would not tolerate an increase in heart rate, i.e., those with cardiovascular disease, should probably receive an NMBA other than pancuronium. The indications for the use of an NMBA must outweigh the risk of tachycardia, and that is based on interpretation of the severity of the patient's underlying cardiovascular disease. For example, a patient with a history of atrial fibrillation now in sinus rhythm and otherwise hemodynamically stable might better tolerate pancuronium than a patient who is hospitalized with cardiogenic pulmonary edema and managed with mechanical ventilation. The clinician should choose an NMBA on the basis of other patient characteristics. Any benzylisoquinolinium compound or aminosteroidal compound could be substituted for pancuronium in these circumstances.

There are no ideal PRCTs that support this recommendation, but there are data suggesting that patients recover more quickly following administration of cisatracurium or atracurium compared with patients receiving other NMBAs if they have evidence of hepatic or renal disease.

> *Recommendations: The majority of patients in an ICU who are prescribed an NMBA can be managed effectively with pancuronium. (Grade of recommendation = B)*
>
> *For patients for whom vagolysis is contraindicated (e.g., those with cardiovascular disease), NMBAs other than pancuronium may be used. (Grade of recommendation = C)*
>
> *Because of their unique metabolism, cisatracurium or atracurium is recommended for patients with significant hepatic or renal disease. (Grade of recommendation = B)*

Monitoring

Monitoring neuromuscular blockade is recommended (Table 5).[12,14,43–55] Monitoring the depth of neuromuscular blockade may allow use of the lowest NMBA dose and may minimize adverse events. No PRCT has reported that reducing the dose of an NMBA can prevent persistent weakness. Despite this lack of evidence and the lack of a standardized method of monitoring, assessment of the depth of neuromuscular blockade in ICU patients is recommended.[43]

Visual, tactile, or electronic assessment of the patient's muscle tone or some combination of these three is commonly used to monitor the depth of neuromuscular blockade. Observation of skeletal muscle movement and respiratory effort forms the foundation of clinical assessment; electronic methods include the use of ventilator software allowing plethysmographic recording of pulmonary function to detect spontaneous ventilatory efforts and "twitch monitoring," i.e., the assessment of the muscular response by visual, tactile, or electronic means to a transcutaneous delivery of electric current meant to induce peripheral nerve stimulation (PNS).

Table 5.
Monitoring the Degree of Neuromuscular Blockade[a]

Monitoring Method	Study Design	Reference	Level of Evidence
TOF vs. clinical assessment to guide dosing	Prospective, randomized, single-blind	14	2
TOF vs. clinical assessment to compare depth of neuromuscular blockade	Prospective, nonrandomized	43	4
Complications with various monitoring methods	Retrospective, nonrandomized cohort	44	4
Use of TOF in comparing NMBAs	Multicenter, double-blind, PRCT	12	2
Methods of monitoring NMBAs	Editorial	45	6
Methods of monitoring NMBAs	Review	46	6
Comparison of common NMBAs/pharmacology	Review	25	6
Frequency of NMBA monitoring methods	Nonrandomized, historic, descriptive	47	4
Comparison of NMBA monitoring methods	Editorial	48	6
Comparison of NMBA monitoring methods	Expert opinion	49	6
Comparison of NMBA monitoring methods	Expert opinion	50	6
Technical aspects and problems in NMBA monitoring	Review	51	6
Technical problems with NMBAs monitoring	Review	52	6
Technical problems with NMBA monitoring	Review	53	5
Methods of assessing depth of NMBA	Prospective, randomized, blinded	54	2
Patient assessment during NMBA use	Review	55	6

[a]TOF = train-of-four, NMBA = neuromuscular blocking agent, PRCT = prospective, randomized, controlled trial.

Since the last practice guidelines were published, only two studies have examined the best method of monitoring the depth of neuromuscular blockade, and none have compared the efficacy or accuracy of specific techniques. The first study was a prospective, randomized, single-blinded trial of 77 patients in a medical ICU who were administered vecuronium based on either clinical parameters (patient breathed above the preset ventilatory rate) or TOF monitoring, with a goal of one of four twitches.[44] PNS resulted in a significantly lower total dose and lower mean infusion rate of NMBA as well as a faster time to recovery of neuromuscular function and spontaneous ventilation.

A second study sought to compare the depth of blockade induced by atracurium either by "best clinical assessment" (i.e., maintenance of patient-ventilator synchrony and prevention of patient movement) or TOF monitoring (with a goal of three of four twitches). Analysis of the 36 medical ICU patients in this prospective, nonrandomized trial revealed no difference in the total dose, mean dose, or the mean time to clinical recovery.[43] This may have been due to sample size or study design.

An additional study examining the results of the implementation of a protocol using PNS to monitor the level of blockade in patients receiving a variety of NMBAs found a reduction in the incidence of persistent neuromuscular weakness.[49]

Other methods of electronic monitoring of the depth of blockade are fraught with difficulties; TOF monitoring of PNS remains the easiest and most reliable method available,[43,44,46–50] despite its shortcomings and technical pitfalls.[51–53] Currently, there is no universal standard for twitch monitoring. The choice of the number of twitches necessary for "optimal" blockade is influenced by the patient's overall condition and level of sedation. The choice of the "best" nerve for monitoring may be influenced by site accessibility, risk of false positives, considerations for the effect of stimulation on patient visitors, and whether faint twitches should be included in the assessment of blockade.[54–56] Despite these gaps in research-generated knowledge, evidence-based practice appears to be influencing the increasing frequency with which PNS is utilized.[47] The low correlation of blockade measured peripherally compared with that of the phrenic nerve and diaphragm underscores the importance of three issues: (1) more than one method of monitoring should be utilized, (2) poor technique in using any device will invariably produce inaccurate results, and (3) more clinical studies are necessary to determine the best techniques.

Recommendations for Monitoring Degree of Blockade

Even though the patient may appear quiet and "comfortable," experienced clinicians understand the indications and therapeutic limits of NMBAs. Despite multiple admonitions that NMBAs have no analgesic or amnestic effects, it is not uncommon to find a patient's degree of sedation or comfort significantly overestimated or even ignored. It is difficult to assess pain and sedation in the patient receiving NMBAs, but patients must be medicated for pain and anxiety, despite the lack of obvious symptoms or signs. In common practice, sedative and analgesic drugs are adjusted until the patient does not appear to be conscious and then NMBAs are administered. There have been no studies of the use of electrophysiologic monitoring in assessing adequacy of sedation or analgesia.

In a phenomenological study of 11 critically ill adult trauma patients who required therapeutic NMBA, patients compared their feelings of vagueness to dreaming.[56] Few patients recalled pain or painful procedures. Family members understood the rationale for the use of the drugs and remembered being encouraged to touch and talk with patients. The use of effective pain and sedation protocols and a liberalized visiting policy may have affected the findings.

Recommendations: Patients receiving NMBAs should be assessed both clinically and by TOF monitoring (Grade of recommendation = B), with a goal of adjusting the degree of neuromuscular blockade to achieve one or two twitches. (Grade of recommendation = C)

Before initiating neuromuscular blockade, patients should be medicated with sedative and analgesic drugs to provide adequate sedation and analgesia in accordance with the physician's clinical judgment to optimize therapy. (Grade of recommendation = C)

Complications

Skeletal muscle weakness in ICU patients is multifactorial, producing a confusing list of names and syndromes, including acute quadriplegic myopathy syndrome (AQMS), floppy man syndrome, critical illness polyneuropathy (CIP), acute myopathy of intensive care, rapidly evolving myopathy, acute myopathy with selective lysis of myosin filaments, acute steroid myopathy, and prolonged neurogenic weakness (Table 6).[57,58]

There are probably two adverse events related to prolonged paralysis following discontinuation of NMBAs. We define the first, "prolonged recovery from NMBAs," as an increase (after cessation of NMBA therapy) in the time to recovery of 50–100% longer than predicted by pharmacologic parameters. This is primarily due to the accumulation of NMBAs or metabolites. By comparison, the second, AQMS, presents with a clinical triad of acute paresis, myonecrosis with increased creatine phosphokinase (CPK) concentration, and abnormal electromyography (EMG). The latter is characterized by severely reduced compound motor action potential (CMAP) amplitudes and evidence of acute denervation. In the beginning, these syndromes are characterized by neuronal dysfunction; later (days or weeks), muscle atrophy and necrosis may develop.[59]

Prolonged Recovery from NMBAs. The steroid-based NMBAs are associated with reports of prolonged recovery and myopathy.[57,60] This association may reflect an increased risk inferred by these NMBAs or may reflect past practice patterns in which these drugs may have been more commonly used.[61] Steroid-based NMBAs undergo extensive hepatic metabolism, producing active drug metabolites. For instance, vecuronium produces three metabolites: 3-des-, 17-des-, and 3,17-desacetyl vecuronium.[62] The 3-desacetyl metabolite is estimated to be 80% as potent as the parent compound. The 3-desacetyl vecuronium metabolite is poorly dialyzed, minimally ultrafiltrated, and accumulates in patients with renal failure because hepatic elimination is decreased in patients with uremia. Thus, the accumulation of both 3–desacetyl vecuronium and its parent compound, vecuronium, in patients with renal failure contributes to a prolonged recovery by this ICU subpopulation. Other explanations have been proposed. One suggests that the basement membrane of the neuromuscular junction acts as a reservoir of NMBAs, maintaining NMBAs at the nAChRs long after the drug has disappeared from the plasma.[63]

Drug–drug interactions that potentiate the depth of motor blockade (Table 7) may also prolong recovery. The specific interaction of NMBAs and exogenous corticosteroids is discussed later.[57,62–65]

Physiologic changes of the nAChRs are enhanced when patients are immobilized or denervated secondary to spinal cord injury, and perhaps during prolonged NMBA drug-induced paralysis. The nAChRs may be triggered to revert to a fetal–variant structure (Figure 3), characterized by an increase in total number, frequent extrajunctional proliferation, and resistance to nondepolarizing NMBAs. The proliferation and distribution of these altered receptors across the myomembrane may account for tachyphylaxis and the neuromuscular blocking effects of these drugs.

AQMS. AQMS, also referred to as postparalytic quadriparesis, is one of the most devastating complications of NMBA therapy and one of the reasons that indiscriminate use of NMBAs is discouraged (Table 8).[65,66] This entity must be differentiated from other neuromuscular pathologies (Table 6) seen in an ICU and requires extensive testing. Reports of AQMS in patients receiving NMBAs alone are quite limited; no experimental model has been able to produce the histopathology of this syndrome by administering NMBAs. Afflicted patients demonstrate diffuse weakness that persists long after the NMBA is discontinued and the drug and its active metabolites are eliminated. Neurologic examination reveals a global motor deficit affecting muscles in both the upper and lower extremities and decreased motor reflexes. However, extraocular muscle function is usually preserved. This myopathy is characterized by low-amplitude CMAPs, and muscle fibrillations but normal (or nearly normal) sensory nerve conduction studies.[63,67] Muscle biopsy shows prominent vacuolization of muscle fibers without inflammatory infiltrate, patchy type 2 muscle fiber atrophy, and sporadic myofiber necrosis.[64] Modest CPK increases (0 to 15-fold above normal range) are noted in approximately 50% of patients and are probably dependent on the timing of enzyme measurements and the initiation of the myopathic process. Thus, there may be some justification in screening patients with serial CPK determinations during infusion of NMBAs, particularly if the patients are concurrently treated with corticosteroids. Also, since AQMS develops after prolonged exposure to NMBAs, there may be some rationale to daily "drug holidays" (i.e., stopping the drugs for a few to several hours and restarting them only when necessary). However, no one has demonstrated that drug holidays decrease the frequency of AQMS. Other factors that may contribute to the development of the syndrome include nutritional deficiencies, concurrent drug administration with aminoglycosides or cyclosporine, hyperglycemia, renal and hepatic dysfunction, fever, and severe metabolic or electrolyte disorders.

Evidence supports, but occasionally refutes,[14] the association of concurrent administration of NMBAs and cor-

Table 6.
Weakness in ICU Patients: Etiologies and Syndromes[a]

1. Prolonged recovery from NMBAs (secondary to parent drug, drug metabolite, or drug–drug interaction)
2. Myasthenia gravis
3. Lambert-Eaton syndrome
4. Muscular dystrophy
5. Guillain-Barré syndrome
6. Central nervous system injury or lesion
7. Spinal cord injury
8. Steroid myopathy
9. Mitochondrial myopathy
10. HIV-related myopathy
11. Acute myopathy of intensive care
12. Disuse atrophy
13. Critical illness polyneuropathy
14. Severe electrolyte toxicity (e.g., hypermagnesemia)
15. Severe electrolyte deficiency (e.g., hypophosphatemia)

[a]ICU = intensive care unit, NMBAs = neuromuscular blocking agents, HIV = human immunodeficiency virus.

Table 7.
Drug–Drug Interactions of Neuromuscular Blocking Agents (NMBAs)

Drugs that Potentiate the Action of Nondepolarizing NMBAs	Drugs that Antagonize the Actions of Nondepolarizing NMBAs
Local anesthetics	Phenytoin
Lidocaine	Carbamazepine
Antimicrobials (aminoglycosides, polymyxin B, clindamycin, tetracycline)	Theophylline
Antiarrhythmics (procainamide, quinidine)	Ranitidine
Magnesium	
Calcium channel blockers	
β-Adrenergic blockers	
Immunosuppresive agents (cyclophosphamide, cyclosporine)	
Dantrolene	
Diuretics	
Lithium carbonate	

Figure 3. Acetylcholine Receptor. The mature nicotinic acetylcholine receptor (AChR) (left) with its glycoprotein subunits arranged around the central cation core. Two molecules of acetylcholine bind simultaneously to the two alpha subunits to convert the channel to an open state. The immature, or fetal-variant, receptor is shown on the right, with a single subunit substitution which follows major stress such as burns or denervation. These immature receptors are characterized by 10-fold greater ionic activity, rapid metabolic turnover, and extrajunctional proliferation. (Reprinted, with permission, from Martyn JAJ, White DA, Gronert GA, et al. Up-and-down regulation of skeletal muscle acetylcholine receptors. *Anesthesiology.* 1992; 76:825.)

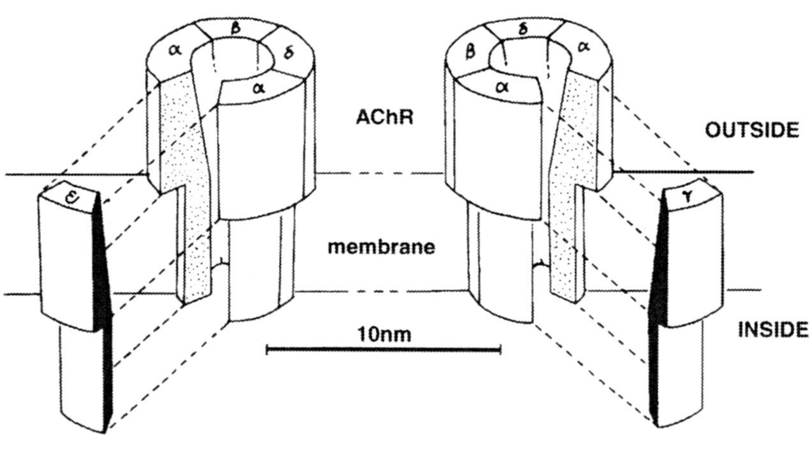

ticosteroids with AQMS.[59,63,68,69] The incidence of myopathy may be as high as 30% in patients who receive corticosteroids and NMBAs. While no period of paralysis is risk free, NMBA administration beyond one or two days increases the risk of myopathy in this setting.[63] Similarly, there is an inconsistent correlation with the dose of corticosteroids, but total doses in excess of 1 g of methylprednisolone (or equivalent) probably increase the risk. Afflicted patients manifest an acute, diffuse, flaccid weakness and an inability to wean from mechanical ventilation. Sensory function is generally preserved.[63] Muscle biopsy shows extensive type 2 fiber atrophy, myonecrosis, disarray of sarcomere architecture, and an extensive, selective loss of myosin. Experimental evidence in animals shows that denervation for ≥24 hours induces profound negative nitrogen balance and increases expression of steroid receptors in muscle. Such denervation sensitizes muscle to even normal corticosteroid concentrations, and evidence suggests that the combination of denervation and high-dose corticosteroids precipitates myosinolysis.

Acute myopathy in ICU patients is also reported after administration of the benzylisoquinolinium NMBAs (i.e., atracurium, cisatracurium, doxacurium).[24,34,69] Common to all these reports is the coadministration of benzyliso-quinolinium NMBAs and large doses of corticosteroids, aminoglycosides, or other drugs that affect neuromuscular transmission.

Recommendations: For patients receiving NMBAs and corticosteroids, every effort should be made to discontinue NMBAs as soon as possible. (Grade of recommendation = C)

Drug holidays (i.e., stopping NMBAs daily until forced to restart them based on the patient's condition) may decrease the incidence of AQMS. (Grade of recommendation = C)

Other nerve and muscle disorders have been recognized in the last decade in ICU patients (Table 6). For instance, CIP is a sensory and motor polyneuropathy identified in elderly, septic patients or those with MODS.[58,66,70] EMG testing reveals decreased CMAP, fibrillation potentials, and positive sharp waves.[60,63,64] CIP is primarily an axonopathy and may be related to microvascular ischemia of the nerve but is not directly related to the use of NMBAs. Recovery from ICU myopathy requires a protracted (weeks or months) hospitalization. One economic analysis of 10 patients who developed AQMS showed the median additional hospital charge to be $66,000 per patient.[65] As for any critically ill patient, particularly immobilized patients, deep venous thrombosis (DVT) prophylaxis and physical therapy to maintain joint mobility are important.

Patients receiving NMBAs are also at risk of developing keratitis and corneal abrasion. Prophylactic eye care is highly variable and recommendations may include methylcellulose drops, ophthalmic ointment, taping the eyelids shut to ensure complete closure, or eye patches. In a study of 69 paralyzed or heavily sedated patients by Lenart and Garrity,[71] there was strong evidence that the use of an artificial tear ointment prevented corneal exposure. In this randomized study, patients served as their own controls.

Myositis Ossificans (Heterotopic Ossification). Myositis ossificans can develop in patients who are paralyzed for long periods of time, but inflammation is not characteristic of the ailment. The name is misleading be cause the process involves connective tissue (not muscle). The name originates from the ossification that occurs within the connective tissue of muscle but may also be seen in ligaments, tendons, fascia, aponeuroses,

Table 8.
Potential Complications of Neuromuscular Blockade Use in the ICU[a]

Complications and Contraindications of Succinylcholine in the ICU	General Complications Associated with NMBAs in the ICU
Loss of airway	Awake, paralyzed patient–anxiety and panic
Hyperkalemia	Risk of ventilator disconnect or airway mishap
Plasma pseudocholinesterase deficiency	Autonomic and cardiovascular effects (i.e., vagolytic)
	Decreased lymphatic flow
	Risk of generalized deconditioning
	Skin breakdown
	Peripheral nerve injury
	Corneal abrasion, conjunctivitis
	Myositis ossificans
	Risk of prolonged muscle weakness, AQMS
	Potential central nervous system toxicity

[a]NMBA = neuromuscular blocking agent, AQMS = acute quadriplegic myopathy syndrome.

and joint capsules. The acquired form of the disease may occur at any age in either sex, especially around the elbows, thighs, and buttocks. The basic defect is the inappropriate differentiation of fibroblasts into osteoblasts and is usually triggered by trauma and muscle injury, paraplegia or quadriplegia, tetanus, and burns. Treatment consists of promoting an active range of motion around the affected joint and surgery when necessary.

Tachyphylaxis. For reasons mentioned earlier, tachyphylaxis to NMBAs can and does develop.

Coursin and colleagues[31] administered doxacurium to four patients who developed tolerance to atracurium infusions (range, 16 to 40 μg/kg/min). Patients were successfully blocked with infusion rates of doxacurium 0.25–0.75 μg/kg/min.

Tschida, et al.[72] described a patient whose atracurium requirement escalated from 5 to 30 μg/kg/min over 10 days. The patient was successfully blocked with a pancuronium infusion of 10–50 μg/kg/min for a period of five days.

Fish and Singletary[33] describe a patient who was inadequately blocked with a 60-μg/kg/min infusion of atracurium but adequately paralyzed for seven days with 2.3-mg/kg/hr infusion of vecuronium. Tachyphylaxis then developed to vecuronium which prompted discontinuation of NMBAs. Two days later, 50–μg/kg/min atracurium infusions were required with high-dose midazolam and fentanyl infusions to achieve adequate oxygenation and acceptable airway pressures.

Recommendations: Patients receiving NMBAs should have prophylactic eye care (Grade of recommendation = B), physical therapy (Grade of recommendation = C), and DVT prophylaxis. (Grade of recommendation = C)

Patients who develop tachyphylaxis to one NMBA should try another drug if neuromuscular blockade is still required. (Grade of recommendation = C)

Economics

There have been few formal pharmacoeconomic evaluations of NMBAs. In one of these economic evaluations, medication-related cost savings were found when voluntary prescribing guidelines for NMBAs were initiated in the operating room of a university hospital.[73] In another study that involved randomization to one of three NMBAs, there were no significant cost differences between atracurium, vecuronium, and rocuronium for surgeries lasting two hours or less, but vecuronium and rocuronium were economically advantageous if the duration of surgery was two to four hours.[74] In a third retrospective study, long-acting NMBAs (e.g., D-tubocurarine and pancuronium) were associated with prolonged postoperative recovery compared with shorter-acting agents (e.g., atracurium, mivacurium, and vecuronium). The authors noted in the discussion section of the paper that based on intrainstitutional recovery room costs, delays in recovery times seen with the longer-acting agents offset the expected savings in drug costs.[75] For patients transferred to the ICU, this may not be a major problem.

Two pharmacoeconomic investigations involving NMBAs in the ICU evaluated the costs associated with prolonged recovery following discontinuation of nondepolarizing NMBAs. In one study, overall costs were lower when TOF monitoring was employed.[76] In another study, patients who had prolonged motor weakness after discontinuing NMBAs were compared with a control group[77]; ICU and hospital costs were substantially higher in the patients with prolonged weakness.

A study involving 40 academic medical centers with patients undergoing coronary artery bypass graft surgery found no significant differences in duration of intubation or duration of ICU or hospital stay among patients who received pancuronium (n = 732), vecuronium (n = 130), or both (n = 242) agents.[78] It is unknown if these results pertain to subgroups of patients, such as those with renal or hepatic dysfunction. If the results of this study are confirmed, the choice of agent could be based solely on cost minimization using medication purchase cost information and equipotent dosage regimens.

A prospective, randomized trial comparing TOF to standard clinical assessment showed decreased NMBA usage and faster return of spontaneous ventilation with TOF monitoring.[14] TOF has the potential to decrease costs associated with NMBA use in ICUs.

Appendix B describes the basic steps involved in conducting a cost-effectiveness analysis of the NMBAs. Consequently, intrainstitutional data and assumptions can be used to perform the analysis along with local value judgments involved in selecting the appropriate agent(s).

Recommendations: Institutions should perform an economic analysis using their own data when choosing NMBAs for use in an ICU. (Grade of recommendation = C)

References

1. Society of Critical Care Medicine and American Society of Health–System Pharmacists. Sedation, analgesia, and neuromuscular blockade of the critically ill adult: revised clinical practice guidelines for 2002. *Am J Health-Syst Pharm.* 2002; 59:147–9.
2. Coakley JH, Nagendran K, Yarwood GD, et al. Patterns of neurophysiological abnormality in prolonged critical illness. *Intensive Care Med.* 1998; 24:801–7.
3. Prielipp RC, Coursin DB. Applied pharmacology of common neuromuscular blocking agents in critical care. *New Horizons.* 1994; 2:34–47.
4. De Lemos JM, Carr RR, Shalansky KF, et al. Paralysis in the critically ill: intermittent bolus pancuronium compared with continuous infusion. *Crit Care Med.* 1999; 27:2648–55.
5. Tobias JD, Lynch A, McDuffee A, et al. Pancuronium infusion for neuromuscular block in children in the pediatric intensive care unit. *Anesth Analg.* 1995; 81:13–6.
6. Segredo V, Caldwell JE, Wright PM, et al. Do the pharmacokinetics of vecuronium change during prolonged administration in critically ill patients? *Br J Anaesth.* 1998; 80:715–9.
7. Appadu BL, Greiff JM, Thompson JP. Postal survey on the long–term use of neuromuscular block in the intensive care unit. *Intensive Care Med.* 1996; 22:862–6.
8. Khuenl-Brady KS, Sparr H, Pühringer F, et al. Rocuronium bromide in the ICU: dose finding and pharmacokinetics. *Eur J Anaesthesiol Suppl.* 1995; 11:79–80.
9. Sparr HJ, Wierda JMKH, Proost JH, et al. Pharmacodynamics and pharmacokinetics of rocuronium in intensive care patients. *Br J Anaesth.* 1997; 78:267–73.
10. McEwin L, Merrick PM, Bevan DR. Residual neuromuscular blockade after cardiac surgery: pancuronium vs rocuronium. *Can J Anaesth.* 1997; 44:891–5.
11. Stene J, Murray M, de Ruyter M, et al. Selective rocuronium pharmacodynamics and kinetics during ICU infusion. *Anesthesiology.* 1998; 89:A477. Abstract.
12. Murray MJ, Coursin DB, Scuderi PE, et al. Double-blind, randomized, multicenter study of doxacurium vs. pancuronium in intensive care unit patients who require neuromuscular–blocking agents. *Crit Care Med.* 1995; 23:450–8.
13. Khuenl-Brady KS, Reitstatter B, Schlager A, et al. Long-term administration of pancuronium and pipecuronium in the intensive care unit. *Anesth Analg.* 1994; 78:1082–6.
14. Rudis MI, Sikora CP, Angus E, et al. A prospective, randomized, controlled evaluation of peripheral nerve stimulation versus standard clinical dosing of neuromuscular blocking agents in critically ill patients. *Crit Care Med.* 1997; 25:575–83.
15. Prielipp RC, Coursin DB, Scuderi PB, et al. Comparison of the infusion requirements and recovery profiles of vecuronium and cisatracurium 51W89 in intensive care unit patients. *Anesth Analg.* 1995; 81:3–12.
16. Hull CJ. Pharmacokinetics and pharmacodynamics of the benzylisoquinolinium muscle relaxants. *Acta Anaesthesiol Scand Suppl.* 1995; 106:13–7.
17. De Wolf AM, Freeman JA, Scott VL, et al. Pharmacokinetics and pharmacodynamics of cisatracurium in patients with end-stage liver disease undergoing liver transplantation. *Br J Anaesth.* 1996; 76:624–8.
18. Pearson AJ, Harper NJ, Pollard BJ. The infusion requirements and recovery characteristics of cisatracurium or atracurium in intensive care patients. *Intensive Care Med.* 1996; 22:694–8.
19. Boyd AH, Eastwood NB, Parker CJ, et al. Comparison of the pharmacodynamics and pharmacokinetics of an infusion of cisatracurium (51W89) or atracurium in critically ill patients undergoing mechanical ventilation in an intensive therapy unit. *Br J Anaesth.* 1996; 76:382–8.
20. Newman PJ, Quinn AC, Grounds RM, et al. A comparison of cisatracurium (51W89) and atracurium by infusion in critically ill patients. *Crit Care Med.* 1997; 25:1139–42.
21. Schramm WM, Papousek A, Michalek-Sauberer A, et al. The cerebral and cardiovascular effects of cisatracurium and atracurium in neurosurgical patients. *Anesth Analg.* 1998; 86:123–7.
22. Schramm WM, Jesenko R, Bartuneka A, et al. Effects of cisatracurium on cerebral and cardiovascular hemodynamics in patients with severe brain injury. *Acta Anaesthesiol Scand.* 1997; 41:1319–23.
23. Grigore AM, Brusco LJr, Kuroda M, et al. Laudanosine and atracurium concentrations in a patient receiving long-term atracurium infusion. *Crit Care Med.* 1998; 26:180–3.
24. Davis NA, Rodgers JE, Gonzalez ER, et al. Prolonged weakness after cisatracurium infusion: a case report. *Crit Care Med.* 1998; 26:1290–2.
25. Reeves ST, Turcasso NM. Nondepolarizing neuromuscular blocking drugs in the intensive care unit: a clinical review. *South Med J.* 1997; 90:769–74.
26. Miller RD. Use of neuromuscular blocking drugs in intensive care unit patients. *Anesth Analg.* 1995; 81:1–2.
27. Bion J, Prielipp RC, Bihari D, et al. Cisatracurium in intensive care. *Curr Opin Anesthesiol.* 1996; 9:S47–51.
28. Werba A, Schultz AM, Hetz H, et al. Benzylisochinoline muscle relaxants in clinical practice. *Acta Anaesthesiol Scan Suppl.* 1997; 111:109–10.
29. Marik PE, Kaufman D. The effects of neuromuscular paralysis on systemic and splanchnic oxygen utilization in mechanically ventilated patients. *Chest.* 1996; 109:1038–42.
30. Prielipp RC, Robinson JC, Wilson JA, et al. Dose response, recovery, and cost of doxacurium as a continuous infusion in neurosurgical intensive care unit patients. *Crit Care Med.* 1997; 25:1236–41.
31. Coursin DB, Meyer DA, Prielipp RC. Doxacurium infusion in critically ill patients with atracurium tachyphylaxis. *Am J Health Syst-Pharm.* 1995; 52:635–9.
32. Manthous CA, Chatila W. Atracurium and status epilepticus. *Crit Care Med.* 1995; 23:1440–2.
33. Fish DN, Singletary TJ. Cross-resistance to both atracurium- and vecuronium-induced neuromuscular blockade in a critically ill patient. *Pharmacotherapy.* 1997; 17:1322–7.
34. Meyer KC, Prielipp RC, Grossman JE, et al. Prolonged weakness after infusion of atracurium in two intensive care unit patients. *Anesth Analg.* 1994; 78:772–4.
35. Manthous CA, Chatila W. Prolonged weakness after the withdrawal of atracurium. *Am J Resp Crit Care Med.* 1994; 150:1441–3.

36. Branney SW, Haenal JB, Moore FA, et al. Prolonged paralysis with atracurium infusion: a case report. *Crit Care Med.* 1994; 22:1699–701.
37. Rubjo ER, Seelig CB. Persistent paralysis after prolonged use of atracurium in the absence of corticosteroids. *South Med J.* 1996; 89:624–6.
38. Hoey LL, Joslin SM, Nahum A, et al. Prolonged neuromuscular blockade in two critically ill patients treated with atracurium. *Pharmacotherapy.* 1995; 15:254–9.
39. Prielipp RC, Jackson MJ, Coursin DB. Comparison of neuromuscular recovery after paralysis with atracurium versus vecuronium in an ICU patient with renal insufficiency. *Anesth Analg.* 1994; 78:775–8.
40. McClelland M, Woster P, Sweasey T, et al. Continuous midazolam/atracurium infusions for the management of increased intracranial pressure. *J Neurosci Nurs.* 1995; 27:96–101.
41. Anandaciva S, Koay CW. Tetanus and rocuronium in the intensive care unit. *Anaesthesia.* 1996; 51:505–6.
42. Freebairn RC, Derrick J, Gomersall CD, et al. Oxygen delivery, oxygen consumption, and gastric intramucosal pH are not improved by a computer-controlled, closed-loop, vecuronium infusion in severe sepsis. *Crit Care Med.* 1997; 25:72–7.
43. Strange C, Vaughan L, Franklin C, et al. Comparison of train–of–four and best clinical assessment during continuous paralysis. *Am J Resp Crit Care Med.* 1997; 156:1556–61.
44. Frankel H, Jeng J, Tilly E, et al. The impact of implementation of neuromuscular blockade monitoring standards in a surgical intensive care unit. *Am Surg.* 1996; 62:503–6.
45. Sladen RN. Neuromuscular blocking agents in the intensive care unit: a two-edged sword. *Crit Care Med.* 1995; 23:423–8.
46. Ford EV. Monitoring neuromuscular blockade in the adult ICU. *Am J Crit Care.* 1995; 4:122–30.
47. Kleinpell R, Bedrosian C, McCormick L. Use of peripheral nerve stimulators to monitor patients with neuromuscular blockade in the ICU. *Am J Crit Care.* 1996; 5:449–54.
48. Murray MJ. Monitoring of peripheral nerve stimulation versus standard clinical assessment for dosing of neuromuscular blocking agents. *Crit Care Med.* 1997; 25:561–2.
49. Tavernier B, Rannou JJ, Vallet B. Peripheral nerve stimulation and clinical assessment for dosing of neuromuscular blocking agents in critically ill patients. *Crit Care Med.* 1998; 26:804–5.
50. Barnette RE, Fish DJ. Monitoring neuromuscular blockade in the critically ill. *Crit Care Med.* 1995; 23:1790–1.
51. Rudis M, Guslits B, Zarowitz B. Technical and interpretative problems of peripheral nerve stimulation in monitoring neuromuscular blockade in the intensive care unit. *Ann Pharmacother.* 1996; 30:165–72.
52. Tschida SJ, Loey LL, Bryan KV. Inconsistency with train-of-four monitoring in a critically ill paralyzed patient. *Pharmacotherapy.* 1995; 15:540–5.
53. Tschida SJ, Loey LL, Mather D. Train-of-four: to use or not to use. *Pharmacotherapy.* 1995; 15:546–50.
54. Martin R, Bourdua I, Theriault S, et al. Neuromuscular monitoring: does it make a difference? *Can J Anesth.* 1996; 43:585–8.
55. Luer JM. Sedation and chemical relaxation in critical pulmonary illness: suggestions for patient assessment and drug monitoring. *AACN Clin Issues.* 1995; 6:333–43.
56. Johnson KL, Cheung RB, Johnson SB, et al. Therapeutic paralysis of critically ill trauma patients: perceptions of patients and their family members. *Am J Crit Care.* 1999; 8:490–8.
57. Watling SM, Dasta JF. Prolonged paralysis in intensive care unit patients after the use of neuromuscular blocking agents: a review of the literature. *Crit Care Med.* 1994; 22:884–93.
58. Nates J, Cooper D, Day B, et al. Acute weakness syndromes in critically ill patients—a reappraisal. *Anaesth Intensive Care.* 1997; 25:502–13.
59. Road J, Mackie G, Jiang T, et al. Reversible paralysis with status asthmaticus, steroids, and pancuronium: clinical electrophysiological correlates. *Muscle Nerve.* 1997; 20:1587–90.
60. Lacomis D, Giuliani MJ, Van Cott A, et al. Acute myopathy of intensive care: clinical, electromyographic, and pathological aspects. *Ann Neurol.* 1996; 40:645–54.
61. Elliot J, Bion J. The use of neuromuscular blocking drugs in intensive care practice. *Acta Anaesthesiol Scand Suppl.* 1995; 106:70–82.
62. Leatherman J, Fluegel W, David W, et al. Muscle weakness in mechanically ventilated patients with severe asthma. *Am J Resp Crit Care Med.* 1996; 153:1686–90.
63. David W, Roehr C, Leatherman J. EMG findings in acute myopathy with status asthmaticus, steroids and paralytics: clinical and electrophysiologic correlation. *Electromyogr Clin Neurophysiol.* 1998; 38:371–6.
64. Faragher MW, Day BJ, Dennett X. Critical care myopathy: an electrophysiological and histological study. *Muscle Nerve.* 1996; 19:516–8.
65. Latronico N, Fenzi F, Recupero D, et al. Critical illness myopathy and neuropathy. *Lancet.* 1996; 347:1579–82.
66. Bolton CF. Muscle weakness and difficulty in weaning from the ventilator in the critical care unit. *Chest.* 1994; 106:1–2.
67. Barohn RJ, Jackson CE, Rogers SJ, et al. Prolonged paralysis due to nondepolarizing neuromuscular blocking agents and corticosteroids. *Muscle Nerve.* 1994; 17:647–54.
68. Zochodne DW, Ramsay DA, Shelley S. Acute necrotizing myopathy of intensive care: electrophysiologic studies. *Muscle Nerve.* 1994; 17:285–92.
69. Marik PE. Doxacurium-corticosteroid acute myopathy: another piece to the puzzle. *Crit Care Med.* 1996; 24:1266–7.
70. Hund E, Fogel W, Krieger D, et al. Critical illness polyneuropathy: clinical findings and outcomes of a frequent cause of neuromuscular weaning failure. *Crit Care Med.* 1996; 24:1328–33.
71. Lenart SG, Garrity J. Eye care for the mechanically ventilated patient receiving neuromuscular blockade or propofol. *Mayo Clin Proc.* In press.
72. Tschida SJ, Hoey LL, Nahum A, et al. Atracurium resistance in a critically ill patient. *Pharmacotherapy.* 1995; 15:533–9.
73. Gora-Harper ML, Hessel E, Shadick D. Effect of prescribing guidelines on the use of neuromuscular blocking agents. *Am J Health-Syst Pharm.* 1995; 52:1900–4.

74. Loughlin KA, Weingarten CM, Nagelhout J, et al. A pharmacoeconomic analysis of neuromuscular blocking agents in the operating room. *Pharmacotherapy.* 1996; 16:942–50.
75. Ballantyne JC, Chang Y. The impact of choice of muscle relaxant on postoperative recovery time: a retrospective study. *Anesth Analg.* 1997; 85:476–82.
76. Zarowitz BJ, Rudis MI, Lai K, et al. Retrospective pharmacoeconomic evaluation of dosing vecuronium by peripheral nerve stimulation versus standard clinical assessment in critically ill patients. *Pharmacotherapy.* 1997; 17:327–32.
77. Rudis MI, Guslits BJ, Peterson EL, et al. Economic impact of prolonged motor weakness complicating neuromuscular blockade in the intensive care unit. *Crit Care Med.* 1996; 24:1749–56.
78. Butterworth J, James R, Prielipp RC, et al. Do shorter-acting neuromuscular blocking drugs or opioids associate with reduced intensive care unit or hospital length of stay after coronary artery bypass grafting? *Anesthesiology.* 1998; 88:1437–46.

Appendix A—Summary of Recommendations

1. NMBAs should be used for an adult patient in an ICU to manage ventilation, manage increased ICP, treat muscle spasms, and decrease oxygen consumption only when all other means have been tried without success.[1] (Grade of recommendation = C)
2. The majority of patients in an ICU who are prescribed an NMBA can be managed effectively with pancuronium. (Grade of recommendation = B)
3. For patients for whom vagolysis is contraindicated (e.g., those with cardiovascular disease), NMBAs other than pancuronium may be used. (Grade of recommendation = C)
4. Because of their unique metabolism, cisatracurium or atracurium is recommended for patients with significant hepatic or renal disease. (Grade of recommendation = B)
5. Patients receiving NMBAs should be assessed both clinically and by TOF monitoring (Grade of recommendation = B), with a goal of adjusting the degree of neuromuscular blockade to achieve one or two twitches. (Grade of recommendation = C)
6. Before initiating neuromuscular blockade, patients should be medicated with sedative and analgesic drugs to provide adequate sedation and analgesia in accordance with the physician's clinical judgment to optimize therapy. (Grade of recommendation = C)
7. For patients receiving NMBAs and corticosteroids, every effort should be made to discontinue NMBAs as soon as possible. (Grade of recommendation = C)
8. Drug holidays (i.e., stopping NMBAs daily until forced to restart them based on the patient's condition) may decrease the incidence of AQMS. (Grade of recommendation = C)
9. Patients receiving NMBAs should have prophylactic eye care (Grade of recommendation = B), physical therapy (Grade of recommendation = C), and DVT prophylaxis. (Grade of recommendation = C)
10. Patients who develop tachyphylaxis to one NMBA should try another drug if neuromuscular blockade is still required. (Grade of recommendation = C)
11. Institutions should perform an economic analysis using their own data when choosing NMBAs for use in an ICU. (Grade of recommendation = C)

Appendix B—Determination of Cost Effectiveness Using Intrainstitutional Data[a]

1. For each adverse effect (e.g., prolonged recovery) of any given neuromuscular blocking agent (NMBA), add all associated costs together and multiply this figure by the probability of the occurrence of the adverse effect. If adverse effects A, B, and C are associated with an NMBA, then

   (Drug cost + cost A1) (probability of occurrence expressed as a decimal) = $U

   (Drug cost + cost B1) (probability of occurrence expressed as a decimal) = $V

   (Drug cost + cost C1) (probability of occurrence expressed as a decimal) = $W

2. Calculate the product of the drug cost multiplied by the probability of occurrence of no adverse effects expressed as a decimal; add this product to the cost multiplied by the probability factor for each adverse effect calculated in step 1.

   (Drug cost) (probability of occurrence of no adverse effects) + $U + $V + $W = average cost of all pathways for agent

   Note: The probabilities of all adverse effects plus the probability of no adverse effects associated with the NMBA must add up to 1.

3. Determine the cost effectiveness of the agent by dividing the total costs associated with the agent by the probability of occurrence of no adverse effects expressed as a decimal.

   Example using pancuronium:

   a. [$224 (drug cost for 4 days of therapy) + $1000 (estimated cost of 1 extra day of ICU stay due to prolonged paralysis resulting from renal dysfunction)] [0.07 (estimated probability of renal dysfunction)] = $85.68 [$224 (drug cost for 4 days of therapy) + $1000 (estimated cost of 1 extra day of ICU (intensive care unit) stay due to prolonged paralysis resulting from hepatic dysfunction)] [0.04 (estimated probability of hepatic dysfunction)] = $48.96
   b. [$224 (drug cost for 4 days of therapy, assuming no adverse effects) × 0.89 (estimated probability of no adverse effects)] + $85.68 + $48.96 = $334.00
   c. Cost effectiveness of pancuronium = 334.00/0.89 (probability of no adverse effects) = $375.28

[a]Note that the term "adverse effects" includes problems such as prolonged paralysis resulting from decreased medication elimination due to impaired organ function. If a neuromuscular blocking agent is eliminated by more than one organ (e.g., kidney and liver), prolonged paralysis may result from impaired elimination due to a combination of organ problems. For example, one adverse effect may be prolonged paralysis associated with renal dysfunction, while another adverse effect may be prolonged paralysis associated with hepatic dysfunction, while a third adverse effect may be prolonged paralysis associated with combined renal and hepatic dysfunction.

Developed through the Task Force of the American College of Critical Care Medicine (ACCM) of the Society of Critical Care Medicine (SCCM), in collaboration with the American Society of Health-System Pharmacists (ASHP), and in alliance with the American College of Chest Physicians; and approved by the Board of Regents of ACCM and the Council of SCCM on November 15, 2001 and the ASHP Board of Directors on November 17, 2001.

Members of the 2001–2002 Commission on Therapeutics are William L. Greene, Pharm.D., BCPS, FASHP, *Chair;* Mary Lea Gora-Harper, Pharm.D., BCPS, *Vice Chair;* Kate Farthing, Pharm.D.; Charles W. Ham, Pharm.D., M.B.A.; Rita K. Jew, Pharm.D.; Rex S. Lott, Pharm.D.; Keith M. Olsen, Pharm.D., FCCP; Joseph J. Saseen, Pharm.D., BCPS; Beth A. Vanderheyden, Pharm.D., BCPS; Amy M. Blachere, R.Ph., *Student Member;* Jill E. Martin, Pharm.D., FASHP, *Board Liaison*; Dennis Williams, Pharm.D., FASHP, FCCP, FAPHA, BCPS, *Liaison Section of Clinical Specialist;* and Cynthia L. LaCivita, Pharm.D., *Secretary.*

Members of the Neuromuscular Blockade Task Force are Michael J. Murray, M.D., Ph.D., FCCM, *Chair,* Professor and Chair of Anesthesiology, and Dean, Mayo School of Health Sciences, Mayo Clinic Jacksonville, FL; Stanley Nasraway, Jr., M.D., FCCM, *Executive Director of Task Force,* Associate Professor, Surgery, Medicine, and anesthesia, Tufts-New England Medical Center, Boston, MA; Jay Cowen, M.D., Director, Medical Intensive Care Unit, LeHigh Valley Hospital, Allentown, PA; Heidi F. DeBlock, M.D., Department of Surgery, Albany Medical Center, Albany, NY; Brian L. Erstad, Pharm.D., FCCM, Department of Pharmacy Practice & Science, College of Pharmacy, University of Arizona, Tucson, AZ; Anthony W. Gray, Jr., M.D., FCCM, Section of Pulmonary and Critical Care, Medicine and Surgical Critical Care, Lahey Clinic Medical Center, Burlington, MA; Judith Jacobi, Pharm.D., FCCM, BCPS, Critical Care Pharmacy Specialist, Methodist Hospital–Clarian Health Partners, Indianapolis, IN; Philip D. Lumb, M.B., B.S., FCCM, Professor and Chairman, Department of Anesthesiology, Keck School of Medicine of USC, Los Angeles, CA; William T. McGee, M.D., M.H.A., Critical Care Division, Departments of Medicine & Surgery, Baystate Medical Center, Springfield, MA; William T. Peruzzi, M.D., FCCM, Associate Professor of Anesthesiology, Northwestern University School of Medicine, Chief, Section of Critical Care Medicine, Northwestern Memorial Hospital, Chicago, IL; Richard C. Prielipp, M.D., FCCM, Section Head, Critical Care and Department of Anesthesiology, Wake Forest University School of Medicine, Medical Center Boulevard, Winston-Salem, NC; Greg Susla, Pharm.D., FCCM, Clinical Center Pharmacy Department, National Institutes of Health, Bethesda, MD; Ann N. Tescher, R.N., Clinical Nurse Specialist, Mayo Clinic, Rochester, MN; Cynthia L. LaCivita, Pharm.D., Clinical Affairs Associate, *ASHP Staff Liaison*; Deborah L. McBride, Director of Publications, *SCCM Staff Liaison.*

Reviewers: American College of Chest Physicians; American Academy of Neurology; American Association of Critical Care Nurses; American Nurses Association; American Pharmaceutical Association; American College of Clinical Pharmacy; Joe Dasta, Pharm.D.; Doug Fish, Pharm.D.; Erkan Hassan, Pharm.D.; H. Mathilda Horst, M.D.; Carlayne E. Jackson, M.D.; Karen Kaiser, R.N.; Kathleen M. Kelly, M.D.; Carl Schoenberger, M.D.; Lori Schoonover, R.N.; and Gayle Takaniski, Pharm.D.

The recommendations in this document do not indicate an exclusive course of treatment to be followed. Variations, taking into account individual circumstances, may be appropriate.

The bibliographic citation is as follows: Society of Critical Care Medicine and American Society of Health-System Pharmacists. Clinical practice guidelines for sustained neuromuscular blockade in the adult critically ill patient. *Am J Health Syst Pharm.* 2002; 59:179–95.

Clinical Practice Guidelines for the Management of Pain, Agitation, and Delirium in Adult Patients in the Intensive Care Unit

Objective: To revise the "Clinical Practice Guidelines for the Sustained Use of Sedatives and Analgesics in the Critically Ill Adult" published in *Critical Care Medicine* in 2002.

Methods: The American College of Critical Care Medicine assembled a 20-person, multidisciplinary, multi-institutional task force with expertise in guideline development, pain, agitation and sedation, delirium management, and associated outcomes in adult critically ill patients. The task force, divided into four subcommittees, collaborated over 6 yr in person, via teleconferences, and via electronic communication. Subcommittees were responsible for developing relevant clinical questions, using the Grading of Recommendations Assessment, Development and Evaluation method (http://www.gradeworkinggroup.org) to review, evaluate, and summarize the literature, and to develop clinical statements (descriptive) and recommendations (actionable). With the help of a professional librarian and Refworks® database software, they developed a Web-based electronic database of over 19,000 references extracted from eight clinical search engines, related to pain and analgesia, agitation and sedation, delirium, and related clinical outcomes in adult ICU patients. The group also used psychometric analyses to evaluate and compare pain, agitation/sedation, and delirium assessment tools. All task force members were allowed to review the literature supporting each statement and recommendation and provided feedback to the subcommittees. Group consensus was achieved for all statements and recommendations using the nominal group technique and the modified Delphi method, with anonymous voting by all task force members using E-Survey (http://www.esurvey.com). All voting was completed in December 2010. Relevant studies published after this date and prior to publication of these guidelines were referenced in the text. The quality of evidence for each statement and recommendation was ranked as high (A), moderate (B), or low/very low (C). The strength of recommendations was ranked as strong (1) or weak (2), and either in favor of (+) or against (–) an intervention. A strong recommendation (either for or against) indicated that the intervention's desirable effects either clearly outweighed its undesirable effects (risks, burdens, and costs) or it did not. For all strong recommendations, the phrase "We recommend …" is used throughout. A weak recommendation, either for or against an intervention, indicated that the tradeoff between desirable and undesirable effects was less clear. For all weak recommendations, the phrase "We suggest …" is used throughout. In the absence of sufficient evidence, or when group consensus could not be achieved, no recommendation (0) was made. Consensus based on expert opinion was not used as a substitute for a lack of evidence. A consistent method for addressing potential conflict of interest was followed if task force members were coauthors of related research. The development of this guideline was independent of any industry funding.

Conclusion: These guidelines provide a roadmap for developing integrated, evidence-based, and patient-centered protocols for preventing and treating pain, agitation, and delirium in critically ill patients. (*Crit Care Med.* 2013; 41:263–306)

Key Words: agitation; analgesia; critical care medicine; delirium; evidence-based medicine; GRADE; guidelines; intensive care; outcomes; pain; protocols; sedation

Statements and Recommendations

1. Pain and Analgesia
   a. Incidence of pain
      i. Adult medical, surgical, and trauma ICU patients routinely experience pain, both at rest and with routine ICU care (B).
      ii. Pain in adult cardiac surgery patients is common and poorly treated; women experience more pain than men after cardiac surgery (B).
      iii. Procedural pain is common in adult ICU patients (B).
   b. Pain assessment
      i. We recommend that pain be routinely monitored in all adult ICU patients (+1B).
      ii. The Behavioral Pain Scale (BPS) and the Critical-Care Pain Observation Tool (CPOT) are the most valid and reliable behavioral pain scales for monitoring pain in medical, postoperative, or trauma (except for brain injury) adult ICU patients who are unable to self-report and in whom motor function is intact and behaviors are observable. Using these scales in other ICU patient populations and translating them into foreign languages other than French or English require further validation testing (B).
      iii. We do not suggest that vital signs (or observational pain scales that include vital signs) be used alone for pain assessment in adult ICU patients (–2C).
      iv. We suggest that vital signs may be used as a cue to begin further assessment of pain in these patients, however (+2C).
   c. Treatment of pain
      i. We recommend that preemptive analgesia and/or nonpharmacologic interventions (e.g., relaxation) be administered to alleviate pain in adult ICU patients prior to chest tube removal (+1C).
      ii. We suggest that for other types of invasive and potentially painful procedures in adult ICU patients, preemptive analgesic therapy and/or nonpharmacologic interventions may also be administered to alleviate pain (+2C).

iii. We recommend that intravenous (IV) opioids be considered as the first-line drug class of choice to treat non-neuropathic pain in critically ill patients (+1C).

iv. All available IV opioids, when titrated to similar pain intensity endpoints, are equally effective (C).

v. We suggest that nonopioid analgesics be considered to decrease the amount of opioids administered (or to eliminate the need for IV opioids altogether) and to decrease opioid-related side effects (+2C).

vi. We recommend that either enterally administered gabapentin or carbamazepine, in addition to IV opioids, be considered for treatment of neuropathic pain (+1A).

vii. We recommend that thoracic epidural anesthesia/ analgesia be considered for postoperative analgesia in patients undergoing abdominal aortic aneurysm surgery (+1B).

viii. We provide no recommendation for using a lumbar epidural over parenteral opioids for postoperative analgesia in patients undergoing abdominal aortic aneurysm surgery, due to a lack of benefit of epidural over parenteral opioids in this patient population (0,A).

ix. We provide no recommendation for the use of thoracic epidural analgesia in patients undergoing either intrathoracic or nonvascular abdominal surgical procedures, due to insufficient and conflicting evidence for this mode of analgesic delivery in these patients (0,B).

x. We suggest that thoracic epidural analgesia be considered for patients with traumatic rib fractures (+2B).

xi. We provide no recommendation for neuraxial/ regional analgesia over systemic analgesia in medical ICU patients, due to lack of evidence in this patient population (0, No Evidence).

2. Agitation and Sedation

a. Depth of sedation vs. clinical outcomes

i. Maintaining light levels of sedation in adult ICU patients is associated with improved clinical outcomes (e.g., shorter duration of mechanical ventilation and a shorter ICU length of stay [LOS]) (B).

ii. Maintaining light levels of sedation increases the physiologic stress response, but is not associated with an increased incidence of myocardial ischemia (B).

iii. The association between depth of sedation and psychological stress in these patients remains unclear (C).

iv. We recommend that sedative medications be titrated to maintain a light rather than a deep level of sedation in adult ICU patients, unless clinically contraindicated (+1B).

b. Monitoring depth of sedation and brain function

i. The Richmond Agitation-Sedation Scale (RASS) and Sedation-Agitation Scale (SAS) are the most valid and reliable sedation assessment tools for measuring quality and depth of sedation in adult ICU patients (B).

ii. We do not recommend that objective measures of brain function (e.g., auditory evoked potentials [AEPs], Bispectral Index [BIS], Narcotrend Index [NI], Patient State Index [PSI], or state entropy [SE]) be used as the primary method to monitor depth of sedation in noncomatose, nonparalyzed critically ill adult patients, as these monitors are inadequate substitutes for subjective sedation scoring systems (−1B).

iii. We suggest that objective measures of brain function (e.g., AEPs, BIS, NI, PSI, or SE) be used as an adjunct to subjective sedation assessments in adult ICU patients who are receiving neuromuscular blocking agents, as subjective sedation assessments may be unobtainable in these patients (+2B).

iv. We recommend that EEG monitoring be used to monitor nonconvulsive seizure activity in adult ICU patients with either known or suspected seizures, or to titrate electrosuppressive medication to achieve burst suppression in adult ICU patients with elevated intracranial pressure (+1A).

c. Choice of sedative

i. We suggest that sedation strategies using nonbenzodiazepine sedatives (either propofol or dexmedetomidine) may be preferred over sedation with benzodiazepines (either midazolam or lorazepam) to improve clinical outcomes in mechanically ventilated adult ICU patients (+2B).

3. Delirium

a. Outcomes associated with delirium

i. Delirium is associated with increased mortality in adult ICU patients (A).

ii. Delirium is associated with prolonged ICU and hospital LOS in adult ICU patients (A).

iii. Delirium is associated with the development of post-ICU cognitive impairment in adult ICU patients (B).

b. Detecting and monitoring delirium

i. We recommend routine monitoring of delirium in adult ICU patients (+1B).

ii. The Confusion Assessment Method for the ICU (CAM-ICU) and the Intensive Care Delirium Screening Checklist (ICDSC) are the most valid and reliable delirium monitoring tools in adult ICU patients (A).

iii. Routine monitoring of delirium in adult ICU patients is feasible in clinical practice (B).

c. Delirium risk factors

i. Four baseline risk factors are positively and significantly associated with the development of delirium in the ICU: preexisting dementia, history of hypertension and/or alcoholism, and a high severity of illness at admission (B).

ii. Coma is an independent risk factor for the development of delirium in ICU patients (B).

iii. Conflicting data surround the relationship between opioid use and the development of delirium in adult ICU patients (B).

iv. Benzodiazepine use may be a risk factor for

the development of delirium in adult ICU patients (B).

- v. There are insufficient data to determine the relationship between propofol use and the development of delirium in adult ICU patients (C).
- vi. In mechanically ventilated adult ICU patients at risk of developing delirium, dexmedetomidine infusions administered for sedation may be associated with a lower prevalence of delirium compared to benzodiazepine infusions (B).

d. Delirium prevention

- **i.** We recommend performing early mobilization of adult ICU patients whenever feasible to reduce the incidence and duration of delirium (+1B).
- **ii.** We provide no recommendation for using a pharmacologic delirium prevention protocol in adult ICU patients, as no compelling data demonstrate that this reduces the incidence or duration of delirium in these patients (0,C).
- **iii.** We provide no recommendation for using a combined nonpharmacologic and pharmacologic delirium prevention protocol in adult ICU patients, as this has not been shown to reduce the incidence of delirium in these patients (0,C).
- **iv.** We do not suggest that either haloperidol or atypical antipsychotics be administered to prevent delirium in adult ICU patients (–2C).
- **v.** We provide no recommendation for the use of dexmedetomidine to prevent delirium in adult ICU patients, as there is no compelling evidence regarding its effectiveness in these patients (0,C).

e. Delirium treatment

- **i.** There is no published evidence that treatment with haloperidol reduces the duration of delirium in adult ICU patients (No Evidence).
- **ii.** Atypical antipsychotics may reduce the duration of delirium in adult ICU patients (C).
- **iii.** We do not recommend administering rivastigmine to reduce the duration of delirium in ICU patients (–1B).
- **iv.** We do not suggest using antipsychotics in patients at significant risk for torsades de pointes (i.e., patients with baseline prolongation of QTc interval, patients receiving concomitant medications known to prolong the QTc interval, or patients with a history of this arrhythmia) (–2C).
- **v.** We suggest that in adult ICU patients with delirium unrelated to alcohol or benzodiazepine withdrawal, continuous IV infusions of dexmedetomidine rather than benzodiazepine infusions be administered for sedation to reduce the duration of delirium in these patients (+2B).

4. Strategies for Managing Pain, Agitation, and Delirium to Improve ICU Outcomes

- **a.** We recommend either daily sedation interruption or a light target level of sedation be routinely used in mechanically ventilated adult ICU patients (+1B).
- **b.** We suggest that analgesia-first sedation be used in mechanically ventilated adult ICU patients (+2B).
- **c.** We recommend promoting sleep in adult ICU patients by optimizing patients' environments, using strategies to control light and noise, clustering patient care activities, and decreasing stimuli at night to protect patients' sleep cycles (+1C).
- **d.** We provide no recommendation for using specific modes of mechanical ventilation to promote sleep in mechanically ventilated adult ICU patients, as insufficient evidence exists for the efficacy of these interventions (0, No Evidence).
- **e.** We recommend using an interdisciplinary ICU team approach that includes provider education, preprinted and/or computerized protocols and order forms, and quality ICU rounds checklists to facilitate the use of pain, agitation, and delirium management guidelines or protocols in adult ICUs (+1B).

Since these guidelines were last published, we have made significant advances in our understanding of how to provide physical and psychological comfort for patients admitted to the ICU.[1] The development of valid and reliable bedside assessment tools to measure pain, sedation, agitation, and delirium in ICU patients has allowed clinicians to manage patients better and to evaluate outcomes associated with both nonpharmacologic and pharmacologic interventions.[2,3] Our expanded knowledge of the clinical pharmacology of medications commonly administered to treat pain, agitation, and delirium (PAD) in ICU patients has increased our appreciation for both the short- and long-term consequences of prolonged exposure to these agents.[4–6] We have learned that the methods of administering and titrating these medications can affect patient outcomes as much as drug choice.[7–16] For most ICU patients, a safe and effective strategy that ensures patient comfort while maintaining a light level of sedation is associated with improved clinical outcomes.[9–13,16–20]

Ensuring that critically ill patients are free from pain, agitation, anxiety, and delirium at times may conflict with other clinical management goals, such as maintaining cardiopulmonary stability while preserving adequate end-organ perfusion and function.[21,22] Management goals may be further complicated by the growing number of "evidence-based" bundles and clinical algorithms, some of which have been widely adopted by regulatory agencies and payers.[23–30] Finally, tremendous worldwide variability in cultural, philosophical, and practice norms, and in the availability of manpower and resources, makes widespread implementation of evidence-based practices challenging.[31–36]

The goal of these clinical practice guidelines is to recommend best practices for managing PAD to improve clinical outcomes in adult ICU patients. We performed a rigorous, objective, transparent, and unbiased assessment of the relevant published evidence. We balanced this evidence against the values and preferences of ICU patients, family members, caregivers, and payer and regulatory groups, and important ICU clinical outcomes, to develop relevant statements and recommendations that can be applied at the bedside.

The scope of these guidelines includes short- and long-term management of PAD in both intubated and nonintubated adult medical, surgical, and trauma ICU patients. These guidelines only briefly address the topic of analgesia and sedation for procedures, which is described in more detail in the American Society of Anesthesiologists guidelines on conscious sedation.[37] The American College of Critical Care Medicine (ACCM) is currently developing separate guidelines on analgesia and sedation for pediatric ICU patients.

This version of the guidelines places a greater emphasis on the psychometric aspects of PAD monitoring tools. It includes both pharmacologic and nonpharmacologic approaches to manage PAD in ICU patients. There is also greater emphasis placed on preventing, diagnosing, and treating delirium, reflecting our growing understanding of this disease process in critically ill patients. These guidelines are meant to help clinicians take a more integrated approach to manage PAD in critically ill patients. Clinicians should adapt these guidelines to the context of individual patient care needs and the available resources of their local health care system. They are not meant to be proscriptive or applied in absolute terms.

Methods

The ACCM's 20-member multidisciplinary task force, with expertise in PAD management, was charged with revising the 2002 "Clinical Practice Guidelines for the Sustained Use of Sedatives and Analgesics in the Critically Ill Adult."[1] Subcommittees were assigned one of the four subtopic areas: pain and analgesia, agitation and sedation, delirium, and related ICU outcomes. Each subcommittee developed relevant clinical questions and related outcomes, identified, reviewed, and evaluated the literature, crafted statements and recommendations, and drafted their section of the article.

To facilitate the literature review, subcommittees developed a comprehensive list of related key words. A professional librarian (C.K., University of Cincinnati) expanded and organized this key word list; developed corresponding medical subject heading (MeSH) terms (Supplemental Digital Content 1, http://links.lww.com/CCM/A590); searched relevant clinical databases; and created an electronic, Web-based, password-protected database using Refworks software (Bethesda, MD). Eight databases were included in all searches: PubMed, MEDLINE, Cochrane Database of Systematic Reviews, Cochrane Central Register of Controlled Trials, CINAHL, Scopus, ISI Web of Science, and the International Pharmaceutical Abstracts. Search parameters included published (or in press) English-only manuscripts on adult humans (> 18 yr), from December 1999 (the search limit for the 2002 guidelines) through December 2010. Studies with less than 30 patients, editorials, narrative reviews, case reports, animal or in vitro studies, and letters to the editor were excluded. Biweekly automated searches were continued beyond this date, and relevant articles were incorporated into the guidelines through July 2012, but studies published after December 2010 were not included in the evidence review and voting process. The 2002 guideline references were also included in the database, and targeted searches of the literature published before December 1999 were performed as needed. Over 19,000 references were ultimately included in the Refworks database.

The statements and recommendations in this 2012 version of the guidelines were developed using the Grading of Recommendations, Assessment, Development and Evaluation (GRADE) methodology, a structured system for rating quality of evidence and grading strength of recommendation in clinical practice (http://www.gradeworkinggroup.org).[38–40] Subcommittees worked with members of the GRADE Working Group (R.J., D.C., H.S., G.G.) to phrase all clinical questions in either "descriptive" or "actionable" terms. They structured actionable questions in the Population, Intervention, Comparison, Outcomes format and classified clinical outcomes related to each intervention as critical, important, or unimportant to clinical decision making. Only important and critical outcomes were included in the evidence review, and only critical outcomes were included in developing recommendations.

Subcommittee members searched the database for relevant articles and uploaded corresponding PDFs to facilitate group review. Two subcommittee members independently completed a GRADE evidence profile summarizing the findings of each study and evaluated the quality of evidence. The quality of evidence was judged to be high (level A), moderate (level B), or low/very low (level C), based on both study design and specific study characteristics, which could result in a reviewer either downgrading or upgrading the quality of the evidence (Table 1). If multiple studies related to a particular outcome demonstrated disparate results, and no published systematic reviews on the topic existed, a meta-analysis of the relevant literature was performed by a member of the GRADE Working Group (R.J.).

Table 1.

Factors That Affect the Quality of Evidence[a]

Level of Evidence	Quality of Evidence	Type of Evidence	Definition
A	High	High quality RCT	Further research is unlikely to change our confidence in the estimate of effect.
B	Moderate	RCT with significant limitations (downgraded),[b] or high-quality OS (upgraded)[c]	Further research is likely to have an important impact on our confidence in the estimate of effect and may change the estimate.
C	Low	OS	Further research is very likely to have an important impact on our confidence in the estimate of effect and is likely to change the estimate.

RCT = randomized controlled trial; OS = observational study.

[a]Adapted from Guyatt, et al.[40]

[b]RCTs with significant limitations: 1) study design limitations (planning, implementation bias); 2) inconsistency of results; 3) indirectness of evidence; 4) imprecision of results; 5) high likelihood of reporting bias.

[c]High-quality OS: 1) large magnitude of treatment effect; 2) evidence of a dose-response relationship; 3) plausible biases would decrease the magnitude of an apparent treatment effect.

Subcommittees collectively reviewed the evidence profiles for each question, and using a nominal group technique, determined the overall quality of evidence (for both descriptive and actionable questions), the strength of recommendation (for actionable questions only), and drafted evidence summaries for review by other task force members. The strength of recommendations was defined as either *strong* (1) or *weak* (2), and either *for* (+) or *against* (–) an intervention, based on both the quality of evidence and the risks and benefits across all critical outcomes (Table 2).[41,42] A *no recommendation* (0) could also be made due to either a lack of evidence or a lack of consensus among subcommittee members. Consensus statements based on expert opinion alone were not used when evidence could not support a recommendation. A *strong* recommendation either in *favor* of (+1) or *against* (–1) an intervention implied that the majority of task force members believed that the benefits of the intervention significantly outweighed the risks (or vice versa) and that the majority of patients and providers would pursue this course of action (or not), given the choice. A *weak* recommendation either in *favor* of (+2) or *against* (–2) an intervention implied that the benefits of the intervention likely outweighed the risks (or vice versa), but that task force members were not confident about these trade-offs, either because of a low quality of evidence or because the trade-offs between risks and benefits were closely balanced. On the basis of this information, most people might pursue this course of action (or not), but a significant number of patients and providers would choose an alternative course of action.[40,43,44] Throughout these guidelines, for all strong recommendations, the phrase "We recommend …" was used, and for all weak recommendations, "We suggest …" was used.

Group consensus for all statements and recommendations was achieved using a modified Delphi method with an anonymous voting scheme.[41,45] Task force members reviewed the subcommittees' GRADE Evidence Summaries, and statements and recommendations, and voted and commented anonymously on each statement and recommendation using an on-line electronic survey tool (E-Survey, http://www.esurvey.com, Scottsdale, AZ). Consensus on the *strength of evidence* for each question required a majority (> 50%) vote. Consensus on the strength of recommendations was defined as follows: a recommendation in *favor* of an intervention (or the comparator) required at least 50% of all task force members voting in *favor*, with less than 20% voting *against*; failure to meet these voting thresholds resulted in *no recommendation* being made. For a recommendation to be graded as *strong* rather than *weak*, at least 70% of those voting had to vote for a *strong* recommendation, otherwise it received a *weak* recommendation. This method for reaching consensus has been proposed by the GRADE Working Group and was adopted by the 2008 Sepsis Guidelines Panel to ensure fairness, transparency, and anonymity in the creation of guideline recommendations.[46,47] Polling results and comments were then summarized and distributed to all PAD guideline task force members for review. When one round of voting failed to produce group consensus, additional discussion and a second and/or third round of voting occurred. Polling for all questions was completed by December 2010. Distribution of the final voting tallies along with comments by task force members for each statement and recommendation is summarized in Supplemental Digital Content 2 (http://links.lww.com/CCM/A591).

Task force members completed required, annual, conflict of interest statements. Those with significant potential conflicts of interest (e.g., manuscript coauthorship) recused themselves from reviewing and grading evidence and from developing a subcommittee's evidence statements and recommendations for related questions. All task force members voted anonymously on the final strength of evidence and strength of recommendations for all questions. No industry funding or support was used to develop any aspect of these guidelines.

Psychometric Analyses. These guidelines include statements and recommendations about using a variety of bedside behavioral assessment tools used to 1) detect and evaluate pain, 2) assess depth of sedation and degree of agitation, and 3) detect delirium in critically ill adult patients who are unable to communicate clearly. To date, a comparative assessment of the psychometric properties (i.e., reliability and validity) and feasibility related to the use of these tools in ICU patients has not been published. *Scale reliability* refers to the overall accuracy of the use of a scale in replicating pain, sedation, or delirium scores over time (i.e., test–retest reliability) or between raters (i.e., inter-rater reliability).[48] *Validity* refers to the conclusions that can be drawn from the results of a test or scale (e.g., does a delirium assessment tool actually detect delirium?).[49] Content, criterion, and discriminant validation are specific strategies of validity testing. A tool can be shown to be both reliable and valid when used for a specific purpose with specified individuals in a given context.[48,49] *Feasibility*

Table 2.

Factors That Affect the Strength of Recommendations[a]

Considerations	Effect on Strength of Recommendation
Quality of evidence	Lower quality of evidence reduces the likelihood of a strong recommendation, and vice versa
Uncertainty about the balance between desirable and undesirable effects	Higher degree of uncertainty about the balance between risks and benefits reduces the likelihood of a strong recommendation, and vice versa
Uncertainty or variability in values and preferences	Wide variability in values and preferences across groups reduces the likelihood of a strong recommendation, and vice versa
Uncertainty about whether the intervention represents a wise use of resources	A higher the overall cost of treatment reduces the likelihood of a strong recommendation, and vice versa

[a]Adapted from Guyatt, et al.[40]

refers to the ease with which clinicians can apply a particular scale in the clinical setting (e.g., in the ICU).

The task force evaluated and compared the psychometric properties of behavioral pain scales (BPSs) used in adult ICU patients and compared their analyses to a previously published process.[50] Similar scoring systems were not available to evaluate and compare the psychometric properties of sedation and delirium scales, which have different validation strategies from those used for pain scales. With input from three psychometric testing experts (D.S., C.J., C.W.), the task force developed similar scoring systems to assess and compare sedation and delirium scales.[48]

The psychometric properties of pain, sedation, and delirium scales were evaluated based on: 1) item selection and content validation, 2) reliability, 3) validity, 4) feasibility, and 5) relevance or impact of implementation on patient outcomes. Psychometric raw scores ranged from 0 to 25 for pain scales, 0 to 18 for sedation scales, and 0 to 21 for delirium scales. Weighted scores were established for each criterion to address variations in scores and to facilitate the interpretation of results, resulting in a total weighted score 0 to 20 for all three domains. The details of each of the three psychometric scoring systems used are summarized in Supplemental Digital Content 3 (http://links.lww.com/CCM/A592). Scales with weighted scores ranging from 15 to 20 had very good psychometric properties, 12 to 14.9 had moderate psychometric properties, 10 to 11.9 had some acceptable psychometric properties which required validation in additional studies, and 0 to 9.9 had very few psychometric properties reported and/or unacceptable results. Scales with moderate to very good psychometric properties (i.e., weighted score ≥ 12) were considered to be sufficiently valid and reliable scales for use in adult ICU patients. The quality of evidence for each individual scale was also evaluated using categories similar to those used in the GRADE system, with modifications adapted for the psychometric analyses. All studies were reviewed, and all scales were scored independently by two reviewers.

Pain and Analgesia. *Incidence of pain in ICU patients.* The International Association for the Study of Pain defines pain as an "unpleasant sensory and emotional experience associated with actual or potential tissue damage, or described in terms of such damage."[51] This definition highlights the subjective nature of pain and suggests that it can be present only when reported by the person experiencing it. Most critically ill patients will likely experience pain sometime during their ICU stay[52] and identify it as a great source of stress.[53–56] However, many critically ill patients may be unable to self-report their pain (either verbally or with other signs) because of an altered level of consciousness, the use of mechanical ventilation, or high doses of sedative agents or neuromuscular blocking agents.[57] Yet, the ability to reliably assess patient's pain is the foundation for effective pain treatment. As the International Association for the Study of Pain also states, "the inability to communicate verbally does not negate the possibility that an individual is experiencing pain and is in need of appropriate pain-relieving treatment."[58] Therefore, clinicians must be able to reliably detect pain, using assessment methods adapted to a patient's diminished communication capabilities. In such situations, clinicians should consider patients' behavioral reactions as surrogate measures of pain, as long as their motor function is intact.[59] Detection, quantification, and management of pain in critically ill adults are major priorities and have been the subject of research for over 20 yr.[60] Despite this fact, the incidence of significant pain is still 50% or higher in both medical and surgical ICU patients.[61,62]

In addition to experiencing pain at rest[61] and pain related to surgery, trauma, burns, or cancer, patients also experience procedural pain.[63–70] This was highlighted in the first practice guideline published on acute pain management 20 yr ago by the Agency for Health Care Policy and Research.[71] Pain related to procedures is ubiquitous, and inadequate treatment of procedural pain remains a significant problem for many ICU patients.[68]

The negative physiologic and psychological consequences of unrelieved pain in ICU patients are significant and long-lasting. For many years, ICU patients have identified pain as their greatest concern and a leading cause of insufficient sleep.[72] More recently, studies on ICU-discharged but still-hospitalized patients showed that 82% (n = 75)[56] remembered pain or discomfort associated with the endotracheal tube and 77% (n = 93) remembered experiencing moderate to severe pain during their ICU stay.[73] One week after discharge from the ICU, 82% (n = 120) of cardiac surgery patients reported pain as the most common traumatic memory of their ICU stay; 6 months later, 38% still recalled pain as their most traumatic ICU memory.[74] Granja and colleagues[75] noted that 17% (n = 313) of patients remembered experiencing severe pain 6 months after an ICU stay and 18% were at high risk of developing posttraumatic stress disorder (PTSD). Schelling and colleagues[25] conducted a long-term follow-up (median, 4 yr) questionnaire study of 80 patients who had been treated in the ICU for acute respiratory distress syndrome. In comparison with normal controls, both medical and surgical patients who recalled pain and other traumatic situations while in the ICU had a higher incidence of chronic pain (38%) and PTSD symptoms (27%), and a lower health-related quality of life (21%).

The stress response evoked by pain can have deleterious consequences for ICU patients. Increased circulating catecholamines can cause arteriolar vasoconstriction, impair tissue perfusion, and reduce tissue-oxygen partial pressure.[76] Other responses triggered by pain include catabolic hypermetabolism resulting in hyperglycemia, lipolysis, and breakdown of muscle to provide protein substrate.[77] Catabolic stimulation and hypoxemia also impair wound healing and increase the risk of wound infection. Pain suppresses natural killer cell activity,[78,79] a critical function in the immune system, with a decrease in the number of cytotoxic T cells and a reduction in neutrophil phagocytic activity.[80] Acute pain may be the greatest risk factor for developing debilitating chronic, persistent, often neuropathic pain.[81] Unrelieved acute pain in adult ICU patients is ubiquitous and far from benign, with both short- and long-term consequences. Adequately identifying and treating pain in these patients require focused attention.

Pain assessment in ICU patients. Treating pain in critically ill patients depends on a clinician's ability to perform a reproducible pain assessment and to monitor patients over time to determine the adequacy of therapeutic interventions to treat pain. A patient's self-report of pain is considered the "gold standard," and clinicians should always attempt to have a patient rate his or her own pain first. Chanques and colleagues[82] demonstrated that a 0–10 visually enlarged horizontal numeric rating scale was the most valid and feasible of five pain intensity rating scales tested in over 100

ICU patients. Yet when critically ill patients are unable to self-report their pain, clinicians must use structured, valid, reliable, and feasible tools to assess patients' pain.[83] It is essential that pain in ICU patients be assessed routinely and repetitively in a manner that is efficient and reproducible. No objective pain monitor exists, but valid and reliable bedside pain assessment tools that concentrate primarily on patients' behaviors as indicators of pain do exist.

Although reviews of behavioral pain assessment tools have been published, an updated discussion is needed about their development, validation, and applicability to ICU patients.[50,84] A detailed, systematic review of the processes of item selection and psychometric properties of pain scales (i.e., validity and reliability) may encourage clinicians to adopt pain scales and to standardize their use in ICU patients. Recent studies have demonstrated that implementing behavioral pain scales improves both ICU pain management and clinical outcomes, including better use of analgesic and sedative agents and shorter durations of mechanical ventilation and ICU stay.[2,3,85]

Treatment of pain. Opioids, such as fentanyl, hydromorphone, methadone, morphine, and remifentanil, are the primary medications for managing pain in critically ill patients (Table 3).[62] The optimal choice of opioid and the dosing regimen used for an individual patient depends on many factors, including the drug's pharmacokinetic and pharmacodynamic properties.[52] The use of meperidine is generally avoided in ICU patients because of its potential for neurologic toxicity.[52]

Several other types of analgesics or pain-modulating medications, such as local and regional anesthetics (e.g., bupivacaine), nonsteroidal anti-inflammatory medications (e.g., ketorolac, ibuprofen), IV acetaminophen, and anticonvulsants, can be used as adjunctive pain medications to reduce opioid requirements (Table 4). However, their safety profile and effectiveness as sole agents for pain management have not been adequately studied in critically ill patients. Pharmacologic treatment principles extrapolated from non-ICU studies may not be applicable to critically ill patients.[52] IV acetaminophen has been recently approved for use in the United States and has been shown to be safe and effective when used in conjunction with opioids for postoperative pain in surgical ICU patients following major or cardiac surgery.[80,86–89] Neuropathic pain, poorly treated with opioids alone, can be treated with enterally administered gabapentin and carbamazepine in ICU patients with sufficient gastrointestinal absorption and motility.[90,91]

Methods of dosing analgesics are another treatment consideration. The choice of intermittent vs. continuous IV strategies may depend on drug pharmacokinetics, frequency and severity of pain, and/or the patient's mental status.[92] Enteral administration of opioids and other pain medications should be limited to patients with adequate gastrointestinal absorptive capacity and motility. Regional or neuraxial (spinal or epidural) modalities may also be used for postoperative analgesia following selected surgical procedures.[93,94]

Complementary, nonpharmacologic interventions for pain management, such as music therapy and relaxation techniques, may be opioid-sparing and analgesia-enhancing; they are low cost, easy to provide, and safe. Although a multimodal approach to pain management in ICU patients has been recommended, few studies have been published on the effectiveness of nonpharmacologic interventions in these patients.[52,95]

Pain occurs commonly in adult ICU patients, regardless of their admitting diagnoses. Pain can preclude patients from participating in their ICU care (e.g., early mobilization, weaning from mechanical ventilation). Thus, clinicians should frequently reassess patients for pain and carefully titrate analgesic interventions to prevent potential negative sequelae due to either inadequate or excessive analgesic therapy. Clinicians should perform routine and reproducible pain assessments in all critically ill patients, using either patient self-report or systematically applied behavioral measures. Pain management can be facilitated by identifying and treating pain early rather than waiting until it becomes severe.[52]

Table 3.

Pharmacology of Opiate Analgesics[1,128,440,472]

Opiates	Equi-Analgesic Dose (mg) IV	Equi-Analgesic Dose (mg) PO	Onset (IV)	Elimination Half-Life	Context-Sensitive Half-Life	Metabolic Pathway
Fentanyl	0.1	N/A	1–2 min	2–4 hr	200 min (6 hr infusion); 300 min (12 hr infusion)[a]	N-dealkylation CYP3A4/5 substrate
Hydromorphone	1.5	7.5	5–15 min	2–3 hr	N/A	Glucuronidation
Morphine	10	30	5–10 min	3–4 hr	N/A	Glucuronidation
Methadone	N/A[c]	N/A[c]	1–3 d	15–60 hr	N/A	N-demethylation CYP3A4/5, 2D6, 2B6, 1A2 substrate
Remifentanil	N/A	N/A	1–3 min	3–10 min	3–4 min	Hydrolysis by plasma esterases

PO = oral; N/A = not applicable; IBW = ideal body weight.

[a]After 12 hrs, and in cases of end-organ dysfunction, the context-sensitive half-life increases unpredictably.

[b]May increase dose to extend dosing interval; hydromorphone 0.5 mg IV every 3 hrs, or morphine 4–8 mg IV every 3–4 hrs.

[c]Equianalgesic dosing tables may underestimate the potency of methadone. The morphine- or hydromorphone-to-methadone conversion ratio increases (i.e., the potency of methadone increases) as the dose of morphine or hydromorphone increases. The relative analgesic potency ratio of oral to parenteral methadone is 2:1, but the confidence intervals are wide.

[d]QTc is the Q-T interval (corrected) of the electrocardiographic tracing.

Table 3. *(continued)*

Pharmacology of Opiate Analgesics[1,128,440,472]

Active Metabolites	Intermittent Dosing	IV Infusion Rates	Side Effects and Other Information
None	0.35–0.5 µg/kg IV q0.5–1 hr	0.7–10 µg/kg/hr	Less hypotension than with morphine. Accumulation with hepatic impairment.
None	0.2–0.6 mg IV q1–2 hr[b]	0.5–3 mg/hr	Therapeutic option in patients tolerant to morphine/fentanyl. Accumulation with hepatic/renal impairment.
6- and 3-glucuronide metabolite	2–4 mg IV q1–2 hr[b]	2–30 mg/hr	Accumulation with hepatic/renal impairment. Histamine release.
N-demethylated derivative	IV/PO: 10–40 mg q6–12 hr IV: 2.5–10 mg q8–12 hr	Not recommended	May be used to slow the development of tolerance where there is an escalation of opioid dosing requirements. Unpredictable pharmacokinetics; unpredictable pharmacodynamics in opiate naïve patients. Monitor QTc.[d]
None	N/A	Loading dose: 1.5 µg/kg IV Maintenance dose: 0.5–15 µg/kg/hr IV	No accumulation in hepatic/renal failure. Use IBW if body weight >130% IBW.

Pain and Analgesia: Questions, Statements, and Recommendations.

1. Incidence of Pain

   a. *Question:* Do adult ICU patients experience *non-procedural* pain in the ICU and, if so, what events or situations are related to pain? (descriptive) *Answer:* Adult medical, surgical, and trauma ICU patients routinely experience pain, both at rest and with routine ICU care (B). Pain in adult cardiac surgery patients is common and poorly treated; women experience more pain than men after cardiac surgery (B). *Rationale:* Medical, surgical, and trauma ICU patients experience significant pain, even at rest.[61,63,73] Therefore, all adult patients in any ICU should be evaluated for pain. Pain at rest should be considered a major clinical diagnostic syndrome. In cardiac surgery patients, pain related to the surgery, coughing, respiratory care procedures, and mobilization remains prevalent and poorly treated; women experience more pain than men after cardiac surgery.[73,96–98] Therefore, activity pain in cardiac surgery patients must be assessed and treated. Pain management should be individualized according to the patient's experience of pain, with special attention to its occurrence in women.[97]

   Question: What is the pain experienced by adult ICU patients undergoing procedures? (descriptive) *Answer:* Procedural pain is common in adult ICU patients (B).

   Rationale: Pain associated with nonsurgical procedures such as chest tube removal or wound care is prevalent in adult ICU patients.[68,99] Generally at a moderate level,[68] pain is influenced by preprocedural pain levels and the administration of analgesics.[100] Less than 25% of patients receive analgesics before the procedures.[68] Procedural pain varies with age[64,66] and is greater in non-Caucasians than in Caucasians.[64,66,68] Differences in procedural pain between nonsurgical and surgical patients vary according to procedure.[64,66] Hemodynamic changes are not valid correlates of procedural pain.[99] Available information suggests that preemptive analgesia has benefits, but the risks of procedural pain and the lack of preemptive treatment are unclear.

2. Pain Assessment

   a. *Question:* Should pain assessments be routinely performed in adult ICU patients? (actionable)

   Answer: We recommend that pain be routinely monitored in all adult ICU patients (+1B).

   Rationale: Routine pain assessments in adult ICU patients are associated with improved clinical outcomes. Pain assessment, especially if protocolized, has been significantly associated with a reduction in the use of analgesic medications, ICU length of stay (LOS), and duration of mechanical ventilation.[3,62] Pain assessment is essential for appropriate treatment, especially when part of a comprehensive pain management protocol. Although the quality of evidence is moderate, a strong recommendation for performing routine pain assessments in all ICU patients is appropriate, as the benefits strongly outweigh the risks.

   b. *Question:* What are the most valid and reliable behavioral measures of pain in critically ill adult patients who are unable to self-report? (descriptive)

   Answer: The Behavioral Pain Scale (BPS) and the Critical-Care Pain Observation Tool (CPOT) are the most valid and reliable behavioral pain scales for monitoring pain in medical, postoperative, or trauma (except for brain injury) adult ICU patients who are unable to self-report, and in whom motor function is intact and behaviors are observable.

Table 4.

Pharmacology of Nonopiate Analgesics[1,91,132,440]

Nonopiates (Route)	Onset	Elimination Half-Life	Metabolic Pathway	Active Metabolites
Ketamine (IV)	30–40 sec	2–3 hr	N-demethylation	Norketamine
Acetaminophen (PO) Acetaminophen (PR)	30–60 min variable	2–4 hr	Glucuronidation, sulfonation	None
Acetaminophen (IV)	5–10 min	2 hr	Glucuronidation, sulfonation.	None
Ketorolac[a] (IM/IV)	10 min	2.4–8.6 hr	Hydroxylation, conjugation/ renal excretion	None
Ibuprofen (IV)	N/A	2.2–2.4 hr	Oxidation	None
Ibuprofen (PO)	25 min	1.8–2.5 hr	Oxidation	None
Gabapentin (PO)	N/A	5–7 hr	Renal excretion	None
Carbamazepine immediate release (PO)	4–5 hr	25–65 hrs initially, then 12–17 hr	Oxidation	None

PO = orally; PR = rectally; max = maximum; IM = intramuscular; N/A = not applicable.
[a]For patients > 65 yr or < 50 kg, 15 mg IV/IM every 6 hrs to a maximum dose of 60 mg/day for 5 days.

Using these scales in other ICU patient populations and translating them into foreign languages other than French or English require further validation testing (B).

Rationale: A total of six behavioral pain scales were analyzed: BPS; BPS—Non-Intubated (BPS-NI); CPOT; Non-Verbal Pain Scale (NVPS), both initial and revised (NVPS-I, NVPS-R); Pain Behavioral Assessment Tool (PBAT); and the Pain Assessment, Intervention, and Notation (PAIN) Algorithm. Table 5 summarizes their psychometric scores. Observational studies, although somewhat limited, provide consistent evidence that the BPS (3–12 total score) and CPOT (0–8 total score) scales have good psychometric properties in terms of: inter-rater reliability,[101–109] discriminant validity,[101,102,104,107,109,110] and criterion validity,[103–105,109,110] in medical, postoperative, and trauma ICU patients. A CPOT score of greater than 2 had a sensitivity of 86% and a specificity of 78% for predicting significant pain in postoperative ICU adults exposed to a nociceptive procedure.[111,112] Investigators suggested a similar cutoff score for the BPS (> 5), on the basis of descriptive statistics in nonverbal ICU adults during nociceptive procedures compared with patients at rest.[62] The CPOT and BPS can be successfully implemented in the ICU following short, standardized training sessions.[2,85] Their regular use can lead to better pain management and improved clinical outcomes in ICU patients.[2,3,85] The BPS-NI is derived from the BPS and adapted for nonintubated ICU patients,[113] but it has been tested in a group of only 30 patients so far, and replication studies are needed to support its psychometric properties. More studies are also necessary to examine the psychometric properties of the NVPS,[114] NVPS-R,[115] PBAT,[116] and PAIN.[117]

c. *Question:* Should vital signs be used to assess pain in adult ICU patients? (actionable)

Answer: We do not suggest that vital signs (or observational pain scales that include vital signs) be used alone for pain assessment in adult ICU patients (–2C). We suggest that vital signs may be used as a cue to begin further assessment of pain in these patients, however (+2C).

Rationale: Observational studies with major limitations provide inconsistent evidence of the validity of vital signs for the purpose of pain assessment in medical, postoperative, and trauma ICU patients. Even if there is a trend for vital signs to increase when critically ill patients are exposed to painful procedures, these increases are not reliable predictors of pain.[66,101,105,107,110] Vital signs have been reported to increase both during nociceptive and non-nociceptive procedures[109] or to remain stable during nociceptive exposure.[99] Vital signs do not correlate with either patients' self-report of pain[105,110] or behavioral pain scores.[101,107] But because vital signs may change with pain, distress, or other factors, they can be a cue to perform further pain assessments in these patients.[118]

3. Treatment of Pain

a. *Question:* Should procedure-related pain be treated pre-emptively in adult ICU patients? (actionable)

Answer: We recommend that preemptive analgesia and/or nonpharmacologic interventions (e.g., relaxation) be administered to alleviate pain in adult ICU patients prior to chest tube removal (+1C). We suggest that for other types of invasive and potentially painful procedures in adult ICU patients, preemptive analgesic therapy and/or nonpharmacologic interventions may also be administered to alleviate pain (+2C).

Rationale: Our strong recommendation is that patients undergoing chest tube removal should be preemptively treated for pain, both pharmacologically and non-pharmacologically. Significantly lower pain scores were reported by patients if they received IV morphine plus relaxation,[119] topical

Table 4. *(continued)*

Dosing	Side Effects and Other Information
Loading dose 0.1–0.5 mg/kg IV followed by 0.05–0.4 mg/kg/hr	Attenuates the development of acute tolerance to opioids. May cause hallucinations and other psychological disturbances.
325–1000 mg every 4–6 hr; max dose ≤ 4 g/day	May be contraindicated in patients with significant hepatic dysfunction.
650 mg IV every 4 hrs – 1000 mg IV every 6 hr; max dose ≤ 4 g/day	
30 mg IM/IV, then 15–30 mg IM/IV every 6 hr up to 5 days; max dose = 120 mg/day × 5 days	Avoid nonsteroidal anti-inflammatory drugs in following conditions: renal dysfunction; gastrointestinal bleeding; platelet abnormality; concomitant angiotensin converting enzyme inhibitor therapy, congestive heart failure, cirrhosis, asthma. Contraindicated for the treatment of perioperative pain in coronary artery bypass graft surgery.
400–800 mg IV every 6 hr infused over > 30 mins; max dose = 3.2 g/day	Avoid nonsteroidal anti-inflammatory drugs in following conditions: renal dysfunction; gastrointestinal bleeding; platelet abnormality; concomitant angiotensin converting enzyme inhibitor therapy, congestive heart failure, cirrhosis, asthma. Contraindicated for the treatment of perioperative pain in coronary artery bypass graft surgery.
400 mg PO every 4 hrs; max dose = 2.4 g/day	
Starting dose = 100 mg PO three times daily; maintenance dose = 900–3600 mg/day in 3 divided doses	Side effects: (common) sedation, confusion, dizziness, ataxia. Adjust dosing in renal failure pts. Abrupt discontinuation associated with drug withdrawl syndrome, seizures.
Starting dose = 50–100 mg PO bid; maintenance dose = 100–200 mg every 4–6 hr; max dose = 1200 mg/day	Side effects: (common) nystagmus, dizziness, diplopia, lightheadedness, lethargy; (rare) aplastic anemia, and agranulocytosis; Stevens–Johnson syndrome or toxic epidermal necrolysis with HLA-B1502 gene. Multiple drug interactions due to hepatic enzyme induction.

valdecoxib,[120] IV sufentanil, or fentanyl[121] prior to chest tube removal. According to these studies, the desirable consequences outweigh undesirable effects. One can reasonably assume that most ICU patients would want their pain preemptively treated with nonpharmacologic and/or pharmacologic interventions prior to other painful procedures as well.

b. *Question:* What types of medications should be administered for pain relief in adult ICU patients? (actionable)

Answer: We recommend that IV opioids be considered as the first-line drug class of choice to treat non-neuropathic pain in critically ill patients (+1C). All available IV opioids, when titrated to similar pain intensity endpoints, are equally effective (C). We recommend that either enterally administered gabapentin or carbamazepine, in addition to IV opioids, be considered for the treatment of neuropathic pain (+1A). We suggest that nonopioid analgesics be considered to decrease the amount of opioids administered (or to eliminate the need for IV opioids altogether) and to decrease opioid-related side effects (+2C).

Rationale: For non-neuropathic pain, evidence supports using an opiate-based regimen to decrease pain intensity.[87,90,91,122–136] Apart from drug cost and resource utilization, all opioids administered IV appear to exhibit similar analgesic efficacy and are associated with similar clinical outcomes (e.g., duration of mechanical ventilation, LOS) when titrated to similar pain intensity endpoints. For non-neuropathic pain, nonopioids such as IV acetaminophen,[87] oral, IV, or rectal cyclooxygenase inhibitors,[122,123,135] or IV ketamine[132,137] can be used in addition to opioids. Using nonopioids may also decrease the overall quantity of opioids administered and the incidence and severity of opioid-related side effects. In patients with neuropathic pain, IV opioid use plus oral gabapentin or carbamazepine provides superior pain relief in mechanically ventilated patients compared to IV opioid use alone.[90,91] A lack of direct comparisons between opioids and nonopioids hinders conclusions regarding the effect of nonopioid analgesics, particularly in ICU patients.

c. *Question:* What mode of analgesic delivery (i.e., either neuraxial or parenteral) is recommended for pain relief in critically ill adults who have undergone either thoracic or abdominal surgery or who have traumatic rib fractures (including both mechanically ventilated and nonmechanically ventilated ICU patients)? (actionable)

Answer: We recommend that thoracic epidural anesthesia/analgesia be considered for postoperative analgesia in patients undergoing abdominal aortic surgery (+1B). We provide no recommendation for using a lumbar epidural over parenteral opioids

Table 5.

Psychometric Scores for Pain Scales

	Scales					
Psychometric Criteria Scored	Critical Care Pain Observation Tool	BPS	BPS Nonintubated	Nonverbal Pain Scale[a]	Pain Behavioral Assessment Tool	Pain Assessment and Intervention Notation
Item selection description	2	2	2	1	2	1
Content validation	2	0	0	1	1	1
Limitations presented	1	0	0	1	1	1
Internal consistency	2	1	2	I = 1/Rev = 2	0	0
Inter-rater reliability	2	2	2	2	0	0
Inter-rater reliability tested with nonresearch team	1	1	1	1	1	1
Intra-rater reliability tested if inter-rater reliability is low or inconsistent	0	0	N/A	I = N/A /Rev = 0	0	0
Total number of participants	2	2	1	2	2	1
Criterion validation: correlation with "gold standard"	1	2	0	0	1	0
Criterion validation: sensitivity	1	0	0	0	0	0
Criterion validation: specificity	2	0	0	0	0	0
Discriminant validation	2	2	2	2	2	0
Feasibility	1	1	0	0	0	0
Directives of use	1	0	1	0	1	1
Relevance of scale in practice	0	1	0	0	0	1
Total score (range: 0–25)	20	14	11	I = 11/Rev = 12	11	7
Weighted score[b] (range: 0–20)	14.70	12.00	10.20	I = 9.2/Rev = 8.7	7.50	5.90
Quality of psychometric evidence (based on weighted score)	M	M	L	VL	L	VL

BPS = Behavioral Pain Scale; I = initial; Rev = revised; N/A = not applicable; M = moderate; L = low; VL = very low.

[a]Nonverbal pain scale has two versions: I and Rev.

[b]Weighted score range (0–20): Very good psychometric properties(Very good): 15–20; Good psychometric properties (M): 12–14.9; Some acceptable psychometric properties, but remain to be replicated in other studies (L): 10–11.9; Very few psychometric properties reported, or unacceptable results (VL): < 10.

for postoperative analgesia in patients undergoing abdominal aortic aneurysm surgery, due to a lack of benefit when these routes of administration are compared in this patient population (0,A). We provide no recommendation for the use of thoracic epidural analgesia in patients undergoing either intrathoracic or nonvascular abdominal surgical procedures, because of insufficient and conflicting evidence for this mode of analgesic delivery in these patients (0,B). We suggest that thoracic epidural analgesia be considered for patients with traumatic rib fractures (+2B). We provide no recommendation for neuraxial/regional analgesia over systemic analgesia in medical ICU patients, due to lack of evidence in this patient population (0, No Evidence).

Rationale: High-quality evidence suggests that thoracic epidural anesthesia/analgesia in patients undergoing abdominal aortic surgery when the epidural catheter is placed preoperatively provides superior pain relief to parenteral opioids alone; rare complications of thoracic epidurals in these patients include postoperative heart failure, infections, and respiratory failure.[138,139] High-quality evidence demonstrates no benefit with lumbar epidural compared with parenteral opioids in these patients.[139–141] Several shortcomings in research design make it difficult to recommend the use of thoracic epidural analgesia in patients undergoing either intrathoracic or nonvascular abdominal surgical procedures.[142–149] Epidural analgesia administered to patients with rib fractures improved pain control, especially during coughing or deep breathing, lowered the incidence of pneumonia, but increased the risk of hypotension.[150,151] No evidence supports using neuraxial/regional analgesia in medical ICU patients.

Agitation and Sedation. *Indications for sedation.* Agitation and anxiety occur frequently in critically ill patients and are associated with adverse clinical outcomes.[152–156] Sedatives are commonly administered to ICU patients to treat agitation and its negative consequences.[157] Prompt identification and treatment of possible underlying causes of agitation, such as pain, delirium, hypoxemia, hypoglycemia, hypotension, or withdrawal from alcohol and other drugs, are important. Efforts to reduce anxiety and agitation, including maintenance of patient comfort, provision of adequate analgesia, frequent reorientation, and optimization of the environment to maintain normal sleep patterns, should be attempted before administering sedatives.

Sedatives can be titrated to maintain either light (i.e., patient is arousable and able to purposefully follow simple commands) or deep sedation (i.e., patient is unresponsive to painful stimuli). Multiple studies have demonstrated the negative consequences of prolonged, deep sedation, and the benefits of maintaining lighter sedation levels in adult ICU patients.[10,14,15,20,158] The use of sedation scales, sedation protocols designed to minimize sedative use, and the use of nonbenzodiazepine medications are associated with improved ICU patient outcomes, including a shortened duration of mechanical ventilation, ICU and hospital LOS, and decreased incidences of delirium and long-term cognitive dysfunction.[7–10,12,13,18,19,159–162]

Clinical pharmacology of sedatives. Historically, benzodiazepines (i.e., midazolam and lorazepam) and propofol have commonly been used to sedate ICU patients. The 2002 guidelines recommended midazolam only for short-term sedation, lorazepam for long-term sedation, and propofol for patients requiring intermittent awakenings.[1] Recent surveys assessing sedation practices demonstrate that midazolam and propofol remain the dominant medications used for ICU sedation, with decreasing lorazepam use, and rare use of barbiturates, diazepam, and ketamine in the ICU.[62,163–166] Dexmedetomidine, approved in the United States shortly before completion of the 2002 guidelines, is now more commonly administered for ICU sedation.[166–168] The clinical pharmacology of sedatives prescribed for ICU patients is summarized in Table 6.

Benzodiazepines. Benzodiazepines activate γ–aminobutyric acid A ($GABA_A$) neuronal receptors in the brain. They have anxiolytic, amnestic, sedating, hypnotic, and anticonvulsant effects, but no analgesic activity.[169,170] Their amnestic effects extend beyond their sedative effects.[171] Lorazepam is more potent than midazolam, which is more potent than diazepam. Midazolam and diazepam are more lipid soluble than lorazepam, resulting in a quicker onset of sedation and a larger volume of distribution than for lorazepam. Elderly patients are significantly more sensitive to the sedative effects of benzodiazepines.[171] Benzodiazepines can cause respiratory depression and systemic hypotension, especially when administered in conjunction with other cardiopulmonary depressants, particularly opioids.[172] Benzodiazepine-induced cardiopulmonary instability is more likely to occur in critically ill patients with baseline respiratory insufficiency and/or cardiovascular instability.[172] Tolerance to benzodiazepines develops with long-term administration.

All benzodiazepines are metabolized by the liver. Benzodiazepine clearance is reduced in patients with hepatic dysfunction and other disease states, in elderly patients, and when administered with other medications that inhibit cytochrome P_{450} enzyme systems and/or glucuronide conjugation in the liver.[173–175] The elimination half-life and duration of clinical effect of lorazepam are also increased in patients with renal failure.[176,177] The active metabolites of midazolam and diazepam may accumulate with prolonged administration, especially in patients with renal dysfunction.[178] Benzodiazepine clearance decreases with age.[175,179,180]

Delayed emergence from sedation with benzodiazepines can result from prolonged administration of benzodiazepines (due to saturation of peripheral tissues), advanced age, hepatic dysfunction, or renal insufficiency.[171,175,181] Because of the greater potency and slower clearance of lorazepam, emergence from short-term sedation (1–2 days) with lorazepam may be longer than with midazolam. However, comparative studies on the prolonged use of these drugs in ICU patients suggest greater variability and longer time to awakening with midazolam than with lorazepam.[171,175,182–184] Diazepam has a prolonged duration of action due to saturation of peripheral tissues and active metabolites that can accumulate in patients with renal insufficiency.[185]

Parenteral formulations of lorazepam contain propylene glycol as a diluent, which can cause toxicity in ICU patients.[186–190] Propylene glycol toxicity manifests as metabolic acidosis and acute kidney injury. Because these conditions occur frequently in critically ill patients, their possible association with lorazepam administration may be overlooked. Although initially thought to accumulate only in patients receiving very high lorazepam doses via continuous infusion (i.e., 15–25 mg/hr), current evidence suggests that total daily IV doses as low as 1 mg/kg can cause propylene glycol toxicity.[191] The serum osmol gap has been used as a reliable screening and surveillance tool; an osmol gap greater than 10–12 mOsm/L may help identify patients receiving lorazepam who have significant propylene glycol accumulation.[187,191]

Propofol. Propofol is an IV sedative that binds to multiple receptors in the central nervous system to interrupt neural transmission, including $GABA_A$, glycine, nicotinic, and M_1 muscarinic receptors.[192–194] Propofol has sedative, hypnotic, anxiolytic, amnestic, antiemetic, and anticonvulsant properties, but no analgesic effects.[195,196] In ICU patients, propofol's amnestic effects at light sedation levels are less than that of benzodiazepines.[197] Propofol is highly lipid soluble and quickly crosses the blood-brain barrier, resulting in the rapid onset of sedation. Because of its high lipid solubility, propofol also rapidly redistributes into peripheral tissues. This rapid redistribution, combined with high hepatic and extrahepatic clearance, results in a rapid offset of effect following short-term propofol administration. Because of its short duration of sedative effect, propofol may be useful in patients requiring frequent awakenings for neurologic assessments and it may facilitate daily sedation interruption protocols.[183,198,199] However, long-term propofol administration can lead to the saturation of peripheral tissues and prolonged emergence.[198]

Propofol causes dose-dependent respiratory depression and hypotension due to systemic vasodilation. These effects may be more pronounced when propofol is administered with other sedative and opioid medications. Cardiopulmonary instability with propofol administration is more likely to occur in patients with baseline respiratory insufficiency and/or cardiovascular instability. Other side

Table 6.

Clinical Pharmacology of Sedative Medications[1]

Agent	Onset After IV Loading Dose	Elimination Half-Life	Active Metabolites	Loading Dose (IV)	Maintenance Dosing (IV)	Adverse Effects
Midazolam	2–5 min	3–11 hr	Yes[a]	0.01–0.05 mg/kg over several minutes	0.02–0.1 mg/kg/hr	Respiratory depression, hypotension
Lorazepam	15–20 min	8–15 hr	None	0.02–0.04 mg/kg (≤ 2 mg)	0.02–0.06 mg/kg q2–6 hr prn or 0.01–0.1 mg/kg/hr (≤10 mg/hr)	Respiratory depression, hypotension; propylene glycol-related acidosis, nephrotoxicity
Diazepam	2–5 min	20–120 hr	Yes[a]	5–10 mg	0.03–0.1 mg/kg q0.5–6 hr prn	Respiratory depression, hypotension, phlebitis[e]
Propofol	1–2 min	Short-term use = 3–12 hr long-term use = 50 ± 18.6 hr	None	5 µg/kg/min over 5 min[b]	5–50 µg/kg/min	Pain on injection[f], hypotension, respiratory depression, hypertriglyceridemia, pancreatitis, allergic reactions, propofol-related infusion syndrome; deep sedation with propofol is associated with significantly longer emergence times than with light sedation
Dexmedetomidine	5–10 min	1.8–3.1 hr	None	1 µg/kg over 10 min[c]	0.2–0.7 µg/kg/hr[d]	Bradycardia, hypotension; hypertension with loading dose; loss of airway reflexes

[a]Active metabolites prolong sedation, especially in patients with renal failure.
[b]Administer IV loading dose of propofol only in those patients in whom hypotension is unlikely to occur.
[c]Avoid IV loading doses of dexmedetomidine in hemodynamically unstable patients.
[d]Dexmedetomidine maintenance infusion rate may be increased to 1.5 µg/kg/h as tolerated.
[e]Phlebitis occurs when diazepam is injected into peripheral veins.
[f]Pain at the injection site occurs commonly when propofol is administered through peripheral veins.

effects include hypertriglyceridemia, acute pancreatitis, and myoclonus.[200–204] Propofol is dissolved in a 10% lipid emulsion containing egg lecithin and soybean oil, which can precipitate allergic reactions in patients with either egg or soybean allergies. Some generic formulations of propofol contain sulfite preservatives, which may also cause allergic reactions.[196]

Propofol administration is rarely associated with developing propofol infusion syndrome (PRIS). The signs and symptoms of PRIS vary but may include worsening metabolic acidosis, hypertriglyceridemia, hypotension with increasing vasopressor requirements, and arrhythmias. Acute kidney injury, hyperkalemia, rhabdomyolysis, and liver dysfunction have also occasionally been reported with PRIS.[205,206] Possible PRIS mechanisms include mitochondrial dysfunction, impaired fatty acid oxidation, diversion of carbohydrate metabolism to fat substrates, and propofol metabolite accumulation.[207] PRIS is usually associated with prolonged administration of high propofol doses (> 70 µg/kg/min), but it may also occur with low-dose infusions.[208,209] The incidence of PRIS with propofol infusions is approximately 1%.[210] Mortality from PRIS is high (up to 33%) and may occur even after discontinuing the infusion.[202] The variable presentation, lack of diagnostic specificity, and infrequent occurrence of PRIS make detection of this potentially life-threatening condition difficult. Early recognition and discontinuation of propofol in patients with suspected PRIS are critically important. Management of patients with PRIS is otherwise supportive.

Dexmedetomidine. Dexmedetomidine is a selective α_2-receptor agonist with sedative, analgesic/opioid sparing, and sympatholytic properties, but with no anticonvulsant properties.[211,212] Dexmedetomidine produces a pattern of sedation that differs considerably from other sedative agents. Patients sedated with dexmedetomidine are more easily arousable and interactive, with minimal respiratory depression.[213,214] The onset of sedation occurs within 15 mins and peak sedation occurs within 1 hr of starting an IV infusion of dexmedetomidine.[167,215] Sedation onset may be hastened by administering an initial IV loading dose of dexmedetomidine, but this is more likely to cause hemodynamic instability in critically ill patients.[216] Dexmedetomidine is rapidly redistributed into peripheral tissues and is metabolized by the liver.[217] In patients with normal liver function, the elimination half-life is approximately 3 hrs.[215] Patients with severe hepatic dysfunction have impaired dexmedetomidine clearance, can experience prolonged emergence, and may require lower dexmedetomidine doses.[218] Although dexmedetomidine has only been approved in the United States for short-term sedation of ICU patients (< 24 hrs) at a maximal dose of 0.7 μg/kg/hr (up to 1.0 μg/kg/h for procedural sedation), several studies demonstrate the safety and efficacy of dexmedetomidine infusions administered for greater than 24 hrs (up to 28 days) and at higher doses (up to 1.5 μg/kg/hr).[216,219–222]

The most common side effects of dexmedetomidine are hypotension and bradycardia.[223] IV loading doses can cause either hypotension or hypertension.[215,224] Because dexmedetomidine does not significantly affect respiratory drive, it is the only sedative approved in the United States for administration in nonintubated ICU patients, and infusions can be continued as needed following extubation.[225–227] However, dexmedetomidine can cause a loss of oropharyngeal muscle tone which can lead to airway obstruction in nonintubated patients, so continuous respiratory monitoring for both hypoventilation and hypoxemia in these patients is indicated.[225] Dexmedetomidine's opioid-sparing effect may reduce opioid requirements in critically ill patients.[219,220,224,228] The mechanism of action for the analgesic properties of dexmedetomidine remains controversial.[229] Although α_2 receptors are located in the dorsal region of the spinal cord and in supraspinal sites, dexmedetomidine's nonspinal analgesic effects have been documented.[230] One recent study suggests that ICU patients receiving dexmedetomidine may have a lower prevalence of delirium than patients sedated with midazolam.[220]

Agitation and Sedation: Questions, Statements, and Recommendations.

1. Depth of Sedation and Clinical Outcomes

   Question: Should adult ICU patients be maintained at a light level of sedation? (actionable)

   Answer: Maintaining light levels of sedation in adult ICU patients is associated with improved clinical outcomes (e.g., shorter duration of mechanical ventilation and a shorter ICU LOS) (B). Maintaining light levels of sedation increases the physiologic stress response, but is not associated with an increased incidence of myocardial ischemia (B). The association between depth of sedation and psychological stress in these patients remains unclear (C). We recommend that sedative medications be titrated to maintain a light rather than deep level of sedation in adult ICU patients, unless clinically contraindicated (+1B).

   Rationale: Thirteen studies examined the direct relationship between sedative depth and clinical outcomes in ICU patients, including duration of mechanical ventilation, ICU LOS, measures of physiologic stress, and assessments of post-ICU psychological stress.[10,14,15,20,158,231–238] Five studies demonstrated that deeper sedation levels are associated with longer durations of mechanical ventilation and ICU LOS.[10,14,15,20,158] Three studies demonstrated evidence of increased physiologic stress in terms of elevated catecholamine concentrations and/or increased oxygen consumption at lighter sedation levels,[232,235,236] whereas one study did not.[233] The clinical significance of this is unclear, because no clear relationship was observed between elevated markers of physiologic stress and clinical outcomes, such as myocardial ischemia, in these patients.[232–234]

   Four studies examined the relationship between depth of sedation and post-ICU psychological stress.[20,231,237,238] One showed that a protocol of daily sedation interruption did not cause adverse psychological outcomes,[231] whereas another found a low incidence of such events in patients who were lightly sedated.[20] A third study showed that deeper sedation levels were associated with a lower incidence of recall, but that delusional memories did not correlate with lighter levels of sedation.[238] However, in the fourth study, periods of wakefulness were associated with recall of stressful ICU memories.[237] The overall quality of evidence evaluating the relationship between depth of ICU sedation and post-ICU psychological stress is low, and these study results are conflicting. Thus, the overall benefits of maintaining a light sedation level in ICU patients appear to outweigh the risks.

2. Monitoring Depth of Sedation and Brain Function

   a. Sedation scales

      Question: Which subjective sedation scales are the most valid and reliable in the assessment of depth and quality of sedation in mechanically ventilated adult ICU patients? (descriptive)

      Answer: The Richmond Agitation-Sedation Scale (RASS) and Sedation-Agitation Scale (SAS) are the most valid and reliable sedation assessment tools for measuring quality and depth of sedation in adult ICU patients (B).

      Rationale: Several subjective sedation scales exist for monitoring depth of sedation and agitation in adult ICU patients, and their psychometric properties are well described. But the cumulative degree of psychometric properties tested and the quality of evidence vary widely among scales. We reviewed the psychometric properties of ten subjective sedation scales, each developed for evaluating the depth and quality of sedation in adult ICU patients: 1) Observer's Assessment of Alertness/Sedation Scale (OAA/S); 2) Ramsay Sedation Scale (Ramsay); 3) New Sheffield Sedation Scale (Sheffield); 4) Sedation Intensive Care Score (SEDIC); 5) Motor Activity Assessment Scale (MAAS); 6) Adaptation to the Intensive Care Environment (ATICE); 7) Minnesota Sedation Assessment Tool (MSAT); 8) Vancouver Interaction and Calmness Scale (VICS); 9) SAS; and 10) RASS. We reviewed 27 studies including 2,805 patients[2,239–264]: 26 were observational studies and one used a blinded and randomized format to evaluate videos of previously scored patient sedation levels.[253] Table 7 summarizes the psychometric scores for all ten sedation scales.

The RASS and SAS yielded the highest psychometric scores (i.e., inter-rater reliability, convergent or discriminant validation) and had a robust number of study participants. Both scales demonstrated a high degree of inter-rater reliability, which included ICU clinicians.[240,262,263] Both scales were able to discriminate different sedation levels in various clinical situations.[246,250,258,261] Moderate to high correlations were found between the sedation scores of these scales and either electroencephalogram (EEG) or bispectral index (BIS) values.[244,246,258] In addition, the RASS consistently provided a consensus target for goal-directed delivery of sedative agents, demonstrating feasibility of its usage.[2,246,254]

We found that the ATICE, MSAT, and VICS had good quality of psychometric evidence, but some psychometric properties (e.g., convergent or discriminant validation) have not been tested.[242,243,249,259,260] The MAAS, SEDIC, Sheffield, Ramsay, and OAA/S scales had a lower quality of evidence; replication studies and psychometric testing of reliability and validity for determining the depth and quality of sedation in ICU patients are needed.[239,241,242,245,247–249,251–253,255,261,262,264]

In summary, our comparative assessment of the psychometric properties of sedation scales revealed RASS and SAS to be the most valid and reliable for use in critically ill patients, whereas ATICE, MSAT, and VICS are moderately valid and reliable. Additional testing of the remaining scales is needed to better assess their reliability and validity in determining depth of sedation in critically ill patients.

b. Neurologic monitoring

i. *Question:* Should objective measures of brain function (e.g., auditory evoked potentials [AEPs], bispectral index [BIS], Narcotrend Index [NI], Patient State Index [PSI], or state entropy [SE]) be used to assess depth of seda-

Table 7.

Psychometric Scores for Sedation Scales

	Sedation Scale			
Psychometric Criteria Scored	**Observer's Assessment of Alertness/Sedation Scale**	**Ramsay Sedation Scale**	**New Sheffield Sedation Scale**	**Sedation Intensive Care Score**
Item selection description	0	0	2	1
Content validation	0	0	0	0
Limitations presented	0	0	1	0
Interrater reliability	0	1	2	2
Interrater reliability tested with nonresearch team	0	1	1	1
Interrater reliability tested if interrater reliability is low or inconsistent	N/A	0	N/A	N/A
Total number of participants	1	2	0	1
Criterion validation	1	2	0	0
Discriminant validation	0	0	0	2
Feasibility	0	0	0	0
Directives of use	1	0	1	0
Relevance of scale in practice	0	0	0	0
Total score (range: 0–18)	3	6	7	7
Weighted score[a] (range: 0–20)	3.7	7.7	8.5	10.5
Quality of psychometric evidence (based on weighted scores)	VL	VL	VL	L

N/A = not applicable; VL = very low; L = low; M = moderate; VG = very good.

[a]Weighted score range (0–20): Very good psychometric properties (VG): 15–20; Good psychometric properties (M): 12–14.9; Some acceptable psychometric properties, but remain to be replicated in other studies (L): 10–11.9; Very few psychometric properties reported, or unacceptable results (VL): < 10.

tion in *noncomatose*, adult ICU patients who are not receiving neuromuscular blocking agents? (actionable)
Answer: We do not recommend that objective measures of brain function (e.g., AEPs, BIS, NI, PSI, or SE) be used as the primary method to monitor depth of sedation in noncomatose, nonparalyzed critically ill adult patients, as these monitors are inadequate substitutes for subjective sedation scoring systems (–1B).

ii. *Question:* Should objective measures of brain function (e.g., AEPs, BIS, NI, PSI, or SE) be used to measure depth of sedation in adult ICU patients who *are* receiving neuromuscular blocking agents? (actionable)
Answer: We suggest that objective measures of brain function (e.g., AEPs, BIS, NI, PSI, or SE) be used as an adjunct to subjective sedation assessments in adult ICU patients who are receiving neuromuscular blocking agents, as subjective sedation assessments may be unobtainable in these patients (+2B).

iii. *Question:* Should EEG monitoring be used to detect nonconvulsive seizure activity and to titrate electrosuppressive medication to obtain burst suppression in adult ICU patients with either known or suspected seizures? (actionable)
Answer: We recommend that EEG monitoring be used to monitor nonconvulsive seizure activity in adult ICU patients with either known or suspected seizures, or to titrate electrosuppressive medication to achieve burst suppression in adult ICU patients with elevated intracranial pressure (+1A).
Rationale: We reviewed 18 studies comparing objective monitors of sedation to sedation scoring systems in adult ICU patients.[244,248,258,265–279] Objective monitors included both raw and processed EEG and AEP monitors. Processed EEG monitors (i.e., conversion of a raw EEG signal to an index by an algorithm) included the Bispectral Index (BIS) and Bispectral Index XP (BIS-XP SE), NI,

Table 7. *(continued)*
Psychometric Scores for Sedation Scales

Psychometric Criteria Scored	Sedation Scale					
	Motor Activity Assessment Scale	Adaptation to the Intensive Care Environment	Minnesota Sedation Assessment Tool	Vancouver Interaction and Calmness Scale	Sedation-Agitation Scale	Richmond Agitation-Sedation Scale
Item selection description	0	2	2	2	1	2
Content validation	0	1	1	1	1	0
Limitations presented	0	1	1	1	1	0
Interrater reliability	2	2	2	2	2	2
Interrater reliability tested with nonresearch team	1	1	1	1	1	1
Interrater reliability tested if interrater reliability is low or inconsistent	N/A	N/A	N/A	N/A	N/A	N/A
Total number of participants	2	2	2	2	2	2
Criterion validation	1	0	0	0	2	2
Discriminant validation	0	0.5	1	2	2	2
Feasibility	0	0	0	0	0	1
Directives of use	1	1	1	1	1	1
Relevance of scale in practice	0	0	0	0	0	1
Total score (range: 0–18)	7	10.5	11	12	13	14
Weighted score[a] (range: 0–20)	11	12.3	13	14.3	16.5	19
Quality of psychometric evidence (based on weighted scores)	L	M	M	M	VG	VG

and the PSI. The overall evidence is conflicting. Fifteen studies of moderate quality found that objective sedation monitors based on either AEP or processed EEG signals, including BIS, NI, SE, and PSI, may be useful *adjuncts* to subjective sedation assessments in critically ill patients.[244,248,258,266,267,271–273,276,278–283] However, most of these studies reported that electromyographic signals negatively affected the correlation between the objective measure in question and sedation scores. Five additional studies of moderate quality found no benefit in using objective monitors over subjective scoring systems to assess depth of sedation.[268–270,277,284] In most studies, objective monitors distinguished only between deep and light levels of sedation, but their values correlated poorly with specific sedation scores and were negatively influenced by electromyographic signal artifact. Several studies demonstrated that continuous EEG monitoring is useful for detecting nonconvulsive seizure activity in ICU patients either with known seizure activity or who are at risk for seizures (e.g., traumatic brain injury, intracerebral hemorrhage, cerebral vascular accidents, patients with an unexplained depressed level of consciousness).[275,281] Continuous EEG monitoring may also be useful in titrating electrosuppressive medications to achieve burst suppression in critically ill patients with increased intracranial pressure.[275,281]

3. Choice of Sedative

Question: Should nonbenzodiazepine-based sedation, instead of sedation with benzodiazepines, be used in mechanically ventilated adult ICU patients? (actionable)

Answer: We suggest that sedation strategies using nonbenzodiazepine sedatives (either propofol or dexmedetomidine) may be preferred over sedation with benzodiazepines (either midazolam or lorazepam) to improve clinical outcomes in mechanically ventilated adult ICU patients (+2B).

Rationale: In general, the choice of sedative agent used in ICU patients should be driven by: 1) specific indications and sedation goals for each patient; 2) the clinical pharmacology of the drug in a particular patient, including its onset and offset of effect and its side effect profile; and 3) the overall costs associated with using a particular sedative. Outcomes studies of the effects of sedative agents in ICU patients typically compare a benzodiazepine (either midazolam or lorazepam) to a nonbenzodiazepine (either propofol or dexmedetomidine) for sedation. At the time of our literature review, only two low-quality studies had been published comparing clinical outcomes in ICU patients receiving propofol vs. dexmedetomidine for sedation.[285,286] No studies have compared clinical outcomes in ICU patients sedated with either ketamine or other sedative agents. Several studies we reviewed suggested that the sustained use of benzodiazepine-based sedative regimens is associated with adverse clinical outcomes, such as prolonged dependence on mechanical ventilation, increased ICU LOS, and the development of delirium.[29,183,220,286–293] These findings had not been consistently reported, however.[197,222,285,294–297]

We reviewed 13 studies of 1,551 ICU patients comparing clinical outcomes in patients sedated with either benzodiazepines (midazolam or lorazepam) or nonbenzodiazepines (propofol or dexmedetomidine) and found no consistent differences in ICU LOS.[183,197,220,222,285,286,292–298] However, our meta-analysis of six trials ranked as moderate to high quality suggested that sedation with benzodiazepines may increase ICU LOS by approximately 0.5 days compared with nonbenzodiazepine sedation ($p = 0.04$) (Fig. 1).[183,197,220,222,292,295–297] Limited data suggested that mechanical ventilation is prolonged with benzodiazepine-based sedation.[183,220,292,298] There was no apparent difference in mortality with benzodiazepine vs. nonbenzodiazepine sedation.[220,222,285,295] Six trials evaluated the influence of benzodiazepine-based sedation on the cost of ICU care;[194,222,286,294,299,300] only one study found that benzodiazepine-based sedation (i.e., midazolam infusion) was associated with higher ICU costs than sedation with dexmedetomidine.[300]

When we compared outcome studies in ICU patients sedated with propofol vs. either midazolam or lorazepam, we found several studies demonstrating that propofol use may be associated with a shorter duration of mechanical ventilation, but this effect varied across patient populations,[183,197,291,292,294–297] and did not necessarily translate into a shorter ICU LOS. There was no apparent difference in the incidence of self-extubation with propofol vs. benzodiazepine sedation.[183] A separate systematic review evaluated 16 randomized, controlled trials comparing clinical outcomes in ICU patients receiving either propofol or another sedative agent.[291] When this meta-analysis was restricted to a comparison of propofol and midazolam, there was no difference in mortality, a slight reduction in the duration of mechanical ventilation with propofol, but no difference in ICU LOS. The relationship between using either propofol or benzodiazepines for sedation and the development of delirium is unclear. Only two relevant studies have been published comparing the incidence of delirium in ICU patients receiving propofol vs. benzodiazepines for sedation.[285, 286] In both studies, patients were randomized to receive propofol, midazolam, or dexmedetomidine for sedation, and the incidence of delirium was similar in patients receiving either propofol or midazolam, but the quality of evidence was low.

We reviewed five studies comparing outcomes in ICU patients receiving either dexmedetomidine or a benzodiazepine (either midazolam or lorazepam) for sedation.[220,222,285,286,293] Three of the four studies evaluating duration of mechanical ventilation showed no difference between these groups.[222,285,286] However, the largest study did demonstrate a significant reduction in the time to liberation from mechanical ventilation with dexmedetomidine (3.7 days) compared with midazolam (5.6 days).[220] Dexmedetomidine was not associated with a lower incidence of self-extubation compared with benzodiazepines.[222] Four of the five studies showed no difference in ICU LOS.[220,222,285,286] Five studies, including a subgroup analysis from the Maximizing Efficacy of Targeted Sedation and Reducing Neurological Dysfunction trial, evaluated the development of delirium in patients receiving either dexmedetomidine or a benzodiazepine for sedation.[220,222,285,286,298] Delirium was reported in

Study or Subgroup	Benzodiazepine Mean	Benzodiazepine SD	Benzodiazepine Total	Non-Benzodiazepine Mean	Non-Benzodiazepine SD	Non-Benzodiazepine Total	Weight	Mean Difference IV, Random, 95% CI
Hall 2001-72+, M/P, SD	9.14	3.99	10	8.46	4.83	4	1.0%	0.68 [−4.66, 6.02]
Hall 2001-24-72, M/P, SD	6.31	5.94	17	6.59	8.34	21	1.4%	−0.28 [−4.83, 4.27]
Pandharipande 2007, L/D, IQR	9	6.66	51	7.5	10.36	52	2.5%	1.50 [−1.86, 4.86]
Carson 2006, L/P, IQR	10.4	7.47	64	8.3	7.4	68	4.2%	2.10 [−0.44, 4.64]
Hall 2001-24, M/P, SD	2.48	1.99	26	2.95	3.9	21	7.8%	−0.47 [−2.31, 1.37]
Riker 2009, M/D, SD, median	7.6	5.35	122	5.9	5.18	244	17.5%	1.70 [0.55, 2.85]
Searle 1997, M/P, SD	3.9	1.7	20	3.7	1.7	21	20.5%	0.20 [−0.84, 1.24]
Huey-Ling 2008, M/P, SD	3.1	1.12	28	2.8	1.13	32	45.1%	0.30 [−0.27, 0.87]
Total (95% CI)			**338**			**463**	**100.0%**	**0.57 [0.03, 1.10]**

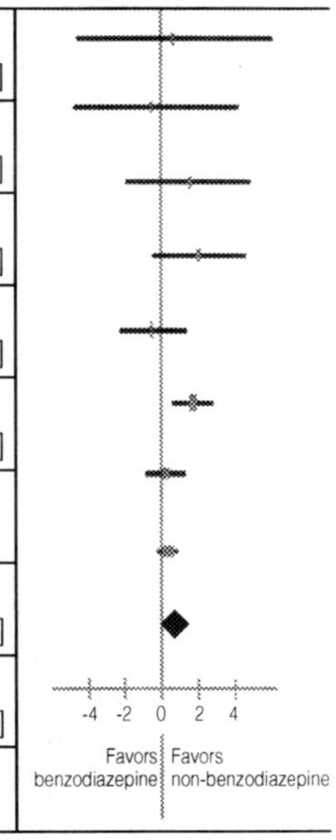

Heterogeneity: $Tau^2 = 0.08$; $Chi^2 = 8.03$, df = 7 ($p = 0.33$), $I^2 = 13\%$
Test for overall effect Z = 2.08 ($p = 0.04$)

Figure 1. ICU length of stay meta-analysis of high and moderate-quality studies comparing benzodiazepine to nonbenzodiazepine sedation. CI = confidence interval; IQR = interquartile range. L/D = lorazepam vs. dexmedetomidine; L/P = lorazepam vs. propofol; M/P = midazolam vs. propofol; M/D = midazolam vs. dexmedetomidine; SD = standard deviation.

terms of frequency of occurrence, prevalence, and delirium-free days. Three studies favored dexmedetomidine,[286,288,300] although only one was of high quality.[220] The subgroup analysis trial favored dexmedetomidine over lorazepam in septic patients only.[298] One trial showed no relationship between benzodiazepine use and delirium.[222] One very low-quality trial suggested a higher rate of delirium with dexmedetomidine, but suffered from serious methodological flaws including imprecision in the measurement of delirium.[285]

The results of two high-quality, randomized, double-blind, comparative trials of dexmedetomidine vs. either midazolam or propofol for ICU sedation were published after the guideline task force had completed its voting and developed its recommendations.[301] The relevant outcomes in both studies included duration of mechanical ventilation, and ICU and hospital LOS. Except for a longer duration of mechanical ventilation with midazolam use, no differences between groups were seen. These results are consistent with both our analysis of previously published data and subsequent recommendation for benzodiazepine-based vs. nonbenzodiazepine-based sedation.

In summary, the current literature supports modest differences in outcomes with benzodiazepine-based vs. nonbenzodiazepine-based sedation. Our meta-analysis of moderate to high-quality trials indicates that benzodiazepine sedation is associated with an increased ICU LOS. Moderate to high-quality data favor using propofol over lorazepam[183] and dexmedetomidine over midazolam[220] to limit the duration of mechanical ventilation. The clinical significance of the comparative deliriogenic effects of benzodiazepines remains uncertain, with one high-quality trial indicating benzodiazepines pose higher risks than dexmedetomidine.[220] Additional recommendations to prevent or treat delirium can be found in the Delirium section of these guidelines. Dexmedetomidine may offer an advantage in ICU resource consumption compared to midazolam infusions in health care institutions that are efficient in transferring patients out of the ICU.[300] Despite the apparent advantages in using either propofol or dexmedetomidine over benzodiazepines for ICU sedation, benzodiazepines remain important for managing agitation in ICU patients, especially for treating anxiety, seizures, and alcohol or benzodiazepine withdrawal. Benzodiazepines are also important when deep sedation, amnesia, or combination therapy to reduce the use of other sedative agents is required.[166,302]

Delirium

Epidemiology of Delirium in ICU Patients. Delirium is a syndrome characterized by the acute onset of cerebral dysfunction with a change or fluctuation in baseline mental status, inattention, and either disorganized thinking or an altered level of consciousness.[303–309] The cardinal features of delirium are: 1) a disturbed level of consciousness (i.e., a reduced clarity of awareness of the environment), with a reduced ability to focus, sustain, or shift attention; and 2) either a change in cognition (i.e., memory deficit, disorientation, language disturbance), or the development of a perceptual disturbance (i.e., hallucinations, delusions).[310] A common misconception is that delirious patients are either hallucinating or delusional, but neither of these symptoms is required to make the diagnosis. Other symptoms commonly associated with delirium include sleep disturbances, abnormal psychomotor activity, and emotional disturbances (i.e., fear, anxiety, anger, depression, apathy, euphoria). Patients with delirium may be agitated (hyperactive delirium), calm or lethargic (hypoactive delirium), or may fluctuate between the two subtypes. Hyperactive delirium is more often associated with hallucinations and delusions, while hypoactive delirium is more often characterized by confusion and sedation, and is often misdiagnosed in ICU patients.

Delirium in critically ill patients is now recognized as a major public health problem, affecting up to 80% of mechanically ventilated adult ICU patients, and costing $4 to $16 billion annually in the United States alone.[311–314] Over the past decade, the study of delirium in ICU patients has expanded significantly.[315–319] But the underlying pathophysiology of delirium in critically ill patients remains poorly understood.[320–322]

Impact of Delirium on ICU Patient Outcomes. Delirium, as a manifestation of acute brain dysfunction, is an important independent predictor of negative clinical outcomes in ICU patients, including increased mortality, hospital LOS, cost of care, and long-term cognitive impairment consistent with a dementia-like state.[313,320–324] ICU team practices affect the incidence of delirium and its consequences.[220,222,325–329] Critical care professionals strive to understand which aspects of delirium are predictable, preventable, detectable, and treatable.

Preventing, Detecting, and Treating Delirium in ICU Patients. Delirium may be a disease-induced syndrome (e.g., organ dysfunction in severe sepsis), for which timely management of the cause or causes is essential in order to reduce the incidence, severity, and duration of delirium. Iatrogenic (e.g., exposure to sedative and opioid medications) or environmental (e.g., prolonged physical restraints or immobilization) factors may also contribute to delirium in ICU patients. ICU patients should be evaluated for identifiable and avoidable risk factors, and therapeutic interventions should be assessed in terms of their likelihood of either causing or exacerbating delirium in individual patients. Delirium prevention strategies can be categorized as nonpharmacologic (e.g., early mobilization), pharmacologic, and combined pharmacologic/nonpharmacologic approaches. Monitoring critically ill patients for delirium with valid and reliable delirium assessment tools enables clinicians to potentially detect and treat delirium sooner, and possibly improve outcomes.

Patients are frequently given various medications to reduce the severity and duration of delirium once it has occurred. Although no double-blind, randomized, placebo-controlled trials which are adequately powered have established the efficacy or safety of any antipsychotic agent in the management of delirium in ICU patients, administration of antipsychotic medications is endorsed by various international guidelines,[330–339] and most critical care specialists use these medications to treat delirious patients.[164] In the previous version of these guidelines, the recommended use of haloperidol for the treatment of delirium was a Level C recommendation based only on a case series. These data did not meet the evidence standard for this version of the guidelines. No recent prospective trials have verified the safety and efficacy of haloperidol for the treatment of delirium in adult ICU patients. Data on the use of other antipsychotics in this patient population are similarly sparse. A recent Cochrane Review on using antipsychotics for the treatment of delirium did not address the issue of antipsychotic use in ICU patients.[340] Robust data on haloperidol in non-ICU patients that could potentially be applied to the ICU patient population are lacking. Further research is needed to determine the safety and efficacy of using antipsychotics in general, including haloperidol, to treat delirium in ICU patients.

Delirium due to Drug and/or Alcohol Withdrawal. During their ICU stay, critically ill patients may develop a subcategory of delirium related to either drug or alcohol withdrawal, which usually manifests as a hyperactive type of delirium. Withdrawal symptoms may result from abrupt discontinuation of: 1) illicit or prescription drugs that patients were taking chronically; 2) sedatives or opioids administered as part of routine ICU care; or 3) chronic ethanol use. An exhaustive review of the pathophysiology, diagnosis, and treatment of drug and alcohol withdrawal is beyond the scope of these guidelines. Clinicians are referred to other clinical practice guidelines for more detail.[341–343]

Patients with long-term exposure to high-dose opiates or sedatives may develop physiologic dependence, and abrupt discontinuation may cause drug withdrawal symptoms.[344] Signs and symptoms of acute opiate withdrawal include sweating, piloerection, mydriasis, lacrimation, rhinorrhea, vomiting, diarrhea, abdominal cramping, tachycardia, hypertension, fever, tachypnea, yawning, restlessness, irritability, myalgias, increased sensitivity to pain, and anxiety. The onset of symptoms can occur < 12 hrs following discontinuation of opioids, or be precipitated by either the administration of the opioid antagonist, naloxone, or mixed agonist/antagonists such as nalbuphine.[345,346] Prolonged benzodiazepine use in ICU patients may lead to withdrawal symptoms when the drug is abruptly discontinued, manifesting as anxiety, agitation, tremors, headaches, sweating, insomnia, nausea, vomiting, myoclonus, muscle cramps, hyperactive delirium, and occasionally seizures.[344] Reversing the sedative effects of benzodiazepines following long-term exposure with the benzodiazepine receptor antagonist flumazenil may induce symptoms of benzodiazepine withdrawal.[347,348] Adult ICU patients receiving dexmedetomidine infusions for up to 7 days have developed withdrawal symptoms, most commonly nausea, vomiting, and agitation, within 24–48 hrs of discontinuing dexmedetomidine.[349] In the largest study to date looking prospectively at the effects of sedation of ICU patients with dexmedetomidine vs. midazolam, the incidence of withdrawal following discontinuation of dexmedetomidine was 4.9% vs. 8.2% in midazolam-treated patients ($p = 0.25$).[220] Signs and symptoms of opioid and sedative withdrawal in critically ill patients may be overlooked or attributed to other causes, such as alcohol or illicit drug withdrawal.

In the past decade, little was published on the pathophysiology and incidence of drug withdrawal from opioids and sedative agents administered to adult ICU patients. Most studies are retrospective and include patients who have received a variety of sedative and analgesic agents, making it difficult to determine specific incidences and risk factors for drug withdrawal in these patients.[344,350] One small prospective study assessed adult ICU patients for signs and symptoms of withdrawal following discontinuation of sufentanil infusions used concurrently with either midazolam or propofol infusions.[351] Patients in the sufentanil/midazolam group were sedated for 7.7 days vs. 3.5 days for the sufentanil/propofol group. Withdrawal symptoms occurred more frequently in the midazolam group (35% vs. 28% with propofol). Although specific recommendations are lacking for the prophylaxis or treatment of opioid or sedative withdrawal in ICU patients, opioids and/or sedatives administered for prolonged periods (i.e., days) should be weaned over several days in order to reduce the risk of drug withdrawal.

Ethanol (ETOH) dependence is present in 15%–20% of all hospitalized patients.[352] Between 8% and 31% of hospitalized patients with ETOH dependence, especially surgical and trauma patients, will go on to develop Alcohol Withdrawal Syndrome (AWS) during their hospital stay, with signs and symptoms of neurologic and autonomic dysfunction.[353–355] Symptoms of AWS range from mild to life-threatening.[356] Up to 15% of hospitalized patients with AWS experience generalized tonic-clonic seizures, and 5% develop delirium tremens (DTs), a life-threatening combination of central nervous system excitation (agitation, delirium, and seizures) and hyperadrenergic symptoms (hypertension, tachycardia, arrhythmias).[357] ICU patients with severe AWS may exhibit prolonged ventilator dependence and extended ICU stays as a result of persistent delirium.[353–355]

Prior ethanol dependence is often underestimated in ICU patients, making identification of patients at risk for AWS or DTs difficult. Screening tools for AWS or DTs have not been fully validated in the critical care setting. Differentiating between delirium due to alcohol withdrawal vs. other causes may be difficult. Symptom-oriented treatment of AWS symptoms with drug dosing as needed to specifically target agitation, psychosis, and autonomic hyperactivity decreases the severity and duration of AWS, and medication requirements in ICU patients.[358] Benzodiazepines are considered the mainstay of alcohol withdrawal treatment, despite uncertainty about their effectiveness and safety.[320] To date, no published studies have compared the safety and efficacy of treating symptoms of severe AWS with dexmedetomidine vs. benzodiazepines. Diagnosis and management of delirium due to AWS in ICU patients remains challenging. It is beyond the scope of these guidelines to describe the validity of alcohol withdrawal measurement tools, of alcohol withdrawal prevention, or of its treatment in the critical care setting.

Delirium: Questions, Statements, and Recommendations.

1. Outcomes Associated With Delirium in ICU Patients

   Question: What outcomes are associated with delirium in adult ICU patients? (descriptive)

   Answer: Delirium is associated with increased mortality (A), prolonged ICU and hospital LOS (A), and development of post-ICU cognitive impairment in adult ICU patients (B).

   Rationale: Numerous prospective cohort studies have demonstrated that patients who develop delirium are at increased risk for adverse outcomes both in the ICU and after discharge. This risk is independent of preexisting comorbidities, severity of illness, age, and other covariates that might be merely associative. Eleven prospective cohort studies examined the relationship between delirium while in the ICU and mortality at various time points: ICU discharge (n = 5), hospital discharge (n = 4), 30 days (n = 1), 3 months (n = 1), 6 months (n = 3), and 12 months (n = 1).[318,319,321,322,359–365] All studies classified delirium as present on one or more ICU days; three studies also examined the relationship between delirium duration and mortality.[320,321,366] Delirium was an independent predictor of mortality in 11 of 15 studies, including the three studies with a high quality of evidence.[320,321,366] Duration of delirium (after adjusting for coma and in some cases psychoactive medication exposure) was significantly associated with 6- and 12-month mortality rates. In two cohort studies, duration of delirium consistently portended a 10% increased risk of death per day (after adjusting for covariates and appropriately treating delirium as a time-dependent covariate).[320,321]

   Nine prospective cohort studies examined the relationship between one or more days of delirium in the ICU and ICU and/or hospital LOS, as well as duration of mechanical ventilation.[318,319,322,323,360,361,363,364,367] Delirium was an independent predictor of duration of mechanical ventilation in four studies[360,363,364,367] and of ICU LOS in four studies.[318,319,364,367] Both of these outcome variables are particularly at risk for immortal time bias, which is introduced when the exposure to a treatment or independent variable (in this case, delirium) can change daily during the actual outcome measurement (in this case, either duration of mechanical ventilation or ICU LOS).[368] It is therefore important that the predictive relationship between delirium and hospital LOS was also strong in seven of nine studies,[318,319,322,323,361,364,367] including three high-quality studies that accounted for immortal time bias.[318,322,368]

   Two prospective cohort studies examined the relationship between delirium in the ICU and subsequent cognitive impairment. One study of moderate quality described an association between the presence of delirium on one or more ICU days and a higher incidence of cognitive dysfunction at hospital discharge.[322] In a recent prospective cohort study of moderate quality, increasing duration of delirium in ICU patients was associated with significantly greater cognitive impairment in these patients at 3 and 12 months.[324]

2. Detecting and Monitoring Delirium

   a. *Question:* Should ICU patients be monitored routinely for delirium with an objective bedside delirium instrument? (actionable)

   Answer: We recommend routine monitoring for delirium in adult ICU patients (+1B).

   Rationale: Delirium is common in both mechanically ventilated[14,220,222,308,360,369,370] and nonmechanically ventilated ICU patients.[309,359,371–379] ICU personnel often underestimate the presence of delirium in patients because it frequently presents as hypoactive rather than hyperactive delirium.[372,380] Delirium can be detected in both intubated and nonintubated ICU patients using valid and reliable tools. In most studies, delirium detection was improved when caregivers used a valid and reliable delirium assessment tool,[367] also allowing them to reassure frightened and disoriented patients.[381] Delirium monitoring rationale includes: 1) most informed patients at moderate to high risk want to be monitored for delirium; 2) high-quality cohort data relating delirium to critical outcomes shows high delirium "miss rates" in the absence of monitoring; 3) clinicians have successfully implemented ICU delirium monitoring programs on a large-scale, using assessment tools recommended in these guidelines; and 4) policy makers can adopt delirium assessment as part of routine, high-quality care in most ICUs.[254,372,374,382,383] Based on moderate evidence, we issue a strong recommendation that ICU patients at moderate to high risk for delirium (e.g., patients: with a baseline history of alcoholism, cognitive impairment, or hypertension; with severe sepsis or shock; on mechanical ventilation; or receiving parenteral sedative and opioid medications) should be routinely monitored, at least once per nursing shift, for the development of delirium using a valid and reliable delirium assessment tool.

b. *Question:* Which instruments available for delirium monitoring have the strongest evidence for validity and reliability in ventilated and nonventilated medical and surgical ICU patients? (descriptive)

Answer: The Confusion Assessment Method for the ICU (CAM-ICU) and the Intensive Care Delirium Screening Checklist (ICDSC) are the most valid and reliable delirium monitoring tools in adult ICU patients (A).

Rationale: Five delirium monitoring tools were evaluated for use in ICU patients: Cognitive Test for Delirium (CTD), CAM-ICU, Delirium Detection Score (DDS), ICDSC, and Nursing Delirium Screening Scale (Nu-DESC). Table 8 compares their psychometric properties. Both the CAM-ICU[308,359,371–374,384–387] and ICDSC[309,371] demonstrate very good psychometric properties (i.e., validity and reliability), and are explicitly designed for use in ICU patients both on and off mechanical ventilation. Translated into over 20 languages, these tools are currently in use worldwide.[315] The CAM-ICU and ICDSC have shown high inter-rater reliability when tested by ICU nurses and intensivists.[308,309,373] They both demonstrated high sensitivity and specificity when tested against the American Psychiatric Association's criteria for delirium.[319,359,379] Predictive validation of the presence of delirium, as detected with the CAM-ICU or ICDSC, was associated with clinical outcomes such as increased ICU and hospital LOS[318,319,322,323,360,361,363,364,367] and higher risk of mortality.[318,319,321,322,359–365] Based on our review of the literature, both the CAM-ICU and ICDSC are valid, reliable, and feasible tools to detect delirium in ICU patients.[254,309] While the CTD[388–390] and Nu-DESC[379] reached the minimum weighted psychometric score of 12 in our analysis, some psychometric properties remain to be tested for these tools, including inter-rater reliability in a nonresearch setting and clinical feasibility. Further psychometric testing of the DDS[347] is needed in order to better assess its overall validity, reliability, and feasibility as a delirium monitoring tool in critically ill patients.

Since completing our review and analysis of the literature in 2010 on delirium monitoring tools, several additional studies have been published analyzing the sensitivity, specificity, and reliability of delirium assessment tools in clinical practice.[391–394] A meta-analysis of five ICU delirium screening tools found that the CAM-ICU and ICDSC were the most sensitive and specific tools for detecting delirium, consistent with our recommendation.[392] A separate meta-analysis of studies comparing the CAM-ICU to the ICDSC also found a high degree of sensitivity and specificity for both tools.[393] Additional studies are needed to assess the performance of delirium monitoring tools in routine clinical practice across different types of ICU patients.[391,394]

c. *Question:* Is implementation of routine delirium monitoring feasible in clinical practice? (descriptive)

Answer: Routine monitoring of delirium in adult ICU patients is feasible in clinical practice (B).

Rationale: Moderate-quality evidence suggests that routine monitoring of delirium is feasible in clinical practice. Numerous implementation studies including over 2,000 patients across multiple institutions showed delirium monitoring compliance rates in excess of 90%. Practicing ICU nurses and physicians demonstrated high inter-rater reliability with trained experts using several of the recommended delirium monitoring tools.[254,372,374,382,383] Although studies show that implementation of delirium monitoring is feasible in the ICU, lack of physician buy-in is a significant barrier.[395] Successful strategies for overcoming this hurdle requires a focus on human factors and changing ICU culture.[316] A more recent study of delirium monitoring implementation (published after evidence was graded for this topic), that included over 500 ICU patients (medical, surgical, and cardiac) and over 600 ICU nurses over a 3-yr period, reinforces the conclusion that routine delirium monitoring is feasible in clinical practice.[394]

3. Delirium Risk Factors

a. *Question:* What baseline risk factors are associated with the development of delirium in the ICU? (descriptive)

Answer: Four baseline risk factors are positively and significantly associated with the development of delirium in the ICU: preexisting dementia; history of hypertension and/or alcoholism; and a high severity of illness at admission (B).

Rationale: The following baseline risk factors have been reported as significant in two or more multivariable analyses: preexisting dementia[329,375,396]; history of baseline hypertension[318,397]; alcoholism, defined as ingestion of two to three or more drinks daily[318,396]; and a high severity of illness at admission.[318,328,329,398] Although age has been identified as one of the most significant risk factors for delirium outside the ICU, only two studies reported it to be significant in ICU patients,[328,398] while four studies reported it as insignificant.[318,375,396,399] More research is needed to confirm the relationship between age and the development of delirium in ICU patients.

Table 8.

Psychometric Scores for Delirium Monitoring Tools

Psychometric Criteria Scored	Delirium Monitoring Tools: Confusion Assessment Method for the ICU	Intensive Care Delirium Screening Checklist	Cognitive Test for Delirium	Nursing Delirium Screening Scale	Delirium Detection Score
Item selection description	2	1	2	1	1
Content validation	1	0	2	0	0
Limitations presented	1	1	1	0	1
Interrater reliability	2	2	2	2	2
Interrater reliability tested with nonresearch team	1	1	0	0	0
Interrater reliability tested if interrater reliability is low or inconsistent	N/A	N/A	N/A	N/A	0
Total number of participants	2	2	2	2	2
Criterion validation: sensitivity	2	2	2	2	0
Criterion validation: specificity	2	1	2	2	2
Predictive validation	2	2	0	1	0
Feasibility	1	0	0	0	0
Directives of use	1	1	1	1	1
Relevance of scale in practice	1	1	0	0	0
Total score (range: 0–19 or 21)	18/19	14/19	14/19	11/19	9/21
Weighted score[a] (range: 0–20)	19.6	16.8	13.0	12.4	8.2
Quality of psychometric evidence (based on weighted scores)	VG	VG	M	M	VL

VG, very good; M = moderate; VL = very low; NA = not applicable.

[a]Weighted score range (0–20): Very good psychometric properties (VG): 15–20; Good psychometric properties (M): 12–14.9; Some acceptable psychometric properties, but remain to be replicated in other studies (Low): 10–11.9; Very few psychometric properties reported, or unacceptable results (VL): < 10.

b. *Question:* Is coma a risk factor for the development of delirium in the ICU? (descriptive)

Answer: Coma is an independent risk factor for the development of delirium in ICU patients. Establishing a definitive relationship between various subtypes of coma (i.e., medication-related, structural, neurological, medical) and delirium in ICU patients will require further study (B).

Rationale: Several reports have shown coma to be an independent risk factor for delirium in ICU patients.[318,399] One study further classified coma into three categories: medical coma (i.e., due to a primary neurological condition), sedative-induced coma, and multifactorial coma (both medical and sedative-induced coma).[318] In this study, sedative-induced coma and multifactorial coma were significantly associated with the development of delirium, but medical coma was not.[318]

c. *Question:* Which ICU treatment-related (acquired) risk factors (i.e., opioids, benzodiazepines, propofol, and dexmedetomidine) are associated with the development of delirium in adult ICU patients? (descriptive)

Answer: Conflicting data surround the relationship between opioid use and the development of delirium in adult ICU patients (B). Benzodiazepine use may be a risk factor for the development of delirium in adult ICU patients (B). There are insufficient data to determine the relationship between propofol use and the development of delirium in adult ICU patients (C). In mechanically ventilated adult ICU patients at risk for developing delirium, dexmedetomidine infusions administered for sedation may be associated with a lower prevalence of delirium compared to benzodiazepine infusions administered (B).

Rationale: Study designs including opioids varied greatly. Some reported individual medications used,[288,328,397,398] while others provided only the medication class,[363] and still others combined opioids with sedatives or other analgesics.[318,329,396] Study results also varied considerably. Most studies reported either an increased risk of delirium with opioids or no association.[288,318,328,329,363,396–398] One study[400] found that opioids reduced the risk of delirium in burn patients. Only one high-quality study explicitly addressed the association between propofol and delirium risk in ICU patients, and found no significant relationship.[328] Benzodiazepines were included in several delirium risk factor studies. As with opioids, study designs varied greatly. Some moderate-quality studies reported a strong relationship between benzodiazepine use and the development of delirium,[288,328] while others found no significant relationship.[318,363,396–399] Two randomized controlled trials comparing sedation with benzodiazepines vs. dexmedetomidine reported a lower prevalence of delirium (~20%) in patients randomized to receive dexmedetomidine.[220,298] Although these data do not prove that benzodiazepines are causal or that dexmedetomidine is protective, this literature suggests that benzodiazepines may be a risk factor for the development of delirium in the ICU. Whether dexmedetomidine reduces the risk of ICU patients developing delirium is now under study.

4. Prevention of Delirium

a. *Question:* Should a nonpharmacologic delirium protocol be used in the ICU to reduce the incidence or duration of delirium? (actionable)

Answer: We recommend performing early mobilization of adult ICU patients whenever feasible to reduce the incidence and duration of delirium (+1B).

Rationale: Early mobilization was initially studied in the critical care setting as a nonpharmacologic intervention aiming to improve functional outcomes. In the first multicenter randomized controlled trial of early mobility,[326] and in a subsequent implementation study,[401] investigators also noted striking reductions in the incidence of delirium, depth of sedation, and hospital and ICU LOS, with an increase in ventilator-free days. These studies suggest that early and aggressive mobilization is unlikely to harm ICU patients, but may reduce the incidence and duration of delirium, shorten ICU and hospital LOS, and lower hospital costs. While more broadly targeted, high-quality non-pharmacologic protocols have shown favorable results in non-ICU hospitalized patients,[402] such multifaceted interventions have not been adequately studied in the ICU setting.

b. *Question:* Should a pharmacologic delirium prevention protocol be used in the ICU to reduce the incidence or duration of delirium? (actionable)

Answer: We provide no recommendation for using a pharmacologic delirium prevention protocol in adult ICU patients, as no compelling data demonstrate that this reduces the incidence or duration of delirium in these patients (0, C).

Rationale: One prospective, unblinded, randomized controlled trial assessed a nocturnal pharmacologic regimen for maintaining sleep-wake cycles in hospitalized patients following gastrointestinal surgery, with questionable value and applicability to critical care practice.[403] A more recent prospective, placebo-controlled, blinded, randomized study did show benefit to administering low doses of haloperidol prophylactic to elderly surgical ICU patients in order to prevent delirium.[404] However, these patients were not very ill, and most were not mechanically ventilated. More study is needed to determine the safety and efficacy of using a pharmacologic delirium prevention protocol in ICU patients.

c. *Question:* Should a combined nonpharmacologic and pharmacologic delirium prevention protocol be used in the ICU to reduce the incidence or duration of delirium? (actionable)

Answer: We provide no recommendation for the use of a combined nonpharmacologic and pharmacologic delirium prevention protocol in adult ICU patients, as this has not been shown to reduce the incidence of delirium in these patients (0, C).

Rationale: One before/after study evaluated the impact of a multidisciplinary protocol for managing PAD in ICU patients. Patients managed with this protocol had a reduced incidence of subsyndromal delirium but not delirium, improved pain control, and a 15% reduction in their total ICU costs.[327,405] Subsyndromal delirium in ICU patients is defined as patients who have less than four points on the ICDSC; patients with subsyndromal delirium have worse clinical outcomes than those without delirium.[319] Further research is needed to determine whether a combined nonpharmacologic and pharmacologic protocol reduces the incidence or duration of full-blown delirium in ICU patients.

d. *Question:* Should haloperidol or atypical antipsychotics be used prophylactically to prevent delirium in ICU patients? (actionable)

Answer: We do not suggest that either haloperidol or atypical antipsychotics be administered to prevent delirium in adult ICU patients (–2C).

Rationale: No high-quality studies with sufficient sample size or effect size demonstrate a benefit of administering prophylactic antipsychotics to the general ICU population. A recent moderate-quality trial demonstrated that low-dose IV haloperidol prophylaxis may reduce the prevalence of delirium in low acuity elderly postoperative patients who are admitted to the ICU.[404] Whether these data can be applied to a more diverse population of sicker ICU patients is uncertain. A well-designed, but underpowered, multicenter, randomized controlled trial of delirium prophylaxis with either haloperidol or ziprasidone vs. placebo did not show any benefit with either treatment group as compared to placebo.[370] One moderate-quality study suggested that a single dose of sublingual risperidone administered immediately postoperatively to cardiac surgery patients reduced the incidence of delirium.[406] Further research is needed to better define the safety and efficacy of typical and atypical antipsychotics for delirium prevention in ICU patients.

e. *Question:* Should dexmedetomidine be used prophylactically to prevent delirium in ICU patients? (actionable)

Answer: We provide no recommendation for the use of dexmedetomidine to prevent delirium in adult ICU patients, as there is no evidence regarding its effectiveness in these patients (0, C).

Rationale: One cardiovascular ICU study ($n = 306$) addressed the issue of dexmedetomidine and delirium prophylaxis in ICU patients.[407] Delirium lasted 2 days in the dexmedetomidine group compared with 5 days in the morphine group ($p = 0.03$), but delirium prevalence was not significantly reduced (9% vs. 15%, respectively, $p = 0.09$). Until more data become available, we provide no recommendation for delirium prophylaxis with dexmedetomidine, given the risks of treatment without clear benefit.

5. Treatment of Delirium

a. *Question:* Does treatment with haloperidol reduce the duration of delirium in adult ICU patients? (descriptive)

Answer: There is no published evidence that treatment with haloperidol reduces the duration of delirium in adult ICU patients (No Evidence).

b. *Question:* Does treatment with atypical antipsychotics reduce the duration of delirium in adult ICU patients? (descriptive)

Answer: Atypical antipsychotics may reduce the duration of delirium in adult ICU patients (C).

Rationale: In a single small prospective, randomized, double-blind, placebo-controlled study ($n = 36$), ICU patients with delirium who received quetiapine had a reduced duration of delirium.[408] Patients with delirium who were being treated with haloperidol were randomized to additionally receive either quetiapine 50 mg or placebo every 12 hrs. The quetiapine dose was increased by 50 mg if more than one dose of haloperidol was given in the previous 24 hrs. All patients were allowed to receive IV haloperidol 1–10 mg every 2 hrs as needed. The use of haloperidol was not significantly different between the groups. Comparable data are not available for treatment with haloperidol alone. Sufficiently powered, carefully designed, multicenter, placebo-controlled trials are needed to address the hypothesis that antipsychotics are beneficial in the treatment of delirium in critically ill patients.

c. *Question:* Should treatment with cholinesterase inhibitors (rivastigmine) be used to reduce the duration of delirium in ICU patients? (actionable)

Answer: We do not recommend administering rivastigmine to reduce the duration of delirium in ICU patients (–1B).

Rationale: Rivastigmine, a cholinesterase inhibitor, may be useful in treating delirium in demented elderly patients. However, rivastigmine was compared to placebo in critically ill patients in an investigation stopped for futility and potential harm[409] This multicenter trial was halted after 104 patients were enrolled because the rivastigmine-treated patients had more severe and longer delirium, with a trend toward higher mortality. In another study (published after the evidence analysis for this recommendation), perioperative rivastigmine was administered for delirium prophylaxis in patients undergoing elective cardiac surgery ($n = 120$, patients > 65 yr), and had no effect on the incidence of postoperative delirium in these patients.[410]

d. *Question:* Should haloperidol and atypical antipsychotics be withheld in patients at high risk for torsades de pointes? (actionable)

Answer: We do not suggest using antipsychotics in patients at significant risk for torsades de pointes (i.e., patients with baseline prolongation of QT interval, patients receiving concomitant medications known to prolong the QT interval, or patients with a history of this arrhythmia) (–2C).

Rationale: Torsades de pointes is a dangerous complication associated with antipsychotic administration. Original case reports warned of this arrhythmia in patients receiving IV haloperidol[411,412] and its association with a prolonged QT interval.[413,414] Although torsades has also been described without QT prolongation.[415,416] Torsades has also occurred in patients receiving atypical antipsychotics, such as ziprasidone[417] and risperidone,[418] and recent reports have warned of drug interactions that could heighten this risk.[419] Although the quality of evidence is low, the morbidity and mortality associated with this complication is high.

e. *Question:* For mechanically ventilated, adult ICU patients with delirium who require continuous IV infusions of sedative medications, is dexmedetomidine preferred over benzodiazepines to reduce the duration of delirium? (actionable)

Answer: We suggest that in adult ICU patients with delirium unrelated to alcohol or benzodiazepine withdrawal, continuous IV infusions of dexmedetomidine rather than benzodiazepine infusions be administered for sedation in order to reduce the duration of delirium in these patients (+2B).

Rationale: Two randomized controlled trials comparing sedation with benzodiazepines vs. dexmedetomidine reported a significant daily reduction (~20%) in delirium prevalence in patients receiving dexmedetomidine.[220,370,420] These data are inconclusive about whether benzodiazepines raised the risk of delirium, or dexmedetomidine reduced the risk, and further investigations are needed to address this question. But data from these two clinical trials (which included a high percentage of patients at risk for delirium), coupled with delirium risk factor data from observational trials, suggest that benzodiazepines may be a risk factor for the development of delirium in the ICU. These findings led to this recommendation for using dexmedetomidine rather than benzodiazepines for sedation in ICU patients with delirium not due either to benzodiazepine or ethanol withdrawal. There are insufficient data to make recommendations regarding the risks and benefits of using other non-benzodiazepine sedatives, such as propofol, to reduce the duration of delirium in ICU patients.

Management of PAD to Improve ICU Outcomes

Use of Integrated PAD Protocols to Optimize ICU Patient Care. Our ability to effectively manage PAD in critically ill patients enables us to develop potential management strategies that reduce costs, improve ICU outcomes, and allow patients to participate in their own care.[9–13,16–20] Yet the application of these guideline recommendations poses significant challenges to critical care practitioners. A successful strategy is to implement an evidence-based, institutionally-specific, integrated PAD protocol, and to assess, treat and prevent PAD, using an interdisciplinary team approach. Protocols facilitate the transfer of evidence-based "best practices" to the bedside, limit practice variation, and reduce treatment delays.[2,3] A protocolized approach can also significantly improve patient outcomes and serve as a guide for quality assurance efforts.[13,327,421,422]

In spite of these recognized advantages, widespread adoption of integrated PAD protocols is lagging. Only 60% of ICUs in the United States have implemented PAD protocols, and even when instituted, protocol adherence is low, which negatively impacts patient outcomes.[163,199] Despite > 20 yr of emphasis on the importance of systematic pain assessment and management, data suggest that: 1) preemptive analgesia for painful procedures is used only 20% of the time in ICU patients; 2) pain and discomfort remain leading sources of patient stress; and 3) at least 40% of ICU patients still report experiencing moderate to severe pain.[2,60,73,423] Medication-induced coma has long been thought of as a "humane" therapeutic goal for many ICU patients. But this strategy leads to increased mortality, prolonged duration of ventilation and ICU LOS, and possibly long-term neuropsychological dysfunction and functional decline of patients.[75,238,287,318,424–426] In spite of the published benefits of ICU sedation strategies that minimize the use of sedatives and depth of sedation in patients, adoption of these sedation practices is not widespread.

ICU protocols that combine routine pain and sedation assessments, with pain management and sedation-minimizing strategies (i.e., daily sedative interruption or protocols that otherwise target light levels of sedation), along with delirium monitoring and prevention, may be the best strategy for avoiding the complications of over sedation. Protocols can also facilitate communication between bedside nurses and other members of the ICU team, helping them to define appropriate pain and sedation management goals, and to assess the effectiveness of treatment strategies for each individual patient.[3,14,62,259, 427,428] Although the impact of routine delirium monitoring on ICU outcomes has never been rigorously evaluated, early recognition of delirium may nevertheless facilitate patient reassurance, help to identify reversible causative factors, and permit implementation of effective delirium treatments. Early detection and treatment of delirium may in turn allow for a patient to be conscious, yet cooperative enough to potentially participate in ventilator weaning trials and early mobilization efforts. However, delirium can only be assessed in patients who are able to sufficiently interact and communicate with bedside clinicians. Optimal pain management and a light level of sedation are essential for this to occur.

Defining Depth of Sedation. Although there are obvious benefits to minimizing sedation in critically ill patients, no clear consensus exists on how to define "light" vs. "deep" sedation. The overarching objectives for the management of pain, agitation, and delirium in ICU patients should be to consistently focus on patient safety and comfort, while avoiding short- and long-term complications associated with either excessive or inadequate treatment. Traditionally, the goals of ICU analgesia and sedation have been to facilitate mechanical ventilation, to prevent patient and caregiver injury, and to avoid the psychological and physiologic consequences of inadequate treatment of pain, anxiety, agitation, and delirium. Avoiding complications of over-sedation, such as muscle atrophy and weakness, pneumonia, ventilator dependency, thromboembolic disease, nerve compression, pressure sores, and delirium, are also important.[11,325,326,429] A more precise definition of light vs. deep sedation is offered to guide the creation and implementation of sedation protocols that provide sufficient patient comfort without inducing coma.

Central to these guidelines are the principles that: 1) pain, depth of sedation, and delirium should be frequently monitored using valid and reliable assessment tools; 2) patients should receive adequate and preemptive treatment for pain; 3) patients should receive sedation only if required; and 4) that sedatives should be titrated to allow patient responsiveness and awareness that is demonstrated by their ability to purposefully respond to commands (i.e., a combination of any three of the following actions upon request: open eyes, maintain eye contact, squeeze hand, stick out tongue, and wiggle toes).[15,16,326] This degree of responsiveness and awareness goes beyond patients being merely "sleepy but arousable" and is essential for the evaluation of pain through patient self-report, for assessing patients' readiness to wean and extubate, for performing delirium assessments, and for implementing early mobility efforts. It remains unclear as to whether it's better to titrate sedation to a goal that allows patients to be consistently awake, cooperative, and calm, or to provide deeper sedation with a daily awakening trial.[16,430] In the final analysis, both strategies have been shown to reduce the incidence of deep sedation and its associated risks.[431]

Outcomes: Questions, Statements, and Recommendations.

1. Sedation Strategies to Improve Clinical Outcomes

a. *Question:* Should a protocol that includes either daily sedative interruption or a light target level of sedation be used in mechanically ventilated adult ICU patients? (actionable)

Answer: We recommend either daily sedation interruption or a light target level of sedation be routinely used in mechanically ventilated adult ICU patients (+1B).

Rationale: Five unblinded randomized controlled trials involving 699 patients evaluated daily sedation interruption.[14–16,432,433] All but one[432] were restricted to medical ICU patients; a single pilot trial targeted light sedation as the comparator.[16] One low-quality trial suggested harm, but suffered from serious methodological issues.[433] Data suggest daily sedation interruption reduces the time that patients spend on the ventilator (or increases ventilator-free days in survivors) and ICU LOS.

An alternative strategy using protocols to maintain light sedation (without daily sedation interruption) was described in 11 unblinded studies involving 3,730 patients. The data suggest this approach reduces the amount of time that patients spend on the ventilator (or increases ventilator-free days for survivors).[7–13,18,19,434] The effect of protocolization on ICU LOS was inconsistent with little data suggesting any detrimental effect.[7–13,17–19,327,434] Conflicting data in two studies were likely related to the similarity of control group sedation practices to those offered by the intervention.[18,19] Healthcare systems that employ bedside care models with 1:1 nurse-to-patient ratios or institutions where sedation minimization is a goal may not benefit.[435] Data are insufficient to draw firm conclusions on the effect of either daily sedation interruption or protocolization to maintain a level of light sedation on ventilator-associated pneumonia (VAP), delirium prevalence, patient comfort, or cost of ICU care.

In summary, daily sedation interruption is associated with clinical benefit in medical ICU patients, but the benefits remain uncertain in those who are alcohol-dependent or not admitted to a medical ICU service. Studies investigating the efficacy and safety of this strategy in surgical, trauma, neurologic, and neurosurgical patients are needed. Protocolized management strategies (e.g., hourly titration) to avoid deep sedation are also associated with clinical benefit, but it remains unclear whether combining sedation protocolization with daily sedative interruption would lead to additional benefits.[16]

b. *Question:* Should analgesia-first sedation (i.e., analgosedation) or sedative-hypnotic-based sedation be used in mechanically ventilated ICU patients? (actionable)

Answer: We suggest that analgesia-first sedation be used in mechanically ventilated adult ICU patients (+2B).

Rationale: Providing analgesia-first sedation for many ICU patients is supported by the high frequency of pain and discomfort as primary causes of agitation and by reports implicating standard hypnotic-based sedative regimens as having negative clinical and quality-of-life outcomes. Four unblinded studies including 630 medical and surgical ICU patients examined an analgesia-first approach.[436–439] Data from one moderate-quality study suggested that analgesia-first sedation is associated with longer ventilator-free time during a 28-day period, and shorter ICU LOS.[439] Otherwise, no consistent advantages of analgesia-first sedation over sedative-hypnotic-based sedation were found. Optimal analgesia and sedation were achieved during 97% of the time with either strategy.[436,438] One trial did not demonstrate any harm from the intervention on rates of self-extubation or VAP, but the incidence of agitated delirium was higher in the analgesia-first sedation group.[439] Data on delirium, self-extubation, VAP, mortality, or cost of ICU care are insufficient to draw firm conclusions about the influence of this intervention.

High-quality study data are scarce in support of using one opiate over another in ICU patients receiving analgesia-first sedation.[127,134,407] Clinicians should rely on pharmacology, safety, and cost-effectiveness when making opioid treatment decisions.[440] Analgesics that are short-acting and easily titratable may offer an advantage by facilitating frequent neurologic evaluations.

The benefits of analgesia-first approach must be balanced by the potential for opiates to interfere with respiratory drive, reduce gastric motility, and complicate the provision of enteral nutrition.[134,441] Possible pain recurrence and withdrawal upon analgesic discontinuation should be anticipated.[130] Furthermore, 18% to 70% of patients treated with analgesia-first strategies will require supplementation with other traditional sedative agents.[436–439]

Although data suggest potential additional benefits with analgesia-first sedation, the ultimate role of this strategy remains unclear because one moderate-quality study[439] required a 1:1 nurse-to-patient ratio and the availability of patient "sitters," and no rigorous published studies have specifically compared analgesia-first sedation with conventional GABA-based sedation strategies. Preliminary data suggest that analgesia-first sedation strategies do not have a negative impact on long-term psychological function.[442] These data should be confirmed and expanded to explore the influence of analgesia-first sedation on outcomes such as delirium, self-extubation, VAP, mortality, and cost of ICU care, and on long-term cognitive function. Although these studies administered an opioid as the primary analgesic, future studies in critically ill patients should evaluate a multimodal analgesic approach using a combination of opioids and nonopioid analgesics.[52]

c. Sleep promotion in ICU patients

i. *Question:* Should nonpharmacologic interventions be used to promote sleep in adult ICU patients? (actionable)

Answer: We recommend promoting sleep in adult ICU patients by optimizing patients' environments, using strategies to control light and noise, clustering patient care activities, and decreasing stimuli at night to protect patients' sleep cycles (+1C).

Rationale: Sleep deprivation is detrimental in humans, and sleep disruption is common in ICU patients.[443,444] They have few complete sleep cycles, numerous awakenings due to environmental disruptions (noise, light, and physical stimulation), and infrequent rapid-eye-movement sleep.[443,445–448] Sleep deprivation impairs tissue repair and cellular immune function, and may affect the healing response.[449] In critically ill patients, sleep deprivation may contribute to the development of delirium[450–454] and increased levels of physiologic stress.[455,456]

Sleep science in the ICU has not advanced in the past decade. Because few studies identify pharmacologic effects of sedatives on sleep in critically ill patients, we focused on nonpharmacologic interventions to promote sleep in the ICU. Two recently published studies ($n > 30$, prospective cohort, before/after study design) demonstrated that implementing quiet time on both day and night shifts and clustering patient care activities reduce disturbances and promote both observed and perceived sleep in adult ICU patients.[457,458] Another descriptive study further confirmed that mechanically ventilated ICU patients do not have uninterrupted periods for sleep to occur.[459] From these findings, we hypothesized that nurses should select time periods to promote sleep by avoiding routine ICU care activities (such as the daily bath), turning down the lights, and reducing ambient noise during these periods. In three studies suggesting scheduled rest periods, the periods most likely to be uninterrupted in the ICU were 2–4 AM,[458] 12–5 AM,[457] and around 3 AM.[459] Another study, using indirect evidence from nursing home patients, suggested that the amount of daytime light exposure may affect a hospitalized elderly patient's quality and consolidation of sleep at night.[460] These findings must be validated in an ICU patient population. Further research is needed to support the positive effects of using eye patches or ear plugs to limit the aversive effects of noise and light.[461] High doses of sedative agents and mechanical ventilation disrupt sleep patterns in critically ill patients.[459,462] There is no evidence that light levels of sedation promote sleep in the ICU.

ii. *Question:* Should specific modes of mechanical ventilation be used to promote sleep in ventilated ICU patients? (actionable)

Answer: We provide no recommendation for using specific modes of mechanical ventilation to promote sleep in adult ICU patients, as insufficient evidence exists for the efficacy of these interventions (0, No evidence).

Rationale: Two small studies ($n < 30$) have demonstrated that modes of mechanical ventilation that reduce the risk of central apnea events may improve the quality of sleep in adult ICU patients.[463,464] Larger, well-designed prospective clinical trials are needed to validate these findings.

2. Strategies to Facilitate Implementation of ICU Analgesia, Sedation, and Delirium Guidelines

Question: Should an interdisciplinary educational and behavioral strategy be used to facilitate the implementation of sedation protocols and guidelines in adult ICUs? (actionable)

Answer: We recommend using an interdisciplinary ICU team approach that includes provider education, preprinted and/or computerized protocols and order forms, and quality ICU rounds checklists to facilitate the use of PAD management guidelines or protocols in adult ICUs (+1B).

Rationale: The bulk of data from 12 unblinded studies involving 2,887 patients suggests that one or more interventions, along with the protocol implementation to provide patient comfort in the ICU, reduces the duration of mechanical ventilation (or increases ventilator-free days for survivors).[7–10,12,13,18,19,159–162] Interventions to implement protocols had inconsistent impact on ICU LOS, with little data suggesting harm within the 11 studies involving 2,707 patients.[7–10,12,13,18,19,159,160,162] There was no evidence for harm with this intervention when the incidence of self-extubation was examined. Lastly, data were insufficient to support a recommendation based on the time patients spent within their defined sedation goal or on patient or nurse satisfaction. Data suggest that the primary benefit of using one or more interventions (e.g., education, additional staff, electronic reminders) is to limit time on mechanical ventilation, but the overall benefit is uncertain. Low risk and minimal cost are associated with implementing one or more strategies to improve the use of an integrated sedation protocol in the ICU.

Tools for Facilitating the Application of These Recommendations to Bedside Care

Closing the gap between the evidence highlighted in these guidelines and ICU practice will be a significant challenge for ICU clinicians[465,466] and is best accomplished using a multifaceted, interdisciplinary approach.[4,467] The recommendations supported by clinical practice guidelines should be adapted to local practice patterns and resource availability, and used as a template for institution-specific protocols and order sets. Successful implementation will require augmentation with education, engagement of local thought leaders, point-of-use reminders, and caregiver-specific practice feedback, together with continuous protocol evaluation and modification.[7–10,12,13,18,19,159–162,468] Incorporating electronically based guidelines into clinical decision-support tools may facilitate bedside knowledge transfer and application.[465,466] To support this effort, we have developed a pocket card summarizing these guideline recommendations (Fig. 2) and a template for a PAD care bundle (Fig. 3).[469]

Care bundles have facilitated translation of practice guidelines to the bedside to manage a number of complex ICU problems, including VAP, catheter-associated bloodstream infections, and sepsis.[470,471] A care bundle includes elements most likely to improve patient outcomes. Elements should be: easy to implement, beneficial, supported by sound scientific and clinical reasoning, and relevant across patient populations and healthcare systems.[31] Adherence to each bundle element should be measurable and linked to one or more specific patient outcomes. Quality assurance data should facilitate caregiver feedback and allow rapid-cycle improvement to further customize bundles. This PAD Care Bundle is based on systematically identifying and managing PAD in an integrated fashion, and assessing the effectiveness of these strategies (Fig. 3).

Summary

The goal of these guidelines is to define best practices for optimizing the management of PAD in adult ICU patients. These guidelines were developed by performing a rigorous, objective, transparent, and unbiased assessment of the relevant published evidence based on the GRADE methodology. Statements and recommendations were developed by taking into consideration not only the quality of the evidence but also important clinical outcomes and the values and preferences of ICU stakeholders. We believe that these guidelines provide a practical roadmap for developing evidence-based, best practice protocols for integrating the management of PAD in critically ill patients.

Acknowledgments

Special thanks to Charles P. Kishman, Jr, MSLS, Information Services Librarian (University of Cincinnati, Cincinnati, OH), for his invaluable contributions to these guidelines. Mr. Kishman was instrumental in helping us to develop our search strategies, creating and maintaining the large Web-based guidelines database, and for creating and managing the guidelines bibliography. Additional thanks to Christopher D. Stave, MLS (Lane Medical Library, Stanford University School of Medicine, Stanford, CA); Psychometric experts David Streiner, PhD (University of Toronto, Department of Psychiatry, Toronto, Ontario, Canada; and McMaster University, Department of Clinical Epidemiology and Biostatistics, Hamilton, Ontario, Canada), Celeste Johnston, RN, DEd (School of Nursing, McGill University, Montreal, Quebec, Canada), and Carolyn Waltz, RN, PhD, FAAN (School of Nursing, University of Maryland, Baltimore, MD); GRADE Working Group members Gordon H. Guyatt, MD (Departments of Medicine and Clinical Epidemiology and Biostatistics, McMaster University, Hamilton, ON, Canada), Holger Schunemann, MD, PhD (Department of Clinical Epidemiology & Biostatistics, McMaster University Health Sciences Centre, Hamilton, ON, Canada), and Deborah Cook, MD (Department of Medicine, Clinical Epidemiology & Biostatistics, McMaster University, Hamilton, ON, Canada); Patricia Rohr, Medical Editor (Stanford University School of Medicine, Stanford, CA); Ina Lee, PharmD, Neuro-ICU clinical pharmacist (University of Washington/Harborview Medical Center, Seattle, WA); and to Kathy Ward and Laura Kolinski (Society of Critical Care Medicine, Mount Prospect, IL) for their technical assistance with these guidelines.

References

1. Jacobi J, Fraser GL, Coursin DB, et al. Task Force of the American College of Critical Care Medicine (ACCM) of the Society of Critical Care Medicine (SCCM), American Society of Health-System Pharmacists (ASHP), American College of Chest Physicians: Clinical practice guidelines for the sustained use of sedatives and analgesics in the critically ill adult. *Crit Care Med.* 2002; 30:119–41.
2. Chanques G, Jaber S, Barbotte E, et al. Impact of systematic evaluation of pain and agitation in an intensive care unit. *Crit Care Med.* 2006; 34:1691–9.
3. Payen JF, Bosson JL, Chanques G, et al. DOLOREA Investigators: Pain assessment is associated with decreased duration of mechanical ventilation in the intensive care unit: A post Hoc analysis of the DOLOREA study. *Anesthesiology.* 2009; 111:1308–16.
4. Vasilevskis EE, Ely EW, Speroff T, et al. Reducing iatrogenic risks: ICU-acquired delirium and weakness—Crossing the quality chasm. *Chest.* 2010; 138:1224–33.
5. Riker RR, Fraser GL. Altering intensive care sedation paradigms to improve patient outcomes. *Crit Care Clin.* 2009; 25:527–38, viii.
6. Arnold HM, Hollands JM, Skrupky LP, et al. Optimizing sustained use of sedation in mechanically ventilated patients: Focus on safety. *Curr Drug Saf.* 2010; 5:6–12.
7. Arabi Y, Haddad S, Hawes R, et al. Changing sedation practices in the intensive care unit—Protocol implementation, multifaceted multidisciplinary approach and teamwork. *Middle East J Anesthesiol.* 2007; 19:429–47.
8. Arias-Rivera S, Sánchez-Sánchez Mdel M, Santos-Díaz R, et al. Effect of a nursing-implemented sedation protocol on weaning outcome. *Crit Care Med.* 2008; 36:2054–60.
9. Brattebø G, Hofoss D, Flaatten H, et al. Effect of a scoring system and protocol for sedation on duration of patients' need for ventilator support in a surgical intensive care unit. *BMJ.* 2002; 324:1386–9.
10. Brook AD, Ahrens TS, Schaiff R, et al. Effect of a nursing-implemented sedation protocol on the duration of mechanical ventilation. *Crit Care Med.* 1999; 27:2609–15.
11. De Jonghe B, Bastuji-Garin S, Fangio P, et al. Sedation algorithm in critically ill patients without acute brain injury. *Crit Care Med.* 2005; 33:120–7.
12. Quenot JP, Ladoire S, Devoucoux F, et al. Effect of a nurse-implemented sedation protocol on the incidence of ventilator-associated pneumonia. *Crit Care Med.* 2007; 35:2031–6.
13. Robinson BR, Mueller EW, Henson K, et al. An analgesia-delirium-sedation protocol for critically ill trauma patients reduces ventilator days and hospital length of stay. *J Trauma.* 2008; 65:517–26.
14. Girard TD, Kress JP, Fuchs BD, et al. Efficacy and safety of a paired sedation and ventilator weaning protocol for mechanically ventilated patients in intensive care (Awakening and Breathing Controlled trial): A randomised controlled trial. *Lancet.* 2008; 371:126–34.
15. Kress JP, Pohlman AS, O'Connor MF, et al. Daily interruption of sedative infusions in critically ill patients undergoing mechanical ventilation. *N Engl J Med.* 2000; 342:1471–7.
16. Mehta S, Burry L, Martinez-Motta JC, et al. Canadian Critical Care Trials Group: A randomized trial of daily awakening in critically ill patients managed with a sedation protocol: A pilot trial. *Crit Care Med.* 2008; 36:2092–9.
17. Adam C, Rosser D, Manji M. Impact of introducing a sedation management guideline in intensive care. *Anaesthesia.* 2006; 61:260–3.

A

- Agitation in critically ill patients may result from inadequately treated pain, anxiety, delirium, and/or ventilator dysynchrony.
- Detection and treatment of pain, agitation, and delirium should be reassessed often in these patients.
- Patients should be awake and able to purposely follow commands in order to participate in their care unless a clinical indication for deeper sedation exists.
- For a comprehensive list of Guideline Statements, Recommendations and GRADES, see back of card.

Assess and Treat	Statements and Recommendations
PAIN	• Pain assessment should be routinely performed in all ICU patients (1B). • Self report is preferred over the use of behavioral pain scales to assess pain in ICU patients who are able to communicate (B). • The BPS and CPOT are the most valid and reliable behavioral pain scales for use in ICU patients who cannot communicate (B). • Vital signs should not be used alone to assess pain, but they may be used adjunctively for pain assessments (2C). • Preemptively treat chest tube removal with either analgesics and/or non-pharmacologic therapy (1C). • Suggest preemptively treating other types of procedural pain with analgesic and/or non-pharmacologic therapy (2C). • Use opioids as first line therapy for treatment of non-neuropathic pain (1C). • Suggest using non-opioid analgesics in conjunction with opioids to reduce opioid requirements and opioid-related side effects (2C). • Use gabapentin or carbamazepine, in addition to intravenous opioids, for treatment of neuropathic pain (1A). • Use thoracic epidural for postoperative analgesia in abdominal aortic surgery patients (1B). • Suggest thoracic epidural analgesia be used for patients with traumatic rib fractures (2B).
AGITATION	• Depth and quality of sedation should be routinely assessed in all ICU patients (1B). • The RASS and SAS are the most valid and reliable scales for assessing quality and depth of sedation in ICU patients (B). • Suggest using objective measures of brain function to adjunctively monitor sedation in patients receiving neuromuscular blocking agents (2B). • Use EEG monitoring either to monitor non-convulsive seizure activity in ICU patients at risk for seizures, or to titrate electrosuppressive medication to achieve burst suppression in ICU patients with elevated intracranial pressure (1A). • Target the lightest possible level of sedation and/or use daily sedative interruption (1B). • Use sedation protocols and checklists to facilitate ICU sedation management (1B). • Suggest using analgesia-first sedation for intubated and mechanically ventilated ICU patients (2B). • Suggest using non-benzodiazepines for sedation (either propafol or dexmedetomidine) rather than benzodiazepines (either midazolam or lorazepam) in mechanically ventilated adult ICU patients (2B).
DELIRIUM	• Delirium assessment should be routinely performed in all ICU patients (1B). • The CAM-ICU and ICDSC delirium monitoring tools are the most valid and reliable scales to assess delirium in ICU patients (A). • Mobilize ICU patients early when feasible to reduce the incidence and duration of delirium, and to improve functional outcomes (1B). • Promote sleep in ICU patients by controlling light and noise, clustering patient care activities, and decreasing stimuli at night (1C). • Avoid using rivastigmine to reduce the duration of delirium in ICU patients (1B). • Suggest avoiding the use of anti psychotics in patients who are at risk for torsades de pointes (2B). • Suggest not using benzodiazepines in ICU patients with delirium unrelated to ETOH/benzodiazepine withdrawal (2B).

Figure 2. A, Pocket card operationalizing the PAD guideline recommendations (front side) (*continued*).

18. Bucknall TK, Manias E, Presneill JJ. A randomized trial of protocol-directed sedation management for mechanical ventilation in an Australian intensive care unit. *Crit Care Med.* 2008; 36:1444–50.
19. Elliott R, McKinley S, Aitken LM, et al. The effect of an algorithm-based sedation guideline on the duration of mechanical ventilation in an Australian intensive care unit. *Intensive Care Med.* 2006; 32:1506–14.
20. Treggiari MM, Romand JA, Yanez ND, et al. Randomized trial of light versus deep sedation on mental health after critical illness. *Crit Care Med.* 2009; 37:2527–34.
21. Griffiths RD, Jones C. Seven lessons from 20 years of follow-up of intensive care unit survivors. *Curr Opin Crit Care.* 2007; 13:508–13.
22. Milbrandt EB, Angus DC. Bench-to-bedside review: Critical illness-associated cognitive dysfunction—Mechanisms, markers, and emerging therapeutics. *Crit Care.* 2006; 10:238.

B

Summary of PAD Guidelines

PAIN AND ANALGESIA

1. ICU patients routinely experience pain at rest and with ICU care (B). Pain in cardiac surgery patients, especially women, is poorly treated (B). Procedural pain is common in ICU patients (B).
2. Perform routine pain assessment in all patients (1B). In motor intact patients unable to self report, we suggest using behavioral pain scales rather than vital signs to assess pain (2C). The BPS and CPOT are the most valid and reliable behavioral pain scales (B). Vital signs should only be used as a cue for further pain assessment (2C).
3. For non-neuropathic pain, use intravenous opioids as first line analgesic therapy (1C); use non-opioid analgesics to reduce opioid side effects (1C); and use either gabapentin or carbamazepine in conjunction with intravenous opioids for neuropathic pain (1A).
4. Suggest preemptively treating procedural pain (2C), especially chest tube removal (1C).
5. Use thoracic epidural analgesia for abdominal aortic surgery (1B), and suggest also using for traumatic rib fractures (2B). No evidence guides the use of lumbar epidural analgesia for abdominal aneurysm surgery (OA), or thoracic epidural analgesia for either intrathoracic or nonvascular abdominal surgical procedures (OB). No evidence guides the use of regional vs. systemic analgesia in medical ICU patients (0).

AGITATION AND SEDATION

1. Maintaining lighter levels of sedation in ICU patients is associated with improved clinical outcomes (B); light levels of sedation should be maintained in these patients (1B).
2. The RASS and SAS scales are most valid and reliable instruments for assessing adequacy and depth of sedation (B).
3. Use Brain Function monitors only as adjuncts to subjective sedation scales in unparalyzed patients (1B), but suggest using brain function monitors to primarily monitor depth of sedation in patients receiving neuromuscular blocking agents (2B).
4. Use EEG monitoring to monitor non-convulsive seizure activity in ICU patients at risk for seizures, and to titrate burst suppression therapy in ICU patients with elevated intracranial pressure (1A).
5. Use either daily sedative interruption or titrate sedative medications to maintain light levels of sedation (1B). Suggest using Analgesia-first sedation (2B). Suggest using non-benzodiazepines rather than benzodiazepine infusions for sedation (2B). Use sedation protocols and daily checklists to integrate and to facilitate management of pain, sedation, and delirium in ICU patients (1B).

DELIRIUM

1. Delirium is associated with increased mortality (A), prolonged ICU and hospital LOS (A), and post-ICU cognitive impairment (B).
2. Delirium risk factors include: pre-existing dementia, HTN, history of alcoholism, and a high severity of illness at baseline (B); coma (B); and benzodiazepine use (B). Mechanically ventilated ICU patients at risk for delirium have a lower delirium prevalence when treated with dexmedetomidine rather than with benzodiazepines (B).
3. Routinely monitor ICU patients for delirium (1B). The CAM-ICU and ICDSC are the most valid and reliable instruments for this purpose (A).
4. Pursue early mobilization to reduce the incidence and duration of delirium (1B).
5. Suggest not using either haloperidol or atypical antipsychotics prophylactically to prevent delirium (2C).
6. Promote sleep in adult ICU patients by optimizing patients' environments, using strategies to control light and noise, to cluster patient care activities, and to decrease stimuli at night in order to protect patients' sleep cycles (1C).
7. Do not use rivastigmine to reduce the duration of delirium in ICU patients (1C).
8. Suggest withholding antipsychotics in patients with baseline QT prolongation, a history of Torsades de Pointes, or in those receiving concomitant medications known to prolong the QT interval (2C).
9. When sedation is required in delirious ICU patients, suggest using dexmedetomidine rather than benzodiazepine infusions for sedation in these patients, unless delirium is related to either alcohol or benzodiazepine withdrawal (2B).

Figure 2 (*continued*). B, Pocket card summarizing specific pain, agitation, and delirium (PAD) guideline statements and recommendations (back side). BPS = Behavioral Pain Scale; CPOT = Critical-Care Pain Observation Tool; RASS = Richmond Agitation and Sedation Scale; SAS = Sedation-Agitation Scale; EEG = electroencephalography; CAM-ICU = Confusion Assessment Method for the ICU; ICDSC = ICU Delirium Screening Checklist; ETOH = ethanol; LOS = length of stay; HTN = hypertension.

23. Larson MJ, Weaver LK, Hopkins RO. Cognitive sequelae in acute respiratory distress syndrome patients with and without recall of the intensive care unit. *J Int Neuropsychol Soc.* 2007; 13:595–605.
24. Jones C, Griffiths RD, Humphris G, et al. Memory, delusions, and the development of acute posttraumatic stress disorder-related symptoms after intensive care. *Crit Care Med.* 2001; 29:573–80.
25. Schelling G, Stoll C, Haller M, et al. Health-related quality of life and posttraumatic stress disorder in survivors of the acute respiratory distress syndrome. *Crit Care Med.* 1998; 26:651–9.

A

	Pain	Agitation	Delirium
ASSESS	Assess pain ≥4x/shift & prn Preferred pain assessment tools: • Patient able to self-report →NRS (0-10) • Unable to self-report →BPS (3-12) or CPOT (0-8) Patient is in significant pain if NRS ≥4, BPS > 5, or CPOT ≥3	Assess agitation, sedation ≥4x/shift & prn Preferred sedation assessment tools: • RASS (-5 to +4) or SAS (1 to 7) • NMB → suggest using brain function monitoring Depth of agitation, sedation defined as: • *agitated* if RASS = +1 to +4, or SAS = 5 to 7 • *awake and calm* if RASS = 0, or SAS = 4 • *lightly sedated* if RASS = -1 to -2, or SAS = 3 • *deeply sedated* if RASS = -3 to -5, or SAS = 1 to 2	Assess delirium Q shift & prn Preferred delirium assessment tools: • CAM-ICU (+ or -) • ICDSC (0 to 8) Delirium present if: • CAM-ICU is positive • ICDSC ≥4
TREAT	Treat pain within 30' then reassess: • Non-pharmacologic treatment–relaxation therapy • Pharmacologic treatment: – Non-neuropathic pain → IV opioids ± non-opioid analgesics – Neuropathic pain → gabapentin or carbamazepine, + IV opioids – S/p AAA repair, rib fractures → thoracic epidural	Targeted sedation or DSI (*Goal: patient purposely follows commands without agitation*): RASS= -2–0, SAS = 3–4 • If *under sedated* (RASS >0, SAS >4) assess/treat pain → treat w/sedatives prn (non-benzodiazepines preferred, unless ETOH or benzodiazepine withdrawal is suspected) • If *over sedated* (RASS <-2, SAS <3) hold sedatives until at target, then restart at 50% of previous dose	• Treat pain as needed • Reorient patients; familiarize surroundings; use patient's eyeglasses, hearing aids if needed • Pharmacologic treatment of delirium: – Avoid benzodiazepines unless ETOH or benzodiazepine withdrawal is suspected – Avoid rivastigmine – Avoid antipsychotics if ↑ risk of Torsades de pointes
PREVENT	• Administer pre-procedural analgesia and/or non-pharmacologic interventions (e.g., relaxation therapy) • Treat pain first, then sedate	• Consider daily SBT, early mobility and exercise when patients are at goal sedation level, unless contraindicated • EEG monitoring if: – at risk for seizures – burst suppression therapy is indicated for ↑ ICP	• Identify delirium risk factors: dementia, HTN, ETOH abuse, high severity of illness, coma, benzodiazepine administration • Avoid benzodiazepine use in those at ↑ risk for delirium • Mobilize and exercise patients early • Promote sleep (control light, noise; cluster patient care activities; decrease nocturnal stimuli) • Restart baseline psychiatric meds, if indicated

Figure 3. A, ICU pain, agitation, and delirium (PAD) care bundle.[469] **B**, ICU PAD care bundle metrics; NRS = Numeric Rating Scale; BPS = Behavioral Pain Scale; CPOT = Critical-Care Pain Observation Tool; nonpharmacologic therapy = relaxation therapy, especially for chest tube removal; IV = intravenous; AAA = abdominal aortic aneurysm; NMB = neuromuscular blockade; RASS = Richmond Agitation and Sedation Scale; SAS = sedation-Agitation Scale; brain function monitoring = auditory evoked potentials (AEP), Bispectral Index (BIS), Narcotrend Index (NI), Patient State Index (PSI), or State Entropy (SE); DSI = daily sedation interruption (also referred to as Spontaneous Awakening Trial [SAT]); ETOH = ethanol; nonbenzodiazepines, propofol (use in intubated/mechanically ventilated patients), dexmedetomidine (use in either intubated or nonintubated patients); SBT = spontaneous breathing trial; EEG = electroencephalography; ICP = intracranial pressure; CAM-ICU = Confusion Assessment Method for the ICU; ICDSC = ICU Delirium Screening Checklist (*continued*).

B

	Pain	Agitation	Delirium
ASSESS	• % of time patients are monitored for pain ≥4x/shift • Demonstrate local compliance and implementation integrity over time in the use of ICU pain scoring systems	• % of time sedation assessments are performed ≥4x/shift • Demonstrate local compliance and implementation integrity over time in the use of ICU sedation scoring systems	• % of time delirium assessments are performed Q shift • Demonstrate local compliance and implementation integrity over time in the use of ICU delirium assessment tools
TREAT	• % of time ICU patients are in significant pain (i.e., NRS ≥4, BPS ≥6, or CPOT ≥3) • % of time pain treatment is initiated within 30" of detecting significant pain	• % of time patients are either optimally sedated or successfully achieve target sedation during DSI trials (i.e., RASS = -2–0, SAS = 3–4) • % of time ICU patients are *under sedated* (RASS >0, SAS>4) • % of time ICU patients are either *over sedated* (*non-therapeutic coma*, RASS <-2, SAS <3) or fail to undergo DSI trials	• % of time delirium is present in ICU patients (CAM-ICU is positive or ICDSC ≥ 4) • % of time benzodiazepines are administered to patients with documented delirium (not due to ETOH or benzodiazepine withdrawal)
PREVENT	• % of time patients receive pre-procedural analgesia therapy and/or nonpharmacologic interventions • % compliance with institutional-specific ICU pain management protocols	• % failed attempts at SBTs due to either over or under sedation • % of patients undergoing EEG monitoring if: – at risk for seizures – burst suppression therapy is indicated for ↑ ICP • % compliance with institutional-specific ICU sedation/agitation management protocols	• % of patients receiving daily physical therapy and early mobility • % compliance with ICU sleep promotion strategies • % compliance with institutional-specific ICU delirium prevention and treatment protocols

Figure 3 (*continued*). A, ICU pain, agitation, and delirium (PAD) care bundle.[469] **B**, ICU PAD care bundle metrics; NRS = Numeric Rating Scale; BPS = Behavioral Pain Scale; CPOT = Critical-Care Pain Observation Tool; nonpharmacologic therapy = relaxation therapy, especially for chest tube removal; IV = intravenous; AAA = abdominal aortic aneurysm; NMB = neuromuscular blockade; RASS = Richmond Agitation and Sedation Scale; SAS = sedation-Agitation Scale; brain function monitoring = auditory evoked potentials (AEP), Bispectral Index (BIS), Narcotrend Index (NI), Patient State Index (PSI), or State Entropy (SE); DSI = daily sedation interruption (also referred to as Spontaneous Awakening Trial [SAT]); ETOH = ethanol; nonbenzodiazepines, propofol (use in intubated/mechanically ventilated patients), dexmedetomidine (use in either intubated or nonintubated patients); SBT = spontaneous breathing trial; EEG = electroencephalography; ICP = intracranial pressure; CAM-ICU = Confusion Assessment Method for the ICU; ICDSC = ICU Delirium Screening Checklist.

26. Swaiss IG, Badran I. Discomfort, awareness and recall in the intensive care—still a problem? *Middle East J Anesthesiol.* 2004; 17:951–8.
27. Hopkins RO, Weaver LK, Collingridge D, et al. Two-year cognitive, emotional, and quality-of-life outcomes in acute respiratory distress syndrome. *Am J Respir Crit Care Med.* 2005; 171:340–7.
28. Jones C, Griffiths RD, Slater T, et al. Significant cognitive dysfunction in non-delirious patients identified during and persisting following critical illness. *Intensive Care Med.* 2006; 32:923–6.
29. Jones C, Bäckman C, Capuzzo M, et al. Precipitants of post-traumatic stress disorder following intensive care: A hypothesis generating study of diversity in care. *Intensive Care Med.* 2007; 33:978–85.
30. Davydow DS, Gifford JM, Desai SV, et al. Posttraumatic stress disorder in general intensive care unit survivors: A systematic review. *Gen Hosp Psychiatry.* 2008; 30:421–34.
31. Rello J, Lode H, Cornaglia G, et al. VAP Care Bundle Contributors: A European care bundle for prevention of ventilator-associated pneumonia. *Intensive Care Med.* 2010; 36:773–80.
32. Tufano R, Piazza O, De Robertis E. Guidelines and the medical "art." *Intensive Care Med.* 2010; 36:1612–3.
33. Bellomo R, Stow PJ, Hart GK. Why is there such a difference in outcome between Australian intensive care units and others? *Curr Opin Anaesthesiol.* 2007; 20:100–5.
34. Rello J, Lorente C, Bodí M, et al. Why do physicians not follow evidence-based guidelines for preventing ventilator-associated pneumonia? A survey based on the opinions of an international panel of intensivists. *Chest.* 2002; 122:656–61.
35. Hicks P, Cooper DJ. The Australian and New Zealand Intensive Care Society (ANZICS) Board and Clinical Trials Group Executive Committee: The Surviving Sepsis Campaign: International guidelines for management of severe sepsis and septic shock: 2008. *Crit Care Resusc.* 2008; 10:8.

36. Orford NR, Faulkner C, Flintoff W, et al. Implementation and outcomes of a severe sepsis protocol in an Australian tertiary hospital. *Crit Care Resusc.* 2008; 10:217–24.
37. American Society of Anesthesiologists Task Force on Sedation and Analgesia by Non-Anesthesiologists. Practice guidelines for sedation and analgesia by non-anesthesiologists. *Anesthesiology.* 2002; 96:1004–17.
38. Schünemann HJ, Jaeschke R, Cook DJ, et al. ATS Documents Development and Implementation Committee: An official ATS statement: Grading the quality of evidence and strength of recommendations in ATS guidelines and recommendations. *Am J Respir Crit Care Med.* 2006; 174:605–14.
39. Guyatt G, Gutterman D, Baumann MH, et al. Grading strength of recommendations and quality of evidence in clinical guidelines: Report from an American college of chest physicians task force. *Chest.* 2006; 129:174–81.
40. Guyatt GH, Oxman AD, Vist GE, et al. GRADE Working Group: GRADE: An emerging consensus on rating quality of evidence and strength of recommendations. *BMJ.* 2008; 336:924–6.
41. Cross H. Consensus methods: A bridge between clinical reasoning and clinical research? *Int J Lepr Other Mycobact Dis.* 2005; 73:28–32.
42. Allen J, Dyas J, Jones M. Building consensus in health care: A guide to using the nominal group technique. *Br J Community Nurs.* 2004; 9:110–4.
43. Guyatt GH, Oxman AD, Kunz R, et al. GRADE Working Group: Going from evidence to recommendations. *BMJ.* 2008; 336:1049–1051.
44. Guyatt GH, Oxman AD, Kunz R, et al. GRADE Working Group: What is "quality of evidence" and why is it important to clinicians? *BMJ.* 2008; 336:995–8.
45. McGinnis PQ, Wainwright SF, Hack LM, et al. Use of a Delphi panel to establish consensus for recommended uses of selected balance assessment approaches. *Physiother Theory Pract.* 2010; 26:358–73.
46. Jaeschke R, Guyatt GH, Dellinger P, et al. GRADE Working Group: Use of GRADE grid to reach decisions on clinical practice guidelines when consensus is elusive. *BMJ.* 2008; 337:a744.
47. Dellinger RP, Levy MM, Carlet JM, et al. International Surviving Sepsis Campaign Guidelines Committee; American Association of Critical-Care Nurses; American College of Chest Physicians; American College of Emergency Physicians; Canadian Critical Care Society; European Society of Clinical Microbiology and Infectious Diseases; European Society of Intensive Care Medicine; European Respiratory Society; International Sepsis Forum; Japanese Association for Acute Medicine; Japanese Society of Intensive Care Medicine; Society of Critical Care Medicine; Society of Hospital Medicine; Surgical Infection Society; World Federation of Societies of Intensive and Critical Care Medicine. Surviving Sepsis Campaign: International guidelines for management of severe sepsis and septic shock. 2008. *Crit Care Med.* 2008; 36:296–327.
48. Streiner DL, Norman GR, Joint Author. *Health Measurement Scales: A Practical Guide to Their Development and Use.* Fourth Edition. Oxford, Oxford University Press, 2008.
49. American Educational Research Association, American Psychological Association, National Council on Measurement in Education, Joint Commission Standards for Educational and Psychological Testing: Standards for Educational and Psychological Testing. Washington, DC, American Educational Research Association, 1999.
50. Pudas-Tähkä SM, Axelin A, Aantaa R, et al. Pain assessment tools for unconscious or sedated intensive care patients: A systematic review. *J Adv Nurs.* 2009; 65:946–56.
51. Pain terms: A list with definitions and notes on usage recommended by the IASP subcommittee on taxonomy. *Pain.* 1979; 6:249.
52. Erstad BL, Puntillo K, Gilbert HC, et al. Pain management principles in the critically ill. *Chest.* 2009; 135:1075–86.
53. Ballard KS. Identification of environmental stressors for patients in a surgical intensive care unit. *Issues Ment Health Nurs.* 1981; 3:89–108.
54. So HM, Chan DS. Perception of stressors by patients and nurses of critical care units in Hong Kong. *Int J Nurs Stud.* 2004; 41:77–84.
55. Hweidi IM. Jordanian patients' perception of stressors in critical care units: A questionnaire survey. *Int J Nurs Stud.* 2007; 44:227–235.
56. Rotondi AJ, Chelluri L, Sirio C, et al. Patients' recollections of stressful experiences while receiving prolonged mechanical ventilation in an intensive care unit. *Crit Care Med.* 2002; 30:746–52.
57. Shannon K, Bucknall T. Pain assessment in critical care: What have we learnt from research. *Intensive Crit Care Nurs.* 2003; 19:154–62.
58. International association for the study of pain | IASP taxonomy. Available at: http://www.iasp-pain.org/AM/Template.cfm?Section=Pain_Defi..isplay.cfm&ContentID=1728#Pain. Accessed October 2010.
59. Anand KJ, Craig KD. New perspectives on the definition of pain. *Pain.* 1996; 67:3–6; discussion 209.
60. Puntillo KA. Pain experiences of intensive care unit patients. *Heart Lung.* 1990; 19(5 Pt 1):526–33.
61. Chanques G, Sebbane M, Barbotte E, et al. A prospective study of pain at rest: Incidence and characteristics of an unrecognized symptom in surgical and trauma versus medical intensive care unit patients. *Anesthesiology.* 2007; 107:858–60.
62. Payen JF, Chanques G, Mantz J, et al. Current practices in sedation and analgesia for mechanically ventilated critically ill patients: A prospective multicenter patient-based study. *Anesthesiology.* 2007; 106:687–95; quiz 891.
63. Stanik-Hutt JA, Soeken KL, Belcher AE, et al. Pain experiences of traumatically injured patients in a critical care setting. *Am J Crit Care.* 2001; 10:252–9.
64. Stotts NA, Puntillo K, Stanik-Hutt J, et al. Does age make a difference in procedural pain perceptions and responses in hospitalized adults? *Acute Pain.* 2007; 9:125–34.

65. Stotts NA, Puntillo K, Bonham Morris A, et al. Wound care pain in hospitalized adult patients. *Heart Lung.* 2004; 33:321–32.
66. Arroyo-Novoa CM, Figueroa-Ramos MI, Puntillo KA, et al. Pain related to tracheal suctioning in awake acutely and critically ill adults: A descriptive study. *Intensive Crit Care Nurs.* 2008; 24:20–7.
67. Puntillo K, Ley SJ. Appropriately timed analgesics control pain due to chest tube removal. *Am J Crit Care.* 2004; 13:292–301; discussion 302; quiz 303.
68. Puntillo KA, White C, Morris AB, et al. Patients' perceptions and responses to procedural pain: Results from Thunder Project II. *Am J Crit Care.* 2001; 10:238–51.
69. Puntillo KA. Dimensions of procedural pain and its analgesic management in critically ill surgical patients. *Am J Crit Care.* 1994; 3:116–22.
70. Puntillo KA. Effects of interpleural bupivacaine on pleural chest tube removal pain: A randomized controlled trial. *Am J Crit Care.* 1996; 5:102–8.
71. Availability of clinical practice guidelines on acute pain management: Operative or medical procedures and trauma and urinary incontinence in adults—AHCPR. *Fed Regist.* 1992; 57:12829–31.
72. Jones J, Hoggart B, Withey J, et al. What the patients say: A study of reactions to an intensive care unit. *Intensive Care Med.* 1979; 5:89–92.
73. Gélinas C. Management of pain in cardiac surgery ICU patients: Have we improved over time? *Intensive Crit Care Nurs.* 2007; 23:298–303.
74. Schelling G, Richter M, Roozendaal B, et al. Exposure to high stress in the intensive care unit may have negative effects on health-related quality-of-life outcomes after cardiac surgery. *Crit Care Med.* 2003; 31:1971–80.
75. Granja C, Gomes E, Amaro A, et al. JMIP Study Group: Understanding posttraumatic stress disorder-related symptoms after critical care: The early illness amnesia hypothesis. *Crit Care Med.* 2008; 36:2801–9.
76. Akça O, Melischek M, Scheck T, et al. Postoperative pain and subcutaneous oxygen tension. *Lancet.* 1999; 354:41–2.
77. Hedderich R, Ness TJ. Analgesia for trauma and burns. *Crit Care Clin.* 1999; 15:167–84.
78. Beilin B, Shavit Y, Hart J, et al. Effects of anesthesia based on large versus small doses of fentanyl on natural killer cell cytotoxicity in the perioperative period. *Anesth Analg.* 1996; 82:492–7.
79. Pollock RE, Lotzová E, Stanford SD. Mechanism of surgical stress impairment of human perioperative natural killer cell cytotoxicity. *Arch Surg.* 1991; 126:338–42.
80. Peterson PK, Chao CC, Molitor T, et al. Stress and pathogenesis of infectious disease. *Rev Infect Dis.* 1991; 13:710–20.
81. Puntillo KA, Miaskowski C, Summer G. Pain. *In*: Pathophysiological Phenomena in Nursing: Human Responses to Illness. Third Edition. Carrieri-Kohlman V, Lindsey AM, West CM (Eds). St. Louis, MO, Saunders, 2003, pp 235–55.
82. Chanques G, Viel E, Constantin JM, et al. The measurement of pain in intensive care unit: Comparison of 5 self-report intensity scales. *Pain.* 2010; 151:711–21.
83. Puntillo K, Pasero C, Li D, et al. Evaluation of pain in ICU patients. *Chest.* 2009; 135:1069–74.
84. Li D, Puntillo K, Miaskowski C. A review of objective pain measures for use with critical care adult patients unable to self-report. *J Pain.* 2008; 9:2–10.
85. Arbour C, Gélinas C, Michaud C. Impact of the implementation of the Critical-Care Pain Observation Tool (CPOT) on pain management and clinical outcomes in mechanically ventilated trauma intensive care unit patients: A pilot study. *J Trauma Nurs.* 2011; 18:52–60.
86. Darce K. Cadence wins FDA nod to sell IV pain treatment | intravenous acetaminophen will be marketed for hospital patients. *San Diego Union-Tribune News.* Nov. 2, 2010.
87. Memis D, Inal MT, Kavalci G, et al. Intravenous paracetamol reduced the use of opioids, extubation time, and opioid-related adverse effects after major surgery in intensive care unit. *J Crit Care.* 2010; 25:458–62.
88. Pettersson PH, Jakobsson J, Owall A. Intravenous acetaminophen reduced the use of opioids compared with oral administration after coronary artery bypass grafting. *J Cardiothorac Vasc Anesth.* 2005; 19:306–9.
89. Candiotti KA, Bergese SD, Viscusi ER, et al. Safety of multiple-dose intravenous acetaminophen in adult inpatients. *Pain Med.* 2010; 11:1841–8.
90. Pandey CK, Bose N, Garg G, et al. Gabapentin for the treatment of pain in Guillain-Barré syndrome: A double-blinded, placebo-controlled, crossover study. *Anesth Analg.* 2002; 95:1719–23, table of contents.
91. Pandey CK, Raza M, Tripathi M, et al. The comparative evaluation of gabapentin and carbamazepine for pain management in Guillain-Barré syndrome patients in the intensive care unit. *Anesth Analg.* 2005; 101:220–5, table of contents.
92. Erstad BL, Chopda S, Esser MJ. Prescribing of analgesics in trauma patients. *Am J Ther.* 1997; 4:27–30.
93. Bernards CM, Shen DD, Sterling ES, et al. Epidural, cerebrospinal fluid, and plasma pharmacokinetics of epidural opioids (part 2): Effect of epinephrine. *Anesthesiology.* 2003; 99:466–75.
94. Richman JM, Liu SS, Courpas G, et al. Does continuous peripheral nerve block provide superior pain control to opioids? A meta-analysis. *Anesth Analg.* 2006; 102:248–57.
95. Cepeda MS, Carr DB, Lau J, et al. Music for pain relief. *Cochrane Database Syst Rev.* 2006; CD004843.
96. Yorke J, Wallis M. Factors affecting the site and intensity of pain experienced by cardiac surgical patients in the critical care unit. *Nurs Monogr.* 2002; 2002:49–55.
97. Yorke J, Wallis M, McLean B. Patients' perceptions of pain management after cardiac surgery in an Australian critical care unit. *Heart Lung.* 2004; 33:33–41.
98. Milgrom LB, Brooks JA, Qi R, et al. Pain levels experienced with activities after cardiac surgery. *Am J Crit Care.* 2004; 13:116–25.
99. Siffleet J, Young J, Nikoletti S, et al. Patients' self-report of procedural pain in the intensive care unit. *J Clin Nurs.* 2007; 16:2142–8.

100. Puntillo KA, Wild LR, Morris AB, et al. Practices and predictors of analgesic interventions for adults undergoing painful procedures. *Am J Crit Care.* 2002; 11:415–29; quiz 430.
101. Aïssaoui Y, Zeggwagh AA, Zekraoui A, et al. Validation of a behavioral pain scale in critically ill, sedated, and mechanically ventilated patients. *Anesth Analg.* 2005; 101:1470–6.
102. Ahlers SJ, van Gulik L, van der Veen AM, et al. Comparison of different pain scoring systems in critically ill patients in a general ICU. *Crit Care.* 2008; 12:R15.
103. Ahlers SJ, van der Veen AM, van Dijk M, et al. The use of the Behavioral Pain Scale to assess pain in conscious sedated patients. *Anesth Analg.* 2010; 110:127–33.
104. Gélinas C, Fillion L, Puntillo KA, et al. Validation of the Critical-Care Pain Observation Tool in adult patients. *Am J Crit Care.* 2006; 15:420–7.
105. Gélinas C, Johnston C. Pain assessment in the critically ill ventilated adult: Validation of the Critical-Care Pain Observation Tool and physiologic indicators. *Clin J Pain.* 2007; 23:497–505.
106. Marmo L, Fowler S. Pain assessment tool in the critically ill post-open heart surgery patient population. *Pain Manag Nurs.* 2010; 11:134–40.
107. Payen JF, Bru O, Bosson JL, et al. Assessing pain in critically ill sedated patients by using a behavioral pain scale. *Crit Care Med.* 2001; 29:2258–63.
108 Marmo L, Fowler S. Pain assessment tool in the critically ill post-open heart surgery patient population. *Pain Manag Nurs.* 2010; 11:134–40.
109. Young J, Siffleet J, Nikoletti S, et al. Use of a Behavioural Pain Scale to assess pain in ventilated, unconscious and/or sedated patients. *Intensive Crit Care Nurs.* 2006; 22:32–9.
110. Gélinas C, Arbour C. Behavioral and physiologic indicators during a nociceptive procedure in conscious and unconscious mechanically ventilated adults: Similar or different? *J Crit Care.* 2009; 24:628.e7–628.17.
111. Gélinas C, Fillion L, Puntillo KA. Item selection and content validity of the Critical-Care Pain Observation Tool for non-verbal adults. *J Adv Nurs.* 2009; 65:203–16.
112. Gélinas C, Harel F, Fillion L, et al. Sensitivity and specificity of the Critical-Care Pain Observation Tool for the detection of pain in intubated adults after cardiac surgery. *J Pain Symptom Manage.* 2009; 37:58–67.
113. Chanques G, Payen JF, Mercier G, et al. Assessing pain in non-intubated critically ill patients unable to self report: An adaptation of the Behavioral Pain Scale. *Intensive Care Med.* 2009; 35:2060–7.
114. Odhner M, Wegman D, Freeland N, et al. Assessing pain control in nonverbal critically ill adults. *Dimens Crit Care Nurs.* 2003; 22:260–7.
115. Kabes AM, Graves JK, Norris J. Further validation of the nonverbal pain scale in intensive care patients. *Crit Care Nurse.* 2009; 29:59–66.
116. Puntillo KA, Morris AB, Thompson CL, et al. Pain behaviors observed during six common procedures: Results from Thunder Project II. *Crit Care Med.* 2004; 32:421–7.
117. Puntillo KA, Miaskowski C, Kehrle K, et al. Relationship between behavioral and physiological indicators of pain, critical care patients' self-reports of pain, and opioid administration. *Crit Care Med.* 1997; 25:1159–66.
118. Herr K, Coyne PJ, Key T, et al. American Society for Pain Management Nursing: Pain assessment in the nonverbal patient: Position statement with clinical practice recommendations. *Pain Manag Nurs.* 2006; 7:44–52.
119. Friesner SA, Curry DM, Moddeman GR. Comparison of two pain-management strategies during chest tube removal: Relaxation exercise with opioids and opioids alone. *Heart Lung.* 2006; 35:269–76.
120. Singh M, Gopinath R. Topical analgesia for chest tube removal in cardiac patients. *J Cardiothorac Vasc Anesth.* 2005; 19:719–22.
121. Joshi VS, Chauhan S, Kiran U, et al. Comparison of analgesic efficacy of fentanyl and sufentanil for chest tube removal after cardiac surgery. *Ann Card Anaesth.* 2007; 10:42–5.
122. Rapanos T, Murphy P, Szalai JP, et al. Rectal indomethacin reduces postoperative pain and morphine use after cardiac surgery. *Can J Anaesth.* 1999; 46:725–30.
123. Hynninen MS, Cheng DC, Hossain I, et al. Non-steroidal anti-inflammatory drugs in treatment of postoperative pain after cardiac surgery. *Can J Anaesth.* 2000; 47:1182–7.
124. Machata AM, Illievich UM, Gustorff B, et al. Remifentanil for tracheal tube tolerance: A case control study. *Anaesthesia.* 2007; 62:796–801.
125. But AK, Erdil F, Yucel A, et al. The effects of single-dose tramadol on post-operative pain and morphine requirements after coronary artery bypass surgery. *Acta Anaesthesiol Scand.* 2007; 51:601–6.
126. Krishnan K, Elliot SC, Berridge JC, et al. Remifentanil patient-controlled analgesia following cardiac surgery. *Acta Anaesthesiol Scand.* 2005; 49:876–9.
127. Dahaba AA, Grabner T, Rehak PH, et al. Remifentanil versus morphine analgesia and sedation for mechanically ventilated critically ill patients: A randomized double blind study. *Anesthesiology.* 2004; 101:640–6.
128. Karabinis A, Mandragos K, Stergiopoulos S, et al. Safety and efficacy of analgesia-based sedation with remifentanil versus standard hypnotic-based regimens in intensive care unit patients with brain injuries: A randomised, controlled trial [ISRCTN50308308]. *Crit Care.* 2004; 8:R268–R280.
129. Chinachoti T, Kessler P, Kirkham A, et al. Remifentanil vs morphine for patients in intensive care unit who need short-term mechanical ventilation. *J Med Assoc Thai.* 2002; 85(Suppl 3):S848–S857.
130. Soltész S, Biedler A, Silomon M, et al. Recovery after remifentanil and sufentanil for analgesia and sedation of mechanically ventilated patients after trauma or major surgery. *Br J Anaesth.* 2001; 86:763–8.
131. Breen D, Wilmer A, Bodenham A, et al. Offset of pharmacodynamic effects and safety of remifentanil

in intensive care unit patients with various degrees of renal impairment. *Crit Care.* 2004; 8:R21–R30.

132. Guillou N, Tanguy M, Seguin P, et al. The effects of small-dose ketamine on morphine consumption in surgical intensive care unit patients after major abdominal surgery. *Anesth Analg.* 2003; 97:843–7.
133. Frakes MA, Lord WR, Kociszewski C, et al. Efficacy of fentanyl analgesia for trauma in critical care transport. *Am J Emerg Med.* 2006; 24:286–9.
134. Carrer S, Bocchi A, Candini M, et al. Short term analgesia based sedation in the Intensive Care Unit: Morphine vs remifentanil + morphine. *Minerva Anestesiol.* 2007; 73:327–32.
135. Maddali MM, Kurian E, Fahr J. Extubation time, hemodynamic stability, and postoperative pain control in patients undergoing coronary artery bypass surgery: An evaluation of fentanyl, remifentanil, and nonsteroidal antiinflammatory drugs with propofol for perioperative and postoperative management. *J Clin Anesth.* 2006; 18:605–10.
136. Guggenberger H, Schroeder TH, Vonthein R, et al. Remifentanil or sufentanil for coronary surgery: Comparison of postoperative respiratory impairment. *Eur J Anaesthesiol.* 2006; 23:832–40.
137. Schmittner MD, Vajkoczy SL, Horn P, et al. Effects of fentanyl and S(+)-ketamine on cerebral hemodynamics, gastrointestinal motility, and need of vasopressors in patients with intracranial pathologies: A pilot study. *J Neurosurg Anesthesiol.* 2007; 19:257–62.
138. Park WY, Thompson JS, Lee KK. Effect of epidural anesthesia and analgesia on perioperative outcome: A randomized, controlled Veterans Affairs cooperative study. *Ann Surg.* 2001; 234:560–9; discussion 569.
139. Nishimori M, Ballantyne JC, Low JH. Epidural pain relief versus systemic opioid-based pain relief for abdominal aortic surgery. *Cochrane Database Syst Rev.* 2006; CD005059.
140. Rigg JR, Jamrozik K, Myles PS, et al. MASTER Anaethesia Trial Study Group: Epidural anaesthesia and analgesia and outcome of major surgery: A randomised trial. *Lancet.* 2002; 359:1276–82.
141. Peyton PJ, Myles PS, Silbert BS, et al. Perioperative epidural analgesia and outcome after major abdominal surgery in high-risk patients. *Anesth Analg.* 2003; 96:548–54.
142. Luketich JD, Land SR, Sullivan EA, et al. Thoracic epidural versus intercostal nerve catheter plus patient-controlled analgesia: A randomized study. *Ann Thorac Surg.* 2005; 79:1845–9; discussion 1849.
143. Ali M, Winter DC, Hanly AM, et al. Prospective, randomized, controlled trial of thoracic epidural or patient-controlled opiate analgesia on perioperative quality of life. *Br J Anaesth.* 2010; 104:292–7.
144. Jottard KJ, van Berlo C, Jeuken L, et al. ERAS Group: Changes in outcome during implementation of a fast-track colonic surgery project in a university-affiliated general teaching hospital: Advantages reached with ERAS (Enhanced Recovery After Surgery project) over a 1-year period. *Dig Surg.* 2008; 25:335–8.
145. Rudin A, Flisberg P, Johansson J, et al. Thoracic epidural analgesia or intravenous morphine analgesia after thoracoabdominal esophagectomy: A prospective follow-up of 201 patients. *J Cardiothorac Vasc Anesth.* 2005; 19:350–7.
146. Wahlander S, Frumento RJ, Wagener G, et al. A prospective, double-blind, randomized, placebo-controlled study of dexmedetomidine as an adjunct to epidural analgesia after thoracic surgery. *J Cardiothorac Vasc Anesth.* 2005; 19:630–5.
147. Turker G, Goren S, Bayram S, et al. Comparison of lumbar epidural tramadol and lumbar epidural morphine for pain relief after thoracotomy: A repeated-dose study. *J Cardiothorac Vasc Anesth.* 2005; 19:468–74.
148. Beattie WS, Badner NH, Choi P. Epidural analgesia reduces postoperative myocardial infarction: A meta-analysis. *Anesth Analg.* 2001; 93:853–8.
149. Block BM, Liu SS, Rowlingson AJ, et al. Efficacy of postoperative epidural analgesia: A meta-analysis. *JAMA.* 2003; 290:2455–63.
150. Bulger EM, Edwards T, Klotz P, et al. Epidural analgesia improves outcome after multiple rib fractures. *Surgery.* 2004; 136:426–30.
151. Carrier FM, Turgeon AF, Nicole PC, et al. Effect of epidural analgesia in patients with traumatic rib fractures: A systematic review and meta-analysis of randomized controlled trials. *Can J Anaesth.* 2009; 56:230–42.
152. Fraser GL, Prato BS, Riker RR, et al. Frequency, severity, and treatment of agitation in young versus elderly patients in the ICU. *Pharmacotherapy.* 2000; 20:75–82.
153. Atkins PM, Mion LC, Mendelson W, et al. Characteristics and outcomes of patients who self-extubate from ventilatory support: A case-control study. *Chest.* 1997; 112:1317–23.
154. Vassal T, Anh NG, Gabillet JM, et al. Prospective evaluation of self-extubations in a medical intensive care unit. *Intensive Care Med.* 1993; 19:340–2.
155. Fraser GL, Riker RR, Prato BS, et al. The frequency and cost of patient-initiated device removal in the ICU. *Pharmacotherapy.* 2001; 21:1–6.
156. Conti J, Smith D. Haemodynamic responses to extubation after cardiac surgery with and without continued sedation. *Br J Anaesth.* 1998; 80:834–6.
157. Cohen D, Horiuchi K, Kemper M, et al. Modulating effects of propofol on metabolic and cardiopulmonary responses to stressful intensive care unit procedures. *Crit Care Med.* 1996; 24:612–7.
158. Kollef MH, Levy NT, Ahrens TS, et al. The use of continuous i.v. sedation is associated with prolongation of mechanical ventilation. *Chest.* 1998; 114:541–8.
159. Mascia MF, Koch M, Medicis JJ. Pharmacoeconomic impact of rational use guidelines on the provision of analgesia, sedation, and neuromuscular blockade in critical care. *Crit Care Med.* 2000; 28:2300–6.
160. Marshall J, Finn CA, Theodore AC. Impact of a clinical pharmacist-enforced intensive care unit sedation protocol on duration of mechanical ventilation and hospital stay. *Crit Care Med.* 2008; 36:427–33.

161. DuBose JJ, Inaba K, Shiflett A, et al. Measurable outcomes of quality improvement in the trauma intensive care unit: The impact of a daily quality rounding checklist. *J Trauma.* 2008; 64:22–7; discussion 27.
162. Devlin JW, Holbrook AM, Fuller HD. The effect of ICU sedation guidelines and pharmacist interventions on clinical outcomes and drug cost. *Ann Pharmacother.* 1997; 31:689–95.
163. Mehta S, McCullagh I, Burry L. Current sedation practices: Lessons learned from international surveys. *Crit Care Clin.* 2009; 25:471–88, vii.
164. Patel RP, Gambrell M, Speroff T, et al. Delirium and sedation in the intensive care unit: Survey of behaviors and attitudes of 1384 healthcare professionals. *Crit Care Med.* 2009; 37:825–32.
165. Salluh JI, Dal-Pizzol F, Mello PV, et al. Brazilian Research in Intensive Care Network: Delirium recognition and sedation practices in critically ill patients: A survey on the attitudes of 1015 Brazilian critical care physicians. *J Crit Care.* 2009; 24:556–62.
166. Wunsch H, Kahn JM, Kramer AA, et al. Use of intravenous infusion sedation among mechanically ventilated patients in the United States. *Crit Care Med.* 2009; 37:3031–9.
167. Szumita PM, Baroletti SA, Anger KE, et al. Sedation and analgesia in the intensive care unit: Evaluating the role of dexmedetomidine. *Am J Health Syst Pharm.* 2007; 64:37–44.
168. Tan JA, Ho KM. Use of dexmedetomidine as a sedative and analgesic agent in critically ill adult patients: A meta-analysis. *Intensive Care Med.* 2010; 36:926–39.
169. Young CC, Prielipp RC. Benzodiazepines in the intensive care unit. *Crit Care Clin.* 2001; 17:843–62.
170. Greenblatt DJ, Harmatz JS, Shader RI. Clinical pharmacokinetics of anxiolytics and hypnotics in the elderly. Therapeutic considerations (Part I). *Clin Pharmacokinet.* 1991; 21:165–77.
171. Barr J, Zomorodi K, Bertaccini EJ, et al. A double-blind, randomized comparison of i.v. lorazepam versus midazolam for sedation of ICU patients via a pharmacologic model. *Anesthesiology.* 2001; 95:286–98.
172. Shafer A. Complications of sedation with midazolam in the intensive care unit and a comparison with other sedative regimens. *Crit Care Med.* 1998; 26:947–56.
173. Swart EL, Zuideveld KP, de Jongh J, et al. Population pharmacodynamic modelling of lorazepam- and midazolam-induced sedation upon long-term continuous infusion in critically ill patients. *Eur J Clin Pharmacol.* 2006; 62:185–94.
174. Swart EL, de Jongh J, Zuideveld KP, et al. Population pharmacokinetics of lorazepam and midazolam and their metabolites in intensive care patients on continuous venovenous hemofiltration. *Am J Kidney Dis.* 2005; 45:360–71.
175. Swart EL, Zuideveld KP, de Jongh J, et al. Comparative population pharmacokinetics of lorazepam and midazolam during long-term continuous infusion in critically ill patients. *Br J Clin Pharmacol.* 2004; 57:135–45.
176. Greenblatt DJ, von Moltke LL, Ehrenberg BL, et al. Kinetics and dynamics of lorazepam during and after continuous intravenous infusion. *Crit Care Med.* 2000; 28:2750–7.
177. Greenblatt DJ, Ehrenberg BL, Gunderman J, et al. Kinetic and dynamic study of intravenous lorazepam: Comparison with intravenous diazepam. *J Pharmacol Exp Ther.* 1989; 250:134–40.
178. Bauer TM, Ritz R, Haberthür C, et al. Prolonged sedation due to accumulation of conjugated metabolites of midazolam. *Lancet.* 1995; 346:145–7.
179. Greenblatt DJ, Abernethy DR, Locniskar A, et al. Effect of age, gender, and obesity on midazolam kinetics. *Anesthesiology.* 1984; 61:27–35.
180. Ochs HR, Greenblatt DJ, Divoll M, et al. Diazepam kinetics in relation to age and sex. *Pharmacology.* 1981; 23:24–30.
181. Oldenhof H, de Jong M, Steenhoek A, et al. Clinical pharmacokinetics of midazolam in intensive care patients, a wide interpatient variability? *Clin Pharmacol Ther.* 1988; 43:263–9.
182. Pohlman AS, Simpson KP, Hall JB. Continuous intravenous infusions of lorazepam versus midazolam for sedation during mechanical ventilatory support: A prospective, randomized study. *Crit Care Med.* 1994; 22:1241–7.
183. Carson SS, Kress JP, Rodgers JE, et al. A randomized trial of intermittent lorazepam versus propofol with daily interruption in mechanically ventilated patients. *Crit Care Med.* 2006; 34:1326–32.
184. Spina SP, Ensom MH. Clinical pharmacokinetic monitoring of midazolam in critically ill patients. *Pharmacotherapy.* 2007; 27:389–98.
185. Ariano RE, Kassum DA, Aronson KJ. Comparison of sedative recovery time after midazolam versus diazepam administration. *Crit Care Med.* 1994; 22:1492–6.
186. Yaucher NE, Fish JT, Smith HW, et al. Propylene glycol-associated renal toxicity from lorazepam infusion. *Pharmacotherapy.* 2003; 23:1094–9.
187. Barnes BJ, Gerst C, Smith JR, et al. Osmol gap as a surrogate marker for serum propylene glycol concentrations in patients receiving lorazepam for sedation. *Pharmacotherapy.* 2006; 26:23–33.
188. Arroliga AC, Shehab N, McCarthy K, et al. Relationship of continuous infusion lorazepam to serum propylene glycol concentration in critically ill adults. *Crit Care Med.* 2004; 32:1709–14.
189. Reynolds HN, Teiken P, Regan ME, et al. Hyperlactatemia, increased osmolar gap, and renal dysfunction during continuous lorazepam infusion. *Crit Care Med.* 2000; 28:1631–4.
190. Wilson KC, Farber HW. Propylene glycol accumulation during continuous-infusion lorazepam in critically ill patients. *J Intensive Care Med.* 2008; 23:413; author reply 414–3; author reply 415.
191. Yahwak JA, Riker RR, Fraser GL, et al. Determination of a lorazepam dose threshold for using the osmol gap to monitor for propylene glycol toxicity. *Pharmacotherapy.* 2008; 28:984–91.
192. Barr J, Donner A. Optimal intravenous dosing strategies for sedatives and analgesics in the intensive care unit. *Crit Care Clin.* 1995; 11:827–47.

193. Barr J. Propofol: A new drug for sedation in the intensive care unit. *Int Anesthesiol Clin.* 1995; 33:131–54.
194. Cox CE, Reed SD, Govert JA, et al. Economic evaluation of propofol and lorazepam for critically ill patients undergoing mechanical ventilation. *Crit Care Med.* 2008; 36:706–14.
195. McKeage K, Perry CM. Propofol: A review of its use in intensive care sedation of adults. *CNS Drugs.* 2003; 17:235–72.
196. Marik PE. Propofol: Therapeutic indications and side-effects. *Curr Pharm Des.* 2004; 10:3639–49.
197. Weinbroum AA, Halpern P, Rudick V, et al. Midazolam versus propofol for long-term sedation in the ICU: A randomized prospective comparison. *Intensive Care Med.* 1997; 23:1258–63.
198. Barr J, Egan TD, Sandoval NF, et al. Propofol dosing regimens for ICU sedation based upon an integrated pharmacokinetic-pharmacodynamic model. *Anesthesiology.* 2001; 95:324–33.
199. Tanios MA, de Wit M, Epstein SK, et al. Perceived barriers to the use of sedation protocols and daily sedation interruption: A multidisciplinary survey. *J Crit Care.* 2009; 24:66–73.
200. Riker RR, Fraser GL. Adverse events associated with sedatives, analgesics, and other drugs that provide patient comfort in the intensive care unit. *Pharmacotherapy.* 2005; 25(5 Pt 2):8S–18S.
201. Walder B, Tramèr MR, Seeck M. Seizure-like phenomena and propofol: A systematic review. *Neurology.* 2002; 58:1327–32.
202. Iyer VN, Hoel R, Rabinstein AA. Propofol infusion syndrome in patients with refractory status epilepticus: An 11-year clinical experience. *Crit Care Med.* 2009; 37:3024–30.
203. Parviainen I, Uusaro A, Kälviäinen R, et al. Propofol in the treatment of refractory status epilepticus. *Intensive Care Med.* 2006; 32:1075–9.
204. Voss LJ, Sleigh JW, Barnard JP, et al. The howling cortex: Seizures and general anesthetic drugs. *Anesth Analg.* 2008; 107:1689–1703.
205. Fong JJ, Sylvia L, Ruthazer R, et al. Predictors of mortality in patients with suspected propofol infusion syndrome. *Crit Care Med.* 2008; 36:2281–7.
206. Diedrich DA, Brown DR. Analytic reviews: Propofol infusion syndrome in the ICU. *J Intensive Care Med.* 2011; 26:59–72.
207. Kam PC, Cardone D. Propofol infusion syndrome. *Anaesthesia.* 2007; 62:690–701.
208. Merz TM, Regli B, Rothen HU, et al. Propofol infusion syndrome: A fatal case at a low infusion rate. *Anesth Analg.* 2006; 103:1050.
209. Chukwuemeka A, Ko R, Ralph-Edwards A. Short-term low-dose propofol anaesthesia associated with severe metabolic acidosis. *Anaesth Intensive Care.* 2006; 34:651–5.
210. Roberts RJ, Barletta JF, Fong JJ, et al. Incidence of propofol-related infusion syndrome in critically ill adults: A prospective, multicenter study. *Crit Care.* 2009; 13:R169.
211. Khan ZP, Ferguson CN, Jones RM. alpha-2 and imidazoline receptor agonists. Their pharmacology and therapeutic role. *Anaesthesia.* 1999; 54:146–65.
212. Bhana N, Goa KL, McClellan KJ. Dexmedetomidine. *Drugs.* 2000; 59:263–8; discussion 269.
213. Triltsch AE, Welte M, von Homeyer P, et al. Bispectral index-guided sedation with dexmedetomidine in intensive care: A prospective, randomized, double blind, placebo-controlled phase II study. *Crit Care Med.* 2002; 30:1007–14.
214. Belleville JP, Ward DS, Bloor BC, et al. Effects of intravenous dexmedetomidine in humans. I. Sedation, ventilation, and metabolic rate. *Anesthesiology.* 1992; 77:1125–33.
215. Venn RM, Karol MD, Grounds RM. Pharmacokinetics of dexmedetomidine infusions for sedation of postoperative patients requiring intensive care. *Br J Anaesth.* 2002; 88:669–75.
216. Dasta JF, Kane-Gill SL, Durtschi AJ. Comparing dexmedetomidine prescribing patterns and safety in the naturalistic setting versus published data. *Ann Pharmacother.* 2004; 38:1130–5.
217. Dyck JB, Maze M, Haack C, et al. The pharmacokinetics and hemodynamic effects of intravenous and intramuscular dexmedetomidine hydrochloride in adult human volunteers. *Anesthesiology.* 1993; 78:813–20.
218. Cunningham FE, Baughman VL, Tonkovich L, et al. Pharmacokinetics of dexmedetomidine (DEX) in patients with hepatic failure (HF). *Clin Pharmacol Ther.* 1999; 65:128.
219. Venn RM, Grounds RM. Comparison between dexmedetomidine and propofol for sedation in the intensive care unit: Patient and clinician perceptions. *Br J Anaesth.* 2001; 87:684–90.
220. Riker RR, Shehabi Y, Bokesch PM, et al. SEDCOM (Safety and Efficacy of Dexmedetomidine Compared With Midazolam) Study Group: Dexmedetomidine vs midazolam for sedation of critically ill patients: A randomized trial. *JAMA.* 2009; 301:489–99.
221. Shehabi Y, Ruettimann U, Adamson H, et al. Dexmedetomidine infusion for more than 24 hours in critically ill patients: Sedative and cardiovascular effects. *Intensive Care Med.* 2004; 30:2188–196.
222. Pandharipande PP, Pun BT, Herr DL, et al. Effect of sedation with dexmedetomidine vs lorazepam on acute brain dysfunction in mechanically ventilated patients: The MENDS randomized controlled trial. *JAMA.* 2007; 298:2644–53.
223. Gerlach AT, Murphy CV, Dasta JF. An updated focused review of dexmedetomidine in adults. *Ann Pharmacother.* 2009; 43:2064–74.
224. Venn RM, Bradshaw CJ, Spencer R, et al. Preliminary UK experience of dexmedetomidine, a novel agent for postoperative sedation in the intensive care unit. *Anaesthesia.* 1999; 54:1136–42.
225. Venn RM, Hell J, Grounds RM. Respiratory effects of dexmedetomidine in the surgical patient requiring intensive care. *Crit Care.* 2000; 4:302–8.
226. Martin E, Ramsay G, Mantz J, et al. The role of the alpha2-adrenoceptor agonist dexmedetomidine in postsurgical sedation in the intensive care unit. *J Intensive Care Med.* 2003; 18:29–41.
227. Venn M, Newman J, Grounds M. A phase II study to evaluate the efficacy of dexmedetomidine for seda-

tion in the medical intensive care unit. *Intensive Care Med.* 2003; 29:201–7.

228. Elbaradie S, El Mahalawy FH, Solyman AH. Dexmedetomidine vs. propofol for short-term sedation of postoperative mechanically ventilated patients. *J Egypt Natl Canc Inst.* 2004; 16:153–8.
229. Panzer O, Moitra V, Sladen RN. Pharmacology of sedative-analgesic agents: Dexmedetomidine, remifentanil, ketamine, volatile anesthetics, and the role of peripheral Mu antagonists. *Anesthesiol Clin.* 2011; 29:587–605, vii.
230. Al-Metwalli RR, Mowafi HA, Ismail SA, et al. Effect of intra-articular dexmedetomidine on postoperative analgesia after arthroscopic knee surgery. *Br J Anaesth.* 2008; 101:395–9.
231. Kress JP, Gehlbach B, Lacy M, et al. The long-term psychological effects of daily sedative interruption on critically ill patients. *Am J Respir Crit Care Med.* 2003; 168:1457–61.
232. Kress JP, Vinayak AG, Levitt J, et al. Daily sedative interruption in mechanically ventilated patients at risk for coronary artery disease. *Crit Care Med.* 2007; 35:365–71.
233. Hall RI, MacLaren C, Smith MS, et al. Light versus heavy sedation after cardiac surgery: Myocardial ischemia and the stress response. Maritime Heart Centre and Dalhousie University. *Anesth Analg.* 1997; 85:971–8.
234. Mangano DT, Siliciano D, Hollenberg M, et al. Postoperative myocardial ischemia. Therapeutic trials using intensive analgesia following surgery. The Study of Perioperative Ischemia (SPI) Research Group. *Anesthesiology.* 1992; 76:342–53.
235. Plunkett JJ, Reeves JD, Ngo L, et al. Urine and plasma catecholamine and cortisol concentrations after myocardial revascularization. Modulation by continuous sedation. Multicenter Study of Perioperative Ischemia (McSPI) Research Group, and the Ischemia Research and Education Foundation (IREF). *Anesthesiology.* 1997; 86:785–96.
236. Terao Y, Miura K, Saito M, et al. Quantitative analysis of the relationship between sedation and resting energy expenditure in postoperative patients. *Crit Care Med.* 2003; 31:830–3.
237. Samuelson KA, Lundberg D, Fridlund B. Stressful experiences in relation to depth of sedation in mechanically ventilated patients. *Nurs Crit Care.* 2007; 12:93–104.
238. Samuelson K, Lundberg D, Fridlund B. Memory in relation to depth of sedation in adult mechanically ventilated intensive care patients. *Intensive Care Med.* 2006; 32:660–7.
239. Binnekade JM, Vroom MB, de Vos R, et al. The reliability and validity of a new and simple method to measure sedation levels in intensive care patients: A pilot study. *Heart Lung.* 2006; 35:137–43.
240. Brandl KM, Langley KA, Riker RR, et al. Confirming the reliability of the Sedation-Agitation Scale administered by ICU nurses without experience in its use. *Pharmacotherapy.* 2001; 21:431–6.
241. Chernik DA, Gillings D, Laine H, et al. Validity and reliability of the Observer's Assessment of Alertness/Sedation Scale: Study with intravenous midazolam. *J Clin Psychopharmacol.* 1990; 10:244–51.
242. De Jonghe B, Cook D, Griffith L, et al. Adaptation to the Intensive Care Environment (ATICE): Development and validation of a new sedation assessment instrument. *Crit Care Med.* 2003; 31:2344–54.
243. de Lemos J, Tweeddale M, Chittock D. Measuring quality of sedation in adult mechanically ventilated critically ill patients. the Vancouver Interaction and Calmness Scale. Sedation Focus Group. *J Clin Epidemiol.* 2000; 53:908–19.
244. Deogaonkar A, Gupta R, DeGeorgia M, et al. Bispectral Index monitoring correlates with sedation scales in brain-injured patients. *Crit Care Med.* 2004; 32:2403–6.
245. Devlin JW, Boleski G, Mlynarek M, et al. Motor Activity Assessment Scale: A valid and reliable sedation scale for use with mechanically ventilated patients in an adult surgical intensive care unit. *Crit Care Med.* 1999; 27:1271–5.
246. Ely EW, Truman B, Shintani A, et al. Monitoring sedation status over time in ICU patients: Reliability and validity of the Richmond Agitation-Sedation Scale (RASS). *JAMA.* 2003; 289:2983–91.
247. Haberthür C, Lehmann F, Ritz R. Assessment of depth of midazolam sedation using objective parameters. *Intensive Care Med.* 1996; 22:1385–90.
248. Hernández-Gancedo C, Pestaña D, Peña N, et al. Monitoring sedation in critically ill patients: Bispectral index, Ramsay and observer scales. *Eur J Anaesthesiol.* 2006; 23:649–53.
249. Hogg LH, Bobek MB, Mion LC, et al. Interrater reliability of 2 sedation scales in a medical intensive care unit: A preliminary report. *Am J Crit Care.* 2001; 10:79–83.
250. Masica AL, Girard TD, Wilkinson GR, et al. Clinical sedation scores as indicators of sedative and analgesic drug exposure in intensive care unit patients. *Am J Geriatr Pharmacother.* 2007; 5:218–31.
251. Nassar AP Jr, Neto RCP, de Figueiredo WB, et al. Validity, reliability and applicability of portuguese versions of Sedation-Agitation Scales among critically ill patients. *Sao Paulo Medical Journal.* 2008; 126:215–9.
252. Olleveant N, Humphris G, Roe B. A reliability study of the modified new Sheffield Sedation Scale. *Nurs Crit Care.* 1998; 3:83–8.
253. Olson D, Lynn M, Thoyre SM, et al. The limited reliability of the Ramsay scale. *Neurocrit Care.* 2007; 7:227–31.
254. Pun BT, Gordon SM, Peterson JF, et al. Large-scale implementation of sedation and delirium monitoring in the intensive care unit: A report from two medical centers. *Crit Care Med.* 2005; 33:1199–1205.
255. Ramsay MA, Savege TM, Simpson BR, et al. Controlled sedation with alphaxalone-alphadolone. *Br Med J.* 1974; 2:656–9.
256. Rassin M, Sruyah R, Kahalon A, et al. "Between the fixed and the changing": Examining and comparing reliability and validity of 3 sedation-agitation measuring scales. *Dimens Crit Care Nurs.* 2007; 26:76–82.

257. Riker RR, Fraser GL, Cox PM. Continuous infusion of haloperidol controls agitation in critically ill patients. *Crit Care Med.* 1994; 22:433–40.
258. Riker RR, Fraser GL, Simmons LE, et al. Validating the Sedation-Agitation Scale with the Bispectral Index and Visual Analog Scale in adult ICU patients after cardiac surgery. *Intensive Care Med.* 2001; 27:853–8.
259. Weinert CR, Calvin AD. Epidemiology of sedation and sedation adequacy for mechanically ventilated patients in a medical and surgical intensive care unit. *Crit Care Med.* 2007; 35:393–401.
260. Weinert C, McFarland L. The state of intubated ICU patients: Development of a two-dimensional sedation rating scale for critically ill adults. *Chest.* 2004; 126:1883–90.
261. Sessler CN, Gosnell MS, Grap MJ, et al. The Richmond Agitation-Sedation Scale: Validity and reliability in adult intensive care unit patients. *Am J Respir Crit Care Med.* 2002; 166:1338–44.
262. Riker RR, Picard JT, Fraser GL. Prospective evaluation of the Sedation-Agitation Scale for adult critically ill patients. *Crit Care Med.* 1999; 27:1325–9.
263. Ryder-Lewis MC, Nelson KM. Reliability of the Sedation-Agitation Scale between nurses and doctors. *Intensive Crit Care Nurs.* 2008; 24:211–7.
264. Schulte-Tamburen AM, Scheier J, Briegel J, et al. Comparison of five sedation scoring systems by means of auditory evoked potentials. *Intensive Care Med.* 1999; 25:377–82.
265. Lu CH, Man KM, Ou-Yang HY, et al. Composite auditory evoked potential index versus bispectral index to estimate the level of sedation in paralyzed critically ill patients: A prospective observational study. *Anesth Analg.* 2008; 107:1290–4.
266. Lu CH, Ou-Yang HY, Man KM, et al. Relative reliability of the auditory evoked potential and Bispectral Index for monitoring sedation level in surgical intensive care patients. *Anaesth Intensive Care.* 2008; 36:553–9.
267. Arbour R, Waterhouse J, Seckel MA, et al. Correlation between the Sedation-Agitation Scale and the Bispectral Index in ventilated patients in the intensive care unit. *Heart Lung.* 2009; 38:336–45.
268. Walsh TS, Ramsay P, Lapinlampi TP, et al. An assessment of the validity of spectral entropy as a measure of sedation state in mechanically ventilated critically ill patients. *Intensive Care Med.* 2008; 34:308–15.
269. Haenggi M, Ypparila-Wolters H, Bieri C, et al. Entropy and bispectral index for assessment of sedation, analgesia and the effects of unpleasant stimuli in critically ill patients: An observational study. *Crit Care.* 2008; 12:R119.
270. Roustan JP, Valette S, Aubas P, et al. Can electroencephalographic analysis be used to determine sedation levels in critically ill patients? *Anesth Analg.* 2005; 101:1141–51, table of contents.
271. Olson DM, Thoyre SM, Peterson ED, et al. A randomized evaluation of bispectral index-augmented sedation assessment in neurological patients. *Neurocrit Care.* 2009; 11:20–7.
272. Weber F, Steinberger M, Ritzka M, et al. Measuring depth of sedation in intensive care patients with the electroencephalographic Narcotrend Index. *Eur J Anaesthesiol.* 2008; 25:123–8.
273. Hernández-Gancedo C, Pestaña D, Pérez-Chrzanowska H, et al. Comparing Entropy and the Bispectral index with the Ramsay score in sedated ICU patients. *J Clin Monit Comput.* 2007; 21:295–302.
274. Weatherburn C, Endacott R, Tynan P, et al. The impact of bispectral index monitoring on sedation administration in mechanically ventilated patients. *Anaesth Intensive Care.* 2007; 35:204–8.
275. Friedman D, Claassen J, Hirsch LJ. Continuous electroencephalogram monitoring in the intensive care unit. *Anesth Analg.* 2009; 109:506–23.
276. Consales G, Chelazzi C, Rinaldi S, et al. Bispectral Index compared to Ramsay score for sedation monitoring in intensive care units. *Minerva Anestesiol.* 2006; 72:329–36.
277. Tonner PH, Wei C, Bein B, et al. Comparison of two bispectral index algorithms in monitoring sedation in postoperative intensive care patients. *Crit Care Med.* 2005; 33:580–4.
278. Adesanya AO, Rosero E, Wyrick C, et al. Assessing the predictive value of the bispectral index vs patient state index on clinical assessment of sedation in postoperative cardiac surgery patients. *J Crit Care.* 2009; 24:322–8.
279. Trouiller P, Fangio P, Paugam-Burtz C, et al. Frequency and clinical impact of preserved bispectral index activity during deep sedation in mechanically ventilated ICU patients. *Intensive Care Med.* 2009; 35:2096–104.
280. Arbour R. Impact of bispectral index monitoring on sedation and outcomes in critically ill adults: A case series. *Crit Care Nurs Clin North Am.* 2006; 18:227–41, xi.
281. Riker RR, Fraser GL, Wilkins ML. Comparing the bispectral index and suppression ratio with burst suppression of the electroencephalogram during pentobarbital infusions in adult intensive care patients. *Pharmacotherapy.* 2003; 23:1087–93.
282. de Wit M, Epstein SK. Administration of sedatives and level of sedation: Comparative evaluation via the Sedation-Agitation Scale and the Bispectral Index. *Am J Crit Care.* 2003; 12:343–8.
283. Mondello E, Siliotti R, Noto G, et al. Bispectral Index in ICU: Correlation with Ramsay Score on assessment of sedation level. *J Clin Monit Comput.* 2002; 17:271–7.
284. Frenzel D, Greim CA, Sommer C, et al. Is the bispectral index appropriate for monitoring the sedation level of mechanically ventilated surgical ICU patients? *Intensive Care Med.* 2002; 28:178–83.
285. Ruokonen E, Parviainen I, Jakob SM, et al. "Dexmedetomidine for Continuous Sedation" Investigators: Dexmedetomidine versus propofol/midazolam for long-term sedation during mechanical ventilation. *Intensive Care Med.* 2009; 35:282–90.
286. Maldonado JR, Wysong A, van der Starre PJ, et al. Dexmedetomidine and the reduction of postoperative delirium after cardiac surgery. *Psychosomatics.* 2009; 50:206–17.

287. Samuelson KA, Lundberg D, Fridlund B. Light vs. heavy sedation during mechanical ventilation after oesophagectomy—A pilot experimental study focusing on memory. *Acta Anaesthesiol Scand.* 2008; 52:1116–23.
288. Pandharipande P, Cotton BA, Shintani A, et al. Prevalence and risk factors for development of delirium in surgical and trauma intensive care unit patients. *J Trauma.* 2008; 65:34–41.
289. Pandharipande P, Ely EW. Sedative and analgesic medications: Risk factors for delirium and sleep disturbances in the critically ill. *Crit Care Clin.* 2006; 22:313–27, vii.
290. Arroliga AC, Thompson BT, Ancukiewicz M, et al. Acute Respiratory Distress Syndrome Network: Use of sedatives, opioids, and neuromuscular blocking agents in patients with acute lung injury and acute respiratory distress syndrome. *Crit Care Med.* 2008; 36:1083–8.
291. Ho KM, Ng JY. The use of propofol for medium and long-term sedation in critically ill adult patients: A meta-analysis. *Intensive Care Med.* 2008; 34:69–79.
292. Fong JJ, Kanji S, Dasta JF, et al. Propofol associated with a shorter duration of mechanical ventilation than scheduled intermittent lorazepam: A database analysis using Project IMPACT. *Ann Pharmacother.* 2007; 41:1986–91.
293. Esmaoglu A, Ulgey A, Akin A, et al. Comparison between dexmedetomidine and midazolam for sedation of eclampsia patients in the intensive care unit. *J Crit Care.* 2009; 24:551–5.
294. Anis AH, Wang XH, Leon H, et al. Propofol Study Group: Economic evaluation of propofol for sedation of patients admitted to intensive care units. *Anesthesiology.* 2002; 96:196–201.
295. Hall RI, Sandham D, Cardinal P, et al. Study Investigators: Propofol vs midazolam for ICU sedation: A Canadian multicenter randomized trial. *Chest.* 2001; 119:1151–9.
296. Huey-Ling L, Chun-Che S, Jen-Jen T, et al. Comparison of the effect of protocol-directed sedation with propofol vs. midazolam by nurses in intensive care: Efficacy, haemodynamic stability and patient satisfaction. *J Clin Nurs.* 2008; 17:1510–7.
297. Searle NR, Côté S, Taillefer J, et al. Propofol or midazolam for sedation and early extubation following cardiac surgery. *Can J Anaesth.* 1997; 44:629–35.
298. Pandharipande PP, Sanders RD, Girard TD, et al. MENDS Investigators: Effect of dexmedetomidine versus lorazepam on outcome in patients with sepsis: An a priori-designed analysis of the MENDS randomized controlled trial. *Crit Care.* 2010; 14:R38.
299. Barrientos-Vega R, Mar Sánchez-Soria M, Morales-García C, et al. Prolonged sedation of critically ill patients with midazolam or propofol: Impact on weaning and costs. *Crit Care Med.* 1997; 25:33–40.
300. Dasta JF, Kane-Gill SL, Pencina M, et al. A cost-minimization analysis of dexmedetomidine compared with midazolam for long-term sedation in the intensive care unit. *Crit Care Med.* 2010; 38:497–503.
301. Jakob SM, Ruokonen E, Grounds RM, et al. Dexmedetomidine for Long-Term Sedation Investigators: Dexmedetomidine vs midazolam or propofol for sedation during prolonged mechanical ventilation: Two randomized controlled trials. *JAMA.* 2012; 307:1151–60.
302. Carrasco G, Cabré L, Sobrepere G, et al. Synergistic sedation with propofol and midazolam in intensive care patients after coronary artery bypass grafting. *Crit Care Med.* 1998; 26:844–51.
303. Meagher DJ, Leonard M, Donnelly S, et al. A longitudinal study of motor subtypes in delirium: Relationship with other phenomenology, etiology, medication exposure and prognosis. *J Psychosom Res.* 2011; 71:395–403.
304. Gupta N, de Jonghe J, Schieveld J, et al. Delirium phenomenology: What can we learn from the symptoms of delirium? *J Psychosom Res.* 2008; 65:215–22.
305. American Psychiatric Association. Delirium, dementia and amnestic and other cognitive disorders. *In*: Diagnostic and Statistical Manual of Mental Disorders, 4th ed. Washington, DC, American Psychiatric Association, 1994, pp 123–33.
306. American Psychiatric Association. Diagnostic and Statistical Manual of Mental Disorders. Washington, DC, American Psychiatric Association, 1994.
307. American Psychiatric Association. Practice guideline for the treatment of patients with delirium. *Am J Psychiatry.* 1999; 156:1–20.
308. Ely EW, Inouye SK, Bernard GR, et al. Delirium in mechanically ventilated patients: Validity and reliability of the confusion assessment method for the intensive care unit (CAM-ICU). *JAMA.* 2001; 286:2703–10.
309. Bergeron N, Dubois MJ, Dumont M, et al. Intensive Care Delirium Screening Checklist: Evaluation of a new screening tool. *Intensive Care Med.* 2001; 27:859–64.
310. American Psychiatric Association. *American Psychiatric Association Practice Guidelines for the Treatment of Psychiatric Disorders. Compendium 2006.* Arlington, VA, American Psychiatric Association, 2006, pp 72–4.
311. Changing intensive care to improve life afterward—WSJ.com. Available at: http://online.wsj.com/article/SB10001424052748704081604576144321242020948.html. Accessed November 2011.
312. Hospitals fight a form of delirium that often strikes ICU patients—The Washington Post. Available at: http://www.washingtonpost.com/national/health/hospitals-fight-a-form-of-delirium-that-often-strikes-icu-patients/2011/03/23/AF518nMD_story.html. Accessed November 2011.
313. Milbrandt EB, Deppen S, Harrison PL, et al. Costs associated with delirium in mechanically ventilated patients. *Crit Care Med.* 2004; 32:955–62.
314. McNicoll L, Pisani MA, Zhang Y, et al. Delirium in the intensive care unit: Occurrence and clinical course in older patients. *J Am Geriatr Soc.* 2003; 51:591–8.
315. Morandi A, Pandharipande P, Trabucchi M, et al. Understanding international differences in terminology for delirium and other types of acute brain dysfunction in critically ill patients. *Intensive Care Med.* 2008; 34:1907–15.

316. Pun BT, Ely EW. The importance of diagnosing and managing ICU delirium. *Chest.* 2007; 132:624–36.
317. Skrobik Y. Delirium prevention and treatment. *Crit Care Clin.* 2009; 25:585–91, x.
318. Ouimet S, Kavanagh BP, Gottfried SB, et al. Incidence, risk factors and consequences of ICU delirium. *Intensive Care Med.* 2007; 33:66–73.
319. Ouimet S, Riker R, Bergeron N, et al. Subsyndromal delirium in the ICU: Evidence for a disease spectrum. *Intensive Care Med.* 2007; 33:1007–13.
320. Shehabi Y, Riker RR, Bokesch PM, et al. SEDCOM (Safety and Efficacy of Dexmedetomidine Compared With Midazolam) Study Group: Delirium duration and mortality in lightly sedated, mechanically ventilated intensive care patients. *Crit Care Med.* 2010; 38:2311–8.
321. Pisani MA, Kong SY, Kasl SV, et al. Days of delirium are associated with 1-year mortality in an older intensive care unit population. *Am J Respir Crit Care Med.* 2009; 180:1092–7.
322. Ely EW, Shintani A, Truman B, et al. Delirium as a predictor of mortality in mechanically ventilated patients in the intensive care unit. *JAMA.* 2004; 291:1753–62.
323. Ely EW, Gautam S, Margolin R, et al. The impact of delirium in the intensive care unit on hospital length of stay. *Intensive Care Med.* 2001; 27:1892–900.
324. Girard TD, Jackson JC, Pandharipande PP, et al. Delirium as a predictor of long-term cognitive impairment in survivors of critical illness. *Crit Care Med.* 2010; 38:1513–20.
325. Needham DM, Korupolu R, Zanni JM, et al. Early physical medicine and rehabilitation for patients with acute respiratory failure: A quality improvement project. *Arch Phys Med Rehabil.* 2010; 91:536–42.
326. Schweickert WD, Pohlman MC, Pohlman AS, et al. Early physical and occupational therapy in mechanically ventilated, critically ill patients: A randomised controlled trial. *Lancet.* 2009; 373:1874–82.
327. Skrobik Y, Ahern S, Leblanc M, et al. Protocolized intensive care unit management of analgesia, sedation, and delirium improves analgesia and subsyndromal delirium rates. *Anesth Analg.* 2010; 111:451–63.
328. Pandharipande P, Shintani A, Peterson J, et al. Lorazepam is an independent risk factor for transitioning to delirium in intensive care unit patients. *Anesthesiology.* 2006; 104:21–6.
329. Pisani MA, Murphy TE, Araujo KL, et al. Benzodiazepine and opioid use and the duration of intensive care unit delirium in an older population. *Crit Care Med.* 2009; 37:177–83.
330. Martin J, Heymann A, Bäsell K, et al. Evidence and consensus-based German guidelines for the management of analgesia, sedation and delirium in intensive care—Short version. *Ger Med Sci.* 2010; 8:Doc02.
331. Michaud L, Büla C, Berney A, et al. Delirium: Guidelines for general hospitals. *Wiadomosci Psychiatryczne.* 2008; 11:283–99.
332. Silva JA, Romera MA, Chamorro C, et al. Sedoanalgesia in neurologically ill patients: Guidelines revisited. *Stroke.* 2008; 39:e67; author reply e68.
333. Tropea J, Slee JA, Brand CA, et al. Clinical practice guidelines for the management of delirium in older people in Australia. *Australas J Ageing.* 2008; 27:150–6.
334. Kessler P, Martin J. [Optimisation of sedation practice in ICU by implementing of S2e Guidelines]. *Anasthesiol Intensivmed Not-fallmed Schmerzther.* 2008; 43:38–43.
335. Playfor S, Jenkins I, Boyles C, et al. United Kingdom Paediatric Intensive Care Society Sedation; Analgesia and Neuromuscular Blockade Working Group: Consensus guidelines on sedation and analgesia in critically ill children. *Intensive Care Med.* 2006; 32:1125–36.
336. Potter J, George J. Guideline Development Group: The prevention, diagnosis and management of delirium in older people: Concise guidelines. *Clin Med.* 2006; 6:303–8.
337. Truman B, Shintani A, Jackson J, et al. Implementation of the SCCM guidelines for sedation and delirium monitoring in the ICU. *Am J Respir Crit Care Med.* 2003; 167:A969.
338. American College of Critical Care Medicine of the Society of Critical Care Medicine, American Society of Health-System Pharmacists, American College of Chest Physicians. Clinical practice guidelines for the sustained use of sedatives and analgesics in the critically ill adult. *Am J Health Syst Pharm.* 2002; 59:150–78.
339. O'Mahony R, Murthy L, Akunne A, et al. Guideline Development Group: Synopsis of the National Institute for Health and Clinical Excellence guideline for prevention of delirium. *Ann Intern Med.* 2011; 154:746–51.
340. Lonergan E, Britton AM, Luxenberg J, et al. Antipsychotics for delirium. *Cochrane Database Syst Rev.* 2007; CD005594.
341. Mayo-Smith MF, Beecher LH, Fischer TL, et al. Working Group on the Management of Alcohol Withdrawal Delirium, Practice Guidelines Committee, American Society of Addiction Medicine: Management of alcohol withdrawal delirium. An evidence-based practice guideline. *Arch Intern Med.* 2004; 164:1405–12.
342. Ashton H. The diagnosis and management of benzodiazepine dependence. *Curr Opin Psychiatry.* 2005; 18:249–55.
343. Nicholls L, Bragaw L, Ruetsch C. Opioid dependence treatment and guidelines. *J Manag Care Pharm.* 2010; 16(1 Suppl B):S14–S21.
344. Cammarano WB, Pittet JF, Weitz S, et al. Acute withdrawal syndrome related to the administration of analgesic and sedative medications in adult intensive care unit patients. *Crit Care Med.* 1998; 26:676–84.
345. American Pain Society. Principles of Analgesic Use in the Treatment of Acute Pain and Cancer Pain. Sixth Edition. Glenview, IL, American Pain Society, 2008.
346. Preston KL, Bigelow GE, Liebson IA. Antagonist effects of nalbuphine in opioid-dependent human volunteers. *J Pharmacol Exp Ther.* 1989; 248:929–37.
347. Kamijo Y, Masuda T, Nishikawa T, et al. Cardiovascular response and stress reaction to flu-

mazenil injection in patients under infusion with midazolam. *Crit Care Med.* 2000; 28:318–23.

348. Breheny FX. Reversal of midazolam sedation with flumazenil. *Crit Care Med.* 1992; 20:736–9.
349. Hospira Inc. FDA package insert for dexmedetomidine. Available at: http://www.precedex.com/wp-content/uploads/2010/11/Precedex_PI.pdf. Accessed October 2010.
350. Brown C, Albrecht R, Pettit H, et al. Opioid and benzodiazepine withdrawal syndrome in adult burn patients. *Am Surg.* 2000; 66:367–70; discussion 370.
351. Korak-Leiter M, Likar R, Oher M, et al. Withdrawal following sufentanil/propofol and sufentanil/midazolam. Sedation in surgical ICU patients: Correlation with central nervous parameters and endogenous opioids. *Intensive Care Med.* 2005; 31:380–7.
352. Moore RD, Bone LR, Geller G, et al. Prevalence, detection, and treatment of alcoholism in hospitalized patients. *JAMA.* 1989; 261:403–7.
353. Foy A, Kay J. The incidence of alcohol-related problems and the risk of alcohol withdrawal in a general hospital population. *Drug Alcohol Rev.* 1995; 14:49–54.
354. Spies CD, Neuner B, Neumann T, et al. Intercurrent complications in chronic alcoholic men admitted to the intensive care unit following trauma. *Intensive Care Med.* 1996; 22:286–93.
355. Spies CD, Nordmann A, Brummer G, et al. Intensive care unit stay is prolonged in chronic alcoholic men following tumor resection of the upper digestive tract. *Acta Anaesthesiol Scand.* 1996; 40:649–56.
356. Bayard M, McIntyre J, Hill KR, et al. Alcohol withdrawal syndrome. *Am Fam Physician.* 2004; 69:1443–50.
357. Turner RC, Lichstein PR, Peden JG Jr, et al. Alcohol withdrawal syndromes: A review of pathophysiology, clinical presentation, and treatment. *J Gen Intern Med.* 1989; 4:432–44.
358. Spies CD, Otter HE, Hüske B, et al. Alcohol withdrawal severity is decreased by symptom-orientated adjusted bolus therapy in the ICU. *Intensive Care Med.* 2003; 29:2230–8.
359. Lin SM, Liu CY, Wang CH, et al. The impact of delirium on the survival of mechanically ventilated patients. *Crit Care Med.* 2004; 32:2254–9.
360. Micek ST, Anand NJ, Laible BR, et al. Delirium as detected by the CAM-ICU predicts restraint use among mechanically ventilated medical patients. *Crit Care Med.* 2005; 33:1260–5.
361. Thomason JW, Shintani A, Peterson JF, et al. Intensive care unit delirium is an independent predictor of longer hospital stay: A prospective analysis of 261 non-ventilated patients. *Crit Care.* 2005; 9:R375–R381.
362. Norkiene I, Ringaitiene D, Misiuriene I, et al. Incidence and precipitating factors of delirium after coronary artery bypass grafting. *Scand Cardiovasc J.* 2007; 41:180–5.
363. Lin SM, Huang CD, Liu CY, et al. Risk factors for the development of early-onset delirium and the subsequent clinical outcome in mechanically ventilated patients. *J Crit Care.* 2008; 23:372–9.
364. Lat I, McMillian W, Taylor S, et al. The impact of delirium on clinical outcomes in mechanically ventilated surgical and trauma patients. *Crit Care Med.* 2009; 37:1898–905.
365. Han JH, Shintani A, Eden S, et al. Delirium in the emergency department: An independent predictor of death within 6 months. *Ann Emerg Med.* 2010; 56:244–52.e1.
366. Ely EW, Dittus R. Reply letter: Pharmacological treatment of delirium in the intensive care unit. *JAMA.* 2004; 292:168–9.
367. Spronk PE, Riekerk B, Hofhuis J, et al. Occurrence of delirium is severely underestimated in the ICU during daily care. *Intensive Care Med.* 2009; 35:1276–80.
368. Shintani AK, Girard TD, Eden SK, et al. Immortal time bias in critical care research: Application of time-varying Cox regression for observational cohort studies. *Crit Care Med.* 2009; 37:2939–45.
369. Girard TD, Pandharipande PP, Carson SS, et al. Feasibility, efficacy, and safety of antipsychotics for intensive care unit delirium: The MIND randomized, placebo-controlled trial. *Crit Care Med.* 2010; 38:428–37.
370. Girard TD, Pandharipande PP, Carson SS, et al. MIND Trial Investigators: Feasibility, efficacy, and safety of antipsychotics for intensive care unit delirium: The MIND randomized, placebo-controlled trial. *Crit Care Med.* 2010; 38:428–37.
371. van Eijk MM, van Marum RJ, Klijn IA, et al. Comparison of delirium assessment tools in a mixed intensive care unit. *Crit Care Med.* 2009; 37:1881–5.
372. Guenther U, Popp J, Koecher L, et al. Validity and reliability of the CAM-ICU Flowsheet to diagnose delirium in surgical ICU patients. *J Crit Care.* 2010; 25:144–51.
373. Ely EW, Margolin R, Francis J, et al. Evaluation of delirium in critically ill patients: Validation of the Confusion Assessment Method for the Intensive Care Unit (CAM-ICU). *Crit Care Med.* 2001; 29:1370–9.
374. Soja SL, Pandharipande PP, Fleming SB, et al. Implementation, reliability testing, and compliance monitoring of the Confusion Assessment Method for the intensive care unit in trauma patients. *Intensive Care Med.* 2008; 34:1263–8.
375. Pisani MA, Murphy TE, Van Ness PH, et al. Characteristics associated with delirium in older patients in a medical intensive care unit. *Arch Intern Med.* 2007; 167:1629–34.
376. Roberts B, Rickard CM, Rajbhandari D, et al. Multicentre study of delirium in ICU patients using a simple screening tool. *Aust Crit Care.* 2005; 18:6, 8–9, 11.
377. Balas MC, Deutschman CS, Sullivan-Marx EM, et al. Delirium in older patients in surgical intensive care units. *J Nurs Scholarsh.* 2007; 39:147–54.
378. Plaschke K, von Haken R, Scholz M, et al. Comparison of the confusion assessment method for the intensive care unit (CAM-ICU) with the Intensive Care Delirium Screening Checklist (ICDSC) for delirium in critical care patients gives high agreement rate(s). *Intensive Care Med.* 2008; 34:431–6.

379. Luetz A, Heymann A, Radtke FM, et al. Different assessment tools for intensive care unit delirium: Which score to use? *Crit Care Med.* 2010; 38:409–18.

380. Peterson JF, Pun BT, Dittus RS, et al. Delirium and its motoric subtypes: A study of 614 critically ill patients. *J Am Geriatr Soc.* 2006; 54:479–84.

381. Misak C. ICU psychosis and patient autonomy: Some thoughts from the inside. *J Med Philos.* 2005; 30:411–30.

382. Riekerk B, Pen EJ, Hofhuis JG, et al. Limitations and practicalities of CAM-ICU implementation, a delirium scoring system, in a Dutch intensive care unit. *Intensive Crit Care Nurs.* 2009; 25:242–9.

383. Devlin JW, Fong JJ, Howard EP, et al. Assessment of delirium in the intensive care unit: Nursing practices and perceptions. *Am J Crit Care.* 2008; 17:555–65; quiz 566.

384. Tobar E, Romero C, Galleguillos T, et al. Confusion Assessment Method for diagnosing delirium in ICU patients: Cultural adaptation and validation of the spanish version. *Med Intensiva.* 2010; 34:4–13.

385. Smith HA, Boyd J, Fuchs DC, et al. Diagnosing delirium in critically ill children: Validity and reliability of the Pediatric Confusion Assessment Method for the intensive care unit. *Crit Care Med.* 2011; 39:150–7.

386. Hudetz JA, Patterson KM, Byrne AJ, et al. Postoperative delirium is associated with postoperative cognitive dysfunction at one week after cardiac surgery with cardiopulmonary bypass. *Psychol Rep.* 2009; 105(3 Pt 1):921–32.

387. Larsson C, Axell AG, Ersson A. Confusion assessment method for the intensive care unit (CAM-ICU): Translation, retranslation and validation into Swedish intensive care settings. *Acta Anaesthesiol Scand.* 2007; 51:888–92.

388. Hart RP, Best AM, Sessler CN, et al. Abbreviated cognitive test for delirium. *J Psychosom Res.* 1997; 43:417–23.

389. Hart RP, Levenson JL, Sessler CN, et al. Validation of a cognitive test for delirium in medical ICU patients. *Psychosomatics.* 1996; 37:533–46.

390. Kennedy RE, Nakase-Thompson R, Nick TG, et al. Use of the cognitive test for delirium in patients with traumatic brain injury. *Psychosomatics.* 2003; 44:283–9.

391. van Eijk MM, van den Boogaard M, van Marum RJ, et al. Routine use of the confusion assessment method for the intensive care unit: A multicenter study. *Am J Respir Crit Care Med.* 2011; 184:340–4.

392. Neto AS, Nassar AP Jr, Cardoso SO, et al. Delirium screening in critically ill patients: A systematic review and meta-analysis. *Crit Care Med.* 2012; 40:1946–51.

393. Gusmao-Flores D, Figueira Salluh JI, Chalhub RA, et al. The confusion assessment method for the intensive care unit (CAM-ICU) and intensive care delirium screening checklist (ICDSC) for the diagnosis of delirium: A systematic review and meta-analysis of clinical studies. *Crit Care.* 2012; 16:R115.

394. Vasilevskis EE, Morandi A, Boehm L, et al. Delirium and sedation recognition using validated instruments: Reliability of bedside intensive care unit nursing assessments from 2007 to 2010. *J Am Geriatr Soc.* 2011; 59(Suppl 2):S249–S255.

395. Devlin JW, Fong JJ, Fraser GL, et al. Delirium assessment in the critically ill. *Intensive Care Med.* 2007; 33:929–40.

396. Van Rompaey B, Elseviers MM, Schuurmans MJ, et al. Risk factors for delirium in intensive care patients: A prospective cohort study. *Crit Care.* 2009; 13:R77.

397. Dubois MJ, Bergeron N, Dumont M, et al. Delirium in an intensive care unit: A study of risk factors. *Intensive Care Med.* 2001; 27:1297–304.

398. Pandharipande PP, Morandi A, Adams JR, et al. Plasma tryptophan and tyrosine levels are independent risk factors for delirium in critically ill patients. *Intensive Care Med.* 2009; 35:1886–92.

399. Ely EW, Girard TD, Shintani AK, et al. Apolipoprotein E4 polymorphism as a genetic predisposition to delirium in critically ill patients. *Crit Care Med.* 2007; 35:112–7.

400. Agarwal V, O'Neill PJ, Cotton BA, et al. Prevalence and risk factors for development of delirium in burn intensive care unit patients. *J Burn Care Res.* 2010; 31:706–15.

401. Needham DM, Korupolu R, Zanni JM, Pradhan P, Colantuoni E, Palmer JB, Brower RG, Fan E. Early physical medicine and rehabilitation for patients with acute respiratory failure: A quality improvement project. *Arch Phys Med Rehabil.* 2010; 91:53.

402. Inouye SK, Bogardus ST Jr, Charpentier PA, et al. A multicomponent intervention to prevent delirium in hospitalized older patients. *N Engl J Med.* 1999; 340:669–76.

403. Aizawa K, Kanai T, Saikawa Y, et al. A novel approach to the prevention of postoperative delirium in the elderly after gastrointestinal surgery. *Surg Today.* 2002; 32:310–4.

404. Wang W, Li HL, Wang DX, et al. Haloperidol prophylaxis decreases delirium incidence in elderly patients after noncardiac surgery: A randomized controlled trial. *Crit Care Med.* 2011; 40:731–9.

405. Awissi DK, Bégin C, Moisan J, et al. I-SAVE study: Impact of sedation, analgesia, and delirium protocols evaluated in the intensive care unit: An economic evaluation. *Ann Pharmacother.* 2012; 46:21–8.

406. Prakanrattana U, Prapaitrakool S. Efficacy of risperidone for prevention of postoperative delirium in cardiac surgery. *Anaesth Intensive Care.* 2007; 35:714–9.

407. Shehabi Y, Grant P, Wolfenden H, et al. Prevalence of delirium with dexmedetomidine compared with morphine based therapy after cardiac surgery: A randomized controlled trial (DEXmedetomidine COmpared to Morphine-DEXCOM Study). *Anesthesiology.* 2009; 111:1075–84.

408. Devlin JW, Roberts RJ, Fong JJ, et al. Efficacy and safety of quetiapine in critically ill patients with delirium: A prospective, multicenter, randomized, double-blind, placebo-controlled pilot study. *Crit Care Med.* 2010; 38:419–27.

409. van Eijk MM, Roes KC, Honing ML, et al. Effect of rivastigmine as an adjunct to usual care with

haloperidol on duration of delirium and mortality in critically ill patients: A multicentre, double-blind, placebo-controlled randomised trial. *Lancet.* 2010; 376:1829–37.

410. Gamberini M, Bolliger D, Lurati Buse GA, et al. Rivastigmine for the prevention of postoperative delirium in elderly patients undergoing elective cardiac surgery—A randomized controlled trial. *Crit Care Med.* 2009; 37:1762–8.
411. Hunt N, Stern TA. The association between intravenous haloperidol and torsades de pointes. Three cases and a literature review. *Psychosomatics.* 1995; 36:541–9.
412. Sharma ND, Rosman HS, Padhi ID, et al. Torsades de pointes associated with intravenous haloperidol in critically ill patients. *Am J Cardiol.* 1998; 81:238–40.
413. Metzger E, Friedman R. Prolongation of the corrected QT and torsades de pointes cardiac arrhythmia associated with intravenous haloperidol in the medically ill. *J Clin Psychopharmacol.* 1993; 13:128–32.
414. Tisdale JE, Rasty S, Padhi ID, et al. The effect of intravenous haloperidol on QT interval dispersion in critically ill patients: Comparison with QT interval prolongation for assessment of risk of torsades de pointes. *J Clin Pharmacol.* 2001; 41:1310–8.
415. Perrault LP, Denault AY, Carrier M, et al. Torsades de pointes secondary to intravenous haloperidol after coronary bypass grafting surgery. *Can J Anaesth.* 2000; 47:251–4.
416. Tisdale JE, Kovacs R, Mi D, et al. Accuracy of uncorrected versus corrected QT interval for prediction of torsade de pointes associated with intravenous haloperidol. *Pharmacotherapy.* 2007; 27:175–82.
417. Heinrich TW, Biblo LA, Schneider J. Torsades de pointes associated with ziprasidone. *Psychosomatics.* 2006; 47:264–8.
418. Tei Y, Morita T, Inoue S, et al. Torsades de pointes caused by a small dose of risperidone in a terminally ill cancer patient. *Psychosomatics.* 2004; 45:450–1.
419. Pham CP, de Feiter PW, van der Kuy PH, et al. Long QTc interval and torsade de pointes caused by fluconazole. *Ann Pharmacother.* 2006; 40:1456–61.
420. Pandharipande PP, Girard T, Sanders RD, et al. Comparison of sedation with dexmedetomidine versus lorazepam in septic ICU patients. *Critical Care.* 2008; 12:P275.
421. Banerjee A, Girard TD, Pandharipande P. The complex interplay between delirium, sedation, and early mobility during critical illness: Applications in the trauma unit. *Curr Opin Anaesthesiol.* 2011; 24:195–201.
422. Sessler CN, Pedram S. Protocolized and target-based sedation and analgesia in the ICU. *Crit Care Clin.* 2009; 25:489–513, viii.
423. Ethier C, Burry L, Martinez-Motta C, et al. Canadian Critical Care Trials Group: Recall of intensive care unit stay in patients managed with a sedation protocol or a sedation protocol with daily sedative interruption: A pilot study. *J Crit Care.* 2011; 26:127–32.
424. Weinert CR, Sprenkle M. Post-ICU consequences of patient wakefulness and sedative exposure during mechanical ventilation. *Intensive Care Med.* 2008; 34:82–90.
425. Roberts BL, Rickard CM, Rajbhandari D, et al. Factual memories of ICU: Recall at two years post-discharge and comparison with delirium status during ICU admission—A multicentre cohort study. *J Clin Nurs.* 2007; 16:1669–77.
426. Nelson BJ, Weinert CR, Bury CL, et al. Intensive care unit drug use and subsequent quality of life in acute lung injury patients. *Crit Care Med.* 2000; 28:3626–30.
427. Shehabi Y, Botha JA, Boyle MS, et al. Sedation and delirium in the intensive care unit: An Australian and New Zealand perspective. *Anaesth Intensive Care.* 2008; 36:570–8.
428. Martin J, Franck M, Fischer M, et al. Sedation and analgesia in German intensive care units: How is it done in reality? Results of a patient-based survey of analgesia and sedation. *Intensive Care Med.* 2006; 32:1137–42.
429. Schweickert WD, Gehlbach BK, Pohlman AS, et al. Daily interruption of sedative infusions and complications of critical illness in mechanically ventilated patients. *Crit Care Med.* 2004; 32:1272–6.
430. Mehta S, Burry L, Cook D, et al. Daily sedation interruption in mechanically ventilated critically ill patients cared for with a sedation protocol: A randomized trial. *JAMA.* 2012 [E-pub ahead of print].
431. Fraser GL, Riker RR. Comfort without coma: Changing sedation practices. *Crit Care Med.* 2007; 35:635–7.
432. Anifantaki S, Prinianakis G, Vitsaksaki E, et al. Daily interruption of sedative infusions in an adult medical-surgical intensive care unit: Randomized controlled trial. *J Adv Nurs.* 2009; 65:1054–60.
433. de Wit M, Gennings C, Jenvey WI, et al. Randomized trial comparing daily interruption of sedation and nursing-implemented sedation algorithm in medical intensive care unit patients. *Crit Care.* 2008; 12:R70.
434. MacLaren R, Plamondon JM, Ramsay KB, et al. A prospective evaluation of empiric versus protocol-based sedation and analgesia. *Pharmacotherapy.* 2000; 20:662–72.
435. O'Connor M, Bucknall T, Manias E. International variations in outcomes from sedation protocol research: Where are we at and where do we go from here? *Intensive Crit Care Nurs.* 2010; 26:189–95.
436. Breen D, Karabinis A, Malbrain M, et al. Decreased duration of mechanical ventilation when comparing analgesia-based sedation using remifentanil with standard hypnotic-based sedation for up to 10 days in intensive care unit patients: A randomised trial [ISRCTN47583497]. *Crit Care.* 2005; 9:R200–R210.
437. Park G, Lane M, Rogers S, et al. A comparison of hypnotic and analgesic based sedation in a general intensive care unit. *Br J Anaesth.* 2007; 98:76–82.
438. Rozendaal FW, Spronk PE, Snellen FF, et al. UltiSAFE Investigators: Remifentanil-propofol analgo-sedation shortens duration of ventilation and length of ICU stay compared to a conventional regimen: A centre randomised, cross-over, open-label study in the Netherlands. *Intensive Care Med.* 2009; 35:291–8.

439. Strøm T, Martinussen T, Toft P. A protocol of no sedation for critically ill patients receiving mechanical ventilation: A randomised trial. *Lancet.* 2010; 375:475–80.
440. Devlin JW, Roberts RJ. Pharmacology of commonly used analgesics and sedatives in the ICU: Benzodiazepines, propofol, and opioids. *Crit Care Clin.* 2009; 25:431–49, vii.
441. Nguyen NQ, Chapman MJ, Fraser RJ, et al. The effects of sedation on gastric emptying and intragastric meal distribution in critical illness. *Intensive Care Med.* 2008; 34:454–60.
442. Strøm T, Stylsvig M, Toft P. Long-term psychological effects of a no-sedation protocol in critically ill patients. *Crit Care.* 2011; 15:R293.
443. Redeker NS. Sleep in acute care settings: An integrative review. *J Nurs Scholarsh.* 2000; 32:31–8.
444. Fontana CJ, Pittiglio LI. Sleep deprivation among critical care patients. *Crit Care Nurs Q.* 2010; 33:75–81.
445. Lawson N, Thompson K, Saunders G, et al. Sound intensity and noise evaluation in a critical care unit. *Am J Crit Care.* 2010; 19:e88–e98; quiz e99.
446. Dunn H, Anderson MA, Hill PD. Nighttime lighting in intensive care units. *Crit Care Nurse.* 2010; 30:31–7.
447. Tembo AC, Parker V. Factors that impact on sleep in intensive care patients. *Intensive Crit Care Nurs.* 2009; 25:314–22.
448. Xie H, Kang J, Mills GH. Clinical review: The impact of noise on patients' sleep and the effectiveness of noise reduction strategies in intensive care units. *Crit Care.* 2009; 13:208.
449. Krachman SL, D'Alonzo GE, Criner GJ. Sleep in the intensive care unit. *Chest.* 1995; 107:1713–20.
450. Sanders RD, Maze M. Contribution of sedative-hypnotic agents to delirium via modulation of the sleep pathway. *Can J Anaesth.* 2011; 58:149–56.
451. Weinhouse GL, Schwab RJ, Watson PL, et al. Bench-to-bedside review: Delirium in ICU patients—Importance of sleep deprivation. *Crit Care.* 2009; 13:234.
452. Sanders RD. Hypothesis for the pathophysiology of delirium: Role of baseline brain network connectivity and changes in inhibitory tone. *Med Hypotheses.* 2011; 77:140–3.
453. Trompeo AC, Vidi Y, Locane MD, et al. Sleep disturbances in the critically ill patients: Role of delirium and sedative agents. *Minerva Anestesiol.* 2011; 77:604–12.
454. Figueroa-Ramos MI, Arroyo-Novoa CM, Lee KA, et al. Sleep and delirium in ICU patients: A review of mechanisms and manifestations. *Intensive Care Med.* 2009; 35:781–95.
455. Novaes MA, Knobel E, Bork AM, et al. Stressors in ICU: Perception of the patient, relatives and health care team. *Intensive Care Med.* 1999; 25:1421–6.
456. Stein-Parbury J, McKinley S. Patients' experiences of being in an intensive care unit: A select literature review. *Am J Crit Care.* 2000; 9:20–7.
457. Li SY, Wang TJ, Vivienne Wu SF, et al. Efficacy of controlling night-time noise and activities to improve patients' sleep quality in a surgical intensive care unit. *J Clin Nurs.* 2011; 20:396–407.
458. Dennis CM, Lee R, Woodard EK, et al. Benefits of quiet time for neuro-intensive care patients. *J Neurosci Nurs.* 2010; 42:217–24.
459. Tamburri LM, DiBrienza R, Zozula R, et al. Nocturnal care interactions with patients in critical care units. *Am J Crit Care.* 2004; 13:102–12; quiz 114.
460. Shochat T, Martin J, Marler M, et al. Illumination levels in nursing home patients: Effects on sleep and activity rhythms. *J Sleep Res.* 2000; 9:373–9.
461. Gabor JY, Cooper AB, Crombach SA, et al. Contribution of the intensive care unit environment to sleep disruption in mechanically ventilated patients and healthy subjects. *Am J Respir Crit Care Med.* 2003; 167:708–15.
462. Cooper AB, Thornley KS, Young GB, et al. Sleep in critically ill patients requiring mechanical ventilation. *Chest.* 2000; 117:809–18.
463. Bosma K, Ferreyra G, Ambrogio C, et al. Patient-ventilator interaction and sleep in mechanically ventilated patients: Pressure support versus proportional assist ventilation. *Crit Care Med.* 2007; 35:1048–54.
464. Parthasarathy S, Tobin MJ. Effect of ventilator mode on sleep quality in critically ill patients. *Am J Respir Crit Care Med.* 2002; 166:1423–9.
465. Shaneyfelt TM, Centor RM. Reassessment of clinical practice guidelines: Go gently into that good night. *JAMA.* 2009; 301:868–9.
466. Clancy CM, Slutsky JR. Guidelines for guidelines: We've come a long way. *Chest.* 2007; 132:746–7.
467. Devlin JW, Tanios MA, Epstein SK. Intensive care unit sedation: Waking up clinicians to the gap between research and practice. *Crit Care Med.* 2006; 34:556–7.
468. Brattebø G, Hofoss D, Flaatten H, et al. Effect of a scoring system and protocol for sedation on duration of patients' need for ventilator support in a surgical intensive care unit. *Qual Saf Health Care.* 2004; 13:203–5.
469. Pisani MA, Araujo KL, Van Ness PH, et al. A research algorithm to improve detection of delirium in the intensive care unit. *Crit Care.* 2006; 10:R121.
470. DePalo VA, McNicoll L, Cornell M, et al. The Rhode Island ICU collaborative: A model for reducing central line-associated bloodstream infection and ventilator-associated pneumonia statewide. *Qual Saf Health Care.* 2010; 19:555–61.
471. Castellanos-Ortega A, Suberviola B, García-Astudillo LA, et al. Impact of the Surviving Sepsis Campaign protocols on hospital length of stay and mortality in septic shock patients: Results of a three-year follow-up quasi-experimental study. *Crit Care Med.* 2010; 38:1036–43.
472. Muellejans B, López A, Cross MH, et al. Remifentanil versus fentanyl for analgesia based sedation to provide patient comfort in the intensive care unit: A randomized, double-blind controlled trial [ISRCTN43755713]. *Crit Care.* 2004; 8:R1–R11.

Juliana Barr, MD, FCCM[1]; Gilles L. Fraser, PharmD, FCCM[2]; Kathleen Puntillo, RN, PhD, FAAN, FCCM[3]; E. Wesley Ely, MD, MPH, FACP, FCCM[4]; Céline Gélinas, RN, PhD[5]; Joseph F. Dasta, MSc, FCCM, FCCP[6]; Judy E. Davidson, DNP, RN[7]; John W. Devlin, PharmD, FCCM, FCCP[8]; John P. Kress, MD[9]; Aaron M. Joffe, DO[10]; Douglas B. Coursin, MD[11]; Daniel L. Herr, MD, MS, FCCM[12]; Avery Tung, MD[13]; Bryce R. H. Robinson, MD, FACS[14]; Dorrie K. Fontaine, PhD, RN, FAAN[15]; Michael A. Ramsay, MD[16]; Richard R. Riker, MD, FCCM[17]; Curtis N. Sessler, MD, FCCP, FCCM[18]; Brenda Pun, MSN, RN, ACNP[19]; Yoanna Skrobik, MD, FRCP[20]; Roman Jaeschke, MD[21]

[1]VA Palo Alto Health Care System, Palo Alto, CA, and Stanford University School of Medicine, Stanford, CA.
[2]Tufts University School of Medicine, Maine Medical Center, Portland, ME.
[3]Department of Physiological Nursing, University of California, San Francisco, CA.
[4]VA-GRECC (Geriatric Research Education Clinical Center) for the VA Tennessee Valley Healthcare System, Vanderbilt University Medical Center, Nashville, TN.
[5]Ingram School of Nursing, McGill University and Centre for Nursing Research/Lady Davis Institute, Jewish General Hospital, Montreal, QC, Canada.
[6]The Ohio State University, College of Pharmacy, Columbus, OH, and The University of Texas, College of Pharmacy, Austin, TX.
[7]Scripps Clinical Center, Scripps Health, La Jolla, CA.
[8]Department of Pharmacy Practice, Northeastern University Special and Scientific Staff, Division of Pulmonary, Critical Care, and Sleep Medicine, Tufts University of Medicine, Boston, MA.
[9]Department of Medicine, Section of Pulmonary and Critical Care, University of Chicago, Chicago, IL.
[10]Department of Anesthesiology and Pain Medicine, University of Washington/Harborview Medical Center, Seattle, WA.
[11]Departments of Anesthesiology and Internal Medicine, University of Wisconsin School of Medicine and Public Health, Madison, WI.
[12]Shock Trauma Center, Division of Trauma Critical Care Medicine, University of Maryland, Baltimore, MD.
[13]Department of Anesthesia and Critical Care, University of Chicago, Chicago, IL.
[14]Department of Surgery, Division of Trauma and Critical Care, University of Cincinnati, Cincinnati, OH.
[15]University of Virginia, School of Nursing, Charlottesville, VA.
[16]Baylor University Medical Center, Dallas, TX.
[17]Tufts University School of Medicine, Maine Medical Center, Portland, ME.
[18]Department of Internal Medicine, Virginia Commonwealth University Heath System, Richmond, VA.
[19]Department of Allergy, Pulmonary, and Critical Care Medicine, Vanderbilt University Medical Center, Nashville, TN.
[20]Université de Montréal, Montréal, Canada.
[21]Departments of Medicine and Clinical Epidemiology and Biostatistics, St. Joseph's Hospital and McMaster University, Hamilton, Ontario, Canada.

Supplemental digital content is available for this article. Direct URL citations appear in the printed text and are provided in the HTML and PDF versions of this on the journal's Web site (http://journals.lww.com/ccmjournal).

To minimize the perception of bias in these Guidelines, individual Task Force members with a significant conflict of interest on a particular topic were recused from grading the literature, writing evidence summaries, and developing specific statements and recommendations on that topic. Final decisions regarding strength of evidence and strength of recommendations for all questions were voted on anonymously by all Task Force members. Voting distributions for all statements and recommendations can be found on line at http://journals.lww.com/ccmjournal. We refer readers to the Methods Section of these Guidelines for more details.

Supporting Organizations: American College of Critical Care Medicine (ACCM) in conjunction with Society of Critical Care Medicine (SCCM) and American Society of Health-System Pharmacists (ASHP).

Mr. Dasta has consultancies with Hospira, Axel Rx, Cadence Pharmaceuticals, and Pacira Pharmaceuticals and has received honoraria/speaking fees from the France Foundation (speakers bureau CME program) sponsored by Hospira. Dr. Devlin has received honoraria/speaking fees, consultancies, and grants from Hospira. Dr. Ely has received honoraria/speaking fees from GSK and Hospira; and has received grants from Hospira, Pfizer, and Aspect. Dr. Herr has received honoraria/speaking fees from Hospira. Dr. Kress has received honoraria/speaking fees from Hospira; and has received a grant from Hospira (unrestricted research). Ms. Pun has received honoraria/ speaking fees from Hospira. Dr. Ramsay has received honoraria/speaking fees from Hospira and Masimo; and has received a grant from Masimo. Dr. Riker has consultancies with Masimo; and has received honoraria/speaking fees from Orion. Dr. Sessler has received honoraria/speaking fees from Hospira and consulting fees from Massimo. The remaining authors have not disclosed any potential conflicts of interest.

These guidelines have been reviewed and endorsed by the American College of Chest Physicians and the American Association for Respiratory Care; are supported by the American Association for Respiratory Care; and have been reviewed by the New Zealand Intensive Care Society.

For information regarding this article, E-mail: barrj@stanford.edu

The American College of Critical Care Medicine (ACCM), which honors individuals for their achievements and contributions to multidisciplinary critical care medicine, is the consultative body of the Society of Critical Care Medicine (SCCM) that possesses recognized expertise in the practice of critical care. The College has developed administrative guidelines and clinical practice parameters for the critical care practitioner. New guidelines and practice parameters are continually developed, and current ones are systematically reviewed and revised.

Index

Index

A

B

C

D

E

F

G

H

M

Q

R

S

T

U

V

W